WOMEN'S PRIMARY HEALTH CARE

WOMEN'S PRIMARY HEALTH CARE

Office Practice and Procedures

SECOND EDITION

Editors

VICKI L. SELTZER, M.D.
Vice President for Women's Health Services
North Shore–Long Island Jewish Health System
Chairman, Departments of Obstetrics and Gynecology
North Shore University Hospital and Long Island Jewish
* Medical Center*
Professor, Obstetrics and Gynecology and Women's Health
Albert Einstein College of Medicine
New Hyde Park, New York

WARREN H. PEARSE, M.D.
The Jacobs Institute of Women's Health
Washington, D.C.

McGraw-Hill
Health Professions Division
New York   St. Louis   San Francisco
Auckland   Bogotá   Caracas   Lisbon   London
Madrid   Mexico City   Milan   Montreal   New Delhi
San Juan   Singapore   Sydney   Tokyo   Toronto

McGraw-Hill

A Division of The McGraw·Hill Companies

WOMEN'S PRIMARY HEALTH CARE
Office Practice and Procedures
Second Edition

1 2 3 4 5 6 7 8 9 0 DOCDOC 99

ISBN 0-07-058044-8

This book was set in Times Roman by Bi-Comp, Inc.
The editors were Martin J. Wonsiewicz, Steven Melvin, and Muza Navrozov.
The production supervisor was Catherine H. Saggese.
The index was prepared by Geraldine Beckford.
Color insert was done by Joan O'Connor.
R. R. Donnelley and Sons was printer and binder.

The book is printed on acid-free paper.

Cataloging-in-Publication Data is on file for this title at
the Library of Congress

To my wonderful family: Richard, Jessica, and Eric Brach, and Marian Seltzer; and to the memory of my father.

Vicki L. Seltzer

To my father, Harry A. Pearse, M.D.: Obstetrician, poet, and religious historian.

Warren H. Pearse

Contents

PART V
OFFICE DIAGNOSTIC PROCEDURES

PART VI
PSYCHIATRIC AND PSYCHOSOCIAL ISSUES
AND SOCIETAL VIOLENCE

PART VII
GENERAL HEALTH

COLOR PLATES

Color Plates appear between pages 984 and 985.

Contributors*

Mohamed S. Aziz, M.D. [53]
Fellow, Cytopathology
Long Island Jewish Medical Center
New Hyde Park, New York

Angeles Badell, M.D. [40]
Former Chief and Professor
Division of Rehabilitation Medicine
Long Island Jewish Medical Center
New Hyde Park, New York

Susanne L. Bathgate, M.D. [7]
Assistant Professor
Department of Obstetrics and Gynecology
The George Washington University
Washington, D.C.

Elise Belilos, M.D. [72]
Division of Rheumatology
Winthrop University Hospital
Clinical Assistant Professor of Medicine
State University of New York at Stony Brook
Mineola, New York

Fred Benjamin, M.D. [24, 66]
Visiting Professor, Obstetrics and Gynecology
  and Women's Health
Albert Einstein College of Medicine
Bronx, New York

Henny Billett, M.D. [70]
Director of Clinical Hematology
Weiler Hospital
Associate Professor of Medicine
Albert Einstein College of Medicine
Bronx, New York

W. Kenneth Blaylock, M.D. [80]
Chief of Dermatology Service
Hunter Holmes McGuire Veterans Administration
  Medical Center
Richmond, Virginia

Vincent R. Bonagura, M.D. [73]
Chief, Division of Allergy and Immunology
Schneider Children's Hospital
Professor of Pediatrics, Microbiology,
  and Immunology
Albert Einstein College of Medicine
New Hyde Park, New York

Jessica L. Brach [20]
Student, Princeton University
Princeton, New Jersey

Mara Pearse Burke [21]
Ethics Program Manager
American Academy of Ophthalmology
Iowa City, Iowa

Joanna M. Cain, M.D. [5, 38]
University Professor and Chair
Department of Obstetrics and Gynecology
Penn State Geisinger Health System
Milton S. Hershey Medical Center
Hershey, Pennsylvania

Steven Carsons, M.D. [72]
Chief, Division of Rheumatology and Allergy
Winthrop University Hospital
Associate Professor of Medicine
State University of New York at Stony Brook
Mineola, New York

Robert C. Cefalo, M.D., Ph.D. [18]
Clinical Professor, Assistant Dean
University of North Carolina School of Medicine
Chapel Hill, North Carolina

* Numbers in brackets refer to chapter(s) written or cowritten
by the contributor.

David Chelmow, M.D. [34, 35]
Associate Professor and Chief
Division of General Obstetrics and Gynecology
Department of Obstetrics and Gynecology
Tufts University School of Medicine
Boston, Massachusetts

Frank A. Chervenak, M.D. [88]
Director of Obstetrics
Director of Maternal-Fetal Medicine
Professor of Obstetrics and Gynecology
Cornell Medical School
New York, New York

Ronald A. Chez, M.D. [90, 91]
Professor, Obstetrics and Gynecology
Professor, Community and Family Health
University of South Florida
Tampa, Florida

PonJola Coney, M.D. [18]
Professor and Chair
Department of Obstetrics and Gynecology
Southern Illinois University School of Medicine
Springfield, Illinois

Jeffrey L. Cornella, M.D. [44, 50]
Assistant Professor
Obstetrics and Gynecology
Mayo Graduate School of Medicine
Director, Division of Urogynecology
   and Pelvic Reconstructive Surgery
Mayo Clinic Scottsdale
Scottsdale, Arizona

John M. Cosgrove, M.D. [54]
Director of Surgery
North Shore University Hospital at Forest Hills
Associate Professor of Clinical Surgery
Albert Einstein College of Medicine
Forest Hills, New York

Susan M. Cox, M.D. [31]
Associate Professor, Obstetrics and Gynecology
Assistant Dean for Professional Education
The University of Texas Southwestern Medical
   Center at Dallas
Dallas, Texas

Stephen L. Curry, M.D. [36]
Professor and Chairman, Obstetrics and Gynecology
University of Connecticut School of Medicine
Farmington, Connecticut

David R. Dantzker, M.D. [61]
President, North Shore–Long Island Jewish
   Health System
Professor of Medicine, Albert Einstein College
   of Medicine
Great Neck, New York

Alan H. DeCherney, M.D. [34, 35]
Professor and Chair
Department of Obstetrics and Gynecology
UCLA School of Medicine
Los Angeles, California

Sylvia A. M. Delaney [33]
Clinical Nurse Specialist/Lactation Consultant
Long Island Jewish Medical Center
New Hyde Park, New York

Leo J. Dunn, M.D. [19]
Professor Emeritus
Department of Obstetrics and Gynecology
Virginia Commonwealth University
Richmond, Virginia

Debra Eisenberger, M.D. [68]
Maimonides Medical Center
Brooklyn, New York

Sherman Elias, M.D. [32]
Professor and Head
Department of Obstetrics and Gynecology
University of Illinois at Chicago
Chicago, Illinois

Roselyn Payne Epps, M.D., M.P.H. [11]
Professor Emerita
Department of Pediatrics and Child Health
Howard University College of Medicine
National Cancer Institute
Bethesda, Maryland

Avital Fast, M.D. [79]
Professor and Chairman
Department of Physical Medicine
   and Rehabilitation Medicine

Albert Einstein College of Medicine
Bronx, New York

Arianna F. Faucetta [20]
Student, Columbia University
New York, New York

Arthur L. Frank, M.D., Ph.D. [85]
Vice President for Medical Education
Topperman Professor of Medical Education
Professor of Occupational and Environmental
  Medicine
Professor of Cell Biology and Environmental
  Sciences
University of Texas Health Center at Tyler
Tyler, Texas

Lisa M. Freese, M.S. [7]
Adjunct Instructor, Department of Obstetrics
  and Gynecology
The George Washington Unviersity
Washington, D.C.

Fredric D. Frigoletto, Jr., M.D. [42]
Chief of Vincent Memorial Obstetrics Division
Massachusetts General Hospital
Charles Montraville Green and Robert Montraville
Green Professor of Obstetrics and Gynecology
Harvard Medical School
Boston, Massachusetts

Stanley A. Gall, M.D. [6]
Professor and Chairman
Department of Obstetrics and Gynecology
University of Louisville School of Medicine
Louisville, Kentucky

Albert B. Gerbie, M.D. [4]
Professor Emeritus, Obstetrics and Gynecology
Northwestern University Medical School
Northwestern Memorial Hospital
Chicago, Illinois

Thomas Glynn, Ph.D. [11]
The American Cancer Society
Washington, D.C.

Neville H. Golden, M.D. [57]
Director, Eating Disorder Center
Schneider Children's Hospital

Associate Professor of Pediatrics
Albert Einstein College of Medicine
New Hyde Park, New York

Steven R. Goldstein, M.D. [51]
Professor of Obstetrics and Gynecology
Director, Gynecologic Ultrasound
New York University School of Medicine
New York, New York

Helen Greco, M.D. [58]
Chief, Division of Gynecology
Long Island Jewish Medical Center
Assistant Professor
Obstetrics and Gynecology and Women's Health
Albert Einstein College of Medicine
New Hyde Park, New York

David B. Hale, M.D., Ph.D. [10, 76]
Assistant Professor of Emergency Medicine
Regions Hospital
St. Paul, Minnesota

Ralph W. Hale, M.D. [10, 76]
Executive Vice President
The American College of Obstetricians
  and Gynecologists
Washington, D.C.

Michael A. Hamilton, M.D. [9, 75]
Director
Duke University Diet and Fitness Center
Department of Community and Family Medicine
Duke University Medical Center
Durham, North Carolina

Charles B. Hammond, M.D. [8]
E. C. Hamblen Professor and Chairman
Department of Obstetrics and Gynecology
Duke University Medical Center
Durham, North Carolina

Julia R. Heiman, M.D. [46]
Professor of Psychiatry and Behavioral Sciences
Associate Director for Psychotherapy Programs
Director, Reproductive and Sexual Medicine Clinic
University of Washington
Seattle, Washington

Arthur L. Herbst, M.D. [26]
Joseph Bolivar DeLee Professor and Chairman
Department of Obstetrics and Gynecology
University of Chicago
Chicago, Illinois

Joseph A. Hill, M.D. [42]
Director
Reproductive Medicine Division
Associate Professor of Obstetrics, Gynecology,
   and Reproductive Biology
Brigham and Women's Hospital
Harvard Medical School
Boston, Massachusetts

Paula J. Adams Hillard, M.D. [15, 25]
Professor
Department of Obstetrics and Gynecology
Associate Professor
Department of Pediatrics
Director of Women's Health
University of Cincinnati College of Medicine
Cincinnati, Ohio

Eileen Hilton, M.D. [69]
President, CEO
Biomedical Research Alliance of New York
Associate Professor of Medicine
Albert Einstein College of Medicine
Great Neck, New York

Jacqueline A. Horton, Sc.D. [23]
Senior Study Director, Westat
Rockville, Maryland

Judith Hsia, M.D. [60]
Associate Professor of Medicine
The George Washington University
Washington, D.C.

J. Stephen Hudgins, M.D. [82]
Private Practice
Christiansburg, Virginia

Edward H. Illions, M.D. [41, 49]
Director
Division of Reproductive Endocrinology
Associate Professor
Obstetrics and Gynecology
University of Florida Health Science Center
Jacksonville, Florida

Donna D. Johnson, M.D. [30]
Assistant Professor of Obstetrics and Gynecology
Medical University of South Carolina
Charleston, South Carolina

Ronald Kanner, M.D. [71, 77]
Chairman
Department of Neurology
Long Island Jewish Medical Center
Professor of Neurology
Albert Einstein College of Medicine
New Hyde Park, New York

Bruce G. Kay, M.S., R.Ph. [86]
Director of Pharmacy Services
Long Island Jewish Medical Center
Affiliated Associate Clinical Professor of Pharmacy
St. John's University College of Pharmacy
New Hyde Park, New York

Abbas E. Kitabchi, M.D., Ph.D., F.A.C.E., A.A.C.E. [67]
Director
Division of Endocrinology and Metabolism
Professor of Medicine and Biochemistry
University of Tennesse, Memphis
Memphis, Tennessee

Eric S. Knochenhauer, M.D. [43]
Assistant Professor
Division of Reproductive Biology
   and Endocrinology
Department of Obstetrics and Gynecology
University of Alabama at Birmingham
Birmingham, Alabama

Thomas G. Kwiatkowski, M.D. [78]
Chairman
Department of Emergency Medicine
Long Island Jewish Medical Center
Associate Professor of Emergency Medicine
Albert Einstein College of Medicine
New Hyde Park, New York

Geraldine Lanman, M.D. [14]
Associate Professor of Medicine
Albert Einstein College of Medicine
Lake Success, New York

John W. Larsen, M.D. [7]
Oscar I. and Mildred S. Dodek Professor
Interim Chairman
Department of Obstetrics and Gynecology
The George Washington University
Washington, D.C.

Lee A. Learman, M.D., Ph.D. [91]
Medical Director, Women's Health Center
San Francisco General Hospital
Assistant Clinical Professor
Department of Obstetrics, Gynecology
  and Reproductive Sciences
University of California, San Francisco
San Francisco, California

Gretchen M. Lentz, M.D. [46]
Assistant Professor of Obstetrics and Gynecology
Acting Director of Women's Health Care Center
University of Washington
Seattle, Washington

Zalman Levine, M.D. [16]
Department of Obstetrics and Gynecology
  and Women's Health
Albert Einstein College of Medicine
Bronx, New York

Anne Y. F. Lin, Pharm.D. [86]
Chair and Professor, Pharmacy Practice
Wilkes University School of Pharmacy
Wilkes-Barre, Pennsylvania

Peter LoGalbo, M.D. [73]
Section Head, Allergy, Schneider Children's
  Hospital
Assistant Professor, Albert Einstein College
  of Medicine
New Hyde Park, New York

Frederick Neil Lukash, M.D. [84]
Assistant Clinical Professor of Surgery
Albert Einstein College of Medicine
Manhasset, New York

Marc Manley, M.D., M.P.H. [11]
Special Assistant for Tobacco Policy
National Cancer Institute
Rockville, Maryland

John H. Mattox, M.D. [29]
Chairman
Department of Obstetrics and Gynecology
Good Samaritan Regional Medical Center
Professor, Clinical Obstetrics and Gynecology
University of Arizona
Phoenix, Arizona

Laurence B. McCullough, Ph.D. [88]
Professor of Medicine and Ethics
Baylor College of Medicine
Center for Medical Ethics and Public Issues
Houston, Texas

Howard Minkoff, M.D. [68]
Chairman
Department of Obstetrics and Gynecology
Maimonides Medical Center
Distinguished Professor
Obstetrics and Gynecology
SUNY Health Sciences Center at Brooklyn
Brooklyn, New York

Rodrique Mortel, M.D. [64]
Professor, Obstetrics and Gynecology
Penn State Geisinger Cancer Center
The Milton S. Hershey Medical Center
Hershey, Pennsylvania

Susan M. Mou, M.D. [28]
Chief of Obstetrics and Gynecology
Highland Hospital
Associate Professor and Associate Chair
University of Rochester School of Medicine
Rochester, New York

Alan S. Multz, M.D. [61]
Director
Medical Intensive Care Unit, Department
  of Medicine
Long Island Jewish Medical Center
Assistant Professor of Medicine
Albert Einstein College of Medicine
New Hyde Park, New York

Peter A. Mychajliw, D.D.S. [83]
Chief, General Dentistry
Long Island Jewish Medical Center
Assistant Professor of General Dentistry, SUNY
  at Stony Brook
Stony Brook, New York

David Myssiorek, M.D. [81]
Section Head, Head and Neck Surgery
Department of Otolaryngology
Associate Professor Clinical Otolaryngology
Albert Einstein College of Medicine
New Hyde Park, New York

Cathy Nonas, R.D., M.S. [9, 75]
Administrative Director
Van Itallie Center for Nutrition
  and Weight Management
Obesity Research Center
St. Luke's-Roosevelt Hospital Center
New York, New York

Linn H. Parsons, M.D. [59]
Assistant Professor, Obstetrics and Gynecology
Wake Forest University School of Medicine
Winston-Salem, North Carolina

Warren H. Pearse, M.D.
The Jacobs Institute of Women's Health
Washington, D.C.

Richard C. Pees, M.D. [64]
Associate Professor
Obstetrics and Gynecology
Penn State Geisinger Health System
The Milton S. Hershey Medical Center
Hershey, Pennsylvania

Jeanne Petrek, M.D. [65]
Director
Surgical Program, Lauder Breast Center
Memorial Sloan-Kettering Cancer Center
Associate Professor of Surgery, Cornell School
  of Medicine
New York, New York

Roy M. Pitkin, M.D. [74]
Professor Emeritus, Obstetrics and Gynecology
University of California, Los Angeles
Los Angeles, California

Kanti R, Rai, M.D. [70]
Chief, Division of Hematology and Oncology
Long Island Jewish Medical Center
Professor of Medicine
Albert Einstein College of Medicine
New Hyde Park, New York

William Rennie, M.D. [78]
Director, Academic Affairs
Department of Emergency Medicine
Long Island Jewish Medical Center
Associate Professor
Clinical Emergency Medicine
Assistant Professor
Anatomy and Structural Biology
Albert Einstein College of Medicine
New Hyde Park, New York

Robert Resnik, M.D. [30]
Professor of Reproductive Medicine
University of California, San Diego School
  of Medicine
San Diego, California

Martha C. Romans [22]
Director
Jacobs Institute of Women's Health
Washington, D.C.

Nelson G. Rosen, M.D. [54]
Department of Surgery
Long Island Jewish Medical Center
New Hyde Park, New York

Allan Rosenfield, M.D. [17]
Joseph R. DeLamar Professor of Public Health
Professor of Obstetrics and Gynecology
Dean, Columbia University School of Public Health
New York, New York

Leonard Rossoff, M.D. [69]
Section Head, Pulmonary Division
Long Island Jewish Medical Center
Associate Professor of Medicine
Albert Einstein College of Medicine
New Hyde Park, New York

Nanette K. Rumsey, M.D. [4]
Clinical Instructor
Obstetrics and Gynecology
Northwestern University Medical School
Northwestern Memorial Hospital
Chicago, Illinois

Carolyn D. Runowicz, M.D. [16]
Professor and Director
Division of Gynecologic Oncology

Albert Einstein College of Medicine
  and Montefiore Medical Center
Bronx, New York

Kenneth J. Ryan, M.D. [87]
Professor Emeritus of Obstetrics, Gynecology
  and Reproductive Biology
Harvard Medical School
Brigham and Women's Hospital
Boston, Massachusetts

Issac Sachmechi, M.D. [66]
Chief of Endocrinology
Queens Hospital Center
Assistant Professor of Medicine
Mount Sinai School of Medicine
New York, New York

James J. Sciubba, D.M.D., Ph.D. [83]
Chairman
Department of Dental Medicine
Long Island Jewish Medical Center
Professor
Oral Pathology and Biology
State University of New York at Stony Brook
New Hyde Park, New York

Vicki L. Seltzer, M.D. [2, 3, 13, 65]
Vice President for Women's Health Services
North Shore–Long Island Jewish Health System
Chairman
Departments of Obstetrics and Gynecology
North Shore University Hospital and Long
  Island Jewish Medical Center
Professor
Obstetrics and Gynecology and Women's Health
Albert Einstein College of Medicine
New Hyde Park, New York

Jeffrey Selzer, M.D. [12, 56]
Director of Community Psychiatry and Substance
Abuse Programs
Hillside Hospital, Long Island Jewish
  Medical Center
Assistant Professor, Psychiatry
Albert Einstein College of Medicine
New Hyde Park, New York

Lee P. Shulman, M.D. [32]
Professor of Obstetrics and Gynecology
  and Molecular Genetics
Director of Reproductive Genetics
University of Illinois at Chicago
Chicago, Illinois

Audrey F. Sofair, M.D. [79]
Assistant Professor of Rehabilitation Medicine
Albert Einstein College of Medicine
Bronx, New York

Mark Spitzer, M.D. [39, 47, 48]
Residency Program Director
Department of Obstetrics and Gynecology
North Shore University Hospital
Manhasset, New York

John F. Steege, M.D. [37]
Professor and Chief,
Division of Gynecology
University of North Carolina at Chapel Hill
Chapel Hill, North Carolina

Nada L. Stotland, M.D., M.P.H. [55]
Professor of Psychiatry, Professor of Obstetrics
  and Gynecology
Rush Medical College
Chicago, Illinois

Kris Strohbehn, M.D. [34, 35]
Assistant Professor
Division of Pelvic and Reconstructive Surgery
Department of Obstetrics and Gynecology
Tufts University School of Medicine
Boston, Massachusetts

Albert L. Strunk, J.D., M.D. [89]
Vice President, Fellowship Activities
The American College of Obstetricians
  and Gynecologists
Washington, D.C.

Hamid Taheri, M.D. [60]
Division of Cardiology
Department of Medicine
The George Washington University School
  of Medicine
Washington, D.C.

Candice A. Tedeschi, O.G.N.P. [39]
Coordinator of DES Screening Center
Long Island Jewish Medical Center
New Hyde Park, New York

Henry A. Thiede, M.D. [44, 50]
Professor Emeritus, Obstetrics and Gynecology
University of Rochester School of Medicine
  and Dentistry
Rochester, New York

Robert J. Thompson, M.D. [41, 49]
Professor
Department of Obstetrics and Gynecology
University of Florida Health Science Center
Jacksonville, Florida

Melody Toth, M.S., ATC [76]
Head Trainer for Women
Women's Athletic Training Room
Honolulu, Hawaii

John D. Wagner, M.D. [62]
Head, Section of Dialysis
Long Island Jewish Medical Center
Clinical Associate Professor of Medicine
Albert Einstein College of Medicine
New Hyde Park, New York

Patricia G. Wasserman, M.D. [53]
Chief, Division of Cytopathology
Long Island Jewish Medical Center
Assistant Professor of Pathology
Albert Einstein College of Medicine
New Hyde Park, New York

Carol S. Weisman, Ph.D. [1]
Professor
Department of Health Management and Policy
  and Department of Obstetrics and Gynecology
University of Michigan School of Public Health
Ann Arbor, Michigan

Sandra Wellner, M.D. [40]
Clinical Assistant Professor
Department of Obstetrics and Gynecology
University of Maryland School of Medicine
Baltimore, Maryland

Claudia L. Werner, M.D. [31]
Assistant Professor, Obstetrics and Gynecology
The University of Texas Southwestern Medical
Center at Dallas
Dallas, Texas

Carolyn Westhoff, M.D. [27]
Associate Professor
Department of Obstetrics and Gynecology
  and School of Public Health
Columbia University College of Physicians
  and Surgeons
New York, New York

Lucille C. Xenophon, M.D. [52]
Assistant Professor of Radiology
Albert Einstein College of Medicine
New Hyde Park, New York

Renée L. Young, M.D. [63]
Chief of Gastroenterology
Omaha Veterans Administration Hospital
Associate Professor, Internal Medicine
University of Nebraska Medical Center
Omaha, Nebraska

James P. Youngblood, M.D. [45]
Professor and Chairman
Department of Obstetrics and Gynecology
University of Missouri-Kansas City
Kansas City, Missouri

J. Benjamin Younger, M.D. [43]
Professor Emeritus, Department of Obstetrics
  and Gynecology
University of Alabama at Birmingham
Birmingham, Alabama

Gerald D. Zahtz, M.D. [81]
Chief, Division of Ambulatory Otolaryngology
Long Island Jewish Medical Center
Associate Professor of Clinical Otolaryngology
Albert Einstein College of Medicine
New Hyde Park, New York

Preface

Early in the evolution of the medical profession, the scientific base was so small that a doctor could easily provide the complete range of medical and surgical services to the entire family. During the latter part of the twentieth century, the rapid proliferation of scientific knowledge and technology caused many physicians to narrow their focus and subspecialize. Subspecialization has resulted in exceptional advances in the quality of care and in the sophisticated and successful therapies that we can offer patients for problems ranging from infertility to coronary artery occlusion.

On the other hand, because of the explosion in knowledge and technology, too many physicians have lost sight of the comprehensive needs of the individual woman, by concentrating only on a particular disease process. Clearly, an essential component of medical care is our ability to offer our patients the highest quality care for complex medical problems; however, we will ultimately not be as effective if we are unable to address the overall health needs of women.

Our first goal is to help our patients stay healthy by educating and counseling them about general health strategies and behaviors which promote wellness. Second, we should involve them in programs of early detection. In this way, problems (whether physical, psychiatric, or psychosocial) can be identified at an early stage, when intervention and treatment are most likely to result in cure or optimally address the problem. While it is essential that physicians be able to treat complex disease, this is less effective if we are not able to promote wellness.

The focus of this book is on the primary and preventive ambulatory health care needs of women. It stresses the role of physicians as educators and promoters of women's wellness. It is as important for the subspecialist as it is for the generalist, since a woman with a narrowly focused problem will often see only one specialist physician over a period of time. Conversely, some women will see many physicians—each for a particular problem that the subspecialist is ideally qualified and most capable of treating—but these women may have no one who is overseeing their total health care needs. Therefore, whether we consider ourselves "generalists" or "subspecialists," we must understand the general health care needs of women and work with them to address their primary and preventive health care needs.

It is clear that no one physician can be all things to all people. For most disease processes, there will come a point at which a given physician believes that the specific problem will be best handled by someone with special expertise. The depth of information in this text extends only to that which would be expected to be handled in a general ambulatory situation.

This book is organized in eight parts, each of which focuses on a distinct aspect of women's health. Part I is an overview of women's health today, addressed in its societal context. Part II reviews a series of preventive health strategies, since preventive care will make a major contribution to improving women's health. Part III addresses women's health needs as they change across the lifespan, first from the perspective of the physician, and then from the perspective of the patient. Part IV reviews reproductive health care and disorders of the reproductive system. Although planning for pregnancy and the diagnosis of pregnancy are addressed, general obstetric care is not, as it is outside the intended scope of this book. Part V discusses common office diagnostic procedures. Psychiatric and psychosocial issues are discussed in Part VI. Part VII encompasses the scope of nonreproductive health care needs of women, and Part VIII addresses other important issues.

This book is intended to assist the clinician in providing quality preventive and primary care to women in the office setting. Its main emphasis is on the fact that women receive the best health care when their physicians, be they generalists or subspecialists, have a well-rounded approach to health care and understand women's general health care needs.

WOMEN'S PRIMARY HEALTH CARE

Part I

Women's Health in Perspective

CHAPTER 1

Women's Health in Perspective

Carol S. Weisman

THE SOCIAL CONTEXT
OF WOMEN'S HEALTH
Education • Paid Employment •
Poverty • Marriage and Parenthood •
Caregiving Roles

WOMEN'S HEALTH ACROSS
THE LIFE SPAN
Adolescence and Early Adulthood • Young
Adulthood • Middle Adulthood • Later
Adulthood

THE CHANGING HEALTH CARE SYSTEM
Health Insurance • Safety Net Services •
Managed Care • Quality Assessment in
Women's Health

OPPORTUNITIES FOR IMPROVING
WOMEN'S HEALTH

The *standard of health* among American women
is so low that few have a correct idea of *what a
healthy woman is.*
—Catharine Beecher, *Letters to the People
on Health and Happiness,*
1855 (Cott, 1986)

Concerns about the status of women's
health in the United States are nothing
new, but how women's health has been
addressed by health care providers and policymakers has changed dramatically over time.
Scholars still struggle to understand what combination of biological attributes, sociocultural conditions, personal health behaviors, and health
care variables produces healthy women. Emerging concepts of women's health across their life
span, combined with developments in the health

care delivery system, provide challenges and opportunities to improve health care for American women.

This chapter is an overview of the social context of women's health. It puts in perspective
some key women's health issues across their life
span, and aspects of the evolving health care delivery system that affect how women seek health
care and how health care providers are responding to their needs.

The Social Context of Women's Health

Shifting concepts of women's health may be attributed to a host of factors, including epidemiological patterns, advancements in biomedical research and technology, changes in women's social
and economic status, evolving professional interests and health care institutions, and recurring
women's health movements and political action.[47]
From an early focus—some would say preoccupation—on the female reproductive system and
the maternal function, concepts of women's
health have evolved to include an array of health
issues beyond reproduction. These issues include
conditions unique to women, as well as conditions that women and men share but may experience differently, due to biological, psychosocial,
or cultural factors. Currently, a multi-issue, life
span perspective has replaced earlier perspectives on women's health.

Women in the United States have a life expectancy that is about six years longer than it is for
men. In 1996, the average life expectancy at birth
for women was 79.1 years and 73.1 years for men.
The gender gap is greater among blacks, whose

3

life expectancy is shorter, than among whites. In 1996, the average life expectancy at birth for black women was 74.2 years and 66.1 years for black men.[32] *

Yet longer life for women is not necessarily equated with better health. Women, as compared with men, generally report lower perceived health status, more acute conditions and chronic diseases, more disability, and more time lost from regular activities because of health problems at all life stages. Women also consume more health care services than men across most of their life span.† The reasons for these general patterns have been debated for some time. Researchers have hypothesized greater underlying morbidity in women, greater predisposition to health care–seeking behaviors in women, and traditions or biases of health care institutions. The apparent gender differences in health, however, also can be understood in terms of some basic social inequalities between women and men.

Gender is a fundamental social cause of health and illness that influences an individual's access to such health-producing resources as a safe environment, adequate nutrition, education, paying jobs, social network and community involvement, and health information and services. Historically, women obtain less formal education than men, are less likely to be employed for pay, earn less income than men, are more likely to be exposed to violence in their homes, and have greater caregiving responsibilities for children and other family members. The Institute for Women's Policy Research concludes that there is substantial variation in women's status across states, as reflected in indicators of economic autonomy (including access to health insurance), political participation, reproductive rights, and other dimensions.[22]

The social and economic roles of women have changed dramatically throughout the twentieth century, with the most profound shifts occurring after World War II, and affecting the postwar baby boom and younger generations of women. Women's levels of education, employment, and income rose, narrowing, but not eliminating, the gender gap in social status. Marriage and fertility rates declined, affecting the pattern of women's social ties across the life span. Because these trends have not been uniform across all subgroups of the female population, however, they have provoked much debate and speculation about their effects on women's health. Today, women of lower socioeconomic status (measured by educational level or family income) and specific ethnic groups (blacks, some Hispanics, and Native Americans) have higher fertility rates, patterns of earlier childbearing, poorer birth outcomes, and worse health status compared with women of higher socioeconomic status and white or Asian women.[50] ‡

Education

In general, higher levels of education are associated with more healthful behaviors, greater use of preventive health services, and better health status. This is likely due to the effects of education on health-related knowledge, as well as on access to jobs, income, health insurance, safe housing and neighborhoods, and other health-producing resources. Education is a key indicator of socioeconomic status because it is so closely linked with these factors.

---

* Ethnic designations vary across studies. In this chapter, the terms used are consistent with the original data sources.

† While women comprise about 52 percent of the adult U.S. population, they account for 60 percent of all visits to physicians' offices, 61 percent of visits to outpatient departments in nonfederal hospitals, a majority of outpatient mental health visits, 60 percent of all discharges (including deliveries) from nonfederal short-stay hospitals, over 72 percent of nursing home residents, and 71 percent of elderly persons receiving home health-agency services.[13,15,25,30,37,41]

‡ The female population of the United States is increasingly culturally diverse. In 1996, 73 percent of the female population was white, 12 percent was non-Hispanic black, 10 percent was Hispanic, 4 percent was Asian or Pacific Islander, and 1 percent was Native American.[45] Hispanics are the fastest growing segment of the female population. The knowledge base regarding the impact of cultural diversity on the health patterns of women is limited but growing.

Women's educational attainment has increased steadily, to where it now meets or exceeds that of men; however, it still varies by ethnicity. Between 1970 and 1993, the percentage of women age 25 and over with at least 12 years of schooling increased dramatically, from 55 to 81 percent among white women, from 32 to 71 percent among black women, and from 34 to 53 percent among women of Hispanic origin.[10] In 1993, 20 percent of white women and 12 percent of black women had at least four years of college. In the 1990s, women were a majority of both full-time and part-time students enrolled in colleges and universities, and in the period 1991 to 1992, women outnumbered men among recipients of all postsecondary degrees except at the doctoral level. Men still outnumber women as recipients of many professional degrees, but women's share of first professional degrees awarded in dentistry, medicine, and law has increased substantially since the mid-1970s. In the period 1991 to 1992, women earned 32 percent of the degrees awarded in dentistry, 36 percent of those awarded in medicine, and 43 percent of those awarded in law.[10]

Paid Employment

The increase in women's labor force participation may be the most important trend in women's status in the twentieth century. (Labor force participation is defined as holding a paying job or looking for one.) Despite early concerns that this trend would produce a decline in women's health, the preponderance of evidence suggests that employment is generally beneficial to women's health due to its economic and psychosocial benefits.[18] Nevertheless, some job-related stresses—such as exposure to unsafe working conditions, workplace sexual harassment, lack of childcare, or heavy job demands combined with low levels of job control—may be associated with risks to women's health.

In 1994, U.S. women suffered 2.2 million occupational injuries, resulting in 19.5 bed days per 100 working women, compared with 28.3 bed days per 100 working men. Between 1990 and 1992, 1068 women died as a result of work-related injuries that occurred primarily in the retail trade and service industries. The leading cause of work-related death in women is homicide: in the period 1990 to 1992, 44 percent of women's work-related deaths were due to homicide, compared to 13 percent among men.[30]

Increasing female labor force participation is a long-term trend. In 1900, approximately 20 percent of women ages 20 to 64 were in the labor force. While about 30 percent of working-age women were in the labor force by 1940, accounting for 24 percent of the total U.S. labor force, the war effort raised women's expectations about participation in work outside the home. The female labor force participation rate climbed steadily from about 30 percent of working-age women in 1950 to 59 percent in 1994, when women ages 16 and over accounted for 46 percent of all U.S. workers. Labor force participation of working-age women is now remarkably similar across ethnic groups: in 1994, 59 percent of white women, 59 percent of black women, and 53 percent of women of Hispanic origin were in the labor force. Unemployment rates, however, were twice as high for black and Hispanic women as for white women.[20]

Women's occupational distribution varies by ethnicity. In 1996, 78 percent of employed white women ages 25 to 64 were in white-collar jobs (e.g., executive, managerial, professional, sales, and administrative support), compared with 68 percent of Asian or Pacific Islanders, 59 percent of non-Hispanic blacks, and 52 percent of Hispanics. The latter two groups were more likely than white and Asian women to be employed in service jobs (e.g., private household, protective services). White women were less likely than all other groups to be employed in blue-collar jobs (e.g., precision production, craft and repair, machine operations.)

Most employed women work full-time, although they remain more likely than men to work part-time. (In 1994, 28 percent of women and 11 percent of men worked part-time.) Perhaps most noteworthy, women now combine paid employment with marriage and childrearing at unprecedented rates: in 1994, over 60 percent of married women, 68 percent of women with children under age 18, and 57 percent of women with children under 3 years of age were in the labor force. One-half of married-couple families with children had working mothers; only 28 percent of married-couple families with children had a father in the labor force and a mother not in the labor force.[20]

Employed women of all ethnic groups continue to earn less than employed men at all educational levels, although the earnings gap has narrowed, especially among younger workers. In 1994, women full-time workers ages 16 and over earned 76 percent of what men earned, up from 63 percent in 1979.[20] Factors that account for the gender gap in earnings include women's concentration in low-paying jobs, their intermittent employment patterns due to childbearing and caregiving, and gender discrimination.

Another economic benefit of employment important to health is access to private health insurance. Women's employment patterns, however, ensure that they are less likely than men to have health insurance through their own employers. For example, women's greater likelihood of working part-time and their generally shorter employment tenure than men are associated with less employer-based health insurance. As a result, women under the age of 65 are less likely than men to have health insurance through their own employment, more likely to be insured as dependents on their spouse's employment-based policies, and more likely to be insured through publicly funded programs, especially Medicaid.[53]

Poverty

Despite gains in education, employment, and earnings, women are more likely than men to live in poverty. In 1993, 15 percent of women ages 18 and over lived in poverty, compared with 10 percent of men; among persons ages 65 and over, women were nearly twice as likely as men to be poor.[10] Goldin argues that the "feminization of poverty" is the result of a combination of factors, including women's earnings being lower than men's, high divorce rates, and the failure of fathers to provide child support.[16] Among women, poverty status varies by ethnicity: in 1993, 12 percent of white women ages 18 and over were poor, compared with 15 percent of Asian women, 29 percent of women of Hispanic origin, and 32 percent of black women.[10]

Even among women in the labor force for at least 27 weeks in 1993, 6 percent of white women lived in poverty, compared with 17 percent of black women and 15 percent of Hispanic women. Families maintained by women in 1993 were more likely to be poor: 26 percent of families maintained by women with children under the age of 18 were living in poverty, as compared to 16 percent of families with children maintained by men and 7 percent of married-couple families with children.[20] Among the elderly (persons ages 65 and over), 15 percent of women and 8 percent of men were poor in 1993, and men were more than twice as likely as women to be receiving income from pensions.[10]

Marriage and Parenthood

Patterns of marriage and childbearing also have been changing. Both women and men increasingly delay marriage or remain unmarried. In 1993, the median age at first marriage was 24.5 years for women and 26.5 years for men, up from 20.8 years for women and 23.2 years for men in 1970. In 1993, 19 percent of women ages 18 and over had never married (17 percent of white women, 35 percent of black women, and 23 percent of Hispanic women).[10] In American culture, childbearing is less and less associated with marital status. Births among unmarried women have been increasing: the percent of live births to unmarried women increased from about 11 percent in 1970 to 32 percent in 1996. The percent of births to unmarried mothers varies by ethnicity, with the lowest percent among mothers of Chinese or Japanese origin and the highest percent among non-Hispanic black mothers.[32]

U.S. fertility rates have been declining: between 1960 and 1996, the fertility rate declined from 118.0 to 65.3 live births per 1000 women ages 15 to 44. Fertility rates remain higher for non-white women than for white women. In 1996, the fertility rate was 64.7 live births per 1000 white women, 70.7 for black women, and 104.9 for Hispanic women. Women also have been delaying childbearing. Between 1960 and 1996, for example, the proportion of women ages 35 to 39 who had never had a live birth increased from 12 to 18.5 percent, and about 17 percent of women ages 40 to 44 in 1996 had not given birth. Birth rates to teenagers finally began to decline during the 1990s.[32]

There also is evidence that more women are choosing not to have children. According to the 1995 National Survey of Family Growth, about 18 percent of women ages 40 to 44 had no birth children and 15 percent expected none in the future.[1]

Unintended pregnancy rates, however, remain unacceptably high. According to the 1995 National Survey of Family Growth, an estimated 49 percent of pregnancies among U.S. women ages 15 to 44, and an estimated 30 percent of live births, are unintended (mistimed or unwanted at the time of conception).[1] Unintended pregnancy has been associated with risks to the woman's health, delayed initiation of prenatal care, poor birth outcomes, and an increased number of abortions.[17]

Caregiving Roles

In American culture, caring for children and other family members remains largely the responsibility of women. This normative role imbalance has been mitigated only modestly by women's increased labor force participation. Informal (unpaid) caregiving includes day-to-day care of healthy persons, as well as arranging for the health care of children and aging parents, and providing home health care to family members who are ill or disabled. The "sandwich generation" phenomenon refers to midlife adults—mainly women—caring for dependent children and aging parents simultaneously.

Over 70 percent of persons caring for disabled elderly are women,[40] and the aging population portends an increased burden on women to care for aging parents. By one estimate, the aging of the baby-boom generation will mean that in 2050, one-third of individuals between the ages of 60 and 74 will have a surviving parent.[7] Women also predominate among legal surrogates designated to make health care treatment decisions for incapacitated, terminally ill patients.[42]

The stresses associated with caregiving can have detrimental effects on women's health. The greatest caregiving burdens are thought to accrue to mothers who do not have access to adequate childcare or support from a spouse, and to midlife or older women who are caring for aging parents, sometimes concurrently with caring for their own children. In the 1993 Commonwealth Fund Survey of Women's Health, for example, married women ages 65 and younger whose husbands were involved in housework and childcare reported fewer depressive symptoms and higher self-esteem than women whose husbands did not share these responsibilities.[24] Among women caregivers of elderly parents, depressive symptoms and social withdrawal are among the most common problems.[7]

Women's Health Across the Life Span

An awareness of women's health across their life span—from childhood through adulthood—is needed to provide appropriate health services to women in all age groups and to develop approaches for preventing or delaying the onset of diseases and disabilities in older age groups. For example, healthy behaviors (such as regular exercise, adequate nutrition, and smoking cessation) and comprehensive clinical screening services at earlier ages can reduce the burden of chronic diseases and disability at later ages. The life span perspective also helps place reproductive health care in the context of women's overall health.

Unfortunately, health statistics are not reported consistently by gender and age groups, making summaries of health issues across the life span difficult. In addition, women in the same age group differ widely in their life circumstances due to many factors including variations in socioeconomic status and ethnicity. The following overview highlights some key women's health issues for four life stages: adolescence and early adulthood (ages 15 to 24), young adulthood (ages 25 to 44), middle adulthood (ages 45 to 64), and later adulthood (ages 65 and over).*

Adolescence and Early Adulthood

In adolescence and early adulthood, the leading causes of death in U.S. women are not disease-related. Deaths from unintentional injuries, mostly motor vehicle crashes, are the leading cause of mortality for women ages 15 to 24, followed by homicide and suicide (Table 1-1). Among young black women in this age group, homicide was the leading cause of death in 1993, and firearm-related injuries ranked higher than motor vehicle crashes as a cause of death.[30] This overall mortality pattern for women ages 15 to 24 suggests the importance of risk-taking behaviors (including substance abuse), exposure to violent situations, and mental health problems for the health of young women.

Nearly one-half of motor vehicle-related deaths, suicides, and homicides involve alcohol consumption, and use of alcohol and illicit drugs typically begins in adolescence or early adulthood.[21] According to the 1996 National House-

TABLE 1-1 Leading Causes of Death in U.S. Women Ages 15 to 24, by Race, in 1993 (Deaths per 100,000 resident population)

	White	Black	Hispanic
Unintentional injuries:			
Motor vehicle crashes	17.1	10.6	10.5
Firearm-related injuries	5.2	18.3	7.8
Homicide	4.2	22.0	7.8
Suicide	4.3	2.7	2.9
HIV/AIDS	0.5	4.7	—

SOURCE: National Center for Health Statistics (1996).

hold Survey on Drug Abuse, 21 percent of women ages 18 to 25 reported heavy alcohol use (5 or more drinks on one occasion at least once in the last month), 9 percent reported use of marijuana, and 1.4 percent reported use of cocaine.[32] Tobacco use also begins early in life: in 1995, 22 percent of women ages 18 to 24 were current smokers.[32]

Younger women also have greater exposure to violence, including sexual violence, than older women. Women ages 20 to 24 have the highest incidence of rape.[21] According to the 1995 National Survey of Family Growth, 20 percent of women ages 15 to 44 reported that they had been forced to have sexual intercourse at least once in their lifetimes, and among women whose first intercourse occurred under age 15, 22 percent reported that the intercourse was not voluntary.[1] Major depression, posttraumatic stress disorder, and alcohol and substance abuse are more common among women who have experienced sexual assault.[15]

Adolescence and early adulthood are times of intense social pressure on young women to adopt normative sexual roles and to initiate sexual activity. As a result, this is a period of high risk for unintended pregnancy and sexually transmitted diseases (STDs), both of which may have long-term impacts on women's health and well-being. According to the 1995 National Survey of Family Growth,[1] the average age at first intercourse was

---

* In standard practice, the term "reproductive years" refers to ages 15 to 44 years or 18 to 44 years, depending on whether adolescents are included. This term is misleading because these age ranges do not coincide with the typical ages of onset and termination of fertility in U.S. women, and because approximately 15 percent of U.S. women do not bear children in their lifetimes.[30]

17.8, and about 50 percent of women ages 15 to 19 had never had sexual intercourse. Unintended births (that is, births that were mistimed or unwanted at conception) were more prevalent among women under the age of 25 (65 percent of live births among women age 20 or under and 38 percent among women ages 20 to 24) than among those age 25 and over (about 20 percent of live births). Women with unintended pregnancies receive later and less adequate prenatal care, are more likely to smoke or consume alcohol during pregnancy, and may be at higher risk for depression during and after pregnancy and for domestic violence during pregnancy.[8] Unintended pregnancy also contributes to abortion rates, and the majority of women who have abortions are under the age of 25.[21]

Of the approximately 13 million annual cases of STDs in the United States, other than human immunodeficiency virus (HIV) infection, about 86 percent occur in persons ages 15 to 29.[21] The most prevalent STD in women is chlamydia. STDs are transmitted more readily from men to women than from women to men and often are asymptomatic in women, which may lead to delays in treatment. The health consequences of STDs for women are serious, because STDs may lead to reproductive cancers, pelvic inflammatory disease, infertility, ectopic pregnancy, and perinatal mortality and morbidity. While improving routine STD screening of women often is emphasized, primary prevention approaches, including health education, use of barrier methods of contraception, and empowerment of women to negotiate the conditions of sexual relationships and to control their sexuality, also are needed.

Emerging understandings of female adolescence and early adulthood in American culture frequently portray this as a period of intense psychosocial pressures in which young women's body image, sexual identity, self-esteem, and sense of self in relation to others are key developmental issues. Depression is more common in young women than in young men, and is associated with suicide among adolescents.[28] Eating disorders (anorexia and bulimia nervosa) are relatively rare, but are more common in women than in men and typically appear during adolescence or early adulthood. Although these conditions are not well understood, they have been associated with low self-esteem, distorted body image, psychological stress, and preoccupation with physical fitness, athletic performance, or training in dance.[21]

The nutritional and exercise habits established in childhood and adolescence can have important consequences for subsequent health status, including the development of osteoporosis later in life. Overweight adults (measured by the body mass index) also are at increased risk for hypertension, heart disease, and diabetes. For women ages 20 and over, the prevalence of being overweight and having a sedentary lifestyle (i.e., no self-reported leisure-time physical activity in the past 2 weeks) is inversely associated with socioeconomic status.[32]

Young Adulthood

In young adult women, ages 25 to 44, the leading overall causes of death in 1993 included cancer, unintentional injuries (62 percent from motor vehicle crashes), heart disease, HIV infection, and homicide.[30] Differences by race/ethnicity are apparent for several causes of death among 25- to 44-year-olds: the cancer death rate for black women (39.3 per 100,000 population) was 47 percent higher than for white women; HIV infection was the leading cause of death among black women in this age group; and the homicide death rate was nearly five times as great among black women as among white women.[30] Most homicide deaths are caused by firearms.

HIV/AIDS is a growing concern in this age group. Forty-five percent of all AIDS cases in women in 1996 were diagnosed among those ages 30 to 39. Seventy-eight percent of AIDS cases reported in women in 1996 were among nonwhites, mostly African-Americans.[32] Most women contract HIV through heterosexual contact rather than through injecting drugs.[21]

Concerns related to childbearing and impaired fertility also are prominent in this age group. Because of a trend toward later childbearing among U.S. women, more women now have their first babies after age 25. In 1996, 65 percent of women ages 20 to 24 had never given birth, compared with 44 percent of women ages 25 to 29 and 26 percent of women ages 30 to 34.[32] Pregnancy complications are more common among women ages 35 and over, compared with women under the age of 35, and maternal mortality rates are highest among women ages 35 and over, and are higher in non-white women than in white women. In 1996, the maternal mortality rate in women ages 35 and over was 14.9 deaths per 100,000 live births in white women and 49.9 per 100,000 live births in black women.[32]

Due to delayed childbearing among other factors, women in the later stage of early adulthood are most likely to experience impaired fertility. According to the 1995 National Survey of Family Growth, about 12 percent of women ages 25 to 44 had impaired fecundity; among women ages 35 to 44 with no children, 26 percent had impaired fecundity and 21 percent had used infertility services of some type. Among married women ages 35 to 44 with no children, 30 percent were infertile (i.e., had not used contraception and had not become pregnant in 12 months or more).[1]

Recent research on depression in women sheds light on some of the dynamics of the condition in this age group and around reproductive events. Major depression occurs most frequently in women ages 25 to 44, but studies suggest that the age of onset increasingly occurs in the adolescent and early adult years.[15,21] Women are at increased risk of depression during pregnancy and following childbirth. About 10 percent of pregnant women have major depression, which is often associated with marital problems, unwanted pregnancy, or a history of depression; postpartum major depression occurs in 10 to 15 percent of new mothers and is thought to be associated with psychosocial stressors and previous psychiatric history.[49]

Middle Adulthood

The health concerns of women in middle adulthood (ages 45 to 64) are generating growing interest because the first baby boomers turned age 45 in 1991 and began the transition to menopause. The cumulative effects of the life experiences of this cohort and of their earlier investments in health (including prevention) and risk behaviors (such as smoking) will have important consequences for the pattern of chronic conditions and disabilities in this life stage and beyond.

For women in middle adulthood, chronic diseases are the major causes of death and disability. The two leading causes of death in 1993 were cancer and heart disease, which accounted for 65 percent of all deaths in women in this age group.[30] Death rates for both of these causes were higher in black women than in white women. Among cancer causes of death, breast cancer is predominant before age 55, with lung cancer surpassing it among 55- to 64-year-olds.[33] Other leading causes of death for women in this age group are cerebrovascular disease, chronic obstructive pulmonary disease (COPD), and diabetes mellitus.

In the 1993 Commonwealth Fund Survey of Women's Health, the most frequent health problems reported by midlife women (defined as ages 40 to 64) were arthritis (31 percent), high blood pressure (25 percent), anxiety or depression (17 percent), urinary tract infections (18 percent), and urinary incontinence (10 percent). Cancer and heart disease were each reported by 9 percent of women in this age group.[52] In addition, it is estimated that approximately half of all women ages 50 and over have osteopenia of the hip and 20 percent have osteoporosis of the hip; the percentage of women with osteoporosis increases with each decade of life after age 50.[30]

The 1994 National Health Interview Survey shows that it is in midlife (ages 45 to 64) when the impact of chronic disease on women's functioning increases substantially. Twenty-four percent of women in this age group reported some activity limitation due to chronic conditions, and

17 percent reported limitations in their major usual activity; these figures compare with 10 and 7 percent, respectively, among women ages 18 to 44. On average, women ages 45 to 64 reported 23.8 days per year of restricted activity due to acute and chronic conditions, compared with 15.7 days for women ages 25 to 44. Nearly 18 percent of women ages 45 to 64 reported that their health status was only fair or poor, more than double the percent among women ages 25 to 44.[2]

The average age of menopause in U.S. women is approximately 51, and the length of the peri-menopausal transition has been estimated at nearly 4 years.[29] For many women, the perimeno-pause is a period in which either symptoms of menopause or concerns about preventing post-menopausal bone loss or heart disease bring them into contact with health care providers and to use hormonal or nonhormonal therapies. In the 1993 Commonwealth Fund Survey of Wom-en's Health, 24 percent of women ages 40 to 64 reported using hormone replacement therapy (HRT) at the time of survey, and current use was associated with higher education and in-come, being white, having private health insur-ance, and using preventive health services.[52] Less is known about long-term use of HRT and its correlates. One study estimates that 20 percent of U.S. women who experienced menopause be-tween 1970 and 1992 used HRT for at least 5 years, whereas 25 percent used HRT for at least one month but less than 5 years; higher education and being white were associated with increased duration of HRT use.[6]

Later Adulthood

The first members of the baby boom generation (born between 1946 and 1964) will reach age 65 in 2011, and the percentage of the U.S. female population ages 65 and over will increase from about 15 percent in 1995 to nearly 22 percent by 2030. The number of women over age 65 in the population will nearly double in the same time period. These trends mean that the health con-cerns of older women, including their chronic conditions and disabilities, will be more prevalent and will demand increased attention from health care providers.

The women who will swell the ranks of older Americans, however, are baby boomers who dif-fer demographically from earlier generations of women. In addition to being proactive health care consumers, they are better educated, spent more time in the paid labor force, earned more income, married later, divorced more often, had their children later, and had fewer children than previous generations.[52] Because higher levels of education and paid employment are known to be associated with better health status among women, the baby boom generation could trans-form the health profile of older American women in ways that cannot yet be anticipated. On the other hand, the tendency of women to outlive their husbands, to have fewer financial resources than men, and to live alone in older age could mitigate these effects.

For older adult women, ages 65 and over, the leading causes of death are cancer and heart dis-case.* In 1993, cancer was the leading cause among women ages 65 to 74, and heart disease was the leading cause among women ages 75 and over.[30] Among cancer causes of death, lung cancer is the leading cause up to age 84, when both breast cancer and colorectal cancer sur-pass it.[33]

Leading chronic conditions among women ages 65 and over are arthritis, high blood pres-sure, and heart disease (see Table 1-2). In the 1993 Commonwealth Fund Survey of Women's Health, the major chronic conditions reported by women ages 65 and over included arthritis and hypertension (each reported by about 50 percent of women), followed by heart disease, depression or anxiety, cancer, emphysema and asthma, hip fractures, and stroke. Thirteen percent reported

---

* Increasing life expectancy and research on the oldest old (those ages 85 and older) are providing new information about women's health and psychosocial attributes in later adulthood. At present, however, many health statistics are reported for the "65 and over" age category only.

TABLE 1-2 Leading Chronic Conditions in U.S. Women, by Age, in 1994 (Conditions per 1000 persons)

Under Age 45	Ages 45–64	Ages 65 and Over
Chronic sinusitis (135.5)	Arthritis (297.0)	Arthritis (553.5)
Hay fever or allergic rhinitis (99.2)	High blood pressure (224.5)	High blood pressure (395.8)
Deformity or orthopedic impairment of the back (71.5)	Chronic sinusitis (210.2)	Heart disease (299.4)
Migraine headaches (67.1)	Heart disease (111.0)	Hearing impairment (238.0)
Asthma (60.0)	Hay fever or allergic rhinitis (133.4)	Cataracts (192.4)

SOURCE: 1994 National Health Interview Survey (Adams and Marano, 1995).

being told by their physician that they had osteoporosis. The co-occurrence of chronic diseases was not uncommon: 18 percent of women ages 65 to 85 reported no chronic conditions, 31 percent had one chronic condition, 27 percent had two, and 24 percent had three or more.[14]

Twenty-eight percent of women ages 65 to 85 in the 1993 Commonwealth Fund Survey reported that disability, handicap, or chronic disease limited their participation in usual activities, and the amount of impairment, as reflected in measures of needing help with the activities of daily living or instrumental activities of daily living as well as inability to participate fully in usual work activities, increased with the number of chronic conditions reported.[14] In the 1994 National Health Interview Survey, the average number of days per year of restricted activity due to acute and chronic conditions was 37.2 among women ages 65 and over, compared with 30.9 among men.[1] Overall, about one in four women ages 65 to 74 and nearly one in three ages 75 and over rate their health as "fair" or "poor."[32]

Comorbidities may produce mental health problems in older women, but also complicate the diagnosis of these problems. While the prevalence of depression among older women is not known, estimates range up to 50 to 60 percent for mild depression and 1 to 3 percent for severe depression.[21] Loss of a spouse or of physical health, as well as caregiver burden, are key risk factors for depression in this age group. The incidence of dementing disorders, including Alzheimer's disease, increases with age, and these conditions are a major cause of disability in the elderly, and diminish the capacity of women to live independently at older ages.[21]

The Changing Health Care System

At the same time that awareness of women's health issues across their life span is growing, changes in the U.S. health care system are affecting how women's primary health care is delivered. While new perspectives on women's health suggest the need to integrate services across organ systems and life stages, trends in health care delivery do not necessarily facilitate this objective. Key trends include the restructuring of both public and private health insurance; threats to the survival of the health care safety net; the growth and increasing diversity of managed care plans; and quality assessment initiatives in women's health.

Health Insurance

Health insurance is a major factor affecting women's access to and use of health care services. Currently, the United States remains one of the few developed nations to lack universal health insurance, and women's ability to obtain health insurance depends upon their employment status, marital status, age, and income level. Health insurance trends affecting women include the decline in employer-based health insurance and in dependent coverage, private health insurance reform, and, because women are more dependent than men on public health insurance programs, the restructuring of Medicaid and Medicare.

Approximately 62 percent of women ages 18 to 64 in 1993 had employer-based health insurance, but about 39 percent of these women were dependents on the policy of a family member, primarily the spouse. About 10 percent of women had privately purchased insurance, 12 percent had public insurance (primarily Medicaid), and 16 percent were uninsured. Low-income and non-white women were more likely than others to be publicly insured or uninsured.[53] Despite the expansions of Medicaid coverage for pregnant women between 1988 and 1994 and Medicaid's coverage of about 40 percent of all U.S. births, an estimated one-third of poor and near-poor women were uninsured in the period 1990 to 1992. During the same period, nearly 28 percent of women enrolled in Medicaid lost eligiblity, and almost two-thirds of these women became uninsured.[38] Among persons ages 65 and over, women are nearly twice as likely as men (10.4 versus 5.5 percent) to supplement Medicare with Medicaid or other public assistance.[30]

Among insured women, the structure of benefits affects access to and use of care. One study of women ages 15 to 44 found that as a consequence of inadequate insurance coverage of reproductive and preventive services, women's out-of-pocket expenses for health care are 68 percent higher than those for men in the same age group. For example, women pay 56 percent of the cost of contraceptives out-of-pocket,[51] and in 1993, most large indemnity health plans with prescription benefits did not cover contraceptives.[3] A study of the Medicare benefit structure found that coverage is less adequate for chronic diseases that are more prevalent in older women than for those that are more prevalent in older men.[39]

Continued access problems associated with women's ability to obtain health insurance and with inadequate benefits for women's services present major challenges.

Safety Net Services

The health care safety net for women consists of organizations with a legal obligation or commitment to provide basic services to the uninsured or underinsured. Demand on these organizations is likely to grow as the number of uninsured women increases due to erosion of employer-based health insurance and to reduced access to Medicaid as a result of welfare reform.*

In addition to public hospitals, academic medical centers, community-based health clinics, adolescent health clinics, migrant worker programs, and programs of public health departments, several types of publicly funded programs provide some basic women's health services. These include Title X family planning clinics, Title V maternal and child health programs, Title XV breast and cervical cancer screening programs, and feminist community-based women's health centers. Many women rely on these organizations for specific reproductive health services or for routine care at some point in their lives. According to the 1995 National Survey of Family Growth, for example, 26 percent of women ages 15 to 24 reported having used a family planning clinic for their first contraception-related visit.[1]

Safety net providers, however, currently confront financial difficulties. Cutbacks in programs such as Title X funding for family planning programs reduce major sources of revenue for these providers. In addition, increased competition from Medicaid managed care organizations reduces safety net providers' revenues from Medicaid reimbursements and their ability to cross-

* The Personal Responsibility and Work Opportunity Reconciliation Act of 1996 severed the automatic link between welfare and Medicaid eligibility. As a result of this legislation, there is likely to be variation across states in how Medicaid eligibility is defined and in how enrollment procedures are administered, with the prospect of some needy women and children, including legal immigrants, not receiving Medicaid benefits.[34]

subsidize care. Together, these trends jeopardize safety net providers' capacity to continue to serve the uninsured unless they can develop new sources of revenue or negotiate contracts with managed care organizations. While the integration of safety net services into mainstream organizations may improve the quality and comprehensiveness of care for women in the long-run, the financial failure of the safety net could, in the short-run, leave many uninsured, underinsured, adolescent, and minority women medically "homeless."

Managed Care

The rapid growth and increasing diversity of managed care plans is transforming women's health care, although there has been little research comparing types of managed care arrangements in terms of their impact on women's health. By 1997, over 160 million persons were enrolled in some form of managed care, including health maintenance organizations (HMOs), preferred provider organizations (PPOs), and point-of-service plans.[19] Additionally, more than 40 percent of Medicaid recipients and 10 percent of Medicare beneficiaries were in managed care plans.[36] Older forms of managed care, represented by staff and group-model HMOs operating their own facilities, were being replaced by more loosely structured types of plans that operate as organizations without walls. In theory, managed care held great promise for women's health care, not only because of reduced out-of-pocket costs to women, but also because of its emphasis on coordination of services and preventive care.

Historically, women's primary health care has been highly fragmented, particularly because of the tendency for reproductive health services, including routine and preventive services, to be provided separately from other components of health care.[9] As a consequence, many women used more than one source of basic care, often concurrently, and did not have access to primary care that was comprehensive, coordinated, and

based on a sustained partnership between provider and patient. The fragmentation of basic health care for women helps explain the recent popularity of primary care women's health centers that provide basic reproductive and nonreproductive services in a "one-stop shopping" format:[48] * Managed care plans that similarly coordinate primary care for women hold the promise of comprehensive care delivered more efficiently, with reduced redundancies and gaps in services and reduced burdens for women.

Managed care also may pose risks to women's health, including possible reduced access to specialists (including specialist and subspecialist obstetrician-gynecologists and mental health providers), incentives to underserve for chronic conditions affecting women, reduced time during visits for provider-patient communication and counseling (which women appear to value more than men), and discontinuities in care associated with voluntary or involuntary plan switching. In addition, some managed care plans serving Medicaid enrollees may be unprepared for the special needs of low-income women. Concerns have been raised, for example, about plans' capabilities to provide care for chronic conditions, disabilities, mental illness, and substance abuse in the low-income population, and to provide links to needed social services.[36]

Managed care plans vary widely in structure and in performance, as reflected in the Health Plan Employer Data and Information Set

---

* According to the National Survey of Women's Health Centers (defined as organizations providing clinical services designed for and marketed to women), there were an estimated 3,600 women's health centers in the United States in 1993, serving 14.5 million women. These included both hospital-sponsored and nonhospital centers of various types: reproductive health centers, primary care centers, birth or childbearing centers, breast care centers, and various other specialty centers. Primary care centers were 12 percent of all centers and included a mix of hospital-sponsored centers, community-based not-for-profit centers, and for-profit centers owned by physician groups, nurse groups, and others. Primary care centers often feature a multidisciplinary "one-stop shopping" model and the availability of women providers.[47]

(HEDIS) developed by the National Committee for Quality Assurance (NCQA). For example, in 1997, the proportion of enrolled women ages 21 to 64 who had received one or more Pap tests in the last 3 years ranged from 24 to 100 percent across plans, with a mean of 70 percent.[43] Research is needed to determine what accounts for this variation and the extent to which the structure or management of plans (as opposed to patient characteristics or other factors) are responsible for these rates.

Comparing types of managed care plans in their treatment of women presents important challenges because of the need for case-mix adjustments and because multiple dimensions of plans are likely to impact service delivery and patient satisfaction levels. These include plans' benefits structures, rules for accessing care (including the use of "gatekeepers," and procedures for referrals to specialists and out-of-plan services), methods of provider payment and evaluation, and the nature of contractual arrangements.[26] A major challenge for research is identifying the characteristics of plans associated with high-quality care for women.

Quality Assessment in Women's Health

The growth of managed care has stimulated efforts to define quality and develop measures that can be used for quality assessment and improvement. Another stimulus is the growing number of women in clinical trials and the need for appropriate outcome measures (e.g., patient satisfaction and quality of life) for women. No consensus currently exists on a definition of quality in women's health care, and measurement of process and outcomes of care relevant to women is not well developed. A number of initiatives to improve quality measurement in women's health care are underway.

The Women's Health Measurement Advisory Panel was convened by the NCQA in 1997 to recommend measures for development for HEDIS. The panel prioritized conditions affect-

ing women, searched the literature for measures associated with these conditions that might be adapted for HEDIS, explored gender differences in satisfaction with care in the patient survey component of HEDIS, and facilitated development of several new measures. The latter included a patient-reported measure of the adequacy of counseling about options for the management of hormonal changes associated with menopause and about measures for preventing unintended pregnancy. Already in the set of measures being tested for possible inclusion in HEDIS were measures of screening for chlamydia, timely follow-up after abnormal Pap smears and mammograms, and risk-adjusted low birth-weight rates.

In addition, the HEDIS Membership Satisfaction Survey is being combined with items developed by the Consumer Assessments of Health Plans (CAHPS) project. This project developed instruments that measure consumers' experiences and satisfaction with health plans across a range of delivery system models and populations. The combined instrument, which will be included in HEDIS in 1999, may provide opportunities to identify gender differences in how health care is experienced and evaluated.[27]

The Foundation for Accountability (FACCT), an alliance of corporate and government purchasers, consumer organizations, providers, researchers, delivery systems, and managers, develops measures of quality that emphasize consumers' experiences with health care. Among the clinical areas in which measures are being developed is breast cancer.

Finally, a number of organizations have compiled indicators of women's health status and health care use at the state level for purposes of identifying variation across states and monitoring trends. These include the Jacobs Institute of Women's Health's *State Profiles in Women's Health* (1998), the Women's Research and Education Institute's project on the health of midlife women,[11] and the Institute for Women's Policy Research.[22]

Opportunities for Improving Women's Health

Few today would argue that health care alone produces healthy women, or that all of women's health concerns can be resolved through the health care delivery system. Status inequalities between women and men and the diverse socio-economic circumstances of women's lives expose them to health risks—such as inadequate health information, domestic violence, nonconsensual sexual encounters, and the stresses associated with caregiving roles—that will require social policy as well as medical remedies. Women's health advocacy addresses both the need for improved health information and services and the need to protect women from unsafe or over-used services.

Nevertheless, women's access to quality health care is a key determinant of their health as well as a timely social issue. With the growth of managed care, the role of the primary care provider has assumed particular significance as the coordinator of women's health care. Primary health care providers can contribute to improving the standard of health for women in a number of ways, including ensuring that health care providers are adequately trained, during basic and continuing education, to deliver comprehensive primary care to women; supporting the development of women-centered delivery models that integrate the full range of services women need to maintain or improve their health across their life span; educating patients and the public about health-promoting behaviors and appropriate use of health services; and participating with consumers, purchasers, researchers, and policymakers in quality initiatives in women's health care.

Physicians who assume the role of primary care provider for women, whatever their specialty, have a responsibility to ensure that their patients receive comprehensive, high quality clinical care and that patients are linked to the information and nonmedical services needed to maintain or improve their health. Women tend to be highly motivated, information-seeking consumers, but they rely on their physicians to be informed about their health problems, to interpret the results of research for them, to advise them on appropriate use of health services, and to treat them with respect and sensitivity. With this in mind, primary care physicians could view each encounter as an opportunity not only to provide clinical services, but to review women's social and life circumstances, to learn about women's barriers to obtaining health care, to screen for problems that women might have difficulty raising (e.g., alcohol use, domestic violence, depressive symptoms, urinary incontinence), to provide guidance on healthy lifestyle and self-care, and to discuss preventive strategies that anticipate potential health problems in the next life stage.

Primary care physicians cannot do it alone. Team approaches to women's health care that incorporate the services of nurses, psychologists, social workers, peer counselors, and others—as well as written material and other information sources for patients—are helpful in fulfilling these objectives. Above all, engaging women as partners in their health care is essential for producing healthy women.

References and Selected Readings

1. Abma JC, et al: Fertility, Family Planning, and Women's Health: New Data from the 1995 National Survey of Family Growth. *Vital and Health Statistics,* Hyattsville, MD: National Center for Health Statistics, 1997, Series 23, No. 19.
2. Adams PF, Marano MA: Current Estimates from the National Health Interview Survey, 1994. *Vital and Health Statistics,* National Center for Health Statistics, 1995, Series 10, No. 193.
3. Alan Guttmacher Institute: *Uneven and Unequal: Insurance Coverage and Reproductive Health Services,* New York: Alan Guttmacher Institute, 1994.
4. American Medical Association: *Physician Characteristics and Distribution in the US: 1997–1998 ed,* Chicago: 1997, American Medical Association.
5. American Psychological Association: *Research Agenda for Psychosocial and Behavioral Factors in Women's Health.* Washington, DC: American Psychological Association, 1996.
6. Brett KM, Madans JH: Use of postmenopausal hormone replacement therapy: Estimates from a nation-

ally representative cohort study. *Am J Epidemiol* 145:536–545, 1997.

7. Brody EM: Women as Unpaid Caregivers: The Price They Pay, Chap. 5 in Friedman E (ed): *An Unfinished Revolution: Women and Health Care in America.* New York: United Hospital Fund, 1994.

8. Brown SS, Eisenberg L (eds): *The Best Intentions: Unintended Pregnancy and the Well-Being of Children and Families.* Washington, DC: National Academy Press, 1995.

9. Clancy CM, Massion CT: American women's health care: A patchwork quilt with gaps. *J Am Med A* 268:1918–1920, 1993.

10. Costello C, Kivimae Krimgold B: *The American Woman 1996–1997 Where We Stand: Women and Work,* New York: WW Norton, 1996.

11. Costello CB, Griffith JE, Wilbon A, Redfearn A: *The Health of Mid-Life Women in the States.* Washington, DC: Women's Research and Education Institute, 1998.

12. Cott NF: *Root of Bitterness: Documents of the Social History of American Women,* Boston: Northeastern University Press, 1986.

13. Dey AN: Characteristics of Elderly Home Health Care Users: Data from the 1993 National Home and Hospice Care Survey. *Advance Data From Vital and Health Statistics,* Hyattsville, MD: National Center for Health Statistics, 1996, No. 272.

14. Fried LP: Older Women: Health Status, Knowledge, and Behavior. in Falik MM, Collins KS, (eds): *Women's Health: The Commonwealth Fund Survey,* Baltimore: Johns Hopkins University Press, pp 175–204, 1996.

15. Glied S, Kofman S: Women and Mental Health: Issues for Health Reform. New York: The Commonwealth Fund Commission on Women's Health, 1995.

16. Goldin C: *Understanding the Gender Gap: An Economic History of American Women,* New York: Oxford University Press, 1990.

17. Gonen J: Managed Care and Unintended Pregnancy: Testing the Limits of Prevention, *Insights* Washington, DC: Jacobs Institute of Women's Health, 1997, No. 3.

18. Hartmann HI, Kuriansky JA, Owens CL: Employment and Women's Health, in Falik MM, Collins KS, (eds), *Women's Health: The Commonwealth Fund Survey,* Baltimore: Johns Hopkins University Press, pp 296–323, 1996.

19. Health Insurance Association of America: *Source Book of Health Insurance Data.* Washington, DC: Health Insurance Association of America, 1998.

20. Herz DE, Wootton BH: Women in the Workforce: An Overview, in Costello C, Kivimae Krimgold B (eds): pp 44–78, *The American Woman 1996–97,*

Where We Stand: Women and Work, New York: WW Norton, 1996.

21. Horton JA: *The Women's Health Data Book, 2nd ed,* Washington, DC: Jacobs Institute of Women's Health, 1995.

22. Institute for Women's Policy Research: *The Status of Women in the States,* Washington, DC: IWPR, 1996.

23. Legato MJ: Research on the Biology of Women Will Improve Health Care for Men, Too, *Chronicle of Higher Education,* 1998, May 15:B4–B5.

24. Lennon MC: Depression and Self-esteem among Women, Chap. 8 in Falik MM, Collins KS, (eds): *Women's Health: The Commonwealth Fund Survey,* Baltimore, MD: Johns Hopkins University Press, 1996.

25. Lipkind KL: National Hospital Ambulatory Medical Care Survey: 1993 Outpatient Department Summary. *Advance Data from Vital and Health Statistics,* Hyattsville, MD: National Center for Health Statistics; 1996. No. 276.

26. McGlynn EA: The effect of managed care on primary care services for women *Women's Health Issues* 8:1–14, 1998.

27. McGlynn EA: Quality of Care for Women: Where are We Now and Where are We Headed? Paper presented at the Jacobs Institute of Women's Health Symposium on Quality in Women's Health: Taking the Measure of Managed Care; July 23, 1998; Washington, DC.

28. McGrath E, Puryear Keita G, Strickland BR, Felipe Russo N: *Women and Depression: Risk Factors and Treatment Issues,* Washington, DC: American Psychological Association, 1990.

29. McKinlay SM, Brambilla DJ, Posner JG: The normal menopause transition, *Maturitas* 14:103–115, 1992.

30. National Center for Health Statistics: *Health United States, 1995.* Hyattsville, MD: US Department of Health and Human Services, 1996.

31. National Center for Health Statistics: *Healthy People 2000 Review 1997.* Hyattsville, MD: Public Health Service, 1997.

32. National Center for Health Statistics: *Health United States, 1998 with Socioeconomic Status and Health Chartbook,* Hyattsville, MD: US Department of Health and Human Services, 1998.

33. Ries LAG, Kosary CL, Hankey BF, et al: (eds): *SEER Cancer Statistics Review, 1973–1994,* Bethesda, MD: National Cancer Institute. National Institutes of Health; 1997. Pub. No. 97–2789.

34. Rosenbaum S, Darnell J: An Analysis of the Medicaid and Health-Related Provisions of the Personal Responsibility and Work Opportunity Reconciliation Act of 1996 (P.L. 104–193). Washington, DC: Kaiser Commission on the Future of Medicaid; 1997.

35. Ruzek SB: *The Women's Health Movement: Feminist*

Alternatives to Medical Control. New York: Praeger, 1978.

36. Salganicoff A: Medicaid and managed care: Implications for low-income women. *J A M Women's A* 52:78–80, 1997.

37. Schappert SM: National Ambulatory Medical Care Survey: 1994 Summary. *Advance Data from Vital and Health Statistics.* Hyattsville, MD: National Center for Health Statistics; 1996. No. 273.

38. Short PF: Medicaid's Role in Insuring Low-Income Women. New York: Commonwealth Fund, 1996.

39. Sofaer S, Abel E: Older women's health and financial vulnerability: Implications of the Medicare benefit structure. *Women and Health.* 16:47–67, 1990.

40. Stone R, Cafferata GL, Sangle J: Caregivers of the frail elderly: A national profile. *Gerontologist* 27:616–626, 1987.

41. Strahan GW: An Overview of Nursing Homes and Their Current Residents: Data from the 1995 National Nursing Home Survey. *Advance Data from Vital and Health Statistics,* Hyattsville, MD: National Center for Health Statistics; 1997. No. 280.

42. Sulmasy DP, Terry PB, Weisman CS, et al: The accuracy of substituted judgments in patients with terminal diagnoses. *Ann Intern Med* 128:621–629, 1998.

43. Thompson JW, Bost J, Ahmed F, et al: The NCQA's quality compass: Evaluating managed care in the United States. *Health Aff* 17:152–158, 1998.

44. U.S. Bureau of the Census: *Statistical Abstract of the United States; 1995.* Washington, DC: US Government Printing Office, 1995.

45. US Bureau of the Census: Population Projections of the United States by Age, Sex, Race, and Hispanic Origin, 1995–2050. Washington, DC: Bureau of the Census; 1996.

46. Weisman CS: Changing definitions of women's health: Implications for health care and policy. *Matern Child Health J* 1:179–189, 1997.

47. Weisman CS: *Women's Health Care: Activist Traditions and Institutional Change,* Baltimore: Johns Hopkins University Press, 1998.

48. Weisman CS, Curbow B, Khoury AJ: The National Survey of Women's Health Centers: Current models of women-centered care. *Women's Health Issues* 5:103–117, 1995.

49. Weissman MM, Olfson M: Depression in women: Implications for health care research. *Science* 269:799–801, 1995.

50. Wingard DL: Patterns and Puzzles: The Distribution of Health and Illness Among Women in the United States. Chap. 2 in Burt Ruzek S, Olesen VL, Clarke AE (eds), *Women's Health: Complexities and Differences,* Columbus: Ohio State University Press, 1997.

51. Women's Research and Education Institute: *Women's Health Insurance Costs and Experiences.* Washington, DC: Women's Research and Education Institute, 1994.

52. Woods NF: Midlife Women: Health Care Patterns and Choices, in Falik MM, Collins KS, (eds): *Women's Health: The Commonwealth Fund Survey.* Baltimore: Johns Hopkins University Press, pp 145–174, 1996.

53. Wyn R, Brown ER: Women's Health: Key Issues in Access to Insurance Coverage and to Services Among Non-Elderly Women. Chap. 11 in Andersen RM, Rice TH, Kominski GF, (eds): *Changing the US Health Care System: Key Issues in Health Services, Policy, and Management.* San Francisco: Jossey-Bass, 1996.

Part II

Prevention

CHAPTER 2

Prevention

Vicki L. Seltzer

In the distant past, doctors saw only ill patients and utilized whatever modalities were available to assist them. During the past several years it has become increasingly clear, however, that physicians can do an enormous amount for their patients by utilizing preventive strategies and helping patients modify high-risk behaviors.

It has been estimated that one-half of premature deaths, one-third of acute disabilities, and one-half of chronic disabilities are preventable. The health care team can play a leading role in reducing morbidity and mortality by identifying current or potential high-risk behaviors and emphasizing the importance of healthy life styles to their patients.

Patient safety is one example of an area in which the health care team can have an important impact. Motor vehicle accidents are the leading cause of death for women ages 13 to 39 years, and they contribute substantially to morbidity and mortality in all age groups. By simply reminding each patient of the importance of seat belt use for themselves, their passengers, and their families at each visit, and by emphasizing the risks of drinking and driving, the health care team can reduce the likelihood of fatalities.

While auto safety is an important preventive issue for most of the women we see, other safety measures that should be addressed may be more age-specific or season-specific. For instance, during winter, warnings about falls on the ice can be emphasized; in the summer, risks of excess sun exposure and skin cancer should be stressed. For those patients who bicycle, the health care team should encourage bicycle helmet use.

Another important preventive strategy relates to patients' behavior and habits. Cigarette smoking contributes substantially to morbidity and mortality. The health care team should be committed to working with women in individual or group programs for smoking cessation, and in counseling adolescents about the risks of smoking before they initiate this habit. Alcohol and drug use are also major contributors to morbidity and mortality. Physicians must be alert to signs of substance use and abuse, must ask direct questions, and must be willing and able to counsel their patients, or to refer them when appropriate. Alcohol and drug use are serious and common problems for women in the United States, and physicians can play a role in reducing women's risk.

Exercise and diet are other areas that physicians should discuss with their patients. Proper dietary and exercise habits can substantially reduce the risk of many illnesses and disabilities. Decreasing the number of calories from fat, increasing the fiber content of the diet, maintaining dietary balance and reasonable body weight, and identifying a fitness program that fits a woman's lifestyle and in which she is willing to participate regularly are important issues for the physician and patient to discuss.

With increasing frequency, sexual behaviors are placing women at risk. In addition to causing lower genital tract infection, sexual practices are placing an increasing number of women at risk for human immunodeficiency virus (HIV) infection and for hepatitis. Women must be counseled regarding safe sexual practices. The physician must not assume that because a woman is a particular age, of an upper socioeconomic status, or married, that she is not at risk for sexually transmitted disease. Although these discussions are sometimes uncomfortable for the physician and/or the patient, morbidity and mortality can be prevented, and health care providers should be committed to addressing these issues. Acquired immunodeficiency syndrome (AIDS) is currently the fourth leading cause of death in the United States of women ages 19 to 39 years. The incidence of sexually transmitted hepatitis is increasing. Despite the difficulty that the physician and/or patient may have, if the physician discusses these issues with true concern for the well-being of the woman, most patients will respond by accepting the importance of the subject and appreciating the physician's concerns.

Prevention of unwanted pregnancy and preconception counseling are other preventive health care areas in which physicians can make major contributions.

Women's psychosocial needs are often overlooked by the health care team. Here again, physician intervention can substantially reduce morbidity and mortality. Treatable problems relating to depression, anxiety, and other disorders should be addressed. Women who are subject to domestic violence need to be identified and helped.

Cancer prevention and screening for premalignant and early invasive disease are important responsibilities for women's primary care providers. The mortality from invasive cervical cancer has fallen dramatically in the United States owing to Pap smear screening programs. Breast cancer is now diagnosed in earlier, more readily treatable, stages because of screening. Many cases of lung cancer are completely preventable with successful smoking cessation programs and behavior modification. The dramatic rise in incidence of skin cancer can be arrested by physicians educating patients about skin cancer and its prevention. Primary care physicians are in ideal positions to work with patients in screening and prevention programs to reduce cancer mortality.

Unfortunately, infections for which immunizations are available are still a cause of morbidity and even mortality. Clearly, adherence to immunization schedules can greatly reduce this problem, and primary care physicians need to make certain that their patients are being immunized.

For older women, physicians must work with their patients to provide accurate information about the prevention of osteoporosis and heart disease. Education regarding hormone replacement therapy, exercise, calcium supplementation, and diet is important.

This section of the book emphasizes prevention. The vital components of preventive health care and women's wellness are discussed. The section begins with a review of the main causes of morbidity and mortality in women and has tables for preventive and screening strategies that are targeted to women in various age groups and various high-risk categories. This review is followed by a chapter that discusses the importance of a detailed personal, social, and family history when providing preventive care. Each of the subsequent chapters in this section focuses on a particular aspect of preventive care, the sum total of which serves to reduce morbidity and mortality for our patients.

It is clear that providing health care to women is not merely an issue of treating illness; at least as important, is preventing illness. Preventing illness requires emphasizing patient education so that women can play a role in maintaining their own health. Via dialogue and counseling, physicians can have a substantial impact on preventive care.

CHAPTER 3

Preventive Health Care and Screening during the Stages of a Woman's Life

Vicki L. Seltzer

A primary role of the physician is to help women stay healthy. If disease does occur, it must be diagnosed as early as possible to afford the greatest likelihood of cure or long-term control of the problem, thereby reducing the risk of substantial secondary morbidity. The screening and prevention strategies that are most important for any given woman depend on her individual risk factors (genetic, environmental, and behavioral). They change as the woman ages and evolves through the phases of her life. This chapter discusses a series of preventive and screening strategies that can be used to optimize patients' well-being. The recommendations are based (with some modifications) on the original report of the American College of Obstetricians and Gynecologists (ACOG) Task Force on Primary and Preventive Health Care and on the updated recommendations in the Primary Care Review series, which were developed under the direction of the ACOG Committee on Primary Care.

In the distant past, emphasis in health care was almost exclusively on the treatment of disease rather than on prevention. However, it has become apparent that physicians can make an enormous impact on their patients' health through preventive strategies. For instance, it is estimated that one-half of premature deaths, one-third of acute disabilities, and one-half of chronic disabilities can be prevented by reducing behavioral risk factors and by preventive health care.

While essentially all medical organizations agree that screening and prevention result in a substantial reduction in morbidity and mortality, for many different medical problems debate continues regarding the ideal frequency of screening, which studies should be employed, when they should be started, and who should be screened. The recommendations in this chapter follow fairly closely those of the ACOG Task Force on Primary and Preventive Health Care and the updated Primary Care Review series. They focus on sensible, cost-effective screening and preventive strategies that can be targeted to what is most appropriate to the individual patient's needs. Clearly, our scientific knowledge, screening modalities, available therapies, and preventive capabilities continue to evolve rapidly. As this occurs, recommendations for preventive and screening interventions also will change.

Other organizations have suggested screening strategies that also can be utilized. They may vary somewhat from those of ACOG. Such variations occur because insufficient data are available regarding the benefits of certain interventions as well as the ideal frequency. While it is reasonable to use any one of a variety of strategies, physicians should have some general program for screening and preventive care that they employ regularly in their practices.

The tables in this chapter focus on the needs of the typical patient who is coming to her physician for routine health care. The tables assume that the patient is "ongoing" and that the initial history, physical examination, risk assessment, diagnostic testing, and counseling were done in the past. The tables also assume that the woman has no underlying medical problems; if she does, further interventions may be required, and the frequency of certain testing might need to be increased.

TABLE 3-1 Leading Causes of Mortality and Morbidity Ages 13 to 18 Years

Mortality	Morbidity
Motor vehicle and other accidents	Acne
Homicide	Asthma
Suicide	Chlamydia
Cancer	Depression
Heart disease	Dermatitis
HIV infections	Headaches
	Infective, viral, and parasitic diseases
	Influenza
	Injuries
	Nose, throat, ear, and upper respiratory infections
	Sexual assault
	Sexually transmitted diseases
	Urinary tract infections

SOURCE: Adapted with permission from The American College of Obstetricians and Gynecologists (1997).[2]

TABLE 3-2 Periodic Health Assessment and Preventive Care for Women Ages 13 to 18 Years

I. Screening
   A. Review problem list and continuity-of-care records
   B. Periodic history: reason for visit; interval medical, surgical, and family history; dietary/nutritional assessment; exercise; tobacco, alcohol, other drugs; abuse/neglect; sexual practices
   C. Periodic physical: height, weight, BP; Tanner staging of secondary sexual characteristics; general physical examination; pelvic examination (yearly when sexually active or by age 18 years)
   D. Laboratory tests
      1. Pap test—yearly when sexually active or by age 18 years
      2. Hemoglobin—testing is particularly important for women of Caribbean, Latin American, Asian, Mediterranean, or African descent, or with a history of excessive menstrual flow
      3. Bacteriuria testing—periodic testing particularly for women with diabetes mellitus
      4. Sexually transmissible infection (STI) testing—for women with a history of multiple sexual partners or with a sexual partner with multiple contacts; women who have a partner with an STI; women with a repeated history of STIs; women who attend an STI clinic; routine screening for chlamydial and gonorrhea (GC) infection for all sexually active adolescents and other asymptomatic women at risk for infection
      5. HIV testing—for high risk women; for women seeking treatment for STIs; for women with a past or present history of drug use by injection; current or past history of prostitution; women whose past or present sexual partners are HIV-positive or bisexual or who inject drugs; women with recurrent genital tract disease; women born, or with long-term residence, in an area with a high prevalence of HIV infection; women transfused between 1978 and 1985; women younger than age 50 who have invasive cervical cancer; women who are pregnant or planning for pregnancy
      6. Genetic testing/counseling—for women exposed to teratogens; for women contemplating pregnancy who have a partner or family member or who themselves have a history of a genetic disorder or birth defect; for women contemplating pregnancy who are of African, Eastern European Jewish, Mediterranean, or Southeast Asian ancestry
      7. Rubella titer—women lacking evidence of immunity
      8. Cholesterol—for women with familial lipid disorders; family history of premature coronary heart disease; history of coronary heart disease
      9. Lipid profile—periodic screening for women with an elevated cholesterol level; a history of a parent or a sibling with a high blood cholesterol level or with documented coronary artery disease at a very young age; presence of diabetes mellitus; smoker
      10. Tuberculosis skin test—regular testing for teens; for women infected with HIV; for close contacts of persons known or suspected to have TB; persons with medical risk factors known to increase the risk of disease if infection has occurred; foreign-born persons from countries with high TB prevalence; medically underserved; low-income populations; alcoholics and IV drug users; residents of long-term care facilities, correctional institutions, mental institutions, and nursing homes; health professionals working in high-risk health care facilities
      11. Fasting glucose test—every 3–5 years for family history of diabetes mellitus (one first- or two second-degree relatives); obesity; history of gestational diabetes mellitus; hypertensive; members of high-risk ethnic groups
      12. Hepatitis C virus test for high-risk individuals
II. Evaluation and Counseling
   A. Sexuality
      1. Development
      2. High-risk behaviors
      3. Preventing unintended pregnancy (postponing sexual involvement; contraceptive options)
      4. Sexually transmissible infections (partner selection; barrier protection)
   B. Fitness
      1. Hygiene (including dental); fluoride supplementation
      2. Dietary/nutritional assessment
      3. Exercise: discussion of program
      4. Folic acid supplementation (0.4 mg/day)
   C. Psychosocial evaluation: interpersonal/family relationships, sexual identity, personal goal development, behavioral/learning disorders, abuse/neglect, satisfactory school experience
   D. Cardiovascular risk factors: family history, hypertension, dyslipidemia, obesity, diabetes mellitus
   E. Health/risk behaviors
      1. Injury prevention—safety belts and helmets, recreational hazards, firearms, hearing
      2. Skin exposure to ultraviolet rays
      3. Suicide: depressive symptoms
      4. Tobacco, alcohol, other drugs
III. Immunizations
   A. Tetanus-diphtheria booster once between ages 13 and 16 years
   B. Measles, mumps, rubella (MMR) for all women unable to show proof of immunity
   C. Hepatitis B vaccine: for those not previously immunized
   D. Varicella vaccine if no previous evidence of immunity
   E. Hepatitis A vaccine for high-risk individuals

SOURCE: Adapted with permission from The American College of Obstetricians and Gynecologists, 1997.[2]

TABLE 3-3 Leading Causes of Mortality and Morbidity in Women Ages 19 to 39 Years

Mortality	Morbidity
Motor vehicle and other accidents	Asthma
Cancer	Back
HIV infections	Breast disease
Heart disease	Deformity or orthopedic impairment
Homicide	Depression
Suicide	Diabetes
	GYN disorders
	Headache/migraines
	Hypertension
	Infective, viral, and parasitic diseases
	Influenza
	Injuries
	Nose, throat, ear, and upper respiratory infections
	Sexual assault/domestic violence
	Sexually transmitted diseases
	Skin rash/dermatitis
	Substance abuse
	Urinary tract infections
	Vaginitis

SOURCE: Adapted with permission from The American College of Obstetricians and Gynecologists, 1997.[2]

TABLE 3-4 Periodic Health Assessment and Preventive Care for Women Ages 19 to 39 Years

I. Screening
 A. Review problem list and continuity-of-care records
 B. Periodic history: reason for visit; interval medical, surgical, and family history; dietary/nutritional assessment; exercise; tobacco, alcohol, other drugs; abuse/neglect; sexual practices
 C. Physical examination including pelvic exam
 D. Laboratory tests
  1. Pap test—after three consecutive normal annual tests, in low-risk woman, physician and patient discretion as to whether this must continue to be annual
  2. Hemoglobin: testing is particularly important for women of Caribbean, Latin American, Asian, Mediterranean, or African descent, or with a history of excessive menstrual flow
  3. Bacteriuria testing: periodic testing particularly for women with diabetes mellitus
  4. Mammography: women aged 35 and older with a family history of premenopausally diagnosed breast cancer in a first-degree relative (may need to begin earlier depending upon the age at diagnosis)
  5. Fasting glucose test: every 3–5 years for family history of diabetes mellitus (one first- or two second-degree relatives); obesity; history of gestational diabetes mellitus; hypertensive; members of high-risk ethnic groups
  6. Cholesterol every 5 years beginning at age 20
  7. Lipid profile: periodic screening for women with an elevated cholesterol level, a history of a parent or a sibling with a blood cholesterol level of 240 mg/dl or higher; a history of a sibling, parent, or grandparent with documented premature (aged less than 55 years) coronary artery disease; presence of diabetes mellitus; smoker; obesity; other risk factors
  8. Sexually transmissible infection (STI) testing: for women with a history of multiple sexual partners or with a sexual partner with multiple contacts; women who have a partner with an STI; women with a repeated history of STIs; women who attend an STI clinic; in addition, perform routine screening for chlamydial and gonorrhea (GC) infection for all asymptomatic women at risk for infection
  9. HIV testing: for high risk women; for women seeking treatment for STIs; for women with a past or present history of drug use by injection; current or past history of prostitution; women whose past or present sexual partners are HIV-positive or bisexual or who inject drugs; women with recurrent genital tract disease; women born, or with long-term residence, in an area with a high prevalence of HIV infection; women transfused between 1978 and 1985; women younger than age 50 years who have invasive cervical cancer; women who are pregnant or planning for pregnancy
  10. Genetic testing/counseling: for women who are exposed to teratogens or who contemplate pregnancy at age 35 years or beyond; patient, partner, or family member with a history of a genetic disorder or birth defect; persons of African, Eastern European Jewish, Mediterranean, or Southeast Asian ancestry
  11. Rubella titer: women lacking evidence of immunity
  12. Tuberculosis skin test: for women infected with HIV; for close contacts of persons known or suspected to have TB; persons with medical risk factors known to increase the risk of disease if infection has occurred; foreign-born persons from countries with high TB prevalence; medically underserved; low-income populations; alcoholics and IV drug users; residents of long-term care facilities, correctional institutions, mental institutions, and nursing homes; health professionals working in high-risk health care facilities; schools may require testing
  13. Thyroid-stimulating hormone: periodic screening of individuals with a strong family history of thyroid disease and patients with autoimmune diseases (there is some evidence that subclinical hypothyroidism may be related to unfavorable lipid profiles)
  14. Hepatitis C virus test for high-risk individuals
II. Evaluation and Counseling
 A. Sexuality
  1. High-risk behaviors
  2. Contraceptive options: discussions to include genetic counseling, prevention of unwanted pregnancy
  3. Preconception counseling for desired pregnancy
  4. Sexually transmissible infections—partner selection, barrier protection
  5. Sexual function
 B. Fitness
  1. Hygiene (including dental)
  2. Dietary/nutritional assessment
  3. Exercise: discuss program
  4. Folic acid supplementation (0.4 mg/day)
  5. Calcium supplementation
 C. Psychosocial evaluation: interpersonal/family relationships, domestic violence, job satisfaction, lifestyle/stress, sleep disorders
 D. Cardiovascular risk factors: family history, hypertension, dyslipidemia, obesity, diabetes mellitus, lifestyle
 E. Health/risk behaviors
  1. Injury prevention: safety belts and helmets, occupational hazards, recreational hazards, firearms, hearing
  2. Breast self-examination
  3. Skin exposure to ultraviolet rays
  4. Suicide: depressive symptoms
  5. Tobacco, alcohol, other drugs
III. Immunizations
 A. Tetanus-diphtheria booster every 10 years
 B. Measles, mumps, rubella—for all women unable to show proof of immunity
 C. Hepatitis B vaccine—for all high risk women; intravenous drug users; current recipient of blood products; health-related job with exposure to blood products; household or sexual contact with hepatitis B virus carriers; history of prostitution; history of sexual activity with multiple partners in last 6 months; schools may require vaccination
 D. Influenza vaccine: residents of chronic care facilities; women with chronic cardiopulmonary disorders; women with metabolic diseases including diabetes mellitus, hemoglobinopathies, immunosuppression, or renal dysfunction; women who will be in the second or third trimester of pregnancy during the epidemic season
 E. Pneumococcal vaccine: women with factors for influenza vaccine plus sickle cell disease, Hodgkin's disease, asplenia, alcoholism, cirrhosis, multiple myeloma, and other chronic illnesses
 F. Varicella vaccine: women with no evidence of immunity
 G. Hepatitis A vaccine for high-risk individuals

SOURCE: Adapted with permission from The American College of Obstetricians and Gynecologists, 1997.[2]

TABLE 3-5 Leading Causes of Mortality and Morbidity in Women Ages 40 to 64 Years

Mortality	Morbidity
Cancer	Arthritis/osteoarthritis
Heart disease	Asthma
Cerebrovascular disease	Back
Motor vehicle and other accidents	Breast disease
COPD	Carpal tunnel
Diabetes	Cardiovascular disease
	Deformity or orthopedic impairment
	Depression
	Diabetes
	Headache
	Hypertension
	Infective, viral, and parasitic diseases
	Influenza
	Injuries
	Menopause
	Nose, throat, and upper respiratory infections
	Obesity
	Skin conditions/dermatitis
	Substance abuse
	Urinary tract infections
	Urinary tract (other) (includes urinary incontinence)
	Vision impairment

SOURCE: Adapted with permission from The American College of Obstetricians and Gynecologists, 1997.[2]

TABLE 3-6 Periodic Health Assessment and Preventive Care for Women Ages 40 to 64 Years

I. Screening
   A. Review problem list and continuity-of-care records
   B. Periodic history: reason for visit; interval medical, surgical, and family history; dietary/nutritional assessment; exercise; tobacco, alcohol, other drugs; abuse/neglect; sexual practices; urinary incontinence
   C. Physical examination including pelvic exam
   D. Laboratory tests
      1. Mammography: annual
      2. Bacteriuria testing: periodic testing particularly for women with diabetes mellitus
      3. Fecal occult blood test: beginning at ages 40–50 years
      4. Sigmoidoscopy: starting at age 50 years average-risk women should have either a sigmoidoscopy every 5 years, or a colonoscopy every 10 years, or a barium enema every 5 to 10 years
      5. Colonoscopy—for women with a personal history of inflammatory bowel disease or colonic polyps or colon cancer; or a family history of familial polyposis coli, colorectal cancer, or cancer family syndrome
      6. Hemoglobin: periodic testing
      7. Sexually transmissible infection (STI) testing: for women with a history of multiple sexual partners or with a sexual partner with multiple contacts; women who have a partner with an STI; women with a repeated history of STIs; women who attend an STI clinic; in addition perform routine screening for chlamydial and gonorrhea (GC) infection for all asymptomatic women at risk for infection
      8. Human immunodeficiency virus testing: for high risk women; for women seeking treatment for STIs; for women with a past or present history of drug use by injection; current or past history of prostitution; women whose past or present sexual partners are HIV-positive or bisexual or who inject drugs; women with recurrent genital tract disease; women born, or with long-term residence, in an area with a high prevalence of HIV infection; women transfused between 1978 and 1985; women younger than age 50 who have invasive cervical cancer; women who are pregnant or planning pregnancy
      9. Tuberculosis skin testing: for women infected with HIV; for close contacts of persons known or suspected to have TB; persons with medical risk factors known to increase the risk of disease if infection has occurred; foreign-born persons from countries with high TB prevalence; medically underserved; low-income populations; alcoholics and IV drug users; residents of long-term care facilities, correctional institutions, mental institutions, and nursing homes; health professionals working in high-risk health care facilities
      10. Pap test: after three consecutive normal annual tests, in a low-risk woman, physician and patient discretion as to whether this must continue to be annual
      11. Cholesterol—every 5 years
      12. Lipids: periodic screening for women with an elevated cholesterol level, a history of a parent or a sibling with a blood cholesterol level of 240 mg/dl or higher; a history of a sibling, parent, or grandparent with documented premature (aged less than 55 years) coronary artery disease; presence of diabetes mellitus; smoker; obesity; other high-risk factors
      13. Fasting glucose test: every 3 years, beginning at age 45 years; testing should begin earlier for high risk women
      14. TSH: periodic screening of individuals with a strong family history of thyroid disease and patients with autoimmune diseases (there is some evidence that subclinical hypothyroidism may be related to unfavorable lipid profiles)
      15. Genetic testing/counseling for women considering pregnancy
      16. Hepatitis C virus test for high-risk individuals
II. Evaluation and counseling
   A. Sexuality
      1. High-risk behaviors
      2. Contraceptive options: discussions to include genetic counseling, prevention of unwanted pregnancy
      3. Preconceptional counseling for desired pregnancy
      4. Sexually transmissible infections: partner selection, barrier protection
      5. Sexual function
   B. Fitness
      1. Hygiene (including dental)
      2. Dietary/nutritional assessment
      3. Exercise (discussion of program)
      4. Folic acid supplementation (0.4 mg/day before age 50 years)
      5. Calcium supplementation
   C. Psychosocial evaluation: family relationships, domestic violence, job/work satisfaction, retirement planning, lifestyle/stress, sleep disorders
   D. Cardiovascular risk factors: family history, hypertension, dyslipidemia, obesity, diabetes mellitus, lifestyle
   E. Health/risk behaviors
      1. Hormone replacement therapy
      2. Injury prevention: seat belts and helmets, occupational hazards, recreational hazards, sports involvement, firearms, hearing
      3. Breast-self-examination
      4. Skin exposure to ultraviolet rays
      5. Suicide: depressive symptoms
      6. Tobacco, alcohol, other drugs
III. Immunizations
   A. Tetanus-diphtheria booster every 10 years
   B. Influenza vaccine for all women annually beginning at age 55 years and for anyone who wishes to reduce the chance of becoming ill with influenza; (prior to age 55 years it should be given to residents of chronic care facilities; women with chronic cardiopulmonary disorders; women with metabolic diseases including diabetes mellitus, hemoglobinopathies, immunosuppression, or renal dysfunction; and women who will be in the second or third trimester of pregnancy during the epidemic season)
   C. Measles, mumps, rubella (MMR): for all women unable to show proof of immunity
   D. Hepatitis B vaccine: intravenous drug users; current recipient of blood products; health-related job with exposure to blood products; household or sexual contact with hepatitis B virus carriers; history of prostitution; history of sexual activity with multiple partners in last 6 months; other high-risk individuals
   E. Pneumococcal vaccine: women with factors for influenza vaccine plus sickle cell disease, Hodgkin's disease, asplenia, alcoholism, cirrhosis, or multiple myeloma, and other chronic illnesses
   F. Varicella vaccine: women with no evidence of immunity
   G. Hepatitis A vaccine for high-risk individuals

SOURCE: Adapted with permission from The American College of Obstetricians and Gynecologists, 1997.[2]

TABLE 3-7 Leading Causes of Mortality and Morbidity in Women Ages 65 Years and Older

Mortality	Morbidity
Heart disease	Arthritis/osteoarthritis
Cancer	Back
Cerebrovascular diseases	Breast cancer
COPD	Cardiovascular disease
Pneumonia and influenza	COPD
Diabetes	Deformity or orthopedic impairment
Motor vehicle and other accidents	Degeneration of macula and posterior pole
	Diabetes
	Hearing and vision impairment
	Hypertension
	Hypothyroidism and other thyroid diseases
	Influenza
	Nose, throat, and upper respiratory infections
	Osteoporosis
	Skin lesions/dematoses/dermatitis
	Urinary tract infections
	Urinary tract (other) (includes urinary incontinence)
	Vertigo

SOURCE: Adapted with permission from The American College of Obstetricians and Gynecologists, 1997.[2]

TABLE 3-8 Periodic Health Assessment and Preventive Care for Women Ages 65 Years and Older

I. Screening
   A. Review problem list and continuity-of-care records
   B. Periodic history: reason for visit; interval medical, surgical, and family history; dietary/nutritional assessment; exercise; tobacco, alcohol, other drugs; abuse/neglect; sexual practices; current medication use; urinary incontinence
   C. Physical examination including pelvic exam
   D. Laboratory tests
      1. Pap test: physician and patient discretion regarding frequency of testing in low-risk woman after three consecutive normal tests (note that cervical cancer is not uncommon in older women)
      2. Urinalysis
      3. Mammography annually
      4. Cholesterol every 3–5 years before age 75 years
      5. Lipid profile: periodic screening for women with an elevated cholesterol level, a history of a parent or a sibling with a blood cholesterol level of 240 mg/dl or higher; a history of a sibling, parent, or grandparent with documented premature (aged less than 55 years) coronary artery disease; presence of diabetes mellitus; smoker; obesity; other risk factors
      6. TSH: every 3–5 years
      7. Periodic CBC, BUN, creatinine, and fasting glucose
      8. Sexually transmissible infection (STI) testing: for women with a history of multiple sexual partners or with a sexual partner with multiple contacts; women who have a partner with an STI; women with a repeated history of STIs; women who attend an STI clinic
      9. HIV testing: for high-risk women; for women seeking treatment for STIs; past or present history of drug use by injection; current or past history of prostitution; women whose past or present sexual partners are HIV-positive or bisexual or who inject drugs; women with recurrent genital tract disease; women born, or with long-term residence, in an area with a high prevalence of HIV infection; women transfused between 1978 and 1985
      10. Tuberculosis skin test: for women infected with HIV; for close contacts of persons known or suspected to have TB; persons with medical risk factors known to increase the risk of disease if infection has occurred; foreign-born persons from countries with high TB prevalence; medically underserved; low-income populations; alcoholics and IV drug users; residents of long-term care facilities, correctional institutions, mental institutions, and nursing homes; health professionals working in high-risk health care facilities
      11. Fecal occult blood test
      12. Sigmoidoscopy: for the average-risk woman sigmoidoscopy every 5 years, or colonoscopy every 10 years, or barium enema every 5–10 years
      13. Colonoscopy: for women with a personal history of inflammatory bowel disease or colonic polyps or colon cancer; or a family history of familial polyposis coli, colorectal cancer, or cancer family syndrome
      14. Hepatitis C virus test for high-risk individuals
II. Evaluation and Counseling
   A. Sexuality
   B. Fitness: hygiene (general and dental), dietary/nutritional assessment, exercise (discussion of program)
   C. Psychosocial evaluation: neglect/abuse, lifestyle/stress, depression/sleep disorders, family relationships, job/retirement satisfaction
   D. Cardiovascular risk factors: hypertension, dyslipidemia, obesity, diabetes mellitus, sedentary lifestyle
   E. Health/risk behaviors
      1. Hormone replacement therapy
      2. Injury prevention: safety belts and helmets, prevention of falls, occupational hazards, recreational hazards, firearms
      3. Visual acuity/glaucoma
      4. Hearing
      5. Breast self-examination
      6. Skin exposure to ultraviolet rays
      7. Suicide: depressive symptoms
      8. Tobacco, alcohol, other drugs
III. Immunizations
   A. Tetanus-diphtheria booster every 10 years
   B. Influenza vaccine (annually)
   C. Pneumococcal vaccine: at age 65 years if it has not been administered previously; may need to be repeated after several years
   D. Hepatitis B vaccine: intravenous drug users; current recipient of blood products; health-related job with exposure to blood products; household or sexual contact with hepatitis B virus carriers; history of prostitution; history of sexual activity with multiple partners in last 6 months; other high-risk individuals
   E. Hepatitis A vaccine for high-risk individuals
   F. Varicella vaccine: women with no evidence of immunity

SOURCE: Adapted with permission from The American College of Obstetricians and Gynecologists, 1997.[2]

References and Selected Readings

1. American Academy of Family Physicians, Commission on Public Health and Scientific Affairs: *Age Charts for Periodic Health Examinations.* Kansas City, MO: AAFP, 1990. Reprint no. 510.
2. American College of Obstetricians and Gynecologists: *Primary Care Review for the Obstetrician-Gynecologist, Primary and Preventive Care,* Washington, DC: 1997.
3. American College of Obstetricians and Gynecologists: *The Obstetrician-Gynecologist and Primary-Preventive Health Care.* Washington, DC: 1993.
4. American College of Physicians: *Clinical Efficacy Report.* Philadelphia: 1987.
5. Canadian Task Force on the Periodic Health Examination: The periodic health examination. *Can Med Assoc J* 121:1193–1254, 1979.
6. Hayward RS, Steinberg EP, Ford DE, et al: Preventive care guidelines: 1991. *Ann Intern Med* 114:758–783, 1991.
7. US Department of Health and Human Services, Public Health Service: *Healthy People 2000: National Health Promotion and Disease Prevention Objectives.* Washington: US Government Printing Office, 1991.
8. US Preventive Services Task Force: *Guide to Clinical Preventive Services:* Report of the US Preventive Services Task Force, 2nd. ed. Williams & Wilkins, 1996.

CHAPTER 4

The Importance of a Detailed Personal, Social, and Family History

Albert B. Gerbie
Nanette K. Rumsey

Effective preventive care, as well as treatment of specific medical problems, is best achieved if appropriate emphasis is placed on a detailed history. In addition to providing the foundation on which we treat patients, obtaining a through medical history is one of the first steps in initiating and establishing the doctor-patient relationship. Time spent with the patient bespeaks genuine interest on the part of the clinician, and this engenders trust. A trusting relationship increases patient receptivity to education and increases the probability of patient compliance.

A clinician's skill, knowledge, and experience are most evident in the taking of a patient's history. By eliciting historical data, the clinician can focus the physical examination, order appropriate laboratory tests, and formulate a differential diagnosis. All of these steps will lead to a plan for long-term treatment and preventive care.

The history should include all medically significant facts up to the time a patient appears. Each symptom must be given its own weight. The physician must know when to question more deeply for further details. While the physician will usually aid or guide the patient through questions, one must avoid the power of suggestion in influencing the patient. Any symptom—trivial, remote, or the one of most concern to the patient—may be the actual key to the problem. Table 4-1 outlines the medical history that the physician needs to elicit. Clearly, the focus is broad with the intent of offering the patient more than the treatment of isolated ailments.

Specific examples that illustrate the importance of a thorough medical history are endless. Eliciting a history of past steroid use or an intensive care admission for asthma, signals the need for careful pre- and postoperative pulmonary and adrenocortical evaluation. Eliciting a history of excessive bleeding from dental extraction in the patient or her family may uncover a blood dyscrasia (e.g., von Willebrand's disease), thereby avoiding catastrophic, perioperative bleeding complications. Taking a thorough immunization history and making a careful risk assessment identifies the 10% of reproductive-age women who are still susceptible to rubella. It also identifies those women needing hepatitis B and varicella vaccinations.

No physician should assume that someone else is supervising the patient's general medical status. To make certain that there are neither duplications nor omissions, each physician should discuss who is providing the primary preventive care and screening services. Furthermore, each physician should make certain to update critical parts of the medical history each and every year. A change in the family history from one year to the next may have life and death consequences for the patient.

One cannot overemphasize the family history. It is a critical part of preventive healthcare for our patients and for their future offspring. Unfortunately, it is frequently obtained in a routine,

TABLE 4-1 **Medical History**

I. Biographical Data

II. Source of History

III. Chief Complaint and Present Illness

IV. Past Medical History
   A. Allergies
   B. Medications
   C. Illness/Hospitalizations
   D. Surgery
   E. Trauma
   F. Bleeding tendencies
   G. Transfusion history
   H. Immunizations

V. Obstetric and Gynecologic History
   A. Menstrual history
   B. Sexual history
   C. Contraception
   D. Vaginal and pelvic infections
   E. Pap smear history
   F. Gynecologic surgery or procedures
   G. Urologic history
   H. Breast disease, prior mammography
   I. Pregnancies
   J. DES exposure

VI. Family history
   A. Breast, gynecologic, colon, or other cancers
   B. Genetic diseases, congenital anomalies, twinning, preeclampsia
   C. Hypertension, diabetes, cardiovascular disease, etc.
   D. Psychiatric and social

VII. Social History
   A. Habits: alcohol, tobacco, illicit drugs
   B. Marital status
   C. Living arrangements
   D. Education
   E. Occupation
   F. Avocations
   G. Diet/exercise
   H. Possible exposure to abuse or neglect

VIII. Review of Systems
   A. Head and neck
   B. Cardiovascular/respiratory
   C. Gastrointestinal
   D. Genitourinary
   E. Neurologic
   F. Psychiatric

cursory fashion. To record the family history as "negative" or "noncontributory" may give an erroneous impression. One should specifically ask about the age, sex, and health of parents, siblings, and other close relatives. The age and cause of death of deceased relatives should be recorded. Abortions and perinatal deaths should be noted. Genetic and ethnic histories are also important, especially with respect to preconception counseling.

The family history is actually a leading tool in clinical genetics and can provide important clues regarding the patient's illness. One must remember that the first principle of genetic counseling is to obtain an accurate genetic history, which includes an accurate diagnosis of the disease in question.

Carrier screening usually refers to identification of carriers (heterozygotes) of autosomal or sex-linked recessive disorders, although the scope of carrier screening is increasing. In obstetrics, carrier screening provides prospective parents with reproductive alternatives such as prenatal diagnosis (with options of preparation for care, termination of pregnancy, or treatment of affected fetuses), artificial insemination, or deferral of child bearing. Ideally, carrier screening is based on these criteria: availability of a simple, accurate, inexpensive carrier test; an ethnic, racial, or geographic heritage of increased risk for a specific genetic disorder; and the availability of treatment or reproductive options for the identified carriers. Modern obstetrics applies these principles to diseases such as Tay-Sachs, sickle-cell, cystic fibrosis, thalassemia, hemophilia, and Canavan's. Molecular genetics has increased the reliability and the number of diseases for which patients may be screened.

Outside the realm of obstetric prenatal diagnosis, there is a growing focus on the genetics of a multitude of diseases. By taking careful family histories of our female patients, we may identify family clusters of colon, breast, ovarian, and other gynecologic neoplasms, thereby allowing preventive care for entire families.

One of the first hereditary cancer syndromes

to be identified was hereditary nonpolyposis co-lorectal cancer (HNPCC), which includes the subsets of Lynch Syndrome I and Lynch Syndrome II (implicated genes: *MSH2, MLH1, PMS1,* and *PMS2*). As HNPCC has autosomal dominant inheritance, early age of onset, and a proclivity to include other cancers, including endometrial and ovarian, gynecologists and all clinicians must obtain detailed medical histories so that proper screening can be initiated for this and all hereditary cancer syndromes. Although most colorectal cancer is not part of a hereditary cancer syndrome, it is indeed a common cancer for both men and women and, again, clinicians must obtain a detailed family history to initiate ideal screening at the appropriate age.

More recently identified and cloned were the genes *BRCA1* and *BRCA2*. Mutations in these genes place patients at risk for breast and ovarian cancer. How best to approach and screen potential carriers of mutations of *BRCA1* and *BRCA2* remains to be determined. If we obtain a detailed family history, and that history identifies family members with an early age of onset of breast or ovarian cancer (certainly before age 40 years), bilateral breast cancer, two or more first-degree relatives with breast or ovarian cancer, and/or Jewish ancestry, the clinician should consider the possibility that the patient is a carrier of a mutation in *BRCA1* and/or *BRCA2* genes. The clinician must keep informed of how best to approach such patients and have ready access to genetic counselors so that proper screening and follow-up can be initiated.

In addition to screening for genetic diseases, the family history should include inquiries about premature coronary artery disease in first-degree relatives, diabetes, hypertension, and hypercholesterolemia. The physician should never lose sight of his or her role in providing preventive care and education to the patient and her entire family.

A discussion of coronary artery disease in women deserves special attention. Many women do not realize that the number one killer of women is heart disease. By screening our patients and by obtaining a detailed family history, we can identify patients at risk for heart disease and we can provide the opportunity for patient education. If a detailed family and personal history are obtained, we can decrease the risk of heart disease by even further emphasizing discussions regarding diet, exercise, smoking cessation, obesity prevention, alcohol moderation, and the need for and frequency of cardiac testing. To be a successful provider of primary and preventive care for women, our job is to heighten a patient's awareness of all of her medical risk factors, including coronary artery disease, and provide her with an opportunity to eliminate or decrease her risk. Patients will frequently modify unhealthy behaviors if physician interest is demonstrated to them, and counseling is provided.

A detailed family and personal history may also help identify women with significant risk factors for osteoporosis. With our current knowledge of the devastation that osteoporosis can cause, and with the availability of preventive and therapeutic modalities, the clinician should not miss the opportunity to identify women at risk for this significant disease.

Just as there are myriad examples that illustrate the importance of a detailed family history, there are also endless examples of the critical importance of a detailed personal and social history. Obtaining a good psychosocial history is important in establishing patient rapport. Furthermore, taking this history can uncover maladaptive behaviors and identify support systems, both of which are important to patient compliance and outcome; for example, home bedrest for an obstetric complication might be doomed to failure if family support is unavailable. In obtaining this personal and social history, it is important to use great tact to avoid embarrassing the patient and to reduce the possibility that the patient may repress or suppress facts. It is also important that physicians learn to overcome their embarrassment in asking about this critical part of the medical history. Many patients can easily sense a clinician's discomfort, and this may hamper the patient's ability to be forthright in answering the questions.

Specific components of the social history should include questions about tobacco use, alcohol intake, drug use, domestic violence, mental health history such as depression, and any history of sexually transmitted diseases. It cannot be stressed enough that specific and direct questions must be asked of the patient. In these sensitive areas, patients will often not volunteer their concerns.

It is beyond this chapter's scope to provide a detailed discussion of how to approach the issue of domestic violence. This issue is discussed in depth in Chap. 59. In general, the physician should ask short questions that are direct and nonthreatening. To just ask the patient "Have you been in a relationship with a person who threatened or physically hurt you?" may be all that is needed to initiate a conversation that might change, or even save, that patient's life. In addition, it is recommended that educational material on domestic violence be provided to the patient in a confidential setting such as the physician's office bathrooms, so that a patient can obtain this information without the knowledge of the abuser. The message to convey is that domestic violence is a common problem, that it is unacceptable, and that help resources are available for the patient.

Tobacco use is another area that must be specifically addressed with the patient. It is known that a physician's advice to the patient about smoking cessation can increase cessation rates by as much as 30 percent. It is incumbent on the physician who provides primary care to women to ask about tobacco use. The clinician should stress the importance of smoking cessation and identify the adverse health effects of cigarette use. The physician should also recommend ways that will assist the patient in smoking cessation. The clinician should be familiar with local stop-smoking programs in the patient's area and with the smoking cessation materials that are available through such organizations as the American College of Obstetricians and Gynecologists, the American Cancer Society, and the American Lung Association. It is important that the clinician address this issue with the patient at each visit, that the clinician provide continued opportunities for initiating smoking cessation, and that the clinician address the possibility of relapse.

Another very important aspect of the history is the topic of mental health. How to obtain a focused history that identifies psychiatric disorders is discussed in Chap. 55. Psychiatric and psychosocial problems result in significant morbidity and sometimes mortality. It is important that these problems be identified as promptly as possible, and this can often be achieved by the primary care physician during the course of obtaining a detailed history.

For instance, clinical depression, specifically major depressive disorder, has an overall lifetime prevalence of 17 percent. However, it is twice as likely to occur in women as it is in men. In addition to decreasing personal, family, and work satisfaction and productivity, a major depressive disorder can be a life-threatening illness; suicide is the eighth leading cause of death in the United States. Knowing these statistics, all primary care providers of women should develop a knowledge and comfort level for probing for depressive disease in their patients.

You can obtain an accurate and honest sexual history from both adults and teenagers if you speak to them in an open, respectful, and friendly manner. When inquiring about sexually transmitted diseases (human immunodeficiency virus, chlamydia, gonorrhea, syphilis, etc.), the physician should ask about the number of sexual partners, contacts with bisexual partners, prostitution, blood transfusions, long-term residence or birth in an area endemic for HIV, the presence of invasive cervical cancer before the age of 50 years, and the presence of IV drug use by the patient or her sexual partner.

There are characteristic historical and physical findings that suggest substance abuse (Table 4-2). Brief, simple questionnaires have been devised to assess specifically for problems with alcohol (Table 4-3). The T-ACE questionnaire is one of

TABLE 4-2 Characteristics That May Be Associated with Substance Abuse

Behavioral and Personal	Medical	Obstetric
Noncompliance with appointments	Drug overdose or withdrawal	No or little prenatal care
Poor historian	Septicemia	Preterm delivery
Slurred speech or staggering gait	Bacterial endocarditis	Premature rupture of the membranes
Bizarre or inappropriate behavior	Sexually transmitted diseases	Birth outside hospital
Psychiatric history	HIV seropositivity	Abruptio placentae
Child abuse or neglect	Tuberculosis	Sudden infant death syndrome
Domestic violence	Hepatitis	Fetal growth retardation
Alcohol- or drug-abusing partner	Pancreatitis	Fetal distress
Family history of substance abuse	Lymphedema	Intrauterine fetal death
Prostitution	Anemia	Congenital anomalies
Incarceration	Cerebrovascular accident	Fetal alcohol syndrome
Frequent emergency room visits	Myocardial ischemia or infarction	Neonatal abstinence syndrome
Chronic unemployment	Poor dental hygiene	
	Poor nutritional status	

SOURCE: From Verp MS: Genetic counseling and screening, in Lin C, Verp MS, Sabbagha RE (eds): *The High Risk Fetus.* New York: Springer-Verlag, 1993, p. 166.

the most sensitive for eliciting a history of alcohol consumption, risk drinking, and long-term alcohol abuse diagnoses.

In obtaining the patient's psychosocial history, it is also important to identify the patient's living arrangements, level of formal education, occupation, marital status, sexual orientation, and ethnic and cultural background. These features of the social history may identify stress levels. Recognizing high stress may explain why the clinician has been ineffective in such areas as tobacco cessation, and it may help identify a patient who is the victim of domestic violence or the patient who is at increased risk for a major depressive disorder. Occupational histories may reveal environmental hazards or exposures particularly relevant to pregnancy. Last, and of utmost importance, all of these demographic features of the social history may give clues to the amount and type of education needed to insure patient compliance. Good patient compliance always improves patient outcomes.

TABLE 4-3 The T-ACE Questionnaire Used to Assess the Possibility of a Drinking Problem[a,b,c]

1. How many drinks does it take to make you feel high? (TOLERANCE)
2. Have people ANNOYED you by criticizing your drinking?
3. Have you felt you ought to CUT DOWN on your drinking?
4. Have you ever had a drink first thing in the morning to steady your nerves or get rid of a hangover? (EYE-OPENER)

[a] Question 1: ≥2 drinks is two points.

[b] A yes answer to questions 2 through 4 is one point each.

[c] A total score of ≥2 is positive for problem drinking.

SOURCE: Modified from Sokol RJ, Martier SS, Ager JW: The T-ACE questions: Practical prenatal detection of risk drinking. *Am J Obstet Gynecol* 160:863, 1989.

Even a patient's postoperative satisfaction and mental health can be predicted if the physician takes this thorough social history. In *The Woman Patient: Medical and Psychological Interfaces,* Roeske identified factors that increased a woman's chance of having mental health problems within three months to three years after a hysterectomy (Table 4-4). Many of these risk factors would be uncovered only by obtaining a detailed, but sensitive, history. These risk factors for adverse outcome after a hysterectomy underscore the importance of viewing patients in a social context—viewing them not just as patients, but as employers, workers, students, sisters, lovers, wives, and daughters. Only with such a broad focus can clinicians provide true primary and preventive care for women.

A thorough assessment of the personal, social, and family history provides the foundation needed to offer women high-quality preventive and primary care, as well as optimal treatment and counseling.

TABLE 4-4   Risk Factors for Mental Health Difficulties after a Hysterectomy

Gender identity (importance of uterus to a feminine self-concept)

Prior adverse reactions to stress

Personal or family history of depression or other mental illness

Multiple somatic complaints (especially low back pain)

History of multiple surgeries or hospitalizations

Desire for children/more children

Fear that surgery will decrease sexual desire or satisfaction

Partner with a negative view of hysterectomy, marital discord

Age less than 35 years at time of surgery

Lack of vocation or outside interests

Negative cultural or religious views of hysterectomy

SOURCE: From Roeske NCA: Hysterectomy and other gynecological surgeries: A psychological view, in Normal MT, Nadelson CC (eds): *The Woman Patient: Medical and Psychological Interfaces.* New York: Plenum Press, 1978.

References and Selected Readings

1. Barbieri RL, et al, (eds): *Depressive Disorders in Women: Diagnosis, Treatment and Monitoring.* Washington, DC: Association of Professors of Gynecology and Obstetrics, 1977.
2. Brooten KE, Chapman S: *Malpractice: A guide to avoidance and treatment.* Orlando: Grune & Stratton, 1987.
3. Chang G, Wilkins-Hang L, et al: Alcohol use and pregnancy: Improving identification. *Obstet Gynecol* 91:892, 1998.
4. Chen L, Karlan BY: Early detection and risk reduction for familial gynecologic cancers. *Clin Obstet Gynecol* 41:200, 1998.
5. Dennerstein L, DeSenarclesn M, (eds.): *The Young Woman: Psychosomatic Aspects of Obstetrics and Gynecology.* Amsterdam: Excerpta Medica, 1983.
6. Droegemueller W, Herbst AL, Mishell DR, Stenchever MA: *Comprehensive Gynecology.* St. Louis: CV Mosby, 1987.
7. Grimes DA: Declining surgical caseload of the obstetrician-gynecologist. *Obstet Gynecol* 67:760, 1986.
8. Judge RD, Zuidema GD, Fitzgerald FT: Clinical Diagnosis, 4th ed. Boston: Little, Brown, 1982.
9. Mayfield D, McLeod G, Hall P: The CAGE questionnaire: Validation of a new alcoholism screening instrument. *Am J Psychiatry* 131:1121, 1974.
10. Olopade OI: The human genome project and breast cancer. *Women's Health Issues* 7:209, 1997.
11. Parsons LH: Domestic Violence, in Precis: An Update in Obstetrics and Gynecology, vol I. Danvers: the American College of Obstetricians and Gynecologists, 1998.
12. Pearse WH, Mendenhall RC, Radecki SE, et al: Manpower for obstetrics-gynecology III. Contributions to total female medical care. *Am J Obstet Gynecol* 144:332, 1982.
13. Roeske NCA: Hysterectomy and other gynecological surgeries: A psychological view, in Notman MT, Nadelson CC (eds): *The Woman Patient: Medical and Psychological Interfaces.* New York: Plenum Press, 1978.
14. Scott N, MacGregor SN, Chasnoff IJ: Substance abuse in pregnancy, in Lin C, Verp MS, Sabbagha RE (eds): *The High Risk Fetus.* New York: Springer-Verlag, 1993, p 570.
15. Seltzer, VL: Obstetrician-gynecologists: Women's health care physicians. *Obstet Gynecol* 91:1, 1998.
16. Shepherd JE, Muto MG: Testing for genetic susceptibility to ovarian and breast cancer. *Contemp OB/GYN* 43:88, 1998.
17. Simpson JL, Elias S: *Essentials of Prenatal Diagnosis:* New York: Churchill Livingstone, 1993.

18. Sokol RJ, Martier SS, Ager JW: The T-ACE Questions: Practical prenatal detection of risk drinking. *Am J Obstet Gynecol* 160:863, 1989.

19. Verp MS: Genetic counseling and screening, in Lin C, Verp MS, Sabbagha RE (eds): *The High Risk Fetus.* New York: Springer-Verlag, 1993, p 166.

20. Verp MS: Substance abuse in pregnancy, in Lin C, Verp MS, Sabbagha RE (eds): *The High Risk Fetus.* New York: Springer-Verlag, 1993, p 570.

21. Wilson JR: Scientific advances, social trends, and the education and practice of obstetrician-gynecologists. *Am J Obstet Gynecol* 162; 1135, 1990.

CHAPTER 5

Cancer Epidemiology, Screening, and Prevention

Joanna M. Cain

A major role of the primary care provider is to work with patients to reduce their risk of developing a malignancy and to involve patients in screening programs so that if a malignancy develops it can be identified in an early, more treatable form. Cancer is, in part, a genetic disease propelled by either inherent underlying genetic instability, or destabilization due to environmental stimulation, or damage at the cellular level. There is no way to prevent, nor to identify, all exposure to potential carcinogens in the air, the food we eat, or the sun. Fur-thermore, until better methods are identified for restructuring the genes with which we are born, we cannot avoid risks associated with our own known or spontaneously occurring genetic changes. However, the careful application of the information gleaned from epidemiologic and screening studies can be used to help patients to decrease their risk for malignancy.

Lung Cancer

Epidemiology and Prevention

Lung cancer, the leading cause of cancer death in American women, is the disease associated with the most clear-cut interaction with preventable carcinogens. Both tobacco and asbestos have been implicated in different histologic types of lung cancer.[10–12] As the number of women who smoke has increased, so has the incidence of lung cancer in women. Between 80 and 90 percent of lung cancers are associated with cigarette smoking. Although the incidence of smoking by men in the U.S. is declining, the incidence in women continues to be high. The physician's role in preventive health care clearly is counseling and support for smoking cessation.[19] Asbestos-free workplaces and asbestos-abatement programs are national initiatives worthy of physician support and patient education. Lung cancer is a disease that, like most cancers, increases in incidence with age.[26] It represents 11 percent of cancers in women.

Screening

Multiple guidelines have been published to evaluate the likelihood that a particular screening test or procedure will be cost-efficient as well as effective.[37] The incidence of the disease should be high in the population, and screening should have a major clinical impact. Screening for a cold virus is not worthwhile because its clinical impact is relatively small, even if the frequency of colds is high. In addition, the preclinical phase does not allow us to intervene to prevent the cold. For a program of cancer screening to be worthwhile, it must identify a premalignant or preclinical phase so that screening can significantly improve survival. Lung cancer, as an example, is an important clinical problem with subsequent disability and death rates that warrant early intervention. Whether or not there is the capability to identify a significant early malignant or premalignant phase with screening programs that can ultimately improve survival is still an open question.

Screening studies focused on chest radiograms and sputum cytology have failed to show a survival advantage at the present time. These studies included randomization between screening and usual care[14] and between cytology and chest radiographs versus radiographs alone in male smokers over age 45.[23] While the first study showed a tendency toward earlier stage disease in the cancers found in the screened group, in neither that group nor the second was there any difference in mortality. These studies were done in a generally younger population. The highest incidence of lung cancer, however, is in men age over 65 and over, so these studies do not reflect directly the potential benefits of such screening. Furthermore, the studies excluded women, and the natural history of the disease as well as screening in that population has not been adequately described. While no advisory group recommends screening for lung cancer at this time, it must be acknowledged that the potential benefits or lack of benefits for women or the elderly are unknown.

Recommendation

Encourage patients not to smoke and assist then with smoking cessation. Specific screening for lung cancer is not currently recommended.

Colorectal Cancer

Epidemiology

For women in the United States, colorectal cancer represents a very common malignancy. This is a cancer that can have a significant inherited tendency. One affected first-degree relative can increase the risk twofold.[38] There are also familial syndromes that carry an increased risk of breast, endometrial, ovarian, and colorectal cancers.[1] Therefore, careful family histories, including both maternal and paternal lines and several generations of family relationships, are important to assess risk and to identify patients with a higher potential incidence of colorectal or other malignancies. This higher potential incidence suggests that screening in such populations might be more effective, although definitive studies are not feasible given the relatively small numbers of such patients.

Prevention

There is clear evidence that dietary factors play a role in the development of colon cancers.[35] Recent literature is replete with theories about the presence of toxins, versus transit time, versus stimulation from a high dose of a single food type as the mechanical initiating event for these cancers, and yet the cause remains a mystery. Epidemiologic data give some guidelines in that diets high in fiber and low in fat can considerably decrease the incidence of disease.[29]

Screening

Colon cancer, like lung cancer, is an important clinical problem with subsequent disability and death rates that warrant early intervention. Furthermore, there is a premalignant lesion detectable[13] as an adenoma or neoplastic change. Finally, one potential screening test is relatively cheap and specific for blood in the stool (95 percent), although not specific for colon cancer itself.[34] Fecal occult blood testing (FOBT) is only 50 to 78 percent[11, 34] sensitive for the diagnosis of colon cancer. Because of its low cost and general patient acceptability (versus invasive procedures), FOBT has the best characteristics of screening tests. However, as noted, it tests for blood, not cancer.

Sigmoidoscopy is another potential means of screening, but a major impediment to its utility is poor patient acceptance.[2] Studies of sigmoidoscopy as a screening tool have been compromised by patient failure to comply. Furthermore, the pattern of colon cancer epidemiologically seems to be shifting to a higher incidence in the right colon, an area not accessed by sigmoidoscopy.[6]

Rectal examinations can diagnose the approximately 10 percent of bowel cancers that occur in the distal rectum.[17] They obviously will fail to diagnose the 90 percent of colorectal cancers that are higher. Yet women commonly have routine screening pelvic examinations on a yearly basis, and the inclusion of a rectal examination for women adds no cost and minimal increased discomfort to the exam.

Serum screening tests hold promise for more specific detection of all cancers, although the presently available serum measure of carcinoembryonic antigen has lacked specificity and has been too costly to promote as a screening tool.[3] The obvious problems as such tests develop will be cost, specificity, and sensitivity, with the potential for overtreatment of patients with false-positive tests.

Recommendation

Rectal examination at the time of pelvic examination for all women. Fecal occult blood screening tests yearly after 40 years of age. In addition, beginning at age 50: either flexible sigmoidoscopy every 5 years, colonoscopy every 10 years, or double contrast barium enema every 5 to 10 years. Patients should begin screening earlier and be screened more often if they have high-risk factors such as a strong family history of colorectal cancer or polyps, a genetic predisposition to colorectal cancer, a personal history of chronic inflammatory bowel disease, or a personal history of adonomatous polyps or colorectal cancer.

Breast Cancer

Breast cancer is discussed extensively elsewhere in this text. It is the most common cancer in women in the United States, occurring in approximately 180,000 women each year, and resulting in approximately 44,000 mortalities annually.

Screening

In terms of screening, although there is variation among the guidelines espoused by different organizations, one set of guidelines for women who are not deemed to be "high risk" recommends:

1. Monthly breast self-examination.
2. Physician examination every 3 years until 40 years of age and then annually. (*Note:* Many physicians recommend that, even prior to age 40, breast examination by a health care provider should be performed yearly.)
3. Annual mammograms beginning at age 40.

Women who are at high risk for breast cancer, particularly at an early age, may require a more aggressive screening program and an earlier initiation of screening.

Recommendation

Careful evaluation of patient risk factors, including a family history, is important for each patient. Based on such evaluation, screening recommendations for breast cancer may need revision for individual patients. For the typical "normal risk" patient, the screening guidelines discussed above are suggested.

Skin Cancer

Epidemiology, Prevention, and Screening

The skin is the largest human organ and has the highest exposure to direct carcinogens, particularly sunlight. It is not surprising, then, that squamous cell and basal cell skin cancers are the most common form of cancer. They are not, however, usually associated with major disability or death.

Malignant melanoma of the skin is associated with increased mortality if not diagnosed early. There has been an increase in incidence, thought to be due to increased sun exposure.[28] Physicians should counsel patients regarding sun exposure and the use of sun block. In addition, skin self-examination and information regarding classic signs of melanoma are important health maintenance approaches for these cancers.

Vulvar cancer is a form of skin cancer, and, as such, is considered in this section. Squamous cell cancer of the vulva has its highest incidence in elderly women, although during the past several years there has been increased incidence in younger women. Educating women regarding the disease, its symptoms, and proper self-evaluation or professional evaluation is beneficial.

Malignant melanoma of the vulva is a rare disease but with a significant mortality if not diagnosed early. The epidemiologic precursors of vulvar melanoma have not been elucidated. Removal of vulvar moles, because of the higher relative risk for malignancy, has been proposed by numerous authors. The actual effect of this on decreasing the incidence of vulvar cancer is unknown.[16]

Recommendation

Teaching of skin self-examination, including vulvar skin, should be a routine part of wellness care. All suspicious lesions must be removed and evaluated by a pathologist.

Cervical and Lower Genital Tract Cancer

Epidemiology

Cervical cancer rates have declined steadily in the United States since the 1950s. Even in the last 30 years, the expected number of cases has declined from 20,000 in 1960 to 13,000 in 1991,[36] with a lifetime risk of five per 10,000. The epidemiology of cervical invasive disease, however, retains the same risk factors delineated 30 years ago, at which time it was thought to have an infectious disease component and to be more common in women who had multiple sexual partners, early age of onset of sexual activity, and low socioeconomic status.[5] Women whose sexual partner has or has had multiple partners also are at increased risk for cervical cancer. The search for a sexually transmitted agent involved in this process led to the identification of human papilloma virus (HPV) as integral to the development of such cancers.[18] Other carcinogenic cofactors implicated include smoking and nutritional factors. Furthermore, concurrent human immunodeficiency virus (HIV) infection is associated with a higher incidence of both preinvasive lesions and invasive cervical cancer. Advancing age is a significant risk factor, with the peak incidence between 45 and 60 years of age.[33] There is a twofold higher risk of cervical cancer in African-American, Hispanic-American, and Native American groups. See Table 5-1 for a summary of risk factors.

TABLE 5-1   Risk Factors for Cervical Cancer

Strong:	Age
	Multiple sexual partners
	Early age of initial sexual intercourse
	Human papilloma virus infection
	Human immunodeficiency virus infection
	Low socioeconomic group
	Sexual partners who have had multiple sexual partners
Moderate:	Smoking
	Nutritional factors
	Herpes simplex infections (questionable)

Prevention

Clearly, changes in sexual practices that encourage later initiation of sexual intercourse, and limiting partners will decrease risk for cervical and lower genital tract cancers. Consistent use of condoms may lower risk for premalignant and malignant cervical lesions as well as for transmission of both HPV and HIV.

Screening

The Papanicolaou smear test described by Papanicolaou and Traut in the 1940s[27] remains the classic screening test. Although it was never subjected to randomized controlled trials, the test is widely credited for the decline in invasive cervical cancer. The Pap smear's success is dependent on important screening characteristics of the disease. For most cervical squamous cancers, there is a clearly defined, preinvasive process. The disease is curable if detected at a premalignant or an early stage. The cost of Pap smear screening is low, and its specificity and sensitivity adequate. Repetition of Pap smears decreases the false-negative rate.

The interval of screening remains somewhat controversial. Because most cervical dysplasia and invasive cancer is related to the onset of sexual activity, screening should begin at that time—even if that is 14 years of age. Because of the large number of young adults who are sexually active by 18 years of age, recommendations have been made to initiate standard screening by age 18.

Once screening has been initiated, the interval between tests is controversial. Ideally, if a Pap smear can identify a preinvasive lesion, the patient can have colposcopy, treatment, and follow-up and never develop cancer. Therefore, in theory, annual Pap smears should reduce the incidence of invasive cervical cancer further by identifying almost all cervical lesions when they are preinvasive. For this reason, a substantial percentage of physicians strongly recommend an annual Pap test and pelvic examination. The 1993 American College of Obstetricians and Gynecologists Committee Opinion on routine cancer screening indicates that after a woman has had three or more consecutive, satisfactory annual Pap smear tests with normal findings, the Pap test may be performed less frequently at the discretion of the physician. It is clear that longer intervals of screening—at 5 years, for example— result in an increase in invasive cancers developed during the interval, but also in a decrease in the cost of screening. There are many arguments in favor of more frequent screening. These include the problem of false-negative smears, the concern about compliance problems and exceeding the interval, and the question of whether presumed historic patterns of progression are valid in all lesions. A study done by Shy and coworkers[32] showed a marked increase in invasive cancers when the interval of screening extended beyond three years.

Cessation of routine Pap smear screening is problematic as well. Ideally, one could assume that by age 65 most women have accumulated a significant history of Pap smear screening to guide further decision making. Unfortunately, studies of women over age 65 show that 25 to 55 percent have never been screened.[22] Furthermore, of those previously screened, one study found that only 26 percent had been regularly screened. It could be a great error to assume that a woman age 65 or older has been screened and to fail to assess or recommend such screening. Screening in the older woman must be assessed individually based on past history of disease and screening, present exposure changes [new partner(s) or the partner having new partner(s)], and symptoms. Cervical cancer is not uncommon in women over the age of 65.

Finally, the issue of screening intervals for women following hysterectomy needs to be addressed. In this circumstance, a screen for vaginal cancers every three years is suggested by various authors. Of concern are data suggesting that a substantial number of women will still have a cervix or cervical tissue after a "hysterectomy."[22] Appropriate screening for these patients can be assessed by careful review of present pelvic examination, review of the pathology for risk factors (e.g., a hysterectomy performed for dysplasia or invasive cancer obviously merits an aggressive screening schedule), and the patient's present risk behaviors.

Patients with known HIV infection, regardless of age, should receive regular Pap smear screening.[21]

The issue of concurrent HPV subtype testing with Pap screening is one of interest to practitioners and patients. As a screening tool, such tests may be very sensitive and specific for HPV, yet not detect (nor are they intended to detect) cervical intraepithelial neoplasia (CIN) or invasive cancer. Therefore, this would not be a screen for the present status of the cervix but, as proposed by some authors, a screen for potential future neoplastic behavior of the cervix. As such, some studies have used HPV testing as a triage for referral for further evaluation or recommendations for screening interval.[31] At present, there are no controlled trials demonstrating the added usefulness and cost-effectiveness of HPV testing for cervical dysplasia or invasive cancer.

Recommendation

All women who are, or who have been, sexually active, or who have reached age 18 should undergo an annual Pap test and pelvic examination. After a woman has had three or more consecutive, satisfactory annual examinations with normal findings, if she is low risk, the Pap test may be performed less frequently at the discretion of her physician. Most physicians recommend continued annual Pap smears.

Ovarian Cancer

Epidemiology

Epithelial ovarian cancer is the most common ovarian malignancy, and is highly fatal, even if relatively rare. In the United States, the lifetime risk for women is 1.6 percent. However, risk substantially increases in postmenopausal women. Risk factors for the disease include a family history of ovarian cancer, a personal history of breast cancer, older age, and activity of the ovary over time. Both nulliparity and late menopause seem to confer a higher likelihood of developing this malignancy.

Prevention

Prevention would be the first choice for this cancer and there is evidence that suppression of ovarian function with birth control pills substantially diminishes the risk of this disease.[1] Clearly for any given woman the risks and benefits of oral contraceptives must be assessed, and it is not recommended at present that the average woman use oral contraceptives for the sole purpose of reducing ovarian cancer risk.

Another potential method of prevention for women who are at very high risk of ovarian cancer is removal of the ovaries. The degree of protection conferred by this mechanism for patients with hereditary ovarian cancer syndromes is incomplete. Extra-ovarian "ovarian carcinoma" (peritoneal carcinomatosis) has been reported in a small number of women who had a bilateral oophorectomy because of a hereditary risk. Despite this, recommendations for prophylactic oophorectomy for individuals at clearly documented very high risk for hereditary ovarian cancer are suggested by many groups. For women with one first-degree relative with ovarian cancer, the risk of developing the disease is 5 percent. Prophylactic oophorectomy as an independent operation is not recommended for these women. With two first-degree relatives the risk of developing ovarian cancer is 7 percent. However, some women in this latter group will have a genetic mutation that may confer a significantly higher risk for development of both breast and ovarian cancer. If a woman inherits a mutation in the most common genes associated with hereditary breast and ovarian cancer, *BRCA1* or *BRCA2*, she may have a risk for developing the disease of up to 44 percent.[15] A *BRCA1* mutation confers a higher risk of ovarian cancer than does a *BRCA2* mutation. Prophylactic oophorectomy is appropriate for these women.

Screening

Screening for ovarian cancer remains controversial for multiple reasons. First, the incidence in the general population is too low for any but the most specific and low-cost screens to be cost-effective. Second, the presence of a premalignant phase is suggested by some retrospective and pathologic work, but would need to be a prolonged phase to accommodate a reasonable interval between screenings. The concurrent finding of adjacent areas of benign epithelium and transitional epithelium next to malignant epithelium does not insure a premalignant phase in the development of the malignancy. Routine pelvic examination, vaginal and abdominal ultrasound, Doppler studies, and serum marker studies (particularly Ca-125) have been studied, but cost-effective screening for the entire population remains elusive. Ca-125 is not a specific marker for ovarian cancer; in addition, levels may be normal in women who have ovarian cancer. Furthermore, in younger women the level of Ca-125 can vary throughout the menstrual cycle. Vaginal ultrasound has been widely promoted as a screening tool, but the studies done failed to deal with the issue of cost versus benefit. They also are structurally difficult because of the failure to assess concurrent control groups or the lack of long-term differences in mortality. In addition, most women who have had surgery because of abnormal findings on screening studies did not have ovarian cancer.

Those most likely to benefit from such screening are the groups at higher risk because of hereditary factors. Even in these women, where every six-month evaluation with pelvic exam, Ca-125, and ultrasound has been proposed, there is no evidence yet of an increase in overall survival for women who are screened. Furthermore, such studies depend solely on historic controls for assessment of efficacy, which will make effective evaluation of these screening methods difficult, if not impossible. Further discussion regarding the use of these diagnostic tools and ovarian cancer can be found in the chapter on malignant and premalignant diseases of the genital tract.

Recommendation

At present, there is no clear benefit for screening for ovarian cancers in any age population. However, the increased incidence of the disease in patients who have a hereditary predisposition suggests that screening these women may be beneficial. Participation in such screening should be understood to be of uncertain, but potential, benefit at present. Finally, women who have specific genetic syndromes that place them at extraordinarily high risk for ovarian cancer require very careful evaluation, and the current recommendation for these women is prophylactic bilateral oophorectomy at the completion of childbearing or at least by age 35.

References and Selected Readings

1. ACOG Committee Opinion: Routine Cancer Screening 128:1–5, 1993.
2. American Cancer Society: American Cancer Society report on cancer related health check ups. *Cancer* 30:194–240, 1980.
3. Bates SE: Clinical application of serum tumor markers. *Ann Int Med* 115:623–628, 1991.
4. Biesecker BB, Boehnke M, Calzone K, et al: Genetic counseling for families with inherited susceptibility to breast and ovarian cancer. *JAMA* 269:1970–1974, 1993.
5. Brinton LA, Fraumeri F: Epidemiology of uterine cervical cancer. *J Chronic Dis* 39:1051–1065, 1986.
6. Cady B, Stone MD, Wayne J: Continuing trends in the prevalance of right-sided lesions among colorectal carcinoma. *Arch Surg* 128:505–509, 1993.
7. Cecchini S, Palli D, Casini A: Cervical intraepithelial neoplasia III: An estimate of screening error rates and optimal screening interval. *Acta Cytol* 29:329–333, 1985.
8. Collins FS: Medical and ethical consequences of human genome project. *J Clin Ethics* 2:260–267, 1991.
9. Daling JR, Chu J, Weiss NS, et al: The association of condyloma acuminata and squamous carcinoma of the vulva. *Br J Cancer* 50:533–535, 1984.
10. DeVos IH, Lamont DW, Hole DJ, Gillis CR: Asbestos and lung cancer in Glasgow and the west of Scotland. *BMJ* 306:1503–1506, 1993.
11. Diehl AK: Screening for colorectal cancer. *J Fam Pract* 12:625–632, 1981.
12. Eddy DM: Screening for lung cancer. *Ann Int Med* 111:232, 1989.

13. Fleischer DE, Goldberg SB, Browning TH, et al: Detection and surveillance of colorectal cancer. *JAMA* 261:580–585, 1989.
14. Fontana RS, Sanderson DR, Woolner LB, et al: Lung cancer screening: The Mayo program. *J Occup Med* 28:746–748, 1986.
15. Frank TR, Manley SA, Olun Funmilaya IO, et al: Sequence analysis of *BRCA1* and *BRCA2*: Correlation of mutations with family history and ovarian cancer risk. *J Clin Oncol* 16:2417–2425, 1998.
16. Friedman RJ, Rigel DS, Kopf AW: Early detection of malignant melanoma: The role of physician examination and self-examination of the skin. *Cancer* 35:130–134, 1985.
17. Hertz REI, Deddish MR, Day E: Value of periodic examination in detecting cancer of the rectum and colon. *Postgrad Med* 27:290–294, 1960.
18. Kiviat N, Koutsky L: Specific human papilloma virus types as the causal agents of most cervical intraepithelial neoplasia: Implications for current views and treatment. *J Natl Cancer Inst* 85:934–935, 1993.
19. Kondo AT: The thoracic surgeon's role in smoking cessation and prevention. *Semin Thorac Cardiovasc Surg* 5:184–188, 1993.
20. Lynch H, Kullander S (eds): Cancer Genetics in Women. Boca Raton: CRC Press, 1987.
21. Mandelblatt J, Fahs M, Garibaldi K, et al: Association between HIV infection and cervical neoplasia: Implications for clinical care of women at risk for both conditions. *AIDS* 6:173–178, 1992.
22. Mandelblatt J, Gopal I, Wistreich M: Gynecologic care of elderly women. *JAMA* 256:367–370, 1986.
23. Melamed MR, Flehinger BJ, Zaman MB, et al: Screening for early lung cancer: Results of the Memorial Sloan Kettering Study in New York. *Chest* 86:44–47, 1984.
24. Miller AB, Baines CJ, To T, Wall C: Canadian national breast cancer screening study, I: Breast cancer detection and death rate among women aged 40–49. *Can Med Assoc J* 147:1459–1476, 1992.
25. Muller C, Mandelblatt J, Schechter CB: *Cost and Effectiveness of Cervical Cancer Screening in the Elderly*. Office of Technology Assessment, Paper 4, Washington: U.S. Government Printing Office, 1990.
26. O'Rourke MA, Feussner JR, Feigel P, Laszlo J: Age trends of lung cancer stage at diagnosis: Implications for lung cancer screening in the elderly. *JAMA* 258:921–927, 1987.
27. Papanicolaou GN, Traut HF: Diagnosis of uterine cancer by the vaginal smear. New York: Commonwealth Fund, 1943.
28. Pollack SV. Skin cancer in the elderly. *Clin Geriatr Med* 3:715–718, 1987.
29. Reddy BS, Engle A, Simi B, Goldman M: Effect of dietary fiber on colonic bacterial enzymes and bile acids in relation to colon cancer. *Gastroenterology* 102:1475–1482, 1992.
30. Rodney WM, Beaber RJ, Johnson R, Quan M: Physician compliance with colorectal cancer screening (1978–1983): The impact of flexible sigmoidoscopy. *J Fam Pract* 20:265–269, 1985.
31. Sheets E, Crum C: Current status and future clinical potential of human papillomavirus infection and epithelia neoplasia. *Curr Opin Obstet Gynecol* 5:63–66, 1993.
32. Shy K, Chu J. Mandelson M, et al: Papanicolaou smear screening interval and risk of cervical cancer. *Obstet Gynecol* 74:838–843, 1989.
33. Silverberg E, Lubera JA: Cancer statistics 1989. *Cancer* 39:3–7, 1989.
34. Simon J: Occult blood screening for colorectal cancer: A critical review. *Gastroenterology* 88:820–837, 1985.
35. Weisberger JH: Cancer's relevant mechanisms, and prevention of large bowel cancer. *Semin Oncol* 18:316–336, 1991.
36. Wilkinson EJ: Pap smears and screening for cervical neoplasia. *Clin Obstet Gynecol* 33:817–821, 1990.
37. Wilson JMG, Junger G: Principles of early disease detection. *Public Health Pap* 34:27–32, 1968.
38. Winawer SJ, Zauber AG, Stewart E, O'Brien MJ: The natural history of colorectal cancer. *Cancer* 67:1143–1149, 1991.

CHAPTER 6

Adult Immunization

Stanley A. Gall

ORGANIZED PHYSICIAN PROGRAMS FOR VACCINE DELIVERY

COST EFFECTIVENESS OF VACCINES

VACCINE ADMINISTRATION

CONTRAINDICATIONS AND MISCONCEPTIONS CONCERNING ADULT IMMUNIZATIONS

IMMUNIZATION FOR HEALTHY ADULTS

Adolescents and young adults (15 to 24 years) • Adults (25 to 64 years) • Adults (65 years or older)

IMMUNIZATION FOR SPECIAL ADULT GROUPS

Pregnant Women • College students and other at risk groups • Immunization of immunocompromised adults

IMMUNIZATION AND OTHER MEASURES FOR INTERNATIONAL TRAVEL

Tetanus and Diphtheria • Poliomyelitis • Viral Hepatitis B • Viral Hepatitis A • Measles, Mumps, Rubella • Yellow Fever • Meningococcal Meningitis • Typhoid Fever • Cholera • Japanese Encephalitis

W hile routine immunization is an integral part of pediatric practices, routine immunization has not been widely incorporated into the health care of adult patients. The result is that adolescents and adults continue to become infected with vaccine-preventable diseases.

The reasons for this seemingly inappropriate lack of attention to adult immunization are several-fold. First, most patients do not perceive a need for immunization and do not ask their physician for immunization advice or schedules. Second, many physicians have not incorporated a routine in their offices to make certain that their patients have been immunized according to an accepted schedule. Lastly, reimbursement for immunizations is not universally provided and patients often do not perceive that they are receiving added value when paying additional fees for immunization.

Vaccination has proved to be the most effective, cost-efficient means to prevent infectious diseases. The pioneering work of Edward Jenner in the eighteenth century using cowpox to prevent smallpox was the first rational, controlled effort to prevent human disease by vaccination. The first "man-made" vaccine was the attenuated virus vaccine developed by Louis Pasteur in 1885. Inactivated vaccines were introduced in the 1890s.

The technology of cultivating virus in tissue culture, developed in the late 1940s, revolutionized the field of vaccine development. This led to an inactivated polio vaccine in 1955, and a live-attenuated oral polio vaccine in 1962. Live-attenuated vaccines against measles, mumps, and rubella were introduced in the late 1960s.

The technology of vaccine production improved with vaccines composed of highly purified capsular polysaccharides against three invasive bacterial pathogens, *Streptococcus pneumoniae*, *Neisseria meningitidis*, and *Haemophilus influenzae* type B, introduced between 1974 and 1984. In 1986, the first vaccine for human use obtained from recombinant DNA technology was introduced for hepatitis B virus.

Despite impressive accomplishments with immunization programs, infectious diseases continue to kill many people for a number of reasons. First, vaccines for several important infectious agents such as *Escherichia coli* and *Plasmodium falciparum* are unavailable. Second, there are numerous logistical problems in the distribution and administration of vaccines. Third, there is insufficient funding for vaccine research and for vaccine administration. Fourth, and probably most important, the general public often fails to understand and comply with recommended vaccine policies.

An important public misconception is the risk-to-benefit ratio that is derived from vaccination. The public perception is that vaccination is essentially risk-free and provides complete protection against disease. Vaccination does have some risks. Rare neurologic sequelae associated with the whole pertussis vaccine have resulted in a dramatic decrease in pertussis vaccine use and increased litigation.

In most circumstances, the benefits of appropriately indicated vaccination overwhelmingly outweigh the risks. Vaccination could reduce the unnecessary occurrence of vaccine-preventable diseases such as polio, diphtheria, tetanus, pertussis, measles, mumps, rubella, influenza, pneumococcal pneumonia, and hepatitis B virus if health care providers for adolescents and adults would provide vaccinations as a routine part of their practice. Patients with special lifestyle behaviors may present additional health problems. International travelers to certain countries may be at increased risk of exposure to vaccine-preventable diseases not present in the United States. In addition, foreign students, immigrants, and refugees either may bring diseases with them or may be exposed to vaccine-preventable diseases in the United States.

Organized Physician Programs for Vaccine Delivery

An immunization program is an important part of primary care. The immunization history of all new patients, and a periodic review of the immunization status of established patients, is the starting point. Because the incidence of childhood diseases has been markedly reduced by immunization, a considerable number of adults have missed both immunization and natural infection. Because some diseases, such as measles, are more serious when they occur in the adult, the clinician should insure that patients are protected.

Unfortunately, an accurate immunization history is often difficult to obtain. The patient may have received immunizations from several sources in the past, and patients often do not keep accurate personal histories. The most reliable way to determine the patient's immunization history is from information obtained from the patient and her previous physician(s). As a general rule, if there is doubt about previous immunizations, assume the patient is not immunized.

The American College of Physicians (ACP) recommends a general review of a patient's health status at age 50. That includes a review of immunizations; lifestyle activities with a concentration on nutrition, exercise, smoking, and alcohol and other drug uses; current illnesses; and medications. The review is used to develop an appropriate plan to address the deficiencies discovered. This is a newer program and its success has not been evaluated, but it makes good sense and is strongly encouraged.

After obtaining a history, the physician must determine who should be immunized and then establish a mechanism for offering necessary vaccines. Experience indicates that all patients need immunization except those whose history indicates prior immunization, or those who have a specific contraindication. The actual mechanisms for a successful vaccine program can be simple. The patient can fill out an immunization questionnaire and discuss it with the office nurse, who can indicate which vaccines are needed. Reminder notices can be by postcard or with other correspondence sent out by the office or clinic. Many approaches are successful, but they must be initiated and supported with enthusiasm by the physicians involved.

Cost-Effectiveness of Vaccines

There are currently more than 50 types of vaccines available in the United States, and some research is available to determine whether these vaccines are worthwhile; that is, do they have positive cost-effectiveness and cost-benefit ratios?

In the analysis of cost-effectiveness and cost-benefit, net medical care costs and net health benefits from the vaccination program are studied. Net medical care costs usually include the cost of the vaccine and its administration and the cost of treating vaccine-related complications, minus the medical care savings due to prevention of disease. Net health benefits from a vaccination program include reductions in morbidity and mortality from prevention of disease offset by any morbidity and mortality associated with vaccine side effects. Net health benefits may include gains in productivity from reduced absences from work.

Net medical care costs, net health benefits, and net health benefits expressed in dollar terms can all be used to evaluate a vaccination program. If the net benefits exceed costs, or if the ratio of benefits to costs is >1, the vaccination program is considered worthwhile on an efficiency basis. Also, net health care costs per unit of health benefit can be calculated for different medical programs, with the lowest cost per unit of health improvement being the most cost-effective.

Cost-effectiveness and cost-benefit analyses demonstrate that immunization programs against measles, pertussis, poliomyelitis, and rubella are cost-effective. Pneumococcal and influenza vaccination programs are reasonably cost-effective, especially in older adults. Studies analyzing hepatitis B screening for health care workers and other groups at risk demonstrate that a vaccine program is cost-effective. The cost-benefit analyses of other vaccines used in adult immunizations have not yet been studied.

Vaccine Administration

The package insert that accompanies the vaccine from the manufacturer should be consulted for each specific vaccine. The recommended route of administration should be followed. Adult vaccines are usually administered via the intramuscular (IM), subcutaneous (SC), or the intradermal (ID) routes. The injections are usually given in the deltoid muscle in adults. The buttock is not recommended as a vaccination site because of possible injury to the sciatic nerve, and studies with the hepatitis B vaccine have shown its immunogenicity is significantly lower when given in the buttock rather than in the deltoid.

The recommended dose for each vaccine varies. A vaccine's package insert provides dose specifics. There is no advantage to splitting the dose into two injections, and data suggest that the resulting protection could be compromised.

Most of the widely used vaccines are safe and effective when given on the same day (Table 6-1). Inactivated vaccines can be given simultaneously at separate sites. Consideration should be given to separate days of administration when using vaccines known to cause pronounced local or systemic side effects (e.g., cholera and typhoid vaccines).

The antibody response to simultaneously administered live-virus vaccines seems to result in appropriate titers for each without an increase in adverse reactions. Theoretical considerations suggest that live viruses not given on the same day should be given at least 1 month apart to prevent inhibition of the immune response. An inactive and a live virus may be given simultaneously at separate sites as long as the recommendations on the package insert are followed. Data suggest that vaccination with cholera and yellow fever vaccines, either simultaneously or within 3 weeks of each other, can interfere with the levels of antibody produced by each vaccine. Therefore, these two vaccines should be given at least 3 weeks apart.

Immune globulin and various disease-specific immunoglobulins contain antibodies that can in-

TABLE 6-1 Vaccine Schedules for Adults[a,b]

Vaccine	Primary Schedule and Boosters	Indications	Contraindications and Precautions	Special Considerations
Tetanus-diphtheria toxoid	Two doses IM 4 weeks apart. A third dose 6 to 12 months after second dose. Booster every 10 years.	All adults	1. History of neurologic or immediate hypersensitivity following a previous dose. 2. History of severe local reaction after previous dose. 3. Do not give routine or emergency toxoids for 10 years. 4. Pregnancy not a contraindication.	
Measles vaccine	One dose SC. Revaccination recommended prior to starting college.	1. Adults born before 1957 are immune. 2. For others, if no documented evidence of vaccination, give two doses of vaccine separated by at least 1 month. 3. Revaccination with MMR recommended for students entering college, health care workers, and international travelers.	Pregnancy, immunocompromised patients, history of anaphylactic reaction following egg ingestion or receipt of neomycin.	1. MMR is vaccine of choice. 2. Live-virus vaccine. 3. Persons vaccinated between 1963 and 1967 with a killed measles vaccine should be revaccinated with live measles vaccine.
Mumps vaccine	One dose SC.	1. All adults without documentation of live vaccine or documented disease should be vaccinated. 2. Susceptible travelers. 3. No contraindication to older persons receiving vaccine.	Pregnancy, immunocompromised persons, history of anaphylactic reaction following egg ingestion or receipt of neomycin.	1. MMR is vaccine of choice if recipient is likely to be susceptible to measles and rubella as well as mumps. 2. Live-virus vaccine.
Rubella	One dose SC.	1. Adults lacking documentation of live vaccine or laboratory evidence of immunity. 2. Particularly for reproductive-age women and persons who work in hospitals, colleges, or on military bases. 3. Susceptible travelers should be immunized.	Pregnancy, immunocompromised persons, history of anaphylactic reaction following receipt of neomycin.	1. A theoretical risk to fetus if vaccinated in first 3 months of pregnancy is so small as to be negligible. 2. MMR is the choice of vaccine if patient is susceptible to measles and mumps too.

TABLE 6-1 Vaccine Schedules for Adults[a,b] (*Continued*)

Vaccine	Primary Schedule and Boosters	Indications	Contraindications and Precautions	Special Considerations
Varicella	Two SC doses 1 month apart—live-attenuated vaccine.	Women who are IgG negative or who have a negative history for chicken pox.	Contraindicated in pregnancy.	Long-term efficacy not determined.
Polio	1. E-IPV is preferred for primary adult vaccination. Two doses SC 4 to 8 weeks apart; third dose 6 to 12 months after second dose. 2. For adults who have completed primary vaccination and who need a booster, either E-IPV or OPV can be given.	1. Persons traveling outside of U.S. and all health care workers. 2. If an incomplete series of vaccinations was given as a child, the entire series with either OPV or E-IPV should be given.	1. Avoid in pregnant women unless immediate protection is needed. 2. If immediate protection is needed, OPV is recommended. 3. OPV should not be given to immunocompromised persons or to individuals with immunocompromised family members. E-IPV is recommended in those situations. 4. OPV has been associated with paralytic polio on rare occasions.	1. E-IPV = Enhanced-potency inactivated poliovirus vaccine. 2. OPV = Oral poliovirus vaccine (live) 3. E-IPV may not induce a protective immune response in immunocompromised individuals.
Hepatitis B	1. Two IM doses 4 weeks apart with third dose 5 months after the second. 2. Protection lasts 7 years. 3. Screening with HbsAB should be done before booster given.	1. Adults at increased risk of occupational environmental, social, or family exposure. 2. All health care workers should be vaccinated. 3. All individuals at risk for sexually transmitted diseases should be vaccinated.	Pregnancy category C.	1. Prevaccination serologic screening for susceptibility may or may not be cost-effective. 2. The vaccine produces neither therapeutic nor adverse effects on HBV-infected persons.
Hepatitis A	Two IM doses 6 months apart. Protection lasts at least 10 years. No recommendation for booster at this time.	Travelers, homosexuals, intravenous drug abusers, food handlers, employees of day care centers, health care workers.	Pregnancy category C.	Inactivated vaccine Havrix 1440 ELU per dose in two-dose schedule. VAQTA 50 U per dose in a two-dose schedule.
Influenza	Annual vaccination with current vaccine. Either whole- or split-virus vaccine may be used.	1. Adults with high-risk conditions, residents of nursing homes or other chronic care facilities. 2. All health care personnel. 3. Healthy person 65 years of age or older.	History of anaphylactic hypersensitivity to egg ingestion is a contraindication.	Inactivated whole-virus and split-virus vaccine.

(continued)

TABLE 6-1 Vaccine Schedules for Adults[a,b] *(Continued)*

Vaccine	Primary Schedule and Boosters	Indications	Contraindications and Precautions	Special Considerations
		4. Pregnant women in second or third trimester during influenza season.		
Rabies	1. Preexposure prophylaxis—two doses IM or ID one week apart, third dose 3 weeks after second. Booster every 2 years if exposure continues. 2. Postexposure prophylaxis—clean wound. If not previously vaccinated: give rabies immune globulin—half at bite site; half IM; 5 doses of rabies vaccine IM on each of days 0, 3, 7, 14, 28. 3. Persons who have received preexposure prophylaxis, or postexposure prophylaxis, or have a previously documented antibody titer considered adequate: 2 doses rabies vaccine—one each on days 0 and 3.	1. Veterinarians, animal handlers, certain laboratory workers, and visitors to countries where rabies is a threat. 2. If substantial risk to rabies, preexposure vaccination should be given before pregnancy.	1. Certain steroids and immunosuppressive agents can interfere with the development of active immunity. 2. History of anaphylaxis to a previous dose of rabies vaccine is a contraindication to further rabies vaccination.	1. HDCV: human diploid cell vaccine. Rabies vaccine, absorbed. (RVA) 2. Complete preexposure prophylaxis does not eliminate the need for additional therapy with rabies vaccine after a rabies exposure. 3. For postexposure prophylaxis, rabies vaccine should always be administered IM, not ID.
Yellow Fever	One dose SC 10 days to 10 years before travel. Booster every 10 years.	Selected persons traveling or living in area where yellow fever exists.	1. Avoid vaccinating pregnant women unless individual must travel to highly endemic areas. 2. Immunocompromised persons, history of hypersensitivity to egg ingestion.	1. 17D = Live-attenuated. 2. Some countries request a valid international certification of vaccination showing receipt of vaccine.
Cholera	Two 0.5 ml doses SC or IM or two 0.2 ml doses ID 1 week to 1 month apart. Booster doses 0.5 ml IM or 0.2 ml ID every 6 months.	The World Health Organization no longer recommends cholera vaccination for international travels to cholera-endemic areas.	1. No safety data on use in pregnancy. 2. Persons who have had severe local or systemic reactions to a previous dose should not be vaccinated.	1. Inactivated bacterial vaccine. 2. Some countries still require a complete series of vaccination. 3. Cholera and yellow fever vaccines should be administered at least 3 weeks apart.

TABLE 6-1 Vaccine Schedules for Adults[a,b] (*Continued*)

Vaccine	Primary Schedule and Boosters	Indications	Contraindications and Precautions	Special Considerations
Meningo-coccus	One dose IM. The need for booster doses is unknown.	Travelers to countries recognized as having epidemic meningococcal disease.	Pregnancy, unless there is substantial risk of infection.	Polysaccharide vaccines (bivalent A and C, tetravalent A, C, and Y, W-135).
Plague	Three IM doses: first dose, second dose 1 month later, third dose 5 months after second dose. Booster doses at 1 to 2-year intervals if exposure continues.	Selected travelers to countries where exposure to rodents and fleas is likely. Field and laboratory workers working with *Yersina pestis*.	1. Pregnancy, unless there is a substantial risk of exposure. 2. Persons with known hypersensitivity to vaccine constituents.	1. Inactivated bacterial vaccine. 2. Prophylactic antibiotics may be indicated following definite exposure.
Pneumo-coccal	One IM dose. Revaccination should be considered every 6 years.	1. Adults at increased risk of pneumococcal disease. 2. All adults 65 years and older.	Pregnancy category C.	1. Inactivated bacterial vaccine. 2. Pneumococcal and influenza vaccines can be given simultaneously at separate sites.
Typhoid	Two doses 4 or more weeks apart. Booster dose every 3 years.	Travelers to areas where there is a recognized risk of typhoid.	Severe local or systemic reaction to a previous dose.	Inactivated bacterial vaccine.

[a]When it is necessary to use an approved vaccine or toxoid in pregnancy, waiting until the second or third trimester, when appropriate, is a reasonable precaution.

[b]Always read the package insert prior to using a vaccine, especially if it is used infrequently.

SOURCE: Modified from: *Guide for Adult Immunization,* 2nd ed. Philadelphia: American College of Physicians, 1990.

terfere with live-attenuated virus vaccines (Table 6-2). Passively acquired antibodies to measles, mumps, and rubella can interfere with the active replication of the vaccine virus and limit the antibody response by the patient. It is recommended that at least 6 weeks and preferably 3 months elapse between administration of passive immune globulin and active immunization. The response to oral polio and yellow fever vaccines is not inhibited by immune globulin. Additionally, inhibition of active immunity after an inactivated vaccine is not observed. These two vaccines can be given simultaneously or at any time after immune globulin. If a live vaccine has been administered and immune globulin is indicated, the minimal interval between them is 2 weeks. The patient subsequently must be tested to confirm seroconversion or the need for revaccination.

Contraindications and Misconceptions Concerning Adult Immunizations

Serious reactions such as anaphylaxis are rare. When serious hypersensitivity reactions occur, they are almost always a reaction to a component of the vaccine, such as residual animal proteins, antibiotics, preservatives, or stabilizers. Egg protein is the most common allergic component found in vaccines made from embryonated chicken eggs or chicken embryonal cultures (measles, mumps, influenza, and yellow fever vaccines). Persons who eat eggs may receive these vaccines, but they are contraindicated for patients with a history of anaphylaxis to eggs or egg protein.

Occasionally, patients will have an anaphylactic reaction to the MMR (measles, mumps, rubella) vaccine. This is seen in those who have

TABLE 6-2   Immunobiologicals[a,b]

Immune Globulins	Schedule	Indications	Major Precautions and Contraindications	Special Considerations
Hepatitis A	Preexposure prophylaxis: 1 IM dose of 0.02 ml/kg for risk of ≤3 months. IM dose 0.06 ml/kg for risk of >3 months. Vaccine preferred.	1. Household and sexual contacts with persons with Hepatitis A. 2. Staff and parents of diapered attendees in day care center outbreaks.	Pregnancy not a contraindication to vaccination if it is necessary.	Immunoglobulin can interfere with the antibody response to administered live-virus vaccines.
Hepatitis B	0.06 ml/kg IM as soon as possible after exposure followed by a second dose 1 month later, except when HBV vaccine is given.	1. Following percutaneous or mucous membrane exposure to blood known to be HbsAg-positive, sexual exposure, or a bite from a person with acute HBV or a chronic carrier. 2. Perinatally for infants born of HBsAg-positive mother.		HBV vaccine should be given if person at risk for HBV.
Measles	Postexposure prophylaxis: 0.25 ml/kg IM (maximum 15 ml) given within 6 days of exposure.	Exposed susceptible contacts of measles cases.	IG should not be used to control measles outbreaks.	1. IG given within 6 days of exposure can prevent or modify measles. 2. Recipients of IG should receive live measles vaccine 3 months later.
Tetanus	250 units IM	Part of management of a nonclean, nonminor wound in a person whose history of tetanus vaccination is unknown.		
Rabies	20 IU/kg half infiltrate around wound, half IM.	Part of postexposure prophylaxis of persons with rabies exposure who lack history of rabies vaccination.		Rabies immune globulin is usually given with the first dose of vaccine, but it can be given up to 8 days after vaccination.
Varicella	1. Persons ≤50 kg: 125 units/10 kg IM. 2. Persons >50 kg: 625 units.	1. Immunocompromised persons likely to have close and prolonged exposure to a contact case. 2. Perinatal prophylaxis and treatment of mothers and prophylaxis of infants born of mothers with varicella.	1. VZIG is not indicated for healthy, normal adults exposed to varicella. 2. Not a treatment for Herpes zoster.	An acceptable alternative to VZIG is to treat varicella if it occurs with high-dose IV acyclovir.

[a]When it is necessary to use an approved vaccine or toxoid in pregnancy, waiting until the second or third trimester, when appropriate, is a reasonable precaution.

[b]Always read the package insert prior to using a vaccine, especially if it is used infrequently.

SOURCE: Modified from: *Guide for Adult Immunization,* 2nd ed. Philadelphia: American College of Physicians, 1990.

sensitivity to either neomycin or streptomycin, as the two antibiotics are present in the MMR vaccine. Vaccination is contraindicated in those patients. Currently, no licensed vaccine contains any penicillin, so patients allergic to penicillin can be vaccinated. On occasion, a patient may experience a severe systemic reaction to cholera, typhoid, or plague vaccines. These reactions are most likely toxic reactions and are true hypersensitivity. Obviously, revaccination should be avoided if possible.

Immunization with live virus vaccines should be avoided in individuals who are immunocompromised as the result of disease or medical therapy. Oral polio vaccine is contraindicated if any member of the family is immunocompromised because the usual spread of polio virus is via the fecal-oral route. The MMR vaccine can be given to members of the same family because, although recipients can shed vaccine virus, infection is not transmitted to others. The use of oral or topical doses of corticosteroids likely to cause systemic effects contraindicates the use of live virus vaccines.

Most patients who do not receive vaccines do so because of misconceptions concerning adult immunization and *not* because of contraindications to the vaccination.[1] The following list addresses some of the more common misconceptions:

1. Reaction to a previous vaccination consisting of only mild to moderate local tenderness, redness, and/or swelling or fever <40.5°C is not a contraindication to vaccination.
2. Mild, acute upper respiratory or gastrointestinal illness with fever <38.0°C is not a contraindication to vaccination.
3. Current antimicrobial therapy or convalescence from a recent illness is not a contraindication to vaccination.
4. Pregnancy in another household contact is not a contraindication to vaccination.
5. Recent exposure to an infectious disease is not a contraindication to vaccination.
6. Breast-feeding is not a contraindication to vaccination.

7. Personal history of "allergies," including allergy to penicillin or other antibiotics, but not anaphylactic reactions to neomycin (MMR vaccine) or streptomycin (oral polio vaccine) is not a contraindication to vaccination.
8. Family history of "allergies," adverse reactions to vaccination, or seizures is not a contraindication to vaccination.

Immunization for Healthy Adults

Adolescents and Young Adults (15 to 24 Years)

Most adolescents and young adults have completed a primary three-dose series of diphtheria and tetanus toxoid by this age. However, if immunization was either incomplete or not done in childhood, the three-dose series should be given. The first two doses should be given at least 4 weeks apart and a third dose 6 to 12 months after the second dose. Those who have completed the entire primary three-dose series should receive a booster dose every 10 years. The combined tetanus and diphtheria toxoids (for adult use) (Td) should be used. Persons whose immunization history is unknown should be considered unvaccinated and receive the full three-dose primary series of Td.

All persons born after 1956 should have received measles vaccine unless they provide documentation of physician-diagnosed measles or laboratory evidence of immunity. Persons born in the U.S. before 1957 almost always were infected with mumps virus and can therefore be considered immune. Because of an outbreak of measles in 1989 in school and college settings, a two-dose live-virus MMR vaccine is recommended. It is advisable that young adults attending college or other post-high school institutions either have documentation of having received two doses of live-virus MMR after their first birthday or have evidence of immunity.

Persons vaccinated with killed-measles virus vaccine (1963 to 1967) or with a measles vaccine of unknown type should receive two doses of live-measles vaccine one month apart.

Persons are considered immune to rubella only if they have a record of immunization or laboratory evidence of immunity.

Influenza vaccination is recommended for those who provide essential community service, such as health care workers including physicians, military personnel, and college students living in dormitories.

Varicella vaccine is now available and should be included in the routine immunization schedule. At present, approximately 20 percent of adolescents remain susceptible to varicella. If the patient or her mother cannot remember whether the patient has had chickenpox, the patient needs to have a varicella IgG determination. If the test is negative, the patient should receive varicella vaccine. For a susceptible person >13 years of age, two doses separated by 4 to 8 weeks are recommended.

Hepatitis B immunization is recommended for all health care workers, institutionalized patients, and patients at risk for sexually transmitted diseases. All pregnant patients should be screened for hepatitis B surface antigen. Immunization consists of two IM doses four weeks apart, and a third dose five months after the second dose. Protection lasts 7 years.

Until recently, the primary methods for preventing hepatitis A have been hygienic measures and passive immunization with immune globulin (Ig) to provide short-term preexposure or postexposure protection. A hepatitis A vaccine has been introduced that can provide long-term protection against hepatitis A infection. Hepatitis A vaccine is indicated for travelers, homosexuals, drug-injecting persons, persons working with nonhuman primates, persons with chronic liver disease, those who have clotting factor disorders, workers in food-service establishments and all food handlers, persons working in day care centers, all persons in health care institutions or offices, elementary and secondary schools and colleges, and any worker exposed to sewage. For persons ≥17 years old two injections are recom-

mended, with the doses separated by 6 months. Preexposure protection should be accomplished with hepatitis A vaccine. Postexposure prophylaxis in those individuals who have not received hepatitis A vaccine should be administered as a single dose of hepatitis A Ig (0.02 mg/kg) intramuscular as soon as possible, but not more than 2 weeks after exposure. Hepatitis A vaccine should be administered at the same time as the Ig, but at a different anatomic site.

Adults (25 to 64 Years)

All adults should have completed a primary series of diphtheria and tetanus toxoids. If needed, it should be completed as soon as possible. For those who have completed their primary series, a booster of Td should be administered every 10 years.

All adults born in 1957 or later who do not have a medical contraindication should receive one dose of measles vaccine unless they have documented evidence of immunity or documentation of physician-diagnosed disease. Health care workers and physicians are at a greater risk of exposure to measles and should be vaccinated. The clinical diagnosis of rubella is nonspecific, and laboratory documentation of immunity is required. Rubella vaccine should not be administered during pregnancy, but should be given after delivery.

Influenza vaccine is often recommended for all individuals in this age group on a yearly basis. While younger adults usually will not manifest influenza pneumonia, they will manifest upper respiratory symptomatology as well as a "flu" syndrome. Many businesses provide influenza vaccine to all employees, as it decreases absenteeism. Those who definitely should receive influenza vaccine include all health care workers who have patient contact; all persons who have a chronic disease, especially pulmonary; all day care workers; all school teachers; and anyone who is active in meeting other persons. Influenza vaccine may be administered from October through March (influenza season), but it is preferable to administer it in the early months of the influenza season.

Pneumococcal vaccine (pneumovax) should be provided for persons with chronic disease states such as diabetes mellitus, and certainly for all persons with chronic cardiopulmonary conditions. The vaccine is a single injection with repeat injections every 6 years.

Hepatitis B immunization is recommended for all health care workers, institutionalized patients, and patients at risk for sexually transmitted diseases. All pregnent patients should be screened for hepatitis B surface antigen.

See previous discussion regarding hepatitis A vaccine, varicella vaccine, and other vaccines.

Adults (65 Years or Older)

Adults 65 years or older are more susceptible to infectious diseases, especially of the lower respiratory tract. This may be caused by a decline in host defense mechanisms primarily affecting cell-mediated immunity.

Adults in this age group should receive influenza vaccine annually. They should receive a single dose of pneumococcal vaccine, with revaccination every 6 years.

Tetanus and diphtheria boosters should be up-to-date, with revaccination every 10 years. More than half of the cases of tetanus are reported in persons 60 years of age or older. The elderly are capable of mounting a strong antibody response to Td.

See previous discussion regarding other vaccines.

Immunization for Special Adult Groups

Pregnant Women

For many of the vaccines, the risks associated with immunization in pregnancy are largely theoretical, and the advantages outweigh the potential risks of adverse reactions. As a general rule, live-virus vaccines should not be used in pregnancy unless specifically indicated (e.g., yel-

low fever vaccine before travel to an endemic area).

Prenatal screening should be done for rubella, hepatitis B, and varicella. Rubella vaccination should be deferred until postpartum. It is advisable to administer MMR (measles, mumps, rubella) vaccine postpartum when the patient is rubella susceptible. Varicella vaccine can be given at the same time postpartum. There is no contraindication to vaccination with hepatitis B vaccine in pregnancy in those women for whom it is clearly indicated.

Women of childbearing age should be immune to poliomyelitis, measles, mumps, rubella, tetanus, and diphtheria before becoming pregnant. A careful history of illnesses and immunizations may clarify the immune status.

Those vaccines that are safe to administer in pregnancy can be administered in any trimester. There is no evidence that teratogenicity occurs with vaccines judged safe for pregnancy. It is wise to defer vaccination until the second trimester when the risk of spontaneous abortion is significantly decreased.

Pregnant patients who have not received tetanus and diphtheria vaccine should receive two doses of Td given 4 to 8 weeks apart. This should be followed by a third dose 6 to 12 months later. If the series was not completed earlier, or if it has been 10 or more years since a patient's last dose, a booster should be given.

Influenza vaccine is now recommended for women who will be in the second or third trimester of pregnancy during the influenza season. Pneumococcal vaccine is pregnancy category C, and is recommended only for pregnant women who need it. It has been suggested that pregnant women with severe asthma and bronchitis might be appropriate candidates. Influenza and pneumococcal vaccines can be given at the same time at different anatomical sites.

MMR vaccine is not indicated in pregnancy. Rubella vaccine should be administered postpartum or may be given to nonpregnant women who do not plan to become pregnant within three months.

Pregnant women in the United States should be immune to polio virus; however, immunization during pregnancy is recommended only when the risk of exposure is high. The risk for polio is largely from international travel to endemic areas.

Two vaccines are available to prevent poliomyelitis: oral live-virus vaccine and an inactivated polio vaccine. For an unimmunized pregnant woman at high risk of exposure to poliovirus, a single dose of oral polio vaccine is recommended if less than four weeks are available and immediate protection is needed. If time permits, two doses of inactivated vaccine at 1- to 2-month intervals are recommended. Pregnant women at high risk of exposure and who received polio vaccinations more than 10 years before, should receive a one-time booster of inactivated polio vaccine.

Yellow fever vaccine is an attenuated live-virus vaccine but it is not known to be teratogenic. Vaccination is indicated if a pregnant woman must travel to areas where yellow fever is endemic.

As should be done for any patient, before ever vaccinating a pregnant woman, read the package insert carefully for contraindications.

College Students and Other At-Risk Groups

College students are at risk for several vaccine-preventable diseases because of crowding in dormitories, importation of disease from foreign students or after foreign travel, and age-group susceptibility. Several states have laws requiring students to document their immunization status, and some colleges require proof of immunization prior to matriculation. An MMR vaccine (two doses) should be administered to students traveling abroad or entering college unless proof of immunization can be determined.

Td should be given as a booster vaccine if more than 10 years have passed since primary immunization. If the primary three-dose series for tetanus and diphtheria has not been completed, it should be completed.

Hepatitis B vaccination is strongly recommended for groups of college students at increased risk for infection. These include: heterosexually active students with multiple sexual partners or those who are at risk for a sexually acquired disease; homosexual or bisexual males; and students with sexual contacts with students from endemic areas. Serologic screening prior to immunization is not cost-effective.

It is highly advisable for all college students to be immunized with influenza vaccine. While influenza pneumonia is uncommon, other "flu"-like symptoms are common, causing discomfort and absence from classes.

Immunization of Immunocompromised Adults

Patients may be immunocompromised by therapies that cause immune system failure or because they have endogenous diseases that cause immune system failure. In approaching prevention of infection in immunocompromised patients, three principles are important: (1) prevention of infection is better than treatment; (2) the need for preventive efforts is determined by the epidemiology of the exposure to infection; and (3) the likelihood of both acquiring and preventing infection is directly related to the net state of immunosuppression.

Immunosuppressed patients should receive their annual influenza vaccine despite suboptimal antibody response. Pneumococcal vaccine should be given, with revaccination in 6 years. *Haemophilus influenzae*, type B conjugate vaccine is of unproven benefit in immunocompromised patients, but should be considered in patients with anatomic or functional asplenia.

Asymptomatic HIV-positive patients may be vaccinated with MMR.

Immunization and Other Measures for International Travel

More than 10 million Americans travel outside of the United States annually, and more than half visit areas where tropical diseases are endemic. The physician's advice regarding immunizations is influenced by the specific itinerary; entry or exit requirements of the countries being visited for yellow fever or cholera vaccination; the type of accommodations; duration of travel; the patient's status regarding routine immunization; and special requirements for people who live within a particular country.

These immunizations are frequently given: tetanus, diphtheria, polio, hepatitis A, measles, mumps, and rubella. Additionally, yellow fever, typhoid, cholera, hepatitis B, meningococcus, rabies, Japanese encephalitis, and plague may be required immunizations based on exposure risk.

Tetanus and Diphtheria

Primary adult immunization is by IM injections of tetanus toxoid (in combination with diphtheria at 0, 1, and 6 to 12 months). A booster injection is recommended every 10 years.

Poliomyelitis

Polio is endemic in several areas of the world and major outbreaks occurred in Senegal in 1986 and Taiwan in 1983. Both oral polio vaccine (OPV) and inactivated polio vaccine (IPV) contain the three viral serotypes. Because OPV has been associated with paralytic polio on rare occasion (1 in 2.6 million doses), enhanced-potency IPV vaccine is preferred for primary vaccination of the previously unimmunized adult. If the traveler has completed the primary series, a one-time booster of either OPV or IPV is advised. Because IPV does not stimulate immunity for several weeks, previously unimmunized travelers entering an endemic area within 30 days should be given OPV or enhanced-potency IPV.

Viral Hepatitis B

Routine immunization against hepatitis B virus should be strongly considered. Persons who may be exposed to blood or blood products, and persons living in close contact or having sexual contact with infected persons, should receive immunization. Hepatitis immunization consists of three IM injections at 0, 1, and 6 months.

Viral Hepatitis A

Active immunization against hepatitis A is now available. Vaccine should be advised for travelers leaving the United States. The vaccine protocol is two doses separated by six months.

Measles, Mumps, Rubella

MMR vaccine should be given to the international traveler who was born after 1957, who has not previously received two doses, and who does not have evidence of immunity.

Yellow Fever

Yellow fever vaccination is required for travel in equatorial Africa and parts of South America. Travelers lacking documentation of immunization may be quarantined 10 days and/or required to receive injection before entry.

Yellow fever vaccine contains attenuated virus and is administered subcutaneously. It is prepared from eggs and is contraindicated in persons with a true egg allergy. It is also contraindicated in immunosuppressed persons and in pregnancy (unless travel to high-risk areas is essential). Protection becomes active 10 days after immunization and continues for 10 years.

Meningococcal Meningitis

Neisseria meningitidis is endemic in parts of sub-Saharan Africa, India, and Southeast Asia. Recently, Saudi Arabia required proof of meningococcal vaccination for all pilgrims traveling to certain parts of the country. The vaccine is a polyvalent polysaccharide vaccine. Antibody development usually takes 4 weeks, so a person should be immunized at least one month before travel to an endemic area. After immunization, a person is considered protected for 3 years.

Typhoid Fever

Typhoid vaccine is indicated for travelers who are likely to be exposed to contaminated food and water, or who will be living in rural areas for a prolonged time. Typhoid vaccine is a killed-bacteria vaccine, and the primary series of two shots given 1 month apart is thought to be protective for 3 years. A single booster is given to travelers immunized more than 3 years prior to travel. Typhoid vaccine is 70 to 90 percent effective in protecting against infection.

Cholera

Cholera is most prevalent in Asia and Africa. Following natural infection, immunity will last for only 3 to 9 months. Therefore, illness may develop many times. A sterile suspension of phenol-killed *Vibrio cholerae* is used for vaccination. The vaccine reduces the incidence of clinical disease by about 50 percent for 3 to 6 months. Optimal immunization requires two injections 4 weeks apart. A single booster injection should be considered if the traveler continues in a high risk situation for more than 6 months.

Japanese Encephalitis

This is a mosquito-borne viral illness endemic to Southeast Asia, Japan, Korea, India, and the Philippines. Epidemics occur during the rainy season (June to September). The killed virus vaccine is 75 to 90 percent effective after two injections 1 to 4 weeks apart. The vaccine is not available in the United States for civilian use but may be obtained upon arrival in Asia.

Conclusion

The concept of immunization and an immunization program should become an important part of a primary care physician's practice. It provides an excellent opportunity to provide primary preventive care. The primary care initiative published by the American College of Obstetricians and Gynecologists stresses immunizations as an important function of the primary care physician. Patients and physicians should view immunization against infectious disease as a cost-effective health measure.

References and Selected Readings

1. ACOG Task Force on Primary and Preventive Health Care: Primary care review for the obstetrician gynecologist. The American College of Obstetricians and Gynecologists 1:3–10, 1997.
2. American College of Physicians Task Force on Adult Immunization and Infectious Disease Society of America: *Guide for Adult Immunization*. 3d ed. Philadelphia: American College of Physicians, 1994.
3. Grahenstein JD: *Immunization Delivery: A Complete Guide. Facts and Comparisons.* St. Louis, MO: 1997, pp 1–183.
4. Recommendation of the Advisory Committee on Immunization Practice. The American Academy of Pediatrics. The American Academy of Family Physicians and the American Medical Association: Immunization of adolescents. *MMWR* 45(RR-13):1–16, 1996.
5. Recommendations of the Advisory Committee on Immunization Practices and the Hospital Infection Control Practices Advisory Committee: Immunizations of health care workers. *MMWR* 46(RR-18):1–43, 1997.
6. Lemon SM, Thomas DL: Vaccines to prevent viral hepatitis. *N Engl J Med* 336:196–204, 1997.
7. Mulley AG, Silverstein MD, Dienstag JL: Indicators for use of hepatitis B vaccine base on cost-effectiveness analysis. *N Engl J Med* 307:644–652, 1982.
8. Nichol KL, Lind A, Margolis K: The effectiveness of vaccination against influenza in healthy working adults. *N Engl J Med* 333:889–893, 1995.
9. Recommendations of the Advisory Committee on Immunization Practices (ACIP): Prevention and control of influenza. *MMWR* 147(RR-6).1–26, 1998.
10. Recommendation of the Advisory Committee on Immunization Practices: Prevention of pneumococcal disease. *MMWR* 46(RR-8):1–24, 1997.
11. Prevention of hepatitis A through active or passive immunization. *MMWR* 45:RR-15:1–30, 1996.
12. Tenninberg AM, Biassaid JE, Van Lieu J: Varicella vaccine for health care workers at a university hospital: An analysis of costs and benefits. *Infect Control Hospital Epidemiol* 18:405–411, 1997.
13. Recommendations of the Advisory Committee on Immunization Practices: Update: Vaccine side effects, adverse reactions, contraindications and precautions. *MMWR* 45(RR-12):1–35, 1996.
14. Weber DJ, Rutala WA, Weigle K: Selections and use of vaccines for health care workers. *Infect Control Hosp Epidemiol* 18:682–687, 1997.

CHAPTER 7

Preconception Counseling

John W. Larsen
Susanne L. Bathgate
Lisa M. Freese

Traditionally, the assumption has been that the likelihood of a successful pregnancy outcome is greatest when the mother-to-be is healthy and her pregnancy is kept free of hazards. Ideally, good health is the woman's natural state, and pregnancy is easily achieved and maintained with little cause for concern. Unfortunately, 3 to 5 percent of live births are affected by birth defects, and many more pregnancies end prematurely or are compromised in some way by maternal or fetal disorders. Physicians are challenged to improve the outcome of pregnancy for both mother and baby. Physicians can improve obstetric outcome through actions that they take prior to conception.

It has become popular in recent years to discuss preconception counseling as a specialized, goal-oriented physician encounter designed as a custom tune-up just prior to a very deliberate effort to conceive. This type of visit follows the traditional pattern of history, physical exam, diagnostic testing, and therapy for various conditions. A matrix of maternal disorders, fetal problems, and possible medical actions is contained in Table 7-1.

When Table 7-1 is considered on an item-by-item basis, it is clear that many of the potential problems can and should have been considered and prevented in the course of routine health care many years in advance of a possible pregnancy. The earliest basis for preconception care is early pediatric care. For instance, routine childhood immunization against rubella, varicella, and hepatitis B eliminates concern regarding these potential perinatal pathogens in the reproductive years.

Education concerning sexually transmitted diseases (STDs), smoking, alcohol, and drugs may come from the family, school, and doctor's office. While cynics observe that human failing in these areas is abundant, an ounce of prevention can still be more potent than a pound of cure. Consider this in the extreme, but not rare, context of a pregnant teenager who is HIV-positive. Many still have no knowledge of the disease, or think it is somehow limited to homosexual men.

A logical, but underutilized, access point for the physician to introduce the topic of preconception care is the young woman's first gynecologic visit. Although that visit may be principally for the purpose of symptom evaluation (e.g., vaginitis or dysmenorrhea) or contraception, there still can be a positive exchange regarding the value of a healthy body for successful reproduction. Depending on the circumstances involved, this communication can be as short as a few words or expanded to include discussion of a pertinent linked topic, such as contraception methods that prevent STDs, thereby preserving tubal function.

Good nutrition is integral to supporting a healthy pregnancy. An appropriate diet can be explained before conception and continued through pregnancy. This is particularly true regarding a therapeutic diet for disorders such as diabetes or phenylketonuria (PKU). Women who are overweight may wish to lose excess weight before pregnancy, but should not attempt further weight loss

TABLE 7-1 Preconception Matrix

Condition	Potential Problem	Action
	Infections	
Toxoplasmosis	Acute maternal infection during pregnancy can cause fetal damage.	Check for antibody. • If positive, it is protective • If negative and the patient is attempting to conceive, counsel her to avoid soiled cat litter and to avoid ingestion of meat that has not been previously frozen or thoroughly cooked.
Rubella	Acute maternal infection during pregnancy can cause fetal damage.	Check for antibody • If positive, it is protective. • If negative, immunize promptly. Defer pregnancy attempt for six weeks after vaccination, although a vaccine-induced fetal anomaly is unlikely.
Cytomegalovirus (CMV)	Acute infection or chronic infection can cause fetal damage. Risk is much greater when first infection occurs during pregnancy	Check for antibody. • If positive, check for viral shedding during pregnancy. Follow course of pregnancy with serial ultrasound and consider amniocentesis. • If negative, counsel to avoid direct contact with CMV. Important for health care and day care contacts to wear latex gloves.
Hepatitis B	Acute or chronic infection during pregnancy can lead to fetal or neonatal infection. Baby may become lifetime HBsAg carrier.	Check for HBsAg • If negative, consider immunization. • If HBsAg is positive, counsel patient about possible in utero transmission, and prepare to immunize the child at birth.
Syphilis	Acute or chronic infection during pregnancy can cause fetal damage.	Check for antibody. • If positive and no prior adequate therapy, treat with antibiotics according to protocol.
Gonorrhea	Can cause cervicitis, salpingitis, infertility, prematurity, postpartum sepsis, or localized infection. Gonococcal ophthalmia neonatorum can cause blindness in the newborn.	Diagnose by swab of endocervix for culture or nucleic acid amplification test. Treat with ceftriaxone or other appropriate antibiotic for resistant strains.
Chlamydia	Can cause cervicitis, salpingitis, infertility, neonatal conjunctivitis, or neonatal pneumonia.	Diagnose by swab of endocervix for nucleic acid amplification test or culture. Treat with tetracycline (if the woman is not pregnant), erythromycin, or other appropriate antibiotics.
Human immunodeficiency virus (HIV)	Can increase maternal risk for other infections. Transmission to fetus approximately 15–25% if not treated during pregnancy, decreased to 8% with antepartum therapy.	Check for antibody. • If positive, counsel regarding ultimate outcome. • Consider contraception rather than pregnancy. • Employ antiviral therapy under protocol.
Genital herpes	Viral shedding at parturition can colonize baby, causing disseminated infection and damage.	Counsel regarding risk and plan cesarean section if infection active at parturition. Consider acyclovir for suppression at term.

TABLE 7-1 Preconception Matrix (*Continued*)

Condition	Potential Problem	Action
Varicella	Acute maternal infection may cross placenta causing disseminated disease with residual damage in baby. Maternal varicella pneumonia can be fatal.	If no prior history of clinical varicella, consider antibody testing and immunization prior to pregnancy. Consider zoster immune globulin for maternal prophylaxis following significant exposure of a susceptible woman who is pregnant or attempting to conceive.
Tuberculosis	Congenital tuberculosis is rare. Maternal disease may become symptomatic during pregnancy. Treatment with isoniazid has potential neurotoxicity for mother and baby.	Skin test if negative history. Chest x-ray followed by completion of chemotherapy, if appropriate, prior to conception.
	Maternal Diseases	
Diabetes (insulin-dependent)	Poor control increases rate of spontaneous abortion, fetal anomalies, and fetal macrosomia.	Check for acute and chronic complications of diabetes, including measurement of renal function. Counsel regarding risks and need for preconception strict control of diabetes to lower abortion rate, anomaly rate, and during pregnancy to prevent macrosomia. Control may be measured by blood-glucose monitoring and hemoglobin A1C levels.
Hyperthyroidism	Thyroid storm can be fatal. Thyroid suppression therapy can cause fetal goiter. Long-acting thyroid stimulator leads to neonatal thyrotoxicosis.	Stabilize with propylthiouracil and possible surgery before pregnancy. Avoid I-131 when pregnancy is being considered.
Seizures	Various antiseizure medications can cause fetal anomalies.	Wean off medication if possible. If not, counsel regarding risk and adjust dose to lowest effective range. Change of medication may be considered.
Cystic fibrosis	Pregnancy can be fatal if pulmonary function is marginal. Male and female infertility is common.	Assess pulmonary function and counsel. When forced expiratory volume is ≤30%, mortality is 50% in two years. Consider contraception rather than pregnancy.
Phenylketonuria (PKU)	Mental retardation and anomalies in fetus if maternal phenylalanine level is in toxic range.	Low phenylalanine diet before and during pregnancy.
Spina bifida	Fetal risk for neural tube defects; pregnancy may hamper maternal function (varies depending on the extent of preconception deficit).	Begin folic acid 1 mg qid one month before conception and continue during pregnancy.
Heart disease	Pregnancy can be fatal if preconception cardiac function is marginal. If maternal or paternal congenital heart disease is present, risk for fetal congenital heart disease is about 4%.	Reevaluate cardiac function and counsel. May need contraception. If at risk for inherited congenital heart disease, then consider fetal echocardiogram during pregnancy.
Renal disease including transplant	Pregnancy can be fatal if marginal renal function preconception. Premature delivery is likely, particularly if pregnancy-induced hypertension occurs.	Reevaluate renal function, including success of prior pregnancy, if any. Counsel; may need contraception.

(*continued*)

TABLE 7-1 Preconception Matrix (*Continued*)

Condition	Potential Problem	Action
Cystic acne	Maternal treatment with oral Accutane (13-*cis*-retinoic acid) during pregnancy can cause multiple severe malformations.	Counsel, confirm negative pregnancy test, and advise simultaneous use of two effective forms of contraception before starting 13-*cis*-retinoic acid. Patient's written consent includes commitment not to become pregnant for at least one month after treatment has been stopped.
Smoking	Decreases fertility and may lead to lower birth weight.	Counsel to stop or severely limit. Consider nicotine-weaning program preconception.
Narcotics/street drugs	Addiction of fetus, brain damage, and prematurity. Placental abruption more frequent among users of crack cocaine. Associated risks for STDs and needle-transmitted infections.	Counsel to stop. Consider methadone program if appropriate.
Alcohol	Fetal alcohol syndrome associated with steady use throughout pregnancy. Risk increases with increased consumption.	Stop alcohol use.
Hypertension	Growth restriction and superimposed pregnancy-induced hypertension. Angiotensin-converting enzyme (ACE) inhibitors can cause fetal skull hypoplasia, renal damage, or stillbirth. Associated renal or cardiac compromise may be detrimental to pregnancy.	Alter antihypertensive therapy if necessary. Evaluate for renal or cardiac end organ damage.
Systemic lupus erythematosus	Conception during active flare more likely to result in active disease during pregnancy. Associated renal or cardiac compromise may be detrimental to pregnancy. Sjögren's antibodies may cause fetal heart block.	Evaluate for renal or cardiac end organ damage. Counsel regarding complications including superimposed pregnancy-induced hypertension, prematurity. Evaluate for antiphospholipid antibodies and Sjögren's antibodies.
History of thromboembolic disease, especially during prior pregnancy	Increased incidence of thrombosis in pregnancy.	Evaluate for hereditary disorders of anticoagulation. Consider anticoagulation with heparin or related drug early in pregnancy. Do not anticoagulate with warfarin during pregnancy.
Inflammatory bowel disease (IBD)	Increased incidence of active disease during pregnancy if conception occurs during active disease.	Evaluate disease status and treat aggressively to achieve quiescence prior to conception. Risk of occurrence of IBD in offspring is about 1%.
Iron deficiency anemia	Worsening anemia in pregnancy.	Replete iron stores prior to pregnancy with dietary sources and iron supplementation.
Family History, Ethnicity, or Genetic Susceptibility		
Congenital heart disease (CHD)	CHD in fetus.	Counsel and consider fetal echocardiogram during pregnancy.
Neural tube defect (NTD)	NTD in fetus.	Begin folic acid preconception, counsel regarding maternal serum alpha-fetoprotein (MSAFP), sonar, and amniocentesis during pregnancy.
African/Hispanic	Sickle cell disease or other hemoglobinopathy.	Screen by hemoglobin electrophoresis.[a]

TABLE 7-1   Preconception Matrix (*Continued*)

Condition	Potential Problem	Action
Southeast Asian/Filipino	α-Thalassemia in fetus.	Screen for carrier status.[a]
French Canadian/Cajun	Tay-Sachs disease.	Screen for carrier status.[a]
Jewish	Tay-Sachs disease.	Screen for carrier status.[a]
	Gaucher's disease.	Screen for both carriers and mildly affected adults[a,b]
	Niemann-Pick disease A&B.	Screen for carrier status[a,b]
	Canavan's disease.	Screen for carrier status[a,b]
Mediterranean	β-Thalassemia in fetus.	Screen for carrier status.[a]
North European Caucasian	Cystic fibrosis.	Screen for carrier status.[a,b]

[a] Counsel regarding prenatal diagnosis by CVS or amniocentesis if both partners are carriers.
[b] Laboratory tests for these disorders may not identify all carriers.

after conception. Underweight women should correct dietary deficiencies prior to pregnancy. A woman who is sedentary may begin exercise in moderation prior to conception.

Daily folic acid supplementation may be wise for all women of reproductive age. As little as 0.4 mg of folic acid daily has been shown to significantly decrease the occurrence of neural tube defects (NTDs). Because roughly 50 percent of pregnancies are "planned," daily dosing by a multivitamin tablet containing folic acid would ensure the benefit whether or not a pregnancy is deliberate.

The physician's office setting may also encourage education that promotes preconception counseling through a variety of patient brochures, video educational aides, and physician-extender support staff. A nurse, a physician's assistant, or a genetic counselor can expand on topics that may be particularly pertinent to the individual patient. This type of office visit may be a good opportunity to screen for genetic traits according to ethnicity (Table 7-1), such as sickle trait, thalassemia minor, or carrier status for Tay-Sachs disease or cystic fibrosis.

A genetic counselor can be particularly helpful in situations that require study of the family tree for disease or carrier identification, or for explaining statistical risks for fetal damage due to disease, genetic factors, or environmental hazards. For some disorders, such as cystic fibrosis, the discussion of statistics may focus on the incomplete sensitivity of carrier detection. (Currently, who should be screened for cystic fibrosis carrier status is controversial. This is an important concern, and the reader is advised to keep up with the evolving literature.) The genetic counselor's work generally is easier if the patient is not yet pregnant. Even if invasive testing [such as chorionic villus sampling (CVS) or amniocentesis] is recommended for diagnosis during pregnancy, this advice is given with less decision-stress during contemplation of pregnancy than in the first or second trimester of pregnancy.

Beyond urging healthy women to stay that way, the physician's mission is to give preconception advice concomitant with the diagnosis and management of certain medical conditions that will affect a subsequent pregnancy. A representative selection of such conditions is included in Table 7-1. Women with chronic or relapsing infections (such as genital herpes or persistent hepatitis B antigenemia) need to know about the possible changes in their perinatal management. Women who are diagnosed with potentially fatal disorders, such as advanced insulin-dependent diabetes, sickle cell disease, cystic fibrosis, severe renal damage, or HIV infection, may wish to avoid pregnancy completely.

Physicians giving ongoing medical care to patients with chronic medical disorders, such as diabetes, hypertension, renal disease, seizure disorders, hyperthyroidism, autoimmune disorders, and asthma, should introduce the issue of pregnancy and make certain that appropriate detailed information is provided to the patient. This may require referral to an obstetric generalist, medical geneticist, or maternal-fetal medicine subspecialist, as appropriate to individual circumstances.

When pregnancy is being considered, the physician should review all medications, including nonprescription agents. Certain medical treatments, such as 13-*cis*-retinoic acid for acne, antiseizure medications, antithyroid medications, and chemotherapy for cancer, can be hazardous to the fetus. Women who require such treatment should be advised to use effective contraception while under medical treatment, or in the case of seizure disorders or hyperthyroidism, only to get pregnant when medical control has been optimized, and the risks of therapy have been understood and accepted.

In many urgent or emergent situations, it is easy to say that preconception counseling is extraneous to the problem at hand or "not medically necessary." It is very important for primary care physicians to realize that preconception advice can and should be integrated into the broad spectrum of health services for women as a part of overall preventive care.

References and Selected Readings

1. Creasy RK, Resnick R: *Maternal-Fetal Medicine: Principles and Practice,* 3d ed. Philadelphia: WB Saunders, 1994.
2. *Genetic Testing for Cystic Fibrosis.* NIH Consensus Statement 15(4):1–37, 1997.
3. *Immunization during Pregnancy.* Washington, DC: American College of Obstetricians and Gynecologists, 1991. Technical Bulletin #160.
4. Kitzmiller JL, Gavin LA, Gin GD, et al: Preconception care of diabetes: Glycemic control prevents congenital anomalies. *JAMA* 265:731–736, 1991.
5. McGregor JA, Mark S, Crawford GP, Levin MJ: Varicella zoster antibody testing in the care of pregnant women exposed to varicella. *Am J Obstet Gynecol* 157:281–284, 1987.
6. Nora JJ, Fraser FC, Bear J, et al: *Medical Genetics,* 4th ed. Philadelphia: Lea & Febiger, 1994.
7. Recommendations for the use of folic acid to reduce the number of cases of spina bifida and other neural tube defects. *MMWR* 41:107, 1992.
8. Sever JL, Larsen JW, Grossman JH: *Handbook of Perinatal Infections,* 2d ed. Boston: Little, Brown, 1989.
9. *Teratology,* Washington, DC: American College of Obstetricians and Gynecologists, 1997. Education Bulletin #236.
10. *The Obstetrician-Gynecologist and Primary-Preventive Health Care.* Washington, DC: American College of Obstetricians and Gynecologists, 1993.
11. Werler MM, Shapiro S, Mitchell AA: Periconceptional folic acid exposure and risk of occurrent neural tube defects, *JAMA* 269:1257–1261, 1993.
12. 1998 Guidelines for treatment of sexually transmitted diseases. *MMWR* 47:1–116, 1998.

CHAPTER 8

Cardiovascular Prevention

Charles B. Hammond

HYPERTENSION
Dietary Management • Drug Therapy
for Hypertension

OBESITY

PLASMA LIPIDS

DIABETES MELLITUS

CIGARETTE SMOKING

SEDENTARY LIFESTYLE

**THE CARDIOPROTECTIVE EFFECTS
OF REPLACEMENT ESTROGEN**

**THERAPEUTIC OPTIONS FOR
CARDIOPROTECTION**

In 1995, the average life expectancy for women in the United States was 79.7 years.[1] Mortality rates, which are shown in Fig. 8-1, clearly illustrate that cardiovascular disease is the major health concern for postmenopausal women. One in 2 women will die of ischemic coronary heart disease (ICHD) or stroke, but only 1 in 25 women will die of breast cancer.[2] This year, more than 100,000 American women under age 65 will die of ICHD, clearly a premature shortening of expected longevity.[3,4] Many more women will experience significant morbidity due to ICHD and require considerable interventive care.

Although there has been a gradual and pronounced decrease in cardiovascular deaths in this country, the decrease has not occurred equally between men and women. Since 1984, cardiovascular death rates for men have dropped, while the rates for women have increased.[1] The incidence of ICHD and stroke is rare in premenopausal women. However, heart disease is the most frequent cause of death in women over the age of 50.

One can speculate why the rates of ICHD are generally lower in women than men. Women have a more favorable risk profile in that their HDL cholesterol levels are higher, triglyceride levels are lower, and they have less upper-body obesity than men. On the other hand, women have a less favorable risk profile because of more obesity, higher blood pressure, higher cholesterol and fibrinogen levels, and more diabetes. It seems that the simplest explanation for this difference between men and women in ischemic coronary heart disease is the effect of estrogen. Estrogen has been noted to improve the lipid profile, to have a direct vasodilatory effect, and perhaps have other helpful factors. After menopause, estrogen levels decline, and women rapidly approach males in the rate of ICHD.[5]

ICHD often presents differently in men and women. In the Framingham Study, angina was the most frequent initial symptom of this disease in women (47 percent).[6] Myocardial infarction was the most frequent initial symptom in men (46 percent). The exercise EKG appears to have lower specificity in women than in men. Women, particularly African-American women, have higher risk of morbidity and mortality than men following a myocardial infarction. Compared to men, women undergoing coronary artery bypass graft surgery have more advanced disease, a higher perioperative mortality rate, less relief of angina, and less graft patency, but similar 5– and 10–year survival rates. Women undergoing percutaneous transluminal coronary angioplasty have lower rates of clinical and angiographic success than men, but also a lower rate of restenosis

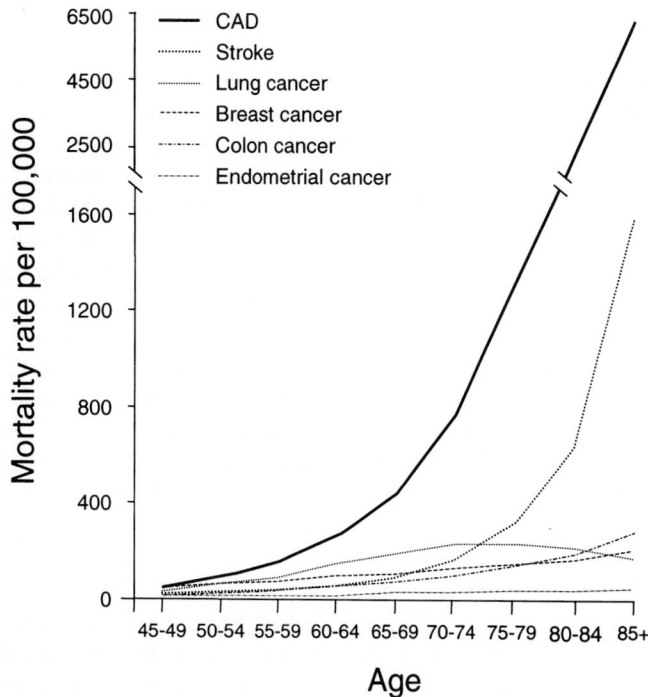

Figure 8-1. Mortality rates in women.

and a better long-term outcome. Women may benefit less and have more frequent serious bleeding complications from thrombolytic therapy than do men. These and other differences dramatize the difference between men and women in coronary ischemic disease, but in both sexes it is quite clear that prevention is far better than active treatment after the disease has occurred.[1] This chapter puts in perspective the various types and successes of ischemic cardiovascular disease prevention. Known clinical areas that impact on the development of ICHD include hypertension, obesity, dyslipidemias, diabetes mellitus, a sedentary lifestyle, and cigarette smoking. We consider each of these issues.

Hypertension

Hypertension is a very common disease in the United States. More women have hypertension than men, perhaps owing, at least in part, to the higher prevalence of hypertension in older patients and the longer survival of women.[7] Renovascular hypertension from fibromuscular dysplasia is seen more commonly in women, but other causes of secondary hypertension occur with relatively equal frequency between the sexes. Benefits of treatment for severe hypertension have been dramatic in both women and men. However, in clinical trials of the treatment of mild-to-moderate hypertension, women have had a smaller decrease in morbidity and mortality than men. Both the effectiveness and the adverse effects of various antihypertensive drugs appear to be comparable in women and in men. Older women benefit at least as much as men from treatment.[1]

An elevated arterial blood pressure is probably the most important public health problem in developed countries. It is common, asymptomatic, readily detectable, usually easily treatable, and often leads to lethal complications if left untreated.

The prevalence of hypertension depends on both the racial composition of the population studied and the criteria used to define the problem. In a Caucasian suburban population, such as that of the Framingham Study, nearly one-fifth of individuals have blood pressures greater than 160/95, while almost one-half have pressures greater than 140/90. An even higher prevalence has been documented in the non-Caucasian population.[6] In women, the prevalence is also closely related to age, with a substantial increase occurring after age 50 years.

Patients with arterial hypertension and no definable cause are said to have primary, essential, or idiopathic hypertension. This problem of essential hypertension accounts for up to 95 percent of patients with hypertension. While not clearly understood as to mechanism, it is obvious that patients with hypertension die prematurely; the most common cause of death is ischemic coronary heart disease, with stroke and renal failure also frequent.[8]

Cardiac compensation for the excessive workload caused by increased systemic pressure is at first sustained by concentric left ventricular hypertrophy characterized by an increase in wall thickness. Ultimately, the function of this chamber deteriorates, the cavity dilates, and symptoms and signs of heart failure appear. Angina pectoris may also occur because of the combination of accelerated coronary arterial disease and increased myocardial oxygen requirements as a consequence of the increased myocardial mass. Most deaths due to hypertension result from myocardial infarction or congestive heart failure. In addition to effects on the heart, there are neurologic effects and effects on the kidney.

Virtually every patient with diastolic arterial pressure that persistently exceeds 90 mmHg, or any patient over 65 years of age with a systolic arterial pressure over 160 mmHg, is a candidate for diagnostic studies and for subsequent treatment.[8] Diagnostic assessment of patients with hypertension is discussed elsewhere in this book. Efforts should be made to exclude pheochromocytoma, Cushing's syndrome, renovascular hypertension, and primary aldosteronism; plasma renin activity measurements may be useful. While decisions about treatment should be individualized because of the potential side effects of therapy, a reasonably good general guideline is that all patients with a diastolic pressure repeatedly above 90 mmHg should be treated unless specific contraindications exist. Patients with isolated systolic hypertension (levels greater than 160 mmHg) also should be treated if they are over the age of 65 years. Patients with labile hypertension or isolated systolic hypertension who are not treated should have regular follow-up exams at six-month intervals to detect a progressive and/or sustained hypertension. Finally, if coronary artery disease or associated cardiovascular risks are present, then antihypertensive treatment of a patient with even lower blood pressure might be warranted.

General measures for the treatment of hypertension should be considered for all patients, including relief of stress, dietary management, regular aerobic exercise, weight reduction (if needed), and control of other risk factors that may contribute to the development of arteriosclerosis.

Dietary Management

Dietary management of hypertension has several considerations. Initially, there was documented efficacy of sodium restriction and volume contraction in lowering blood pressure. For this reason patients were previously instructed to drastically curtail their sodium intake. Newer investigations suggest this is not necessary. However, meta-analyses of previous dietary studies in patients with hypertension have documented a 5 mmHg reduction in systolic pressure and a 2.6 mmHg reduction in diastolic pressure when sodium intake is reduced to approximately 75 mEq/day. In addition, several reports have documented that while sodium restriction has little if any direct action on blood pressure, it significantly potentiates the efficacy of nearly all antihypertensive agents.[8]

Thus, because there is no apparent risk to mild sodium restriction, the most practical approach now is to advise mild dietary sodium restriction (up to 5 g NaCl per day), which can be achieved by eliminating all additions of salt to food that is prepared normally.

Caloric restrictions should be urged for patients who are overweight. Some obese patients show a significant reduction in blood pressure simply as a consequence of weight loss. A restriction in the intake of cholesterol and saturated fats is also usually recommended, as this diet modification may diminish the incidence of arteriosclerotic complications. Reducing or eliminating alcohol intake is beneficial, and regular exercise is indicated within the limits of the patient's cardiovascular status. Not only is exercise helpful in controlling weight, but there is also evidence that physical conditioning itself may lower arterial pressure. Probably the most significant additional step that can be taken is to convince the smoker to give up her cigarettes.

Drug Therapy for Hypertension

Many agents are available for the treatment of hypertension. To effectively utilize them, the sites and mechanisms of their actions should be understood. In general, there are six classes of drugs: diuretics, antiadrenergic agents, vasodilators, calcium-entry blockers, angiotensin-converting enzyme (ACE) inhibitors, and angiotensin-receptor antagonists. Medical management of hypertension is discussed in detail elsewhere in this text.

The *thiazides* are the most frequently used and extensively investigated agents. Their early effect is related to sodium diuresis and volume depletion. Some investigators have also reported reduction in peripheral vascular resistance. Traditionally, thiazide diuretics have formed the cornerstone of most therapeutic programs and are usually effective in three to four days. Furthermore, they have been shown to reduce mortality and morbidity in long-term trials. However, in recent years there has been increasing resistance to their routine use, primarily because of the adverse metabolic effects thiazides can cause, which include hypokalemia, hyperuricemia, carbohydrate intolerance, and hyperlipidemia.

The *antiadrenergic agents* act at one or more sites—centrally on the vasomotor center and neurons, where they modify catecholamine release, or in target tissues, where they block adrenergic receptor sites. These drugs may produce a greater postural effect than other drugs, and orthostatic hypotension is a somewhat frequent side effect. Alpha-adrenergic receptor blockers block the action of norepinephrine at alpha-adrenergic receptor sites. These compounds block both presynaptic (alpha$_2$) and postsynaptic (alpha$_1$) alpha receptors, and the former action accounts for the tolerance which develops. Beta-adrenergic receptor blockers are available that block sympathetic effects on the heart and should be more effective in reducing cardiac output and in lowering arterial pressure when there is increased cardiac sympathetic nerve activity. In addition, these drugs block the adrenergic nerve-mediated release of renin from the renal juxtaglomerular cells, and this action may be an important component of their blood pressure-lowering action. Beta-adrenergic blockers are particularly useful when employed in conjunction with vascular smooth muscle relaxants, which tend to evoke a reflex increase in heart rate, and with diuretics, the administration of which often results in the elevation of circulating renin activity.

Vasodilators are agents that are effective both orally and parenterally, which act mainly on arterial resistance rather than on venous capacitance vessels, as evidenced by the lack of postural effects. Unfortunately, the effect of these agents on peripheral resistance is partially negated by a reflex increase in sympathetic discharge that raises heart rate and cardiac output. A serious side effect of one of these agents, hydralazine, in doses exceeding 300 mg per day, has been the production of a lupus erythematosus-like syndrome.

ACE inhibitors are drugs known to possess an additional action resulting in the inhibition of renin secretion. Others suggest they inhibit the enzyme-converting angiotensin I into angiotensin II, which is the angiotensin-converting enzyme (ACE). Angiotensin receptor antagonists are drugs that have similar effects to those of ACE inhibitors. However, instead of blocking the production of angiotensin II, they competitively inhibit its binding to the angiotensin II A_{T1}, receptor subtype.

Calcium channel blockers are divided into three categories: the phenylalkylamine derivatives, the benzothiazepines, and the dihydropyridines. All three modify calcium entry into cells by interacting with specific binding sites on the alpha$_1$ subunit of the L-type voltage-dependent calcium channel. There are a variety of concerns regarding these agents, including slowing of atrial ventricular conduction, negative ionatrophic actions, and an increase in the incidence of acute coronary events with long-term therapy in hypertensive patients. Accordingly, one should be familiar with the specifics of each.

It is obvious that the control of hypertension provides cardiovascular protection from atherosclerotic ischemic coronary disease.

Obesity

Obesity remains the oldest identified risk factor for cardiovascular disease in men and women, and most studies report a positive correlation between obesity and coronary heart disease. Seventy percent of coronary disease in obese women and 40 percent of coronary disease in all women is attributed to being overweight, and is potentially preventable. In the United States, 25 percent of Caucasian and 44 percent of African-American females are overweight by more than 20 percent of their desirable weight.[9]

Obesity itself does not seem to be the lone culprit in coronary disease; rather, the culprits seem to be obesity with the associated disease factors of hypertension, hyperlipidemia, hyperinsulinemia, insulin resistance, or diabetes mellitus. The age- and smoking-adjusted relative risk of

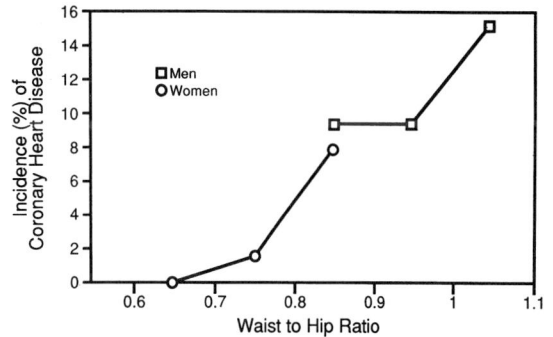

Figure 8-2. Fat distribution as a prognostic factor in coronary disease.

coronary artery disease is 3.3 times higher among severely obese women and 80 percent increased in mildly to moderately obese women.

It is also known that body fat distribution is a better prognostic marker of obesity than actual weight. Centralized body fat ("apple shaped") is a strong prognostic factor for coronary disease in both men and women (Fig. 8-2).[10] Such fat distribution is much more strongly associated with coronary disease than gluteal body fat ("pear shaped") and is also correlated with the findings of hypertension, dislipidoses, and diabetes mellitus. Waist to hip ratio thus serves as a marker that correlates well to this disease. The mechanism by which such centralized obesity confers increased coronary risk is not yet fully understood, although it appears to be the result of different responses of upper body versus lower body lipidocytes in free fatty acid metabolism.

It is estimated that weight reduction, coupled with changes in lifestyle, such as participation in formal exercise programs, is beneficial in favorably modifying plasma lipids. Maintaining body weight at an ideal level is estimated to reduce the overall risk of coronary disease by 30 to 50 percent.[11]

Plasma Lipids

Unfavorable changes in plasma lipids are regarded as a major causative mechanism for the development of coronary artery disease in men and women, and such changes are common.[12,13] Numerous studies have shown that a 1 percent increase in plasma-total cholesterol or low-density lipoprotein cholesterol increases the risk of coronary artery disease by 2 percent. Most of these studies, plus similar studies of high-density lipoprotein cholesterol were done in men, but some recent studies in women show similar results.

Plasma-total cholesterol is an independent risk factor for coronary disease. Evidence is clear that individuals who have total cholesterol levels greater than 260 mg/dl are considered at high risk.[11] Elevated plasma levels of triglycerides are also associated with an increased risk of coronary disease but are not thought to be independent risk factors.[14] Plasma levels of LDL-C and HDL-C are independent and causative risk factors of coronary disease in both men and women. Values of 130 to 159 mg/dl of the former are associated with moderate increased risk, and levels of above 160 mg/dl are associated with high risk.[5] In women, elevated HDL-C levels above the median range (55 mg/dl) can neutralize the adverse effects of high total cholesterol and LDL-C levels. It is estimated that about one-third of postmenopausal women are at moderate risk and one-fourth are at high risk of coronary disease, as indicated by HDL-C levels lower than 45 mg/dl.[5]

While unfavorable plasma lipid ratios at young ages can be found in persons with congenital and acquired hyperlipidemias, and these individuals are at significant risk of dying from coronary disease at a young age, unfavorable changes are more commonly found at midlife and in the aging population. The effect is positively correlated with advancing age. More recent studies suggest that postmenopausal women have greater increases in LDL-C and greater decreases in HDL-C than age-adjusted premenopausal controls.[15]

A number of studies have investigated the effect of cholesterol-lowering therapy on reducing the risk of coronary disease, but only a few included women as part of the trial.[16,17] Accordingly, results to date in women remain somewhat speculative. Normalization of elevated lipid levels retards the progression of coronary atherosclerotic lesions and may even regress some existing plaques.

Diabetes Mellitus

Hyperinsulinemia, chronic hyperglycemia, insulin resistance, and diabetes mellitus are independent risk factors for coronary disease morbidity and are direct causative factors of premature mortality from coronary disease.[18,19] Diabetes mellitus accelerates atherosclerosis and increases the risk of acute coronary disease, particularly in women.[20] Age-adjusted relative risk for coronary disease in patients with diabetes mellitus is in the range of 2 to 3 in men and 3 to 7 in women.[11] Blood glucose levels are a graded independent risk factor for cardiovascular disease in women, even in a relatively normal blood sugar range. Early-onset diabetes mellitus exposes the patient to further increased risk.[20]

Whether tightly controlling glucose levels in women with diabetes mellitus can decrease the risk of coronary artery disease remains to be fully determined. Programs directed at reducing plasma glucose levels in patients with noninsulin-dependent diabetes mellitus have also used measures to control obesity, promote exercise, and to favorably affect plasma lipids levels. While these measures lowered the risk of coronary artery disease, it is impossible to conclude whether they were solely due to control of blood glucose and/or insulin levels.[21] Due to the association of other risk factors (hypertension and hyperlipidemia), and improvement of these, which is known to be protective for coronary disease, it would seem that at least part of the mechanism of improvement may be due to improvement in these parameters.

Cigarette Smoking

Cigarette smoking remains the single most important preventable risk factor for cardiovascular disease in women.[22-24] In women, cigarette smoking is directly responsible for 21 percent of all mortality from cardiovascular disease and 50 percent of all acute coronary events before the age of 55.[25,26] In women under age 65, the proportion of deaths from coronary disease directly attributable to smoking rose from 26 percent in 1965 to 41 percent in 1985.[26] Although smoking in the United States in the last decade has decreased overall, smoking initiation has increased by 1 percent per year among young women. It is now estimated that almost 30 percent of all women in the United States smoke, and that in the near future the number of women smokers will exceed that of men.[27]

It is now known that cigarette smoking relates positively to the risk of fatal coronary disease in a dose-related manner. The greater the number of cigarettes smoked, the greater the relative and attributable risk.

Smoking exerts its adverse coronary influence via several mechanisms. Nicotine releases catecholamines and stimulates the sympathetic nervous system with a responsive increase of free fatty acids and LDL-C.[28] Nicotine has also been shown to increase platelet aggregation and plasma fibrinogen levels.[29] All of these can contribute to an increased risk of coronary thrombosis.[5] Cigarette smokers have a higher incidence of insulin resistance, and plasma lipids demonstrate an unfavorable profile, while premenopausal women who smoke cigarettes may have lower estrogen levels and thus may reduce or eliminate the protective effect of estrogens on the cardiovascular system. There are a variety of other mechanisms proposed. Women who are ex-smokers decrease their risk after two to three years of cessation of smoking, and return to a comparable risk of nonsmokers.[11]

Sedentary Lifestyle

It would appear that the effect of physical exercise on the risk of cardiovascular disease in women is not yet as clear as it is in men.[30] In men, the relative risk of death from coronary disease is higher (1.9) in sedentary compared with active controls.[31] Sectional studies have shown that middle-aged women who have higher levels of physical activity had lower weight, lower systolic and diastolic blood pressures, a more favorable lipid profile, and a lower fasting glucose.[32] Longitudinal studies, however, have been somewhat less clear.

Mechanisms that potentially allow physical exercise to decrease the incidence of coronary atherosclerotic disease include the improvement of functional work capacity, lowering of heart rate and blood pressure, weight reduction, improvement of the lipid profile, diminished platelet adhesiveness and aggregation, enhanced fibrinolysis, and a decreased adrenergic response to stress. Estimated reduction of acute coronary disease in men with the maintenance of an active lifestyle is between 30 and 55 percent.[11]

The Cardioprotective Effects of Replacement Estrogen

It seems that the risk of coronary atherosclerotic disease and its morbidity and mortality increase fairly rapidly in women after menopause. As one reviews the number of observational studies on the use of replacement estrogen/hormonal replacement therapy (ERT/HRT), it appears from the studies alone, and in meta-analysis, that hormonal therapy significantly reduces the likelihood of women having cardiovascular disease.[5,33-45] (Fig. 8-3). Some have suggested that these studies may have selective bias in that women who take estrogen are "healthier." Several large, prospective, randomized trials are under way that should answer this important question.

Several studies have involved estrogen use in postmenopausal women with angiographically defined coronary artery disease.[46,47] Women who used estrogen had significantly less coronary stenosis than women who did not use estrogen; they also had reduced rates of secondary coronary

Relative risk

Stampfer et al, 1985

Wilson et al, 1985

Bush et al, 1987

Petitti et al, 1987

Boysen et al, 1988

Criqui et al, 1988

Henderson et al, 1988

van der Giezen et al, 1990

Wolf et al, 1991

Falkeborn et al, 1992

Psaty et al, 1994

Folsom et al, 1995

0   0.5   1.0   2.0   10

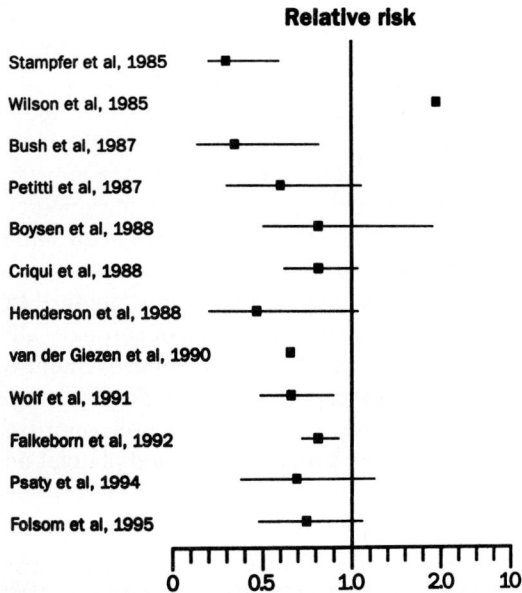

Figure 8-3. Summary of observational studies of ERT/HRT and CVD.

events. Moreover, those patients with the most advanced coronary artery disease benefited the most from ERT.[48]

The HERS study has provided an initial report that documents a reduction in coronary mortality among women after a previous coronary event.[49] However, in the initial year of this study, the women who had preexisting coronary disease did have a higher risk of coronary death, which was then lost, and a protective effect was gained after the first year if the medication was continued. Little is known of the mechanisms by which this might occur in this important randomized, prospective, and placebo-controlled trial. It is unfortunate that the study was terminated before some of the answers were obtained.

The effects of ERT/HRT are not uniform in the context of restenosis and angioplasty outcome. Two studies present interesting differences. In one study, estrogen had no effect on restenosis following angioplasty but had a significant effect (reduction to 0.5) on the rate of

restenosis following atherectomy.[50] A second study on the long-term outcome of angioplasty produced similar discrepancies.[51] Although HRT shows no effect on the occurrence of myocardial infarction after angioplasty, it produces a highly significant benefit when seven-year mortality is the end point.

The precise mechanisms of ERT/HRT in protecting women are only now being elucidated. It appears that there are plasma-lipid-dependent effects and also plasma-lipid-independent factors (Fig. 8-4). It appears that *estrogen* therapy benefits both.

Concern remains regarding the impact of progestin upon the beneficial effects of estrogen on coronary atherosclerotic disease. The postmenopausal estrogen/progestin interventions (PEPI) trial confirmed that estrogen, taken alone or in combination with progestin, produced an improved lipid profile and lower fibrinogen levels, and that these changes are large enough to be clinically relevant.[52] The study also demonstrated that the unopposed estrogen has a greater effect on HDL cholesterol than a regimen that includes progestin. In addition, the use of progestin with estrogen slightly reduces, but does not eliminate, the lowering of LDL seen with estrogen alone.

Finally, studies have addressed the effect of estrogen on the endothelium. The ability of the artery to dilate when it should, rather than to constrict, is one of its more important properties. Endothelium modulates whether the coronary arteries can dilate when needed as opposed to undergoing an inappropriate constriction. Acetylcholine can be perfused into coronary arteries to evaluate the function of the endothelium.

Studies with nonhuman primates have shown that estrogen deprivation causes coronary arteries to constrict when stimulated with acetylcholine, and that estrogen replacement returns endothelial function and vascular dilatation to normal.[53] Some progestins have been shown to at least partially block this beneficial effect of estrogen.[54]

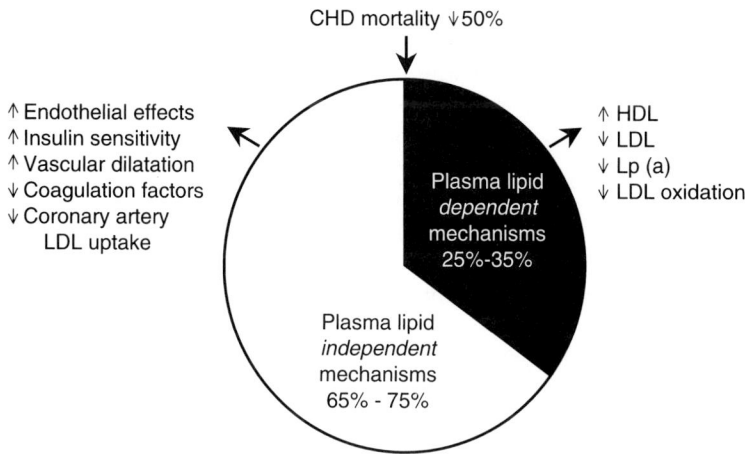

Figure 8-4. ERT/HRT mechanisms of cardioprotection and impact on mortality.

CHD mortality ↓50%

↑ Endothelial effects
↑ Insulin sensitivity
↑ Vascular dilatation
↓ Coagulation factors
↓ Coronary artery LDL uptake

↑ HDL
↓ LDL
↓ Lp (a)
↓ LDL oxidation

Plasma lipid *dependent* mechanisms 25%-35%

Plasma lipid *independent* mechanisms 65% - 75%

Therapeutic Options for Cardioprotection

Given estrogen's cardioprotective effects, an important question is how ERT/HRT compares with other pharmaceutical interventions that primarily affect plasma lipoprotein concentrations. Several recent studies suggest that, for certain patients, hormonal therapy could be an effective alternative to treatment with the statins.[55,56] Moreover, one of the studies suggested there may be an additive effect with estrogen and Pravastatin (Fig. 8-5). Patients who have severe hypercholesterolemia, however, often require a statin.

Drug therapy for elevated cholesterol ("statins"), particularly in women, has remained controversial, primarily because of insufficient evidence that drug therapy enhances survival. Two recent reports, however, prove that there are significant treatment benefits.[57,58]

Antioxidant vitamins are commonly taken by postmenopausal women with the expectation that they may provide some cardioprotection. Whether, and to what extent, they might do so is based largely on observational data.[59] Observational studies have suggested an increased intake of vitamins A, C, and E; beta-carotene; flavinoids; and folic acid, by diet or supplement, reduced cardiovascular event rates. As an exam-

ple, Stampfer and coworkers reported a protective effect on the risk of human coronary artery disease with vitamin E consumption in the Nurses' Health Study.[60] However, when subjected to randomized controlled trials, only vitamin E, in doses of 400 to 800 International Units (IU) daily, significantly reduced the rate of recurrent myocardial infarction. Another mechanism, at least for folic acid therapy, may be beneficial in cardioprotection by way of lowering plasma concentrations of homocysteine.

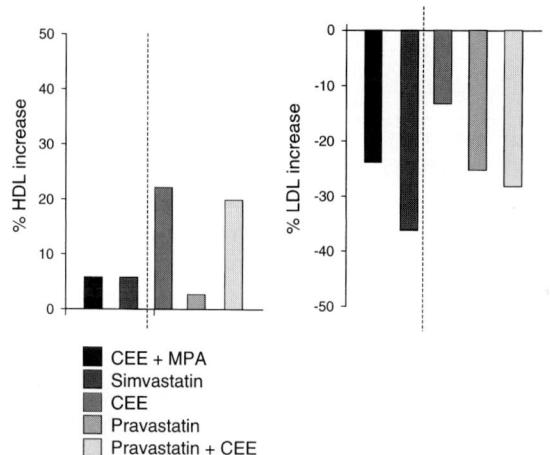

CEE + MPA
Simvastatin
CEE
Pravastatin
Pravastatin + CEE

Figure 8-5. Effect of ERT and statins on lipids.

TABLE 8-1 Strategies for Risk Reduction in Cardiovascular Disease

Risk Factor	Goal	Strategy	Estimated Reduction in Risk
Weight	Maintenance of ideal body weight	Balanced diet	35–55% lower compared with obese (≥20% above desirable weight)
Lipids	Total cholesterol ≤200 mg/dl; HDL-C ≥55 mg/dl; LDL-C ≤130 mg/dl	Low-fat diet, lipid-lowering medications, weight reduction, modifications in life-style	2–4.7% reduction per 1% decrease in total cholesterol or 1% increase in HDL-C
Hypertension	<140 mmHg systolic and <90 mmHg diastolic blood pressure	Weight reduction, salt-restricted diet, hypotensive drug therapy	2–3% decline in risk for each reduction of 1 mmHg in diastolic blood pressure
Glucose intolerance	Normoglycemia and normoinsulinemia	Early detection of abnormality, weight reduction, controlled diet, hypoglycemic therapy	Unknown
Cigarette smoking	Cessation of smoking	Prevention, education	50–70% reduced risk compared with current smokers
Sedentary lifestyle	Active life-style	Life-style modifications	45% lower risk, (data obtained for men)
Diet	Balanced diet, mild alcohol consumption	Life-style modifications	25–45% lower risk for those who consume small amount of alcohol daily
Estrogen deficiency	Equivalent of plasma E_2 50–200 pg/ml	Estrogen replacement after the menopause	50% lower risk in users compared to nonusers; effect of added progesterone is unknown
Progesterone or progestogens	Reduce the risk of the add-on progesterone/progestogen to estrogen replacement in postmenopausal women	Use of C-21 progesterone or progestogen, lowest necessary dose to transform the endometrium to secretory type	Unknown; low-dose medroxyprogesterone acetate does not seem to significantly reduce the beneficial effect of estrogen
Time of day	Decrease elevated risk of acute coronary events in awakening hours	Life-style modifications, prophylactic low-dose aspirin, β-adrenergic blockers	Unknown
Acute thrombosis	Reduce the risk	Prophylactic low-dose aspirin	33% lower risk in users compared with nonusers (data obtained for men)
Stress	Reduce the risk	Life-style modifications	Unknown
Family history	Early detection of risk	Preventive medicine	Unknown

SOURCE: Gorodeski GI, Utian WH: Epidemiology and risk factors of cardiovascular risk in postmenopausal women, in Lobo RA (ed): *Treatment of the Postmenopausal Woman.* New York, Raven Press, 1994. With permission.

Aspirin is another option for coronary prevention in postmenopausal women. In a study of high-risk patients, prolonged aspirin treatment (of one month or more) offered significant protection against myocardial infarction, stroke, and death. Such therapy reduced vascular events by about 25 percent. Benefit was seen in those over 65 years of age and was equal in men and women.[61]

The selective estrogen-receptor modulator raloxifene is being recommended for some postmenopausal women, instead of the more traditional hormonal replacement therapy.[12] Because coronary heart disease is the leading cause of death among postmenopausal women, it is important to know how raloxifene compares with traditional therapy in terms of affecting the lipid/lipoprotein level. In comparisons of raloxifene with conjugated equine estrogen (CEE), raloxifene seems somewhat less effective in reducing plasma LDL concentrations.[62,63] Conjugated equine estrogen has significant beneficial effects on increasing HDL concentrations, an effect that is not observed with raloxifene. CEE results in a modest increase of plasma triglycerides, which is not seen with raloxifene treatment. However, no adverse effects on coronary heart disease inhibition have been shown from these modest increases in plasma triglyceride concentration.

Animal studies using a nonhuman primate show similar changes in lipid profiles between conjugated estrogen and raloxifene. The effects of raloxifene on decreasing LDL concentration are somewhat less than those of conjugated equine estrogen, and raloxifene has no effect on HDL.[64] The extent of coronary artery atherosclerosis was also quantified in this primate system. Treatment with conjugated equine estrogen resulted in a 70 percent decrease in plaque size compared with postmenopausal monkeys given placebo.[64] Neither low- nor high-dose raloxifene had any measurable effect on coronary artery atherosclerosis.

In summary, it would appear that long-term therapy with estrogen is indeed a useful protectant for coronary atherosclerotic disease in postmenopausal women. This is true in all of the categories of risk previously listed, including obesity, hypertension, smoking, sedentary lifestyle, dislipidemias, and diabetes mellitus. It is this author's opinion that all of these serve as indications to consider such therapy.

It is also clear that many lifestyle changes can have a significant beneficial effect in regard to coronary artery health (Table 8-1). These lifestyle changes should be stressed to all women as they consider ways of reducing their risk of this important disease.

References and Selected Readings

1. Komaroff AL, Robb-Nicholson C, Woo B: Women's health, in Fauci AS, Brunwald E, et al, (eds): *Har-rison's Principles of Internal Medicine.* New York: McGraw-Hill, 1998, pp 21–22.

2. *1997 Heart and Stroke Statistical Update.* Dallas, Texas: American Heart Association, 1997.

3. National Center for Health Statistics. *Vital Statistics of the United States.* 1992, Vol II—Mortality, Part A. Hyattsville, MD: US Department of Health and Human Services, Public Health Service; 1996. DHHS publication 96-1101.

4. Miller EC, et al (eds): *SEER Cancer Statistics Review 1973–1993.* National Cancer Institute, 1997.

5. Gorodeski Gi, Utian WH: Epidemiology and risk factors of cardiovascular disease in postmenopausal women, in Lobo RA (ed): *Treatment of the Postmenopausal Woman: Basic and Clinical Aspects,* New York: Raven Press, 1994, pp 199–221.

6. Marabito J: Women and cardiovascular disease: Contributions from the Framingham heart study. *JAMA* 50:35, 1995.

7. MacMahon S, Peto R, Cutler J, et al: Blood pressure, stroke and coronary heart disease. *Lancet* 335:765–774, 1990.

8. Williams G. Hypertensive vascular disease in Fauci AS, Brunwald E, et al (eds): *Harrison's Principles of Internal Medicine,* New York: McGraw-Hill, 1998, pp 1380–1394.

9. Manson JE, Colditz GA, Stampfer MJ, et al: A prospective study of obesity and risk of coronary heart disease in women. *N Engl J Med* 332:882–889, 1990.

10. Larsson B, Bengtsson C, Bjorntorp P, et al: Is abdominal body fat distribution a major explanation for the sex difference in the incidence of myocardial infarction? *Am J Epidemiol* 135:266–273, 1992.

11. Manson JE, Tosteson H, Ridker PM, et al: The primary prevention of myocardial infarction. *N Engl J Med* 326:1406–1416, 1992.

12. Report of the National Cholesterol Education Program Expert Panel on detection, evaluation and treatment of high blood cholesterol in adults. *Arch Intern Med* 148:36–49, 1988.

13. Jacobs DR, Mebane IL, Bangdiwala SI, Cirquin MH, Taylor HA: High density lipoprotein cholesterol as a predictor of cardiovascular disease mortality in men and women: The follow-up study of the Lipid Research Clinics Prevalence Study. *Am J Epidemiol* 131:32–47, 1990.

14. Austin MA: Plasma triglyceride as a risk factor for coronary heart disease. *Am J Epidemiol* 129:249–259, 1989.

15. Matthews KA, Meilahn E, Kuller LH, Kelsy SF, Cagginia AW, Wing RR: Menopause and risk factors for coronary heart disease. *N Engl J Med* 321:641–646, 1989.

16. Arntzenius AC, Kromhont D, Barth JD, et al: Diet, li-

poproteins and the progression of coronary atherosclerosis. *N Engl J Med* 312; 805–811, 1985.

17. Schuler G, Hambrecht R, Schlierf G, et al: Regular physical exercise and low fat diet. *Circulation* 86:1–11, 1992.

18. Barrett-Connor E, Wingard DL: Sex differential in ischemic heart disease mortality in diabetics. *Am J Epidemiol* 118:489–496, 1983.

19. Ford ES, DeStefano F: Risk factors for mortality from all causes and from coronary heart disease among persons with diabetes. *Am J Epidemiol* 133:1220–1230, 1991.

20. Kannel WB, Wilson PWF, Zhang TJ: The epidemiology of impaired glucose tolerance and hypertension. *Am Heart J* 121:1268–1273, 1991.

21. Manson JE, Rimm EB, Stampfer MJ, et al: Physical activity and incidence of noninsulin-dependent diabetes mellitus in women. *Lancet* 338:774–778, 1991.

22. Bush TL, Comstock CW: Smoking and cardiovascular mortality in women. *Am J Epidemiol* 118:480–488, 1983.

23. Rosenberg L, Kaufman DW, Helmrich SP, Miller DR, Stolley PD, Shapiro C: Myocardial infarction and cigarette smoking in women younger than 50 years of age. *JAMA* 253:2965–2969, 1985.

24. LaCroix AZ, Lang J, Scherr P, et al: Smoking and mortality among older men and women in three communities. *N Engl J Med* 324:1619–1625, 1991.

25. Willett WC, Green A, Stampfer MJ, et al: Relative and absolute excess risks of coronary heart disease among women who smoke cigarettes. *N Engl J Med* 317:1303–1309, 1987.

26. Department of Health and Human Services: *Reducing the health consequences of smoking: 25 years of progress: A report of the Surgeon General.* Washington, DC: US Government Printing Office, 1989. DHHS publication CDC 89-8411.

27. American Heart Association: *1993 Heart and Stroke Facts.* Dallas: American Heart Association National Center, 1993.

28. Mjos OD: Lipid effects of smoking. *Am Heart J* 115:272–275, 1988.

29. Schoenberger JC: Smoking change in relation to changes in blood pressure, weight, and cholesterol. *Prev Med* 11:441–453, 1982.

30. Paffenbarger RS, Hide PHRT, Wing AL, Hseih CC: Physical activity, all-cause mortality and longevity of college alumni. *N Engl J Med* 314:605–613, 1986.

31. Berlin JA, Colditz GA: A meta-analysis of physical activity in the prevention of coronary heart disease. *Am J Epidemiol* 132:612–628, 1990.

32. Sallis JF, Patterson TL, Buono MJ, Nader PR: Relation of cardiovascular fitness and physical activity to cardiovascular risk factors in children and adults. *Am J Epidemiol* 127:933–941, 1988.

33. Stampfer MJ, Willett WC, Colditz GA, Rosner B, Speizer FE, Hennekens CH: A prospective study of postmenopausal estrogen therapy and coronary heart disease. *N Engl J Med* 313:1044–1049, 1985.

34. Wilson PWF, Garrison RJ, Castellio WP: Postmenopausal estrogen use, cigarette smoking, and cardiovascular morbidity in women over 50: The Framingham Study. *N Engl J Med* 313:1038–1043, 1985.

35. Bush TL, Barrett-Connor E, Cowan LD, et al: Cardiovascular mortality and noncontraceptive use of estrogen in women: Results from the Lipid Research Clinics Program Follow-up Study. *Circulation* 75:1102–1109, 1987.

36. Petitti DB, Periman JA, Sidney S: Noncontraceptive estrogens and mortality: Long-term follow-up of women in the Walnut Creek Study. *Obstet Gynecol* 70:289–293, 1987.

37. Boysen G, Nyobe J, Appleyard M, Sorensen PS, Boas J, Somnier F: Stroke incidence and risk factors for stroke in Copenhagen, Denmark. *Stroke* 19:1345–1353, 1988.

38. Criqui MH, Suwarez L, Barrett-Connor E, McPhillips J, Wingard DL, Garland C: Postmenopausal estrogen use and mortality. *Am J Epidemiol* 128:606–614, 1988.

39. Henderson BE, Paganini-Hill A, Ross RK: Estrogen replacement therapy and protection from acute myocardial infarction. *Am J Obstet Gynecol* 159:312–317, 1988.

40. Van der Giezen AM, Schopman-Guerts van Kessel JG, Schouten EG, Slotboom BJ, Kok FJ, Collete HJ: Systolic blood pressure and cardiovascular mortality among 13,740 Dutch women. *Prev Med* 19:456–465, 1990.

41. Wolf PH, Madans JH, Finucane FF, Higgins M, Kleinman JC: Reduction of cardiovascular disease-related mortality among postmenopausal women who use hormones: Evidence from a national cohort. *Am J Obstet Gynecol* 164:489–494, 1991.

42. Falkeborn M, Perrson I, Adami HO, Bergstrom R, Eaker E, Lithell H: The risk of acute myocardial infarction after oestrogen-progestogen replacement. *Br J Obstet Gynaecol* 99:821–828, 1992.

43. Psaty BM, Heckbert SR, Atkins D, Lemaltre R, Koepsell TD, Wahl PW: The risk of myocardial infarction associated with the progestins in postmenopausal women. *Arch Intern Med* 154:1333–1339, 1994.

44. Folsom AR, Mink PJ, Sellers TA, Hong CP, Zheng W, Potter JD: Hormonal replacement therapy and morbidity and mortality in a prospective study of postmenopausal women. *Am J Public Health* 85:1128–1132, 1995.

45. Eaker ED, Castelli WP: Differential risk for coronary heart disease among women in the Framingham Study, in Eaker E, Packard B, Wenger N, Clarkson

T, Tyroler HA (eds): Coronary Heart Disease in Women. New York: Haymarket Doyma, 1987, pp 122–130.

46. Sullivan JM, Vander Zwaag R, Hughes JP, Maddock V, Kroetz FW, Ramanathan KB: Estrogen replacement and coronary artery disease: Effect on survival in postmenopausal women. *Arch Intern Med* 150:2557–2562, 1990.

47. Sullivan JM, Vander Zwaag R, Lemp EF: Postmenopausal estrogen use and coronary atherosclerosis. *Ann Intern Med* 108:358–363, 1988.

48. Newton KM, LaCroix AZ, McKnight B, et al: Estrogen replacement therapy and prognosis after first myocardial infarction. *Am J Epidemiol* 145:269–277, 1997.

49. Hulley S, Grady D, Bush T, Furberg C, et al: Randomized trial of estrogen plus progestin for secondary prevention of coronary disease in postmenopausal women: The Heart and Estrogen Replacement Study (HERS). *JAMA* 280(7)605–613, 1998.

50. O'Brien JE, Peterson ED, Keeler GP, et al: Relation between estrogen replacement therapy and restenosis after percutaneous coronary interventions. *J Am Coll Cardiol* 28:1111–1118, 1996.

51. O'Keefe JH, Kim SC, Hall RR, Cochran VC, Lawhorn SL, McCallister BD. Estrogen replacement therapy after coronary angioplasty in women. *J Am Coll Cardiol* 29:1–5, 1997.

52. The Writing Group for the PEPI Trial: Effects of estrogen or estrogen/progestin regimens on heart disease risk factors in postmenopausal women. *JAMA* 273:199–208, 1995.

53. Adams MR, Register JC, et al: Medroxyprogesterone acetate antagonizes inhibitory effects of conjugated equine estrogens on coronary artery atherosclerosis. *Arterioscler Thromb Vasc Biol* 17:217–221, 1997.

54. Clarkson TB: Effects of progesterones, progestins, and estrogens on atherosclerosis and other metabolic parameters. *Arterioscler Thromb Vasc Biol* 17:222–223, 1997.

55. Darling GM, Johns JA, McCloud PI, Davis SR: Estrogen and progestin compared with simvastatin for hypercholesterolemia in postmenopausal women. *N Engl J Med* 337:595–601, 1997.

56. Davidson MH, Testolin LM, Maki KC, von Duvillard S, Drennan KB: A comparison of estrogen replacement, Pravastatin, and combined treatment for the management of hypercholesterolism in postmenopausal women. *Arch Intern Med* 157:1186–1192, 1997.

57. Pedersen TR: Randomised trial of cholesterol lowering in 4444 patients with coronary heart disease: the Scandinavian Simvastatin Survival Study (4s). *Lancet* 344:1383–1389, 1994.

58. Gotto LT, et al: Presentation at Annual meeting of the American Heart Association; 1997; Orlando, FL.

59. Jha P, Flather M, Lonn E, Farkouh M, Yusuf S: The antioxidant vitamins and cardiovascular disease. *Ann Intern Med* 123:860–872, 1995.

60. Stampfer MJ, Hennekens CH, Manson JE, Colditz GA, Rosner B, Willett WC: Vitamin E consumption and the risk of coronary disease in women. *N Engl J Med* 328:1444–1449, 1993.

61. Antiplatelet Trialists' Collaboration. Collaborative overview of randomised trials of antiplatelet therapy—I: Prevention of death, myocardial infarction, and stroke by prolonged antiplatelet therapy in various categories of patients. *Br Med J* 308:81–106, 1994.

62. Raloxifene [package insert]. Indianapolis, Indiana: Eli Lilly, 1998.

63. Walsh BW, Kuller LH, Wild RA, et al: Effects of raloxifene on serum lipids and coagulation factors in healthy postmenopausal women. *JAMA* 279:1445–1451, 1998.

64. Clarkson TB, Anthony MS, Jerome CP: Lack of effect of raloxifene on coronary artery atherosclerosis of postmenopausal monkeys. *J Clin Endocrinol Metab* 83:721–726, 1998.

CHAPTER 9

Nutrition and Maintaining a Healthy Weight

Michael A. Hamilton
Cathy Nonas

cal activity at each visit can help prepare women for these transitions, and for the many other life events that seem to affect weight: illness, the stresses of personal life and the workplace, marriage, retirement, and so on. Understanding the factors that influence weight, the variability in weight between different ethnic and age groups, and the health consequences of weight abnormalities enables the clinician to be a more effective and compassionate counselor to his or her patients.

Factors Determining Weight

What one weighs is determined by three major factors: genes, nutrition, and physical activity. However, socioeconomic status, race, age, and such diverse factors as tobacco use, alcohol, stress, and medications powerfully influence weight and body fat distribution.

Genes

The biological basis for weight in humans was recently highlighted by the discovery of leptin, a hormone secreted by fat cells which decreases food intake and increases energy expenditure in animals. A deficiency of leptin in the *ob* mouse (a mouse with defective expression of the *ob* gene) leads to obesity, which can be reversed by administration of leptin. In contrast to the *ob* mouse, obese humans have more than normal amounts of leptin, suggesting that human obesity

The physician is in a unique position to help women have a healthy nutritional status, and achieve and maintain a healthy weight, from childhood well into the elder years. The clinician who delivers primary care to women will probably emphasize the issues of nutrition and weight during three major transitions: puberty, pregnancy, and menopause. At times other than these three important transitions, the clinician may not stress nutrition and weight with his or her patient, unless there is an obvious problem. Yet addressing weight, nutrition, and physi-

may result from an insensitivity to leptin, analogous to insulin resistance in type II diabetes. Because receptors to leptin are found in several tissues, including the ovary, leptin may prove to play many roles.

In addition to the *ob* gene, several other genes have been identified that affect weight in animal models of obesity. As many as 20 to 50 genes affecting weight may ultimately be identified. It is estimated that 30 to 40 percent of the variability in weight among individuals is determined by heredity, which affects such factors as resting metabolic rate, appetite, satiety, body fat distribution, and perhaps predisposition to physical activity. The remaining variance in weight (60 percent) is mostly attributable to environment; that is, food intake and physical activity. Contrary to common belief, early family environment (i.e., childhood) plays only a minor role in a person's weight as an adult.

Diet

Intuitively, we know that food intake in excess of energy expenditure leads to weight gain, and that the reverse leads to weight loss. Epidemiologic studies suggest that over the last 15 years average daily caloric intake has increased by about 200 calories, contributing significantly to the sharp rise in the prevalence of obesity in this country since the 1980s. In spite of evidence that increased caloric intake alone, irrespective of nutrient choice, is a major determinant of weight, we are nevertheless confronted each year by a new diet that promotes one nutrient above all others, or blames one nutrient for all problems, especially weight. The fact remains that calories do count, no matter from which nutrient they come, and that attention to calories (i.e., portion size) is the most important strategy to significantly influence weight. The primacy of calories with respect to weight is demonstrated by the following patient, a woman who was admitted to a hospital for almost 100 days (Fig. 9-1).

She was placed on a daily intake of about 1800 calories, which was calculated to maintain her body weight without gain or loss. During the first 38 days of her hospitalization, she was placed on a low-fat diet, 10 percent of calories from fat and 75 percent of calories from carbohydrate. During the remaining time, she was placed on a high-fat diet, 70 percent of calories from fat and 15 percent of calories from carbohydrate. As can be seen from her hospital weight graph, there was essentially no change in her weight on these two very different diets. However, high-fat diets do have adverse effects on lipid metabolism, insulin sensitivity, and body composition (high-fat diets favor the deposition of visceral fat and seem to increase the percentage of total body fat, even in the absence of weight gain). For these reasons, high-fat diets are discouraged.

Physical Activity

Over the last 100 years, human ingenuity has produced a multitude of inventions to help us accomplish a great deal with minimal physical effort (it has been estimated that today we expend 800 fewer calories per day in physical activity than we did in 1970). Over this period of time food intake initially decreased, but not sufficiently to offset the decrease in daily energy expenditure. However, in the last decade, this downward trend in food intake reversed course, and we now consume approximately 200 kcal more per day. In addition, the greater availability of lower-cost food items high in fat and simple sugars, such as snack/fast foods, has produced an environment particularly "toxic" to those who are sedentary and also predisposed genetically to overweight and obesity.

Other Factors

While diet, physical activity, and genes are the major determinants of weight, other factors play a significant role as well:

1. *Socioeconomic status:* In the United States, women living in conditions of lesser

Figure 9-1. The unchanging energy need when a hospitalized patient is fed liquid diets varying widely in fat-to-carbohydrate ratio. The patient was a 64-year-old woman fed 7322 kJ/d. CHO, carbohydrate. For details, *see* Hirsch J, Hudgins LC, Leibel RL, Rosenbaum M: Diet composition and energy balance in humans. *Am J Clin Nutr.* 67(Suppl): 552S, 1998. Reproduced with permission from the American Society for Clinical Nutrition.

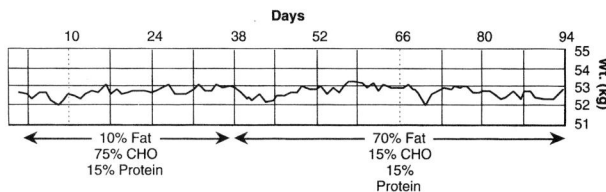

income have a greater prevalence of overweight and obesity as compared to women in the higher socioeconomic levels.

2. *Tobacco use:* Smoking cessation is associated with an average weight gain of approximately seven pounds, but sometimes much more in those who are predisposed to obesity.

3. *Alcohol:* The effects of alcohol on total weight are complex and even confusing. However, alcohol is associated with the development of central obesity, thus increasing cardiovascular risk.

4. *Medications:* Certain medications are associated with weight gain—antihistamines (especially cyproheptadine), tricyclic antidepressants, steroids, exogenous insulin and oral sulfonylureas, lithium, valproic acid, and phenothiazines.

5. *Endocrine:* Glucocorticoidism (Cushing's syndrome or exogenous use of glucocorticoids) leads to weight gain; androgenicity, as seen in polycystic ovary syndrome, is associated with a central or upper-body distribution of fat.

6. *Emotional:* Even in the absence of a clinically significant psychological disorder, most people have the potential to eat more or to eat less for emotional reasons, during periods of stress and unhappiness, as well as during periods of success, achievement, and happiness. Those with bulimia nervosa and binge eating disorder, however, may respond to stress by overeating that is clearly excessive.

7. *Food availability:* Access to inexpensive, high fat, high sugar foods, particularly "snack" foods, increases the risk of weight gain, especially in those with limited income.

Assessment of Weight

Weight, height, and waist circumference are simple but effective measurements to assess weight and the associated risks of weight abnormalities.

Body mass index (BMI) has replaced "ideal" body weight as a descriptor of weight and body fatness. Body mass index is defined as weight in kilograms divided by height in meters squared. It can also be calculated from pounds and inches (Table 9-1).

There are several advantages to assessing BMI rather than ideal body weight: BMI normalizes for height; it is correlated with independent measures of body fat and with the incidence and prevalence data of weight-related morbidities and mortality; and the term is emotionally neutral as opposed to "ideal" body weight.

BMI does not distinguish between fat and muscle tissues; therefore, a very muscular person may have a high BMI. There is also considerable variability in percent body fat at a given BMI. One study found that in subjects with a BMI between 28 and 30, mean percent body fat was 28 percent but the range varied between 15 and 41 percent. Nevertheless, in general, a woman with a BMI greater than 25 probably has an excess of body fat.

Normal BMI is between 18.5 and 24.9. The

TABLE 9-1 Calculating Body Mass Index (BMI) from Pounds and Inches

Method 1		Method 2 (this method is more usable with calculators)
$$\frac{703 \times \text{weight in pounds}}{\text{height in inches}^2} = \text{BMI}$$	*or*	1. $703 \times$ weight in pounds $= a$ 2. $a \div$ height (in inches) $= b$ 3. $b \div$ height (in inches) $=$ BMI

Each BMI unit is equivalent to about 5 to 7 pounds.

different levels of overweight and obesity are defined as follows:

Classification	BMI
Overweight	25–29.9 kg/m²
Class I obesity	30–34.9 kg/m²
Class II obesity	35–39.9 kg/m²
Class III obesity	>40 kg/m²

At a BMI of greater than 25 kg/m², health risk increases moderately. At a BMI of 30 kg/m² or above, health risk increases sharply, particularly for the metabolic consequences of obesity: diabetes, dyslipidemia, hypertension, and cardiovascular disease. However, BMI should not be used as the only criterion to predict health risk, because persons with a greater percentage of lean tissue may be quite healthy. One study suggests that persons who have a higher BMI (>27 kg/m²), but who are fit as determined by exercise stress testing, do not have an excess risk of cardiovascular mortality compared to persons with a normal BMI who also are fit.

Health Consequences of Weight Gain, Obesity, and Body Fat Distribution

The health consequences of weight gain and obesity include an increased risk of diabetes mellitus, hypertension, and abnormalities of the lipid profile, which together increase the risk of cardiovascular disease. Gallstone disease is also more common in women who are obese, but weight loss, particularly rapid weight loss and extremely low fat diets, may also increase the risk of gallstone formation. Menstrual ab-

normalities, infertility, and polycystic ovary syndrome are also associated with obesity. Obstructive sleep apnea, which is less common in women than men, can lead to increases in pulmonary artery pressure and right heart failure, and, in addition, may increase the risk of a motor vehicle accident because of the somnolence associated with this disorder.

Persons who have upper-body obesity (android, abdominal, or apple-shaped obesity) as opposed to lower-body obesity (gynoid, hip/thigh, or pear-shaped obesity) are at greater risk for the metabolic complications of obesity, such as reduced insulin sensitivity, hyperinsulinemia, impaired glucose tolerance, hypertension, dyslipidemia with elevated triglycerides, low HDL cholesterol, and increased numbers of small, dense LDL particles, all of which increase the risk of cardiovascular disease. Upper-body or abdominal fat consists of two compartments, the subcutaneous compartment and, within the abdominal cavity, the visceral compartment. The presence of large amounts of visceral fat appears to confer the greatest health risk. Fat cells in the visceral cavity are larger than subcutaneous fat cells, and are more metabolically active. These fat cells exhibit enhanced lipolysis which results in an increased flow of free fatty acids through the portal system, leading to hyperinsulinemia and the metabolic abnormalities listed earlier. Ethnicity, however, appears to influence the relative risk of visceral fat compared to subcutaneous fat. For example, in African-American women, the presence of increased subcutaneous abdominal fat may carry a greater health risk than visceral fat.

TABLE 9-2 Measuring Waist Circumference

Waist circumference is an indirect indicator of visceral fat. Waist circumference is measured horizontally at the level of the uppermost lateral border of the iliac crest with the patient standing. A waist circumference >35 in. in women (>40 in. in men) increases the likelihood that the patient has an excess of visceral fat that is sufficient to increase health risk.

African-American women have also been found to have a slightly lower resting metabolic rate (by about 80 to 120 kcal/day) compared to Caucasian women matched for body composition. For a given BMI, African-American women have a slightly lower all-cause mortality compared to Caucasian women.

Factors that increase the risk of visceral fat deposition include heredity, high-fat diet, lack of physical activity, alcohol intake, and elevated levels of glucocorticoid and androgenic steroids. There may be a relationship between stress, increased cortisol levels, and the development of increased visceral fat. Testosterone levels are increased in women with significant visceral obesity, whereas in men with visceral obesity, testosterone levels are diminished.

A woman with a waist circumference (Table 9-2) greater than 35 in. has a greater likelihood of having a significant amount of visceral fat. Other than waist circumference, there are no reliable and inexpensive tools to assess the degree of visceral obesity. The CAT scan and the MRI are the best tools for assessing visceral fat. An MRI or CAT scan slice at the L4/L5 level can provide an indirect indicator of total visceral versus subcutaneous abdominal fat.

Weight Trends in the United States

Childhood through Adolescence

The prevalence of severe obesity in childhood increased from 5 to 10 percent between National Health and Nutrition Examination Survey (NHANES) II (1976 to 1980) and NHANES III (1988 to 1994). During that same period, the prevalence of overweight and obesity in adolescent girls increased from 15 to 22 percent. These trends pose a serious health risk to women because childhood and adolescent overweight and obesity are risk factors for adult overweight and obesity. For example, one study found that among 36-year-old obese women, 30 percent experienced the onset of their obesity during adolescence. The future social well-being of young women also may be negatively affected by overweight and obesity; one study showed that obese older adolescents and young women were less likely to marry, more likely to have less education, and more likely to live in conditions of lesser income and poverty compared to their peers who were normal weight at baseline. In men, stature has a similar social impact as obesity in women.

Although eating disorders are on the rise, they are nevertheless rare compared to the increasing prevalence of obesity in young women. In spite of their youth, young women who become obese develop a health risk pattern similar to older obese adults. One study compared cardiovascular risk factors in obese (BMI $\geq$30 kg/m^2) and lean (BMI = 21 kg/m^2) adolescent girls. The obese girls who had upper-body obesity had higher basal insulin and serum triglyceride levels and lower serum HDL cholesterol levels. The obese girls who had lower-body obesity had higher serum HDL cholesterol levels. Finally, with an increase in obesity there is an increase in type II diabetes in children.

Adulthood

In adults, the prevalence of overweight and obesity increased from 25 percent to almost 35 percent between NHANES II (1976 to 1980) and NHANES III (1988 to 1994). Based on the new U.S. BMI criteria, overweight and obesity (BMI >25 kg/m^2) have increased from 40.8 to 49.6 percent in women of all races and ethnic groups, adjusted for age. The largest increases in the prevalence of overweight and obesity have oc-

TABLE 9-3 Prevalence of Different BMI Categories in Women between 1960 and 1994, Adjusted for Age

Period (survey)	BMI			
	25–29.9	30–34.9	35–39.9	>40
1960–62 (NHES I)	23.6	10.4	3.3	1.3
1971–74 (NHANES I)	23.6	10.5	3.8	1.9
1976–80 (NHANES II)	24.3	10.2	4.2	2.1
1988–94 (NHANES III)	24.7	14.2	6.8	3.9

SOURCE: Flegal KM, Carrol MD, Kuczmarki RJ, Johnson CL: Overweight and obesity in the United States: Prevalence and trends, 1960–1994. *Obes Res* 22:41–44, 1998. Reproduced with permission.

curred in the heavier BMI categories; that is, BMIs greater than 30 kg/m². In contrast, prevalence in the 25 to 29.9 kg/m² BMI category (Table 9-3) has increased only slightly.

The prevalence of overweight and obesity by age shows a progressive increase up to the age of 60, with a slight decrease thereafter (Table 9-4). Longitudinal studies following individuals over time for up to 10 years show the same trend of increasing weight up to the age of 60 years.

African-American and Mexican-American women have a greater prevalence of overweight and obesity than Caucasian women in most age

TABLE 9-4 Prevalence of Different BMI Categories by Age Groups in Women in NHANES III (1988 to 1994)

BMI	Age group (years)					
	20–29	30–39	40–49	50–59	60–69	70–79
25–29.9	30.6	40.9	42.4	44.1	45.4	43.1
30–34.9	8.6	14.1	15.5	20.2	17.4	15.9
35–39.9	4.3	7.3	6.5	9.6	8.7	5.2
>40	1.8	4.4	5.0	5.7	3.7	3.9

SOURCE: Flegal KM, Carrol MD, Kuczmarki RJ, Johnson CL: Overweight and obesity in the United States: Prevalence and trends, 1960–1994. *Obes Res* 22:41–44, 1998. Reproduced with permission.

TABLE 9-5 Prevalence of Different BMI Categories by Race-Ethnic Groups between NHANES II (1976 to 1980) or NHANES (1982 to 1984) and NHANES III (1988 to 1994)

Race-Ethnic Groups	NHANES II	NHANES III
Non-Hispanic Caucasian		
BMI 25–29.9	22.9	23
BMI 30–34.9	9.1	12.7
BMI >35	5.6	9.8
Non-Hispanic African-American		
BMI 25–29.9	30.5	29.2
BMI 30–34.9	18.1	19.2
BMI >35	11.9	18.1
Mexican-American		
BMI 25–29.9	34.7	33.4
BMI 30–34.9	15.5	21.3
BMI >35	9.9	12.9

SOURCE: Flegal KM, Carrol MD, Kuczmarki RJ, Johnson CL: Overweight and obesity in the United States: Prevalence and trends, 1960–1994. *Obes Res* 22:41–44, 1998. Reproduced with permission.

and BMI categories (Table 9-5). This may reflect the conditions of lesser income in African-American and Mexican-American women (income is inversely related to weight in women). Biological factors may also play a role; African-American women have a slightly lower resting metabolic rate compared to Caucasian women.

Pregnancy Many women report gaining significant weight following pregnancy. Because weight commonly increases with age and because of methodologic difficulties in correctly assessing pre- and postpregnancy weights, the effect of parity on weight is difficult to analyze. During pregnancy, a weight gain of 12.5 kg is considered typical, but commonly varies with mean increases between 10.7 kg and 15.2 kg. Excessive weight gain during pregnancy, however, increases the risk for subsequent obesity in the mother, particularly weight gain during the first trimester. Other factors associated with greater retention of weight 1 year after delivery include a larger initial weight before pregnancy, smoking cessation during pregnancy, and less-structured eating habits following delivery. Women engaging in higher levels of physical activity are less likely to retain weight following pregnancy.

In the Stockholm pregnancy and weight development study, 1423 women were studied from conception to 12 months after delivery. The mean weight increase was 0.5 kg. A small percentage of these women (1.5 percent) had a mean increase of 10 kg, and 13 percent had an increase of between 5 and 10 kg. Most (56 percent) had an increase of up to 5 kg. Thirty percent lost weight.

The effect of obesity on pregnancy and perinatal complications may be even more closely related to the existing complications of obesity that antedated the pregnancy than to the obesity itself. On the other hand, overweight adversely affects fertility, with increased rates of infertility for women who have BMIs above 25. Upper-body obesity, as reflected by the waist/hip ratio, is also associated with a decrease in the ability to conceive.

Contrary to popular opinion, lactation seems to have only a slight effect on weight 1 year following pregnancy, albeit women may respond differently to lactation with respect to weight.

In view of the health risks associated with overweight and obesity, weight recommendations during pregnancy should be individualized based on the woman's initial weight before pregnancy, and on her and her family's history of obesity and/or metabolic complications of obesity. Evidence suggests that heavier women do not require the same amount of weight gain during pregnancy as women who are lean.

Menopause It is commonly thought that women gain significant weight at menopause. This may reflect a slight decrease in resting metabolic rate due to cessation of ovulation, resulting in a slight weight gain over time. However, several studies have shown relatively small weight gains during the menopausal years. One study followed women prior to menopause between the ages of 42 and 50 years, and then 3 years later. Those who remained premenopausal and those who had natural menopause gained similar amounts of weight, a mean of 2.25 kg. Another

study using data from the NHANES I epidemiologic follow-up found that women ages 45 to 55 years had an increase in their BMI of 0.3 kg/m^2 (approximately 2 lb). In a study of the same population, the greatest incidence of overweight (14 percent) occurred between the ages of 35 and 44 years, and then declined. Therefore, the greatest risk for weight gain appears to occur before menopause.

However, at menopause, even in the absence of weight gain, there is a change in body fat distribution, with a shift in the distribution of fat from the lower body to the upper body. One study followed premenopausal women for seven years and found that even in the absence of any weight gain, there was an increase of 30 percent in visceral fat. Those women who experienced this increase in visceral fat had increases in fasting insulin levels and deterioration in glucose tolerance. By contrast, women who did not have any increase in visceral fat during the follow-up had no deterioration in glucose and insulin metabolism. It is well known that women have a lower risk of cardiovascular disease before menopause, but begin to assume the same risk as men after menopause. This increase in cardiovascular risk may be partly due to the increased deposition of visceral fat and its associated metabolic abnormalities, hyperinsulinemia, higher triglycerides, lower HDL cholesterol, and increased numbers of small, dense, LDL cholesterol particles. Studies suggest that physical activity and a low-fat diet can reduce the risk of developing visceral obesity at menopause and that hormone replacement therapy attenuates the development of visceral obesity at menopause, lowers LDL cholesterol, and raises HDL cholesterol. Physical activity can also help to minimize the loss of lean tissue and the associated decrease in resting metabolic rate that occurs with aging.

Postmenopause Weight appears to increase until the age of approximately 60, and then slightly decline. This weight decline does not reflect a loss of fat tissue; instead it reflects the loss of lean tissues, including skeletal muscle, skeleton, and brain. The causes for these changes in body composition partly reflect lower levels of physical activity in older women.

Physical activity appears to minimize the loss of lean tissue with aging. One study showed that endurance-trained older women were closer to their younger endurance-trained counterparts in terms of fat mass when compared to older sedentary women; total fat mass was 5.5 kg greater in the trained older woman as compared to the younger endurance-trained woman, but was 12.2 kg greater in older women who were sedentary. Therefore, physical activity may play an important role in preventing the body composition changes associated with aging. Physical activity, particularly weight-bearing activities such as walking and climbing stairs, slows the process of demineralization, attenuating the risk of osteoporosis.

Maintaining a Healthy Weight

General Principles

Based on the rate of increase in the prevalence of obesity in the last decade, it has been estimated (hopefully erroneously) that by year 2030, almost 100 percent of the U.S. population will be overweight or obese. Therefore, the prevention of weight gain assumes even greater importance for the future health of women. It is a paradox that while overweight and obesity are more common than normal weight (approximately 60 percent of the population has a BMI >25 kg/m^2), we live in a society in which the "ideal woman" is thinner and more muscular than ever, and in which there is rampant dissatisfaction with body image, an important factor in the development of eating disorders, particularly in young women.

It is important for the primary care physician to distinguish between those women who need to lose weight for health reasons, and those who wish to lose weight for aesthetic purposes. The woman who wants to lose weight for cosmetic reasons can certainly benefit from a healthy diet and moderate exercise, but she should not be placed on a restrictive diet. On the other hand,

the woman who has a strong family history of diabetes or high blood pressure may be an appropriate candidate for a more aggressive program of diet and exercise, especially if her weight is increasing and approaching a BMI of 25 kg/m^2.

While epidemiologic studies indicate that the healthiest BMI is between 20 and 25 kg/m^2, with the lowest mortality ratio around 22 kg/m^2, it makes no sense to apply this standard to every woman without considering her current weight, her weight history since adolescence, her family's weight history, and her and her family's medical history. Clearly, if a woman has a normal BMI, she should be encouraged to maintain her weight. If her BMI is slowly rising and has moved into the BMI range of 25 to 29.9 kg/m^2, this trend should be pointed out and she should be reminded of the health, social, and quality of life consequences of increasing weight. This advice should be tempered by an assessment of her nutrition habits and her level of physical activity. There are many young women who eat a very healthy diet and who are physically active whose BMI is approaching 30 kg/m^2. Furthermore, if her waist circumference is less than 35 in. and she has no evidence of the comorbidities associated with obesity, such as hypercholesterolemia, hypertension, or a family history of such diseases, there is very little reason to advise anything but weight maintenance. On the other hand, a family history of diabetes or a waist/hip ratio that indicates a significant likelihood of increased visceral fat should prompt recommendations for at least weight maintenance and preferably weight loss.

With a BMI greater than 30 kg/m^2, the health risks of further weight gain are too compelling to ignore. Lifestyle modification, including recommendations for a healthy diet and moderate physical activity, should be advised. Because a 5 to 10 percent loss from initial weight is associated with significant health benefit in terms of the metabolic consequences of overweight and obesity, a modest weight loss should be encouraged, with an initial goal of 5 percent and additional weight loss in incremental steps. At a BMI greater than 30 kg/m², pharmacological therapy may be instituted in conjunction with a program for lifestyle modification. It may sometimes be appropriate to institute pharmacological agents at a BMI as low as 27 kg/m², if the woman has one or more comorbid complications of weight gain and obesity: diabetes, hypertension, dyslipidemia, or arthritis that interferes with physical activity.

Women with a BMI of 35 kg/m² or more with comorbidities, or 40 kg/m² or greater even without comorbidities, have a significantly greater mortality risk. Lifestyle modification is necessary. Pharmacologic treatment may be indicated, and the option of surgery, either gastric restriction or gastric bypass, may be appropriate.

Principles of Nutrition and Physical Activity

Maintenance of a healthy weight must include a healthy lifestyle, no matter what the woman's age. The elements of good nutrition are easily understood through the use of the food pyramid (Fig. 9-2). The food pyramid's basic premise is that fats should be used sparingly, while vegetables and fruits should be increased significantly, and a variety of *high-fiber* starches should become the foundation of a healthy diet. The principles contained within the concept of this pyramid apply to all age groups from youth to adulthood. However, Americans have not been able to follow these guidelines. As a whole, Americans eat too few vegetables and fruits, and too many starches that are low in fiber. Our diets have a slightly lower percent of fat than a decade ago, not because of a reduction in the absolute amount of fat consumed, but because the total caloric intake is higher. We may be trying, but, gram for gram, we are eating the same amount of fat now as we did when the campaign to reduce fat was started.

Although the pyramid is an appropriate guideline for everyone, there are certain nutrients that are age-specific. For example, dietary calcium is important in all stages of a woman's life, but during pregnancy and menopause the need for calcium increases. The daily caloric requirements of older adults are less compared to teenagers; and protein requirements may need to be adjusted depending on a person's general health or specific medical condition such as chronic renal failure.

As one ages there is a decrease in resting metabolic rate, which accompanies the loss of lean tissue. With aging, women may need to readjust their food intake to match the decrease in metabolic rate and avoid weight gain. However, older women who are physically active are less likely to lose lean tissue and may appropriately have a higher food intake and still maintain their weight. Table 9-6 lists nutritional requirements for women at different ages, and during pregnancy and lactation.

Not noted in the table, but particularly important, is that recent data suggest that women may be able to decrease the likelihood of neural tube defects in their offspring by the periconceptional use of folic acid supplements. Women who are planning pregnancy are advised to take a multivitamin supplement with 0.4 mg of folic acid and to consume a diet high in folic acid.

Calcium is a particularly important mineral for women. Osteoporosis is a common problem for postmenopausal women, and adequate calcium intake starting early in life can help to diminish a woman's likelihood of developing osteoporosis. Ideally, to prevent osteoporosis, a woman needs to maximize peak bone mass earlier in life and then decrease the rate of bone loss later in life. This can best be achieved by sufficient calcium intake and exercise from an early age, continuing as a woman ages. Estrogen replacement therapy for the postmenopausal woman reduces bone loss. Even postmenopausal women who are receiving hormone replacement therapy need to take calcium. Postmenopausal women who are not on hormone replacement therapy should have an intake of 1500 mg of calcium daily. Women may need additional vitamin D supplementation, particularly if they have fat malabsorption or minimal exposure to sunlight.

Iron supplements are also important for women, particularly those who have heavy menses and for women who are pregnant or who have had multiple pregnancies. Iron requirements are greater for these women in order to prevent iron-deficiency anemia.

Women should have well-balanced diets based on good nutritional principles, and should not rely on taking vitamin and mineral supplements as a substitute for a diet with proper nutritional content.

Physical activity during all stages of life is a

vital component of good health. The recommendations for physical activity are that both women and men should exercise at moderate intensity for 30 min. on most days of the week. Furthermore, it appears that the 30 min. can be broken into smaller segments, such as three 10-min. sessions. The normal activities of daily living can also contribute significantly to physical activity. Walking and climbing stairs whenever possible (for those who are able) are the most accessible activities. Standing, strolling, or pacing are always preferable to sitting. Refusing help to

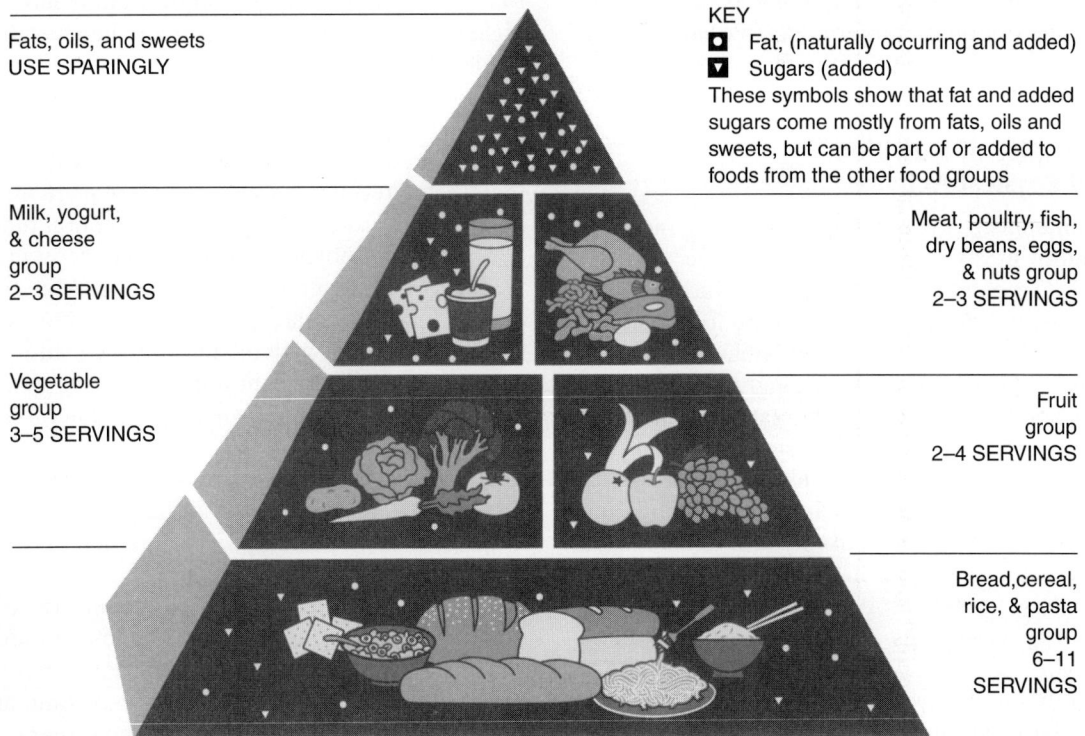

KEY
◻ Fat, (naturally occurring and added)
▼ Sugars (added)
These symbols show that fat and added sugars come mostly from fats, oils and sweets, but can be part of or added to foods from the other food groups

Fats, oils, and sweets
USE SPARINGLY

Milk, yogurt, & cheese group
2–3 SERVINGS

Meat, poultry, fish, dry beans, eggs, & nuts group
2–3 SERVINGS

Vegetable group
3–5 SERVINGS

Fruit group
2–4 SERVINGS

Bread,cereal, rice, & pasta group
6–11 SERVINGS

What is a Serving?
   Bread Group: 1 slice of bread; 1 ounce of ready-to-eat cereal; and 1/2 cup of cooked cereal, rice, or pasta.
   Vegetable Group: 1 cup of raw leafy vegetables; 1/2 cup of other vegetables, cooked or chopped raw; and 3/4 cup of vegetable juice.
   Fruit Group: 1 medium apple, banana, orange, etc.; 1/2 cup of chopped, cooked, or canned fruit; and 3/4 cup of fruit juice.
   Milk Group: 1 cup of milk or yogurt; 1.5 ounces of natural cheese; and 2 ounces of processed cheese.
   Meat Group: 2–3 ounces of cooked lean meat, poultry, or fish. Each 1/2 cup of cooked dry beans, 1 egg, or 2 tablespoons of peanut butter counts as 1 ounce of lean meat, poultry, or fish.

Figure 9-2. A guide to daily food choices. (Source: USDA, 1992).

TABLE 9-6 Food and Nutrition Board, National Academy of Sciences—National Research Council Recommended Dietary Allowances,[a] Revised 1989

Category	Age (years) or Condition	Weight[b] (kg)	Weight[b] (lb)	Height[b] (cm)	Height[b] (in)	Protein (g)	Fat-Soluble Vitamins Vita-min A (μg RE)[c]	Vita-min D (μg)[d]	Vita-min E (mg α-TE)[e]	Vita-min K (μg)	Water-Soluble Vitamins Vita-min C (mg)	Thia-min (mg)	Ribo-flavin (mg)	Niacin (mg NE)[f]	Vita-min B6 (mg)	Fo-late (μg)	Vitamin B12 (μg)	Minerals Cal-cium (mg)	Phos-phorus (mg)	Mag-nesium (mg)	Iron (mg)	Zinc (mg)	Iodine (μg)	Sele-nium (μg)
Females	11–14	46	101	157	62	46	800	10	8	45	50	1.1	1.3	15	1.4	150	2.0	1,200	1,200	280	15	12	150	45
	15–18	55	120	163	64	44	800	10	8	55	60	1.1	1.3	15	1.5	180	2.0	1,200	1,200	300	15	12	150	50
	19–24	58	128	164	65	46	800	10	8	60	60	1.1	1.3	15	1.6	180	2.0	1,200	1,200	280	15	12	150	55
	25–50	63	138	163	64	50	800	5	8	65	60	1.1	1.3	15	1.6	180	2.0	800	800	280	15	12	150	55
	51+	65	143	160	63	50	800	5	8	65	60	1.0	1.2	13	1.6	180	2.0	800	800	280	10	12	150	55
Pregnant						60	800	10	10	65	70	1.5	1.6	17	2.2	400	2.2	1,200	1,200	300	30	15	175	65
Lactating	1st 6 months					65	1,300	10	12	65	95	1.6	1.8	20	2.1	280	2.6	1,200	1,200	355	15	19	200	75
	2nd 6 months					62	1,200	10	11	65	90	1.6	1.7	20	2.1	260	2.6	1,200	1,200	340	15	16	200	75

[a] The allowances, expressed as average daily intakes over time, are intended to provide for individual variations among most normal persons as they live in the United States under usual environmental stresses. Diets should be based on a variety of common foods in order to provide other nutrients for which human requirements have been less well defined. See text for detailed discussion of allowances and of nutrients not tabulated.

[b] Weights and heights of Reference Adults are actual medians for the U.S. population of the designated age, as reported by NHANES II. The median weights and heights of those under 19 years of age were taken from Hamill et al. (1979) (see pages 16–17). The use of these figures does not imply that the height-to-weight ratios are ideal.

[c] Retinol equivalents. 1 retinol equivalent = 1 μg retinol or 6 μg β-carotene. See text for calculation of vitamin A activity of diets as retinol equivalents.

[d] As cholecalciferol. 10 μg cholecalciferol = 400 IU of vitamin D.

[e] α-Tocopherol equivalents. 1 mg d-α tocopherol = 1 α-TE. See text for variation in allowances and calculation of vitamin E activity of the diet as α-tocopherol equivalents.

[f] 1 NE (niacin equivalent) is equal to 1 mg of niacin or 60 mg of dietary tryptophan.

SOURCE: Reprinted with permission from: Recommended Dietary Allowances, National Academy Press. Copyright 1989 by the National Academy of Sciences. Courtesy of the National Academy Press, Washington, DC.

accomplish the common physical tasks of living (e.g., opening doors, carrying packages and suitcases) is especially important for women as they age, because younger persons seem to be more willing to help older persons, the older they get.

Counseling lifestyle modification with respect to nutrition and physical activity is time-consuming, and many clinicians are ill-prepared to effectively counsel patients about lifestyle. Most communities have resources and organizations that can effectively help. Women seem to be more receptive to joining such organizations, but often because of body image and self-esteem issues, are hesitant to join clubs, which attract younger, thinner, more physically active women. Increasingly, groups are being formed that address the needs of older women and women with moderate or greater degrees of overweight. The clinician should be aware of these community groups and encourage patients to participate.

There is no doubt that discussing lifestyle changes, particularly when the clinician is unfamiliar with the topic, is time-consuming and difficult to do correctly. The intent of this chapter is not to add another task to a growing list of patient care needs that the clinician is struggling to provide. However, it is important to address the issue of nutrition and physical activity even in the global sense, and to offer encouragement to change, to improve, to seek help. Tables 9-7 and 9-8, provide small lists of ways in which the clinician can make suggestions for improvement.

Maintaining a Healthy Weight: Childhood through Adolescence

Childhood obesity has increased in the last decade, in part because children have increased their food consumption and decreased their level of physical activity. Several studies show that the hours spent television watching are directly related to increasing weight. By the end of high school, the average child has seen almost 19,000 h of television. Children not only watch too much television and play too many computer

TABLE 9-7 Ways to Outwit Human Ingenuity and Increase Energy Expenditure

- Move the phone away from the bedside. Use a cordless phone and pace while talking.
- Move the television out of the kitchen or the dining room.
- Eat only in one room (the one without the television).
- Park the car at the end of the parking lot, furthest from the entrance to the building. Select a specific parking space and use it consistently (it will usually be free because it is the most distant spot).
- Use light weights for arm and leg movement during television watching.
- Don't use the rollers on luggage.
- In airports, walk instead of sitting and waiting for the flight.
- Avoid all forms of passive transportation; e.g., escalators, moving walkways, carts that whisk people from hotel reception areas to their rooms, etc.
- Play ball with the children instead of watching them in the playground.
- Above all, don't let other people do anything physical that you could do yourself. Don't let others rob you of an opportunity to add even a little physical activity to your life.

TABLE 9-8 Ways to Healthier Eating

- Introduce one new vegetable or fruit per week. Try different ways of incorporating these into the meal. Be creative; read healthy recipes from magazines devoted to low-fat lifestyles.
- Make a diary of all foods eaten as they are eaten. This can be done selectively, 1 or 2 days per week, on weekends, or only during high-risk times of the day—for example, after dinner.
- Add skim milk powder to soups and salad dressings, even to peanut butter, to increase calcium intake.
- Offer sliced fruit with or instead of cookies or cake.
- Half the dinner plate should be vegetables made without added fat.
- Get a food scale and learn what common servings look like; for example, 4 oz of meat, 2 oz of cheese, etc.

and video games, but they tend to engage in these sedentary activities while snacking, often on sweet, high-fat foods.

During puberty, a young girl will lay down fat while a young man will lay down more lean tissue. Both genders grow, although at different rates. It is important to allow this period of growth to proceed normally. Excessive caloric restriction in adolescents is discouraged. Young women who are overweight or obese should be encouraged to engage in moderate exercise and to increase their intake of healthier foods; for example, fruits and vegetables as a substitute for high-fat, carbohydrate foods. If a young woman increases her level of physical activity and also improves her nutrition, she may grow out of this overweight stage. Restrictive diets should be reserved for those pubescent girls whose health and quality of life are severely compromised from obesity.

Portion size is important. The supersizing of food is a marketing concept that has increased the caloric consumption of Americans. Often a large size soda is 32 oz, versus a small one which is 16 oz, a difference of 160 "empty" calories. A can of soda is 12 oz and most bottles are 20 oz. Thirty years ago, the average bottle of soda was 6.5 oz. Substituting low-fat for high-fat foods also helps; for instance, replacing high-fat chips with pretzels is a modest, but practical, way to reduce calories.

In spite of the obvious health threat of fast foods and oversized portions, prohibiting a teenager from going to a fast food restaurant, or requiring her to eat only salad at a fast food restaurant, can result in a rebellious teenager who may act out by consuming greater amounts of prohibited junk foods, often secretively.

However, children may be willing to eat their favorite food accompanied by a salad. For example, if the french fries are important to a child, the small size can be ordered (rather than the supersize, thereby saving 330 calories) along with a salad. The object of desire in a children's meal may be a special glass or inexpensive toy that can often be bought separately.

Adolescence is a crucial time for bone development. Unfortunately, adolescents tend to consume too little calcium and folate. Although some teenagers drink milk, many do not. Suggesting fruit shakes using milk or milk powder, or mixing skim milk powder into soups or peanut butter are helpful ways to enrich the diet with calcium. Suggesting fruits instead of juices and adding vegetables to stews and pasta sauces is one way to increase folate and fiber.

The challenge in changing eating behavior is to create an environment that is natural, consistent, and reasonable. Disordered eating may be encouraged by unfairly restricting a child's access to food. For example, it is cruel to have soft drinks in the house only for the adults or for some of the children but not for the overweight child. If soft drinks are available in a home, they should be available to all members of the household. On the other hand, soft drinks and other appealing foods (which are usually high in fat and sugar) should not be used as a reward or inducement for approved behavior. Making policy decisions about food that affect the overweight child requires consistent messages about health and nutrition that apply to all members of a household. Eating in only one room in the house, for example, is a policy that is good for the whole family. Hopefully that room has no television in it. Sugar-coated cereals are another example where policy can make the difference. If no one in the family is allowed to have sugar-coated cereals as a meal or demi-meal, but all can enjoy it as a snack with low-fat milk—in that one room in the house without a television set—then the child has the choice to eat or not, and the snack becomes a reasonable, low-fat, high-calcium choice.

The risks of an eating disorder must be considered before advising weight loss to young women. Although obesity in childhood and adolescence poses a risk for adult obesity, it is also true that young women in adolescence are at an age of greater risk for eating disorders. Therefore, it is important that they not be shamed because of weight gain or because they choose foods that are fattening. It is better to improve the environ-ment by increasing healthy food choices as a fam-ily, and to encourage extracurricular school activ-ities such as dance, movement, or gym. If the adolescent is overweight but not obese, it may be more important to prevent further weight gain than to focus single-mindedly on weight loss. A pattern of disordered eating or rigid dieting alter-nating with weight gain can develop if more natu-ral eating and physical habits are not established. Therefore, it is important that the clinician not subject the child or adolescent to the anxieties and pressures of the family with respect to weight, but to instead suggest changes that pro-mote a healthier lifestyle for the whole family and not the child alone.

Maintaining a Healthy Weight: Adulthood

Pregnancy The issue of weight gain during pregnancy is complicated. Too much or too little weight gain may compromise the health of the fetus. Because women enter pregnancy at dif-fering weights, they require flexibility with re-spect to recommendations for weight gain during pregnancy. In 1990, the Institute of Medicine sug-gested a total weight gain of 28 to 40 lb for those women whose prepregnancy BMIs are under 20. Women whose prepregnancy BMIs are greater than 29 kg/m² should gain approximately 15 to 25 lb during pregnancy. Individuals with a normal prepregnancy weight should gain approximately 25 to 35 pounds during pregnancy. Weight rec-ommendations also vary by trimester. There should be little weight gain in the first trimester; most of the weight gain of pregnancy should oc-cur in the second and third trimesters.

The need for vitamins and minerals increases during pregnancy. At this time, a woman is pre-scribed a multivitamin specifically for pregnancy, which will be particularly high in calcium, iron, and folate. However, this does not obviate the need for a healthy diet, nor does it reduce the need for exercise. Eating generous quantities of fruits and vegetables and increasing fiber in the diet not only help improve nutrition, but can

reduce the risk of constipation and hemorrhoids, both of which are common during pregnancy. The old adage of eating for two is not correct, but if the mother does not eat appropriately, the fetus will take what nutrients it can and leave the mother with less. Eating a healthy, low-fat diet increases the quality of nutrition while main-taining an appropriate caloric intake.

If a woman is exercising already, then except for exercises that are dangerous or excessive, she can usually continue exercising at the same level throughout the pregnancy. When the pregnant woman exercises, core body temperature should not exceed 38°C, because hyperthermia may be associated with neural tube defects. In addition, she should avoid exercises in the supine position, and should avoid deep flexion and extension. If she hasn't been exercising, there are books and exercise groups that specialize in enhancing safe exercise during pregnancy.

For most lactating women there does not need to be too great an increase in food intake, because energy requirements during lactation are met partly from the mobilization of stored body fat (primarily in the hips and thighs) that occurred during pregnancy. The need for liquids is signifi-cant because of lactation, and water is obviously the best choice compared to sodas. Vitamin and mineral requirements also increase for lactating women, and supplements are usually recom-mended.

Perimenopause, Menopause, and Postmeno-pause There is a redistribution of fat to the visceral area, which is associated with an in-creased risk for the cardiovascular complications of obesity; that is, diabetes, dyslipidemia, and hypertension. In some women, it seems more difficult to maintain weight even with constant exercise and healthy eating habits.

At menopause, the resting metabolic rate is reduced because of the absence of a luteal phase; metabolic rate normally rises slightly during the luteal phase, and the lack of this physiologic event may make a significant difference in weight over a number of years. The role of hormone replacement therapy in body weight has not been well studied, but seems to vary among women. Studies suggest that hormone replacement therapy attenuates the increase in visceral fat that occurs at menopause.

Women who maintain moderate to high levels of physical activity gain less weight than those who do not. Overweight may be protective of bone, and obese women may have a lesser risk of osteoporosis. African-American women have denser bones than non-Hispanic Caucasian women or Asian women, and therefore osteoporosis is of less concern in this population.

Physical activity improves the cardiovascular risk profile and may have beneficial effects on mood and quality of life. A low-fat diet is also protective against weight gain and cardiovascular disease. Physical activity (both aerobic and weight training) lets women enter old age with greater functional ability to cope with the activities of daily living, such as getting out of chairs, bathing, and bathroom hygiene. While the ability to perform these activities is taken for granted by younger people, those who are older may define their quality of life by the ease with which they can care for themselves unassisted.

Calcium is usually consumed in foods in insufficient quantities to be effective against osteoporosis; therefore, calcium supplementation is necessary in the older woman. Vitamin E supplements may also be necessary for some women in small amounts (400 IU per day). It is important that the physician inquire about the patient's use of vitamins and minerals, as well as prescription drugs, because vitamins such as E can interfere with blood clotting, and therefore cause undue bleeding postsurgery.

Drug interactions are a concern, especially in older people who are more likely to take multiple medications. Aspirin may compete with folate, hindering the body's use of this vitamin. In addition, aspirin and vitamin E can cause bleeding. Tetracycline and calcium taken at the same time bind to each other, reducing the absorption of both.

The nutritional adequacy of the diet in older women may suffer because of age-related changes in taste and smell. Weight loss may be the first sign of inadequate food intake, because many older persons are isolated from family and friends who would normally monitor and encourage food intake. Spicy foods, if tolerated, can be helpful in restoring interest in food.

References and Selected Readings

1. Björkelund C, Lissner L, Andersson S, et al: Reproductive history in relation to relative weight and fat distribution. *Int J Obes Relat Metab Disord,* 20:213–219, 1996.
2. Bray GA: Fat distribution and body weight. *Obes Res* 1,3,203–219, 1993.
3. Brown WJ, Dobson AJ, Mishra G: What is a healthy weight for middle aged women? *Int J Obes Relat Metab Disord* 22:520–528, 1998.
4. Colditz GA: Economic costs of obesity. *Am J Clin Nutr* 55:503S–507S, 1992.
5. Flegal KM, Carrol MD, Kuzmarki RJ, Johnson CL: Overweight and obesity in the United States: Prevalence and trends, 1960–1994. *Obes Res* 22:39–47, 1998.
6. Foster GD, Kendall PC: The realistic treatment of obesity: Changing the scales of success. *Clin Psychol Rev* 14(8):701–736, 1994.
7. Garfinkel L: Overweight and cancer. *Ann Intern Med* 103(6 pt 2):1034–1036, 1985.
8. Givens JR: Reproductive and hormonal alterations in obesity, in Björntorp P, Brodoff B (eds): *Obesity.* Philadelphia: JB Lippincott, 1992.
9. Haarbo J, Marslew U, Golfredsen A, Christiansen C: Postmenopausal hormone replacement therapy prevents central distribution of body fat after menopause. *Metabolism* 40:1323–1326, 1991.
10. Heymsfield SB, Gallagher D, Poehlman ET, et al: Menopausal changes in body composition and energy expenditure. *Exp Gerontol* 29(3/4):377–389, 1994.
11. Hirsch J, Hudgins LC, Leibel RL, Rosenbaum M: Diet composition and energy balance in humans. *Am J Clin Nutr* 67(Suppl):551S–555S, 1998.
12. James WPT: A public health approach to the problem of obesity. *Int J Obes Relat Metab Disord* 19(suppl 3):S37–S45, 1995.
13. Kuczmarski RJ, Flegal KM, Campbell SM, Johnson CL: Increasing prevalence of overweight among U.S. adults. *JAMA* 272:205–211, 1994.
14. Lew EA, Garfinkel L: Variations in mortality by weight among 750,000 men and women. *J Chron Dis* 32:563–576, 1979.

15. Manson JE, Willett WC, Stampfer MJ, et al: Body weight and mortality among women. *N Engl J Med* 333:677–684, 1995.

16. NIH Consensus Development Panel: Health implications of obesity: National Institutes of Health Consensus Development Conference Statement—NIH Consensus Development Panel on the Health Implications of Obesity. *Ann Intern Med* 103:1073–1077, 1985.

17. Olson CL, Shumaker HD, Yawn BP: Overweight women delay medical care. *Arch Fam Med* 3:888–892, 1994.

18. Rossner S: Obesity and pregnancy, in Bray G, Bouchard C, James WPT (eds); *Handbook of Obesity.* New York; Marcel Dekker, 1998, pp 775–790.

19. Serdula MK, Ivery D, Coates RJ, Freedman DS, Williamson DF, Byers T: Do obese children become obese adults? A review of the literature. *Prev Med* 22(2):167–177, 1993.

20. Stunkard AJ, Sorensen TIA, Hanis C, et al: An adoption study of human obesity. *N Engl J Med* 314:193–198, 1986.

21. Troiano RP, Flegal KM, Kuczmarski RJ, et al: Overweight prevalence and trends for children and adolescents: The National Health and Nutrition Examination Surveys, 1963 to 1991. *Arch Pediatr Adolesc Med* 149:1085–1091, 1995.

22. Williamson DF, Pamuk E, Thun M, et al: Prospective study of intentional weight loss and mortality in never-smoking overweight US white women aged 40–64 years. *Am J Epidemiol* 141:1128–1141, 1995.

CHAPTER 10

Exercise

David B. Hale
Ralph W. Hale

GENERAL FITNESS
CARDIOVASCULAR FITNESS
INJURY PREVENTION
WEIGHT CONTROL
MUSCLE STRENGTH
EFFECTS ON MENSTRUATION
    AND REPRODUCTION
BONE DENSITY
OTHER BENEFITS
PELVIC STRUCTURES

During the last 20 to 30 years, there has been a sudden increase in emphasis on exercise as a key aspect of a healthy lifestyle. When exercise is combined with proper nutrition and preventive health care measures, there can be an increase in the quality as well as the quantity of life. As a result of this emphasis on exercise, women have become more involved in active exercise, extending from general fitness to elite athletic activity. This change in women's lifestyles has been accompanied by an increasing need for basic information, and women frequently turn to their physician for this information.

General Fitness

Fitness, or conditioning, is a term used to describe the changes in cardiovascular endurance, muscle strength, coordination, and flexibility that result from an organized, repetitive exercise program. In some instances, it also includes weight control. The major component of fitness is determined by the type of exercise program selected and the ultimate goal of the program. However, for any program to be successful it must be repetitive and it must be directed. A variety of exercises within the limits of a specific type of activity can often make training more enjoyable. It is important to recognize that "cross-training" can increase the risk of injury and is not advisable for the recreational athlete. The goal should be maintaining a specific program rather than multiple programs. Because most current programs emphasize aerobic conditioning, the cardiovascular component becomes the key factor.

The energy source for exercise is dependent on carbohydrates and fats. Glucose is the principal sugar used, and this is either available in the blood or stored in the body as glycogen for later use. Muscle mass is the primary storage area for glycogen, and during exercise enzymatic breakdown occurs that releases the glucose for active cellular metabolism.[12] As exercise continues, there is also a release of lactic acid, which is a by-product of anaerobic metabolism.[18] Resynthesis of lactate to glucose can occur, and some physiologists and coaches use lactate measurements to measure conditioning.[3–5]

Fatty acids stored within the body as fats comprise the largest potential energy stores. They become most important in exercise of longer duration and of low-to-moderate intensity. When intensity increases, the amount of energy obtained from fats decreases.[2] The key factor in this energy cycle is the amount of oxygen available to complete the cycle. Because cellular oxygen is essential for utilization of carbohydrates and fats, any program that increases the presence of cellular oxygen prolongs the ability of the muscle to function. When the amount of oxygen available is depleted, the energy cycle continues, but becomes anaerobic. Although anaerobic training is utilized in some short, high-intensity athletic programs, in the usual aerobic program it signals the end of a meaningful exercise session.

In general, repetitive exercise programs increase the efficiency of the body's utilization of these energy sources, which increases endurance. As training continues, there is an enhanced oxidative capacity as the result of increased capillary density within muscle fibers. Mitochondrial size and enzyme activity also increase fatty acid utilization. The net result is an increased extraction/utilization of oxygen from the blood. These changes are considered peripheral adaptations and account for at least 50 percent of the body's adaptation to exercise.[15]

Ultimately, the longer an exercise session continues, the less efficient it becomes. Thus, for individuals to perceive that they are "in condition," the initial program must be repetitive over long periods as opposed to infrequent, long, individual sessions. It takes approximately 12 weeks in any program to achieve a significant fitness level.[1]

Cardiovascular Fitness

The goal of most exercise programs is to obtain a degree of cardiovascular fitness. This is interpreted as the ability to sustain physical activity over a prolonged period. The level of activity and the length of time varies with individual goals. Some persons seek to become elite athletes, but most simply wish to improve their general fitness.

The usual format consists of an aerobic activity performed for 30 minutes, three or four times a week. In response to this repeated exercise, the body increases its ability to utilize the aerobic energy cycle. The name given to this phenomenon is *aerobic capacity*. The most common method of determining the level of aerobic capacity is to determine the maximum oxygen uptake over a given period of time. The result is called the V_{O_2max}, and is measured utilizing a controlled environment such as a laboratory. V_{O_2max} is calculated by using the Flick equation. A general understanding of this formula helps in understanding some of the adaptations that occur during exercise:

$$V_{O_2max} = (\text{stroke volume} \times \text{heart rate})$$
$$\times (C_aO_2 - C_vO_2).$$

C_aO_2 and C_vO_2 are the oxygen saturation of the arterial and mixed venous blood. This is a peripheral vascular change and demonstrates the body's ability to extract and utilize oxygen. As an athlete trains, the heart increases stroke volume and decreases rate. Both of these adaptations are central vascular changes and reflect improved cardiac performance. The final result is referred to as *aerobic capacity*. Aerobic capacity increases in response to sustained repetitive exercise. As aerobic capacity/cardiovascular fitness improves, the V_{O_2max} increases. Except for monitoring heart rate changes, there is no easy way to evaluate V_{O_2max}. Fortunately, heart rate and V_{O_2max} are directly related.

As an athlete's cardiovascular status improves, higher exertion levels are required to increase the heart rate to training levels. This directly correlates with improved V_{O_2max}. A practical way of measuring aerobic capacity is to utilize the heart rate change. Because the heart rate increases as oxygen deprivation increases, it provides a method to determine the amount of oxygen and resulting glycolysis that is being utilized as a result of exercise.[1] The goal of exercise is to reach and maintain a specific heart rate over a minimum time period. By utilizing this method, each exercise session can be monitored to achieve the desired goal. The formula utilized for this determination is: $(220 - \text{age}) \times 60$ to

TABLE 10-1 **Target Heart Rates**

	Ranges	
Age	Minimum 60%	Maximum 80%
20	120	160
30	114	152
40	108	144
50	102	136
60	96	128
70	90	120

80%. The resulting number is the target heart rate range. For example, a 40-year-old female has a target heart rate range of 108 to 144 beats per minutes [(220 − 40) = 180 × 0.6 or 0.8]. See Table 10-1 for target heart rate ranges of other age groups.

The exercise program can be tailored to the individual's specific needs. Once the target range is reached, it should be maintained for 20 to 30 min (not including warmup and cooldown periods) and this program should be repeated three to four times a week.[8]

Remember that before each exercise program there should be 3 to 5 min of gradually increasing activity to reduce the potential for muscle injury. This is referred to as the "warmup" period. By the completion of exercise there has been a vasodilation in the muscles and skin, and sudden stopping can result in extensive distal vascular pooling, which could cause a relative central hypovolemia. Thus, a period of 5 to 15 min at the completion of exercise should be devoted to the gradual reduction of intensity. This is referred to as the "cooldown" period.[21] During this cooldown period, hot baths, hot showers, or any other activity that could contribute to peripheral vascular pooling should be avoided.

There are three key aspects of any exercise program designed to obtain cardiovascular fitness: specificity, progression, and overload.[14] Specificity refers to designing a program that results in attainment of the goals. For example, if the goal is cardiovascular fitness, the exercise should be aerobic and not designed to increase muscle strength. If the goal is to run a marathon, then training for a short jog is insufficient. Progression refers to starting at a low level of intensity and increasing to a higher level of intensity over time. There is no ideal time length for this to occur, and it varies greatly from individual to individual. A method of measuring progression is to use the target heart rate. As conditioning (i.e., cardiovascular fitness) occurs, an increased intensity of activity is required to reach the target rate. The concept of overload refers to the necessity of increasing the demand on the body over and above that which is usual. Because the cardiovascular system is not stable, it responds to the demands placed upon it by increasing or decreasing activity over a period of time. Thus, for any exercise program to succeed, it must exceed the current level of performance and stress the system. The target heart rate remains an excellent measurement tool to evaluate the level of stress attained.

Coordination, balance, and flexibility may occur as the result of an exercise program. As muscles work in a group in a repetitive program, they become more efficient as a group. This helps the individual perform activities with less difficulty. Although this is rarely an initial goal of exercise, it is an important benefit.

A word of caution: Any level of conditioning is reversible and often occurs faster than developing the conditioning.[4,17] A long-term commitment to exercise is necessary if conditioning is to persist.

Injury Prevention

All exercise programs can be harmful if they are improperly performed. Any of these signs signal the need for an abrupt halt until adequate reevaluation occurs[1]:

- Sudden pain, especially if sharp and specific
- Excessive fatigue, acute or chronic
- Respiratory problems
- Nausea and/or vomiting

- Dizziness or light-headedness
- Chronic muscle or joint pain
- Any heart rate irregularity or pain
- Frequent severe headaches
- Recurrent epistaxis

Weight Control

Exercise can help maintain as well as reduce weight. Weight-reduction programs that are combined with exercise are more effective than any dieting program by itself.[20]

When utilizing exercise as part of a weight-control program, remember that weight loss is a slow process. Depending on the intensity of exercise, it is necessary to expend approximately 3500 calories for each pound of fat lost. Thus, the time span for significant weight reduction can be very lengthy. In addition, as fat is lost, muscle is produced. Per unit volume, muscle is approximately twice the weight of fat. Thus, in the initial phases of exercise, weight may increase slightly before a significant decrease occurs. A helpful guide during this period of time is the fit of clothes. If fat is lost, they should become looser, even while weight is stable.

Remember that any exercise program that is part of weight control is based on maintaining a stable or reduced caloric intake. If additional calories are consumed because of the exercise, minimal or no weight reduction occurs.

A word of caution: Strenuous dieting in association with exercise is to be avoided. The resulting energy loss will increase the exhaustion felt with exercise, and usually will lead to cessation of the exercise program.

Muscle Strength

For a muscle to strengthen, it is essential that it work repetitively against a fixed resistance, which causes fibers to hypertrophy. It is this hypertrophy that causes an increased work capacity or strength. For muscle strength to occur, a program for the specific muscle group must be developed.

Strength-training programs designed for one muscle group do not affect other unstressed groups. The classic example is the tennis player with one large strong arm used to hold the racquet, while the other arm has less muscle mass and is much weaker.

Depending on the program, there may also be some cardiovascular effects. However, if the main goal is cardiovascular fitness, aerobic exercise should be performed; if the goal is strength, a specific strength program is necessary.

An ancillary use of muscle strength is for "toning," which is accomplished by developing specific muscle groups to improve one's appearance. Body builders use this form of weight training.

Effects on Menstruation and Reproduction

The most common effect of exercise on the female reproductive system is to initiate changes in the menstrual cycle. This was first reported in long-distance runners and occurred as oligomenorrhea. Menstrual changes may vary from a sudden cessation of menses to a gradual reduction over an extended period. The exact mechanism is unknown, but probably relates to changes in the hypothalamic-pituitary axis.[16]

It is known that both oligomenorrhea and amenorrhea are related to the amount of exercise. The amount and intensity can vary from individual to individual, but it appears that a minimum exercise expenditure equivalent to running 20 miles per week is needed.[7] On the other hand, some women can exercise far more extensively without any noticeable changes. If changes occur, a reduction in activity usually results in a return of normal menses within two to three months.

However, when presented with a patient who is experiencing the onset of amenorrhea of several months duration associated with strenuous exercise, the initial evaluation should establish whether she is pregnant. If she is not pregnant, the next step is to determine if she has adequate estrogen production. Withdrawal bleeding should be accomplished with oral me-droxyprogesterone 10 mg twice a day for 3 days. (If she menstruates, no further action is needed other than periodic treatment with progesterone to induce withdrawal bleeding at three-month intervals.) If she does not have withdrawal bleeding, intramuscular progesterone should be given to eliminate the possibility of any absorption problem. If no bleeding occurs, then obtain a prolactin and a serum estrogen level. An abnormal prolactin level requires further evaluation. Patients with serum estrogen levels of less than 50 picograms (pg) should be given supplemental estrogen therapy for 30 to 60 days followed by oral medroxyprogesterone to induce withdrawal bleeding. Failure to menstruate at that time usually indicates a need to increase estrogen supplement. If repeat dosing in 30 to 60 days still fails to cause menstruation, further evaluation is needed.

Other areas of concern are the impact of exercise on menarche, dysmenorrhea, infertility, and the breast. These areas are all currently being investigated. Thus far, there are no consistent findings, and the reader is referred to specific references on these topics for greater detail.[1,6] Unfortunately, anecdotal experiences are quoted far more commonly than scientific studies. It appears that the menarche may be delayed if intense exercise is started several years prior to menarche. However, no adverse effects have been noted due to this delay. Dysmenorrhea may or may not be increased. It is theoretically possible that release of prostaglandins during exercise increases dysmenorrhea. On the other hand, many women report a relief from dysmenorrhea once they begin an active exercise program.

The effect of exercise on fertility is still controversial. Obviously, a woman who becomes amenorrheic is usually infertile. However, it is unknown whether this amenorrhea will subsequently impact fertility. Some very preliminary evidence suggests that those who would have infertility problems anyway may be more susceptible, but this has not been proven.[7]

It is rare for any exercise program to cause significant injury to the breast. Minor abrasions can occur if an ill-fitting support is used, but no long-term effects have been documented.

Bone Density

Bone density has been shown to increase in women who are involved in an active exercise program.[10] Pressure on the bone results in increased calcium deposition due to increased osteoblastic activity. Thus, a moderate exercise program can be helpful as an adjunct to supplemental estrogen therapy in postmenopausal women. It can also be a primary therapy in menopausal women who do not take estrogens. Exercise designed to help prevent osteoporosis involves use of large muscles attached to the long bones. It is necessary that stress be placed on the bone to ensure that adequate bone strength is maintained; this facilitates conservation or replacement of calcium. Fortunately, most aerobic exercise programs involve use of enough large muscle mass to accomplish this stress and to help reduce the incidence of osteoporosis. Because osteoporosis probably begins to develop when a woman is in her 40s and 50s, it should be emphasized that exercise at this age is an important step in preventing later problems. However, in women over 60, light-to-moderate aerobic exercise apparently can still have a positive effect in improving bone density. When combined with hormonal replacement therapy and adequate calcium intake, bone density will improve.[11]

Other Benefits

Several recent studies have shown other benefits to an ongoing exercise program. A study in Norway concluded that women who exercised regularly reduced their incidence of breast cancer, especially in premenopausal women. The mechanism is unknown, but may be related to reduced body fat.[19]

In another study, investigators found a reduction in mortality in women who exercised regularly. This reduced mortality from cardiovascular and respiratory illness was seen with as little as moderate activity once per week.[9]

Pelvic Structures

Some physicians are concerned about the effect of an exercise program on the bladder and supporting structures. There is no evidence that any permanent damage can result from exercise programs or elite athletic programs. Some women notice transient urinary incontinence while competing, especially in high-impact sports. Follow-up studies, however, fail to reveal any significant increase in long-term incontinence.[13]

Summary

Exercise should be a regular part of an individual's daily activities. Whether it is a 2- to 3-mile vigorous walk or a high-intensity, elite athletic program, exercise will have long-term benefits on the lifestyle and health of the individual. Humans throughout history have never been a sedentary species. Activity has always been central to living. Modern appliances and conveniences, however, have reduced the need for exercise, and we must now help our patients maintain fitness.

References and Selected Readings

1. American College of Obstetricians and Gynecologists: *Women and Exercise.* American College of Obstetricians and Gynecologists; October 1992. Technical Bulletin 173, Washington, DC.
2. Ahlbory G, Felig P, Hagenfeldt L, et al: Substrate turnover during prolonged exercise in man: Splanchnic and leg metabolism of glucose, free fatty acids, and amino acids. *J Clin Invest* 53:1080–1090, 1974.
3. Cheetham ME, Boobis LH, Brooks S, Williams C: Human muscle metabolism during sprint running. *J Appl Physiol* 61:54–60, 1986.
4. Coyle EF, Hemmert MK, Coggan AR: Effects of detraining on cardiovascular responses to exercise: Role of blood volume. *J Appl Physiol* 60:95–99, 1986.
5. Gollnick PD: Energy metabolism and prolonged exercise, in Lamb DR, et al (eds): *Perspectives in Exercise Science and Sports Medicine.* Indianapolis: Benchmark Press, 1988, pp 14–15.
6. Hale RW (ed): *Caring for the Exercising Woman.* New York: Elsevier, 1991.
7. Hale RW, Kosasa T, Kruger J, Pepper S: A marathon: The immediate effect of female runners luteinizing hormone, follicle stimulating hormone, prolactin, testosterone and cortisol levels. *Am J Obstet Gynecol* 146:550–556, 1983.
8. Hartley LH: General principles of exercise prescription, in Strauss RH (ed): *Sports Medicine.* Philadelphia: WB Saunders, 1984, pp 45–56.
9. Kushi LH, Fee RM, Falsom AR, Mink PJ, Anderson KE, Sellers TA: Physical activity and mortality in postmenopausal women. *JAMA* 277:1287–1292, 1997.
10. McCulloch RG, Bailey DA, Houston CS, Dogg BL: Effects of physical activity, dietary calcium intake and selected lifestyle factors on bone density in young women. *CMAJ* 142:221–227, 1990.
11. National Institutes of Health Consensus Conference: Osteoporosis. *JAMA* 252:799–802, 1984.
12. Newsholme EA: The regulation of intracellular fuel supply during sustained exercise. *Ann NY Acad Sci* 301:81–91, 1977.
13. Nygaard IE: Does prolonged high impact activity contribute to later urinary incontinence? A retrospective cohort study of female olympians. *Obstet Gynecol* 90:118–122, 1997.
14. Prins J, Hale RW: Exercise programs and the prescription of exercise, in Hale RW (ed): *Caring for the Exercising Woman.* New York: Elsevier, 1991, pp 42–50.
15. Prins J: Basic exercise physiology, in Hale, R (ed): *Caring for the Exercising Woman.* New York: Elsevier, 1991, pp 9–11.
16. Russell JB, Mitchell D, Musey PI, Collins DC: The relationship of exercise and anovulatory cycles in female athletes: Hormonal and physical characteristics. *Obstet Gynecol* 63:452–456, 1984.
17. Salten B, Blomquist G, Mitchell JH, et al: Response to exercise after bed rest and after training. *Circulation* (suppl), 7:8, 1968.
18. Sherman MS, Lamb DR: Nutrition and prolonged exercise, in Lamb DR, Murray R (eds): *Perspectives in Exercise and Sports Medicine,* vol 1, *Prolonged Exercise.* Indianapolis: Benchmark Press, 1988, pp 213–217.
19. Thume, Brenn T, Lund F, Gaard M: Physical activity and the risk of breast cancer. *N Engl J Med* 336:1269–1275, 1997.
20. Tremblay A, Despres JP, et al: Effect on intensity of physical activity on body fatness and fat distribution. *Am J Clin Nutr* 51:153–157, 1990.
21. Wilmore JH. *The Wilmore Fitness Program: A Personalized Guide to Total Fitness and Health.* New York: Simon & Schuster, 1981, pp 75–123.

CHAPTER 11

Tobacco Use

Marc Manley
Roselyn Payne Epps
Thomas Glynn

CLINICAL INTERVENTIONS
ASK About Smoking at Every Opportunity •
ADVISE All Smokers to Stop • ASSIST the
Patient in Stopping • ARRANGE Follow-up
Visits
OFFICE ORGANIZATION
SPECIAL ISSUES IN TOBACCO CONTROL
Weight Gain • Lack of Social Support for
Stopping • Preventing Tobacco Use
among Youth

Cigarettes are the leading factor contributing to preventable death in the United States. Cigarettes are associated with more than 400,000 deaths each year, which is more than alcohol, illegal drugs, car crashes, homicides, suicides, and AIDS combined. For women and men, smoking is a known cause of cancer of the lung, larynx, oral cavity, esophagus, pancreas, bladder, and kidney; it also causes coronary heart disease, atherosclerotic peripheral vascular disease, chronic obstructive pulmonary disease, intrauterine growth retardation, and low birthweight. Smoking also contributes to cervical cancer, infertility, peptic ulcer disease, and skin wrinkling. Smokeless tobacco use causes oral cancer and other oral lesions. Environmental tobacco smoke, a known human carcinogen, causes lung cancer in nonsmoking adults and respiratory illness in children.

An epidemic of lung cancer is now occurring among women. Lung cancer deaths have surpassed breast cancer deaths as the most common fatal cancer among women. The number of lung cancer deaths is rising rapidly among women, while remaining constant among men. Women who smoke face a risk of lung cancer 12 times the risk of nonsmoking women. Approximately 80 percent of lung cancer deaths among women are attributable to smoking.

In 1995, 47 million Americans, or 24.7 percent of the adult population, smoked cigarettes; 27.0 percent of men smoked compared with 22.6 percent of women. The highest levels of smoking were among people ages 25 to 44. Until the mid-1990s, smoking rates were decreasing for both men and women; now these rates have leveled off.

This chapter provides physicians, nurses, other health care providers, and their associates with the necessary information to institute effective smoking cessation techniques in their practices. The interventions described are simple and brief, taking as little as 3 min. They are based on large clinical trials supported by the National Cancer Institute (NCI), which clearly indicate that physicians and other health care professionals can significantly reduce the prevalence of smoking if they provide smoking cessation interventions.

Clinical Interventions

The NCI recommendations for clinical interventions consist of four activities, each beginning with the letter "A":

- *Ask* all patients about smoking
- *Advise* smokers to stop
- *Assist* their efforts with self-help materials, a quit date, and possibly nicotine gum or the transdermal patch
- *Arrange* follow-up

This intervention plan (often referred to as the "4 A's") describes a general approach to smoking that can be used in almost any outpatient encounter, whether 30 s or 30 min are available to the clinician. Each element of the intervention is described below.

Ask about Smoking at Every Opportunity

A nurse or other staff member should routinely ask patients "Do you smoke?" or "Are you still smoking?" at each visit, usually while measuring vital signs. Once it is known that a person smokes (or previously smoked), an identifier should be placed prominently on the patient's chart to remind the physician and staff to discuss smoking at each visit.

Advise All Smokers to Stop

A clear statement of advice (e.g., "As your physician, I must advise you to stop smoking now.") is essential. Many patients do not recall receiving this advice from their physician; the statement must be easy to understand and memorable. Personalization of the message by referring to the patient's clinical condition, social roles, personal interests, or family history may add to the effectiveness of the advice. Motivations to stop smoking vary greatly from patient to patient. A list of reasons different people might give for stopping is provided in Table 11-1.

Assist the Patient in Stopping

A patient's level of interest in stopping smoking usually is evident in discussions with the physician. If it is not, ask the patient if he or she wants

TABLE 11-1 Good Reasons to Stop Smoking

For teenagers	For asymptomatic adults
Bad breath	Twice the risk of heart
Stained teeth	disease
Cost	Six times the risk of em-
Lack of independence—	physema
controlled by cigarettes	Cost of cigarettes
Sore throats	Cost of sick time
Cough	Bad breath
Dyspnea (might affect	Less convenient and so-
sports)	cially unacceptable
Frequent respiratory in-	Wrinkles
fections	For symptomatic adults
For pregnant women	Upper respiratory infection
Increased rate of sponta-	Sore throat
neous abortion and fe-	Gum disease
tal death	Dyspnea
Increased risk of low	Cough
birthweight	Angina
For parents	Claudication
Increased coughing and	For any smoker
respiratory infections	Money saved by stopping
among children of	Feel better
smokers	Improved ability to exercise
Poor role model for	More likely to enjoy retire-
child	ment, grandchildren, etc.
For new smokers	
Easier to stop now	

SOURCE: Adapted from Glynn T, Manley M: *How to Help Your Patients Stop Smoking: A National Cancer Institute Manual for Physicians.* Bethesda, MD: National Institutes of Health, 1989. NIH Publication No. 89-3064.

to stop. For those patients who do not want to stop, nagging rarely helps. Physicians must accept the patient's decision, must make sure that the patient is making an informed decision, and must maintain the patient's trust and confidence so that smoking can be discussed at future visits.

For those patients who express a sincere desire to stop smoking, the physician should help them set a specific date. There is evidence that patients who set a "quit date" are more likely to make a serious attempt to stop. This date should be soon (generally within 4 weeks), but not immediate, giving the patient the necessary time to prepare to stop.

Once a patient has selected a specific date to stop, information must be provided so that the patient can prepare for that date. For patients who can read, this is easily accomplished by providing them with a self-help brochure. Effective brochures provide the patient with necessary information about smoking cessation (e.g., symptoms and time course of withdrawal, tips about stopping, good reasons for stopping, answers to common questions). Effective brochures are available from several professional and voluntary organizations, including the American Cancer Society, the American Lung Association, and the National Cancer Institute.

Nicotine replacement therapy should be considered for almost all patients who wish to stop smoking. In clinical trials, nicotine replacement products and bupropion each roughly doubled the rates of successful cessation when combined with advice and information from a physician or other health professional.

The use of nicotine replacement therapy during pregnancy is not officially approved. However, blood nicotine levels are generally lower among patch and gum users than among smokers, and the harmful compounds contained in tobacco smoke are avoid.

The transdermal nicotine patch delivers nicotine through the skin. It is relatively easy for patients to use, placing minimal demands on their need for compliance. Several studies suggest that the patch reduces craving for cigarettes, a principal cause of smoking relapse. Some brands of nicotine patches are now available without a prescription.

Patients should be provided with an information sheet on the patch and instructed in its proper use. The patient who does not stop smoking cannot use the patch. All patches, regardless of brand, should be applied once every 24 h, usually in the morning, to a nonhairy, clean, dry skin site on the upper torso or arm. Skin sites should be changed daily, and the same site not reused for at least 1 week. Most brands of patch recommend a higher initial dose of nicotine (21 to 22 mg for the 24-h patches, 15 mg for the 16-h patch) for the first few weeks of treatment. Patients can then be given a lower dose patch for subsequent weeks. Two brands have a third and lowest dose patch for the final weaning period. Manufacturers commonly recommend 6 to 8 weeks of treatment. Patients weighing less than 100 lb may begin treatment with a lower-dose patch.

The most common side effect of the nicotine patch is mild, transient itching or burning after application. Erythema, sometimes accompanied by edema, may also occur at the patch site. The nicotine patch is contraindicated for patients who have hypersensitivity or an allergy to nicotine, have serious arrhythmias or severe or worsening angina, or have had a recent myocardial infarction.

An alternative form of nicotine replacement is nicotine polacrilex gum. It should not be used like chewing gum. Instead, it should be chewed intermittently and then held in contact with the oral mucosa, where the nicotine is absorbed. Patients need careful instruction in the use of this unusual drug-delivery system or they will derive no benefit from it. The office staff can review its use with the patient. When the gum is used appropriately, withdrawal symptoms are reduced.

Two other forms of nicotine replacement have been approved by the Food and Drug Administration: the nicotine nasal spray and the nicotine inhaler. The nicotine nasal spray delivers 0.5 mg of nicotine with each spray. Patients use one spray in each nostril every 1 to 2 h, to a maximum of 40 doses per day. The manufacturer recommends eight weeks of initial treatment, followed by a gradual tapering for another 4 to 6 weeks. The most common adverse reaction to the spray is nasal irritation, which occurs in nearly all patients during the first 2 days.

The nicotine inhaler allows patients to titrate their own dose of nicotine. Patients use the inhaler frequently, taking about 80 inhalations over 20 min. Each cartridge of the inhaler delivers 4 mg of nicotine, and 6 to 16 cartridges are used per day for up to 12 weeks. Gradual tapering can follow, if needed. Common local side effects include mouth and throat irritation.

The antidepressant bupropion has also been approved as a pharmacologic aid to smoking cessation. Bupropion hydrochloride is provided in sustained-release tablets of 150 mg. One tablet daily is used for 3 days, then increased to 2 per day, and used for 7 to 12 weeks. Because the use of bupropion is associated with a dose-dependent risk of seizures, over 300 mg per day should not be prescribed for smoking cessation. Bupropion is contraindicated in patients with seizure disorders, a history of anorexia nervosa or bulimia, and in patients who took a monoamine oxidase (MAO) inhibitor in the previous 14 days.

Arrange Follow-up Visits

When patients know that their progress will be reviewed, their chances of successfully stopping improve. This monitoring may include a letter or telephone call from the office staff just before the quit data, which reinforces the decision to stop. Most relapses occur in the first weeks after cessation, and a person who comes to the office after being a nonsmoker for 1 to 2 weeks has a much-improved chance of remaining abstinent. For this reason, it is critical that patients be contacted during their first two weeks of abstinence to reinforce their decision to stop. Follow-up visits consist of an assessment of the patient's progress, a discussion of any problems encountered or anticipated, and a discussion of nicotine gum or patch use, if prescribed.

It is important to set up a second follow-up visit with the physician or staff member in 1 to 2 months. Studies show that the quit rate improves as the number of follow-up visits increases.

Office Organization

Some simple changes in office procedures significantly increase the physician's effectiveness in treating patients who smoke. The goal is to ensure that all patients who smoke are routinely identified, monitored, and appropriately treated. Office organizational procedures include selecting an office coordinator, making the office tobacco-free, systematically identifying and monitoring smokers, and involving staff members with the intervention and follow-up.

To act as a coordinated team, all members of the office staff must know their roles. The team approach is facilitated by naming a smoking cessation coordinator who will incorporate the intervention into the day-to-day activities of the practice with the help of the other staff members, maintain the staff members' commitment to the program, and ensure that the system is operating smoothly.

The team approach emphasizes staff identification of all patients who smoke. When patients are identified as smokers, their charts should be marked in a prominent manner. The typical identifier is a brightly colored permanent sticker or stamp, but this can be a removable sticker that is put on the chart at each visit. The regular use of these chart reminders has been shown to significantly increase cessation rates in office practices.

Staff members also should attach a progress card or flow sheet to the chart, thereby providing an easy way for the entire team to keep informed about the patient's current smoking status and allowing for brief cessation advice to become a routine part of every office visit for this patient. It is important that all staff members understand and implement this kind of charting system.

A staff member often schedules the follow-up visits, makes the contact just prior to the "quit date," and is the person who conducts some or all follow-up visits. Staff members also can review with patients their self-help materials and instructions for use of nicotine polacrilex gum or transdermal patches, if prescribed.

Steps for making an office tobacco-free include posting no-smoking signs, removing ashtrays, displaying tobacco cessation information prominently, and eliminating tobacco advertising from the office, either by subscribing to magazines that do not carry this advertising or by crossing out the tobacco advertisements with bright markers.

Special Issues in Tobacco Control

Weight Gain

The issue of weight gain is important to many patients who try to stop smoking. Some patients cite weight gain as the reason for relapse after previous attempts to stop. Most patients gain less than 10 lb after cessation. Some patients gain no weight after cessation, but a small percentage gain large amounts of weight.

Advice to a patient who is concerned about preventing weight gain can include two approaches. First, high-calorie foods should be avoided. Carrot and cinnamon sticks are time-honored, low-calorie foods that patients should have available whenever the urge to eat occurs. Recommend to patients that they pay attention to caloric intake to avoid weight gain. Second, recommend to weight-conscious smokers that they exercise more, even if this exercise is nothing more than walking. This tactic may help prevent weight gain and provide the patient with activity that is usually incompatible with smoking, thus supporting smoke-free behavior.

Lack of Social Support for Stopping

Social factors are frequently given as a reason for relapse, particularly when the patient is confronted by situations and friends who provide strong cues or prompts for smoking. During the time of a brief office visit, major changes in the social skills and support of a patient cannot be expected. However, all patients should be encouraged to tell their family, friends, and coworkers of their decision to stop smoking. Patients with little support for stopping can be referred to group cessation programs, if they are willing to attend. Referral to a counselor or other health professional also may be useful.

It is often difficult for a smoking patient to stop if the patient's spouse also smokes and is unwilling to stop. The unwilling spouse should be encouraged to join in the quit attempt. If this is not successful, the smoking spouse should at least be encouraged to smoke only outside the home.

Preventing Tobacco Use among Youth

Youth are another group who can benefit from the advice and assistance of physicians. Because most smokers become addicted during childhood and adolescence, advice from physicians during these periods is critical. Although any adolescent is a potential smoker, those at highest risk of becoming addicted have a smoking parent, low self-esteem, poor academic performance, and engage in other risky behaviors such as alcohol and drug use. It is challenging, but essential, to provide these young people with anticipatory guidance that is appropriate for their age and developmental stage. Some physicians have used cigarette advertisements to initiate discussions with adolescents, showing them the deceptive nature of the ads. When rapport with a young person is established, a physician can provide reasons for avoiding tobacco use that are relevant to an adolescent and can also help the patient practice refusal skills. Adolescents who are already regular smokers should be advised and assisted like an adult. However, adolescents are often much more concerned with the immediate effects of smoking, such as odors and poor athletic performance, and often are not influenced by risks of cancer and other diseases, which might not appear for many years.

Finally, children of any age should be protected from exposure to environmental tobacco smoke. Parents who smoke should be advised to stop and to keep their children in smoke-free environments, both at home and at daycare and other settings.

Summary

There is an enormous potential public health impact to be derived from clinical interventions with smoking patients. Even with very modest expectations of cessation rates, 100,000 clinicians using effective intervention can produce more than 3 million new ex-smokers each year. This, in conjunction with other tobacco control efforts in communities, will result in a marked reduction in the morbidity and mortality caused by smoking and control of one of the most important public health issues of our time.

References and Selected Readings

1. Fiore MC, Bailey WC, Cohen SJ, et al: *Smoking Cessation: Clinical Practice Guideline No. 18.* Rockville, MD: US Department of Health and Human Services, Agency for Health Care Policy and Research, April 1996. AHCPR Publication No. 96-0692.
2. Epps RP, Manley MW: A physician's guide to preventing tobacco use during childhood and adolescence. *Pediatrics* 88(1):140–144, 1991.
3. Fiore MC, Jorenby DE, Baker TB, Kenford SL: Tobacco dependence and the nicotine patch: Clinical guidelines for effective use. *JAMA* 268(19):2687–2694, 1992.
4. Glynn T, Manley M: *How to Help Your Patients Stop Smoking: A National Cancer Institute Manual for Physicians.* Bethesda, MD: National Cancer Institute, National Institutes of Health, 1989. NIH Publication No. 89-3064.
5. Manley M, Epps RP, Glynn T: The clinician's role in promoting smoking cessation among clinic patients. *Med Clin North Am* 76(2):477–494, 1992.
6. Hurt RD, Sachs DP, Glover ED, et al: A comparison of sustained-release bupropion and placebo for smoking cessation. *N Engl J Med* 337:1195–202, 1997.
7. Centers for Disease Control and Prevention. Cigarette smoking among adults—United States, 1994. *MMWR* 45:588–590, 1996.

CHAPTER 12

Alcohol and Drug Use in Women: A Major Contributor to Premature Morbidity and Mortality

Jeffrey Selzer

EPIDEMIOLOGY

DIAGNOSIS

ETIOLOGY

MEDICAL COMPLICATIONS

Cigarettes • Alcohol • Opiates • Cocaine

THE EFFECTIVENESS OF SUBSTANCE ABUSE TREATMENT

S ubstance use disorders include abuse and dependence on alcohol, cigarettes, pharmaceutically produced drugs, and illicit drugs. This type of illness may be the most preventable cause of premature death and disability in the United States today. It is also a type of illness that places an enormous burden on the health care system due to its protean medical consequences. The economic effects of substance use disorders are not only felt in higher health care costs, but also in lost productivity, crime and criminal justice costs, and increased use of social service benefits. In 1990, the total cost of tobacco, alcohol, and illicit drug use to the United States economy exceeded 238 billion dollars.[9] Finally, the personal suffering of patients and those close to them is profound and incalculable.

In general, American women are less likely than men to be afflicted by substance use disorders. Recently, however, sex differences have been less striking, particularly in the youngest members of the population. This narrowing of the "gender gap" certainly applies to experimental drug use by preadolescents and adolescents. At the other end of the age spectrum, a landmark study by the National Center on Addiction and Substance Abuse, appropriately titled *Under the Rug,* uncovered the extent of substance abuse (especially alcohol and prescription drugs) in women over age 59.[6] Unfortunately, due to stereotyped notions of addictions, and of women addicts in particular, not only do women deny substance use problems, but their physicians do as well. This lack of recognition of substance abuse as a "woman's problem" has also involved the research community, which has historically studied male populations and inadequately addressed women as a special population.

Women with substance use disorders are commonly seen in primary care settings, including obstetrical/gynecological practices. As often as all patients with substance use disorders go undetected, women are even less often diagnosed correctly.[5] Women with substance use disorders typically have responsible social roles and behave appropriately, in contrast to the "fallen woman" stereotype. Even after a correct diagnosis is made, primary care interventions or referrals are usually not made. This may be due to a misperception about the effectiveness of treatment for substance abuse and a lack of realization regarding the positive impact a primary care physician can have using brief, but repeated, interventions with medical authority.

Epidemiology

Surveys consistently find men more likely to use alcohol and illicit drugs than women, while women use pharmaceutical drugs with abuse potential more often than men.

As with men, nicotine and alcohol are the most commonly used drugs of abuse by women. Although rates of smoking have been declining for men since the 1960s, the rate of smoking by women has not decreased. A consequence of this is that lung cancer is now the most common cause of cancer death in women. For the general adult population, 25 percent of women smoke compared with 30 percent of males. However, there may be more female than male smokers in high school- and college-age populations. Clearly, a goal for all who come into contact with young women is prevention of cigarette smoking. Indeed, this may prevent other drug abuse, as nicotine is an important "gateway drug" to other drug use. An individual who reaches age 21 without smoking is almost free of later risk of smoking.

Alcohol use disorders are more common in men than women by a ratio ranging from 4:1 to 3:1. As with other drugs of abuse, the ratio may be narrowing for younger populations. Rates of problem drinking in college women have increased as have the volumes of alcohol consumed by college women. It has been estimated that 6 percent of the adult female population has a diagnosable alcohol use disorder at some point in their lives (in contrast to 14 percent of males). This percentage is significantly higher in outpatient primary care practices. A number of studies indicate that 1 to 2 women in 10 who are seen in outpatient practices are likely to be actively alcohol dependent.[3]

Alcohol-dependent women are also more likely to be overrepresented on inpatient hospital services compared to their numbers in the general population. Less than 25 percent of alcohol-dependent patients in a mixed gender sample of inpatients are correctly identified as having an alcohol-dependence diagnosis. Factors associated with physician underdiagnosis are female sex, higher education and income, and private insurance—all factors keeping with the stereotype many physicians have of alcohol-dependent patients.

An exception to the rule that men are drug abusers more often than women comes in the nonmedical use (unprescribed or not according to prescription) of pharmaceutically manufactured drugs. The overall nonmedical use of pharmaceuticals is 1.2 percent of women during one month, with higher rates in women aged 18 to 25 and, perhaps, the highest rates in women over 59. Women who misuse or abuse pharmaceutical drugs often do so in combination with alcohol. The greater prevalence of prescription drug abuse in women may reflect greater exposure to these compounds, as women are given more prescriptions for psychoactive medication than are men.

In the 1993 National Institute on Drug Abuse (NIDA) Household Survey, 5 percent of women aged 18 to 35 acknowledged using an illicit drug during the month prior to the survey. Although women are less likely to have ever used or currently use illicit drugs, here, too, the gender gap is closing in the younger population. For both men and women, cannabis is the most commonly used illicit drug. Although rates of illicit drug use are stabilizing or decreasing in the population aged 18 to 34, they are increasing among those aged 12 to 17. Cases of illicit abuse or dependence are more equally distributed among women and men than are alcohol abuse or dependence. The male to female ratio for illicit drug dependence is 1.6:1.

Women of lower socioeconomic status tend to use illicit drugs more frequently than women with greater material resources. As with alcohol, women who use illicit drugs are overrepresented in primary care settings. An important social consequence of female parity in illicit drug use is a greater rise in federal and state female prisoners as compared to men.[10]

Diagnosis

The transition from experimentation to unharmful drug use to drug abuse to drug dependence is difficult to define. Some drug taking is so highly toxic that almost no level of use is without adverse consequence. Certain drugs may have such high "addictive potential" or likelihood of experimentation leading to dependence, that any use is problematic (e.g., cocaine). Finally, it is not clear that the threshold for when an amount of drug use becomes detrimental is equal for men and women. Research has shown that women are more susceptible to a variety of health consequences of alcohol than men at comparable "doses" of alcohol. More research is necessary to determine whether there is differential toxicity from drugs other than alcohol.

The Diagnostic and Statistical Manual of Mental Disorders

The *Diagnostic and Statistical Manual of Mental Disorders, 4th edition* (DSM-IV)[1] defines psychoactive substance abuse and dependence by criteria that have become accepted as the international standard. These diagnostic criteria apply to all psychoactive drugs with abuse potential so that abuse and dependence are diagnosed similarly for every class of drug. Classes of drugs differ from each other, however, in the disorders which are "substance-induced." For example, only certain drugs of abuse have withdrawal symptoms associated with them, and the withdrawal symptoms are specific for a class of drug.

Two features of the diagnostic criteria deserve special attention. The absolute quantity of a substance used is unimportant in making a diagnosis. Physicians often focus on absolute quantity, forgetting that the *consequence* of whatever quantity is used is most important. Furthermore, patients often cannot reliably remember the quantities that they consumed, or they may be made defensive by detailed questions about quantity. The only mention of quantity in the diagnostic criteria is in assessing whether tolerance (criterion 1) or loss of control over amount consumed (criterion 3) has developed; even here, the items ask only about relative quantities. The other important aspect of these diagnostic criteria is that "substance dependence" is not defined solely by "physiological dependence" (either evidence of tolerance or withdrawal). Although the presence of tolerance and, particularly, of withdrawal may have important clinical consequences, neither is sufficient or necessary to make a diagnosis of substance dependence. Indeed, certain substances (e.g., cannabis) have not yet had clear withdrawal phenomena described, but produce clinically important dependence by DSM-IV diagnostic criteria.

Substance dependence is a pattern of repeated drug use and preoccupation with drug use despite significant drug-related adverse consequences. The person's life becomes organized by drug acquisition and drug taking. The diagnostic criteria for substance dependence are shown in Table 12-1.

Substance abuse is defined as a pattern of harmful consequences due to substance use. Unlike substance dependence, there is no tolerance or withdrawal, nor is there compulsive use. The person is not as preoccupied with the drug but finds herself in trouble when she uses it. Once a patient meets diagnostic criteria for drug dependence, she no longer meets criteria for drug abuse. The diagnostic criteria for drug abuse are shown in Table 12-2.

Etiology

Substance use disorders arise when an addictive drug is taken by a susceptible woman in a setting that facilitates initial and subsequent drug use. This conceptualization of the illness resulting from interaction between agent, host, and environment derives from the biopsychosocial model of illness. This model fits other chronic, multifac-

TABLE 12-1 Criteria for Substance Dependence

A maladaptive pattern of substance use, leading to clinically significant impairment or distress, as manifested by three (or more) of the following, occurring at any time in the same 12-month period:

(1) tolerance, as defined by either of the following:
 (a) a need for markedly increased amounts of the substance to achieve intoxication or desired effect
 (b) markedly diminished effect with continued use of the same amount of the substance
(2) withdrawal, as manifested by either of the following:
 (a) the characteristic withdrawal syndrome for the substance
 (b) the same (or a closely related) substance is taken to relieve or avoid withdrawal symptoms
(3) the substance is often taken in larger amounts or over a longer period than was intended
(4) there is a persistent desire or unsuccessful efforts to cut down or control substance use
(5) a great deal of time is spent in activities necessary to obtain the substance (e.g., visiting multiple doctors or driving long distances), use the substance (e.g., chain-smoking), or recover from its effects
(6) important social, occupational, or recreational activities are given up or reduced because of substance use
(7) the substance use is continued despite knowledge of having a persistent or recurrent physical or psychological problem that is likely to have been caused or exacerbated by the substance (e.g., current cocaine use despite recognition of cocaine-induced depression, or continued drinking despite recognition that an ulcer was made worse by alcohol consumption)

Specify if:
 With Physiological Dependence: evidence of tolerance or withdrawal (i.e., either Item 1 or 2 is present)
 Without Physiological Dependence: no evidence of tolerance or withdrawal (i.e., neither Item 1 nor 2 is present)

SOURCE: American Psychiatric Association: *Diagnostic and Statistical Manual of Mental Disorders, 4th ed.* (DSM-IV). Washington, DC: APA Press, 1994, p 181.

TABLE 12-2 Criteria for Substance Abuse

(A) A maladaptive pattern of substance use leading to clinically significant impairment or distress, as manifested by one (or more) of the following, occurring within a 12-month period:
 (1) recurrent substance use resulting in a failure to fulfill major role obligations at work, school, or home (e.g., repeated absences or poor work performance related to neglect of children or household)
 (2) recurrent substance use in situations in which it is physically hazardous (e.g., driving an automobile or operating a machine when impaired by substance use)
 (3) recurrent substance-related legal problems (e.g., arrests for substance-related disorderly conduct)
 (4) continued substance use despite having persistent or recurrent social or interpersonal problems caused or exacerbated by the effects of the substance (e.g., arguments with spouse about consequences of intoxication, physical fights)
(B) The symptoms have never met the criteria for Substance Dependence for this class of substance.

SOURCE: American Psychiatric Association: *Diagnostic and Statistical Manual of Mental Disorders, 4th ed.* (DSM-IV). Washington, DC: APA Press, 1994, pp 182–183.

The "agent" in drug abuse is, of course, the drug of abuse. Although structurally dissimilar, drugs of abuse typically all have rapid onsets of action in the central nervous system and produce, at least initially, pleasurable changes in mental status. They also often have rapid offsets of action, leading to acute withdrawal symptoms. The route of administratation can be varied to produce more rapid changes in mental state (e.g., smoking cocaine leads to faster intoxication than does using it intranasally), as can the concentration of the active drug in its vehicle (e.g., drinking rum per unit volume is more effective than drinking beer). All drugs of abuse seem to affect neurotransmission in reward pathways in the midbrain, which involve the ventral tegmental area and the nucleus accumbens.

The host is the woman exposed to the drug of abuse. The most compelling host factor for alcoholism in men has been genetic legacy. The data for women also suggest that genes are im-

torial illnesses such as asthma and hypertension. In this model, neither agent, host, nor environment operates powerfully enough to determine the illness alone. Individuals afflicted with the illness vary in the degree to which these forces act and interact to produce the illness.

portant, but not as important as for men. As with men, family-history-positive women show less sensitivity to the motor-impairment effects of alcohol at low-to-moderate doses. This may cause vulnerable women to receive fewer cues to curb use when blood alcohol levels are in a low-to-moderate range. Women with substance use disorders typically suffer from anxiety and depression more often than their male counterparts. Women with substance use disorders are more likely to report having been victims of sexual assault in childhood than women who are not addicted. Finally, studies in adolescents show that attitude about harmfulness of a drug is an important determinant of whether experimentation will occur; girls are less likely to use a drug if they believe its use is harmful.

The environment is the setting where agent and host come together. Environmental factors apply not only to ease of access to the drug but also to factors in the environment that affect the woman's emotional life and influence the likelihood that she will use a drug. Although simple measures such as raising price, strictly enforcing laws about age of access to legal drugs, and discouraging illicit drug sales may reduce drug use, there are serious questions from drug abuse researchers as to the extent to which resources to reduce drug supply are overspent. Manufacturers of legal drugs have targeted advertising to women to suggest that the user will be more independent and attractive. In the case of cigarettes, the frequent reference to "slimness" and "thinness," combined with the use of slender models in advertising, appeal to the belief among girls and young women that cigarettes are helpful in weight-control efforts. For illicit drug use, poverty and living with an active drug-using partner have been consistent environmental factors associated with addiction in women.

Medical Complications

Cigarettes

Cigarette smoking is related to approximately 400,000 deaths annually. Although women are aware of the link between lung cancer and cigarette smoking, they may not be aware that lung cancer is now the most common cause of cancer death in women. In addition to cancer, cigarette smoking is the most common factor in chronic obstructive pulmonary disease. Coronary artery disease is the leading cause of death in older women, although the link between fatal cardiac disease and smoking has been less publicized than the link with lung disease. Smoking also has endocrine effects with smokers reaching menopause earlier, and an increased risk for osteoporosis.

Cigarette smoking results in obstetrical complications ranging from reduced fertility to increased rates of spontaneous abortion to premature babies with low birthweights and reduced head circumferences. Finally, children who grow up exposed to cigarette smoke passively have higher rates of respiratory and middle ear illness than children not exposed to passive smoke.

Alcohol

Alcohol may account for 100,000 deaths annually in the United States. There is increasing evidence that the health risks of excessive alcohol use are greater for women than for men, and that excessive use for women is about half the quantity considered excessive for men.[8] This phenomenon of women experiencing more accelerated and profound medical consequences of alcohol has been called "telescoping." Women develop cirrhosis, peptic ulcer that requires surgery, myopathy, and cardiomyopathy at lower levels of alcohol intake than men. This phenomenon may be due to higher blood-alcohol levels in women following ingestion of a given quantity of alcohol. Women have relatively reduced activity of gastric alcohol dehydrogenase to begin alcohol metabolism, and have less body water in which to distribute unmetabolized alcohol. Due to greater susceptibility to negative effects of alcohol, the National Institute on Alcohol Abuse and Alcoholism sets a limit of one drink per day for women as "moderate drinking" where two drinks per day is the limit for men.

Reports linking alcohol consumption with breast cancer have been inconsistent. As with men, moderate intake reduces the risk of coronary artery disease. Alcohol-dependent persons are also more likely to smoke and to smoke heavily. The two drugs synergize in complications such as oral and esophageal cancers.

Fetal alcohol syndrome (FAS) is considered among the most common causes of birth defects associated with mental retardation. Although there is no known, safe level of alcohol use during pregnancy, teratogenic effects are dose related. Neonates with FAS exhibit growth retardation, abnormalities of the face, and central nervous system effects such as mental retardation. A set of other detrimental effects of alcohol ingestion during pregnancy termed "fetal alcohol effects," includes other congenital abnormalities and learning disabilities.

Opiates

Most of the negative consequences of opiate use relate to the use of these drugs by injection. Although lethal overdose is possible, most morbidity and mortality is related to infectious agents and contaminants associated with injection drug use. In some areas, most new cases of HIV positivity are in women who inject heroin or are sexual partners of men who inject heroin. Although pregnancy outcomes for women who inject heroin are worse for multiple reasons (e.g., lack of prenatal care), there has been no specific teratogenic effect for heroin or other opiates described. There is, however, a well-described neonatal withdrawal syndrome associated with opiate use during pregnancy. Although heroin use interferes with the menstrual cycle, the belief among some users that it protects against pregnancy is incorrect.

Cocaine

Cocaine use is associated with morbidity in the central nervous system (e.g., psychiatric disor-

ders, cerebrovascular disease, and seizures), the cardiovascular system (cardiac ischemia, arrhythmias, acute hypertensive emergencies), and other organ systems (e.g., intestinal ischemia). Cocaine use has been associated with an increased incidence of sexually transmitted diseases. Female adolescents who use cocaine are not only more likely to be sexually active, but are also more likely to have multiple partners and less likely to use condoms.[10] Obstetrical complications such as an increased risk of spontaneous abortions and abruptio placentae have been associated with cocaine use. As with opiates, negative outcomes for babies may also be associated with a constellation of unfortunate factors common in cocaine-using women, rather than due to specific teratogenic effects of cocaine.

The Effectiveness of Substance Abuse Treatment

There is a growing body of evidence that attests to the effectiveness of substance abuse treatment.[7] The most stringent criterion for success is complete abstinence. This criterion is often unrealistic, given the chronic and relapsing nature of substance use disorders. What has been shown is that treatment consistently leads to a *reduction* in drug use if not complete abstinence, better general health, improved social function, and reduced threats to public health and safety caused by drug abuse (e.g., criminal behavior). Factors associated with better outcomes are absence of psychiatric symptoms, better social supports, and longer time in treatment. Furthermore, compliance with treatment suggestions and relapse rates are similar for other chronic illnesses that require behavioral change, such as diabetes, hypertension, and asthma.

There is little evidence to suggest that women have a different prognosis after entering treatment than do men. Specialized programs for women have developed because of reports of discomfort in mixed-gender programs from some women. Limited research has shown that women-only programs lead to greater decreases in alcohol use and increases in social functioning compared with mixed-gender programs.[10] There are less data on the treatment of illicit drug use in women than there are data for the treatment of alcohol dependence. Women in treatment for illicit drug dependence are more often coerced into treatment by legal sanctions than are alcohol-dependent women. For both types of women, drug-using significant others make a successful outcome harder to achieve, and a focus of treatment is to establish drug-free social networks.

Summary

Substance use and abuse are major contributors to morbidity and mortality in women. The primary care physician has the opportunity to reduce premature morbidity and mortality by educating patients about risks and primary prevention, being vigilant about detection of affected patients, helping patients to become involved in treatment, and offering support and assistance for these women.

References and Selected Readings

1. American Psychiatric Association: *Diagnostic and Statistical Manual of Mental Disorders,* 4th ed. *DSM-IV:* Washington, DC: APA Press, 1994.
2. Blume S: Understanding addictive disorders in women, in Graham AW, et al (eds): *Principles of Addiction Medicine,* 2nd ed. Chevy Chase, MD: American Society of Addiction Medicine, 1998.
3. Cyr MG, Moulton AW: Substance abuse in women. *Obstet Gynecol Clin North Am* 17(4): 905–925, 1990.
4. Fielding JE: Smoking: Health effects and control. *N Engl J Med*, 313(8): 491–498, 1985.
5. Moore RD, et al: Prevalence, detection and treatment of alcoholism in hospitalized patients. *JAMA,* 261(3): 403–407, 1989.
6. National Center on Addiction and Substance Abuse at Columbia University: *Under the Rug: Substance Abuse and the Mature Woman.* New York, NY: CASA, 1998.
7. O'Brien CP, McLellan AT: Myths about the treatment of addiction. *Lancet* 347 : 237–240, 1996.
8. O'Connor PG, Schottenfeld RS: Patients with alcohol problems. *New Eng J Med* 338(9): 592–602, 1998.
9. Rice DP: Cited in *Substance Abuse: The Nation's One Health Problem,* Princeton, NJ: Robert Wood Johnson Foundation, 1993.
10. Stein MD, Cyr MG: Women and substance abuse. *Med Clin North Am* 81(4): 979–998, 1997.

CHAPTER 13

Driving while Intoxicated—A Major Cause of Fatalities

Vicki L. Seltzer

The eighth leading cause of death in the United States is motor vehicle accidents.[1] Motor vehicle accidents are the number one cause of death for females between the ages of 13 and 39[2], and are a common cause of death for all age groups.

In 1993, 44 percent of total traffic fatalities in the U.S. were alcohol-related.[3] There were 1.6 million people arrested in the United States in 1992 for driving while under the influence of alcohol or drugs. Of course, it is not only the intoxicated drivers who are at risk for morbidity and mortality, but also their passengers, pedestrians, bicyclists, and drivers of other vehicles.

In addition to fatalities, more than three million Americans each year sustain nonfatal injuries from motor vehicle accidents.[4] It is not uncommon for these injuries to result in permanent impairment.

Alcohol is not the only substance that increases the risk of motor vehicle crashes and fatalities. Marijuana, cocaine, and tranquilizers have been identified in the blood of 10 to 32 percent of drivers who are in automobile accidents.[3]

Alcohol-related traffic accidents (and accidents related to the use of other substances) clearly represent a major risk to our patients. However, aggressive education and intervention programs can have a beneficial effect in reducing risky behaviors and resultant accidents. Although this is still a serious problem in the United States, it is important to note that alcohol-related traffic fatality rates between 1979 and 1990 declined by more than 10 percent.[5] This suggests that national advocacy and education programs

such as Mothers Against Drunk Driving (MADD) and Students Against Drunk Driving (SADD) can change behavior. Because health care providers can have a significant impact on patient behavior, we must play a role in community and patient education regarding this important issue.

Health care providers should counsel patients about the risks associated with driving while under the influence of alcohol and/or drugs. Patients must be made aware that it is not just the driver who is at risk, but also passengers. Patients must also be made aware that although the legal definition of alcohol intoxication in the U.S. varies by state and has typically been defined as a blood alcohol content of 0.08 or 0.10 g/dl[4], much lower blood alcohol levels are also associated with an increased risk of motor vehicle accidents and fatalities.

As health care providers focus on reducing morbidity and mortality from motor vehicle accidents, it is important to identify individuals who are problem drinkers or who use drugs. The CAGE questionnaire is a simple, four-question tool, which is commonly used in primary care practices to identify alcohol abusers.[6] The patient is asked to respond to four questions:

C: Have you ever felt you ought to *C*ut down on your drinking?

A: Have people *A*nnoyed you by criticizing your drinking?

G: Have you ever felt bad or *G*uilty about your drinking?

E: Have you ever had a drink first thing in the

morning to steady your nerves or to get rid of a hangover (*E*ye opener)?

A problem with this simple screen is that it does not always identify individuals who drive while intoxicated. Therefore, in addition to whatever simple screening tools the health care provider uses to identify individuals with alcohol dependency and drug-related problems, it is helpful to also ask these directed questions:

- Do you ever drive after you had a drink or used drugs?
- Do you ever drive after taking tranquilizers or other medications that may impair your abilities (be specific)?
- Are you ever the passenger of a driver who was drinking or using drugs or medications?

Obviously, depending upon the response of the patient, further counseling or intervention may be necessary.

An important related issue is seatbelt use. Failure to use proper vehicle occupant protection (seatbelts, appropriately used infant and child safety seats, and helmets for bicyclists and motorcyclists) is the other leading preventable cause of traffic injury and fatality. Again, counseling by the physician can play an important role.

Pregnant women must also be counseled regarding the importance of proper seatbelt use. One of the leading causes of death for pregnant women is motor vehicle accidents. This can be reduced by seatbelt use. There is no evidence that seatbelt use increases the likelihood of fetal injury; in fact, the leading cause of fetal death in motor vehicle accidents is death of the mother.[7] Pregnant women should be told how important it is to wear their seatbelts, and taught how to use seatbelts properly, according to the guidelines of The American College of Obstetricians and Gynecologists.[8] The lap-belt portion of the seatbelt should be placed under the pregnant woman's abdomen, across her upper thighs. The shoulder belt should be positioned between the breasts.

Motor vehicle accidents represent a major cause of morbidity and mortality for women in the United States. Physician counseling and intervention can reduce the scope of this problem. Physicians can play a role by identifying patients at increased risk for DWI accidents, by counseling all patients about the magnitude of this problem and how it may affect them, and by having patients who require treatment treated. Discussing proper seatbelt use is also important.

References and Selected Readings

1. National Center for Health Statistics: *Annual Summary of Births, Marriages, Divorces, and Deaths: United States, 1993.* Hyattsville, MD: Public Health Service, 1994. Monthly vital statistics report; vol. 42 no. 13 (Suppl).
2. The American College of Obstetricians and Gynecologists: *Primary Care Review for the Obstetrician-Gynecologist,* Washington, DC: ACOG, 1997.
3. Report of the US Preventive Services Task Force: *Guide to Clinical Preventive Services,* Baltimore, MD: Williams & Wilkins, 1996.
4. National Highway Traffic Safety Administration: *Traffic Safety Facts 1994.* Washington, DC: Department of Transportation, 1995. Publication DOT HS 808 292.
5. Zobeck TS, Grant BF, Stinson FS, Bertolucci D: Alcohol involvement in fatal traffic crashes in the United States 1979-90. *Addiction* 89:227–31, 1994.
6. Ewing JA: Detecting alcoholism: The CAGE questionnaire. *JAMA* 252:1905–7, 1984.
7. Cunningham FG, MacDonald PC, Gant NF, Leveno KJ, Gilstrap LC: *Williams Obstetrics,* 19th ed. Norwalk, CT: Appleton & Lange, 1993, p 262.
8. The American College of Obstetricians and Gynecologists: *Automobile Passenger Restraints for Children and Pregnant Women.* Washington, DC: ACOG, 1991. Technical bulletin no. 151.

CHAPTER 14

Safety and Accident Prevention

Geraldine Lanman

Accidents are significant causes of mortality—and certainly of morbidity—in the United States. In fact, after cardiovascular diseases and malignancies, they are the leading cause of death in the United States, regardless of age. Accidents cause more deaths than infectious diseases, pulmonary diseases, diabetes, and liver or kidney problems. In women, the importance of accidents as a cause of death varies by age; from ages 13 through 39 accidents are the leading cause of death. Although accidents are by no means uncommon in middle-aged women, the frequency of accidents as a cause of death diminishes with age until 55, when it starts to climb again, doubling every 5 years until age 85, when it triples in number. Motor vehicle accidents constitute the majority of the accidents; the remainder are assaults, burns, toxic ingestion, and electrical, household, and sports injuries.

In caring for our patients, we physicians can be far more than just "medical people." We can help our patients by anticipating problems and risks, and then educating and advising them about our concerns without causing needless alarm. While there are many ways of identifying risks and still more of advising people of them, the direct face-to-face method is the most effective. Brochures and other educational aids are best used to augment and enhance, rather than substitute for, counseling.

Leaving the advice for the "wrap-up" session at the end of a visit sometimes leaves the patient overwhelmed and confused. In addition, the patient may believe that what you are telling her is something you identified during the course of the physical examination and that you are withholding information from her. The best time to identify issues and initiate advice about safety is during the initial conversation, while the history is being obtained. This can then be reinforced at the wrap-up consultation after the physical examination. At subsequent visits, because the patient's condition may change, recurrent issues of safety and accident prevention can be reinforced and new ones introduced.

Use the following suggestions to integrate safety issues into the patient's history. When obtaining the surgical history, make certain to inquire about injuries. Previous injuries will provide an idea of the person's risk, particularly as pertains to driving. This is an important time to emphasize seat belt use. Also ask about other types of accidents. In older women, make certain to ask about falls. Discuss potential household injuries that represent a significant hazard, particularly in women. Advise about caustic agents, bathtub falls (particularly in the elderly), loose rugs, furniture or clutter obstructing frequently traveled paths (e.g., between the bed and the bathroom, particularly at night), stairs, kitchen utensils, stoves, and sports and recreation equipment. Are there joint instability or limb weakness problems that might predispose to falls? In the winter, warn about injuries on the ice. During the other seasons, yard and garden equipment may cause injuries.

Discuss the details of the woman's occupation to understand its risks, and to advise about any special precautions to be borne in mind. For example, hepatitis and HIV should be emphasized with health care workers, tetanus shots with construction workers, and TB exposure with school teachers. Carefully explore substance abuse issues in relation to occupation and the jeopardy coworkers and others are placed in by those who abuse a substance while working.

Ask about eyeglass frames. Are they shatterproof? Do dentures fit? Oversize dentures are a major choking hazard in the elderly.

With allergies, ask specifically about bee stings. Caution the person with this allergy to keep an Epi-Pen in her purse, desk, and house. With medications, be sure to ask about over-the-counter drugs, so that any possible adverse drug interactions can be discussed.

Look into the possibility that the patient who is a smoker may smoke in bed, and caution about the risk of fire. Alcohol and drug use should be discussed, with particular emphasis on driving or involvement in other dangerous activities while not completely mentally alert. A substantial proportion of motor vehicle accidents are the result of persons driving under the influence of alcohol or drugs.

Safety is an important issue. It is more likely that many of our patients will suffer injury or death from preventable accidents than from many of the other medical issues we physicians diligently address. As physicians entrusted by patients with their care, it is our obligation to evaluate potential safety risks for each patient and to offer safety advice.

Part III

Varying Health Care Needs during the Phases of a Woman's Life

The general health care needs of a woman vary during the phases of her life. This section of the book identifies the breadth of important physical and psychosocial issues that physicians can help women with during their transition through the life phases.

Chapters in this section focus on the special needs of the adolescent, the reproductive-age woman, the menopausal woman, and the woman who is beyond the menopausal years. The first five chapters address women's health care needs over the years as seen from the physician's perspective. The next four chapters are written by women who span the age ranges, and discuss what women want and need from their physicians during different phases of their lives.

This section of the book is brief because each of the medical issues identified is reviewed in greater depth elsewhere in the text. It serves to emphasize the broad scope of health care needs that we can and should address with our patients, and how these vary at different times.

The physician has the greatest overall impact upon women's health by focusing attention on women's general well-being and appropriate preventive interventions in the various stages of life.

CHAPTER 15

Special Needs of the Adolescent

Paula J. Adams Hillard

Adolescent Development

The concept of adolescence as a life stage is a relatively modern concept, resulting from the evolution of what is now an extended interval between physical maturity and the acceptable age for marriage and childbearing. Adolescence encompasses the years from the onset of physical development through early young adulthood; a very broad definition is the transition from the preteen years (9 to 10 years) through the early 20s. All adults acknowledge that childhood, until about age 10 to 12, is "different" from adulthood. However, that adolescent development takes place in a number of spheres (physical, cognitive, psychosocial, and sexual) is less well recognized by the average adult.

Adolescent development can be divided into three intervals, which roughly correspond to chronological age: early adolescence (ages 10 to 13), middle adolescence (ages 14 to 17) and late adolescence (ages 18 to 22). One problem that clinicians and parents encounter with adolescents is that development in each of these spheres is occuring simultaneously, but at different rates. Development may be dyssynchronous; for example, a physically mature 13-year-old may still be a concrete thinker. While it is recognized that adolescents typically display behavior that is "difficult," the complex reasons for this difficulty are much less understood by the average parent or even the clinician. Many of the difficulties of adolescence can be better understood as relating to the developmental tasks that the adolescent must accomplish in each of these spheres, and within a social, cultural, and economic climate that frequently is not conducive to healthy development.

Physical Development

The physical transition to adolescence, known as puberty, generally proceeds in an orderly fashion, beginning in girls between the ages of 8 and 11. The sequence of breast and pubic hair growth, and the processes of adrenarche, thelarche, and menarche, are well described elsewhere in this text. A description of the staging of breast and pubic hair development was first published by Marshall and Tanner in 1969—the Tanner staging. What is less well recognized is that pubertal development is beginning earlier; one observational study of more than 18,000 girls noted that at age 7, 7 percent of Caucasian girls, and 27 percent of African-American girls had evidence of breast budding or pubic hair growth, and by age 8 (an age that had previously been cited as the lower limit of normal for the onset of puberty), the percentages were 15 percent and 48 percent, respectively. The typical sequence of pubertal growth involves accelerated linear growth (height), breast budding, the appearance of pubic hair, peak growth velocity, and menarche, although African-American girls are somewhat more likely than Caucasian girls to experience pubarche before thelarche. Menarche, the most obvious and quantifiable marker for puberty, occurs at an average age of 12.9 for Caucasian girls and 12.2 for African-American girls in the U.S. Menarche typically occurs when a girl has reached Tanner breast stage 3 to 4, occuring approximately 2 years after the onset of breast budding. Aberrations from the normal sequence or timing of pubertal development should be evaluated to rule out pathologic conditions of precocious or delayed puberty. These aberrations include: pubertal growth prior to age 7, absence of breast budding by age 12, no menarche by age 15 or 16, or onset of vaginal bleeding prior to breast or pubic hair development.

Cognitive Development

The ability to think abstractly is a major marker of adult cognitive function. Piaget postulated that individuals progress during adolescence from concrete to formal operational thinking, with the onset of the ability to think abstractly beginning at about age 12. The ability to generate abstractions, generate hypotheses, consider contrary-to-fact situations, generate all possibilities from a specific situation, approach a problem systematically, and use combinatory logic develops gradually during adolescence, and is not typically achieved until an adolescent is age 15 or 16. Some adults do not consistently use abstract thinking. The incomplete cognitive development of adolescents leads to a number of characteristic aspects of adolescent thinking: the inability to prioritize solutions to problems; the concept of having an imaginary audience (assuming that

what is important to them is important to everyone else, or that everyone is aware of their own personal and intimate thoughts/feelings); apparent hypocrisy (the ability to conceptualize rules but the inability to apply them consistently to themselves); and the "personal fable" (the feeling of "specialness" or invulnerability). These aspects of adolescent development are developmentally normal, but can lead to frustration for clinicians and parents.

The early and middle adolescent who becomes prematurely sexually active is often an ineffective contraceptor, in part because of these aspects of cognitive development: the inability to conceptualize the consequences of her actions (9 months in the future); the inability to successfully choose and use a method of contraception consistently; and the feeling that "it (pregnancy) can't happen to me."

Psychosocial Maturation

The adolescent's development of self within a social context includes the tasks of effectively separating from parents and family by gaining independence, the achievement of a realistic vocational goal, the achievement of a mature level of sexuality, and the consolidation of a realistic and positive self-image. Early adolescents will typically begin to demonstrate their desire to separate from the family in ways that include temper outbursts and tantrums. In addition, they will also demonstrate a desire to be alone, with much preoccupation with the developing physical changes of puberty. By middle adolescence, individuals are identifying with a mixed-gender peer group. The influence of this peer group can be either a positive or negative one. This time has been described as an opportunity for an individual to try out different identities with their peers until they find one with which they are comfortable. In middle adolescence, limits are tested by challenging parental and societal beliefs and opinions. By late adolescence, the peer group becomes less important and individual choices more comfortable.

Sexuality

Children and adolescents are sexual beings. Normal infants and prepubertal children explore the pleasurable sensations of self genital contact. Sexuality does not begin suddenly at adolescence. However, with the growing physical maturity of adolescents, and the cultural influences of our society, adolescence as a time of heightened sexual awareness and libido is a normal occurrence—not only for boys, but also for girls. The early adolescent typically engages in sexual fantasies, but socially has few opportunities for real interactions with members of the opposite gender. By middle adolescence, group dating and social activities are most common; a girl typically compares a boyfriend to her idealized version of a partner, and a boy often compares the physical attributes of his girlfriend to the ideal. By late adolescence, a more mature relationship with mutual concern for the partner's feelings and welfare is usually possible, with the development of true intimacy in an adult manner.

An understanding of these aspects of normal adolescent development is essential for the clinician who sees adolescents and evaluates, manages, and treats their gynecologic and general medical problems. Failing to understand that an adolescent may look physically mature, but has not yet accomplished the developmental tasks necessary for adulthood and maturity can lead the clinician to inappropriate decisions and recommendations, with resultant negative consequences for the individual's health and growth.

Communication

Adolescents appreciate clinicians who take a genuine interest in their health and well-being, which is manifest with a friendly, open, and respectful manner. A nonjudgmental attitude is also important, as are clear, concise statements of fact. Each clinician develops her or his own style of communication; however, the language should be understandable and not patronizing. It is important to avoid giving a sermon or lecture, and to listen for verbal cues while observing nonverbal communication. An interactive session, in which communication flows in two directions, is more likely to generate useful information for both the clinician and the adolescent.

Confidentiality The concept of confidentiality is an absolutely essential tenet of adolescent health care. Numerous studies demonstrate that without assurances of confidentiality, some adolescents are not honest or forthcoming about issues dealing with sexuality, depression, substance use, or sexually transmitted diseases (STDs) in particular. The caveat that must be conveyed is that confidentiality must occasionally be breached if suicide, homicide, or abuse are at issue.

The concept of confidentiality should be discussed with parents and reinforced with the adolescent individually. This can be done in a manner that helps parents recognize and respect the adolescent's growing independence, but that also encourages parents and teens to communicate with one another. Clinicians can facilitate communication without breaching confidentiality; they can suggest that certain issues should be shared, and offer suggestions for ways in which that can be accomplished. Clinicians can offer to bear the news (for example, of the diagnosis of an STD) to a parent, provided that they are given the appropriate permission by the patient. Clinicians who develop this skill will recognize that adolescents live their lives within the context of the family, and that parents can be allies in encouraging healthy behaviors. However, the clinician will also readily recognize that the judgments involved in making these decisions are frequently difficult ones.

If there are issues that the adolescent insists be kept confidential, the clinician should behave in a way that minimizes the health risks to the adolescent. This is most commonly the case for an adolescent who is sexually active and requests contraception. The clinician often makes the judgment that the risks of an unintended pregnancy warrant the provision of contraception, and that the risks of STDs merit information about safer sex using condoms. There is no evidence that the provision of information about sexual activity increases the risk that an adolescent will become sexually active. On the contrary, providing information through sexuality education programs and encouraging the postponement of sexual activity have been shown to be beneficial. To my knowledge, no clinician who provided nonnegligent medical care/contraception to an adolescent without parental consent has been successfully sued. However, certain medical situations, including abortion, are covered by specific state laws that require either parental notification or consent; clinicians must be aware of the laws that apply in their state, including mandatory reporting of child sexual abuse or intercourse with an adolescent younger than a defined age of consent.

In general, adolescents who have reached the age of majority—usually 18 or 21—may consent to treatment; medical care of younger individuals usually requires parental consent. There are exceptions, however, to this general rule. True medical emergencies constitute one exception. The concept of emancipation is also recognized. "Emancipated minors" are those individuals, such as those in the military, who are living independently, are self-supporting, and are not dependent on parents. In addition, there are situations that affect public and individual health in which the states encourage the minor to consent to treatment, such as pregnancy, substance use and abuse, and STDs. In all states, adolescents can consent to evaluation and treatment of STDs confidentially; they can also consent to treatment for alcohol and other substance use in nearly all states.

Some states have specific minor treatment statutes, which express the age at which an adolescent can give consent as if she were an adult. Other states have statutes of precedent for the concept of "mature minors" in which treatment is allowed if the young person (usually 14 to 15 years or older) understands the

proposed treatment, understands the risks, the physician believes the adolescent can give the same degree of consent as an adult, and the treatment does not pose serious risk. The clinician should consider the patient's age, maturity, nature of illness, and risks of therapy, and make judgments accordingly. This determination is not always easy; the clinician can ask him/herself if the adolescent makes most decisions about her daily affairs; balances school work, employment, and social activities; comes and goes independently; makes her own appointments with the doctor; states her needs and follows through with recommendations; understands the benefits and risks of proposed treatments; and communicates clearly to the physician and others about these alternatives. In general, the clinician who provides medical treatment based on the good faith judgment of emancipation or maturity will not be held liable. These agreements and consents for treatment should be documented and held confidential. With the above-noted exceptions for abuse, homicide, and suicide, parents should not be informed without the minor's permission. Physicians must, of course, be knowledgeable regarding the laws with which they must comply in their own states.

Pediatricians recognize that children exist within the context of their families. At times, the adolescent patient who is seeing the gynecologist may insist on confidentiality, thereby excluding parents who may well be allies in encouraging healthy lifestyles and behaviors. Adolescents whose parents are aware of their oral contraceptive use have been reported to be more reliable pill-takers, which suggests that parents can assist with and encourage compliance with contraception. Thus, encouraging the adolescent to involve parents or other significant adults in their decision making should be a priority for the clinician. The adolescent will often approve the sharing of general health information with the parent, such as the statement that "Your daughter doesn't have any major gynecologic health problems."

The Gynecologic Visit

The Committee on Adolescent Health of the American College of Obstetricians and Gynecologists (ACOG) has proposed that "an adolescent's initial visit to an obstetrician/gynecologist for health guidance, screening, and provision of preventive services should take place around age 13 to 15." This new guideline for care allows the opportunity for an ob/gyn to provide preventive guidance. Additional guidelines for preventive guidance come from a multidisciplinary group under the auspices of the AMA, which published *Guidelines for Adolescent Preventive Services* (GAPS) that outlines specific recommendations for routine annual health visits, screening, preventive guidance, and health care.

There is much evidence that the health risks of adolescents are related to risk-taking behaviors such as smoking, alcohol and other substance abuse, premature sexual activity, and morbidity/mortality due to accidental and intentional injuries or depression and suicide. Most adolescents engage in some risk-taking activities, and many engage in several such activities. The age at which adolescents initiate these activities is frequently during early adolescence. Adolescents who are sexually active are more likely to engage in other risk-taking behaviors.

By age 15, about 20 percent of adolescents in the United States have already initiated sexual intercourse. Fifty percent of 17-year-olds have had intercourse. The first ob/gyn visit at age 13 to 15 allows the detection of teens who have had intercourse, and to determine whether it was involuntary. It also provides the opportunity to discourage risk-taking by the majority of teens who are not yet sexually active.

The initial ob/gyn visit allows the opportunity to assess the extent to which an adolescent is engaging in these risk-taking behaviors, to screen for the onset of sexual intercourse, to offer health guidance and preventive health messages (encouraging the postponement of sexual involvement), and to offer contraceptive services to those teens who need them. Informa-tion about emergency contraception should be provided.

Most of the time this first visit does *not* include a pelvic examination. Most teens at the age of 13 to 15 have a normal gynecologic history with regular menses, only mild dysmenorrhea, and have not initiated sexual intercourse. These teens do not need an exam, but can be given information about the examination for future reference and seen yearly for the provision of further health guidance and screening. Those teens whose gynecologic history is abnormal should be encouraged to undergo a pelvic examination, preferably at the time of the initial visit, or within the near future. This includes those with evidence of androgen excess or hirsutism, with severe or disabling dysmenorrhea, with vulvovaginal symptoms, or who have had intercourse and thus merit STD testing.

Visit Structure

After many years of working with adolescents and their parents, I have developed a workable model of a structured first visit to an ob/gyn. This structure encourages and facilitates communication between the adolescent and her mother, yet upholds the importance of confidentiality. It serves as a model to encourage the teen to learn about appropriate interactions with the health care system as she grows, develops, and matures into an adult who is responsible for her health. This model includes helping teens learn to make and keep their own appointments, to communicate effectively about their health concerns and needs, and, eventually, to take financial responsibility for their health care. This model also allows for the provision of health guidance to the mother/caretaker about parenting an adolescent. Using this model, the clinician can facilitate appropriate parent/teen interaction and communication. Figure 15-1 illustrates the structure of the first ob/gyn visit.

The clinician meets first with both the parent (usually the mother) and the adolescent. At this time, the structure and purpose of the visit should

PATIENT AND PARENT/GUARDIAN
Outline Structure of Visit/Confidentiality
Past Medical History
Family History

PATIENT
Health History/Risk-Taking Behaviors
Confidentiality/Patient Concerns
Health Guidance

PARENT
Parental Concerns
Guidance about Adolescent Development

Physical Exam as Indicated

Summarize Findings and Recommendations
Determine Parental Involvement
Determine Method of Notification

PATIENT AND PARENT
Summarize Findings and Recommendations

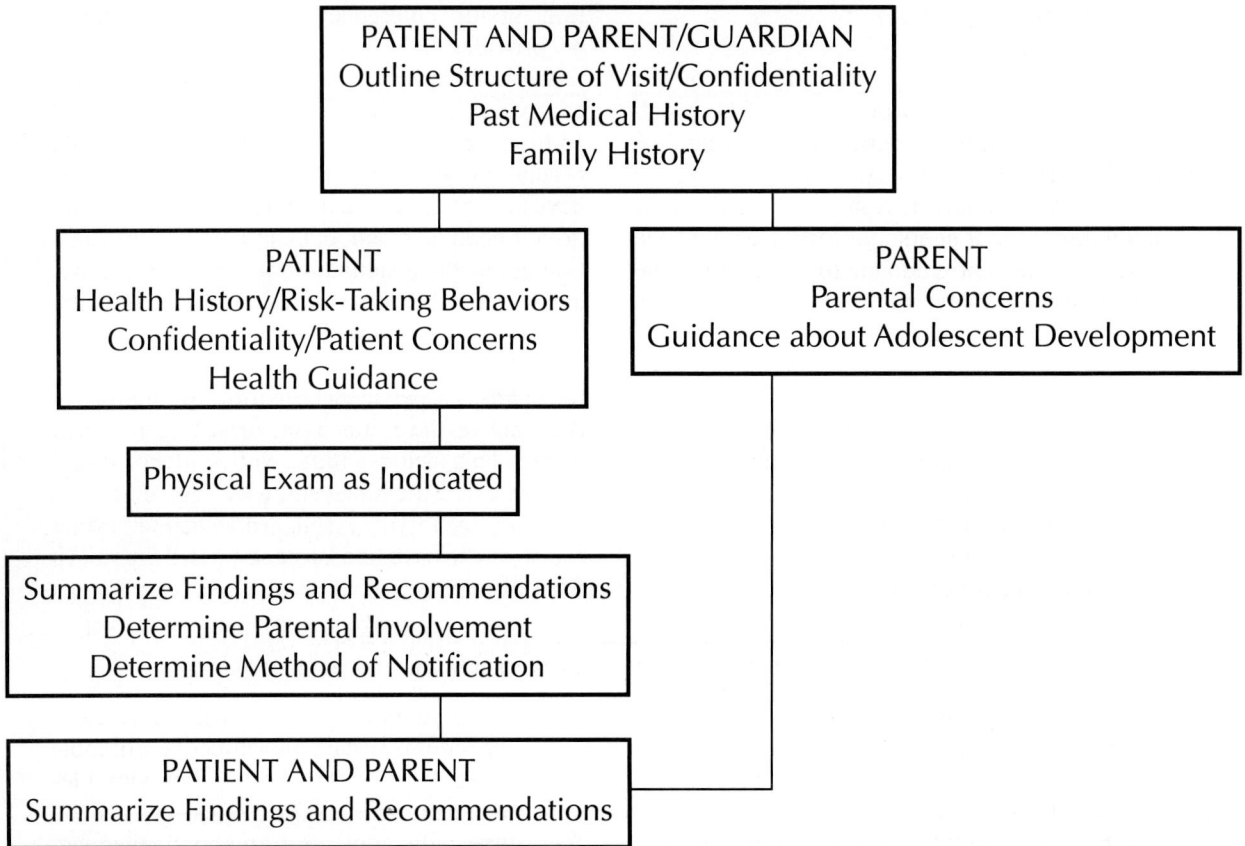

Figure 15-1 First gynecologic visit.

be explained—screening, preventive guidance, establishing a health care relationship, and allowing for a discussion of any concerns or questions about health. The concept of confidentiality should be explained in a way that encourages parent-teen communication, while acknowledging the growing maturity and independence of the teen and not alienating the parent. During this initial phase of the visit, the clinician obtains information about the menstrual and pubertal history, past medical history, and family history. In the early teenage years, the mother is the best source of accurate information about these aspects of the medical history.

The clinician should address questions to the teen herself, but observe the interactions between parent and teen. Who answers the ques-

tions? How articulate and knowledgeable is the teen? Is there discord, argument, or frank confrontation between the two? Are they respectful of one another, demonstrating good rapport and communication? Is the mother encouraging her teen to accept increasing responsibility in caring for her own health, or is she quite protective or overprotective in her maternal role?

After getting this initial information, the clinician should tell the mother to wait in the waiting area (not just outside the office door), and the teen should be seen alone. The concepts of confidentiality and the caveats outlining the situations in which confidentiality must be breached (homicidal or suicidal ideation or abuse) are restated. The term confidential/confidentiality may be misinterpreted as having to do with self-esteem (confidence); preferable terms are "private" or "privacy." A social and sexual history are then obtained from the teen. The social history should include an assessment of the teen's functioning in school, extracurricular activities including athletics, and her functioning with peers and with family. Questions about the risk-taking activities of peers: (smoking, alcohol and other drug use, and sexual activity) give important information about the peer pressures to which the teen is exposed, and provide a less threatening entree into the assessment of risk-taking behaviors of the individual herself. The sexual history should ascertain information about dating behaviors—does she have anyone who is a special friend or is she in a relationship? and "Tell me about your partner." Gender-neutral questions comfort teens who are struggling with questions about their sexual identify. Ascertaining the partner's age is helpful, because a much older partner may signify an increased risk of sexual coercion, pressure, or potential for abuse or assault. A sexual history should include questions about the type and range of sexual activities—from holding hands, to kissing, to touching (breast and genital) with and without clothing, to oral sex (receptive and donor), and to intercourse (vaginal and anal). It should be ascertained whether these activities are engaged in voluntarily or as a result of pressure, coercion, or force. Past efforts to protect from STDs and pregnancy should be determined, and the teen's knowledge base about these issues assessed. The consistency of hormonal contraceptive and condom use should be determined. If the teen is sexually active, determine whether her parents are aware of this and encourage her to discuss this fact with her parents.

A review of symptoms is important—including questions about gynecologic and endocrine function and symptoms of gastrointestinal/genitourinary (GI/GU) disease. Asking these questions with the adolescent alone respects her privacy and conveys to her that the clinician considers her own assessment of these issues to be important. Suicide is a significant cause of death among ado-

lescents. Physicians who see adolescents must be alert to the signs of depression and the frequency of suicidal ideation, and must make appropriate inquiries about thoughts, plans, and means of committing suicide. Referrals for mental health care or even immediate hospitalization may be necessary in adolescents who have a well-conceived plan and the means to commit suicide.

Because disordered eating can have a major impact on general and gynecologic health, the teen should be asked about weight loss or gain, her feelings about current weight (feeling "too fat" when she is of normal or low weight), and efforts to diet or nondietary measures to lose weight (bingeing, purging, laxatives). Injury-prevention messages—not riding/driving after alcohol use, bicycle/skateboard/skating helmet use—can be conveyed verbally or with health promotion brochures. ACOG has promoted a campaign—Stay Alert/Stay Safe—with brochures and tips to help teens avoid sexual violence and date rape by recognizing the possibility and minimizing the risks of unsafe situations. Other health promotion measures—the importance of regular exercise, healthy diet with adequate calcium intake and lower fat—can also be transmitted with teen-appropriate patient education brochures available from ACOG, the American Academy of Pediatrics, or other health education sponsors.

After a discussion of these issues (which should be interactive rather than a lecture), give the teen patient an opportunity to ask any health or sex-related questions and to discuss any concerns. Information about the pelvic examination can also be given verbally or by written brochure. Tell her that oral contraceptives can be prescribed without an examination (but encourage an examination in the near future).

The clinician's style of interaction is especially important with teens, as they will quickly "tune out" a clinician who is condescending, judgmental, uses medical terminology without explanation, or who does not show a genuine interest in their health. At age 14, adolescents need to know the facts, including information about anatomy, menstruation, conception and pregnancy, abstinence as the only sure method to prevent STDs/pregnancy, birth control methods including emergency contraception, and STDs, including HIV. One question that allows an assessment of the adolescent's previous instruction about these topics is to ask whether she has had a health class or class in human sexuality and to ask her to talk about the content of that class. With regard to sexual decision making, it is appropriate for the clinician to encourage abstinence or the postponement of sexual involvement until the teen is developmentally ready to be responsible about her sexuality. However, the clinician should not address abstinence to the exclusion of the appropriate provision of information about contraception and STDs. School-based and religious community–based programs frequently supplement the information provided by clinicians and parents. The most useful programs for teens focus on helping them develop the skills necessary to successfully negotiate sexual decision making—*how* to say no, and to recognize what sexual behaviors one is saying *no* to. For example, saying no to having intercourse, but yes to holding hands and kissing. Helping adolescents to deal with their sexuality in healthy and appropriate ways is a goal that is the shared responsibility of parents, caring adults, schools, religious institutions, clinicians, and society as a whole.

The first visit allows the clinician to address the prevalent myths about sex, contraception, and health. It is not unusual to hear these statements:

"You can't get pregnant the first time you have sex."

"You can't get pregnant if you have sex standing up."

"I haven't gotten pregnant so far, so I won't in the future."

"Birth control pills mess up your insides."

"Birth control pills make you fat."

"Birth control pills make you infertile."

"If you haven't had sex by age [17] you'll never be normal."

"You can't get STDs from clean (or nice) people."

The physician should establish rapport by showing a genuine interest in the teen's life, interests, and activities. A respectful attitude, an interactive style, and the avoidance of lecturing are important. In taking a sexual history, it is important to be precise and expect concrete responses, asking, "Have you had sex?" rather than, "Are you sexually active?", which is open to misinterpretation. The clinician should attempt not to appear shocked; adolescent dress styles, body piercing, fads in hair color and style may be intended to both express individuality and to distance oneself from adults.

Generalizing a statement or placing a behavior within a normative context can be helpful: "Many people find it difficult to talk about sex" or "Most of us find it hard to remember to take a pill every day." The interaction with the adolescent will provide enough information on which to make a decision about whether a pelvic examination is indicated. If the clinician decides that this is appropriate, an explanation can be given to the teen who can then elect whether to "get it over with" at the same visit or to schedule a second visit. Encourage the former option after ascertaining what the teen has heard about the exam from her girlfriends or mother and correcting any misinformation about the exam. She should be offered the choice of having her mother or other support person present with her during the exam. The mother should also be given an explanation of the necessity for the examination, even if it is in the most vague or general terms to protect the teen's confidences, and even if the teen elects not to have her mother present during the exam.

After talking with the teen, a private conversation with the parent can give additional historical information. Information about disordered eating, or even frank bulimia or anorexia nervosa, may only be forthcoming from the mother who reports an unhealthy focus on excessive exercise, diet, elimination of fat, or bingeing/purging behaviors. During this conversation, the clinician can also get information about parenting skills. If this is a first child, the parents will not have had the practical experiences of parenting a teenager. In addition, health guidance regarding parenting of a teen is almost always welcomed by the parent of an early/midteen. Parents should be informed of the importance of parental monitoring of the adolescent's friends (and their behaviors) and activities.

Encourage parents and responsible adults to discuss responsible sexual decision making, healthy sexuality, abstinence, the role of the media in influencing adolescents, parents' values and beliefs, and the necessity for preparation and readiness for parenting. Parents frequently have questions and concerns about their adolescent's behaviors. A parent can be encouraged to make a "contract" with their daughter for a "free" ride home from anywhere if she or her ride have been drinking or using drugs. The "free" ride means that a lecture or discussion about the risks of drinking/driving will *not* take place that evening, but at a later time when the parent is less angry and the teen is sober.

If an examination takes place during this first visit, its goal should be to identify disease (such as signs of androgen excess or evidence of STDs). The examination should be accomplished in an atraumatic manner that leaves the adolescent feeling empowered about her mastery of her body rather than feeling violated by a painful procedure forced upon her. If the findings are normal, emphasize this fact to the teen. If the findings suggest evidence of STDs, then the findings of lab tests such as a wet prep showing WBCs should first be presented to the adolescent privately. The clinician and patient can then discuss how this information can be shared with the parent. The teen can be encouraged to talk to the mother on her own, or the clinician can offer (with the teen's permission) to tell the mother jointly with the teen or privately with the mother alone. A final meeting with the adolescent and her mother in which findings and plans are shared (to the extent that the adolescent has granted permission to do so) provides closure and builds

an alliance. This can be a positive experience, and can provide the clinician a window of opportunity to help the teen avoid the common health risks of adolescence. Adolescents, particularly younger teens, may listen to the clinician's authoritative advice about postponing sexual intercourse. The clinician can take a proactive stance with the mothers of adolescents, encouraging appropriate parenting and informing them about the health needs of their daughters.

Obstetricians/gynecologists are in a particularly good position to provide this health guidance which may prevent the sequelae of adolescent risk-taking behaviors that present to the ob/gyn, such as pelvic inflammatory disease, infertility, and ectopic pregnancies. After this initial visit to an ob/gyn, the adolescent will recognize that if she has questions, concerns, or gynecological health problems, she can receive confidential and caring health care. The establishment of this relationship is one of the most important consequences of the first gynecological visit. An annual visit should take place, providing a regular opportunity for health guidance, screening, provision of contraception, and treatment of disease.

Specific Medical Issues
Normal and Abnormal Menses

One of the most common gynecological concerns and problems of adolescence is that of abnormal menstrual bleeding. An understanding of the concept of the parameters of normal menstrual cycles is essential for diagnosis of the abnormal. Early menstrual cycles are typically anovulatory. However, they are basically at least irregularly regular. Prospectively collected data indicate that although the interval from the first menstrual period to the second period can be quite long, subsequent cycles generally fall within a range of 21 to 45 days. Only a minority of cycles fall outside of this range. Individual adolescents with widely varying cycles or long intervals of amenorrhea should be evaluated for possible endocrine abnormalities, including hypoestrogenemia associated with eating disorders or excessive exercise, androgen excess disorders such as polycystic ovarian disease, thyroid dysfunction, or other more unusual causes such as hyperprolactinemia and pituitary microadenomas. The accurate diagnosis of these disorders permits appropriate therapy and can prevent significant morbidity from prolonged or heavy menses.

Dysmenorrhea

Because early menstrual cycles are typically anovulatory, they are frequently associated with minimal or no dysmenorrhea or menstrual molimina. The onset of ovulatory cycles with associated dysmenorrhea or mittelschmerz can lead to office or emergency department visits. If the pain is not recognized as related to the menstrual cycle (by either the patient, her parents, or the clinician), other diagnoses such as that of a "ruptured cyst" may be invoked. This may be based on the appearance of a cystic ovarian follicle on ultrasound, perhaps accompanied by a small amount of peritoneal fluid. While true cyst rupture can occur, it is relatively infrequent, and most of these diagnoses represent exaggerations of physiological events. Adolescents and parents may be unaware that nonsteroidal anti-inflammatory medications currently available over the counter provide excellent pain relief, which is often superior to that provided by ASA or acetaminophen.

Pelvic Pain

While chronic pelvic pain is, fortunately, infrequent during adolescence, attention to the diagnosis and management may allow the earlier diagnosis of medically treatable conditions such as endometriosis. The adolescent who has severe, persistent dysmenorrhea or noncyclic pelvic pain in spite of using oral contraceptives to treat pain coupled with nonsteroidal anti-inflammatory medications, can be evaluated with laparoscopy. Pelvic endometriosis has been reported to occur in 50 to 75 percent of adolescents meeting this definition of pelvic pain.

Menorrhagia

Adolescents who present with menstrual bleeding heavy enough to cause symptoms or anemia should be evaluated for the presence of bleeding abnormalities, although the majority will be found by exclusion to have anovulatory bleeding. Pregnancy-related complications should always be ruled out with a pregnancy test, regardless of the individual's acknowledgement of sexual activity, as the consequences of missing this diagnosis can be life-threatening. Evaluate adolescents who present at menarche or with significant anemia (Hgb ≤ 10) with a CBC and differential to rule out leukemias or other hematologic problems such as ITP, and with coagulation studies including bleeding time to screen for problems including von Willebrand disease. Consideration should also be given to checking thyroid and liver function. After these lab studies are obtained, treatment consists of high-dose combination oral contraceptives in a tapering regimen, followed by a withdrawal bleed, and then ongoing oral contraceptive therapy. Medical therapy can almost always lead to the avoidance of a D&C in this age group.

Sexual Activity

The age of onset of sexual intercourse has declined over the last 25 years. In 1970, fewer than 50 percent of 19-year-olds had initiated intercourse. By 1992, more than 50 percent of 17-year-olds were sexually experienced. Although the vast majority of adolescent pregnancies are unintended, adolescent birth rates are declining. However, adolescent pregnancy and abortion rates in the United States are higher than in any other developed country. Nearly 75 percent of adolescents report using contraception at the time of first intercourse, with condom use accounting for the largest increase in usage.

The most commonly used method of contraception among teens is oral contraceptives; condom use is the second most popular method. Although adolescent pregnancy is a significant societal and individual problem, women over the age of 20 make up 70 to 80 percent of the numbers of nonmarital births, unintended pregnancies, and abortions. The problem of contraceptive compliance is a significant one both for adolescents and for older women. Most adolescents have used some method of contraception in an attempt to prevent pregnancy. However, the consistent and ongoing use of oral contraceptives is problematic, as exemplified by a failure rate of oral contraceptives of up to 15 percent in typical use by teens. Similarly, condom use by adolescents is typically sporadic and inconsistent. Studies examining what has been termed "microbehaviors" around oral contraceptive and condom use reveal that fewer than 40 percent of adolescents take a pill daily; in comparison, 59 percent of the best pill-users in this study, women over 30, took a pill daily. Only about a third of adolescents used a condom with every act of intercourse; 40 percent of women over 30 did. The relatively high failure rates of these methods that require daily or perfectly consistent use leads to the consideration of longer-acting and less compliance-dependent methods of contraception for teens.

Depot medroxyprogesterone acetate, given intramuscularly every three months, was used by 10 percent of adolescents, as reported in the 1995 National Survey of Family Growth Statistics. While this method is growing in popularity, in part because it obviates the need for daily compliance, ongoing use continues to be problematic. Several studies report continuation rates at the end of one year that are low, with studies reporting as few as 25 percent of users continuing to use the method at the end of one year. Side effects are frequently cited as the primary reason for method discontinuation.

The implantable subdermal levonorgestrel-containing rods, Norplant, were initially quite popular, and continue to show promise for providing long-term contraception for up to 5 years of use. Studies report continuation rates of 80 to 90+ percent at the end of one year, with commensurately low pregnancy rates. When this method was first introduced, some patients did

not have sufficient information about possible side effects. The occurrence of unexpected side effects coupled with difficulty in removing the devices by clinicians who did not have extensive experience led to legal challenges that continue to taint this method. This is unfortunate, because the method has many benefits.

Counseling that encourages postponement of sexual involvement, provides information about contraceptive options (including emergency contraception), encourages responsible sexual activity (if there will be sexual activity) with the use of appropriate contraceptive methods to prevent pregnancy and to create barriers that decrease the risk of STDs, and provides realistic expectations about the possible side-effects of contraception, will result in improved and successful prevention of pregnancy and STDs by more adolescents. Clinicians should plan to see adolescents every 3 to 6 months to counsel about the continuation of the chosen contraception method, assess side effects and their effect on compliance, provide reassurance about nuisance effects and reinforce effective use, renew prescriptions if needed, recommend an alternative formulation of pills or alternative contraceptive method if needed, take a sexual history and counsel about condom use, and screen for STDs.

STDs

When one controls for rates of sexual activity, the adolescent age group is at the greatest risk for nearly all STDs, with resultant significant acute morbidity, complications, and long-term sequelae. Recent studies report that as many as 29 percent of sexually active inner-city teens test positive for chlamydia, prompting the authors to recommend screening every 6 months. The 1997 Youth Risk Behavior Survey indicated that 16 percent of adolescents reported four or more sexual partners. In the same survey, 43 percent reported that they did not use a condom at last intercourse. Pelvic inflammatory disease (PID) is an unfortunate sequela of undiagnosed STDs, and adolescents typically delay seeking treatment for genital symptoms, increasing their risk for ascending infections and PID.

Clinicians play an important role in the control of STD rates among adolescents. Clinicians can promote primary prevention with abstinence counseling, urging condom use for sexually active teens, and promoting responsible decision making. In addition, they play an important role in the suspicion, diagnosis, and management of STDs among both asymptomatic and symptomatic adolescents. At annual visits, clinicians can routinely address issues related to sexuality and STDs in a consistent and repetitive manner. The role of the clinician as STD educator for individual teens, for the general public, and for parents of adolescents, can increase adolescents' recognition of disease.

Summary

A primary goal of clinicians in adolescent medicine is to facilitate adolescents' healthy transition to adulthood without major reproductive morbidities or sequelae. Preventive guidance, screening, and appropriate reproductive health care of the common gynecological problems of adolescence will help to accomplish this goal. An awareness of the common comorbidities of adolescence—substance use and abuse, depression and suicide, eating disorders, and sexual risk-taking—allows the clinician to identify these problems early, to provide counseling and referral when needed, and to treat if disease occurs.

References and Selected Readings

1. Abma J, Chandra A, Mosher W, Peterson L, Piccinino L: Fertility, family planning, and women's health: New data from the 1995 National Survey of Family Growth. National Survey of Family Growth, National Center for Health Statistics. *Vital Health Stat* 23(19):1–125, 1997.
2. American College of Obstetricians and Gynecologists ACOG: *Confidentiality in Adolescent Health Care.* Washington, DC: 249:1, 1998 Educational Bulletin.
3. Biro FM, Rosenthal SL: Adolescents and sexually transmitted diseases: Diagnosis, developmental issues, and prevention. *J Pediatr Health Care* 9:256–262, 1995.
4. Centers for Disease Control CDC: Youth Risk Behavior Surveillance—United States, 1997. *MMWR* 47:1–89, 1998.
5. Claessens E, Cowell CA: Acute adolescent menorrhagia. *Am J Obstet Gynecol* 139:277, 1981.
6. Committee on Adolescence, American Academy of Pediatrics: The adolescent's right to confidential care when considering abortion. *Pediatrics* 97:746–751, 1996.
7. Council on Scientific Affairs of the AMA: Confidential health services. *JAMA* 269:1420–1424, 1993.
8. Elders MJ, Albert AE: Adolescent pregnancy and sexual abuse. *JAMA* 280(7):648–649, 1998.
9. Elster AB, Kuznets NJ: *AMA guidelines for adolescent preventive services (GAPS): Recommendations and rationale.* Baltimore, MD: Williams & Wilkins, 1994.
10. Emans SJ, Goldstein DP, *Pediatric and Adolescent Gynecology,* 4th ed. Philadelphia: Lippincott-Raven, 1998.
11. Hatcher RA, Trussell J, Stewart F, et al: *Contraceptive Technology.* 17th ed. New York: Ardent Media, 1998.
12. Herman-Giddens ME, Slore EJ, Wasserman RC, et al. Secondary sexual characteristics and menses in young girls seen in office practice: A study from the pediatric research in office settings network. *Pediatrics* 99:505–512, 1997.
13. Hillard PA: Contraceptive use and attitudes among U.S. women. *Womens Health Issues* 4:138–143, 1994.
14. Hillard PJ: Oral contraception noncompliance: The extent of the problem. *Adv Contracept* 8(Suppl 1):13–20, 1992.
15. Hillard PJ: Family planning in the teen population. [Review]. *Curr Opin Obstet. Gynecol* 5:798–804, 1993.
16. Marshall WA, Tanner JM: Variations in patterns of pubertal changes in girls. *Arch Dis Child* 44:291–303, 1969.
17. NICHD. Androgens and women's health. *Clinician* 12:1–30, 1994.
18. Rosenthal SL, Cohen SL, Burklow KA, Hillard PA: Family involvement in the gynecological care of adolescents. *J Adolesc Ped Gynecol* 9:59–65, 1996.
19. Sanfilippo JS, Muram D, Lee PA, Dewhurst J: *Pediatric and Adolescent Gynecology* 2nd ed. Philadelphia: WB Saunders, 1994.
20. Strasburger VC, Brown RT: *Adolescent Medicine.* Philadelphia: WB Saunders, 1997.
21. The Alan Guttmacher Institute: *Sex and America's Teenagers.* New York: The Alan Guttmacher Institute, 1994.
22. Treloar AE, Boynton RE, Behn BG, Brown BW: Variation of the human menstrual cycle through reproductive life. *Int J Fertil* 12:77–126, 1970.

CHAPTER 16

Health Care Needs of the Reproductive-Age Woman

Zalman Levine
Carolyn D. Runowicz

REPRODUCTIVE HEALTH ISSUES
Contraception • Conception • Sexually
Transmitted Diseases
GENERAL MEDICAL ISSUES
Cancer • Endocrine • Immunizations •
Occupational • Cardiovascular

For women of reproductive age, a large gap often exists between a patient's self-recognized health care needs and her epidemiological needs. Patient-initiated needs generally focus on specific reproductive issues such as contraception, menstrual abnormalities, and pregnancy, while the epidemiological needs of the reproductive-age female focus more broadly on a host of screening, prevention, and counseling concerns. Therefore, for the ambulatory care goals in this age group to be realized, the health care provider must initiate such care for these women.

Recently, preventive medicine has achieved a high degree of visibility. The practice of preventive medicine should ideally include primary prevention, such as immunization, which prevents disease from occurring; secondary prevention, such as breast examinations, which detects already existing disease that has not yet become clinically apparent; and tertiary prevention, such as aspirin after a stroke, which prevents progression of an already apparent disease. Prevention also includes counseling to identify and help eliminate risk factors for a disease.

Motivating asymptomatic patients to actively seek preventive care often requires considerable effort on the part of the physician, particularly when the preventive care includes what may be perceived as an unpleasant procedure such as a pelvic exam, or demands a behavioral change, such as the cessation of smoking, and when the intervention has only long-term benefits. Establishing a supportive physician-patient relationship, educating the patients and the public, and encouraging realistic patient expectations have all been shown to improve the success of preventive care.[1-3]

Reproductive Health Issues

The most pressing health care needs of the reproductive-age female, both preventive and curative, often relate to the reproductive system. Usually in good health, the 18- to 50-year-old patient generally presents to her physician with a need, often focused on contraception, infertility, menstrual abnormalities, or pregnancy.

Contraception

Unwanted pregnancies, which are a huge problem in the United States, can be prevented with effective contraception.[4] The use of contraception involves not only contraceptive efficacy, but a host of other factors, such as culture, religion, social circumstances, and values. Proper counseling should include a discussion of these factors, as well as of the methods available.

Screening prior to prescribing contraception should include a medical history designed to uncover potential contraindications, such as recurrent thromboembolic disease, which is a contraindication to the combined oral contraceptive pill. A family history of ovarian cancer might suggest a potential noncontraceptive benefit of the oral contraceptive such as a reduced risk of epithelial ovarian neoplasia.[5, 6] A review of systems and social history should also be obtained to identify risk factors and to explore lifestyle preferences. Physical examination and laboratory studies should focus on identifying potential contraindications to the use of a particular method—such as evidence of active cervicitis or abnormal liver function tests. Using this information, the clinician can help the patient choose an effective and safe method of contraception based on her individual risk profile. A discussion of pregnancy prevention should also include the Yuzpe method of emergency contraception.[7]

Conception

Pregnancy and its related issues play a central role in the health care needs of the reproductive-age woman. Multiple and complex medical and social issues must be addressed by the physician and the patient with respect to preconceptional counseling, pregnancy, postpartum care, and, when applicable, infertility and recurrent pregnancy loss.

Strong evidence exists for the preconceptional use of folic acid to decrease the incidence of neural tube defects.[8, 9] All women contemplating pregnancy should be advised to ingest 400 μg (0.4 mg) folic acid daily, and to continue this regimen throughout at least the first trimester of pregnancy. Women with a history of previous children with neural tube defects should take 4 mg folic acid daily.[10]

Preconceptionally, the reproductive-age female contemplating pregnancy should be screened with a careful history, review of systems (ROS), and physical exam to identify medical and gynecologic problems that can impact pregnancy, such as diabetes, hypertension, systemic lupus erythematosis, valvular heart disease, and uterine leiomyoma. If this screening process reveals underlying disease, the status of the disease should be appropriately assessed prior to the pregnancy; for example, a 24-h urine sample should be obtained in the diabetic patient to quantify any proteinuria due to nephropathy. The patient's immunization status should be reviewed, and appropriate immunization offered prior to planning a pregnancy.[11, 12] To identify risks for teratogenicity, preconceptional counseling should also include a history of medication use and of toxic occupational and recreational exposures. The patient should be counseled regarding risk factors and lifestyle changes to help ensure a successful pregnancy. Couples with genetic risks should be counseled appropriately or referred for genetic counseling services for in-depth assessment. Patients aged 35 years and older should be advised of genetic disorders associated with advanced maternal age.

Evaluate patients with infertility—defined as failure to conceive after one year of unprotected intercourse—for an etiology. Patients with recurrent pregnancy loss should be evaluated for such problems as Mullerian anomalies, antiphospholipid antibody syndrome, abnormal karyotype, thyroid disorders, and infections such as mycoplasma or syphilis.

Women desiring an elective termination of pregnancy should be counseled regarding the techniques currently available in the United States. The best procedure is based on the patient's individual medical circumstance and influenced by the patient's cultural and religious beliefs, social supports, reasons for desiring a termination, and anxieties regarding the decision.

Sexually Transmitted Diseases

The incidence of sexually transmitted diseases (STDs) in the United States is on the rise.[13] This rise results in increasing long-term population risks of pelvic inflammatory disease, tuboovarian abscess, chronic pelvic pain, infertility, and ectopic pregnancy.

Prevention of STDs is rooted in education.[14, 15] Physicians must discuss the short- and long-term dangers of STDs, and emphasize their easy transmissibility and prevention.

Screening should be done on the basis of risk factors. Cultures from the vagina or cervix are most useful in cases of gonorrhea and chlamydia infection.[11] Most states require a syphilis test prior to marriage and also during pregnancy.[11] Many ethical and legal issues surround testing for the presence of human immunodeficiency virus (HIV). However, testing for HIV should be encouraged among populations that have a known high prevalence of the disease,[11] and for women who are contemplating becoming pregnant or who are pregnant.

The patient diagnosed with an STD should be treated and counseled regarding the need for treatment of her partner and future condom use. Those who test positive for HIV should be counseled and referred for further evaluation and therapy. Those who have frequently recurring genital herpes simplex virus can be offered suppressive therapy. Patients with a positive rapid plasma reagin (RPR) must be further evaluated with a treponeme-specific serologic test and treated for syphilis, as appropriate.

General Medical Issues

Overwhelmingly, the medical health care needs of the reproductive-age female center on prevention, rather than on treatment of disease. The clinician knowing the importance of establishing health habits that can significantly affect the patient's future incidence of disease, must educate the patient on disease prevention and risk-reduction behaviors.

Cancer

Screening programs for many common cancers have been shown to significantly decrease mortality, and more sophisticated screening, using genetic markers, is now emerging.[16] Prevention of cancer through diet, lifestyle, and therapies is an important objective for patients. The role of the primary care provider in screening and cancer prevention in the reproductive-age female involves both gynecologic and nongynecologic malignancies.

Breast Now the most common malignancy in U.S. women, breast cancer affects 1 in 9 females over an 85-year lifetime, and is second to lung cancer as a cause of death in women due to malignancy. Breast cancer increases in incidence with increasing age, with a risk of 1/2500 in women ages 20 to 30, 1/238 in women ages 30 to 40, and 1/66 in women ages 40 to 50. Breast cancer incidence rates for women increased about 4 percent per year from 1982 to 1987; between 1990 and 1994, the incidence stabilized at about 110 per 100,000.[17]

Cancer counseling must include an assessment of the individual patient's risks for cancer. However, most women with breast cancer do not have identifiable risk factors beyond age and gender.

Most palpable breast cancers are discovered by the patient on breast self-examination, and some by the physician on routine physical examination. Therefore, in addition to the complete patient and family histories that should be performed, screening should include instruction in the breast self-exam, which reproductive-age patients should perform during the first 7 days following the onset of menses on a monthly basis. In addition, a physical examination by the physician should be performed annually—or perhaps semiannually for high-risk patients.

Increased use of mammography has resulted in breast cancers being found earlier in their development, when they are smaller and at less-advanced stages. The American Cancer Society (ACS) recommends annual mammography for women beginning at age 40, a recommendation that we strongly endorse.[18] Women with high-risk factors for the early development of breast cancer may need to begin radiologic screening at an earlier age.[19]

With the availability of genetic testing for

BRCA 1 and *2* mutations, the health care provider must be prepared to counsel the patient about genetic testing or to refer the patient to a genetic counselor. Genetic testing is recommended if the probability of finding a mutation is > 10 percent.[20] Because this issue is quite complex, serious consideration regarding referral of the woman to an established genetic screening center of excellence is appropriate.

For women with *BRCA 1* or *2* mutations or with pedigrees strongly suggestive of a *BRCA 1* or *2* mutation, the current recommendations include monthly breast self-examination beginning in their late teens, annual or semiannual clinical examinations starting at age 25 to 35, and annual mammograms starting at age 25 to 35.[19]

Cervix In counseling a reproductive-age female regarding her risk of cervical cancer, the fundamental concept of its sexual transmission must be stressed. Early age at first intercourse, multiple partners, and high-risk male partners have each been independently shown to increase the risk of cervical cancer, and are probably surrogate markers for a sexually transmissible agent. More than 90 percent of invasive cervical cancers and their precursor lesions contain human papillomavirus (HPV) DNA.[21, 22]

Environmental and lifestyle factors play significant roles in the epidemiology of cervical cancer as well. Cigarette smoking increases the risk of cervical cancer by as much as 50 percent.

The use of barrier methods of contraception decreases the risk of cervical cancer, which decrease is presumably related to decreased sexual transmission of virus and other cofactors.

Since its description by Dr. George Papanicolaou in the 1930s and its initiation for widespread screening in the 1940s, the Pap smear has developed into an effective cancer screening technique, and has resulted in a significant reduction in mortality from cervical cancer. Various recommendations regarding screening protocols exist, with all recommending that patients begin screening with annual Pap smears at age 18, or with the onset of sexual activity if that occurred

earlier than age 18. Annual screening is recommended for women with risk factors, as noted above. Low-risk women can increase this interval after three negative smears.

As with the primary prevention of sexually transmitted diseases, cervical cancer prevention must include strong educational initiatives aimed at safe sexual practices, at lifestyle changes, and at regular Pap screening. High-risk women should be encouraged to use condoms regularly.

Ovary Because ovarian cancers are usually detected at an advanced stage of the disease, they have the highest fatality-to-case ratio of all gynecologic malignancies. Furthermore, no screening technique has yet been shown to improve early detection, nor the capability to reduce morbidity and mortality for the general population.

The incidence of epithelial ovarian cancer—90 percent of all ovarian cancers—increases with age, with more than 80 percent found in postmenopausal women and fewer than 1 percent occurring before the age of 21. Only 7 percent of epithelial ovarian neoplasms in premenopausal women are malignant.[23] For women in the United States, the lifetime risk of ovarian cancer is 1.6 percent with 90 percent being sporadic, and 10 percent hereditary. Care of women who have *BRCA 1* or *BRCA 2* mutations is discussed elsewhere in this book.

In the case of ovarian cancer, strong epidemiologic data show a decreased risk with increasing parity and with oral contraceptive use. This protective effect of oral contraceptive use was recently retrospectively shown to apply, as well, to women with hereditary cancer syndromes.[5]

Endometrial The most common gynecologic malignancy in the United States, endometrial carcinoma, primarily affects postmenopausal women. However, certain risk factors increase its incidence in premenopausal women, including obesity, diabetes, and chronic anovulation due, for example, to polycystic ovarian syndrome, with consequent unopposed endogenous estrogen stimulation. Tamoxifen use also increases the risk of endometrial cancer, as does a personal history of breast, colon, or ovarian cancer.[24] Oral contraceptive pill use and pregnancy decrease the risk of endometrial carcinoma.[25] Because endometrial carcinoma typically presents in an early stage with abnormal vaginal bleeding, mass screening of the asymptomatic public has not been shown to be cost-effective or to reduce mortality.

Colon Ranking third after lung and breast cancers as a cause of cancer-related mortality in women, colorectal cancer affects men and women in equal numbers, with an overall per-person lifetime risk of 7 percent in the United States.[17] The risk of colon cancer is minimal for the average-risk reproductive-age woman. The need for screening begins at age 50, according to the American Cancer Society Screening (ACS) guidelines, which were updated in 1997.[26] However, the incidence of colon cancer rises even in the premenopausal population in the presence of certain risk factors, and for these patients screening must begin at an earlier age.[27]

Skin Basal cell and squamous cell carcinoma are sun-induced cancers associated with chronic sun exposure. Melanoma is particularly associated with sun exposure as a child; it typically affects patients older than age 70, but has been rising in incidence among younger patients.[28] Screening consists of careful physical examination of the skin by the physician, with attention to nevi with irregular borders, color changes, itching, and bleeding. Primary prevention includes limiting exposure to the sun either by avoiding the outdoors at midday, or by using an appropriately rated sunblock formulation.

Endocrine

Thyroid Both hypo- and hyperthyroidism are more common in females than in males; hypothyroidism tends to be diagnosed in women over the age of 60, but has a slow, insidious onset and may exist subclinically in reproductive-age women. Postpartum thyroid dysfunction occurs in 4 to 7 percent of women.[29] Current screening guidelines begin for the low-risk woman at age 50 with measurement of TSH, but premenopausal

women with a review of systems suggestive of disease should undergo thyroid testing.[30]

Diabetes In 1997, the American Diabetes Association modified its recommendations for diabetes testing in asymptomatic, undiagnosed patients.[65] All women should be tested at age 45, with repeat testing every 3 years, if normal. Testing at a younger age and at more frequent intervals should be performed for high-risk patients, which include those with obesity; family history of a first-degree relative with diabetes; hypertension; history of gestational diabetes or of a baby weighing > 9 lb; HDL cholesterol ≤ 35 mg/dl; triglyceride level ≥ 250 mg/dl; membership in a high-risk ethnic population such as African-American, Hispanic, Asian, or Native American; or previous impaired glucose testing.[31] The preferred method of testing is the fasting plasma glucose (FPG) performed after at least 8 h of fasting; FPG ≥ 126 mg/dl establishes the diagnosis of diabetes, <110 is normal, and 110 to 125 is considered "impaired."

Osteoporosis Most of the adult bone mass is laid down during adolescence, but bone mineral content rises through ages 25 to 30. Women achieve peak bone mass of both trabecular and cancellous bone by age 30; bone loss begins shortly thereafter.[32] Although osteopenia and osteoporosis do not become epidemiologically significant until the postmenopausal years—with the exception of young women using long-term steroids or heparin, and of those with hypogonadism with low endogenous estrogen production—reproductive-age women can begin lifestyle changes that will have long-term effects on fracture rates. Such prevention includes exercising and diets high in calcium and low in protein, phosphorous, fat, sodium, and caffeine, all of which either increase urinary excretion of calcium or decrease its intestinal absorption. Calcium intake of 1.0 to 1.5 g per day, particularly during adolescence and the 20s, increases peak bone mass and decreases the risk of future fractures. Calcium supplementation should be encouraged to ensure adequate daily intake. Alcohol and smoking are both associated with decreased peak bone mass and with increased rates of bone loss and of osteoporosis.

Immunizations

Immunizations have been effective in the control of many infectious diseases; thus, immunization history and administration of vaccines must be a routine component of the primary care of the reproductive-age female.[11]

Occupational

A careful occupational history should be used as a screen to detect potentially hazardous exposures. Such exposures can lead to respiratory syndromes such as hypersensitivity pneumonitis and occupational asthma; musculoskeletal syndromes such as chronic back pain, tendonitis, and synovitis; and reproductive problems including infertility and fetal effects by exposure to such things as ionizing radiation, lead, and mercury.[33] Animal studies have associated noise exposure with embryotoxicity, and it is a known cause of sensorineural hearing loss in adults.[34] Motor vehicle accidents are a common cause of death in reproductive-age women, and seat belt use has had a beneficial effect on the case-fatality ratio of motor vehicle accidents.[35] Patients should therefore be routinely counseled regarding seat belt use.[35]

Cardiovascular

Although uncommonly diagnosed in the reproductive-age female, cardiovascular disease is the overall leading cause of death among women, and its incidence can be significantly affected by lifestyle interventions.[36] Cigarette smoking, obesity, hypercholesterolemia, diabetes, and hypertension are all identified risk factors for cardiovascular disease, and are all influenced by habits that often form before or during the reproductive-age years. Counseling about diet and exercise should comprise a prominent part of the health care of reproductive-age females. Early

embracement of the American Heart Association Step I Diet of ≤30 percent fat, <7 percent saturated fat, and <200 mg/day of cholesterol creates lifestyle habits that will serve to prevent the later development of obesity, hypercholesterolemia, diabetes, and heart disease—as does the incorporation of 30 to 60 min of moderate-intensity activity into the young patient's daily routine.[11, 36]

Summary

It is an important to provide women with a comprehensive health program that fulfills their needs during their reproductive-age years. Because most women in this age group are generally in good health, the focus needs to be on prevention, screening, and the development of healthy lifestyles and risk-reduction behaviors.

References and Selected Readings

1. Ely JW, Goerdt CJ, Bergus GR, et al: The effect of physician characteristics on compliance with adult preventive care guidelines. *Fam Med* 30(1):34–39, 1998.
2. Scutshfield FD: Clinical preventive services: The physician and the patient. *Clin Chem* 38:1547–1551, 1992.
3. McCormick WC, Inui TS: Geriatric preventive care: Counseling techniques in practice settings. *Clin Geriatr Med* 8(1):215–228, 1992.
4. Mishell DR: Contraception. *N Engl J Med* 320:777–787, 1989.
5. Narod SA, Risch H, Moslehi R, et al: Oral contraceptives and the risk of hereditary ovarian cancer. *N Engl J Med* 339:424–428, 1998.
6. Whittemore AS, Harris R, Itnyre J, Collaborative Ovarian Cancer Group: Characteristics relating to ovarian cancer risk: Collaborative analysis of 12 U.S. case-control studies. II. Invasive epithelial ovarian cancers in white women. *Am J Epidemiol* 136:1184–1203, 1992.
7. Yuzpe AA, Smith RP, Rademaker AW: A multicenter clinical investigation employing ethinyl estradiol combined with di-norgestrel as a postcoital contraceptive agent. *Fertil Steril* 37:508–513, 1982.
8. Centers for Disease Control: Recommendations for the use of folic acid to reduce the number of cases of spina bifida and other neural tube defects. *MMWR* 41(RR-14); 1–7, 1992.

9. American College of Obstetricians and Gynecologists: Folic acid for the prevention of recurrent neural tube defects. Washington, DC: ACOG, 1993. ACOG Committee Opinion No. 120.

10. Centers for Disease Control: Use of folic acid for prevention of spina bifida and other neural tube defects—1983–1991. *MMWR* 40:513–516, 1991.

11. American College of Obstetricians and Gynecologists: Guidelines for women's health care. Washington, DC: ACOG, 1996.

12. American College of Obstetricians and Gynecologists: *Primary—Preventive Care Criteria Set.* Washington, DC: ACOG, 1996. ACOG Criteria Set 19.

13. Catchpole MA: The role of epidemiology and surveillance systems in control of sexually transmitted diseases. *Genitourin Med* 1996; 72:321-9.

14. The NIMH Multisite HIV Prevention Trial: Reducing HIV sexual risk behavior. *Science* 280:1889–1894, 1998.

15. Osujih M: The "other" sexually transmitted diseases: A case for public health education. *J R Soc Health* 117:351–4, 1997.

16. Blackwood MA, Weber BL: *BRCA1* and *BRCA2*: From molecular genetics to clinical medicine. *J Clin Oncol* 16:1639–1641, 1998.

17. *American Cancer Society Facts and Figures—1998.* Atlanta, GA: American Caner Society, 1998.

18. Smart CR, Hendrick RE, Rutledge JH 3rd, Smith RA: Benefit of mammography screening in women ages 40–49 years; current evidence from randomized controlled trials. *Cancer* 75:1619–1626, 1995.

19. Burke W, Daly M, Garber J, et al: Recommendations for follow-up care of individuals with an inherited predisposition to cancer. *JAMA* 277:997–1003, 1997.

20. Statement of the American Society of Clinical Oncology: Genetic testing for cancer susceptibility. *J Clin Oncol* 14:1730–1736, 1996.

21. Fisher B, Costantino JP, Wickerham DL, et al: Tamoxifen for prevention of breast cancer: Report of the National Surgical Adjuvant Breast and Bowel Project R1 Study. *J Natl Cancer Instit* 90:1371–1388, 1998.

22. National Institutes of Health Consensus Conference on Cervical Cancer. *J Natl Cancer Inst Monogr* (21):1–148, 1996.

23. Kurman RJ (ed): *Blaustein's Pathology of the Female Genital Tract,* 4th ed. New York: Springer-Verlag, 1994.

24. Fisher B, Costantino JP, Redmond CK, et al: Endometrial cancer in tamoxifen-treated breast cancer patients: Findings from the National Surgical Adjuvant Breast and Bowel Project (NSABP) B-14. *J Natl Cancer Inst* 86:527–537, 1994.

25. The Centers for Disease Control Cancer and Steroid Hormone Study: Oral contraceptive use and the risk of endometrial cancer. *JAMA* 249:1600–1604, 1983.

26. Byers T, Levin B, Rothenberg D, et al: American Cancer Society guidelines for screening and surveillance for early detection of colorectal polyps and cancer: Update 1997. *CA Cancer J Clin* 47:154–160, 1997.

27. Khullar SK, DiSario JA: Colon cancer screening: Sigmoidoscopy or colonoscopy. *Gastrointest Endosc Clin N Am* 7:365–386, 1997.

28. Quinn AG: Ultraviolet radiation and skin carcinogenesis. *Br J Hosp Med* 58(6):261–264, 1997.

29. Ecker JL, Musci TJ: Treatment of thyroid disease in pregnancy. *Obstet Gynecol Clin North Am* 24(3):575–589, 1997.

30. Brody MB, Reichard RA: Thyroid screening: How to interpret and apply the results. *Postgrad Med* 98(2):54–56, 1995.

31. American Diabetes Association: Clinical practice recommendations 1997. *Diabetes Care* 20 (suppl 1):1997.

32. Center J, Eisman J: The epidemiology and pathogenesis of osteoporosis. *Baillieres Clin Endocrinol Metab* 11(1):23–62, 1997.

33. Smith EM, Hammonds-Ehlers M, Clark MK, Kirchner HL, et al: Occupational exposures and risk of female infertility. *J Occup Environ Med* 39(2):138–147, 1997.

34. Hallberg LR, Jansson G: Women with noise-induced hearing-loss: An invisible group? *Br J Audiol* 30(5):340–345, 1996.

35. Robertson LS: Reducing death on the road: The effects of minimum safety standards, publicized crash tests, seat belts, and alcohol. *Am J Public Health* 86(1):31–34, 1996.

36. Woods SE: Primary prevention of coronary heart disease in women. Should asymptomatic women 50 years of age take aspirin regularly? *Arch Fam Med* 3(4):361–364, 1994.

CHAPTER 17

Reproductive Health

Allan Rosenfield

The International Conference on Population and Development, held in Cairo in 1994, and attended by representatives of almost every nation in the world, established a broad reproductive health agenda for the world, with the empowerment of women being a centerpiece. For probably the first time, a United Nations–sponsored world congress focused attention on the health and well-being of women as a primary goal of development. While there was much debate at the conference as to the definition of reproductive health, reproductive health encompasses a broad range of services for women of reproductive age, including the provision of, and education about, contraception; the prevention, screening, and treatment of sexually transmitted diseases (STDs), including HIV/AIDS; pregnancy-related care that is focused on a reduction in the high rates of maternal mortality in poorer developing countries; treatment of the complications of an unsafely performed abortion and the provision of safe abortion services in those countries where abortion is legal; and counseling about healthy lifestyles and the benefits of preventive care. These and related programs are indeed of high priority—yet, the effective provision of such comprehensive reproductive health services is an elusive, often neglected target throughout the world, including in the United States.

The provision of family planning services is a critically important part of reproductive health care. For many years, the topic was too controversial to be included in the routine care of women. Margaret Sanger, the founder of what eventually became the Planned Parenthood Federation of America, was imprisoned in the 1920s as a result of her efforts to make contraceptive services available. In a few states, it was illegal to provide contraception as late as the 1960s. The Supreme Court ended this anachronism in 1965, when it ruled, in *Griswold et al. v. Connecticut,* that couples in the privacy of their homes could use contraceptives.[1] Since that time, family planning services have become more readily available throughout the United States. However, although women have better access to contraception, they would benefit by a more active program of counseling and education regarding a variety of issues related to their reproductive health.

Closely related to contraceptive services are education, counseling, and screening aimed at the prevention of STDs and lower reproductive tract infections. The management of these conditions is a major component of primary reproductive health services. Morbidity secondary to chlamydia or herpes is a significant source of concern to many women. The incidence of STDs has increased significantly, as have ectopic pregnancies. Finally, there is great concern about HIV/AIDS, and many women wish confidential counseling, education, and testing. Primary care physicians need to be knowledgeable about these diseases and to take the initiative in discussing them with their patients.

Teen pregnancy remains a major social problem in the United States, requiring a number of creative initiatives beyond access to services. School-based clinic programs, out-of-school programs, effective sexuality education, and other efforts are of great importance if we are to have an impact on this serious problem.

Without question, the most controversial and difficult topic relates to abortion and the provision of abortion services.[2] Worldwide, the World Health Organization estimates that somewhere between 50,000 and 100,000 maternal deaths each year are the consequence of a botched, usually illegal, abortion procedure.[3] Through most of the nineteenth century, British common law held in the United

States, ruling that abortion prior to quickening (between 17 and 20 weeks' gestation) was legal. This changed in the late 1800s, when major efforts were made to make abortion at all stages of pregnancy illegal. By the turn of the century, every state had laws against abortion.

During the first half of the twentieth century, abortion remained illegal, except for so-called therapeutic abortions, almost all of which were provided to private patients.[4] Efforts aimed at change at the state level began in the late 1960s, and a small number of states legalized abortion by the early 1970s, culminating in 1973 with the landmark Supreme Court decision *Roe v. Wade,* which legalized abortion throughout the country, establishing the trimester framework.[5]

While the great majority of physicians in the United States believe that a woman should have the right to terminate a pregnancy, there is an increasing severity in the shortage of abortion providers, with a majority of counties in the United States having no providers.[6] Although the goal clearly is to prevent unintended pregnancy, safe abortion services must be made available.

Prevention of STDs and their early diagnosis and treatment; education of women regarding contraception and the prevention of unintended pregnancy and infectious disease; making available to all women the range of contraceptive and reproductive services and providing preventive, screening, counseling and general health care are the major components of providing primary health care for reproductive-age women.

References and Selected Readings

1. *Griswold v. Connecticut,* 381 US 479 (1965).
2. Rosenfield A: Women's reproductive health. *Am J Obstet Gynecol* 169:128–133, 1993.
3. World Health Organization: *Abortion: A Tabulation of Available Data on the Frequency and Mortality of Unsafe Abortion,* 2nd ed. Geneva: WHO, 1994.
4. Hall RE: Therapeutic abortion, sterilization and contraception. *Am J Obstet Gynecol* 91:518–532, 1965.
5. *Roe v. Wade,* 410 US 113 (1973).
6. Henshaw S, Van Vort J: Abortion services in the United States, 1987 and 1988. *Fam Plann Perspect* 22:102–142, 1990.

CHAPTER 18

Menopause: Acceptance and Understanding of Its Impact

PonJola Coney
Robert C. Cefalo

**BODY RESPONSES TO ESTROGEN
   DEFICIENCY**
Central Nervous System Responses •
Physical Responses • Sexual Responses •
Osteoporosis • Cardiovascular Heart
Disease • Alzheimer's Dementia
**RISKS OF HORMONE REPLACEMENT
   THERAPY**
MANAGEMENT OF MENOPAUSE
Behavioral • Pharmacologic • General
Considerations (What to Tell the Patient)

M enopause is the second most common and predictable endocrine-metabolic event that occurs in the human female. Puberty is the first. The usual age for the last menstrual period is 50 ± 1.5 years. The classic clinical features of amenorrhea and hot flashes often obviate the necessity for a battery of testing to obtain a diagnosis. The climacteric characterizes the period prior to the cessation of menstruation when symptoms and changes in quantity and duration of menstrual flow may appear, reflecting some instability and decline in ovarian function. As life expectancy of the human female increases (it is now 84 years in the United States), the impact of menopause on the quality of a woman's life and health assumes even greater interest and importance. The physician who is the primary care provider for a woman as she reaches the perimenopausal years and beyond has an extremely important role to play. By making certain

that a woman is properly educated about and prepared for the changes that are likely to occur, and that she understands what preventive measures are important, and that the physician and the woman are cooperative partners in health care decisions, the primary care physician can make a substantial positive impact on the woman's physical and emotional well-being.

Body Responses to Estrogen Deficiency

Central Nervous System Responses

The most common affective phenomena seen at the time of the menopause are referable to the central nervous system and include, in order of frequency, hot flashes, fatigue, depression, headache, palpitations, and anxiety. As many as 30 percent of women display some significant degree of stress in response to the menopause. Reports suggest that approximately 16 percent of women are free of noticeable affective symptoms at the menopause.

The hot flash is a sensation of heat that is recurrent and often accompanied by sweating, flushing, anxiety, and chills. The hot flash usually lasts from two to five minutes, and may be associated with an increase in body temperature. Hot flashes can begin as soon as estrogen levels begin to decline in the climacteric. Some women endure hot flashes for as long as 10 years, and they can be disruptive to a sense of well-being and to daily function. Hot flashes are the primary reason women seek medical therapy for menopause.

They are most prevalent in the first two or three years postmenopause, and tend to be more intense and to last longer in women who undergo surgical menopause. Hot flashes do not show a consistent correlation with estrogen or gonadotropin levels. Kronenberg's epidemiologic survey of menopausal women with hot flashes revealed that how long they last is quite variable and that the pattern may change, becoming less frequent and less intense for some women, but continuing for many years for others. In the survey, 50 percent of women who experienced hot flashes said that the hot flashes began before menopause in the presence of regular menstrual cycles; others said that the hot flashes began more than two years after menopause. Hot flashes in this group varied considerably among women, with a frequency of 5 to 50 per day and lasting from 1 to 5 minutes. The surveyed women reported other affective discomforts during hot flashes, such as irritability or a sense of panic. Some women reported specific triggers of hot flashes, including stressful situations, caffeine, alcohol, confining space, and external heat.

Physical Responses

Estrogen deficiency can have substantial effects on the skin. Epidermal and skin-fold thickness diminish, and there are decreases in tensile strength, compressibility, turgor, and total skin collagen after the menopause. Estrogen binding to its receptor is greatest in the uterus, followed by face skin, breast skin, thigh skin, lung cells, and adipose tissue. Estrogen's effect on the vascular system, with its potential to modulate arteriolar and venous tone and to alter blood flow, can also influence skin physiology. With estrogen deficiency, breast tissue will lose some form and fullness, distribution of body hair changes, and pubic hair becomes sparse. Although hirsutism may develop, it is not pathologic. It reflects secretion of androgens primarily, instead of estrogen by the ovary.

In the absence of significant levels of circulating estrogen, the menopausal vaginal epithelium may become thin and dry, which may lead to vaginitis and sexual dysfunction. Lack of lubrication and regression of the upper vagina may lead to dyspareunia. Urethral cellular changes coincide with vaginal changes, and urinary symptoms may appear. Pelvic tissues may lose tone and predispose to prolapse.

Sexual Responses

Sexual response and libido gradually decline with age in both men and women. No obvious relationship between libido decline and menopause has been shown.

Osteoporosis

Bone loss begins before menopause and may be accelerated after menopause. Postmenopausal osteoporosis affects more than 20 million American women. One-third of women with osteoporosis suffer vertebral and hip fracture. Prior to fracture, no symptoms are associated with osteoporosis. The key to management is prevention. Lindsay was the first to show the protective effect of estrogen on bone preservation.

More recently, Stevenson randomized 66 early postmenopausal women to either continuous transdermal estrogen (0.05 mg) with norethisterone acetate or oral continuous premarin (0.625 mg) with norgestrel. Thirty women were untreated and served as controls. Bone density was measured by dual photon absorptiometry in the spine and three femoral sites. The untreated group lost 2.4 percent bone from the spine, 3.1 percent from the femoral neck, and 2.1 percent from the trochanteric region. The treated groups did not lose bone at any site, and there were slight gains in bone tissue for both transdermal and oral estrogen users at all sites. Estrogen promotes a decrease in osteoclastic resorption. It is more effective on trabecular bone than cortical bone, and will decrease hip and spinal fractures with long-term therapy.

Cardiovascular Heart Disease

Cardiovascular heart disease (CHD) is the chief cause of death in women and men in the western world. Before menopause, CHD mortality is lower in women than in men; after menopause, mortality in women rises to approach that of men. CHD risk is substantially increased in young women after spontaneous and surgically induced menopause. A tremendous amount of experimental evidence—observed, retrospective, and prospective—exists to support the beneficial or protective effects of estrogen against CHD. The exact magnitude of the associated protection is not clear. In 1983, the Lipid Research Clinics Study reported the all-cause mortality in estrogen users to be only half that of nonusers. The one contradictory report was from the Framingham Study, which did not suggest any such cardiovascular benefit. In the Framingham Study, estrogen use was associated with an increased incidence of stroke and CHD, despite a more favorable cardiovascular risk profile in the estrogen users. It is not difficult to draw the conclusion that estrogen probably protects against heart disease and stroke. Overviews of more than 30 reports, both retrospective and observed, estimate a reduction in CHD risk with the use of hormone replacement therapy.

Prospective cohort studies generally show that estrogen use reduces CHD. The largest cohort study is the Nurses' Health Study, which followed 48,000 menopausal women for 10 years and found the relative risk to be reduced at 0.89 for "ever" used and 0.56 for "current" users of estrogen. Evidence from epidemiologic studies indicates that estrogen reduces the risk of CHD by approximately 50 percent.

Data suggest that increased high-density lipoprotein (HDL) cholesterol (C) levels might be the biological mechanism by which estrogen confers protection. HDL-C is further subdivided into HDL and HDL subfractions. Sex hormones are known to alter lipid profiles. Estrogen therapy increases the HDL-C subfraction. HDL-C is the only hormone-sensitive risk factor marker known, at this time, to predict CHD risk. Within months after menopause, serum concentrations of total cholesterol rise by 6 percent, low-density lipoprotein (LDL) cholesterol by 11 percent, and triglycerides by 9 percent, with a gradual fall in HDL cholesterol. Treatment with oral estrogen lowers total serum cholesterol and LDL cholesterol and raises HDL. Estrogen typically lowers LDL by 15 to 19 percent and raises HDL by 16 to 18 percent.

The cardioprotective effect of estrogen appears to go far beyond the lipoprotein action. Estrogen may modulate vasomotor tone by increasing the production of nitric oxide (a vasodilator). Estrogen also enhances endothelial function and increases blood flow in vascular compartments. Estrogen may reduce coronary stenosis and increase survival after myocardial infarction and coronary surgery.

Alzheimer's Dementia

Estrogen may slow the progression and prevent the impairment associated with senile dementia and Alzheimer's disease. Estrogen has been shown to improve memory, orientation, space and time, and calculation tasks in patients with mild-to-moderate dementia.

Risks of Hormone Replacement Therapy

It is well-established that unopposed estrogen therapy in the presence of a uterus increases the patient's relative risk for endometrial cancer up to eightfold. Therefore, progestins are used in addition to estrogen when giving hormone replacement therapy to a woman who has a uterus. The potential risk that concerns the patient the most, however, is the risk for breast cancer. In a large Gallup poll survey of women to determine their perception of their most serious health risk, 46 percent incorrectly believed that the most serious health risk for women is breast cancer.

The association between HRT and breast cancer risk continues to be investigated. This potential association is discussed in detail elsewhere in this book. Some studies have shown an association, others have shown no association, and yet others have shown an association in particular subsets of women. A very important point to emphasize, however, is that most women have a much greater risk from cardiovascular disease (for which HRT reduces the risk) than for breast cancer (for which data on the effects of HRT are somewhat unclear). It should be emphasized to patients that for most women the benefits of HRT appear to substantially outweigh any potential risks. Obviously, care for any woman should be appropriately individualized.

Management of Menopause

Behavioral

An exercise program to improve physical fitness decreases all-cause mortality from a number of disease processes, including coronary heart disease, hypertension, diabetes, colon cancer, and possibly depression. Walking is the best exercise to prevent bone loss. Exercise stimulates HDL production.

Women should also be educated regarding the importance of good nutrition, calcium supplementation, smoking cessation, and drinking only in moderation. They should be told that appropriate weight reduction (for the overweight) and moderate exercise retards bone loss and improves the cardiovascular profile.

Pharmacologic

In addition to behavior modifications—and potentially more important for many women—is the pharmacologic management of menopausal symptoms and effects. The most crucial pharmacologic agent is estrogen. This very important topic is discussed at length later in the text.

General Considerations (What to Tell the Patient)

Education about the menopause is the first and best prescription to give a patient. She should be given comprehensive and accurate information regarding what we know about the menopause, and this information should be provided in a neutral manner. The patient should be armed with accurate information and given full opportunity to make her own decision regarding intervention. She should be told that therapies and recommendations continually change based on ongoing research.

Summary

Menopause is a universal and physiologic event. For some women it represents a psychological and biological crisis, and counseling and education by health care providers, as well as therapeutic interventions, can have a substantial beneficial effect. Symptoms can become severe, disabling, and intolerable for some, and the decision for medical intervention should be made between the patient and her physician. For those who desire medical therapy, epidemiologic data favor the use of estrogen to protect against accelerated bone mass loss; to reduce the incidence and severity of heart disease; to possibly decrease the risk of colorectal cancer and dementia; to improve psychological function; and to generally improve the quality of life. The evidence continues to grow and demonstrate that hormone replacement therapy can largely prevent or mitigate the disorders of aging for women. Despite the association in the literature of HRT with a modestly increased risk for breast cancer, the risk for death is decreased. For most women, HRT is not associated with a statistically significantly increased risk for breast cancer. Although for most women the benefits of hormone replacement therapy substantially outweigh any potential risk, there is currently no absolute consensus among medical professionals as to what the universal practice should be. The patient, her understanding of the benefits and risks, and her participation in the decisions regarding management are instrumental in the approach to menopause. The physician, working with the patient, can contribute greatly to the patient's well-being at this important time in her life.

References and Selected Readings

1. Bilezikian JP, Silverberg SJ: Osteoporosis: A practical approach to the perimenopausal woman. *J Women's Health* 1:21–27, 1992.
2. Block E: Quantitative morphological investigations of the follicular system in women. *Acta Anat* 14:108–23, 1952.
3. Bush TL, Cowan LD, Barrett-Connor E, et al: Estrogen use and all-cause mortality: Preliminary results from the Lipid Research Clinics Program follow-up study. *JAMA* 249:903–906, 1983.
4. Calaf I, Alsina J: Benefits of hormone replacement therapy—overview and update. *Int J Fertil Womens Med* 42(suppl):329–346, 1997.
5. Chen M-J, Longnecker MP, Morgenstern H, et al: Recent use of hormone replacement therapy and the prevalence of colorectal adenomas. *Cancer Epidemiol Biomarkers Prev* 7:227–230, 1998.
6. Cutler WB, Garcia CR: The menopausal transition and beyond, in *The Medical Management of Menopause and Premenopause,* Philadelphia: JB Lippincott, 1984, p 31.
7. Dupont WD, Page DL: Menopausal estrogen replacement therapy and breast cancer. *Arch Intern Med* 151:67–72, 1991.
8. Feldman BM, Voda AA, Gronseth E: The prevalence of hot flashes and associated variables among perimenopausal women. *Res Nurs Health* 8:261–268, 1985.
9. Gordon T, Kanel W, Hjortland M, McNamara P: Menopause and coronary heart disease. The Framingham Study. *Ann Intern Med* 89:157–216, 1978.
10. Henderson BE, Ross RK, Lobo RA, et al: Re-evaluating the role of progestogen therapy after the menopause. *Fertil Steril* 49:95–155, 1988.
11. Hirvoen E, Malkonen M, Manninen V: Effects of different progestogens on lipoproteins during postmenopausal replacement therapy. *N Engl J Med* 304:560–563, 1981.
12. Hughes BD, Dallal GE, Krall EA, et al: A controlled trial of the effect of calcium supplementation on bone density in postmenopausal women. *N Engl J Med* 323:878–883, 1990.
13. Kronenberg F: Hot flashes: Epidemiology and physiology, in *Multidisciplinary Perspectives on Menopause,* vol 592. New York: New York Academy of Science, 1990 p 52.
14. Lindsay R, Hart DM, Aitken JM, et al: Long-term prevention of postmenopausal osteoporosis by estrogen: Evidence for an increased bone mass after delayed onset of estrogen treatment. *Lancet* 1:1038–1041, 1976.
15. Etidronate for postmenopausal osteoporosis: *Med Lett Drugs Ther* 32:111, 1990.
16. McBee WL, Dailey ME, Dugan E, Shumaker SA: Hormone replacement therapy and other potential treatments for dementias. Endocrinol Metab Clin North Am 26:329–345, 1997.
17. Meldrum DR: Treatment of hot flashes, in Daniel R, Mishecc JR (eds): *Menopause Physiology and Pharmacology,* Chicago: Mosby Year Book, 1987, p 141.
18. Nachtigall LE, Nachtigall RH, Nachtigall RD, Beckman EM: Estrogen replacement therapy. I. A 10-year prospective study in the relationship to osteoporosis. *Obstet Gynecol* 53:277–281, 1979.
19. Nachtigall MJ, Smilen SW, Nachtigall RD, et al: Incidence of breast cancer in a 22-year study of women receiving estrogen-progestin replacement therapy. *Obstet Gynecol* 80:827–830, 1992.
20. Prelevic GM, Jacobs HS: New developments in postmenopausal hormone replacement therapy. *Curr Opin Obstet Gynecol* 9:207–212, 1997.
21. Sarrel P, Rousseau M, Mazure C, Glazer W: Ovarian steroids and the capacity to function at home and in the workplace, in *Multidisciplinary Perspectives on Menopause,* vol 592. New York: New York Academy of Science, 1990.
22. Sellers TA, Mink PJ, Cerhan, JR et al: The role of hormone replacement therapy in the risk for breast cancer and total mortality in women with a family history of breast cancer. *Ann Intern Med* 127:973–980, 1997.
23. Stampfer MJ, Colditz GA, Willett WC, et al: Postmenopausal estrogen and cardiovascular disease: 10-year follow-up from Nurses Health Study. *N Engl J Med* 325:756–762, 1991.
24. Stampfer MJ, Willett WC, Colditz GA, et al: A prospective study of postmenopausal estrogen therapy and coronary heart disease. *N Engl J Med* 313:1044–1049, 1985.
25. Stevenson JD, Cust MP, Gangar KF, et al: Effects of transdermal versus oral hormone replacement therapy on bone density in spine and proximal femur in postmenopausal women. *Lancet* 335:265–269, 1990.
26. Stolier AJ, Mera R, Schapira D: The impact of current use of hormone replacement therapy on prognostic factors and surgical treatment of new breast cancers. *Oncol Reports* 5:61–64, 1998.
27. Van Keep PA, Ser DM, Greenblatt RB, Kopera H:

Workshop report, in *Female and Male Climacteric: Current Opinion,* Baltimore: University Park Press, 1978.

28. Wahl P, Walden C, Knopp R, Hoover J: Effect of estrogen/progestin potency on lipid/lipoprotein cholesterol. *N Engl J Med* 308:862–867, 1983.

29. The Writing Group for the PEPI Trial:Effect of hormone therapy on bone mineral density (results from the postmenopausal estrogen progestin intervention (PEPI) trial). *JAMA* 276:1389–1395, 1996.

CHAPTER 19

Health Care Needs of the Older Woman

Leo J. Dunn

MEETING THE NEEDS OF THE ELDERLY

MEDICATIONS

DEPRESSION

HYPERTENSION

PELVIC FLOOR DYSFUNCTION—
  URINARY INCONTINENCE
Urge Incontinence • Stress Incontinence •
Overflow Incontinence • Therapy

ADVANCE DIRECTIVES AND POWER
  OF ATTORNEY

The older-age segment of the population of the United States will progressively increase as we move forward in the new millennium. The transition from a young and growing nation with an age distribution that was pyramidal into a more even distribution of ages that is rectangular in shape is now progressing, slowly reshaping toward an inverted pyramid as the age distribution favors the elderly. This transition carries with it major implications regarding health and its costs. An elderly population has many differences including gender distribution, quantity of services needed, incidence of chronic disease, ability to give self-care, and the need for assisted daily living. In direct proportion to age, the cost of providing care to this population is very high. Health care systems have estimated that the annual revenues in the senior citizen health market are $124 billion per year if assisted-living, skilled nursing, and home care industries

are combined. They estimate that whereas the proportion of our population over age 65 is currently 12 percent, it will be 20 percent by the year 2030, a 1 percent increase every 4 years. In preparation for that trend, the number of adult day care centers increased 113 percent in the 5 years ending in 1995, and assisted-living facilities and hospital geriatric assessment programs are increasing at the rate of 2 to 5 percent per year.

The definition of elderly is not static and not uniform. Physicians who practice obstetrics and gynecology commonly focus on the onset of menopause as a transition that reflects aging. The average age of menopause is approximately 51. Others use as a reference age 65 because it denotes the usual time at which most individuals become eligible for retirement and when most persons may enroll for Medicare health coverage. This definition may also be modified as the age of retirement is being moved upward. Laws now have eliminated forced retirement from most occupations. Textbooks of geriatric medicine appear to utilize the age of 75 and above as a definition. Therefore, there is no sentinel event in life that would distinguish those we consider aged, and definitions are arbitrary and subject to change.

The focus on menopause as a signal that the process of aging should be addressed in women is perhaps not unreasonable, as many important physiological changes can be noted at that time. It is an opportunity to initiate preventive measures if they have not already commenced, which is important to emphasize. It is likely that there will be two major directions in health care in the future that are of importance to this population. One is the focus on maintenance of health and prevention of disease, and the second is on standardization of the management of disease, especially chronic disorders.

The focus upon preventive medicine has been widely popularized as a mission of managed care, as it has been introduced as a potential system of health care throughout the nation. As this process has evolved, great emphasis has been placed upon the need to promote healthy living habits and to eliminate those behaviors that are known to increase risk for disease. The most commonly used measurement of the effectiveness of managed care organizations has been their capability to apply screening services such as mammography, and to provide preventive services such as immunization, to their population of patients. The outcome and potential benefit from this direction is more difficult to demonstrate than its utilization. Research is also being directed towards prevention. For example, the Women's Health Initiative, funded by NIH, is the largest clinical trial ever conducted in the world, and it is entirely focused on methods of prevention including the use of hormone replacement therapy, calcium intake, and low-fat diets to prevent disease.

On the other hand, it is recognized that the major cost factor to payers is the care of individuals with chronic diseases. One trend in managed care has been the assignment of populations of patients to primary care physicians who are expected to provide for as many of their needs as possible. A contrasting trend has been the carving out of populations with chronic disorders to be cared for by physicians with expertise in the care of those disorders, usually specialists. Both of these trends are based upon considerations of cost, but contain other implications for medical practice of the future.

Individual physicians should anticipate that measurements devised for evaluating the effectiveness of these programs eventually will be used as measures of the quality of care provided by them. The diligence with which a physician provides preventive services to those who are well, and provides services designated as essential for those with chronic diseases, may constitute the measures of quality of practice in the foreseeable future. The data systems that would permit such analyses in an accurate, timely, and affordable manner are a major thrust in the current milieu of change.

Cardiovascular disease is not only the most frequent major illness of women after menopause, it is the major cause of death. What influence can a primary care physician have upon this disease? Whereas some risk factors are not currently amenable to preventive services, such as a genetic influence and the influence of race, many other risk factors can be affected. Risk factors for cardiovascular disease include smoking, obesity, lack of physical exercise, poor management of environmental stress, and excessive use of alcohol, all of which are lifestyle issues known to be susceptible to counseling by physicians. Public awareness has been demonstrated by surveys that have shown that over 90 percent of women are aware of these diseases, indicating that public education measures have been effective. However, the same surveys indicate that only one-third of these women could recall their physician ever mentioning the diseases. The Joint National Committee on the Detection, Evaluation, and Treatment of High Blood Pressure indicates that only 27 percent of hypertensives in the United States have their disease under control. Prevention, detection, and treatment of the most common and lethal group of diseases for women at menopause can be greatly influenced by primary care physicians.

The primary care physician provides continuity of care to his or her patient throughout the menopause and into that phase of life designated as geriatric care. The management of menopause, hormone replacement therapy, and recommendations for health maintenance during this phase of life are covered elsewhere. It is an important responsibility and opportunity for the primary care physician, who can influence significantly each woman's future health by actions taken at this time.

The disorders that may affect women in their later years include all organ systems, and many acute and chronic diseases. They are discussed in several chapters throughout this book. A few specific disorders of substantial importance to women in this age group are highlighted in this chapter, as well as some general considerations regarding the care of the elderly woman. The physician must realize that in this nation, where women outlive men and where families are often widely scattered, one is often dealing with an aging woman who lives alone. The potential for isolation and its variety of effects on the individual should be explored at regular health visits.

Meeting the Needs of the Elderly

Physicians frequently identify patient needs that require the use of community resources. It is often difficult for individual practitioners to be aware of those resources so that they may incorporate them into their efforts to maintain patients' health and well-being.

Governmental concern regarding the aging population in the United States has been demonstrated in several ways, including the Older Americans Act of 1965. Its purpose was to provide social services to the elderly through a community-based network and to establish the Administration on Aging as an advocate for the elderly. The six Titles of the Act describe its philosophy and services:

Title I states that the policy objectives for services to older persons include income, health, housing, long-term care, and transportation.

Title II establishes the Administration on Aging and authorizes the Federal Council on Aging to advise the president.

Title III authorizes supportive nutrition and home-care service programs, most of which are through home-delivered meals and congregate meals.

Title IV provides federal funding for training,

research, and demonstration activities in the field of aging.

Title V awards funds to national organizations and state agencies to create jobs for low-income older workers in a variety of community service activities.

Title VI is a specific program for older Indians and native Hawaiians to provide supportive and nutritional services.

A variety of national programs are available for elderly citizens who qualify, including:

- Food stamp programs
- Congregate nutrition and home-delivered meals program
- Native American services
- Federal commodity donations
- Social Security
- Supplemental Security Income
- Medicare
- Medicaid
- Federal assisted housing programs
- Employment and training programs for older Americans

Other programs that may be available within a community include adult day care services; senior centers; transportation services; older-American volunteer programs; in-home health aides and personal care services; homemaker and chore services; respite and caregiver support services; and minor home repair services. Information about such services can be obtained by contacting the Agency on Aging.

The Nutrition Screening Initiative provides two levels of screening to be applied by a health professional. The Level I Screen uses a nomogram to compute the formula to determine the body mass index (BMI). A BMI <22 or >27, or a weight change of plus or minus 10 pounds in 6 months, is indicative of a possible nutrition problem. A series of questions on eating habits, living environment, and functional status are also provided to aid in identifying persons who require nutritional assessment.

The Level II screen also uses the BMI criteria used in Level I, but adds anthropometric measurements, such as midarm muscle circumference and triceps skinfold. It also requires determination of serum albumin and cholesterol. The questions provided for assessment ask about drug use, symptoms of oral or dental disease, eating habits, living environment, functional status, and mental and cognitive status. Patients with anthropometric measurements ≤10th percentile or a skinfold >95th percentile, a serum albumin below 3.5 g/dl or a cholesterol <160 mg/dl or >240 mg/dl require further nutritional assessment.

Medications

Physicians who care for the elderly are aware of the importance of the pharmacologic aspects of their care. Older patients are more likely than others to be taking multiple medications, which they often obtain from a variety of sources. Therefore, at each visit it is advisable to ask for a recitation of what medications the patient is now using. A more accurate method is to encourage the patient to bring a list from home, including the correct name and prescribed dose, or to bring in their containers of medicines, which can provide an amazing display of pharmaceuticals.

A common experience is the failure of the patient to take the medication as prescribed. It has been estimated that as many as 50 percent of elderly patients take their medications incorrectly. Written instructions to the patient are often more helpful than the usual directions typed on the container itself. Arikian and co-workers, in their review of the economics of hormone replacement therapy (HRT), noted that although 10 years of continuous therapy was advocated for the prevention of osteoporosis, utilization and compliance were major impediments in achieving protection for a population. In their evaluation, only 10 percent of women in a susceptible age range received prescriptions for HRT, 20 to 30 percent of those never filled the prescription, 20 percent of those who filled the prescriptions stopped within nine months, and 10 percent of those who continued took the medication sporadically. The reasons behind these failures are of pragmatic importance and include unresolved fears, misunderstandings, and the need for more user-friendly packaging.

A general concern in the use of medications by the elderly is a narrowed therapeutic index, as their tolerance decreases and their responses become altered. In addition, the use of many medications increases the risk of drug interactions. Because patients may obtain their medications from different pharmacies, they should be encouraged to take their full medication list with them when they fill any prescription so that the pharmacist may check for potential problems.

Depression

Women are more subject to depression than are men, with a reported ratio of 2 : 1. Although a common perception is that depression increases in frequency with age, the mean incidence of the disorder is about age 40. It is a condition recognized in adolescence and that can occur at any age, including postmenopausal and later years. It is not correct to consider symptoms of depression as an expected event associated with the aging process. Situational changes in anyone's life that involve personal loss—whether economic, social, companionship, health, or loss of a loved one—can give rise to symptoms common to depression. These symptoms are more akin to grief reactions than to true depression. The frequency with which one might face such situations does increase with age, and this may explain the perception of depression as part of the aging process. Although depression is not an uncommon problem in older women, it also may be overdiagnosed. Avoidance of misdiagnosis is important; therefore, a careful interview to expose the life events that may have caused the patient's symptoms is a necessary part of evaluation. The topic of depression is discussed in depth in Chap. 55.

Not every patient with depression is placed on medication. The importance of counseling and interpersonal interventions, whether or not the woman is placed on medication, cannot be overstated. Some medications currently considered effective for depression are tricyclic and heterocyclic antidepressants, selective serotonin reuptake inhibitors, and monoamine oxidase inhibitors. The older patient may have conditions that are affected by antidepressants, such as glaucoma, constipation, cardiac arrhythmias, and some neurologic conditions. Patients who have had strokes or who have dementia such as Alzheimer's disease may have untoward effects from these drugs, such as delirium.

Particularly in the elderly, it is obvious that initiation of pharmacotherapy for depression requires very close follow-up. Because some medications may interfere with cardiac conduction and rhythm, patients receiving these medications require a pretherapy baseline ECG and periodic repeat studies to evaluate the QRS complex. The patient should be told what to expect from the medication, how soon improvement may be noted, and what risks and side effects are likely. A decision should be made regarding psychiatric consultation. The need for psychiatric consultation depends on the patient's symptoms and the breadth of the primary care physician's experience. Patients with severe symptoms, those who are unresponsive to medication, or those who have recurrences, should have in-depth psychiatric evaluation. Any patient who is a significant suicide risk requires immediate psychiatric intervention.

Hypertension

In most countries, hypertension does not usually make its appearance in later life, but late-onset hypertension is found in the United States. Because cardiovascular diseases are of such impor-

tance in the elderly, and because hypertension is a major cause of these disorders, all primary care physicians should make an effort to control abnormal elevations of either systolic or diastolic blood pressure. The Joint National Committee on Detection, Evaluation, and Treatment of High Blood Pressure, funded by the National Institutes of Health, has provided important guidelines. These are discussed in Chap. 60.

Both a personal and family history regarding coronary heart disease, cardiovascular disease, stroke, diabetes, dyslipidemia, renal disease, and gout should be taken of a patient diagnosed as hypertensive. Specific information should be obtained regarding the duration of the hypertension, previous antihypertensive therapy, weight gain, diet, alcohol use, smoking, and the use of medications that might cause blood pressure elevation.

During the physical examination the physician should document the presence of sustained hypertension in both arms; measure height and weight; perform a funduscopic examination for retinal vascular changes; and examine the neck for carotid bruits, distended veins, or thyroid enlargement. Physical examination should include examination of the heart for size, rate, rhythm, and sounds, as well as auscultation of the abdomen for bruits and palpation for kidney enlargement or abnormal aortic pulsations. Peripheral pulses should be assessed, a neurologic examination performed, and any edema described.

Routine laboratory tests include urinalysis, complete blood count, a fasting blood glucose, potassium, calcium, creatinine, uric acid, lipid profile, and ECG. Some tests done for specific indication include urinary microscopic and albumin determination, echocardiography, and plasma renin/urinary sodium determination. The management of patients with hypertension is discussed in Chap. 60.

The medical literature offers supportive evidence that when blood pressure is controlled, there is a distinct reduction in stroke incidence and a definite but lesser reduction in coronary heart disease. These benefits are seen in older patients whose blood pressure is adequately controlled; they are not limited to younger age groups.

Isolated systolic hypertension (ISH) was once considered a natural consequence of vascular rigidity and an inevitable consequence of aging. Studies have shown that treatment of ISH does decrease the risk of stroke, and therefore should not be overlooked.

Pelvic Floor Dysfunction— Urinary Incontinence

A major problem for aging women is urinary incontinence. Although this has been the primary focus for investigation and treatment, it is only one manifestation of the broader entity referred to as "pelvic floor dysfunction" (PFD). PFD includes a variety of manifestations of loss of anatomical support and pelvic nerve damage that most commonly are initiated by childbirth and worsened by aging. Well-known anatomical manifestations include cystourethrocele, rectocele, enterocele, and uterine prolapse. Functional loss with urinary incontinence and fecal incontinence are among the most troublesome manifestations. The inability to control urine or feces loss may make the difference between relatively independent living at home and the need for institutional care. The economic difference is considerable as well.

The most frequent problem is urinary incontinence. Incontinence has been estimated by the Agency for Health Care Policy and Research (AHCPR) to affect 15 to 30 percent of noninstitutionalized persons over age 60, and more than 50 percent of 1.5 million nursing home residents. The agency estimates that the cost of caring for these individuals exceeds $10 billion annually. The AHCPR has published a clinical practice guideline for "Urinary Incontinence in Adults." Although these guidelines are subject to revision with time, they are the basis for the following information.

Several types of incontinence have been identified:

Urge Incontinence (Fig. 19-1)

Definition: The involuntary loss of urine associated with an abrupt and strong desire to void.

Symptoms: Patients usually complain that they cannot get to the bathroom quickly enough, they leak urine when hearing or touching running water, or they void very frequently day or night and may have bed wetting.

Physical Findings: No specific, characteristic findings.

Laboratory Findings:

- Involuntary detrusor contractions are most common.
- Urethral instability with involuntary urethral relaxation.
- Detrusor hyperactivity with impaired bladder contractility has also been described.

Stress Incontinence (Fig. 19-2)

Definition: The involuntary loss of urine during coughing, sneezing, laughing, or other physical activities that increase intra-abdominal pressure.

Symptoms: Patients usually complain of urine loss with coughing, sneezing, laughing, rising from a chair, or during exercise.

Physical Findings: Hypermobility or significant displacement of the bladder neck demonstrable by the "Q-tip test." Visible loss of urine with coughing induced as part of the examination.

Laboratory Findings: No test is absolutely diagnostic. Dynamic urethral profilometry frequently demonstrates the dominance of intravesical pressure over intraurethral pressure during coughing.

Overflow Incontinence

Definition Involuntary loss of urine associated with overdistension of the bladder.

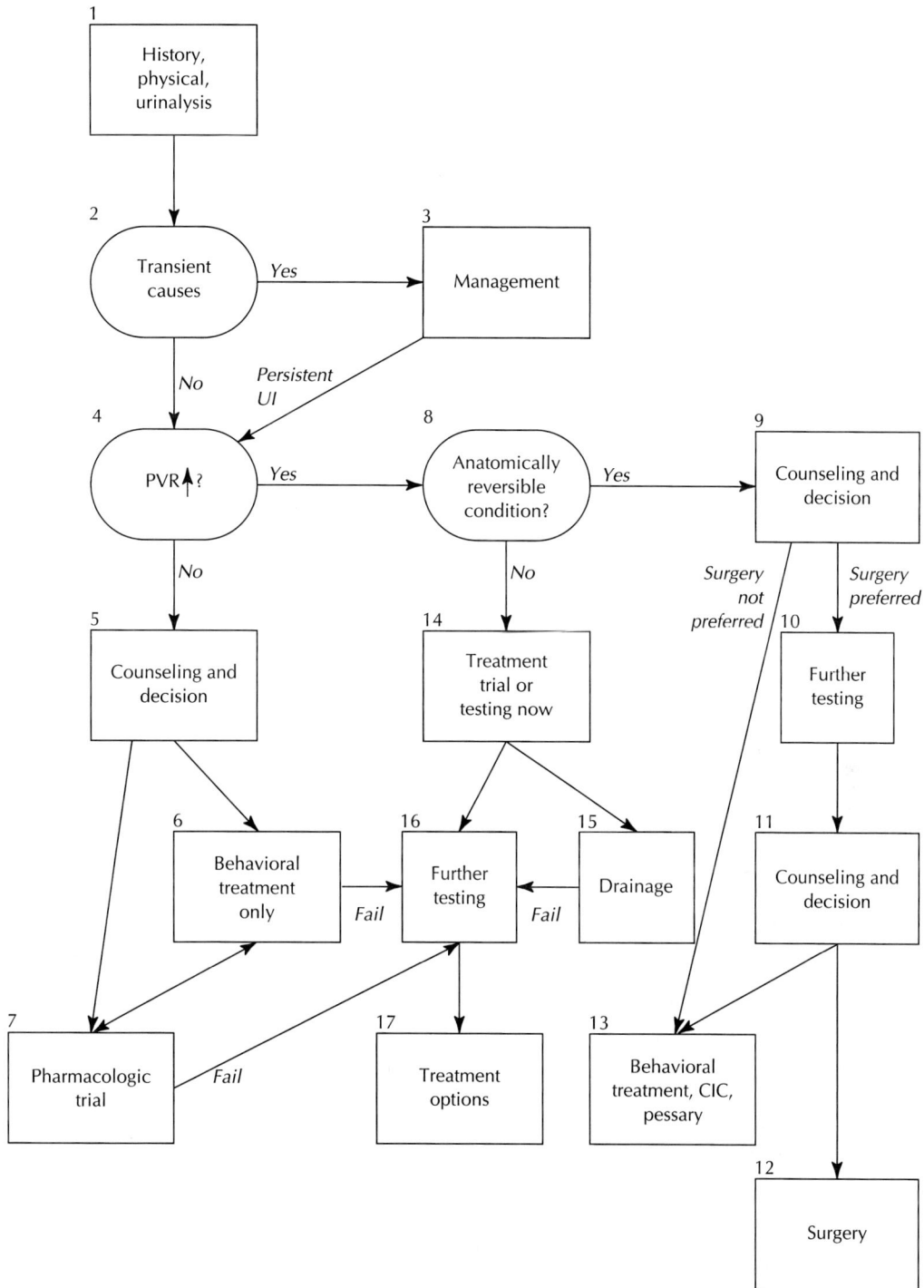

Figure 19-1. Female urge incontinence. (From *Urinary Incontinence in Adults—Quick Reference Guide for Clinicians,* U.S. Department of Health and Human Services, 1992.) Key: PVR = Post void residual; UI = Urinary incontinence; CIC = Clean intermittent catheterization.

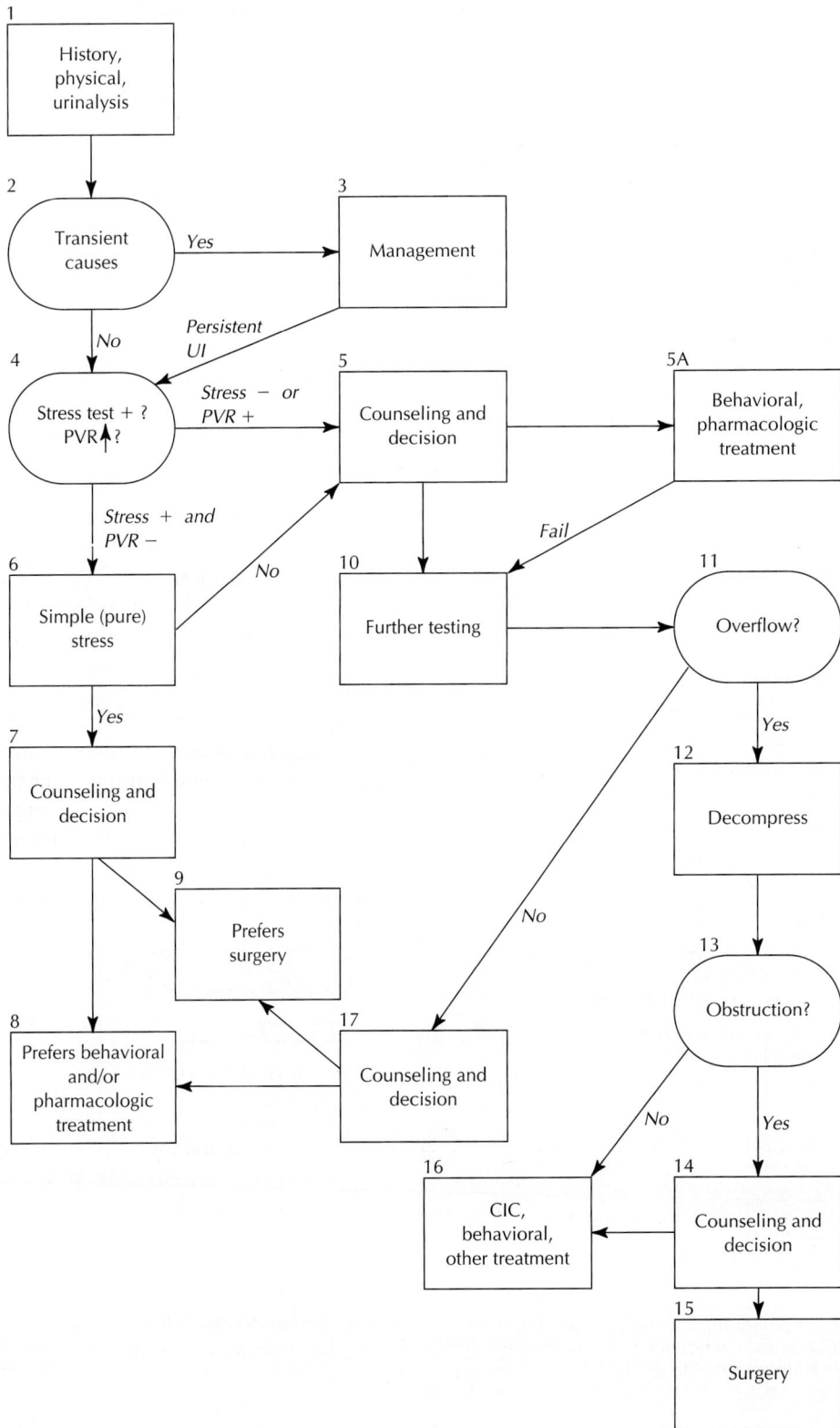

1 History, physical, urinalysis

2 Transient causes — Yes → 3 Management

No

Persistent UI

4 Stress test + ? PVR↑? — Stress − or PVR + → 5 Counseling and decision → 5A Behavioral, pharmacologic treatment

Stress + and PVR −

6 Simple (pure) stress — No → 5 Counseling and decision

5 → 10 Further testing

5A → Fail → 10 Further testing

10 Further testing → 11 Overflow?

6 Simple (pure) stress — Yes → 7 Counseling and decision

7 Counseling and decision → 9 Prefers surgery

7 Counseling and decision → 8 Prefers behavioral and/or pharmacologic treatment

11 Overflow? — Yes → 12 Decompress

11 Overflow? — No → 17 Counseling and decision

12 Decompress → 13 Obstruction?

17 Counseling and decision → 9 Prefers surgery

17 Counseling and decision → 8 Prefers behavioral and/or pharmacologic treatment

13 Obstruction? — No → 16 CIC, behavioral, other treatment

13 Obstruction? — Yes → 14 Counseling and decision

14 Counseling and decision → 16 CIC, behavioral, other treatment

14 Counseling and decision → 15 Surgery

160

Symptoms Patients usually complain that they lose small amounts of urine day and night, feel that they must void but cannot, void small amounts of urine and still feel full, void frequently at night, spend a long time at voiding and produce only a weak or dribbling stream.

Physical Findings Usually none except for palpation of a urine-filled bladder. If neuropathy is the cause, neurologic examination may show sensory or motor deficits. If obstruction is the cause, vaginal relaxation or obstructing tumors may be demonstrated.

Laboratory Findings A cystometrogram would be expected to show an atonic bladder of large capacity. A postvoid residual urine volume would be expected to be large. When obstructive pathology is present, a voiding uroflowmetry study should show an obstructive pattern.

Therapy

Not uncommonly, patients will have mixed forms of urinary incontinence (usually urge and stress together), or they may have such complicating conditions as cystitis, respiratory disease, excessive fluid intake, use of diuretics, mental impairment, or emotional problems. A thorough evaluation is necessary before considering a method of therapy.

Treatment methods include behavioral, pharmacologic, and surgical.

Algorithims have been proposed by the AHCPR for the management of urge incontinence and stress incontinence as follows:

Behavioral Methods

- Bladder retraining
- Timed voiding
- Prompted voiding
- Pelvic muscle exercises

Adjunctive techniques include:

- Biofeedback
- Vaginal cones
- Electrical stimulation

Pharmacologic Therapy

Urge Incontinence Drugs that have been used include propantheline, oxybutynin, tricyclic antidepressants, and terodiline. These have varying degrees of success and have significant side effects. Physicians prescribing them should be familiar with the risks and benefits before advocating their use.

Stress Incontinence Drugs that have been used to treat urethral sphincter insufficiency as a cause of stress incontinence are phenylpropanolamine and estrogen. The risks, benefits, and contraindications should be carefully evaluated by the physician for each patient before using these drugs.

Surgical Therapy The various procedures devised for treatment of incontinence, their indications, contraindications, complications, risks and benefits are described elsewhere. However, the basic requirements are that the patient has had a work-up sufficiently complete to arrive at an accurate diagnosis and that there has been a trial of nonsurgical therapy of sufficient vigor and duration to assure that surgery is necessary. The operating surgeons should be entirely familiar with the patient's problem and should possess the skill necessary to perform a variety of procedures so that the correct one suited to the patient's specific need can be performed.

Advance Directives and Power of Attorney

Although it is beyond the scope of this chapter to provide details on the issues of advance directives and power of attorney, they are important considerations, especially for the elderly. Laws relating to these issues, such as living wills, vary by

---

Figure 19-2. Female stress incontinence. (From *Urinary Incontinence in Adults—Quick Reference Guide for Clinicians,* U.S. Department of Health and Human Services, 1992.)

state. Patients should be informed and encouraged to take action on these issues well in advance of need. The medical implications are substantial, and care in the absence of such documents can become quite problematic for physicians, institutions, and families. Many medical societies provide such information, which can be displayed in an office and made available to each patient.

References and Selected Readings

1. Arikian S, Bootman JL, Fish L(ed): *The Economics of Hormone Replacement Therapy.* Philadelphia, PA: Medical Education Systems, 1998.
2. *Cardiovascular Disease in Women: APGO Educational Series on Women's Health Issues, Medical Education Collaborative.* Golden, CO: 1998.
3. Furrow, et al: *Health Law,* St. Paul, MN: West Publishing, 1995.
4. National Institutes of Health: *Report of the Joint National Committee on Prevention, Detection, Evaluation, and Treatment of High Blood Pressure.* Washington, DC: National High Blood Pressure Education Program, National Heart, Lung, and Blood Institute, 1997. NIH Publication 98-4080.
5. *Nutrition Interventions Manual for Professionals Caring for Older Americans.* American Academy of Family Physicians, The American Dietetic Association, and National Council on the Aging, 1992.
6. Snow C: Senior services. *Mod Healthcare* 27(24):26, 1997.
7. *Urinary Incontinence in Adults—Quick Reference Guide for Clinicians.* Washington, DC: US Department of Health and Human Services, 1992.

CHAPTER 20

The Patient's Perspective: What a Teenage Woman Expects from Her Physician

Jessica L. Brach
Arianna F. Faucetta

During the last decade there has been an increasing awareness of the unique health care needs of women, and of the necessity to deliver a complete range of care that addresses reproductive health, general physical health, preventive care, and psychosocial well-being. Simultaneously, there has been a growing realization of the importance of providing to adolescent and teenage females health care services that are carefully targeted to the particular needs and concerns of this group.

During a female's teenage years, which are the bridge between childhood and maturity, her body and mind undergo substantial changes. Coping with these changes can be difficult. Proper help and guidance are necessary to make these transitional years as smooth and stable as possible. One of the individuals who can and should significantly aid a teenage girl in these developing years is her physician.

Medical expertise on the part of the physician is assumed; it is a wide range of other factors, central to the type of relationship a teenager has with her physician, that determines the long-term value of the interaction to the patient. Various essential elements are expected by a teenage woman in relating to her physician. Concern, interest, and compassion are the foundation of a supportive interaction; it is important that these aspects be present in a relationship between a patient and her physician for the relationship to be most constructive. To be fully beneficial to the patient, a young woman's relationship with her physician must also be based on trust, honesty, and knowledge. In this relationship, a teenager also expects confidentiality. Often a teenager needs to discuss a sensitive topic, but has no one in whom she feels comfortable confiding. If a physician makes it clear to the patient that sensitive issues will be addressed on a confidential basis, a teenager will likely be more forthcoming and the physician will be better able to provide needed care.

Teenagers may not yet be adults, but they are also not children anymore. They rightfully expect a physician to respect their intelligence and provide accurate, informative answers. Some doctors might avoid difficult subjects or hide behind lengthy and circuitous explanations because they feel that the teenager is not sufficiently mature to handle the situation. This often constitutes a disservice to the teenager and adversely affects her health care. A teenage woman needs informative answers and clear explanations. She will be making many choices about her lifestyle during her teenage years, and it is imperative that she be fully informed. A doctor's ability to provide honest, educational answers can greatly influence a teenage woman's decisions and positively affect her present and future life.

It is often difficult for a physician to ascertain what information is appropriate for an individual adolescent. What is appropriate depends on the adolescent's level of education, social environment, and a variety of personal issues. While not all teenage girls face the same problems, many of their concerns are similar, and the same facts and information are likely to be important to each of them. Although a doctor may not be certain whether a particular teenage girl is sexually active, information concerning protection against sexually transmitted diseases (STDs), avoiding unintended pregnancy, and maintaining healthy relationships is always important. Emergency contraception may be an issue particularly for sexually active teens, but it is also a concern for rape victims. Information on how to deal with possible emergencies is also generally useful; patients want to know whom to contact and how to reach them in case of a problem that will not wait.

Physicians may wish to begin difficult conversations with a teen by first discussing sensitive topics in a general fashion, and then becoming increasingly specific depending upon the teenager's responses. In offering information on highly personal subjects, physicians might have to walk a fine line; but it is clear that no harm can come from people being well informed. Physicians should be ready and willing to discuss difficult topics openly, but must concurrently be aware of the stresses, strains, and pitfalls in a teenage woman's world. It is impossible for doctors to be fully beneficial to teenagers without a significant comprehension of the lives of their patients. It is important that the teenager be invited to continue to discuss these matters with her physician confidentially, at any time in the future. Knowledge, understanding, and access can only serve to assist teenagers in making good decisions and in helping protect themselves.

Teenagers do not react well to being talked down to or lectured. This is one reason teenage females are notorious for fighting with their parents. While doctors must endeavor to provide their patients with comprehensive current health care information, physicians must do so with demonstrated respect for their adolescent and teenage patients' abilities. Many teenage girls are, in their minds, if not always in fact, beyond the point at which they need their doctor to speak privately to their parents after a consultation. Usually, they do not want the physician to speak with their parents at all about particular issues. If a teenager is to become more self-sufficient and deal with her own health in a responsible manner and without intervention of adult family members, she must be provided with sufficient information to do so.

Another point that should not be ignored is that physicians should not assume that teenagers know what may seem to the physician to be obvious about health care. Teenagers are frequently extraordinarily underinformed if not wholly misinformed. Some have parents who are not well-educated about basic health matters, or who are so uncomfortable discussing sensitive issues that they avoid them entirely. Some school systems do not cover many personal health topics appropriately. Some teenage patients, unsurprisingly, may not have bothered to pay attention. And some preposterous stories persist despite their lack of any serious foundations. For all these reasons, a physician with teenage patients must be prepared to be the teenager's primary source of reliable health-related information.

Teenagers may well have health care needs or questions that don't fall within their primary physician's expertise. However, because most teenage girls see only one physician (who may be an internist, a gynecologist, a pediatrician, or a family practitioner), physicians who provide care for teenage women must have a well-rounded background in medicine. They must make certain that the teenager is receiving preventive care and education, reproductive health care as needed, and general medical care, and that significant psychosocial issues are not ignored. If specific questions are beyond a doctor's knowledge, that doctor must know to whom to refer the patient.

Adolescent females commonly experience some degree of confusion concerning their roles and their fit; they are sometimes teenage girls, sometimes teenage women, and sometimes both. Teenage years can be difficult, and it is essential that a doctor be able to distinguish between the minor anxieties of being a teenage girl and the major psychosocial problems (such as depression, eating disorders, or abuse) that too many people that age experience. Most teenage girls suffer a certain degree of displeasure with their bodies or other aspects of themselves. This can be the stimulus for a program of healthy dieting and exercise, but it can just as easily be the precursor of dangerous eating disorders. The better a doctor gets to know a patient, the more likely it is that the physician will notice features of or changes in a patient's behavior that could be important warning signals.

Being a good doctor to a teenage girl is not significantly different from being a good doctor to a woman of any age. The prescription for the doctor is simple to state, though not nearly so easy to follow: be knowledgeable, interested, respectful, informative, and approachable; know your patient, build a relationship of trust, and fully inform the patient; trust in the patient's ability to understand choices and consequences and to make decisions, but do not assume much about the quantity or sophistication or accuracy of your teenage patient's medical and health care knowledge. In following this prescription, the physician will materially help the teenage patient learn to become the primary protector of her own health.

CHAPTER 21

The Patient's Perspective: What the Reproductive-Age Woman Wants and Needs from Her Physician

Mara Pearse Burke

What does a woman in her reproductive years want and need from her physician? The answer is simple: she wants "good" medical care. That little word "good," however, is deceptively complex. In the traditional sense of the physician-patient relationship, practicing "good" medicine meant doing what was in the best interest of the patient. The patient trusted her physician to place her welfare above all other things. The woman in her reproductive years wants and needs what any patient wants and deserves from a physician—justified trust that her physician will lead her to the best information regarding her condition and will provide fair access to the remedies and technologies that may aid in the maintenance of her health.

In the current health care environment, where the traditional provision of medical care has changed so much in the past few years, many patients believe that "good" medical care means something far different than it did in years past. However, that is not really true. Common practices may have changed, but the definition of "good" has not changed. In today's environment, medical care is often delivered in a different format and patients must take a realistic view of how external forces, such as evolving economics, advancing technology, and societal change, influence the provision of good medical care. The provider of professional services always has some potential degree of conflict of interest with the vulnerable patient. That is why trust and trustworthiness are of primary importance to the patient, regardless of the form or economic structure under which those services are delivered. In the fee-for-service format, the patient must be

confident that she will not be offered unnecessary services, and in the capitated format, the patient must trust that she will be offered necessary services. For most physicians and their patients, the balance of "good" medicine and trust is the solid foundation of their physician-patient relationship.

Webster's defines "trust" as "assured reliance on the character, ability, strength, or truth of someone or something", "one in which confidence is placed", and "to permit [one]... to do something without fear or misgiving." Physicians and patients engage in a special relationship based on this element of trust; trust is the reason why a patient will submit her body to the inspection, questioning, and probing of a stranger. In the early twentieth century, that trust was naturally assumed by patients. Today, that trust is not so often assumed; instead, it must be earned by the corporate entities that provide care to patients, whether they be insurance companies or professional organizations, and by the individual practitioners within those organizations. Today, informed patients question recommended treatments, and the medical profession, in general, is not held in unquestioned esteem.

Physician visits in a woman's reproductive years are different than at any other time in her life. She, of course, has the need for preventive care, screening, and attention to general medical problems. She also has special concerns above and beyond those of other healthy patients, and thus has special requirements for her relationship with her health care provider. The unique concerns of the woman contemplating or experiencing pregnancy, the physical and emotional factors surrounding birth or miscarriage, and the physical and psychological changes in preparation for menopause require that the woman have social and psychological support as well as technically competent medical care. That support should be a mandatory component of health care, in whatever form health care must take in response to economic, social, and scientific changes.

When a positive physician-patient relationship develops, the patient has confidence in the physician's technical knowledge, skills, and experience. Physicians earn the trust of their patients by their own actions: by being their patients' advocates and by adhering to the principles that have attributed virtue to the profession of medicine. Physicians, and the entities hiring them, should recognize the perceived value placed upon medical care by the public and the honorable tradition of the profession created by their predecessors. Patients trust their physicians to appropriately inform them of options and to offer timely advice; to sustain their rights as patients and as women; to appropriately delegate care to others in whom the physicians have placed their own trust; to be abreast of current research and new technologies; to engage in collegial relationships with other professionals involved in their patient' care; and to acknowledge their own limitations in instances where they may not be the best care provider for the patient. In this way, total competence, in both technical and moral aspects, is assumed by the patient and the physician-patient relationship remains strong.

The physician-patient relationship, founded in trust, is strengthened by open communication between the two parties. Communication is the key element in patient autonomy and thus of true informed consent. The more the patient knows, the more she can control her well-being and make informed decisions about the course of her medical care. Effective communication is, of course, a two-way street. Physicians who openly and fully communicate with their patients trust them to use information wisely in their decision making and to share relevant information with them. Additionally, physicians must effectively listen and interpret correctly their patients' communication.

Ultimately, what the reproductive-age woman wants and needs from her physician is a trustworthy, competent, caring physician practicing "good" medicine, acknowledging the boundaries of medical science, using judgment to apply wisdom appropriately, and attending patients with honesty and empathy. Ideally, that care encompasses prevention, education, screening and early detection, concern for psychosocial needs, and the scope of reproductive health and general medical concerns.

Selected Readings

Bayles MD: The Professions: *Ethical Issues in Professional Life.* Callahan JC (ed): New York: Oxford University Press, 1988.

Drane JF: Becoming a Good Doctor, *The Place of Virtue and Character in Medical Ethics.* Kansas City, MO: Sheed & Ward, 1988.

Monagie JF, Thomasma DC: *Medical Ethics, A Guide for Health Professionals.* Rockville, MD: Aspen Publications, 1988.

Pellegrino ED, Thomasma DC: *For the Patient's Good. The Restoration of Beneficence in Health Care.* New York: Oxford University Press, 1988.

Reiser SJ: *Medicine and the Reign of Technology.* Cambridge, UK: Cambridge University Press, 1978.

Rothman DJ: *Strangers at the Bedside.* New York: Basic Books, 1991.

Willis D (ed): The changing character of the medical profession. *Milbank Q.* 66:1–202, 1988.

CHAPTER 22

The Patient's Perspective: What the Perimenopausal Woman Wants and Needs from Her Physician

Martha C. Romans

Newspaper headlines have trumpeted that the generation of women born during the baby boom of the late 1940s to early 1950s is now entering menopause. Some 15 million women strong, this generation has shaped consumer, social, and economic trends for decades. What do they expect of their physicians as they move through menopause? This chapter provides some answers to that question.

Most women in the United States experience menopause between the ages of 45 and 55. However, many women begin to experience changes in their menstrual cycles in their early 40s, and for some the transition is not fully complete until their late 50s. Thus, the term *perimenopause* describes women somewhere along a continuum of about 20 years.

A pollster recently described women in this middle-age range as the "great negotiators." They juggle multiple roles as wives, mothers, daughters, and employees. With respect to the health care system, they often serve as the primary care managers for their partners, children, and aging parents, in addition to themselves. Whereas younger women may be more assertive, and older women may be more willing to "put up with it," women in the middle are the negotiators, trying to work with and through the health care system to get what they or their loved ones need.

During the perimenopausal years, women begin to shift their focus from reproductive health care to other nonreproductive health issues. General health and wellness, and prevention of chronic disease and disability, become more viable concerns.

Women in midlife take prevention seriously and look to their health care provider to recommend routine screenings, to counsel about lifestyle issues, and to become familiar with their family histories. Opportunities for positive interventions abound, as approximately 21 percent of adult women in the United States smoke, 26 percent report they are overweight, and 31 percent report no leisure-time physical activity. Significant numbers of women in the perimenopausal age group have one or more risk factors for cardiovascular disease, including high blood pressure, high cholesterol, and diabetes. Pap screening rates are lower among women over age 45, compared to women 18 to 44 years of age, and breast cancer screening rates, highest among women 40 to 49 years of age, are lower among women over 50 and lower still among women over 65.[1]

The current era is often referred to as the "information age." Perimenopause is also an "information age," and women's desire for information about menopause and willingness to discuss it openly have never been greater. Women are prime consumers of health information; one has only to look at the popular media for the omnipresent health advice column to know this is true. Apart from health care professionals, women derive health information from a variety of sources including friends and family members, books, magazines, television, newsletters and newspapers, and, increasingly, the Internet. These information sources often reinforce important messages regarding diet, exercise, and the role of health screenings. However, reliance on sources such as the popular media can skew women's perceptions of the major risk factors that they face, or create confusion when contradictory research reports appear. For example, media coverage of breast cancer, while important, has resulted in women overestimating their risk for breast cancer, while underestimating their risk for heart disease and lung cancer, which are less well covered, but which pose a greater risk of death for most women than breast cancer.

In addition to women's great interest in and access to information about health care matters, this generation possesses a determination to be active decision makers with respect to their care. In light of this, the role of the physician takes on a somewhat different character. The physician becomes the arbiter of science, the expert who can efficiently weigh the various claims and reports and help a woman make sense of them in terms of her history, her values, and her choices.

Probably no issue better illustrates the gulf that sometimes exists between practitioners and the public than questions regarding the role of hormone replacement therapy. Whereas many physicians enthusiastically endorse hormone replacement therapy for treatment of menopausal symptoms, and for longer-term use to prevent osteoporosis and decrease the risk of heart disease and cognitive difficulties, women have been more reluctant to embrace it. Their concerns are many; some believe that menopause is a normal change, and that exogenous hormones are unnatural and may be dangerous; other believe the side effects they experience are too uncomfortable and that "it's not worth it." Some women prefer "natural" alternatives, ranging from changes in lifestyle to use of alternative products, some tried and true, some of questionable efficacy. What is certain is that our knowledge is still evolving, and that every perimenopausal woman should be counseled about the risks and benefits surrounding the use of hormone replacement therapy.

The goal of counseling should not be to persuade a woman to accept a specific recommendation, but rather to educate a woman so that she can make an informed decision. This decision should be based on the woman's personal history, her "risk tolerance," to borrow a phrase from the field of finance, and other values. Informed choices about therapy include an understanding of the purpose and duration of treatment, whether short- or long-term, and the expected benefits and risks. Such extensive counseling may be somewhat more difficult to achieve due to increasing physician time constraints, but it need not be accomplished in a single visit. Just as menopause itself involves a gradual transition, the dialogue between a woman and her physician about strategies for protecting her health and well-being during the perimenopausal and menopausal years should begin before the first hot flash, and continue beyond the cessation of her menstrual periods.

Women in their reproductive years use a variety of practitioners for their primary care: some rely on an obstetrician-gynecologist, others use an internist or family practitioner, while still others seek concurrent care, that is, they use an obstetrician-gynecologist for certain services and a primary care physician for other needs. In the perimenopausal years, this fragmentation of care may become more pronounced, with more visits to more practitioners, increasing the likelihood that needed care may be postponed or foregone.

When provided a choice, many women prefer a comprehensive woman's health center at which most of her basic health care needs are met in a single visit. Beyond patient convenience, comprehensive centers can offer education and counseling services and access to a range of providers, including physicians, psychologists, nurses and nurse practitioners, and dieticians, working together as part of an integrated team. These centers recognize that individual practitioners are unlikely to be competent in every aspect of care, that the various disciplines can combine to take care of the whole patient, and that the woman herself is a crucial member of the health care team.[2,3]

Women entering menopause today want information in order to make informed choices, convenient access to care, and assistance with preventing illness and disability. They are better informed than their mothers were, and convinced that they play a fundamentally important role on the health care team.

References and Selected Readings

1. Horton JA (ed): *State Profiles on Women's Health.* Washington, DC: Jacobs Institute of Women's Health, 1998.
2. Schaps MJ, Linn ES, Wilbanks GD, Wilbanks ER: Women-centered care: Implementing a philosophy. *Women's Health Issues* 3:52–54, 1993.
3. Weisman CS, Curbow B, Khoury AJ: The national survey of women's health centers: Current models of women-centered care. *Women's Health Issues* 5:103–117, 1995.

CHAPTER 23

The Patient's Perspective: What the Postmenopausal Woman Wants and Needs from Her Physician

Jacqueline A. Horton

Most women rate their health as good to excellent during their middle years. The normal aging process often is associated with the development of chronic disease, and sometimes with disability. However, women today are living longer, healthier lives than ever before. Therefore, the emphasis for many women as they age is on preventive measures to reduce risk factors for the development of disease. This chapter reflects the perspective of a woman in good health who receives primary care from a gynecologist. However, what a healthy older woman wants from her physician is not very different from what a woman with medical problems wants.

What I expect from my primary care physician is a partnership. I have chosen my gynecologist as my primary care physician because he is a caring, thoughtful physician who addresses my questions and my occasional medical problems with a wonderful sense of humor and concern, as well as medical skill. I have reached that point in my life where I want to be consulted as an active partner in the decision-making process about my health. I know that the medical literature is filled with information concerning the risks associated with health behaviors and with the consequences of lifestyle choices, both good and bad. I want my physician to personalize those statistics and consult with me and advise me on a course of action that will maximize *my* health and minimize *my* particular risk. I want to be fully informed of the consequences of my decisions, but I want them to be decisions that are made by me with the advice and counsel of a physician I trust.

Because I am relatively healthy, I would like my physician to focus on preventive health measures to delay the onset of chronic diseases. It would be wonderful if his practice had wellness counseling, such as nutrition counseling, available onsite. Prenatal and parenting classes are often part of an obstetrician's practice. Meeting with a nurse or other health professional is often incorporated into the routine prenatal visit. It would be ideal if this model of preventive counseling was also available for the older woman.

It may come as a surprise to my gynecologist that I rarely think of myself as postmenopausal. In fact, I do not know of any of my peers who use that frame of reference. I know that there are physiologic changes that take place as one ages, and that certain medical conditions are more prevalent with advancing years. The need for added medical intervention occurs more frequently in the older person. However, these events often occur slowly over a period of time and may not occur at all until many years after menopause. I am pleased that my physician does not define me only by my stage of reproductive function, and I appreciate that he sees me as a total person, albeit of a certain age.

Perhaps most of all, I want to be alone in the office when I visit my primary care physician. I do not want a case manager looking over my shoulder and deciding whether or not I need a test. I definitely do not want Congress in the office with me deciding if I can or cannot have a surgical procedure. If I have a lump in my breast, I want to be free to decide with my doctor that I can have a mastectomy, even though a simple lumpectomy may be currently in vogue. It is my body, and I do not want it subject to legislation.

I would like to be able to receive all of the care that I need in one location. I often put off getting a mammogram because it means a separate visit to another office where I may have another long wait before I am seen. Why can't I get my blood drawn in my primary care physician's office? Why do I have to go to another part of town for an x-ray? Who took those conveniences away?

I am old enough to remember when I was the only person my physician had to be concerned with when I was in his care. Isn't it too bad that this is no longer the case? I have a living will, but I wonder if my physician and my family will be able to honor it. Or, will someone decide that I really didn't mean what I said and go to court to challenge my wishes? I am able to make decisions about my life for myself. I want to trust my physician to be honest with me and to be my advocate. I want to be able to trust him to carry out my wishes when I am no longer able to do so. I want him to support my family in doing so.

I want my physician to know that for many women life after menopause is really not that different than it was before menopause. For many women, menopause is often not a landmark event. Isn't that great?

Part IV

Reproductive Health and Disorders of the Reproductive System

CHAPTER 24

Anatomy, Physiology, Growth, and Development

Fred Benjamin

ANATOMY
Vulva • Vagina • Uterus • Fallopian Tubes or Oviducts • Ovaries

PHYSIOLOGY OF MENSTRUATION
Hypothalamic Cycle • The Anterior Pituitary Cycle • The Ovarian Cycle • The Endometrial Cycle

PRIMARY AMENORRHEA
Definition • Clinical Approach • Causes of Primary Amenorrhea • Diagnosis • Treatment

NORMAL AND ABNORMAL SEXUAL DEVELOPMENT
Normal Sexual Development and Sexual Differentiation • Abnormal Sexual Development and Reproductive Tract Congenital Anomalies

T he ability of the health care provider to dispense proper primary care for women presupposes a basic knowledge of female anatomy, the normal growth and development of the reproductive organs, and the physiology of menstruation.

Anatomy

The female genital reproductive organs consist of the reproductive tract (the vulva, vagina, cervix, uterus, fallopian tubes, and ovaries) and the breasts. However, because the urinary and gas-trointestinal tracts develop in close embryologic relationship with the genital organs, and because they remain in close contact with the reproductive structures and share many pathologic and clinical presentations with each other, knowledge of the anatomy of all of these interrelated organs is also necessary.

Vulva

The vulva is the composite name for the female external genitalia (Fig. 24-1). It includes the mons pubis or veneris, the labia majora and minora, the clitoris, the entrance to the vagina, the hymen, the vestibule, the urethra, and the perineum.

The mons is a fatty pad covered by hair-bearing skin; it lies over the upper part of the symphysis pubis. Extending backward from the mons are the labia majora, which are folds of skin overlying fat pads on either side of the vaginal orifice that merge posteriorly in the midline; laterally they are covered with hair, but their medial surfaces are smooth. Between the labia majora and vaginal orifice are two delicate flaps of skin called the labia minora, which vary in size considerably so that they may be hidden by the labia majora or may project beyond them. Anteriorly, they split at the clitoris to supply it with a prepuce superiorly and a frenulum inferiorly. Posteriorly, they form a fold of skin called the fourchette. The depression between the fourchette and the hymen is the fossa navicularis. The hymen is a thin membrane covering the entrance to the vagina. It has one or more apertures

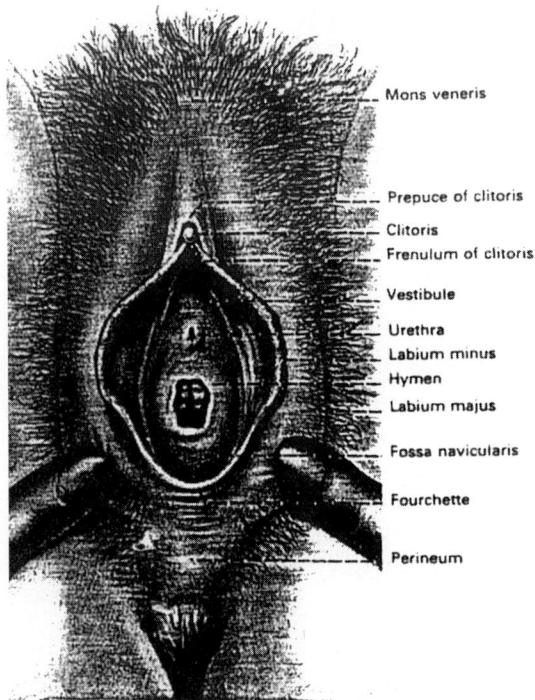

Mons veneris

Prepuce of clitoris

Clitoris

Frenulum of clitoris

Vestibule

Urethra

Labium minus

Hymen

Labium majus

Fossa navicularis

Fourchette

Perineum

Figure 24-1. External organs of reproduction of women. In nulliparous women, the vaginal orifice is not so readily visible because of the close apposition of the labia minora. (With permission from Tindale VR (ed): *Jeffcoate's Principles of Gynecology,* 5th ed. Oxford, England: Butterworth-Heinemann, 1987, p 16.)

tissue, which is richly supplied with nerves that make it the most erotically sensitive area of the vulva. The vestibular bulbs are two elongated collections of erectile tissue that pass from the root of the clitoris to either side of the vaginal orifice; they are analogous to the corpus spongiosum or bulb of the penis.

Bartholin's glands (also known as "the greater vestibular glands") are the analogs of Cowper's glands in the male. They are located on the posterolateral aspects of the vaginal orifice at 4 and 8 o'clock. Each gland is about the size of a pea, and has a duct about 1 cm in length that runs downward and inward to open into the groove between the hymen and the labia minora. The gland is racemose and produces a colorless mucoid secretion, mainly in response to sexual stimulation. Skene's glands, or the paraurethral glands, correspond to the prostate gland in the male. They are branched tubular glands that lie next to the distal urethra. They have a duct that runs for 1 cm parallel to the long axis of the urethra, eventually opening into the distal urethra. The perineum is the tissue between the vaginal orifice anteriorly and the anus posteriorly. It consists of nonhairy skin and subcutaneous tissue. Its length anteroposteriorly, which ranges from 2 to 5 cm or more, is directly related to the resistance it offers and the injury it sustains during the delivery of a child.

to allow the outflow of menstrual blood. Unless the hymen is particularly elastic, it is nearly always torn by coitus, but being relatively avascular, bleeding is usually slight. During childbirth, it is torn more extensively so that only small remnants or tags called carunculae myrtiformes remain. The vestibule is the space between the labia minora and extends from the clitoris anteriorly to the fourchette posteriorly; the vagina and urethral openings are seen in it. The clitoris, the homologue of the penis, is a small organ that lies in front of the symphysis pubis, almost hidden by the anterior portions of the labia majora. It consists of a glans, prepuce, body, and two crura that attach it to the pubic bones, and erectile

Vagina

The vagina is an elastic fibromuscular tube that extends upward and downward from the vulva to the uterus (Figs. 24-2 and 24-3). Normally, the walls of the vagina are in apposition and flattened anteroposteriorly so that on cross-section it has an H-shaped appearance. The vagina has a blind upper end except for the external os of the cervix. The cervix protrudes down below the vault, forming four areas: the posterior fornix, which is capacious; the anterior fornix, which is shallow; and two lateral fornices. The result is that the anterior vaginal wall is about 8 cm long, the posterior wall

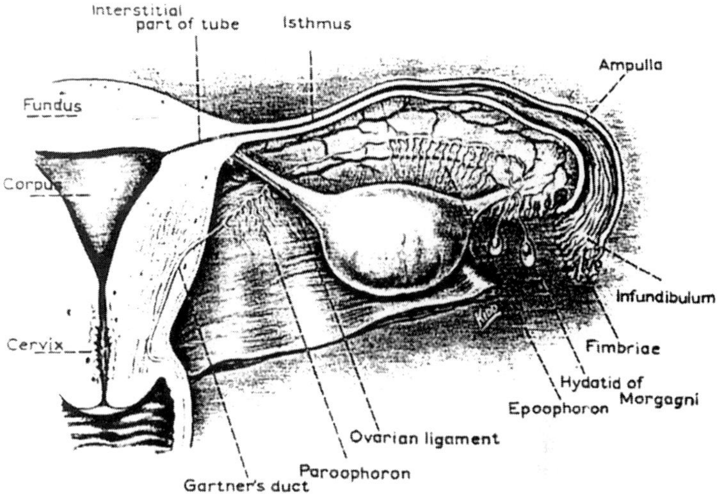

Figure 24-2. The uterus and broad ligament from behind. (With permission from Tindale VR (ed): *Jeffcoate's Principles of Gynecology,* 5th ed. Oxford, England: Butterworth-Heinemann, 1987, p 26.)

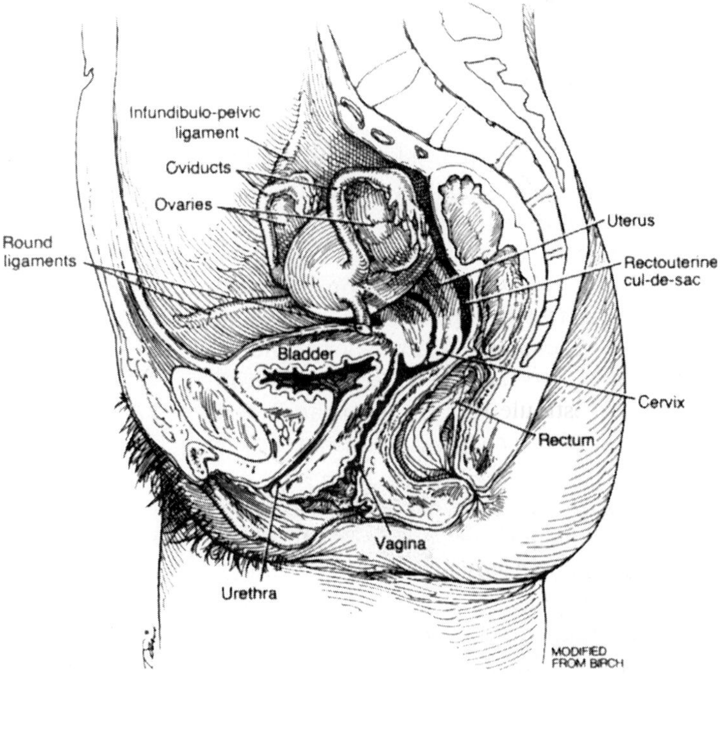

Figure 24-3. Sagittal section of pelvis of an adult woman that is illustrative of relations of the pelvic viscera. (With permission from Pritchard JA, MacDonald PC, Gant NF (eds): *Williams Obstetrics,* 17th eds., Norwalk, Conn: Appleton and Lange, 1988, p 11.)

10 cm, and the diameter 3.5 cm. However, the length and width vary considerably in different women; functionally, its elasticity and the tone and contractions of the surrounding muscles enable the vagina to accommodate readily to coitus. Folds of vaginal mucous membrane running circumferentially, called rugae, contribute to the ability of the vagina to distend.

The vagina is lined by stratified squamous epithelium, which also covers the vaginal portion of the cervix up to the external os. The superficial zones of the epithelium contain glycogen, which is acted upon by a normal inhabitant of the vagina, Döderlein's bacillus (or the lactobacillus) to produce lactic acid, resulting in an acid pH of the vagina of about 4.5. This acidity is of major clinical importance and accounts for the excellent resistance of the vagina to infection with common bacteria.

The upper third of the vagina is supported by the cardinal ligaments and parametria, the middle third by the levator ani muscles and the lower portion of the cardinal ligaments, and the lower third by the urogenital and pelvic diaphragms. When a woman is standing, the axis of the vagina is close to horizontal. The tissues surrounding the vagina and the vaginal wall itself are extremely vascular. The blood supply is mainly from the vaginal artery, but branches of the uterine artery and internal pudendal artery also contribute, as do small branches from the middle and inferior rectal arteries.

The vagina undergoes considerable anatomic and physiologic change from the neonatal period through puberty, the reproductive years, and menopause. The vagina of the newborn child has a well-developed, glycogen-rich epithelium with an acidic pH, due to estrogen from the mother that has crossed the placenta. With the drop in estrogen, the epithelium becomes atrophic after about two weeks, and the pH of the vagina remains at an alkaline level of about pH 7 until puberty, when it reverts to its estrogenized state. The pH becomes even more acidic during pregnancy. After menopause, some thinning of the tissue occurs, the vaginal wall becomes smooth, glycogen and Döderlein's bacilli wane, and the pH rises.

The anatomic relations of the vagina are important in connection with clinical examination, injuries, childbirth, and surgery (Figs. 24-2 and 24-3). Anteriorly, the lower portion of the vagina is related to the urethra and the upper portion to the bladder. Posteriorly, the upper end of the vagina is in contact with the peritoneal cul-de-sac of Douglas, the middle portion is related to the ampulla of the rectum, and the lower third to the perineal body. Laterally, the upper third of the vagina is related to the lower portion of the cardinal ligaments, which are inserted into the lateral fornices. Below the fornices are the levator ani muscles and the tissues of the paracolpos; lower down is the ischiorectal fossa. On either side of the vaginal introitus are the sphincter vaginae or bulbocavernosus muscles, the vestibular bulbs, Bartholin's glands and their ducts, and the triangular ligaments with their muscles.

Uterus

The uterus is a thick-walled hollow muscular organ shaped like a pear. The tapering end is the cervix, which projects into the vagina. The nulliparous uterus is about 8 to 9 cm long, 6 cm wide, and about 4 cm thick. The length of the cavity on sounding is, therefore, about 6 cm. The organ weighs 40 to 50 g. The multiparous uterus weighs about 70 to 80 g.

When seen from the front, the cavity is triangular in shape. The uterus is made up of a body (or corpus) and a cervix. The narrowed area between the cervix and the body is called the isthmus. The part of the body above the insertion of the fallopian tubes is called the fundus; the area where the tube is inserted is termed the cornu of the uterus.

The uterus has three layers: the outer serosal layer consists of the visceral peritoneum; the middle layer is the muscular layer (myometrium); the inner layer is the endometrium, which, depending on the phase of the menstrual cycle, varies from 1 to 6 mm in thickness. The endometrium is divided into three layers: the superficial stratum compactum; the intermediate stratum spongiosum; and the innermost layer, the stratum basalis, which lies on and often penetrates somewhat into the myometrium. Only the superficial and intermediate layers respond to the hormonal changes of the menstrual cycle and are shed with menstruation. They are therefore referred to as the "functional zone" of the endometrium.

The blood supply of the uterus is furnished by the uterine arteries, derived from the hypogastric arteries, and by the ovarian arteries, which come off the aorta directly.

Fallopian Tubes or Oviducts

The fallopian tubes (oviducts) extend from the cornua of the uterus outward in the free upper edge end of the broad ligament toward the ovaries (Fig. 24-2). The lumen of each tube opens into the uterine cavity at its proximal end and into the peritoneal cavity at its distal end. This is the only communication between the peritoneal cavity and the outside, which explains the susceptibility of women to pelvic peritonitis arising from an ascending infection.

The fallopian tubes are between 10 and 14 cm long, and each is divided into four anatomic sections:

1. The interstitial or intramural segment is the part that transverses the uterine wall and is about 2 cm long;
2. The isthmus begins as the tube leaves the uterus; it is straight and narrow (1 to 2 mm in its inside diameter), 4 cm long, and has the most highly developed muscular wall;
3. The ampulla is the widest portion of the tube (6 mm in its inside diameter) and is 6 cm long (fertilization normally takes place in the ampulla, and 80 percent of ectopic tubal pregnancies occur in this area);
4. The infundibulum is the most distal, trumpet-shaped end of the tube; it bears the opening into the peritoneal cavity, the "abdominal ostium." About 20 to 25 finger-like projections protrude from the fimbriated end of

the tube and surround the abdominal ostium; one of the longest of these is attached to the ovary and is called the fimbria ovarica.

The mucosa of the tubes have numerous folds, or plicae, which are most prominent in the ampullary portion. The mucous membrane has three different types of cells: columnar ciliated cells, columnar secretory cells, and narrow peg cells situated between the ciliated and secretory cells.

Ovaries

The two ovaries are mainly solid structures, light gray in color. During the reproductive years, they measure approximately 3.5 cm × 2.5 cm × 1.5 cm, and each weighs about 5 g. After the menopause, the ovaries become smaller and firmer, and clinically are nonpalpable. The ovaries are attached to the back of the broad ligament by the mesovarium, and are attached to the cornu of the uterus by the ovarian ligament. The part of the ovary that is attached to the mesovarium is called the hilum, and all nerves and vessels enter and leave at this area. In the hilum are groups of hilus cells, which are analogous to the interstitial Leydig cells of the testis.

The ovary is divided into an outer zone, called the cortex, and an inner zone, the medulla. Follicles are located mainly in the cortex, the medulla being composed largely of connective tissue and blood vessels. The ovary is the only intraabdominal organ not covered by the peritoneum. In early life, it is covered by a single layer of cuboidal cells derived from the coelomic epithelium, the primitive peritoneum. This layer is often called the "germinal epithelium;" however, it does not give rise to germ cells, and preferably should be labeled the "surface epithelium" of the ovary.

Physiology of Menstruation

Menstruation is a phenomenon unique to the human species and the higher apes. Its purpose is the periodic preparation for fertilization and pregnancy. The physiology of menstruation consists of the integration of four interdependent activities:

1. The hypothalamus secretes gonadotropin-releasing hormone (GnRH);
2. The anterior pituitary gland, in response to the stimulus of GnRH, secretes follicle-stimulating hormone (FSH) and luteinizing hormone (LH);
3. These two hormones then act on the ovaries to cause the development of the follicles, ovulation, and the secretion of the two major ovarian hormones, estrogen and progesterone;
4. Estrogen and progesterone cause growth and development of the endometrium in preparation for embedding of the fertilized ovum.

Each of these four aspects of the menstrual cycle will be considered in turn.

The Hypothalamic Cycle

The hypothalamus secretes hormones that have been identified as small polypeptides. These substances pass through the pituitary portal system to the anterior pituitary to stimulate it to synthesize and secrete its hormones. The hypothalamic hormone responsible for FSH and LH secretion is GnRH, a decapeptide containing 10 amino acids. GnRH is not secreted at a steady rate, but in a pulsatile fashion, one pulse occurring every one to three hours. Many of the menstrual disorders, such as amenorrhea and dysfunctional uterine bleeding, are basically due to aberrations in the pulsatility of GnRH.

The Anterior Pituitary Cycle

In response to GnRH, the anterior pituitary synthesizes and secretes FSH and LH. FSH causes growth and development of the graafian follicle, and in concert with LH results in estrogen production. LH, through its surge at midcycle, causes

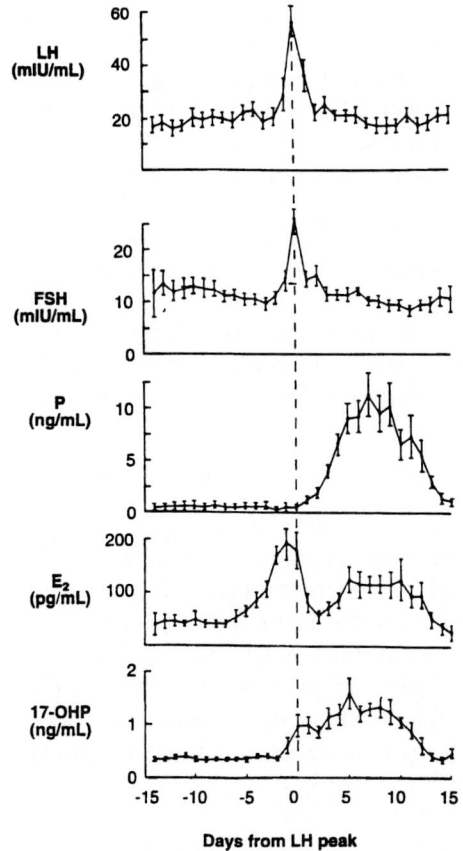

Figure 24-4. Mean values of LH, FSH, progesterone (P), estradiol (E_2) and 17-hydroxyprogesterone (17 OHP) in daily serum samples of 9 women during ovulatory menstrual cycles. Data from different cycles combined with the use of the day of the mid-cycle LH peak as the reference day (Day 0). The vertical bars represent one standard error of the mean. (From Thorneycraft IH, Mischell DR Jr, Stone SC, et al: The reaction of serum 17-hydroxyprogesterone and estradiol-17β levels during the human menstrual cycle. *Am J Obstet Gynecol* III:947, 1971. With permission.)

ovulation and the subsequent development of the corpus luteum (Fig. 24-4).

The Ovarian Cycle

The ovary is endowed with a peak of about 6 million ova at 20 weeks of gestation, but this number is reduced to about 1 million at birth and about 300,000 at puberty. The store of germ cells continues to be depleted by atresia until the process finally is completed about 40 years later at menopause.

Ovulation does not take place until full maturation of the hypothalamic pituitary axis after puberty. Beginning at that time, with each menstrual cycle, a large number of follicles begin to develop. With few exceptions, only one of these undergoes full development. This total development consists of three phases: the follicular phase, ovulation, and the formation of the corpus luteum.

The follicular phase begins with the primordial follicle, which is an oocyte arrested in the diplotene stage of the first meiotic division, surrounded by a single layer of granulosa cells. This development then proceeds through ovulation and the formation of the corpus luteum. The ovarian follicles undergo significant development throughout life, beginning in the fetus during intrauterine life, and continuing throughout life until menopause. However, the vast majority of these developing follicles become blighted at various stages of their development through atresia, a process in which a follicle grows and enlarges but fails to ovulate; instead, it degenerates and becomes replaced by fibrous tissue. The follicles that do ovulate rupture; the ovum is extruded and is picked up by the fimbriated end of the fallopian tube and transported to the uterus. The ruptured follicle develops into a corpus luteum, which secretes progesterone as well as estrogen. If pregnancy occurs, the corpus luteum persists, and there is no menstruation until after delivery. If pregnancy does not occur, the corpus luteum degenerates after its life span of about 14 days, and menstruation ensues.

The Endometrial Cycle

At the beginning of the menstrual cycle, the endometrium is only about 1 mm thick—much of it, except for the basal layer, having been shed with the menstrual flow. The developing follicle now produces estrogens, which cause the endometrium to grow; the glands lengthen, but do not become convoluted nor do they secrete. These endometrial changes prior to ovulation are called the proliferative, or follicular, or preovulatory phase of the cycle. Following ovulation and the formation of the corpus luteum, the endometrium, under the influence of progesterone, exhibits coiled and tortuous glands that secrete a clear fluid; this phase of the cycle is called the luteal or secretory phase. When the corpus luteum degenerates and the estrogen and progesterone wane, the endometrial vessels go into spasm, probably as a result of the release of prostaglandins. This results in necrosis of the endometrium and the shedding of the superficial and intermediate layers of the endometrium (the strata compactum and spongiosum, respectively) causing the menstrual flow. The basal layer remains behind to grow and to develop and form the new endometrium for the next cycle. At its peak, the endometrium has grown to a thickness of about 6 mm.

The mean duration of the menstrual flow is 4 ± 2 days, and the mean length of the cycle is 28 ± 7 days. The mean blood loss with each menstrual period is 35 ml; if the mean blood loss is regularly more than 80 ml, iron deficiency anemia will develop.[2]

Primary Amenorrhea

Definition

The mean age for the appearance of the first menstrual period (the menarche) is 12.8 years. Girls who do not have their first period by age 15 will usually be evaluated by that time.

Clinical Approach

A useful clinical approach to the patient with primary amenorrhea is to carry out a general physical examination, when it will be found that all of the patients fall into one of three clinical categories:

1. Those with absent secondary sex characteristics—i.e., no breast development and (usually) no pubic nor axillary hair;
2. Patients with well-developed breasts and pubic and axillary hair;
3. Those with evidence of androgenization—i.e., hirsutism and possibly an enlarged clitoris.

By using this simple classification, the differential diagnosis becomes logical and easy, because each of these three types of situations has its own specific causes.

Causes of Primary Amenorrhea (Table 24-1)

Patients with absent secondary sex characteristics Failure of breast development is due to absence of ovarian estrogen production. In the overwhelming majority of patients, this results from failure of gonadal development and formation of streak ovaries—i.e., gonadal dysgenesis. Occasionally, however, the ovaries are normal, and their failure is secondary to hypothalamic or pituitary disease, with resulting absent stimulation of the ovaries. The differential diagnosis between these two types of ovarian failure is readily made by an FSH assay; in primary ovarian failure, the FSH is high (above 40 mIU/ml), whereas in secondary ovarian failure, it is low or absent.

Primary amenorrhea with well-developed secondary sex characteristics In these patients, the ovaries function normally, with good estrogen production. The amenorrhea usually is due to a developmental defect in the müllerian ducts, resulting in absence or obstruction of the vagina or uterus. Occasionally, however, an apparent female with primary amenorrhea and well-developed breasts actually has androgen insensitivity syndrome (also known as the testicular feminization syndrome). This condition can be suspected clinically by the absence of pubic and axillary hair, and the diagnosis can be established by the finding of an XY karyotype. Other rare causes of primary amenorrhea with well-developed breasts include nutritional amenorrhea, systemic disease, and hyperprolactinemia (although these conditions usually cause secondary rather than primary amenorrhea).

TABLE 24-1 **Clinical Presentations and Causes of Primary Amenorrhea**

Absent Secondary Sex Characteristics	Well-Developed Secondary Sex Characteristics	Virilization
Primary ovarian failure (gonadal dysgenesis)[a]	Congenital uterovaginal anomaly[a]	Congenital adrenal hyperplasia (CAH)[a]

Secondary ovarian failure
  Pituitary failure
  Hypothalamic failure (Kallmann's syndrome)
	Stein-Leventhal syndrome/polycystic ovarian disease (PCOD)	True hermaphrodite

	Testicular feminization syndrome; androgen insensitivity syndrome (AIS)	Male pseudohermaphrodite, developmental type
	Hyposensitive ovary syndrome/"Savage" syndrome	Incomplete testicular feminization (AIS)

	Many of the causes of secondary amenorrhea occur at or before puberty
	  Hypothalamic; psychogenic
	  Nutritional
	  Systemic disease
	  Medical endocrine disease
		Stein-Leventhal syndrome/polycystic ovarian disease (PCOD)
		Rare virilizing tumors before or at puberty
		  Ovarian
		  Adrenal

[a] Most common cause (all others are rare causes of primary amenorrhea).

Primary amenorrhea with androgenization Practically all patients with primary amenorrhea, hirsutism, and an enlarged clitoris have congenital adrenal hyperplasia. Very rare and unusual causes of primary amenorrhea with androgenization are polycystic ovarian disease (this more often presents as secondary amenorrhea), various types of pseudohermaphroditism, and masculinizing ovarian or adrenal tumors.

Diagnosis

When a girl of 16 or 17 has not started menstruating, diagnosis of the cause of the condition can be made by determining in which of the three clinical categories the patient fits. Most of those with absent breast development have primary ovarian failure due to gonadal dysgenesis. If the secondary sex characteristics are normal, most have a congenital anomaly of müllerian duct development. In the majority of cases, those with hirsutism have congenital adrenal hyperplasia. Only in the rare case where these three diagnoses are ruled out should a workup be done to determine which of the other rarer conditions (mentioned above in the discussion of the causes of primary amenorrhea) is present.

Treatment

The mainstay of the treatment of primary and secondary ovarian failure is estrogen replacement therapy (with the addition of a progestational agent to prevent the development of endometrial hyperplasia or carcinoma). The treatment of müllerian duct anomalies is reviewed later in this chapter. Congenital adrenal hyperplasia is managed by corticosteroid therapy with excellent clinical results.

Normal and Abnormal Sexual Development

Because the interpretation of congenital anomalies of the reproductive tract requires an understanding of the developmental processes involved, this basic embryology is reviewed briefly to highlight aspects of the embryology that are essential to an understanding of the various clinical abnormalities.

Normal Sexual Development and Sexual Differentiation

Basically, the sex of an individual depends on the chromosomes which that individual possesses. This is determined at conception according to whether the ovum, which is always X-bearing, is fertilized by an X-bearing sperm, to form an XX or female chromosomal pattern, or by a Y-bearing sperm, to form an XY or male chromosomal pattern. However, although the sex is determined from the very moment of conception, for the first two months of embryonic life there is no real difference between the male and female embryonic form, all the genital structures being the same and having the potential of developing into male or female body form.

Thus, the primitive genital ridge from which the gonad develops appears at about the fourth week of embryonic life, but it is only at the seventh week in the male, and the ninth week in the female, that this genital ridge begins to differentiate into a testis or an ovary. Until then the ridge is the same in both sexes and consists of a peripheral cortex and a central medulla. In the male, the medulla predominates and the cortex atrophies—and this becomes a testis. In the female, the opposite occurs, the cortex predominating and the medulla atrophying—and this becomes an ovary.

What makes the undifferentiated gonad develop into a testis or an ovary? A single gene situated on the short arm of the Y chromosome with a 1A1 DNA sequence is the essential factor necessary for the development of the testis. It is called the sex-related Y gene (SR-Y gene) or the testis-determining factor (TDF) gene. Without the presence of this gene, the testis will not develop, and the gonad will develop into an ovary. It was previously thought that the H-Y gene and its antigen, the H-Y antigen, was the TDF. We now know that it is involved in spermatogenesis and not in testis determination; it is, in fact, situated on the long arm of the Y chromosome.

The undifferentiated gonad contains three distinct specialized tissues: primordial germ cells that will become either oogonia or spermatogonia; specialized epithelium that will become either granulosa cells or Sertoli cells; and specialized mesenchyme or stromal cells that will become either theca cells or Leydig cells. Although germ cells do not induce gonadal development and simply take the form of the gonad in which they find themselves, becoming either oogonia or spermatogonia, should they fail to arrive the gonads do not develop and form mere fibrous streaks. This results in the clinical disorder of gonadal dysgenesis or Turner's syndrome and its variants.

As is true of the gonads, the extragonadal genital structures are at first the same in both the male and female embryos. The internal structures are the müllerian (paramesonephric) ducts and the wolffian (mesonephric) ducts. At about the 12th week in the male the wolffian duct predominates and the müllerian duct atrophies; the wolffian duct develops into the epididymis, vas deferens, and seminal vesicles. At about the same time in the female, the wolffian duct atrophies, and the müllerian duct develops into the fallopian tubes, uterus, and upper part of the vagina.

Likewise, the external genital structures in both sexes originally are the same; by looking at a fetus before the 10th week—for example, after a spontaneous abortion—it cannot be determined whether it is male or female. These external structures, which appear at about the fourth week, are the genital tubercle, the genital or labioscrotal folds, and the urogenital membrane. At about the 12th week, the genital tubercle develops into the penis in the male and clitoris in the female; the labioscrotal folds develop into the scrotum in the male and the labia majora in the female; and the urogenital membrane forms the penile portion of the urethra in the male and the labia minora in the female.

The differentiation of the external and internal genital organs along male lines is entirely dependent on two substances produced by the fetal testicle, namely, testosterone produced by the Leydig cells and the müllerian inhibiting factor (MIF) secreted by the Sertoli cells. Testosterone causes the genital tubercle to develop into the penis and the labioscrotal folds into the scrotum. It causes the urogenital sinus to furnish the penile portion of the urethra and the prostate, and also causes the wolffian duct to develop into the epididymis, vas deferens, and seminal vesicles. The MIF causes atrophy of the müllerian duct. On the other hand, in the absence of testes and the consequent lack of testosterone and MIF, the müllerian duct develops into the uterus, tubes, and upper part of the vagina.

Abnormal Sexual Development and Reproductive Tract Congenital Anomalies

A knowledge of the embryology as described above permits a ready understanding of the clinical states resulting from abnormalities in sexual development.

Chromosomal defects   Two of the clinical conditions the physician may encounter that are due to sex chromosomal defects are gonadal dysgenesis (Turner's syndrome) and Klinefelter's syndrome.

Gonadal dysgenesis (Turner's syndrome) can occur in a male or female. In the male, if there is a defect in the short arm of the Y chromosome, there is absence of the testis-determining factor and failure of testicular development, the testes presenting as mere streaks. Because there is no testosterone and no müllerian-inhibiting factor, these patients present as females, with a vulva, vagina, uterus, and streak gonads; they are indistinguishable phenotypically from the usual female gonadal dysgenesis.

In the female, any abnormality in the second X chromosome (whether it is absent altogether, i.e., XO, or present but abnormal) results in total failure of development of the ovaries, and they become fibrous streaks.

Both male and female Turner's syndromes

present with female genitalia, but with primary amenorrhea and absent secondary sex characteristics. Both are treated with replacement estrogens; however, if the karyotype is male—that is, if there is a Y chromosome—it is essential to remove the streak gonads because there is a high incidence of malignancy.

Klinefelter's syndrome affects males with an extra X chromosome, that is, XXY. They present as phenotypic males. However, having an extra X chromosome, they tend to have some feminine characteristics. There is a whole spectrum of clinical presentations, ranging from an apparently normal male who is only diagnosed in the course of an infertility work-up, to a male who is tall and eunuchoidal with somewhat enlarged breasts and small testes. They are all infertile, having either azoospermia or marked oligospermia.

Gonadal defects The most striking gonadal defect is the well-known but very rare situation where both ovarian and testicular tissue are present—the true hermaphrodite. With the presence of both ovarian and testicular tissue a wide range of clinical presentations has been encountered. In the majority of cases there is a phallus, so most of these patients are reared as boys. However, when puberty arrives there is much confusion because in most cases, a greater or lesser degree of breast development occurs. Diagnosis is made by karyotyping and by evaluating the external and internal genitalia. Eventually, laparoscopy or laparotomy with biopsy of the gonads usually are required to make a definitive diagnosis.

Extragonadal defects This category includes all congenital defects where the chromosomes and gonads are normal but the extragonadal structures—that is, the external genitalia and/or the internal genitalia (derived from the müllerian and wolffian ducts)—resemble those of the opposite sex. These patients are called pseudohermaphrodites.

Male pseudohermaphrodites are males (with an XY chromosomal makeup and testes), but there are varying degrees of incomplete masculinization of the external and/or internal geni-

talia. The clinical presentation can range from a simple hypospadias, to a small penis, bifid scrotum (i.e., failure of fusion of the labioscrotal folds), to undescended testes, to almost complete feminization, as seen in the "testicular feminization syndrome" or "androgen insensitivity syndrome." In this syndrome, the male pseudohermaphrodite looks like a normal female, with breast development but no pubic nor axillary hair. Because this patient is XY, there will be no menstruation. If a patient presents with any or all of these features, the differential diagnosis is from a female pseudohermaphrodite or a true hermaphrodite, and the main key to the diagnosis is the karyotype; an XY pattern will show that the patient is a male pseudohermaphrodite.

Female pseudohermaphrodites are females with an XX karyotype and ovaries, but with some degree of masculinization of the external genitalia. The usual way this is shown is by enlargement of the clitoris, but in advanced cases there may be a single urogenital sinus.

The vast majority of these cases are due to congenital adrenal hyperplasia (CAH), but on rare occasion the condition is due to exogenous masculinizing hormone taken by the mother during pregnancy, or when an ovarian or adrenal tumor during pregnancy produces the androgens.

Evaluations, diagnosis, and treatment of the intersexual state (hermaphroditism) When a patient (usually a newborn child) presents with ambiguous genitalia, the main method of evaluating the patient and making a diagnosis is by carrying out a karyotype and by performing appropriate hormone assays. The karyotype indicates whether the patient is a male or female pseudohermaphrodite, or the very rare true hermaphrodite. The dehydroepiandrosterone sulfate (DHEA-S) and 17-hydroxyprogesterone (17-OHP) enable a diagnosis of CAH to be made. In some cases, the diagnosis cannot be made by these tests alone, and a laparotomy and inspection of the internal genitalia, and biopsy of the gonads may be necessary.

Treatment of the young child depends on what the anticipated pubertal changes will be (male or female), and whether the patient will be able to function best as a male or female. Obviously, the size of the phallus is an important determining factor. It is much easier by plastic surgery to create a suitable vagina than a penis. If the phallus is inadequate, the child should be feminized, and a vaginoplasty should be done. In that case, one must make sure that the patient will not have a male puberty. If there is any testicular tissue, it must be removed. If the diagnosis is CAH, it must be properly treated with cortisone so that the child does not masculinize at puberty.

If the patient is an older child or an adult, the most important factor is whether the individual is psychosexually oriented in a masculine or feminine way. It is essential that the patient be treated appropriately so that the individual can live a life dictated by their psychosexual orientation. This may require both surgery and hormonal manipulation. If this is not done, major psychological problems are inevitable.

Müllerian duct anomalies A large number of different congenital anomalies result from developmental defects in müllerian ducts. In practically all of these cases, however, the ovaries are normal; therefore, these patients have well-developed secondary sex characteristics. Owing to the close embryologic relationship between the müllerian and wolffian ducts, anomalies of the kidneys and ureters must be sought, because they are present in about 25 to 30 percent of the cases.

A simple classification of all the müllerian duct anomalies has been proposed by Jones[4]: 1. agenesis; 2. problems of vertical fusion: (a) obstructive and (b) nonobstructive; 3. problems of lateral fusion: (a) obstructive and (b) nonobstructive.

1. Agenesis of the Müllerian Ducts: Part or all of the vagina may be absent, and often the uterus also is absent; this disorder is sometimes called the Rokitansky-Küster-Hauser syndrome.
2. Problems of Vertical Fusion: The most common clinical presentation is a transverse vaginal septum. If complete, it will cause obstruction to the outflow of menstrual blood after puberty, and surgical excision is required. If incomplete, surgery may be required later because of dyspareunia.
3. Problems of Lateral Fusion: Varying degrees of failure of lateral fusion of the müllerian ducts may occur. The extreme form is total lack of fusion, resulting in a double vagina and uterus (uterus didelphys). In some cases, there is full development of one side and rudimentary development of the other. If there is no obstruction of menstrual outflow, there are usually no overt symptoms. Should obstruction be present, menstrual outflow is impaired and surgical management is usually mandatory.

The condition that may be encountered in the office setting is hematocolpos resulting from obstruction at or near the outlet of the vagina. This could be due to a problem of vertical fusion of the lower ends of the müllerian ducts, to an imperforate hymen, or to failure of canalization of the area where the müllerian ducts join the sinovaginal bulb. The patient presents with one of three symptoms: primary amenorrhea; cyclic or continuous pelvic pain; or difficulty in urinating culminating in acute retention of urine. The condition must be suspected in any young girl who complains of any of these symptoms soon after puberty.

References and Selected Readings

1. Crowley WF Jr, Filicori M, Spratt DI, et al: The physiology of gonadotrophin-releasing hormone (GnRH) secretion in men and women. *Recent Prog Horm Res* 41:501, 1988.
2. Hallberg L, Hillson L: Determination of menstrual blood loss. *Scand J Clin Lab Invest* 16:244, 1964.
3. Hallberg L. Hogdahl AM, Nilsson L, Rybo L: Menstrual blood loss—a population study variation at different ages and attempts to define normality. *Acta Obstet Gynecol Scand* 45:320, 1966.
4. Jones HW Jr: Anomalies of the müllerian ducts, in Rosenwacks Z, Benjamin F, Stone ML (eds): *Gynecology: Principles and Practice.* New York: Macmillan, 1987.
5. Knobil E: The neuroendocrine control of the menstrual cycle. *Recent Prog Horm Res* 36:53, 1980.

CHAPTER 25

Pediatric Gynecology

Paula J. Adams Hillard

ANATOMY AND BACTERIOLOGY OF THE VULVOVAGINAL AREA IN PREPUBERTAL GIRLS

THE HISTORY OF GYNECOLOGIC SYMPTOMS

EXAMINATION OF THE PREPUBERTAL GIRL

SPECIFIC GYNECOLOGIC CONDITIONS

Vulvovaginal Symptoms • Vaginal Bleeding • Hymenal and Vaginal Abnormalities • Pelvic Mass

Anatomy and Bacteriology of the Vulvovaginal Area in Prepubertal Girls

Gynecologic problems in prepubertal girls are, fortunately, infrequent. However, the gynecologist who sees primarily adults must recognize that the anatomy, physiology, and etiologies of common symptoms (e.g., vaginal discharge) differ in this age group, due to the different hormonal milieu and growth factors. The anatomy of prepubertal girls includes the hairless labia majora, which lack fat; small labia minora; a clitoris generally measuring less than 0.5 cm in length and width; a thin and reddened vestibule and vaginal mucosa (due to the unestrogenized state); and a short distance between the vaginal vestibule and the anus, resulting in the potential for bacterial overgrowth with a primary vulvitis and secondary vaginitis.

The hymen itself may have differing configurations, ranging from a crescentic shape to annular. The margin is generally thin and delicate, although congenital septa, notches, or hymenal tags may be visualized. Recent studies note that superior and lateral notches are not uncommon and should be considered a normal variant, but that notches between the 5 and 7 o'clock position on the inferior hymen suggest prior trauma. In particular, hymenal transections that extend across the hymen onto the vestibule are observed only in situations of trauma. Accidental trauma is more likely to result in injuries to the anterior vulva, whereas penetrating injuries from sexual abuse most commonly result in injuries to the posterior fourchette.

As a general guideline, the transverse diameter of the hymenal orifice measures approximately 1 mm for each year of age for children between 3 and 6 years old, although this measurement depends on examination techniques, measurement techniques, and the child's relaxation, and should not be used to establish a diagnosis of sexual abuse. A discussion of acquired abnormalities of the hymen resulting from sexual abuse is beyond the scope of this chapter. Evaluations of children suspected of being sexually abused should be performed only by individuals who are experienced in this type of examination.

The normal bacterial flora of prepubertal girls is not as well established as it is in older individuals. One study found an average of nine bacterial species, including four aerobic and facultatively anaerobic species and five obligately anaerobic species. Younger girls more frequently have enteric organisms than do adolescents. In general, lactobacilli are infrequent prior to pubertal estrogen stimulation of the vaginal epithelium.

The History of Gynecologic Symptoms

The history of gynecologic symptoms in prepubertal girls is obtained primarily from the mother or primary caregiver, with supplemental and confirming information from the girl herself, depending on her age and verbal skills. Specific information should be obtained about symptoms such as vaginal discharge or itching. Information about onset, timing, and duration; exacerbating or alleviating factors; previous evaluation or treatment and its success or failure; and degree of disability should be recorded, including the child's exact phrases or descriptions. Associated systemic symptoms such as abdominal pain, headaches, enuresis, or disturbed behaviors should suggest the possibility of abuse, a possible cause for any child with vulvovaginal symptoms. Questions about inappropriate touching or sexual abuse can be turned into a "teachable moment" for the child; if she denies anyone touching her private parts, the clinician can ask "What would you do if someone tried to do that?", providing the answers of "Say no, get away, then tell."

The child herself should be engaged in conversation, with specific questions that allow her to know the importance of the information that she supplies. Allowing her to ask questions and answering them honestly will help enlist her cooperation with the examination.

If the chief complaint is vulvar irritation or vaginal discharge, the questions listed in Table 25-1 can be helpful. Vaginal bleeding is sometimes described as menses, although the presence of other pubertal development prior to age 7 should be evaluated as precocious puberty, and vaginal bleeding in the absence of pubertal growth requires a careful history (Table 25-2) and complete vaginal examination (which may need to be performed under anesthesia) to rule out tumor or other serious, but rare, abnormalities.

TABLE 25-1 Historical Information with Vulvovaginal Symptoms

Timing of onset: whether gradual or abrupt
Nature of symptoms: itching, burning, odor, pain, pain with urination
Associated symptoms: dysuria, urgency
Hygiene measures: baths, bubble baths, showers, soaps
Topical treatments and efficacy: petroleum jelly, zinc oxide, antifungals, triple antibiotic ointment, estrogen cream
Systemic treatments and efficacy: antibiotics
Recent infections in patient or family: diarrheal illness, URI with strep, pinworms
Masturbation
Behavioral symptoms suggesting abuse: enuresis, vague abdominal pain, headaches, nightmares, avoidance of certain situations or individuals

Examination of the Prepubertal Girl

The examination should include a general assessment, including height and weight, assessment of heart and lungs, and abdominal palpation. The breast evaluation should involve careful palpation for beginning breast budding. Examination of lymph nodes is important, as is palpation of the inguinal area for hernia or an inguinal gonad. The gynecologic exam includes a careful visualization of external genitalia, selective visualization of vagina and cervix (as needed), and rectal exam with abdominal palpation. This exam can almost always be accomplished in the office if the clinician establishes rapport and proceeds slowly and gently. A child who is markedly anxious, who has been abused, or who has experienced a traumatic exam may need to have an examination under anesthesia. Positions that

TABLE 25-2 Historical Information with Vaginal Bleeding

History of vaginal (or other body orifice) foreign body
History of trauma
History of breast or pubic hair growth
Use of hormonal medications (prescribed for patient or family member)
Vaginal discharge or symptoms of vulvovaginitis
Pain

facilitate the examination include: the mother's lap (for infants and toddlers); frog-leg position; astride the mother's lap with mother (clothed) resting her feet in stirrups; knee-chest; or lithotomy in stirrups (for the older child). Explanations of what the child can expect are helpful for most children although anxiety provoking for some; many girls will do better with distractions from nurse or mother. On occasion, the mother's anxiety is transmitted to the child; careful explanations to the mother (such as explaining that a speculum will not be used) may prevent this, but occasionally a child does better with an exam when an overly anxious, histrionic mother is asked to leave the room.

During inspection of the labia, hymen, and vaginal vestibule, a strong light is helpful; an otoscope with light or a magnifying lens can be used. Topical lidocaine jelly can be used to allow better visualization of the hymen, unless cultures are planned. The lower vagina, and frequently upper vagina and cervix, can be visualized with the child in the knee-chest position. An adult otoscope is frequently sufficient, although other instruments, such as specially designed vaginoscope, hysteroscope, or veterinary otoscope, have been used.

When vaginal discharge is present, cultures should be obtained using a small, male urethral swab. Alternatively, a double-catheter technique has been described in which the tubing from a butterfly catheter is threaded into the cut-off end (~4 in.) of a red-rubber urethral catheter. The catheter within a catheter technique is well tolerated, with a few ccs of sterile irrigating fluid injected into the vagina, aspirated, and sent for culture. In addition, after cultures are obtained, the vagina can be irrigated with copious amounts of saline, allowing small pieces of toilet paper (the most common foreign body) to be flushed from the vagina. *Cultures* for gonorrhea and chlamydia, rather than indirect tests, LCR, or PCR, are recommended in the evaluation of suspected sexual abuse.

A rectal examination with abdominal palpation should be a part of the examination when vaginal discharge is present and if there is vaginal bleeding or abdominal pain. Vaginal discharge may be related to the presence of a firm object (such as a penny, bean, or doll's shoe) which the child has placed in the vagina. Vaginal bleeding or pain are uncommonly the result of a rare vaginal or ovarian tumor.

After the examination, the clinician should discuss the evaluation, examination, diagnosis, treatment, and timing of return visit to assess efficacy of therapy. When sexual abuse is suspected, referral to the appropriate social service agency for reporting and appropriate evaluation and assessment is mandatory.

Specific Gynecologic Conditions

Vulvovaginal Symptoms

Vulvovaginal inflammation and discharge are most frequently due to a mixed bacterial infection. Infections due to a single organism, such as gonorrhea, chlamydia, group B strep, or shigella are distinctly unusual, and more likely to be associated with an acute onset of symptoms, rather than the typically insidious, intermittent, and chronic symptoms of a mixed infection. Girls who are toilet trained and out of diapers rarely develop vulvovaginal candidiasis, although patients have frequently been treated with antifungal agents without success.

With vulvovaginitis, examination reveals inflammation, erythema, a discharge, odor, and often signs of less-than-optimal perineal hygiene. Smegma, or even stool, may be present in the interlabial folds. The first line of management consists of emphasizing hygiene with daily baths and cleansing of the interlabial folds, and instruction on appropriate toileting (wiping front to back; parental supervision of toileting). If symptoms do not resolve, cultures should be taken, the possibility of sexual abuse assessed, and a broad-spectrum antibiotic prescribed if cultures indicate a mixed infection. Culturing a specific bacterial organism should lead to appropriately targeted antibiotic therapy. In addition, the topical application of estrogen cream, applied sparingly twice a day to the interlabial area for a period of several weeks, leads to increased cornification of the vaginal and vestibular epithelium, making them more resistant to the bacterial flora which are normally present in the area. The persistence of a discharge (as opposed to recurrence of symptoms after clearing) suggests the possibility of a foreign body; vaginal irrigation should be repeated and a repeat examination performed. Ongoing attention to vulvar hygiene is necessary to prevent recurrence of symptoms, which is common with a mixed bacterial infection.

Chronic vulvar irritation can lead to the agglutination of the labia minor with resultant labial fusion/adhesions. Minor degrees of agglutination are common, and need not be specifically treated. Adhesions that result in urinary symptoms—dribbling, UTIs, pooling of urine behind the adhesions—or individuals with symptoms of pain or vulvar irritation, should be treated. Treatment consists of applying topical estrogen cream sparingly bid for 2 to 6 weeks. Treatment results in thinning of the adhesions, often with resultant separation. If the labia do not separate spontaneously with this treatment, the clinician can often apply topical 2% lidocaine to the external and internal surfaces with a Q-tip, and, by placing only gentle pressure, separate the labia with minimal trauma. The resultant raw surfaces should be treated with topical estrogen for a few more days, and there may be a small amount of spotting or bleeding from the area. Rarely, the child who has experienced a previous traumatic and painful labial separation will not even allow the clinician to examine the area; an examination and labial separation under anesthesia may be required. The key to treatment is to prevent recurrent adhesions; the daily topical application of an emollient ointment, such as A&D ointment, is required until pubertal development leads to estrogenization of the labia.

Another vulvar condition, which can be confused with an inflammatory lesion, is vulvar lichen sclerosis, which can occur in women and girls of all ages. Examination reveals an abnormal appearance to the labia, with thin, white,

"cigarette paper" skin changes in a keyhole appearance surrounding the vaginal introitus and anus. Linear areas of fissuring, or "blood blisters," may be seen, and there can be significant pain, itching, and irritation. While previous clinical observations suggested that the condition is likely to resolve with puberty, recent longitudinal studies suggest that this is not invariably the case. Treatment consists of the application of topical steroids, using a medium-high potency steroid initially (Betamethasone valerate 0.1% ointment) or high-potency steroid (Temovate 0.05% cream), and tapering to a low-dose steroid such as hydrocortisone for use on a chronic basis to prevent scarring.

Vaginal Bleeding

Vaginal bleeding may be the first sign of precocious puberty, although it is more commonly associated with inflammatory conditions, such as an acute group B strep vulvovaginitis, or skin conditions, such as lichen sclerosus (see Table

TABLE 25-3 Causes of Vaginal Bleeding in Prepubertal Girls

Vulvar and external
Vulvitis with excoriation
Trauma (e.g., straddle injury)
Lichen sclerosus
Condylomas
Molluscum contagiosum
Urethral prolapse
Vaginal
Vaginitis
Vaginal foreign body
Trauma (abuse, penetration)
Vaginal tumor
Uterine
Precocious puberty
Ovarian tumor
Exogenous estrogens
Topical
Enteral

SOURCE: Reproduced with permission from Hillard PA: Benign diseases of the female reproductive tract: Symptoms and signs, in Berek JS, Adashi EY, Hillard PA (eds): *Novak's Gynecology*, 12th ed. Baltimore: Williams & Wilkins, 1996.

25-3). The failure to find a specific cause with examination of the external genitalia should prompt a careful visual inspection of the vagina, and examination or imaging studies to rule out vaginal or ovarian pathology/tumors, such as a sarcoma botryoides or an estrogen-producing granulosa cell tumor. A history of bleeding must prompt questioning/evaluation for possible sexual abuse as well. Vulvovaginitis is a frequent cause of vaginal spotting, while frank bleeding is more likely related to a more serious condition such as precocious puberty or tumor. If there has been vulvar or perineal trauma from a straddle injury, an examination under anesthesia is indicated unless the complete extent of any lacerations or hematoma can be evaluated.

Hymenal and Vaginal Abnormalities

During childhood, abnormalities of the hymen may be noted by a caregiver. The diagnosis of vaginal agenesis or imperforate hymen should be made cautiously in the prepubertal girl. Parents should be informed of a possible abnormality, with the plan to reexamine the child after the onset of puberty, when breast development indicates estrogen stimulation, which will be manifest with an increasing "fimbrial" appearance of the hymen. The hymen, which originally appeared imperforate, may in reality be microperforate, or even normal in appearance, once estrogen stimulation occurs. While an imperforate hymen should not be corrected with incision until after puberty begins, the former concept that suggested delay until the vagina is well distended with blood, giving the typical thin blue-domed appearance, can result in significant dysmenorrhea and retrograde menses/endometriosis. Thus, the optimal timing for repair is after pubertal growth has begun but prior to menarche. The diagnosis of imperforate hymen must be absolutely certain prior to surgical correction, as a vaginal septum or vaginal agenesis can have a similar appearance.

Surgical errors can be avoided if the diagnosis of vaginal agenesis or vaginal septum has been confirmed with imaging studies. An ultrasound can serve as the initial screening procedure, confirming the presence or absence of a uterus. When more complex anomalies are suspected on the basis of the ultrasound, such as uterine septa, duplication, or vaginal septa with obstruction, an MRI is frequently the most helpful diagnostic test, allowing the planning of what may be complex surgical correction.

Pure vaginal agenesis with Mayer-Rokitansky-Küster-Hauser syndrome or androgen insensitivity syndrome can be treated with the surgical creation of a neovagina. However, many gynecologists who specialize in the care of adolescents favor the use of progressive dilation with graduated plastic dilators (the Frank technique), as it is associated with fewer complications and a more satisfactory result. In either case, the therapy should be delayed until the adolescent is motivated to use dilators (usually midadolescence, age 15 to 16). Even the surgical techniques require the use and wearing of dilators and should not be undertaken until the individual is willing to cope with the necessary therapeutic measures. Psychological counseling should occur concurrently with the medical therapy for vaginal anomalies, in an effort to help the young woman (and her family) understand the diagnosis, and cope with feelings of inadequacy, concerns about femininity, or grief about the inability to have children.

Pelvic Mass

The presence of a pelvic mass in the pediatric age group is cause for concern, and deserves careful evaluation to rule out neoplasm. Fewer than 5 percent of ovarian malignancies occur in children and adolescents, and ovarian tumors account for approximately 1 percent of all tumors in these age groups. In girls younger than 9 years of age, a high percentage of the ovarian neoplasms were found to be malignant—80 percent in one study. Because neoplastic tumors are rare, data are usually reported from referral centers. Some reports include only neoplastic masses, whereas others

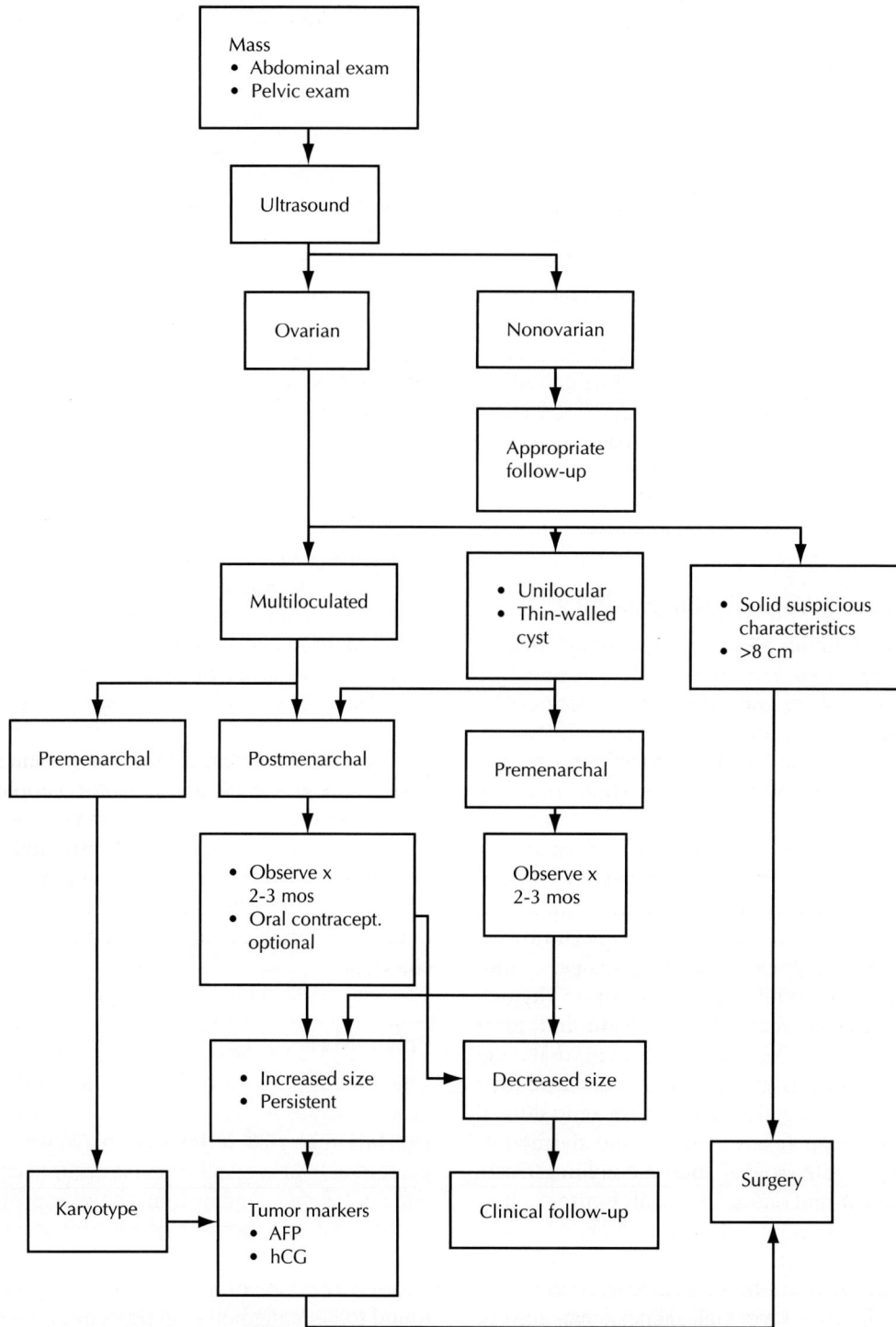

Figure 25-1. Management of pelvic masses in premenarchal and adolescent girls. [Reproduced with permission from Hillard PA: Benign diseases of the female reproductive tract: Symptoms and signs, in Berek JS, Adashi EY, Hillard PA (eds): *Novak's Gynecology*, 12th ed. Baltimore: Williams and Wilkins, 1996.]

TABLE 25-4   Causes of Pelvic Mass by Age

Infancy	Prepubertal	Adolescent	Reproductive	Perimenopausal	Postmenopausal
Functional ovarian cyst Germ cell	Germ cell tumor	Functional cyst Pregnancy Dermoid/other germ cell tumors Obstructing vaginal/uterine anomalies Epithelial ovarian tumors	Functional cyst Pregnancy Uterine fibroids Ovarian epithelial tumors	Fibroids Ovarian epithelial tumors Functional cysts	Ovarian tumor (malignant or benign) Bowel, malignant tumor or inflammatory Metastases

SOURCE: Reproduced with permission from Hillard PA: Benign diseases of the female reproductive tract: Symptoms and signs, in Berek JS, Adashi EY, Hillard PA (eds): *Novak's Gynecology*, 12th ed. Baltimore: Williams & Wilkins, 1996.

include nonneoplastic pelvic masses. In one series of ovarian masses in women under age 20 nonneoplastic masses made up two-thirds of the total; even in girls younger than 10 years of age, 60 percent in this series were nonneoplastic, and two-thirds of neoplastic masses were benign.

Contrary to previous teaching, functional ovarian masses/cysts do occur throughout the prepubertal age group and resolve spontaneously. They can be associated with hormonal production and sexual precocity. In young girls, the growth of a pelvic mass leads to the mass becoming abdominal in location, and thus palpable on abdominal examination. Ovarian masses can be confused with other abdominal masses occurring in children, such as Wilms' tumor or neuroblastoma. Acute pain may be associated with ovarian torsion.

When a mass is discovered, ultrasound imaging will determine if the mass is solid, a unilocular cyst, or a multilocular cyst. Solid masses are neoplastic and should prompt surgical removal. Germ cell tumors, both benign and malignant, are the most common ovarian tumors in this age group, and may be associated with the production of tumor markers such as AFP or hCG. An algorithm for the management of pelvic masses in premenarchal and adolescent girls is noted in Fig. 25-1. The clinician who does an exploratory laparotomy for an individual in this age group should be prepared to do an appropriate cancer staging procedure, although a conservative procedure with unilateral oophorectomy (and complete surgical staging) is indicated, unless the malignancy has spread to the abdominal organs. The diagnoses of ovarian masses are different for the pediatric/prepubertal age group than are for adolescents and older women (Table 25-4). Additional imaging studies such as CT scanning, MRI, or Doppler flow studies may help suggest the diagnosis.

A multilocular cyst is frequently benign, although the index of suspicion for neoplasm is higher than it is for a unilocular cyst, which is almost always benign. Conservatism and observation with repeat ultrasound examinations for a brief interval of two to three months is appropriate. For benign masses, surgical therapy should be avoided if possible. Preservation of ovarian tissue is a priority to ensure future endocrine function and fertility. Recurrence rates after cyst aspiration are as high as 50 percent.

References and Selected Reading

1. American Medical Association: *Diagnostic and Treatment Guidelines on Child Sexual Abuse.* Chicago: American Medical Association, 1992.
2. Berenson AB, Heger AH, Hayes JM, Bailey RK, Emans SJ: Appearance of the hymen in prepubertal girls. *Pediatrics* 89:387–394, 1992.
3. Carpenter SE, Rock JA: *Pediatric and adolescent gynecology.* New York: Raven, 1992.
4. Emans SJ, Goldstein DP: The gynecologic examination of the prepubertal child with vulvo-vaginitis: use

of the knee-chest position. *Pediatrics* 65:758–760, 1980.

5. Emans SJ, Goldstein DP: *Pediatric and adolescent gynecology,* 4th ed. Philadelphia: Lippincott-Raven, 1998.

6. Hammerschlag MR, Alpert S, Onderdonk AB, et al: Anaerobic microflora of the vagina in children. *Am J Obstet Gynecol* 131:853–856, 1978.

7. Herman-Giddens ME: Vaginal foreign bodies and child sexual abuse. *Arch, Pediatr, Adolesc Med* 148:195–200, 1994.

8. Herman-Giddens ME, Slore EJ, Wasserman RC, et al: Secondary sexual characteristics and menses in young girls seen in office practice: A study from the pediatric research in office settings network. *Pediatric* 99:505–512, 1997.

9. Hillard PA: Benign diseases of the female reproductive tract: Symptoms and signs, in Berek JS, Adashi EY, Hillard PA (eds): *Novak's Gynecology,* 12th ed. Baltimore, MD: Williams & Wilkins, 1996, pp 331–398.

10. Lampkin BC, Wong KY, Kalinyak KA, et al: Ovarian malignancies in children and adolescents. *Surg Clin North Am* 65:1386, 1985.

11. Lindenman E. Shepard MK, Pescovitz RH: Mullerian agenesis: An update. *Obstet Gynecol* 90:307–312, 1997.

12. Marshall WA, Tanner JM: Variations in patterns of pubertal changes in girls. *Arch Dis Child* 44:291–303, 1969.

13. Muram D: Child sexual abuse—genital tract findings in prepubertal girls. I. The unaided medical examination. *Am J Obstet Gynecol* 160:328–333, 1989.

14. Muram D: Vaginal bleeding in childhood and adolescence. *Obstet Gynecol Clin North Am* 17:389–408, 1990.

15. Norris HG, Jensen RD: Relative frequency of ovarian neoplasms in children and adolescents. *Cancer* 30:719, 1972.

16. Pokorny SF: Child abuse and infections. *Obstet Gynecol Clin North Am* 16:401–415, 1989.

17. Pokorny SF: Configuration of the prepubertal hymen. *Am J Obstet Gynecol* 157:950–956, 1987.

18. Pokorny SF: *Pediatric and Adolescent Gynecology*: New York: Chapman & Hall, 1996.

19. Pokorny SF: Prepubertal vulvovaginopathies. *Obstet Gynecol Clin North Am* 19:39–58, 1992.

20. Pokorny SF: The genital examination of the infant through adolescence. *Curr Opin Obstet Gynecol* 5:753–757, 1993.

21. Pokorny SF, Pokorny WJ, Kramer W: Acute genital injury in the prepubertal girl. *Am J Obstet Gynecol* 166:1461–1466, 1992.

22. Pokorny SF, Stormer J: Atraumatic removal of secretions from the prepubertal vagina. *Am J Obstet Gynecol* 156:581–582, 1987.

23. Sanfilippo JS, Muram D, Lee PA, Dewhurst J: *Pediatric and Adolescent Gynecology,* 2d ed. Philadelphia: WB Saunders, 1994.

24. Van Winter JT, Simmons PS, Podratz KC: Surgically treated adnexal masses in infancy, childhood, and adolescence. *Am J Obstet Gynecol* 170:1780–1789, 1994.

CHAPTER 26

The Pap Smear

Arthur L. Herbst

**IMPORTANT CONSIDERATIONS
        IN THE OBTAINING OF A CERVICAL
        PAP SMEAR**

**METHODS OF REPORTING
        SMEAR RESULTS**

HPV TESTING

**CHARACTERISTICS OF THE
        CONVENTIONAL SMEAR AND
        FALSE-NEGATIVE RESULTS**

AutoPap   •   PAPNET   •   ThinPrep

FREQUENCY OF PAP SMEAR SCREENING

Important Considerations in Obtaining a Cervical Pap Smear

Because of its accessible location at the top of the vagina, the cervix is uniquely situated for careful monitoring to prevent the development of invasive cancer. Cervical cytology or the Pap smear provides an important mechanism for the implementation of an effective cervical cancer prevention program. It is important to realize that the Pap smear is a screening test that provides the clinician with useful information. It does not establish a diagnosis, and a negative smear report may occur in spite of the presence of neoplastic disease.

The Pap smear samples the so-called transformation zone of the cervix, which is an area usually located on the cervix that is formed by the squamocolumnar junction, that is, the junction of squamous epithelium on the exocervix with co-

lumnar epithelium that predominates in the endocervix. Columnar epithelium on the exocervix normally undergoes a process called squamous metaplasia, and it is this area that is known as the normal transformation zone. During reproductive years, the junction is just outside the external os and moves further outward during pregnancy. In the postmenopausal woman, it usually recedes into the endocervical canal. To obtain an adequate and proper Pap smear, the entire transformation zone, including both the exocervix (portio of the cervix) and the endocervix, must be sampled (Figs. 26-1 and 26-2).

The following describes the general technique that should be used in obtaining a PAP smear; the pertinent points are summarized in Table 26-1. It is important that the cervix and upper vagina be clearly visualized, and that no surgical lubricant be used. Gently remove excess mucus and discharge. If the patient has severe vaginitis, treat it and take the Pap smear during a subsequent visit, if the patient is reliable and will keep the following appointment. Ideally, the portio of the cervix (Fig. 26-1) and the endocervix (Fig. 26-2) are separately sampled. The separate specimens can be submitted on two slides, because knowing whether abnormal cells exist in the endocervix is an important point in management of the abnormal Pap smear (see Chap. 47). It is also possible to place the separate samples on the same slide so that the location of the abnormal cells can be clearly identified, or at least give separate reports concerning the endocervical sample, in order to impart the most useful information to the clinician. Figure 26-3 shows a type of slide in use at the University of Chicago that permits separation of the

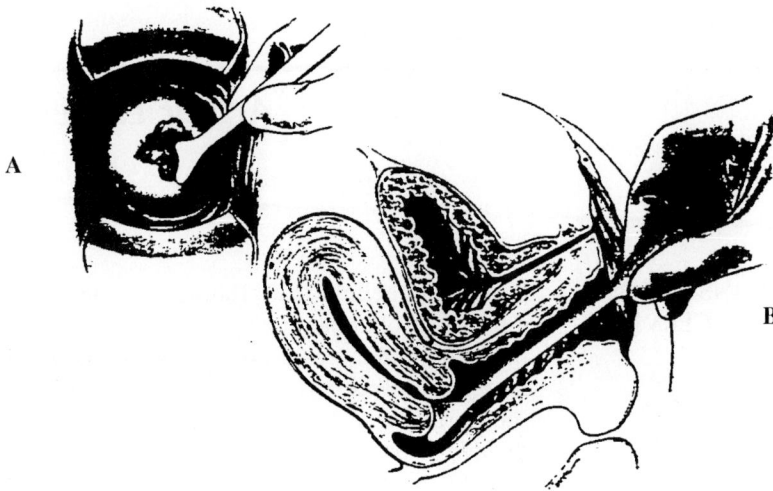

Figure 26-1 *A* and *B,* Scrape of the exocervix. [Reprinted with permission from Herbst AL: Intra-epithelial neoplasia of the cervix, in Droegemueller W, Herbst AL, Mishell DR, Stenchever MA (eds): *Comprehensive Gynecology,* 3d ed. St. Louis: Mosby Yearbook, 1997.]

specimens from the cervix, endocervix, and also from the vagina, if desired.

Methods of Reporting Smear Results

A number of different classifications have been utilized to report the results of cervical cytology. Traditionally, terms used to describe the varying degrees of premalignant changes of the cervix have been from slight to moderate dysplasia, to more severe lesions of moderate to severe dysplasia, and the most severe premalignant change of carcinoma in situ. This system employs *four* levels of abnormalities and is a traditional system that has been in use for a number of years (Table 26-2).

There have been a number of studies done to estimate the risk of progression of premalignant lesions to a more advanced change or to actual malignancy. Table 26-3 shows the results abstracted from a summary article by Oster,[14] which

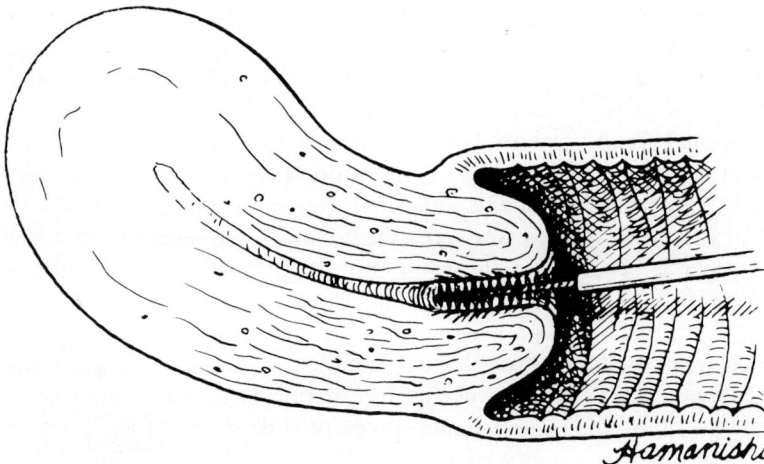

Figure 26-2 Sampling of the endocervix.

TABLE 26-1 General Technique to Use to Obtain a Pap Smear

- Patient should avoid douching or intercourse on day of exam.
- The Pap smear is obtained prior to the bimanual exam.
- No lubricant should be used on the speculum, which should be moistened with warm water, if needed.
- Visualize the entire cervix.
- Remove any excess discharge prior to taking the smear, and take any indicated cultures.
- When taking the Pap smear, the endocervix and the exocervix should be separately sampled (Fig. 26-1). The endocervical brush ideally is rotated 90–120 degrees for an adequate sample. Greater rotation predisposes to bleeding.
- The slide is immediately fixed; if spray fixative is used, hold it at least 12 in. from the slide to avoid cellular artifact.
- In DES-exposed females, separately sample the vagina, particularly the upper one-third of the vagina.

TABLE 26-2 Traditional Classification of Papanicoulaou Smear

- Normal
- Metaplasia
- Inflammation
- Minimal atypia-koilocytosis
- Mild dysplasia (CIN I)
- Moderate dysplasia (CIN II)
- Severe dysplasia—carcinoma in situ (CIN III)
- Invasive carcinoma

combines a number of different studies reported from various centers throughout the world. The results are consistent with the concept that low-grade lesions can often regress, while the risk of progression increases with higher-grade lesions. As shown in Table 26-3, the risk of progression to invasive cancer is lower for mild dysplasia and

becomes quite large for patients with carcinoma in situ. These are cytologic studies; it should be emphasized that these estimates are not based on biopsy, which is required for treatment decisions.

New terminology was introduced in the 1970s, which divided the premalignant abnormalities into *three* grades of severity: mild cervical intraepithelial neoplasia (comparable to mild dysplasia [CIN I]); an intermediate level of abnormality comparable to moderate dysplasia [CIN II]; or severe intraepithelial neoplasia (comparable to severe dysplasia and carcinoma in situ) [CIN III]. In 1988, a further adaptation of cytologic terminology was introduced, (known as the "Bethesda System" (Table 26-4), which made a number of

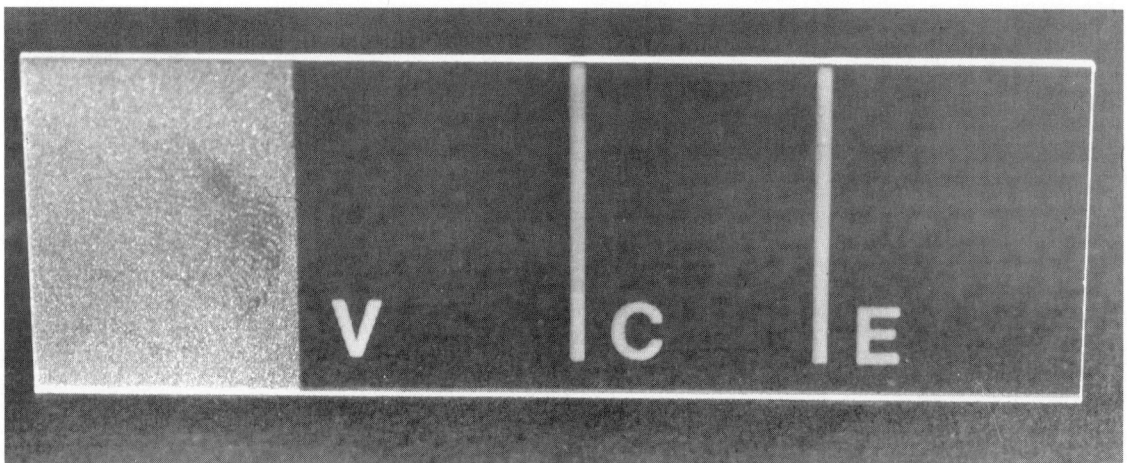

Figure 26-3 Three-part Pap smear slide.

TABLE 26-3 Natural History of CIN

Subjects (N)	Regress	Persist	Progression CIN III	Progression Invasive
4504 CIN I	57%	32%	11%	1%
2247 CIN II	43%	35%	22%	5%
767 CIN III	32%	?<56%	—	12%[a]

[a]Limited follow-up in some series.
Limited to report of cytology and/or biopsy alone. Excludes cone and destructive therapy.
SOURCE: From Oster AG: *Int J Gynecol Pathol* 12:186, 1993.

TABLE 26-4 The Bethesda System for Reporting Cervical/Vaginal Cytologic Diagnoses

Format of the Report:
a. A statement on Adequacy of the Specimen for Evaluation
b. A General Categorization which may be used to assist with clerical triage (optional)
c. The Descriptive Diagnosis

Adequacy of the Specimen
Satisfactory for evaluation
Satisfactory for evaluation but limited by ... (specify reason)
Unsatisfactory for evaluation ... (specify reason)

General Categorization (Optional)
Within normal limits
Benign cellular changes: See descriptive diagnoses
Epithelial cell abnormality: See descriptive diagnoses

Descriptive Diagnoses
Benign cellular changes
  Infection
    Trichomonas vaginalis
    Fungal organisms morphologically consistent with *Candida* spp
    Predominance of coccobacilli consistent with shift in vaginal flora
    Bacteria morphologically consistent with *Actinomyces* spp
    Cellular changes associated with herpes simplex virus
    Other

Reactive changes
  Reactive cellular changes associated with:
    Inflammation (includes typical repair)
    Atrophy with inflammation ("atrophic vaginitis")
    Radiation
    Intrauterine contraceptive device (IUD)
    Other

Epithelial Cell Abnormalities
  Squamous Cell
    Atypical squamous cells of undetermined significance: Qualify[a]
    Low-grade squamous intraepithelial lesion encompassing:
      HPV[b]
      Mild dysplasia/CIN 1
    High-grade squamous intraepithelial lesion encompassing:
      Moderate and severe dysplasia
      CIS/CIN 2 AND CIN 3
    Squamous cell carcinoma
  Glandular Cell
    Endometrial cells, cytologically benign, in a postmenopausal woman
    Atypical glandular cells of undetermined significance: Qualify[a]
    Endocervical adenocarcinoma
    Endometrial adenocarcinoma
    Extrauterine adenocarcinoma
    Adenocarcinoma, not otherwise specified (NOS)

Other malignant neoplasms: Specify
Hormonal evaluation (applied to vaginal smears only)
  Hormonal pattern compatible with age and history
  Hormonal pattern incompatible with age and history: Specify
  Hormonal evaluation not possible due to: Specify

[a]Atypical squamous or glandular cells of undetermined significance should be further qualified as to whether a reactive or a premalignant/malignant process is favored.

[b]Cellular changes of human papillomavirus (HPV)—previously termed koilocytosis atypia, or condylomatous atypia—are included in the category of low-grade squamous intraepithelial lesion.

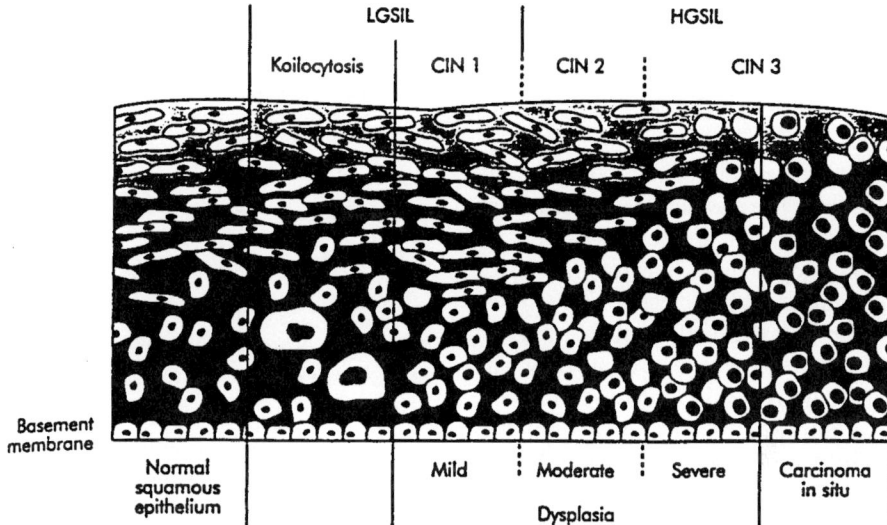

Figure 26-4 Diagram of cervical epithelium showing various terminologies used to characterize progressive degrees of cervical neoplasia. [Reprinted with permission from Herbst AL: Intraepithelial neoplasia of the cervix, in Droegemueller W, Herbst AL, Mishell DR, Stenchever MA (eds): *Comprehensive Gynecology*, 3d ed. St. Louis: Mosby Yearbook, 1997.]

changes and included only *two* levels of abnormalities. The mild changes are known as low-grade squamous intraepithelial lesions (LGSIL), while the severe type is known as high-grade squamous intraepithelial lesions (HGSIL). Figure 26-4 depicts these three systems and shows how the various terminologies overlap. An additional change was that the Bethesda System assigned the diagnosis of koilocytosis to the category of LGSIL, which means that when this diagnosis is made, it is equivalent to mild dysplasia, or CIN I.

Two other terms were introduced with the Bethesda System and these are *ASCUS* (atypical squamous cells of undetermined significance) and *AGCUS* (atypical glandular cells of undetermined significance). ASCUS is frequently used to describe a smear that contains some atypicality, but that does not have changes sufficiently severe to warrant a diagnosis of low-grade SIL. There is disagreement and debate on the importance and premalignant risk of smears carrying this diagnosis. In general, an ASCUS

diagnosis should occur in no more than 3 to 5 percent of smear reports from a given laboratory and tends to be more frequent in those populations with a higher frequency of premalignant dysplastic changes, such as sexually transmitted disease clinics. Close communication between the clinician and cytologist is of help in determining what steps should be taken in the management of cases of ASCUS smears (see Chap. 47).

A much less frequent, but even less well understood term is that of atypical glandular cells of undetermined significance (AGCUS). As the term implies, there is abnormality noted in the glandular cells and the degree of this abnormality is of uncertain significance. Occasionally, such diagnosis occurs in cases that have only inflammation, while in other instances, premalignant glandular *and* premalignant squamous lesions have been identified. Some cytology laboratories modify the AGCUS diagnosis with the term "favor neoplasia" or "favor reactive." The former requires more diligent follow-up and evaluation, while the reactive category is most likely due to inflammation.

Another problem for the clinician has been the term koilocytosis. In general, this describes a cell that is usually infected with human papillomavirus (HPV). Unfortunately, the diagnosis is sometimes made in the absence of the stringent morphologic criteria that are required. Specifically, to be a koilocyte a cell must contain cytoplasmic vacuolization *with* nuclear abnormalities, such as nuclear enlargement, binucleation, or hyperchromasia. In the absence of nuclear abnormalities, a diagnosis of koilocytosis must not be made. It is important to know that normal glycogenated squamous epithelial cells and some inflammatory cells can contain cytoplasmic vacuolization, but these cells do not have *nuclear* abnormalities and are not koilocytes, and, therefore, do not qualify for that diagnosis under the Bethesda System, even though they erroneously, in some instances, are so labeled. This leads to an incorrect diagnosis of LGSIL. When this occurs, there is overdiagnosis and the risk of overtreatment.

HPV Testing

HPV has been strongly associated with cervical intraepithelial neoplasia and cervical cancer. Studies of cervical cancer indicate the presence of HPV in about 85 to 90 percent of cases. HPV infection is noted most frequently in patients with multiple sexual partners, as well as in those patients with sexually transmitted disease. Molecular techniques allow the typing of HPV, and over 70 human types have been identified. Various studies have led to some of these types being considered as high-risk (oncogenic), while others are considered low-risk for malignant or premalignant changes. Table 26-5 shows different types that fit into each of these categories. In general, HPV types 6 and 11 are considered low-risk and are often associated with benign condyloma, whereas HPV types 16 and 18, as well as others, are identified as high-risk types.

TABLE 26-5 Oncogenic Potential of HPV Types

Potential	HPV Types
Nononcogenic	6, 11, 42, 43, 44
Oncogenic	16, 18, 31, 33, 39, 45, 51, 52, 56, 58, ?59, ?68

There have been innumerable studies to evaluate whether knowing the presence of a specific HPV type in an individual might predict whether or not that individual will develop a significant or high-grade premalignant lesion. Some investigations have indicated that HPV testing can be predictive,[9] particularly in assessing or triaging individuals with low-grade or ASCUS smears, while others have concluded that such testing of multiple HPV types is not useful.[10] My opinion is that in view of the lack of specificity, as well as conflicting results regarding HPV testing, it is not worthwhile to routinely conduct such testing in the management of patients. Clinical decision-making should be based on morphologic (biopsy) criteria, as well as on characteristics including reliability and history. The National Cancer Institute is currently conducting a randomized trial to determine the optimal way to manage low-grade Pap smear reports and to identify the value of HPV testing in these situations. The results of these studies should be available in a few years.

Characteristics of the Conventional Smear and False-Negative Results

Cervical cytology is very useful, but not a perfect screening test. False-negative results do occur, and are estimated to be in the range of 5 to 25 percent in most series. A false-negative rate refers to the number of smears that are reported as normal out of a population of abnormal smears. Thus, if a laboratory during the course of a week has 100 abnormal smears, but correctly identifies only 75 of the 100, the false-negative rate is 25 percent. Similarly, if 90 of the abnormal slides are correctly identified, the false-negative rate is 10 percent. Certain characteristics of the slide predispose to an increase in the likelihood of a false-negative reading. The average conventional smear contains approximately 300,000 to 500,000 cells and, depending upon the cytology laboratory, the average cytotechnician might spend 5 to 10 minutes reviewing the slide. However, a number of slides are difficult to interpret, because they often have a few abnormal cells—sometimes less than 100—or the abnormal cells are very small and difficult to spot, or the smear has a great deal of inflammation or blood which obscures the abnormal cells. Taking Pap smears properly can reduce the latter problem.

To reduce the false-negative rate and improve the accuracy of Pap smear reading, a number of new technologies have been introduced in recent years. Three of these are briefly described. Either they involve the use of a computer to aid in the diagnosis (PAPNET or AutoPap) or use an alternative liquid-based preparation that produces a monolayer (ThinPrep). The FDA has approved all three for use in the United States. The AutoPap and ThinPrep systems are currently approved for primary screening, and the PAPNET system is approved for rescreening in the United States, but is approved for primary screening in countries outside the United States, including Canada.

AutoPap

The AutoPap system uses the computer to sort slides into a negative or positive category. Those slides assigned to the negative group are considered to be free of abnormalities and are not further reviewed, which improves laboratory efficiency. Those assigned to the positive group are reviewed by the cytotechnician for abnormalities, although many of the slides in this group ultimately may be found to be negative. The system improves laboratory reliability and allows increased productivity.

PAPNET

The PAPNET system is an interactive system, which displays the 128 computer-selected most abnormal cells on a video screen. These cells can be reviewed in a few minutes by the cytotechnologist and can be simultaneously located on the slide for direct visualization and review. It is possible that all 128 computer-identified cells do not display a premalignant abnormality, in which case the smear is assigned a normal reading. Conversely, the computer is capable of identifying slides that contain only a few abnormal cells or the very small cells that can lead to false-negative results. The system is labor-intensive due to its interactive characteristics, but does produce very accurate and precise results.

ThinPrep

For the ThinPrep system, the smear is taken from the cervix and placed into a liquid-based medium, which is then processed through a filter. The resulting sample includes cells from both the endocervix and exocervix. After filtration, a representative sample is placed on a slide, which permits visualization in a thin or monolayer form. This enhances the cytotechnologist's ability to read the smear and reduces the problem of unsatisfactory smears, particularly due to inflammation. The technique produces a clean preparation, which is more efficiently read by the cytotechnologist.

All of these tests, in their trials before the FDA, were shown to enhance the effectiveness of Pap smear screening. Various cost-effectiveness studies have been done and there is some controversy concerning the cost effectiveness of these techniques, and the degree to which these techniques can reduce mortality. These studies are reimbursed in many situations, but not all are covered by all provider health plans. Additional information concerning these new technologies will be becoming available in the next few years, and other similar technologies will likely be introduced to enhance precision of Pap smear interpretation.

Frequency of Pap Smear Screening

The frequency with which Pap smear screening should be done has been a subject of debate. Certain countries advocate Pap screening only every three years. However, it is undeniable that the leading predisposing cause of the development of cervical cancer in the United States is lack of Pap smear screening, particularly of certain indigent populations. It is not uncommon to find a patient with a diagnosis of cervical cancer who has not had a Pap smear in the previous ten years. The unfortunate few who have had more frequent Pap smear screening have, unfortunately, had smears with false-negative results. It is very unusual, though not impossible, for an invasive lesion to develop in an individual who has regular, annual Pap smear screening. The American College of Obstetricians and Gynecologists Committee on Gynecologic Practice recommends that all women who are sexually active or have reached the age of 18 years should undergo an annual Pap smear screening and pelvic examination. If a woman has three or more consecutive examinations with normal findings, it is then recommended for low-risk women that the Pap smear be done less frequently at the physician's discretion. If any high-risk factors are present, it is extremely important that the patient have an annual Pap smear. Such high-risk factors include women with multiple sexual partners or whose male partners have had multiple partners, those whose sexual partners have had partners with cervical cancer, and those with HPV infections. Any woman who is immunosuppressed, such as those who have received organ transplants

or have been infected with the HIV virus, must have regular Pap smear screening. Any individual who has a history of cervical intraepithelial neoplasia or any cervical, endometrial, vaginal, or vulvar carcinoma should have at least an annual Pap smear.

Summary

This chapter outlines the important features of taking the Pap smear. It summarizes various considerations for the clinicians who are involved in interpreting the Pap smear report, as well as understanding its strength and weakness. The Pap smear has been extraordinarily effective when used regularly, reducing the incidence of cervical cancer. At the same time, it is not a perfect test and new technologies are being introduced that can enhance the accuracy of Pap smear interpretation. Nonetheless, the most important public health factor in the prevention of cervical cancer for women is that they receive a regular Pap smear screening. This should be done at a minimum annually for those women who fit into high-risk categories, and should be done regularly for all women.

References and Selected Readings

1. American College of Obstetricians and Gynecologists: *Committee Opinion: Recommendations Frequency of Pap Test Screening.* Washington, DC: ACOG, 1995. Number 152.
2. American College of Obstetricians and Gynecologists: *Ambulatory Care Criteria Set.* Washington, DC: ACOG, 1995. Number 6.
3. American College of Obstetricians and Gynecologists: *Committee Opinion, New Pap Test Screening Techniques.* Washington, DC: ACOG, 1998. Number 206.
4. Cox JT, Lorincz AT, Schiffman MH, et al: Human papillomavirus testing by hybrid capture appears to be useful in triaging women with a cytologic diagnosis of atypical squamous cells of undermined significance. *Am J Obstet Gynecol* 172:946, 1995.
5. DeMay RM: *The Art & Science of Cytopathology.* Chicago: American Journal of Clinical Pathologists Press, 1996.

6. Hatem F, Wilbur DC: High-grade lesions following negative smears: False-negatives or rapid progression? *Diagn Cytopathol* 12:135, 1995.

7. Herbst AL: The Bethesda System for cervical/vaginal cytologic diagnoses: A note of caution. *Obstet Gynecol* 76:449, 1990.

8. Herbst AL: Intraepithelial neoplasia of the cervix, in Droegemueller W, Herbst AL, Mishell DR, Stenchever MA (eds.): *Comprehensive Gynecology,* 3d ed. St. Louis: Mosby Yearbook, 1997.

9. Herbst AL: The Bethesda System for cervical/vaginal cytologic diagnoses Podratz KC (ed.): *Clin Obstet Gynecol* 35: 22–27, 1992.

10. Kaufman RH, Adam E, Icenogle J, et al: Relevance of HPV screening in management of cervical intraepithelial neoplasia. *Am J Obstet Gynecol* 176:87, 1997.

11. Kennedy AW, Salimeri SS, Wirth SL, et al: Results of the clinical evaluation of atypical glandular cells of undertermined significance (AGCUS) on routine cervical cytology screening. *Gynecol Oncol* 63(1):14, 1996.

12. Kurman RJ, Henson DE, Herbst AL, et al: Interim guidelines for management of abnormal cervical cytology. *JAMA* 271:1866, 1994.

13. Montz FJ, et al: Natural history of the minimally abnormal Papanicolaou smear. *Obstet Gynecol* 80:385, 1992.

14. Ostor AG: Natural history of cervical intraepithelial neoplasia: A critical review. *Int J Gynecol Pathol* 12:186, 1993.

15. Syrjanen K, Kataja V, Yliskoski M, et al: Natural history of cervical human papillomavirus lesions does not substantiate the biologic relevance of the Bethesda System. *Obstet Gynecol* 79:675, 1992.

Contraception and Abortion

Carolyn Westhoff

There are 60 million women aged 15 to 44 in the United States. Most of these women spend at least 20 years at risk of unintended pregnancy; that is, being sexually active with a male partner and not seeking pregnancy. Due to inaccurate ideas about their fertility, due to fears of the most effective contraceptive methods, and due to difficulty obtaining birth control methods just when they are needed, American women experience over three million unintended pregnancies each year. One-half of these pregnancies end in abortion.[34,72]

The primary care provider can help patients reduce the likelihood of unintended pregnancy by proactively asking every patient about their contraceptive needs and experience. Waiting for the reproductive-age woman to raise the issue of contraception can be a serious problem for the many who are shy about this sensitive topic. Many women avoid effective methods because of mistaken beliefs about side effects that need to be corrected. Many women discontinue highly effective methods because their partners are worried about side effects; therefore, for providers who take care of both women and men, asking male patients as well as female patients about their contraceptive concerns can help the couple practice more effective contraception. Finally, parents of young adults often believe that talking about contraception will encourage their children to have sex; parents also usually believe that their adolescent children will take the initiative to come to them for help if pregnancy occurs. The clinician needs to correct these incorrect ideas and encourage their patients who are parents to educate their children about contraception.

Young women state that contraception is one of the issues that they most want to discuss with a clinician, but this issue is often left unaddressed. Too often, both doctors and patients wait for the other to initiate discussion of potentially embarassing topics such as birth control. Do not wait for the patient to ask. Tell each patient that family planning services are available; decide for your practice what you can offer directly, what you can learn, and what you will refer out; then tell your patients what these services are. Take care to include testing for and treatment of sexually transmitted diseases (STDs) in this list of services. Specifically tell your patients that confidential reproductive health care is available, and offer to help your patients to involve, as appropriate, their parents or partners.

Condoms

Most male condoms are latex and may be lubricated with either a nonoxynol-9 based spermicide or with an inert lubricant. The pore size of latex condoms is small enough to block passage of sperm as well as any sexually transmitted pathogens. Male condoms made of polyurethane are also available in some areas and have similar STD prevention benefits. Male condoms made of lamb cecum effectively prevent transmission of sperm, but may be less effective against STDs, and thus are not recommended for STD prevention. Female condoms are made of polyurethane, lubricated with an inert fluid supplied with each package, and prevent passage of both sperm and of STDs.[50,78]

All condoms prevent pregnancy by blocking access of sperm to the upper reproductive tract of the female. The addition of spermicide may improve protection in case of leakage or breakage, but there are no empirical data that quantify the additional effect of the spermicide. Typical users of condoms report about 10 pregnancies per 100 couples in the first year of condom use. Actual failure rates experienced by condom users vary greatly depending on correct and consistent use. Two frequent reasons for unplanned pregnancy among condom users include not using the condom during the early minutes of intercourse leading to insemination by the preejaculatory fluid, and also failure to use condoms during an imperfectly calculated safe period. Condom slippage and breakage are also reasons for unintended pregnancy. Any of these occurrences can be remedied by use of emergency contraception.

The only medical risk associated with condom use is latex allergy. This is an increasingly common problem that can be manifested by local irritation or systemic symptoms.[87] Systemic symptoms, although rare, may indicate a risk of anaphylaxis and require complete abstinence from latex exposure. Local symptoms, such as irritation, itching, and discharge, may indicate allergy, but are more likely due to other factors, such as inadequate lubrication, or irritation from exposure to the spermicide or its vehicle. Patients with these complaints should be encouraged to use a water-based lubricant, and to try brands of condoms without spermicide. In addition, even though condom use protects against STDs, vaginal symptoms in a condom user may indicate a genital tract infection, which should be sought by examination. Conversely, when evaluating a patient for an irritating discharge, consider spermicide irritation as a possible cause.

Hormonal Methods

Combination Oral Contraceptives

It has been estimated that the birth control pill has been used by about 80 percent of American women born since 1935, and is typically used for an average of 5 years. While it is most often used by women in their 20s, oral contraceptive (OC) use is appropriate for women throughout their reproductive years. There are many formulations available. Essentially all of the combination pills contain 21 active pills followed by 7 days of placebo. This pattern of active pills followed by placebo was developed to mimic the bleeding pattern of a physiological menstrual cycle, but the contraceptive effect can be equally achieved by other patterns, including continuous active pills. Today's active pills contain from 20 to 35 μg of ethinyl estradiol, and a wide variety of different progestins. Monophasic formulations contain the same fixed hormone combination in every active tablet; in multiphasic formulations, the dose of one or both hormones may change several times over 21 days. Most of the different formulations that are typically used are approximately equally safe and effective, although women may strongly prefer particular formulations due to individual differences in minor side effects. These differences are usually not predictable nor easily explained, and women's consequent pill preferences should be respected.

Birth control pills prevent pregnancy through multiple simultaneous mechanisms of action. First, the continuous estrogen inhibits follicle-stimulating hormone (FSH) release, thus diminishing the development of ovarian follicles (and decreasing endogenous estrogen production). Second, the continuous progestin prevents the occurrence of a midcycle luteinizing hormone (LH) surge, which would otherwise stimulate ovulation if a dominant follicle were present (thus preventing endogenous progesterone production). Third, the progestin thickens cervical mucus, which prevents the ascent of sperm to the upper genital tract. Finally, the progestin prevents development of an endometrium that would be suitable for implantation if a fertilized ovum reached the uterus.

Today's low-dose pills are highly effective, and the typical failure rates reported for the first year of use are about 3 percent. As with most other methods, the failure rate varies according to correct and consistent use.[69] One of the main reasons for unintended pregnancy is that oral contraceptive users are too quick to discontinue the method when they experience small problems or when they anticipate a short period of abstinence. For instance, some women incorrectly interpret the amenorrhea that can normally occur in many OC users as a sign of pregnancy and discontinue the pills. Such women often become pregnant immediately after discontinuing the OCs.

Another common reason for pregnancy in OC users is difficulty in refilling a prescription; clinicians should be liberal in giving refills to satisfied OC users. Annual refills are reasonable, and a woman should be able to obtain additional refills easily.

Drug interactions are a rare cause of OC failure.[15] Those drugs that activate hepatic enzymes can lead to rapid inactivation of the oral hormones and thus permit ovulation and pregnancy to occur. Antiseizure medications, including phenobarbital, phenytoin, primidone, and carbamazepine, may have this effect, and barbiturates used for other indications are suspect. The only antibiotics clearly shown to have this effect are rifampin and possibly griseofulvin. The suspicion that other antibiotics decrease the effectiveness of OCs through a possible modification of the enter-

ohepatic circulation has not been clearly substantiated despite many studies of this question.

The widespread fear of OCs is completely out of proportion to any risks. The main fears focus on cancer and cardiovascular diseases. New studies have evaluated today's low-dose pills with respect to both venous and arterial events.[29] We now know that the risks of stroke and heart attack are not increased for appropriately selected OC users.[13] Strokes are very rare in reproductive-age women, and are mainly secondary to hypertension;[64] similarly, myocardial infarctions in young women are mainly associated with cigarette smoking and other identifiable predispositions.[47,55] The risk of venous thromboembolism (VTE)—whether presenting as a deep vein thrombosis in the leg, or as a pulmonary embolism, or as a cerebral vein thrombosis—is still increased with the use of combined OCs.[36–38] In healthy young women who are not pregnant and not using OCs, the risk of a venous thrombosis is about 1 case per 10,000 women per year. For OC users, the risk is about 3 cases per 10,000 women per year. Fortunately, these events are rarely fatal. Women who are at a high risk of VTE due to obesity (body mass index (BMI) > 30), or due to a genetic predisposition, will have those risks magnified by OC use, but these events are very rare even in high-risk groups. There is growing evidence that most of the VTE risk seen with OCs may be concentrated in the first two years of OC use.[61] The magnitude of the VTE risk has decreased as the estrogen dose of OCs decreased; however, recent studies do not show any additional decrement in risk for OCs containing 20 μg of estrogen when compared to those containing 30 to 35 μg of estrogen. Recent studies also suggested that the risk of DVT varied according to the type of progestin used in the OCs.

Fear of cancer is another reason that women and their doctors avoid the OCs. Breast cancer increased in the U.S. during the same years that OC use became widespread. Because breast cancer can be a hormonally mediated disease, a possible relationship between OCs and this cancer is of concern. Studies have long agreed that OCs do not increase the most common breast cancers, those diagnosed after age 50 or after menopause. Controversy has centered on the possible effect of OCs on the less-common breast cancer that is diagnosed in the premenopausal years. The urgency to resolve this issue led to a large number of epidemiological studies throughout the world in the 1980s and 1990s. A combined analysis of these studies that included over 50,000 cases of breast cancer and 100,000 controls has provided a comprehensive assessment of the question.[6] In that analysis, current and recent OC users had slightly more breast cancer diagnosed than non-users. Past users and never users had similar risks of breast cancer. The cancers diagnosed in OC users were more likely to be localized than those diagnosed in nonusers, and OC users had a deficit of more advanced breast cancers. These findings suggest that OC users, who have to remain in contact with the health care system to have their prescriptions renewed, have earlier diagnosis due to more surveillance. Alternatively, OC use might accelerate the growth of well-differentiated cancers, bringing such women to medical attention sooner than nonusers. The cumulative number of breast cancer cases by age 50 (the end of the reproductive years) is the same for users and never users. In addition, OC dose or duration of use has no effect on breast cancer risk; nor do OCs modify the excess risk that is due to a positive family history. These results should be reassuring to the many women who are very worried about the possible effect of OCs on breast cancer risk.

Almost every other type of cancer has been suspected of having an association with OCs. Carefully done studies have excluded most of these associations. Whether OCs are a cofactor in the development of squamous, or the more rare, adenocarcinoma of the cervix, remains unclear.[5] Studies may never completely disentangle the complex effects of confounding factors such as sexual behavior, HPV infection, and smoking.[31] Because periodic cervical screening is routinely recommended and widely available, OC users will benefit from early detection as much as other women in the population. Hepatic adenoma and hepatocellular carcinomas were associated with high-estrogen-dose OCs in the past. Because these conditions are so rare, it is difficult to determine whether there is any extra risk associated with today's low-dose pills. It has been shown that OCs do not increase the risk of hepatic cancer in women who are chronic carriers of hepatitis B.[18]

Ovarian and endometrial cancer are both greatly reduced in women who have used OCs.[75] Studies have consistently agreed on this effect, and have shown that the magnitude of reduced risk increases with more years of OC use. In addition, the effect lasts long after OCs are discontinued, and may prove to be lifelong. It is biologically plausible that these observed reductions in risk are due to true protective effects of OCs, because OC use inhibits endometrial proliferation and decreases ovarian activity, including ovulation. Women who are worried about cancer may want to know that 10 years of OC use is associated with an 80 percent reduced risk of these two gynecological cancers.[28] This reduced risk has also been observed among women with an inherited predisposition to ovarian cancer.[42]

There are many short-term noncontraceptive benefits that accrue to women taking OCs. Menstrual cycle control is improved for women of all ages. Withdrawal bleeds become very predictable in their timing, and the duration and amount of flow typically decrease substantially. These benefits are most important to women at the extremes of the reproductive years, who are the most likely to experience irregular and heavy or prolonged menses. Combined OCs are also the best treatment for dysmenorrhea, with gradually increasing improvement seen over the first 6 months of use.[39,41] OCs should be considered for treatment of these menstrual problems even for women who do not need contraceptive protection, such as those who have had a sterilization procedure or those who are not sexually active.

A more recently recognized OC benefit is improvement in acne. This occurs because the estrogen in the OCs causes an increase in sex hormone binding globulin (SHBG), which, in turn, leads to a decrease in free androgens, thus decreasing acne.[74] Like the improvement in dysmenorrhea, this is not an overnight effect, but rather an improvement that increases gradually over several months. Only one OC is currently approved for this indication (Ortho Tri-Cyclen), although most estrogen-containing OCs will have the same effect.

In addition to these major and clearly demonstrated benefits of OCs, epidemiologic and clinical studies over the years have indicated numerous other noncontraceptive effects that are probably direct results of the physiologic actions of the OC. These include decreased ovarian cysts, decreased endometriosis, decreased salpingitis, decreased ectopic pregnancy, decreased benign breast disease, and increased bone density.

The decision about whether combination OCs are suitable for use by a particular woman can be determined primarily by medical history. The main contraindications are the existence of definite or suspected vascular disease, including past or present stroke, coronary disease, or venous thromboembolism; because these are serious conditions, the history should be easy to identify. Serious vascular disease that has not yet led to a clinical event is a relative contraindication for combined OCs, but is somewhat more difficult to identify. Long-standing diabetes mellitus, or long-standing and poorly controlled hypertension are good indicators of vascular disease. Also, women older than 35 years who smoke have a markedly increased risk of myocardial infarction, presumably due to vascular damage that has accrued during many years of smoking. None of these women are good candidates for use of combined oral contraceptives, even in the absence of clinical events. Because pregnancy is also a greater risk for women with these medical problems, it is important to find some other highly effective contraceptive method.

Only a few other conditions are contraindications to estrogen-containing OCs. Whether OCs

affect the prognosis of current or past breast cancer is uncertain,[52] but all clinicians agree that hormonal contraceptive methods should not be used by these women. Women with current abnormal liver function may not metabolize OCs predictably, and should not use them. Women with current gallbladder disease may become worse with OCs and should not use them; however, after cholecystectomy a woman can again consider OCs.

Women who have migraine and use OCs may be at increased risk of thrombotic stroke, but their absolute risk remains extremely low.

A blood pressure measurement should be obtained prior to starting OCs.[84] There is some controversy regarding which aspects of the physical examination are essential prior to initiating OC use. Commonly, a general physical examination including breast and pelvic exams will be performed shortly before a woman begins taking OCs. A Pap smear is usually obtained as are any appropriate cultures. On the other hand there are some who feel that women should have easier access to OCs to reduce the rate of unintended pregnancies.

Selecting a particular OC for a patient should not be difficult. Her past use of OCs and her beliefs about OCs should be the primary guide. Any OC she liked using in the past is usually the best first choice. Any OC she disliked in the past should be avoided. Similar weight should be given to the experience of her friends or family members. For new OC users who have no preferences, I prescribe a monophasic combination pill that contains 30 to 35 μg of ethinyl estradiol. This estrogen dose is usually associated with less breakthrough bleeding than the 20 μg pills, and monophasics often seem a little simpler to the patients. Packs with 28 pills (nearly always 21 active pills and 7 placebos) are preferable to 21-day packs because they reinforce daily pill-taking behavior and reduce questions about when to start the next pack. With these packs, the patient starts a new pack as soon as the first one is empty. Examples of initial OC choices that I might typically prescribe include Brevicon,

Demulen 35, Desogen*, Levlen*, Lo-Estrin 1.5/30, Lo-Ovral, Modicon*, Nordette, Norinyl 1/35, Ortho-cept*, Ortho-cyclen*, Ortho-Novum 1/35,* and Ovcon-35. The asterisked brands allow a flexible starting day; the others are packaged for a Sunday start. Many of these pills have multiphasic counterparts, which are also fine. There are also now several OCs with 20 μg of ethinyl estradiol including Alesse*, Lo-Estrin 1/20, and Mircette*; using these provides patients with the lowest effective dose.

Pills are usually initiated during the next menstrual period. Starting the pack on the first day of menstrual flow is simple and gives the quickest onset of contraceptive protection. Any day very early in the cycle is acceptable, so that a woman who doesn't have her pills on the first day shouldn't have to wait an entire month to begin—just begin a day or two later.[12,33] Many brands are packaged for a Sunday start, which is also fine.

In general, the OCs are effective after taking them for seven days. During those first seven days, patients should abstain from intercourse or use condoms for protection. If a patient takes emergency contraception and wants to use OCs as her long-term method, she can begin a new pack of OCs the day after she completes the emergency contraception. Once begun, the rule is one pill each and every day; when the pack is empty, begin a new pack the next day regardless of bleeding. Emphasize to patients that pill taking should be daily, and not be linked to bleeding. All women should be told to expect changes in their bleeding patterns, particularly during the first three cycles of pill use. The occurrence or absence of bleeding during pill use should not modify the simple pattern of one pill a day, every day. If a period is missed, the patient should be evaluated for possible pregnancy, but she can continue using OCs during the short interval until this is assessed.

Daily pill-taking (for any indication) is difficult for most patients, and how to achieve this goal should be discussed with each patient. While choosing a regular hour can help develop this habit and enhance pill effectiveness, patients should know that it is always OK to take the daily pill whenever it is remembered, not just at the specified hour. If a pill is forgotten, the patient should take two the next day with no loss of contraceptive effectiveness. If the patient misses two pills, she should double up for two days. If a patient misses three or more days of pills, she should discard the partially used pack, and just begin a new pack on Sunday—regardless of bleeding. This approach is arbitrary, but effective and simple to explain and to remember. Any patient who misses two or more active pills should use condoms (or abstinence) until the active pills are taken again for seven consecutive days.[35] If patients have had intercourse during the days that they missed pills, then use of emergency contraception is usually indicated.

As with any new oral medication for any indication, women may experience a variety of minor side effects during the first month or two of OC use. Some patients will experience breast tenderness, nausea, headaches, appetite changes, and changes in mood or sense of well-being. The latter complaints are often expressed as just not feeling right on the pill. Patients should be reassured in advance that these symptoms are typically transient and not dangerous. The only problems that require immediate assessment are those that might be symptoms of an emerging cardiovascular problem; these are exceedingly rare in this age group, but should be attended to promptly.

Patients who find that minor problems persist for 2 or 3 months may want to consider changing to a different OC formulation. Persistent problems with headaches or nausea are often improved with use of a pill containing 20 μg of estrogen or by using a progestin-only pill ("POP"). The so-called POP pills (Ovrette, Micronor, Nor-Q-D) contain a small amount of progestin in every pill, no estrogen, and no placebo tablets. The progestin-only pills are useful for any woman with contraindications to estrogen-containing pills, as well as for women with the above side effects. Like all progestin-only contraceptives, these pills are usually associated with increased menstrual irregularity, about which a patient needs to be forewarned.

Side effects and discomforts other than nausea or headaches are often best improved by trying an OC with a different progestin. Similar to the difficulties of any chronic treatment, there is no recipe that will assure each patient the best pill immediately. Individualized changing of OCs every 2 or 3 months will lead to finding an acceptable pill for almost all women. A majority of women will do fine with the first pill they try; the rest will usually succeed with the second or third pill. Multiple, ongoing minor complaints with pill use despite changing brands often reflect some underlying worries about pill safety that should be explored and resolved.

Breakthrough bleeding and spotting during the first three months of OC use are frequent. Smokers have higher rates of breakthrough bleeding, presumably due to changes in estrogen metabolism.[51] Forgetting occasional pills is the main reason for irregular bleeding, but this problem may also be due to unrelated causes such as cervical infections or neoplasia, and thus a pelvic exam is a necessary part of evaluating irregular bleeding.

Follow-up for the satisfied OC user can be very limited. Patients should receive the periodic examinations that are needed for their age group, but extra examinations are not necessary except to evaluate problems. All of the medical problems that are prevalent in young women will be seen in OC users. OC discontinuation is often a quick response to a young woman with any medical complaint. Clinicians should not take this action prior to making an appropriate evaluation of the medical problem; in most cases, OC use is coincidental and not causal. If OC discontinuation is planned, then alternative acceptable contraception should be initiated immediately.

Injections

A depot preparation of medroxyprogesterone acetate (DMPA), Depo-Provera is the only in-jectable contraceptive currently available in the United States. It contains 150 mg of hormone, and is given as a deep intramuscular injection every 12 to 13 weeks. It is highly effective, with failures well below 1 percent per year. It works by inhibition of ovulation. While repeat injections are required every 3 months to assure continuous contraceptive protection, the average user will not ovulate again until 6 months following an injection, and some users will not experience an ovulation for over 1 year following even a single injection. This long duration of action, combined with an inability to actively reverse its action, means that DMPA is not a suitable contraceptive for any woman planning a pregnancy within the next 18 months.[32]

Along with other progestin-only contraceptives, DMPA does not appear to have many serious risks. Its approval in the United States was delayed for years due to concern about risk of breast cancer; this concern derived from results of animal studies. In the meanwhile, human use has been widespread in other countries, and a WHO case-control study of cancer in users of hormonal contraception provides reassurance about the safety of DMPA with regard to cancer.[59] Although data are scanty, DMPA also appears to be free of any excess cardiovascular risks.[85] The main current controversy regarding use of DMPA is whether the temporary, and apparently reversible, bone loss sometimes seen among users will lead to adverse clinical effects in later years.[9] As with combined oral contraceptives, DMPA use protects against endometrial cancer.

The main nuisance side effects associated with DMPA use are overwhelmingly the various changes in menstrual pattern. During initial use, women may have extended periods of bleeding and unpredictable menstrual patterns. After use of 1 year or more, and frequently sooner, the majority of DMPA users become nearly or completely amenorrheic. Satisfaction with use of DMPA depends on specific counseling about the anticpated menstrual changes. Headache is also a widely reported symptom associated with

DMPA, and patients should consider this possibility before beginning the method. Cross-sectional studies report that women who use DMPA weigh more than women using other contraceptives; however, the only prospective study of this issue did not show any weight differences after 1 year between young women selecting DMPA or Norplant or oral contraceptives.[40] There are anecdotal reports of depression in DMPA users, but a large prospective study did not find adverse mood changes.[79] Studies consistently show small adverse effects of DMPA on lipid profiles, but there is no known clinical significance to these findings.

Depo-Provera is an excellent choice for women who need a highly effective birth control method and who cannot remember to take a daily pill, or those who may not be candidates for combination oral contraceptives due to smoking or hypertension. There have been suggestions that patients with epilepsy or with sickle cell anemia may do particularly well with this method. As with the combination oral contraceptive, avoid using DMPA in women with breast cancer or in women with overt cardiovascular disease.

As with the oral contraceptive, women can be evaluated for their suitability to use DMPA based on a medical history and counseling. No special physical examination nor any special laboratory tests are needed prior to initiating DMPA.[84] All women should undergo routine age-appropriate physical examination and screening tests on a periodic basis, but no change in such routine evaluation is needed for use of DMPA.

The injection is best initiated during the first 7 days of a woman's menstrual cycle when pregnancy protection will begin immediately following injection. Repeat injections can be scheduled every 12 weeks. This is not a suitable method for women who will be upset by the menstrual disturbances, or for women who will have difficulty returning for regular repeat injections.

DMPA users who complain about frequent bleeding can be managed with a pack of oral contraceptives or with estrogen alone (such as Premarin 1.25 mg daily) for 3 weeks to stabilize the endometrium. These are basically temporizing measures for a woman who is tired of the daily bleeding or spotting that may occur. The bleeding may return when the additional treatment is stopped. If a woman decides to discontinue DMPA due to bleeding abnormalities, she must appreciate that both irregular bleeding and amenorrhea may persist for months until the DMPA has been completely utilized. Despite the potentially tiresome quality of these symptoms, most women tolerate these bleeding irregularities quite well. Although the magnitude of blood loss is usually small, checking for anemia is indicated with persistent bleeding, as is a pelvic examination to check for other reasons for the bleeding. Women with headache can best be managed with over-the-counter analgesics; however, any marked change in the quality or severity of headache merits the same evaluation as for a woman not using DMPA.

Implants

The use of subcutaneous silastic implants to deliver contraceptive hormones allows the continuous release of a minimal therapeutic dose. The currently available implant, Norplant, consists of six implants that each contain levonorgestrel, a progestin. The daily hormone dose is less than the lowest dose delivered by any oral contraceptives. The Norplant system is effective for at least 5 years of use. Recent U.S. data indicate failure rates well below 1 percent each year, and below 2 percent over the full 5 years.[56] The continuous hormone released by the system inhibits ovulation in most users, particularly during the first 3 years of use. In addition, as with other progestin-containing contraceptives, there is a thickening of the cervical mucus, which prevents the ascent of sperm, and changes in the endometrial lining, both of which would contribute to contraceptive effectiveness even if ovulation were to occur. New implant systems that employ fewer capsules will be available imminently. These may prove to be preferable to clinicians because of quicker insertion and removal; however, their clinical features will be very similar to the existing six-rod system.

The implants are inserted through a small incision or puncture into a shallow subcutaneous plane; all of the implants can be inserted through a single puncture. The upper arm is chosen because it is accessible and inconspicuous. The thin skin in this area facilitates identifying the implants at the time of removal. A careful, superficial insertion is a requirement for easy removal. Both insertion and removal can be done in an office setting with local anesthesia. The puncture site can be closed with a steri-strip and covered with a compression dressing to minimize bruising. Patients are usually pleased by how easy and painless the insertion process is. Onset of contraceptive protection occurs as soon as 48 h after insertion of the implants, and reversal of protection may be equally quick after removal of the implants. One of the main differences between implants and injections is the easy reversibility of the implants.

Implants are a new part of the contraceptive armamentarium, and thus there are not yet many years of studies that evaluate their risks. Current information indicates that Norplant implants do not generally result in serious risks, and can be used safely by most women.[46] As with the other progestin-only contraceptives, disruption of the menstrual bleeding pattern is the most common side effect in implant users, and is reported by at least two-thirds of users.[56] The total amount of blood loss is usually less than that lost with physiologic cycling; however, the pattern of blood loss changes. There is a marked lack of predictability with an increase in the total number of bleeding days and an increase in the frequency of bleeding episodes. A small proportion of users experience prolonged amenorrhea. Any imaginable bleeding pattern is possible, and, unfortunately, there is no test or treatment trial that can predict the bleeding pattern a woman will experience while using one of the progestin-only hormonal contraceptives. The menstrual disruption is greatest during the first 6 months of use;

thereafter, many women regain some pattern to their bleeding. In addition to the bleeding changes, many implant users report headache, weight gain, and an increase in acne.[40] Local problems at the insertion site, such as pain, paresthesia, or infection are extremely rare. As with DMPA, prospective evaluation has shown no change in depressive symptoms.[80] International and U.S. prospective studies indicate no differences in the overall pattern of morbidity or mortality among implant users when compared to the general population.[21]

Contraceptive implants are suitable for almost any woman who wants a highly effective, low-maintenance contraceptive method. As with the other hormonal methods, no special examination or laboratory tests are required prior to starting this method.[84] There are a few women who would be excluded from using implantable contraception by medical history. Women who use medicines that activate hepatic enzymes may not achieve contraceptive effectiveness with implants due to accelerated metabolism of the hormones; this problem is mainly limited to epileptics. In addition, women with past or present breast cancer are not considered candidates for any hormonal contraception.

Implantable contraception is usually initiated during the first seven days of the menstrual cycle; however, if a woman is already using a highly effective method of contraception, then the implants could be inserted at any time in the cycle, with an expectation that contraceptive effectiveness will begin within 48 h. A pressure dressing on the insertion site for 24 to 48 h minimizes bruising, and some reduction in vigorous activity for that extremity is appropriate. No other special care is required after insertion. During the years that the implants are used, no special follow-up is required above the usual periodic examinations. If a patient complains of persistent bleeding, especially if it begins after the first 6 months, it is important to evaluate the patient for other causes of irregular bleeding or spotting, including cervical infection or cervical neoplasia. Short-term management of prolonged bleeding can be achieved by use of combination oral contraceptives or estrogen replacement to stabilize the endometrium. A patient who does well with this supplementation may want to consider switching to oral contraception as a long-term method. If a patient using implants has regular menses (during use of the implant) followed by amenorrhea, she must be evaluated for pregnancy.[54] Essentially all of the few pregnancies in Norplant users occurred in the women who reported a regular menstrual cycle; presumably these women had become ovulatory.

Emergency Contraception

Every reproductive-age female should understand that emergency contraception (EC) is available. EC includes those techniques that can be used after unprotected intercourse to prevent pregnancy by the delay of ovulation, or through interference with fertilization or implantation. Situations that indicate use of EC include broken or slipped condoms, misplaced diaphragms, missed pills, incomplete withdrawal, miscalculations of rhythm methods, and rape. In addition, many acts of consensual intercourse are not planned in advance and occur without any protection.[24,26]

The main type of EC is known as the Yuzpe regimen and consists of two doses of oral contraceptive hormones taken 12 h apart. The standard dose is 100 μg of ethinyl estradiol and 0.50 mg of DL-norgestrel or 0.25 mg of levonorgestrel. The FDA has indicated that the use of this regimen for EC is safe and effective, and has recently approved a prepackaged kit that is labeled for this indication. Another approach is to use progestin-only pills (2 doses of 0.75 mg of DL-norgestrel 12 h apart).[63] If either of these regimens is initiated within 72 h of unprotected intercourse, the risk of pregnancy is reduced substantially. In studies of women receiving emergency contraception within this time frame, only 1 to 3 percent of women became pregnant after using this treatment; without EC about four times as many preg-

nancies would have been expected.[66-68] There is no specific information available that explains why EC failures occur.

An EC kit that is specifically packaged and labeled for this use (Preven) is now available in the United States by prescription only. In addition to prescribing EC in a kit form, it is also possible to use oral contraceptives containing levonorgestrel that have not been prepackaged for emergency contraceptive use. The appropriate oral contraceptive brands, along with the number of active tablets needed for each of the two doses, are Ovral (2); Lo-ovral (4); Nordette (4); Levlen (4); Triphasil (4 yellow); Trilevlen (4 yellow); Alesse (5); and Ovrette (20 pills per dose; this is a progestin-only pill). Emergency contraception using pills needs to be instituted within 72 h of unprotected intercourse.

If an intrauterine contraceptive device (IUD) is inserted in the uterus within 7 days of unprotected intercourse, it will probably prevent implantation. Some clinicians recommend an IUD as EC for that reason. I do not recommend this approach because IUDs are expensive and are intended to be a long-term method of contraception—their use in an emergency situation might prevent the woman from making a considered assessment of whether the IUD is an appropriate long-term method for her. Nonetheless, in the occasional patient who is already considering an IUD, it might be inserted at a time when EC is needed, thus addressing both the immediate and the long-term contraceptive needs of the woman.

The main side effect of the EC pill regimen is nausea in up to 50 percent of women, and vomiting in up to 20 percent of women; this may occur less frequently with the progestin-only pills.

Many believe that EC should be provided in advance with written instructions for when and how to use it if the need arises. A randomized trial showed that women given an advance prescription for EC used it appropriately during one year of follow-up, and there was a trend toward fewer pregnancies among these women compared to those who were instructed to ask for EC when needed.[23]

Allow the patient to time her doses sensibly. Unless it is already close to the 72-h mark, there is no need to take the first dose at 3 PM because this would require most patients to set the alarm for 3 AM to take the second dose. Instead, plan the first dose for a time when she is likely to be awake for the second dose.

Women who are suscepible to nausea may benefit from using an antiemetic 30 min before each dose of the EC. Diphenhydramine in a single 50-mg dose is available over the counter and may be adequate to prevent this side effect. Vaginal bleeding occurs in 95 percent of women within 21 days of using EC. The timing of the bleeding is variable and often is earlier or later than the next period was expected to be. If there is no bleeding at 21 days, then the woman needs to have a pregnancy test.

Patients do need explicit instructions to use the method with confidence. Because EC has been known as the "morning-after pill," many women are unaware that it is highly effective for at least 72 h postintercourse. When EC fails to prevent pregnancy, there is no demonstrated risk to the embryo if the patient then wishes to continue the pregnancy.

Intrauterine Contraceptives (Copper and Hormonal)

IUDs are the most underutilized contraceptive methods in the U.S. The only IUD that ever had to be removed from the U.S. market was the Dalkon Shield, which was specifically associated with an excess of septic abortions. In the early 1980s, several articles appeared showing that women with tubal infertility were more likely to be past users of IUDs.[7,10] This excess risk was concentrated among women with multiple partners and women using the Dalkon Shield. Despite the lack of association between other IUDs and infertility in women with a single partner, most of the other IUDs disappeared from the U.S. market consequent to this adverse publicity.

Several things have changed since the early 1980s. First, we have become much more aware of sexually transmitted diseases, and now take appropriate histories and do relevant testing. Also, we now have relatively quick and inexpensive tests available for chlamydia, which in the past could only be diagnosed by cell culture techniques. A study of 20,000 women obtaining IUDs in WHO clinical trials, showed that all of the excess pelvic inflammatory disease (PID) occurred in the first month after insertion; after the first month there was no excess of PID in these IUD users.[14] This report indicates that the risk of upper genital tract infection derives from inserting instruments (and the IUD itself) through an already infected cervix. With this knowledge and the availability of screening tests for STDs, we can now minimize the risk of infection by evaluating patients prior to IUD insertion. A recent U.S. controlled trial of prophylactic antibiotic use at the time of IUD insertion showed extremely low rates of infection in both groups, and no benefit of antibiotics.[77] In addition to the reassuring data about infection risk, today's copper IUDs have even higher effectiveness and a longer duration of action (up to 10 years) than those previously available.

The main mechanism of action of today's IUDs is the prevention of fertilization. This perhaps surprising effect occurs because the presence of the foreign body in the endometrial cavity causes a sterile inflammation that inhibits ascent of sperm to the fallopian tubes where fertilization normally occurs. This effect is particularly strong with copper-containing IUDs because copper both intensifies the inflammatory reaction in the uterus and because copper has a direct adverse effect on sperm motility.[88] The progestin-containing IUDs do not cause an equally intense inflammatory reaction, but the progestin causes marked thickening of the cervical mucus, which creates a mechanical barrier that prevents the ascent of sperm. In the rare event that fertilization does occur in the presence of an IUD, the IUD may still prevent pregnancy by interference with movement of the zygote to the uterus or prevention of implantation.

The main IUD available today in the United States is the copper-T 380A (Paragard) which is effective for up to 10 years, and which has a failure rate of less than 1 percent per year, with a cumulative 10-year failure rate of only 3 percent. The progesterone-containing IUD (Progestasert) needs annual replacement and has an annual failure rate of about 2 percent. IUDs protect against both extrauterine and intrauterine pregnancies. If a copper IUD user experiences a pregnancy, the probability that the pregnancy is ectopic is about 5 percent, but because the total number of pregnancies is so greatly reduced, the total number of ectopic pregnancies is also greatly reduced. With the current progesterone-containing IUDs, a pregnancy that occurs with the device in place may be ectopic more than 10 percent of the time; but again, because the total number of all pregnancies is greatly reduced, the number of ectopics is also reduced when compared to women using no contraception or using less effective methods of contraception.[58] The contraceptive effect of IUDs is immediately reversible when the IUD is removed, and women who discontinue IUDs conceive at the same rate as women who discontinue other birth control methods.[82]

The main side effect of IUD use is increased menstrual flow and increased dysmenorrhea.[57] These symptoms are more noticeable for women using copper-containing IUDs, and increased bleeding is the main reason for discontinuing this method. Copper-containing IUDs do not cause changes in copper homeostasis, nor are there any short-term or long-term systemic effects. There has been concern that the long-term presence of a foreign body might increase risk of neoplasia, but well-done studies have shown that IUD users experience rates of endometrial and cervical cancer that are as low as or lower than the rates experienced by women using other birth control methods.[30,44] In contrast to inert or copper-containing IUDs, the hormonal IUDs decrease menstrual flow and cramps. This effect is particularly noted with a longer-acting IUD with levonorgestrel that is used in Europe.[3] Women using this IUD also experience a marked decrease in pelvic inflammatory disease when compared to women using other methods, presumably because the potent progestin makes the cervical mucus impenetrable to microbes as well as to sperm, and perhaps because the thin endometrial lining is less prone to infection.[65]

Women who want a highly effective, convenient, long-acting contraceptive without hormones are particularly good candidates for a copper IUD. A copper IUD is less suitable for women who have heavy periods or cramps without an IUD; such women may consider using a hormonal IUD; however, systemic hormonal contraception is probably their best choice. Women who have current or recent STDs, or women with a documented history of PID are not suitable IUD users due to their risk of recurrent infection. The most well-described specific risk is that of inserting an IUD through an infected cervix;[14] this problem can be avoided by bacteriologic testing of the cervix prior to any IUD insertion. There is no good information about the natural history of a new sexually transmitted infection that might be acquired by a woman while using an IUD. Women at risk of infection should, of course, first be using condoms to prevent transmission of such infections. Women with HIV are not considered suitable candidates for IUD use.

Evaluation of a woman prior to IUD insertion includes obtaining the relevant history, as well as any history of previous IUD use. As with other methods, a history of successful use predicts future success, whereas any history of problems with an IUD needs to be explored. A previous IUD expulsion is not an absolute contraindication, but this woman will have a higher risk of experiencing another expulsion. A pelvic examination must be done prior to deciding whether an IUD is appropriate. This examination is needed to rule out infection and to identify anatomical abnormalities that might make insertion or retention of an IUD difficult. A stenotic cervix from previous treatment makes insertion more difficult, possibly requiring a local anesthetic and rarely requiring the use of dilators. Embryologic anomalies of the uterus, or more common abnormalities such as leiomyoma, increase the risk of expulsion. Women with submucous leiomyoma may also have heavy or prolonged bleeding while using an IUD. An anemic woman should have evaluation and treatment before beginning IUD use because of the expected increase in menstrual flow that would exacerbate preexisting anemia. The possibility of STDs should be considered before IUD insertion. Abnormal bleeding or an abnormal Pap needs to be evaluated and treated prior to IUD insertion.

IUDs are most commonly inserted during menstruation. Insertion of an IUD requires a speculum, tenaculum, sound, and scissors to trim the string. After the uterine position and size have been determined by sounding, the IUD is placed in the uterine cavity and the insertion instruments are removed. IUD manufacturers package illustrated instructions with each IUD, and there are videotapes available to demonstrate insertion.

Follow-up for patients with an IUD consists of a bimanual pelvic examination about six weeks after insertion to rule out early expulsion or uterine infection. Thereafter, unless a patient has symptoms, she only needs routine examinations. However, the need for an examination whenever a new sexual partnership begins should be emphasized with these patients.

Patients with an IUD should be advised to check for its presence after each menses by inserting a finger into the vagina and palpating the string at the cervix. If the string is not palpable, the patient should use backup contraception until the clinician can confirm the presence of the IUD. If the patient feels the hard tip of the stem of the IUD, this indicates partial expulsion, and the IUD must be removed. Along with a new partner, examination is indicated for pelvic pain to rule out infection or expulsion, for unusual discharge to rule out infection, and for amenorrhea to rule out pregnancy. If patients with a copper IUD are intolerant of the increased menstrual symptoms, it is appropriate to consider a progesterone IUD. Because the progesterone IUD

needs to be replaced annually, it is not usually the first choice for a woman who desires an IUD. Properly counseled and selected IUD users are typically highly satisfied with the method, and discontinuation is uncommon.

Spermicides

Spermicides can be used alone or as adjuncts to barrier contraceptive methods. All of the spermicide preparations available in the United States use nonoxynol-9 (N-9) as the active ingredient. N-9 is a detergent that is spermicidal. It is also microbicidal in vitro for many of the sexually transmitted pathogens. Preparations differ in the total dose and concentration of N-9, in the type of vehicle used, and in the mode of delivery. All are intended to deliver a dose of N-9 to the vaginal fornices that will be available in this location to inactivate sperm if ejaculation occurs during a few hours after application. Preparations of N-9 include cream or jelly, which are intended to be used with a diaphragm or cervical cap, and foams, suppositories, and films, which can be used alone or with condoms. A sponge impregnated with N-9 is no longer marketed due to manufacturing issues.

There are no comparative trials regarding the relative contraceptive efficacy of the different preparations. The reported typical user 1-year failure rates for spermicides used as the sole contraceptive method are about 20 to 25 percent.[69] All of the spermicide preparations are short-acting with the intent of providing protection for a single act of intercourse that takes place within minutes to hours following the application of the spermicide. Foams provide immediate protection after application, but suppositories and films need to melt and disperse in the vagina, and thus may not be active until 20 min after application.

Although laboratory studies indicate that spermicides are active against sexually transmitted pathogens, clinical studies are inconsistent regarding their effect on protecting users against infection.[43] Most human studies were trials that enrolled commercial sex workers, treated them with an N-9 preparation (along with latex condoms), and followed them for six months to one year to assess the occurrence of various infections. In several studies, there was a double-blind placebo control group. The largest study to date found no evidence of protection against genital lesions; in fact, there was an increase in genital ulcers, and there was no protection against gonorrhea, chlamydia, or HIV seroconversion among users of an N-9 film.[49] Existing studies have assessed only a few N-9 formulations, and whether there will prove to be an important STD-protective effect is still uncertain. The existing literature does not support recommending spermicides for STD protection.

The only medical drawback to use of spermicides is hypersensitivity reactions. As much as 10 percent of the population may have allergic irritation due to these preparations.

There is no medical evaluation or laboratory testing needed prior to recommending spermicides to a patient. This method can be a reasonable choice for people who have infrequent intercourse and who do not wish to use one of the long-term methods. In addition, it is a female-controlled method that may be useful for women whose partners will not use a condom. Spermicides can also be useful for oral contraceptive users who need a backup method due to missed pills. The only problem to watch for in spermicide users is local irritation in either partner that may be due to hypersensitivity. This problem may be due to the vehicle rather than due to the N-9, and it may improve by changing formulations.

Diaphragm and Cervical Cap

Latex rubber caps of various sizes have been used to cover the cervix for contraceptive purposes since the nineteenth century. In the United States, diaphragms consist of a soft, thin, latex bowl with an embedded flexible metal rim that measures from 60 to 105 mm in diameter (in 5-mm increments) and that covers the entire up-

per vagina. When the diaphragm is correctly inserted, the cervix rests in a puddle of spermicidal cream or jelly in the bowl. Clinical trial estimates of failure rates are 16 percent per year.[70,71] As with other coitally related birth control methods, there are wide variations in failure rates depending on personal factors that influence correct and consistent use. There are no estimates of diaphragm effectiveness if used without spermicide, but its main mechanism of action may be that it holds the spermicide over the cervix, maximizing the effectiveness of the spermicide.

The cervical cap is a smaller rubber device that fits over the cervix itself. The Prentif cavity rim cap is the only one available in the United States; it is available in four sizes with diameters from 18 to 25 mm. The cap is labeled for use with spermicide and has reported failure rates identical to the diaphragm when used in this fashion.[48] Many cap users forgo spermicide, and because a well-fitted cap tends to adhere to the cervix by suction, it may have good contraceptive effect without spermicide due to this tight barrier. However, the cap is supposed to be used with spermicide.

Both caps and diaphragms tend to protect against upper genital tract infections that gain entry via the cervical mucosa, including gonorrhea and chlamydia.[1] Women who are diaphragm users have a lower risk of cervical cancer,[45] which may be a consequence of the device blocking cervical infection with oncogenic strains of HPV. There is an increase in urinary tract infection risk among diaphragm users.[17,20]

Both the diaphragm and the cervical cap must be individually fitted. Reusable fitting sets are available from the manufacturers of the devices. If the pelvic examination reveals marked prolapse of the uterus or relaxation of the introitus, it may not be possible to fit a diaphragm successfully. A woman who has not yet begun sexual activity may not be able to be fitted. A woman who is immediately postpartum, or who is breastfeeding, also may not be comfortable with a diaphragm. Most women, however, can be easily fitted. During digital examination, the distance from the pubic arch to the posterior fornix should be estimated, and a diaphragm approximating that distance can be selected and inserted. A woman should be fitted with the largest comfortable size so that the diaphragm will stay in place (that is, covering the cervix) during intercourse. Because the upper vagina expands during sexual arousal, a relatively small diaphragm may be displaced. The potential space of the vagina may become larger after childbirth or after a substantial weight loss; thus, these are appropriate times to reassess the fit of the device.

Abortion

First Trimester: Surgical

There are about 1.4 million induced abortions in the United States each year. Approximately 90 percent are surgical procedures performed in the 12 weeks following the last normal menstrual period. Early surgical abortion is statistically safer for a woman than continuing a pregnancy until term, does not impair future fertility, and does not have adverse medical effects.[25] Early surgical abortion is performed using the technique of vacuum aspiration. This procedure can be done in an office or clinic setting with local anesthesia given as a paracervical block. An oral analgesic or antianxiety agent can be given as an adjunct to the local anesthetic. Some women prefer sedation or general anesthesia; however, most complications are related to anesthesia use, thus local anesthesia is safer, as well as adequate, for pain relief. First trimester abortions are typically performed in a single visit with mechanical dilatation of the cervix preceeding insertion of a cannula into the uterine cavity for aspiration of the products of conception. Aspiration is accomplished by attaching the cannula to an electric vacuum pump or to a syringe for manual vacuum aspiration (MVA).[11] Transvaginal sonography is sometimes used prior to the procedure to locate and date the pregnancy, and inspection of the aspirated material is performed to document completion of the abortion. Patients are usually observed briefly for pain and bleeding, and are usually discharged from care within 1 h after completing the procedure.

The main risks of early vacuum aspiration abortion are bleeding, which may require reaspiration in less than 2 percent of patients, and endometrial infection in less than 5 percent of patients. To decrease the risk of infection to less than 1 percent, most women receive antibiotic prophylaxis with doxycycline after the procedure. Patients may receive antibiotics up to 7 days following the procedure. Major complications include uterine perforation or bleeding requiring hospitalization and transfusion; these events occur in only 1 per 1000 early abortion procedures.[34] A few women with serious medical problems may benefit from having the abortion procedure done in the hospital. For instance, women receiving chronic oral anticoagulation may need admission for a switch to heparin therapy for the time of the procedure. The safety of abortion is greatest when performed very early; that is, by 8 weeks of pregnancy. This is particularly true for women with common medical problems, such as diabetes and hypertension, that are adversely affected by the hormonal and cardiovascular changes of pregnancy.

Prior to abortion, the medical history must be reviewed to identify any contraindications for an outpatient procedure. The hematocrit should be checked to assess the patient's reserve and to identify any unsuspected problems, and Rh-negative patients should be identified to prevent isoimmunization by administration of RhoGAM. Routine evaluation of vital signs and heart and lungs, as well as a pelvic examination, are all needed immediately prior to the procedure.

Patients can expect some bleeding and cramps during the week following an early abortion. Bleeding or pain that is in excess of a usual menstrual flow may indicate retained tissue or clots in the uterus that sometimes requires reaspiration. Patients should be advised to call about these symptoms. A 1 week follow-up appointment is routinely given, but few problems are detected at this time. Patients who are interested in a hormonal method of contraception can initiate any of these on the same day or within 7 days of an abortion procedure; there is no need for the patient to wait for follow-up or for the next menstrual period.

First Trimester: Medical

Abortion using a medical treatment rather than surgery is still a new and little-used approach in the United States, although there is substantial experience in other countries. Mifepristone, an orally administered progesterone receptor antagonist, has been used routinely for abortion up to 49 days of gestation (counting from the begining of the last normal menstrual period) in Europe for more than a decade. Although it can be effective when used alone, most protocols include a dose of mifepristone followed 2 days later by an oral or vaginal dose of misoprostol, a prostaglandin that causes uterine contractions.[60] Administration of the mifepristone is followed by few or no symptoms except for the usual pregnancy-related symptoms such as fatigue or nausea.[83] Administration of the misoprostol is followed rapidly by intense uterine cramping that typically lasts 2 to 6 h. In most cases, expulsion of the products of conception occurs promptly and predictably during this period of cramping. The intensity of the cramps varies greatly among women. Most women have subsequent bleeding that is heavier and continues longer than their menses.

Follow-up examination reveals complete abortion in over 95 percent of women. An aspiration procedure may be required in the other 5 percent due to incomplete abortion with bleeding, failure of expulsion, or, in about 1 percent, a pregnancy that is continuing to grow. Alternative protocols are being investigated that consider different doses of mifepristone, different regimens for prostaglandin, including self-administration of the prostaglandin at home, as well as use of medical abortion later in the first trimester.[53]

An alternative approach to medical abortion is the use of methotrexate, a folic acid antagonist approved for use as chemotherapy. A single injection of methotrexate followed 3 to 5 days later by misoprostol has been reported to be an effective technique for abortion up to 49 days following the last menstrual period.[8,81] A drawback of this approach is that the duration of cramping and bleeding may be more prolonged and the timing of the symptoms and the expulsion are less predictable than with mifepristone. Some patients require multiple doses of the misoprostol before the abortion is complete. An advantage of this approach is that the medications are inexpensive and available, and that this treatment can be effective for early or unsuspected ectopic pregnancy.

All medical abortion techniques require medical familiarity with the diagnosis of early pregnancy, excellent counseling skills, and familiarity with surgical techniques for emptying the pregnant uterus. Prescription of the medications used in medical abortion should be done by practitioners with broad training in abortion care. A physician who provides medical abortion but not surgical abortion needs to have an explicit relationship with a backup physician who can provide surgical care for the occasional patient with a failed or incomplete abortion. Nonetheless, if these conditions are met, medical abortion can be provided by a wide range of practitioners who do not currently provide surgical abortion care. This possibility may help alleviate the current shortage of abortion providers that forces many women to travel great distances to find this kind of care.

Second Trimester

About 10 percent of all abortions in the U.S. are performed after 12 weeks gestational age. Most of these are performed from 13 to 14 gestational weeks, and the number performed decreases with each additional week of gestation; only 1 percent of abortions are performed after 20 gestational weeks.[84] Abortions in the second trimester are performed with either surgical techniques or by-administering medications that cause uterine contractions and expulsion of the pregnancy.

The majority of second trimester abortions are performed surgically.[27] Vacuum aspiration, the same technique used in the first trimester, is also the procedure of choice for women seeking an abortion early in the second trimester.

The major risks of any surgical abortion include perforation of the uterus with possible damage to other organs, and hemorrhage that requires transfusion or surgical intervention. These major problems occur in about 1 per 1000 procedures, and may be more common in women who have had multiple cesarean section operations. Less serious problems include infection and the need for repeat emptying of the uterus due to an incomplete abortion. Overall, abortion risks increase with advancing gestational age. Until about 20 weeks of gestation, the surgical approaches to abortion are safer than continuing a pregnancy to term. After 20 weeks, the safety of an abortion procedure, whether medical or surgical, is often similar to continuing the pregnancy to term, although in each case this will depend on the medical condition of the woman.[25]

Medical methods of abortion in the second trimester are often used when no physician trained in the surgical techniques is available. Instillation of hypertonic saline solution or of a prostaglandin into the amniotic cavity causes uterine contractions leading to abortion. Prostaglandins can also be administered vaginally or intramuscularly.[2] The disadvantages of these techniques include the need for hospitalization for the 24 to 48 h required for the process to be completed. Because the placenta is often not expelled promptly, it may be necessary for the woman to undergo curettage after expulsion of the fetus. There are additional medical complications that can occur due to systemic effects of the saline or the prostaglandin, and the experience for the woman of a prolonged medical abortion in the second trimester is very different from the experience of a surgical abortion at the same gestational age.

For any woman seeking abortion, the process is both safer and simpler at early gestational ages; therefore, it is a priority to arrange care as soon as the woman's plan has been established. Of course, it is important for all women who need contraception to have appropriate education, information, and access. This would likely reduce the number of abortions that are performed.

References and Selected Readings

1. Alexander NJ. Barriers to sexually transmitted diseases. *Sci Am* 3:31–41, 1996.
2. American College of Obstetricians and Gynecologists (ACOG) Committee on Technical Bulletins: *Methods of Midtrimester Abortion.* Washington, DC: ACOG, 1987. ACOG technical bulletin 10.
3. Andersson JK, Rybo G: Levonorgestrel-releasing intrauterine device in the treatment of menorrhagia. *Br J Obstet Gynecol* 97:690–694, 1990.
4. Bracken MB: Oral contraception and congenital malformation in offspring: A review and meta-analysis of prospective studies. Obstet Gynecol 76:552–557, 1990.
5. Brinton LA, Huggins GR, Lehman HF, et al: Long-term use of oral contraceptives and risk of invasive cervical cancer. *Int J Cancer* 38:339–344, 1986.
6. Collaborative Group on Hormonal Factors in Breast Cancer: Breast cancer and hormonal contraceptives: Collaborative reanalysis of individual data on 53,297 women with breast cancer and 100,239 women without breast cancer from 54 epidemiological studies. *Lancet* 347:1713–1727, 1996.
7. Cramer DW, Schiff I, Schoenbaum SC, et al: Tubal infertility and the intrauterine device. *N Engl J Med* 312:941–947, 1985.
8. Creinin MD, Vittinghoff E, Schaff E, Klaisle C, Darney PD, Dean C: Medical abortion with oral methotrexate and vaginal misoprostol. *Obstet Gynecol* 90:611–616, 1997.
9. Cundy T, Cornish J, Roberts H, Elder H, Reid I: Spinal bone density in women using depot medroxyprogesterone contraception. *Obstet Gynecol* 92:569–573, 1998.
10. Daling JR, Weiss NS, Metch BJ, et al: Primary tubal infertility in relation to the use of an intrauterine device. *N Engl J Med* 312:937–941, 1985.
11. Edwards J, Carson SA: New technologies permit safe abortion at less than six weeks gestation and provide timely detection of ectopic gestation. *Am J Obstet Gynecol* 176:1101–1106, 1997.
12. Elomaa K, Rolland R, Brosens I, et al: Omitting the first oral contraceptive pills of the cycle does not automatically lead to ovulation. *Am J Obstet Gynecol* 179:41–46, 1998.

13. Farley T, Collins, Schlesselman J: Hormonal contraception and risk of cardiovascular disease: An international perspective. *Contraception* 57:211–230, 1998.

14. Farley T, Rosenberg MJ, Rowe PJ, Chen JH, Meirik O: Intrauterine devices and pelvic inflammatory disease: An international perspective. *Lancet* 339:785–788, 1992.

15. Fazio A: Oral contraceptive drug interactions: Important considerations. *South Med J* 84:997–1002, 1991.

16. Fihn SD, Boyko EJ, Normand EH, et al: Association between use of spermicide-coated condoms and *Escherichia coli* urinary tract infection in young women. *Am J Epidemiol* 144:512–520, 1996.

17. Fihn SD, Latham RH, Roberts P, Running K, Stamm WE: Association between diaphragm use and urinary tract infection. *JAMA* 254:240–245, 1985.

18. Forman D, Vincent TJ, Doll R: Cancer of the liver and the use of oral contraceptives. *BMJ* 292:1357–1361, 1986.

19. Fotherby K: Metabolic interrelationships, cardiovascular disease, and sex steroids. *Contraception* 57:183–187, 1998.

20. Foxman B, Frerichs RR: Epidemiology of urinary tract infection: I. Diaphragm use and sexual intercourse. *Am J Public Health* 75:1308–1313, 1985.

21. Fraser I, Tiitinen A, Affandi B, et al: Norplant consensus statement and background review. *Contraception* 57:1–9, 1998.

22. Gans Epner JE, Jonas HS, Seckinger DL: Late-term abortion. *JAMA* 280:724–729, 1998.

23. Glasier A, Baird D: The effects of self-administering emergency contraception. *N Engl J Med* 339:1–4, 1998.

24. Glasier A: Drug therapy: Emergency postcoital contraception. *N Engl J Med* 337:1058–1064, 1997.

25. Gold RB: *Abortion and Women's Health: A Turning Point for America?* New York/Washington DC: The Alan Guttmacher Institute, 1990.

26. Grimes DA: Emergency contraception—expanding opportunities for primary prevention. *N Engl J Med* 337:1078, 1997.

27. Grimes DA, Schulz KF, Cates W, Tyler CW: Mid-trimester abortion by dilatation and evacuation; A safe and practical alternative. *N Engl J Med* 296:1141–1145, 1977.

28. Gross TP, Schlesselman JJ: The estimated effect of oral contraceptive use on the cumulative risk of epithelial ovarian cancer. *Obstet Gynecol* 83:419–424, 1994.

29. Hannaford P: The collection and interpretation of epidemiological data about the cardiovascular risks associated with the use of steroid contraceptives. *Contraception* 57:137–142, 1998.

30. Hill D, Weiss N, Voigt L, Beresford S: Endometrial cancer in relation to intra-uterine device use. *Int J Cancer* 70:278–281, 1997.

31. Irwin KL, Rosero-Bixby L, Oberie MW, et al: Oral contraceptives and cervical cancer risk in Costa Rica: Detection bias or causal association? *JAMA* 259:59–64, 1988.

32. Kaunitz AM: Injectable contraception. *Clin Obstet Gynecol* 32:356–368, 1989.

33. Killick SR, Bancroft K, Oelbaum S, Morris J, Elstein M: Extending the duration of the pill-free interval during combined oral contraception. *Adv Contracep* 6:33, 1990.

34. Koonin LM, Smith JC, Ramick M, Strauss LT, Hopkins FW: Abortion surveillance—United States, 1993 and 1994. *MMWR* 46:37–83, 1997.

35. Letterie GS, Chow GE: Effect of "missed" pills on oral contraceptive effectiveness. *Obstet Gynecol* 79:979, 1992.

36. Lidegaard O, Edstrom B, Kreiner S: Oral contraceptives and venous thromboembolism: A case-control study. *Contraception* 57:291–301, 1998.

37. Lidegaard O, Kreiner S: Cerebral thrombosis and oral contraceptives: A case-control study. *Contraception* 57:303–314, 1998.

38. Martinelli I, Sacchi E, Landi G, Taioli E, Duca F, Mannucci P: High risk of cerebral-vein thrombosis in carriers of a prothrombin-gene mutation and in users of oral contraceptives. *N Engl J Med* 338:1793–1797, 1998.

39. Milsom I, Andersch B: Effect of various oral contraceptive combinations on dysmenorrhea. *Gynecol Obstet Invest* 17:284–292, 1984.

40. Moore L, Valuck R, McDougall C, Fink W: A comparative study of one-year weight gain among users of medroxyprogesterone acetate, levonorgestrel implants, and oral contraceptives. *Contraception* 52:215–220, 1995.

41. Nabrink M, Birgersson L, Colling-Saltin A, Solum T: Modern oral contraceptives and dysmenorrhea. *Contraception* 42(3):275–282, 1990.

42. Narod SA, Risch H, Moslehi R, et al: Oral contraceptives and the risk of hereditary ovarian cancer. *N Engl J Med* 339:424–428, 1998.

43. Niruthisad S, Roddy RE, Chutivonges S: Use of nonoxynol-9 and reduction in the rate of gonococcal and chlamydia cervical infections. *Lancet* 339:1371–1375, 1992.

44. Parazzini F, La Vechia C, Negri E: Use of intrauterine device and risk of invasive cervical cancer [letter]. *Int J Epidemiol* 21:1030–1031, 1992.

45. Peters RK, Thomas D, Hagan DG, Mack TM, Henderson BE: Risk factors for invasive cervical cancer among Latinas and non-Latinas in Los Angeles County. *J Natl Cancer Inst* 77:1063–1077, 1986.

46. Petitti D, Siscovick D, Sidney S, et al: Norplant im-

plants and cardiovascular disease. *Contraception* 57:361–362, 1998.

47. Petitti D, Sidney S, Quesenberry C: Oral contraceptive use and myocardial infarction. *Contraception* 57:143–155, 1998.

48. Richwald GA, Greenland S, Gerber MM, Potik R, Kersey L, Comas MA: Effectiveness of the cavity-rim cervical cap: Results of a large clinical study. *Obstet Gynecol* 74:143–148, 1989.

49. Roddy R, Zekeng L, Ryan K, et al: A controlled trial of nonoxynol-9 film to reduce male to female transmission of sexually transmitted diseases. *N Engl J Med* 339:504–510, 1998.

50. Rosenberg MJ, Davidson AJ, Chen JH, Judson FN, Douglas JM: Barrier contraceptives and sexually transmitted diseases in women: A comparison of female-dependent methods and condoms. *Am J Public Health* 82:669–674, 1992.

51. Rosenberg MJ, Waugh MS, Stevens C: Smoking and cycle control among oral contraceptive users. *Am J Obstet Gynecol* 174:628–632, 1996.

52. Sauerbrei W, Blettner M, Schmoor C, Bojar H, Schumacher M: The effect of oral contraceptive use on the prognosis of node-positive breast cancer patients. *Eur J Cancer* 34:1348–1351, 1998.

53. Schaff EA, Stadalius LS, Eisinger SH, Franks P: Vaginal misoprostol administered at home after mifepristone (RU486) for abortion. *J Fam Pract* 44:353–360, 1997.

54. Shoupe D, Mishell D, Bopp B, Fielding M: The significance of bleeding patterns in Norplant implant users. *Obstet Gynecol* 77:256–260, 1991.

55. Sidney S, Siscovick D, Petitti D, et al: Myocardial infarction and use of low-dose oral contraceptives. *Circulation* 98:1058–1063, 1998.

56. Sivin I, Mishell DR Jr, Darney P, Wan L, Christ M: Levonorgestrel capsule implants in the United States: A 5-year study, *Obstet Gynecol* 92:337–344, 1998.

57. Sivin I, Greenslade F, Schmidt F, Waldman S: *The Copper T 380 Intrauterine Device: A Summary of Scientific Data.* New York: Population Council, 1992.

58. Sivin I: Dose- and age dependent ectopic pregnancy risks with intrauterine contraception. *Obstet Gynecol* 78:291–298, 1991.

59. Skegg D, Noonan E, Paul C, Spears GFS, Meirik O, Thomas DB: Depot medroxyprogesterone acetate and breast cancer. *JAMA* 273:799–804, 1995.

60. Spitz IM, Bardin CW, Benton L, Robbins A: Early pregnancy termination with mifepristone and misoprostol in the United States. *N Engl J Med* 338:1241–1247, 1998.

61. Suissa S, Blais L, Spitzer W, et al: First-time use of newer oral contraceptives and the risk of venous thromboembolism. *Contraception* 56:141–146, 1997.

62. Stubblefield P: Self-administered emergency contraception—A second chance. *N Engl J Med* 339:41–42, 1998.

63. Tasks Force on Postovulatory Methods of Fertility Regulation: Randomised controlled trial of levonorgestrel versus the Yuzpe regimen of combined oral contraceptives for emergency contraception. *Lancet* 352:428–433, 1998.

64. Thorogood M: Stroke and steroid hormonal contraception. *Contraception* 57:157–167, 1998.

65. Toivonen J, Luukkainen T, Allonen H: Protective effect of intrauterine release of levonorgestrel on pelvic infection: Three years' comparative experience of levonorgestrel- and copper-releasing intrauterine devices. *Obstet Gynecol* 77–261, 1991.

66. Trussel J, Rodriguez G, Ellerston C: New estimates of the effectiveness of the Yuzpe regimen of emergency contraception. *Contraception* 57:363–369, 1998.

67. Trussel J, Ellerston C, Rodriguz G: The Yuzpe regimen of emergency contraception: How long after the morning after? *Obstet Gynecol* 88:150–154, 1996.

68. Trussel J, Ellerston C, Stewart F: The effectiveness of the Yuzpe regimen of emergency contraception. *Fam Plann Perspect* 26:58–64, 1996.

69. Trussel J: Contraceptive efficacy. *Arch Dermatol* 131:1064–1068, 1995.

70. Trussel J, Sturgen K, Stricker J, Dominik R: Comparative contraceptive efficacy of the female condom and other barrier methods. *Fam Plann Perspect* 26:66–72, 1994.

71. Trussel J, Strickler J, Vaughan B: Contraceptive efficacy of the diaphragm, the sponge, and the cervical cap. *Fam Plann Perspect* 25:100–105, 1993.

72. Trussel J, Hatcher RA, Cates W, Stewart FH, Kost K: Contraceptive failure in the United States: An update. *Stud Fam Plann* 21:51–54, 1990.

73. Ursin G, Peters RK, Henderson BE, d'Ablaing III G, Monroe KR, Pike MC: Oral contraceptive use and adenocarcinoma of cervix. *Lancet* 344:1390–1394, 1994.

74. van der Vange N, Blankenstein MA, Kloosterboer HJ, Haspels AA, Thijssen JHH: Effects of seven low-dose combined oral contraceptives on sex hormone binding globulin, corticosteroid binding globulin, total and free testosterone. *Contraception* 41:345, 1990.

75. Vessey MP, Painter R: Endometrial and ovarian cancer and oral contraceptives—Findings in a large cohort study. *Br J Cancer* 71:1340–1342, 1995.

76. Walker A: Newer oral contraceptives and the risk of venous thromboembolism. *Contraception* 57:169–181, 1998.

77. Walsh T, Grimes D, Frezieres R, et al: Randomised controlled trial of prophylactic antibiotics before insertion of intrauterine devices. *Lancet* 351:1005–1008, 1998.

78. Weller SC: A meta-analysis of condom effectiveness

in reducing sexually transmitted HIV. *Soc Sci Med* 36:1635–1644, 1993.

79. Westhoff C, Truman C, Kalmuss D, et al. Depressive symptoms and Depo-Provera. *Contraception* 57:237–240, 1998.

80. Westhoff C, Truman C, Kalmuss D, et al: Depressive symptoms and Norplant contraceptive implants. *Contraception* 57:241–245, 1998.

81. Wiebe ER: Abortion induced with methotrexate and misoprostol: A comparison of various protocols. *Contraception* 55:159–163, 1997.

82. Wilson J: A prospective New Zealand study of fertility after removal of copper intrauterine contraceptive devices for conception and because of complication: A four-year study. *Am J Obstet Gynecol* 160:391–396, 1989.

83. Winikoff B, Ellerston C, Elul B, Sivin I: *Acceptability and Feasibility of Early Pregnancy Termination by Mifepristone-Misoprostol: Results of a Large Multicenter Trial in the United States.* Population Council, 1998.

84. WHO: *Improving Access to Quality Care in Family Planning: Medical Eligibility Criteria for Contraceptive Use.* New York: WHO, Family and Reproductive Health, 1996.

85. WHO Collaborative Study of Cardiovascular Disease and Steroid Hormone Contraception: Cardiovascular disease and use of oral and injectable progestogen-only contraceptives and combined injectable contraceptives. *Contraception* 57:315–324, 1998.

86. WHO Collaborative Study of Neoplasia and Steroid Contraceptives: Breast cancer and depot-medroxy-progesterone acetate: A multinational study. *Lancet* 338:833–838, 1991.

87. Yassin MS, Lieri MB, Fischer TJ, O'Brein KO, Cross J, Steinmetz C: Latex allergy in hospital employees. *Ann Allergy Asthma Immunol* 72:245–249, 1994.

88. Zipper JA, Tatum HJ, Pastene L, Medel M, Rivera M: Metallic copper as an intrauterine contraceptive adjunct to the "T" device. *Am J Obstet Gynecol* 105:1274–1278, 1969.

CHAPTER 28

Gynecologic Infections

Susan M. Mou

SITES OF GYNECOLOGIC INFECTIONS
Vaginitis • Mucopurulent Cervicitis •
Pelvic Inflammatory Disease • Bartholin's
Duct Cysts/Abscesses • Necrotizing Fasciitis

COMMON SEXUALLY TRANSMITTED ORGANISMS
N. Gonorrhoeae • Chlamydia •
Syphilis • Mycoplasma • Human
Papilloma Virus • Herpes •
Chancroid • Lymphogranuloma
Venereum • Donovanosis • Molluscum
Contagiosum • Pediculosis Pubis •
Scabies

COMMON SYSTEMIC DISEASES THAT MAY BE TRANSMITTED VIA THE VAGINAL ROUTE
HIV • Hepatitis B • Toxic Shock
Syndrome

Many diseases are transmitted to women by infection via the vaginal route. The site of the ultimate infection may be any one of a variety of organs, or multiple sites may become infected. The patient may present with an infection of the vulva (vulvitis, Bartholin's abscess), vagina (vaginitis), cervix (cervicitis), or uterus (endometritis). An organism may then ascend further (with or without prior clinical symptoms in any of the aforementioned areas) to involve one or both fallopian tubes (salpingitis) or tubes and ovaries (salpingo-oophoritis). It is rare for the ovaries to be infected (oophoritis) without accompanying tubal infection. In addition to being foci of local disease, the lower genital tract is a route of entry for organisms that cause life-threatening systemic disease (e.g., HIV and hepatitis B).

Sites of Gynecologic Infections

Vaginitis

Vaginitis is a common problem for which women seek medical care. Prior to discussing the usual forms of vaginitis, it is important to understand the normal flora of the vagina. Postpubertally, the vagina contains multiple organisms, with a concentration of less than 1×10^7 organisms per gram of vaginal secretion. Lactobacilli are the predominant organisms. The ratio of anaerobes to aerobes is 2:1 to 5:1. Group B streptococci can be cultured from the vagina in 20 to 30 percent of normal women. There are three primary vaginal infections for which women commonly seek care: bacterial vaginosis, candidiasis, and trichomoniasis.

Bacterial vaginosis Bacterial vaginosis is a disruption of the normal vaginal flora, with an overgrowth of anaerobes. Some women are symptomatic, complaining of increased vaginal discharge and a foul-smelling fishy odor (especially after intercourse, when alkaline semen mixes with the vaginal discharge). Other women are asymptomatic, but on physical examination, bacterial vaginosis will be evident. The majority of women who have bacterial vaginosis are sexually active and between the ages of 15 and 44. The lactobacilli that are predominant in a healthy vagina are replaced by anaerobes, with the ratio of anaerobes to aerobes increasing up to 100:1. The vaginal pH is elevated. The number of organisms per gram of vaginal fluid increases to 1×10^{11}.

The diagnosis of bacterial vaginosis can be

made clinically with three of four of Amsel's criteria present. These are as follows:

1. Vaginal fluid collected from the side walls of the vagina with a pH greater than 4.5;
2. A thin, homogenous discharge that looks like skim milk and may roll out of the vagina onto the perineum;
3. A positive amine (Whiff) test (performed by adding 10% KOH to vaginal secretions on a glass slide); and,
4. Clue cells present on a wet preparation of vaginal secretions. The clue cells are epithelial cells coated with bacteria. More than 20 percent of the epithelial cells need to be clue cells for this element of the clinical diagnosis.

Gram stain criteria also have been described for bacterial vaginosis and consist of an absence of lactobacilli with many anaerobic morphotypes present. It is not necessary to culture for *Gardnerella* because up to 40 percent of healthy women may have *Gardnerella* as normal flora. Similarly, culture for anaerobes is not necessary because anaerobes can be normal vaginal flora. It is the overgrowth that is associated with bacterial vaginosis.

There are multiple treatment regimens for bacterial vaginosis. Metronidazole, 500 mg orally, twice daily for 7 days is effective about 85 percent of the time. An alternate oral regimen of one 2-g dose is slightly less effective. Oral clindamycin can be used in a dose of 300 mg twice daily for 7 days. Alternatively, topical regimens with fewer potential side effects also are effective. A 2% clindamycin vaginal cream can be used nightly for seven nights. Alternatively, metronidazole gel, 0.75%, applied intravaginally twice daily for five days is effective. The FDA has approved metronidazole 750-mg extended-release tablets daily for 7 days and nightly intravaginal metronidazole gel 0.75% for 5 days, but there are no published comparisons of these last two regimens to the previously mentioned oral and topical regimens.

Neither vaginal medications designed to lower vaginal pH nor douching cure bacterial vaginosis. Treatment of sexual partners is advised only when patients have recurrent bacterial vaginosis, as it has not been proven of benefit.

While bacterial vaginosis was once considered a benign nuisance condition, there is now evidence that it is associated with postabortal infections; posthysterectomy infections; postpartum endometritis; preterm labor; delivery of low birthweight infants; and chorioamnionitis.[6] Pregnant patients at risk for preterm delivery, especially with a previous history of preterm delivery, may be screened and treated in the early second trimester for bacterial vaginosis with an oral regimen as described above.

Lower dose treatment of symptomatic, low-risk pregnant women is also advocated by the Centers for Disease Control and Prevention to relieve symptoms.[1] Metronidazole, one 2-g oral dose, oral clindamycin 300 mg twice daily for 7 days, or metronidazole gel 0.75% twice daily for 5 days can be used for the lower risk women.

Candidiasis   Vulvovaginal infections caused by *Candida* species are very common in women. *C. albicans* is responsible for the infection in 80 to 90 percent of patients; the remaining 10 to 20 percent are due to *C. glabrata, C. tropicalis,* and other *Candida* species. The role of asymptomatic colonization and infection of other sites (such as the oral cavity and gastrointestinal tract) in subsequent symptomatic vaginal infections are not fully understood at this time. It is known that patients who have depressed cell-mediated immunity, those with high blood-glucose levels, and those who have recently received antimicrobials, are at increased risk for vulvovaginal candidiasis.

Patients usually complain of vulvar, and sometimes vaginal, pruritus, burning, dysuria, and dyspareunia. Some patients note a vaginal discharge. Physical examination reveals vaginal and/or vulvar edema and erythema, which signify a vulvitis. A discharge will be nonodorous to sweet-smelling, possibly thick and white. The vaginal pH is usually less than 4.5.

Microscopic examination of a wet mount of

vaginal secretions at $100\times$ magnification shows branching hyphae and spores. Leukocytes usually are absent, and lactobacilli are present. Visualization of the hyphae and spores may be aided by addition of 10% KOH. *C. glabrata* will be seen with spores present without branching pseudohyphae. Yeast culture can be done on Sabouraud's medium, but is clinically indicated only when, on the basis of signs and symptoms, candida is suspected but no confirmation can be made on potassium hydroxide preparation.

Local therapy is usually employed, including imidazole compounds such as clotrimazole, miconazole, and butoconazole. Nystatin is also useful. Triazoles, including terconazole, may also be used. In patients who do not respond to local therapy, oral fluconazole may be effective. There is no need to treat sexual partners unless a male partner has balanitis.

In patients with recurrent candidiasis, which is defined as four or more symptomatic vulvovaginal candidiasis episodes in one year, a 1% aqueous solution of gentian violet to the vagina and vulva twice weekly for 2 weeks is effective. Alternatively, 10 to 14 days of a topical agent followed by 6 months of daily 100-mg ketoconazole can be used. Oral treatment with ketoconazole, 200 to 400 mg daily for 7 to 14 days, with monitoring of liver function tests, is an alternative regimen for recurrent candidiasis.

Trichomoniasis   Trichomoniasis is the third of the most common etiologic agents of vaginitis. *Trichomonas vaginalis,* a flagellated protozoan, causes this communicable infection. The asymptomatic carrier rate in women is about 10 percent. Symptomatic patients may complain of dysuria, vaginal discharge, and/or pruritis.

The diagnosis of trichomoniasis can be made at the time of pelvic examination. A thin, yellow-green, sometimes foul-smelling discharge is usually present. The vaginal pH is elevated to between 5 and 7. Vulvar irritation is often present. Motile trichomonads can be seen on saline suspension of vaginal discharge. The wet mount is 50 to 60 percent sensitive, while cultures are usually more than 89 percent sensitive.[5]

Cultures can be done with Trichicult's or Diamond's culture media. InPouch TV,[3] a culture system that can be used at the bedside and then examined under the microscope daily without opening the culture, is also helpful in diagnosis.

Treatment consists of oral metronidazole, 2 g once, or metronidazole 500 mg two times per day for 7 days. Partners should be referred for treatment at the same time. Follow-up is necessary for women who do not become asymptomatic after treatment.

Other causes of abnormal vaginal discharge as well as cervicitis and upper tract disease are discussed in the next section.

Mucopurulent Cervicitis

Mucopurulent cervicitis is a clinical entity characterized by a yellow endocervical exudate, visible either in the endocervical canal or an endocervical plug specimen, and by polymorphonuclear leukocytes in the endocervical exudate. Mucopurulent cervicitis is found in reproductive-age women. It should not be diagnosed during the bleeding phase of the menstrual cycle. Mucopurulent cervicitis may be caused by *Chlamydia trachomatis, Neisseria gonorrhoeae,* herpes simplex virus, or other vaginal organisms. The first two organisms cause 50 to 70 percent of mucopurulent cervicitis.

Clinically, women may be asymptomatic, or they may complain of dyspareunia, postcoital spotting, or abnormal discharge. Patients may have tenderness on palpation of the cervix during a pelvic exam. Criteria for diagnosis include yellow or green mucopurulent endocervical secretion(s) when viewed on a white cotton-tipped swab (positive swab test); cervicitis as determined by a friable cervix and/or erythema or edema in the cervical ectropion; and 10 or more polymorphonuclear leukocytes per microscopic oil immersion field on a Gram stain smear of endocervical secretions. Cultures, a DNA probe, PCR, or LCR for *Neisseria gonorrhoeae* and *Chlamydia trachomatis* should be performed at the same time. Herpes simplex virus infection usually can be diagnosed clinically. It also can be detected about 50 percent of the time on Papanicolaou smears or by viral culture.

Treatment of mucopurulent cervicitis ideally should be based on the results of tests for *C. trachomatis* and *N. gonorrhoeae*. However, if the likelihood of infection with either organism is high, or if the patient is unlikely to follow through once culture results are available, outpatient treatment should be initiated empirically. Treatment for *C. trachomatis* and *N. gonorrhoeae* should also be prescribed empirically for patients with mucopurulent cervicitis in populations with a high prevalence of these infections. If prevalence of both infections is low, and if compliance is high, test results may be awaited. If the prevalence of *N. gonorrhoeae* is low but the likelihood of chlamydia is high, treatment for chlamydia only may be prescribed. Follow-up should be specific for the organisms cultured or otherwise detected. Sex partners of patients treated presumptively should receive the same treatment as the woman with mucopurulent cervicitis. See later sections on chlamydia and gonorrhea for treatment specifics.

Pelvic Inflammatory Disease

Pelvic inflammatory disease (PID) encompasses a spectrum of disease, including endometritis, salpingitis, oophoritis, tubo-ovarian abscess, and pelvic peritonitis. The two most common organisms that cause PID are *N. gonorrhoeae* and *C. trachomatis*. However, many other vaginal microorganisms, such as E. coli and other gram-negative enteric organisms, Bacteroides species, anaerobic cocci, Prevotella species, *Haemophilus influenzae, Streptococcus agalactiae, Gardnerella vaginalis,* and possibly *Mycoplasma hominis* and *Ureaplasma urealyticum,* are potential etiologic agents for PID.

The severity of PID varies greatly, ranging from asymptomatic to life-threatening diffuse peritonitis and florid sepsis. A high index of suspicion on the part of the physician is necessary. Risk factors for PID include young age, multiple sexual partners, attendance at a sexually trans-

mitted disease (STD) clinic, recent insertion of an intrauterine device, vaginal douching, cigarette smoking, and recent gonorrhea or chlamydia infection.[11] Barrier methods of contraception and, to a lesser extent, oral contraceptives reduce the risk of PID.

The most common presenting symptom is lower abdominal pain, which is usually bilateral. Gonococcal and chlamydial PID typically present during the first half of the menstrual cycle. Abnormal bleeding; abnormal vaginal discharge; fever; nausea; vomiting; new onset breakthrough bleeding on oral contraceptives, Norplant, or Depo-Provera; and new onset dysmenorrhea and dyspareunia may also be present. Some questions to ask the patient include: Have you noticed a change in your vaginal discharge? Do you have spotting after intercourse? (This may also be suggestive of cervical cancer or cervical intraepithelial neoplasia.) Have you noticed a sudden onset of pain with sexual intercourse?[7]

Diagnosis The diagnosis is usually made by employing clinical criteria. Laparoscopy is the gold standard for diagnosis, but may not be necessary or indicated, may not be available universally, and may miss early endometritis. Clinical criteria have a positive predictive value of 65 to 90 percent as compared to laparoscopy.[1] Empirical treatment of PID is recommended by the Centers for Disease Control and Prevention (CDC) when there is lower abdominal tenderness, adnexal tenderness, and cervical motion tenderness, and no other detectable cause, such as ectopic pregnancy, appendicitis, bowel diseases, endometriosis, ovarian torsion, bleeding into a corpus luteum, or functional pain. Additional diagnostic criteria are oral temperature >38.3°C; abnormal cervical/vaginal discharge, elevated erythrocyte sedimentation rate or C-reactive protein; and documented *N. gonorrhoeae* or *C. trachomatis* infection.

Cultures, DNA probes, PCR, or LCR should be obtained from the endocervix and rectum for *N. gonorrhoeae,* and from the endocervix for *C. trachomatis*. In acutely ill patients, aerobic and anaerobic blood cultures may be obtained, but are frequently negative, even in the presence of infection. The CDC denotes the following definitive criteria for PID, which are present in selected cases: (a) endometrial biopsy showing histologic diagnosis of endometritis; (b) transvaginal ultrasound or other imaging showing thickened, fluid-filled tubes with or without a tuboovarian complex (TOC) or free fluid; or (c) laparoscopic abnormalities showing PID (erythema, edema of the tubes, pelvic adhesions, free pus in the pelvis, a tuboovarian complex or a tuboovarian abscess).

Treatment Appropriate treatment (Table 28-1) varies, depending on the clinical presentation and the severity of illness. Many experts believe that all patients with PID should be hospitalized. Certainly most adolescents with PID should be hospitalized, owing to the likelihood of poor compliance and the sequelae of PID. Mild PID is treated by some on an outpatient basis if clinical follow-up within 72 h of antibiotic therapy initiation can be assured. Hospitalization may be required when the diagnosis is uncertain; pelvic abscess is suspected; the patient is pregnant; the patient has HIV infection; severe illness or nausea and vomiting preclude outpatient therapy; the patient is unable to tolerate an outpatient regimen; or when the patient has failed to respond to outpatient therapy.[1] In those who fail to respond to outpatient antibiotics, the diagnosis should be reassessed.

Patients with tuboovarian abscesses need anaerobic antibiotic coverage and hospitalization, and may need laparoscopic follow-up if they do not respond clinically. A ruptured tuboovarian abscess is a surgical emergency and may be fatal if not promptly treated.

Treatment of sexual partners Sexual partners should be referred for evaluation and empirical treatment of *C. trachomatis* and *N. gonorrhoeae* and for screening for other STDs. Treatment of the infected patient and her partner ideally should be simultaneous.

Follow-up Some recommend rescreening for *N. gonorrhoeae* and *C. trachomatis* 4 to 6 weeks after therapy is completed. PCR and LCR must

TABLE 28-1   Antibiotic Therapy in PID

Outpatient	
Regimen A	Ofloxacin 400 mg orally 2 times per day for 14 days *plus* Metronidazole 500 mg orally 2 times per day for 14 days *or*
Regimen B	Ceftriaxone 250 mg IM once *or* Cefoxitin 2 g IM *plus* 1 g probenecid orally concurrently *or* other parenteral third-generation cephalosporin (e.g., ceftizoxime or cefotaxime) *plus* doxycycline, 100 mg orally 2 times per day for 14 days
	NOTE: Azithromycin for the treatment of PID is not recommended due to insufficient clinical trials showing efficacy.
Parenteral[a]	
Regimen A	Cefotetan, 2 g IV every 12 h *or* Cefoxitin, 2 g IV every 6 h *plus* Doxycycline, 100 mg IV or orally every 12 h
Regimen B	Clindamycin, 900 mg IV every 8 h *plus* gentamicin, loading dose 2 mg/kg body weight IV or IM, followed by a maintenance dose (1.5 mg/kg) every 8 h. Peak and trough gentamicin levels are needed. Single, daily gentamicin dosing may be substituted.
Alternative Parenteral Regimens	
Regimen A	Ofloxacin 400 mg IV every 12 h *plus* metronidazole 500 mg IV every 8 h *or* Ampicillin/Sulbactam 3 g IV every 6 h *plus* doxycycline 100 mg IV or orally every 12 h *or* Ciprofloxacin 200 mg IV every 12 h *plus* doxycycline 100 mg IV or orally every 12 h *plus* metronidazole 500 mg IV every 8 h[1]

[a] Parenteral regimens should continue until the patient is afebrile and nontender for 48 h; then oral doxycycline or clindamycin is continued until 14 days of therapy are completed.

be delayed until 1 month after therapy is completed, if these testing modalities are used, because residual organism fragments may cause false-positive results.

Tubal scarring and damage from PID can result in long-term sequelae of chronic pelvic pain, recurrent disease, ectopic pregnancy, and infertility. Westrom and coworkers[15] found that 8 percent of women had tubal occlusion and infertility after a single episode of PID, 19.5 percent after two episodes, and 40 percent after three or more episodes of PID. Previous serologic evidence of chlamydia infection is associated with increased infertility and an increased incidence of ectopic pregnancies.[11]

Pyometra Pyometra is the accumulation of purulent material in the endometrial cavity. It usually occurs as the result of interference with the normal drainage of the uterus. Most often, this obstruction is due to malignant disease, such as cervical or endometrial cancer. However, other causes have been identified, including polyps, leiomyomata, scarring after cervical surgery such as conization, radiation, cervicitis, congenital anomalies, and puerperal infection.

The diagnosis may be difficult. It is essential to consider pyometra in the differential diagnosis of a tender midline pelvic mass, because therapy is different from that for salpingo-oophoritis. Classically, women with pyometra present with vaginal discharge, fever, and abdominal pain, and sometimes bleeding. Physical examination reveals an enlarged uterus, and the presence of endometrial cavity fluid can be confirmed by ultrasound.

A thorough pelvic examination is necessary if pyometra is suspected. Dilatation of the cervix and gentle curettage of the cervix and uterine cavity with histologic examination, as well as aerobic and anaerobic culturing, are important in evaluating the patient. In patients with malignancy, treatment of the malignancy by hysterectomy also removes the pyometra. In patients with such benign conditions as leiomyomata or polyps causing obstruction of the endocervical canal and resultant pyometra, removal of the uterus or the obstructing lesion will resolve the condition. However, in many situations this may not be necessary or desirable.

Many women with pyometra prefer to preserve the uterus if possible (e.g., young women with pyometra following surgery for cervical dysplasia). Cervical dilatation, prolonged drainage of the uterus with a catheter, and broad-spectrum antibiotics covering the usual genital tract flora may resolve the problem. Sometimes the myometrial infection cannot be eradicated, and hysterectomy may be necessary even in young women.

Left untreated, pyometra may result in spontaneous perforation and then sepsis. Broad-spectrum antibiotics with good anaerobic coverage, surgical exploration, and hysterectomy are necessary in patients with ruptured pyometra. Without aggressive therapy, ruptured pyometra is fatal. Even with surgical exploration and antibiotics, death may occur.

Bartholin's Duct Cysts/Abscesses

An acute abscess of the Bartholin's gland and duct may occur as the result of infection; from trauma, such as improperly placed mediolateral episiotomy; or after a posterior colporrhaphy where sutures can ligate or injure the duct. Infectious agents causing the abscess include *N. gonorrhoeae, C. trachomatis,* and facultative and obligate anaerobes that are normal vaginal/perineal flora. In older women, cancer of the Bartholin's duct or gland must be considered in the differential diagnosis, although this is uncommon. Bartholin's duct cysts may follow acute abscess formation or may be found incidentally during routine pelvic examination. Patients with symptomatic cysts present with pain on walking, sitting, or with intercourse.

Diagnosis Examination of the vulva reveals a tender, cystic-feeling mass in the area of the Bartholin's duct and gland. It must be differentiated from a hydrocele, from Skene's glands, which are more anterior, and from such solid tumors as fibromas, fibromyomas, lipomas, and hidradenomas.

Treatment An acute abscess must be incised and drained. Marsupialization is sometimes difficult with the acute abscess. Local anesthetic should be sufficient for incision and drainage; however, some patients require brief general anesthesia. Cultures for aerobes and anaerobes, and screening by culture, DNA probe, LCR, or PCR, for *N. gonorrhoeae* and *C. trachomatis* should be obtained at the time of incision and drainage. The incision should be made inside the vaginal mucosa but outside the hymenal ring. Systemic broad-spectrum antibiotics that cover *N. gonorrhoeae, C. trachomatis,* and normal vaginal flora may be administered after cultures are obtained; when culture results are available, the antibiotics may be adjusted to provide the best coverage for infecting organism(s). Sitz baths postoperatively are helpful.

A Bartholin's abscess/cyst also may be treated with insertion of a Word catheter. The bulb is inflated with 2 to 3 ml normal saline. The catheter is removed three to four weeks later, after epithelialization of the incision has occurred. Both marsupialization and Word catheter insertion are usually performed under local anesthesia in an outpatient setting, but may occasionally need to be done in an operating room. These procedures avoid exicising the gland and preserve its secretory function.

Marsupialization is performed by making a wedge-shaped vertical incision in the vaginal mucosa, draining the cyst and breaking up any loculations with a Kelly clamp, and everting the cyst wall edges to the vaginal mucosa with number 2-0 delayed absorbable interrupted sutures. Sitz baths are helpful postoperatively. No wick or packing is necessary. Cysts may recur in 10 to 15 percent of patients.

Excision of a Bartholin's duct cyst should be reserved for recurrent cysts that are refractory to other therapies and that are symptomatic. This procedure should be done in the operating room.[9]

Necrotizing Fasciitis

Necrotizing fasciitis is a relatively uncommon but life-threatening soft tissue infection that may progress rapidly. The risk of necrotizing fasciitis increases in patients over 50 years of age, and those with histories of arteriosclerosis, diabetes, obesity, smoking, previous radiation therapy, and operative trauma. Hypertension, renal failure, immunosuppression, and vascular disease are also thought to be risk factors for necrotizing fasciitis.[13]

Diagnosis Patients with necrotizing fasciitis of-

ten appear acutely ill with severe systemic toxicity. However, occasionally there is surprisingly little evidence of generalized toxicity. Fever is usually present. There may be erythema, edema, and tenderness of the overlying or adjacent skin. Thick pus is usually not present in the wound; however, there is a thin "dishwater" appearance to wound drainage. Examination of the wound may show necrotic edematous-appearing tissue. The fascia may appear gray. When blunt dissection with a finger or probe is performed, the fascia feels soft, and the adjacent subcutaneous tissue does not bleed.

Laboratory data may show an increased leukocytosis, anemia from hemolysis or hemoconcentration due to third-spacing of intravascular fluid into the wound, and/or hypocalcemia. Radiographic studies may show soft tissue gas. Culture of debrided tissue usually shows a polymicrobial infection. Histology of debrided tissue shows leukocyte infiltration, thrombosis of microvasculature, and focal necrosis of the fascia.

Treatment Immediate surgical debridement in an operating room is necessary. The necrotic tissue has to be excised back to margins that bleed easily. Delay in surgical debridement can increase the mortality rate to almost 100 percent. Polymicrobial etiology is common, with both aerobes and anaerobes being present in wound cultures; thus, broad-spectrum antibiotics are indicated until culture results are available. Patients who succumb to necrotizing fasciitis usually die in septic shock.

Common Sexually Transmitted Organisms

Patients who have one STD are at high risk for simultaneous or subsequent infection with others, and should be screened appropriately.

N. Gonorrhoeae

Gonococcal infections may be symptomatic or asymptomatic; both can cause infertility and increase the risk of ectopic pregnancy. Screening of high-risk women has been the mainstay of *N. gonorrhoeae* control in the United States. *N. gonorrhoeae* is found most commonly in 15 to 29-year-olds. The primary site in women is usually the endocervix, although the urethra, Bartholin's, Skene's and periurethral glands may be involved. In women with endocervical infection, a large number also have coexistent rectal infection. Pharyngeal infection also should be considered in the evaluation. Symptoms of gonococcal infection that may prompt a visit to a health care provider and that should be elucidated in the history include vaginal discharge, dysuria, pelvic pain, dyspareunia, menorrhagia, and intermenstrual bleeding.

Diagnosis Mucopurulent discharge may or may not be present on pelvic examination. After cleansing the cervix to remove exudate, culture should be obtained from the endocervix by inserting a swab 1 to 2 cm into the internal os and rotating it for 5 to 10 seconds. Alternatively, DNA probes can be used for diagnosis with one swab needed for both *N. gonorrhoeae* and *C. trachamatis* probes. If prompt transport and prompt incubation of the culture are not possible, DNA probes may be a good alternative method of diagnosis. However, because DNA probes are usually "batched" by labs, the turnaround time for results may be up to one week. PCR and LCR are also used for detecting *N. gonorrhoeae* with high sensitivity and specificity.

Treatment Uncomplicated *N. gonorrhoeae* is treated with antibiotics. The cost of the antibiotic, side effects, resistance, anatomical site of infection, and possible concurrent infection with *C. trachomatis* or syphilis must all be considered when choosing an appropriate antibiotic. The 1998 CDC STD guidelines recommend, for uncomplicated gonorrhea, cefixime 400 mg orally, or ceftriaxone 125 mg IM, or ciprofloxacin 500 mg orally, or ofloxacin 400 mg orally; *plus* azithromycin 1 g orally once or doxycycline 100 mg orally bid for 7 days. Presumptive chlamydia treatment with azithromycin or doxycycline is useful in patients who may not return for labora-

tory results and/or where there is a high prevalence of coexistent gonoccocal and chlamydia infections. Co-treatment may also delay development of antimicrobial-resistant *N. gonorrhoeae.* Already, some communities have quinolone-resistant *N. gonorrhoeae,* and quinolones should only be used if the resistant strains comprise <1 percent of strains isolated. In pregnancy, quinolones and tetracyclines are contraindicated; substitute erythromycin or ampicillin for the doxycycline in the treatment protocol. Cephalosporins are safe in pregnancy. Spectinomycin 2 g can be substituted for cephalosporins if a patient is unable to tolerate the latter and erythromycin may be substituted for tetracycline. Pharyngeal infection is effectively treated over 90 percent of the time with the ceftriaxone or ciprofloxacin regimens. Incubating syphilis can be treated with ceftriaxone or the 7-day course of doxycycline or erythromycin used to treat *C. trachomatis.*

Alternative regimens for uncomplicated gonorrhea include spectinomycin for patients allergic to cephalosporins and quinolones. This regimen does not treat incubating syphilis or pharyngeal gonorrhea. Ceftizoxime, cefotaxime, cefotetan, and cefoxitin are also active against *N. gonorrhoeae.* Alternate quinolone regimens are enoxacin 400 mg orally, lomefloxacin 400 mg orally, and norfloxacin 800 mg orally. Azithromycin needs to be given in a 2-g dose, but is expensive and can cause gastrointestinal distress at this dose, so it is not recommended for the treatment of uncomplicated gonorrhea. Other antimicrobials are effective, and the above guidelines are not an exhaustive list of antibiotics usable to treat gonorrhea.

Screening for HIV should be offered at the time of diagnosis of gonorrhea. Screening for syphilis and other STDs should be performed when *N. gonorrhoeae* is diagnosed. Patients who do not receive a β-lactam or tetracycline derivative should have the serologic test for syphilis repeated in one month.

Sexual partners need to be referred for evaluation and treatment if patients are symptomatic. In asymptomatic patients, sexual contacts within the last 60 days should be examined and treated. If the last sexual intercourse took place before this time period, then the most recent sex partner needs evaluation and treatment.

Disseminated gonococcal infection requires hospitalization, and was alluded to in the section on PID.

Chlamydia

Chlamydial genital infection is common among adolescent and young adult women. Screening of asymptomatic sexually active teenagers and women 20 to 24 is recommended. Other women at risk obviously should be screened as well. Those who do not use barrier contraception or who have new or multiple partners should be screened at the time of routine periodic examinations.

It is generally believed that treatment of asymptomatic cervical infection will reduce the likelihood of upper genital tract disease and such sequelae as infertility and ectopic pregnancy, although few studies have been performed to confirm this. Routine screening and treatment has been shown in a health maintenance organization to decrease the subsequent likelihood of PID and thus reduce overall health care costs. Treatment prevents transmission to partners and may prevent vertical transmission at birth.

Diagnosis Women may be asymptomatic or may have mucopurulent cervicitis with symptoms of vaginal discharge, postcoital bleeding, and/or dyspareunia. Upper genital tract infection may go unrecognized or may produce subtle symptoms of infection, such as abnormal bleeding, dyspareunia, vaginal discharge, low-grade fever, or mild abdominal pain. Endocervical culture, DNA probe, fluorescent antibody tests, immunoassay tests, PCR, or LCR, may be performed for diagnosis. When culturing the endocervix, endocervical cells need to be obtained because chlamydia is an obligate intracellular organism. The endocervix should first be sampled for the Papanicolaou smear (exfoliative cytology), unless this was recently performed; then it should be sam-

pled with a cotton-tipped swab for *N. gonorrhoeae;* and lastly, for chlamydia testing, the endocervix should sampled with a Dacron-tipped, plastic-shaft swab. If only chlamydia testing is performed, the endocervix should be cleansed with a swab initially, and then a second sample obtained. A sterile cytobrush may facilitate procurement of endocervical cells. In patient populations with a high prevalence of chlamydia infections, the rapid tests for chlamydia are sufficiently sensitive and specific. However, in patient populations with a low prevalence of chlamydia, there may be a high number of false-positive results. Thus, in children and in alleged assault evaluations, culture should be employed for diagnosis whenever possible. Introital specimens evaluated by LCR may also be used for routine screening in high-risk populations.

Treatment Uncomplicated chlamydia cervicitis may be treated with doxycycline, 100 mg orally twice daily for 7 days, or azithromycin, 1 g orally (single dose).[1] Cost and compliance should determine which regimen is employed. Alternative regimens include ofloxacin, 300 mg twice daily for 7 days; erythromycin base, 500 mg four times daily for 7 days; or erythromycin ethylsuccinate, 800 mg orally four times daily for 7 days.[1] Additionally, amoxicillin, 500 mg orally three times daily for 7 to 10 days, may be used if erythromycin is not tolerated in pregnant women.[2] If 500 mg of erythromycin base is not tolerated four times daily for 7 days, alternative erythromycin regimens during pregnancy include erythromycin base, 250 mg orally four times a day for 14 days; erythromycin ethylsuccinate, 800 mg orally four times a day for 7 days; or erythromycin ethylsuccinate, 400 mg orally four times a day for 14 days.

When azithromycin or doxycycline are used for treatment, no "test of cure" repeat chlamydia screening is necessary. Patients treated with erythromycin, pregnant and nonpregnant, need retesting for chlamydia more than 3 weeks after the therapy is completed. Partners should be treated and abstinence from sexual intercourse encouraged until therapy is complete. Azithromycin 1 g orally in pregnant women is probably safe, but effectiveness data are insufficient to recommend its routine use in pregnant women.

Syphilis

Presentation, diagnosis, and treatment of early syphilis Syphilis, caused by *Treponema pallidum,* is a sexually transmitted disease that can manifest a myriad of signs and symptoms, ranging from asymptomatic to neurologic impairment in neurosyphilis, or visceral gummas in tertiary syphilis. Syphilis also can be transmitted vertically, causing congenital syphilis and stillbirth. *T. pallidum* gains systemic access through minute abrasions in skin or mucosal surfaces and begins to replicate locally, extending to systemic disease.

Primary syphilis Dark-field microscopy of a moist primary chancre or regional lymph node aspiration can be used for the diagnosis. The chancre is a painless, firm ulcer with raised edges, and often is asymptomatic. The chancre heals spontaneously in three to eight weeks.

Secondary syphilis Serological testing with rapid plasma reagin (RPR) or the Venereal Disease Research Laboratory (VDRL) test usually is positive (80 to 90 percent). Confirmatory testing with microhemagglutination assay for antibodies to *T. pallidum* (MHA-TP) or fluorescent treponemal antibody-absorption (FTA-ABS) is necessary after the nonspecific serologic antibody tests.

About six weeks after primary syphilis, almost all untreated patients will progress to secondary syphilis. Multiple symmetrical skin lesions may develop, as well as any of these: lymphadenopathy, hepatitis, nephrosis, alopecia, or condyloma latum. Serologic testing is positive. The untreated secondary syphilis lesions resolve after 3 to 12 weeks. Following secondary syphilis, there is a syphilis of less than one year's duration, termed "early-latent."

All of the above types of syphilis can be treated with benzathine penicillin G, 2.4 million units IM in a single dose. Pencillin-allergic nonpregnant patients may be treated with doxycycline, 100 mg orally two times a day for 2 weeks, or tetracycline, 500 mg orally four times a day for 2 weeks, or, with a higher failure rate, erythromycin, 500 mg orally 4 times a day for 2 weeks. A single dose of ceftriaxone is not effective for treating syphilis, but a regimen producing 8 to 10 days of treponemicidal blood levels may be used.[1]

Follow-up of patients with early syphilis The serologic test titers should be repeated and a clinical exam performed at 3 and 6 months posttreatment. All patients should be screened for HIV. Titers should decline fourfold by three months with primary and secondary syphilis, and by 6 months with early latent syphilis. Patients with continuing signs or symptoms of persistent infection or reinfection, or with a fourfold increase in serologic titer, should have their HIV status rechecked and a lumbar puncture performed to examine the cerebrospinal fluid (CSF) for signs of infection. Retreatment should be with benzathine penicillin G, 2.4 million units IM for three weekly injections, unless neurosyphilis is present. As is the case for any patient being treated for syphilis, pregnant patients may develop a Jarisch-Herxheimer reaction after penicillin, with fever, headaches, myalgia, and flushing, but this should not be a reason to delay therapy. Patients should be instructed to watch for decreased fetal activity and preterm labor. Penicillin-allergic pregnant patients should be hospitalized for desensitization to penicillin, then treated with penicillin. Follow-up of pregnant patients should consist of HIV testing and monthly serologic titers until antibody titers decrease appropriately.[1] Early latent syphilis is rarely diagnosed and requires a documented seroconversion in the last year, or unequivocal primary or secondary syphilis in the last year, or a sex partner with primary or secondary or early latent syphilis in the last year.

Late latent syphilis or latent syphilis of unknown duration Late latent syphilis or latent syphilis of unknown duration includes patients who have had syphilis for more than one year on the basis of documented seroconversion or who have latent syphilis of unknown duration. These patients are asymptomatic. They need to be evaluated for evidence of tertiary disease. A CSF examination is necessary for patients that meet any of these criteria:

- Neurologic or ophthalmic signs or symptoms
- Other evidence of active syphilis (e.g., aortitis, gumma, iritis)
- Treatment failure
- HIV-positive
- Serum nontreponemal titer ≥1:32, unless the duration of infection is known to be <1 year
- Nonpenicillin therapy planned, unless the duration of infection is known to be <1 year[1]

Treatment consists of

- Benzathine penicillin G, 7.2 million units total, administered in three doses of 2.4 million units IM each, at one-week intervals.
- For penicillin-allergic nonpregnant patients (after neurosyphilis is excluded): doxycycline, 100 mg twice daily for 2 weeks if <1 year infection or for 4 weeks if duration of infection is unknown or >1 year, or tetracycline 500 mg four times a day for 2 weeks if duration of infection is <1 year or for 4 weeks otherwise.

Penicillin-allergic pregnant patients need to be hospitalized and desensitized.[1] *Follow-up:* Quantitative nontreponemal serologic testing should be repeated at 6 months and 12 months. If titers increase, if a titer ≥1:32 does not decline fourfold (two dilutions) within 12 to 24 months, or if the patient develops signs or symptoms of syphilis, the patient needs to be evaluated for neurosyphilis and retreated as necessary.

Tertiary (late) syphilis Tertiary (late) syphilis develops only after a latency of many years, and occurs in only 20 to 30 percent of untreated patients. Tertiary syphilis encompasses patients with gumma and cardiovascular syphilis. A CSF examination is necessary at the time of diagnosis. Consult with an expert.

Recommended treatment is benzathine penicillin G, 7.2 million units IM total, given in three doses of 2.4 million units at 1-week intervals.[1] Penicillin-allergic patients should receive doxycycline or tetracycline as in late-latent syphilis. Penicillin-allergic pregnant patients need to be desensitized.

Neurosyphilis Ophthalmic or auditory symptoms or cranial nerve palsies can occur at any stage of syphilis and warrant a CSF examination. Syphilitic eye disease, such as uveitis, neuroretinitis, or optic neuritis is frequently associated with neurosyphilis. Patients with syphilis and eye disease should be treated as if they have neurosyphilis.

The CDC-recommended treatment regimen is 18 to 24 million units aqueous crystalline penicillin G daily, administered as 3 to 4 million units IV every 4 h for 10 to 14 days, or, in a compliant patient, 2.4 million units procaine penicillin IM daily plus probenecid, 500 mg orally four times per day, both for 10 to 14 days. In addition, some physicians recommend benzathine penicillin, 2.4 million units IM, after completion of the above regimen, to have therapy last as long as the therapy for late latent syphilis. Penicillin-allergic patients need to be desensitized and treated as above.

If CSF pleocytosis was present initially, follow-up CSF should be examined every 6 months until there is a normal cell count. If the cell count has not decreased by 6 months, or if there is an abnormal cell count at 2 years, retreatment needs to be considered.

HIV and syphilis All patients with syphilis should be screened for HIV infection as well as for other STDs. Syphilis in HIV-infected patients requires special care owing to reported treatment failures, occurrence of neurosyphilis, and bizarre nontreponemal titers. The reader is referred to the *1998 Centers for Disease Control—Sexually Transmitted Disease Guidelines* for specifics.

Partner evaluation Sexual partners of all patients with syphilis (any stage) should be evaluated serologically and clinically. Sexual transmission only occurs with mucocutaneous lesions. The CDC recommend that

- Persons who are exposed to a patient with primary, secondary, or latent (duration <1 year) syphilis within the preceding 90 days might be infected even if seronegative, and should be treated presumptively.
- Persons who are sexually exposed to a patient with primary, secondary, or early latent syphilis >90 days before examination should be treated presumptively if serologic test results are not available immediately and the opportunity for follow-up is uncertain.
- For purposes of partner notification and presumptive treatment of exposed partners, patients who have syphilis of unknown duration and who have high nontreponemal serological test titers (≥1:32) may be considered to have early syphilis.
- Former and current sex partners of patients with late syphilis should be evaluated clinically and serologically for syphilis.[1]

The time periods before treatment used for identifying at-risk partners are 3 months plus duration of symptoms for primary syphilis, 6 months plus duration of symptoms for secondary syphilis, and 1 year for early latent syphilis.

Mycoplasma

Mycoplasma and ureaplasma are organisms that have no cell wall but that can grow in cell-free media. The presence of *Mycoplasma genitalium* is of uncertain clinical significance. *M. hominis* is present in about 50 percent of public clinic patients and 20 percent of private obstetric patients. *U. urealyticum* is present in 80 percent of women in public clinics and in 50 percent of private patients.[10] Both of the latter species are present more often in women with bacterial vaginosis. Along with other organisms, both have been found in patients with intra-amniotic infection, pelvic inflammatory disease, and postpartum en-

dometritis. Ureaplasma has been associated with low birthweight infants, infertility, and habitual abortion.

Cultures for these organisms should not be obtained routinely in clinical practice. However, if cultures are needed, the vaginal mucosa rather than the endocervical canal should be cultured. Genital mycoplasma can be cultured from specimens transported by an anaerobic transport device within 2 to 3 h of obtaining the specimen. Special mycoplasma transport broth contains antibiotics and cannot be used for any other cultures. Rapid delivery to the laboratory is important.[8]

Because mycoplasma usually are associated with other organisms, broad-spectrum antibiotics are usually employed to treat associated pathogens. *U. urealyticum* is treated with tetracyclines or erythromycins. *M. hominis* is susceptible to clindamycin. *M. hominis* is not susceptible to erythromycins, and some isolates are resistant to tetracycline. Upper genital tract infections should be treated with an antibiotic that is effective against these organisms.

Human Papilloma Virus

Human papilloma virus (HPV) causes a broad spectrum of disease, ranging from subclinical infection in 70 percent of infected patients to overt genital warts in 30 percent of patients. HPV prevalence is greatest between ages 15 and 35. As with trichomoniasis and bacterial vaginosis, HPV is associated with other sexually transmitted diseases. Human papilloma virus can be detected by cytology, histology, and DNA probes. HPV is associated with squamous genital tract malignancies. HPV usually occurs multicentrically in the cervix, vagina, vulva, and perianal regions.

Some condylomas are seen grossly on physical examination; others are visible with colposcopy. Cytology, histology, HPV antigen detection, and HPV DNA molecular hybridization also may be used to detect HPV.

Treatment of HPV is difficult, with recurrences and failure to treat all involved areas common.

The goal should be to rule out significant neoplasia, to eradicate exophytic warts, and to decrease symptoms. The goal is not to remove all HPV completely, because this usually cannot be achieved.

In patients with external symptomatic disease, once colposcopic evaluation (of the vulva, vagina, and cervix) and biopsy (of the lesion and of other areas as needed) have been performed to rule out the presence of a malignancy or a premalignant lesion, trichloroacetic acid (TCA) or bichloroacetic acid 80 to 90% may be applied to warts. Patients are retreated every week for up to 6 weeks. An alternative regimen that can be used at home is purified podophyllin resin, podofilox (Condylox) 0.5% solution or gel, which may be applied to obvious lesions twice daily for 3 days, followed by no treatment for 4 days. This cycle may be repeated up to four times. Podophyllin 10 to 25% in compound tincture of benzoin, can also be used externally only, but treatment must be performed by the health care provider. It must be washed off in 1 to 4 h, and can be repeated weekly up to six times. As with podofilox, ≤0.5 ml of solution can be used in daily treatment, and ≤ 10 cm^2 of tissue per day can be treated. Podofilox and podophyllin are *contraindicated* in pregnancy. External vulvar lesions may be treated at home with a local immune response modifier, imiquimod 5% (Aldara) 3 times a week for up to 16 weeks; imiquimod should not be used in pregnant patients.

5-Fluorouracil 5% is sometimes used to treat vulvar and vaginal lesions; however, it may cause severe ulceration of normal tissue. Treatment with cryotherapy, laser, LEEP procedures, and interlesional interferon also may be helpful.

Cervical warts must be examined for coexistent dysplasia or carcinoma before treatment. Cervical warts can be treated with cryotherapy, LEEP, or TCA. Because of the role of HPV as a cocarcinogen for lower genital tract squamous carcinoma, all women with HPV should be followed regularly with Papanicolaou smears and, when indicated, colposcopy.

Herpes

Herpes simplex is the most common cause of genital ulcers. After an incubation period of three to five days, 2- to 4-mm vesicles appear, and subsequently become painful ulcerations. Genital herpes may be caused by two serotypes, HSV-1 and HSV-2. HSV-2 is most common in genital disease.

Diagnosis of acute genital herpes is made by recognizing clinical lesions and culturing unroofed vesicles or ulcers. Cytology with a Papanicolaou smear or a Tzanck smear has lower sensitivity.

Treatment for primary herpes in the immunocompetent patient is any one of the following: acyclovir 400 mg orally 3 times daily for 7 to 10 days; or acyclovir 200 mg orally five times daily for 7 to 10 days; or famciclovir 250 mg orally three times daily for 7 to 10 days; or valacyclovir 1 g orally twice daily for 7 to 10 days. Patients systemically ill with herpes should be treated with intravenous acyclovir, 5 to 10 mg/kg body weight, every 8 h for 5 to 7 days or until clinical resolution occurs. Treatment for recurrent herpes in immunocompetent patients may be acyclovir 200 mg orally five times a day for 5 days; or acyclovir 400 mg orally three times a day for 5 days; or acyclovir 800 mg orally two times a day for 5 days; or famciclovir 125 mg orally two times a day for 5 days; or valacyclovir 500 mg orally two times a day for 5 days. Daily suppressive therapy in patients with six or more recurrences per year may also be used. Safety and efficacy have been shown with therapy for as long as 5 years, but after 1 year a trial without acyclovir should be allowed to assess the patient's recurrence rate. Daily suppressive therapy dosing is acyclovir 400 mg orally twice daily; or famciclovir 250 mg twice daily; or valacyclovir 500 mg daily; or valacyclovir, 1000 mg daily.

HIV-infected women and other immunosuppressed women who have an acute herpes infection may need an increased acyclovir dosage of 400 mg three to five times daily until clinical resolution occurs; intravenous therapy should also be considered. High-dose valacyclovir has been associated with TTP or hemolytic uremic syndrome, but low doses for genital HSV should be safe. Famciclovir 500 mg bid may also be used in the immunocompromised.

Resistant herpes strains may respond to foscarnet, 40 mg/kg body weight IV every 8 h until clinical resolution.[1]

HIV and other STDs may be transmitted more easily when open ulcers are present; thus, patients with herpes should be counseled and appropriate screening performed.

Chancroid

Chancroid has an incubation period of 1 to 14 days. A small papule or pustule erodes into an ulcer, which usually is deep, painful, and indurated. The ulcerated area is softer than that present in syphilis or granuloma inguinale. Painful adenopathy is present in 30 to 60 percent of patients. Diagnosis of chancroid is usually clinical, with one or more painful genital ulcers present, no *Treponema pallidum,* and no HSV clinical symptoms or positive tests. Tender inguinal adenopathy with a painful ulcer is suggestive, and suppurative inguinal adenopathy is almost pathognomonic of chancroid. Laboratory confirmation is difficult, but can be made by culture of *Haemophilus ducreyi,* using direct inoculation of ulcer exudate onto selective blood agar media with vancomycin and then incubation at 33°C with 5% CO_2. Cytologic examination of the ulcer base exudate with a Giemsa or Gram stain will show gram-negative rods, but this is not very sensitive or specific. Biopsy of the ulcer base shows three zones: one of neutrophils, red blood cells, and fibrin; one of blood vessel formation and endothelial cell proliferation; and one deeper level with plasma cell and lymphocyte infiltrate.

Treatment regimens include azithromycin, 1 g orally in one dose; ceftriaxone, 250 mg IM; or erythromycin base, 500 mg orally four times a day for 7 days; or ciprofloxacin, 500 mg orally, twice daily for 3 days. Patients with chancroid should be screened for HIV, syphilis, and other STDs.

Lymphogranuloma Venereum

Lymphogranuloma venereum (LGV), caused by *Chlamydia trachomatis,* serotypes L1, L2, or L3, is endemic in tropical areas. There are three stages of this disease. The incubation period for the first stage is 5 to 7 days. A pustule or papule forms and rapidly ulcerates. In women, this is commonly on the vaginal wall, vulva, posterior fourchette, or posterior lip of the cervix. Fifty percent are asymptomatic and heal spontaneously. Stage II presents with a tender, firm, lymph node collection (bubo). Proctitis may be found with anal involvement. Infrequently, systemic symptoms of fever, headache, and meningismus occur. These lesions resolve in 2 to 3 months. Stage III results from fibrosis of lymphatic tissue with elephantiasis, rectal strictures, and perineal fistulas. Diagnosis is by a serologic complement fixation test or microimmunofluoresence test. Alternatively, tissue culture of an aspirate from an enlarged lymph node can be used for diagnosis. Histologic identification of chlamydia elementary or inclusion bodies in secretions or infected tissue also may be used. The differential diagnosis includes other sexually transmitted ulcerative diseases, Hodgkin's disease, non-Hodgkin's lymphoma, cat scratch fever, and bacterial lymphadenitis. Treatment is with doxycycline, 100 mg orally twice daily for 21 days. The CDC also recommends an alternative regimen of erythromycin base, 500 mg orally 4 times per day for 21 days. Pregnant and lactating women should be treated with erythromycin.[1] As in all sexually transmitted diseases, when one is present the woman is at risk of infection with multiple other STDs. She should be tested for these, and also counseled.

Donovanosis

Granuloma inguinale (donovanosis) is caused by *Calymmatobacterium granulomatis,* and is endemic in tropical regions. The incubation time is 8 to 80 days. Single or multiple genital ulcers occur; these ulcers are painless, irregular, and hard, with a rolled border and a clean base. Labial lesions are most common, but cervical and vaginal lesions may occur. Lymph nodes are not enlarged, but a "psuedobubo," which is a deep granuloma, may mimic a fluctuant node. If left untreated, sequelae include lymphatic obstruction and elephantiasis. Diagnosis is by histologic evidence of short, pleomorphic rods in ulcer border biopsies. Giemsa, Wright's, Dieterle, or Warthin-Starry staining enhances diagnosis by identification of intracytoplasmic inclusion bodies (Donovan bodies) within histiocytes. Pap smears may reveal Donovan bodies in women who have cervical lesions. Treatment can be trimethoprim-sulfamethoxazole, one double-strength tablet orally two times daily for at least 3 weeks, or doxycycline 100 mg orally two times daily for a minimum of 3 weeks. Therapy continues until all lesions are completely healed. Alternate protocols arc ciprofloxacin 750 mg bid for 3 weeks or erythromycin base 500 mg qid for 3 weeks. Gentamicin 1 mg/kg IV every 8 h can be added if there is no response in the first few days of therapy with any of the preceding four regimens.

Molluscum Contagiosum

Molluscum contagiosum is caused by an unclassified pox virus. It is seen most often in children. However, it is also a sexually transmitted disease in adults, occurring in adults on the lower abdomen, thighs, genitalia, or buttocks. The incubation period is 1 week to 6 months; if untreated in immunocompetent hosts, the infection remits spontaneously in about 6 months to 3 years. Diagnosis is by clinical recognition of dimpled papules. Confirmation is by biopsy or staining a smear of the caseous material from the dimple, in which inclusion bodies of virions can been seen. Treatment is by mechanical removal of the lesion with liquid nitrogen, direct curettage, or trichloroacetic acid. Disseminated molluscum contagiosum is seen in immunocompromised patients.

Pediculosis Pubis

Phthirius pubis, the crab louse, is usually spread through sexual contact. Patients with this problem commonly complain of itching. Small hemorrhages in the skin from lice bites may be visible. Patients may see the lice moving. Microscopic examination of nits or adult lice is diagnostic. Treatment is with lindane 1% shampoo, used for 4 min and then washed off; permethrin 1% cream rinse, used for 10 min and then rinsed off; or pyrethrins with piperonyl butoxide for 10 min and then rinsed off. Lindane should not be used in pregnant or lactating women or in children under age 2. Machine washing and drying (hot cycles) or dry cleaning of bedclothes and clothing are recommended. Eyelash involvement should be treated with occlusive ophthalmic ointment to eyelids twice daily for 10 days. Patients should be reevaluated in 1 week.

Scabies

Scabies is caused by *Sarcoptes scabiei,* variety hominis, and is transmitted both by sexual contact and by contact with infected bedding, clothes, or other fomites. Patients complain of intense itching, usually worse at night. Linear burrows 5 to 10 mm long with tiny brown and white specks at the ends (the mites) are pathognomonic. A scraping of the burrow examined microscopically can confirm the diagnosis. Treatment is with 5% permethrin cream applied from the neck down and washed off after 8 to 14 h or 1% lindane 1 oz of lotion or 30 g of cream applied from the neck down and washed off after 8 h. Lindane should not be used in pregnant or lactating women, in children less than 2 years old, after a bath, or in individuals with extensive dermatitis, as it may cause seizures. An alternative therapy is 10% crotamiton applied from the neck down for two nights and washed off 24 h after the second application. Bedding and clothes should be machine washed and dried (hot cycles) or dry cleaned. Pruritus may persist for several weeks, even with adequate therapy.

Common Systemic Diseases That May Be Transmitted via the Vaginal Route

HIV

Human immunodeficiency virus (HIV), the virus that causes AIDS as a late manifestation, is another sexually transmitted virus. HIV testing should be offered to all women at risk, including, but not limited to, women with other STDs; women whose partners are infected with the HIV virus; women whose partners are bisexual or drug users; women who are drug users; women with multiple sexual partners; and women whose partners have multiple sexual partners. HIV infection is discussed extensively in Chap. 68.

Hepatitis B

Hepatitis B is sexually transmitted. One-third to two-thirds of the 200,000 to 300,000 new cases that have occurred annually in the United States in the past 10 years were due to sexual transmission.[1] Hepatitis B virus (HBV) infection can result in death due to fulminant disease, jaundice, chronic HBV, and long-term sequelae, including cirrhosis of the liver and hepatocellular carcinoma.

The use of HBV vaccine should be advised for women at risk of acquiring HBV. This includes, but is not limited to, health care workers; persons with multiple sex partners; sex partners of HBV carriers; sex partners of injecting drug users; injecting drug users; and women whose partners have multiple partners. Advisory Committee on Immunization Practices (ACID) recommends HBV vaccination for persons who have had more than one sex partner in the last 6 months, men and women with another STD diagnosis, and sexually active homosexual and bisexual men. Older patients ($\geq$age 25) may have a higher incidence of past infection as measured by anti-HB$_C$; those immune due to vaccination have a positive anti-HBs. Depending on the patient population, the physician needs to determine whether serologic screening for past infection/immunization is cost-effective before vaccination.

Vaccination dosage   The vaccination dosage is 1 ml of HBV vaccine IM in the *deltoid* at 0, 1, and 6 months. Depending on the vaccine manufacturer, the dose for adolescents (11 to 19 years) is either 0.5 or 1 ml. Universal vaccination is recommended for newborns and the 12-year-olds not previously vaccinated.

Exposure to HBV through sexual contact   Patients sexually exposed to HBV should receive 0.06 ml/kg of HBIG IM once within 14 days of last exposure, plus the first (0) dose of HBV vaccine, followed by the 1- and 6-month vaccine doses. Pregnancy is not a contraindication to HBV or HBIG. As patients age, there may be less of an antibody response to HBV vaccine. Repeat dosing is recommended if seroconversion does not occur after the first vaccine series.

Sequelae   Of the young adults who survive HBV, 6 to 10 percent become carriers; and over 25 percent of the carriers develop chronic active hepatitis with cirrhosis. An HBV carrier's risk of liver cancer is 12 to 300 times higher than that of non-HBV carrier adults.

Toxic Shock Syndrome

Toxic shock syndrome (TSS) is caused by infection or colonization with bacteriophage-specific strains of *Staphylococcus aureus* in a body cavity or on a foreign object in a body cavity. The strain of *S. aureus* that causes TSS makes an epidermal toxin, TSST-1. This toxin and staphylococcal enterotoxin B (SEB), and possibly other toxins, cause clinical symptoms.

Toxic shock syndrome may occur with menstruation, particularly when tampons are used, and has also been associated with vaginal infections, vaginal delivery, cesarean section, spontaneous abortion, diaphragm and sponge contraceptive use, CO_2 laser treatment of condyloma acuminatum, salpingitis, and postoperatively.

Diagnosis In 1980, the CDC compiled the following diagnostic criteria. The patient should have the first four of the following criteria and three or more organ system criteria:

- Temperature >38.9°C (102°F)
- Erythematous rash
- Hypotension
- Desquamation of palms and soles 1 to 2 weeks after illness onset

Three or more of the following systems:

- Gastrointestinal: vomiting or diarrhea
- Muscular: myalgia or elevated creatine phosphokinase (2× upper limit of normal)
- Mucous membrane: hyperemia of vagina, oropharynx, or conjunctivae
- Renal: elevated blood urea nitrogen; elevated creatinine (≥2× upper limit of normal); more than 5 WBC in a high-power field in urinary sediment without a UTI
- Hematologic: low platelet count (<100,000/mm^3)
- Hepatic: elevated SGPT ≥2× upper limit of normal
- Neurologic: disorientation or alteration in consciousness without focal neurologic signs
- Negative tests for Rocky Mountain spotted fever, leptospirosis, and measles
- Negative throat, blood, and CSF cultures[4]

The differential diagnosis includes any systemic illness associated with fever, rash, hypotension, and multiorgan system involvement.

Cultures to be obtained include those from body cavities (vagina, cervix, and throat), blood, any lesions, and wounds. Cultures of foreign objects, such as tampons, diaphragms, or sponges, should be obtained when applicable.

Treatment Hospitalization is necessary. Fluid replacement is the most important aspect of supportive care. Penicillinase-resistant penicillins,

such as nafcillin or oxacillin, are the drugs of choice.

TSS may recur in up to 30 percent of menstrual-related cases. The recurrence rates may drop to 5 percent if the patient receives β-lactamase-resistant antibiotics early in the course of the disease. Tampons should be avoided by women with a history of TSS.

References and Selected Readings

1. Centers for Disease Control: 1998 Sexually transmitted diseases treatment guidelines. *MMWR* 47, 18–106, 1998.
2. Crombleholme WR, Schacter J, Grossman MA, et al: Amoxicillin therapy for chlamydia trachomatis in pregnancy. *Obstet Gynecol* 75:752, 1990.
3. Draper D, Parker R, Patterson E, et al: Detection of trichomonas vaginalis in pregnant women with the In-Pouch TV culture system. *J Clin Microbiol* 31(4):116–118, 1993.
4. Duff P: Staphyloccal infections, in Gleicher N (ed): Principles and Practice of Medical Therapy in Pregnancy, 2d ed, New York: Appleton & Lange, 1992.
5. Eschenbach DA, Hillier SL: Advances in diagnostic testing for vaginitis and cervicitis. *J Reprod Med* 34(8):555–564, 1989.
6. Eschenbach DA: Bacterial vaginosis and anaerobes in obstetric-gynecologic infection. *Clin Infect Dis* 16(Suppl 4):S282, 1993.
7. Faro S: Infection and infertility. *Infect Dis Obstet Gynecol* 1:51–57, 1993.
8. Hill B: Techniques for isolating pelvic bacterial pathogens, in Mead PB, Hager WD (eds): *Infection Protocols for OB/GYN*. Montvale, NJ: Medical Economics, 1992, pp 265–271.
9. Mattingly RF, Woodruff JD: Surgical conditions of the vulva, in Mattingly RF, Thompson JD (eds): *Operative Gynecology*. Philadelphia: JB Lippincott, 1985, pp 694–696.
10. McCormack WM: Genital mycoplasmas, in Mead PB, Hager WD (eds): *Infection Protocols for OB/GYN*. Montvale, NJ: Medical Economics, 1992, pp 217–219.
11. McCormack WM: Current concepts: Pelvic inflammatory disease. *N Engl J Med* 330:115–119, 1994.
12. *Med Lett Drugs Ther* 36:113, 1994.
13. Piper JM, Mitchell EF, Ray WA: Prenatal use of metronidazole in birth defects: No association. *Obstet Gynecol* 82(3):348–352, 1993.
14. Thompson CD, Brekken AL, Kutteh WH: Necrotizing fasciitis: A review of management guidelines in a

large obstetrics and gynecology teaching hospital. *Infect Dis Obstet Gynecol* 1:16–22, 1993.

15. Westrom L, Joesoef R, Reynolds G, et al: Pelvic inflammatory disease and fertility: A cohort study of 1,844 women with laparoscopically verified disease and 657 control women with normal laparoscopic results. *Sex Transm Dis* 19:185–192, 1992.

16. Witkin SS, Jeremias J, Ledger WJ: Recurrent vaginitis as a result of sexual transmission of IgE antibodies. *Am J Obstet Gynecol* 159:32, 1988.

CHAPTER 29

Disorders of Menstruation

John H. Mattox

PRECOCIOUS PUBERTY
PRIMARY AMENORRHEA
SECONDARY AMENORRHEA
OLIGOMENORRHEA
PREMENSTRUAL SYNDROME
DYSMENORRHEA
ABNORMAL UTERINE BLEEDING
Presentation and Management • Most
Common Etiologies of Bleeding in the Various
Age Groups

Menstrual disorders are a common problem. They are sometimes associated with serious underlying pathology. It is important, as part of a woman's routine health evaluation, to inquire about her menstrual cycles. The first menstrual period usually occurs around 12 years of age but the range is between 9 and 16 years. The interval between normal menstrual cycles typically varies from 25 to 34 days. Cycles shorter than 3 weeks or longer than 40 days may indicate some abnormality in ovulation. The length of flow on the average is 5 ± 2 days. Menses may last as little as two, or as long as eight days and be within normal limits. A normal menstrual cycle correlates very highly with ovulation occurring; when the clinical parameters are exceeded on either end, this usually indicates ovulatory dysfunction.

Precocious Puberty

The appearance of sexual development before 8 years of age characterizes precocious puberty (PP). Seventy to 80 percent of cases of PP are due to an early "awakening" of the hypothalamic-pituitary-ovarian axis—idiopathic PP. The clinical presentation of precocious puberty in the female is almost always isosexual. The onset of secondary sexual characteristics is predominantly estrogen-dependent. Heterosexual precocity resulting in virilization of the female is unusual and is not discussed in this chapter; it is discussed elsewhere in this text.

Any secondary sex characteristics appearing before the age of 8 years warrant a clinical evaluation that involves trying to exclude serious disease such as neoplasms of the brain, adrenal, or ovary, or some disorder of the thyroid. While the complete premature onset of puberty is the most dramatic, there are partial presentations that also generate significant concern. Premature thelarche is usually an isolated event and is mainly self-limiting. It is not unusual to see breast changes related to maternal estrogen production in the newborn for up to 6 months following delivery.

Until recently, the cause of breast development in early childhood (premature thelarche) was unknown and was thought to be due to temporary increased sensitivity of estrogen receptors in breast tissue, because no increase in circulating estrogen could be detected in most of these cases. However, more sensitive assays have demonstrated a subtle, but real, increase in estradiol, and ultrasound has shown an increase in ovarian size with small follicle cysts. The Gn-RH pulse pattern is not quiescent in these girls as it is normally in the prepubertal period, but neither is it as active as it is in girls with true precocious puberty. The resultant increased estrogen production is very slight. It is enough to cause some isolated breast development, but it is not sufficient to cause any other features of puberty.

Premature pubarche or premature adrenarche can also occur as isolated events but may also hail the beginning of abnormal androgen secretion. Some investigation of all of these partial forms is warranted. This should begin with a focused history, a physical examination looking for other signs of secondary sexual maturation, and a bone age determination; an advanced bone age indicates that there may be a more serious underlying disease.

The most common type of isosexual precocious puberty is constitutional (idiopathic), and is found in 70 to 80 percent of cases. Early activation of the hypothalamic-pituitary-ovarian unit is responsible and denotes premature secretion of Gn-RH. Besides the obvious phenotypical manifestations, there are major psychosocial issues associated with this problem. The parents are often very distressed, and the child may experience problems relating to peers. The behavioral precocity needs to be addressed, and may be the more poignant reason for instituting therapy. While in the beginning of constitutional sexual precocity anovulation is more common, ovulatory cycles can be established, putting these children at potential risk for pregnancy. If ovulation can be documented with a well-timed serum progesterone test, no other studies are likely to be necessary; ovulation does not occur during any pathological or disease states associated with precocious puberty. A thorough history, which includes information about the mother's pregnancy, developmental milestones, family history regarding the onset of puberty, and the possibility that the child may be ingesting sex steroid hormones, is critical. The physical assessment should include documentation of the stage of pubertal development using Tanner's system for grading the breast and pubic hair progression.

As the diagnosis of idiopathic or constitutional precocious puberty is a diagnosis of exclusion, some testing is desirable, as is illustrated in Table 29-1. It should be recognized that some of the cases are associated with serious central nervous system (CNS) problems, hypothyroidism, or neoplasms of the adrenal or ovary; therefore, the

TABLE 29-1 A Basic Evaluation for Isosexual Sexual Precocity

Possible Site of Problem	Test(s)
CNS Lesions	MRI
Thyroid	TSH, ultrasensitive
Adrenal	DHEAS
Ovary	FSH, E_2

NOTE: Bone age assessment using x-rays of the wrist helps in assessing severity.

therapy is guided by the etiology. If all other etiologies have been excluded, and it is determined that the problem is idiopathic, Gn-RH analog therapy is used for the curtailment of physical and behavioral symptoms. The drug can be administered by injection or nasal spray. A 3-month depot preparation is available.

Important clinical issues regarding precocious puberty are reviewed in Table 29-2. Because most clinicians have limited experience with this problem, the optimum management usually requires either close consultation with, or referral to, a qualified endocrinologist. Depending on the consultant's training and clinical experience, this individual could be a medical, reproductive, or pediatric endocrinologist.

Primary Amenorrhea

The female pubertal sequence usually follows a predictable, chronological pattern initiated by

TABLE 29-2 Important Clinical Issues regarding Precocious Puberty (PP)

The onset of secondary sex characteristics, usually isosexual, before 8 years of age requires evaluation.

Premature thelarche and premature pubarche are most often isolated and self-limiting problems; some evaluation is required, and follow-up is essential to exclude more serious pathology.

The etiology in the majority of females with PP is an earlier onset of hypothalamic-pituitary-ovarian function.

The location of possible pathology resulting in PP includes the brain, adrenal, thyroid, and ovary.

the onset of a growth spurt and breast changes. The absence of breast-budding by age 14 and no menses by age 16, primary amenorrhea (PA), constitute reasons for concern. Although this chapter distinguishes between the clinical evaluation and management of primary amenorrhea, secondary amenorrhea, and oligomenorrhea, the clinical reality is that this separation is arbitrary and that there is often overlap.

Primary amenorrhea may be due to delayed physiological menarche. Other possible reasons include a genetic cause impacting ovarian or gonadal function, a congenital anomaly involving the vagina and/or uterus, or a central problem influencing hypothalamic function and Gn-RH pulsatile secretion. A clinical evaluation should be directed to different compartments: the uterovaginal tract, ovary, pituitary, CNS-hypothalamus, and other systemic problems.

An average healthy female in the United States usually has menarche by the age of 12.5 years; it is not unusual, however, for menarche to be delayed until 15 or 16 years of age. A major consideration influencing the onset of menses is the female having reached a certain body mass with a proportional amount of fat-to-lean body tissue. Any disease state, a psychosocial problem, or physical stress (particularly that which results in a sudden increase or decrease in weight) can result in the delay of menstrual function.

Congenital abnormalities associated with primary amenorrhea can be as minor as an imperforate hymen or as major as the complete absence of the müllerian structures (the uterus and vagina). Patients with the latter frequently have renal anomalies and skeletal defects along with the underlying vaginal agenesis. The diagnosis of anatomic defects is readily evident on performing a careful physical examination. A lack of sensitivity of androgen receptors, more commonly known as *testicular feminization syndrome,* should also be included in this category. Patients with androgen insensitivity have some secondary sex characteristics and a 46,XY karyotype. Any female patient with a Y-bearing gonad should have it removed because of the increased risk of neoplasia.

Gonadal causes comprise a substantial number of the cases in this category. Turner's syndrome, 45,X, is the most common of the primary gonadal causes. Numerous anomalies have been associated with this problem, and there is individual variation. The major medical problems for these individuals are a high incidence of heart disease, particularly coarctation of the aorta, and renal anomalies. Occasionally, some learning disorders are found in such individuals. The FSH is elevated (>40 mIU/ml). Along with the characteristic 45,X karyotype, a 46,XX and a 46,XY (*Swyer's syndrome*) are characterized by an elevated FSH level. The key physical finding is the absence of secondary sex characteristics, defining the need for karyotypic analysis.

Pituitary causes of primary amenorrhea are uncommon, although isolated gonadotropin deficiencies have been reported. Any patient with a diagnosis of amenorrhea should have a serum prolactin, the elevation of which would require the investigator to exclude a tumor. Whenever a pituitary cause of amenorrhea is considered, careful evaluation dictates that hypothyroidism or hypoadrenalism be excluded.

CNS causes of primary amenorrhea should focus on either a primary or a secondary process inhibiting the pulsatile secretion of Gn-RH. The patient with *Kallmann's syndrome*, Gn-RH deficiency associated with an inability to smell (anosmia), presents with the absence of secondary sex characteristics and a low FSH level. A simplified review of the most common clinical problems in patients who present with primary amenorrhea is presented in Table 29-3.

When considering therapy, disorders of the outflow tract may require surgical correction to allow for either the exit of menstrual flow, as in the case of imperforate hymen, or the creation of a new vagina for sexual function when vaginal agenesis is present. Prior to the latter procedure, a trial of vaginal dilators should be considered. Those females with a Y chromosome require gonadectomy, as approximately one-third will

TABLE 29-3   Common Diagnoses in Patients with Primary Amenorrhea

Diagnosis	Secondary Sex Characteristics	Serum FSH	Karyotype
Delayed menarche	Yes	Normal	46,XX
Gonadal dysgenesis	No	Elevated	45,X (Turner's syndrome) 46,XX; 46XY (Swyer's syndrome)
Uterovaginal anomaly	Yes[a]	Normal	46,XX; 46,XY (testicular feminization)
Gn-RH deficiency (Kallmann's syndrome)	No	Low	46,XX

[a]Partial in cases of androgen insensitivity, in which case patients have breast development.

develop gonadal neoplasia. Individuals with other genetic problems present a fascinating clinical picture, and there is a strong temptation to perform a laparoscopy. However, this almost never adds any additional information that can be used in the patient's clinical management.

For those individuals who will not have functioning ovaries, hormone replacement therapy, usually esterified or conjugated estrogens, 1.25 mg daily, with medroxyprogesterone acetate, 5 mg, calendar days 1 through 13, are sufficient to ensure body function and tissue integrity.

There are many psychosocial issues that need to be addressed when managing patients with these complicated endocrinopathies, and on occasion extensive counseling is required. Important clinical issues regarding primary amenorrhea are reviewed in Table 29-4. Optimum management by the primary care provider can often be enhanced by liberal dialogue and interaction with a reproductive endocrinologist.

Secondary Amenorrhea

After a previously menstruating individual misses three consecutive periods (if she is oligomenorrheic) or 6 months pass without a period, she has met the definition of secondary amenorrhea. When pregnancy has been excluded, clinical evaluation should be directed to different compartments: CNS-hypothalamus, pituitary, ovary, and the uterovaginal tract. Other systemic problems should be considered in the differential diagnosis, and will need to be ruled out if no other etiology is identified. The most common problem resulting in secondary amenorrhea is

TABLE 29-4   Important Clinical Issues regarding Primary Amenorrhea

The absence of breast budding by age 14 or lack of menses by age 16 requires evaluation.

Delayed menarche is the most common explanation for primary amenorrhea and is self-limiting.

A careful history (including family history) and a physical examination, documenting the state of development of the secondary sex characteristics and pelvic structures, usually suggests the diagnosis.

Gonadal (usually ovarian) failure is the most common pathological etiology in primary amenorrhea patients.

An elevated FSH (>40 mIU/ml) requires that a karyotype be performed.

A normal FSH requires that an MRI be obtained.

Two principles of therapy for women with no ovarian function are most important: (1) providing hormone replacement and (2) addressing future fertility potential (adoption or oocyte donation).

The most common hormone replacement regimen is conjugated estrogen, 1.25 mg daily, and medroxyprogesterone acetate, 5 mg, calendar days 1 to 13.

Y-bearing gonads should be removed.

hypothalamic dysfunction and includes weight-change-related disorders, severe psychological stress, and exercise-induced problems. Pituitary causes include neoplasms, the most common being a tumor that either directly or indirectly results in hyperprolactinemia. Premature ovarian failure, the cessation of periods before age 40, is another important cause, and is characterized by an elevated serum FSH of >40 mIU/ml. Intrauterine scarring can be sufficiently extensive to result in amenorrhea. Characteristically, these patients have either had a D&C following a pregnancy episode or have had severe endometritis.

While secondary hypothalamic amenorrhea can be associated with CNS lesions such as craniopharyngioma, glioma, other tumors, head trauma, and external irradiation, the overwhelming majority of patients with this problem have a neurobiochemical disorder affecting Gn-RH secretion. The diagnosis of hypothalamic amenorrhea is usually suggested by the history and reinforced after the evaluation of the pituitary, ovary, and endometrium have revealed no significant abnormalities. Amenorrhea associated with dramatic or sudden significant changes in weight (plus or minus 15 percent from ideal body weight) is often associated with hypothalamic amenorrhea. Anorexia nervosa (more than a 25 percent loss of ideal weight) is the most extreme form of weight loss associated with amenorrhea, and the patient needs to be referred to an appropriate counseling and support environment. At the other end of the spectrum is pseudocyesis, a strong desire for pregnancy, with mild to moderate weight gain. Pregnancy is excluded by a negative pregnancy test, and pseudocyesis is self-limiting. Hypothalamic amenorrhea associated with significant forms of exercise, such as long-distance running, usually is accompanied by loss of body weight. However, there is also a stress component if these individuals are participating in organized competition. In addition, there is a decrease in the percent of body fat below 22 percent, which seems necessary to maintain normal menses.

Any woman who has a disorder of ovulation including amenorrhea should have at least one serum prolactin test and pregnancy must be excluded. In addition, a serum-ultrasensitive TSH level should be part of the evaluation. With any persistent prolactin elevation when pregnancy, hypothyroidism, the use of medication known to elevate prolactin levels, and chest wall trauma have been excluded, the patient should be evaluated for a prolactin-secreting tumor. The basic assessment is a radiologic study, usually MRI.

The diagnosis of premature ovarian failure requires ordering a serum FSH level, which should be greater than 40 mIU/ml in ovarian failure. If ovarian failure is suspected, it must be remembered that disorders of other endocrine systems such as the adrenal, thyroid, parathyroid, and islet cells should be assessed. An SMA 20 or the equivalent, along with an ACTH-stimulation test measuring the changes in cortisol, will usually point toward any associated endocrinopathy.

Karyotypic analysis is important to order in women who are under 30 years of age because XY mosaicism can be present and necessitate gonadectomy. Any patient who has the appearance of hirsutism or androgen excess should have a serum testosterone and DHEAS.

A very common cause of secondary (and occasionally primary) amenorrhea is *polycystic ovarian syndrome* (PCOS). This is a hyperestrogenic and hyperandrogenic syndrome associated with anovulation. The basic pathogenesis of the disorder is an increase in LH, which stimulates the theca interna of the follicle to produce increased amounts of androstenedione. The three cardinal symptoms of PCOS are menstrual disorders [amenorrhea, oligomenorrhea, or dysfunctional uterine bleeding (DUB)], which are present in about 90 percent of the cases; hirsutism, which occurs in 70 percent; and infertility, which is the presenting symptom in 75 percent of patients with PCOS. The diagnosis is made by the clinical features and by the presence of an elevated serum LH (or reverse FSH/LH ratio). After exclusion of pregnancy, the amenorrhea, oligomenorrhea, and/or DUB are usually treated by endometrial sampling and then either cycles of medroxyprogesterone each month, or a monophasic birth control pill. Women who wish to become pregnant may be treated with clomiphene to induce ovulation.

Another cause of amenorrhea and/or oligomenorrhea is congenital adrenal hyperplasia (CAH). The "acquired" or "adult onset" form of this disease closely resembles PCOS in its clinical presentation. Although it is a common autosomal genetic disorder, clinically it is a far less frequent cause of oligomenorrhea than PCOS. The basic defect in CAH is an enzymatic failure in the production of cortisol. The resultant increase in ACTH stimulates the adrenal to produce increased amounts of androgens, causing hirsutism and oligomenorrhea. The diagnosis is made by considering the family history, clinical presentation, and laboratory findings, including elevated DHEAS, and 17-OHP. The obvious, logical, and specific treatment is oral cortisone administration. This replaces the cortisol that is lacking, suppresses the ACTH of the anterior pituitary, and prevents the excess secretion of androgens by the adrenal cortex. In this way, both the oligomenorrhea and the hirsutism are ameliorated.

The most probable diagnoses and the basic evaluation of these problems are shown in Table 29-5.

TABLE 29-5 Most Probable Diagnoses in Patients with Secondary Amenorrhea

Diagnosis	Study
Pregnancy	HCG determination
Hypothalamic dysfunction	History; other studies negative
Pituitary tumor	Prolactin; MRI
Premature ovarian failure	FSH > 40 mlU/ml (screen for other endocrinopathies)
Intrauterine scarring	Hysterogram or hysteroscopy
Polycystic ovarian syndrome	LH : FSH ratio (3 : 1)
Adult onset CAH	DHEAS; 17-OHP

The more precise the diagnosis, the more accurate is the plan of therapy. For some women with hypothalamic amenorrhea, all that may be needed to correct the amenorrhea is adequate nutrition, stress reduction, and/or moderation in exercise. If any of these conditions is coexistent with an extreme form of behavior, consultation with a psychiatrist is important.

Individuals with either primary or secondary amenorrhea usually have estrogen deficiency and require hormone replacement. In young acyclic patients, particularly if androgen excess is present, hormone therapy is most likely provided by a birth control pill; one with minimal androgen activity should be utilized. Alternatively, a commonly prescribed hormone replacement regimen in patients with amenorrhea is conjugated estrogens 1.25 mg or equivalent, daily, with medroxyprogesterone acetate, 5 mg, on calendar days 1 to 13. This program provides the needed hormone to prevent osteoporosis and sufficient hormone to keep the other tissues and the vascular system intact. Clomiphene citrate is indicated in women who have some evidence of ovarian function and who desire pregnancy. The initial dose is 50 mg per day from cycle day 5 to 9. In acyclic individuals, after endometrial hyperplasia has been ruled out, progesterone-induced withdrawal bleeding is required before therapy can begin. In women who weigh more than 175 lb, 100 mg as the starting dose should be considered.

Bromocriptine (Parlodel), a dopamine agonist, is effective in treating prolactin-secreting adenomas. As the majority of patients will have a microadenoma, they should be quite responsive to this medication. Starting with a small dose, 1.25 mg po at bedtime with a snack, and increasing the dose until euprolactinemia is achieved, is the simplest way to provide therapy. There is still significant debate about whether every patient with a microadenoma should be treated with medication, or whether they can just be observed.

Intrauterine scarring is strongly suggested by history, and in most patients the history includes a prior pregnancy episode followed by severe endometritis or a postpregnancy hemorrhage that requires curettage. Pelvic irradiation in large doses directed to the uterus can result in obliteration of the endometrial cavity. In addition to the significant history, the diagnosis could be made, and often the problem treated as well, by performing a hysteroscopy; the hysterosalpingogram can also be of utility. Hormone therapy may be indicated to stimulate uterine lining growth.

Table 29-6 reviews important clinical issues in patients with secondary amenorrhea. If there are any atypical clinical presentations, inconsistent laboratory findings, or if the patient fails to respond promptly to therapy, consider consulting with a reproductive endocrinologist.

Oligomenorrhea

Most of what has been discussed in the section on secondary amenorrhea applies to the differential diagnosis, evaluation, and treatment of oligomenorrhea as well. The symptom of oligomenorrhea, infrequent uterine bleeding at unpredictable times, is arbitrarily characterized as occurring at intervals of greater than 45 days. It signifies an underlying disorder of ovulation and therefore represents a malfunction of the hypothalamic-pituitary-ovarian axis. A small percentage of women will never have normal menses following menarche because the axis does not completely mature. Oligomenorrhea can represent an intrinsic axis disorder such as premature ovarian failure or an extrinsic problem interfering with normal axis function such as hypothyroidism. The more common problems can be detected by utilizing the tests listed in Table 29-7.

Other systemic or metabolic problems (e.g., severe hepatic or renal disease) can be associated with oligomenorrhea; however, the clinical management is usually focused on the primary disease and the menstrual disorder becomes a secondary issue.

Hypomenorrhea, either in amount or in duration (less than 3 days), is more likely to represent an underlying uterine cavity disorder but can be associated with oligo-ovulation. The same tests,

TABLE 29-6 Important Clinical Issues in Patients with Secondary Amenorrhea

After pregnancy has been excluded, hypothalamic causes of secondary amenorrhea are identified over 50 percent of the time.

Hypothalamic-related amenorrhea is most strongly suggested by the history of rapid weight changes, excessive exercise, or serious psychological stress. Laboratory and radiologic studies are usually negative; an FSH is normal.

Any patient with a disorder of ovulation should have a serum prolactin.

About one-third of patients with amenorrhea and hyperprolactinemia will have a tumor; hypothyroidism and prolactin-elevating medications should be excluded.

A serum FSH >40 mIU/ml strongly suggests ovarian failure; the diagnosis should not be made based on one test; hypothyroidism, hypoadrenalism, and associated autoimmune disorders should be excluded.

Patients with oligoamenorrhea and hirsutism should be screened with a serum testosterone and DHEAS.

Women with premature ovarian failure should have a karyotype if <30 years old.

Uterine bleeding following a progesterone challange does not exclude ovarian failure.

Intrauterine scarring (synechiae) is usually preceded by a history of uterine curettage associated with a pregnancy episode and/or infection.

If a patient is not responding to ovulation induction, she may have ovarian failure or a nonprolactin-secreting pituitary tumor.

Hormone replacement therapy, oral estrogen 0.625 to 1.25 mg daily (women <50 years old may need the higher dose), with medroxyprogesterone acetate, 5 mg calendar days 1 through 13 (if the uterus is present), is one of the most widely used regimens in these situations.

With hypothalamic amenorrheic patients desiring pregnancy, starting clomiphene, 50 mg daily (a higher dose if the patient weighs more than 80 kg), for 5 days is the initial ovulation-inducing therapy.

Neither clomiphene or menotropin therapy has been successful in inducing ovulation in patients with premature ovarian failure.

also including a hysterogram, would adequately evaluate this symptom. The evaluation and management of these disorders are similar to those for amenorrhea.

TABLE 29-7 Tests Commonly Utilized to Identify Potential Problems in Patients with Oligomenorrhea

Test	Significance
hCG	Any oligomenorrheic patient can have an occasional ovulatory cycle. Pregnancy should be excluded prior to any evaluation.
FSH	If it is elevated, ovarian failure may be present; the FSH level is usually normal with other intrinsic or extrinsic axis disorders.
Prolactin (PRL)	Any patient with a disorder of ovulation should have a PRL. When elevated, the etiology should be identified.
TSH	The current "ultrasensitive" test can screen for hypo- and hyperthyroidism; although a less likely cause of axis dysfunction, thyroid disease should be considered.
Testosterone, DHEAS, and 17-OHP	These tests are only necessary if the patient has symptoms of androgen excess or is very obese.
LH/FSH ratio	LH/FSH ratio is inverted in women with PCO, usually 3:1.

Premenstrual Syndrome

Most women having ovulatory cycles experience alterations in their body's sensation, and sometimes their mood, prior to the onset of menses. This symptom aggregate is termed *molimina*. If the number and severity of the symptoms increase to the point where they interfere with daily existence, this is considered *premenstrual syndrome* (PMS). The general approach of the primary care provider is to make the patient who has premenstrual symptoms more comfortable and functional. Predominant somatic symptomatology can include the feeling of bloatedness, breast pain, headache, pelvic pain, and alterations in bowel function. The major psychological symptoms can include mood alterations such as irritability, aggressive tendencies, anxiety, de-

pression, extreme lethargy, sleep disorders, crying spells, diminished libido, and loss of concentration. Feeling bloated seems to be the most common somatic complaint, while depression is the most common psychological complaint.

The incidence of PMS is reported to be between 5 and 95 percent of the population; 2 to 3 percent of women of child-bearing age have a severe form. The *Diagnostic and Statistical Manual of Mental Disorders,* 4th ed. (DSM-IV), 1995, lists the criteria that must exist to make the psychiatric diagnosis of premenstrual dysphoric disorder (PMDD). While this classification has added more objectivity, both physicians and patients more frequently use the term PMS. It is important to differentiate PMDD from a concurrent or underlying serious psychiatric disorder. Usually this requires a consultation from a psychiatrist.

There is no single, currently understood, biochemical etiology that satisfactorily explains the entire symptom complex associated with PMS. Part of the difficulty relates to this multifaceted disease and the investigational limitations in dealing with disorders of brain function and neurotransmitter metabolism. Numerous hypotheses have been tested, including progesterone deficiency, progesterone allergy, hypoglycemia, vitamin B_6 deficiency, inappropriate aldosterone secretion, inappropriate prostaglandin activity, endorphin dysfunction, and disorders of monoamine oxidase or dopamine metabolism. It also is readily apparent to the health care provider who has cared for a number of PMS patients that there can be a serious anxiety or depressive disorder which includes the premenstruum, or which is intensified around the time of ovulation or in the luteal phase.

Following the initial history and physical, including the pelvic examination, the most practical approach is to have the patient record her symptomatology on a daily basis, identifying both somatic and psychological complaints and quantitating the severity, usually on a scale of 1 to 4, with 4 being the most intense. Concurrently, she should document basal body temperature measurements, which should serve to localize the major symptomatology to the luteal phase. Coexisting medical problems should be considered, and laboratory tests that address those possible problems obtained.

The patient requires constant support and affirmation that improvement will occur, but it is important to identify those symptoms that are most bothersome. It is also critical for the patient to understand that there is no single medicine that will take away all the symptoms, but that the approach is to try to alleviate the most bothersome ones. The health care provider, on the other hand, must strongly avoid a multiple pharmacologic approach, as this avenue often creates more problems that it solves.

Following clinical evaluation and after concluding that PMS is the most likely diagnosis, several therapies can be considered. This is an opportune time to motivate the patient towards a more healthy diet and to include a moderate amount of exercise. A multiple-feeding, high-protein dict and the elimination of caffeine and alcohol have been very effective for certain patients. Vitamin B_6 (pyridoxine) 50 mg daily, has also had a salutary effect on this condition. Table 29-8 lists some other medical therapies. If depression or other substantial psychiatric problems are a component of the woman's problems, these must be addressed. Formal psychiatric consultation is sometimes needed.

Important clinical issues about PMS are reviewed in Table 29-9.

Dysmenorrhea

Dysmenorrhea, lower abdominal-pelvic crampy pain with menses and usually with a constellation of other symptoms, is classified as primary or secondary and can be incapacitating. The major tenet when considering this diagnosis is the accurate identification or, more specifically, the exclusion of pelvic disease.

Primary dysmenorrhea (PD) usually appears shortly after the menarche and is associated with

TABLE 29-8 Possible Medications for PMS Symptoms[a]

Symptoms	Oral Drugs
Bloating or fluid retention	Spironolactone, 50 mg A.M.
General, multiple symptoms	Low-dose estrogen birth control pill
Sleep disorder	Dalmane 15–30 mg hs
Anxiety, mood swings, crying	Xanax, 0.25–0.5 mg tid
Depression	Prozac, 10–20 mg qd
Breast tenderness	Danazol, 200 mg qd

Symptoms	Injectable Drugs
Severe PMS (not responsive to oral therapy)	Gn-RH analog with or without add-back therapy

[a] Usually required during luteal phase only except for birth control pills. Some contraceptive measures should be used to avoid taking the medication during pregnancy. The pharmacology of these medications should be reviewed before usage.

ovulatory cycles. Characteristically, it is not caused by or associated with demonstrable pelvic pathology such as adhesions, infection, or endometriosis. The pain is crampy in nature and may sometimes radiate to the back or thighs. Other symptoms, such as nausea, emesis, headache, fatigue, and diaphoresis, have been associated with

TABLE 29-9 Premenstrual Syndrome (PMS)

Premenstrual symptoms may be incapacitating for a small number of women.

A thorough clinical evaluation should occur prior to making the diagnosis of PMS.

A daily diary kept by the patient recording her symptoms is the cornerstone of diagnosis and management.

General health improvement measures addressing exercise, diet, and reduction of alcohol and caffeine will produce improvement in most patients.

Medications are prescribed to relieve the most bothersome symptom(s).

Formal psychiatric consultation may be necessary for certain patients.

dysmenorrhea. The severity may be correlated with the amount and duration of menstrual flow.

While the exact etiology of the pain is unknown, the role of endogenous prostaglandins seems to be important. Women with clinically significant dysmenorrhea have elevated prostaglandin levels in menstrual fluid, increased uterine tone, and increased frequency of uterine contractions, believed secondary to prostaglandins. Once severe cyclic pain is anticipated, there may be an associated fear and anxiety, which, as in other forms of pain, has been shown to intensify the perception of pain.

The diagnosis can usually be made after taking a detailed history about the character of the pain associated with menstruation and the lack of abnormal physical findings during the pelvic examination. If there is any concern about a possible pelvic finding or a limited exam because of obesity, a pelvic ultrasound should be obtained. Currently, there is no significant value to ordering a screening battery of laboratory tests. A hemoglobin or a serum ferritin might prove beneficial if anemia secondary to excessive menstrual flow is suspected with dysmenorrhea; other tests should be obtained as clinically warranted.

As this problem is often seen in younger women who may have not had prior interaction with a health care professional, it is particularly important to approach the patient with sensitivity and a sympathetic demeanor. Sufficient time should be allowed in the office to avoid giving the patient the impression that she is being rushed through the visit. This visit may also present an opportunity to discuss the need for maintaining physical activity, correcting dietary deficiencies, and considering some relaxation therapy. The initial medical therapy in women who do not desire any contraception is a prostaglandin synthetase inhibitor (PGSI). Over-the-counter ibuprofen, with a usual dose of 400 mg three times per day, will provide adequate relief for many patients. Higher doses of more potent agents may be utilized if over-the-counter medication is not effective. It is important for the patient to understand that the medication is being taken not only

for the relief of discomfort, but also for reduction of the production of prostaglandins, and therefore it needs to be taken continuously through the entire episode for optimum relief. Low-estrogen-containing birth control pills are effective therapy for primary dysmenorrhea in approximately 90 percent of patients. If the patient does not respond to the birth control pills or PGSI, it is appropriate to consider a diagnostic laparoscopy, as the presence of pelvic pathology (i.e., advanced endometriosis) has been identified in a teenage population that has not been responsive to medical therapy.

The primary care provider must consider secondary dysmenorrhea (SD) as a symptom, requiring an attempt to identify some pelvic pathology. Women presenting with SD are usually over 20 years of age and have experienced a significant period of time during which the pain associated with menstruation was manageable. Historically, the patient will relate that the pain has gradually progressed over some time and is becoming more incapacitating and less likely to be relieved with over-the-counter analgesics. There is frequently a concomitant change in the pattern of menstrual flow either in the duration or the amount.

While the list of possible pelvic diseases causing secondary dysmenorrhea can be seen in Table 29-10, the most likely candidates are endometriosis, adenomyosis, and chronic pelvic infection. The same detailed inquiry into the nature of the pain will usually point to one of the diagnoses. There are often significant pelvic findings at the time of the bimanual examination (e.g., uterine enlargement or a fixed retroflexed uterus). Char-

TABLE 29-10 **Possible Causes of Secondary Dysmenorrhea**

Endometriosis
Adenomyosis
Chronic upper genital tract infection
Adhesions
Cervical stenosis
Accentuated by stress, fatigue, or pelvic somatization

acteristically, mild analgesic therapy and oral contraceptive steroids have not been effective in relieving the discomfort. The assessment of the endometrial cavity, either with hysterosalpingo-gram or hysteroscopy, and of the pelvic structures, utilizing a diagnostic laparoscopy, should be incorporated into the clinical evaluation. The rational approach to therapy depends on a specific diagnosis and using whatever medical or surgical therapies are necessary to make the patient more comfortable; on rare occasions, a hysterectomy may be indicated. The most vexing problem for the clinician is the patient with chronic pelvic pain that is accentuated at the time of menses. It is thought that this condition might be due to pelvic nerve hypersensitivity, a form of pelvic somatization. If after a complete workup, pelvic disease has been excluded, it may be necessary for the patient to be referred to an individual or clinic specializing in the management of chronic pain. Important clinical issues about dysmenorrhea are reviewed in Table 29-11.

Abnormal Uterine Bleeding

Abnormal uterine bleeding (AUB) is a frequent complaint of patients and a major reason for the

TABLE 29-11   Dysmenorrhea

Primary dysmenorrhea (PD) usually presents shortly after menarche in the absence of any abnormal pelvic findings and is customarily improved with PGSI or birth control pills

A sudden acute episode of PD can be alleviated by a para-cervical block injecting 2 ml of 0.25% Marcaine at 12, 4, and 8 o'clock.

Any patient with PD who does not adequately respond to medical therapy should be considered a potential candidate for diagnostic laparoscopy.

Patients with secondary dysmenorrhea usually have some accompanying pelvic pathology; the most common problems are endometriosis, adenomyosis, and pelvic inflammatory disease (PID) with concomitant pelvic adhesions.

Dysmenorrhea may be intensified by stress, fatigue, and pelvic somatization.

TABLE 29-12   Differential Diagnosis of Abnormal Uterine Bleeding

Pelvic Pathology (Organic)
  Endocervical or endometrial polyps
  Leiomyoma
  Malignancy of the cervix, endometrium, or myometrium
  Premalignant lesions of the endometrium (hyperplasia)
  Chronic endometritis
  Adenomyosis
  Endometriosis
  Pelvic inflammatory disease (PID)
  Functional ovarian tumors
  Neoplastic ovarian tumors

Hormone-related (Nonorganic)
  Endogenous
    Anovulatory cycles
    Ovulatory cycles
  Exogenous
    Hormone replacement therapy
    Birth control pill therapy

Systemic Problems
  Disorders of hypocoagulation
  Severe liver or renal disease
  Thyroid disease (usually hypofunction)

Disorders of Pregnancy
  Ectopic pregnancy
  Threatened abortion, incomplete abortion, complete abortion, missed abortion
  Gestational trophoblastic disease

performing of gynecologic procedures. Making an accurate diagnosis and ruling out serious etiologies are important. Table 29-12 reviews the differential diagnosis of abnormal uterine bleeding and Table 29-13 reviews the possible causes of anovulation in reproductive-age women. When a woman complains of vaginal bleeding, it is important to rule out the possibility that the origin is actually from another site (e.g., bowel, urinary tract, vulva).

Benign organic causes of abnormal bleeding such as endocervical polyps are usually not difficult to diagnose and manage. Gynecologic malignancy (particularly of the uterus and cervix) often presents with abnormal uterine bleeding. The major clinical dilemmas are created by nonorganic, hormonally related causes of bleeding, 80 percent of which are associated with anovulatory

TABLE 29-13 Possible Etiologies of Anovulation in Reproductive Age Women

Peripheral Etiologies
  Liver and renal disease
  Neoplasms producing androgen, estrogen, or chorionic
    gonadotropin
  Obesity

Central Etiologies
  Hypothalamic: malnutrition, anorexia, substantial weight
    loss, exercise-associated, systemic disease, psychogenic
    factors
  Kallmann's syndrome (Gn-RH deficiency)
  Hypothalamic-pituitary damage
  Hyperprolactinemia-galactorrhea—e.g., due to medica-
    tions, pituitary tumors, hypothyroidism, associated with
    empty-sella syndrome.

Other Endocrine Etiologies
  Congenital adrenal hyperplasia (CAH)
  Thyroid disorders
  Polycystic ovarian syndrome
  Cushing's syndrome
  Acromegaly

cycles. Pregnancy-related disorders are common causes of abnormal uterine bleeding but are easy to diagnose. Hormone replacement and birth control pill therapy, as well as certain systemic diseases (e.g., disorders of blood coagulation, severe liver disease, and thyroid dysfunction) can also result in AUB.

While the same general approach as outlined in Table 29-14 can be used in any patient regardless of age, stronger emphasis is placed on specific tests as the risk of certain diseases varies in different age groups. The exclusion of a premalignant or malignant endometrial lesion is the major reason to sample the endometrium. In anovulatory cycles, the management of AUB focuses on:

- Controlling an acute bleeding episode
- Ruling out the presence of a malignancy
- Preventing unpredictable bleeding
- Treatment to prevent the occurrence of endometrial hyperplasia

Presentation and Management

In an ovulating woman, normal menstrual periods occur approximately 14 days following ovula-

tion. Women who are ovulating and experiencing regular menstrual periods may have menorrhagia (duration of flow longer than 7 days) or hypermenorrhea (excessive bleeding with normal duration). An estimated blood loss of more than 80 ml during a menstrual period is considered excessive uterine flow. *Metrorrhagia* is variably defined as abnormal bleeding between periods (intermenstrual bleeding) or irregular, usually excessive, bleeding with no definable cycle.

When conditions of pregnancy are excluded, a simplistic separation of the causes of abnormal uterine bleeding are those associated with pelvic pathology and those that are a result of the hormonal effect on the endometrium. There are a small number of patients who have systemic disease, such as a disorder of coagulation or severe liver disease, in whom the uterine bleeding problem is secondary. In these instances, although the bleeding may be a problem, it is usually not the major issue.

Dysfunctional uterine bleeding (DUB) is abnormal endometrial shedding caused by an endocrine dysfunction. Seventy to 80 percent of DUB is associated with anovulation, and this is more likely to be seen when the hypothalamic-pituitary-ovarian axis begins to mature during

TABLE 29-14 Evaluation of Abnormal Uterine Bleeding

Basic Assessment
  Problem-oriented history
  General physical and pelvic exam
  Pap smear
  CBC
  hCG
  Endometrial biopsy (if patient is not pregnant)

As Indicated
  Transvaginal ultrasound with endometrial thickness
    measured
  Prolactin
  TSH, ultrasensitive
  Platelet count, PTT, bleeding time
  AST, ALT
  Hysterogram or hysteroscopy
  D&C, laparoscopy
  Other studies as warranted

adolescence, as well as in women from 40 to 50 years of age. About 20 percent of abnormal uterine bleeding occurs in the peripubertal period, 30 percent during the prime reproductive years, and 50 percent during peri- and post-menopause.

There is a group of conditions associated with ovulatory cycles that are usually not clinically dramatic and are self-limiting. A persistent corpus luteum, a short luteal phase, and an irregular shedding of the endometrium have all been associated with unpredictable endometrial bleeding; uterine lining asynchrony is more likely to require hormone therapy to correct.

A constitutional illness producing DUB is uncommon; a factor VIII deficiency, leukemia, and other problems of coagulation are clinical examples in which interference with blood clotting is manifested by abnormal uterine bleeding.

Most Common Etiologies of Bleeding in the Various Age Groups

Although almost all of the etiologies listed in Tables 29-12 and 29-13 are possible in all age groups, certain problems are more likely to be seen depending on the patient's age. These age-related problems are discussed in the following sections.

Adolescence As the hypothalamic-pituitary-ovarian axis begins to function, it takes an average of approximately 2 years for it to mature completely. During this transition, menstrual cycles are frequently anovulatory. If cycles do not normalize within 5 years of menarche, it is unlikely that they will normalize through the remainder of menstrual life. This lack of normalization occurs in less than 10 percent of women.

The patient's history should include specific items that address the onset of pubertal changes. It is important to determine whether the adolescent has become sexually active. Depending on the history and the severity of bleeding, a recto-abdominal examination or abdominal ultrasound may be all that is necessary for an adolescent who is definitely not sexually active. Pap smears are not usually obtained until sexual activity is initiated, and an endometrial biopsy is almost never necessary. With *severe, acute episodes* of DUB, screening for a clotting disorder and an examination (possibly under anesthesia) to exclude malignancy are warranted. With an acute episode of bleeding in a nonpregnant adolescent, a progestin-dominant birth control pill administered every 8 h will usually control the bleeding over 3 to 4 days; the pill should be continued in the usual dosage for three to six cycles. In milder cases, medroxyprogesterone acetate 5 to 10 mg, calendar days 1 through 13 for 3 to 6 months, should achieve normal bleeding. Because of the self-limiting nature of the problem, it is unusual to require hormonal treatment for a longer period of time. If contraception is needed, birth control pills will serve the dual role of providing contraception and correcting the abnormal bleeding.

Organic causes are unusual in this age group. However, the presence of endometriosis has been documented in teenagers. In this situation pelvic pain, not abnormal bleeding, tends to be the presenting complaint.

Reproductive Age It is not unusual for a normal menstruating female to have one or two anovulatory cycles per year, which may be associated with abnormal bleeding. If cycles are usually regular and pregnancy and other obvious considerations are ruled out, a brief evaluation and pelvic examination will assure both the physician and the patient that nothing serious is wrong and that the problem need only be monitored. It is not necessary to do a full-scale work-up after a single episode for a woman in this age group. However, if the situation becomes repetitive, it must be investigated. There are women who, under normal circumstances, have either very heavy flow during their menses, resulting in anemia, or who have menstrual periods lasting 7 to 8 days, placing them at risk for iron deficiency. It has been well-documented that the use of prostaglandin synthetase inhibitors during the time of menses will reduce the flow; oral iron therapy is also recommended.

Patients in this age group who have a history of menometrorrhagia of more than two cycles duration require a basic assessment as outlined in Table 29-14. If the pelvic examination is limited for any reason, a pelvic ultrasound using an endovaginal probe is the preferred method of accessing pelvic structures. The assessment of the myometrium and endometrial thickness can help to exclude intramural myomas and make the diagnosis of endometrial hyperplasia or cancer less likely if the total endometrial thickness is under 5 mm. As the risk of malignancy is low in women under age 30, selective endometrial biopsy is preferable and depends on the presence of other risk factors. A pregnancy episode should always be considered when abnormal bleeding occurs in this age group, and a quantitative hCG test is mandatory.

Hypothyroidism can be seen in this group, and an ultrasensitive TSH should be performed; coagulation studies are less likely to be productive.

An endometrial sampling can be performed in the office. If desired, a paracervical block with 2 ml of 1% Lidocaine at 12, 4, and 8 o'clock may be used. The Pipelle disposable suction cannula will help determine uterine depth as well as provide an adequate sampling approximately 97 percent of the time. As endometrial polyps or submucous myomas will not be diagnosed with this technique, some patients with chronic or recurring DUB may require a hysterogram or hysteroscopic evaluation of the endometrial cavity to make a precise diagnosis.

In the absence of pelvic pathology, pregnancy, or serious endocrine or systemic problems, the most convenient therapy for the patient is to use the low-dose monophasic birth control pill. The hormones will override the "inappropriate messages" being sent to the endometrium and will induce regular menstrual bleeding. Clearly, for each woman the risks and benefits of the birth control pill should be assessed. However, it should be noted that the birth control pill has many noncontraceptive benefits, including a reduction in the risk of developing ovarian and endometrial cancer and pelvic inflammatory dis-

TABLE 29-15   Noncontraceptive Advantages of Birth Control Pills

Birth Control Pills Reduce Incidence of
Iron deficiency anemia
Ovarian cancer
Endometrial cancer
Irregular bleeding
Pelvic inflammatory disease
Ectopic pregnancy
Premenstrual syndrome
Dysmenorrhea
Breast fibroadenomas

ease (Table 29-15). An alternate hormonal therapy is medroxyprogesterone acetate, 5 to 10 mg, calendar days 1 through 13. This helps prevent endometrial hyperplasia, although the patient must be counseled that some form of contraception is necessary as she can rely neither on her past history of anovulatory cycles nor on the current medication as adequate protection against unwanted pregnancy.

The clinician will readily intuit that organic causes of uterine bleeding are more common in this age group than in the adolescent. The likelihood of serious pathology being present increases as women become older, although this does occur in younger women as well. Adnexal masses, usually ovarian lesions, may require diagnostic surgery, depending on the size and character of the mass. Ovarian unilocular cysts less than 5 cm in diameter are usually functional and usually disappear with observation. An ovarian mass that is multilocular on ultrasound exam or persistent after 8 weeks requires further investigation.

If the work-up makes malignancy quite unlikely, diagnostic laparoscopy with cyst resection answers most questions. As more and more experience is gained with this technique, larger ovarian lesions are managed in this fashion. The only way to properly diagnose and stage endometriosis is with a diagnostic laparoscopy. Because fertility potential may be part of the clinical evaluation, chromotubation at the same time is appropriate.

Adenomyosis usually occurs in parous females in their late 30s and 40s. In addition to abnormal uterine bleeding, the uterus is often slightly enlarged and globular, and it may be tender. Not every woman with adenomyosis is symptomatic; therefore, her clinical presentation should interfere with her lifestyle before surgical intervention is considered. Hormone therapy can be considered on a trial basis but is usually ineffective; the patient's age and her desire to maintain fertility will determine if hysterectomy is the best course.

Endometriosis and ovarian cysts also may result in abnormal vaginal bleeding in women in this age group, and they may require laparoscopy for diagnosis. Following a thorough evaluation, when no serious pathology is present and neoplasia has been ruled out, endometrial ablation as a therapy for dysfunctional uterine bleeding is beginning to emerge as a procedure of choice. As it gains popularity, there have been refinements in the technique beginning with the laser destruction, rollerball ablation, and the recent release of the thermal balloon. Preliminary studies have shown that the latter is clinically efficacious and easier to perform. Using this modality, it is conceivable that the number of hysterectomies performed because of abnormal uterine bleeding will continue to decline.

Perimenopause As ovarian function wanes and the cyclic production of estrogen and progesterone varies, the incidence of abnormal uterine bleeding increases. While the more common problem is ovarian insufficiency, the incidence of organic lesions is also increased. Disorders of coagulation are rare at this time in life, and the possibility of pregnancy is lessened. The algorithm suggested in Table 29-14 provides a satisfactory way to approach these patients and, as a general statement, every woman with AUB should have an evaluation of the endometrial cavity and a pelvic ultrasound. If any endometrial abnormality exists, a diagnostic hysteroscopy should be considered. If an adnexal abnormality is suggested on sonography, laparoscopy should be performed concomitantly.

Because hormone-related problems are the most common problems, some type of management to promote regular uterine bleeding should be considered. Once premalignant and malignant lesions and pregnancy are ruled out, give consideration to using a low-dose birth control pill; not only will this provide appropriate support for the endometrium, vascular system, and bones, but it may help to reduce the risk of ovarian and endometrial cancer. Current practice is that prescribing a birth control pill up until age 50 if there are no contraindications is acceptable; smoking is the most serious contraindication necessitating that birth control pills not be prescribed after the age of 34. Whether or not a woman should be required to forego birth control pills exactly at age 50 if there are no risk factors and she is tolerating the medication satisfactorily is a point of debate, but most doctors recommend that this patient be given hormone replacement therapy rather than the birth control pill. As part of the routine health maintenance there should be periodic monitoring of the serum cholesterol, fasting blood sugar, TSH, and blood pressure. Although continuous estrogen therapy with cyclic progestin therapy is probably the most efficacious for the patient at this time, there will be withdrawal bleeding and the patient needs to be counseled and reassured.

Postmenopause Women with postmenopausal bleeding should be considered to have pelvic cancer unless proven otherwise. Approximately 20 percent of women with postmenopausal bleeding who are not receiving hormone replacement therapy do have a premalignant lesion or cancer. In addition, it is important to remember that serious pelvic disease and hormone replacement therapy can exist concomitantly; therefore, all patients should undergo an evaluation if unpredictable bleeding occurs. The clinician should assume that organic pelvic pathology exists until all possibilities have been excluded. Therefore, the liberal use of endometrial sampling, pelvic ultrasound, hysteroscopy, and even diagnostic laparoscopy should be considered in patients who have unexplained abnormal uterine bleeding in this age group. With women on long-term hormone therapy the assessment of the endometrium with ultrasound becomes even more valuable; incorporating this adjunct can help to reduce the number of times an endometrial sampling is required. However, endometrial measurements should never be used as a substitute for a biopsy. Hormone replacement therapy in this group can be modified to continuous therapy: the most popular regimen is 0.625 mg conjugated or esterified estrogen and 2.5 mg medroxyprogesterone daily. Endometrial thickness will be less with this treatment, and the regular withdrawal bleeding episodes will be avoided in most of the patients after adjusting to the medication, which may take up to 1 year. I perform an endometrial biopsy for an endometrial stripe >4 mm.

References and Selected Readings

1. Bayer SR, DeCherney AH: Clinical manifestations and treatment of dysfunctional uterine bleeding. *JAMA* 269:1823, 1993.
2. Brenner PF: Precocious puberty in the female, in Lobo R, Mishell D, Paulson R, Shoupe D, (eds): *Infertility, Contraception and Reproductive Endocrinology*, 4th ed. Malden, MA; Blackwell Science, 1997, pp 278–300.
3. Breyer P, Haider A, Pescovitz OH: Gonadotropin-releasing hormone agonist in the treatment of girls with central precocious puberty. *Clin Obstet Gynecol* 36:764, 1993.
4. Caufriez A: Menstrual disorders in adolescence: Pathophysiology and treatment. *Horm Res* 36:156, 1991.
5. Classen EA, Cowell CL: Acute adolescent menorrhagia. *Am J Obstet Gynecol* 87:603, 1981.
6. Freeman E, Rickels K, Sandheimer SJ, Polansky M: Ineffectiveness of progesterone suppository treatment for premenstrual syndrome. *JAMA* 264:349, 1990.
7. Frische RE, MacArthur JW: Menstrual cycles: Fatness as a determinant of minimum weight for height necessary for the maintenance or onset. *Science* 185:945, 1974.
8. Ingram JM: The bicycle stool in the treatment of vaginal agenesis: A preliminary report. *Am J Obstet Gynecol* 140:867, 1981.
9. Kauppila A: The changing concepts of medical treatment of endometriosis. *Acta Obstet Gynecol Scand* 72:324, 1993.
10. Mahnmood TA, Templeton A: Prevalence and genesis of endometriosis. *Hum Reprod* 6:544, 1991.
11. Mattox JH: Normal and abnormal uterine bleeding, in Mattox JH (ed): *Core Textbook of Obstetrics and Gynecology*, 10th ed. St. Louis, MO: Mosby-Yearbook, 1998, pp 395–413.
12. Meyer, et al: Thermal balloon and rollerball ablation to treat menorrhagia: A multicenter comparison. *Obstet Gynecol* 92:98, 1998.
13. Mortola JF: Applications of gonadotropin-release hormone analogues in the treatment of premenstrual syndrome. *Clin Obstet Gynecol* 36:753, 1993.
14. Rebar RW, Cedars MI: Hypergonadotropic forms of amenorrhea. *Endocrinol Metab Clin North Am* 21:173, 1992.
15. Reindollar RH, Novak M, Tho SPT, McDonough PG: Adult onset amenorrhea: A study of 262 patients. *Am J Obstet Gynecol* 155:531, 1986.
16. Stenchever, MA: Primary and secondary dysmenorrhea and premenstrual syndrome, in Herbst AL, et al. (eds): *Comprehensive Gynecology*, 3rd ed., St. Louis, MO: Mosby-Yearbook, 1997.
17. Tanner JM: *Growth in Adolescents,* 2d ed. Oxford, England: Blackwell Scientific, 1962.
18. Vale RF: Endometrial ablation for dysfunctional uterine bleeding: Role of GNRH agonists. *Int J Gynaecol Obstet* 41:3, 1993.
19. Wilmore JH: Eating and weight disorders in the female athlete. *Int J Sport Nutr* 1:107, 1991.

CHAPTER 30

Planning for Pregnancy

Donna D. Johnson
Robert Resnik

MATERNAL STATUS
Advanced Maternal Age • Medical Disorders • Reproductive History

GENETICS
Genetic Counseling • Prenatal Diagnostic Tests • Screening Tests

GENERAL HEALTH HABITS
Medications • Nutrition • Sexually Transmitted Diseases • Illicit Drug Use • Smoking • Alcohol • Exercise • Immunizations • Environment

An uncomplicated pregnancy and the birth of a healthy child are the primary goals of every expectant couple. However, many prospective parents do not realize that preparation prior to conception optimizes their chances for a normal pregnancy. Often the only contact the couple has with the medical community is during the woman's annual checkup. If a woman is contemplating a pregnancy, the primary care provider should identify any historical or physical factors that may affect the offspring of the couple. The physician can then encourage the patient to alter any behavior that may affect the pregnancy or the fetus. In addition, a woman with underlying medical problems should maximize her physical well-being prior to conception.

The best method of identifying any risk factors associated with an adverse pregnancy outcome is by performing a thorough history, physical examination, *and general health assessment.* The medical history should include any medical illness, current medication, vaccinations, and dietary habits. The obstetric history should contain details of previous preterm deliveries, pregnancy complications, repetitive first trimester losses, second trimester losses, and intrauterine fetal demises. The gynecologic history should identify any previous abnormal cervical cytology and treatment, and any risk factors for sexually transmitted diseases. In addition to medical problems, the family history should incorporate questions designed to identify any genetic disorder or congenital malformation in either the paternal or maternal family. Also, ethnicity of the potential parents should be noted. The social history should include questions regarding tobacco, alcohol, or illicit drug use. A history of exposure to potentially toxic agents and infectious diseases in the workplace and home should also be obtained.

Maternal Status

Preconception counseling begins with an overall assessment of general health status. As part of this evaluation, attention is directed to a complete review of systems in order to determine the presence of any issues that may influence reproductive outcome. Although it is beyond the scope of this chapter to discuss all of the potential medical problems that may influence pregnancy, a few are mentioned briefly as examples of the type of information women require to make informed choices prior to conception.

Advanced Maternal Age

It is clear that many women, for professional and personal reasons, are delaying their childbearing until later in their reproductive years. Recent studies strongly suggest that healthy, nonsmoking women over the age of 35 years may ultimately anticipate a good pregnancy outcome, assuming the fetus does not have a genetic disorder.[2] However, women need to be aware of the issues that they may confront by delaying their childbearing. First, it is well known that fecundity decreases with advancing maternal age. Further, the risk of chromosomal disorders increases with advancing maternal age. At age 35 the risk of trisomy 21 is approximately 1/260, and at age 40 this risk increases to 1/75. When one considers all chromosomal abnormalities, including trisomy 21, the risk is approximately doubled.[13] Balancing this negative counseling is that other types of congenital malformations, including neural tube defects, do not increase in frequency with advancing maternal age as long as they are not associated with chromosomal defects.

Once beyond the first trimester, and with genetic studies indicating a normal fetus, maternal and neonatal outcomes in this group of women are largely favorable. However, older obstetric patients are more likely to have hypertension, Type II diabetes mellitus, uterine leiomyomata, and increased cesarean section rates.

Medical Disorders

Diabetes mellitus Probably more than any other disorder, the experience of women with diabetes mellitus illustrates the benefits of preconceptional counseling. Meticulous metabolic control during pregnancy, combined with tests of fetal well-being and fetal lung maturity, drastically reduced perinatal mortality among infants of diabetic women from 1970 to the present. However, the high frequency of congenital malformations among infants of diabetic women remained an uncontrolled problem until it was demonstrated that good metabolic control and normalization of blood glucose prior to pregnancy and during the critical periods of embryogenesis could reduce the risk to the level of that found in the general population.[6] This crucial observation serves to emphasize the singular importance of preconceptional counseling.

Congenital heart disease Another example of the role of preconceptional counseling is found in women who have cardiac disorders in which pregnancy carries a significant risk of maternal mortality. For example, women with pulmonary hypertension alone, or Eisenmenger's syndrome of pulmonary hypertension and an uncorrected right-to-left shunt, are subject to a maternal mortality risk of 30 to 50 percent. Those with Marfan's syndrome should undergo echocardiographic examination prior to pregnancy inasmuch as their risk of aortic dissection is much higher if the diameter of the aortic root exceeds 40 mm. Women with artificial heart valves should understand the risk of the various types of anticoagulation prior to conception. Women with mechanical valves require anticoagulation to prevent valve clotting and strokes. Those with biological valves do not require anticoagulants, but the valve has a limited life span of about 10 years. This information is useful to the woman with heart disease who is considering pregancy.

Chronic renal disease It has long been known that women with chronic, underlying renal disease have an increased risk of delivering preterm, frequently growth-restricted infants, and of developing superimposed preeclampsia. Women with chronic renal disease anticipating a pregnancy should have their renal function thoroughly evaluated prior to conception inasmuch as various derangements of renal function are correlated with increasingly poor fetal outcome. For example, among patients without hypertension and a serum creatinine of 1.4 mg/dl or less, pregnancy outcome is quite favorable and further deterioration of renal function is unusual. However, in the presence of hypertension or a serum creatinine of 1.5 mg/dl or higher, the prognosis for a healthy pregnancy outcome is more guarded. There is a small risk of deterioration of renal function as well as a significant perinatal morbidity, largely due to preterm delivery. Clearly, women who have undergone renal transplantation also need to be counseled regarding the effects of various immunosuppressive drugs on fetal outcome. They also need to understand the criteria most commonly associated with a favorable pregnancy result.

These are but three examples of the importance of providing women with adequate and precise information prior to conceiving, rather than placing them in the position of having to make difficult choices after they have become pregnant.

Similar counseling is required for virtually all medical disorders inasmuch as the disease entities themselves or the medication utilized to treat the disorder may have a significant impact on the patient or her fetus.

Reproductive History

The nonpregnant state provides the physician an excellent opportunity to evaluate causes of previous poor pregnancy outcomes. First, the cause for recurrent first trimester losses may be evaluated after two or three spontaneous abortions, depending on maternal age and degree of anxiety. Cytogenetic studies of couples with a history of repetitive spontaneous abortions reveal that there is approximately a 5 percent risk of karyotypic abnormalities. Although this problem is not correctable, genetic screening tests in successive pregnancies may be offered. Next, müllerian anomalies, as well as submucosal fibroids, have been implicated as a cause of recurrent spontaneous abortions, and they can best be detected by a hysterosalpingogram or hysteroscopy. Advanced techniques in operative hysteroscopy may provide patients with the opportunity to have some of these malformations readily corrected. In addition, luteal phase defects can be excluded with serum progesterone levels or an endometrial biopsy. Finally, several autoimmune factors, such as lupus anticoagulant and anticardiolipin antibody, have been implicated as a cause of repetitive spontaneous abortions. Although treatment remains controversial, physicians can be alerted to the potential problems

associated with these antibodies, such as preeclampsia, stillbirth, and intrauterine growth restriction.

Although second trimester losses may be due to a structurally or karyotypically abnormal fetus, most are associated with maternal causes such as preterm labor, an incompetent cervix, a placental abnormality, uterine anomalies, drug abuse, or infection. Physicians should obtain an accurate history as well as review previous medical records to clarify etiology. Clarification of the diagnosis of an incompetent cervix versus preterm labor is important. Although the classic history of an incompetent cervix (painless dilatation and delivery) is rarely obtained, other historical facts, such as DES exposure, previous obstetric laceration, or cone biopsy may make a diagnosis of cervical incompetence more likely. Efforts to define cervical incompetence clinically with hysterosalpingograms, Hegar's dilators, and Foley catheters have been proposed but are not widely accepted. Ultrasonographic evaluation of the cervix and lower uterine segment during pregnancy may provide additional information. Anticipating the problem of an incompetent cervix can result in timely diagnosis and intervention, and lead to a successful pregnancy outcome.

Some third trimester complications in a previous pregnancy may warrant further workup when a patient is planning another pregnancy. For example, a woman who had early onset severe preeclampsia may have persistent hypertension or renal disease. A woman who had a previous pregnacy complicated by insulin-requiring gestational diabetes may now have overt diabetes. Each evaluation must be individualized and based on the patient's prior history.

Genetics

Genetic Counseling

The most valuable tool for identifying couples at risk for transmitting an inherited disorder to their fetus is a thorough history. To simplify the recorded history, physicians may construct a pedigree that includes first-degree relatives (parents, siblings, and offspring), second-degree relatives (grandparents, uncles, aunts, nephews, and nieces), and third-degree relatives (first cousins). Questions should identify family members with congenital anomalies; mental retardation; learning disabilities; blindness; deafness; chronic medical illnesses such as anemia and skin disorders; and genetic disorders such as cystic fibrosis, myotonic dystrophy, and Huntington's chorea. A careful review of the reproductive history, as well as possible drug or toxin exposure, is important.

A more extensive discussion of genetic counseling and testing is found in Chap. 32.

Because some gene mutations are concentrated in specific ethnic populations, ethnic origin should be documented. Ashkenazi Jews and French Canadians are frequently carriers of Tay-Sachs disease. The carrier frequency is 1/27 and 1/30 to 1/50 for the respective populations. Like many other enzyme deficiencies, the carrier status of the parents can be determined by DNA mutation analysis or enzyme activity levels.

Similarly, hemoglobinopathies are more frequent in specific groups. Approximately 1 in 10 African-Americans is positive for sickle cell trait. α-Thalassemia is most frequently encountered in Southeastern Asians. β-Thalassemia is encountered in many ethnic groups; however, Italians and Greeks have the highest carrier frequency. Prenatal diagnostic techniques are now available, and screening tests, such as red cell indices and hemoglobin electrophoresis, should be offered preconceptionally.[13]

Nowhere in medicine has the impact of molecular genetics been more evident than cystic fibrosis screening. Currently, over 70 cystic fibrosis mutations can be identified. Our ability to determine carrier status for an individual depends on the carrier frequency of specific mutations in their ethnic group. In Caucasians, the sensitivity is 80 percent. Screening for the cystic fibrosis carrier status is recommended for individuals with a positive family history and for the partner of an individual with cystic fibrosis. There is some

controversy regarding which couples currently planning pregnancy should be screened.

Parental ages should be documented. In addition to decreased fertility and an increased rate of spontaneous abortions and underlying medical illness, a woman of advanced maternal age is at risk for problems related to autosomal trisomies and sex chromosome aberrations. Although many women are aware of their increased risk for a child with Down syndrome, they do not realize what their risk is for problems related to other chromosomal abnormalities secondary to nondisjunction. Any woman who will be 35 years or older at the time of delivery should be offered genetic counseling and prenatal diagnosis. With the exception of aneuploidy, paternal age over 55 years is not associated with any chromosomal abnormality. However, fathers in their fifth decade of life are at increased risk of offspring with new autosomal dominant mutations such as Marfan's syndrome and neurofibromatosis. Because these mutations are random, diagnostic tests for specific autosomal dominant mutations are not warranted.

Couples who are first cousins have one-eighth of their genes in common. Consequently, they are at higher risk for having a child who is homozygous for a deleterious autosomal recessive gene. Although prenatal diagnosis is not beneficial for these couples, counseling should be provided. Genetic counseling may be very emotional and often difficult for patients to comprehend. Counselors should use simple terms, visual aids, and written information to reinforce concepts. Most importantly, the information should be relayed in an objective manner.[13]

Prenatal Diagnostic Tests

Amniocentesis performed at 15 to 18 weeks of gestation is the most commonly used prenatal genetic diagnostic test. The advantage of this procedure is its safety. Although the exact fetal loss rate is debated, the overall risk of abortion appears to be less than 1 percent. The disadvantage of this test is that a woman is often into the mid-second trimester before the results are available. If a couple chooses to terminate their pregnancy based on the information obtained, the procedure may be technically difficult or physically uncomfortable for the patient.

As an alternative to a traditional amniocentesis, an early amniocentesis may be performed at 11 to 14 weeks gestation. An early amniocentesis is performed in the same manner as a traditional amniocentesis except that a smaller aliquot of amniotic fluid (1 ml/week of gestation) is removed. Because the chorion and amnion often do not fuse until after the 14th week of gestation, the procedure is technically more difficult and is associated with a greater percentage of unsuccessful procedures. The associated fetal loss rate appears to be greater than with a traditional amniocentesis.

Another method, chorionic villus sampling (CVS), may be performed in the first trimester. Placental chorionic villi tissue is obtained either transabdominally or transvaginally with ultrasound guidance. Although the results are available earlier, this procedure is associated with a one- to threefold higher fetal loss rate than is traditional amniocentesis. Several studies have raised the possibility of limb reduction defects in the offspring after CVS. The overall risk appears to be 1/1000 to 1/3000 for CVS procedures. The risk and severity of limb reduction is associated with the timing of the CVS, with the lower risk being after nine completed weeks of gestation. The information obtained from CVS and amniocentesis is the same except that amniotic α-fetoprotein analysis cannot be performed on CVS samples.[5]

Percutaneous umbilical blood sampling provides the quickest results. Chromosomal studies are available within 72 h. However, this technique is difficult prior to 20 weeks of gestation. The fetal loss rate is dependent on the experience of the physician and the indication for the procedure.

Screening Tests

Trisomy 21 (Down syndrome) occurs in approximately 1 of 800 live births. Although the risk of giving birth to a child with trisomy 21 increases with maternal age greater than 35 years, most affected infants are born to women who are younger. Low maternal serum α-fetoprotein (MSAFP) can detect approximately 20 percent of fetuses with trisomy 21. High maternal serum human chorionic gonadotropin and low conjugated estriol have also been associated with trisomy 21. Studies suggest that a combination of age and these three maternal serum biochemical markers may detect 60 to 70 percent of affected pregnancies without greatly increasing the number of invasive tests. Routine screening for trisomy 21 in all pregnancies is now available.[11]

General Health Habits

Medications

Many prescribed and over-the-counter drugs are known to be teratogenic. Medications known to be potentially teratogenic include angiotensin converting enzyme (ACE) inhibitors, antiepileptics, antimetabolites, coumadin, isotretinoin, and lithium. When taking any medication, a woman contemplating a pregnancy and her physician should assess the potential risk to a fetus and the importance of the medications to the patient's well-being. If the medication is needed for only a short duration, such as isotretinoin, the patient may delay childbearing until after the treatment is completed. Although medical illnesses, such as epilepsy, may require a woman to take teratogenic drugs throughout her lifetime, these patients should be informed of such risks prior to conception. In other medical conditions, patients may be able to change from medications associated with malformations to safer alternatives. For example, a patient with chronic hypertension may be changed from an ACE inhibitor to another effective antihypertensive medication. Medications, such as large doses of vitamin A, which are not essential to maternal well-being should be discontinued. Prior to taking any medication a woman should consult her physician regarding the potential effects on a fetus. Prior to advising the patient, the physician should be aware of the teratogenic potential of the medication. Although the drugs mentioned above are not all-inclusive, they are pharmacologic agents that have received extensive study.[3]

Nutrition

Inadequate nutrition is often a confounding variable in adverse pregnancy outcomes. Yet, scientific data in humans are frequently lacking regarding the role that specific nutrients play in normal pregnancy. In addition to encouraging all women to eat a well-balanced diet prior to pregnancy, the physician should also make some specific dietary recommendations. Recent studies have indicated that dietary supplementation with 0.4 mg of folic acid reduces the incidence of neural tube defects (NTD) by 50 percent. If a patient has had an infant with a NTD, she should take 4 mg of folic acid each day. Folic acid supplementation should be instituted several months prior to conception and continued through the first trimester.[4]

The physician can calculate a woman's body mass index (BMI) by dividing her weight in kilograms by the square of her height in meters.[2] Women with a BMI less than 19.8 kg/m^2 are underweight. Women with a low pregnancy weight are at significant risk for having low birthweight infants and should have extensive nutritional counseling to ensure an adequate caloric intake. On the other hand, women with a BMI greater than 29 kg/m^2 are considered obese. Maternal obesity is associated with an increased incidence of diabetes, hypertension, and fetal macrosomia. Encourage patients to modify their weight appropriately prior to conception to optimize their pregnancy outcome.[9]

Sexually Transmitted Diseases

In the past several decades, there has been a striking increase in the occurrence of sexually transmitted diseases in the United States. A resurgence of old infections, such as *Neisseria*

gonorrhoeae, has been noted, in addition to the recognition of new diseases, such as acquired immunodeficiency syndrome (AIDS). Patients who are at high risk for sexually transmitted diseases should be screened prior to pregnancy. Chlamydial and gonococcal infections often coexist in the same patient, and both are associated with similar perinatal complications. Although still requiring extensive investigation, other sexually transmitted diseases have also been associated with prematurity. Bacterial vaginosis and *Trichomonas vaginalis* have received more attention in recent years.

Syphilis can be directly detrimental to the fetus. High-risk patients should be screened with a nonspecific serological test such as the rapid plasma reagin (RPR) prior to pregnancy. Positive results should be confirmed by specific antitreponemal tests [fluorescent treponemal antibody absorption (FTA-ABS) test], and patients who require treatment should receive immediate therapy.

No treatment can eradicate herpes simplex virus, human papilloma virus, or HIV, and these sexually transmitted diseases may adversely affect pregnancy outcomes. The patient should be cautioned about the effects of perinatal transmission. As AIDS becomes an increasing health concern, women at risk for HIV infection deserve special consideration. Prior to conception all women should be offered HIV screening tests. The vertical transmission of HIV has been reduced dramatically by administering AZT during pregnancy, and HIV-positive patients should be counseled accordingly. In addition, further significant progress is being made in the ability to reduce vertical transmission of HIV.

Illicit Drug Use

As many as 10 to 15 percent of pregnant women may use illicit drugs. Because women often do not volunteer information regarding substance abuse, the physician should ask directed questions about the type, frequency, and quantity of substances abused. Questions should not be posed in a judgmental or confrontational manner. If a patient admits to using illicit drugs, random urine toxicology screens with the patient's permission may be useful in assessing the type and frequency of use. Drug users rarely abuse a single substance. Once a problem with drug addiction is identified, the physician should explore other aspects of the patient's health associated with substance abuse. In addition, the safety of the social environment to which a newborn child will be taken should be evaluated. Ideally, substance abuse should be identified prior to pregnancy, and women should be referred to a drug rehabilitation program before conception. Continued substance abuse during pregnancy has been associated with placental abruption, growth retardation, congenital anomalies, central nervous system damage, and drug withdrawal in the neonate. The physician should be familiar with the potential pregnancy complications and adverse fetal effects of each drug.[1]

Smoking

In addition to affecting general health and reproductive capabilities, cigarette smoking adversely affects pregnancy. In pregnancy, an increased incidence of placenta previa, abruptio placenta, premature rupture of the membranes, and low birthweight infants are associated with tobacco use. Although over 2500 chemicals are present in tobacco smoke, carbon monoxide and nicotine appear to be the major components that cause health problems. Smoking cessation programs that use adjunctive therapy with transdermal nicotine patches have reported success rates of 50 percent. Although the use of transdermal nicotine patches is controversial in pregnancy, replacing cigarette usage with the patch reduces fetal exposure to carbon monoxide and other toxins. The physician and the patient must weigh the potential harm of the transdermal patches to the fetus against the risk of continued cigarette use during pregnancy. If a patient cannot stop smoking prior to pregnancy, she should be encouraged to decrease the amount she smokes to less than 10 cigarettes per day.[8]

Alcohol

Because alcohol consumption is popular and legal in our society, many women do not realize the substantial risk that alcohol consumption may confer to the fetus. Fetal alcohol syndrome (FAS) may result from heavy drinking during pregnancy; it consists of growth deficiency, developmental delay, and structural abnormalities. Although children born to mothers who consume even moderate amounts of alcohol during their pregnancy may not have the complete syndrome, many may exhibit some features. Excluding genetic causes, alcohol consumption during pregnancy is the major identifiable cause of mental retardation in the United States. Because the amount of alcohol consumption that is safe in pregnancy has not been established, encourage women who are contemplating pregnancy to abstain from alcohol.[1]

Exercise

As general awareness of the cardiovascular benefits of exercise increases, more women will engage in fitness programs. In addition, exercise can assist women in controlling weight as well as improving flexibility and coordination. Although extremely vigorous exercise programs may cause menstrual irregularities, women who are attempting to become pregnant can engage in moderate activity without increasing the likelihood of menstrual disorders. After conception, the patient may need to modify her exercise program. Exercises performed in the supine position and deep flexion or extension should be avoided. Because of the possible association of neural tube defects and hyperthermia, core body temperature should not exceed 38°C. Basic principles of fitness programs, such as avoiding unlevel surfaces and avoiding dehydration, should also be followed. In general, the physician and patient can compose an individual exercise program based on a clinical understanding of the physiological adaptations in pregnancy and common sense.[14]

Immunizations

All women of reproductive age should be immune to measles, mumps, rubella, tetanus, diphtheria, and poliomyelitis by virtue of natural infection or vaccination. However, in recent years, an increasing number of postpubertal females in the United States are seronegative for rubella. Because rubella infection during pregnancy may be devastating to the fetus, the rubella status of women should be documented prior to pregnancy. Susceptible women should be immunized. The patient should avoid pregnancy for a minimum of 3 months after her inoculation. In general, live-attenuated viral vaccines of any type should be avoided during pregnancy and immediately prior to conception.

Hepatitis B infection during pregnancy can also be detrimental to the mother as well as the fetus. Women who are at high risk for hepatitis B should be immunized. High-risk groups include intravenous drug users, health care workers who may be exposed to body fluids, household contacts of chronic hepatitis B carriers, and recipients of clotting factors. Although this immunization is considered safe during pregnancy, ideally, patients should be immune prior to pregnancy. In general, vaccines derived from toxoids or inactivated organisms may be used in pregnancy if needed.

In 1995, a live-attenuated varicella (chicken pox) immunization became available for use in the United States. More than 95 percent of Americans are immune. However, varicella may be associated with serious complications in the adult, and may lead to congenital malformations if it occurs during pregnancy. If a patient is contemplating pregnancy and has no history of varicella infection, consider obtaining a varicella IgG titer. If the patient is nonimmune, the vaccine may be administered in two doses 4 to 8 weeks apart. After immunization, pregnancy should be avoided for 3 months.[15]

Environment

As more women are employed outside of the home, physicians providing conception counseling should be aware of the potential exposure to teratogens and infectious agents in the workplace. Doctors should ask the patient about her occupation, hobbies, and environment. Although most occupations do not pose a risk to the pregnant woman or to the fetus, some hazards do exist. For example, gardeners and veterinarians who come in contact with cat feces are at higher risk for toxoplasmosis infections. Child care providers and elementary school teachers are at greater risk for cytomegalovirus and parvovirus exposure. If a patient is at higher risk for an infectious disease that may affect her pregnancy outcome, her immunity status may be determined prior to conception. Practical advice may be given to a nonimmune female to decrease her susceptibility, and she should be told to report any exposure or symptoms immediately. Women employed in the biomedical industry are often exposed to radiation, organic solvents, and heavy metals.

The intent of this discussion is to increase physician awareness of risks, not to outline every possible risk. Ideally, all hazardous materials should be avoided in pregnancy. However, we do not live in a risk-free environment. Consequently, efforts should be made to minimize exposure to agents that may contribute to adverse pregnancy outcomes. In addition to the references provided, other information resources include teratogen registries, occupational health experts, and several government agencies.

References and Selected Readings

1. Andres RL, Jones KL: Social and illicit drug use during pregnancy, in Creasy RK, Resnik R (eds): *Maternal Fetal Medicine,* 3d ed. Philadelphia: WB Saunders, 1994.

2. Berkowitz GS, Skovron ML, Lapinski RH, et al: Delayed childbearing and the outcome of pregnancy. *N Engl J Med* 59–664, 1990.

3. Briggs GC, Freeman RK, Yaffe SJ: *Drugs in Pregnancy and Lactation: A Reference Guide to the Fetal and Neonatal Risks.* Baltimore: Williams and Wilkins, 1998.

4. Centers for Disease Control: Recommendations for use of folic acid to reduce number of spina bifida cases and other neural tube defects. *JAMA* 259:1233, 1993.

5. Centers for Disease Control: Chorionic villus sampling and amniocentesis: Recommendations for prenatal counseling. *MMWR* 44(RR-9):1, 1995.

6. Fuhrmann K, Reiher H, Semmler K, et al: Prevention of congenital malformations in infants of insulin-dependent diabetic mothers. *Diabetes Care* 6:219, 1983.

7. Genetic testing for cystic fibrosis. *NIH Consens Statement* 15(4):1, 1997.

8. Lando HA, Gritz ER: Smoking cessation techniques. *J Am Med Womens Assoc* 52:31, 1996.

9. King JC, Weininger J: Nutrition during pregnancy. *Semin Perinatol* 13:162, 1989.

10. Klirsfeld D: HIV disease and women. *Med Clin North Am* 82(2):335, 1998.

11. MacDonald ML, Wagner RM, Slotnick RN: Sensitivity and specificity of screening for Down syndrome with alpha-fetoprotein, hCG, unconjugated estriol; and maternal age. *Obstet Gynecol* 77:63, 1991.

12. Rayburn WF: Treatment of sexually transmitted diseases: 1998 recommendations by the Center for Disease Control and Prevention. *J Repro Med* 43(6): 471, 1998.

13. Scioscia AL, Resnik R: Preconception counseling. *Curr Probl Obstet Gynecol Fertil* 14:42, 1991.

14. Sternfield B: Physical activity and pregnancy outcome. *Sports Med* 1:33, 1997.

15. Venture A: Varicella vaccination guidelines for adolescents and adults. *Am Fam Physician* 55(4):1220, 1997.

CHAPTER 31

Diagnosis of Pregnancy

Claudia L. Werner
Susan M. Cox

PREGNANCY TESTS
CLINICAL APPLICATIONS

Every encounter with a female patient of reproductive age should promptly bring to mind the question, "Could she be pregnant?" A pregnancy test should always be considered before ordering diagnostic tests that use radiolabeled compounds or ionizing radiation, and before initiating therapies that have the potential to harm the unborn child. Despite the low or even debatable risks of many procedures and therapeutic interventions to early pregnancy, medicolegal considerations make the liberal use of pregnancy testing a wise consideration. Furthermore, early pregnancy diagnosis allows the timely initiation of prenatal care, which will have a favorable impact on the outcome for both mother and child.

The diagnosis of pregnancy is usually based on a delay or cessation of menses and the presence of a positive pregnancy test. Unfortunately, many women do not keep careful track of their menstrual periods and may be unaware that they have missed one or more periods. Also, spotting in early pregnancy may be misinterpreted as a period. Therefore, it is incumbent on the physician caring for a reproductive-age woman to elicit the most accurate information possible about the date of the last normal menstrual period, any missed periods or abnormal bleeding, sexual activity, and contraceptive method. The physician should then obtain a pregnancy test if indicated by the history or physical examination.

This chapter reviews the symptoms and signs of pregnancy and the available diagnostic tests. Common symptoms of pregnancy include "morning sickness," frequent urination, fatigue, and the perception of fetal movement. These are symptoms, as opposed to clinical signs. The signs of pregnancy (Table 31-1) are categorized as "presumptive," "probable" or "positive."

In women with regular, predictable, cyclic menstruation, the abrupt cessation of menses is highly suggestive of pregnancy. This is especially true if there is associated fatigue, morning sickness, and/or breast tenderness. The physical exam may reveal softening and enlargement of the pregnant uterus, bluish discoloration of the vagina and cervix (Chadwick's sign), and softening of the cervix and lower uterine segment (Hegar's sign).

The probable signs of pregnancy include an enlarged abdomen and uterus, palpable Braxton-Hicks contractions, ballottement of the fetus, and a positive pregnancy test. None of these is a positive (as opposed to probable) sign of pregnancy because all can be mimicked by a variety of other conditions; for example, the uterus may be enlarged by leiomyomata and the pregnancy test may be positive secondary to various ovarian tumors (i.e., embryonal carcinoma, choriocarcinoma, and immature teratoma).

The positive, or definitive, signs of pregnancy include identification of fetal heart tones, examiner-detected fetal movements, and recognition of the fetus via ultrasound or incidental x-ray. Fetal heart motion is audible by Doppler at 10

TABLE 31-1 Signs of Pregnancy

Presumptive
  Cessation of menses
  Skin changes
  Chadwick's sign
  Breast changes

Probable
  Enlarged abdomen
  Fetal outline on physical examination
  Positive pregnancy test
  Anatomic changes in cervix
  Ballottement
  Braxton-Hicks contractions
  Changes in uterine shape/size

Positive
  Identifiable fetal heart tones
  Examiner-detected fetal movement
  X-ray or ultrasound detecting fetus

to 12 weeks gestation and by auscultation with a fetoscope at 18 to 20 weeks. Generally, fetal movements can be palpated by 20 weeks gestation. A gestational sac can be visualized by 6 weeks and fetal cardiac activity by 8 weeks using ultrasound techniques. (Gestational age is generally measured in weeks from the first day of the last normal menstrual period.)

Pregnancy Tests

The basis for all current pregnancy tests is the presence of human chorionic gonadotropin (hCG), which can be detected in maternal serum 8 to 11 days after fertilization and in the maternal urine soon thereafter. Levels of hCG peak approximately 65 days after conception, and fall gradually in the second and third trimesters. A variety of techniques are available for the detection of this glycoprotein hormone, including agglutination inhibition tests, radioimmunoassays, and ELISA (enzyme-linked immunosorbent assays). All use mono- or polyclonal antibodies directed against hCG in urine or serum samples.

Agglutination inhibition, utilized by the older and less-sensitive urine slide tests, makes use of anti-hCG, which is added to the urine sample.

This is followed by the addition of erythrocytes or latex particles coated with hCG. In the presence of pregnancy, no agglutination occurs because all the antibody has been complexed with the hCG in the patient's urine, and is unavailable. Agglutination, which is seen as clumping of particles within the sample, occurs if hCG is absent (i.e., the patient is not pregnant). Sensitivity varies from 250 to 3000 mIU/ml of hCG. Therefore, most tests are positive one week after a missed menses.

ELISA tests determine the quantity of hCG present by binding the sample hCG to monoclonal antibodies attached to a solid phase. A second enzyme-linked antibody is used to "sandwich" the hCG. A dye color change occurs when substrate for the enzyme is added to samples that contain hCG. Based on the amount of dye released, hCG can be quantitated. This technique is sensitive to levels of hCG in the 10 to 25 mIU/ml range, and is usually performed in less than 1 hr.

Radioimmunoassays are the most commonly used tests to accurately quantitate serum levels of hCG. By targeting the β subunit of the hCG glycoprotein, cross-reactivity with LH (luteinizing hormone) is avoided, allowing very sensitive and specific measurements. The assay is based upon the competitive displacement of a radiolabeled ligand, $[^{125}I]hCG$, from antibody directed against the beta subunit of hCG. The amount of unbound ligand is proportional to the amount of hCG present in the patient's serum. Unbound radioactivity is quantified and standard curves are used to calculate results. Serum levels as low as 2 to 4 mIU/ml can be detected. Serum β-hCG can therefore be positive several days before menstruation is delayed. This assay is commonly used to rule out early pregnancy prior to invasive or radiographic procedures. However, highly sensitive urine pregnancy tests can now rule out early pregnancy reliably. The use of radioimmunoassay is probably not necessary or cost-effective for most routine pregnancy testing. It can be reserved for special circumstances where hCG quantification is useful. Such situations include evaluation for early pregnancy complications (discussed in greater detail below); monitoring of medical therapy for ectopic pregnancy; and monitoring treatment for gestational trophoblastic neoplasia.

The urine and serum pregnancy test kits presently in widespread clinical use combine immunochromatography with the principles basic to ELISA tests. These test kits consist of convenient plastic test devices across which urine or serum samples are allowed to diffuse. Antibody reaction with hCG results in a color change and/or appearance of a symbol in the "window." Results usually are available in 3 to 5 min. These kits can detect levels of hCG in serum or urine as low as 25 mIU/ml. They can become positive any time from one week postconception (synchronous with the earliest secretion of hCG by the blastocyst) to the time of expected menses. This level of detection represents optimal sensitivity because detection of hCG levels under 25 mIU/ml leads to false-positive test results.

Numerous home urine pregnancy test kits are available and are popular and widely used. Older versions utilize hemagglutination inhibition, while newer ones utilize immunochromatography as described above. There have been reports of false-positive and, much more commonly, false-negative home test results. The causes of these include older, less sensitive technology, failure to follow package directions correctly, or misinterpretation of results. Therefore, it is prudent for the clinician to confirm reported home test results. Additionally, clinicians should make patients aware that home pregnancy tests detect hCG but do not guarantee that a normal gestation is present or that it is intrauterine. A careful history and physical examination are always indicated as soon as possible after a positive pregnancy test.

Clinical Applications

ELISA-based urine pregnancy testing is sensitive enough to detect nearly all early gestations in-

cluding abnormal ones.[7] Serum pregnancy testing becomes positive no earlier than one week postconception, offering only a narrow, if any, temporal advantage over urine tests. Concerns that the physiologic variation in urine concentration seen throughout the day affects the sensitivity of urine pregnancy tests in detecting early or abnormal gestations are not supported by clinical studies.[4] In fact, urine and serum hCG levels are similar, and nearly equivalent for the purpose of pregnancy testing.[2] Incorrect dating of the menstrual period is a more common and likely cause of a false-negative test result in early pregnancy, and a repeat urine pregnancy test one to two weeks later should settle the question. The routine testing of serum hCG to confirm a negative, sensitive urine test is usually unnecessary.

If an abnormal early gestation is suspected by history and/or clinical presentation, and a positive urine pregnancy test is obtained, a quantitative serum hCG is useful. The serum hCG level at which an intrauterine pregnancy is visible by sonography (the so-called "discriminatory zone") is 6000 to 6500 mIU/ml for transabdominal and 1000 to 2000 mIU/ml for transvaginal sonography. These discriminatory zone values vary somewhat between centers due to variations in equipment and experience. If the hCG level is higher than the discriminatory zone, the lack of a gestational sac in the uterus by sonography should prompt evaluation for an abnormal (i.e., nonviable intrauterine or ectopic) gestation. In a clinically stable patient with a serum hCG level below the discriminatory zone for sonography, a second quantitative serum hCG may be obtained 48 h later. In normal early gestations, the serum hCG level doubles, on average, every 48 h until a level of 10,000 mIU/ml is reached.[6] Abnormal intrauterine and ectopic gestations generally show a longer doubling time, with the majority rising less than 66 percent in the 48 h.[5] An abnormally slow rise in the serum hCG level warrants further evaluation, often by dilatation and curettage and/or laparoscopy, to rule out an ectopic gestation. Clinicians should remember that 15 percent of normal intrauterine gestations demonstrate a slower than expected rise in hCG. Additionally, interassay variation in results can be in the 10 to 15 percent range and may also affect results. Therefore, the uterus should not be instrumented solely on the basis of an inadequate rise in serial serum hCG measurements if the pregnancy is wanted. Conversely, abnormal gestations can demonstrate normally rising serum hCG levels, so a normal doubling time does not completely rule out an ectopic or abnormal intrauterine gestation. As always in medical practice, clinical judgment in assessing the history, physical exam, data, and imaging are critical to optimal decision making and management.

Another clinical option to screen for abnormal gestations is the measurement of a single serum progesterone.[8,9] A serum progesterone level less than 5 ng/ml is indicative of a nonviable gestation (intrauterine or ectopic); a progesterone level greater than 25 ng/ml indicates a normal pregnancy.[9] Between these two values is a large indeterminate range. However, a progesterone level less than 5 ng/ml at presentation essentially rules out the presence of a viable pregnancy, and may obviate the need for serum hCG quantification and/or sonography.

Summary

The diagnosis of pregnancy is generally based upon the patient's history, physical exam, and pregnancy test detecting serum or urine hCG. Sensitive urine pregnancy tests in common clinical use are adequate in nearly all clinical situations to rule pregnancy in or out. In addition, quantitative serum hCG levels, serum progesterone levels, and sonography can be used adjunctively to help distinguish between normal and abnormal early gestations. The possibility of pregnancy should be considered whenever the health care provider cares for a woman of reproductive age. By always considering the possibility of pregnancy, clinicians avoid unintentional exposure of the fetus to potentially harmful agents and procedures. Additionally, a diagnosis of pregnancy allows the initiation of prenatal care, and the timing and modification of necessary therapeutic interventions in ways that maximize benefits and minimize risks to the patient and to her unborn child.

References and Selected Readings

1. Buster JE, Carson SA: Endocrinology and diagnosis of pregnancy, in Gabbe SG, Niebyl JR, Simpson JL (eds). *Obstetrics: Normal and Problem Pregnancies,* 3d ed. New York: Churchill Livingstone, 1996, pp 31–64.
2. Chard T: Pregnancy tests: A review. *Hum Reprod* 7:701, 1992.
3. Cunningham FG, MacDonald PC, Leveno KJ, et al: Pregnancy: Overview, organization, and diagnosis, in (eds). *Williams Obstetrics,* 20th ed. Stamford, CT: Appleton & Lange, 1997, pp 22–35.
4. Ikomi A, Matthews M, Kuan AM, Henson G: The effect of physiological urine dilution on pregnancy test results in complicated early pregnancies. *Br J Obstet Gynaecol* 105:462, 1998.
5. Kadar N, Caldwell BV, Romero R: A method of screening for ectopic pregnancy and its indications. *Obstet Gynecol* 58:162, 1981.
6. Kadar N, Freedman M, Zacher M: Further observations on the doubling time of human chorionic gonadotropin in early asymptomatic pregnancies. *Fertil Steril* 54:783, 1990.
7. Kingdom JCP, Kelly T, MacLean AB, McAllister EJ: Rapid one step urine test for human chorionic gonadotrophin in evaluating suspected complications of early pregnancy. *BMJ* 302:1308, 1991.
8. Matthews CP, Coulson PB, Wild RA: Serum progesterone levels as an aid in the diagnosis of ectopic pregnancy. *Obstet Gynecol* 68:390, 1986.
9. Stovall TG, Ling FW, Carson SA, Buster JE: Serum progesterone and uterine curettage in the differential diagnosis of ectopic pregnancy. *Fertil Steril* 57:456, 1992.

Genetic Testing

Lee P. Shulman
Sherman Elias

chapter reviews genetic information and technology as applied to the care of obstetrical and gynecologic patients This is a rapidly changing field, and the health care team needs to watch for new recommendations as they evolve.

Genetic Counseling

Genetic counseling plays a central role in genetic testing. Whenever genetic testing is being considered, both physician and patient have a shared responsibility. The physician must effectively communicate and promote a patient-physician relationship characterized by trust and honesty. The patient must provide complete and accurate information concerning her health and that of her family. Decisions should be based on information provided and the personal beliefs of the patient, not those of the counselor. Testing should be performed for the benefit of the patient, and the results communicated within a framework that guarantees the woman's confidentiality in all but exceptional situations. Accordingly, genetic counseling facilitates the genetic testing process and serves to improve the overall quality of medical care.[2]

Physicians who care for women must be increasingly aware of the benefits and responsibilities of genetic counseling in modern obstetrical care. Twenty years ago, Hsia and Hirschhorn defined genetic counseling as ". . . the process whereby an individual or family obtains information about a real or possible genetic problem."[23] To provide accurate and empathetic genetic counseling, it is essential to understand

Advances in the elucidation of the structure and actions of DNA have permitted intensive study of human genes. Indeed, the last decade has witnessed the delineation of novel modes of genetic transmission that were only discovered as a result of the intensive study of the molecular structure of certain genes. With this expanding knowledge of molecular biology, genetic technology has become an important part of all areas of clinical medicine. Genetic testing was initially limited to obstetrical practice, specifically with regard to prenatal counseling and diagnosis. However, delineation of genes and factors associated with gynecologic disease has made genetics an increasingly important segment of the screening and diagnosis for benign and malignant disease in women. This

the components of the genetic counseling process.

Who Provides the Genetic Counseling?

Genetic counseling cannot and should not be exclusively provided by a single specialist, but rather should be approached as an interdisciplinary responsibility. In certain situations (e.g., advanced maternal age, a first-degree relative with a neural tube defect), a primary care physician can provide the necessary counseling; in fact, the primary care physician may be better suited to provide such counseling because he or she is aware of the various family circumstances and socioeconomic factors affecting the gravida. However, in more complex situations, the primary care physician may lack the specific knowledge, time commitment, availability of specific diagnostic tests, or skills required for genetic counseling. In such situations, referral to a center with a medical genetics team is appropriate. Such a team might include a physician, a medical geneticist, genetic counselors, a social worker, a psychiatrist or psychologist, a child development specialist, and clergy. In addition, any potential prenatal problems or queries regarding specific patients can be directed to the medical genetics team for consultation.[35]

Gathering Genetic Information

Good genetic counseling requires certainty of diagnosis; even the best counseling cannot compensate for an inaccurate diagnosis. Questionnaires that may facilitate the counseling procedure can be obtained from several sources [e.g., American College of Obstetricians and Gynecologists (ACOG)]. The initial step in providing genetic counseling is to obtain an accurate personal and family history. Information about the woman's family may be obtained by the woman's health care provider or the genetic counselor. If the patient agrees, it may prove useful to include other relatives, especially parents or older siblings, who may be able to provide additional rele-

vant information about the health of family members.

The family history should include information about the health status of the patient and, at least, her biological parents, other first-degree (siblings and offspring), second-degree (aunts, uncles, nieces, nephews, and grandparents) and third-degree (first cousins) relatives. All untoward pregnancy outcomes (miscarriages, abortions, stillbirths, anomalous infants) should be noted and details sought if the person providing the history is unsure of specific diagnoses. Also, the ethnic origin of both parents should be ascertained. It is also important to determine whether or not consanguinity exists in the family. Exposure to drugs (both legal and illegal), toxic chemicals, and radiation should be documented and, if possible, quantified.

Obtaining medical records, examining affected relatives, and performing certain laboratory tests may serve to confirm or dispute certain diagnoses. Despite the most intensive efforts, however, a precise diagnosis cannot always be established. Some women and families will receive a measure of satisfaction and relief in knowing that all reasonable steps have been taken; others may express considerable dissatisfaction and even anger that a precise diagnosis could not be obtained.[11,35]

Risk Counseling

Once established, interpretation of genetic risk must be communicated in understandable and meaningful terms. The perception of genetic risk will vary widely from patient to patient, and the counselor must recognize that risk-perception is a complex phenomenon. The counselor should explain the consequences of the specific genetic problem, understanding that the perception of risk is highly dependent upon the individual's subjective experiences and expectations. For example, one person may perceive a cleft lip as a major tragedy, while another person may readily accept an affected child. Explanation of both the risk and the genetic disorder should be developed in small, discrete steps with frequent pauses to allow the patient time to ask questions as they arise.

Once the woman is aware of her risks, a discussion of the available options serves to make the counseling process more relevant and meaningful. If the counseling involves an obstetrical situation, encouraging the father to participate may facilitate the decision-making process. Indeed, including partners or other significant individuals may prove useful to the entire process, if this is acceptable to the patient. This component of the counseling process, irrespective of the specific circumstances, must provide information about the condition, its prospects, further diagnostic and treatment possibilities (including availability of pregnancy termination, if applicable), and available support services and organizations, including training and education.

To avoid confusion, the relevant medical and genetic information should be reinforced with a letter to the patient, the referring physician, and others to whom the patient wishes the letter be sent. The number and frequency of follow-up visits will vary with each patient and will depend on the specific circumstances of each case. All patients should understand that any extended family counseling must be initiated by them and that confidentiality will be strictly respected.[2,35]

Strategies for Genetic Counseling

The most widely used and promoted technique of genetic counseling is so-called "nondirective genetic counseling," which was endorsed by the World Health Organization (WHO) in 1969. The counselor makes clear from the outset that the counseling process is strictly educational and that no decisions will be made for the counselees. The counselor attempts to remain impartial and objective in providing information that will allow the counselees to make their own decisions. Although this form of counseling may appear to be passive or, at times, indifferent, counselors usually do interject their own biases by either verbal or nonverbal messages. Examples of such messages include shifting in one's chair, the repe-

tition of certain unpleasant symptoms of the disease in question, and the raising of one's eyebrows. Although the interjection of the counselor's own views may occur, nondirective counseling is a crucial part of the process that provides information so that patients can make rational decisions about their lives based on facts and not opinions.

Physicians providing counseling need to be cognizant of the psychological and social impact on their patients of the information they provide. This is particularly important when dealing with abnormal results, when women and families are under considerable stress, and decisions may be affected by emotional instability. The counselor must recognize the psychological defenses (e.g., repression, denial, anger, isolation of affect) that underlie all genetic counseling sessions; failure to do so may impede the entire process. Individuals who experience a major life stress, such as an abnormal pregnancy outcome, usually manifest clearly identifiable sequential coping responses before attaining psychological homeostasis. These coping responses usually divide into stages with the initial responses often being shock and disbelief, followed by fear and anger. Failure to resolve the problems frequently leads to depression. Most patients eventually abandon old modes of thought and behavior, and attempt adaptive changes, which ultimately lead to psychological homeostasis.[35]

Assessment of Genetic Counseling

Although it is difficult to ascertain whether a counselor has provided effective genetic counseling, the question to be asked is whether the counseling increased the patients' awareness of their genetic status, the risk of having a handicapped child, and the options available to the patients so that the decision that was made was "genetically informed." This question places genetic counseling in the important role of enhancing individual reproductive liberty, instead of imposing the beliefs of the counselor or society-at-large upon the patients.

Antenatal Diagnosis of Genetic Disorders

Once a careful personal and family history have been obtained, clinicians then decide whether the offering of further prenatal screening or diagnosis is warranted. The offering of further screening or diagnostic tests can be made because of personal history (e.g., advanced maternal age), family history (e.g., previous child with cystic fibrosis), ethnicity (sickle cell disease in African-Americans), or positive screening outcomes (maternal serum screening for fetal neural tube defects and chromosome abnormalities). Any positive historical information should, if possible, be verified by medical records.

Prenatal Cytogenetic Studies

The most common reason for women to consider prenatal testing is an increased risk for fetal chromosome abnormalities, usually because of advanced maternal age (≥35-years-old at estimated date of delivery). Ultrasonography and maternal serum analyte screening have increased the use of prenatal genetic studies among women previously recognized as low-risk by history alone (see below). Although such screening has, until recently, been available only during the second trimester, advances in ultrasonography and the development of new serum analytes have permitted the development of first trimester fetal chromosome screening protocols. First-trimester screening is not yet a part of routine obstetrical care, but such screening is being used in Europe and within the United States under an investigational protocol sponsored by the National Institutes of Health.

The most common methods to obtain fetal tissue for prenatal cytogenetic testing are chorionic villus sampling (CVS), amniocentesis, and fetal blood sampling.[36] Determination of which method to use is based primarily on the gestational age of the fetus at the time of prenatal diagnosis. ACOG has concluded that first-trimester CVS is a safe and reliable alternative to conventional mid-trimester amniocentesis.[3]

Advanced maternal age Advanced maternal age is the most common indication for prenatal cytogenetic studies. The overall incidence of Down syndrome is 1 per 800 liveborns, with increasing frequency with advancing maternal age. Trisomy 18 (Edward syndrome), trisomy 13 (Patau syndrome), 47,XXX, and 47,XXY (Klinefelter syndrome) also increase in frequency with advancing maternal age; however, 45,X (Turner syndrome), 47,XYY, and structural chromosome aberrations are not associated with maternal age.[21]

The prevalence of chromosome abnormalities is also dependent on the gestational age at which prenatal testing is performed. For example, the risk of a fetal chromosome abnormality for a 35-year-old woman is 1/118 at the time of first-trimester CVS, 1/141 at the time of mid-trimester amniocentesis, and 1/202 at birth. This reflects the disproportionate likelihood that fetuses lost spontaneously between the time of prenatal testing (10 to 18 weeks' gestation) and birth will have chromosome abnormalities. Indeed, 5 percent of stillbirth infants demonstrate chromosome abnormalities.

In the United States, the definition of advanced maternal age has generally been accepted as 35 years old at the estimated date of delivery. It is at this age that women are routinely informed of the availability of prenatal diagnosis.[8] However, the choice of a particular age is largely arbitrary because the risk for a chromosomally abnormal child increases year-to-year. Accordingly, when requests for prenatal cytogenetic testing come from younger women, such requests should not be simply dismissed; rather such women should be provided with counseling concerning risks of fetal abnormalities, available prenatal screening protocols for "low-risk" women, and risks and benefits of prenatal testing, if elected, despite the ostensibly unfavorable risk/benefit ratio.

Previous offspring with aneuploidy Following the birth of a child with a chromosome abnormality, the likelihood that subsequent progeny will be affected has traditionally been considered increased, even if parental complements are normal. Data concerning neonatal trisomy 21, as summarized by Hook, demonstrate that if the mother of the affected pregnancy was less than 30 years old, the recurrence risk was 1.4 percent; if she was 30 years old, the recurrence risk was 0.5 percent.[22] For counseling purposes the chance of recurrence for Down syndrome can be rounded to 1 percent over baseline risk. Although this represents a considerable increase in risk for women under the age of 35, this increase is less apparent for women over the age of 35. The recurrence risk in older women may also be influenced by maternal age at diagnosis of the first affected pregnancy or infant, because women older than 35 years who had their first affected pregnancy under age 30 are more likely to have greater underlying predisposition to recurrence compared with older mothers who had their first affected pregnancy after age 35.

Information concerning other aneuploids is limited, but data from three collaborative studies suggest a risk of 1 to 2 percent for either the same or a different chromosome abnormality.[29,41,43] Thus, prenatal diagnosis should be offered to parents of a child with a chromosome abnormality. Even in cases where chromosome abnormalities do not presage an increased risk for future pregnancies (e.g., 45,X, triploidy), women should be offered prenatal diagnosis as a result of the emotional and psychological impact of the previously affected pregnancy.

Structural chromosome rearrangements The diagnosis of a structural chromosome rearrangement in a pregnancy or newborn infant should initiate an evaluation of parental chromosome complements. If both parents are found to have normal complements, then women should be offered prenatal diagnosis in subsequent pregnancies with an estimated risk of 1 to 2 percent over baseline.[9]

If one or both parents are found to have a rearrangement, then risk for future abnormal offspring is dependent on the type of rearrangement. Specific recurrence risks are found in Table 32-1. The most common type of translo-

TABLE 32-1 Risks for Chromosomally Unbalanced Offspring to Carriers of Balanced Chromosome Rearrangements

Rearrangement	Carrier Gender	Risk of Abnormal (Unbalanced) Offspring
Robertsonian	Male	2–4%
Robertsonian	Female	~11–15%
Reciprocal	Male	~11%
Reciprocal	Female	~11%
Inversion	Male	4%
Inversion	Female	8%

SOURCE: From Boué and Gallano, 1984[17] and Daniel et al, 1989.[18]

cation is the Robertsonian variety. In cases of balanced rearrangements, two D (chromosomes 13, 14, and 15) or G (chromosomes 21 and 22) group chromosomes, all of which are acrocentric, lose their minute short arms and have fusion of their long arms. Accordingly, phenotypically normal individuals with balanced Robertsonian translocations appear to have 45 chromosomes. Although all combinations of the aforementioned chromosomes have been observed, the most common Robertsonian translocation involves chromosomes 14 and 21. Those translocations involving the same, or homologous, chromosomes are characterized by near-universal adverse pregnancy outcomes. In such cases, the only possible outcomes involve monosomy or trisomy for the particular chromosome. Because most monosomic complements are lethal, risk for a trisomic conceptus with parental homologous Robertsonian rearrangements approaches 100 percent.

Reciprocal translocations involve exchange of chromosome material between two, and sometimes more, nonhomologous chromosomes. Because of their individual rarity, specific empirical data for most reciprocal translocations do not exist. What is known is that reciprocal translocations that result in short unbalanced segments are more likely to result in abnormal offspring than those that result in long unbalanced segments, which are more likely to lead to spontaneous loss.[33]

Inversions are another type of rearrangement that lead to abnormal offspring. If the inversion involves the central portion of the chromosome (centromere), the inversion is known as pericentric; if the inversion segment does not involve the centromere, it is known as paracentric. As with reciprocal translocations, specific empirical data do not exist; however, parental pericentric inversions are associated with considerable increased risk for abnormal offspring (Table 32-1). Risk is also influenced by length of inversion segment. Individuals with inversions involving relatively long segments are more likely to produce anomalous offspring than those with pericentric inversions involving shorter segments. However, both very short and very long inversions can yield large imbalances in the conceptus; such large imbalances are more likely to be lethal.[17]

Certain inversions, such as one involving chromosome 9 with breakpoints p11 and q11, are common variants in the general population and do not lead to substantial increased risk for adverse perinatal outcome.[28] Clinical queries concerning specific inversions should be directed to geneticists or cytogeneticists.

Maternal serum analyte screening Maternal serum α-fetoprotein (MSAFP) screening is an integral part of prenatal care in the United States. Second-trimester MSAFP screening is offered to women at low risk for fetal structural defects and chromosome abnormalities. Through carefully structured screening protocols, maternal serum analyte screening effectively detects those women at increased risk for open neural tube defects, and those at increased risk for other congenital fetal structural abnormalities (e.g., omphalocele, gastroschisis) and for chromosome abnormalities (e.g., Down syndrome, trisomy 18).

Over the past decade other analytes have been added to the initial MSAFP protocol in order to improve screening efficacy for fetal chromosome abnormalities. These are the use of double [MSAFP and human chorionic gonadotropin (hCG)] or triple analyte [MSAFP, hCG, and unconjugated estriol (uE3)] screening for determining risk for fetal Down syndrome and other aneuploidies during the second trimester.[15,32]

Those women found to be at increased risk for fetal chromosome abnormalities should be offered ultrasonography and, if ultrasound confirms gestational number and age, genetic counseling and prenatal diagnosis (usually amniocentesis).[35] Although maternal serum screening is not a diagnostic test, it should be offered with counseling as the implications of undergoing or foregoing screening may have considerable impact on pregnancy outcome. Accordingly, women who are considering or eligible for such screening should be provided counseling concerning abnormalities detectable by serum screening, possible screening outcomes, and diagnostic procedures that may be offered in case of positive screening outcomes.

Further study of other second trimester (e.g., inhibin-A) and first trimester analytes (e.g., PAPP-A, β-hCG) may allow for more sensitive second trimester screening and expansion of screening into the first trimester, thus allowing at-risk women to consider CVS.

Ultrasound Advances in high-resolution ultrasonography have led to a dramatic increase in the capability to detect fetal structural abnormalities and abnormal biometric measurements associated with cytogenetic abnormalities. Studies evaluating fetuses with fetal anomalies detected by second trimester ultrasound found aneuploidy rates to be from 2 to 76 percent, depending on the specific structural defect and the presence of isolated or multiple anomalies.[19] Accordingly, the offering of prenatal cytogenetic studies for most detected structural abnormalities in all trimesters is warranted.

The encouraging prospect of using nuchal translucency thickness measurements as a screening technique for Down syndrome and other chromosome abnormalities is promising. Numerous studies[30,38] have demonstrated a marked increased risk for fetal chromosome abnormalities when a prominent nuchal translucency of at least 2.5 mm is detected during the first trimester. When such a finding is encountered, it is appropriate to offer counseling and prenatal diagnosis. However, an ongoing study of more than 100,000 pregnancies has shown that the use of nuchal translucency is effective as a screening tool, detecting approximately 80 percent of fetuses with Down syndrome while offering 5 percent of the population prenatal diagnosis (false-positive rate).[42]

Limitations to this protocol are primarily based on operator experience, mechanical quality, and reproducibility of results. It has been proposed by some that first-trimester maternal serum analyte analysis can be combined with nuchal translucency and, possibly, fetal heart rate measurement to better screen the general obstetric population for fetal chromosome abnormalities.[24,31,39]

Prenatal Genetic Studies

An important role of the counseling process is to ascertain whether women and couples are at increased risk for fetal genetic disorders. Such risk is identified as a result of a previously affected child, family members with a genetic disorder, or belonging to a particular racial or ethnic group associated with a particular genetic disorder.

If a specific genetic disorder is detected within a family pedigree, written confirmation of the diagnosis is critical so that appropriate counseling, screening, or diagnosis can be offered. Once confirmation has been achieved, determination as to the possibility of prenatal diagnosis must be made before further counseling can be provided. As the list of genetics disorders amenable to prenatal diagnosis continues to expand, physicians are encouraged to contact a genetics center to determine whether prenatal diagnosis is feasible and what parental/familial studies are necessary. If prenatal diagnosis by DNA analysis is possible, CVS or amniocentesis can obtain fetal tissue for the appropriate molecular studies. For

selected conditions amenable only to special molecular or enzyme analyses (e.g., amniocentesis for fragile X syndrome), either amniotic fluid cells or chorionic villi may specifically be needed for the test.

Hemoglobinopathies

Hemoglobinopathies result in maternal anemia and other complications of pregnancy. There are 2 to 2.5 million people in the United States with inherited abnormalities of hemoglobin structure or synthesis. The effects of hemoglobinopathies vary from asymptomatic maternal anemia to significant morbidity and mortality. As pregnancy tends to exacerbate the anemias associated with hemoglobinopathies, maternal screening and prenatal testing are appropriate for obtaining important maternal and fetal information. As with other screening/diagnostic processes, counseling should precede all steps.

β-Thalassemia is seen in almost all populations, but the groups at greatest risk are people of Mediterranean, North African, Southeast Asian, Indian, or Pakistani descent. Hemoglobin S (sickle cell) is primarily found in people of African ancestry. Hemoglobin C is found in people of African ancestry, as well as people originating from Mediterranean regions. Hemoglobin E occurs primarily in people from Southeast Asia. Specific hemoglobinopathies and associated hemoglobin abnormalities are found in Table 32-2.[6,14]

A complete blood count with red cell indices should be performed on all pregnant women to screen for thalassemia traits. In the absence of iron deficiency anemia, microcytosis (mean cell volume ≤ 80 fl), hypochromia, and low hemoglobin values are suggestive of a thalassemia syndrome. In such cases, iron supplementation can be offered, as iron deficiency anemia is far more common than thalassemia. If the woman fails to respond to such therapy, or if there is a high index of suspicion, a hemoglobin electrophoresis is helpful to detect heterozygous β-thalassemia. In women with consistently low mean corpuscu-

TABLE 32-2 Hemoglobin Abnormalities and Associated Disorders

Hemoglobin Abnormalities	Resultant Hemoglobin	Clinical Signs/Symptoms
3/4 α chains	α-Thalassemia-2	None
2/4 α chains	α-Thalassemia-1	α-Thalassemia minor—mild anemia
1/4 α chains	Hemoglobin H	Severe hemolytic anemia
0/4 α chains	Bart's hemoglobin	Fetal hydrops/stillbirth
β-Chain reduced	β^+-Thalassemia	Mild anemia
β-Chain absent	β°-Thalassemia	Severe anemia (Cooley's anemia)
Sickle cell trait	Hb AS	Mild anemia
Sickle cell disease	Hb SS	Severe anemia
β-Chain abnormality	Hb AC	Mild anemia
β-Chain abnormality	Hb CC	Moderate anemia

lar volume and normal iron and electrophoresis studies, heterozygous α-thalassemia can be detected by use of DNA-based testing to assess the number of α chains present.[14]

Sickle cell screening is generally achieved by use of solubility tests such as Sickledex. Such tests, however, are inadequate as a primary screening procedure because of their inability to identify important transmissible hemoglobin gene abnormalities affecting fetal outcome. For example, a negative solubility test may occur in individuals with β-thalassemia trait or Hb C trait. Although solubility tests may detect individuals with Hb AS/SS, groups at risk for Hb S are also at risk for other hemoglobinopathies, with resultant compound heterozygote offspring at potential increased risk for serious hemoglobinopathies. Accordingly, hemoglobin electrophoresis is the appropriate initial laboratory determination for individuals at risk for a hemoglobin disorder, although solubility tests are still valuable for the rapid assessment of individuals at specific risk for sickle cell disease (e.g., in an emergency room setting).[14]

Although universal screening by hemoglobin electrophoresis is not indicated, physicians should try to identify couples who would potentially benefit from such screening. Because of the genetic basis of hemoglobinopathies, carrier testing of couples and not individuals is strongly

recommended. If a couple is found to be at increased risk for a hemoglobinopathy, prenatal diagnosis can be offered. CVS, amniocentesis, or fetal blood sampling can be used to obtain fetal cells for prenatal genetic diagnosis, as sickle cell disease, α/β-thalassemia, and most other hemoglobinopathies are amenable to diagnosis by DNA molecular diagnosis using polymerase chain reaction DNA amplification technology.

It must be emphasized that normal diagnostic outcomes do not guarantee a "normal" baby, as these tests exclude only specific conditions. If results are positive, consideration of pregnancy management options is warranted and should be done with a complete understanding of potential outcomes, including developmental and therapeutic possibilities.

Cystic Fibrosis

Cystic fibrosis (CF) is an autosomal recessive disease primarily affecting North American Caucasians of European ancestry. CF is characterized by gastrointestinal, pancreatic, pulmonary, and hepatic dysfunction. Carrier frequency in the United States. is 1/25 among this ethnic group. Until the mid-1980s, only counseling was available to assess risk for affected offspring. Later, the gene responsible for CF was localized to chromosome 7, allowing the use of closely linked genetic marker DNA sequences for diagnosis. Although this method had a greater sensitivity and specificity than microvillar enzymes, DNA was required from the affected relative. More recently, the CF gene was cloned and sequenced, allowing for direct mutational analysis. The most common mutation, ΔF508, is responsible for 75 percent of CF mutations. The number of recognized CF mutations is now over 600; however, these mutations represent only 90 to 92 percent of all CF mutations. Certain populations (e.g., Spanish) still have detectable CF mutation rates of less than 50 percent.[1,20]

In couples where either partner is affected with CF or there is a positive family history (first-, second-, or third-degree relative), mutational screening using DF508 and other common CF mutations should be offered. As current screening modalities will detect only one-half to two-thirds of carrier couples, and 6 percent of couples will be found to have only one partner with a detectable mutation with no possibility for complete diagnostic testing, in-depth counseling must be provided throughout the screening and diagnosis process.[20] As result of these diagnostic limitations, CF screening of the general population is still not recommended at the time this chapter is being written.[1] However, such population-based screening will likely become standard of care in the foreseeable future.

Tay-Sachs

Tay-Sachs disease (TSD) is an autosomal recessive disorder in which GM_2 gangliosides accumulate as result of a deficiency of the enzyme hexosaminidase A (Hex A). It most commonly occurs in individuals of eastern/central European Jewish (Ashkenazi) ancestry with carrier frequencies being approximately 1/30, compared to the general population carrier frequency of 1/300. The carrier frequency among Cajun and French-Canadian individuals is higher than the general population as well.[5]

Carrier screening is done by measuring serum levels of Hex A; Hex A activity is usually less than 55 percent in carriers, whereas Hex A activity is usually 60 percent or more in noncarriers. Carrier screening for women taking oral contraceptives or who are pregnant may lead to many false-positive results as a result of interference by estrogen in the serum assay. Accordingly, carrier screening for such women should be done by Hex A leukocyte analyses. Carrier screening by enzyme activity, and not DNA analysis, is recommended as several Hex A mutations are responsible for disease expression. When serum tests are inconclusive, leukocyte analyses are, again, recommended. DNA analyses are recommended only when serum and leukocyte analyses provide inconclusive results or when a low-risk partner tests "screen positive."[5,25]

Hex A screening for TSD should be offered to all couples of Ashkenazi, French-Canadian, or Cajun ancestry, as well as to those individuals with an affected family member. When only one member of a couple is at increased risk, that individual should be offered screening; if that individual is found to be a carrier, then the partner should be offered screening. During pregnancy, screening both partners simultaneously may be warranted so that results are available in a timely fashion and all pregnancy management options are possible. If any screening outcome is found to be ambiguous, consideration of DNA analysis is warranted. Only if both partners are found to be carriers should further genetic counseling and prenatal testing be offered.[5]

Fragile X

Fragile X syndrome (Fra X) is the most common inherited form of mental retardation, affecting 1/1500 males and 1/2500 females. The condition derives its name from the demonstration of a fragile site (Xq27–28) on the long arm of the X chromosome in metaphases from folate-deprived culture medium. The condition was originally thought to be transmitted in an X-linked fashion; however, certain clinical incongruities precluded confirmation of a classic X-linked inheritance pattern.[4]

The molecular cloning of the Fra X gene

(*FMR-1*) helped delineate the genetic basis of Fra X. Nearly all mutations involve expansion of a triplet repeat, which consists of the bases cytosine-guanine-guanine (CGG). The number of repeats varies in unaffected individuals; those with less than 50 are considered normal, whereas 50 to 200 repeats are considered a premutation. Greater than 200 repeats constitutes a full mutation that results in phenotypic Fra X. The *FMR-1* gene almost always becomes methylated and thereby inactivated in cases of full mutation. Thus, the number of CGG repeats helps determine the methylation pattern and, thereby, the activity or inactivity of the gene, with inactivity being associated with phenotypic expression of Fra X.[45]

Transmission of Fra X depends on the number of CGG repeats and the gender of the affected parent. When a female carries the premutation and the repeats exceed 90, premutation genes are likely to expand and result in an affected child. Males may transmit the premutation to their offspring, but expansion of the repeat sequence in offspring has not been demonstrated.[4] The role of CGG in premutant/mutant gene determination and methylation activities serves to explain the apparent X-linked transmission incongruities observed in many Fra X families.

Screening and diagnosis is centered on determining the number of CGG repeats and methylation patterns in potential carriers and affected individuals. Although general population-based screening is not yet recommended, Fra X screening should be offered to couples with a family history of mental retardation or Fra X. In addition, children with developmental delay of uncertain etiology should be offered Fra X screening. If either partner is found to have a full or premutation, prenatal genetic testing by amniocentesis should be offered; analysis of chorionic villi is reliable for determining the number of CGG repeats but may not be reliable for assessing methylation of the *FMR-1* gene.[4]

Pregnancy Loss

Approximately 50 to 75 percent of all pregnancies end in spontaneous loss. Most of these losses

are unrecognized as they occur at or prior to expected menses. Of clinically diagnosed pregnancies, 15 to 20 percent are lost in the first or early second trimester. Early pregnancy loss is a common but sporadic event, with subsequent pregnancy usually resulting in a live birth. However, some women experience recurrent pregnancy loss, defined as the loss of three or more *consecutive* pregnancies. Such loss occurs in 0.5 to 1.0 percent of pregnant women; studies have shown that women with two successive spontaneous losses have a recurrence risk of 25 to 45 percent.[13,16,34]

Recurrent pregnancy loss is a difficult and frustrating problem for couples and clinicians alike. In up to 50 percent of couples experiencing multiple loss, no specific etiology is identified. For the other 50 percent of couples, none of the traditional etiologies or therapeutic options have been established by well-designed studies. Regardless, many couples benefit from a thorough evaluation of various structural, endocrinologic, immunologic, and chromosomal factors that may lead to an increased risk of pregnancy loss.[13]

A complete assessment of family and personal medical history is necessary prior to performing any diagnostic tests. With regard to genetic abnormalities, *parental blood karyotypes* will provide the necessary information concerning the presence or absence of balanced chromosome rearrangements. Parental karyotypic abnormalities are found in approximately 2 to 3 percent of couples with recurrent pregnancy loss. This rate can be higher if history reveals anomalous infants or stillbirths; however, the presence of phenotypically normal children does not preclude a parental chromosome rearrangement. Balanced translocations account for the highest frequency of chromosome abnormalities in couples experiencing recurrent pregnancy loss, with reciprocal translocations being more frequent than Robertsonian translocations. Other, less frequent findings include inversions, ring chromosomes, and marker chromosomes.

In couples with normal karyotypes, a chromosomal cause for recurrent loss can essentially be excluded. In those couples in whom a chromosome rearrangement is detected, in-depth counseling should be provided. Couples should be informed that although certain very rare rearrangements may preclude normal offspring (e.g., 21q;21q Robertsonian rearrangement), the vast majority of parental rearrangements can result in normal offspring, either with chromosomally normal offspring or phenotypically normal children with balanced rearrangements similar to their parent (Table 32-1). The overall risk of miscarriage in couples with reciprocal rearrangements is approximately 25 to 50 percent, with the risk of miscarriage for couples with a nonhomologous Robertsonian translocation being about 25 percent.[16]

The recognition of a parental rearrangement may help abate the emotional trauma of recurrent loss. Nonetheless, the toll of recurrent loss and the risk of abnormal offspring may lead some couples to consider gamete donation or adoption. As with other genetic counseling issues, nondirective counseling and empathetic support for patient decisions are vital components of the process; if gamete donation or adoption is selected, appropriate referral is warranted.

Approximately 50 percent of all spontaneous losses are chromosomally abnormal, with greater than 50 percent of early losses being chromosomally abnormal. However, most of these abnormalities are nondisjunctional in nature and are associated with loss or gain of whole chromosomes. Although some data suggest that subsequent pregnancy losses may have a higher risk for aneuploidy, the subject remains controversial. Accordingly, routine cytogenetic testing of abortus specimens is not indicated[13]; however, consideration of cytogenetic analysis in cases of fetal demise at or after 20 weeks gestation is warranted and may provide critical information as to the cause of fetal death or stillbirth.[10]

Gynecologic Cancer

Cancer is in part a genetic disease. Over the past several decades, insights into the genetic basis of cancer have come from diverse medical and scientific fields. It is now widely accepted that solid tumors arise from a multistep process involving gene mutations and clonal selection of variant progeny cells. This is followed by increasingly aggressive growth properties and uninhibited cellular proliferation, with subsequent invasion of neighboring tissues, blood and lymphatic vessels, and distant metastases. Although the vast majority of mutations are somatic in nature (i.e., occur only in tumor cells), an increasing number of genes (i.e., germinal) have been implicated in inherited susceptibility to certain cancers. It is these germinal mutations that hold promise for assessing risk for development of malignancies. This section reviews genetic screening for breast-ovarian cancer, one of the cancer syndromes for which germinal mutations are identified.

An estimated 5 to 7 percent of breast and ovarian cancers are attributable to inherited mutations in two highly penetrant autosomal dominant susceptibility genes, *BRCA1* and *BRCA2*. Earlier data indicated that women who inherit the *BRCA1* gene have a greater than 80 percent lifetime risk for developing breast cancer and an estimated 45 percent risk of developing ovarian cancer by age 70[7], although more recent studies suggest that these risks are lower.[40] *BRCA1* appears to confer a higher risk for ovarian cancer than *BRCA2*, but *BRCA2* confers a higher risk for breast cancer in men. In all, *BRCA1* and *BRCA2* account for almost 80 percent of all heritable cases of breast cancer; other genes including *p53, H-ras* and the ataxia-telangiectasia gene are responsible for most of the remaining cases.[7]

BRCA1, BRCA2, and *p53* are tumor-suppressor genes that increase risk for tumorigenesis when mutations inactivate or deactivate the genes and, thus, alter or eliminate their protein products. The two-step cancer model of Knudson[26] calls for two steps, or hits, to occur in tumorigenesis. If the first step has been inherited, the likelihood of cancer is far greater than if two random, or somatic, hits are required for the promotion of tumorigenesis. Accordingly, inherited mutations in *BRCA1* or *BRCA2* would serve as the first "hit" and, in many cases, render the gene inactive. A second somatic "hit" would then promote development of cancer. Such germinal mutations would provide critical clinical information for assessing risk for breast-ovarian cancer development.

However, many issues serve to cloud the efficacy of screening using the BRCA genes. The vast majority of cases of breast cancer are isolated and not associated with ovarian cancer; *BRCA1* and *BRCA2* mutations are found in only a small percentage of women with isolated, post-menopausal breast cancer. Numerous mutations exist throughout both genes, with certain mutations more common in specific populations. In addition, the interaction of other genes and proteins in the breast-ovarian tumor pathway have not yet been delineated. For example, a certain mutation (*BRCA1 185delAG*) has been identified in women at high risk for developing breast cancer as well as in 1 to 2 percent of Ashkenazi Jews.[44] With little information concerning other mutations in the Ashkenazi Jewish community, and the frequency of this mutation in the general population, the presence of this mutation may not have the adverse connotation in an Ashkenazi Jewish woman and, conversely, its absence may not have the reassuring effect in a woman with a strong family history of breast-ovarian cancer.

In addition, as functional mutations are widely scattered throughout the *BRCA1* gene, identifying specific mutations in an affected family member is needed before screening other family members. Screening usually begins with DNA analysis of an affected individual, limiting the ability to screen the general population. Further compounding the issue is the lack of clear therapeutic options for those women found to have positive or negative mutational analyses.[7]

Accordingly, *BRCA1* and *BRCA2* screening in the general population is not currently recommended. Consideration of screening is recommended for individuals at a marked increased risk for breast-ovarian cancer as result of personal or family history. Because the issues surrounding screening and its results are complicated and can create considerable uncertainty and angst, screening should be performed by experienced clinicians and investigators who can provide detailed and empathetic genetic counseling throughout the process. Indeed, the standard of care should emphasize genetic services, genetic information, education, and counseling rather than testing procedures alone.[7] The most important part of the screening process involves a detailed review of a personal and family history, for this provides critical information as to the risk for developing cancer and the need for further screening, testing, or therapy.

References and Selected Readings

1. American College of Obstetricians and Gynecologists, Committee on Obstetrics: *Maternal and Fetal Medicine: Current Status of Cystic Fibrosis Carrier Screening.* Washington, DC: ACOG, 1991. ACOG Committee Opinion 101.

2. American College of Obstetricians and Gynecologists, Committee on Ethics: *Ethical Guidance for Patient Testing.* Washington, DC: ACOG, 1995. ACOG Committee Opinion 159.

3. American College of Obstetricians and Gynecologists, Committee on Genetics: *Chorionic Villus Sampling.* Washington, DC: ACOG, 1995. ACOG Committee Opinion 160.

4. American College of Obstetricians and Gynecologists, Committee on Genetics: *Fragile X Syndrome.* Washington, DC: ACOG, 1995. ACOG Committee Opinion 161.

5. American College of Obstetricians and Gynecologists, Committee on Genetics: *Screening for Tay-Sachs Disease.* Washington, DC: ACOG, 1995. ACOG Committee Opinion 162.

6. American College of Obstetricians and Gynecologists, Committee on Genetics: *Genetic Screening for Hemoglobinopathies.* Washington, DC: ACOG, 1996. ACOG Committee Opinion 168.

7. American College of Obstetricians and Gynecologists, Committee on Genetics: *Breast-ovarian Cancer Screening.* Washington, DC: ACOG, 1996. ACOG Committee Opinion 176a.

8. American College of Obstetricians and Gynecologists, ACOG: *Guidelines for Women's Health.* Washington, DC: ACOG, 1996.

9. American College of Obstetricians and Gynecologists, *Antenatal Diagnosis of Genetic Disorders.* Washing-

ton, DC: ACOG, 1987. ACOG Technical Bulletin 108.

10. American College of Obstetricians and Gynecologists, *Diagnosis and Management of Fetal Death.* Washington, DC: ACOG, 1993. ACOG Technical Bulletin 176b.

11. American College of Obstetricians and Gynecologists, *Preconceptional Care.* Washington, DC: ACOG, 1995. ACOG Technical Bulletin 205.

12. American College of Obstetricians and Gynecologists, *Genetic Technologies.* Washington, DC: ACOG, 1995. ACOG Technical Bulletin 208.

13. American College of Obstetricians and Gynecologists, *Early Pregnancy Loss.* Washington, DC: ACOG, 1995. ACOG Technical Bulletin 212.

14. American College of Obstetricians and Gynecologists, *Hemoglobinopathies in Pregnancy.* Washington, DC: ACOG, 1996. ACOG Technical Bulletin 220.

15. American College of Obstetricians and Gynecologists, *Maternal Serum Screening.* Washington, DC: ACOG, 1996. ACOG Technical Bulletin 228:

16. Boué J, Boué A, Lazar P: Retrospective and prospective epidemiological studies of 1,500 karyotyped spontaneous abortions. *Teratology* 12:11, 1975.

17. Boué A, Gallano P: A collaborative study of the segregation of inherited chromosome structural rearrangements in 1,356 prenatal diagnosis. *Prenat Diagn* (Spec iss)4:45, 1984.

18. Daniel A, Hook EB, Wulf G: Risks of unbalanced progency at amniocentesis to carrier of chromosome rearrangement: Data from United States and Canadian laboratories. *Am J Med Genet* 33:14, 1989.

19. D'Ottavio GD, Rustico V, Pecile A, et al: Malformations and karyotype, in Chervenak FA, Kurjak A, (eds); *Current Perspectives on the Fetus as a Patient.* London: Parthenon, 1996, p. 213.

20. Elias S, Annas GJ, Simpson JL: Carrier screening for cystic fibrosis: Implications for obstetric and gynecologic practice. *Am J Obstet Gynecol* 164:1077, 1991.

21. Ferguson-Smith MA, Yates JRW: Maternal age-specific rates for chromosome aberrations and factors influencing them: Report of a collaborative European study on 59,965 amniocentesis. *Prenat Diagn* 4:5, 1984.

22. Hook EB: Chromosome abnormalities: Prevalence, risks and recurrences, in Brock DH, Rodeck CH, Ferguson-Smith MA (eds): *Prenatal Diagnosis and Screening.* Edinburgh: Churchill Livingstone, 1992, p 351.

23. Hsia YE, Hirschhorn K: What is genetic counseling? in Hsia YE, Hirschhorn K, Silverberg RL, et al (eds): *Counseling in Genetics.* New York: Alan R Liss, 1979.

24. Hyett JA, Noble PL, Snijders RJM, et al: Fetal heart rate in trisomy 21 and other chromosomal abnormalities at 10–14 weeks gestation. *Ultrasound Obstet Gynecol* 7:237, 1996.

25. Kaback M, Lim-Steele J, Dabholkar D, et al: Tay-Sachs disease-carrier screening, prenatal diagnosis and the molecular era. An international perspective, 1970–1993. The International TSD Data Collection Network. *JAMA* 270:2307, 1993.

26. Knudson A. Mutation and cancer: Statistical study of retinoblastoma. *Proc Natl Acad Sci U S A* 68:820, 1971.

27. Koster T, Rosendaal FR, de Ronde H, et al: Venous thrombosis due to poor anticoagulant response to activated protein C: Leiden Thrombophilia Study. *Lancet* 342:1503, 1993.

28. Mikkelsen M, Poulsen H, Tommerup N: Genetic risk factors in human trisomy 21, in Hassold TJ, Epstein CJ (eds): *Progress in Clinical and Biological Research. Molecular and Cytogenetic Studies of Non-Disjunction.* vol 311. New York: Alan R. Liss, 1989, p 183.

29. Mikkelsen M, Stene J: Previous child with Down's syndrome and other chromosome aberrations, in Murken JD, Stengel-Rutkowski S, Schwinger E, (eds): *Prenatal Diagnosis: Proceedings of the Third European Conference on Prenatal Diagnosis of Genetic Disorders.* Stuttgart: F Enke, 1979, p 22.

30. Nicolaides KH, Azar G, Byrne D, Mansur C, Marks K: Fetal nuchal translucency: Ultrasound screening for chromosomal defects in first trimester of pregnancy. *BMJ* 304, 867, 1992.

31. Noble PL, Wallace Em, Snijders RJ, et al (1997): Maternal serum inhibin-A and free beta-hCG concentrations in trisomy 21 pregnancies at 10 to 14 weeks gestation. *Br J Obstet Gynaecol* 104:367, 1997.

32. Phillips OP, Elias S, Shulman LP, Andersen RN, Morgan CD, Simpson JL: Maternal serum screening for fetal Down syndrome in women less than 35 years of age using alpha-fetoprotein, human chorionic gonadotropin, and unconjugated estriol: A prospective two-year study. *Obstet Gynecol* 80:353, 1992.

33. Phillips OP, Tharapel AT, Shulman LP, Simpson JL, Elias S: Segregation analysis and genetic counseling when both parents carry balanced chromosomal translocations. *Fertil Steril* 56:646, 1991.

34. Regan L: A prospective study of spontaneous abortion, in Beard RW, Sharp F, (eds): *Early Pregnancy Loss.* London: Springer-Verlag, 1988, p 23.

35. Shulman LP: Perspectives on counseling in maternal serum alpha-fetoprotein screening, in Elias S, Simpson JL (eds): *Maternal Serum Screening for Fetal Genetic Disorders.* New York: Churchill Livingstone, 1992, p 121.

36. Shulman LP, Elias S: Amniocentesis and chorionic villus sampling. *West J Med* 159:260, 1993.

37. Shulman LP, Elias S, Phillips OP, et al: Amniocente-

sis performed at 14 weeks gestation or earlier. Comparison with first-trimester transabdominal chorionic villus sampling. *Obstet Gynecol* 83:543, 1994.

38. Shulman LP, Emerson DS, Felker RE, et al: High frequency of cytogenetic abnormalities in fetuses with cystic hygroma diagnosed in the first trimester. *Obstet Gynecol* 80:80, 1992.

39. Shulman LP, Emerson DS, Tharapel AT, et al: First-trimester detection of fetal trisomy 13 distinguished only by persistent fetal tachycardia. *Int J Gynecol Obstet* 57:317, 1997.

40. Simard J, Tonin P, Durocher F, et al: Common origins of *BRCA1* mutations in Canadian breast and ovarian cancer families. *Nat Genet* 8:392, 1994.

41. Simoni G, Fraccaro M, Arsianian A, et al: Cytogenetic finding in 4,952 prenatal diagnoses: An Italian collaborative study. *Hum Genet* 60:63, 1982.

42. Snijders RJ, Johnson S, Sebire NJ, et al: First-trimester ultrasound screening for chromosomal defects. *Ultrasound Obstet Gynecol* 7:216, 1996.

43. Stene J, Stene E, Mikkelsen M: Risk for chromosome abnormality at amniocentesis following a child with a non-inherited chromosome aberration. *Prenat Diagn* 4 (Spec iss):81, 1984.

44. Struewing JP, Abeliovich D, Perez T, et al: The carrier frequency of the BRCA1 185delAG mutation is approximately 1 percent in Ashkenazi Jewish individuals. *Nat Genet* 11:198, 1995.

45. Warren ST, Nelson DL: Advances in molecular analysis of fragile X syndrome. *JAMA* 271:536, 1994.

Lactation

Sylvia A. M. Delaney

Breastfeeding is the optimal method of feeding infants: a simple, low-cost, effective maternal and child health measure. A variety of breastfeeding promotion activities have been implemented at national, state, and local levels over the past decade and a half. Government agencies' and health professionals' efforts are beginning to influence the rate of breastfeeding initiation. The latest U.S. figures on in-hospital initiation rates of breastfeeding for 1997 are at an all-time high of 62.4 percent with the largest increase seen among women who traditionally have breast-fed the least: African-American mothers, mothers younger than 20 years of age, and W.I.C. (Women, Infants and Children supplemental food program) participants. The percentage of mothers who continue to breastfeed for 6 months has increased to 26 percent.[18]

One goal of the U.S. Healthy People 2000: National Health Promotion and Disease Prevention Objectives is to increase to at least 75 percent the proportion of mothers who breastfeed their babies in the early postpartum period, and to at least 50 percent those who continue breastfeeding for the first 6 months. In addition to these objectives, the revised (December 1997) American Academy of Pediatrics policy statement on breastfeeding recommends that breastfeeding should continue for at least 12 months, and for as long as mutually desired after that.[1] The challenge is to all perinatal health care providers to promote and support breastfeeding, especially among women least likely to breastfeed: the poor, the young, and the less-educated.

Ongoing restructuring of the health care system continues to affect the ability to provide adequate in-hospital assistance to establish breastfeeding with neonates and their mothers. Providers of perinatal care must accept the challenge to redesign services to better educate, care for, and support breastfeeding families. A team approach is necessary, as is providing consistent and current education on lactation management for both health care providers and their patients. Though it is the right and the privilege of every new mother to choose the method of infant feeding, it is hoped that every obstetric practitioner will educate her. Consistency in approach regarding the promotion of breastfeeding by all staff in the prenatal period has been shown to affect positively the initiation rates of breastfeeding.

Benefits

The health benefits for both mother and baby make it easy to promote breastfeeding. Nutritionally, breast milk contains all that the baby needs for the first several months. It is a perfect combination of nutrients, enzymes, immunoglobulins, and antibodies for the infant. On average, mothers of exclusively breastfed single babies produce 600 to 850 ml of milk per day. No other supplements (water, juice, other foods) are generally necessary during the first several months.[1] The nutrients in breast milk provide what the growing infant requires for optimal growth and development.

Immunologically, breast milk provides protection against disease to the neonate and growing infant that cannot be duplicated or obtained from other sources. Disease prevention is one of the most important reasons to promote the mother's breastfeeding her baby.[1,4,6–8] The frequency of infectious and allergic disorders of the alimentary and respiratory tracts in infancy are lower in fully breast-fed than in formula-fed babies.[6,23] Increased breastfeeding incidence in a population has been causally associated with declines in infant morbidity.[24] Human milk feeding has also been suggested to have a preventive effect against sudden infant death syndrome(SIDS).

Breastfeeding also contributes to the mother's long-term health maintenance. The early postpartum effects of more rapid uterine involution and more efficient use of nutrient stores accumulated during pregnancy may lead to an earlier return to prepregnancy weight. Recent research suggests that breastfeeding may improve bone remineralization. Also, reduced rates of ovarian cancer and premenopausal breast cancer have been noted in women who breastfed.

In addition, the greater physical contact between breastfeeding mother and baby enhances their attachment. The infant is nurtured while being fed.

Health care dollar savings may occur because both breastfeeding mother and breastfed baby may have lower incidences of illness, resulting in fewer outpatient contacts and fewer hospitalizations. In addition, several hundred dollars can be saved by the family of the breastfed infant that does not purchase infant formula during the first year of life.

Prenatal Education and Assessment

A positive attitude toward breastfeeding should be reinforced with each prenatal contact with the health care provider. Reassurance that education, assistance, and support are available do much to encourage a woman to consider breastfeeding. Allowing her to discuss her concerns regarding breastfeeding is also essential to resolve her misconceptions, reduce her fears, and promote her confidence in her ability to so nurture her infant. A woman who really wants to breastfeed will be more successful in doing so. One must also be aware of cultural factors that may enhance or decrease her motivation and support. Involving her family or support person in her education may also be important.

Attendance at a good prenatal breastfeeding class helps motivate the prospective parents and provides an understanding of what to expect in the early postpartum period. Perhaps most important for them is to be reassured of the availability of assistance both in the hospital and following discharge. Knowing where and how they can obtain help improves the chances that they will be successful. Helping the mother choose a knowledgeable and supportive pediatrician on whom she can rely for advice once the baby is born is essential.

A consistent perinatal message should aim to

1. Educate to empower choice
2. Dispel myths—know and teach facts, not attitudes or opinions
3. Assume that she will breastfeed
4. Use no formula company literature or giveaways
5. Provide consistent support and correct information

During the early prenatal contact, a thorough breast and nipple examination should be done. Ascertaining pregnancy-related breast changes can be done through exam and discussion.[9] Prior breast surgeries need not prevent most women from breastfeeding. Flat or inverted nipples should be noted, and referral to a lactation consultant for appropriate intervention during the prenatal period could be important in preventing or reducing latch-on difficulties. Most women need to be reassured that their breasts and nipples are normal and adequate for successful breastfeeding. Nipple and breast conditioning exercises are neither necessary nor recommended. It is always appropriate to discuss Breast Self-Exam (BSE) and the need to continue this during pregnancy and lactation.

Consideration of breastfeeding while taking a complete medical history promotes discussion of potential or existing health problems or behaviors that may affect breastfeeding. Very few medical contraindications to breastfeeding exist. In the United States, women who are HIV+ are advised not to breastfeed.[17] Some other infections that make breastfeeding contraindicated are active herpes in the breast area, active cytomegalovirus, and active TB when the mother is still infectious. If the mother is positive for hepatitis B virus surface antigen (HbsAg), the infant must receive hepatitis B virus immune globulin and vaccine.

Extensive information regarding drug transmission through breast milk is readily available from up-to-date reliable sources.[5,10] Most medications do not pose a risk through breastfeeding, but it is always wise to check. An informed health care provider should discuss safe drug use with the breastfeeding mother and be reassured that she will not take any medications without first consulting him or her.

Hospital Practices and Initiation of Breastfeeding

Practices that promote the early initiation of breastfeeding, continued frequent nursing, nonrestrictive policies allowing mothers and babies to remain together, breastfeeding education and

assistance during the early postpartum period, and postdischarge follow-up services are all essential components of a comprehensive breastfeeding program. Many hospital maternity services now employ lactation consultants, most of them registered nurses who are certified (I.B.C.L.C.) by the International Board of Lactation Consultant Examiners, and who are experts in lactation management. These health care professionals offer education and support to staff as well as to breastfeeding families, and are important members of the perinatal health care team.

Breastfeeding should be initiated as soon as possible after delivery of the well newborn, whether the birth is vaginal or by cesarean section.[1,20,21] During the first hour after birth, the neonate is usually in an awake and alert state, often searching for something on which to suck. Separation of mother and baby at this time should be avoided whenever possible. Encouraging the new mother to initiate breastfeeding soon after delivery is important, as is providing her with some basic positioning assistance. She should be prepared prenatally to expect to breastfeed shortly after delivery and to continue frequent feedings.

The baby who begins breastfeeding within the first hour after birth is likely to continue to breastfeed without difficulty from then on, and to breastfeed longer in months.[22] Though not every newborn will immediately latch on to the breast, most will do so more easily at that time. The benefits to mother and baby are significant: more rapid uterine involution for the mother, and the provision of antibody-rich colostrum to enhance the infant's immune system. The close contact is comforting to the newborn, and enhances attachment for both mother and child. The support person can be enlisted to help hold the baby to the breast and taught to watch for the infant's swallowing once the milk ejection has occurred at that first feed.

Restrictions are no longer part of current breastfeeding standards of practice.[1] Mothers are encouraged to breastfeed their infant frequently from the beginning, and to respond to the infant's feeding readiness cues before the infant is stressed by hunger. These cues may be moving of extremities, hands to mouth, increased alertness, and movements in an otherwise quiet and undemanding baby. It is neither necessary nor advisable to wait for the baby to cry to begin the feeding.

Mothers are encouraged to breastfeed every 2 to 3 hours or on demand, whichever comes first, during the first weeks. Most newborns do not necessarily "demand" appropriately. The parents can be taught how to rouse the infant to breastfeed until the infant begins to respond to its hunger cues, to demand to feed 8 to 12 times in 24 h. Parents must know that breastfeeding a newborn only every 4 hours or on a limiting schedule may not provide enough milk for the baby's growth.

Part of the assistance that the new breastfeeding mother should receive in the hospital includes teaching her to:

- Assume comfortable positions that will minimize nipple trauma and permit optimal milk transfer to her infant.
- Observe the nursing baby for nonnutritive and nutritive sucking. It is essential that she be able to identify that the breastfeeding infant is in fact sucking and swallowing. This will not tell her how much the baby is getting, but it will reassure her that she is producing colostrum or milk and that the baby is effective in obtaining it. In time, the swallowing becomes audible as the volume of milk increases.
- Breastfeed her infant frequently and without restrictions. Babies vary in efficiency in obtaining the milk, and mothers vary in speed of milk let-down. The mother will fairly quickly determine how long her baby needs to be sucking for the infant to obtain an adequate feeding. She should allow the baby to remain on the breast as long as the baby continues to swallow, and not for an arbitrarily prescribed number of minutes.
- Wake her infant for feedings during the first week if the baby does not "demand"

to feed adequately. Once the baby has regained its birthweight and appears to be thriving, she can rely more on her baby's demand.
- Avoid any supplementation with formula or water. If she is confident that her baby is swallowing, and she is willing to feed the baby frequently, there is no reason for routine use of bottles. The mother who breastfeeds frequently during her hospital stay is better equipped with the knowledge and strategies needed to continue to breastfeed when she is discharged home. Early introduction of bottles can lead to nipple confusion on the baby's part and to the baby's preferring the quick, easy flow from the bottle. If supplementation must occur, attempts should be made to obtain the mother's expressed milk to feed her baby.
- Know her resources for postdischarge support. She can be provided with concise written information that will enhance what she has been taught, and will guide her to access help once she is home. Again, including her support person in her teaching greatly encourages continued participation and the reassurance that she will need once she is home. Early contact with her pediatrician should be planned.
- Be confident in her body's ability to continue to nurture her baby through her breastfeeding. The new mother is very vulnerable to everyone's advice and questioning. Praise and reassurance by a caring and knowledgeable health care provider can make the difference in her succeeding.
- Be reassured that once breastfeeding is established with her body and with the baby, she will be able to offer the baby supplements of expressed breast milk. The increasing number of new mothers returning to work during the first few months mandates their being taught how to combine breastfeeding while home with feeding expressed breast milk by the caregiver when the mother is away. Efficient double electric breast pumps allow many mothers to continue to breast milk feed for many months, even when employed outside the home.

- Be knowledgeable about how to assess her infant's adequate intake during the first few days at home. On average, her milk supply will increase between days 3 and 7 postdelivery. During that time, for 2 to 3 days, her breasts may become heavier, warmer, fuller, engorged, and may possibly leak milk. If the baby is an efficient nurser, her breasts should feel softer after a feeding, and the infant should be seen and heard gulping milk and be content after a feeding. The baby's output should increase during this time, so that, from 1 to 2 days after her milk has come in, her baby should have 6 to 8 wet diapers, and at least 4 stools per 24 h during the first few weeks. Frequent wet and soiled diapers are signs of an adequately fed infant. The parents should be instructed regarding reasonable amounts to expect, and to contact the pediatrician if the baby is not having sufficient urinary output or bowel movements.

Breastfeeding Challenges

Though breastfeeding can be easily established, pain free, and without difficulty for most mothers and babies, some mothers will experience some challenge to continuing to breastfeed in the early days postpartum, either while in the hospital or after discharge home. Prompt identification and quick, effective treatment of difficulties encountered could intercept certain events that lead to early weaning. The most common problems, with strategies to assure trouble-free exclusive breastfeeding and to prevent premature weaning, are discussed below. It is very important to reassure the new mother that breastfeeding difficulties, if they do occur, are temporary, and that before long breastfeeding her infant will be a pleasant and fulfilling experience.

Proper Latch On

Most women sustain some degree of nipple trauma in the early breastfeeding period. It was once thought that limiting the infant's sucking time at the breast would prevent nipple irritation. However, it is not the length of time that the baby is at the breast that causes nipple soreness. Rather, it is how the baby's mouth is positioned on the breast that leads to skin breakdown. Teaching the mother how to properly place the baby on the breast from the very beginning is essential to the prevention of nipple trauma.

For proper and nontraumatic latch on, the baby's rooting reflex should be stimulated (at the center of the lower lip) to elicit a wide open mouth. When this occurs, the mother should be taught to quickly place the baby's open mouth onto her breast tissue well beyond the nipple. She can be reminded that the baby is to "breast" feed, and not to "nipple" feed. She should bring the baby to the breast, and not try to get her breast into the baby's mouth. This approach more effectively assures correct placement of the infant on the areolar tissue of her breast, and not only on the nipple tip. Proper latch on is also important to assure efficient transfer of milk. If the baby is only nipple feeding, it will cause undue nipple soreness and reduced milk transfer.

When a new mother reports nipple tenderness that persists beyond the first minute of latch on, it is essential that her technique be examined and incorrect positioning be immediately corrected. Nipple skin breakdown is painful and unnecessary in most instances, and should be prevented.

Strategies that help a new mother breastfeed pain-free include assuring her comfort by providing her with pillows and supports for her back, arms, and legs. She should be taught to pick up and hold her breast so that her nipple is centered on the baby's tongue. She should turn the infant's body in toward her, removing excessive blankets and clothing between them.

Correcting the infant's improper attachment to the breast allows the mother to continue to breastfeed while assuring the prevention of further nipple breakdown. Her discomfort should diminish day by day. Continued excessive nipple pain must be evaluated by an expert in lactation management. There is no substitute for direct observation of a breastfeeding.

Comfort measures that have been reported to decrease the mother's nipple discomfort include applying colostrum or breast milk to her nipples and warm compresses or wet tea bags. Recently the use of purified, hypoallergenic lanolin cream has resulted in quicker healing and more comfortable breastfeeding for many mothers. Care must be taken to recommend only products that contain a minimum number of ingredients, and these must be pure and safe for breastfeeding infants.

Engorgement

Frequent and efficient breastfeeding does much to prevent the extreme discomfort of engorgement that commonly occurs between the third and seventh days postpartum. During the 2 to 3 days of increased lactogenesis, edema in the breast tissue plus full milk ducts can lead to excessive congestion and pain in the breasts. Often during this time, the nipples become cracked and bleed due to the infant's inability to completely attach to the areolar tissue.

An engorged breast must be relieved; it is considered a lactation emergency. Diligent attention to frequently relieving the breast fullness is imperative. Using wet heat around the breast, such as warm showers or compresses, helps to relieve some of the swelling and allows an easier milk flow. Cold compresses may be more effective in some instances; if the woman finds that the heat does not relieve the congestion, she should try cold.

If the infant is unable to attach to the severely engorged breast, the use of a piston-type electric breast pump is recommended to begin the flow of milk and relieve areolar engorgement. The infant can then properly attach to the breast to continue the release of breast milk. If areolar engorgement is not reduced, the baby is more likely to attach only to the nipple and cause uncomfortable breakdown. Frequent nursing or pumping of the breast at this time is mandatory to assure continued adequate milk production

and minimal breast and nipple trauma. Mothers often use the abundance of engorement as an opportunity to initiate breast milk collection and storage for future use. It is not advisable to feed the infant via bottles during the engorgement period. The mother needs the infant to breastfeed as often as possible.

Once the breast fullness disappears, mothers often worry that they have "lost" their milk. They should be reassured that the swelling has subsided and that their milk will continue to be produced as long as there is stimulation and breast milk removal. A basic principle that helps them understand the process is that breast milk production is dependent on breast milk removal.

Mastitis

Mastitis differs from engorgement in that it is usually unilateral and is an inflammatory process involving breast tissue. The treatment for early, very mild, noninfectious mastitis is simply heat, rest, and emptying of the breast. Frequent removal of milk from the affected breast often prevents further symptoms.

When there is an infection, the mother may have flu-like symptoms including fever; a hot, hard, and inflamed area on the breast; and malaise. She must be treated quickly with an appropriate broad-spectrum antibiotic; she can continue to breastfeed while taking antibiotics. Prevention of a breast abscess is paramount. Again, she must be diligent to effect frequent milk transfer, especially from the affected breast.

Once a woman has suffered a bout of mastitis, she is more likely to suffer a repeat bout during the current breastfeeding experience. She can be taught to prevent future episodes by becoming alert to any potential nonemptying of milk ducts, and intervening quickly.

Insufficient Milk

Insufficient milk production is the most common reason given by women who prematurely discontinue breastfeeding. Though one must always be alert to anatomic or physiologic conditions that could prevent a woman from actually making enough milk for her baby, almost all women are capable of supplying all the milk that their baby needs for optimal growth and development.

Conditions that can affect a woman's milk-producing capability include immature breast development, removal of milk-producing tissue through surgical breast reduction, or breast surgery that severed the lactiferous sinuses and/or the fourth intercostal nerve. Excessive maternal smoking and/or alcohol consumption can also have a negative effect on her milk supply.

True insufficient milk production does not require that the mother discontinue breastfeeding. She can continue breastfeeding while providing whatever supplement the infant requires for adequate weight gain. Supplementation can be done through the use of a cup, or a supplementer nutrition system, which is worn around her neck with a feeding tube taped to her areola along her nipple. The supplement is delivered to the infant via the feeding tube when the infant sucks at the breast. She may also feed the infant the supplement through a baby bottle. The risk with that approach is that the infant may quickly become accustomed to the rapid and easy flow from the bottle and then refuse to feed at the breast. The mother must be informed of that risk.

Perceived Insufficiency

Most often, the insufficient milk production is perceived to be so by the mother rather than real. Infrequent breastfeeding is a most common but preventable cause of insufficient milk supply. The mother must know that it is normal, and often necessary, to breastfeed her newborn at least 8 to 12 times per 24 h. If she expects to breastfeed only every 4 h, she will conclude that she is not making enough milk to get the baby to feed only every 4 h. Giving supplemental bottles at the beginning may interfere with her body's ability to make all the milk the baby needs. Wherever possible, it is best to delay the introduction of supplemental bottles beyond the first

few weeks. It is best also to feed the baby only expressed breast milk in the bottle, once it is introduced.

An infant who breastfeeds ineffectively can also lead to the mother producing an insufficient milk supply. If the baby is extracting a minimal amount of milk from her breast, the mother's supply will quickly be reduced. Observation of the breastfeeding by an experienced health care professional is necessary to determine the cause of low supply so that appropriate efforts can then begin to improve the breastfeeding, increase the mother's milk, and assure adequate weight gain in the infant.

Frequent Feedings

It is helpful to reassure the new mother during the first few weeks that extreme breastfeeding frequency will subside. As time goes on, she will find that her thriving infant will eventually require fewer feeds and begin to have longer sleep periods at night. The newborn benefits greatly from the extra holding and stimulation that accompanies frequent breastfeeding.

Encouraging the new mother to get some sleep whenever the baby naps helps her to make it through the first few weeks. The efficiency of milk production and transfer increases as the weeks pass by, and eventually the baby takes all it needs in a shorter breastfeeding episode. Reassuring her that breastfeeding will not always be as time-consuming helps the mother get through the intense first few weeks. Enlisting the aid of the father and other family members to help with household tasks and to hold the baby gives her an opportunity to get some rest.

Mother's Diet

Although a mother's balanced nutritional intake is vital to her well-being, occasional lapses in proper eating should not affect the nutritional quality of her breast milk. She would have to be malnourished for her milk to become inadequate for her baby.[14] There are very few restrictions on the diet of a breastfeeding woman. Occasionally, the mother may discover that her baby is sensitive to a particular food she eats, and eliminating that food for the interim should keep the infant more comfortable. A diet based on the USDA pyramid, including a variety of foods, textures, flavors, and colors, and consistent with the cultural eating habits of the new mother, is recommended. Encouraging her to continue to take prenatal vitamin supplements and to drink sufficient liquids, especially water, is also important. Of course, the breastfeeding mother must not be using harmful drugs, and should avoid alcohol and tobacco use.

Postdischarge Support and Resources

In this day of short maternity stays, it is essential to have a system of postdischarge breastfeeding support in place. Many hospital lactation programs provide these services through phone consults, return outpatient visits, home care programs, and breastfeeding mothers' support groups. Availability of local skilled follow-up resources should be discussed with new parents prior to their discharge from the hospital. Volunteer breastfeeding organizations (e.g., La Leche League) and local W.I.C. clinics are in place in many areas and are a good source of breastfeeding education and support. Home care services are also a referral option for breastfeeding mothers. Open and frequent communication with the pediatrician should always be encouraged. Collaboration among the health care professionals provides the greatest degree of education and support for the new family.

Working Mothers

A growing number of new mothers return to their employment or school within several weeks of the infant's birth. Though some will choose to discontinue breastfeeding at that time, all should be encouraged to maintain whatever breastfeeding they can for as long as possible. Even continuing the early morning and evening breastfeedings is extremely beneficial to both infant and mother.

The widespread availability of efficient electric breast pumps has allowed more women to prolong breast milk feeding during the recommended first year. Many women pump their breasts at their work or school to maintain their milk supply.

It is not easy for a mother to be separated from her infant and to continue to breastfeed, but many women do so, and do so well. Some women pump their breasts at work or school and bring the expressed breast milk home for the caregiver to feed the infant the next workday. Some women pump ahead and fill their freezer during their maternity leave—this is especially effective in providing them with extra breast milk for those times when their work schedule prevents them from pumping as much as they should. It also makes them familiar with and comfortable in using their breast pump.

There are many safe, effective, and efficient breast pumps available. The ideal pump should not cause any nipple or breast trauma while effecting quick removal of milk from the breast. And though the breast pump market has grown in recent years, there are still widely available pumps that cause nipple cracking and bleeding or do not effectively remove breast milk. Caution should be exercised in recommending pumps.

Women who pump frequently do best with electric piston-type breast pumps that use intermittent suction and exert similar pressure and frequency as a breastfeeding baby. The most efficient pumps allow women to express milk from both breasts at one time, thereby decreasing pumping time and increasing their milk yield. Generally, battery-operated breast pumps are not a good choice because of their limitations in speed and pressure. A mother should obtain a pump in consultation with a knowledgeable health care provider. Obtaining a breast pump from a toy or baby store is not the best strategy to assure proper fit and appropriate selection. Many hospital lactation programs and private lactation consultants sell and rent breast pumps.

Collection and Storage of Breast Milk

Breast milk can be stored in a refrigerator for 3 to 5 days, and can be frozen for 3 to 5 months. It is preferable to obtain and store expressed milk in a hard plastic container. It is not recommended to use plastic bags as containers for expressed breast milk.

Breast milk collection is also important for the mother of a preterm or ill infant who is unable to breastfeed. The mother should pump eight times per 24 h to establish and maintain a milk supply until the infant is mature or well enough to feed directly. Her breast milk will be valuable to the compromised infant.

The mother of a well, efficiently breastfeeding baby should be encouraged to breastfeed rather than to pump whenever possible. The baby is truly the most effective "pump." The mother can begin collection for storage by pumping any residual milk or if the infant skips a feeding on a breast. Pumping in the beginning is not to be considered a true determinant of what she is actually producing. Some mothers have found that pumping the second breast while the baby is feeding on the first is an effective way to quickly obtain a collection. Mothers need to be reassured that their removing their breast milk will lead to their producing more milk.

References and Selected Readings

1. American Academy of Pediatrics Work Group on Breastfeeding: Breastfeeding and the use of human milk. *Pediatrics* 100:1035–1039, 1997.
2. American Academy of Pediatrics: Practice parameter. Management of hyperbilirubinemia in the healthy term newborn. *Pediatrics* 94:558–565, 1994.
3. Auerbach KG, Riordan J. Breastfeeding and Human Lactation, 2nd ed. Boston: Jones & Bartlett, 1998.
4. Beaudry M, Dufour R, Marcoux S: Relation between infant feeding and infections during the first six months of life. *Pediatr* 126:191–197, 1995.
5. Briggs GG, Freeman RK, Yaffe SJ: Drugs in Pregnancy and Lactation. 5th ed. Baltimore: Williams & Wilkins, 1998.
6. Cunningham ASA, Jelliffe DB, Jelliffe EFP: Breast-feeding and health in the 1980s: A global epidemiologic review. *Pediatr* 118:659–665, 1991.
7. Dewey KG, Heinig MJ, Nommsen-Rivers LA: Differences in morbidity between breast-fed and formula-fed infants. *J Pediatr* 126:696–702, 1995.
8. Duncan B, Ey J, Holberg CJ, Wright AL, Martinez FD, Taussig LM: Exclusive breast-feeding for at least four months protects against otitis media. *Pediatrics* 91:867–872, 1993.
9. Gartner LM, Newton ER: Breast-feeding: Role of the obstetrician. *ACOG Clin Rev* 3:1–2, 14–15, 1998.
10. Hale T: *Medications and Mothers' Milk* 7th ed. Amarillo, TX: Pharmasoft, 1998.
11. Healthy People 2000: *National Health Promotion and Disease Prevention Objectives*. Washington, DC: Government Printing Office, pp 379–380, 1990.
12. Howard CR, Schaeffer SJ, Lawrence RA: Attitudes, practices and recommendations by obstetricians about infant feeding. Birth 24:240–246, 1997.
13. Humenick SS, Hill PD, Wilhelm S: Postnatal factors encouraging sustained breast-feeding among primiparas and multiparas. *Perinatal* 6:33–45, 1997.
14. Institute of Medicine: National Academy of Sciences: Nutrition during lactation. Washington, DC: National Academy Press, 1991.
15. Lawrence RA: The clinician's role in teaching proper infant feeding techniques. *J Pediatr* 126:S112–S117, 1995.
16. Lawrence RA, Lawrence RM: Breastfeeding: A guide for the medical profession. 6th ed. St. Louis: CV Mosby, 1999.
17. Montgomery D, Splett P: Economic benefit of breast-feeding infants enrolled in WIC. *J Am Diet Assoc* 97:379–385, 1997.
18. Naylor AJ, Creer AE, Woodward-Lopez G, Dixon S: Lactation management education for physicians. *Semin Perinatol* 18:525–531, 1994.
19. Neifert M: Early assessment of the breast-feeding infant. *Contemp Pediatr* 13:142–166, 1996.
20. Righard L, Alade MO: Effect of delivery room routines on success of first breast-feed. *Lancet* 336:1105–1107, 1990.
21. Stuart-Macadam P, Dettwyler KA: eds. Breast-feeding: Biocultural Perspectives. New York: Aldine de Gruyter, 1995.
22. Taylor PM, Maloni JA, Brown DR: Early suckling and prolonged breast-feeding. *Am J Dis Child* 140:151–154, 1986.
23. Wang YS, Wu SY: The effect of exclusive breast-feeding on development and incidence of infection in infants. *J Hum Lact* 12:27–30, 1996.
24. Wright AL, Bauer M, Naylor A, Sutcliffe E, Clark L: Increasing breast-feeding rates to reduce infant illness at the community level. *Pediatr* 101:837–844, 1998.

CHAPTER 34

Disorders of the Ovary and Fallopian Tube

David Chelmow
Kris Strohbehn
Alan H. DeCherney

ANATOMY AND PHYSIOLOGY

PHYSIOLOGIC OVARIAN DISORDERS

DIFFERENTIAL DIAGNOSIS OF THE ADNEXAL MASS

WOMEN OF REPRODUCTIVE AGE: THE PHYSIOLOGIC CYST

Small Ovarian Cysts in Postmenopausal Women • The Palpable Mass in the Menopausal Woman • The Scan-detected Mass

BENIGN OVARIAN NEOPLASMS

Benign Cystic Teratoma (Dermoid Cyst) • Cystadenomas • Solid Benign Tumors • Endometriomas

BENIGN DISORDERS OF THE FALLOPIAN TUBE

DISORDERS OF TUBAL TRANSPORT

PARATUBAL CYSTS

ECTOPIC PREGNANCY

TUBO-OVARIAN ABSCESS

HYDROSALPINX

Disorders of the ovary and fallopian tube can cause significant problems in prepubertal, reproductive-age, and postmenopausal women. Many of these disorders can be managed by the primary care provider. All can be *detected* by the primary care provider, and attention should be focused during the routine history and physical exam on screening for these problems so that appropriate management or referral can be initiated. The range of possible disorders spans physiologic, infectious, anatomic, and neoplastic.

Anatomy and Physiology

The ovaries lie in the pelvis, usually immediately lateral and posterior to the fundus of the uterus. Their size varies with the stage of the woman's life. In a woman of reproductive age, ovaries each measure approximately 1.5 by 2.5 by 4.0 cm; postmenopausal ovaries measure approximately 2.0 by 2.0 by 1.0 cm. Premenopausal ovaries are frequently palpable on bimanual pelvic examination, while normal postmenopausal ovaries are seldom palpable. The ovaries are mobile, suspended from the uterus by the uteroovarian ligaments, and from the pelvic sidewall by the infundibulopelvic ligaments. These two ligaments are fibrovascular bundles that contain the vascular supply to the ovaries. Occasionally, an ovary can twist on this vascular pedicle, leading to ovarian torsion, an acute emergency.

Approximately every 28 days in the reproductive-age woman, the ovary develops a single, dominant follicle containing an ovum, and releases it into the peritoneal cavity. The follicle is picked up by the fimbriated end of the tube and passed down the tube to the endometrial cavity.

This process of ovulation is the result of a complex combination of hypothalamic, pituitary, and ovarian interactions.

Prior to ovulation, the main steroid produced by the ovary is estradiol. Estradiol, along with two pituitary hormones, luteinizing hormone (LH) and follicle-stimulating hormone (FSH), stimulates a single follicle to grow, frequently to several centimeters in diameter. In response to a surge of LH in combination with several other factors, the follicle ruptures, releasing the ovum. For the next 14 days, the cells that originally formed the follicular cyst become a corpus luteum cyst and begin producing large amounts of a second ovarian hormone, progesterone. If the egg is not fertilized, the corpus luteum stops producing progesterone, the corpus luteum cyst involutes, and the woman menstruates 14 days after ovulation. As intermediates in ovarian steroid production, androgens, including testosterone, are made. Ovulation usually begins around age 13, and continues, on average, until age 51, when the woman undergoes menopause. After menopause, the ovary no longer produces significant amounts of estrogen or progesterone.

The fallopian tube, a 7- to 10-cm long tubular structure, emerges from the uterine cornua bilaterally. The distal end has frondlike, delicate fimbria, which help guide the ovum into the tube after it is released from the follicular cyst. Fertilization of the ova by sperm occurs in the tube approximately two days after ovulation. The ovum slowly travels down the tube until it reaches the uterus, approximately seven days after ovulation. Unlike the ovary, the tube is not hormonally active. Its main purpose is to facilitate egg transport and fertilization.

Physiologic Ovarian Disorders

During the reproductive years, either ovary produces an egg monthly, as well as cyclic production of estrogen, progesterone, and androgen. Most physiologic disorders are manifested by irregular or absent ovulation. In a reproductive-age woman, chronic anovulation usually presents as irregular or absent vaginal bleeding, mild hirsutism, and infertility. These patients are frequently obese. Characteristically, they have ovaries with many small follicular cysts visible on ultrasound, which has led to this syndrome being called polycystic ovarian syndrome (PCO), formerly known as Stein-Leventhal syndrome. This naming has somewhat confused understanding of this syndrome, as it implies that the ovary is the source of the problem. Actually, the polycystic ovary is the result of chronic disruption of androgen metabolism, and is not necessarily the cause. Recently, it has become clear that insulin resistance is also a frequent part of the syndrome. PCO patients usually present with a long history of irregular, infrequent menses, often since menarche. Their initial complaint frequently relates to the mild androgenization, especially hair growth and acne, that often accompanies the syndrome. True virilization, with temporal hair loss, voice change, and clitoromegaly is not consistent with this syndrome and requires further evaluation. Their physical exam is frequently normal except for having a weight in excess of their ideal body weight, oily skin, and increased body hair growth.

Patients fitting this description do not need an extensive work-up. The evaluation of any reproductive-age woman with irregular bleeding or amenorrhea does require a pregnancy test. PCO patients can ovulate, albeit infrequently; because many do not believe that they can become pregnant, they often do not use contraception and can present with an unexpected pregnancy. Prolactin and TSH should be checked in the oligomenorrheic and amenorrheic woman to eliminate a pituitary adenoma as a possible cause. The main concern in providing care for these patients is the protection of the endometrium from the effects of unopposed estrogen. These patients frequently develop endometrial hyperplasia and are at much higher risk for the eventual development of endometrial cancer. If the patient has had more than a year of anovulation, office endometrial biopsy should be performed to evaluate for hyperplasia or cancer. The patient with anovulation and normal endometrial pathology should be cycled with monthly progesterone. This is frequently done by administering medroxyprogesterone (Provera) 10 mg daily the first 10 to 14 days of the month. Contraception counseling should be done as well. In the patient who also needs contraception, oral contraceptive pills or depot medroxyprogesterone (DepoProvera) provides a combined solution. Oral contraceptives also suppress ovarian androgen production and frequently improve the patient's hirsutism, although usually a prolonged period of time (greater than 6 months) is necessary before improvement is noted. Patients desiring pregnancy should be referred to a gynecologist, as they will frequently need ovulation induction to become pregnant.

At around age 40, ovulation becomes less frequent, and less estrogen is produced by the ovary. Eventually ovulation ceases, with most women having their last menses between ages 48 and 55. This time period is the menopause, and is manifested by hypoestrogenic symptoms including hot flashes, vaginal dryness, sleep disturbances, and mood changes. It is a physiological process and is addressed in Chap. 43. Menopause is only considered pathologic if it occurs prior to age 40, when it is termed "premature ovarian failure." There are a number of causes of premature ovarian failure, including gonadal dysgenesis, especially Turner's syndrome, chemotherapy, and radiation therapy. Some autoimmune disorders including hypoparathyroidism, rheumatoid arthritis, thyroiditis, and myasthenia gravis have also been implicated, with antiovarian antibodies noted in some cases. The evaluation of a patient with suspected premature ovarian failure should include FSH measurement to confirm an ovarian rather than central cause, and if the FSH is elevated to postmenopausal levels, a karyotype and screening for autoimmune disease (Table 34-1).

Differential Diagnosis of the Adnexal Mass

Ovarian enlargement can be abnormal at any age, and if found, always requires further evalua-

TABLE 34-1 Laboratory Evaluation of Premature Ovarian Failure

Karyotype
Calcium
Phosphorus
AM cortisol
TSH
Free T_4
Rheumatoid factor
Antinuclear antibody

SOURCE: Adapted from Speroff and coworkers, 1994.[4]

tion. Ovarian cancer, which has a 1.5 percent cumulative lifetime risk has recently received a large amount of media attention and is of concern to many women. The ovaries, with their deep intraabdominal location, pose great diagnostic difficulties. Benign and malignant diseases can result in ovarian enlargement, and their location makes thorough evaluation difficult.

The routine physical examination of all women should include a pelvic examination once the woman has turned 18 or becomes sexually active. This examination should include careful bimanual palpation of the uterus and ovaries. Rectovaginal examination is frequently necessary to palpate ovaries, and frequently normal-sized ovaries cannot be palpated even by careful examination. Although a number of methods, including ultrasound and tumor markers, have been studied as potential screening tools for ovarian cancer, none have been shown to be cost-effective. In particular, Ca-125 has received tremendous attention in the lay press, but it is not effective as a routine screening tool, and should not be used as such. Physical examination is frequently the only way in which asymptomatic ovarian masses and cancers are identified.

The presence of a pelvic mass does not ensure that the mass is gynecologic in origin. The pelvis contains gastrointestinal and genitourinary organs, which can cause masses that may be difficult to differentiate from ovarian masses. Table 34-2 lists a number of nongynecologic sources of

TABLE 34-2 Pelvis Masses from Sites Other Than the Ovary or Fallopian Tube

Nongynecologic	Gynecologic
Colon cancer	Uterine leiomyoma
Diverticulitis	Uterine sarcoma
Diverticular abscess	Adenomyosis
Appendiceal abscess	Cervical cancer
Distended bladder	Vaginal cancer
Bladder cancer	Pyometra
Mesenteric cysts	Hematocolpos
Metastatic cancer	Uterine anomaly
Omental cysts	Pregnancy
Pelvic kidney	
Stool	
Retroperitoneal tumor	

pelvic masses. Patients should be examined after emptying their bladder. In addition to making the exam more uncomfortable and the anatomy more difficult to discern, a distended bladder can mimic a pelvic mass. Chronically obstipated patients, particularly those taking methadone or other narcotics, can have a stool-filled sigmoid that can mimic a pelvic mass. In these patients, a rectovaginal exam is particularly important. Repeating the exam in several days or after an enema can also eliminate confusion.

Many patients are difficult to examine either because of obesity or discomfort during the exam. If the patient is asymptomatic, it is probably not cost-effective to perform ultrasound to visualize the ovaries. If the patient has pelvic symptoms and an adequate pelvic exam cannot be performed, or a mass is suggested on physical exam, a pelvic ultrasound is usually performed to evaluate the pelvic anatomy. Although CT scans are frequently performed, they are considerably more expensive and often do not visualize the adnexa as well as ultrasound.

A number of symptoms suggest the presence of a pelvic mass. Unfortunately, many masses including cancers can be asymptomatic, which emphasizes the importance of a pelvic exam-

ination as a routine part of the woman's physical exam. Women who have ovarian cancer often present with feelings of pelvic pressure, bloating, dull pelvic pain, or bladder pressure. In most instances, pain begins gradually and progressively increases. In unusual instances, patients can present with extremely large abdominal masses that originated in the pelvis. Advanced pelvic masses can present with increased abdominal girth, masses that are palpable even to the patient, or obstructed bowel or ureter.

Although most symptoms related to ovarian masses are chronic, there are two important instances where acute events can happen that can present as surgical abdomens. The first is adnexal torsion. Torsion occurs when an ovarian mass rotates on its pedicle, the infundibulopelvic ligament. The fallopian tube can also torse, either with the ovary or separately. This rotation occludes the blood supply to the ovary and can lead to infarction. Commonly, bleeding occurs into the cyst and ovary, and can cause substantial blood loss.

Torsion can occur at any age, and is more common during pregnancy. It seldom occurs spontaneously, and usually requires the presence of a preexisting adnexal mass to incite the torsion. Torsion presents as the sudden onset of severe abdominal pain, often with low-grade fever, nausea, and vomiting. Physical exam is usually remarkable for an enlarged, exquisitely tender unilateral adnexal mass. These patients may be so uncomfortable that adequate physical examination is impossible. Ultrasound typically shows a complex adnexal mass. Doppler ultrasound may show very reduced to absent blood flow. Torsion is a surgical emergency and requires immediate laparotomy or laparoscopy. In the reproductive-age woman, conservative surgery is possible, with reduction of the torsion and cystectomy of any ovarian abnormality. If the ovary is clearly infarcted, it is removed. After the reproductive years, torsion is usually treated by salpingoophorectomy.

The second ovarian condition that can appear

as a surgical emergency is cyst rupture. Any non-solid adnexal mass has the potential to rupture and release its contents into the peritoneal cavity. In some instances, particularly with dermoid cysts (benign cystic teratomas), the contents can be very irritating and can cause a severe chemical peritonitis. Most cyst ruptures occur in reproductive-age women, and are usually related to the midcyle rupture of follicular cysts.

Patients with cyst rupture often describe the sudden onset of severe abdominal pain, frequently beginning in a single location and gradually spreading. Low-grade fever is very common. Physical examination can be remarkable for signs of peritoneal irritation, adnexal tenderness on pelvic exam, and cervical motion tenderness. Laboratory analysis can show a mild elevation of the white blood cell count without a left shift. Differential diagnosis depends on the patient's age and can be quite broad, including appendicitis, torsion, ectopic pregnancy, pyelonephritis, or gastroenteritis. Ultrasound can be helpful, revealing an adnexal mass or free fluid in the cul-de-sac. Culdocentesis, the transvaginal aspiration of fluid from the pouch of Douglas, can also be extremely helpful, usually yielding serous or serosanguinous fluid in cases of cyst rupture.

Most cyst ruptures can be managed with pain control until the irritating fluid has been resorbed through the peritoneum. Laparoscopy is usually diagnostic if noninvasive methods are inconclusive; it is absolutely required when the patient's condition and differential diagnosis demand an immediate answer. Some cysts, especially corpus luteum cysts, can hemorrhage. This occurs most frequently in patients who are pregnant or who are receiving anticoagulants. Hemorrhagic cysts are often found during a surgical procedure to rule out ectopic pregnancy. If a hemorrhaging corpus luteum is suspected and intrauterine pregnancy is confirmed by ultrasound, the situation can often be managed by following serial hematocrits and observation, with surgical intervention reserved for the small subset of patients with a persistently falling hematocrit.

Women of Reproductive Age: The Physiologic Cyst

Among reproductive-age women, the overwhelming majority of ovarian cysts are physiologic in nature, related to the normally occurring cysts of the menstrual cycle. During the early part of the menstrual cycle, a single dominant follicle is selected and progressively grows. Under normal circumstances, this cyst grows to 1 to 2 cm in diameter and ruptures approximately 14 days prior to the onset of menses, releasing an egg into the peritoneal cavity. Many women are aware of this happening, and report monthly midcycle mild unilateral discomfort as the follicular cyst expands and ruptures, a phenomenon known as "mittelschmerz."

As mentioned previously, follicular cyst rupture can cause sudden, severe pain. The patient with suspected follicular cyst rupture can be managed conservatively, provided she is hemodynamically stable. Pain control can usually be achieved with oral analgesics. The pain from cyst rupture usually resolves over the course of 48 h. The stable patient with the presumed diagnosis of follicular cyst rupture should be reexamined 48 h after the initial event, assuming that nothing has occurred to prompt earlier evaluation or intervention. If by this time the pain is not substantially improved, further evaluation, often with laparoscopy, is warranted. A small subset of patients will have recurrent symptomatic cyst rupture. Use of a monophasic oral contraceptive pill containing 35 μg of ethinyl estradiol suppresses most ovulations and gives these patients relief.

Another frequent problem is that sometimes either a follicular or corpus luteum cyst may persist. In some instances, this will cause discomfort, including dull abdominal pain or pressure. More frequently, a cyst or mass is noted on routine examination or as an incidental finding on a pelvic ultrasound done for other reasons. Most of these cysts are physiologic, and a careful workup can differentiate most physiologic cysts from nonphysiologic cysts without invasive or expensive testing.

Physiologic cysts have a characteristic appearance on physical examination that usually sets them apart from nonphysiologic cysts (Table 34-3). When a cyst is present on physical examination, a pelvic ultrasound will often be obtained. This is particularly important when physical examination has any component which suggests that the mass may not be physiologic. Common ultrasonic findings more likely characteristic of benign or malignant ovarian cysts are listed in Table 34-4.

Cysts that can be easily palpated on pelvic exam and meet the criteria described in Table 34-3 do not require immediate ultrasound examination. As these cysts are thought to be physiologic, and related to the menstrual cycle, they can be managed by observation. Most of these cysts will spontaneously resolve over the next one or two menstrual cycles. It is a misconception that starting oral contraceptives will "treat" the cyst, or hasten its resolution; however, in patients thought to be frequent cyst formers, oral contraceptives do have a place in preventing the development of new cysts. The new lower-dose oral contraceptives do not reliably suppress all ovulation, and cysts can form in some patients while on these pills. Progestin-only contraceptives, particularly Norplant, may not decrease the incidence of cyst formation. The low levels of progestin do not inhibit follicular recruitment, but do inhibit the midcycle LH surge necessary for ovu-

TABLE 34-3 Physical Examination Characteristics of Physiologic and Nonphysiologic Ovarian Cysts

Physiologic	Nonphysiologic
Discrete	Irregular
Smooth	Multicystic
Simple (single cyst)	>5 cm
≤5-cm Diameter	Solid components
Fluid-filled	Fixed
Mobile	Bilateral
Unilateral	

NOTE: Presence of any single characteristic listed under nonphysiologic makes the mass suspicious for not being physiologic.

TABLE 34-4 Typical Ultrasonic Characteristics of Benign and Suspicious Ovarian Cysts

Benign	Malignant
Simple	Complex
Unilateral	Bilateral
Thin-walled	Thick-walled
Fluid-filled	Solid components
No internal echoes	Internal echoes
Smooth capsule	Papillations
	Excrescensces
	Ascites

lation. Reproductive-age patients with cysts persistent through two menstrual cycles and with ultrasonographically benign appearing cysts need individualized management. Surgical evaluation of these cysts is usually performed, although close follow-up of benign appearing lesions with frequent ultrasounds and pelvic exams can be done, with intervention if growth or change occurs.

Ca-125, a tumor marker, has received much recent attention. Ca-125 levels are elevated in many women who have certain histologic types of ovarian cancer, particularly serous cystadenocarcinomas. Ca-125 is also elevated with endometriosis and several bowel conditions, and varies with the menstrual cycle. Conversely, the test is not very specific and can be normal in many premenopausal women with early ovarian cancer. Given its lack of sensitivity and specificity, Ca-125 is usually not useful in the initial evaluation of premenopausal women with adnexal masses, and often leads to diagnostic confusion. Several other tumor markers are under investigation as screening tests, but none have been found to be reliable because of poor sensitivity and specificity.

Masses that seem to be neoplastic, and particularly those that are suggestive of malignancy, require immediate attention. The first line of treatment for ovarian cancer is surgical. It is also important to note that while high-quality ultrasound evaluation of an ovarian mass is usually accurate in distinguishing benign from malignant lesions, it is not completely diagnostic. There may be a substantial number of ovarian masses which appear benign on ultrasound evaluation but are not.

Small Ovarian Cysts in Postmenopausal Women

By definition, menopausal women do not have menstrual cycles, and therefore do not have physiologic cysts. Nonetheless, wider use of the new imaging modalities has shown that ovarian cysts can be quite common. Some series of transabdominal ultrasound have shown cysts in 2 to 3 percent of postmenopausal women; using the more sensitive endovaginal probe, cysts have been demonstrated in 10 to 15 percent of menopausal women. This is also the age group with the highest incidence of ovarian malignancy. Adnexal masses in this age group are clearly not normal, but neither are they necessarily cancer. Attempting to detect cancer while minimizing surgery on patients with benign lesions remains one of the most challenging problems of gynecology.

The Palpable Mass in the Menopausal Woman

No proven screening modalities for ovarian cancer are available, and current recommendations for average-risk women only include yearly pelvic exams. Unfortunately, annual pelvic exams detect most ovarian cancers at an advanced stage (stage III or IV), resulting in poor five-year survival rates. The ovary normally shrinks after the menopause to approximately 1 by 2 cm. It is rarely palpable on pelvic exam in any but the thinnest, most relaxed patient. Palpable ovaries in women who are more than a few years postmenopausal are often abnormal. Although not necessarily malignant, they do require thorough evaluation. As in premenopausal women, most small adnexal masses are not symptomatic, but others may present as bloating, increased abdominal girth, or pelvic pressure. Many are detected during the evaluation of vague urinary or gastrointestinal symptoms. If a mass is palpated, an ultrasound should be performed. Masses with any of the characteristics of malignancy noted in Table 34-4 need immediate surgical evaluation.

The Scan-Detected Mass

A diagnostic dilemma occurs when small, simple cysts, are identified as incidental findings on ultrasound studies done for other reasons on a postmenopausal woman. Occasionally, these cysts represent early cancers, but most are benign. Close observation is reasonable if the patient is asymptomatic and the cyst's ultrasound appearance is simple, unilateral, thin-walled, and under 5 cm in diameter without internal echoes, solid components, or ascites, and if the Ca-125 is normal. The frequency of observation is usually individualized, but often entails a repeat examination in one month. If no change is detected, ultrasound and pelvic exam can be repeated every 3 months for a year, then every 4 to 6 months for 1 to 2 years. If at any time the cyst grows or changes characteristics, surgical exploration is imperative. Some practitioners also follow Ca-125 levels in these patients. Management of these cysts with laparoscopy is advocated by some, but remains controversial. Surgical excision is warranted in the patient who does not desire or will not comply with close observation.

Benign Ovarian Neoplasms

There are a large number of different benign neoplasms of the ovary (Table 34-5). All are of

TABLE 34-5 Benign Ovarian Masses

Benign cystic teratomas

Physiologic cysts (follicular and corpus luteum cysts)

Cystadenomas

Fibromas

Thecomas

Brenner tumors

Endometriomas

concern for several reasons. First, they can cause symptoms, including pain, pressure, and bloating. Some can grow to be quite large. Second, there is the small chance that they can cause an acute emergency either by rupturing or inciting torsion. Third, they must be differentiated from malignancy.

Benign Cystic Teratoma (Dermoid Cyst)

The most frequently encountered benign ovarian neoplasm is the mature cystic teratoma, also called a dermoid cyst. Excluding physiologic cysts, mature cystic teratomas comprise approximately 10 to 25 percent of all ovarian neoplasms. They are most frequently found in reproductive-age women, but can be found in all age groups from pediatric to postmenopausal. They are often small and asymptomatic, found on routine pelvic examination, or identified because of their characteristic appearance on plain film or ultrasound done for other reasons. Once they reach a 6- to 10-cm size they can cause abdominal pain, pressure, swelling, or a mass detectable by the patient.

Mature cystic teratomas are derived from germ cells. Histologically, they contain mature elements derived from all three embryonic cell types: ectoderm, mesoderm, and endoderm. Ectodermal tissues predominate, and recognizable hair, teeth, cartilage, and bone are frequently found. These structures give a characteristic appearance on x-ray or ultrasound. These cysts are usually surgically removed to prevent torsion or rupture (causing a severe chemical peritonitis). In reproductive-age patients, the dermoid cyst is removed by cystectomy, with preservation of the normal ovarian tissue. Many physicians are managing these cysts with laparoscopic removal. In peri- and postmenopausal women, oophorectomy is performed as there is a small risk of malignant transformation of squamous elements within the cyst.

Cystadenomas

Cystadenomas are the benign counterparts of the epithelial ovarian malignancies. Their histology may be serous or mucinous. The serous tumor usually is uniloculated, whereas mucinous tumors are frequently multiloculated and can grow to be extremely large. Rupture of a benign mucinous cystadenoma can lead to pseudomyxoma peritonei, diffuse intraperitoneal spread of the benign tumor.

Solid Benign Tumors

Fibromas, thecomas, and Brenner tumors are solid benign tumors found in women of all ages. In unusual instances, fibromas and thecomas can be associated with ascites and pleural effusions, a situation called Meigs' syndrome. There are rare reports of malignant Brenner tumors.

Endometriomas

Endometriomas are found in reproductive-age women. They can be associated with pelvic pain and infertility. They can be unilateral or bilateral and appear on ultrasound as complex cysts with internal echoes consistent with hemmorhage. They are discussed at length in Chap. 35.

Benign Disorders of the Fallopian Tube

The differential diagnosis of tubal disease is much more limited than ovarian disorders. Physiologic disorders are limited to structural tubal disorders preventing egg, sperm, and zygote transport. Most enlargements of the tube are benign in nature. They are in the differential diagnosis of adnexal masses, and must be differentiated from ovarian neoplasms. Primary fallopian tube malignancy is the rarest of the gynecologic cancers, comprising less than 1 percent. It is, however, a common site to which other gynecologic malignancies metastasize.

Disorders of Tubal Transport

Tubal disease is one of the most common sources of infertility, and is implicated in 25 to

40 percent of female infertility. Establishment of tubal patency is essential early in the infertility work-up, and can be done by hysterosalpingo-gram or by chromotubation at the time of laparoscopy. Tubal obstruction is most frequent after episodes of salpingitis. Chlamydia infection has been implicated as a source of major tubal damage after clinically asymptomatic infection. Even in cases where obstruction is not complete, damage to the ciliated lining of the fallopian tube can result in defects in transport of ga-metes. The risk of ectopic pregnancy is greatly elevated in patients with tubal damage. Karta-gener's syndrome, with reversed direction of cilia movement, is a true functional disorder of the fallopian tube. Interestingly, it does not absolutely prevent fertility.

Paratubal Cysts

The fallopian tube can give rise to thin-walled, simple, clear, fluid-filled cysts known as paratubal cysts. These cysts are usually quite small, but can grow as large as 20 cm. Pedunculated cysts arising from the fimbria are called hydatid cysts of Mor-gagni. These cysts are usually incidental findings on ultrasound or at gynecologic surgery. They are almost without exception benign, and seldom cause problems, except rare torsions and cyst ruptures. The main difficulty is in differentiating them from ovarian neoplasms.

Ectopic Pregnancy

The fallopian tube is the most common location for ectopic pregnancy. Ectopic pregnancy should be considered first in the differential diagnosis of a reproductive-age woman with an adnexal mass because it is the only part of the differential that has the potential to be immediately lethal. A diagnosis of ruptured ectopic pregnancy is vir-tually impossible in the presence of a negative sensitive urine pregnancy test. Ectopic pregnancy should be suspected in any woman with vaginal

bleeding, pain, and a positive pregnancy test. It is discussed at length in Chap. 64.

Tubo-ovarian Abscess

Tubo-ovarian abscess can result as a complica-tion of acute salpingitis, which is discussed in Chap. 28. These masses can be quite large, as they can combine tube, ovary, and a phlegmon of matted bowel. On physical exam they present as an enlarged, tender adnexal mass. Frequently, the patient is in such discomfort that even a large mass is not palpable. Ultrasound will show a complex adnexal mass, and the patient is usually febrile and has significant abdominal tenderness. Management in the reproductive-age woman is discussed elsewhere. Tubo-ovar-ian abscess is very unusual in the postmeno-pausal woman and merits surgical management because of the association with ovarian neo-plasms.

Hydrosalpinx

Hydrosalpinx is a common sequelae of acute sal-pingitis. These are usually small, but can be as large as 5 to 10 cm and are sometimes incidental findings on pelvic exam. They are formed from the dilated tubes created by tubal abscesses, now filled with sterile serous fluid. Most often they are incidental findings on pelvic ultrasound or at gynecologic surgery. On ultrasound, they appear as complex multicystic masses with internal ech-oes. They are usually not symptomatic, and only need to be removed if necessary to differentiate them from ovarian neoplasms. Once formed, they are frequently present for the duration of the patient's life.

References and Selected Readings

1. DiSaia PJ, Creasman WT: The adnexal mass and early ovarian cancer, in *Clinical Gynecologic Oncology,* 5th ed. St. Louis, MO: CV Mosby, 1997, pp 253–281.
2. Droegemueller W: Benign gynecologic lesions, in

Mishell DR, Stenchever MA, Droegemueller W, Herbst AI, (eds): *Comprehensive Gynecology,* 3d ed. St Louis: Mosby-Yearbook, 1997, pp 467–516.

3. Rulin MC: Controversies in the management of adnexal masses. *Clin Obstet Gynecol* 36:361–456, 1993.

4. Speroff L, Glass RH, Kase NG: *Clinical Gynecologic Endocrinology and Infertility,* 5th ed. Baltimore: Williams & Wilkins, 1994.

5. Stenchever MA: Differential diagnosis of major gynecologic problems by age groups: Vaginal bleeding, pelvic pain and pelvic mass, in Mishell DR, Stenchever MA, Droegemueller W, Herbst AI, (eds): *Comprehensive Gynecology,* 3d ed. St. Louis: Mosby-Yearbook, 1997, pp 159–165.

CHAPTER 35

Endometriosis

Kris Strohbehn
David Chelmow
Alan H. DeCherney

ndometriosis is a disease almost exclusively of reproductive-age women. It has classically been described as extrauterine growth of endometrial glands and stroma. A newer definition includes histologic evidence of ectopic endometrium associated with evidence of either cellular activity and progression (such as adhesions) or interference with normal physiologic processes (such as decreased tubal motility).[3, 5] Endometriosis is a benign condition that affects 5 to 15 percent of all reproductive-age women. It is found in up to 40 percent of patients who have chronic pelvic pain or infertility. Recently, Koninckx[10] suggested that inconspicuous peritoneal findings are common in most if not all women; he emphasized that as many as one-third of women with findings of endometriosis by laparoscopy are asymptomatic. Konickx implied that the findings, when subtle and asymptomatic, may not represent a true disease, but a normal physiologic finding. Despite its benign classifica-

tion, and despite it clearly not being a cancer, symptomatic endometriosis has some characteristics of a cancer: it grows progressively while under the influence of normal ovarian function; it frequently recurs despite treatment; and it appears in sites distant from its origin.

The age at onset is usually the late 20s but endometriosis may present in any reproductive-age woman. Postmenopausal women rarely get endometriosis, even those on hormonal replacement therapy. Endometriosis has been described in male patients on high-dose estrogen agonists, such as tamoxifen, for prostate cancer.

Endometriosis most frequently occurs in the pelvis and on its peritoneal surfaces. It may rarely involve the lung, brain, and prior surgical scars, such as episiotomy scars. Regions in the pelvis that are commonly affected include the ovaries, and the serosal surfaces of the uterus, bladder, bowel, and rectosigmoid. Endometriosis can invade the stroma of the ovary resulting in a cyst, called an *endometrioma*. Endometriomas are present in approximately one-third of women surgically evaluated for endometriosis. The cysts are filled with a "chocolate" fluid composed of hemosiderin deposits, old blood, and debris. The cysts are usually lined with endometrial stroma and glands, but the normal architecture may be absent. Hemosiderin-laden macrophages may be the only histologic confirmation of endometriosis.

Symptoms

The most frequent presenting symptoms are dysmenorrhea, chronic pelvic pain, dyspareunia, and infertility (Table 35-1). Characteristically, pain from endometriosis occurs in the latter half of the cycle, usually a few days prior to the onset of the next period. The chronology of pain and other symptoms can be established by having the patient keep a menstrual calendar, recording her symptoms in relationship to her cycle. Over time, the pain may become noncyclic, but it is often worst in the premenstrual period. Spotting of dark menstrual blood several days prior to the onset of the normal period is frequently described. Deep dyspareunia and dysmenorrhea are common, and many women have referred pain localized to the lower back.

Rarely, an acute abdomen results when an endometrioma causes ovarian torsion; an endometrioma can also rupture or leak resulting in a chemical peritonitis and acute pain. Occasionally, patients complain of cyclical hematuria or hematochezia when endometriosis involves the mucosa of the bladder or rectum. Rarely, endometriosis occurs in other extrapelvic regions with bizarre symptoms, such as catamenial pneumothorax or hemothorax when endometriosis involves the lung; cyclical seizures when it involves the central nervous system; or pain that mimics an inguinal hernia when it tracks along the round ligament. The patient may also complain of a painful nodule on the skin of the abdomen, vulva, or vagina.

TABLE 35-1 **Symptoms of Endometriosis**

Common Symptoms
  Dysmenorrhea
  Chronic pelvic pain
  Low-back pain
  Deep dyspareunia
  Infertility
  Premenstrual spotting
Rare Symptoms
  Acute pelvic pain
  Painful skin nodule: vaginal, vulvar, inguinal, or abdominal
  Cyclical hematuria
  Cyclical hematochezia
  Catamenial pneumo- or hemothorax
  Cyclical seizures

The extent of disease often contrasts significantly with symptoms. Approximately one-third of all patients with surgical evidence of endometriosis are asymptomatic. Frequently, the patient with extensive endometriosis has minimal pain. Conversely, patients with minimal objective findings often complain of severe pain.

Another common presenting symptom is infertility. Often, patients who are otherwise asymptomatic may be unable to conceive because of endometriosis. The causes of infertility from endometriosis are probably multifactorial.[4] Inflammation, pelvic, and peritubal adhesions may reduce or obstruct tubal transport. Immunologic factors, including cytokines and enhanced macrophage activity in the peritoneal fluid, may prevent normal sperm function and conception. Increased prostaglandin activity may inhibit the motility of the tubal cilia and smooth muscle, preventing normal ovum transport. Impaired ovulatory function has also been suggested.

Differential Diagnosis

Endometriosis is important to consider in the differential diagnosis of several symptoms, such as pelvic pain, dysmenorrhea, and infertility (Table 35-2).

Among patients with pelvic pain, the differential diagnosis must include other gynecologic sources. Pelvic pain can be caused by pelvic inflammatory disease, as well as adhesions resulting from other inflammatory processes including surgery and nongynecologic intra-abdominal infections. Sexually active patients with pelvic pain should have genital chlamydia and gonorrhea cultures obtained.

Pregnancy should always be considered in the differential diagnosis of pelvic pain.

Many neoplastic processes can lead to progressive, chronic pelvic pain. Benign processes such as leiomyomata uteri may cause pelvic pain. This presentation is rare unless the myomas outgrow their blood supply, which results in central tumor necrosis and pain. Ovarian neoplasms, both ma-

TABLE 35-2   Causes of Chronic/ Subacute Pelvic Pain

Gynecologic
    Endometriosis
    Adenomyosis
    Pelvic inflammatory disease
        Acute/chronic salpingitis
        Chronic endometritis
    Leiomyomata uteri
    Ectopic pregnancy
    Threatened spontaneous abortion
    Adnexal cyst

Gastrointestinal
    Diverticulitis
    Inflammatory bowel disease
        Crohn's disease
        Ulcerative colitis
    Hernias
    Chronic constipation

Urinary
    Acute/chronic cystitis (infectious)
    Interstitial cystitis

Other
    Abdominal wall trigger points
    Adhesions

lignant and benign, may also present primarily with pelvic pain, due to local infiltration of nerves, ovarian torsion, and chemical peritonitis. If there is any doubt regarding the diagnosis, it is prudent to rule out adnexal neoplasia.

Other nongynecologic sources of pelvic pain include gastrointestinal sources such as diverticulitis, inflammatory bowel disease, appendicitis, and irritable bowel syndrome. In addition, the genitourinary system must be considered; acute cystitis should be ruled out by performing a urinalysis. If the patient has accompanying symptoms of urinary urgency with a negative urinalysis, interstitial cystitis should be suspected. Because some patients with interstitial cystitis have minimal urinary symptoms, a cystoscopy under general anesthesia with hydrodilatation should be considered if surgical evaluation for endometriosis is planned.

The symptoms of dysmenorrhea usually include only gynecologic sources in the differential.

Most commonly, dysmenorrhea presents in patients with endometriosis or fibroids. Dysmenorrhea is particularly common with submucosal leiomyoma, and a hysteroscopy with endometrial sampling is advised if the patient is having irregular bleeding.

The differential diagnosis for patients presenting with infertility includes problems with the male (abnormal semen analysis, which accounts for up to 40 percent of infertility among couples); tubal disease from causes other than endometriosis, such as infection; anovulation; cervical factors due to thick mucus, sperm antibodies, or cervical stenosis; luteal-phase deficiencies due to progesterone deficiency; and, finally, endometriosis.

Diagnosis

Physical Examination

Clinical findings on physical exam that may raise the examiner's suspicion include pelvic tenderness, especially in the cul-de-sac. Nodularity and tenderness may be encountered in the region of the uterosacral ligaments and posterior uterus, which will be more apparent during rectovaginal examination. The rectovaginal examination is a valuable part of the pelvic exam and can help define a retroflexed, fixed uterus. This finding is very suggestive of endometriosis, although it can also be encountered with gynecological malignancies. A palpable adnexal mass may represent an endometrioma, particularly if it has decreased mobility. Any persistent palpable mass requires further evaluation with ultrasound or surgery. If the sonographic appearance is other than that of a simple cyst, surgical evaluation is warranted to rule out malignancy. Many patients with endometriosis will have normal pelvic exams.

Laparoscopy

The definitive diagnosis of endometriosis can only be made surgically, usually by diagnostic laparoscopy, and sometimes by exploratory laparotomy. The characteristic endometriotic lesion is described as a "powder-burn lesion," which represents a small (2 to 10 mm) collection of blood and debris, endometrial glands and stroma within an area of fibrosis. There is a wide range in the gross appearance of endometriosis and the findings are often subtle. The surgeon must be thorough in inspecting the intraperitoneal cavity when endometriosis is suspected. The spectrum of gross appearance of endometriosis includes clear vesicles, white adhesions, red papules, and the characteristic dark-purple lesions. Given the wide range of gross findings, a confirmatory biopsy is often performed.

Cystoscopy with hydrodilatation should be performed concomitantly, if the patient has urinary urgency or hematuria, to rule out interstitial cystitis. In addition, cystoscopy with hydrodilatation may be considered if there are negative laparoscopic findings in a patient with chronic pelvic pain. Some physicians perform cystoscopy with hydrodilatation even in the presence of endometriotic lesions, as patients may have concomitant endometriosis and interstitial cystitis.

CA-125

The serum tumor marker CA-125 is often elevated in patients with endometriosis. Because an elevated CA-125 level can be found in other disease and physiologic processes, including infection, menses, pregnancy, and neoplastic processes, the utility of CA-125 levels for the diagnosis or management of endometriosis is limited and not recommended at present. Other serum markers are being investigated.

Classification

The staging of endometriosis is surgical and not part of an office evaluation. The current staging is included for office reference, so that the extent of disease may be understood and discussed with the patient when she presents with surgically con-firmed endometriosis. Figure 35-1 outlines the 1996 American Society for Reproductive Medicine Revised Classification of Endometriosis. Current debate illustrates that the current staging system has limitations due to poor correlation in some series between stage of disease, symptoms of pain, and pregnancy rates; variable intra- and interobserver reproducibility in some series; and a lack of inclusion of extrapelvic endometriosis. Because of this debate, an international panel is investigating the limitations. The panel's recommendations for future classification schemes will likely incorporate more clinical information, such as mapping pain distribution and physical findings.[6]

Pathology

The histologic appearance of endometriosis is similar to the stromal and glandular components of endometrium. Frequently, biopsies of endometriosis fail to reveal endometrial tissue, but hemosiderin-laden macrophages are usually present.

Pathophysiology

There are many theories regarding the etiology of endometriosis. Three theories currently predominate: The first theory is that retrograde menstruation percolates through the fallopian tubes, leading to the deposition of endometrial tissue in the pelvis. A second theory proposes that coelomic metaplasia of "totipotential cells" of the peritoneum can differentiate into any type of tissue, including endometrial tissue. The third theory postulates that both explanations may play a role in endometriosis. Endometrial tissue and fluid settle in the cul-de-sac and pelvis, which may lead to metaplastic changes in these inflamed regions of the peritoneum.

None of these theories explains why many patients with endometriosis have lymphatic involvement, nor how endometriosis can spread to such distant organs as the lung or brain. It has

AMERICAN SOCIETY FOR REPRODUCTIVE MEDICINE
REVISED CLASSIFICATION OF ENDOMETRIOSIS

Patient's Name _____ Date _____

Stage I (Minimal) - 1-5
Stage II (Mild) - 6-15
Stage III (Moderate) - 16-40
Stage IV (Severe) - >40
Total _____

Laparoscopy _____ Laparotomy _____ Photography _____
Recommended Treatment _____
_____

Prognosis _____

PERITONEUM	ENDOMETRIOSIS	<1cm	1-3cm	>3cm
	Superficial	1	2	4
	Deep	2	4	6
OVARY	R Superficial	1	2	4
	Deep	4	16	20
	L Superficial	1	2	4
	Deep	4	16	20

	POSTERIOR CULDESAC OBLITERATION	Partial	Complete
		4	40

	ADHESIONS	<1/3 Enclosure	1/3-2/3 Enclosure	>2/3 Enclosure
OVARY	R Filmy	1	2	4
	Dense	4	8	16
	L Filmy	1	2	4
	Dense	4	8	16
TUBE	R Filmy	1	2	4
	Dense	4*	8*	16
	L Filmy	1	2	4
	Dense	4*	8*	16

*If the fimbriated end of the fallopian tube is completely enclosed, change the point assignment to 16.

Denote appearance of superficial implant types as red [(R), red, red-pink, flamelike, vesicular blobs, clear vesicles], white [(W), opacifications, peritoneal defects, yellow-brown], or black [(B) black, hemosiderin deposits, blue]. Denote percent of total described as R___%, W___% and B___%. Total should equal 100%.

Additional Endometriosis: _____

Associated Pathology: _____

To Be Used with Normal Tubes and Ovaries

To Be Used with Abnormal Tubes and/or Ovaries

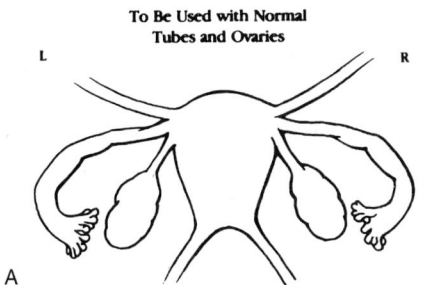

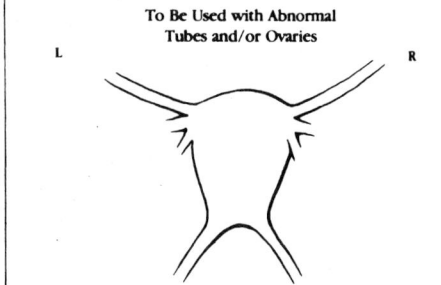

Figure 35-1 American Society for Reproductive Medicine Revised Classification of Endometriosis. (Reprinted by permission from American Society for Reproductive Medicine: Revised American Society for Reproductive Medicine Classification for Endometriosis: 1996. *Fertil Steril* 67:817–821, 819–820, 1997.)

STAGE I (MINIMAL)

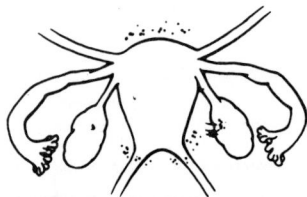

PERITONEUM			
Superficial Endo	–	1-3cm	· 2
R. OVARY			
Superficial Endo	–	< 1cm	· 1
Filmy Adhesions	–	< 1/3	· 1
		TOTAL POINTS	4

STAGE II (MILD)

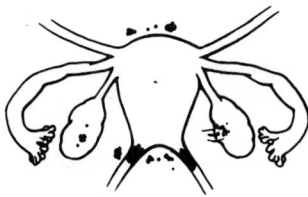

PERITONEUM			
Deep Endo	–	>3cm	· 6
R. OVARY			
Superficial Endo	–	< 1cm	· 1
Filmy Adhesions	–	< 1/3	· 1
L. OVARY			
Superficial Endo	–	< 1cm	· 1
		TOTAL POINTS	9

STAGE III (MODERATE)

PERITONEUM			
Deep Endo	–	>3cm	· 6
CULDESAC			
Partial Obliteration			· 4
L. OVARY			
Deep Endo	–	1-3cm	· 16
		TOTAL POINTS	26

STAGE III (MODERATE)

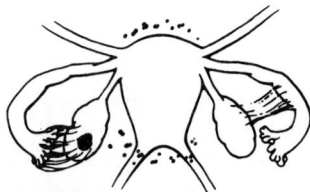

PERITONEUM			
Superficial Endo	–	>3cm	-4
R. TUBE			
Filmy Adhesions	–	< 1/3	· 1
R. OVARY			
Filmy Adhesions	–	< 1/3	· 1
L. TUBE			
Dense Adhesions	–	< 1/3	· 16*
L. OVARY			
Deep Endo	–	< 1 cm	-4
Dense Adhesions	–	< 1/3	-4
		TOTAL POINTS	30

STAGE IV (SEVERE)

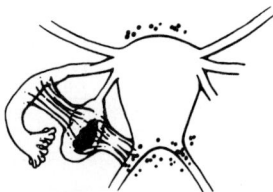

PERITONEUM			
Superficial Endo	–	>3cm	-4
L. OVARY			
Deep Endo	–	1-3cm	· 32**
Dense Adhesions	–	< 1/3	· 8**
L. TUBE			
Dense Adhesions	–	< 1/3	· 8**
		TOTAL POINTS	52

*Point assignment changed to 16
**Point assignment doubled

STAGE IV (SEVERE)

PERITONEUM			
Deep Endo	–	>3cm	· 6
CULDESAC			
Complete Obliteration			· 40
R. OVARY			
Deep Endo	–	1-3cm	· 16
Dense Adhesions	–	< 1/3	· 4
L. TUBE			
Dense Adhesions	–	>2/3	· 16
L. OVARY			
Deep Endo	–	1-3cm	· 16
Dense Adhesions	–	>2/3	· 16
		TOTAL POINTS	114

Determination of the stage or degree of endometrial involvement is based on a weighted point system. Distribution of points has been arbitrarily determined and may require further revision or refinement as knowledge of the disease increases.

To ensure complete evaluation, inspection of the pelvis in a clockwise or counterclockwise fashion is encouraged. Number, size and location of endometrial implants, plaques, endometriomas and/or adhesions are noted. For example, five separate 0.5cm superficial implants on the peritoneum (2.5 cm total) would be assigned 2 points. (The surface of the uterus should be considered peritoneum.) The severity of the endometriosis or adhesions should be assigned the highest score only for peritoneum, ovary, tube or culdesac. For example, a 4cm superficial and a 2cm deep implant of the peritoneum should be given a score of 6 (not 8). A 4cm deep endometrioma of the ovary associated with more than 3cm of superficial disease should be scored 20 (not 24).

In those patients with only one adnexa, points applied to disease of the remaining tube and ovary should be multiplied by two. **Points assigned may be circled and totaled. Aggregation of points indicates stage of disease (minimal, mild, moderate, or severe).

The presence of endometriosis of the bowel, urinary tract, fallopian tube, vagina, cervix, skin etc., should be documented under "additional endometriosis." Other pathology such as tubal occlusion, leiomyomata, uterine anomaly, etc., should be documented under "associated pathology." All pathology should be depicted as specifically as possible on the sketch of pelvic organs, and means of observation (laparoscopy or laparotomy) should be noted.

B

Figure 35-1 (Continued).

been proposed that lymphatic or hematogenous transport of endometrial tissue can occasionally cause endometriosis. There is also evidence for enhanced cellular-mediated activity of macrophages in the peritoneal fluid of some patients with endometriosis. This, combined with evidence for a familial predisposition for endometriosis, suggests that immunologic and genetic components play a role in the genesis of endometriosis.

Treatment

The goals of treatment for patients suffering with endometriosis depend primarily on reversing the presenting symptoms. When the chief complaint is pain, dysmenorrhea, or dyspareunia, the obvious goal is to alleviate this pain. Patients with infertility due to endometriosis will have treatment targeted at conception. Patients with an adnexal mass usually require surgical evaluation and treatment. Treatment options for endometriosis range from observation when the disease is mild, to medical and surgical options when the disease is more severe.

Patients with known mild endometriosis and infertility may be as successful in their efforts at conception without medical or surgical intervention. Therefore, a period of 6 to 12 months without further infertility therapy is often recommended unless the patient is approaching the end of her child-bearing potential.

Medical

If the chief complaint is pelvic pain, nonsteroidal anti-inflammatory agents (NSAIDs) often improve the pain over a 3-to 6-month course of treatment. There is a large placebo effect, reaching as high as 40 percent, when treating patients with pelvic pain and endometriosis.[5] If the goal of medical therapy for endometriosis is to halt progression, then the estrogen-dominant and fluctuating hormonal environment leading to proliferation of the heterotopic endometrial tissue must be stopped. This can be accomplished

in two ways: by achieving a hypoestrogenic, hypoprogestational "pseudomenopausal" state, or by increasing the hormonal environment, causing a "pseudopregnancy" state. Several medical options are listed in Table 35-3.

Pregnancy itself may palliate the pain associated with endometriosis. Decidualization of heterotopic endometrial tissue occurs during pregnancy, although many patients have recurrent symptoms following resumption of ovulation.

Many clinicians start with an empirical trial of a pseudogestational agent, such as an oral contraceptive, or a progestational agent in combination with NSAIDs without surgical confirmation of the diagnosis. Pseudomenopausal agents have traditionally not been used without surgical

TABLE 35-3 Medical Therapy for Endometriosis

Drug	Side Effects
Nonsteroidal anti-inflammatory agents (NSAIDs)	
Examples: ibuprofen, naproxyn sodium	Gastritis, nephrotoxicity
Pseudogestational agents	
Continuous oral contraceptive pills (any monophasic combination pill containing 20–35 µg estrogen)	Bloating, headaches, mood swings, weight gain, hypertension
Progestational agents	
Medroxyprogesterone (IM, Depot form, or PO)	Mood swings, weight gain, increased appetite
Pseudomenopausal agents	
Danazol	Weight gain, fluid retention, decreased breast size, hot flushes, irritability, acne, ↑ LDL, ↓ HDL, hirsutism, deepening of the voice
GnRH agonist	
Leuprolide, goserelin	Hot flushes, vaginal dryness, emotional lability, headaches, depression, osteoporosis
Nafarelin spray	Same as leuprolide and goserelin and nasal irritation

confirmation of disease, but some clinicians now prefer to try these agents before surgery.

A "pseudopregnancy" state can be achieved by using a combined monophasic estrogen-progesterone contraceptive preparation. A low-dose combined estrogen (20 to 35 μg)/progesterone pill is preferred. A continuous regimen is employed to maintain a nonfluctuating hormonal milieu. The patient is instructed to take 1 pill daily and start the subsequent pack of pills after taking the first 21 pills, without using the placebo pills at the end of the cycle. She should become amenorrheic on the continuous hormonal regimen, thus removing the stimulus for heterotopic endometrial tissue growth. Breakthrough bleeding is common on this regimen, but is lessened by emphasizing that the patient take the pill at the same time of the day. If the patient has breakthrough bleeding, Droegemueller[7] recommends doubling the dose for 5 days to stop the bleeding and then resuming the previous dose. An alternative is to add additional estrogen for 5 days. Side effects are those that are commonly found with oral contraceptive preparations, including headaches, hypertension, weight gain, mood swings, and bloating.

A progestational agent alone can also achieve a pseudopregnancy state. Progesterone can be prescribed as a daily oral agent or as an intramuscular agent (Table 35-3). Side effects include mood swings, irritability, weight gain, increased appetite, and fatigue. Breakthrough bleeding is common, and can be managed with the temporary supplementation of an estrogen. Among patients with infertility, the conception rate is approximately 30 percent after completing 6 to 12 months of the above regimens.

Two types of medication are currently available to achieve a pseudomenopausal state. Historically, this was first accomplished in the 1970s when danazol was introduced. It is a combined androgen agonist and antagonist that causes anovulation by suppressing luteinizing hormone (LH) and follicular stimulating hormone (FSH). Danazol affects multiple sites necessary for normal reproductive function, including the hypo-

thalamus, pituitary gland, ovaries, endometrium, and sex hormone binding globulin levels. The endometrial glands become atrophic, thus diminishing the symptoms.

The side effects of danazol are related primarily to its androgenic properties. These include weight gain, irregular bleeding, depression, hirsutism, acne, an adverse change in the lipid profile [increased low-density lipoproteins (LDL) and decreased high-density lipoproteins (HDL)], and decreased breast size. Rarely, an irreversible deepening of the voice occurs. Given the particularly undesirable side effects, danazol use has largely been replaced by gonadotropin-releasing hormone (Gn-RH) agonists.

Gn-RH agonists have been used to treat endometriosis with equal efficacy to that of danazol. These preparations result in a hypogonadotrophic state through the binding of Gn-RH receptors on the pituitary gland. After an initial stimulatory effect, the pituitary hormones FSH and LH are suppressed, leading to anovulation; amenorrhea and atrophy of the endometrial glands result.

The most common side effects of Gn-RH agonists are vaginal dryness, hot flushes, and progressive bone demineralization, similar to that found in a menopausal woman. Because of concerns of long-term adverse effects, including osteoporosis, Gn-RH agonists are typically only used for six months. Various estrogen add-back regimens have been proposed to prevent osteoporosis, cardiovascular changes, and urogenital atrophy. Most add-back regimens include estrogen and progesterone in combination therapy to maintain amenorrhea. A compilation of studies of various add-back regimens with progestins alone, combined estrogens and progestins, and with etidronate was reviewed by Gargiulo et al.[8]

Success rates for the two pseudomenopausal regimens are similar. Approximately 40 percent of patients successfully conceive after therapy, but these rates are not better than simple observation among patients with mild to moderate disease. Pain is improved in 80 to 90 percent of patients after treatment, although the pain recurs in 15 to 30 percent of patients within 2 years of completing therapy. For a patient who is not attempting conception, a pseudogestational state can be initiated after 6-months of treatment with danazol or Gn-RH agonist therapy. Continuous oral contraceptives or progesterone therapy can be initiated, as described above. Alternatively, add-back hormone replacement can be started to reduce long-term sequelae of hypoestrogenism, but this approach may be costly.

Surgical

Historically, surgical treatment by excision or electrocautery were the only options available for treating endometriosis. Technological advances in fiberoptics, pelviscopic equipment, and laser propagation have improved surgical options for treating endometriosis. Laser vaporization offers theoretical advantages over electrocautery. The chances of damage to underlying organs are less because of decreased penetration and decreased thermal destruction. In practice, however, laser has not been shown to have improved outcomes compared to electrocautery, and is more costly.

Patients with suspected severe endometriosis or an uncertain diagnosis should have a definitive diagnosis made surgically.

Patients with severe endometriosis are more likely to benefit from surgical treatment than are patients with mild or moderate disease. If severe endometriosis is encountered at the time of diagnostic laparoscopy, treatment can be performed at the time of diagnosis.

If a patient has completed her child-bearing, definitive cure is possible with hysterectomy and bilateral salpingo-oophorectomy. In addition, presacral neurectomy and ablation of the uterosacral ligaments has been performed to alleviate pain and dysmenorrhea successfully in some patients, while preserving fertility.

Combined Therapy

Combination therapy with surgery and medical treatment has some theoretical advantages. Because some endometriosis may be present microscopically without gross evidence of disease, these areas would be missed during surgery. Some investigators have suggested medical treatment with danazol or a Gn-RH agonist following surgery. One theoretical disadvantage with this approach is that the patient then must delay her attempts to conceive, with greater potential for adhesion formation from the surgery.

Summary

Patients with endometriosis present with a myriad of symptoms including pelvic pain, dyspareunia, dymenorrhea, and infertility—or with no symptoms at all. Once the diagnosis is established surgically, medical treatment and follow-up in the office setting are appropriate. In selected cases, empiric medical therapy for endometriosis might be considered prior to surgical evaluation. If the diagnosis is in doubt, however, surgical evaluation is warranted.

References and Selected Readings

1. American College of Obstetricians and Gynecologists: Washington, DC: *Endometriosis.* ACOG, 1993. ACOG Technical Bulletin No. 185.
2. Adamson GD, Nelson HP: Surgical treatment of endometriosis. *Obstet Gynecol Clin North Am.* 24:375–409, 1997.
3. Audebert A, Backstrom T, Barlow DH: Endometriosis, 1991: A discussion document. *Hum Reprod* 7:432–435, 1992.
4. Brosens IA: Pathology and medical treatment of endometriosis-associated infertility, in Seibel MM (ed): *Infertility: A Comprehensive Text,* 2d ed. Norwalk, CT: Appleton and Lange, 1997, pp 189–202.
5. Cirkel U: Medical treatment of symptomatic endometriosis. *Hum Reprod* 11:89–101, 1996.
6. Damario MA, Rock JA: Classification of endometriosis. *Semin Reprod Endocrinol* 15:235–44, 1997.
7. Droegemueller W: Endometriosis and adenomyosis, in Mishell DR, Stenchever MA, Droegemueller W, Herbst AI (eds.): *Comprehensive Gynecology,* 3d ed. St. Louis: Mosby-Yearbook, 1997, pp 517–546.
8. Gargiulo AR, Hornstein MD: The role of GnRH agonists plus addback therapy in the treatment of

endometriosis. *Semin Reprod Endocrinol* 15:273–284, 1997.

9. Loy RA, DeCherney AH: Surgery for endometriosis, in Gershenson DM, DeCherney AH, Curry SL (eds): *Operative Gynecology.* Philadelphia: WB Saunders, 1993, pp 569–584.

10. Koninckx PR: Is mild endometriosis a disease? Is mild endometriosis a condition occurring intermittently in all women? *Hum Reprod* 9:2202–2205, 1994.

11. Metzger DA: Treating endometriosis pain: A multidisciplinary approach. *Semin Reprod Endocrinol* 15:245–250, 1997.

12. Olive DL, Schwartz LB: Endometriosis. *N Engl J Med* 328: 1759–1769, 1993.

13. Ryan IP, Taylor RN: Endometriosis and infertility: New concepts. *Obstet Gynecol Surv* 52:365–371, 1997.

14. Speroff L, Glass RH, Kase NG: *Clinical Gynecologic Endocrinology and Infertility,* 5th ed. Baltimore: Williams & Wilkins, 1994, pp 853–872.

CHAPTER 36

Other Disorders of the Vulva, Vagina, Cervix, and Uterus

Stephen L. Curry

This chapter reviews common disorders of the vulva, vagina, cervix, and uterus with an emphasis on medical management. Infectious disorders, premalignant lesions, and cancers are discussed elsewhere in the text. A complete history remains the mainstay of proper diagnosis and treatment. The patient should first describe her problem or concern, which is followed by a focused history. For vulvar problems the use of douches, deodorants, powders, and creams, along with questions about use of synthetic underwear, perineal pads, and tight slacks are important areas to investigate. A careful assessment of menstrual history, abnormal bleeding, and pelvic pain is critical. Pain should be evaluated as to timing in relation to the menstrual period, location, and intensity.

This is often a good time to begin educating the patient with vulvar symptoms about avoiding aggressive rubbing with toilet paper, bath towels, or wash cloths. She should wear cotton underwear and avoid tight slacks to prevent vulvar problems.

In carrying out the physical examination, it is critically important to palpate and visualize the entire vulva and to observe carefully the entire vaginal surface as the speculum is removed. Because the lower third of the vagina and the entire vulva have their lymphatic drainage through the groin, it is also important to evaluate all these areas during the complete examination.

Vulvar Vestibulitis

The patient with vulvar vestibulitis will present, usually in her third or fourth decade of life, complaining of the sudden onset of severe posterior vulvar burning and/or pain, which is significantly exacerbated during and immediately after intercourse. Eventually the pain becomes constant. On careful examination with the colposcope or a magnifying glass, one can see erythema around the vestibular gland openings. These glands are most prominent from approximately the 4 o'clock to the 8 o'clock locations, just outside the hymenal ring and extending slightly down the perineum in the midline. Application of mild acetic acid used for colposcopic examination of the cervix often creates a frost-like well-circumscribed area. Many investigators have attempted to show that this inflammation is secondary to bacterial or viral infections, but to date, no etiology is known. Some authors consider the disorder to be a combination of etiologies, including chronic yeast infection, chronic vaginitis, and atrophic vulvitis.

In many patients, the condition will spontaneously regress in 6 months to 1 year. Application of dilute trichloroacetic acid every other week for 8 weeks, followed by 6 weeks of vulvar rest, appears to benefit a significant number of patients. Some authors recommend weekly 5-fluorouracil (5-FU) cream for 6 months. Those women who do not have spontaneous regression of the problem, or who do not respond to medical management, may be treated with a vestibulectomy. This is an outpatient procedure that requires careful mapping of the involved area to ensure the best result. The patient should be warned that even under the best circumstances the response rate does not exceed 80 percent. Maximum response results from excising the posterior hymeneal ring, dissecting deep into the fat to remove the glands, mobilizing the posterior vagina to bring it out to the skin, and using the finest possible suture. Laser treatment of this condition has not been successful. There is no evidence of any long-term sequela from vulvar vestibulitis.

Vulvar Dystrophy

Recently there has been a move to drop the word dystrophy and describe two lesions, lichen sclerosis and hyperplastic epithelium. To date, there is not universal agreement on this nomenclature. The classic presentation of vulvar dystrophy is the onset of vulvar pruritis and/or burning in the perimenopausal or postmenopausal period. However, lichen sclerosis can occur at any age. The vulva is hormonally responsive, and one might expect that because the changes appear to be due to estrogen deprivation, as is seen in other organs at or around the menopause, estrogen

TABLE 36-1 Vulvar Drying Regimen

No unprescribed creams or medications
No douches, deodorants, or powders
Cotton underwear or no underwear
No tight slacks or pantyhose
No rubbing with toilet paper, towels, or washcloths
Liberal use of hair dryer to perineum

replacement therapy should help; but it does not. Whether the failure of response is an indication that low levels of androgens produced throughout the menstrual years most affect the vulva, or that the estrogen receptors in the vulva are lost, is not yet well understood.

It is likely that these conditions begin with a thinning of the vulvar epithelium, which may go on to become symptomatic. This is called lichen sclerosis in both the old and new terminology. At the opposite end of what may be a spectrum or a separate disorder is hyperplastic epithelium. There are also those individuals who have a mixed pattern; this favors the disorders being a spectrum rather than separate entities as now is being proposed. The correct diagnosis can only be made with a biopsy. In addition, biopsy is necessary to rule out the presence of malignancy.

The standard treatment at this time is a high-potency steroid cream or ointment applied twice a day for a minimum of 4 to 6 weeks. Clobetasol propionate is most commonly used. Cream may cause stinging, whereas the ointment usually does not. It is critical for the patient to follow the vulvar drying regimen as shown in Table 36-1.

Other therapies include testosterone cream, subepithelial injections of hydrocortisone, or, rarely, surgical removal. The literature documents a high rate of recurrence with surgical removal.

Patient education is critical. These are long-term chronic conditions. She should understand that therapy will take weeks to work, she should continuously follow the drying regimen as much as possible, and she should reinstitute therapy the minute she suspects a recurrence. The patient needs to know that although these vulvar changes are not premalignant, patients with long-term vulvar irritation may be at risk for cancer of the vulva.

Vulvodynia

Chronic vulvar irritation, previous vulvar surgery (including laser treatment of the vulva), and long-term effects of vulvar viral infections can lead to a diffuse vulvar burning or pain without any visible evidence of changes in the vulvar epithelium. Occasionally there will be a diffuse mild erythema. These patients often respond well to 3 months of treatment with a low-dose amitriptyline, imipramine, or desipramine. The patients who respond most likely have a neuritis of the pudendal nerve or its branches. If the patient has not responded within 3 months, it is unlikely that she will respond to this treatment, in which case local blocks or more aggressive therapy may need to be considered.

Hydradenitis

Hydradenitis occurs most commonly in the fourth and fifth decade of life. Initially presenting as small abscesses on the vulva, it eventually becomes a deep-seated inflammation of the apocrine glands. It is thought that some patients with significant hydradenitis may be unable to mobilize an appropriate immune response to staphylococcus infections of the skin. They often have lesions of the vulva and in the axillary regions. Early lesions can be treated with hot soaks and regular washing with hexachlorophene soap. Deep-seated lesions should be aggressively opened and cleaned with curettage, allowing secondary healing. In the axillary regions, complete removal with skin grafting may be the best treatment for some patients; however, on the vulva, patients usually respond to more conservative treatment. Long-term bathing with hexachlorophene soap has been beneficial. Rarely do these patients respond to oral or local antibiotics.

There is some indication that progression can be prevented by placing the patient on birth control pills until menopause, thus potentially decreasing the secretions of the apocrine glands. Obviously, the patient's risk factors for the use of the birth control pill and potential contraindications must be assessed.

Condylomata Acuminata

Condyloma acuminata (venereal warts) occur most commonly on the female vulva, and can also be seen on the vagina, cervix, or in the perirectal area. They are the result of exposure to human papilloma virus (HPV) types 6 and 11, 3 months or more prior to the appearance of the warts. They can be small focal finger-like projections or massive fungating lesions. Often in the vagina and on the cervix they present as flat white lesions. The clinician must always be aware of the possibility of premalignancy or malignancy, although, following biopsy, initially conservative therapy may be appropriate, especially for the small finger-like projections on the vulva in young women. On the other hand, in a 45-year-old woman with a large condyloma on the perineum, strong consideration should be given to complete excision in order to rule out the possibility of an underlying carcinoma.

Once it is proven that the diagnosis is condyloma, treatment should begin with the simplest and least costly regimen and then proceed depending on response. Initially painting the external warts with 80% bichloracetic acid—or vaginal or cervical warts with 50% bichloracetic acid—results in a response rate approaching 80 percent. Weekly applications for 4 weeks should provide the best response. A new therapy is the use of Aldara cream, which is applied three times a week for 3 months. This can be accomplished by a reliable patient at a slightly increased cost, but with low side effects.

If there is no evidence of regression then one must consider more aggressive therapy. The next step is to either locally excise or freeze the warts, or to treat the warts with laser. All appear to be equally effective, and thus one must consider cost in choosing the most appropriate treatment. A patient with massive or persistent warts should be referred to a clinician with special expertise in this condition.

There are two special considerations, those being massive cervical or vaginal warts during pregnancy and the very resistant warts. In the former case, it is recommended that the patient be treated with 50% bichloracetic acid between weeks 34 and 36 to assure maximum regression at the time of delivery. Rarely is cesarean section required. In the case of very resistant warts, one must be sure that immunodeficient disorders, such as AIDS, have been ruled out, and then experimental treatments such as interferon or immunization may be considered.

Condyloma acuminata are a result of viral exposure through sexual contact, and therefore consideration should be given to having the partner evaluated and treated. Use of condoms can be effective in preventing recurrences. Rarely does this disorder result in any long-term consequences.

Other Vulvar Conditions

Hematoma of the vulva may result from either blunt trauma or spontaneous rupture of varicose veins, although such cases are rare. Treatment should be conservative unless there is evidence that the hematoma is expanding. An attempt at evacuation may lead to further complications, including infection. If continued bleeding is a concern, the hematoma should be opened and packed. It is rare for the physician to find a true bleeding point.

Uncommonly, benign tumors can present as vulvar masses, including such entities as lipomas and fibromas. These lesions usually need to be removed for cosmetic reasons and patient comfort, and to confirm the diagnosis of a benign lesion.

Gartner's Duct Cysts of the Vagina

These remnants of the mesonephric system most often present with difficulty visualizing the cervix with a speculum in a completely asymptomatic female. On palpation there is a soft, elongated cystic structure either at 3 or 9 o'clock in the vagina, extending from the junction of the lower and middle third of the vagina to the vaginal fornix. Rarely, these can be so dilated that they obstruct intercourse or create mild pelvic discomfort. There are also reported cases of infected Gartner's duct cysts. The most appropriate management for these rare complications is marsupialization.

Fibroids of the Vagina

Very rarely a smooth, round, firm, freely movable mass is noted anteriorly. These are benign fibroids and can almost always be enucleated in the outpatient setting using local anesthesia and a small incision. If necrosis has occurred, they may feel soft and diffuse, but the diagnosis is almost always the same because it is extremely rare for any other neoplasm to present in this location.

Nabothian Cysts of the Cervix

During the teenage years the cervix everts so that the columnar epithelium, with its glands and crypts of the endocervix, is present on the exocervix. There is an aggressive attempt to cover this columnar epithelium with squamous epithelium by a process called squamous metaplasia. As the glandular epithelium is covered with the squamous epithelium some of the glands and crypts are trapped, yet continue to secrete mucus. This becomes a nabothian cyst. It appears as a small, yellow, fluid-filled cyst on the exocervix at the time of speculum examination. It is a completely benign condition without any short- or long-term risk. It does clue the clinician that this is an area of squamous metaplasia and thus the best place to take a scraping for the Pap smear. No treatment for nabothian cysts is necessary.

Endocervical Polyps

Endocervical polyps must be distinguished from pedunculated leiomyomata. The vast majority of endocervical polyps are benign; however, they should be removed and sent for pathologic evaluation. In perimenopausal women, there is a potential for the endocervical polyp to be a result of prolonged unopposed estrogen, and thus consideration should be given to evaluating the endometrium to rule out adenocarcinoma. Small polyps can be removed by simply biopsying or twisting them off. Larger polyps are removed by placing a suture around the base and then cutting the stalk distal to the suture.

Leiomyomata Uteri

Leiomyomata uteri (fibroids) are the most common pathologic condition of the female genital tract. Fibroids can occur anywhere along the tract, including the vulva, vagina, and cervix; however, the vast majority are in the uterine fundus. One of five women and as many as one of three African-American women has at least one myoma in her uterus. They are classically described by their location as being submucosal (protruding into the endometrial cavity), intramural (within the myometrium), subserosal (on the external surface), or pedunculated (either intraperitoneally or within the endometrial cavity). They appear to be the result of a common mutation of a single gene. However, some others propose a multifactoral causation. There continues to be controversy about the hormone responsiveness of fibroids, with the latest data showing that by careful ultrasound measurement during pregnancy there is no consistent pattern. The vast majority regress after menopause and other than appearing as "onion skin" calcifications on x-ray, are not related to any complications or concerns.

Of great importance is differentiating fibroids from ovarian neoplasms. In the past, it was not uncommon for a patient with ovarian cancer to have been told on exam that she had fibroid tumors of her uterus. Ultrasound and laparoscopy have significantly decreased this problem, but the outpatient clinician must always keep this differential in mind, and if there is any question, take further steps to differentiate the two. No longer is it acceptable to refer a patient for hysterectomy just because she has a fibroid uterus. Treatment of fibroids is individualized, on the basis of symptoms and physical findings.

The most common symptom in a woman with fibroids is abnormal bleeding, most often menorrhagia, and/or metrorrhagia. The mechanisms by which the uterus stops bleeding include coagulation, vascular spasm, retraction of the spiral arterioles, and contraction of the myometrium. The latter two create a slowing of blood flow, and thus easier ability of the first two to cause cessation of bleeding. Submucosal fibroids can result in the inability of the spiral arterioles to retract completely and create an endometrial surface that is distant from adequate blood supply. Thus, menorrhagia or metrorrhagia, or more often both, are seen with submucosal fibroids. Intramural fibroids result in a distortion of the normally uniform myometrium, and thus interrupt myometrial contraction, resulting in increased blood flow to the endometrium during the period instead of a slowing of the flow.

The patient presenting with abnormal bleeding could also have an internally pedunculated fibroid, endometrial hyperplasia, or endometrial cancer. Endometrial evaluation should be the first step. This has traditionally been done by endometrial biopsy. In addition, currently endovaginal ultrasound is typically performed. This can be followed at the same time by fluid instillation into the endometrial cavity to first measure the endometrial stripe and then with the fluid evaluate for polyps, a pedunculated fibroid, or irregular surface indicating a submucosal fibroid. All of the above can usually be removed by hysteroscopic resection.

Pedunculated fibroids must always be removed. They may present as a mass in the vagina or cervix dilating the cervix. These can be removed by placing a suture around the base of the pedicle as high as possible and then removing the fibroid distal to the suture. This can often be done as an outpatient procedure, and should rarely be immediately followed by hysterectomy as the chronically open cervical os could result in significant postoperative infection. If possible, it is best to wait six to eight weeks before performing a necessary hysterectomy.

Often abnormal bleeding secondary to submucosal or intramural fibroids will respond to conventional birth control pills. Depo-Provera administered every 3 months appears to be a useful conservative treatment. Not all patients with abnormal bleeding secondary to fibroids are anemic; some fibroids make erythropoietin. If the patient is severely anemic, Gn-RH agonist treatment is a good mechanism for stopping the bleeding in order to increase the hematocrit prior to any more definitive therapy. Although most fibroids shrink during treatment with a Gn-RH agonist, they rapidly return to their original size when the medication is stopped.

Therefore, the algorithm for fibroids and abnormal bleeding is to first insure that the bleeding is secondary to the fibroids. Next, evaluate for anemia and if significant use Gn-RH agonist therapy. Rule out pedunculated or submuscosal fibroids that can be resected hysteroscopically and then begin conservative medical treatment. Myomectomy or hysterectomy may be needed, but usually more conservative measures are effective.

Pain as a presenting symptom in a patient with myomas is most likely secondary to hypovascular necrosis, sometimes related to torsion of an external pedunculated fibroid, but more commonly a subserosal fibroid at the top of the fundus. The latter occurs most often during or immediately after pregnancy and at the time of menopause. The subserosal fibroids have a tenuous blood supply normally, and when there is a further decrease in blood supply, necrosis occurs. On x-ray

these fibroids show onion skinning as they have become necrotic a layer at a time.

The patient with an acutely necrosing fibroid will present with an acute abdomen, elevated temperature, and high WBC. Often no pelvic mass is appreciated and pelvic ultrasound may or may not demonstrate a fibroid. During pregnancy, conservative therapy with appropriate pain control is warranted. Menopausal patients are often diagnosed at the time of exploration for an acute abdomen.

Massive fibroids in a very young patient may require myomectomy to preserve future childbearing ability. This is best accomplished at the end of a short course of Gn-RH agonist therapy, as the uterus is smaller and bleeding is lessened. Rarely do the fibroids rapidly recur.

Occasionally, patients with massive fibroids will present with pyelonephritis, severe constipation, or lower abdominal discomfort. More often the complaint is nonspecific pelvic heaviness or low-back pain. Because these neoplasms are so slow-growing, the patient usually has no complaints even after she is told about the large uterus. If symptoms do occur, usually myomectomy or hysterectomy should be discussed, but unless some vital organ is being affected, patient choice comes first. Often, if surgery is being considered, a vaginal approach can be facilitated by pretreatment with a Gn-RH agonist.

Infertility and myomas remains a controversial topic. Submucosal fibroids may interfere with implantation; intramural fibroids may distort the intramural fallopian tube; low-lying fibroids may obstruct descent of the fetus during labor. Individual patient evaluation, planning, and therapy is the best option as there are very little hard data. In general, infertility patients who have fibroids do not necessarily need a myomectomy.

In the past, rapid growth of fibroids had been considered an indication for hysterectomy, with the potential of growth being secondary to leiomyosarcoma. Research has shown that this is very rare prior to the menopause. Growth of fibroids postmenopausally is extremely uncommon and should warrant immediate evaluation, first ruling out ovarian cancer and then considering hysterectomy, as there is no good mechanism to diagnose leiomyosarcoma except with pathologic evaluation of the entire uterus.

In summary, fibroids are exceedingly common, rarely require hysterectomy, and can be followed conservatively until the menopause when they most often regress. Symptomatic patients will often benefit from conservative therapy. When surgery is indicated, depending upon a woman's age and reproductive concerns, decisions regarding myomectomy or hysterectomy should be individualized.

Adenomyosis Uteri

Also known as endometriosis interna, this is a condition in which the normal endometrial glands and stroma have invaded or somehow become trapped in the myometrium. During the menstrual cycle these cells respond to hormonal stimulation similar to the normal endometrium; however, at the time of the period they have no place to go, and thus necrosis and bleeding occur within the myometrium. This patient will complain of heavy painful periods that have gotten worse as each month goes by. On examination during a menstrual period the patient will usually have an enlarged, boggy, tender uterus.

This condition is rare in the nulligravid patient, and thus there may be a relationship to parturition. When histology is the method of diagnosis,

only about 70 percent of the patients will have a retrospective history of symptoms.

Historically, the diagnosis has been made by careful history and pelvic exam, at the same time excluding any other pathology. More recently, MRI is an excellent modality for confirming adenomyosis prior to definitive therapy. There are no known risks or long-term sequela secondary to adenomyosis; thus, conservative therapy using oral contraceptives or Gn-RH agonists is first-line therapy. Hysterectomy is only considered in refractory cases. Perimenopausally this condition will regress.

References and Selected Readings

1. Kaufman RH, Friedrich EG, Gardner HL: *Benign Diseases of the Vulva and Vagina,* 3rd ed. Chicago: Year Book Medical Publishers, 1989.
2. Baggish MS, Miklos JR: Vulvar pain syndrome: A review. *Obstet Gynecol Surv* 50:618, 1995.
3. McKay M: Dysesthetic "essential" vulvodynia, treatment with amitriptyline. *J Reprod Med* 38:9, 1993.
4. Proceedings of the 11th International Congress of the International Society for the Study of Vulvar Disease. *J Reprod Med* 38:1, 1993.
5. Dalziel KL, Wojnarowska F: Long-term control of vulval lichen sclerosus after treatment with potent topical steriod cream. *J Reprod Med* 38:25, 1993.
6. Stewart EA, Nowak RA: New concepts in the treatment of uterine leiomyomas. *Obstet Gynecol* 92:624, 1998.
7. Azziz R: Adenomyosis: Current perspectives. *Obstet Gynecol Clin North Am* 16:221, 1989.
8. Moghissi KS: Hormonal therapy before surgical treatment for uterine leiomyomas. *Surg Gynecol Obstet* 172:497, 1991.

CHAPTER 37

Chronic Pelvic Pain and Dyspareunia

John F. Steege

THE GENERAL APPROACH
RECOGNIZING THE PROBLEM
EDUCATING THE PATIENT
FACTORS THAT CAN BE DIAGNOSED
    BY PHYSICAL EXAMINATION
    AND/OR LAPAROSCOPY
Endometriosis • Pelvic Adhesions • Pelvic
Support Problems • Levator Muscle Spasm
CAUSES OF PAIN IN THE
    "LAPAROSCOPY-NEGATIVE"
    PATIENT
DYSPAREUNIA

T he problems of chronic pelvic pain and dyspareunia are among the most challenging
problems addressed by the primary care
physician. Women so affected are often frustrated by the chronicity of the problems and the
apparent lack of clear solutions. The complexities
of psychosocial and sexual factors, as well as the
frequent involvement of nongynecologic, organ
systems in symptom production, often make it
difficult for the patient and the clinician to understand the problem. This chapter summarizes the
clinical guidelines for the evaluation and treatment of these problems.

The General Approach

When evaluating the problems of chronic pelvic
pain and dyspareunia, it often best serves the
patient to maintain a careful balance between
pursuit of physical factors and consideration of
psychological concerns. Given the usual constraints of time, skill, and inclination, clinicians
sometimes either pursue organic therapies beyond the limits of their utility or prematurely
assume that psychological factors are responsible
for the problem if a clear organic etiology is not
evident. Examples of the former include the repeated prescription of various vaginal medications for vaginal symptoms occurring in the absence of pathology or pathogens, or the repeated
lysis of intraperitoneal adhesions in the chronic
pain sufferer. An example of the latter is immediately referring the patient with dyspareunia for
psychotherapy upon learning of her past history
of being sexually abused.

These approaches spring from our traditional
Western cultural predilection to separate mind
and body. Recent theories of pain perception and
sexual functioning attempt to integrate psychological and physical processes very closely. The
scientific underpinnings of this approach lie in
our expanding understanding of the biochemical
pathways involved in the regulation of mood,
libido, and pain perception. Although our understanding of these pathways remains primitive,
the field has progressed to the point that clinical
evaluation and treatment should take its findings
into account. For example, it no longer makes
sense for the gynecologist to describe a "negative
laparoscopy" and conclude that no physical
cause for pain exists. At the same time, the mental health clinician should not ask for the patient
to be "cleared gynecologically" before beginning
psychotherapy or other forms of counseling.
Rather, the evaluation and treatment should be
interactive and collaborative in an ongoing
fashion.

Recognizing the Problem

Chronic pain is best viewed as a rather different illness from acute pain. It is by nature multifactorial, often making it necessary to treat with several modalities at once. For example, one might simultaneously offer suggestions for improving chronic constipation, diminishing the freqency of postcoital urinary tract infections, and resolving depression by taking a serotonergic antidepressant. One surrenders the intellectual satisfaction of figuring out which component is the most significant, but the chance of good outcome is enhanced.

When treating the patient with chronic pain, the clinician must recognize that pain is not necessarily proportional to the amount of organic disease present. This absence of correlation has been documented for both endometriosis and pelvic adhesions, the two forms of organic pathology most frequently present in patients with chronic pelvic pain. The clinical query must be restructured to determine whether or not treatment of visible organic changes will be sufficient therapy, or whether the patient will need other treatments for other components of her chronic pain syndrome.

How can the clinician recognize when a patient has developed a chronic pain syndrome? While there are exceptions to every generalization, some reliable hallmarks include:

- Duration of pain longer than 6 months.
- Incomplete relief by medical or surgical therapies.
- Discontinuation of some physical function (e.g., athletics, coitus, household tasks).
- Signs of depression (e.g., sleep disturbance, weight loss, loss of appetite).
- Significant alterations in family roles (e.g., emotional support of children or extended family, financial decision-making). Basically, if your patient or her family considers your patient's problem to be the most significant problem the *family* faces, then family dynamics have likely changed in important ways.

Questions that might be included in your history to bring out these issues are listed in Table 37-1. Recognizing this pattern impels a shift to a multifactorial diagnostic and treatment approach.

Educating the Patient

With rare exceptions, the patient with chronic pain or dyspareunia believes—or at least strongly wishes—that a single diagnosable and treatable cause must exist. Once a patient's problem is recognized as being complex and chronic, it is worth taking time to educate the patient and at least one member of her family about the nature of chronic pain. Expectations should be made more realistic, and their participation solicited in the development of a management plan to treat whatever portion of the pain cannot be resolved. This goes beyond suggesting that she must "learn to live with it," and might include the notions that no single cause is likely to be found; several contributing factors may need simultaneous treatment; it probably will not be possible to tell how much of the problem is physical and how much is psychological; and regardless of how a problem has started, when it becomes severe, mental health help often aids the patient and her family in the effort to reduce the discomfort itself as well as its impact.

With this background in mind, the following sections will summarize the historical questions, physical examination findings, and treatment suggestions appropriate for various factors commonly involved in chronic pelvic pain and dyspareunia.

Factors That Can Be Diagnosed by Physical Examination and/or Laparoscopy

Endometriosis

The severity of pain associated with endometriosis does not correlate (either directly or inversely)

TABLE 37-1   Questions Relevant to the Hallmarks of a Chronic Pain Syndrome

1. Duration >6 months	How long has the pain been present? How long (months) did it take to get to its worst level? What was going on in your life when it got worse?
2. Incomplete relief by medical/surgical treatments	On a scale of 1–10, how much did each treatment help? For how long after surgery did the pain remain improved? When the pain returned, what did you notice first? Next?
3. Discontinuation of some physical functions	What have you stopped doing because of the pain? When? What activities have you continued despite the pain? On the 1–10 scale, what happens to the pain when you do (some activity)? Are you considering stopping work? (. . . applying for disability?) Regarding sex, has frequency decreased? Is there more pain than pleasure? What were things like sexually before the pain?
4. Signs of depression	Does the pain wake you up? Do you wake up early and can't get back to sleep, not particularly because of the pain? Do you have crying spells? Feelings of great sadness? Loss of appetite? Gain or loss of weight? Loss of sexual interest? Suicidal feelings?
5. Altered family dynamics	Who disciplines the kids? (. . . helps with their homework, pays the bills, makes vacation plans, decides what to buy?) Has this changed because of the pain? Is your pain the biggest problem the family faces?

with the amount of endometriosis present, when one compares one patient with another. Within the experience of an individual patient, increased pain often means increased disease, with the site of the pain usually corresponding fairly accurately to the location of the disease. However, in the patient who starts to show the hallmarks of a chronic pain syndrome, pain may progress when organic pathology is stable. Questions aimed at diagnosing a chronic pain syndrome become appropriate (Table 37-1).

A typical historical scenario for a person who develops symptoms due to endometriosis might include a gradual increase in the duration of the strongest menstrual cramps (e.g., increasing from 1 to 3 or 4 days), appearance of premenstrual pain, and cylic dyspareunia, which gradually becomes continuous but remains worst perimenstrually. Painful defecation is less common, as is a more internal, visceral discomfort on urination.

Another very important set of factors may increase the pain associated with endometriosis. Understanding that pelvic examinations (as well

as ultrasounds and other scans) are at best a crude indicator of the extent of disease, the woman with known endometriosis is left with her pain as the only real indicator of the extent of her disease. She also understands that it may require uncomfortable and expensive hormonal therapies, multiple surgeries, may cause infertility, and may ultimately require hysterectomy and the removal of both ovaries. All of these events may occur rapidly or may extend over many years. That the clinical course of most cases of endometriosis is rather indolent is scant comfort to the affected woman and her partner who understand the disease. Fear, anxiety, and a sense of helplessness may contribute to pain intensity, depression, and sexual dysfunction.

Physical examination findings are most often lacking entirely in early cases of endometriosis, or may be limited to cul-de-sac tenderness without palpable nodularity. In the nulliparous woman, when oral contraceptives and prostaglandin inhibitors are either ineffective or their impact diminishes over time, endometriosis must be suspected, even in the absence of palpable pathology. (Other forms of intrinsic uterine pathology such as adenomyosis become more likely in the multiparous woman in her 30s or older.) While the possibility of endometriosis should certainly be reviewed when appropriate, expensive and difficult hormonal treatments (medroxyprogesterone, danocrine, gonadotropin-releasing hormone agonists) should not be initiated in the absence of a clear diagnosis. Laparoscopy offers the opportunity for diagnosis as well as treatment in the form of laser ablation, electrocautery, or excision. Given the highly variable progression of endometriosis over time, when symptoms persist or worsen despite treatment, a repeat laparoscopy a year or more later clarifies how aggressive the disease is in a particular patient. Most often, indolent disease does not change its behavior and become rapidly aggressive. This information is often invaluable for realistic planning of childbearing attempts and treatment, and serves to adjust vigilance and anxiety to appropriate levels. When more advanced disease is documented, stronger hormonal regimens should be started, and advanced laparoscopic surgery for reduction of the bulk of the disease should be considered.

The couple struggling with this disease also has to deal with the discomforts that are sometimes experienced during sexual intercourse. Dyspareunia is associated primarily with cul-de-sac disease, but may also occur when an ovary is adhered to the cul-de-sac or posterior broad ligament, especially in the case of a retroverted uterus. A woman experiencing this pain (and her partner) may understandably feel anxious about its recurrence, and may fear that the pain signals further tissue damage or progression of the disease. Sexual response may diminish as a result, which only aggravates the discomfort. Vaginal lubrication may then decrease or stop, and the normal physiologic, vaginal expansion that occurs with sexual arousal may cease, leaving the tender cul-de-sac closer to the vaginal introitus, and thus more easily struck during coitus. The more pain, the less sexual response—and the less

response, the more pain. Counseling suggestions appropriate for this problem are discussed below.

Pelvic Adhesions

Since the beginnings of abdominal surgery, postoperative adhesion formation has been a problem. Many have questioned the idea that adhesions cause pain, noting that the degree of adhesive disease does not correlate with pain intensity. However, recent studies suggest that, as in the case of endometriosis, the location of pain often corresponds well to the location of adhesions. Given the complexities of pain perception described above, this allows for the possibility that in cases of chronic pain, adhesions may be an important component of the problem in many individuals. Comprehensive treatment should certainly include attention to as many factors in the pain problem as possible, sometimes including attempts at adhesiolysis.

The pain associated with adhesions often starts within weeks of the physical insult responsible (e.g., pelvic infection, surgery). In most instances, pain duration varies from moments to an hour or so, and may be related to physical activity. Over time (beyond three or four months after its beginnings), pain episodes may progress in severity and duration, even if the physical pathology remains stable. Such a pattern should prompt careful inquiry regarding other factors such as constipation, muscular deconditioning, and the development of a chronic pain syndrome as described above. When one is involved in the ongoing care of such a problem from its start, the transition to a chronic pain syndrome can be subtle. When years separate the suspected insult from the beginning of the pain, other factors besides adhesions must be investigated.

Physical findings are often limited to pain roughly corresponding to the site of the adhesions (right, left, or midline). Over time, pain originating with adhesions may spread, as intestinal, muscular, and chronic pain syndrome factors are added to the mix. Depression and chronicity of pain, with a resultant lower pain threshold, serve to make the physical findings less distinct and treatment necessarily more complex. The inability to accurately diagnose pelvic or abdominal adhesions by ultrasound or other imaging techniques makes laparoscopy essential to the diagnosis and treatment of the problem in many cases. Preoperative laboratory screening should include studies to exclude more acute causes for pain, such as inflammatory conditions (e.g., sedimentation rate, cervical cultures for chlamydia and gonorrhea, urine culture). Bowel studies, such as endoscopy or barium enema, should be limited to those women exhibiting signs (e.g., hematochezia, mucus), as opposed to only symptoms, of bowel disease.

Laparotomy for pain attributed to adhesions should continue to be reserved for patients who have intestinal obstruction refractory to medical management. However, a number of studies of laparoscopic adhesiolysis suggest that pain relief may be obtained in 70 to 80 percent of cases. In especially refractory or difficult situations, repeating laparoscopy at time intervals as short as one week may be effective. Ultimately, effective management of the problem of recurrent adhesions is likely to be solved only with a multimodal approach, combining adhesion-preventing agents such as Ringer's lactate at the time of original laparoscopy, with second-look procedures at short intervals, allowing the reapplication of such agents. At this time, such procedures remain experimental.

Pelvic Support Problems

Pelvic relaxation commonly occurs in the fifth and sixth decades of life or later, while most chronic pelvic pain problems occur in the third and fourth decades. Nevertheless, in some women pelvic relaxation may be accompanied by feelings of heaviness, pressure, dropping sensations, and aching. Treatment is primarily surgical, ideally employing preoperative estrogen replacement in the case of the postmenopausal woman.

Levator Muscle Spasm

Levator muscle spasm may develop by itself or, more commonly, in reaction to another pelvic discomfort. Along with occasional pain with defecation or during intercourse, the patient may note a sense of pelvic heaviness or the sensation of something "falling out" even when pelvic support is normal. Such sensations often resolve promptly upon reclining, worsen during the course of the day, and are frequently accompanied by progressive loss of sexual response.

Diagnosis of this problem is primarily made by the history described above, corroborated by pelvic examination that demonstrates levator plate tenderness. Kegel exercises, consciously "letting it all fall out," reclining at intervals during the day, and hot baths may help. Muscle relaxants are helpful in duress, but physical therapy approaches such as the above should be attempted first. Of course, relief of the primary pelvic pathology may result in spontaneous resolution of the spasm, but it can remain as an ongoing problem for some women, even when the precipitating cause is successfully treated.

Causes of Pain in the "Laparoscopy-Negative" Patient

A variety of other etiologies (Table 37-2) for pelvic pain may occur in the absence of any laparoscopically observable cause. Of course, any of these disorders may occur in the presence of visible pathology as well. In many instances, the musculoskeletal and urinary tract problems listed may accumulate over time, as a person's distress over problems such as endometriosis or adhesions increases. A careful chronologic history of the various pain components may shed light on this pattern.

Dyspareunia

Some of the more common contributing factors that may cause or exacerbate dyspareunia are

TABLE 37-2 Possible Causes for Pelvic Pain in "Laparoscopy-Negative" Patients

Gastrointestinal tract
   Constipation
   Irritable bowel syndrome
   Inflammatory bowel disease
   Diverticulitis
Urinary tract
   Urethral syndrome
   Interstitial cystitis
Musculoskeletal, neurologic
   Pelvic floor tension myalgia (levator spasm)
   Piriformis syndrome
   Nerve entrapment
   Ventral hernia
   Rectus tendon strain
   Myofascial pain
   Back/pelvic postural changes
Gynecologic
   Pelvic vascular congestion
   Cervical stenosis
   Endometritis

TABLE 37-3 Factors Contributing to the Development of Sexual Dysfunction

Vulvar
   Vulvar vestibulitis syndrome
   Chronic monilial vulvitis
Vaginal
   Repeated or chronic vaginitis
   Urethritis/urethral syndrome
   Interstitial cystitis
   Cervicitis
   Diminished lubrication due to insufficient arousal
   Levator spasm
   Treatment with progestins or Gn-RH analogs
Deep pelvic
   Uterine retroversion (rare cases)
   Pelvic relaxation
   Endometriosis
   Adhesions
   Adenomyosis
   Pelvic congestion syndrome
   Lack of vaginal expansion due to insufficient arousal

listed in Table 37-3. An individual may certainly be afflicted with more than one cause, given that many of the problems listed are quite common.

Further, the presence of one problem may predispose a woman to the development of other problems in the list. For example, vaginitis may recur often enough to create anxiety, which in turn, alters sexual response often enough to diminish vaginal lubrication during coitus. The resulting vaginal dryness may cause coitus-related urinary tract infection, leading to treatment with antibiotics that bring on more episodes of vaginitis. As this unhappy scenario unfolds, deep dyspareunia begins as diminished sexual response, eliminating the vaginal expansion and uterine elevation that usually accompanies sexual response, allowing previously asymptomatic culde-sac endometriosis to be more easily struck during intercourse. These discomforts (or similar ones due to different types of pelvic pathology) and the anticipation of their regular recurrence

cause a protective contraction of the vaginal introital muscles at the start of a coital attempt, resulting in involuntary spasm (vaginismus) over time.

To follow our prototypic patient a bit further, let us suggest that the stress of these problems aggravates a previously mild case of irritable bowel syndrome. Loss of orgasmic response may add to the problems by adding symptoms of chronic pelvic heaviness attributed to venous overfilling, or the pelvic congestion syndrome. Over time, levator spasm may begin, adding to the "falling out" sensation that the patient experiences. Laparoscopy then reveals her endometriosis, and because childbearing is complete, she undergoes laparoscopically assisted vaginal hysterectomy, removal of both ovaries, and laser treatment of the endometriosis.

Postoperatively, some tender granulation tissue at the vaginal apex requires several treatments with silver nitrate cautery. The emotional environment surrounding attempts at intercourse has become strained. Her sexual response fails to return, helping to perpetuate the vicious cycle of pain-decreased sexual response–more pain.

After this problem has continued for 6 months to a year, she begins to note some trouble sleeping. She has some difficulty getting to sleep, but also notes that she sometimes wakes up at 4 AM and can't get back to sleep. Fatigue increases, and she stops exercising. Some low-back pain

TABLE 37-4 Counseling Suggestions for Sexual Dysfunction

Introital Dyspareunia

(First eliminate tissue conditions such as vestibulitis, vaginitis)
  Supplemental lubrication
    Vegetable oil (don't use with latex contraceptive products)
    Commercially available lubricants
  Vaginal relaxation exercises
    Demonstrate during pelvic examination first; patient practices contraction-relaxation cycles (Kegel exercises with short contraction, long relaxation phases) alone, then with partner present, then with partner's finger inserted;
    then "bridge over" into intercourse, doing only what is comfortable (the "no pain" contract)
  Position changes
    Suggest cross-wise position for intercourse (with both partners on their sides facing one another) to allow careful vaginal entry, and to allow the woman to have control over the degree of vaginal penetration.

Deep Dyspareunia

  Correct pelvic pathology to the degree clinically possible, but try to avoid extirpative surgery as much as possible, unless otherwise clinically indicated
  Suggest "no-pain contract," i.e., "don't do anything that hurts," proceeding with deeper entry only if sexual arousal is present and deeper entry is comfortable
  Suggest cross-wise position, as above
  Supplemental lubrication, as needed

General Considerations

  Refer for professional counseling if
    More than one sexual dysfunction is present (e.g., vaginismus and premature ejaculation);
    Significant marital discord is present;
    The dysfunction has been present for over a year before help is sought;
    The suggestions made seem difficult to implement

starts, and she wonders if the endometriosis has recurred. . . .

Every practicing gynecologist has seen patients with at least some portion of this story. The situation may seem hopeless and overwhelming for the patient and the physician at its end point. Nevertheless, significant help can often be rendered, with time and patience, by the gynecologist, either alone or in collaboration with a skilled counselor. History-taking should emphasize the chronology of events, in the hope of understanding a sequence such as that described above. Discussing this with the patient can help make it seem more manageable by breaking it down into a sequence of smaller problems. Indeed, understanding the chronology of events and each of the sequentially contributing factors may improve the patient's and physician's abilities to address and alleviate the problems.

A brief listing of useful office counseling suggestions is listed in Table 37-4. More complete discussions of the topic are in the references cited.

References and Selected Readings

1. Bachmann GA, Leiblum SR, Grill J: Brief sexual inquiry in gynecology practice. *Obstet Gynecol* 73:425–427, 1989.
2. Carlson KJ, Miller BA, Fowler FJ Jr: The Maine Women's Health Study: II. Outcomes of nonsurgical management of leiomyomas, abnormal bleeding, and chronic pelvic pain. *Obstet Gynecol* 83:566, 1994.
3. Fedele L, Parazzini F, Bianchi S, et al: Stage and localization of pelvic endometriosis and pain. *Fertil Steril* 53:155–158, 1990.
4. Lamont JA: Female dyspareunia. *Am J Obstet Gynecol* 136:282–285, 1980.
5. Reiter RC: Occult somatic pathology in women with chronic pelvic pain. *Clin Obstet Gynecol* 33:154–160, 1990.
6. Reiter RC, Gambone JC: Demographic and historic variables in women with idiopathic chronic pelvic pain. *Obstet Gynecol* 75:428–432, 1990.
7. Sinaki M, Merritt JL, Stillwell GK: Tension myalgia of the pelvic floor. *Mayo Clin Proc* 52:717–722, 1977.
8. Steege JF, Ling FW: Dyspareunia: A special type of

chronic pelvic pain. *Obstet Gynecol Clin North Am* 20:779–793, 1993.

9. Steege JF, Metzger DA, Levy BS: *Chronic Pelvic Pain: An Integrated Approach*. Philadelphia: WB Saunders, 1998.

10. Steege JF, Stout AL: Resolution of chronic pelvic pain following laparoscopic adhesiolysis. *Am J Obstet Gynecol* 165:278–283, 1991.

11. Steege JF, Stout AL, Somkuti S: Chronic pelvic pain: Toward an integrative model. *Obstet Gynecol Surv* 48:95–110, 1993.

12. Stout AL, Steege JF, Dodson WC, et al: Relationship of laparoscopic findings to self-report of pelvic pain. *Am J Obstet Gynecol* 164:73–79, 1991.

13. Stovall TG, Ling FW, Crawford DA: Hysterectomy for chronic pelvic pain of presumed uterine etiology. *Obstet Gynecol* 75:676–679, 1990.

14. Walker EW, Katon W, Harrop-Griffiths J, et al: Relationship of chronic pelvic pain to psychiatric diagnoses and childhood sexual abuse. *Am J Psychiatry* 145:75–80, 1988.

CHAPTER 38

Premalignant and Malignant Gynecologic Lesions

Joanna M. Cain

VULVA

Vulvar Squamous Changes • Pigmented Lesions and Nevi • Paget's Disease • Vulvar Biopsy • Management of Vulvar Intraepithelial Neoplasia (VIN) and Invasive Carcinoma • Management of Malignant Melanoma

VAGINA

Normal Vaginal Examination • Vaginal Squamous Changes • Vaginal Biopsy • Management

CERVIX

Normal Cervix • Cervical Abnormalities • Cervical Biopsy • Management • Follow-up

UTERUS

Management

OVARIES

Normal Ovaries • Ovarian Masses • Biopsy • Management

FALLOPIAN TUBES
GESTATIONAL TROPHOBLASTIC DISEASE

Molar Pregnancy • Choriocarcinoma

T his chapter is structured by anatomic site and provides the following for each site:

1. Introduction to common premalignant and malignant gynecologic pathology
2. Standard techniques of evaluation for diagnosis
3. Decision-making flow charts (Figs. 38-1 to 38-4)
4. Information about management of premalignant and malignant gynecologic lesions

Vulva

The skin of the vulva must sustain integrity in the face of multiple insults from body moisture, urine, fecal material, trauma, and infections with local or introduced pathogens. Considering the biological challenge it faces, it is surprising that vulvar abnormalities are not the most common abnormalities in women. Vulvar cancer only comprises 5 percent of all gynecologic malignancies. In considering premalignant and malignant changes in vulvar tissue it is valuable to remember the axiom for all gynecologic tissues that can be visually inspected: *If it looks abnormal, it should be biopsied.* This is the only way that the clinician can avoid misdiagnosing a premalignant problem or a vulvar cancer.

Vulvar Squamous Changes

The normal color of the vulvar skin is uniform over the labia majora but may vary over the labia minora. There is an obvious change from the pink, unpigmented vaginal mucous membrane to the labia minus at the introitus. The vulvar skin becomes thicker, more stratified, more pigmented, and more keratinized the farther it is from the introital area. Normal vulvae should be symmetric in their distribution of pigment changes, underlying fat, and thickness of skin. Changes in pigmentation, thickness, or symmetry should be sought at every examination. Lentiginous changes in the vulva are normal and fairly common.

The most common premalignant change in vulvar skin is vulvar intraepithelial neoplasia (VIN). The physical appearance of VIN can vary from mild whitening of the epithelium with no change in texture to lesions with a tan to brown appearance and to lesions that mimic condylomata. It is for this reason that any change of appearance warrants further evaluation and usually biopsy.

VIN has been associated with the human papilloma virus (HPV).[6,17] VIN is most commonly associated with women in the 20- to 30-year age range, while invasive squamous cancers are more commonly seen in older women.[17,35] Verrucous cancer, one of the rarer subtypes of squamous cancers that occurs more frequently in older women, has a gross appearance very similar to that of condylomata acuminata.[24] That these cancers may appear either mimicking condylomata or in concert with apparent HPV infection, argues for a high index of suspicion and biopsy rather than presumption of diagnosis and treatment of HPV.

Colposcopy of the vulva can reveal some of the features of neoplasia seen in lesions on the mucous membranes. Obviously, these features are more likely to be present the closer the lesion is to the introital area, because keratinization may obscure the underlying vascular structures. Changes suggestive of VIN are white epithelium, mosaicism and punctation, and irregular surface structure.[19]

Invasive squamous cancers generally share the characteristic of being more friable and more frequently associated with loss of skin integrity or ulceration. As noted, the verrucous subtype does not share these characteristics, as it mimics condylomata. In addition, most invasive cancers are unilateral, thus destroying the symmetry described earlier. Invasive cancers are associated with thickening and irregularity of the epithelium. Colposcopically, these lesions can display the hallmarks of invasion such as atypical, aberrant blood vessels and marked irregularity of the

topography of the lesion. Colposcopic evaluation is rarely required, however, because these lesions stand out as different even in vulva with squamous hypertrophy or other vulvar conditions.

Pigmented Lesions and Nevi

Lentiginous changes are present on the vulva as a normal finding. It is important to note that such changes occur in the basal layer and as such should not disturb in any way the texture of the skin in the area. Nevi also are present on the vulva as a normal finding. However, for the proportionate area of skin represented by vulvar tissue (2 percent), a disproportionate number of malignant melanomas (3 to 5 percent) occur in this area.[25] This has led some authors to suggest removal of all nevi, although the actual benefit in terms of prevention of melanoma is unknown. Certainly, the number of admittedly uncomfortable biopsies with benign findings would be likely to be excessive.

Given these caveats, it is important to document the presence of any presumed nevi on the vulvar skin and to chart the appearance of these areas over time. Any adverse change in appearance warrants removal of the area. In addition, the changes associated with malignant melanoma in other areas of the skin should always be evaluated. These include asymmetry within the lesion/nevus itself; an irregular border; marked color change, including different shades in the same lesion; a diameter greater than 6 mm or size changes; and any evidence of an inflammatory response with weeping, bleeding, or itching. Finally, as distinct from lentigo, the skin is elevated in the area of melanoma.

Paget's Disease

Another change in the vulvar skin of importance is the erythematous and often raised and rough surface associated with Paget's disease.[4,15] This can be unilateral or bilateral, but again presents with a departure from previous evaluation and certainly from normal skin appearance. It often appears pink and white, and is sometimes said to have a "cake frosting" appearance. This lesion can be difficult to differentiate from chronic skin irritation due to multiple etiologies, such as urinary incontinence.

Vulvar Biopsy

The next step in evaluating all these abnormalities is vulvar biopsy or wide local excision of the area. The decision regarding whether one biopsy, multiple biopsies, or wide local excision is appropriate depends on the area involved, the number of lesions, and the type of potential premalignant or malignant condition that the appearance portends. For a large lesion or multiple affected areas, it must be borne in mind that a single biopsy with a benign or a premalignant diagnosis does not preclude invasive cancer elsewhere on the vulva. As a general rule, a single lesion up to 1 cm can be easily excised in the office setting. Multiple lesions require multiple biopsies. In addition, lesions that are suspicious for melanoma are best served by an initial wide excision that is deep enough to allow for pathological measurement of depth of invasion. If the lesion suspicious for melanoma is too large for adequate local excision, the biopsy technique must be adequately deep to permit proper measurement of depth of invasion.

Two techniques are appropriate in this area and are summarized below:

PUNCH BIOPSY

Equipment

- Local antiseptic solution
- Local anesthetic and 30-gauge needle
- Topical anesthetic if lesion is on mucosal area
- Keyes punch (disposable): 6-, 8-, or 10-mm, depending on size and depth of lesion
- Iris scissors
- Fine surgical forceps
- Silver nitrate sticks
- Gauze sponges

Note: Have available Monsel's solution, needle holder, 3-0 suture

Procedure After adequate preparation of the area, infiltrate the skin with local anesthetic (if on mucosal area, pretreat area with topical anesthetic). Place the punch over the area and press firmly while twirling the punch between thumb and forefinger. Remove the punch and grasp the specimen below the skin level with forceps. Cut the base cleanly with the iris scissors. Put the specimen in fixative. Cauterize the base or suture as clinically indicated.

Precautions for the Patient The area is at risk for infection and bleeding. Some spotting and bleeding can be expected for 24 h. Ice packs may be applied to control swelling and for comfort for the first 24 h as necessary. Wound care should include 1 or 2 sitz baths per day for 2 days and longer if the area is not closed. The area should not be rubbed or wiped but patted dry or dried with a hand-held hair dryer on a low temperature. Any evidence of increasing pain, erythema, fever, or increased bleeding should be reported promptly.

WIDE LOCAL EXCISION

Equipment

- Local antiseptic solution
- Local anesthetic and 30-gauge needle
- Topical anesthetic if lesion is on mucosal area
- No. 15 scalpel (disposable)
- Iris scissors
- Fine surgical forceps
- Needle holder (fine)
- Hemostat
- Suture: 2-0, 3-0, or 4-0 subcuticular (cutting needle)
- Gauze sponges
- Sterile perineal pad

Note: Optional: purple sterile surgical pen, surgical assistant (extremely helpful)

Procedure After adequate preparation of the area, infiltrate the area with local anesthetic (use topical pretreatment if on mucosal area). Outline the area to be resected prior to preparation or at this time, if necessary. Excise the perimeter from inferior to superior. Grasping one edge, dissect the area to be removed from the underlying subcutaneous tissue with the scalpel at a depth appropriate for the lesion type. Put the specimen in fixative, with a suture at 12 o'clock if orientation is important. Grasp areas of major bleeding with the hemostat and tie. Close the incision in layers with 2-0 for the deep subcutaneous layer and 3-0 or 4-0 for the skin closure, using either a subcuticular or an interrupted closure.

Precautions for the Patient These are the same as for the punch biopsy, with the following exceptions: Ice should be applied to the perineum for 24 h. (A damp sterile perineal pad cooled in the freezer makes a good ice pad to use at home.) After 24 h, sitz baths twice a day for 1 week are recommended. Any evidence of increasing pain, erythema, fever, or increased bleeding should be reported promptly.

Management of Vulvar Intraepithelial Neoplasia and Invasive Carcinoma [Fig. 38-1]

The underlying phenomenon of VIN is the assumed connection between the propensity to form VIN and infection with HPV. That the virus appears to infect the field—including the perineum, potentially the distal anal squamous area, the vagina, and the cervix at the time of the initial exposure—underlies the clinical pattern of behavior of these lesions. Despite adequate treatment with local excision, laser ablation, or topical solutions such as 5-fluorouracil, these lesions have a 30 to 50 percent chance of recurrence. Because women with VIN and invasive vulvar cancers are at higher risk for cervical and vaginal lesions as well, they must also have an evaluation of the cervix and vagina, usually by colposcopy. Certain patient behaviors or conditions seem to be related to the development of such neoplasias, including smoking and the use of immunosuppressive drugs or immunosuppres-

sion associated with infection with human immunodeficiency virus (HIV). Greater age does increase the likelihood of finding invasive disease, so excision is the best choice for therapy.[9,10] No matter how young or old the patient, under no circumstances should a lesion be presumed to be VIN and treated with ablative therapy without adequate biopsies and careful histologic evaluation to rule out the presence of microinvasive or invasive cancer.

Patient Counsel The obvious preventive counsel for patients without the disease is to avoid infection with HPV and HIV a priori. For patients with VIN, smoking cessation and avoidance of infection with the virus are important topics to cover. In addition, patient vulvar self-examination and report of any new lesions is important in follow-up. Appropriate follow-up includes inspection and colposcopy every 3 months for the first year, every 6 months for the next, and then yearly if no other lesions appear. Continued support for smoking cessation and avoidance of sexually transmitted diseases is appropriate.

Invasive squamous cancers and verrucous cancers are appropriately treated by surgical excision. The extent of surgical excision may vary by the lesion size, location, histologic appearance—including depth of invasion and the presence or absence of involvement of regional inguinal lymph nodes—and local structures. As an example, some early invasion (less than 1 mm with no other prognostic risk factors) may be treated by wide radical excision, whereas a 1-cm lesion with a spray pattern located in the midline may require full radical vulvectomy and bilateral groin lymph node dissection. Large lesions that compromise surrounding structures such as the pubic arch or the urethra or rectum may be better treated with chemoradiation and potential subsequent excision. Choices of therapy come under the expertise of the gynecologic oncologist and require such consultation.

Overall, squamous cancers of the vulva are found at earlier stages and associated with excellent long-term cure rates (Table 38-1). Follow-

Squamous Lesions

Small (<1 cm)   Large (≥1 cm or multiple lesions)

Biopsy

Completely excise   Representative biopsies of most
                                                         worrisome areas

VIN I, II   **VIN III**   **Invasive cancer**
▲ Assess for immunocompro-   ▲ Colposcopy.   ▲ Early, well-differentiated,
  mise, smoking, and expo-   ▲ To rule out early cancer,   <1 mm, with no suspicious
  sure to HPV.   excise if thick, irregular sur-   areas for vascular or lym-
▲ Colposcopy.   face and/or marked variabil-   phatic spread or spray
▲ Treat residual areas with   ity in appearance or if there   pattern.
  excision or local ablation   is any question regarding   ▲ Wide local radical excision.
  except in some chronically   the possibility of cancer.
  immunosuppressed patients   ▲ If homogeneous appearance
  where close follow-up can   and biopsy are representa-   **Invasive cancer**
  be anticipated.   tive, consider ablation of   ▲ Treatment depends on size
▲ >45 years of age, best Rx   remaining lesions. If   and site.
  by complete excision for   > age 45, excision is   ▲ Standard Rx: radical vulvec-
  pathology.   preferred.   tomy and groin node dissec-
                                                                  tion (less extensive surgery
                                                                  may be appropriate).

                           Follow-up   **Follow-up**
                    ▲ Clinical visits   ▲ Clinical visits
                      Every 3 months the first   Every 3 months for the first
                      year.   year.
                      Every 6 months the second   Every 4 months the second
                      year.   year.
                      Annually thereafter.   Every 6 months, to 5 years.
                    ▲ Teach vulvar self-examination.   Annually thereafter.
                    ▲ Counsel to avoid risk factors.   ▲ Note association with cervi-
                    ▲ Note association with cervi-   cal and vaginal neoplasia
                      cal and vaginal neoplasia   and need for screening.
                      and need for screening.

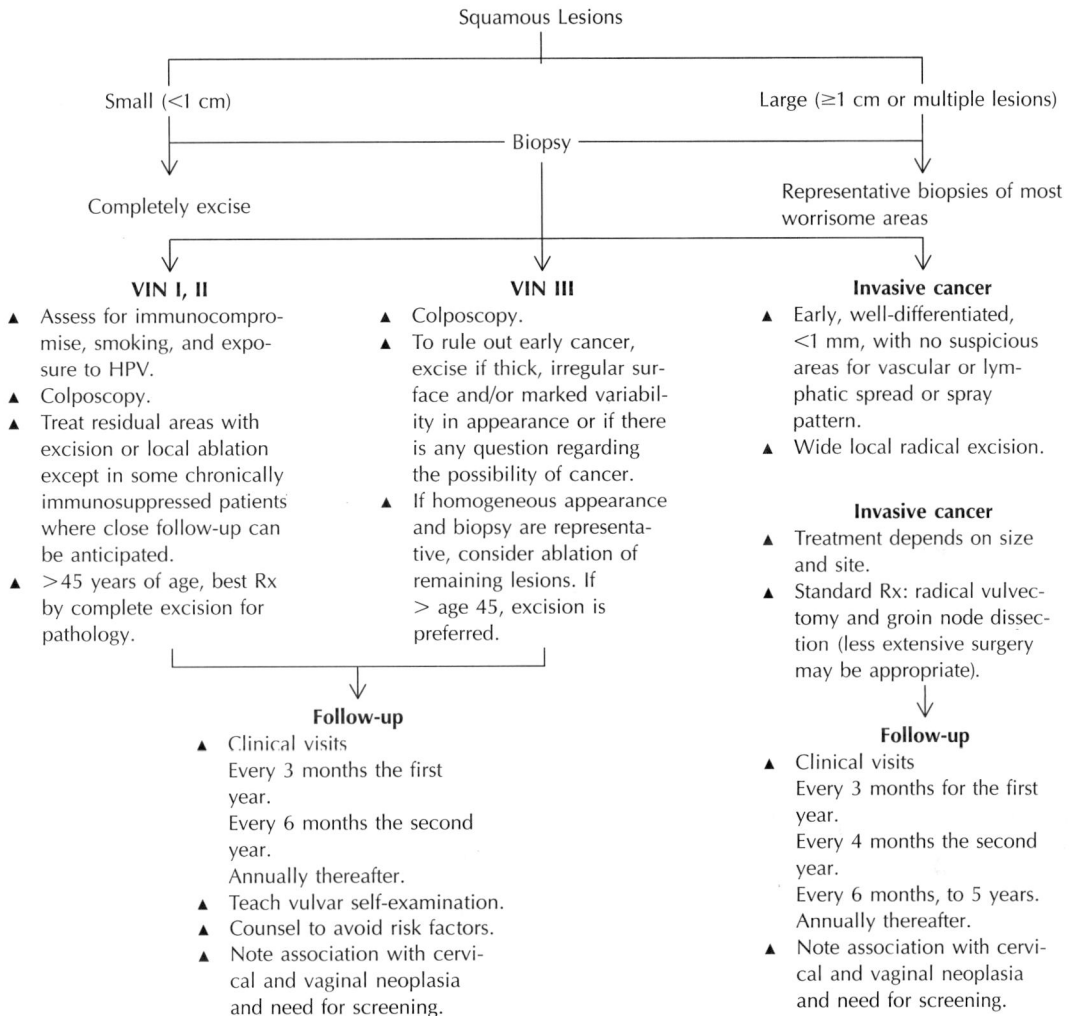

Figure 38-1   Decision flowchart for vulvar cancer.

up for patients includes an evaluation every 3 months for the first year, then follow-up depending on the prognostic factors of the original lesion. These patients are also at risk for the development of VIN or neoplasia elsewhere in the genital tract or the anorectal area, and clinical evaluation of these areas is required during follow-up.

Management of Malignant Melanoma
As opposed to the squamous cancers, malignant melanomas derive their prognosis from depth of invasion and are rarely found in favorable depth.[14,25] The standard therapy remains either vulvectomy or wide local radical dissection, both with regional node dissection. Other forms of therapy such as radiation, chemotherapy, and

TABLE 38-1   Common Invasive Disease and Treatment

Type of Cancer	Most Common Type	Most Common Stage	5-Year Survival	Common Treatment[a]	Common Side Effects of Treatment
Vulvar	Squamous	I	90%	Radical vulvectomy and bilateral groin node dissection (less extensive surgery may be appropriate for many lesions)	Wound breakdown, leg lymphedema
Vaginal	Squamous	Rare	Variable	Radiation or radical surgery	
Cervical	Squamous	I	75 to 90%	Radical hysterectomy with lymph node dissection	Ureteral fistula (1.6%), bowel and bladder dysfunction
				Radiation therapy	Ureteral fistula (1.6%), long-term bowel, rectal, and bladder dysfunction, including fistula
Endometrial	Adenocarcinoma	I	75 to 90%	Staging laparotomy with total abdominal hysterectomy, bilateral salpingo-oophorectomy, and node sampling	
				May require adjuvant radiation therapy	Radiation may result in bladder and bowel changes
Ovarian	Epithelial carcinoma	III	30%	Staging laparotomy with tumor debulking, TAH-BSO, omentectomy, multiple biopsies, possible bowel resection	
				Chemotherapy given after initial exploration	Chemotherapy side effects depend on which agents are used

[a]Treatment depends on histopathology and clinical risk factors.

immunotherapy, remain of little benefit for most of the these patients. Again, selection of therapy is the expertise of the gynecologic oncologist, and these patients require such consultation.

Vagina

Normal Vaginal Examination

The normal vagina should have a pale-pink appearance that demonstrates a good subdermal blood supply throughout. The texture of the walls should be smooth with circular rugae. The under-lying tissue should be symmetrical and should not contain cystic or firm structures. The suburethral area should be rubbery, consistent throughout its length and not firm. On inspection it is important to note that either the traditional Graves or the Pedersen metal speculum will obscure the vaginal mucosa underneath, and adequate inspection requires either the use of a clear plastic speculum or careful inspection of the anterior and posterior walls on withdrawal of the speculum. It is also important to note that Pap smears can identify vaginal neoplasia. If the Pap smear is abnormal but there is no cervical pathology, the vagina requires careful inspection, including colposcopy, to rule it out as the site of the abnormality.

Vaginal Squamous Changes

The same changes that are seen in the medial vulva when neoplastic lesions are present are seen in the vagina. Because the vagina is not keratinized, colposcopy can identify lesions that are clinically inapparent. Application of 1% acetic acid to the area of colposcopic view and sequential inspection with colposcopy from cephalad to caudad offers a method that should prevent skipping a clinically inapparent lesion. Of practical assistance, given the softness of the vaginal walls and their tendency to collapse into the field of view, a condom (with both ends open) or finger of a large surgical glove applied over the speculum before insertion can assist in the lateral retraction of tissue. Again, the classic changes of whitening of the epithelium or pigment change as well as vascular changes (from punctation to atypical or abnormal vessels) identify the areas for biopsy. Invasive squamous cancers may be friable, may be ulcerated, and have a consistency that is different from the surrounding mucosa. Such lesions should be biopsied regardless of the colposcopic appearance or Pap smear results. Again, remember the axiom: *If it looks abnormal it should be biopsied.*

Cystic areas can be seen in the wall of the vagina. These may be associated with epithelialized islands of adenosis in patients with a history of diethylstilbestrol (DES) exposure or may be remnant cysts. The hallmarks of colposcopic vascular changes associated with DES exposure[36] or with neopolasia must be sought before conservative management is proposed. In addition, for DES patients a drawn map of lesions is of great assistance to the patient and the physician in the long-term management of such lesions. While clear cell adenocarcinoma of the vagina is less common contemporarily, the clinical appearance is of importance. One of the differences between adenocarcinomas and squamous carcinomas in

the vaginal mucosa is the fact that these lesions often may not be palpably different from the surrounding tissue and therefore are more likely to be missed at early stages. In addition, adenocarcinomas may have a papillary and cystic appearance as well as the ulcerative and friable nature associated with squamous cancers. Again, the importance of careful inspection of the entire vagina, including the anterior and posterior surfaces, cannot be overstated.

Vaginal Biopsy

Vaginal biopsy presents particular difficulties because of the soft and mobile nature of vaginal tissue. Wide local excision requires significant surgical assistance and rarely is an option for the office setting.

Equipment
- Local antiseptic solution
- Local and topical anesthetic solution
- Skin hook
- Allis clamp, long
- Kevorkian or Shubert biopsy forceps
- No. 15 blade scalpel
- Long forceps or Crile clamp
- Long Metzenbaum scissors
- Long hemostat
- Long needle holder
- Gauze sponges
- Sponge stick
- Chromic or Dexon suture material, 2-0 or 3-0 atraumatic
- Silver nitrate and Monsel's solution

The appropriate mixture of equipment depends on the area of the vagina involved and the accessibility of the lesion. The above list is provided because all of these instruments have been found to be of assistance at one time or another, depending on the extent of the lesion.

Procedure   In general, lesions near the introitus can be managed much as described in the section on vulvar biopsies. Lesions near the cervix can be managed as described under "Cervix" (see text following below). It is the lesions in the deep vaginal fornices and sidewalls, which are difficult to grasp, that present a greater clinical challenge. Such lesions can be managed with topical application of anesthetic (and infiltration as needed) and grasping with an Allis or skin hook to tent the area so as to enable the use of a biopsy forceps, scalpel, or Metzenbaum scissors. Adequate exposure of the area is important, and readjustment of the speculum or addition of the sidewall support as described previously can be very helpful. There is a tendency, however, to overdistend the vagina in the region, which leads to an inability to tent the vaginal wall. This can be solved by merely releasing the pressure slightly on the speculum.

Precautions for the Patient This area is at risk for infection and bleeding. Spotting and bleeding can be expected for 24 hours. No vaginal intercourse, tampons, or douching should be permitted for at least 24 hours for small biopsies, and longer depending on the size of the biopsy. Any increasing pain, bleeding, or fever should be promptly reported.

Management

The most common neoplastic lesions in the vagina are vaginal intraepithelial neoplasia (VAIN) and invasive squamous cancer.[2] VAIN can be treated with a multiplicity of options, including wide local excision, laser ablations, and topical measures such as 5-fluorouracil. Of these, the only option that adequately evaluates the lesion for the presence of early invasive disease is the wide local excision. For this reason, if the biopsy suggests a carcinoma in situ or there is any clinical or pathologic question of invasion, the local excision is usually the best option.

Invasive vaginal cancer is rare, and the appropriate management is predicated on the depth of invasion, the location of the lesion, and the cell type. The majority of vaginal cancers are treated primarily with radiation, although radical surgery is appropriate in some patients with limited le-

sions. Such choices come under the expertise of gynecologic oncologists and require such consultation.

Patient Counsel While vaginal cancer and intraepithelial neoplasia have not received the study that vulvar and cervical lesions have, the avoidance of infection with HPV and HIV is appropriate in prevention. For patients with such lesions, particularly intraepithelial neoplasia, support for smoking cessation, as well as prevention of infection with other sexually transmitted pathogens, may be of value.

Cervix

Cervical neoplastic changes are far more common than either vaginal or vulvar changes. For this reason, any woman's primary care physician should be aware of the issues involved in the management of premalignant and malignant lesions of the cervix. The hallmark symptom of invasive cervical cancer, postcoital bleeding, is important to note because lesions may not be clinically apparent, and this symptom should warrant further investigation even if the Pap smear is read as negative. The false-negative rate of one Pap smear may be as high as 10 to 30 percent[10] and cannot be taken as proof that no malignancy exists. In the face of this classic symptom of malignancy, further evaluation is warranted.

Normal Cervix

The normal cervix has a uniform pale-pink appearance with a smooth surface. Occasional nabothian cysts can be seen with mucoid material covered by a smooth surface epithelium. These can vary in size, but should not be friable or irregular in appearance. The endocervix generally appears velvety red. Previous trauma to the cervix from biopsy or cervical lacerations should present a white appearance with a distribution consistent with the trauma, most often linear. The substance of the cervix is moderately firm and consistent throughout. The shape of the cervix should be symmetrical, except in those circumstances in which significant cervical trauma or previous surgery can be documented.

Cervical Abnormalities

Because of early detection of many neoplastic changes of the cervix by Pap smear, these changes may be apparent only colposcopically. Therefore, any patient with a Pap smear consistent with CIN or invasive cancer (unless a tissue diagnosis of invasive cancer has already been obtained)—and often patients with a smear interpreted as atypical squamous cells of undetermined significance—must undergo colposcopic evaluation. The colposcopic hallmarks of a neoplastically active epithelium are described in Chap. 47. The adequacy of view of the most biologically active zone, the *transformation zone,* must be carefully assessed and documented. A careful map should be drawn for further evaluation and management. Areas of abnormality should be biopsied for diagnosis. It is essential that the transformation zone can be visualized totally because almost all cervical cancers begin in this region. If the whole transformation zone cannot be visualized colposcopically, the physician cannot be certain that invasive cancer is not present.

Any gross lesion of the cervix requires biopsy, preferably at the time of first notation. Some patients may prefer rescheduling, but a Pap smear obtained at the time of notation of such a lesion is not adequate either to make a diagnosis of the etiology of the lesion or to plan therapy. A negative Pap smear does not alter the mandatory requirement for biopsy of any abnormal lesion noted clinically.

Of importance in the evaluation of the cervix are lesions that occur in the endocervical area. These may present with no gross external abnormality and merely a thickening of the cervical diameter. The ability of Pap smears to detect such lesions is diminished because of their site in the substance of the endocervix. Because of these difficulties, the diagnosis of endocervical lesions can be clinically challenging. The endo-cervical curettage is often the only way to diagnose such cancers, and, even so, may miss the lesion. A high index of suspicion is therefore appropriate.

Cervical Biopsy

This discussion confines itself to routine biopsy of the cervix. Loop excision is discussed in Chap. 47 on colposcopy.

Equipment
- Antiseptic solution
- Topical anesthetic solution
- Shubert, Kevorkian, Tischler biopsy forceps
- Kevorkian curette
- Silver nitrate sticks, Monsel's solution

Note: Optional: tenaculum, paracervical block material (see endometrial biopsy, Chap. 48).

Procedure After identification of the area either visually or colposcopically, topical anesthetic can be applied to the area. In patients with previous traumatic experiences with cervical biopsy, consideration of a paracervical block may be appropriate. In general, simple cervical biopsy is well tolerated. The area for biopsy is located and biopsy forceps chosen based on the site. For some lesions at the transformation zone, the need to grasp the endocervical area may suggest a Kevorkian biopsy forceps as the best choice. If there is difficulty due to excess cervical mobility, use of the tenaculum can be quite helpful. As with all biopsies, the area of highest clinical suspicion should be biopsied first, particularly if discomfort or unusual bleeding occurs. This will assure that the most important area is evaluated. An endocervical curettage is performed with the Kevorkian curette.

Precautions for the Patient There may be spotting and bleeding for 24 h following the procedure. No douching, use of tampons, or intercourse are permitted for 24 h. If fever, increased bleeding, or pelvic pain occurs, this should be reported promptly.

Gross Lesion or Colposcopic Lesion (with Adequate Colposcopy)

↓

Biopsy

CIN I		CIN II and III		Invasive cervical cancer		
Reliable	Unreliable or difficult to follow (or desires therapy)	+ECC Extent of lesion(?) Invasion(?)	Clearly defined lesion, no endocervical extension.	<3 mm No lymphatic or vascular invasion, not multiple areas.	Confined to cervix	Extends outside cervix
					Radical hysterectomy and node dissection or radiation.	Possible lymph node sampling and staging surgery.
						Radiation with possible chemotherapy.
Observe q 3 mo.	Rx with excision or ablation	Cone biopsy	Excision or ablation	Hysterectomy, possibly extended cone biopsy if fertility an issue (with close follow-up and planned hysterectomy).		

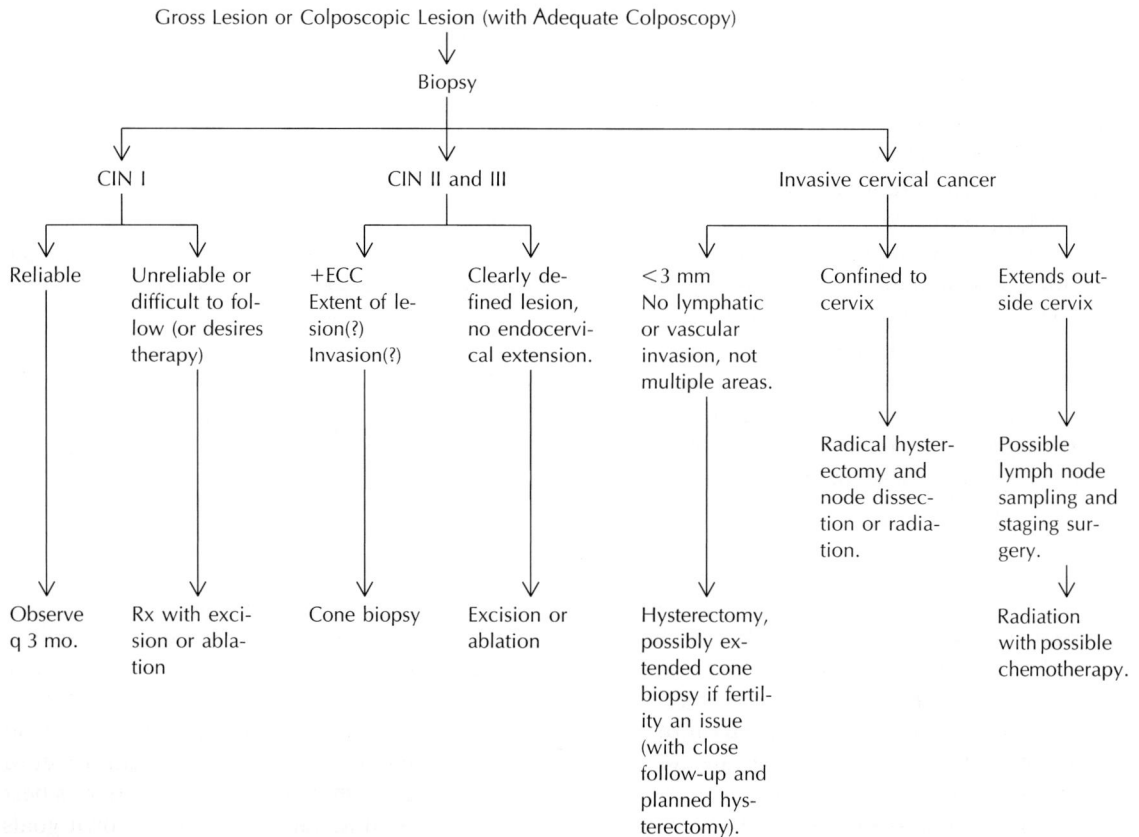

Figure 38-2   Decision flowchart for cervical cancer.

Management [Fig. 38-2]

Management of preinvasive cervical disease is discussed in Chap. 47.

For patients with CIN III and negative endocervical evaluation who have completed desired childbearing or are perimenopausal, a hysterectomy may be the most appropriate choice, because it produces a slightly lower chance of recurrence. For these patients as well, the importance of careful compliance with a proposed screening and evaluation management plan cannot be overstated. In particular, even with a hysterectomy, these patients are at risk for vaginal neoplasias and require Pap follow-up of the vaginal apex.

Squamous carcinoma of the cervix generally presents as a stage I lesion.[18,34] Despite the fact that the new FIGO staging defines subgroups based on a depth of invasion of 5 mm or a width of invasive disease of 7 mm, these are generally not the criteria used to define microinvasive disease for purposes of planning therapy. In the United States, the generally accepted criteria are those proposed by the Society of Gynecologic Oncologists (SGO), which recognizes microinvasion as lesions with less than 3 mm of depth of invasion from the basement membrane and with no vascular or lymphatic invasion or confluent tongues. The reason for this caution is the possibility of lymph node involvement at the FIGO microinvasion stage, generally held to be 1 to 5 percent, depending on risk factors.[1] Even using the SGO definition, lymph node involvement may, on rare occasion, occur.

For those patients meeting the criteria set by the SGO for microinvasion, the most common recommendation is hysterectomy, although cone biopsy can be considered in very specific circumstances in young women wishing to preserve childbearing capacity for the immediate future. In general, a hysterectomy would then be recommended when childbearing was completed, although some European-based studies suggest that cone biopsy alone may be adequate. The rate of recurrence of cancer in the cervix is slightly higher in the group managed conservatively than in groups managed by hysterectomy, although generally the risk is less than 5 percent.[26]

For patients with invasion beyond this limit (i.e., not microinvasion but still restricted to the cervix), two options for therapy of equivalent efficacy as measured by 5-year survival rates are available. One option is radical hysterectomy and lymph node dissection, and the other is primary radiation therapy. Removal of the ovaries is not necessary for therapy unless they are diseased. Both options have potential complications, with surgical side effects being the risk of ureteral fistula (1.6 percent) and potential long-term bladder and bowel dysfunction (rarely requiring therapy). These side effects occur because radical hysterectomy entails the removal of the parametrial tissue in the broad ligaments and the uterosacral ligaments, and this removal disrupts the normal nerve supply to the bladder and the rectum; the surgery also requires the complete dissection of the ureter to remove the surrounding parametrium and a wide margin of upper vaginal mucosa. Radiation side effects tend to be long-term (beyond the initial mild nausea and diarrhea) and include the risk of ureteral fistula (1.6 percent), permanent and progressive bowel and bladder injury (occasionally requiring surgical management), and vaginal atrophy and stenosis. Because of the time differential in side effects, surgery is generally recommended for women who are good surgical candidates, and particularly if they are young and/or sexually active.

All other stages of cervical cancer and some subtypes of stage I cervical cancer are treated primarily with radiation therapy. The barrel-shaped stage I cervical cancer often is treated primarily with radiation therapy with a subsequent hysterectomy planned, depending on the lesion and the response.[32]

For patients who present with massive pelvic disease (stage III or IVA), radiation therapy may be augmented with chemotherapy to increase the response rate. Patients with these advanced stages of disease may present with ureteral obstruction and, if so, are best served by nephrostomy to restore renal function during therapy, with the potential for conversion to internal stents if further therapy is required. This can allow these patients an appropriate trial of chemoradiation therapy to control their disease and prolong a disease-free interval. This is different from the choice that might be made in a patient with secondary ureteral obstruction with massive recurrence of disease after adequate primary therapy has failed. In that circumstance, if no other therapy offers reasonable benefit, relief of the renal failure may not be in the patient's best interest. In that setting, the patient's own goals with a terminal illness and her comfort (which is potentially augmented by the renal failure) are the primary objectives.

Adenocarcinoma of the cervix is treated in the same fashion as squamous carcinoma of the cervix, although there is some evidence in the literature that the response to therapy may not be as good as with the squamous counterparts.[3] Particular cell types of high metastatic potential include glassy cell cancers and small cell cancers (particularly those with markings for neuroendocrine or oat cell subtypes). These cancers, with their high propensity for early local and distant spread, may be treated by different combinations of all the modalities. At present, therapy has been individualized for such patients, and no one pattern of therapy seems to offer an advantage over another. It is important to note that even microinvasive tumors of these high-risk histologic types behave in atypical fashions, and conservative therapy for them is not appropriate.

Follow-up

For invasive cancers, follow-up should include examinations and Pap smears every three months for at least 1 to 2 years. Following that, the interval for follow-up is dependent on the cell type and stage, with shorter intervals both initially and long-term, depending on the pattern of potential metastases.

Uterus

Endometrial cancers tend to be diagnosed in early stages because of their identifying symptom, uterine bleeding. The majority of these malignancies occur in postmenopausal age groups, but they can occur in women in their 30s or younger. Predisposing factors include large adipose tissue layers (presumed to increase endogenous estrogen), unopposed exogenous estrogen, and, in very rare instances, a genetic component. Patients with previous breast cancer may have a slightly higher rate of endometrial cancers, particularly if receiving adjuvant tamoxifen.

The hallmark of these cancers is postmenopausal or irregular bleeding. Uterine size or shape may not be altered in the presence of malignancy; therefore, the absence of such change on physical examination does not rule out a premalignant or malignant condition.

The presence of rapid growth in an area of presumed myoma, particularly in a postmenopausal woman, may be characteristic of the rare uterine malignancy sarcoma, although this occurs in less than 1 percent of myomas. It is the pattern of rapid growth that is of concern rather than the presence of myomas. Slow growth over many years would not be a significant concern.

Suspected involvement of the cervix in the patient with endometrial cancer often dictates a different surgical or radiation and surgery choice of management. Because of this, careful description of the cervical appearance, including its shape and size, is important.

Screening with Pap smears is ineffective for this malignancy, as 50 percent or more are not detected with Pap smears. The finding of endometrial cells on a Pap smear of a woman who is postmenopausal or not near a normal menstrual flow may be a warning of underlying pathology and should warrant further investigation. A negative Pap smear, logically, does not rule out this malignancy.[42]

When abnormal bleeding occurs, an office evaluation of the endometrium and endocervix is warranted. Office biopsies with various instruments have been reported to have sensitivities and specificities that range from 80 to 98 percent.[11,27,39] The addition of hysteroscopy may be warranted in some circumstances to identify polypoid lesions or anatomic abnormalities, such as submucous myomas, that might be the cause of the abnormal bleeding. It is neither warranted nor required in all cases of abnormal uterine bleeding. The procedure for office endometrial evaluation is discussed in Chap. 48.

Management [Fig. 38-3]

If the pathology of an office endometrial biopsy shows hyperplasia, most physicians feel that a formal D&C must be performed to rule out the presence of a synchronous endometrial cancer. Evidence suggests that the use of progestins in patients who only have simple hyperplasia will decrease the incidence of subsequent endometrial cancers; therefore, its use may be considered in such women.

Atypical endometrial hyperplasia may represent a premalignant lesion. In a perimenopausal woman, the association with concurrent or subsequent endometrial cancer is high enough to warrant removal of the uterus.[28,29] In younger women who desire preservation of the uterus, a conservative approach with higher-dose progestins and follow-up biopsies may be considered if the patient is likely to be compliant with close follow-up.

Endometrial Biopsy
ECC

Nondiagnostic but clinically suspicious.	Atypical adenomatous hyperplasia.	Grade I, confined to uterine fundus.	Cervix involved, any grade.	Grade II, III, papillary serous, clear cell, adenosquamous, confined to fundus.
D&C +/− hysteroscopy.	▲ Hysterectomy +/− oophorectomy. ▲ Conservative treatment (with progestins and rebiopsy) is an option with young patients, once cancer has been ruled out by D&C.	▲ Hysterectomy and bilateral salpingo-oophorectomy. ▲ Open uterus +/− frozen section at surgery; if question of deep invasion or higher grade, sample lymph nodes.	Options depend on evaluation by gynecologic oncologist; may include varying forms of radiation + surgery or radical hysterectomy.	Staging laparotomy with TAH/BSO/lymph node dissection; possible omentectomy with multiple biopsies. May need further treatment based on findings.

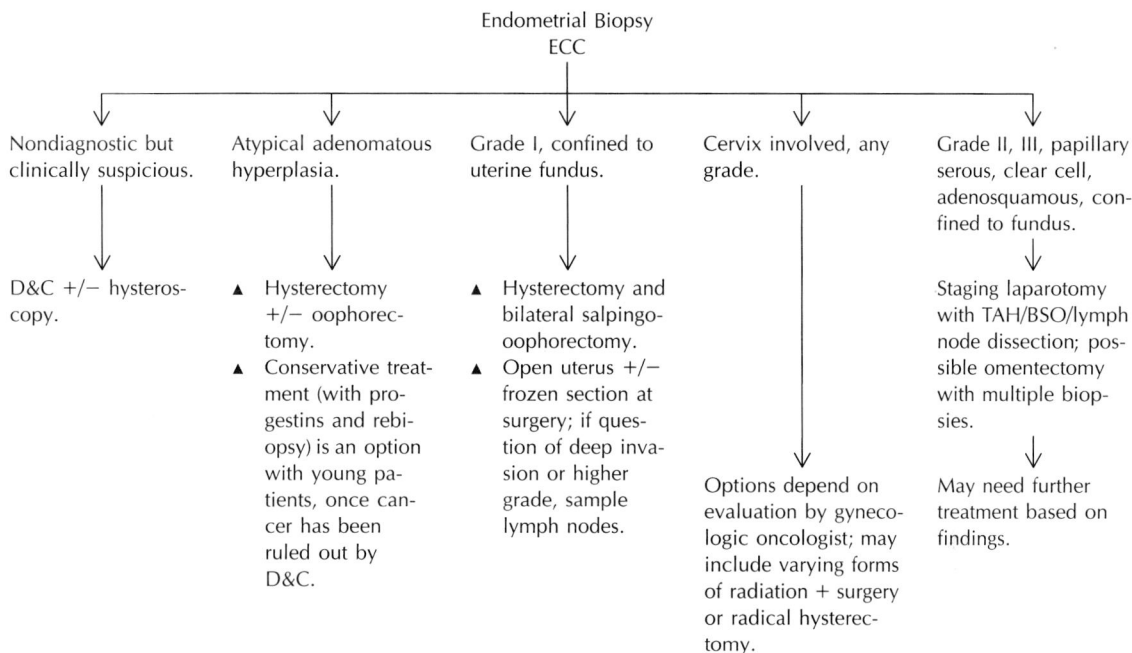

Figure 38-3 Decision flowchart for endometrial cancer.

Adenocarcinoma of the endometrium is generally well differentiated—most often stage I—and highly curable. It is important to recognize the differences among subtypes, however, as their behaviors vary widely from the usual and should be treated differently. Most important is recognizing that papillary serous endometrial cancer invades earlier and has a high propensity to spread as though it were a primary ovarian cancer. This cancer requires an approach analogous to ovarian cancer, which is discussed later in the chapter. In addition, clear cell and adenosquamous cancers also have a higher likelihood of spread.

The standard treatment for endometrial cancers is removal of the uterus, cervix, tubes, and ovaries (because of a greater propensity to spread to this region). Lymph node sampling and full lymphadenectomy are based on the grade, the depth of invasion at surgery, and the histologic type. Full staging biopsies are reserved for cell types such as papillary serous or for histologic or surgical findings that place the patient at risk

for spread of disease. The surgeon should be able to provide all of these options at the time of surgery as well as to differentiate among the various prognostic factors associated with the cell type and the surgical findings.[16]

Uterine sarcomas may present as rapid growth of a uterine "fibroid" in a postmenopausal woman. However, more frequently they present with vaginal bleeding, and an endometrial biopsy returns copious, fleshy, often gray, material. These cancers vary prognostically according to histologic type, mitotic activity, and extent of disease, although they generally confer a much poorer outcome than endometrial adenocarcinoma.[30] Their primary management is surgically tailored to the presentation and the histologic type.

Ovaries

Ovarian cancers are the most fatal of all the gynecologic malignancies.[39] Whether or not they have a premalignant phase and, if so, how long a phase that might be, is a matter of great interest as the existence of such a phase might allow for the development of a screening system for the disease. Although there has been much interest in serum cancer-related antigens (particularly Ca-125) and ultrasound in screening for these cancers, there is presently no evidence to support the cost and/or efficacy of any screening method.[23,40] The management of both benign and malignant ovarian neoplasms begins with the diagnosis of a pelvic mass.

Normal Ovaries

Normal ovaries in premenopausal and menopausal women differ in shape and consistency. The premenopausal, ovulatory woman usually has ovaries that are palpable, somewhat almond-shaped, with a length of 3 to 5 cm and width of 2 to 3 cm. The normal ovary produces cystic structures on a cyclic basis, some of which can persist through a cycle. These tend to be mobile, nontender, and less than 5 cm in diameter. The postmenopausal ovary undergoes progressive atrophy. Thus the ovary 1 year after menopause will be different than the ovary from 20 years after menopause. The idea of a nonpalpable ovary being the hallmark of the menopausal ovary merely refers to the small size (1- to 1.5-cm diameter of the senescent ovary). The postmenopausal ovary can be occasionally felt in extremely thin women, and the ovary may be slightly larger if menopause has been fairly recent. (Adherence to the criteria of surgery for every palpable postmenopausal ovary is therefore not warranted.)

Ovarian Masses

The problem of management of ovarian masses is complicated by the fact that biopsy of the ovary is generally discouraged and direct access for evaluation is required. Management must then depend on the likelihood of malignancy for certain presentations at different ages as well as

the likelihood of complications from suspected benign ovarian masses. Furthermore, ovarian masses must be differentiated from the multiple surrounding structures that can present as pelvic masses but require entirely different management plans. Clinical examination and evaluation form the major means of providing the plan and differ according to age groups. The differential diagnosis and triage of masses in the premenarchal female will not be included in this discussion, except for the comment that pelvic masses in this young group of patients invariably represent a condition that warrants further investigation.

Ovarian Masses in Premenopausal Women Premenopausal cycling women may have cystic areas of the ovary on a routine basis. The persistence of a cyst of greater than 5 cm requires further evaluation. The concurrent nonovarian conditions that need to be differentiated from these include hydrosalpinx, hydatid cysts, and pedunculated fibroids.[8] As with most medical investigations, the history and physical examination can provide most of the major clues as to the cause of the mass. For example, an ovarian mass in a woman who has a history of multiple episodes of sexually transmitted diseases may suggest a tuboovarian abscess or hydrosalpinx, whereas an ovarian mass in a patient with increasing dyspareunia and dysmenorrhea may suggest the presence of an endometrioma. In these examples, it is important to note that the patient's wishes for present or future fertility may play a substantial role in the therapy chosen. Of course, if there is a significant likelihood of malignancy, surgery is mandatory.

As noted in Fig. 38-4, in the premenopausal population ultrasound, particularly vaginal ultrasound, may be an appropriate next step in narrowing the differential diagnosis. The use of ultrasound in the premenopausal patient is more likely to result in information that allows for the conservative management of these patients, thus justifying the added cost of such procedures. In particular, the findings that corroborate hydrosalpinx with a normal ovary or a simple cyst suggestive of a physiologic cyst may allow a choice for close observation. The addition of serum tests for cancer antigens such as Ca-125 can be problematic at this point in evaluation because of the increased unreliability in premenopausal cycling women and because of the potential for Ca-125 elevation in the presence of other conditions, particularly endometriosis, but also infections. For that reason, unless the clinical differential diagnosis at this point in the evaluation includes malignancy, Ca-125 may not be of value.

The clinical characteristics of a malignant process of the ovary in this population are important. In particular, persistence and growth of an ovarian mass through a normal menstrual cycle are potentially worrisome. Additionally, the finding of internal septations, excrescences, and large bilateral cysts on ultrasound are correlated with a higher likelihood of malignancy. For these lesions the inclusion of Ca-125 in the evaluation may be of some benefit with the caveat that malignancy, particularly mucinous and low-malignant-potential epithelial cancers, can have normal Ca-125s in 50 percent of patients or more. If the lesions have clinical criteria suggestive of possible malignancy, despite a normal Ca-125, further evaluation with surgery is warranted.

Rapid growth of an ovary, often with pain and the ultrasound finding of primarily solid consistency, is suggestive of a germ cell malignancy. Germ cell malignancies occur more commonly in younger patients and are usually confined to one ovary. Examples of germ cell tumors are the dysgerminoma (which is not usually an aggressive malignancy), the immature teratoma, endodermal sinus tumor, and embryonal cancers (which are extremely aggressive malignancies). The benign cystic teratoma (dermoid) is a very common benign germ cell tumor. Germ cell malignancies may also have an elevated Ca-125, but the tumor markers more commonly associated with germ cell tumors are alpha-fetoprotein, beta-hCG, and, potentially, LDH. This clinical pattern requires more rapid intervention.

Gonadal stromal tumors are rare ovarian neoplasms that are often hormonally active. The granulosa cell tumor is associated with increased estrogen production and therefore may cause abnormal vaginal bleeding, endometrial hyperplasia, or endometrial cancer. Although uncommon, granulosa cell tumors are seen in postmenopausal women as frequently as in premenopausal women. The arrhenoblastoma often produces androgen and is associated with masculinization.

Ovarian Masses in Postmenopausal Women
The differential diagnosis of ovarian masses in postmenopausal women is substantially different than it is with women in their 20s, 30s, and 40s because of the absence of physiologic cysts in the older age group and the fact that the incidence of epithelial ovarian malignancy in ovarian masses steadily rises as age progresses. For these reasons, a significant ovarian mass generally warrants surgical exploration in postmenopausal women. Ultrasound or CT scan may be of assistance, but is not usually considered completely diagnostic. The possibility of other malignancies, such as pancreatic cancer, gastric or bowel cancer, metastatic breast cancer, inflammatory conditions such as Crohn's disease, or chronic diverticulitis, should be elicited from the history and physical examination. A history of previous conditions such as pelvic inflammatory disease (PID) with persistence of a known or suspected hydrosalpinx should also be sought. In such circumstances, the utility of a CT scan or ultrasound might be increased. The finding of a large mass with associated ascites or cul-de-sac nodularity is highly suggestive of ovarian malignancy. Ca-125 is warranted, as are other tumor markers for colon or breast cancer, if any of these cancers is suspected in these patients. The finding of a normal Ca-125 does not change the management when the possibility of malignancy is suspected.

Biopsy

Not appropriate for ovarian lesions.

Management [Fig. 38-4]

The surgical management of an ovarian mass depends on the patient's age, the suspected diag-

Ovarian Mass

Cycling premenopausal women

Postmenopausal women

≤5 cm, clinically benign. Repeat exam after next cycle.

>5 cm and/or persistent.

Found on CT or ultrasound for other reason—rule out benign reasons (e.g., old hydrosalpinx).

No symptoms.

Symptoms suggest endometriosis or inflammatory condition.

Mobile; consider ultrasound.

Nonmobile, suggestive of solid areas or cul-de-sac nodularity.

Symptoms, ascites, or lesions with increased potential for malignancy.

Consider laparoscopy for confirmation of diagnosis.

Dermoid or nonfunctional benign cyst.

Draw Ca-125.

Cystectomy

<40 years of age; draw blood for serum markers for germ cell malignancies; draw Ca-125.

Staging laparotomy, debulking, possible TAH/BSO/omentectomy, possible bowel resection.

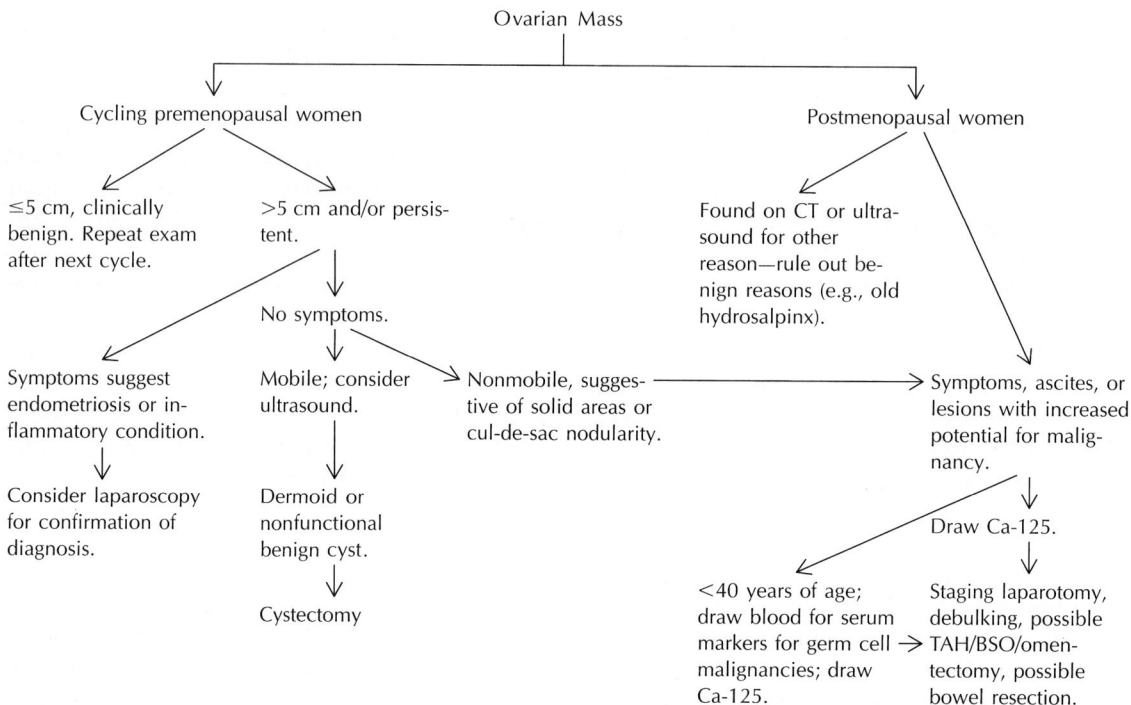

Figure 38-4   Decision flowchart for ovarian mass.

nosis, and the associated radiographic, ultrasound, or serum findings if warranted.

Premenopausal masses, particularly those suspected to be benign and requiring confirmatory histology, may be appropriate for laparoscopic management. Drainage of what grossly appears to be a "physiologic" cyst, however, presents particular difficulties. The major problem is that a benign gross appearance does not disprove the presence of malignancy. In addition, the laparoscopic drainage or rupture of malignant "cysts" may be correlated with an increased likelihood of more advanced disease,[31,33] particularly if there is a delay between the drainage or cyst removal with rupture and definitive surgery. For this reason, the choice of evaluating a patient with a persistent ovarian mass needs to be made judiciously with corresponding counsel to the patient that appropriate surgical treatment and staging should be done concurrently if a malignancy is found. If there is sufficient presurgical suspicion

of cancer or intraoperative laparoscopic suspicion, a biopsy or drainage should not be attempted; it does not serve to further a diagnosis and potentially increases the likelihood of spread of the disease. The diagnoses of endometriosis, pedunculated fibroid, or hydrosalpinx and associated PID may or may not require a corresponding laparoscopically directed biopsy.

The definitive therapy for ovarian malignancy is a full staging laparotomy.[7,21] The utility of laparoscopic staging is fundamentally compromised by the inability to assess adequately all areas of the abdomen, including the mesenteric folds, as well as the inability to adequately debulk tumor that is present. Both accurate initial staging and aggressive surgical debulking of epithelial ovarian malignancies have prognostic and therapeutic correlates with the patient's survival. These should never be compromised by the use of technology that has not been proven adequate for the circumstances. Studies are currently underway to evaluate the use of laparoscopic surgery for patients with ovarian cancer. At present, standard care is surgery via a full open laparotomy through a vertical or muscle-cutting incision. For all but the malignancies restricted to one ovary and of low grade, a hysterectomy and bilateral salpingo-oophorectomy are standard parts of the staging laparotomy. Dependent on the findings at the time of surgery, the ultimate therapy may differ.

The majority of these cancers present with widespread peritoneal disease and with higher grades of tumor. The standard therapy following adequate staging and debulking is chemotherapy. A number of regimens and cytotoxic drugs may be employed, including those restricted to the protocol setting. At present, active agents for ovarian epithelial carcinoma include cisplatin, carboplatin, cyclophosphamide (Cytoxan), ifosfamide, paclitaxel (Taxol),[13] hexamethamelamine, melphalan, and other agents with slightly lower response rates. Standard first-line therapy includes one of the platinum compounds, and with this regimen in the Netherlands registry, an improvement in overall survival for ovarian malignancies can be documented. Currently most physicians in the United States believe that platinum plus paclitaxel is the most effective combination of agents for ovarian cancer, and that this combination should be used as first-line therapy following primary surgery for advanced epithelial ovarian cancer. Optimal therapy for epithelial ovarian cancer focuses on accuracy and adequacy of initial surgical management and then on aggressive chemotherapy. The Ca-125 serum levels find their best use in the setting of evaluating responses to ongoing therapy.

Germ cell malignancies have a presentation that differs from the epithelial malignancies. Their proper surgical and chemotherapeutic management differ as well. In general, these malignancies present as stage I disease; that is, confined to the ovary. Because this disease is more common in young women, the issue of preserving childbearing ability is relevant. In this disease, the likelihood of spread to the uterus or other

ovary is smaller, and if those organs are grossly normal, they can be retained at the time of staging laparotomy. Following primary surgery, women who have stage I dysgerminomas do not require additional therapy. However, without further treatment (chemotherapy) most germ cell malignancies (endodermal sinus tumor, embryonal tumor, primary ovarian choriocarcinoma, immature teratoma) are usually fatal. Appropriate surgical staging and treatment planning are critical to survival for patients with these malignancies. Present aggressive chemotherapy regimens have altered response rates from less than a 10 percent 5-year survival to greater than 90 percent 5-year survivals for many germ cell tumors.

The issue of quality of life is a frequent problem in patients with progressive malignancy and may be one in which primary care physicians can play an important role assisting their patients. There are multiple issues with which it is important to become familiar, including a durable power of attorney and the "living will" or advance directive documents, as well as ethical concerns surrounding the concept of quality of life and treatment planning.[9]

Fallopian Tubes

These are very rare tumors. They are usually not diagnosed preoperatively, but rather the diagnosis is made either at the time of surgery or by the pathologist. The staging that is utilized is the ovarian cancer staging, and both surgery and subsequent chemotherapy follow the guidelines used for ovarian malignancy.

Gestational Trophoblastic Disease

This set of diseases is unique to pregnancy as it requires some combination of maternal ovum and paternal sperm to initiate the changes. These diseases include varieties of hydatidiform mole, invasive mole, and choriocarcinoma. Gestational trophoblastic disease (GTD) was the first such malignancy reported to have been cured by chemotherapy. With appropriate management virtually all of these malignancies can be cured, and this makes it important to recognize the classic symptoms and initiate standard evaluation and management. The types most likely to be encountered by primary care physicians are complete mole and partial mole. Complete moles have no identifiable fetal components and are characterized by trophoblastic overgrowth. The usual karyotype is a 46,XX, where both components are paternally derived. This is in contrast to the rarer partial mole where the trophoblastic changes are similar, but fetal tissues or fetal development is present. This karyotype is usually triploid, with two components being paternally derived.

Molar Pregnancy

Presenting Signs and Symptoms A majority of patients with molar pregnancy present with two features. The first is a delay in menses related to the pregnancy and the second is the presence of vaginal bleeding. Bleeding occurs in about 97 percent of patients with the most common type of GTD, complete molar pregnancy. In complete mole, the classic presentation also includes a uterine size larger than dates (although present only in about half of patients); early preeclampsia (in about a quarter) that is usually associated with high hCG levels; hyperemesis gravidarum (in about a quarter of patients)—also associated with high serum hCG levels; and the rarer (<7 percent) hyperthyroidism. In addition, patients may present initially or after evacuation of a mole with transportation of molar tissue to the pulmonary vasculature with tachypnea and tachycardia. Finally, patients may have concurrent ovarian enlargement (theca lutein cysts) of greater than 6 cm correlated with high serum hCG levels.

Evaluation Initial evaluation of a suspected molar pregnancy should include a careful physical examination with particular attention to neurologic function, pulmonary status, size of liver, size of the uterus, and the presence or absence of ovarian enlargement. Occasionally, the classic,

small, grape-like clusters can be seen in the cervical os or in the vagina. Additionally implants of a similar appearance might be seen in the cervical stroma or vagina. If GTD is suspected, biopsy of these lesions is not performed because of the associated risk of severe hemorrhage from these ectopic sites of abnormal trophoblast.

Initial evaluation requires the measurement of a serum beta-hCG and performance of a pelvic ultrasound. The hCG will be elevated out of proportion for the gestational age, and the ultrasound will show a classic "Swiss cheese" appearance consistent with a molar pregnancy. In partial moles, the placental site will usually show classic changes despite the presence of a fetus. Evaluation for hepatic, cerebral, and pulmonary metastases varies, depending on risk factors identified by the patient's history and the findings of physical examination, laboratory values, and ultrasound. Consulation with a gynecologic oncologist is appropriate after the diagnosis is made.

Management These tumors are usually treated initially by suction and, occasionally, by sharp evacuation after careful evaluation for the significant medical complications that can occur with possible attendant hyperthyroidism, preeclampsia, and anemia. The potential for transportation of trophoblastic tissue with pulmonary embolization also exists at the time of evacuation. In general, patients with recognized molar gestations should have their evacuation done at a center that has experience in such uterine evacuations. Management alternatives include hysterectomy in patients who do not desire preservation of fertility. Patients who have metastatic disease must receive chemotherapy in addition to having evacuation of the mole, or a hysterectomy.

Follow-up Follow-up after initial evacuation (or hysterectomy) for a molar pregnancy should be serial beta-hCG measurements on a weekly basis until normal for 3 weeks, then monthly until normal for 6 months, then bimonthly for the remainder of the year. Because of the concern about detecting recurrence, prevention of pregnancy during this follow-up time is advisable. The use of oral contraceptives, diaphragm, or an IUD after normalization of hCG levels are all options for patients. If the hCG fails to decline with either a plateau of values or an increase in level, the patient should be referred for evaluation and probable chemotherapy.

Choriocarcinoma

Malignant trophoblastic disease is preceded by hydatidiform mole in 50 percent of cases, by an antecedent normal pregnancy in 25 percent of cases, and by an abortion or ectopic pregnancy in the other 25 percent of cases. In a woman who has a history of a previous hydatidiform mole, it is usually not difficult to make the diagnosis when malignant trophoblastic disease occurs because the physician's index of suspicion is high. However, if the pregnancy event that preceded malignant trophoblastic disease was an abortion, a seemingly normal pregnancy, or an ectopic pregnancy, there is often a delay in making the diagnosis. In a few instances, the antecedent pregnancy was many years before.

To make a timely diagnosis the physician needs to have an index of suspicion in any woman with a previous pregnancy who has abnormal bleeding. For instance, hemoptysis in a young woman who has had a previous pregnancy may be from trophoblastic disease metastatic to the lungs. A woman who has bleeding a few weeks, many months, or even years following a pregnancy could have gestational trophoblastic neoplasia in her uterus. Metastatic gestational neoplasia can also be found in the brain, liver, gastrointestinal (GI), or genitourinary (GU) systems. If a patient is not pregnant, a positive beta subunit will provide very important assistance in making the diagnosis. Because gestational trophoblastic neoplasia is often curable, it is important for the primary care physician to appropriately consider this when formulating a differential diagnosis.

References and Selected Readings

1. Alvarez RD, Soong SJ, Kinney WK, et al: Identification of prognostic factors and risk groups in patients found to have nodal metastases at the time of radical hysterectomy for early stage squamous cell carcinoma of the cervix. *Gynecol Oncol* 35:130, 1989.
2. Ball HG, Berman ML: Management of primary vaginal carcinoma. *Gynecol Oncol* 14:154–163, 1982.
3. Berek JS, Hacker NF, Fu YS, et al: Adenocarcinoma of the uterine cervix: Histologic variables associated with lymph node metastases and spread. *Obstet Gynecol* 65:46–49, 1985.
4. Bergen S, DiSaia PJ, Liao SY, Berman ML: Conservative management of extramammary Paget's disease of the vulva. *Gynecol Oncol* 33:151–156, 1989.
5. Berget A, Lenstrup C: Cervical intraepithelial neoplasia examination, treatment, and follow-up. *Obstet Gynecol Surv* 40:545–551, 1985.
6. Boden E, Rylander E, Evander M: Papilloma virus infection of the vulva. *Acta Obstet Gynecol Scand* 68:179–184, 1989.
7. Buchsbaum HJ, Lifshitz S: Staging and surgical evaluation of ovarian cancer. *Semin Oncol* 1:227–230, 1984.
8. Cain JM: Pelvic mass: Detection, diagnosis and management, Stenchever M (ed): *Office Gynecology*. St. Louis: Mosby Year-Book, 430–440, 1991.
9. Cain JM, Stacy L, Jusenius K, Figge D: The quality of dying: Financial, psychological, and ethical dilemmas. *Obstet Gynecol* 76:149–152, 1990.
10. Cecchini S, Palli D, Casini A: Cervical intraepithelial neoplasia III: An estimate of screening error rates and optimal screening interval. *Acta Cytol* 29:329–333, 1985.
11. Chambers JT, Chambers SK: Endometrial sampling: When? Where? Why? With what? *Clin Obstet Gynecol* 35:28–39, 1992.
12. Chafe W, Richards A, Morgan L, Wilkinson E: Unrecognized invasive carcinoma in vulvar intraepithelial neoplasia. *Gynecol Oncol* 31:154, 1988.
13. Advanced Ovarian Trials Group: Chemotherapy in advanced ovarian cancer: An overview of randomized clinical trials. *Br Med J* 303:884–893, 1991.
14. Chung AF, Woodruff JW, Lewis JL: Malignant melanoma of the vulva: A report of 44 cases. *Obstet Gynecol* 45:638, 1975.
15. Creasman WT, Gallagher HS, Rutledge F: Paget's disease of the vulva. *Gynecol Oncol* 3:133–148, 1975.
16. Creasman WT, Morrow CP, Bundy BN, et al: Surgical pathologic spread patterns of endometrial cancer. *Cancer* 60:2035, 1987.
17. Daling JR, Chu J, Weiss NS, et al: The association of condylomata acuminata and squamous carcinoma of the vulva. *Br J Cancer* 50:533–535, 1984.
18. Delgado G, Bundy BN, Zaino R, et al: Prospective surgical-pathology study of disease free survival with stage IB cervical cancer: A Gynecologic Oncology Group study. *Gynecol Oncol* 38:352–357, 1990.

19. Giuntoli RL, Atkinson BF, Ernst CS, et al: *Atkinson's Correlative Atlas of Colposcopy, Cytology and Histopathology*. Philadelphia: JB Lippincott, 1987.

20. Hendrickson M, Ross J, Eifel P, et al: Uterine papillary serous carcinoma: A highly malignant form of endometrial adenocarcinoma. *Am J Surg Pathol* 6:93, 1982.

21. Hoskins WJ, Bundy BN, Thigpen JT, Omura GA: The influence of cytoreductive surgery on recurrence-free interval and survival in small volume stage III epithelial ovarian cancer: A Gynecologic Oncology Group study. *Gynecol Oncol* 47:159–166, 1992.

22. Hsiu JG, Given FT, Kemp GM: Tumor implantation after diagnostic laparoscopic biopsy of serous ovarian tumors of low malignant potential. *Obstet Gynecol* 68:902–903, 1986.

23. Jacobs IJ, Oram DH, Bast RC: Strategies for improving the specificity of screening for ovarian cancer with tumor associated antigens Ca-125, Ca-15-3, and TAG 72.3. *Obstet Gynecol* 80:396–399, 1992.

24. Japaze H, Dinh TV, Woodruff JD: Verrucous carcinoma of the vulva: Study of 24 cases. *Obstet Gynecol* 60:462–466, 1982.

25. Karlen JR, Piver S, Barlow JJ: Melanoma of the vulva. *Obstet Gynecol* 45:181–184, 1975.

26. Kolstad P: Follow-up study of 32 patients with stage Ia1 and 411 patients with Stage IA2 squamous cell carcinoma of the cervix. *Gynecol Oncol* 33:265–267, 1989.

27. Koss LG, Schreiber K, Oberlander SG, et al: Detection of endometrial carcinoma and hyperplasia in asymptomatic women. *Obstet Gynecol* 64:1–11, 1984.

28. Kurman RJ, Kaminski PF, Norris HJ: Behavior of endometrial hyperplasia: A long-term study of "untreated" hyperplasias in 170 patients. *Cancer* 56:403, 1985.

29. Kurman RJ, Norris HJ: Evaluation of criteria for distinguishing atypical endometrial hyperplasia from well-differentiated carcinoma. *Cancer* 49:2547, 1982.

30. Leibsohn S, Mishell DR, d'Ablaing G, Schlaerth JB: Leiomyosarcomas in a series of hysterectomies performed for presumed uterine leiomyomata. *Am J Obstet Gynecol* 162:968, 1990.

31. Maiman M, Seltzer V, Boyce J: Laparoscopic excision of ovarian neoplasms subsequently found to be malignant. *Obstet Gynecol* 77:563–566, 1991.

32. Maruyama Y, Van Nagall JR, Yoneda J, et al: Dose response and failure pattern for bulky and barrel shaped IB cervical carcinoma treated by combined photon irradiation and extrafascial hysterectomy. *Cancer* 63:70–76, 1989.

33. Menczer J, Voliovitch Y, Modan B, et al: Some epidemiologic aspects of carcinoma of the vulva in Israel. *Am J Obstet Gynecol* 143:893–896, 1982.

34. National Institutes of Health: Consensus statement on cervical cancer. *Gynecol Oncol* 66:351–361, 1997.

35. Report of the Committee on Terminology of the International Society for the Study of Vulvar Disease. New nomenclature for vulvar disease. *J Reprod Med* 35:483–484, 1990.

36. Robboy SJ, Szyfelbein WM, Goeliner JR: Dysplasia and cytologic findings in 4,589 young women enrolled in the diethylstilbestrol-adenosis (DESAD) project. *Am J Obstet Gynecol* 140:579–586, 1981.

37. Sheets E, Crum CP: Current status and future clinical potential of human papilloma virus infection and epithelial neoplasia. *Curr Opin Obstet Gynecol* 5:63–66, 1993.

38. Silverberg E, Boring C, Squires T: Cancer statistics. *Cancer* 40–49, 1990.

39. Vuopala S: Diagnostic accuracy and clinical applicability of cytological and histological methods for investigating endometrial carcinoma. *Acta Obstet Gynecol Scand* (suppl) 56:1–72, 1977.

40. Willson JR: Ultrasonography in the diagnosis of gynecologic disorders. *Am J Obstet Gynecol* 164:1064–1067, 1991.

41. Yoonessi M, Hart WR: Endometrial stromal sarcomas. *Cancer* 40:898, 1977.

42. Zucker PK, Kasdon EJ, Feldstein ML: The validity of pap smear parameters as predictors of endometrial pathology in menopausal women. *Cancer* 56:2256–2263, 1985.

CHAPTER 39

Nonmalignant DES-Related Changes

Mark Spitzer
Candice A. Tedeschi

D iethylstilbestrol (DES), a nonsteroidal estrogen, was used from 1941 through 1971 in the United States and through 1978 in Europe to prevent miscarriage. DES was marketed by many companies under more than 70 different names. The peak years of its use were the late 1940s and early 1950s, after which its popularity declined. In some parts of the United States, DES continued to be prescribed widely through November, 1971. An estimated 5 to 10 million Americans received DES during pregnancy (DES mothers) or were exposed to the drug in utero (DES daughters and sons). The drug was banned from use during pregnancy after its use was associated with clear-cell adenocarcinoma of the vagina and cervix. While this form of cancer is rare (risk between 1.4:1000 to 1.4:10,000 women exposed to DES in utero), the benign changes associated with DES are common. DES-associated changes are most common if the mother took DES during the first 18 weeks of pregnancy, which is the period of fetal life when the genital tract is being formed.

Pertinent Questions to Ask during History Taking

It is estimated that only half of those exposed to DES in pregnancy are aware of their exposure. By asking a patient certain questions, the physician can identify women who may have had in utero DES exposure. Such questions include:

- Did your mother take medication during her pregnancy with you?
- Did your mother have a history of miscarriages or threatened miscarriages?
- Has any other health care provider told you about any vaginal or cervical changes seen or felt during prior examinations?

Knowledge of DES-associated problems together with a complete obstetric and gynecologic history should raise the practitioner's level of suspicion regarding DES exposure. Today, with the declining number of unidentified DES-exposed women, these questions are frequently asked only after DES-associated problems have been identified.

Epithelial Changes

Adenosis is the presence of normal glandular epithelium on the vaginal wall. Studies differ in their estimation of the number of DES-exposed women with adenosis; estimates range from 35 percent to 90 percent. Each woman differs in the amount of adenosis she may have. Investigators from the National Cooperative Diethylstilbesterol Adenosis (DESAD) Project[16] reported that DES daughters with vaginal epithelial changes were generally found to be exposed in utero to larger total doses of DES administered over longer periods of time and beginning at an earlier gestational age than were daughters without changes. Adenosis was observed in 73 percent of subjects initially exposed during the first 2 months of pregnancy, but in only 7 percent of those initially exposed in the 17th week of pregnancy or later.[9] The most common vaginal walls affected are the anterior and posterior. Adenosis may extend from the fornices and along the entire length of the vagina. This is important because the vaginal walls are frequently covered by the blades of the vaginal speculum; therefore, these changes may be missed. Adenosis regresses spontaneously through the process of squamous metaplasia. Often, by the time a woman reaches her 30s, her adenosis has resolved, but the rate of regression varies.

Structural Changes of the Upper and Lower Genital Tract

Eighteen to 33 percent of DES-exposed women have a variety of structural changes of the cervix and vagina. The most common of these are vaginal and cervical ridges, pseudopolypoid formation, cervical hood or cockscomb cervix, absent pars vaginalis, and apical narrowing of the vagina. The endocervical canal may be about a third smaller. As many as 53 percent of DES-exposed women have abnormal hysterosalpingograms.[11] The most common abnormalities are a T-shaped uterus; a hypoplastic uterus; constriction of the upper, middle, or cornual uterine regions; and irregular uterine margins. Any of these structural changes may be associated with a higher risk of fertility problems or difficulties maintaining a pregnancy.

Cervical ectropion and gross malformations of

the vagina and cervix may also improve over time and disappear in some DES daughters.[2] Cervical ectropion has been found to decrease or disappear in about three-fourths of DES daughters observed up to 5 years, and cervical-vaginal ridges, decrease or disppear in about half of them.

Pregnancy-Associated Problems

The issue of infertility has not been resolved. Some studies show a doubling in the rate of primary infertility in DES-exposed women; others do not. If several of the largest pregnancy outcome studies are evaluated, it seems that once pregnancy has been achieved, DES-exposed women may be at greater risk for pregnancy problems. These problems include ectopic pregnancy, spontaneous abortion, and premature delivery. It is estimated that, when compared to unexposed women, DES daughters are 8.6 times more likely to have an ectopic pregnancy.[20] Ectopic pregnancies are most commonly located in the isthmic portion of the fallopian tube and are unrelated to a previous history of PID. DES daughters are 1.8 times more likely to have a spontaneous abortion and 4.7 times more likely to have a preterm birth.[20] They also have an increased risk of premature cervical effacement, particularly in the second trimester. Among DES-exposed women who have a structural abnormality of the vagina, cervix, or uterus, the relative risk for ectopic pregnancy rises to 13.5, for spontaneous abortion to 2.6, and for preterm birth to 9.6.[20] Infertile women with a history of in utero DES exposure also exhibit a significantly impaired implantation rate following in vitro fertilization, and the outcome for achieving pregnancy with assisted reproductive technology remains poor.[17]

Other Problems Which May Be Associated with DES Exposure

In addition to having an increased risk of invasive clear-cell adenocarcinoma of the vagina and cervix, DES daughters may also have an increased risk of intraepithelial squamous neoplasia of the cervix and vagina. The DESAD study found that the prevalence of dysplasia in DES daughters was twice that in women who had not been exposed to DES.[18] However, using colposcopy to identify areas of dysplasia may be very difficult because of the marked colposcopic changes due to metaplasia, which are frequently found in DES-exposed women. White epithelium, punctation, and mosaic patterns are all very common on the cervix and vagina of DES-exposed women; dysplastic changes may be admixed with the metaplasia. Colposcopy in DES-exposed women should be done by an experienced colposcopist, and preferably by the same one each time, so that findings different from the patient's normal metaplastic changes can be recognized.

Despite the potential increased risk for dysplasia, caution is advised when deciding on a mode of treatment. Any mode of surgical treatment (e.g., conization, cautery, or cryosurgery) may be associated with cervical stenosis in a substantial percentage of DES-exposed women. Nearly 30 percent of DES daughters who have had cervical cauterization or cryosurgery have experienced at least one subsequent pregnancy loss.[8] Treatment of a cervical ectropion for mucorrhea should be discouraged. Treatment with laser vaporization may be less associated with stenosis, but the risk is still present.

Some evidence suggests that there may be as much as a twofold increased risk for breast cancer among DES mothers.[5] There is also some evidence that there may be an increased prevalence of autoimmune diseases among DES daughters. The relative prevalence rate of autoimmune diseases among exposed women is 1.8, with the strongest association being with Hashimoto's thyroiditis.[14] Others have not confirmed this association.

The DES-exposed population is aging. At this time, it is unknown what additional or increased risk this aging group of women may have.

Health Care Guidelines

The following guidelines have been suggested in the care of DES-exposed women:

DES mothers:

In light of the possible increased risk for breast cancer, women who received DES during pregnancy should be encouraged to do monthly breast self-examinations, have an annual breast physical examination, and follow established recommendations for screening mammography.

DES daughters:

1. Annual pelvic examinations including a careful 360-degree palpation of the vagina, feeling for any induration and nodularity; a cervical Pap smear; and a 4-quadrant vaginal Pap smear.
2. Annual colposcopy to monitor DES-associated changes. This is particularly important if the woman has a history of an abnormal Pap smear. If it is not possible to perform a colposcopy, use half-strength Lugol's iodine solution to stain the vaginal walls. Nonstaining areas of the vagina may indicate adenosis or dysplasia.
3. Routine biopsies are not necessary. They should be reserved for specific indications such as abnormal Pap smears or visualized lesions. If abnormalities are found and the primary care physician does not have expertise with this problem, the primary care physician may need to consult with, or refer the woman to, a physician experienced with treating DES-exposed women.
4. If a DES-exposed woman thinks she may be pregnant, it is important to order a pregnancy test as early as possible. A pelvic ultrasound should be done at 6 to 7 weeks gestation to rule out an ectopic pregnancy. Because of the increased risk for spontaneous abortions, ectopic pregnancies, early cervical effacement, and premature labor, DES daughters should be followed as obstetric high-risk patients.
5. Because of the potential risk of premature cervical effacement, a careful palpation of the cervix should be done every 1 to 2 weeks during pregnancy to monitor the length of the cervix. If effacement occurs, bedrest is recommended. Routine cerclage is not recommended unless there is a history of proven cervical incompetence. Most women can be conservatively managed dur-

ing pregnancy with good outcome.[12] Practitioners are encouraged to refer women with known in utero exposure to centers that have focused on the follow-up, treatment, and education of these women.

6. Currently, data are insufficient to adequately advise DES daughters on the potential risk of hormonal contraceptives, ovulatory agents, and hormone replacement therapy.

Summary

Nonmalignant changes in DES-exposed women are much more common than malignant ones. Adenosis and structural changes of the cervix and vagina are common findings; however, clinical problems such as an increased risk of ectopic pregnancy, premature deliveries, and premature effacement of the cervix may be of greater concern. DES-exposed women are at risk for cervical and vaginal dysplasia. Careful adherence to health care guidelines will help ensure optimal care for these women.

References and Selected Readings

1. American College of Obstetricians and Gynecologists: Washington, DC: ACOG Committee Opinion, *Diethylstilbestrol,* 131:1, 1993.

2. Antonioli DA, Burke L, Friedman EA: Natural history of diethylstilbestrol-associated genital tract lesions, cervical ectopy, and cervico-vaginal hood. *Am J Obstet Gynecol* 137:847–853, 1980.

3. Barnes AB, Colton T, Gundersen J, et al: Fertility and outcome of pregnancy in women exposed in utero to diethylstilbestrol. *N Engl J Med* 301:609–613, 1980.

4. Cousin L, Karp W, Lacey C, Lucas WE: Reproductive outcome of women exposed to diethylstilbestrol in utero. *Obstet Gynecol* 56:70–76, 1980.

5. Giusti RM, Iwamoto K, Hatch EE: Diethylstilbestrol revisited: A review of the long-term health effects. *Ann Intern Med* 122:778–788, 1995.

6. Haney AF, Hammond MG, Soules MR, Creasman WT: Diethylstilbestrol-induced upper genital tract abnormalities. *Fertil Steril* 31:142–146, 1979.

7. Herbst AL, Hubby MM, Azizi F, Makii MM: Repro-

ductive and gynecological/surgical experience in diethylstilbestrol-exposed daughter. *J Obstet Gynecol* 141:1019–1028, 1981.

8. Herbst AL, Senekjian EK, Frey KW: Abortion and pregnancy loss among diethylstilbestrol-exposed women. *Semin Reprod Endocrinol* 7:124–129, 1989.

9. Herbst AL, Poskanzer DC, Robboy SJ, Friedlander L, Scully RE: Prenatal exposure to stilbestrol. *N Engl J Med* 292:334–339, 1975.

10. Kaufman RH, Adam E: Genital tract anomalies associated with in utero exposure to diethylstilbestrol. *Isr J Med Sci* 14:353–362, 1978.

11. Kaufman RH, Adam E, Noller KL, et. al: Upper genital tract changes and infertility in diethylstilbestrol-exposed women. *Am J Obstet Gynecol* 154:1312–1318, 1986.

12. Levine RU, Berkowitz KM: Conservative management and pregnancy outcome in diethylstilbestrol-exposed women with and without gross genital tract abnormalities. *Am J Obstet Gynecol* 169:1125–1129, 1993.

13. Mangan CE, Borow J, Burtnett-Rubin MM, et al: Pregnancy outcome in 98 women exposed to diethylstilbestrol in utero, their mothers, and unexposed siblings. *Obstet Gynecol* 59:315–319, 1982.

14. Noller KL, Blair PB, O'Brien PC, Melton LJ, et al: Increased occurrence of autoimmune disease among women exposed in utero to diethylstilbestrol. *Fertil Steril* 49:1080–1082, 1988.

15. Noller KL, O'Brien PC, Colton T, et al: Medical and surgical disease associated with in utero exposure to diethylstilbestrol, in Noller KL (ed): *Clinical Practice of Gynecology.* New York: Elsevier, 1990, pp 1–7.

16. O'Brien PC, Noller KL, Robboy SJ, et al: Vaginal epithelial changes in young women enrolled in the National Cooperative Diethylstilbestrol Adenosis (DESAD) Project. *Obstet Gynecol* 53:300–308, 1979.

17. Pal L, Shifren JL, Isaacson KB, et al: Outcome of IVF in DES-exposed daughters: Experience in the 90s. *J Assist Reprod Genet* 9:513–519, 1997.

18. Robboy SJ, Noller KL, O'Brien P: Increased incidence of cervical and vaginal dysplasia in 3,980 diethylstilbestrol-exposed young women. *JAMA* 252:2979–2983, 1984.

19. Schmidt G, Fowler WC Jr: Cervical stenosis following minor gynecological procedures on DES-exposed women. *Obstet Gynecol* 56:333–335, 1980.

20. Swan SH: Pregnancy outcome in DES-daughters, in Giusti RM (ed): Report of the NIH workshop on long-term effects of exposure to diethylstilbestrol (DES). Washington, DC: US Department of Health and Human Services, Public Health Service, National Institutes of Health, 1992, pp 42–49.

CHAPTER 40

The Care of Women with Physical Disabilities

Angeles Badell
Sandra Welner

DISABILITIES CAUSED BY NEUROLOGIC IMPAIRMENTS AND BY MUSCULOSKELETAL DISORDERS

GYNECOLOGIC CARE AND THE DISABLED WOMAN

Office Design and Equipment • Sexuality • Contraception • Pregnancy • Sexually Transmitted Diseases • Infertility • Menopause, Osteoporosis, and Hormone Replacement

EMOTIONAL ADJUSTMENT

SOCIAL ISSUES

According to the National Health Interview Survey (NHIS)[1] in 1990, there were 33.8 million persons, 13.7 percent of the total U.S. noninstitutionalized population, who were very limited in physical activity because of a chronic health condition. The prevalence of disability is fairly consistent between genders for persons under age 65. Limitation in activity increases with age, and by the age range of 65 to 69, 33.5 percent of females were limited in activity. The NHIS survey data document the extent of the need for primary health care for the physically challenged.

Disability is defined as any long- or short-term reduction of a person's activity as a result of an acute or chronic condition. Limitations in mobility are a common means by which a person's activity is reduced. Affected individuals are often in need of medical rehabilitation for aerobic conditioning.

The first part of the chapter describes health problems related to the most frequent type of disabilities, that is, disabilities caused by neurologic impairments and by musculoskeletal disorders. Related issues are discussed in depth in chap. 79. The second part of the chapter addresses sexual and reproductive health issues as they relate to women with physical disabilities.

Disabilities Caused by Neurologic Impairments and by Musculoskeletal Disorders

Individuals affected by traumatic brain injury (TBI), stroke, or any other static or progressive central nervous system disorder have decreased or limited mobility in the body as a whole or in individual body parts. Particularly pertinent for health care are the deficits affecting oral, pharyngeal, and esophageal motions, as well as laryngeal and respiratory movements. These problems should alert the physician to the need for prevention and treatment of such disorders as chronic malnutrition, deficits in dental hygiene, gastroesophageal reflux, recurrent atelectasis, aspiration pneumonia, chronic constipation, and related disorders.

Spinal cord injuries (SCI) cause complete or incomplete sensory and motor deficits below the level of injury, as well as neurogenic bowel and bladder incontinence. The high cord levels of quadriplegia affect respiratory function, and may require assisted ventilation. Persons with low cervical quadriplegia above T6 share a high risk for episodes of autonomic dysreflexia (autonomic hyperreflexia). Autonomic dysreflexia is a serious and relatively common problem in individuals with spinal cord injuries above T6. It is induced by noxious stimuli acting below the level of the lesion. The symptoms are uncontrolled sympathetic activity. The associated hypertension may become life-threatening. Management calls for the use of rapid-onset, short-duration sympathetic outflow blockers and a search for and removal of the noxious causative factors. One particular cause of autonomic dysreflexia may be acute abdominal disease. The symptomatology and physical findings of an acute abdomen in SCI patients can be masked by the lack of ability to perceive abdominal pain, and abnormal abdominal and leg muscle tone changes may be noted.

Neurogenic bowel incontinence in SCI patients often results in constipation, and impaction can cause autonomic dysreflexia. The person with SCI needs to be trained in the management of constipation and the use of techniques to trigger evacuation at predetermined times to avoid socially unacceptable incontinence. The physiatrist who manages the training of the patient should be contacted for guidance in difficult cases.

Another serious potential problem in SCI patients is renal disease. Chronic bladder, ureteral, and eventually renal damage may occur. This course of events can be prevented by attention to adequate hydration and periodic bladder emptying with clean intermittent catheterization. A low-grade bladder infection is not uncommon and may not always require chronic antibiotic treatment. Continued urologic follow-up is a must for all SCI patients.

A major health issue related to all SCI patients is skin care. The most serious skin problems are caused by decubitus ulcers, which are caused by prolonged pressure, usually on areas with an underlying bony prominence. The rehabilitation management of the paraplegic includes education in avoiding traumatic and thermal injuries and the provision of equipment that can reduce the effect of pressure. However, all precautions may fail, and the examination of the skin is basic in all individuals with sensory deficits.

The pharmacologic management of spasticity is of particular concern. The most frequently used antispastic medications are baclofen, diazepam, and dantrolene sodium. Modifications of the dosage may be required if the severity of spasticity changes or if the side effects demand a change.

Pain is often the cardinal symptom associated with musculoskeletal impairments. Joint inflammation results in decreased mobility, causing secondary muscle atrophy and a progressive cycle of pain and disability. The appropriate pharmacologic management of rheumatic and other musculoskeletal disorders should be complemented with attention to the deleterious effects of prolonged rest, muscle atrophy, and aerobic deconditioning. Physically challenged persons who do not participate in regular aerobic conditioning activities are at risk for early onset of osteoporosis, obesity, hypertension, and atherosclerotic heart disease. The primary care physician should be alert to the early onset of these health problems, as well as to the need for anticipatory preventive care.

Gynecologic Care and the Disabled Woman

Office Design and Equipment

A number of key points are important in designing an office to cater to women with physical limitations. The office should have accessible doorways, adequate spacing of furniture, and no projecting obstacles. An important feature of the gynecologic exam is an accessible table.[2] This table should lower to 19 in. in height to facilitate the transfer of patients from wheelchairs, and should have safety and security features to allow an adequate exam of the mobility-impaired individual. When low tables are not available and the patient needs to be lifted to a higher table, adequate personnel must be available to allow safe and dignified transfer.

Patients with extreme spasticity may be more easily examined in the knee-chest position, with an assistant holding the spastic legs away from the perineum to allow access for the speculum. When patients are examined in bed, a rolled blanket can be used to elevate the pelvis. Because of the different angle of the pelvis in relation to the speculum in this position, the speculum inserted handle downward may not expose a mid-position or anteverted cervix. It often is helpful to reverse the speculum so that the blade that ordinarily pushes down is now pushing up, exposing the cervix.

In elderly or spinal cord-injured patients, lidocaine gel applied liberally to the perineal surface while talking to the patient before the exam may be of great benefit in decreasing perineal pain. In spinal cord-injured patients, application of lidocaine gel has been reported to decrease the incidence of spasticity.[3] As with all female patients, it is important to empty the bladder prior to the pelvic exam. However, this is particularly important for women with spinal cord injuries, because a full bladder and constipation can trigger spasticity and even autonomic dysreflexia.

If hip mobility is difficult, which is quite common in elderly women, patients may need to have one leg abducted and one knee flexed. If this maneuver is performed gently and slowly, adequate visualization usually can be achieved.

Sexuality

Some physiologic changes seen in women with disabilities include loss of innervation to the vagina; inadequate lubrication; decreased vaginal accommodation; and reduced, delayed, or absent orgasmic sensation.[4] For the woman who becomes disabled later in life, sexual identity adjustments can be extremely difficult. A newly disabled woman often feels that she has not changed and, on an emotional level, may not accept that her body has changed. The disabled woman may

experience some anxiety about her ability to satisfy her partner. Her sexual partner, who may perceive her as fragile, may be afraid to touch her or to find ways to achieve their mutual satisfaction. If a disabled teenager or adult woman feels undesirable, she may become vulnerable to exploitation, particularly in sexual relations.[5] For example, before the woman became disabled, she may have refused to participate in unprotected sexual intercourse; now she may feel that if she does not consent to participate, no one else will approach her. She may hesitate to discuss such fears with her physicians, who should give her the opportunity to express her concerns.

Open communication is especially important when dealing with sexual difficulties, so that problems can be clearly identified and solutions explored. A careful history may differentiate between an impairment in genital functioning and a situational dysfunction.

Contraception

Primary care physicians should explore contraceptive options when caring for the disabled woman. Choice should depend on the patient's mobility status, as well as on her dexterity and coordination. Patients with certain chronic diseases may have special considerations. Combination oral contraceptives used by spinal cord-injured women have traditionally been thought to be associated with a high incidence of thrombosis and should be avoided.[6] Patients with lupus may have an increased risk of developing thrombosis when using oral contraceptives.[7] Packaging is important when selecting oral contraceptives for a patient because of potential problems with dexterity. The simplest package is the best.

Two kinds of IUDs are available in the United States: Progestasert and Paraguard. These methods are useful for monogamous women with no history of pelvic infections in the past and whose pelvic sensation is intact. The use of condoms should be encouraged. Barrier methods such as the diaphragm may be difficult for two reasons: Dexterity and range of motion can interfere with proper insertion, and sensory loss in the pelvis may preclude the patient's ability to detect proper positioning of the device. Medroxy-progesterone acetate in a Depo form is safe and effective if repeated administrations are given every three months. The Norplant system also appears to be safe, and is effective for 5 years in most women. However, the irregular menstrual bleeding that can occur, and arm position difficulties in women with range of motion impairments, may decrease the suitability of this method.

Pregnancy

Pregnancy in women with physical disabilities may range from routine to complex. Complications reported to be increased in disabled women include urinary tract infections, pyelonephritis, decubitus ulcers, and premature labor. Some disabilities result in pelvic deformities that may necessitate cesarean section.

Pregnancy in the spinal cord-injured woman is also associated with the life-threatening syndrome autonomic dysreflexia, which can masquerade as preeclampsia.[8] Patients with autonomic dysreflexia are reacting to distension of the visceral organs resulting in activation of the autonomic nervous system. A noxious stimulus dilates large blood vessels above the level of the lesion and constricts blood vessels below the level of the lesion. There is profuse sweating, headaches, and severe muscle spasms. These patients may have seizures and hemorrhagic stroke, and the mortality risk is substantial.[3,9]

Medical issues surrounding postpartum care in a woman with mobility impairments include thrombophlebitis, urinary tract infections, constipation, decubitus ulcers, and poor episiotomy healing.[9]

The pregnant woman who is disabled may encounter a significant amount of societal prejudice because in others' eyes, her disability would make it impossible for her to be a competent mother. This in fact is not the case.[10]

Sexually Transmitted Diseases

All sexually active women are at risk for contracting a sexually transmitted disease (STD). In a woman with a disability, this infection may go undetected for a number of different reasons. Sensory deficits in the pelvis may not specifically alert the patient to the usual symptoms of infection. She may have to learn to recognize such vague cues as an increase in spasticity and upper abdominal discomfort. A woman with mobility impairment may be reluctant to seek assistance even if she suspects an infection because of transportation difficulties or privacy concerns.

When prescribing antibiotics for a woman with physical limitations, consider her dexterity and coordination. Remember to designate easy-opening packaging for patients whose finger dexterity is impaired. If a patient has a vision impairment, ask that a family member or friend assist her in monitoring her temperature. Some patients who have dysphagia may benefit from unit-dose packaging of liquid medications.

Infertility

The infertility concerns of the woman with a physical disability are not different from those of any other woman. Fertility usually is not affected by physical disability. Tubal factors, ovulation dysfunction, sperm-mucus interaction, and male factors all require the same thorough evaluation as performed for any other woman. If a couple has been attempting pregnancy for a year or more without success, an infertility work-up is appropriate.

Menopause, Osteoporosis, and Hormone Replacement

Women with disabilities are living longer. Therefore, the impact of aging in people with underlying disabilities requires significantly more consideration than in the past. Women with mobility impairment have a higher risk of osteoporosis. In some cases, it is useful to evaluate this bone loss with quantitative digitized radiography measurements.[11] Long-term steroid use in patients with autoimmune disorders may compound osteopenia.[12] Calcium supplementation with vitamin D must be included in all regimens unless significant impairment in creatinine clearance or calcium excretion is present.

Women with physical disabilities are less likely to participate in exercise; they are thus at risk for cardiovascular deconditioning and excessive weight gain, and at higher risk for cardiovascular morbidity and mortality. Menopausal women lose the protective effects of estrogen on the cardiovascular, urologic and skeletal systems, and on the skin. Estrogen replacement therapy is an important preventive intervention for these conditions. Unfortunately, this therapy has been inappropriately linked with thrombosis episodes in data derived from research on high-dose oral contraceptives. Many studies of coagulation function in estrogen replacement therapies have found no significant alterations.[13,14] Even in patients with a history of thrombotic events in the distant past, a transdermal form of estrogen therapy can sometimes be used safely.[15]

Emotional Adjustment

A woman may have different emotional adjustment problems, depending on her age at the onset of the disability. The young girl who has had a congenital impairment or one that developed at a very early age may have incorporated her existing, accepted limitation into her identity. Though many women may accept such challenges with a positive outlook and strive for excellence within their capacities, others may feel that they will never be able to reach the achievement levels of their unaffected counterparts.

A woman or teenager who becomes physically challenged later in life experiences many losses that she is reminded of daily. These may be exacerbated by other adults and teenagers who may feel uncomfortable around the disabled individual. This could lead to blatant rejection by long-standing friends and coworkers, which, in turn, may result in severe isolation and depression. The physician needs to understand the patient's perception of these losses and how they affect her functioning. Such understanding is crucial in directing appropriate support and intervention, if required. Key areas for focus include dissolution of long-standing friendships, leaving work with its activities and coworkers, and the need to adapt her lifestyle to accommodate newly acquired, and often frustrating, physical limitations.

Grief and loss are natural and appropriate feelings. The clinician should not attempt to negate, discount, or ignore these emotions. Careful attention, however, is mandatory to prevent this normal frustration and sadness from developing into a pathologic paralyzing, isolating, and possibly even suicidal depression. The health care provider must be empathetic and understanding to these women and must address their individual needs and concerns in a supportive manner. If the clinician senses that the patient's depression is becoming unstable or exacerbated, and the primary care physician cannot manage the problem, the patient should be immediately referred to an appropriate specialist. However, the primary care physician must maintain a strong, supportive relationship with the patient. This continuity is crucial in the emotional healing stage.

Social Issues

The physician's attention to the disability should not impair the value assessment of the person who is disabled. Handicaps are barriers that society and the environment place in the path of any person. Individuals with disabilities are not intrinsically handicapped, and many are able to overcome societal and environmental obstacles.

Being sensitive to the person's needs and what can be done to reduce and eliminate handicaps that could affect the function of physically challenged individuals is what the 1990 Americans with Disabilities Act is all about.[16]

References and Selected Readings

1. *Disability Statistics Abstract*—University of California, San Francisco. Published by U.S. Department of Education. National Institute of Disability and Rehabilitation Research (NIDRR), 1992.
2. Wheelchair Accessible Powermatic Examination Table, US Patent No. 5507050.
3. Colachis SC III: Autonomic hyperreflexia with spinal cord injury. *J Am Para Soc* 15:171–186, 1991.
4. Yarkony GM: Spinal cord-injured women: Sexuality, fertility and pregnancy, in Goldstein PJ, Stern BJ(eds): *Neurological Disorders of Pregnancy.* Mount Kisco: Futura, 1992, pp 203–222.
5. Welner SL: Caring for the woman with a disability, in Wallis LA(ed): *Textbook of Women's Health.* Philadelphia: Lippincott-Raven, 1998, pp 87–92.
6. Sipski ML, Alexander CJ: Sexual function and dysfunction after spinal cord injury. *Traum Spinal Cord Inj* 3:811–828, 1992.
7. Liang MH, Carlson EW: Female hormone therapy and the risk of developing or exacerbating systemic lupus erythematosus or rheumatoid arthritis. *Proc Assoc Am Physicians* 108:25–28, 1996.
8. McGregor JA, Meeuwsen J: Autonomic hyperreflexia: A mortal danger for spinal cord-damaged women in labor. *Am J Obstet Gynecol* 151:330–333, 1985.
9. Cross LL, Meythaler JM, Tuel SM, Cross AL: Pregnancy following spinal cord injury. *West J Med* 154:607–611, 1991.
10. Verduyn WH: Spinal cord-injured woman: Pregnancy and delivery. *Paraplegia* 24:231–240, 1986.
11. Scialli AR, Gestila KJ, Simon JA: Luprolide acetate in bone mineral density measured by quantitative digitized radiography. *Fertil Steril* 59:674–676, 1993.
12. Olbricht T, Benker G: Glucocorticoid-induced osteoporosis: Pathogenesis, prevention and treatment, with special regard to the rheumatic diseases. *J Intern Med* 234:237–244, 1993.
13. Alkjaersig N, Fletcher A, DeZiegler D, et al: Comparison of transdermal and oral administration. *J Lab Clin Med* 3:224–228, .
14. Lobo RA: Estrogen and the risk of coagulopathy. *Am J Med* 92:283–285, 1992.
15. Stampfer MJ, Colditz GA, Willett WC, et al: Postmenopausal estrogen therapy and cardiovascular disease. *N Engl J Med* 325:756–762, 1991.
16. Batavia A, DeJong G, Eckenhoff EA, Haterson RS: After the Americans with Disabilities Act: The role of the rehabilitation community. *Arch Phys Med Rehabil* 71:114, 1990.

CHAPTER 41

Office Evaluation of the Infertile Couple

Edward H. Illions
Robert J. Thompson

Approximately 12 to 15 percent of married U.S. couples are infertile, and many seek medical evaluation initially through their primary care network.[43] Managed care systems now direct most medical care through primary care "gatekeepers," thus making it essential that these physicians remain current in the assessment of the infertile couple and recognize appropriate candidates for referral to infertility specialists. Heightened public awareness of infertility and an increased prevalence of infertility have combined to place further demands on primary care physi-

cians offering these services. Interestingly, many managed care networks exclude infertility evaluation and/or treatment, further stressing the relationship between patient and physician. This chapter evaluates various etiologies of infertility and presents useful algorithms to manage affected couples.

Demographics

Infertility is characterized by the inability of a sexually active, noncontracepting couple to conceive within 1 year. Data supporting this one-year interval indicate that known conception rates in couples attempting to conceive are 50 percent at 3 months, 75 percent at 6 months, and 88 percent at 1 year.[21,32] Couples never having conceived identifies those with primary infertility, while secondary infertility describes those couples with at least one previous conception.

The probability that a couple will achieve a conception within one menstrual cycle is called fecundability (0.20 to 0.25), and approximates conception rates achieved with some aggressive contemporary treatment modalities. Given the increased pregnancy loss in the infertile population, terms that describe *live* birth rates per menstrual cycle (fecundity) are better suited for this discussion.

Although the percentage of married couples considered infertile has not changed, the actual number of infertile patients seeking care has

History
↓
Physical (Baseline lab tests)
Cervical cultures
RPR
Lab tests to evaluate general health

Prolactin
Thyroid function tests
Rubella

Female

Ovulation monitoring
Basal body temperature chart

Monophasic
LH kits
Transvaginal sonography (TVS)
Hormonal evaluation and treatment

Biphasic

Postcoital test (PCT)

Normal → Midluteal Progesterone Endometrial Biopsy (EMBx)

Abnormal → Repeat PCT
Consider in vitro sperm–mucus penetration assay
Immune factor
Cervical factor
Male factor

Hysterosalpingogram (HSG)

Normal uterus and tubes → Laparoscopy after basic evaluation*

Abnormal uterine cavity or tubes → Laparoscopy and/or hysteroscopy → Surgical correction*

In-phase biopsy
Progesterone ≥10 ng/ml

Out-of-phase biopsy
Progesterone <10 ng/ml

Luteal phase defects (LPD)?

Repeat EMBx

Out-of-phase (LPD)
In-phase

LPD Treatment
Clomid, Progesterone, Parlodel

Empirical therapy for unexplained infertility*

Male

Semen analysis

Oligospermic
Mild → Rule out varicocele
Severe (<5 million/ml) → Hormonal evaluation

Normal

Azoospermic → Seminal fructose

Absent → Vasogram
Testicular biopsy
Rectal sonogram

FSH low (<5 mIU/ml) → Rule out hypothalamic–pituitary dysfunction

FSH normal → Testicular biopsy
Vasogram

Present → Hormonal evaluation

FSH high (>40 mIU/ml) → Testicular failure

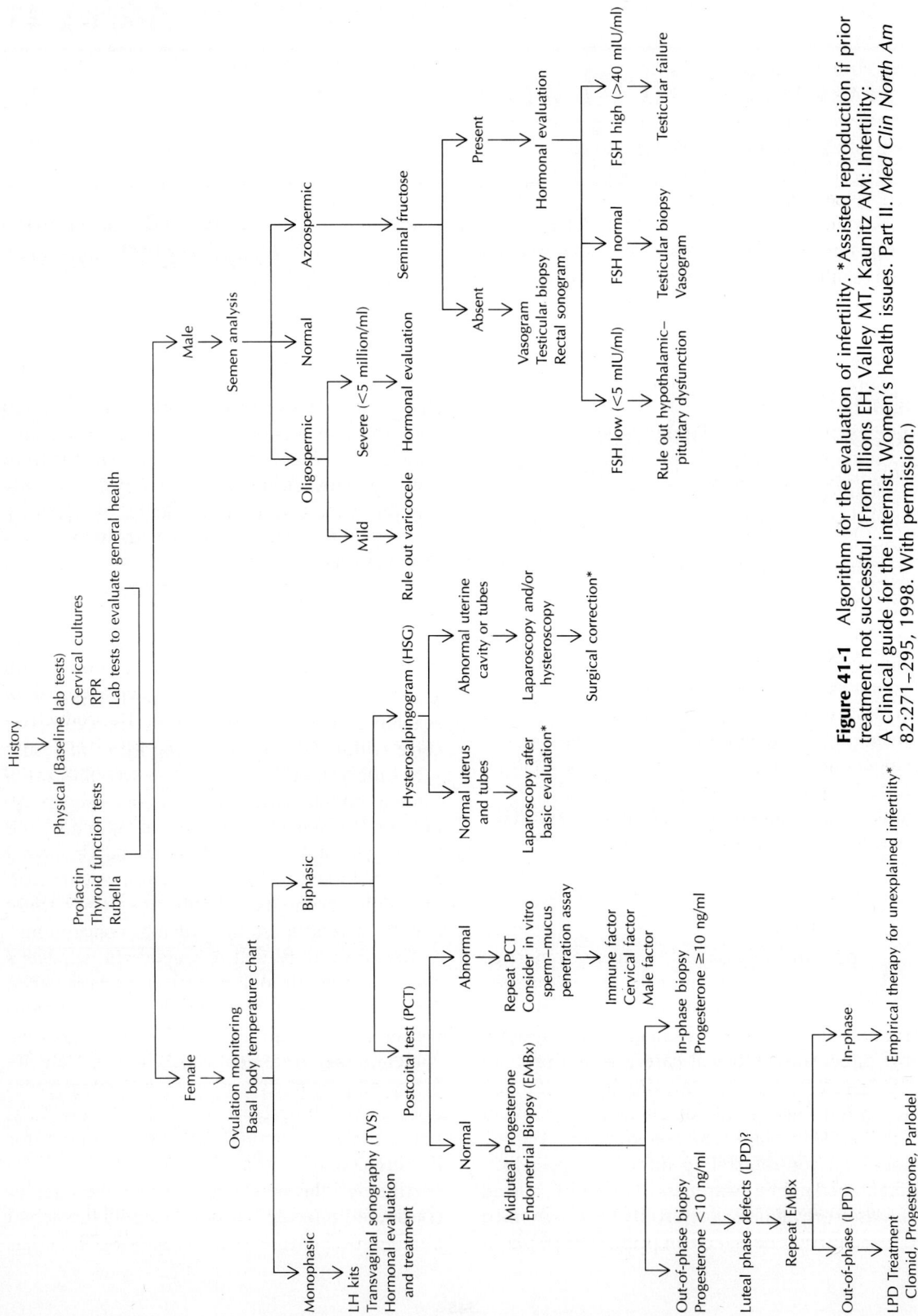

Figure 41-1 Algorithm for the evaluation of infertility. *Assisted reproduction if prior treatment not successful. (From Illions EH, Valley MT, Kaunitz AM: Infertility: A clinical guide for the internist. Women's health issues. Part II. *Med Clin North Am* 82:271–295, 1998. With permission.)

greatly increased from 600,000 visits in 1968 to 1.35 million visits in 1988.[42] Many factors account for this marked increase, including postponement of childbearing secondary to career issues; increased social awareness and publicity for infertility services; decreased numbers of adoptable infants; increased availability of services; drastic improvements in physician knowledge related to infertility; and new aggressive treatments such as assisted reproductive technology (ART).

Preconception Counseling

A detailed history obtained at the initial patient visit may identify various risk factors that must be addressed prior to attempting conception. The primary care physician in this setting may favorably affect pregnancy outcome by systematically screening the patient's reproductive and family history.

Reproductive History

Prior obstetrical complications such as early pregnancy loss, premature labor, intrauterine fetal demise, pregnancy-induced hypertension, and fetal malpresentation may suggest recurrent risk factors. Prompt identification of these conditions may demonstrate an underlying, yet correctable, disorder such as uterine malformation, maternal endocrinopathy, antepartum infection, or maternal autoimmune disease, which, when corrected, may ultimately reduce the risk of recurrence.

Family History

A detailed family history may identify the need for carrier screening. Preconception recognition of carrier status for genetic diseases allows pertinent counseling prior to the first pregnancy. Proper preconception identification of carriers enables the physician to educate and prepare the couple. Well-informed couples can then decide on the proper course of action, which may include completion of certain diagnostic tests, assisted reproductive technology (ART), or even permanent sterilization.

Medical Conditions and Pregnancy

A variety of medical problems may coexist in the pregnant patient. Some diseases are exacerbated by pregnancy, whereas other medical conditions place the pregnant patient at increased risk during gestation and occasionally into the immediate postpartum period. The use of certain medications may also increase fetal risk.

Reproductive-age women should be screened for a variety of infectious diseases, and susceptible individuals immunized to reduce perinatal transmission and congenital birth defects. Congenital rubella syndrome may occur if a pregnant woman contracts rubella. First trimester infection affects 50 to 80 percent of fetuses, often causing cataracts, heart defects, cranial microcalcifications, and deafness.[38] Hepatitis B virus (HBV) vaccination should be offered to nonimmune women at risk for exposure. Infants born to HBV affected women are at increased risk of becoming HBV chronic carriers.[1] Reproductive-age women at risk for tuberculosis (TB) or cytomegalovirus (CMV) should be screened and counseled when indicated. Hospital workers and child care attendants are at increased risk for HBV, TB, and CMV. Women who handle cat feces and/or raw meat should be screened for toxoplasmosis and offered preconception counseling when indicated by test results. Confidential human immunodeficiency virus (HIV) screening should be offered to all reproductive-age women, because retroviral therapy will reduce vertical transmission to the fetus.[9] When indicated, patients should be screened for sexually transmitted diseases such as syphilis (*Treponema pallidum*), gonorrhea (*Neisseria gonorrhoeae*), and chlamydia (*Chlamydia trachomatis*). Maternal syphilis infection may result in fetal demise with hydrops. Similarly, varicella infection in the peripartum period may cause congenital varicella syndrome in the neonate. Varicella-zoster immune globulin (VZIG) may reduce the severity of maternal disease and neonatal transmission.[7,8]

Nutritional Assessment

Inadequate caloric intake and unusually restrictive diets may pose significant risk to a developing fetus. Early identification of eating disorders may permit adequate preconception counseling with subsequent reduction in maternal and fetal risk. Patients contemplating pregnancy can reduce the risk of neural tube defects by consuming at least 0.4 mg of folic acid daily.[58] However, pregnant women with previously affected offspring should consume 4 mg daily of folic acid.[10] Women should initiate prenatal vitamins with folic acid at least one month prior to attempting conception and continue therapy throughout the first trimester.

Social Issues and Environmental Factors

A detailed social evaluation may uncover domestic issues that impact on the timing of conception and affect ongoing pregnancies. Domestic abuse must be addressed, because at-risk women are more likely to be abused during pregnancy. These situations increase the risk of placental separation and bleeding, premature labor and delivery, and uterine rupture.[4]

Certain environmental factors such as heavy metals, pesticides, and organic solvents pose threats to a developing fetus; however, larger risks exist with cigarette smoking, alcohol consumption, and illicit drug usage.[82] In addition, nicotine and its metabolites negatively impact on spermatogenesis, fallopian tube function, and cervical mucus production, thereby representing common environmental toxins. Effective preconception counseling may significantly reduce their use. Preconception counseling is discussed at length elsewhere in this book.

Age-Related Decline in Fecundity

Reproductive potential initially declines in the mid-30s, with a marked decrease in fecundity beyond age 40.[73] The current trend in our society to delay childbearing diminishes the time available to complete an infertility evaluation when necessary and to conceive. In addition to career and financial considerations, other associated factors in delaying childbearing include decreased frequency of intercourse, increased contraceptive use, and a progressive rise in the occurrence of such conditions as leiomyomata uteri (fibroids) and endometriosis.[35] Nevertheless, the principal reason for diminished reproductive potential in this age group relates to declining ovarian function.[46]

Ovarian function begins to wane well in advance of natural menopause. While the average age of menopause in this country is 51.4, follicle stimulating hormone (FSH) levels steadily rise approximately 8 to 10 years earlier, reflecting diminished ovarian reproductive capability.[29,64] Age-related declines in levels of certain ovarian peptides such as inhibin may be involved in the progressive rise in FSH.[26,80] These serum alterations indicate a diminished functional capability of the follicular apparatus within the aging ovary, a term collectively known as *ovarian reserve.*

FSH values obtained in the early proliferative phase of menstrual cycles are useful determinants of ovarian reserve when evaluated according to preset limits.[59] The clomiphene citrate challenge test (CCCT) provides a more expanded assessment of ovarian reserve via determinations of FSH and estradiol on cycle days 3 and 10 of a clomiphene cycle. The incidence of abnormal tests rises with age, reflected by a 9 percent pregnancy rate when infertile patients had abnormal CCCT values, versus 43 percent in those with normal ovarian reserve.[60]

A 1982 evaluation of 2193 nulliparous women whose husbands had complete azoospermia further underscores that diminishing ovarian reserve is the chief determinant of reduced fertility rates in aging women. In the absence of known tubal disease, and with male factor controlled via donor insemination, differences in cumulative pregnancy rates reflected an age-related decline in ovarian function.[16] (Table 41-1)

Similarly, pregnancy rates in in vitro fertiliza-

TABLE 41-1 Effect of Advanced Maternal Age on Pregnancy Rates

Age	Cumulative Pregnancy Rates (%)	Monthly Pregnancy Rates (%)
<30	74	10.5
31–35	61	9.1
>35	54	6.5

SOURCE: From Illions EH, Valley MT, Kaunitz AM: Infertility: A clinical guide for the internist. Women's health issues. Part 2. *Med Clin North Am* 82:271–295, 1998. With permission.

tion (IVF) cycles demonstrate an age-related decline in fecundity. Clinical pregnancy rates per transfer decrease notably beyond age 40.[50,74] Lastly, data from egg donation programs point to declining ovarian function, suggested by poor oocyte and embryo quality, as the prime cause for lowered pregnancy rates and high spontaneous abortion rates in this age group.[55,56]

The Evaluation and Consultation

Both partners should be present at the initial infertility appointment. The physician's schedule should allow ample time for an in-depth history, physical exam, and consultation that details the overall direction of the impending infertility work up. An initial visit so constructed will greatly mitigate the anxiety experienced by most infertile couples. Implicit in the successful outcome of this initial office visit is the philosophy that infertility is a "couple's disorder." Combined male and female factors are found in approximately one-third of infertile couples, documenting the multiplicity of causes and the necessity for a thorough evaluation.

Evaluation of the Female

History Ovulatory dysfunction is suggested by irregular menses, and the absence of premenstrual symptoms (molimina), whereas the presence of regular menses and molimina indicates ovulation in approximately 98 percent of patients. More than 60 percent of individuals with complete amenorrhea fail to ovulate. In addition, patients with infrequent menses (e.g., three to four per year) are similarly oligo-ovulatory. In such patients, a 6-month period of medical ovulatory assistance is prudent prior to beginning a lengthy work-up. Age of menarche and thelarche should be elicited, in addition to current cycle characteristics (duration, flow, and molimina). Psychological stress, excessive weight loss from dieting, and strenuous exercise may result in ovulatory dysfunction, ostensibly through altered Gn-RH pulsatility. Headaches and visual complaints occasionally accompany a pituitary tumor, especially if galactorrhea exists. Hirsutism, acne, and oily skin indicate androgen excess that may disrupt ovulation.

Distorted peritoneal and tubal anatomy may result in altered ovum pick-up and hinder tubal transport of gametes. A history of abdominal surgery suggests the possibility of pelvic adhesions. Episodes of sexually transmitted diseases may render fallopian tubes nonfunctional because of endosalpingeal damage or peritubal adhesions. Complaints of dysmenorrhea, dyspareunia, chronic pelvic pain, and premenstrual spotting suggest endometriosis or adhesions.

Structural abnormalities of the cervix leading to poor mucus production account for 3 to 5 percent of infertility. A history of a cone biopsy, cryosurgery, laser, loop electrosurgical excision procedure (LEEP), or multiple D&Cs suggest a cervical role. A prior surgical procedure on the cervix may result in stenosis or decreased mucus production. In addition, intrauterine exposure to diethylstilbestrol (DES) may result in anatomic and functional anomalies of the cervix.

Irregular vaginal bleeding may point to abnormalities within the uterine cavity. A history of menstrual cycle irregularities may indicate the presence of submucosal myomas or intrauterine polyps. In addition, hypomenorrhea or amenorrhea occurring after a curettage of an infected uterus suggests intrauterine synechiae (Asherman's syndrome). DES-exposed individuals may have structural anomalies of the uterus that result in T-shaped or hypoplastic cavities.

Although many environmental toxins reduce

fertility in laboratory animals, their relation to human infertility is difficult to quantify. However, the potential detrimental effects on human reproduction by nicotine, alcohol, marijuana, and other illicit drugs are well recognized.[23,68]

Prior poor obstetric outcomes, particularly spontaneous or induced abortions, midtrimester losses, and postpartum complications should be elicited. A sexual history should include coital frequency and technique. In general, coitus occurring two to three times throughout the week is adequate for conception. Too frequent ejaculations can deplete the sperm numbers, whereas infrequent ejaculation may adversely affect sperm motility. The use of vaginal lubricants such as K-Y jelly or postcoital douching should be discouraged, because both practices are potentially spermicidal.

The Physical Exam   The general physical exam allows additional time to gain a personal history by separating the couple. Such delicate topics as prior relationships may be explored at this time. A detailed physical exam should be performed early, and may influence the direction of the work-up.

The physician should evaluate overall body habitus, weight, height, and limb length. Eunuchoidal proportions suggest hormonal deficiency, whereas short stature is frequently characteristic of genetic abnormalities. Signs of androgen excess are suggested by hirsutism, temporal balding, a male escutcheon pattern, acne, oily skin, and clitoromegaly. The thyroid gland should be palpated for enlargement and nodularity. Inadequate sexual development may be indicated by poor breast development. One should test for galactorrhea. Surgical scars on the abdomen may suggest underlying intraabdominal adhesions that might hinder tubal and ovarian reproductive function. Amenorrheic females with clinical signs of androgen excess may warrant an evaluation for hypercortisolism.

External genitalia should be evaluated for developmental abnormalities and clitoromegaly. A blind vaginal pouch in an individual presenting with a primary amenorrhea may indicate either müllerian agenesis or androgen insensitivity. Cervical abnormalities may be the first clue to DES exposure, prompting additional studies to evaluate the uterine cavity and fallopian tubes. Painful adnexa to lateral cervical motion is suggestive of salpingitis, especially if an odiferous cervical discharge is present. A retroverted or immobile uterus and uterosacral nodularity suggest endometriosis. Bilateral ovarian enlargement, especially if associated with menstrual irregularities, may indicate polycystic ovarian syndrome. An enlarged irregular uterus accompanied by menorrhagia suggests leiomyomata (uterine fibroids), while a tender, symmetrically enlarged uterus is often associated with adenomyosis. The pelvic exam should include a determination of estrogen support, a Pap smear, and a wet prep for cervical and vaginal infections. An endocervical sample should be taken for gonococci and chlamydia.

Evaluation of Ovulation

Ovulatory dysfunction accounts for approximately 25 percent of all causes of infertility. Ovulatory status should be assessed prior to performing more invasive tests. A thorough understanding of the menstrual cycle is essential when evaluating and treating infertile couples.

Regulation of the Menstrual Cycle   The menstrual cycle consists of three phases: follicular, periovulatory, and luteal. Each segment has a distinct hormonal pattern reflected by histologic alterations throughout the female genital tract. Histologic evaluation of the endometrium, combined with serum hormone levels, routinely assesses the presence and quality of ovulation.

The menstrual cycle is regulated by a complex interaction of hypothalamic-releasing factors and anterior pituitary glycoproteins that direct ovarian follicle development (folliculogenesis) and ovarian hormone production (steroidogenesis). Follicular-phase pulsatile-release of gonadotropin-releasing hormone (Gn-RH) every 60 to 90 min directs gonadotropin production and secretion from the anterior pituitary. These gonadotropins recruit a cohort of follicles within the ovary; however, only one follicle attains dominance by the midproliferative phase of each menstrual cycle. Early follicular development is gonadotropin independent whereas the final stages, including ovulation and luteal hormonal support, depend upon adequate levels and frequency of gonadotropin exposure.[19] The exact mechanism(s) governing dominant follicle selection remains enigmatic. The mid to late proliferative phase of the menstrual cycle is characterized by rising estradiol levels that reflect the gonadotropin-induced mitotic activity of the granulosa cells within the dominant follicle.

The periovulatory period is marked by an abrupt rise in serum estradiol levels to approximately 200 pg/ml for 48 to 50 h, which initiates the LH surge. This midcycle gonadotropin surge causes resumption of meiosis, luteinization of theca-granulosa cells, and proteolytic enzyme activation, which culminates in separation of the oocyte-cumulus mass from the remaining granulosa cells and dissolution of the follicular wall. The actual extrusion of the oocyte occurs 32 to 34 h after initiation of the LH surge, and marks entry into the luteal phase. Progressive increases in progesterone and 17-hydroxyprogesterone levels at this time alter the endometrial lining of the uterus in preparation for implantation of an embryo. Failure to conceive effectively withdraws support from the corpus luteum, and luteolysis ensues approximately 12 to 16 days after the LH surge. The duration of the luteal phase in primates is constant and its continuation depends on adequate LH support. With the late luteal decline in both gonadal steroids and inhibin, endometrial vascular changes ensue resulting in menstruation.

Ovulation reliably occurs in the presence of cyclic menses.[65] However, detailed histories, even when combined with basal body temperature charting, describe ovulation only within a three-day window.[39] Currently, more accurate ovulatory tests allow physicians to tell patients how to precisely time coital activity, and enable precise luteal phase testing.

Four different means of detecting ovulation

were recently reviewed. Late luteal endometrial biopsies served as the gold standard to compare the accuracy of each test. The biopsies were in agreement (within 2 days) with transvaginal sonography 96 percent of the time, whereas serum LH levels were the next most accurate test (85 percent). Basal body temperature charting was in agreement with late luteal endometrial biopsies 77 percent of the time, whereas chronologic dating based on the next menstrual cycle agreed only 65 percent of the time.[61] Table 41-2 lists various tests that allow physicians to accurately monitor ovulation. A detailed discussion of ovulatory tests is presented in Chap. 49.

Specific Ovulatory Disorders Often simultaneous evaluation of tubal and male factors in conjunction with ovulatory dysfunction is advisable, because 30 percent of couples have multiple causes of infertility. Amenorrheic patients or patients with few menstrual cycles annually usually do not need to undergo an initial extensive evaluation for ovulatory dysfunction. These patients are usually best served by medical ovulation induction. Treated patients who successfully ovulate, but still fail to conceive, may then complete the infertility evaluation. Some common disorders associated with ovulatory dysfunction are

TABLE 41-2   Tests to Determine Ovulation

Test	Criteria
Basal body temperature	Luteal evaluation (0.5°F) for at least 11 days
Cervical mucus	Abundant watery discharge, ferning pattern on glass slide, distensibility of mucus
Endometrial biopsy (late luteal phase)	Histology within 2 day of chronologic cycle-day based on LH surge
Menstrual history	Most cycles 23–40 days
Midluteal progesterone	Values >10 ng/ml
Urinary LH kits	Color change 12–24 h before ovulation

SOURCE: From Illions EH, Valley MT, Kaunitz AM: Infertility: A clinical guide for the internist. Women's health issues. Part 2. *Med Clin North Am* 82:271–295, 1998. With permission.

androgen excess, galactorrhea, significant weight reduction, and various endocrinopathies.

Primary amenorrhea is the failure to undergo menarche by age 14 in the absence of any secondary sexual development or by age 16 regardless of the status of secondary development. Secondary amenorrhea is defined as the absence of menses for 6 months in a previously menstruating female. Gonadal dysgenesis accounts for 30 to 40 percent of all cases of primary amenorrhea. A variety of chromosomal disorders, most commonly 45X, result in formation of dysgenetic gonads presumably secondary to accelerated follicular atresia. Chief presenting signs include primary amenorrhea and sexual infantilism; however, classic Turner's syndrome (45X) may include short stature, web neck, high-arched palate, epicanthal folds, low-set prominent ears, increased carrying angle of the arm (cubitus valgus), wide-set nipples and coarctation of the aorta. Mosaic Turner's occasionally undergo pubertal change and even menstruate when follicular atresia rates slow.

Müllerian agenesis accounts for 20 to 22 percent of all cases of primary amenorrhea, and is characterized by congenital absence of those pelvic organs derived from müllerian origin (upper vagina, cervix, uterus, and fallopian tubes). Secondary sexual development occurs because ovarian function is normal. Individuals with androgen insensitivity, the third most common cause of primary amenorrhea (10 to 11 percent), have a 46XY karyotype and functioning testes; therefore serum testosterone levels are in the normal male range (300 to 900 ng/dl). In this setting, androgen resistance, secondary to an androgen receptor defect, yields a female phenotype and absent to sparse body hair.

Hyperprolactinemia Elevated prolactin levels account for approximately 20 percent of all cases of secondary amenorrhea. Elevated prolactin levels alter Gn-RH pulsatility, which results in ovulatory dsyfunction. The patients may experience anovulation, oligo-ovulation, or a luteal phase defect, depending upon the degree of hypothalamic derangement. A variety of medications, most notably antipsychotic agents, promote hyperprolactinemia. Hyperprolactinemia may also result from physiologic events (pregnancy, stress, exercise, coitus) or demonstrable pathology such as pituitary adenomas, renal failure, hypothyroidism, or hypothalamic lesions. Table 41-3 is a more complete listing of the various etiologies of hyperprolactinemia.

After excluding physiologic causes, pituitary microadenomas (prolactinomas) are the single most common cause of hyperprolactinemia. Prolactin levels greater than 100 ng/ml require comprehensive radiographic imaging of the pituitary sella (magnetic resonance imaging with gadolinium).[41] Virtually 100 percent of women with prolactin levels in excess of 200 ng/ml harbor a prolactin-producing adenoma.[5] The vast majority of patients with pituitary adenomas respond well to medical therapy with a dopamine agonist (bromocriptine), while surgery is reserved for refractory cases. Long-term longitudinal studies of patients with idiopathic hyperprolactinemia and microadenomas indicate that most have an indolent course with 30 percent of untreated patients

TABLE 41-3 Causes of Hyperprolactinemia

Physiologic	Pathologic
Sleep-associated elevation	Prolactinoma
High protein content at lunch	Acromegaly
	Nonsecreting pituitary tumor
Exercise	Craniopharyngioma
Stress	Nelson's syndrome
Coitus	Empty sella syndrome
Late follicular and luteal phase of menstrual cycle	Primary hypothyroidism
	Chest wall lesions
Pregnancy	Trauma to pituitary stalk
Pharmacologic	Renal failure
	Pseudocyesis
Ovarian steroids	Cushing's disease
Tricyclic antidepressants	Infiltrative disorders: tuberculosis, sarcoidosis, and histiocytosis
Metoclopramide	
Cimetidine	
Opiates	
Phenothiazines	
α-Methyldopa	
Anesthesia	
Reserpine	

SOURCE: From Illions EH, Valley MT, Kaunitz AM: Infertility: A clinical guide for the internist. Women's health issues. Part 2. *Med Clin North Am* 82:271–295, 1998. With permission.

regaining ovulatory function.[37] Patients with long-standing untreated hyperprolactinemia risk the sequelae of hypoestrogenism. Oral contraceptives and other hormonal preparations may be used for those hypoestrogenic women not interested in conceiving.

Luteal Phase Defects Luteal phase dysfunction is a relatively uncommon cause of infertility accounting for only 3 to 5 percent of all cases. Luteal phase defect (LPD) arises from either subnormal progesterone levels (inadequate luteal phase) or shortened duration of progesterone action on the endometrium (shortened luteal phase). Elevated prolactin levels, hypothalamic disorders secondary to weight loss, stress, or exercise, and occasionally hyperandrogenism, may disrupt follicular development and hence luteal function. An endometrial biopsy performed 10 to 12 days after ovulation is considered the gold standard for diagnosis. Luteal phase temperature elevations by basal body thermometer of less than 11 days points to luteal phase defect. Inadequate luteal phase is likely when midluteal serum progesterone levels fall below 10 ng/ml.[26] Both entities, however, need confirmation by endometrial biopsy in the late luteal phase of the menstrual cycle. Luteal phase dysfunction is confirmed when each of two late luteal endometrial biopsies demonstrates greater than a two-day histologic lag. The controversy involving the interpretation of midluteal progesterone levels, however, preclude the use of progesterone levels as the sole determinant for LPD diagnosis.

Treatment of luteal phase defect involves correction of the underlying disorder. In euprolactinemic patients with normal androgen levels, clomiphene citrate or progesterone administration is utilized. Clomiphene citrate (50 to 100 mg per day) is administered on cycle days 5 to 9 of the menstrual cycle to improve folliculogenesis. Pregnancy rates with clomiphene citrate are reported to be between 25 and 50 percent. However, pregnancy rates are greatest when repeat biopsy confirms correction of the histological lag.[12] Progesterone therapy yields similar results.[44] FDA approval of a new 8% progesterone gel (Crinone) increases the available routes of administration. Previously, patients were restricted to intramuscular administration or progesterone suppositories. Crinone is locally absorbed in the endometrium and readily adheres to the vaginal mucosa. Crinone-treated patients have lower serum progesterone levels than parenterally treated patients; however, pregnancy rates are similar.[17] Patients failing to respond to clomiphene and/or progesterone therapy frequently respond to gonadotropin therapy, whereas hyperprolactinemic individuals are best treated with bromocriptine.

Androgen Excess Elevated androgen levels may disrupt ovulation through direct effects on the ovarian follicles.[66] Elevated androgen levels can result from increased ovarian or adrenal production or any condition that lowers the sex hormone-binding globulin levels. The resulting decrease in androgen-binding sites elevates free androgen levels, increasing their intracellular availability. Circulating serum levels of free androgens often double (from 1 percent to 2 percent) in the hirsute patient with ovulatory dysfunction, accounting for clinical expression. Nonetheless, total testosterone and dehydroepiandrosterone sulfate (DHEAS) remain the clinically important first-line tests in the evaluation of hyperandrogenism. Total testosterone levels in excess of 200 ng/dl or DHEAS levels over 600 μg/dl suggest an androgen-producing tumor in the ovary or adrenal respectively.[67] Rapid elevations of androgens secondary to an androgen-producing tumor cause clitoromegaly, deepening of the voice, change in body habitus, and temporal balding, collectively known as *virilizaton*. Androgen-producing tumors, however, are rare. Cushing's syndrome, late-onset congenital adrenal hyperplasia, and ovarian hyperandrogenism are all associated with hyperandrogenic anovulation.

Hirsute individuals with normal circulating levels of androgens have idiopathic hirsutism. Increased androgen effects arise from either increased enzymatic conversion of testosterone to more active metabolites (5α-reductase) or ultrasensitive androgen receptors in the hair follicles.

After idiopathic hirsutism, ovarian hyperandrogenism represents the next most common androgen-excess disorder causing ovulatory dysfunction. Ovarian hyperandrogenism (OHA), also known as polycystic ovarian syndrome (PCO), causes chronic anovulation and infertility through increased ovarian production of testosterone. The subsequent elevated intrafollicular androgen levels within each ovary results in increased rates of follicular atresia and anovulation. The causative factors for ovarian hyperandrogenism remain enigmatic; however, many researchers implicate abnormal ovarian steroid feedback by the gonads to the hypothalamus.[81] The ensuing cascade of events results in tonic LH stimulation of the ovarian stromal compartment leading to excess androgen production. Peripheral androgen conversion to estrogens perpetuates the abnormal steroid feedback to the hypothalamus. Hirsutism (terminal coarse hair), acne, and oily skin are the clinical correlates of elevated androgen effects.[15] Although the majority of patients with OHA are obese, approximately one-third of patients are lean.[30]

Recent evidence suggests that the majority of patients with OHA have hyperinsulinism secondary to peripheral insulin resistance.[22] Insulin resistance may be confirmed by obtaining serial serum insulin levels after an oral glucose load. Lipid screening is suggested in this population given their lower high-density lipoprotein levels (HDL) and higher low-density lipoprotein to high-density lipoprotein ratios (LDL/HDL).[78] Patients with idiopathic hirsutism and ovarian hyperandrogenism achieve a 40 to 50 percent pregnancy rate with ovulation induction regimens. Clomiphene citrate is the usual drug of choice with ovulatory rates ranging between 70 and 80 percent.[27] Parenteral therapy with gonadotropins is reserved for those candidates failing clomiphene therapy. Recently, insulin-sensitizing agents such as glucophage (Metformin) and troglitazone (Rezulin) have proven effective in partially correcting the PCO-induced metabolic abnormalities.[75] Metformin treatment of hyperinsulinemic anovulatory women reduces free testosterone levels by 44 percent, significantly lowers insulin levels, and promotes ovulation.[48]

Medical Endocrine Disorders Thyroid disorders, hypercortisolism, and diabetes are endocrine disorders that are frequently associated with ovulatory dysfunction. Hypothyroidism has been linked to infertility, spontaneous abortions, stillbirths, and congenital anomalies.[71] Although thyroid abnormalities are rare, a few simple blood tests will uncover this correctable condition. Hypothyroid patients may complain of weight gain, lethargy, decreased energy level, constipation, and cold intolerance. Hypothyroidism affects ovulation via abnormal androgen and estrogen feedback to the hypothalamus and through mild elevations in prolactin levels.[71] Levothyroxin therapy promptly corrects thyroid function with subsequent return of ovulation in the majority of patients. Hyperthyroidism infrequently affects ovulation, except in severe cases.

The vast majority of patients with hypercortisolism are anovulatory. Cushing's syndrome should be considered in those individuals manifesting any of the following: dorsocervical hump; supraclavicular fat pads; hirsutism; truncal obesity; moon facies; facial plethora; proximal muscle wasting; easy bruisability; hypertension; glucose intolerance; or violaceous abdominal striae. Initial screening tests include multiple 24-h urines for urinary-free cortisol, an overnight dexamethasone suppression test, and diurnal cortisol levels. Hypercortisolemic individuals should then undergo localization tests to determine its source. ACTH-producing pituitary adenomas (Cushing's disease) are typically found and can be treated via transphenoidal resection of the tumor.[33] Cushing's syndrome secondary to nonpituitary causes are more difficult to locate and treat.

Late-onset congenital adrenal hyperplasia may mimic PCO and accounts for 1 to 5 percent of all hirsutism in reproductive-age women.[6] Elevated androgens in this autosomal recessive disorder inhibit ovulation in women and spermatogenesis in men. A screening baseline 17-hydroxyprogesterone level obtained in the proliferative phase of the menstrual cycle followed by a one-hour ACTH stimulation test will confirm the diagnosis. Treatment with glucocorticoids often restores menstrual function. Prenatal diagnosis is available to at-risk couples through either chorionic villus sampling or amniocentesis. High-risk individuals should be treated with glucocorticoids during early pregnancy to minimize or prevent masculinization of an affected female fetus in utero. Treatment can be stopped if antenatal testing identifies a male or unaffected female infant.

Uncontrolled diabetes mellitus disrupts ovulation either by direct effects on the ovary or through an adrenal-related increase in androgen and cortisol levels. Meticulous glucose control can restore ovulation and prevent the threefold increase in congenital malformations that accompanies elevated blood glucose levels in early pregnancy.[51]

Hypothalamic Dysfunction Stress, weight loss, exercise, and certain medications can disrupt GnRH pulsatility. Altered hypothalamic function in this setting results in anovulation. Unlike most other causes of ovulatory dysfunction, these individuals often are hypoestrogenic. Untreated individuals remain at risk for osteoporosis and cardiovascular disease in the future. Behavioral and lifestyle modifications directed toward the underlying disorder often restore ovulation. The hypoestrogenism often precludes use of clomiphene citrate for ovulation induction. Parenteral gonadotropin therapy for ovulation induction is recommended in those individuals not responding to nonmedical therapy.

Female Tubal and Peritoneal Factors

Tubal blockage and peritoneal factors that adversely affect tubal function account for approximately 30 percent of female infertility. A dramatic rise in the incidence of sexually transmitted diseases with subsequent tubal damage has greatly contributed to the concomitant increase in both the risk of ectopic pregnancy and tubal factor infertility in the last two decades.[2,77] The initial offending agent is most commonly chlamydia, followed by *Neisseria gonorrhoeae*. Subsequent cases of salpingitis are often polymicrobial, underscoring the need for multiagent screening and treatment targeted towards these offending agents, specifically anaerobes. Prompt recognition and treatment is warranted because the incidence of tubal infertility increases with each subsequent infection.[77]

Tests to evaluate tubal patency yield limited information regarding overall reproductive function of the fallopian tubes, due to their inability to predict the adequacy of tubal transport mechanisms and ovum capture by the fimbria. A hysterosalpingogram (HSG) may be the initial screening test for tubal patency, with laparoscopy representing the gold standard for evaluation of tubal and peritoneal factors. The HSG, along with semen analysis and tests to determine ovulatory status, are all performed early in the evaluation of the infertile couple. This fluoroscopic examination, performed in the proliferative phase of the menstrual cycle, involves the introduction of radiopaque dye into the uterine cavity. Abnormalities of the uterine cavity alone comprise only 3 to 5 percent of all causes of infertility; however, they are often easily correctable. The HSG also aids in the diagnosis of proximal tubal disease and assesses ampullary tubal architecture thereby predicting, in part, successful surgical repair.

Evaluation of the Uterine Cavity

HSG correctly identifies most uterine filling defects, with false negative rates ranging from 8 to 24 percent and false positive rates reported between 6 and 25 percent.[52] Many false positive results occur secondary to tubal spasm. Myomas, endometrial polyps, intrauterine adhesions, congenital anomalies of the uterus, and foreign bodies are readily identified by HSG but rarely cause infertility. Intrauterine pathology may cause infertility by hindering implantation or sperm ascent, or by obliteration of the tubal ostia. Additionally, intrauterine synechiae (Asherman's syndrome), sometimes seen after curetting an infected postpartum uterus, obliterate the cavity resulting in amenorrhea and/or infertility. Infections after HSG are uncommon (1 to 3 percent) and may be prevented with antibiotic prophylaxis.[69] Patients with previously diagnosed pelvic inflammatory disease (PID) are high-risk; they may be best evaluated initially via laparoscopy and hysteroscopy.

Patients with abnormal uterine cavities by HSG should undergo hysteroscopy for definitive diagnosis and/or surgical correction. When warranted, hysteroscopic resection of polyps, myoma, and intrauterine adhesions can increase conception rates.[34]

Transvaginal sonography with saline infusion of the uterine cavity (sonohysterography) allows detailed evaluation of the uterine cavity. Infusion of approximately 10 cc of physiologic sterile saline under aseptic technique enables detailed sonographic evaluation and measurements of any uterine pathology. Sonohysterographic findings correlate highly with hysteroscopic results.[53] A more detailed discussion on sonohysterography can be found elsewhere in this book.

Evaluation of Tubal Patency

HSG may identify either proximal and/or distal tubal pathology. Proximal tubal blockage may occur secondary to salpingitis isthmica nodosa (SIN), inflammatory changes from ascending infection, cornual myomas, endometriosis, or tubal diverticuli. SIN has a characteristic "fingerprint" pattern in the isthmic region and increases the risk of both tubal factor infertility and ectopic pregnancies.[25]

Distal tubal disease is the most commonly encountered tubal abnormality, and arises from ascending infection or prior surgery. Distal tubal pathology varies, and may include patent tubes with minimal agglutination (phimosis) to complete obstruction with loss of all normal distal tubal architecture (hydrosalpinx). Patients with HSG-documented tubal pathology should undergo laparoscopic evaluation. Distal blockage may favorably respond to laparoscopic neosal-

pingostomy (opening the distal end); however, pregnancy rates correlate with tubal thickness, extent of mucosal damage, and presence of peritubal disease.

Surgical correction may involve hysteroscopic tubal cannulation for proximal disease, laparoscopic adhesiolysis and neosalpingostomy for distal occlusions, and laparotomy when laparoscopic repair is not possible. Patients with evidence of both proximal and distal tubal disease (bipolar tubal disease) are not surgical candidates and are best served by referral for in vitro fertilization (IVF). In general, patients with poor prognosis for surgical repair should be referred for IVF.[54]

Evaluation of Peritoneal Factors

Laparoscopy, although more invasive than HSG, identifies endometriosis and peritubal adhesions with greater precision, as both often escape detection under fluoroscopy.[32] Laparoscopy allows direct visualization of the pelvic viscera and surrounding structures, and is mandated when HSG is abnormal and/or inconclusive. The HSG and laparoscopy are equally sensitive in identifying distal tubal disease, whereas laparoscopy more aptly demonstrates nonobstructive tubal pathology (peritubal disease) while allowing for surgical correction.[70]

Endometriosis is characterized by the ectopic location of endometrial glands and stroma, and most often involves dependent pelvic structures. Endometriosis is more prevalent in infertile women (38.5 percent) than fertile women (5.2 percent).[76] Endometriosis-related infertility occurs when adhesions restrict tubal motility or obstruct the distal fallopian tube. Either event affects ovum capture, fertilization, and subsequent embryo transport. Severe endometriosis causes marked distortion of pelvic anatomy through formation of ovarian endometriomas and dense pelvic adhesions. Infertile patients with only minimal peritoneal endometriosis present a dilemma. In this setting, infertility persists despite seemingly normal tubal function. Infertility results from subtle ovulatory dysfunction and/or alterations in the peritoneal fluid environment. Increased numbers of peritoneal macrophages, especially those that phagocytose sperm, are reported.[45] Other studies suggest that altered T-cell and B-cell function, alterations in the immune system, and effects on local prostaglandin function are significant factors.[18,24]

Treatment is based on the severity of the condition. Patients with minimal endometriosis may be treated surgically, medically, or managed expectantly. Because pregnancy rates are similar in all three groups, a period of observation is often appropriate[49,57] depending upon the clinical circumstance.

Patients with extensive endometriosis benefit from surgical correction (by laparoscopy or laparotomy) if normal pelvic anatomy is restored. Pregnancy rates after surgery correlate with the severity of endometriosis by stage.[3] Whereas 70 percent of patients with stage I or II endometriosis conceive within two years of surgery, only 30 to 40 percent of those with severe endometriosis (stage III or IV) achieve that goal.[11] Patients with severe endometriosis and dense pelvic adhesions who fail surgical correction should undergo IVF.

Evaluation of the Cervix

A functional cervix is necessary to achieve pregnancy via natural coitus. The cervix filters out bacteria and debris, acts as a conduit for mobile sperm to reach the upper genital tract, and functions as a sperm reservoir.[40]

Adequate cervical mucus production is proportional to local estrogen levels. Therefore, while cervical mucus production is scant in hypoestrogenic individuals, appropriately rising midcycle estradiol levels are associated with the production of abundant acellular, nonviscous cervical mucus. Maximal sperm transport occurs under these conditions, and cervical mucus is initially assessed with a postcoital test (PCT) (discussed in Chap. 49). Poor PCT results may be due to bad timing of the test in the menstrual cycle, poor cervical mucus production, or sperm

antibodies. Patients with a history of prior cervical cone biopsy, cryosurgery of the cervix, or multiple dilatations and curettages are also at risk for decreased cervical mucus production. The postcoital test indirectly measures cervical mucus competency by assessing sperm-mucus interaction; however, poorly designed studies, inconsistent methodology, and variable interpretations have generally invalidated its use. Moreover, postcoital test results fail to correlate with pregnancy rates.[20]

Antisperm antibodies represent an infrequent cause of infertility and adversely affect PCT results by inhibiting sperm motility. Genital tract antibodies directed against sperm membranes (IgG or IgA) impair sperm function (capacitation and/or acrosomal reaction) and inhibit fertilization.

Currently, cervical factor infertility is treated by completely bypassing the cervix and instilling washed sperm directly into the uterine cavity [intrauterine insemination (IUI)]. IUI therapy has improved pregnancy rates per cycle except in cases of immunological-associated infertility (antisperm antibodies).[13] In general, cervical factor aberrations account for only 3 to 5 percent of all infertility etiologies.[64]

Evaluation of the Male

Infertility in 30 to 40 percent of couples is due to male factors. This underscores the importance of interviewing the couple together, and concomitantly evaluating both partners at the initial visit. A number of conditions may result in male infertility (Table 41-4).

Anatomy and Physiology of the Male The testis is the site for both steroidogenesis and sperm production. These processes involve a coordinated effort of the hypothalamic-pituitary-testicular axis, and, unlike the female, allow the male to constantly produce mature gametes. Normally, about 74 days are required for an immature germ cell to develop and appear in the ejaculate as a mature spermatozoan.

Gn-RH is secreted from the hypothalamus in

TABLE 41-4 **Causes of Male Infertility**

Category	Incidence (%)	Example
Idiopathic	70–75	
Primary testicular disorders	10–13	Klinefelter's syndrome, orchitis, cryptorchidism
Genital tract obstruction	8–10	Congenital (Young's syndrome) or acquired infection
Agenesis of vas deferens (malformation)	1–5	Congenital (cystic fibrosis)
Antisperm antibodies	4–6	Fertilization failures, motility disorders
Hypothalamic-pituitary	1	Kallmann's syndrome, CNS tumors, infiltrative disorders
Coital disorders	1	Ejaculatory failure, hypospadias, retrograde ejaculation

a pulsatile fashion and results in synthesis and release of gonadotropins (FSH and LH) from the anterior pituitary. Lutenizing hormone binds with its receptors in testicular Leydig cells and stimulates the production of testosterone. Follicle stimulating hormone enhances this effect and also increases Leydig cell LH receptors. Increasing levels of testosterone inhibit LH secretion. FSH stimulates Sertoli cells of the seminiferous tubules and, with high intratesticular testosterone levels, generates spermatogenesis. Inhibin produced by the stimulated Sertoli cells inhibits pituitary FSH secretions.

Normal testicular size depends directly on seminiferous tubule volume, and therefore reflects the presence of a functioning germinal epithelium. A testicular length less than 4 cm or inadequate volume (less than 18 cc) may suggest a volume of seminiferous tubules inadequate for normal sperm production.

After ejaculation, mature sperm undergo various surface changes called *capacitation*. These changes can also be induced in vitro. Upon reaching the zona pellucida of the oocyte, spermatozoa undergo an acrosomal reaction that allows the release of various enzymes from the acrosome of the sperm head. These enzymes enable the sperm to effectively penetrate the oocyte via digestion of the zona pellucida. Fertilization occurs in the distal oviduct once fusion of the two pronuclei is completed.

History Upon completion of a general medical history, the male should be questioned about his previous fertility and prior test results. A sexual history should include questions on coital technique, timing, and frequency; erectile or ejaculatory dysfunction; and frequency of ejaculation. Symptoms of inadequate androgens are suggested by a history of cryptorchidism; hypospadias; lack of pubertal development; a loss of libido; decreased frequency of shaving; and erectile and ejaculatory dysfunction. A history of recent drug usage (sulfasalazine, nitrofurantoin, chemotherapeutic agents, alcohol abuse, and illicit drugs) and exposure to environmental toxins should be elicited. Excessive cigarette and marijuana usage is associated with subnormal spermatogenesis. Exposure to heavy metals and ionizing radiation is often deleterious to spermatogenesis, as is testicular exposure to excessive heat. Pubertal or postpubertal mumps orchitis often results in irreparable testicular damage. A history of surgery (abdominal or genital) or genital trauma is elicited. Subfertile males with a history of chronic sinusitis and/or respiratory infections may have concomitant sperm motility disorders. In addition, liver disease and chronic renal failure adversely affect Leydig cell testosterone production and seminiferous tubule function. Diabetes mellitus, spinal cord injuries, and retroperitoneal lymph node dissection may result in retrograde ejaculation, as evidenced by a small semen volume and the presence of sperm in a postejaculatory urine. A past history of genital infections or recent testicular pain, dysuria, and penile discharge must be elicited and may indicate an active prostatitis, urethritis, or epididymitis.

Physical Examination A complete physical exam should be performed. The physician must carefully note any signs of hypogonadism;

namely, decreased facial and body hair, eunuchoidal body proportions, underdevelopment of the external genitalia, and gynecomastia. The external genitalia should be evaluated for hypospadias and testicular size and consistency. Testicular dimensions are normal when linear length exceeds 4 cm and testicular volume is at least 18 cc measured with a Prader orchiometer. The epididymis should be palpated for swelling, nodularity, and tenderness. Presence of the vas deferens is confirmed by careful palpation of the spermatic cord while a valsalva maneuver aids in detection of a varicocele. A rectal examination should be done to determine prostate size and tenderness.

The Semen Analysis Regardless of the history and physical exam findings, all males should undergo a semen analysis as the initial screening test. Due to marked variability in semen analysis results, multiple specimens are desirable at 2- to 4-week intervals. The male should be carefully counseled regarding a proper collection technique. After abstaining from ejaculation for at least 48 h (longer than 72 h is not necessary) a masturbated specimen is collected in a wide-mouth jar. Ideally, the semen should be analyzed within one hour of collection. Transported semen specimens must be kept at body temperature.

The semen is evaluated for volume, sperm concentration, viscosity, sperm motility, and morphology. The normal parameters, as suggested by the World Health Organization, are listed in Table 41-5.[8]

TABLE 41-5 Normal Semen Analysis

Volume	2 ml or more
Concentration	20 million/ml or more
Viscosity	Liquefaction in under 30 min
Motility	50% or more with forward progression or 25% or more with rapid progression within 60 min of ejaculation
Morphology	Over 50 to 60% oval (normal forms)
Cellularity (leukocytes)	Less than 1 million/ml

Consistent volumes below 2 ml should prompt an investigation for ductal obstruction, absence of the seminal vesicles, or retrograde ejaculation. A combination of the findings on physical exam, rectal probe sonography, and seminal fructose (from the seminal vesicles) will delineate an obstruction or absence of the seminal vesicles. Retrograde ejaculation is suspected in individuals with low seminal volumes and sperm in a postejaculate urine specimen. Persistent severe oligospermia or azoospermia with normal collection techniques mandates an endocrine evaluation in the male.

When overall motility and/or directional motion is diminished, the physician should consider the possibility of either a genital infection or a varicocele. Leukocytospermia and a seminal culture will confirm the presence of bacteria and infection, whereas palpation of the genitals identifies varicoceles. Scrotal Doppler studies may be needed to uncover subclinical varicoceles. Cigarette smoking, marijuana, environmental toxins, and androgen-deficient states may also decrease sperm motility, as can epididymal dysfunction. Antisperm antibodies may also impair sperm motility. Rarely, a hereditary disorder in ciliary action can adversely affect sperm motility along with chronic pulmonary problems (immotile cilia syndrome).

Evaluation of sperm morphology is somewhat subjective, relying on the expertise of the technician. Overall, normal forms exceeding 50 percent are considered adequate. Kruger has developed strict criteria for sperm morphology.[28] Under his system, adequate in vitro fertilization pregnancy rates exist when at least 14 percent of sperm have normal morphology. IVF success rates fall drastically when less than 4 percent normal morphology exists.

Endocrine Evaluation of the Male An endocrine evaluation should be done in cases of moderate to severe oligospermia (less than 5 to 10 million/ml) or azoospermia. FSH, LH, TSH, prolactin, testosterone, and estradiol levels should be obtained. An elevated TSH suggests hypothyrodism, which is easily treated. FSH and LH values that exceed 40 mlU/ml indicate primary testicular failure, which is refractory to treatment. Low FSH and LH are associated with hypothalamic-pituitary dysfunction, and further evaluation is necessary. Radiographic imaging with MRI or CT in conjunction with a Gn-RH stimulation test often aids in delineating hypothalamic from pituitary disorders. Gonadotropin or pulsatile Gn-RH therapy may be successful. Rarely, FSH may be normal while LH and testosterone levels are high, suggesting partial androgen resistance. Skin fibroblast cultures for androgen receptors are necessary to confirm the diagnosis. Occasionally, only FSH is elevated and may indicate germinal cell failure (Sertoli-cell–only syndrome).

The vast majority of men have a normal endocrine profile. In such individuals, hormonal therapy with gonadotropins, thyroid replacement, testosterone, or clomiphene citrate does not improve male fertility. In such cases, additional studies to exclude ductal obstruction are indicated. Because fructose is produced in the seminal vesicles, its presence in semen excludes ductal obstruction and absence, or atresia of the seminal vesicles. In males with azoospermia or severe oligospermia (less than 1 million/ml), treatment of the male for infertility is frequently not beneficial. However, assisted reproductive technologies (ART) provide promising results, and include intrauterine insemination, usually in hyperstimulated ovarian cycles, in vitro fertilization, and intracytoplasmic sperm injection.

Unexplained Infertility

Approximately 10 percent of infertile couples have no discernible cause for their infertility and are said to have unexplained infertility.[31] Most infertility clinics perform a detailed history and physical examination, multiple semen analyses, an HSG, evaluation of luteal function, a baseline hormonal panel, and laparoscopy. Subtle defects in this population may include subtle ovulatory dysfunction, sperm function abnormalities, and/or aberrations in ovum pick-up, which escape detection by currently utilized tests. Certain specialized tests, including ultrasound, antisperm antibodies, and sperm function assays, may uncover previously undetected abnormalities. Individuals with unexplained infertility may also have gamete disorders or fertilization defects that only IVF could uncover.[47]

Given that the basic battery of infertility testing lacks the appropriate sensitivity to identify all disorders in this population, certain empiric regimens are utilized to correct these subtle defects. It is necessary for physicians to initially verify the completeness and accuracy of all previous testing, especially if performed elsewhere. For such couples, three to five cycles of superovulation combined with IUI increase conception rates.[14] Superovulation (controlled ovarian hyperstimulation) involves ovarian stimulation to develop multiple follicles within each ovary by using either oral clomiphene citrate or injectable gonadotropins.

Approximately 23 to 25 percent of couples with unexplained infertility will conceive after three cycles of superovulation and IUI with gonadotropins, which compares favorably with one IVF cycle.[62] Superovulation IUI is widely accepted, and we use it as the initial treatment regimen for patients with unexplained infertility. Couples failing to conceive after three to five cycles are candidates for advanced assisted reproductive technologies.

Advanced Assisted Reproductive Technologies

Assisted reproductive technologies involve all procedures whereby human gametes (oocytes and sperm) are artificially combined either in the lab (in vitro fertilization) or within the fallopian tube [gamete intrafallopian transfer (GIFT)]. Other advanced ART techniques exist [zygote intrafallopian transfer (ZIFT)]; however, these are beyond the scope of this text. ART referrals are made for couples with severe tubal disease, advanced endometriosis, refractory ovulatory dysfunction, severe male factor, and for patients with unexplained infertility failing to conceive with superovulation and IUI. These patients benefit from referral to a center where advanced training in reproductive technology exists. The most recently published data from the Society for Advanced Reproductive Technology (SART) compares success rates for various ART techniques in terms of delivery rates per retrieval: IVF 22.5 percent, GIFT 27 percent, and ZIFT 27.9 percent.[63]

Summary

Infertility is a common condition that primary care practitioners may increasingly encounter. Because primary and secondary infertility are not infrequent findings in the general population, the clinician should have a thorough understanding of the various etiologies, diagnostic tests, and treatment algorithms. Preconception counseling is an essential part of the infertility evaluation. A simple and cost-effective work-up for the evaluation of infertility has been suggested; it includes an initial evaluation of the ovulatory status of the female combined with a semen analysis. Evaluation of tubal and peritoneal factors are likewise performed early in the work-up of the couple. Ovulatory dysfunction can be evaluated further by such specialized tests as urinary LH monitoring, transvaginal sonography, and late luteal endometrial biopsies. Secondary testing may include evaluation of sperm–mucus interactions and specialized tests of sperm function. A small subset of patients will have completely normal testing, and can be treated by superovulation and intrauterine insemination for a few cycles. Some peritoneal and tubal disorders require surgical correction; others may require assisted reproductive technologies.

In spite of a detailed work-up and advanced therapeutic modalities, some patients still fail to conceive. Owing to the intense psychological stress, these couples may be offered no treatment for a few cycles. Spontaneous pregnancies have been reported in such individuals. Finally, adoption should be discussed as a viable alternative for patients failing to conceive with assisted reproduction technologies. Intense counseling is often required for such individuals.

References and Selected Readings

1. American College of Obstetricians and Gynecologists: *Preconceptional care.* Washington, DC: ACOG, 1995. ACOG Technical Bulletin 204.
2. American College of Obstetricians and Gynecologists: *Gonorrhea and chlamydial infections.* Washington, DC: ACOG, 1994. ACOG Technical Bulletin 190.
3. American Fertility Society: Revised American Fertility Society classification of endometriosis. *Fertil Steril* 43:351, 1985.
4. American Medical Association, Council on Scientific Affairs: Violence against women, relevance for medical practitioners. *JAMA* 267:3184, 1992.
5. Blackwell RE: Hyperprolactinemia: Evaluation and management. *Endocrinol Metab Clin North Am* 21(1): 105, 1992.
6. Brody BL, Wentz AC: Late onset congenital adrenal hyperplasia: A gynecologist's perspective. *Fertil Steril* 48:175, 1987.
7. Brunell PA, Cherry J, Ector WL, et al: Expanded guidelines for use of varicella-zoster immune globulin. *Pediatrics* 72:886, 1983.
8. Centers for Disease Control: Varicella-zoster immune globulin for the prevention of chickenpox. *Ann Intern Med* 100:859, 1984.
9. Centers for Disease Control: Recommendations of the US Public Health Sevice task force on the use of zidovudine to reduce perinatal transmission of human immunodeficiency virus. *MMWR* 43:1, 1994.
10. Centers for Disease Control: Use of folic acid for prevention of spina bifida and other neural tube defects: 1983–1991. *MMWR* 40:513, 1991.
11. Cook AS, Rock JA: Surgical management of endometriosis. *Semin Reprod Endocrinol* 9:138, 1991.
12. Daley DC, Walters CA, Soto-Albors CE, Riddick DH: Endometrial biopsy during treatment of luteal phase defects is predictive of therapeutic outcome. *Fertil Steril* 40:305, 1983.
13. Dodson WC, Haney AF: Controlled ovarian hyperstimulation and intrauterine insemination for treatment of infertility. *Fertil Steril* 55:457, 1991.
14. Dodson WC, Whitesides DB, Hughes CL Jr, et al: Superovulation with intrauterine insemination in the treatment of infertility: A possible alternative to gamete intrafallopian transfer and in vitro fertilization. *Fertil Steril* 48:441, 1987.
15. Falcone T, Bourque J, Granger L, et al: Polycystic

ovary syndrome. *Curr Probl Obstet Gynecol Fertil* 16:69, 1993.

16. Federation CECOS, Schwart D, Mayaux NJ: Female fecundity as a function of age: Results of artificial insemination in 2193 nulliparous women with azoospermic husbands. *N. Engl J Med* 306:404, 1982.

17. Gibbons WE, Toner JP, Hamacher P, Kolm P: Experience with a novel vaginal progesterone preparation in a donor oocyte program. *Fertil Steril* 69(1): 96, 1998.

18. Gleicher N, El-Roeiy A, Confino E, et al: Is endometriosis an autommune disease? *Obstet Gynecol* 70:115, 1987.

19. Goegeon A: Dynamics of follicular growth in the human: A model from preliminary results. *Hum Reprod* 1:81, 1986.

20. Griffith CS, Grimes DA: The validity of the postcoital test. *Am J Obstet Gynecol* 162:615, 1990.

21. Guttmacher AF: Factors affecting normal expectancy of conception. *JAMA* 161:855, 1956.

22. Guzick DS: Cardiovascular risk in women with polycystic ovarian syndrome. *Semin Reprod Endocrinol* 14:45, 1996.

23. Hembree WC, Zeidenberg P, Mahas GG: Marijuana's effect on human gonadal function, in Mahas GG (ed): *Marijuana: Chemistry, Biochemistry and Cellular Effects.* New York: Springer-Verlag, 1976, pp 521–532.

24. Hirsch MB, Mosher WD: Characteristics of infertile women in the United States and their use of infertility services. *Fertil Steril* 47:618, 1987.

25. Jenkins CS, Williams SR, Schmidt GE: Salpingitis isthmica nodosa: A review of the literature, discussion of clinical significance, and consideration of patient management. *Fertil Steril* 60(4): 599, 1993.

26. Johansson EDB: Progesterone levels in peripheral plasma during the luteal phase of the normal human menstrual cycle measured by a rapid competitive protein binding technique. *Acta Endocrinol (Copenh)* 61:592, 1969.

27. Kettel ML, Himmel WP: Ovulation induction in estrogenized anovulatory patients. *Semin Reprod Endocrinol* 14:309, 1996.

28. Kruger TF, Acosta AA, Simmons KF, et al: Predictive value of abnormal sperm morphology in in vitro fertilization. *Fertil Steril* 49:112, 1998.

29. Lee SJ, Lenton EA, Sexton L, et al: The effect of age on the cyclical patterns of plasma LH, FSH, oestradiol and progesterone in women with regular menstrual cycles. *Hum Reprod* 3:851, 1988.

30. Lobo RA: The syndrome of hyperandrogenic chronic anovulation, in Mishell DR, Davajan V, Lobo RA (eds): *Infertility, Contraception and Reproductive Endocrinology,* 3d ed. Boston: Blackwell Scientific, 1991, p 447.

31. Lobo RA: Unexplained infertility. *J Reprod Med* 38:241, 1993.

32. Maathuis JB, Horbach JGM, Van Hall EV: A comparison of the results of hysterosalpingography and laparoscopy in the diagnosis of fallopian tube dysfunction. *Fertil Steril* 23:428, 1972.

33. Mampalam TJ, Tyrrell JB, Wilson CB: Transphenoidal microsurgery for Cushing's disease: A report of 216 cases. *Ann Intern Med* 109:487, 1988.

34. March CM. Hysteroscopy for infertility Baggish, in MS, Barbot J, Valle RF, (ed): *Diagnostic and Operative Hysteroscopy: A Test and Atlas.* Chicago: Year Book Medical, 1989, p 136.

35. Maroulis GB: Effect of aging on fertility and pregnancy. *Semin Reprod Endocrinol* 9:165, 1991.

36. Mars R, Lobo R, Campeau J, et al: Correlation of human follicular fluid inhibin activity with spontaneous and induced follicle maturation. *J Clin Endocrinol Metab* 58:704, 1984.

37. Martin TL, Kim M, Malarkey WB: The natural history of idiopathic hyperprolactinemia. *J Clin Endocrinol Metab* 60:855, 1985.

38. Miller E, Cradock-Watson JE, Pollock TM: Consequences of confirmed maternal rubella at successive stages of pregnancy. *Lancet* 2:781, 1982.

39. Moghissi KS: Accuracy of basal body temperature for ovulation detection. *Fertil Steril* 27:1415, 1976.

40. Moghissi KS: Cervical mucus changes and ovulation prediction and detection. *J Reprod Med* 31:748, 1986.

41. Molitch M: Disorders of the pituitary lactotroph, in Adashi EY, Rock JA, Rosenwaks Z (eds): *Reproductive Endocrinology, Surgery, and Technology.* Philadelphia: Lippincott-Raven, 1996, p 1303.

42. Mosher WD, Pratt WF: The demography of infertility in the United States, in Asch RH, Studd JW, (eds): *Annual Progress in Reproductive Medicine.* Pearl River, NY: Parthenon, 1993, pp 37–43.

43. Mosher WD, Pratt WF: Fecundity and infertility in the United States: Incidence and trends. *Fertil Steril* 56:192, 1991.

44. Murray DL, Reich L, Adashi EY: Oral clomiphene citrate and vaginal progesterone suppositories in the treatment of luteal phase dysfunction; A comparative study. *Fertil Steril* 51:35, 1989.

45. Musacato JJ, Haney AF, Weinberg JB: Sperm phagocytosis by human peritoneal marophages: A possible cause of infertility in endometriosis. *Am J Obstet Gynecol* 144:503, 1982.

46. Navot D, Bergh PA, Williams MA, et al: Poor oocyte quality rather than implantation failure as a cause of age-related decline in female infertility. *Lancet* 337:1375, 1991.

47. Navot D, Muasher SJ, Oehninger S, et al: The value of in vitro fertilization for the treatment of unexplained infertility. *Fertil Steril* 49:854, 1988.

48. Nestler JE, Jakabowicz DJ: Decreases in ovarian cytochrome P450c 17α activity and serum-free testosterone after reduction of insulin secretion in polycystic ovary syndrome. *N Engl J Med* 335(9):617, 1996.

49. Olive DL, Kee KL: Analysis of sequential treatment protocols for endometriosis-associated infertility. *Am J Obstet Gynecol* 154:613, 1986.

50. Padilla SL, Garcia JE: Effect of maternal age and number of in vitro procedures on pregnancy outcome. *Fertil Steril* 52:270, 1989.

51. Reece EA, Hobbins JC: Diabetic embryopathy: Pathogenesis, prenatal diagnosis and prevention. *Obstet Gynecol Surv* 41:325, 1986.

52. Rice, Karasick S. Goldfarb AF: Peritoneal adhesions in infertile women: Diagnosis with hysterosalpinography. *AJR Am J Roentgenol* 152:111, 1989.

53. Romano F, Cicinelli E, Anastasio PS, Epifani S, et al: Sonohysterography versus hysteroscopy for diagnosing endouterine abnormalities in fertile women. *Int J Gynaecol Obstet* 45(3):253, 1994.

54. Rosen GF: Treatment of endometriosis-associated infertility. *Infertil Reprod Med Clin North Am* 3:728, 1992.

55. Rotsztejn DA, Asch RH: Effect of aging on assisted reproductive technologies (ART): Experience from egg donation. *Semin Reprod Endocrinol* 9:272, 1991.

56. Sauer MV, Paulson RJ, Lobo RA: A preliminary report on oocyte donation extending reproductive potential to women over 40. *N Engl J Med* 323:1157, 1990.

57. Schenken RS. Malinak LR: Conservative surgery versus expectant management for the infertile patient with mild endometriosis. *Fertil Steril* 37:183, 1982.

58. Schwarz RH, Johnston RBJ: Folic acid supplementation when and how. *Obstet Gynecol* 88:886, 1996.

59. Scott RT, Hofmann GE: Prognostic assessment of ovarian reserve. *Fertil Steril* 63:1, 1995.

60. Scott RT, Leonardi MR, Hofmann GE, et al: A prospective evaluation of clomiphene citrate challenge test screening in the general infertility population. *Obstet Gynecol* 82:539, 1993.

61. Shoupe D, Mishell DR, Lacarra M, et al: Correlation of endometrial maturation with four methods of estimating day of ovulation. *Obstet Gynecol* 73:88, 1989.

62. Simon A, Avidan B, Mordel N, et al: The value of menotropin treatment for unexplained infertility prior to an in vitro fertilization attempt. *Hum Reprod* 6:222, 1991.

63. Society for Assisted Reproductive Technology and the American Society for Reproductive Medicine: Assisted reproductive technology in the United States and Canada: 1995 results generated from the American Society for Reproductive Medicine Society for Assisted Reproductive Technology Registry. *Fertil Steril* 69(3): 389, 1998.

64. Speroff L, Glass RH, Kase N: Female infertility, in *Clinical Gynecologic Endocrinology and Infertility,* 5th ed. Baltimore: Williams & Wilkins, 1994, p 809.

65. Speroff L, Glass RH, Kase N: Regulation of the menstrual cycle, in *Clinical Gynecologic Endocrinology and Infertility,* 5th ed. Baltimore: Williams & Wilkins, 1994, p 219.

66. Speroff L, Glass RH, Kase NG: Anovulation and the polycystic ovary, in *Clinical Gynecologic Endocrinology and Infertility,* 5th ed. Baltimore: Williams & Wilkins, 1994, p 457.

67. Speroff L, Glass RH, Kase NG: Hirsutism, in *Clinical Gynecologic Endocrinology and Infertility,* 4th ed. Baltimore: Williams & Wilkins, 1989, p 233.

68. Stillman RJ, Rosenberg MJ, Sachs RP: Smoking and reproduction, in Wallach EE, Kempers RD (eds): *Modern Trends in Infertility and Contraception Control.* Chicago: Year Book Medical, 1988, p 31.

69. Stumpf PF, March CM: Febrile morbidity following hysterosalpingography: Identification of risk factors and recommendations for prophylaxis. *Fertil Steril* 33:487, 1980.

70. Swart P, Mol BW, van der Veen F, et al: The accuracy of hysterosalpingography in the diagnosis of tubal pathology: A meta-analysis. *Fertil Steril* 64:486, 1995.

71. Thomas R, Reid RL: Thyroid disease and reproductive dysfunction: A review. *Obstet Gynecol* 70:789, 1987.

72. Tietze C, Guttmacher AF, Rubin S: Time required for conception in 1727 planned pregnancies. *Fertil Steril* 1:338, 1950.

73. Tietze C: Reproductive span and rate of reproduction among Hutterite women. *Fertil Steril* 8:89, 1957.

74. van Kooij RF, Looman CWN, Habbema JDF, et al: Age-dependent decrease in embryo implantation rate after in vitro fertilization. *Fertil Steril* 66:769, 1996.

75. Velazquez EM, Mendoza S, Hamer T, Sosa F, Glueck CJ: Metformin therapy in polycystic ovarian syndrome reduces hyperinsulinemia, insulin resistance, hyperandrogenemia, and systolic blood pressure, while facilitating normal menses and pregnancy. *Metabolism* 43:647, 1994.

76. Verkauf BS: Incidence, symptoms, and signs of endometriosis in fertile and infertile women. *J Fla Med Assoc* 74:671, 1987.

77. Westrom L: Effect of acute pelvic inflammatory disease on fertility. *Am J Obstet Gynecol* 121:707, 1974.

78. Wild RA, Painer PC, Coulson PB: Lipoprotein lipid concentration and cardiovascular risk in women with polycystic ovary syndrome. *J Clin Endocrinol Metab* 61:946, 1985.

79. World Health Organization: *Laboratory Manual for the Examination of Human Semen and Sperm—*

Cervical Mucus Interaction. Cambridge: Cambridge University Press, 1992.

80. Yen SSC: Prolactin in human reproduction, in Yen SSC, Jaffe RB (eds): *Reproductive Endocrinology,* 3 ed. Philadelphia: WB Saunders, 1991, p 389.

81. Yen SSC: Chronic anovulation caused by peripheral endocrine disorders, in Yen SSC, Jaffe RB (eds): *Reproductive Endocrinology,* 3d ed. Philadelphia: WB Saunders, 1991, p 597.

82. Zuckerman B, Frank DA, Hinson R: Effects of maternal marijuana and cocaine use on fetal growth. *N Engl J Med* 320:762, 1989.

CHAPTER 42

Diagnosis and Management of Spontaneous and Recurrent Abortion

Joseph A. Hill
Fredric D. Frigoletto, Jr.

DIFFERENTIAL DIAGNOSIS OF VAGINAL
BLEEDING IN EARLY PREGNANCY
SPONTANEOUS ABORTION
RECURRENT ABORTION
Etiology • Evaluation • Therapy

S pontaneous abortion is a common reason why women of reproductive age seek medical attention. Of the more than 5 million clinically recognizable pregnancies established each year in the United States, 70 percent or less result in a viable infant.[14] The majority of spontaneous abortions result from fetal chromosomal abnormalities, and occur in the first trimester of pregnancy. A significantly smaller number are the potential results of a maternal condition, such as a uterine abnormality, endocrine deficiency, immunologic factor, genital tract infection, or environmental factors such as smoking, caffeine, or alcohol consumption.

Women of reproductive age who experience vaginal bleeding other than at the time of expected menses should be considered to have a pregnancy-related problem until proven otherwise. First trimester vaginal bleeding occurs in 30 to 40 percent of pregnancies, and one-half of these end in abortion. Generally, those that proceed to abortion are preceded by heavier bleeding and cramping. Although vaginal bleeding other than menses is commonly a consequence of pregnancy, other conditions should be considered.

Differential Diagnosis of Vaginal Bleeding in Early Pregnancy

The possible causes of vaginal bleeding in early pregnancy can be divided into those etiologic factors that are solely pregnancy-related and those that are pregnancy-associated (i.e., not caused by pregnancy but which can occur during pregnancy) as listed in Table 42-1.

A quantitative pregnancy test (using β-hCG) should be performed on all women of reproductive age with abnormal vaginal bleeding. This test determines whether women are having bleeding during pregnancy; it does not distinguish whether this bleeding is a direct result of the pregnancy. A thorough history will often enable the clinician to arrive at the proper diagnosis. Determining the date of the last menstrual period is important, as implantation bleeding occurs around cycle day 21, while ectopic pregnancies usually do not become symptomatic until 6 to 8 weeks of gestation. Bleeding tends to become heavy in cases of spontaneous abortion, while ectopic pregnancies more likely present with spotting.[13] Passage of tissue suggests spontaneous abortion; however, passage of decidual tissue may occur in ectopic pregnancies, mimicking spontaneous abortion. Crampy lower abdominal pain and vaginal bleeding in a women who is pregnant suggests an inevitable abortion.

TABLE 42-1 Etiologies of Vaginal Bleeding in Early Pregnancy

Pregnancy Related	Pregnancy Associated
Implantation bleeding	Vulvitis
Abortion	Vaginitis
Ectopic pregnancy	Cervicitis
Molar pregnancy	Carcinoma of vagina, cervix
	Foreign body
	Polyp
	Thrombocytopenia
	von Willebrand's disease
	Anticoagulant therapy
	Disseminated intravascular coagulation

In ectopic gestations, the pain may be described as cramping, but more commonly will be sharp and constant, often associated with peritoneal signs resulting from the accumulation of blood in the abdomen and pelvis. Hemorrhage may also result in referred shoulder pain. Often an ectopic pregnancy is very difficult to diagnose in early pregnancy (before 5 weeks of gestation), because it is difficult to determine whether an intrauterine pregnancy exists by ultrasound assessment before 5 weeks of gestation or when the β-hCG level is <2000 mIU/ml. In cases of a ruptured corpus luteum cyst during pregnancy, spotting associated with pain may mimic an ectopic pregnancy. Furthermore, free fluid in the posterior cul-de-sac may be seen on ultrasound after the release of the cyst fluid, which in appearance is ultrasonically indistinguishable from blood seen in the cul-de-sac after a ruptured or unruptured but bleeding ectopic pregnancy. Sophisticated ultrasound techniques with quantitative serum β-hCG determinations have largely replaced culdocentesis as a diagnostic modality.[7,10] Serial quantitative β-hCG titers can be helpful in these cases to determine whether an abnormal pregnancy exists. If the β-hCG titer does not rise by 66 to 100 percent after 48 hours, then an abnormal pregnancy (ectopic or poten-

tial abortion) may be present.[8] A quantitative β-hCG titer >2000 mIU/ml warrants an ultrasound examination to look for an intrauterine pregnancy. If no intrauterine pregnancy is seen, an ectopic gestation is strongly suggested. Abnormally high β-hCG titers associated with vaginal bleeding may be the result of a molar pregnancy, although multiple gestation is another possibility. Possible risk factors for ectopic pregnancy include prior ectopic pregnancy; a history of pelvic inflammatory disease; pelvic adhesions; prior ruptured appendix; prior tubal surgery; contraceptive failures with intrauterine devices (IUDs) or oral contraceptives; prior tubal ligation; diethylstilbestrol (DES) exposure; and a history of recurrent abortion. One method of assessment to rule out ectopic pregnancy is demonstrated in Fig. 42-1.

Spontaneous Abortion

In approximately 70 percent of human conceptions, fetal viability is not achieved, with an estimated 50 percent of pregnancies lost prior to the first missed menses.[12] The actual rate of pregnancy loss after implantation may be as high as 31 percent.[14] Spontaneous abortion is defined as the loss of a clinically recognized (blood test or ultrasound) pregnancy prior to 20 weeks of gestation, and occurs in 10 to 15 percent of all clinically established pregnancies. Approximately 60 percent of first trimester pregnancy losses are chromosomally abnormal, with trisomies being the most common abnormality, especially trisomy 16 followed by trisomy 22, 21, 15, 14, 18, and 13. Monosomy X (45X) and triploidy (69 chromosomes) are also found; tetraploidy (92 chromosomes) occurs less commonly.

Spontaneous abortions are subdivided into threatened abortion, inevitable abortion, incomplete abortion, complete abortion, missed abortion, and recurrent abortion. Threatened abortion refers to viable clinical pregnancies accompanied by vaginal bleeding. Inevitable abortion occurs during pregnancy in the presence

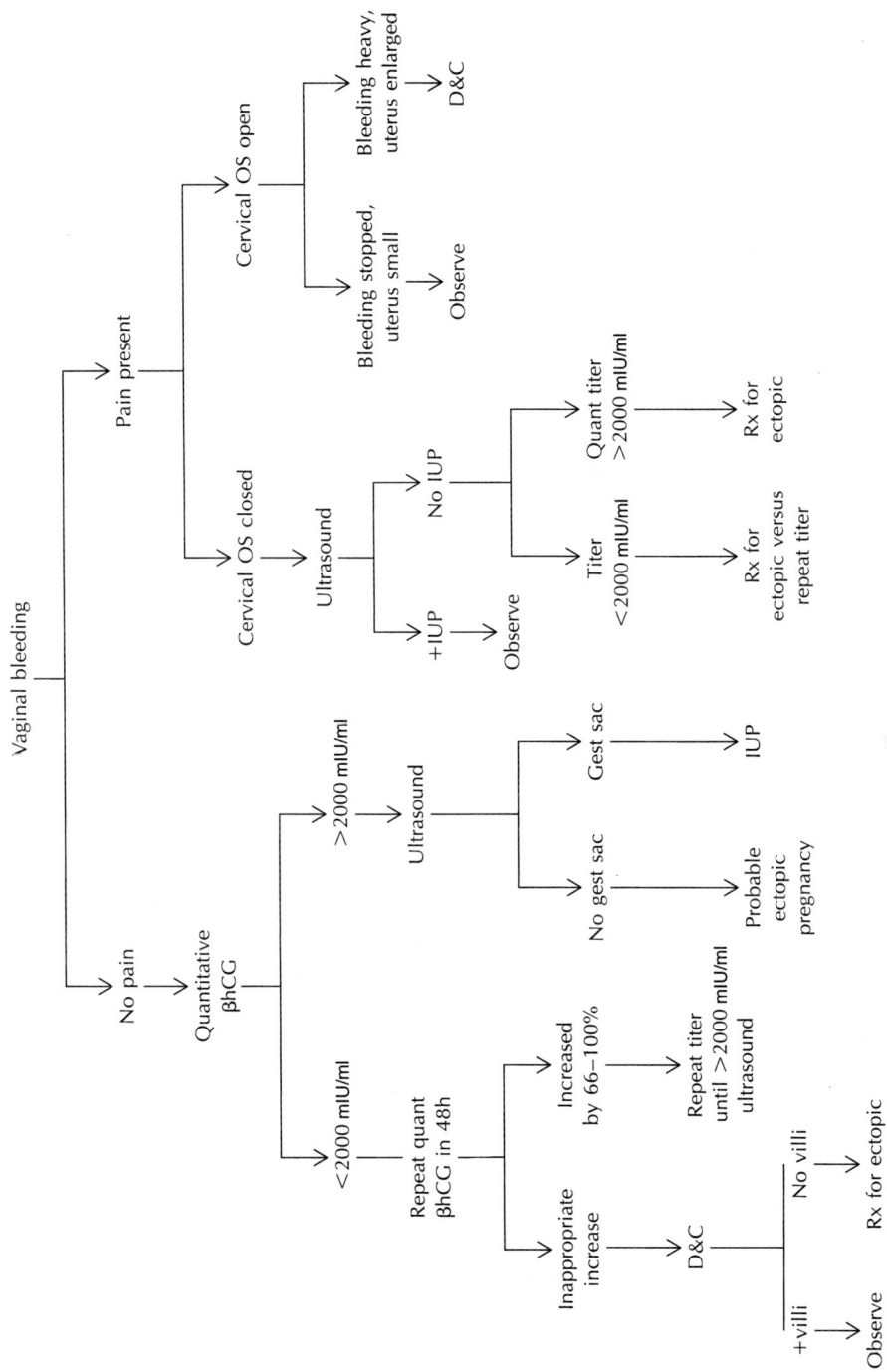

Figure 42-1 An algorithm for ruling out ectopic pregnancy. IUP, intrauterine pregnancy.

of a dilated internal cervical os, or in cases with ruptured membranes. An incomplete abortion occurs when some, but not all, fetal placental tissue has passed through the internal cervical os; a compete abortion is when all fetal placental tissue has been spontaneously passed through the internal cervical os. A missed abortion is a pregnancy in which the fetus is no longer viable in the absence of vaginal bleeding. Symptoms of pregnancy (nausea, breast tenderness) may or may not be present at the time of a pregnancy loss. Pelvic examination and ultrasound assessment will usually lead to the proper diagnosis.

Recurrent Abortion

Recurrent abortion has been traditionally defined as the occurrence of three or more clinically recognized pregnancy losses prior to 20 weeks of gestation, and occurs in approximately 1 in 300 pregnancies.[1] A clinical investigation of pregnancy loss, however, should be initiated after two spontaneous abortions, as the recurrence risks are very similar between individuals with two and three prior losses. It is important to understand the calculated risks for recurrent abortion based on epidemiologic surveys, especially when reviewing the literature on potential success rates with various therapies. These surveys indicate that after one spontaneous abortion the recurrent risk is approximately 15 to 18 percent; after two, 25 to 30 percent; after three, 30 to 35 percent; and approximately 40 percent after four consecutive clinical losses.[1,12]

Etiology

Parental chromosomal abnormalities remain the only uncontested cause of recurrent abortion, and occur in approximately 3 to 4 percent of couples seeking evaluation. Other associations with recurrent pregnancy loss have been made, including müllerian or anatomic anomalies (10 percent), endocrinologic abnormalities (17 percent), infections (5 percent), and autoimmunity (4 percent). The potential cause in the majority

of cases, however, remains unexplained (60 percent), even after a thorough evaluation (Table 42-2).[5,6]

The most common inborn parental chromosomal abnormality contributing to recurrent abortion is balanced translocation. Pericentric chromosomal inversion and sex chromosome mosaicism have been associated with recurrent abortion, but are more controversial. Other genetic causes of abortion include multifactorial factors, inheritance of autosomal recessive genes and X-linked disorders.

Anatomic causes can be divided into both congenital and acquired lesions. Congenital anomalies include incomplete müllerian fusion or septum resorption defects, diethylstilbestrol (DES) exposure, and uterine artery anomalies. Women with a septate uterus may have a 60 percent risk for spontaneous abortion. Second trimester losses are seen; however, first trimester abortions may be caused if the embryo implants on the intrauterine septum, because the endometrium overlying the septum is poorly developed and blood supply to this area is often limited. When abnormal placentation occurs, the pregnancy may end in an abortion. DES exposure in utero can lead to uterine developmental anomalies, most commonly hypoplasia, which may be associated with both first and second trimester abortions. DES-exposed women may also have a pre-

TABLE 42-2   Investigative Measures Potentially Useful in the Evaluation of Recurrent Spontaneous Abortion

1. Parental peripheral blood karyotypes
2. Intrauterine structural study (sonohysterogram)
3. Luteal phase endometrial biopsy
4. Thyroid stimulating hormone (TSH)
5. Anticardiolipin and antiphosphatidyl serine antibodies
6. Lupus anticoagulant
7. Interferon-γ production in response to trophoblast stimulation (Embryotoxic Factors-Lymphocyte [ETF-L] Assay)
8. Cervical cultures for *mycoplasma*, ureaplasma, *chlamydia*

disposition to develop an incompetent cervix and premature labor. Isolated cases of uterine artery anomalies have been reportedly associated with recurrent abortion, most likely due to compromised blood flow to the implanting blastocyst and developing placenta. Acquired anatomic lesions that are potentially predisposing to recurrent abortion include uterine synechiae (adhesions) and submucous or intramural leiomyomata (fibroids). These associations with abortion are tenuous, but theoretical mechanisms that may be involved include interference with blood supply compromising implantation.

Endocrinologic abnormalities associated with recurrent abortion include luteal phase insufficiency, thyroid disorders, and uncontrolled diabetes mellitus. The early maintenance of pregnancy is dependent on progesterone production by the corpus luteum until the placenta takes over progesterone production between seven and nine weeks of gestation. Spontaneous abortion could ensue if the corpus luteum fails to produce sufficient quantities of progesterone; progesterone delivery to the uterus is compromised; or progesterone utilization within endometrial-decidual tissue is disordered. Thyroid disorders, most commonly hypothyroidism, have also been associated with recurrent abortion, most likely due to ovulation disorders leading to corpus luteum insufficiency. The mechanism of abortion in women with diabetes mellitus is unclear, but in advanced cases may be due to compromised blood flow to the developing conceptus.

Maternal infections have been tenuously associated with recurrent abortion. The most commonly reported association between infection and pregnancy loss has been cervical colonization with mycoplasma, ureaplasma, and chlamydia. Causal mechanisms are poorly described, but one theoretical possibility may involve immunologic activation.

Other factors, including immunologic phenomena involving allogeneic immunity and autoimmunity, have also been associated with reproductive failure.[3] Environmental factors such as heavy metal toxicity; carbon tetrachloride and trichloroethylene benzene; drugs such as folic acid antagonists, nicotine, caffeine, ethanol, and inhalation anesthetic agents; ionizing radiation; and chronic medical illnesses, such as cardiac and renal diseases or any other disorder that compromises uterine blood supply, are associated with spontaneous pregnancy loss. Thrombocytosis (platelet count greater than 1 million) has also been associated with recurrent abortion, presumably due to clotting and occlusion of the placental vasculature. It is important to reassure patients that exposure to video display terminals (VDTs) and microwave ovens do not cause abortion.

Evaluation

Diagnostic evaluation of couples experiencing recurrent abortion should begin with a general history that includes medical, surgical, genetic, and psychological factors. A description and sequence of all prior pregnancies are important, as is whether histologic and karyotypic assessments of prior abortions were performed. The practitioner should also ask about chronic illnesses, uterine instrumentation, infection, and DES exposure, as well as exposure to drugs, radiation, and possible environmental pollutants.

A general physical examination of the woman should include an investigation for signs of metabolic illness. On pelvic examination the examiner should search for signs of infection, DES exposure, or previous cervical laceration, and on bimanual examination, for irregularity of the size, shape, and contour of the uterus.

Laboratory measurements that are potentially useful (Table 42-2) include a peripheral blood karyotype of both partners; a sonohysterogram followed by hysteroscopy and laparoscopy, if indicated; a luteal phase endometrial biopsy, ideally 10 days following the luteinizing hormone (LH) surge or after cycle day 24 of an idealized 28-day cycle (if the biopsy is out of phase by 3 or more days according to established criteria, then repeat assessment in a subsequent cycle is often suggested before making the diagnosis of luteal phase insufficiency; in cases of an abnormal biopsy, a serum prolactin and androgen profile should also be considered); thyroid stimulating hormone (TSH); an autoimmune evaluation consisting of anticardiolipin and antiphosphatidyl serine antibodies, and lupus anticoagulant (an aPTT or Russell viper venom time); potentially an alloimmune evaluation consisting of assessment of interferon-γ production to trophoblast (ETF-L assay); and cervical cultures for mycoplasma, ureaplasma, and chlamydia may also be considered.

Therapy

Therapy should include appropriate measures for the specifically identified problem. For individuals with an intrauterine abnormality, hysteroscopic resection is recommended. For luteal phase insufficiency consisting of a 3- or 4-day lag, therapy consisting of progesterone vaginal suppositories 50 mg bid beginning 3 days after the LH surge through 10 weeks of gestation is in order. For defects ≥5 days out of phase, ovulation induction should be considered.

Hypothyroidism and hyperprolactinemia should be treated with thyroid replacement and a dopamine agonist, respectively. Meticulous control of diabetes mellitus is also warranted. An infectious etiology should be treated with an appropriate antibiotic in both partners, with repeat cervical culture to confirm eradication. A presumed allogenic abnormality (positive ETF-L assay) is treated with potentially immunosuppressive doses of vaginal progesterone (100 mg bid) beginning 3 days after the LH surge until 20 weeks of gestation, although this has not been tested as yet in an appropriately designed clinical trial.

For individuals with autoimmunity as evidenced by a positive lupus anticoagulant or sustained moderate- or high-titer anticardiolipin or antiphosphatidyl serine IgG or IgM antibodies, low-dose aspirin (81 mg) and heparin (5,000 to 10,000 units bid or alternatively, low molecular-weight heparin 2500 to 5000 units once daily)

should be considered. Immunotherapy with either donor leukocytes or intravenous immunoglobulin has not been substantiated to be efficacious in treating reproductive failure.

For individuals with recurrent abortion of unknown etiology, expectant management consisting of synchronized ovulation and sperm deposition may be helpful, as desynchronized fertilization has been hypothesized to contribute to early pregnancy loss due to chromosomal abnormalities. Early diagnosis and close monitoring during the first trimester may also be psychologically therapeutic. Serial hCG determinations should be performed. Once the β-hCG attains 1000 to 5000 mIU/ml at 5 to 6 weeks gestation, an intrauterine pregnancy should be confirmed by ultrasound, recognizing that women with recurrent spontaneous abortion have a 2 to 4 percent risk of ectopic gestation.

The prognosis for a subsequent live birth (Table 42-3) in couples with a history of recurrent abortion is not necessarily dismal. Most chromosomally abnormal pregnancies abort prior to achieving fetal cardiac activity. Recent evidence suggests that once fetal cardiac activity has been ultrasonically detected between 5 and 6 weeks of gestation, the risk of subsequent loss is approximately 23 percent. While this is significantly higher than the 4 percent incidence in the general population, knowledge that a 77 percent chance of fetal viability exists once fetal cardiac activity has been detected can be tremendously reassuring to the couple who has experienced multiple miscarriages, and it helps to set a more realistic prognosis for pregnancy success.

TABLE 42-3   **Prognosis for Live Birth**

Etiology	Percent Success
Genetic (chromosomal)	up to 90
Anatomical	60–70
Endocrinological	90
Immunological	70–90
Unknown (other)	30–90

Summary

The diagnosis of early pregnancy disorders depends on an accurate assessment of the patient's history, physical examination, and appropriate laboratory tests. Understanding the potential pathophysiologic mechanisms involved in each diagnosis as outlined in this chapter, together with a caring empathetic attitude, will enable women's health care providers to manage effectively the most commonly encountered disorders potentially contributing to early pregnancy loss.

References and Selected Readings

1. Alberman E: The epidemiology of repeated abortion, in *Early Pregnancy Loss: Mechanisms and Treatment.* New York: Springer-Verlag, 1988, pp 9-17.
2. Boue J, Boue A, Lasar P: Retrospective and prospective epidemiologic studies of 1,500 karyotyped spontaneous abortions. *Teratology* 11:11–26, 1975.
3. Johnson PM, Ramsden GH: Recurrent miscarriage. *Baillieres Clin Immunol Allergy* 2:607–624, 1992.
4. Hill JA: Recurrent pregnancy loss, in Creasy R, Resnick R (eds): *Maternal Fetal Medicine.* New York: WB Saunders, 1998.
5. Hill JA, Polgar K, Harlow BL, Anderson DJ: Evidence of embryo- and trophoblast-toxic cellular immune response(s) in women with recurrent spontaneous abortion. *Am J Obstet Gynecol* 166:1044–1052, 1992.
6. Hill JA: Recurrent Abortion, in Berkowitz RS, Barbieri RL (eds): *Gynecology: Principles and Practice,* 5th ed. St. Louis; MO: Mosby Year-Book, 1994.
7. Kadar N, DeVore G, Romero R: Discriminatory hCG zone: Its use in the sonographic evaluation for ectopic pregnancy. *Obstet Gyencol* 58:156, 1981.
8. Kadar N, Freedman M, Zackar M: Further observation on the doubling time of human chorionic gonadotropin in early asymptomatic pregnancy. *Fertil Steril* 34:783, 1980.
9. Laufer MR, Ecker JL, Hill JA: Pregnancy outcome following ultrasound-detected fetal cardiac activity in women with history of multiple spontaneous abortion. *J Soc Gynecol Invest* 1:138–142, 1994.
10. Nyberg DA, Filly RA, Mahoney BS, et al: Early gestation: Correlation of hCG levels and sonographic identification. *Am J Roentgenol* 144:951–954, 1985.
11. Triplett DA: Obstetrical implications of antiphospholipid antibodies. *Clin Obstet Gynecol* 6:507–518, 1992.
12. Warburton D, Fraser FC: Spontaneous abortion rate in man: Data from reproductive histories collected in a medical genetics unit. *Am J Hum Genet* 16:1–28, 1963.
13. Weckstein LN: Clinical diagnosis of ectopic pregnancy. *Clin Obstet Gynecol* 3:236–244, 1987.
14. Wilcox AJ, Weinberg CR, O'Connor JF, et al: Incidence of early loss of pregnancy. *N Engl J Med* 319:189–194, 1990.

CHAPTER 43

Menopause

Eric S. Knochenhauer
J. Benjamin Younger

Physiology of Menopause

Menopause refers to the cessation of menstruation due to the depletion of ovarian follicles. Most definitions require that women be amenorrheic for at least 6 months with physical or laboratory evidence of estrogen depletion before they are termed "menopausal." Prior to actual ovarian failure, there is a decline in ovulatory function with fewer follicles present. Thus, there is a decline in ovarian estrogen and inhibin production. With falls in ovarian hormones, there is less negative feedback on the pituitary and hypothalamus, and there is a detectable rise in follicle stimulating hormone and lutenizing hormone. A serum follicle-stimulating hormone (FSH) level is the most sensitive test to confirm menopause.

The physiologic period of waning ovarian function is called the climacteric. This period is variable in length, but generally lasts for several years before atresia of all estrogen-producing follicles has occurred. During the climacteric, noncyclic uterine bleeding due to anovulation or to sporadic ovulation may occur.

In the United States, menopause is said to occur normally between ages 45 and 55 (95 percent confidence interval), with the median age being

51. Menopause prior to age 40 is termed premature menopause; after age 55 it is termed late menopause. The onset of menopause is genetically related; contrary to myths, it is not related to age at menarche, number of pregnancies, age of last pregnancy, oral contraceptive use, or use of infertility medications. It is also not related to race, socioeconomic status, height, or weight. Menopause may occur earlier in women who have a history of tobacco use.

Ovarian failure and its sequelae have gained much attention in the United States primarily because one-third of all women in the United States are postmenopausal. The average life span of women will approach 85 in the year 2000, in contrast to an average life span of 50 in the 1900s (Fig. 43-1). In the next 20 years, approximately 40 million American women will enter menopause.[1]

In a 1996 survey, approximately one-third of perimenopausal,[2] and at most one-fourth of postmenopausal women, currently took hormone replacement therapy (HRT).[2,3] Most women remain uninformed of the benefits of HRT,[2,4,5] and some physicians remained unconvinced of the benefits and therefore do not raise the issue.[4]

Changes Associated with Estrogen Decline

Numerous physical and psychological symptoms have been attributed to the decline and discontinuance of ovarian function in midlife. These symptoms include vasomotor symptoms, genital atrophy, osteoporosis, menopausal skin changes, cardiovascular disease, psychiatric disorders, and changes in sexual satisfaction. Cross-cultural research on menopause (i.e., examining these symptoms in different cultures) reveals that there is a large discrepancy in the prevalence of symptoms in different cultures.[6] In some cultures, it is uncommon for women to experience any symptoms.[6] However, among women who experience

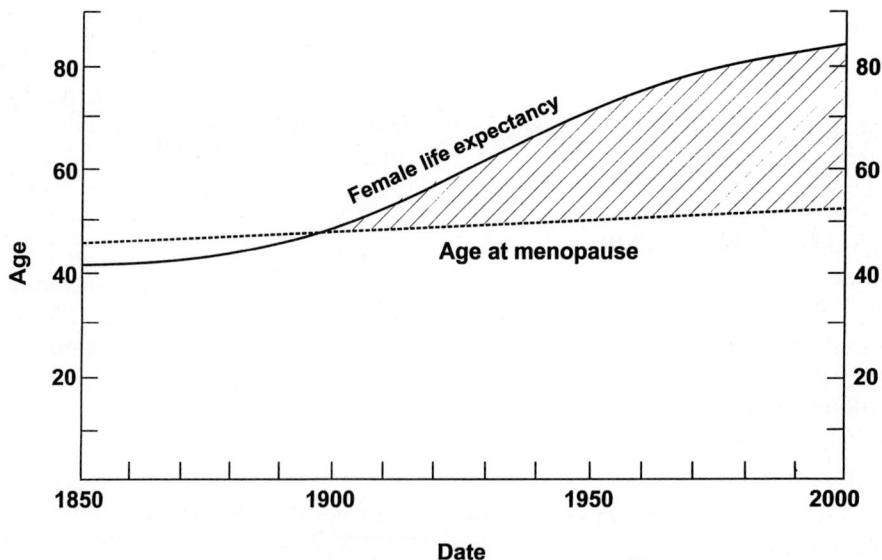

Figure 43-1 Female life span. [From Cope E: Physical changes associated with the postmenopausal years, in Campbell S (ed): *Management of the Menopause and Postmenopausal Years.* Lancaster, England: MTP Press, 1976, p 33, reprinted with permission.]

menopause, these symptoms adversely affect their quality of life.[7]

Vasomotor Symptoms

Vasomotor symptoms, or hot flushes, are the most common perimenopausal symptoms that compel women to seek medical attention. Seventy-five percent of women experience hot flushes. The average duration of these symptoms is 2 to 3 years. Eighty percent of women who experience the symptoms complain about them for more than 1 year, and 25 percent for up to 5 years.

These symptoms, which include sudden increases in central skin temperature as well as perspiration, are apparently due to deregulation of the temperature-regulating center in the hypothalamus. Both peripheral vasodilatation (a sympathetic adrenergic inhibitory action) and perspiration (a sympathetic cholinergic stimulatory action) occur. The flush, which generally lasts from a few minutes to 20 min, typically is preceded by a premonition—a flash.

Although the precise etiology of vasomotor symptoms is unclear, it is apparently related to decreases in estrogen and inhibin levels, not to absence of estrogen. It is theorized that a decline below a certain level exerts more effect on the hypothalamic thermostat, thus affecting autonomic nervous system control of peripheral vasculature. Once the central nervous system has adjusted to decreased estrogen levels, vasomotor symptoms cease.

About one-third of women with vasomotor symptoms find these symptoms severe enough to require medical assistance. The symptoms, which may occur up to 15 times daily, may awaken the individual, producing sleep deprivation, and may cause sweating, necessitating a change of clothing. Hot flushes may begin before menopause, but generally are more severe after cessation of menses.

Exogenous estrogen therapy,[8] progestogen therapy,[9] and, to a lesser extent, vasodilator therapy have been shown to decrease the incidence of vasomotor symptoms. Flushes may not respond optimally to estrogen replacement therapy for up to one month; however, there is usually some decrease in frequency within the first few days of use.

Genital Atrophy

Genital atrophic changes associated with hypoestrogenism are a significant problem for many women. Clinically, the atrophic vagina has a pale appearance and loses its elasticity. The epithelium is thin and friable, and with the lack of colonization by acidophilic bacteria, it no longer produces glycogen. The vagina, vulva, and external urethra may become colonized by gastrointestinal bacteria and develop an inflammatory response, causing tissue crythema and denudation, a purulent discharge, and bleeding. Intercourse may aggravate these inflammatory changes. At times, the vaginal walls actually may agglutinate, making intercourse very uncomfortable. The symptoms related to genital atrophy include vaginal and vulvar itching and burning, dyspareunia, vaginal bleeding, dysuria, urinary frequency, and urinary urgency.[10] The sexual dysfunction,[11] which many women do not report, may lead to decreased sexual activity and have psychological effects on both partners. The most effective therapy for atrophic vaginitis or urethritis is estrogen, which increases the local blood supply and in part reverses these changes[12] (see "Individualization of Care" later in this chapter).

Osteoporosis

Osteoporosis, defined as a reduction of bone mass per unit volume, significantly affects more than one-third of older women. This often leads to fractures, which, in addition to causing pain and disabilities, result in direct and indirect cost of over 3.8 billion dollars annually in the United States. Annually 1.6 to 1.7 million fractures occur in the United States.[13]

Bone strength or bone mineral content is a

function of numerous factors (Table 43-1) that, when deficient, may predispose one to develop osteoporosis. Osteoporosis is rare in African-American women,[14,15] and it is more common in thin Caucasian or Asian women than in large, muscular women. Osteoporosis may be somewhat less common in women who have maintained healthy lifestyles. Smoking, excessive alcohol use, sedentary lifestyle, and steroid use appear to be contributing factors in women who develop osteoporosis. Figure 43-2 illustrates the relationship between bone calcium content (bone strength) and age in women. All of the above-mentioned factors appear to affect the slopes of the lines of increase and decrease in bone calcium content. They affect the peak calcium content, present in the mid-30s, and affect the likelihood of the individual's bone calcium content reaching the "fracture point" later in life.

There is well-documented accelerated bone calcium loss beginning prior to the time of ovarian failure. The calcium loss is primarily from the trabecular (spongy) bone of the vertebral bodies, long bone shafts and heads, and the pelvis. There is now abundant evidence indicating that exogenous estrogen therapy reduces the risk of postmenopausal (type I) osteoporosis and fractures. Numerous studies have shown decreased fracture rates in estrogen-treated women as compared with untreated women.[16] Increased calcium and hydroxyproline urinary excretion occurring

TABLE 43-1   Factors Contributing to Bone Strength

Heredity
Activity (weight-bearing exercise)
Race
Dietary intake of calcium, vitamin D, and other nutrients
Good general health
Normal functioning endocrine glands (thyroid, parathyroid, and ovaries)
Normal function of kidneys and GI tract
Estrogen status of the woman

after menopause have been shown to be normalized by estrogen treatment. In addition, serial bone densitometry studies show a halt in bone density loss in estrogen-treated patients but not in untreated controls.[16] Other therapies, including high-dose calcium, have not been shown to affect this early postmenopausal loss of bone mass.[17] The use of calcium, with or without vitamin D, has been shown to decrease bone loss and fractures.[17–19]

Menopausal Skin Changes

The skin changes associated with aging include increased fragility and wrinkling, as well as some changes in sensation. These changes may increase around the time of menopause. A decline in skin collagen content paralleling the decline in bone density in postmenopausal women has been illustrated[20] with a loss of up to 3 percent per year.[21] With a decline in collagen, skin slackness increases.[22] Estrogen therapy slows the loss of collagen.[21] Menopausal women treated with estrogen develop thicker skin, which is less prone to wrinkling,[23] slow the development of slackness,[22,24] and complain less of dry skin.[23] With declining estrogen production, relative signs of androgen excess may develop, including hirsutism, acne, and temporal balding.

Cardiovascular Disease

In the United States, heart disease—specifically coronary artery disease (CAD)—is the leading cause of death for postmenopausal women.[1] Although the disease tends to strike men earlier in life, the overall chance of dying from heart disease is essentially equal in women and men. However, when plotted on a logarithmic scale, the death rate from CAD in women does not increase after menopause as one would expect if estrogen deficiency was an important etiologic factor.[25] The primary risk factors for coronary artery disease are tobacco use, hypertension, and elevated serum cholesterol or unfavorable lipoprotein profiles. Secondary factors include diabe-

Figure 43-2. Relationship of bone mass to age in women.

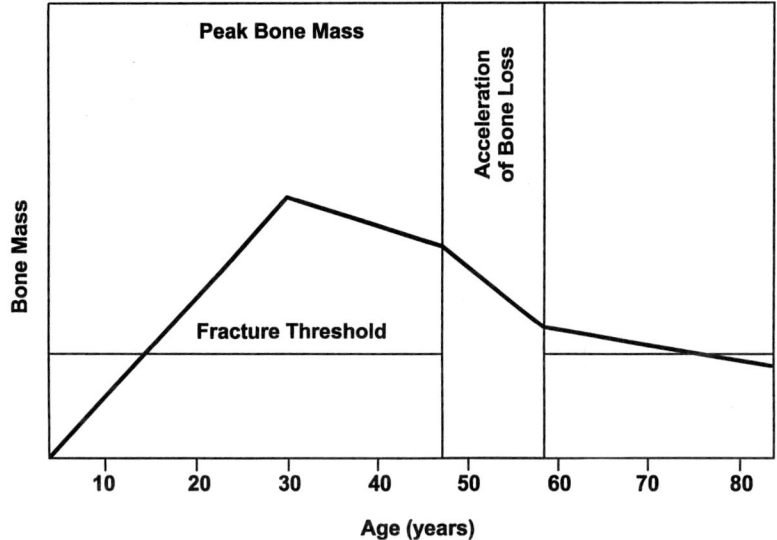

tes mellitus, obesity, and sedentary lifestyle. The modification of these risks through education, lifestyle changes, and medical therapy appears to reduce the incidence of the disease.

Numerous epidemiologic studies indicate that hormone replacement, particularly estrogen replacement, after ovarian failure substantially reduces the incidence of coronary artery disease. Meta-analyses of these data have shown relative risk of myocardial infarction (fatal and nonfatal) in ever-users of postmenopausal estrogens to be between 0.55 and 0.65.[25,26] However, not all epidemiological studies agree,[25] including the Framingham cohort study.[27] One study noted that there was an increase in CAD only in women with surgical menopause and not in women with natural menopause.[28] The mechanisms by which estrogen may affect coronary artery disease include its favorable effect on cholesterol and lipoproteins and its local relaxing effect on vascular smooth muscle. In theory, there appears to be some attenuation of both of these favorable effects of estrogen by synthetic progestins administered with estrogen; however, the actual impact of the commonly used progestins is unknown. Two European case-referent studies continued to demonstrate a decrease in the risk of CAD in women with both estrogen and progestin replacement therapy.[25] However, there are few studies that confirm the cardiovascular benefits of estrogen/progestin regimens.

Ovarian failure may also be an important determining factor in coronary artery disease in women. The incidence of the disease in women prior to menopause is much lower than that in men of the same age.[25] Surgical removal of the ovaries produces an increase in coronary artery disease similar to that seen in men.[28] As opposed to natural menopause, using exogenous estrogens protects oophorectomized patients from developing CAD.[28] It also appears that natural menopause may increase a woman's susceptibility to the disease. The incidence of coronary artery disease in women clearly increases with age after menopause, whereas little to no increase is seen prior to ovarian failure. In addition, women with CAD have a significant reduction in CAD death with estrogen replacement.[25] A randomized placebo-controlled study of estrogen (0.625 mg equine estrogens) and medroxyprogesterone acetate (2.5 mg) did not provide any benefit to women with established CAD.[29]

More remains to be learned about hormone replacement therapy and heart disease. Currently, several randomized clinical trials are under way with CAD as the end point. These studies will ultimately quantify the benefit of estrogen replacement therapy with far more certainty than present case-controlled and cohort studies. For example: What are the optimal regimens, doses, and administration routes for both estrogen and progestin? Will there be a protective effect in obese women who have higher levels of endogenous estrogens after menopause and who are not likely to need hormone replacement therapy for other reasons?

Psychological Disorders

A number of symptoms (anxiety, depression, irritability, fatigue, insomnia, emotional lability, and changes in libido) may occur around the time of menopause. Whether a person will exhibit the symptoms is variable; some individuals will show minimal or no symptoms, while others will have symptoms that they find disabling. The etiology of these symptoms is incompletely understood and appears to be multifactorial. In addition to the hormonal and metabolic changes that occur with menopause, age-related social and economic changes may affect an individual's lifestyle and self-image (Table 43-2). A great deal of variability exists among both men and women in the ability to withstand these changes. Estrogen decline may indirectly cause or worsen these

TABLE 43-2 Life Events That Often Occur Around the Time of Menopause and That May Affect Mental Status

Empty nest (children leaving home)

Interpersonal changes (changes in friends)

Employment changes

Marital changes

Relocation

Financial changes

Loss of family or friends

Health concerns

symptoms by increasing the risk of developing a sleep disturbance and adversely affecting overall feelings of well-being. The use of HRT in menopausal patients has been demonstrated to help improve symptoms such as nervousness,[13] depression,[13] anxiety,[30] and insomnia .[13] However, estrogen therapy alone is insufficient treatment in women who meet the criteria for major depression.[10,31] In addition, progestin therapy may increase depressive symptoms.[31] The mechanism by which estrogen affects mood is not understood, although estrogen receptors have been located in the hypothalamus,[32] limbic forebrain,[32] cerebral cortex,[32] and the pituitary gland.[33] The management of patients with these symptoms varies. Disorders such as thyroid disease, other chronic disease states, and clinical depression should be considered as possible causes of the symptoms; when indicated, investigational studies should be undertaken. Women having mild symptoms with no obvious organic cause should be well counseled and made aware that these symptoms generally resolve with time as long as the patient maintains a healthy lifestyle. Those whose symptoms affect their ability to function and to maintain a healthy lifestyle frequently will benefit from psychological counseling, antidepressant therapy, and, rarely, other psychiatric care.

As longevity of women increases, so does the prevalence of senile dementia. It is estimated that up to 50 percent of women 85 years or older may suffer from Alzheimer's disease.[34] Estrogen has been shown to protect neurons in vitro from oxidative stress-induced cell death.[35] In addition, estrogen produces a reduction in the levels of the amyloid precursor, which accelerates the deposition of the β-protein component of senile plaques.[34,36] Overall, patients with mild to moderate dementia have demonstrated improvement of memory, orientation to place and time, and mental calculations. Estrogen replacement therapy has also been demonstrated to reduce the number of women who develop Alzheimer's disease. In a community-based study of 1124 menopausal women, the onset of Alzheimer's disease was significantly later in women who had taken estrogen as compared to those who had not.[3] The relative risk of the disease was 5.8 per cent in estrogen users as compared to 16.3 percent in nonusers ($p < .01$).[3] Progestins may reduce the improvement seen with estrogen alone.[34] Currently there are few studies investigating hormonal replacement therapy and the development of Alzheimer's disease. Although current studies appear promising, they are not conclusive.

Symptoms Not Directly Related to Estrogen Depletion

Androgens and Menopause

Recently, much has been presented in the lay press concerning the use of androgens, such as dehydroepiandrosterone (DHEA), as an energy boost and sexual aid. As a brief review, androgens are produced by both the ovary and the adrenal gland. Androgenic hormones include testosterone (T), androstenedione (A), and DHEA and its sulfate (DHEAS). Approximately half of peripheral T is produced from a conversion of a weaker androgen, A. The adrenal gland produces large quantities of an even weaker androgen, DHEA, and DHEAS may be converted to A and then to either T or estrogen.[40]

Circulating levels of both total and free T decline 50 percent between the third and fifth decade of life.[41,42] In addition, DHEAS levels decline with age.[43] A crossover, controlled study demonstrated that testosterone enanthate increased sexual motivation, arousal, and frequency when compared to HRT alone.[44] Myers and colleagues[45] assessed the effect of estrogen, estrogen and androgens, and placebo on sexual function (episodes of intercourse, masturbation, and orgasm). The frequency of intercourse did not increase; however, the number of masturbatory episodes and resulting orgasms did increase. Of note, the 5 mg of methyltestosterone used was 2 to 4 times the dose commonly used in the United States.[45] This has been confirmed by other authors.

The addition of androgens to estrogen replacement therapy may possibly aid in the treatment of menopausal women's psychological symptoms (i.e., anxiety and depression), and may help prevent bone reabsorption as compared to estrogen alone.[42] It has shown no therapeutic benefit with vasomotor or endometrial protection.[46] However, androgens may have a negative impact upon lipoproteins,[46] and high-dose androgen therapy can be toxic to the liver. Side effects of androgen therapy include hirsutism, acne, temporal balding, deepening voice, and clitorimegaly.[42,46] Deepening of the voice and clitorimegaly have been noted only with injection replacement therapy and not oral replacement therapy. Hirsutism, acne, and balding tend to be reversible; however, clitorimegaly and deepening voice are not. Hirsutism and acne have developed with methyltestosterone doses as low as 1.25 mg.[46]

Libido

When a women complains of decreased libido, more than androgen levels need to be considered. Libido and sexual function are determined by emotional, environmental, and endocrine factors.[47] However, an age-independent association between menopause and a decline in sexual and coital frequency has been observed.[48] In addition, an increase in libido does not always result in increased sexual activity. A good medical history is important. Identification of estrogen-deficient changes aid in the choice of therapy. Women with less vaginal atrophy tend to be more sexually active.[49] Due to embarrassment, older women may find it easier to admit to vasomotor symptoms, but not to sexual dysfunction.

Hormone Replacement Therapy

There are essentially five indications for the use of HRT: treatment of vasomotor symptoms; treatment of atrophic vaginitis; reduction of cardiovascular disease; prevention of osteoporosis; and management of menopausal-related psychosomatic complaints.

It is apparent from the previous discussion that estrogen deficiency may produce numerous adverse effects. Some of these, such as urogenital atrophy, vasomotor symptoms, loss of skin thickness and elasticity, and sleep disturbances may affect quality of life. Others, such as osteoporosis and coronary artery disease may affect not only quality of life, but also longevity. Because women live much longer today and spend at least one-third of their lives after menopause (Fig. 43-1), estrogen deficiency and its treatment have become much more significant issues than they were in the early 1900s.

Although the idea of "glandular therapy" can be traced back to ancient Egyptian times, the first real attempts to treat symptoms of ovarian failure with "ovarian secretions" did not occur until 1885. It was not until the 1920s and 1930s that estrogens in the urine of pregnant mares were discovered to be active when given to humans, and that estrogens could be produced synthetically in forms that could be absorbed and remain active when given orally (diethylstilbestrol and ethinyl estradiol). Although the pharmacologic development of estrogen and progesterone preparations has proceeded rapidly, it may still be in its adolescence.

Benefits

It is now clear that estrogen given to postmenopausal females in doses that produce serum levels of active estrogens (estrone or estradiol) biologically equivalent to the lowest levels seen in women of reproductive age will effectively treat vasomotor symptoms and genital atrophy, will prevent up to one-half of cases of osteoporosis, and will possibly decrease mortality from coronary artery disease by 40 to 50 percent.[50] In addition, hormone replacement therapy likely decreases the risk of Alzheimer's disease, osteoarthritis, colon cancer, tooth loss, and skin aging.[50]

Endometrial Effects—Rationale for Progestin Therapy

Numerous epidemiologic studies have shown an increase in adenocarcinoma of the endometrium

with use of exogenous estrogens without progestin after menopause (Table 43-3). This increase appears to be related to potency, dose, and duration of use. Careful analysis of some of these studies reveals that the risk is probably overestimated, owing to more aggressive diagnosis and to the fact that, like prostate cancer in men, many women may harbor low-grade, somewhat dormant endometrial cancers that become apparent when stimulated by estrogen. Studies have not shown an increase in death from endometrial cancer in estrogen users, presumably because most of these cancers are low-grade and confined

TABLE 43-3 Risk Estimates from Case Control Studies of Unopposed Estrogen Replacement Therapy and Endometrial Cancer

Study		Relative risks[a]	
Author	Year	Ever-users	Long-term users
Smith	1975	4.5	—
Ziel	1975	7.6	13.9
Mack	1976	5.6	8.8
Gray	1977	3.1	11.6
McDonald	1977	2.0	7.9
Wigle	1978	2.2	5.2
Horwitz	1978	12.0	—
Hoogerland	1978	2.2	6.7
Antunes	1979	6.0	16.0
Weiss	1979	7.5	8.2
Hulka	1980	—	4.2
Shapiro	1980	3.9	6.0
Jelovsek	1980	2.4	4.8
Spengler	1981	3.2	8.6
Stavraky	1981	4.2	14.4
Kelsey	1982	—	8.2
LaVecchia	1982	2.7	—
Henderson	1983	1.4	3.1

[a]Risk relative to never users.

SOURCE: From Peterson HB, et al: Genital neoplasia, in Mishell, D. (ed). *Menopause and Pharmacology.* St. Louis: CV Mosby, 1987. Reprinted with permission.

to the uterus when diagnosed. There is a high cure rate with hysterectomy.

Experimental evidence indicates that administration of estrogen without progesterone to postmenopausal women, even in low doses, will produce early forms of hyperplasia in 20 to 35 percent within a year's time.[51,52]

Like progesterone production in ovulatory women, exogenous progestins prevent hyperplasia in postmenopausal women receiving estrogens. In addition, administration of progestins decreases the incidence of endometrial cancer. This protective effect also appears to be related to progestin dose, potency, and duration of use (see "Hormone Replacement Regimens" later in this chapter).

Other Cancer Risks

There have been reports *suggesting* a linkage of exogenous hormonal therapy with cancers of the ovary, uterine cervix, liver, and malignant melanoma.[30] However, no currently published study establishes any link between these cancers and exogenous estrogen use. In addition, estrogen replacement therapy has been shown to decrease the risk of colon cancer.[54]

Cancer of the breast is the most frequent cancer in women, and the second leading cause of cancer death. The median age at which breast cancer develops is 69, but 80 percent of women are affected after the age of 40. There is an abundance of indirect evidence that estrogen and/or progesterone have roles in breast cancer etiology. Most breast cancers occur in women who have had ovarian function. Early menarche, low parity, and late menopause increase breast cancer risk, whereas early removal of the ovaries decreases it.[55] Breast glandular tissue has estrogen and progesterone receptors that have a proliferative effect when stimulated. Ductal breast carcinoma also may exhibit receptors. Cancers exhibiting receptor activity respond favorably to oophorectomy and to therapy aimed at decreasing ovarian estrogen production. From these observations one might expect that prolonged exposure to estrogen would increase the risk of the disease. In a large population-based cohort study of more than 23,000, the relative risk (RR) of breast cancer was not statistically elevated with a relative risk of 1.1 and a 95 percent confidence interval overlapping 1.0 (1.0 to 1.2).[30]

Surprisingly, the data available on breast cancer and menopausal hormone replacement have not clearly defined an association.[56] Numerous epidemiological studies show varying results; however, the majority show a relative risk no greater than 1.7, and most show a relative risk very close to 1 or 1.1.[57,58] Several meta-analyses suggest that the risk may be related to dose and duration of use, and is possibly increased when hormone replacement is given to patients with additional risk factors for breast cancer (e.g., strong family history, which in itself gives a relative risk from 2.5 to 3.5).[57] Data from a meta-analysis by Dupont and Page of epidemiological studies are presented in Fig. 43-3. Risk has not been consistently shown to increase with the amount of estrogen received,[57] as measured by length of use (Table 43-4), average daily dose, or cumulative dose.

The FDA Advisory Committee has agreed that long-term use of estrogen is associated with a modest increase in breast cancer risk of a magnitude of 1.3 to 1.5; however, the risk may be significantly lower if lower doses of estrogen are used consistently. Higher doses and longer duration of exogenous estrogen use may be associated with increased breast cancer risk. In addition, the risk may increase further when women already at high risk for breast cancer take exogenous estrogen.

The association of the progestin component of estrogen-progestin use and the risk of breast cancer is not clear from the available data. Progesterone and progestins cause glandular proliferation in normal breast tissue and could theoretically increase the risk of carcinogenic events. However, high-dose progestin therapy may suppress the growth of some breast cancers. With incomplete data on how progestins affect breast cancer risk, and because progestins adversely af-

Figure 43-3 Relative risk of breast cancer with conjugated estrogen therapy by dosage. *A.* Patients treated with 0.625 mg conjugated estrogens. *B.* Patients treated with 1.25 mg conjugated estrogens. (From Dupont and Page,[71] reprinted with permission.)

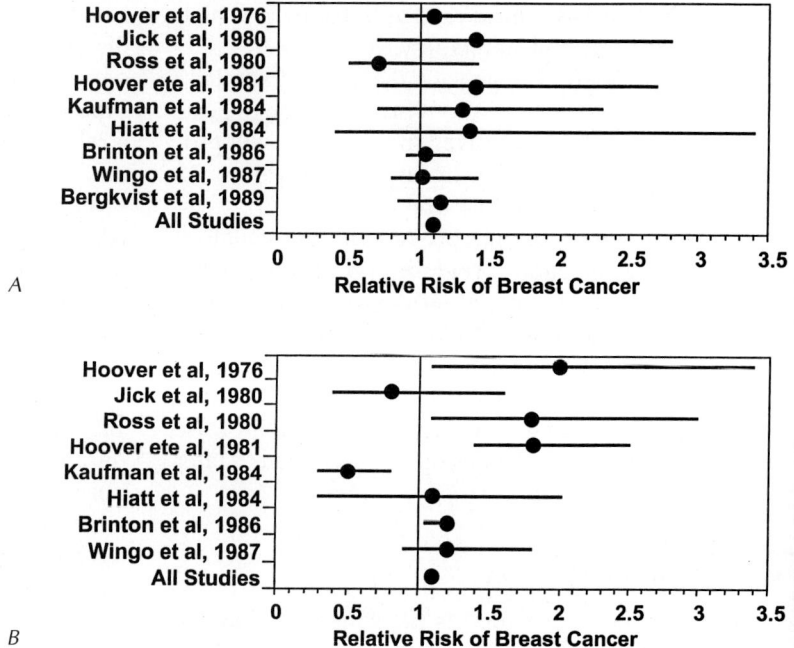

fect the favorable effect of estrogen on lipoproteins and cause most of the side effects associated with hormone replacement, we favor not administering progestins to patients without uteri solely for their presumed protective effect on the breast. However, if a women has a uterus and is receiving hormone replacement therapy, most clinicians believe that a progestin is required.

Adami found no association of HRT and cervical cancer (RR = 0.8; 0.5 to 1.2), decreased risk of developing liver or biliary tract cancer (RR = 0.4; 0.2 to 0.7), pancreatic cancer (RR = 0.8; 0.5 to 1.2), large bowel cancer (RR = 1.0; 0.8 to 1.2), or malignant melanoma (RR = 1.5; 1.0 to 2.1).[30]

There are no known relationships between menopausal hormone replacement therapy and cervical, lung, gastrointestinal, hematologic, or lymphomatous malignant neoplasms. A few epithelial (especially endometroid) ovarian cancers and osteoblastic sarcomas may have estrogen receptors, which would contraindicate estrogen therapy. There is some debate as to whether such therapy is contraindicated in patients with mela-

nomas, because estrogen may stimulate melanocytes.

Benign Breast Problems

Fibrocystic breast changes respond variably to menopausal hormone replacement. The presence of premenopausal fibrocystic changes or cyclic mastalgia does not always indicate that the problem will be exacerbated by postmenopausal hormone replacement. However, some women with previous breast symptoms, and a few who have never had breast symptoms, will develop mastalgia and/or fibrocystic changes when treated. As with other hormone-related effects, breast symptoms usually are dose-related, and mastalgia frequently worsens during the estrogen/progestin days of cyclic therapy.[57] In addition, both the length of therapy and dose have been positively correlated with an increase in the risk of developing fibrocystic disease and mastalgia.[64,65]

TABLE 43-4 Relative Risks of Breast Cancer in Women With and Without Ovaries by Duration of Use of Estrogens

Reference	Year of Use	Relative Risks Ovaries Removed	Ovaries Retained
Kaufman et al. (55)	<1	0.4	0.9
	1–4	0.8	0.9
	5–9	1.1	0.7
	≥10	0.5	1.3
McDonald et al. (56)	1–5	1.3	0.9
	≥6	1.2	0.7
Brinton et al. (57)	<5	1.0[a]	1.0[a]
	5–9	1.2	1.1
	10–14	1.6	1.3
	≥15	1.4	1.7
Wingo et al. (58)	<1	1.6	0.8
	1–4	1.3	0.9
	5–9	1.1	0.7[b]
	10–14	1.5	
	≥15	1.7	
Buring et al. (59)	<5[c]	0.9	1.1
	≥5[c]	1.3	1.3

[a]P-value of test for trend: 0.03.

[b]This category is 5 yr of use.

[c]Duration at entry into cohort study in 1976; women followd to 1980.

Other Effects (Coagulation, Hypertension, Vascular Disease, and Gallbladder Disease)

By directly or indirectly stimulating liver enzymes, estrogen may increase the production of serum globulins, including angiotensinogen, sex hormone binding globulin, and others. It favorably affects fat and cholesterol metabolism in the liver, tilting the balance toward increases in high-density lipoprotein cholesterol and triglycerides, and decreases in total cholesterol and low-density lipoprotein cholesterol, including apolipoproteins. It decreases antithrombin III activity, but apparently has little effect on other clotting factors. Progestins exert no effect on clotting factors, but act against the beneficial effect of estrogens on cholesterol and lipoproteins. Estrogen also increases the cholesterol content of bile, and may increase the incidence of cholesterol-containing gallstones in some individuals.

All of these effects appear to be related to hormone dose, potency, and route of administration. The formulations generally recommended for postmenopausal replacement produce blood levels of biologically active estrogen at or below those seen in the follicular phase of reproductive-aged women. All orally administered compounds tend to exert more effect on the liver because of their entry through the portal circulation. However, there is apparently little clinical significance of this effect with doses equivalent to 0.625 mg of conjugated estrogens in women with normal hepatic and renal function. Two recent studies report a slight increase in the risk of thromboembolism in hormone replacement therapy users as compared to nonusers,[66,67] although the overall risk may be no greater than 1 in 5000.[67] No epidemiologic study has shown an increase in hypertension or other vascular disease. The low-dose regimens used in hormone replacement therapy apparently produce a greater beneficial effect by favorably affecting cholesterol and lipoproteins and by directly causing vasodilation. There does appear to be a rare susceptible individual who will develop coagulation problems; however, there is no laboratory test known to recognize which individuals might have this increased susceptibility. Transcutaneous and premucosal administration of estrogen have less effect on liver metabolism, and antithrombin III activity has not been shown to change with therapy. However, there is not enough evidence as yet to say that the presently available patch and creams are totally safe in these susceptible individuals.

Hormone Replacement Regimens

Hormones in Replacement Therapy

Computer modeling studies, assuming a 40 percent reduction in relative risk for coronary disease, a 54 percent reduction in hip fracture risk, and a 30 percent increase in breast cancer risk, also indicate that most American women would extend life expectancy with the use of HRT.[68] However, controversies remain in the absence of a clinical trial. By defining the specific menopausal symptoms, a more rational therapy can be selected.

Estrogens

The most commonly used oral estrogen preparation is conjugated equine estrogens (Premarin). Tablet strengths are 0.3, 0.625, 0.9, 1.25, and 2.5 mg. Esterified estrogen preparations (Estratab, Mentest) principally contain estrone and equilin sulfate. Esterified estrogen tablet strength is similar to conjugated equine estrogens, although they are not biochemical equivalents. Estradiol is the principal estrogen produced by the premenopausal ovary. 17β-estradiol (Estrace) is conjugated and metabolized to estrone. Estradiol has a short half-life and BID dosing may be appropriate. Estrone (Ogen, Orthotest) contains purified estropipate.

Although there is not sufficient information regarding which treatment regimens produce the maximum benefit with minimal side effects, several regimens have emerged that, based on current experience, should be beneficial to most women. Unopposed estrogen therapy appears to be the optimal regimen for patients who have undergone hysterectomy; but for women with a uterus, a progestin is important to reduce the risk of endometrial hyperplasia and cancer. Fig. 43-4 represents the blood levels produced by daily administration of two doses of oral conjugated estrogens, one dose of oral micronized estradiol, and two estradiol transdermal patches.[69,70] The estradiol and estrone levels produced by most of these regimens, as well as by equivalent doses of other oral medications, either are lower than or biologically equivalent to blood levels seen in reproductive-aged women. Intramuscularly administered estrogen and once-a-week oral estrogens produce higher peak blood levels of estrogen than do the above-mentioned regimens, and probably should be avoided.

In the United States, the progestin used in most low-dose hormone replacement therapy regimens is medroxyprogesterone acetate (MPA). This progestin is less potent than nortestosterone derivatives. It is available in 2.5-, 5-, and 10-mg doses. The 10-mg dose is adequate for endometrial suppression when given cyclically for 12 days per month with doses equivalent to 1.25 mg of conjugated estrogens or less. MPA 5 mg given cyclically with 0.625 mg of conjugated estrogens does not always produce histologic evidence of endometrial suppression, but in one study, the combination was shown to prevent the development of hyperplasia.[71] Doses of 2.5 mg and 5 mg of MPA and less than 1 mg of norethindrone produce endometrial suppression when given daily in combination with the oral estrogen regimen. Norethindrone or norethindrone acetate 5 mg given cyclically will suppress the endometrium and may produce fewer progesterone-related side effects than MPA. Unfortunately, 5 mg of norethindrone acetate may have a more pronounced adverse effect on cholesterol and lipoproteins than MPA.

Fig. 43-5 depicts the most frequently used estrogen/progesterone regimens. The rationale for cyclic therapy is based on a normal reproductive cycle. During the estrogen-only days, the endometrium exhibits some proliferative effect. When the progestin is added, the endometrium is suppressed; when withdrawn, if adequate endometrial build-up is present, bleeding will occur. Administration of estrogen every day with no days off may produce less withdrawal bleeding and may possibly have a more beneficial effect on the bone and heart. The absence of withdrawal bleeding does not signify a lack of endometrial suppression by the progestogen, but usually implies a lesser response of the endometrium to estrogen. The disadvantages of cyclic therapy include both bleeding and the progestin-related side effects of bloating, GI disturbances, and premenstrual symptoms.

Continuous combined regimens utilize the

Figure 43-4 Serum estradiol and estrone levels as affected by menopause and estrogen replacement. FP, follicular phase; LP, luteal phase. (From Chetkowski et al.[65] and Powers et al.,[66] reprinted with permission.)

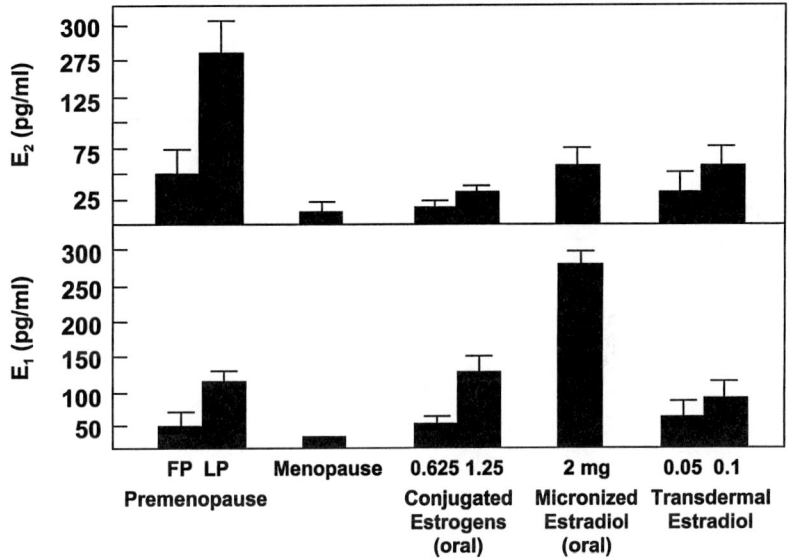

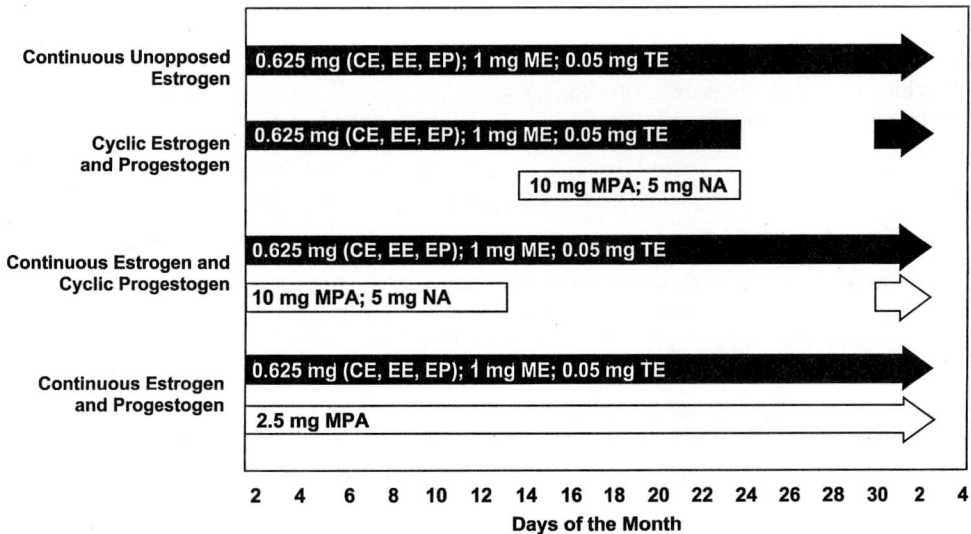

Figure 43-5 Hormone replacement regimens. Filled bars (■): estrogen. CE, conjugated estrogens; EE, esterified estrogens; ME, micronized estradiol; EP, estradiol pipate; TE, transdermal estradiol. Clear bars (□): progestogen. MPA, medroxyprogesterone acetate; NA, norethindrone. Dosages are the most commonly recommended and have been shown to inhibit bone calcium loss or to suppress endometrium. Continuous unopposed estrogen is used in women who have had a hysterectomy.

same estrogen doses, with 2.5 mg of MPA or a nortestosterone derivative (generally 1 mg or less). The advantages of these regimens include absence or very low incidence of progestin-related side effects and the potential for amenorrhea due to the progestogen's ability to inhibit endometrial proliferation. Unfortunately, more than 50 percent of women will experience breakthrough bleeding during the first four to six months of these regimens. The breakthrough bleeding decreases with time, and fewer than 10 percent will have breakthrough bleeding after six months.

Numerous other treatment plans have been used in clinical practice. Although most of these regimens should produce beneficial effects, no specific advantage of any one regimen over those mentioned above has been demonstrated in controlled clinical trials. Table 43-5 lists the advantages and disadvantages of each route of HRT administration.

Individualization of Care

All women should be counseled or given information regarding diet, nutrition, exercise, weight control, smoking, certain drugs, excess alcohol intake, and such safety factors as seat-belt use. This emphasis on preventive care is an important part of the primary care physician's relationship with patients. This counseling should include issues related to menopause when women are in their 40s, and should be emphasized further as women approach their menopausal years. Most women want and should be given information about ovarian failure and the climacteric. Individual risks can be assessed by a history, physical exam, and selected tests. In addition to an appropriate gynecologic examination, an assessment of cholesterol profile (i.e., HDL, LDL) and bone densitometry (dual-energy absorptiometry (DEXA) should be performed in high-risk women.[1,16]

TABLE 43-5 **Routes of Administration**

Type	Advantages	Disadvantages
Oral	Effective against physical and emotional symptoms High protection against osteoporosis Easily discontinued	Nausea Breast tenderness Breakthrough bleeding if tablet omitted Unsuitable if hypertensive
Transdermal	Equally effective against physical and emotional symptoms Effective against osteoporosis (85–90%) Easily changed Simple to stop Few side effects	Local skin reactions
Subcutaneous	Excellent relief from physical and emotional symptoms High protection against osteoporosis	Wrong doses difficult to modify Difficult to remove Requires minor surgical procedure
Local (vaginal treatment)	Easily applied Eliminates vaginal dryness and irritation	No protection against osteoporosis, hot flushes, or night sweats

Primary care providers should be well informed about hormone replacement and should try to present the facts with as little bias as possible. The following include the authors' perceptions regarding to whom, how, and when hormone replacement should or should not be recommended.

Who Should Receive Hormone Replacement?

When absolute contraindications do not exist, all women who present with vasomotor symptoms or genital atrophic symptoms, all women with documented osteoporosis, all women at risk for osteoporosis, and women at risk for coronary artery disease should be considered as potential candidates for hormone replacement. A pro and con list should be constructed for each individual. This should include her potential benefits, potential risks, and the presence or absence of side effects once therapy is started. From this list, decisions regarding individual therapy can be made.

Contraindications

Absolute contraindications to maintenance hormone replacement therapy are uncommon. Lists of contraindications have included active or recent history of breast cancer or endometrial cancer, undiagnosed vaginal bleeding, active liver or gallbladder disease, and active thrombophlebitis or a history of recurrent thrombotic events. Women with these problems may occasionally be candidates for temporary treatment with low-dose estrogen cream for symptomatic atrophic symptoms, as other treatments usually are ineffective for this problem. A prior breast cancer is considered a contraindication for estrogen replacement therapy, although if a patient is severely symptomatic, some physicians will prescribe hormone replacement with the patient's thorough, informed consent. Women with a strong family history of breast cancer (numerous direct family members) should be considered at

increased risk and should be given hormone replacement only when its therapeutic benefits are indicated. An endometrial cancer with a good prognosis (low-grade with minimal invasion and negative nodes) is not considered a contraindication to hormone therapy by many experts, although the PDR may still list it as an absolute contraindication. If a patient who has been treated for endometrial cancer is severely symptomatic and wishes to receive estrogen replacement, thorough informed consent is important, as it is for all patients.

It is doubtful that women who have had previous thromboses related to a fracture or a temporary stasis condition have any contraindication to low-dose hormone replacement. Because the transcutaneous administration route has no apparent effect on antithrombin III activity, it may be the best option for these patients.

There is little evidence to support the belief that women who have benign breast disease, when exposed to exogenous estrogen, have an increased risk of cancer. However, this risk may increase in women who have biopsy-proven premalignant breast lesions and take estrogen. The presence of fibrocystic changes or previous mastalgia are not contraindications to hormone replacement. Some women with mastalgia on cyclic combination therapy will benefit from a continuous combined regimen utilizing a lower progestin dose. Women receiving hormone replacement, like all women, should receive thorough surveillance for breast cancer.

How Should Hormone Replacement Be Administered?

Generally, doses of 0.625 mg conjugated estrogens, or equivalent oral doses of other estrogens or, 0.05 mg of estradiol per transcutaneous patch should be given for prophylaxis against osteoporosis, cardiovascular disease, and vaginal atrophic symptoms. These dosages are also effective for vasomotor symptoms in most patients. However, if women continue to have vasomotor symptoms on these regimens, the estrogen dose may be temporarily increased incrementally, or the route of administration may be changed. If vasomotor symptoms are not improved after these changes, other causes of vasomotor symptoms should be considered (e.g., dysautonomia, thyroid disease, or infectious diseases). For reasons discussed, unopposed estrogen should be given only to women who have undergone hysterectomy.

Vaginal estrogen cream should be reserved for treatment of women with acute symptoms related to vaginal atrophy. Doses of 0.5 to 1 mg of estrogen cream daily will reverse atrophy within one to three months. Estrogen cream in these doses used once or twice weekly can prevent atrophic symptoms or their recurrence. This regimen may be useful for the patient who has had previous problems with atrophy but has contraindications to or side effects from other maintenance therapies. In our experience, this approach rarely causes endometrial proliferation and does not require supplemental progestogen. However, it will probably not benefit the bones or the heart. The previously mentioned oral or transcutaneous regimens, with the addition of a progestin given either cyclically or continuously, should be optimal for a woman with a uterus. Which regimen to initiate will depend on the patient's and the physician's preference (see "Hormone Replacement Regimens" earlier in this chapter).

When and for How Long Should Hormone Replacement Be Administered?

Women at low risk for osteoporosis, or who have no worrisome vasomotor symptoms, can begin therapy as soon as 6 months after the last menstrual period. By then, sporadic ovulation and its resultant bleeding is less likely to occur. For women with worrisome vasomotor symptoms that start before the last menstrual period and for those at significant risk for osteoporosis, earlier hormone replacement may be preferred. Because the low-dose regimens do not prevent ovulation, early initiation may be accompanied by what is perceived as abnormal uterine bleeding.

One proposed option for these women is the very low-dose oral contraceptive (for those women for whom it is not contraindicated) containing 20 to 30 mg ethinyl estradiol and a relatively low-potency progestin. The oral contraceptive can be stopped 2 weeks before each physician visit, at which time a symptom diary can be reviewed and a serum FSH can be measured. An FSH greater than 50, although not absolutely specific, generally suggests ovarian failure; thereafter, a lower dose replacement regimen may be substituted. Women who have a history of tobacco use, hypertension or vascular disease, and women who do not tolerate oral contraceptives, may be candidates for and may tolerate cyclic therapy or very low-dose (0.3 mg conjugated estrogens) replacement prior to their last menstrual period. Evaluation of the bleeding that may occur when low-dose therapy is given prior to menopause should be individualized.

We believe that when hormone replacement is given to retard osteoporosis or heart disease, the therapy should be continued as long as the prophylactic benefit is desired.

Bone Density Assessment

Several techniques for bone density measurement have been advocated to determine when or if patients will develop significant osteoporosis, and whether interventional or prophylactic therapy is indicated. Dual-energy x-ray absorptiometry (DEXA) may be used to measure local bone density in the vertebral bodies, hips, radius, and elsewhere. With a special set-up, the technique may be used to interpret total bone content. DEXA appears to be as accurate or more accurate than previously recommended nuclear dual-photon absorptiometry (DPA) and computed tomography (CT) interpretations.[16] The DEXA scans also are less expensive and can be performed more rapidly than CT or DPA studies. Single-photon absorptiometry is also easy to perform; however, it can only be used to measure the density of structures containing primarily cortical bone in the distal axial skeleton. It is thus not recommended for screening the early menopausal patient who is likely to lose trabecular bone first. Neither DEXA nor DPA can measure the true volume of the bone. Although volumetric density of trabecular bone can be measured by quantitative computed tomography, the exposure to radiation is much higher, thereby making this technique less useful.

Biochemical markers of bone reabsorption such as urinary hydroxyproline and urinary calcium-to-creatinine ratio are not adequately sensitive or specific.[16] More recently developed markers such as hydroxylysyl pyridinoline and lysyl pyridinoline,[72] N-telopeptides of type 1 collagen,[73] and C-telopeptide of type 1 collagen[74] hold more promise. However, more studies are needed.

The cost effectiveness of bone density measurement is doubtful in women at low risk for osteoporosis who are compliant with preventive measures. Should a relatively healthy, active, early menopausal female with minimal family history of osteoporosis who eats a well-balanced diet (with a gram of calcium daily), and who takes estrogen replacement, undergo bone density measurements? Her risk of developing osteoporosis is low and it is unlikely that the test will influence her management. Assessment of bone density does appear to be reasonable in patients at high risk for osteoporosis or in patients who are at minimal risk and are trying to make a decision whether or not to use hormone replacement solely as a prophylactic measure against osteoporosis. It is debatable whether to recommend serial bone density studies to high-risk patients who are on maximum prophylactic therapy (diet, calcium, exercise, and hormone replacement). A few of these patients may benefit from slightly higher doses of estrogen or progestins than are usually suggested, or they may be candidates for bisphosphonate therapy in addition to hormone replacement therapy if they do develop significant bone loss. The cost-effectiveness of performing serial studies on all patients at increased risk is doubtful; therefore, recommendations should be individualized.

Side Effects of Hormone Replacement Therapy and Their Management

Uterine bleeding is the most common side effect of hormone replacement in menopause. Withdrawal bleeding after the progestin days of a cyclically administered estrogen/progestin regimen occurs in 60 to 90 percent of women on these regimens. Bleeding is more common in younger menopausal women and when higher-dose estrogen regimens are used. Because cyclic menses are not acceptable to many menopausal women, continuous combined estrogen/progestin regimens have been introduced to maintain constant endometrial suppression. However, a significant number of women (40 to 60 percent) experience varying degrees of bleeding for several months after initiation of continuous combined therapy. This is apparently due to an abnormal endometrial response to the hormones. Endometrial histologic evaluation of these patients usually reveals small amounts of tissue with inconsistent microscopic findings, and no evidence of neoplasia or hyperplasia. Management of this problem may require only simple observation, as the bleeding will usually resolve with time (several weeks to several months) or with change of therapy.

In the protocol we utilize, we believe that endometrial evaluation usually is not indicated prior to hormone therapy, in patients with withdrawal bleeding after cyclic therapy, or in patients having breakthrough bleeding the first few months after initiating continuous combined therapy. A screening biopsy should be strongly considered before initiating therapy if a patient has a long history of anovulation or other risk factors for endometrial cancer. Likewise, patients with bleeding other than the normal withdrawal bleeding, unexplained increase in bleeding that continues for several months, or women who are taking continuous combined therapy who have persistent bleeding (greater than 4 to 6 months duration) should undergo endometrial evaluation. A thin-appearing endometrium (less than 5 mm total thickness) has been shown in almost all cases, when biopsied, to represent atrophic or suppressed endometrium. This does not totally rule out the presence of a small neoplasm as a cause for the bleeding. A few cases of carcinoma have been found within atrophic endometrium. Therefore, persistent bleeding after 4 to 6 months of combined therapy indicates the need for biopsy regardless of sonographic findings. A sonographically depicted endometrial stripe greater than 5 mm in diameter usually represents estrogen-stimulated endometrium, and warrants histologic evaluation. Hyperplasia and neoplasia cannot be ruled out sonographically.[75] Sonograms may be useful in managing the patient on continuous combined therapy to exclude the possibility of excess estrogen stimulation or the presence of a large intrauterine abnormality, thus allowing one to avoid biopsy when breakthrough bleeding occurs early in the therapy.

Fluid retention, gastrointestinal symptoms, psychological effects, or other side effects may occur in 10 to 20 percent of postmenopausal women placed on hormone replacement. Bloating and a feeling of fluid retention are not uncommon complaints. These symptoms are most likely to occur during the estrogen/progestin days of cyclic therapy and are, for the most part, progestin-dose related. Gastrointestinal dysfunction (flatulence, constipation, and diarrhea) are rare complaints that may be due to the effects of the progestin on gastrointestinal motility. Finally, a few patients develop depression and a premenstrual-like syndrome. Psychological symptoms may occur with estrogen alone, but are most frequently seen during the estrogen/progestin days of cyclic therapy. These side effects may not be related to therapy, and other causes should be considered. If the symptoms are thought to be due to cyclic progestin use, continuous combination therapy or other therapeutic regimens with lower progestin dosage may be useful.

Alternatives to Estrogen Replacement Therapy

Alternatives to estrogen may also be used by women. These alternatives can be divided into nonestrogenic medical therapies and nonpharmacologic therapies.

Bisphosphonates are analogs of pyrophosphate that inhibit bone reabsorption. Etidronate was the original bisphosphonate used for treatment of osteoporosis; however, osteomalacia is a risk with etidronate's continuous use.[76] Alendronate, 10 mg/day, increased bone density in menopausal women over 2 years without the risk of osteomalacia.[77] Other fracture preventive treatments are under investigation including calcitonin, calcitrol, other anabolic steroids, progestins, fluoride, growth hormone, parathyroid hormone, and bone growth factors.[16,78] Women who have osteoporosis and are taking hormone replacement therapy may be advised to take alendronate in addition.

Centrally acting α-adrenergic agents such as clonidine and α-methyldopa have shown some effectiveness against vasomotor symptoms. The side effect of these medications is hypotension, and blood pressure should be monitored. Other side effects of clonidine include fatigue, irritability, headache, nausea, and dizziness.[79] Transdermal clonidine reduced hot flashes in up to 80 percent of women with fewer side effects.[80] A belladona alkaloid (Bellergal) has been used for vasomotor symptoms; however, there are no good controlled studies to document effectiveness and this compound has numerous contraindications and risks.

There is no good substitute for estrogen for the reversal or prevention of vaginal atrophy. However, vaginal acidification, or creams containing antimicrobial agents such as sulfa or clindamycin, may decrease vaginal itching and burning.

Complementary therapies include relaxation techniques, massage, herbal medicines, homeopathy, and acupuncture. Little is known about the use of these therapies in the United States. The use of herbal therapies for postmenopausal symptoms has not been infrequent. Up to 12 percent of women in one study used some form of herb for this medicinal purpose.[78] Few studies have been performed with regard to safety or efficacy[81] of this type of treatment. Dietary phytoestrogens (lignans and isoflavonoids) may decrease vasomotor symptoms, provide some protection against osteoporosis, and may aid in the prevention of CAD and certain types of cancer.[82] Again, however, little is known of the benefits or risks of these dietary compounds and no recommendation can be made at this time.

Patients who are not receiving estrogen replacement therapy—as well as those who are—should be counseled regarding the importance of a well-balanced, low-fat diet, calcium supplementation, exercise, moderate use of alcohol, and cessation of smoking.

Premature Ovarian Failure

Cessation of menses due to depletion of ovarian follicles prior to the age of 40 is termed premature ovarian failure. While causes for the disorder are variable, most cases are idiopathic, with the ovaries exhibiting the same anatomical and functional appearance seen with natural menopause. Patients with premature ovarian failure exhibit the same symptoms and physiologic changes as those undergoing age-appropriate ovarian failure. Diagnosis is made by: a negative pregnancy test, a negative progesterone withdrawal test, and an elevated FSH level (greater than 30 to 50, depending on the laboratory). The progesterone withdrawal test involves intramuscular injection of progesterone in oil, or 7 to 10 days of oral progestin. Bleeding thereafter suggests estrogen production and endometrial stimulation. No bleeding implies hypoestrogenism. A few patients with a presumed diagnosis of ovarian failure will periodically experience ovulation. Therefore, reproductive failure is not absolute. In addition, some patients (particularly young patients) who have physical and laboratory evidence of ovarian failure after chemotherapy will regain ovarian function.

Hormone replacement appears to be quite important in patients with premature ovarian failure. There is a substantial increase in coronary artery disease and osteoporosis in these patients

that is preventable by estrogen administration. Patients who experience ovarian failure secondary to chemotherapy regimens should receive hormone replacement therapy if not contraindicated, stopping therapy periodically to remeasure FSH levels. If a patient has ovarian failure secondary to chemotherapy for breast cancer, tamoxifen therapy may be the best choice. However, it may be wise to monitor the endometrium as proliferative disorders, including endometrial cancer, may occur.

In addition, tamoxifen will decrease bone calcium loss when given to early postmenopausal women[83] and may protect against heart disease possibly by decreasing cholesterol and low density lipoproteins.[84] Tamoxifen does very little for vasomotor symptoms, and may actually worsen atrophic symptoms in a few individuals.

Assisted Reproductive Technologies in the Menopausal Patient

Donor In Vitro Fertilization

The first birth from in vitro fertilization (IVF) was in 1978. Because of the initial low pregnancy rates, IVF was considered a therapy for women with nonsurgically reparable tubal disease. As the IVF pregnancy rate has increased, its use expanded to treat a variety of nontubal causes of infertility. Donor oocyte IVF (D-IVF) was created to treat infertility in women with no or poor ovarian function. In D-IVF, a woman donates her oocytes (the donor) to a patient who does not have adequate ovarian function (the recipient). The donor's oocytes are then inseminated with the spermatozoa of the recipient's husband, and the resultant embryos are transferred to the recipient's uterus.

The first live birth from D-IVF was reported in 1984.[85] Initially, D-IVF was offered to women with premature ovarian failure (POF) who were similar in age (20 to 37 years) to those undergoing standard IVF. This was partly due to the belief, later proven incorrect, that the age-related decrease in fecundity was secondary to both uterine and ovarian causes. Current additional indications for the use of D-IVF are women who are menopausal, have genetic disorders, or have a poor response to gonadotropin stimulation. As expected, with the expansion of indications, the use of D-IVF has increased by approximately 500 percent between 1990 and 1994. In 1994, there were 163 programs in the United States and Canada offering D-IVF and these programs collectively performed 3119 D-IVF cycle starts, with 2758 transfers and 1139 clinical pregnancies for a 41 percent pregnancy rate.[86] Currently, the most common reasons for the use of D-IVF are previously failed IVF (32 percent), POF (23 percent), menopause (16 percent), and transitional menopause (14 percent).[87] The number of cycles performed each year is restricted only by the number of willing donors available.

The success rate of D-IVF depends on many factors, one of the most important being the chronological age of the oocyte. Prior to D-IVF, it was unclear whether decreased fecundity in women older than 40 was the result of ovarian or uterine aging. However, from the results of D-IVF it is now clear that ovarian aging is by far the most important determinant of the age-related decline in fecundity. Currently, pregnancy rates with D-IVF approach and may exceed that of standard IVF. In addition, recipients who used parous donors had a higher pregnancy rate than those who used nulliparous donors. A birth rate of 25 to 35 percent per cycle in D-IVF is a reasonable expectation of success, depending upon the age of the donor.

States that have adopted legislation have granted oocyte donation the same legal status as sperm donation. How old is too old? Most programs have an age limit (usually 45 to 49 years), but some others do not. The oldest reported recipient became pregnant at 62 years of age. Nonetheless, pregnancy over the age of 40 years has increased risks for both the mother and child including gestational diabetes, postpartum hemorrhage, fetal distress, prematurity, low birthweight, cesarean section, and induction of labor. Congenital and genetic abnormalities are

increased in this group, but only if the woman uses her own oocytes. There is no increased risk of genetic and congenital abnormalities with the use of donor oocytes.

An issue to consider is the length of time the recipient mother would be expected to care for her D-IVF child. For example, we would expect that a 35-year-old woman would live longer than a 50-year-old woman, and thus would nurture and care for her child longer. The present life expectancy of women in the United States is greater than 78 years, meaning that the 50-year-old woman could theoretically provide an average of 28 years of mothering, if she remained healthy. How old is too old to be an effective parent? Older parents tend to have more time to spend with their offspring, but they may not be present for them later in their adulthood. Is it age discrimination to deny this service to women based on age? These issues remain unresolved.

Summary

It should be emphasized that menopause does not signify a change from "young" to "old" but is simply an event, and that there are many productive years ahead. The psychosocial aspect of the climacteric should be discussed, depending on the patient's symptoms, and psychological treatment or referral should be considered when indicated. Sexuality should also be discussed, emphasizing both physical and psychological factors, and emphasizing that ovarian failure does not imply sexual decline. Lastly, hormone replacement should be discussed with each patient, presenting the perceived benefits in her case and the potential risks or side effects.

References and Selected Readings

1. Thacker HL: Current issues in menopausal hormone replacement therapy [review]. *Cleve Clin J Med* 63:344–353, 1996.
2. Schneider HPG: Cross-national study of women's use of hormone replacement therapy (HRT) in Europe. *Int J Fertil Womens Med* 42 (2):365–375, 1997.

3. Tang M, Jacobs D, Stern Y, et al: Effect of oestrogen during menopause on risk and age at onset of Alzheimer's disease. *Lancet* 348:429–432, 1996.

4. Samsioe G: Hormone replacement therapy in Europe. *Int J Fertil Womans Med* 40:124–128, 1995.

5. Draper J, Roland M: Perimenopausal women's views on taking hormone replacement therapy to prevent osteoporosis. *Br Med J Bull* 300:786–788, 1990.

6. Robinson G: Cross-cultural perspectives on menopause [review]. *J Ner Ment Dis* 184:453–458, 1996.

7. Wiklind I, Karlberg J, Mattsson LA: Quality of life of postmenopausal women on a regimen of transdermal estradiol therapy: A double-blind placebo-controlled study. *Am J Obstet Gynecol* 168:824–830, 1993.

8. Coope J, Campbell S (eds): Double-blind crossover study of estrogen replacement therapy, *Management of the Menopause and Postmenopausal Years.* Lancaster, England: MTP Press, 1976, p 167.

9. Schiff I, Tulchinsky D, Cramer D, et al: Oral medroxyprogesterone in the treatment of postmenopausal symptoms. *JAMA* 244:1443, 1980.

10. Sherwin BA: Hormones, mood, and cognitive functioning in postmenopausal women. *Obstet Gynecol* 87:20–26, 1996.

11. Stenberg A, Heimer G, Ulmsten U, et al: Prevalence of genitourinary and other climacteric symptoms in 61-year-old women. *Maturitas* 24:31–36, 1996.

12. Belchetz PE: Hormonal treatment of postmenopausal women. *N Engl J Med* 350:1062–1071, 1994.

13. Gambrell RD Jr: Estrogen-progestogen replacement and cancer risk. *Hosp Pract* 3:81–100, 1990.

14. Lucky MM, Meier DE, Mandelie JP: Radial and vertebral bone density in white and black women: Evidence for racial differences in premenopausal bone homeostasis. *J Clin Endocrinol Metab* 69:762, 1989.

15. Weistein RS, Bell NH: Diminished rates of bone formation in normal black adults. *N Engl J Med* 319:1968, 1988.

16. Wark JD: Osteoporotic fractures: Background and prevention strategies [review]. *Maturitas* 23:193–207, 1996.

17. Dawson-Hughes B, et al: A controlled trial of the effect of calcium supplementation on bone density in postmenopausal women. *N Engl J Med* 323:878–883, 1990.

18. Chapuy MC, et al: Vitamin D3 and calcium to prevent hip fractures in elderly women. *N Engl J Med* 327:1637–1642, 1992.

19. Reid IR, et al: Effect of calcium supplementation on bone loss in postmenopausal women. *N Engl J Med* 328:460–461, 1993.

20. Brincat M, Kabalan S, Studd J, et al: A study of the decrease of skin collagen content, skin thickness, and bone mass in the postmenopausal woman. *Obstet Gynecol* 70:840, 1987.

21. Brincat M, Moniz CF, Kabalan S, et al: Decline in skin collagen content and metacarpal index after the menopause and its prevention with sex hormone replacement. *Br J Obstet Gynaecol* 94:126–129, 1987.

22. Pierard GE, Letawe C, Dowlati A, et al: Effect of hormone replacement therapy for menopause on the mechanical properties of skin. *J Am Geriatr Soc* 43:662–665, 1995.

23. Dunn LB, Damesyn M, Moore AA, et al: Does estrogen prevent skin aging? Results from the First National Health and Nutrition Examination Survey (NHANES I). *Arch Dermatol* 133:339–342, 1997.

24. Maheux R, Naud F, Rioux M, et al: A randomized, double-blind, placebo-controlled study on the effects of conjugated estrogens on skin thickness. *Am J Obstet Gynecol* 170:642–649, 1994.

25. Barrett-Connor E: The menopause, hormone replacement, and cardiovascular disease: The epidemiologic evidence [review]. *Maturitas* 23:227–234, 1996.

26. Grady D, Rubin SM, Pititti DB, et al: Hormone therapy to prevent disease and prolong life in postmenopausal women. *Ann Intern Med* 117:1016, 1992.

27. Wilson WC, Garrison RJ, Castelli WP: Postmenopausal estrogen use, cigarette smoking, and cardiovascular morbidity in women over 50. *N Engl J Med* 313:1038–1043, 1985.

28. Colditz GA, Willett WC, Stampfer MJ, Rosner B, Speizer FE, Hennekens CH: Menopause and the risk of coronary heart disease in women. *N Engl J Med* 316:1105–1110, 1987.

29. Hulley S, Grady D, Bush T, et al: Randomized trial of estrogen plus progestin for secondary prevention of coronary heart disease in postmenopausal women. *JAMA* 280:605–613, 1998.

30. Adami HO, Persson I, Hoover R, Schairer C, Berqkvist L: Risk of cancer in women receiving hormone replacement therapy. *Int J Cancer* 44:33–39, 1989.

31. Pearlstein TB: Hormones and depression: What are the facts about premenstrual syndrome, menopause, and hormone replacement therapy? [review]. *Am J Obstet Gynecol* 173:646–653, 1995.

32. Pfaff DW, Schwartz-Giblin S, McCarthy MM, et al: Cellular and molecular mechanisms of female reproductive behaviors, in Knobil E, Neill JD, Greenwald GS, et al (eds.): *The Physiology of Reproduction,* 2d ed. New York: Raven, 1994.

33. Spangers SA, West NB, Brenner RM, et al: Regulation and localization of estrogen and progestin receptors in the pituitary of steroid-treated monkeys. *Endocrinology* 126:1133–1142, 1990.

34. Paganini-Hill A: Oestrogen replacement therapy and Alzheimer's disease. *Br J Obstet Gyneacol* 103:80–86, 1996.

35. Behl C, Widmann M, Trapp T, et al: 17-β estradiol protects neurons from oxidative stress-induced cell

death in vitro. *Biochem Biophys Res Commun* 216:473–482, 1995.

36. Honjo H, Tanaka K, Kashiwagi T, et al: Senile dementia—Alzheimer's type and estrogen. *Horm Metab Res* 27:204–207, 1995.

37. Davis SR, Burger HG: Clinical review 82: Androgens and the postmenopausal woman [review]. *J Clin Endocrinol Metab* 81:2759–2763, 1996.

38. Zumoff B, Strain GW, Miller LK, Rosner W: Twenty-four-hour mean plasma concentration declines with age in normal premenopausal women. *J Clin Endocrinol Metab* 80:1429–1430, 1995.

39. Kaunitz AM: The role of androgens in menopausal hormonal replacement [review]. *Endocrinol Metab Clin North Am* 26:391–397, 1997.

40. Judd HL: Hormonal dynamics associated with the menopause. *Clin Obstet Gynecol* 19:775–798, 1976.

41. Sherwin BB, Gelfand MM, Brender W: Androgen enhances sexual motivation in females: A prospective, crossover study of sex steroid administration in surgical menopause. *Psychosom Med* 47:339–351, 1985.

42. Hutchinson K: Androgens and sexuality. *Am J Med* 98:1–111S, 1995.

43. Hickok L, Toomey C, Speroff L: A comparison of esterified estrogens with and without methyltestosterone: Effects on endometrial histology and serum lipoproteins in postmenopausal women. *Obstet Gynecol* 82:919, 1993.

44. Meldrum D: Changes in circulating steroids with aging in post-menopausal women. *Obstet Gynecol* 57:624–628, 1981.

45. Hallstrom T: Sexuality in the climacteric. *Clin Obstet Gynecol* 4:227–239, 1977.

46. Nachtigall LE: Sexual function in menopause and postmenopause [review]. *Curr Ther Endocrinol Metab* 6:632–650, 1997.

47. Calaf I, Alsina J: Benefits of hormone replacement therapy—overview and update [review]. *Int J Fertil Womens Med* 42:Suppl 2:329–346, 1997.

48. Schiff I, Komarov H, Cramer D, et al: Endometrial hyperplasia in women on cyclic or continuous regimens. *Fertil Steril* 37:79, 1982.

49. Woodruff JD, Pickar JH, The Menopausal Study Group: Incidence of endometrial hyperplasia in postmenopausal women taking conjugated estrogens (Premarin) with medroxyprogesterone acetate or conjugated estrogens alone. *Am J Obstet Gynecol* 170:1213–1223, 1994.

50. Calle EE, Miracle-McMahill HL, Thun MJ, et al: Estrogen replacement therapy and risk of fatal colon cancer in a prospective cohort of postmenopausal women. *J Natl Cancer Inst* 87:517–523, 1995.

51. Thomas DB, Lilnenfeld AM (eds): Epidemiologic and related studies of breast cancer etiology, in *Reviews in Cancer Epidemiology*. New York: Elsevier North-Holland, 1980, pp 153–217.

52. Ewertz M: Hormone therapy in the menopause and breast cancer risk—A review. [review]. *Maturitas* 23:241–246, 1996.

53. Thomas DB: Steroid hormone and medications that alter cancer risks. *Cancer* 62:1755–1767, 1988.

54. Colditz GA, Egan KM, Stampfer MJ: Hormone replacement therapy and risk of breast cancer: Results from epidemiologic studies. *Am J Obstet Gynecol* 168:1473–1480, 1993.

55. Kaufman DW, Miller DR, Rosenberg L, et al: Noncontraceptive estrogen use and the risk of breast cancer. *JAMA* 252:63–67, 1984.

56. McDonald JA, Weiss NS, Darling JR, Francis AM, Polissar L: Menopausal estrogen use and the risk of breast cancer. *Breast Cancer Res Treat* 7:193–199, 1986.

57. Brinton L, Hoover R, Fraumeni JF Jr: Menopausal oestrogen and breast cancer risk: An expanded case-control study. *Br J Cancer* 54:825–832, 1986.

58. Wingo PA, Layde PM, Lee NC, Rubin G, Ory HW: The risk of breast cancer in postmenopausal women who have used estrogen replacement therapy. *JAMA* 257:209–215, 1987.

59. Buring JE, Hennekens CH, Lipnick RJ, et al: A prospective cohort study in postmenopausal hormone use and risk of breast cancer in US women. *Am J Epidemiol* 125:939–947, 1987.

60. Berkowitz GS, Kelsey JL, Holford TR, et al: Estrogen replacement therapy and fibrocystic breast disease in postmenopausal women. *Am J Epidemiol* 121:238–245, 1985.

61. Trapido EJ, Brinton LA, Schairer C, Hoover R: Estrogen replacement therapy and benign breast disease. *J Natl Cancer Inst* 73:1101–1105, 1984.

62. Jick H, Derby L, Myers M, et al: Risk of hospital admission for ideopathic venous thromboembolism among users of postmenopausal oestrogens. *Lancet* 348:981, 1996.

63. Daly M, Vessey M, Hawkins M, et al: Risk of venous thromboembolism in users of hormone replacement therapy. *Lancet* 348:977, 1996.

64. Col NF, Eckman MH, Karas RH, et al: Patient-specific decisions about hormone replacement therapy and mortality. *JAMA* 277:1140–1147, 1997.

65. Chetkowski RJ, Meldram DR, Steingold KA, et al: Biological effects of transdermal estradiol. *N Engl J Med* 314:1615, 1986.

66. Powers MS, Schenkel L, et al: Pharmacokinetics and pharmacodynamics of transdermal dosage forms of 17-β estradiol: Comparison with conventional oral estrogens used for hormone replacement. *Am J Obstet Gynecol* 152:1099, 1985.

67. Luciano AA, DeSouza MJ, Roy MP, et al: Evalua-

tion of low dose estrogen and progestin therapy in postmenopausal women. A double-blind prospective study of sequential versus continuous therapy. *J Reprod Med* 38:207, 1993.

68. Uebelhart D, et al: Effect of menopause and hormone replacement therapy on the urinary excretion of pyridinium cross-links. *J Clin Endocrinol Metab* 72:367–373, 1991.

69. Hanson DA, et al: A specific immunoassay for monitoring human bone reabsorption: Quantitation of 1 collagen cross-linked N-telopeptides in urine. *J Bone Miner Res* 7: 1251–1258, 1992.

70. Bonde M, Quist P, Fledelius C, et al: Applications of an enzyme immunoassay for a new marker of bone reabsorption (crosslaps): Follow-up on hormonal replacement therapy and osteoporosis risk assessment. *J Clin Endocrinol Metab* 80:864–868, 1995.

71. Dupont WD, Page DL: Menopausal estrogen replacement therapy and breast cancer. *Arch Intern Med* 151:67–72, 1991.

72. Grey AB, Stapleton JP, Evans MC, et al: The effect of the antioestrogen tamoxifen on bone mineral density in normal late postmenopausal women. *Am J Med* 99:636–641, 1995.

73. Bagdade JD, Wolter J, Subbaiah PV, Ryan W: Effects of tamoxifen treatment on plasma lipids and lipoprotein composition. *J Clin Endocrinol Metab* 70:1132, 1990.

74. Harris ST, Watts NB, Jackson RD, et al: Four-year study of intermittent cyclic etidronate treatment of postmenopausal osteoporosis: Three years of blinded therapy followed by one year of open therapy. *Am J Med* 95:557–567, 1993.

75. Chestnut CH, McClung MR, Ensrud KE, et al: Alendronate treatment of the postmenopausal osteoporotic women: Effect of multiple dosages on bone mass and bone remodeling. *Am J Med* 99:144–152, 1995.

76. Nagamani M, Keiver ME, Smith ER: Treatment of menopausal hot flashes with transdermal administration of clonidine. *Am J Obstet Gynecol* 156:561, 1987.

77. Israel D, Youngkin EQ: Herbal therapies for perimenopausal and menopausal complaints [review]. *Pharmacotherapy* 17:970–984, 1997.

78. Adlercreutz H, Mazur W: Phyto-oestrogens and western diseases [review]. *Ann Med* 29:95–120, 1997.

79. Trounson A, Leeton J, Besanko M, Wood C, Conti A: Pregnancy established in an infertile patient after transfer of a donated embryo fertilized in vitro. *Br Med J* 286:835–838, 1983.

80. Society for Assisted Reproductive Technology and the American Society for Reproductive Medicine: Assisted reproductive technology in the United States and Canada: 1994 results generated from the American Society for Reproductive Medicine/Society for Assisted Reproductive Technology Registry. *Fertil Steril* 66:697–705, 1996.

81. Sauer MV, Paulson RJ, Ary BA, Lobo RA: Three hundred cycles of oocyte donation at the University of Southern California: Assessing the effect of age and infertility diagnosis on pregnancy and implantation rates. *J Assist Reprod Genet* 11:92–96, 1994.

82. Darner MC, Epstein YM, Treiser SL, Comito CE, Rosenburg HS, Dzingala L: The effects of prior gravidity on the outcomes of ovum donor and own oocyte cycles. *Fertil Steril* 65:578–582, 1996.

83. Kessel B: Alternatives to estrogen for menopausal women [review]. *Proc Soc Exp Biol Med* 217:38–44, 1998.

84. Laufer LR, Erlick Y, Meldrum DR, Judd HL: Effect of clonidine on hot flashes in postmenopausal women. *Obstet Gynecol* 60:583, 1992.

85. Paulson RJ, Sauer MV: Regulation of oocyte donation to women over the age of 50: A question of reproductive choice. *J Assist Reprod Genet* 11:177–182, 1994.

CHAPTER 44

Urogynecology

Jeffrey L. Cornella
Henry A. Thiede

Anatomy

The Lower Urinary Tract

Important clinical generalizations, which apply
to an understanding of urogynecology and urinary continence, include:

1. The female bladder and urethrovesical
    junction are supported by the anterior vagi-
    nal wall. Anatomic relaxation and its surgi-
    cal correction involve vaginal weakness, de-
    tachment, and resultant descent. Routine
    operations for female stress urinary inconti-
    nence stabilize the vagina and the ur-
    ethrovesical junction.

2. Postoperative traction placed on one ana-

tomic portion of the vagina may cause relaxation in other anatomic areas. Excessive
elevation of the anterior vaginal wall may
predispose the patient to subsequent enterocele formation. Similarly, excessive traction of the posterior vagina by fixation to
the sacrospinous ligament may increase the
propensity for cystocele formation.[66,14]
3. Anatomic relaxation does not necessarily
result in symptoms. Patients may have significant prolapse and be asymptomatic.
Other patients may be free of vaginal relaxation, yet experience sensations of pressure, urgency, and frequency of urination.

The Urinary Bladder

The wall of the bladder consists of an outer ad-
ventitial layer of connective tissue, a smooth muscle layer, and an inner layer of mucous membrane that lines the interior. The detrusor
comprises a single unit of large-diameter, in-
terlacing, smooth muscle cells. Contraction results in a reduction of all dimensions of the bladder lumen.

The bladder neck consists of muscle that is
histologically, histochemically, and pharmacologically distinct from the detrusor proper. Although the human female bladder neck does not
possess a true anatomic sphincter, there is a functional contribution to the maintenance of continence.

The Urethra

Strohbehn et al. showed that the multilayered
appearance of the urethra on MRI T_2-weighted
sequences matched its histologic layers and previous description by DeLancey.[74] DeLancey reviewed 22 paraurethral anatomic dissections and
1500 slides to identify structures that influence
urethral position and resistance.[21] The position
of each of these structures along the urethra was
determined. Two anatomic areas appear to make
the most salient contribution to urinary continence:

1. The midurethra extends for approximately

20 to 60 percent of total urethral length
and includes the region of the striated urethral sphincter (rhabdosphincter) and muscular attachment of urethral supports.
2. The urogenital diaphragm with the deep
transverse perineal musculature (urethrovaginal sphincter muscle and compressor
urethrae muscle) is found from 54th to
76th percentile of the urethral length.

The smooth muscle of the urethra is found
throughout its length without specific condensa-
tions. The majority of these slender muscle bundles are oriented obliquely or longitudinally and
may serve to shorten or widen the urethra during
micturition. The pubovesical muscle is an extension of the detrusor muscle into the proximal
midurethra and is identified separately from the
striated urethral muscle.[74] It is unlikely that the
competence of the female bladder neck and proximal urethra is solely the result of smooth muscle activity.[36]

The striated internal urethral sphincter wraps
around the urethra as a 1.5-cm band, extending
from the 18th to the 64th percentile of urethral
length. This rhabdosphincter is anatomically separate from the adjacent periurethral striated
muscle of the anterior pelvic floor. The muscle
fibers are of the slow twitch variety, able to exert
tone upon the urethral lumen over prolonged
periods of time. The internal sphincter is the site
of maximum resting urethral pressure.

The maximum dynamic (during coughing) urethral pressure in the normal female corresponds
to the area of the deep transverse perineal musculature. Pressure increases in this area are partially reflexive and may precede transmitted abdominal pressure by 200 to 300 milliseconds.[17]
This area may be considered the external striated
sphincter of the female.

The upward and downward motion of that portion of the urethra that lies above the urogenital
diaphragm is under voluntary control. Jeffcoate
and Roberts have ascribed this mobility to connections of the vagina to the levator ani muscles.
DeLancey has described this as the vaginolevator

attachment or muscular attachment of the urethral supports.

Muscular Attachment of the Urethral Supports (Paravaginal Attachment)

Fibers connect the vagina to the pubococcygeus portion of the levator ani muscle and its fascia. As the urethra and vagina are intimately connected at this point, this vaginolevator attachment significantly affects the urethra. At the upper end of the vaginolevator fibers, the direct interdigitation of collagen and smooth muscle from the vaginal wall with the levators is no longer present, but the connection of the vagina with the superior fascia of the levator ani continues as the arcus tendineus fasciae pelvis. This paravaginal attachment can be disrupted during a vaginal delivery, resulting in a paravaginal defect and anterior wall descent. The reattachment of this defect is called a paravaginal defect repair.

Neurology

Innervation of the Detrusor and Urethral Smooth Muscle

The sympathetic innervation of the bladder and the associated thoracolumbar visceral afferent fibers are concerned with the filling and storage phases of micturition. The parasympathetic innervation and accompanying sacral afferent fibers are important for normal voiding.

The pelvic and hypogastric nerves supply the bladder and urethra with efferent parasympathetic and sympathetic neurons, and both convey afferent sensory neurons from these organs to the spinal cord. The parasympathetic efferent supply is classically described as originating in the intermediolateral region of the gray matter of the sacral spinal cord segments S2-4, and is ultimately conveyed by the pelvic nerve.[76] The efferent sympathetic nerves to the bladder and urethra are thought to originate in the intermediolateral nuclei of spinal cord segments T11-12,

and are ultimately conveyed by the hypogastric nerves.

Ganglia that innervate the bladder and urethral smooth musculature generally lie close to or within these structures, and give rise to "short neurons," which comprise the bulk of the nerves that actually innervate these structures.[25] The innervation of the bladder is thus remarkably complex, with reflexes that not only travel to and from the spinal cord, but also to and from individual ganglia at a subspinal level.

There is clear evidence that acetylcholine acting as a transmitter from parasympathetic efferents is responsible for detrusor contraction during micturition (Kuru). It is suggested that sympathetic mediated inhibition of the bladder depends, not on direct effects from noradrenergic fibers on the detrusor, but on indirect inhibition of excitatory parasympathetics within the ganglia of the pelvic plexus.

Sacral visceral afferents have been shown to be evenly distributed throughout the bladder. They appear to convey touch, pain, and bladder distension, and are essential to complete micturition.

Innervation of Urethral Striated Muscle

Somatomotor innervation of the rhabdosphincter has traditionally been believed to be conveyed exclusively by the pudendal nerves. This concept may need some revision in view of accumulating data that this structure may be partially autonomically innervated.

Pathophysiology of Stress Urinary Incontinence

The Role of Partial Denervation of the Pelvic Floor

In a remarkable study performed in 1953 by Berglas and Rubin, x-ray myography showed that, at rest, the levator plate has an almost horizontal course.[5] The uterus and vagina are situated over the levator plate posteriorly, and not over the levator hiatus as had been previously deduced by examination of cadaveric specimens. During a sudden rise of the intraabdominal pressure in a normal patient, the thrust is directed backward and downward, which pushes the rectum, vagina, and uterus against the levator plate. Adequate function of the levator plate depends upon the proper activity of the nervous system. Impairment of the structural and functional integrity of the levator plate allows it to sag downward. This directly correlates with resultant prolapse, as the total area of the muscular hiatus increases with levator inclination.

Histochemical studies of pelvic floor muscle biopsies and pelvic floor single-fiber electromyography have demonstrated evidence of muscle fiber damage in the pelvic floor of women suffering from genital tract prolapse and urinary stress incontinence.[67] There is evidence of local partial denervation accompanied by reinnervation of the posterior pubococcygeus muscle.[34] Smith performed single-fiber electromyography of the pubococcygeus in 69 asymptomatic women and 105 women with stress incontinence or genitourinary prolapse.[67]

These studies suggest that partial denervation of the pelvic floor is a normal accompaniment of aging and is increased by childbirth.[60] Women with stress incontinence or genitourinary prolapse have a significant increase in denervation of the pelvic floor compared with asymptomatic women. Tetzschner et al. assessed pudendal nerve function serially during pregnancy and after delivery. Results showed that pudendal nerve terminal motor latency did not increase significantly during pregnancy, but increased significantly after delivery.[80] Meyer et al. described vaginal delivery leading to stress incontinence, bladder neck hypermobility, decreased intervaginal and intra-anal pressures, and shortening of the urethral functional length.[53] Fynes et al. noted in a prospective study that cesarean delivery performed in late labor is not protective of the anal sphincter mechanism, due to the effects of the first stage and early second stage of delivery on pudendal nerve conduction.[33] The mechanism was noted to be neuropathic in this study.

In a separate study, Smith evaluated the terminal pudendal nerve conduction in asymptomatic and stress-incontinent women.[68] Women with stress incontinence of urine had delayed conduction to both the striated urethral muscle and the pelvic floor muscle, indicative of denervation injury. Women with normal urinary control and genitourinary prolapse had similar conduction times to the urethral sphincter striated muscle as normal women, but showed clear evidence of denervation damage to the pelvic floor muscle.

Proposed Continence Mechanisms

Continence in the female is maintained by a summation of several factors or mechanisms which act in concert.[13] As these factors diminish, the patient may reach a threshold at which pressure acting on the bladder results in loss of urine. Treatment attempts to add or restore factors to the point of patient satisfaction with reduction of symptoms.

These factors contribute to continence in the female:

1. Proper innervation of the urethra maintaining striated muscle function and viscoelastic properties;
2. Proper innervation of the bladder neck maintaining the functional pressure of the urethrovesical junction;
3. A supported urethrovesical junction which, upon straining, arrests the descent of the urethrovesical junction;
4. Proper innervation and muscular function of the deep transverse perineal muscles which act as an external sphincter and provide reflexive increased pressure coincident with coughing;
5. Submucosal vascularity of the urethra and surface tension of the mucosa;
6. A stable and properly functioning detrusor.

Under normal conditions, continence is maintained as a result of efficient transmission of intraabdominal pressure, rising to the proximal three-quarters of the urethral length. Factors that may predispose to failure of adequate pressure transmission include a low resting urethral closure pressure (i.e., urethral pressure minus bladder pressure); urethral pressure instability; extreme abdominal pressure variations; excessive sustained response to stress; and a shortened dysfunctional urethra.[16]

These, in turn, may be directly affected by the levator muscular support and function.[22] Impaired mechanical function due to loss of anatomic connections or neurologic function may result in defective pressure transmission and resultant urine loss. In addition, delivery and the effects of aging can result in loss of the striated muscle surrounding the posterior urethra.[58]

A lack of these factors can contribute to incontinence in the female. Additional conditions that contribute to incontinence include:

1. Chronic serial coughing with resultant serial lowering of urethral pressure;
2. Obesity with presumed resultant increased abdominal pressures;
3. Denervation of the pelvic floor and pudendal nerve compromise;
4. Damage of the pelvic plexus secondary to pelvic surgery or a pelvic mass;
5. Anatomic abnormalities, such as fistulas or diverticula;
6. Urinary tract infection (cystitis).

Differential Diagnosis of Female Urinary Incontinence

1. Stress urinary incontinence
2. Bladder instability or detrusor instability
3. Mixed urinary incontinence
4. Detrusor hyperreflexia (neurologic in etiology)
5. Overflow incontinence
6. Vesicovaginal, urethrovaginal, or ureterovaginal fistula
7. Urethral instability
8. Pharmacologic incontinence
9. Spurious incontinence

Office Evaluation of Incontinence

History

The evaluation of urinary incontinence, and other urogynecologic problems, involves the assessment of multiple symptoms and objective findings with subsequent formation of an overall impression. The more complex the problem, the more important objective testing becomes in the evaluation of the patient. While mixed-incontinence symptoms alone are a poor predictor of the type of incontinence, objective testing should include a thorough and detailed history. As our methods of testing become more precise in the future, the predictive validity of some aspects of the medical history may improve.

The historical data should include the following as a minimum:

1. The impact of the urine loss upon the patient's life, socially and personally;
2. Indicators of stress incontinence or bladder instability;
3. Past urologic evaluations, treatment measures, and previous pelvic surgery;
4. Medical diagnoses or medications that may be affecting the urinary tract;
5. Cognitive level and capacity.

If the patient feels her urine loss is a significant problem for her, additional evaluation and treatment is appropriate. An equal amount of urine loss in a patient who does not perceive it as a problem would most likely not receive further evaluation and therapy. Education about incontinence allows patients to make informed choices when options are presented.

Symptoms of only stress incontinence or only urge incontinence (bladder instability) are more predictive than a mixture of symptoms. However, the vast majority of patients present with mixed symptoms, especially those beyond the fifth decade of life. The physician must then primarily rely on objective parameters for a diagnosis.[77] The pure symptom of nonsustained, immediate urine loss with coughing, laughing, and sneezing is predictive of stress incontinence. The same symptom with a background of mixed symptoms can be found with a final diagnosis of detrusor instability or mixed incontinence. There may be clinical criteria that have a high correlation with objective diagnosis by multichannel urodynamic testing. As an example, Videla and Wall reviewed 652 patients who presented for evaluation of lower urinary tract complaints. If the patients had a predominant complaint of stress incontinence, a positive stress test, a residual volume less than 50 cc, and a functional bladder volume of 400 cc as determined by a 24-h frequency chart, stress incontinence was confirmed in 94 percent of patients.[82] Only 15 percent of the stress-incontinent patients also had objective detrusor instability.

Most patients will give a history of en route urine loss (a symptom usually associated with control loss or bladder instability). The majority of these patients will not have bladder instability on routine multichannel urodynamic testing. This is partially explained by the fact that detrusor instability may not show up on a given cystometrogram, but may be demonstrated objectively by other means, such as ambulatory urodynamic monitoring or a repeat cystometrogram on an alternate day.[88] Spontaneous complete bladder emptying and true nocturnal enuresis are rare and more predictive of bladder instability. There is a difference between awakening and subsequent urine loss in bed and urine loss in bed when asleep. Only the latter should be considered as true nocturnal enuresis.

It is important to ask the patient about previous evaluations and treatment successes or failures. Some previously utilized unsuccessful medications may be successful when given at different dosages. Unsuccessful pelvic floor exercise experiences may be made successful by proper instruction. Patients with failed previous operations should be considered in a complex group and undergo urodynamic evaluation. Previous operative notes should be reviewed for technique and suture type.

Medical problems may affect a patient's tendency to experience incontinence. Diabetes may result in a propensity to develop urinary tract infections or may result in sacral neuropathy with resultant bladder effects. Chronic coughing may cause an asymptomatic patient to be symptomatic. Multiple sclerosis, Parkinson's disease, or cerebral vascular accidents may result in incontinence. Medications such as α blockers may decrease urethral resistance and make an asymptomatic patient experience incontinence. Anticholinergic agents may inhibit bladder emptying and result in overflow incontinence.

Physical Examination

The office examination is a very important objective assessment in the formation of an overall diagnostic impression. The examination should be thorough, consistent, and accompanied by discussion emphasizing the reproduction of symptoms. If the office examination is inconsistent with the patient's description of symptoms, additional evaluation is indicated. If the patient's symptoms are consistent with the findings on physical examination, the practitioner may, at his or her discretion, order additional testing, if it is felt to be beneficial to form the best and most accurate impression. The physician may choose to repeat portions of the vaginal examination on an alternate day, as relaxation may vary depending upon activities.

Physical examination should include these assessments as a minimum:

1. Degree of pelvic floor relaxation and vaginal descent;
2. Degree of urethrovesical junction descent with straining;
3. Vaginal integrity and estrogenization;
4. Bimanual and rectal examination to rule out pelvic mass and to assess anal sphincter tone;
5. Neurologic examination of the perineum and lower extremities;
6. Amount of urine loss on stress testing.

Standing Examination The patient is asked to present with a subjectively full bladder. The physical examination begins in the standing position. The patient stands over a pad with a wide stance as the examiner looks for evidence of prolapse with straining and coughing. The labia are then separated and the patient is asked to give a single, hard cough. If urine loss is absent, coughing is extended to two hard coughs, then three in a row. If urine loss is noted, a distinction is made between immediate, nonsustained urine loss, and loss that occurs after a one- to three-second delay and is somewhat sustained. The latter is suggestive of bladder instability and the former of stress urinary incontinence. These are impressions that should almost always be confirmed by additional objective testing prior to any consideration of surgery.

If prolapse is present, an additional standing examination with fingers in the rectum and vagina is repeated at the time of bimanual examination.

Sitting Examination The neurologic examination starts in the sitting position. The spinal center for micturition is in sacral segments 2, 3 and 4. (This can be considered subservient to the pontine micturition center). The lower extremities are mainly innervated by the lower lumbar segments. Therefore, it is possible to have a lesion in this area and preserve the sacral area, giving a lower motor neuron lesion picture to the extremities and an upper motor lesion picture to the bladder. The patellar reflex arc involves the second to fourth lumbar segments. The ankle reflex involves the lumbar 5 and sacral 1 and 2 segments.

Supine Examination The patient is then sent to empty her bladder, and on return is asked to assume the dorsal lithotomy position. Attention is directed to the perineum. A cotton swab is used to test fine-touch sensation in the saddle area. Pinprick and dullness are also tested in the same area. Reflexes, which involve S2, S3, and S4, are the anal wink or anocutaneous reflex and the bulbocavernosus reflex.[30] The former is tested by stimulating the perianal skin with the swab or a pinprick stimulus to the mucocutaneous junction of the anus. The bulbocavernosus reflex involves visualizing or palpating lightly with a finger in the vaginal introitus; a contraction of the bulbocavernosus muscle is stimulated by tapping or squeezing the clitoris, or, if these measures fail, by stimulating the bladder base with gentle traction on a Foley balloon. Bulbocavernosus reflexes should be tested bilaterally, as a unilateral lesion may exist. Local damage to the anal sphincter from surgery or childbirth may influence interpretation of the response to stimulus.

The patient is then asked to volitionally contract the anal sphincter (corticoregulatory tract) and to contract the circumvaginal muscles. The latter is assessed with an examining finger in the vagina, noting appropriateness of response and strength and symmetry of contraction. It is essential that the speculum used for the examination can be taken apart to form a retracting blade (Sims), which can be used to examine the anterior and posterior walls separately. The intact speculum is initially used to examine the vaginal apex or cervix for descent. The speculum is withdrawn slightly as the patient is asked to strain, while observing the response of the apex. The amount of descent is graded. The speculum is then taken apart and the anterior wall is retracted while observing the posterior wall's response to straining. A bulge and descent in the superior aspect of the posterior wall is termed a rotation rectocele, and involves detachment from the upper sidewall of the pelvis. Relaxation due to thinning of the posterior wall is also termed a rectocele. The amount of relaxation is graded. The speculum is used to gently retract the posterior wall of the vagina. It should be noted that this compromises one of the continence mechanisms and lowers the urethral pressure.[89] One should test for coughing loss in the supine position without the speculum in place. The patient is asked to cough and strain; relaxation and descent are noted.

There are three areas of relaxation that may involve the anterior wall.[2] The anterior wall may be detached from the area of the cervix or high apex (cervicovaginal detachment or level I detachment).[20] The anterior wall may be detached paravaginally (lower vaginal lateral detachment or level II detachment); elevation of the anterior lateral sulci with a forceps results in full correction or partial correction of this relaxation. The anterior wall may be thinned in the midline above the urethrovesical junction forming what is termed a transverse cystocele. In addition, a small but important relaxation may result in midline rotation of the urethrovesical junction without any of the defects described above. The physician notes and grades the defects and judges the degree of urethrovesical junction rotation. The latter is best accomplished by insertion of a sterile cotton swab into the urethra, which has been lubricated with xylocaine jelly. Degrees of rotation are measured from a horizontal reference of zero. Rotation with straining greater than 30 degrees is considered abnormal.

In 1996, the International Continence Society, the American Urogynecologic Society, and the Society of Gynecologic Surgeons established the standardization of terminology of female pelvic organ prolapse.[11] It was developed to enhance both clinical and academic communication regarding individual patients and populations of patients. It consists of an objective specific-site system for describing, quantifying, and staging pelvic support defects in women. It utilizes six points [two on the anterior wall (Aa, Ba), two in the superior vagina (C, D), and two on the posterior wall (Bp, Ap)] with a reference-distance on the hymen. (Aa is 3 cm proximal to the urethral meatus and Ap is 3 cm proximal to the hymen on the midline posterior wall.) Ba is the most dependent position (of any part) of the anterior wall, and Bp the most dependent portion (of any part) of the posterior wall. Describing the distance of these points (positive, or minus in the case of prolapse beyond the introitus), allows quantification of the pelvic organ support. The genital hiatus, perineal body, and total vaginal length are also measured.

If the anterior lateral sulci are completely elevated and a bulge is noted above the urethrovesical junction (often accompanied by loss of vaginal rugae), this is termed a transverse cystocele.

A bimanual examination is then accomplished. Initially, the vaginal mucosa is carefully palpated to rule out any vaginal lesions not observed on speculum examination. The urethra is palpated to rule out any overt tenderness or abnormality, such as a diverticulum. A bimanual exam of the pelvis is done. The rectal finger is then added to the exam. The patient is then asked to stand and the rectovaginal exam is repeated to assess the components of relaxation.

Before proceeding, it is important to educate the patient regarding the evaluation of incontinence. She should understand the purpose of testing and its impact on future management decisions.

Simple Office Testing

In general, the value of simple office filling tends to be underestimated, and the sophistication of formal urodynamic testing tends to be overestimated.[87] Simple office filling is extremely valuable in forming the overall impression or diagnosis. Wall et al. demonstrated that simple bladder filling had a sensitivity of 64 percent and a specificity of 86.8 percent for detrusor instability, with a positive predictive value of 83.3 percent and a negative predictive value of 70.2 percent. The demonstration of stress incontinence during simple bladder filling had a sensitivity of 88.1 percent and a specificity of 77.1 percent, with a positive predictive value of 82 percent and a negative predictive value of 84.4 percent when compared to multichannel testing.[87] Additionally, simple bladder filling offers an examination on an alternate day of formal testing, which may increase the sensitivity of diagnosis. Often, simple office testing shows a residual urine which more truly reflects the patient's status, as compared with residual examinations at cystoscopy or multichannel testing, which may be spuriously elevated.

The patient is asked to empty her bladder and the amount voided is recorded. If the patient has no need of subacute bacterial endocarditis (SBE) prophylaxis, a sterile catheter is used for a residual urine determination. The urine obtained can be used for urinalysis and, if indicated, culture and sensitivity testing. The physician may reflect upon the summation of the voided urine and residual amount against the background of urine loss demonstrated during initial examination.

A catheter-tipped syringe minus the plunger is then attached to the catheter, and simple office filling of the bladder follows, using sterile water filling at a rate between 75 and 100 ml per minute. Urine cytology may be indicated in patients over age 50, especially if they have symptoms of urgency. In this case, the bladder is filled with normal saline instead of water. The volumes at first sensation, fullness, and maximum fullness are then recorded. The last value is referred to as the maximum cystometric capacity on a simple office filling. This may exceed that which is later demonstrated at urodynamic testing, again demonstrating the value of this separate examination. The patient is then asked to give a single cough, then incrementally add coughs to the number five or to the point of urine loss. Whether the patient loses urine with a single cough or multiple coughs is recorded as a rough indicator of severity at a given bladder volume. Immediate, non-sustained, or projectile loss of urine is suggestive of stress incontinence. Delayed loss, which is sustained or cannot be volitionally inhibited, is suggestive of control loss or an uninhibited detrusor contraction. Throughout this process it is important to ascertain from the patient whether or not the observed losses are representative of her symptoms. The patient may give no history of stress incontinence symptoms, yet demonstrate significant loss with straining on office testing. This allows an opportunity to educate the patient regarding this component of loss and its contribution to her overall incontinence.

Patients with prolapse should be further stress-tested in the supine and standing positions with the prolapse reduced. Care must be taken not to press on the anterior vaginal wall with prolapse reduction, but rather to address pressure to the vaginal apex or high posterior wall. Stress incontinence may be masked by the vaginal relaxation pressing on or kinking the urethra at the time of straining. When the relaxation is surgically corrected (or elevated with a pessary), urine loss is unmasked and becomes symptomatic. If surgery is considered, it is incumbent upon the examiner to perform this aspect of testing. If incontinence is not addressed at surgery, the patient may have immediate stress incontinence postoperatively, or within several months of surgery. Incontinence and vaginal relaxation are interrelated and must be addressed concomitantly in the assessment and treatment of patients. Similarly, if a small enterocele is noted at examination and not corrected at incontinence surgery, the patient may return several months later with a large, symptomatic enterocele. The best care of the patient dictates that all vaginal relaxation should be corrected at incontinence surgery to avoid this occurrence.

Urodynamic Testing

Urodynamic testing refers to multichannel pressure-testing, uroflowmetry, sphincter electromyography, and cystourethroscopy. Multichannel pressure-testing includes cystometrogram testing, pressure-flow studies, valsalva leak-point pressures, and urethral profilometry. Descriptions of these techniques can be found in Chapter 50. The following section is concerned with the indications, benefit, and meaning of urodynamic testing.

The Significance of Urodynamic Testing

Urodynamic testing is technician dependent. The skill of the examiner and the quality of the interaction with the patient are of paramount importance. It is incumbent upon the referring physician to find practitioners who have significant training in the performance of urodynamic testing and knowledge of female urogynecologic pathophysiology. A given gynecologist or urologist may not have this training and knowledge. Experience and knowledge are more important than the particular specialty of the clinician.

Urodynamic testing is technician dependent because the patient's symptoms must be reproduced during the testing in order to arrive at a conclusion. The symptoms are temporally related to the findings on the recording. In this way, an impression is reached regarding the pathophysiologic occurrence responsible for the patient's symptoms. If the symptoms are not reproduced, data may be reported which are not relevant or are, in fact, misleading. All symptoms may not be reproduced at the time of testing. As an example, a given cystometrogram may not demonstrate detrusor instability in a patient which is demonstrated on a repeat cystometrogram or ambulatory testing.

Cystourethroscopy is also observer dependent. A dysfunctional bladder neck may or may not always be evident to a given observer. Borderline impressions often require other testing for confirmation, such as a standing, at-rest cystogram, to rule out a severely dysfunctional or type III urethra.

Indications for Urodynamic Testing and Cystourethroscopy The indications for urodynamic testing are:

1. Neurologic conditions such as multiple sclerosis or Parkinson's disease.
2. Symptoms of urge incontinence suggestive of severe bladder instability or detrusor hyperreflexia.
3. Urinary retention with or without a history of detrusor hyperreflexia.

A case can be made for routine performance of urodynamic testing prior to surgery. The purpose is to rule out occult detrusor instability and assess bladder contractility, both of which have prognostic implications. Some patients also demonstrate cough-induced bladder instability on testing. These patients would be at risk for continued incontinence following an operation. If one does not wish to perform urodynamic studies on all preoperative patients undergoing an incontinence procedure, then consider the following as imperative indications:

1. Any patient who has had a previous incontinence operation, vaginal colporrhaphy, or radical pelvic surgery.
2. Any patient with a history of pelvic irradiation.
3. Any patient who does not demonstrate urethrovesical junction rotation greater than 20 degrees in the presence of stress urinary incontinence signs and symptoms.
4. Patients who have a urethral diverticulum.
5. Patients with equivocal findings on simple office testing or significant postvoid residual volumes (>100 ml).
6. Elderly patients, because of the prevalence of detrusor instability and low urethral closure pressure.
7. A history of multiple vaginal surgeries and/or vaginal prolapse.

Cystourethroscopy should also be performed on preoperative patients to assess the urethra and to rule out a lesion of the bladder mucosa. It is further indicated for patients with:

1. A history of recurrent pyuria.
2. A history of asymptomatic hematuria.
3. New onset of irritative bladder symptoms.
4. History suggesting interstitial cystitis, painful bladder syndromes, or chronic infectious cystitis.

Treatment of Stress Urinary Incontinence

Education of the incontinent patient is extremely important, and often underestimated in terms of its benefit to the patient. It offers an opportunity to make the patient an informed partner regarding her care. This fosters additional motivation and understanding, which aids in the success of the conservative approach. If additional testing is required, patients feel more comfortable knowing what to expect in the urodynamic laboratory. Studies have also suggested that patients feel better knowing that there are options, possible improvement that can be acquired through therapy, and that they are not alone in experiencing their problem.

Education itself can result in improvement through bladder retraining, description of timed voiding, reemphasis of pelvic floor exercises, and adjunctive therapy measures. The use, benefits, and untoward symptoms of medications can be discussed. Patients feel that they have an opportunity to more fully express their feelings, frustrations, and have questions answered.

If patient numbers warrant, it can be highly beneficial to establish a weekly or biweekly class in incontinence. Ideally, a follow-up class may also be established. If a physical therapist is not available, nurses can work with patients one-on-one to ensure that they are performing circumvaginal exercises appropriately.

Conservative Treatment of Urinary Incontinence

There has been a resurgence of interest in the conservative treatment of incontinence. As the methods of performing and investigating conservative methods have improved, it has become evident that they are more beneficial than previously appreciated.

As an example, for years patients were told to perform pelvic floor exercises without testing to see whether the particular patient knew how, or which muscles to contract. The number of contractions performed during the day was also often inadequate. Bump demonstrated that 25 percent of uninstructed patients actually produce a reaction that may increase urine loss (such as valsalva) when asked to contract their pelvic floor muscles.[10] If conservative methods are to be successful, a motivated and properly instructed patient is essential.

Pelvic Floor Exercises Pelvic floor exercises were performed as early as the mid-nineteenth century, although Kegel, reporting in 1948, was the first to investigate the long-term effects utilizing somewhat objective methods with the aid of a perineometer. The results of past studies are variable, with poor follow-up, infrequent urodynamic testing, and lack of standardized methods and descriptive terms. More recently, studies have been published utilizing objective methods. It appears that pelvic floor exercises, when properly performed, are a useful adjunct in mild to moderate incontinence.

Mouritsen studied the long-term effect of pelvic floor exercises on female incontinence.[54] Seventy-six women underwent a 3-month exercise program and were followed for one year. At the 12-month evaluation, 30 percent were considered cured, and 17 percent improved. Patients with severe incontinence did not benefit from the therapy, while 72 percent of patients with mild incontinence experienced a cure. Patients in this study were instructed in self-digital biofeedback.

Some studies have suggested that formal biofeedback increases the success rate of pelvic floor exercises. Burgio studied a group of 11 women treated with digital biofeedback, compared to a group of 13 women with bladder-sphincter biofeedback. The latter group had a 76 percent decrease in incontinence compared with a 51 percent decrease in the former group.[12] The more enthusiastic and involved the instruction, the greater the success. It is not possible to have intensive, recurrent biofeedback sessions for all patients.

The following recommendations and interventions, which increase in scope, should be considered:

1. Assessment of circumvaginal muscle contraction during physical examination for strength and the absence of improper contraction of surrounding muscle (such as the gluteal and rectus muscles);
2. Feedback to the patient during physical examination regarding her ability to contract appropriate muscles;
3. Written instructions given to the patient on the proper performance of pelvic floor exercises, including frequency and number of contractions. The patients should be instructed to perform 4 sets of 20 contractions per day, consistently, for at least 8 weeks;

4. Follow-up visitation with the patient regarding compliance, benefit of digital pelvic floor exercise biofeedback, and changes in symptomatology;
5. Instruction by a therapist on biofeedback and the proper performance of circumvaginal exercises;
6. Continued biofeedback with a home unit, and symptom and therapy diary over weeks to months;
7. Continued biofeedback with visitations to a therapist biweekly for single or group sessions over months;
8. Weekly sessions with a therapist for biofeedback over months.

Functional Electrical Stimulation Electrical stimulation has been used throughout the last three decades in the treatment of stress urinary incontinence. It has been employed either to aid in the treatment of bladder instability or to increase sphincteric/outlet resistance. Devices have included implanted electrodes, electronic pessaries, anal electrodes, and intravaginal electrodes of various types.

The goal of electrical stimulation in the treatment of stress urinary incontinence is to increase the strength of the pelvic and periurethral muscles. Animal studies have shown that urethral pressure increases with intravaginal probes are secondary to direct stimulation of efferent motor axons. Electrical stimulation of the pelvic floor muscles results in reflexive contraction of paraurethral musculature and reflexive detrusor inhibition. There is unproven speculation that electrical stimulation may result in enhanced sprouting of previously damaged axons, or a conversion of fast to slow twitch axons in paraurethral muscles. Patients with stress incontinence may benefit from the feedback of electrically induced muscle contractions, thus learning how to contract the appropriate muscles when performing pelvic floor exercises.

Studies in humans and animals have shown detrusor inhibition with electrical stimulation.[21] Possible mechanisms include direct stimulation of pudendal afferents and secondary reflex spinal inhibition, and improved reflex inhibition of the detrusor with improved striated pelvic muscle strength. Although methods of acute inhibition are fairly well postulated, carryover effects are more difficult to explain. These could be explained by spinal opioid activation or reactivation of functionally lost reflexes.

A study by Bent et al. of patients with stress, urgency, and mixed incontinence groups has shown significant subjective patient improvement (52 percent in mixed, 70 percent in urgency, and 71 percent in pure stress incontinence), while objective parameters of improvement have remained unchanged. Additional studies are needed to determine success rates and physiologic effects.[4] If a patient is able to perform Kegel exercises, functional electrical stimulation may not be required. Bo and Talseth demonstrated that voluntary muscle contraction increased urethral pressure more significantly than functional electrical stimulation.[9] In addition, electrical stimulation may not cause a typical pelvic floor contraction or "Kegel contraction" in the majority of women.[8]

Surgical Treatment of Stress Urinary Incontinence

There are a number of features of urethral function that distinguish symptom-free women from patients with genuine stress urinary incontinence, including maximum urethral pressure at rest or closure pressure, intraabdominal pressure variations, sustained response to stress (drop in urethral pressure from sustained coughing), and pressure-transmission ratios.

The aims of incontinence surgery have been variously defined as tightening of the pubocervical fascia; elevation of the bladder neck; increasing urethral resistance; and increasing urethral functional length. Postoperative urodynamic studies have not shown consistent increases in urethral pressure or functional length in patients cured of incontinence. Most studies have shown that there is no increase in urethral resting or closure pressure. Surgical success does appear to be urodynamically associated with increased pressure transmission to the urethra.[46]

It appears that the pressure-transmission ratio has an all-or-none effect in the determination of stress incontinence. The exact cause of the impairment in a given woman may not be completely apparent. The ability to maintain positive pressure in the urethra during stress may be a result of multiple factors acting in concert. These include a functional rhabdosphincter, anatomic support of the urethrovesical junction, a healthy estrogenized urethral lumen, and proper function of the levator musculature as described earlier.

Surgery for urinary incontinence results in support to the urethrovesical junction, arrest of downward descent with straining, and increased pressure transmission to the urethra. The classic pubovaginal sling causes obstruction to the urethra coincident with coughing and increased pressure transmission to the urethra. Recent modifications result in less obstruction.

The distribution of pressure transmission along the urethra following successful colposuspension is quite different from that seen in healthy women.[38] In healthy women, the maximum transmission ratios are at or just distal to the resting profile peak, which is at the mid-distal urethra. In women made continent by colposuspension, maximum transmission is achieved within the proximal half of the functional urethra. Thus, most incontinence operations do not restore a woman to a fully physiologic state.

The Paravaginal Defect Repair The paravaginal defect repair, or vaginolevator shelf procedure, by virtue of its close reapproximation to normal anatomy, may restore the extrinsic continence mechanism to a degree somewhat comparable to that of the normal female. Support of the urethrovesical junction is reestablished and attachment to the levator musculature may again allow movement and increased function. In the majority of cases, patients are able to void almost immediately following surgery. Full function may be subclinically compromised in those patients who have sustained significant damage to the pudendal nerve.

Shull and Baden reported a six-year experience with the paravaginal defect repair for stress incontinence. One hundred forty-nine patients were treated, and 97 percent were reported as having excellent results with no further subjective stress incontinence.[65] However, Colombo et al. in a prospective comparison of the Burch urethropexy and paravaginal defect repair reported a 100 percent and 61 percent cure rate respectively at six months.[15] The overall patient number was limited to 29 patients.

The Marshall-Marchetti-Krantz Procedure The Marshall-Marchetti-Krantz (MMK) procedure has been successful in the treatment of urinary stress incontinence as a primary operation, and in patients with failure of previous surgical treatment.[48]

Considering the limitation of mobility following this procedure, and the high position of the anterior wall, it is unlikely that the continence mechanism is commensurate with that of the normal female. MMK may work by a combination of slight obstruction, creating positive pressure transmission by an unknown mechanism, and additional features that act at the urethrovesical junction subsequent to its elevation. An extremely rare complication is the development of osteomyelitis of the pubic bone.[41] This complication is treated with debridement and ambulatory intravenous antibiotics. So-called osteitis pubis following urethropexy should be considered osteomyelitis until proven otherwise.

The Burch Colposuspension The clinical effects of the Burch colposuspension and anterior vaginal repair for correction of stress urinary incontinence were assessed by Van Geelen in a superbly performed prospective study.[81] A full clinical examination, including simultaneous urethrocystometry, was performed with patients in the supine, sitting, and standing positions. This objective testing was accomplished preoperatively, 3 months, 12 months, and 24 months after operation. Total follow-up of patients was 5 to 7 years. Neither surgical anterior repair nor Burch colposuspension affected the resting variables of the urethral sphincter mechanism. After Burch colposuspension, the transmitted intraabdominal pressure to the urethra significantly increased in all recording positions in all women who were successfully treated. After successful anterior colporrhaphy, the increase in pressure transmission from the abdomen to the urethra was less prominent. The objective success rate of the Burch procedure was 85 percent at 2 years, compared to the anterior colporrhaphy, which was 45 percent. At 5 years, the subjective cure rate for the Burch procedure was 76 percent, and 31 percent for the anterior colporrhaphy. This and other studies have reaffirmed that anterior colporrhaphy (Kelly-Kennedy type) should not be used as the primary operation for stress incontinence.[6,17,15]

It is possible that bladder neck elevation not only allows improved pressure transmission, but also promotes greater efficiency of the pelvic floor reflex with accentuation of urethral closure by active means. Downward pressure on coughing from abdominal viscera may compress the urethra. Slight obstruction may also occur with a Burch procedure, as urodynamic studies have shown increased urethral resistance with a reduction in peak flow rate and an increase in voiding detrusor pressure.[37]

The Pubovaginal Sling Procedure The classic pubovaginal sling procedure results in obstruction at the urethrovesical junction with descent of the bladder neck on coughing. Slings placed distal to this site will result in failure even though the urethra is compressed with coughing. This transient obstruction results in increased pressure transmission to this area with stress. Beck reported that in 97 percent of 151 patients cured by a fascia lata sling procedure, the pressure-transmission ratio was greater than 100 percent.[3] The use of fascia lata significantly decreases risks of vaginal erosion and infection in comparison to synthetic materials.

Slings should not be used exclusively by a surgeon as a primary incontinence operation. The literature supports the fact that increased morbidity is seen with the sling in comparison to Burch urethropexy. In addition, long-term Burch

studies of 5 to 10 years reveal a high persistent cure rate of greater than 75 to 80 percent.[6,15] Decisions for the type of incontinence procedure should be based on clinical criteria such as a history of multiple incontinence operations, poor tissues, a scarified urethra, high-stress states expected after surgery (coughing, lifting, etc.), not on a single laboratory parameter such as low urethral pressure.

The Modified Pereyra Procedure (Raz Needle Suspension Procedure) This procedure provides support to the urethrovesical junction and allows compression of the urethra with stress. There is no attachment to levator musculature or restoration of reactive function. This procedure does result in positive pressure transmission to the urethra. A recent prospective study by Bergman and Elia compared the modified Pereyra procedure to the Burch procedure with an objective 5-year follow-up. This revealed 43 percent and 82 percent cure rates, respectively.[6] This is representative of multiple prospective and retrospective studies in the 1990s that have shown significantly decreased cure rates from the Raz procedure in comparison to reported cure rates from the Burch procedure and Marshall-Marchetti-Krantz procedure. The operation most commonly fails at the vaginal attachment. Thus, bone-anchors, which strengthen the superior abdominal attachment, have not been shown to decrease this failure rate.[63] There is a trend in the United States and other countries to abandon the procedure.

Operative Recommendations

Preoperative testing and assessment are described in the text above. The minimum preoperative evaluation of an incontinent patient includes: history, physical examination, urinalysis, urine culture, residual urine determination, and objective demonstration of stress urinary incontinence.

Stress Urinary Incontinence (Immediate, Non-sustained Objective Loss with Pure Symptoms)

I. Rotational descent of the urethrovesical junction
   A. No previous operations for urinary stress incontinence = retropubic urethropexy
   B. Previous operation for stress urinary incontinence
      1. Urodynamic testing, cystourethroscopy.
         a. Nondysfunctional urethra; pressures ≥20 cm H_2O
            i. Normal urethral coaptation = retropubic urethropexy
            ii. Abnormal urethral coaptation suggesting a severely dysfunctional or type III urethra; perform standing rest cystogram; if positive for type III urethra = pubovaginal sling procedure
            iii. Obvious scarred urethra = pubovaginal sling procedure
II. No rotational descent
   A. Multichannel urodynamic testing, cystourethroscopy
      1. Low urethral pressure dysfunctional urethra = consideration of pubovaginal sling if mobility can be developed at operation, or consideration of artificial sphincter (rare)

Stress Urinary Incontinence with Symptoms of Detrusor Instability

I. Conservative treatment (oxybutynin, imipramine, tolterodine, etc.)
   A. Unstable bladder symptoms respond
      1. Persistent genuine stress incontinence. Obtain urodynamic testing and enter genuine stress incontinence (GSI) algorithm above
      2. Patient satisfaction without wish for further evaluation
   B. Unstable bladder symptoms do not respond

   1. Obtain multichannel urodynamic testing and cystourethroscopy
      a. Severe detrusor instability = conservative treatment with medication, bladder retraining, timed voiding, biofeedback, circumvaginal exercises, and functional electrical stimulation
      b. No evidence of detrusor instability or other pathology = repeat cystogram on alternate day; if negative, consider ambulatory testing, if available, or consider GSI algorithm

Severe Vault Prolapse without History of Stress Incontinence

I. Obtain residual urine determination and test full bladder for stress incontinence in standing position with manual prolapse reduction
   A. Genuine stress incontinence demonstrated with vaginal route of repair indicated = modified Pereyra procedure at time of vault repair
   B. Genuine stress incontinence demonstrated with abdominal route of repair indicated = retropubic urethropexy and paravaginal repair at the time of vault repair

Bladder Instability

The most common cause of urinary incontinence in elderly women is the unstable bladder, which is the result of uninhibited bladder contractions.[23] It is also a significant contributor or the second most common cause of urinary incontinence in younger women of the fifth, sixth, and seventh decades. Symptoms suggesting possible bladder instability, such as en route urine loss, frequency, urgency, nocturia, and urgency incontinence, are common components of the patient's complaints. Rare components of the history suggestive of detrusor instability are true nocturnal enuresis and spontaneous complete bladder emptying. It is important for the physician who takes care of women to have an understanding of this condition. The reader is referred to an excellent review of bladder instability by L. Lewis Wall.[83]

Urinary urgency indicates a strong desire to void. Urgency incontinence is loss of urine (without straining) accompanied by a sensation of urgency. Detrusor instability refers to contractions noted at cystometry that are coincident with the reproduced symptoms of urgency. If control loss is secondary to a neurologic condition, it is referred to as detrusor hyperreflexia. Unstable bladder is usually used to describe the nonneurologic condition of presumed detrusor instability, which may be demonstrated on a given cystometrogram.

Patients experience symptoms coincident with increased tone and pressure of the bladder. The patient may experience a feeling of urgency without urine loss. As the pressure of the uninhibited contraction increases, the outlet resistance is overcome and the patient loses urine. This may or may not be preceded by relaxation of the urethral sphincter.

The pathophysiology of detrusor instability is poorly understood. Elbadawi and Resnick have added insight to that aspect of the pathophysiology, which involves myogenic changes seen in the aging detrusor.[26] Bladder cell junctions undergo transformations that more readily allow electrical propagation of a stimulus. Outlet obstruction is very rare in the female (although it can be induced by urethropexy), and the vast majority of patients with urgency incontinence have no evidence of increased outlet resistance. Neurologic examination of the S234 area is unremarkable. Cystourethroscopy is usually negative or may show mild to moderate trabeculations. A single cystometrogram may or may not show evidence of uninhibited contractions. The sensitivity of testing is increased with provocative maneuvers such as periodic heel bouncing and coughing during cystometry and the use of ambulatory monitoring. Patients who have low level contractions ($<15\ cmH_2O$) are more likely to have symptoms of urgency and frequency without urine loss, while patients with higher level contractions ($>15\ cmH_2O$) have a greater tendency to experience incontinence.

Patients who have objectively demonstrated mixed urinary incontinence are at risk of continued bladder instability when treated with operation. Uncontrolled moderate to severe detrusor instability may preclude the option of urethropexy.

Behavioral Therapy of Detrusor Instability

One of the most underestimated and poorly utilized beneficial forms of treatment in routine practice is bladder retraining. A significant percentage of patients experiencing urgency and frequency symptomatology may benefit from changes in voiding habits. The goal of bladder retraining is to suppress micturition until a set time, thus regaining control of the inhibitory reflexes or abilities.[86]

The patient voids at regular intervals and avoids entering the bathroom in the interim. The time intervals are gradually increased to a goal of 2 or $2\frac{1}{2}$ h. When the patient reaches the given time interval, she enters the bathroom and attempts to void (whether or not she has the urge to void or can void). The important considerations are attempting micturition and avoiding the restroom at unassigned times, even if it results in urine loss. With time, most patients will experience less frequency, less urgency incontinence, and more control of micturition. At night, the patient attempts to sleep as much as possible or void once per night. The frequency of changing the time intervals can vary. Most workers recommend voiding at a set interval for 1 week before increasing the time between voids.

Gradual increases in time intervals are important for success as well as motivation and confidence in the therapy. Occasionally, a patient will state consistently and more emphatically than most, that she will not be able to control the bladder. If the patient continues with this attitude, it will often become a subconscious self-fulfilling prophecy.

Pharmacologic Treatment of Detrusor Instability

Pharmacologic therapy for bladder instability relates to four classes of medication: anticholinergics, antispasmodics, tricylic antidepressants, and calcium antagonists.[85] The latter have not been commonly used in the United States for this purpose.

Anticholinergics or antimuscarinics are better utilized initially at lower dosages than are commonly prescribed. This will reduce the frequency of untoward symptoms such as dry mouth and blurred vision. It is important to combine these medications with timed voiding to achieve the highest success. The medications allow the bladder to fill fuller before reaching the trigger volume of urgency loss. Once this volume is reached, the patient will have the same tendency for uncontrolled loss (unless retarded with concomitant bladder retraining). If the patient voids every two hours, the higher trigger volume is not reached and the patient reduces or eliminates the episodes of detrusor instability loss.

Tricyclic antidepressants have some anesthetic bladder properties, anticholinergic effects, and stimulate α receptors in the region of the bladder neck. The medication most commonly used has been imipramine hydrochloride. The dosage used in adults is 10 to 25 mg three times per day. This may produce sedation in some patients. The medication works especially well for nocturnal enuresis or nocturia/nocturnal en route loss. In this setting, it would be used as a one-time bedtime dosage of 25 mg. The elderly are sensitive to medication and an initial 10 mg nightly dose should be used for several days in this group to assess tolerance. Stress to patients that the medication is in the antidepressant class, but that much larger doses are required when used for depression. Imipramine should not be used in conjunction with monoamine oxidase inhibitors.

Antispasmodics have a direct relaxant effect on the bladder in addition to anticholinergic and anesthetic properties.

Some recommended drugs and dosages are recorded in Table 44-1.

Urinary Retention

Acute urinary retention is defined as an acute inability to void. It is rare in women with the exception of patients in the immediate postpartum or postoperative state. Causes include pelvic mass, acute presentation of neurological events, and psychogenic reactions. This discussion is limited to chronic urinary retention.

Chronic urinary retention is often insidious, usually becoming apparent during investigation of urgency incontinence symptoms or in patients later discovered to have overflow incontinence. Most females with retention have no evidence of obstruction, but rather have decreased contractility of unknown etiology. Residual urine testing reveals a significant amount of urine remaining in the bladder after voiding. A value greater than 100 ml is considered abnormal by many investigators. Evaluation to rule out any neurologic contribution is essential.

Differential Diagnosis

The differential diagnosis of chronic urinary retention includes nonneurogenic hypocontractility of unknown etiology; detrusor hypocontractility with concomitant detrusor instability (often noted in the elderly); neurogenic causes such as multiple sclerosis or Parkinson's disease; conditions that damage the pelvic plexus (radical pelvic surgery, pelvic masses, anterior-posterior resections); conditions that affect the spinal cord area of S234 (nerve compression or tumor); and conditions that result in neuropathy, such as diabetes. Cystoceles may cause retention from kinking of the urethra secondary to prolapse. This must be documented objectively, as there are many patients with complete vault prolapse and severe cystocele who are able to empty their bladders to a normal residual volume (without maneuvers such as prolapse reduction).

TABLE 44-1

Class	Drug	Dosage
Anticholinergics	Propantheline	15–30 mg po qid
	Hyoscyamine	0.125–0.25 mg q 6 hrs
Antispasmodics	Oxybutynin	2.5 mg po bid—10 mg po qid
	Dicyclomine	20 mg po qid
	Flavoxate	200 mg po qid
Antimuscarinics	Tolterodine	1–2 mg po bid

History and Physical Examination

Patients with chronic urinary retention may present with decreased force of stream, frequency of urination, urinary incontinence, recurrent urinary tract infections, or nocturia. Most patients who present with frequency and a sensation of not emptying completely, on objective examination are found to be emptying their bladder well. The residual urine determination becomes important, not only in determining if the patient has true retention, but in reassuring those who are emptying their bladder normally, before recommendations of bladder retraining.

On examination, the patient may or may not have a palpably distended bladder. A neurologic examination of the lower extremities and perineum is accomplished (see earlier section on Physical Examination). An absent bulbocavernosus reflex or decreased saddle sensation suggests a possible neurologic lesion. A bimanual examination, including rectal examination, is carried out to detect any suggestion of a pelvic mass. This may be repeated after voiding, depending on difficulty of examination. A sterile catheter is then placed for residual urine determination after voiding. A value less than 100 ml is considered essentially normal. The urine is sent for urinalysis and culture, as cystitis can result in retention. If the residual determination is abnormal, bladder filling is then accomplished to detect any change in sensation of the bladder. If the bulbocavernosus reflex was absent or equivocal, a Foley catheter is used for residual, so tension can be placed on the bladder base with the Foley balloon to increase the likelihood of obtaining the reflex.

Urodynamic Testing

Urodynamic testing should be considered in any patient who has evidence of a neurologic etiology for retention (in addition to a complete neurologic evaluation). The factors to be assessed include normal relaxation of the pelvic floor musculature with voiding, normal coordination of the external sphincter with voiding (lack of dyssynergia), the lack of outlet obstruction, and the true detrusor pressure at the time of voiding. The lack of a detrusor contraction in the urodynamic setting is a common occurrence in normal patients and cannot be equated with a contractility. Many patients are unable to generate a contraction in this setting secondary to stress or the presence of even a small urethral catheter. If the patient is able to generate a contraction and a significantly elevated detrusor pressure is noted in the presence of a low urinary flow rate, obstruction is suggested.

Treatment

Treatment of chronic retention is directed toward the inciting disorder or condition. Often it will not be possible to reverse the conditions causing retention and self-intermittent catheterization becomes the therapy of choice. If the patient is able to catheterize herself, this often becomes readily acceptable despite early reservations in some patients. Catheterization often immediately reduces or eliminates symptoms of frequency, incontinence, nocturia, and problems related to urinary tract infections from stasis of urine. A clean method is utilized, the patient washing the catheter in soap and water after each use, followed by intermittent boiling of the catheter.

There are no pharmacologic agents available that can reliably increase bladder contractility. Cholinergic agents are not efficacious and often result in side effects. The patient is better served with a trial of an α-blocking agent such as prazosin. This results in relaxation of the bladder neck and upper urethra and aids some patients in bladder emptying when they can generate a partial contraction, for example, a patient with chronic urinary retention following radical pelvic surgery.

Urethral dilatation is not helpful when there is no evidence of stenosis (a rare condition in the female). Many patients with retention have been treated with multiple urethral dilatations without success. If a sterile, lubricated cotton swab can be easily passed through the urethra, any significant stenosis is extremely unlikely. Questionable patients can be evaluated by cystourethroscopy to fully visualize the urethra and bladder neck.

In the past, sphincterotomy was occasionally performed in females for retention. This often resulted in urinary incontinence. Patients who suffer from a combination of detrusor instabilty and retention are best treated with a combination of self-intermittent catheterization and an antimuscarinic agent to suppress incontinence.

Patients who have a neurogenic basis for their retention should be followed by a specialist. As an example, patients with multiple sclerosis often experience a combination of detrusor hyperreflexia and detrusor external sphincter dyssynergia. Detrusor external sphincter dyssynergia is an uninhibited bladder contraction combined with an uninhibited sphincter contraction. The latter may result in retention and high bladder pressures. Other women with multiple sclerosis may demonstrate hypocontractility and retention without dyssynergia. If some of these patients

are treated with anticholinergic agents without proper assessment, symptoms may improve in the face of silent increased bladder pressures, which may result in reflux and upper tract damage. After proper assessment, patients may benefit from a combination of intermittent catheterization and an anticholinergic agent.

Action Steps in Urinary Retention

1. History and physical examination (including careful neurologic examination).
2. Residual urine determination (obtained in a relaxed office setting; this may need to be repeated on more than one occasion).
3. Rule out urethral stenosis or obstruction (rare).
4. Rule out other conditions or medications associated with retention.
5. Obtain urinalysis and culture (respond as indicated and reassess).
6. Consider cystourethroscopy and urodynamic testing.
7. In the absence of a neurologic condition or other overt genitourinary (GU) pathology requiring treatment, teach self-intermittent catheterization.
8. In the presence of a neurologic condition, refer to a GU specialist for an outline of treatment and evaluation schedule following full assessment.
9. Avoid cholinergic agents and unnecessary dilatation.
10. When indicated, consider a trial of an α-blocking agent and double voiding

Incontinence in the Elderly

Incontinence is not only more prevalent in the elderly, but it may also have characteristics that are different from those experienced in patients of a younger age.[60] These characteristics are just beginning to be recognized, and additional studies are needed comparing symptoms and pathophysiology in patients of different ages. This will allow more appropriate treatment of elderly patients, and will further emphasize the importance of addressing multiple factors, which when added together, increase the margin of continence.

The percentage of patients with mixed incontinence increases as the population ages. Some workers give percentages of 55 percent mixed, 20 percent pure stress, and 15 to 20 percent pure urgency loss. This reflects a decreasing incidence of pure stress incontinence in comparison with younger age groups, transitioning to higher incidences of mixed and pure urgency incontinence. The elderly also manifest a condition described by Resnick as detrusor hyperactivity with impaired contractility.[50] Elderly patients also tend to have incontinence of multifactorial etiology.

History in an elderly incontinent patient must include a list of medical problems, medications, and past pelvic operative history. Bowel history is additionally important, as previous colorectal surgery or chronic constipation can contribute to urinary symptomatology. Nocturia increases with age and is related to changes in fluid hydrostasis, cardiac function, and renal filtration.

Physical examination should include pelvic examination to rule out a pelvic mass, rectal examination to rule out constipation or impaction, and neurologic examination to rule out spinal or pelvic floor abnormalities.

Urine culture results should be interpreted in conjunction with urinalysis results to detect pyuria or hematuria in the absence of infection, or to suggest contamination. Cytology should be performed in patients with asymptomatic sterile hematuria, pyuria, or recurrent urinary tract infections.

Urodynamic and office testing should be sensitive to the high incidence of detrusor hyperactivity with impaired contractility in the elderly population.

Urethral Diverticulum

It is important for the generalist to have a working understanding of this condition, which can be present more commonly than is recognized.[1] Diverticula may be multiple or single, with an average size of 2 to 3 cm in diameter. The wall of the sac is fibromuscular, and the lining consists of granulation tissue, or squamous/transitional epithelium. The exact prevalence rates are unknown, but reports have ranged from 1.8 to 4.7 percent.[75] The incidence appears to be higher in individuals of African-American descent, at a possible ratio of 6:1. Reports in the literature have been few, with some of the largest series appearing from the Mayo Clinic and Johns Hopkins.

It is postulated that acquired urethral diverticula are secondary to obstructed and infected paraurethral glands, which subsequently rupture into the lumen.[42] Congenital diverticula may be secondary to remnants of Gartner's ducts. Diverticula are usually located in the middle third of the urethra, with the neck or mouth of the diverticula connecting dorsolaterally. Tender cystic swelling may or may not be palpated in this area.

Symptoms

Symptoms are often nonspecific and may contribute to the difficulty of diagnosis if the diverticulum is not considered part of the differential. The most common complaints are frequency of urination and dysuria. Also commonly associated with diverticula are recurrent and refractory cystitis, dyspareunia, urgency, and incontinence. Post-micturitional dribbling and expression of fluid on palpation of a suburethral swelling are highly suggestive of diverticula. Ten to 20 percent of patients with diverticula may be asymptomatic.[47]

Diagnosis

Suspicion of the entity is one of the most useful adjuncts in diagnosis, as the diverticulum may or may not be palpable. Diverticula can be missed on laboratory evaluation and may require more than one test to visualize. A significant percentage are missed on cystourethroscopic examination due to the location of the orifice, the folds of the urethra, and because most scopes do not balloon or distend the urethra on examination. Properly performed dye tests with the use of a Davis or Tratner catheter are valuable, as the diverticulum may have more than one connection to the urethra. This becomes important when considering repair. Contrast is injected under pressure, filling the urethra and diverticulum. Vaginal ultrasound appears to be more sensitive than many diagnostic modalities. MRI is also an excellent method of diagnosis, and may show greater involvement by the diverticula than appreciated on other testing methods. Although MRI may be precluded by expense, it could be considered cost-effective to prevent a diverticulum from being incompletely removed at operation. The voiding cystourethrogram is a useful adjunct. Urethral profilometry is less helpful as pressure diminutions correlate poorly with the location of the diverticulum.

Treatment

The treatment of urethral diverticula is either observation in asymptomatic patients or surgical removal in symptomatic patients. The proper surgical removal of urethral diverticula is challenging and carries risks of local complications such as fistula formation, recurrence, and urinary incontinence. The challenge is to avoid these complications while removing all of the diverticulum wall, closing all ostia, and preserving surrounding tissue to aid in a multilayer closure. The repair is made additionally difficult by the surrounding inflammation and friability of the tissue. Marsupialization is only useful for the distal aspect of the urethra due to risks of urethral damage and subsequent incontinence.

One of the largest experiences is reported by Lee; it consisted of 85 patients who were approached via an anterior vaginal wall incision.[47] Two additional supporting layers can be provided by imbricating the pubocervical fascia with a side-to-side (vest-over-pants) repair. A personal examination was accomplished in 76 patients with a follow-up period of 2 to 15 years.

The remaining nine patients were contacted by telephone or letter. Eighty-two percent of patients experienced immediate relief of symptoms. One patient experienced a postoperative fistula, two patients experienced urinary incontinence, two patients experienced urethral-pain syndromes, and eight patients experienced a recurrent diverticulum.

Urethral and Bladder Leiomyoma

The largest series from a single institution is from the Mayo Clinic.[18] Urethral and bladder leiomyomas may present as a urethral or bladder mass. The mass is usually more indurated than a diverticulum. Genitourinary leiomyomas have been routinely surgically removed in the past. Similarities with uterine leiomyoma should be considered and an asymptomatic bladder leiomyoma may undergo observation.

Urethral Syndrome and Painful Bladder Syndrome

Urethral syndrome is a term used to describe chronic symptoms of urethral pain, urgency, dysuria, and frequency of urination without pathologic findings.[62] These symptoms may be present separately or in combination. Patients who are given this term to describe their condition are usually in the third to fourth decades of life. Similar reversible symptoms in postmenopausal patients responsive to estrogen administration are not termed urethral syndrome. The etiology of the condition is not apparent, with studies focusing on urethral spasm, irritation, infection, and allergic causes. The vast majority of patients have no evidence of overt infection, although *Chlamydia trachomatis* has been isolated in a small percentage of patients. Other proponents of an infectious etiology have suggested that low count bacterial infections may be responsible. The majority of studies have shown no increased incidence of infection in urethral syndrome patients when compared to controls.

Objective studies to date have not supported the concept of spasm or urethral striated-muscle hypersensitivity. The internal sphincter is relatively small and difficult to study without precise needle electrode studies. Studies can be difficult to interpret, especially because ambulatory monitoring has shown that urethral pressure variations are normal in the female and vary throughout the day.

Physical examination and office assessment include pelvic examination, wet preparation of vaginal secretions, and urethral palpation.

The diagnosis of urethral syndrome is currently a diagnosis of exclusion. Tests include urinalysis, urine culture, and consideration of urethral cultures for chlamydia and/or gonorrhea. Cystourethroscopic examination is helpful in reassuring the patient, and enables the physician to rule out occult cystitis or interstitial cystitis. If a urethral diverticulum is suspected, additional testing can be considered, as described in this chapter. An additional consideration is skin testing to rule out unrecognized allergies. This is similar to comparable testing in the condition of vulvar vestibulitis syndrome.

Treatment is difficult and often centers on attempting to make individual symptoms better. Several treatments have arisen which do not have a solid pathophysiologic basis, yet may result in improved symptoms in a significant percentage of patients. As an example, empiric gentle urethral dilatations (a series of three over several weeks to months) have been symptomatically helpful in many patients. Regardless of the treatment, a significant percentage of patients continue to experience symptoms for months to years. Other patients experience spontaneous resolution of symptoms without therapy. Treatment has also included empiric doxycycline treatment, urethral estrogen administration, diazepam for spasm, and, in selected patients, psychiatric evaluation. Some researchers believe that the symptoms of urethral syndrome are actually a manifestation of painful bladder syndrome.[73]

The term "painful bladder syndrome" refers to painful conditions of the bladder when no abnormality is apparent on investigation. Patients complain of a combination of urgency, vague suprapubic discomfort, nocturia, and frequency of urination. Cystoscopic examination should be performed to rule out interstitial cystitis. This may require hydrodistension under anesthesia. The etiology and pathogenesis of interstitial cystitis is still undetermined. A much greater understanding of interstitial cystitis and other painful bladder syndromes is needed.

Asymptomatic Hematuria

This discussion is limited to asymptomatic microhematuria in the nonadolescent patient. Numerous studies have documented the necessity for urologic investigation of patients with asymptomatic hematuria.[19,42] Howard et al. reported an experience in 1980 with 246 patients with asymptomatic hematuria.[35] A urologic neoplasm was noted in 10 percent of patients, while an additional 12 percent had other significant urological lesions. In a recent 10- to 20-year follow-up assessment of 191 patients, Howard et al. noted that all patients were free of genitourinary malignancies.[40] Seventy-eight percent of these patients had persistent microscopic blood cells in the urine throughout their follow-up. This suggested a low yield for routine IVP and cystourethroscopy. This is supported by three additional major series totaling 428 patients with a 2- to 20-year follow-up and no evidence of upper tract malignancy appearance.[40] The urologic investigation of asymptomatic hematuria by urinalysis, urine cytology, IVP, and cystoscopy has been challenged. Kolin and Silverstein suggested that the initial diagnostic approach to asymptomatic hematuria include cystoscopy and renal ultrasound. Some investigators have suggested diagnostic follow-up only in patients who demonstrate gross hematuria, recurrent urinary tract infections, or changes in voiding characteristics.

Mariani et al. evaluated 1000 consecutive adults with asymptomatic hematuria in the absence of proteinuria. A percentage of these patients had one episode of gross hematuria in the absence of diagnostic symptoms such as cystitis. The majority of patients received IVP, serum creatinine, culture, cytology, and cystoscopy. Lesions that could account for hematuria were detected in 88.3 percent of patients, with life-threatening lesions diagnosed in 9.1 percent. In 22.8 percent, patients had lesions requiring minimal observation. The incidence of life-threatening lesions was noted to increase with age and was higher in men.[52] In the patient group with life-threatening lesions, 18.6 percent had at least one urinalysis with less than three red blood cells per high-power field within six months of diagnosis.

The incidence of low-grade microscopic hematuria (less than two red blood cells per high-power field) ranges from 9 to 18 percent. In a population-based study performed at the Mayo Clinic, 13 percent of patients were noted to have some degree of hematuria without statistically significant differences between various population groups.[69] The majority of investigators may not evaluate patients who have less than three red blood cells per high-power field. Measures taken to define a safe and acceptable lower limit of hematuria have not been successful.

In our practice, we consider three red blood cells per high-power field on two to three properly collected specimens as asymptomatic hematuria. Higher levels of red blood cells on one urinalysis would additionally be acceptable for this diagnosis. Urine cytology is performed along with screening studies for bacteria or infection. In the absence of infection, we proceed with cystoscopy and ultrasound of the urinary tract. Additional follow-up is by urinalysis and urine cytology every 6 to 12 months, depending upon the index of suspicion. Patients are instructed to return for symptoms such as gross hematuria or irritative voiding symptoms. A creatinine study and IVP is considered within the current standard of care, although in the future, additional parameters may need to be present to indicate cost-effectiveness and desirability of radiologic contrast studies. This also reflects a 0.03 percent incidence of life-threatening anaphylactic contrast medium reactions with excretory urograms.

Some investigators have suggested that asymptomatic microhematuria may warrant investigation for parenchymal renal disease. Smith reviewed the records of 125 patients with isolated asymptomatic hematuria and elevated serum creatinine and the records of 83 comparison patients with no hematuria and elevated serum creatinine from a previous population-based study.[69] The results showed that disease was detected no more frequently in patients with elevated creatinine in asymptomatic hematuria than those with elevated creatinine without asymptomatic hematuria. The investigators concluded that exhaustive diagnostic testing to detect renal parenchymal disease cannot be advised in asymptomatic elderly patients with low-grade (grade 1) microhematuria unless more specific indications are present. The degree of microhematuria in this particular study was the presence of one or more erythrocytes per high-power field.

Vesicovaginal Fistula

Vesicovaginal fistulas are somewhat rare in affluent societies, occurring most commonly following operation or radiation. In developing countries, obstetric fistula secondary to poor labor management practices are most common. When obstetric fistulas are encountered in affluent countries, the etiology usually relates to forceps or instrumented delivery rather than pressure necrosis from neglected labor. In the United States, approximately 5 percent of fistulas result from obstetric damage. An additional 10 percent are from irradiation, and 85 percent are related to pelvic operative procedures.[78] Symmonds, in a large referral practice at the Mayo Clinic, noted an unchanging rate of 25 to 30 fistulas per year. The majority of these were complex, with 10 percent involving ureters or bladder, 10 percent were noted in conjunction with additional ureteral or bowel fistulas, and 52 percent of the patients had at least one prior attempt at operative repair.[78]

In a Mayo Clinic experience of 600 fistulas, 75 percent occurred after hysterectomy, with more than 50 percent resulting from a simple total abdominal hysterectomy. The majority of vesicovaginal fistulas are noted after benign pelvic surgery via an abdominal approach.

The office practitioner may encounter a fistula in the recent postoperative patient less than 30 days from operation, the previously operated patient who presents with incontinence and occult fistula, or a patient who has had irradiation therapy months to years in the past. The majority of early postoperative patients will demonstrate urinary leakage per vagina in the first 2 weeks following surgery, although an additional group of patients will first demonstrate urine loss several weeks after operation.

Diagnosis

The patient with a vesicovaginal fistula describes constant urine loss per vagina following operation. Alternatively, the patient may present with a long-standing history of urinary incontinence and previous operation.[44] In these patients, bona fide urinary stress incontinence may be present, but augmented by a small amount of urine loss from an occult fistula. Patients have received an operation for incontinence with elevation of the urethrovesical junction, not recognizing the presence of a small communication between the bladder and vagina. To avoid incorrect diagnosis, a tampon dye test should be considered part of the evaluation in patients who describe a constant small amount of leakage, patients with previous history of irradiation, or patients with a history of incontinence and no overt evidence of loss per urethra on stress testing.

Although cystoscopy is an important part of fistula evaluation, the absence of a fistula on visual inspection does not rule out its presence. Patients with occult fistulas have had negative cystoscopic examinations performed by very skilled endoscopists. The majority of fistulas following total abdominal hysterectomy tend to be high in the apex of the vagina in a supratrigonal

location. A lack of surrounding inflammation in folds may make the small defect difficult to delineate on cystoscopic inspection.

The tampon dye test is accomplished in the following manner: The patient is assessed by speculum visualization of the vagina and pelvic examination. Colposcopic examination of the vaginal apex may be helpful in the detection of a small occult fistula, as colposcopy provides magnification and improved lighting. A small fistula may have erythema surrounding the vaginal opening, which aids in detection. Approximately 300 to 350 cc of methylene blue-stained saline is placed in the bladder after its initial drainage with a catheter. Three separate 4 × 4 gauzes, or pledgets, are then placed into the vagina. The patient is then asked to walk, do deep-knee bends, go up and down stairs, and finally void after approximately 20 to 30 min. The patient is immediately examined after voiding by removal of the gauze pledgets. The first gauze pledget will be stained from urination; however, the voiding contraction may increase the sensitivity of fistula detection. The successive gauze pledgets are then examined for evidence of dye. An occult fistula often presents at the apex, and thus the second gauze pledget is free of dye, with the final pledget being stained.

It should be understood that this does not rule out a ureterovaginal fistula.[49] Ureterovaginal fistulas can be detected by giving the patient indigo carmine dye with a concomitant tampon test over a longer duration of time or by accomplishing retrograde contrast studies. The latter studies are often helpful even when a vesicovaginal fistula has been detected to rule out a secondary ureterovaginal fistula.

If a vesicovaginal fistula is evident on vaginal examination or tampon testing, the timing of cystoscopy depends on consideration of operative repair.[79] If the patient is several weeks postoperative, it may be additional weeks to months before timing of repair. The cystoscopy is best done just prior to the time of operative repair to note the position of the ureteral orifices relative to the fistula and rule out any additional abnormalities.

If the ureteral orifices are 0.5 cm from the edge of the fistula or if the communication is noted lateral to the ureters, ureteral catheters may be considered at the time of operation.

Management

Surgeons have different opinions concerning the timing of operative repair. Most small fistulas benefit from an initial trial of bladder catheter decompression to allow the possibility of spontaneous healing. Some studies have suggested a benefit from low suction applied to the catheter drainage. Fifteen to 20 percent of small posthysterectomy vesicovaginal fistulas may heal spontaneously with prolonged catheter drainage of the bladder. If spontaneous healing of the fistula has not occurred by 6 to 8 weeks, the possibility of healing is remote and the urinary catheter should be removed.[78] Classic opinion regarding timing of repair is after a waiting period of 2 to 6 months, which allows tissues to become less inflamed and edematous. Other investigators have suggested that delay is not required. The exact time for repair depends on the size of the fistula and integrity of surrounding tissues. Symmonds advocated that a definitive repair should be deferred for 2 to 4 months depending on the quality of tissues and the condition for which the operation was accomplished. In-dwelling catheterization during this time period should be avoided, as it may promote infection and further delay operative repair. In addition, social pressure to repair a fistula prematurely should be resisted. Postradiation fistulas are at significant risk of recurrence due to poor vascularity of the tissues. The surgical delay in these instances may approach 1 to 2 years to ensure the integrity of surrounding tissue.

Operative Repair

The surgeon needs to be familiar with all operative techniques for fistula repair, and needs to tailor the operation to the patient. The approach should allow accessibility, wide mobilization of tissues, excision of scar tissue, and a repair that results in the greatest likelihood of success. Practitioners should recognize that the majority of vesicovaginal fistulas are able to be repaired vaginally with an excellent cure rate.

The possibility of infection is minimized by prophylactic antibiotic administration, avoiding tissue necrosis by careful handling of the tissues, complete hemostasis, and postoperative bladder drainage. The first attempt at operative repair provides the best opportunity for success, making the experience of the surgeon and the technique utilized important.

The vaginal repair consists of a vertical vaginal incision followed by wide mobilization of the tissues. Scar is excised, and healthy, pliable tissues are approximated without tension, usually resulting in a transverse bladder closure. Fine suture material is utilized, which inverts the bladder epithelium. A secondary suture row extends beyond the initial closure layer. The vagina is closed in the opposite direction so that suture layers are not superimposed. Cul-de-sac peritoneum or a Martius flap may be effective in interposing tissue between the bladder and the vaginal mucosal suture line. Regardless of the type of flap utilized, it will not provide success if the bladder suture lines break down due to excessive tension, decreased vascularity, or a poor watertight closure. Ureterovaginal fistulas, urethrovaginal fistulas, and large obstetrical fistulas are beyond the scope of an office text; however, references are provided for the interested practitioner.[27,28]

Urinary Tract Infections

This discussion is limited to acute, sporadic urinary tract infections. Consultation should be considered in selected patients with a history of diabetes, vesicoureteral reflux, renal calculi, obstructive uropathies, immunocompromise, parenchymal renal disease, a chronic indwelling catheter, current pregnancy, severe acute pyelonephritis, or documented recurrent infections without prior history of urologic investigation.[43]

Acute uncomplicated urinary tract infections are responsible for six to seven million office visits per year in the United States. Adult women as a group experience the majority of urinary tract infections in the population at large, with related health expenditures exceeding 1 billion dollars. Approximately 43 percent of females aged 14 to 61 claim to have experienced a past bladder infection. In addition, the tendency for reinfection may increase with increasing age. Evans noted a 3.5 percent incidence of significant bacteriuria in teenagers, which rose to 10 percent in patients over the age of 70.[29] Higher rates are noted in nursing home populations. Mabeck reported that 85 percent of patients experience 0.32 infections per year, while 15 percent experience 2 per year. He also noted that treated patients experience future recurrence at the same rate as patients whose symptoms resolve without treatment.

Evans reported that 5.7 percent of abacteriuric women complained of dysuria.[29] It may be important to document infection by culture in patients who experience recurrent infections. Many asymptomatic younger women may have periods of occult significant bacteriuria that subsequently resolve without consequence. Significant bacteriuria is common in females, yet the meaning of this term is complex.[38] The amount of bacteria that should be considered significant varies depending on the organism, concurrent use of antibiotics, and associated pathology. Coagulase negative staphylococcus bacteria grow slowly and counts of 10,000 to 100,000 cfu/ml are considered significant. Gram-negative enteric bacteria and enterococci grow rapidly and more commonly fit the Kass criteria of 100,000 cfu/ml as diagnostic of infection. A small percentage of patients with true infections will have very small organism counts.

This indicates that in addition to host defenses, the characteristics of the organism, and not just its foreign presence, are important in the overall virulence. Fimbriae allow enteric gram-negative bacteria to have increased adherence to mucosal surfaces. Additional virulence factors may be resistance to human serum complement, production of bacterial hemolysin, and ability to bind and use host iron. Increased susceptibility to recurrent infections in females is conferred by intrinsic host factors including nonsecretor genotype and estrogen.[39]

Recurrent infections are usually from different strains of bacteria. Recurrent significant bacteriuria with the same strain would suggest persistence of infection, rather than true recurrent infections. This is rare, and the vast majority of infections encountered in practice are recurrent. Stamm noted this fact in supporting the importance of host susceptibility. Additionally supportive are the relationship between the onset of infections and age and the tendency for urinary tract infections to cluster.[71]

There is evidence that vaginal colonization of enteric pathogens is a significant factor in patients with a history of recurrent infectious cystitis.[70] Fecal bacteria colonize in an ascending fashion and in sexually active individuals who experience recurrent infections, and may be intercourse associated, although the magnitude of this association is unclear. In the majority of females, intercourse results in the transfer of bacteria into the bladder, but it takes on significance in patients predisposed to vaginal colonization and/or decreased host defense factors. Diaphragm spermicide use appears to markedly affect vaginal flora and increase the tendency to develop infections.[71]

It is unusual for long-term, recurrent urinary tract infections to produce renal damage. High-risk groups include patients with diabetes, increased age (elderly), vesicoureteral reflux, immunosuppression, or a pregnancy.[51]

Diagnosis

Diagnosis includes history, microscopic examination of the urinary sediment, and quantitative urine culture.[56] The presence of one bacterium in each high-power field of an uncentrifuged specimen corresponds to 100,000 cfu/ml of urine. Approximately 30 percent of patients with bacteriuria based on symptoms and microscopy will have sterile urine cultures.[32]

The reliability of cultures from the female is 80 percent, which is the most accurate reflection of the amount and type of bacteriuria. Twenty percent of patients with significant enterobacter bacteriuria will have less than 1000 organisms on culture. An equal percentage of patients with sterile urine may show up to 10,000 organisms in the voided specimen. If the patient is asymptomatic and bacteriuria is detected, two to three consecutive cultures are desirable. However, a single catheterized specimen showing 100,000 organisms is considered diagnostic in an asymptomatic individual. Two consecutive specimens in a symptomatic individual are considered desirable by some experts, but the taking of two consecutive specimens is not commonly performed. Most vaginal and periurethral organisms are gram-positive and their isolation suggests contamination. Contamination is also suggested by isolation of unusual or multiple organisms in a voided specimen in the absence of pyuria.

Pyuria reflects an inflammatory response in the genitourinary system. Associated causes are infection (typical and atypical), foreign bodies, stones, trauma, neoplasms, contamination, glomerulonephritis, and tubulointerstitial disease. Pyuria in the absence of infection requires urologic investigation to rule out these associated causes. Some patients demonstrate pyuria on a voided specimen from vaginal leukocyte contamination. A wet preparation of the vaginal secretions would show a significant amount of white blood cells. A catheterized specimen may be free of pyuria in these patients, and unnecessary urologic testing would be avoided.

Clean catch specimens are the standard office sampling method, although some investigators have suggested that it may not reduce contamination over voided non-clean catch specimens.[50] Leisure et al. made the comparison in 100 asymptomatic women; 64 total contaminants were noted in each of the groups. In addition, 10 women had sterile non-clean catch cultures and contaminated clean catch cultures. Regardless of the method, urine specimens should be promptly cultured or refrigerated to avoid false-positive results.

Treatment

The microorganism most commonly responsible for uncomplicated infections is E. coli, with six serotype strains predominating. *Staphylococcus saprophyticus* is the second most common pathogen in young women of childbearing age. Five to 10 percent of cases will involve *Proteus* or other gram-negative bacteria or enterococci.[45] *Staphylococcus saprophyticus* may also be encountered. Kunin notes that enteric gram-negative rods and enterococci take on a greater role in complicated infections, although *E. coli* is still commonly present.

The efficacy and benefit of an antimicrobial drug depends on the agent's ability to concentrate at the site of infection, bacterial effects (organism susceptibility), frequency of resistance, side effects, and cost.[45] Bacteriostatic agents are acceptable for uncomplicated infections, while bacteriocidal drugs may be needed in complicated cases. Individuals predisposed to the latter condition are those with congenital abnormalities, foreign bodies, diabetes, or neurologic problems.

The object of management in uncomplicated infections is to avoid persistence of significant bacteriuria or infection, and to eradicate reversible bacteriuric-related symptoms. The importance of clearing low levels of bacteriuria depends on the age of the patient, associated medical conditions, and individual history. There appears to be no definite advantage in treating asymptomatic bacteriuria in the nonpregnant female. In addition, in some groups, such as in the elderly, it may be difficult to clear the bacteriuria.

Recommendations for the office practitioner include the following as minimum treatment:

1. Three-day treatment with nitrofurantoin (Macrodantin), trimethoprim-sulfamethoxazole, or agents that concentrate primarily

in the urinary tract, have excellent efficacy, and are relatively low cost;

2. Single-dose therapy only in uncomplicated patients, and those without pregnancy, diabetes, or history of acute pyelonephritis;
3. Office microscopy or other methods to detect pyuria, bacteria, and microscopic hematuria. Pyuria is defined as 10 leukocytes/ml and is present in the vast majority of women with urinary tract infections.

If the patient has acute symptoms of infection with pyuria and bacteria, the practitioner may choose not to obtain a culture. This should only be considered in the patient with less than two infections per year or the patient who has been thoroughly investigated and is under close urologic follow-up. Anatomic abnormalities of the urinary tract detected by cystoscopy and excretory urography are found in less than 5 percent of young women with recurrent uncomplicated cystitis.[71]

Recently, such considerations as cultures for patients suffering from infrequent sporadic episodes, urinalysis, susceptibility testing, the indications for urologic investigation, treating for greater than 5 days, and posttreatment cultures have been challenged.[32]

Fowler recommends the following in uncomplicated infections:

1. Treatment for 3 to 5 days with nitrofurantoin (Macrodantin), sulfamethoxazole, or penicillin-G;
2. Avoidance of susceptibility testing;
3. Posttreatment cultures in urologic referral practices, patients with *Proteus mirabilis* as the cause of bacteriuria, or in patients with complicated infections;
4. Avoiding prophylactic treatment until the frequency and bacteriology of the infections have been determined;
5. Initiating treatment in symptomatic patients with pyuria before urine culture results are known;
6. Awaiting culture results before initiating treatment in symptomatic patients who do not manifest pyuria (a majority of pa-

TABLE 44-2

Drug	Dosage
Nitrofurantoin	50–100 mg q 6–8 h
TMP-SMX	1 to 2 tabs q 12 h
Noroxin	400 mg q 12 h
Floxin	200–300 mg q 12 h
Ampicillin	250–500 mg q 6–8 h
Cephalexin	250–500 mg q 6–8 h
Tetracycline	250–500 mg q 6–8
Fosfomycin	3 g po single dosage

tients without pyuria do not have infection).

Some recommended drugs and dosages for 3- to 5-day therapy, and one-day therapy of uncomplicated urinary tract infections are listed in Table 44-2. Published data suggest that a 3-day regimen is more effective than a single-dose regimen for all microbials tested.[72]

Single-dose therapy can be considered for trimethoprim-sulfamethoxazole, trimethoprim, sulfonamide, fosfomycin, and tetracyclines at increased dosage.[57] Fihn noted higher failure rates at 13 days with single-dose trimethoprim-sulfamethoxazole.[31]

Prophylactic therapy can be utilized in patients with a chronic history of recurrent (nonpersistent) urinary tract infections. Low-dosage antimicrobials that lack deleterious effects on the bowel flora are utilized, including nitrofurantoin (100 mg), trimethoprim-sulfamethoxazole (1 tab), trimethoprim (50 mg), cephalexin (250 mg), and cinoxacin (250 mg) in daily use. If efficacious, alternate-day use may be considered for a trial period.

References and Suggested Readings

1. Andersen MJF: The incidence of diverticula in the female urethra. *J Urol* 98:96–98, 1967.
2. Baden WF, Walker TA: Physical diagnosis in evaluation of vaginal vault relaxation. *Clin Obstet Gynecol* 15:1055, 1972.

3. Beck RP, et al: Intra-urethral-intravesical cough-pressure spike differences in 267 patients surgically cured of genuine stress incontinence of urine. *Obstet Gynecol* 72:302–306, 1988.

4. Bent AE, Sand PK, Ostergaard DR, Brubaker LT: Transvaginal electrical stimulation in the treatment of genuine stress incontinence in detrusor instability. *Int Urogynecol J* 4:9–13, 1993.

5. Berglas B, Rubin IC: Study of the supportive structures of the uterus by levator myography. *Surg Gyn Ob* 97:677, 1953.

6. Bergman A, Elia G: Three surgical procedures for genuine stress incontinence and colon: Five-year follow-up of a prospective randomized study. *Am J Obstet Gynecol* 173(1):66–71, 1995.

7. Bergman A, Koonings PP, et al: Primary stress urinary incontinence in pubic relaxation: Prospective randomized comparison of three different operations. *Am J Obstet Gynecol* 166:97, 1989.

8. Bo K, Maanum M: Does vaginal electrical stimulation cause pelvic floor muscle contraction? A pilot study. *Scand J Urol Nephrol* 179:39–45, 1996.

9. Bo K, Talseth T: Change in urethral pressure during voluntary pelvic floor muscle contraction and vaginal electrical stimulation. *Int Urogynecol J Pelvic Floor Dysfunct* 8(1):3–6, 1997.

10. Bump RC, Hurt WG, et al: Assessment of Kegel pelvic exercise performance after verbal instruction. *Am J Obstet Gynecol* 165:322–329, 1991.

11. Bump RC, Mattiasson A, Bo K, et al: The standardization of terminology of female pelvic organ prolapse and pelvic floor dysfunction. *Am J Obstet Gynecol* 175:10–17, 1996.

12. Burgio KL, et al: The role of biofeedback in Kegel exercise training for stress urinary incontinence. *Am J Obstet Gynecol* 154:58, 1986.

13. Burgio KL, et al: Urinary incontinence in the elderly. *Ann Intern Med* 104:507–515, 1985.

14. Colombo M, Milanik R: Sacrospinous ligament fixation and modified McCall culdoplasty during vaginal hysterectomy for advanced uterovaginal prolapse. *Am J Obstet Gynecol* 179:13–20, 1998.

15. Columbo M, Milani R, Vitobello D, Maggioni A: A randomized comparison of Burch colposuspension and abdominal paravaginal defect repair for female stress urinary incontinence. *Am J Obstet Gynecol* 175(1): 78–84, 1996.

16. Constantinou CE: Resting stress urethral pressures as a clinical guide to the mechanism of continence in the female patient. *Urol Clin North Am* 12:247–258, 1985.

17. Constantinou CE, et al: Spacial distribution and timing of transmitted in reflexly generated urethral pressures in healthy women. *J Urol* 127:964–969, 1982.

18. Cornella JL: Leiomyoma of the female urethra and bladder: Report of twenty-three patients and review of the literature. *Am J Obstet Gynecol* 176:1278–1285, 1997.

19. Corwin HL, Silverstein MD: The diagnosis of neoplasia in patients with asymptomatic microscopic hematuria: A decision analysis. *J Urol* 139:1002, 1988.

20. DeLancy JOL: Anatomic aspects of vaginal eversion after hysterectomy. *Am J Obstet Gynecol* 166:1717–1724, 1992.

21. DeLancey JOL: Correlative study of paraurethral anatomy. *Obstet Gynecol* 68:91, 1986.

22. DeLancey JOL: Structural aspects of the extrinsic continence mechanism. *Obstet Gynecol* 72:296, 1988.

23. DuBeau CE, Resnick MM: Evaluation of the causes and severity of geriatric incontinence: A critical appraisal. *Urol Clin North Am* 18:243–256, 1991.

24. Elbadawi A: Interstitial cystitis: A critique of current concepts with a new proposal for pathologic diagnosis and pathogenesis. *Urology* 49:14–40, 1997.

25. Elbadawi A: Neuromorphologic basis of vesicourethral function: I. Histochemistry, ultrastructure, and function of intrinsic nerves of the bladder and urethra. *Neurourol Urodyn* 1:3, 1982.

26. Elbadawi A: Pathology and pathophysiology of detrusor incontinence. *Urol Clin North Am* 22(3):499–512, 1995.

27. Elkins TE, et al: Transvaginal mobilization and utilization of the anterior bladder wall to repair vesicovaginal fistulas involving the urethra. *Obstet Gynecol* 79:455–460, 1992.

28. Elkins TE, et al: Vesicovaginal fistula revisited. *Obstet Gynecol* 72:307–312, 1988.

29. Evans DA, et al: Bacteriuria in a population-based cohort of women. *J Infect Dis* 138:768–773, 1978.

30. Fall M, et al: Electrical stimulation. *Urol Clin North Am* 18:393–407, 1991.

31. Fihn SD, et al: Trimethoprim-sulfamethoxazole for acute dysuria in women: Double-blind, randomized trial with single dose versus ten-day treatment. *Ann Intern Med* 108:350, 1988.

32. Fowler JE: Urinary tract infection in women. *Urol Clin North Am* 13:673–683, 1986.

33. Fynes M, Donnelly VS, O'Connell PR, O'Herlitty C: Cesarean delivery and anal sphincter injury. *Obstet Gynecol* 92:496–500, 1998.

34. Gilpin SA: The pathogenesis of genitourinary prolapse and stress incontinence of urine. A histological and histochemical study. *Br J Obstet Gynecol* 96:15, 1989.

35. Golin AL, Howard RS: Asymptomatic microscopic hematuria. *J Urol* 124:389, 1980.

36. Gosling JA: Structure of the lower urinary tract and pelvic floor. *Obstet Gynecol* 12:285, 1985.

37. Hilton P, Stanton SL: A clinical and urodynamic assessment of the Burch colposuspension for genuine stress incontinence. *Br J Obstet Gynecol* 90:934, 1983.

38. Hilton P, Stanton SL: Urethral pressure measurement by microtransducor: The results in symptom-free women and in those with genuine stress incontinence. *Br J Obstet Gynecol* 90:919–933, 1983.

39. Hooton TM, Stamm WE: Diagnosis and treatment of uncomplicated urinary tract infection. *Infect Dis Clin North Am* 11(3):551–581, 1997.

40. Howard RS, Golin AL: Long-term follow-up of asymptomatic microhematuria. *J Urol* 145:335–336, 1991.

41. Kammerer-Doak DN, Cornella MD, Magrina MD, Stanhope CR, Smilack J: Osteitis pubis after Marshall-Marchetti-Krantz urethropexy: A pubic osteomyelitis. *Am J Obstet Gynecol* 179:586–590, 1998.

42. Karram MM: The urethral syndrome. *Am Urogyn Soc Quarterly Rep* 8:3, 1990.

43. Karram MM: Lower urinary tract infection, *Urogynecology and Urodynamics,* 3rd ed.

44. Keettel WC: Surgical management of urethrovaginal and vesicovaginal fistulas. *Am J Obstet Gynecol* 131:425, 1978.

45. Kunin CM: *Detection, Prevention, and Management of Urinary Tract Infections.* Philadelphia, PA: Lea and Febiger, 1987.

46. Langer R, et al: The value of simultaneous hysterectomy during Burch colposuspension for urinary stress incontinence. *Obstet Gynecol* 72:866–869, 1988.

47. Lee RA: Diverticulum of the female urethra: Postoperative complications and results. *Obstet Gynecol* 61:52–58, 1983.

48. Lee RA, Symmonds RE: Repeat Marshall-Marchetti Krantz procedure for recurrent stress urinary incontinence. *Am J Obstet Gynecol* 122:219, 1975.

49. Lee RA, Symmonds RE: Ureteral vaginal fistula. *Am J Obstet Gynecol* 109:1032–1035, 1971.

50. Leisur MK, et al: Does a clean-catch urine sample reduce bacterial contamination [letter]? *N Engl J Med* 328:289, 1993.

51. Mabeck CE: Treatment of uncomplicated urinary tract infection in non-pregnant women. *Postgrad Med J* 48:69–75, 1972.

52. Mariani, AJ, et al. The significance of adult hematuria: 1000 hematuria evaluations including a risk, benefit, and cost effective analysis. *J Urol* 141:350–355, 1989.

53. Meyer S, Schreyer A, DeGrandi P, Hohfeld P: The effects of birth on urinary continence mechanisms and other pelvic floor characteristics. *Obstet Gynecol* 92:613–618, 1998.

54. Mouritsen L, et al: Long-term effect of pelvic floor exercises on female urinary incontinence. *Br J Urol* 68:32–37, 1991.

55. Murakima S, et al: Strategies for asymptomatic microscopic hematuria: A perspective study of 1034 patients. *J Urol* 144:99–101, 1990.

56. Ostergard DR, Bent AE (eds): *Urogynecology and Urodynamics* Baltimore, MD: William & Wilkins, 1991, pp 306–329.

57. Patel SS, Balfour JA, Bryson HM: Fosfomycin tromethamine. A review of its antibacterial activity, pharmacokinetic properties, and therapeutic efficacy as a single-dose oral treatment for acute uncomplicated lower urinary tract infections. *Drugs* 53(4):637–656, 1997.

58. Perrucchini D, DeLancey JOL: The number and diameter of female urethral muscle fibers as a product of aging. *Neurourol Urod* 16:407, 1997.

59. Resnick MM, Yalla SV: Detrusor hyperactivity with impaired contractile function: An unrecognized but common cause of incontinence in elderly patients. *JAMA* 257:3076, 1987.

60. Resnick NM, Yalla SV, et al: The pathophysiology of urinary incontinence among institutionalized elderly persons. *N Engl J Med* 320:1, 1989.

61. Rosenzweig BA, Bhatia NN, et al: Dynamic urethral pressure profilometry, pressure-transmission ratio: What do the numbers really mean? *Obstet Gynecol* 77:586–590, 1991.

62. Schmidt RA: The urethral syndrome. *Urol Clin North Am* 12:349–354, 1985.

63. Schultheiss D, Hafner K, Oelke M, Grunewald V, Jonas U: Does bone anchor fixation improve the outcome of percutaneous bladder neck suspension in female stress urinary incontinence? *Br J Urol* 82:192–195, 1998.

64. Scotti RJ, Ostergard DR: The urethral syndrome. *Clin Obstet Gynecol* 27:515–529, 1984.

65. Shull BL, Baden WF: A six-year experience with paravaginal defect repair for stress urinary incontinence. *Am J Obstet Gynecol* 160: 1432–1440, 1989.

66. Shull BL, et al: Preoperative and postoperative analysis of site-specific pelvic support defects in 81 women treated with sacrospinous ligament suspension and pelvic reconstruction. *Am J Obstet Gynecol* 166:1764–1771, 1992.

67. Smith ARB, et al: The role of partial denervation of the pelvic floor and the etiology of genitourinary prolapse and stress incontinence: A neurophysical study. *Br J Obstet Gynecol* 96:24, 1989.

68. Smith ARB, et al: The role of pudendal nerve damage in the etiology of genuine stress incontinence in women. *Br J Obstet Gynecol* 96:29, 1989.

69. Smith RF, et al: Renal insufficiency in community patients with mild asymptomatic microhematuria. *Mayo Clin Proc* 64:409–414, 1989.

70. Stamey TA, et al: The role of vaginal colonization with enterobacteriaceae in recurrent urinary infections. *J Urol* 113:214–217, 1975.

71. Stamm WE, et al: Urinary tract infections: From

pathogenesis to treatment. *J Infect Dis* 159:400–406, 1989.

72. Stapleton A, Stamm WE: Prevention of urinary tract infection. *Infect Dis Clin North Am* 11(3):719–733, 1997.

73. Stone AR: Treatment of voiding complaints and incontinence in painful bladder syndrome. *Urol Clin North Am* 18:317–325, 1991.

74. Strobehn K, Quint LE, Prince MR, Wojno KJ, De-Lancey JOL: Magnetic resonance imaging anatomy of the female urethra: A direct histologic comparison. *Obstet Gynecol* 88:750–756, 1996.

75. Summitt RL: Urethral diverticula. *Am Urogyn Soc Quarterly Rep* 11:3, 1993.

76. Summitt RL, et al: The pathophysiology of genuine stress incontinence. *Int Urogynecol J* 1:12–18, 1990.

77. Summitt RL, et al: Urinary incontinence: Correlation of history and brief office evaluation with multichannel urodynamic testing. *Am J Obstet Gynecol* 166:1835–1844, 1992.

78. Symmonds RE: Prevention and management of genitourinary fistula. *J Obstet Gynecol* 21:13–24, 1979.

79. Tancer ME: The post total hysterectomy vesicovaginal fistula. *J Urol* 123:839–840, 1980.

80. Tetzschner T, Sorenson M, Lose G, Christiansen J: Delivery and pudendal nerve function. *Int Urogynecol J Pelvic Floor Dysfunct* 8(2):66–68, 1997.

81. Van Geelen JM, et al: The clinical and urodynamic effects of anterior vaginal repair in Burch colposuspension. *Am J Obstet Gynecol* 159:137–144, 1988.

82. Videla FL, Wall LL: Stress incontinence diagnosed without multi-channel urodynamic studies. *Obstet Gynecol* 91(6):965–968, 1998.

83. Wall LL: Diagnosis and management of urinary incontinence due to detrusor instability. *Obstet Gynecol Surv* 45:15–475, 1990.

84. Wall LL: The management of detrusor instability. *Clin Obstet Gynecol* 33:367–377, 1990.

85. Wall LL: The unstable bladder. *Te Linde's Operative Gynecol Updates* 1:1–13, 1992.

86. Wall LL, Davidson TG: The role of muscular re-education by physical therapy in the treatment of genuine stress urinary incontinence. *Obstet Gynecol Surv* 47:322–331, 1992.

87. Wall LL, Wiskind AK, Taylor PA: Simple bladder filling with a cough stress test compared with subtracted cystometry with a diagnosis of urinary incontinence. *Am J Obstet Gynecol* 171(6):1472–1477, 1994.

88. Webb RJ, et al: Ambulatory monitoring and electronic measurement of urinary leakage in the diagnosis of detrusor instability and incontinence. *Br J Urol* 68:148–152, 1991.

89. Zivkovic F, Tamussino K, Haas J: Contribution of the posterior compartment to the urinary continence mechanism. *Obstet Gynecol* 91:229–233, 1998.

CHAPTER 45

Other Pelvic Floor Dysfunctions

James P. Youngblood

CYSTOCELE
PARAVAGINAL DEFECT
RECTOCELE
ENTEROCELE
UTERINE PROLAPSE
THE RELAXED INTROITUS
ANORECTAL INCONTINENCE

A ny discussion of pelvic floor dysfunction must emphasize that a careful medical history is paramount. A woman may be uncomfortable volunteering the information that she has severe leakage of urine on straining or coughing and must wear a pad, either socially or continuously when active. She also may be hesitant to volunteer that she must use digital pressure on the posterior vagina to evacuate a large rectocele. A woman is often embarrassed to relate that she has, at the worst, fecal and gas incontinence, or, at the least, severe fecal urgency. She may be hesitant to say that sexual intercourse is uncomfortable because of a protruding cervix, or that coitus is less enjoyable because of reduced sensation due to a relaxed introitus. Direct questioning is of great importance, and many of these problems and concerns will not be brought out unless the physician asks specific questions.

Almost all pelvic floor dysfunction is related to childbirth trauma, and frequently is progressive with age. A very small percentage of these problems may be congenital and/or hereditary. A brief description of each anatomical defect is presented, as well as its major symptoms, the physi-cal findings, and the possible treatment regimen(s).

Cystocele

Cystocele is a herniation of the posterior bladder into the anterior vagina. It may be minimal, moderate, or extremely large in size. By itself it seldom causes genuine stress urinary incontinence, but may contribute to it. It may be completely asymptomatic, but the large cystocele may cause an inability to empty the bladder, requiring digital pressure on the anterior vaginal wall to empty. Stasis of urine is not uncommon in the presence of a large cystocele, and this may lead to chronic or recurrent cystitis. Frequent episodes of cystitis in a patient with this anatomical problem usually are an indication for anterior colporrhaphy.

Paravaginal Defect

This defect has been well described by A. Cullen Richardson,[4] and may involve the right, left, or both anterior paravaginal sulci. If a paravaginal defect exists, the urethra will descend and rotate anteriorly when there is increased intraabdominal pressure, as may occur with severe coughing, sneezing, or straining. Genuine stress urinary incontinence may then result. Milder forms of stress urinary incontinence may be treated with pelvic floor and perineal exercises, such as Kegel's exercises. More severe stress incontinence may require surgical intervention, such as paravaginal defect repair, retropubic urethral suspension, or one of the various types of needle suspensions. Stress incontinence is more completely addressed in Chap. 44.

Rectocele

A rectocele is an outpouching of the anterior rectal wall into the posterior vagina. It, too, may be minimal, moderate, or very large. The major symptom associated with a rectocele is an inability to evacuate the contents of the rectum, even with straining. Unfortunately, hard straining causes the rectocele to become larger; the larger the rectocele becomes, the more difficult evacuation becomes—a vicious cycle. If the rectocele is very large, the patient may need to resort to using pressure with her fingers on the posterior vagina to evacuate. The fact that this maneuver must be used is rarely volunteered by the patient and must be elicited by careful questioning. The severely symptomatic rectocele requires surgical intervention with a posterior colporrhaphy.

Enterocele

An enterocele is a herniation of the peritoneum of the posterior cul-de-sac that dissects down the rectovaginal septum, often far enough to protrude through the vaginal introitus. This is a true hernia, lined by peritoneum, and often containing small bowel. A smaller enterocele may be asymptomatic and also difficult to detect. Frequently, it is detected only at the time a patient is having a posterior colporrhaphy. A large enterocele may be difficult to distinguish from a rectocele, but careful rectovaginal examination while the patient is straining may reveal its existence. Incarceration or strangulation of bowel is seldom encountered with an enterocele, but its existence almost always requires surgical intervention.

Uterine Prolapse

The cause of uterine prolapse is still not clearly and completely understood, but certainly has to do with childbirth trauma, which relaxes the cardinal and uterosacral ligaments, allowing descent of the uterus. Aging and atrophy contribute to the problem, and therefore it may progress with age. Symptoms with a milder prolapse may be minimal, but the patient with significant prolapse who is still menstruating may have a wide range of complaints. These may include low-back pain, both premenstrually and during menstruation, as well as dysmenorrhea and dyspareunia. Uterine prolapse is usually described as first degree when the cervix descends nearly to the introitus; second degree when the cervix descends and protrudes through the introitus; and third degree, or total procidentia, when there is a complete evagination of the cervix and uterus. Frequently, procidentia afflicts the elderly and, in the nursing home setting, becomes a very serious care problem.

Symptomatic uterine prolapse may be treated simply with the placement of a pessary. The author has had the greatest degree of success with the use of a simple ring pessary, which is fitted to the individual patient. However, especially in the elderly, this requires an intact perineum to retain the pessary. A pessary is most satisfactory when the patient is able to care for it herself by removing, cleaning, and replacing it. If necessary, periodic visits to the gynecologist will accomplish the same thing. The patient should be routinely examined within 2 or 3 days of initial placement to make certain that the pessary has not caused vaginal ulceration or other problems, and she should be examined regularly thereafter. In addition to the simple ring, a wide variety of other types of pessaries can be used; these should be suited to the individual anatomic requirements.

For the patient who is in appropriate medical condition for a surgical procedure, vaginal hysterectomy and careful culdoplasty usually are indicated for the severely symptomatic uterine prolapse. In the very elderly, poor-risk patient with procidentia who is unable to retain a pessary, a Le Fort colpocleisis under local anesthesia may still be an option.

The Relaxed Introitus

Sexual dysfunction is a frequent complaint with this finding. Counseling alone may obviate the problem; however, surgical intervention may be indicated in a patient who is having an unsatisfactory sexual experience because of excessive vaginal introitus relaxation. Generally speaking, a carefully done perineorrhaphy will alleviate the problem. It should be emphasized, however, that this procedure probably should not be done in the relatively satisfied patient, as many women with what appears anatomically to be an extremely relaxed introitus will have a very satisfactory sexual relationship.

Anorectal Incontinence

Often in a multiparous woman, a history of fecal or gas incontinence may be elicited. Incontinence may result from sphincter damage or nerve injury, or both. Risk factors for these injuries can be identified. Clinical evaluation, anorectal physiology, and endoanal ultrasonography allow accurate planning of subsequent surgery.[1] Not so often recognized is fecal urgency, which may occur in up to one-third of multiparas who have not experienced obvious birth injury.

Usually, chronic anal sphincter separation is readily obvious, but not so obvious may be a small rectovaginal or rectoperineal fistula. These problems require surgical intervention.

Recent literature indicates that fecal urgency is a much more common problem than previously recognized. Often physical therapy and/or other bowel training are necessary to alleviate these symptoms. Fortunately, considerable research is ongoing regarding the dysfunctions of the poste-rior compartment of the female pelvis, and it is hoped that effective therapies will continue to evolve.

Any or all of these pelvic floor defects may occur singly or in combination with any other. It is not uncommon for them all to be present in the same patient, requiring a total vaginal hysterectomy, careful culdoplasty, anterior and posterior colporrhaphy and perineorrhaphy, as well as a retropubic, paravaginal, or periurethral operation. Again, it must be emphasized that careful history and physical examination are of paramount importance in restoring pelvic floor anatomy. This will enable the physician to determine the type and extent of the defect(s) so that the ideal surgical repair can be performed to address the individual woman's problem.

References and Selected Readings

1. Cook TA, Mortensen NJ: Management of faecal incontinence following obstetric injury. *Brit J Surg* 85:293–299, 1998.
2. Crawford LA, Quint EH, Pearl ML, DeLancey JOL: Incontinence following rupture of the anal sphincter during delivery. *Obstet Gynecol* 82(4):527–531, 1993.
3. DeLancey JOL: Functional anatomy of the female lower urinary tract and pelvic floor [review]. *Ciba Found Symp* 151:57–69, 1990.
4. Madoff RD, Williams JG, Caushaj PF: Fecal incontinence: Review article, current concepts. *N Engl J Med* 326(15):1002–1007, 1992.
5. Richardson AC, Edmonds PB, Williams NL: Treatment of stress urinary incontinence due to paravaginal fascial defect. *Obstet Gynecol* 57(3):357–363, 1981.
6. Shull BL: Clinical evaluation of women with pelvic support defects. *Clin Obstet Gynecol* 36(4):939–951, 1993.
7. Sultan AH, Kamm MA, Hudson CN, et al: Anal sphincter disruption during vaginal delivery. *N Engl J Med* 329(26):1905–1911, 1993.

Sexuality

Julia R. Heiman
Gretchen M. Lentz

T he role of sexuality in women's lives has been addressed only as a peripheral topic in health care, with the exception of managing sexually transmitted diseases and contraception. This estrangement from sexual behavior and its determinants was not as problematic for busy physicians and their patients until the last decade when several factors became obvious. First, HIV/AIDS would be prevented only by sexual behavior change, and the cheapest, most reliable prevention method, other than abstinence, is still the *male* condom. These factors forced healthy sexual behavior to be redefined and understood in a psychosocial context that took gender roles into account as major influences in determining sexual practices.[1,2] Second, the exponential increase in available medications combined with an aging population has resulted in health practitioners prescribing more medications, many of which negatively impact sexual functioning.[3] Thus, many sexual health problems are iatrogenically caused by well-intentioned physicians. Third, the post-World War II cohort of baby boomers is aging in comparably good health, is active in health care decisions, and is invested in a good quality of life that includes at least middle-aged sexual capabilities. And fourth, medicine is changing with primary care taking on a more central role in assisting patients with quality of life issues.

Physicians and other health care professionals typically have not been well trained to deal with sexuality issues, and as a result may ignore the topic entirely, lack basic knowledge for patients, or make unproductive suggestions that prove unhelpful. This chapter provides information about the basic aspects of women's sexuality, and offers guidelines for current assessment and treatment strategies for common sexual problems that women face throughout their lifetimes.

Sexual Development and Sexuality during Different Life Stages

Biological and psychosocial influences interact throughout sexual development and changes in human sexuality. One researcher has identified three separate but interacting "threads" of sexual development: sexual differentiation in male or female and gender identity, sexual responsiveness, and the capacity for close dyadic relationships.[4] This chapter focuses on sexual responsiveness and treatment for sexual relationship problems with only brief attention to gender/sexual identity and dyadic relationship problems.[5-8]

Prenatal through Childhood

Sexual development begins prenatally when the fetus begins the process of differentiating into male or female. Even at this level, there is an interaction between biological (genetic, neuroendocrinological) and environmental factors, the environment being the mother's psychophysiological condition, especially during sensitive periods for sexual development.

Multiple factors appear to influence sexual orientation. There has been interest and some evidence of genetic influences in the development of same-sex preferences, though most of the work has been with gay men. The Xq28 gene locus of the X chromosome has 83 percent concordance in gay brothers (22 percent concordance in gay-heterosexual brothers).[9] Based on far fewer studies, the current consensus for women is that environment plays a stronger role in the development of female than male homosexuality. Bailey et al. used a national registry to identify 1912 female twins between 17 and 50 years of age. While the rates of lesbianism were higher in the twins of lesbians, there was no difference between identical and fraternal twins, suggesting that genes were not a differentiating factor.[10]

Sexual behavior, usually in the form of sex play or masturbation, appears to be common in childhood.[11] Normative frequencies of sex play are difficult to document, and research relies on parental or adult retrospective accounts for estimates. All of the data we cite are from the United States unless otherwise specified. It is normal for children to be curious about their own or others' bodies, and they may engage in observable sexual behaviors, particularly when they are under age 6. As children grow older and are socialized into

the cultural emphasis on privacy and sexual inhibition in social situations, observable sexual behavior decreases.[6,11] The prevalence of sex play is probably quite high. For example, college females were surveyed and asked to recall normal childhood sexual experiences.[12] Most of the women (85 percent) reported a childhood sexual game experience, 44 percent reported cross-gender play, and 56 percent recalled same-gender play, usually with someone their own age. On average, the experience occurred between ages 7 and 8 with 43 percent stating that the experience caused sexual excitement. Another retrospective study of college-aged men and women found that 59 percent recalled sexual contact before age 13, which consisted of primarily exposure of one's own body, looking at someone else's body, and genital or nongenital fondling.[115] Although sexually abused children have been reported to display more sexualized behaviors than nonabused peers, the difference appears to be one of intensity and frequency, not behavioral incidence.[13] Genital self-stimulation begins before the end of a child's first year and by the age of 10, far fewer girls than boys have masturbated,[14] though there are scant recent data on this topic.

Childhood sex play, as distinct from childhood sexual abuse, may have very little bearing on later adjustment, including sexual attitudes, self acceptance, relationships with peers and parents, antisocial behavior, drug use, pregnancy, and sexually transmitted disease (STD) rates. An 18-year longitudinal project found no significant associations between childhood sex play and these variables.[15] In the same study, 77 percent reported that their child (n = 96 boys, 88 girls) had engaged in sex play before age 6.

Adolescence

Gender identity and sexual preferences begin to solidify as puberty begins[17-20] and sexuality, whether it is acted upon or not, becomes more prominent in the adolescence peer subculture. The likelihood of a girl being interested in sex at puberty may depend on her hormonal status, but the likelihood of her actually engaging in sexual activity with a partner is more related to her peer group.[16]

Adolescence presents challenges for girls in terms of body changes and social pressures to fit in with a group or subgroup. Active struggles with body image may stimulate dieting, and eating disorders can be the result. Although girls usually are sexually active later than boys, the majority of teenagers have had sexual intercourse by the time they are out of high school (18 years old). Based upon data for women who were born between 1962 and 1964, the percentage of women who were sexually active at age 14 was under 10 percent, while the percentage sexually active at age 17 was 35 to 40 percent for Caucasian women and 50 to 60 percent for African-American women.[21] These figures are higher than those for earlier cohorts, and need to be updated periodically given cultural shifts. Wyatt's community sample of African-American and Caucasian women between ages 18 and 36 found that education was a major factor in delaying first coitus.[22] If education was held constant, ethnicity was not the strongest predictor of first coitus (mean age 16.7 for African-Americans, 17.2 for Caucasian), but perceiving parents as more influential than peers and being in love and ready for sex predicted older age at first coitus.[22] It is clear that sexual activity may be occurring in young teens, and the possibility of pregnancy or STDs must be addressed at quite early ages for preventive health care.

Menstrual Cycle

Across the menstrual cycle, women's sexual desire is quite variable, and the cycle can affect sexuality. Adams and Gold[23] demonstrated an increased frequency of female-initiated sexual behavior at midcycle in normal women, although no endocrine markers of cycle phase were used. When Bancroft et al. used repeated hormonal assays to control cycle phase and control for mood and energy self-ratings, they found a sexual activity pattern across 55 women with a peak at midfollicular (or postmenstrual) and smaller peak at midluteal (premenstrual) phases.[24]

Pregnancy and Postpartum

For some couples, pregnancy is a time during which coitus is avoided due to fear of harming the baby or female self-perception of unattractiveness. Some studies report a progressive decline in desire, frequency of intercourse, and response through the pregnancy.[25-27] Retrospective data by Naeye[28,29] suggested that coitus could induce preterm births. However, later studies failed to show a harmful effect of coitus on pregnancy outcome.[30,31] Kurki and Ylikorkala[32] reported that vaginal intercourse in pregnancy was not related to bacterial vaginosis and did not predispose women to preterm birth. Thus, though there are certain obstetrical conditions where coitus should be avoided (placenta previa, abruptio placenta, premature labor and premature rupture of membranes), health practitioners can generally relieve patients' anxieties about the safety of maintaining sexual activities with their partners during pregnancy.

Postpartum sexuality and sexual problems have been studied infrequently. Clinical experience shows women often experience problems within the first 6 weeks after delivery, but it is less commonly recognized that these problems may continue long beyond the early postpartum recovery period. Women are often counseled about the safety of resuming sexual intercourse six weeks postpartum, but are not prepared for the potential physical problems, such as dyspareunia, that may occur. Furthermore, little is known about how the demands of being a new mother affect sexual desire and response.

A 1993 survey in England showed that 25 percent of the women surveyed indicated that more than six weeks was necessary for their perineum to feel "normal" again.[33] In this same study, 17 percent of over 2000 women surveyed had difficulty with sexual intercourse at 6 weeks postpartum.[33] A 1997 questionnaire by Glazener contacted 1391 postpartum women from a general obstetric clinic with a 90 percent response rate (1249 women).[35,36] The median time to restarting sexual intercourse was 6 weeks (range 1 to 60) and 53 percent had problems in the first 8 weeks. The problems women cited included perineal soreness (28.1 percent), excessive fatigue (20.7 percent) and disinterest in sex (8.7 percent), with some women reporting more than one problem. Of the 49 percent of women who had problems in the 12 to 18 months after delivery, the most common were perineal pain (19.7 percent), tiredness (35.9 percent), and lack of sexual interest (21.4 percent). It is important to acknowledge that postpartum sexual problems are quite common and can last much longer than previously recognized. One of the problems with all of these studies is that data were not collected pre-pregnancy on rates of dyspareunia or lack of interest in sex.

Glazener's survey also showed that women who breast-fed their babies were significantly less interested in intercourse than those who bottle-fed.[36] Glazener hypothesized that the hyperprolactinemia of breast feeding combined with amenorrhea and decreased estrogen, progesterone, and androgen levels might be involved in the decreased sexual interest. Alder et al. showed that breast-feeding women in comparison to bottle-feeding women, had significantly lower levels of androstendione and testosterone.[37] However, well-controlled studies have not been performed to sort out loss of interest in sexual relations from mood changes, hormone levels, tiredness, and body image changes postpartum. Furthermore, little is known about possible partner issues with sexuality after childbirth. Partner issues include fatigue, fear of harming the woman or causing pain with intercourse, cultural or religious issues, or jealousy towards the baby.

On the other end of the spectrum, 56.8 percent of 812 patients had no problems with intercourse by 8 weeks post delivery.[36] A recent study, which followed patients and their partners longitudinally, reported 89 percent of 570 women had resumed intercourse by 4 months postpartum.[27] It appears from the literature that most couples have resumed intercourse by 12 weeks postpartum, although at a lower frequency than before birth.[38]

Health practitioners could be helpful by being alert to these issues, educating patients antenatally, and advising patients. This remains an issue for physicians; Glazener's[36] survey found that doctors discussed postpartum contraception 76 percent of the time, but postpartum intercourse only 34 percent of the time. Due to the high frequency of postpartum sexual function problems, health providers should routinely add sexual health discussion to the postpartum visit.

Menopause

Many factors contribute to sexual changes during a woman's 40s and 50s. A decrease in sexual activity is the typical pattern, often with some change in sexual desire. This is driven by a number of factors. Aging is associated with the slowing of sexual response and decreases in the intensity of response.[39] For example, a random sample of 436 women in the United Kingdom found that advancing age was inversely associated with intercourse frequency, orgasmic frequency, and the enjoyment of sexual activity.[40] Sexual enjoyment also decreased with the duration of the relationship and with the partner's increasing age. A complete lack of orgasm in the past 3 months was reported in 5 percent of the 35- to 39-year-olds and 35 percent of the 55- to 59-year-olds.

Decreasing responsiveness, as indicated by slower arousal and less intense and less frequent orgasms, may be reversible if it is caused by reduction in functioning of genital smooth muscle tissue. There is now an oral medication (sildenafil citrate, Viagra) for men that improves smooth muscle erectile functioning through the selective inhibition of cyclic-GMP (guanosine monophosphate) catabolism in cavernosal smooth-muscle cells.[41] Because women have similar tissue, the usefulness of sildenafil for female sexual dysfunction has been hypothesized.[42] Along with other vasodilators that have been shown to be successful for male genital response, sildenafil is currently undergoing clinical trials with women. The predominant focus is on the postmenopausal woman.

Aging is also a psychosocial issue, and middle-aged women often report feeling less desirable. In addition, a menopausal woman's partner is usually middle-aged as well and may suffer from sexual problems or be absorbed in his own aging issues. For both individuals in the couple, multiple changes in roles are occurring over these years, particularly around family life and work, requiring multiple adjustments and a different sense of future. Sexuality may be a lower priority. If both individuals within the couple agree to this, there is no particular problem. Difficulties arise when one person is wanting more of a sexual relationship and their partner is no longer interested in sex and only pursuing help for the partner's sake.

What are the hormonal changes to accompany menopause and what are their consequences to sexual functioning?

- Estrogen decreases result in decreased vaginal lubrication, a thinner, less elastic vaginal lining, and atrophic vaginitis in postmenopausal women, potentially causing coital pain and subsequent loss of desire.[43]
- Very low levels of estrogen may be associated with depressive symptoms and indirectly affect sexual desire and well-being.[44]
- Administering estrogen does not necessarily increase sexual desire or activity but does improve vaginal lubrication and atrophic conditions, and in some women depressive symptoms (along with other nonsexual symptoms such as hot flashes, headaches, insomnia, and possibly certain types of memory losses).[45]
- More consistently sexually active women, through masturbation or partner sex, have less vaginal atrophy even if not taking hormone replacement therapy.[43]
- Androgens have been shown to increase desire and pleasure for masturbation but not necessarily for coitus or for orgasm during coitus.[46,47]

Hormone replacement therapy (HRT) improves a variety of symptoms for women, which contributes to a feeling of well-being, which in turn contributes indirectly to interest in sex. Similarly, the loss of sexual desire caused by oophorectomy in premenopausal women may be restored with testosterone or testosterone-estrogen combinations.[47,48] The safety issues of estrogens are addressed elsewhere, but key concerns for women are abnormal vaginal bleeding and endometrial cancer, and the fear of developing breast cancer.

Many selective estrogen-receptor modulating (SERM) drugs are in development and coming to market. Raloxifene was the first to be marketed, and is approved for the prevention of osteoporosis. At the time this chapter was written, there were no published data on raloxifene's effects on mood or sexual desire. However, the adverse event data from trials on osteoporosis showed no change from placebo on depression or vaginitis.

Androgens have a more direct effect on sexual desire and arousal and also improve the overall sense of well-being.[45,48,114] However, the most important issue is the long-term health effects of taking androgens, particularly in terms of how they impact the cardiovascular system. To date there are no well-controlled studies on this point. The use of androgens may also be questionable in cases in which a woman has had an estrogen-dependent tumor.

Dehydroepiandrosterone (DHEA) and dehydroepiandrosterone sulfate (DHEAS) are the most abundant steroids in the body; they are primarily from the adrenal gland. DHEA levels peak in the reproductive years and gradually fall with age. It is not clear whether the age-related decrease in DHEA (termed "adrenopause") is just a manifestation of aging or if it represents an endocrine deficiency state like menopause. It had been suggested that DHEA replacement might possibly have positive effects on the cardiovascular system, cognition, weight control, immune function, osteoporosis, diabetes, and even cancer prevention.[49] Unfortunately, evidence of long-term efficacy is lacking, and the FDA has no approved indications for DHEA.

Some clinical studies have been done evaluating DHEA and its biological impact. Mortola[50] gave 12 obese postmenopausal women DHEA over a 1-month period. No beneficial effects were seen, and the women became androgenized on a dose of 1600 mg/day. Morales[51] studied 30 men and women and evaluated sexual function. Fifty mg/day of DHEA or placebo was given in a double-blinded crossover fashion. No change in libido was seen, although 84 percent of the women reported an increased sense of well-being. There were no androgenizing side effects, but HDL levels did decline slightly.

Hysterectomy

There is controversy regarding the impact of hysterectomy, particularly the role of the cervix, on sexual response.[52-56] It is possible that decreased total vasocongestion and lack of uterine contractions with orgasm could alter the sexual response. Furthermore, the role of the nervous system in female sexual response is very poorly described and might be affected by pelvic surgery. Radical hysterectomy for cervical cancer treatment can result in bowel and bladder dysfunction, probably from disruption of autonomic nerve supply. Unfortunately, there is no information on nerve injury and sexual response.

A 1993 study compared women in their mid-50s with and without hysterectomy in regard to sexual function. The 97 women with hysterectomy had more sexual satisfaction, and 22 percent complained of a sexual problem. Of the 249 without a hysterectomy, 34 percent reported a sexual problem.[52] A Finnish study prospectively studied supracervical hysterectomy (cervix left in situ) versus total abdominal hysterectomy (cervix removal) and followed the patients for one year after surgery. Diminished or absent libido was reported preoperatively by 26.4 percent of supracervical hysterectomy patients and 28 percent of total abdominal hysterectomy patients, and postoperatively in 31.4 percent and 35.4 percent, re-

spectively.[54] This was not statistically significant. The frequency of orgasms was similar in the two groups preoperatively, but postoperatively the total abdominal hysterectomy group had a significant decrease in frequency of orgasms, while the supracervical hysterectomy group had no change. Coital frequency did not change in either group.[55] Dyspareunia was relieved significantly in both groups, but even more so in the supracervical hysterectomy group (28.6 percent preoperatively to 6.3 percent postoperatively) compared to the total abdominal hysterectomy group (30.8 percent to 15.6 percent respectively).[55] Others have refuted any benefit to retaining the cervix for a woman having a hysterectomy; in addition, one must consider the risk of cancer in the cervical stump. Emotional sequelae and depression have also been reported posthysterectomy, primarily related to issues of a lost body part, lost ability to reproduce, and perceived sexuality changes.[56]

Sexual History, Evaluation, and Physical Exam

A general medical history and detailed gynecologic history are important for proper evaluation of sexual problems (see Table 46-1). Current and past medical problems of related concern include diabetes mellitus, neurological conditions (such as multiple sclerosis) and/or injuries, and endocrine disorders (such as hyper or hypothyroidism, hyperprolactinemia, and adrenal disorders). Urinary incontinence, especially incontinence with intercourse, can be extremely embarrassing for women and can affect sexual activity. Psychiatric disorders and conditions that may be associated with sexual dysfunction include depression, anxiety, stress, chronic fatigue, alcohol abuse, or other recreational drug abuse. Interpersonal factors include child/adult sexual and physical abuse, relationship issues, and partner health and sexual functioning. Surgical history, including hysterectomy, other pelvic surgery (particularly surgery for cancer), and surgical trauma, can im-

TABLE 46-1   Sexual Function History: Key Factors

General health

Endocrine: diabetes mellitus, adrenal disorders, hyper- or hypothyroidism

Neurologic: spinal cord injury, multiple sclerosis, Parkinson's disease, head injury, stroke, psychomotor epilepsy

Cardiovascular: cardiac disease, vasculopathy

Surgical: vulvectomy, female circumcision

Degenerative: arthritis, COPD, advanced stages of cancer

Psychiatric disorders

Depression

Anxiety

Bipolar—manic-depressive

Psychological and interpersonal factors

Past sexual trauma, relationship issues, partner problems

Hormonal status

Menopause

Prescription drugs

Tricyclic antidepressants, selective serotonin reuptake inhibitors, MAOIs, antihypertensives, benzodiazepines, neuroleptics

Recreational drugs

Alcohol, marijuana, cocaine, heroin, barbiturates

---

pact sexuality. Vulvar surgery, such as radical vulvectomy, vulvar wide excision, or female circumcision, results in a 2 to 3 times greater incidence of sexual dysfunction. Gynecologic history taking should include questions covering the life span experiences that affect sexuality including menstruation, pregnancy, postpartum, aging, and menopause. Pregnancy causes obvious body changes, and aging and menopause can create difficult psychosocial issues in terms of a women's self-image and views of sexuality.

Many medications are known to affect sexual function. They can affect desire and arousal, or delay or inhibit orgasm. Frequent medications taken by women include tricyclic antidepressants, monoamine oxidase inhibitors, selective serotonin reuptake inhibitors, antihypertensives, diuretics, benzodiazepines, and neuroleptics; all have been reported to adversely affect sexual function. Oral contraceptives may impact sexual desire.[57–60] Questions about nonprescription medications should be asked, including about use of dehydroepiandrosterone (DHEA), anabolic steroids, and herbal treatments.

History taking in women complaining of sexual dysfunction involving pain requires specific detailed attention. A 1989 study from a gynecologic clinic found that dyspareunia was the most common sexual complaint.[61] Long-term pain problems and diffuse symptoms are more difficult to treat because there are often coexistent or secondary psychosocial issues, and usually prior evaluations and treatments have been unsuccessful. However, a comprehensive history, systematic physical exam, directed diagnostic tests, and psychological evaluation may lead to beneficial therapy.

A complete history of the pain includes timing, location, severity, quality, onset, and association with bodily functions. Timing of the pain can be with clitoral stimulation, penetration at the introitus, with penile thrusting, during orgasm, or after intercourse. Pain sites can include the clitoris, vulva or vulvar vestibule, vagina, cervix and uterus, bladder, rectum, or deep within the pelvis, and should all be checked during the physical examination. Most of the time patients have difficulty localizing the painful areas, except to specify introital pain versus deep pelvic pain. Questions about onset of pain include onset prior to first coitus, postpartum, after a surgical procedure, with a new partner, or with an associated life event, such as menopause, cancer therapy, or psychological problems.

Endometriosis is defined as the presence of endometrial-type stroma and glands outside the endometrial cavity or myometrium. It affects 7 to 10 percent of the premenopausal population. Dyspareunia, dysmenorrhea, and abnormal uterine bleeding are the most frequent symptoms. The pain is usually described as deep pelvic pain.

Vaginal discharge, itching, burning, or irritation may indicate a vaginal or urinary tract infection. Urinary and gastrointestinal symptoms should be screened for because interstitial cystitis, urethral syndrome, inflammatory bowel conditions, and irritable bowel syndrome are often overlooked as potential causes of pain with intercourse. Women with vaginismus often have pain, or fear of pain, with both pelvic exam and coitus. They may give a history of difficulty or pain with inserting a tampon or using vaginal medications.

Urogenital atrophy or atrophic vaginitis is a condition that occurs during or after the menopause from declining estrogen levels, and results in vaginal and/or urinary tract symptoms. Vaginal atrophy eventually affects most postmenopausal women not using estrogen replacement therapy.[62–64] Many postmenopausal women experience vaginal dryness and lack of adequate lubrication with sexual activity that lead to discomfort with intercourse. Other symptoms may include vaginal burning, itching, irritation, or bleeding, as well as urinary urgency and frequency. Vaginal atrophy can also result from pelvic radiation, lactation, antiestrogen therapy, or extreme athletic conditioning. It is often difficult to assess the role of the menopause, hormone depletion, and hormone replacement in female sexual dysfunction. Part of the reason is that many factors are responsible for sexuality and purely age-related changes in sexuality may be attributed to hormonal changes at the menopause.

A careful physical exam can often help identify the etiology of pain. Abdominal exam may reveal tenderness suggesting an intraabdominal process needing evaluation. A pelvic exam starts with careful inspection of the vulva (Table 46-2). Perineal scarring might result from an episiotomy or other surgical procedures, and may be tender. The vulvar vestibule may be erythematous or have small erythematous macules. Q-tip touching of this area of the vestibule may elicit exquisite tenderness, while the surrounding vulva and inner vagina are unaffected suggesting vulvar vestibulitis. A fistulous tract in the perineum or vagina may occasionally be discovered and be tender on exam. Vaginal scarring or stenosis may be found, and may be the result of anterior and posterior colporrhaphy, radiation, or severe infection after vaginal surgery. Vaginal infections

TABLE 46-2 Gynecologic Examination

Perineal scarring or tenderness

Vulvar vestibule erythema or tenderness with Q-tip touch

Vaginal stenosis or scarring

Vaginal atrophy

Vaginal or cervical discharge

Pelvic floor muscle tension

Cervical motion tenderness

Bimanual exam findings of pelvic mass, tenderness, or uterosacral ligament nodularity

can readily be diagnosed on examination, and wet mount should be performed in evaluating women with sexual pain disorders.

Vaginal atrophy is readily diagnosed by simple inspection and the observing of decreased vaginal rugation, vaginal dryness, and pale mucosa, sometimes with petechiae and friability. A vaginal pH may be elevated above 5.0, and a vaginal smear for cytologic maturation index may reveal few superficial cells and an abundance of parabasal/basal cells.

Cervical evaluation for discharge and cervical motion tenderness and bimanual exam will assess for common clinical problems that might contribute to sexual pain disorders, including endometriosis, pelvic inflammatory disease, and pelvic masses. An ultrasound should be performed if there is unexplained pelvic pain or a pelvic mass. Pelvic relaxation can be visualized with a split speculum inspection of the vagina when asking the patient to perform the Valsalva maneuver. Pelvic floor muscle tenderness or tension can be assessed by palpation.

Women with a history of physical trauma such as a prior pelvic fracture; difficult childbirth related to a large baby, shoulder dystocia, forceps, or vacuum extraction; neurologic disease; or complaint of lack of sensation in the genital area, require a thorough neurologic exam. Beyond the standard neurologic exam, careful light touch and pinprick evaluation of the sacral dermatomes 2 to 4 can evaluate sensation. The bulbocavernosus and anal wink reflexes can be elicited. Muscle bulk of the levator ani muscle complex can reveal potential denervation injury with loss of muscle bulk and function. Pudendal nerve injuries have been documented postpartum and postpelvic surgery, although correlation with sexual function has not been evaluated.

The physical exam itself can be instructive in the treatment of some sexual pain disorders, particularly vaginismus. This is one opportunity to show the patient that examination does not have to be uncomfortable, and that she may control the degree of discomfort by stopping the examination. Speculum size adjustment and pace of the examination may need to be altered for patient comfort. Several different exam sessions may be necessary. Attempts at vaginal examination with a single digit usually reveal involuntary muscle spasm, patient discomfort with pressure on the perineal or pubococcygeus muscles, and, in severe cases, involvement of thigh adductors, rectus abdominis, and gluteal muscles.

Sexual and Physical Interpersonal Trauma

The estimated prevalence of sexual and physical trauma histories is quite high. Among U.S. women, estimates vary from 15 to 62 percent for sexually coerced experiences prior to age 18.[66-68] Approximately 1 of 5 women have experienced a completed rape.[69,70] Although there is no unitary sexual abuse "syndrome," when women with and without histories of these traumas are compared, childhood-adolescent abuse has been shown to be associated with a variety of adult physical complaints, psychiatric problems, and sexual and relationship difficulties.[71,72] The effect of sexual abuse on a woman's sexuality varies, but usually impacts at least 50 percent of the survivors by either more sexual experience with more partners, more STDs, and earlier consensual intercourse, or problems with sexual desire, pain during sex, or responsiveness.[71,73] Similarly, an experience of rape is usually accompanied by a variety of symptoms in the short term and the possibility of longer-term sexual and interpersonal problems in a subgroup of women. The response to rape as an adult appears to depend on a variety of premorbid social and psychological factors in addition to the actual characteristics of the rape in terms of severity and context. Careful attention to a history of physical or sexual abuse is needed to provide adequate care, especially if the woman also presents with multiple medical and/or pain complaints. The usual question to ask is whether a patient ever experienced unwanted or forced sexual contact.

Disability or Chronic Illness and Sexuality

While sexual counseling of individuals with a physical disability or chronic illness is based on the same concepts and treatment approaches as for other women, the clinician needs to understand the disability or chronic illness and what it means to the woman. Obtaining the general history is the same as previously described. In addition, specific questions should be asked regarding the impact of the disability or illness on sexual function. Lefebvre[74] describes "bridge statements," or questions that help ease into sensitive topics for discussion:

- Has anyone talked to you about how your injury [illness] can affect your ability to have sex [or a sexual relationship]?
- Since your injury [illness], has your relationship with your significant other changed? Has there been any change in your physical relationship?
- How has your injury [illness] changed the kinds of things you and your significant other do together? Does he treat you any differently now? How has your sexual relationship been affected?
- How has your libido changed? How has it affected the way you feel sexually about your partner?

More specific topics can then be addressed after the provider and patient have established good rapport. Issues to discuss might include timing of sexual activity, preparation for sexual activity, stimulation for arousal and lubrication, expansion of sexual repertoire, medication timing and management, contraception, and precautions to prevent injury.[76]

Lesbian Health

Estimates of the incidence of female homosexuality approximate 2 to 5 percent of the general population.[75] Controversy exists regarding whether lesbians face unique health care problems. Looking at the World Health Organization's definition of health—"a state of complete physical, mental, emotional, and social well-being, and not merely the absence of disease or infirmity"—it is reasonable to argue in favor of acknowledging some different health issues for lesbian women than for heterosexual women. Emotional and social well-being are central issues in a predominantly heterosexual and sometimes homophobic society.

Although most of the physical health problems are the same as those of heterosexual women,[81] the lesbian's interactions with the health care system may be different, with possible health consequences for her. Eighty-four percent of lesbians surveyed had experienced a general reluctance to seek health care.[77] One study showed the average time between Pap smears was 8 months for heterosexual women and 21 months for lesbians.[78] Another study found that bisexual women were more likely than lesbians to have yearly Papanicolaou smears (70.2 percent vs. 55.6 percent).[79] A 1985 survey found that 58 percent of lesbians sought gynecologic care only if symptomatic.[80] One factor that might influence health care utilization is concern about physicians' attitudes toward homosexuality. Johnson et al.[81] found that 40 percent of homosexual women surveyed thought their health care would be adversely affected if their physician knew they were homosexual. In contrast to the work cited above, Johnson's well-educated group did seek routine care.

Two studies mentioned concerns about higher rates of alcohol dependency among lesbians.[81,82] However, these reports did not address incidence. Rough estimates cite the incidence of alcoholism to be 25 to 35 percent among lesbians, which is five to seven times that of heterosexual women.[83,84]

In terms of gynecological health, lesbians actually have lower rates of several diseases. Sexually transmitted diseases, including gonorrhea, syphilis, chlamydia, and pelvic inflammatory disease are less common in lesbians.[79]

In Johnson's questionnaire, there were no differences in past oral contraceptive use, endometriosis, menstrual dysfunction, or breast disease.[79] Abnormal Papanicolaou smears were present in 2.9 percent of the women in one study,[79] and a squamous intraepithelial lesion (SIL) rate of 2.7 percent was found in a study of 148 lesbians.[85] While an exact comparison group of heterosexual women is not available, a study of 382,660 women showed an abnormal Papanicolaou rate of 6 percent overall. Within that group, there was a 3.4 percent incidence of a squamous intraepithelial lesion or worse.[117] Estimates that 80 percent of lesbians had heterosexual intercourse in the past indicates they are at risk for dysplasia and need appropriate screening.[82]

One survey found the incidence of sexual dysfunction in lesbians to be 23 percent.[81] One study of married heterosexual couples found 63 percent of the women reported sexual dysfunction.[86] While the exact prevalence of sexual dysfunction among lesbians is not known, the data available indicate the incidence may be lower than among married heterosexual couples.[81,86] The approach to treating sexual dysfunctions among lesbians is, in general, similar to heterosexual women providing that the clinician is comfortable, appropriately trained, and attentive to differences in sexual patterns.

Sexual Dysfunctions: Diagnosis and Treatment

Sexual dysfunctions are frequently reported by women across the life span. A·random sample in the early 1990s by Laumann et al. reported on the sexual behavior and satisfaction of 1,622 U.S. women between the ages of 18 and 59.[75] These women were 75 percent Caucasian, 12 percent African-American, and 7 to 9 percent Hispanic, with a range of educational, economic, and religious backgrounds. The most common sexual problem women reported was lack of sexual interest, which was reported by 33 percent of those surveyed. The next most frequently reported sexual problems, all defined as problems experienced for several months or more during the prior year, were orgasmic inability (24 percent), sex not pleasurable (21 percent), inadequate lubrication (19 percent), and pain during sex (14 percent).

Clinic-based data show higher frequencies of dysfunctions. In an outpatient gynecologic clinic, a sample of 329 healthy, 18- to 73-year-old women being followed for routine care, reported orgasmic problems (58 percent), frequent intercourse pain (18 percent), and anxiety or inhibition during sex (38 percent).[87] Of interest, in spite of the high incidence of specific sexual dysfunctions, 68 percent of the entire sample reported being relatively satisfied with the overall sexual relationship.

The current official system for diagnosing sexual dysfunctions is the American Psychiatric Association's (APA) *Diagnostic and Statistical Manual of Mental Disorders,* 4th ed. (DSM-IV).[88] It provides a framework for classifying sexual dysfunctions that is individually and physically symptom-based rather than interpersonally based, making it easier for communication with medical specialties but omitting a great deal of information. Table 46-3 summarizes the dysfunctions based on DSM-IV criteria. For all of the categories of sexual dysfunction (desire, arousal, orgasm, pain), it is important to first clarify

TABLE 46-3   Female Sexual Dysfunctions

Sexual desire disorders

  Hypoactive sexual desire disorder: persistent or recurrent absence or deficit of sexual fantasies and desire for sexual activity; take into account factors that affect sexual functioning such as age, sex, life context; rule out other psychiatric disorders such as major depression, anxiety.

  Sexual aversion disorder: persistent or recurrent aversion to and avoidance of genital contact with a sexual partner; rule out other psychiatric disorders such as major depression, anxiety, or obsessive-compulsive disorder.

Sexual arousal disorder

  Partial or total lack of physical response as indicated by lack of lubrication and vasocongestion of genitals.

  Persistent lack of subjective sense of sexual excitement and pleasure during sex (this criterion is omitted from DSM-IV, but it is important for clarification).

Orgasmic disorder

  Persistent delay or absence of orgasm. Lack of coital orgasm is usually considered a normal variation of female sexual response if the woman is able to experience orgasm with a partner using other, noncoital methods. Take sexual experience into account.

Sexual pain disorders

  Dyspareunia: recurrent genital pain before, during, or after intercourse; rule out physical disorder, vaginismus, and lack of lubrication.

  Vaginismus: recurrent involuntary spasm of the outer third of the vagina interfering with or preventing coitus; rule out physical disorder or other psychiatric disorder (rare).

Sexual dysfunctions not otherwise specified

  Examples: genital pain during noncoital activities; lack of pleasure during sex.

Sexual satisfaction

  A woman may be satisfied despite the preceding symptoms, but the partner may be dissatisfied; the problem may be a difference in desire rather than hypoactivity of one partner.

NOTE: Modified DSM-IV[88] classification with expansion.

whether the dysfunction reported is *lifelong* or *acquired,* whether it is *global* (across all partners and situations) or *situational,* and then to check for the presence and primary/secondary occurrence of each of the other categories.

Sexual Desire Disorders

Hypoactive sexual desire disorder is the persistent or recurrent absence or deficit of sexual fantasies and desire for sexual activity. There are no norms for sexual desire across ages, so it is difficult to diagnose "abnormal" behavior. This is a frequent complaint in as many as 30 to 50 percent of women attending sex therapy clinics.

The physical factors mentioned in the sexual history and evaluation section apply to this disorder, including medical illnesses, menopausal status, depression, medication use, and drug abuse. Vaginal atrophy and lack of adequate lubrication can result in painful intercourse, which, in turn, impacts desire. Medications such as tricyclic antidepressants, monoamine oxidase inhibitors, selective serotonin reuptake inhibitors, lithium, and some antipsychotics have been reported to decrease sexual interest. Likewise, psychological and interpersonal factors may play a role. Chronic stress and fatigue from work or family dysfunction, difficulty with aging and lifestyle changes, or relationship problems often affect sexual desire. Furthermore, a partner might perceive the lack of lubrication as disinterest or nonarousal.

Sexual aversion disorder is less common and probably often included with hypoactive desire disorder in clinical epidemiological studies.

Regarding treatment, medical illnesses need evaluation and specific treatment. Medications suspected to alter sexual interest can often be changed or the dosage reduced. Depression can be screened for and treated, recognizing that many antidepressants alter libido. Psychotherapy has been shown to be as effective as medications for some depressed patients, and combined psychotherapy and medication appear to be at least as, if not more, effective than medication alone.[89] Depressed patients should be advised regarding these different options for treatment.

Menopause and hormonal deficiencies should be addressed, particularly if the desire disorder is not lifelong and correlates with the perimenopausal or postmenopausal years. While controversy exists on the role of hormones in sexual desire, hormonal changes can affect a woman's general sense of well-being, which, in turn, can impact desire. Estrogen, progesterone, and testosterone production all decrease in menopause. Bachmann et al. noted that there was no correlation of gonadotropin levels to sexual drive.[90] Estrogen replacement therapy (ERT) suppresses pituitary gonadotropin production, which further decreases ovarian testosterone production after the menopause. Furthermore, estrogen replacement increases sex hormone binding globulin (SHBG) levels, which decreases the bioavailability of androgens and estrogens. Treatment with conjugated equine estrogens has been reported to improve libido in some studies and to have no effect in other studies. Dennerstein[59] showed improvement in sexual desire, enjoyment, orgasmic frequency, and overall mood in women receiving estrogen. Another Dennerstein study[91] found that posthysterectomized women did not have improved libido on estrogen. Campbell and Whitehead[92] found estrogen therapy had no effect on libido when looking at secondary outcomes of masturbation, orgasm, frequency of intercourse, and coital satisfaction. Studd's[93] 1977 study of estradiol implants in postmenopausal women showed no improvement of sexual response unless combined with androgens.

It is important to note that no study of estrogen replacement in postmenopausal women has been shown to decrease libido. Furthermore, no study clearly proves that estrogen alone directly improves desire. However, the estrogen effects to improve the overall sense of well-being, probably do improve sexual desire secondarily.

Androgens have been studied as a treatment for decreased libido in women. At the menopause, estrogens and progesterone production cease almost completely. Testosterone production from the ovary declines 28 percent and adrenal production of testosterone declines too, although more gradually with aging. Sherwin et al.[48] associated decreased androgen levels with decreased libido, even without physical symptoms of vaginal dryness and pain with coitus. Greenblatt's[94] 1950 double-blind study of menopausal women given diethylstilbestrol (DES), DES plus methyltestosterone (5 mg), methyltestosterone alone (5 mg), or placebo found improvement in libido in 12.3 percent, 23.5 percent, 42.0 percent, and 1.8 percent respectively. Overall, 65 percent of the women given androgen reported improvement in libido. Studd et al.[93] found improvement in sexual response in women treated with estradiol and testosterone implantable pellets. In 1985, Sherwin et al.[48] did a prospective double-blind crossover study in surgically menopausal women with injectable estradiol valerate, testosterone enanthate alone, or testosterone enanthate in combination with estradiol as compared to placebo. Estrogen alone had no effect on desire, arousal, or number of orgasms. However, the androgen groups had greater sexual desire, level of arousal, and sexual fantasies compared to placebo or estrogen alone. Interestingly, they did not have any change in frequency of intercourse or number of orgasms compared to use of estrogen alone or placebo. A later study by Sherwin,[47] evaluating similar groups, again showed significant improvement in desire, and also significantly greater frequency of intercourse and orgasm. More recent work by Davis[95] involved a 2-year, single-blind randomized trial in 34 postmenopausal women. Women seeking therapy for decreased libido were excluded. Women were given either estradiol (50 mg implants) or estradiol (50 mg) plus testosterone 50 mg implants. All measures of sexuality improved in both groups (activity, satisfaction, pleasure, orgasm, relevancy). There was a trend toward significance with estrogen plus testosterone versus estrogen alone in terms of libido, but it did not reach statistical significance. While these patients were not seeking treatment for low libido, they all had improvements in sexual function which persisted over two years.

Overall, the cumulative data on androgen replacement therapy seem to suggest improved sexual function in women who have had a surgical menopause. The data are less clear in women who have natural menopause.

Androgens given to women have been reported to cause increased facial hair, acne, and male pattern baldness at oral doses of 1.25 mg a day of methyltestosterone. Less often, voice deepening or hoarseness and virilization have been reported. Clitoromegaly has been reported in studies of injectable androgens. Hepatic toxicity is known to occur with high doses of androgens, but has not been reported in recommended estrogen-androgen replacement doses.[96] Greater concern exists regarding the addition of androgens to estrogen replacement and potential reduction in the beneficial cardiovascular effects of estrogen. Oral estrogen reduces total cholesterol, increases cardioprotective high-density lipoproteins (HDL), and slightly increases triglycerides.[97] Estrogen-androgen replacement decreases cardioprotective HDL, but also decreases triglycerides. The long-term impact on cardiovascular disease is unknown. However, not all of estrogen's beneficial effects on cardiovascular disease are lipid related. Some effect may be mediated through the vascular system with vasodilation. Long-term, randomized studies need to be done to address the impact on cardiac risks of androgen use in women.

Currently, there are no data to support using DHEA for low sexual desire. The reported improvements in overall well-being and energy levels need to be substantiated, and if true, might impact sexuality secondarily.

Sexual Arousal Disorders

Sexual arousal disorder is currently defined as a lack of physical response as indicated by lack of lubrication and vasocongestion of the genitals.[88] Although not included in the DSM-IV criteria, one should also be attentive if a woman reports persistent lack of a subjective sense of sexual excitement and pleasure during sex.

Complaints about sexual arousal are uncommonly reported in women unless they are accompanied by other symptoms such as dyspareunia, lack of lubrication, or orgasmic difficulty. Since the 1998 release of sildenafil for the treatment of male erectile disorder, there has been increased attention to the potential importance of identifying genital vasculogenic disorders in women that might be labeled vaginal engorgement insufficiency or clitoral erectile insufficiency disorders.[42] Whether changes in objectively measured vasocongestion will correspond to a subjectively reported sexual disorder remains to be confirmed or refuted by research.

When lubrication is an issue, topical lubricants such as KY jelly or Astroglide remain useful options. Menopausal symptoms may respond to oral or topical estrogen for women in whom this is an appropriate choice. Similarly, other genital vasculogenic agents or more central agents, such as those currently being used in men, may be helpful for women with sexual arousal disorders.

Sildenafil (Viagra) is a selective inhibitor of cyclic guanosine monophosphate (cGMP)-specific phosphodiesterase type 5. Increased levels of cGMP lead to smooth-muscle relaxation in the corpus cavernosum, allowing inflow of blood in the presence of sexual stimulation. It has been shown to significantly improve erectile function in men compared to placebo, and, theoretically, it could have an effect in women. Sexual arousal in women is associated with clitoral erection, vasodilation, and increases in vaginal blood flow as measured by indirect techniques like vaginal photoplethysmography, thermal clearance, and clearance of radioactive xenon.[99,100] Increased vasocongestion might result from Viagra ingestion, leading to improved genital stimulation. Studies are not yet available, and it is speculative as to whether sildenafil would be effective for women.

Psychological issues such as poor self-esteem, discomfort with sexual responsiveness, and worries about contraception are common individual issues. Partner-related issues include sexual dysfunction of the partner, and inadequate sexual stimulation from or a lack of attraction to the partner. If a woman has long-standing lubrication difficulty not associated with another primary sexual dysfunction such as genital pain or anorgasmia, a referral for psychosocial consultation or therapy might be recommended.

Orgasm Disorders

Orgasmic disorders refer to the persistent delay or absence of orgasm. Lack of coital orgasm is generally considered a normal variation of female sexual response if the woman is able to experience orgasm with a partner using other, noncoital methods. Sexual experience needs to be taken into account, as a woman often becomes more orgasmic with experience. Orgasm disorders are quite common, with nearly 25 percent of U.S. women reporting this as a problem in the past year, as did nearly 60 percent of women seeking routine care in an ob/gyn clinic.[75,87]

Physical factors impacting orgasm include diseases, injuries, or surgeries that might have interfered with neurovascular pelvic functioning. Medications, including those for hypertension, cardiac disorders, and psychiatric disorders, can impact arousal and orgasmic response. Antidepressants are particularly common prescriptions for women to take, and a number of them have sexual side effects, specifically orgasm delay or inhibition. Psychological and interpersonal factors are also very common in women who experience orgasm problems. Growing up with messages that sex was shameful and men's pleasure only, or a history of unpleasant earlier sexual experiences, sexual trauma, and emotionally unreliable parental figures are frequently reported by women with orgasmic problems. In addition, a partner's sexual skills, expectations about sex, and personal enjoyment of sex can be contributing factors, especially if the couple has difficulty communicating about sexual desires and preferences. Male partners often feel responsible for the woman's orgasm and inadvertently pressure their partners to experience orgasm, which may prolong rather than help the difficulty.   For lifelong, generalized orgasmic disorder, there is rarely a physical cause. It is best treated using masturbation programs, sex therapy, or both.[101] Books are available teaching the key principles and to help the woman deal with related issues of body image, relaxation, tolerance of sexual arousal tension, sexual expressiveness, touching, and acceptance of her own sexuality. If the woman needs therapy, individual, couples, or group therapy can be helpful; it usually lasts from 6 to 15 sessions. These treatments have a good success rate, with 85 to 90 percent of women becoming orgasmic alone, and about 70 to 75 percent orgasmic with a partner. Situational or intermittent orgasmic disorders are more likely to be related to nonsexual stresses and relationship issues, and may take longer to deal with in treatment.

When orgasmic disorders are due to medication issues, reducing or changing medications is often the first effort, if this can be done safely. In the case of antidepressant medications, peripheral anticholinergic activity or adrenergic blockade can be the source of the dysfunction. Typically, the increased availability of serotonin and decreased dopamine impact sexual response, although the mechanisms are incompletely described.[103,104] Among antidepressants, those that least impact sexual functioning appear to be buproprion (Wellbutrin) and nefazodone (Serzone). For the shorter-acting SSRIs (e.g., paroxetine, sertraline), with stable patients, a drug holiday can be considered by going off medication from Friday morning until Sunday noon. Buspirone (Buspar), an antianxiety agent that reduces adrenergic α_1 activity and decreases serotonin, has been recommended for inclusion with an SSRI to counteract the sexual side effects.[105]

Pain Disorders

Dyspareunia or painful sexual intercourse is a common complaint and frequently has an organic basis. Laumann et al. reported that 14 percent of women 18 to 59 years old stated that they had experienced pain during sex in the prior year.[75] A 1993 study by Rosen et al. of 329 outpatient gynecologic patients aged 18 to 79 found that 18 percent had pain with intercourse.[87] As discussed earlier, a careful history including possible physical, psychological, and interpersonal factors (e.g., relationship distress, guilt, shame, or traumatic

sexual history) is important. In addition, a thorough examination is critical.

If organic factors are identified, specific treatment can be initiated. However, not all of the factors are curable. If vaginal scarring or vaginal stenosis is found after episiotomy or other vaginal surgery, initial therapy can include work with gradual vaginal stretching using dilators and massage. For postmenopausal women, vaginal estrogen cream is usually indicated to improve vaginal pliability. If the scar tissue includes thick, fibrous bands, this may not be successful, and surgical reconstruction may be necessary. It is worthwhile trying conservative approaches first. The pain sensitivity may remain postoperatively and require time to resolve plus desensitization techniques. Massage to the area, pelvic floor physical therapy, and low-dose tricyclic antidepressants may all be helpful. It is important to recognize that tricyclic antidepressants may affect desire as can the pain condition itself. Coital position changes may relieve dyspareunia.

Vulvar vestibulitis is frequently unrecognized and patients are often extremely relieved just to find a clinician who can identify the condition and offer treatment. Vulvar vestibulitis is defined as a chronic, persistent clinical syndrome characterized by severe pain on touch to the vestibular area or with attempted vaginal entry. This condition is poorly understood and treatment is not always curative. Overall, studies have been small with variable treatment outcomes. Reports involving topical steroids have had mixed results. Interferon injections are expensive, painful, and time-consuming but have been shown to be effective.[106] Tricyclic antidepressants often help alleviate the pain.[107] Low oxalate diets have not been effective. Some studies have shown cure or improvement rates of 50 to 89 percent with surgery.[108–110]

Urogenital atrophy affected 48.8 percent of 2045 postmenopausal women at some time according to a British study.[110] Vaginal atrophy can result in vaginal dryness and painful intercourse. In Rosen's study, 44 percent of postmenopausal women "often" complained of lack of vaginal lubrication, 17 percent "often" reported dyspareunia, and 18 percent "sometimes" reported dyspareunia.[87] Atrophic vaginal tissues can lead to vaginal dryness, soreness, bleeding, and painful intercourse and sometimes vaginismus. The best treatment to reverse vaginal atrophy is topical estrogen. Systemic estrogens can restore vaginal tissues, but the effects of topical estrogen may be more rapid. Furthermore, some women who take systemic hormones continue to have atrophic vaginitis symptoms if inadequate therapeutic levels of estrogen reach the vaginal mucosa. Estradiol vaginal cream 0.01%, conjugated estrogens vaginal cream, or dienestrol cream 0.01% are all effective treatments. Initial therapy can start with daily vaginal application at bedtime for 2 to 4 weeks, and then reducing to 2 to 3 times per week as atrophy resolves. Eventually, application 1 to 2 times per week is all that is needed for maintenance. Usually patients note improvement in 3 to 6 weeks.

Randomized trials have shown that the estradiol-releasing vaginal ring (Estring) is as effective as estrogen vaginal creams.[61,111] The ring contains a core of 2 mg of 17β-estradiol surrounded by a 55-mm silicone ring; the ring allows for a low-dose, slow release of estradiol over 90 days. It has the advantage of eliminating the irregular administration intervals and messiness of creams, as well as allowing for a constant absorption rate in the vagina.

Both the estrogen creams and the ring carry the same contraindications for use as systemic estrogens. Contraindications include pregnancy, undiagnosed genital bleeding, estrogen-dependent neoplasms, active thrombophlebitis or a history of hormone-induced thromboembolic disorders, and active liver disease.

Many nonprescription vaginal lubricants and moisturizers are available. Astroglide, Replens, KY jelly, Lubrin, and Moist Again are examples. They can be very helpful in relieving discomfort with intercourse while waiting for estrogens to restore the vaginal mucosa, or for minor vaginal dryness. They are sometimes needed long term to reduce pain with friction from inadequate vaginal lubrication associated with aging.

Vaginismus is defined as involuntary spasm of the pelvic floor muscles (levator ani muscles) and perineal muscles. This reflex muscle spasm involving the outer third of the vagina is triggered by fear of anticipation of vaginal penetration or actual penetration. It may be triggered by coitus, pelvic examination, or even trying to insert tampons or vaginal medication. The condition can be primary with the patient never allowing coitus. This may involve underlying factors of sexual abuse or sexual aversion. Vaginismus can also develop secondarily from repeated dyspareunia. Once the reflex muscle spasm is established, it is difficult to interrupt the response.

The evaluation and diagnosis as described earlier relies on history and examination revealing involuntary perineal and levator ani muscle spasm. Lamont[113] classified a group of 80 patients by degrees of vaginismus. Twenty-seven (34 percent) had first-degree vaginismus, defined as perineal and levator ani spasm, relieved with reassurance during physical examination. Twenty-one (26 percent) had second-degree vaginismus with perineal spasm throughout examination. Eighteen (22.5 percent) had third-degree vaginismus with levator spasm and elevation of the buttocks, and 10 (12.5 percent) demonstrated levator and perineal spasm, adduction of the thighs, and withdrawal. Four patients refused pelvic examination.

Treatment for vaginismus requires both physical and psychological approaches. Weekly 1-h sessions for 10 to 14 weeks can address sexual attitudes, knowledge, interpersonal problems, and involve the partner with treatment. Both the psychological and mechanical treatment teach the patient vaginal comfort. Muscle relaxation, massage, Kegel exercises, and gradual vaginal dilatation may be utilized. Vaginal dilatation is considered central to treatment. The woman controls the pace and duration of vaginal dilatation. As the woman graduates to larger dilators, the partner can become involved with the process using traditional dilators, the patient or partner's finger, or other devices. Eventually, the couple can advance to coital attempts. Additional desensitization to vaginal penetration may be needed if phobia persists.

Lamont[113] reported success in the 66 patients that attempted treatment. In the management of these patients, relaxation, self- and mutual pleasuring exercises, Kegel exercises, and physical examination played an important role in successful treatment. Four patients (6 percent) had no success, and three of those had primary vaginismus and had unconsummated relationships. Nine patients (14 percent) had technical success and 53 (80 percent) success with pleasure.

Specific organic causes, such as vaginitis, endometriosis, pelvic inflammatory disease, irritable bowel syndrome, urethral syndrome, interstitial cystitis, and others, should be evaluated and treated as indicated. With all of the sexual pain disorders, it is not uncommon to treat the underlying organic cause with success and find that the pain continues. It is often a muscle-tension problem from the pain-tension-pain cycle that still remains. Specialized pelvic floor physical therapy can be extremely helpful in breaking the cycle and improving the patient's awareness of the pelvic floor musculature's role in pain. Also, psychological counseling, with or without the partner, is frequently helpful even if organic causes are identified. There are other issues involved that need attention, either primarily contributing to the pain disorder, or secondarily from the potentially disrupted relationship with long-term dyspareunia.

Screening and Referral Strategies

Many primary care providers have limited time available and need quick screening strategies and good referral sources and techniques.

For screening, a good strategy is to have a quick checklist for a patient to indicate whether they are having any difficulty with sexual desire, arousal, orgasm, or pain during or after sex; and if "yes" to any of these items, does she wish to discuss it? An interview could follow up on a patient's responses. Direct questions in an interview could be used in place of a checklist, but usually in more general terms, such as whether a patient has "any current sexual concerns or problems."

Decisions about referral are usually straightforward and include: diagnostic uncertainty or complexity that would benefit from consultation; the clinician's lack of expertise; time factors; and patients dealing with recovery from a routine or complex treatment who might benefit from someone to help them come to terms with limitations, disfigurement, and loss. A common example is recovery from aggressive cancer treatments and finding a quality of life that includes sexuality.

In referring a patient, it is crucial to identify and have a list of competent experts who can deal well with sexual issues with patients. A further key to a successful referral is how it is presented to the patient. Stressing the special expertise of the clinician to whom the referral is made is important. For the nonmedical referral, such as the psychiatrist, psychologist, or social worker, it is helpful to stress that they are trained to work with how physical and psychosocial factors interact to influence sexual functioning and satisfaction. Addressing these issues may have implications for patients' relationships and broader health concerns.

References and Selected Readings

1. Amaro H: Love, sex and power: Considering women's realities in HIV prevention. *Am Psychol* 50:421–427, 1995.
2. Ehrhardt AA, Wasserhert JN: Age, gender and sexual risk behaviors for sexually transmitted diseases in the United States, in Wasserhert JN, Aral KK, Holmes KK, Hitchcock PJ (eds): *Research Issues in Human Behavior and Sexually Transmitted Diseases in the AIDS Era.* Washington, DC: American Society for Microbiology, 1991, pp 97–121.
3. Crenshaw TL, Goldberg JP: *Sexual Pharmacology: Drugs That Affect Sexual Function.* New York: Norton, 1996.
4. Bancroft J: *Human Sexuality and Its Problems,* 2nd ed. London: Churchill Livingstone, 1989.
5. Ehrhardt AA, Meyer-Bahlburg HFL: Psychosexual development: An examination of the role of prenatal hormones, in *Sex Hormones and Behavior.* Symposium 62, Ciba Foundation Excerpts Medica, Amsterdam: 1979, pp 41–50.
6. Money J, Ehrhardt AA: *Man and Woman, Boy and Girl: Differentiation and Dimorphism of Gender*

Identity from Conception to Maturity. Baltimore: Johns Hopkins University Press, 1972.

7. Miller WL, Levine LS: Molecular and clinical advances in cogenital adrenal hyperplasia. *J Pediatr* 111:1–17, 1987.

8. Hines M, Collaer L: Gonadal hormones and sexual differentiation of human behavior. Developments from research on endocrine syndromes and studies of brain structure. *Ann Rev Sex Res* 4:1–48, 1993.

9. Hamer DH, Hu S, Magnuson VL, Hu N, Pattatucci AML: A linkage between DNA markers on the X chromosome and male sexual orientation. *Science* 261:321–327, 1993.

10. Bailey JM, Pillard RC, Neale MC, Agyei Y: Heritable factors influence sexual orientation in women. *Arch Gen Psychiatry* 50:217–223, 1993.

11. Friedrich WN, Grambsch P, Broughton D, Kuiper J, Beilke RL: Normative sexual behavior in children. *Pediatrics* 88:456–464, 1991.

12. Lamb S, Coakley M: "Normal" childhood sexual play and games: Differentiating play from abuse. *Child Abuse Negl* 17:515–526, 1993.

13. Friedrich WN, Grambsch P, Damon L, et al: Child sexual behavior inventory: Normative and clinical comparisons. *Psychol Assess* 4:303–311, 1992.

14. Elias J, Gebhardt P: Sexuality and sexual learning in childhood, reprinted in Rogers RS (ed): *Sex education—Rationale and Research*. London: Cambridge University Press, 1969, pp 143–154.

15. Okami P, Olmstead R, Abramson PR: Sexual experiences in early childhood: 18-year data from the UCLA Family Lifestyles Project. *J Sex Res* 34:339–347, 1997.

16. Udry JR, Talbert LM, Morris NM: Biosocial foundations for adolescent female sexuality. *Demography* 23:217–229, 1986.

17. Marshall EA, Tanner JM: Variations in patterns of pubertal changes in girls. *Arch Dis Child.* 44:291–303, 1969.

18. de Ridder CM, Thijssen JHH, Bruning PF, Van den Brande JL, Zonderland ML, Erich WBM: Body fat mass, body fat distribution, and pubertal development: A longitudinal study of physical and hormonal sexual maturation of girls. *J Clin Endocrinol Metab* 75:442–446, 1992.

19. Frische RE, Revelle R: Height and weight at menarche and a hypothesis of critical body weights and adolescent events. *Science* 9:169–172, 1970.

20. Graber JA, Brooks-Gunn J, Warren MP: The antecedents of menarche age: Heredity, family environment, and stressful life events. *Child Dev* 66:346–359, 1995.

21. Hofferth SL: Trends in adolescent sexual activity, contraception and pregnancy in the United States, in Bancroft J, Reinisch J (eds): *Adolescence and Pu-berty. Third Kinsey Symposium*. New York: Oxford University Press, 1988.

22. Wyatt GE: Reexamining factors predicting Afro-American and white American women's age at first coitus. *Arch Sex Behav* 4:271–298, 1989.

23. Adams D, Gold A: A rise in female-initiated sexual activity at ovulation and its suppression by oral contraceptives. *N Engl J Med* 299(21):1145–1150, 1978.

24. Bancroft J, Sanders D, Davidson DW, Warner P: Mood, sexuality, hormones and the menstrual cycle. III. Sexuality and the role of androgens. *Psychosom Med* 45:509–516, 1983.

25. Reamy K: Sexuality in pregnancy: A prospective study. *J Reprod Med* 27:321–327, 1982.

26. Perkins RP: Sexuality in pregnancy: What determines behavior? *Obstet Gynecol* 59:189–198, 1982.

27. Hyde JS, DeLamater JD, Plant EA, Byrd JM: Sexuality during pregnancy and the year postpartum. *J Sex Res* 33:143–151, 1996.

28. Naeye RL: Coitus and associated amniotic-fluid infections. *N Engl J Med* 301:1198–2000, 1979.

29. Naeye RL: Factors that predispose to premature rupture of the fetal membranes. *Obstet Gynecol* 60:93–98, 1982.

30. Reamy K, White S: Sexuality in pregnancy and puerperium: A review. *Obstet Gynecol Surv* 40:1–13, 1985.

31. Toth M, Witkin SS, Ledger W, Thaler H: The role of infection in the etiology of preterm birth. *Obstet Gynecol* 71:723–726, 1988.

32. Kurki T, Ylikorkola O: Coitus during pregnancy is not related to bacterial vaginosis or preterm birth. *Am J Obstet Gynecol* 169:1130–1134, 1993.

33. Greenshields W, Hulme H: *The Perineum in Childbirth. A Survey of Women's Experiences and Midwives' Practices*. London: National Childbirth Trust, 1993, pp 1–95.

34. Sleep J, Grant A: West Berkshire perineal management trial: Three-year follow-up. *BMJ* 295:749–751, 1987.

35. Glazener CMA, Abdalla MI, Stroud P, Naji SA, Templeton AA, Russell IT: Postnatal maternal morbidity: Extent, causes, prevention and treatment. *Br J Obstet Gynaecol* 102:282–287, 1995.

36. Glazener CMA: Sexual function after childbirth: Women's experiences, persistent morbidity and lack of professional recognition. *Br J Obstet Gynaecol* 104:330–335, 1997.

37. Alder EM, Cook A, Davidson D, West C, Bancroft J: Hormones, mood and sexuality in lactating women. *Br J Psychiatry* 148:74–79, 1986.

38. Robson KM, Brant HA, Kumar R: Maternal sexuality during first pregnancy and after childbirth. *Br J Obstet Gynecol* 88:882–889, 1981.

39. Masters WH, Johnson VE: *Human Sexual Response.* Boston: Little, Brown, 1966.

40. Hawton K, Gath D, Day A: Sexual function in a community sample of middle-aged women with partners: Effects of age, marital, socioeconomic, psychiatric, gynecological, and menopausal factors. *Arch Sex Behav* 23:375–395, 1994.

41. Goldstein I, Lue TF, Padma-Nathan H, Rosen RC, Steers WD, Wicker PA: Oral sildenafil in the treatment of erectile dysfunction. *N Engl J Med* 338:1397–1404, 1998.

42. Goldstein I, Berman JR: Vasculogenic female sexual dysfunction: Vaginal engorgement and clitoral erectile insufficiency syndromes. *Int J Impot Res* 10:S84–S90, 1998.

43. Leiblum S, Bachman G, Kemmann E, et al: Vaginal atrophy in the post-menopausal woman: The importance of sexual activity and hormones. *JAMA* 249:2195–2198, 1983.

44. Zweifel JE, O'Brien W: A meta-analysis of the effect of hormone replacement therapy upon depressed mood. *Psychoneuroendocrinology* 22:189–212, 1997.

45. Sherwin BB: The psychoendocrinology of aging and female sexuality. *Ann Rev Sex Res* 2:181–199, 1991.

46. Meyers LS, Dixen J, Morreisette D, et al: Effects of estrogen, androgen, and progestin on psychophysiology and behavior in post-menopausal women. *J Clin Endocrinol Metab* 70:1124–1131, 1990.

47. Sherwin BB, Gelfand MM: The role of androgen in the maintenance of sexual functioning in oophorectomized women. *Psychosom Med* 49:397–409, 1987.

48. Sherwin BB, Gelfand MM, Brender W: Androgen enhances sexual motivation in females: A prospective, crossover study of sex steroid administration in the surgical menopause. *Psychosom Med* 47:339–351, 1985.

49. Yen SSC, et al: Replacement of DHEA in aging men and women: Potential remedial effects. *Ann N Y Acad Sci* 774:128–142, 1995.

50. Mortola J, Yen SSC: The effects of dehydroepiandrosterone on endocrine-metabolic parameters in postmenopausal women. *J Clin Endocrinol Metab* 71:696–704, 1990.

51. Morales AJ, Nolan JJ, Nelson JC, Yen SCC: Effects of replacement dose of dehydroepiandrosterone in men and women of advancing age. *J Clin Endocrinol Metab* 78:1360–1367, 1994.

52. Darling CA, McKay J, Smith YM: Understanding hysterectomies: Sexual satisfaction and quality of life. *J Sex Res* 30:324–335, 1993.

53. Carlson KH, Miller BA, Fowler FJ: The Maine women's health study: I. Outcomes of hysterectomy. *Obstet Gynecol* 83(4):556–564, 1994.

54. Kilkku P, Grönroos M, Hirvonen T, Rauramo L: Supravaginal uterine amputation vs. hysterectomy: Effects on libido and orgasm. *Acta Obstet Gynecol Scand* 62:147–152, 1993.

55. Kilkku P: Supravaginal uterine amputation vs. hysterectomy: Effects on coital frequency and dyspareunia. *Acta Obstet Gynecol Scand* 62:141–145, 1983.

56. Drummond J, Field P: Emotional and sexual sequelae following hysterectomy. *Health Care Women Int* 5:261–271, 1984.

57. Grounds D, Davies B, Mowbray R: The contraceptive pill, side effects and personality: Report of a controlled double blind trial. *Br J Psychiatry* 116:169, 1970.

58. Leeton J, McMaster R, Worsley A: The effects on sexual response and mood after sterilization of women taking long-term oral contraception: Results of a double blind cross-over study. *Aust N Z J Obstet Gynecol* 18:194, 1978.

59. Dennerstein L, Burrow G, Wood C, et al: Hormones and sexuality: Effect of estrogen and progesterone. *Obstet Gynecol* 56(3):316–322, 1980.

60. Bancroft J, Sherwin BB, Alexander GM, Davidson DW, Walker A: Oral contraceptives, androgens, and the sexuality of young women: I. A comparison of sexual experience, sexual activity, and gender role in oral contraceptive users and nonusers. *Arch Sex Behav* 20:105–120, 1991.

61. Bachmann G, Notelovitz M, Nachtigall L, Birgerson L: A comparative study of a low-dose estradiol vaginal ring and conjugated estrogen cream for post-menopausal urogenital atrophy. *Prim Care* Update OB/GYNs 4(3):109–115, 1997.

62. Ravnikar VA: Compliance with hormone replacement therapy: Are women receiving the full impact of hormone replacement therapy preventative health benefits? *Womens Health Issues* 2:75–82, 1992.

63. Ravnikar VA: Compliance with hormone therapy. *Am J Obstet Gynecol* 156:1332–1334, 1987.

64. Utian WH, Schiff I: NAMS-Gallup survey on women's knowledge, information sources, and attitudes to menopause and hormone replacement therapy. *Menopause* 1:39–48, 1994.

65. Task Force for the International Society for the Study of Vulvar Disease: Burning vulva syndrome. Report of the ISSVD Task Force. *J Reprod Med* 29:457, 1984.

66. Russell DEH: The incidence and prevalence of intrafamilial and extrafamilial sexual abuse of female children. *Child Abuse Negl* 7:133–146, 1982.

67. Wyatt GE: The sexual abuse of Afro-American and white-American women in childhood. *Child Abuse Negl* 9:507–519, 1985.

68. Wyatt GE, Newcomb M: Internal and external mediators of women's sexual abuse in childhood. *Child Abuse Negl* 58:758–767, 1990.

69. Kilpatrick DG, Saunders BE, Veronen LJ, Best CL, Von JM: Criminal victimization: Lifetime prevalence, reporting to police, and psychological impact. *Crime Delinq* 33:478–489, 1987.

70. Wyatt GE: The sociocultural context of African-American and white-American women's rape. *J Sociocultural Issues* 48:77–91, 1992.

71. Saunders BE, Villeponteaux LA, Lipovsky JA, Kilpatrick DG, Veronen LJ: Child sexual assault as a risk factor for mental health disorders among women: A community sample. *J Interp Viol* 7:189–204, 1992.

72. Koss MP, Heslet L: Somatic consequences of violence against women. *Arch Fam Med* 1:53–59, 1992.

73. Fergusson DM, Horwood LJ, Lynsky MT: Childhood sexual abuse, adolescent sexual behaviors, and sexual revictimization. *Child Abuse Negl* 21:789–803, 1997.

74. Lefebvre KA: Performing a sexual evaluation on the person with disability or illness, in Sipski ML, Alexander CJ (eds): *Sexual Function in People with Disability and Chronic Illness: A Health Professional's Guide.* Gaithersburg, MD: Aspen Publishers, 1997, pp 19–44.

75. Laumann EO, Gagnon JH, Michael RT, et al: *The Social Organization of Sexuality: Sexual Practices in the United States.* Chicago: University of Chicago Press, 1994.

76. Brash McGreer K, Whipple B, Weisberg M: Supporting sexual health in women with disability: Living with physical disability or chronic illness. *Med Asp Hum Sex* 1:13–19, 1998.

77. Stevens P, Hall J: Stigma, health beliefs and experiences with health care in lesbian women. *Image—J Nurs Sch* 20(2):69–73, 1988.

78. Adams ML: You're all right so long as you act nice. *Fireweed* Spring: 1989, pp 53–67.

79. Johnson SR, Smith EM, Guenther SM: Comparison of gynecologic health care problems between lesbians and bisexual women. *J Reprod Med* 32(11):805–811, 1987.

80. Smith EM, Johnson SR, Guenther SM: Health care attitudes and experiences during gynecologic care among lesbians and bisexuals. *Am J Public Health* 75:1086–1087, 1985.

81. Johnson SR, Guenther SM, Laube DW, Keettel WC: Factors influencing lesbian gynecologic care: A preliminary study. *Am J Obstet Gynecol* 140(1):20–27, 1981.

82. Johnson SR, Palermo JL: Gynecologic care for the lesbian. *Clin Obstet Gynecol* 27(3): 724–731, 1984.

83. Diamond D, Wilsnack S: Alcohol abuse among lesbians: A descriptive study. *J Homosex* 4(2):123, 1978.

84. Saghir MT, Robins E: Homosexuality: IV. Psychiatric disorders and disability in the female homosexual. *Am J Psychiatr* 127:64, 1970.

85. Robertson P, Schachter J: Failure to identify venereal disease in a lesbian population. *Sex Transm Dis* 8:75, 1981.

86. Frank E, Anderson C, Rubinstein D: Frequency of sexual dysfunction in "normal couples." *N Engl J Med* 229:111, 1978.

87. Rosen RC, Taylor JF, Leiblum SR, Bachmann GA: Prevalence of sexual dysfunction in women: Results of a survey of 329 women in an outpatient gynecologic clinic. *J Sex Marital Ther* 19:172–188, 1993.

88. American Psychiatric Association: *Diagnostic and Statistical Manual of Mental Disorders,* 4th ed. Washington, DC: American Psychiatric Association, 1993.

89. Elkin I, Shea T, Watkins JT, et al: National Institute of Mental Health treatment of depression collaborative research program: General effectiveness of treatments. *Arch Gen Psychiatry* 46:971–982, 1989.

90. Bachman G, Leiblum S, Sandler B, et al: Correlates of sexual desire in post-menopausal women. *Maturitas* 7:211–216, 1985.

91. Dennerstein L, Wood C, Burrows GD: Sexual response following hysterectomy and oophorectomy. *Obstet Gynecol* 49:92–96, 1997.

92. Campbell S, Whitehead M: Oestrogen therapy and the menopausal syndrome. *Clin Obstet Gynecol* 4:31–47, 1977.

93. Studd JWW, Collins WP, Chakravarti S, et al: Oestradiol and testosterone implants in the treatment of psychosexual problems in the postmenopausal woman. *Br J Obstet Gynaecol* 84:314–315, 1977.

94. Greenblatt RB, Barfield WE, Garner JF, et al: Evaluation of an estrogen, androgen, estrogen-androgen combination, and a placebo in the treatment of the menopause. *J Clin Endocrinol Metab* 10:1547–1558, 1950.

95. Davis SR, McCloud P, Strauss BJ, Burger H: Testosterone enhances estradiol's effects on postmenopausal bone density and sexuality. *Maturitas* 21:227–236, 1995.

96. Phillips E, Bauman C: Safety surveillance of esterified estrogens—methyltestosterone (Estratest and Estratest HS) replacement therapy in the United States. *Clin Ther* 19:1070–1084, 1997.

97. Bush TL, Barrett-Connor E, Cowan LD, et al: Cardiovascular mortality and noncontraceptive use of estrogen in women: Results from the Lipid Research Clinics Follow-up Study. *Circulation* 75:1102–1109, 1987.

98. Honore EK, Williams JK, Adams MR, Ackerman D, Wagner JD: Methyltestosterone does not diminish the beneficial effects of estrogen replacement on coronary artery reactivity in cynomolgus monkeys. *J North Am Menopause Soc* 3(1):20–26, 1996.

99. Levin RJ, Wagner G, Ottesen B: Simultaneous monitoring of human vaginal haemo dynamics by three independent methods during sexual arousal, in Hoch Z, Lief HI, (eds): *Sexology: Excerpta Medica.* Amsterdam: Elsevier, 1982, pp 114–120.

100. Levin RJ: The mechanisms of human female sexual arousal. *Ann Rev Sex Res* 3:1–49, 1992.

101. Heiman J, Meston M: Empirically validated treatment for sexual dysfunction. *Ann Rev Sex Res* 8:148–194, 1997.

102. Heiman JR, LoPiccolo J: *Becoming Orgasmic: A Sexual and Personal Growth Program for Women,* 2nd ed. New York: Simon & Schuster, 1988.

103. Meston CM, Gorzalka BB: Psychoactive drugs and human sexual behavior: The role of serotonergic activity. *J Psychoactive Drugs* 24:1–40, 1992.

104. Steele TE, Howell EF: Cyprohepatadine for imipramine-induced sexual anorgasmia. *J Clin Psychiatry* 6:326–327, 1986.

105. Gitlen MJ: Psychotropic medication-included sexual dysfunction, in Dunner DL (ed): *Current Psychiatric Therapies II.* Philadelphia: WB Saunders, 1997, pp 385–391.

106. McKay M: Dysesthetic ("essential") vulvodynia, treatment with amitryptyline. *J Reprod Med* 38:9, 1993.

107. Friedrich EG: Vulvar vestibulitis syndrome. *J Reprod Med* 32:110, 1987.

108. Marinoff SC: Total vestibulectomy with vaginal advancement in the treatment of vulvar vestibulitis syndrome. Abstract from the ISSVD 12th International Congress, Quebec, 1993.

109. Foster DC, Butts C, Shah K, Woodruff JD: Long-term outcome of perineoplasty for vulvar vestibulitis. *J Womens Health* 4:669–675, 1995.

110. Barlow DH, Cardozo LD, Franus RM, et al: Urogenital aging and its effect on sexual health in older British women. *Br J Obstet Gynaecol* 104:97–91, 1997.

111. Ayton RA, Darling GM, Murkies AL, et al: A comparative study of safety and efficacy of continuous low-dose oestradiol released from a vaginal ring compared with conjugated equine oestrogen vaginal cream in the treatment of postmenopausal urogenital atrophy. *Br J Obstet Gynaecol* 103:351–358, 1996.

112. Masters WH, Johsnon VE: *Human Sexual Inadequacy.* Boston: Little, Brown, 1970.

113. Lamont JA: Vaginismus. *Am J Obstet Gynecol* 131(6):632–636, 1978.

114. Davis SR: The role of androgens and the menopause in the female sexual response. *Int J Impot Res* 10:S82–S83, 1998.

115. Haugaard J: Sexual behaviors between children: Professionals' opinions and undergraduates' recollections. *Fam in Sociocultural; J Contemp Human Srv* 2:81–89, 1996.

116. Steege JF: Dyspareunia and vaginismus. *Clin Obstet Gynecol* 27:750–759, 1984.

117. Lonky NM, Navarre GL, Saunders S, Sadeghi M, Wolde-Tsadik G: Low-grade Papanicolaou smears and the Bethesda system: A prospective cytohistopathologic analysis. *Obstet Gynecol* 85:716–720, 1995.

Part V

Office Diagnostic Procedures

CHAPTER 47

Colposcopy and the Evaluation and Treatment of Abnormal Pap Smears

Mark Spitzer

THE EVALUATION OF THE ABNORMAL PAP SMEAR

THE ATYPICAL SMEAR

PAP SMEARS SUSPICIOUS FOR SQUAMOUS INTRAEPITHELIAL LESIONS

COLPOSCOPY

Abnormal Epithelial Changes • Colposcopic Diagnosis of Invasive Cancer • Criteria for a Satisfactory Colposcopy • Glandular Abnormalities • Management of AGUS Smears • Colposcopy of Vulvar and Vaginal Lesions

TREATMENT OF CERVICAL INTRAEPITHELIAL NEOPLASIA

WHO SHOULD BE TREATED?

TREATMENT OF VULVAR AND VAGINAL LESIONS

S quamous cell cancer of the cervix is the most common female genital malignancy. Worldwide, it is the greatest cancer killer of women under the age of 40. Cervical cancer is less frequent in countries where women have good access to health care, and is more frequent in underdeveloped countries. This is because the premalignant phase of cervical cancer is well-recognized, easily detectable, and easily treated. This chapter focuses on the detection and treatment of premalignant lesions of the cervix, vagina, and vulva.

Squamous cell cervical cancer is considered by many clinicians and investigators to be a sexually transmitted disease. Early age at first intercourse, multiple partners, and partners who have multiple partners are all well-documented risk factors for the development of cervical cancer. In recent years, it has been well-recognized that human papilloma virus (HPV) is a likely candidate as the sexually transmitted carcinogen. There is much epidemiologic, histologic, and microbiologic evidence linking HPV to cervical cancer. However, it is also quite evident that HPV infection alone will not lead to cancer. Several factors—the HPV subtype, certain cofactors such as smoking, the host-immune response, and the time in a woman's life at which she is infected—influence the potential progression to cervical cancer. Further, the colposcopic and histologic appearance of HPV infection (condyloma) and cervical intraepithelial neoplasia (CIN) are very similar and difficult to distinguish. Because HPV infection and milder forms of CIN do not invariably progress to cervical cancer, a rational approach to the diagnosis and treatment of these lesions is essential.

The Evaluation of the Abnormal Pap Smear

Because of the high false-negative rate of Pap smears, negative Pap smears should be repeated annually for at least three years before one can be reliably reassured that no disease is present. After three negative annual Pap smears, a woman without high-risk factors may be able to have her subsequent Pap smears less often than annually.

Since 1988, the Bethesda Classification System has been used for the reporting of cervical cytology in the United States. The Bethesda System divides epithelial changes found on cytology into several categories. Table 47-1 provides a summary of these categories and their approximate equivalents in the World Health Organization (WHO) and Papanicolaou systems.

The Atypical Pap Smear

Historically, the "atypical" category has included a wide range of abnormalities ranging from milder forms of inflammatory atypia, likely to be caused by infection, through squamous atypia, and condylomatous atypia likely to represent low-grade intraepithelial lesions (condyloma, mild dysplasia, CIN-1). In the Bethesda Classification System, the cytologist is asked to predict the etiology of the cytologic changes. Changes most likely related to inflammation with no premalignant potential are called epithelial changes related to inflammation. More marked epithelial changes are called atypical squamous cells of undetermined significance (ASCUS). The cytologist is asked to classify these as likely to be etiologically related to either inflammation or dysplasia.

The incidence of atypical smears has been reported as being in the range of 2 to 10 percent, with some reports indicating an incidence as high as 30 percent or more. This difference is as a result of differences in the patient populations reported, as well as from a marked interobserver variation in the reporting of ASCUS. In most populations, the diagnosis of ASCUS should be expected in no more than 5 percent of the smears. An ASCUS rate higher than this probably represents overreading of benign reactive and inflammatory changes. The reported incidence of dysplasia in patients with atypical smears also varies widely. Dysplasia has been reported in 10 to 40 percent of patients with atypical smears. Even more worrisome are data documenting that

TABLE 47-1 Comparison of Three Classification Systems Historically Used to Report the Results of Cervical Cytology

Papanicolaou System	Descriptive System (WHO)	Bethesda System[a,b]
Class I	Negative Negative with inflammation	Within normal limits Infection (specify type)
	Inflammatory atypia	Epithelial changes related to inflammation
Class II	Squamous atypia	Atypical squamous cells of undetermined significance
	Condylomatous (koilocytotic) atypia	Low-grade squamous intra-epithelial lesion (SIL) with or without cellular changes associated with HPV
	Minimal or Mild Dysplasia (CIN-1)	
Class III	Moderate Dysplasia (CIN-2) Severe Dysplasia (CIN-3)	High grade SIL
Class IV	Carcinoma-in-situ (CIN-3)	
Class V	Positive for malignant cells	Squamous cell carcinoma

[a]The Bethesda System incorporates into each report a statement on specimen adequacy.

[b]The Bethesda System incorporates a separate statement about glandular cells, atypical glandular cells, adenocarcinoma, or other malignant neoplasms when appropriate.

NOTE: It is important to note that the three classification systems overlap each other and that one cannot extrapolate results from the Papanicolaou System to the Bethesda System. To do so would be misleading and may result in errors in patient management.

approximately 30 percent of cervical cancers in women who had a preceding Pap smear had ASCUS as the only cytologic diagnosis preceding the detection of invasion. A variety of approaches have been suggested in the management of atypical Pap smears; however, none of these has been universally accepted as the only correct approach. The interobserver variability among cytologists means that not all clinicians share the same experience in clinically correlating this cytological entity, which results in differing perceptions of the most appropriate response to the ASCUS category.

The traditional approach in the management of atypical Pap smears is to treat based on the presumed cause of inflammation and to repeat the Pap smear at a later date. Patients whose repeat Pap smear is again atypical would undergo evaluation with colposcopy and biopsies, while patients with a negative follow-up smear should have their Pap smears repeated every 4 to 6 months until there have been at least three consecutive satisfactory normal smears. If one of those smears show ASCUS or a more advanced lesion, the patient should undergo colposcopy. While this traditional approach will reduce the burden on colposcopic resources, it may burden the rest of the system with multiple follow-up examinations. It also risks losing women to follow-up and the potential delayed diagnosis of significant cervical lesions. Studies have shown that treatment prior to repeat cytology did not improve the rate of reversion to normal cytology. Finally, the protocol of "treat and repeat" requires patience and reliability on the part of the patient. No amount of reassurance will completely allay the fears of a woman who has been told that her "cancer test" was not normal, but that she merely needs to have it repeated in four months.

Other approaches have been suggested in the management of ASCUS Pap smears. Colposcopy of all patients with atypical Pap smears is an effective method of identifying those patients with dysplasia, reduces the risk of patients lost to follow-up, and quickly reassures the patient; however, because of the significant investment required in time, resources, and trained personnel, this approach often is impractical. The Bethesda Classification System attempts to identify a subset of patients with atypical Pap smears who are at greater risk of cervical dysplasia. This is the category of atypical squamous cells of un-

determined significance suggestive of dysplasia. There are conflicting published data as to the effectiveness of this approach. This, along with the considerable interobserver variability among cytologists in interpreting this category, makes this approach impractical.

Intermediate triage tools also have been used to determine which patients need evaluation with colposcopy. In my opinion, the most successful of these tools are cervicography and HPV-DNA testing. Cervicography is a photographic method that provides a "colposcopic-type" view of the cervix, which is then interpreted for the practitioner by an expert in colposcopy. Cervicography has been shown to be effective in distinguishing atypia caused by dysplasia from other types of atypia. However, the initial experience with this method indicated that it had a high false-positive rate.

Because of the relationship of HPV to cervical cancer, testing for HPV-DNA has been proposed as a possible tool to identify women with ASCUS Pap smears who are at higher risk for cervical dysplasia. Women who test positive for high-risk HPV-DNA types would be evaluated with colposcopy, while those who are HPV-negative or have only low-risk HPV-DNA types would be followed with repeat testing in 6 months. This approach has been shown to detect most cases of dysplasia while reducing the number of colposcopies that need to be done.

Finally, there are certain situations that present clinical dilemmas. Women with ASCUS Pap smears whose colposcopy is repeatedly negative should not have any additional intervention. One approach is to manage these women with the help of HPV testing. HPV-DNA-positive women could be followed with cytology every 6 months while those who are HPV-negative could be followed annually.

Patients with atypical smears should be considered at high risk for CIN. Because no single method of triage is perfect, further study is necessary to find the best alternative. Until the best system is found, the evaluation of patients with atypical smears should not be considered complete until they have had a negative colposcopy, three consecutive negative Pap smears, and/or a negative cervigram or HPV-DNA test. The indications for HPV-DNA testing are an area of controversy, and trials are currently in progress to further analyze and define its role.

Pap Smears Suspicious for Squamous Intraepithelial Lesions

These smears must be evaluated on the assumption that the patient has a premalignant condition. The instrument used for this evaluation is the colposcope. It is a stereoscopic binocular microscope with illumination.

Colposcopy

The ultimate goal of colposcopy is to assess the size of a patient's lesion or lesions, their distribution, and the severity of the patient's disease, while determining that there is no evidence of microinvasive or invasive cancer. If these facts can be established, the patient can then be managed with conservative forms of treatment, and more radical approaches can be avoided. However, it is important to note that colposcopy is not a diagnostic test. Rather it is a triage technique that helps the colposcopist to identify the most suitable sites to biopsy. Histology remains the definitive diagnostic test. Colposcopy focuses on evaluation of the transformation zone. The transformation zone is the area of the cervix, and occasionally the vagina, that originally was covered by columnar epithelium and through a process called squamous metaplasia has changed to squamous epithelium. It extends outward from the squamocolumnar junction. The importance of the transformation zone is that almost all squamous cell carcinomas of the cervix begin in the transformation zone. If the entire transformation zone has been visualized and evaluated, the area at risk has been evaluated, and the most severe lesion has been seen.

The technique of colposcopy involves washing the cervix with 3 to 5% acetic acid. After treatment with acetic acid, areas with a greater nuclear density, such as benign metaplastic epithelium and dysplastic epithelium, will reflect light rather than transmitting it to the underlying stroma. The reflected light will therefore appear white rather than pink or red. Neovascularization will cause vascular changes of mosaic patterns, punctations, and atypical vessels in some lesions. These changes, taken together and graded for their severity, can be used to predict which areas have the most significant histologic abnormality, and will help to direct the colposcopist's decisions regarding the optimal locations for colposcopic biopsies. A good colposcopist should be able to recognize colposcopic patterns and to predict the histologic equivalents of these patterns. However, limiting the number of biopsies is one of the most common errors in colposcopy, which may result in the failure to diagnose significant disease. All but the most expert colposcopists should take biopsies from all significant lesions. In addition, a thorough endocervical curettage (ECC) should be performed in all nonpregnant patients to exclude occult disease in the endocervical canal and to detect adenocarcinoma.

Mature squamous epithelium remains pink after the application of acetic acid. It is covered by a fine network of uniformly thin and evenly distributed subepithelial blood vessels. Certain benign changes, such as inflammation and mucosal thinning due to inadequate estrogen stimulation, may make the vascular markings appear more pronounced. However, these are easily distinguished from the bizarre vascular patterns of early carcinoma. The endocervical mucosa around the external os appears red prior to the application of acetic acid, and has been called eversion, ectropion, or ectopy. Its surface presents longitudinal ridges and multiple villus-like projections. After the application of acetic acid, the tips of these villi may turn white, indicating the earliest manifestations of metaplasia.

The squamocolumnar junction is the line separating these two types of epithelial cells. It is frequently identified by a thin rim of acetowhite epithelium. The acetowhiteness seen at the squamocolumnar junction and in the remainder of the transformation zone is less intense and more translucent than acetowhiteness seen in dysplastic and neoplastic lesions, and it has a less distinct border (Fig. 47-1; see also color Plate 1). Other manifestations of the transformation zone seen during colposcopy include endocervical gland openings and nabothian cysts, which present as dome-like structures raised above the cervix and which are filled with a mucinous content behind a thin semitransparent wall, giving the cyst a yellow color. Large blood vessels found over the dome of the cyst are arranged in a characteristic branching pattern. It is this branching pattern that distinguishes these benign vessels from neoplastic atypical vessels (Fig. 47-2; see also color Plate 2).

Abnormal Epithelial Changes

Colposcopy identifies the area of cervical epithelium with the most advanced histological abnormality. By noting the colposcopic features characteristic of these lesions, each characteristic can be judged and graded based on the likelihood that it represents a high-grade versus a low-grade lesion. The individual criteria that distinguish

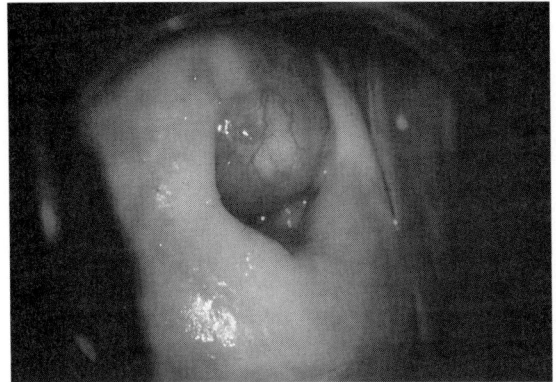

Figure 47-2 Nabothian cyst. Note the large blood vessels over the dome of the cyst. These can be distinguished from neoplastic vessels because they branch. (See color Plate 2.)

low-grade from high-grade lesions are the epithelial thickness, its contour, the degree of acetowhiteness, the presence of vascular changes, the border of the lesion, and its location within the transformation zone.

The most common colposcopic manifestation of CIN is acetowhiteness. Acetowhite epithelium appears white only *after* the application of acetic acid. Acetowhiteness must be distinguished from leukoplakia, which appears white *before* the application of acetic acid (Fig. 47-3; see also color Plate 3). Leukoplakia is caused by hyperkeratosis

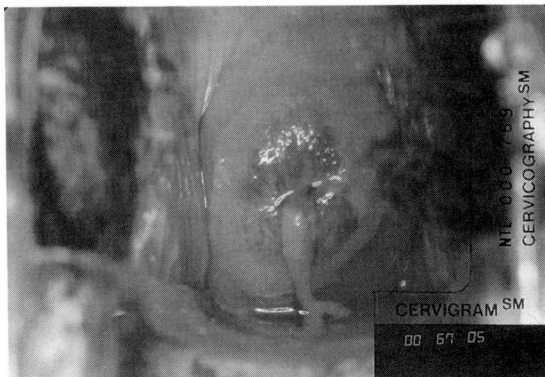

Figure 47-1 Normal transformation zone—columnar epithelium can be seen in the endocervical canal. Mature squamous epithelium is seen on the ectocervix. The metaplastic epithelium in the transformation zone in this woman is seen as a rim of acetowhite epithelium immediately surrounding the endocervical mucosa. A faint, mosaic pattern can be seen. (See color Plate 1.)

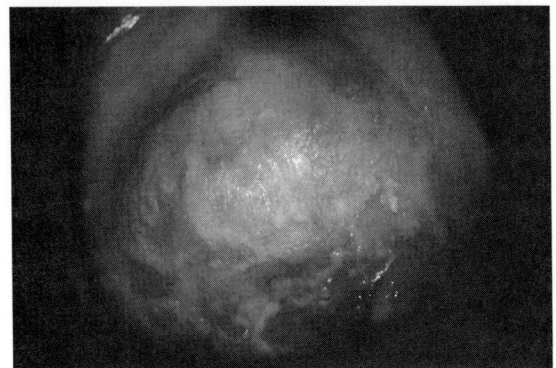

Figure 47-3 Leukoplakia: A thick layer of keratin can be seen on the anterior lip of the cervix. The surface is white, shiny, and irregular prior to the application of acetic acid. (See color Plate 3.)

and is important only because it obscures the underlying epithelium. Because it is impossible to evaluate the underlying epithelium colposcopically, leukoplakia always should be biopsied.

Acetowhiteness can range in intensity. Metaplastic epithelium is semitransparent. A snow-white, shiny epithelium is found in low-grade lesions (Fig. 47-4; see also color Plate 4). Intermediate lesions have a grayish-white, but still shiny, epithelium, and high-grade lesions have a dull grayish to oyster shell-white epithelium (Fig. 47-5; see also color Plate 5).

The sharpness of the peripheral margin is another feature that is used to grade epithelial abnormalities. Squamous metaplastic lesions turn white after the application of acetic acid, but their borders tend to be diffuse and to blend into the adjacent squamous epithelium. True dysplastic lesions have a sharp and well-demarcated border. In low-grade lesions, this border may be feathered or finely scalloped, or may be angular and irregularly shaped, similar to geographic features on a map (Fig. 47-4). Significant satellite lesions, not contiguous with the rest of the transformation zone, are most commonly low-grade lesions. Intermediate- and high-grade lesions usually have straight and sharp peripheral margins (Fig. 47-5). The highest grade lesions have edges that

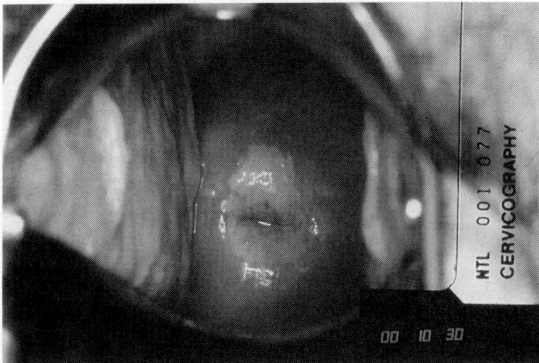

Figure 47-5 Acetowhite epithelium—high grade. This is a well-demarcated, dense acetowhite epithelium on the anterior lip of the cervix. Note the straight edges of this high-grade lesion. Also, there is dense acetowhite epithelium extending into the endocervical canal on the posterior lip of the cervix. (See color Plate 5.)

detach from the underlying stroma and curl back upon themselves (Fig. 47-6; see also color Plate 6). This is due to the poor cell-to-cell cohesiveness in these lesions. Lesions that show an internal margin between two different colposcopic patterns almost always are high-grade, with the peripheral area representing a minor-grade le-

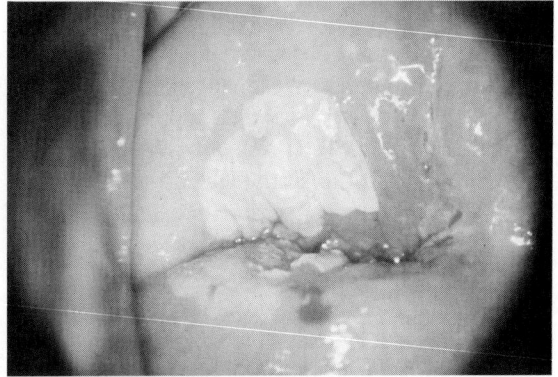

Figure 47-4 Acetowhite epithelium—low grade. The lesion on the anterior lip of the cervix is snow-white in color and has an irregular geographic border. These are both characteristics of a low-grade dysplastic lesion. (See color Plate 4.)

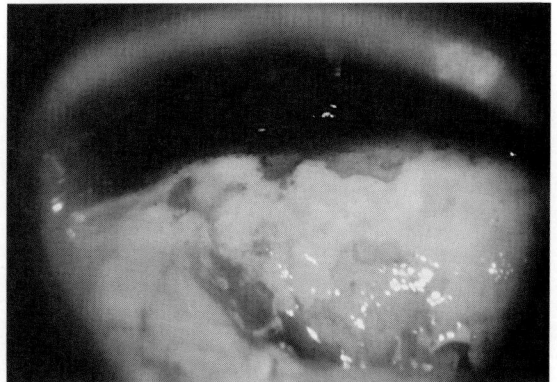

Figure 47-6 Peeling margins. In high-grade lesions, the desmosomal attachment of the epithelium to the underlying stroma is weakened. The epithelium appears to peel away. At both the upper and lower portion of this lesion, the dense, high-grade acetowhite epithelium has been peeled away exposing the underlying stroma. (See color Plate 6.)

sion and the central area a high-grade lesion (Fig. 47-7; see also color Plate 7).

Another colposcopic feature to consider when grading lesions is the epithelial thickness and contour. Condylomatous lesions have a micropapillary contour (Fig. 47-8; see also color Plate 8), while dysplastic lesions are more likely to be flat. Low-grade lesions are flat with their surface at the same level as the adjacent squamous epithelium. Lesions with a definite thickness above the adjacent squamous epithelium are more likely to be high grade (Fig. 47-9; see also color Plate 9).

Another colposcopic feature used to grade epithelial abnormalities is the vascular pattern. Vascular patterns in benign epithelium are seen when the hairpin capillary at the core of an endocervical villus that is undergoing metaplasia has not completely regressed. Abnormal vascularity, punctations, and mosaic patterns occur when the stromal papilla and their blood vessels persist in the neoplastic epithelium with neovascularization. Persistent blood vessels reach the epithelial surface and then become visible as colposcopic abnormalities.

Punctation is seen as multiple red dots spaced over a demarcated area of acetowhite epithelium.

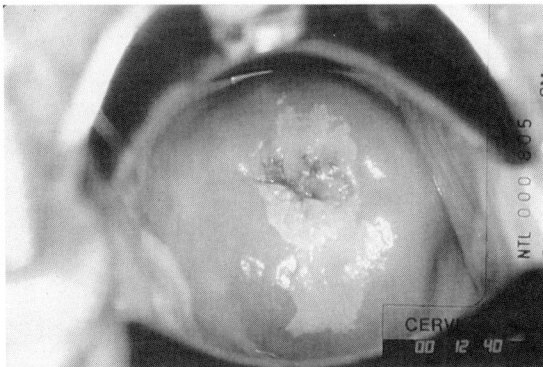

Figure 47-7 Internal margins. A low-grade acetowhite lesion with a geographic border is seen on both the anterior lip and the posterior lip of the cervix. However, on the posterior lip of the cervix, within the larger lesion is a dense, oyster shell-white lesion with a clearly demarcated border. Such lesions with internal margins are almost always high-grade lesions. (See color Plate 7.)

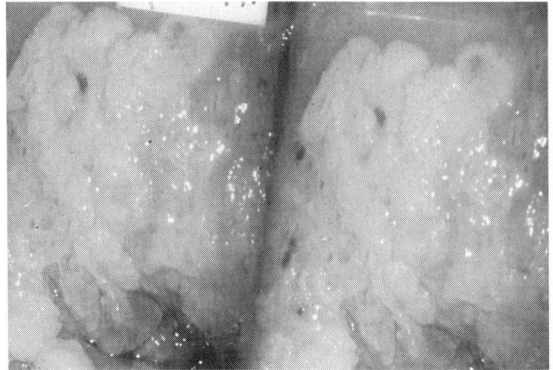

Figure 47-8 Cervical condyloma. This is a raised hyperkeratotic acetowhite lesion with papillary features characteristic of overt cervical HPV infection. (See color Plate 8.)

A true punctation has an acetowhite background with well-demarcated borders. Red dots on a pink or red mucosa usually are manifestations of an inflammatory condition such as Trichomonas or some other type of vaginitis (Fig. 47-10; see also color Plate 10).

Mosaic patterns are characterized by round or polygonal, tile-like fields of acetowhite epithelium, each encircled by a blood vessel. Mosaic patterns develop when the persistent superficial vessels run horizontally, forming a honeycomb pattern, and enclose islands of white epithelium between their anastomotic branches. A true neo-

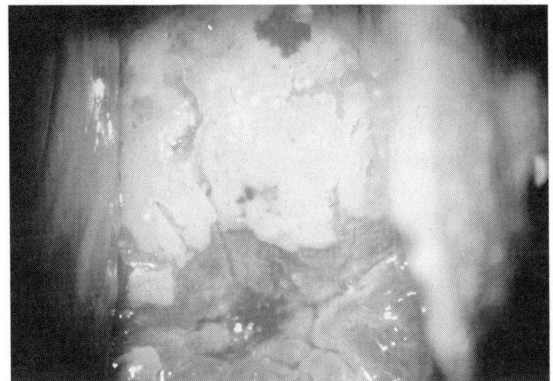

Figure 47-9 Acetowhite epithelium. Biopsies should be taken from the inner margin of this dense acetowhite lesion. This is the most immature area and likely to be the highest grade lesion. (See color Plate 9.)

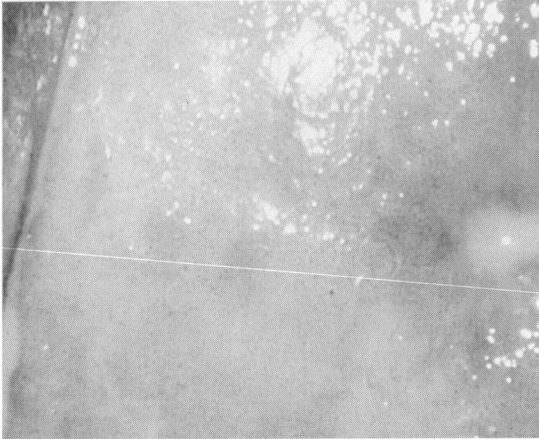

Figure 47-10 Inflammatory punctations. The cervix is covered with intensely red punctations, but there is no well-defined acetowhite epithelium. This pattern is often found associated with vaginitis or cervicitis and is distinguished from true punctations because they are not found within an acetowhite layer. (See color Plate 10.)

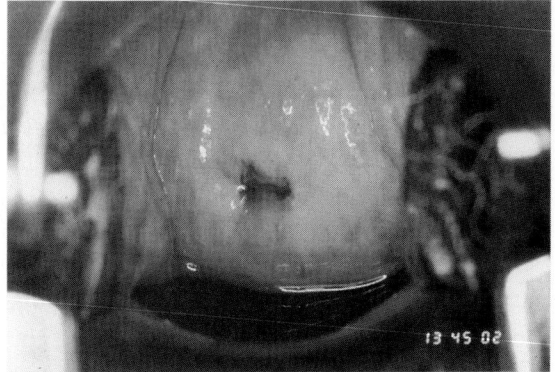

Figure 47-11 Fine punctations. A faint acetowhite lesion is seen on the anterior lip of the cervix. Careful inspection will reveal fine punctations. This is characteristic of metaplastic or low-grade lesions. (See color Plate 11.)

plastic mosaic pattern is always associated with well-demarcated acetowhite epithelium, just as in true punctations.

Mosaic patterns and punctations may be fine or coarse. Fine punctation patterns are distinguished from coarse ones by the caliber of the vessels, the intercapillary distance, and the regularity of the pattern. Fine punctations appear as small red dots closely and regularly spaced in the field of acetowhite epithelium (Fig. 47-11; see also color Plate 11). In coarse punctations, the individual vessels may be dilated, the distance between the dots is increased, and the pattern is irregular (Fig. 47-12; see also color Plate 12). In extreme cases, the punctations may be seen to rise above the surface epithelium, and they may begin to take on bizarre appearances (Fig. 47-13; see also color Plate 13). Fine punctations and fine mosaic patterns are associated with low-grade lesions, while coarse punctations and mosaic patterns are associated with high-grade lesions. Fine mosaic patterns are characterized by thin vessels separating small, regularly spaced acetowhite tiles. The pattern may be poorly developed (Fig. 47-14; see also color Plate 14). In

a coarse mosaic pattern, the vessel caliber is large. The acetowhite tiles frequently are raised above the surface epithelium. In the highest-grade lesions, there is frequently punctation in the center of the mosaic tile. This pattern is almost always indicative of a high-grade lesion (Fig. 47-15; see also color Plate 15).

The most extreme form of abnormal vascular pattern is the presence of atypical vessels. Atypical vessels may be comma-shaped or may have other bizarre appearances, such as sharp bends,

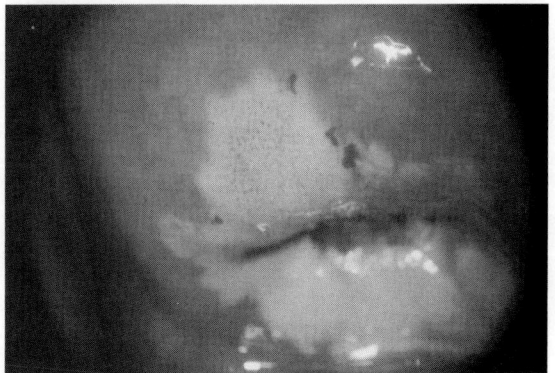

Figure 47-12 Coarse punctations. Acetowhite epithelium with a coarse punctation pattern. Note that the dots vary in size and intensity, and their pattern is irregular. This is typical of a high-grade lesion. (See color Plate 12.)

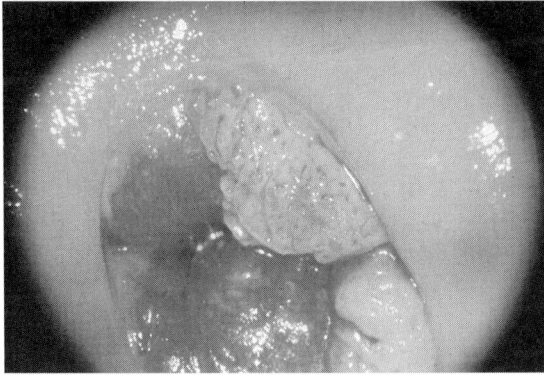

Figure 47-13 Coarse punctations. In addition to having a large caliber and large intercapillary distances (distance between punctations), these punctations rise above the surface epithelium and are beginning to take on comma shapes suggestive of atypical vessels. (See color Plate 13.)

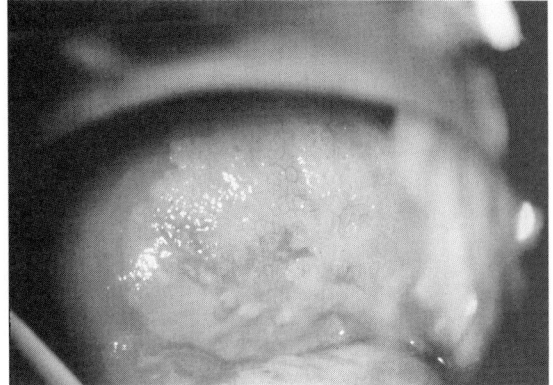

Figure 47-15 Coarse mosaic. Acetowhite epithelium with a coarse mosaic pattern. Note that the mosaic tiles are large and irregular in size and shape. The vessels surrounding the mosaic tiles have a central vessel. This is highly suggestive of a high-grade lesion. (See color Plate 15.)

turns, or spirals. The vessel caliber may suddenly constrict or dilate, or the vessel may change course abruptly. Vessels are sometimes seen to plunge beneath the surface of the epithelium only to resurface in a serpentine manner (Fig. 47-16; see also color Plate 16). Most characteristically, these vessels do not branch. Atypical vessels are the earliest colposcopic manifestation of invasive cancer (Fig. 47-17; see also color Plate 17).

The final colposcopic feature that is used to distinguish among epithelial abnormalities is

their location. High-grade intraepithelial lesions show changes that are dysplastic and immature all the way to the surface of the epithelium. Given an identical neoplastic stimulus, the most immature epithelium is likely to have the greatest de-

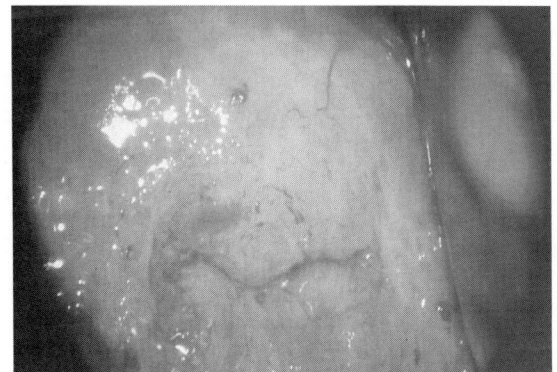

Figure 47-16 Atypical vessels. Atypical vessels have a variety of bizarre patterns. Sharp turns, comma-shaped vessels, and other bizarre patterns are seen in this colpophotograph. Several serpentine vessels are seen which rise above the epithelium and then plunge below it only to resurface again. Although atypical vessels may be found in benign as well as malignant lesions, when they are seen, invasive cancer must always be excluded by a biopsy. (See color Plate 16.)

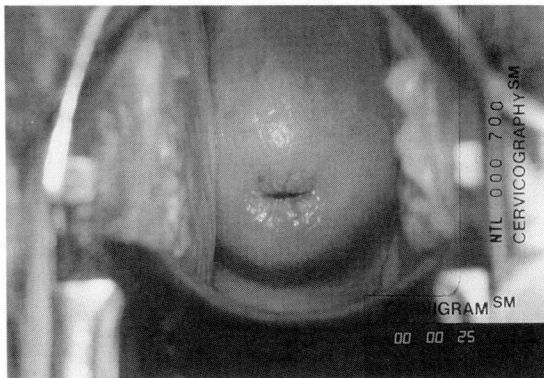

Figure 47-14 Mosaic pattern. A large acetowhite lesion with a poorly developed mosaic pattern. Such a pattern is often seen in metaplastic epithelium. (See color Plate 14.)

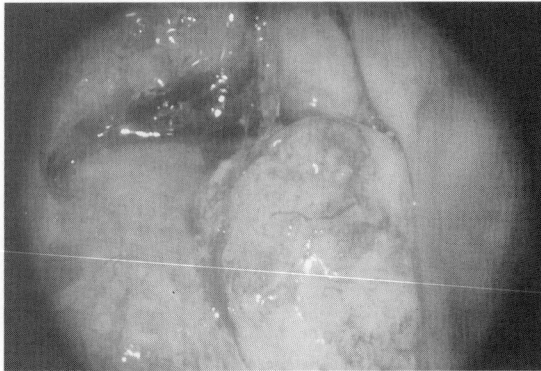

Figure 47-17 Atypical vessels. The prominent vessel in the center of the colpophotograph is one of several atypical vessels on this cervix. Note the varying caliber of this large vessel. Another characteristic of atypical vessels is that they do not branch. (See color Plate 17.)

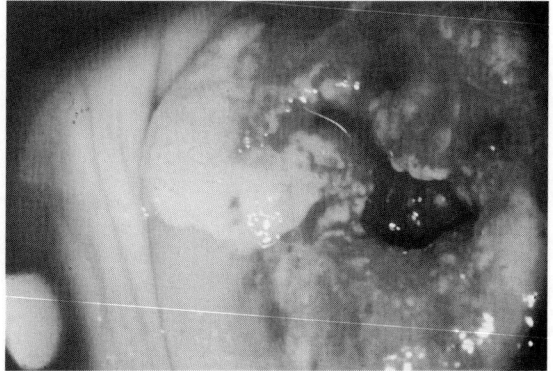

Figure 47-18 Invasive cancer. This is a bloody cervix with ulceration. There is a grossly visible acetowhite lesion with comma-shaped atypical vessels. (See color Plate 18.)

gree of histologic change. The most immature squamous epithelium is found closest to the squamocolumnar junction. Therefore, on any cervix, biopsies should always be taken of lesions closest to the squamocolumar junction.

Colposcopic Diagnosis of Invasive Cancer

The colposcopic diagnosis of invasive cancer is the most important, and frequently the most difficult, diagnosis to make. While low-grade and high-grade intraepithelial lesions show distinctive colposcopic patterns, the colposcopic appearance of invasive cancer may be nonspecific and may resemble benign conditions such as chronic cervicitis. Because early invasive cancer is seen infrequently, even by experienced colposcopists, it is a very easy diagnosis to miss. Some features of invasive cancer are atypical vessels, a yellow color, a gelatinous appearance of the lesion surface, markedly irregular contour (because of ulceration, granularity, or necrosis, or exophytic, or endophytic lesions), and multiple areas of superficial bleeding (Fig. 47-18; see also color Plate 18). There may be surface hemorrhages and atypical vessels. Because the intense inflammatory response may obscure the cyto-

logic diagnosis of cancer, colposcopic recognition of these lesions is important and may be the only opportunity the clinician has to make an early diagnosis. For this reason, biopsy of any suspicious areas is essential.

Criteria for a Satisfactory Colposcopy

Colposcopy is a tool used to establish the location of the patient's most significant disease while excluding the possibility of invasive cancer. A directed biopsy (or more commonly, multiple biopsies) should be taken to establish the diagnosis. If the diagnosis can be established and cancer can be ruled out, the patient can be managed with conservative forms of treatment, and more aggressive treatment can be avoided. To avoid delays in the diagnosis of invasive cancer, certain criteria have been established to define a satisfactory colposcopy. Rigid adherence to these criteria will help avoid delay of the diagnosis and inadequate treatment of invasive cancer. To be certain that the worst lesion has been seen, the entire transformation zone must be visualized, and the entire lesion must be visualized. An ECC should be done unless the patient is pregnant, and it should not demonstrate any evidence of neoplastic disease. Finally, the biopsy findings should not be significantly less severe than the cytologic and colposcopic findings. Such a discrepancy implies that the biopsy may not have been taken from the worst lesion. When all these criteria are met, and invasive cancer has been ruled out, the colposcopy is deemed to be satisfactory, and the patient can be treated with a conservative ablative modality such as cryotherapy or laser vaporization. If these criteria are not met, then invasive cancer has not been definitely ruled out, and the patient must undergo a cone biopsy. A cone biopsy removes the entire transformation zone, which can then be submitted for histologic evaluation to definitely rule out invasive cancer. Excision of the transformation zone also serves to treat the disease.

An important step in resolving noncorrelating cytology and histology is communication with the pathologist. The colposcopist and pathologist must agree on terminology and serve each other's needs. Standardization of terminology was one of the principal contributions of the Bethesda Classification System. The colposcopist must provide the pathologist with an adequate history and description of the clinical findings. The pathologist should thoroughly describe his or her findings, including any deficiencies in the sample (e.g., failure to sample the transformation zone, absence of underlying stroma, obscuring inflammation on a cytological specimen). All noncorrelating cytology/histology should be reviewed by the pathologist to confirm the original diagnosis and to determine whether cellular changes in the Pap smear can be explained by the histological findings.

Glandular Abnormalities

The frequency of cervical adenocarcinoma has risen during the last two decades. There is added concern because adenocarcinoma is responsible for the majority of the increase in cervical cancer among women under the age of 35, and glandular cancers may be rapidly progressive. Unfortunately, both cytology and colposcopy are less sensitive at detecting glandular abnormalities than their squamous counterparts. As many as half

of adenocarcinoma or adenocarcinoma-in-situ (AIS) lesions are detected after referral for associated squamous abnormalities. Also, although it appears that AIS is a preinvasive stage of cervical adenocarcinoma, the existence of earlier grades of glandular dysplasia is less conclusive.

Cytology is a poor predictor of glandular disease. Its poor sensitivity is related to the more irregular shedding of abnormal glandular cells, the smaller size of the lesions, and their endocervical location. Many invasive adenocarcinomas show less-marked cytologic abnormalities than do glandular dysplasias, and it may be difficult to distinguish the cytology of early, well-differentiated adenocarcinoma from normal.

The colposcopic changes associated with glandular dysplasias are nonspecific and difficult to identify. The lesions may be focal, multicentric, or diffuse, and although they may be found in any area of glandular epithelium, they most commonly develop adjacent to the squamocolumnar junction. The colposcopic appearance of AIS is also nonspecific. It may appear as a normal ectopy, or as villi that are fused, or as villi whose acetowhiteness is slightly more pronounced. As a result, AIS is often discovered incidently during conization for squamous disease.

The colposcopic appearance of adenocarcinoma differs markedly from that of squamous disease. The typical changes of mosaic patterns and punctation are not seen. The cervix has a dull, pale, orange-to-dark yellow appearance prior to the application of acetic acid. Vascular changes are described as willow branch-like, root-like, loop-like, and linear. Acetowhite epithelium is less prominent than with squamous neoplasia, and gland openings are larger and are not surrounded by white rims as is seen in metaplastic epithelium.

Because of the absence of a well-recognized continuum of glandular dysplasias, the spectrum of cytologic abnormalities identified by the Bethesda Classification System is also more limited. Glandular abnormalities are classified as atypical glandular cells of undetermined significance (AGUS) (subdivided into AGUS favoring a reactive process and AGUS favoring a neoplastic process), AIS, and adenocarcinoma. Because of the combination of the poor sensitivity of cytology and the lack of cytologic categories for glandular disease, the AGUS diagnosis represents a mixture of benign and neoplastic conditions. Also, because the interobserver variability for AGUS is even greater than it is for ASCUS, the percentage of benign and neoplastic abnormalities can vary significantly among laboratories. Consequently, every clinician should be familiar with the clinical correlation of their individual laboratory before acting on a noncorrelating AGUS smear.

More than half of AGUS smears are associated with benign conditions such as inflammatory changes, microglandular hyperplasia, intrauterine devices, and benign endocervical polyps. Approximately 25 percent or more of women with AGUS smears will have AIS, adenocarcinoma, or glandular involvement of CIN. The remaining cases of AGUS are associated with benign or malignant endometrial lesions, or lesions of the fallopian tubes, ovaries, gastrointestinal tract, or breast. Proper evaluation of these lesions must consider the patient's age and clinical findings and should include confirmation of the cytologic findings by a second pathologist before embarking on an extensive and invasive diagnostic workup.

Management of AGUS Smears

All women, regardless of age, who have an AGUS smear, should undergo colposcopy of the cervix and vagina. The evaluation should include an ECC even if the endocervical canal looks normal through the colposcope. In patients with risk factors for endometrial or ovarian cancer (age, personal or family history, or physical examination; and in those whose atypical glandular cells appear to be of endometrial or ovarian origin), appropriate diagnostic evaluation should be considered, including sonography, endometrial biopsy, hysteroscopy, and dilatation and curettage or laparoscopy. For women in whom the colpos-

copic evaluation and ECC are negative, and who have AGUS smears favoring neoplasia of endocervical origin, a deep conization should be done (2.0 to 2.5 cm long). Prior to such a conization, the potential for cervical stenosis and future fertility problems should be discussed with the patient.

In women with AGUS favoring a reactive process, the source of the atypicality should be sought. Cervicitis should be treated, polyps should be removed, and consideration should be given to removal of an IUD if the AGUS smear persists. All women with AGUS smears should be followed with repeat Pap smears every 4 to 6 months until a minimum of four negative follow-up Pap smears have been obtained.

Any woman whose smear suggests AIS or adenocarcinoma must have colposcopy with directed biopsies and an ECC. If the etiology is not identified, the vagina should be evaluated with the help of Lugol's staining and palpation. The Pap smear should also be reviewed by a second cytopathologist because several benign conditions such as cervicitis, microglandular hyperplasia, Arias-Stella reaction, adenomatoid proliferation, and mesonephric remnants can all mimic the cytologic finding of AIS or adenocarcinoma on Pap smears. If the cytologic findings are confirmed, all women should undergo a deep conization unless invasive cancer is confirmed by the colposcopically directed biopsy. The standard treatment for patients with AIS confirmed by conization is simple hysterectomy. However, for women who desire to become pregnant in the future and whose cone margins are free of neoplasia, very close follow-up without hysterectomy may be offered if they are informed and are willing to accept the risk. Follow-up of these patients should include cytology every 4 months for 2 years and then annually. A good endocervical brush specimen or an ECC should be included with each visit.

Colposcopy of Vulvar and Vaginal Lesions

The colposcopic features of vulvar and vaginal intraepithelial lesions are similar to those on the cervix. Because metaplasia is uncommon on the vagina, except in DES-exposed women, mosaic and punctation patterns are almost always indicative of condyloma or intraepithelial neoplasia. Because of the large surface area of the vagina and its many folds, colposcopy of the vagina is difficult. Multicentric disease is common on the vulva. Because dysplastic lesions of these areas are uncommon, colposcopy for disease of the vagina and vulva may need to be referred to an expert, unless the primary care physician has experience with these problems.

Treatment of Cervical Intraepithelial Neoplasia

Once the diagnosis has been established and colposcopy is satisfactory, the patient's disease may be treated by ablation or excision of the transformation zone. If the colposcopy is not satisfactory, the transformation zone must be excised to establish the diagnosis and to exclude the possibility of invasive cancer.

Whether treating the patient with ablation or excision, it is important to treat the entire transformation zone and to treat it to a depth of 7 to 10 mm so that all of the endocervical glands or crypts that may be involved with disease are treated. None of the treatments are 100 percent effective, but any of them, properly applied, provides a cure in 90 to almost 100 percent of patients. Treatment of just the lesion without treating the remainder of the transformation zone, or treatment of the transformation zone, but to an inadequate depth, results in significantly diminished cure rates. The techniques commonly employed in the United States are cryosurgery, laser surgery, loop electrosurgical excision, and cold-knife conization. For a single, small, low-grade lesion, some very experienced physicians will remove the lesion entirely by colposcopically directed biopsy, and not treat the remainder of the transformation zone.

Cryosurgery freezes the transformation zone with a liquid nitrous oxide or carbon dioxide probe. In well-selected patients, most authors report cure rates in excess of 90 percent following one treatment. Cryosurgery can be done on an outpatient basis and requires no anesthesia, although pretreatment with a nonsteroidal anti-inflammatory agent may help prevent the cramps that are associated with the procedure. Cryosurgery does, however, have some limitations. Because the probe size and shape need to approximate the size and shape of the lesion and the transformation zone, women who have a very large lesion, a very large transformation zone, or whose cervix is significantly distorted after obstetric trauma may be poor candidates for cryosurgery.

Several technical points must be kept in mind to obtain an optimal freeze. After insertion of an adequately sized speculum, including a vaginal side-wall retractor to prevent the vagina from making contact with the cryosurgery probe, a water-soluble lubricant jelly is applied to the probe to allow for efficient heat transfer. The probe is then applied to the cervix and the freezing initiated. The freeze should continue until an ice ball forms and its margins extend 5 mm beyond the edge of the lesion. Two freezes, each 3 min long, with a 3-min wait in between, usually is sufficient. The pressure gauge on the nitrous oxide tank must be observed to insure that the gas pressure is adequate to chill the probe sufficiently at all times. A tank of adequate size should be chosen to insure that adequate pressures are maintained throughout the procedure. Because the actual depth of destruction is usually only between 2 and 5 mm, cryosurgery may be less effective in ablating lesions that extend to the endocervical glands or into the endocervical canal. For this reason, cryosurgery may be less effective in curing CIN-3. Cryosurgery should never be utilized if colposcopy was not satisfactory (i.e., it should not be utilized if the transformation zone was not fully visualized, if the entire lesion could not be seen colposcopically, or if the cytological findings or colposcopic findings were significantly worse than that which could be demonstrated on histological evaluation).

Carbon dioxide laser surgery is probably the most versatile of the treatment modalities. Large lesions, irregular cervices, and high-grade lesions can all be managed by this modality. Laser can be done safely in an outpatient setting and under local anesthesia with minimal discomfort to the patient and with excellent cure rates. The disadvantages of laser surgery include a small but significant incidence of bleeding associated with the procedures, expensive equipment, and the significant amount of training and experience required to achieve good results, especially in an outpatient setting.

Loop electrosurgical excision, also known as large loop excision of the transformation zone (LLETZ), is becoming increasingly popular in the United States. A large unipolar electrocautery wire loop is used to excise the transformation zone in one piece. The procedure can be used in place of ablative techniques such as cryosurgery and laser vaporization, and can be tailored as an alternative to excisional cone biopsy. It can be done under local anesthesia in an outpatient setting and has the major advantage of providing a specimen for histologic evaluation. Because LLETZ provides a histologic specimen, some practitioners use it instead of punch biopsy during colposcopic examination of patients with cytologic evidence of CIN. The use of this approach in women whose cytologic results are only mildly abnormal may result in many unnecessary excisions.

The LLETZ technique is as follows: A wire loop is chosen of a shape and size that will excise the entire transformation zone, preferably in one pass. The loop is attached to an electrosurgical generator, and the patient is grounded to that generator. A large speculum is placed in the vagina and attached to a smoke-evacuation device. Lateral side-wall retractors are placed to avoid injury to the vaginal wall. A local anesthetic is injected into the cervix. The wire loop is then slowly plunged into the cervical stroma 3 to 5 mm lateral to the edge of the transformation zone on one side of the cervix, to a depth of 7 mm. It is then slowly passed under the transformation

zone until the entire transformation zone is removed 3 to 5 mm lateral to the transformation zone on the other side of the cervix. The electrosurgical generator power setting should be set with sufficient power to allow the probe to pass easily without drag, but not so high that the specimen is damaged. Approximately 30 watts of power is sufficient in most cases. One disadvantage of this procedure is the possibility of bleeding, but it is usually minimal and can be controlled with electrocautery using a ball electrode or thickened ferric subsulfate solution. Also, there is a small incidence of thermal damage to the cone specimen.

Cold-knife conization, which is an alternative method for cervical conization, is not discussed in this chapter because it is usually performed in the operating room, not in the office.

Who Should Be Treated?

After a complete colposcopic examination with biopsies and ECC, patients with high-grade squamous intraepithelial lesions (CIN-2 and -3, moderate-to-severe dysplasia, carcinoma-in-situ) in whom invasive cancer has been ruled out should be treated. Patients with satisfactory colposcopy and a negative ECC may be treated by ablation of the transformation zone. Cryosurgery, laser vaporization, and LLETZ are all good alternatives for this treatment, although cryosurgery may be slightly less effective in CIN-3. When the colposcopy is not satisfactory, a cone biopsy must be performed. This acts as a combination of diagnosis and treatment. Techniques for cone biopsy that can be utilized in an office setting include laser excisional conization and LLETZ.

When the colposcopically directed biopsy shows a low-grade lesion (condyloma, CIN-1, mild dysplasia), the alternatives are expanded. When the colposcopy is satisfactory, cryosurgery, laser vaporization, and LLETZ are all viable alternatives for treatment. However, because the vast majority of these lesions will never progress to invasive cancer and many will regress, close observation with cytology and colposcopy without treatment is another alternative. When deciding whether or not to treat such patients, some of the factors to consider are the woman's age and parity, the size of the lesion, whether the lesion has persisted for a long time or whether it is newly discovered, previous treatment, her immune status, and her reliability. While there is no evidence that cryosurgery, laser surgery, or LLETZ adversely affects fertility or the ability of a woman to carry a pregnancy to term, in cases of young, nulliparous women, the alternative of watchful waiting should be favored in reliable patients who do not have other risk factors. In patients with large or persistent lesions, and in patients who cannot be relied on to continue close follow-up, the alternative of treatment should be favored. Also, in patients with a history of in utero DES exposure, therapy should be avoided when possible because of the great risk of cervical stenosis following treatment in such patients. If the colposcopy is not satisfactory, a cone biopsy should be performed. In young and nulliparous women, referral for colposcopy to an expert colposcopist should be considered prior to conization.

It is important to remember that the goal of treatment for women with intraepithelial disease of the cervix is the prevention of cancer, not the treatment of a viral infection. No treatment currently available is capable of eradicating the viral presence from the lower genital tract. Therefore, it is expected that viral presence may persist despite treatment and that flat condylomata may reappear on the mature squamous epithelium of the cervix following treatment. This does not necessarily represent a treatment failure. Once the transformation zone has been destroyed, reappearance of flat condylomata on the cervix does not necessarily need to be retreated. Such patients can be managed by careful cytologic and colposcopic follow-up. However, if the recurrent lesion is a high-grade intraepithelial lesion, these patients must be retreated, preferably using an excisional technique to assure that the margins are nega-tive and that the lesion has been completely excised.

Treatment of Vulvar and Vaginal Lesions

Because the progressive potential of low-grade vulvar and vaginal intraepithelial lesions and condylomata is so low, excessively aggressive treatment of these lesions to prevent cancer usually is not warranted once high-grade, premalignant lesions in these areas have been ruled out. Because the disease is often multifocal and because colposcopy of the vagina and vulva are more difficult than cervical colposcopy, such patients should be evaluated by an expert colposcopist to confirm that there is no disease that is more advanced. After such an evaluation, patients with low-grade disease may be followed carefully with colposcopy and cytology. High-grade lesions should be treated. The most effective and versatile therapeutic modality for this treatment is the carbon dioxide laser. The laser can eradicate the disease with excellent precision while preserving the adjacent tissue. Loop electrosurgical excision is effective, but depth control is more difficult, and proper depth control is crucial to avoid scarring caused by an overly deep excision. Unless invasive cancer has been ruled out, it is essential that therapy be by excision rather than ablation, so that the pathologist can evaluate the entire specimen.

Summary

The evaluation of women with abnormal Pap smears should follow a careful, stepwise approach. By using the protocols outlined above, significant disease can be recognized and treated, and unnecessary treatment can be avoided.

Finally, it must be recognized that one does not become an expert colposcopist by evaluating the small number of patients that present to the average practitioner during the course of a routine practice. During the first several hundred cases, the beginning colposcopist should always continue to obtain consultation from more experienced colleagues, especially whenever difficult or unusual cases present themselves.

References and Selected Readings

1. Carter R: *Practical Colposcopy,* 2d ed. New York: Fisher, 1984.
2. Coppleson M, Pixley E, Reid B: *Colposcopy: A Scientific and Practical Approach to the Cervix, Vagina, and Vulva in Health and Disease,* 3d ed. Springfield, IL: Charles C Thomas, 1986.
3. Follen MM, Levine RU, Carillo E, et. al: Colposcopic correlates of cervical papillomavirus infection. *Am J Obstet Gynecol* 157:809–814, 1987.
4. Giuntoli RL, Atkinson BF, Ernst CS, et. al: *Atkinson's Correlative Atlas of Colposcopy Cytology, and Histopathology.* Philadelphia: JB Lippincott, 1987.
5. Kolstad P, Stafl A: *Atlas of Colposcopy,* 3d ed. Baltimore: University Park Press, 1982.
6. Spitzer M, Krumholz BA, Seltzer VL: The multicentric nature of disease related to human papillomavirus infection of the female lower genital tract. *Obstet Gynecol* 73:303–307, 1989.
7. Spitzer M, Krumholz BA: Human papillomavirus related diseases in the female. *Urol Clin North Am* 19:71–82, 1992.
8. Spitzer M, Chernys AE, Seltzer VL: The outpatient use of large loop excision of the transformation zone in an inner-city population. *Obstet Gynecol* 82:731–735, 1993.
9. Spitzer M, Krumholz BA: Intraepithelial neoplasms of the lower genital tract, in Jacobs AJ, Gast M, (eds): *Practical Gynecology: A Clinical Manual.* Stamford, CT: Appleton & Lange, 1994, pp 135–147.

CHAPTER 48

Endometrial Evaluation, Sampling, and Hysteroscopy as Office Procedures

Mark Spitzer

CYTOLOGIC SCREENING DEVICES

HISTOLOGIC SAMPLING

TRANSVAGINAL SONOGRAPY

SALINE-INFUSION SONOGRAPHY

HYSTEROSCOPY

The need for a safe, accurate, and simple method of sampling the endometrium has become increasingly important. Financial constraints, patient demands, and advances in technology have all pushed endometrial sampling from a procedure that usually was performed in the hospital to one now commonly performed in the office. Much of the literature regarding office endometrial sampling focuses on the ability of this technique to screen and accurately detect endometrial hyperplasia and carcinoma. However, there are many other indications for endometrial sampling in the office including evaluation of infertility, menstrual disorders, cytology suggesting endometrial pathology, follow-up of patients receiving hormonal therapy, and the evaluation of postmenopausal and perimenopausal bleeding.

The ideal technique for endometrial sampling should be safe and easy to use. It should be well tolerated by the patient, preferably with either local anesthesia or no anesthetic at all. It should have minimal limitations on its use, and should provide a diagnostic specimen in the vast majority of cases.

The most common indication for office endo-metrial sampling is to screen for or to diagnose endometrial carcinoma or hyperplasia. The gold standard for the diagnosis of these lesions has always been a dilatation and curettage (D&C) done in the operating room under general anesthesia. However, the need for hospitalization, general anesthesia, and a formal D&C is not well supported in the literature. One very large study compared D&C to an office biopsy technique (Vabra) and found that the office technique was safer, cheaper, more convenient, and provided an adequate and equally diagnostic specimen.[8] In another study, endometrial lesions were missed in 10 percent of preoperative D&Cs.[23] In one study, a curettage was found to have sampled less than a quarter of the endometrium in 16 percent of cases, less than half of the endometrial cavity in 60 percent, and less than three-quarters in 84 percent.[16] Other studies have found a 2 to 6 percent false-negative rate in the diagnosis of endometrial hyperplasia and cancer based on D&C.[19,22] Even as a therapeutic technique for the treatment of menorrhagia, several well-designed studies showed that the reduction in menstrual blood loss usually does not extend beyond the first month following the procedure.[10,15] Nevertheless, the D&C is the standard to which the endometrial biopsy is compared.

Two of the basic indications for endometrial sampling are screening for endometrial carcinoma or hyperplasia and for the diagnosis of other endometrial pathology. Different devices have been developed for each indication, and must be considered separately.

Cytologic Screening Devices

The simplest screening device for endometrial carcinoma is the Pap smear. However, while the Pap smear is a relatively sensitive screen for early cervical cancer, it detects endometrial cancer in only 25 to 67 percent of women in whom the disease is present, and detects endometrial hyperplasia in as few as 20 percent of women in whom the disease is present. Therefore, as many as 75 percent of women with endometrial cancer will have completely normal Pap smears, and the presence of a normal Pap smear is obviously not sufficient evaluation to rule out endometrial cancer in a woman with abnormal bleeding.

Other devices that have been used for cytologic screening of endometrial cancer include the Endocyte, Accurette, and the Mi-Mark sampler. The Endocyte and Accurette devices are inserted into the endometrial cavity through a protective sleeve, which is then partially retracted. The specimen is collected and then withdrawn through the sleeve. With the Mi-Mark sampler, a plastic helix is inserted into the endometrial cavity and then withdrawn.

These devices are also less than ideal. While cytologic devices are easy to use, inexpensive, and cause minimal discomfort to the patient, their effective use is dependent on the availability of cytologists with expertise in evaluating endometrial cytologic samples. These devices tend to underdiagnose hyperplasia by about 20 percent. Furthermore, endometrial polyps, which can be a significant cause of abnormal bleeding, usually go undetected. Finally, the utility of screening for endometrial cancer in the absence of irregular bleeding has been questioned. Because of their limitations in diagnosing endometrial pathology other than carcinoma, cytologic devices are not ideal tools in such diagnosis.

Histologic Sampling

Histologic sampling of the endometrial lining is more accurate than cytology in detecting endometrial hyperplasia and cancer, uterine polyps, and other endometrial pathologies. It may also be therapeutic in some instances. Newer devices have greatly reduced the discomfort associated with the procedure and have increased patient acceptance.

Most descriptions of office D&Cs include the use of paracervical blocks, analgesics, and tranquilizers when deemed appropriate. Although the instrumentation and technique of office D&C is similar to a D&C done in the operating room, patient discomfort may limit one's ability to do an adequate curettage. Therefore, the vast majority of office endometrial sampling does not use this technique.

The earliest endometrial sampling tools were reusable stainless steel curettes. The Novak curette is a prototype of this instrument. These instruments are 3- to 4-mm tubes with an opening near the distal end, and an attachment for a suction apparatus at the proximal end. The Novak curette uses a syringe to provide suction, and has a sawtooth arrangement at the distal opening. This was a source of patient discomfort, and the syringe was inconvenient to use. The Vabra aspirator uses a rigid plastic tube instead of stainless steel, and a suction pump rather than a syringe. The Vakutage uses a preevacuated glass collection bottle instead of the suction pump, and is entirely self-contained.

The newest and most commonly used endometrial sampling devices are flexible polypropylene sheaths such as the Pipelle, the Z-sampler, the Explora, and the Endosampler. These devices are approximately 3 mm in diameter with a 2.4-mm perforation near their distal end. Within the cannula is an internal piston that creates the suction necessary to sample the endometrial cavity. The advantages of this type of device are that it can pass through most endocervical canals without dilatation or the use of a tenaculum, and because there is less discomfort associated with its use than with the rigid devices, paracervical block and analgesia are not needed. The Pipelle is also more convenient to use and costs less than the Vabra.

The adequacy of an endometrial biopsy technique relates to the clinical findings in the patient being sampled, when the uterus is being sampled, and the indication for sampling. Inadequate samples are more common in women who have just finished their menstrual period or who have had a prolonged period of bleeding resulting in a denuded endometrium. Patients with a thinned endometrium resulting from the progestational effect of oral, injectable, or subdermal contraceptives, or those with an atrophic endometrium resulting from a hypoestrogenic state, may also have an inadequate sample. Endometrial sampling is much more likely to be sufficient when the endometrial change is global (e.g., diffuse endometrial hyperplasia or when it is done to date the endometrium), than when there is focal change (e.g., endometrial polyp or a focal endometrial carcinoma). This is because the Pipelle samples an average 4 percent of the endometrium (with a range of 0 to 12 percent). When it is used to date the endometrium, the Pipelle adequately samples the endometrium 99 percent of the time. When evaluating for abnormal uterine bleeding, one study found that the Pipelle produces adequate samples 87 percent of the time in premenopausal women and 77 percent of the time in postmenopausal women.[17] The accuracy of the other devices is comparable.

The diagnostic accuracy of endometrial sampling depends on the standard to which it is compared. Because only a fraction of the endometrium is sampled even in a thorough D&C, it may miss focal disease such as an endometrial polyp or a focal carcinoma in up to 10 percent of cases.[23] When histologic findings obtained by Pipelle are compared to those found at hysterectomy in patients with known endometrial carcinoma, studies show that the sensitivity of Pipelle sampling is 83 to 97 percent.[9,18] The differences are attributed to variations in sampling technique and the focality of lesions. In one study, of the 11 endometrial cancers missed by Pipelle sampling, 5 were confined to a polyp, and 3 others occupied less than 5 percent of the endometrium.[9] When compared to D&C, Pipelle detects the vast majority of endometrial hyperplasia and carcinoma.

It is also able to detect polyps in most cases. If, based on history or clinical findings, a woman appears to be at risk for significant endometrial pathology but the endometrial sampling does not provide the diagnosis, the clinician needs to perform additional studies.

Disadvantages of endometrial biopsy techniques include the need to use a tenaculum to stabilize the cervix so that the instrument can be passed through the cervical canal, failed procedures when cervical stenosis is encountered, and some degree of patient discomfort necessitating analgesia or paracervical block in certain patients.

The indications for endometrial biopsy were mentioned briefly and are discussed in detail in other chapters. Endometrial biopsy is contraindicated during pregnancy. When the patient has severe clotting disorders, it should not be done in an office setting. Salpingitis, endometritis, and acute PID may be exacerbated by endometrial biopsy. Relative contraindications or limitations to endometrial biopsy include cervical stenosis and extreme anteflexion or retroflexion of the uterus. Also, in a patient who is bleeding heavily, it may be difficult to obtain an adequate endometrial sample because the Pipelle will fill with blood rather than endometrial curettings. Finally, in a patient with a large fibroid uterus, the size of the cavity or the presence of submucous myomas may impede one's ability to sample the cavity adequately.

The best time to do an endometrial biopsy in a premenopausal woman is in the midluteal phase of the cycle. In addition to being able to date the endometrium and identify luteal phase defects, the documentation of a secretory endometrium can confirm ovulation and exclude many types of dysfunctional bleeding. However, cramps associated with the procedure are more common and more severe when the procedure is done during the late luteal phase.

The technique for endometrial biopsy or cytologic aspiration is essentially the same regardless of which sampling device is used. Informed consent should be obtained prior to the procedure.

A prostaglandin inhibitor such as ibuprofen may be given prior to the procedure; however, when using a device such as the Pipelle, this usually is not necessary. It is also usually not necessary to use a paracervical block. Antibiotic prophylaxis is usually not indicated, but may be needed in patients at high risk, such as those with prosthetic heart valves. The patient is placed on the examination table in the dorsal lithotomy position. A recent Pap smear report should be available. If it is not, one should be performed provided the patient is not bleeding excessively. A bimanual examination is done to assess the uterine size, position, and axis. A bivalve speculum is inserted into the vagina. The cervix is visualized, then cleaned using an antiseptic solution. The anterior lip of the cervix is grasped with a single-tooth tenaculum for stabilization. This is necessary when using the more rigid sampling devices, although it may not be necessary when using the more flexible Pipelle. Injecting 1 ml of 1% lidocaine into the anterior lip of the cervix or the topical application of 10% benzocaine gel may reduce the discomfort associated with this part of the procedure. If an endocervical curettage is planned, it is done at this point. A Kervorkian curette is often used to sample the endocervix.

The endometrial sampling is then performed. The sampling device is inserted through the endocervical canal and into the uterus. Although the patient may feel a cramping sensation when the instrument passes through the internal os, it usually is not necessary to dilate the cervix when using the Pipelle. It is also usually not necessary to sound the uterus prior to biopsy because most of the newer sampling devices are marked along their length so that they may also function as uterine sounds. If the cervix is stenotic and needs to be dilated, a paracervical block may be used. The block is done by injecting 2 to 3 ml of 1% lidocaine without epinephrine in three to four sites just below the mucosa at the junction of the uterine reflection and the posterior vaginal vault. The sampling instrument is then passed all the way to the fundus, and suction is applied. When using the Pipelle, this is done by withdrawing the

piston to its full length. The suction device is then rotated inside the endometrial cavity while it is slowly withdrawn. It usually is not necessary to repeat the procedure. If the sample seems inadequate, the procedure may be repeated; however, the second sample is usually not as good as the first.

The lower abdominal cramps experienced during the procedure usually pass within several minutes. If pain persists after a few minutes, prostaglandin inhibitors may be given. A small number of patients may experience a vasovagal reaction during or after the procedure. For this reason, patients should not be allowed to get up off the examination table unattended following the procedure. If such a reaction does occur during the procedure, it should be halted temporarily until the reaction passes. If it occurs after the procedure, the patient should remain on the examination table until the symptoms pass. When the reaction is prolonged, vital signs should be monitored and the legs elevated. It is rarely necessary to administer atropine for a symptomatic bradycardia. Following the procedure, the patient should be instructed not to engage in intercourse for several days—at least as long as any bleeding persists. Infection or perforation associated with office endometrial biopsy is rare; however, the patient should report any symptoms of fever, chills, increasing pain, significant bleeding, or other problems to the physician.

Transvaginal Sonography

The poor sensitivity of all blind endometrial sampling methods is due mainly to their failure to detect endometrial polyps, submucosal myomas, and other focal endometrial disease. Office endometrial biopsy may also be precluded by cervical stenosis or may be nondiagnostic because of insufficient tissue. It is estimated that in women with postmenopausal bleeding, 25 percent will have insufficient tissue on endometrial biopsy, and in another 3 percent, cervical stenosis will prevent its performance. Ultrasound is a safe, readily available, noninvasive modality that may be used to screen the entire endometrium for such focal changes.

Instruments used in diagnostic ultrasonography operate at frequencies between 2 and 10 MHz. The higher the frequency, the greater the resolution of the image, but the lesser the depth of penetration. Because of the proximity of pelvic structures to the vaginal vault, most vaginal transducers can operate at 5 to 7.5 MHz. This frequency provides excellent detail for structures up to 6 to 8 cm from the probe tip at the vaginal vault. The uterus and the endometrium are well within range of transvaginal sonography. A detailed description of transvaginal sonography is provided in Chap. 51.

Sonographically, the two endometrial surfaces are separated by a thin echogenic line. During the follicular phase of the cycle, the endometrium is hypoechoic. There is a characteristic, pencil-thin line at the myometrial-endometrial interface. Combined with the hyperechoic line that separates the endometrial surfaces, they form a triple-stripe characteristic of follicular phase endometrium. Following ovulation, the endometrium gradually becomes more hyperechoic, and eventually the line separating the opposing surfaces of the endometrium disappears.

In postmenopausal women, the overall thickness of the endometrium is correlated with the risk of endometrial cancer. Endometrial cancer is very rare in a woman whose endometrial echo measures 4 mm or less in maximum anteroposterior thickness read on a longitudinal view. The false-negative rate for this cutoff is <1 percent. The measurement is made from the outer edge of the endometrial stripe to the opposite outer edge. Any endometrial fluid is excluded from the measurement.

In women with postmenopausal bleeding and an endometrial thickness of 5 to 10 mm, the endometrial cancer risk is 6.6 percent; from 11 to 15 mm, 31 percent; from 16 to 20 mm, 48 percent; and >20 mm, 62 percent.[3,11,12,20] The endometrial thickness tends to be greater in women taking cyclic hormone replacement therapy (HRT) (4

to 8 mm) and in those receiving combination HRT (5 mm), but the cutoff for excluding cancer should not be changed.

One investigator reported that the presence of fluid in the endometrial cavity was associated with endometrial carcinoma in as many as half the cases.[21] However, in each case the combined endometrial thickness exceeded 4 mm,[21] so the endometrial thickness remains a better indicator of cancer risk than the presence of fluid. The most common cause of intracavitary fluid is cervical stenosis. If possible, women with endometrial fluid should have an endometrial sampling.

Saline-Infusion Sonography

This technique, also called sonohysterography, evolved because of the well-recognized benefit of a fluid-filled endometrial cavity in identifying and describing intracavitary abnormalities. Saline-infusion sonography (SIS) can be helpful in women with a thickened, irregular, unmeasurable, or poorly visualized endometrium on conventional transvaginal sonography. SIS can also be used to help clarify the etiology of a thickened or bizarre-appearing endometrium in women receiving tamoxifen therapy.

In SIS, the normal premenopausal endometrium appears symmetrical when it is surrounding anechoic saline. Endometrial polyps, which may present as a thickened endometrium on unenhanced sonography, are easily identified when surrounded by hypoechoic fluid. Submucosal fibroids, which may be difficult to locate on conventional sonography because they transmit sound poorly, attenuate the beam and have ill-defined borders, are more easily defined on SIS. Long-term use of tamoxifen can induce changes in the subendometrial layer, which is often confused with endometrial thickening. This distinction is more easily made with SIS.

Hysteroscopy

Hysteroscopy allows direct visualization of the endometrial cavity. The physician is able to evaluate the topography of the uterine lining and use the information to help make rational decisions on medical or surgical approaches to the patient's problem. It has been used for the evaluation and treatment of endometrial lesions for many years. Recently, improved technology including fiber optics has allowed hysteroscopy to move from the operating room to the office. In most women, it can be done without cervical dilatation or local anesthetics. Because hysteroscopy is frequently associated with some degree of patient discomfort, its use in the office probably should be restricted to physicians who have already gained sufficient experience with hysteroscopy in the operating room. The experienced hysteroscopist can complete a diagnostic hysteroscopy using CO_2 gas in less than 10 minutes.

Because of its ability to identify focal lesions, panoramic hysteroscopy coupled with endometrial sampling, is able to identify the correct histologic diagnosis 98 percent of the time, as compared with 85 percent for a prior or concomitant D&C.[6,13] However, conditions such as chronic cervicitis, adenomatous hyperplasia, and atrophic change, which affect the entire endometrium, can be missed. It is therefore advisable to sample the endometrium regardless of the hysteroscopic impression.

Some indications for office hysteroscopy include abnormal uterine bleeding, postmenopausal bleeding, suspected leiomyomata with bleeding, the evaluation of infertility with bleeding, patients in whom uterine anomalies may be suspected, patients with suspected endometrial polyps, and women who have abnormal uterine bleeding and a negative D&C.

The most commonly used and most versatile hysteroscope for office use is a rigid, panoramic hysteroscope with a 30-degree viewing angle and a sheath measuring 3 mm in diameter. The procedure described here assumes the use of this instrument. However, advances in instrumentation have also improved the flexible hysteroscope. The flexible tip on these instruments rotates 100 degrees in two directions, facilitating directed biopsy. The light source is a 100- to 300-watt halo-gen or xenon lamp. Office hysteroscopy usually uses CO_2 gas as a distension medium. Low molecular-weight distension media, such as lactated Ringer's solution, are far too messy for office use because they require such large volumes of fluid. High molecular-weight distension media, such as Dextran 70, require significantly less volume; however, they are also messy and difficult to use in an office setting. The flow rate for CO_2 should not exceed 100 ml per minute, and the pressure should remain below 100 mm Hg. The total volume of CO_2 used in a patient with patent fallopian tubes should be below 600 to 700 ml CO_2. The total volume of Dextran 70 needed is rarely more than 100 ml, and should never be more than 300 ml because of the risk of pulmonary edema and blood dyscrasia.

Prior to hysteroscopy, the patient should be assessed as to her ability to cooperate during the procedure. A pregnancy test and cervical cultures for gonorrhea and chlamydia should be checked. Premedication with a prostaglandin inhibitor 30 minutes prior to the procedure is helpful. The procedure is done with the patient in the dorsal lithotomy position. A paracervical block is administered. The cervix is dilated if necessary, and the hysteroscope inserted into the cervical canal. The flow of the distension medium is started, and the hysteroscope is advanced slowly, allowing the distension medium to dilate the internal os.

When the hysteroscope enters the uterus, the cavity should be inspected to assess its general shape, the presence of any foreign bodies, synechiae, polyps, myomas, or septa. The appearance of the endometrium should also be checked, looking for irregularities suggestive of hyperplasia or cancer. The anterior and posterior walls of the uterus can be inspected by rotating the hysteroscope clockwise and counterclockwise. The left and right cornua and tubal ostia are examined by rotating the hysteroscope into the proper position at the fundus. If no lesions are seen, the hysteroscope is slowly removed so that the cavity can be reexamined on the way out; then the endometrium is sampled, using an endometrial sampling device as described earlier. If a lesion is seen, it can sometimes be removed through the hysteroscope; however, operative hysteroscopy requires a larger diameter hysteroscope, operative instruments, and possibly anesthesia. It may be beyond the skill level of many office practitioners. Postoperatively, the patient is given a prostaglandin inhibitor for any mild cramps that may follow the procedure and is told to avoid intercourse for several days—at least until any bleeding stops. She should call the physician if she experiences any fever, severe pain, heavy bleeding, or other problems. Potential complications of operative hysteroscopy are the same as those for D&C and include bleeding, infection, and perforation. However, these complications are rare.

References and Selected Readings

1. Apgar BS, DeWitt D: Diagnostic hysteroscopy. *Am Fam Physician* 46:19S–36S, 1992.
2. Brown FH, Kammeyer SE: Office gynecologic procedures. *Prim Care* 13:493–511, 1986.
3. Botsis D, Kassanos D, Pyrgiotis E, Zouras PA: Vaginal sonography of the endometrium in postmenopausal women. *Clin Exp Obstet Gynecol* 19:189–192, 1992.
4. Chambers JT, Chambers SK: Endometrial sampling: When? Where? Why? With what? *Clin Obstet Gynecol* 35:28–39, 1992.
5. Gimpelson RJ: Office hysteroscopy. *Clin Obstet Gynecol* 35:270–281, 1992.
6. Gimpleson RJ, Rappdo HO: A comparative study between panoramic hysteroscopy with directed biopsies and dilatation and curettage. *Am J Obstet Gynecol* 158:489–492, 1988.
7. Goldchmit R, Katz Z, Blickstein I, et al: The accuracy of endometrial sampling with and without sonographic measurement of endometrial thickness. *Obstet Gynecol* 82:727–730, 1993.
8. Grimes DA: Diagnostic dilatation and curettage: A reappraisal. *Am J Obstet Gynecol* 142:1–6, 1982.
9. Guido RS, Kanbour A, Ruhn M, Christopherson WA: Pipelle endometrial sampling sensitivity in the detection of endometrial cancer. *J Reprod Med* 40:553–555, 1995.
10. Haynes PJ, Hodgson H, Anderson ABM, Turnbull AC: Measurement of menstrual blood loss in patients complaining of menorrhagia. *Br J Obstet Gynaecol* 84:763–768, 1977.
11. Karlsson B, Granberg S, Wikland M, Ryd W, Norstrom A: Endovaginal scanning of the endometrium compared to cytology and histology in women with postmenopausal bleeding. *Gynecol Oncol* 50:173–178, 1993.
12. Karlsson B, Granberg S, Wikland M, et al: Transvaginal ultrasonography of the endometrium in women with postmenopausal bleeding—A Nordic multicenter study. *Am J Obstet Gynecol* 172:1488–1494, 1995.
13. Loffer FD: Hysteroscopy with selective endometrial sampling compared with D&C for abnormal uterine bleeding: The value of a negative hysteroscopic view. *Obstet Gynecol* 73:16–20, 1989.
14. Malinova M, Pehlivanov B: Transvaginal sonography and endometrial thickness in patients with postmenopausal uterine bleeding. *Eur J Obstet Gynecol Reprod Biol* 58:161–165, 1995.
15. Nilsson L, Rybo G: Treatment of menorrhagia. *Am J Obstet Gynecol* 110:713–720, 1971.
16. Stock RJ, Kanbour A: Prehysterectomy curettage. *Obstet Gynecol* 45:537–541, 1975.
17. Stovall TG, Ling FW, Morgan PL: A prospective, randomized comparison of the Pipelle endometrial sampling device with the Novak curette. *Am J Obstet Gynecol* 165:1287–1289, 1991.
18. Stovall TG, Photopulos GJ, Poston WM, Ling FW, Sandles LG: Pipelle endometrial sampling in patients with known endometrial cancer. *Obstet Gynecol* 77:954–956, 1991.
19. Stovall TG, Solomon SK, Ling FW: Endometrial sampling prior to hysterectomy. *Obstet Gynecol* 73:405–409, 1989.
20. Taipale P, Tarjanne H, Heinonen U-M: The diagnostic value of transvaginal sonography in the diagnosis of endometrial malignancy in women with peri- and postmenopausal bleeding. *Acta Obstet Gynecol Scand* 73:819–823, 1994.
21. Van Den Bosch T, Vandendoel A, Van Schoobroeck D, Wranz PAB, Lombard CJ: Combining vaginal ultrasonography and office endometrial sampling in the diagnosis of endometrial disease in postmenopausal women. *Obstet Gynecol* 85:349–352, 1995.
22. Vuopala S: Diagnostic accuracy and clinical applicability of cytological and histological methods for investigating endometrial carcinoma. *Acta Obstet Gynecol Scand* 70(Suppl):22–25, 1977.
23. Word B, Gravlee LC, Wideman GL: The fallacy of simple uterine curettage. *Obstet Gynecol* 12:642–643, 1958.

tre of ovulation in
ate luteal phase
perature rise per-

CHAPTER 49

Office Procedures for Infertility Patients

Edward H. Illions
Robert J. Thompson

BASAL BODY TEMPERATURE GRAPH
URINARY LH KITS
TRANSVAGINAL SONOGRAPHY
ENDOMETRIAL BIOPSY
CERVICAL FACTOR TESTING
TUBAL AND PERITONEAL FACTORS
Hysterosalpingogram
OFFICE HYSTEROSCOPY
ENDOCRINE TESTING
Clomiphene Citrate Challenge Test

Much of the basic infertility evaluation can be performed with simple office tests and procedures. The clinician should have a good understanding of the basic tests needed to evaluate ovulation, sperm-mucus interactions, intrauterine pathology, and tubal and peritoneal abnormalities.

Basal Body Temperature Graph

Four basic office tests can be utilized to evaluate ovulation. A basal body temperature graph is the initial screening test for ovulation. Some controversy exists regarding the interpretation of this test; however, a sustained luteal temperature elevation is indicative of ovulation. The test is not useful in predicting ovulation. The couple should be advised to initiate basal body temperature charts on the first day of a menstrual cycle. The patient should record her temperatures each morning before any activity or consuming any liquid or food. It is helpful if patients keep their basal body thermometer by the bedside as a reminder to record their temperature at the same time every morning. The temperature will typically rise as much as 0.5°F within 1 to 3 days after the urinary LH surge, and remain elevated for the duration of the luteal phase. Typical luteal phase elevation is 14 days plus or minus 2 days. A biphasic pattern is indicative of ovulation in most patients, whereas an adequate luteal phase is demonstrated when the temperature rise persists for at least 11 days. However, 10 percent of ovulatory patients will demonstrate a monophasic basal body temperature chart.

Urinary LH Kits

Many commercially available kits exist to measure urinary LH. Because the onset of the LH surge occurs 32 to 36 hours prior to ovulation, the test is useful for timing coitus and artificial insemination, as well as for scheduling postcoital tests and endometrial biopsies. The patient should be instructed to start checking her urine on day 10 or 11 of her cycle. Urine samples taken in the late afternoon or early evening are quite accurate. OvuSTICK and OvuQUICK utilize a control surge guide on day 1 or daily, respectively, increasing the accuracy of the tests. A significant LH surge is noted when the daily test turns bluer than the control surge guide. This indicates the onset of the LH surge as measured by levels in the urine greater than 40 mIU/ml, with ovulation occurring the following day.

Transvaginal Sonography

Transvaginal sonography of the female pelvis provides the physician great accuracy when evaluating folliculogenesis and predicting ovulation. Daily scanning may commence on day 12 of a normal cycle, or a single scan can be performed 1 day after the LH surge. Follicular size typically is measured in at least two diameters, with the periovulatory follicles measuring in excess of 18 mm. The patient should be positioned in stirrups at the end of the exam table. A high-resolution vaginal probe is covered with a sterile condom, and gel is applied to enhance resolution and visualization of the pelvic structures. Transvaginal sonography also detects a rare entity—luteinized unruptured follicle (LUF)—and is a necessity in ovulation-induction cycles.

In recent years, sonohysterography (saline-infusion sonography) has allowed physicians to more accurately evaluate the uterine cavity. As an absolute prerequisite, the sonographer should be well versed in all aspects of transvaginal sonography. Transvaginal sonohysterography is indicated in any patient in whom a detailed evaluation of the uterine cavity is necessary. This procedure readily identifies submucosal myomas, endometrial polyps, and intrauterine synechiae (Asherman's syndrome). The actual location of any intrauterine pathology is readily identified, and this procedure allows for detailed and accurate measurements of polyps and myomas. Sonohysterography has clinical utitlity when screening IVF patients. The detection of intrauterine pathology prior to an assisted reproductive technologies (ART) cycle allows for hysteroscopic confirmation and surgical correction. In addition, instillation of an ultrasound contrast agent (Albunex, Molecular Biosystems, Inc., San Diego, CA) allows sonographic documentation of tubal patency.

Endometrial Biopsy

The endometrial biopsy is currently the gold standard for diagnosis of luteal phase defects. The couple should utilize barrier contraception during the test cycle or have a sensitive quantitative β-HCG performed one day prior to the endometrial sampling. The biopsy should be performed between the 10th and 12th postovulatory day as determined by urinary LH surge kits. A description of the technical aspects of office endometrial sampling is found in Chap. 48. A histologic lag of greater than two days indicates a luteal phase defect. Confirmation of a luteal phase defect must be present on at least two sampled cycles.

Cervical Factor Testing

The postcoital test is an essential part of the basic infertility evaluation. The postcoital test (Sims-Huhner test) is performed the morning after an LH surge. The couple should be instructed either to have intercourse the night before or at least two to three hours prior to the test.

After placing the patient on the exam table, a speculum is inserted to allow visualization of the cervix. An attempt is made to quantify both the amount and viscosity of the cervical mucus, as this is a direct reflection of estrogen effect on the cervix. Cervical mucus is obtained from the external os utilizing an 18-gauge angiocath on a 1-ml tuberculin syringe. Recovery of cervical mucus in the syringe allows for accurate determinations of its amount. Cervical mucus elasticity (spinnbarkeit) may be determined by slowly moving the syringe away from the external os. Periovulatory cervical mucus should allow for at least 8 to 10 cm of spinnbarkeit. Cervical mucus is placed on two glass slides. A cover slip is placed over one of the specimens; the other is allowed to air dry. The air-dried specimen is evaluated for the presence of ferning indicative of an adequate estrogen effect on cervical mucus. The other slide is microscopically analyzed for the presence and number of motile sperm per high-powered field. Although much controversy exists as to normal threshold values, visualization of more than five motile sperm per high-powered field is reassuring. Slides with absent sperm should alert the physician to possible problems with coital technique, whereas the presence of shaking and immobilized sperm may indicate immunologic disorders. Periovulatory cervical mucus is relatively acellular; therefore, the presence of many leukocytes or red blood cells (RBC) may indicate a cervicitis.

Great emphasis was placed on the Sims-Huhner test in the past. Treatment was directed towards the improvement of mucus or sperm characteristics after in vivo and in vitro tests revealed poor mucus-sperm interaction. Recently, controversy over the interpretation of test results, as well as the outcome of therapeutic efforts, has led to a diminished emphasis on this test. Therapy is now directed at bypassing the cervix and its mucus abnormalities with intrauterine insemination of washed sperm.[1, 2]

Tubal and Peritoneal Factors

Hysterosalpingogram

Hysterosalpingography (HSG) is a fluoroscopic examination that allows assessment of the uterine cavity and tubal patency. An HSG should be performed in the midproliferative phase of the patient's cycle, no sooner than two days after the cessation of her menses. Contraindications to performing an HSG include dye allergy, active pelvic infection, or a past medical history of pelvic inflammatory disease. Patients with a prior history of genital infections may undergo an HSG if recent WBC, erythrocyte sedimentation rate (ESR), and cervical cultures for gonorrhea and

chlamydia are normal. Antibiotic prophylaxis is indicated in these patients to prevent the 1 to 3 percent incidence of HSG-associated infections. No premedication is required, and the patient is positioned on the exam table in stirrups. A pelvic examination is useful to ascertain uterine position; then a speculum is placed intravaginally. A tenaculum is applied to the anterior cervical lip to stabilize the uterus during the exam. An intrauterine catheter is placed in the lower segment to allow injection of radiopaque dye with concomitant image intensification fluoroscopy. Typically, only 2 to 3 ml of dye is necessary to fill the uterine cavity, and a slow injection technique aids in demonstrating intrauterine abnormalities. Fallopian tubes are then assessed for patency, and a final postinjection film is obtained to document free intraperitoneal spillage of dye. Most HSG studies can be completed with as little as 10 to 12 ml of contrast material. Failure to visualize either tube may indicate tubal spasm, and is usually treated with intravenous administration of 1 mg of glucagon followed by reinjection of the radiopaque dye. Postglucagon visualization of the fallopian tubes confirms a diagnosis of tubal spasm. Most contrast media are water-based and allow for better mucosal detail than the oil-based dyes previously used. Oil-based dyes, in addition, have been implicated in granuloma formation and oil embolization.

Office Hysteroscopy

Hysteroscopic evaluation of the uterine cavity is indicated in patients with prior abnormal HSGs, as well as in DES-exposed patients. Carbon dioxide (CO_2) is the usual distension medium and allows for good visibility during these diagnostic procedures. The patient is examined during the midproliferative phase of her cycle. The technical aspects of office hysteroscopy are discussed elsewhere in this text. Office CO_2-hysteroscopy allows for the detection of intrauterine congenital anomalies, polyps, myomas, and intrauterine synechiae, while avoiding the expense of an operating room and anesthesia. Operative hysteroscopy for correction of these defects is best performed in an operating room with adequate anesthesia.

Endocrine Testing

Clomiphene Citrate Challenge Test

A Clomiphene Citrate Challenge test (CCCT) is an indirect measure of ovarian reserve. It is easily performed as an outpatient, and may predict the response to ovulation induction. Serum FSH, LH, and estradiol levels are obtained on days 3 and 10 of the patient's cycle after receiving clomiphene citrate 100 mg on days 5 through 9 of that same cycle. Gonadotropin levels are increased transiently after clomiphene citrate administration; however, rising estradiol and inhibin from stimulated follicles have a negative feedback effect on the pituitary to prevent an elevated FSH by day 10. Normal values for this test vary with the gonadotropin reference preparation utilized; however, FSH values below 25 mIU/ml are considered normal in most centers.

Summary

The simple office tests and procedures reviewed in this chapter will assist in the accurate assessment of ovulatory status, sperm-mucus interaction, and the tubal and peritoneal factors involved in infertility. Office endocrine testing may aid in uncovering hypothalamic or pituitary dysfunction.

References and Suggested Readings

1. Collins JA, So Y, Wilson FH, Wrixon W, Casper RF: The postcoital test as a predictor of pregnancy among 355 infertile couples. *Fertil Steril* 41:703, 1984.
2. Griffith CS, Grimes DA: The validity of the postcoital test. *Am J Obstet Gynecol* 162:615, 1990.

CHAPTER 50

Cystourethroscopy and Urodynamics

Jeffrey L. Cornella
Henry A. Thiede

CYSTOURETHROSCOPY
Dynamic Urethroscopy • Cystoscopy
URODYNAMIC TESTING
Uroflowmetry • Cystometry • Urethral
Profilometry • Cystograms and
Videocystourethrography

Cystourethroscopy

Since Philipp Bozzini developed the first instrument to inspect the bladder in 1806, endoscopy has been a cornerstone of urinary tract assessment. Today endoscopic visualization allows examination of the lower and upper urinary tracts. Cystoscopic assessment of subtle lesions requires a significant amount of experience and is beyond the scope of this chapter. This discussion instructs in basic cystourethroscopic technique and familiarizes the office practitioner with common terms and findings, because urogynecologic problems are so common and of such great concern for women, and ones for which they are often evaluated in the office setting with the studies described below.

Dynamic Urethroscopy

Dynamic urethroscopy refers to visualization of the urethra during maneuvers to reproduce symptoms. Robertson emphasized the benefit of assessment during bladder filling and stressful maneuvers in making accurate diagnoses.[2] Robertson describes the use of a zero-degree 24-French direct endoscope. Carbon dioxide or water can be used for distension with careful visualization of the urethra on initial insertion. During visualization of the urethrovesical junction, the patient is asked to cough, perform the Valsalva maneuver, and contract the pelvic floor musculature. The response of the junction is noted, including "telescoping" or inappropriate opening and descent of the junction with coughing. Normally the endoscopist will see gradual closure of the junction and vesical neck with bladder filling and increased muscular tone. This correlates with increased EMG activity (Fig. 50-1). The pink mucosa is examined for erythema, atrophy, and the ostia of urethral diverticula. A dysfunctional urethrovesical junction and bladder neck may be noted in the patient who has had multiple operations or in those individuals who have experienced neurologic damage of the pelvic plexus. This may result in a scarified appearance or an open, flaccid appearance at rest.

The normal urethra may balloon during visualization if the patient experiences a detrusor contraction. This gives a sharp circular appearance to the lumen.

Cystoscopy

Cystoscopy is generally performed only after acute cystitis or significant bacteriuria has been excluded. Anesthetic jelly is placed into the urethra and left in place for 5 to 10 min, but is not essential in most patients. A cystoscope (8 to 24 F available) is inserted after removal of the obturator, followed by systematic bladder inspection. A 70-degree lens is used to examine the

Urethral Closure Pressure (cmH$_2$O)

Integrated EMG

Time (sec)

Intravesical Pressure (cmH$_2$O)

Volume (ml CO$_2$)

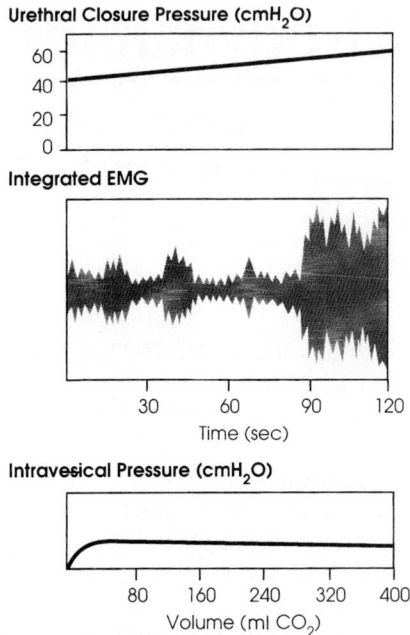

Figure 50-1 In this normal individual, urethral closure pressure and pelvic floor EMG activity gradually increase with bladder filling as intravesical pressure remains stable. (Adapted with permission from Ostergard DR, Bent AE (eds): *Urogynecology and Urodynamics.* Williams & Wilkins.[2])

bladder mucosa throughout 360 degrees, noting vascularity, underlying muscular patterns, and trigonal appearance.

The smooth wall of the bladder may be affected by changes in the underlying musculature. Hypertrophy results in muscle bundles creating an impression beneath the mucosa resembling a cord or trabeculation. This may give an interwoven pattern of ridges. Pockets may form between the trabeculations called cellules. If cellules penetrate the underlying musculature completely, they form sacculations called diverticula.

The mucosa of the bladder may become inflamed secondary to infection. Often a similar appearance is noted in carcinoma in situ and may require repeat cystoscopy after antibiotic therapy to confirm resolution of the abnormal appear-

ance. The vascularity of the bladder may show submucosal hemorrhages or glomerulations suggesting cystitis or the possibility of mild interstitial cystitis. Classic Hunner's ulcers may be seen with cracks in the mucous membrane and stellate scarring in more advanced cases.

Examination of the trigone notes the position of the ureteral orifices, efflux of urine, the absence of ureteroceles, and the underlying trigonal mucosal appearance, which often varies from the appearance of the other mucosal areas. The bladder is examined at various stages of filling. In the half-filled state the configuration of the ureteral orifices are noted. Interstitial cystitis may require filling to capacity or hydrodistention for diagnosis.

Urodynamic Testing

Pertinent considerations regarding urodynamics in the office setting are discussed in this chapter. The reader is referred to Chap. 44 (Urogynecology) for indications for urodynamic testing, significance, and instruction on methods of simple office-filling of the bladder. The goal of urodynamic testing is to reproduce urological symptoms during physiologic monitoring of bladder emptying and storage. Only in this manner can pertinent conclusions be reached that have clinical implications for patient treatment.

Uroflowmetry

Flowmetry must also reproduce the normal voiding experience of the patient. If the flow rate and pattern are normal, it is unlikely that a significant emptying abnormality exists.[5] Peak flow rates and flow times are dependent on the volume voided. It is important that the patient has at least 150 cc within the bladder to aid interpretation. It is unclear whether lesser volumes can be interpreted. Volume-rate nomograms aid this interpretation. Flow patterns can suggest obstruction, decreased contractility, or decreased outlet resistance. Maximum flow rates in females are 20 to 25 cc/sec as described in the literature. Measured parameters include peak flow rate, average flow rate, time to peak flow, voiding time, flow time, residual urine determination, and voided volume. Urethral relaxation is noted to precede detrusor contraction by 1 to 2 sec (Fig. 50-2). Flow rates can vary in an individual from one episode to another, especially at different starting volumes. It is also important that the patient assumes the sitting position and should be so instructed.

Cystometry

Cystometry is utilized to assess bladder sensation, capacity, activity, and compliance. Filling

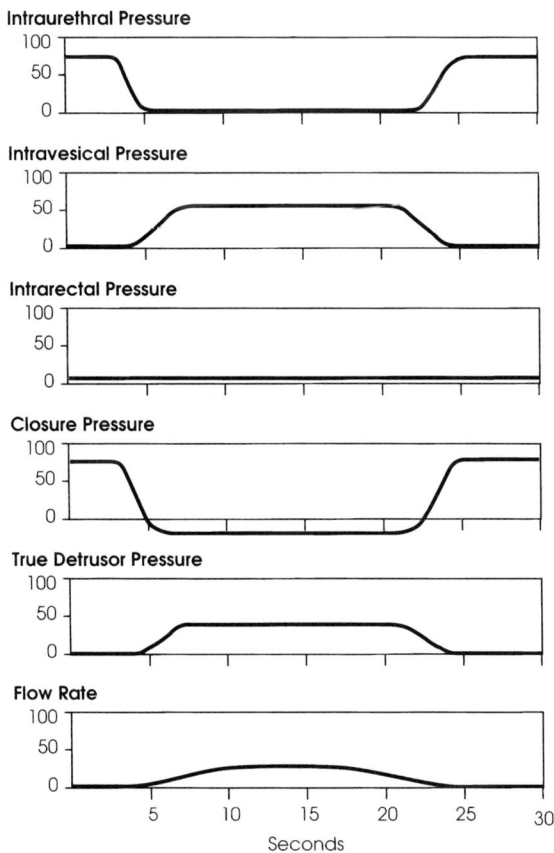

Intraurethral Pressure

Intravesical Pressure

Intrarectal Pressure

Closure Pressure

True Detrusor Pressure

Flow Rate

Seconds

Figure 50-2 In this normal female, urethral relaxation precedes vesical contraction. (Adapted with permission from Ostergard DR, Bent AE (eds): *Urogynecology and Urodynamics.* Williams & Wilkins.[2])

cystometry refers to changes in bladder pressure during filling. The normal bladder shows little pressure change during the majority of physiologic filling. The qualitative classification of bladder abnormalities is not significantly different whether carbon dioxide or water is used as the distending medium.[5] There are quantitative differences noted between the two mediums in assessing sensation of the bladder. Quantitative capacities are reduced when gas is used as the distending medium. Fluid is administered at body or room temperature via a small catheter and at a constant rate to reduce artifact. Medium-fill cystometry refers to a filling rate of 80 to 100 cc/minute. The bladder capacity of the average female is 350 to 500 ml of fluid.

Filling cystometry thus demonstrates a low-pressure plateau in the normal state, which is referred to as the tonus limb of the cystometrogram. Artifacts can be created by filling the bladder too quickly, resulting in a spurious recording which is not reflective of the normal physiologic state. This affects the viscoelastic properties of the bladder and raises the pressure early in the cystometrogram. This is followed by the flat tonus limb of the pressure curve, but at a higher artifactual pressure.

Communication between the technician and the patient is essential in the interpretation of the tracing. A volitional contraction may be identical in appearance to a nonvolitional contraction that the patient is unable to inhibit. It is only with honest communication that the tracing can be interpreted during reproduction of symptoms. First sensation of filling, fullness, and the feeling of strong desire to void (imminent micturition) are recorded. Increases in intravesical pressure may be reflective of detrusor contractions or increased muscular wall tension. The patient is asked to describe any concomitant sensations to aid in interpretation and diagnosis. The normal rise in bladder pressure during filling is less than 6 to 10 cm of water pressure. The final phase of bladder filling occurs when the elastic properties of the wall have reached their limit.[5] For this to fully have meaning, the bladder must be filled at

Figure 50-3 This normal female is able to inhibit the terminal contraction during cystometry. The intra-abdominal pressure when subtracted from the intravesical pressure gives true detrusor pressure. The closure pressure is determined by subtracting intravesical pressure from intraurethral pressure. (Adapted with permission from Ostergard DR, Bent AE (eds): *Urogynecology and Urodynamics.* Williams & Wilkins.[2])

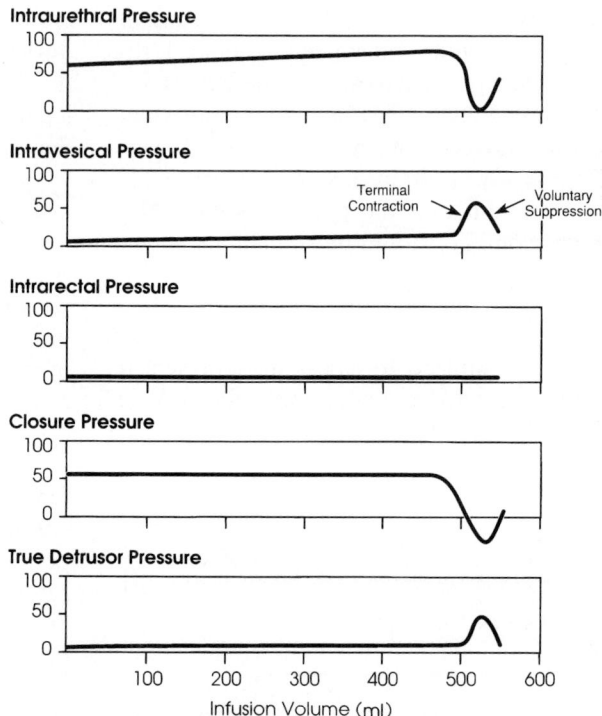

a standardized rate. The patient should be able to inhibit contractions at this volume (Fig. 50-3). Uninhibited spontaneous contractions at any pressure level are significant if symptoms are reproduced (Fig. 50-4). Some studies have elicited greater amounts of high-threshold contractions (>15 cmwater) when diuresis cystometry is utilized (physiologic filling combined with a diuretic).[6] Often, provocative maneuvers such as heel bouncing, testing in the semistanding position, and coughing are used to stimulate the appearance of symptomatic bladder instability or uninhibited detrusor contractions (Fig. 50-5). A small uninhibited phasic rise in true detrusor pressure accompanied by urgency or incontinence as a reproduction of symptoms suggests bladder instability. This may or may not be preceded by a decrease in urethral closure pressure.

Abnormalities are suggested by a reduced bladder capacity in the presence of increased pressure, or an increased bladder capacity in the presence of extremely low pressures. The latter may suggest a flaccid bladder or a sensory neuropathic condition. The former may suggest an inflammatory condition or severe bladder instability.

The second portion of cystometry is voiding cystometry. Care should be taken to avoid compromise of pressure-flow studies by the size of the intravesical catheter. A smaller catheter can be placed for this portion of the study (<8 F). The patient may or may not be able to generate a void at the end of filling. Stress or discomfort may result in central inhibition of the void. The measurement of true detrusor pressure at maximum flow is evaluated on the pressure flow study. This is helpful in determining outlet resistance and strength of detrusor contractions during a volitional void.

True detrusor pressure is determined by subtracting abdominal pressure measurements from bladder pressure measurements. The former are

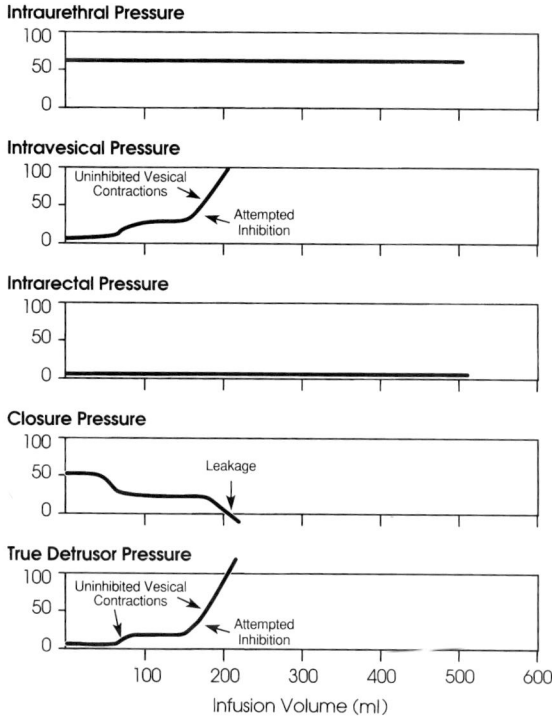

Figure 50-4 Uninhibitable bladder contractions at relatively low bladder volumes. A drop in urethral closure pressure precedes the detrusor contraction. (Adapted with permission from Ostergard DR, Bent AE (eds): *Urogynecology and Urodynamics.* Williams & Wilkins.[2])

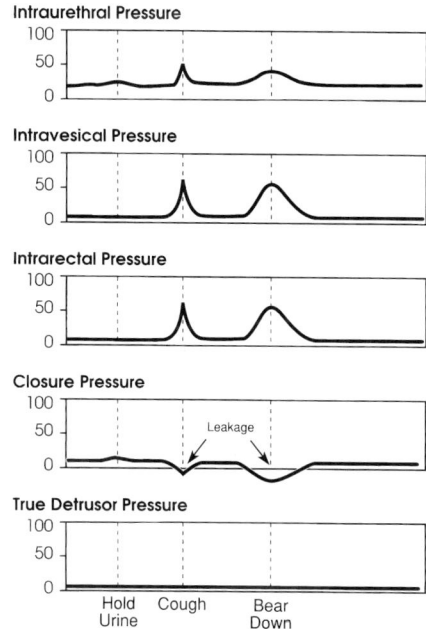

Figure 50-5 Dynamic evaluation of the urethral sphincter with negative closure pressure and resultant stress incontinence demonstrated on provocative coughing. (Adapted with permission from Ostergard DR, Bent AE (eds): *Urogynecology and Urodynamics.* Williams & Wilkins.[2])

obtained from rectal or vaginal catheters. Urethral closure pressure is determined by subtracting bladder pressure from urethral pressure. This is best measured by a single small lumen catheter with two sensors, six centimeters apart. When both transducers are placed within the bladder, coughing should result in equal pressure excursions on the graph. The catheter is then withdrawn at a constant rate (profilometer controlled) of 1 mm per second and the pressure differential is measured at rest and during coughing.

The EMG combines with the cystometrics to aid in diagnosis. In the normal patient, detrusor contraction is accompanied by coordinated relaxation of the urethral sphincter (Fig. 50-6). Some patients exhibit discoordination of this mechanism. As an example, patients with severe multiple sclerosis often have detrusor external-sphincter dyssynergia as a component of their urologic picture. This discordance between the external sphincter and the detrusor results from an uninhibited bladder contraction accompanied by an uninhibited urethral sphincter contraction. Increased EMG activity is inappropriately noted at the time of increased true detrusor pressure. Dyssynergia may result in increased intravesical pressure when sustained throughout the void (Fig. 50-7).

Urethral Profilometry

Urethral profilometry consists of static and dynamic urethral pressure profiles. The latter refers to pressure-transmission ratios (maximum ure-

Pressure (cmH₂O)

Integrated EMG

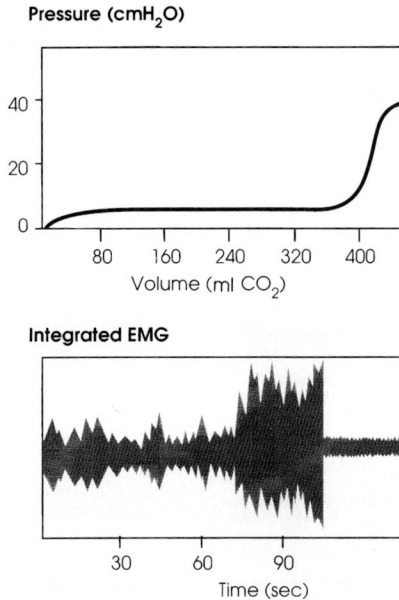

Figure 50-6 EMG activity during a normal cystometry. There is a gradual increase in activity due to increased sphincter tone during filling. Note quiescence of EMG activity coincident with bladder contraction. (Adapted with permission from Ostergard DR, Bent AE (eds): *Urogynecology and Urodynamics*. Williams & Wilkins.[2])

Intraurethral Pressure

Intravesical Pressure

Intrarectal Pressure

Closure Pressure

True Detrusor Pressure

Flow Rate

Figure 50-7 Obstruction on voiding is noted with increased intravesical pressure. This outlet obstruction may result from stenosis or if EMG activity shows an uninhibitable external sphincter contraction, from neurogenic dyssynergia. (Adapted with permission from Ostergard DR, Bent AE (eds): *Urogynecology and Urodynamics*. Williams & Wilkins.[2])

thral pressure divided by bladder pressure × 100). A discussion of pressure-transmission ratios and their meaning can be found in Chap. 44 (Urogynecology) under surgical treatment of stress urinary incontinence. This discussion is limited to resting or static urethral pressure profiles.

The urethral closure pressure is the urethral pressure that exceeds the bladder pressure. The normal value in the young female is 60 cm of water pressure. Urethral closure pressures decrease with age. Abnormally decreased urethral closure pressures are noted in stress-incontinent patients. Pressures decrease in these patients with standing, filling of the bladder, and serial coughing.

Resting urethral pressure profiles are measured with a microtransducer catheter oriented to the 3 or 9 o'clock position of the urethra (Fig. 50-8). Perfusion catheters may also be used, al-

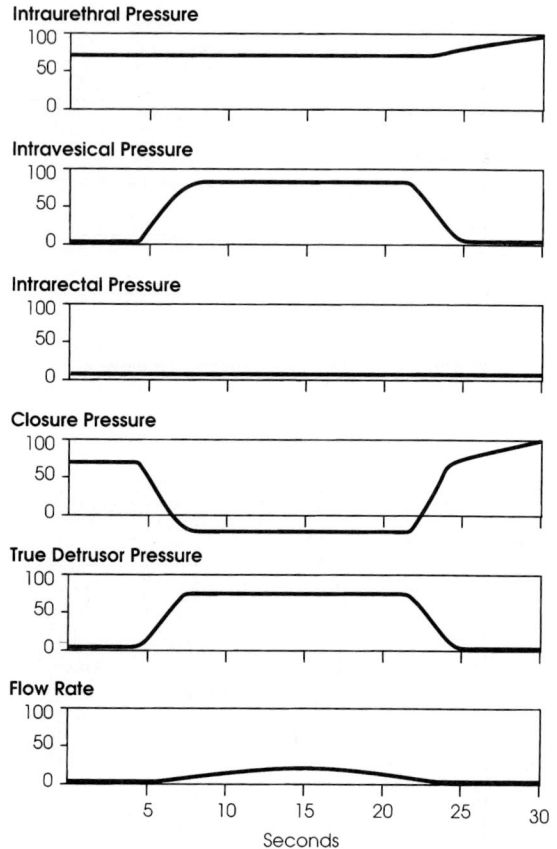

though some clinicians would state that increased artifact is produced with perfusion measurement.

Many investigators have studied the results of incontinence operations on resting closure pressures. The vast majority of the studies show no evidence of significant restoration of resting urethral pressure following retropubic urethropexy. The clinical utility of this study is low in females and much overlap exists between continent and

Intraurethral Pressure

Intravesical Pressure

Intrarectal Pressure

Closure Pressure

True Detrusor Pressure

Urethral Length (cm)

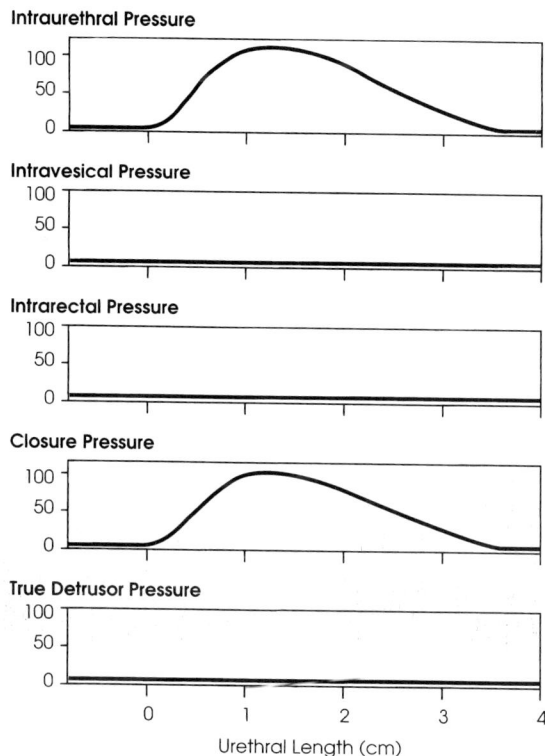

Figure 50-8 Urethral closure pressure tracing in the normal female. (Adapted with permission from Ostergard DR, Bent AE (eds): *Urogynecology and Urodynamics*. Williams & Wilkins.[2])

incontinent patients with given urethral closure pressures.

Some investigators have suggested that low urethral closure pressures are predictive of increased risk of failure after retropubic urethropexy. Less than 20 cm of water pressure was selected as the cutoff point in the definition of low urethral pressure by Sand.[3] He noted that in patients under age 50, there was a 54 percent failure rate following Burch colposuspension in patients with low urethral pressures as compared to an 18 percent failure rate in patients with >20 cmH$_2$O pressure. Richardson performed Burch colposuspension in 29 patients with low urethral pressures evaluated with preoperative and postoperative urodynamic testing. The success rate

was 78 percent cured and 7 percent improved with a 15 percent failure rate. Richardson noted that if urethral mobility is present, urethropexy is a reasonable alternative in low urethral pressure patients.[1]

Sand also reported on uninhibited urethral relaxation as a cause of incontinence.[4] Uninhibited urethral relaxation is a sudden drop in urethral pressure resulting in leakage in the absence of detrusor contraction or provocative maneuvers. Its existence as a pathologic entity is debated. Normal women on ambulatory testing have demonstrated urethral pressure variations throughout the day. Versi stated that urethral pressure variations which are greater than one-third the resting pressure fall outside the 99 percent confidence limit in studied patients and should be considered abnormal.[7]

Cystograms and Videocystourethrography

The static cystogram provides information about the bladder neck and urethra. This is especially helpful in the patient with a questionable dysfunctional or type III urethra. Contrast is placed within the bladder and the patient is radiographed in the standing, at-rest position. A type III urethra is suggested by a square, wide column of dye filling the upper urethra in the absence of a bladder contraction. Versi demonstrated that the prevalence of bladder neck incompetence (opening with coughing) was approximately 48 percent.[8] In a related study the incidence of open bladder neck at rest was 21 percent in patients presenting to a urodynamic clinic.[9]

Videocystourethrography combines pressure-testing and fluoroscopy to assess bladder and urethral function. This can be extremely helpful in understanding complex pathologic conditions.

References and Selected Readings

1. Richardson DA, et al: Surgical management of stress incontinence in patients with low urethral pressure. *Gynecol Obstet Invest* 31:106–109, 1991.
2. Robertson JR: Dynamic urethroscopy. In Ostergard

DR, Bent AE (eds): *Urogynecology and Urodynamics*. 3d ed. Philadelphia: Williams & Wilkins, 1991.

3. Sand PK, et al: The low pressure urethra as a factor in failed retropubic urethropexy. *Obstet Gynecol* 69:399–402, 1987.

4. Sand PK, et al: Uninhibited urethral relaxation: An unusual cause of incontinence. *Obstet Gynecol* 68:645–648, 1986.

5. Wein AJ, et al: Office urodynamics. *Urol Clin North Am* 15:609–623, 1988.

6. van Venrooij GE, et al: Urodynamics and incontinence II: The diagnostic value of diuresis cystometry. *Int Urogynecol J Pelvic Floor Dysfunct* 1:191–195, 1990.

7. Versi E, Cardozo L: Urethral instability: Diagnosis based on variations of the maximum urethral pressure in normal climacteric women. *Neurourol Urod* 5:535–541, 1986.

8. Versi E, et al: Distal urethral compensatory mechanisms in women with an incompetent bladder neck who remain continent, and the effect of the menopause. *Neurourol Urod* 9:579–590, 1990.

9. Versi E: The significance of an open bladder neck in women. *Br J Urol* 68:42–43, 1991.

CHAPTER 51

Office Use of Endovaginal Ultrasound

Steven R. Goldstein

TECHNIQUE OF VAGINAL SCANNING
ORIENTATION
OFFICE APPLICATIONS
Complex Adnexal Masses • Perimenopausal
Uterine Bleeding • Postmenopausal
Patients • Vaginal Bleeding in Pregnancy

When real-time ultrasound scanners were first introduced, they were transabdominal and had barely enough resolution to do little more than identify a breech versus vertex presentation, measure biparietal diameter, or localize a placenta. Their use was limited almost exclusively to the obstetrician. A complete exam was extremely limited, consisting only of several Polaroid pictures. Gynecologic imaging, initially with static arm scanners, and then later with small-headed sector scanners, initially seemed more complex. The equipment was large and expensive.

Over time, obstetric scanning has become increasingly more sophisticated; the standard obstetric exam now necessitates an understanding of cross-sectional body anatomy. The gynecologic ultrasound exam requires only an understanding of the anatomy, histology, and physiology of the pelvic organs. The gynecologist performs pelvic examinations daily and pelvic operations frequently, and is usually well educated in the technique of endovaginal ultrasound. Frequently, the obstetrician gynecologist is the appropriate person to be performing imaging of the pelvis.

Clearly an important advance to this end was the introduction of the vaginal probes in the mid-1980s. They are smaller and less expensive than the early equipment, and very adaptable to use by the physician at the time of the bimanual pelvic exam, particularly because the urinary bladder is already empty. The procedure requires very little time once the operator is adequately trained. Occasionally, some clinical situations require adjunctive full bladder transabdominal views.

I predicted over a decade ago that vaginal probe ultrasound would become an integral part of the overall bimanual exam. I have already integrated it in my own clinical practice. Furthermore, I have seen prototypes of equipment that will be to current ultrasound machines what the laptop is to the computer. Such small, portable, personal ultrasound devices will make the concept of an ultrasound-enhanced pelvic exam simpler.

There are times when the information obtained by an office vaginal probe ultrasound will allow the physician to make an immediate diagnosis. This can eliminate the need to refer the patient for an ultrasound examination elsewhere, to later receive a report of anatomic findings, and subsequently finalize the diagnosis. Consider this example: A 46-year-old woman, P3003, status post tubal ligation, who usually has regular menses, presents with 8 weeks of amenorrhea. The urinary pregnancy test in the office is negative. Palpation reveals a top normal size, parous, anteverted uterus, and a 4 to 5 cm right adnexal mass. The physician sends the woman for a pelvic ultrasound and the report's impression (2 days later) reveals a normal-sized uterus with thickened endometrial echo (11 mm), and a 5.4 × 4.1-

cm complex right adnexal mass. The differential diagnosis includes endometrioma, neoplasia, and hemorrhagic cyst. An endovaginal sonogram performed in the office at the time of the pelvic exam would have revealed her obvious secretory endometrium (Fig. 51-1) coupled with a hemorrhagic corpus luteum cyst showing classic clot retraction (Fig. 51-2), and this would have allowed a diagnosis of delayed ovulation. Depending on the physician's comfort level, this might have been verified with a serum progesterone, and the patient would have been told to expect her menses within a maximum of 2 weeks. Furthermore, once normal menses did ensue, the patient could return in the proliferative phase of her second cycle to document a normal right ovary (Fig. 51-3).

The technical considerations that lend themselves to such an approach are an empty urinary bladder and higher-frequency equipment used in closer proximity to the structures being studied. This results in excellent resolution, not lost with magnification. The drawbacks to the vaginal probe, as compared with traditional transabdominal panoramic views, are the short field of view, the lack of sound enhancement that a filled urinary bladder affords, the limitations of the probe by the confines of the vagina, new orientation for those familiar with traditional transabdominal panoramic views, and the presence of loops of bowel and the confusing echoes that they generate throughout the pelvis. The advantages are that the procedure is very simple once the operator has been adequately trained; further, it is time-efficient for the patient and the physician because it can easily be done by the clinician while the patient is still in the lithotomy position for the bimanual exam. The probe adds very little time to the overall bimanual exam and has very high patient acceptance.

Technique of Vaginal Scanning

The probe is prepared by wiping it clean, washing it with soap and water, and using a spray disinfectant between usages. It is covered with a clean (not sterile) condom, sheath, or finger of a glove. Ultrasound coupling gel is placed inside the condom. Outer lubricant is generally not necessary because a Papanicolaou smear and palpatory bimanual exam (with lubricant) have preceded this procedure. The pelvic organs are imaged to confirm or deny impressions obtained during the

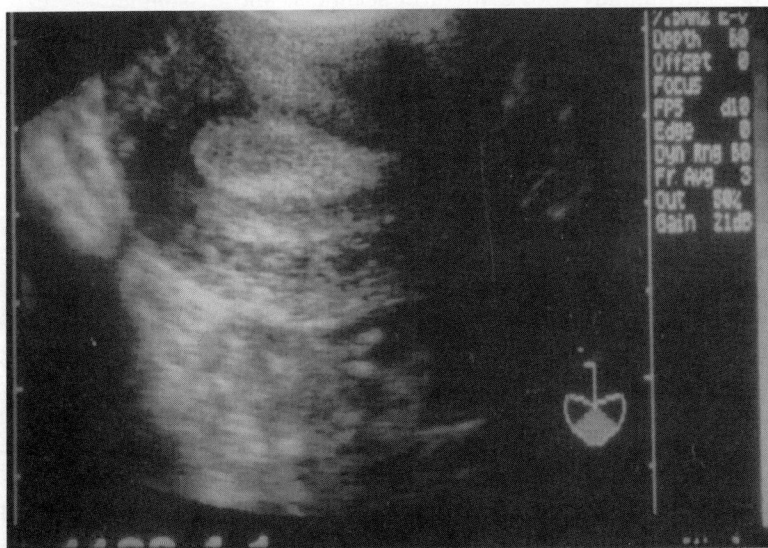

Figure 51-1 Long-axis view of a 46-year-old Para 3003 with 8 weeks of amenorrhea and negative office pregnancy test. Palpatory exam reveals a top normal size uterus and long-axis transvaginal ultrasound exam here reveals a classic secretory endometrium, which is echogenic and surrounded by a well-defined junctional zone that is hypoechoic.

Figure 51-2 Right adnexal cyst measuring 5.4 × 4.1 cm. It was taken at the same time as Fig. 51-1. This is a classic appearance of a hemorrhagic corpus luteum with a "cobweb"-like pattern, which represents bleeding into the site of ovulation and subsequent clot retraction and resorption.

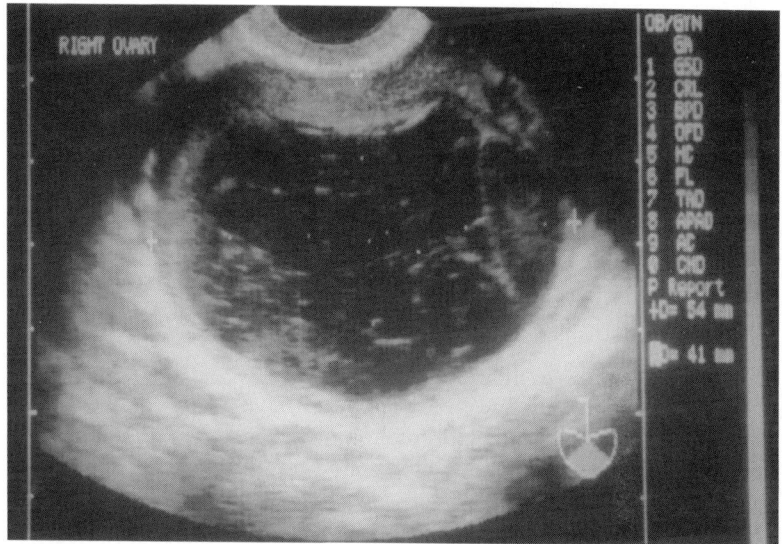

palpatory portion of the exam. Frequent use of the abdominal hand to bring the structure closer to the probe tip improves results.[1]

Once the probe is inserted into the vagina, it is manipulated posteriorly, anteriorly, and obliquely to the right and left to image recognizable anatomical structures. The uterus in long-axis serves as a basic anatomical landmark from which to orient one's eyes and hands. One looks for recognizable endometrial echo surrounded by typical myometrium. The contour of the myometrial border, the homogeneity of the myometrium itself, and a characterization of the endometrium, both subjectively and by measurement, should be carried out (Fig. 51-1). The operator must remember that the uterus is a three-dimen-

Figure 51-3 Same patient as depicted in Figs. 51-1 and 51-2, on Day 2 of the subsequent menstrual cycle. Notice this normal, early proliferative right ovary, which measures 2.3 cm maximum diameter. Notice its relationship to the iliac artery and iliac vein (labeled).

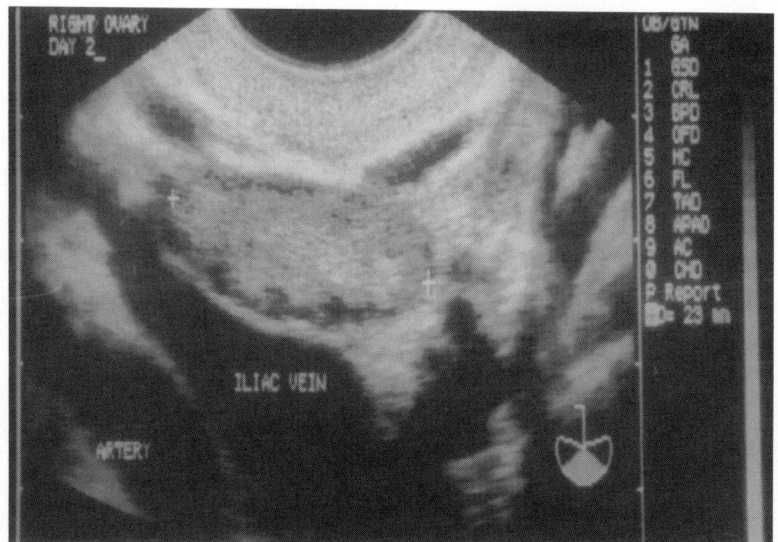

sional structure, and that in the long-axis, one must fan from cornua to cornua. The transducer is then turned 90 degrees to view the uterus in a semicoronal plane. By moving one's hand in an anterior-posterior fashion, this plane is visible from cervix to fundus.

Returning to the long-axis view, one then moves in a sagittal-oblique fashion looking for ovarian structures. These are recognized by their location (in premenopausal patients) immediately adjacent to the iliac vessels. Remember that the iliac artery is smaller and can be seen to pulsate; the iliac vein can often be seen to have flow on real-time scanning. Premenopausal patients without significant pelvic adhesions have ovaries that, by gravity, when in the lithotomy position, are located immediately adjacent to the iliac vessels. Ovaries are also recognized by their appearance. There is a typical gray pattern to the stroma, as well as numerous follicles at various stages of development, depending on the time of the menstrual cycle or whether the patient is taking oral contraceptive pills (Fig. 51-4). When either ovary is found in this long-axis orientation, the transducer handle is again rotated 90 degrees. Assessing the ovary in two planes at right angles to each other allows a three-dimensional assess-

ment of the structure. The method used to find the contralateral ovary is exactly the same.

The complete pelvic ultrasound examination should include assessment of the cul-de-sac and the region anterior to the uterus, where the bladder is often seen to start to fill with a small amount of sonolucent urine. Characterization of the cervical region can be carried out as well.

Orientation

Traditional transabdominal pelvic ultrasound makes use of multiple two-dimensional images (tomograms) to mentally recreate three-dimensional anatomy. In vaginal sonography, such concepts as longitudinal and transverse lose their meaning. Rather, one wants to obtain an "anatomy-derived orientation." A view of a structure and then a corresponding view at right angles to the initial view allows a three-dimensional assessment of that structure.

Office Applications

In my opinion, in the future, a potential office application for vaginal probe ultrasound will be

Figure 51-4 Left ovary patient on monophasic oral contraceptive pills. Note numerous small sonolucencies marked with calipers ranging between 5 and 7 mm. This is the typical pattern of ovarian suppression with birth control pills and follicles usually less than 10 mm.

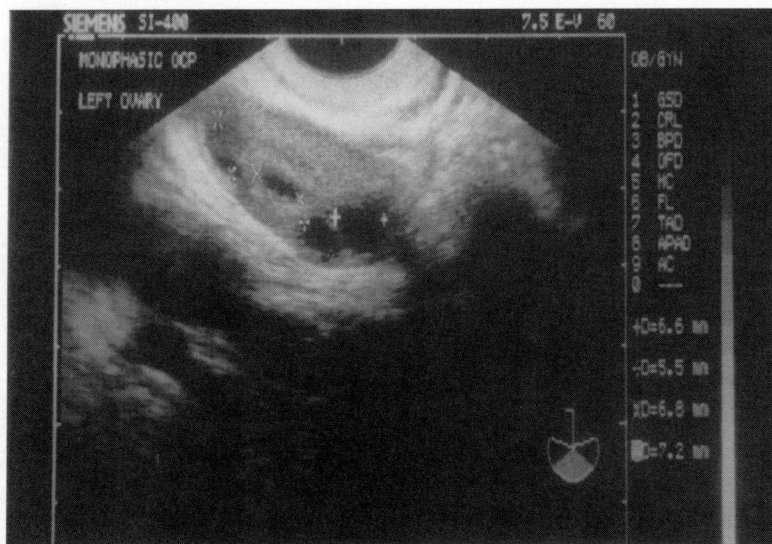

for confirming what appears to be a normal palpatory exam. The uterus is seen in long-axis and is normal in size, shape, and contour. The endometrial echo is visualized and can be correlated physiologically to the finding within the ovary. This procedure will be extremely reassuring to the patient. For some healthy patients, the physician is unable to perform a conclusive palpatory examination, especially on those patients who may be tense and thus involuntarily guarded and on those patients who are obese.

Conversely, physicians may be confronted with definitive or suspected abnormal findings during the palpatory portion of the exam. The uterine contour may be irregular in shape, suggesting the presence of intramural/subserosal myomas. A "fullness" in the adnexa may be thought to represent a hydrosalpinx, but when imaged, it may only represent a prominent loop of bowel. When one encounters what seems to be an enlargement in the adnexa, the vaginal probe may distinguish between a prominent ovary and actual cystic enlargement, which on palpation may be of similar size but during sonography may have internal characteristics that are extremely divergent.

Complex Adnexal Masses

Often, a mass may be appreciated on routine pelvic examination or as part of an imaging study ordered for other reasons. These are often asymptomatic, or can be associated with a range of symptoms from mild to severe. In the past, a mass in the adnexa was described and a sonographic differential diagnosis given. For a septated or "complex" adnexal mass, the list often included endometriosis, hemorrhagic functional cyst, and "possibly but cannot rule out neoplasia." Depending on the size, symptoms, length of time the mass was present, and the degree of anxiety of the patient, such patients often underwent a laparoscopy or exploratory laparotomy. Use of vaginal ultrasound can often help distinguish endometriosis from a hemorrhagic corpus luteum or from neoplasia.

Endometriomas may have a more variable ap-

pearance on transabdominal ultrasound. With the vaginal probe, endometriomas characteristically are unilocular or multilocular masses with diffuse uniform internal echoes throughout (Fig. 51-5). Such an internal echo pattern is optimally appreciated with the vaginal probe, but may be more sonolucent when seen transabdominally. Do not confuse endometriosis with a solid mass, even though it will demonstrate some acoustic enhancement. Such masses are increasingly managed by endoscopic surgical resection.

Hemorrhagic corpora lutea are functional cysts with fresh bleeding into the site of the ovulation (Fig. 51-2). The blood will organize and undergo a "maturation," progressing from diffuse (but more heterogenous than endometriomas) to a reticular "cobweb"-like pattern, and finally clot retraction, after which the cysts may mimic papillary projections with bridging. Such structures (unless accompanied by some coagulation defect) are invariably self-limited and, if recognized, any operative intervention (diagnostic or therapeutic) can be avoided. Follow-up after the second menses in the proliferative phase of the cycle will usually show resolution.

Malignancy will show trends toward certain features that have allowed development of scoring systems to help distinguish them from benign disease (Fig. 51-6). Various systems use vaginal probe assessment of inner-wall structure, wall thickness (mm), septa (mm), and echogenicity to score masses. In one study, the ability of these particular diagnostic techniques to predict malignancy had a specificity of 83 percent, sensitivity of 100 percent, a positive predictive value of 37 percent, and a negative predictive value of 100 percent.[2] The information obtained from preoperative endovaginal ultrasound can assist the physician in making proper operative plans, such as having a gynecologic oncologist available and the amount of operating time expected.

Perimenopausal Uterine Bleeding

Unscheduled uterine bleeding is a major source of concern to women, and accounts for many of

Figure 51-5 Classic endovaginal ultrasound appearance of an endometrioma. This measures 5.6 × 4.2 cm. It is a "solid-appearing" cyst with very fine homogenous internal echoes, sometimes referred to as ground glass.

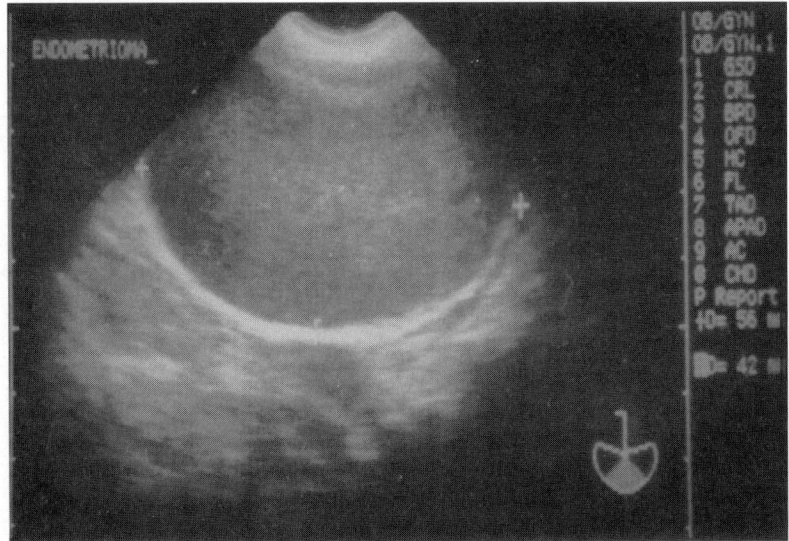

their office visits to the gynecologist. In perimenopausal women, such bleeding may be anovulatory, but concerns about pathology, such as hyperplasia, polyps, submucous myomas, or carcinoma, are heightened, and invasive diagnostic procedures are commonplace. I have used fluid instillation into the uterine cavity to enhance vaginal probe ultrasound imaging of the endometrium in perimenopausal women with irregular vaginal bleeding.[3]

A prospective pilot study was done of 21 women between the ages of 40 and 52. Clinically, they had a sufficient history of irregular vaginal bleeding of uterine origin to be triaged for some form of invasive endometrial sampling. On days 4 to 6 of their cycle, a sonohysterography catheter

Figure 51-6 Stage I papillary serous cystadenocarcinoma in a 71-year-old patient. This ovarian tumor measured 4.0 × 3.4 cm. It is mostly cystic although the solid area in one pole is clearly marked.

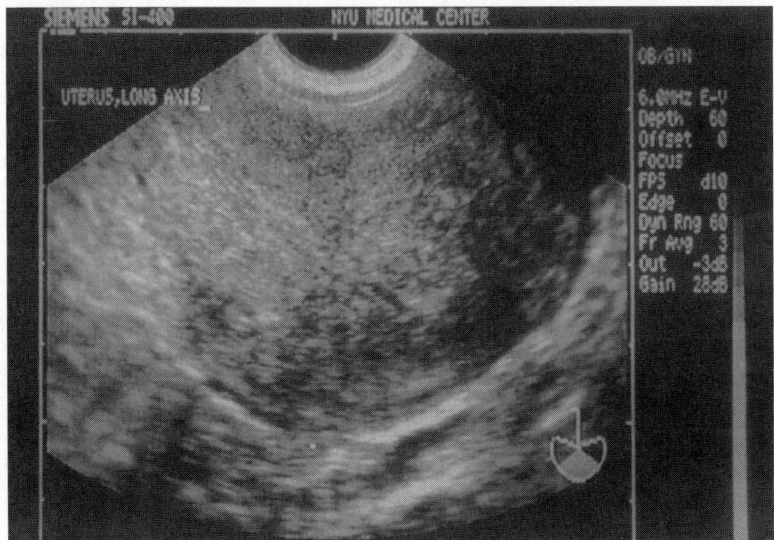

was inserted. Sterile saline was slowly infused under direct ultrasound examination. The procedure was videotaped, and the endometrial cavity was carefully examined, both in the long-axis and coronal views. If present, any polyps or submucous myomas were noted and measured. Invasive endometrial sampling was then carried out. All pathology reports were then reviewed.

Of the 21 patients, 8 had obvious polypoid lesions and were triaged for operative hysteroscopic removal. Hysteroscopic visualization and pathology reports confirmed benign polyps in all eight patients. Three patients had submucous myomas. Two were offered and accepted wire-loop resectoscopic excision. The third had a submucous myoma that extended to the serosal edge of the uterus and was treated expectantly. Nine patients had no obvious anatomical lesion and an endometrial thickness of 4 mm or less. Endometrial biopsy in all nine of these patients revealed early proliferative endometrium. One patient had an endometrial thickness of 8 mm; fractional curettage with hysteroscopy revealed simple hyperplasia without atypia.

This demonstrated that endometrial fluid instillation to enhance vaginal ultrasonography in perimenopausal women could distinguish between patients with minimal tissue whose bleeding is anovulatory and can be treated with hormonal therapy, and those patients with significant amounts and types of tissue requiring curettage. Furthermore, polyps could be distinguished from submucous myomas, which allowed appropriate preoperative triage for operative hysteroscopy when indicated, and eliminated the need for diagnostic hysteroscopy in patients whose bleeding was dysfunctional.

In a subsequent prospective study[4] of 433 perimenopausal women with abnormal uterine bleeding, an algorithm involving ultrasound as the first intervention was utilized for triage. Women were examined on days 4 to 6 of the bleeding cycle, when the endometrium was as thin as one would expect it to be at any time during the month. An initial transvaginal pelvic ultrasound was performed. If a thin distinct endo-

metrial echo was seen and measured ≤5 mm in maximum AP thickness, this was considered to be a reliable sign of lack of significant tissue; the patient was considered as having dysfunctional uterine bleeding and no further work-up was done. If the endometrial echo was >5 mm or not adequately visualized (Fig. 51-7), then the patient underwent saline-infusion sonohysterography. If the saline-infusion sonohysterography revealed a thin distinct endometrium surrounding the fluid instillation measuring ≤3 mm on the anterior and posterior walls, respectively, then this was considered compatible with early proliferative endometrium based on the results of the pilot study, and a diagnosis of dysfunctional anovulatory bleeding was made. If the tissues surrounding the fluid instillation were >3 mm and symmetrical (Fig. 51-8), then blind endometrial sampling was carried out. If there were focally thick abnormal areas of the tissue (Fig. 51-9), or endometrial polyps (Fig. 51-10), or submucous myomas, then the patient was triaged for hysteroscopically directed intervention. Some submucous myomas were followed expectantly.

Overall, 280 women (64 percent) had thin distinct endometrial echos on days 4 to 6. Saline-infusion sonohysterography was used on 153 women of which 71 percent were for thickened endometrial echo and 29 percent were for inability to visualize adequately an endometrial echo. Endometrial polyps were found in 61 patients, which were all removed hysteroscopically and confirmed pathologically. Twenty-two patients had submucous myomas, of which 13 were treated expectantly while 9 had resectoscopic myomectomies. There were 10 patients with symmetrically thick endometrial echos measuring >3 mm single-layer thickness. Blind endometrial sampling revealed proliferative endometrium in five patients and hyperplasia in five other patients. The sonohysterograms were technically inadequate in 2.5 percent of patients, and these patients underwent D&C and hysteroscopy. One of these patients had a submucous myoma, and three had a proliferative endometrium. When subjected to a cost analysis, this ultrasound-based

Figure 51-7 Transvaginal scan of a perimenopausal patient with abnormal uterine bleeding. In this case, no discrete endometrial echo can be visualized and thus cannot be measured. This is an indication for saline-infusion sonohysterography (SIS).

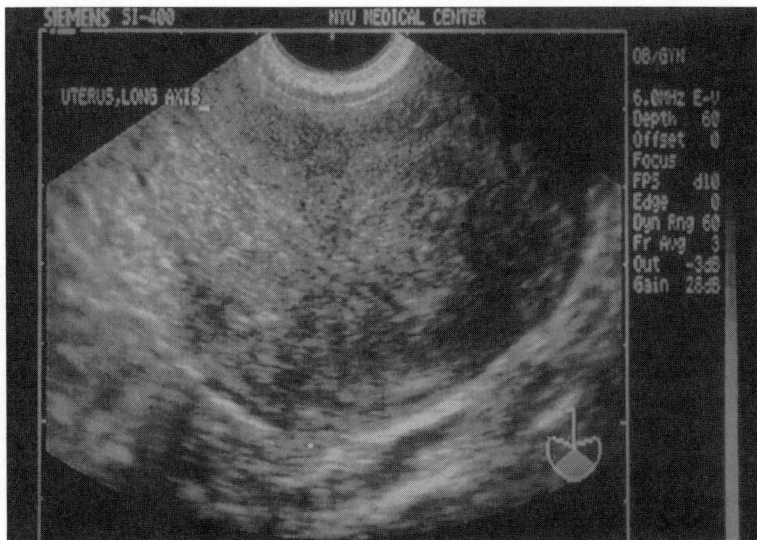

triage for abnormal perimenopausal bleeding was equivalent to initial Pipelle biopsy, but according to our analysis, Pipelle biopsy could miss up to 18 percent of lesions such as polyps, submucous myomas, or focal hyperplasias.

Postmenopausal Patients

After menopause, patients with bleeding or palpable adnexal masses can also be evaluated with the use of vaginal probe ultrasound. In the presence of postmenopausal bleeding, an

Figure 51-8 Saline-infusion sonohysterogram of a perimenopausal patient with abnormal uterine bleeding. The sonolucent fluid has distended the anterior and posterior walls, which measure 7.9 and 5.8 mm, respectively (calipers). This symmetrically thickened endometrium can be sampled blindly. Histology revealed simple hyperplasia.

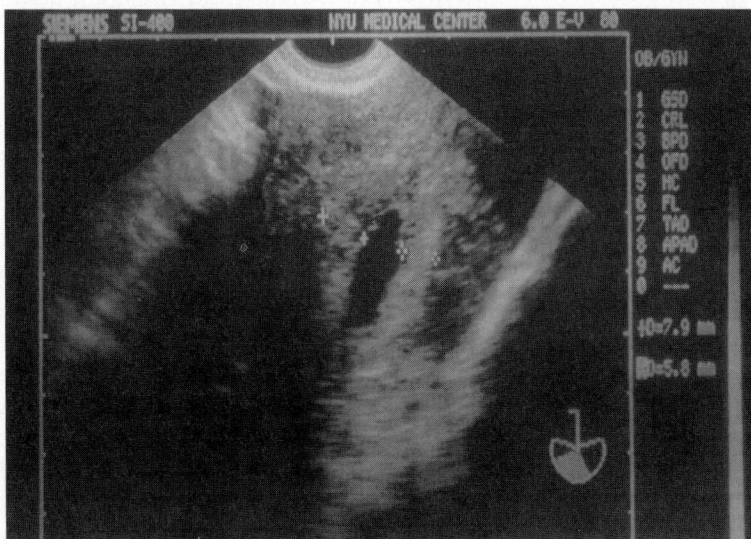

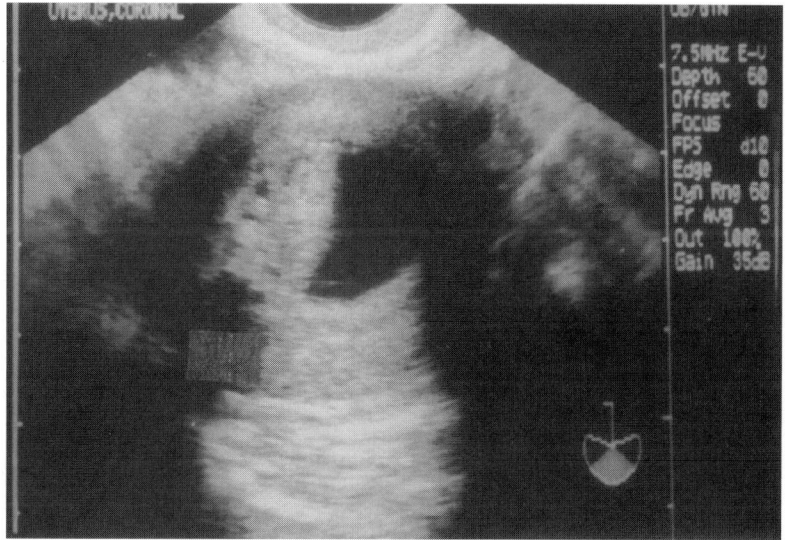

Figure 51-9 Saline-infusion sonohysterogram revealing a markedly thickened and heterogenous irregular endometrium along the right lateral border of the uterus. There was no significant thickening of the tissue along the left lateral border. Histologically this patient manifested complex hyperplasia with atypia, which only involved 50 percent of the uterine cavity.

endometrial echo less than 4 to 5 mm thick has been shown to be associated with a lack of pathologic tissue.[5-7] An endovaginal ultrasound examination can spare such patients the discomfort and expense of endometrial sampling. In the presence of postmenopausal bleeding, an endometrial thickness greater than 5 mm is associated with virtually all pathology tissue types, and sampling is mandatory.

Routine use of the vaginal probe may show cystic adnexal masses in as many as 10 to 15 percent of postmenopausal patients.[8] When these are unilocular and unilateral and less than 3 cm, they have virtually no malignancy. Regardless,

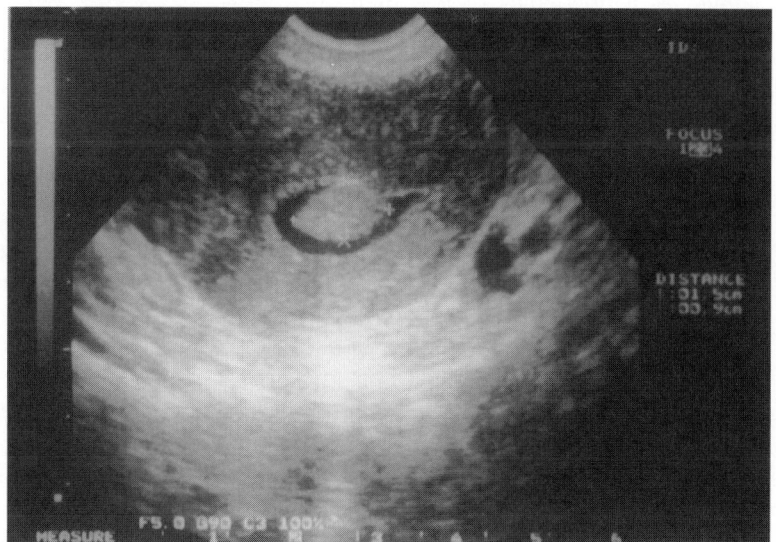

Figure 51-10 Saline infusion sonohysterogram reveals an anterior wall polyp approximately halfway to the fundus. It measures 1.5 × 0.9 cm (calipers). The endometrium seemed to surround the fluid instillation. Here it is unmeasured but clearly thin-compatible with the early proliferative phase as this patient was day 6 of her bleeding cycle.

Figure 51-11 Transvaginal sonogram of a patient with vaginal bleeding and closed cervical os. Crown rump length measures 2.3 cm corresponding to 9 weeks 2 days gestation. Cardiac activity was clearly seen. The yolk sac is normal in size, shape, and appearance. There is no obvious explanation for this patient's clinical diagnosis of "threatened abortion," but such a transvaginal ultrasound appearance with positive cardiac activity is associated with an extremely high pregnancy continuation rate (>95 percent).

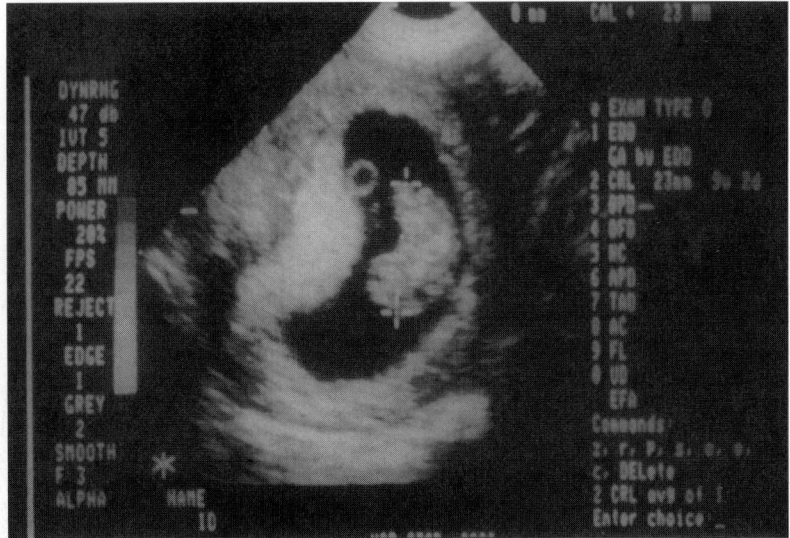

such findings should be initially followed at relatively close intervals to be sure that there is neither progression and enlargement nor development of ascitic fluid.[9]

Vaginal Bleeding in Pregnancy

"Threatened abortion" is a clinical term. It is defined as a pregnancy of less than 20 weeks gestation with vaginal bleeding in the presence of a closed cervical os. In the past, it has been one of the most common indications for performing ultrasound in an early pregnancy. One should realize, however, that all patients with positive pregnancy tests and vaginal bleeding are patients in whom one must rule out an ectopic pregnancy.

Ultrasound findings in the majority of patients with threatened abortions will show a normal-appearing intrauterine gestation (findings will depend on the age of the gestation) with no obvious reason for, or source of, the clinically apparent vaginal bleeding. If a definitive intrauterine gestation is identified (Fig. 51-11), especially in the presence of embryonic cardiac activity, then sonography may not provide the clinician with the cause for the vaginal bleeding, but the seem-

ingly normal findings may be reassuring to the patient.

Occasionally, the uterus shows no gestational sac on initial ultrasound examination and a definite extrauterine pregnancy is diagnosed (Fig. 51-12). This allows one to proceed immediately to therapeutic intervention.

From a clinical perspective, the presence of a definitive intrauterine pregnancy virtually excludes ectopic pregnancy. Heterotopic pregnancy (a simultaneous intrauterine and extrauterine pregnancy) is stated to occur in 1:30,000 spontaneous pregnancies.[10] However, in women undergoing assisted reproductive technologies, this incidence will increase to about 1:6,000[11,12] The ability to definitively diagnose an intrauterine pregnancy will rely on well-established criteria. When no intrauterine gestation is seen on ultrasound, the quantitative human chorionic gonadotropin (hCG) level must be determined and the concept of a discriminatory level used. If the hCG level is less than the discriminatory level, then serial hCG determination must be implemented. Current assays measure the intact hCG molecule. It should rise a minimum of 66 percent every 48 hours or effectively double every 3 days

Figure 51-12 Transvaginal ultrasound that reveals a gestational sac containing a yolk sac and embryonic structure. This, however, is located in the right adnexa. The uterus was visualized in a separate scanning plane and did not contain any sign of gestational sac. This is a definitive ectopic pregnancy and allows definitive intervention.

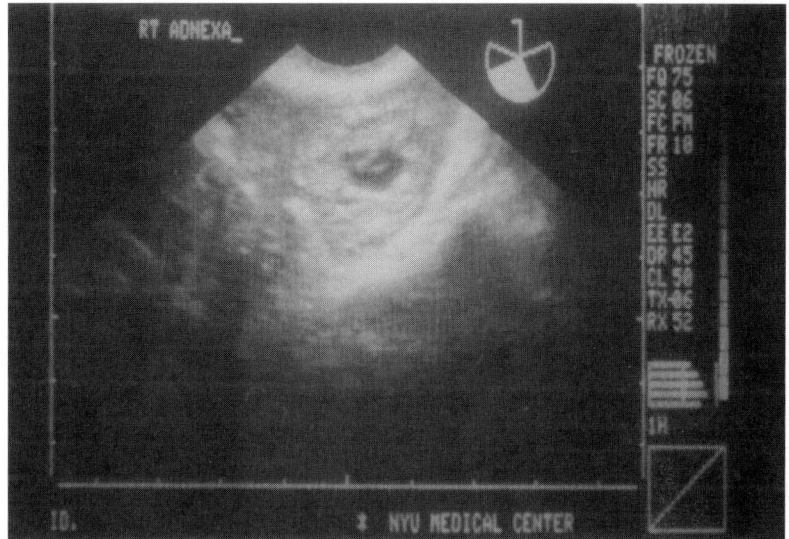

in a normal pregnancy. Once the hCG level surpasses a discriminatory level (usually 1000 to 1500 mIU/ml), an intrauterine gestation should be imaged. The absence of an intrauterine gestation suggests that the pregnancy is not capable of continuing; that is, it represents either a failing intrauterine gestation or an extrauterine pregnancy. Similarly, a subnormal rate of rise of hCG also indicates a failing intrauterine gestation or extrauterine pregnancy. In such cases, because ongoing normal pregnancy has been excluded, curettage and examination of tissue for the presence or absence of chorionic villi may be useful as a next step in triage. The presence of chorionic villi proves an intrauterine gestation. The presence of only decidual tissue raises the index of suspicion for ectopic pregnancy, although, if there has been previous bleeding, complete abortion (possibly tubal) can account for such findings. Follow-up quantitative hCG level, whether rising, plateauing, or falling, may help distinguish ectopic pregnancy from completed abortion.

Some intrauterine fluid collections may look like gestational sacs. The presence of yolk sac precludes a diagnosis of such "pseudosacs." If any doubt exists about the legitimacy or normalcy of a gestational sac before a yolk sac or

embryo is present, follow-up ultrasound scan is warranted.

Finally, extrauterine findings on ultrasound will reflect in vivo findings. This is an important concept in all of ultrasound scanning. The more the clinician appreciates the range of how an entity can look in vivo, the better the clinician can understand why the ultrasound images appear as they do. One should realize that the ability to reliably recognize pregnancy depends not on the location but on the appearance. The more normal in appearance the gestation is, the more likely one will recognize it as a pregnancy, regardless of whether it is located inside or outside the uterus.

Fifteen to 28 percent of ectopic pregnancies develop to the point of yolk sac and/or cardiac activity.[13,14] Obviously, such pregnancies often have normal doubling times of hCG. Furthermore, the familiar gestational sac appearance, with its sonolucent center, is more easily seen on ultrasound. This finding is especially true if there is cardiac activity present. Likewise, not all sonolucent or complex adnexal structures are extrauterine gestations. The ovaries should be identified on the side in question to avoid mistakenly identifying a corpus luteum or corpus luteum cyst as an extrauterine gestation.

Summary

The use of vaginal ultrasound by the office practitioner has tremendous advantages. Diagnoses can more often be made promptly, which leads to more timely therapy or, in the case of normal findings, to relieving patient anxieties. The technique saves time for both the patient and the physician. Vaginal scanning in the office reduces the need for referring patients elsewhere (except for consultation). This reduces the number of errors that occur when information must be transmitted from one source to another. Patients almost uniformly prefer vaginal scanning over the discomfort of a full bladder transabdominal approach. Patients can better understand their care, and the pictures generated on the screen are very helpful in communicating the pathology to them. In addition, ultrasound is a very powerful teaching tool of normal anatomy and physiology. Vaginal scanning allows instant confirmation of the primary obstetric gynecologic physician's anatomical findings at the time of the pelvic examination. It also yields physiologic information that is unavailable by palpation alone.

References and Selected Readings

1. Timor-Tritsch IE: Is office use of vaginal sonography feasible? *Am J Obstet Gynecol* 162:983–985, 1990.
2. Sassone A, Timor-Tritsch I, Artner A: Transvaginal sonographic characterization of ovarian disease: Evaluation of a new scoring system to predict ovarian malignancy. *Obstet Gynecol* 78:70, 1991.
3. Goldstein SR: Use of ultrasonohysterography for triage of perimenopausal patients with unexplained uterine bleeding. *Am J Obstet Gynecol* 170:565–570, 1994.
4. Goldstein SR, Zeltser I, Horan CK, Snyder JR, Schwartz LB. Ultrasonography-based triage for perimenopausal patients with abnormal uterine bleeding. *Am J Obstet Gynecol* 1997; 177:102–108.
5. Goldstein SR, Nachtigall M, Snyder JR, et al: Endometrial assessment by vaginal ultrasonography before endometrial sampling in patients with postmenopausal bleeding. *Am J Obstet Gynecol* 163:119–123, 1990.
6. Nasri MN, Coast GJ: Correlation of ultrasound findings and endometrial histopathology in postmenopausal women. *Br J Obstet Gynaecol* 96:1333–1338, 1989.
7. Granberg S, Wikland M, Karlsson B, et al: Endometrial thickness as measured by endovaginal ultrasonography for identifying endometrial abnormality. *Am J Obstet Gynecol* 164:47–52, 1991.
8. Levine D, Gosink BB, Wolf SI, et al: Simple adnexal cysts: The natural history in postmenopausal women. *Radiology* 184:653–659, 1992.
9. Auslander R, Atlas I, Lissak A, et al: Follow-up a small postmenopausal ovarian cyst using ultrasound and CA-125 antigen. *J Clin Ultrasound* 24:175–178, 1996.
10. DeVoe RW, Pratt JH: Simultaneous intrauterine and extrauterine pregnancy. *Am J Obstet Gynecol* 78:70, 1991.
11. Gamberdella FR, Marrs RP: Heterotropic pregnancy associated with assisted reproductive technology. *Am J Obstet Gynecol* 160:1520–1524, 1989.
12. Dimitry ES, Subak-Sharpe R, Mills M, et al: Nine cases of heterotrophic pregnancies in 4 years of in vitro fertilization. *Fertil Steril* 53:107–110, 1990.
13. Stiller RJ, de Regt RH, Blair E: Transvaginal ultrasonography in patients at risk for ectopic pregnancy. *Am J Obstet Gynecol* 161:930–933, 1989.
14. Fleischer AC, Pennell RG, McKee MS et al: Ectopic pregnancy: Features of transvaginal sonography. *Radiology* 174:375–378, 1990.

CHAPTER 52

Mammography and Other Techniques for Breast Imaging

Lucille C. Xenophon

Screening and Diagnostic Mammography

Mammography is the gold standard method for breast imaging. There are two basic indications for mammography: screening and evaluation of a possible problem (diagnostic). Routine screening is performed for an asymptomatic patient. Diagnostic mammography is performed to evaluate a clinical sign or symptom or to evaluate further an imaging finding identified on a screening mammogram.

A screening mammogram consists of two views per breast—usually a craniocaudad view and a mediolateral oblique view. It is sometimes performed by a technologist without a radiologist on-site. It can be processed in batches and given to a radiologist to interpret afterwards. Screening mammography allows for imaging of higher volumes of patients and allows imaging to be per-

formed outside the hospital or radiology office setting. Mobile units, for example, can provide outreach to medically underserved areas.

There is some disagreement in the United States regarding protocols for the age at which regular mammography screening should be initiated. My recommendation for the typical patient is for a baseline mammogram at age 40 and yearly thereafter. It has been shown by randomized controlled clinical trials that screening mammography can reduce the mortality rate from breast cancer by at least 25 percent for women age 50 or greater. The benefit of screening mammography for women between the ages of 40 and 50 has been a topic of heated debate revolving around issues of medicine, epidemiology, economics, and politics. In 1997, the American College of Radiology recommended annual screening mammography for all asymptomatic women beginning at age 40. Two current individual trials have each reported a statistically significant decrease in breast cancer mortality rate as a benefit of screening women in the 40- to 50-year age range. For patients age 45 to 49 at entry in the Malmo, Sweden trial, a 36 percent mortality reduction has been reported. For women age 39 to 49 at entry in the Gothenberg, Sweden trial, a 45 percent reduction has been reported. In the "Minority Report" of the National Institutes of Health Consensus Statement concerning Breast Cancer Screening for Women Ages 40 to 49, dissenting members of the panel stated that screening mammography in women age 40 to 49 results in earlier detection. Earlier detection usually results in detection of tumors of smaller size and lower stage. It increases the number of treatment options, including breast conservation. The dissenting opinion goes on to state that the increase in detection of ductal carcinoma in situ is a goal of earlier screening because the dissenting panel members believe that detection at this stage leads to a decrease in incidence of invasive cancer. They further state that "Although there is theoretical risk from radiation exposure, if it exists at all, it is very low. There is no measurable harm from the diagnostic doses used for screening mammography." False-positive mammography in younger women—those leading to extra views or biopsy—is thought by this group to be statistically within acceptable limits and should not be a deterrent to screening. Although one would always like to reduce the incidence of false-positive reports, on balance the benefits of early detection of breast cancer outweigh the risk of this problem. Further supporting the need for screening women in the 40 to 50 age range is the generally accepted theory that breast cancers in premenopausal women are more aggressive and faster growing.

Mammographic screening before age 40 may benefit women who are at high risk for breast cancer (e.g., a woman who has a first-degree relative with a history of premenopausal breast cancer). Although there are no established guidelines, it has been suggested that a woman over the age of 25 who is at high risk should be first screened 10 years earlier than the age at which her relative was diagnosed. For example, a patient whose mother was diagnosed with breast cancer at age 36 should begin screening at age 26.

A diagnostic mammogram is performed for problem solving. The need for a diagnostic mammogram is sometimes generated by a finding identified on screening mammography. It is sometimes generated by the referring primary health care provider who orders a mammogram to help assist in evaluating a clinical problem, such as a palpable mass, focal tenderness, new nipple inversion, nipple discharge, or breast skin changes, such as dimpling or unexplained erythema.

In diagnostic mammography, the mammographer plays an active role. The radiologist requests additional views or imaging techniques tailored to address the specific problem. Communication between the referring health care provider and the radiologist is essential. The mammographer must be made aware that there is a clinical issue to be evaluated. Often, anxious patients are only able to report "my doctor felt a lump" but are unable to pinpoint the area of concern. When ordering a diagnostic mammogram, it is extremely helpful to provide the mammographer with a diagram of the breast indicating the location of a palpable mass or skin change. Another method to describe the location of a lesion is to view the breast as a clock face with the patient facing the observer. For example, an upper outer quadrant mass on the right may be described as being in the 11 o'clock position. An upper outer quadrant mass on the left may be described as being in the 1 o'clock position. A mass should also be described in terms of approximate size and distance from the nipple. Improved accuracy of diagnosis can be achieved if the written prescription for mammography indicates, for example, possible 1-cm mass, left 12 o'clock, 2 cm from the nipple. (It is essential to remember that a mammogram is an important component in the evaluation of a breast abnormality, but it is just one component. The false-negative rate of mammograms is 10 to 15 percent. Therefore, if a breast mass is clinically present, it must be further evaluated, even if the mammogram report is normal.)

The Mammography Report

The mammography report is the main form of communication between the mammographer and the referring clinician. The style and verbiage of the report tend to vary from mammographer to mammographer. In an effort to standardize the terminology used in mammography reports, the Breast Imaging Reporting and Data System (BI-RADS™) was developed by the American College of Radiology (ACR). It provides a lexicon of terms to describe findings such as masses and calcifications. The "final assessment category" in the lexicon describes the radiologist's level of suspicion for malignancy.

The radiology report should include the patient's name and date of birth. The basic format includes the following:

Clinical Indication: The mammographer indicates whether the study was performed as a screening exam or whether there was a diagnostic problem such as a palpable mass or imaging abnormality on screening mammography.

Pertinent History: Examples include surgical or radiation history, factors increasing the risk for breast cancer, and history of hormone replacement therapy.

Comparison: Documentation that the current study was compared to prior mammograms.

Images: The views obtained may or may not be described in the report at the discretion of the radiologist.

Findings: The overall density of the breast is described. Any positive findings are reported.

Impression: A summary and interpretation of the important findings.

Recommendations: The recommended time interval for the next follow-up, or recommendation for further evaluation, is made.

Assessment: A number from 0 to 5 is assigned to designate a specific BI-RADS™ category.

Pertinent History

The pertinent history component of the report describes any factor that would place the patient at an increased risk for carcinoma. There is a two to four times increased risk for breast carcinoma if the patient has a first-degree relative (mother, sister) with a history of breast cancer. If the cancer was diagnosed prior to age 50, the risks are higher. A patient who has a personal history of breast cancer is two to four times more likely to develop contralateral breast carcinoma. The lifetime risk for women with the *BRCA1* or *BRCA2* gene mutation is 56 to 87 percent. Patients with biopsy-proven atypical ductal hyperplasia are at increased risk (four to five times) for breast cancer. Lobular carcinoma in situ and well-differentiated ductal carcinoma in situ place the patient at high relative risk (8 to 10 times) for development of breast carcinoma. Women treated with mediastinal radiation therapy for Hodgkin's lymphoma while in their teens or 20s have a significantly increased risk of developing breast carcinoma.

Breast surgical history is described in this section of the mammography report, as is any history of radiation therapy directed to the breast. This history is essential to the analysis of architectural distortion. The possibility of recurrent cancer in the surgical bed is searched for carefully by the mammographer (Figs. 52-1 and 52-2). Surgical scars on the skin are demarcated with radiopaque markers to bring attention to this area. If a woman uses hormone replacement therapy, this fact is included in the report, because hormone usage can increase the glandular tissue/fat ratio, dramatically changing the mammographic appearance of the breasts (Figs 52-3 and 52-4). Significant weight change—plus or minus—can also alter the glandular/fat composition of the breasts, resulting in a change in appearance. Knowing if there has been a history of breast trauma is essential in the interpretation of a new spiculated mass, because a hematoma can mimic carcinoma radiographically. The presence of implants is recorded. Reduction mammoplasty can cause architectural distortion and fat necrosis, and is, therefore, considered to be pertinent history. Systemic illness that may affect mammographic appearance (e.g., thickening of the trabeculae or skin) includes congestive heart failure and renal failure. Burns involving the breast may cause mammographically visible skin thickening and architectural distortion. A history of other carcinoma is reported. Tumors known to manifest in the breast include non-Hodgkin's lymphoma, melanoma, and others.

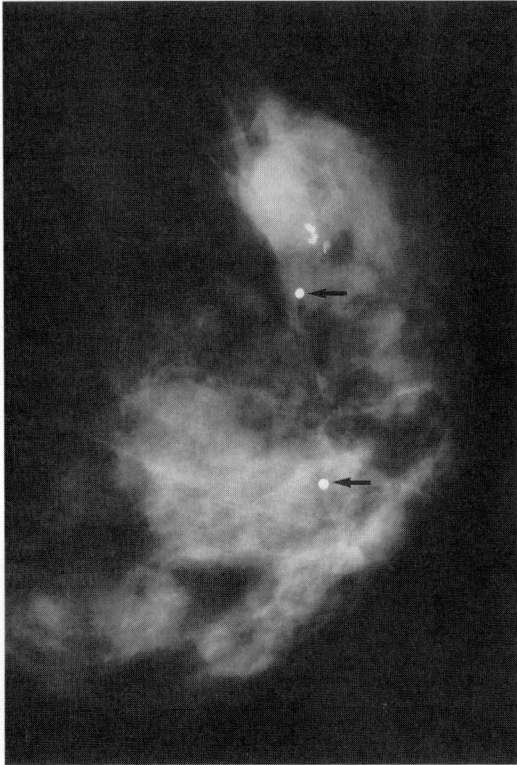

A

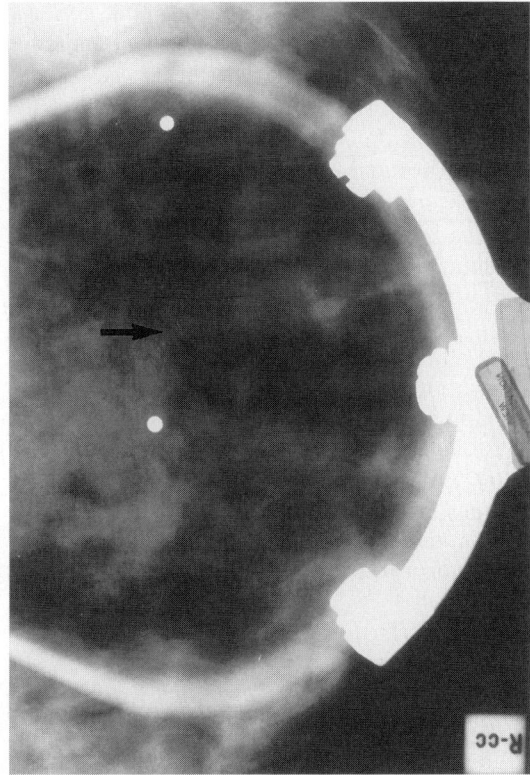

B

Figures 52-1 and 52-2   65-year-old patient, 15 years status post (s/p) lumpectomy and radiation therapy. *A.* The scar site is demarcated by radiopaque markers (arrows). *B.* With magnification, pleomorphic calcifications can be seen at the surgical site (arrow). This is a BI-RADS™ category 5 lesion. Needle localization and biopsy revealed recurrent intraductal carcinoma.

Comparison

Whenever possible, a mammogram should be compared with prior studies. Patients should be encouraged to keep a record of the site(s) where their mammogram was performed in order to be able to retrieve films for comparison. Mammographic signs of cancer can be very subtle. A change in pattern occurring slowly over time may not be easily perceived if the study is read in conjunction only with the study performed the preceding year. Comparison to studies done two years prior and earlier is desirable. Follow-up or work-up of probable benign findings or asymmetric densities can often be obviated if stability over a two- to three-year time

interval can be established. It is important to remember that findings with suspicious features, even if stable over time, are still suspicious and biopsy should be considered.

Images

At least 15 standard mammographic positions are defined by the American College of Radiology. Prior to obtaining an image, the technologist confirms that the patient is not wearing powder, perfume, or deodorant because residue from these products can mimic microcalcifications. The technologist affixes radiopaque markers to the breast to demarcate scars and palpable

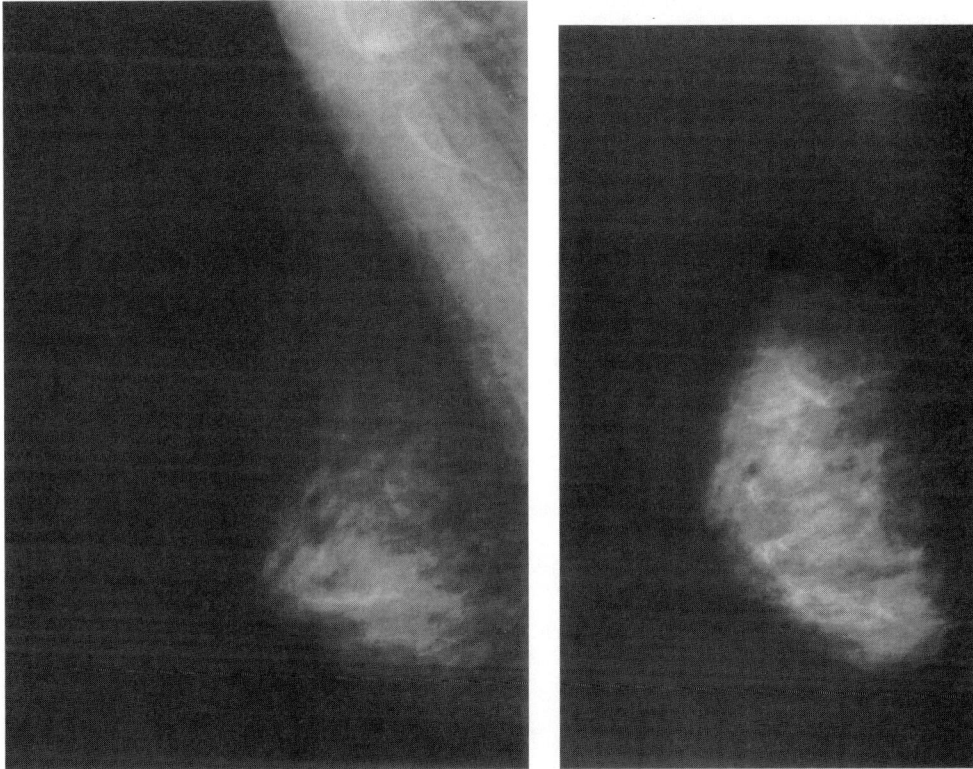

Figures 52-3 and 52-4 52-year-old patient. Mediolateral oblique views were performed 1-year apart. Shortly after the first mammogram, the patient began using exogenous hormones, resulting in a dramatic increase in glandular tissue and change in the mammographic appearance.

masses. Prominent lesions on the skin surface are marked so that the mammographer does not misinterpret a shadow created by the skin lesion as being within the breast parenchyma. In some facilities, the nipple is routinely marked.

The two basic positions for routine screening are the craniocauded (CC) and the mediolateral oblique (MLO) views. To obtain a craniocaudad view, the film cassette is placed under the breast, the breast is compressed between two plastic plates, and the x-ray beam is directed from the top of the breast to the bottom. This view allows evaluation of the breast from medial to lateral. In this view, the goal is to image as much posterior breast tissue as possible. Inclusion of the pectoral muscle assures that this goal has been accom-

plished (Figs. 52-5, 52-6, and 52-7). In the MLO view, the film cassette is located on the lateral aspect of the breast. The breast is compressed between two plates that are oriented 45 to 60 degrees oblique relative to vertical. The x-ray beam is directed from medial to lateral. This view allows evaluation of the breast from superior to inferior. A properly positioned MLO view images the pectoral muscle to the level of the nipple and the nipple is viewed in profile.

In some women, glandular tissue extends laterally beyond the lateral edge of the CC view. In this case, a third view called the exaggerated craniocaudad view (XCCL) is added; the patient is rotated to include the lateral tissue on the film.

Figures 52-5, 52-6, and 52-7 The first craniocaudad view does not include the posterior breast tissue. When properly positioned, a posterior and lateral carcinoma is identified (arrow). Incidentally noted was a subareolar mass, shown to be a cyst by sonography (thin arrow).

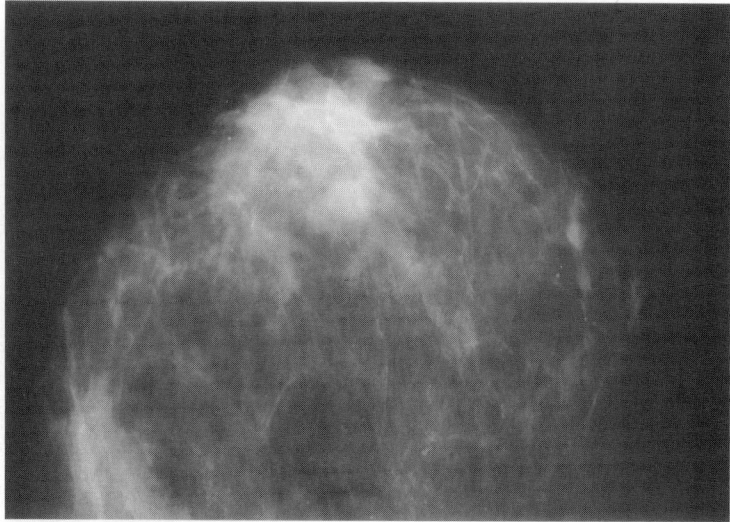

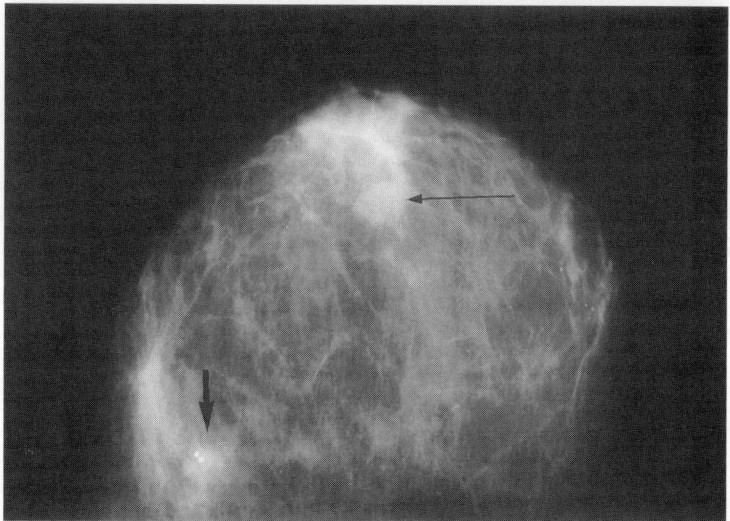

A "spot compression" view uses a compression device smaller than the conventional compression plates to cone down to a small area of interest. This is useful to determine whether a possible lesion is artifactually created by superimposed normal tissue. To analyze the margins of a definite mass or to look more closely at calcium, magnification views are obtained with the spot paddle (Figs. 52-8 and 52-9). Spot images are usually more painful to the patient than full-

paddle images because the forces of compression are concentrated in one small area. A patient in pain will move. Motion leads to image blurring and defeats the purpose of the extra views. If the patient cannot tolerate spot magnification, full-paddle magnification is used.

A mediolateral view (ML) in the 90-degree position (nonangled) is used to triangulate the location of a lesion for preoperative needle localization. It is used to demonstrate "milk of cal-

Figures 52-5, 52-6, 52-7
(*Continued*) Specimen radiograph, following surgical excision, shows the carcinoma.

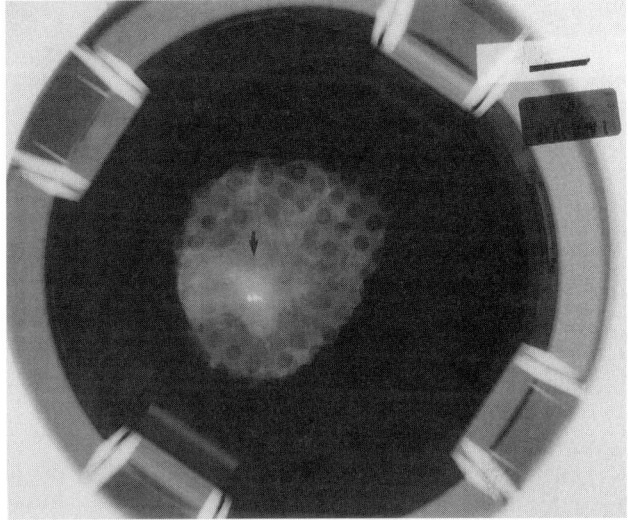

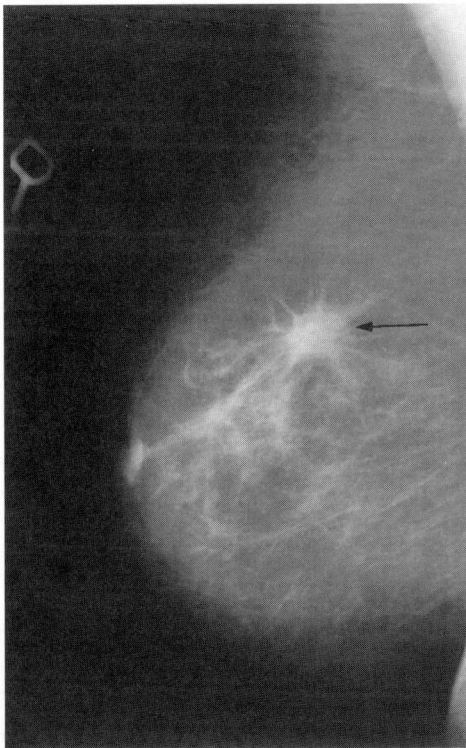

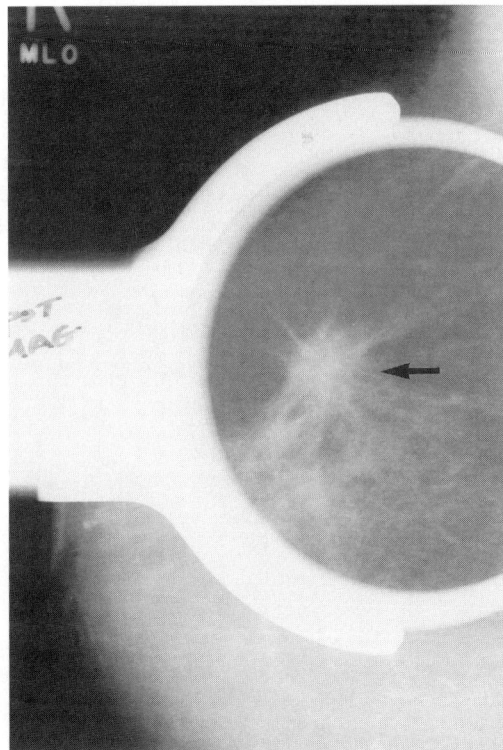

Figures 52-8 and 52-9 Spot magnification view more clearly shows the spiculations of this mass. This is a BI-RADS™ category 5 lesion—highly suspicious for carcinoma.

cium"—calcium that layers in microcysts, has the appearance of sharp menisci, and is considered typically benign. The 90-degree view may help to localize a mass seen only on CC or only on MLO view. Tangential views (TAN) are performed by positioning the breast so that the area of interest is in tangent to the x-ray beam. This is used to help separate an obscured palpable mass from the surrounding breast tissue and is especially useful in a dense breast (Fig. 52-10). It is also used to prove the dermal location of calcium.

Breast implants obscure the breast parenchyma. To allow imaging of as much breast tissue

as possible, the technologist pushes the implant against the chest wall to remove it from the field of view. Prior to performing implant-displaced (ID) views, CC and MLO views are obtained with the implant in the field of view, using minimal compression (Figs. 52-11 and 52-12).

Findings

According to BI-RADS™, the breast composition is described as one of four types:

1. The breast is almost entirely fat. (Fig. 52-13)
2. There are scattered fibroglandular densities.
3. The breast tissue is heterogeneously dense. This may lower the sensitivity of mammography.
4. The breast tissue is extremely dense, which could obscure a lesion on mammography. (Fig. 52-14)

If a lesion can be seen on one view only, it is called a density. A mass has volume. A lesion can be classified as a mass if it can be imaged in two orthogonal planes, which allows it to be described in three dimensions. According to BI-RADS™ criteria, masses are described as follows:

1. Shape—round, oval, lobular, irregular
2. Margins—circumscribed (well defined or sharply defined), microlobulated, obscured, indistinct (ill-defined), spiculated (lines radiating from the margins of a mass)
3. Density—describes the opacity of a lesion relative to the adjacent breast parenchyma. Masses denser than the surrounding breast are regarded with a higher degree of suspicion than low-opacity lesions.

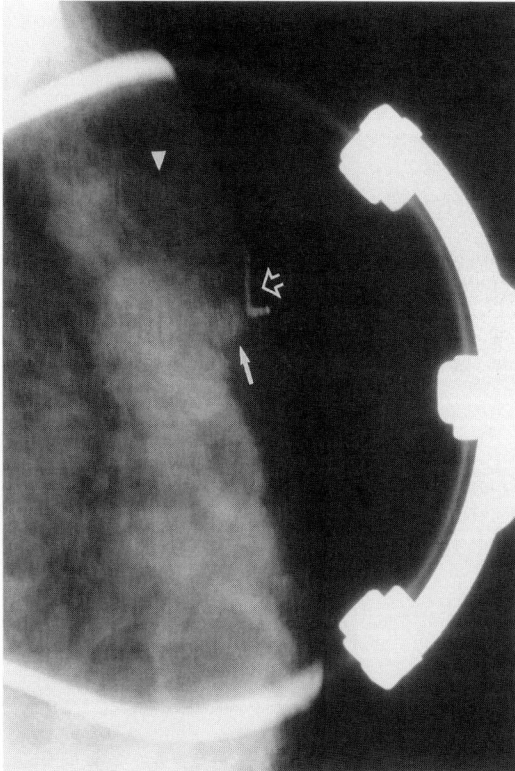

Figure 52-10 A radiopaque marker (open arrow) was placed on a palpable mass. The x-ray beam was directed tangential to the marker. Two nodules were seen (arrows). The tangential view projected the nodules against the subcutaneous fat and away from the dense breast parenchyma.

Calcifications that are described as typically benign by the ACR include calcium with lucent centers such as fat necrosis and skin calcium. Other calcifications in this category are vascular (parallel rows of calcium associated with the soft tissue shadow of a blood vessel), coarse or "pop-

Figures 52-11 and 52-12
Images performed before and after displacement of a breast implant. Even with displacement of the implant, large portions of the breast cannot be imaged.

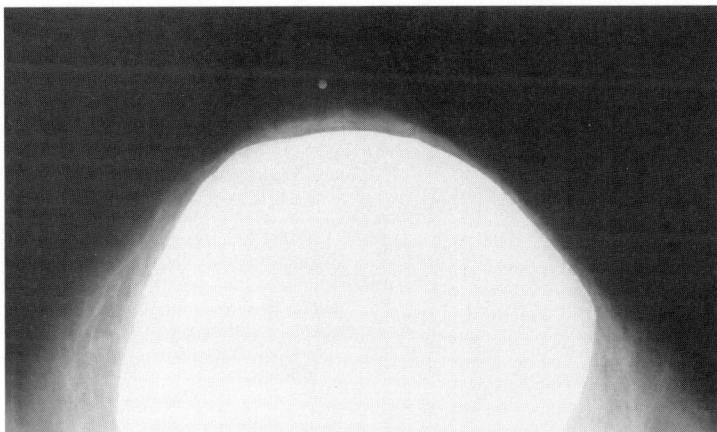

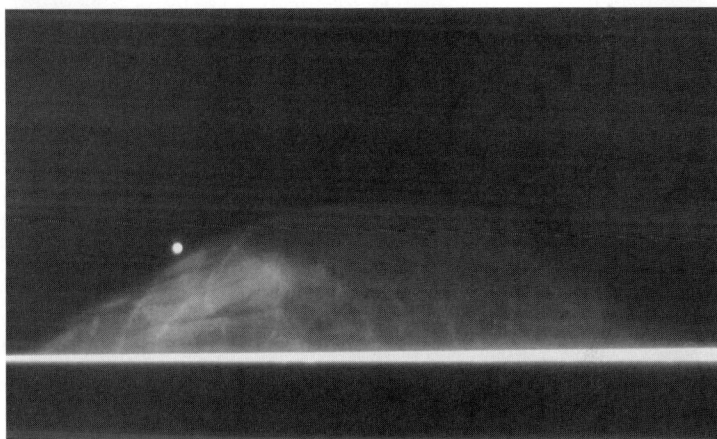

corn-like" (typical of fibroadenoma; Fig. 52-15), large rod-like (described in secretory disease), and rim-like or eggshell calcifications. Milk of calcium appears as menisci of calcium on the 90-degree lateral view and is described by many radiologists as "teacups." It appears indistinct or "smudged" on craniocaudad view.

Calcifications of intermediate concern are described as amorphous or indistinct on all views. Calcifications considered of higher probability for malignancy are described as pleomorphic, fine linear, or fine linear branching (Fig. 52-16).

The distribution of calcium is reported as clustered if the deposits are grouped into a 2-cc or less volume of tissue. Both malignant and benign processes may have this appearance. A linear distribution describes calcium deposits that array in a line. The term segmental implies that multiple linear ducts are involved. Calcium scattered in a large volume of breast tissue is described as regional. Diffuse/scattered calcifications are distributed randomly throughout the breast.

Other findings that may be included in the report are skin changes, such as thickening or retraction, which raise suspicion for malignancy, and asymmetric density. Asymmetric density refers to an area of tissue density seen in only one breast but not seen in the opposite breast. It may represent an island of normal glandular tissue. Comparison to older films is often helpful in eval-

Figure 52-13 The breast density is predominantly fatty. Lesions tend to be more conspicuous in breasts with this pattern.

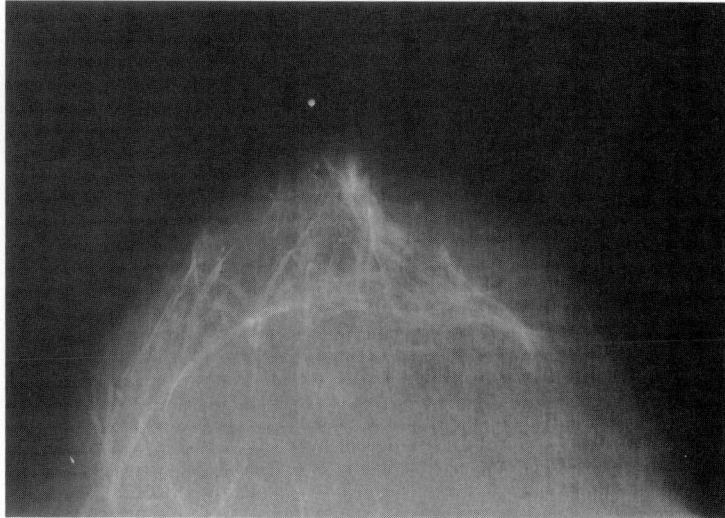

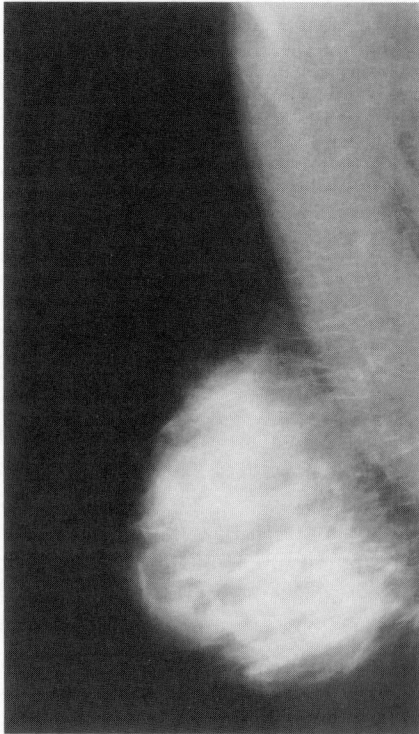

Figure 52-14 Dense breast pattern. Noncalcified masses can easily be obscured.

uating this finding. It can be further evaluated with additional views, physical examination of the breast, and by sonography. Architectural distortion refers to distortion or puckering of the normal breast parenchyma with no visible central mass. It can be a sign of malignancy but can also be seen as a result of trauma or surgery.

The radiologist, at the completion of the report, indicates her or his degree of suspicion for malignancy by assigning one of the following assessment categories:

Category 0—Need Additional Imaging Evaluation: The radiologist recommends additional workup. This is most commonly used in a screening report.

Category 1—Negative.

Category 2—Benign Finding—This is a negative study but the mammographer may wish to describe findings such as implants or stable benign-appearing calcium.

Category 3—Probably Benign Finding—Short Interval Follow-up Suggested: A finding is identified that has a very high probability of being benign. To assure the expected stability over time, a short interval follow-up mammogram is recommended.

Figure 52-15 A "popcorn-like" calcification is typical of a degenerated fibroadenoma.

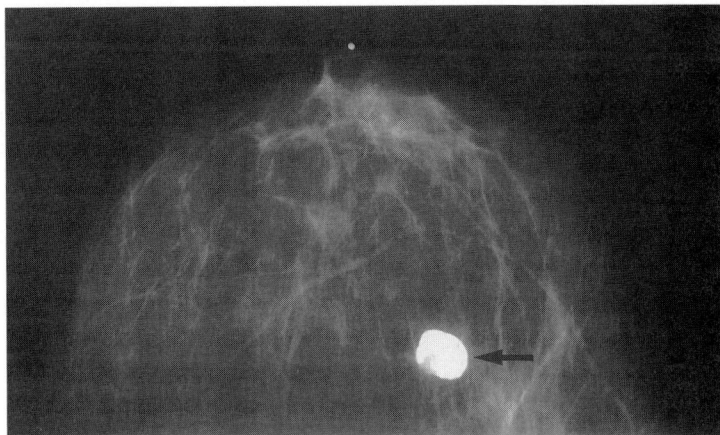

Category 4—Suspicious Abnormality—Biopsy Should Be Considered.

Category 5—Highly Suggestive of Malignancy—Appropriate Action Should Be Taken: These lesions have a high probability of being cancer.

Liberman et al. investigated the positive predictive value of mammographic features described according to the BI-RADS™ lexicon. The study concluded that findings described to have spiculated margins, irregular shape, linear morphology, and/or segmental or linear distribution are the most suspicious for breast carcinoma and should be assessed as Category 5 lesions.

Breast Sonography

Breast sonography is frequently used as an adjunct to mammography. Sonography should not be used for routine screening. It cannot adequately identify microcalcifications, a major imaging sign of malignancy. The advantages of ultrasound are that it uses no ionizing radiation, is usually well tolerated by the patient, and can be rapidly performed. A main goal of sonography is to determine whether a mass is cystic or solid

(Figs. 52-17, 52-18, and 52-19). Sonographic imaging alone cannot exclude carcinoma if a solid or atypical cystic mass is found. Sonography can be used to guide a fine-needle or core biopsy. (Figs. 52-20, 52-21, and 52-22) The mass targeted for sonographic evaluation can either be a palpable finding or a mass identified by mammography. Sonography is also used to evaluate asymmetric densities. If a lesion is seen in only one mammographic view, sonography may help to locate it. Because it does not require use of radiation, sonography is the imaging modality of choice for evaluating a palpable mass in pregnant women or in a woman younger than age 30.

The technical quality of sonographic imaging is dependent on the skill of the sonographer. For high resolution, transducers of 7.5 MHz or higher are used. The patient is imaged in the supine position. Her ipsilateral arm is placed overhead. To image the outer quadrants, the patient is usually asked to roll into an oblique position, with the quadrants of interest raised off the table. For superficial lesions, a gelatinous solid pad is placed on the breast. This improves visualization by reducing near-field artifact. The focal zone is positioned at the level of the lesion or just posterior to it. It is essential for the breast imager to assure that the sonographic finding correlates with the suspicious mammographic or physical finding. It is extremely important to remember that inability to image a palpable mass by mammography or by sonography does not negate the presence of the mass. If a mass is clinically suspicious by physical exam, inability to image it should not delay further management, such as biopsy.

Techniques for Biopsy of Nonpalpable Breast Lesions

Historically, needle-wire localization followed by surgical excision has been the method of breast biopsy for nonpalpable breast lesions appearing suspicious by mammography or sonography. Over the last 10 years, multiple options for breast biopsy, other than conventional surgery, have become available. Choice of biopsy technique is usually based on issues of equipment availability, operator skills, type and location of lesion, cost of procedure, physical ability of the patient to undergo the procedure, acceptance by the medical community, and patient demand. For percutaneous biopsies, most breast imagers use sonographic guidance for masses and stereotactic procedures for microcalcifications or asymmetry.

For all biopsy techniques, if the pathology result does not make sense based on imaging appearance, repeat biopsy or surgical biopsy should usually be performed.

Needle localization followed by surgical biopsy is the chosen method of biopsy in many cases. This method is sometimes chosen if the lesion is difficult to access by percutaneous biopsy. Lesions located against the chest wall or lesions near the nipple would fall into this category. Sometimes surgery is chosen due to preferences of the referring physician or surgeon who may have confidence in the traditional method of biopsy, or who may be unfamiliar with the newer choices. The main advantage of the excisional biopsy is that the entire lesion and surrounding tissue are removed. This theoretically allows for more accurate pathologic diagnosis. It is the method of choice if a radial scar is suspected, because this can mimic intraductal carcinoma pathologically. Radial scars have been associated with tubular carcinoma and some authors believe that it is a precursor to tubular carcinoma. It is also the method chosen if a percutaneous biopsy yields equivocal results or results that are discordant with the expected diagnosis based on imaging. Needle

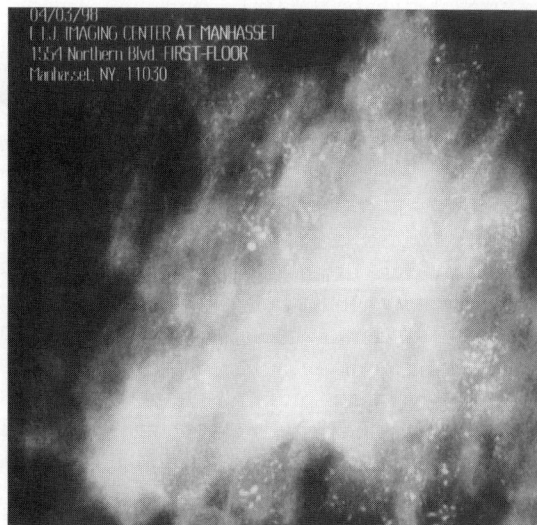

Figure 52-16 Innumerable pleomorphic microcalcifications are identified diffusely in this breast. These are BI-RADS™ category 5. Biopsy revealed ductal carcinoma in situ. Mastectomy was performed.

Figures 52-17, 52-18, and 52-19 A nodule is partially well defined and partially obscured in this dense breast pattern. Sonography revealed a simple cyst. To confirm that the cyst represented the mammographic nodule, aspiration of the cyst was performed.

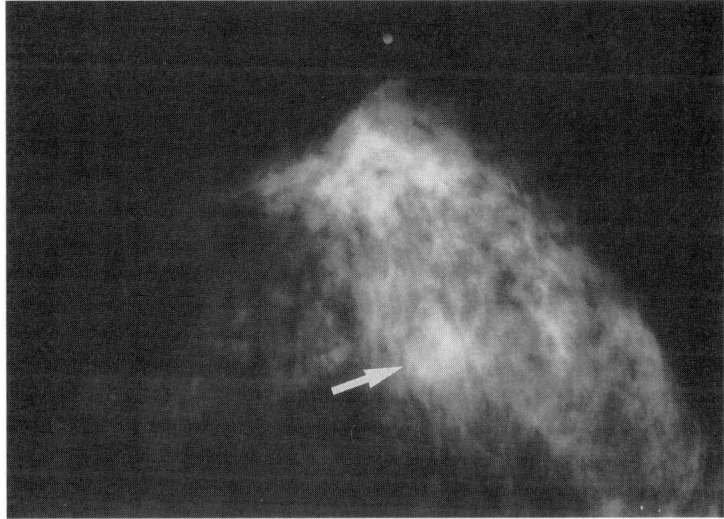

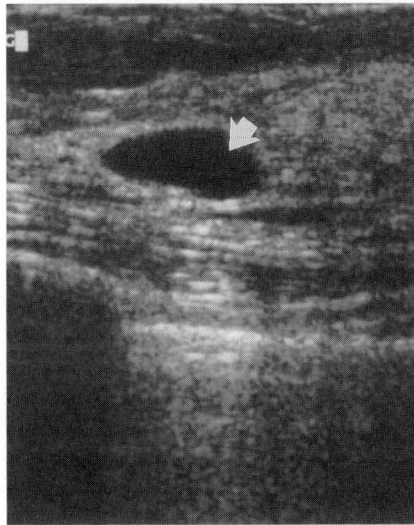

localization followed by surgery is the most expensive biopsy method because it requires operating room time and both surgical and radiological personnel. Compared to most percutaneous biopsy techniques, it has a higher potential for scar and has a greater delay between the time of abnormal imaging and biopsy. The latter can contribute significantly to patient anxiety.

A common method for needle-wire localiza-

tion involves use of a compression plate with fenestrations or open alphanumeric grid. The shortest distance to the targeted lesion is calculated with use of two orthogonal views—usually a CC and a 90-degree lateral. The needle length is chosen. After informed consent, the patient's breast is placed in compression with the compression plate open to the side planned for needle entry. A mammographic film is obtained to identify the target. Using sterile technique, the needle

Figure 52-17, 52-18, and 52-19 (*Continued*) Postaspiration mammography revealed resolution of the mammographic nodule.

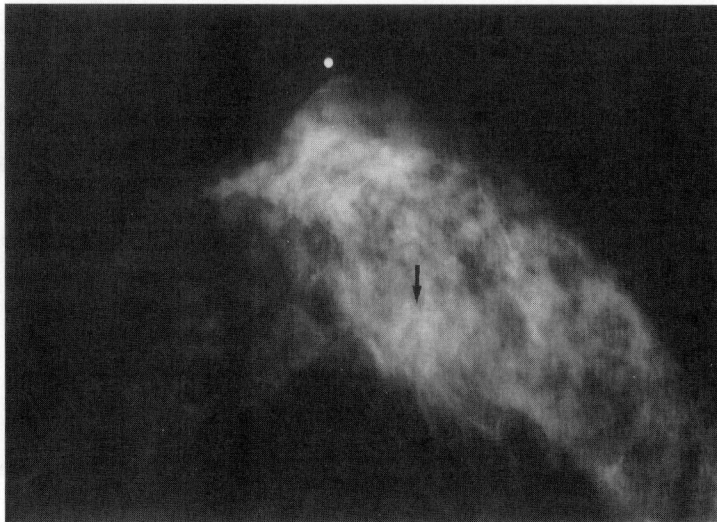

is advanced into the breast. The needle has a hollow core through which a wire passes. The position of the needle-wire apparatus is confirmed in orthogonal planes. When it is determined that the needle is adequately located with respect to the lesion, the wire is advanced. The needle may or may not be removed, depending on the surgeon's preference. The patient is taken to the operating room with the needle and/or wire in situ. After the biopsy is performed, the surgical specimen is usually radiographed to assure that the target tissue has been removed (Figs. 52-23, 52-24, 52-25, 52-26, 52-27, and 52-28).

Fine-needle aspiration (FNA) biopsy can be performed using either sonographic or mammographic guidance, with or without stereotactic technique. It requires minimal equipment, can be done rapidly, and is relatively inexpensive. When compared to gun-fired core biopsy needles, the FNA needle is smaller gauge (21 or 25 G) and is easier to control for sonographically guided procedures. For these reasons, and to avoid the risk of pneumothorax, it is often the chosen percutaneous technique if the breast is very thin or if the target is deep against the chest wall. If the lesion is suspected to be a cyst, FNA is

the procedure of choice; it allows fluid aspiration with minimal breast intervention.

The success of FNA depends on the availability of a skilled cytopathologist. The rate of insufficient samples ranges up to 36 percent. Even under optimal circumstances, FNA samples cannot accurately diagnose atypical ductal hyperplasia, carcinoma in situ, or infiltrating carcinoma because the architecture surrounding the abnormal cells is not evaluated.

Core-needle biopsy is a highly accurate method of biopsy. The procedure is fast and cost-effective when compared to surgery. The goal of core biopsy (either sonographically guided or mammographically guided) is to make a diagnosis percutaneously. If the results are malignant, theoretically the patient will then only need one operation—a lumpectomy or mastectomy, with or without axillary lymph node dissection. In comparison, a surgical biopsy requires an operation to make the diagnosis and a second operation for therapy. Performance of core biopsy may not always result in a single operative procedure because 20 percent of cases diagnosed as ductal carcinoma in situ (DCIS) by core biopsy have an invasive component that can only be determined by repeat biopsy using surgical excision. Other

Figures 52-20, 52-21, and 52-22 Mammography demonstrates a dominant mass in this fatty breast. Sonography revealed that the mass is solid (dark arrow). It has irregular margins. The mass is taller than wider—a sign of malignancy. Sonographically guided needle biopsy was performed, revealing carcinoma.

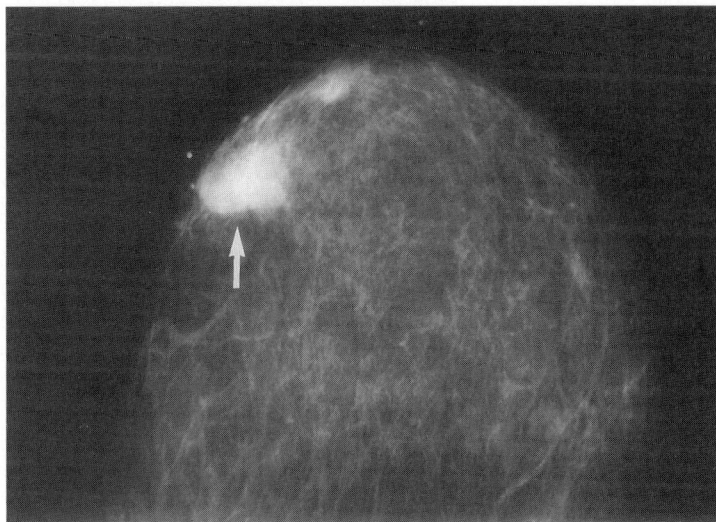

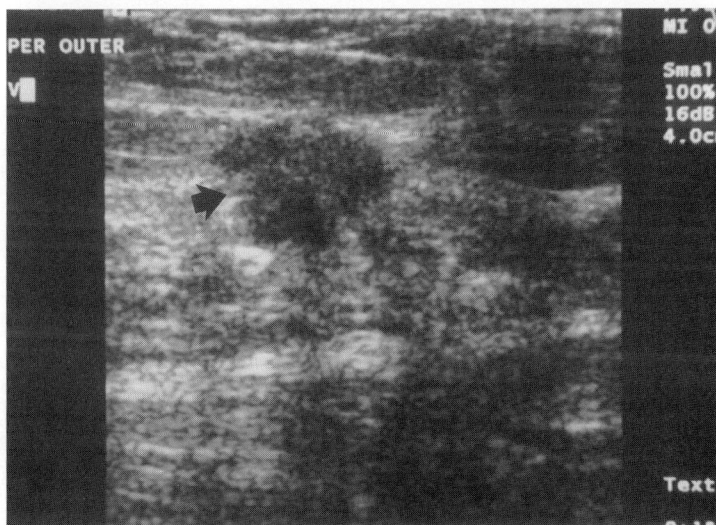

diagnoses requiring reexcision are radial scar and atypical duct hyperplasia. If the lesion is very small, it is possible to remove the entire mass with core biopsy. In this case, it is essential to leave a marker to enable localization for excisional biopsy if warranted by pathology results.

In sonographically guided core biopsy, the needle trajectory is planned so that it traverses the breast parallel to the chest wall to avoid misfire into the pleura or pericardium. After informed consent and using sterile technique, the skin entry site is anesthetized with lidocaine. The mass is continuously observed in real-time. A 14-gauge cutting needle attached to a biopsy gun is advanced into the breast through a small skin nick. The needle is advanced or fired with use of the biopsy gun. The area is scanned to assure that the lesion is traversed by the needle and to assure that the needle tip is safely within breast parenchyma.

Figures 52-20, 52-21, 52-22
(*Continued*) The needle
entered the lesion (white
arrows).

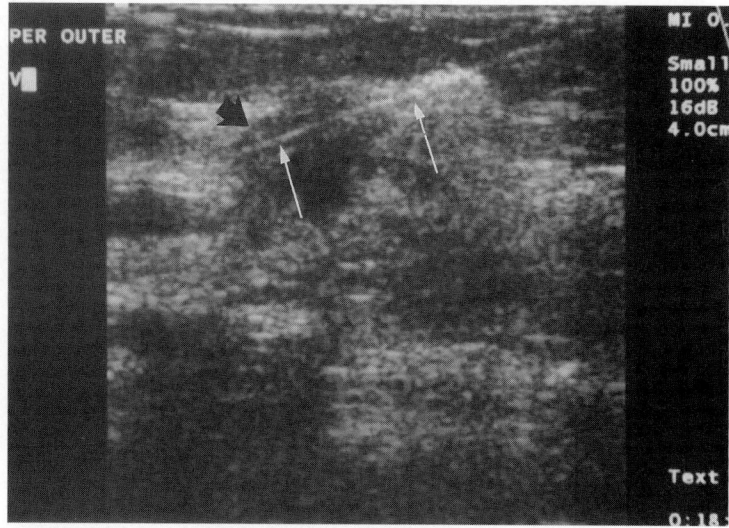

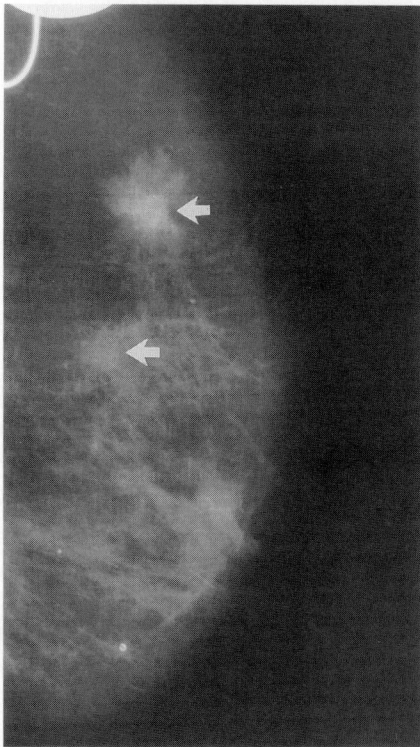

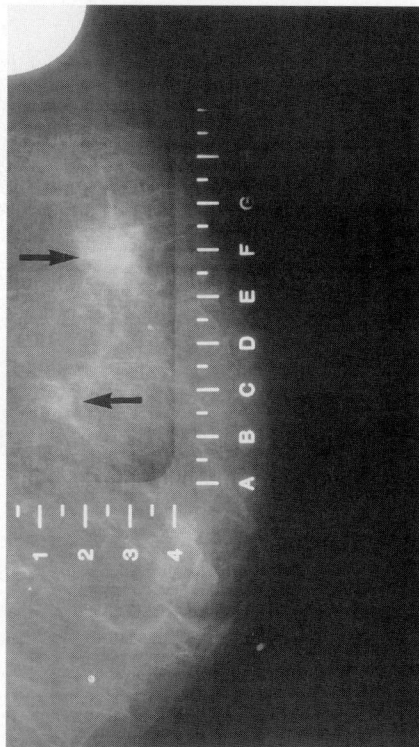

Figures 52-23 to 52-28 Two cancers are identified as spiculated masses in this elderly
patient. Note the presence of a pacemaker in the axilla. The patient's breast is placed in
compression using an alphanumeric grid. The masses are identified.

Figures 52-23 to 52-28
(*Continued*) Needles are
placed into the breast at the
sites of abnormality. The
needle/wire position is
confirmed in orthogonal
views.

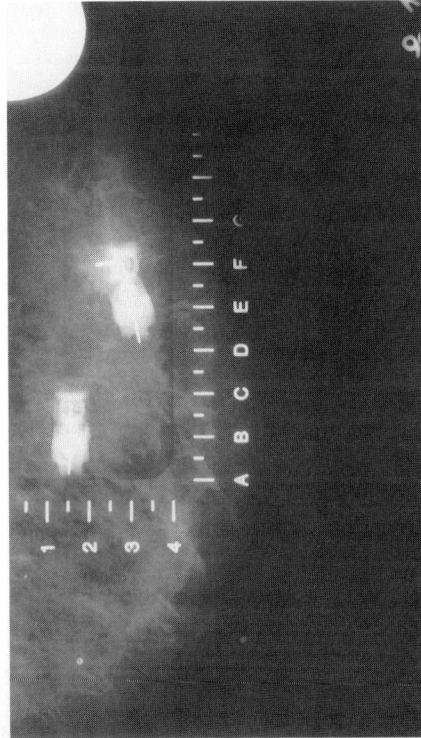

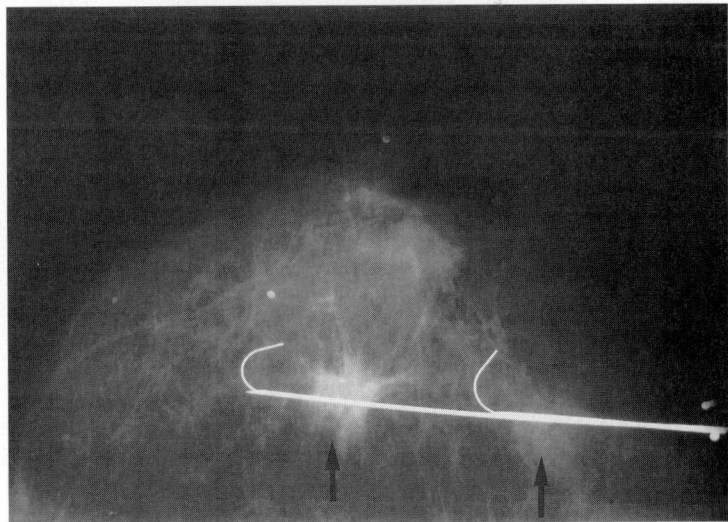

Stereotactic biopsy uses a computer to calculate the three-dimensional location of a lesion using x, y, and z coordinates. To perform this calculation, two images of a lesion are obtained mammographically. The x-ray tube is angled 15 degrees relative to the lesion in one direction and 15 degrees relative to the lesion in the other direction. Stereotactic technique can be used for

Figures 52-23 to 52-28
(*Continued*) Two biopsy specimens were submitted and radiographed. Carcinoma was diagnosed at both sites. Mastectomy was performed.

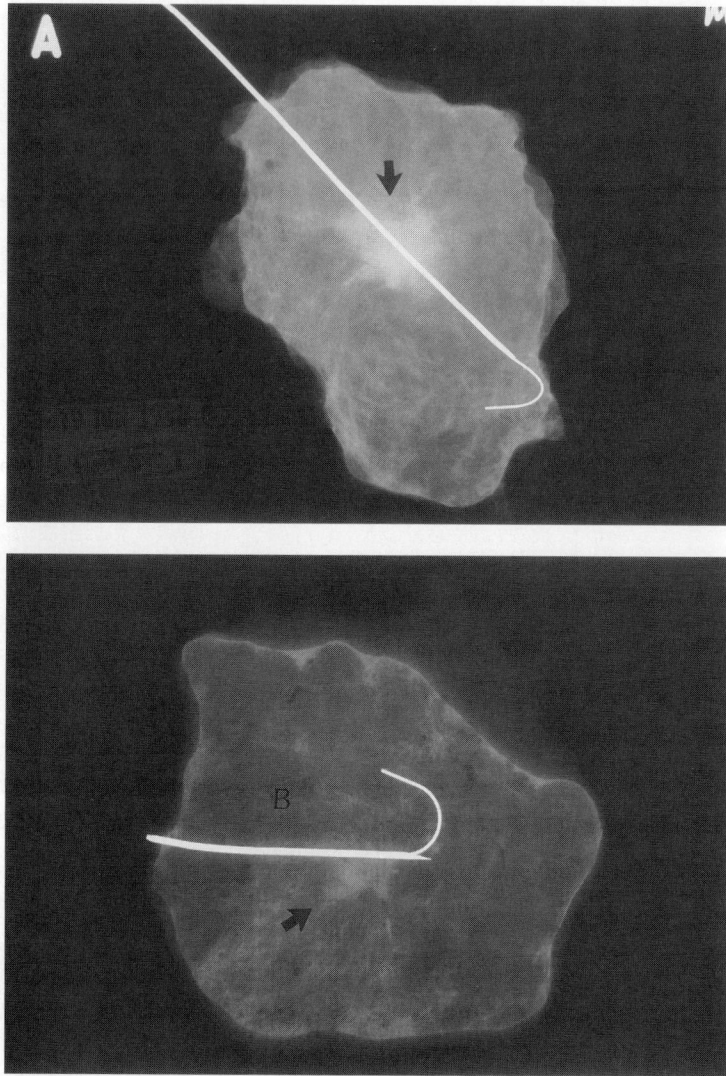

fine-needle, core-needle, or vacuum-assisted core-needle biopsy. The patient can be imaged prone with the use of a special table that has an opening to allow the breast to hang down pendulously. Some mammography machines have an add-on unit attached, allowing the patient to be imaged in the sitting position. The target is identified. After informed consent and using sterile technique, the skin site is anesthe-tized and a small skin nick is made. A 14-gauge needle is advanced to the proper depth. A prefire image is obtained. If correct needle placement relative to the lesion is confirmed, the needle is fired. Several passes can be made. The needle must be removed from the breast to retrieve the specimen after each pass.

A new stereotactic technique, biopsy with a directional vacuum-assisted biopsy instrument

(Mammatome, Biopsys Medical, Irvine, California), uses a gentle vacuum to pull tissue into the probe and to retrieve the specimen (Fig. 52-29). With this new technique, the probe remains in the breast, a vacuum draws the tissue into the probe, and a cutting needle cuts a core of tissue. The probe is turned clockwise after each specimen acquisition, allowing contiguous tissue sampling. The probes for the Mammatome are available in both 14- and 11-gauge. Following a Mammatome biopsy, a metallic clip can be deployed at the biopsy site. This allows for localization in the event that surgical excisional biopsy is needed. The clip directs the attention of the mammographer for future follow-up (Fig. 52-30).

There is debate with regard to the use of stereotactic biopsy for areas of calcium less than or equal to 2 cm. Some clinicians advocate surgical excision because the excised tissue may constitute an acceptable lumpectomy if the surgical margins are clear. Certain lesions, such as faintly visualized microcalcifications and ill-defined masses, are not amenable to stereotactic biopsy methods, because the target may be difficult to identify on digitized images. Needle localization followed by surgical biopsy is usually chosen in these cases. To perform stereotactic biopsy, the breast is held taut by compression plates. If the breast compresses too thinly, there may not be enough depth for the needle to be fired; the needle could pass through the breast. For patients with this body habitus, stereotactic biopsy is usually not an option.

Galactography

Nipple discharge is a common clinical complaint and is most commonly due to benign causes such as papilloma. The least common cause is carcinoma. Women who have nipple discharge all require, at a minimum, clinical evaluation. Most of these women will require further studies. For example, unilateral spontaneous nipple dicharge always requires further evaluation. There may be even greater cause to worry if the discharge is bloody or clear.

Mammography is usually the imaging test of choice, but it often does not reveal an abnormality. Cytologic analysis of the discharge is rarely useful. Galactography (ductography) is an imaging modality dedicated to the evaluation of the breast ductal system (Figs. 52-31 and 52-32). This procedure can be time-consuming, is sometimes difficult to perform, and can be painful to the patient. Ductography requires visualizing the ori-

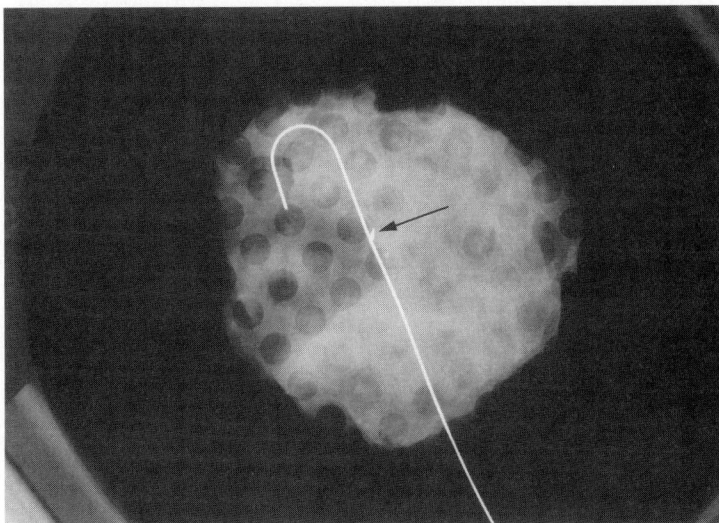

Figure 52-29 Close inspection reveals that a metallic clip (black arrow) has been localized. This was deployed at the time of core biopsy using the Mammotome technique. The Mammotome biopsy pathology results were atypical ductal hyperplasia. This diagnosis, if made by core biopsy, requires that the patient go on to excisional biopsy.

Figure 52-30 Mammotome biopsy probe is seen in stereotactic views. These prefire views indicate that the probe is in good position to obtain a diagnostic specimen.

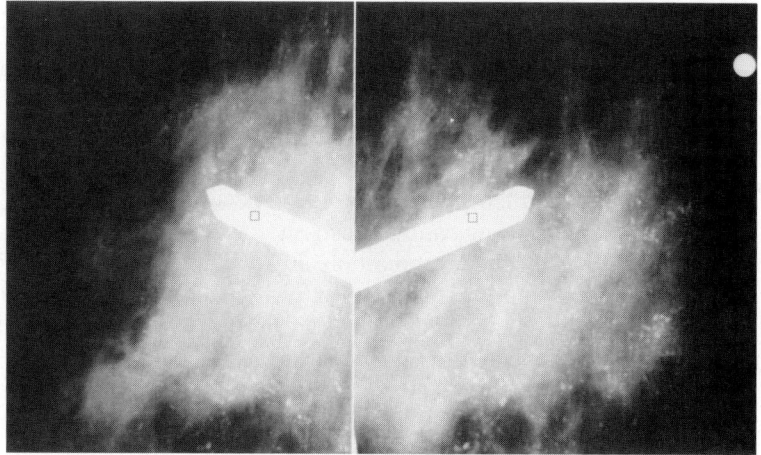

fice of the abnormal duct and cannulating it with a 27-or 28-gauge blunt-tipped catheter. Iodinated contrast is injected and the breast is then imaged mammographically with orthogonal magnification views. The images are not specific; benign and malignant lesions both appear as filling defects in the contrast-filled duct and cannot be reliably distinguished from one another. Lesions can be missed if the duct does not fill with contrast. Air bubbles, if inadvertently introduced during contrast injection, can mimic a lesion. The study is contraindicated in patients with mastitis.

Women who have nipple discharge often ultimately require surgical evaluation.

MRI

Magnetic resonance imaging (MRI) of the breast is most commonly used to evaluate silicone implants suspected to have ruptured. MRI is more accurate than mammography or sonography for evaluation of breast implant integrity. Subglandular implants are located anterior to the pectoralis major muscle. Retropectoral implants are located posterior to the pectoralis major muscle. There are hundreds of types of silicone implants. Most have an outer shell filled with silicone gel. When in situ, scar tissue forms around the shell to create a fibrous capsule. There are two basic types of rupture. Most commonly, intracapsular rupture occurs. The integrity of the implant shell breaks down allowing silicone to leak through. The silicone gel, in this case, is confined by the fibrous capsule. The collapsed implant shell folds upon itself and floats in the gel. On MRI, this classically appears as multiple serpiginous lines and is known as the "linguine" sign (Fig. 52-33). If silicone breaks through both the shell and the fibrous capsule, extracapsular rupture is diagnosed. In this case, free silicone may be identified in breast parenchyma or in lymph nodes.

The use of MRI to diagnose or evaluate breast carcinoma is still in the developmental stage. Even with optimized protocols and the use of dynamic imaging following intravenous contrast, there remains significant overlap in the MRI appearance of benign and malignant lesions. It has been demonstrated that MRI is useful for differentiating a lumpectomy scar from recurrent tumor; scars older than six months usually do not enhance. MRI is highly sensitive in detecting invasive breast cancer and slightly less sensitive for ductal carcinoma in situ. It can detect mammographically and clinically occult cancer, and is therefore potentially useful for staging. The problem is that not all enhancing lesions are cancer. Because it is a very sensitive modality, it results in many false-positive findings. If these

Figure 52-31 and 32 Dilated subareolar ducts are seen. The patient complained of intermittent spontaneous nipple discharge. Image from galactogram shows cannulation of the duct at its orifice (black arrow). The duct is opacified with contrast and multiple filling defects are shown (white arrows). Papillomatosis cannot be differentiated from multifocal carcinoma by imaging alone. At surgery, multiple papillomata were found.

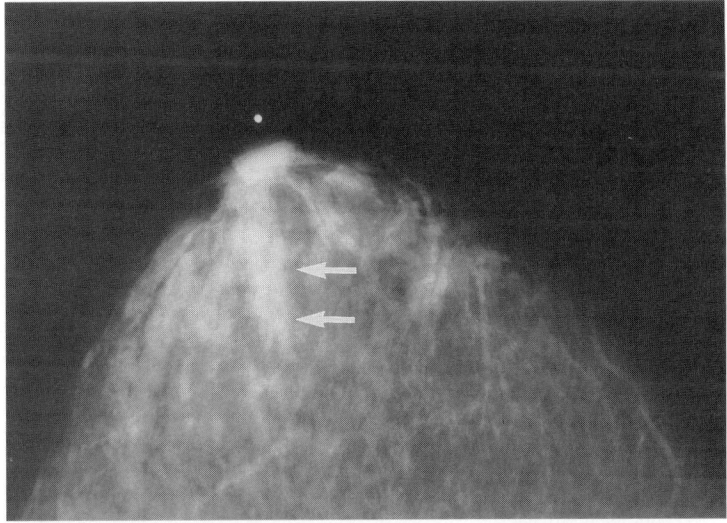

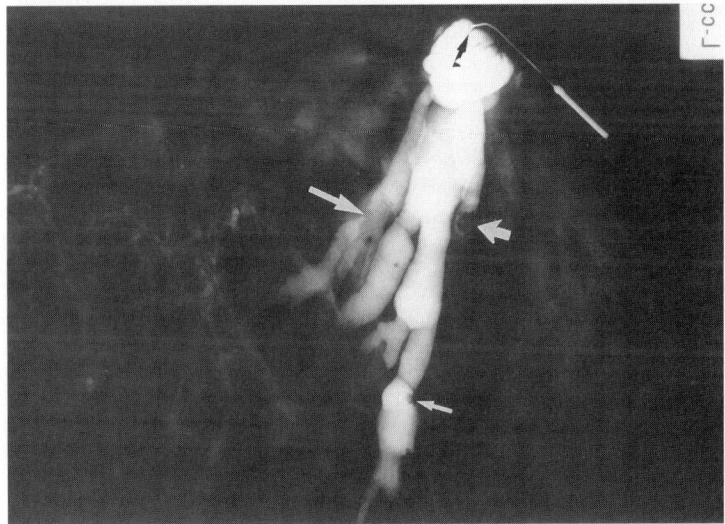

findings are seen only by MRI, biopsy can be difficult because nonferromagnetic (able to be used safely in the bore of the magnet) needle/wire localization systems are not widely available. MRI cannot be used for claustrophobic patients or for patients with pacemakers or ferromagnetic metallic implants. Patients must be physically able to lie prone and immobile in specially designed breast coils. Another disadvantage of MRI in the evaluation of breast cancer is its high cost relative to mammography and sonography.

Digital Mammography

Digital mammography is an exciting new breast-imaging technology that is under clinical investigation. This modality produces images by x-ray exposure, resulting in an electronic signal that

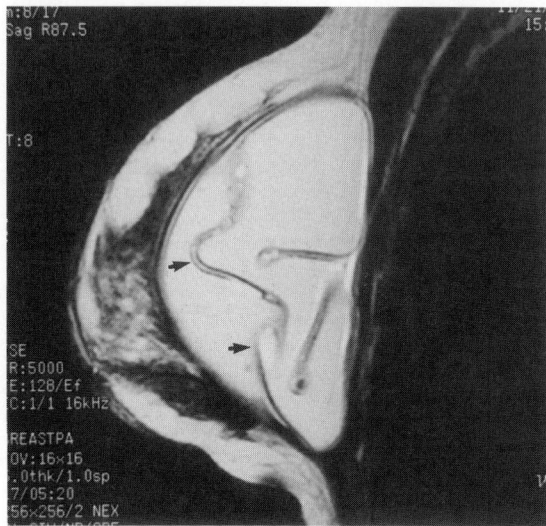

Figure 52-33 Intracapsular rupture of silicone implant. The shell (arrows) of the implant has collapsed and now floats in the silicone, resulting in the "linguine" sign. The fibrous capsule is intact.

can be stored and processed on a computer. The image can be displayed on a monitor or on film. The image can be adjusted by changing the brightness and contrast settings. Theoretically, digital imaging allows for higher sensitivity imaging of dense breasts. Another goal of digital mammography is to resolve densities artifactually created by tissue overlap without need for extra views or unnecessary biopsy. Digital technology enables transmission of images (teleradiology) to distant locations. If the images can be produced with high resolution and with speed, it will allow for off-site interpretation or expert consultation. Finally, and most intriguing, is a proposed theory that a computer will be able to provide second-opinion readings of digitized images.

Acknowledgment

The BI-RADS™ terminology has been reprinted with permission of the American College of Ra-

diology, BI-RADS™, third edition, copyright © 1998 ACR.

References and Selected Readings

1. American College of Radiology (ACR). *Breast Imaging Reporting and Data System* (BI-RADS™). 3rd ed. Reston, VA: American College of Radiology, 1998.
2. Andersson I, Janzon L: Reduced breast cancer mortality in women under 50: Updated results from the Malmo mammographic screening program. *J Natl Cancer Inst Monogr* 22:63–68, 1997.
3. Bjurstram N, Bjorneld L, et al: The Gothenburg breast screening trial: First results on mortality, incidence, and mode of detection for women ages 39–49 years and randomization. *Cancer* 80:2091–2099, 1997.
4. Breast Cancer Screening for Women Ages 40–49. Jan 21–23:15(1):1–35, 1997. NIH Consensus Statement
5. Feig S, D'Orsi CD, et al: American College of Radiology guidelines for breast cancer screening. *Am J Roentgenol* 171:29–33, 1998.
6. Feig S: Digital Mammography. *Radiographics* 18:893–901, 1998.
7. Ford D, Easton DF, et al: Breast Cancer Linkage Consortium: Risks of cancer in *BRCA1*-mutation carriers. *Lancet* 343:692–695, 1994.
8. Frouge C, Tristant H, et al: Mammographic lesions suggestive of radial scars: Microscopic findings in 40 cases. *Radiology* 195:623–625, 1995.
9. Gorczyca DP: MR Imaging of breast implants. *Magn Reson Imaging Clin N Am* 2(4);659–672, 1994.
10. Gundry KR, Berg WA: Treatment issues and core needle breast biopsy: Clinical context. *Am J Roentgenol* 171:41–49, 1998.
11. Hancock SL, Tucker MA, et al: Breast cancer after treatment for Hodgkin's disease. *J Natl Cancer Inst* 85:25–31, 1993.
12. Harvey JA, Moran RE: US-guided core needle biopsy of the breast: Technique and pitfalls. *Radiographics* 18:867–877, 1998.
13. Homer MJ, Smith TJ, Safaii H, et al: Prebiopsy needle localization, *Radiol Clin North Am* 130(1):139–153, 1992.
14. Hoskins KF, Stopfer JE, et al: Assessment and counseling for women with a family history of breast cancer: A guide for clinicians. *JAMA* 273:577–585, 1995.
15. Kelsey L, Gammon M: The epidemiology of breast cancer. *CA Cancer J Clin* 41:146–165, 1991.
16. Khalkhali I, Cutrone J, Mena I, et al: Scintimammography: The complementary role of Tc-99m sestamibi prone breast imaging for the diagnosis of breast carcinoma. *Radiology* 196:421–426, 1995.

17. Liberman L, Fahs MC, Dershaw DD, et al: Impact of stereotaxic core breast biopsy on cost of diagnosis. *Radiology* 195:633–637, 1995.
18. Liberman L, Abramson A, et al: The breast imaging reporting and data system: Positive predictive value of mammographic features and final assessment categories. *Am J Roentgenol* 171:35–40, 1998.
19. Liberman L, Cohen MA, Dershaw DD, et al: Atypical ductal hyperplasia diagnosed at stereotaxic core biopsy of breast lesions: An indication for surgical biopsy. *Am J Roentgenol* 164:1111–1113, 1995.
20. Orel S: High-resolution MR imaging for the detection, diagnosis, and staging of breast cancer. *Radiographics* 18:903–912, 1998.
21. Page DL, Dupont WD: Premalignant conditions and markers of elevated risk in the breast and their management. *Surg Clin North Am* 70(4);831–851, 1990.
22. Parker SH, Burbank F, Jackman RJ, et al: Percutaneous large-core breast biopsy: A multi-institutional study. *Radiology* 193:359–364, 1994.
23. Parker SH, Jobe WE, Dennis MA, et al: US-guided automated large-core breast biopsy. *Radiology* 187:507–511, 1993.
24. Parker SH, Klaus AJ: Performing a breast biopsy with a directional vacuum-assisted biopsy instrument. *Radiographics* 17:1233–1252, 1997.
25. Parker SH: The advanced breast biopsy instrumentation: Another Trojan horse? *Am J Roentgenol* 171:51–53, 1998.
26. Piccoli CW, Feig SA, Vala MA: Breast imaging case of the day. *Radiographics* 18:783–786, 1998.
27. Streuwing JP, Hartge P, et al: The risk of cancer associated with specific mutation of *BRCA1* and *BRCA2* among Ashkenazi Jews. *N Engl J Med* 336:1401–1408, 1997.

CHAPTER 53

Role of Fine Needle Aspiration Cytology in Clinical Practice

Patricia G. Wasserman
Mohamed S. Aziz

Historical Background

Over the past 50 years exfoliated cells have been collected and analyzed from accessible anatomic surfaces, such as the uterine cervix and the bronchus, giving rise to a new diagnostic discipline, cytopathology. George Papanicolaou was a founding contributor to this discipline. In recent years, cytopathology has undergone significant transformation as a result of aspiration of cells by means of a needle and syringe. The wide acceptance of needling of bone marrow as an integral part of the investigation of hematologic disorders served as a model for sampling of other tissues by a technique requiring no anesthesia and avoiding expensive surgical intervention.

The history of fine needle aspiration (FNA) can be traced to the tenth century when the Arabian physician, Abul Kasim (A.D. 936–1013), described needle puncture of the thyroid to diagnose different types of goiters. Kun reported the first FNA in 1847. In 1886, Menetreer used needles to obtain cells and tissue fragments to isolate pneumonic microorganisms and to diagnose pulmonary carcinoma. In those early years, few pathologists practiced needle aspiration cytology, which was performed mainly by clinicians to obtain rapid diagnoses. In 1927, Dudgeon and Patrick from Great Britain proposed the needling of tumors to obtain rapid microscopic diagnoses following their observations of the value of examination of cytological scrape preparations of excised tissue. In the mid 1930s, Martin and Ellis of the Memorial Hospital for Cancer and Allied Diseases in New York maintained an active interest in FNA, but used needles of thicker caliber than those commonly used today. In the 1950s and 1960s, FNA gained popularity in Europe, particularly in Scandinavia, and in the United States a decade later. Currently, FNA biopsy is widely used and has proven to be a safe and reliable diagnostic tool.

Indications, Benefits, and Limitations of FNA

FNA provides several advantages for patients and clinicians. The technique is relatively painless, produces rapid results, and is inexpensive. FNA technique utilizes needles of varying caliber resulting in such terms as "thin needle," "skinny needle," and "aspiration cytology" biopsies. The gauge of the needles is smaller than those used for drawing blood. FNA biopsy is defined as removal of a cell sample from a suspicious mass, using a fine-bore needle, for diagnostic purposes. FNA biopsy is not a substitute for conventional surgical histopathology, but is a valuable supplement.

The procedure can be applied to palpable lesions from organs such as the breast, salivary glands, lymph nodes, and thyroid, as well as superficial masses and nodules of the skin, subcutis, and soft tissues. For deep-seated lesions, radiologically guided FNAs are performed either as inpatient or outpatient procedures by radiologists. Previously inaccessible lesions can now be safely sampled. The needle can be guided by different diagnostic imaging techniques such as fluoroscopy, ultrasound, and computed tomography (CT). All of these imaging techniques are excellent for visualizing and sampling deep-seated lesions. Sensitivity improves with increasing operator experience. Familiarity with each technique plays an important role in the choice of guidance modality.

FNA is a cost-effective diagnostic modality. It generates sensitive and specific diagnoses with a very low false-positive rate. However, a combination of clinical, radiographic, and pathologic information should guide any therapeutic decisions. Kaminsky concluded that the use of FNA biopsy might reduce the cost of diagnostic procedures by as much as 90 percent compared with hospitalization and excisional biopsy. FNA increases the accuracy of preoperative diagnoses so that appropriate work-up can be performed prior to definitive surgery. Many studies have demonstrated that FNA biopsy can significantly reduce the number of surgeries performed for benign breast problems, and hence reduce scarring and disfigurement of the breast. This technique is also extremely useful for the early diagnosis of metastases and recurrence, and for staging of tumors.

FNA is a safe and cost-efficient first diagnostic tool for a palpable mass. It can be performed in the physician's office, in an outpatient setting, or at the patient's bedside. The fast turnaround time allows for an early diagnosis, thus decreasing patient anxiety and facilitating subsequent diagnostic and therapeutic planning. The equipment needed is minimal. Adequate and representative sampling remain the greatest challenges to achieving a correct diagnosis. Technical competence requires considerable hands-on practice. In addition to training and expertise, other factors affect the quality of FNA, including the number of FNAs performed by the clinician, pathologist, or radiologist, and effective communication between the clinician and the cytopathologist. The procedure is deceptively simple but requires considerable skill and experience. The principal sources of error include lack of training and experience, poor FNA technique, poor sample preparation, and the temptation to provide a diagnosis on an inadequate smear.

Preparation for FNA

FNA is relatively painless to the patient. Most clinicians and cytopathologists perform the procedure without the use of local anesthetic, unless the procedure is performed in a highly sensitive area such as the nipple. A local anesthetic also may be administered to apprehensive patients. An informed consent should be obtained. The patient should be alerted that an average of three passes is required to obtain a representative sample.

Equipment Needed for FNA

FNA requires needles, syringes, syringe holder, glass slides, fixatives, and transportation media.

Needles

Standard, disposable needles are suitable for most palpable lesions. The needles routinely used are 1 in. and 1.5 in. long, 22, 23, or 25 gauge. The size and location of the lesion determine the choice of needle length and gauge. The 25-gauge needles are most commonly used for small superficial lesions. The yield from a 25-gauge needle is usually sparser than from a 22- or 23-gauge needle. However, the 25-gauge needle is usually sufficient for aspiration from any cellular and vascular tissues such as lymph nodes, thyroid, and most malignant tumors. For deeper palpable lesions, we usually use a 22-gauge needle. Thicker needles provide no advantages, tend to cause more bleeding, and can be blocked by tissue fragments from the target lesion.

Syringes

Standard, disposable 10-ml plastic syringes are used.

Syringe Holders

The aspiration is aided by the use of a syringe holder. We use the Cameco syringe pistol (Cameco AB, Taby, Sweden). This holder is made to fit a 10-ml disposable syringe. It allows for aspiration with a single hand, letting the other hand fix the lesion in place. Although the use of a syringe holder is recommended, aspiration can be performed by use of a needle and a syringe alone. Even a needle alone can be used, especially for small superficial lesions, as is explained later in this chapter.

Glass Slides

Glass slides should be clean, dry, and free of grease. We use glass slides with a frosted end, as they are suited for immediate labeling.

Fixatives and Transportation Media

Fixation must be matched to the planned staining technique. We use Papanicolaou stain (Pap), Ul-tra Fast Pap stain (UFP), and the rapid Diff-Quick stain (D-Q). Pap stain requires immediate fixation in 95% ethanol. An alcohol-based spray fixative is also used to prepare smears intended for Pap stains; however, alcohol immersion fixation is preferable as it provides a uniform effective smear fixation. The rapid stain (D-Q) is used when assessment of adequacy and rapid interpretation is performed by a cytopathologist who is assisting a clinician or performing the FNA at the bedside or in the office. The rapid stain (D-Q) requires the slide to be completely air dried without fixation.

The rapid drying of small quantities of material before fixation causes air-drying artifacts and creates a potential for misinterpretation of Pap-stained slides. Both air-dried and wet-fixed smears for the Diff-Quick, Pap, and UFP stains provide the best preparations for accurate diagnosis.

Other fixatives and transportation media include 50% ethanol tubes (for needle rinse and cell blocks or cytospin preparations); tissue culture media tubes (Roswell Park Memorial Institute, RPMI medium 1640) (for flow cytometry or immunohistochemistry studies); 10% formalin tubes (for fixation of larger fragments of tissue for histological paraffin embedding); glutaraldehyde tubes (for electron microscopic studies); and sterile containers (for microbiological studies).

Other Equipment

Other materials needed for FNA include a microscope, Coplin jars, alcohol pads, plastic tubes, small forceps, slide trays to carry dry slides, and requisition forms. Organ-specific forms are the best means of communication between clinician and cytopathologist. It is of utmost importance for the cytopathologist to be fully informed of the patient's clinical history and radiographic findings. Diagnostic errors may arise when the cytopathologist attempts to provide a cytologic interpretation with insufficient clinical history. Figure 53-1 is an example of an organ-specific form for breast cytopathology.

CYTOPATHOLOGY BREAST REQUISITION FORM

PATIENT DEMOGRAPHICS

NAME:_____   DOB:_____

SS#: _____   GROUP#:_____

ADDRESS:_____

INSURANCE CARRIER:_____   INSURED SS#_____

HISTORY

PREGNANT: YES   NO   HORMONAL THERAPY: YES   NO   (LIST)_____

MEDICATIONS (LIST)_____

FAMILY HISTORY OF BREAST CANCER: 1_____   2_____   MATERNAL_____   PATERNAL_____

NIPPLE DISCHARGE: YES_____   NO_____   RIGHT_____   LEFT_____

CAN PATIENT IDENTIFY NODULE?_____

PREVIOUS BREAST HISTORY _____

MAMMOGRAM/ULTRASOUND FINDINGS AND DATE_____

PHYSICAL EXAMINATION

LOCATION: RIGHT   LEFT   1 2 3 4 5 6 7 8 9 10 11 12 o'clock

_____CM FROM THE NIPPLE _____CM FROM THE AREOLA

SIZE_____CM.

CLINICAL IMPRESSION:_____

CONSISTENCY: SOFT, FIRM, RUBBERY, MOBILE, FIXED

SHAPE: ROUND, OVAL, ILL-DEFINED

BORDERS: SMOOTH, IRREGULAR

FNA: PALPABLE_____   XR-GUIDED_____   ULTRASOUND-GUIDED_____

NEEDLE SIZE: _____NO. OF PASSES _____NO. OF SLIDES_____

CYTOPATHOLOGY LAB ONLY

_____DO _____UFP _____PAP _____CS _____CB _____TOTAL

SPECIMEN CHARACTERISTICS: VOLUME_____   COLOR_____

ADEQUATE FOR FURTHER EVALUATION   YES_____   NO_____

Figure 53-1 Cytopathology breast requisition form (which provides important clinical information to the cytopathologist).

All of the equipment is placed in a mobile cart, which is used for transportation to the patient.

FNA Technique

The diagramatic steps of the technique are depicted in Fig. 53-2. Clean the skin with alcohol. The lesion is palpated to estimate the size and depth of the mass. This is important for determining the size of the needle to be used and the number of passes to be performed. For a large mass, the aspiration is directed to the periphery, as the center may be necrotic or hemorrhagic. For deep lesions, a larger 22-gauge needle is used to prevent bending and deviation from the lesion. For small superficial lesions, a 25-gauge needle with standard technique or only the needle without aspiration can be used.

A tender lesion indicates the possible need for culture media. The syringe is placed in the syringe holder and the needle firmly attached to the syringe. The lesion is immobilized using the second and third finger of one hand, and the thumb of the same hand is used to guide the syringe. The needle is inserted gently but firmly through skin and subcutaneous tissue and into the mass. An obvious change in consistency of the tissue should be felt when the lesion is entered.

A perpendicular approach into the mass is recommended. Tangential entry is used for special circumstances such as a lymph node attached to a pulsating blood vessel or a superficial skin lesion. After entering the mass, suction is applied to create negative pressure on the retractable arm of the syringe holder or the piston of the syringe. This suction should be maintained throughout the procedure and released only before the needle is withdrawn from the lesion. The negative pressure is needed to pull dislodged cells and tissue fragments into the needle.

While inside the lesion, move the needle in and out in a sewing-cutting motion. This cutting motion is required to obtain an adequate sample, and it serves to cut multiple minute cylinders of cellular tissue with the sharp, blade-like tip of the needle. The type of lesion dictates the movements of the needle; a fibrous lesion requires more force than a soft lesion. Kreula described four parameters relating to the movements of the needle: amplitude, frequency, direction, and duration. He advised that long-needle excursions increase the cellular yield compared with the short fluctuating movements. The speed of the needle traveling inside the lesion is also important. Three strokes per second, with suction maintained throughout, results in a good yield. The direction of the needle within the lesion should be changed to form a cone, with the apex of the cone being the point at which the needle has been inserted into the skin.

Correct timing of suction and cutting strokes is necessary to obtain an adequate sample. Applying negative pressure without moving the needle inside the lesion produces a scanty or inadequate sample. If suction is applied while the needle is not within the lesion, the aspirate will be contaminated with unrepresentative material (e.g., skin, subcutaneous tissue). If a local anesthetic has been used, suction should not be applied while the needle is traversing the infiltrated area. Any anesthetic material introduced into the needle will cause cell lysis, producing an inadequate specimen or even a diagnostic error.

The duration of the needle excursions within the lesion usually lasts for about 10 to 15 seconds. Prolonged aspiration causes sample dilution by blood and may coagulate the specimen. As soon as material is seen entering the hub of the needle, the negative pressure must be released while the needle is still within the target lesion. Allow the return of the plunger of the syringe to the resting position. If the negative pressure is not released before withdrawing the needle, the entire material will be aspirated into the syringe and immediate evaluation will not be possible. The diagnostic material should always remain within the needle. The needle is withdrawn and the sample prepared.

If only fluid is obtained, the cyst should be completely drained. It is very important to reaspirate any residual mass after this is accomplished.

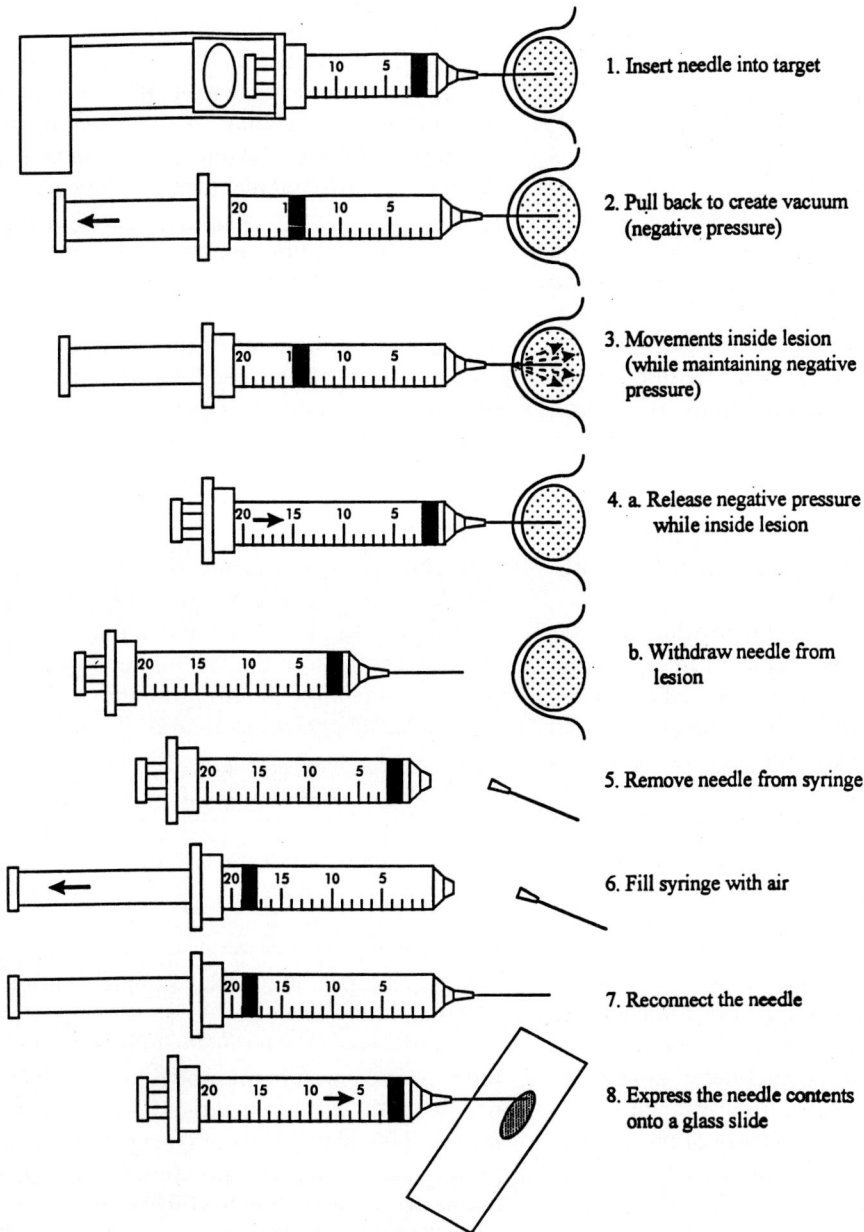

1. Insert needle into target

2. Pull back to create vacuum (negative pressure)

3. Movements inside lesion (while maintaining negative pressure)

4. a. Release negative pressure while inside lesion

   b. Withdraw needle from lesion

5. Remove needle from syringe

6. Fill syringe with air

7. Reconnect the needle

8. Express the needle contents onto a glass slide

Figure 53-2   Steps in FNA technique.

Fine Needle Sampling without Aspiration

Zajdela introduced the concept of sampling without aspiration, which is based on the principle that capillary pressure in a fine needle is adequate to keep dislodged cells within the lumen. This technique is performed by introducing a 23- or 25-gauge needle directly with fingertips without the use of a syringe. The needle is moved back and forth in different directions until material is seen in the hub of the needle (Fig. 53-3). The needle is then removed and the sample is prepared. This technique has the advantage of allowing for enhanced appreciation of the consistency of small superficial lesions. The sample is also less contaminated with blood, so that this technique is useful for vascular superficial targets, such as thyroid nodules. Although this technique usually provides less cellular yield, it is of adequate quality. It is important to maintain stability of the needle within the lesion for a few seconds before withdrawing to allow the capillary pressure to draw the material into the lumen.

Reasons for Obtaining Insufficient Sample

Large lesions are usually associated with central necrosis, hemorrhage, and cystic changes. If the aspirate is taken from the center, no diagnostic cells may be found. In that case, the aspiration should be repeated from the periphery of the lesion. The needle may narrowly miss the lesion so that the sample is obtained from the surrounding inflammatory process and an erroneous diagnosis rendered. A small malignant lesion may be located immediately beneath a large cyst or a benign lesion. If the aspiration is performed on the dominant cyst or the adjacent benign lesion, a diagnosis of a benign process is rendered. This scenario is not uncommon in many breast and thyroid lesions. A malignant tumor associated with a dense fibroblastic reaction may not yield a satisfactory sample, as the malignant cells are firmly bound by collagenous tissue. When aspirating an unexpected cystic lesion, the aspiration should be continued until the cyst is completely evacuated and the area palpated to determine if there is any residual mass. A second pass is required to assess any persisting palpable abnormalities.

Optimal FNA technique is essential for obtaining an adequate sample. Important points to remember are: proper immobilization of the lesion; needle selection; number of passes; site selection for entering the mass; movements of the needle inside the lesion; and the timing of application and release of suction.

How to Prepare the FNA Sample

The aspirated material usually falls into three categories: semisolid, sample with minimal fluid, and sample with excessive fluid. The semisolid material is ideal for preparing a monolayer smear. Although excessive blood and fluid is undesirable, a minimal amount of fluid admixed with the aspirated material is necessary for optimal spreading of the material on the slide. If the aspirated material in the needle hub is seen to consist mainly of thick white material, the aspiration should be continued for a few more seconds until the material is slightly blood tinged.

A one-step technique is used for smear preparation from a semisolid material or a sample with minimal fluid, while a two-step technique is used for a material with excessive fluid. In the following text, the representative slide that is used for microscopic examination is referred to as the *sample slide,* and the second slide used for spreading of the smear is referred to as the *spreading slide.*

The One-Step Smear Preparation Technique

The various steps of this technique are illustrated in Fig. 53-4. The one-step technique is used for a semisolid aspirate to produce a monolayer spread, usually referred to as a bullet-shaped spread. After release of the negative pressure, while the needle is in the mass, the needle is withdrawn and disconnected from the syringe. If

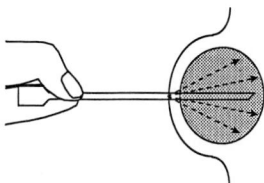

Figure 53-3 Technique of FNA without aspiration.

Figure 53-4 One-step smear preparation technique.

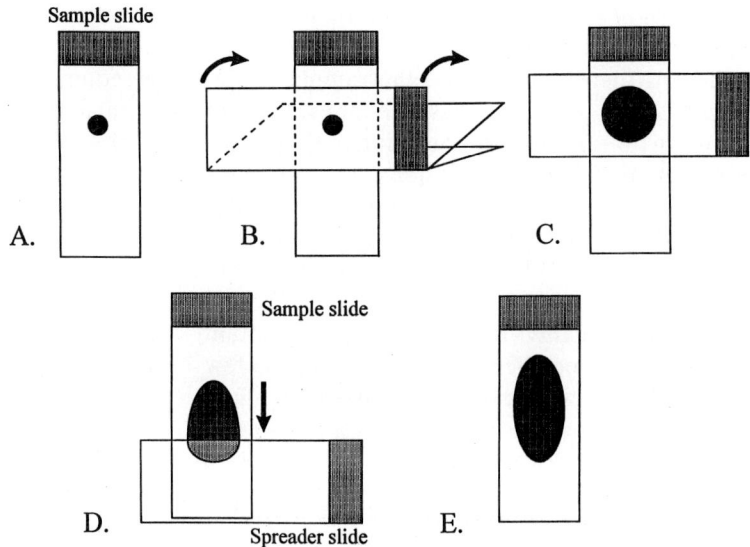

the needle is firmly attached to the syringe, a small forceps should be used to disconnect it. Fill the syringe with air and reconnect the needle. Bring the needle tip into tight contact with the surface of a clean glass slide and express the material at the lower part of the upper-third of the slide near the frosted end. The needle tip should touch the surface of the sample slide to minimize air drying and to prevent sprinkling and loss of the material. If the capillary nonaspiration technique using only a needle is employed, withdraw the needle and connect it to an already air-filled syringe. The aspirated material can be expressed into one to three sample slides, depending upon the volume of the aspirate. If the expressed material seems large for one sample slide, transport some of this material onto a second sample slide using the edge or the deep surface of the spreading slide. Hold the sample slide firmly between the thumb and two fingers of one hand at the frosted end, and use the thumb and two fingers of the other hand to hold the spreading slide. Put the long edge of the spreading slide on the sample slide and lower the slide until it gently touches the material. The material will

slowly begin to spread between the two slides. Pull the spreading slide away from the frosted end of the sample slide in a downward movement in the direction of the edge of the slide, and apply slight pressure on the material. Increase the pressure during the downward pull to spread the sample thinner toward the tail of the bullet-shaped smear. It is important to maintain a constant pressure until the material is completely smeared on the sample slide. Applying the proper amount of gentle pressure is critical to producing an ideal monolayer bullet-shaped smear and to avoid hesitation lines and undesirable artifacts.

Immediately fix all slides in 95% ethanol to be used for Pap staining. If a cytopathologist is performing the aspiration, the cytopathologist should allow a few slides to air dry for rapid staining with D-Q in order to immediately evaluate the adequacy of the specimen. If the sample is inadequate, the procedure should be repeated. Usually one to three passes produces sufficient material.

Always rinse the needle from each pass in a tube containing 50% alcohol. This rinsed material will be used for cytospin preparation, thus assuring that all additional material can be thoroughly examined. If the aspirate contains tissue fragments or thick material, transport it into a small tube containing 10% formalin to be processed as a cell block for histologic examination.

Clinical judgment should be used to determine the need for possible further ancillary studies, such as immunohistochemistry, flow cytometry, hormone receptor studies, EM studies, and culture. Additional passes specifically for such ancillary studies may be required. The aspirated material should be rinsed in the appropriate medium ready for shipment to the laboratory. If the cytopathologist is not present during the procedure, the laboratory can be called to obtain the necessary information regarding media selection for possible ancillary studies. If a lymphoproliferative process is suspected, the laboratory may require additional air-dried unstained slides or fresh material placed in RPMI solution in order to perform immunophenotypic analysis.

Preparation of Smears with Excessive Blood or Fluid

Samples with excessive blood or fluid can cause lysis of the cells, or there may be loss of cell adhesion to the slide during immersion fixation. Resulting artifacts may preclude interpretation. If the material obtained contains excessive blood or fluid, the slide should be tilted to allow the excess fluid to drain onto a piece of gauze or paper. Preparation of the smear should then be completed with the one-step technique using only the thicker material left behind at the sample slide.

Sample Preparation Errors

An adequate sample obtained by FNA can be rendered inadequate by poor sample preparation technique. Sample preparation is as important as the FNA technique itself. Most errors during sample preparation can be avoided by paying attention to the following:

- Air drying artifact in slides prepared for Pap stain is a major factor in producing specimen inadequacy and cytologic misinterpretation.
- The slide should be fixed immediately after preparation by placing it gently into an alcohol jar. The slide should not be forcefully dropped, as this will cause dislodgment of cells from the surface.
- Constant gentle pressure should be applied and maintained while spreading the material on the sample slide to produce the ideal bullet-shaped smear.
- Transport the thicker particles and tissue fragments to the appropriate transportation media.
- Thick smears should be fixed immediately in 90% alcohol and used for Pap staining; if the slide is needed for immediate evaluation using the rapid stain (Diff-Quick), a longer time should be allowed for the smear to dry.
- Occasional clusters of cells on a slide are inadequate for cytologic evaluation; additional passes are required to provide adequate material.
- Clinical judgment is required to plan for possible ancillary studies; additional passes may be required and appropriate transportation media should be used for the aspirated material.
- Practice is the best method to master the FNA technique.

Complications of FNA

FNA tends not to be associated with serious complications even if the target is missed. Needle diameter is a major factor associated with complications. The incidence of complications increases with increasing needle diameter. FNA of deep-seated lesions is more likely to be associated with complications than FNA of superficial lesions.

For superficial lesions, complications are infrequent and almost always minor. Applying local pressure can prevent bleeding. The needle is so thin that even accidental penetration of major vascular structures is not a significant concern. A small hematoma may occasionally form and compression of the area usually helps reduce hematoma formation. Painful ecchymoses may also develop, but usually disappear within a few days. A local infection at the site of FNA is extremely rare and easily controlled by antibiotics.

Other reported transient and rare complications include vasovagal reaction, seizures, nerve damage, infection, and tumor necrosis. Tracheal puncture also may occur, particularly during aspiration of a lesion located within the isthmus of thyroid. The patient may not be aware that this has occurred and the aspirator may find that the syringe suddenly fills with air. Pneumothorax is an unlikely possibility when FNA is performed in the region of the chest, including breast, supraclavicular region, and axilla.

The possibility of dissemination of cancer cells along the needle track initially caused great concern that was aggravated by occasional reports of tumor cell implants at the site of an incisional or core-needle biopsy. Recent reviews of reported cases of needle-track tumor implantation after intra-abdominal thin-needle biopsy concluded that multiple passes and larger needles in the absence of normal parenchyma covering the lesion appear to increase the risk. This risk has been estimated to be less than 0.0045 percent for deep-seated aspirations and even less for aspiration of superficial lesions. The risk of seeding of the needle track following a tissue core-needle biopsy is estimated to be at least 0.4 percent.

Fatalities related to FNA of superficial lesions are almost nonexistent. The clinical value and wide application of FNA cytology far outweigh concerns about the infrequent complications associated with the technique.

FNA Interpretation

Accurate and reliable FNA interpretation can only be achieved if the sample is representative of the lesion and if adequate material is retrieved. Specimen adequacy is the cornerstone of cytologic evaluation. No diagnoses can be rendered if well-preserved representative cells are not present in the examined slide.

The cytopathologist reaches the diagnoses by identifying benign or malignant morphological features on a cytologic sample. The parameters used are characteristic cellular changes such as cell and nuclear size and shape, chromatin pattern, and matrix production. The reader is advised to refer to the many textbooks on FNA cytology for further details on cytologic features of various body sites.

Diagnostic cell samples by FNA can be obtained from virtually any palpable lesion. The targets were expanded to include deep-seated lesions using radiographically guided techniques. With the introduction of new, sophisticated imaging techniques, almost every organ in the body is now accessible to sampling by aspiration. The targets of diagnostic aspirate include breast; thyroid; salivary glands; lymph nodes; skin and soft tissue; lung; pleura; mediastinum; abdominal organs (kidney, adrenals, retroperitoneal space, pancreas, liver, spleen); bone; eye; and central nervous system. The management of breast FNA is described as an example of a clinical application of this valuable technique.

Breast FNA

Numerous surgical breast biopsies are performed in the United States, the majority of which are for benign processes. To reduce the number of avoidable biopsies, clinical, radiologic, and cytologic criteria are defined to better identify the subset of patients who will require further invasive procedures. The diagnostic triad of clinical evaluation, radiologic findings, and FNA biopsy is known as the "triple test." The combined diagnostic accuracy of these three tests is high, with a false-negative rate of 0.5 to 2 percent.

In 1996, The National Cancer Institute sponsored a meeting of experts that defined a "uniform approach to breast FNA biopsy." Criteria and recommendations for training and credentialing of FNA operators, diagnostic terminology, and post-FNA recommendations were standardized.

The accuracy rate of FNA is highly dependent on aspirator proficiency, in addition to the level of interest and training in the technique and first-hand information of the patient's history and clinical presentation. It has been shown that the best results are achieved when expertise is concentrated within a clinic/lab devoted exclusively to FNA cytology.

Breast FNA are reported using one of these five standard nomenclatures: benign; atypical/indeterminate, a term which conveys that the lesion is probably benign, but that malignancy cannot be entirely ruled out; suspicious, a term that conveys a high probability that the lesion is malignant, but that tissue confirmation is required before definitive surgery; malignant; and unsatisfactory, which is usually secondary to scant cellularity, air drying artifact, or obscuring blood or inflammation.

The correlation of clinical, imaging, and cytologic diagnoses, or triple test (TT), has been defined as: benign TT is when all three parameters are unequivocally benign and the patient can be followed clinically; malignant TT is when all three parameters are conclusively malignant and definitive therapy following frozen section confirmation can be entertained; mixed TT includes cases when one or two diagnostic modalities are discrepant and an open biopsy is indicated.

The 1996 NCI conference created a protocol for patient management. First, when a patient presents with a breast lesion, the clinician must decide if the patient is likely to return for continuous follow-up or not. If the patient is not likely to return, an open biopsy is recommended. If the patient is compliant, an FNA is obtained after diagnostic imaging.

The material obtained from the FNA can originate from a solid or a cystic lesion. If the lesion is solid and the FNA is atypical or a mixed triplet is generated, an excisional biopsy is recommended.

A benign triplet can be followed up clinically in six months. An insufficient cytologic diagnosis requires repeat FNA or an excisional biopsy. A malignant FNA may be associated with a mixed triplet or a malignant triplet. In the case of a mixed triplet, definitive therapy after frozen section confirmation is recommended. A malignant triplet requires definitive therapy after histological examination.

A cystic lesion may leave no residual mass. If a mass persists after complete drainage, reaspiration or excision is recommended. The aspirated fluid may be clear or hemorrhagic. Clear fluid can be discarded or sent to the cytology lab where concentration techniques may be performed. If the cytospin product is malignant, a definitive therapy after biopsy is recommended. If the aspirate fluid is hemorrhagic and cloudy, cytospin preparations are performed. A benign cytology requires routine follow-up within 3 to 6 months. A malignant cytology requires definitive therapy after biopsy.

Grant et al. calculated the following breast FNA statistics from a summary of 18 studies: sensitivity = 92.5 percent, specificity = 99.8 percent, positive predictive value = 99.7 percent, negative predictive value = 94.2 percent, and accuracy = 96.5 percent.

Several studies suggest that FNA biopsy should be part of the initial evaluation of every patient with a breast mass. In addition, FNA biopsy is quite useful in the evaluation of recurrence and metastases of breast carcinoma.

References and Selected Readings

1. Al-Mofleh IA: Ultrasound-guided fine needle aspiration of retroperitoneal, abdominal and pelvic lymph nodes: Diagnostic reliability. *Acta Cytol* 36:413–415, 1992.
2. Anderson JB, Webb AJ: Fine-needle aspiration biopsy and the diagnosis of thyroid cancer. *Br J Surg* 74:292–296, 1987.
3. Boccato P, Briani G, Bizzaro N, et al: Cytology in "black and white." *Acta Cytol* 31:643–645, 1987.

4. Grant CS, Goellner JR, Welch JS, et al: Fine-needle aspiration of the breast. *Mayo Clin Proc* 61:377–381, 1986.

5. De May RM: *The Art and Science of Cytopathology,* vol II. Chicago, IL: ASCP Press, 1996.

6. Dudgeon LS, Patrick CV: A new method for the rapid microscopical diagnosis of tumors: With an account of 200 cases so examined. *Br J Surg* 15:250–261, 1927.

7. Grant CS, Goellner JR, Welch JS, et al: Fine-needle aspiration of the breast. *Mayo Clin Proc* 61:377–381, 1986.

8. Kaminsky DB: Aspiration biopsy in the context of the new medicare fiscal policy. *Acta Cytol* 28:333–336, 1984.

9. Kreula J, Bondestan JK, Virkkunen P: Sample size in fine needle aspiration biopsy. *Br J Surg* 76:1270–1272, 1989.

10. Koss LG: Thin needle aspiration biopsy. *Acta Cytol* 24:1–3, 1980.

11. Koss LG: On the history of cytology. *Acta Cytol* 24:475–477, 1980.

12. Mair S, Dunbar F, Becker PJ, DuPless W: Fine needle cytology—Is aspiration suction necessary? A study of 100 masses in various sites. *Acta Cytol* 33:809–813, 1989.

13. Martin HE, Ellis EB: Biopsy by needle puncture and aspiration. *Ann Surg* 92:169–181, 1930.

14. National Cancer Institute Sponsored Conference, Bethesda, MD: The uniform approach to breast fine-needle aspiration biopsy, special communication, *Diagn Cytopathol* 16:295–311, 1997.

15. Editorial. Needlesticks: Preaching to the seroconverted? *Lancet* 340:640–642, 1992.

16. Orell S, Sterrett G, Walters M, Whitaker D: *Manual and Atlas of Fine Needle Aspiration Cytology.* New York, Churchill Livingstone, 1992.

17. Pack HY, Yokota SB, Teplitz RL: Rapid staining techniques in fine needle aspiration. *Acta Cytol* 23:81–82, 1983.

18. Silverman LF, Finley JL, O'Brien KF, et al: Diagnostic accuracy and role of immediate interpretation of fine needle aspiration biopsy specimens from various body sites. *Acta Cytol* 33:791–796, 1989.

19. Smith EH: Complications of percutaneous abdominal fine needle aspiration biopsy: Review. *Radiology* 178:253–258, 1991.

20. Van den Breckel MWM, Castelijns JA, Stel HV, et al: Occult metastatic neck disease: Detection with US and US-guided fine needle aspiration cytology. *Radiology* 180:457–461, 1991.

21. Zajdela A, Zillhardt P, Voillemot N: Cytological diagnosis by fine needle aspiration without aspiration. *Cancer* 59:1201–1205, 1987.

CHAPTER 54

Flexible Sigmoidoscopy

Nelson G. Rosen
John M. Cosgrove

HISTORICAL REVIEW

EQUIPMENT

INDICATIONS

PROCEDURE

Preprocedure Discussion and Testing •
Bowel Preparation • Consent • Antibiotic
Prophylaxis • Special Concerns in
Pregnancy • Procedure • Endosurgical
Procedures: Biopsy and Polypectomy •
Documentation • Postprocedural care

COMPLICATIONS

Colorectal cancer is the most common of all gastrointestinal malignancies. While often thought of as a disease of men, it is the third most common nonskin malignancy in women, resulting in approximately 26,000 deaths annually.[5] An effective screening tool for colorectal cancer is flexible sigmoidoscopy. As most colon cancers arise in benign polyps, a program of endoscopic screening with polyp removal could make a major impact on colon cancer mortality. Unfortunately, a significant gender bias exists against women among patients undergoing colorectal cancer screening.[10] Whether this is a result of physician attitude or patient perception, the result can impact directly on deaths from colorectal cancer. By bringing flexible sigmoidoscopy into the offices of more physicians who provide primary care for women, these obstacles can be overcome.

In addition to its role in cancer detection, the flexible sigmoidoscope is useful in the work-up of all types of lower abdominal and gastrointestinal complaints. It can be used for the diagnosis of ulcerative colitis, Crohn's disease, and irritable bowel syndrome. It can be effective in the evaluation of hematochezia secondary to either primary colorectal pathology or symptomatic rectosigmoid endometriosis. It can even prevent unnecessary surgery in severe cases of psuedomembranous colitis mimicking an acute abdomen.

The use of the flexible fiberoptic sigmoidoscope (FFS) is well within the capability of all primary care physicians. The ability to perform this procedure in the office setting brings a flexibility to the diagnosis and management of colorectal pathology that benefits both patient and physician. Flexible sigmoidoscopy is not to be considered a substitute for colonoscopy and radiographic contrast enema examinations, because it only affords evaluation of the distal colon. It should be considered as a replacement for rigid sigmoidoscopy in cancer screening and evaluation of suspected distal colorectal pathology.

This chapter provides physicians with an overview of flexible sigmoidoscopy. Primary care and other specialty physicians with no prior endoscopic training who wish to incorporate flexible sigmoidoscopy into their office practice can obtain more in-depth information from one of several texts dedicated to flexible sigmoidoscopy.[4,7,12] One-day workshops are available to practitioners interested in performing flexible sigmoidoscopy. Additional postworkshop endoscopy experience proctored by an experienced endoscopist is recommended. Such additional training is helpful for office practice, essential for endosurgical procedures, and may be required by hospital credentialing committees before hospital endoscopy privileges may be granted. Once trained, skill should be maintained by performing a minimum of 15 flexible sigmoidoscopies annually.

Historical Review

The FFS developed through a series of gradual improvements on the first endoscopes of the early nineteenth century. Electric light was first used for endoscopy by Max Nitze of Germany in 1879.[12] The rigid sigmoidoscope was first popularized in the United States by a gynecologist, Howard Kelly, in 1895.[13] Insufflation and distal illumination were later added to bring light closer to the area of interest and keep the bowel from collapsing on itself. Further refinements of the rigid scopes continued, but persistent limitations included poor visibility due to light and optical restrictions, and difficulty maneuvering within the twists and turns of the bowel.

In 1958, Hirschowitz et al. reported their results with the use of a fiberoptic gastroscope.[11] This is credited as being the first application of fiberoptics in the examination of the gastrointestinal tract. Two years later, in Japan, the fiberoptic gastroscope was first used to examine the rectum and colon.[12] The initial image quality was poor, secondary to the low quality of early fiberoptics, but the framework had been created for the eventual endoluminal visualization of the entire colon. Recent developments of flexible sigmoidoscopes include improved distal tip control for increased ease of bowel navigation, and improved fiberoptics. The flexible video sigmoidoscope was developed in the early 1980s by placing a tiny video chip at the tip of the scope and transmitting the images electronically, resulting in thinner endoscopes with improved resolution.

In the 1970s, Wolff and Shinya pioneered colonoscopic polypectomy, demonstrating it to be a safe alternative to open surgical removal.[19,20] This revolutionized modern colorectal cancer diagnosis and screening.

Equipment

Flexible sigmoidoscopes vary in both size and nature of controls. Most manufacturers produce sigmoidoscopes with lengths ranging from 60 to 70 cm. Scopes are constructed by combining many different lumens, to accomplish all the required functions of the scope, under a protective plastic coating. In addition to a channel for the fiberoptics for light and image conveyance, the instrument contains a channel for air insufflation and water irrigation, one for suction, and a lumen for the passage of instruments such as biopsy forceps and snare cauteries (Fig. 54-1). Video scopes have a video camera chip at the tip of the scope and convey the image by wires through the scope to an external video processor. A fiberoptic scope may be used with a video attachment—a camera unit that attaches to the eyepiece of the scope and transmits the image to a processor and monitor. The video scopes are more expensive than the fiberoptic scopes, but offer improved resolution over the fiberoptic scope/video-attachment combination. For routine examinations, fiberoptic scopes are more than sufficient.

In addition to the various scope lumens, there are wires that connect the tip of the scope with pulleys located within the control head of the scope. When these pulleys, called control or deflection wheels or knobs, are turned by the operator, the scope tip deflects. Most scopes deflect in two planes, or four directions, with maximum angles of deflection ranging from 160 to 180 degrees. It is by using this tip deflection that the operator is able to navigate the scope through the twists and turns of the sigmoid colon—a structure that doesn't make the task any easier due to its often floppy attachments to the retroperitoneum.

The proximal ends of the air, irrigation, suction, and biopsy lumens, and the control knobs

Figure 54-1 Diagram of a typical 60-cm flexible fiberoptic sigmoidoscope (FFS).

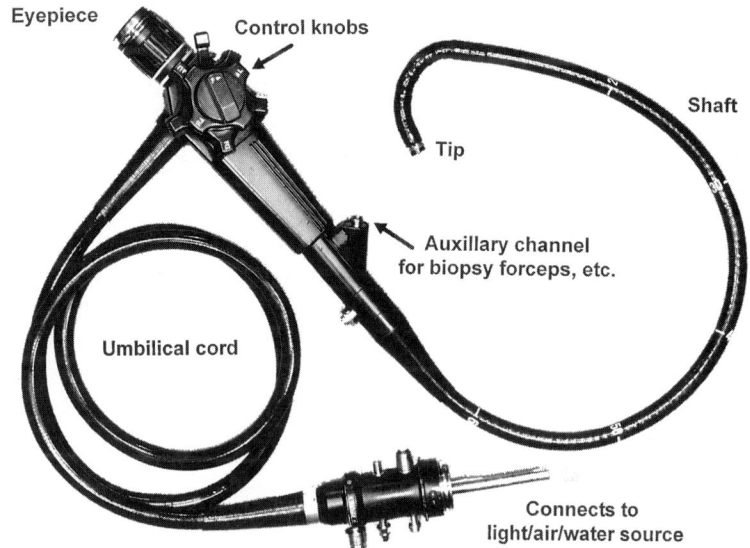

are located on the control head of the scope. This is also where the eyepiece is located. Video attachments connect here, in addition to teaching attachments that allow endoluminal viewing by a second individual. The control head of the scope connects to an external light source and air insufflation unit via the "umbilical" cord. The insufflation unit has a small tank for water for irrigation. Suction is provided by attaching an external suction device to a port on the control head of the scope.

Techniques for cleaning the scope should be included in the scope manual provided by the manufacturer. The scope should be thoroughly cleaned both inside and out. Following this, it must be disinfected using any one of the many commercial solutions available. Most commonly a glutaraldehyde solution (Cidex) is used. Automated cleaning units are available, but are often prohibitively expensive for the office-based practitioner. Disinfection, rather than sterilization, is all that is usually done with the equipment between examinations on routine patients. For use with immunosupressed, neutropenic, or HIV patients, gas sterilization should be performed before and after examinations. The instrument

should also be gas sterilized following use in patients with known hepatitis or other major communicable diseases.

Proper care and maintenance of a FFS is essential to keep it in good working condition. Operators and ancillary staff involved in caring for the instrument should thoroughly familiarize themselves with both the scope and its manual. This practice can be effective in avoiding unnecessary damage to the scope, and in lengthening its operative life.

Indications

For colorectal cancer screening, in addition to digital rectal examination and fecal occult blood testing, the current American Cancer Society guidelines recommend flexible sigmoidoscopy every 5 years, or radiographic double-contrast barium enema exam every 5 to 10 years, or colonoscopy every 10 years for all individuals 50 years of age or older.[1] Screening should be started under age 50 for individuals with a strong family history of colon cancer or polyps; a family history of familial polyposis or nonpolyposis colon cancer syndromes; a personal history of colon cancer or polyps; a personal history of uterine, breast, or ovarian cancer; or a personal history of chronic inflammatory bowel disease. Fecal occult blood testing alone is insufficient as a screening modality. In a large study that compared screening by fecal occult blood testing versus flexible sigmoidoscopy, the sensitivity for the occult blood test was 20.8 percent as compared to 93.8 percent for sigmoidoscopy.[17]

In addition to screening, patients with symptoms suspicious for lower intestinal pathology or asymptomatic patients with guaiac-positive stools should undergo flexible sigmoidoscopy as an initial diagnostic study. Such symptoms include rectal bleeding, anemia, changes in bowel habits or stool character, weight loss, and abdominal pain. While intestinal endometriosis is a rare cause of hematochezia, it has been estimated to occur in as many as 5 percent of reproductive-age females[15] and should be considered in the differential diagnosis of hematochezia. The FFS exam should not be used as the only diagnostic procedure in the evaluation of lower intestinal pathology. It is an excellent initial exam, but is not a substitute for radiographic examination of the colon and full colonoscopy.

Patients with severe diarrhea or other signs of significant colitis will most often benefit from a full colonoscopic evaluation. If a patient has been in an institutional setting or has been receiving antibiotics and is having diarrhea, a sigmoidoscopic exam may be sufficient to diagnose psuedomembranous colitis. Patients with intermittent chronic left lower abdominal pain may have diverticulosis diagnosed via sigmoidoscopy, but should also undergo total colonic evaluation to exclude synchronous pathology.

FFS has been used in the preoperative evaluation of patients with pelvic masses, to help determine bowel involvement. A recent study that evaluated this indication for sigmoidoscopy found that extrinsic bowel compression on FFS exam correlated with attachment of the lesion to the bowel, but did not significantly influence surgical therapy.[14] In that series of 107 women, 18 had extrinsic compression on FFS exam with only 1 of the 18 requiring bowel resection. Beyond routine screening for patients over age 50, we do not recommend FFS exam as a routine part of a preoperative evaluation of a patient with a pelvic mass.

Lower endoscopy is contraindicated in patients with acute diverticulitis due to greater risk of colonic perforation. Lower endoscopy is relatively contraindicated in the early postoperative period following colon and rectal surgery due to risk of anastomotic injury. Early postoperative endoscopic procedures may only be performed safely by either the surgeon involved or by an experienced endoscopist with the responsible surgeon in attendance. Other relative contraindications for lower endoscopy include significant cardiopulmonary disease and a large abdominal aortic aneurysm. Patients with a history of bleeding disorders or known coagulopathy should undergo endoscopic procedures in a hospital endoscopy suite with access to blood products if needed.

Procedure

Preprocedure Discussion and Testing

As in all operative procedures, a discussion with the patient about the nature of the procedure and its possible complications must take place. Patients are always apprehensive about endoscopic procedures. This discussion should reassure the patient and allay fears regarding the procedure. It is important to emphasize that the instrument is flexible and of a much smaller caliber than a normal stool. It may help to show the patient the instrument. The necessity of the bowel preparation should be discussed. Patients should also be counseled that air insufflation may result in crampy discomfort, and to inform the operator of this so that the gas may be suctioned. Patients being considered for endosurgical procedures should have routine coagulation tests performed (platelet count, prothrombin, and activated partial thromboplastin times) and should be instructed to discontinue aspirin or any medications that may affect platelet function for at least seven days prior to the procedure. Menstruation is not a contraindication to endoscopy.

Bowel Preparation

Debate continues regarding what is the optimal bowel preparation for flexible sigmoidoscopy. The goal of bowel preparation is to provide a clean surface in the lower colon and rectum to make viewing possible. The regimen that accomplishes this with the least associated discomfort will be most appreciated by patients and will increase their compliance. One preferred regimen consists of a self-administered phosphate enema (such as a Fleet's enema) approximately 1 to 2 hours before the procedure. This regimen provides a higher percentage of adequate bowel preparations when compared to oral agents such as bisacodyl.[6] Often, this may not be sufficient for full visualization with a 60-cm scope. Oral administration of 8 to 10 ounces of magnesium citrate the night before the examination, followed by two Fleet's enemas the morning of the examination, should provide full visualization with the longest of flexible sigmoidoscopes.

Full oral colonic preparation with solutions such as magnesium citrate or polyethylene glycol is necessary when electrical endosurgery, such as biopsy and snare-cautery, may be used. This is needed to decrease the amount of hydrogen and methane gas within the colon to eliminate the risk of explosion. Full oral preparations may also be necessary for diagnostic procedures in patients with such severe constipation that enemas are not effective.

In patients with active inflammatory bowel conditions, enemas and oral solutions may inflame the bowel mucosa and cause bleeding or exacerbation of the colitis. If the colitis is mild, a gentle tap-water enema may be given. More severe cases may require referral to a surgical endoscopist or gastroenterologist.

Dietary recommendations vary according to individual practitioner preference. A safe recommendation for patients is for a light dinner the evening before the procedure followed by clear liquids on the day of the exam.

Consent

Informed consent, as with any operative procedure, should include a discussion of the reason for the procedure, the nature of the procedure, its complications, their treatment, and alternatives to the procedure. This is ideally performed using a dedicated sigmoidoscopy consent form, as most routine hospital consent forms are too general and often contain information about anesthesia complications and blood transfusions. If endosurgical procedures will be performed, these should be discussed specifically. The most common significant complication to be discussed is the risk of perforation, which occurs in less than 1 in 1000 procedures.[4,9] For polypectomy, overall complication rates have been reported to be up to 1.2 percent, with bleeding (0.6 percent overall) and transmural burn (0.4 percent) being the two most common complications.[16]

Antibiotic Prophylaxis

Patients at risk for bacterial endocarditis should receive intravenous prophylactic antibiotics prior to FFS. Current American Heart Association guidelines should be followed for particular antibiotics and their dosing regimens.

Special Concerns in Pregnancy

In pregnant patients with symptomatic anorectal conditions, sigmoidoscopy is a safe alternative to radiographic colon evaluation.[3] Care should be taken to avoid maternal hypotension or hypoxia due to the sensitivity of the fetus. Patients undergoing endoscopy for hematochezia should be receiving intravenous hydration to avoid hypotension. The supine position should not be used as this position could decrease venous return, resulting in hypotension. All pregnant patients should receive supplemental oxygen. Medications for sedation should be avoided; if necessary, they should be chosen based on risk to the fetus. Endoscopy can often be deferred until after pregnancy for patients with mild abdominal pain or diarrhea, mild hematochezia due to known hemorrhoids, or change in bowel habits. A conservative practice is to reserve sigmoidoscopy for pregnant patients in whom it is clearly necessary. Physicians in doubt about specific indications should consult the opinions of experienced endoscopists and maternal-fetal-medicine specialists.

Procedure

Sigmoidoscopy takes an average of 10 to 20 minutes to perform. The procedure is usually accomplished with only verbal assurance and without sedatives. Extremely apprehensive patients may require a sedative. In these cases, an intravenous catheter should be inserted and a short-acting benzodiazepine, such as midazolam, may be administered either alone or in combination with low-dose meperidine for synergism. In this situation, supplemental oxygen should also be administered and appropriate monitors should be used, including a cardiac monitor, intermittent blood pressure monitoring, and continuous pulse-oximetry. Flumazenil for benzodiazepine reversal and naloxone (Narcan) for opiate reversal should be readily available for any signs of respiratory or cardiovascular depression.

Patient positioning depends on the preference of the endoscopist. The patient may be placed in a left lateral (Sims) position with the right leg flexed and over the left leg (Fig. 54-2). The other option is the inverted position on a sigmoidoscopic tilt-table, where the patient is prone and flexed at the waist and knees and the table is tilted 15 to 20 degrees downward. Either position is usually well tolerated. The advantages of the inverted position include an easy transition for the physician experienced in rigid sigmoidoscopy and slightly better access to the perineum and anus. Advantages of the Sims position include

not requiring a special sigmoidoscopic table and greater comfort in pregnant patients.

Following positioning, the perineum is examined making note of any hemorrhoids, fissures, fistulas, ulcerations, skin tags, or other lesions. Anoscopy may then be performed with a standard metal anoscope. As the flexible sigmoidoscope is effective for examining the anus on scope withdrawal, anoscopy should be performed only when greater scrutiny of the anal canal is required.

With the FFS connected to the light source, suction apparatus (and video device if available), all functions of the device are checked prior to usage. The control head is grasped in the left hand and the control wheels are manipulated to verify tip-deflection control. The shaft of the scope near the tip may be lubricated with any of the available commercial preparations. Lubricants containing local anesthetics may ease discomfort when active disease is present. Lubricating the distal shaft is preferred, as lubrication of the tip of the instrument may blur images.

Before the introduction of the scope, a rectal exam is performed to lubricate the anal canal, relax the sphincter, and check the vault for residual feces. With the FFS control head in the left hand and holding the shaft with the right hand, the tip of the scope is inserted into the anus at a 90-degree angle to facilitate entry (Fig. 54-3). Once the tip is within the anal verge, the tip may be directed up the anal canal and into the rectum. To better examine anorectal pathology, the FFS tip may be retroflexed to look back at the area in question. Once the tip is in the rectum, the principal rule of endoscopy must be observed: *the endoscope may never be advanced unless the lumen is well visualized.* Keeping this principle paramount will avoid many potential complications. As long as the lumen is visualized, the scope may be advanced as far as its working length allows. The shaft of the scope is advanced with the right hand (often with a piece of gauze to improve grip) while the left hand controls the wheels to keep the scope tip in the center of the lumen. Once the scope is advanced as far as

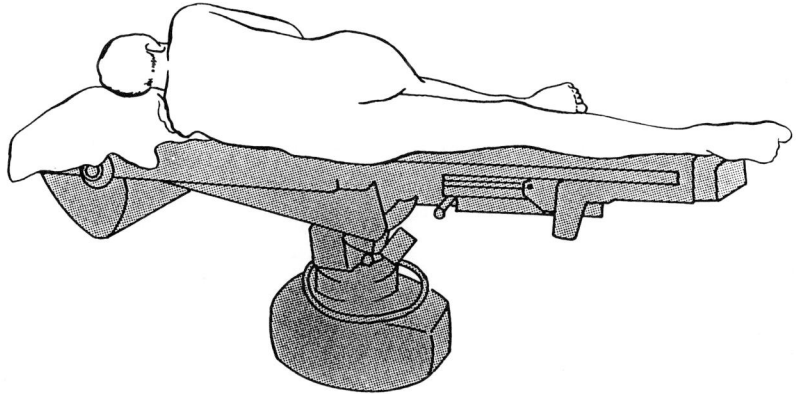

Figure 54-2 Patient positioned in the left lateral (Sims) position. This position may be used on any bed or table and may afford greater patient comfort. (From Katon RM, et al: *Flexible Sigmoidoscopy.* Orlando, FL: Grune & Stratton, 1985. Used with permission.)

possible, it should be completely withdrawn very slowly. It is during withdrawal that a thorough circumferential examination of the colonic mucosa is performed. If the scope cannot be advanced its entire working length, it is best not to expend a great deal of time and effort trying to accomplish this. Average insertion length is about 46 cm.[18] If the insertion length achieved is inadequate, the patient may require referral to a more experienced endoscopist.

If the scope is advanced and the lumen appears to be turning off to one side, manipulate the control wheels to keep the scope in the center of the lumen. This is best accomplished with slow and deliberate turning of the control wheels. If at any time the picture appears to be obscured by enteric contents, these may be gently irrigated and suctioned. Large particles of stool are not amenable to suction and will only clog the device. If the image is obscured due to the scope tip being pressed up against the mucosa (referred to as "red-out"), gently backing the shaft out

Figure 54-3 Technique for facilitating entry of the sigmoidoscope tip to minimize trauma to the region: (A) Incorrect insertion. (B) Correct insertion. A digital rectal examination should be performed prior to scope entry. (From Katon RM, et al: *Flexible Sigmoidoscopy.* Orlando, FL: Grune & Stratton, 1985. Used with permission.)

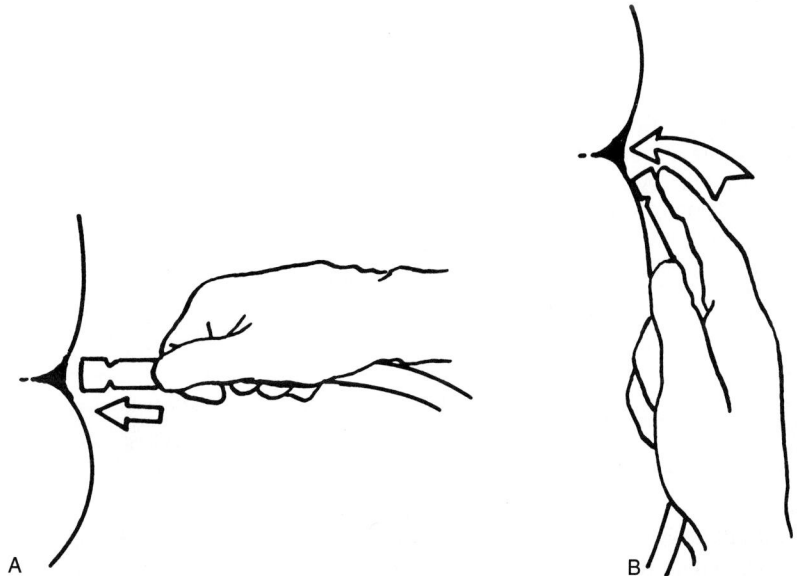

A

B

slightly and insufflating air may be effective in locating the lumen. If the lumen is still not visible, manipulating the control wheels may be effective. The control wheels should be used gently; rapid large deflections are not beneficial and can damage the control cables over time. Twisting the shaft in a clockwise direction may be very helpful in finding the lumen.

A common problem encountered in trying to advance the scope is the formation of an N-loop. In trying to advance the scope through the sigmoid colon, the rectosigmoid flexure can stretch so that further advancement of the shaft stretches this loop and does not advance the scope tip (Fig. 54-4). This may be countered by twisting the instrument shaft in combination with withdrawing the shaft in an effort to telescope the bowel along the shaft of the scope. Such techniques are only safely learned in a proctored endoscopy situation and should be used carefully.

If the patient complains of pain during the exam, it is most probably secondary to bowel distension. Backing out the shaft slightly and suctioning some air are usually all that are necessary to do to increase patient comfort. This discomfort can sometimes be avoided by keeping insufflation to the minimum required to visualize the lumen well.

Endosurgical Procedures: Biopsy and Polypectomy

The primary care endoscopist should have a thorough knowledge of endosurgical procedures including biopsy and polypectomy before undertaking them. These procedures are most safely done in a hospital endoscopy suite because longer postprocedural observation is required. Small biopsies may safely be performed in an office setting. Complications of polypectomy may require in-patient observation and, occasionally, operative intervention. An experienced assistant must be present during biopsy and polypectomy procedures to handle the proximal end of either the biopsy forceps or the snare-cautery, at the direction of the operator. Polypectomy requires the possession of an electrocautery device.

Small polyps (<1 cm) can be biopsied safely using the biopsy forceps. As with any procedure, visibility and exposure are a necessity. With the polyp in view, the operator asks the assistant to advance the biopsy forceps until the forceps may be viewed by the endoscopist. The assistant may then open the jaws of the forceps and advance it, guided by the operator until the desired piece of the polyp is within the forceps jaws. The forceps is then closed by the assistant and retracted slightly, separating the specimen

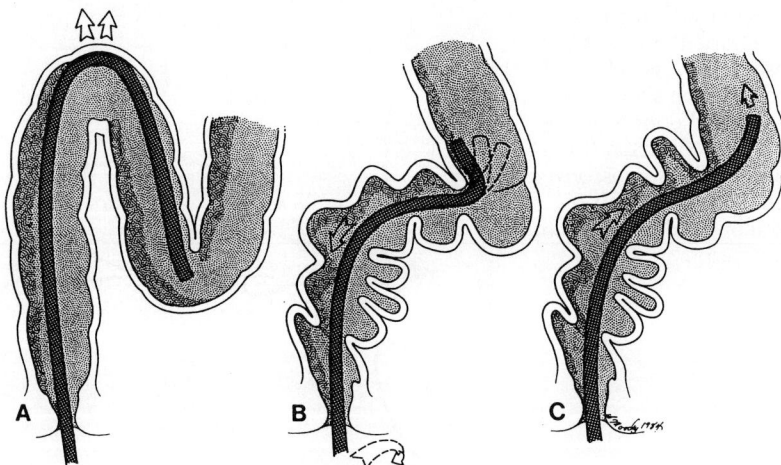

Figure 54-4 The formation of an N-loop (A) can often be dealt with by a combination of withdrawing and twisting the shaft of the scope (B) in an effort to "pleat" the bowel over the scope shaft (C). (From Katon RM, et al: *Flexible Sigmoidoscopy.* Orlando, FL: Grune & Stratton, 1985. Used with permission.)

from the polyp. The biopsy forceps is then removed by the assistant and the specimen is removed from its jaws manually. Biopsy forceps are available in several sizes and with optional cautery attachments.

Polyps with diameters between 1 and 3 cm can be safely removed by snare-cautery. Large pedunculated polyps (>3 cm) should only be removed by experienced endoscopists due to increased risk of complications following removal. Patients with such large lesions will need to undergo full colonoscopy anyway.

Snare-cautery devices consist of a catheter with a wire loop within it. When the loop is advanced beyond the tip of the catheter it may be placed over a polyp, and the wire can be retracted, tightening around the polyp stalk. The ensnared polyp is then removed by applying current and withdrawing the snare wire very gently until the polyp is no longer attached (Fig. 54-5). Current is then discontinued. The scope is withdrawn, holding the polyp to the scope tip by applying suction, and the polyp removed. Polyps should be ensnared at a point on their stalk approximately 1 cm from the bowel wall. Care must

be taken to prevent electrical current from being transmitted to the bowel wall, resulting in transmural burn and increased risk of bowel perforation. This is best done by keeping the forceps, snare, or the polyp that is being removed off of the bowel wall, or using an oscillating motion and not lingering in any one area. If contact is made, smaller areas of contact sustain greater injury than larger areas. When removing multiple polyps, it is best to remove the proximal-most polyp first because the scope must be withdrawn each time. If the stalk has significant bleeding following polypectomy, it can be resnared and cauterized. Small oozing is best managed with observation as most of this bleeding stops. Persistent bleeding may be managed by the use of thermal coagulation probes, tamponade with the scope tip, or application of epinephrine either topically or by injection. Sessile polyps between 1.5 and 3 cm may be removed by snare-cautery by partially snaring the polyp and removing it in piecemeal fashion. All of the techniques for safe electrical endosurgery can only be learned in a proctored endoscopy environment.

Figure 54-5 Technique of polypectomy using snare-cautery. Endosurgical procedures using cautery should be performed in a hospital endoscopy suite.

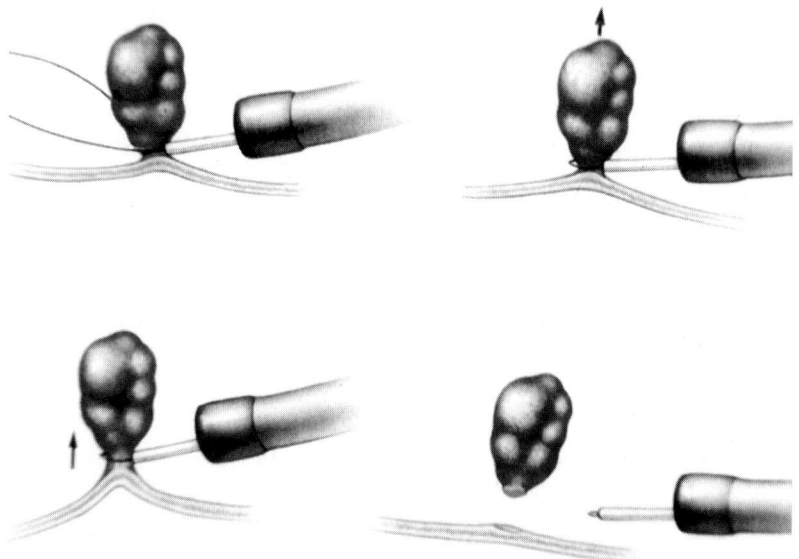

Documentation

Immediately following the endoscopy procedure, all findings should be documented on a dedicated procedure form. This allows all findings to be recorded while the events are fresh in the operator's mind. A small diagram of the colon should be used to make notes of findings and their location. Any endosurgical procedures should be carefully documented.

Postprocedural Care

If no sedatives have been used, the patient should have no procedure-related restrictions beyond the constraints of the initial complaint. When sedatives have been used, the patient should be observed with monitoring for a minimum of 30 minutes. Longer observation times should be used with deeper levels of sedation and depending on the patient's medical history and vital signs. Patients who have undergone endosurgery should be placed on a clear liquid diet and observed for postprocedural bleeding for several hours. If no bleeding is observed, the patient may be discharged on a regular diet. Postprocedural pain never should require pain medication. It is usually due to incomplete evacuation of insufflation air, and usually resolves over time with the patient supine.

Complications

The most common complications of FFS exam are colonic perforation and bleeding. If strictly diagnostic sigmoidoscopy is done, bleeding is an extremely rare complication. Perforation has been reported to occur with incidence ranging from 0.01 to 0.2 percent.[4,7,9] In one study of flexible sigmoidoscopy done specifically by primary care physicians, of 17,167 procedures the overall perforation rate was 0.01 percent.[9] Patients with active inflammatory conditions of the bowel or ischemic colitis are at greater risk for perforation.

Complications of endosurgery include both bleeding and transmural burn. Significant bleed-ing requiring transfusion occurs in up to 0.6 percent of procedures.[4,16] Bleeding may be delayed for as long as two weeks due to the formation of eschar, which falls off over time. Transmural burns can occur in up to 0.4 percent of procedures.[16] They often manifest by the acute onset of abdominal pain several hours following the procedure. If there is no evidence of perforation, these patients should be managed by in-patient observation, bowel rest, and intravenous fluids until the resolution of symptoms. Bowel perforation should be treated by expedient laparotomy. Treatment options for significant persistent bleeding include laparotomy, angiographic embolization, or placement of a selective arterial catheter for local arginine-vasopressin (Pitressin) infusion. A general surgeon should be consulted early, along with the interventional radiology department if a need for angiography is anticipated.

Explosions due to combustible colonic gases and the use of electrocautery have been reported but are extremely rare.[2] This is best prevented by full oral bowel preparation. Due to the rarity of endoscopic explosion, no definitive guidelines for the management of this complication exist. Conservative options range from water-soluble-contrast enema examinations of stable patients to emergency laparotomy for unstable patients.

References and Selected Readings

1. American Cancer Society: *Cancer Facts and Figures 1998*. Atlanta, GA: American Cancer Society, 1998.
2. Becker GL: The prevention of gas explosions in the large bowel during elective surgery. *Surg Gynecol Obstet* 97:463–467, 1953.
3. Cappell MS: The safety and efficacy of gastrointestinal endoscopy during pregnancy. *Gastroenterol Clin North Am* 27:37–71, 1998.
4. Cohen, LB, Basuk PM, Waye JD: *Practical Flexible Sigmoidoscopy*. New York: Ikagu-Shoin, 1995.
5. Donovan JM, Syngal S: Colorectal cancer in women: An underappreciated but preventable risk. *J Womens Health* 7:45–48, 1998.
6. Drew PJ, Hughes M, Hodson R, et al: The optimum bowel preparation for flexible sigmoidoscopy. *Eur J Surg Oncol* 23:315–316, 1997.

7. Dutta SK, Kowalewski EJ (eds): *Flexible Sigmoidoscopy for Primary Care Physicians*. New York: Alan R. Liss, 1987.
8. Fenlon HM, Clarke PD, Ferrucci JT: Virtual colonoscopy: Imaging features with colonoscopic correlation. *AJR Am J Roentgenol* 170:1303–1309, 1998.
9. Groveman, HD, Sanowski RA, Klauber MR: Training primary care physicians in flexible sigmoidoscopy—Performance evaluation of 17,167 procedures. *West J Med* 148:221–224, 1988.
10. Herold AD, Riker AI, Warner EA, et al: Evidence of gender bias in patients undergoing flexible sigmoidoscopy. *Cancer Detect Prev* 21:141–147, 1997.
11. Hirschowitz BI, Curtiss LE, Peters CW, et al: Demonstration of a new gastroscope, the "Fiberscope." *Gastroenterology* 35:50–53, 1958.
12. Katon RM, Keeffe EE, Melnyk CS: *Flexible Sigmoidoscopy*. Orlando, FL: Grune & Stratton, 1985.
13. Kelly HA: A new method of examination of diseases of the rectum and sigmoid flexure. *Ann Surg* 21:468–478, 1895.
14. Lawitz E, Kadakia SC: Utility of preoperative fiberoptic flexible sigmoidoscopy in the evaluation of patients with suspected gynecologic malignancy. *Gastrointest Endosc* 47:350–353, 1998.
15. Miller LS, Barbarevech C, Friedman LS. Less frequent causes of lower gastrointestinal bleeding. *Gastroenterol Clin North Am* 23:21–52, 1994.
16. Nivatvongs S: Complications in colonoscopic polypectomy: Lessons to learn from an experience with 1576 polyps. *Am J Surg* 54(2):61–63, 1988.
17. Rozen P, Ron E, Fireman Z, et al: The relative value of fecal occult blood tests and flexible sigmoidoscopy in screening for large bowel neoplasia. *Cancer* 58:2553–2558, 1987.
18. Selby JV, Friedman GD: Sigmoidoscopy in the periodic health examination of asymptomatic adults. *JAMA* 261:595–601, 1989.
19. Shinya H, Wolff WI: Morphology, anatomic distribution and cancer potential of colonic polyps: An analysis of 7000 polyps endoscopically removed. *Ann Surg* 190:679–683, 1979.
20. Wolff WI, Shinya H: Polypectomy via the fiberoptic colonoscope: Removal of neoplasms beyond the reach of the sigmoidoscope. *N Engl J Med* 288:329–332, 1973.

Psychiatric and Psychosocial Issues and Societal Violence

CHAPTER 55

Psychiatric and Psychosocial Issues in Primary Care for Women

Nada L. Stotland

As much as 50 percent of all patient visits for psychosocial problems—psychiatric illness, or psychiatric complications of other illnesses—are to primary care physicians.[69,74] Primary care physicians sometimes regard these problems as annoyances that drain time and energy from the "real" mission of care, rather than as legitimate medical issues in their own right. This attitude is reinforced by the misperception that psychiatric symptoms are neither deserving of nor responsive to primary care intervention.

Mental illness has also been linked to women's reproductive functions since the time of Hippocrates. "Hysteria" is so termed because ancient Greek physicians believed that unexplained physical symptoms in women were caused by migrations of the uterus out of the pelvis to the afflicted areas of the body. Relationships between psychiatric illness and female reproductive events are still being explored. For instance, "premenstrual dysphoric disorder" is described among the "disorders requiring further study" in the Appendix of the American Psychiatric Association's *Diagnostic and Statistical Manual of Mental Disorders,* 4th ed. (DSM-IV).

Stigma has dogged psychiatric illness for millennia. Currently, people misunderstand the mechanisms of action and effectiveness of psychopharmacologic agents. Lay persons and policymakers alike tend to perceive the "talking therapies" as indulgences for worried or bored well persons, rather than as interventions whose efficacy and cost-effectiveness have been demonstrated repeatedly in the scientific literature, and which compare favorably with many common and well-accepted medical treatments.[2]

Both sophisticated interviewing skills and the understanding of psychosocial issues and their implications are central to the ability to identify, diagnose, and treat psychiatric disorders.[61] These skills are important for the primary care practitioner because psychiatric disorders are common; often cause serious impairment, suffering, complications in medical treatment and recovery, and even mortality; and often can be identified by the astute primary care provider and treated promptly. Often, primary care patients do not complain of problems with their emotions, thinking, or behavior, but of physical symptoms.[74] Their psychiatric problems are manifested in somatic form or as noncompliance with the primary physician's recommendations. Therefore, the primary care physician must not only be familiar with the criteria for diagnosing common psychi-

atric disorders, but also must possess the interviewing skills and psychological expertise necessary to recognize the relevant signs and symptoms, to help the patient acknowledge her psychiatric difficulty, and either to provide counseling or to make an effective referral to a mental health professional.[38] Because psychiatric illnesses so infrequently present in the primary care setting with signs and symptoms that the physician can usefully look up in a table of contents or index, and are so frequently missed in medical evaluation and treatment, this chapter dwells extensively on diagnostic technique before describing illnesses and treatments.[65]

While social context has always been a central factor in susceptibility to disease, in illness behavior, and in the use of medical care, physicians of the past could, and frequently did, take the social context for granted. The physician was familiar with the milieu from which the patient came or was able to infer it from her address, name, dress, or manner. Such assumptions, if they ever were reliable, are reliable no longer. Not only have there been major changes, but the change in women's roles and expectations vary among social subgroups and age groups, from woman to woman, and over the course of a given woman's lifetime. The physician must obtain specific, relevant information from each patient.

Failure to address these issues has direct medical consequences. Stereotypes may prevent physicians from identifying instances of domestic violence and other abuse, situations precipitating depressive reactions, and psychosocial etiologies for gynecologic symptoms, as well as many other conditions. This chapter offers an overview of the interviewing skills necessary to obtain essential data and to establish an effective working relationship with patients in a variety of primary care settings. It includes information about the prevalence and distribution of psychiatric and psychosocial problems in the female patient population. It addresses the psychology of women and psychosocial issues as they present in and complicate primary care. It covers diagnosis, triage, and outpatient management of the major psychiatric illnesses; it suggests criteria and techniques for referring patients to psychiatrists and other mental health professionals, and establishing interdisciplinary collaboration for the coordination of patient care.

The Psychology of Women

In most societies, girls are socialized to be submissive and agreeable; assertiveness is actively discouraged. Despite some recent attempts to deemphasize the gender specificity of children's toys, activities, and clothing, girls and boys are treated differently from birth onwards. They are dressed differently, and live in differently decorated nurseries with different toys. Parents expect different things of them. From infancy, girls are described in terms of physical appearance, boys in terms of physical strength.

In primary school, boys receive more attention than girls. Boys and girls have equivalent self-esteem, and girls' academic achievement is similar to or better than boys'. During preadolescence, however, girls retreat from academic and athletic excellence; their self-esteem, self-assertion, and self-confidence fall significantly. Though women have entered and completed higher education in ever-increasing numbers, women do not achieve equivalent pay or leadership roles in jobs and professions.[24,32,58] Women's typical occupations are those associated with the highest level of stress, because they combine high levels of responsibility with low levels of autonomy and authority. Employed women continue to carry the lion's share of responsibility for family and domestic tasks.[45] Outside employment with appropriate social support, however, is associated with improved mental health status for women.[71] The physician can help women patients recognize sources of stress and encourage them to enjoy their academic and occupational achievements. The physician must also recognize that multiple responsibilities can interfere with women's ability to comply with recommended diagnostic and therapeutic regimens.

Psychosocial Aspects of Reproductive Development

As early as toddlerhood, girls have a positive awareness of their internal genital structures. Their feelings about them, and about themselves as female, derive directly from the attitudes of their parents and other important figures toward women and the availability of positive female role models. Women's development has almost always been construed in terms of reproductive milestones: menarche, first intercourse, childbearing, and menopause. The rhythms of reproductive physiology exert tangible effects on women's development. Puberty brings with it not only changes in body structure, but also the possibility of pregnancy. Bleeding connotes injury and can be frightening to the girl who is not prepared and given emotional support. First intercourse entails bodily penetration that can be both frightening and painful. Upon beginning intercourse, a young woman must either negotiate with her partner and/or a health care provider to prevent pregnancy, or become pregnant.

The pregnant woman literally makes room for another human being in her body, her emotions, and her plans. She must tolerate major changes in her body shape and function. During the first trimester, a woman must recognize the signs and symptoms of pregnancy, and, in some societies, decide whether to continue or terminate it. For women in some cultural subgroups, pregnancy precipitates an assessment of life plans, capacities, resources, and other commitments. In other groups, both in North America and around the world, a pregnancy is simply a given in a woman's life. In either case, pregnancy requires that a woman begin to see herself as a mother.

Childbirth is a powerful, inexorable, demanding physiological event, complicated in industrialized societies by both the comforts and the fears of obstetrical oversight and intervention. At the culmination of this event, a woman is called upon to form an intense, caring relationship with a new, unique, and helpless human being. She may be astounded by the strength of her attachment; she may be surprised, terrified, and guilty because those feelings are lacking; and she may feel each at one point or another. After uncomplicated childbirth, parents and infants are particularly alert and attuned to one another. They begin to establish bonds that are important for infant care and development. If separation is necessary for medical or other reasons, however, normal parents and infants with good social supports can still establish normal relationships. Those who are psychiatrically ill or without social supports may require professional mental health intervention.[7]

Breast-feeding extends the healthy bodily symbiosis between mother and child into the child's infancy. It entails sharing one's time and one's body with the baby while managing other tasks and relationships. The impact of the birth of children after the first child is somewhat attenuated by familiarity, but also complicated by the need to integrate new tasks and a new person into the existing family.

At menopause, a woman must adapt to a self that is no longer capable of childbearing. Some women face this challenge at an earlier age because of infertility or hysterectomy. In Western society, menopause generally coincides with the maturation of a woman's children and their financial and social independence from the family. For women who have not borne children, menopause ends the possibility that childbearing will occur in the future. The end of childbearing capacity may be a loss and/or a relief; the same is true of the end of menstruation. Menopause is also a symbol of aging, a process that is anticipated with some dread in our youth-oriented society.

Psychological Development in Social Context: Implications for Medical Care

There is no such thing as "natural" human behavior outside a social context. Human beings are social creatures; few have survived, and none has developed normally, isolated from other people. Specifically female developmental tasks involve identifying oneself as a female in relation to a particular society that defines femaleness in particular ways. It is difficult and perhaps meaningless to try to differentiate some sort of innate biopsychological sequence of female development from the influences of family and culture. What affects a woman psychologically is not so much the physiologic processes that take place in her body, but the meanings her particular society attaches to them and the ways in which those meanings change her experiences and her options.

As mentioned earlier, menopause, for example, may be regarded as a loss of central life function or as a relief from the burdens of bleeding, contraception, childbearing, and childrearing. Its association with aging is negative in most Western societies, but in other cultures, women are accorded increasing respect, autonomy, and power as they grow older.[28,38]

Psychological symptoms in Western women around the time of menopause may be caused by family stress, such as abandonment by a husband or sudden responsibility for the care of grandchildren or elderly relatives, rather than by hormonal changes per se. Physicians can have a positive effect on the way women approach and experience reproductive milestones in their lives.

Sexual, physical, and emotional abuse characterize the histories and lives of all too many female patients. Despite an increase in awareness and appreciation of the effects of domestic violence, there is still a powerful tendency to ignore the problem or to blame the victim rather than the perpetrator. Victimization is woefully underdiagnosed in the health care setting.[4] This is particularly unfortunate in light of the fact that health care may be the only reason for which the woman is allowed to leave the home, and a unique opportunity for lifesaving interventions.

Lesbian women's health care needs, long neglected, have begun to be recognized. Homosexuality, male or female, is not a disease and does not cause mental illness. Homosexual individuals, however, are subjected to considerable developmental and social stress, as they come to realize that they are different from what their families and society expect, and must either hide their orientation, living a lie, or cope with the responses of society to their "coming out," which not infrequently includes not only discrimination, but harassment and physical attacks.[35] Lesbians are at increased risk of breast and uterine malignancies.[43] Some of the risk may be due to delayed or absent childbearing, but the reluctance of lesbian women to seek health care in settings that they experience as insensitive or insulting may also be a factor.[62]

Physicians have, and bring to their interactions with patients, the same kinds of experiential and attitudinal baggage that everyone else has, with reference to expectations for female behavior, social roles, health, sickness, and treatment. It is essential that physicians make every effort to be aware of their own attitudes and behaviors and how they affect the provision of care. Psychological and social factors are not obstacles to medical care, but intrinsic to it. The attitudes and behaviors of physicians carry tremendous weight, positive or negative, for patients.

Interviewing Techniques for Primary Physicians

General Interviewing Techniques

The ability to encourage patients to explain their complaints and concerns, and to ask the right questions in the right way, is essential both to the identification of psychiatric disorders and to the effective management of the psychosocial factors, notably including compliance with diagnostic and therapeutic regimens, in health care overall. In the rush to obtain diagnostic data and outline the plan of treatment, it is easy to forget that the essence of the dialogue is in listening rather than talking. The medical interviewer, on average, interrupts a patient with specific questions before a minute of her description of her complaint has elapsed.[14] Allowing the patient some uninterrupted minutes to present her problems is actually time-effective. It conveys a sense of genuine interest that is essential to compliance. A primary care physician must create an atmosphere in which a patient feels comfortable revealing intimate, sometimes frightening, often embarrassing problems.

A few moments of spontaneous talking reveals a wealth of useful information about a patient: her level of education; her vocabulary; her medical sophistication; her attitudes towards her body, her symptoms, and medical care; and frank deficits in cognition and reality testing. Her mental status becomes apparent in a more useful way than in a formal mental status examination. Her body habitus, dress, verbal style, and body language can be observed. Is she anxious, depressed, angry, frightened? What are her attitudes towards illness and treatment? Is she a doctor-shopper, never satisfied with her care? Does she seek medical care often and on minimal grounds, or, more commonly and crucially, does she hate to "bother" the doctor, not ask for clarifications of instructions she doesn't understand, and only seek care when her condition is very serious? The physician will want to know, and to inform staff, that a call from such a patient, even when she minimizes her complaints, demands an immediate response.

Physicians worry that encouraging patients to speak freely will open the floodgates: that patients will unburden themselves of problems beyond the scope of the physician's expertise, and the visit will consume more time than is possible. Prescriptions for psychotropic and other medications are sometimes written as a way of ending a visit and giving a patient something tangible to carry away. But it is possible to control the flow and length of an interview without resorting to check-off lists and prescriptions. Inform a patient at the outset how much time you have. Ask her to tell you about her most pressing medical problems; if there are others, you can get to them at the next visit. This counters the natural tendency to "save the worst for last" just when the doctor is becoming impatient. Patients are able to sort the wheat from the chaff when asked to do so.

Getting Comfortable with Uncomfortable Topics

Some topics engender discomfort in nearly everyone. And physicians fear that certain topics will enrage, embarrass, or alienate a patient, or even precipitate a patient's acting on a destructive urge that is brought to light. Physicians are also reluctant to elicit information or problems that they are unsure of their ability to manage. Such topics include sexuality, insanity and other kinds of incapacity, and death. Unspoken collusion between doctor and patient to avoid those topics can result in serious medical omissions and bad outcomes.

Asking a patient about suicidal or homicidal ideas does not increase the risk of dangerous behavior.[30] On the contrary, asking these questions can and does save lives. Questions about sexual behavior or psychiatric symptoms are much more likely to be appreciated by patients than to make them angry. Patients tend to give straightforward answers to straightforward questions. The doctor's office is a place where intimate questions are expected. Therefore, in the rare circumstance that a patient is shocked at a question, it is easy to explain that the doctor asks the question routinely, makes no assumptions, and wants patients to know that the subject is open should there be problems in the future.

The Sexual History Sexual function is often ignored, but should be inquired about at every diagnostic, yearly, postpartum, and postoperative visit. Because society, however open it seems, is full of sexual taboos, it is best to phrase questions in such a way that sexual activities or problems are assumed. The patient can simply correct these assumptions when they are not valid. For example:

What sexual experiences did you have in childhood?
How were/are sexual matters handled in your family?
What is the nature of your current sexual activity, either by yourself or with one or more partners? (This phraseology avoids the pitfalls of

assumptions about the patient's sexual orientation, marital sexual activity, or fidelity.)
What sexual problems and questions have you encountered since your last visit/delivery/surgery?

A patient may be homosexual or bisexual, despite being or having been married. Most lesbian women engage in heterosexual activity. Unwarranted assumptions and negative attitudes drive lesbian patients away from medical care.[48] The same may be true of women engaged in prostitution. Further discussion of sexual history can be found in the section on sexual complaints.

Suicide and Homicide Questions about suicide and homicide flow naturally from a patient's responses or comments about being sad or angry:

Do you get so sad you think about hurting yourself?
Do you get so angry you might hurt someone?

The issues can be introduced by referring to universal feelings:

Everyone has such a bad day sometimes that they wish they just weren't on earth.
Everyone has had the experience of getting so aggravated that they feel they'd like to murder someone.

Most patients will acknowledge those common experiences, and go on to explain why they would not follow through on those kinds of thoughts: "My religion forbids suicide," or "It would hurt my family." If a patient acknowledges the feelings without offering such an explanation, the physician must ask whether she's been tempted to act on them, and then, sequentially, whether she has acted on them, whether the behavior was planned or impulsive, what precipitated it, and what the outcome was, including whether psychiatric or other medical treatment was provided. Risk factors for suicide also include a family history of suicide; alcoholism and/or other substance abuse; psychosis; serious recent loss; and serious, disabling, or chronic illness.[44] Most importantly, the physician must ask whether the patient is currently suicidal or homicidal, whether she has a specific plan for carrying out those intentions, and whether she has the means (a gun or pills, for example) to carry out the plan.

Patients almost always reply sincerely to these questions, so long as they are confident that the questions are in the interest of their care. When a patient is having sucidal or homicidal ideation, whatever her responses to the remaining questions, it is advisable that she be seen by a psychiatrist before leaving the medical care setting. If her physician has any reason whatsoever to suspect that the danger may be imminent, it may be necessary to summon the police or a security guard. The ethos of the medical profession discourages physicians from seeking help. This well-meaning self-reliance is tragically fatal for the patient and/or physician in some avoidable clinical situations. In contemporary America, many people carry firearms and other weapons.

When a patient or someone accompanying her is acutely threatening to the physician or others, the physician must not respond with anger and confrontation; such a response escalates the situation and has been shown to increase the likelihood of bodily injury. It is better to leave the room, and to take other care staff along. On the other hand, a patient who is acutely suicidal MUST NOT BE LEFT ALONE. Suicidal patients can be extremely fast and ingenious, crashing through upper-story windows and using medical equipment to harm themselves. Although it is uncomfortable to intrude on a patient's privacy, a suicidal patient must not be allowed to go to the bathroom alone, and must not be left alone while family members or medical staff get a drink of water or make a brief telephone call. If there is no telephone in the room, it is best to step to the door and call calmly but firmly for help. If it is necessary to leave the room, it is probably best to bring the patient along. Inform the patient of the basis for your concern and of the actions you plan to take: "What you have told me makes me concerned for your safety. In order not to take chances, I have called for help. You will not be left alone until we are certain that you are safe." The patient must be accompanied until she is under the direct care of a psychiatrist. Other mental health professionals defer to psychiatrists, the only medically trained mental health professionals, in these life-and-death matters.

Eliciting Psychotic Symptoms Asking a patient about psychotic symptoms (hallucinations, delusions, ideas of reference) seems like suggesting that she is "crazy"—certainly an insult in our society. Nevertheless, this inquiry is a necessary component of the mental status examination, and is perfectly well tolerated by patients who simply answer in the negative. Patients who have chronic or recurrent psychotic symptoms are accustomed to these questions. Patients with first-time, acute psychotic symptoms are frightened by them, and are generally aware of their need for medical help. Paranoid ideation may appear in the patient's complaints: people are plotting against her, poisoning her food, and so forth. Nonverbal cues to acute psychotic symptoms include fixing one's gaze at some point where there does not appear to be anything to see, and seeming to listen to an inner dialogue rather than attending to the interchange with the physician. Following are suggested questions:

Have you ever seen or heard things that other people couldn't?

What did you see or hear?

Have you ever had the feeling that something you read or heard on radio or TV was directed at you personally? (This is an idea of reference.)

What do you do when these things happen?

Have you seen a mental health professional about these experiences? What was diagnosed and what treatment was provided? What was the outcome?

Is this happening right now?

Because 1 percent of the world's population suffers from schizophrenia, and many others have psychotic episodes complicating alcohol and other substance abuse and other forms of metabolic, infectious, and other toxicity, questions about psychotic symptoms are crucial.[55] However, the presence of psychotic symptoms or illness do not in and of themselves make a patient incompetent to give a history and to make decisions about her care. However, some patients experience "command hallucinations," voices that order them to do things. If a patient is currently experiencing command hallucinations to harm herself or others, that is a psychiatric emergency.

Death and Dying   There is a growing literature on physicians' failure to discuss death and dying with their patients.[40] Patients' fears of being subjected to painful, humiliating, expensive, and ultimately useless medical interventions when they are helpless to refuse, fuel much of the current preoccupation with physician-assisted suicide, powers of attorney, living wills, and other means of extricating dying patients from unwanted medical interventions. In our mainstream culture, physicians are often more reluctant to discuss death than are their patients.[40] (There are other cultures, such as some Native American societies, in which mention, or even thoughts, of negative outcomes, is considered harmful.) Actually, it is not the prospect of death itself that terrifies people, but the prospect of pain, disability, helplessness, and abandonment. Avoidance of the subject exacerbates those very fears. Many patients are more aware of the possibility of death than their physicians and their families realize. It should arise naturally as the physician and patient communicate about the nature of her condition.

The primary physician should reassure the patient that she or he will remain available and active in coordinating the patient's care, even if other specialists assume a major role. Seriously ill patients too often get lost among personnel in a tertiary care setting; they hear conflicting opinions and are unable to distinguish just who is ultimately in charge. The primary physician is invaluable as the mediator, advocate, and inter-preter whom the patient knows and trusts. The patient may understand that she is likely to die of her condition, but she must never be told "There is no more we can do for you." She should be told that she will receive support, advice, and relief of symptoms as long as she lives. The knowledge that the primary physician will "be there" reduces both physical and psychological suffering.[22]

Religion   Many patients experience religious faith as the single most important support in times of stress.[47] Faith and spirituality may or may not be associated with an organized religion or a particular religious community. The physician can ask "Are you a religious person?" and "Does your religious faith help you cope with your illness?" as well as a patient's designated religious denomination. Medical staff can be helpful in soliciting the support of the patient's, or a nearby, religious leader.

When specific religious beliefs, such as the Jehovah's Witnesses refusal to accept blood products, interfere with the medically indicated course of treatment, the situation is painful for both patient and physician. Before attempting to override these prohibitions, it is essential to determine whether the patient's convictions are long-standing and freely held, and what implications violating them would have for her future social relationships and peace of mind. Refusal to accept any or all medical treatment, even when the refusal may or will result in death, is not synonymous with suicidality, which denotes an active wish to kill oneself, nor with psychosis. Many people hold values more important to them than life itself, and those values must be respected. Patients who refuse care should be asked to explain. It is only appropriate to consider overriding their wishes when the patient is unable to understand the nature of her illness and to make a reasonably informed decision. The Jehovah's Witnesses produce educational literature specifically written for the medical community, to help physicians understand the scriptural basis and nature of their unwillingness to accept treatment with blood products.

Domestic Violence Another uncomfortable, but life-and-death, topic is domestic violence and other forms of abuse. There is a tragic tendency to blame the victim: to ask what the rape victim was wearing and why she was walking down a particular street or in the company of a particular person, to fault a woman for remaining in an abusive relationship. It is difficult to comprehend the sense of helplessness engendered in these situations, and the real danger patients are in. These widespread attitudes of blaming the victim make patients reluctant to reveal these experiences. The primary care relationship can create paradoxical difficulties in obtaining this history. The medical care setting is often the only place outside the home to which the abuser allows the patient to go. The abuser often hovers over her, appearing solicitous and staying at her side throughout the medical encounter. She would like to appear "normal;" her association with an abuser taints her as well. Therefore, it often takes weeks, months, or even years of visits before a patient feels comfortable enough to divulge this information. Even when the patient seeks care for injuries caused by domestic violence, it is uncommon for the history to be volunteered or solicited in the medical setting.[67]

Domestic violence respects no boundaries of race, class, or income.[70] Victims of domestic violence are at high risk for being murdered. Every diagnostic interview must include this subject, in dialogue conducted outside the presence of a possible abuser. Some useful questions are:

Do arguments in your house sometimes get physical?
Is anyone in your life hurting you? Show me where on your body you have been hurt.

Opening the subject lets patients know that even if they are not ready to discuss it in the current interview, they can bring it up whenever they are able. Every primary care setting should have printed information about help lines, shelters, and other community resources openly available (sometimes in the ladies' room); the information is usually provided in forms that women can safely carry with them (inside their shoes, rolled into what appears to be a lipstick case). Knowing about resources makes physicians more comfortable bringing up the topic and patients more comfortable dealing with it.

Achieving Doctor-Patient Consensus

The physician who does not determine a patient's beliefs about the cause, diagnosis, necessary work-up, and treatment of her condition should expect that even the most scientifically valid diagnostic and therapeutic plan will be consciously or unconsciously sabotaged. A patient who believes that her abdominal pain is caused by the same kind of duodenal ulcer her mother had 50 years ago will go to one doctor after another until she is made to swallow some chalky fluid and take x-rays, and advised to drink lots of cream. She may die of a treatable malignancy. The gap between the physician's understanding and the patient's beliefs must be exposed and accepted before it can be bridged. The only way to know what the patient understands and accepts is to ask her. Then the physician has the opportunity to address the specific misunderstandings, relevant medical developments, etc., that may convince the patient to adopt the physician's views.

Just as it is unwise to assume that patients accept physicians' diagnoses as rendered, it is folly to assume that patients have complied with recommended treatments, no matter how important or carefully explained. Many life events intervene between the medical visit and the proposed treatment; friends and relatives advocate for alternative approaches, money for tests and medications is required for other purposes. The physician should always ask, at the subsequent visit, "Were you able to get that medication I suggested?" "How did your attempt to cut down on salt/stop smoking/get exercise go?"

It is also safe to assume that patients do not understand or fully integrate most of what they are told at a medical encounter; they are nervous, they are in a stressful environment, medical professionals use medical jargon, the diagnosis is frightening, there is just too much information to absorb. A large proportion of prescription medication, for instance, is taken incorrectly. Patients must be told that they are not expected to have grasped and remembered everything and that they should write down their questions as they come up and either call or bring them to the next appointment. Questions should be solicited at every visit.

Mental Status Examination

Mental status determination provides a baseline, especially important for the aging female population, and in situations where the patient's competence or compliance capabilities are in doubt. It provides crucial data for the diagnosis of major psychiatric and other medical conditions. Dementia and delirium are very common conditions in the general hospital, but, because patients may appear normal on brief bedside visits, they are often unrecognized until there is a crisis. Mental status changes or instability can be the first signs of septicemia or metabolic imbalance. Such changes cause the episodes in which patients pull out their IVs and other equipment and try to walk out of the intensive care unit in the middle of the night.

The mini-mental status examination is an effective, accurate, and efficient technique for determining a patient's cognitive and emotional status, including her ability to take in, process, retain, and respond to information. Questions about what the patient had for breakfast and how she interprets proverbs have proven unhelpful, allowing considerable condensation of the process. It is a good idea to perform some mental status examination at every initial visit and every day, or more often, after general anesthesia, sedation, and major surgery,[81] explaining that this is a routine part of the medical evaluation. Depression may result in false-positives; patients with dementia try to cover up their memory lapses, while depressed patients exaggerate them.

1. What is your name?
2. What is the day? Date? Month? Season? Year? (Hospitalized patients may lose track of the exact date without external cues such as newspapers.)
3. Where are you right now? Hospital? City? State?
4. What is your age? When were you born? (Ask both and look for discrepancies.)
5. Who is president of the United States? Who was president before him?
6. How many nickels are there in a dollar? Subtract 3 from 100 and continue to subtract 3 from each answer. (This is not a test for math; it is a test of concentration. It makes some patients anxious, and anxiety interferes with performance.)
7. What is this? (Show patient a watch and a pen.)
8. Please repeat: "no ifs, ands, or buts."
9. Hand the patient a piece of paper and instruct her: "Take this in your right hand, fold it in half, and set it on the table."
10. Hand the patient a card imprinted with "Close your eyes." Tell her to read it and do what it says. (Remember that a surprising number of people are illiterate or read only a language other than English.)
11. Write a sentence.
12. Copy this design (interlocking pentagons).
13. Please repeat these three items: red balloon, New York, yellow pencil. I will ask you to repeat them again in about five minutes. Then ask.[33]

Psychosocial Aspects of Medical and Obstetric/Gynecologic Conditions

The psychosocial impact of a physiologic condition or disease process cannot be predicted by laboratory values, pathology reports, or physical findings; it is mediated through its meaning to the patient, her significant others, and her society. The patient's beliefs, values, and feelings interact with the availability of human, financial, and other resources; the reactions of family members, sexual partners, and friends; and the effect on employment status.

Emotional Responses to Medical Illness

Chronic and/or severe illness is associated with an increased incidence of clinical depression.[26] Depressive symptoms must not be confused with a patient's acute response to bad news about diagnosis or prognosis, to pain, or to adverse developments in her life. Conversely, signs and symptoms of depression must not be dismissed on the grounds that they are inevitable responses to illness or life situations. Clinical depression is a disease requiring treatment, regardless of the circumstances in which it occurs, just as a broken limb demands treatment even though it is a natural consequence of an encounter between a pedestrian and a speeding truck. When clinical depression complicates or coexists with a medical illness, it causes needless suffering and interferes with motivation, compliance, and recovery.

The vegetative signs and symptoms of medical illness and treatment, such as loss of energy, appetite, and sleep, may confound the diagnosis of clinical depression. However, the diagnostic criteria of guilt, suicidality, and feelings of worthlessness are typically absent in the nondepressed medically ill. Therefore, depression can be diagnosed using the standard diagnostic criteria (elaborated in the next section). The fulfillment of diagnostic criteria predicts a positive response to antidepressant treatment.

Anxiety is the other common psychological complication of illness. Because anxiety can arise from a patient's misunderstanding of her condition and treatment, the communications described in the preceding section can be of benefit. Small adjustments in the treatment approach, based on that communication, can make a big difference to the patient. For example, she might prefer an alternative method of anesthesia, sedation before a procedure, or permission to have a trusted friend or relative remain with her during a test or treatment. Anxiety is a real and painful state. It is a constant struggle for medical professionals to recognize that the surroundings and procedures that are most familiar to them are most frightening to their patients.

Conditions related to reproduction and reproductive organs carry special emotional meanings. Given that a large proportion of pregnancies are unintended; that infertility threatens a woman's image of herself, her relationships, and her future; and that sexually transmitted diseases are rampant and increasingly dangerous; gynecologic symptoms and examinations are fraught with the likelihood of receiving unwelcome news. Perhaps that is one reason so many women fail to obtain regular gynecologic care.

Rape

Rape is both a physical and an emotional trauma. Patients whose psychological needs are not addressed following a rape are at risk for sexual dysfunction and posttraumatic stress disorder. Because rape usually leaves the victim feeling sullied and ashamed, she finds it difficult to discuss and work through. Attempts to discuss the assault with friends and relatives often provoke their anxiety, avoidance, or blame. The responses of the men in a women's life are particularly important. At worst, they may see the victim as a "slut" or as "damaged goods;" these responses are institutionalized in some societies. At best, men can help to restore her sense of goodness, safety, and sexual and romantic desirability.

Typically, a rape victim discards clothing or other items soiled in the assault, and attempts to cleanse her body by douching and bathing. Paradoxically, these responses destroy the legal evidence crucial to the conviction of the perpetrator. A victim may sacrifice a successful job and a satisfying living arrangement in order to remove herself from the places and routines that remind her of the rape or expose her to a second assult.

Avoidance of reminders, nightmares, intrusive memories, irritability, and social isolation are symptoms of posttraumatic stress. The primary care provider must inquire about these symptoms, whether or not the patient complains of emotional sequelae to the rape. When symptoms are present, counseling is advisable and effective.[25]

Primary Care Presentations of Psychosocial and Psychiatric Problems

Increasingly, patients discuss their psychological and psychiatric problems directly with their primary care provider; as more information about mental disorders is made available to the public, more patients recognize their own signs and symptoms. However, psychosocial and psychiatric problems also present under the guise of somatic complaints. Psychosocial and psychiatric problems occur in women of every class and in every situation, from the most fortunate to the most tragic. The primary care physician must be mindful of the diagnostic criteria for psychiatric disorders, and observant of the patient's appearance, behavior, and speech. Familiarity with the patient's ongoing personality style, life circumstances, and previous interactions with physicians is extremely helpful. While patients may experience adverse life events without psychiatric complications, they should be queried about changes in their sleep, appetite, concentration, mood, and level of anxiety, as well as their ability to carry on their usual domestic and employment responsibilities.

A number of psychiatric illnesses can present with somatic symptoms. Conversion disorder ("hysteria"), hypochondriasis, and somatization disorder are classic examples; but depression may present as tiredness, psychosis as somatic delusions, eating disorders as infertility, panic as palpitations and dyspnea, and domestic violence as pelvic pain. These presentations are common and underrecognized.

Psychiatric Disorders: Recognition, Diagnosis, and Management

The Diagnostic System

Contemporary psychiatry uses a system of classification and diagnosis whose validity and reliability compare favorably with those in other areas of medicine. Diagnostic categories and criteria are described in the *Diagnostic and Statistical Manual of Mental Disorders,* which is researched and published by the American Psychiatric Association. The most recent edition, the fourth, was published in 1994, and is commonly referred to as DSM-IV. The DSM-IV is compatible with the International Classification of Diseases (ICD 10), and is the official nomenclature for North America and much of the rest of the world. Its validity and reliability have been achieved by the use of observable behaviors and discrete symptoms tested in field trials, rather than imputed intrapsychic memories, motivations, and conflicts, as diagnostic criteria.[84] The DSM-IV system is far more accessible to primary care physicians than previous diagnostic systems; there is also a version published specifically for the nonpsychiatrist.

Diagnoses in DSM-IV are classified along five axes. Axis I comprises disorders having discrete episodes and exacerbations, producing signs and symptoms that are distressing to the patient. Axis II consists of personality disorders—chronic conditions that skew a patient's inner experience and view of the world, and thereby affect much of her ideas and behavior. Her behaviors tend to provoke responses that corroborate her world view. For example, a person with a dependent personality induces others to take care of her, reifying her experience of helplessness. The symptoms of the patient with a personality disorder are complaints about the world and the people in it, rather than complaints about her own state, which she experiences as a natural reaction to a problematic environment.

Axis III are the patient's nonpsychiatric medical diagnoses. Axis IV indicates the level of stressors in the patient's life, and Axis V the level of life-functioning she has achieved during the past year. As with other medical conditions, the diagnostic category of a psychiatric condition influences, but does not completely determine, a patient's ability to relate to others, fulfill family and social obligations, or care for herself. Both the stressors and the level of functioning are important therapeutic and prognostic indicators.

Definitions

DSM-IV categories and criteria are used throughout this chapter. Because some terms have different meanings in common parlance and in psychiatry, and others are specific to psychiatry, a short glossary follows.

Affect: subjective experience of emotion accompanying an idea or mental representation. The word affect is often used loosely as a generic term for feeling, emotion, or mood.

Agitation: excessive motor activity, usually non-purposeful and associated with internal tension. Examples: inability to sit still, fidgeting, pacing, wringing hands, pulling at clothing.

Ambivalence: the coexistence of contradictory emotions, attitudes, ideas, or desires with respect to a particular person, object, or situation. It suggests psychopathology only when extreme and paralyzing.

Anhedonia: inability to experience pleasure.

Anniversary Reaction: an emotional response to a previous event, occurring at the same time of year as the original event. Often the event involved a loss, and the reaction is a depressed state. The reaction can range from mild to severe and may occur on any anniversary after the event.

Anxiety: apprehension, tension, or uneasiness from anticipation of danger, the source of which is largely unknown or unrecognized, in contrast to fear, which is the emotional response to a consciously recognized and usually external threat or danger. Anxiety may be regarded as pathologic when it interferes with effectiveness in living, achievement of desired goals or satisfaction, or reasonable emotional comfort.

Behavior Therapy: a mode of treatment that focuses on modifying observable and, at least in principle, quantifiable behavior by means of systematic manipulation of the environment and behavioral variables functionally related to the behavior.

Character: the sum of a person's relatively fixed personality traits and habitual modes of response.

Compulsion: an insistent, repetitive, intrusive, and unwanted urge to perform an act that is contrary to one's ordinary wishes or standards. Failure to perform the compulsive act causes anxiety.

Conflict: a mental struggle that arises from the simultaneous operation of opposing impulses, drives, and/or environmental demands.

Conversion: a mechanism by which intrapsychic conflicts are given symbolic external expression in symptoms involving the nervous system such as pain, paralysis, or loss of sensory function.

Delusion: a false belief firmly held despite incontrovertible and obvious proof or evidence to the contrary. The belief is not one ordinarily accepted by other members of the person's culture or subculture.

Denial: a mechanism for allaying anxiety by disavowing thoughts, feelings, wishes, needs, or external reality factors that are consciously intolerable.

Dysphoria: unpleasant mood.

Empathy: insightful awareness, including the significance of the feelings, emotions, and behaviors of another person.

Euphoria: an exaggerated feeling of physical and emotional well-being.

Hallucination: a sensory perception in the absence of an actual external stimulus; this may occur in any of the senses.

Ideas of Reference: incorrect interpretation of casual incidents and external events as having direct reference to oneself.

Loosening of Associations: a disturbance of thinking in which ideas shift from one subject to another in an oblique or unrelated manner; the speaker is unaware of the disturbance.

Mood: a pervasive and sustained emotion that, in the extreme, markedly colors one's perception of the world.

Obsession: a persistent, unwanted idea or impulse that cannot be expunged by logic or reasoning.

Panic: sudden, overwhelming anxiety of such intensity that it produces terror and physiological changes.

Paranoid Ideation: suspiciousness or nondelusional, but unfounded, belief that one is being harassed, persecuted, or unfairly treated.

Personality: the characteristic way in which a person thinks, feels, and behaves; the ingrained pattern of behavior that each person evolves, both consciously and unconsciously, as the style of life or way of being in adapting to the environment.

Pressured Speech: rapid, accelerated, frenzied speech.

Psychomotor: combined physical and mental activity.

Psychosis: a major mental condition in which a person's ability to think, respond emotionally, remember, communicate, interpret reality, and behave appropriately is sufficiently impaired so as to interfere grossly with the capacity to meet the ordinary demands of life.

Secondary Gain: the external gain derived from any illness, such as personal attention and service, monetary gains, disability benefits, and release from unpleasant responsibility.

Thought Disorder: a disturbance of speech, communication, or content of thought, such as delusions, ideas of reference, or loosening of associations.

Disorders Usually First Diagnosed in Infancy, Childhood, or Adolescence

Mental Retardation

Mental retardation is characterized by the onset before age 18 of intellectual function significantly below average (Intelligence Quotient below about 70) that significantly interferes with the individual's performance in her life situation.

This chapter does not address the causes, diagnoses, or mangement of developmental disorders. It is important to note, however, that most medical care requires that a patient have the capacity to retain, process, and act upon information. The possibility that an adolescent or adult patient is retarded is often overlooked. The diagnosis of mild-to-moderate mental retardation is much more common in the school-age population than in adults, but not because the affected individuals disappear or improve. Rather, once free of the intellectual demands of the academic environment, many find a niche in the family and blend into the general population.

An undiagnosed deficit in intelligence or cognition can lead to major disruptions in the primary care process.[31] The physician is bewildered, frustrated, and angry because the patient fails to follow up on a diagnostic or therapeutic regimen that the physician assumes she understands. The highest level of education the patient has attained is a useful piece of information, although patients may inflate the level (uncommonly), may have been unable to finish school despite having normal intelligence, or may have been allowed to continue in mainstream or special classes despite serious disability.

The intelligence relevant to clinical care is that required to comprehend, agree to (or disagree with) and implement medical recommendations, and to take basic care of oneself. A practical assessment by the primary physician suffices in most cases; that is detailed, practical, and verifiable information directly relevant to the issues at hand: "How do people get pregnant?," "How do you get groceries, and what do you eat for dinner?," "What do you do if your blood sugar is 200?" The same approach applies to patients who may have dementia or other disorders that interfere with self-care or consent capacity. The needs of such patients vary according to the circumstances in which they live. The impact of mild-to-moderate intellectual deficits is largely a factor of the fit between the individual and her environment. A relatively slight degree of retardation may be a disaster in a subculture of high intellectual achievement. An easygoing society is more likely to accommodate the affected individual in roles consonant with her abilities.

The primary care physician can be of enormous help to the patient and family in accepting and adapting to her limitations, and recognizing and capitalizing on her abilities. When the impairment puts severe stress on the immediate family, female family members may need support or become patients as well. Families often have particular difficulties dealing with the menstruation and the sexuality, or sexual vulnerability, of women with intellectual deficits. Collaboration with specialists is essential.[50]

Attention Deficit/Hyperactivity Disorder

Another childhood condition that may persist into adulthood is attention deficit/hyperactivity disorder (ADHD). This disorder hampers an individual's ability to sustain attention, follow through, organize, remember, and ignore ordinary distractions. Persons with ADHD have a great deal of difficulty in school, for obvious reasons. Adult life offers more options; patients can adopt active lifestyles in which sustained attention is not necessary. For those whose disorder persists, certain situations will provoke recurrent problems.

Case Example:

A patient with placenta previa was hospitalized on bedrest, but was often noted to be up and moving about her room, precipitating episodes of bleeding. The staff repeatedly explained the dangers of ambulation for the patient and her unborn baby, but to no avail. A psychiatric consultant was called and, upon asking the relevant questions, learned that the patient had never been able to sit still in school and that she had been extremely physically active before she experienced complications of pregnancy. She genuinely desired to comply with the restriction to bedrest. Once the diagnosis of adult ADHD was made, the hospital activity therapist was enlisted to provide the patient with a variety of craft activities that could be performed in bed. There were no further difficulties. After the patient delivered, she happily incorporated her baby into her active life.

Patients with conduct disorder may also come to the clinical attention of the primary care physician. Conduct disorder is a constellation of dangerously destructive, antisocial behaviors, including sexual promiscuity. It is unlikely that a young woman with conduct disorder will comply with the recommendations of the gynecologist; this condition requires specialized management.

Many other kinds of disorders are manifest early in life, but they are beyond the scope of this chapter. Questions mothers may have about their children are best referred to the pediatrician or to a child psychiatrist. The mother's primary practitioner should be alert, when a child exhibits behaviors of concern, for signs and symptoms of stress—disturbances in sleep, appetite, concentration, mood—in the mother. The physician might ask the patient to call or to come for brief visits at short intervals so as to monitor her condition and either provide or refer for counseling if necessary.

Affective, or Mood, Disorders

The affective disorders include clinical depression and mania, which are unipolar mood disorders, and combinations of the two: manic-depression, or bipolar affective disorder. Ups and downs in affective state are normal. The universality of sad and happy experiences helps people to understand something of the experience of depression and mania. By the same token, it is difficult for those not affected to understand that depression and mania are diseases, not mere variations of affect, and are not susceptible to cheering up or calming down by the usual means. The failure of family, friends, and physicians to recognize these conditions for the diseases they are, results in avoidable emotional pain, morbidity, and mortality.

Bipolar Illness

Mania is life-threatening without treatment; patients die from exhaustion and failure to take in sufficient food. Mania is characterized by

1. Elevated, expansive, and/or irritable mood
2. Grandiose ideas and behaviors
3. Excess energy with reduced sleep
4. Pressured speech
5. Racing thoughts
6. Excessive involvement in pleasurable activities with a high risk for adverse consequences: e.g., reckless expenditures, ill-planned ventures, indiscriminate sexual intercourse

7. Distractibility
8. Increase in goal-oriented activity or psycho-motor agitation.

Unipolar mania is rare; bipolar illness is more frequent; and depression affects up to one-fifth of the population at least once in their lives.[3] Manic-depression may begin at any time from adolescence through adulthood. The episodes tend to become more frequent and more severe over time; in some patients, cycles are shortened to days or hours.

Mild hypomania can be chronic or episodic. The hypomanic individual is energetic, confident, and impatient. Although this excess vitality can be wearing on others, the hypomanic's zest is somewhat infectious, and her energy and accomplishments may be the envy of both her peers and her physicians. The hypomanic patient is, therefore, loath to "come down." This disinclination stems both from poor judgment inherent in the disease and from the enjoyable quality of the hypomanic state, often making it difficult to get the patient to seek and comply with care while in the prodromal state.[60] When an episode cannot be averted, the patient may squander her own and family assets and embarrass her family, friends, and herself with her flamboyant and inappropriate, even psychotic, behavior. The primary physician can help the family understand what is happening, as well as intervening with the patient. The treatment itself should be administered by a psychiatrist; neuroleptics, mood stabilizers, lithium, electroconvulsive treatment, and voluntary or involuntary hospitalization may be indicated.[56]

Depression

Clinical depression is two to three times more common in women than in men, from puberty onwards.[44] It has been reliably diagnosed as early as toddlerhood and throughout the remainder of the life span. Young, unmarried mothers of young children are at highest risk.[23] Marriage decreases the risk for men but increases the risk

for women.[52] The criteria for diagnosis of a major depressive episode are at least five of the following signs and symptoms, which must have been present most of the day, every day, for at least 2 weeks. One of the symptoms must be either 1 or 4.

1. Sad or irritable mood
2. Decreased energy
3. Decreased interest in one's usual activities
4. Decreased pleasure in previously pleasurable events and activities
5. Difficulty concentrating
6. Withdrawal from social relationships
7. Psychomotor retardation or agitation
8. Changes in sleep
9. Changes in appetite and weight
10. Loss of libido
11. Helplessness and hopelessness
12. Feelings of worthlessness and guilt
13. Thoughts of death and/or suicide

Typically, depression causes decreased sleep and decreased appetite. The patient is able to get to sleep, but wakens earlier than she wishes, still feeling tired. Anxiety, in contrast, makes it difficult for a patient to fall asleep. Atypical depression, more common in late adolescent women, is associated with increased sleep and food intake. The natural course of a depressive episode is approximately nine months. Each episode, especially if untreated, increases the likelihood of additional episodes.

Because of the confusion between depression as a self-limited, universal experience and depression as a disease, and the stigma associated with mental illnesses, patients and their families may resist the diagnosis. Social attitudes exacerbate the patient's suffering; if she has been socioeconomically fortunate, she and her friends and relatives will regard her sadness as unwarranted; if she has been unfortunate, she and they may consider her illness a natural response and therefore fail to recognize the need for treatment. If friends and relatives fail to offer support, the patient feels worse, but attempts to cheer her up are also problematic, because they inevitably fail. The patient must either pretend to be cheered while feeling hollow inside, or admit that her mood has not improved, which evokes accusations of ingratitude.

Depressive episodes range from very mild to very severe. Untreated severe depression often results in either suicide or death from starvation and lowered immune response. The decision whether to treat a depressed patient, to seek consultation, and/or to refer to a mental health professional depends on the interests and competence of the primary physician, the response to a trial of treatment, the availability of a psychiatrist, the need for assistance with differential diagnosis, and the preferences and condition of the patient. Suicidality and psychosis require urgent psychiatric intervention.

Two-thirds of cases of clinical depression respond to treatment with antidepressant medication and/or psychotherapy. Table 55-1 lists the available antidepressants. The choice among them is based on side effects, cost, half-life, and convenience of administration, with the newer selective serotonin reuptake inhibitors requiring only a single daily dose. Patients who tend to forget or discontinue their medications may be best treated with agents with long half-lives. There is no evidence that any agent is superior to another on the basis of therapeutic effectiveness or speed of onset of therapeutic action. Typically, the vegetative signs improve before the patient's subjective sense of depression. Therefore, it is necessary not only to ask how the patient is feeling overall, but whether she is sleeping better, eating better, and so forth. Pointing out these improvements helps the patient tolerate the wait. The goal of treatment should be complete remission, and changes of dosage or medication, or specialty referral, should be effected if response is partial. Medication should be used for at least the 9 months that the episode is likely to last. The pros and cons of longer treatment are still being debated; many psychiatrists recommend open-ended treatment after the second episode.

The psychotherapeutic modality that has been proven effective for mild-to-moderate depression is cognitive-behavioral therapy.[2] In a specified number of sessions, generally 8 to 12, the therapist helps the patient identify behaviors and thought patterns of hopelessness, helplessness, and self-reproach, and to systematically and willfully replace them with behaviors and thoughts of competence, confidence, self-acceptance, and optimism. Supportive or insight-oriented therapy is an important adjunct to pharmacotherapy. It helps the patient to understand how depression has affected her world view and behavior, how her history and circumstances affect her vulnerability to depression, how to improve her personal relationships and life situation, and how to detect recurrence so that interventions can be resumed.

Mood Disorders Limited to Women

Premenstrual Dysphoric Disorder Some premenstrual physical and emotional symptoms are reported by a majority of women in the United States. The pattern of symptoms varies from country to country. Various constellations of symptoms have been dubbed premenstrual syndrome (PMS), which has therefore become a very loosely defined entity. Similarly, a wide variety of treatment approaches have been attempted, ranging from dietary and supplemental vitamins, to exercise regimens, psychotropic medications, and hormones. Each has been anecdotally reported to be effective, and each has failed to prove effective in scientific trials.

There are several methodological difficulties in the study of premenstrual symptoms:

- Many retrospective accounts cannot be corroborated by prospective daily records.
- The lack of a consistent definition confounds comparisons of older and newer literature, and the literature in general.
- Although the concept of a premenstrual syndrome implies a hormonal etiology, women with premenstrual symptoms have no distinguishable differences in hormone levels

TABLE 55-1 Antidepressant Medication

Drug (Brand Names)	Side Effects	Comments
Tricyclics	All: Quinidine-like slowing of cardiac conduction, weight gain, impotence	Avoid in patients with heart block
Amitriptyline (Elavil)	Moderate orthostatic hypotension, sedation, anticholinergic effects	Good for patients with migraine headaches and Parkinson's diseae
Desipramine (Norpramin, Pertofrane)	Mild sedation, mild insomnia, mild orthostatic hypotension, mild anticholinergic effects	Also used in bulimia; good for patients with associated panic or anxiety
Doxepin (Sinequan)	Sedation, mild anticholinergic effects, orthostatic hypotension	Approved for use in anxiety; used for insomnia, good in patients with peptic ulcer disease and chronic diarrhea
Imipramine (Tofranil, Tofranil PM)	Moderate sedation, moderate orthostatic hypotension, moderate anticholinergic effects	Also used in bulimia; good for patients with associated panic or anxiety
(Nortriptyline (Pamelor, Aventyl)	Moderate sedation, moderate orthostatic hypotension, moderate anticholinergic effects	
Protriptyline (Vivactil)	Mild sedation, moderate insomnia, moderate anticholinergic effects, mild orthostatic hypotension	
Trimipramine (Surmontil)	Sedation, anticholinergic effects, orthostatic hypotension	
MAOIs	All: weight gain, possible impotence, delay in cardiac conduction (rare)	May be better than TCAs in atypical refractory, or bipolar depression
Isocarboxazid	Moderate orthostatic hypotension, moderate insomnia	
Phenelzine (Nardil)	Mild sedation, mild insomnia, orthostatic hypotension	Approved for OCD
Tranylcypromine (Parnate)	Moderate insomnia, mild nausea, orthostatic hypotension	Possible toxic effects; altered mental status, hyperpyrexia, hyperreflexia
Selective Serotonin Reuptake inhibitors	All: Good safety profile; may induce agitation, anxiety, sleep disturbance, tremor, sexual dysfunction, headache, altered GI motility, nausea, dry mouth, sweating, and weight change	Good for patients with panic and anxiety disorders; not potentiated by alcohol
Citalopram		
Fluoxetine (Prozac)		Good for patients with pain syndromes
		Also used in bulimia, OCD, PTSD, PMDD; good for patients with problems of aggression and anger
Fluvoxamine (Luvox)		Also used in PMDD
Paroxetine (Paxil)		Also used in PMDD and premature ejaculation
Sertraline (Zoloft)		Also used in PMDD and premature ejaculation
Other agents		
Amoxapine (Asendin)	Generally less dangerous in overdose, moderate sedation, mild anticholinergic effects, moderate orthostatic hypotension, low delay in cardiac conduction	
Bupropion (Wellbutrin)	Moderate insomnia, low delay in cardiac conduction	May be good for patients with rapid-cycling bipolar disorder. Do not use for bulimic patients
Maprotiline (Ludiomil)	Moderate sedation, mild anticholinergic effects, moderate orthostatic hypotension, delay in cardiac conduction	
Trazodone (Desyrel)	Sedation, moderate orthostatic hypotension, mild nausea, low cardiac conduction delay, priapism (rare)	

SOURCE: Adapted from Schatzberg AF, Nemeroff CB (eds): *Textbook of Psychopharmacology,* 2nd ed. Washington, DC: American Psychiatric Press, 1998.

from the general population of menstruating women.

- Premenstrual physical symptoms must be distinguished from premenstrual psychological symptoms.

It is believed that approximately 4 to 7 percent of menstruating women suffer from premenstrual dysphoric disorder (PDD). Women with prior episodes of depression are at increased risk. PDD and postpartum depression are also related.[36]

Beginning with the publication of DSM-III-R in 1987, the American Psychiatric Association has worked to differentiate a discrete mental illness from the more common PMS, in hopes of standardizing research and improving research into etiology and treatment. Because of the methodological problems mentioned above, the description of the syndrome was placed in the Appendix section of the DSM, with other entities requiring further study. In DSM-III-R, the syndrome was called *late luteal phase dysphoric disorder*. After research failed to corroborate a late luteal incidence, and the symptoms proved compatible with the depressive spectrum, the title was changed in DSM-IV to *premenstrual dysphoric disorder*. The criteria for PDD include:

The confirmation by two months of prospective daily ratings of the following signs and symptoms, occurring only premenstrually, fully remitting menstrually, and interfering markedly with domestic, educational, and/or work responsibilities, and not caused by another psychiatric disorder:

1. Irritable and/or depressed mood
2. Mood lability
3. Difficulty concentrating
4. Anxiety
5. Decreased interest in usual activities

The following is a suggested protocol for the evaluation and treatment of a woman who complains of premenstrual psychological symptoms:

1. Take a complete history, including past psychiatric history, and past sexual, physical, and psychological abuse. The patient may fail to report dysthymia or depression because of fear of stigma, or acceptance of the disorder as a fact of life. It has also been hypothesized that the premenstruum merely mobilizes feelings and behaviors appropriate to adverse circumstances, feelings, and behaviors that are suppressed during the remainder of the cycle. Inquire about the patient's life situation, stressors, and coping techniques.
2. Perform a complete physical examination.
3. Instruct the patient to chart her symptoms on a prospective, daily basis. The use of a calendar with a separate sheet for each day is preferable, so as to lessen the effect of patient expectation on her perception of her state. For the same reason, the menstrual cycle should be charted separately.
4. Suggest that the patient decrease or eliminate caffeine, nicotine, and alcohol, and establish regular exercise, sleep, and dietary habits.
5. If those measures fail to relieve symptoms, and the patient meets criteria for PDD, institute treatment with a selective serotonin reuptake inhibitor. Fluoxetine, sertraline, and paroxetine have proven effective, in the doses generally used for an episode of major depression.[87]
6. Follow the patient over time. Symptoms of abuse, personality disorder, and/or depression may become apparent only on longer acquaintance, when she feels more at ease. If another psychiatric disorder is identified, treat or refer as outlined elsewhere in this chapter.

Postpartum Psychiatric Symptoms The existence of a distinct postpartum psychiatric disorder is still a matter of dispute. The incidence of clinical depression and manic-depression does increase postpartum; diseases such as obsessive-compulsive disorder, other anxiety disorders, and psychotic illness may be relieved, exacerbated, or precipitated in the postpartum period. Early discharge of patients presents a diagnostic challenge; the exhaustion and psychological and social adjustments of the postpartum period are easy to confuse with the prodrome of a psychiatric illness.

Fifty to 80 percent of U.S. women experience a brief, self-limited period of affective lability within a few days of delivery.[72] Though crying is a very common symptom, new mothers often report that they are not so much feeling sad as an intensification of all emotions. Probably hormonal changes, physical exhaustion, and psychosocial adjustments all contribute to this phenomenon. The role of culture is less clear. "Baby blues," as the phenomenon is called, is not reported in all countries. Western perinatal care entails increasingly intense monitoring of a woman through pregnancy and delivery, with an abrupt fall-off of interest, or interest switched to the infant, at hospital discharge. This system may address biological risks, but it does not correspond with the psychological needs of the mother. During pregnancy, there are anxieties, adjustments, and discomforts, but the fetus is cared for automatically. It is only after delivery that the full weight of responsibility for round-the-clock care falls on the new mother. Traditional practices in China and Nigeria, in contrast, focus care heavily on the postpartum, rather than the antepartum period.[12] The adoption of Western obstetrical care does not obliterate long-standing cultural attitudes. Emotional disturbances following childbirth may be less common in those societies.

Frank depressive or psychotic illness may manifest gradually or suddenly within weeks of delivery. Either condition can manifest alone, or psychosis can be a symptom of severe depression. Clinically significant postpartum depression occurs after approximately 10 percent of deliveries. The affected mother is typically increasingly sleepless, agitated, and inattentive to her own nutrition and personal hygiene. She is preoccupied with fears or even delusions about the newborn. Delusions that the baby is evil or dangerous constitute a psychiatric emergency; the mother may commit infanticide. Depression alone impairs the woman's ability to feel affection for and pleasure in her new baby, and compromises her maternal confidence. Friends and relatives may make matters worse by reminding the patient how lucky she is to have a healthy child and how this period should be the happiest of her life.

Alternatively, friends, relatives, and health care providers may mistake serious psychiatric illness for the simple insecurity and exhaustion so common after birth. In either case, the patient may feel increasingly guilty and inadequate. Why can't she weather and enjoy this common human experience? Many cases of postpartum depression go tragically undiagnosed and untreated,[59] leaving the affected women with a lifelong sense of guilt, inadequacy, and loss associated with delivery.

Because postpartum stays are so short, routine telephone contact by a member of the primary care team can provide support, information, and monitoring for obstetric, pediatric, and psychiatric complications during the postpartum period. When a patient or family member reports that she is crying frequently, having difficulty eating and sleeping, feeling guilty, obsessing about the infant, and/or becoming agitated, she must be carefully followed to determine whether the signs and symptoms are abating. If they continue, worsen, and/or interfere with the patient's ability to carry out her daily responsibilities, psychiatric consultation should be obtained. Delusions and fears of harming the newborn are psychiatric emergencies. Women with past histories of postpartum psychiatric illness are at increased risk for subsequent episodes. Their pregnancies and postpartum care should be managed collaboratively with a psychiatrist.[64]

In some instances, psychotropic medication that is to be administered immediately following delivery can be prescribed ahead of time. Breastfeeding should not be ruled out automatically under these circumstances. Although no psychotropic medication has been declared completely safe for the fetus or nursing infant, increasing numbers of follow-up studies have failed to demonstrate adverse effects. The concentrations of fluoxetine and sertraline in breast milk are minimal. The unknown risks of psychotropic medication must be weighted, with the patient, against the negative psychological effects of a depressed or psychotic mother on the fetus and infant, the physiologic advantages of breast-feeding for both mother and newborn, and the psychological importance of breast-feeding to a particular mother. For a depressed mother, especially, the ability to offer her infant the advantages of mother's milk may be comforting.

Anxiety Disorders

Anxiety is defined as a feeling of dread, with the somatic manifestations of fear, in the absence of a stimulus or situation of real danger. Anxiety disorders include panic disorder, agoraphobia, specific phobias, social phobia, obsessive-compulsive disorder, posttraumatic stress disorder, acute stress disorder, generalized anxiety disorder, and anxiety secondary to a general medical condition or substance abuse.

Panic attacks occur in several anxiety disorders, and are of particular importance to the primary practitioner because they often lead patients to seek care in the emergency room, clinic, or office, convinced that they are suffering from a life-threatening cardiac or respiratory disorder. A panic attack is a discrete period of intense fear or discomfort, with the abrupt onset of four or more of the following additional symptoms:

1. Palpitations/increased heart rate/sense of pounding in the chest
2. Diaphoresis
3. Trembling
4. Shortness of breath
5. Choking feeling
6. Thoracic discomfort
7. Nausea or gastrointestinal upset
8. Dizziness/light-headedness/unsteadiness
9. Feelings of unreality
10. Fear of going crazy/losing control
11. Fear of dying
12. Paresthesias
13. Chills or hot flushes

The diagnosis of *panic disorder* requires recurrent panic attacks without a specific trigger situation, and a month or more of concern about future attacks or deleterious consequences of attacks. *Agoraphobia* is defined as anxiety about the prospect of being in a situation where symptoms of panic might occur, a situation where the patient will be unable to escape or obtain help. This anxiety must lead the patient to avoid those situations, to enlist the presence of a companion, and/or to endure the situations despite the discomfort. Panic disorder and agoraphobia can occur separately or in combination.

Specific phobias are unreasonable fears of specific objects or situations, despite the patient's recognition that there is no real danger, that elicit avoidance or discomfort that interferes with relationships and normal functioning. Phobias commonly evident in the primary care setting include fear of blood, injections, or vomiting. *Social phobia* is a chronic, severe fear of situations where the patient will encounter and be observed by others; she imagines that she will humiliate herself in some way. Although she realizes that her fears are out of proportion to the situation, she either endures social situations with considerable psychic pain, or avoids them, incurring deterioration in her functioning or relationships.

Obsessive-compulsive disorder (OCD) is characterized by obsessions—irrepressible, recurrent thoughts, impulses, or images that the patient recognizes as products of her own mind but cannot control. These may occur with compulsions—pointless, repetitive behaviors that a patient feels driven to perform in order to forestall some dreaded event with which they have no reasonable relationship and that significantly intrude upon her life. The disorder can be utterly disabling, with the patient spending nearly all her waking hours in various compulsive rituals. The disease becomes chronic in over half the patients. The condition seems to be related to dysregulation of serotonin in the brain. Both behavioral and psychopharmacologic approaches—clomipramine, fluvoxamine, sertraline, and fluoxetine—have proven effective.

Posttraumatic stress disorder (PTSD) is precipitated by a traumatic event that confronts the individual with actual or threatened death or serious injury to herself or others, resulting in terror, horror, and a sense of helplessness at the time of the event. Symptoms include flashbacks in which the event seems to be reoccuring, upsetting dreams, intrusive thoughts, and subjective distress or physiological reactivity in response to reminders of the event. She may be unable to remember some aspects of the trauma. She is hyperarousable, with irritability, difficulty concentrating, and/or sleep disturbance. The clinician should be alert for this disorder in victims of domestic and nondomestic violence, natural disasters, war, and criminal attacks. *Acute stress disorder* is a briefer, less chronic form of PTSD.

Generalized anxiety disorder is characterized by chronic, irrational, excessive nervousness or worry not caused by any other psychiatric or medical disorder, and causing significant distress or loss of function. Associated with the anxiety are three or more of the following: restlessness, fatigability, difficulty concentrating, irritability, muscle tension, or sleep disturbance. Benzodiazepines are effective, but potentially addictive. Buspirone is a different type of agent, used chronically, but reports of its efficacy are contradictory.

Anxiety is a universal human experience, particularly prevalent among the population of patients seeking medical care. Benzodiazepines are effective anxiolytics. However, these medications are among the most commonly prescribed drugs in the United States, raising concern that they are used too often as a first or only approach.[11] When a patient is in some sort of psychological distress, the primary care physician often feels helpless but compelled to provide some sort of relief. A prescription for a benzodiazepine is sometimes used as a way to provide some tangible intervention, and to end the medical encounter. Some primary care physicians tend to undervalue the power of their listening, talking, and caring. If medication is prescribed at the first appointment, the physician never has the opportunity to observe the impact of the doctor-patient interaction on the patient's anxiety, and fosters the patient's belief that medication is the answer to all problems. On the other hand, some physicians are reluctant to prescribe any psychotropic medication, urging patients to endure psychic discomfort whatever the circumstances. Anxiety should be inquired after like any other symptom:

When did it begin?
Under what circumstances?
What is the patient anxious about?
Is the anxiety getting better or worse?
What brings it on or alleviates it?
How is it affecting the patient's life?

Anxious patients often have misconceptions about their symptoms, diagnoses, or treatment—misconceptions that can readily be allayed with accurate information. A patient may understand congestive heart failure to mean that she is in the throes of cardiac arrest. She may hear that she has a mass and conclude that she has terminal cancer. She may have a morbid fear of needles, in a situation where an alternate approach—an oral sedative preceding surgery—could be used. Reassessment several hours or days after such a discussion often reveals a considerable reduction in anxiety. Antianxiety agents are a second-line approach; useful medications are listed in Table 55-2.

Panic disorder, agoraphobia, obsessive-compulsive disorder, generalized anxiety disorder, PTSD, and specific phobias have been treated successfully both with behavioral psychotherapy and with antianxiety and antidepressant medications. Any of these diseases can be utterly crippling for a patient and tremendously disruptive to her family. Because the treatments are specialized, and because new approaches are rapidly evolving, it is best to consult with, or refer the

TABLE 55-2 Compounds Used for Anxiety

Medication	Trade Name	Rate of Absorption	Half-Life	Active Long-Acting Metabolite	Comments
Benzodiazepines:	The first-line of treatment for patients with generalized anxiety disorder				Metabolism is inhibited by cimetidine, disulfiram, isoniazid, and oral contraceptives resulting in enhanced effects. Benzodiazepine effects are reduced by antacids, tobacco, and rifampin.
Alprazolam	Xanax	Intermediate	Intermediate	No	Preferred in older adults or patients with poor hepatic function.
Chlordiazepoxide	Librium, others	Intermediate	Intermediate	Yes	
Clonazepam	Klonopin	Intermediate	Long	No	
Chlorazepate	Tranxene, others	Intermediate	Short	Yes	
Diazepam	Valium, others	Short	Long	Yes	Half-life increased three or four times in elderly patients
Halazepam	Paxipam		Short	Yes	Preferred in older adults or patients with poor hepatic function.
Lorazepam	Ativan, others	Short	Intermediate	No	Preferred in older adults or patients with poor hepatic function.
Oxazepam	Serax	Short-Intermediate	Intermediate	No	
Prazepam	Centrax	Long	Short	Yes	
Atypical					
Buspirone	BuSpar	Long	Short	Yes	Azaperones have been found to have few side effects and are at little risk of dependence/tolerance.
Selective Serotonin Reuptake Inhibitors: The drug of choice in panic disorder with demonstrated anxiolytic effectiveness.					
Citalopram		Short	Long	No	
Fluoxetine	Prozac	Intermediate	Long	No	
Fluvoxamine	Luvox	Intermediate	Intermediate	Yes	
Paroxetine	Paxil	Long	Long	No	
Sertraline	Zoloft	Long	Long	Yes	
Miscellaneous					
Trazodone	Desyrel, Trazon, Trialodine	Short	Short	Yes	Side effects may include sedation and orthostatic hypotension.
Tricyclic Antidepressants: Proven useful anxiolytics, their side effect profile makes them less useful than the above listed agents.					
Clomipramine	Anafranil	Intermediate	Long	Yes	These four TCA agents' side effects may include: blurred vision, dry mouth, sinus tachycardia, constipation, urinary retention, cognitive dysfunction, postural hypotension, dizziness, drowsiness, reflex tachycardia, sedation, weight gain.
Desipramine	Norpramin	Intermediate	Intermediate	Yes	
Doxepin	Sinequan, Zonalon	Intermediate	Intermediate	Yes	
Imipramine	Tipramine, Tofranil	Intermediate	Intermediate	Yes	
Monoamine Oxidase Inhibitor: These drugs are used only in treatment-resistant patients due to the high risk-benefit ratio.					

SOURCE: Adapted from Schatzberg AF, Nemeroff CB (eds): *Textbook of Psychopharmacology,* 2nd ed. Washington, DC: American Psychiatric Press, 1998.

patient to, a psychiatrist, preferably one who specializes in anxiety disorders. Many academic departments offer clinics and new research protocols for the treatment of these illnesses. The primary practitioner plays a crucial role in coordinating the patient's psychiatric care with other aspects of her health care, and in providing explanations and support to her and to her family.

Psychotic Illnesses

Psychotic illnesses include schizophrenia, paranoia, brief reactive psychoses, and psychotic symptoms secondary to other systemic and/or central nervous system diseases. Despite immense strides in the understanding and treatment of psychoses, these conditions continue to carry terrible stigma. Because insurance coverage and social support systems are inadequate and easily exhausted, psychotic illness can readily reduce a patient from any background to penury and homelessness. Psychosis often coexists with significant general medical and gynecological conditions, increasing both the need for care and the difficulty patients have in accessing social and medical services. As public psychiatric systems shrink,[83] more of these patients commit such crimes as sleeping in cars they find open or stealing food, and find themselves in the rapidly growing prison population.

Although psychotic illness is the most florid psychiatric condition, and the one most caricatured in folklore and the arts, it can be overlooked in the hurried and focused atmosphere of the primary care setting. Open-ended questions are quite effective and efficient in eliciting psychotic signs and symptoms.

One percent of the worldwide population suffers from *schizophrenia*. The sexes are approximately equally affected, although women tend to have later onset (averaging in the early 20s) and somewhat milder cases. Both deinstitutionalization and increasingly effective psychiatric care have resulted in increased numbers of individuals with schizophrenia in primary care settings. Derived from the Greek for "split mind," *schizophrenia* originally referred to the patient's emotional distance from his or her own behaviors and to the preservation of cognitive functions such as orientation and memory despite the intrusion of hallucinations and delusions. "Schizoprenic" is widely and incorrectly used as a synonym for ambivalence; it does not mean being of two minds about something.

The etiology of schizophrenia is both genetic and environmental; there is a genetic substrate and environmental precipitants.[55] Because onset is nearly always in the teens or 20s, first-onset psychosis at a later age should prompt immediate investigation into possible systemic and/or central nervous system etiologies. Some individuals with schizophrenia appear to have been perfectly normal in childhood and early adolescence, while others, in retrospect, were socially distant and "odd." Onset may be insidious, with gradual withdrawal from social contacts, deterioration in functioning, neglect of personal hygiene, and increasingly bizarre ideas and behavior. Sometimes onset is more abrupt; frantic parents may call the primary care physician because their child is psychotic and out of control. In these situations, acute reactions to substances of abuse must be considered in the differential diagnosis.

The diagnostic criteria for schizophrenia include so-called positive symptoms of delusions, hallucinations, disorganized speech or behavior, and negative symptoms of affective flattening and diminished speech, volition, and activity. These symptoms must have persisted for at least six months, and must have markedly affected the patient's social and/or occupational functioning. They must not be the result of a mood, substance use, or other medical disorder. There are many subcategories and degrees of severity of schizophrenia. Many patients, with proper care, can live in the community and support and care for themselves and for their families. The primary care physician can assume responsibility for the care of such patients, in collaboration with a psychiatrist. Schizophrenia in and of itself is not grounds to deny a patient care, or the right to make decisions about her care.

Paranoid is another term that is often misused to connote simple suspiciousness or appropriate fear. Genuine paranoia consists of the conviction, in the absence of logical evidence, that others are consciously and purposely inflicting, or plotting to inflict, harm upon oneself. Paranoid patients may present in primary care settings with seemingly rational complaints about past medical care, or with somatic symptoms for which, upon questioning, they blame conspirators in the home, neighborhood, workplace, or major institution (e.g., the Federal Bureau of Investigation). Because family members, employers, coworkers, and neighbors can and do harass, torment, and injure people at times, and because such treatment can result in directly or psychologically mediated physical symptoms, such complaints must not be discounted out of hand. The paranoid patient is more likely than the abused patient to volunteer her story, to tell it repeatedly and insistently, and to attribute all her troubles to mistreatment by others. When the patient's beliefs do not reach the level of psychosis, but are chronic and pervasive, the diagnosis may be paranoid personality disorder.

Schizoaffective disorder combines signs and symptoms of schizophrenia with those of a depressive or manic condition. A *brief psychotic disorder* is defined as psychotic symptoms and *delusional disorders* lasting at least one full day but not fulfilling criteria for schizophrenia. Patients with delusional disorders frequently present in primary care settings. They have nonbizarre delusions, that is, delusions that could be true: having been deceived in love, having a disease, emanating a bad odor, having the love of a famous figure. Aside from the direct effects of these unfounded beliefs, the patient's functioning does not deteriorate. The primary care physician need neither attempt to disprove the delusion nor pretend to believe it. The dialogue can center, rather, on the patient's distress about the delusion. High-potency neuroleptics such as trifluoperazine and haloperidol may be helpful.

Somatoform Disorders

Patients with somatoform disorders experience and manifest psychological distress in the form of somatic pains, dysfunctions, and disabilities rather than in disturbances of thought, feeling, or behavior. The substitution is completely unconscious; that is, the patient does not con-

sciously create, mimic, or manipulate physical signs of illness. In some cultures, nearly all nonpsychotic psychiatric problems present somatically. Somatoform disorders comprise somatization disorder, conversion disorder, and undifferentiated somatoform disorder.

Somatization Disorder

Somatization disorder is much more common in women than in men, whether for cultural reasons or because of bias in diagnosticians. Onset is before the age of 30, extending over several years, with many physical complaints, resulting in repeated health care-seeking and/or impairment of life functioning. Either the symptoms cannot be explained by a diagnosable medical condition or the complaints and impairment exceed what seem to be justified by objective findings. Sometime during the course of the disorder, the patient will have manifested each of the following:

- Pain related to 4 different anatomical sites or physiologic functions
- Two gastrointestinal symptoms
- One sexual or reproductive symptom
- One pseudoneurological symptom or deficit other than pain.

The precise incidence of somatization disorder is not known, because the patients tend to visit many physicians, each of whom may not be aware of the full spectrum of complaints and treatments. The patients' own perceptions are that they are the unfortunate victims of general sickliness and/or a host of physical illnesses, which their physicians are not always able to diagnose and treat effectively. Although they do not hide their history, their preoccupation with a current complaint may overshadow it; careful inquiries about the criteria listed above must be made. An abdomen criss-crossed with surgical scars is an ominous sign, and one that should give major pause to the clinician contemplating an operative procedure for a subjective complaint.

Unfortunately, the diagnosis of a somatoform disorder can never rule out the possibility of a somatic disorder requiring medical intervention. However, invasive procedures and potent medications should be considered with caution. Neither is it effective to insist that the symptoms are baseless. This is a chronic illness, manageable but not curable. The best approach is to sympathize with the patient about her symptoms (remembering that all symptoms are subjective by definition), minimize complex diagnostic and therapeutic interventions, acknowledge that it is unlikely that the symptoms can be entirely eliminated, and suggest health-promoting behaviors such as good diet and exercise (spelled out in detail for these patients). Rather than attempting to avoid seeing these patients, thereby increasing their neediness and desperation, it is best to schedule frequent, brief, supportive visits in advance. At these visits, the patient should be encouraged and applauded for carrying on with her life despite her symptoms.

Conversion Disorder

Conversion disorder was traditionally known as hysteria. It consists of loss of function or other symptoms related to the senses or voluntary motor system, symptoms not caused by diagnosable medical illness, not deliberately produced by the patient, and related to psychological conflicts or stress. Conversion disorder occurs more frequently in women than in men, often in less socially and psychologically sophisticated patients.[34] The psychological etiology may be complex or relatively transparent. Medical illness must be carefully ruled out; patients with disorders such as multiple sclerosis are often dismissed as hysterical when the early symptoms appear. The prognosis for conversion disorder is directly related to the length of time that the symptom has been present. In an acute situation, a single interview with an expert can often reveal the source of the problem and alleviate the symptom. *Pain disorder* is a related condition in which pain with a significant psychological etiology disrupts the patient's life and brings her to medical attention.

The medical staff is often tempted to trick a patient with an obvious conversion disorder into revealing the normality of the affected body part. Superficially, such maneuvers can be effective. For example, the patient with a conversion paraplegia will manage to ambulate if someone yells "Fire!" However, this duplicity backfires; the source of the patient's distress is not illuminated, the patient is humiliated, and the doctor-patient relationship is undermined. It is preferable to design a face-saving, step-wise course of treatment. For example, the dysphagic patient may be prescribed a dietary regimen, beginning with liquids and progressing incrementally to pureed foods, soft foods, and finally a regular diet. The paralyzed patient can progress from wheelchair to crutches to cane. The family should be instructed to facilitate the course of treatment, but to avoid structuring their lives around the patient's illness.

Hypochondriasis

Hypochondriasis is often confused with somatization disorder. The hypochondriacal patient's preoccupation, however, is not with her physical symptoms per se, but with a nondelusional fear or conviction that she has a serious disease, despite all reassurance. She overinterprets normal bodily sensations as omens of medical disaster. Treatment, as with somatization, is aimed at restoring function rather than eliminating symptoms.

Body Dysmorphic Disorder

A patient with *body dysmorphic disorder* is preoccupied with an imagined or trivial defect in appearance. When there is any reason at all to suspect this diagnosis, a patient should be referred for psychiatric evaluation before undergoing cosmetic surgery; she will not be satisfied with the result of the cosmetic surgery.

Factitious Disorders

This is a complex and mysterious group of disorders in which the patient actively causes or consciously feigns real somatic damage. Often these disorders are loosely ascribed to patients' enjoyment of the invalid role.[84] Everyone wants attention, care, and freedom from onerous responsibilities, but it is only these patients who are willing to harm and hospitalize themselves to obtain them. These patients are extraordinarily adept at producing medical histories and physical findings that guarantee them admission to the hospital. They willingly submit to painful and dangerous diagnostic and therapeutic procedures. They may, however, resist psychiatric examination; few of them have been studied in depth. Patients with factitious disorders may be very appealing to medical staff, mobilizing whole units to worry about them. When the true diagnosis is suspected, staff are conflicted and enraged. Though it is not ethical to do so, they often get the patient out of her hospital room on a pretext and search it in her absence, finding the medical equipment or medications she has used to cause her signs and symptoms. When confronted, she leaves the hospital abruptly, only to take her story to another facility. Persons who deliberately feign illness to gain specific ends that would be desired by any reasonable person, such as release from prison or military service, are *malingerers*.

Disorders of Cognition

Delirium

Delirium consists of deficits in orientation and in the ability to initiate and sustain attention, with changes in memory, language, and/or perception, developing over hours to days, fluctuating during the course of the day, and not due to a preexisting dementia. Delirium is caused by a general medical condition that interferes with brain function or by the use of a legal or illegal mind-altering drug. In the context of an acute care environ-

ment, the onset of delirium may be unnoticed. Because a delirious patient may superficially appear lucid and may make seemingly appropriate responses to brief interchanges in the hospital, regular, formal, mini-mental status examinations must be performed on patients at risk. Changes in mental status may be the crucial first signs of toxic and pathological metabolic states.

Dementia

Dementia is defined as multiple, nonfluctuating cognitive deficits, including memory (registration and recall), aphasia, apraxia, agnosia, or disturbances in organization or abstraction. Alzheimer's disease has an insidious, gradual onset, and a progressive course. Vascular dementia is associated with focal neurological signs and symptoms. Dementia can also be caused by a wide variety of general medical and central nervous system diseases and by prolonged alcohol or substance abuse.

Because women live longer, on average, than men, and are more likely to provide direct care for dependent family members, women are doubly affected by dementia.[46] Patients seen in primary care settings may be suffering from a dementia and/or caring for someone else with dementia. Caring for a cognitively impaired spouse is a grinding, draining task. Most such caregivers suffer clinically significant depression. The primary physician can help the patient and family locate resources. It is crucial to monitor the caregiver's physical and psychological state, and to encourage her strongly to find help and take some time to recuperate.

Dementia leads to difficult decisions: when to respect a patient's autonomy, and when to override decisions she is not competent to make. In these situations, the primary practitioner can draw on previous knowledge about a patient's baseline level of functioning, social supports, philosophy of life, and previously expressed wishes. Patients in the earlier stages of dementia are often terrified and humiliated by their loss of memory and other cognitive lapses, and make great efforts to hide or compensate for them. Again, formal assessment of cognition must be performed. What is particularly important is the patient's ability to keep herself safe, fed, clothed, and housed. The physician may have to decide to contact family members, even over the patient's objections.

Eating Disorders

Most women in our society are preoccupied with slenderness; most are unhappy with their body habitus; and most make constant or repeated efforts to restrict their food intake. Physicians may unwittingly reinforce this preoccupation by praising slim patients and scolding heavier ones. Unfortunately, while physicians have a responsibility to educate patients about good nutrition and about the health effects of being overweight, there is little evidence that physician advice, or any other approach for that matter, can effect lasting weight loss in most overweight patients.

Eating disorders involve other signs and symptoms in addition to changes in eating habits. The syndrome of *anorexia nervosa* includes misperception of one's own bodily state, an intense fear of becoming fat, amenorrhea, excessive and compulsive exercise, the use of body size as an indicator of self-worth, and refusal to acknowledge or address dangerously low body mass. Weight loss may be achieved by food restriction and/or by purging with laxatives or inducing vomiting after eating. Most patients with *bulimia nervosa* have approximately normal weights. The disorder is characterized by episodes in which the patient feels out of control of her eating. She eats inordinate amounts of food during discrete binges, and then compensates by fasting, excessive exercise, vomiting, and/or using diuretics or laxatives. She also measures her self-esteem, chronically low, by her weight.

Overeating is an eating disorder that is often overlooked, even though obesity is a major, and growing, public health problem. Obese patients, unlike those with the other eating disorders, are ostracized. They are often the butt of jokes, and they are discriminated against in all kinds of situations. While underweight patients are viewed as victims of illness, overweight patients are considered infantile and self-indulgent. Unless the patient's weight puts her at medical risk, the best approach may be to ask her how she feels about her weight, to assure her that she will not be lectured about it, and to let her know that advice is available if and when she wants to address the problem. Overweight patients are already ashamed of themselves; the perception that the physician is judgmental may stop the patient from keeping important medical appointments. Morbid obesity is, of course, medically urgent, and must be addressed, although some patients deteriorate psychologically after weight reduction accomplished by medical intervention.[41]

Eating disorders may present directly or indirectly in primary care. Anorexic patients may present to gynecologists complaining of amenorrhea or infertility, without recognizing the connection between their eating disorder and their gynecological symptoms. Dentists and physicians who examine the oral cavity can make a presumptive diagnosis of recurrent self-induced vomiting on the basis of the characteristic pattern of dental enamel erosion. Anorexia (and, to a lesser degree, bulimia) can cause grave metabolic disturbances, and are often associated with serious psychiatric conditions such as clinical depression. Anorexia is still associated with significant mortality. These conditions are best treated by a team of primary physician and psychiatrist.

Substance Use Disorders

The psychiatric diagnostic system includes syndromes associated with the use of alcohol, amphetamines, caffeine, cannabis, cocaine, hallucinogens, inhalants, nicotine, opioids, phencyclidine, sedative/hypnotic/anxiolytics, and polysubstances. The primary practitioner responsible for triage in an emergency room or a similar setting has to be familiar with the signs of acute intoxication and withdrawal from each of these agents. For office and inpatient primary practice, critical issues include education and prevention, alertness to the possibility of substance use and abuse in every single patient, and awareness of the association between substance use and other psychiatric and medical disorders. Questions must be specific and weighted so as to maximize the likelihood of a positive response:

What alcoholic beverages/cigarettes/prescription medications/other drugs do you use?
How often?
How much?
Do you use it to the point of intoxication?
Do you experience withdrawal symptoms when you do not use this substance?
Does the use of the substance cause concern or friction with your significant others?
Has there been a time when you could not remember afterwards what happened while you were using the substance?

The categories of substance-related disorders are: substance dependence, substance abuse, substance intoxication, and substance withdrawal. The diagnosis and treatment of substance abuse disorders in women is complicated by social attitudes that stigmatize women, as compared with men, who abuse substances. There is an assumption that the consumption of substances by women is associated with promiscuous sexual behavior.[63] Substance use puts women at greater risk for sexual victimization; when sexual assaults occur, the male perpetrator who is intoxicated may be viewed as less culpable, while an intoxicated female victim is seen as guiltier.[16] Women addicts may resort to prostitution rather than to more violent criminal activity to obtain drugs. Women in relationships with substance-abusing men are often pressured to join their partners in substance use, and often suffer a host of medical, psychiatric, and social consequences, regardless of socioeconomic class.

Given a dose of alcohol standardized for body weight, women's blood alcohol levels are higher than men's. Social custom dictates that women consume less alcohol than men, but alcohol intake, especially among younger women, has been rising steadily. There are strong associations between substance abuse and low self-esteem, depression, and a history of victimization. Because women are more likely to be prescribed sedatives and minor tranquilizers, they are at risk for overlapping dependencies and addictions.

Sleep Disorders

Both general medical conditions and psychiatric illnesses are frequently associated with sleep disturbances. Primary sleep disturbances include insomnia, hypersomnia, narcolepsy (irresistible attacks of sleep, with brief episodes of sudden loss of muscle tone), breathing-related sleep disorder (sleep apnea), and disorders of circadian rhythm, which may be spontaneous or secondary to changes in time zone or work schedule. Chronic, serious sleep disorders can be evaluated with sleeping electroencephalograms and other parameters in a sleep laboratory. Short-term sleep disturbances are best approached with "sleep hygiene." Many patients do not realize that their lifestyles are causing their sleep problems. Sleep hygiene includes:

- Decrease or cessation of caffeine intake
- Regular exercise—although not immediately before bedtime
- Nutritious diet, with regular meals, and no heavy foods before bedtime
- A regular regimen of calming activities in the hour before bedtime: warm (not hot) bath, low-key reading material, soft music, routine television programs
- Regular bedtime
- Removal of anxiety-producing items (bills, work) from the bedside

Hypnotic agents can be useful in the short term, after a traumatic experience, or to break the wakefulness cycle. However, there is some question as to whether they continue to be useful. Patients tend to become psychologically and physiologically dependent on them.[9]

Impulse Disorders

This is a group of conditions in which the patient experiences increasing tension which is relieved abruptly by the performance of a behavior dangerous to herself or others. Impulse disorders include intermittent explosive disorder (outbursts of aggression without reasonable precipitants), kleptomania (stealing), pyromania (fire-setting), pathologic gambling, and trichotillomania (pulling out one's hair). These diagnoses may be made by a primary physician in whom the patient confides, or after apprehension by the police. These conditions are not treated by primary physicians. The existence of a diagnosable psychiatric disorder does not exonerate the patient from legal culpability.

Adjustment Disorders and Grief Reactions

Adjustment disorders are very common in primary care. An adjustment disorder occurs in response to a specific stress, begins within three months after the stress, and ceases spontaneously within six months after the stress ends. The stress leads to depressed mood, anxiety, behavioral disturbances, or any combination, that causes the patient distress and/or interferes with her functioning. The symptoms must not be the result of any other psychiatric disorder or of uncomplicated bereavement. Adjustment disorders can be treated with brief outpatient psychotherapy, augmented with psychotropic medications if necessary.

Bereavement causes signs and symptoms much like those of a psychiatric disorder: disturbances in sleep and eating, loss of interest and pleasure in usual activities and relationships, and preoccupation with the person who has died. Grief reactions after the death of a close loved one can

normally last a year or more. The stages of grief—denial, anger, bargaining, and acceptance—need not occur, nor occur in a particular order. Grief may recur on anniversaries of the death or of special occasions with the loved one. However, if a patient does not begin to feel better after six months, and is unable to go on with her life, even with some sadness, counseling, and evaluation for clinical depression, are indicated. A protracted grief reaction that does not respond to office counseling requires psychiatric consultation.

Personality Disorders

Personality disorders are persistent, problematic, pervasive disturbances in a patient's perception of, relation to, and reactions to, the world. The patient sees her problems as originating outside herself; in a world of people who are unreliable, hostile, dismissive, and all-powerful. She experiences herself as helpless, justifiably outraged, all-important, and/or unworthy. Unfortunately, the behaviors she exhibits in response to her perceptions often confirm her perceptions. For example, a person who fears abandonment will cling desperately to others, causing them to avoid her.

Personality disorders are organized into clusters. Very often patients manifest signs and symptoms from more than one diagnostic entity in the cluster.

Cluster A: The patient with *schizoid personality disorder* appears detached, with little interest in activities, relationships, and the opinions of others; the *schizotypal personality disorder* causes cognitive distortions and eccentric behaviors as well. Patients with *paranoid personality disorder* perceive others as exploitive and abusive. Patients are unable to confide in, trust, or forgive others.

Cluster B: *Antisocial personality disorder* begins before age 15; patients lack respect for the rights and feelings of others, and engage in illegal activities, aggressiveness, irresponsibility, lying, and lack of remorse. *Borderline personality disor-*

der is perhaps the single greatest challenge for the clinician, causing unstable relationships, affects, self-image, and self-control. Patients with borderline personality disorder have intense and unstable feelings about other people; at a given time, they see some people as benign and others as malignant, but attitudes can alternate without notice. This can wreak havoc in a medical setting with several providers (doctors, nurses, aides, etc.). These patients are recurrently self-destructive. Their anger is frequent, intense, and inappropriate—although they feel it is entirely justified. They feel empty, and, terrified of abandonment, they make frantic attempts to maintain contact. Under stress, they may experience transient paranoid ideation or feelings of unreality. *Histrionic personality disorder* causes a person to want to be the center of attention, using, to achieve this, his/her physical appearance, theatricality, shallow emotional displays, and provocative behavior. She exaggerates the intimacy of her relationships and is highly suggestible. *Narcissistic personality disorder* is associated with grandiosity and grandiose fantasies, a sense of uniqueness and entitlement to special treatment, envy and exploitation of others, arrogance, and lack of empathy.

Cluster C: The patient with *avoidant personality disorder* feels inferior and inept; she avoids situations and relationships in which she might be unsuccessful, ashamed, disliked, or criticized. *Dependent personality disorder* results in submissiveness and an excessive need to be taken care of. The patient relies on others for decisions, opinions, and to initiate activities. Fearful of being alone, she clings to others and seeks immediate replacements when a relationship ends. *Obsessive-compulsive personality disorder* is characterized by preoccupation with details, routine, and perfection. These individuals have trouble parting with possessions and money, and are inflexible in routines and beliefs. They do not delegate readily, and tend to devote themselves exclusively and unnecessarily to work activities, to the exclusion of relationships and relaxation.

Patients with personality disorders arouse strong feelings in care providers. Generally, such patients arouse feelings that mirror their own. The angry patient makes others angry; the depressed patient, depressed; the victim, victimized. Only the sociopathic patient is consciously manipulative; patients with the other disorders are genuinely in psychic pain. The clinician must be on guard to notice his or her own reactions and not to overreact, either by getting angry, avoiding the patient, or acceding to untoward requests, but rather to determine what can reasonably and ethically be offered to the patient and to maintain a steady emotional posture despite the patient's emotional demands. This is best for the patient and for the physician. It is extremely helpful to inquire about the patient's past experiences with physicians. Because these disorders are chronic and pervasive, these experiences are likely to repeat themselves. If the patient extols the virtues of the current physician, in contrast to the terrible failings of previous physicians, the current physician had better expect to be found wanting as well. It is often useful to consult or collaborate, to form a team caring for the patient, in order to obtain corroboration, support, and relief. Well-motivated patients can improve markedly in long-term psychotherapy with an experienced mental health professional.

Sexual and Gender Identity Disorders

It is very difficult to characterize a "normal" level of sexual interest or activity for a gender, situation, or stage of life. At best, we may have an idea of the reported average in a given subculture. For example, women may have been expected in the past to lose sexual desire at menopause, whether or not that was true for a given woman. Now a lack of sexual desire is seen by some as pathological, necessitating hormonal intervention. There are no sexual equivalents to nutritional requirements. One can live without conscious sexual feelings or behavior, or with unfulfilled sexual interests and desires, but not without ingesting food. On the one hand, sexual activity may be extremely difficult to suppress, even under the most adverse circumstances; on the other, sexual feelings and activity are very susceptible to psychological conflicts and social context.

However defined, sexual dysfunction is very common. However, some patients are embarrassed to bring sexual complaints to the primary physician, and some physicians are uncomfortable in assessing and treating them. Inadequate training leaves practitioners drawing more on their own values and experiences than on scientific expertise. Sexual functions in every culture are subject to regulations and taboos. Almost all of the rules apply more stringently to women; it is women who are blamed or even ostracized for being immodestly dressed if sexually attacked; women are held responsible not only for their own, but for men's sexual behavior. The so-called sexual revolution in the United States was associated with some changes in sexual rules and behaviors, but traditional attitudes persist.

Most women are uninformed and uncomfortable about their own genital anatomy. Few women can draw an accurate diagram of the external and internal genitalia, and many have major misconceptions about the mechanisms of menstruation and reproduction. Women often lack the vocabulary to think about and describe sexual concerns, and they have sometimes well-founded fears that their sexual behavior will elicit negative reactions from a physician. It is useful to install a mirror over the examining table and to name anatomical parts aloud as a routine during the gynecologic examination. The patient learns the proper terms without having to reveal her ignorance, and also learns something about the way each body part feels as it is examined. Reducing patients' discomfort with their bodies facilitates the proper use of devices and medications that require insertion by the patient.

The Sexual History

One basic approach to the sexual history is to ask open-ended questions. If the physician is not prepared to ask the necessary questions and to listen nonjudgmentally to a sometimes astonishing array of answers, it may be preferable to refer the patient to a colleague or a specialist in sexual dysfunction. Some physicians fear that inquiries about socially proscribed sexual behaviors will insult and alienate patients, but this is rarely, if ever, the case. A woman who has never masturbated or never engaged in homosexual activity has only to say so. It is particularly important to inquire about sexual abuse and assault. Patients understand that physicians ask a wide range of questions. The physician's questions open subjects that the patient may not be ready to talk about at the given visit, but will be able to bring up at a future visit. Moreover, there is absolutely no other way to get the necessary information.

The Sexual Complaint

The history must include each stage of sexual function: sexual interest, arousal (lubrication), and orgasm. It is important to know under what precise circumstances the problem was first noted and under what circumstances it occurs now. Is the problem lifelong (primary) or of later onset (secondary)? What is the nature of her relationship with the partner, if any, with whom the problems occur? If she has ever had a satisfactory experience, what was it, and how did it come about? What techniques do the sexual partners use, and under what circumstances does sexual activity occur? What approaches to address the problem has the patient already tried? What is her opinion about the cause of the problem, and the appropriate treatment? How does she expect the physician to proceed? The physician need not fulfill the patient's expectations, but must address them.

It is surprising how often the responses to these questions will not only clarify, but even solve, the problem. Patients can be oblivious to the fact that a sexual dysfunction happens with a spouse but not with a lover; or that it began after a difficult birth, with the patient terrified she might conceive again; or that there is no foreplay before intercourse; or that the patient has entirely unrealistic expectations for her sexual performance. Some women are so exhausted by their responsibilities that they fall asleep the moment they go to bed. Many sexual problems can first, and successfully, be addressed with education.

Diagnostic Categories

Sexual dysfunction can be classified as to whether it is due to psychological factors, whether it is lifelong or acquired, and whether it occurs in all situations or only particular ones. Disorders correspond to stages: disorders of desire, arousal, and orgasm. There are also sexual pain disorders and sexual dysfunctions secondary to a general medical condition or substance use (either intoxication or withdrawal). The psychiatric diagnosis of a sexual disorder requires that the condition cause marked distress or interpersonal difficulty for the patient and that the dysfunction not be simply secondary to another psychiatric disorder, such as depression, or medical disorder.

Disorders of sexual desire include hypoactive desire and active aversion to genital contact with a partner. Female sexual arousal disorder is a condition in which the patient does not lubricate and become aroused despite sexual interest and desire. Orgasmic disorders are characterized by the inability to reach orgasm despite normal sexual excitement. There is wide variation among human beings in the amount of sexual stimulation required for desire, arousal, and orgasm. Responses also depend on the circumstances: mood, distractions, energy level, previous experience, age, and privacy. Sexual pain disorders include dyspareunia, or pericoital pain, and vaginismus, involuntary spasm of vaginal musculature preventing intromission.

Medical Causes of Sexual Dysfunction

Poor general health and specific conditions such as anemia, diabetes, and thyroid abnormalities, affect sexual function both directly, through innervation and hormonal changes, and indirectly,

TABLE 55-3 Medications That Cause Sexual Dysfunction

Loss of libido (decreased responsiveness and interest)
  Adrenal steroids
  Alcohol
  Analgesics (narcotics)
  Antiandrogens
  Hallucinogens (chronic use)
  MAOIs
  Risperidone
  Sedative-hypnotics (e.g., barbiturates)
  Stimulants (chronic use, e.g., cocaine, amphetamines)

Impotence
  Alcohol
  Antiandrogens
  Anticholinerigc drugs (e.g., atropine, Pro-Banthine)
  Antihypertensives (especially guanethidine, rauwolfia alkaloids, and methyldopa)
  Antipsychotics (especially thioridazine, haloperidol)
  MAOIs
  Tranquilizers
  Venlafaxine

Increased Libido
  Hallucinogens (e.g., marijuana, LSD)
  L-dopa
  Stimulants (acute use, e.g., cocaine, amphetamines)
  Trazodone (used as treatment for erectile dysfunction)

Retrograde Ejaculation
  Phenothiazine (thioridazine)

Retarded Ejaculation
  Butyrophenone (haloperidol)
  MAOIs
  Risperidone

Orgasmic Dysfunction
  MAOIs
  Selective Serotonin Reuptake Inhibitors
    (may be reversed by Buspirone)
    (also used as treatment for premature ejaculation)
  Tricyclic antidepressants
  Venlafaxine

SOURCE: Adapted from Schatzberg AF, Nemeroff CB (eds): *Textbook of Psychopharmacology*, 2nd ed. Washington, DC: American Psychiatric Press, 1998.

through reducing overall vitality. Medications prescribed for medical or psychiatric conditions can cause sexual dysfunction (Table 55-3), as can obstetrical and gynecological procedures. Infertility treatment is often associated with changes in sexual function secondary to feelings of inadequacy, to medical intrusions on intimacy, and to the need to have intercourse under prescribed conditions. Therefore, a workup for sexual dysfunction must begin with a thorough history, physical examination, and appropriate laboratory studies. Treatment does not end with discovery of a medical or gynecological cause for a sexual dysfunction. Avenues for medical and surgical treatment should be explored, so that women with medical conditions are not denied sexual gratification.

Treatment

Disorders of arousal and orgasm are treated with behavioral desensitization, sensate focus, and improvements and practice in sexual technique. Patients learn to pay attention to their own preferences and responses, to give and receive pleasurable stimulation, and to relax. Some women are uncomfortable with their sexual fantasies and inhibit them. Fantasies play a central role in normal sexual function. To reduce performance pressure, couples may be instructed to avoid intercourse for some weeks, while the partners practice other ways to exchange sexual pleasure. A patient who has never experienced an orgasm is generally advised to begin with private self-stimulation. The primary practitioner can learn these therapeutic techniques or refer patients to a specialized sexual disorders program. Sexuality and the diagnosis and treatment of sexual disorders are discussed in detail in Chap. 46.

Homosexuality

There is no evidence that homosexuality is an illness or is associated with pathological thinking or functioning. Lesbian and bisexual women do suffer from the effects of being made to feel abnormal, from the disapprobation and disappointment of their families, and from disapproval, as well as frequent overt discrimination, harassment, and assault from members of society. It is crucial to remember that most lesbian women have engaged in, and many continue to engage in, heterosexual activity. It is also crucial for primary care physicians to acknowledge and deal with their own prejudices and feelings about sexual orientation so as not to alienate lesbian patients. The simple, routine inquiry about contraceptive needs can signal to the patient that the physician expects her to be heterosexual.[62] Neither the sexual orientation nor the sexual behavior of any patient can be taken for granted, be she a married grandmother or a nun.

Summary

Psychosocial and psychiatric issues are ubiquitous, pervasive, and critical in primary care. The ability to elicit the patient's story, to listen thoughtfully and nonjudgmentally, and to tolerate awkward topics and powerful feelings (one's own and the patient's) is central to accurate diagnosis, compliance, and patient satisfaction. Psychiatric disorders are common, but often overlooked, causing tremendous suffering and disability in patients and pain for their loved ones. Informed treatment by the primary physician, a consulting psychiatrist, or the two in collaboration, can almost always alleviate the patient's symptoms.

References and Selected Readings

1. American College of Obstetricians and Gynecologists: *The Obstetrician-Gynecologist and Primary Preventive Health Care.* Washington, DC: ACOG, 1993.
2. Andrews G, Harvey R: Does psychotherapy benefit neurotic patients? A reanalysis of the Smith, Glass, and Miller data. *Arch Gen Psychiatry* 38: 1203–1208, 1981.
3. Angst J: Epidemiology of depression. *Psychopharmacol* (suppl)106:71–74, 1992.
4. American Medical Association Council on Scientific Affairs: Violence against women: Relevance for medical practitioners. *JAMA* 267(23):3184–3189, 1992.
5. American Psychiatric Association: *Diagnostic and Statistical Manual of Mental Disorders,* 4th ed. Washington, DC: American Psychiatric Press, 1994.
6. American Psychiatric Association, Task Force on DSM-IV: *Diagnostic and Statistical Manual of Mental*

Disorders, 4th ed. Draft criteria. Washington, DC: American Psychiatric Press, 1993.

7. Apfel RJ, Handel MH: *Madness and Loss of Motherhood: Sexuality, Reproduction and Long-Term Mental Illness.* Washington, DC: American Psychiatric Press, 1993.

8. Arms S: *Immaculate Deception: A New Look at Women and Childbirth in America.* Boston: Houghton Mifflin, 1975.

9. Ashton H: Psychotropic-drug prescribing for women. *Br J Psychiatry* 158(Suppl 10):30–35, 1991.

10. Association of University Women: *How Schools Shortchange Girls: A Study of Major Findings on Girls and Education.* Washington, DC: American Association of University Women Education Foundation and the National Education Association, 1992.

11. Baldessrini RJ: Drugs and the treatment of psychiatric disorders, in: Gilman AG, et al: *Goodman and Gilman's The Pharmacological Basis of Therapeutics,* 8th ed. New York: McGraw-Hill, 1990.

12. Bagedahl-Strindlund M: Postpartum mental illnesses: Cross-cultural and social anthropological aspects—A review, in Wijma K, von Schoultz B (eds): *Reproductive Life: Advances in Research in Psychosomatic Obstetrics and Gynecology.* Trenton, NJ: Parthenon, 1992.

13. Becker JV, Kavoussi RJ: Sexual disorders, in Talbott JA, Hales RE, Yudofsky SC (eds). *Textbook of Psychiatry.* Washington, DC: American Psychiatric Press, 1988, pp 587–604.

14. Beckman HB, Frankel RM: The effect of physician behavior on the collection of data. *Ann Intern Med* 101:692–696, 1984.

15. Bleier R: Gender ideology and the brain: Sex differences research, in Notman MT, Nadelson CC (eds): *Women and Men: New Perspectives on Gender Differences.* Washington, DC: American Psychiatric Press, 1991.

16. Blume SB, Russell M: Alcohol and substance abuse in the practice of obstetrics and gynecology, in Stewart DS, Stotland NL (eds): *Psychological Aspects of Women's Health Care,* Washington, DC: American Psychiatric Press, 1993, pp 391–409.

17. Blumenthal SJ: Psychiatric consequences of abortion: Overview of research findings, in Stotland N (ed): *Psychiatric Aspects of Abortion.* Washington, DC: American Psychiatric Press, 1991.

18. Boston Women's Health Collective: *The New Our Bodies, Ourselves: A Book By and For Women.* New York: Simon & Schuster, 1992.

19. Boston Women's Health Collective: *Changing Bodies, Changing Lives.* New York: Simon & Schuster, 1989.

20. Boston Women's Health Collective: *Ourselves and Our Children.* New York: Simon & Schuster, 1988.

21. Boston Women's Health Collective: *Ourselves, Growing Older.* New York: Simon & Schuster, 1991.

22. Brody DS, Khliq AA, Thompson TL: Patients' perspectives on the management of emotional distress in primary care settings. *J Gen Intern Med* 12(7):403–406, 1997.

23. Brown G, Harris TO: *Social Origins of Depression: A Study of Psychiatric Disorder in Women.* London: Tavistock, 1978.

24. Calandra B: Closing the gap, Scott Levin's Pallas Athena 1(1):27–30, 1992.

25. Campbell R, Bybee D: Emergency medical services for rape victims: Detecting the cracks in service delivery. *Womens Health* 3(2):75–101, 1997.

26. Cohen P, Pine DS, Must A, Kasen S, Brook J: Prospective associations between somatic illness and mental illness from childhood to adulthood. *Am J Epidemiol* 147(3):232–239, 1998.

27. Cramer DW: Epidemiology and biostatistics, in Berek JS, Hacker NF (eds): *Practical Gynecologic Oncology.* Baltimore: Williams & Wilkins, 1989.

28. Dubovsky SL, Weissberg MP: Clinical Psychiatry in Primary Care, 3rd ed. Baltimore: Williams & Wilkins, 1986.

29. Datan N: Aging into transitions: Cross-cultural perspectives on women at midlife, in Formanek R (ed): *The Meanings of Menopause: Historical, Medical and Clinical Perspectives.* Hillsdale, NJ: The Analytic Press, 1990, pp 117–132.

30. Dreifus C (ed): *Seizing Our Bodies: The Politics of Women's Health.* New York: Vintage Books, 1978.

31. Earl DT, Blackwelder RB: Management of chronic medical conditions in children and adolescents. *Prim Care* 25(1):253–270, 1998.

32. Faludi S: *Backlash: The Undeclared War Against American Women.* New York: Crown Publishers, 1991.

33. Folstein MF, Folstein SE, McHugh PR: Mini-mental state, a practical method for grading the cognitive state of patients. *Psychiatry Res* 12:189–194, 1975.

34. Ford CV, Folks DG: Conversion disorders: An overview. *Psychosomatics* 26(5):371–382, 1985.

35. Freud S: Femininity Lecture 33 (1931), in the *Standard Edition of the Complete Works of Sigmund Freud,* vol 22. London: Hogarth Press, 1964.

36. Gartrell N: The lesbian as a "single" woman. *Am J Psychother* 35(4):502–516, 1981.

37. Gehlert S, Hartlage S: A design for studying the DSM-IV research criteria of premenstrual dysphoric disorder. *J Psychosom Obstet Gynaecol,* 18(1):36–44, 1997.

38. Gilligan C: *In a Different Voice.* Cambridge, MA: Harvard University Press, 1982.

39. Greene JG: Psychosocial influences and life events at the time of the menopause in Formanek R (ed): *The*

Meanings of Menopause: Historical, Medical, and Clinical Perspectives. Hillsdale, NJ: The Analytic Press, 1990, pp 79–116.

40. Haas AP: Lesbian health issues: An overview, in Dan AJ (ed) *Reframing Women's Health.* London: Sage, 1994, pp 339–356.

41. Hales REL: Dying Patients: A challenge to their physicians and consultation psychiatry. *Mi Med* 145:674–680, 1980.

42. Halmi KA: Eating disorders, in Talbott JA, Hales RE, Yudofsky SC (eds): *Textbook of Psychiatry.* Washington, DC: American Psychiatric Press, 1988, pp 753–766.

43. Hamilton JA: Emotional consequences of victimization and discrimination in "special populations" of women. *Psychiatr Clin North Am* 12:35–35, 1989.

44. Haynes S: *Risk of Breast Cancer Among Lesbians.* Seattle: Fred Hutchinson Cancer Research Center Community Liaison Program, 1994, pp 28–41.

45. Hirschfeld RMA, Goodwin FK: Mood disorders, in Talbott JA Hales RE, Yudofsky SC (eds): *Textbook of Psychiatry.* Washington, DC: American Psychiatric Press, 1988, pp 403–441.

46. Hochschild A: *The Second Shift: Working Parents and the Revolution at Home.* New York: Viking, 1989.

47. Horton JA (ed): *The Women's Health Data Book: A Profile of Women's Health in the United States.* Washington, DC: The Jacobs Institute of Women's Health, 1992.

48. Jacobsen DM: Religious experience and the biopsychosocial, in Browning DS, Jobe T, Evison IS (eds): *Religious and Ethical Factors in Psychiatric Practice.* Chicago: Nelson-Hall, 1990.

49. Johnson SR, Guenther SM, Laube DW, Keettel WC: Factors influencing lesbian gynecologic care: A preliminary study. *Am J Obstet Gynecol* 140(1):20–25, 1981.

50. Kirkpatrick M, Smith C, Roy R: Lesbian mothers and their children: A comparative survey. *Am J Orthopsychiatry* 51(3):545–551, 1981.

51. Martin BA: Primary care of adults with mental retardation living in the community. *Am Fam Physician* 56(2): 485–494, 1997.

52. McEwen BS: Sex differences in the brain: What they are and how they arise, in Notman MT, Nadelson CC (eds): *Women and Men: New Perspectives on Gender Differences,* Washington, DC: American Psychiatric Press, 1991.

53. McGrath E, Keita GP, Strickland BR, Russo NF (eds): *Women and Depression: Risk Factors and Treatment Issues.* Washington, DC: American Psychological Association, 1990.

54. McKinlay SM: The Massachusetts Women's Health Study: A longitudinal study of the health of mid-aged women and the epidemiology of the menopause. *Psychol Women* 16:1–4, 1989.

55. Mendelsohn R: *Male Practice: How Doctors Manipulate Women.* Chicago: Contemporary Books, 1982.

56. Michels R, Marzuk PM: Progress in psychiatry (first of two parts). *N Engl J Med* 329(8):552–560, 1993.

57. Michels R, Marzuk PM: Progress in psychiatry (second of two parts). *N Engl J Med* 329(8):628–638, 1993.

58. Mullen PE, Romans-Clarckson SE, Walton VA, et al: Impact of sexual and physical abuse on women's mental health. *Lancet* 1(8590):841–845, 1988.

59. Nadelson CC: Professional issues for women. *Psychiatr Clin North Am* 12(1):25–33, 1989.

60. Nonacs R, Cohen LS: Postpartum mood disorders: Diagnosis and treatment guidelines. *J Clin Psychiatry* 59(Suppl 2):34–40, 1998.

61. Novacek J, Raskin R: Recognition of warning signs: A consideration for cost-effective treatment of severe mental illness. *Psychiatr Serv* 49(3):376–378, 1998.

62. Odell SM, Surtees PG, Wainwright NW, Commander MJ, Sashidharan SP: Determinants of general practitioner recognition of psychological problems in a multiethnic inner-city health district. *Br J Psychiatry* 171:537–541, 1997.

63. O'Hanlan KA: Lesbian health and homphobia: Perspectives for the treating obstetrician/gynecologist. *Curr Prob Obst Gyn* 18(4):93–136, 1995.

64. Okey JL: Is psychoanalytic theory relevant to the psychology of women? *J Am Acad Psychoanal* 19:396–402, 1991.

65. Oppenheimer E: Alcohol and drug misuse among women: An overview. *Br J Psychiatry* 158(Suppl 10):36–44, 1991.

66. Pariser SF, Nasrallah HA, Gardner DK: Postpartum mood disorders: Clinical perspectives. *J Womens Health* 6(4):421–434, 1997.

67. Pierce C: Failure to spot mental illness in primary care is a global problem. *Clin Psychiatr News* 21(8):5, 1993.

68. Platt FW, McMath JC: Clinical hypocompetence: The interview. *Ann Intern Med* 91:898–902, 1979.

69. Post RD, Willett AB, Frnsk RD, et al: A preliminary report on the prevalence of domestic violence among psychiatric inpatients. *Am J Psychiatry* 137:974–975, 1980.

70. Potter WZ, Rudorfer MV, Manji H: The pharmacologic treatment of depression. *N Engl J Med* 658(9):633–642, 1991.

71. Regier D, Goldberg ID, Taube CA: The de facto US mental health services system: A public health perspective. *Arch Gen Psychiatry* 35:685–693, 1978.

72. Rose DS: Sexual assault, domestic violence, and incest, in Stewart DS, Stotland NL (eds): *Psychological Aspects of Women's Health Care,* Washington, DC: American Psychiatric Press, 1993, pp 447–483.

73. Rosenfeld S: The effects of women's employment:

Personal control and sex differences in mental health. *J Health Soc Behav* 30:77–91, 1989.

74. Rosenthal M, O'Grady P: Affective anxiety disorders, in O'Grady JP (ed): *Obstetrics: Psychological and Psychiatric Syndromes*. New York: Elsevier, 1992.

75. Schatzburg AF, Cole JO: *Manual of Psychopharmacology,* 2d ed: Washington, DC: American Psychiatric Press, 1991.

76. Schurman RA, Kramer PD, Mitchell JB: The hidden mental health network: Treatment of mental illness by nonpsychiatrist physicians. *Arch Gen Psychiatry* 42:89–94, 1985.

77. Stevens PE, Hall JM: A critical historical analysis of the medical construction of lesbianism. *Int J Health Serv* 21(2):291–307, 1991.

78. Stewart DE, Stotland NL (eds): *Psychological Aspects of Women's Health Care*. Washington, DC: American Psychiatric Press, 1993.

79. Stewart DE: Psychiatric admission of mentally ill mothers with their infants. *Can J Psychiatry* 34:34–37, 1989.

80. Stotland NL: The myth of the abortion trauma syndrome [commentary]. *JAMA* 268(15):2078–2079, 1992.

81. Stotland NL (ed): *Psychiatric Aspects of Abortion*. Washington, DC: American Psychiatric Press, 1991.

82. Stotland NL (ed): *Psychiatric Aspects of Reproductive Technology*. Washington, DC: American Psychiatric Press, 1990.

83. Stotland NL, Garrick TR: *Manual of Psychiatric Consultation*. Washington, DC: American Psychiatric Press, 1990.

84. Stotland NL: *Social Change and Women's Reproductive Health Care: A Guide for Physicians and Their Patients*. New York: Praeger, 1988.

85. Stoudemire A: Psychiatry in medical practice. Implications for the education of primary care physicians in the era of managed care: Part I. *Psychosomatics* 37(6):502–508, 1996.

86. Stoudemire GA: Somatoform disorders, factitious disorders, and malingering, in Talbott JA, Hales RE, Yudofsky SC (eds): *Textbook of Psychiatry*. Washington, DC: American Psychiatric Press, 1998, pp 533–556.

87. Tavris C: *The Measurement of Women: Why Women are Not the Better Sex, the Inferior Sex, or the Opposite Sex*. New York: Simon & Schuster, 1992.

88. Williams JH: *Psychology of Women: Behavior in a Biosocial Context,* 2nd ed. New York: WW Norton, 1983.

89. Yonkers KA: Antidepressants in the treatment of premenstrual dysphoric disorder. *J Clin Psychiatry,* 58(Suppl 14):4–13, 1997.

CHAPTER 56

Alcohol and Drug Use in Women: What the Primary Care Physician Can Do

Jeffrey Selzer

SCREENING

BRIEF INTERVENTIONS

SPECIALIZED ADDICTION TREATMENT

PHARMACOLOGIC MANAGEMENT OF
    SUBSTANCE-RELATED DISORDERS

SYNDROMES RELATED TO
    INTOXICATION

Alcohol Intoxication • Opiate
Intoxication • Cocaine and Other Stimulant
Intoxication • Hallucinogen (LSD, Mescaline,
MDMA (''Ecstasy'') & Psilocybin)
Intoxication • Phencyclidine Intoxication

DRUGS FOR THE TREATMENT OF
    WITHDRAWAL SYNDROMES

Alcohol Withdrawal • Sedative-Hypnotic
Withdrawal • Opiate Withdrawal •
Management of Withdrawal in Patients with
Multiple Dependencies

AGENTS TO AID RELAPSE PREVENTION

Medications for Alcohol Dependence •
Medications for Cocaine Dependence •
Medications for Opiate Dependence •
Medications for Nicotine Dependence

PHARMACOTHERAPIES FOR SUBSTANCE
    ABUSERS WITH ADDITIONAL TYPES
    OF PSYCHIATRIC ILLNESS

PREGNANCY AND ADDICTION

Primary care physicians are typically overly pessimistic about their ability to help substance abusers.[9] Studies have shown that even brief interventions in a clinician's office can increase the chance that a patient will successfully quit or cut down her use of a substance. At a minimum, the primary care physician should screen for this relatively common illness, present it as a problem to the patient, and make it part of the problem list. An appropriate referral for treatment should be made if the primary care physician feels that they cannot try an intervention, or if primary care interventions fail.

Screening

Substance use disorders are common enough in primary care practices that primary care physicians should routinely screen for them. There are a number of sets of screening questions that take little time to administer (or for the patient to self-administer) and have sufficient sensitivity to be useful. Although patterns of suggestive laboratory findings have been proposed, particularly for alcohol (e.g., increased MCV and GGT) none have performed as well as brief screening interviews. If a screen is positive, the clinician can follow with a more detailed interview guided by the Diagnostic and Statistical Manual of Mental Disorders, 4th ed. (DSM-IV) diagnostic criteria (see Chap. 12). It is important that these questions be a part of the routine review of history and that the interviewer's tone be concerned, interested, and nonjudgmental.

The CAGE questions developed by Ewing[6] have been validated in patients with alcohol-use disorders across a variety of settings. The questions are as follows:

1. Have you ever felt you ought to *C*ut down on your drinking?
2. Have people *A*nnoyed you by criticizing your drinking?
3. Have you ever felt bad or *G*uilty about your drinking?
4. Have you ever had a drink first thing in the morning to steady your nerves or to get rid of a hangover (*E*yeopener)?

These questions do well in summarizing the main features of the DSM-IV diagnostic criteria. Question 1 assesses loss of control over amount consumed. Question 2 assesses a common social consequence and, with question 3, assesses use despite negative consequences. Question 3 also detects negative psychological consequences. Question 4 detects use of the substance to treat withdrawal symptoms and takes advantage of the fact that withdrawal symptoms are often most distressing in the morning, because for many patients the period of sleep may be the longest time without using the substance. Although screening interviews for drugs of abuse other than alcohol have not been well studied, the CAGE questions have good face validity given that diagnostic criteria for abuse and dependence are identical regardless of the substance.

In a sample of pregnant women, Sokol[13] found that asking patients about guilt about drinking did not add significantly to detecting problem drinking. Sokol found that asking about tolerance, as measured by requiring two or more drinks "to feel high," was more effective in detecting women whose drinking put them at risk for obstetrical complications, including delivering a baby with fetal alcohol syndrome. The question regarding tolerance was combined with the remaining CAGE questions to create the T-ACE questions. Supporters of the T-ACE scale argue that patients are more likely to answer questions about tolerance honestly, and without defensiveness, than they would questions asking about guilt about drinking.

Finally, Cyr and Wartman[4] performed alcohol screening in a population of general medical outpatients coming to an urban teaching hospital. The sample is notable for the generous representation of women in the sample as a whole, and in the alcoholic subsample. Two questions, "Have you ever had a drinking problem?" and "When was your last drink (positive response is within the past 24 hours)?" emerged as the most significant questions for detecting alcohol dependence. When both questions were answered positively, sensitivity was increased further.

Detection of drug use is also possible by laboratory evaluation. Urine is the body fluid used to detect cannabis, cocaine, and opiates, whereas alcohol is detected in blood and breath. A positive finding in itself signifies no more than use of the substance and, therefore, must be followed by a screening and diagnostic interview.

Brief Interventions

Any intervention occurs in the context of a physician-patient relationship. Although the physician should be supportive and tactful, the communication should also be direct about the nature of the illness. Directness is not equivalent to a judgmental, critical approach which may make patients feel scorned and less likely to share openly, or even return to treatment. What is more helpful, rather, is an approach that increases the patient's motivation to change and expresses a sense of hope and optimism to her. As with other chronic relapsing illnesses, setbacks should be seen as part of the course of the illness and as an opportunity to collaboratively examine how the treatment can be changed if necessary. There is a risk that the clinician will convey disillusionment and anger at the time of a relapse. Alcohol-dependent patients usually require three or four attempts at quitting before they are successful.[14]

A brief intervention is a short counseling session focused on helping a person change a specific behavior. The content of an intervention for substance abuse should consider the severity of the patient's situation, and her willingness and ability to make a change in behavior. After assessing a patient's motivation to change, the physician tries to persuade her that change is in her best interest. This is done by taking stock of the pros and cons of substance use and heightening her awareness of detrimental effects. In a patient ambivalent about the need for changing, applying diagnostic labels or making specific treatment recommendations is counterproductive. Rather, educational approaches (e.g., "I wonder if your fatigue and upset stomach may be related to alcohol use?") and realistic targets for change (e.g., "Could you limit yourself to one drink of alcohol per day?") are more effective. The physician should monitor the effect of the recommendation to guard against the patient feeling condemned. The motivation for change and the ability of the patient to take action should be reassessed with subsequent visits. The physician's return to this health problem at every visit emphasizes to the patient that decreasing or eliminating substance use is among the most important actions she can take to improve her health.

Any change in a positive direction, even moving from contemplating a change to taking limited steps to promote change, should be reinforced. For example, a patient who goes from being unwilling to consider that she has a drinking problem to willingness to keep a drinking diary is taking a significant step. For patients who are unable to make any progress or who experience disabling relapses, specialized addiction treatment should be offered. Because this option may be necessary, the primary care physician should know of addiction specialists as she or he would know of other subspecialists.

Specialized Addiction Treatment

Specialized addiction treatment should begin with a comprehensive assessment of not only the patient's degree of substance use and resulting symptoms, but also of comorbid conditions and of supports in the "recovery environment." The American Society of Addiction Medicine has developed Patient Placement Criteria to guide the clinician in placing the patient in the most appropriate level of care.[1] This may range across a spectrum from weekly outpatient treatment, to daily outpatient treatment, to residential treatment, to inpatient hospital treatment. Research has shown that the intensity and variety of services are more important than the setting of services. Given the high rates of psychiatric comorbidity with substance use disorders, particularly in women, successful programs must have considerable psychiatric expertise.

Addiction programs for women must consider the specific needs of women. Because women often have child care responsibilities, this is a helpful and, at times, necessary service if women are to participate in treatment. Programs for women should also have sufficient numbers of women patients so that same-gender group treatment is possible, as patients may feel uncomfortable discussing certain problems, such as histories of sexual abuse, in mixed-gender groups. Programs for women should be prepared to help intervene in relationships with partners who themselves are substance involved and/or abusive. Finally, specialized addiction treatment programs should be prepared to help pregnant patients.

In addition to specialized addiction treatment, community-based twelve-step programs, such as Alcoholics Anonymous, can be a great help to women with addictions. The twelve steps refer to a progression of realizations and tasks that such groups believe are vital to recovery from substance dependence. Twelve-step groups are often mistakenly called "self-help" when they are rather "nonprofessional help." A central tenet of these groups is that a member is "powerless" to recover on her own but gains strength from the group. Because members are "anonymous," longitudinal research has been difficult to perform. What research is available suggests the majority of people who begin to attend twelve-step meetings do not continue; for those who do, the effect is beneficial. A recently completed large study on psychotherapies for alcoholism showed that twelve-step facilitation therapy compared favorably with other types of psychotherapy.

Whatever a patient's involvement with specialized addiction treatment and/or twelve-step groups, she will need ongoing primary care from her referring physician. The primary care physician should, at a minimum, address with the patient the course of her recovery and support it. Although always beneficial, there are times when communication between the addiction treatment program and the primary care physician is essential (e.g., obtaining medical clearance prior to prescribing medication or providing care for a pregnant patient). Because of the addictive potential of certain psychotropics, it is best that the primary care physician not make unilateral decisions about prescribing psychotropics. Further, it may be best for the addiction treatment physician to write psychotropic prescriptions.

Pharmacologic Management of Substance-Related Disorders

There is enormous interest in expanding the role of pharmacotherapy for addictive disorders. Medications have long played an important role in treating syndromes related to intoxication and overdose, as well as those related to withdrawal. The role of medication as an aid to relapse prevention once a women has detoxified is a relatively new area of interest. Primary care physicians may find themselves in emergency situations where prescribing skills are necessary and in less urgent situations where prescribing skills are valuable (and may prevent the recurrence of emergencies). No pharmacologic intervention is a magic bullet for addiction. Psychosocial interventions are vital in all phases of chemical dependency treatment and add to the efficacy of pharmacotherapy.

Syndromes Related to Intoxication

When evaluating a patient for possible intoxication, arriving at an accurate diagnosis is funda-

mental. To this end, the physician must obtain a history while remaining vigilant to the possibility that intoxication syndromes can progress to life-threatening overdose syndromes or withdrawal symptoms. The physical examination of the patient should focus on acute consequences of drug intoxication (e.g., vital signs, neurological signs), and the chronic consequences of drug dependence (e.g., evidence of venipuncture, liver size). Blood and breath analysis can be used to assess drug use within 4 to 12 hours prior to testing; urine toxicology identifies substances used during a 24- to 72-hour period prior to evaluation. Except for alcohol, urine is generally the body fluid used for toxicologic analysis.

Alcohol Intoxication

Alcohol intoxication is characterized by a maladaptive mental state (e.g., increased aggressivity), accompanied by neurologic signs, which include slurred speech, poor coordination, unsteady gait, and impairment of attention and memory. If alcohol levels are high enough (400 to 800 mg%, depending on level of tolerance), stupor, coma, and cardiovascular collapse may result. In general, it is best to manage alcohol intoxication nonpharmacologically to avoid synergism between alcohol and any administered drug. On average, blood-alcohol levels decrease 15 mg% per hour. In patients whose intoxication includes belligerence that does not respond to supportive limit-setting, lorazepam 1 to 2 mg po may be effective. If a patient becomes violent, physical restraint and intramuscular lorazepam may be necessary. Patients who continue to escalate for 1 to 2 hours after these measures are taken may be safely treated with haloperidol 5 mg intramuscularly.

Opiate Intoxication

Opiate intoxication is characterized by a maladaptive mental state (e.g., apathy) accompanied by pupillary constriction (midpoint with meperidine, dilatation if anoxia from severe overdose), central nervous system depression, and respiratory depression. Meperidine, propoxyphene, and pentazocine may present with seizures due to toxic metabolites.

When a patient presents with miosis and respiratory depression, pharmacotherapy must begin immediately. Naloxone HCL, a pure opiate antagonist, effectively reverses the central nervous system effects of opiates. An initial intravenous dose of 0.4 to 0.8 mg will usually reverse respiratory and central nervous system depression in 2 min. Repeat doses may be given every 2 to 3 min if the previous dose is ineffective. While most patients respond after one to four doses, larger doses of naloxone may be necessary for highly potent opiates (e.g., fentanyl). Once a response to naloxone is obtained, an infusion (initial dose 0.4 mg/hr) should be administered for a minimum of 12 hours because the opiates taken in overdose often have a longer duration of action than naloxone's 1 to 2 hours. There are three caveats in the use of naloxone. Other causes of CNS depression should be suspected while treating for opiate overdosage (especially when conventional naloxone doses are ineffective); naloxone must be administered cautiously because an opiate-withdrawal syndrome may be abruptly precipitated; and naloxone should be used with great caution in pregnant patients as its use has been associated with spontaneous abortion, premature labor, and/or stillbirth.[12]

Cocaine and Other Stimulant Intoxication

Intoxication with cocaine and other stimulants is characterized by maladaptive behavioral or psychological changes (e.g., anxiety, paranoid delusions, hallucinations), accompanied by physical signs such as tachycardia, mydriasis, hypertension, perspiration, psychomotor agitation, and dyskinesia. More extreme untoward effects from overdose with these substances can also result: respiratory depression, cardiac arrhythmias, delirium, and seizures. As amphetamine has a longer duration of action than cocaine, untoward behavioral, psychological, and physical effects are more prolonged. Because of the potential for serious physical consequences of cocaine and other stimulant use, a physician treating a patient with this type of intoxication must always evaluate the patient's cardiac and neurologic status and prepare a management plan for medical emergencies including arrhythmias, hypertension, and seizures.

In treating untoward behavioral and psychological effects, attempts should be made to be reassuring and straightforward in a low-stimulation environment, if possible. When pharmacologic measures are necessary, a benzodiazepine, such as lorazepam 2 mg, is often effective. Even for more severe untoward effects, such as psychosis, benzodiazepines are preferable to neuroleptic medication, which may exacerbate cardiovascular complications (e.g., tachycardia) and neurologic complications (e.g., seizures and hyperthermia). If benzodiazepines are ineffective in the management of a behaviorally escalating patient, a high-potency antipsychotic agent, such as haloperidol 5 mg, may be used cautiously. Urine acidification may increase the clearance of amphetamine, but it is not advocated to hasten the clearance of cocaine.

Hallucinogen [LSD, Mescaline, MDMA ("Ecstasy") and Psilocybin] Intoxication

Hallucinogen intoxication is characterized by maladaptive psychological changes (anxiety, paranoia, a conviction that one is going insane), perceptual changes in an alert state (e.g., "intensification" of perception, depersonalization, hallucinations, synesthesia), and physical signs, such as mydriasis and tachycardia. Hallucinogen intoxication can often be managed using a "talk-down" method focused on reassuring the patient that the distressing experiences are drug-induced, temporary, and will be followed by full recovery. If medication is necessary, benzodiazepines will provide welcome sedation and reduction of anxiety. If neuroleptic medication is necessary to control psychotic symptoms and agitation, haloperidol may be used cautiously.

The hallucinogen-persisting perception disorder ("flashback") involves the transient recurrence of perceptual abnormalities that are reminiscent of hallucinogen intoxication in an individual who used hallucinogens in the past. These perceptual episodes may be triggered by drug use (e.g., cannabis), anxiety, or fatigue. Flashbacks may cause much distress, especially if there was a history of distress during the original period of intoxication. Because flashbacks are so brief and usually remit spontaneously, treatment generally involves no more than supportive reassurance. If anticipatory anxiety about flashbacks is particularly intense, benzodiazepines may be useful in carefully selected patients.

Phencyclidine Intoxication

Phencyclidine (PCP) intoxication is characterized by maladaptive behavioral changes (e.g., belligerence, assaultiveness, and impulsivity), accompanied by these physical signs: nystagmus, hypertension, ataxia, muscle rigidity, diminished responsiveness to pain, seizures, and coma. In general, lower doses produce excitation, and higher doses produce dangerous levels of sedation.

The time required for resolution of symptoms varies. Due to enterohepatic recirculation, patients intoxicated with PCP are notorious for the unpredictable reemergence of symptoms after a period of quiescence. It is, therefore, reasonable to require a 12-hour period of observation before releasing a patient.

Nonpharmacologic interventions include close observation for behavioral and physical manifestations in a low-stimulation environment. "Talking-down" techniques have been reported to be less helpful than when used with hallucinogen intoxication. Because of the combination of belligerence and diminished response to pain (PCP has anesthetic properties), patients may struggle violently against restraint. When restraint is necessary, patients who struggle should be observed for the development of rhabdomyolysis.

When pharmacologic agents are used, the aim is usually to produce sedation or relieve psychosis. For general sedation, a benzodiazepine, such as lorazepam, may be used po or IM. Haloperidol is a reasonable neuroleptic agent when psychotic agitation is unresponsive to benzodiazepines. More anticholinergic neuroleptics may act to enhance the anticholinergic properties of PCP itself. If neuroleptics are used, one must remember that PCP itself can produce muscle rigidity and acute dystonias. Urine acidification has been recommended to increase excretion of PCPs in the urine. However, this may also exacerbate a developing metabolic acidosis and increase the risk of renal failure secondary to rhabdomyolysis.

Drugs for the Treatment of Withdrawal Syndromes

In approaching pharmacologic treatments for specific withdrawal syndromes, some general principles are important to bear in mind (see Table 56-1). From a pharmacologic standpoint, an ideal agent for the treatment of withdrawal should have a number of characteristics: It should have efficacy in relieving the complete range of abstinence signs and symptoms for a given type of withdrawal; the agent should have a relatively long duration of action and a gradual offset of

TABLE 56-1 General Principles of Detoxification

Agent factors
1. Efficacy in relieving broad range of signs and symptoms
2. Long duration of action and gradual offset of effects
3. High therapeutic index
4. Multiple routes of administration
5. Low abuse potential

Monitoring treatment
1. Clear targets
2. Serial assessments
3. Modification based on serial assessments

Psychosocial factors
1. Prepare patient
2. Emphasize detoxification as a beginning to treatment

effects; the agent should have a high degree of safety in the dose needed to suppress withdrawal (i.e., high therapeutic index); and it should be available by a variety of routes of administration and have little abuse potential itself.

Other aspects of detoxification, which are not specific to the medication chosen, are equally important and too often overlooked. The clinician should have clear targets for treatment and consider the use of structured rating scales to measure symptom severity. There is no substitute for serial assessment of clinical response to guide treatment; it is dangerous to think of a detoxifying patient as "on autopilot." Orders must be thoughtfully rewritten, often on a daily basis, although protocols may provide useful guidelines.

Patients should be told what to expect from the experience, and every effort should be made to engage patients in a collaboration to alleviate symptoms as much as and as safely as possible. Patients should understand, however, that they will probably not be free of all distress. For those patients with relatively good health and adequate social stability, detoxification can often be accomplished on an outpatient basis. Finally, and most importantly, patients must understand that detoxification is only the beginning of treatment for what are typically chronic problems with substance dependence; detoxification is not a treatment on its own for addiction.

Alcohol Withdrawal

Symptoms of alcohol withdrawal usually occur within 6 to 12 hours after a decrease or cessation in drinking that has been heavy and prolonged (symptoms may occur in a person with significant alcohol levels if levels are falling). Symptoms of alcohol withdrawal include: autonomic hyperactivity; increased muscle tremor (may be hand, eyelids, tongue); insomnia; nausea or vomiting; transient hallucination or illusions; agitation; and anxiety. Generalized seizures as part of alcohol withdrawal are typically nonfocal, one or two in number, and begin 12 to 48 hours after cessation of alcohol use. An alcohol withdrawal delirium

(delirium tremens) occurs most commonly 3 to 5 days after cessation in drinking. As with other deliria, there is a disturbance of consciousness, a change in cognition, or perceptual disturbances. In addition, agitation, belligerence, and elevation in vital signs often occur. The development of an alcohol-withdrawal delirium is more likely in someone with an underlying physical disorder. Therefore, delirium should prompt a reassessment of a patient's general medical status for undiagnosed concurrent conditions.

With proper management, the likelihood of progression from uncomplicated withdrawal to seizures or delirium should be greatly reduced. It is useful to systematically assess a patient, both at entry into a detoxification protocol and as she is detoxified. A simple and widely used tool for this purpose is the Clinical Institute Withdrawal Assessment—Alcohol Scale (see Fig. 56-1).

The scale should be administered every 6 hours until there are at least two consecutive assessments with scores less than 10; at that point, structured evaluation can safely end. Scores above 20 may indicate the need for even closer monitoring. Intermediate scores require judgments based on factors such as the patient's degree of discomfort and past history of withdrawal episodes.

The most consistent error physicians make in medicating withdrawal is undertreatment; that is, doses are too low and dosing intervals are too long. If serial clinical assessments are made, navigating a route between withdrawal and intoxication is relatively straightforward.

Benzodiazepines are the treatment of choice for alcohol withdrawal given that alcoholics are cross-tolerant to them, given their relative safety compared with other sedative hypnotics, and given their consistently demonstrated ability to reduce the frequency of withdrawal seizures and delirium. Because of cross-tolerance, alcoholic patients require benzodiazepine doses that would be high for a nontolerant person.

There are two major classes of benzodiazepines to choose from: longer-acting agents (e.g., chlordiazepoxide and diazepam), which are metabolized by oxidation and glucuronidation, and

Addiction Research Foundation Clinical Institute Withdrawal Assessment for Alcohol

Patient_____ Date_____ Time_____

Blood Pressure: Systolic_____
                 Diastolic_____

1. Autonomic hyperactivity (choose higher score, either pulse or sweating)
   Pulse rate, beats/min, taken for 1 min
   0 <80
   1 81–100
   2 101–110
   3 111–120
   4 121–130
   5 131–140
   6 141–150
   7 >150

   Sweating: observation
   0 No sweat visible
   1 Barely perceptible sweating, palms moist
   2
   3
   4 Beads of sweat obvious on forehead
   5
   6
   7 Drenching sweats

2. Hand tremor: arms extended and fingers spread apart: observation
   0 No tremor
   1 Not visible, but can be felt fingertip to fingertip
   2
   3
   4 Moderate, with patient's arms extended
   5
   6
   7 Severe, even with arms not extended

3. Anxiety: Ask, "Do you feel nervous or anxious?" observation
   0 No anxiety, at ease
   1 Mildly anxious
   2
   3
   4 Moderately anxious
   5
   6
   7 Severe, equivalent to panic state

4. Transient tactile, auditory, or visual disturbances: Ask, "Have you any itching, pins and needles sensations, any burning, any numbness, or do you feel bugs crawling on or under your skin?" "Are you more aware of sounds around you? Are they harsh? Are you hearing things that you know are not there?" "Does the light appear to be too bright? Does it hurt your eyes? Are you seeing anything that is disturbing to you?":
   observation
   0 Not present
   1 Present, but minimal
   2
   3 Moderate
   4 Frequent
   5
   6
   7 Hallucinations almost continuous

5. Agitation: Observe
   0 Normal activity
   1 Somewhat more than normal activity
   2
   3
   4 Moderately fidgety and restless
   5
   6
   7 Paces back and forth during most of interview, or constantly thrashes about

6. Nausea or vomiting: Ask, "Do you feel sick to your stomach or have you vomited?" Include recorded vomiting since last observation
   0 No nausea and no vomiting
   1 Mild nausea with no vomiting
   2
   3
   4 Intermittent nausea with dry heaves
   5
   6
   7 Constant nausea, frequent dry heaves and vomiting

7. Headache: Ask, "Does your head feel different? Does your head feel full? Does it feel like there is a band around your head?" Do not rate for dizziness or lightheadedness. Otherwise, rate severity
   0 Not present
   1 Very mild
   2
   3
   4 Moderate
   5
   6
   7 Severe

Total CIWA-A Score_____
Rater's Initials_____

Figure 56-1 Addiction Research Foundation Clinical Institute Withdrawal Assessment for Alcohol.

shorter-acting agents (e.g., oxazepam and lora-zepam), which are metabolized only by glucuronidation. Both classes of benzodiazepine are available orally and intravenously, although only lorazepam is available for intramuscular administration. The advantage of longer-acting agents is that there is a more gradual decline in blood levels during the taper (leading to greater patient comfort between doses), and possibly greater seizure prophylaxis. The disadvantage of longer-acting agents is that delayed elimination may lead to accumulation and toxicity, particularly in the elderly or in patients with impaired liver or pulmonary function. The advantage of shorter-acting agents is that the elderly metabolize and eliminate these agents well, and there is less chance of toxicity due to a accumulation in patients with liver disease. The disadvantage of shorter-acting agents is that abrupt declines in medication levels between doses may result in breakthrough symptoms and seizures.

Response to treatment should be assessed serially, and medication should be increased or withheld depending on what the clinical situation dictates. If the patient is showing increased signs of withdrawal, the dose of medication should be increased or the dosing interval decreased. Although some degree of sedation is desirable, should the patient become overly sedated, the medication should be held until symptoms of alcohol withdrawal recur. Medication recommendations are summarized in Fig. 56-2.

For patients who develop hallucinations despite the use of sedative-hypnotic substitution therapy, haloperidol 2 to 5 mg may be given as an adjunct. Once hallucinations develop as a feature of delirium, they are relatively refractory to benzodiazepines alone.

In a patient with persistent tachycardia or hypertension, one should first ascertain whether the problem is inadequately treated withdrawal. Although β blockers and clonidine have been used successfully in management of this problem, these agents may decrease vital signs and tremor without providing anticonvulsant benefits.

An alternative strategy to that presented is to "frontload" a patient presenting for detoxification with doses of diazepam or every 1 to 2 hours until sedation is achieved. The long half-life of this medication allows for a slow, smooth offset of effects during the withdrawal period. This technique, however, does not obviate the need for careful serial assessment of the patient during the period of vulnerability for withdrawal complications.

Every alcoholic should be given thiamine to prevent the development of Wernicke's encephalopathy and subsequent Korsakoff's amnestic syndrome. Replacement thiamine should be given immediately and must precede the administration of IV glucose. The dose is typically 100 mg daily. Although less emergent, folate 1 mg and a multivitamin complete the nutritional management. There is not a clear consensus on the need for supplemental magnesium in the absence of a documented deficiency, although there is clinical lore that its use prevents withdrawal seizures. There are promising reports on the use of carbamazepine and valproate in alcohol withdrawal. Although these alternatives may be helpful in special circumstances, the safety and efficacy of benzodiazepines are difficult to surpass.

Sedative-Hypnotic Withdrawal

Symptoms of sedative-hypnotic withdrawal are qualitatively similar to alcohol withdrawal and include: tremor; anxiety; insomnia; anorexia; nausea and vomiting; postural hypotension; and seizures. The symptoms are similar enough to alcohol withdrawal that the CIWA scale can be used to follow the progression of symptoms and the impact of treatment. Sedative-hypnotic withdrawal is a medical emergency that, if untreated, can lead to serious complications (e.g., hyperpyrexia) and death. Symptoms are similar for all sedative-hypnotics, but the time course depends on the half-life of the particular drug involved; short-acting drugs, such as secobarbital, produce withdrawal phenomena that begin 12 to 24 hours after the last dose, whereas withdrawal symptoms due to long-acting drugs, such as diazepam,

Figure 56-2 Medication recommendations for treating alcohol withdrawal.

Patient in Alcohol Withdrawal

<65 years old and NO evidence of liver and/or pulmonary disease	> 65 years old or evidence of liver and/or pulmonary disease
Day 1:	*Day 1:*
Chlordiazepoxide 50–100 mg q 6 hrs	Lorazepam 2 mg q 4 hrs
Day 2:	*Day 2:*
Chlordiazepoxide 50–100 mg q 8 hrs	Lorazepam 1.5 mg q 4 hrs
Day 3:	*Day 3:*
Chlordiazepoxide 50–100 mg q 12 hrs	Lorazepam 1 mg q 4 hrs
Day 4:	*Day 4:*
Chlordiazepoxide 50–100 mg hs	Lorazepam 0.5 mg q 4 hrs

develop more slowly and may reach maximum intensity 1 week after cessation of drug use.

Phenobarbital is an excellent candidate for substitution therapy in sedative-hypnotic withdrawal. It has little abuse potential, therapeutic levels are far lower than lethal levels, and its long duration of action leads to relatively little fluctuation in blood level between doses. Finally, phenobarbital intoxication symptoms—ataxia, slurred speech, and nystagmus—are easy to observe and act upon in a detoxification protocol.

The first step in detoxifying someone who is dependent on sedative-hypnotics is to take a history of use. This history serves as a *guide* to dosing with phenobarbital. The total dose of sedative-hypnotic can then be converted into "phenobarbital equivalents" as specified in Table 56-2.

The total number of phenobarbital equivalents is then added and divided into a tid schedule. Even in extreme degrees of dependency, the daily dose of phenobarbital rarely needs to exceed 500 mg. If a patient is showing signs of acute withdrawal prior to beginning substitution therapy, the first dose of phenobarbital can be given intramuscularly. The patient should be reassessed for withdrawal or intoxication symptoms in 1 to 2 hours in order to make the best choice of the next dose of phenobarbital. Although pentobarbital can be given in serial 200-

mg "challenges" to assess degree of dependence, the advantages of this technique over the speed, simplicity, and safety of direct substitution with phenobarbital are not clear.

After 24 to 48 hours of phenobarbital substitution therapy, the patient should be showing neither signs of sedative-hypnotic withdrawal nor signs of phenobarbital toxicity, and should be able to move into a phenobarbital dose-reduction phase. During this phase, phenobarbital is decreased by 30 mg per day while a tid allocation of the total daily dose is preserved. If the patient develops signs of phenobarbital toxicity (slurred speech, nystagmus, ataxia), the next dose is held and the total daily dose is decreased. If objective signs of withdrawal develop, the daily dose is increased and the patient is restabilized before phenobarbital dose reduction proceeds again.

As with alcohol withdrawal, carbamazepine and valproate have also shown promise in the treatment of sedative-hypnotic withdrawal.

Opiate Withdrawal

Unlike sedative-hypnotic withdrawal, opiate withdrawal may be intensely uncomfortable but it is not typically life-threatening to most adults (newborns and adults with little reserve, such as those with advanced AIDS, are important exceptions). However, ameliorating withdrawal symp-

TABLE 56-2 Phenobarbital Conversion for Sedative-Hypnotic Withdrawal

Class/Generic Name	Dose (mg)	Phenobarbital Equivalence (mg)
Benzodiazepines		
Alprazolam	1	30
Chlordiazepoxide	25	30
Clonazepam	2	30
Clorazepate	7.5	30
Diazepam	10	30
Estazolam	1	30
Flurazepam	15	30
Halazepam	40	30
Lorazepam	2	30
Oxazepam	10	30
Prazepam	10	30
Quazepam	15	30
Temazepam	15	30
Triazolam	.25	30
Barbiturates		
Amobarbital	100	30
Butabarbital	100	30
Butalbital	100	30
Pentobarbital	100	30
Secobarbital	100	30
Other		
Chloral hydrate	500	30
Ethchlorvynol	500	30
Glutethimide	250	30
Meprobamate	800	30
Methyprylon	300	30
Zolpidem	5	30

SOURCE: Adapted from Wesson DR et al: in Lowinson JH, et al. (eds): *Substance Abuse: A Comprehensive Textbook,* 3rd ed., Baltimore: Williams & Wilkins, 1997.

toms may be an important step in engaging an opiate addict in treatment for addiction and in encouraging her to continue treatment for another medical problem.

Opiate withdrawal symptoms typically begin 6 to 24 hours after the last use of a short-acting opiate such as heroin, while they may not appear until 48 to 72 hours after longer-acting opiates such as methadone. Administration of an opiate antagonist, such as naloxone, however, can induce severe withdrawal symptoms precipitously. The symptoms, which have been compared to an episode of a viral upper respiratory and gastrointestinal illness, consist of dysphoria; nausea and vomiting; muscle aches; lacrimation or rhinorrhea; pupillary dilatation; piloerection; diarrhea; diaphoresis; yawning; fever; and insomnia. These symptoms can be assessed and graded with the Objective Opiate Withdrawal Scale (Fig. 56-3).

Methadone is a useful medication for treating opiate withdrawal, and it has FDA approval for this purpose. Practitioners should be aware, however, of how their respective states regulate its use. Typically, its use for *inpatient* detoxication or methadone maintenance is permitted. However, methadone cannot be prescribed in an outpatient setting for the management of opiate withdrawal except in a licensed methadone-maintenance treatment program. Methadone has a long duration of action and can be given orally. When signs of opiate withdrawal are seen (not merely reports of drug craving), a patient is given an initial dose of 15 to 20 mg of methadone. If symptoms persist or worsen, one may give an additional 5 to 10 mg in 1 to 2 hours. Signs of withdrawal are usually well controlled by 40 mg of methadone per day. (This is often not an adequate dose for long-term methadone maintenance, which is a different indication for methadone.) If withdrawal symptoms make oral medication impossible, methadone may be given intramuscularly in 5-mg doses. Once a dose has been found which alleviates withdrawal symptoms, methadone can be gradually tapered by 10 to 20% per day to achieve full detoxication.

An alternative to methadone for opiate withdrawal is clonidine, an α-receptor agonist used primarily as an antihypertensive. Unlike methadone, clonidine is not an opiate agonist to which addicts have cross-tolerance; rather, clonidine suppresses many of the autonomic symptoms of opiate withdrawal due to its central nervous system effects. While autonomic symptoms may be well controlled, patients often complain of greater subjective distress with clonidine than with methadone. Clonidine may be used either as a detoxifying agent for illegal opiates (e.g., in outpatient settings where methadone is not

Objective Opiate Withdrawal Scale (OOWS)

Instructions: Rate the patient on the basis of what you observe during a timed 10-minute period:

Item	Score 1 point for Each Item If	Points
1. Yawning	present	_____
2. Rhinorrhea	3 or more	_____
3. Piloerection (observe patient's arm or chest)	present	_____
4. Perspiration	present	_____
5. Lacrimation	present	_____
6. Mydriasis	present	_____
7. Tremors (hands)	present	_____
8. Hot and cold flashes (shivering or huddling for warmth)	present	_____
9. Restlessness (frequent shifts of position)	present	_____
10. Vomiting	present	_____
11. Muscle twitches	present	_____
12. Abdominal cramps (holding stomach)	present	_____
13. Anxiety (observable manifestations: finger tapping, fidgeting, agitation)	present	_____
TOTAL OOWS (Sum items 1–13)		_____

Figure 56-3 Objective opiate withdrawal scale (OOWS). [Reprinted with permission from Barker SB, et al: *Diagnostic Source Book on Drug Abuse Research and Treatment.* NIDA, 1993 (NIH No. 93-3508).]

permitted) or to alleviate methadone abstinence symptoms in a patient ending methadone maintenance. The major side effects to monitor in a clonidine-assisted detoxification are hypotension and sedation. Hypotension, in particular, may result in doses of clonidine being held or in discontinuation of the procedure. Because clonidine is not a cross-tolerant agent for opiates, adjunctive medication may be necessary to treat certain aspects of withdrawal.

A protocol for clonidine-assisted detoxication is given in Fig. 56-4.

Management of Withdrawal in Patients with Multiple Dependencies

In patients dependent on drugs from several pharmacologic classes, the safest strategy is to suppress the abstinence syndrome for each drug class and detoxify the patient from the most dangerous class of drugs first. This problem appears in patients dependent on both opiates and sedative-hypnotics or alcohol. With these patients, it is best to hold a constant reasonable methadone dose while gradually detoxifying the patient from a sedative hypnotic or alcohol. Management of the sedative or alcohol withdrawal, which may lead to convulsions or death, is clearly more pressing than the discomfort associated with opiate withdrawal. After sedative-hypnotic withdrawal is complete or very well controlled, methadone detoxification can proceed.

Agents to Aid Relapse Prevention

An exciting new area in psychopharmacology is medication to prevent relapse in chemically de-

Figure 56-4 Clonidine detoxification.

Day	Short-acting Opiate (e.g., heroin)	Long-acting Opiate (e.g., methadone)
Day 1	0.1 mg every 4 hrs	0.1 mg every 4 hrs
Day 2–4	0.1–0.2 mg every 4 hrs (depending on symptoms)	0.1–0.2 mg every 4 hrs (depending on symptoms)
Day 5–10	Reduce daily dose by 0.2–0.4 mg/day	Maintain on 0.4–1.2 mg/day
Day 11		Reduce daily dose by 0.2–0.4 mg/day

Adjunctive medication: Oxazepam (in limited supplies) for sleep or agitation; ibuprofen for muscle or bone pain; bismuth subsalicylate for diarrhea

pendent patients once the immediate detoxification period is over. The agents for this indication act by widely differing mechanisms. *Aversive therapy* creates a new biochemistry in which use of a substance produces an unpleasant effect rather than the usual gratifying effect. *Antagonist therapy* prevents the usual gratifying effect, but does not replace it with an aversive experience. *Agonist therapy* replaces the drug of abuse with an agent that stimulates the same receptor system, but that has a safer pharmacologic profile. Agents are also being used on a limited basis to correct hypothesized persistent neurochemical changes induced by drug abuse. Finally, agents are being developed to act on the many intervening processes between substance use and effect (e.g., to act on synaptic transporters).

A psychopharmacologic approach to relapse prevention is not meant to replace psychosocial treatment. There is evidence that psychosocial treatments add to the effectiveness of pharmacologic treatment. In fact, when psychosocial treatments are intensive and relevant to problems of drug dependency, the difference in effectiveness between placebo and medications proposed for relapse prevention is reduced. The physician is often challenged to justify to both the patient and the nonphysician clinician the value of medication in the treatment of drug dependence. This justification must include a clear distinction between the effects of taking prescribed medication and addiction to drugs of abuse.

Medications for Alcohol Dependence

Disulfiram inhibits aldehyde dehydrogenase by binding to it irreversibly and, in doing so, changing the body's response to alcohol. Aldehyde dehydrogenase catalyzes the oxidation of acetaldehyde to acetic acid. Therefore, when alcohol is ingested, acetaldehyde accumulates, leading to an experience that may be extremely dysphoric, but which is usually self-limited and not life-threatening. The acetaldehyde reaction is characterized by palpitations, hypotension, nausea and vomiting, and diaphoresis. In its most severe form (usually associated with high doses of both alcohol and disulfiram), the reaction may lead to cardiovascular collapse and death.

The best work to date suggests that disulfiram may reduce the number of drinking days in those alcoholics who drink while taking it. Placebo-controlled studies suggest that compliance with medication taking rather than the disulfiram itself may be the critical factor in producing a better outcome in alcoholics. Many clinicians feel that among well-motivated patients, disulfiram may be an important disincentive to drink. In particular, there is some research that shows good results when disulfiram is used in a contract with an alcoholic's spouse; the alcoholic agrees to take disulfiram in the spouse's presence and the spouse agrees to cease commenting on the alcoholic's drinking.

Disulfiram is usually prescribed at a dose of

250 mg per day. At this dose, side effects such as lethargy are reduced, yet inhibition of aldehyde dehydrogenase is maintained. Disulfiram may cause a drug-induced psychosis by virtue of its inhibition of dopamine β-hydroxylase. It may also cause changes in the blood levels of other medications (e.g., tricyclic antidepressant and phenytoin levels are increased). Patients should be warned about sources of alcohol beyond beverages (e.g., cosmetic preparations). Acetaldehyde reactions from alcohol ingestion may occur up to 2 weeks after the last dose of disulfiram.

Naltrexone's use in alcohol-relapse prevention derives from the hypothesis that endogenous opiate systems might mediate the reinforcing effects of alcohol. This hypothesis has been tested in animal models, where naltrexone administration led to diminished alcohol consumption.

Positive clinical trials with naltrexone have led to its approval by the FDA for the treatment of alcoholism. In these studies, naltrexone *combined with structured psychosocial treatment* was associated with greater complete abstinence than was placebo, less craving for alcohol when abstinent, and less drinking once drinking began. In these 12-week trials, naltrexone was well tolerated. The recommended dose is 50 mg per day.

Naltrexone may be superior to disulfiram in that there is no added ill-effect once drinking begins, it may limit the severity of binges, and it may diminish preoccupation with alcohol in abstinent alcoholics. Some have suggested that it may allow alcoholics to drink in a controlled way (this is at odds with the goal of almost all treatment programs, however). Naltrexone is a promising new treatment modality that must be evaluated in longer clinical trials and in populations of patients with multiple drug dependencies. It should also be compared with disulfiram in clinical trials.

Medications for Cocaine Dependence

There is tremendous interest in the development of pharmacotherapies for cocaine dependence, given the high relapse rates with psychosocial treatment alone. Although a variety of agents have been reported to be effective in case reports or open pilot studies, the results of double-blind studies have been disappointingly inconsistent. Yet surveys show that a large number of physicians in addiction medicine are prescribing medication to treat cocaine dependence even though no agent has met standards that would qualify for FDA approval.

Antidepressants are the most often prescribed medications for cocaine dependence. Their use is prompted by the frequent presence of symptoms of depression in cocaine addicts and the possibility that antidepressants might correct neurotransmitter deficiencies caused by cocaine use. Desipramine has been the best studied medication. Unfortunately, initial reports of its success in preventing relapse have been followed by studies that questioned its efficacy. Doses typically used are in the same range as in the treatment for depression. Patients who relapse into cocaine use while taking antidepressants should be assessed for the possibility of additive cardiotoxic effects.

Dopamine agonist therapy has been suggested based on the hypothesis that an underlying mechanism in cocaine relapse is compensation for cocaine-induced dopamine depletion. Bromocriptine and amantadine have been the most commonly used medications based on this hypothesis. Although early anecdotal reports and open trials showed promise in relieving cocaine "craving" in newly abstinent addicts, better controlled studies with objective outcomes (e.g., urine toxicology results) have been discouraging.

Neuroleptic medication has also been suggested as a treatment for cocaine addiction given the possibility that its dopamine-receptor blockade may prevent the euphoric response to cocaine. Flupenthixol decanoate has shown some promise in limited clinical trials. However, vast clinical experience in patients with schizophrenia taking neuroleptic medication suggests that currently available neuroleptic medication will not, on its own, diminish cocaine use. Furthermore, if cocaine induces dopamine depletion, patients taking neuroleptics may be at greater risk for dyskinesia and neuroleptic malignant syndrome. There are some data suggesting that cocaine use predisposes to dyskinesia, but less to support worries about neuroleptic malignant syndrome.

Psychomotor stimulants, suggested as a maintenance treatment, have been reported to exacerbate cocaine dependence. Those patients with comorbid attention deficit disorder, however, may benefit from stimulants. Similarly, lithium has not been effective in decreasing cocaine use except in those patients with comorbid bipolar disorder. Anticonvulsants, particularly carbamazepine, have been disappointing in controlled trials after showing initial promise in open studies. The best evidence to date on pharmacotherapy for cocaine dependence suggests that aggressive treatment of comorbid psychopathology improves outcome; the benefits of pharmacotherapy for patients without comorbid psychopathology remain unclear. The development of an effective pharmacotherapy for cocaine dependence is a research priority of the highest order.

Medications for Opiate Dependence

Methadone maintenance remains a controversial therapy for opiate dependence despite three decades of demonstrated efficacy. When properly prescribed, methadone prevents *or reduces* illicit opiate use, craving for illicit opiates, criminal behavior associated with acquisition of illicit opiates, and diseases associated with illicit opiate use (such as HIV-related illness). No other treatment for opiate dependency compares as favorably, nor does any other treatment so successfully retain patients who start treatment. Although the benefits of methadone maintenance may be seen as early as 1 year in treatment, maximum benefits may not be seen until 4 years of treatment.

The pharmacology of methadone makes it a good therapeutic agent for maintenance treatment. Like heroin, it is a μ-receptor agonist. Unlike heroin, it is effective after oral administration and has a long half-life (>24 hours). It effectively suppresses the opiate withdrawal syndrome for up to 36 hours and it also blocks the euphoric effects of other opiates. There are minimal side effects during chronic administration; constipation, excess sweating, and decreased sexual interest are most commonly reported but these rarely lead to discontinuation. When prescribed with careful titration, methadone is neither intoxicating nor sedating and does not interfere with performance of functions that are important for responsible adult roles (e.g., studies have shown that methadone does not impair driving ability).

In the initial phases of methadone maintenance, patients are given daily doses in the 20 to 40 mg range primarily to relieve abstinence symptoms. During the "induction period," a patient is typically given 5- to 10-mg increases over a period of days to weeks, to establish the dose required to prevent craving for opiates and to block the euphoric effects of opiates taken illicitly. Subjective reports and interval history are supplemented by regular and frequent urine toxicologies. Although some patients do well at doses of 40 mg per day, several studies have now found doses of 80 mg per day or higher are more likely to confer benefit. There is research to suggest that most patients will have an optimal treatment response with trough methadone blood levels in the 200 to 400 ng/ml range. Some patients who require relatively higher methadone doses have been shown to have relatively low methadone blood levels at more conventional doses. As with other types of pharmacotherapy, dose should be individually determined by the physician based on the treatment response; the terms "high dose" and "low dose" should be replaced with "proper dose" for each patient.

Two special circumstances merit comment—methadone-maintained patients on medical/surgical units and pregnant patients. For patients admitted to general hospitals, the dose of methadone should be verified by contact with the patient's methadone program. It is best to maintain the patient on that dose throughout the stress of an illness and its treatment rather than to suggest dose reduction. Although the methadone given for maintenance will suppress opiate withdrawal, it will not provide analgesia. Methadone-maintained patients with severe pain should be given nonopiate analgesia or short-acting opioid analgesics as needed (doses may be higher and intervals shorter). Mixed agonist-antagonist drugs, such as pentazocine or buprenorphine, should be avoided as they may precipitate opiate withdrawal.

Women on methadone maintenance who become pregnant should be encouraged to continue methadone maintenance, although some clinicians recommend a lower daily dose during the third trimester. Symptoms of neonatal abstinence must be anticipated and treated following birth. Parents should be reassured that longitudinal studies have shown that methadone-exposed infants develop normally.

Medications for Nicotine Dependence

Nicotine induces the same addictive behavioral patterns (e.g., inability to cut down use) and types of neuroadaptation (e.g., tolerance) as other addictive drugs. Although nicotine intoxication and withdrawal do not lead to the acutely harmful behavioral disturbances that are seen with other drugs of abuse, nicotine is a very important drug of abuse given its health consequences. Relapse-prevention pharmacotherapy for nicotine addiction must address these withdrawal symptoms, which may last for weeks in untreated patients: anxiety, restlessness, difficulty concentrating, and irritability. Effective pharmacotherapy should also decrease craving for nicotine and must compete with multiple conditioned-stimuli for nicotine use (e.g., a morning cup of coffee) to produce this effect. The degree of nicotine dependence may be assessed by the Fagerstrom test (Fig. 56-5).

Nicotine replacement therapies provide a medically safe way to deliver nicotine and then gradually reduce it. Unlike methadone, this is not intended as an indefinite maintenance treatment. Nicotine is currently available without prescription in two forms for replacement therapy: In nicotine polacrilex ("nicotine gum") and as a transdermal patch. Both replacement strategies have been found effective in promoting nicotine abstinence.

Nicotine polacrilex is a resin containing either 2 or 4 mg of nicotine. Because of limited bioavailability of buccal nicotine, only about 50 percent of the nicotine is absorbed. Studies show that this agent works best when patients achieve nicotine blood levels with gum comparable to nicotine blood levels with smoking; this may require 25 pieces of gum per day. Advantages of the gum are its convenience and the degree of patient control over its use. Some have criticized its prn use as akin to smoking cigarettes and point to individuals who have had great difficulty stopping the gum. Some patients have developed temporomandibular joint syndrome from the quantity of chewing and some find its peppery taste offensive.

Nicotine patches are less obtrusive than gum for some patients. They are applied once per day and provide steady nicotine levels, thereby avoiding the peak and trough effects that nicotine polacrilex shares with cigarettes. The patches are available in diminishing strengths, which allow for orderly downward titration. Local skin reactions to the patch are common but usually manageable. Some patients complain of nighttime restlessness and nightmares. Patients should be cautioned to wash their hands after handling nicotine patches because eye irritation can result from inadvertently rubbing nicotine there. Current research suggests little benefit from continuing transdermal nicotine beyond 8 weeks in most patients.

A sustained-release preparation of bupropion also has FDA approval for the treatment of nicotine dependence, and its efficacy is similar to nicotine replacement. The suggested dose is 150 mg bid. Patients should take the medication for two weeks before attempting smoking cessation. For patients who have not benefited from either nicotine replacement or bupropion alone, the combination of nicotine replacement and bupropion has shown safety and greater success than either treatment above.

Figure 56-5 Fagerstrom test for nicotine dependence. (Reprinted with permission from Fagerstrom KO, Heatherton TF, Kozlowski LT: Nicotine addiction and its assessment. *Ear Nose Throat* 69(11):763–767, 1992.)

Questions	Answers	Points
1. How soon after you wake up do you smoke your first cigarette?	Within 5 minutes	3
	6–30 minutes	2
	31–60 minutes	1
	After 60 minutes	0
2. Do you find it difficult to refrain from smoking in places where it is forbidden, e.g., in church, at the library, in cinema, etc?	Yes	1
	No	0
3. Which cigarette would you hate most to give up?	The first one in the morning	1
	All others	0
4. How many cigarettes/day do you smoke?	10 or less	0
	11–20	1
	21–30	2
	31 or more	3
5. Do you smoke more frequently during the first hours after waking than during the rest of the day?	Yes	1
	No	0
6. Do you smoke if you are so ill that you are in bed most of the day?	Yes	1
	No	0

Proposed Scoring Cut-Offs		
0–2	Very low	
3–4	Low	
5	Medium	
6–7	High (Heavy)	
8–10	Very High	

Pharmacotherapies for Substance Abusers with Additional Types of Psychiatric Illness

Studies have consistently demonstrated higher than expected rates of substance abuse in psychiatric patients, and higher than expected rates of other psychiatric illness in patients treated for substance-related disorders. This comorbidity is especially true for women. The following generalizations are supported by clinical experience with this challenging patient population: treatment should be administered by professionals with a skill in both general psychiatry and chemical dependency; insistence on abstinence as a condition for treatment is unrealistic, and some psychiatric symptom stability may be necessary before decreases in substance use are evident; and abstinence is not a requirement for safe and effective pharmacotherapy with most psycho-tropic agents. Agents with abuse potential themselves, such as benzodiazepines, should be avoided whenever possible. Even when comorbid psychopathology is effectively treated, the substance-use disorder tends to persist if not treated as an illness in itself.

Pregnancy and Addiction

Pregnancy offers a unique opportunity to help addicted women, given that motivation to protect the fetus may translate into better self-care. Laws requiring clinicians to report any drug use in pregnancy to child protective services may have the unwanted effect of keeping pregnant drug users away from care for fear of imagined or real legal consequences. Beyond treatment for addiction, services for pregnant addicts should include case management to assure that appropriate prenatal care is received, that the woman has concrete resources to support the newborn, and that the woman is ready for parenting emotionally and based on infant-care knowledge. Good care for these patients requires coordination of the efforts of a number of caregivers (e.g., physician, social worker, drug counselor).

Treatment of alcohol withdrawal in pregnancy is most safely done on an inpatient basis. During treatment for withdrawal, fetal well being should be monitored by external cardiac monitoring. Although benzodiazepine use poses some risk of toxicity to the fetus, there is little evidence that short-term use during an episode of withdrawal has ill effects. Furthermore, the risk of uncontrolled alcohol withdrawal, with possible progression to delirium, poses a far greater threat to the woman and fetus. When intravenous benzodiazepines are necessary, there is a greater possibility of high free bilirubin levels in the fetus as the preservative in the intravenous preparation is a potent uncoupler of bilirubin and albumin.

Disulfiram is contraindicated for relapse prevention in pregnancy as its use has been associated with teratogenic effects. Although there are no adequate studies of naltrexone in pregnancy, preliminary studies have shown large doses of naltrexone are embryocidal in animals.

Sedative-hypnotic withdrawal, like alcohol withdrawal, should be undertaken (or at least begun) on an inpatient basis for pregnant patients. Substituting a long-acting sedative-hypnotic for the shorter-acting drug of abuse followed by a gradual taper is the best practice.

Pregnant women who are using cocaine should clearly detoxify from it, but no medications have been consistently shown to ameliorate the process.

For opiate addicts who are pregnant, my opinion is that stabilization with methadone maintenance is the most successful strategy. "Drug-free" approaches result in frequent relapses and patients leaving treatment. The Center for Substance Abuse Treatment presents the following advantages of methadone maintenance in pregnancy:[12]

- Reduces illegal opioid use as well as use of other drugs
- Helps to remove the opioid-dependent woman from the drug-seeking environment and eliminates the necessary illegal behavior
- Prevents fluctuations of the maternal drug level that may occur throughout the day
- Improves maternal nutrition, increasing the weight of the newborn
- Improves the woman's ability to participate in prenatal care and other rehabilitation efforts
- Enhances the woman's ability to prepare for the birth of the infant and begin home-making
- Reduces obstetrical complications

After a methadone-maintained woman gives birth, monitoring of the infant and treatment of withdrawal should be undertaken by a pediatrician or neonatologist. Treatment protocols using paregoric and phenobarbital have been effective in treating neonatial opiate withdrawal.

References and Selected Readings

1. American Society of Addiction Medicine: *Patient Placement Criteria for the Treatment of Substance-Related Disorders,* Chevy Chase, MD: ASAM, 2nd ed. 1996.
2. Barnes HN, Samet JH: Brief interventions with substance-abusing patients. *Med Clin North Am* 81(4):867–879, 1997.
3. Ciraulo D, Shader R (eds): *Clinical Manual of Chemical Dependence.* Washington, DC: APA Press, 1991.
4. Cyr MG, Wartman SA: The effectiveness of routine screening questions in the detection of alcoholism. *JAMA,* 259(1):51–54, 1988.
5. Dawson NV, et al: The effect of patient gender on the prevalence and recognition of alcoholism on a general medicine inpatient service. *J Gen Intern Med,* 7:38–45, 1992.
6. Ewing JA: Detecting alcoholism, the CAGE questionnaire. *JAMA,* 252(14):1905–1907, 1984.
7. Fiore MC, et al: *Smoking Cessation: Information for Specialists, Clinical Practice Guideline.* Rockville, MD: DHNS 1996. Quick Reference Guide, No. 18. AHCR Pub No. 96–0694.

8. Galanter M, Kleber H (eds): *The American Psychiatric Press Textbook of Substance Abuse Treatment.* Washington DC: APA Press, 1994.
9. Lewis DC: The role of the generalist in the care of the substance-abusing patient. *Med Clin North Am* 81(4):831–843, 1997.
10. Lowinson J, et al (eds): *Substance Abuse, A Comprehensive Textbook* 3rd ed. Baltimore: Williams & Wilkins, 1997.
11. Miller LJ: Treatment of the Addicted Woman in Pregnancy, in Graham AW, et al (eds): *Principles of Addiction Medicine* 2nd ed. Chevy Chase, MD: ASAM, 1998.
12. Mitchell JL, et al: *Pregnant, Substance-Using Women.* Rockville, MD: DHHS, 1993. Pub. No. 93-1998.
13. Sokol RJ, et al: The T-ACE questions: Practical prenatal detection of risk-drinking. *Am J Obstet Gynecol* 160(4):863–868, 1989.
14. Vaillant GE: *The Natural History of Alcoholism.* Cambridge, MA: Harvard University Press, 1983.
15. Wesson DR, et al: *Detoxification from Alcohol and Other Drugs.* Rockville, MD: DHHS 1995. Pub No. 95-3046.
16. Zweben J, Payte J: Methadone maintenance in the treatment of opioid dependence: A current perspective. *West J Med,* 152(5):588–599, 1990.

CHAPTER 57

The Recognition and Management of Eating Disorders

Neville H. Golden

Current fashion trends and societal pressure to be thin have resulted in large numbers of young women who are dieting. It is not surprising that the incidence of eating disorders has increased markedly in the last two decades, particularly in the adolescent age group. Eating disorders are complex biopsychosocial disorders that have significant medical and psychiatric morbidity. Caloric restriction, excessive exercise, and unhealthy weight loss practices can affect many organ systems including the reproductive system.

Diagnostic Criteria

The diagnostic criteria for the two major eating disorders, anorexia nervosa and bulimia nervosa, are listed in Table 57-1.[1] Anorexia nervosa is a condition characterized by excessive weight loss, preoccupation with shape and weight, and an intense fear of becoming fat. Despite their emaciated state, these individuals consider themselves to be fat and restrict their caloric intake, exercise excessively, and abuse diet pills, laxatives, or diuretics in an attempt to lose further weight. By definition, patients have amenorrhea of greater than three months duration.

Bulimia nervosa is characterized by repeated cycles of bingeing followed by inappropriate compensatory behaviors such as self-induced vomiting, excessive exercise, starvation, or use of laxatives or diuretics. A "binge" has two features: consumption of an amount of food that most people would consider to be excessive and a sense of loss of control during the binge. After a binge, patients feel guilty and shameful, and engage in some form of compensatory behavior to bring a sense of relief. Compensatory behavior may be purging by vomiting, using laxatives or diuretics, or starvation or excessive exercise. Cycles of starvation are followed by episodes of

TABLE 57-1 DSM-IV Diagnostic Criteria for Anorexia Nervosa and Bulimia Nervosa[1]

Anorexia Nervosa

A. Refusal to maintain body weight over a minimally normal weight for age and height (e.g., weight loss leading to maintenance of body weight 15% below that expected), or failure to make expected weight gain during period of growth, leading to body weight below 15% of that expected.

B. Intense fear of gaining weight or becoming fat, even though underweight.

C. Disturbance in the way in which one's body weight or shape is experienced, undue influence of body shape and weight on self-evaluation, or denial of the seriousness of current low body weight.

D. In postmenarchal females, amenorrhea, i.e., the absence of at least three consecutive menstrual cycles. (A woman is considered to have amenorrhea if her periods occur only following hormone, e.g., estrogen, administration).

Restricting type: During the episode of anorexia nervosa, the person does not regularly engage in binge eating or purging behavior (i.e., self-induced vomiting or the misuse of laxatives or diuretics).

Binge eating/purging type: During the episode of anorexia nervosa, the person regularly engages in binge eating or purging behavior (i.e., self-induced vomiting or the misuse of laxatives or diuretics).

Bulimia Nervosa

A. Recurrent episodes of binge eating. An episode of binge eating is characterized by both of the following:

  (1) eating in a discrete period of time (e.g., within any 2-hour period), an amount of food that is definitely larger than most people would eat in a similar period of time in similar circumstances; and,

  (2) a sense of lack of control over eating during the episode (e.g., a feeling that one cannot stop eating or control what or how much one is eating).

B. Recurrent inappropriate compensatory behavior to prevent weight gain, such as self-induced vomiting; misuse of laxatives, diuretitcs, or other medications; fasting; or excessive exercise.

C. The binge eating and inappropriate compensatory behaviors both occur, on average, at least twice a week for 3 months.

D. Self-evaluation is unduly influenced by body shape and weight.

E. The disturbance does not occur exclusively during episodes of anorexia nervosa.

Purging type: The person regularly engages in self-induced vomiting or the misuse of laxatives or diuretics.

Nonpurging type: The person uses other inappropriate compensatory behaviors, such as fasting or excessive exercise, but does not regularly engage in self-induced vomiting or the misuse of laxatives or diuretics.

food craving, bingeing, and then purging. Most patients with bulimia nervosa are of normal weight but they can be underweight or overweight. Menses are usually regular, but they may be irregular.

There is a spectrum of eating disorders with obesity at the one extreme, bulimia nervosa in the middle, and anorexia nervosa at the other extreme. While there are clinical differences between anorexia nervosa and bulimia nervosa, patients with these disorders share many similar features. Approximately 40 percent of patients with anorexia nervosa also engage in bulimic behaviors. Furthermore, 10 to 30 percent of patients may cross over from one disorder to the other at some time in the course of their illness.[21]

The vast majority of patients who require intervention do not meet the above diagnostic criteria. Included in this group of patients are those who have not yet lost 15 percent of their body weight, those who induce vomiting to maintain a weight in the normal range, and those who binge and purge regularly, but not at the frequency of twice a week. This group of patients is sometimes given the diagnosis of Eating Disorder Not Otherwise Specified (NOS). These patients suffer from the same degree of psychological distress and still need clinical intervention.

Epidemiology of Eating Disorders

Eating disorders primarily affect young women—only 5 to 10 percent of cases are male. In the United States, between 1 and 2 million women meet strict criteria for bulimia nervosa, and approximately 500,000 women meet diagnostic criteria for anorexia nervosa. The incidence of anorexia nervosa among females 15 to 24 years old has increased over the past 10 to 20 years, but has remained relatively stable among older women and males.[13]

The peak age of onset of anorexia nervosa is in mid adolescence (age 13 to 15 years) and for bulimia nervosa in late adolescence or early adulthood (age 17 to 25 years). Over 90 percent of patients with eating disorders are diagnosed before the age of 25 years. The prevalence of anorexia nervosa in adolescent girls is 1 in 200. For bulimia nervosa the prevalence in young women is 1 to 5 percent.[2]

The eating disorders are more frequently seen in women from middle and upper-middle class socioeconomic groups and, despite previous beliefs, they are found in all ethnic groups. Women who engage in sporting activities where physical appearance is important are at increased risk for the development of an eating disorder. There is also an increased incidence of eating disorders in women with diabetes mellitus. In this subgroup of patients, manipulation of diet and insulin dose in order to lose weight can have a devastating impact on control of the diabetes.

Etiology

The etiology of eating disorders is multifactorial and includes biological, psychological, and sociocultural factors.

Biological Factors

There is an increasing body of literature demonstrating a genetic predisposition to the development of an eating disorder. Studies have consistently demonstrated increased concordance rates for anorexia nervosa in monozygotic, as compared to dizygotic, twins and increased prevalence of eating disorders in female relatives of probands with anorexia nervosa.[22]

In addition, neurotransmitter abnormalities in serotoninergic, dopaminergic, and noradrenalin pathways have been identified in patients with eating disorders, and many patients respond to medications that affect central neurotransmitter levels. Most of these abnormalities resolve with refeeding, which suggests that they are secondary to malnutrition, but some have been found to persist after long-term weight gain, which suggests that they may have predated the development of the eating disorder and may even have predisposed to its onset.[7]

Dieting is common to all of the eating disorders, and prolonged starvation can result in predictable physiological responses. In 1950, Keys et al. demonstrated that self-imposed starvation in previously healthy male volunteers resulted in many of the psychological, as well as the physiologic, disturbances seen in patients with anorexia nervosa. Subjects became preoccupied with food, had dreams about food, and collected recipes. They became progressively more depressed and irritable and lost their sexual drive.[8] Malnutrition may result in altered neurotransmitter pathways as a result of lack of essential dietary substrates (such as tryptophan), which are necessary for the synthesis of neurotransmitters.

Psychological Factors

Individuals with certain psychological traits are more likely to suffer from an eating disorder. Patients with anorexia nervosa tend to be bright, excellent students, and good athletes. Despite apparent successes in academic and athletic pursuits, these individuals feel inadequate. Self-esteem is low and they strive hard to please others at the expense of their own feelings. They tend to be rigid, obsessive, and perfectionistic, and have difficulty separating from their families. They have a tremendous need for control, and a sense of lack of control during the adolescent years causes them to focus on something they can control, namely their diet and body size. Women with anorexia nervosa show little interest in dating and are not usually sexually active.

Patients with bulimia nervosa are less perfectionistic and tend to be more impulsive. They are more likely to be sexually active and may have multiple sexual partners. They are more likely to participate in high-risk behaviors such as alcohol and drug use. Patients with bulimia nervosa are much more aware of their psychological distress and are more amenable to intervention. Childhood sexual abuse is a risk factor for bulimia nervosa, particularly when a coexistent mood disorder or personality disorder is present.

Sociocultural Factors

Societal norms, where thinness is equated with beauty, success, and power, pose tremendous pressures on young women. Large numbers of otherwise normal women in nonclinical samples are dieting and exercising to maintain low body weights. Most women who are dieting do not develop an eating disorder, but historically, changes in the incidence of anorexia nervosa have coincided with changes in fashion trends, with peaks in the 1920s and 1930s and further increases in the 1980s and 1990s.

The etiology of an eating disorder in a particular individual depends on many factors and may be different for different individuals. In a biologically predisposed individual from a high-striving middle-class family, a feeling of loss of control during adolescence may cause her to diet to regain control. Initial weight loss is met with approval by family and friends. Continued dieting leads to neurotransmitter abnormalities and the features of malnutrition that perpetuate the illness. By the time a patient is brought in to a physician for help with the eating disorder, patterns of behavior are well entrenched and the disease has taken on "a life of its own," controlling daily activities of the young woman.

Clinical Manifestations

For both anorexia nervosa and bulimia nervosa, denial of the illness is universal and the presence of an eating disorder may be hidden for months or years. It is not unusual for a young woman to be reluctantly brought to the physician by a concerned family member who has noticed a rapid weight loss. An adolescent may be brought in for evaluation of short stature or delayed puberty. When a young woman does seek help voluntarily, it is usually because of menstrual irregularity, hair loss, or after a frightening event, such as an episode of syncope or hematemesis. Occasionally, a patient seeks medical attention because she is "fed up with the eating disorder."

The presence of amenorrhea (either primary or secondary) in a young woman of low weight should raise the suspicion of an underlying eating disorder. A few pertinent questions can help elucidate the underlying problem. It is important to explore the patient's feelings about her current weight, her desired weight, and concerns about the weight loss. Even the most difficult of patients will openly admit that they feel they are too fat and that they would like to lose further weight. If they deny feeling too fat, an appropriate question would be, "Is there any part of your body that you consider too fat?" The patient usually will admit that she perceives her abdomen, thighs, or buttocks to be too large.

Information should be obtained regarding the amount, duration, rate, and methods of weight loss; the patient's highest and lowest weights; the amount of exercise performed and the duration of amenorrhea. The weight at which menses were lost should be noted because this can help predict the weight necessary for menses to resume. An average 24-hour dietary recall should be obtained. In review of systems, the patient should be asked about cold intolerance, bowel habits, and episodes of hematemesis or fainting. Some assessment should be made regarding coexistent depression and social isolation.

Physical Examination

Patients with anorexia nervosa are hypothermic and wear multiple layers of clothing to keep warm and to hide the weight loss. It is essential to obtain an accurate height and weight. Weight should be measured post-voiding with the patient undressed and wearing only underwear and a hospital gown.

In anorexia nervosa, the most notable findings on physical examination are the features of malnutrition. These include loss of subcutaneous tissue, muscle wasting, and prominence of bony protuberances. The extremities may be cold and blue (acrocyanosis). The skin may be dry and scaly with a yellow discoloration secondary to carotenemia. There may be evidence of easy bruising. The hair may be dry and listless and the nails brittle. Fine downy hair (lanugo) may be present over the back, abdomen, and extremities. There may be evidence of dehydration or, less frequently, dependent edema. Core body temperature may be very low. Bradycardia may be profound with resting heart rates of 30 to 50 beats per minute. There may be hypotension with or without postural changes. The abdomen is scaphoid and the posterior abdominal wall easily felt through the weak abdominal musculature. Stool may be palpable in the left lower quadrant. There may be generalized muscle weakness and evidence of peripheral neuropathy.

Patients with bulimia nervosa may be of normal weight. The three clinical signs to look for on physical examination are parotid hypertrophy, erosion of dental enamel, and scars over the knuckle of the index finger (Russell's sign). Parotid hypertrophy occurs in 10 to 30 percent of patients with bulimia nervosa.[17] It is usually bilateral. The exact etiology is not clear, but it is thought to be secondary to hypertophy as a result of the frequent binges. Erosion of dental enamel is most apparent on the lingual aspects of the anterior teeth and is caused by dissolution of the dental enamel by acidic gastric contents. Calluses over the knuckles are formed by abrasions from

TABLE 57-2 Recommended Laboratory and Ancillary Tests for the Evaluation of Eating Disorders

---
1. Complete blood count
2. Erythrocyte sedimentation rate
3. Urinalysis
4. Chemistry profile
5. Serum amylase—if vomiting
6. Thyroid function tests
7. LH, FSH, estradiol, and prolactin—if amenorrheic
8. Electrocardiogram

---

the incisors when the fingers are used to induce vomiting.

Laboratory Investigation

Recommended laboratory tests to be obtained on initial presentation are listed in Table 57-2. Despite marked cachexia, the laboratory tests are usually normal. The complete blood count may show mild anemia, leukopenia, or thrombocytopenia. In states of malnutrition, the erythrocyte sedimentation rate is characteristically very low and the presence of a mildly elevated sedimentation rate should raise the suspicion of another diagnosis.

Electrolyte disturbances may occur with fluid restriction, vomiting, or laxative or diuretic use. Hypokalemia is seen in those who are vomiting or using laxatives. Hyponatremia can occur when the young woman is water-loading to suppress feelings of hunger or to achieve a desired weight in the doctor's office. Both hypernatremia and hyperkalemia can occur in the presence of dehydration. Hypochloremic alkalosis develops with recurrent vomiting. Serum phosphorus levels are usually normal on presentation but may drop precipitously on refeeding or after a binge. Serum transaminases are elevated in 4 to 38 percent of patients with anorexia nervosa, probably because of fatty degeneration of the liver secondary to malnutrition. In those who are bingeing and purging, serum amylase may be elevated. Total protein and serum albumin are usually normal. Cholesterol levels are elevated.

The urinalysis may show ketones, mild proteinuria, and an alkaline urine. Specific gravity may be high in the presence of dehydration, but low if the patient has been water-loading prior to the visit with the doctor.

Thyroid function tests should be performed to exclude thyroid disease as the etiology of the weight loss, the menstrual irregularity, the dry hair, and the constipation. Disturbances in thyroid function tests are usually a result of malnutrition and should not be treated with thyroid replacement. Low levels of triiodothyronine (T_3) reflect the body's attempt to slow down basal metabolism to conserve energy. Thyroxine (T_4) is preferentially converted to reverse T_3, the metabolically inactive isomer of T_3, so that low levels of T_3 are accompanied by high levels of reverse T_3. Thyroid-stimulating hormone (TSH) levels are usually normal.

In anorexia nervosa, gonadotropins and estradiol levels are characteristically low reflecting suppression of the hypothalamic-pituitary-ovarian axis. Estradiol levels can be later used to monitor reproductive recovery. A normal prolactin level rules out a prolactinoma.

The electrocardiogram usually shows bradycardia and low-voltage complexes, but there may be a prolonged QTc interval, nonspecific ST segment depression, or T wave changes. In a malnourished patient, both relative tachycardia and a prolonged QTc are causes for concern because of the association between a prolonged QTc and potentially fatal ventricular tachyarrythmias.

In normal-weight bulimics, arrythmias may occur secondary to electrolyte and acid-base imbalance due to vomiting, or laxative or diuretic abuse. Bulimics who use ipecac to induce vomiting may develop a cardiomyopathy due to the toxic effect of emetine, the active alkaloid component in syrup of ipecac. The initial cardiac manifestations are tachycardia, a prolonged QTc interval, inverted T waves, and depressed ST segments.[20]

Differential Diagnosis

The diagnosis of an eating disorder is not usually difficult to make, but there are other medical and psychiatric conditions that can mimic both anorexia nervosa and bulimia nervosa. Usually these conditions can be distinguished from an eating disorder by the history, physical examination, and basic laboratory tests.

The differential diagnosis of anorexia nervosa includes inflammatory bowel disease, diabetes mellitus, hyperthyroidism, hypothalamic or pituitary tumors, and occult malignancies. When there is doubt about the diagnosis, an imaging study of the brain (CT scan or MRI) or a gastrointestinal (GI) series can be performed. Any cause of weight loss or excessive exercise may lead to amenorrhea. Athletic amenorrhea, in particular, may be difficult to distinguish from the "female athlete triad" (which is described below) or from a frank eating disorder.

Primary psychiatric illnesses, such as depression or obsessive-compulsive disorder, may result in weight loss because of lack of interest in eating or anxiety related to obsessions and compulsions such as hand washing before meals. Patients with depression or obsessive-compulsive disorder are unable to eat because of their underlying psychiatric illness, and should be distinguished from those who voluntarily refuse to eat in order to lose weight.

In the differential diagnosis of bulimia nervosa, other causes of recurrent vomiting, such as achalasia, Addison's disease, and peptic ulcer disease, should be considered.

The Female Athlete Triad

The female athlete triad consists of amenorrhea, osteopenia, and disordered eating.[15] It is caused by an imbalance between dietary intake and energy expenditure. Competitive athletes who are training several hours each day and whose caloric intake is insufficient develop hypothalamic amenorrhea with resulting hypoestrogenemia. In addition to inadequate caloric intake, some athletes may also be vomiting or using laxatives, diuretics, or diet pills to control their weight. Most of these young women do not meet the classic diagnostic criteria for anorexia nervosa. For example, their weight may be normal, they may not be trying to lose weight, and they usually do not have a distorted body image. They do not, however, increase their caloric intake to compensate for the amount of athletic training.

The female athlete triad is seen in sports in which subjective judging encourages a lean appearance, such as gymnastics, ballet dancing, figure skating, and diving, but it is also seen in long-distance runners, triathlon competitors, and tennis players. Athletes in individual sports are at higher risk than those involved in team sports. The triad occurs not only in elite athletes, but also in recreational athletes whose diet is inadequate. As in the case of the eating disorders, the hallmark is amenorrhea, which should be considered not simply a consequence of training but rather an indicator that there is a potentially serious clinical problem. Osteopenia can be profound (Fig. 57-1), placing these athletes at risk for the development of stress fractures. Women with the female athlete triad should be evaluated for the presence of a coexisting eating disorder.

Medical Complications of Eating Disorders

The medical complications of eating disorders are listed in Table 57-3.[2] Despite regular exercise, low heart rates, and low blood pressures, patients with anorexia nervosa have an impaired cardiovascular response to exercise and reduced physical fitness as measured by decreased oxygen consumption during aerobic exercise.[16] Heart size and blood volume are decreased. Recurrent ipecac use causes ipecac cardiomyopathy with myocardial cell death, and may be fatal. Congestive cardiac failure may occur, especially during the refeeding phase. Pericardial effusions are more likely to occur in those who are severely malnourished and in those who have very low heart rates. Sudden unexpected death can occur as a result of tachyarrhythmias, sometimes related to electrolyte disturbances.

Gastrointestinal complications are frequently found. Feelings of bloating, abdominal distension, and constipation are universal and occur as a result of decreased intestinal motility. Recurrent vomiting causes esophagitis which should be treated medically to relieve pain and discomfort. Mallory-Weiss tears may occur, and rupture of both the esophagus and the stomach have been described. Erosion of dental enamel warrants dental referral and evaluation. There may be mild elevations of liver enzymes secondary to fatty infiltration and focal hepatic necrosis.[14, 18] Gallstones may develop in those who lose weight rapidly.

In an adolescent whose growth is not yet complete, growth retardation and short stature can occur. With appropriate intervention prior to fusion of the epiphyses, catch-up growth can occur, but final adult height may still be lower than genetic potential.

Amenorrhea is one of the cardinal features of anorexia nervosa and is associated with low levels

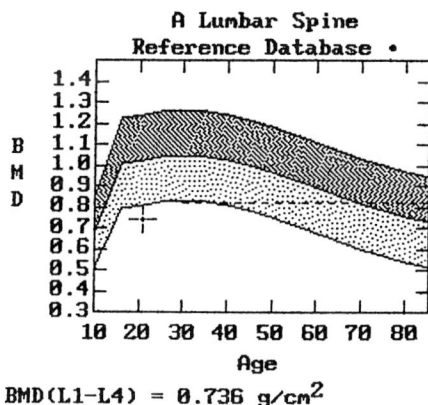

A Lumbar Spine Reference Database •

$BMD(L1-L4) = 0.736 \ g/cm^2$

Figure 57-1 Osteoporosis in a 20-year-old triathlon competitor. The patient had been amenorrheic for 15 months and trained for 2 hours a day, 6 days a week. Bone mineral density of the lumbar spine is 2.8 SD below peak bone mass and is equivalent to the bone mass of an 80-year-old woman.

TABLE 57-3 Medical Complications of Eating Disorders

Fluid and Electrolyte Imbalance	Acute pancreatitis
Hypokalemia	Superior mesenteric artery syndrome
Hyponatremia	Gallstones
Hypochloremic alkalosis	Dermatologic
Elevated BUN	Acrocyanosis
Inability to concentrate urine	Yellow dry skin (hypercarotenemia)
Decreased GFR	Brittle hair and nails
Ketonuria	Lanugo
Cardiovascular	Hair loss
Bradycardia	Russell's sign
Orthostatic hypotension	Pitting edema
Dysrhythmias	Endocrine
Electrocardiographic abnormalities	Growth retardation and short stature
Prolonged QT interval	Delayed puberty
T wave abnormalities	Amenorrhea
Low voltage	Low T_3 syndrome
Conduction defects	Partial diabetes insipidus
Ipecac cardiomyopathy	Hypercortisolism
Mitral valve prolapse	Skeletal
Congestive cardiac failure	Osteopenia
Pericardial effusion	Fractures
Gastrointestinal	Hematologic
Parotid hypertrophy	Bone marrow suppression
Perimolysis and increased incidence of dental caries	Mild anemia
Constipation	Leukopenia
Bloody diarrhea	Thrombocytopenia
Delayed gastric emptying	Low sedimentation rate
Intestinal atony	Impaired cell-mediated immunity
Esophagitis	Neurologic
Mallory-Weiss tears	Seizures
Esophageal or gastric rupture	Myopathy
Perforation/rupture of stomach	Peripheral neuropathy
Barrett esophagus	Cortical atrophy
Fatty infiltration and focal necrosis of liver	

SOURCE: Reprinted with permission of Elsevier Science and The Society for Adolescent Medicine from Fisher M, Golden NH, Katzman DK, et al: Eating disorders in adolescents: A background paper. *Adolesc Health* 16:420–437, 1998.

of luteinizing hormone (LH), follicle-stimulating hormone (FSH), and estradiol. Pulsatile secretion of LH reverts to a prepubertal pattern. The basic mechanism for the amenorrhea appears to be neurotransmitter-mediated alteration in the regulation of Gn-RH secretion by the hypothalamus. Amenorrhea usually develops after weight loss, but 20 to 30 percent of adolescents may have amenorrhea prior to significant weight loss.[3, 4]

Prolonged amenorrhea and hypoestrogenemia are associated with osteopenia, and bone mineral density of the hip and lumbar spine are reduced in anorexia nervosa. The degree of osteopenia is directly related to the age of onset and duration of amenorrhea. Reduction in bone mass occurs after relatively short duration of illness and may not be entirely reversible. The later development of osteoporosis and skeletal fractures depend not only on the rate of bone loss but also on the amount of bone present at skeletal maturity. Approximately 60 percent of peak bone mass is acquired during adolescence and very little bone is deposited after the second decade of life. A woman who develops anorexia nervosa during adolescence may not reach her peak bone mass, placing her at increased risk for the development of fractures. Because she starts off with a lower baseline bone mass, the increased fracture risk persists for many years after recovery from the eating disorder.

Osteopenia is defined as a bone mineral density between 1.0 and 2.5 SD below the mean. In frank osteoporosis, bone mineral density is more than 2.5 SD below the mean and there is disruption of the normal microarchitecture of bone, resulting in pathologic fractures, pain, and disability. Factors contributing to osteopenia and osteoporosis in patients with anorexia nervosa are shown in Table 57-4. Bone is a living structure and the amount of bone deposited depends on the tensile forces applied to it. Low body weight results in decreased bone formation. Nutritional deficiencies of calcium, vitamin D, and dietary protein may all contribute to reduced bone formation. The major dietary source of calcium is milk products. Because these foods are perceived to be of high fat content, calcium consumption is particularly low in this population. In fact, patients with anorexia nervosa have been shown to consume approximately one-third of the recommended dietary intake for calcium. Hypercortisolism, secondary to decreased metabolic clearance of cortisol, is thought to cause increased bone resorption, which will contribute to the osteopenia. Estrogen deficiency is the one factor common to the bone loss seen in postmenopausal women, competitive athletes, women who have undergone oophorectomy, and in women with anorexia nervosa. The effect of estrogen on bone deposition and resorption is mediated via cytokines, particularly interleukin-6. Weight-bearing exercise is protective of bone mass, provided body weight and regular menses are maintained. When patients with eating disorders exercise excessively and become amenorrheic, the protective effect of exercise on bone mass is lost and the fracture risk once more increases.

The major hematologic complication of anorexia nervosa is bone marrow suppression as evidenced by varying degrees of anemia, leukopenia, and, less frequently, thrombocytopenia. Despite the findings of impaired cellular immunity, there does not appear to be an increased risk of infection in this group of patients.

The neurologic complications include episodes of syncope, seizures (on the basis of electrolyte disturbances), a nutritional myopathy, and peripheral neuropathy. Structural brain changes consisting of loss of brain parenchyma and cerebral ventricular dilatation have been found with computed tomography and magnetic resonance imaging. These changes are associated with impairments in attention and concentration, and with subtle deficits in visuospatial abilities and perceptual motor functioning. Results on IQ testing are usually unaffected. The cerebral ventricular dilatation is reversible with nutritional rehabilitation and long-term follow-up, but there do appear to be persistent cerebral gray matter volume deficits after weight recovery.[5,6] The clinical implications of these findings remain to be determined.

TABLE 57-4 **Factors Contributing to Osteopenia in Anorexia Nervosa**

Reduced bone mass

Decreased calcium intake

Hypercortisolism

Estrogen deficiency

Management by the Primary Care Physician

The primary care physician can play a critical role in the management of a woman with an eating disorder. The first important step is identifying the problem. Since the primary care physician is often the only physician who sees the patient, it is important that he or she be vigilant and identify patients with eating disorders as early as possible.

Accurate information presented early in the course of the illness may be enough to prevent the development of a full-blown eating disorder. On the other hand, inaccurate or incomplete information may only serve to perpetuate the problem. For example, in a young woman with anorexia nervosa, it would be a disservice to the patient to symptomatically treat the amenorrhea by prescribing oral contraceptives without addressing the underlying eating disorder. Patients should be given a clear message that they need to gain weight and, if necessary, that they need psychological intervention.

How involved the primary care physician becomes in the management of the patient will depend on the degree of severity of the illness, the level of interest of the practitioner, and time constraints. Participating in the treatment of these patients can be time-consuming but also very rewarding. For patients who have a clear-cut eating disorder, optimal management is interdisciplinary, involving medical, nutritional, and psychiatric intervention. The primary care physician will often be the person who coordinates the treatment efforts. The broad goals of medical intervention are to reverse the unhealthy behaviors such as starvation and purging; to promote weight gain to a weight that will allow for spontaneous resumption of menses; to reverse the medical complications of the eating disorder; and to promote physical health and well-being. From a practical standpoint, it is best to consider three possible clinical situations.

Early or Mild Anorexia Nervosa or Bulimia Nervosa

In this group, the patient is of normal weight (>90 percent of ideal body weight); has no symptoms or signs of excessive weight loss; has a caloric intake above 1000 kcal/day; and is not purging but is preoccupied with weight or is using unhealthy methods for weight control.

In such a patient, the practitioner should establish a weight loss limit and a treatment goal weight (see below). The patient should be educated about the dangers of eating disorders and the potential implications of prolonged amenorrhea. Basic nutritional advice can be given regarding caloric requirements, taking into account age and activity level. To prevent daily weighing and preoccupation with weight, the patient should be advised to give away the scale and should be monitored instead by the practitioner every 2 to 4 weeks, as clinically indicated. Patients should be weighed in a consistent manner—wearing a hospital gown, post-voiding, and using the same scale. Urine specific gravity should be measured for evidence of water-loading or dehydration. The practitioner can easily be fooled by small weight increases following large weight drops. A flowchart such as that shown in Fig. 57-2 will help the physician better appreciate overall trends.

Established or Moderate Anorexia Nervosa or Bulimia Nervosa

A patient fitting into this category is someone whose weight is less than 85 percent of ideal body weight, who has symptoms of excessive weight loss, and who is using unhealthy methods to lose weight (restricting caloric intake to less than 1000 kcal/day, exercising excessively, bingeing, purging, or using laxatives). Such patients are usually amenorrheic.

In this situation, interdisciplinary intervention is warranted. Evaluation and management should address the medical, nutritional, and psychological needs of the patient. No single professional can be proficient in all aspects of the patient's care, and such patients are best managed by a team approach. The team usually comprises a physician, a nutritionist, a psychologist or psychiatrist, and sometimes a social worker. Frequent communication between team members is essential. The patient can still be followed by the primary care practitioner. Nutritional and psychological consultation can be obtained at a spe-

Figure 57-2 Flowchart for office use to monitor progress of patients with eating disorders. Overall trends in weight gain are better appreciated in the busy office setting by using a flowchart.

EATING DISORDER PROGRESS SHEET

Name _____   DOB_____

Date Initial Visit_____   Diagnosis_____

Initial Ht _____(___%)__

Initial Wt_____(___%)_   IBW_____   Goal Weight_____

Menarche_____   LMP_____

Date	Ht.	Wt.	Menses	Urine SG	Diet order

cialized eating disorder center, if available, or from professionals in the community.

Evaluation The psychiatric component of the evaluation examines for coexistent psychiatric illness, and assesses the need for psychotropic medication and individual or family psychotherapy. The nutritionist assesses the patient's nutrient intake, evaluates her attitudes towards food and eating and, when appropriate, performs skinfold measurements to assess changes in the various body compartments. After the assessment, an individualized treatment plan is formulated.

Ongoing Management The primary care practitioner can continue to provide the medical component of ongoing management. Patients with an established or moderate eating disorder should initially be monitored weekly. At each visit the patient should be weighed, examined, and the urine specific gravity checked. A rate of weight gain of approximately 1 pound per week is encouraged. Caloric prescriptions are adjusted at each visit, depending on the amount of weight gained or lost. In a patient who has been restricting calories excessively, prescribed caloric intake should be relatively low initially, but should be gradually increased by increments of 200 to 300 kcal/day at each visit. Prescribed caloric prescriptions can be translated into actual meal plans with the help of the nutritionist.

Patients should be advised to discontinue the unhealthy weight loss activities and counseled about the potential medical dangers of continuing these behaviors. Exercise aimed at "burning off calories" should be curtailed until a medically safe weight is achieved. For those who are amenorrheic for greater than 6 to 12 months, bone densitometry should be performed. If osteopenia is present, estrogen replacement therapy should be considered (see discussion below) and weight-bearing exercise encouraged. Clear criteria for hospitalization should be established early in the course of treatment.

Most patients require individual psychotherapy to address the issues that led to the development of the eating disorder, to build self-esteem, and to develop better coping strategies. For younger patients who still live at home, family therapy may be as useful as individual psychotherapy. Group therapy provides emotional support and allows the patient to feel less alone. Despite limited scientific research on the use of psychotropic medication in anorexia nervosa, there is a role for medication such as the serotonin selective reuptake inhibitors (SSRIs) in those patients who have coexistent depression or obsessive compulsive disorder. In bulimia nervosa, the efficacy of a number of antidepressant medications is well established and their effects can be independent of the effect on the depressive symptoms. In a recent multicenter, randomized, placebo-controlled trial, fluoxetine hydrochloride (Prozac) at a dose of 60 mg per day, reduced the frequency of bingeing and purging. It is widely used for this purpose.[11]

Severe Anorexia Nervosa or Bulimia Nervosa

Included in this group are those who are severely malnourished (less than 75 percent of ideal body weight); those who are dehydrated and have electrolyte disturbances or vital sign instability; those who have uncontrollable bingeing and purging; and those who have medical or psychiatric complications of the eating disorder.

Patients in this category cannot be adequately managed as outpatients and should be admitted to a specialized eating disorders unit. Generally accepted indications for hospitalization are listed in Table 57-5.[2] In clinical practice, the most common reason to hospitalize the patient is failure of outpatient treatment where, despite intervention, the patient continues to lose weight or binge and purge. Hospitalization is effective in achieving weight gain and interrupting binge-purge behaviors. Nutritional rehabilitation needs to be performed slowly and under close medical supervision to prevent sudden unexpected death associated with the "refeeding syndrome."[9] Ideally, intensive individual, family, and group psychotherapy should be provided concurrently.

Specific Clinical Issues
Determination of Treatment Goal Weight

An important role for the physician is to determine what is a healthy goal weight for the individual patient. Treatment goal weight is a topic of tremendous concern for the patient, who already feels too fat and is very reluctant to gain any weight at all. Despite the importance of this issue for both the patient and the physician, few data exist on determination of treatment goal weight, and most clinicians determine "goal weight" empirically.

TABLE 57-5 Indications for Hospitalization in a Patient with an Eating Disorder

Any one or more of the following justifies hospitalization:

1. Severe malnutrition: Weight <75% ideal body weight
2. Dehydration
3. Electrolyte disturbances
4. Cardiac dysrhythmia
5. Physiologic instability
   Severe bradycardia
   Hypotension
   Hypothermia
   Orthostatic changes
6. Arrested growth and development
7. Failure of outpatient treatment
8. Acute food refusal
9. Uncontrollable bingeing and purging
10. Acute medical complication of malnutrition (e.g., syncope, seizures, cardiac failure, pancreatitis, etc.)
11. Acute psychiatric emergencies (e.g., suicidal ideation, acute psychosis)
12. Comorbid diagnosis that interferes with the treatment of the eating disorder (e.g., severe depression, obsessive compulsive disorder, severe family dysfunction)

SOURCE: Reprinted with permission of Elsevier Science and The Society for Adolescent Medicine from Fisher M, Golden NH, Katzman DK et al: Eating disorders in adolescents: A background paper. *J Adolesc Health* 16:420–437, 1998.

Average body weight (taken from standardized tables such as the Metropolitan Life Tables or the National Center for Health Statistics height-weight tables) does not necessarily represent a "healthy" or "ideal body weight." Resumption of menses provides an objective criterion for return to biological health, and the weight necessary for resumption of menses can be considered a rational treatment goal weight. In a prospective study of 100 adolescents with anorexia nervosa (mean age at enrollment 16.9 ± 2.8 years), a weight approximately 90 percent of average body weight (defined as median weight for age and height using the NCHS tables) was the average weight at which resumption of menses occurred. Eighty-six percent of patients

who achieved this weight resumed menses within 6 months. Menses resumed at a weight approximately 5 pounds greater than the weight at which menses were lost.[4]

Based on these data, a treatment goal weight of approximately 90 percent of average body weight for age and height is assigned, but the physician should recognize that the actual weight for biological health needs to be individualized. Some patients will resume menses and function well at a weight lower than 90 percent of average body weight, and others, especially those who were overweight before the onset of the illness, may need to be at a weight higher than 90 percent average body weight.

From a practical point of view, it is reasonable to aim for maintenance at or around 90 percent of average body weight for 3 months. If after 3 months, the patient remains amenorrheic, serum estradiol should be measured. An estradiol level above 30 pg/ml indicates restoration of normal hypothalamic-pituitary-ovarian function and the physician can wait a further 3 months for resumption of menses. An estradiol level below 30 pg/ml indicates that the goal weight needs to be higher and the patient needs to gain further weight.

The Use of Estrogen Replacement Therapy for the Treatment of Osteopenia in Anorexia Nervosa

The use of estrogen replacement therapy in preventing osteoporosis in postmenopausal women is well established, and the sooner after menopause it is initiated the greater the efficacy.[12] In young women with anorexia nervosa, gaining weight and resuming spontaneous menses takes months to years at a time when bone should be accrued to achieve peak bone mass. The obvious question is, should the physician be prescribing estrogen replacement therapy for these young women with anorexia nervosa?

In a retrospective study of 65 women with anorexia nervosa, Seeman et al. showed that the 16 women who had been on oral contraceptives had higher lumbar spine bone mineral density than the 49 women with no contraceptive exposure. Both groups, however, still had lower bone mass than healthy controls.[19] In the only prospective randomized study published to date, Klibanski et al. found that after a mean follow-up period of 1.5 years, there was no significant change in bone mineral density in those treated with estrogen replacement therapy when compared with those who received placebo. Only in the subgroup of patients who were less than 70 percent of ideal body weight, was there a significant difference. In that group, spinal bone mass increased 4 percent in those who received estrogen but decreased 20 percent in those who received placebo.[10] These investigators demonstrated that young women with anorexia nervosa have persistent osteopenia despite estrogen replacement. They also showed that there was a marked improvement in spinal bone mass in those patients who gained weight and spontaneously resumed menses during the study period. Clearly, further studies with a longer follow-up period are needed to clarify the role of estrogen replacement therapy in anorexia nervosa.

Nutritional rehabilitation, weight gain, and resumption of spontaneous menses remain the mainstay of treatment. Calcium supplementation should be prescribed for those whose diets provide less than 1200 to 1500 mg/day. Moderate weight-bearing exercise should be encouraged, but strenuous exercise that may result in stress fractures should be avoided. In those with prolonged amenorrhea (>6 to 12 months' duration), bone densitometry should be performed and estrogen replacement therapy considered.

Summary

Eating disorders are complex biopsychosocial disorders that are prevalent in young women. Primary care physicians have an important role in both diagnosis and management. Amenorrhea in a young woman should be a red flag for the possibility of an underlying eating disorder. Appropriate anticipatory guidance may avert progression of the disorder. For those patients who have an established eating disorder, an interdisciplinary team approach is recommended. The goals of medical intervention are weight gain, reversal of the complications of malnutrition, and resumption of spontaneous menses. Calcium supplementation and weight-bearing exercise should be encouraged. The role of estrogen replacement therapy in the treatment of osteopenia of anorexia nervosa remains unresolved. There may be a place for the use of estrogen replacement therapy in those patients with anorexia nervosa who have prolonged amenorrhea and extremely low body-weight, but such patients should also receive comprehensive treatment for their eating disorder.

References and Selected Readings

1. American Psychiatric Association: *Diagnostic and Statistical Manual for Mental Disorders,* 4th ed: Washington, DC: APA Press, 1994.
2. Fisher M, Golden NH, Katzman DK, et al: Eating disorders in adolescents: A background paper. *J Adolesc Health* 16:420–437, 1995.
3. Golden NH, Shenker IR: Amenorrhea in anorexia nervosa: Etiology and implications. *Adolesc Med: State Art Rev* 3:503–517, 1992.
4. Golden NH, Jacobson MS, Schebendach J, et al: Resumption of menses in anorexia nervosa. *Arch Pediatr Adolesc Med* 151:16–21, 1997.
5. Golden NH, Ashtari M, Kohn MR, et al: Reversibility of cerebral ventricular enlargement in anorexia nervosa demonstrated by quantitative magnetic resonance imaging. *J Pediatr* 128:296–301, 1996.
6. Katzman DK, Zipersky RB, Lambe EK, Mikulis DJ: A longitudinal magnetic imaging study of brain changes in adolescents with anorexia nervosa. *Arch Pediatr Adolesc Med* 151:793–797, 1997.
7. Kaye WH: Persistent alterations in behavior and serotonin activity after recovery from anorexia and bulimia nervosa. Adolescent nutritional disorders: Prevention and treatment. *Ann N Y Acad Sci* 817:162–178, 1997.
8. Keys A, Brozek J, Henschel A, Mickelsen O, Taylor HL: The biology of human starvation. Minneapolis: University of Minnesota Press, 1950.
9. Kohn MR, Golden NH, Shenker IR: Cardiac arrest and delirium: Presentations of the refeeding syndrome in severely malnourished adolescents with

anorexia nervosa. *J Adolesc Health* 22:239–243, 1998.

10. Klibanski A, Biller BMK, Schoenfeld DA, Herzog DB, Saxe VC: The effects of estrogen administration on trabecular bone loss in young women with anorexia nervosa. *J Clin Endocrinol Metab* 80:898–904, 1995.

11. Levine LR, Pope HG, Enas GG, et al: Fluoxetine in the treatment of bulimia nervosa. A multicenter, placebo-controlled trial. *Arch Gen Psychiatry* 49:139–147, 1992.

12. Lindsay R: Estrogen therapy in the prevention and management of osteoporosis. *Am J Obstet Gynecol* 156:1347–1351, 1987.

13. Lucas AR, Beard CM, O'Fallon WM, Kurland LT: 50-year trends in the incidence of anorexia nervosa in Rochester, Minn.: A population-based study. *Am J Psychiatry* 148:917–922, 1991.

14. Mickley D, Greenfeld D, Quinlan DM, Roloff P, Zwas F: Abnormal liver enzymes in outpatients with eating disorders. *Int J Eat Disord* 20:325–329, 1996.

15. Nattiv A, Agostini R, Drinkwater B, Yeager KK: The female athlete triad. The inter-relatedness of disordered eating, amenorrhea and osteoporosis. *Clin Sports Med* 13:405–417, 1994.

16. Nudel DB, Gootman N, Nussbaum MP, et al: Altered exercise performance in patients with anorexia nervosa. *J Pediatr* 58:425–433, 1978.

17. Ogren FP, Huerter JV, Pearson PH, Antonson CW, Moore GF: Transient salivary gland hypertrophy in bulimics. *Laryngoscope* 97:951–953, 1987.

18. Palla B, Litt IF: Medical complications of eating disorders in adolescents. *Pediatrics* 81:613–623, 1988.

19. Seeman E, Szmukler GI, Formica C, Tsalamandris C, Mestrovic R: Osteoporosis in anorexia nervosa: The influence of peak bone density, bone loss, oral contraceptive use and exercise. *J Bone Miner Res* 7:1467–1474, 1992.

20. Schiff RJ, Wurzel CL, Brunson SC, Kasloff I, Nussbaum MP, Frank SD: Death due to chronic syrup of ipecac use in a patient with bulimia. *Pediatrics* 78:412–416, 1986.

21. Strober M, Freeman R, Morrell W: The long-term course of severe anorexia nervosa in adolescents: Survival analysis of recovery, relapse, and outcome predictors over 10–15 years in a prospective study. *Int J Eat Disord* 22:339–360, 1997.

22. Walters EE, Kendler KS: Anorexia nervosa and anorexic-like syndromes in a population-based female twin sample. *Am J Psychiatry* 152:64–71, 1995.

CHAPTER 58

Sexual Assault

Helen Greco

MEDICAL ASSESSMENT

MEDICAL-LEGAL RESPONSIBILITIES

PSYCHOLOGICAL AND EMOTIONAL SUPPORT

Sexual assault occurs when any sexual act is performed by one person on another without that person's consent. According to the U.S. Department of Justice, the annual incidence of sexual assault is 73 per 100,000 females, accounting for approximately 6 percent of all violent crimes.[11] Twenty-five percent of females are raped at some time in their lives.[2] One in 7 women will be raped by her husband.[5] Only 16 percent of rape cases are reported.[5]

Rape is defined as sexual intercourse without the consent of one party, whether from force, threat of force, or incapacity to consent due to physical or mental condition. Acquaintance rape is a variant of sexual assault, and is more widespread than previously thought. The age group with the highest rate of acquaintance rape in the United States is 16- to 24-year-olds.[8] Studies report estimates of violence ranging from 17 to 52 percent among college students, and from 12 to 27 percent among high school students.[3] Seventy-five percent of rape victims knew the person who assaulted them.[1] There is concern throughout the country regarding the substantial number of adolescents who have experienced some form of violence in a dating relationship.

Sexual assault can occur in any age, socioeconomic, or racial group. The very young, the very old, and the handicapped are particularly vulnerable to sexual assault. Statutory rape is defined as sexual intercourse with a person under a specified age. Even if such a person gives consent it is illegal because, by law, the person is defined as being incapable of consenting.

It is very important for health professionals caring for a victim of sexual assault to understand their medical and legal responsibilities, and the psychological and emotional stresses of the "rape-trauma" syndrome, which is also known as the Rape-Related Post Traumatic Stress Disorder (RR-PTSD). Based on U.S. Census reports, 1.3 million women in the United States currently have RR-PTSD, 3.8 million women have previously had RR-PTSD and roughly 211,000 women will develop RR-PTSD each year.[5] When a woman is sexually assaulted, she has lost control of her life, and may have experienced the threat of losing her life. Fear and anxiety may render her helpless. This acute phase may last for hours or days, with loss of the woman's usual coping mechanisms. Her responses may range from complete loss of control to outwardly well-controlled behavior. The signs and symptoms vary in each individual and may include eating and sleep disorders; physical symptoms such as vaginal itch, pain, discharge, headaches, and gastrointestinal disturbances; generalized body aches and pains, such as chest pain, backaches, and pelvic pain; and mood swings, such as anxiety and depression.

The acute phase usually is followed by a reorganization phase that may be characterized by phobias, flashbacks, and nightmares. In addition, there may be gynecologic complaints. This phase may be delayed, occurring months or even years after the event. Therefore, it is imperative that the victim receive appropriate psychological and emotional support and counseling, regardless of the extent of her injuries or her apparent emotional control at the time. The victim's defense mechanisms should not be misinterpreted as indicating that she is able to cope with the particular circumstance. It should always be anticipated that she will demonstrate one or more aspects of the rape-trauma syndrome. In addition, arrangements should be made for immediate family counseling, if appropriate, as well as for follow-up treatment. Forty-six percent of rape victims have considered or attempted suicide.[1]

Medical Assessment

The physician's medical and legal responsibilities are outlined in Table 58-1.

Informed consent must be obtained prior to any examination, collection of specimens, or taking of photographs. After the acute injuries have been addressed, a thorough history and physical examination should be performed. As many as 40 percent of victims sustain injuries, the severity of which will vary according to the violent nature of the attack and how the patient has attempted to protect herself.[4] Approximately 1 percent of injuries require hospitalization and major operative repair; about 0.1 percent are fatal.[4] All examinations must be performed in the presence of a female chaperone, even if the health care provider is female. This person can also reassure the victim, provide support, and help her gain control of her situation. A history and physical examination with collection of indicated data must be done in a compassionate manner; otherwise, the patient may feel victimized again and may experience feelings of guilt and self-depreciation.

The patient should be asked to state in her own words a history of events that occurred. She should be asked to identify her attacker(s) if possible, as well as the date, time, and place, and to describe the specific act(s) performed. The victim should also be asked if she bit, scratched, or

TABLE 58-1 Physician's Responsibilities

Medical

Obtain thorough gynecologic and medical history

Assess and treat physical injuries

Obtain appropriate cultures

Provide counseling and prophylaxis for sexually transmitted diseases (STDs)

Provide preventive therapy for unwanted conception

Assess psychological and emotional status

Provide crisis intervention

Arrange for follow-up medical care and psychological counseling (examination for STDs should be repeated 2 weeks after the assault; testing for syphilis and HIV should be repeated 6, 12, and 24 weeks after the assault)

Legal[a]

Obtain consent for treatment, collection of evidence, the taking of photographs, and the reporting of the incident to the authorities

Provide accurate recording of events

Provide accurate description of injuries

Collection of appropriate samples as well as clothing

Report to authorities, with the victim's consent to do so

Label photographs, articles of clothing, and specimens with the patient's name; seal and store safely

[a]Various jurisdictions have different legal requirements for evidence with which the physician should be familiar. Most emergency rooms have written protocols for handling evidence.

pulled the hair of the assailant. This may aid in identifying the assailant.

Also important is the patient's previous gynecologic history, including her last menstrual period; contraceptive use; last consensual sexual activity; preexisting pregnancy; and/or sexually transmitted disease. Few studies are available to predict the actual risk of acquiring a sexually transmitted diseases (STD) as a result of sexual assault, but *Chlamydia trachomatis* is the STD organism most likely to be acquired.[7] The current risks of acquiring the human immunodeficiency virus (HIV) in this circumstance do not appear to be very high, but this is a serious concern. A study from the Centers for Disease Control and Prevention found that the chance of victims acquiring gonorrhea ranges from 6 to 12 percent, and the chance of acquiring syphilis is up to 3 percent.[7]

A thorough physical examination of the entire body should be performed. Pertinent drawings should be made or photographs taken. Any evidence of abrasions, lacerations, and bruises (especially of the neck, back, buttocks, genitalia, and extremities) should be noted. It is important to examine the vaginal vault completely for lacerations or possible rupture into the abdominal cavity. A flat and upright abdominal radiograph may aid in the latter diagnosis. This can be particularly useful in a young child, a woman who has never before had sexual intercourse, or an elderly woman.

Assessment of the reproductive organs and collection of samples and cultures from the cervix and vagina are very important parts of the physical examination. Baseline serological tests should be done as outlined in Table 58-2. Appropriate slide preparations should be performed to identify any preexisting or recently acquired infections, such as the human papillomavirus, candida infections, and trichomoniasis.

Prophylaxis against infection should be offered (Table 58-3).[6] If appropriate, prophylaxis against unwanted pregnancy (Table 58-4) should be offered as well. Seven percent of rape victims became pregnant or contracted a sexually transmitted disease as a result of the assault.[9] Hormonal postcoital contraception is extremely effective, with a failure rate of 1.6 percent or less when administered within 72 hours of sexual intercourse. Treatment is useless after implantation. The patient should be warned to expect severe nausea from the use of hormones, and told that she will have vaginal bleeding within 21 to 30 days after treatment. Follow-up must be arranged to detect any treatment failures. This treatment should be offered no matter where the patient is in her menstrual cycle, although it should be determined that the victim was not already pregnant prior to the attack.

TABLE 58-2   History and Physical Examination

History
Complete sexual, gynecologic, and general medical history
Pertinent "positive and negative" account of the event
Thorough and objective documentation
Any loss of consciousness at any time during the assault
Has the victim changed clothes, voided, defecated, and/or douched since the incident?
Condom use or ejaculation by the assailant

Physical Examination
General appearance
Assessment of psychological and emotional status
Assess entire body for signs of trauma such as bruises, bites, lacerations, abrasions
Photographs, if appropriate
Condition of external genitalia
Speculum examination of cervix and vagina
Oral and rectal assessment for injury
Collection of samples as indicated, that include the following:
Oral cavity—secretions and culture for chlamydia and gonorrhea
Genitalia—hair combings, hair sample, vaginal secretions, cultures for chlamydia and gonorrhea
Fingernail scrapings
Rectal cultures for chlamydia and gonorrhea
Baseline serology tests for syphilis, hepatitis B antigen, herpes simplex virus, cytomegalovirus, and human immunodeficiency virus (if appropriate), as well as a urine pregnancy test
Search for foreign bodies
Evaluation of all pertinent areas for sperm and acid phosphatase
Collect pertinent clothing
Arrange for follow-up of repeat cultures and serology in 2 and 12 weeks
Tests for HIV serology repeated in 3–6 months

Medical-Legal Responsibilities

Sexual assault is a legal term and not a medical diagnosis. However, the medical report should document, when present, all signs consistent with the use of force.

TABLE 58-3 Prophylaxis Against Infection

Gonorrhea, chlamydia, and trichomonal infections:
Ceftriaxone 125 mg IM PLUS azithromycin 1 g orally in a single dose or doxycycline 100 mg orally twice daily for 7 days, PLUS metronidazole 2 g orally in a single dose

If the patient is pregnant:
Use erythromycin base to substitute for doxycyline, 500 mg orally four times daily for 7 days

Hepatitis B virus vaccination offered

Tetanus Diphtheria Toxoid to be administered when indicated

Documentation of the complete history, physical examination, and emotional condition of the patient is extremely important. Evidence collection should be labeled and sealed. It is also particularly important to make written notes of whether the victim has bathed, brushed her teeth, used mouthwash, defecated, voided, or douched prior to examination. When possible, patients must be encouraged to go immediately to a health care facility. Evidence of coitus will be present in the vagina for up to 48 hours after an assault. However, other orifices may retain such evidence for only up to 6 hours.

Vaginal secretions (and other appropriate areas, as indicated by history) should be investigated for motile sperm, and samples collected for the presence of acid phosphatase. Acid phosphatase is present in high concentration in seminal fluid. Motile sperm may be present in the vagina for up to 8 hours after intercourse but may be present in cervical mucus for as long as

TABLE 58-4 Postcoital Regimen

Ovral: 2 tablets orally stat, then 2 more tablets 12 hours later

Nordette or Lo/Ovral: 4 tablets stat, then 4 additional tablets 12 hours later

Postcoital contraception is also now available, by prescription, packaged for that purpose

SOURCE: Adapted from Schnare.[7]

two to three days. Nonmotile sperm may be noted in the vagina for up to 24 hours and in the cervix for up to 17 days.[12] Even if no sperm are noted, evidence for acid phosphatase should be obtained, because the assailant may have had a vasectomy. Motile sperm may be present in the rectum for an indeterminate amount of time. However, nonmotile sperm can be found up to 24 hours. Acid phosphatase may also be detected in the rectum.[12]

Secretions of a major blood group antigen are found in the saliva of 80 percent of people. Saliva should be obtained from the patient to assess whether she is a secretor, thus aiding in the differentiation of her secretions from those of the assailant.

Fingernail scrapings should be obtained to look for possible skin or blood from the assailant. DNA fingerprinting and specific blood from these materials may assist in the identification of the assailant.

Seminal fluid is rapidly destroyed by salivary enzymes and makes identification difficult after several hours. Staining of clothes and skin by seminal fluid and/or blood may be noted several hours after a crime. Skin washings and clothing should be examined for acid phosphatase.

Psychological and Emotional Support

At all times during the examination and collection of medical and legal evidence, the victim's emotional status should be of foremost concern. Questioning should proceed in a compassionate manner. Although this statement should be obvious, this does not always occur, especially if the woman is drunk, a prostitute, or claiming spouse/date rape. A nonjudgmental manner must be assumed during the examination.

The patient should not be discharged from the health care facility without proper psychological and emotional counseling from health personnel specifically trained to help victims of sexual assault. In addition, follow-up counseling should be scheduled, and an emergency resource made available, should the patient require acute care for psychological symptoms prior to the counseling visit. The latter should be scheduled within 1 to 2 weeks after the medical assessment.

References and Suggested Readings

1. Bureau of Justice Statistics, 1994.
2. Mary Koss, et al: *A Criminological Study.* 1990.
3. Koval JE: Violence in dating relationships. *J Pediatr Health Care* 3:298–304, 1989.
4. Marchbanks PA, Lui KJ, Mercy JA: Risk of injury from resisting rape. *Am J Epdemiol* 132:540–549, 1990.
5. National Victim Center Rape in America Report, 1992.
6. Rayburn WF: Treatment of sexually transmitted diseases. 1998 Recommendations by the Centers for Disease Control and Prevention. *J Reprod Med* 43:471–476, 1998.
7. Schnare S: Postcoital contraception. *Contemp Ob-Gyn* 1(1):4, 1993.
8. Schwarcz SK, Whittington WL: Sexual assault and sexually transmitted diseases: Detection and management in adults and children. *Rev Infect Dis* 12(Suppl b):5682–5689, 1990.
9. Senate Judiciary Committee, 1991.
10. US Department of Justice: *Uniform Crime Reports for the United States, 1987.* Washington, DC: US Government Printing Office, 1987. Publication No. 14.
11. Ward SK, Chapman K, Cohn E, et al: Acquaintance rape and college social scene. *Fam Relations* 40:65–71, 1981.
12. Warner CG: *Rape and Sexual Assault: Management and Intervention.* Germantown, MD: Aspen, 1980.

CHAPTER 59

Domestic Violence: The Lost Right of Sanctuary

Linn H. Parsons

W hile to most people the word "home" implies a place of safety or refuge and the word "intimate" denotes a comfortable supportive relationship, these same terms conjure thoughts of fear and threat of violence for approximately 4 million American women each year. Domestic violence or partner abuse refers to a relationship in which an individual is victimized by a current or past intimate or romantic partner. Victimization is the appropriate term to describe the relationship, yet abused women prefer the term "survivor"— providing a positive connotation regarding their strength and skills in their day-to-day struggle.

What is the role of the physician, as leader of the health care team, in providing assistance and serving as an advocate for survivors of domestic violence?

Scope of the Problem

Prevalence of Partner Abuse

Conservative estimates are that 1 in 4 women will at some time be abused by her partner. Surveys in a variety of medical settings confirm abuse as a common problem in medical practice. Twenty-five to 35 percent of women presenting to emergency rooms have a history of domestic violence. In adolescence, the percent affected may reach 42 percent. Approximately 1 in 4 women on university campuses have experienced physical abuse. Although exact figures are not available, about 25 to 30 percent of young women in colleges have experienced unwanted intercourse. Studies of women who are currently pregnant reveal a 4 to 17 percent prevalence of abuse during pregnancy. As high as 33 percent of women seeking prenatal care report a prior history of domestic violence, and that history is the greatest risk factor for abuse in the current pregnancy. Abuse during pregnancy is associated with an increase in the risk of violence in the postpartum period. Up to 40 percent of women seeking services at abortion clinics have reported a history of abuse. Similar percentages of current and past abuse have been found in primary care office settings.

Characteristics of Domestic Violence

Domestic violence can occur in current or past relationships involving dating, marriage, or cohabitation, and occurs in heterosexual and same-sex relationships. While the perpetrator would have us believe that the relationship is one of loss of control caused by anger, alcohol, drugs, or other factors for which the perpetrator cannot be responsible, the abusive relationship is really one of carefully exercised domination and control. Episodes are not random events, but instead recur and are chronic in nature. The pattern is usually one of increasing frequency and severity. Tactics of the abuser are selected from physical, psychological, and/or sexual behaviors. The impact of these tactics on the survivor and children involved are injury, pain, fear, isolation, loss of self-esteem, and, ultimately, being totally controlled. An examination of these behaviors provides a better understanding of the relationship.

Physical abuse is any behavior or action that threatens the physical well-being of the victim. Direct physical injuries can result from a wide range of behaviors such as pushing, shoving, slapping, kicking, punching, hitting, pinching, pulling hair, throwing objects, use of restraints, choking, or the use of weapons. Actions that indirectly lead to injury of the victim, such as the withholding of medical care or medications, are included. Physical abuse rarely occurs alone, but instead is combined with sexual and/or emotional abuse.

Sexual abuse occurs in about two-thirds of relationships involving physical abuse. Sexual abuse may consist of any activity that is generally thought of as being part of a sexual act or sexual behavior but is not desired by the victim. A wide range of activities, including forced intercourse; forcing the woman to perform sexual acts with which she is uncomfortable or degraded; assault on the genital area; the use of objects vaginally, orally, or anally; or the use of sexually degrading names, are included. Unfaithfulness as a part of this behavior leads to increased risk of sexually transmitted diseases. Refusal to allow contraception and forced intercourse result in a risk of unwanted pregnancy. Control of reproductive behavior, including contraception, sterilization, and pregnancy termination or continuation, can be forms of sexual abuse.

Psychological or emotional abuse may be more subtle, varied, and difficult to identify. Ridiculing or humiliating the partner in public, as well as name calling, yelling, and criticizing are included. Threats and intimidation can occur by destruction of property, injury or destruction of pets, the threat of physical injury to the woman, or the threat of injury to children. Control of money, employment, and access to family and friends are emotionally abusive behavior, which serve to isolate the woman and contribute to an undermining of her self-esteem and the development of fear.

Survivors of domestic violence can be found in all age, racial, educational, occupational, religious, and sexual-orientation groups. One survey of obstetrician/gynecologists found 20 percent of physicians who responded reported a personal family history of violence. No group is immune.

In relationships where violence is present, direct injury of children from abuse occurs in about 50 percent. Yet children experience and are affected by what is going on around them; thus 100 percent of children are affected by the violence in the relationship. Childhood sexual abuse (defined as an unwanted sexual experience before the age of 14) occurs in 1 in 4 girls overall and 1 in 3 in lower socioeconomic groups. A study of teenage mothers revealed that 57 percent had experienced an unwanted sexual act involving contact and that 33 percent had unwanted sexual intercourse prior to pregnancy.

Relationship

The pattern of behavior in the relationship is often characterized as a "cycle of violence." The first phase of the cycle is one of increasing tension. At this point, the woman feels that if she is cautious about her behavior, she will be able to prevent or control the violence. Increasing verbal assault in this phase, as well as emotional abuse, may occur. The cycle ultimately leads to the acute battering phase, when physical, sexual, and emotional abuse may occur. This phase is the most dangerous and attempts to leave may lead to homicide of either partner. The last phase is that of reconciliation. Women may seek to leave a relationship at this time, but the persuasiveness of the partner regarding the partner's remorse and promises of no more violence may lead her to stay. The controlling nature of the relationship is the greatest deterrent to a woman's departure. Myths exist that tend to keep her in the relationship. She is convinced that the battering or abuse is deserved and is her fault. She may also believe this behavior is normal. The slow development of low self-esteem and fear keeps her in check. The two most common reasons for not leaving a relationship are fear and lack of financial resources. Other reasons for staying or returning to the partner include dependence resulting from psychological trauma; physical illness; continued contact because of the perpetrator's access to children; cultural/family/religious beliefs or values; hope that the relationship will improve; lack of social support; and continued love and her identity as partner/wife/mother.

Just as there is no specific profile for a survivor, there is similarly no one profile of an abuser. The abuser will have one face for the public and one for private. He or she may appear to be a most protective, supportive, and available partner. This behavior makes questioning of individuals difficult. Health providers should be alert for behavior used by a perpetrator to control the victim through manipulation of the health care system. Control of medications; canceling appointments; preventing the obtaining of health care; use of multiple doctors; victim-blaming in front of health care providers; arguing with or threatening the health care team; or refusal to leave the patient's side to allow private conversations may indicate a woman in an abusive relationship.

Recognition

Health Consequences of Domestic Violence

Women may present to an emergency facility or primary care office with injuries related to abuse.

Injuries are most commonly to the head, eyes, neck, torso, breasts, abdomen, and genitals. They often have bilateral or multiple injuries. Commonly, a delay exists between the onset of the injury and the woman seeking treatment. Her explanation for the etiology of the injury may be inconsistent with your findings. Any injury during pregnancy, especially one to the abdomen or breasts, should make one suspicious of abuse. A history of repeated trauma may be seen in the record. The primary care provider should be alerted to the possibility of domestic violence when women call or visit frequently for general somatic complaints. Choking sensation, hyperventilation, chest pain, gastrointestinal symptoms, headache, back pain, abdominal pain, or other pain have been associated with past or present partner violence. Women often present with difficulty sleeping, anxiety or panic disorders, depression, attempted suicide, substance and alcohol abuse, or eating disorders (either overeating or anorexia). Survivors may appear hostile or uncooperative and noncompliant with therapy.

An increase in gynecologic complaints has been demonstrated in abused women. Chronic vulvovaginal symptoms or recurrent infections originating from worries regarding sexually transmitted diseases may bring the woman to the office. Sexual problems including dyspareunia are common. Chronic pelvic pain without an apparent pathologic diagnosis raises the possibility of an abuse history. An unusual or extreme response to the pelvic examination should alert the physician to look for a history of physical or sexual abuse.

As maternal mortality from hypertension, hemorrhage, and sepsis has declined, violence has risen to be a leading cause of maternal death.[24] Unintended pregnancy is increased in women with a history of violence. Late entry into prenatal care, missed appointments, and multiple repeated complaints are often seen in abused pregnant women. Substance abuse is increased in pregnancies where there is an abuse history. A link between domestic violence and preterm labor, low birthweight, fetal injury and death, chorioamnionitis, and placental abruption has been seen in some studies. Women with severe anxiety over labor, or fear of loss of control in labor, or those reporting nightmares during pregnancy or postpartum, may be current or past survivors of abuse. Just as in the nonpregnant individual, women reporting any explanation for vaginal bleeding, abdominal pain, or any injury to either themselves or their fetus that is inconsistent with the evidence, should lead the health care team to suspect abuse.

The adolescent who has experienced family violence either by observation or as the direct recipient of abuse may exhibit chronic anxiety, difficulty in controlling anger or aggression, dissociation, or a fantasy life. Depression and hopelessness occur and indeed family violence is an important cause of teenage suicide. Adolescents exhibit relationship problems including learned victim or aggressor roles, delinquency, or school problems. Early marriage and early pregnancy are common. Male adolescents who observed family violence were found more likely to father pregnancies as teenagers. The observation of family violence has been linked with increased risk of teenage suicide, sexual assault perpetration, violent crime, and increased use of drugs and alcohol.

Because of the wide variety of physical and mental health complaints, abused women use pain medications, tranquilizers, and antidepressants three to four times more often than nonabused women. Lack of identification of the history of violence leads not only to excessive use of medication, but also to the inability to appropriately treat the somatic and mental health problems.

Universal Screening: Creating Opportunities for Assistance

Women do not volunteer their history of abuse, nor do they recognize medical problems related to that history. These facts, along with the prevalence of the problem of abuse and the lack of a characteristic "abuse profile," leads to only one logical conclusion regarding abuse screening: everyone must be screened. Just as with any medical problem, failure to identify leads to failure to treat (Table 59-1).

The setting for screening is critical. It should be private and in the absence of any family, partner, or friends. The information should be clearly designated as confidential. If a translator is necessary, it should be someone not involved with the family or patient.

Direct questions regarding abuse have been more successful than nondirect questioning. The volunteering of abuse information is never as successful as direct questioning. Verbal direct questioning has generally been more productive than written questionnaires.

The choice of words during screening is important. Be cautious in interpreting the response to any question containing the word "abuse." The questioner's interpretation of abusive behavior may be quite different from that of the battered woman. The abuse assessment screen (Table 59-2) is a valid and reliable tool and can be used in any setting. Table 59-3 contains questions that may be more useful in ongoing primary care and emergency room settings. Screen for past as well as present violence.

Emotional abuse may be more difficult to identify. Questions may be more lengthy (Table 59-4) because the pattern of behaviors can be varied. Anyone who appears to have low self-

TABLE 59-1 Reasons to Screen for and Assist Survivor of Domestic Violence

Prevalence of abuse: injuries, deaths

History is not volunteered

Women do not recognize that their medical problems may be related to abuse

Inability to treat somatic problems unless history is recognized

Child abuse occurs in 50 percent of relationships, while 100 percent of children are affected by observation of abuse

Cost of health care for injuries, somatic problems

Mental health costs, including depression and suicide

Improper use of medications (pain, anxiety, depression, sleep)

TABLE 59-2   Abuse Assessment Screen

1. Have you ever been emotionally or physically abused by your partner or someone important to you?

2. Within the last year, have you been hit, slapped, kicked, or otherwise physically hurt by someone?

3. Since you've been pregnant, have you been hit, slapped, kicked, or otherwise physically hurt by someone?

4. Within the last year, has anyone forced you to have sexual activities? Has anyone in the past forced you to have sexual activities?

5. Are you afraid of your partner or anyone you listed above?

SOURCE: Adapted from Nursing Research Consortium on Violence and Abuse, 1989.

TABLE 59-3   Abuse Assessment Screen

Primary Care Routine Screening

About 25% of the women in this country are abused by their partners. Because this is such a common problem, I am asking every woman in my practice about domestic violence.

Since the last time I saw you, have you been hit, physically hurt, or threatened by your partner?

Many of my patients tell me they have been hurt by someone close to them. Has this ever happened to you?

Many young women believe that they do not always have a choice about sexual activity. Does this ever happen to you? (Adolescent)

Often the young women who see me have partners who hit them or physically hurt them. Does your partner ever hurt you? Are you ever afraid of your partner? (Adolescent)

Emergency Room Screening

Have you been hit or hurt by anyone?

Have you been threatened or verbally attacked by anyone?

Has anyone forced you to have intercourse or participate in any other sexual activity against your will?

Are you afraid of anyone?

When I see the type of injuries that you have, I often find they have been caused by the woman's partner. You may not be ready to talk with me now, but let me give you some information on partner violence. We are here for you if you want to discuss it.

TABLE 59-4   Screening for Emotional Abuse

1. Does your partner:
   - Belittle or humiliate you?
   - Blame you for problems?
   - Insult or swear at you?
   - Make you cry?
   - Threaten to hit or throw something at you?
   - Threaten to use weapons on you?

2. Is your partner overly jealous or possessive?

3. Does your partner break things that are important to you?

4. Does your partner threaten your children, parents, friends, or pets?

5. Does your partner control you by keeping you from working, going to school, or seeing friends or family?

6. Does your partner control all of the money by not giving you enough money, taking your money, or drinking or gambling away your money?

7. Does your partner lock you in or out of the house/room/car or prevent you from leaving?

8. Does your partner only want you to do things with him/her? (Adolescent)

9. Does your partner want to know where you are all the time? (Adolescent)

10. Does your partner tell you where you can go and who you can be with? (Adolescent)

11. Does your partner criticize what you wear, your weight, how you look? (Adolescent)

esteem or has difficulty in making eye contact with the provider should be questioned more extensively.

Because abuse may begin later in pregnancy or after the baby is born, pregnant women should be questioned during each trimester and postpartum. Increased rates of abuse have been found with more frequent questioning. It is easy to include questions about family violence while asking about alcohol abuse and substance abuse in the initial prenatal history. As you inquire about the woman's alcohol/drug use, the partner's alcohol/drug use can also be discussed. A statement such as, "A new baby requires adjustment. How will/has this affected your relationship with your partner?" may be useful either during pregnancy or postpartum. Screening regularly at annual examinations and frequently during pregnancy increases the chance of eliciting an abuse history. Because of the dynamics of the relationship, the partner may be present during the examination. Techniques such as screening in the restroom, sending the partner to the business office, or separately questioning a partner about family genetic history may lead to opportunities for private questioning of the woman.

Women do not object to being questioned about abuse. Battered women have stated that they wish their doctor or nurse had asked about abuse so that they could divulge their history. Survivors have requested that their health providers not turn their heads but that they directly ask, assess their backgrounds, notice their excuses, and let them know that they always have options and that we will be there for them. Nonabused women are not offended by questioning regarding abuse; to the contrary, they are glad that their physicians care about this problem.

If because of injury, medical history, or patient or partner behavior, you suspect abuse but are unable to elicit a history, other questions may be utilized; for example, "With this particular injury (or medical problem), I find that it has often occurred because a woman has been hit by her partner or another person. I am available to discuss this with you at any time." Although the woman may recognize abuse as a problem, she may not be emotionally ready to leave. She may not believe that there are viable alternatives to staying in the relationship or be unaware of community resources. Failure to divulge the violence history can result from fear of escalating danger and injury or death.

Reaction to Domestic Violence

Physician's Response to Women Who Are Screened Positive for Abuse

The initial response to a woman who divulges her abuse history is critical. While listening in a nonjudgmental fashion, inform her that the violence is not her fault and that she does not deserve to be abused (*validation*). Clearly state that the abuser is responsible for his or her own behavior, and that the pattern of abuse is usually one of worsening behavior. Inform her of your concern and fear for her safety and the safety of her children. Tell her she is not alone and that you and your practice are there for her when she is ready to leave the abuser. Let her know you understand how difficult it is for women in abusive relationships to make changes. Instead of using the word "victim" when referring to her, use the word "survivor." Do not ask her, "Why don't you leave?" This question represents victim-blaming.

For women in a currently abusive relationship, *safety* must first be assessed. If her partner is with her, ask her what assistance she would like you to provide. If she is ready to leave the abusive relationship, you can assist in connecting her with a shelter or other community resources, or by allowing her to call for someone to pick her up. Find out where her children are and if they are safe. If she feels she needs to leave with her partner at this time, find out if there is any way you can assist her in the future. If her partner is not present, does she need to be home by a certain time to prevent violence?

The *danger or safety* assessment is used to assess increased risk of homicide of either partner. The greatest risk of homicide is around a threat or attempt to leave the relationship. Any adolescent in an abusive relationship is also at great risk of homicide. With violence toward an adolescent, the abuser may not be a girlfriend or boyfriend, but may be a parent or family member. An increased risk of homicide has also been associated with an escalation in severity or frequency of the violence, increased isolation of the woman, threatened or attempted suicide, threat of murder, use of a weapon, the presence of weapons in the house, the use of alcohol or drugs, or sexual abuse as part of the violence. Abuse of children has also been associated with an increased risk of homicide. Mandatory reporting statutes regarding child abuse exist in all 50 states. Prior to asking questions regarding injury of the children, the woman should be informed that you are required to report child abuse.

If the survivor is not ready to leave, a *safety plan or exit plan* should be discussed. Advise selection of a trusted friend or relative with whom she can keep an emergency suitcase containing necessary items. Included in this suitcase should be some money, a spare set of keys, social security card, needed documents regarding car/house/safety deposit box/checking account information and checks, a change of clothing for herself, a change of clothing for the children, and items of comfort or play for the children.

Take a thorough history including a violence history. Listen to her chief complaint and provide necessary medical care. If she is injured, address the injuries. Information regarding sexually transmitted diseases and pregnancy prevention should be offered. During your medical evaluation, do not prescribe drugs for pain, sleep, anxiety, or depression except under very close supervision. Narcotics should be used in a limited fashion for acute injuries only. Drugs may impair the ability of the woman to respond in a dangerous situation, lead to addiction, or be used for suicide or suicide attempt.

Mental health services should be offered. Most physicians are not qualified as counselors of abused women. The physician should supply the names of appropriate counselors who have experience in dealing with abused women.

Information about domestic violence should be provided. Women will be surprised to learn that they are not alone. Pamphlets are available from the American College of Obstetricians and Gynecologists (409 12th Street, SW, Washington, DC 20024) and the Family Violence Prevention Fund (383 Rhode Island St., Suite 304, San Francisco, CA 94103). Because such information, if found by a partner, could lead to violence, instruct women not to take this information home with them. Referral information regarding the police, restraining orders, county family services, availability of shelters, community support groups, and emergency telephone numbers should be given (Table 59-5).

Make her aware of your continued availability even if she is not ready to leave the abuser. Assist her with information on how to obtain

TABLE 59-5 Community Resources

Resources	Function
Advocates	Trained persons with knowledge about all resources; serve to guide women through legal process, provide emotional support and guidance. Many communities provide advocates through shelters or social services.
Police	Assist with arrest or other possible actions at site of family violence. Enforce restraining orders. With proarrest or "no-drop" laws, they are key in convictions (prevent need for abused woman testifying or pressing charges). Provide facts on local statutes.
Judges	Issue restraining orders. Make decisions about resources, child custody, mandatory counseling for abuser, court proceedings, sentencing in criminal cases.
Lawyers	Not necessary for restraining order or other civil complaints, but are needed for criminal proceedings.
Shelters	Provide short-term safe house, support groups, advocates, access to family services, and links to other community resources such as job training, housing, medical care.
Clergy	Some are specially trained as counselors. Can assist with safety and planning. Be sure that they do not recommend dangerous interventions such as couples counseling.
Public Agencies	Vocational training, counseling/mental health, other services that vary by community.
Social Services	Coordination of services such as housing, financial resources, food programs, job training, child care, child protection.
Counselors	Mental health providers with special training and experience in domestic violence should be sought.

emergency assistance from your practice, the emergency room, or a shelter on a 24-hour basis.

For women who are currently abused, but who have left their abusive relationship, ask if they are still afraid of their ex-partner and if they are safe. If they have successfully left a violent relationship and are not in danger, the history of abuse may be important in management of their medical problems. Questions regarding the perpetrator, length and type of abuse, and possible history of childhood sexual abuse or physical abuse are important events in a medical history. If the woman has not received counseling for her abuse history, a recommendation for referral to appropriate counselors is indicated.

Documentation

Precise factual documentation in the medical record is essential in domestic violence (Table 59-6). The records can be used in a legal case to establish abuse, thus becoming critical for prevention of further abuse. Legal experts need our help in supporting women's histories by documenting their stories.

The documentation includes Subjective, Objective, Assessment, and Plan (SOAP), just as with any other medical problem. Whenever possible, the patient's own words should be used. Instead of the legal term "alleged," it is better to substitute such words as "the patient states."

The details of the abuse and its relationship to the chief complaint should be documented. In the past medical history and review of systems, include any injuries, medical problems, or psychiatric problems related to domestic violence. A substance abuse history should also be recorded. A thorough sexual history includes information on sexual assault; lack of barrier protection; history of sexually transmitted diseases; pregnancy history, including unplanned pregnancy; and the patient's ability to use birth control. Forced pregnancy, pregnancy termination, and forced contraception or inability to use contraception should be documented. If the use of any psychoactive or analgesic medications is felt related to the abuse, this should also be documented. Include details of social history such as the relationship of the woman to the abuser, her current living arrangement, and the abuser's access to her.

Objective evidence of abuse should be carefully documented. Body maps or drawings indicating areas of new or old injuries are useful. Photographs taken in color that are clearly labeled and that include the patient's face in at least one picture are helpful. Document bruises in different phases of coloration. Standardized kits for sexual assault documentation are available. The Polaroid Corporation provides a manual for instruction on medical photography and conducts training of medical staff in documenting injuries. Written permission should be obtained to take photographs. Any laboratory testing pertaining to the abuse, such as x-rays or results of sexually transmitted disease testing, should be documented.

The safety assessment should be recorded, including that the individual has been informed of

TABLE 59-6   Documentation in the Medical Record

S = • Chief complaint
    • Abuse history in patient's own words
    • Past medical history and review of systems
    • Substance abuse
    • Sexual history
    • Medication use

O = • Injuries (use description, body map, photographs, x-ray)
    • Sexual assult kit if indicated
    • Physical examination
    • Indicated labs, cultures (STDs)

A = • Safety/danger assessment (children, suicide, homicide)
    • Medical assessment

P = • Provision of violence information
    • Community resources, counseling offered
    • Follow-up information
    • Appropriate notifications depending on state (child abuse, mandatory reporting of domestic violence, weapons use)
    • Indicated medical treatment

her increased risk of homicide. Assess her degree of readiness for change.

Document the options which were discussed with the patient and the referrals that were offered. Note any arrangements that were made for follow-up and what discharge information was given to her. Police reports should be filed according to local statutes. If a police report was filed, documentation should be made regarding this including the name of the investigating officer.

In recording the reason for the office visit, avoid diagnostic codes such as domestic violence and spouse abuse. Inclusion of these diagnoses on medical bills or other documentation that may be seen by the perpetrator could further endanger the patient and cause an escalation of violence.

All states require physicians to report child abuse, and most states require physicians to report injuries caused by guns, knives, or other deadly weapons. A few states require mandatory reporting of domestic violence. Those who support these laws feel that just as any other crime, intimate partner violence should be reported and prosecuted. Supporters hope that identification of battered women will lead to protection and utilization of services, and prevention of future violence. No evidence exists to support these laws as beneficial. Instead, mandatory reporting laws may place women at greater risk from the perpetrator. Such laws may prevent women from confiding in their physicians, and interfere with the physician/patient relationship of confidentiality. Mandatory reporting laws could deter providers from screening for abuse. The ultimate goal in assisting women in abusive situations is to allow them to become empowered and to move with our assistance to protect themselves and their families. Substituting one controlling power for another is not beneficial. One newer policy, the "proarrest" approach, has been more successful in achieving convictions while protecting the survivor of the violence. These policies allow for arrest and prosecution of a suspected perpetrator of domestic violence without requiring the victim

to press charges or testify in court. The physician needs to be aware of local and state statutes in order to comply with them.

Overcoming Barriers

Despite the recognition of the prevalence of domestic violence and its consequences, only 25 percent of physicians report routine screening for abuse and only 66 percent screen for abuse in high-risk situations. Family practitioners, internal medicine specialists, and obstetrician/gynecologists report the same barriers to the incorporation of routine screening and prevention in domestic violence. The two most common barriers are lack of time and insufficient training in dealing with psychosocial issues such as domestic violence. Other common barriers include the belief that domestic violence could not occur among their patients, concern that questioning will offend patients, a belief that domestic violence is a "private" issue, and a feeling of helplessness or frustration in not being able to improve the patient's situation. Physicians inquire about many private matters such as sexual practices and risk assessments for HIV, and routinely test for diseases much less common than domestic violence. With the information presented here and some thoughtful planning for a practice, there remains no excuse to prevent assessing for abuse.

Until recently, there has been little organized education regarding domestic violence. Textbooks have not included information on family violence. Medical schools, residencies, and continuing medical education programs are now providing information on partner violence. Information is readily available from many excellent resources. Experts present in the community are eager to assist us in our educational process.

The struggle to find time for all issues impacting our patients is a difficult problem. Advanced preparation is the key that allows the provider to save time. Screening questions should be incorporated into all history forms and asked routinely. Questions may be asked by trained office personnel and not necessarily by the physician. To prepare for those needing services, the physician should become educated in his or her role in intervention. Taking an adequate history, performing the physical examination, and medical intervention and documentation are all part of the physician's responsibility. Validation of the patient is an extremely important role for the physician. Prior to instituting a routine screening policy, office personnel can be trained to assist survivors of partner abuse. They can visit community resources, talk with people at the shelter, obtain information regarding local support groups and counselors experienced in abuse, and find out about the legal resources. County social services can help coordinate the training of office personnel. Following adequate training of all the health care team, routine screening can be put into place. Once abuse is identified, the physician can then complete his or her responsibility during the office encounter (Table 59-7). The trained personnel can then take over to provide resources appropriate to the individual, and provide information on domestic violence. Flexibility in offices is important in dealing with women who may have difficulty keeping appointments for reasons that are beyond their control. The Warshaw and Ganley *Resource Manual for Health Care Providers*[23] is an excellent resource for your office. Schornstein's book[19] provides complete information for the health care team. Philadelphia Physicians for Social Responsibility Program entitled "RADAR: Domestic Violence Intervention for Health Care Professionals," is a winner of the 1988 models that work. The RADAR model can be obtained by calling (301) 594-4310.

Promotion of Healthy Relationships

To stop the cycle of relationship violence in our society, intervention must begin on many different fronts. This chapter has thus far addressed strategies for prevention of future violence in already abusive relationships. Many communities are turning their attention to primary preven-

tion of partner abuse. The education of children regarding their safety, and teaching them the skills to make healthy relationships, is necessary for prevention. Programs teaching teens about choices and learning to communicate in assertive ways without either aggression or passivity may lead to healthier relationships. Teens must learn the warning signs of an abusive relationship and dangerous patterns of behavior and learn to assert their own rights while respecting their partner's rights. The teaching of conflict resolution can lead to more productive interactions.

Levy and Giggans' *"What Parents Need to Know About Dating Violence"* will assist parents

TABLE 59-7 Domestic Violence Intervention Checklist

After universal screening for abuse, this checklist can assist in providing complete services for those who are *screened positive:*

Past or present history:

_____ Validation that abuse is unacceptable/not deserved

_____ Provide information about domestic violence[a]

_____ Take a thorough abuse history

_____ Document the abuse history

_____ Recommend mental health services—supply names of appropriate counselors[a]

_____ Safety assessment: women and children (inform of legal requirement to report child abuse); danger assessment for homicide/suicide[a]

Present history/current abuse add the following:

_____ Documentation of injuries (bodymaps, photographs, x-rays)

_____ Provide medical care: chief complaint, injury care, STD assessment, pregnancy prevention

_____ Do not prescribe drugs (pain, anxiety, sleep, depression) except limited use under close supervision

_____ Provide referral information: police, restraining order, social services, shelter, support groups, etc.[a]

_____ Develop a safety plan/exit plan[a]

_____ Emphasize your continued availability—even if she is not ready to leave abuser

[a]Can be provided by trained office personnel

in teaching their teens. Their list of characteristics of a healthy relationship include the use of give and take and compromise, mutual respect, support and encouragement of one another's ambitions, trust without jealousy, lack of fear, open communication, shared decision making, acceptance of differences, and encouraging outside friends and activities.

Physicians and other health providers in communities can become actively involved in teaching healthy relationship techniques to children and teenagers through schools, religious organizations, or private groups. Materials such as those by Levy and publications from project HART (Healthy Alternatives for Relationships Among Teens, St. Louis, Missouri) can provide resources.

Physician Power and Opposition to Domestic Violence

People listen to physicians and respect their education and viewpoints. Participation through religious organizations, county social services, boards of battered women's shelters, and other community efforts against domestic violence go a long way toward helping survivors.

A statement can be made in every office by placing educational materials in the waiting room and exam rooms. Posters against domestic violence can be placed in every restroom and other areas where patients and staff congregate. These materials could clearly designate the physician as a concerned and caring individual who does not condone violence.

Summary

The incorporation of the basic materials in this chapter in your practice will let you provide services to women who have been in the past or are currently in abusive relationships. This information is necessary to the provision of appropriate medical care. By serving as an advocate, you assist in the empowerment of the survivors. It has been said that silence is collusion with the batterer. We can no longer afford to be in that position.

Adopting routine screening, being prepared to assist survivors, and community involvement against domestic violence by each physician will go a long way toward fulfilling the principles Warshaw and Ganley recommended to guide clinical practice:

1. Regarding the safety of victims and their children as a priority;
2. Respecting the integrity and authority of each battered woman over her own life choices;
3. Holding perpetrators responsible for the abuse and for stopping it;
4. Advocating on behalf of survivors of domestic violence and their children; and
5. Acknowledging the need to make changes in the health care system to improve the health care response to domestic violence.

References and Selected Readings

1. American College of Obstetricians and Gynecologists: *Mandatory Reporting of Domestic Violence.* Washington, DC; ACOG, 1998. ACOG Committee Opinion: Committee on Health Care of Underserved Women, March 1998.
2. Bachman GA, Moeller TP, Benett J: Childhood sexual abuse and the consequences in adult women. *Obstet Gynecol* 71:631–642, 1988.
3. Campbell JC, Pugh LC, Campbell D, Visscher M: The influence of abuse on pregnancy intention. *Womens Health Issues* 5:214–223, 1995.
4. Council on Ethical and Judicial Issues: Physicians and domestic violence: Ethical considerations. *JAMA* 267:3190–3193, 1992.
5. Council on Scientific Affairs of the American Medical Association: Violence against women: Relevance for medical practitioners. *JAMA* 267:3184–3189, 1992.
6. Cunningham RM, Stiffman AR, Doré P: The association of physical and sexual abuse with HIV risk behaviors in adolescence and young adulthood: Implications for public health. *Child Abuse Negl* 18:233–245, 1994.
7. Domino JV, Haber JD: Prior physical and sexual abuse in women with chronic headache: Clinical correlates. *Headache* 27:310–314, 1987.
8. Drossman DA, Leserman J, Nachman G, et al: Sexual and physical abuse in women with functional or

organic gastrointestinal disorders. *Ann Intern Med* 113:828–833, 1990.

9. Gershenson HP, Musick JS, Rueh-Ross HS, Magee V, Rubino KK, Rosenberg D: The prevalence of coercive sexual experience among teenage mothers. *J Interpersonal Viol* 4:204–219, 1989.

10. Glander SS, Moore ML, Michielutte R, Parsons LH: The prevalence of domestic violence among women seeking abortion. *Obstet Gynecol* 91:1002–1006, 1998.

11. Johnson D, Elliott E: Screening for domestic violence in a rural family practice. *Minn Med* 80:43–45, 1997.

12. Levy B (ed): *Dating Violence: Young Women in Danger.* Seattle, WA: Seal Press, 1991.

13. Levy B, Giggans PO: *What Parents Need to Know About Dating Violence.* Seattle, WA: Seal Press, 1995.

14. McFarlane J, Parker B, Soeken K, Bullock J: Assessing for abuse in pregnancy: Severity and frequency of injuries and associated entry into prenatal care. *JAMA* 267:3176–3178, 1992.

15. McGrath ME, Hogan JW, Peipert JF: A prevalence survey of abuse and screening for abuse in urgent care patients. *Obstet Gynecol* 91:511–514, 1998.

16. Mullen PE, Martin JL, Anderson JC, Romans SE, Herbison GP: Childhood sexual abuse and mental health in adult life. *Br J Psychiatry* 163:721–731, 1993.

17. Parsons LH, Zaccaro D, Wells B, Stovall TG: Methods of and attitudes toward screening ob/gyn patients for domestic violence. *Am J Obstet Gynecol* 173:381–387, 1995.

18. Rapkin AJ, Kames LD, Drake LL, Stampler FM, Nabboff BD: History of physical and sexual abuse in women with chronic pelvic pain. *Obstet Gynecol* 76:92–96, 1990.

19. Schornstein SL: *Domestic Violence and Health Care: What Every Professional Needs to Know.* Thousand Oaks, CA: SAGE, 1997.

20. Singer MI, Anglin TM, Song LY, Lunghofer L: Adolescents' exposure to violence and associated symptoms of psychological trauma. *JAMA* 273:477–482, 1995.

21. Smikle CB, Satin AJ, Dellinger CL, Hankins GDV: Physical and sexual abuse: A middle-class concern? *J Reprod Med* 40:347–350, 1995.

22. Walling MK, Reiter RC, O'Hara MW, Milburn AK, Lilly G, Vincent SD: Abuse history and chronic pain in women: I. Prevalences of sexual abuse and physical abuse. *Obstet Gynecol* 84:193–199, 1994.

23. Warshaw C, Ganley AL: *Improving the Health Care Response to Domestic Violence: A Resource Manual for Health Care Providers.* San Francisco: Family Violence Prevention Fund, 1995.

24. Harper M, Parsons L: Maternal deaths due to homicide and other injuries in North Carolina: 1992–1994. *Obstet Gynecol* 90:920–923, 1997.

Part VII

General Health

CHAPTER 60

Cardiovascular Disease

Hamid Taheri
Judith Hsia

CARDIOVASCULAR RISK FACTORS: SCREENING AND MODIFICATION

History • Physical Examination • Laboratory Evaluation • Hypertension • Diabetes Mellitus • Hyperlipidemia • Cigarette Smoking • Exercise • Aspirin • Exogenous Hormone Replacement

EVALUATION OF SIGNS AND SYMPTOMS DURING ROUTINE OFFICE VISITS

Chest Pain • Dyspnea • Palpitations • Syncope • Claudication • Peripheral Venous Disease • Aortic Disease • Myocarditis, Pericarditis, and Endocarditis

PREOPERATIVE EVALUATION

Antibiotic Prophylaxis • Assessment of Operative Cardiac Risk

CARDIAC LIFE SUPPORT

C ardiovascular disease is by far the leading cause of death among women in the United States; more women die from cardiovascular disease, predominantly heart attacks, congestive heart failure (CHF), and strokes, than from the next 16 causes combined. The opportunity for screening and prevention lies in the hands of the primary care physician. In the office, efforts should focus on prevention of cardiovascular disease through risk-factor management and on identification of cardiovascular disease in patients with symptoms.

Cardiovascular Risk Factors: Screening and Modification

Public education efforts have led to a fairly precipitous decline in cardiovascular mortality since the 1960s; however, the rate of decline among women has lagged behind that of men. Despite significant public education efforts, cancer, specifically breast cancer, is widely viewed by women as their greatest health threat, and most women do not sufficiently understand their risk of cardiovascular disease. Consequently, behaviors such as smoking, sedentary lifestyle, inadequate attention to blood pressure (BP) control, and consumption of a high-fat diet, all of which confer added cardiovascular risk, remain widespread.

Traditional cardiovascular risk factors—hypertension, diabetes mellitus, hypercholesterolemia, smoking, and a family history of premature atherosclerosis—are predictive of subsequent myocardial infarction (MI) and stroke. In addition to identification and modification of risk factors, promotion of healthful activities, such as regular exercise, attainment of ideal body weight, and consumption of a high-fiber, low-fat diet, should be encouraged.

History

At the women's initial visit, a history of hypertension, treated or untreated; smoking, past or current; and family history of premature atherosclerosis (that is, a parent or sibling with heart attack or stroke before age 55 for men or 65 for women) should be obtained (Table 60-1). Patients should be asked if they have been told of hypercholester-

TABLE 60-1 Obtaining a Cardiac History

Cardiovascular risk factors
 Hypertension
 Diabetes mellitus
 Hypercholesterolemia
 Family history of premature atherosclerosis
 Cigarette smoking
 Obesity
Cardiovascular symptoms
 Chest discomfort
 Shortness of breath
 Palpitations/syncope
 Claudication
Past hospitalization or evaluation for cardiovascular disease

Regular exercise

Medications

olemia. A history of glucose intolerance, whether treated or not, and symptoms of diabetes mellitus, such as polydipsia and polyuria, should be ascertained. Patients, especially patients who are middle-aged or older, must be asked about additional evidence of cardiac disease, such as chest discomfort, particularly when exertional in nature, dyspnea, syncope, known heart murmurs, and hospitalization for myocardial infarction (MI) or other heart disease. It may also be useful to determine whether previous cardiac evaluation, such as exercise testing, has been performed. Patients should also be asked if they get any regular exercise as a prelude to exercise promotion.

During follow-up visits, a simple query, "Have you developed any problems with high blood pressure, diabetes, or chest discomfort?" is important. Because women often view coronary disease as a problem limited to men, their discounting of cardiac symptoms is commonplace and underscores the necessity for the physician to prompt them in revealing symptoms that may reflect coronary insufficiency and/or cardiac risk.

Physical Examination

Recording of weight and blood pressure (BP) is appropriate at every visit. For risk-factor screening, observation of body habitus to encourage exercise and maintenance of ideal body weight is desirable. Xanthomas (cholesterol-filled nodules) may be found on the eyelids or extensor tendons of the extremities of patients with familial hyperlipidemias. Funduscopic examination may reveal retinal arteriopathy in patients with hypertension or beading of the retinal artery in those with hypercholesterolemia. Auscultation of the chest for rales or diminished breath sounds due to pleural effusion may provide evidence of CHF.

Cardiac examination should start with palpation of the chest to locate the point of maximum impulse (PMI), which should normally be in the midclavicular line of the fifth intercostal space. Lateralization of the PMI may indicate cardiomegaly. Palpation over the sternum identifies a right ventricular lift, characteristic of right heart dilatation and failure, which may be due to pulmonary disease, primary pulmonary hypertension, or intrinsic cardiac disease. During systematic auscultation of the heart, assess the splitting of S2 to screen for heretofore undetected atrial septal defects in which splitting of S2 is fixed rather than narrowing during expiration. An S4 may be heard in older patients or those with hypertension; an S3 may be normal in young patients but reflects left ventricular dysfunction in older patients. Murmurs, both innocent and pathologic, should be recorded.

Assessment of the waist-to-hip ratio permits risk stratification because upper-body fat distribution has been associated with a number of cardiovascular risk factors, including elevated systolic BP, total cholesterol, low-density lipoprotein (LDL) cholesterol, and triglyceride levels, as well as lower high-density lipoprotein (HDL) cholesterol. Examination of the abdomen may reveal hepatomegaly due to right heart failure or a pulsatile abdominal mass in patients with abdominal aortic aneurysms. Flank bruits may also be audible in those with renal artery stenosis.

Peripheral edema may be evident in patients with CHF, and peripheral pulses should be

checked to document the condition of the peripheral arteries.

Laboratory Evaluation

Laboratory screening for cardiac risk factors should include a fasting glucose and lipid profile; that is, total cholesterol, triglycerides, high-density lipoprotein cholesterol (HDL-C), and calculated low-density lipoprotein cholesterol (LDL-C). Glucose and lipid abnormalities are commonly related, with about half of noninsulin-dependent diabetics manifesting lipid abnormalities. Guidelines for frequency of risk-factor screening are described in sections below.

A 12-lead electrocardiogram (ECG) may be obtained as a baseline study for future reference or for prognosis. The yield in normal subjects varies with their age. Among 67,375 young U.S. Air Force personnel, electrocardiographic abnormalities were detected in 3.8 percent. Among 2940 women over 65 years of age, abnormal ECGs were found in 23 percent. Data from the Framingham Study suggest that the development of ECG abnormalities has predictive value for coronary heart disease and sudden death. The relative risk of MI during 12 years of follow-up among women with nonspecific ST segment abnormalities was 1.5 for women younger than 65 years and 1.7 ($p < .05$) for older women. The presence of MI, left ventricular hypertrophy, intraventricular conduction delay, heart block, or nonspecific ST changes on a 12-lead ECG was highly associated with sudden death ($p < .0001$). Therefore, a periodic electrocardiogram in older women appears justified, provided that interpretation of the tracing is performed by a knowledgeable physician. Detection of new abnormalities should trigger further evaluation for ischemic heart disease, such as electron beam computed tomography or exercise thallium testing.

Hypertension

The National Health and Examination Survey estimated that 57.5 million United States residents were hypertensive. By the age of 60, about half the population will have a diastolic pressure >90 mmHg and/or a systolic pressure >140 mmHg. The incidence and severity of hypertension is greater among African-Americans than Caucasians at all ages after adolescence. In the Framingham Study—a large, longitudinal population-based study in Framingham, Massachusetts—increased risk of stroke or coronary heart disease was associated with diastolic pressure exceeding 90 mmHg. Because most hypertensives are asymptomatic, blood-pressure screening should be undertaken at every opportunity.

The sixth report of the Joint National Committee on Prevention, Detection, Evaluation, and Treatment of High Blood Pressure's (JNC VI) classification of adult blood pressure is summarized in Table 60-2. The classification is based on an average of two or more BP readings on two or more occasions.

Large clinical trials of antihypertensive treatment have included both men and women. No

TABLE 60-2 Classification of Blood Pressure in Adults

Category	Systolic Pressure (mmHg)	Diastolic Pressure (mmHg)	Follow-up Recommended
Optimal	<120	<80	
Normal	<130	<85	Recheck in 2 years
High-normal	130–139	85–89	Recheck in 1 year
Hypertension			
Stage 1	140–159	90–99	Confirm within 2 months
Stage 2	160–179	100–109	Refer or Rx within 1 month
Stage 3	≥180	≥110	Refer or Rx immediately or within 1 week

NOTE: When systolic and diastolic pressure fall into different categories, the more severe category applies.

SOURCE: From National Institutes of Health: *National High Blood Pressure Education Program*. Washington, DC: NIH, 1997. NIH Publication No. 98-4080.

significant differences in responses to treatment and outcome have been identified between men and women.

Once a patient has been identified as hypertensive, what is the significance of this finding? A number of studies have demonstrated increased cardiovascular risk in patients with mild hypertension, as well as the protective benefit conferred by antihypertensive therapy against strokes and probably CHF (Table 60-3). Demonstration of protection against MI is less well established. In general, treatment of all patients with diastolic pressures >100 mmHg, many with diastolic pressure of 95 to 100 mmHg, and some with a diastolic pressure of 90 to 95 mmHg, is indicated. The threshold for pharmacological therapy depends in part, on the presence of other risk factors.

Treatment of isolated systolic hypertension, that is, systolic blood pressure >160 mmHg with diastolic pressure <90 mmHg, is indicated in the elderly, in whom the risk of stroke was reduced 36 percent by diuretic treatment in the Systolic Hypertension in the Elderly Program (SHEP).

Following identification of hypertension, patients should be evaluated for underlying causes of hypertension such as renal failure, renal artery stenosis, coarctation of the aorta, endocrinopathies, and for end organ damage. Funduscopic examination and urinalysis should be performed on all hypertensive patients. A baseline 12-lead ECG to document the presence or absence of evidence of left ventricular hypertrophy may be warranted, particularly in African Americans, who have higher prevalence of left ventricular hypertrophy, a higher incidence of stroke, and a higher mortality rate than Caucasian hypertensives.

Renovascular hypertension is often severe, abrupt in onset, and prevalent in smokers and Caucasians. The prevalence in large series has been about 3 percent, although estimates as high as 43 percent have been reported in patients with accelerated or malignant hypertension with marked retinopathy. In young women, fibromuscular dysplasia is the usual cause; in older patients, the cause is usually renal arterial atheroma. Abdominal bruits are audible in about 40 percent of patients, and are moderately specific indicators of renal artery stenosis. Elevated blood urea nitrogen (BUN) or serum creatinine suggests renal parenchymal, rather than renovascular, disease. Asymmetric renal uptake and retention of radioisotope during a captopril renal scan suggests renovascular hypertension; arteriography is the definitive test. Treatment involves either percutaneous or open angioplasty.

When treating patients with hypertension, the objective is to achieve a sustained BP below 140/90 mmHg (Fig. 60-1). In patients with stage 1 or 2 hypertension, lifestyle modification should be attempted for 3 to 6 months before instituting drug treatment. During this interval, close follow-up is warranted to vigorously reinforce the necessity of lifestyle modification and to ensure that hypertension is not progressing to stage 3. Initial steps to lower BP in patients with essential hypertension include weight reduction and dietary sodium restriction. Recently, a high fruit, vegetable, and low-fat dairy diet, which was high in fiber, calcium, potassium, and magnesium was reported to reduce blood pressure. If lifestyle changes are ineffective, drug therapy should be instituted, usually with a single agent. Diuretics and β-adrenergic blockers have established efficacy in large clinical trials and are comparatively inexpensive. Calcium channel antagonists and angiotensin converting enzyme (ACE) inhibitors are reasonable alternatives. In diabetics, ACE inhibitors are preferred because of their renal-protective benefits. If adequate response has not been obtained after 1 to 3 months, the dose may be increased or a different agent tried. A second drug may be added if minimization of side effects by using lower doses of two drugs is desired; newer, convenient formulations of drug combinations are available.

For stage 3 hypertension, chances are slim that BP will be controlled by lifestyle modification alone. Therefore, drug therapy should be instituted earlier, with the understanding that combination drug therapy is likely to be necessary.

TABLE 60-3 Antihypertensive Medications

Drug	Trade Name	Side Effects
Diuretics		Hypokalemia, increase in uric acid
Clorthalidone	Hygroton	
Furosemide	Lasix	
Hydrochlorothiazide	Microzide	
Bumetanide	Bumex	
Metolazone	Zaroxolyn	
β-Adrenergic blockers		
Nonselective		Bronchospasm, depression, bradycardia, masks hypoglycemia in diabetics
Propranalol	Inderal	
Nadolol	Corgard	
β-Selective		Depression, bradycardia, masks hypoglycemia in diabetics
Metoprolol	Lopressor	
Atenolol	Tenormin	
Intrinsic sympathomimetic activity		Less bradycardia
Acebutolol	Sectral	
Pindolol	Visken	
α-β Blockers		Orthostatic hypotension
Labetalol	Normodyne, Trandate	
Carvedilol	Coreg	
α-Receptor blockers		
Prazosin	Minipress	Orthostatic hypotension
Doxazosin	Cardura	
Central α₂-antagonists		Sedation, withdrawal hypotension
Clonidine	Catapres	
α-Methyldopa	Aldomet	
Calcium channel blockers		
Diltiazem	Cardizem, Tiazac, Dilacor	Bradycardia, ankle edema, constipation
Verapamil	Calan, Verelan, Covera, Isoptin	
Nifedipine, nicardipine, nisoldipine	Procardia, Adalat, Cardene, Sular	
Isradipine	DynaCirc	
Amlodipine	Norvasc	
Felodipine	Plendil	
ACE inhibitors[a]		
Captopril	Capoten	Cough, hypotension, hyperkalemia, rise in creatinine, angioedema
Enalapril	Vasotec	
Lisinopril	Prinivil, Zestril	
Benazepril	Lotensin	
Fosinopril	Monopril	
Ramipril	Altace	
Quinapril	Accupril	
Trandolapril	Mavik	
Angiotensin II receptor blockers		
Losartin	Cozaar	Hyperkalemia
Valsartan	Diovan	
Direct vasodilators		
Hydralazine		Fluid retention, reflex tachycardia
Minoxidil		

[a]ACE inhibitors = Angiotensin-converting enzyme inhibitors.

Figure 60-1 Treatment of
Hypertension

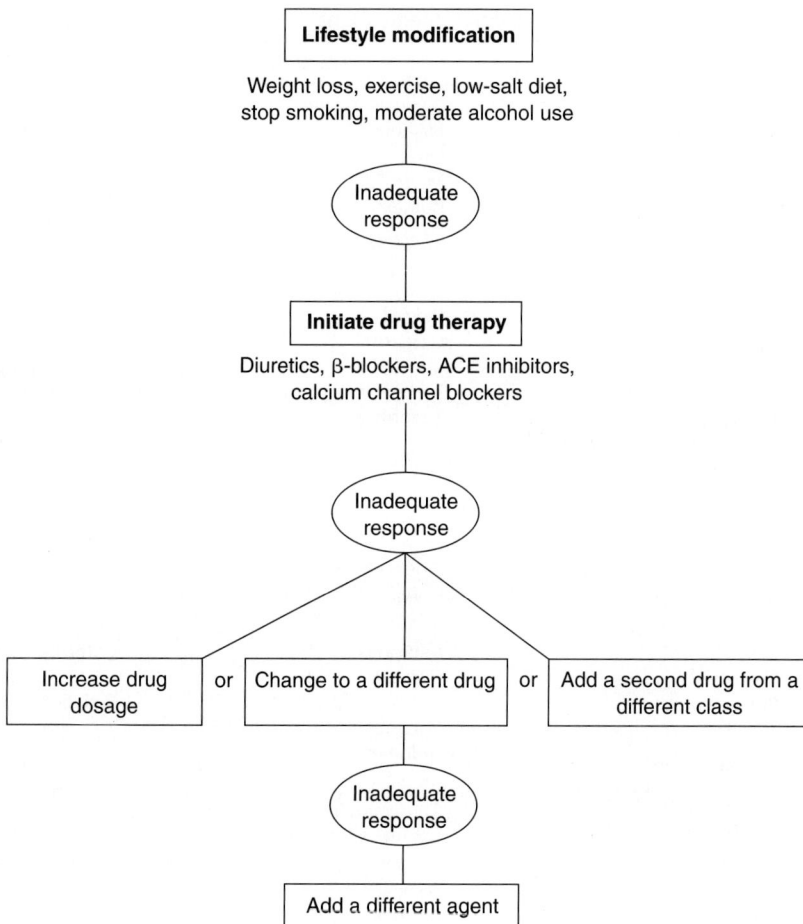

```
          ┌─────────────────────────┐
          │  Lifestyle modification  │
          └─────────────────────────┘
        Weight loss, exercise, low-salt diet,
        stop smoking, moderate alcohol use

                   ╭──────────╮
                   │ Inadequate│
                   │  response │
                   ╰──────────╯

          ┌─────────────────────────┐
          │   Initiate drug therapy  │
          └─────────────────────────┘
        Diuretics, β-blockers, ACE inhibitors,
            calcium channel blockers

                   ╭──────────╮
                   │ Inadequate│
                   │  response │
                   ╰──────────╯
```

| Increase drug dosage | or | Change to a different drug | or | Add a second drug from a different class |

```
                   ╭──────────╮
                   │ Inadequate│
                   │  response │
                   ╰──────────╯

          ┌─────────────────────────┐
          │   Add a different agent  │
          └─────────────────────────┘
```

An ever-growing armamentarium of antihypertensives is available, including diuretics, adrenergic blockers, calcium channel blockers, ACE inhibitors, angiotensin II receptor blockers, and direct vasodilators. Trials have used antihypertensives from a variety of classes, all of which appear to be effective. Cost, dosing convenience, insurance formulary concerns, and side-effect profile influence the choice of an agent. These are particularly important issues because treatment is often lifelong.

Patients with hypertensive emergencies have acute end organ sequelae of hypertension, such as encephalopathy, acute heart failure with pulmonary edema, or dissecting aortic aneurysm. These situations require prompt hospitalization for parenteral antihypertensive therapy.

Diabetes Mellitus

The prevalence of diabetes mellitus in the United States is 2 to 6 percent, with impaired glucose tolerance in as much as 20 percent of the population. The American Diabetes Association suggests fasting 8 h plasma glucose measurement at 3 year intervals in women with major risk factors for diabetes (Table 60-4). Women with fasting

TABLE 60-4   Major Risk Factors for Diabetes

Family history of diabetes (parents or siblings with diabetes)

Obesity (≥20% over desired body weight or BMI ≥27 kg/m²)

Bioethnicity (African-Americans, Hispanics, American Indians, Asians/Pacific Islanders)

Age ≥45 years

Previously identified impaired fasting glucose or impaired glucose tolerance

Hypertension

HDL ≤35 mg/dl (0.9 mmol/l) and/or triglycerides ≥250 mg/dL (2.82 mmol/l)

History of gestational diabetes or delivery of babies over 9 lb

---

plasma glucose ≥110 mg/dl (6.1 mmol/l) should be further evaluated.

Diabetes is clearly associated with increased risk of cardiovascular disease; mortality from coronary disease among diabetics is twice that of nondiabetics. Data from the Diabetes Control and Complications Trial suggests that intensive treatment of insulin-dependent diabetes with three or more daily injections of insulin, or by using an infusion pump, can reduce end organ damage. A study of intensive therapy of individuals with impaired glucose tolerance and noninsulin-dependent diabetes, the Diabetes Prevention Trial, is in progress. In the meantime, diabetics should be identified and receive aggressive weight control, dietary education, and, in many instances, drug therapy. Diabetes is discussed in depth in Chap. 67.

Hyperlipidemia

The prevalence of hypercholesterolemia has fallen in recent years; however, the prevalence of elevated (>240 mg/dl) or borderline (200 to 239 mg/dl) total cholesterol among women is still estimated at 20 and 30 percent, respectively. Hyperlipidemia usually causes no symptoms until coronary, cerebral, or peripheral vascular insufficiency develops. Physical manifestations are comparatively infrequent, so the diagnosis is usually made through blood screening. The lipid profile generally includes total cholesterol, triglycerides, HDL-cholesterol, and calculated LDL-cholesterol.

Nonfasting patients can be screened with random glucose, total, and HDL-cholesterol. Because the triglyceride level depends on recent dietary intake, this value, as well as the LDL level, which is calculated using the triglyceride level, is inaccurate in nonfasting patients. The total cholesterol, however, is not influenced much by food consumed during the preceding few hours and thus may be measured in the nonfasting state.

The National Cholesterol Education Program (NCEP), Adult Treatment Panel II, classification and guidelines are summarized in Table 60-5. Patients with desirable cholesterol levels should have them repeated at 5-year intervals. Fasting lipid profiles should be obtained for those with borderline cholesterol levels; management is discretionary. Patients with undesirable total or LDL-cholesterol levels should receive lipid-lowering management, including education in weight reduction, exercise, and the NCEP "Step One" diet (Table 60-6). Physicians or their office staff can teach the Step One diet; education in the Step Two diet generally requires the assistance of a registered dietitian. After 2 to 3 months of dietary therapy, the fasting lipid profile should be repeated. If lipids are still above the desirable range, drug therapy is indicated.

Patients with known coronary disease should be referred for dietary education and, if necessary, drug therapy to achieve an LDL level <100 mg/dl. The Scandinavian Simvastatin Survival Study investigated the long-term effects of lowering cholesterol on reducing mortality in patients with preexisting coronary heart disease. This study showed that reducing LDL-cholesterol with an HMG CoA reductase inhibitor significantly decreased (35 percent) the risk of major coronary events. This risk reduction was independent of gender or baseline LDL-cholesterol levels.

TABLE 60-5 National Cholesterol Education Program Guideline

	Initiation Level	*Goal of Therapy*	*Goal of Therapy*
	LDL-cholesterol (md/dl)		**Total Cholesterol**
Without CHD			
<2 risk factors	≥160	<160	<240
≥2 risk factors	≥130	<130	<200
With CHD	≥100	≤100	≤160

For patients without known coronary heart disease, NCEP guidelines, which were released in 1993, call for pharmacologic therapy in women if the LDL level remains >190 mg/dl on a diet, or >160 mg/dl on a diet in the presence of two other risk factors (hypertension, diabetes, obesity, HDL <35 mg/dl, or a family history of coronary disease). The AFCAPS/TexCAPS data suggest that a more aggressive management approach may be justified if the HDL-cholesterol is low. AFCAPS/TexCAPS demonstrated a coronary protective benefit of cholesterol lowering in men and women without coronary heart disease who had average LDL-cholesterol levels and moderately low HDL-cholesterol. Thus, the spectrum of individuals who stand to benefit from cholesterol-lowering treatment has expanded.

A wide range of cholesterol-lowering drugs are available, including niacin, resin agents (cholestyramine, colestipol), and HMG-CoA reductase inhibitors (atorvastatin, lovastatin, simvastatin, pravastatin, cerivastatin, fluvastatin). Niacin is inexpensive and raises HDL, as well as lowers LDL to a modest extent, but patients often dislike and will not tolerate the flushing that is common even when niacin is titrated up from a low dose. A new longer-acting niacin, Niaspan, appears to have a lower frequency of flushing. Resin agents' ability to prevent coronary events is well established, as is their safety record. Patients frequently complain of constipation and dislike consuming quantities of granules suspended in liquid several times a day. The HMG-CoA reductase inhibitors have greater LDL-lowering capability, are well tolerated, and are of proven benefit in prolonging life. Asymptomatic transaminase elevation exceeding three times the upper limit of normal occurs in about 0.5 percent of patients taking low-dose HMG-CoA reductase inhibitors. Higher doses are associated with a modest increase in likelihood of transaminase elevation. Therefore, serum AST should be measured at baseline and monitored periodically; frequency of recommended monitoring differs among the

TABLE 60-6 National Cholesterol Education Program Dietary Recommendation

	Step One Diet	**Step Two Diet**
Total fat	<30% of total calories	<30% of total calories
Saturated fatty acids	<10% of total calories	<7% of total calories
Polyunsaturated fatty acids	Up to 10% of total calories	Up to 10% of total calories
Monounsaturated fatty acids	10–15% of total calories	10–15% of total calories
Carbohydrates	50–60% of total calories	50–60% of total calories
Protein	10–20% of total calories	10–20% of total calories
Cholesterol	<300 mg/day	<200 mg/day
Total calories	To achieve and maintain desirable weight	To achieve and maintain desirable weight

various agents. Because these agents are of proven benefit in reducing MI and coronary death, treatment should generally not be withheld because of potential adverse drug effects.

Cigarette Smoking

Cigarette smoking is the foremost preventable factor associated with coronary death in the United States. The risk of coronary disease among smokers is twice that of nonsmokers; cardiac risk is directly related to the number of cigarettes smoked each day. Secondary exposure to cigarette smoke through passive inhalation by nonsmokers increases risk as well. Cigarette smoking also enhances the risk of stroke and peripheral vascular disease.

Smoking cessation should be universally encouraged. Among 35-year-old women, cessation is expected to prolong life expectancy by more than 3 years; 55-year-old women may expect to live 2 extra years. Physician advice to discontinue smoking will induce about 5 percent of patients to stop. Other interventions, such as referral to smoking cessation programs, increase the likelihood of success. Smoking cessation programs often use aversive techniques such as rapid puffing in combination with steps to enhance recognition of situations provoking a desire to smoke, as well as behavioral modification techniques. Bupropion hydrochloride (Zyban, Wellbutrin) is a long-acting antidepressant that has been proven effective as an adjunct in smoking cessation (dosage: 150 mg bid for up to 12 weeks).

Management of physical nicotine dependence in smokers may include prescription of nicotine patches or chewing gum. Transdermal nicotine patches are usually applied daily using the 21-mg size for the first 6 weeks, followed by the 14-mg patch and the 7-mg patch for 2 weeks each. Nicotine chewing gum (Nicorette, 2 mg nicotine polacrilex each) may be prescribed as needed, up to 30 doses per day, although the average consumption is 10 doses daily. Patients usually reduce their use of nicotine chewing gum over several months. Persistent nicotine chewing gum use for more than 6 months suggests that gum dependency has replaced cigarette dependency.

Exercise

Physical activity reduces cardiovascular risk, lowers BP, improves glucose tolerance, assists with maintenance of ideal body weight, and improves the lipid profile. Any amount of aerobic activity appears preferable to no exercise. The American Heart Association recommends three 20-min sessions per week, each preceded by a warm-up and followed by a cooling down period. Patients with previously sedentary lifestyles should start slowly and gradually increase the intensity of their exercise.

For exercise programs to be successful, patients must realize that exercise is a lifelong commitment and thus should choose types and intensities of exercise that are enjoyable or, at least, tolerable. A variety of different exercise activities is desirable to prevent injury from repetitive stress, provide seasonal adaptability, and maintain interest. Women with known coronary disease or suggestive symptoms, such as exertional chest discomfort or dyspnea, should be evaluated for cardiac ischemia before initiating an exercise program. Such evaluation may also be warranted in some asymptomatic patients with cardiac risk factors.

Aspirin

In the Physician's Health Study, aspirin, 325 mg every other day, provided cardiovascular protection in middle-aged and older men. No women were included in that study. A similar placebo-controlled randomized trial in women is currently in progress, but the results will not be available for a number of years. In the meantime, no blanket recommendation is appropriate regarding aspirin for cardiovascular prophylaxis in women. On an individualized basis, physicians may choose to recommend aspirin for women with cardiac risk factors.

Exogenous Hormone Replacement

Long-term follow-up of oral contraceptive users has indicated no increased risk of cardiovascular disease from oral contraceptive use. Nevertheless, it seems prudent to use those preparations with progestins, such as norgestimate or desogestrel, which are least likely to adversely alter lipid profiles. In general, women over 35 years of age who smoke should be counseled against oral contraceptive use unless they can stop smoking. In one report, the risk of MI was increased 30-fold in women over age 35 who smoked and used oral contraceptives.

The relationship between menopause and cardiovascular disease is undergoing extensive evaluation. The Framingham Study identified a striking increase in coronary artery disease (CAD) in postmenopausal women, as compared to premenopausal women. Since 1970, a number of large cohort and case control studies and one small randomized trial have examined estrogen's role in the prevention of cardiovascular disease among postmenopausal women. Three meta-analyses found the relative risk for coronary artery disease to be significantly lower in women who had ever used estrogen, as compared to those who had never used estrogen.

The first controlled trial of hormone replacement for prevention of coronary heart disease was the Heart & Estrogen/Progestin Replacement Study (HERS), which randomized women with preexisting coronary disease to daily placebo or conjugated equine estrogen 0.625 mg plus medroxyprogesterone 2.5 mg (Prempro). Somewhat unexpectedly, during the first year of the study, women assigned to active hormone replacement in HERS had more coronary events than placebo recipients; in contrast, after several years on treatment, women assigned to active hormone replacement had fewer coronary events than placebo recipients, but overall, during 4.1 years of follow-up, no treatment benefit was apparent. Follow-up of the HERS cohort is continuing. The National Institutes of Health (NIH) is currently conducting a trial of hormone replacement in healthy women, the Women's Health Initiative, results of which are expected around 2005.

Although continued research in this field is urgently needed and is vitally important to women's health, most physicians believe that the data that are currently available do suggest that the use of estrogen for postmenopausal women has beneficial cardiac effects.

Evaluation of Signs and Symptoms during Routine Office Visits

Women are less likely than men to seek medical attention for potential cardiac complaints, and they are less likely to be referred for diagnostic testing once they do seek medical attention, despite the fact that cardiovascular mortality in older women actually exceeds that in men of the same age. Gender bias in evaluation as well as treatment of coronary heart disease should be avoided.

Chest Pain

Chest pain is a common complaint, the differential diagnosis of which is summarized in Table 60-7. The quality, location, and duration of chest discomfort should be elicited, along with precipitants and factors providing relief. An antecedent viral illness and positional quality to the chest pain suggest pericarditis. Association of chest discomfort with upper extremity and perioral paresthesias in high-stress situations suggests hyperventilation. Greater age and the presence of cardiac risk factors should increase one's suspicion of coronary disease.

On examination, costochondritis may be diagnosed if chest wall tenderness is present. A pericardial or pleural friction rub suggests pericarditis or pleuritis. A midsystolic click should be audible in patients with mitral valve prolapse, and possibly a holosystolic murmur at the apex as well. Epigastric tenderness suggests gastrointestinal disease.

TABLE 60-7   Differential Diagnosis of Chest Pain

	Location	Quality	Duration	Provoked By	Relieved By
Angina pectoris	Substernal, radiation to arm, neck, jaw	Pressure	Minutes	Exertion, stress	Rest, nitroglycerin
Pericarditis	Substernal	Sharp	Hours	Lying down, inspiration	Sitting forward
Esophageal reflux, spasm	Substernal, epigastric	Pressure	Variable	Recumbency, food	Nitroglycerin
Gastritis, peptic ulcer	Epigastric	Burning	Hours	Food or lack of food	Antacids
Pulmonary embolism, pneumonia	Substernal with dyspnea	Pleuritic	Hours	Inspiration or spontaneous	Specific therapy
Costochondritis	Costosternal joint	Tenderness	Variable	Palpitation	Analgesics
Mitral valve prolapse	Left chest	Sharp	Variable	Spontaneous	β-Blockers
Hyperventilation	Precordial	Pressure	Minutes	Emotional stress	Relief of stress

In the Framingham Study, angina pectoris rather than MI was the predominant presenting symptom for women with coronary heart disease. Classic angina is characterized as substernal heaviness or pressure radiating to the neck, left arm, or jaw and lasting minutes; it is brought on by exercise and relieved by rest. The character of chest symptoms should be ascertained, bearing in mind the mediocre specificity of a diagnosis of coronary disease based on patient history alone. Because the history in both men and women who have coronary artery disease may be rather nonspecific, the decision regarding the need for further evaluation should be as aggressive for women as it is for men. Usually no specific physical findings will be apparent.

A 12-lead ECG may be helpful in identifying pericarditis (Fig. 60-2) or previous MI. Evidence of ischemia is unlikely unless the patient is having symptoms at that time. Echocardiography will identify mitral valve prolapse.

Treadmill testing, nuclear imaging, and coronary angiography remain the mainstays for the diagnosis of CAD. Treadmill testing is well established as a valuable, safe, and comparatively inexpensive means for diagnosing coronary heart disease in men. Its value in women, however, is less certain. In one comparison of treadmill testing in men and women, in which one-third of patients in each group had angiographically documented coronary disease, the false-positive rate in men was 7 percent compared with 22 percent in women ($p < .05$). The false-negative rate—that is, negative treadmill tests in patients with angiographic coronary disease—was 13 percent for men and women. Overall, treadmill results were misleading in 35 percent of women, severely limiting the utility of treadmill testing as a screening tool in women. False-positive exercise tests have been related to phases of the menstrual cycle and to oral contraceptive use, suggesting a relationship between sex hormones and ECG responses to exercise.

Fortunately, nuclear imaging has provided a more accurate noninvasive means of diagnosing coronary heart disease in women. For patients unable to achieve a reasonable exercise level, pharmacologic stress using either dipyridamole, adenosine, or dobutamine appears to have similar diagnostic accuracy to exercise. Using thallium-201 or technetium 99m-based imaging agents in conjunction with exercise or pharmacologic stress, diagnostic accuracy is comparable in men and women when valve plane, breast artifacts, and diaphragmatic attenuation are taken into account by experienced interpreters (Fig. 60-3).

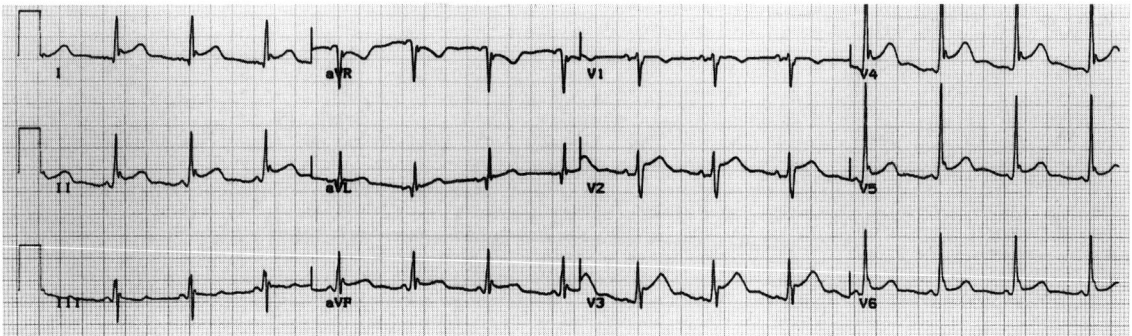

Figure 60-2 Twelve-lead electrocardiogram (ECG) in pericarditis. There is diffuse elevation of ST segments as well as depression of the PR segment in relation to the TP segment.

Stress echocardiography, using either exercise or dobutamine, is also an effective approach to evaluation of patients with suspected coronary disease, provided the quality of the echocardiographic images acquired is adequate. Pulmonary disease and unsuitable body habitus may limit the necessary visualization of the endocardium.

Electron beam computed tomography (EBCT) is a relatively new, noninvasive test that detects the presence of coronary calcification, which is highly correlated with atherosclerotic disease (Fig. 60-4). This test is valuable as a noninvasive, relatively inexpensive method for assessing coronary artery disease in individuals with cardiac risk factors, particularly those who may be asymptomatic. Although EBCT does not

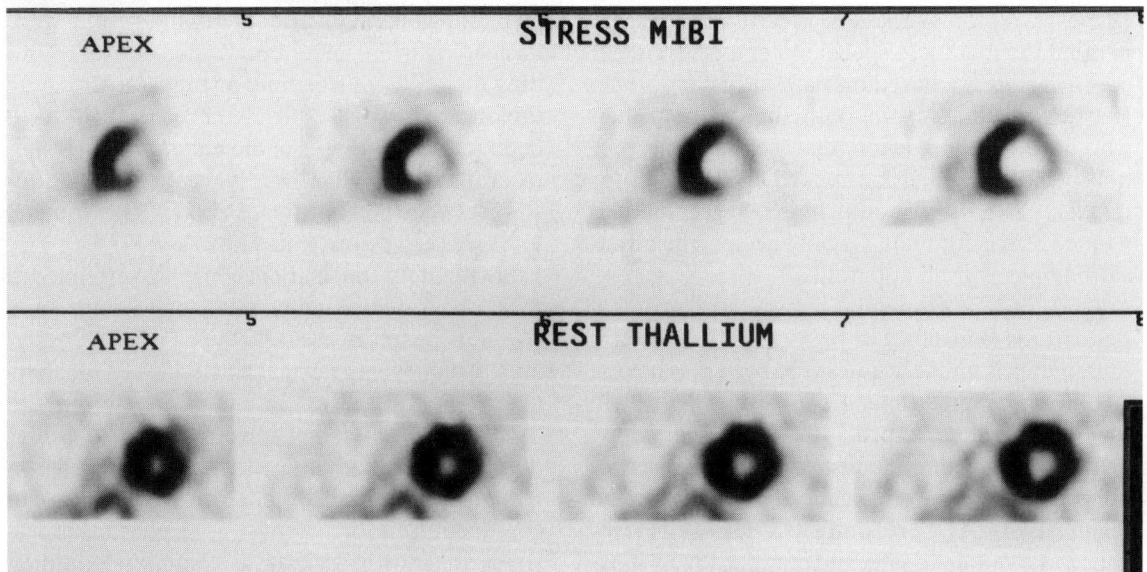

Figure 60-3 Abnormal thallium-201 scintigraphy. Short-axis tomographic images during stress reveal decreased uptake of nuclear contrast in the lateral wall. Uptake is restored following rest, consistent with stress-induced myocardial ischemia.

Figure 60-4 Coronary artery scan of a patient with severe coronary artery disease demonstrating extensive calcification in the left coronary artery.

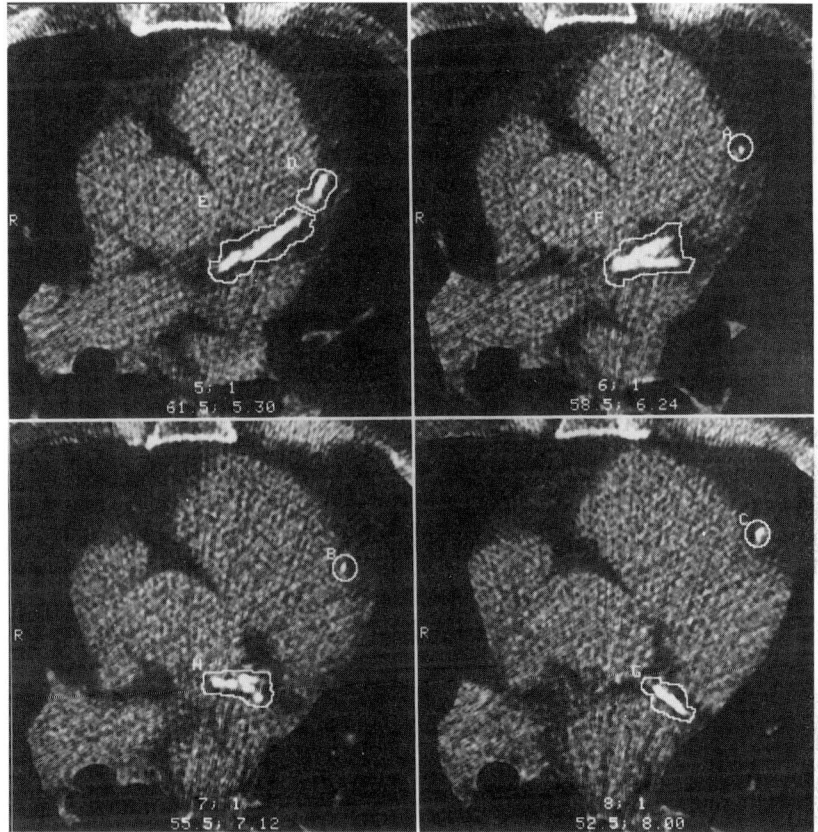

specify the severity of coronary stenoses, the extent of coronary calcification is well correlated with subsequent clinical coronary events. The amount of ionizing radiation is similar to that required for an abdominal "flat plate" x-ray.

Coronary angiography remains the gold standard for diagnosis of coronary heart disease, but does involve ionizing radiation and a small risk of MI, stroke, hemorrhage, vascular damage, or allergy to the contrast agent. Therefore, unless the prior suspicion of coronary disease is reasonably high, noninvasive evaluation should precede angiography. Patients with Prinzmetal's variant angina—that is, coronary artery spasm—may have normal exercise test, nuclear imaging studies, and coronary angiography. Administration of ergonovine during angiography often induces

spasm in such patients, provided they are not receiving vasodilators, such as nitrates or calcium channel blockers, at the time.

Some types of coronary disease warrant more urgent evaluation. Patients with new-onset angina or crescendo angina—that is, increasing frequency and/or severity of angina that may be provoked at a lower level of exertion—should be seen by a specialist that day. Those with unstable angina—that is, pain at rest, including nocturnal angina—should be hospitalized that day. Those with suspected MI—that is, severe chest pain with or without associated dyspnea, diaphoresis, nausea, vomiting, or syncope—should be brought to the closest emergency room by ambulance.

Treatment of chronic coronary disease consists

of medical therapy and/or revascularization. Revascularization can be performed percutaneously by balloon angioplasty with or without coronary stent placement, or through coronary artery bypass grafting. Medical therapy options include aspirin or other antiplatelet agents, such as clopidogrel, β-adrenergic blockers, calcium channel blockers, and nitrates, singly or in combination.

Aspirin for primary and secondary prevention of MI and stroke has been studied predominately in men. Women with documented coronary disease should take aspirin, 325 mg every other day, in the absence of any specific contraindication, such as peptic ulcer disease, gastritis, concurrent warfarin therapy, or known aspirin allergy. In other women, prescription of aspirin for primary prevention is discretionary.

β-Adrenergic blockers (also known as "β-blockers") are highly effective in the treatment of chronic stable angina and have the added benefit in hypertensives of lowering BP concurrently. β-blockers are categorized by their specificity for β-receptor subtype 1 or 2. $β_1$-receptors predominate in the heart, whereas stimulation of $β_2$-receptors induces vasodilation, bronchodilation, and glycogenolysis. The clinical efficacy of β-blockers in angina patients is attributable to these agents' negative chronotropic and inotropic effects. In titrating the dosage of a β-blocker, the treatment goal of freedom from angina or control of BP should be kept in mind; a reasonable starting point is to aim for a resting heart rate of 50 to 60 beats per minute. Once-a-day formulations of β-blockers are available and represent a tradeoff between cost and convenience. The common adverse effects of β-blockers include:

- Exacerbation of heart block in patients with conduction abnormalities
- Bronchoconstriction
- Nightmares, depression, fatigue

β-blockers permit unopposed α-adrenergic stimulation, which is undesirable in patients with coronary spasm. Patients taking ophthalmic preparations of timolol commonly manifest systemic effects of β blockade, such as bradycardia and bronchospasm. $β_1$ selective agents, such as atenolol and metoprolol, are somewhat less likely to cause bronchospasm than nonselective agents, such as propranolol and nadolol. Lipid-soluble β-blockers, such as propranolol and metoprolol, are more likely to cross the blood-brain barrier and cause central nervous system (CNS) side effects such as nightmares, fatigue, and depression.

Calcium channel blockers impede the influx of calcium into cardiocytes and vascular smooth muscle cells. Vasodilation and negative inotropic and chronotropic effects contribute to the efficacy of these agents and also to the profile of adverse effects. Predominant vasodilators, such as nifedipine, have vasodilation-related effects, including peripheral edema, reflex tachycardia, headache, and hypotension. Verapamil and diltiazem are negative inotropes and can also cause atrioventricular (AV) block (Fig. 60-5), which makes them effective for the treatment of some arrhythmias, but disadvantageous in patients with conduction abnormalities. Amlodipine has been generally well tolerated.

For treatment of angina and/or hypertension, amlodipine is very effective with a starting dose of 5 mg/day, increased to 10 mg/day as tolerated. Long-acting diltiazem is another reasonable alternative, particularly well-tolerated in older patients, with a starting dose of 120 mg/day of the sustained-release formation, increased to 240 mg/day as needed. Caution is warranted when prescribing the combination of diltiazem with a β-blocker, as excessive bradycardia may ensue. Other calcium channel blockers include verapamil, felodipine, isradipine, bepridil, nicardipine, nimodipine, nisoldipine, and nifedipine. Calcium channel blockers are effective antianginals in conjunction with nitrates, although the combination of preload and afterload reduction can lead to hypotension.

Nitrates are predominant venodilators and have been the mainstay of antianginal therapy since the nineteenth century. Acute anginal episodes are treated with sublingual nitroglycerin,

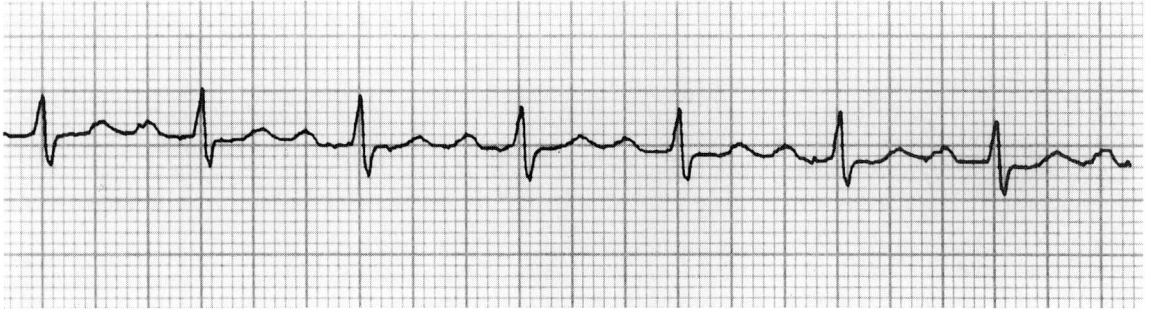

Figure 60-5 Electrocardiogram of a patient with first-degree AV block, PR interval is greater than 200 msec.

0.3 mg, repeated if necessary. Sublingual nitroglycerin is also effective when taken prophylactically before planned angina-provoking activities. Reactions to nitrates are related to their vasodilating effects and include flushing, hypotension, headache, and dizziness. Patients should be instructed to be seated or supine when taking sublingual nitroglycerin to avoid abrupt hypotension with loss of consciousness.

Long-acting nitrate preparations can be oral or topical. Nitrate tolerance will develop in most recipients unless a nitrate-free interval is provided. Nitroglycerin patches in doses ranging from 0.1 to 0.6 mg/h should be applied in the morning and removed at night to avoid tolerance. Oral nitrates are available as isosorbide dinitrate or isosorbide mononitrate. Isosorbide dinitrate is susceptible to substantial first-pass hepatic metabolism and should be prescribed in fairly high doses to ensure adequate bioavailability; e.g., 30 to 40 mg two or three times daily. Isosorbide mononitrate is longer-acting and may be prescribed as 30 to 120 mg once daily.

Combination therapy with aspirin and antianginals from one, two, or three other classes provides effective treatment for most patients.

Dyspnea

Dyspnea can be attributed to a wide variety of causes (summarized in Table 60-8). Distinguishing among these causes may be aided by de-termining the acuteness of dyspnea onset; precipitants; associated cough, fever, and chest pain; orthopnea; paroxysmal nocturnal dyspnea; peripheral edema; a history of past heart or lung disease; cardiac risk factors; and medications.

On physical exam, tachycardia suggests a problem with delivery of oxygenated blood to end organs, because of either pulmonary or cardiac disease or anemia. The presence of a pulsus paradoxus exceeding 10 mmHg suggests either pulmonary disease or pericardial tamponade. Pulsus paradoxus is an exaggerated effect of respiration on the arterial pulse, detectable by inflating a blood pressure cuff to suprasystolic level, then deflating slowly. The difference between the pressure at which Korotkoff sounds first become audible and the pressure at which they are audi-

TABLE 60-8 Causes of Dyspnea

Noncardiac Causes	Cardiovascular Causes
Deconditioning	Congestive heart failure
Anxiety	Aortic valve disease
Anemia	Pericardial tamponade
Pulmonary disease	Mitral valve disease
Pulmonary embolism	
Obstructive airway disease	
Parenchymal disease	
Interstitial disease	

ble throughout the respiratory cycle is the pulsus paradoxus, normally <10 mmHg.

Fever, cough, and localizing pulmonary signs suggest pneumonia. The presence of jugular venous distension, rales, and an S3 suggests cardiomyopathy. A delayed arterial upstroke, single or narrowly split S2, and midpeaking systolic ejection murmur are consistent with aortic stenosis. A diastolic rumble and opening snap in early diastole may be heard in mitral stenosis. A blowing decrescendo diastolic murmur along the upper-right or upper-left sternal border with a wide pulse pressure suggests aortic insufficiency, and a holosystolic murmur at the apex radiating to the axilla suggests mitral insufficiency. A harsh systolic ejection murmur that gets quieter with squatting and louder with valsalva maneuver suggests obstructive hypertrophic cardiomyopathy. A swollen, red, warm, or tender leg raises the possibility of deep venous thrombosis with subsequent pulmonary embolization.

If deconditioning is a consideration, a treadmill test will quantify exercise capacity to a much greater extent than will history. A treadmill test may also provide an opportunity to encourage regular exercise. Pulmonary disease may be evident on chest roentgenography or pulmonary function testing. If pulmonary embolism is suspected, a scintigraphic ventilation/perfusion scan should be obtained promptly. Cardiac diagnoses such as valvular disease or cardiomyopathy are usually confirmed by echocardiography.

Congestive heart failure (CHF) is defined as cardiac function inadequate to meet the metabolic needs of peripheral tissues, most commonly because of valvular disease or ventricular dysfunction. Dyspnea, either exertional or at rest, cough, orthopnea, paroxysmal nocturnal dyspnea requiring a patient to arise from bed to aid breathing, and peripheral edema are characteristic symptoms in CHF. Physical findings may include tachycardia, hypotension, jugular venous distension, hepatojugular reflux, hepatomegaly, rales, pleural effusion, an S3 gallop, and peripheral edema. The severity of CHF is often characterized by the New York Heart Association func-

tional class (Table 60-9). Annual mortality among patients with class III heart failure is about 20 percent, rising to 60 percent in class IV. **Valvular Disease** Recommendations for antibiotic prophylaxis of patients with valvular disease and congenital cardiac malformations are summarized in the preoperative evaluation section of this chapter.

Mitral stenosis in adults results from previous rheumatic fever. Patients commonly present with fatigue and exertional dyspnea or with atrial fibrillation, which exacerbates their difficulty filling the left ventricle through a stenotic mitral valve because of loss of the atrial contraction. Physical findings (diastolic rumble and opening snap) may be subtle, but mitral stenosis is readily diagnosed by echocardiography. Treatment is surgical.

Mitral insufficiency may also be a sequela of rheumatic fever, but it also results from:

- Papillary muscle ischemia or infarction
- Ruptured chordae tendinae
- Endocarditis
- Mitral valve prolapse
- Mitral annular calcification (in older patients)
- Dilatation of the mitral annulus in dilated cardiomyopathy

Mitral insufficiency may present as an asymptomatic holosystolic apical murmur, as atrial arrhythmia, or as CHF. Serial echocardiography will provide a record of changes in ventricular

TABLE 60-9 New York Heart Association Functional Classification

Class I	No limitation; ordinary activity does not cause fatigue, dyspnea
Class II	Slight limitation of physical activity; ordinary activity results in fatigue, dyspnea
Class III	Marked limitation of physical activity; modest activity results in fatigue, dyspnea
Class IV	Dyspnea and fatigue at rest

and atrial dimensions over time. The regurgitant volume assessed by color flow Doppler ultrasound will vary with loading conditions. Medical therapy includes afterload reduction (ACE inhibitors or hydralazine plus nitrates) to improve forward flow and diuresis to reduce pulmonary congestion. In chronic mitral insufficiency, the left ventricle must pump both the cardiac output to the aorta and the regurgitant fraction into the left atrium, resulting in chronic volume overload, which can lead to irreversible ventricular damage. Thus, surgical valve repair or replacement should be undertaken before the development of cardiomyopathy. Determining the optimal time for surgery can be tricky because left ventricular emptying into a low-pressure chamber, the left atrium, can present a misleading appearance of normal intrinsic ventricular contractility.

Mitral valve prolapse (MVP) is a common congenital abnormality in which the mitral valve leaflets are myxomatous, redundant, and prolapse into the left atrium during systole. MVP may occur sporadically or through autosomal dominant inheritance and can be associated with Marfan syndrome, Ehlers-Danlos syndrome, and other connective tissue diseases. Symptoms that can be associated with MVP include chest pains, palpitations, and sometimes neuropsychiatric complaints. Classic physical findings include one or more mid to late systolic clicks, with or without a murmur of mitral insufficiency.

Many patients have been erroneously diagnosed with MVP on the basis of physical findings and/or M-mode echocardiography. Although the prevalence of MVP has been reported to be as high as 6 percent, that estimate will fall with application of stringent two-dimensional echocardiographic criteria for diagnosis. Adverse outcomes associated with MVP include infective endocarditis, severe mitral insufficiency requiring mitral valve replacement, arrhythmias, and cerebral embolic events.

Asymptomatic patients with MVP have an excellent prognosis and require only periodic echocardiography (every 2 to 4 years) and endocarditis prophylaxis. Patients with palpitations,

dizziness, or chest pain should be evaluated to exclude ischemic heart disease or significant arrhythmia with treadmill testing, with or without nuclear imaging, and Holter or event-monitor recording. β-adrenergic blockade is the treatment of choice for chest discomfort. Patients with documented arrhythmias may need to be referred to a cardiologist. Those with mitral insufficiency should be followed with more frequent echocardiography. Afterload reduction may be warranted to enhance forward flow, and a proportion of patients will eventually require mitral valve repair or replacement. Patients with cerebral ischemic events should be evaluated for other causes of cerebral ischemia and may require antiplatelet therapy or anticoagulation.

Aortic insufficiency may result from rheumatic fever, congenital malformation of the leaflets including bicuspid valve, endocarditis, trauma, or aortic annular dilatation due to aortic root disease (Marfan syndrome, Ehlers-Danlos syndrome, hypertension). Patients with acute aortic insufficiency will develop CHF. Those with chronic aortic insufficiency are often asymptomatic for years. Eventually they may develop exertional dyspnea, orthopnea, and fatigue. Physical examination may reveal a wide pulse pressure, systolic ejection murmur, and blowing diastolic murmur along the right or left sternal border in the third or fourth intercostal space. Echocardiography is helpful in determining the number of aortic cusps, severity of aortic insufficiency, and left ventricular dimensions. Afterload reduction will improve forward flow. Timing of aortic valve replacement to precede irreversible ventricular dysfunction from chronic overload should be undertaken with cardiology consultation. Patients with aortic root disease may require β blockade and earlier surgical intervention to prevent aortic rupture.

Aortic stenosis also may be rheumatic in origin, but is usually due to degeneration of either a normal or congenitally malformed aortic valve. Patients may present with asymptomatic murmurs but more often have angina, heart failure, or syncope. The angina may be due either to coexisting coronary disease or to subendocardial ischemia in a hypertrophied heart. Heart failure may reflect ventricular failure, a poor prognostic indicator. Syncope caused by inadequate cerebral perfusion during exertion results from peripheral vasodilation and the inability to increase the cardiac output to meet demand during exercise. Physical findings include a blunted arterial upstroke, harsh systolic ejection murmur, S4, and, in severe aortic stenosis, a single S2. Occasionally an ejection click may be audible shortly after S1. Signs and symptoms of heart failure may be apparent.

Echocardiography will estimate the pressure gradient across the stenotic aortic valve and the cross-sectional valve area. Afterload reduction is of no value in aortic stenosis because the afterload is fixed by the stenotic valve. Preload reducing agents, such as nitrates, are contraindicated because preload must be adequate to generate the interventricular pressures (as high as 300 mmHg) necessary to force blood through the narrowed valve orifice. Once symptomatic, mortality is about 25 percent per year. Valve replacement should be carried out in all symptomatic patients and in asymptomatic patients developing ventricular dysfunction.

Tricuspid and pulmonic insufficiency can be congenital or caused by endocarditis, trauma, carcinoid syndrome, or annular dilatation. Pulmonary hypertension, either primary or secondary to parenchymal disease or recurrent pulmonary embolism, leads to dilatation of the right heart, including the tricuspid annulus. Tricuspid insufficiency due to failure of the tricuspid leaflets to coapt may result, with subsequent development of right heart failure with peripheral edema, jugular venous distension, hepatic congestion, and right-sided S3 (louder with inspiration). Echocardiography will identify the lesion, estimate the severity, and shed light on the etiology. Treatment may include diuretics, digoxin, and afterload reduction.

Use of appetite suppressants for treatment of obesity was a common practice in the past few years. In 1996, the number of prescriptions for these medications exceeded 18 million. Among the most common were fenfluramine and phentermine. Prolonged use of these medications may be associated with pulmonary hypertension and valvular heart disease. Patients who have had prolonged exposure to these medications, particularly those with cardiopulmonary symptoms, should probably have an echocardiogram.

Ventricular Dysfunction As a practical matter, ventricular dysfunction can be categorized as due to systolic dysfunction (that is, impaired emptying) or diastolic dysfunction (impaired filling). These may be present concurrently. Systolic dysfunction may be ascribed to:

- Ischemic cardiomyopathy due to prior myocardial infarction
- Cardiomyopathy due to long-standing hypertension or diabetes
- Alcoholic cardiomyopathy
- Peripartum cardiomyopathy
- Other causes

The patient's history may provide insight into the etiology of systolic dysfunction; symptoms do not distinguish among causes. The severity of ventricular dysfunction (Table 60-9) and the presence of associated abnormalities, such as mitral or tricuspid insufficiency due to cavity and annular dilatation, can be assessed by echocardiography. Coronary angiography is required to confirm the diagnosis of CAD.

Treatment should initially be directed at the underlying cause; for example, alcoholics should stop drinking, and the management of hypertension and diabetes should be optimized. Risk factors for CAD, such as smoking and hyperlipidemia, should be addressed. In symptomatic patients, restriction of physical activity to reduce cardiac work is appropriate. Dietary sodium restriction attenuates salt and water retention. Pharmacologic therapy with inotropic agents (digoxin), vasodilators, and diuretics usually improves functional status. Afterload reduction with ACE inhibitors or hydralazine and nitrates has been shown in controlled trials to prolong life. Cardiomyopathy patients are also prone to develop thrombi in their hypokinetic ventricles with subsequent embolization, and thus are frequently anticoagulated with warfarin. Patients should also be evaluated for risk of arrhythmic death, which is markedly increased in this population as a whole.

Peripartum cardiomyopathy (CM) is an uncommon, but life-threatening form of heart failure occurring in late pregnancy or in the postpartum period. Diagnostic criteria for this entity include:

- Cardiac failure in the last month of pregnancy or within 5 months of delivery
- Absence of other causes for heart failure
- Absence of demonstrable heart disease before the last month of pregnancy
- Evidence of left ventricular systolic dysfunction by echocardiogram

The etiology of peripartum CM remains unclear, although autoimmune mechanisms have been hypothesized. Early diagnosis of heart failure remains a challenge because the signs and symptoms of this condition often resemble those of normal pregnancy. The diagnosis is made most commonly after the thirty-sixth week of gestation until the fourth month postpartum. Recovery of heart function occurs about half the time. Women should be managed with afterload reduction, digoxin, and diuretics as necessary.

Diastolic dysfunction is less commonly identified as a cause of heart failure, but it may be due to:

- Restrictive/constrictive cardiomyopathy due to amyloidosis, hemochromatosis, or chronic pericardial disease.
- Hypertrophic cardiomyopathy
- Hypertensive cardiomyopathy

Restrictive and constrictive cardiomyopathies often present with signs of right failure—edema, jugular venous distension, and hepatomegaly. The liver may be pulsatile. In constrictive pericardial disease, a pericardial knock may be audible early in diastole. Echocardiographic signs of restrictive myocardial disease may include marked biatrial enlargement, thickened ventricular walls, ventricular dilatation, and Doppler evidence of impaired ventricular filling. Amyloidosis is confirmed by biopsy of subcutaneous fat, rectum, or endocardium. Hemochromatosis is suggested by elevated plasma iron and serum ferritin levels and by elevated transferrin saturation. Constrictive pericardial disease is most readily identified by computed tomographic radiography.

Hypertrophic cardiomyopathy is a hereditary disease with autosomal dominant transmission. Occurrence in about half of patients, however, is spontaneous. The left ventricle is abnormally thickened, with the ventricular septum often disproportionately so. This asymmetric septal hypertrophy can cause dynamic outflow obstruction, particularly when left ventricular filling is impaired by dehydration, diuretics, nitrates, upright posture, or arrhythmias. Microscopic examination reveals hypertrophied muscle cells with marked architectural disarray. Dyspnea is the most common symptom, but patients may present with asymptomatic murmurs, angina, or sudden death. Murmur may be absent in patients without outflow obstruction. The presence of a harsh systolic ejection murmur at the lower left sternal border, which is quieter upon squatting, with handgrip, or passive leg elevation, and louder upon standing or during Valsalva maneuver, should raise the possibility of hypertrophic cardiomyopathy. The diagnosis is readily confirmed by echocardiography. Because this is a potentially life-threatening disease, these patients should be referred for negative inotropic therapy, management of arrhythmic risk, and genetic counseling. Volume management is a particular cause for concern in this population; dehydration exacerbates the outflow obstruction. Because of the high blood-flow velocity across the left ventricular outflow tract, patients with hypertrophic cardiomyopathy are at risk for infective endocarditis and should receive appropriate prophylaxis.

Hypertensive cardiomyopathy results from thickening of the left ventricle in response to long-standing hypertension. Treatment should include management of the underlying hypertension, preferably with negative inotropic agents, such as β-blockers, or calcium channel blockers such as verapamil. Diuretics should be used with caution.

Management of CHF Appropriate management of CHF depends on etiology, which is why it is important to determine the underlying cause of heart failure. Some of these causes and their treatment are summarized in general terms in Table 60-10.

The common types of heart failure vary from community to community. Physicians seeing predominately older patients may be faced with a preponderance of ischemic, dilated cardiomyopathies, which can be treated with afterload reduc-

TABLE 60-10 Management of Congestive Heart Failure

Etiology of Congestive Heart Failure	Management
Transient ischemic mitral insufficiency or systolic dysfunction	Nitrates, calcium channel blockers, revascularization
Ruptured chorda tendina	Afterload reduction (ACE inhibitors, nitroprusside), valve repair or replacement
Infectious endocarditis	Antibiotics, afterload reduction, valve replacement
Other mitral or aortic insufficiency	Afterload reduction, diuretics, valve repair or replacement
Mitral or aortic stenosis	Valve replacement or mitral commissurotomy
Cardiomyopathy with systolic dysfunction	Afterload reduction, diuretics, inotropic support (digoxin), Carvedilol (classes I and II only)
Diastolic dysfunction	Negative inotropes (verapamil, β-blocker, disopyramide); avoid diuretics
Atrial fibrillation	Rate control (digoxin, diltiazem, β-blocker); conversion to sinus rhythm

tion using an ACE inhibitor such as enalapril titrated to systolic blood pressure, or symptoms of hypotension (bearing in mind that enalapril causes cough, renal failure, and hyperkalemia), with or without diuretics and digoxin (0.125 or 0.25 mg/day in patients with normal renal function). Digoxin did not improve survival in patients with CHF, but in a randomized trial, did reduce the frequency of hospitalization. Carvedilol (a nonselective β-blocker) has been shown to decrease mortality and need for hospitalization as well as disease progression. Carvedilol is approved for treatment of class I and class II heart failure, and should be used in conjunction with afterload reduction with or without diuretics and digoxin.

In other communities with a high proportion of hypertensives, CHF may be due predominantly to diastolic dysfunction, in which case inotropic agents such as digoxin are deleterious, and diuretics, by reducing preload, may aggravate left ventricular outflow obstruction. Drugs of choice for diastolic dysfunction are negative inotropic agents such as verapamil, β-adrenergic blockers, and disopyramide, titrated to symptoms and outflow obstruction assessed by echocardiography. Remember that for patients with structurally abnormal hearts, drugs are double-edged swords and often have narrow therapeutic windows.

Palpitations

Palpitations are variously described as skipped beats, pounding, or racing of the heart. They may represent paroxysmal atrial tachycardia or any other type of tachycardia, premature atrial or ventricular beats, atrial fibrillation, compensatory or sinus pauses, sudden onset of sinus bradycardia, or complete heart block, or may not be associated with any rhythm disturbance at all. In evaluating patients with palpitations, past cardiac history including MVP and MI should be obtained and questions should be asked regarding any symptoms suggesting thyrotoxicosis. Physical examination may reveal evidence of MVP; that is, a midsystolic click with or without a holosystolic murmur.

If MVP is suspected, an echocardiogram will confirm the diagnosis. Thyroid function tests will assess the possibility of thyrotoxicosis. A 12-lead electrocardiogram may reveal evidence of an accessory atrioventricular pathway such as a delta wave slurring the upstroke of the R wave (Fig. 60-6). Patients with Wolff-Parkinson-White syndrome who note palpitations should be referred for electrophysiologic study, whether or not arrhythmia is documented by other means, because of their increased risk of sudden death. Documenting the presence or absence of arrhythmia is important for other patients. This can be undertaken either through Holter monitoring, if the palpitations occur daily, or event monitoring, if they are less frequent. Event monitors record brief intervals of heart rhythm selected by the patient because of symptoms. These recordings are transtelephonically transmitted for interpretation. This approach enhances the possibility of capturing infrequent arrhythmias.

Syncope

Syncope is loss of consciousness, usually due to inadequate cerebral perfusion. Syncope may be caused by:

- Vasomotor instability
- Drug effects
- Cerebrovascular disease
- Cardiac outflow obstruction
- Brady- or tachyarrhythmias

Vasomotor syncope is common, particularly in young people. Patients may report many past syncopal episodes, which may be precipitated by prolonged standing, fear, heat, the sight of blood, perceived threat, or pain. The autonomically mediated vasodilatation with subsequent fall in blood pressure is usually associated with other vagal symptoms, such as diaphoresis and nausea. If this diagnosis is suspected, referral for tilt-table testing is appropriate. During tilt-testing, patients are maintained upright with arterial pressure and ECG monitoring, with or without intravenous isoproterenol provocation. The upright posture provokes gravitational pooling of blood, reducing stroke volume. In patients with abnormal compensatory responses, bradycardia, hypotension, and syncope may ensue, supporting the diagnosis of vasomotor syncope. Pharmacologic therapy with β-adrenergic blockers, disopyramide, or other agents may be initiated, with repeat tilt-testing on treatment to confirm efficacy.

Drug effects may cause syncope as well. In

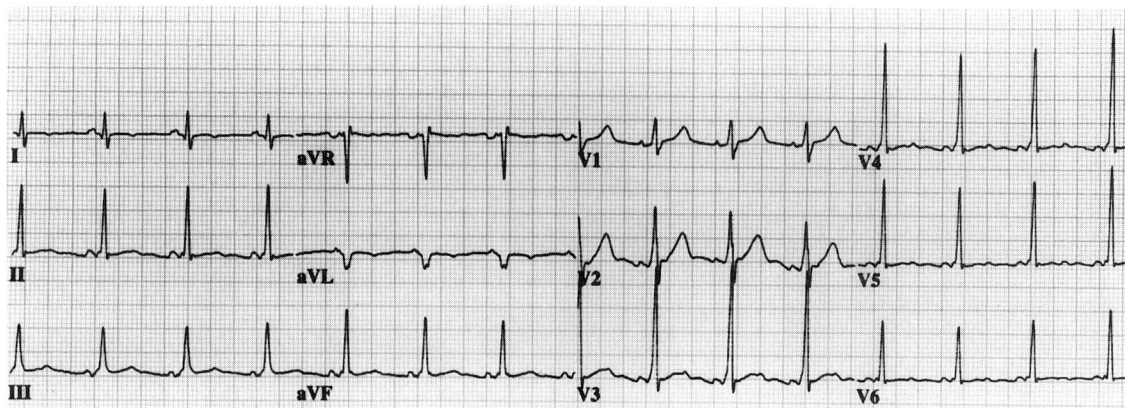

Figure 60-6 Electrocardiogram of a patient with Wolff-Parkinson-White syndrome. Delta wave is present as the slurring of the R wave.

cardiac patients, syncope can be induced by vasodilation following sublingual nitroglycerin consumption, particularly in older patients taking several sequential doses of nitroglycerin. Instructing the patient to use this agent while seated or supine usually solves the problem. Other antihypertensives may cause excessive hypotension, leading to dizziness or syncope as well. Digoxin toxicity may cause any type of brady- or tachyarrhythmia, leading to syncope.

Syncope due to *torsade de pointes,* a life-threatening form of ventricular tachycardia, is usually a result of toxicity from quinidine, procainamide, flecainide, bepridil, disopyramide, propafenone, encainide, or, rarely, amiodarone. Antihistamines such as astemizole (Hismanal), particularly in conjunction with erythromycin, have been associated with torsade de pointes as well. Patients taking these histamine H_1-receptor blockers should be warned not to exceed prescribed doses, and such drugs should *never* be prescribed in combination with erythromycin. Overall, in 2 to 9 percent of patients with syncope, the problem is caused by drug toxicity.

Cerebrovascular disease may lead to syncope. Transient ischemic attacks (TIAs) of the vertebrobasilar system may infrequently cause syncope. Carotid sinus syncope is a form of carotid sinus hypersensitivity leading to loss of consciousness when pressure is applied to the carotid sinus, as when turning the head or wearing a tight collar. Carotid sinus hypersensitivity occurs predominantly in men.

Cardiac outflow obstruction can lead to inadequate cerebral perfusion with loss of consciousness. Characteristically, the cardiac output fails to rise in response to exertion because of fixed outflow obstruction such as aortic stenosis. In general, syncope is a poor prognostic sign in such patients, and should serve as an indication for intervention.

Syncope due to brady- or tachyarrhythmias may be difficult to diagnose, because rhythm disturbances are often intermittent. Among patients with cardiac syncope, about 30 percent will die suddenly within 3 years of follow-up; thus, refer-

ral for further evaluation is appropriate. The specifics of the work-up depend on indications from history, physical examination, and a 12-lead ECG, but may include echocardiography to evaluate for structural heart disease, signal-averaged electrocardiogram to assess the potential of the myocardial substrate for ventricular tachycardia, tilt-table testing to exclude vasomotor syncope, Holter monitoring, event recording, coronary angiography if ischemia is implicated, and/or electrophysiologic testing to assess sinus node, AV node, and His bundle conduction, as well as the inducibility of atrial and ventricular arrhythmias.

In obtaining a history from patients with syncope, a description of events leading up to the syncopal episode, concurrent symptoms, drug regimen, past MI, valvular disease, and past cardiac evaluation may be helpful. Physical examination should include measurement of supine and upright pulse and blood pressure. Attention should be given to signs of aortic stenosis or hypertrophic cardiomyopathy (systolic ejection murmur that gets softer with squatting and louder with upright posture). Electrocardiography may reveal evidence of prior MI, conduction abnormalities, or left ventricular hypertrophy (which may indicate aortic stenosis or hypertrophic cardiomyopathy).

Whether the presenting symptom is syncope or palpitations, the presence of an arrhythmia must be sought and documented either by telemetry, Holter monitoring, or event recording, or during electrophysiologic testing. Once a rhythm abnormality has been identified, specific treatment may be instituted for relief of symptoms or for prognosis. Bradyarrhythmias requiring treatment include high-grade heart block (i.e., complete heart block or distal second-degree AV block [Mobitz II]) and sick sinus syndrome. Symptomatic bradycardia is often an iatrogenic sequela of β-adrenergic or calcium channel blockade, in which case discontinuation of the offending medication suffices. Otherwise, placement of a permanent transvenous pacemaker may be indicated.

Common supraventricular tachyarrhythmias

include atrial fibrillation and flutter, ectopic atrial tachycardias, and reentrant supraventricular tachycardias (Fig. 60-7). Patients with new-onset atrial fibrillation/flutter should be evaluated for causes such as mitral stenosis, pulmonary embolism, thyrotoxicosis, and coronary disease if none is readily apparent. The objectives of treatment are control of ventricular rate, conversion to sinus rhythm, and prevention of thromboembolism.

In *atrial fibrillation,* ventricular rate assessed by electrocardiography or apical (not peripheral) pulse, can be controlled in stable patients using oral or intravenous digoxin, a calcium channel blocker such as diltiazem or verapamil, or a β-adrenergic blocker such as esmolol. Unstable patients should be electrically cardioverted without delay. Patients should be electrocardiographically monitored during this interval. Either electrical or chemical cardioversion to sinus rhythm may be attempted once the ventricular rate is controlled. Patients with atrial fibrillation of less than 3 days duration may be cardioverted to sinus rhythm without prior anticoagulation, according to guidelines suggested by the American College of Chest Physicians. Those with atrial fibrillation of longer duration should be anticoagulated for 3 weeks before cardioversion and for 2 to 4 weeks afterwards. Electrical cardioversion is usually carried out with short-acting anesthesia. Chemical cardioversion can be attempted acutely with

intravenous ibutilide fumarate, a class III antiarrhythmic; attempted maintenance of sinus rhythm may be tried with class 1C agents such as flecainide or propafenone, or class III agents such as amiodarone and sotalol. All of these drugs have serious side effects, including sudden death, and should be administered with monitoring by physicians experienced with their use. Some patients cannot be converted into or maintained in sinus rhythm. Rate control and long-term prophylaxis against thromboembolism are the mainstays of therapy in that group.

Other atrial tachycardias, including *paroxysmal atrial tachycardia,* may be treated with calcium channel or β-adrenergic blockers if clinically warranted. Transvenous ablation of reentrant pathways or automatic foci may be performed by an electrophysiologist as an alternative to drug therapy. Patients with Wolff-Parkinson-White syndrome conduct electrical impulses from the atrium to the ventricle faster than usual by conducting down an accessory pathway, so-called preexcitation. These patients are susceptible to reentrant supraventricular tachycardias and to atrial fibrillation that may be life-threatening if ventricular fibrillation is precipitated by rapid stimulation of the ventricle via the accessory pathway. Drugs such as digoxin and intravenous verapamil are relatively contraindicated in patients with preexcitation, because they may facilitate accessory pathway conduc-

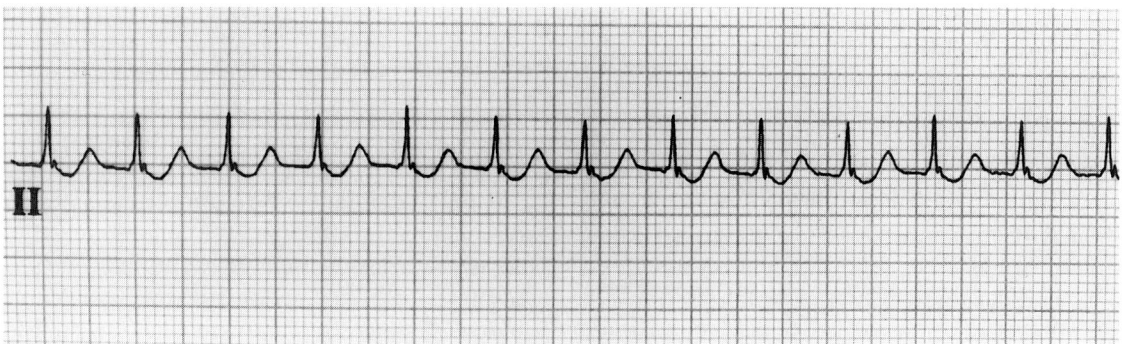

Figure 60-7 Electrocardiographic recording of supraventricular tachyarrhythmia with rate of 150 beats per minute. There is an absence of P wave preceding narrow QRS complexes.

tion. Patients with symptomatic preexcitation should be referred for electrophysiologic testing and accessory pathway ablation.

Ventricular arrhythmias vary in severity from isolated premature ventricular contractions to sudden death. In general, isolated premature ventricular contractions do not require treatment. Indications for treatment of ventricular tachycardia depend on the substrate; patients with normal ventricles and no coronary disease may not need treatment. If the underlying precipitant for ventricular arrhythmia is myocardial ischemia, treatment should be directed accordingly. On the other hand, cardiomyopathy patients at high risk for sudden death may require aggressive arrhythmic therapy and/or implantation of an automatic defibrillator. The latter devices can be placed transvenously and no longer require thoracotomy.

Cardiac arrhythmias vary in severity, and certain arrhythmias can result in sudden death. Many of the arrhythmias are not commonly treated in the office as a component of primary care, and therefore a more detailed discussion regarding this management is beyond the scope of this book.

Claudication

Most leg cramps are not claudication, yet claudication is important to identify, in part because of its close association with CAD. Of patients with peripheral vascular disease but no symptoms referable to the heart, half will have coronary disease and all should be evaluated for this possibility. *Claudication* is the peripheral vascular equivalent of angina, characterized as crampy pain in the buttocks, posterior thigh, or calf, brought on by exertion and relieved by rest. Cardiovascular risk factors, particularly smoking, should be carefully assessed. Physical exam should include palpation of femoral, popliteal, dorsalis pedis, and posterior tibialis pulses bilaterally. Ischemic foot ulcers may be apparent. Initial management is conservative, with good control of hypertension, diabetes, and hyperlip-

idemia. Patients must stop smoking. Modest exercise training is sometimes helpful, enabling muscles to make efficient use of the available blood supply. If patients have pain at rest or persistent claudication after a trial of conservative management, they should be referred to a vascular surgeon.

Peripheral Venous Disease

Venous thrombophlebitis is prevalent following gynecological surgery. Some studies report that 40 percent of deaths following pelvic surgery are attributable to venous thrombosis and pulmonary embolism. Not surprisingly, the frequency of these adverse events increases with the age of the patient, the duration of the surgery, and in those immobilized for prolonged intervals. Other risk factors for venous thrombosis include obesity, malignancy, and hypercoagulable states. Estrogen may also increase risk about three-fold.

Clearly, prophylaxis against deep venous thrombosis or pulmonary embolism is preferable to treatment after the problem has arisen. Prophylaxis regimens include compression stockings, low-dose warfarin, or intravenous or subcutaneous heparin. The suitability of any of these approaches depends on the clinical setting.

Characteristic physical findings of deep venous thrombosis include localized warmth, redness, tenderness, and swelling of the extremity. Tenderness over the femoral veins is more suggestive of proximal venous thrombosis. Clinical signs are not especially specific, so that patients in whom venous thrombosis is suspected should have noninvasive testing.

Impedance plethysmography is widely available and inexpensive. Venous outflow from the leg is occluded with a cuff inflated to 45 to 60 mmHg. Arterial inflow is not affected, so blood accumulates distal to the cuff. When the cuff is suddenly released, blood flows out of the leg. In the presence of venous obstruction, the venous outflow is impaired. This diagnostic test is particularly helpful in patients with proximal vein thrombosis; it is less sensitive for distal thrombosis. Two-dimensional ultrasound (duplex) scanning is even more sensitive and specific than impedance plethysmography; it is noninvasive and comparatively inexpensive. Venography is the gold standard. If embolization of a thrombus from the leg to the pulmonary circulation is suspected, ventilation-perfusion lung scanning is recommended. Usually pulmonary angiography can be avoided.

Once proximal deep venous thrombosis or pulmonary embolism has been confirmed, patients should be treated with either intravenous or subcutaneous heparin. Anticoagulation should be transitioned to warfarin and maintained for at least 3 months. Pregnant women who cannot take warfarin may be transitioned to subcutaneous heparin.

Calf vein thrombosis is generally associated with a good prognosis even when treated conservatively. However, over 10 to 14 days, about 6 percent of affected individuals develop abnormal impedance plethysmographic studies, indicating extension into the popliteal vein. Therefore, either conventional anticoagulation with heparin and warfarin or serial noninvasive evaluation for 10 to 14 days is recommended.

Superficial phlebitis can be managed conservatively with analgesics or anti-inflammatory agents, heat, and elevation.

Aortic Disease

Aortic disease is generally structural, because the aorta predominantly functions as a conduit from the left ventricle to end organs. Structural aortic disease can be categorized as congenital or acquired.

Coarctation of the aorta is a congenital malformation associated with bicuspid aortic valve and with Turner's syndrome. Coarctation is usually identified during childhood because of the loud murmur, unequal extremity blood pressures, and hypertension. The presence and severity of the coarctation and any associated anomalies can be readily confirmed by echocardiography, and the aorta either dilated by bal-

loon angioplasty or surgically repaired. Restenosis occurs in a proportion of patients using either of these treatment approaches. During pregnancy, placental blood flow may be inadequate due to aortic obstruction, and aortic rupture has been reported. Additionally, women with coarctation have an increased likelihood of having offspring with congenital heart disease. Genetic counseling and, if desired and available, fetal echocardiography at 16 to 17 weeks gestation are appropriate.

The other comparatively common group of congenital diseases with aortic manifestations is connective tissue disease, such as Ehlers-Danlos and Marfan syndromes. In Ehlers-Danlos syndrome, echocardiography for detection of associated mitral valve prolapse and appropriate antibiotic prophylaxis usually suffice. Genetic counseling is indicated, and women with subtype IV should avoid pregnancy because of enhanced risk of spontaneous, catastrophic arterial rupture. Mitral valve prolapse is also common in Marfan syndrome. In addition to echocardiography for mitral valve evaluation, all patients with Marfan syndrome should have serial echocardiographic follow-up of their aortic root dimension and should be seen periodically by a cardiologist. Prophylactic aortic surgery is usually carried out to prevent rupture once the aorta reaches 60 mm in diameter. Aortic dissection is a prominent cause of death in patients with Marfan syndrome, and may occur without marked aortic root dilatation. Inheritance of Marfan syndrome is autosomal dominant; thus affected women have a 50 percent chance of transmitting the disease to their offspring. Further, the risk of aortic rupture or dissection is augmented by pregnancy.

The two most common acquired structural abnormalities of the aorta are aortic aneurysm and dissection. Although the differential diagnosis of thoracic or abdominal aortic aneurysm is extensive, most cases are due to atherosclerosis. Abdominal aortic aneurysms are usually detected as asymptomatic, pulsatile abdominal masses. Aneurysm size is readily quantified by abdominal ultrasound, and surgical repair recommended for aneurysms exceeding 6 cm in diameter. Aneurysms less than 6 cm should be followed with serial ultrasound studies.

Thoracic aneurysms are more frequently symptomatic due to compression of intrathoracic structures, leading to cough, hoarseness, stridor, hemoptysis, and obstructive pneumonia. Diagnosis of thoracic aneurysms may be confirmed by MRI, CT scan, or transesophageal echocardiography. Surgical repair is recommended for thoracic aneurysms producing symptoms or for asymptomatic aneurysms exceeding 7 cm in diameter because of the risk of rupture.

Aortic dissection is a dramatic event, presenting with severe, knifelike back or chest pain, hypotension, and, at times, a sensation of impending doom. In contrast to aortic aneurysms, in which the vessel wall remains intact, aortic dissection is caused by a tear in the intima or hemorrhage into the media with immediate propagation of the dissection along the vessel wall. Upper extremity pulses may be absent, and congestive heart failure may result from acute aortic insufficiency. Because the pleura and pericardium enwrap the ascending aorta, aortic rupture can lead to pleural and pericardial effusions. If the dissection extends into the carotid arteries, localizing neurologic signs may be present. Dissection is more common in patients with Marfan syndrome or hypertension. When aortic dissection is suspected, the patient should urgently be transported to an emergency room for diagnosis and management.

Myocarditis, Pericarditis, and Endocarditis

Dilated cardiomyopathy can present as new-onset congestive heart failure or with atrial or ventricular arrhythmias. As many as 10 percent of patients with dilated cardiomyopathy have otherwise structurally normal hearts and normal coronary arteries. In one large series of such dilated cardiomyopathy patients, 12 percent had endomyocardial biopsy-proven myocarditis. In contrast to idiopathic cardiomyopathy, patients with

myocarditis often recover. Congestive heart failure and arrhythmias in myocarditis are responsive to conventional treatment; immunosuppressive therapy has not proven efficacious in randomized trials.

Pericarditis usually presents as substernal or left precordial chest pain, often relieved by leaning forward and exacerbated by cough, deep inspiration, or supine posture. A pericardial friction rub may be audible. A sequence of characteristic electrocardiographic changes includes sinus tachycardia, diffuse ST elevation, and PR depression followed several days later by return of ST and PR segments to baseline with T-wave inversion (Fig. 60-2). Echocardiography may reveal a pericardial effusion. Pericarditis may be idiopathic, infectious, malignant, uremic, or associated with collagen vascular diseases such as systemic lupus erythematosus or rheumatoid arthritis. Idiopathic pericarditis, a self-limited disease, is treated with nonsteroidal anti-inflammatory agents. Patients with bacterial, tuberculous, or fungal pericarditis are acutely ill, and require prompt diagnosis, pericardial drainage, and specific antibiotic therapy. Malignant effusions occur most commonly in patients with known breast or lung cancer, lymphoma, or melanoma. Pericardial effusion with or without symptoms is also prevalent in human immunodeficiency virus infection, occurring in 17 percent of patients during 2 years of follow-up.

Pericarditis due to any etiology may result in pericardial tamponade. Patients with tamponade are severely dyspneic, with tachycardia, jugular venous distension, and an elevated pulsus paradoxicus; they may be hypotensive. Characteristic echocardiographic findings confirm the diagnosis of pericardial tamponade, which may be relieved by either percutaneous or open pericardial drainage.

Bacterial endocarditis is an infection of a native or prosthetic heart valve, usually with characteristic organisms such as staphylococci, streptococci, or enterococci. Patients commonly present with fever and a new heart murmur. Individuals with a structural heart abnormality, such as mitral valve prolapse or ventricular septal defect, have increased susceptibility to endocarditis, as do the elderly, diabetics, and intravenous drug users. The responsible pathogen is identified by blood culture; vegetations and paravalvular abscesses may be identified by echocardiography. Antibiotic therapy is tailored to the specific organism. Indications for valve replacement include persistent sepsis despite adequate antibiotics, embolization, paravalvular abscess, and congestive heart failure due to valvular insufficiency.

Preoperative Evaluation

Antibiotic Prophylaxis

The American Heart Association (AHA) recommends antibiotic prophylaxis in patients with:

- Prosthetic heart valves
- Most congenital cardiac malformations (except ostium secundum atrial septal defects)
- Rheumatic and other acquired valvular disease
- Hypertrophic cardiomyopathy
- Mitral valve prolapse with mitral insufficiency

Prophylaxis is recommended for several obstetrical and gynecological procedures, including:

- Vaginal hysterectomy
- Vaginal delivery in the presence of infection
- Urethral catheterization or urinary tract surgery in the presence of a urinary tract infection
- Incision and drainage of infected tissue

Prophylaxis is generally not recommended for low-risk procedures such as uncomplicated vaginal delivery or dilatation and curettage when there is no evidence of infection. In patients with prosthetic heart valves or previous endocarditis, however, physicians may elect to provide antibiotic prophylaxis even for low-risk procedures.

In the presence of infection, antibiotic therapy should be directed against known or suspected pathogens in addition to providing the standard prophylactic regimen for genitourinary and gastrointestinal procedures. The new American Heart Association prophylactic regimens for GU/GI procedures are summarized in Table 60-11. Recommendations for prophylaxis during dental, oral, and upper respiratory tract procedures are summarized in Table 60-12. Erythromycin is no longer included as an alternative regimen for patients with allergy to penicillin. Newer macrolides (azithromycin and clarithromycin) are alternatives to clindamycin in penicillin-allergic patients. Also the postprocedure dose of amoxicillin has been deleted.

Assessment of Operative Cardiac Risk

Cardiac ischemia during the perioperative period is a primary determinant of operative morbidity and mortality. The objectives of preoperative

TABLE 60-11 American Heart Association (AHA) Guidelines for Antibiotic Prophylaxis in Genitourinary/Gastrointestinal (Excluding Esophageal) Procedures

Situation	Regimen (Adults)
High-risk patients	Ampicillin 2.0 g IM/IV plus gentamicin 1.5 mg/kg IM/IV (not to exceed 120 mg) within 30 min before procedure; followed by ampicillin 1 g IM/IV or amoxicillin 1 g orally 6 h later
High-risk patients allergic to penicillin	Vancomycin 1.0 g IV over 1–2 h plus gentamicin 1.5 mg/kg IV/IM (not to exceed 120 mg) within 30 min of starting procedure
Moderate-risk patients	Amoxicillin 2.0 g orally 1 h before procedure or ampicillin 2.0 g IM/IV within 30 min of starting procedure
Moderate-risk patients allergic to penicillin	Vancomycin 1.0 g IV over 1–2 h complete within 30 min of starting procedure

TABLE 60-12 AHA Prophylactic Regimens for Dental, Oral, Respiratory Tract, or Esophageal Procedures

Situation	Regimen (Adults)
Standard general prophylaxis	Amoxicillin: 2.0 g orally 1 h before procedure
Unable to take oral medications	Ampicillin: 2.0 g IM/IV within 30 min before procedure
Allergic to penicillin	Clindamycin: 600 mg orally 1 h before procedure
	Cephalexin or cefadroxil: 2.0 g 1 h before procedure
	Azithromycin or clarithromycin: 500 mg 1 h before procedure
Allergic to penicillin and unable to take oral medications	Clindamycin: 600 mg IV within 30 min before procedure
	Cefazolin: 1.0 g IM/IV within 30 min before procedure

TABLE 60-13 Assessment of Cardiac Risk Prior to Noncardiac Surgery

Factors	No. of Points
Age >70 years	5
Myocardial infarction within 6 months	10
S_3 gallop or jugular venous distension	11
Significant aortic stenosis	3
Nonsinus rhythm on preoperative ECG	7
>5 premature ventricular contractions/min	7
P_{O_2} <60 or P_{CO_2} >50 mm Hg, or K <3, or HCO_3 <20 mEq/l, or BUN >50, or creatinine >3 mg/dl, or chronic liver disease, or bedridden patient	3
Intraperitoneal, intrathoracic, or aortic operation	3
Emergency operation	4
Total possible points	53

NOTE: Operative candidates with 26 or more Goldman points have a 56% risk of perioperative myocardial infarction, pulmonary edema, ventricular tachycardia, or death.[25]

cardiac evaluation are to assess the risk of MI or cardiac death during and immediately following surgery; to develop a management plan intended to minimize cardiac operative risk; and to evaluate the risks and benefits of surgery and make an assessment regarding the risk/benefit ratio (Table 60-13). In carrying out this assessment, these factors should be kept in mind:

- The type of operation
- Whether it is an emergency or an elective procedure
- The patient's underlying health status

Intraabdominal operations are associated with increased risk, in part because of the comparatively prolonged postoperative course associated with such operations and the fluid and electrolyte shifts that often accompany them. Cardiovascular risk is also related to the complexity and duration of the surgery. There is ample evidence that the likelihood of perioperative MI and cardiac death are increased 2.5- to 4-fold if the operation is performed as an emergency.

History *Age.* Age is a potent predictor of oper-

ative risk, albeit one that is not susceptible to alteration.

Prior MI. Past history of ischemic heart disease predicts cardiovascular operative risk; the likelihood of intra- or postoperative myocardial infarction is 10 to 50 times greater in patients with prior MI than in those without. The 6 months following MI represent a particularly high risk interval. In general, elective surgery should be delayed until 6 months after an MI.

Angina Pectoris. In patients with stable angina—that is, no pain at rest or crescendo anginal pattern—an objective assessment of ischemic burden can be performed prior to elective surgery. Depending on the degree of exercise achieved, blood pressure response, area of ischemic myocardium, and evidence of prior MI, adjustment of the medical regimen or revascularization may be recommended. Evidence that revascularization prior to elective noncardiac surgery prevents perioperative cardiac events is scanty.

Unstable angina. Patients with unstable angina should be hospitalized and generally undergo coronary angiography before elective noncardiac surgery. Whether revascularization or medical therapy is recommended depends on the angiographic findings.

Claudication. About one-half of patients with peripheral vascular disease will have coronary disease whether or not they have angina. Often such patients are unable to achieve a sufficient degree of exercise to develop angina; nonetheless, their coronary atherosclerosis contributes to their operative risk. Therefore, individuals with intermittent claudication should undergo pharmacologic stress nuclear or echocardiographic imaging before undergoing noncardiac surgery.

Cardiac risk factors. Risk factor assessment should be included as part of the preoperative evaluation because one-half of patients with MI have no premonitory angina. Individuals with several risk factors may warrant stress testing as well.

Medications. If patients will be unable to take their oral medications before or after surgery, contingency plans for alternative management of hypertension or diabetes should be developed. Lipid-lowering medications may be withheld during the perioperative period, but other agents, such as clonidine and β-blockers, need to be tapered in advance and possibly replaced with alternatives not susceptible to rebound. Reduced insulin-dosing on the day of surgery should be planned if appropriate.

Physical Examination Physical examination may reveal hypertension, evidence of congestive heart failure, or valvular disease. Congestive heart failure is a particularly adverse prognostic indicator.

Preoperative Testing. Perhaps the most common indication for preoperative cardiac evaluation is an abnormal 12-lead ECG, usually with evidence of prior MI. Upon specific questioning, many patients will have had prior ECGs. The facsimile machine facilitates comparison of current and past tracings. If the ECG abnormality was present at least 3, and preferably 6, months previously, operative risk is reduced. In the absence of an available prior ECG, echocardiography demonstrating normal wall motion may provide a degree of reassurance, although patients with prior MI may have normal or near-normal wall motion, particularly in the thrombolytic era.

Evaluation and Optimization of Preoperative Status. In view of known predisposing factors to cardiac events following surgery, purely elective operations should be deferred in patients with recent MI, uncompensated heart failure, or severe mitral or aortic stenosis. Beyond these few clear-cut situations, a balance must be struck between the urgency and strength of surgical indication and the estimated risk of a perioperative cardiac event. The multicenter study of the Perioperative Ischemia Research Group showed that in patients undergoing noncardiac surgery, perioperative use of β-blocker was associated with a significant reduction of mortality and cardiovascular events.

Optimization of perioperative status should be undertaken in all nonemergency situations. These measures include repletion of serum potassium to >4 mEq/dl and serum magnesium >2 mEq/dl, insulin management, pulmonary toilet, nutritional status, intravascular and total body volume adjustment, including dialysis if necessary, optimization of CHF, and anti-ischemic treatment. In patients with significant cardiac history this often includes intravenous inotropic support for several days with invasive hemodynamic monitoring, diuresis, intravenous nitroglycerin, and aspirin. Usually the consulting cardiologist assumes responsibility for preoperative optimization of patients with cardiac problems with this degree of complexity.

Cardiac Life Support

Although it is extremely uncommon for a patient to require cardiopulmonary support in an office situation, so much more is being done for patients in office settings because of the mandates of managed care that this incidence may increase. The likelihood of a cardiac arrest in the office will vary depending on the patient population seen and the type of practice. Resuscitation carts are not standardized; the contents of such carts at one university hospital are noted in Table 60-14. Cardiac life support is discussed in greater depth in Chap. 78.

Summary

Cardiovascular disease is widespread, yet underdiagnosed and undertreated in women in the United States. A woman's primary care physician should use the opportunity of the office visit to screen for and identify cardiovascular risk factors

TABLE 60-14 **Resuscitation Cart Supplies and Equipment**

Top of cart
  Synchronizing defibrillator

Side of cart
  Cardiopulmonary resuscitation board

Drawer 1

Atropine	0.5 mg/5 ml	4 prefilled syringes
Bretylium	500 mg/10 ml	2 ampules
Calcium chloride	1 g/10 ml	3 prefilled syringes
50% dextrose	25 g/50 ml	1 prefilled syringe
Epinephrine, 1:10,000	1 mg/10 ml	4 prefilled syringes
Heparin, 1:1000	10,000 U/10 ml	1 vial
Isoproterenol	1 mg/5 ml	2 ampules
Norepinephrine (Levophed)	4 mg/4 ml	2 ampules
Lidocaine	100 mg/5 ml	4 prefilled syringes
Naloxone (Narcan)	0.4 mg/1 ml	3 ampules
Normal saline	500 cc	2 bags
Sodium bicarbonate	50 mEq/50 ml	6 prefilled syringes
Valium	10 mg/2 ml	2 prefilled syringes
Magnesium	1 g/2 ml	4 prefilled syringes

  IV additive and blood labels, 3 rubber stoppers, 20 alcohol swabs, vacutainers, pen

Drawer 2
  Subclavian catheter kit, selection of needles and syringes, five preheparinized syringes, cotton 4 × 4 s, sterile gloves, tape, scalpel handle and blades, Kelly clamp, 3.0 silk suture on a needle, tourniquets, betadine and benzoin swabs, padded tongue blade.

Drawer 3
  Bags of normal saline and 5% Dextrose for infusion, IV tubing, premixed dopamine (800 mg/500 ml D5W) and lidocaine (1 g/250 ml D5W) infusions, IV catheters.

Drawer 4
  Nasogastric tube, lubricating jelly, suction cannister and connectors, Yankauer suction-tip catheter, normal saline for irrigation, laryngoscope handle and blades, copper stylet, oral airway, adult McGill forceps, assorted endotracheal tubes, batteries and replacement bulb for laryngoscope.

Drawer 5
  Tracheostomy tray and tubes, cut down tray.

Bottom of cart
  Self-inflating resuscitation bag with oxygen accumulator, adult masks (large and small), oral airway, oxygen tank, tubing, and flow meter.

NOTE: This list includes the items on a resuscitation cart in one university hospital. By evaluating this list, physicians can determine which items might be needed in their individual office situations.

and either treat or refer the woman with cardiovascular disease.

References and Selected Readings

1. American Heart Association: http://www.amhrt.org.scientific/HSstats98
2. The Sixth Report of the Joint National Committee on Prevention, Detection, Evaluation, and Treatment of High Blood Pressure. *Arch Intern Med* 157:2413, 1997.
3. Gueyffier F, Boutitie F, Boissel JP, et al: Effect of antihypertensive drug treatment on cardiovascular outcomes in women and men; a meta-analysis of individual patient data from randomized, controlled trials. The INDANA Investigators. *Ann Intern Med* 126:761, 1997.
4. SHEP Cooperative Research Group: Prevention of stroke by antihypertensive drug treatment in older persons with isolated systolic hypertension: Final results of the Systolic Hypertension in the Elderly Program (SHEP). *JAMA* 265:3255, 1991.
5. Appel LJ, Moore RJ, Obarzanek E, et al. for the DASH Collaborative Research Group: A clinical trial of effects of dietary patterns on blood pressure. *N Engl J Med* 336:1117, 1997.
6. American Diabetes Association: Report of the expert committee on the diagnosis and classification of diabetes mellitus. *Diabetes Care* 21(Suppl 1):S5–S19, 1998.
7. The Diabetes Control and Complications Trial Research Group: The effect of intensive treatment of diabetes on the development and progression of long-term complications in insulin-dependent diabetes mellitus. *N Engl J Med* 329:977, 1993.
8. The Scandinavian Simvastatin Survival Study group: Randomised trial of cholesterol lowering in 4444 patients with coronary heart disease: The Scandinavian Simvastatin Survival Study. *Lancet* 344:1838, 1994.
9. Downs JR, Clearfield M, Weis S, et al: Primary prevention of acute coronary events with lovastatin in men and women with average cholesterol levels: Results of AFCAPS/TexCAPS. *JAMA* 279:1615, 1998.
10. National Institutes of Health: *Second report of the Expert Panel on Detection, Evaluation and Treatment of High Blood Cholesterol in Adults.* Washington, DC: NIH 1993. NIH publication 93-3095.
11. Grady D, Rubin SM, Pettiti DB, et al: Hormone therapy to prevent disease and prolong life in postmenopausal women. *Ann Intern Med* 117:1016, 1992.
12. Hulley SB, Grady D, Bush T, et al. for the HERS Study Group: Randomized trial of estrogen plus progestin for secondary prevention of coronary heart disease in postmenopausal women. *JAMA* 280:605, 1998.
13. Connolly HM, Crary JL, McGoon MD, et al: Valvular heart disease associated with fenfluramine-phentermine. *N Engl J Med* 337:581, 1997.
14. Pearson G, Veille J-C, Rahimtoola S, et al: Peripartum cardiomyopathy: Summary of a National Heart, Lung, and Blood Institute Workshop. *JAMA* (submitted).
15. Kasper EK, Agema WRP, Hutchins GM, et al: The causes of dilated cardiomyopathy: A clinicopathologic review of 673 consecutive patients. *J Am Coll Cardiol* 23:586, 1994.
16. Packer M, Bristow MR, Cohn JN, et al: The effect of carvedilol on morbidity and mortality in patients with chronic heart failure. *N Engl J Med* 334:1349, 1997.
17. Prystowsky EN, Benson DW, Fuster V, et al: Management of patients with atrial fibrillation: A statement for healthcare professionals from the subcommittee on electrocardiography and electrophysiology, American Heart Association. *Circulation* 93:1262, 1996.
18. Wachtel HL, Czarnecki SW: Coarctation of the aorta and pregnancy. *Am Heart J* 72:251, 1996.
19. Williams GB, Gott VL, Brawley RK, et al: Aortic disease associated with pregnancy. *J Vasc Surg* 8:470, 1988.
20. Rudd NL, Nimrod C, Holbrook K, et al: Pregnancy complications in type IV Ehlers-Danlos syndrome. *Lancet* 1:50, 1983.
21. Becker RC, Ansell J: Antithrombotic therapy: An abbreviated reference for clinicians. *Arch Intern Med* 155:149, 1995.
22. Slunsky R: General perioperative prevention of thromboembolism in gynecology with low molecular weight heparin: Clinical experiences with enoxaparin over 7 years. *Zentralbl Gynakol* 117:598, 1995.
23. Dajani AS, Taubert KA, Wilson W, et al: Prevention of bacterial endocarditis: Recommendations by the American Heart Association. *Circulation* 96:358, 1997.
24. ACC/AHA Task Force Report: Guidelines for preoperative cardiovascular evaluation for noncardiac surgery. *J Am Coll Cardiol* 27:910, 1996.
25. Goldman L: Multifactorial index of cardiac risk in noncardiac surgery: Ten-year status report. *J Cardiothorac Vasc Anesth* 1:237, 1987.
26. Emergency Cardiac Care Committee and Subcommittees, American Heart Association: Guideline for cardiopulmonary resuscitation and emergency cardiac care. *JAMA* 268:2171, 1992.

CHAPTER 61

Pulmonary Disorders

Alan S. Multz
David R. Dantzker

the body. The lung has an enormous amount of redundancy, and uses barely 15 to 20 percent of its capacity at rest. Even during strenuous exercise it is rarely called upon to use more than 50 percent of its capacity. For this reason there can be a considerable loss of function before a patient becomes symptomatic, and many lung diseases are, as a result, picked up late in their course. A patient may give a history of sudden onset of symptoms even when the disease has been progressing for a considerable time.

The process of respiration is intimately linked with three other organ systems: cardiovascular, nervous, and musculoskeletal. An abnormality of any of these may present initially in the form of some respiratory complaint. While it is often difficult to identify the origin of the complaint from the history and physical examination alone, simple diagnostic studies exist that can usually focus on the etiology of the problem.

This chapter is not a complete discussion of the pathophysiology, diagnosis, and treatment of pulmonary disease. We do, however, elucidate those factors that suggest that the lungs may be the source of an observed or perceived illness and indicate steps that should be taken to confirm the supposition. We also expand on the more common or important disorders that may be seen by a woman's primary care provider.

Signs and Symptoms of Pulmonary Disease

General Information

The presence of lung disease is usually suspected because of some specific complaint by the pa-

The major function of the lung is the exchange of oxygen and carbon dioxide with the environment, and it accomplishes this effortlessly under normal circumstances. The energy cost of normal breathing is less than 10 percent of the total basal energy requirements of

tient. However, the long latency period between the beginning of disease and the onset of symptoms of many lung diseases requires alertness by the physician in identifying those symptoms that may be early indicators of an abnormality. Particular vigilance must be exercised in those patients whose family history, occupation, social habits, or travel make them particularly prone to the development of lung disease. Smokers should be counseled to stop and helped to do so. Patients who run the risk of environmental exposure to noxious or infectious agents should be educated about those risks, and, when indicated, proper preventive measures or epidemiological screening should be advised, as in the case of tuberculosis exposure.

While respiratory disease may present in a number of ways, there are some complaints that are common enough to be worthy of separate discussion.

Breathing is ordinarily an automatic, unconscious act, and, thus, a sensation of breathlessness or increased difficulty in breathing is often the first complaint. This awareness of difficulty breathing is termed *dyspnea*. Its pathophysiologic basis is unknown, but it probably represents an imbalance or disproportion between the perceived demand for ventilation and what is achieved. This may be due to an abnormality of the lung itself, a heightened input from receptors in the chest wall, or a change in the relationship between the respiratory center drive and minute ventilation. Occasionally, the patient's history may be helpful in clarifying the origin of the dyspnea. Episodic dyspnea associated with wheezing or cough at rest, or following exercise, may be an indication of bronchospasm. Dyspnea causing arousal from sleep may be due to nocturnal asthma, neuromuscular disease, sleep apnea, chronic aspiration, or congestive heart failure. Dyspnea only on exertion may represent lung, heart, or neuromuscular disease, which can often be differentiated only by cardiopulmonary exercise studies. On rare occasions, dyspnea on exercise, or even at rest, may be an initial clue to a slowly developing chronic anemia. While a sense

of breathlessness at rest or during exercise—often described as a reduction in exercise tolerance—may be a manifestation of depression, boredom, or other functional disorders, the complaint of dyspnea should never be ascribed to this until all possible organic sources are ruled out.

Cough has been called "the watchdog of the lungs." It is usually initiated by mechanical or chemical stimulation of the upper or lower airways, and serves as a reflex to protect the lungs against potentially dangerous inhalants. As with dyspnea, the development of a cough may be a manifestation of a functional problem, but ascribing it to that cause should never be done without a full exploration of potentially pathological conditions. Cough is usually indicative of the need for increased clearance of mucus from the lungs, which may result from infectious or noninfectious inflammatory conditions. The most common noninfectious inflammatory condition that stimulates the cough receptors is asthma, and episodic cough may be the first and only symptom of bronchospasm. Cough that occurs predominantly when lying down at night may be secondary to the aspiration of gastric contents or from postnasal drip. Smokers often have a chronic productive or nonproductive cough, but a change in the character of the cough should raise the suspicion of bronchogenic carcinoma. Occasionally, a cough may be due to nonpulmonary disorders. The most common of these is gastroesophageal reflux. A more unusual cause of cough is that seen secondary to tympanic membrane stimulation, often due to an impacted hair.

When cough is productive of blood, it always requires immediate evaluation. While a bleeding site in the upper airway should be excluded, the most common causes of blood-streaked sputum are chronic bronchitis, pneumonia, and (particularly in a smoker) a tumor. Rarely, hemoptysis may be the presenting complaint in a patient with pulmonary embolic disease. The diagnosis of the cause of hemoptysis can usually be made following a history and physical examination and simple chest roentgenogram, but occasionally more complex studies, such as bronchoscopy, may be necessary to determine the source of the bleeding.

The lung parenchyma and visceral pleura are insensitive to painful stimuli, and therefore the presence of chest pain should always indicate disease of parietal pleura, the large airways, the chest wall, or structures located within the mediastinum. Noncardiac chest pain is often difficult to differentiate from cardiac pain. Pericardial and pleural pain are also often difficult to separate from each other. Occasionally, chest pain may be referred from abdominal disease, and often an abnormality in the chest may present as abdominal pain.

Hoarseness indicates intrinsic or neuromuscular disease of the vocal cords. It may be due to such minor problems as overuse, cigarette smoke, or viral infection, or it may indicate more serious disease such as cancer or granulomatous disease of the vocal cords.

The Physical Examination

The physical examination of the chest should be familiar to all physicians, and we will not review it in detail here. Suffice it to say that significant pulmonary disease may be present despite a normal physical examination. On the other hand, a careful physical examination may discover an unsuspected abnormality, or at least assist in directing the workup of a respiratory complaint.

Certain points about the physical examination are worth emphasizing. The normal resting respiratory rate is approximately 8 to 12 breaths per minute. A respiratory rate of greater than 20 almost always suggests some underlying cardiopulmonary disease. When lung disease is suspected, the respiratory rate is an easily obtainable variable that may be a useful confirmatory sign. Patients with obstructive lung disease may show no evidence of wheezing on normal breathing, and yet have dramatically abnormal chest sounds during a forced expiration. A forced expiratory time (the amount of time that one can hear air

moving during a forced expiratory maneuver) of greater than three to four seconds usually suggests significant airway obstruction.

Observation of the breathing pattern may also be very useful. Under normal circumstances the chest wall and abdomen move outward symmetrically during inspiration and inward during expiration. Paradoxical movement of either of these components of the chest wall may indicate the presence of underlying disease. Inward movement of the abdomen during inspiration suggests diaphragmatic dysfunction or excessive respiratory work, whereas inward movement of the intercostal spaces is seen with marked airway obstruction. The inward inspiratory movement of the lower portions of the chest wall (Hoover's sign) is often suggestive of significant lung hyperinflation, and is caused by the horizontal orientation of the depressed diaphragm.

Digital clubbing may occasionally be congenital, but it usually indicates significant underlying lung disease such as carcinoma of the lung, chronic inflammatory disease such as bronchiectasis, cystic fibrosis (CF), lung abscess, or the presence of diffuse interstitial fibrosis. When clubbing is due to cancer or bronchiectasis, it may be accompanied by the full-blown syndrome of hypertrophic osteoarthropathy. This includes, in addition to clubbing, long-bone tenderness and pain, as well as asymmetrical arthritis-like changes in the joints, increased thickness of the soft tissue in the distal third of the arms and legs, and neurovascular changes in the hands and feet. Occasionally, clubbing may be indicative of a nonpulmonary disease, as it can be seen with inflammatory bowel disease, chronic liver disease, and cyanotic congenital heart disease.

Any patient presenting with pulmonary complaints should have a thorough cardiac examination. In addition to the normal areas of attention, one should concentrate on evidence of right-sided heart disease. The presence of a pulsus paradoxus of greater than 10 mmHg often indicates significant obstructive airways disease. Increased neck vein distension, a substernal heave, the murmur of tricuspid insufficiency, or a widely split second sound may all be evidence of cor pulmonale.

Diagnostic Studies

The presence, and often the degree and specific diagnosis of, many common pulmonary diseases can be defined by a few relatively simple laboratory studies. These include spirometry, a measurement of the diffusing capacity for carbon monoxide (DLCO), arterial blood gases, and a chest roentgenogram. A patient who needs more complicated studies usually requires consultation with a pulmonologist or thoracic surgeon.

Simple spirometry is an easy-to-obtain, accurate screening test of lung mechanics. The variables that are usually measured are listed in Table 61-1. Most patients with symptomatic obstructive or restrictive lung disease will have some abnormal spirometric variable. Occasionally, as in the case of asthma, which may be asymptomatic at the time of testing, or early interstitial lung disease, the spirogram may be within normal limits.

The measurement of lung volumes is easy to obtain and an often useful adjunct to simple spirometry. A reduction in one or more of these volumes may point to restrictive or neuromuscular disease, or implicate obesity as the cause of the symptoms (Fig. 61-1).

When asthma is considered and the patient is asymptomatic at the time of testing, one of the many provocative tests meant to induce bronchospasm may be useful. A fall in the expired flow rate after methacholine or histamine inhalation or isocapnic hyperventilation of cold air are sensitive screening tests for hyperactive airways.

Measurement of arterial blood gases can be a good screening study, especially if spirometry is normal. While blood gases may remain normal in the early phases of lung disease, a widened alveolar-arterial gradient for oxygen (O_2) is almost always present in patients with symptomatic disease. O_2 saturation by oximetry may not be a useful substitute for arterial blood gases when the goal is early identification of pulmonary dysfunction. Because of the shape of the oxyhemoglobin dissociation curve, the arterial P_{O_2} must fall into the low seventies before the saturation becomes significantly abnormal and the O_2 saturation does not provide a measurement of Pa_{CO_2}.

An easily obtainable and often useful test in the work-up of the patient who complains of exercise intolerance, especially if spirometry and arterial blood gases are normal, is the diffusing capacity for carbon monoxide (DLCO). The DLCO can be looked upon as an index of the integrity of the pulmonary vascular bed. Therefore, it is commonly decreased in the setting of lung-destructive processes such as emphysema and diffuse interstitial diseases, although it is rarely the only abnormal pulmonary function study in these settings. In patients with pulmonary vascular disease, by contrast, it may be the only abnormality found during a routine pulmonary function screening. An isolated reduction of the DLCO that is found in a dyspneic patient

TABLE 61-1   Spirometric Values

Variable (units)	Symbol	Change with Disease	
		Obstructive Disease	Restrictive Disease
Forced vital capacity (liters)	FVC	D	D
Forced vital capacity in I s (liters)	FEV_1	D	D
Forced vital capacity in I s/forced vital capacity (%)	$FEV_1\%$	D	N
Maximum midexpiratory flow (liters/s)	MMEF	D	N

NOTE: D = decreased; N = normal

Figure 61-1 Lung volume changes in various categories of lung disease. The characteristic alterations in lung volume can often be used to narrow the differential diagnosis of a pulmonary abnormality. RV = residual volume; TV = tidal volume; TLC = total lung capacity; VC = vital capacity; ERV = expiratory reserve volume; IRV = inspiratory reserve volume; FRC = functional residual capacity.

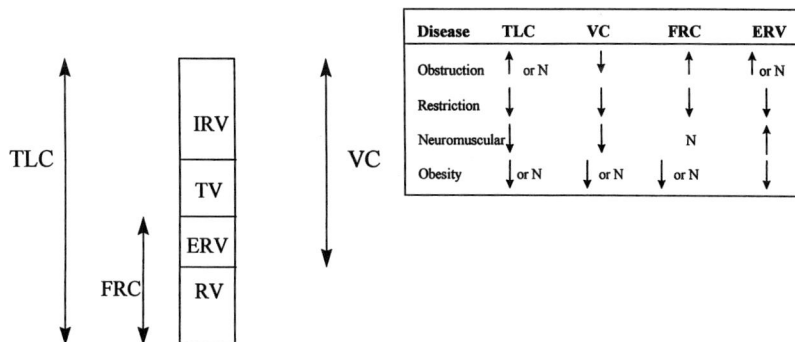

Disease	TLC	VC	FRC	ERV
Obstruction	↑ or N	↓	↑	↑ or N
Restriction	↓	↓	↓	↓
Neuromuscular	↓	↓	N	↑
Obesity	↓ or N	↓ or N	↓ or N	↓

with otherwise normal studies should raise the possibility of pulmonary hypertension, embolic disease, or vasculitis. Unfortunately, the sensitivity of the DLCO is not good enough, even with far advanced pulmonary vascular disease, to rule out the diagnosis.

The standard posteroanterior (PA) and left lateral chest roentgenographs should be a routine part of the work-up for respiratory complaints. When done correctly, they allow visualization of the air-containing lung, blood vessels, large airways, heart and mediastinum, pleura, lymph nodes, and chest wall. Significant improvement in visualization of the thorax can be obtained with computerized tomography (CT). Recent improvements in technology allow complete scanning of the chest with a single breathhold and with much less radiation exposure. This spiral CT technique may eventually replace standard roentgenograms as a screening study. High-resolution CT provides a very sensitive view of the lung parenchyma, and is rapidly becoming a standard part of the work-up of dyspnea that remains unexplained after more routine studies.

When all of the routine tests of lung function are normal, a cardiopulmonary exercise study may be helpful in differentiating organic disease from a functional complaint. By combining continuous recordings of heart rate with measurements of expired gas and minute ventilation dur-

ing a progressive exercise load using a treadmill or exercise bicycle, a clear picture of both cardiac and respiratory response to stress can be assessed. It can differentiate malingering or asthenia from disease, as well as separate a cardiac from pulmonary source of limitation.

Obstructive Lung Diseases

A reduction in inspiratory and expiratory flow rates is the characteristic finding in a number of common lung diseases (Table 61-2). Asthma affects as many as 5 to 10 percent of Americans, and chronic obstructive pulmonary disease (COPD) is one of the most common causes of time lost from work.

TABLE 61-2 **Obstructive Lung Diseases**

Asthma

Chronic obstructive pulmonary disease (COPD)

Bronchiectasis

Cystic fibrosis (CF)

Upper airway disorders

Disorders of the intrathoracic airways

Asthma

Asthma is an obstructive lung disease that is characterized by chronic and persistent inflammation of the airways, manifested by the presence of cellular infiltrates, epithelial disruption, mucosal edema, and mucous plugging. About half of all patients will develop their first symptoms of asthma before the age of five, with many becoming asymptomatic in their late teens. However, most patients who have an apparent resolution of asthma will experience recurrences later in life, and even those who remain relatively symptom-free can often be shown to manifest bronchial hyperreactivity. These "asymptomatic" individuals often develop overt bronchospasm during episodes of infection or inhalation of environmental irritants in the air. The remaining patients with asthma develop their first symptoms as adults, and some will show no abnormalities until their sixth or seventh decade. There does not appear to be any significant difference in sex predominance of this disease. African-Americans and people of poor socioeconomic status are at the highest risk for death from this disease.

Patients with asthma have episodic wheezing, cough, and shortness of breath due to the widespread narrowing of their airways. Such narrowing varies over time and can be ascribed to both inflammation and bronchospasm. The stimulus for the response is often immunologic in origin, but in many cases, there may be no clear-cut immunologic link between bronchospasm and exercise, cold air exposure, or emotional stress.

The asthmatic response has been divided into two stages: immediate and late phase. The *immediate response* is due mainly to bronchial smooth muscle contraction initiated by exposure to some immunological stimulus or irritant. If untreated, the bronchospasm usually goes away on its own after about 30 to 60 min. In about half of patients, with no further stimulus, airway obstruction will occur again after about 4 to 6 h. This *late phase response* is inflammatory in nature and is caused by the recruitment of inflammatory cells and release of mediators in airway walls. The late phase response may last, if untreated, for 24 h or more and makes the airways hyperreactive to a variety of stimuli in addition to the initial offender, thus perpetuating the attack. A patient with a specific allergy to a single agent, such as pollen, who has developed generalized hyperreactivity might therefore go on to develop bronchospasm and airway inflammation in response to any sort of irritant.

Many different types of asthma have been defined (Table 61-3) based on the clinical presentation or the presumed inciting "trigger." However, there is marked overlap in these groups and because, in general, there is a common approach to treatment, differentiation of these different forms is usually important only if there is an easily identifiable extrinsic factor, such as a drug or industrial substance, that needs to be avoided. In general, a careful identification of all substances to which the patient is allergic is unnecessary, because attempts at desensitization do not appear to alter the clinical course of the asthma.

The diagnosis of asthma can often be made on the basis of a history of intermittent dyspnea and wheezing in a patient with an underlying allergic diathesis. Occasionally, patients complain only of episodic cough. Pulmonary function studies in symptomatic patients will confirm the presence of airway obstruction that is usually reversible, at least in part, following acute administration of a bronchodilator. In asymptomatic patients, the diagnosis can be made by stimulating the hyperactive airways with methacholine, histamine, or cold air. Alternatively, the patient can be sent home with a peak flowmeter and asked to keep a diary of peak flows throughout the day. Marked variability in peak flow rate is also diagnostic of asthma. If a diagnosis of occupational asthma is suspected, a similar record of peak flow rates in the workplace is helpful.

An attack of asthma can vary in intensity from a mild increase in wheezing that is easily reversible with an inhaled bronchodilator to the devel-

TABLE 61-3 Types of Asthma

Classification	Initiating Factors
Extrinsic	IgE-mediated allergens
Intrinsic	?
Adult onset	?
Exercise induced	Change in airway temperature
Aspirin sensitivity or triad (associated with nasal polyps)	Aspirin and other nonsteroidal anti-inflammatory drugs
Allergic bronchopulmonary aspergillosis	Airway colonization with Aspergillus
Occupational	Toluene diisocyanates (TDI), cotton dusts (byssinosis), wood dust, animal proteins, etc.

opment of severe unremitting dyspnea that requires hospitalization (status asthmaticus). Severe asthma usually develops in a patient with increased lability of expired flows that are unresponsive to gradually increasing amounts of medication, although, on occasion, the attack will arise suddenly and without warning. Death from asthma is uncommon and usually occurs when increasing symptoms are disregarded and the correct therapy not initiated.

The degree of physiologic disturbance can be best monitored by the measurement of expiratory flow rates in the office or emergency room. These indices are helpful in assessing the response to therapy because they provide immediate quantitative estimates of the obstruction and can be repeated at frequent intervals. One must always remember, however, that these are subjective measurements. Arterial blood gases correlate less well with the degree of mechanical impairment, although the presence of significant hypoxemia, especially if accompanied by hypercapnia, suggests severe obstruction and indicates the need for hospitalization. The presence of a significant paradoxical pulse is also an indicator of severe airways obstruction.

During pregnancy, patients with asthma must be carefully observed. About a third of the patients will have worsening of their asthma, in a third the asthma will remain the same, and in a third it will actually improve. Pregnant patients already have some compromise of respiratory function due to incursion of the uterus on thoracic space, and thus asthma may have even greater physiologic consequences in the mother as well as the fetus. Hypoxemia, severe respiratory alkalosis that subsequently produces a reduction in utcrine artery blood flow, and hence placental blood flow, and a decrease in cardiac output that may accompany severe airway obstruction, may potentially interfere with fetal well-being. Thus, vigorous treatment of the pregnant asthmatic is important. Other than the leukotriene inhibitors, the other classes of medications used to treat asthma are acceptable for use in pregnancy.

On rare occasions the symptoms of asthma may be fictitious with airway obstruction produced by abduction of the vocal chords. This syndrome of "pseudoasthma" is probably a hysterical conversion syndrome and is often difficult to diagnose. Patients are typically treated with increasing amounts of medication before the true diagnosis is suspected. It may sometimes be recognized by the presence of stridor instead of true wheezing, and a diagnosis can be made if a reduction of peak inspiratory flow on the flow volume loop is seen during an attack. Speech therapy may be useful as a symptomatic therapy in these patients.

The management of chronic asthma in adults is summarized in Table 61-4.

TABLE 61-4 Management of Chronic Asthma in Adults

Type	Characteristics	Therapy	Medications	Alternatives
Mild intermittent	Symptoms 2 times/week Exacerbations brief Asymptomatic between exacerbations	No daily medication; inhaled β_2-agonists as needed for symptoms	Albuterol MDI Metaproterenol MDI Terbutaline MDI Isoetharine MDI	Pirbuterol MDI Bitolterol MDI Epinephrine MDI
Mild persistent	Symptoms >2 times/ week but <1 time/day	One daily medication: Anti-inflammatory; in-haled corticosteroids or cromolyn or nedo-cromil; inhaled β_2-agonists as needed for symptoms	Triamcinolone (TAA) Beclomethasone (BDP) Budesonide (BUD) Flunisolide (FP) Fluticasone (FLU)	Zafirlukast or Zileuton age >12 Montelukast age >6 Sustained-release theophylline (not preferred)
Moderate persistent	Daily symptoms; daily use of inhaled short-act-ing β_2-agonist, exacer-bations 2 times/week; may last days	Daily medication: Anti-inflammatory inhaled corticosteroids with or without a long-acting inhaled β_2-agonists; leukotriene antago-nists; inhaled β_2-agonists as needed	TAA, BDP, BUD FP, or FLU Salmeterol Montelukast Zafirlukast Zileuton	Sustained-release theophylline Long-acting β_2-agonists tablets
Severe persistent	Continual symptoms, limited physical activ-ity, frequent exacerba-tions	Daily medications: As in moderate persistent with the addition of oral corticosteroids	TAA, BDP, FP, FP or FLU; Salmeterol, Mon-telukast, Zafirlukast, Zi-leuton; Prednisone or Medrol	Sustained-release the-ophylline, Ipratropium bromide

MDI = metered dose inhaler

National Asthma Prevention Program: *Guidelines for the Diagnosis and Management of Asthma.* Bethesda, MD: National Heart, Lung and Blood Institute, 1997. Publication no. 97-4051C.

Chronic Obstructive Pulmonary Disease

Normal subjects have a slow decline in pulmo-nary function with increasing age. Patients with chronic obstructive pulmonary disease (COPD) have an exaggeration of this decline. The pro-gressive decrease in pulmonary function in pa-tients with COPD may also be punctuated by acute exacerbations secondary to infection, the development of heart failure, or poor patient compliance with prescribed medications.

COPD affects middle-aged and older individ-uals, although, on rare occasions, COPD can be demonstrated in patients by the time they reach their fifth decade. The patients are almost invariably cigarette smokers, although, under rare circumstances, patients with an inherited

deficiency of α_1-antiprotease develop obstruc-tive lung disease even in the absence of cigarette smoking. As the number of female cigarette smokers continues to rise, we can expect to see more women afflicted with clinical manifes-tations of COPD.

The diagnosis of COPD can usually be made on the basis of a history of cough and sputum production with gradually increasing functional impairment and dyspnea on exertion in a ciga-rette smoker. The physical examination is consis-tent with airway obstruction, and pulmonary function studies demonstrate reduced expiratory flow rates, which may or may not respond to an acute trial of bronchodilators. The degree of improvement in flow rates, however, unlike that seen with asthmatics, is usually modest—on the order of 15 to 25 percent.

Arterial hypoxemia is almost inevitable as the disease progresses; in some patients, hypercapnia may also develop. Patients who develop significant hypoxemia are prone to the development of pulmonary hypertension and right-sided heart failure, the constellation known as *cor pulmonale*. On occasion, these patients may have acceptable oxygenation during the day but develop significant desaturation at night. The finding of cor pulmonale in a patient with good daytime oxygen saturation should lead to a sleep study to rule out nocturnal hypoxemia.

Patients with COPD are clinically diverse, depending, in part, on the underlying pathological changes that are present. Almost all patients with significant symptomatic COPD have *emphysema,* which is defined as an abnormal enlargement of the air spaces distal to the terminal bronchials accompanied by destructive changes in the alveolar walls. As with other forms of COPD, the primary etiologic factor in the development of emphysema is cigarette smoke, which appears to work by increasing the number of inflammatory cells in the lung, enhancing the release of proteases, and impairing the activity of normally active antiproteases. However, other factors must also be operative because as few as 10 to 15 percent of smokers develop clinical evidence of emphysema.

The earliest manifestation of COPD appears to be inflammatory changes in the small peripheral airways. These changes are also related to cigarette smoke and are probably the abnormalities most amenable to therapy.

Chronic bronchitis is a chronic inflammatory condition of the large airways characterized by cough and sputum production. As with the other two abnormalities mentioned above, cigarette smoke is the primary etiologic factor in the development of chronic bronchitis, although exposure to other pollutants may play a role. While almost all heavy smokers will develop the symptom complex of chronic bronchitis, very few of them go on to develop airway obstruction. Therefore,

there is a poor correlation between the presence of chronic bronchitis and the development of emphysema or small airways disease.

Bronchiectasis

Bronchiectasis is an abnormal and persistent dilatation of the bronchi due to destructive changes in the elastic and muscular walls of the airway. It may be localized or widespread depending on the underlying etiology, and is found as a consequence of a variety of clinical disorders (Table 61-5). Prior to the introduction of antibiotics and immunization for common viral illnesses, infection was the most common cause of bronchiectasis. In underdeveloped countries, it is still commonly seen as a consequence of severe necrotizing lung infection, predominantly gram-negative pneumonia. In the United States, bronchiectasis is commonly associated with other systemic disorders that lead either to reduced immunological capacity or an abnormality in lung clearance of secretions. Deficiencies in secretory IgA as well as IgG subclasses and infection with HIV are considered potential predisposing factors.

The most common inherited abnormality of lung clearance is *cystic fibrosis* (CF), a generalized disorder of exocrine gland function, which also impairs clearance of secretions in a variety of other organs. CF is associated with abnormal chloride transport and is one of the most common genetic disorders, occurring in about 1 in 200

TABLE 61-5   **Causes of Bronchiectasis**

Cystic fibrosis

Hypogammaglobulinemia

HIV

Immotile cilia syndrome (Kartagener's syndrome)

Severe bacterial or viral infection

Exposure to corrosive gases

Allergic bronchopulmonary *Aspergillosis*

Unilateral hyperlucent lung (Swyer-James-Macleod syndrome)

α_1-Antitrypsin deficiency

births in Caucasians. It is inherited in an autosomal recessive pattern, and the abnormal gene is
located on the long-arm of chromosome 7. Infertility in men is a common manifestation with approximately 95 percent of all males affected unable to bear children. Females with CF have
reduced fertility, in part because of the thickness
of the cervical mucus. However, many women
with CF have become pregnant and carried the
fetus to term. Women with CF should understand
the increased risks involved in becoming pregnant, which are worsened if the patient is also malnourished or suffering from advanced disease.

Immotile cilia syndrome, which may include,
in addition to bronchiectasis, situs inversus, nasal
polyps, and recurrent sinusitis, is another cause
of abnormal lung clearance. It is inherited in an
autosomal recessive pattern. This syndrome is
noteworthy because of its association with male
and female infertility. In women, the diagnosis
of immotile cilia syndrome is easiest to make
with a nasal biopsy and electron micrography to
evaluate ciliary ultrastructure.

The diagnosis of bronchiectasis is suggested by
historical evidence of long-standing cough, and
the production of large quantities of purulent as
well as, occasionally, foul and/or bloody sputum,
along with the physical findings of persistent
crackles over the affected lung zones. With
chronic disease, clubbing and cor pulmonale
may be seen. A definitive diagnosis is often made
on the basis of a chest radiograph, although
occasionally high-resolution CT scanning is
necessary. A definitive etiology of bronchiectasis
requires additional testing, looking for the presence of immunodeficiency, abnormal structure
of ciliated cells, or an elevated sweat chloride
(>80 mEq/l) in the case of CF.

Treatment

For the most part, specific therapy aimed at underlying pathophysiologic abnormalities is unavailable for most patients with obstructive lung
diseases. The use of α_1-antiprotease replacement
in patients who have a hereditary absence of this

important antiprotease is now being studied, but
its ability to prevent the development of emphysema is unknown. Intravenous immunoglobulin
replacement in patients with immune deficient
states is helpful in reducing the rate of infection.
Gene replacement therapy for the cystic fibrosis
transmembrane conductance regulator (CFTR),
the protein missing in patients with CF, is also
under intense investigation. The best specific
treatment for COPD is smoking cessation. Following cessation of smoking, the rate of decline
of pulmonary function in susceptible smokers is
reduced to that of a nonsmoker over a period of
3 to 4 years. Counseling by health care professionals along with the use of transdermal nicotine
patches and behavioral modification increase the
success of cessation attempts.

The main treatment modalities for these patients are directed at amelioration of symptoms
and correction of the physiologic consequences
of the various disorders that are involved.
Bronchodilators Drugs that can affect smooth
muscle tone or decrease bronchial hyperreactivity may be divided into five categories (Table
61-6). The sympathomimetic drugs are the most
potent bronchodilators, and the development of

TABLE 61-6 Drugs That Decrease Bronchial Smooth Muscle Tone and Inflammation

Sympathomimetics
  Epinephrine
  β_2-specific agents
    Metaproterenol, Albuterol, Pirbuterol, Biltoterol, Fenoterol, etc.
Anticholinergic agents
  Atropine
  Ipratropium bromide
Methylxanthines
  Theophylline
  Aminophylline
Corticosteroids
  Sodium cromoglycate and Nedocromil
Leukotriene antagonists: Zileuton, Zafirlukast, Montelukast

noncatecholamine, β_2-specific agents has improved their specificity as well as increased the duration of action to 4 h or more. In general, aerosolization is the preferred route of administration because of the lower total dose required and the rapidity of onset of action. Significant side effects of these drugs are rare, but tolerance may develop with repeated and excessive use. For this reason, present recommendations require that inhaled β-agonists be used intermittently to control the symptoms of bronchospasm.

A long-acting inhaled β-agonist, salmeterol, is useful in chronic persistent asthma, and for those with exercise induced or nocturnal symptoms. This is a twice-a-day medication with a duration of action of about 12 h. Due to its long onset of action, 60 to 90 min, this medication will not produce a rapid improvement in acute symptomatology. Salmeterol has not yet been studied in pregnancy.

There appear to be minimal problems with the use of inhaled β-agonists in pregnant patients, although a higher incidence of pregnancy-induced hypertension was found with frequent use. Because the control of asthma is so important in pregnancy, inhaled β-agonists should be prescribed in the same way as for nonpregnant patients.

Anticholinergic agents were the first clinically available bronchodilators, but their use declined because of concerns about side effects, specifically decreased lower airway secretions. This is no longer believed to be a problem, and inhaled anticholinergic agents have been shown to be quite effective in COPD and in selective patients with exacerbations of asthma. The use of the anticholinergic agent ipratropium bromide has markedly reduced anticholinergic side effects because its systemic absorption from the airways is poor. Use of ipratropium bromide in pregnancy has not been associated with a significant increase in adverse fetal outcome. A commercially available combination of albuterol and ipratropium bromide is now available for those patients who are being treated with both classes of inhaled bronchodilators.

Methylxanthines, such as theophylline, are less effective bronchodilators than sympathomimetics and anticholinergic agents, but their availability as long-acting oral preparations may be useful when nocturnal symptoms develop because of the loss of activity of the more short-acting inhaled bronchodilators. Because of the significant toxicity that may develop from high blood levels of methylxanthine, considerable controversy exists as to their risk-benefit ratio. In general, blood levels of 8 to 10 mg/ml are a reasonable compromise between efficacy and toxicity. In pregnancy, blood levels in the fetus are similar to those in the mother, and theophylline appears in breast milk. For all of these reasons, it is probably best to consider methylxanthine a second-line drug in most patients, and its use in pregnancy should be approached with care and careful monitoring of blood levels.

Corticosteroids are a required part of the treatment of most patients with asthma. With the exception of patients who are only intermittently symptomatic, corticosteroids are usually indicated to reduce the inflammatory phase of the disease and prevent symptoms. They are safest and most effectively used as an inhaled medication. In patients with acute exacerbations of asthma, it is usually necessary to give steroids as oral, or occasionally intravenous, medications in equivalent dosages of 40 mg of prednisone per day or more. Their early use in acute exacerbations can be an important way of preventing the requirement for hospitalization. Corticosteroids, administered via any route, block both the immediate response and the late response in asthmatics.

The use of corticosteroids in COPD is more controversial. In one study, corticosteroid therapy for acute exacerbation of COPD was shown to increase the rate of improvement of airway function, although not the duration of hospitalization. However, this has been disputed by other well-controlled studies. A prospective study from the Veteran's Cooperative Study Group is in the process of being analyzed, and it may provide some new information regarding this question.

The chronic utilization of corticosteroids for patients with COPD is even more controversial, and should be reserved only for those patients who can be shown to demonstrate objectively a significant improvement in airway obstruction when they are prescribed.

Corticosteroid use during pregnancy is also controversial, although there are now numerous reports that have shown successful administration without adverse fetal effects. Increased incidence of cleft-palate malformations has been demonstrated only in rabbits; not in humans. Because of the complications of persistent asthma during pregnancy, our opinion is that its control with corticosteroids is preferable to continuing symptoms.

Inhaled sodium cromolyn, as well as the newer drug nedocromil, have been shown to prevent bronchospasm in some asthmatics, probably due to the anti-inflammatory effect of the medication. These drugs are not helpful, however, in the management of an acute asthmatic attack. Cromolyn has been used in pregnant patients, and although there are no large studies of its use in pregnant patients, there is currently no evidence that its use results in adverse effects. Nedocromil has not been studied in pregnancy.

The leukotriene inhibitors are the newest class of drugs used to treat asthma (zileuton, zafirlukast, and montelukast). The anti-inflammatory effect is on mediators released in arachidonic acid metabolism. The leukotrienes are potent inducers of inflammation and tissue damage. Two of the three agents available (zafirlukast and montelukast) work specifically on leukotriene D_4. The other available agent (zileuton) appears to have a role in the treatment of asthma that is seen in the setting of aspirin sensitivity and nasal polyps. These drugs have not been demonstrated to be safe in pregnancy.

Antibiotics Antibiotics are a mainstay in the therapy of acute exacerbations of bronchiectasis. Antibiotics are less clearly indicated in acute exacerbations of asthma or COPD, because bacterial infection is rarely implicated. In patients with bronchiectasis, especially with CF, the specific organisms responsible are usually *Staphylococ-*

cus aureus or *Pseudomonas spp*. Antibiotics in these patients should, therefore, be chosen to cover these two organisms. In patients with asthma and COPD, antibiotics should be used when there is other evidence of infection, such as the development of fever, an infiltrate that appears on x-ray, or a change in the character or quantity of sputum. In these patients, it is usually difficult to identify the specific offending organism, and the empirical use of broad-spectrum antibiotics, such as amoxicillin/clavulanic acid, trimethoprim sulfamethoxazole, cefuroxime, or levofloxacin, is appropriate. In patients with underlying obstructive pulmonary disease who have developed pneumonia, the present recommendations for community-acquired pneumonia are use of the third-generation cephalosporin with or without the addition of a macrolide, depending on underlying clinical circumstances. With the rise in penicillin-resistant *Streptococcus pneumoniae,* a fluoroquinolone may be substituted for the macrolide for the patient with a community-acquired pneumonia. In pregnant patients, penicillin, cephalosporins, and erythromycin (with the exception of erythromycin estolate) are considered safe for use.

Oxygen Significant hypoxemia should always be corrected by oxygen therapy with the goal of maintaining an oxygen saturation of about 90 percent. In patients with COPD, especially those who develop hypercarbia with acute exacerbations or those who have chronic hypercarbia, the use of even low concentrations of oxygen may lead to an increase in the partial pressure of CO_2 in the blood. This is an expected occurrence and is normally not a problem unless the Pa_{CO_2} rises progressively or signs of CO_2 narcosis develop.

In patients with COPD, chronic hypoxemia below the level of 60 torr may indicate the need for chronic oxygen therapy. This has been shown to reduce both morbidity and mortality in these patients.

Upper Airway Obstruction

Upper airway obstruction is a rare clinical entity associated with abnormalities in any anatomical site proximal to the major bronchi, including the nose, pharynx, larynx, and trachea. Patients usually present complaining of difficulty breathing. Important findings on physical examination include stridor, inspiratory and possibly expiratory wheezes, and necessity for use of the accessory muscles of respiration. If left untreated, respiratory failure may ensue with rapid development of cyanosis that is inevitably followed by cardiopulmonary arrest. The more serious abnormalities associated with the development of this clinical entity are listed in Table 61-7. They include pharyngeal infection; glottic obstruction due to a malignancy, foreign body, epiglottitis, or endotracheal intubation trauma; or laryngeal obstruction due to malignancy, connective tissue disorders, or involvement in neurologic disease.

Relapsing polychondritis is a rare disease of unknown etiology that involves the upper airway. It is seen in the 40- to 60-year-old age group, and is more prevalent in females. Laryngotracheal involvement is a bad sign in this disease, and more than 50 percent of the deaths reported due to this illness are from a respiratory cause.

Management depends on the clinical setting. Paradoxical breathing, tachycardia, and cyanosis in the presence of stridor suggest a medical emergency requiring immediate tracheostomy or cricothyrotomy. In a conscious and stable patient, a judicious search for the cause of the upper airway obstruction may be pursued. Heliox, a mixture of helium and oxygen, may have a role in the treatment of non-life-threatening upper airway obstruction. Because of its decreased density, it decreases turbulence by creating a more laminar type of airflow pattern.

TABLE 61-7   Causes of Upper Airway Obstruction

Disorders of the Pharynx
  Enlarged tonsils
  Ingestion of corrosive material
  Syphilitic gumma
  Mucosal destruction
  Deep neck infections
  Retropharyngeal abscess
  Ludwig's angina
  Trauma/intubation injury
  Foreign bodies

Disorders of the Glottis
  Glottic obstruction
  Angioneurotic edema
  Intubation trauma
  External neck trauma
  Epiglottitis/croup

Disorders of the Larynx
  Congential malformations
  Cartilaginous tumors
  Relapsing polychondritis
  Arthritis of the arytenoid joint
  Malignant tumors
  Benign tumors
  Sarcoidosis
  Tuberculosis
  Histiocytosis X
  Vocal cord paralysis—unilateral or
    bilateral

Sleep Disorders

Complaints related to sleep are commonly encountered by the primary care physician, because sleep is an important basic need of all human beings. There are many sleep-related disorders (Table 61-8). Those that cause sleep-related breathing disorders include obstructive sleep apnea, periodic breathing, and central sleep apnea. Abnormalities of breathing during sleep may also be seen in other diseases of the respiratory system

TABLE 61-8   Examples of Sleep-Related Disorders

Insomnia

Narcolepsy

Periodic limb movement disorder (PLMs)

Restless legs syndrome

Drug-dependent sleep disorder

Breathing disorders
  Obstructive sleep apnea
  Periodic breathing
  Central sleep apnea
  Hypoventilation secondary to neuromuscular, pulmonary,
    or chest wall disease

including alveolar hypoventilation syndromes, respiratory neuromuscular disorders, chest wall abnormalities, and pulmonary diseases such as asthma, COPD, CF, and idiopathic pulmonary fibrosis (IPF). The clinical consequences of sleep disorders are due to either a change in the quality or quantity of sleep, a change in the structure of sleep, nocturnal hypoxemia, or asphyxia. Their clinical manifestations include recurrent awakenings; unsatisfying or restless sleep; morning headaches; daytime somnolence; personality disorders; intellectual impairment; nocturnal cardiac arrhythmias; and the development of pulmonary hypertension or cor pulmonale, polycythemia, or even chronic respiratory failure.

Of all the aforementioned disorders, obstructive *sleep apnea* is probably the most important. It occurs during the deep phases of sleep when decreased skeletal muscle tone, perhaps combined with reduced respiratory drive, allows occlusion of the pharyngeal airway. Sleep apnea represents the leading cause of daytime sleepiness and may play a causative role in automobile accidents in this group of patients because of daytime hypersomnolence. Both snoring and obstructive sleep apnea have been identified as risk factors in the development of cardiovascular morbidity.

The diagnosis should be suggested by patient history and clinical manifestations (Table 61-9). Sleep apnea is most common in obese people. Its incidence increases with increasing age and is unusual in women before menopause. However,

TABLE 61-9 Clinical Manifestations That Suggest Obstructive Sleep Apnea

Restless sleep
Loud snoring
Grunting or gasping
Excessive daytime somnolence
Abnormal mentation
Personality changes
Impotence
Morning headaches
Witnessed apneas

young, obese women who are still menstruating, but who have complaints consistent with the diagnosis of sleep apnea, are just as likely as their male counterparts to have the disease. Excessive daytime sleepiness is the most common complaint and may significantly limit the ability to perform activities of daily living, even to the point of disability. Snoring is the most common nocturnal symptom and indicates upper airway narrowing during sleep. Nocturnal cardiac arrhythmias are common in these patients, as is systemic hypertension. A small but significant percentage of patients with obstructive sleep apnea may go on to develop pulmonary hypertension and cor pulmonale. Patients suspected of sleep apnea should be referred to a certified sleep laboratory for confirmation of the diagnosis.

The management of sleep apnea is guided by the severity of the disease. In mild to moderate cases, patients can be managed by avoidance of alcohol or other agents that depress upper airway muscle activity, by weight reduction, a dental appliance, laser-assisted uvuloplasty or by medical-surgical correction of nasal narrowing. In severe cases, more aggressive measures such as nasal continuous positive airway pressure (CPAP), tracheostomy, or uvulopalatopharyngoplasty (UPPP) may be necessary, in addition to supplemental oxygen therapy. Drug therapy has not proven useful.

Restrictive Lung Diseases

The restrictive lung diseases comprise a wide variety of disorders. Their common characteristic is the restrictive ventilatory defect that is seen on pulmonary function testing. The major physiological abnormality associated with these disorders is a decreased vital capacity (VC) with normal expiratory flow rates. With time, as the underlying disease becomes more severe, all lung volumes will decrease, and the total lung capacity (TLC) will follow the trend started by the VC. Other abnormalities include a reduction in the single-breath diffusing capacity (DLCO), chronic hyperventilation, and an increased alveolar-arterial Pa_{O_2} difference.

Interstitial lung disease is a vast topic and consists of diseases of known etiology, those due to occupational and environmental inhalants, and those of yet unknown causes. They are summarized in Tables 61-10 and 61-11. The scope of this chapter does not permit a discussion of every interstitial lung disease, but a few of "unknown etiology" merit consideration in a little more detail.

Idiopathic Pulmonary Fibrosis

Idiopathic pulmonary fibrosis (IPF) is a disorder limited to the lung. Because it has no known cause, its diagnosis is one of exclusion. Hamman and Rich initially described a group of patients who presented with interstitial infiltrates, dyspnea, and cor pulmonale and died within a 6-month period.

The disease as we have come to know it has a more variable clinical course. Patients who present with IPF are usually between 40 and 70 years of age and often exhibit dyspnea on exertion, nonproductive cough, and bibasilar end-inspiratory dry crackles on examination. It is not uncommon to find clubbing of the fingers. The chest roentgenograph commonly reveals a diffuse reticulonodular interstitial infiltrate, although in its late stages honeycombing may be seen. High-resolution chest CT may show peripheral infiltrates with central sparing and may serve to rule out other clinical entities in the differential diagnosis, such as asbestosis. Pulmonary function studies reveal characteristic findings of

---

TABLE 61-10   Interstitial Lung Diseases of Known Etiology: Occupational and Environmental Inhalants

Inorganic dusts	**Drugs**
Silica	Chemotherapeutic agents
Silicates such as asbestos and talc	Busulfan
Asbestos	Bleomycin
Aluminum	Cyclophosphamide
Carbon	Methotrexate
Beryllium	Nitrosoureas (BCNU)
Hard metals	Procarbazine
Organic Dusts	Mitomycin
Farmer's lung	Antibiotics
Bagassosis	Nitrofurantoin
Mushroom worker's lung	Sulfonamides
Humidifier lung, air conditioner lung	Penicillin
Maple-bark stripper's lung	Others
Sequoiosis	Diphenylhydantoin
Bird breeder's lung	Drugs inducing lupus-like syndrome
Gases, Fumes, Vapors (Aerosols)	Gold salts
Gases	Amiodarone
Oxygen	Poisons
Sulfur dioxide	Paraquat
Fumes	Radiation
Oxides to zinc, copper, manganese, cadmium, iron,	External
magnesium, nickel, brass, selenium, tin, and an-	Internal
timony	
Vapors	
Mercury	
Thermosetting resins	
Toluene diisocyanate (TDI)	

SOURCE: From Crystal RG, Gadek JE, Ferrars VJ, et al: Interstitial lung disease: Current concepts of pathogenesis, staging and therapy. *Am J Med* 70:542–568, 1981. With permission.

TABLE 61-11 Interstitial Lung Disease of Unknown Etiology

Idiopathic pulmonary fibrosis

Chronic interstitial disease associated with collagen-
  vascular disorders
   Progressive systemic sclerosis
   Systemic lupus erythematosus
   Polymyositis-dermatomyositis
   Rheumatoid arthritis
   Sjögren's syndrome
   Overlap syndrome

Sarcoidosis

Histiocytosis-X (eosinophilic granuloma)

Goodpasture's syndrome

Idiopathic pulmonary hemosiderosis

Wegener's granulomatosis

Lymphocytic infiltrative disorders
   Lymphomatoid granulomatosis
   Immunoblastic lymphadenopathy

Vasculitides
   Churg-Strauss syndrome
   Hypersensitivity pneumonitis
   Overlap

Inherited disorders
   Tuberous sclerosis
   Neurofibromatosis
   Familial pulmonary fibrosis

Ankylosing spondylitis

Diffuse amyloidosis of the lung

Chronic eosinophilic pneumonia

Lymphangioleiomyomatosis

Whipple's disease

Weber-Christian disease

SOURCE: From Crystal RG, Gadek JE, Ferrars VJ, et al: Interstitial lung disease: Current concepts of pathogenesis, staging and therapy. *Am J Med* 70:542–568, 1981. With permission.

restrictive lung disease with reduced lung volumes and a reduced DLCO. The mean survival is between 4 and 6 years.

The major pathologic abnormality of IPF is an increased amount of fibrous tissue in the alveolar septae or in the intra-alveolar tissue in the septae. Depending on the type of IPF, the fibrous tissue may be present in focal parts of the lung or spread out in a diffuse pattern. There are usually increased numbers of inflammatory cells noted in the areas of fibrosis. The two most common clinical variants of IPF are *desquamative interstitial pneumonitis* (DIP) and *usual interstitial pneumonitis* (UIP). These diseases are likely to represent different stages of the same entity, with DIP being the earlier, and possibly more treatable, disease.

All known causes of interstitial lung disease must first be excluded before a diagnosis of IPF can be accepted. This is best done with a careful history and search for evidence of systemic disease. It may be necessary to perform a lung biopsy to make the diagnosis. Should this be required, open or thorascopic lung biopsy is the procedure of choice so that a larger tissue specimen may be obtained. Other studies, such as gallium-67 (Ga-67) lung scans or bronchoalveolar lavage (BAL), have not proven useful in the diagnosis or long-term management of IPF.

When attempting to suppress the inflammatory response and prevent progression to fibrosis, corticosteroids are the treatment of choice. A clinical response is judged by subjective data as well as serial pulmonary function studies and exercise testing. Other immunosuppressive agents have been used to treat IPF, with cyclophosphamide being the second-line of therapy should a second agent be necessary. However, controlled studies have not clearly demonstrated their efficacy in patients unresponsive to corticosteroids. Single lung transplantation has been successfully performed in end-stage patients with IPF.

Sarcoidosis

Sarcoidosis is another disease of unknown etiology. It was first described in the late nineteenth century and was soon recognized as a multisystem granulomatous inflammatory disease. The most common organs involved are the lungs, lymph nodes, skin, eyes, and liver.

Sarcoidosis is found worldwide and is essentially a disease of young people. Seventy percent of the patients with sarcoidosis are under the age of 40 when they first become symptomatic. In the United States, sarcoidosis has a greater incidence in African Americans. In the Caucasian population, it has an equal gender distribution, but in the African-American population it predominates in females.

The characteristic histologic finding on biopsy is the presence of noncaseating granulomas, which may be found virtually anywhere in the body. Prior to a diagnosis of sarcoidosis, a variety of other diseases that may also be characterized by the presence of granulomas must be excluded, including infections with mycobacteria or fungi, malignancy, mineral dust exposures, brucellosis, hypersensitivity pneumonitis, and Wegener's granulomatosis. This is best accomplished by a thorough history, special staining of biopsied tissue, and immunologic procedures.

Sarcoidosis has many clinical manifestations, depending on which organ system is involved (Table 61-12). The lung is the most common organ involved. Frequently, the patient is asymp-

TABLE 61-12 Common Manifestations of Sarcoidosis by Organ System

Nervous system	*Cardiac*
Blindness	Arrhythmias
Hypopituitarism	Conduction disturbances
Polyneuropathy	Left ventricular failure
Subacute meningitis	*Musculoskeletal*
Eye	Arthritis, tenosynovitis
Keratoconjunctivitis	Myopathy
Optic neuritis	*Skin*
Uveitis	Erythema nodosum
Liver-spleen	Lupus pernio
Intrahepatic cholestasis	Lymphadenopathy
Splenomegaly	Maculopapular lesions
Upper respiratory tract	*Endocrine*
Laryngeal sarcoid	Hypercalcemia
Tracheitis	Diabetes insipidus
Pulmonary	Panhypopituitarism
Interstitial lung disease	*Lymph node involvement*
Lymphadenopathy	
Airways obstruction	
Cavitation	

tomatic, and the diagnosis is suspected from a chest roentgenograph obtained for some other reason. Pulmonary symptoms include dyspnea, with or without exertion, as well as a nonproductive cough and nonspecific chest pains. Laboratory evaluation may reveal hypercalcemia, hypergammaglobulinemia, abnormal liver function studies, or an elevated angiotensin-converting enzyme (ACE) level, although the latter is not specific for sarcoidosis.

Radiographic manifestations are divided into stages: Stage 0 has a normal chest roentgenograph; stage 1 has lymph node enlargement without pulmonary parenchymal disease. Stage 2A has a combination of lymph node and diffuse pulmonary disease; stage 2B shows diffuse pulmonary disease without lymph node enlargement. Finally, stage 3 has radiographic changes indicating pulmonary fibrosis ("honeycombing"). The largest review of sarcoidosis patients suggested a distribution of 8 percent for stage 0, 51 percent for stage 1, 29 percent for stage 2, and 12 percent for stage 3.

When diffuse pulmonary disease is present, it tends to have an upper-lobe prevalence. Pulmonary function studies are consistent with a restrictive ventilatory defect showing decreased lung volumes and a reduced DLCO. However, sarcoidosis frequently causes an additional obstructive ventilatory defect attributable to granulomatous involvement of the airways. When an obstructive defect is present, it suggests a worse overall prognosis.

It is worthwhile to mention briefly some clinical manifestations of sarcoidosis in other organ systems. One common skin lesion associated with sarcoidosis is erythema nodosum, which when biopsied, does not reveal granulomas. Rather, it reveals a vasculitis. When seen in sarcoidosis, it implies a more benign clinical course. Ocular involvement is common and may present as an anterior or posterior uveitis. Myocardial sarcoidosis has become increasingly important because of its association with sudden death due to involvement of the conduction system. Central nervous system (CNS) sarcoidosis presents most commonly as aseptic meningitis or a neuropathy, and rarely as a space-occupying lesion.

The natural history of sarcoidosis is not predictable, although patients with radiological stage 3 disease or multiple system involvement have a worse prognosis. Unfortunately, there are no conventional tests that can predict its course or prognosis. Serial chest roentgenographs, ACE levels, and Ga-67 lung scans have not proven useful prognostic tools in long-term prospective trials. Pulmonary function studies are the best test to follow in this illness. The VC correlates best with dyspnea and the response to treatment. Because sarcoidosis is usually self-limited, patients should only be treated if they have significant and symptomatic lung disease or granulomatous involvement of organs, such as the brain, eye, or heart, where the physical presence of granulomas may lead to significant organ dysfunction. Hypercalcemia is another clear indication for treatment.

Corticosteroids are the therapy of choice in sarcoidosis, with dosage guided by symptoms and pulmonary function studies. Despite adequate treatment, a small percentage of patients will continue to deteriorate. Other immunosuppressive agents have been tried in an uncontrolled fashion in patients who fail a trial of corticosteroids, without reproducible success.

Hypersensitivity Pneumonitis Hypersensitivity pneumonitis (HP) results from recurrent exposures and sensitization to organic dusts (Table 61-13). It results in a diffuse mononuclear inflammatory response in the alveoli, bronchioles, and interstitium, which may organize into granulomas and eventually produce fibrosis. The pathological changes are felt to result from the formation of antigen-antibody complexes in the lung.

There are two common modes of presentation. The first is an acute reaction characterized by the abrupt onset of fever, chills, malaise, cough, chest tightness, and wheezing. On examination, crackles are audible in both lungs, and cyanosis may be present. These symptoms usually subside over hours or days. Mild hypoxemia and a restric-

tive ventilatory defect are found, and the chest roentgenograph shows fleeting, nodular interstitial infiltrates in the lower and midlung fields. Removal from the inciting source usually leads to complete resolution of the problem. The chronic form results from repetitive acute exposures or continued subacute antigen exposure. This type is characterized by irreversible lung damage with pulmonary fibrosis. Symptoms include dyspnea on exertion and hyperventilation, with the eventual development of cor pulmonale and respiratory failure. Pulmonary function studies reveal a mixed obstructive and restrictive defect with a reduced DLCO. Arterial blood gases frequently demonstrate hypoxemia and a widened alveolar-arterial O_2 gradient, while the chest roentgenograph shows progressive fibrotic disease with loss of volume, particularly in the upper lung zones, and no hilar adenopathy. The serum may be tested against known antigens, but a positive study is evidence only of exposure, not active disease.

The therapy for HP is avoidance of exposure to the antigen, because the risk of development of chronic disease increases as the number of acute episodes exceeds five. Corticosteroid treatment is rarely needed, but may accelerate recovery and improve gas exchange in symptomatic individuals. The prognosis for recovery from acute episodes is usually excellent.

Connective Tissue Disorders

Connective tissue disorders frequently involve the lung and may manifest themselves roentgenographically as a chronic interstitial pattern that cannot be differentiated from IPF (Table 61-11). In addition to interstitial lung disease, these disorders may affect the respiratory muscles, predispose to infection or aspiration, involve the pleura or pleural space, or present as a pulmonary vasculitis with pulmonary hypertension.

Rheumatoid Arthritis While rheumatoid arthritis (RA) has a female predominance, pulmonary disease associated with RA has a male predominance. Diffuse interstitial pneumonitis and

TABLE 61-13   Examples of Allergic Extrinsic Alveolitis

Disease or Occupation	Exposure Material	Specific Allergen
Farmer's lung	Mold, hay, grain, silage	Micropolyspora faeni *Thermoactinomyces spp.*
Bird breeders	Bird droppings Dander, feathers	Avian proteins Feathers
Humidifier lung	Forced air ventilation	Amebae *Thermoactinomyces spp.*
Bagassosis	Moldy sugar cane	*Thermoactinomyces sacchari*
Malt workers	Moldy sprouting barley	*Aspergillus clavatus*
Woodworkers	Moldy logs	*Alternaria spp., Rhizopus spp.,* *Saccharomyces spp.*
	Moldy redwood sawdust	*Graphium spp.* *Aureobasidium spp.*
Mushroom workers	Mushroom compost Mushroom spores	*Thermoactinomyces spp.* *Micropolyspora faeni*
Rodent handlers	Urine, dander	Rodent protein
Chemical workers	Plastic manufacture	Methyl isocyanate, TDI

fibrosis indistinguishable from IPF may be seen, which can progress to honeycombing. Symptoms are usually dyspnea on exertion and a dry cough. Other pulmonary manifestations of RA include pleurisy with or without effusion; necrobiotic nodules with or without cavities; pulmonary hypertension due to pulmonary vasculitis; Caplan's syndrome (rheumatoid pneumoconiosis); bronchiolitis obliterans with or without organizing pneumonitis; or upper airway obstruction from rheumatic involvement of the arytenoid cartilage.

Progressive Systemic Sclerosis   (PSS), or ***Scleroderma,*** is a systemic disease characterized by skin changes, microvascular abnormalities, and esophageal dysfunction. Interstitial pulmonary fibrosis is the most common pulmonary manifestation, and has been reported in 14 to 90 percent of all clinical cases. Pulmonary function studies frequently show a restrictive ventilatory defect with a decreased DLCO in spite of a normal chest roentgenograph. A low DLCO in this disease is a predictor of mortality. Progressive asymmetric basal interstitial infiltrates spread upward and in late stages produce honeycombing. D-Penicillamine may be useful in treating the interstitial lung disease associated with PSS. Other pulmonary complications described with PSS include pulmonary hypertension from medial hypertrophy of pulmonary arteries; aspiration pneumonitis due to involvement of the esophagus; increased incidence of carcinoma of the lung; and a "pulmonary-renal" syndrome. Pleural involvement due to scleroderma is very rare.

Systemic Lupus Erythematosus   (SLE) is a systemic disease of unknown etiology that is characterized by autoimmune damage to tissue. Lung manifestations include pleuritis with or without pleural effusion, atelectasis, diaphragmatic dysfunction with loss of lung volume, alveolar hemorrhage syndrome, secondary pulmonary infections from immunosuppression, acute lupus pneumonitis, and bronchiolitis obliterans with or without organizing pneumonitis. Interstitial lung disease is an uncommon manifestation of this connective tissue disorder. The chronic interstitial pneumonitis, when seen, presents with nonproductive cough, dyspnea, and pleuritic chest pain. Drug-induced SLE, due most commonly to INH, procainamide, and hydralazine, may produce many of the same thoracic manifestations as SLE, although the symptoms are usually mild and reversible when the drug is stopped.

Polymyositis/Dermatomyositis Lung involvement, in the form of interstitial pneumonitis, is seen in about 5 to 10 percent of patients with polymyositis/dermatomyositis (PM/DM). The infiltrates are alveolar and interstitial in nature and start at the bases. Other pulmonary manifestations of PM/DM include hypercapnic respiratory failure secondary to muscle weakness and recurrent aspiration pneumonias.

Sjögren's Syndrome (SS) is a systemic disease manifested by xerostomia, recurrent swelling of the parotid glands, and keratoconjunctivitis sicca. This disease had been associated with interstitial lung and is clinically indistinguishable from IPF. Histologically, however, it is a lymphocytic interstitial pneumonitis. This lymphocytic pneumonitis is frequently difficult to differentiate from lymphoma or pseudolymphoma.

Lymphangioleiomyomatosis

Lymphangioleiomyomatosis (LAM) is a devastating disease that affects young women during their reproductive years. Both its etiology and pathogenesis are unknown, but it is believed to be a hormonally related disorder because it is frequently exacerbated by menses and pregnancy. This disorder shares pathological and clinical features with tuberous sclerosis, a genetic defect that is inherited with an autosomal-dominant pattern.

Clinically, it presents with dyspnea on exertion, cough, chest pain usually due to recurrent hemoptysis, unilateral or bilateral chylous pleural effusions, or hemoptysis. Chylous pleural effusions are seen in about 75 percent of patients and hemoptysis in about 50 percent. A chest roentgenograph usually reveals a coarse reticular interstitial pattern but with normal or large-appearing lung volumes. Cystic changes and honeycombing are common findings. Pulmonary function testing reveals evidence of airway obstruction due to obstruction of air flow from smooth muscle bundles in the alveolar walls or a mixed picture of restriction with obstruction. There is almost always a reduction of the DLCO. A diagnosis requires an open lung biopsy, although CT scanning of the chest may be diagnostic if the characteristic thin-walled cystic air spaces that suggest LAM are seen. LAM may also present with extrapulmonary manifestations, particularly in the renal and intra-abdominal areas. Treatment, including oophorectomy, medroxyprogesterone, tamoxifen, or combination therapy, has been attempted in LAM without much success. Single- or double-lung transplantation has been performed successfully in females with LAM. For patients with LAM, pregnancy and the use of any exogenous estrogen preparations should be strongly advised against.

Eosinophilic Granuloma

Eosinophilic granuloma (EG) is a rare disorder that presents with chronic interstitial lung disease and spontaneous pneumothoraces in smokers. EG is a disease of adults between the ages of 20 and 50, and has a Caucasian predominance. A slight female predominance (3:2) appears to exist for this disease.

Clinically, this disease presents with cough, dyspnea, and spontaneous pneumothoraces. Extrapulmonary manifestations include bone lesions and diabetes insipidus due to pituitary gland involvement. CT of the chest has characteristic findings of upper-lobe cystic and nodular lesions; the nodular lesions help distinguish this disease from LAM, which does not have this feature. Prognosis is good for EG, and treatment includes cessation of cigarette smoking. In patients in whom the disease does not spontaneously resolve, a trial of corticosteroids may be of benefit.

Takayasu's Arteritis

Two other rare diffuse lung diseases warrant mention due to their female predominance. They are Takayasu's arteritis (TA) and eosinophilic myalgia syndrome (EMS). TA is a chronic inflammatory disease that primarily affects the aorta and other large arteries. It has a predilection for Asians with a female to male ratio of 8.5 : 1, and is a disease of young people. Corticosteroid therapy is the treatment of choice for TA, producing symptomatic improvement in days to weeks.

Eosinophilic Myalgia Syndrome

EMS is a systemic inflammatory disease characterized by myalgias and eosinophilia that results from ingestion of L-tryptophan. L-Tryptophan has been used as a natural remedy for insomnia, depression, and premenstrual syndrome (PMS), as well as for other health reasons. Pulmonary complications develop in 50 to 60 percent of patients with EMS and include pulmonary infiltrates, hypoxemia, pleural disease, and pulmonary hypertension. EMS has a female predominance, with the onset of symptoms usually within one to nine months following initial ingestion. Discontinuation of the L-tryptophan and administration of corticosteroid agents rapidly improves this disease.

Catamenial Pneumothorax

Catamenial pneumothorax (CP) is associated with about 5 percent of all spontaneous pneumothoraces seen in women under the age of 50. This illness is almost exclusively associated with menses, and has a right-sided predilection. In addition to pneumothorax, women may also present with hemoptysis, hypoxemia, and atelectasis. Drugs that suppress ovulation, including Danazol, medroxyprogesterone, or gonadotropin-releasing hormone analogs, are the treatment of choice.

Pulmonary Vascular Disease

The pulmonary vascular bed is normally a low-resistance, low-pressure system that receives blood from the right ventricle, predominantly due to the reciprocating change in intrathoracic pressure. The right ventricle, in turn, serves mainly as a capacitance chamber and under normal circumstances is able to generate only relatively low pumping pressure. The maximum pressure that the right ventricle can produce under normal circumstances is a mean pressure of about 40 mmHg. If the resistance in the pulmonary vascular bed goes up acutely, such that higher pressures must be generated by the right ventricle in order to permit forward flow, the right ventricle will fail and cardiac output will drop drastically. If the resistance in the pulmonary vascular bed increases gradually, as it does with chronic diseases, the right ventricle has time to hypertrophy and can eventually generate systemic pressures.

A large variety of conditions and diseases can lead to a rise in pulmonary vascular resistance and thus the development of pulmonary hypertension (Table 61-14). Many of these are discussed elsewhere in this chapter or the book; in

TABLE 61-14 Causes of Pulmonary Hypertension

Postcapillary pulmonary hypertension (increased venous pressure)
    Left ventricular failure
    Mitral valve failure
    Pulmonary veno-occlusive disease

Obliterative or obstructive pulmonary hypertension (loss of pulmonary vessels)
    Pulmonary emboli
    Primary pulmonary hypertension
    Parenchymal lung disease
    Vasculitis

Hyperkinetic pulmonary hypertension (increased pulmonary flow)
    Atrial and ventricular septal defects
    Patent ductus arteriosus
    Peripheral arteriovenous shunts

Reactive pulmonary hypertension (vasoconstriction)
    High altitude
    COPD
    Persistent or intermittent hypoventilation
        Neuromuscular disease
        Sleep apnea

this section, we confine our comments to two diseases that are often difficult to diagnose. One of these is relatively common, pulmonary embolic disease, and the other relatively rare, primary pulmonary hypertension.

Pulmonary Embolism

The pulmonary vascular bed acts as a filter for the circulation. Thus, any substance that gets into the venous blood embolizes to the lung. The response to this embolization depends on the composition of the embolic material. Embolization of air or amniotic fluid leads to an alteration in the alveolar capillary membrane and results in a picture typical of the adult respiratory distress syndrome. Talc granules or cotton fibers injected during illicit drug use lead to slowly progressive inflammatory disease of the pulmonary capillaries and pulmonary hypertension. The consequence of the most commonly embolized material, thromboemboli, depends on the degree and rapidity with which the pulmonary vascular bed is occluded as well as the underlying cardiac status of the patient. The symptoms may vary from mild dyspnea and tachycardia to cardiopulmonary arrest.

More than 80 percent of pulmonary thromboemboli originate in deep veins of the iliofemoral system. Other sources of clot include the inferior vena cava, the right side of the heart and, less commonly, the upper extremities. The diagnosis of deep venous thrombosis (DVT) is a difficult one to make because 50 percent of the patients have neither the signs nor the symptoms of venous occlusion. On the other hand, in patients presenting with the classic findings of thrombophlebitis, pain and swelling in the legs, only 50 percent will be found on objective examination to actually have DVT. While DVT is often underdiagnosed in hospitalized patients, it is also often overdiagnosed in the ambulatory arena, where a clinical misdiagnosis can lead to inappropriate and high-risk therapy. For this reason, a diagnosis of thrombophlebitis should always be confirmed by objective study. For disease in the

lower legs, the best techniques are Doppler/duplex ultrasound studies or impedance plethysmography. When these are nondiagnostic, a contrast venogram may be required. Ultrasound can also be useful in diagnosing a mural thrombus in the heart and upper extremity clots.

The diagnosis of pulmonary embolic disease can be difficult, especially in the ambulatory population, because the presenting symptoms and signs are both nonspecific and insensitive. About 80 percent of patients will complain of dyspnea, which in a slightly smaller percentage is accompanied by pleuritic chest pain. Hemoptysis is seen in less than 20 to 30 percent of patients with pulmonary emboli. While tachypnea is almost invariable and tachycardia is common, obvious thrombophlebitis, evidence of acute right ventricular strain, or positive findings during auscultation of the heart and lungs, are seen in less than 40 percent of cases. However, patients who present without dyspnea, pleuritic chest pain, or tachypnea are unlikely to have acute pulmonary embolism. A low-grade fever is common, but persistent fever with marked leukocytosis is unusual in embolic disease and more likely to suggest pneumonia. Perhaps the most important clue to the presence of pulmonary embolic disease is identification of patients at high risk for a DVT. These conditions are listed in Table 61-15.

TABLE 61-15 Patients at High Risk for Pulmonary Emboli

Prolonged bedrest or immobility

Congestive heart failure or low flow states

Malignancy

Postoperative (greater than 30 min of general anesthesia)

Lower extremity trauma or surgery

Pregnancy

Abnormal clotting
   Antithrombin III, protein S, and protein C deficiencies
   Thrombocytosis
   Heparin-associated thrombocytopenia
   Activated protein C resistance (factor V Leiden factor)
   Anticardiolipin antibody
   Antiphospholipid antibody

A chest x-ray and electrocardiogram (ECG) may be reasonable diagnostic aids in a patient presenting with chest pain and shortness of breath, but both of them serve more to rule out other causes of these symptoms than to help make a diagnosis of pulmonary embolic disease. The same thing can be said for the measurement of arterial blood gases. While studies have suggested that a patient with both normal alveolar-arterial O_2 and a normal Pa_{CO_2} has less than a 5 percent chance of having had a pulmonary embolism, no pattern of blood-gas abnormality is specific enough to make the diagnosis of embolic disease. Thus, clinical presentation and routine laboratory studies may suggest a diagnosis of pulmonary embolism, but confirmation will require more specific investigation.

The most important diagnostic test is the ventilation-perfusion lung scan. Patients with a normal ventilation-perfusion scan are effectively eliminated from the diagnosis while a high-probability scan, described as the presence of segmental or larger defects on the perfusion scan with normal ventilation, is virtually diagnostic. Any other combination of matched or mismatched defects should be considered an indeterminate scan and requires further diagnostic testing. If the patient is hemodynamically unstable, this test should be a pulmonary angiogram, which is still considered the gold standard in the diagnosis of pulmonary emboli. In all other cases, the next step is to look for the presence of DVT. Clearly, patients with objective evidence of DVT and an indeterminate scan require no further testing and can be treated for embolic disease. Unfortunately, in as many as 30 to 40 percent of patients with a pulmonary embolism, these studies may be negative because the clot has already embolized. These patients will require either a CT pulmonary angiogram (CTPA), a pulmonary angiogram, or repeated noninvasive testing to look for the development of further clots in the leg. There are data to suggest that the specificity and sensitivity of CTPA is close to that of pulmonary angiography, particularly for central pulmonary emboli. Studies have also suggested that in patients suspected of hav-

ing had a pulmonary embolism, repetitive negative noninvasive tests for DVT preclude the need for anticoagulation because the goal of therapy is the prevention of further clots rather than the treatment of the embolism. A schema for the diagnosis of pulmonary embolism is shown in Fig. 61-2.

The treatment of DVT and pulmonary embolism consists of anticoagulation, initially with intravenous heparin sufficient to prolong the activated partial thromboplastin time (aPTT) to 1.5 to 2 times the patient's baseline values. Once the aPTT is therapeutic, warfarin can be started with the goal of prolonging the international normalized ratio (INR) to a level between 2 and 3. Patients who are hypercoagulable, such as those with anticardiolipin or antiphospholipid antibodies, require higher levels of anticoagulation. Warfarin should not be used in early pregnancy due to teratogenic effects, and it must be stopped several weeks prior to anticipated delivery due to the fetal risk of intracranial hemorrhage. Pregnant patients require heparin when anticoagulation therapy is utilized during these periods. In addition, for patients who have had serious side effects from warfarin, continued heparinization is required. This can be done on an ambulatory basis using controlled doses of subcutaneous injections. The use of low molecular-weight heparin is acceptable as an alternative for those patients who require anticoagulation and who, for whatever reason, may not be able to take either warfarin or unfractionated heparin. The dose is 1 mg/kg/day in divided doses and no laboratory monitoring is necessary.

Most patients require continuing anticoagulation for 3 months. For those patients in whom the risk for embolic disease remains at the end of 3 months, or in whom recurrent embolic episodes have been demonstrated, a longer term of anticoagulation is required.

For most patients, there is no indication for the use of fibrinolytic drugs. Extensive studies have demonstrated that the outcome of patients with pulmonary emboli treated with fibrinolytic drugs is no different from those treated with hep-

Figure 61-2 Algorithm for a clinically suspected pulmonary embolism.

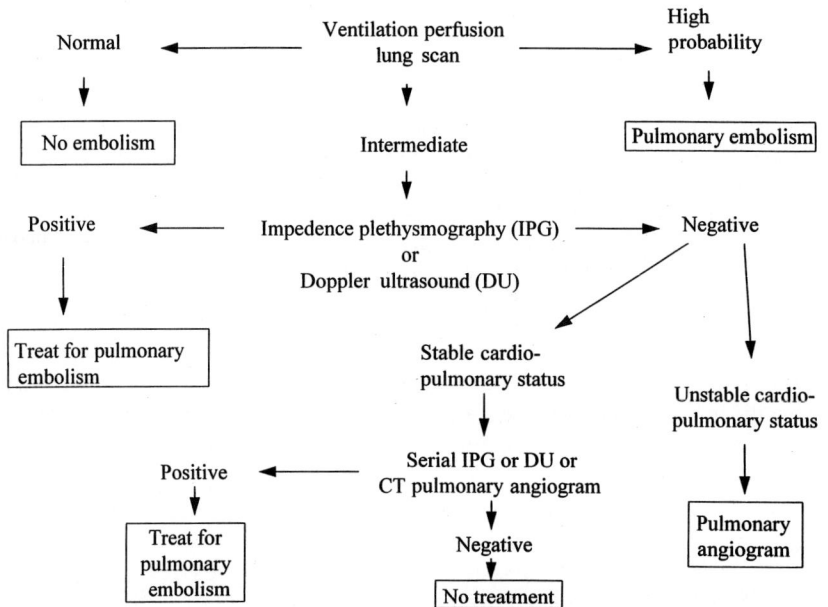

arin, although resolution of the clot is faster. Thus, it has become common practice to reserve fibrinolytic therapy for patients with massive embolization and evidence of cardiovascular compromise, because fibrinolytic therapy carries a higher risk of hemorrhagic side effects. Recently, it has been suggested that patients who are "hemodynamically stable," but who have echocardiographic evidence of right-sided heart involvement, may benefit from thrombolytic therapy with the goal of improving right ventricular function. This is not yet accepted practice.

The best way to treat thromboembolic disease is to prevent its occurrence. Appropriate prophylaxis of high-risk patients is safe and efficient. Different patients may require different types of prophylaxis (Table 61-16).

Primary Pulmonary Hypertension

Primary pulmonary hypertension is a disease of unknown etiology that can occur in patients at any age but is most common in the third and fourth decades. In children there is no gender predominance, but in adults, the female-to-male ratio is about 2:1. These patients often present to the physician complaining of vague symptoms of decreased exercise tolerance or shortness of breath. Often the physical examination is normal, and the symptoms are dismissed initially as functional. In time, the patient's complaints progress, and chest pain, cor pulmonale, and syncope on exertion may develop. By this time, the physical examination is often diagnostic of the presence of pulmonary hypertension with the development of a right ventricular heave and tricuspid insufficiency. Once the pulmonary artery pressures get high enough, the diagnosis can often be suspected by an echocardiographic assessment of the right ventricle and an estimate of a right ventricular systolic pressure. It is confirmed by right catheterization and the exclusion of other causes of pulmonary hypertension.

The prognosis for patients with primary pulmonary hypertension is dismal, with only 20 percent survival 3 years after diagnosis. In about 25 percent of patients, pulmonary vasodilation is possible using either prostacyclin or a calcium channel blocker. Chronic anticoagulation is recommended because low-grade thrombosis and

TABLE 61-16   Preventing Deep Venous Thrombosis

Risk Group	Recommendations
Hip or knee replacement	Low-dose warfarin Low molecular-weight heparin Intermittent pneumatic compression
Neurosurgery	Intermittent pneumatic compression with or without unfractionated heparin
General surgery	Unfractionated heparin Low molecular-weight heparin
Medical admission to the hospital	Unfractionated heparin Low molecular-weight heparin Intermittent pneumatic compression

small pulmonary arteritis are thought to contribute to the progressive increase in pulmonary vascular resistance. These treatment approaches, however, should only be thought of as bridges to lung transplantation, the only long-term successful therapy presently available.

Pneumonia

Pneumonia is a common cause of morbidity and mortality in women. While pneumonia can affect anyone at any age, it is more frequent in older patients and those with other comorbid conditions (Table 61-17). The diagnosis of pneumonia is relatively easy to make and confirm, but it is usually difficult or impossible to define the specific pathogen responsible for the infection. Even with extensive testing and careful pathologic follow-up, a clear etiologic diagnosis of pneumonia can be made less than 50 percent of the time. For this reason, the treatment of pneumonia is usually empiric, based on what is known about its epidemiology.

The patient with pneumonia typically has a history of cough with fever and sputum production, which may be accompanied by pleuritic or nonpleuritic chest pain. Occasionally, pneumonia may present with minimal pulmonary symptoms; the patient complains, instead, of upper abdominal pain or diarrhea. The physical findings of crackles or consolidation on examination of the thorax are typical, although early in the course of pneumonia the physical examination may be entirely normal. Clinical features are rarely useful or reliable in trying to determine the specific etiology, although on occasion the history may be helpful. For example, a travel history to the river valleys of the Midwest, or the central valleys of California, or to Arizona may suggest a fungal disease. Occupational exposure, a recent hospitalization, or a nursing home stay may also raise the specter of an unusual infecting agent.

Once the diagnosis of pneumonia is suspected, a posterior-anterior and lateral chest radiograph should be obtained for confirmation of a pulmonary infiltrate. While the x-ray is rarely specific enough to be diagnostic, occasional findings may be useful in determining the approach to treatment. Obtaining sputum for Gram's stain and culture is a common recommendation, although it is rare that either of these procedures provides useful information leading to the diagnosis of a specific pathogen. Similarly, serologic testing may be useful from an epidemiologic standpoint, but it is rarely helpful in the clinical approach to the patient because both acute and convalescent titers are usually required to define recent infection. From a diagnostic and therapeutic standpoint, the most important considerations are the clinical severity of the illness, the presence or absence of coexistent conditions as stated in

Table 61-17, and the presence of advanced age, defined in this context as being older than 65 years.

Once the diagnosis of pneumonia is made, two questions should be considered. The first is whether or not the patient is ill enough to require hospitalization. Table 61-18 lists some criteria that may confirm the need for hospitalization. This chapter does not discuss the in-hospital treatment of pneumonia, which is discussed in Chap. 69.

In those patients not requiring hospitalization, a second question serves to divide the patients based on age and the presence of a comorbid illness. This differentiation assists in selecting the most likely organism involved, and in defining therapy. For patients less than 60 to 65 years of age without any comorbid illnesses, the most common organisms, in order of occurrence, are shown in Table 61-19. For patients older than 60 to 65 years of age or with one of the comorbid illnesses listed in Table 61-17, a slightly different order of occurrence is found (Table 61-20). Patients who have been in a nursing home have an increased incidence of methicillin-resistant *S. aureus, Mycobacterium* tuberculosis, vancomycin-resistant *Enterococcus spp.,* and viral pneumonias. Regardless of the age and comorbid status of the patient, the presence of penicillin-resistant *Streptococcus pneumoniae* presents a major problem to clinicians, with resistant rates

around the country between 10 and 20 percent. This has been accompanied by macrolide-resistance rates exceeding those of the penicillin-resistant bacteria.

Based on this approach, treatment of pneumonia can be initiated empirically. Our recommendations for women treated for pneumonia on an ambulatory basis are discussed below. For younger patients with no comorbid conditions, treatment is started with either a macrolide or fluoroquinolone; if the patient is allergic to macrolides and/or fluoroquinolones, tetracycline. While erythromycin is an effective initial therapy, some of the newer macrolide agents have a broader spectrum and are quickly becoming the initial choice of outpatient management of pneumonia in this group of patients. For older patients or those with comorbid illness, our first choices

TABLE 61-18   **Decision to Hospitalize a Patient for Pneumonia**

Age over 65 years

Comorbid conditions (see Table 61-17)

Physical findings suggesting sepsis or extrapulmonary spread of infection

White blood cell count of less than 4000 or greater than 30,000 or an absolute neutrophil count of <1000

Requirement for supplemental oxygen or mechanical ventilation

Chest radiograph demonstrating multilobar involvement, cavitary disease, or pleural effusion

Significant anemia (a hematocrit <30%)

TABLE 61-17   **Comorbid Conditions Associated with Increased Risk and Poor Outcome of Pneumonia**

Chronic obstructive pulmonary disease

Diabetes mellitus

Renal insufficiency

Congestive heart failure

Chronic liver disease

Altered mental status

Postsplenectomy

Alcohol abuse or malnutrition

TABLE 61-19   **Common Pathogens in Patients <60 Years of Age with No Comorbid Illnesses Who Can Be Treated in an Outpatient Setting**

	Miscellaneous Organisms
Streptococcus pneumoniae	*Legionella spp.*
Mycoplasma pneumoniae	*Staphylococcus aureus*
Respiratory viruses	*Mycobacterium tuberculosis*
Chlamydia pneumoniae	Anaerobic gram-negative
Haemophilus influenza	bacillae

TABLE 61-20   Common Pathogens in Patients Being Treated As Outpatients for Pneumonia Who Are >60 Years of Age or Who Have a Comorbid Illness

Streptococcus pneumoniae	**Miscellaneous**
Respiratory viruses	*Moraxella catarrhalis*
	Legionella spp.
Haemophilus influenzae	*Tuberculosis*
Aerobic gram-negative organisms	*Fungi*
Staphylococcus aureus	

include a second-generation cephalosporin, tri-methoprim-sulfamethoxazole, or a β-lactamase inhibitor combination. In this group of patients, the macrolide is added as a second drug if there is a significant suspicion of *Legionella*.

Most patients with pneumonia continue to have fever for 2 to 3 days following therapy. However, if fever persists or symptoms do not begin to show some resolution, repeat evaluation is necessary, and hospitalization should be considered if the patient shows any signs of worsening. A total duration of therapy of 10 to 14 days is usually sufficient. A repeat chest x-ray should be taken probably 4 to 6 weeks following completion of antibiotic therapy. A persistent infiltrate this long after therapy should raise the suspicion of abnormal underlying lung pathology and lead to a more extensive work-up. In particular, an obstructing bronchial lesion in patients with a smoking history should be ruled out.

Certain patients who are at high risk for pneumonia should be considered for prophylaxis. In many patients, pneumococcal pneumonia may be preventable by immunization with a polyvalent pneumococcal polysaccharide vaccine. While this has proven to be effective in normal hosts, unfortunately it is not particularly effective in immuno-compromised patients. Even in patients with COPD, the efficacy of pneumococcal vaccine has been questioned. Yearly influenza vaccinations should be given to patients at high risk and to all older patients, because this decreases the at-tack rate of influenza as well as the morbidity and mortality due to secondary bacterial pneumonia.

Tuberculosis is preventable with prophylactic therapy, which should be provided for all patients who have a positive tuberculin test and an increased risk for reactivation. Indications for prophylaxis in patients with a positive skin test are shown in Table 61-21.

Lung Cancer

Although cardiac disease remains the most frequent cause of death in American women, mortality due to cancer continues to rise. Lung cancer is the most common cause of cancer mortality in both American women and men. In men, the incidence of lung cancer has either leveled off or declined. In women, overall rates continue to rise. Since the 1950s, the rate in women has risen over 400 percent. In 1992, lung cancer accounted for about 146,000 deaths. All projections for the future suggest that lung cancer mortality will continue to rise. Although it is expected that the rate of lung cancer in men will plateau through the 1990s, it is projected that the rate for women will continue to rise into the early 2000s before a decline and plateau are seen.

TABLE 61-21   Indications for Antituberculosis Chemoprophylaxis in a Patient with Positive Tuberculin Skin Test

Recent skin test converters

Patient less than 35 years of age from high-endemic area

History of tuberculosis without adequate treatment in the past

Chest roentgenogram consistent with prior tuberculosis

High risk of activation of latent disease
  HIV infection
  Alcohol and drug abuse
  Silicosis
  Chronic renal failure
  Malnutrition
  Diabetes mellitus
  Immunosuppressive therapy
  Malignancy

Risk Factors

The cause of lung cancer is multifactorial and includes cigarette smoking, occupational exposures, environmental factors, and diet. The most important and most modifiable of these factors is cigarette smoking. Tobacco is associated with approximately 90 percent of all lung cancers. The reduction of risk in males parallels the lower rates of male smoking, as the increasing rate in women correlates with their increasing use of cigarettes. Smoking cessation decreases lung cancer risk, but there is a long latency period from cessation to normalization of risk. The risks of lung cancer are increased in cigar and pipe smokers in relation to user inhalation practices. Smokeless tobacco has not been proven to be a risk factor for lung cancer.

Occupational carcinogens have also been identified as causes of human lung cancer. The most important of these are asbestos and radon. Smoking in these cohorts, especially in those with asbestos exposure, serves to augment the carcinogenic potential of such agents. Passive smoke accounts for the major environmental factor. Studies have confirmed that there is an increased risk of lung cancer from passive inhalation of cigarette smoke, which is directly proportional to the concentration of smoke in the environment.

Classification of Lung Cancer

Bronchogenic carcinoma of the lung is classified by histologic type. It is best divided into small-cell carcinoma and nonsmall-cell carcinoma, which includes squamous cell carcinoma, adenocarcinoma (which includes the subtype of bronchoalveolar cell carcinoma), large-cell carcinoma, and adenosquamous carcinoma. The most common cell types are squamous and adenocarcinoma, which account for about 60 percent of all carcinomas of the lung.

Symptoms and Clinical Features of Lung Cancer

At the time of presentation, nearly 90 percent of all patients with lung cancer are symptomatic. Symptoms like dyspnea, hemoptysis, cough, or chest pain may be related to the primary tumor, while evidence of hoarseness, dysphagia, and superior vena cava syndrome are usually due to regional spread. Lung cancer not infrequently presents with complaints referable to metastatic spread, particularly to bone or the central nervous system. Constitutional complaints may be nonspecific, such as anorexia, weight loss, weakness and fevers, or they may be a result of paraneoplastic endocrine or metabolic abnormalities. The more common of these paraneoplastic syndromes include Cushing's syndrome (usually associated with small-cell carcinoma), Lambert-Eaton myasthenic syndrome (LEMS) (a myasthenia-like syndrome associated with small-cell carcinoma), hypercalcemia (due to a PTH-like substance and associated with squamous cell carcinoma), and the syndrome of inappropriate ADH secretion (SIADH).

Initial assessment of the patient suspected of having lung cancer should consist of a complete history and physical examination, with the review of systems focusing on symptoms and signs suggestive of metastatic disease. The most important imaging study is the standard posteroanterior and lateral roentgenogram of the chest. There is considerable overlap in the radiographic abnormalities among the various cell types of bronchogenic carcinoma of the lung. However, central lesions are more characteristic of squamous cell or small-cell carcinoma, while peripheral lesions are usually adenocarcinoma, or, if particularly large in size, large-cell carcinoma. Other radiologic techniques become more useful in the staging of lung cancer and include computerized tomography (CT) of the chest and brain and nuclear imaging procedures, such as bone scanning.

There are two primary modalities for diagnosing the primary lesion in bronchogenic carcinoma: fiberoptic bronchoscopy and percutaneous needle biopsy. The sensitivity of bronchoscopy for central lesions is between 90 and 95 percent. For peripheral tumors of greater than 2 cm diameter, the sensitivity is between

60 and 75 percent, although some investigations have increased the yield significantly with bronchoalveolar lavage. Percutaneous needle biopsy has a greater sensitivity than bronchoscopy for solitary peripheral nodules, especially if the lesions are less than 2 cm. However, there is a significant complication rate of pneumothorax with this procedure (20 to 25 percent), and about 5 percent of these patients may require placement of a chest tube.

Once a tissue diagnosis is made, the staging process begins. There is an International Staging System of Lung Cancer done via the TNM system (T = primary tumor; N = regional lymph nodes; M = presence or absence of distant metastases). If a CT scan was not obtained as part of the initial diagnostic work-up, it is essential that one be done to assess the mediastinum for adenopathy. If significant adenopathy is present, then either mediastinoscopy or thoracoscopy is required to determine if they are involved. The chest CT should be extended down to the level of the adrenal glands to rule out what is usually asymptomatic involvement of this site.

If the physical examination or routine laboratory studies are suggestive, the search for distant metastases may include an abdominal or a head CT scan. The presence of a pleural effusion itself does not imply metastatic disease unless the cytology is positive.

The most important determinant of survival is the extent of the disease. Seventy-five percent of patients with squamous cell carcinoma die of complications of the thoracic tumor, and only 25 percent demonstrate extrathoracic spread at autopsy. Forty percent of the patients with adenocarcinoma and large-cell carcinoma die of intrathoracic complications, whereas 55 percent have evidence of distant metastases. Thirty percent of patients with small-cell carcinoma die of local tumor complications and 70 percent of disseminated carcinomatosis. Approximately 50 percent of patients with small-cell carcinoma, adenocarcinoma, or large-cell carcinoma have brain metastases at autopsy.

The treatment of nonsmall-cell carcinoma depends on the extent of the disease and the physiologic ability of the patient to withstand lung resection. Surgery is the only curative method available. Patients whose disease is confined to a single lung and its regional lymph nodes, and who are physiologically resectable, should always be considered for surgery. If the tumor has spread to the chest wall, diaphragm, or pericardium, even with ipsilateral mediastinal involvement, patients may be considered surgical candidates with the use of adjuvant or neoadjuvant therapies. Adjuvant or neoadjuvant therapies consist of chemotherapy, radiation therapy, or a combination of the two modalities. Patients with greater involvement or distant metastasis are not curable and may be treated with radiation, chemotherapy, or combination therapy, or given only symptomatic treatment.

For small-cell carcinoma, combination chemotherapy is the primary treatment of choice. Chest radiation has not been shown to be of benefit in extensive disease, but may be beneficial in combination with chemotherapy to patients with limited disease. For those patients with very localized disease, surgery as an adjuvant to aggressive chemotherapy may be beneficial, with 5-year survival rates approaching those seen in stage I nonsmall-cell carcinoma. Prophylactic whole-brain irradiation has been studied and has not been proven to be of any value in reducing the number of brain metastases found at autopsy.

Pulmonary Carcinoid

Pulmonary carcinoid, which was previously referred to as a bronchial adenoma, is a tumor thought to arise from the neuroendocrine system. This tumor has a slight female predominance, and the mean age at presentation is 45 years. This tumor is not related to cigarette smoking, and the diagnosis is not always easy to distinguish from small-cell carcinoma. It may present with cough, wheezing, or hemoptysis. Management is with complete surgical resection unless there is evidence of unresectability. Chemotherapy and radiation elicit a variable to poor response to treatment.

The Asymptomatic Coin Lesion

The *asymptomatic coin lesion* is defined as a mass up to about 6 cm in diameter. About three-fourths of these patients will be asymptomatic on presentation. Malignant disease is diagnosed in these patients about 50 percent of the time, and the likelihood of malignancy increases as age increases. A lesion greater than 3.5 cm and with a spicular contour suggests a malignant process. The pattern of calcification does not always exclude malignancy, but concentric lamellated rings, for instance, are almost always associated with benign lesions. Stability of the abnormal lesion over time, particularly 2 years or more, is more likely to be associated with a benign course and nature of disease. Unless the lesion can be shown to be stable or the pattern of calcification is clearly benign, the most expeditious approach is to remove the lesion as long as the patient is physiologically able to tolerate surgery.

References and Selected Readings

1. American Thoracic Society: Standards for the diagnosis and treatment of patients with chronic obstructive lung disease (COPD) and asthma. *Am Rev Respir Dis* 136:225–244, 1987.
2. Bone R, Dantzker DR, George R, et al: *Pulmonary and Critical Care Medicine.* St. Louis, MO: CV Mosby, 1993.
3. Matthay RA (ed): Lung cancer. *Clin Chest Med* 14:1, 1–200, 1993.
4. Cannon GW, Zimmerman G: *The Lung in Rheumatic Diseases.* New York: Marcel Dekker, 1990.
5. Alpern RJ: Southwestern Internal Medicine Conference: Vasculitis—It's time to reclassify. *Am J Med Sci* 309:235–48, 1995.
6. Prakash UBS: Pulmonary manifestations in systemic disease, in Baum GL, Wollinsky E (eds): *Textbook of Pulmonary Diseases,* 5th ed. Boston: Little, Brown, 1993, pp 1471–1746.
7. Cooper JAD (ed): Drug-induced pulmonary disease. *Clin Chest Med* 11:1, 1–189, 1990.
8. Rosenow EC III: Drug-induced pulmonary disease. *Dis Mon* 40:253–310, 1994.
9. Glynn TJ, Manley MW: *How to Help Your Patient Stop Smoking: A National Cancer Institute Manual for Physicians.* Bethesda, MD: Department of Health and Human Services, National Institutes of Health, National Cancer Institute, Division of Cancer Prevention and Control, Smoking, Tobacco and Cancer Program 1989. NIH Publication No. 89-3064.
10. Chediak AD, Krieger BP: Obstructive sleep apnea syndrome, in Bone RC (ed): *Pulmonary and Critical Care Medicine.* St. Louis, MO: CV Mosby, 1996.
11. Lieberman J: *Sarcoidosis.* Orlando, FL: Grune & Stratton, 1985.
12. Sharma OP (ed): Sarcoidosis. *Clin Chest Med* 18:4;663–874, 1997.
13. Moser KM: Venous thromboembolism. *Am Rev Respir Dis* 141:235–249, 1990.
14. Goldhaber SZ: Pulmonary embolism. *N Engl J Med* 339:2, 93–104, 1998.
15. National Asthma Education and Prevention Program: *Guidelines for the Diagnosis and Management of Asthma.* Bethesda, MD: US Department of Health and Human Services, National Heart, Lung and Blood Institute, 1997. Publication No. 97-4051C.
16. Niederman MS, Buss JB, Campbell GD, et al: Guidelines for the initial management of adults with community-acquired pneumonia: Diagnosis, assessment of severity and initial antimicrobial therapy. *Am Rev Respir Dis* 148:1418–1426, 1993.
17. Niederman MS (ed): Pulmonary disease in pregnancy. *Clin Chest Med* 13:4;555–740, 1992.
18. Occupational and environmental medicine: The internist's role. *Ann Intern Med* 113:974–982, 1990.
19. The PIOPED investigators: Value of ventilation/perfusion scan in pulmonary embolism. *JAMA* 263:2753–2754, 1990.
20. Rich S, Dantzker DR, Ayres SM, et al: Primary pulmonary hypertension: A national prospective study. *Ann Intern Med* 107:216–223, 1987.
21. Schwarz ML, King TE: *Interstitial Lung Disease.* Toronto: Decker, 1988.
22. Iseman MD, Huitt GA (eds): Tuberculosis. *Clin Chest Med* 18:1;1–168, 1997.

CHAPTER 62

Renal Disorders

John D. Wagner

Symptomatic Urinary Tract Disease

Urinary Tract Infections

Up to 50 percent of women experience a urinary tract infection (UTI) during their lifetime. Hence, UTIs are among the most common reasons why women seek medical care, with many experiencing recurrent infections. UTIs are divided into those that affect the lower tract (cystitis/urethritis) and those that affect the upper tract (acute pyelonephritis).

Patients with lower UTIs present with a variety of symptoms, including small-volume urinary frequency, nocturia, dysuria (the pain of which women may describe as "internal"), and lower abdominal discomfort. Patients with acute pyelonephritis may have some of these symptoms, as well as flank pain and fever. Depending on the severity of the infection, patients with upper tract infections may have nausea, vomiting, and prostration.

Although it is possible for the physician to render a diagnosis of simple cystitis based on a telephone conversation, using laboratory techniques, it is apparent that symptoms and signs occasionally do not clearly distinguish the anatomic site of infection. What appears to be simple cystitis really represents occult upper tract infection in some cases. Having the patient come to the office allows the physician to evaluate whether systemic toxicity, fever, or flank tenderness are absent. At that time, a urine reagent strip incorporating tests for nitrite and leukocyte esterase is approximately 85 percent reliable in confirming the presence of bacteriuria and/or pyuria in a freshly voided specimen. A high urine pH (greater than 7.5) suggests the presence of urea-splitting organisms.

If symptoms are compelling but the dipstick test is negative, microscopy can be performed to look for pyuria (more than five white blood cells on a high-power view of a centrifuged sediment). One should be aware that the degree of centrifugation and thickness of the urine sediment under the coverslip is subject to significant variability. Hence, pyuria defined by this technique does not correlate well with the technique of direct quantification of urinary white cells per cubic millimeter. Nonetheless, its simplicity has established it as the conventional standard.

Additional facts worth eliciting from patients with cystitis are whether UTIs have occurred in the past, the relationship of sexual activity to the onset of UTIs, the likelihood of pregnancy, clues to anatomic or functional disorders of the urinary tract, and whether the patient uses a diaphragm. If a nonpregnant woman has been symptomatic for 2 days or less, has no complicating drug allergies, no known urinary tract disease, and no prior UTIs for 6 months, one can initiate therapy without urine culture if the urinalysis is consistent with a UTI. The most common organisms causing UTIs are *E. coli,* other coliform bacteria, and *Staphylococcus saprophyticus.*

The enthusiasm for single-dose therapy has waned given the significant number of treatment failures. A notable exception is the relatively new oral antibiotic fosfomycin, which is given as a single dose. Three- to five-day courses of other oral antibiotics in uncomplicated lower tract disease offer a high cure rate. For women who are diabetic and/or pregnant, or whose symptoms have been present more than 2 days, a longer course of therapy is prudent (7 to 14 days). If not obtained initially, cultures need not be obtained unless the patient's symptoms fail to respond.

The reasons that an infection fails to respond to therapy include noncompliance with medication, upper tract infection, antibiotic resistance, or incorrect diagnosis. The pelvic exam will exclude some of the other potential diagnoses. These include periurethral inflammation from vaginitis or local lesions such as herpes. The 3-day course of antibiotics chosen for cystitis is not effective in the treatment of gonococcal or nongonococcal urethritis. Interstitial cystitis is a non-infectious bladder disorder associated with urinary frequency, nocturia, and suprapubic discomfort as the bladder distends. Hematuria may be the predominant urinary finding, and cystoscopy usually serves to confirm the diagnosis. Occasionally, passage of urinary stones or clots will provoke urinary frequency and dysuria. Usually, the urinalysis demonstrates hematuria as the predominant cellular abnormality.

The antibiotics used for 3 day therapy for an uncomplicated UTI include trimethoprim alone, combination sulfamethoxazole-trimethoprim, cephalosporins (such as cephalexin), nitrofurantoin, fluoroquinolones (ciprofloxacin, norfloxacin, ofloxacin, and others), and amoxicillin-clavulanate. Fluoroquinolones should not be used in pregnancy and sulfa drugs should be avoided late in pregnancy. Given the level of resistant organisms in the community, ampicillin is not recommended unless a sensitive organism is proven by culture. If a urine culture was done initially or is done because of an initial lack of response, the antibiotics can be adjusted according to sensitivity.

Non-toxic-appearing women with low-grade temperature or flank pain (presumed pyelonephritis) who otherwise are in good overall health, may also be treated with oral antibiotics if noncompliance is not an issue. The presence of nausea and vomiting usually preclude this approach. Infecting organisms are usually the coliforms responsible for cystitis, and the antibiotics chosen are largely the same. However, one prescribes a longer course (14 days) to treat pyelonephritis. If the patient worsens on therapy, or fails to respond within 3 days, parenteral therapy is advisable.

The laboratory evaluation of the patient with presumed pyelonephritis includes a urinalysis as well as urine culture, hemogram, BUN, creatinine, and glucose. Pregnancy should be excluded if appropriate. Laboratory investigation in excess of the urinalysis yields information that may be useful should the patient fail to respond as expected to the antibiotic course.

Other disorders that can mimic acute pyelonephritis include perirenal abscess; infected renal cyst (particularly seen in patients with polycystic kidney disease, an autosomal dominant disorder in adults); renal abscesses; non-renal infections with musculoskeletal back pain and fever; rare presentations of acute glomerulonephritis; renal infarction from thromboembolism or renal vein thrombosis; hemorrhage into a renal cyst; renal colic or obstruction from stones; blood clots; papillary necrosis; or neoplasms. Unusual presentations of lung or intraperitoneal disorders can sometimes mimic acute pyelonephritis.

The primary care practitioner must decide whether the patient is likely to have pyelonephritis that can be managed as an outpatient with oral antibiotics. If the diagnosis is in doubt and/ or if the appropriateness of oral therapy is in doubt, then an inpatient approach is preferable. Pyelonephritis can be diagnosed readily when flank pain, fever, lower tract symptoms, and pyuria are present. The urine culture and response to antibiotics will confirm the diagnosis. Some of the other disorders in the differential diagnosis will be apparent from the history and other features of the disease (for example, circulatory congestion in a patient with acute glomerulonephritis).

Women with lower tract infections, or a single, rapidly treatable episode of pyelonephritis, do not need to undergo radiological or cystoscopic evaluation of the urinary tract unless other symptoms prompt such an investigation. These women only rarely demonstrate anatomic disorders, and these do not usually lead to a different therapeutic approach. Patients whose UTIs do not readily respond to therapy or perhaps who have had prior episodes of pyelonephritis should undergo imaging studies. If azotemia is present, it is prudent to begin with a renal ultrasound. Urinary tract infection associated with obstruction requires prompt urological intervention to relieve the obstruction; stones, congenital abnormalities, and tumors are among the causes of such obstruction. Infected renal cysts, renal, or perirenal abscesses may require prolonged antibiotic therapy and drainage. Abnormalities of bladder emptying might be uncovered by additional studies. Rarely, radiocontrast imaging demonstrates evidence of renal infarction, a disorder manifested by flank pain and fever, although cultures are negative unless endocarditis has caused the infarction.

Women whose urological evaluation is unrevealing and whose urine cultures are negative may need to undergo evaluation for noninfectious renal parenchymal inflammatory disease (acute glomerulonephritis or interstitial nephritis) or for extrarenal disease producing the patient's symptoms. One might suspect nephritis in women with evidence of a multiorgan disorder, particularly when blood tests demonstrate unexplained renal insufficiency, or urinalysis reveals red blood cell casts and proteinuria.

For women with frequent UTIs, various strategies have been proposed to reduce the recurrence rate. Adjunctive measures include increasing fluid intake, switching from a diaphragm to another method of contraception, and increased care to avoid fecal contamination of the vagina. Estrogen therapy has been proposed as beneficial in preventing UTIs in postmenopausal women. Patients with recurrent cystitis might be offered the option of self-treatment at the earliest sign of a lower UTI; low-dose prophylaxis on a three times weekly schedule, or postcoital prophylaxis. Drugs for prophylaxis include trimethoprim with or without sulfa.

Urolithiasis

About 1 in 30 women are affected by kidney stones (roughly half the rate of men). The clinical manifestations range from a women plagued by severe pain to an incidental finding on x-rays done for another purpose. Colicky flank pain radiating anteriorly to the groin may be a presenting symptom. The patient may complain of urinary frequency and dysuria, particularly if the stone is lodged in the distal ureter. Alternatively, she may observe hematuria. Symptoms of infection may coexist with stone symptoms.

Historical clues to the presence of stones include passage of gravel or prior stones, a family history of stone disease, in postmenopausal women a gouty diathesis, coexisting inflammatory bowel disease, or dietary habits favoring intake of large amounts of certain foods, or brewed tea. Women regularly exposed to a hot climate or who exert themselves strenuously on a frequent basis without adequate hydration create favorable conditions for stone formation. High calcium intake in the absence of a metabolic predisposition to unusually efficient gut calcium absorption (absorptive hypercalciuria) should not lead to urolithiasis.

If the woman's pain is intolerable, the diagnosis of urolithiasis is often made in the Emergency

Room. The differential diagnosis includes the multitude of causes of an acute abdomen, and the patient requires an expeditious evaluation. If the patient appears stable and is afebrile, and etiologies of the pain that require immediate treatment (e.g., ectopic pregnancy) have been ruled out, an outpatient evaluation is usually appropriate. Mild costovertebral angle tenderness may be present, but physical findings are usually nonspecific.

A urinalysis will reveal hematuria. The dipstick should suffice as a screen for hematuria, but microscopy is needed to confirm the presence of red blood cells and to allow a search for crystals. Red blood cell casts should not be present, and if seen, suggest another diagnosis. Pyuria may be variably present. Concomitant urinary tract infection should be excluded by culture. While cystine crystals are diagnostic of cystinuria, an autosomal recessive disease, uric acid, calcium oxalate, or phosphate crystals may be seen in normal women. However, marked crystalluria is suggestive of urolithiasis. Low urine pH favors uric acid stones; high pH favors calcium phosphate stones. A concentrated urine metabolically predisposes to all types of stones.

Blood screening with a blood urea nitrogen (BUN), serum creatinine, potassium, chloride, total CO_2, calcium, and uric acid provides information about whether renal function is normal (obstruction may result in azotemia), and whether certain metabolic risk factors for stone formation are present (hypercalcemia, hyperuricemia, renal tubular acidosis). The definitive diagnosis of stone disease is made either if the woman collects the passed stone or by radiological imaging.

A plain film of the abdomen (KUB) serves to indicate if a calcium-containing stone is present (most stones fall into that category); pure uric acid stones are radiolucent. Infection stones (struvite) and cystine are radiodense, but less so than calcium oxalate. In the absence of allergy, azotemia, or pregnancy, an intravenous pyelogram is usually indicated to localize the stones and to exclude obstruction. Ultrasonography and CT scanning also contribute to the evaluation of stone disease. Ultrasound is particularly useful in women in whom radiocontrast or x-rays are undesirable.

If radiologic imaging confirms stone disease, urological intervention should be sought for relief of complete obstruction or when stone size greater than 5 mm makes spontaneous passage unlikely. The patient can be instructed to strain her urine. If at all possible, retrieved stones should be sent for analysis. The stone analysis should include information about what comprises the center of the stone as well as its outer layers.

Oral hydration and analgesics may allow outpatient management, but severe pain prompts hospitalization. Stones that are likely to be uric acid (radiolucent on x-ray) may shrink and pass if the urine is alkalinized. The alkalinizing agent of choice is potassium citrate, although some patients cannot tolerate this drug because of gastrointestinal intolerance or hyperkalemia. Sodium bicarbonate is an alternative alkalinizing agent, but it increases calcium excretion and may predispose to calcium stone formation. If spontaneous passage of the stone is not an option, the present urologic techniques of percutaneous stone extraction and lithotripsy allow stone removal without the morbidity and inconvenience attendant with an open procedure.

Apart from defining the chemical nature of the stone, it is important to delineate the metabolic risk factors for stone formation, an oft-neglected aspect of stone management. Although it is simple to do the testing, one needs to interpret the results with care. A 24-hour collection of urine for volume, pH, sodium, uric acid, and calcium might serve as an initial screening test for patients with known uric acid or calcium stone disease. If a radiologically identified stone is not densely calcified, a qualitative cystine screen can be done as well.

Depending on the results of the initial screen, one may want to also measure urinary oxalate, citrate, phosphate, and magnesium. For hypercalciuric patients, some would proceed further with urinary testing on calcium-restricted diets followed by measurement of calcium excretion after an oral load. Therapeutic intervention to reduce the risk for stone disease may be best achieved by those clinicians with specific expertise in this subject. However, in most patients, encouragement of at least 2 liters of daily water intake spread throughout the course of the day into the evening is appropriate. This will result in the passage of a dilute urine containing lower concentrations of all stone constituents.

Non-stone Causes of Renal Colic

Renal colic can also be produced by the passage of blood clots or sloughed renal papilla. The intravenous pyelogram will demonstrate papillary necrosis or may indicate tumor-associated urinary tract bleeding. Papillary necrosis is seen in patients with severe acute pyelonephritis, sickle cell disease, analgesic abuse, and diabetes mellitus. It is important to recognize when papillary necrosis is associated with infection and obstruction. Such patients require relief of obstruction and antibiotic therapy, presumably in a hospital setting. Identifying clots from a bleeding tumor will prompt referral to the urologist. Occasionally, the upper tract bleeding site is not evident from the usual radiological studies. Some of these patients have glomerular renal disease; some have vascular anomalies. Input from a nephrologist may be helpful.

Other causes of renal colic have been mentioned above. Bleeding into a renal cyst, particularly in a patient with polycystic kidney disease, may produce flank symptoms, although one would not expect radiation to the groin. An obscure disorder, loin pain hematuria syndrome, manifests as expected. Its cause is unclear. Variable obstruction from intrinsic or extrinsic lesions of the urinary tract may cause flank pain which waxes and wanes. Renal infarction was mentioned earlier.

Occasionally, women present with poorly localizing symptoms of urinary tract pain, which might be confused as musculoskeletal back pain, irritable bowel disease, or another non-renal disorder. In the assessment of abdominal, back, or pelvic complaints, one must keep in mind the possibility of renal obstructive lesions. Retroperitoneal disease may result in no discernible abnormalities on urinalysis, and unilateral obstruction may not change renal function enough to produce a recognized elevation in BUN or creatinine. Occasionally, the renal etiology is inadvertently discovered during x-ray studies designed to elucidate skeletal or gastrointestinal pathology. Inflammatory masses from diverticular disease, Crohn's disease, retroperitoneal fibrosis, or metastatic retroperitoneal deposits are some of the causes of obstructive uropathy. Renal obstruction may also occur secondary to gynecologic disorders. By maintaining an index of suspicion, one can make the diagnosis of renal obstruction by any of a variety of imaging studies: IVP, ultrasound, CT, nuclear renography.

Edema

Women who complain of edema challenge the clinician to distinguish between a variety of ailments. The presence of lower extremity edema, which may worsen towards the end of the day, is consistent with either local anatomic disease or total body salt and water overload. Local disease may stem from chronic venous insufficiency, arthritic knee effusions, or from more ominous acute phlebitis or neoplastic lymphatic obstruction. Upper extremity, trunk, or facial puffiness should be absent; the legs may be asymmetrically edematous. Recumbency may not eliminate the edema, although the swelling may diminish. The edema of renal disease is generalized, although the total salt and water accumulation may be such that the patient notices only the effect of gravity in inducing lower extremity swelling.

The edema of renal parenchymal disease may be on the basis of intravascular congestion leading to interstitial extravasation of salt and water, or it may be on the basis of the nephrotic syndrome leading to hypoalbuminemia and a redistribution of salt and water to the extravascular space. In either case, renal sodium retention results in a period of positive sodium and water balance. An example of intravascular congestion is acute poststreptococcal glomerulonephritis. Affected patients classically have symptoms and signs of vascular congestion (dyspnea, hypertension, increased jugular venous pressure, pulmonary crackles). An example of nephrotic syndrome is minimal change disease, which induces heavy proteinuria (more than $3.5 \text{ g}/1.73 \text{ m}^2/\text{day}$) and hypoalbuminemia. Diseases leading to renal failure can provoke edema by diminishing the filtered load of sodium to the renal tubules as the glomerular filtration rate falls. An incomplete ability to balance salt excretion with intake results in a positive sodium balance. The increase in total body salt and water produces edema, vascular congestion, and hypertension.

Both heart and liver failure can activate renal sodium retention. One should attempt to elicit historical clues pointing to these disorders in approaching the patient with edema. Stigmata of chronic liver disease and a palpably abnormal liver make the case for cirrhotic edema. Differentiating circulatory congestion on the basis of cardiac failure from renal disease can be difficult on examination, although one should take note of the history and findings of S3 gallops and significant cardiac murmurs.

Certain commonly taken medications can be associated with edema, notably estrogen preparations and nonsteroidal anti-inflammatory agents. An entity known as idiopathic edema or cyclic idiopathic edema is a waxing and waning sodium retentive state described only in females, some of whom took diuretics. In these women who took medication, cessation of diuretic use provoked an exaggerated renal avidity for sodium. In some of the women described, the patients took the diuretic initially not for true edema, but inappropriately for weight reduction.

The diagnosis of renal edema gains support by the finding of elevated levels of blood urea nitrogen and creatinine; proteinuria of 200 mg/ dl or more on a random urine specimen; 24-h excretion rates of 2 g or more of protein (3.5 g/ 1.73 m^2 body surface area in nephrotic syndrome); hypoalbuminemia in association with such proteinuria; and urine sediment activity (red cells with or without white blood cells and cellular casts). Patients with nephrotic syndrome classically have hyperlipidemia as well. Further evaluation of such evidence of renal parenchymal disease may benefit from the participation of a nephrologist.

Nonspecific Symptoms Related to Electrolyte Disturbances and Azotemia

The symptoms associated with advanced azotemia or electrolyte disorders are numerous and nonspecific. Blood tests incorporating a BUN, creatinine, sodium, potassium, chloride, and total CO_2 should be obtained in patients with somatic complaints whose etiology are unclear.

The differential diagnosis and treatment of acute renal failure are presented in Tables 62-1 and 62-2. Some of the etiologies of chronic renal failure and the treatment of chronic renal failure are presented in Tables 62-3 and 62-4.

TABLE 62-1 Etiologies of Acute Renal Failure

Prerenal
  Volume depletion
  Congestive heart failure
  Cirrhosis
  NSAID or ACE inhibitor therapy
  Renal artery stenosis

Intrinsic Renal Disease
  Glomerulonephritis
  Drug-induced interstitial nephritis
  Acute tubular necrosis
  Embolic disease
  Postpartum renal failure

Postrenal
  Obstruction secondary to urinary tract, retroperitoneal, or
    pelvic tumors
  Obstruction secondary to urolithiasis
  Obstruction secondary to extrinsic inflammatory masses
    (retroperitoneal fibrosis, abscesses)
  Neurogenic bladder
  Congenital obstruction diagnosed in adulthood

TABLE 62-2 Treatment of Acute Renal Failure Based on Etiology

Prerenal Etiology
  Treat dehydration, excessive diuresis, other causes of a diminished effective arterial blood volume
  If related to cardiac or liver disease, address primary problem while providing supportive therapy.
  If medication related, discontinue drug
  If related to renal artery stenosis, angioplasty or surgical revascularization

Intrinsic Renal Disease
  If etiology appears to be inflammatory renal disease, assess for evidence of multisystem disorder by careful history, physical, and laboratory testing. Renal biopsy may be useful.
  Discontinue unnecessary medications.
  Supportive care.
  Identify and treat infections

Postrenal Etiology
  Utilize surgical or interventional radiological techniques to bypass or eliminate obstruction (upper tract obstruction); bladder catheterization (lower tract)

Chronic renal failure may remain asymptomatic until the glomerular filtration rate falls to less than 10 percent of normal. The degree of azotemia found at such low levels of function depends on factors such as the magnitude of dietary protein intake, but a BUN of 100 mg/dl accompanying a serum creatinine of about 8 mg/dl roughly correlates to a glomerular filtration

TABLE 62-3 Some Etiologies of Chronic Renal Failure

Systemic Disease Affecting the Kidney
  Diabetes mellitus
  Hypertension
  Systemic lupus
  Vasculitis
  HIV-associated nephropathy

Renal Parenchymal Disease
  Chronic glomerulonephritis with or without specific etiology (focal and segmental glomerulosclerosis, membranous nephropathy)
  Polycystic kidney disease
  Chronic interstitial nephritis (analgesic abuse, chronic hypercalcemia, idiopathic)
  Long-standing renal obstruction

TABLE 62-4 Treatment of Chronic Renal Failure

Address underlying systemic disease (such as immunosuppressive therapy for lupus)
Control blood pressure (ACE inhibitors are preferred in glomerular disorders if not contraindicated)
Avoid agents that might interfere with renal function when possible (such as NSAIDs)
Low-protein diets may be helpful in proteinuric renal disease
Monitor for secondary hyperparathyroidism and treat
Epoetin therapy for anemia of chronic renal failure
Dialysis or transplantation at appropriate time

---

rate (GFR) at which symptoms might develop. Diseases that cause acute renal failure may induce symptoms at lower levels of BUN and creatinine.

Features of advanced azotemia include anorexia, lassitude, weight loss, muscular cramps, hiccupping, pruritus, twitching, headache, nausea, vomiting, chest pain from pericarditis, and bone pain from renal osteodystrophy. If azotemia is moderate (BUN less than 50), and one is uncertain if vague symptoms are likely to be on the basis of uremia, a 24-h urine for creatinine and urea excretion will allow the determination of creatinine and urea clearances. As renal function approaches low levels, the creatinine clearance tends to overestimate the glomerular filtration rate. By averaging the urea and creatinine clearances, one may get a truer picture of the level of function. With clearances less than 15 ml/min/1.73 m^2, renal failure may account for the symptoms enumerated above, although they need not be present. However, because they are nonspecific symptoms, evidence of other possible etiologies should not be overlooked. Some patients with symptomatic azotemia will need immediate referral to a nephrologist.

Headache, anorexia, muscular twitching, somnolence, nausea, and vomiting are manifestations of hyponatremia. The degree of symptoms depends on the rapidity with which hyponatremia develops, and the absolute level of serum sodium. Usually women with serum sodium levels greater than 130 mEq are not symptomatic from hyponatremia. Symptoms are more likely at values of 125 mEq or less, and symptomatic or significant hyponatremia requires immediate medical intervention.

To evaluate the asymptomatic, mildly hyponatremic patient, one should confirm the abnormality with a repeat serum sodium and get a serum and urine osmolality as well. One should assess the volume status of the patient. If she is hypovolemic from vomiting, diarrhea, or diuretics, salt and water repletion should correct the disorder.

In patients with euvolemic hyponatremia, one should exclude adrenal and thyroid insufficiency, cirrhosis, and renal failure by history and physical examination. A BUN and creatinine will exclude renal insufficiency. Additional lab testing can exclude the other diagnoses if necessary. Medications that can cause hyponatremia include thiazide diuretics, certain psychotropic drugs, anticonvulsants, and chemotherapeutic agents. If appropriate, medications can be changed. Certain neoplasms, lung, and CNS disorders can yield the syndrome of inappropriate antidiuretic hormone. A thorough history and physical examination should direct any additional investigations for these possibilities.

Hypervolemic hyponatremia is present in patients with edematous disorders: congestive heart failure, cirrhosis, and nephrotic syndrome. Diuretics and fluid restriction may be appropriate therapy.

Although neurological symptoms may accompany hypernatremia, the water losses that invariably account for this disorder are usually what brings the patient to medical attention. Diarrhea, vomiting, excessive diuretic use, and uncontrolled glycosuria in diabetic patients are the usual causes. Management often requires parenteral fluids in an inpatient setting.

A disturbance in thirst and renal concentration in elderly women may result in varying degrees of hypernatremia. Central or nephrogenic diabetes mellitus rarely provokes hypernatremia, when the urinary losses exceed the ability of the patient to replace fluid orally. These patients have large urine volumes (in excess of 2 liters per day). Investigation of these disorders requires inpatient testing.

Hypo- or hyperkalemia can lead to muscle weakness and arrhythmias, usually with values of potassium <3 or >6 mEq/l. Patients with these symptoms require urgent intervention to normalize potassium levels. Women with mild asymptomatic hypokalemia (>3.0 mEq) with underlying cardiac disease can be given a potassium supplement while an explanation for their problem is sought. Diuretic use is the usual cause. Other possibilities include extrarenal losses from diarrhea, or vomiting, or renal losses from osmotic diuresis from glycosuria, or from rare endocrine and renal tubular disorders. Urine electrolytes (sodium, potassium, and chloride) will help direct the diagnostic approach. For example, surreptitious vomiting or laxative abuse might be suggested by unexplained hypokalemia accompanied by a low urine chloride.

Certain drugs (potassium-sparing diuretics, angiotensin-converting enzyme inhibitors, nonsteroidal anti-inflammatory agents); renal failure; diabetes or sickle cell induced tubular defects; or renal obstruction are among the causes of hyperkalemia. Potassium levels of 6.0 mEq/l or more require immediate attention. Patients with lesser values also should receive prompt care if the disorder is confirmed. In the meantime, potassium supplements should be discontinued.

Acid-base disorders in primary care usually present in association with obvious related problems. For example, patients with uncontrolled diabetes may develop ketoacidosis, characterized by polyuria, polydipsia, malaise, and other symptoms. Occasionally, one comes across minor abnormalities in the total CO_2 content of an electrolyte profile. For example, diuretics may induce a mild metabolic alkalosis producing a slightly higher CO_2 value. Pregnancy usually results in a lower value related to a chronic respiratory alkalosis. The differential diagnosis of acid-base disorders is extensive. If the CO_2 consistently deviates from normal by more than 2 mEq/l, one may wish to have the patient evaluated for a metabolic or respiratory acid-base disturbance of consequence such as renal tubular acidosis, chronic respiratory alkalosis from heart failure or intrinsic lung disease, chronic hypercapnia from neuromuscular disorders, etc.

Urinary Frequency

Patients occasionally present with complaints of passing urine frequently. One needs to distinguish between problems of bladder function and frequent voiding related to the passage of atypical amounts of urine. Nocturia may or may not accompany daytime frequency.

If the urinary concentrating mechanism is intact, and if patients drink less than 2 liters of fluid a day, urine output should also be less than 2 liters a day. If fluid intake diminishes in the evening, an intact renal concentrating mechanism will increase the urinary concentration such that the average patient should have less urine to pass during the night than during the day. Hence, patients usually do not need to urinate after retiring to sleep. The first voided urine of the morning should reflect urinary concentration (urine specific gravity more than 1.015). The need to pass larger amounts of urine obligates more frequent voiding. If larger volumes of urine are passed throughout the 24-h period, nocturia will result.

In evaluating patients with urinary frequency, symptoms suggestive of local bladder problems are usually not difficult to elicit if present. Infection or inflammation, bladder outlet dysfunction, or extrinsic bladder compression may result in small volume, frequent voids throughout the day and night. Besides the genitourinary exam, urinalysis and urine culture may be helpful. Patients whose symptoms and examination do not clearly point to a lower tract etiology may be experiencing polyuria. A 24-h urine volume should be helpful, particularly if the patient is willing to record the volume of each void. The urine should be assayed for osmolality, protein, creatinine, and sodium. If the urinalysis indicates glycosuria or if the patient is diabetic, the 24-h urine can also be used to quantify the glycosuria.

Causes of polyuria include solute diuresis from glycosuria (diabetic patients), or diuretic use, water diuresis from increased fluid intake unrelated to renal disease, or solute diuresis consequent to kidneys that are unable to concentrate maximally to maintain fluid balance. Patients who habitually drink large volumes of fluid may be difficult to differentiate from those whose obligatory renal salt and water losses drive the thirst mechanism. The latter group of patients includes patients with central or nephrogenic diabetes insipidus. The search for such disorders is prompted by the finding of polyuria (more than 2 liters of urine output per day), particularly if accompanied by hypernatremia (diabetes insipidus patients), hyponatremia (compulsive water drinking patients), or a urine specific gravity less than 1.010 measured on the first voided urine of the day. Patients with urinary frequency without polyuria, infection, or known bladder pathology might be further studied with urodynamics.

Screening and Management of Abnormal Findings

Although urinalysis is one of the most frequently performed laboratory tests, its true value in altering patient outcome when used to screen truly asymptomatic patients is not established. Perhaps up to 18 percent of unselected patients will have abnormalities on reagent strip testing in a general practice setting. The ease with which such testing is done has to be compared to the difficulty in consistently obtaining the complete and accurate histories from patients that would allow one to be certain that a patient is in fact asymptomatic. Hence, I believe it is reasonable to offer reagent strip testing of urine on a yearly basis unless it is shown conclusively that false-positive results outweigh the benefits.

The reagent strip should include tests for pH, protein, heme pigment, nitrite, and leukocyte esterase. Strip testing of specific gravity is also available if one prefers that to the other techniques of measurement of this parameter. The sensitivities of the reagent chemicals for the detection of clinically significant hematuria, pyuria, and bacteriuria are high. Urine microscopy can be reserved for specimens with dipstick abnormalities or for patients with symptoms.

The specimen should be examined microscopically when freshly voided, in order to observe formed elements before degradation. Ten ml of urine should be centrifuged for 5 minutes at about 2500 rpm. After decanting all but 0.1 ml of supernatant, resuspend the sediment, and place under a coverslip. The relationship of formed elements per unit volume in unspun urine to that seen per high-power field is quite variable. Despite this imprecision, the number of cells observed by this method forms the basis for determining which women need further evaluation for hematuria and pyuria.

Hematuria (Table 62-5)

Microscopic hematuria, defined as more than three to five red blood cells on multiple high-power views of centrifuged urine, will cause a positive dipstick reaction. Although ingested substances (such as phenazopyridine) occasionally render a reddish tinge to urine and lead to patient concern, the dipstick should remain negative. If the reagent strip indicates the presence of heme, one needs to perform microscopy to confirm that red cells are present. The povidone disinfectant solution used to cleanse the meatus can cause a false-positive result.

Myoglobin released from the breakdown of muscle will also cause a positive reaction, but red cells are usually absent (unless renal parenchymal injury has resulted). Strenuous muscular activity, such as long distance running, or viral illnesses may provoke rhabdomyolysis. One can confirm the identity of the compound causing a positive dipstick as myoglobin by obtaining a urine myoglobin test. If myoglobinuria seems likely, one should also obtain a blood urea nitrogen, serum creatinine, and electrolyte panel. If the patient appears ill, notes a reduced urine

TABLE 62-5   Evaluation of Hematuria

1. Confirm with microscopy and repeat urinalysis (patient should submit specimen after refraining from exercise and, if feasible, when not febrile).

2. Exclude urinary tract infection with culture if pyuria is present without RBC casts.

3. (a) If RBC casts and/or more than 200 mg/dL protein, check BUN, creatinine, and electrolytes, and 24-hour urine protein and creatinine. If new azotemia is present, evaluate quickly for systemic or primary renal inflammatory disease (may require renal biopsy). If patient has stable renal function, order serologic work-up and assess need for biopsy as indicated by history and physical (differential diagnosis may include vasculitis, lupus, poststreptococcal glomerulonephritis).

   (b) Isolated hematuria without casts or heavy proteinuria: Image kidneys (IVP unless contraindicated). If anatomic or stone disease, evaluate further as indicated.

4. Normal imaging: In young patients obtain 24-h urine for calcium and uric acid. Treat confirmed hyperuricosuria (allopurinol) or hypercalciuria (thiazides) if present to remit hematuria. Obtain hemoglobin electrophoresis in patients at risk for sickle hemoglobinopathy.

5. For other than young women or for those with persistent hematuria without other explanation: cystoscopy

6. If cytoscopy is negative, consider more detailed imaging studies (such as CT, retrograde pyelography, or angiography), urinalysis of family members to exclude familial hematuria syndromes, TB skin testing and urine cultures for acid-fast bacilli, and renal biopsy. The order in which one chooses to do any of these studies depends on the patient's history and physical, and one's index of suspicion.

output, or manifests azotemia, she may require immediate hospitalization.

If red blood cell casts accompany microscopic or gross hematuria, the patient has renal parenchymal inflammatory disease until proven otherwise. Proteinuria, particularly at a level greater than 200 mg/dl, is highly suggestive of renal inflammatory disease as well.

In evaluating a woman who presents because of what turns out to be hematuria, one must perform a careful review of systems in search of clues to the possibility of a multisystem disorder. For example, the diagnosis of systemic lupus erythematosus first might come to light because of urinary tract manifestations. At that point, careful questioning might reveal the presence of joint, skin, and constitutional symptoms. The physical examination should be particularly thorough, with a focus on how sick the patient appears, whether hypertension or fever is present, and whether she manifests salt and water overload (edema is present, and/or there are abnormalities on the lung examination).

Laboratory evaluation should include a chemistry profile and a complete blood count with platelet count. Results should be available in a timely fashion. Patients who appear sick, who exhibit obvious multisystem disease, or who manifest renal insufficiency may require immediate hospitalization.

If there is doubt as to the source of the urinary tract bleeding, quantification of a 24-h urine for protein is useful in identifying patients in whom glomerular disease is highly likely. More than 2 g of proteinuria per 24 h is particularly suggestive of glomerular disease. Definitive diagnosis of a glomerular disease may require the input of a nephrologist. Furthermore, if glomerular disease is excluded, further evaluation of the etiology of hematuria is probably in order.

If red blood cell casts or heavy proteinuria are not present, then the anatomic site of urinary tract bleeding is unclear. One should exclude urinary tract infection if pyuria is present. Tuberculosis of the urinary tract may manifest as "sterile" pyuria with hematuria, although this is indeed a rare diagnosis. Mycobacterial culture of the urine should be sought if other diagnoses are not forthcoming.

In the absence of pyuria or dysuria, or if the predominant urinary finding is hematuria with or without urinary tract pain, one needs to investigate the gross anatomy of the urinary tract. Persistence of microscopic hematuria should be confirmed with additional specimens.

Neoplastic processes usually occur in middle age, but should be sought in any female with unexplained hematuria. One should exclude renal insufficiency by chemistry profiling and then proceed to an intravenous pyelogram if not contraindicated by allergy. One may choose to substitute renal ultrasound or CT without intravenous contrast if contraindications to IVP are present (such as allergy or renal insufficiency).

If evaluation of the upper urinary tract is negative, evaluation of the lower tract with cystoscopy and cytology is usually appropriate. The discovery of primary urinary tract neoplasia prompts urologic consultation. The finding of nonobstructive stone disease can be evaluated further before referral if one wishes. Occasionally, one discovers previously unsuspected anatomic abnormalities such as congenital ureteropelvic obstruction or polycystic kidney disease during the course of investigation of hematuria. Anatomic urinary tract disease usually prompts urological consultation. Polycystic disease, usually inherited as an autosomal dominant disease when diagnosed in adults, may lead to urinary tract infection, pain, hypertension, and renal insufficiency. Nephrologic input in the care of such patients is useful.

Papillary necrosis is another hematuria-producing renal disorder that is readily identified on intravenous pyelogram. Risk factors include sickle cell disease, diabetes mellitus, analgesic abuse, and obstructive uropathy. Infection and secondary renal obstruction from sloughed renal papillae may complicate the disease and require management. Hence, such patients often do not present with simple asymptomatic hematuria.

Occasionally, women exhibit hematuria despite normal gross anatomy of the urinary tract and no evidence for renal inflammatory disease (that is, urinary casts, heavy proteinuria, and renal insufficiency are not present). Some of these patients have occult glomerular disease such as IgA nephropathy or thin basement membrane disease. Applicable at-risk populations with sickle cell disease or trait can develop microhematuria from renal medullary microinfarcts. Sickle cell screening may be helpful in identifying patients at risk for this disorder. Hypercalciuria and/or hyperuricosuria without gross calculous disease have also been implicated in causing hematuria. Twenty-four-hour urine measurement of calcium and uric acid excretion will clarify whether microhematuria might stem from an excess of these minerals. Angiography may indicate vascular anomalies as the cause of urinary tract bleeding.

Some of these hematuria producing conditions are not specifically treated and the probability of a yield from extensive evaluation is difficult to predict. How aggressively to pursue a diagnosis of hematuria is usually decided on a case-by-case basis. Urologic and nephrologic input are helpful.

Proteinuria (Table 62-6)

Normal urinary protein excretion does not exceed 150 mg per day. The urinary dipstick detects albumin in concentrations from 30 mg/dl to more than 300 mg/dl. Depending on how concentrated the urine is, the dipstick might read up to 100 mg/dl on random specimens. Protein excretion can increase beyond the upper limit of normal with exercise or fever, even in women without renal parenchymal disease. Certain younger individuals manifest postural proteinuria, whereby the upright position is associated with increased levels of urinary protein. Recumbency returns the protein excretion to the normal range. "Overflow" proteinuria occurs when an increased production of filtered proteins overwhelms the ability of the nephron to prevent their appearance in the excreted urine. This situation occurs in patients with multiple myeloma who excrete light chains. Glomerular proteinuria occurs when the glomerular filtration barrier fails to restrain the passage of serum proteins from the blood to Bowman's space. This protein leakage occurs in diseases affecting the glomerulus, such as various forms of glomerulonephritis and diabetic nephropathy.

Women with elevated BUN and/or creatinine, diabetes mellitus, or persistent proteinuria on reagent-strip testing of more than 30 mg/dl warrant

TABLE 62-6 Evaluation of Isolated Proteinuria

1. If urinalysis indicates more than 100 mg/dl proteinuria on random specimen or any degree of proteinuria is associated with azotemia, check BUN, creatinine, glucose, and 24-h urine protein. Urine collection should be obtained with patient refraining from exercise. Ideally, patient should not have fever or decompensated congestive heart failure at time of collection.

2. Exclude postural proteinuria: divide 24-h collection into ambulatory and recumbent time periods. If proteinuria is absent during recumbency, reassure patient that she has benign findings.

3. Evaluate diabetic patient with microalbumin to creatinine on random urine specimen. If elevated, obtain 24-hour urine collection.

4. Consider immunoelectrophoresis of blood and urine to evaluate proteinuria further in middle-aged and older women. If monoclonal gammopathy is found, consider multiple myeloma, amyloidosis, other dysproteinemias.

5. If proteinuria is less than 2 g, and hypertension, renal insufficiency, and diabetes are absent, image kidneys to look for renal scarring or obstruction. If imaging study is normal, observe patient over time to assess whether proteinuria is increasing and/or azotemia is developing.

6. Differential diagnosis of more than 3 g of proteinuria in a nondiabetic female includes diseases causing nephrotic syndrome (hypoalbuminemia, hyperlipidemia, lipiduria) such as minimal change disease, membranous nephropathy, focal and segmental glomerular sclerosis, and amyloidosis. Renal biopsy may be warranted.

7. If diabetes is present in patients with abnormal protein excretion, assess for presence of retinopathy (supports diagnosis of diabetes as cause of renal disease). Optimize glycemic control, control hypertension (use ACE inhibitor if not contraindicated), and consider prescribing low-protein diet.

the collection of a 24-h urine for measurement of protein and creatinine. Dividing the 24-h period into daytime and recumbent collections serves to distinguish nonpathologic postural proteinuria from fixed proteinuria. Patients with orthostatic proteinuria excrete all their urinary protein when in the upright position. These women should have periodic assessments that include measurement of blood pressure, urinalyses, and

24-h urine protein excretions. One would expect them to remain normotensive, urine sediments should stay benign, and their protein excretion pattern should not change. If fixed proteinuria, hypertension, and abnormal urinalysis or azotemia became manifest, nephrologic evaluation is advisable.

Immunoprotein electrophoresis of blood and urine identifies those women with overflow proteinuria related to monoclonal gammopathy, and these tests might be obtained in patients with unexplained proteinuria, particularly if unexplained anemia is present. Patients with monoclonal immunoproteins in blood or urine should be referred for further evaluation. The differential diagnosis includes multiple myeloma and primary amyloidosis.

Women who do not have evidence of systemic disease and who have abnormal urine protein excretion rates less than 2 g per day as their sole urinary abnormality (no red cells, white cells, cellular casts, azotemia, hypertension, or edema) can be followed with periodic surveillance for systemic disease or additional renal disorders (hypertension, edema, azotemia, active urine sediment). An increase of protein excretion into the nephrotic range or the development of additional signs and symptoms should prompt a re-evaluation.

Females with nephrotic-range proteinuria (3.5 g protein excretion/1.73 m^2/day) may or may not have normal renal function, normotension, and an acellular urinary sediment. Most of these patients have some form of primary or secondary glomerular disease. Often they are diagnosed with the aid of a renal biopsy. The input of a nephrologist should be sought for such patients.

Pyuria

Women who have no urinary tract symptoms may have pyuria. It is important to exclude vaginal contamination of the specimen. Some of these patients have silent bacterial infections; some have interstitial renal disease. Genitourinary mycobacterial disease rarely presents as "sterile" pyuria. Appropriate cultures may elucidate whether infection is the cause of pyuria. One should also obtain a chemistry profile to assess whether azotemia is present. If it is, one proceeds to investigate for causes of azotemia as outlined above.

The need to treat asymptomatic bacteriuria unassociated with known urinary tract disorders is unclear. Pregnant women have an increased risk of symptomatic urinary tract infection. These patients should receive antibiotics.

BUN, Creatinine, and Electrolytes

Blood testing of truly asymptomatic nonpregnant women is also an ill-defined area. In the absence of some evidence of possible urinary system disease, the outpatient determination of BUN, creatinine, and electrolytes is not clearly cost-effective, but certainly any abnormalities uncovered might be meaningful. I believe that it is reasonable to screen for azotemia or electrolyte disorders in truly asymptomatic women at least once before age 40, and perhaps every few years after age 40. Women with diseases known to affect the kidney, such as systemic lupus or diabetes mellitus, obviously need more frequent testing. Women who will need repetitive therapy with medications, the pharmacodynamics of which would either alter renal function or cause toxicity in the setting of renal disease, would also benefit from blood testing. For example, chronic therapy with nonsteroidal anti-inflammatory agents might influence renal function, which should therefore be assessed.

Familial Disorders

Autosomal-dominant polycystic kidney disease (ADPKD) is one of the most common genetic disorders in the United States, with about 500,000 affected individuals. On average, 50 percent of offspring of an affected parent inherit the disease. One may screen adult children by means of renal ultrasound, which will demonstrate the characteristic cysts even before the kidneys are palpably enlarged. Rarely, ultrasound criteria for PCKD are not met before the fourth decade. Renal CT scanning may help resolve matters. If imaging studies fail, genetic studies may be helpful if an aggressive diagnostic strategy is believed to be warranted.

End-Stage Renal Disease

There are more than 100,000 women in the United States on dialysis, with 33,835 initiating dialysis in 1996. The rate of end-stage renal disease of 225 women per 1 million is slightly less than 70 percent of the rate of men. Women on dialysis need routine gynecologic care no less than the general female population. Unfortunately, the overwhelming financial and physical demands made on the dialysis patient may make it difficult for her to seek care outside the dialysis unit setting.

Dialysis patients should undergo screening for breast, cervical, and ovarian neoplasms on a schedule similar to nondialysis patients. The incidence of endometrial cancer may be increased fourfold compared to nonuremic patients. However, dysfunctional utcrine bleeding is also common. Evaluation of such bleeding by endometrial biopsy or dilatation and curettage might be particularly appropriate in patients aged 40 or more.

Anovulatory menstrual cycles, secondary amenorrhea, and infertility are common. One can treat menstrual irregularities with hormonal manipulation similar to patients with normal renal function. However, hypertension may be aggravated by the use of estrogens. Hyperprolactinemia may accompany advanced renal failure, although levels are usually less than 100 ng/ml. Levels above this warrant investigation. Galactorrhea may result from hyperprolactinemia, but as in nonuremic subjects, other causes should also be sought. Bromocriptine has been used in dialysis patients, but intradialytic hypotension may make this therapy problematic.

Women with Renal Transplants

There are more than 31,000 women with functioning renal transplants in the United States. Immunosuppressed transplant recipients are at heightened risk for the development of neoplasms. Cervical carcinoma in situ has a 14-fold increase in incidence; vulvar and vaginal cancers are 34 times more likely to occur in this group than in the general population. Colposcopic identification of papillomavirus is more common in transplant recipients than in controls.

Infections in renal transplant recipients are a major cause of morbidity. Symptomatic urinary tract infections should be diagnosed and treated. Reactivation of genital herpes occurs and responds to acyclovir or similar agents.

Fertility returns in women of childbearing age after transplantation. A high percentage of pregnancies that enter midtrimester end successfully. However, women should enter pregnancy understanding the potential risks to maternal and fetal health. To ensure stable graft function and to allow for minimal immunosuppressive dosing, one usually advises that pregnancy not be attempted for a 2-year period after transplant. Absence of hypertension and renal disease (proteinuria, renal insufficiency) is desirable.

Preeclampsia occurs more frequently than in patients without renal disease. A variety of neonatal problems have been described including preterm delivery, growth retardation, depressed hematopoiesis, and CMV infections.

Ectopic pregnancy occurs in patients with renal transplants as in other women. Because of the pelvic location of the transplant, symptoms pointing to other pathology may be attributed erroneously to the transplant. One must remain vigilant to all possibilities.

The choice of contraceptive method is difficult for the transplant recipient. Estrogen-containing contraceptives have been used, but they may have effects on immune function, aggravate hypertension, and increase the risk for thromboembolism in patients. Cyclosporine levels need to be monitored because of drug interactions. An intrauterine device in an immunosuppressed host predisposes to chronic pelvic infection, and hence an IUD is best avoided.

References and Selected Readings

1. Coe FL, Parker JH, Asplin JR: The pathogenesis and treatment of kidney stones. *N Engl J Med* 327:1141–1152, 1992.

2. Grossman S, Hou S: Obstetrics and gynecology, in Daugirdas JT, Ing TS (eds): *Handbook of Dialysis,* 2d ed. Boston: Little, Brown, 1994.

3. Hooton TM, Stamm WE: Diagnosis and treatment of uncomplicated urinary tract infection. *Infect Dis Clin North Am* 11:551–581, 1997.

4. Greenberg A: Urinalysis, in Greenberg A (ed): *Primer on Kidney Diseases,* 2d ed. San Diego: Academic Press, 1998.

5. Pak CY: Southwestern Internal Medicine Conference: Medical management of nephrolithiasis—A new simplified approach for general practice. *Am J Med Sci* 313:215–219, 1997.

6. Stamm WE, Hooton TM: Current concepts: Management of urinary tract infections in adults. *N Engl J Med* 329:1328–1334, 1993.

CHAPTER 63

Gastrointestinal Disorders

Renée L. Young

Abdominal Pain—An Approach to the Differential Diagnosis

History taking remains the most important tool in the evaluation of abdominal pain. Chronic or nonacute abdominal pain is rarely immediately life-threatening. Acute abdominal pain, on the other hand, may represent a situation that is an immediate threat to the woman's life. Thus, it is very important to determine the exact duration of the abdominal pain. Distinguishing features of some of the most common and important causes of abdominal pain are reviewed below.

Diseases of the Gallbladder, Biliary Tree, and Pancreas

Biliary Colic *History* Biliary colic is usually a steady, midepigastric or right upper-quadrant pain that is not crampy, but rather continuous in nature. Biliary colic is more common in the evening or at night, although it is not restricted to these times. This pain is frequently referred to the back at the angle of the right scapula. Nausea and vomiting are associated with biliary colic, especially when it is related to acute cholecystitis or acute pancreatitis.

Physical Examination Tenderness at Murphy's point, often accompanied by rebound tenderness and right upper-quadrant spasm, is suggestive of biliary colic. Significant negative findings include absence of rectal tenderness, and absence of lower abdominal pain or tenderness.

Diagnostic Studies Laboratory findings such as elevated white blood cell count and liver enzymes are suggestive of, but not specific for, biliary colic. Imaging studies such as ultrasound or radionuclide scanning may be helpful (see under Gallbladder Disease below).

Acute Cholecystitis Right upper-quadrant pain that lasts more than 3 to 4 h accompanied by tenderness and rebound in the right upper quadrant, a rising white blood cell count, and ultrasound evidence of thickening of the gallbladder wall, all support the diagnosis of acute cholecystitis rather than biliary colic. Biliary colic usually lasts less than 2 to 3 h; the pain of acute cholecystitis persists longer than this.

Acute Pancreatitis Acute cholecystitis and biliary colic must be distinguished from acute gallstone pancreatitis (see Pancreatitis). The most prominent symptoms in acute pancreatitis include nausea, vomiting, and epigastric discomfort that radiates to the back. Physical examination findings usually include diffuse abdominal tenderness, often extending into the lower abdomen. Patients with acute pancreatitis may also have discomfort on rectal examination. Serum levels of amylase and lipase are typically elevated, and ultrasound should depict an edematous pancreas.

Acute Appendicitis

The classic symptom of acute appendicitis is periumbilical pain that moves to the right lower quadrant, usually severe and steady, made worse with moving, especially after the appendix has ruptured. Frequently patients are constipated and anorexic. Exceptions to these classic presentations of appendicitis include the case of a retrocecal appendix, which is usually associated with diarrhea; and situations in which an inflamed appendix is overlying the ureter, which will give rise to ureteral colic-type pain when appendicitis is present.

Physical findings of right lower-quadrant tenderness at McBurney's point with rebound, and rectal tenderness on the right, are the findings most consistent with acute appendicitis.

The white cell count is usually elevated; however, in the immunocompromised patient this will not always be the case. Ultrasonography may reveal the characteristic doughnut, which represents the edematous appendix. An important condition to consider in a granulocytopenic patient with signs of apparent appendicitis during intensive chemotherapy is typhlitis. In patients with typhlitis, ultrasound usually shows a thickened cecum, and the patient should be treated with IV antibiotics and observation.

Ischemic Bowel Disease

Acute Ischemia Ischemic bowel disease is much more common in older patients, particularly in patients over the age of 60. Classically, the patient gives a history of severe abdominal pain followed by the passage of a large bloody stool. However, the passage of the bloody stool is not essential for this diagnosis, and frequently the abdominal pain is a rather nonspecific pain, which can be diffuse or localized in the right or left lower quadrants.

It is imperative to distinguish ischemic small bowel disease, which is typically occlusive in origin, from ischemic colitis, which is typically nonocclusive. Mesenteric ischemia from occlusive disease can be related to arterial thrombus, embolus, venous thrombosis, or vasculitis. Occlusive ischemia or acute mesenteric ischemia generally presents with one or a combination of the following: periumbilic pain out of proportion to tenderness, nausea, vomiting, distension, GI bleeding, or altered bowel habits. Nonocclusive ischemia, ischemic colitis, usually is related to hypotension, heart failure, or arrhythmia. It more frequently presents with severe lower abdominal pain, rectal bleeding, and hypotension.

The most impressive physical finding is the lack of an abnormal physical manifestation in the face of severe abdominal symptoms. The abdomen is soft. Plain abdominal films are helpful and can demonstrate either the absence of intestinal gas or a thickened bowel wall with thumb printing suggestive of submucosal edema. Computed tomography of the abdomen will also show the edematous bowel wall and can demonstrate air in the portal vein. Sigmoidoscopy will demonstrate submucosal hemorrhage, friability, and ulcerations, often with sparing of the rectum, in ischemic colitis. Full colonoscopy should not be undertaken in patients suspected of ischemic colitis, because of the risk of perforation. If embolic occlusion is suspected, early arteriography and surgical embolectomy should be considered.

Speed is of the essence when treating occlusive ischemia. Occlusive ischemia will require vascular surgery if reversible; however, when necrotic bowel is found, this requires bowel resection and often leaves the patient with short-bowel syndrome. Conservative management with NPO and IV fluids, and correction of hypotension, heart failure, or arrhythmia, is the preferred approach to ischemic colitis.

Chronic Mesenteric Insufficiency "Abdominal angina," which is a dull, crampy, periumbilical pain associated with eating and that lasts several hours after eating, is the hallmark of chronic mesenteric insufficiency. Patients typically have lost weight because they are afraid to eat. This type of chronic abdominal pain requires evaluation with mesenteric arteriography for possible bypass graft surgery.

Abdominal Aortic Aneurysm

If the physician waits for the typical triad of a pulsating abdominal mass, abdominal pain, and hypotension to develop in the patient with an abdominal aortic aneurysm (AAA), a good outcome is unlikely. Unfortunately, abdominal aneurysms often produce no symptoms at all until they are ruptured. The chances of rupture increase with the size of the aneurysm. If a pulsatile mass in the abdomen is found on physical examination, further diagnostic studies should be undertaken to evaluate for an aneurysm.

Plain films may show the calcified outline of an aneurysm, but ultrasound is more sensitive and specific. CT scan with contrast is also an excellent tool for diagnosing an aneurysm. Vascular surgeons should be consulted once an aneurysm is detected. Operative excision and replacement graft are indicated for AAA greater than 5 to 6 cm in diameter, as well as for rapidly expanding aneurysms regardless of the size.

Diverticular Disease

Diverticula are herniations or sac-like protrusions of the mucosa through the muscularis at the points of nutrient artery penetration. The presence of diverticula is termed diverticulosis. Inflammation of these herniations leads to diverticulitis. Some patients with diverticulosis have recurrent bouts of left lower-quadrant pain in the absence of diverticulitis, which is called painful diverticular disease without diverticulitis. Diverticula tend to increase in incidence with increasing age and tend to be more common in the left colon than in the right colon. They are usually asymptomatic, but in the case of diverticulitis, present with abdominal pain, fever, and altered bowel habits.

Laboratory evaluation when diverticulitis is present reveals a leukocytosis, frequently with an increase in band forms. Although diverticular disease can be diagnosed with barium enema or colonoscopy, neither of these tests should be undertaken in the presence of acute diverticulitis because the rate of perforation is high when diverticula are inflamed.

If the patient is known to have diverticular disease, treatment should be started with high-fiber diet/fiber supplementation (e.g., Metamucil, Citrucel, Konsyl). For acute diverticulitis, treatment is with antibiotics that cover gram-negative organisms and bowel flora. Depending on the extent of patient illness, these patients may be treated on an ambulatory basis with oral antibiotics. Diverticula can bleed, sometimes profusely. Patients suspected of having diverticular hemorrhage should be admitted to the hospital. Complications of diverticulitis include pericolic abscess, perforation, fistula, and stricture.

Irritable Bowel Syndrome

This is a very common diagnosis and is more frequent in women. Irritable bowel syndrome is characterized by altered bowel habits, abdominal pain, and the absence of other detectable organic pathology. It is therefore a diagnosis of exclusion. There are at least three variants of this syndrome: alternating constipation and diarrhea; spastic colon that presents as chronic abdominal pain with or without constipation; and chronic painless diarrhea. Frequently, the patient presents before the age of 30. She may complain of bloating and diffuse abdominal pain, pasty stools, or ribbon or pencil-thin stools. Patients frequently have mucus but no blood in their stools. Because this is a diagnosis of exclusion, other organic pathology needs to be excluded. Further information regarding irritable bowel syndrome can be found in the last section of this chapter.

Intestinal Obstruction

Intestinal obstruction is generally caused by adhesions from a previous operation, but sometimes an incarcerated hernia will be the etiology. Occasionally, intestinal obstruction presents in patients who have never had abdominal operations. Malignancy, both intraintestinal and extraintestinal, can cause intestinal obstruction. Occasionally, an appendiceal abscess or other intraperitoneal infection will lead to obstruction. Volvulus, a twisting of the intestine (usually cecum or sigmoid), can also account for the problem.

Intestinal obstruction is generally defined as a blockage of the intestine that prevents passage of intestinal contents. When the patient presents with obstruction, this requires hospitalization and surgical evaluation. Intestinal obstruction leads to early dehydration and fluid and electrolyte loss, and requires immediate medical attention and resuscitation of the patient.

The exact clinical presentation of the patient depends upon where the obstruction is located. Higher obstructions, such as in the small intestine, frequently present with early vomiting, whereas obstructions that are more distal, such as in the colon, may present with constipation. The most classic presentation is colicky abdominal pain along with vomiting and scars from a previous operation, all suggesting intestinal obstruction. Physical examination of the abdomen may reveal high-pitched abdominal tinkles or rushes. A succussion splash can frequently be heard with small intestinal obstruction; strangulation or bowel necrosis must be suspected when the abdomen becomes tender.

Diagnosis still depends on characteristic history and physical examination to provide the best clues, but abdominal x-rays provide another important diagnostic study. Radiologic films in the standing, supine, and left lateral decubitus positions will show air or gas accumulation in the bowel. CT scan of the abdomen may be helpful to look for malignancy. Occasionally, endoscopic exams or barium studies are performed to further define the etiology and site of the obstruction.

Management of the intestinal obstruction depends on the etiology of the obstruction. Generally total obstruction requires surgical intervention, as do many cases of partial obstruction.

The presence of alimentary tract dilatation anywhere along its course raises the possibility of obstruction or a functional hypoperistaltic adynamic state. The former is frequently referred to as intestinal obstruction or mechanical obstruction, whereas the latter is referred to as adynamic ileus or ileus. Classically, mechanical obstruction results in bowel dilatation due to the accumulation of air and fluid proximal to the point of obstruction, but diminished bowel caliber occurs distal to the point of obstruction with little or no air and fluid present. On x-ray films there is often a sharp cut-off point below which there is no air or dilatation and above which there is a dilated air-filled intestine. Adynamic ileus is often metabolic or toxic in origin, in which case it is global in effect, often involving both large and small bowel and resulting in dilatation of both colon and small bowel with air-fluid levels. Focal areas of ileus may also occur in small bowel or colon. It is sometimes difficult to determine on x-ray films whether the condition is an obstruction or an ileus. Both conditions, however, require hospitalization, fluid resuscitation, and nasogastric tube decompression. Obstruction will more likely require surgical intervention as well.

Gynecologic Problems

Gynecologic pathology is a common cause of pelvic and, often, abdominal pain. Acute pain may be secondary to an ectopic pregnancy, a ruptured ovarian cyst, torsion of the adnexa, pelvic infection, a tubo-ovarian abscess, or an infarcted myoma. Chronic or subacute pain may be secondary to chronic salpingitis, an adnexal mass, endometriosis, pelvic adhesions, uterine leiomyomata or adenomyosis, or advanced malignancy.

Esophageal Diseases

Gastroesophageal Reflux Disease

Gastroesophageal reflux disease (GERD) is the term used to describe symptoms or damage secondary to reflux of gastric contents into the esophagus. Presentations of GERD vary widely and can be classified into typical symptoms, atypical symptoms, and complications. However, neither the severity of the symptoms nor the pattern can be used to predict the presence or absence of esophagitis. GERD occurs commonly in both men and women, but there are certain clinical circumstances in which women may be more prone to develop symptomatic reflux disease.

Pregnancy, oral contraceptive use, and certain rheumatologic diseases predispose women to develop symptoms of GERD.

Typical symptoms of gastroesophageal reflux disease are heartburn and regurgitation. Other symptoms include dysphagia or bitter/sour taste in the mouth. Endoscopic evidence of esophagitis is only found in approximately one-third of patients complaining of these symptoms. An increased frequency of the symptoms of heartburn and regurgitation are very common in pregnant women, and this is thought to be secondary to increased gastric pressure from increased abdominal pressure relating to the pregnancy. Another frequent, but less readily reported, manifestation of reflux in women is "reflux dyspareunia," symptomatic reflux during intercourse.

Some atypical symptoms of gastroesophageal reflux disease include angina-like chest pain, hoarseness, bronchospasm, and hiccups. Chest pain caused by GERD should be evaluated after life-threatening cardiac disease has been ruled out. Chronic hoarseness associated with reflux is secondary to inflammation of the vocal cords. Nocturnal episodes of nonallergic asthma preceded by reflux symptoms are very suggestive of reflux disease. Protracted hiccups have also been reported in reflux patients.

Complications of GERD can also be a presentation of this disease. These complications include erosive or ulcerative esophagitis and dysphagia secondary to peptic strictures. Another complication is the frequent association with metaplasia of the epithelium referred to as Barrett's esophageal mucosa. Barrett's esophagus typically appears after chronic untreated reflux disease. Approximately 10 to 20 percent of patients with chronic symptoms of heartburn and regurgitation already demonstrate changes consistent with Barrett's esophagus at the time of initial endoscopy.

The pathophysiology of gastroesophageal reflux disease is a topic of ongoing investigation. The mechanisms that normally prevent damage from gastroesophageal reflux are multiple. The role that a particular defect in these mechanisms plays varies with the individual situation and is not always easily identified. However, knowledge of the mechanisms that are involved in a particular case of GERD are often helpful in establishing a therapeutic regimen. Reflux disease is generally considered to result from prolonged contact of refluxed gastric acid with the esophageal epithelium. Factors that determine reflux injury to the esophagus include both offensive and defensive ones. The principle offensive factor is potency of the refluxate, which is primarily related to its acid and pepsin concentration. Defensive factors consist of a three-tiered system including antireflux barriers, luminal clearance mechanisms, and epithelial resistance.

The antireflux mechanisms are not totally protective. Even normal individuals, without evidence of reflux injury, reflux approximately once per hour with increasing episodes following meals. Reflux episodes occur more frequently in patients with reflux esophagitis than in normal individuals. There is a strong correlation between the duration of contact of the acidic gastric contents with the esophagus and the extent of esophageal damage. Intraesophageal pH monitoring has shown the percentage of time below pH 4 is higher in patients with complicated esophagitis.

Mechanisms for esophageal clearance include gravity, but this is only operational in the upright position. Elevation of the head of the bed does not decrease the frequency of reflux events in the recumbent position, but it does reduce the duration of contact of acidic contents with esophageal mucosa. Esophageal peristalsis and saliva are two other factors involved in esophageal acid clearance. Gravity, peristalsis, and secretion of saliva are less operative in the recumbent position; therefore, the potential for acid contact with the epithelium is greatest during sleep.

The esophageal epithelial resistance factors provide another level of defense against reflux damage by limiting esophageal damage during contact with acid.

The role of hiatus hernia in gastroesophageal

reflux disease is debated. Studies in the past have concluded that hiatus hernia does not play a causal role in the production of GERD. Although only 50 to 60 percent of patients with hiatus hernia have endoscopic evidence of esophagitis, up to 90 percent of patients with esophagitis have a hiatus hernia, implying that there is a contributing factor. The hiatus hernia may, in fact, impair lower esophageal sphincter (LES) function during straining. Displacement of the LES from the abdomen to the chest leads to mechanical alterations as well. This is an area of ongoing investigation, and there is not yet general agreement about the role that hiatus hernia plays in the pathophysiology of gastroesophageal reflux disease. A simple clinical point to remember is that most people with a hiatus hernia are asymptomatic. If the patient is having symptoms, that patient should be evaluated for gastroesophageal reflux disease.

There is also no general agreement about the role of delayed gastric emptying in gastroesophageal reflux disease; however, the greater gastric residual volumes found in patients with delayed gastric emptying does increase the number of lower esophageal sphincter relaxations, allowing further gastroesophageal reflux to occur.

Gastroesophageal reflux disease is more common in patients with Zollinger-Ellison syndrome because of the overwhelming hypersecretion of acid. The hypersecretory state, however, is not a mechanism in the great majority of patients with GERD.

Scleroderma, which is more common in the female patient, presents a combined alteration of the clearance mechanisms and of the antireflux barrier. Scleroderma patients have fewer reflux events, but the reflux events have significantly longer duration in comparison with patients who have esophagitis of similar severity and no connective tissue disease. Lower esophageal sphincter pressure is reduced and the loss of this LES barrier, along with impairment of esophageal clearance, may result in severe reflux disease.

Initial diagnosis of gastroesophageal reflux disease is made by history. A 24-h esophageal luminal pH recording is the most sensitive test to determine whether reflux is present. Endoscopy (esophagogastroduodenoscopy) is sensitive in detecting mucosal changes caused by reflux disease. Esophageal biopsies can be taken at the time of endoscopy; these often detect microscopic esophagitis not seen grossly. Esophageal biopsies should also be taken to check for dysplasia associated with Barrett's esophagus. Although barium swallow can detect esophageal strictures and gross esophagitis, there are frequent false-positives for reflux disease, because many people reflux during barium studies and do not have gastroesophageal reflux disease.

Therapy of gastroesophageal reflux disease has multiple tiers. For mild disease, patients can be instructed in weight reduction; sleeping with the head of the bed elevated 30 to 60 degrees; no meals taken for 1 to 2 h before recumbency; and avoidance of smoking, caffeine, alcohol, chocolates, fatty foods, spicy foods, peppermints, and specific foods that cause heartburn. The patient with documented esophagitis or any complications of GERD will require more intensive medical therapy. The proton pump inhibitors (examples: omeprazole, lansoprozole) are currently the best medications available for treatment of esophagitis and symptomatic reflux disease. Acid suppression can also be obtained with the H_2-receptor antagonist (examples: ranitidine, cimetidine, famotidine, nizatidine) but are inferior to the proton pump inhibitors for controlling GERD. A prokinetic agent, such as cisapride or metoclopramide, may be added for second-line therapy in addition to acid suppression in patients with esophagitis or other complications of GERD.

Other therapy to be considered for gastroesophageal reflux disease would be surgical therapy, including Nissen fundoplication. Currently this procedure is available to some patients laparoscopically. The decision regarding whether to proceed to surgical intervention should be considered carefully, putting into perspective such factors as severity of the disease, underlying medical condition, and the effect of long-term medication versus surgical intervention. Esophageal strictures related to GERD will need to be dilated.

Other Forms of Esophagitis

Not all forms of esophagitis are related to gastroesophageal reflux disease. Pill-related esophagitis can be caused by any medication; the most commonly offending agents include doxycycline, tetracycline, aspirin, nonsteroidal anti-inflammatory drugs, potassium chloride, quinidine, ferrous sulfate, and clindamycin. Pill-esophagitis is more commonly seen in patients who take pills with small sips of water, in patients who recline after swallowing their pill, and in individuals with anatomic defects, such as an enlarged left atrium or ectatic aorta, that impinge on the esophagus and cause the pills to "hang up" in these areas. Pill-related esophagitis is usually diagnosed endoscopically. The primary treatment is withdrawing the offending drug and providing acid suppression with H_2-receptor antagonist, omeprazole, or antacids. If this is a recurrent problem, it predisposes the patient to strictures, and if strictures are present, they need to be dilated.

Immunocompromised patients, such as patients with AIDS, are predisposed to develop other forms of esophagitis. Patients with malignancy, diabetes, hypoparathyroidism, hemoglobinopathies, systemic lupus erythematosus, and corrosive esophageal injury are also predisposed to develop infectious etiologies of esophagitis. These include both herpes esophagitis and candida esophagitis. Esophagitis can also be caused by cytomegalovirus and varicella zoster virus, as well as herpes virus I or II. These patients can present with dysphagia, odynophagia, fevers, bleeding, and oral thrush (particularly in candida esophagitis). Diagnosis is generally by endoscopy with brushings for cytology or culture and/or biopsies for culture.

Herpes and varicella esophagitis are treated with acyclovir. CMV is treated with ganciclovir. Candida esophagitis can be treated with oral nystatin or clotrimazole, ketoconazole, or amphotericin, depending on the severity of the disease.

Peptic Ulcer Disease

Ulcerations most commonly occur in the duodenal bulb (duodenal ulcer) and stomach (gastric ulcer). However, peptic ulcer disease (PUD) may also occur in the esophagus, pyloric channel, distal to the duodenal bulb in the second or third portions of the duodenum, in the jejunum, or in relation to a Meckel's diverticulum. The precise mechanisms underlying ulcerogenesis are still debated, but simply stated, it results from an imbalance between "aggressive" factors (gastric acid, pepsin, *Helicobacter pylori*) and "defense" factors involved in mucosal resistance (gastric mucus, bicarbonate, microcirculation, prostaglandins, and the mucosal barrier).

There are numerous risk factors and associations with PUD: heredity, smoking, gastrinoma (Zollinger-Ellison syndrome), hypercalcemia (hyperparathyroidism), and mastocytosis. The prevalence of peptic ulcers has shifted from male predominance to comparable prevalence in both sexes. These changing trends in ulcer occurrence reflect declining rates in young men and increasing rates in older women.

Most recently, *Helicobacter pylori,* a spiral urease-producing organism that colonizes gastric mucosa in 80 to 100 percent of persons with duodenal ulcers and in 70 to 80 percent of those with gastric ulcers, has been implicated in the pathophysiology of ulcers, especially with ulcers that are not associated with nonsteroidal anti-inflammatory drugs (NSAIDs). This organism is also found in normal individuals with increasing prevalence with increasing age. Its exact role in ulcer pathogenesis is still under investigation, but recent literature strongly supports treatment for *H. pylori* in cases of documented gastritis and peptic ulcer disease. Irradication of *H. pylori* is associated with a decrease in ulcer recurrence.

The World Health Organization has classified *H. pylori* as a carcinogen because it is associated with both adenocarcinoma of the stomach and with gastric lymphomas.

Nonsteroidal anti-inflammatory drug use also predisposes to PUD. Rheumatoid arthritis and degenerative joint disease predominate in women. Women with these arthritic conditions frequently develop PUD from NSAID use. Chronic salicylate or NSAID use may account for over 30 percent of gastric ulcers and is associated with an increased risk of bleeding and perforation.

The hallmark of PUD is a burning, gnawing, epigastric discomfort. This presentation is common in both gastric and duodenal ulcers, although the pattern can differ in each case. The classic presentation of a duodenal ulcer is that of periodic gnawing epigastric discomfort with onset 1 to 2 h after eating, usually relieved by food or antacids. Nighttime pain is common, often occurring between midnight and 4:00 AM. Pain may also be relieved with vomiting. On the other hand, the classic presentation of a gastric ulcer is persistent epigastric pain not relieved by food, antacids, or vomiting. In fact, food frequently exacerbates the abdominal discomfort; as a consequence, patients tend to lose weight.

Upper gastrointestinal hemorrhage is a less frequent but important presentation of PUD. Ten percent of duodenal ulcer patients present with bleeding without a prior history of ulcer pain. Bleeding is an especially common presentation of PUD in the elderly. Among patients with nonsteroidal anti-inflammatory drug-related ulcerations, abdominal discomfort may be minimized by the analgesic properties of the NSAID. Ulcer bleeding may present as hematemesis or melena; or, if low-grade, the sole manifestation may be either iron deficiency or a hematest-positive stool.

Other presentations of PUD besides pain and bleeding include gastric outlet obstruction, perforation, or penetration causing acute pancreatitis, the latter as a consequence of penetration through to the pancreas.

The diagnosis of PUD can be made either by upper gastrointestinal endoscopy or upper GI barium examination. In the past, the standard diagnostic tool for PUD was the upper GI barium study. More recently, endoscopy has become an effective and commonly used tool. Endoscopy is particularly accurate and superior to the barium examination in detecting diffuse mucosal abnormalities such as gastritis. It is preferable to barium studies for diagnosis of gastric ulcers because endoscopy has the added benefit of allowing a biopsy to be obtained. Gastric ulcers may be malignant, and therefore should always be biopsied.

Helicobacter pylori can be diagnosed with a variety of tests that vary in cost and invasiveness. Antibody testing can be used to diagnose previous or current infection, but cannot be used to follow-up on eradication. Endoscopic biopsy is accurate but costly, especially if endoscopy is not also needed for diagnosis of PUD. Breath tests are an excellent choice to follow-up on eradication of the organism.

The primary objectives of treatment of PUD are to relieve symptoms and heal the ulcer. Gastric ulcers need to be followed endoscopically with biopsies until healed. The previous use of dietary restrictions for treatment of PUD is unnecessary given the drugs now available. Nonsteroidal anti-inflammatory drugs should be stopped to promote healing, and smoking should be curtailed as it also prevents healing. H$_2$ antagonists (such as cimetidine, ranitidine, famotidine, or nizatidine) are the most widely used medications for healing PUD. Antacids are also effective in healing peptic ulcers, but they need to be taken frequently, which decreases patient compliance. The proton pump inhibitors (omeprazole and lansoprazole) are the most powerful acid suppressants available and are frequently used to heal PUD.

Eradication of *H. pylori* from the stomach decreases the subsequent ulcer relapse rate. If *H. pylori* has been documented, then drugs to eradicate *H. pylori* should be given as well as an acid-suppressing drug. The optimum regime for the eradication of *Helicobacter* continues to undergo definition. The gold standard anti-Helicobacter therapy regimen is triple-therapy consisting of a two-week course of amoxicillin (500 mg po qid), bismuth (Peptobismol 2 tabs qid), and metronidazole (250 mg qid). However, there are many other combinations of drugs to eradicate *Helico-*

bacter. Patients should be instructed carefully when prescribing these medications to prevent formation of resistant organisms.

Most studies on eradication of *H. pylori* have documented higher eradication rates with 10 to 14 days of triple therapy. Compliance increases with shorter duration of therapy and less frequent medications per day. Metronidazole resistance is well documented. Other acceptable anti-Helicobacter therapies include (10 to 14 days of therapy):

Metronidazole: 500 mg bid		Clarithromycin: 500 mg bid
Omeprazole: 20 mg bid	*or*	Lansoprazole: 30 mg bid
Clarithromycin: 250 mg bid		Amoxicillin: 1 g bid

There are multiple other antibiotic and acid-suppressing drug combinations used in eradication of *H. pylori*.

A surgery referral is necessary for complications such as persistent or recurring bleeding, obstruction, perforation, or intractability. One should always exclude gastrinoma by obtaining a serum gastrin if the patient has a history of intractable or recurrent PUD despite optimal treatment.

Pancreatitis

Acute Pancreatitis

Acute pancreatitis is an inflammatory disease that can range in severity from mild edema to severe pancreatic and peripancreatic necrosis.

There are four major theories of pathogenesis; each theory is only partly supported, however, by research and clinical data. The four major theories are: secretion against an obstructed duct, bile reflux into the pancreatic duct, duodenal reflux into the pancreatic duct, and intracellular protease activation.

The most common causes of acute pancreatitis in the United States are excessive alcohol consumption and cholelithiasis. In women, the most frequent cause of pancreatitis is gallstones. Less common etiologies include abdominal trauma; hereditary pancreatitis; infection (mumps, hepatitis viruses, coxsackievirus); medications (azathioprine, 6-MP, sulfonamides, thiazides, furosemides, estrogens, tetracycline, valproic acid, pentamidine); vasculitis (lupus, necrotizing angiitis, thrombotic thrombocytopenia purpura); penetrating peptic ulcer; obstruction of the ampulla of Vater or pancreatic duct by tumor; pancreas divisum; postoperative or postendoscopic retrograde cholangiopancreatography (post-ERCP); metabolic (hypertriglyceridemia, hypercalcemia, renal failure); and hereditary pancreatitis.

One usually diagnoses acute pancreatitis on the basis of the clinical symptoms of abdominal pain associated with chemical evidence of pancreatic inflammation in the form of elevated serum concentrations of pancreatic enzymes such as amylase and lipase. The pain is most typically epigastric in location. It is described as a steady, boring midepigastric pain often radiating to the back. Nausea and vomiting are frequent associations. Physical exam may yield a low-grade fever up to 101°F. However, if the temperature is higher than this, one must consider an alternate diagnosis or complications of pancreatitis. Patients with pancreatitis may present with volume depletion, manifested as hypotension or shock. The abdomen is frequently distended and bowel sounds may be diminished or absent. Epigastric tenderness may be severe, and localized rebound may be elicited.

Less frequent physical findings associated with pancreatitis include Cullen's sign (a blue discoloration in the periumbilical area due to hemorrhage in the pancreatic bed) and Turner's sign (a blue, red, purple, or green-brown discoloration of the flanks due to tissue catabolism of hemoglobin).

The association of hyperamylasemia with acute pancreatitis has been recognized for many years but is not pathognomonic, as amylase is produced in other structures, and when those structures are inflamed, they may also produce both an elevated amylase and abdominal pain. Duodenal perforation and mesenteric infarction may also give rise to abdominal pain and elevations of amylase. Hyperamylasemia is occasionally associated with salivary gland inflammation, diabetic ketoacidoses, anorexia nervosa, bulimia, HIV infection, macroamylasemia, ectopic pregnancy, and fallopian tube torsion.

In acute pancreatitis, the magnitude of the amylase elevation is often three times or more greater than normal. However, a normal serum amylase does not absolutely exclude the diagnosis of acute pancreatitis, and the degree of elevation does not predict the severity of pancreatitis. Amylase levels typically return to normal in uncomplicated pancreatitis in 48 to 72 h.

The serum lipase level is more specific for pancreatic disease, although it is also present in other organs, including the duodenum, liver, tongue, and other parts of the intestine. In patients with acute pancreatitis, lipase usually remains elevated longer than amylase, often remaining elevated for 7 to 14 days.

Radiographic imaging studies are of great value in a patient suspected of having pancreatitis. Abdominal radiographs are abnormal in about half of the patients with acute pancreatitis, but they are nonspecific for pancreatitis. Common findings include total or partial ileus (sentinel loop) and spasm of the transverse colon. Abdominal radiographs are very useful for excluding other etiologies of abdominal pain associated with elevated amylase levels, such as an intestinal perforation.

Ultrasonography is used to evaluate the patient with acute pancreatitis. Although it may fail to visualize the pancreas because of overlying intestinal gas, it may detect gallstones, or edema, or enlargement of the pancreas. It is most useful in evaluating the biliary tract and especially for identifying gallstones, but ultrasonography may define features, such as thickening of the gallbladder wall and pericholecystic fluid collections, which are suggestive of cholecystitis, or reveal dilatation of the bile ducts, which is suggestive of obstruction by stone or tumor.

Computed tomography scanning is superior to ultrasound in evaluating the pancreas because it is not limited by the presence of bowel gas. CT scan can often confirm the diagnosis of pancreatitis by finding an edematous pancreas, and it is also useful for predicting and identifying late complications.

Endoscopic retrograde cholangiopancreatography is not routinely indicated in the evaluation of patients during an attack of acute pancreatitis. It does, however, have an important role in specific situations. For example, endoscopic sphincterotomy and stone extraction can be performed on those patients suspected of having gallstone pancreatitis who are not clinically improving within 24 h after admission. ERCP is also used for the preoperative evaluation of patients suspected of having traumatic pancreatitis to localize the site of the pancreatic duct disruption. In patients with no identifiable cause of acute pancreatitis, once the attack of pancreatitis has subsided, ERCP may be performed in order to define such causes as occult common bile duct stones, pancreatic or ampullary carcinoma, or other causes of obstruction.

The differential diagnosis of acute pancreatitis should include other causes of severe acute abdominal pain, which may or may not be accompanied by an elevation of amylase, such as intestinal perforation (especially from PUD), ectopic pregnancy, tubo-ovarian abscess, torsion of the adnexa, ruptured ovarian cyst, acute cholecystitis, acute intestinal obstruction, mesenteric ischemia, renal colic, myocardial ischemia or infarction, aortic dissection, connective tissue disorders, pneumonia, and diabetic ketoacidosis.

Treatment for acute pancreatitis generally involves hospitalization and supportive measures such as analgesia (meperidine), IV fluids and colloids, no oral alimentation (NPO), and correction of hypocalcemia. Fulminant pancreatitis requires aggressive fluid support and meticulous management of cardiovascular collapse, respiratory insufficiency, and pancreatic infection. These patients require hospitalization and usually need consultations from gastroenterologists and surgeons.

Chronic Pancreatitis

The differentiation between acute and chronic pancreatitis is based on clinical criteria. Following recovery from acute pancreatitis there is restoration of normal pancreatic function. In chronic pancreatitis there is permanent loss of function, and pain usually predominates. Chronic pancreatitis may present either as recurrent episodes of acute inflammation superimposed on a chronically damaged pancreas or as a more chronic and persistent syndrome of pain and malabsorption.

The most common etiology of chronic pancreatitis in the United States is alcoholism. Less common causes include hypertriglyceridemia, hypercalcemia, hereditary pancreatitis, hemochromatosis, and cystic fibrosis. In approximately one-quarter of patients with chronic pancreatitis, no specific etiology is identified.

Pain is the cardinal symptom of chronic pancreatitis. Weight loss, steatorrhea, and other signs of malabsorption are frequent associations. Physical exam is commonly unremarkable except for signs of malabsorption. There are no specific laboratory tests for chronic pancreatitis. Both the serum amylase and lipase levels are often normal. Steatorrhea typically occurs late in the course of chronic pancreatitis.

Abdominal x-rays can reveal pancreatic calcification, especially when the etiology of the chronic pancreatitis is alcohol abuse. Ultrasound or CT scan of the abdomen may reveal dilatation of the pancreatic duct or the presence of pancreatic pseudocysts. ERCP is helpful in showing the characteristic ductal changes of chronic pancreatitis—irregular dilatation of the main pancreatic duct and pruning of its branches.

It is very important, but often difficult, to distinguish chronic pancreatitis from pancreatic carcinoma, as both can present with recurrent attacks of abdominal discomfort.

Treatment of these patients is frequently difficult and discouraging. The main goals should be to control pain and correct malabsorption. Intermittent attacks should be treated much like acute pancreatitis. Narcotics can be given for severe pain, but subsequent addiction is very common. Surgery may control pain if there is a ductal stricture. Subtotal pancreatectomy may also control pain, but at the cost of exocrine insufficiency and diabetes. Malabsorption is managed with a low-fat diet and adequate pancreatic enzyme replacement.

Gallbladder Disease

Cholelithiasis

In the United States, there are approximately 1 million new cases of cholelithiasis per year. There are three major types of gallstones: cholesterol, pigment, and mixed stones. In the United States, 80 percent of stones are cholesterol stones or mixed, and 20 percent are pigmented stones.

There is an increased incidence of gallstones in American Indians, the obese, and diabetics; in relation to ileal disease or resection; during pregnancy; in association with estrogen or oral contraceptive use; in type IV hyperlipidemia; and in patients with cirrhosis. Females predominate in a ratio of 4 to 1. In the United States, Native and Mexican Americans have the highest incidence of disease. Caucasians have an intermediate prevalence, and African and Asian Americans have the lowest incidence.

Pregnancy is an independent risk factor for the development of gallstones. The incidence of gallstones increases with each trimester and increases with parity. The history of gallstones in pregnancy and postpartum does not reflect the natural history of other gallstones. There is a high incidence of postpartum clearance of stones. Conservative management is often the rule for symptomatic gallstones in pregnant women.

In the evaluation of women for abdominal pain, gallstones are frequently found. However, gallstones are the cause of this pain only in a minority of cases.

Because most gallstones are silent, the majority will be diagnosed in asymptomatic patients

undergoing ultrasound or radiogrpahic studies for another reason. Symptoms tend to occur when the stones produce inflammation or obstruction of the cystic or common bile ducts. The major symptoms associated with cholelithiasis are: nausea and vomiting; biliary pain, which is usually constant rather than colicky; and postprandial right upper-quadrant or epigastric pain, which typically occurs 30 to 60 min after meals, lasts for several hours, and occasionally radiates to the right scapula or back. Physical exam may be unremarkable or show epigastric or right upper-quadrant tenderness.

Accompanying an attack of biliary colic there are usually mild and transient elevations in bilirubin and alkaline phosphatase. Because only 10 percent of gallstones are radiopaque, ultrasonography is the best diagnostic test. To opacify the gallbladder an oral cholecystogram requires a functioning gallbladder; today, oral cholecystogram is used less frequently than ultrasound.

The differential diagnosis of gallbladder pain includes PUD, gastroesophageal reflux disease, the irritable bowel syndrome, and other inflammatory processes in the right upper quadrant such as hepatitis or pancreatitis.

Because one cannot improve symptoms in asymptomatic patients, asymptomatic cholelithiasis should not be an indication for surgical intervention. Elective cholecystectomy should be reserved for symptomatic patients, those with previous complications of cholelithiasis, and those asymptomatic patients who are at an increased risk of complications. Oral dissolution agents (chenodeoxycholic acid, ursodeoxycholic acid) completely dissolve radiolucent stones in approximately half of suitable patients, but are ineffective in dissolving large radiopaque or pigmented stones. Only a small number of patients meet the four criteria and are eligible for dissolution therapy. The four criteria are: those with radiolucent gallstones less than 20 mm in diameter; functioning gallbladder by oral cholecystogram; noncalcified gallstones; and when surgery is relatively contraindicated. Unfortunately, recurrence is inevitable when these agents are stopped. Pregnancy is a contraindication for dissolution therapy.

Acute Cholecystitis

Acute cholecystitis (acute inflammation of the gallbladder) is usually caused by cystic duct obstruction by an impacted stone. Over 90 percent of acute cholecystitis is associated with gallstones, with distension of the gallbladder due to obstruction of the cystic duct being the primary event. The bile may either be sterile or infected secondarily. Gram-negative organisms such as *Escherichia coli, Klebsiella,* and enterococcus are the most common organisms isolated in cases of acute cholecystitis. If the bile is infected, this can lead to abscess formation and perforation. Approximately 10 percent of the time acute cholecystitis occurs in the absence of gallstones (acalculous cholecystitis). This is generally associated with prolonged acute illness, prolonged fasting, or intravenous hyperalimentation that leads to gallbladder stasis. The differential diagnosis of acalculous cholecystitis includes carcinoma of the gallbladder or common bile duct and vasculitis.

The most common presenting symptoms of acute cholecystitis are abdominal pain, nausea, vomiting, and fever; usually onset of symptoms is acute. The pain is typically in the right upper quadrant with localized tenderness. In 20 percent of patients, there is a palpable right upper-quadrant mass that is the distended gallbladder.

Laboratory evaluation usually reveals a mild leukocytosis with increased polymorphonuclear cells and band forms. There is typically a mild elevation of bilirubin, aspartate aminotransferase (AST), alanine aminotransferase (ALT), and alkaline phosphatase.

Ultrasonography is useful for demonstrating gallstones, but may not confirm the diagnosis of acute cholecystitis. Ultrasound findings suggestive of acute cholecystitis include gallbladder wall thickening, gallbladder sludge, pericholecystic fluid, marked distension of the gallbladder, and the demonstration of a positive Murphy's sign during direct probing of the gallbladder at the time of ultrasonography. Radionuclide biliary imaging (HIDA or DISIDA scans) is highly sensitive and specific in the diagnosis of cystic duct obstruction. Both radionuclide studies and ultrasonography are very accurate; however, the choice of imaging studies remains controversial. Ultrasound is often selected as the initial test because it can be performed quickly, is less expensive, and provides information about nonbiliary structures.

The differential diagnosis of acute cholecystitis should include acute pancreatitis, appendicitis, pyelonephritis, PUD, hepatitis, and hepatic abscess.

The initial management of acute cholecystitis is supportive and includes IV fluids, antibiotics, NPO, and parenteral analgesics (meperidine or other narcotics); a nasogastric tube should be inserted if the patient has nausea and vomiting. Surgical cholecystectomy, either open or laparoscopic, is the definitive treatment and should be performed as soon as is feasible, generally within 24 to 48 h of admission. Delayed surgery is reserved for patients who would be at high risk if they had emergency surgery or when the diagnosis is in doubt. Urgent surgery is indicated for patients with complications, such as perforation of the gallbladder or empyema, or for those patients who fail to respond to initial medical therapy, or for those patients who deteriorate while receiving medical therapy.

Complications related to acute cholecystitis include empyema, hydrops, gangrenous gallbladder, perforation, fistulization, and gallstone ileus.

Chronic Cholecystitis

Chronic cholecystitis is usually caused by gallstones; this is a much more difficult diagnosis to make than acute cholecystitis. In fact, many physicians think chronic cholecystitis is a pathologic rather than a clinical entity.

Symptoms and signs are often nonspecific, including fatty food intolerance, abdominal pain, and dyspepsia. Laboratory tests are often normal. Ultrasonography usually shows gallstones within a contracted gallbladder; sometimes a thickened gallbladder wall may be demonstrated.

The diagnosis is usually made following the exclusion of other etiologies of right upper-quadrant discomfort such as PUD, esophagitis, and the irritable bowel syndrome.

Inflammatory Bowel Disease

Chronic inflammatory disorders of unknown etiology involving the GI tract are subdivided into two principal categories. Ulcerative colitis is a diffuse mucosal inflammatory process generally limited to the colon. It invariably affects the rectum and may extend proximally in a symmetrical uninterrupted pattern to involve part or all of the large intestine. By contrast, Crohn's disease is a patchy transmural inflammation that can affect any part of the gastrointestinal tract from the mouth to the anus. It most commonly involves the small bowel alone, the colon alone, or both the large and the small bowel simultaneously. The peak occurrence of either of the inflammatory bowel diseases lies between ages 15 and 35, but onset may occur at any age. There is a secondary peak between 55 and 65 years. Depending on the study, there may be an increased incidence of inflammatory bowel disease (IBD) in women.

Ulcerative Colitis

This disease is characterized by inflammation confined to the mucosa. It is not a transmural process. The rectum is almost always involved with inflammation extending continuously. Skip areas do not occur. Typical histologic features include epithelial damage, inflammation, crypt abscesses, and loss of goblet cells.

The most common clinical manifestation of ulcerative colitis is bloody diarrhea. Other manifestations include passage of mucus, fever, abdominal pain, tenesmus, and weight loss. There is a wide spectrum of severity at presentation that may extend to toxic megacolon, which is a surgical emergency. Other possible clinical fea-

tures at presentation include anemia, hypokalemia, hypoalbuminemia, and dehydration.

Acute colitis can be diagnosed on a limited sigmoidoscopic examination; full colonoscopy should not be undertaken during the acute phase as the risk of perforation is high. Endoscopic features of ulcerative colitis include mucosal erythema and granularity, friability of the mucosa, hemorrhage, exudate, ulceration, and pseudopolyp formation.

Complications of ulcerative colitis include toxic megacolon and colonic perforation. There is also an increased risk of colon cancer in patients with ulcerative colitis; this risk is related to the extent and duration of colitis. Patients with long-standing extensive ulcerative colitis should be enrolled in a screening colonoscopy program in which colonoscopy with multiple biopsies is performed at regular intervals to detect dysplasia, an early marker of carcinoma.

Crohn's Disease

Any part of the GI tract can be involved in this inflammatory process. However, the terminal ileum or colon are the most frequently involved parts. Unlike ulcerative colitis, this is a transmural inflammation. The bowel wall becomes very thickened. Involvement is discontinuous; skip lesions, which feature intervening segments of inflamed and normal intestine, are quite common. Characteristic histologic features include transmural inflammation, granulomas, fissures, and fistulas.

Typical clinical manifestations of Crohn's disease include diarrhea (often not bloody), abdominal pain, weight loss, fatigue, and fever. Acute ileitis can often mimic appendicitis. Other presentations of Crohn's disease include anorectal fissures, fistulas, and abscesses. If the colon is involved, the diagnosis can be made with sigmoidoscopy or colonoscopy. Often an upper GI and small bowel series is required to make the diagnosis because the small bowel is frequently involved. Complications include obstruction; fistulas (to bowel, bladder, vagina, or skin); abscess formation; bile salt malabsorption leading to cholesterol gallstones; oxalate kidney stones; amyloidosis; and intestinal malignancy.

The differential diagnosis of either ulcerative colitis or Crohn's disease should include infectious colitis; ischemic bowel disease; diverticulitis; radiation-induced colitis; bleeding colonic lesions such as neoplasm; and irritable bowel disease.

Any of the infectious etiologies of colitis can present in a manner indistinguishable from inflammatory bowel disease. These infections include shigella, salmonella, campylobacter, *Yersinia,* gonorrhea, lymphogranuloma venereum, *Clostridium difficile* toxin, tuberculosis, and amebiasis.

There are a number of important extraintestinal manifestations of ulcerative colitis and Crohn's disease: skin: aphthous ulcerations, erythema nodosum, and pyoderma gangrenosum; eye: episcleritis, iritis, and uveitis; joint: peripheral arthritis (monoarticular, asymmetric, large joints; no synovial destruction, no subcutaneous nodules, seronegative), ankylosing spondylitis, and sacroileitis (associated with HLA B27); liver: fatty liver, cholangiocarcinoma, and primary sclerosing cholangitis; hematologic: autoimmune hemolytic anemia and a thrombotic tendency that may lead to deep venous thrombosis and pulmonary embolism.

There are several major categories of drug therapy for inflammatory bowel disease. Symptomatic agents include antidiarrheals, antispasmodics, and, occasionally, cholestyramine. Antiinflammatory compounds include oral sulfasalazine; topical sulfasalazine; oral 5-aminosalicylic acid and its analogs; topical 5-ASA and 4-ASA; corticosteroids, including both oral and parenteral forms; immunosuppressives, such as azathioprine and 6-mercaptopurine; and antibiotics, such as metronidazole. Other agents, such as cyclosporin and methotrexate, are undergoing evaluation.

Surgery is indicated in ulcerative colitis when a patient fails medical management, has bowel perforation or impending perforation, high-

grade dysplasia, or carcinoma. Resection in Crohn's disease is not curative and has a high incidence of post-operative recurrence. Some indications for surgical management in Crohn's include: perforation, nonhealing fistulae, or stricture.

The course of IBD in pregnancy is usually reflective of the disease at conception. If the disease is quiescent at conception, it most likely will remain inactive during the pregnancy. The best advice to give women with IBD who wish to become pregnant is to stabilize IBD before becoming pregnant. Many cases of Crohn's disease actually improve during the course of pregnancy. Sulfasalazine can interfere with folate absorption and pregnant women have increased requirements for folic acid. Folate supplementation should be prescribed to compensate for the abnormal absorption in patients taking sulfasalazine. Pregnant women should, of course, minimize their medication use; however, IBD needs to be controlled in pregnancy to have a healthy outcome for mother and child.

Malabsorption

Intestinal malabsorption of ingested nutrients often produces diarrhea, specifically, steatorrhea, or fat in the stools. Specific deficiencies (vitamins A, D, E, and K, B_{12}, folate, and iron) are other manifestations of malabsorption. Although the three major nutrients—fat, carbohydrate, and protein—may all be malabsorbed, clinical symptoms are generally recognized due to the malabsorption of either carbohydrate or fat.

Different symptoms provide clinical clues as to the substance malabsorbed. Steatorrhea means that fat is not absorbed; anemia may be a clue that iron, B_{12}, or folate is not being absorbed; edema suggests protein as the malabsorptive substance; milk intolerance suggests lactose malabsorption. Steatorrhea is the hallmark of malabsorption. These patients present with diarrhea. These stools are generally greasy, bulky, putty-like, foul-smelling stools. They are not watery or bloody. Fat absorption requires an intact liver, pancreas, small bowel, and lymphatic function. There are many intricate tests in the evaluation of malabsorption, but the most important step is to suspect malabsorption when a patient presents with diarrhea and weight loss.

The initial evaluation of a patient with malabsorption should involve documenting steatorrhea. The most cost-effective method to document steatorrhea is a qualitative fecal fat determination on a single stool collection. The qualitative fecal fat determination done on a single stool collection is about 90 percent sensitive and specific for detecting steatorrhea. The 72-h stool collection is very costly and inconvenient, and should not be included in the initial evaluation of these patients. When collecting stools for evaluation of fat, it is important to remember that the patient needs to be on a full fat diet. Collecting stools for fat from patients who are fasting or being fed intravenously could lead to false-negative results.

Once significant steatorrhea has been documented, a small bowel biopsy is the most cost-effective way to proceed with the evaluation. A small bowel biopsy could be characteristic and diagnostic for celiac sprue, Whipple's disease, abetalipoproteinemia, or agammaglobulinemia. Patchy diseases that may show a normal biopsy due to sampling error include intestinal lymphoma, intestinal lymphangiectasia, amyloidosis, eosinophilic enteritis, systemic mastocytosis, and parasitic infections. These may require repeat biopsy to secure the diagnosis.

The D-xylose test involves D-xylose, which is a five-carbon sugar that is incompletely absorbed in the duodenum and jejunum. It is used as a small intestinal absorption test. This test is helpful in those mucosal diseases in which a patchy distribution of the histologic lesion may invalidate the endoscopic biopsy. Careful administration and collection of serum levels or 5-h urine collections should be undertaken if this test is performed, because less than meticulous administration and collection in performing this test will result in uninterpretable results. Abnormalities could result from small bowel diseases as listed earlier. There are other causes of an abnormal D-xylose test besides malabsorptive diseases, including abnormal renal function, bacterial overgrowth leading to breakdown of xylose in the bowel, poor hydration, congestive heart failure, or the use of nonsteroidal anti-inflammatory drugs.

Other tests employed in the evaluation of malabsorption include the lactose tolerance test by breath and hydrogen analysis to diagnose both lactose intolerance and bacterial overgrowth. Small bowel x-rays may also be helpful to find defects as clues to the cause of malabsorption. The Schilling test for B_{12} absorption is another useful test and abnormalities can be seen with intrinsic factor deficiency, bacterial overgrowth, or ileal dysfunction.

Protein-losing enteropathy may result from several causes of the malabsorption. It is associated with hypoalbuminemia and can be detected by measuring stool α-antitrypsin.

These evaluations for patients with malabsorption frequently require a referral to a gastroenterologist. Many of the specific tests required for the diagnosis are not readily available at all institutions.

Therapy is directed at the underlying disease. Some of the more common etiologies of malabsorption and the appropriate therapy are presented in Table 63-1.

Motility Disorders

Gastrointestinal motility testing is a developing area of gastrointestinal investigation. Although esophageal manometry and rectal manometry are available in most institutions, small bowel motility studies are available in only a few centers. Patients with motility disturbances need to be referred to a gastroenterologist, preferably one whose subspeciality is motility disturbance. Some of the more common gastrointestinal motility problems are discussed below.

TABLE 63-1 Disease States Causing Malabsorption

Disease State	Examples	Treatment
Insufficient pancreatic enzyme activity	Chronic pancreatitis Pancreatic carcinoma Pancreatic resection Cystic Fibrosis	Low-fat diet, pancreatic enzyme replacement
Insufficient intraluminal bile acid activity	Intrahepatic cholestasis Extrahepatic cholestasis Intestinal stasis syndromes Ileal resection Ileal Crohn's disease	Treat the underlying disease, antibiotics if bacterial overgrowth present, bile salt-binding agents may help, cholestyramine
Intramural small bowel disease	Celiac sprue Tropical sprue Whipple's disease Intestinal lymphangiectasia Abetalipoproteinemia Eosinophilic enteritis	Gluten-free diet Antibiotics and folic acid Antibiotics Low-fat diet and medium-chain triglycerides Low-fat diet and medium-chain triglycerides Steroid therapy
Malabsorption due to multiple defects	Zollinger-Ellison Sclerodema Postgastrectomy Radiation enteritis	Treat the underlying disease

Esophageal Motor Disorders

These patients typically present with dysphagia. Investigation should be undertaken first to rule out other etiologies of dysphagia such as gastroesophageal reflux disease, tumor, or stricture.

Achalasia (failure of the smooth muscles of the esophagus to relax) has a number of etiologies including primary (idiopathic) or secondary causes. Secondary causes include Chagas' disease, lymphoma, carcinoma, ischemia, neurotropic viruses, drugs, toxin, postvagotomy radiation, and chronic intestinal pseudo-obstruction. The manometric findings include hypertensive lower esophageal sphincter, inadequate relaxation of the LES, and loss of peristalsis in the smooth muscle portion of the esophageal body. Diagnosis can be suspected if there is absence of the gastric air bubble on a chest x-ray.

Helpful studies include a barium swallow showing a dilated esophagus with distal beak-like narrowing and air fluid levels. Endoscopy should be done to exclude tumor. Esophageal manometry should be done to confirm the diagnosis. Treatment involves a trial of calcium antagonists, pneumatic balloon dilatation, or surgical Heller myotomy of the lower esophageal sphincter. Endoscopic injection of *Botulinum* toxin is another alternative for treatment in certain patients with achalasia.

Patients with scleroderma may also have an esophageal motor disturbance. They are usually diagnosed with scleroderma before GI manifestations of the disease occur. These patients have gastroesophageal reflux disease and should be treated for this. Their manometric findings include incompetent lower esophageal sphincter leading to reflux esophagitis and stricture, and aperistalsis due to atrophy of the esophageal smooth muscle and fibrosis of the muscle.

Gastric Motor Disorders

The most common cause of gastroparesis in the United States is diabetes mellitus. Gastroparesis generally presents with recurrent episodes of nausea and vomiting postprandially. It also can present with blood sugars that are difficult to control in diabetic patients because of the uneven emptying of the stomach and resultant highs and lows in blood sugars. Diabetic gastroparesis can also present with abdominal distension or abdominal discomfort. Endoscopy or barium studies should be done to exclude gastric outlet obstruction causing delayed gastric emptying secondary to peptic ulcer disease or malignancy. Low-level intestinal obstruction or partial obstruction should also be excluded. Gastric emptying studies through nuclear medicine provide good documentation of the delayed gastric emptying. Another cause of gastroparesis is eating disorders such as anorexia nervosa. It is not unusual to see temporary gastroparesis related to a viral infection; these tend to resolve spontaneously but can be associated with permanent gastroparesis. Gastroparesis is generally treated with a prokinetic agent such as cisapride or metoclopramide. Frequent, smaller meals also help treatment. Intravenous erythromycin is reserved for patients with refractory gastroparesis. Domperidone, yet to be released, is another oral agent for gastroparetics.

Small Bowel Dysmotility

Ambulatory small bowel motility testing is available at very few centers. Patients are generally referred for small bowel studies when they have such disease states as diabetic enteropathy, chronic idiopathic intestinal pseudo-obstruction, primary pseudo-obstruction from visceral myopathy, or visceral neuropathy.

Anorectal Manometry

Anal and rectal motility tests are usually undertaken in the evaluation of fecal incontinence. Childbirth may sometimes result in a sphincter defect that may be detected with anal manometry. Other etiologies of fecal incontinence in which anal rectal manometry may be useful include neurologic disease; central nervous system process, such as dementia, stroke, brain tumors,

spinal cord lesions, Tabes dorsalis, and multiple sclerosis; peripheral nervous system process, such as cauda equina lesions, polyneuropathies, traumatic neuropathies, or altered rectal sensation in which the site of the lesion is not known; musculoskeletal diseases such as myasthenia gravis; myopathies such as muscular dystrophy; smooth muscle dysfunctions such as abnormal rectal compliance and internal and anal sphincter weakness; anatomic derangement such as congenital anomalies of the anorectum, fistula, and rectal prolapse; anorectal trauma secondary to injury, surgery, or childbirth; and miscellaneous disease (such as severe diarrhea, irritable bowel syndrome, hypoparathyroidism).

Anal manometry generally gives the measurement of basal and squeeze pressure in the anal canal. Rectal balloon manometry gives measurement of rectal sensation, compliance, inhibitory reflex, and contractile responses. Other tests to consider in the evaluation of rectal-anal function are electromyography, nerve conduction studies, mucosal electrosensitivity, and reflex or stimulation radiographic tests (defacography, balloon proctography, anal endosonography). Often these tests are available at a motility center and often these centers provide biofeedback information as a treatment for fecal incontinence. These tests as a group can provide useful information to determine whether a patient would be helped by any surgical intervention.

Gastrointestinal Malignancies

Malignancies of the gastrointestinal tract are relatively common. Common to most of the GI malignancies are clinical presentations consisting of weight loss; iron deficiency; or gastrointestinal dysfunction such as dysphagia, altered bowel habits, or abdominal pain.

Esophageal Cancer

Common clinical features of esophageal carcinoma include progressive dysphagia (typically first with solids, followed by liquids), weight loss, hoarseness from laryngeal nerve involvement, pulmonary aspiration (either from obstruction or tracheal esophageal fistula), and occasionally chest pain from mediastinal spread of the tumor.

Esophagoscopy is the most sensitive and specific test for diagnosing tumors of the esophagus; pathologic confirmation of the tumor is performed by a combination of endoscopic biopsies and cytologic examination of mucosal brushings. Barium swallow is another tool used for diagnosis of esophageal tumors; however, esophagogastroduodenoscopy (EGD) still should be done to provide a pathology specimen. A CT scan of the chest is valuable for assessing local and nodal spread. Endoscopic ultrasound is a new modality for staging tumors of the esophagus.

Squamous cell carcinomas are most commonly in the upper two-thirds of the esophagus; adenocarcinoma occurs more frequently in the distal third of the esophagus, often arising in a region of metaplastic columnar epithelium. Proximal gastric adenocarcinomas frequently extend directly into the esophagus, and sometimes it is difficult to judge whether the adenocarcinoma is of esophageal or gastric origin. Lymphomas and melanomas occur in the esophagus, but these are rare.

The 5-year survival is about 10 percent for esophageal cancers, and this has not changed in approximately 4 decades. Depth of penetration of the esophageal wall, lymph node involvement, weight loss, and age of the patient are major prognostic factors for patients with localized esophageal cancer.

Therapy depends on the extent of spread of the tumor. For patients with localized cancer who are medically fit, resection is the best choice of therapy, resulting consistently in 5-year survival rates of 10 to 20 percent. Radiation therapy alone should not be recommended to patients with squamous cell carcinoma of the esophagus, because a combination of chemotherapy and radiation therapy is superior. If a contraindication to chemotherapy exists, however, radiation therapy alone can provide effective palliation for a few weeks to months. Combination chemotherapy

usually involving 5-FU plus cisplatin can provide a partial response; unfortunately, these responses are short lived.

Palliative measures include laser ablation, dilatation, luminal prosthesis to bypass the tumor, and gastrostomy or jejunostomy tube feedings for nutritional support.

Physicians should be aware of the risk factors associated with esophageal tumors. Long-term gastroesophageal reflux disease with Barrett's mucosa is associated with an increased incidence of adenocarcinoma. Ethanol abuse and smoking (with the combination being synergistic) are major risk factors for squamous cell carcinoma of the esophagus, and physicians should counsel all their patients regarding the risks associated with the use of these substances. Other risk factors include previous lye ingestion, radiation exposure, other head and neck cancers, achalasia, tylosis, Plummer-Vinson Syndrome, and vitamin A deficiency.

Gastric Cancer

Gastric carcinoma commonly presents with upper abdominal discomfort, which is frequently associated with weight loss, anorexia, nausea, and evidence of acute or chronic GI blood loss (iron deficiency anemia in two-thirds of patients; fecal occult blood in 80 percent).

The exact cause of gastric carcinoma is unknown. It is currently thought that *Helicobacter pylori* may play a role. There are several dietary factors that correlate with an increased incidence of stomach cancer, including the ingestion of nitrates, smoked foods, and heavily salted foods. A genetic component is suggested by an increased incidence in relatives of affected patients. Other risk factors include atrophic gastritis, adenomatous gastric polyps, pernicious anemia, and Ménétrier's disease.

EGD is the most sensitive and specific test to diagnose gastric cancer, and it can also provide pathologic confirmation by biopsy. Barium examination of the stomach is unable to provide pathologic confirmation. Adenocarcinoma is the pathology found in approximately 90 percent of gastric carcinomas. Lymphoma accounts for about 7 percent of gastric malignancies and leiomyosarcoma is considerably less frequent.

The conventional treatment for early gastric carcinoma is resection, as it is the only potentially curative modality available. Feasibility of resection is dependent on the stage of the tumor. Adjuvant radiation therapy has been shown to improve survival in combination with adjuvant chemotherapy.

Small Bowel Tumors

Tumors of the small intestine are uncommon, and represent less than 5 percent of all GI neoplasms. They typically present with bleeding, abdominal pain, or intestinal obstruction. There is an increased incidence of lymphomas in patients with celiac sprue (gluten-sensitive enteropathy).

The barium small bowel series is the best diagnostic test, and its sensitivity in finding a tumor may be increased with the use of enterolysis, which is direct small bowel installation of contrast. CT is useful to evaluate the extent of tumor, especially in the case of lymphomas. Angiography is frequently used when there is an undetermined site of bleeding, and this can be used to detect a plexus of tumor vessels.

Most small bowel tumors are benign. These include adenomas, which are most frequently found in the duodenum; leiomyomas, which are intramural benign tumors; and lipomas, which are most frequently found in the ileum. Of the malignant tumors of the small bowel, 50 percent are adenocarcinomas. Lymphomas are the second most frequent malignant tumors of the small intestine. Treatment usually involves surgical excision and adjuvant chemotherapy for lymphomas.

Colorectal Cancer

Adenocarcinoma of the colon and rectum is predominantly a disease of the Western world.

There are approximately 70,000 deaths annually in the United States that are attributed to colorectal cancer. This tumor is common in North America and Europe, and less common in developing nations. Over the past 20 years, a proximal migration of the location of colorectal cancer has been noted with an increase in frequency in the transverse and right colon, and a slight decrease in frequency in the sigmoid and rectum.

Theories explaining the high prevalence of this tumor in the Western world include diet high in animal protein and animal fat, decreased fiber in the diet, and hereditary factors. It is increasingly clear that genetic predisposition plays a role in a substantial number of patients with colorectal cancer. Hereditary factors in colon cancer are most obviously manifested in those with inheritable polyposis syndromes (Gardner's syndrome, Turcot syndrome, and familial polyposis coli). These syndromes are inherited and are characterized by the presence of hundreds to thousands of colonic adenomas with or without extracolonic tumors. The nonpolyposis hereditary carcinoma groups (Lynch I and Lynch II) suggest the presence of a genetic predisposition among certain populations in the Western world. Lynch first described a cancer family syndrome involving a colon in which there was no familial polyposis and 75 percent of the carcinomas involved the ascending colon. He later described a second family colon cancer syndrome that included carcinomas of the breast, ovary, and endometrium in women, and bowel and urologic malignancy in both sexes. In these syndromes, discrete polyps, but not polyposis, may precede the cancers.

Recent advances have now made genetic testing available for many of the GI malignancies. Counseling should be undertaken before any testing is considered, as testing may have profound implications on the psyche, affect insurance coverage, and have broad implications for other family members.

Occurrence of colorectal cancer is approximately equal in both sexes. Occurrence below the age of 40 is unusual but the incidence increases dramatically between the ages of 50 and 90. Most colorectal cancers are believed to arise from adenomatous polyps. Patients with one colorectal carcinoma have an increased risk of developing a second carcinoma either simultaneously (synchronous carcinomas) or subsequently (metachronous carcinomas). In addition to the previously mentioned risk factors, the incidence of carcinomas dramatically increases in patients with ulcerative colitis, approximately 20 percent at 20 years when pancolitis exists.

The clinical picture of adenocarcinomas of the colon and rectum is quite variable. Presentations include occult or gross bleeding, weight loss, generalized malaise or fatigue, iron deficiency anemia, obstruction of the colon, and metastatic disease including liver metastases. A common presentation in colon cancer is a change in bowel habits or a change in the caliber of the stool or increasing constipation. Distal cancers are more likely to present with narrowing of the stool, whereas cancers in the right colon are more likely to present with anemia and fatigue. Rectal tumors frequently present with change in the caliber of the stool, fecal urgency, rectal bleeding, frequency, tenesmus, and, occasionally, tumor prolapse outside the rectum.

Bleeding from carcinomas may be slow and intermittent or profuse. In a nonacute patient who presents with occult or gross rectal bleeding, the best evaluation is a colonoscopy; however, sometimes a proctosigmoidoscopy combined with an air-contrast barium enema is performed. The advantage of colonoscopy is that it can provide important biopsies for diagnosis.

There are routine screening procedures available for the early detection of colorectal cancer. Between the ages of 40 and 50 for the average-risk-group patient, yearly digital rectal examinations and testing the stool for the presence of occult blood should be undertaken. In addition to continuing yearly digital rectal examinations and fecal occult blood testing (FOBT), for the average-risk patient beginning at age 50, screening should include flexible sigmoidoscopy every 5 years, colonoscopy every 10 years, or double-contrast barium enema every 5 to 10 years. For high-risk patients, screening can begin earlier and continue more aggressively.

When colorectal cancer is suspected because of clinical signs, or when a screening test for occult blood is positive, prompt diagnostic evaluation should be undertaken endoscopically with colonoscopy. If colonoscopy is unavailable, refused by the patient, or technically difficult, then an air-contrast barium enema and flexible sigmoidoscopy should be done.

Fecal occult blood testing with a hemoccult-type guaiac test is convenient, inexpensive, and readily available, but not specific for colon cancer. Bleeding from any part of the GI tract can test positive on these cards. Other sources of GI blood loss would include epistaxis, upper GI tract bleeding, hemorrhoids, gingival bleeding, or ingestion of aspirin or nonsteroidal anti-inflammatory agents. Exogenous peroxidase activity from red meat or uncooked fruits and vegetables can also lead to false-positive tests. These false-positives can be avoided if the patient is instructed to avoid rare red meat and peroxidase-containing vegetables and fruits (cauliflower, radishes, cantaloupe, turnips, broccoli) for the three days prior to the collection of the stool for occult blood testing. Nonsteroidal anti-inflammatory drugs, aspirin, and vitamin C should also be avoided during the testing period. Two stool samples on each of three consecutive stools should be tested.

These screening recommendations are for the woman at average risk. Patients in high-risk groups for colon cancer (including patients with long-standing ulcerative colitis, previous colorectal cancer, previous adenomas, familial polyposis or Gardner's syndrome, and familial colon cancers) are generally followed by a gastroenterologist with more frequent surveillance for colon cancer. The physician should also remember that women who have had breast, ovarian, or endometrial cancer are also at increased risk for colon cancer.

Patients who have had a colon cancer resected

should have colonoscopy performed at 6 months to 1 year following surgery, followed by yearly colonoscopies for 2 years. If the results are negative, then, in general, colonoscopies should be performed at least every 3 years. This, of course, would be combined with yearly fecal occult blood testing. In the patient who has had a preoperative elevated carcinoembryonic antigen (CEA) level, postoperative CEA levels should be followed three times at 4- to 6-month intervals, then five times at yearly intervals.

Current treatment for adenocarcinoma of the colon is surgical, either palliative or curative. Staging of colon cancer is helpful prognostically. Staging is usually done by the Duke's classification or a derivative. Duke's A tumors are limited to the mucosa; B_1 tumors have penetration of the muscular mucosa; B_2 tumors penetrate through the serosa; C_1 (fewer than four lymph nodes), B_1 with positive nodes; C_2 (more than four lymph nodes), B_2 with positive nodes. Controlled studies showed that adjuvant therapy with 5-FU and levamisole for Duke's C colorectal carcinoma, and adjuvant radiotherapy for rectal cancer, improved 5-year survival.

Pancreatitic Cancer

Clinical features suggestive of pancreatic cancer include painless jaundice, weight loss, abdominal pain, back pain, and anorexia. Clinical suspicion should be heightened, especially if the patient has had a recent (within 1 to 2 years) diagnosis of diabetes.

Pancreatic cancer is the fourth most common cause of cancer death in the United States and the incidence appears to be increasing, particularly in women. The peak incidence occurs in the seventh decade. Seventy percent of pancreatic cancers are found in the head of the pancreas and 30 percent are found in the tail and body of the pancreas. There is a very high incidence of local invasion or metastatic disease at the time of initial diagnosis. Pathology generally shows adenocarcinoma. There are other types of pancreatic tumors, but these are significantly less common.

Gastrinomas, insulinomas, and VIPomas (tumors producing vasoactive intestinal peptide) most frequently present because of the clinical effects of the hormones being secreted by these islet cell tumors.

There is a clear association between chronic pancreatitis and pancreatic cancer. In addition, alcohol consumption plays a causative role in pancreatic cancer, as does cigarette smoking.

Ultrasound is useful for evaluation, and is sensitive for lesions over 2 cm in the head and body of the pancreas. CT is somewhat more sensitive, and can frequently identify lesions in the tail of the pancreas that ultrasound cannot. Endoscopic retrograde cholangiopancreatography is the most sensitive test for carcinoma in the pancreatic head; pancreatic duct abnormalities can be seen in the majority of patients regardless of the location of the tumor. Pathologic confirmation is obtained by aspiration of biliary secretions during ERCP or percutaneous needle biopsy of the mass under ultrasound or CT guidance. Endoscopic ultrasound (EUS) is another imaging modality to find and stage pancreatic cancers. Some EUS units can also provide pathologic biopsy information.

Surgical resection for partial pancreatectomy or Whipple's procedure is potentially curative; however, careful selection is mandatory. Contraindications include visceral metastases, extrapancreatic serosal implantation, periportal or periaortal adenopathy, or invasion of the superior mesenteric artery or vein. The majority of patients will have obvious metastases or micrometastasis at the time of diagnosis; the tumor is resectable in only 10 to 20 percent of patients and curable in less than 5 percent. Palliative relief of biliary obstruction can be provided by endoscopic or transhepatic stent placement. There are ongoing trials evaluating radiation therapy, specialized radiation techniques (including labeled monoclonal antibody), and chemotherapy. One promising new chemotherapeutic entity is gemcitabine, a well-tolerated agent that has improved quality of life in certain pancreatic cancer patients.

Biliary Tract Cancers

Biliary tract cancers are less common than pancreatic cancers and usually present with one or a combination of the following: obstructive jaundice, pruritus, right upper-quadrant pain, weight loss, anorexia, nausea, and vomiting.

Cholangiocarcinoma is adenocarcinoma of the bile duct epithelium. Predisposing factors for this tumor include primary sclerosing cholangitis, ulcerative colitis, chronic *Clonorchis sinensis* infestations, and choledochal cysts. This tumor is usually unresectable at the time of diagnosis and frequently presents with obstructive jaundice, but occasionally with hemobilia. Diagnosis is made with a combination of either ultrasound or CT and ERCP. Biliary fluid can be sent for cytology and CT-guided biopsies are frequently needed for tissue diagnosis.

Ampullary carcinoma is a tumor of the papilla of Vater or ampullary involvement of duodenal adenocarcinoma. These patients present with obstructive jaundice or GI bleeding and can have silver stools as a clinical presentation. Direct visualization using EGD or a side-viewing endoscope, accompanied with biospy, are best for diagnosis.

Gallbladder carcinoma may be found incidentally at laparotomy or autopsy. The advanced tumor usually presents in patients in the seventh to eighth decade of life, with right upper-quadrant pain, a palpable mass, jaundice, and weight loss. Preoperative diagnosis can be made by ultrasound or CT.

Treatment of these biliary duct cancers is similar to treatment for carcinoma of the head of the pancreas. The cure rate of advanced or symptomatic tumors is usually less than 5 percent.

Hepatocellular Carcinoma

Hepatocellular carcinoma is one of the most common and deadly malignancies in the world. There are substantial geographic differences in its prevalence, with the highest incidence in areas where hepatitis B virus infections are endemic. In the United States, the peak incidence is in the fifth and sixth decades, but in endemic areas the peak incidence is often 10 to 20 years earlier.

There is a strong correlation with chronic hepatitis B infection, suggesting a causative role of this virus in the majority of cases. In the Western world, the most common associations are alcoholic cirrhosis and other forms of cirrhosis, the use of anabolic steroids, and the administration of Thorotrast (a radiologic contrast agent used in the 1940s and 1950s). Inherited hemochromatosis, hepatitis C, schistosomiasis, $alpha_1$-antitrypsin deficiency, and chronic methotrexate ingestion are all associated with hepatocellular carcinoma. Oral contraceptives, aflatoxin ingestion, and exogenous androgens have each been suggested as being associated with hepatocellular carcinoma in noncirrhotic livers. There are no convincing data at present that demonstrate that oral contraceptive use increases the risk of hepatocellular carcinoma. Tumors that have been most frequently associated with oral contraceptive use include hepatic adenomas and focal nodular hyperplasia.

Hepatocellular carcinoma in cirrhotic patients frequently presents as decompensation of underlying liver disease, weight loss, right upper-quadrant pain, and jaundice. Physical exam can reveal a tender, enlarged liver and a palpable liver mass. Ascites may be present, and when associated with hepatocellular carcinoma it is frequently blood tinged. A bruit or hepatic friction rub may be auscultated over the liver. Besides abnormal liver function tests, an elevated serum α-fetoprotein (AFP) is suggestive of this tumor.

A mass in the liver can be demonstrated with ultrasound, CT, or MRI. Pathologic confirmation by radiologically guided percutaneous liver biopsy is necessary. Radionuclide scanning and angiography may be undertaken in the preoperative evaluation, because the only chance for cure in patients with hepatocellular carcinoma is hepatic resection. Unfortunately, only a very small percentage of patients with hepatocellular carcinoma are candidates for resection. Cirrhosis often limits the extent of hepatic resection, because the diseased liver has limited functional reserve. A small minority of patients are actually cured by a hepatic resection, and most patients die from recurrent or metastatic disease. Liver transplantation has been tried for hepatocellular carcinoma, but this approach remains highly controversial.

Gastrointestinal Carcinoid Tumors

Carcinoid tumors are rare tumors of the gastrointestinal tract. Carcinoids are members of the neuroendocrine or amine precursor uptake and decarboxylation (APUD) tumors. This family also includes other rare tumors, such as islet cell carcinoma of the pancreas and medullary carcinoma of the thyroid. These cells produce biogenic amines and polypeptide hormones, which account for the striking clinical displays of excessive hormonal production.

The carcinoid tumor has been found in almost every organ derived from the primitive entoderm as well as from teratomas. In the gastrointestinal tract, 95 percent of all GI carcinoids take origin in one of these sites: the colon, the appendix, the rectum, and the small intestine. However, they have been found in such unusual locations as the esophagus, bile duct, ampulla of Vater, and Meckel's diverticulum.

Carcinoid tumors of the appendix are fairly common neoplasms. It is not known what percentage of the population have carcinoid tumors of the appendix that are asymptomatic. Frequently, these tumors are not even noticed until the pathologist finds them after appendectomy. The vast majority are exceedingly small. It is generally accepted that those carcinoids of the appendix less than 2 cm in diameter can be treated with simple appendectomy. For carcinoids of the appendix, only those ≥2 cm in their largest dimension should be considered for a more radical operation such as right hemicolectomy.

Carcinoids of the rectum are found most typically in middle-aged adults, but these individuals are also the most likely people to undergo screening proctoscopic examination. These carcinoids are usually not palpated by the examining finger and are generally asymptomatic. Carcinoids of the rectum less than 1 cm rarely metastasize; however, those greater than 2 cm usually have metastasized by the time of diagnosis. If the tumor is 2 cm or larger, the patient, in general, should have a cancer operation. Those carcinoids of the rectum between 1 and 2 cm will require clinical judgement based on patient age, operative risk, and the necessity for and the acceptability of a permanent colostomy.

Carcinoids of the small bowel are more common in the distal compared to the proximal small intestine. They tend to congregate in the distal ileum where almost 40 percent are located within 2 feet of the ileal cecal valve. The most common clinical presentation for small bowel carcinoids is abdominal pain that is periodic and consistent with intermittent bowel obstruction. The lack of physical signs, nondescript nature of the symptoms, negative x-ray findings, and frequently long duration of symptoms often lead to the erroneous diagnosis of a psychosomatic problem. These tumors are often unresectable at initial surgery. This tumor spreads locally and can encase the mesenteric artery. The liver is another frequent site of spread. These carcinoids tend to grow slowly, and the liver appears to adapt to its presence. Patients can present relatively asymptomatic with large hepatic masses and near-normal liver function tests. Accepted therapy of these tumors is local resection if possible. The malignant carcinoid syndrome is a striking, unusual syndrome that is directly related to tumor bulk in an area that drains into the systemic circulation. It is common in patients with hepatic metastases, and is generally a manifestation of late-stage disease. Flushing is the hallmark, and diarrhea is a frequent manifestation. More unusual manifestations include carcinoid asthma and pellagra.

Although its exact role in producing symptoms has been disputed, serotonin and particularly its metabolite, 5-hydroxyindoleacetic acid (5-HIAA) provides an important biological marker for this disease. 5-HIAA is measured through collection of a 24-h urine sample.

The characteristic flush of the carcinoid syndrome has the appearance of a sunburn involving the face, neck, and upper trunk. It typically lasts for seconds to minutes and can be precipitated by almost anything that changes vascular tone, such as emotional stress, exertion, a large meal, or sexual intercourse. Especially common are flushing with first morning exertions. This carcinoid flush is usually associated with carcinoids of the ileum, and has also been classified as the "midgut flush." The most dramatic manifestation of the malignant carcinoid syndrome is the carcinoid crisis. These patients have greatly elevated 5-HIAA levels and have flushes described as the "foregut flush." This is a much more intense flush than that of the midgut variety and it is also associated with conjunctival injection and facial edema. After repeated bouts of flushing, patients may actually take on a cyanotic hue and lionesque appearance. This type of flush is usually associated with gastric or pulmonary carcinoids.

Management of the patient with advanced and metastatic carcinoid tumors usually involves a combination of chemotherapeutic agents, octreotide, and, in some instances, hepatic arterial infusion. It should be kept in mind, however, that this is a very indolent disease. For many patients no treatment is the best treatment.

Differential Diagnosis of Jaundice

Jaundice is an abnormal yellow discoloration in the skin, sclera, or mucus membranes that develops as a result of an elevated concentration of bilirubin in the sera. The concentration of bilirubin is determined by the rate of bilirubin formation from breakdown of heme-containing compounds and the rate of bilirubin elimination via hepatic uptake, conjugation, and secretion into bile.

Generally, jaundice is not physically evident until the serum bilirubin concentration exceeds 3 mg/dl. The measurement of serum bilirubin is conventionally by the diazo reaction (van den Bergh reaction). Conjugated bilirubin will react "directly" with diazo reagents. Total bilirubin measurement requires the addition of other compounds, which facilitates the reaction of unconjugated bilirubin with the diazo reagent. Indirect bilirubin fraction is calculated by subtracting the direct bilirubin concentration from the total. Direct and indirect bilirubin concentrations are not entirely equivalent to those of conjugated and unconjugated bilirubin, respectively, but in general, an increase in the direct bilirubin concentration reflects increase in the serum concentration of conjugated bilirubin and an increase in the concentration of indirect bilirubin reflects increase in the concentration of unconjugated bilirubin. More sophisticated testing methods are used to measure the concentrations of unconjugated monoglucuronidated and diglucuronidated bilirubin, as well as conjugated bilirubin-albumin complexes. These sophisticated methods may occasionally be helpful in determining isolated disorders of bilirubin and metabolism from other causes of jaundice, but the conventional diazo method for measurement of serum bilirubin is what is used in the vast majority of patients.

In considering the differential diagnosis of jaundice, either an increase in bilirubin formation or a decrease in hepatic clearance may lead to jaundice. This differential can be further simplified by dividing into three broad categories: isolated disorders of bilirubin metabolism; liver disease; and obstruction of the bile ducts. Table 63-2 reviews the more common etiologies in the differential diagnoses of jaundice. Many of the conditions listed under liver disease and obstruction of the bile ducts are discussed in other sections. Further discussion of the isolated disorders of bilirubin metabolism is included in this section.

There are isolated disorders of bilirubin metabolism that have decreased hepatic clearance leading to jaundice.

Gilbert's syndrome is a hereditary disorder of decreased hepatic clearance of bilirubin leading to unconjugated hyperbilirubinemia. It is fairly common, and is seen in about 5 percent of caucasian adults in the United States. This frequently presents in an otherwise healthy patient in the second or third decade of life, frequently pre-

TABLE 63-2   Differential Diagnosis of Jaundice

Isolated Disorders of Bilirubin Metabolism
  Increased production (hemolysis, blood transfusion, hematoma)
  Decreased hepatic clearance
    Decreased uptake or conjugation of bilirubin (Gilbert's syndrome, Crigler-Najjar syndrome, physiological jaundice of the newborn, drugs)
    Decreased canalicular secretion (Dubin-Johnson syndrome, Rotor syndrome)
Liver Disease
  Hepatocellular dysfunction—acute or chronic
    Viral hepatitis; hepatotoxins (ethanol, acetaminophen); drugs; ischemia; metabolic disordes (Reye's syndrome, Wilson's disease, hemochromatosis); pregnancy-related (acute fatty liver of pregnancy, eclampsia); autoimmune hepatitis
  Cholestatic
    Primary biliary cirrhosis; graft versus host disease; drugs; infiltrative disorders (granulomatous disease such as sarcoid, lymphoma, mycobacterial infections, Wegener's); amyloidosis; malignancy; miscellaneous conditions including benign recurrent intrahepatic cholestasis; estrogens; anabolic steroids; total parenteral nutrition; bacterial infections; pregnancy-related such as hyperemesis gravidarum, intrahepatic cholestasis of pregnancy; pregnancy.
Obstruction of the Bile Ducts
  Choledocholithiasis
  Bile duct disease
    Neoplasms
    Inflammation (primary sclerosing cholangitis, AIDS cholangiopathy)
  Biliary compression
    Neoplasms (pancreatic carcinoma, hepatoma, metastatic lymphadenopathy)
  Pancreatitis

senting with mild scleral icterus. The diagnosis of Gilbert's syndrome is established by demonstration of repeated normal liver function tests in an asymptomatic patient with a mild elevation of unconjugated bilirubin and no evidence of hemolysis. Liver biopsy is unnecessary. It is most important to establish the diagnosis of Gilbert's syndrome as reassurance to the patient and also to avoid unnecessary investigations or even surgical interventions.

Crigler-Najjar syndrome (congenital nonhe-

molytic jaundice) is uncommon and also leads to unconjugated neonatal hyperbilirubinemia. There are two types of this syndrome. In Type I, the majority of patients develop kernicterus and die in the neonatal period. Type II Crigler-Najjar syndrome patients may reach adulthood. These patients have bilirubin concentrations between 5 and 50 mg/dl, all of which is unconjugated.

Examples of hereditary conjugated hyperbilirubinemias are Dubin-Johnson and Rotor syndromes. Dubin-Johnson syndrome is uncommon, and has autosomal recessive inheritance. The plasma bilirubin concentration is usually less than 7 mg/dl, and about half of this is conjugated. The bilirubin concentration frequently rises with exogenous estrogen, so some of these patients are not detected until they start using birth control pills. There is no specific therapy except avoidance of exogenous estrogens. A classic diagnostic test is the slow disappearance of sulfobromophthalein, with a frequent secondary rise at 1 to 2 h. Rotor syndrome is a very rare autosomal recessive disorder of excretion or storage of conjugated bilirubin. The plasma bilirubin concentration is usually less than 7 mg/dl and about half of this is conjugated. Affected patients classically have a very slow disappearance of the plasma sulfobromophthalein without a secondary rise. There is no treatment available and affected individuals have a normal prognosis.

The most common causes of increased bilirubin production leading to jaundice are hemolysis, ineffective erythropoiesis, or resorption of a hematoma. Patients with hemolytic anemia are prone to jaundice, as are patients with hereditary or acquired megaloblastic anemia from either folate or vitamin B_{12} deficiency. Jaundice may also follow massive transfusion. Major trauma with subsequent resorption of hematomas can also cause an increase in bilirubin production.

Important clues regarding the etiology of jaundice can be obtained through the patient's history and physical examination. In a jaundiced patient who is otherwise asymptomatic, has a normal physical examination, and normal serum activities of alkaline phosphatase and transaminases, jaundice is unlikely to be due to liver disease or biliary obstruction. Further testing for specific disorders such as isolated defects in bilirubin metabolism or hemolysis is warranted. On the other hand, if the history and physical examination are abnormal and laboratory studies suggest the possibility of obstruction of the biliary tree, an imaging study is appropriate either to confirm the presence of biliary tract obstruction and localize an obstruction or to exclude it. The least invasive imaging studies are abdominal ultrasound and computed tomography of the abdomen. Ultrasound has the advantage of being noninvasive, portable, and least expensive; however, bowel gas may obscure the common bile duct and it is difficult to perform in obese individuals. Abdominal CT scan is another noninvasive test with higher resolution than ultrasound, and it is also not as operator-dependent as ultrasound. However, it is not available in portable form and it can only visualize calcified gallstones. Intravenous contrast is typically required for abdominal CT and this is potentially nephrotoxic. Other biliary imaging studies include endoscopicretrograde cholangiopancreatography or percutaneous transhepatic cholangiography. These permit direct visualization of the biliary tree as well as the pancreatic ducts (for ERCP). They are more invasive than ultrasound or CT and require consultation with a gastroenterologist or invasive radiologist.

A decision tree for the evaluation and management of jaundice would list history, physical examination, and routine laboratory tests at the top. If the alkaline phosphatase or transaminases are normal, then the direction of investigation should be turned to evaluation for hemolysis and hereditary hyperbilirubinemias. On the other hand, if the alkaline phosphatase or transaminases are abnormal, and the clinical likelihood of biliary obstruction is low, one should proceed to biochemical studies for specific liver diseases. This might eventually require a liver biopsy for definitive diagnosis. If the clinical likelihood of biliary obstruction is high, one should consider having an ERCP or percutaneous transhepatic

cholangiogram performed with therapeutic intervention accompanying the procedure. If the clinical likelihood of biliary obstruction is low, then one should proceed with evaluation by a less invasive test, such as abdominal ultrasound or CT scan. If dilated bile ducts are found, then the patient should be evaluated for ERCP or percutaneous transhepatic cholangiogram. If the abdominal ultrasound or CT scan shows nondilated bile ducts, further biochemical studies should be done looking for specific disease states.

Findings that are suggestive of obstructive jaundice include a history of abdominal pain, fever, prior biliary surgery, and older age. Physical exam findings might include a high fever, abdominal tenderness, palpable abdominal mass, or abdominal scar. Laboratory studies suggestive of obstructive jaundice include predominant elevation of serum bilirubin and alkaline phosphatase, elevated serum amylase, and a prothrombin time that is normal or normalizes with vitamin K administration.

On the other hand, findings more consistent with cholestatic liver disease include a history of anorexia, malaise, or myalgias, or possibly symptoms suggestive of a viral prodrome. Other history to consider in the evaluation of cholestatic liver disease includes known infectious exposure, receipt of blood products or use of intravenous drugs, exposure to known hepatotoxin, or family history of jaundice. Physical examination findings supporting cholestatic liver disease include ascites, asterixis, encephalopathy, and other stigmata of chronic liver disease (such as prominent abdominal veins and spider angiomata). Laboratory investigation might show a predominant elevation of the serum transaminases, prolonged prothrombin time that does not easily correct with vitamin K administration, or blood tests indicative of specific liver diseases.

Liver Disorders

Acute Hepatitis

Acute viral hepatitis is a syndrome of liver injury resulting from viral infection of the liver which, by definition, persists for less than 4 months. The clinical features of acute viral hepatitis are similar regardless of the etiology. Symptoms such as nausea, anorexia, abdominal pain, malaise, arthralgia, and fever are common to all the etiologies of viral hepatitis. Findings on physical examination are also similar in the various forms of viral hepatitis. A detailed history may be suggestive, but is usually not conclusive for identifying the precise etiology. The viral etiologies of viral hepatitis can, therefore, only be distinguished by a series of sensitive and specific serological assays. Liver biopsy is usually not useful in acute hepatitis. In the majority of patients with acute viral hepatitis, the disease is asymptomatic and may only be detected in retrospect when antibodies are detected. In all cases, acute hepatitis is associated with elevation in serum aminotransferase activity; serum alkaline phosphatase, γ-glutamyl transferase, and bilirubin levels may be elevated.

Hepatitis related to hepatic viruses A, B, C, D, and E is discussed in the following section (Table 63-3). Hepatitis may also be caused by other viruses such as Epstein-Barr virus (mononucleosis), cytomegalovirus, and herpes simplex virus.

Some etiologies of acute hepatitis, including viruses, can lead to chronic hepatitis, which is a term applied to liver disease that is protracted and necroinflammatory in nature. As a general rule,

chronic hepatitis is defined as abnormal liver enzyme activity for at least a 6-month period. Such ongoing inflammation of the liver has the potential of culminating in cirrhosis. In addition to viruses, there are multiple other etiologies of chronic hepatitis including drugs, alcohol, Wilson's disease, α_1-antitrypsin deficiency, hemochromatosis, autoimmunity, primary biliary cirrhosis, and primary sclerosing cholangitis. In some instances, no specific etiology can be uncovered.

Hepatitis A Hepatitis A (HAV), usually the least severe form of viral hepatitis, is caused by a small RNA virus. The epidemiology of hepatitis A is based on fecal-oral spread, and typically occurs as an outbreak. In the United States, epidemics are often traced to a common food source or to situations, such as institutional living or day care, that facilitate this manner of spread. For those same reasons, hepatitis A is common among children in developing countries. It is generally an acute and self-limited illness, and although fulminant hepatic failure has been recorded, it is rare. Virus appears in the bloodstream at about the same time that symptoms commence, and can persist for up to 12 weeks. Virus does not persist thereafter; there is no chronic carrier state for hepatitis A. The detection of elevated titers of IgM anti-HAV indicates acute disease. A second antibody (IgG anti-HAV) appears approximately 3 months later and indicates immunity. Generally, no specific therapy is required other than supportive therapy. Corticosteroids may be useful if, as may occur rarely, there is a prolonged cholestatic phase. γ-Globulin provides short-term protection to close contacts. Hepatitis A vaccine is now available and recommended especially when traveling to high risk areas.

Hepatitis B Hepatitis B (HBV) is a 42-μm DNA virus that consists of a central core that contains DNA, DNA polymerase, hepatitis B core antigen (Hb$_c$Ag), and hepatitis B$_e$ antigen (HB$_e$Ag). This core is surrounded by an envelope of surface protein, hepatitis B surface antigen (HB$_s$Ag). The interpretation of HBV serological tests is complex but clinically important. There

TABLE 63-3 Comparison of Features of the Three Common Forms of Acute Viral Hepatitis

	Hepatitis A	Hepatitis B	Hepatitis C
Virus	HAV	HBV	HCV
Source	Fecal-oral	Blood-borne	Blood-borne
Incubation	15–50 days	50–150 days	15–150 days
Chronicity	No, 0%	Yes, 10%	High, 50%
Antigens	HAV Ag	HB$_s$Ag Hb$_c$Ag Hb$_e$Ag	HCV Ag
Antibodies	Anti-HAV	Anti-HB$_s$ Anti-HB$_c$ Anti-HB$_e$	Anti-HCV

are a few general guidelines for interpretation of these tests; complex cases often may need to be referred for interpretation. HB_sAg, the earliest marker, typically appears 4 to 12 weeks after infection. This is followed in sequence by the appearance of HB_eAg, IgM anti-HB_c and subsequently, IgG anti-HB_c. HB_sAg indicates the presence of virus and that the patient is infected. Anti-HB_s means the patient is immune. The detection of HB_eAg provides evidence of active viral replication. This replication stage can also be quantitated by an HBV DNA assay. The detection of IgM anti-B_c through an early antibody response does not indicate protection. IgM anti-HB_c alone can be used to screen for acute hepatitis, but this strategy could miss the very early stages of hepatitis B infection when HB_sAg alone will be detected. As the infection is resolving, there is seroconversion of HB_eAg to anti-HB_eAg, and seroconversion of HB_sAg to anti-HB_s follows from a few weeks to several months later. IgM anti-HB_c eventually disappears after the acute phase of the disease; however, IgG anti-HB_c persists for years or perhaps for a lifetime.

Therapy for acute hepatitis B infection relies on supportive measures alone. The identification of chronic hepatitis B is based on the persistence of hepatitis B surface antigen for more than 6 months. Chronic disease can be treated with α-interferon (5 million units per day for 3 to 6 months), but only a small percentage of patients will be cured with interferon therapy.

A hepatitis B virus vaccine is available that is safe, cost-effective, and the most effective means of preventing this disease. All individuals at risk should be vaccinated.

Hepatitis C Hepatitis C (HCV) is a 55-μm RNA virus. There are several strains of this virus, some of which may differ in biological effects. This virus is transmitted parenterally and accounts for almost 95 percent of all cases of transfusion-related non-A, non-B hepatitis. The incubation period is 4 to 12 weeks, but can be longer. Serum aminotransferase levels can be 10 to 20 times normal, but often demonstrate rather characteristic fluctuations in an individual patient.

Approximately 50 percent of infected patients progress to develop chronic active hepatitis. Chronic infection can evolve to cirrhosis over a 10- to 20-year period, accompanied by a significant risk for the later development of hepatocellular carcinoma.

The hepatitis C antibody assay does not distinguish acute from chronic disease. Initial tests approved for the detection of hepatitis C detected antibody directed against a single epitope on HCV; second-generation tests are available that detect four antibodies with improved sensitivity. RNA testing is now available to give an estimation of the virus load involved in a particular infection.

α-Interferon, 3 million units 3 times a week for 24 weeks, is the current standard therapy for chronic HCV. However, recurrences and treatment failures are common. Newly released is ribavirin. Combination therapy with ribavirin and interferon is currently used in nonresponders and patients who relapse. There is currently no vaccine available to prevent hepatitis C.

Hepatitis D Hepatitis D (HDV) virus is a very small RNA virus that is a parasite of hepatitis B virus. The delta virus attaches itself to an HBV and uses its surface antigen coating to survive and multiply. This binding by delta virus may, in turn, prevent the detection of HB_sAg. Hepatitis D virus should be suspected in patients with chronic hepatitis B who have negative HB_sAg test results and persistent aminotransferase abnormality. Currently the only serologic marker for delta hepatitis virus is hepatitis D virus antibody (HDV Ab).

Because delta hepatitis virus requires hepatitis B virus for replication, only populations at risk for B virus can be infected. HBV and HDV can be acquired simultaneously (coinfection) or sequentially (superinfection). Superinfection usually results in a chronic carrier state. Coinfection, in contrast, results in acute disease with resolution.

α-Interferon is not active against this infection. The best strategy against this disorder is to prevent hepatitis B infection by vaccination.

Hepatitis E Hepatitis E (HEV) is another RNA virus that is spread by fecal-oral contamination. This virus has been responsible for waterborne epidemics, and, for the most part, instances in the United States have been restricted to those who acquired infection in the course of overseas travel. This is usually an acute, self-limited disease that often has a prominent cholestatic phase. Pregnant women who acquire HEV have a high rate of fulminant hepatic failure. Serologic tests are not commercially available. There is no known therapy and no vaccine.

Chronic Liver Disease

Chronic Hepatitis Chronic hepatitis is a term applied to all liver disease that is protracted, generally greater than 6 months in duration, and necroinflammatory in nature. This disorder has the potential to develop into cirrhosis and to result in primary hepatocellular carcinoma. Chronic hepatitis is the consequence of numerous stimuli, differing mechanisms and sequelae, and responses to treatment that vary widely.

There are three primary clinical circumstances that warrant consideration of the diagnosis of chronic hepatitis: First, persons with a previous history of acute viral hepatitis may continue to have elevated serum enzyme levels for longer than 6 months (see ''Acute Hepatitis'' above for further details). Second, patients may present with overt cirrhosis with portal hypertension or hepatic failure, or with hepatocellular carcinoma. These individuals generally escape detection of the initial acute hepatitis because of the asymptomatic nature of the process. Third, the majority of patients with chronic hepatitis are identified when routine biochemical screening tests reveal abnormal aminotransferase activity.

A liver biopsy is required for a conclusive diagnosis of chronic hepatitis. There can be a wide variety of lesions of varying severity. Liver biopsy is important not only for diagnosis but for prognosis. The etiology of chronic hepatitis is heterogeneous in origin, consisting of viral, autoimmune, hepatotoxic, and metabolic disorders. It is imperative to distinguish the etiology of chronic hepatitis because prognosis and therapy vary accordingly.

The first step in any clinical evaluation involves obtaining a careful history. This should include family, social, travel, occupational, and medical history. Questions should address intravenous drug use; use of alcohol; sexual behavior; family history of liver, lung, neurologic, endocrine, or autoimmune diseases; travel; place of birth; workplace exposure to hepatotoxic chemicals; a complete medication summary including those medications used in the past; transfusions; needle sticks; acupuncture; tattooing; and previous history of jaundice or hepatitis. It is important to ask about current and past medications. The list of medications associated with chronic hepatitis is large and continues to grow. Some of the more common drugs implicated are listed in Table 63-4.

Physical examination should look for signs of chronic liver disease and of portal hypertension. Portal hypertension can manifest as ascites, esophageal varices, prominent hemorrhoids, caput medusa, and splenomegaly. Other stigmata of chronic liver disease include liver nails, palmar erythema, telangiectasias, or spider angioma.

Laboratory evaluation should include biochemical tests directed at defining the presence of liver disease such as total and direct serum bilirubin, AST, ALT, alkaline phosphatase, total serum proteins, serum albumin, protime, and hepatitis serologies as described in the earlier

TABLE 63-4 **Drugs Implicated as Causes for Chronic Hepatitis**

Methyldopa
Sulfonamides
Nitrofurantoin
Dantrolene
Oxyphenistatin
Papaverine
Propylthiouracil
Isoniazid

section on acute viral hepatitis. Other specialized tests are conducted once it has been concluded that chronic hepatitis probably exists. These tests help identify the specific disease process inducing the chronic hepatitis. Examples include ordering a ceruloplasmin when evaluating for Wilson's disease or ordering a protein electrophoresis and Pi typing when looking for α_1-antitrypsin deficiency. Serum iron, transferrin saturation, and serum ferritin are used to further define hemochromatosis. Evaluation of chronic hepatitis is often best handled by a gastroenterologist. Liver biopsy may provide important pathologic clues for diagnosing the etiology of chronic hepatitis. Treatment will depend on the etiology of the chronic hepatitis.

Hemochromatosis Hemochromatosis is an autosomal recessive disorder of iron metabolism that leads to increased total body iron and excessive iron deposition in several organs. It can be either primary or secondary (e.g., due to excessive transfusion or excessive intake of iron, thalassemia, or other ineffective erythropoiesis/hemolysis syndromes). The classic tetrad of presentation is diabetes, cirrhosis, congestive heart failure, and bronze skin, all reflective of areas of iron deposition such as the pancreas, heart, liver, and skin. Hepatomegaly is almost invariably present. Hepatocellular carcinoma complicates the disease approximately 20 percent of the time. Iron studies show increased iron levels, transferrin saturation, and ferritin. Liver biopsy is still a standard of care for establishing the diagnosis, and is useful for distinguishing primary from secondary forms. In hemochromatosis, the total body iron is increased 5- to 10-fold, and the standard of care is phlebotomy. One unit of blood will phlebotomize the equivalent of 250 mg of iron. Chelation therapy can be used for those patients who do not tolerate phlebotomy.

Wilson's Disease Wilson's disease is an autosomal recessive inherited disorder of copper metabolism that leads to accumulation of copper in tissues, including the liver, brain, eyes, skeleton, and kidneys. The clinical presentation is variable, but tends to be either hepatic or neurologic.

Kayser-Fleischer rings are diagnostic. They may be absent when the patient presents with liver disease, but are always present when patients present with neurologic disease. Serum ceruloplasmin is typically low, as is serum copper. Urine copper excretion is increased and liver copper is always elevated. Treatment is with copper chelation therapy, penicillamine.

α_1-Antitrypsin Deficiency α_1-Antitrypsin deficiency is an inherited deficiency of serum protease inhibitor, variably associated with emphysema and liver disease. The protease inhibitor phenotype ZZ is the phenotype associated with clinical liver and lung disease. Orthotopic liver transplantation has been successful with patients with advanced liver disease.

Alcoholic Liver Disease Alcoholic liver disease has three major clinical pathologic settings: alcoholic fatty liver; alcoholic hepatitis; and alcoholic fibrosis and cirrhosis. The clinical picture of cirrhosis is related to three separate entities: portal hypertension; loss of parenchymal function; and extrahepatic injury produced by alcoholism. In advanced cirrhosis, the chief manifestations result from portal hypertension, expressed as esophageal, gastric, or duodenal varices; splenomegaly; hypersplenism; and ascites. Hepatic encephalopathy is easily precipitated because of the distorted portal venous flow and inadequate parenchymal hepatic function. In patients with ascites, bacterial peritonitis is an easily overlooked and frequently fatal complication. The key to treatment is abstinence from alcohol and treatment of the complications of portal hypertension.

Primary Biliary Cirrhosis Primary biliary cirrhosis (PBC) is a progressive, nonsuppurative, destructive intrahepatic cholangitis. PBC is characterized by gradual, progressive destruction of medium-sized intrahepatic bile ducts. It more commonly affects middle-aged women, but can be diagnosed in women from ages 20 to 60. Typically, it presents as asymptomatic elevation in the alkaline phosphatase, and it can present with pruritus, progressive jaundice, cirrhosis, or liver failure. Clinical manifestations more specific for primary biliary cirrhosis are xanthelasma and xanthomata and skin hyperpigmentation. Patients can have associated connective tissue diseases including Sjögren's syndrome and collagen vascular diseases. Diagnosis generally rests on the presence of an antimitochondrial antibody (AMA) and specific changes on liver biopsy. Patients frequently have high serum cholesterol levels, and jaundice is usually a late finding.

There is no effective cure for PBC, but ursodeoxycholic acid improves biochemical markers and slows histological progression. Liver transplantation is another form of treatment. Cholestyramine should be given for pruritus.

Diarrhea: Differential Diagnosis and Treatment

Diarrhea can be defined as the "too frequent passage of too liquid stool." As a symptom, diarrhea can manifest as an increase in stool frequency, an increase in stool volume, or a decrease in stool consistency.

History and Differential Diagnosis

The frequency of bowel movements varies considerably in the general population, from three stools per week to three stools per day being normal, and it is considerably influenced by diet. In individuals on a typical American diet, diarrhea is defined as a stool weight in excess of 150 to 200 g per 24 h. In obtaining the history it is important to determine what is normal for each patient; recent changes often prove to be most significant. The clinical history is of paramount importance. If the duration of diarrhea is short, meaning less than 3 weeks, the diarrhea is most often infectious and the illness self-limiting. Chronic diarrheas, those of greater than 3 weeks duration, need complete investigation. Two major clinical distinctions need to be made when evaluating a patient complaining of diarrhea: Is the diarrhea inflammatory or noninflammatory? Is the diarrhea secretory or osmotic? Based on

the answers to these questions four major clinical categories of diarrhea can be distinguished: osmotic; secretory; inflammatory; and functional (see also Inflammatory Bowel Disease and Irritable Bowel Syndrome). This clinical categorization of diarrhea can be accomplished on the basis of clinical evaluation and two simple diagnostic tests.

On history, inflammatory diarrhea is characterized by frequent mucoid or bloody stools, at times accompanied by tenesmus, fever, and abdominal pain. Microscopic examination of a stool specimen typically reveals many fecal leukocytes and red blood cells. In contrast, in noninflammatory diarrhea, the diarrhea is watery, frequently of large volumes (over 1 liter per day) and blood and pus are absent. Abdominal pain and fever are also usually absent. The importance of examination of the stool smear for both the presence of fecal leukocytes and red blood cells is clear. White blood cells in the stool indicate the existence of an inflammatory process somewhere in the gastrointestinal tract.

There are several mechanisms involved in producing inflammation-induced diarrhea. The epithelium is stimulated to secrete by a variety of substances made by neutrophils, activated enteric nerves, and immune cells. Inflammatory reaction products may also lead to mucosal destruction, increased permeability, and nutrient malabsorption and maldigestion. Etiologies of inflammatory diarrhea include ulcerative colitis and Crohn's disease, antibiotic-associated colitis, radiation colitis, diverticulitis, and such infectious causes as shigella, campylobacter, salmonella, *E. coli,* and amoebiasis.

If diarrhea appears to be noninflammatory, the next step in the evaluation is to determine whether the diarrhea is osmotic or secretory. The distinction is best made by measuring fecal sodium and potassium concentrations and osmolality, and then calculating the stool "anion gap." When requesting the stool osmolality assay, it is important to perform the test on a fresh stool sample. If the stool is allowed to sit for a period of time, bacteria begins to act on the stool, changing the osmolality. The sum of the measured sodium and potassium concentrations is multiplied by 2 to account for anions in the stool. If the stool osmolality exceeds what can be accounted for by the measured electrolytes, then an osmolar gap exists and the diarrhea is defined as osmotic diarrhea. In secretory diarrheas, in contrast, stool osmolality is related almost entirely to the concentration of sodium and potassium and their related anions and an osmotic gap does not, therefore, exist. Secretory diarrhea tends to be of large volume, often greater than 1 liter per day, and continues during fasting, while osmotic diarrhea tends to be of smaller volume and ceases with fasting.

Osmotically induced diarrhea results when nonabsorbable ions or solutes are ingested or produced in the intestinal lumen. Because these solutes are not absorbed, they exert an osmotic force on the enterocytes resulting in water being drawn into the lumen and excreted. Causes of osmotic diarrhea include the ingestion of poorly absorbed solutes (prune juice, magnesium sulfate- and phosphate-containing laxatives, antacids, sorbitol, and sulfates), disaccharidase deficiency (e.g., lactase deficiency), maldigestion, pancreatic insufficiency, and any disorder of digestion or absorption that results in the intraluminal accumulation of unabsorbed carbohydrate.

Stimuli that drive the epithelium to actively secrete water and electrolytes result in secretory diarrhea. Infectious agents may cause secretory diarrheas by any one of four mechanisms: the elaboration of an enterotoxin, such as occurs with cholera and *E. coli;* the direct invasion of the intestinal epithelium, such as occurs with salmonella, shigella, and campylobacter; the elaboration of cytotoxic substances, such as occurs with *Clostridium difficile,* some shigella species, and enterohemorrhagic *E. coli;* and through an enteroadherent mechanism associated with a variety of *E. coli.* In addition to these bacterial agents, a number of protozoal agents and viruses may also be responsible. Examples include *Giardia, Cryptosporidia,* and *Microsporidia.* Peptides secreted by a variety of tumors can also cause secretory diarrhea. Examples include calcitonin from medullary carcinoma of the thyroid, serotonin from carcinoid tumors, gastrin in the Zollinger-Ellison syndrome, and vasoactive intestinal peptide (VIP) from ganglioneuromas. A number of luminal detergents also act as intestinal secretagogues, including bile acids, long-chain fatty acids, and certain laxatives. When the terminal ileum has been resected or severely damaged, such as in inflammatory bowel disease, unabsorbed bile salts and fatty acids are delivered into the colon where they act as potent intestinal secretagogues and result in the colonic secretion of electrolytes and water.

In the United States, the most common infectious causes of acute diarrhea are campylobacter, salmonella, shigella, enterohemorrhagic *E. coli, Giardia,* and a number of viruses. *Giardia* and bacteria should be sought initially by stool culture and three stool exams for ova and parasites. If this does not establish a diagnosis, a distal duodenal or jejunal biopsy and aspirate should then be obtained to further exclude *Giardia.* When an acute diarrhea develops, especially in a hospitalized patient, two specific etiologies must be considered: *Clostridium difficile* colitis (pseudomembranous colitis) or medication effects. Medication effects may be direct side effects (examples include methyl xanthines, β blockers, antacids, antibiotics) or related to vehicles such as sorbitol and mannitol, which are common in various elixirs.

Treatment of Diarrhea

Treatment, of course, depends on the etiology of the diarrhea, but should be mainly directed to preventing dehydration and restoring lost volume. This is frequently achieved with intravenous fluids; in many circumstances the same goal could be achieved with oral fluid and electrolyte therapy. The sodium substrate-coupled absorptive pathway is preserved in many diarrheal disorders and appropriate formulated solutions (such as Pedialyte or Gatorade) can take advantage of this intact absorptive pathway. Home remedies such as soda and fruit juices are suboptimal because they are generally deficient in electrolytes and poor replacements for diarrheal losses. Commercially available oral rehydration solutions are formulated to take advantage of the glucose sodium-coupled transport mechanism to stimulate sodium and thus water absorption. They are strongly recommended for use in adults, as well as in children.

Constipation

Constipation is one of the most common gastrointestinal symptoms of patients seen in the general physician's office. A majority of patients suffer from constipation at some point in their lives; however, it usually does not become a chronic, recurrent problem.

There is no one definition of constipation, but one accepted definition of constipation is less than two or three bowel movements per week, or extreme straining with more than 25 percent of evacuation efforts. Simple measures, such as dietary changes and fiber supplementation, suffice in managing most patients.

A careful history is by far the most important method of delineating the problem. Important points in the patient's history include the onset of constipation and its duration. Severe constipation that has been lifelong, often dating from early childhood, suggests a congenital abnormality such as Hirschsprung's disease. Not infrequently, onset after an illness or traumatic event, such as surgery, will be noted. Diet and medications are also critical points to be examined. The use of medications, particularly laxatives, narcotics, and anticholinergics must be ascertained. The nature of the bowel movement must be outlined in some detail, including the frequency and timing of evacuation; time spent on the commode; alternate methods of evacuation (squatting, digitally assisted evacuation); color, consistency, and size of the stools; abdominal discomfort; and bleeding. Gynecologic disorders, including urinary incontinence, cystocele, uterine prolapse,

previous hysterectomy, endometriosis, and rectocele, and obstetric history are also factors to consider. Prior surgeries and anal-rectal complaints must be discussed. Child abuse or spouse abuse, sexual orientation, and anal receptive intercourse may all be significant factors.

On physical examination, the degree of abdominal distension and neurological examination, including sensation in the pelvic saddle area, must be assessed. The exam should also include a Valsalva maneuver as the physician checks for rectal prolapse. Especially in the parous woman, a large rectocele bulging into the vagina would be strongly suggestive of the etiology of constipation.

After a careful history and physical examination (including evaluation to make certain that the woman is not pregnant), a sigmoidoscopy and barium enema are usually done to rule out mechanical obstruction. Laboratory evaluation to rule out metabolic and endocrine disorders including hypercalcemia, hypothyroidism, and hypokalemia should be undertaken. If a history of infrequent defecation is noted, colonic transit may be measured by using radiopaque markers for assessment of transit time. No enemas or laxatives should be used during the transit study, and a written diary of bowel movements should be kept while markers are being evaluated by x-ray studies. A majority of patients assessed will show abnormal colonic transit. Patients with slow transit can further be subdivided into three groups. Most commonly colonic inertia is seen; transit seems to be delayed in the right colon or even throughout the entire colon. The left colon and rectosigmoid seem to be the areas of delay in hindgut dysfunction. In outlet dysfunction, markers reach the rectum rapidly, but stay there for long periods of time.

Anorectal manometry should be used to rule out short-segment Hirschsprung's disease in those patients in whom rectal retention seems to be the primary problem. Defecography (evacuation proctography) may also be used to assess relaxation and contractions or to identify rectoceles or intussusceptions that may interfere with evacuation. Defecography generally should be reserved for those patients whose symptoms indicate difficulty in evacuation of the rectum. In patients in whom colonic inertia is diagnosed by colonic transit studies, esophageal, gastric, and small intestinal motility should be evaluated to rule out one of the forms of chronic intestinal pseudo-obstruction.

Most patients with constipation may be successfully treated with a conservative bowel management program consisting of a high-fiber diet, plenty of liquids, fiber supplementation (psyllium), and stool softener. A rigorous trial with this approach, and the occasional judicious use of laxatives such as milk of magnesia or enemas, is necessary for at least 3 to 6 months. Only a very small group of patients will not respond and will have no other identifiable etiology for their constipation. When anatomic abnormalities are found, such as a rectocele, these patients should be evaluated for surgical correction.

Colonic inertia rarely responds to cholinergic agents, but cisapride, a synthetic prokinetic agent, is helpful in alleviating constipation in some cases of colonic inertia. Surgery is quite useful in limited, clearly defined groups of patients, especially in those with short-segment Hirschsprung's disease.

Irritable Bowel Syndrome

This is a disease more commonly reported in women. They are often middle-aged or younger, and tend to be affluent. Affected patients have symptoms consisting primarily of abdominal discomfort and altered consistency of the stool, either recurrent diarrhea or recurrent constipation, or most commonly, alternation between the two. This is a diagnosis of exclusion. The diagnosis requires that no anatomic or histologic explanations for the symptoms are found. Synonyms for irritable bowel syndrome include spastic colon, spastic colitis, and functional bowel disease. The term colitis actually should not be used because it implies inflammation, and these patients do not have an inflammatory process.

The actual presentation varies from patient to patient, but usually includes abdominal distress which may vary from week to week in the same patient. These patients frequently complain of abdominal distension, flatulence, cramping, and belching. Their abdominal discomfort is most typically in the lower quadrants, but is also seen in the left upper-quadrant. It tends to be a diffuse type of discomfort, and is not localized to one specific area. Patients with irritable bowel syndrome (IBS) generally do not have pain that awakens them at night, and if diarrhea is one of their symptoms, the diarrhea is not nocturnal. Stool pattern and consistency are commonly diagnostic in their variability. Patients most frequently describe alternating constipation and diarrhea.

Patients presenting with IBS typically have numerous other complaints such as gastroesophageal reflux, dysphagia, heartburn, chest pain, and nausea. There are many investigators who believe that IBS is not just a disease of the GI tract, but much more widespread throughout the body.

A number of factors have been associated with IBS. Symptoms may be induced with stress, alcohol, medications, dietary products, or psychological factors. Certain medications are more likely to induce IBS symptoms and they include antibiotics, narcotics, diuretics, and cardiac medication. A previous history of sexual abuse or history of psychiatric disorders has been documented in a subset of patients with IBS. Other investigators believe that the majority of patients with IBS have normal psychological profiles, and it is only in a small subset of patients that seek repeated medical attention that there is a history of abnormal psyche involved.

Typically patients will not have a bowel movement for several days followed by the frequent passage of hard stool, then passage of stools that the patient frequently describes as being worm-like, long, and accompanied by mucus. Bleeding is not a part of irritable bowel syndrome.

Physical exam is usually unremarkable except for perhaps lower-quadrant tenderness to deep palpation. Because this syndrome is a diagnosis of exclusion, it is important to examine the colon with either a flexible sigmoidoscopy and barium enema or colonoscopy. Organic problems need to be excluded such as diverticular disease, inflammatory bowel disease, and microscopic or collagenous colitis.

This group of patients has documented abnormal motility tests in various parts of the gastrointestinal tract including the esophagus, small bowel, and colon. It is still debatable whether there is an underlying myoelectric abnormality in patients with irritable bowel syndrome. Studies suggest that the volume of gas within the gastrointestinal tract in patients with irritable bowel syndrome is normal, but that the response to measured volumes of gas is abnormally perceived.

The mainstay of treatment of irritable bowel disease is a high-fiber diet, and fiber supplementation such as bulking mucoloids (psyllium). The addition of antispasmodics is sometimes beneficial, whereas therapy with antispasmodics alone or with antidiarrheal agents is usually unsatisfactory. Reassurance is a key factor in the treatment process of patients with this disorder. Stress management and mental health intervention should be considered in some patients.

References and Selected Readings

1. Borum ML: Gastrointestinal diseases in women. *Med Clin North Am* 82(1):21–50, 1998.
2. Fauci A, et al: *Harrison's Principles of Internal Medicine,* 14th ed. New York: McGraw-Hill, 1997.
3. McIntyre N, Benhomon JP, Bircher J, Rizzetto M, Rodes J (eds): *Oxford Textbook of Clinical Hepatology.* Oxford: Oxford University Press, 1991.
4. Sherlock S, Dooley J (eds): *Diseases of the Liver and Biliary System,* 10th ed. Oxford: Blackwell Scientific, 1997.
5. Sleisenger MH, Fordtran JS (eds): *Gastrointestinal Disease: Pathophysiology, Diagnosis, Management,* 5th ed. Philadelphia: WB Saunders, 1993.
6. Yamada T (ed): *Textbook of Gastroenterology,* 2d ed. Philadelphia: JB Lippincott, 1995.

CHAPTER 64

The Acute Abdomen

Richard C. Pees
Rodrique Mortel

The term acute abdomen is used when a patient presents with abdominal pain of sudden onset, or abdominal pain of gradual onset that increases in intensity over time. The pain may become diffuse, or remain localized. Frequently, it is associated with nausea and emesis. Patients with an acute abdomen present a true diagnostic challenge. The underlying pathology may require immediate surgical intervention, or a period of close observation.

The perception and interpretation of pain are subjective, and may be influenced by the patient's cultural, socioeconomic, and educational background. The level of anxiety and discomfort will be expressed differently in a stoic versus an hysterical individual. The diagnostic task can be made easier if there is a clear understanding of abdominal anatomy, neuroanatomy, and pathophysiology of disease.

There are several categories of abdominal pain: *Visceral pain* usually is poorly localized and is perceived as dull, burning, diffuse, waxing and waning, and/or crampy. Visceral pain fibers have their nerve endings in the parenchyma and walls of the various abdominal organs. They are sensitive to dilatation/distension, stretch, and ischemia, and are relatively insensitive to burning, cutting, compression, and crushing. Visceral pain frequently results in an autonomic response consisting of nausea, emesis, diaphoresis, hypotension, tachycardia, and diarrhea.[11]

Somatic pain usually is perceived as sharp, knife-like, and well localized. Somatic pain fibers are located in the mesentery and parietal peritoneum. The abdomen is a continuum, and pathology in one organ system frequently produces pain at distant locations.

Referred pain: As an example, the patient will perceive shoulder pain from subdiaphragmatic irritation secondary to a ruptured and/or bleeding ovarian cyst, intra-abdominal bleeding or infection, or air under the diaphragm.

History

The evaluation of a patient with an acute abdomen requires answers to several questions. The ultimate goal is to characterize the nature, onset, location, severity, duration, quality, effect of activity, and radiation patterns of the abdominal pain. Answers to these questions, coupled with a knowledge of neuroanatomy and abdominal anatomy, will result in the development of an appropriate list of differential diagnoses.[3,14] A description of the sequence of events leading up to the onset of the pain is extremely helpful. It is also important to know whether the pain necessitated a change in the woman's lifestyle or activity. Particular attention should be paid to the pain patterns because they may provide important clues to the etiology.

It is essential to ascertain when the pain started and whether it was gradual or sudden in onset. The effect on the pain from oral intake, meals, changes in position, urination, and defecation should be assessed. Questions should be directed to determine where the pain is located; whether the pain is sharp, dull, knife-like, burning, tearing, crampy, or ripping; how long the pain has been present; if there are any radiation patterns; if there have been any previous episodes of such pain; and if the pain is increasing or decreasing in intensity.

Pain that is sharp and sudden in onset tends to imply a potentially catastrophic event or disease process such as a ruptured viscus, ovarian cyst or mass, or ruptured ectopic pregnancy. If the pain began suddenly and is of severe intensity, it is important to know if it began during intercourse or vigorous physical activity. Pain that is the result of inflammation usually is more gradual in onset, initially not as severe, and usually associated with a temperature elevation. If generalized peritonitis is present, the patient will be lying quite still and tend to be in the fetal position with her legs drawn up toward the chest. Movement tends to exacerbate the intensity of the pain when peritonitis is present.

Crampy pain is associated with muscular contraction, and is frequently seen in individuals with a partial small bowel obstruction, early complete bowel obstruction, ureteral calculi, or biliary calculi. The location and radiation patterns of the pain will provide clues as to the particular organ

system involved. Epigastric and/or periumbilical pain is suggestive of small bowel origin; suprapubic pain implies large bowel, bladder, or reproductive organ origin; and flank/groin pain points to ureteral or kidney origin. Pancreatic pain usually is first perceived in the epigastric region, and later radiates along the costal margins to the back.

The duration of pain is also important. Pain that has been present for several hours and is intensifying implies a more severe process. The patient should be asked if there is any activity that exacerbates the pain. If the pain is relieved by simple measures such as antacids, and there are no additional or associated symptoms, then the problem may be less serious and may not require emergency therapy. If associated symptoms of diaphoresis, nausea, emesis, diarrhea, or chest discomfort are present, further evaluation is mandatory to rule out such catastrophic events as myocardial infarct, pulmonary infarct, ruptured viscus, or severe peptic ulcer disease.

It is imperative that a complete menstrual history be obtained, including the date of the last menstrual period and whether it was normal in flow, duration, and timing. If the patient is sexually active, the method of birth control being used and whether it is being used regularly and correctly need to be ascertained.

The patient needs to be questioned about the associated symptoms of nausea; emesis; diarrhea; constipation; last bowel movement; passage of flatus; chest pain or discomfort; shortness of breath; urinary tract symptoms (frequency, dysuria, burning, hematuria); hematemesis; hemoptysis; bloody or mucoid stools; loss of appetite; and anorexia. Emesis frequently occurs with small bowel obstruction, cholecystitis, appendicitis, and pancreatitis. It occurs within three to five hours following the onset of appendiceal pain, is present early and frequently in small bowel obstruction, and appears late or not at all in large bowel obstruction.[3]

Anorexia is common with pancreatitis and appendicitis. Failure to pass flatus is common with complete bowel obstruction. Diarrhea, on the other hand, is common in individuals suffering from gastroenteritis, colitis, and irritable bowel syndrome, and cyclically in those with endometriosis.

Additional inquiry should include a past history of abdominal surgery; drug allergies; prior similar episodes of this type of pain; current medications; any recent change in medications or ingestion of illegal substances; recent consumption of alcohol; and any history of abdominal trauma. A general review must address the cardiac, pulmonary, and metabolic systems, as well as connective tissue disorders. A myocardial infarct can present with upper epigastric pain and diaphoresis. Pneumonia and pulmonary emboli can cause diaphragmatic irritation and upper abdominal pain as well as shortness of breath, diaphoresis, fever, and tachycardia. Lupus and sickle cell crisis can precipitate an episode of acute abdominal pain.[1,11]

Persistent abdominal pain demands a thorough evaluation. A detailed history is critical in determining the cause of the acute abdomen. It should be remembered that a prior history of pelvic inflammatory disease (PID) does not rule out other etiologies for the pain.

Physical Examination

The examination of the patient with an acute abdomen begins by observing how the patient is sitting or lying. Observe whether the patient is lying quietly, knees or hips flexed, pacing about, or agitated. Observe whether she appears pale, flushed, or diaphoretic. Examine the abdomen for surgical incisions, distension, erythema, and/or cutaneous lesions. Evaluate for tachycardia, hypotension, hypertension, tachypnea, and fever. Tachycardia implies a sympathetic reaction to severe pain via the release of catecholemines, hypovolemia, or severe dehydration. Hypotension is suggestive of sepsis or hypovolemia. Tachypnea may imply pneumonia, pulmonary emboli, or sepsis. Fever over 103°F implies sepsis, pelvic abscess, pelvic inflammatory disease, pneumonia,

early appendicitis, or pyelonephritis. Subnormal temperatures may imply late sepsis, bowel gangrene, viscus perforation, pancreatitis, appendicitis, or pelvic inflammatory disease.[1,11,14]

Following visual inspection of the abdomen and review of the vital signs, direct examination of the abdomen is performed. The objective is to define the area of pathology and arrive at a diagnosis. Have the patient isolate the area of most intense pain by asking her to outline this area with her finger. Then auscultate the abdomen. Gently lay the stethoscope on the abdomen and listen to the quality of the bowel sounds. A silent abdomen or one with markedly decreased bowel sounds implies a complete bowel obstruction, severe peritonitis, or a potentially ruptured viscus. High pitched and increased bowel sounds may imply an early bowel obstruction. The presence of a murmur may imply the presence of arterial stenosis, aneurysm, or other vascular disease. A sense as to the degree of tenderness can also be gained by gently placing pressure on the stethoscope while auscultating the abdomen.

Palpation of the abdomen should begin away from the point or area of maximum pain. Begin by applying light pressure and then gradually increase this downward pressure. Evaluate for direct, rebound, and referred tenderness. Also evaluate for the presence or absence of guarding, rigidity, and masses. Rigidity may imply a ruptured viscus; rebound tenderness points toward an inflammatory process or peritonitis such as appendicitis, pancreatitis, cholecystitis, salpingo-oophoritis, or diverticulitis. Direct tenderness implies an early inflammatory process, ruptured ovarian cyst/mass, or ectopic pregnancy—ruptured or unruptured. Percuss the abdomen to detect tympany, which may imply a ruptured viscus or free air; dullness; and ascitic waves.

During the physical examination, the following maneuvers may be helpful in detecting an inflammatory process involving the peritoneum. If by flexing the thigh against the abdomen (iliopsoas sign), by rotating the flexed thigh internally (obturator sign), or by having the patient bounce on her heels (heel tap sign), severe pain is elicited, then the diagnosis of appendicitis, salpingo-oophoritis, diverticulitis, or peritonitis may be suspected. Likewise, if pushing in and under the right costal margin while asking the patient to take a deep breath causes her to stop the inspiration because of severe pain (Murphy's sign), then cholecystitis may be suspected.

Bimanual pelvic and rectal examination is essential. Is there discharge coming from the cervical os? Is the uterus enlarged, or are there unilateral or bilateral adnexal masses? Is there tenderness on cervical motion, or other pelvic tenderness? Is there a rectal tumor/mass?

Examination of the heart, lungs, flanks, extremities, head, and neck is required to complete a thorough evaluation of a patient with an acute abdomen.

Laboratory Testing

The results of these tests are often helpful in the evaluation of the patient:

CBC with differential
Urinalysis
Amylase
Liver function tests
Renal function tests
Electrolytes
Serum or urine pregnancy test
Abdominal/pelvic ultrasound

Additional tests that may be of some help are:

Acute abdominal x-ray series to include pulmonary diaphragms
CT scan of abdomen/pelvis
Chest x-ray

Depending on the clinical level of suspicion regarding various potential etiologies in the differential diagnosis, a variety of other studies may also be appropriate.

Differential Diagnosis

At this point in the evaluation, a differential diagnosis should be possible (Table 64-1). This differential is developed through the knowledge of anatomy, pathophysiology, and the physical examination.

TABLE 64-1 **Differential Diagnosis of the Acute Abdomen**

Right Upper Quadrant	Left Upper Quadrant
Pneumonia	Gastritis
Pulmonary emboli	Pulmonary emboli
Hepatitis	Pancreatitis
Hepatic/subdiaphragmatic abscess	Pyelonephritis
	Renal calculi
Pyelonephritis	Diverticulitis
Renal calculi	Splenic flexure syndrome
Peptic ulcer disease	Splenic rupture
Biliary disease	Myocardial infarction
Myocardial infarction	Mononucleosis
Pancreatitis	Pneumonia
Appendicitis	Gastric ulcer disease
Congestive heart failure	Perforation
Perforation	Abdominal aortic aneurysm
Abdominal aortic aneurysm	Ischemic bowel
Ischemic bowel	Intraperitoneal bleeding
Intraperitoneal bleeding	
Fitz-Hugh-Curtis syndrome	
Right Lower Quadrant	**Left Lower Quadrant**
Appendicitis	Diverticulitis
Cholecystitis	Ureteral calculi
Diverticulitis	Colonic perforation
Cecal perforation	Volvulus
Ectopic pregnancy	Salpingo-oophoritis
Salpingo-oophoritis	Ectopic pregnancy
Ruptured ovarian mass/cyst	Ruptured ovarian mass/cyst
Tubo-ovarian abscess	Tubo-ovarian abscess
Adnexal torsion	Adnexal torsion
Mittleschmerz	Mittleschmerz
Ureteral calculi	Abdominal aortic aneurysm
Mesenteric adenitis	Ischemic bowel
Regional enteritis	Intraperitoneal bleeding
Meckel's diverticulum	
Abdominal aortic aneurysm	
Ischemic bowel	
Intraperitoneal bleeding	

The following discussion is directed to the more common causes of an acute abdomen. Appendicitis and ectopic pregnancy are discussed in some depth.

Generalized Peritonitis

These patients are lying quietly with their knees drawn up toward the chest. Movement makes the pain worse. The pain is relatively rapid in onset, usually localized at first, and then it becomes diffuse. Tachycardia, hypotension, dehydration, hypoactive bowel sounds, and fever are present. Rebound tenderness is present to both percussion and palpation. WBC is elevated early, liver function tests are normal or mildly elevated, and amylase may be elevated. Management consists of identifying the cause, intravenous fluids, antibiotics, and, on occasion, a Foley catheter and nasogastric tube. Surgery is usually required.

Perforated Ulcer

There is usually a history of prior ulcer disease. The pain is sudden in onset and sharp, usually starting in the epigastric area and then spreading over the entire abdomen. Shoulder pain may also be present. Nausea and emesis are common. The patient lies supine and avoids any undue motion. The abdomen is rigid and board-like with rebound in all quadrants. The bowel sounds are hypoactive to absent; tachycardia, tachypnea, hypotension, and shallow respirations are all present. Serum amylase and WBC are elevated. Fever is usually present. The acute abdominal x-ray series is diagnostic, with free air under the diaphragm. Surgery is required.

Pancreatitis

This is a disease that is most common in patients 30 to 50 years old, and is usually associated with chronic alcoholism or biliary tract disease. Nausea, emesis, and anorexia are common. The pain usually begins over the epigastric area and rapidly increases in intensity. It radiates directly through to the back and around both costal margins. The patient appears acutely ill and lies quietly. There is severe tenderness to percussion and palpation, tachycardia, tachypnea, and fever. The amylase and WBC are elevated. Treatment includes hospitalization, intravenous fluids, nasogastric tube, and perhaps surgical drainage if a pseudocyst forms. Abdominal ultrasound and CT scan are very helpful in making the diagnosis.

Diverticulitis

This problem is commonly seen in the fifth or sixth decade of life. The patient usually has a history of diverticulosis. Left lower-quadrant tenderness and perhaps a mass are present. Nausea is common. WBC is elevated and the urinalysis contains many WBCs. Patients with diverticulitis occasionally are clinically misdiagnosed as having ovarian cancer. CT scan is the most useful diagnostic test. Hospitalization is usually required.

Cholecystitis

This problem most commonly occurs in women in their 30s to 60s. The pain most commonly starts a few hours after a large meal. Fatty foods tend to make the episodes of pain worse. Nausea and emesis are common, while anorexia is uncommon. The pain begins in the right upper quadrant and may radiate to the scapula or shoulder. Mild elevation of temperature (99 to 101°F), WBC, and the serum bilirubin are common. There may be mild abdominal distension. Deep inspiration increases the pain, and there may be a right upper-quadrant mass. Ultrasound is diagnostic. Hospitalization and IV antibiotics may be required. Surgical removal of the gallbladder is usually required.

Small Bowel Obstruction

The pain usually begins suddenly, is sharp and colicky in nature, and starts periumbilically. The patient is usually pain-free between attacks. There is usually a prior history of abdominal surgery. Nausea and emesis are common. Emesis is frequent in a high obstruction; early emesis is greenish in color and later becomes brownish with fetid odor. Bowel sounds are high pitched and come in rushes early; later the bowel sounds are hypoactive or absent. Lower abdominal cramping suggests a distal obstruction. Tachycardia, hypotension, increased hematocrit (from dehydration), elevated WBC, and fever (99 to 103°F) are present. Acute abdominal series is diagnostic and reveals dilated loops of bowel with air-fluid levels and no gas in the distal colon. Progression of crampy abdominal pain and progression from hyperactive to absent bowel sounds with abdominal distension suggests bowel strangulation, perforation, and general peritonitis. Hospitalization, intestinal tube suction, intravenous hydration, antibiotics, and surgical exploration are required.[3] If nonsurgical management of small bowel obstruction is selected and does not succeed, it is essential that the physician be vigilant to insure that surgery is undertaken before bowel perforation occurs.

Large Bowel Obstruction

This disease process usually occurs in those over the age of 40. There is a gradual onset of pain, constipation, absence of flatulence, and abdominal distension. Nausea and emesis occur late, if at all. Tachycardia, tachypnea, and severe pain are absent unless perforation occurs. The hematocrit and WBC are frequently normal. The abdomen is distended and tympanic. Common causes are carcinoma, diverticulitis, volvulus, and a history of prior abdominal surgery. Acute abdominal x-ray series and/or CT scan are diagnostic. A left lower-quadrant mass may be felt on abdominal and rectal examination. Hospitalization and surgical management are required.

Pelvic Inflammatory Disease

This category includes salpingitis, salpingo-oophoritis, and tubo-ovarian abscess. The initial episode may be mild and go unrecognized, or it may produce severe symptoms. There is usually a history of recent sexual activity or a new partner. The pain usually begins as mild, and then intensifies over the course of 24 h. In severe cases, the pain is bilateral. Nausea and gradual loss of appetite are common. There may be a low-grade fever in mild cases, or a fever over 103°F in severe cases and in cases of tubo-ovarian abscesses. The patient usually lies still and shuffles when she walks. There is bilateral (occasionally unilateral) lower-quadrant direct and rebound tenderness. There may or may not be a mass present. WBC is generally elevated, and the pelvic examination produces cervical motion tenderness and adnexal tenderness. The bowel sounds are hypoactive. A pelvic ultrasound is diagnostic in cases of tubo-ovarian abscess. Hospitalization and intravenous antibiotics are essential if tubal damage is to be minimized and fertility preserved. Recurrent episodes are common; if a tubo-ovarian complex forms, surgical removal is often required.

Adnexal Torsion

The history will reveal prior intermittent attacks of lower-quadrant crampy pain. The onset of the pain usually coincides with an abrupt change in position or with vigorous activity and is sudden and unilateral. This pain becomes constant and more severe over the course of a few hours. As the process progresses, nausea and emesis are common, and a low-grade fever and leukocytosis develop. This sequence of events should lead to the suspicion of tissue hypoxia and infarction. Physical examination will reveal unilateral tenderness, and usually a mass. Treatment is often surgical removal of the affected adnexa. However, if there has been no tissue necrosis, then the adnexa can often be untwisted at the time of surgery, and salvaged. Common causes of adnexal torsion include large (>10 cm) ovarian masses/cysts, dermoid cysts, or a corpus luteum of pregnancy. Torsion of a pedunculated myoma results in the same symptoms and physical findings, and frequently requires surgical removal of the pedunculated myoma.

Appendicitis

Appendicitis is a common disease, and occurs over 250,000 times per year in the United States. It is slightly more common in males than in females, with a peak incidence in the teens and 20s. The incidence declines thereafter, and is relatively uncommon in the 40s and 50s. The diagnosis of appendicitis is extremely difficult in the very young and very old. Under the best of circumstances, when the individual fulfills all the classic symptoms and signs of appendicitis, the diagnostic accuracy as confirmed by surgical and pathological findings is only 70 to 90 percent.[5–7] The symptoms vary according to the location of the appendix, coexisting disease, age of the patient, and whether perforation has occurred.[3] For example, a retrocecal appendix may cause right upper-quadrant pain; a pregnant uterus will cause rotation of the point of maximum tenderness from appendicitis upward toward the right upper quadrant.[15]

Classic abdominal pain in appendicitis usually begins in the periumbilical region and migrates toward the right lower quadrant. Atypical abdominal pain is also quite common.[1] Nausea, emesis, and anorexia are frequently associated symptoms. Physical examination reveals right lower-quadrant direct and rebound tenderness. Bowel sounds may be hypoactive. A mild fever may be present and the WBC may be elevated or normal early in the course of the disease. The hematocrit is usually normal. The urinalysis is usually normal or may reveal a few WBCs if the inflammatory process overlies the ureter. A rectal examination is essential in the evaluation of a patient with suspected appendicitis and may reveal a mass. Acute abdominal x-ray series are not very useful. Abdominal ultrasound and CT

scanning are more diagnostic. A barium enema may also be of value.

The differential must include acute gastroenteritis; Meckel's diverticulum; mesenteric adenitis; salpingitis; ruptured ovarian cyst/endometrioma/mass; ectopic pregnancy; torsion of the adnexa; Mittelschmerz; regional enteritis; and ureteral calculi.[1] Ovarian events often can be differentiated from appendicitis by taking a good menstrual and sexual history, performing a culdocentesis, and obtaining a pelvic ultrasound study. Ureteral calculi usually produce severe colicky pain, and urinalysis reveals multiple red and white cells. An acute abdominal x-ray series may reveal the calculi, or the CT scan will reveal a dilated ureter and the calculi.

Surgical exploration is necessary. Laparoscopic evaluation results in earlier diagnosis, lower morbidity, and quicker return to full functional status. Early laparoscopic evaluation can yield a negative appendectomy rate of 2.2 percent.[5–7]

Ectopic Pregnancy

The incidence of ectopic pregnancy in the United States increased approximately fourfold between 1970 and 1989, and then decreased by 30 percent between 1989 and 1992.[8] Ectopic pregnancy occurs in 19.7/1000 pregnancies. Although the maternal mortality rate has decreased by 90 percent, mortality from ectopic pregnancies accounts for 10 percent of maternal deaths.[4] Extrauterine pregnancy is 50 times as likely to result in a maternal death as is a therapeutic first trimester abortion, and 10 times as likely to result in a maternal death as is a full-term vaginal delivery. The usual causes of death in a women with an ectopic pregnancy are related to hemorrhage, infection, delay in diagnosis, misdiagnosis, and anesthesia complications.[2] The substantial decrease in mortality is related to earlier detection, use of a more sensitive radioimmunassay for β-HCG, development of sensitive vaginal ultrasound, and a higher index of suspicion.[9]

Certain risk factors are known to be associated with an increased incidence of ectopic pregnancy. The most significant is that of previous salpingitis. Any infection that causes damage to the tubal epithelium increases the probability that a fertilized ovum will implant at a site other than the endometrial cavity.[9] Laparoscopically proven PID increases the risk of a subsequent ectopic pregnancy sixfold, and a history of a prior ectopic pregnancy increases the risk by 10-fold.[2] Other possible risk factors include endometriosis, prior or current IUD usage, advanced maternal age, progestin-only birth control pills, transmigration of the fertilized ovum, tubal reconstructive surgery, and assisted reproductive techniques.

The classical presentation is one of pelvic pain, an adnexal mass, and amenorrhea. Only a small percent of women present with this classic triad. Common presenting symptoms and signs are listed in Table 64-2.[10,12]

The history is suggestive of pregnancy, potentially including such factors as breast tenderness, nausea, urinary frequency, fatigue, unprotected intercourse, and an abnormal last menstrual period. If the patient takes oral contraceptives, there may be a history of missing a few pills. The last menses is usually later and shorter than normal. A spotty type of bleeding is often present. The examination may reveal an adnexal mass or tenderness. Usually direct tenderness is present; if rupture has occurred, there is rebound tenderness. Commonly, the WBC is normal; the hematocrit is normal unless significant hemorrhage has occurred. Use of a sensitive radioimmunoassay for β-HCG is essential for early diagnosis. If the HCG titer is above 1500 mIU/ml, the transvaginal ultrasound usually detects an intrauterine gestational sac if one is present. More than 6500 mIU/ml is necessary to detect an intrauterine gestational sac when using an abdominal transducer.[9] The probability of an ectopic pregnancy with a positive culdocentesis and positive β-HCG is 86 to 99 percent. A positive culdocentesis is the return of nonclotting blood (hematocrit >35 percent) from the posterior cul-de-sac.[10] Positive culdocentesis can also be present with ruptured ovarian cysts, retrograde menstruation, endometriosis, adnexal torsion, and intra-abdominal bleeding of unknown origin.

Once the diagnosis of ectopic pregnancy is made, the two treatment options are medical and surgical.

Medical treatment of ectopic pregnancy is a more recent development, and is becoming a more common form of treatment of ectopic pregnancy. It consists of the use of methotrexate and citrovorum factor rescue. Contraindications for medical therapy include an uncertain diagnosis; a gestational sac >3.5 cm; presence of fetal cardiac activity; poor patient compliance; active peptic ulcer disease; abnormal SGOT; active hepatic or renal disease; active bleeding; abdominal or pelvic pain; and hemodynamic instability.

Surgical options consist of laparoscopy or laparotomy. Laparoscopy is possible if the patient is hemodynamically stable, the size of the ectopic is <6 cm, hemoperitoneum is absent or small, an interstitial pregnancy is not present, and the surgeon has the necessary laparoscopic skills.[10] Linear salpingostomy, segmental resection, or

TABLE 64-2   Presentation of Ectopic Pregnancy

Symptoms		Signs	
Abdominal pain	80–95%	Abdominal tenderness	85–98%
Abnormal bleeding	50–85%	Adnexal tenderness	85–95%
Amenorrhea	30–70%	Peritoneal signs	70–75%
Symptoms of pregnancy	20–30%	Adnexal mass	30–50%
Syncope/faintness	6–40%	Enlarged uterus	6–30%
Shoulder pain	5–22%	Shock	2–20%
Passage of tissue	6–10%		

salpingectomy are all acceptable methods with either laparoscopy or laparotomy. β-HCG titers must be followed until they are <10 mIU/ml.

Most ectopic pregnancies are located in the fallopian tube: ampullary, 78 percent; isthmic, 12 percent; interstitial, 2 to 3 percent; fimbrial, 5 percent; ovarian, <0.5 percent; cervical, <0.5 percent; and abdominal, 0.1 to 0.2 percent. Rupture usually occurs at 6 to 8 weeks in isthmic ectopic pregnancies, 8 to 10 weeks in ampullary ectopic pregnancies, and 8 to 16 weeks in interstitial ectopic pregnancies. If the patient is Rh-negative, then RhoGam must be administered.

Systemic and Other Disorders

Other problems, including systemic diseases, may cause an acute abdomen. The more common causes are familial Mediterranean Fever; lower lobe pneumonia; pseudomembranous colitis; pyelonephritis; sickle cell crisis; diabetic ketoacidosis; lead poisoning; and porphyria.[3,11]

References and Suggested Readings

1. Diethelm AG, Stanley RJ: The acute abdomen, in Sabiston DC Jr (ed): *Sabiston Textbook of Surgery.* Philadelphia, PA: WB Saunders 1991, pp 736–755.
2. Trott AT: Nontraumatic acute abdominal pain, in Rosen P, et al, (ed): *Emergency Medicine.* St. Louis, MO: CV Mosby, 1983, pp 1025–1035.
3. Shea DJ, et al: Abdominal pain, in Schwartz GR (ed): *Principles and Practice of Emergency Medicine.* Malvern, PA: Lea and Febiger, 1992, pp 374–388.
4. MacFadyen BV, et al: Laparoscopic management of the acute abdomen, appendix, and small and large bowel. *Surg Clin North Am* 72(5):1169–1183, 1992.
5. Graham A, et al: Laparoscopic evaluation of acute abdominal pain. *J Laparoscopic Surg* 1(3):165–168, 1991.
6. Maxwell JM: Appendicitis: Improvements in diagnosis and treatment. *Am Surg* 57(5):282–285, 1991.
7. Varner M: General medical and surgical diseases in Scott JR (ed): Pregnancy, in *Danforth's Obstetrics and Gynecology.* Philadelphia, PA: JB Lippincott, 1990, pp 495–534.
8. Mischell, et al: Ectopic pregnancy, *Comprehensive Gynecology,* 3rd ed. St Louis: CV Mosby, 1997, pp 432–433.
9. Coudon RE, et al: Appendicitis, in *Sabiston Textbook of Surgery.* Sabiston DC Jr (ed): Philadelphia, PA: WB Saunders, 1991, pp 884–898.
10. _____ Ectopic pregnancy—United States. *MMWR* 41:591–595, 1992.
12. DeCherney A, et al: Ectopic pregnancy, in *Sciarra Gynecology and Obstetrics.* Philadelphia, PA: JB Lippincott, vol 2, chap 25, pp 1–17, 1991.
13. Montgomery-Rice V, et al: New options for the diagnosis and treatment of ectopic pregnancy. *Female Patient,* 18:31–46, 1993.
14. Seigler A: Salpinotomy and salpingectomy: Indications and techniques for tubal pregnancy, in *Sciarra Gynecology and Obstetrics.* Philadelphia, PA: JB Lippincott, vol 1, chap 68, pp 1–8, 1991.
15. Stabile I, et al: Ectopic pregnancy: A review of incidence, etiology and diagnostic aspects. *Obstet Gynecol Surv* 45(6):335–347, 1990.
16. Stovall T, et al: Methotrexate treatment of unruptured ectopic pregnancy: A report of 100 cases. *Obstet Gynecol* 77(5):749–753, 1991.

CHAPTER 65

The Breast

Vicki Seltzer
Jeanne Petrek

Embryology, Development, and Anatomy

The mammary glands begin to develop in the 6-week embryo, when an ectodermal ridge (the milk line) begins as a bilateral thickening extending from the axilla to the groin. This ridge eventually atrophies, with the exception of bilateral small portions in the pectoral regions that become the breasts. During the fifth embryonic month, each breast develops 15 to 20 solid cords (primary milk ducts) which branch. The ends of the primary milk ducts dilate. The ducts become hollow during the seventh and eighth month. At the same time, a small depression develops in the skin that corresponds to the nipple.

Nearing the onset of puberty, the first change in the breast is the formation of the breast bud. The areola subsequently enlarges, and then the nipple begins to grow outwards. A few years later there is progressive subareolar growth, so that the areola is raised above the breast outline, producing the appearance of a secondary mound. In the adult breast, the level of the areola has recessed to the level of the surrounding breast tissue so that only the nipple protrudes. It appears that estrogen is responsible for the initial stages of breast development, but that further development of the lobules requires adult levels of progesterone. Other hormones that play a role in breast development are prolactin, insulin, growth hormone, and corticosteroids.

Because the adult breast develops as a skin appendage within the superficial fascia, its anterior boundary is the superficial portion of the superficial fascia and its posterior boundary is the deep layer of the superficial fascia. The breast is at the level of the second to sixth ribs, its medial boundary being the sternum and its lateral border the midaxillary line. The upper and medial two-thirds of the breast lie on the fascia above the pectoralis major muscle, and the lower outer one-third of the breast rests on the serratus anterior muscle. The upper, lateralmost portion of the breast, the tail of Spence, extends into the axilla and then passes through an opening in the axillary fascia (the foramen of Langer). A disproportionately large percentage of the breast tissue is in the upper outer quadrant; therefore, a large proportion of both benign and malignant lesions arise in that area.

The nipple, which contains smooth muscle, is raised approximately 5 to 10 mm above the areolar skin; the areola, which is a darkly pigmented ring of epithelium surrounding the nipple, contains many small openings of Montgomery's glands (sebaceous glands).

The breast is comprised of approximately 12 to 20 lobes, which are arranged like spokes of a wheel. Lobes contain their own excretory duct, which has its own opening into the nipple surface. Collecting ducts extend from the surface of the nipple to the lactiferous sinus, a dilated sinus that contains secretions from the segmental duct, which in turn has received secretions from the subsegmental duct. Each lobe of the breast is comprised of many lobules, each containing 10 to 100 acini. The acini are arranged around an intralobular ductule that ultimately drains into the subsegmental duct. The lobule contains the epithelial units that are ultimately responsible for milk production.

Ten to 15 percent of the breast tissue is epithelium, the rest being stroma. Cooper's ligaments are the supporting framework of the breast lobes.

Two major arteries provide most of the blood supply for the breast. More than 50 percent of the vascular supply is from the anterior perforating branches of the internal mammary artery. The other major component of blood supply to the breast is from the axillary artery via the lateral thoracic and thoracoacromial arteries. Most of the superficial veins of the breast drain into the internal mammary vein. The deep venous drainage corresponds roughly to the arterial supply.

The lymphatics of the breast have great clinical significance, because breast cancer can spread via the lymphatics. Most of the lymphatic drainage is to the ipsilateral axillary nodes. Some of the medial breast has drainage through the intercostal spaces and into the internal mammary nodes inside the thorax. Lesser areas of drainage include supraclavicular and anterior cervical lymphatics.

Physiology

During pregnancy, alveolar growth and early colostrum production are stimulated by steroids produced by the placenta and ovary, human placental lactogen (HPL), growth hormone, insulin, and cortisol. Although prolactin is elevated, the high concentrations of circulating estrogen and progesterone exert an inhibitory effect during pregnancy. Within the first few days postpartum, this inhibition is no longer present, circulating estrogen and progesterone levels fall, the role of prolactin predominates, and milk is produced. Suckling of the infant elevates prolactin levels. If a woman does not breast-feed, her prolactin level decreases to normal at approximately one week postpartum. In the woman who is breast-feeding, by 6 to 12 weeks postpartum, prolactin levels fall to prepregnancy values. High prolactin seems to be a requirement for the initiation of lactation, but subsequent lactation can proceed without these high levels.

Benign Breast Lesions

Although the clinician, when performing a breast examination, places the greatest emphasis on the early detection of malignancy or on the identification of premalignant lesions, it is more likely that benign pathology will be identified. Therefore, the clinician must be familiar with the spectrum of benign entities that may be encountered.

In 1985, the Cancer Committee of the College of American Pathologists arrived at a consensus statement on the relative risk for invasive breast cancer based on pathologic examination of benign breast tissue.[25] The Committee agreed that the following histologic reports are not associated with any increased risk of malignancy: adenosis (sclerosing or florid); apocrine metaplasia; cysts (macro and/or micro); duct ectasia; fibroadenoma; fibrosis; mild hyperplasia (more than two but not more than four epithelial cells in depth); mastitis; periductal mastitis; and squamous metaplasia.

Women who were classified as having a slightly increased risk were defined as those whose risk would be 1.5 to 2 times greater than baseline. Women were placed in this category if they had a papilloma with a fibrovascular core or if they had hyperplasia which was moderate or florid, solid or papillary. This level of risk in itself is not clinically significant.

Women were identified as having five times the risk of breast cancer if they had either ductal or lobular atypical hyperplasia. They identified these as borderline lesions, with some features of carcinoma in situ (CIS), but not enough to make an unequivocal diagnosis of CIS.

Fibrocystic Changes

Probably the most common benign problem that the physician sees relates to patients with fibrocystic changes, those who complain of painful and/or "lumpy" breasts. This term is used by many patients as a catchall term for benign breast disease, as opposed to a term like fibroadenoma, which describes a specific histologic entity. The consensus statement discouraged the use of the term fibrocystic disease;[25] it is not a disease at all, and is more appropriately called fibrocystic changes or condition. The incidence of fibrocystic changes is uncommon before the age of 21, occurs in greater numbers of women in the reproductive years coming for routine health care, and has an incidence that continues to increase during the late premenopausal years, being most common in the fifth decade of life.

Patients with fibrocystic changes most commonly complain of bilateral breast tenderness, often beginning 7 to 14 days prior to the onset of menses, and this problem may be even more common in anovulatory women. It is essential, when the diagnosis of fibrocystic changes is made, that the presence of malignancy be considered and that every effort be made to rule it out. Fibrocystic changes are usually bilateral and diffuse. If a dominant lesion is present, a diagnosis must be made. Mammography and/or ultrasound can be utilized to make certain that the lesion is cystic and that there are no radiographic findings suggestive of malignancy. Ultrasound may be useful in demonstrating the presence of cystic lesions, whereas mammography, where indicated, is more sensitive in identifying early, non-palpable malignancies. If a lesion is clearly cystic, and there is no suggestion of malignancy, aspiration of the fluid should be performed. If the fluid is not bloody, and if the cyst completely collapses and does not recur, the patient can be carefully followed.

In a patient with a questionable physical exam, it is helpful to reexamine the breasts one week after the onset of her next period to make certain that these changes regress. Obviously patients who have bilateral fibrocystic changes may also be harboring a subclinical malignancy, so even when the clinical diagnosis of fibrocystic changes seems clear, it is important that standard protocols to rule out malignancy are not inadvertently omitted. Mammography certainly should be done when indicated, and in some circumstances a biopsy will be needed if there is any remaining question of malignancy.

If the patient has symptomatic fibrocystic changes, she may wish to be treated. It has been suggested that she avoid caffeine and other methylxanthines (which are present in coffee, tea, chocolate, and many soft drinks), because fibrocystic changes may be correlated with caffeine consumption and the amount of caffeine consumed.[11] Although some studies[66,70] have supported such a correlation, there have been several reports that have failed to demonstrate such a link.[33,60,82] While the issue is by no means resolved, there is a widespread clinical recommendation that women who have symptomatic fibrocystic changes avoid these compounds. Wearing a tight fitting brassiere may also be helpful. The use of oral contraceptives may alleviate symptoms, but the risks and benefits must be considered for the individual patient. It is usually recommended that patients who are using oral contraceptives solely to decrease the symptoms of fibrocystic changes do so for a limited time (e.g., six months), but at least one-third of the patients subsequently develop recurrent symptoms.

It is rare for women to require prescription medication for treatment of fibrocystic changes. Provera from days 15 to 25 of the cycle has been shown to relieve symptoms, although patients sometimes have side effects, and at least one-third of the women develop recurrent symptoms when they discontinue the medication. Danazol may reduce the discomfort of fibrocystic changes, but patients often report unacceptable side effects. Tamoxifen has also been suggested for this problem,[92] although fibrocystic changes is not an approved indication for its use.

Fibroadenoma

Another common benign breast problem is the fibroadenoma that is most often found in patients between the late teenage years and age 40. It is rare in postmenopausal women. These are usually mobile, rubbery, well-delineated lesions.

Despite being benign, fibroadenomas almost always undergo core biopsy or are removed. This is done for several reasons, the most important one being to make certain that the diagnosis is correct and that there is no evidence of malignancy. In addition, upon occasion the fibroadenoma can become large and distort the breast. If the patient becomes pregnant, fibroadenomas can grow rapidly, and even infarct. Also, patients usually want to have the lesion removed.

Intraductal Papilloma

Intraductal papilloma is a benign papillary lesion that is not very common. It is usually solitary, but in about 10 percent of cases it is multiple. It often causes a serous or bloody discharge. Approximately 50 percent of the patients have a palpable subareolar mass. The mean age of patients with this lesion is 48,[71] although there is great variability.

Mammary Duct Ectasia

Mammary duct ectasia is an uncommon benign inflammatory problem in which subareolar ducts are dilated and there is periductal mastitis. Patients may present with nipple discharge, which may range from grumous to serous to bloody. Ductal fibrosis may result in nipple flattening or inversion, and it is important to distinguish this from breast cancer.[71]

Mastitis

Mastitis is a relatively uncommon postpartum complication, occurring in 1 to 5 percent of postpartum women.[77] Approximately 11 percent of patients with postpartum mastitis subsequently develop a breast abscess, most commonly due to *Staphylococcus aureus*.[77] It may be difficult to distinguish between inflammatory breast cancer and postpartum mastitis, which can lead to a delay in the diagnosis of malignancy.

Fat Necrosis

The usual etiology of this rare condition is trauma, although the patient may not remember or be unaware of the causative injury. The patient presents with a breast mass that may be tender. The importance of the condition is that it must be differentiated from carcinoma, and it may be confusing. This is the only benign lesion that can cause skin dimpling. Furthermore, on mammography, it appears as a spiculated area.

Oversized, Underdeveloped, and Asymmetrical Breasts

Many women consult their physicians because they consider their breasts to be overly large, or unduly small, or asymmetrical, and these problems are often of considerable concern to many women. Studies have uniformly failed to identify any endocrine abnormality, and when endocrine manipulation has been tried it has always been unsuccessful. The only exception is underdeveloped breasts due to primary ovarian failure (such as that related to gonadal dysgensis or Turner's syndrome, or secondary to pituitary failure); in such cases, estrogen therapy is highly successful and achieves full breast development. With this exception, the only treatment available for excessively large or small breasts, or markedly asymmetrical breasts, is corrective plastic surgery.

Accessory Nipples

Accessory nipples, sometimes associated with accessory breasts, can occur anywhere along the milk line from the neck to the groin. They may be single or multiple. They require no therapy except for explanation, many women thinking that they are moles or skin growths.

Nipple Discharge

Approximately 5 percent of women who seek medical care for breast complaints will have nipple discharge. It is a more common complaint among patients with benign tumors (approximately 10 to 15 percent) than in women with malignancies (approximately 3 percent). In any event, the physician should make certain when a woman presents with this complaint that no malignant or premalignant pathology exists.

When a woman complains of a nipple discharge, the first step in the evaluation is a careful history. This should include the color of the discharge, whether it is from a single duct, whether it is bilateral, its frequency and duration, and whether it is intermittent. One of the most important facts about nipple discharge is whether it is spontaneous. Most premenopausal women, and some postmenopausal women taking hormone replacement therapy, can produce a small amount of discharge when squeezing the nipple or the breast just behind it.

The physician, on physical examination, should attempt to determine and record the duct or ducts that are involved, what the color and character of the discharge are, and whether the patient has any abnormalities on physical exam, particularly a mass in the subareolar region.

There is some difference of opinion regarding whether cytology of the discharge should be obtained.[47,59] Unfortunately, cytologic evaluation of nipple discharge is known to have both a high false-positive and false-negative rate. Therefore, therapeutic decisions should not be made only on the basis of cytologic evaluation. In addition, nipple discharge cannot be determined to be due to a benign etiology merely on the basis of benign cytology.

If the patient has not had a recent mammogram, such testing is appropriate, unless she is a patient under age 30 with no history or physical findings that are at all suspicious. (For instance, it would not be appropriate to obtain a mammogram for a 25-year-old with bilateral milky discharge.)

Galactorrhea can be distinguished clinically from other types of discharge, and must be, because the evaluation is different. Galactorrhea is usually from multiple ducts, bilateral, milky, and nonspontaneous. This is not uncommon in parous women, and also may be found in patients using phenothiazines, drugs that deplete dopamine, and hormones. It may be secondary to mechanical stimulation. The potential presence of a prolactin-secreting tumor should be considered.

It is important to distinguish a nipple lesion that is eczematous and bloody from a blood-tinged nipple discharge, because the former may be Paget's disease of the nipple.

If the patient has a breast mass and a nipple discharge, both must be fully evaluated. The nipple discharge may be occurring because of the mass, but they may be unrelated. Seltzer et al. demonstrated that in the absence of a mass, the likelihood that nipple discharge is related to malignancy increases with the patient's age.[84]

Nipple discharge may be grumous, purulent, milky, watery, serous, serosanguinous, or grossly bloody. Grumous discharge is usually associated with duct ectasia. Watery or serous discharge is most commonly associated with cancer or papillomas. Bloody or blood-tinged discharge may be related to malignancy, but it is more commonly related to benign lesions. Other than for patients with galactorrhea, the diagnosis and treatment of nipple discharge usually involves surgery.

Epidemiology of Breast Cancer

Breast cancer is the most common malignancy diagnosed in women in the United States, with an estimated 175,000 new cases of invasive cancer diagnosed in 1999. In 1999, breast cancer resulted in approximately 43,300 deaths in U.S. women, and 400 deaths in U.S. men. Breast cancer is the second most common cause of cancer death in U.S. women, surpassed only by lung cancer.

Although the incidence of breast cancer in the United States had been rising, much of this seemed attributable to the greater use of screening mammography and early detection. In 1982, 15,000 women were diagnosed with breast cancers less than 2 cm in diameter; by 1986 this had risen to 39,000. This suggested that perhaps some of the increase in reported cases of breast cancer might have been due to their earlier detection, resulting from improved mass screening efforts. The age-adjusted incidence rate for breast cancer among U.S. women showed a gradual rise that began around 1981, climbing to a high of 113.1 new cases per 100,000 women in 1987. The incidence remained fairly constant from 1987 through 1992, although slightly lower rates were measured in 1993 and 1994.[76]

In this section, risk factors for breast cancer are reviewed (Table 65-1). However, it is essential to underscore that one in eight women born in the United States today will develop breast cancer. The incidence of breast cancer (whether age-adjusted or unadjusted) shows international variation, with the United States, Canada, and Northern Europe having the highest rates in the world.[51] Approximately 75 percent of U.S. women with breast cancer have no other known risk factors, and therefore all U.S. women must be screened aggressively.

Another long-recognized factor that significantly increases breast cancer risk is family history, even if the risk appears unrelated to a genetic syndrome. If a woman has a first-degree relative with breast cancer (mother or sister), her risk becomes quite significant. If the breast cancer was premenopausal and/or bilateral, this further increases risk. Having multiple relatives affected also increases risk. Close relatives may also share similar environmental and even reproductive breast cancer risk factors.

TABLE 65-1   **Risk Factors for Breast Carcinoma**

Age
Previous cancer in the contralateral breast
Residence in North America or Northern Europe
Family history
Nulliparity
First birth age 35 or older
Previous biopsy with premalignant histology
Early menarche
Late menopause
Obesity
High-fat, low-fiber diet
Radiation exposure
Caucasian
Upper socioeconomic status
Residence in cold climate
Urban residence
Other primary cancer in ovary, endometrium, or colon

Approximately 10 percent of breast cancers are attributable to specific, inherited, single-gene mutations. Among these specific mutations, roles have been identified for mutations in *BRCA1* and *BRCA2*. The *BRCA1* gene encodes a tumor-suppressor protein that acts to inhibit tumor. Various alterations within the *BRCA1* gene may be responsible for as much as half of all breast cancers resulting from a single-gene mutation, and perhaps as many as 80 percent of patients in whom there is a family history of early onset breast cancer and ovarian cancer.

BRCA2 gene mutation also results in an elevation in breast cancer risk. It is not associated with as great an increased risk of ovarian cancer, but does also predict an increased breast cancer risk among men who carry the mutated gene.[6,31,105]

Another risk factor for breast cancer, and almost all other cancers, is age. The older a woman becomes, the greater her likelihood of developing breast cancer. Therefore, women should continue to be screened throughout their lives. On the other hand, breast cancer is not completely unknown in women in their teens and 20s, so any mass in the breast, even in young women, must be evaluated, and malignancy ruled out.

Having had a cancer in the contralateral breast also places a woman at greatly increased risk for a new primary breast cancer.

Menstrual and reproductive history are significant factors.[50] Women who have an early menarche or late menopause are at increased risk. Kuale,[54] in his analysis of Scandinavian women, suggested that for each year of decrease in age at menarche there is an average increase in breast cancer risk of 4 percent, and that for each year of increased age at menopause there is a 3.6 percent increase in risk. Having a first child before the age of 18 reduces the risk of breast cancer to one-third the risk of a woman who has her first child at age 35 or later.[49] On the other hand, having multiple pregnancies is not protective. Earlier studies had suggested that breast-feeding might reduce breast cancer risk, but this is debated.

Several authors support diet as a significant factor in increasing breast cancer risk. Wynder[106] and many others have presented laboratory data and experimental evidence to support the association of high-fat diets and breast cancer. Researchers in his group have demonstrated that rats initiated with mammary gland carcinogens have an increased rate of breast cancer if they consume a high-fat diet. In addition, he demonstrated an almost linear relationship between the daily dietary fat intake in a country and its death rates from breast cancer. Nevertheless, after decades of study, only a few dietary constituents have shown an independent association with risk of breast cancer, and none of them have shown it consistently. It has been suggested that findings regarding proving the role of dietary fat in breast cancer risk among humans have been flawed by an inability to correctly classify individuals with respect to fat intake. However, more recent studies using improved dietary assessment methods have also consistently failed to incriminate dietary fat as an established risk factor. Some investigators have suggested that dietary fat indirectly influences risk by determining obesity, which is a risk factor, particularly among postmenopausal women.[45,61,102]

Wyngaarden reviewed work done by Toniolo that analyzed data on the consumption of total fat, saturated fat, and animal protein, and suggested that breast cancer risk could be reduced by diminishing fat intake to less than 30 percent of daily caloric intake, diminishing saturated fat to less than 10 percent of total calories, and diminishing animal protein intake to less than 6 percent of total calories.[107] Others have suggested that breast cancer risk can be reduced by increasing the fiber content of the diet, and by increasing consumption of foods rich in vitamins A and C.

Willett[101] and others have suggested that alcohol consumption may increase breast cancer risk. However, Harris[42] and others found that there is no compelling evidence to substantiate this. Recent studies demonstrate a slight (up to 25 percent) increase in risk of breast cancer among women who consume two alcoholic drinks or more per day. The relationship between alcohol intake and breast cancer is still not fully defined.

Although there has been evidence that caffeine consumption exacerbates fibrocystic changes of the breast, it does not appear to increase the likelihood of developing breast cancer.[73]

Other factors that seem to increase breast cancer risk include radiation exposure (e.g., survivors of the Hiroshima and Nagasaki atomic bombs, those with multiple chest fluoroscopies for tuberculosis, and those treated with x-rays for acute postpartum mastitis).[56] The strength of the association of radiation and breast cancer risk is related, first and foremost, to young age at radiation exposure, level of radiation exposure, and length of time after exposure. Findings suggest that exposure to radiation at a young age when estrogen stimulation begins (menarche or beyond) may initiate the process that ultimately leads to breast cancer.[49]

Additional factors that appear to increase risk include residence in the north, urban residence, upper socioeconomic status, and other primary cancer in the ovary, endometrium, or colon.

The issue of breast cancer risk and exogenous hormone use has been one of some controversy. In 1986, the Cancer and Steroid Hormone study of the Centers for Disease Control and the National Institute of Child Health and Human Development[96] analyzed case-control data for 4711 women ages 20 to 54 with newly diagnosed breast cancer and 4676 controls. The study found that as compared to women who had never utilized birth control pills, those who had, had a relative risk of breast cancer of 1.0. In addition, for women who had used oral contraceptives they reported that breast cancer risk was not affected appreciably by the formulation used, the type of estrogen, the type of progestin, the duration of use, nor the time since they were last used. This study was reassuring to women using the pill and to their physicians, because oral contraceptives are so widely utilized and because they have had such a major positive influence on women's reproductive choices. Another study by Miller[65] found that up to age 45, breast cancer risk did not appear to be increased by the use of oral contraceptives before age 25 or before the birth of the first child, even if the duration of use was 5 or more years. Murray[67] evaluated oral contraceptive use in women with a family history of breast cancer and found that for women with a first-degree family history there was no evidence that even long-term use of oral contraceptives increased breast cancer risk.

A few studies have been published that suggest that for certain subsets of women, the use of oral contraceptives may increase their breast cancer risk. Pike suggested that use of the birth control pill before the age of 25[74] or before the first full-term pregnancy[75] could increase a woman's breast cancer risk. Chilvers[19] investigated women diagnosed with breast cancer before the age of 36, and found a significant trend in breast cancer risk with duration of oral contraceptive use.

In general, in evaluating whether there is any relationship between exogenous hormones and breast cancer, there has been either no association or, occasionally, a weak association.[97] A recent meta-analysis of 54 epidemiologic studies has identified a weak association between breast cancer and current and recent oral contraceptive users.[16] These investigators identified a small increase in breast cancer risk among current oral contraceptive users (these may be older women using oral contraceptives in the perimenopausal period). A similar, albeit much weaker, effect was also seen for women who had stopped use of oral contraceptives within the previous 10 years. It is also possible that this effect is related to the known effect of increased risk with delay of first full-term pregnancy. It should be noted that this study found that breast cancers detected among oral contraceptive users were less advanced than those detected in women of the study not using oral contraceptives.

There are data that suggest that oral contraceptives do not increase breast cancer risk, and conflicting data that suggest that for certain subsets of women it does increase risk. Further research into this question must continue. In the meantime, women and their physicians must remember that in addition to making an enormous contribution to providing women with the capability to control their reproductive lives, the birth control pill has important side benefits, such as reducing the risk of salpingo-oophoritis and the risk of ovarian and endometrial cancer.

Another concern has been whether the use of estrogen for postmenopausal women increases breast cancer risk. Again, the data are somewhat controversial. On the one hand, there is a significant body of data that suggests that exogenous estrogen use for postmenopausal women does not increase breast cancer risk.[29,40,90] On the other hand, there have been a few articles suggesting that exogenous postmenopausal estrogen use may increase breast cancer risk for some subgroups of women.[13,80] The relationship between hormone replacement therapy and risk of breast cancer may relate to such factors as the duration of use and the dose, or level of hormones during use, as well as the recency of hormone replacement therapy.[12] This issue continues to be evaluated carefully by many investigators, and is the subject of multiple reviews and meta-analyses.[12,22,87,90,92] However, in assisting patients in making risk-benefit decisions on the use of postmenopausal exogenous estrogens, the positive impact on cardiovascular disease, prevention of osteoporosis, and clinical symptomatology often outweigh the as yet incompletely defined issue of the role of exogenous estrogen in breast cancer risk.

Screening for Breast Cancer

Women should be involved in a program for the early detection of breast cancer that includes mammography, breast self-examination, and examination by a health care provider.

Mammography and Other Breast-Imaging Techniques

At present, mammography is the best technique available for the early detection of breast cancer. It does, however, have a false-negative rate of approximately 10 percent, making breast self-examination and clinical breast examination essential supplemental modalities. If a mass is present in a woman's breast, despite the presence of a normal mammogram, it is essential that the etiology of the mass be determined. A normal mammogram must not convey a false sense of security. Burns reported that 7 percent of women with breast cancer in her study had a delay in diagnosis because of a negative mammogram.[14] Patients in her series ranged from 28 to 66 years of age, and had a mean delay of 45 weeks in having their cancers diagnosed. Mammography is not perfect, but it has made a remarkable contribution to the early diagnosis and ultimate reduced likelihood of mortality for women with breast cancer. Although there is not completely uniform agreement on when mammography should be performed, our recommendation is for annual mammography from age 40 onward.

Although breast x-rays have been performed for more than 70 years, modern mammography has existed only since 1969, the year the first x-ray units dedicated to breast imaging were available. In 1962, the Health Insurance Plan of Greater New York (HIP), under contract with the National Cancer Institute (NCI), undertook a research study to determine whether periodic screening using mammography as well as clinical examination could result in a reduction in mortality from breast cancer, and what contribution mammography would make.[93] Sixty-two thousand women ages 40 to 64 were included in this study (31,000 matched pairs). Women in the study group had an initial mammography and breast examination, and these were planned to be repeated annually for three years, although many women did not return as advised. Women in the control group received their usual medical care. One-third of the cancers were detected on mammography alone but were not identified on physical exam; 79 percent of the women in this group did not have axillary node involvement. Approximately one-fifth of the cancers were detected by both mammography and clinical examination; 52 percent of these were no longer localized. Approximately two-fifths of women who had breast cancer identified by physical examination did not have the cancer identified by mammography.

Despite the lack of sophistication of mammography in these earlier years of its use and development, and the fact that mammography had a false-negative rate at that time that was three-to fourfold greater than that which exists today, the women in the study group had a one-third reduction in mortality from breast cancer after seven years of follow-up. After almost 20 years of follow-up, this reduction in mortality persisted.[86]

In part due to the lack of sophistication of mammography at that stage of its development, the HIP study was unable to demonstrate conclusive findings for women in their 40s. Fortunately, subsequent studies by the Breast Cancer Detection Demonstration Projects (BCDDP), in addition to several other studies, have clearly shown that women under the age of 50 derive significant benefit from screening mammography. The American Cancer Society now recommends yearly mammography for women in their 40s.

Smart and Beahrs reported the results of 280,000 volunteers from 27 Breast Cancer Detection Demonstration Projects supported by the NCI and the American Cancer Society (ACS). In this report, 44 percent of the cancers detected at the first screening were suspicious on mammography alone and not by physical examination, and this rose to 49 percent at the second screen. More than one-quarter of the cancers diagnosed were noninfiltrative. In addition, 15 percent of the infiltrative cancers were less than 1 cm in size. Seventy percent of the women with disease had negative lymph nodes. Of note is that only in 7.4 percent of instances was physical examination suspicious for malignancy in the presence of a normal mammogram.

Two advances that occurred between the time of the HIP study and the BCDDP were that mammography had become more accurate and that the radiation exposure was reduced. At present, mammography is underutilized in the United States, and only a fraction of women are having their evaluations at regular intervals.

In 1997, the American Cancer Society changed its breast cancer detection guidelines to include yearly screening mammography for all women 40 years of age and older. The society's decision was based upon the evidence that one in 66 women in their 40s will develop breast cancer. About 18 percent of all breast cancers occur now in women in their 40s (this is partly due to the population bulge of the baby boomers reaching middle age). Thirteen percent of the 43,300 women expected to die of breast cancer in 1999 will be in their 40s.

Mammography and other breast imaging techniques are discussed further in Chap. 52.

Physical Examination

Although mammography is the most sensitive technique for the early diagnosis of breast cancer, physical examination by the health care provider does play an important complementary role. The Breast Cancer Detection Demonstration Project found that 8.7 percent of breast cancers in their series were diagnosed by physical examination alone, when mammographies had been read as normal.[2] Other series have reported an even greater frequency of breast cancers detected by physical examination alone in the presence of normal mammography. Therefore, careful regular physical examinations of the breasts by the health care team are essential for the early detection of breast cancer.

In addition, if the physician finds an abnormality on physical examination, the physician must not be lulled into a false sense of security by a normal mammogram. Because 8 to 15 percent of women with breast cancer have normal mammograms, the etiology of the abnormal physical findings should be determined, and the physician should avoid placing excessive reliance on a normal mammogram in this situation. The mammogram is a very powerful tool, but it cannot, with absolute certainty, rule out breast cancer. Therefore, not only is it important that women have regular breast exams by their health care provider, but it is also important that when an abnormality is identified on physical examination the reason for this finding should be determined, even in the presence of a normal mammogram.

The American Cancer Society guidelines for physical examination for the detection of breast cancer in women with no symptoms are: women 20 years of age and older should perform breast self-exam every month; women ages 20 to 39 should have a physical exam of the breasts performed by a trained health care professional, usually a physician, every 3 years; and women 40 and older should have a physical exam of the breasts performed by a trained health care professional every year, and a mammogram every year.

Our suggestion regarding clinical breast examinations by a health care provider for women between the ages of 20 and 39 is a bit different. Most women in this age group are receiving regular health care for Pap smears and other medical needs, and it is appropriate for them to also have annual breast examinations when they come for other care. Although breast cancer incidence continues to rise with age, it is certainly not rare prior to the age of 40, and it is optimal to begin annual clinical breast exams much earlier.

In addition, women who are at higher-than-average risk may need to be examined more often than annually. Of course, any woman with a breast complaint should be examined, regardless of when her most recent prior examination took place.

Although there are some individual variations in the performance of breast examination, we describe one technique. The physician should begin by obtaining pertinent epidemiological information such as reproductive history, family history, and so forth. The physician should then determine whether the patient has any breast complaints (e.g., nipple discharge, presence of a mass, pain, etc.). The first step in the breast examination is inspection. This is usually done with the arms raised overhead, then with tension on the pectoralis muscles (which can be accom-

plished by having the patient place her hands on her hips and press inward), and finally with the patient relaxed and leaning forward. The physician is looking for skin and contour changes such as retraction, edema, or erythema, and for nipple changes such as retraction, eczema, or erosion. The breasts are then examined with the patient in both the sitting and supine positions. The examination must be systematic, with a thorough evaluation of all breast tissue for masses. This is commonly done in concentric circles, starting with the outermost breast tissue. The physician should attempt to elicit nipple discharge and should examine the axilla carefully for nodes.

The breast examination should be documented in the medical record.

Teaching Breast Self-Examination

Women should be taught how to perform breast self-examination and encouraged to do so. This can be reenforced while the clinical breast examination is being performed.

The patient should be instructed that if she does note any abnormalities, she must report them to her physician so that the doctor can promptly perform an evaluation. The woman should understand that breast self-examination is complementary to mammography, and that although mammography is usually much more sensitive than self-examination, the latter may identify a breast cancer that was missed on mammography. In addition, a breast cancer may develop in the interval between radiographic examinations, and therefore monthly self-examination may result in earlier diagnosis.

Staging

Staging refers to the grouping of patients according to the extent of their disease. Staging is either clinical, meaning before surgical treatment, or pathologic, based on findings on the specimen and any testing. Staging is important in determining the kind of pretreatment evaluation; determining the choice of treatment for an individual; assessing the patient's prognosis; and comparing the results of different treatment programs.

Currently, staging of cancer is determined by the American Joint Committee on Cancer (AJCC), which is jointly sponsored by the American Cancer Society, The National Cancer Institute, The College of American Pathologists, and The American Colleges of Physicians, Radiologists, and Surgeons. The AJCC is a clinical and pathological staging system, and is based on the TNM system in which the T refers to tumor, the N to nodes, and the M to metastasis. The current edition, the fourth, published in 1992, differs from previous versions.

Clinical staging is based on all information prior to definitive treatment and includes the findings on physical exam, imaging studies (mammography and ultrasound), operative findings, and findings of biopsy material. Clinical stage is useful in selecting and evaluating therapy.

Pathologic staging (pTNM) includes all data used for clinical staging and surgical resection, as well as pathological exam of the primary cancer and axillary lymph nodes. The pathologic stage provides the most precise data to estimate prognosis and to evaluate end results.

The current system does not address present-day issues and clinical decision-making such as the patient's suitability for breast-conserving treatment or the risk of distant metastases with or without systemic therapy. Attempts are under way to develop more useful staging systems.

Stage 0 means that the cancer is in situ only. Stage I cancers are less than 2 cm with no suspicious lymph nodes and no suspicion of distant metastases.

Stage IIA are patients who have cancers less than 2 cm but who have suspicion of cancer in the axillary lymph nodes, although the lymph nodes are not fixed to each other and are not fixed to any other structures. Also included in Stage IIA are cancers that are more than 2 cm but not more than 5 cm in greatest dimension but the axillary lymph node exam is negative. In Stage IIB, the cancer is also between 2 and 5 cm,

but there can be suspicion of cancer in the lymph nodes, although the lymph nodes are not fixed to each other (matted) nor fixed to any other structures (such as the pectoralis minor muscle). Also included in IIB are cancers greater than 5 cm in greatest dimension, but with the lymph node exam normal.

In Stage IIIA, a tumor that has lymph nodes that are matted or fixed to each other is included, regardless of the size of the cancer. Also included in Stage IIIA are cancers that are greater than 5 cm with an exam that suggests cancer in the lymph nodes, in which the lymph nodes are not fixed to each other or to any other structures.

Stage IIIB includes any cancer of any size with direct extension to the chest wall or skin. Extension to skin may have the appearance of "peau d'orange," ulceration of the skin or satellite skin nodules, as well as inflammatory breast cancer, as noted clinically. With those special skin changes, the cancer may be of any size, and the lymph node involvement may be none, or of any degree, and it is still Stage IIIB. Also included in Stage IIIB are cancers of any size if there is metastasis found in the internal mammary lymph nodes.

Stage IV only includes patients with distant metastasis. Ipsilateral supraclavicular lymph node metastasis is considered distant metastasis.

Staging is very important for considering what kind of diagnostic tests are obtained before definitive treatment. Mammography of the opposite breast is important in all women. Furthermore, if breast-conservation therapy is being planned, current mammography of the breast with a breast cancer diagnosis is essential. There is controversy involving the extent of metastatic work-up for women who appear to have early disease, especially as it relates to a cost-benefit analysis. Because bones are the most common first-diagnosed site of metastatic disease for breast cancer, a bone scan is often performed, especially as a baseline. Nevertheless, it is not indicated for Stage 0 breast cancer, and a bone scan is not usually performed before treatment of Stage I or Stage II breast cancer. The exception may be where the plan is to do a mastectomy for Stage I/ II patients. In this case, it becomes more important to rule out any small possibility of metastatic disease before a major operation. Other tests, including computed tomography scans of the chest, abdomen, and pelvis, are obtained if there is clinical suspicion or abnormalities on screening blood values. A chest x-ray is always obtained, because it is useful to diagnose pulmonary metastasis, and it is almost always done as part of a preoperative anesthetic evaluation.

Surgical Procedures

Cyst Aspiration

Cysts in the breast are a common occurrence. The cyst is typically found as a smooth, round, slippery mass, and can be distinguished from solid masses with a similar palpatory sensation by the simple technique of cyst aspiration. This finding on physical exam feels similar to a common lesion, the fibroadenoma, or to medullary breast cancer, a rare lesion.

Palpable cysts are drained for four reasons: to establish the diagnosis of a cyst; to provide a quick diagnosis; occasionally to provide relief of pain if the cyst is causing pressure; and to provide for an optimal clinical breast exam free of the interfering mass.

The key issue in the evaluation and management of a cystic breast lesion is to make certain that a malignancy is not present, either in that location or elsewhere in the breasts. If the patient has not had her appropriate mammography screening, it is preferable to do this prior to aspirating the cyst so as to avoid distortion of the mammography films. In addition, a sonogram is often done to confirm the fact that the lesion is, indeed, cystic. In many situations, it may be more expeditious to omit the sonogram.

To perform cyst aspiration, the cyst is stabilized between two fingers of the nondominant hand, and a 20-gauge needle and syringe are used to aspirate the cyst. Several conditions must be satisfied for a cyst aspiration to be considered

adequate treatment. The cyst must fully collapse and there must be no residual mass following aspiration. The cyst fluid must be clear or cloudy. If it is brown or red, this is suggestive of previous bleeding into the mass. Finally, the cyst must not repeatedly reaccumulate.

If the cyst does not completely collapse, if it repeatedly reaccumulates, or if the cyst fluid is bloody, a breast biopsy is indicated. Many physicians believe that it is unnecessary to send the aspirated fluid for cytology if it is not bloody, because the potential for finding malignant cells in this situation is extremely low when the cyst fully collapses and does not repeatedly reaccumulate.

Fine-Needle Aspiration Biopsy, Needle Localization, and Stereotaxic Core Biopsy

These procedures are discussed in detail in Chaps. 52 and 53.

Incisional and Excisional Biopsy

Chapters 52 and 53 described techniques for fine-needle aspiration and stereotaxic biopsy. Core biopsies may also be obtained using an instrument such as a TruCut needle. Incisional biopsy may be performed for a patient with a breast malignancy to confirm a diagnosis prior to definitive therapy as well as to obtain tissue for hormone receptor analysis. An advantage of the Tru-Cut needle is that it can be easily and rapidly employed to ascertain a diagnosis in many patients who have a clinically palpable malignancy. If the histological analysis shows malignancy, treatment planning can be initiated with the patient. On the other hand, in a patient with a suspicious lesion, if no malignancy is identified utilizing this technique, it is essential to perform an excisional biopsy to confirm that there is no malignancy. Under other circumstances, incisional biopsy may be done with a scalpel. If it is possible that the patient will be undergoing further surgery, the incision must be made within the boundaries of the area that would subsequently be removed, with a secondary goal being to achieve an optimal cosmetic result.

Surgery for Breast Cancer

The first major advance in the treatment of breast cancer was made in 1882, when William Halsted, a professor of surgery at Johns Hopkins, developed and refined the technique of radical mastectomy. In his first 50 operations, Halsted reported a local-regional combined recurrence rate of only 24 percent. This represented an enormous improvement when compared to any of the therapies that preceded it. The operation was eventually met with widespread general acceptance. However, removal of the pectoralis muscles resulted in significant cosmetic and functional problems. As with all malignancies, once it became clear that an operation existed that could cure this disease (the radical mastectomy), the natural progression was to see whether cure could be achieved with a less radical procedure and possibly fewer adverse effects. It was ultimately demonstrated that mastectomy and axillary dissection with preservation of the pectoralis muscle could, for most women, achieve an equivalent opportunity for cure without quite the same likelihood of functional and cosmetic problems as followed the radical mastectomy. At the same time during these decades, and as was the case with other cancers, there was a trend of women presenting for treatment with smaller primary tumors.

During the 1970s there was a major evolution in the surgical therapy for breast cancer in the United States. Until 1970, approximately half of all American women with breast cancer were treated by radical mastectomy. By 1976, only one-quarter were treated with this approach, with most of the remaining patients having mastectomy and axillary dissection with preservation of the pectoralis muscles. During the 1980s there was more rapid evolution toward lumpectomy, axillary dissection, and radiation as widely accepted primary approaches to treatment.

Although until this time most physicians in the United States considered surgical therapy to be the primary therapy for breast cancer, the concept of treating breast cancer with radiation was not a novel approach, and had been used in Europe and Canada with good results since the 1930s.[52] One of the problems that many of the early series encountered was related to much of the work being done with orthovoltage radiation, which was the only therapy that was available. This resulted in difficulty treating the local disease adequately without excessive adverse effects on normal tissue. Therefore, in many of the early studies there was an excessive rate of local recurrence, along with postradiation sequela to the normal breast (including shrinkage and deformity of the breast mound and telangiectasia of breast skin). During the 1960s, when several studies began to evaluate results with megavoltage therapy, local recurrence rates were diminished and cosmetic effects improved. Radiation therapy for the primary treatment of early breast cancer became somewhat more rapidly accepted in other areas of the world. However, in the early 1980s, two major studies were published that almost immediately began to exert an influence in providing American women with the option of breast-conserving treatment.[38,100]

In 1981, Veronesi reported on 701 Italian women with breast cancer less than 2 cm in size and with no palpable axillary lymph nodes who were treated at the National Cancer Institute in Milan from 1973 to 1980. The patients were randomized to be treated either with a Halsted radical mastectomy or a quadrantectomy, axillary dissection, and radiation to the residual ipsilateral breast tissue. Actuarial survival curves showed no difference in the two groups in disease-free or overall survival.[99]

In 1985, Fisher[38] reported data on a randomized trial initiated in 1976 in which 1843 American women with stage I and II breast cancers up to 4 cm in size were treated by total mastectomy, segmental mastectomy alone (i.e., removal of tumor with only sufficient surrounding tissue to ensure negative margins), or segmental mastectomy followed by breast irradiation. All patients underwent axillary dissection. Patients with positive nodes received adjuvant chemotherapy. Disease-free survival after segmental mastectomy plus radiation was not significantly different from that with total mastectomy. If patients were treated with segmental mastectomy, postoperative radiation was important in reducing the likelihood of local recurrence. It is important to note that slightly more than 1 percent per year of patients developed recurrent tumor in the irradiated breast and underwent salvage mastectomy.

In June 1990, the National Institutes of Health convened a Consensus Development Conference on Treatment of Early-Stage Breast Cancer.[26] The conference concluded that treatment that conserves the breast is an appropriate primary treatment for the majority of women with stage I and II breast cancer, and that because it preserves the breast and provides survival equivalent to total mastectomy and axillary dissection, it is preferable. Whether patients select total mastectomy or excision of the tumor with a margin (lumpectomy, segmental mastectomy) followed by radiation, determining the lymph node status (usually by axillary dissection) is important in either case.

Patients should be carefully counseled regarding their treatment options, with consideration given to their specific needs. Because a major goal of breast-conserving therapy is to attain a good cosmetic result, the patient must be advised if there are features that would result in a poor cosmetic result, such as a large tumor in a small breast. It is important to remember that the patient should not make a decision about therapy that would reduce the potential for cure. Therefore, women who have either gross multifocal disease or diffuse microcalcifications found on mammography would usually not be candidates for treatment that preserves the breast. At the consensus conference there was controversy regarding certain clinical or pathologic situations in which it was thought that therapy that preserved the breast might potentially have an adverse impact on the likelihood of local recurrence. Some examples of these controversial areas included extensive intraductal carcinoma (EIC) within and adjacent to the primary tumor,

possibly extensive lymphatic involvement, and patients under 35 to 39 years of age. In addition, there was some concern about women with very large tumors, because most of the prospective data evaluating lumpectomy were obtained for women with tumors less than or equal to 4 cm in largest diameter.

In 1992, the American Colleges of Surgeons, Radiology, and Pathologists and the Society of Surgical Oncology held a conference on Standards for Breast Conservation Treatment. The result was published in *CA: A Cancer Journal for Clinicians,* and is available as a booklet from the American Cancer Society. The booklet comprehensively discusses philosophical and practical considerations of breast and axillary surgery and radiation.[15]

Given that the goal of lumpectomy, axillary dissection, and radiation is to attain maximum cosmetic results while achieving a high probability of local control and survival rates at least as good as those found with total mastectomy and axillary dissection, the consensus conference made recommendations regarding surgical technique and radiation therapy to assist in achieving these ends.

Some surgical recommendations relate to those factors that would ultimately result in optimal cosmetic effect. They noted that particularly for lesions in the upper quadrants, arcuate incisions with the skin lines with thick flaps centered over the lesion are preferable to radial incisions. Except when tumors are quite superficial, overlying skin does not require excision. Meticulous hemostasis is important, drains are rarely needed, and the surgeon should refrain from suture reapproximation of breast tissue if possible, and leave the "dead space" cavity.

Regarding the amount of tissue to be removed and the margins, approximately 1 cm of normal margin should be removed. The removal of excessive tissue adversely affects the cosmetic result. Conversely, the surgeon should remove the tumor so that the margins are grossly negative (or further resection is indicated) and should attempt to achieve microscopically negative margins (although it was believed that current data are inadequate to indicate whether a small focus of microscopic disease at a margin increases the risk of local failure after appropriate radiation). It is important to ink the resection margins and mark the excised tissue to assist the pathologist with proper orientation.

Both for staging and to prevent axillary recurrence, an axillary dissection is important in most women. However, some women may have no suspicious palpable lymph nodes, and thereby may not necessarily require an axillary dissection for local control. Furthermore, elderly women may not require accurate staging; their treatment will be the same regardless of microscopic cancer found in the lymph nodes. These women do not have the same indications as the other patients for axillary dissection.

A great deal of investigation is ongoing with dye and tracer techniques to accurately find the "sentinel" lymph node . . . the lymph node predictive of the rest of the axillary lymph nodes. If the sentinel lymph node does not contain metastases, the rest of the lymph nodes are also presumed to be normal, and an axillary dissection can be avoided.

The consensus conference also made recommendations regarding radiation therapy. At present, all patients who have lumpectomy and axillary dissection should have radiation following the surgery. Although some patients can be cured with this limited surgery alone, it is not known which, if any, subgroups of patients can be safely treated with limited surgery without radiation.

Patients should routinely receive 4500 to 5000 cGy to the whole breast using megavoltage radiation. Most trials have utilized boost irradiation as well, although the precise indications for this are not fully defined. Patients with focal microscopic disease at the margins of resection have been treated either with boost irradiation or mastectomy, and no data presently exist to refute the need for this. Boost irradiation is either by electron beam or, less commonly, by implantation, with doses of 1000 to 1500 cGy.

Reconstructive Surgery

Reconstruction following mastectomy became more frequent during the late 1970s, and even more commonplace during the 1980s. The transition from radical mastectomy to mastectomy with preservation of the pectoralis muscle made reconstructive surgery somewhat simpler. Simultaneously, major advances in plastic surgery occurred during this period.

The timing of reconstructive surgery is occasionally an issue that evokes some controversy. Often it can be done at the time of mastectomy, especially in earlier stage patients. However, depending on the extent of disease and the therapy to be utilized postoperatively (chemotherapy, chest wall radiation), physicians sometimes prefer to have the reconstructive procedure delayed.

Breast reconstructive surgery is discussed further in Chap. 84.

Histopathology of Breast Cancer

The most common type of primary invasive breast cancer is infiltrating ductal carcinoma, which accounts for 70 to 80 percent of invasive breast cancers. The next most common variety, infiltrating lobular carcinoma, accounts for only 5 to 8 percent of invasive breast cancers. It is clinically important that this lesion is more commonly multicentric and/or bilateral.

Three percent of breast cancers are medullary carcinomas, and 2 percent are mucinous (colloid) carcinomas; each of these usually are reported to have a better prognosis than infiltrating ductal carcinoma. Approximately 1 percent of breast cancers are tubular carcinomas. Pure tubular carcinomas have a very good prognosis, but they are sometimes intermingled with other histologic types. Adenoid cystic carcinoma is a rare, slowly growing tumor with a good prognosis, and is a variant of ductal carcinoma. Secretory carcinoma, also called juvenile carcinoma, is an extremely rare tumor that has been seen in prepubertal girls and, on rare occasion, in adults, and has a good prognosis.

One to 2 percent of breast cancers are inflammatory carcinomas. This is not a specific histologic subtype, but is distinguished by extensive invasion of dermal lymphatics that clinically can be confused with mastitis. This tumor has a very poor prognosis.

Cystosarcoma phyllodes is a lesion with both epithelial and mesenchymal components. It is distinguished from a fibroadenoma by the fact that cystosarcoma phyllodes has increased cellularity and overgrowth in the stromal component. It is more commonly found in older patients than is the fibroadenoma, is more likely to be a single lesion, and is commonly larger. This lesion can be categorized as benign, borderline, or malignant, depending upon its histologic features. Cystosarcoma phyllodes can usually be treated by excision with a wide margin.[81] It is important to make certain that the tumor is completely excised with a wide margin of grossly normal tissue, or it is likely to recur locally. Although these lesions are generally not aggressive, patients with borderline or malignant lesions may rarely develop metastatic disease.[81]

Paget's disease of the breast usually first appears as a painless sore on the nipple (not the areola). Reddening and thickening commonly then appear. The lesion has Paget's cells (which have large nuclei and abundant cytoplasm), and in the vast majority of patients there is an underlying breast cancer, either intraductal and/or invasive cancer.

There are two types of in situ breast cancers, intraductal (ductal carcinoma in situ) and lobular carcinoma in situ. Intraductal carcinoma starts within the ducts and does not extend beneath or through the basement membrane. It has a wide spectrum of presentation and is usually detected on screening mammography, although it may also present as a palpable mass or may be discovered incidentally. This lesion is often multicentric, and may occasionally present with bloody nipple discharge. Pure intraductal carcinoma has become very common since the advent of population mammographic screening. The number of intraductal carcinomas diagnosed in the United States is now about one-quarter that of the number of invasive breast cancers. Clustered micro-

calcifications on screening mammography is the most common reason for its coming to medical attention.

Following treatment—excision with negative margins that is usually followed by radiation—patients with pure intraductal carcinoma should have a 99 percent survival rate free of distant disease, because this is a preinvasive cancer. It is classified as Stage 0 breast cancer.

Lobular carcinoma in situ is a preinvasive lesion that appears to begin in the mammary lobule as opposed to in the duct. As distinguished from intraductal carcinoma in situ that may present with a mass, lobular carcinoma in situ does not. It is usually either an incidental finding or it may produce mammographic abnormalities. Lobular carcinoma in situ is often multicentric and/or bilateral. It predicts a higher risk of breast cancer in the future, which affects either breast equally, even when LCIS is diagnosed in only one breast.

Prognostic Factors

A variety of factors will have an impact on any individual patient's likelihood of cure (Table 65-2). One of the most significant factors affecting prognosis and length of survival is the presence of metastatic disease at the time of diagnosis. The SEER data[1] indicated that for caucasian American women with breast cancer, between 1980 and 1985, the 5-year survival for women with tumor confined to the breast was 91 percent, for women with regional node involvement it was

TABLE 65-2 **Prognostic Factors**

Lymph node involvement

Tumor size

Receptor status

Distant metastases

Peritumoral lymphatic and blood vessel invasion

Histology

Nuclear grade

Ploidy

Protease cathepsin D

69 percent, and for those with distant metastatic disease it was 19 percent. The number of nodes involved is important; in addition, particularly if only one node is involved, it is significant to note whether this is a micrometastasis or whether the node is grossly replaced by tumor. For women with negative nodes, peritumoral lymphatic and blood vessel invasion adversely affect prognosis.[55]

Axillary lymph node metastases are used to determine whether adjuvant chemotherapy is necessary in the treatment of breast cancer. Nevertheless, the recurrence rate at 5 years of 15 to 20 percent in patients with lymph-node-negative disease has led to greater scrutiny of "negative" lymph nodes. Micrometastases undetected with standard routine lymph node sectioning, but found with multiple sectioning, serial sectioning, and additional staining, has been reported. In a review of multiple studies, it is found, depending upon the study and the methods, in as much as 33 percent of such cases with lymph-node-negative disease that microscopic cancer may indeed be present. Follow-up consistently shows these small metastases to be important in prognosis and thus in therapeutic decisions.[28]

Although size is correlated with lymphatic metastases, size of the primary breast cancer is also a prognostic factor. Women with tumors less than 1 cm in largest diameter and with negative lymph nodes have a 10-year survival of approximately 90 percent.

Histology is important in determining prognosis. Although these lesions are all uncommon, women with adenoid cystic, colloid, tubular, or secretory breast cancers have an enhanced prognosis. On the other hand, women with inflammatory or undifferentiated cancers have a poor prognosis. Nuclear grade is another important prognostic factor; high nuclear grade being associated with an unfavorable prognosis.

The value of DNA flow cytometry as a prognostic factor has been explored. In Clark's series of patients with node-negative breast cancers, DNA flow-cytometric measurements were performed to assess ploidy and the fraction of cells in the synthesis phase of the cell cycle (S phase). Women who had tumors that were diploid had a significantly better disease-free 5-year survival than did those with aneuploid tumors. In addition, in patients with diploid tumors, those with low S-phase fractions had a better 5-year disease-free survival than did those with high S-phase fractions.[21] Unfortunately, one of the main problems with using DNA flow cytometry is sampling error. The tumor is composed of heterogeneous elements, and only the smallest fraction can be submitted for analysis.

Adjuvant Chemotherapy

It has been demonstrated that the potential curability of a malignancy by chemotherapy is inversely related to tumor burden, and that if a primary malignancy has been removed, chemotherapy may be able to ablate any residual micrometastases.[41]

Adjuvant systemic therapy is the administration of chemotherapy or the use of ablative or additive endocrine therapy after primary treatment of breast cancer. The goal is to kill or inhibit clinically occult micrometastases. Death from breast cancer results from growth of micrometastases present at distant sites (beyond the treated breast and axilla). These metastases, rarely diagnosed on radiographic and nuclear scans at the time of initial breast cancer diagnosis, account for treatment failure in breast cancer patients who receive only surgery and/or radiation to the breast and regional lymph nodes.

Contemporary adjuvant systemic therapy trials were begun in the late 1960s and early 1970s. Initial studies accrued women with positive axillary lymph nodes who had a high risk of distant recurrence, thereby justifying the use of toxic chemotherapy. Trials using endocrine therapy, the antiestrogen tamoxifen, were initiated in the mid-1970s. The 1980s brought studies of doxorubicin-based chemotherapy regimens, clinical trials of systemic therapy in women with negative lymph nodes, studies in the combination of

ISBN 0-07-058044-8

90000

9 780070 580442

chemotherapy and endocrine therapy, and a renewed interest in ovarian ablation using the new luteinizing hormone-releasing hormone (LHRH) antagonist. The 1990s will almost certainly be known as the decade for studies of chemotherapy dose-intensity, including trials of extremely high-dose chemotherapy with autologous bone marrow transplantation or stem cell transplantation. There have also been clinical trials of preoperative chemotherapy designed to reduce the tumor in the breast and make it amenable to breast conservation. More than 100 randomized clinical trials of breast cancer systemic therapy have now been completed. Many of these studies have even had 15 to 20 years of patient follow-up.

In early data collected from 23 institutions treating women with breast cancer, 10-year survival for breast cancer patients with positive nodes was 25 percent. There was a 38 percent survival rate for women with one to three positive nodes and a 14 percent survival rate for women with four or more positive nodes.[34] Because the likelihood of recurrence for breast cancer patients with positive nodes was so high, the importance of identifying adjuvant systemic chemotherapy that could improve survival for women with breast cancer was clear.

As far as specific landmark studies, in a seminal study published in the mid-1970s, Fisher found that for premenopausal women with four or more positive nodes, adjuvant thiotepa following radical mastectomy could reduce the likelihood of treatment failure.[33] At the same time in Italy, Bonadonna[7] started evaluating Cytoxan, methotrexate, and 5-fluorouracil (CMF) as adjuvant therapy over two years for women with breast cancer and positive axillary nodes. He showed that CMF improved relapse-free survival and total survival for premenopausal women.[9] Response to CMF was dose-dependent, and many of the postmenopausal patients received a reduced dose. When postmenopausal patients received an equivalent dose, they also demonstrated a comparable response to that seen in premenopausal patients.[9]

In further studies, Fisher, in the National Surgical Adjuvant Project for Breast and Bowel Cancers (NSABP), utilized L-phenylalanine mustard (P) either alone, or combined with 5-fluorouracil (PF), or combined with 5-fluorouracil and methotrexate (PFM), to provide adjuvant therapy for breast cancer patients with positive nodes. He found that adjuvant chemotherapy prolonged relapse-free survival and reduced mortality in premenopausal women, and that PF improved relapse-free survival and overall survival in postmenopausal patients.

During the past several years, data have become available on the role of adjuvant chemotherapy and/or hormonal therapy when lymph nodes do not contain metastatic disease. In 1988, the National Cancer Institute (NCI) mailed a clinical alert to physicians regarding the benefits of adjuvant therapy for patients with node-negative breast cancer.[64] In this clinical alert, the NCI revealed preliminary data from three trials that had completed their planned accrual of patients, but only had a median follow-up of 3 to 4 years. Each of the three landmark studies had demonstrated that adjuvant systemic chemotherapy had resulted in a statistically significant improvement in disease-free survival, and although none of the three studies had yet had their results printed in peer-reviewed journals, the potential impact of the findings was so great that the NCI believed it necessary to immediately inform physicians.

The first study, NSABP-13, included women under 71 years of age with node-negative, estrogen receptor (ER)-negative (<10 fmol) breast cancer and tumor of any size. Primary therapy was either by total mastectomy and axillary dissection or by segmental resection and axillary dissection with radiation. Patients were randomly assigned to receive either observation or chemotherapy.[36] When the paper was ultimately published, Fisher indicated that they found no survival advantage for women who received adjuvant therapy versus those who did not during four years of follow-up (87 percent vs. 86 percent, $p = .8$). However, they did find a significant prolongation of disease-free survival for women who

received adjuvant therapy when compared with those who did not (80 percent vs. 71 percent, $p = .003$). They found that treatment was advantageous both for women up to the age of 49, who had the incidence of treatment failure reduced by 24 percent, and for women over the age of 50, who had treatment failure reduced by 50 percent.

The second study involved patients under the age of 71 with negative nodes and tumors of any size that were ER-positive. Thus the criteria for entry into NSABP-13 and NSABP-14 were the same, except that while the women in NSABP-13 had negative ER, those in NSABP-14 had positive ER. Patients in this randomized, double-blind study received either a placebo or tamoxifen 10 mg orally twice-a-day for 5 years.[35] A total of 2644 women were enrolled. As in NSABP-13, NSABP-14 found no survival advantage during four years of follow-up (93 percent for the treated group and 92 percent for the placebo group). However, disease-free survival was significantly prolonged when women who received tamoxifen were compared to women who did not (83 percent vs. 77 percent; $p < .00001$). In women through the age of 49, treatment failure was reduced by 44 percent over placebo. In women 50 or older, there was a 14 percent reduction in treatment failure at 4 years.

The third study of lymph-node-negative patients that was brought to the attention of physicians in the NCI clinical alert was the Intergroup Study (INT 0011). For eligibility, tumors that were ER-positive needed to be greater than 3 cm in largest diameter; tumors that were ER-negative could be any size. Women were either observed or treated with CMFP (cyclophosphamide, methotrexate 5-FU, and prednisone). This chemotherapy course was repeated every 28 days, and six courses of chemotherapy were given. At the time of publication of the NCI clinical alert, 422 patients had been randomized and had a median follow-up of 3 years. At this time, 84 percent of patients who received CMFP were free of disease, as were 67 percent of controls ($p = .0001$). Therapy was effective in both premenopausal and postmenopausal women. It

was also effective whether patients were ER-positive or ER-negative.

A fourth trial that had been simultaneously ongoing was conducted by the Ludwig Breast Cancer Study Group.[95] Patients with negative lymph nodes who had both positive and negative receptor status were included. At a median follow-up of 42 months, there was no statistically significant difference in survival but disease-free survival was improved. Both premenopausal and postmenopausal women were helped by this regimen, but patients with no or low estrogen-receptor content in the primary tumor had the greatest likelihood of deriving benefit from therapy.

In June 1990, the NIH held a Consensus Development Conference,[26] which concluded that adjuvant therapy reduces the rate of recurrence for negative lymph node patients by approximately one-third, although the majority are cured by local therapy alone. Because so many questions remain to be answered, the conference recommended that all women who are candidates for clinical trials be offered the opportunity to participate. However, if a patient either is not interested in participating or is not a candidate for protocol, the conference indicated that it is important that the risks and benefits of adjuvant systemic therapy be explained to the patient as it pertains to the specifics of her tumor. For instance, for some women, the risk of recurrence is so small (e.g., women with small tumors, positive receptor status, low nuclear grade, a favorable histological subtype, and/or favorable outcome of DNA flow cytometry) that the risk and expense of treatment may outweigh the potential benefit. On the other hand, women with node-negative breast cancer but with other factors that might lead to poor prognosis are at greater risk of recurrence and therefore might have greater potential benefit from chemotherapy. When tamoxifen is utilized, the optimal period, according to the 1992 meta-analysis published in *Lancet,* is 5 years.[30]

It is clear that extensive research is needed so that accurate risk-profile systems can be devel-

oped and the individual patient with breast cancer and negative lymph nodes can understand her risk of recurrence, as well as the potential benefit that she can expect to derive from adjuvant therapy. At present, the consensus conference concluded that patients with tumors less than or equal to 1 cm with negative lymph nodes have such a good prognosis that they do not require adjuvant systemic therapy outside clinical trials. In a 20-year survival study, results showed that patients with cancers 1 cm in diameter or smaller have a 10 to 15 percent chance of ever having a recurrence, whereas those with tumors 3 cm or larger have a 50 percent or greater chance of disease recurrence without adjuvant chemotherapy.[79] In addition to refining risk profiles, the conference concluded that future research must investigate such issues as improving systemic chemotherapy regimens, duration of treatment, chemotherapy and hormonal therapy combinations, and the optimal sequence and timing for radiation therapy and systemic adjuvant therapy.

A great degree of certainty of the disease-free survival and overall survival benefits of adjuvant therapy in node-negative patients comes from the breast cancer meta-analysis published in *Lancet* in 1992.[30] Quantitatively, the improvements in disease-free survival and overall survival were similar in the node-negative and node-positive patients—approximately a one-third reduction in expected recurrence rate. These data indicate that systemic adjuvant therapy provides important reductions in recurrence and mortality in node-negative patients, at least those with a relatively high risk of recurrence based on prognostic factors.

During the past 20 years, studies have addressed the question of what is the optimal adjuvant therapy regimen (Tables 65-3 and 65-4). Studies that compare single agents to combination therapy are under way. A potential problem with combination therapy is that doses of each agent in the combination often must be reduced because of overlapping toxicity. Administration of each of the agents in a combination regimen

sequentially, and at optimal dose, instead of in their combination, is currently under investigation. Longer duration versus shorter duration chemotherapy is being investigated, and some issues have been settled. For CMF-based regimens, 6 months of treatment is as effective as 1 year.

Perioperative chemotherapy—given at the time of or just after surgery—offers several theoretical advantages in that drugs may kill circulating tumor cells that conceivably were dislodged at the time of surgery. On the other hand, this timing may decrease healing capability.

Currently, patients who require chemotherapy but who are lower risk are usually given a 6-month course of CMF, which is eight cycles. Higher risk patients are usually given an Adriamycin-based regimen, with the "Bonnadonna" regimen (named after the medical oncologist in Milan, Italy where the publications originated) being the most common. It consists of four cycles of Adriamycin followed by the standard course of CMF as in lower-risk cancers. Recently, the trend has been to give Adriamycin and Cytoxan for four cycles followed by Taxol for four cycles to the higher risk patients. Stem cell transplant is truly investigational because it so far has failed to prove its worth after more than a decade of usage and study.

Treatment side effects, long-term toxicity, and the decrease in the quality of life are additional important gauges of adjuvant treatment and need to be further studied. Side effects as recorded by a nurse or physician often underestimate the incidence and severity of side effects because these end points may not be sought in a formal prospective fashion. The accurate assessment of side effects is necessary when comparing the overall efficacy of two treatments that are similar in their breast cancer mortality reduction. An accurate side effect profile is also important for women to make an informed decision about adjuvant treatment, especially patients with a low risk of disease recurrence.

Certain "side effects" of tamoxifen may contribute to its overall net benefit. The estrogen-

TABLE 65-3 Adjuvant Therapy for Women with Negative Lymph Nodes

Tumor Size	Hormone Receptor Status	Menopausal Status	
		Premenopausal	Postmenopausal
≤1[a]	ER+	None	None
	ER−	None	None
>1 cm	ER+	Chemotherapy (e.g., CMF) usually followed by tamoxifen[b]	Either tamoxifen alone or chemotherapy[d] (e.g., CMF) followed by tamoxifen[b]
	ER−[c]	Chemotherapy (e.g., CMF)	Chemotherapy (e.g., CMF)

[a]In general, for all cancers <1 cm with negative lymph nodes, the long-term risk of distant metastases without chemotherapy is less than 9 percent. It is usually the case that the side effects of tamoxifen or any chemotherapy are not worth the benefit.

[b]The recommended course of tamoxifen currently is 5 years for adjuvant treatment.

[c]Five percent or less of ER− cancers are thought to respond to tamoxifen.

[d]Depending on age and comorbid status, older women may not have enough estimated benefit from chemotherapy to justify the more serious side effects in the elderly.

like properties may result in reduced serum cholesterol and a more favorable lipid profile, and may reduce the risk of cardiovascular disease. The estrogen-like properties of tamoxifen also may stabilize and sometimes increase bone density. Individual trials, as well as the 1992 *Lancet* meta-analysis,[30] show a 40 percent reduction in the risk of contralateral breast cancer with tamoxifen therapy.

The side effects of tamoxifen are menopausal symptoms with at least 50 to 60 percent of patients reporting hot flashes. Clinically significant eye toxicity in the form of retinopathy is rare if, indeed, it exists at all. Tamoxifen use, much like unopposed estrogen therapy, is clearly related to increased incidence of endometrial cancer, with as much as a 2 percent estimate of developing this disease in a 5- to 10-year course of treatment.

In the past several years, there have been more and more indications for prescribing tamoxifen. The course of treatment is almost always five

TABLE 65-4 Adjuvant Therapy for Women with Positive Lymph Nodes

Tumor Size	Hormone Receptor Status	Menopausal Status	
		Premenopausal	Postmenopausal
Any tumor size[a]	ER+	Chemotherapy (e.g., a doxorubicin-based program) usually followed by tamoxifn	Chemotherapy (e.g., a doxorubicin-based program or CMF) followed by tamoxifen
	ER−	Chemotherapy (e.g., a doxorubicin-based program)	Chemotherapy (e.g., a doxorubicin-based program or CMF)

[a]If the lymph nodes have cancer, tumor size is of no prognostic value. Rather, the increasing number of positive lymph nodes is directly proportional to the worse prognosis.

years. Among its many uses, tamoxifen is given to most women after chemotherapy whose cancer had positive hormone receptors. The only exception may be for women who maintain their menstrual cycles after chemotherapy. Due to feedback inhibition, the serum estradiol of such an individual may greatly rise, and it is unknown whether this effect, in the face of concomitant tamoxifen, is desirable.

In 1998, research on 13,000 study subjects was published, demonstrating that tamoxifen "prevented" about half the number of breast cancers that appeared in the group randomized to the placebo.[39] Because these results were achieved within 4 years, it is reasonable to wonder whether this effect was merely suppression or treatment of early existing subclinical cancers, and not really prevention. This is borne out as tamoxifen reduced the occurrence of hormone receptor positive cancers by 70 percent, but no difference in the occurrence in hormone receptor-negative cancers was seen between the tamoxifen and the placebo groups. As one might expect there was a statistically significant increase (2.5-fold) in endometrial cancers in the group taking tamoxifen, all of which were diagnosed as stage I in this research protocol. There was also a doubling of the occurrence of thrombophlebitis and pulmonary embolus in the tamoxifen group.

Continuing research in similar but smaller protocols in England and Italy has thus far found no prevention benefit, according to news releases in *Lancet.*[94] Therefore, the overall effectiveness of tamoxifen for prevention of breast cancer, especially as related to various high-risk indications, is unknown. The ability of tamoxifen and of raloxifene to reduce breast cancer risk, as well as potential side effects of each, is currently being evaluated in the "STAR" trial.

Carcinoma In Situ

There are two types of carcinoma in situ of the breast, ductal carcinoma in situ (DCIS) and lobular (LCIS).

Ductal carcinoma in situ, also called intraductal carcinoma, had, until recently, been considered a fairly uncommon lesion. However, with the advent of widespread mammography screening, resulting in early diagnosis, the capability to diagnose these preinvasive lesions has increased dramatically. The diagnosis of DCIS in the United States increased 200 percent between 1983 and 1992.[32]

Historically, patients with ductal carcinoma in situ were treated by mastectomy. This was particularly appropriate then, because patients presented with large palpable tumors. Currently, the majority of intraductal carcinomas are small and mammographically detected. Because breast conservation has been proven to be effective for invasive cancer, preserving the breast, with or without radiotherapy, has been explored for successful treatment of preinvasive cancers.

Between 1983 and 1992, the proportion of patients with DCIS who were treated with mastectomy markedly declined (from 71 percent to 43 percent) while the proportion treated with lumpectomy increased (from 25 percent to 53 percent). In 1992, 30 percent of patients were treated with lumpectomy alone and 23 percent were treated with lumpectomy and breast radiation.[103]

There are a few series in which patients with DCIS have been randomized to receive excision with negative margins or the same kind of excision with radiotherapy. Each of these series have had some patients who developed local recurrence, and no series has a very long follow-up. There is some suggestion that if the breast is conserved, postoperative radiation will reduce or delay the risk of recurrence.[83]

Schnitt et al. recommend that, when possible, patients should be encouraged to participate in clinical trials because there is so much that is unknown about the optimal treatment and outcome of these lesions. They believe that the extent of disease is important in determining treatment.[83] If disease is multifocal or greater lengths of ducts are involved, mastectomy may be appropriate. Some investigators believe that axillary sampling is indi-

cated in extensive intraductal cancer.[88] If there is very minimal unifocal disease, and the margins of resection are negative, some investigators believe that these patients can be treated by wide local excision. Others believe that it is optimal to add radiation. In any event, patients must be followed very carefully if they elect to have breast-conserving treatment, because there is a significant subsequent risk for either in situ or invasive disease, with at least 1 percent per year developing recurrence in the breast.

The National Surgical Adjuvant Breast and Bowel Project (NSABP) Protocol B-17 evaluated the efficacy of radiation for DCIS. It randomized 403 women with DCIS to be treated with lumpectomy alone; 104 (26 percent) had ipsilateral breast cancer recurrence compared with 47 (11 percent) of 411 treated with lumpectomy and breast radiation. Nevertheless, it is not clear that women with small lengths of ducts involved (less than 1 cm) and, in particular, with unaggressive subtypes such as noncomedo and particularly those who are older, always require radiation. That issue specifically requires more investigation, because there may be some small groups of women with DCIS in whom radiation is not indicated.

Whereas mammography assists greatly in identifying lesions that prove to be ductal carcinoma in situ, it is not as helpful in identifying lobular carcinoma in situ, mainly because LCIS does not contain calcifications. Hutter indicates that one-quarter to one-third of patients with lobular carcinoma in situ will develop invasive cancer in the next 20 years, which may be in either breast.[46] Some of the invasive cancers will be lobular, but most will be ductal. When LCIS is found on biopsy, as opposed to DCIS, it is not useful to reoperate for "clean" margins.

Recommendations for treatment of LCIS have ranged from careful follow-up to bilateral total mastectomy with reconstructive surgery. Recent trends are clearly toward a more conservative approach, and tamoxifen chemoprevention should be considered.

Breast Cancer in Pregnancy

Approximately 3 percent of breast cancers occur in women who are pregnant.[78] In the past, it was assumed that breast cancer that was diagnosed during pregnancy or the puerperium had an extremely poor prognosis. It subsequently became apparent that one of the significant factors resulting in poor prognosis is delay in diagnosis. It is not uncommon during this time period for a breast cancer to be incorrectly attributed, by the patient or the physician, to physiologic and morphologic changes associated with pregnancy or lactation. It is essential that breast cancer be appropriately considered in the differential diagnosis when a breast abnormality is identified during pregnancy, and that a biopsy be performed if appropriate. Nugent[69] found that when he compared 5-year survival for breast cancer in pregnant and nonpregnant women, when appropriate controls were instituted for stage and other important factors, there were no statistically significant differences. The pregnant patients had a 57 percent 5-year survival, and the nonpregnant patients a 56 percent 5-year survival. He believed that the issues adversely affecting the prognosis for breast cancer in pregnancy included its more advanced stage, young patient age, and the large number of estrogen-receptor negative tumors. It is these factors, rather than the pregnancy itself, which cause the poor prognosis.

It has been stated by some investigators that interruption of pregnancy does not improve the likelihood of survival. However, this is a somewhat complex issue. In certain circumstances, a decision may be made to abbreviate the metastatic work-up because a woman is pregnant. In others, her therapeutic options may be limited with regard to radiation and/or adjuvant chemotherapy. In addition, the woman must consider the possibility of developing a recurrence while the child is still young, and whether other relatives would be willing and able to raise the child if the natural mother was deceased. The decision to terminate a pregnancy if breast cancer occurs during its course requires that consideration be

given to a wide range of medical and personal issues.

In general, if a woman has breast cancer during her pregnancy and she plans to continue the pregnancy, she will be treated with mastectomy. On the other hand, if a pregnancy has progressed to the stage of fetal viability and the patient strongly wishes to be treated with surgery that preserves her breast, she may have an early delivery and lumpectomy and axillary dissection, followed by radiation.[3] At present, there are only a small number of patients treated in this fashion. It is of theoretical concern that the ducts are enlarged and interanastamosing during pregnancy and lactation, and may allow greater intraductal extension of cancer cells.

In recent years, it has become apparent that many subsets of women with breast cancer will benefit from adjuvant chemotherapy. Many authors recommend that pregnant women be strongly considered for adjuvant chemotherapy, with appropriate consideration of the risks and benefits.[3] Chemotherapy during the first trimester of pregnancy is associated with what might be considered a prohibitive risk of fetal anomalies and spontaneous abortions. Chemotherapy later in pregnancy is less commonly associated with adverse effects in fetal development. However, the potential for adverse long-term outcome must be considered. Although this is clearly a complex issue, the benefits of a specific adjuvant chemotherapy regimen for the mother with her particular tumor characteristics must be evaluated, the risks to the fetus of the specific drugs at the particular time in pregnancy must be weighed, and a decision must be made by the patient with the guidance of her physician given her individual circumstances.

As more women are deferring pregnancy until later in life, consideration must be given to the issue of pregnancy following treatment for breast cancer. There is some consensus that a minimum of two years should elapse before a woman who has been treated for breast cancer should consider becoming pregnant.[17] After that time, consideration must be given to the woman's risk of developing recurrent disease. If nodes were negative and the tumor small, her risk of recurrence is low, and she may decide to become pregnant. For the woman who has a greater likelihood of recurrence, for instance because of positive nodes, she must give stronger weight to the effects on her growing family if she develops recurrent disease. In addition, the question of the effects of pregnancy on estrogen-receptor positive tumors and on the patients treated with irradiation without mastectomy require further definition.[53]

Treatment of Advanced and Recurrent Breast Cancer

TNM stage III breast cancer is considered locally advanced disease. Patients are usually treated with a multimodality approach. One approach is to begin with chemotherapy, followed by mastectomy, followed once again by chemotherapy to complete the program, and then chest wall radiation. If the patient's primary tumor disappears after the initial chemotherapy, the patient's chances of survival are much greater. The amount of residual disease in the mastectomy specimen is also of prognostic significance, as is the number of positive nodes following initial chemotherapy.

Hortobagyi[44] reported the results of 174 patients with noninflammatory stage III breast cancer; 48 were IIIA and 126 were IIIB. All patients were initially treated with three cycles of combination chemotherapy, 5-fluorouracil, Adriamycin, and cyclophosphamide. This was followed by local therapy with total mastectomy and axillary dissection, radiotherapy, or both. Chemotherapy was then continued. The median follow-up was 59 months. The five-year disease-free survival rate was 84 percent for patients with stage IIIA disease and 33 percent for patients with stage IIIB disease. The authors projected that at 10 years, 56 percent of patients with stage IIIA disease and 26 percent of patients with stage IIIB disease would be alive.

Jacquillat[48] treated 98 patients with stage III breast cancer with neoadjuvant chemotherapy (vinblastine, thiotepa, methotrexate, Adriamycin, 5-fluorouracil, prednisone) with or without hormonochemotherapy, followed by external and interstitial radiotherapy, and subsequently with consolidation chemotherapy with or without hormonochemotherapy. The 3-year disease-free survival was 62 percent. In their series, the main predictor of disease-free survival was whether there was greater than 75 percent tumor regression following the initial chemotherapy.

Because many patients with stage III breast cancer could have had the opportunity for earlier diagnosis but avoided doing so, Berger[5] studied the compliance rate of these patients with aggressive multimodal therapy. They reported 100 percent overall compliance at 2 months, 82 percent at 6 months, and 75 percent at 1 year. They concluded that although their patients were medically indigent and had initially neglected their disease, once therapy began, despite the complexity and discomforts of the treatment, there was good compliance, and that complex regimens for locally advanced breast cancer are both feasible and effective.

Inflammatory breast cancer also is treated with multimodality therapy beginning with systemic treatment. The prognosis is very poor, but fortunately only 1 to 2 percent of breast cancers are inflammatory tumors. Chevallier[18] reported an overall 3-year survival of only 38 percent, and found that these eight factors affected prognosis: lymph node involvement; size of initial edema; extent of initial erythema; erythema present at the end of initial chemotherapy; tumor size at the end of induction chemotherapy; erythema present at the end of radiotherapy; residual breast tumor at the end of maintenance chemotherapy; and performance of a radical mastectomy. He treated patients with three or four courses of induction chemotherapy followed by locoregional irradiation therapy, and then maintenance chemotherapy only if induction chemotherapy was successful.

The issue of breast recurrence following breast-conserving primary therapy is becoming increasingly important. Kurtz[55] studied 1593 women with stage I and II breast cancer who had been treated initially by macroscopic complete tumor excision and radiotherapy. He reported an actuarial freedom from mammary recurrence of 93 percent at 5 years, 86 percent at 10 years, 82 percent at 15 years, and 80 percent at 20 years. Although 79 percent of recurrences were in the vicinity of the tumor bed, as the time from treatment lengthened, an increasing percentage of the tumors were located elsewhere in the breast and may have been new tumors. Only 10 of 181 women with recurrence had distant metastases either concurrently or previously. For women who developed an operable recurrence, the uncorrected overall survival was 69 percent at 5 years and 57 percent at 10 years. If recurrence occurred more than five years after initial treatment, the prognosis was 84 percent. Kurtz reported that survival after recurrence was independent of the type of salvage operation, but that locoregional control was 88 percent at 5 years if the breast recurrence was treated by salvage mastectomy, but only 64 percent if the patient had a breast-conserving salvage procedure.

Local recurrence after breast-conserving surgery and radiation has a better prognosis than does chest wall recurrence following primary treatment by mastectomy. Mangno[62] retrospectively reviewed 162 patients treated for breast cancer by mastectomy who subsequently had isolated chest wall recurrences. There was a 34 percent 5-year cumulative survival. The five prognostic factors that influenced survival were length of disease-free interval, axillary node status, primary T stage, and number and size of recurrences. If a woman had three or more of these five favorable prognostic factors, her 5-year survival was 75 percent.

Despite improvements in primary and adjuvant therapy, a percentage of women initially diagnosed with early stage disease will experience systemic recurrence in the next 20 to 25 years. It is estimated that 24 to 30 percent of women with node-negative disease, and at least 50 to 60 percent of women with positive nodes

at diagnosis, will experience relapse despite adjuvant therapy if they do not die of other causes.[98]

Between 1983 and 1987, 7 percent of women newly diagnosed with breast cancer presented with distant metastases.[104] In the case of distant metastatic disease, the response to therapy, and the short-term prognosis, depends upon many factors.

The site of recurrence or metastatic disease is important in determining prognosis. The development of visceral metastases is usually associated with a shorter disease-free interval after treatment for the metastases and a subsequent decreased survival. Brain metastases have a particularly poor prognosis; these patients have a median survival as short as three to six months. On the other hand, women with metastatic disease confined to the bone frequently have indolent disease and survive, on average, for 4 to 5 years with treatment.

African-American and Hispanic women are likely to have a shorter survival after development of metastases, in part because of differences in the stage at presentation, but also because of poor prognostic factors. However, a wide range of survival times is observed in all groups of women and individual patient factors should be considered when planning treatment and discussing prognosis.

Response to therapy will also depend upon tumor burden and disease-free interval.

Therapy for recurrent disease almost always includes chemotherapy and/or hormonal therapy. Surgery or radiation may be utilized in addition to systemic therapy under certain circumstances. Emergency radiotherapy may be lifesaving in cases of superior vena caval syndrome (respiratory distress, venous distension of the chest wall and neck, puffiness of the face and neck, and central nervous system effects such as visual and mental disturbances and headaches), spinal cord compression, or bronchial obstruction.[20]

Fifty to 70 percent of patients with estrogen-receptor-positive tumors will respond to endocrine therapy, but only 10 percent of those who are receptor-negative will.[43] Women with recurrent breast cancer that is not life-threatening (e.g., not with superior vena caval syndrome or spinal cord compression) who have estrogen-receptor-positive tumors (or, if receptors cannot be measured, disease with characteristics suggestive of hormonal responsiveness such as a long disease-free interval) may be treated initially with hormonal therapy. This would usually be tamoxifen for postmenopausal women and usually for premenopausal women as well, although sometimes oophorectomy is recommended. High-dose medroxyprogesterone acetate may produce responses in some patients.[4] Patients who have previously responded to tamoxifen but then suffer a relapse may respond to other hormonal agents. In some circumstances, chemohormonal therapy may be useful either as primary or secondary therapy for recurrent disease.

Many chemotherapeutic agents are active in the treatment of metastatic breast cancer. Overall, first-line combination chemotherapy utilizing the most commonly employed combination for patients with metastatic disease, such as CMF, doxorubicin (Adriamycin)-based regimens, and paclitaxel (Taxol), induces a response rate of 50 percent and an overall duration of survival of approximately 1 year. Obviously there is enormous variation, depending upon such characteristics as the location of the recurrence, tumor volume, and the disease-free interval. Although second-line chemotherapy, such as mitomycin, vinorelbine, or Xeloda, has a lower likelihood of inducing a response, and a shorter duration of response, it often can be utilized with success. Colozza[23] reported a 43 percent remission rate with a median survival of 11.5 months in 44 evaluable patients with recurrent breast cancer previously treated with combination chemotherapy and currently receiving doxorubicin and mitomycin. A new class of drug, Herceptin, is now available. This specifically inhibits the growth of cancer cells with more HER-2/neu, an oncogene which causes production of a protein that stimulates cell growth.

Women with metastatic breast cancer may live comfortably for several years, and it is important that their routine health needs receive regular

attention. In addition, women with breast cancer are at high risk to develop primary endometrial, ovarian, and colon cancers, and they should be appropriately screened for these diseases.

References and Selected Readings

1. National Cancer Institute: *1988 Annual Cancer Statistics Review.* Washington, DC: NCI, 1988.
2. Baker LH: Breast cancer detection demonstration project: Five-year summary report. *CA Cancer J Clin* 32:1–35, 1982.
3. Barnavon Y, Wallack MK: Management of the pregnant patient with carcinoma of the breast. *Surg Gynecol Obstet* 171:347–352, 1990.
4. Becher R, Miller AA, Hoffken K, et al: High-dose medroxyprogesterone acetate in advanced breast cancer. *Cancer* 63:1938–1943, 1989.
5. Berger D, Braverman A, Sohn C, et al: Patient compliance with aggressive multimodal therapy in locally advanced breast cancer. *Cancer* 61:1453–1456, 1988.
6. Bilmovia MM: The woman at increased risk for breast cancer: Evaluation and management strategies. *CA Cancer J Clin* 45:263–278, 1995.
7. Bonadonna G, Brusamolino E, Valagussa P, et al: Combination chemotherapy as an adjuvant treatment in operable breast cancer. *N Engl J Med* 294:405–410, 1976.
8. Bonadonna G, Valagussa P: Current status of adjuvant chemotherapy for breast cancer. *Semin Oncol* 14:8–22, 1987.
9. Bonadonna G, Valagussa P: Dose-response effect of adjuvant chemotherapy in breast cancer. *N Engl J Med* 304:10–15, 1981.
10. Bowlin SJ, Leske MC, Varma A, et al: Breast cancer risk and alcohol consumption: Results from a large case-control study. *Int J Epidemiol* 26:915–923, 1997.
11. Boyle CA, Berkowitz GS, LiVoisi VA: Caffeine consumption and fibrocystic breast disease: A case-control epidemiologic study. *J Natl Cancer Inst* 72:1015–1019, 1984.
12. Brinton LA, Schairer C: Estrogen replacement therapy and breast cancer risk. *Epidemiol Rev* 25:66–79, 1993.
13. Brinton LA, Hoover RN, Szklo M, et al: Menopausal estrogen use and risk of breast cancer *cancer* 47:2517–2522, 1981.
14. Burns PE: False-negative mammograms delay diagnosis of breast cancer. *N Engl J Med* 299:201–202, 1978.
15. Standards for breast-conservation treatment: *CA Cancer J Clin* 42:134–162, 1992.
16. Callee EE, Heath CW Jr, Miracle-McMahill HL, et al: Breast cancer and hormonal contraceptives: Collaborative reanalysis of individual data on 53,297 women with breast cancer and 100,239 women without breast cancer from 54 epidemiological studies. *Lancet* 346:1713–1727, 1996.
17. Carbone PP: Pregnancy after breast cancer (Q&A). *JAMA* 255:1062, 1986.
18. Chevallier B, Asselain B, Kunlin A, et al: Inflammatory breast cancer: Determination of prognostic factors by univariate and multivariate analysis. *Cancer* 60:897–902, 1987.
19. Chilvers C, McPherson K, Peto J: Oral contraceptive use and breast cancer in young women. *Lancet* 1:973–982, 1989.
20 Chu FCH: Radiation therapy in the management of locally advanced and disseminated breast cancer. *Cancer* 45:1075–1078, 1980.
21. Clark GM, Dressler LG, Owens MA: Prediction of relapse or survival in patients with node-negative breast cancer by DNA flow cytometry. *N Engl J Med* 320:627–633, 1989.
22. Colditz GA, Egan KM, Stampfer MJ: Hormone replacement therapy and risk of breast cancer: Results from epidemiologic studies. *Am J Obstet Gynecol* 168:1473–1480, 1993.
23. Colozza M, Tonato M, Rignani F: Low-dose doxorubicin combination chemotherapy for patients with metastatic breast carcinoma previously treated with cyclophosphamide, methotrexate, and 5-fluorouracil. *Cancer* 62:262–265, 1988.
24. Consensus Conference: Adjuvant chemotherapy for breast cancer. *JAMA* 254:3461–3463, 1985.
25. Consensus Meeting: Is "fibrocystic disease" of the breast precancerous? *Arch Pathol Lab Med* 110:171–173, 1986.
26. National Institutes of Health Consensus Development Conference: Consensus Statement. 8:4–8, 1990.
27. Cooper R: Combination cytotoxic chemotherapy in hormone-resistant breast cancer. *Proc Am Assoc Ca Res* 10:15, 1969.
28. Dowlatshahi K, Fan M, Snider HC, et al: Lymph node micrometastases from breast carcinoma: Reviewing the dilemma. *Cancer* 80:1188–1197, 1997.
29. Dupont WD, Page DL, Rogers LW, et al: Influence of exogenous estrogens, proliferative breast disease, and other variables on breast cancer risk. *Cancer* 63:948–957, 1989.
30. Early Breast Cancer Trialists' Collaborative Study Group: Systemic treatment of early breast cancer by hormonal, cytotoxic, or immune therapy. *Lancet* 339:1–71, 1992.
31. Easton DF, Bishop DT, Ford D, et al: The breast cancer linkage consortium. Genetic linkage analysis

in familial breast and ovarian cancer: Results from 214 families. *Am J Hum Genet* 52:678–701, 1993.

32. Ernster VL, Barclay J, Kerlikowske K, et al: Incidence of and treatment for ductal carcinoma in situ of the breast. *JAMA* 275:913–918, 1996.

33. Ernster VL, Mason L, Goodson WH, et al: Effects of caffeine-free diet on benign breast disease: A randomized trial. *Surgery* 91:263, 1982.

34. Fisher B, Slack N, Datrych D, et al: Ten-year follow-up results of patients with carcinoma of the breast in a co-operative clinical trial evaluating surgical adjuvant chemotherapy. *Surg Gynecol Obstet* 140:528–534, 1975.

35. Fisher B, Costantino J, Redmond C, et al: A randomized clinical trial evaluating tamoxifen in the treatment of patients with node-negative breast cancer who have estrogen receptor-positive tumors. *N Engl J Med* 320:479–484, 1989.

36. Fisher B, Redmond C, Dimitriv NV, et al: A randomized clinical trial evaluating sequential methotrexate and fluorouracil in the treatment of patients with node-negative breast cancer who have estrogen receptor-negative tumors. *N Engl J Med* 320:473–478, 1989.

37. Fisher B, Redmond C, Poisson R, et al: Eight-year results of a randomized clinical trial comparing total mastectomy and lumpectomy with or without irradiation in the treatment of breast cancer. *N Engl J Med* 320:822–828, 1989.

38. Fisher B, Bauer M, Margolese R, et al: Five-year results of a randomized clinical trial comparing total mastectomy and segmental mastectomy with or without radiation in the treatment of breast cancer. *N Engl J Med* 312:665–673, 1985.

39. Fisher B, Costantino JP, Wickerham DL, et al: Tamoxifen for prevention of breast cancer: Report of the national surgical adjuvant breast and bowel project P-1 study. *J Natl Cancer Inst* 90:1371–1388, 1998.

40. Gambrell RD: Proposal to decrease the risk and improve the prognosis of breast cancer. *Am J Obstet Gynecol* 150:119–132, 1984.

41. Goldie HJ: Scientific basis for adjuvant and primary (neoadjuvant) chemotherapy. *Semin Oncol* 14:1–7, 1987.

42. Harris RE, Wynder EL: Breast cancer and alcohol consumption. *JAMA* 259:2867–2871, 1988.

43. Henderson IC, Hayes DF, Come S, et al: New agents and new medical treatments for advanced breast cancer. *Semin Oncol* 14:34–64, 1987.

44. Hortobagyi GN, Ames FC, Buzdar AU, et al: Management of stage III primary breast cancer with primary chemotherapy, surgery, and radiation therapy. *Cancer* 62:2507–2516, 1988.

45. Hunter DJ, Willet WC: Diet and body build: Diet,

body size, and breast cancer. *Epidemiol Rev* 15:110–132, 1993.

46. Hutter RP: The management of patients with lobular carcinoma in situ. *Cancer* 53:798–802, 1984.

47. Ibarra J: Bloody discharge from the nipple: The utility of cytology. *JAMA* 261:2202, 1989.

48. Jacquillat C, Baillet F, Weil M, et al: Results of a conservative treatment combining induction (neoadjuvant) and consolidation chemotherapy, hormonotherapy, and external and interstitial irradiation in 98 patients with locally advanced breast cancer (IIIA-IIIB). *Cancer* 61:1977–1982, 1988.

49. Kelsey J: A review of the epidemiology of human breast cancer. *Epidemiol Rev* 1:74–109, 1979.

50. Kelsey JL, Gammon MD, John EM: Reproductive and hormonal risk factors: Reproductive factors and breast cancer. *Epidemiol Rev* 15:36–47, 1993.

51. Kelsey JL, Horn-Ross PL: Breast cancer: Magnitude of the problem and descriptive epidemiology. *Epidemiol Rev* 15:7–16, 1993.

52. Keynes G: Conservative treatment of breast cancer. *BMJ* 2:643–649, 1937.

53. Kinne D: Pregnancy after breast cancer (Q&A). *JAMA* 255:1061–1062, 1986.

54. Kuale G, Heuch I: Menstrual factors and breast cancer risk. *Cancer* 62:1625–1631, 1988.

55. Kurtz JM, Amalric R, Brandome H, et al: Local recurrence after breast-conserving surgery and radiotherapy. *Cancer* 63:1912–1917, 1989.

56. Land CE, Boice JD, Shore RE, et al: Breast cancer risk from low-dose exposure to ionizing radiation: Results of parallel analysis of three exposed populations of women. *J Natl Cancer Inst.* 65:353–376, 1980.

57. Lee AKC, DeLellis RA, Silverman ML: Prognostic significance of peritumoral lymphatic and blood vessel invasion in node-negative carcinoma of the breast. *J Clin Oncol* 8:1457–1465, 1990.

58. Leis H: Nipple discharge: Surgical significance. *South Med J* 81:20–26, 1988.

59. Love SM: Bloody nipple discharge. *JAMA* 260:2296, 1988.

60. Lubin F, Rom E, Wax Y, et al: Case-control study of caffeine and methylxanthines in benign breast disease. *JAMA* 253:2388–2392, 1985.

61. Lund E: The research tide ebbs for the dietary fat hypothesis in breast cancer. *Epidemiology* 5:387–388, 1994.

62. Mango L, Bignardi M, Micheletti E, et al: Analysis of prognostic factors in patients with isolated chest wall recurrence of breast cancer. *Cancer* 60:240–244, 1987.

63. Meirik O, Farley TMM, Lund E, et al: Breast cancer and oral contraceptives: Patterns of risk among parous and nulliparous women—Further analysis of

Swedish-Norwegian material. *Contraception* 29:471–475, 1989.

64. Merz B: Clinical alert gives breast cancer data, revised recommendations. *JAMA* 260:153–154, 1988.

65. Miller DR, Rosenberg L, Kaufman DW, et al: Breast cancer risk in relation to early oral contraceptive use. *Obstet Gynecol* 68:863–868, 1986.

66. Minton JP: Methylxanthines in breast disease, in Schwartz GF, Marchant D (eds): *Breast Disease, Diagnosis and Treatment.* New York: Symposia Specialists, 1980, p 143.

67. Murray PP, Stadel BV, Schlesselmann JJ: Oral contraceptive use in women with a family history of breast cancer. *Obstet Gynecol* 73:977–983, 1989.

68. Noguchi S, Miyauhi K, Nishizawa Y, et al: Management of inflammatory carcinoma of the breast with combined modality therapy including intra-arterial infusion chemotherapy as an induction therapy. *Cancer* 61:1483–1493, 1988.

69. Nugent P, O'Connell TX: Breast cancer in pregnancy. *Arch Surg* 120:1221–1224, 1965.

70. Odenheimer DJ, Zunzunegui MV, King MC, et al: Risk factors for benign breast disease: A case control study of discordant twins. *Am J Epidemiol* 120:565–571, 1984.

71. Osuch JR: Benign lesions of the breast other than fibrocystic change. *Obstet Gynecol Clin N Am* 14:703–710, 1987.

72. Page DL, Dupont WD, Rogers LW, et al: Intraductal carcinoma of the breast: Follow-up after biopsy only. *Cancer* 49:751–758, 1982.

73. Phelps HM, Phelps CE: Caffeine ingestion and breast cancer. *Cancer* 61:1051–1054, 1988.

74. Pike MC, Henderson BE, Krailo MD: Breast cancer in young women and the use of oral contraceptives. *Lancet* 11:926–930, 1983.

75. Pike MC, Henderson BE, Casangrande JT, et al: Oral contraceptive use and early abortion as risk factors for breast cancer in young women. *Br J Cancer* 43:72–76, 1981.

76. Reis LAG, Kosary CL, Hankey BF, et al (eds): *SEER Cancer Statistics Review: 1973-1994.* Bethesda, MD: National Cancer Institute, 1997. NIH Pub No. 97-2789.

77. Rench MA, Baker CJ: Group B streptococcal breast abscess in a mother and mastitis in her infant. *Obstet Gynecol* 73:875–878, 1989.

78. Ribeiro G, Jones DA, Jones M: Carcinoma of the breast associated with pregnancy. *Br J Surg* 73:607–609, 1986.

79. Rosen PP, Groshen S, Saigo PE, et al: A long-term follow-up study of survival in stage I (TiNoMo) breast carcinoma. *J Clin Oncol* 7:355, 1989.

80. Ross PK, Paganini A, Gerkins VR, et al: A case control study of menopausal estrogen therapy and breast cancer. *JAMA* 243:1635–1639, 1980.

81. Salvardor B, Cusumano F, Del Bo R: Surgical treatment of phyllodes tumors of the breast. *Cancer* 63:2532–2536, 1989.

82. Schairer C, Brinton LA, Hoover RN: Methylxanthines and benign breast disease. *Am J Epidemiol* 124:603, 1986.

83. Schnitt SJ, Silen W, Sadowsky NL, et al: Ductal carcinoma in situ. *N Engl J Med* 318:898–903, 1988.

84. Seltzer MH, Perloff LJ, Kelley RI, et al: The significance of age in patients with nipple discharge. *Surg Gynecol Obstet* 131:519–522, 1970.

85. Shaaban MM, Morad F, Hassan A: Treatment of fibrocystic mastopathy by an anti-estrogen tamoxifen. *Int J Gynaecol Obstet* 18:348–350, 1980.

86. Shapiro S, Venet W, Strax P, et al: *Current Results of the Breast Cancer Screening Randomized Trial: The Health Insurance Plan (HIP) Screening for Breast Cancer* Toronto: Sam Hyber Press, 1988.

87. Sillero-Aernas M, Delgado-Rodriguez M, Rodrigues-Canteras R, et al: Menopausal hormone replacement therapy and breast cancer: A meta-analysis. *Obstet Gynecol* 79:286–294, 1992.

88. Silverstein MJ, Rosser RJ, Gierson ED, et al: Axillary lymph node dissection for intraductal breast carcinoma is it indicated? *Cancer* 59:1819–1824, 1987.

89. Smart CR, Beahrs OH: Breast cancer screening results as viewed by the clinician. *Cancer* 43:851–856, 1979.

90. Smith HO, Kammerer-Doak DN, Barbo DM, Sarto GE: Hormone replacement therapy in the menopause: A pro opinion. *CA Cancer J Clin* 46:343–363, 1996.

91. Snyder RE: Specimen radiography and pre-operative localization of nonpalpable breast cancer. *Cancer* 46:950–956, 1980.

92. Steinberg KK, Thacker SB, Smith SJ, et al: A meta-analysis of the effect of estrogen replacement therapy on the risk of breast cancer. *JAMA* 265:1985–1990, 1991.

93. Strax P, Venet L, Shapiro S: Value of mammography in reduction of mortality from breast cancer in mass screening. *Am J Nat Cancer Inst Rad* 117:686–689, 1973.

94. Tamoxifen prevention claim will not be allowed in USA. *Lancet* 352:883, 1998.

95. The Ludwig Breast Cancer Study Group: Prolonged disease-free survival after one course of perioperative adjuvant chemotherapy for node-negative breast cancer. *N Engl J Med* 320:491–496, 1989.

96. The Cancer and Steroid Hormone Study of the Centers for Disease Control and The National Institute of Child Health and Human Development: Oral con-

traceptive use and the risk of breast cancer. *N Engl J Med* 68:863–868, 1986.

97. Thomas DB: Oral contraceptives and breast cancer: Review of the epidemiologic literature. *Contraception* 43:597–642, 1991.

98 Valagussa P, Bonadonna G, Veronesi U: Patterns of relapse and survival following mastectomy. *Cancer* 41:1170, 1978.

99. Veronesi U, Banfi A, Salvadori B, et al: Breast conservation is the treatment of choice in small breast cancer: Long-term results of a randomized clinical trial. *Eur J Cancer* 26:668, 1990.

100. Veronesi U, Saccozzi R, Del Vecchio M, et al: Comparing radical mastectomy with quadrantectomy, axillary dissection, and radiotherapy in patients with small cancers of the breast. *N Engl J Med* 305:6–11, 1981.

101. Willett WC: Moderate alcohol consumption and the risk of breast cancer. *N Engl J Med* 316:1174–1180, 1987.

102. Willet WC, Hunter DJ, Stampfer MJ, et al: Dietary fat and fiber in relation to risk of breast cancer; An 8-year follow-up. *JAMA* 268:2037–2044, 1992.

103. Winchester DP, Menk HR, Osteen RT, et al: Treatment trends for ductal carcinoma in situ of the breast. *Ann Surg Oncol* 2:207–213, 1995.

104. Wingo PA, Tong T, Bolden S: Cancer Statistics 1995. *CA Cancer J Clin* 45:12, 1995.

105. Wooster R, Bignell G, Lancaster J, et al: Identification of the breast cancer susceptibility gene *BRCA2*. *Nature* 378:789–792, 1995.

106. Wynder EL: Dietary factors related to breast cancer. *Cancer* 46:899–904, 1980.

107. Wyndgaarden JB: From the National Institutes of Health. *JAMA* 261:2481, 1989.

Endocrine Disorders

Fred Benjamin
Issac Sachmechi

THYROID DISEASE
Thyroid Anatomy and Physical
Examination • Thyroid Physiology •
Thyroid Function Tests •
Hypothyroidism • Hyperthyroidism •
Enlargement of the Thyroid Gland
(Thyromegaly, Goiter)

PITUITARY DISORDERS
Physiology • Hypothalamic-Pituitary
Diseases • Hypopituitarism •
Hyperpituitarism • Posterior Pituitary
Disorders

ADRENAL DISEASE
Anatomy and Physiology of the Adrenal
Glands • Adrenal Cortical Hypofunction •
Hyperfunction of the Adrenal Cortex •
Pheochromocytoma

CARCINOID SYNDROME
Etiology and Pathology • Symptoms •
Diagnosis • Treatment

HIRSUTISM
Causes of Hirsutism • Diagnosis •
Treatment

**PARATHYROID DISORDERS AND
BONE METABOLISM**
Hypercalcemia/Hyperparathyroidism •
Hypocalcemia/Hypoparathyroidism

The physician responsible for the primary
health care of women frequently encounters disorders that are basically endocrine
in origin. Many of these diseases occur in men

as well, but the clinical presentation is often different in women and of particular importance to
the female patient. For example, a large number
of the endocrinopathies affect menstrual function so that the woman's chief complaint is
frequently a menstrual disorder. Likewise,
hormonal disorders associated with hyperandrogenism are often of much more concern to
women because the manifestations include the
disturbing symptom of hirsutism.

This chapter reviews the commonly occurring
endocrine disorders that are encountered in
women, how they present to the primary care
physician, and the manner in which they can be
recognized, diagnosed, and treated in the office
setting. Thyroid disease, pituitary disorders, adrenal disorders, pheochromocytoma, carcinoid
syndrome, hirsutism, metabolic bone disease,
and parathyroid disorders are all considered.
However, some concerns that have a large endocrine component, such as the physiology of menstruation, menstrual disorders, normal and abnormal sexual development, the special needs of
adolescents, infertility, and the menopause are
reviewed elsewhere in this book and are not discussed in this chapter.

Thyroid Disease

Thyroid disease is of particular importance in the
primary health care of women because practically all thyroid disorders, both benign and malignant, are much more common in women than
in men. Hyperthyroidism is about 5 times, and

hypothyroidism about 10 times more frequent in females than in males.

Thyroid disease usually presents itself to the clinician in one of four ways: hypothyroidism; hyperthyroidism; enlargement of the thyroid gland (thyromegaly or goiter); or a thyroid nodule. An understanding of these disorders presupposes a basic knowledge of the anatomy, physical examination, and physiology of the thyroid gland, as well as an understanding of the thyroid function tests.

Thyroid Anatomy and Physical Examination

Embryologically the thyroid gland is formed from the thyroglossal duct that migrates from the pharynx down into the neck. The gland consists of two lobes, one on either side of the trachea, each being 2 to 3 cm in length and 1 cm in width; the lobes are joined by a narrow isthmus which crosses the trachea just below the cricoid cartilage. Physical examination of the thyroid gland should begin by inspection both before and during swallowing. Palpation is best accomplished with the patient seated and the clinician standing behind her. With the first three fingers on either side of the trachea at the level of the cricoid cartilage, the thyroid gland is readily identified by its movement up and down with swallowing. Normally it is readily palpated, and may even be visible in thin patients.

Histologically, the thyroid is composed of rounded follicles lined by cuboidal cells and filled with colloid, the storage form of thyroglobulin, which is secreted by the thyroid cells. Iodide is incorporated into the amino acid tyrosine in thyroglobulin at one site to form monoiodotyrosine, or at two sites to form diiodotyrosine. Monoiodotyrosine and diiodotyrosine are then joined to form the active hormones triiodothyronine (T3) or tetraiodothyronine or thyroxine (T4); monoiodotyrosine plus diiodotyrosine form triiodothyronine, and diiodotyrosine plus diiodotyrosine form tetraiodothyronine.

The thyroid gland secretes 20 times more T4 than T3, but 30 percent of the T4 is converted in the periphery to T3, and 40 percent to inactive reverse T3. The action of thyroid in the body is mainly due to T3, because the thyroid hormone receptors have a 10-fold higher affinity for T3 than T4. However, the blood level of T3 is not a good reflection of thyroid function because T3 has a much shorter half-life than T4 (7 h versus 7 days) and because T3 is formed mainly in the periphery.

Thyroid Physiology

Thyroid hormone production within the thyroid gland is stimulated by thyroid-stimulating hormone (TSH) secreted by the anterior pituitary gland. If the thyroid levels increase, TSH secretion is inhibited, a negative feedback mechanism. Thyroid hormone has two major functions: it increases protein synthesis in all body tissues (T3 and T4 enter cells, bind to nuclear receptors, and influence the formation of RNA), and it increases oxygen consumption.

Thyroid Function Tests

Total Serum T4 (Thyroxine) This is measured very accurately by radioimmunoassay (RIA), but this assay measures both the free (active) T4 and the bound T4. Thyroid-binding globulin is increased by pregnancy, estrogen therapy, and hypothyroidism, and is decreased by androgen, hyperthyroidism, and obesity. The normal level is about 5 to 12 μg/dl.

Total Serum T3 This is measured by radioimmunoassay (RIA) and is normally about 80 to 200 ng/dl.

Free T4 and Free T3 Theoretically these determinations are the most valuable tests because they measure the active forms of thyroid hormone. However, these assays are difficult and expensive, and are therefore only really required in situations where changes in thyroid-binding globulin are expected; for example, when a woman is pregnant or is taking birth control pills.

Thyroid-Stimulating Hormone Thyroid-stim-

ulating hormone used to be measured by RIA, but the drawback was insensitivity in the lower ranges. The development of monoclonal antibodies to TSH of high specificity has allowed the development of a super sensitive TSH assay that is useful in testing both hypo- and hyperthyroid states.[7] The normal values are 0.4 to 4.8 μU/ml.

TRH Stimulation Test When a bolus of 500 μg TRH is given to a normal person, the serum TSH increases 2 to 5 times above baseline and by at least 6 μU/ml 30 min after the injection. In hyperthyroidism, there is a blunted or absent response to TRH. This test was used to diagnose mild hyperthyroidism, but has now been replaced by the new super-sensitive monoclonal antibody TSH assay.

Thyroid Antibodies Two thyroid antibodies are used in studying patients with thyroid disease: antithyroglobulin antibodies and antimicrosomal antibodies. They are both positive in most patients with Hashimoto's thyroiditis and in patients with Graves' disease.

Radioactive Iodine Uptake and Scan A tracer dose of radioactive iodine (RAI) is given and a count is taken over the thyroid gland 6 and 24 h later. The main value of the scan is to determine whether a thyroid nodule is active or "hot" (i.e., benign) or inactive or "cold" (i.e., a tumor, potentially malignant). The main value of uptake is to determine if it is high-uptake thyrotoxicosis (i.e., Graves' disease, multinodular toxic, or toxic nodule), or low-uptake thyrotoxicosis (i.e., thyroiditis).

Hypothyroidism

Etiology The most common type of hypothyroidism is "primary hypothyroidism" where the disorder is in the thyroid gland itself. "Secondary hypothyroidism" is rare and is due to lack of secretion of TSH by the pituitary or inadequate production of TSH-RH by the hypothalamus. The most common cause of primary hypothyroidism is Hashimoto's thyroiditis, an autoimmune disease that results in gradual destruction of the thyroid gland; it is 10 times more common in women than in men.[9] The second most common cause of primary hypothyroidism is posttherapeutic, following RAI therapy or surgery.

Symptoms Fatigue, lethargy, weakness, cold intolerance, weight gain, constipation, joint pains, and menorrhagia are common symptoms; forgetfulness, intellectual impairment, and even frank psychosis (called "myxedema madness") may occur.

Signs Weight gain, dry skin, bradycardia, cardiac enlargement and pericardial effusion, edema, slow relaxation of deep tendon reflexes, and hypercholesterolemia may occur. There may be loss of pubic, axillary, and scalp hair, and hair of the lateral aspects of the eyebrows.

Diagnosis The thyroid gland may or may not be enlarged. The key to the diagnosis is an elevated TSH, and, in the later stages, a low T4. In the most common type of hypothyroidism, Hashimoto's thyroiditis, antithyroglobulin and antimicrosomal antibodies are usually present.

Treatment Thyroid replacement, usually for life, is required. Three forms of thyroid hormone have been used: 1. Desiccated thyroid from animal sources (e.g., Thyrolar). This is not recommended because it is not standardized, and contains variable proportions of T3 and T4. The dose is 1 to 3 gr/day. 2. Synthetic T3, i.e., triiodothyronine (e.g., Cytomel). This is also not recommended because it has a short half-life of 7 h; accordingly, the serum concentrations are labile and are difficult to monitor, and at times there is hyper- and at other times hypothyroidism. 3. Synthetic thyroxine, i.e., T4 or tetraiodothyronine (e.g., Synthroid) is the best choice for therapy. It has a long half-life of 7 days, and therefore the serum levels are stable and can be monitored at any time of the day. The average dose required is 0.1 to 0.15 mg/day (100 to 150 μg). In older patients, the treatment should be started with 0.025 mg (i.e., 25 μg/day) and gradually increased by 25 μg every 4 weeks; rapid treatment may result in cardiac failure because of the cardiac effects that may have been present as a result of the hypothyroidism. In younger patients, the starting dose can be higher than 50 μg/day.

Response to treatment should be monitored by serum TSH levels; the aim is to achieve normal TSH levels (0.4 to 4.8 μU/ml) with normal or slightly elevated T4 values (5 to 12 μg/dl)

Hyperthyroidism

Etiology By far the most common cause of hyperthyroidism is Graves' disease (or toxic diffuse goiter), an autoimmune disease that is characterized by hyperthyroidism with goiter, exophthalmos, and pretibial myxedema. It is due to circulating thyroid-stimulating immunoglobulins or thyroid-stimulating antibodies that specifically stimulate the TSH receptors. The exophthalmos and pretibial myxedema are due to the autoimmune disease, the imunoglobulins causing inflammatory changes in these areas. Other less common causes of hyperthyroidism are as follows: (1) toxic solitary nodule or toxic multinodular goiter occurs when one or more nodules function autonomously, producing thyroid hormones; they are treated surgically or with radioactive iodine; (2) various forms of thyroiditis often begin with a hyperthyroid phase; (3) T3 thyrotoxicosis; here there are symptoms of hyperthyroidism. The T3 is elevated but the T4 is normal or low; (4) secondary hyperthyroidism due to overproduction of TSH by a tumor of the pituitary, embryonal carcinoma or choriocarcinoma (due to the TSH-like properties of chorionic gonadotropin), or to struma ovarii, tumor of the ovary producing thyroid hormones; (5) factitious thyrotoxicosis, due to exogenous thyroid intake.

Symptoms The more frequent symptoms of hyperthyroidism are nervousness, increased sweating, heat intolerance, palpitations, fatigue, weight loss, and frequent bowel movements.

Signs The common signs are goiter, tremor, warm moist skin, and tachycardia. In addition, in Graves' disease there are exophthalmos and pretibial myxedema.

Diagnosis Diagnosis is made by the symptoms and signs, a high T4 and low TSH (and, if the T4 is normal, an elevated T3).

Treatment *Propranolol (Inderal)* For the acute symptoms due to the adrenergic stimulation effects of hyperthyroidism (tremor, tachycardia, diaphoresis, and mental symptoms) the β-adrenergic antagonist, propranolol, is very effective. It is used in thyroid storm and as an adjunctive therapy with antithyroid medications. The dose is 10 mg twice daily to 80 mg four times daily.

Thiourea Drugs Propylthiouracil and methimazole interfere with thyroid hormone synthesis (by blocking the organification of iodide).[3] A maintenance dose of 100 to 300 mg of propylthiouracil daily, or methimazole, 10 to 30 mg daily, is given for 1 to 2 years. There is a high recurrence rate of 50 to 80 percent on discontinuing the medication, but there is less posttherapy hypothyroidism than with RAI or surgery. Propylthiouracil is preferred during pregnancy because it crosses the placenta much less readily than methimazole.

Radioactive Iodine Radioactive iodine (^{131}I) is usually used in patients past their childbearing years, because of concerns about possible effects to any subsequent offspring, such as birth defects and neoplasia. However, extensive studies have failed to show such effects. Accordingly, there has been an increasing tendency to use RAI in younger patients, because it is easy to administer, can be given to outpatients, avoids surgery, is 100 percent effective if given in adequate dosage, and has no complications except hypothyroidism. Hypothyroidism has an increasing incidence as time goes by, eventually reaching as high as 80 percent.

Surgery In experienced hands surgery is safe and effective and achieves euthyroidism rapidly. It is particularly indicated if the thyroid is very large; if the patient is young and should not receive radioactive iodine; if the patient has a toxic adenoma or toxic multinodular goiter; and during pregnancy if the disease is not adequately controlled.

Iodine In pharmacological doses iodide (3 drops of saturated potassium iodide tid or qid) rapidly inhibits the release of T4 and T3, inhibits the organification of iodine for a few days to a week, and decreases the vascularity of the thyroid

gland. It is very helpful for situations in which a rapid response is required, such as in thyroid storm or thyrotoxic patients undergoing emergency surgery.

Thyroid Storm This is a life-threatening emergency that can occur in patients with Graves' disease and is usually precipitated by infection, trauma, surgery, or toxemia of pregnancy. There is a sudden onset of acute thyrotoxicosis with fever, marked weakness, restlessness, confusion, and even coma, cardiovascular collapse, and shock. It is treated with iodine, propylthiouracil, propranolol, IV hydration and electrolytes, and, if necessary, cortisone.

Enlargement of the Thyroid Gland (Thyromegaly, Goiter)

Most pathologic states of the thyroid gland present as a diffuse or nodular enlargement of the gland. The various forms of hyperthyroidism and hypothyroidism discussed previously may have goiter. Other causes of thyroid enlargement are the following:

Euthyroid Goiter This is a simple, endemic, nontoxic, or colloid goiter. There is enlargement of the thyroid gland due to diminished thyroid hormone production, but there is no evidence of clinical hypothyroidism. It can be due to iodine deficiency, increased demand for thyroid hormone (at puberty, during pregnancy, or the menopause), or due to foods or medications that block the synthesis of thyroid hormone. Compensatory TSH elevations occur, preventing hypothyroidism, but causing enlargement of the thyroid gland in the process. An attempt should be made to identify the cause and to treat it (e.g., iodine deficiency). Levothyroxine may be necessary to suppress the TSH and decrease the goiter. Surgery may be necessary for very large goiters.

Silent Thyroiditis Mild transient enlargement of the thyroid may occur in the postpartum period, lasting from a few weeks to a few months. It may be associated with mild hyperthyroidism, but usually recovers spontaneously. The cause is

undetermined but may be an autoimmune phenomenon.

Subacute Thyroiditis A form of thyroiditis, also known as de Quervain's or granulomatous or giant-cell thyroiditis, is a painful condition that often follows some viral respiratory illness. Thyroid follicules are disrupted and stored hormone is released, causing hyperthyroid symptoms. The radionuclide thyroid uptake is characteristically very low (1 to 2 percent at 24 h) early in the course of this disorder. The hyperthyroidism is self-limited, lasting only a few weeks. Treatment includes aspirin for pain and propranolol to reduce symptoms. If pain is protracted, prednisone is used for 2 to 3 weeks. Usually there is full recovery.

Thyroid Nodule This is defined as a palpably discrete swelling within an otherwise apparently normal gland. It is usually a benign lesion, but could be malignant. The initial test that should be performed in a euthyroid patient with a solitary thyroid nodule is fine-needle aspiration.[16]

Thyroid Cancer Thyroid cancer usually presents as a symptomless lump in the neck. There are four types of thyroid cancer: papillary carcinoma is the most common (70 percent) and the least aggressive; follicular, which accounts for about 15 percent of cases; medullary, which accounts for about 5 percent of cases; and anaplastic, which is rare. Diagnosis is made by biopsy, and treatment is surgical. Suppressive doses of thyroid hormone may be given to prevent regrowth, and in some cases postoperative radioiodine may be advised.

Pituitary Disorders

Physiology

Some knowledge of the basic physiology of pituitary function is essential for an understanding of the causes, work-up, and management of pituitary disorders.

Seventy-five percent of the mass of the pituitary gland comprises the anterior pituitary, and 25 percent the posterior pituitary. The posterior

pituitary is an extension of the hypothalamus, and consists of nerve tissue that serves as a storage site for two peptide hormones synthesized by the hypothalamus, namely, vasopressin and oxytocin. The anterior pituitary synthesizes and secretes six major polypeptide hormones: adrenocorticotropic hormone (ACTH); thyroid-stimulating hormone (TSH); luteinizing hormone (LH); follicle-stimulating hormone (FSH); prolactin (PRL); and growth hormone (GH). ACTH, TSH, LH, and FSH act by stimulating other endocrine glands, whereas GH and PRL act directly on target tissues. In the past, it was thought that the pituitary was the "conductor" of the whole "endocrine orchestra" or the "master gland." It is now known that the pituitary is not the "master" but the "slave"—it is completely subservient to the hypothalamus, which secretes small polypeptide hormones that are necessary to stimulate the pituitary to synthesize and secrete large polypeptide hormones. Practically all of the hypothalamic and pituitary hormones are secreted in a pulsatile fashion, one pulse occurring every, 1 to 3 h; additionally, ACTH, GH, and PRL have a circadian rhythm with increased secretion between midnight and early morning.

Hypothalamic-Pituitary Diseases

Patients with hypothalamic-pituitary diseases present clinically in three ways: hypofunction of one or more of the pituitary hormones; hyperfunction of one or more of the hormones; and/or symptoms such as headaches, visual disturbances, or neurologic signs due to a tumor or other hypothalamic pituitary lesions (e.g., inflammatory, granuloma, or lymphoma that is causing hypo- or hyperfunction).

Hypopituitarism

Etiology Anterior pituitary deficiency is due to a decrease of one or more of the hormones, and may be caused by lesions of the pituitary itself, the pituitary stalk, or the hypothalamus. Causative tumors include micro- or macroadenomas,

craniopharyngiomas, pinealomas, and hamartomas. Other problems that may cause hypopituitarism are shock (especially postpartum, which can cause Sheehan's syndrome), inflammatory lesions, infiltrative disorders (such as hemochromatosis), and iatrogenic factors (e.g., radiation or surgery).

Symptoms and Signs The onset of the disease may be sudden, but is usually slow and insidious. The hormonal decrease often occurs in a definite order: gonadotropins are usually the first to decrease, resulting in amenorrhea (and impotence and oligospermia in men); growth hormone disappears next; the last hormones to be lost are usually TSH, which leads to hypothyroidism, and ACTH, which leads to hypoadrenalism, with resultant hypotension, fatigue, and intolerance to stress and infection.

Diagnosis When hypopituitarism is suspected or diagnosed, an underlying hypothalamic-pituitary lesion should be sought by visual fields and neurologic examinations, and by imaging techniques (sella x-ray, CT scan, and/or MRI). The specific hormone deficiencies must be diagnosed, with early emphasis on ACTH and TSH, which can be life-threatening. Assays required are serum FSH, LH, testosterone, estradiol, PRL, T4, TSH and cortisol.[1] The most efficient method of evaluating pituitary function is by testing the pituitary reserve for several hormones simultaneously: 0.1 unit regular insulin/kg, TRH 200 μg and Gn-RH 100 μg are administered together IV over about 20 seconds. Glucose, cortisol, GH, TSH, PRL, LH, FSH, and ACTH are then measured at frequent intervals for 3 h.

Treatment Treatment consists of replacing the specific hormone(s) that is/are deficient. The target gland hormone(s) rather than the pituitary hormone is used (i.e., thyroid hormone, cortisone, estrogen, or testosterone). However, in the case of Gn-RH deficiency, if infertility is the problem and ovulation induction is required, pituitary FSH and LH (or the LH surrogate HCG) are used. GH replacement in adults improves body composition, physical performance, lipid profiles, cardiovascular morbidity, and quality of

life. Isolated deficiencies of Gn-RH, ACTH, TSH, or HGH may occur, but more than one, or all of the hormone deficiencies may coexist and must be sought.

Hyperpituitarism

Excessive secretion of any of the pituitary hormones may occur, resulting in hyperpituitarism. Excess secretion of growth hormone results in gigantism or acromegaly, excess ACTH secretion causes Cushing's disease, and excess secretion of PRL causes hyperprolactinemia. In most of these situations, the hormone is overproduced by a pituitary tumor. For many years, three types of pituitary tumors have been recognized, depending on the type of staining of the granules in the cells of the tumor as seen by ordinary light microscopy. Tumors with basophilic-staining granules produce excessive amounts of ACTH resulting in Cushing's disease; tumors with acidophilic-staining granules produce excessive amounts of growth hormone; the third type of pituitary tumor, and by far the most common type, is the chromophobe adenoma, so-called because neither basophilic nor acidophilic granules are seen in the cells. As a result of the development of the radioimmunoassay for prolactin, it is now known that these tumors produce excessive amounts of prolactin. In fact, the rate of prolactin turnover is so great and so rapid that the small granules containing prolactin do not have time to coalesce into the larger granules that are necessary for basophilic or eosinophilic staining. These tumors, previously called chromophobe adenomas, are now called prolactinomas.

Acromegaly and Gigantism   Excess of GH before closure of the epiphyses results in gigantism; much more commonly, the hypersecretion occurs later in life, resulting in acromegaly.

Acromegaly is characterized by coarsening of the facial features, thickening of the skin, enlargement of the hands and feet, and protrusion of the jaw, which is called prognathism. Diagnosis is made by the characteristic appearance, and by elevation of serum GH, which is not suppressed by glucose administration.

Treatment methods include transsphenoidal resection of the causative adenoma, radiotherapy, and/or bromocriptine.

Cushing's Disease   Hypercortisolism due to excess pituitary ACTH secretion is called Cushing's disease; all other types of hypercortisolism are referred to as Cushing's syndrome. Treatment modalities for Cushing's disease are transsphenoidal removal of the basophil adenoma and radiotherapy.

Pituitary Hyperthyroidism   Occasionally, hyperthyroidism is due to a pituitary adenoma that secretes TSH. Its management consists of surgical removal of the tumor, irradiation, bromocriptine, or octerotid.

Hyperprolactinemia   By far the most common type of hyperpituitarism is excess secretion of prolactin, which is due to prolactin secreted by the most common pituitary tumor, the prolactinoma. Most of these tumors are less than 1 cm in diameter and are termed microadenomas.

Although the most important cause of hyperprolactinemia and/or galactorrhea is a pituitary tumor or other lesion of the hypothalamus (generically called the Forbes-Albright syndrome), there are several other causes, namely, tranquilizers, narcotics, antihypertensive drugs, birth control pills, stimulation of the nipples or breasts, hypothalamic-pituitary dysfunction, hypothyroidism, chest lesions, chronic renal disease, and certain nonpituitary prolactin-producing tumors (e.g., of the lung or kidney).

Symptoms Because there are receptors for prolactin in many tissues of the body, hyperprolactinemia can cause one or more of several symptoms: galactorrhea, oligomenorrhea, infertility, hirsutism, or osteoporosis.

Diagnosis Diagnosis is made by finding an elevated serum prolactin level, above the upper limit of normal (20 ng/ml in most laboratories). A serum prolactin assay should be carried out in all cases of galactorrhea and a screening prolactin assay should be done in all patients complaining

of infertility, oligomenorrhea, hirsutism, or osteoporosis.

If the prolactin is elevated, the patient is not on any medications, and the TSH and chest findings are normal, the pituitary and hypothalamic area should be imaged by conventional radiology, or by CT scan or MRI.

Treatment In most cases, the nonsurgical treatment of hyperprolactinemia is very satisfactory.[13] If a nonpituitary cause is found, it should be treated; for example, discontinuation of the causative drug, treatment of hypothyroidism that may be present, or therapy for any underlying treatable chest or renal disease. In most other situations, the mainstay of treatment is bromocriptine [i.e., 2-bromo-α-ergocriptine (Parlodel), a long-acting dopamine agonist], which directly inhibits the pituitary lactotropes from secreting prolactin. It is effective in functional hyperprolactinemia as well as in cases with micro- or macroadenoma. In cases of microadenoma, the medication should be discontinued every 1 to 2 years, with measurement of the prolactin levels 6 weeks later, because there is a permanent remission in 10 percent of cases after 1 year and 20 percent after 2 years of bromocriptine treatment. In addition, in half of those patients in whom the prolactin level rises again after discontinuing the bromocriptine, the levels are much lower than they were before treatment, and it may not be necessary to reinitiate bromocriptine therapy. There is a high incidence of side effects with bromocriptine: gastrointestinal (nausea, vomiting, and abdominal cramps), as well as symptoms due to hypotension caused by inhibition of sympathetic nerve activity with resultant relaxation of the splanchnic and renal vascular beds, dizziness, and syncope. Bromocriptine should be started in a small dosage (half of a 2.5-mg tablet) at night, and then gradually increased to twice daily administration until the prolactin levels are in the normal range. Vaginal administration obviates the gastrointestinal symptoms and, because of the slower absorption from the gut and slower metabolism by the liver, necessitates only once daily administration. Cabergolin, a long-acting dopaminergic drug, is available. Cabergolin, given in a dose of 0.5 mg, one-half tablet twice weekly, has fewer gastrointestinal side effects.[7]

Surgery for macroadenomas has a high morbidity and mortality rate, and an 80 percent recurrence rate. There is a 40 percent recurrence with microadenomas. Accordingly, surgery is reserved for patients who cannot tolerate the side effects or expense of prolonged bromocriptine treatment. Radiotherapy requires considerable expertise and may be associated with several complications, so it has assumed only a minor role in the treatment of prolactinomas.

Women with infertility due to hyperprolactinemia can achieve a pregnancy in most cases by normalizing the prolactin levels with bromocriptine. The therapy is usually discontinued during pregnancy, but studies have shown that it causes no teratogenic or other side effects. Only 5 percent of microadenomas and 20 percent of macroadenomas enlarge during pregnancy and, if this occurs, treatment with bromocriptine is very satisfactory.

Posterior Pituitary Disorders

The posterior pituitary is a direct extension of the hypothalamus, and serves as a storehouse and site of release of two hormones synthesized by the supraoptic and paraventricular nuclei of the hypothalamus, namely oxytocin and arginine-vasopressin. Oxytocin has two physiologic effects, ejection of milk and stimulation of uterine contractions; however, there are no significant clinical disease states associated with excess endogenous oxytocin secretion. The major function of arginine-vasopressin is the regulation of osmolality and blood volume. It does this by being a powerful vasoconstrictor and an antidiuretic hormone, and is therefore called the antidiuretic hormone or ADH. When plasma osmolality rises ADH release increases; conversely, water-loading inhibits ADH release, thereby increasing diuresis.

The only significant posterior pituitary disease seen clinically is deficiency of ADH, resulting in

excretion of excessive quantities of very dilute urine, the disease being known as diabetes insipidus (DI).

Diabetes Insipidus *Etiology* The major cause of diabetes insipidus is a hypothalamic-pituitary disorder resulting in deficient secretion of ADH, known as central or ADH-sensitive DI. Occasionally ADH secretion is normal, but the kidney is ADH-resistant, a condition known as nephrogenic diabetes insipidus (NDI). This discussion is limited to the major type of DI, central DI. A variety of hypothalamic and posterior pituitary diseases can cause central DI: primary or idiopathic, hypophysectomy, cranial lesions, granulomatous disease, infections, and vascular lesions.[10]

Symptoms The only symptoms of DI are polydipsia and polyuria. The patient may consume enormous quantities of fluid, and large volumes (up to 30 l) of very dilute urine may be excreted daily.

Diagnosis Diabetes insipidus must be distinguished from other causes of polyuria, including chronic renal disease, diabetes mellitus, and compulsive water-drinking. Measurement of circulating levels of ADH by radioimmunoassay would appear to be the most specific method of making a diagnosis. However, this assay is difficult and not generally available; the water-deprivation test is simple and reliable, and makes the RIA ADH assay unnecessary. The water-deprivation test should be performed with the patient under close supervision. A normal response is one in which the maximum urine osmolality after dehydration exceeds the plasma osmolality and does not increase more than an additional 5 percent after injection of vasopressin.

Treatment If an underlying cause is found, it should be treated. Aqueous vasopressin can be administered by injection (subcutaneously or intramuscularly) 5 to 10 units, but this is not very practical because it has to be given every 6 h. Synthetic vasopressin (Pitressin) may be given bid or qid as a nasal spray. Vasopressin tannate in oil IM (0.3 to 1 ml) may control symptoms for up to 96 h. In partial or mild DI, various diuretics (especially thiazide) may be helpful as may be ADH-releasing drugs such as chlorpropamide or carbamazepine.

Adrenal Disease

Anatomy and Physiology of the Adrenal Glands

The adrenal gland consists of an outer cortex that synthesizes and secretes steroid hormones and an inner medulla that is part of the sympathetic autonomic nervous system, the cells of which synthesize the catecholamines, dopamine, norepinephrine, and epinephrine, all of which are derived from tyrosine. Unlike other sympathetic neurons that secrete mostly norepinephrine, the adrenal medulla secretes mostly epinephrine, which is about 5 to 10 times more potent than norepinephrine.

The adrenal cortex consists of three zones:

1. An outer zone, the zona glomerulosa, secretes the mineralocorticoids, the most potent of which is aldosterone. Mineralocorticoids cause retention of sodium and excretion of potassium. Aldosterone secretion is not under the control of ACTH, but is stimulated mainly by renin (via angiotension II) and to some extent by hyperkalemia.

2. A middle zone, the zona fasciculata, which secretes mainly the glucocorticoid cortisol, is under the control of ACTH. During stress (including trauma, infection, and exercise) cortisol is secreted and is life-saving; it makes increased amounts of glucose and fatty acids available for energy, and attenuates defense mechanisms, thereby protecting against their potentially dangerous overactivity. The increased cortisol levels during stress cause vasodilation to protect against possible dangerous vasoconstriction.

3. An inner zone, the zona reticularis, synthesizes mainly the sex steroids, androgens and estrogens. The zona reticularis is also under the control of ACTH.

The main diseases of the adrenal gland are those that involve either hypofunction or hyperfunction of the adrenal cortex.

Adrenal Cortical Hypofunction

Adrenal cortical hypofunction is usually due to disease of the adrenal cortex itself, when it is known as primary adrenocortical insufficiency or Addison's disease. Occasionally the adrenal cortex is normal, but due to a deficiency of ACTH a secondary adrenal cortical insufficiency occurs; this is known as secondary adrenal insufficiency.

Addison's Disease (Primary Adrenocortical Insufficiency) *Etiology* In about 75 percent of cases of Addison's disease, there is atrophy of the adrenal cortex without any obvious local disease. This has been called "idiopathic" Addison's disease, but in 75 percent of cases, it is probably due to an autoimmune process because it is often associated with other autoimmune diseases such as hypo- or hyperthyroidism, hypoparathyroidism, primary ovarian failure, diabetes mellitus, or pernicious anemia. In the remaining 25 percent of cases, there is destruction of the adrenal cortex by tuberculosis, amyloidosis, or neoplasm.[14]

Symptoms Weakness, fatigue, anorexia, nausea, vomiting, diarrhea, and abdominal pain occur, with weight loss. Dizziness and syncopal attacks may occur.

Signs Inability to concentrate the urine, together with changes in electrolyte balance, result in severe dehydration, hypotension, and collapse. Reduced cortisol levels cause increased ACTH and β-lipoprotein, which stimulates the melanocytes and produces hyperpigmentation of the skin and mucous membranes. Pigmentation is not present in secondary adrenocortical insufficiency.

Diagnosis The disease can be suspected from the symptoms and signs. In primary failure, there is a high plasma ACTH level, and in secondary adrenal failure, a low plasma ACTH level. The specific diagnosis can be made by performance of an ACTH stimulation test: plasma cortisol levels normally range from 5 to 25 μg/dl; following an IV injection of 0.25 μg of ACTH, the plasma cortisol level doubles in 30 to 60 min, whereas in Addison's disease, the levels are low and do not rise following IV ACTH.

Treatment With appropriate cortisol replacement therapy the prognosis is very good and patients can lead normal lives. Patients may also need mineralocorticoids.

For acute adrenocortical insufficiency, dehydration and hyponatremia are treated with IV fluids and electrolytes, and IV hydrocortisone. For chronic insufficiency hydrocortisone 20 mg is given in the morning and 10 mg in the afternoon, with adjustment of the dose as necessary. In addition to mineralocorticoids, fludrocortisone once a day should be given to patients with Addison's disease or primary adrenal insufficiency.

Secondary Adrenal Insufficiency This is due to Sheehan's syndrome, or to pituitary or hypothalamic tumors, infections, or trauma. The treatment is the same as for Addison's disease, except that these patients do not need mineralocorticoid supplementation.

Hyperfunction of the Adrenal Cortex

Hyperfunction of the adrenal cortex may involve any of the three zones: hyperfunction of the zona fasciculata causes production of excess cortisone, which results in Cushing's syndrome; hyperfunction of the zona reticularis is associated with excess androgen production, which results in adrenal virilism called the adrenogenital syndrome; and hyperfunction of the outer zone, the glomerulosa, causes excess aldosterone production, which results in hyperaldostronisim. However, there may be some overlapping of these three areas of hyperfunction.

Cushing's Syndrome Cushing's syndrome is a generic term that includes all the clinical syndromes that result from chronic excess cortisol stimulation.

Etiology Excess cortisol activity or Cushing's syndrome in its broad sense has several causes:

1. Hypersecretion of ACTH by the anterior pituitary. This is usually referred to as Cushing's disease. In many of these cases, a basophil adenoma or chromophobe adenoma is the source of the excess ACTH and the tumor can be visualized by CT scan or MRI. However, a microadenoma may be difficult to see, and sometimes, despite the finding of excess ACTH, no histological abnormality can be identified;
2. Occasionally, excess ACTH or cortisone may be administered exogenously or may be produced by a nonpituitary tumor such as carcinoma of the lung;
3. Cushing's syndrome may also result from cortisol production by an adenoma or carcinoma of the zona fasciculata of the adrenal cortex.

Symptoms The patient may complain of weakness and fatigue due to muscle wasting, and may have obesity, or acne and hirsuitism, or excessive bruising. Women often have oligomenorrhea.

Signs The patient may show truncal obesity with moon face, buffalo hump, and supraclavicular fat pads, with thin extremities due to muscle wasting. The skin may show acne, hirsutism, bruising, and purple striae. The patient may have hypertension, diabetes, or osteoporosis.

Diagnosis Normally there is a circadian rhythm of cortisol secretion, the plasma level being about 15 μg/dl in the morning (6 to 8 AM) and 5 μg/dl in the evening (6 PM). The presence of such diurnal variation rules out Cushing's syndrome and its absence is diagnostic of the disease. Likewise, the administration of 1 mg of dexamethasone at bedtime yields a 7 to 8 AM serum cortisol of less than 5 μg/dl; lack of such suppression is diagnostic for Cushing's syndrome in most cases. Administration of 1 mg CRF (corticotropin-releasing factor) and measurement of serum cortisol 30 minutes later and ACTH 15 minutes later can be helpful in the differential diagnosis of Cushing's disease from ectopic Cushing's. The patient with Cushing's disease will respond to CRF, but the patient with ectopic ACTH will not respond. Inferior petrosal sinus sampling with CRF stimulation is essential for the accurate differential diagnosis of ACTH-dependent Cushing's syndrome.[9]

Treatment If the pituitary gland is the source of the excess ACTH secretion (i.e., it is a case of Cushing's disease), transsphenoidal exploration of the pituitary should be carried out, and if a tumor is found it should be excised. If it is a microadenoma there is about an 80 percent success rate, but macroadenomas frequently recur. If no tumor is found, then treatment choices are total hypophysectomy, irradiation of the pituitary, or adrenalectomy.

Adenomas and carcinomas of the adrenal gland have to be removed surgically. Because the remainder of the adrenal cortex will have been suppressed and therefore have become atrophic, supplementary cortisol must be given during surgery and the postoperative period.

Hyperaldosteronism Aldosterone, a potent mineralocorticoid, is produced by the zona glomerulosa, the outer zone of the adrenal cortex. It causes retention of sodium and water, and excretion of potassium. When secreted in response to stimuli such as hypertension or edematous disorders (such as cardiac failure or the nephrotic syndrome) it is called secondary aldosteronism.

When excess aldosterone is produced by a lesion of the adrenal itself (usually an adenoma, but occasionally a carcinoma or hyperplasia) it is called primary aldosteronism or Conn's syndrome.[6] In many cases, the only manifestation is a mild to moderate hypertension, but the patient may have hypernatremia, hypervolemia, and hypokalemic alkalosis resulting in weakness, paresthesias, and tetany. A CT scan of the adrenal often reveals a small adenoma.

If the diagnosis of primary aldosteronism is made, both adrenals should be explored for possible multiple adenomas. The prognosis is good when an adenoma is identified and removed. If the hyperaldostronism is due to adrenal hyperplasia, surgery is not indicated. The hyperaldosteronism can usually be controlled by spironolactone.

Adrenogenital Syndrome (Adrenal Virilism)
When there is excess secretion of androgens by the inner reticularis zone of the adrenal cortex, the condition is called the adrenogenital syndrome or adrenogenital virilism. Very occasionally this is due to an adrenal adenoma or carcinoma. In most cases, it is caused by an enzyme block in the synthesis of hydrocortisone, in which case it is known as congenital adrenal hyperplasia (CAH).

Congenital Adrenal Hyperplasia Congenital adrenal hyperplasia is an important disease for several reasons: it is one of the most frequent autosomal genetic disorders in humans, being transmitted via an autosomal recessive inheritance pattern; it is the most common of all the intersexual states—of all infants born with ambiguous genitalia 40 to 50 percent have CAH; it is the most common cause of heterosexual precocious pseudopuberty in girls; it is the main disorder that must be excluded before a diagnosis of polycystic ovarian disease (PCOD) can be made; and, lastly, it is the next most common cause of hirsutism and acne after PCOD and constitutional hirsutism.

Etiology and Pathogenesis The basic defect in this syndrome is a failure in the production of hydrocortisone due to an enzyme block in its biosynthetic pathway. In most cases (about 90 percent), the block is at the stage of 17α-hydroxyprogesterone (17-OHP), because the enzyme 21-hydroxylase, which is essential for the conversion of 17-OHP into desoxycorticosterone, and hence to hydrocortisone, is defective, The deficiency of hydrocortisone results in absence of inhibition of the output of ACTH by the pituitary, and the excess ACTH stimulates the adrenal to secrete increased amounts of androgens, because the adrenal pathways to androgens (the δ-5 pathway through dehydroepiandrosterone-sulfate [DHEAS] and the δ-4 pathway through progesterone) are not blocked. The blood contains not only increased amounts of DHEAS but also increased amounts of 17α-hydroxyprogesterone, and the urine contains not only increased amounts of 17-ketosteroids, which are the excretion product of DHEAS, but also large amounts of pregnanetriol, which is the excretion product of 17-OHP.

There are also two other possible enzyme blocks. In one type, a hypertensive form, the 21-hydroxylase is competent, but the deficiency is at the next step, 11-hydroxylase, which is necessary for the conversion of desoxycorticosterone to hydrocortisone. This results in the production of excessive amounts of desoxycorticosterone, which is a potent hypertensive agent. The third block is very rare. Here the block is very early in the biosynthetic pathway. Pregnenolone cannot be converted into progesterone because of a deficiency of 3β-ol-dehydrogenase. This results in profound adrenocortical insufficiency and early death; unless this deficiency is very mild, these cases are not seen clinically.

Clinical Presentations There are three different clinical presentations of CAH, depending on the severity of the block; the more severe the block the earlier in life the condition manifests itself clinically. The three clinical presentations are: a severe form that presents at birth as a child with ambiguous genitalia, a female pseudohermaphrodite; a moderately severe form which presents in late childhood as heterosexual precocious pseudopuberty; and, a mild or attenuated form (also called "cryptic," or "late onset," or "adult onset," or "acquired form") where the child appears normal at birth and throughout infancy and childhood, but presents in her late teens or early 20s simulating a case of PCOD.

The severe form presents at birth. There is greatly increased production of androgens even in fetal life, so that the development of the genital organs is disturbed in utero. The ovaries, tubes, uterus, and upper part of the vagina are basically unaffected because adrenal function is not present at their formative stage, and particularly because androgens have no influence on their development. However, the external genitalia, the development of which is completed later and which are influenced by androgens, become malformed. The clitoris is enlarged, and there may be a single urogenital sinus. The child is born

with ambiguous genitalia and as a female pseudo-hermaphrodite.

In addition, about a third of these patients have a salt-losing state, as in Addison's disease, and they present with neonatal vomiting, diarrhea, and collapse due to loss of sodium and water, with a resultant profound electrolyte imbalance. This is due to deficiency of 21-hydroxylase in both the zona glomerulosa and the zona fasciculata. It is very important to recognize this condition in the neonate because it can be treated and the whole clinical picture can be altered.

The second clinical presentation is a moderately severe form that presents in late childhood as a heterosexual precocious pseudopuberty. The child is normal at birth but in late childhood develops a precocious puberty along male lines. As a result of the excess androgens there is a preliminary stimulation of growth so that at first the patient is taller than her peers, but ends up being short in stature due to premature closure of the epiphyses due to the androgens. So, the patient presents not only with precocious pubic and axillary hair, but also with hirsutism all over the body and acne. She also has all the other signs of a precocious puberty along male lines—a muscular body and deep voice, together with primary amenorrhea and absent breast development.

The third clinical presentation is the mild, attenuated, late-onset form, which is the most common type. The child appears normal at birth and throughout childhood. However, in her late teens or early 20s she presents with acne, hirsutism, oligomenorrhea, and possibly an enlarged clitoris, a clinical picture very similar to that seen in cases of PCOD.

Diagnosis The diagnostic approach must be directed to the type of clinical presentation. In the severe form that presents at birth with an enlarged clitoris, the main differential diagnosis is from a male pseudohermaphrodite of the developmental type (i.e., a male with a small penis, hypospadias, a bifid scrotum, and undescended testes); Reifenstein syndrome; or, very rarely, a true hermaphrodite. The differential diagnosis also includes a female pseudohermaphrodite due to exogenous male hormone taken by the mother in pregnancy or endogenous masculinizing hormone during fetal life other than CAH; that is, an androgen-producing ovarian or adrenal tumor. The main diagnostic measures required to make a diagnosis are karyotyping and endocrine assays. However, the most important initial laboratory test is the measurement of the serum electrolytes, because one-third of these patients have a deficiency of aldosterone, and this is a life-threatening disease that can easily be corrected.

In the moderately severe and the late onset mild forms that occur in childhood and in the late teens, respectively, the diagnosis is made by the finding of an elevated DHEAS and particularly by an elevation of the 17-OHP level, which is specific for CAH. In severe cases, the 17-OHP will be markedly elevated, and will be elevated all the time. However, in the moderately severe and mild cases it may only be slightly elevated or it may only be elevated in the early morning when the circadian rhythm of the adrenal hormones is at its peak, or it may not be elevated at all and may require an ACTH stimulation test to uncover it.

Accordingly, the following procedure should be used to make a diagnosis of CAH: a basal follicular morning serum 17-OHP and progesterone (P) should be obtained. If this 17-OHP is above 8 ng/ml, the diagnosis of CAH is established; if it is below 2 ng/ml, CAH is very unlikely. If it is above 2 but less than 8 ng/ml, an ACTH stimulation test should be done. A level above 20 ng/ml 30 min to 1 h, after an intravenous injection of 0.25 mg ACTH (Cortrosyn, Organon) is diagnostic for CAH.

Treatment The logical and specific treatment is cortisone. This replaces the cortisone that is lacking, suppresses the excess ACTH secretion by the anterior pituitary, and prevents the oversecretion of androgens by the adrenal cortex. With this treatment, the patient with severe CAH can be prevented from developing a heterosexual precocious pseudopuberty, and the patient with a heterosexual precocious pseudopuberty can be

restored to normal femininity—the breasts develop, the uterus grows, ovulation and menstruation occur, and fertility is present. The usual daily dose of oral cortisone required is 25 mg cortisone acetate, or 5 mg prednisone, or their equivalents. The dose should be sufficient to suppress the 17-OHP to below 2 ng/ml; however, if the dose suppresses the morning blood cortisol to below 2 μg/dl the dose should be reduced to avoid an inability to react to stress. Patients with a salt-losing syndrome should additionally be given fludrocortisone (e.g., Florinef 0.1 to 0.2 mg po daily) and serum electrolyte levels and blood pressures should be monitored closely. Fluids and sodium must be given as necessary.

Pheochromocytoma

Pheochromocytoma is a tumor of chromaffin cells, which are cells of the sympathetic nervous system that secrete catecholamines—dopamine, norepinephrine, and epinephrine.[5]

Etiology In 80 percent of cases the tumors are in the adrenal medulla, but they may be found in any other chromaffin tissues such as the ganglia of the sympathetic chain. They are usually about 5 cm in diameter, and 95 percent are benign.

Symptoms and Signs The clinical manifestations are variable and depend mainly on the relative amounts and patterns of norepinephrine and epinephrine secretion. About 90 percent of patients have hypertension, which may be paroxysmal or continuous, and they may have headaches, palpitations, tremors, and hot flushes.

Diagnosis Diagnosis is suspected from the symptoms and signs. It is made by imaging techniques including CT scan and MRI. It is also made by measuring the main urinary excretion product of the catecholamines, namely, vanilmandelic acid (VMA); normally there is less than 10 mg VMA per 24-h urine. The clonidine suppression test may be useful in distinguishing patients with pheochromocytoma from patients whose hypersecretion of norepinephrine is physiologic.[11] Normal plasma metanephrines exclude the diagnosis of pheochromocytoma.[13]

Treatment Patients with biochemical evidence of pheochromocytoma should have preoperative management with an oral α-adrenergic blocking effect. Phenoxybenzamine, an α blocker, with the subsequent addition of propanolol, a β blocker, may be used to reduce the symptoms and in preparation for surgery. However, surgery is the treatment of choice for most patients with pheochromocytoma, after adequate preoperative preparation.[12]

Carcinoid Syndrome

Carcinoid syndrome is a syndrome in which the patient experiences recurrent bouts of flushing of the skin, and abnormal cramps with diarrhea. It is usually due to secretion of vasoactive substances by carcinoid tumors of the intestine.

Etiology and Pathology

The usual etiology of the carcinoid syndrome is tumor formation that arises from enteroendocrine cells in the ileum, pancreas, thyroid, gonads, or bronchi. These cells produce vasoactive substances including serotonin, histamine, prostaglandins, and polypeptide hormones. Histamine causes vasodilation and hence results in flushing. Serotonin stimulates smooth muscle and hence causes diarrhea and abdominal cramps.

Symptoms

The most prominent symptoms are flushing of the skin (especially the head and neck), abdominal cramps, and recurrent diarrhea. Some patients develop bronchial spasm leading to asthmatic-like wheezing.

Diagnosis

The condition should be suspected from the aforementioned symptoms. The diagnosis is confirmed by testing for increased urinary excretion of the serotonin metabolite, 5-hydroxyindoleacetic acid (5-HIAA). Liver scan and imaging techniques may be used to demonstrate the causative tumor, and laparotomy is usually required.

Treatment

Treatment is difficult and often unsatisfactory. Resection of some carcinoid tumors may be feasible. Radiation therapy is unsuccessful and no effective chemotherapy is available. However, even with metastatic carcinoid tumors, long-term survival up to 15 years is fairly common. Numerous palliative medications have been tried for the symptoms of flushing and diarrhea, including phenothiazine, prednisone, and peripheral serotonin antagonists such as cyproheptadine. Success with these drugs is variable.[20]

Hirsutism

There are two types of body hair in the adult female: vellus (fine, soft, nonpigmented) and terminal (coarse, pigmented). Hirsutism refers to the presence of increased numbers of terminal hairs in an area associated with male-pattern hair growth; that is, on the face, chest, lower back, lower abdomen, and inner thighs. Hirsutism in women is a common and unpleasant condition. It is always due to excess androgen activity. However, although the most common, it is only one of the clinical manifestations of hyperandrogenism, the others being acne, oligomenorrhea, enlargement of the clitoris, hoarseness of the voice, temporal recession of scalp hair, and increased masculinity. Except for acne and hirsutism, the other symptoms are uncommon, and usually signify markedly increased androgen production.

Causes of Hirsutism

Although there are a large number of causes of hirsutism, the problem as encountered by the clinician is a fairly simple one, because in practice, 95 percent of cases of hirsutism are due to one of only four causes:[4] polycystic ovarian disease is by far the most common cause of hirsutism, being responsible for about 80 percent of cases; CAH is the cause in 5.5 percent; hyperprolactinemia is the cause in 3.5 percent; and end organ hyperresponsiveness is the cause in 6.8 per-

cent. There are numerous other rare causes of hirsutism (such as ovarian and adrenal tumors, Cushing's syndrome, acromegaly, the taking of dilantin, and hermaphroditism), but all of these together are responsible for only 5 percent of all cases of hirsutism.

PCOD The basic defect in this syndrome revolves around an increase in LH. LH normally acts on the theca interna of the follicle to induce the synthesis of androstenedione, which diffuses into the follicular fluid where it is aromatized to estrogen. The increased LH in PCOD stimulates the theca interna to produce increased amounts of the androgen androstenedione, which results in hirsutism.

CAH The basic defect in CAH is an enzyme deficiency resulting in decreased production of cortisol. The ACTH rises and stimulates the zona reticularis of the adrenal cortex to produce increased amounts of androgens, which results in hirsutism.

Hyperprolactinemia Numerous studies have shown that in as many as 40 percent of cases of hyperprolactinemia there are increased levels of DHEAS and free testosterone, and in about 20 percent there are clinical manifestations of these excess androgens such as acne and hirsutism. These increased androgens may be due to a direct action of prolactin on the adrenals and ovaries, or due to anovulation and PCOD caused by the hyperprolactinemia.

End Organ Hyperresponsiveness In this cause of hirsutism, the plasma levels of all the androgens are normal, and therefore this was formerly called "idiopathic," "familial," or "constitutional" hirsutism. It is now known, however, that end organ hyperresponsiveness is due either to increased androgen receptors, or, more commonly, to increased activity of 5α-reductase, resulting in increased peripheral production of dihydrotestosterone, the most potent of all of the androgens. There are increased serum and urinary levels of 3α-androstanediol glucuronide, a metabolite of dihydrotestosterone, which is directly related to the rate of conversion of testosterone to dihydrotestosoterone; the upper level

of normal of this metabolite in serum is approximately 200 ng/dl; in end organ hyperresponsiveness it is above 400 ng/dl.

Diagnosis

The clinician needs to obtain the laboratory tests for only four diseases in order to diagnose the etiology of 95 percent of cases of hirsutism. To diagnose PCOD, FSH, LH, and androstenedione level tests are required. In PCOD, there is an inverse FSH/LH ratio and/or an increased LH, and the androstenedione is elevated. To diagnose CAH, asssays of DHEAS and 17-OHP should be done, and they are both elevated. For hyperprolactinemia, only a prolactin level is needed. End organ hyperresponsiveness is diagnosed by finding that all tests are normal, and confirmation can be achieved by a serum 3α-androstenediol glucuronide determination.

If the serum testosterone is above 200 ng/dl, or if the DHEAS is above 7000 ng/ml, an ovarian or adrenal tumor should be suspected.

Treatment

The hirsuitism due to PCOD can be treated specifically by suppressing the elevated LH with the combination birth control pill, or by treatment with medroxyprogesterone acetate (Provera). CAH and hyperprolactinemia are treated specifically with cortisone or bromocriptine, respectively. For end organ hyperresponsiveness one of the antiandrogens is often used: spironolactone or cimetidine, which are available in the United States (FDA approved but not specifically for hirsutism); or cyproterone acetate (CPA), which is not approved for use in the United States but has been used successfully in Europe. Another newer form of therapy is the use of a Gn-RH analog with estrogen.[18] Although all of these modalities will prevent further hair growth, the hair already present will not fall out, and will have to be removed by shaving, waxing, tweezing, or electrolysis (i.e., electrocoagulation of the dermal papillae).

Parathyroid Disorders and Bone Metabolism

The homeostatic regulation of calcium metabolism involves calcium fluxes in and out of bone, changes in calcium absorption from the intestine, and calcium excretion in the urine. All of this is controlled primarily by parathyroid hormone (PTH), an 84-amino acid single-chain polypeptide secreted by the parathyroid glands. Secretion of PTH from the parathyroid glands is regulated by serum calcium levels through a classic negative feedback mechanism—a low serum calcium level stimulates PTH secretion, while a high level suppresses it. PTH stimulates the renal tubules to reabsorb calcium and also stimulates the kidneys to produce 1-25-dihydroxyvitamin D which enhances the absorption of calcium from the gut. These mechanisms maintain normal serum calcium levels between 8.8 and 10.4 mg/dl.

Hypercalcemia/Hyperparathyroidism

Etiology Hypercalcemia, a serum calcium of greater than 10.5 mg/dl, is most often due to primary hyperparathyroidism, but may be due to malignancy (especially breast), medications (thiazides, lithium, vitamin A and D preparations, calcium, and antacids), immobilization (especially with Paget's disease), thyrotoxicosis, adrenal insufficiency, sarcoidosis, and acute renal failure (especially in the diuretic phase).[17] Primary hyperparathyroidism is usually due to a single parathyroid adenoma (which is found in more than 80 percent of cases); in the remaining cases hyperplasia, multiple adenomas, and, occasionally, carcinoma may be found.

Symptoms Many patients are asymptomatic, the disorder being discovered on routine serum chemistry screening. When symptoms do occur they may be gastrointestinal or renal; ureteric colic due to a stone; or bone pain, especially when osteitis fibrosa cystica, the bone disease of severe hyperparathyroidism, occurs.

Diagnosis The hallmark of the diagnosis of primary hyperparathyroidism is hypercalcemia,

without appropriate suppression of PTH levels. Because of the technical difficulty in locating the source of the excess PTH at surgery, several imaging techniques have been used and proven effective: ultrasound, CT scan, MRI, and thallium scan of the neck, or sestamibi scan of the parathyroids.[15]

Treatment Medical management of primary hyperparathyroidism using measures such as increased fluid intake, additional sodium chloride, and oral phosphate have been tried, but with little success. Ultimately, surgery is required for most cases of primary hyperparathyroidism and may be totally curative if there is a well-defined single adenoma. However, when there is hyperplasia, or supernumery, or ectopic glands, there may be persistent disease despite multiple operations.[11,15,17]

Hypocalcemia/Hypoparathyroidism

Hypocalcemia is defined as a total serum calcium level of less than 8.8 mg/dl in the presence of normal serum albumin.

Etiology The major cause of hypocalcemia is hypoparathyroidism, which can be primary (due to deficient PTH secretion) or secondary (where the end organs are insensitive to circulating PTH).[2] There are many other causes that must be ruled out, but if hypocalcemia is accompanied by hyperphosphatemia the diagnosis is almost certainly hypoparathyroidism. Among the other etiologies are hypo- or hypermagnesemia, chronic renal failure (with accompanying hyperphosphatemia), metastatic carcinoma (which may cause hypo- or hypercalcemia), and acute pancreatitis. Primary hypoparathyroidism is often due to surgical damage or removal of the parathyroid glands during thyroidectomy or radical neck dissection, or removal of the glands for hyperparathyroidism. Infection, metastatic tumor, or infiltration by granuloma may occasionally be the cause of damage to the parathyroid glands. Secondary hypoparathyroidism, also known as pseudohypoparathyroidism (PHP), is an uncommon inherited disorder.[22]

Symptoms The hypocalcemia may cause carpopedal spasm, paresthesias, and muscle cramps, and occasionally tetany and convulsions.

Signs Most signs are due to the hypocalcemia. Chvostek's sign consists of contraction of the facial muscles when the facial nerve is gently tapped. The occurrence of carpopedal spasm within 3 min of impeding the return of blood from the forearm with a blood pressure cuff is known as Trousseau's sign. Hyperreflexia may be seen, and the teeth may reveal enamel hypoplasia and caries.

Diagnosis The serum calcium is low. The PTH is low in primary hypoparathyroidism and high in pseudohypoparathyroidism. Renal function must always be evaluated, because hypocalcemia may be due to renal disease.

Treatment In severe, acutely symptomatic hypocalcemia, intravenous calcium chloride or calcium gluconate should be given. The mainstay of the treatment of chronic hypocalcemia is oral calcium. Calcium carbonate is the preferred form because it contains more elemental calcium than most other calcium salts. Up to 2 g of elemental calcium may be required daily. In hypoparathyroidism, vitamin D, either as calciferol (50,000 to 100,000 units daily) or Rocaltrol (0.25 to 0.5 μg/day) should be given in addition to elemental calcium supplementation. Serum calcium levels should be monitored and maintained at or near 8 mg/dl.

References and Selected Readings

1. Abboud CF: Laboratory diagnosis of hypopituitarism. *Mayo Clin Proc* 61:35, 1986.
2. Ahn TG, et al: Familial isolated hypoparathyroidism: A molecular genetic analysis of eight families with 23 affected persons. *Medicine* 65:73, 1986.
3. Allanic H, et al: Antithyroid drugs and Graves' disease: A prospective randomized evaluation of the efficacy of treatment duration. *J Clin Endocrinol Metab* 70:675, 1990.
4. Benjamin F, Deutsch S, Sapertein H, Seltzer VL: Prevalence of and markers for the attenuated form of congenital adrenal hyperplasia and hyperprolactinemia masquerading as polycystic ovarian disease. *Fertil Steril* 46:215, 1986.

5. Benowitz NL: Pheochromocytoma. *Adv Intern Med* 35:195, 1990.

6. Bravo EL: Primary aldosteronism. *Urol Clin North Am* 16:481, 1989.

7. Colao A, De Sarno A, Sarnaicharo F, et al: Prolactinomas—resistant to standard dopamine agonists respond to chronic cabergoline treatment. *J Clin Endocrinol Metab* 82:876–883, 1997.

8. Caldwell G, et al: A new strategy for thyroid function testing. *Lancet* 1:1117, 1985.

9. Findling JW, Hehoe ME, Shaker JL, Raff H: Routine inferior petrosal sinus sampling in the differential diagnosis of adrenocorticotropin (ACTH)-dependent Cushing's syndrome; Early recognition of the occult ectopic ACTH syndrome. *J Clin Endocrinol Metab* 73:408–413, 1991.

10. Gesundheit N, et al: Thyrotropin-secreting pituitary adenomas: Clinical and biochemical heterogenecity—case reports and follow-up of nine patients. *Ann Intern Med* 111:827, 1989.

11. Grossman F, Goldstein DS, Hoffman A, Keiser HR: Glucagon and clonidine testing in the diagnosis of pheochromocytoma. *Hypertension* 17:733–741, 1991.

12. Kidd A, et al: Immunologic aspects of Graves' and Hashimoto's disease. *Metabolism* 29:80, 1980.

13. Lenders JW, Keiser HR, Goldstein DS, et al: Plasma metanephrines in the diagnosis of pheochromocytoma. *Ann Intern Med* 123:101–109, 1995.

14. Maesaka JK, et al: Hyponatremia and hypouricemia: Differentiation from SIADH. *Clin Nephrol* 33:174, 1990.

15. Mallette LF: The hypercalcemias. *Semin Npehrol* 12:159–190, 1992.

16. Mazzaferri E: Management of a solitary thyroid nodule. *N Engl J Med* 328:553–559, 1993.

17. Potts JT Jr: Management of asymptomatic hyperparathyroidism. *J Clin Endocrinol Metab* 70:1489, 1990.

18. Sheps SG, et al: Recent developments in the diagnosis and treatment of pheochromocytoma. *Mayo Clin Proc* 65:88, 1990.

19. Vance ML: Treatment of hyperprolactinemia. *J Clin Endocrinol Metab* 68:336, 1989.

20. Vinik AT, Renor IP: Carcinoid tumors. *Dabetalogia Creatica* 23–24, 123–138, 1994.

21. Vita JA, et al: Clinical clues to the cause of Addison's disease. *Am J Med* 78:461, 1985.

22. Whyte MP: Hypocalcemia, in Nordin BEC, Need AG, Morris HA (eds): *Metabolic Bone and Stone Disease,* 3rd ed. Edinburgh; Churchill Livingstone, 147–162, 1993.

23. Winzelberg GG: Parathyroid imaging. *Ann Intern Med* 237:893, 1989.

Diabetes Mellitus

Abbas E. Kitabchi

DIAGNOSIS OF DIABETES MELLITUS
Indications and Criteria for Screening Tests for
DM 2 • Performance of OGTT (Oral
Glucose Tolerance Test)

ASSESSMENT OF GLYCEMIC CONTROL
Glycohemoglobin

**TREATMENT REGIMEN OF PATIENTS
WITH DIABETES**
Education • Diet Therapy • Treatment of
DM 2 • Treatment of DM1 • Outpatient
Management of Patients with Diabetes

**COMPLICATIONS OF INTENSIVE
INSULIN THERAPY—
HYPOGLYCEMIA**

Diabetes mellitus (DM) is a clinical disorder characterized by abnormal metabolism of carbohydrate, fat, and protein, that results in inappropriate hyperglycemia. It may be due to either a deficiency in secretion of insulin, or ineffectiveness of insulin, or both. According to the latest statistics in the United States, there are 1 million Americans with type 1 diabetes and 15 million Americans with type 2 diabetes, of whom about 50 percent are unaware of their disorder. In addition, there are approximately 20 million Americans with impaired glucose tolerance (IGT), the group that has a high risk for developing type 2 diabetes.[1]

Table 67-1 shows the most recently revised classification of diabetes and hyperglycemia.[2] The new criteria replace the previously named "adult onset," or "noninsulin-dependent," or "ketosis-independent" diabetes, and only uses the term type 2 diabetes (DM 2). Similarly, the previously designated "juvenile onset," or "insulin-dependent," or "ketosis-prone," diabetes is replaced by type 1 diabetes (DM 1). Table 67-1 depicts not only the two major types of spontaneous diabetes (i.e., type 1 and type 2), but also gestational diabetes and other types that are associated with endocrinopathies. It also provides a new terminology for the formerly named "chemical diabetes," which is now known as impaired glucose tolerance (IGT). Of all of these forms of diabetes, by far the most frequent in the United States is type 2, which constitutes more than 90 percent of all diabetic cases. Table 67-2 provides the clinical characteristics of these two major forms of diabetes.[3]

DM 2 is ethnic group-related.[4,5] The prevalence of the disease is: in Pima Indians (35 percent), in Native Americans (17 percent), in Hispanics (12 percent), and in African-Americans (5 percent), as compared to 2.5 percent for the general population of the United States. The incidence of DM 2 increases with age, number of family members with a history of diabetes, and other risk factors, which are summarized in Table 67-3. A 60-year-old Pima Indian, for example, has an approximately 60 percent chance of being diabetic.

Table 67-4 summarizes some statistics on the microvascular complications of diabetes[6], and Table 67-5 depicts its macrovascular complications.[6] DM 2 is more often associated with macrovascular, and DM 1 more often with microvascular, complications. According to the latest statistics from the American Diabetes Association (ADA), more than $98 billion in direct and indirect costs were spent on diabetes and its com-

TABLE 67-1 **Classification of Various Hyperglycemias**

Diabetes Mellitus (DM)
 Type 1 DM
  Immune-mediated
  Idiopathic
 Type 2 DM
  Individuals with insulin resistance who usually have
   relative, rather than absolute, insulin deficiency
   (obese or nonobese).
 Other Types of DM
  Pancreatic disease and pancreatic surgery, including
   tropical calcific DM
  Endocrinopathies (Cushing's syndrome, acromegaly,
   hyperaldosteronism, pheochromocytoma)
  Drug-induced
 Gestational DM (GDM)
 Maturity Onset DM of the Young (MODY)

Impaired Glucose Tolerance (IGT)

SOURCE: Adapted from Harris MI, Goldstein DE, Flegal KM, et al: Prevalence of diabetes, impaired fasting glucose and impaired glucose tolerance in US adults: The third national health and nutrition survey, 1988–1994. *Diabetes Care* 21:518–524, 1998.

plications in 1996.[7] This included the costs of management and therapy, as well as loss of wages associated with the disease. In certain ethnic groups, DM 2 has reached epidemic proportions in the United States. Because DM 2 is a leading cause of death in this country, and is related to lifestyle, an effort to modify lifestyle to reduce the incidence of these disorders is important.

DM 1, however, is more often associated with ketosis and is characterized by insulinopenia. It is believed to be an autoimmune-related disease that may be initiated as a result of viral infection or a toxic component in the environment with the following chronologic events: introduction of pancreatropic virus into the pancreas with production of an antigen; processing of antigen by macrophages to a peptide that fits into class II molecules on the membrane of the macrophage (DR_3, DR_4); further engagement of this peptide in T lymphocyte for CD_4 activation; production of two cytokines, interleukin-1 (IL1)

and tumor necrosis factor-α (TNFα) from macrophages; production of interferon-γ (INFγ) from lymphocytes; and production of these compounds collectively results in destruction of β cells, and when more than 90 percent of β cells are destroyed, the clinical presentation of DM 1 emerges. DM 1 is strongly associated with the human leukocyte antigen (HLA), particularly with DR_3 and DR_4 genes. More specifically, DQ locus (DQW32) has been identified as a susceptibility gene for DM 1. The deficiency of insulin and excess counterregulatory hormones (such as cortisol, catecholamines, glucagon, and growth hormone) in uncontrolled diabetes brings about a series of metabolic decompensations resulting in a breakdown of protein in muscle (proteolysis), which brings about an excess of amino acids, which are used in gluconeogenesis; a breakdown of triglycerides in fat tissue, leading to increased free fatty acid (lipolysis); and a breakdown of glycogen to glucose (glycogenolysis) and increased gluconeogenesis (glucose production from noncarbohydrate precursors), both of which lead to hyperglycemia. Decreased insulin availability in the presence of increased glucagon and increased free fatty acids lead to excessive ketone production, which can eventually result in severe metabolic ketoacidosis and, if not treated, coma and death. Table 67-6 correlates these clinical conditions with various metabolic defects.[3]

Type 2 diabetes, which is also heterogeneous, is not an autoimmune disease, but is characterized by the presence of insulin resistance. The disease may be insidious at the start, with normal fasting blood glucose at the expense of hyperinsulinemia, but postprandial hyperglycemia, which is the characteristic of impaired glucose tolerance. This postprandial hyperglycemia in certain susceptible individuals may cause glucose toxicity in β cells of the pancreas leading to decreased insulin production, insulinopenia, and frank DM 2. The hyperinsulinemic stage may be variable, from a short period to a long duration, before the appearance of clinical diabetes. The hyperinsulinemia is an effort on

TABLE 67-2 Major Characteristics of Diabetes Mellitus Types 1 and 2

Features	Type 1 DM	Type 2 DM
Age at onset	Usually <40	Usually >40
Proportion of all DM	About 10%	About 90%
Seasonal trend	Fall and winter	None
Appearance of symptoms	Acute or subacute	Slow or subacute
Metabolic ketoacidosis	Frequent	Rare[a]
Obesity at onset	Uncommon	Common
β-Cells	Decreased	Variable
Insulin	Decreased or absent	Variable
Inflammatory cells in islets	Present initially	Absent
Family history of DM	Uncommon	Common
Concordance in identical twins	30–50%	90–95%
HLA association	Yes	No
Antibody to islet cells (ICA)	Yes	Uncommon
Insulin autoantibodies (IAA)	Yes (in younger age)	No
"64K" GAD[b] antibodies	Yes	No
Treatment	Insulin and diet Pancreas transplantation	Diet, weight reduction, exercise, OAA,[c] insulin

[a]Except in African-Americans.

[b]Glutamic acid decarboxylase (GAD).

[c]Oral antidiabetic agents.

SOURCE: Adapted from Kitabchi AE, Fisher JN: Diabetes mellitus, in Conn R (ed): *Current Diagnosis.* Philadelphia: WB Saunders, 1991, pp 766–774.

the part of the pancreas to maintain fasting euglycemia in IGT by excess secretion of insulin, and, therefore, the ratio of insulin to glucose at this stage remains elevated, denoting endogenous insulin resistance. Although the pathogenesis of DM 2 has not been fully elucidated, insulin-resistance is the hallmark of the disease, with subsequent reduction of insulin secretion and insulinopenia. Obesity is a strong contributing factor, as 85 percent of DM 2 patients are obese.

A subclassification of DM 2 is MODY (Maturity Onset Diabetes of the Young), which occurs in the young age group and is transmitted via autosomal dominant inheritance, with possible alteration of a glucokinase gene in the pancreas. It is important to note that concordance of DM 2 in identical twins is about 95 percent, whereas concordance for DM 1 in identical twins is between 30 to 50 percent (Table 67-2).

Diagnosis of Diabetes Mellitus

Based on the latest consensus report,[2] there are now three accepted methods by which DM is diagnosed in nonpregnant adults. Two of the methods consist of the use of a single blood-glucose determination, and the third method involves the use of a 2-h oral glucose tolerance test (OGTT) with 75 g glucose for those individuals whose fasting blood-glucose level is >100 but <126 mg/dl. The first two methods consist of having either a fasting blood-glucose level equal

TABLE 67-3 Population At Risk for Type 2 Diabetes Mellitus

1. Persons with classic signs and symptoms of diabetes (polyuria, polydipsia, polyphagia, and unexplained loss of weight).

2. Obesity (particularly upper-body adiposity) with BMI ≥27 or ≥120% of ideal body weight.

3. Primary relatives with history of Type 2 DM.

4. Ethnic groups (i.e., African-Americans, Hispanics, Native Americans, Asian Americans)

5. GDM or history of having a neonate weighing >9 pounds.

6. Having HDL cholesterol ≤35 mg/dL and/or triglyceride ≥250 mg.

7. Previous IGT or IFG

8. History of coronary artery disease and/or hypertension (≥140/90 mm Hg).

9. Persons ingesting high doses of glucocorticoids.

SOURCE: Adapted from The Expert Committee on the Diagnosis and Classification of Diabetes Mellitus: Report on the diagnosis and classification of diabetes mellitus. *Diabetes Care* 20:1183–1197, 1997.

to or greater than 126 mg/dl on two separate occasions or a random blood-glucose level that is unequivocally elevated (greater than 200 mg/dl) in a subject who has the classical signs

TABLE 67-4 Microvascular Complications of Diabetes Mellitus

Eye (Retinopathy)	Leading cause of new cases of blindness in adults. (Increased risk: 20×) Relative risk for cataracts and glaucoma increased 2–3×.
Kidney (nephropathy)	Occurs in 35 percent of Type 1, and 20 percent of type 2 patients. Accounts for 30 percent of new cases of end stage renal disease (ESRD) each year. (Increased risk: 25×)
Nerve (neuropathy)	Common in both Type 1 and Type 2 patients. Important cause of morbidity.

SOURCE: Harris MI: Undiagnosed NIDDM: Clinical and public health issues. *Diabetes Care* 16:642–652, 1993.

TABLE 67-5 Macrovascular Complications of Diabetes Mellitus

Coronary heart disease	Increased in men, 4× in women. Responsible for 50 to 60 percent of adult deaths.
Cerebrovascular disease	Risk for stroke increased 6×.
Peripheral vascular disease	Present in 8 percent at diagnosis, 45 percent at 20 years. Foot or ankle ulcers occur in 15 percent. 40 to 50 percent of nontraumatic amputations. (Increased risk: 40×) 50 percent 3-year survival of the other limb after amputation.

SOURCE: Adapted from Harris MI: Undiagnosed NIDDM: Clinical and public health issues. *Diabetes Care* 16:642–652, 1998.

and symptoms of diabetes (polydipsia, polyuria, polyphagia, and unexplained weight loss).

Indications and Criteria for Screening Tests for DM 2

In general, as DM 1 patients present themselves with a decompensated metabolic condition, the early screening is not recommended at this time. Such screening, however, is under consideration for first-degree relatives of DM 1 patients for investigational purposes. On the other hand, with the recent reports on the results of both the Diabetes Control and Complications Trial (DCCT),[8] indicating that control of blood glucose can significantly reduce complications of diabetes in DM 1 patients, and the Kumamoto Study[9] showing similar reduction of risk of microangiopathy in DM 2, it is important that people at high risk be screened for DM 2 in order to appropriately treat or prevent complications of diabetes. Table 67-7 depicts the 1997 criteria for diagnosis of diabetes, IGT, impaired fasting blood glucose (IFG) and new recommendations for screening of DM in pregnancy. In addition, the ADA now recommends that all individuals ≥45 years of age should be screened for DM and that those individuals at high risk

TABLE 67-6   Correlation of Uncontrolled Diabetic Syndromes with Various Metabolic Defects

Metabolic Defects	Chemical Abnormalities	Clinical Symptoms
Carbohydrate Metabolism		
1. Diminished uptake of glucose by muscle, adipose, and liver cells	Hyperglycemia	Polyuria, polydipsia, polyphagia, fatigue, weakness, pruritus
2. Overproduction of glucose (via glycogenolysis and gluconeogenesis) by the liver	Hyperglycemia	Blurred vision Diminished mentation
Protein Metabolism		
1. Diminished uptake of amino acids and diminished synthesis of protein	Negative nitrogen balance Elevated levels of branched-chain amino acids and blood urea nitrogen	Loss of muscle mass and weakness
2. Increased proteolysis	Elevated serum potassium	
Fat Metabolism		
1. Increased lipolysis	Elevated plasma fatty acids and glycerol	Loss of adipose tissue Nausea and vomiting
2. Decreased lipogenesis		Loss of adipose tissue
3. Increased production of triglycerides	Hypertriglyceridemia	Exudative xanthoma (skin lesions) Lipemia retinalis Pancreatitis (abdominal pain)
4. Decreased removal of ketones and increased ketone production	Elevated plasma and urine ketones	Hyperventilation, metabolic acidosis, abdominal pain, acetone on breath

SOURCE: Adapted from Kitabchi AE, Fisher JN: Diabetes mellitus, in Conn R (ed): *Current Diagnosis.* Philadelphia: WB Saunders, 1991, pp 766–774.

(Table 67-3) should be screened before the age of 45.

Performance of OGTT

As stated under the methods of diagnosis of DM, the screening tests used to detect DM consist of fasting blood glucose, random blood glucose, or OGTT.

Table 67-8 summarizes the conditions under which an OGTT should be performed.[10] Meticulous attention should be given to the adequate intake of carbohydrates (CHO) by the patient (>150 grams of CHO/day × 3 days prior to the study), use of no drugs, and no prolonged bed confinement or stress. It should be emphasized that OGTT is not recommended for those individuals who have had a diagnosis of DM by either fasting blood glucose or random blood glucose, because the ingestion of the glucose load may precipitate diabetic ketoacidosis (DKA) or a hyperglycemic hyperosmolar nonketotic state (HHNS).

Assessment of Glycemic Control

For many years it was assumed that urine glucose testing was a good indicator of glycemic status control, but recent studies suggest a poor relationship between blood glucose and urine glucose by numerous dipstick/test tapes, including the glucose oxidase-containing dipstick/test tapes.[11] The only acceptable method for assessment of glycemic control is determination of

TABLE 67-7 New Criteria for Diagnosis of DM and IGT

DM
   FPG ≥126 mg/dl on two separate occasions
   Casual BG ≥200 mg/dl with symptoms of DM (polyuria, polydipsia, unexplained weight loss)
   2 HPPG ≥200 mg/dl on OGTT

Impaired Glucose Tolerance (IGT)
   2 HPPG ≥140 but <200 mg/dl on OGTT

Impaired Fasting Glucose (IFG)
   FPG ≥110 but <126 mg/dl

Gestational DM (GDM)
   Same criteria as before (i.e., following 100 g OGTT, plasma glucose reaching or exceeding any of the following two values: 105, 190, 165, 145 for fasting, 1 hr, 2 hr, 3 hr respectively). Screen high risk subjects: all women >25 years; >120% IBW; family history of DM; ethnic groups at high risk; previous GDM; morbid obstetrical history or neonate birth weight >9 pounds

Screen for DM in all individuals >45 years and if normal, repeat at 3-year intervals. Screen at age <45 in high risk individuals (see Table 67-2).

FPG = Fasting Plasma Glucose; 2HPPG = 2 h Postprandial Glucose
SOURCE: Adapted from The Expert Committee on the Diagnosis and Classification of Diabetes Mellitus: Report on the diagnosis and classification of diabetes mellitus. *Diabetes Care* 20:1183–1197, 1997.

TABLE 67-8 Preparations and Procedures for Performance of OGTT

1. Administer only to otherwise healthy ambulatory subjects.
2. Allow at least 3 days of unrestricted diet and physical activity prior to the test. The diet should include at least 150 g of carbohydrates per day.
3. Subject should have fasted for 10–14 h.
4. Test should be performed in the morning.
5. Administer 75 g of oral glucose for adults, 100 g for pregnant adults, and 1.75 g/kg/body weight for children, up to a maximum of 75 g.
6. Subjects should remain seated and nonsmoking during the test, and should use no caffeine.
7. Venous plasma glucose determinations are drawn fasting and every 30 min for 2 h in nonpregnant adults.
8. Venous plasma glucose determinations are drawn fasting and every hour for 3 h in pregnant adults.
9. Test should not be performed on subjects with previously diagnosed DM (by fasting or random blood glucose), as it may induce marked hyperglycemia.

SOURCE: Adapted from Kitabchi AE, et al: Diabetes mellitus, in Ling FW, Laube DW, Nolan TE, Smith RP, Stovall TG (eds): *Primary Care in Gynecology*. Baltimore: Williams & Wilkins, 1996, pp. 279–298.

blood glucose with the use of direct enzymatic methods (i.e., glucose oxidase). In addition to the standard laboratory method, many meters are now available that use strips containing glucose oxidase enzyme for direct measurement of glucose in whole blood. The accuracy of such machines has been well documented. Those with an easier method of analysis (no wiping of blood from the strip) and memory have become more acceptable to patients and health care providers. Urine tests for "ketone bodies" still remain a useful and quick way to assess ketosis. We advise patients to check their urine for ketones when their blood glucose continues to remain above 250 mg/dl, and, if moderate ketones are present, to seek immediate medical advice. Self glucose-monitoring (SGM) systems are now an accepted method of monitoring for those patients who must adjust their medication and activities based on their blood glucose.

Glycohemoglobin

Glycohemoglobin is a product of a ketoamine reaction between glucose in the blood and N-terminal amino acids of the β chains of hemoglobin; it consists of hemoglobin A_{1a}, A_{1b}, and A_{1c}. Because the life of red blood cells is about 120 days, the glycohemoglobin level generally reflects the glycemic state over the last 12 weeks.[12] A more specific form of glycohemoglobin (HbA_{1c}), although more difficult to assay, is more specific for the stable form of glycohemoglobin and is now recommended for assessment of chronic glycemic control. The normal level of this compound is between 4 and 6 percent (depending on the laboratory method used), and, therefore, values up to 7 percent are considered good for patients with diabetes, while values above 10 percent are considered poor control. A falsely decreased level of glycosylated hemoglobin can be found in patients with severe anemia or shortened red blood cell life, such as seen in

patients with hemolytic anemias or hemoglobinopathies. Conversely, falsely elevated levels of glycosylated hemoglobin can be found in patients with uremia and hemoglobin-F elevation.

Although SGM is a useful method for monitoring day-to-day glucose variations, HbA_{1c} provides an accurate reflection of an average level of blood glucose in the past few weeks. HbA_{1c}, however, cannot demonstrate the severe fluctuations that a brittle diabetic may experience during such a period. In that situation, daily SGM is the most useful method of monitoring. Obtaining HbA_{1c} levels every 3 months is the standard method for follow-up of patients with DM 1 or DM 2.

Treatment Regimen of Patients with Diabetes

Education

It is incumbent upon those who manage patients with diabetes to provide appropriate education for the patients. This should either be done in the physician's office, or the patient can be referred to a facility or an organization with enough expertise that its program has been approved by the American Diabetes Association (ADA) and certified by the American Association of Diabetes Educators (AADE).

Table 67-9 summarizes the goals and methods of therapy for patients with diabetes. Table 67-10 provides general guidelines for management of patients with diabetes. Because education is by far the most important aspect of management, Table 67-11 summarizes the pertinent points of the educational program that every patient and family member needs to know. It cannot be overstated that a well-informed patient (regardless of level of education) is essential for good care. Therefore, any physician attempting to manage a diabetic patient should ideally have access to a team of health care professionals, including a nutritionist, a diabetes educator, and a mental health professional, in addition to the physician. In some locales, the patient may not

TABLE 67-9 Goals and Methods of Therapy of Patients with Diabetes Mellitus

Goals of Therapy
  Normalize metabolism
  Normalize physical well being
  Normalize psychological well being
  Avoid complications:
    Acute complications
    Long-term complications
Methods of Therapy
  Education
  Diet/meal planning
  Exercise
  Antidiabetic agents
    Oral antidiabetic agents
      Sulfonylureas
      Repaglidine
      α-Glucosidase inhibitor
      Biguanide
      Thiazolidinedione
  Insulin

have access to such individuals, in which case the physician will need to fill these roles. In the DCCT studies, the team approach was proven to contribute enormously to the successful management of DM 1. Table 67-12 provides the guidelines I emphasize to patients in my educational program. They are very similar, but not identical, to the ADA guidelines.

Diet Therapy

The most important step after the diagnosis and education of a patient with diabetes is discussion of diet. Although many patients have traditionally been frightened by the thought that their diabetes has "sentenced" them to a miserable and unpalatable diet, adherence to such old beliefs is no longer justified.

With the availability of a large number of innovative recipes it is imperative that the health care team uses a common sense approach to the meal plan and impresses on the patient that the ADA diet is similar to any other common sense meal plan.

TABLE 67-10 General Guidelines for Management of DM

1. Establish diagnosis of DM and emphasize educational components. Do not perform OGTT if diagnosis of DM is already established.
2. Classify DM as type 1 or type 2.
3. Inform patient of diagnosis and refer to DM education classes (to learn signs and symptoms, complications, SGM, DM medications, sick days, etc.)
4. Place patient on ADA diet with appropriate caloric, sodium, and lipid restrictions.
5. Identify cardiac risk factors.
6. Determine status of kidney function (serum creatinine, 24-h urine microalbumin), and check annually thereafter.
7. Evaluate for presence of neuropathy (refer to neurologist when necessary).
8. Establish extent of fundoscopic lesion (refer to ophthalmologist[a]).
9. Check feet, pulses, and toe nails at each visit.
10. Use SMBG for daily diabetic control and check urine only for ketones.
11. Follow chronic glycemic control by HbA_{1c} approximately every 2 months in the office, and perform complete physical annually.

[a]At diagnosis of type 2 DM, at 5 years if type 1 DM

TABLE 67-11 Educational Component for DM Teaching

1. Overview of DM
2. Establishment of metabolic goals (see Table 67-12)
3. Emphasize psychological adjustment
4. Family involvement and social support
5. Nutrition
6. Exercise
7. Work and recreational activities
8. Medications (oral antidiabetic versus insulin preparations)
9. Monitoring, keeping records, and proper use of results
10. Relationshp of nutrition, exercise, and medication
11. Reduction of vascular risk factors (e.g., smoking)
12. Prevention, detection, and treatment of acute complications
13. Prevention, detection, and treatment of chronic complications
14. Foot, skin, and dental care
15. Benefits, risks, and management for improving glycemic control
16. Sick days
17. Various strategies for travel
18. Preconception care, pregnancy, and DM in pregnancy
19. Use of health care system and community resources.
20. Provision of identification tag (MedicAlert) to be worn around the neck.

The most important aspects of this meal plan regimen are moderation, avoidance of large amounts of refined sugar, and a decrease in the size of food portions. In my practice, I emphasize that my patients follow a diet consistent with both the ADA and American Heart Association (AHA) diets; that is, 50 to 55 percent carbohydrates (mostly complex carbohydrates and less refined sugar), 15 to 20 percent protein, and 30 percent fat, of which no more than 10 percent should be saturated fat, plus an adequate amount of fiber (20 to 30 g/day). Probably the most important aspects of a diet to emphasize are timeliness of the food intake in relation to medication, moderation in consumption of any food group, and food servings of smaller portions.

My team proposes that calorie requirements be based on simplified calculation of ideal body weight (IBW) and caloric requirement based on IBW, as depicted in Table 67-13, where dietary composition is also listed.

Treatment of DM 2

Table 67-14 provides more specific guidelines for the management of patients with DM 2. As stated above, diet is the backbone of DM management. My approach to overweight diabetic individuals consists of three major strategies: weight loss, low-fat diet (≤30 percent kcal from fat with low-saturated fat), and physical exercise. Obese patients should be advised to reduce their weight

TABLE 67-12   Metabolic Goals in DM

	Normal Value	Goal Value for DM
Fasting Blood Glucose	70–110 mg/dl	80–120 mg/dl
Pregnant	69–90 mg/dl	69–90 mg/dl
Postprandial Blood glucose (2 h)	<140 mg/dl	<180 mg/dl
Pregnant (1 h)	<140 mg/dl	100–120 mg/dl
Glycosylated Hemoglobin HbA$_{1c}$	4–6%	<7%[a]
Total Cholesterol	<200 mg/dl	<200 mg/dl
HDL Cholesterol Men	>45 mg/dl	>35 mg/dl
Women	>45 mg/dl	>45 mg/dl
LDL Cholesterol	<130 mg/dl	<100 mg/dl
Triglycerides	<150 mg/dl	<150 mg/dl
Body Mass Index[b]	20–25	20–25

[a] In certain groups of patients

[b] BMI >27 is defined as obese.

SOURCE: Adapted from Kitabchi AE, et al: Diabetes mellitus, in Ling FW, Laube DW, Nolan TE, Smith RP, Stovall TG (eds): *Primary Care in Gynecology*. Baltimore: Williams & Wilkins, 1996, pp 279–298.

to the ideal body weight as detailed in Table 67-13.

Weight reduction in overweight individuals is associated with improved triglyceride levels, insulin sensitivity, total cholesterol and low-density lipoprotein (LDL) cholesterol, increased high-density lipoprotein (HDL) and improved glucose, and decreased insulin resistance. Although

TABLE 67-13   Calculation for Ideal Body Weight (IBW) and Body Mass Index (BMI), and Recommendation for Proper Dietary Composition

Ideal Body Weight (IBW)	
Women	100 lb for first 5 feet + 5 lb for each additional inch
Men	106 lb for first 5 feet + 6 lb for each additional inch
Body Mass Index (BMI)	Wt (kg)/height (M)^2; normal value 20–25; obese > 27
Calorie Requirements	
Basal requirement	Ideal body weight (lb) × 10
Average activity	Add 30% to basal requirement
Strenuous activity	Add 100–200% to basal requirement
Weight loss	Subtract 500 calories/day to lose 1 lb/week
Pregnancy	Add 300 calories/day
Lactation	Add 500 calories/day
Dietary Composition	
Carbohydrate	50–55% of total calories
Protein	15–20% of total calories
Fat	30% of total calories (<10% saturated fat)
Fiber	30 g soluble fiber

SOURCE: Adapted from Kitabchi AE, et al: Diabetes mellitus, in Ling FW, Laube DW, Nolan TE, Smith RP, Stovall TG (eds): *Primary Care in Gynecology*. Baltimore: Williams & Wilkins, 1996, pp 279–298.

TABLE 67-14   General Guidelines for Management of Type 2 (DM 2) Diabetes

1. Place patient on ADA reducing diet (50% CHO, 30% fat, 20% protein, high fiber) with 3 meals a day to achieve and maintain ideal body weight or to reduce weight by 5–15% in 3 months (if ≥130% above ideal body weight).

2. Encourage risk factor interventions (smoking, exercise, lipids, etc.).

3. While on diet, check fasting blood glucose by finger stick daily for 2 months. If diet is effective, FBG will gradually decline during this period. If FBG does not decline or increases, consider use of oral antidiabetic agents (OAA) if:
    a. Patient has had diabetes for less than 10 years.
    b. Patient does not have severe hepatic or renal disease.
    c. Patient is not pregnant.
    d. Patient is not allergic to sulfonylurea

4. Patients with FBG (on diet) ≥250 mg/dl (after adequate dietary restriction) are not suitable candidates for monotherapy of OAA.

5. While on OAA check patient for FBG and 2 HPPBG every 2 months (with daily FBG and 2 HPPBG monitoring at home); if 2 HPPBG <200 mg/dl, omit OAA and place on diet alone and follow every 1–2 months. If FBG >200 mg/dl consistently, place patient on insulin.

6. Insulin dosage should be calculated on actual body weight (0.5–1.0 U/kg body wt).

7. If total insulin requirement is less than 30 U/day, may try to give the entire dose as NPH or Lente before a major meal and check for glycemic control (Goal: FBG <140, 2 HPP <200, and no BG <60 mg/dl).

8. If the goal is not achieved by a single insulin injection, insulin may be given as a mixture of Regular: NPH (50:50) bid, 30 min before breakfast and 30 min before supper.

9. Very obese NIDDM may require more insulin/kg body weight, and greater percentage of total insulin as regular insulin than less obese DM 2.

10. If above regimen fails to control blood glucose, consider multiple regular insulin injections before each meal with bedtime NPH or Lente insulin.

NOTE: Refer insulin-resistant patients (requiring >200 U insulin/day) to a diabetologist.

the greater the weight loss the greater the improvement, even with a weight loss of 5 percent of original body weight an improvement in lipid disorders has been observed.

Physical exercise helps not only with weight reduction, but regular exercise has been shown to also improve insulin sensitivity and dyslipidemia in those people who are in high-risk groups for cardiovascular and microvascular diseases. ***Oral Antidiabetic Agents (OAA)*** Sulfonylureas Although up to 1995 the major OAA in the U.S. consisted of various forms of sulfonylureas (SU), the burgeoning of numerous oral agents with different useful properties (and some side effects) has made decisions about prescribing the proper medication for DM 2 patients by health care providers challenging. Table 67-15 depicts various forms of SU, whereas Table 67-16 lists the available nonsulfonylurea preparations and

their dosage and properties. In general SU's mechanism of action is twofold: insulin stimulation (i.e., insulin secretogogue) and extrapancreatic effect including possible effect on metabolism of insulin. Fifty percent of patients who are on a diet and SU respond satisfactorily to the medication, but there is also a 3 to 5 percent failure to SU per year.[13] The more recent preparation of SU, glimepiride (Amaryl), has the advantage of a longer half-life with one dose a day efficacy without the undesirable side effects on water and electrolytes that chlorpropamide exhibits.[14].

Other Insulin Secretogogue Another class of insulin secretogogue that is not an SU is repaglinide (Prandin), which has the advantage of having a short duration of action. It has to be taken with each meal, and therefore, when the patient is not planning to take a meal, the medicine is not

TABLE 67-15 Available Oral Antidiabetic Agents (OAA)

Generic Name	Brand Name	Daily Dosage (mg)	Duration of Action (h)	Comments
First-Generation Sulfonylureas				
Tolbutamide	Orinase	500–3000	6–12	Metabolized by liver to inactive product; excreted by kidneys; taken 2–3 times a day
Chlorpropamide	Diabinese	100–500	60	Metabolized by liver (~70%) to less active metabolites and excreted intact (~30%) by kidney; can potentiate antidiuretic hormone action; taken once a day
Tolazamide	Tolinase	100–1000	12–24	Metabolized by liver to both active and inactive products; excreted by kidneys; taken 1–2 times a day
Second-Generation Sulfonylureas				
Glipizide	Glucotrol	2.5–20	12–24	Metabolized by liver to inert products; excreted by kidneys; taken 1–2 times a day
	Glucotrol XL	5–20	24	Controlled-release preparation produces sustained plasma levels, taken once daily
Glyburide	DiaBeta Micronase	1.25–20	16–24	Metabolized by liver to mostly inert products; excreted in bile and by kidneys; taken 1–2 times a day
	Glynase Pres Tab	0.75–12	12–24	Small particle size facilitates rapid absorption
Glimepiride	Amaryl	1–4	24	Metabolized by liver; excreted 60% renal, 40% bile; lower incidence of hypoglycemia; taken once a day

SOURCE: Kitabchi & Bryer-Ash (with permission) (21)

taken. Long-term experience with this relatively new drug is limited.

α-Glucosidase Inhibitor Acarbose (Precose) is an α-glucosidase inhibitor that acts on the jejunal part of the intestine to inhibit breakdown of complex carbohydrates (except lactose), and therefore, delays intestinal absorption of glucose with concomitant reduction of insulin secretion.[15] Acarbose is effective in reducing postprandial hyperglycemia in DM 2, and especially those with higher HbA_{1c} (i.e., >12 percent). It is more effective in combination with a sulfonylurea.[15] The major side effect is dose-related flatulence, which can be reduced with gradual increase in dosage starting with 25 mg dose per day with the breakfast meal for one week and then adding 25 mg to each meal at weekly intervals. If the desired

effect is not obtained, incremental addition of 25 mg for each meal at weekly increments for total doses of 50 mg tid will provide the optimal effect. Acarbose has to be taken with the first bite of each meal. It should not be used in patients with liver disease.

Biguanide The only biguanide available in the U.S. is metformin (Glucophage), which is as effective as SU. Its reduces hepatic glucose output, and it has a salutary effect on weight reduction and lipids.[16, 17] Recent work suggests that metformin and troglitazone have additive effects.[18] Metformin's side effect is GI-related, but if the dosage is given in stepwise fashion (i.e., 500 mg/dl with gradual increase to 1000 mg bid), the GI side effects will be less bothersome. The greatest potential side effect is lactic acidosis, which is

TABLE 67-16   Other Antidiabetic Agents

Generic Name	Brand Name	Daily Dosage (mg)	Duration of Action (h)	Comments
Meglitinides: Repaglinide	Prandin	0.5–4	~1	Taken only with meals. It is an insulin secretogogue, but it is unrelated to sulfonylureas.
Biguanides: Metformin	Glucophage	1,500–2,550	~5.5[a]	Not metabolized; excreted by kidneys; may be used alone or in combination with sulfonylureas
α-Glucosidase Inhibitors: Acarbose	Precose	25–150	~2	Slows absorption of poly- and disaccharides from jejunum by inhibiting α-glucosidase; taken with first bite of meal; main action is on postprandial glucoses
Thiazolidinediones: Troglitazone	Rezulin	200–600	24	Decreases insulin resistance
Rosiglitazone	Avandia	2–8	24	Decreases insulin resistance

[a]Plasma half-life.
SOURCE: Obtained from Kitabchi and Bryer-Ash with permission (21).

more prevalent in conditions associated with hypoxia or renal diseases. The absolute contraindications in those patients are serum creatinine of >1.4 mg/dl for females and >1.5 mg/dl for males, as well as other conditions associated with metabolic acidosis. Metformin is especially suited for obese hyperinsulinemic individuals with insulin resistance, as the drug produces some weight loss and decreases hepatic glucose production.

Thiazolidinediones Troglitazone (Rezulin) is one of the approved thiazolidinedione preparations. It is a class of antidiabetic compound that is marketed as an insulin sensitizer, as it stimulates the family of nuclear receptors (PPARγ),[19] but is ineffective in the absence of residual insulin. Recent reports on abnormal liver function, and reports of severe liver failure in some patients that resulted in five deaths, has prompted the FDA to provide guidelines for the use of Rezulin, including contraindications to its use in the presence of any abnormal liver function test. The patients should be followed *every month* for eight months with hepatic enzyme profiles, every two months for an additional two times, and at certain intervals thereafter. Any sign or symptom or detection of liver enzyme abnormality should alert the patient to seek medical advice, and patients should be taken off Rezulin immediately. Rezulin is also effective in patients with insulin-resistance such as IGT,[20] as it stimulates peripheral glucose utilization. In treatment of an insulin-requiring patient with DM 2, troglitazone addition produces dramatic decreases in insulin dosage requirement.

Rezulin is not recommended as monotherapy. The effects of Rezulin and metformin are additive, as they each work at different metabolic sites (i.e., metformin decreases hepatic glucose production and troglitazone stimulates peripheral glucose utilization).[18]

A second thiazolidinedione, rosiglitazone (Avandia), has just been approved. It appears to have less hepatotoxicity and higher potency.

Insulin Therapy Table 67-17 lists various preparations of insulin and their bioavailability.[21]

Studies at certain centers suggest that the combination of an evening dose of insulin (NPH or combined NPH plus regular) at supper or bedtime, followed by a morning dose of OAA, may be effective in the control of hyperglycemia in DM 2.[22] Although this method of therapy is not uniformly accepted, in difficult situations where

TABLE 67-17 Characteristics of Human Insulins Available in the United States

	Insulin Type	Onset	Peak Action	Duration
Ultrashort-acting	Lispro	minutes	45 min	3–4 h
Short-acting	Regular, Velosulin	15–30 min	1–3 h	5–6 h
	Semilente	30–60 min	4–6 h	12–16 h
Intermediate-acting	Lente, NPH	1–3 h	6–10 h	16–20 h
Long-acting	Ultralente	4–6 h	8–20 h	24–28 h
Mixture	(70/30, 50/50)	30 min	Biphasic	16–20 h

SOURCE: Adapted from Kitabchi AE, Bryer-Ash M: NIDDM: New Aspects of Management. *Hosp Pract* 32:135–164, 1997.

DM 2 patients are reluctant to use multiple insulin injections, it may be worth a trial.

The newly available preparations of combined intermediate (NPH) and regular insulin (70/30; 50/50) may be important adjuncts to the therapy of patients with DM who are unable to mix regular and NPH insulin, or in certain DM 2 patients who may use these preparations alone or in conjunction with OAAs. The newest form of insulin is an ultrashort-acting preparation which is a recombinant form of modified insulin called Lispro (Table 67-17). This is particularly useful in patients with variable meal schedules. Lispro provides more effective reduction in postprandial hyperglycemia and less delayed hypoglycemia than regular insulin.

Implications of DCCT Studies in the Management of DM 2 Patients Although the DCCT studies showed an impressive reduction in complications of DM 1 patients with intensive therapy, which was also confirmed by the Kumamoto study for DM 2, it must be emphasized that whereas control of hyperglycemia in both types of DM patients is of paramount importance, prevention of DM 2 in those individuals at high risk (Table 67-3) is of crucial importance. Methods such as lifestyle modification and certain insulin sensitizers may be of great benefit in preventing or delaying development of diabetes. The two most important components of such management are still diet and exercise, but as DM 2 is more prevalent in minority groups, such measures must be culturally and ethnically acceptable to these patients.

Treatment of DM 1

Table 67-18 recommends steps in the management of patients with DM 1. All modes of treat-

TABLE 67-18 General Guidelines for Management of Type 1 (DM 1) Diabetes

1. Place patient on ADA diet (50% CHO, 30% fat, 20% protein) suitable for growth, development, and maintenance of ideal body weight. Give at least 3 meals a day plus bedtime snack (see below).
2. Do not give oral hypoglycemic agents for type 1 DM.
3. All patients must receive at least bid insulin (with short- and intermediate-acting insulins).
4. Give insulin based on actual body weight (0.5–0.8 U/kg body wt.), 40–60% of total as intermediate-acting and 60–40% as regular insulin.
5. Goal of therapy: FBG 70–120 mg/dl and 2 HPP ≤180 mg/dl with no blood glucose below 60 mg/dl.
6. Split dosage of intermediate-acting insulin to give about half of it in the morning and remaining at supper or HS.
7. If bid insulin does not achieve the therapeutic goal, consider injection of regular insulin before each meal with intermediate- or long-acting insulin at bedtime.
8. Regular insulin must be given 30 min before each meal or snack. Adjust regular insulin based on AC blood glucose and/or grams of CHO intake.
9. If regular insulin is prescribed at HS, be sure to give snack (if BG ≤200 mg/dl).
10. See patient for follow-up initially every 2 weeks, then every 1–3 months for glycemic control, dietary compliance, and chronic complications.

NOTE: Refer brittle diabetic (i.e., wide swing of hypo- and hyperglycemia) to a diabetologist.

Figure 67-1 A simplified representation of baseline and postprandial insulin secretion in a 70-kg subject (total of 49 U/day).

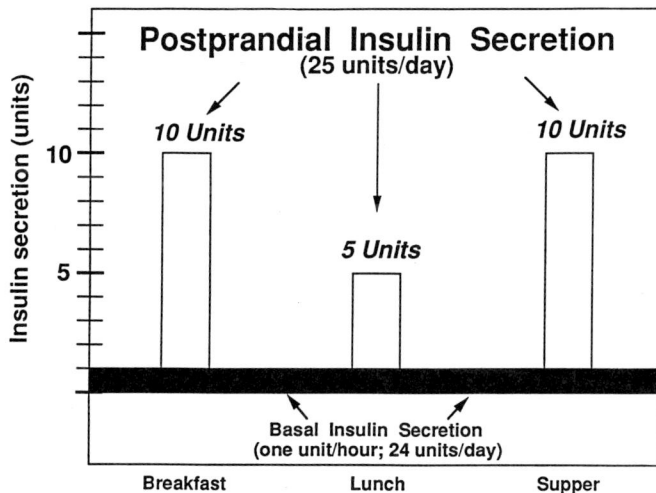

ment, however, must be individualized, and a general approach needs to be tailored to the needs of the individual taking into consideration activity, dietary preference, workplace, and family support.

Various studies suggest that the human pancreas in adults secretes basal insulin and C-peptide in equimolar concentrations.[23] It is estimated that the basal rate of insulin secretion is 1 unit/h daily for a total of about 24 units/day. In addition, the pancreas, through a multiple mechanism of cephalic and gastric phases, secretes postprandially approximately 25 units per day. This is shown graphically in Fig. 67-1 for the three meals (realizing that this is an approximation and that the secreted amounts are influenced by multifactorial events). The total estimated daily secretion of insulin is 49 units in a 70-kg person, which calculates to about 0.7 units of insulin/kg. As can be seen from the figure, about half of this insulin has a low steady level (resembling intermediate-NPH or long-acting ultralente insulin), while the remaining 25 units are secreted on demand as a fast-acting insulin (resembling a regular or Lispro insulin preparation).

Based on this assumption, I suggest in Table 67-18 a dosage of insulin in DM 1 that simulates the pancreas (i.e., 50 percent intermediate- or long-acting and 50 percent regular insulin) of which two-thirds of the dose (combined NPH and regular insulin) is given before breakfast and the remaining one-third (combined NPH and regular insulin) before supper. As stated, however, there are tremendous individual variabilities for combined insulin therapy. As an example, Fig. 67-2, depicts various proposed schedules for insulin injections that can be used in DM 1 patients.

In general, human insulin is preferred to other animal sources of insulin, because animal insulins are more immunogenic than the human form of insulin. Also, in general, regular insulin produces less insulin antibodies than intermediate- or long-acting preprations (even human preparations). Note, however, that in a patient who is allergic to insulin, the allergic response can occur even with human insulin.

Even with the advent of intensive therapy, no DM 1 patient can achieve euglycemic control—even with excellent dietary compliance—with one insulin injection per day. Almost all such patients require two injections (i.e., before breakfast and before supper), and the majority require three injections of insulin (morning, sup-

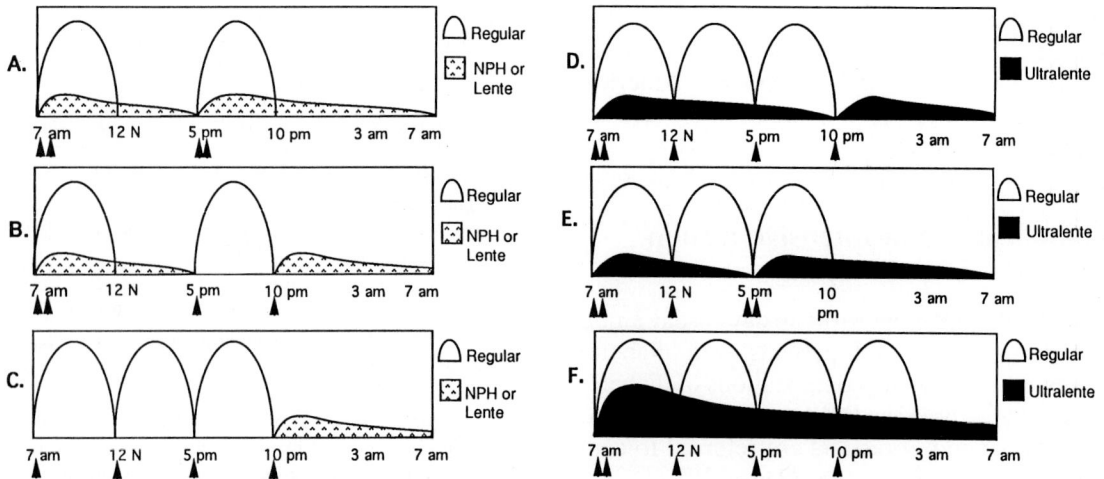

Figure 67-2 Proposed methods of insulin injection schedule in DM 1 patients. The Ultralente insulin dose in F is twice as much as in D or E.

per, and bedtime). Some patients may need small doses of regular insulin at lunch (Fig. 67-2).

Hypoglycemia is one of the most serious side effects of intensive therapy. As a result, intensive therapy in young children (<13 years) or older DM 1 patients with multiorgan complications or hypoglycemic unawareness is not recommended.[8].

Outpatient Management of Patients with Diabetes

Until 1993, there were no clear studies to correlate hyperglycemia with the complications of diabetes in DM 1, but the recent report of the DCCT studies[8] as well as Kumamoto studies[9] clearly demonstrate the benefit of glycemic control. All physicians who manage patients with diabetes should have a definite numerical goal for glycemic control and emphasize this target range to the patient, in addition to the other factors mentioned earlier. The desired level of HbA_{1c} should also be discussed. Although 7.2 percent was the approximate average of the HbA_{1c} of DCCT patients on intensive therapy, it is important to note that the studies showed any reduction in HbA_{1c} was beneficial in reducing the complications.

Because permission for admission of patients to the hospital for diabetes control is difficult to obtain from health insurance carriers in the absence of acute metabolic decompensation (i.e., DKA, HHNS, or hypoglycemia), outpatient care is the prevailing method of management. I recommend that DM 1 patients be seen at least every 2 months and that patients do a minimum of two blood glucoses per day (SGM), and, importantly, that they communicate with the health care team when repeated levels of hypoglycemia or hyperglycemia are experienced.

I particularly encourage patients to fax their glucose data to me so that I can advise them on proper adjustment of their insulin. In such cases, a quarterly visit may be adequate for a more stable patient. A similar schedule should also be followed for DM 2 patients, as these patients may need just as much behavior modification and support for their control of diet and weight as DM 1 patients require for their insulin, particularly in coordination with the nutritionist and mental health professionals (who are knowledgeable regarding diabetes). No therapy can substitute for a highly motivated patient, who is assured by a compassionate and knowledgeable health care provider team that help is available; the major responsibility for care, however, rests on

the shoulders of the patient. In general, I recommend that health care providers for patients with DM familiarize themselves with the American Diabetes practice recommendations, which are updated annually.[24]

Complications of Intensive Insulin Therapy—Hypoglycemia

This chapter has dealt with the day-to-day ambulatory management of patients with diabetes. Management of acute complications of diabetes, such as hypoglycemia, DKA and HHNS, has not been discussed but readers are referred to comprehensive reviews on this subject.[25-27]

Because hypoglycemia is becoming more frequent with the use of intensive insulin therapy, it should be emphasized that patients prone to hypoglycemia must carry on their person not only a MedicAlert identification, but also a glucagon injection kit and glucose tablets (or a tube of Write-A-Cake icing, which requires no refrigeration). The preferred method of therapy for hypoglycemia in an alert patient is a glass of milk, which provides longer-lasting euglycemia than a glass of orange juice or sugar cubes. Obviously an unconscious patient at home needs either parenteral administration of glucagon (subcutaneous or IM) or sugar paste on the gums (but not in the mouth) by another person prior to taking the patient to the emergency room, where IV glucose may be administered.

References and Selected Readings

1. Harris MI, Goldstein DE, Flegal KM, et al: Prevalence of diabetes, impaired fasting glucose and impaired glucose tolerance in U.S. adults: The third national health and nutrition examination survey, 1988–1994. *Diabetes Care* 21:518–524, 1998.
2. The Expert Committee on the Diagnosis and Classification of Diabetes Mellitus: Report on the diagnosis and classification of diabetes mellitus. *Diabetes Care* 20:1183–1197, 1997.
3. Kitabchi AE, Fisher JN: Diabetes mellitus, in Conn R (ed): *Current Diagnosis*. Philadelphia: WB Saunders 1991, pp 766–774.
4. American Diabetes Association: *Diabetes 1996 Vital Statistics*. Alexandria, VA: ADA, 1996.
5. National Institute of Diabetes and Digestive and Kidney Diseases: *Diabetes Statistics*. Bethesda, MD: NIDDK, 1995. NIH Publication H96-3926.
6. Harris MI: Undiagnosed NIDDM: Clinical and public health issues. *Diabetes Care* 16:642–652, 1993.
7. The American Diabetes Association: Economic consequences of diabetes mellitus in the U.S. in 1996. *Diabetes Care* 21:296–309, 1998.
8. The DCCT Research Group: The effect of intensive treatment of diabetes on the development and progression of long-term complications in insulin-dependent diabetes mellitus. *N Engl J Med* 329:977–986, 1993.
9. Ohkubo Y, Kishikawa H, Araki E, et al: Intensive insulin therapy prevents the progression of diabetic microvascular complications in Japanese patients with non-insulin-dependent diabetes mellitus: A randomized prospective 6-year study. *Diabetes Res Clin Pract* 28:103–117, 1995.
10. Kitabchi AE, et al: Diabetes mellitus, in Ling FW, Laube DW, Nolan TE, Smith RP, Stovall TG (eds): *Primary Care in Gynecology*. Baltimore: Williams & Wilkins, 1996 pp 279–298.
11. Morris LR, McGee JA, Kitabchi AE: Correlation between plasma and urine glucose in diabetes. *Ann Intern Med* 94:469–471, 1981.
12. Bunn HF: Glycosylated hemoglobins and diabetes mellitus. *Res Staff Physician* 12:53–57, 1978.
13. Lebovitz HE: Oral antidiabetic agents, in Kahn CR, Weir GC (eds): *Joslin's Diabetes Mellitus*. Philadelphia: Lea & Febiger 1994, pp 508–529.
14. Draeger E: Clinical profile of glimepiride. *Diabetes Res Clin Pract* 28:138–146, 1995.
15. Coniff RF, Shapiro JA, Seaton TB, Bray GA: Multicenter, placebo-controlled trial comparing acarbose (Bay g5421) with placebo, tolbutamide and tolbutamide plus acarbose in non-insulin-dependent diabetes mellitus. *Am J Med* 98:443–451, 1995.
16. Stumvoll M, Nurjhan N, Perriello G, Dailey G, Gerich JE: Metabolic effects of metformin in non-insulin-dependent diabetes mellitus. *N Engl J Med* 333:550–554, 1995.
17. DeFronzo R, et al: Efficacy of metformin in patients with NIDDM. *N Engl J Med* 333:541–549, 1995.
18. Inzucchi SE et al: Efficacy and metabolic effects of metformin and troglitazone in type II diabetes mellitus. *N Engl J Med* 338:867–872, 1998.
19. Saltiel AR, Olefsky JM: Thiazolidinediones in the treatment of insulin resistance and type II diabetes. *Diabetes* 45:1661–1669, 1996.
20. Nolan JJ, Ludvik B, Beersdsenp JM, Olefsky J: Improvement in impaired glucose tolerance and insulin

resistance in obese subjects treated with troglitazone. *N Engl J Med* 331:118–193, 1994.

21. Kitabchi AE, Bryer-Ash M: NIDDM: New aspects of management. *Hosp Pract* 32:135–164, 1997.

22. Shank ML, Del Prato SD, DeFronza RA: Bedtime insulin/daytime glipizide: Effective therapy for sulfonylurea failures in NIDDM. *Diabetes* 44:165–172, 1995.

23. Kitabchi AE, Duckworth WC, Stentz FB: Insulin synthesis, proinsulin and C-peptide, in Rifkin H and Porte D (eds): *Diabetes Mellitus,* 4th ed. New York: Elsevier Science, 1990 pp. 71–88.

24. American Diabetes Association Clinic Practice Recommendations: Gestational diabetes. *Diabetes Care* 21:S60–S61, 1998.

25. Kitabchi AE, Umpierrez GE, Murphy MB: Treatment of patients with diabetic ketoacidosis (DKA) or hyperglycemic hyperosmolar, nonketotic state (HHNS) in Rakel RE (ed): *Conn's Current Therapy,* Philadelphia: WB Saunders, 1999, pp 555–561.

26. Kitabchi AE, Fisher JN, Murphy MB, Rumbak MJ: Diabetes ketoacidosis and hyperglycemic hyperosmolar nonketotic state, in Kahn CR, Weir G, (eds): *Joslin's Diabetes Mellitus Textbook,* 13th ed. Philadelphia: Lea & Febiger, 1993, pp 738–770.

27. Pourmotabbed G, Kitabchi AE: Hyperglycemia, in Ling FW, Duff P (eds): *Obstetrics and Gynecology: Principles for Practice.* Stamford: Appletone & Lange (in press).

HIV Infection in Women

Howard Minkoff
Debra Eisenberger

EDUCATION AND PREVENTION
DIAGNOSIS OF HIV INFECTION
PRIMARY CARE OF HIV INFECTION
PREGNANCY AND THE HIV-POSITIVE WOMAN
GYNECOLOGIC CARE OF THE HIV-POSITIVE WOMAN
Candidiasis • Sexually Transmitted Diseases • Cervical Disease • Contraceptive Options for Seropositive Women

The World Health Organization estimates that by the year 2000 there will be 6 million HIV-infected pregnant women and 5 to 10 million infected children. Women accounted for over 40 percent of the 16,000 new HIV infections that occurred every day in 1997. AIDS is the third leading cause of death of reproductive-age women in the United States, and is the leading cause in many large cities. Children who acquire the virus do so, in the overwhelming majority of cases, via mother-to-child transmission. In the face of this epidemic, providers of health care to women will be called upon to perform several vital functions: educate their patients about prevention; diagnose and treat HIV infection; and provide obstetric and gynecologic care focused on the unique needs of HIV-infected women.

Education and Prevention

HIV is only one of a number of sexually transmitted diseases (STDs) that bring women to the attention of physicians. It is estimated that there are over 300 million STDs annually worldwide and approximately 13 million Americans will acquire an STD next year. The consequences of those diseases will range from infertility to death from AIDS. Because most women who see an obstetrician/gynecologist see no other provider in a given year, and because issues of sexual and reproductive health are part of the purview of these providers, obstetricians/gynecologists, as well as all other women's primary health care providers, have an obligation to be involved, in a routine manner, in emphasizing the prevention message. These efforts are especially important until an effective AIDS vaccine is developed.

To craft an optimal prevention method, a provider must have a basic understanding of the modes of transmission of HIV. Increasingly, women are acquiring HIV heterosexually, with the AIDS cases attributable to heterosexual contact rising by 146 percent between 1990 and 1994.[1] Intravenous drug use also continues to be a key vector for transmission. Heterosexual contact in the United States is intimately linked to intravenous drug use. Approximately an equal number of women acquire HIV from sharing needles and from sex. Many of the women who acquire the virus sexually do so from a drug-using partner. The reduction of risk to intravenous drug users through the adoption of needle exchange programs or the cleaning of needles (so-called "harm reduction") has been clearly demonstrated. These approaches reduce the incidence of HIV without increasing drug use.

Women's primary health care providers must

emphasize a safer sex message. Absolutely safe sex would involve abstinence or mutual monogamy with an uninfected partner. Bisexuals or intravenous drug users are examples of "high risk" partners. Realistically, however, it is unlikely that many women will know the HIV status of sexual partners and, particularly in high prevalence communities, any casually known partner poses a risk. Therefore, women have to rely on other safety techniques. Although noninsertive sex is also very safe, it is not widely accepted. Therefore, most safer sex strategies, to a greater or lesser extent, rely on condoms. The utility of condoms in the prevention of STDs, particularly HIV, has been widely heralded. The evidence for their efficacy comes from prostitute studies, discordant couple studies, and in vitro experiments. The latter have even demonstrated efficacy in the prevention of transmission of hepatitis B, which is a smaller virus than HIV. Most evidence of efficacy is limited to latex condoms, however, because natural skin condoms have much wider variation in pore size. The role of viricidal agents such as nonoxynol-9 has still not been resolved. Although they have the potential to inactivate a virus should a condom break, there is concern that chronic frequent usage could result in vaginal ulcerations. Recent evidence has not sustained the argument that regular use of nonoxynol is associated with lower rates of HIV seroconversion in high-risk women.

Diagnosis of HIV Infection

Serologic tests for antibody to HIV became accessible clinical tools in 1985. Given the limited treatment options available for the care of HIV-infected women and children in the early 1980s, the driving force behind testing at that time was to allow women to make informed reproductive choices. Shortly thereafter, however, researchers[2] demonstrated that serostatus did not substantively alter reproductive choice. Despite that fact, it was still believed that each woman had the right to all information germane to her individual decision and that HIV tests should be made available. The strategy utilized to provide access at that time was to selectively offer the test. Women who volunteered a history of "risk" behavior had the advantages and disadvantages of the test discussed at their prenatal visit. The failure of that approach to engage many women in the process of learning their serostatus soon became apparent. Several researchers compared HIV serosurveys with anonymously collected patient histories and found that a large percentage of infected individuals had not acknowledged any risk behaviors.[3] Apparently, because a history of intravenous drug use or sex with bisexual men was perceived to be stigmatizing, many women chose not to acknowledge those behaviors when the sole advantage was perceived to be access to a test.

In response to these reports, many clinicians, particularly those in high-prevalence communities, started to universally offer the test. As expected, it was then found that many women who at the time of pretest counseling acknowledged no risk, but whose test result confirmed an HIV infection, did indeed know their risk factor but had chosen not to discuss it until their serostatus had been established.[4]

As therapeutic interventions for both the mother and child were developed in the late 1980s, and advanced dramatically in the late 1990s, many clinicians came to believe that a nondirectional "offering" of the test was too passive a process. It was suggested that the imprimatur of the physician should be given to the test through the substitution of a "recommendation" for an "offer."[5]

It is currently recommended that all prenatal patients take an HIV test. There are clinicians who believe that the time has come to go even further. Some, who advocate either mandatory or "right of refusal" approaches to testing do so based on their belief that substantive medical advantage is available to children whose serostatus is known, and that children cannot speak for themselves and attain those advantages by opting to have an HIV test.[6] Consequently, there has been a debate between those who prioritize fetal/neonatal beneficence and those who champion

maternal autonomy. Current guidelines promulgated by the American College of Obstetricians and Gynecologists advocate testing but still strongly recommend that informed consent remain part of the pretest process. However, the field is evolving rapidly, in part due to evidence that the overwhelming number of neonatal infections can be prevented if the mother's serostatus is known. This knowledge has driven some states (e.g., New York) to mandate testing. Federal law is moving in a similar direction, with AIDS funding threatened in states that do not either demonstrate high testing rates or dropping neonatal infection rates and that do not institute mandatory testing.

The posttest counseling session for a seropositive woman should be planned before the woman arrives for her result.[7] In general, it can be anticipated that women will react to learning this diagnosis in much the same way that they have reacted to other stressful events in their lives. It is important to allow them sufficient time during the session to work through some of these initial reactions. The initial counseling session often lasts between 45 and 75 min.

The content of the counseling that a seropositive woman receives must be sufficient to assure an informed decision regarding reproductive choice. Information about the perinatal transmission of the virus, the consequence of pregnancy on the natural history of HIV disease, the natural history of pediatric HIV disease, and the therapeutic options for the woman should be described in lay language. If abortion is still an option, depending upon the woman's due date and the state's legal limit for abortion, it should be discussed. The woman's decision, whether or not she chooses abortion, should be supported and liaison with psychosocial supports should be established.

Primary Care of HIV Infection

The management of HIV infection has undergone dramatic changes in the last few years, holding the promise of substantive improvements in the quality and quantity of life for the infected individual. Thus, once a woman has been identified as HIV infected and has received appropriate counseling and emotional and social support, the physician must turn attention to a baseline medical evaluation of the patient.[8] A history and physical examination that includes mental status, fundoscopic, pelvic, genital, and rectal examination should be performed to ascertain the presence of any HIV-related stigmata.

Baseline laboratory studies should also allow the clinician to assess both the patient's susceptibility to infection (immune status, viral load studies) and any evidence of prevalent infections (e.g., syphilis). Therefore, a complete blood count, CD4 lymphocyte studies, viral load assessments, and serologic tests for syphilis, hepatitis B and C, and toxoplasma (even women chronically infected with *Toxoplasma gondii* can transmit it to their fetus in the setting of HIV[9]) should be obtained. The patient also needs a tuberculin skin test (PPD).

The laboratory results will inform decisions regarding preventive strategies such as the use of tuberculosis prophylaxis and *Pneumocystis carinii* pneumonia prophylaxis (generally instituted when the patient's CD4 count is $<200/mm^3$). Appropriate vaccinations with hepatitis vaccine, pneumonia vaccine, and influenza vaccine can be given as necessary. Any sexually transmitted diseases that are diagnosed should also be treated.

It is at this point that decisions regarding the use of antiretrovirals should be made.[10,11] Although there are only two classes of antiretrovirals (reverse transcriptase inhibitors—nucleosides and nonnucleosides—and protease inhibitors) there are an expanding number of agents available with many interactions between them. Although the paradigm of care can be briefly summarized—treat anyone with a viral load in the 5000 to 10,000 range and start treatment with a protease and two nucleosides—management of the HIV-infected individual is extremely complex and should be in the hands of an expert. Each regimen has its own set of side

effects and potential complications. For example, when a patient is placed on AZT the provider should be aware that the most common complications are anemia, thrombocytopenia, and granulocytopenia, all of which are generally reversible. Nausea, headache, myalgias, and myopathy are often reported, but may be transient. Patients should be followed with CBCs and serum chemistries. Several simple reviews are available to assist the clinician who wishes to contribute to the care of these patients.[11] Many aspects of care are still unsettled, such as the optimal second-line drugs to use when primary therapy has failed, and when and how to use phenotypic and genotypic studies of drug resistance.

A key part of the management of infected women is to assess their immune and viral status in an ongoing manner. CD4 counts can indicate where the patient is in the course of her disease, while viral loads may offer some sense of the rate of decline of their status. Both may be substantially altered by aggressive antiretroviral therapy. These tests should be performed at baseline, and then again after therapy has been instituted, in order to gauge the success of the regimen that has been instituted. Similarly, if the woman is pregnant, tests should be obtained several times during pregnancy and after the initiation of therapy in order to monitor the success of the treatment. One critically important determinant of the success of any regimen is adherence. Resistance to therapy develops rapidly in the setting of substandard therapy. Patients must be informed of the importance of strict compliance with their entire regimen, although these can be quite difficult to maintain. There is some preliminary evidence that some women may have a failure of therapy as defined by a rising viral load, but not have a concomitant drop in CD4 count. This may suggest that the viral mutation that allowed the virus to replicate in the setting of antiretroviral therapy has resulted in a less virulent strain of virus.

Although management of the protean infectious diseases that occur in the setting of HIV infection is well beyond the scope of this chapter and falls more appropriately within the purview of a specialist in infectious diseases, the primary care physician should be familiar with the manifestations of diseases that are clinically significant and that require consultation and/or referral. These complications can be broadly categorized into infectious, neoplastic, and neurologic.

Infectious complications range from local fungal infections (thrush, esophageal candidiasis) through a wide array of pulmonary, gastrointestinal, and other infections caused by parasites (*Pneumocystis carinii* pneumonia, *toxoplasma gondii,* cryptosporidium species), fungal organisms (*candida albicans, cryptococcus neoformans, histoplasma capsulatum*), bacterial organisms (mycobacterial infections, salmonella, *treponema pallidum*), and viruses (herpes simplex virus, cytomegalovirus, varicella zoster, human papilloma virus). These infections may present as pneumonia, watery diarrhea, or as neurologic impairment.

AIDS-defining neoplastic complications include Kaposi's sarcoma, B-cell lymphomas, and primary central nervous system lymphoma. In some other neoplasias, such as oral and anal squamous cell carcinoma and Hodgkin's disease, a link with AIDS has been suspected. Treatment of AIDS-associated neoplasia should be under the guidance of a hematologist/oncologist and be appropriate for the specific neoplasm.

Management of neurologic complications are extremely complex. Neurologic dysfunction in patients with AIDS may be a consequence of HIV infection of the central nervous system (AIDS dementia) or of toxic metabolic disorders. It may also result from infectious or neoplastic complications of AIDS.

Pregnancy and the HIV-Positive Woman

The "golden rule" for physicians caring for pregnant women with any medical complication is to provide optimal care in a fashion that is unmodi-

fied by gender or childbearing considerations, unless there is compelling evidence that such care poses an unacceptable risk to the fetus. If fetal risks are substantial, then the counsel of the mother is sought in order to best balance the maternal/fetal risks and benefits assoicated with an alternative approach. The same principle holds in the case of the HIV-infected woman. Even with the large number of medications now available for HIV-infected women, there are very few examples of HIV therapies that need to be modified because of pregnancy. Thus, the clinician's first responsibility is to assure that standard interventions are in place. One exception might be vaccinations. Some of these can be associated with a viremia that may pose a risk to the fetus should it occur during pregnancy. In addition, testing should be performed to detect sexually transmitted diseases such as syphilis, gonorrhea, and chlamydia. Tuberculosis should be ruled out, and baseline toxoplasmosis titers should be obtained.

As previously noted, the timing of initiation of many of the therapeutic agents used in the management of HIV infection is determined by an individual's CD4 count and viral load. These counts, therefore, must be followed closely during pregnancy. Although some component of the decline of CD4 counts during pregnancy may be attributable to pregnancy per se, it should not be assumed that the prognostic significance of a low count is less reliable than in nonpregnant populations. Similarly, viral loads do not appear to be influenced by trimester of pregnancy, and remain a reliable guide to the status of an individual's disease and response to therapy even in the setting of pregnancy.

Standard approaches to prophylaxis against *Pneumocystis carinii* pneumonia should be utilized during pregnancy. Women whose CD4 counts drop below 200/mm^3 should receive Bactrim therapy. Pentamidine is a useful second-line therapy for those intolerant of Bactrim. It has the advantage of less-frequent side effects and extremely low blood levels, though access to the aerosol form may not be readily available to all

women and its use can be associated with breakthrough. Bactrim is readily available and highly effective. Although adverse maternal reactions are common (most often rash), neonatal consequences have not been serious, and kernicterus has not been reported in settings in which sulfa derivatives were not also used during the neonatal period. The specific agent that is used is probably less important than that some therapy is prescribed during gestation.

As was previously mentioned, it is currently recommended that nonpregnant individuals whose viral loads are over 5000 to 10,000 copies/ml receive antiretroviral therapy. Some clinicians have even suggested that anyone with any detectable viral level should be started on therapy. Certain unique considerations have a bearing in regards to the use of antiretrovirals during pregnancy, including possible adverse fetal effects and potential beneficial effects on vertical transmission. Studies of teratogenicity in animals are, on the whole, reassuring, although one study reported that among rats exposed to zidovudine (ZDV) throughout their lives, approximately 10 percent of the female rats had nonmetastasizing vaginal tumors at the time of their deaths. Several factors may mitigate the significance of these findings. First, rats excrete ZDV and its metabolites in their urine whereas humans do not. Second, rats soil the vaginal vault with urine. Some concern has been raised, however, as a result of data reported from studies on mice performed at the National Cancer Institute. That report suggested that mice exposed to high-dose rates of AZT in the third trimester birthed pups that were subsequently found to have high rates of liver, lung, skin, and genitourinary tumors in midlife. Although other investigators have reported conflicting findings, the NCI data should chasten those who would dismiss all concerns regarding these therapies, and they reinforce the need for thorough counseling and long-term follow-up. In regard to monitoring of the mother on AZT, it is only necessary to measure the blood count on a monthly basis and assess liver functions intermittently. The

only abnormality that occurs with any frequency is anemia.

In 1994, the results of ACTG Protocol 076 were released. The results showed that a regimen of ZDV given during pregnancy and labor and to the newborn for 6 weeks resulted in a 70 percent reduction in transmission risk of HIV (from 25 percent in the placebo group to 8 percent in the ZDV group).[12] More recently, ACTG 185 demonstrated that similar results could be seen even among women who had previous exposure to AZT or who had CD4 counts below 200/mm³. The ZDV regimen from ACTG 076 is being successfully integrated into clinical practice in the United States and Europe, and is being accompanied by dramatic declines in perinatal transmission rates in these countries. The 076 regimen consists of AZT 100 mg 5 times a day (or 200 mg 3 times a day or 300 mg twice a day) in the antepartum period beginning after 14 weeks gestation. In the intrapartum period, a loading dose of 2 mg/kg over the first hour followed by a maintenance dose of 1 mg/kg/h thereafter is administered, and in the neonatal period the infant receives an AZT syrup for 6 weeks at a dose of 2 mg/kg every 6 h. Preliminary data regarding the safety of this regimen have been reassuring. More than 1000 children have been tracked for four years with no demonstrated increase in risks of neurodevelopmental delay or carcinogenesis.

The vast majority of perinatal HIV-1 infection occurs in the developing world. Unfortunately, the ACTG 076 ZDV regimen is too costly and logistically complex for many nonindustrialized countries to implement on a widespread scale, and its efficacy in a breast-feeding population is unknown. An ideal preventive intervention would be cheap, nontoxic to mother and fetus, easy to administer, only need to be given once or for a limited period of time, and have utility in preventing postpartum transmission. The results of ACTG 076 have spurred the worldwide evaluation of multiple other modalities to reduce transmission. Several studies are currently ongoing to determine whether more abbreviated, affordable regimens would have utility in countries

where costs make the utilization of the full regimen unrealistic. Recently, preliminary reports from Thailand have suggested that short-course therapy (treatment beginning at 36 weeks of gestation) can have a beneficial effect on rates of transmission.[13]

Other potential interventions to reduce transmission have focused on reduction of maternal viral load; enhancement of maternal and infant HIV-1-specific immune response; prophylaxis of the newborn; and attempts to reduce peripartum and postpartum exposure to the virus. The future challenge for researchers is to utilize the increasing understanding of the pathogenesis of perinatal HIV-1 transmission to design preventive regimens that will be applicable on a global basis.

Within the last year data have been presented that strongly suggest that *elective* cesarean section (no labor and no rupture of membranes) in conjunction with ZDV can reduce transmission to approximately 2 percent. Thus, in countries where the risks of surgery are not prohibitive, the routine use of elective cesarean section in conjunction with ZDV therapy should be considered.[14]

The possibility that fetal scalp electrodes and scalp clips can act as potential vectors of viral transmission continues to be raised. This concern is based upon the presence of virus that has been documented in the vaginal secretions and the prolonged contact that the fetus might have in the hours before birth, after the membranes have ruptured, with those viral particles. Some component of fetal protection at that point could be intact skin. Thus, piercing that skin to obtain a scalp blood sample, or placing an electrode into the skin, poses a theoretical risk of inoculating the fetus with virus. There are, however, scant empirical data that address this concern. Invasive procedures that breach the infant skin barrier could provide another mechanism for viral entry. In a large French cohort, invasive procedures (particularly amniocentesis and amnioscopy) were associated with increased transmission risk; other obstetric-related risk factors were premature membrane rupture, hemorrhage in labor,

and bloody amniotic fluid.[15] Other investigators have reported that infants who underwent the types of invasive procedures described above were no more likely to become infected than infants not so exposed, but the size of those cohorts were too small to have the requisite statistical power to rule out the level of risk generally associated with needle stick injuries. Thus, clinicians must continue to balance the theoretical risk of these procedures with the clinical benefit to be derived from their performance. In any event, "routine" use of invasive procedures should be avoided.

Given the demonstration that short courses of ZDV[13] and operative delivery can both play important roles in reducing the transmission rate of HIV, it is important to attempt to identify HIV-infected patients even if they have not been tested prior to labor.[16] There are new, rapid-testing modalities that are being introduced into clinical settings. It has been suggested that these tools may have a role in the intrapartum period for those patients who had no earlier opportunity to learn their serostatus.[16]

In the postpartum period, universal precautions should be extended to the neonate. Additionally, there is an ever-increasing body of evidence that breast-feeding can be associated with viral transmission and should be proscribed (in developed countries). Because new protocols for management of pediatric and adult HIV are constantly under development, appropriate referral of mother and child to physicians with expertise in the management of HIV disease should be made before their discharge from the hospital.

Gynecologic Care of the HIV-Positive Woman

Candidiasis

Clinicians were aware of an association between vaginal candidiasis and depressed immune function long before the HIV epidemic began. For example, it has been known for several decades that there is an increased prevalence of candidia-

sis associated with iatrogenic immunocompromise and with pregnancy.[17] The latter observation has led some investigators to suggest that women's high susceptibility to candidial overgrowth is related to elevated progesterone levels as is also observed in the luteal phase of the menstrual cycle.[18] Oral contraceptive use has also been linked to vaginal candidiasis. That interaction has been primarily attributed to the estrogen effects seen in oral contraceptive users.[19] Antibiotic use and diabetes are also known to predispose to vaginal moniliasis.[17] Even in the absence of predisposing factors, vaginal candidiasis is quite common, with up to 75 percent of all women having at least one episode of candidial vaginitis during their reproductive years.[17] Colonization, which may or may not be associated with clinical signs or symptoms, has been found in up to 25 percent of women.[17]

A woman's immunologic defense against *C. albicans* is primarily cell-mediated.[18] Because an increased frequency of vaginal candidiasis is found to accompany even the mild cell-mediated immunocompromise associated with pregnancy, it is not surprising that candidial infections have also been described in association with HIV infection. In fact, an association between candidial infections and both the stage and prognosis of HIV disease was noted in some of the earliest reports on HIV infections.[19]

The relationship between HIV and *Candida* among women in particular has been the subject of a growing body of research. In 1982, in one of the first reports on AIDS in women, Masur et al. reported oral or esophageal candidiasis in four of five patients with the syndrome.[20] In 1987, Rhoads and colleagues reported on chronic vaginal candidiasis in women with relatively advanced immunocompromise.[21] Among 29 women with HIV, 7 (24 percent) were found to have chronic recurrent vulvovaginal candidiasis. The severity of the infection in those women (symptoms and discharge for at least one year and requiring almost constant use of intravaginal antifungal agents for suppression) was more remarkable than the percentage infected. Of the

seven women with chronic vaginal candidiasis, six had severe depletion of CD4 cells, with counts below 100/mm³, and were diagnosed with AIDS. None of the HIV-positive women without mucocutaneous candidiasis developed AIDS over the study period.

More recently, a clinical continuum of candidiasis that is linked to progressive immunocompromise has been described.[22] Mean CD4 counts among women with vaginal candidiasis only were generally still in the normal range, while among women with thrush but not esophageal candidiasis average CD4 counts were 230/mm³. CD4 counts among women with esophageal candidiasis averaged 30/mm³. In another study of 97 HIV-infected women, vaginal candidiasis was present more commonly in the women with CD4 counts <100/mm³.[23] It is important to be aware that the rate of vulvovaginal candidiasis seen in HIV-infected women prior to immune compromise may not exceed the background level among HIV-negative women.

The precise frequency with which cutaneous candidial infections occur in HIV-infected women is still incompletely defined. The CDC has reported the results of their spectrum of disease project, which assessed the diagnosed manifestations of HIV infection among 7000 patients in the United States. In the study, 20 percent of women with CD4 counts of less than 500/mm³ reported candidiasis or chronic or recurrent candidial vulvovaginitis.[24] It has been speculated that the low rate of infections in that cohort, compared to others in the literature,[25] may be explained in part by the fact that medical facilities for HIV-infected women may not have provided gynecologic care. Women surveyed in the CDC study may therefore have had limited access to gynecologic care, or may have received their gynecologic care at sites that did not report data to the study.[26]

There have been increasing reports of non-*albicans* species that may be refractory to the azole therapeutics; these have been suggested as etiologic factors in recurrent candidiasis.[27,28] There is little information available about the prevalence of these yeast species among HIV-infected women, or whether they are linked to refractory disease.

Finally, although it has been suggested that women with vaginal candidiasis are appropriate candidates for HIV testing, the utility of that approach is questionable.[29] Recurrent vulvovaginal candidiasis occurs with some frequency in the HIV-seronegative population, making it an extremely nonspecific marker of HIV infection in low (HIV)-prevalence communities.

Management of vaginal candidiasis, at least in the early stages of HIV disease, isn't substantively different than it is for HIV-uninfected women. Although no therapeutic failure rates have been published, an initial attempt at topical therapy (e.g., clotrimazole, miconazole, terconazole, and boric acid vaginal suppositories [600 mg twice daily for two weeks]) would appear to be warranted for the symptomatic individual. Single-dose fluconazole for the treatment of acute vaginal candidiasis should be used sparingly because of reports of fluconazole resistance of HIV-infected patients.[30] It is reasonable to assume that among relatively immunocompetent women cure rates should not be markedly lower than that seen in seronegative women. When a women has recurrent or refractory disease, a variety of treatment options are available. If an oral agent is necessary, fluconazole is associated with fewer elevations of transaminases than ketoconazole. Long-term use may be associated with the development of resistance.[31]

Sexually Transmitted Diseases

Sexually transmitted diseases (STDs) have been clearly implicated in the transmission of HIV. Genital ulcer diseases (syphilis, chancroid, herpes simplex virus) are thought to increase the risk of both HIV acquisition and transmission, and non-ulcerative diseases, such as trichomonas, have also been implicated in the facilitation of viral transmission.

It has also been reported that the natural history of many sexually transmitted diseases may be modified by HIV infection. Disseminated or

chronic severe herpes infections, for example, have been reported in association with advanced HIV disease when immunosuppression is more marked.[32] Quinnan et al. summarized several studies that noted an increased prevalence and severity of herpes simplex (HSV) and herpes zoster in other immunosuppressed populations, such as those receiving bone marrow transplants.[33] In one of the first descriptions of HIV infection in women, researchers in Rhode Island found that among 200 HIV-positive women, 20 had chronic recurrent genital or generalized mucocutaneous herpes simplex. Severe genital herpes was more common in this group of women than had been observed in similar groups of men.[25] In prospectively followed cohorts, higher genital tract shedding rates of herpes simplex virus have been found among HIV-infected women who were HSV seropositive than among HIV-uninfected women who were HSV seropositive.[34]

Another study found that among HIV-infected patients, those with CD4 counts of $<50/mm^3$ had a significantly higher risk of HSV ulceration. Despite that observation, the authors did not recommend anti-HSV prophylaxis for patients with low CD4 counts, but did suggest appropriate empirical therapy when individuals presented with ulcers.[35] Other authors have also recommended that the indications for the use of suppressive acyclovir be the same for HIV seropositive patients as HIV seronegative patients.[36] An example of an indication for therapy is for individuals whose recurrences are very frequent (more than six per year). Restricting the use of suppressive acyclovir to such individuals might help limit acyclovir-resistant strains of HSV. Self-treatment with acyclovir is a common practice among patients with recurrent herpes. Whether such practice can contribute to the development of HSV resistance in HIV-infected patients has not been the subject of controlled trials.

Several authors have commented on interactions between syphilis and HIV. Coincident infection with the causative organisms of AIDS and syphilis is not unusual. In Baltimore STD clinics for example, 24.3 percent of patients with a reactive syphilis serology were HIV-infected compared to 3.5 percent of patients with a nonreactive test for syphilis. In heterosexual women without a history of intravenous drug use (IVDU), the risk of HIV was 6.8 times greater among those with a positive syphilis serology.[37] Additionally, syphilis may follow a more fulminant course among HIV-infected individuals, and the laboratory diagnosis may be more complicated with increased rates of both false-negative and false-positive reactions.[38] Syphilitic infection of the central nervous system, which usually occurs after years of infection, has been documented with primary syphilis in HIV-infected individuals. Johns et al. reported four cases of neurosyphilis in HIV-infected patients. They warned of an increased propensity of the disease to progress to neurosyphilis and a shortened latency before the onset of symptomatic neurosyphilis.[39]

In 1990, Musher, Hamill, and Baughn completed an extensive survey of the alterations in the course of syphilis in the presence of HIV.[40] They reported that some evidence of neurologic involvement, including asymptomatic CSF abnormalities and cranial nerve dysfunction, was noted in 39 of 40 patients with HIV and syphilis. Nonneurologic manifestations of syphilis (such as dermatologic, rheumatologic, or hepatic) were found to be no more severe in HIV-infected patients. (They did, however, report one study of prolonged skin rash in secondary syphilis in a small number of patients with HIV.) Musher and colleagues also raised the question of whether some cases of congenital syphilis in infants born to women who were reportedly treated for syphilis may have been related to HIV.[40]

Standard therapies for syphilis may not be ideal in the setting of HIV infection because of the increased risk of neurosyphilis (treatment failures have been reported for penicillin and ceftriaxone in HIV-positive patients with latent or asymptomatic neurosyphilis)[41] and because of the poor penetration of benzathine penicillin into cerebrospinal fluid. Treatment failure is difficult to document; CNS involvement may be present even with negative tests for *T. pallidum*. Other measures of CSF abnormality (alterations in glu-

cose, protein, cell counts) should lead to suspicion of neurologic involvement. Alternative therapies are higher dose and longer treatments with benzathine penicillin, daily injections of penicillin G for 14 days, amoxicillin with probenicid, or ceftriaxone.[42] Evaluation of cerebrospinal fluid for evidence of neurosyphilis is recommended in all HIV-infected individuals with positive treponemal tests.[43] If the cerebrospinal fluid is negative, treatment is with three intramuscular doses of benzathine penicillin, 2.4 million units weekly. If the cerebrospinal fluid is abnormal, the patient should receive intravenous aqueous penicillin, 2.4 million units every 4 h for 10 to 14 days.

Interpretation of serological tests for nontreponemal and treponemal antibodies must be made with caution. Biological false-positives [positive rapid plasma reagin (RPR) with negative fluorescent treponemal antibody absorption (FTA-ABS) tests] have been noted to be more common in those with HIV, although the phenomenon is relatively rare. Of 4863 patients in two STD clinics, 4 percent of HIV-positive patients had biological false-positive (BFP) reactions, as opposed to 0.8 percent of HIV-negative patients (odds ratio, 5.0; 95 percent confidence interval, 1.9 to 12.7).[44] HIV-infected patients with BFPs were also noted to have higher titers on their RPR.[45]

Another concern is that specific serologic tests for syphilis may become falsely negative in individuals with HIV infection.[46] Negative specific serology does not exclude a past history of syphilis infection in patients with AIDS. Ten percent of AIDS patients in one study showed negative FTA-ABS and treponema pallidum hemagglutination (TPHA) within three years after known syphilis infection. In the same study, a significantly greater proportion of HIV-infected patients showed decreasing titers of specific antibody, compared with HIV-negative controls.[46]

Haas and coworkers observed a decrease in TPHA-FTA with declining T cells in patients with a prior history of syphilis.[47] Similarly, loss of positive treponemal antibody has been found in patients previously infected with syphilis,

though none of these patients had a generalized loss of antibody (e.g., to toxoplasma and mumps.). The authors of this study report that serologic testing may miss patients with persistent syphilis infection.[48] Conversely, even with adequate treatment, RPR titers may not fall as expected.[40] Careful history-taking about exposure to and treatment of STDs and complete medical and sexual histories may reveal past infection in HIV-positive patients undetected by standard screening tests.

Very little data have been published on the course and response to therapy of *N. gonorrhoeae* and *Chlamydia trachomatis,* although there has been a suggestion of an altered presentation of disseminated gonoccocal disease.[49] The course of PID among HIV-infected women has been the subject of several reports. Given the similar etiology (sexual transmission) of HIV and PID, it is not surprising that the reported prevalence of HIV in a population of women with PID is higher than that among other women in the same community. In Brooklyn, the prevalence of HIV among women hospitalized with PID was 13 percent compared to 2 percent among women giving birth in the same hospital. In this population, in contrast to the two previous studies, there was a trend towards a higher rate of syphilis among HIV-positive women, though HIV seropositivity was not associated with a higher frequency of other STDs.[50]

It is less clear whether women coinfected with HIV have a different course of PID than seronegative women. Studies to date have been limited to in-patients and cannot address issues such as the relative likelihood of need for admission based on serostatus. Hoegesberg et al. reported in a small study that women admitted with PID were significantly less likely to have a leukocytosis if they were HIV seropositive. On admission, 40 percent of the HIV-positive patients and 89 percent of the HIV-seronegative women had a white blood cell count of $\geq 10,000/mm^3$ ($p < .001$). HIV-infected women were twice as likely to have a tubo-ovarian abscess and three times as likely to fail antibiotic therapy, although these

differences did not reach statistical significance. The microbiological etiology did not differ with serostatus, but the power of the study to detect such differences was limited by the small sample size.[50] Most subsequent evaluations have confirmed that HIV infection does not appear to have a dramatic effect on the course of PID. Currently, the CDC recommends that HIV-infected women who develop PID should be followed closely with early hospitalization and IV antibiotic therapy.[51]

Cervical Disease

Human papilloma virus (HPV)-associated cervical intraepithelial lesions have an increased frequency and severity among women who are immunocompromised. The *tat* gene of HIV is known to upregulate the E6 and E7 regions of HPV, regions that normally inhibit tumor-inactivating genes. Though this increased risk is widely reported, the magnitude of the risk varies greatly in the small case series and cohort studies published to date. The variability of the increased risk reported may be due to the unstable nature of estimates made using small numbers, or it may arise from geographical differences in risk of cervical neoplasia, differences in the risk for sexually transmitted infections among HIV-infected women (for example, HIV-infected prostitutes may be at higher risk for HPV than are HIV-infected intravenous drug-using women), and differences in disease stage among different groups of HIV-infected women (if women with more advanced disease are more likely to develop cervical dysplasia). Controlled studies have shown that the odds ratio of HIV-infected women having CIN are about five to six times greater than the odds of HIV-uninfected women.[52]

It has also been widely reported that the prevalence and severity of cervical dysplasia are linked to the degree of immune compromise, and hence is most notable among those with advanced HIV disease. Higher rates of dysplasia, for example, are seen in women with symptomatic HIV disease or AIDS, in women with low CD4 counts, or CD4/CD8 ratios less than 1.[53] An association of immunosuppression or symptomatic HIV disease with increased severity of cervical cytologic abnormalities is also suggested by the work of various investigators.[54]

HPV is etiologically linked to cervical dysplasia. Studies of HIV-infected women indicate that HPV infection is common, with some reports finding that one-third to one-half of women carried the virus.[55] Several comparative studies have been performed that have demonstrated an increased prevalence of HPV in women infected with HIV-1 or HIV-2.[55,56] Vermund et al. reported similar rates of HPV carriage in uninfected and immune-competent HIV-infected women, with a three- to fivefold increase in HPV infection associated with immune suppression.[56] The increase in HPV infection may arise from higher rates of HPV infection among HIV-infected women, or may be due to higher rates of expression, and therefore higher rates of detection, among immune-compromised HIV-infected women. Incidence rates have also been assessed and have been found to be higher among HIV infected women and, within a cohort of HIV-infected women, the rates are highest in the lowest strata of CD4 counts.[57]

The clinical course may be marked by more progression and less regression.[58,59] Maiman reported CIN recurrence rates of 39 percent and 9 percent ($p < .01$) in HIV-positive and HIV-negative women, respectively.[60] While other groups have also found that persistent or recurrent disease is more common among HIV-infected women,[61] still others have failed to detect increased rates of recurrence or progression after standard treatment,[62] or find higher recurrence rates for vulvar and vaginal condyloma only.[63] These differences may arise due to differences in degree of immunosuppression in the groups of HIV-infected women followed, or to differences in stage of cervical disease at time of treatment.

The adequacy of Papanicolaou smear screening in HIV-infected women remains controver-

sial. An early report by Maiman indicated that a high proportion of cervical pathology among 32 HIV-infected women was not detected on Papanicolaou smear.[64] In a similar study of 68 HIV-infected women, all of whom received Papanicolaou smears, colposcopy, and biopsy, the sensitivity of Papanicolaou smears relative to biopsy was 38 percent.[65] In an unpublished study of 300 HIV-infected women followed with Papanicolaou smears, colposcopy, and biopsy (as indicated by colposcopy), the sensitivity of Papanicolaou smears (with respect to biopsy) was 76 percent and the specificity was 95 percent.[66] Larger controlled studies have shown sensitivity and specificity rates for Papanicolaou smears similar to those reported for uninfected women.[67] At present, neither the CDC nor ACOG advocate routine colposcopy for HIV-infected women;[68,69] Papanicolaou smear screening at least once yearly is recommended. Colposcopic examination is warranted following a single Papanicolaou smear showing cytologic atypia.

Contraceptive Options for Seropositive Women

The fertility of women appears to be unaffected by HIV serostatus, at least until the latter stages of disease. For all other HIV-infected women, decisions regarding contraception need to be made on the basis of safety and effectiveness of the contraceptive method, and whether the health effects of the method may be influenced by HIV infection. The impact of the method on HIV infection, if such information becomes available, would be another important consideration.

Condoms Condoms have been widely recommended to avoid further HIV transmission, but when avoidance of pregnancy is a major concern, barrier methods alone may not confer optimal protection. Although condoms are highly effective for contraception if used consistently and correctly, some couples do not consider them an acceptable contraceptive choice. Supplemental methods may be indicated to assure effective contraception.

Although Goedert et al. found no evidence of accelerated progression to AIDS among seropositive couples who practiced unprotected intercourse,[70] the possibility that such behavior may introduce more virulent viral strains or, through antigenic stimulation, activate viral replication, cannot be ruled out. The use of condoms can also reduce the risk of secondary infections with other STDs.

Condom use should be urged for all HIV-positive individuals.

Hormonal Contraceptives Variation in humoral and cell-mediated immune activity related to gender has been reported. Although the natural history of HIV disease has not been demonstrated to vary with gender, any medication that affects immune status could theoretically contribute to a difference between women and men in disease progression. Gonadal steroids; adrenal glucocorticoids; pituitary hormones, including growth hormone and prolactin; thymic hormones; and factors elaborated by activated lymphocytes all influence immune function, with ovarian production of estrogen playing a central role.[71] Sex steroid-mediated immunodepression is also postulated to explain the immune system downregulation noted to occur during pregnancy, which may act to prevent rejection of developing fetal tissue.

Among oral contraceptive (OC) users, an absence of fluctuation in natural killer (NK) activity has been noted, but other studies have failed to demonstrate any effect on NK activity,[72] lymphocyte subpopulations,[73] or IgG and IgM levels.[74] However, a decrease in cell-mediated immunity, as represented by response to phytohemagglutinin associated with OC use, has been documented.[75]

Steroid hormone levels have been implicated in HIV disease progression. Mulder et al. have reported that decreased levels of dehydroepiandrosterone (DHEA), an adrenal steroid intermediary in estrogen and testosterone metabolism, may be a marker for impaired immune status

in asymptomatic HIV-infected men.[76] It has been proposed that this steroid may modify host-resistance mechanisms, in this case resulting in a protective effect.[77] The influence of DHEA and other steroid hormones on immune function in HIV-infected individuals is still being clarified, and it is not known how such influences change as a function of menstrual cycle or with pregnancy in HIV-infected women.

It is also unclear whether the effect of estrogen is to increase T-suppressor cell function, decrease T-helper or T-cytotoxic cell function, decrease some other cytotoxic lymphoid element, or produce a combination of the above effects. It seems that estrogen is immunoenhancing at low doses and immunosuppressive at higher doses.[78]

At present, the potentially multiple biological effects of steroid hormone-containing contraceptives remain incompletely understood. Possible mechanisms by which OC use might affect progression of HIV disease in seropositive women are inhibition of cell-mediated immunity, with possible simultaneous enhancement of susceptibility to opportunistic infections, and suppression of stimulation of CD4 cells, which may lead to decreased viral expression. The estrogen component of OCs may also be associated with a variety of perturbations of the immune system including decreased natural killer cell activity and neutrophil function, potentiation of the production of systemic antibody, and decreased local antibody responses.

Pending confirmed evidence of risk, there is at present no justification for modifying standard recommendation for the use of hormonal contraception in the setting of HIV infection. However, clinicians must be wary about the potential effects of proteases on the pharmacokinetics of oral contraceptives.

IUDs Because of concerns about increased risk of upper genital tract infections among IUD users, IUDs are not recommended for women at risk of STDs including HIV. Multiple concerns have been raised over their use among HIV-infected women. A theoretical risk of decreased efficacy due to reduced local inflammatory response among women with advanced immunosuppression has been raised. Anemia may be exacerbated by the increased menstrual blood flow associated with IUD use, and tailed IUDs may provide a route for ascending infection leading to PID that may be more severe in immunocompromised patients.

IUDs with progesterone may be more appropriate for seropositive women. A decrease in blood loss and duration of menstruation and thickening of cervical mucus were all noted in users of progesterone IUDs. However, the immunosuppressive effects of progesterone may pose another cause for concern, and could outweigh any benefit that may accrue from decreased incidence of ascending infections and anemia. Also, it may be undesirable to subject infected women to the increased frequency of procedures with their attendant risk of infection necessitated by the shorter duration of use permitted with hormonal IUDs. The IUD may also render a seropositive woman more infectious secondary to the increased volume and duration of menses and to any contribution which increased genital inflammation may make to transmission. There are, however, no data substantiating these hypothetical concerns.

Tubal Ligation Tubal ligation offers a very effective means of contraception, but may not be an option for all women due to its irreversible nature. The appropriateness of surgical sterilization should be assessed without excess focus on serostatus.

Summary

The last several years have borne witness to dramatic improvements in prognosis for the HIV-infected woman. To realize the potential advantages of the rich amalgam of new therapies, women need the assistance of their primary care providers. These women's care requires compassion, energy, and expertise. Providers must assist women in all stages of the illness; encouraging them to learn their status, minimizing gyneco-

logic disorders, preventing perinatal transmission of HIV, and maintaining their general health and well being. Despite the daunting nature of these challenges, no other aspect of medicine can, by requiring a total commitment of knowledge and concern, so thoroughly fulfill physicians' social, ethical, and medical obligation to their patients and their community.

References and Selected Readings

1. Fowler MG, Melnick SL, Mathieson BJ: Women and HIV: Epidemiology and global overview. *Obstet Gynecol Clin North Am* 24:705–730, 1997.

2. Selwyn PA, Carter RJ, Schoenbaum EE, Robertson VJ, Klein RS, Rogers MF: Knowledge of HIV antibody status and decisions to continue or terminate pregnancy among intravenous drug users. *JAMA* 261:3567–3571, 1989.

3. Landesman S, Minkoff HL, Holman S, McCalla S, Sijin O: Sero survey of human immunodeficiency virus infection in parturients. *JAMA* 258:2701–2703, 1987.

4. Minkoff HL, Landesman SH, Delke I, et al: Routinely offered prenatal HIV testing (letter). *N Engl J Med* 319:1018, 1988.

5. American College of Obstetricans and Gynecologists: Human Immunodeficiency Virus Infection. ACOG: 162:1–11, 1992. Technical Bulletin (revised).

6. Minkoff H, Willoughby A: Pediatric HIV disease, zidovudine in pregnancy and unblinding heelstick surveys: Reframing the debate on prenatal HIV testing. *JAMA* 274:1165–1168, 1995.

7. Holman S, Sunderland A, Brethard M: Counselling of the HIV infected pregnant woman. *Clin Obstet Gynecol* 32:486–491, 1989.

8. AIDS Institute, N.Y.S. Dept of Health: Criteria for the medical care of adults with HIV infection. (appendix) 1:109–111, 1993.

9. Minkoff H, Remington J, Holman S, Ramirez R, Goodwin S, Landesman S: Vertical transmission of toxoplasma by HIV-infected women. *Am J Obstet Gynecol* 176:555–559, 1997.

10. Minkoff H, Augenbraun M: Antiretroviral therapy of the pregnant women. *Am J Obstet Gynecol* 176:478–489, 1997.

11. Carpenter CCJ, Fischl MA, Hammer SM, et al: Antiretroviral therapy for HIV infection in 1998: Updated recommendations of the international AIDS society—USA panel. *JAMA* 280:78–86, 1998.

12. Connor EM, Sperling RS, Gelber R, et al: Reduction of maternal-infant transmission of human immunodeficiency virus type 1 with zidovudine treatment. *N Engl J Med* 331:1173–1180, 1994.

13. CDC: Administration of zidovudine during late pregnancy and delivery to prevent perinatal HIV transmission—Thailand 1996–1998. 48(8):151–154, 1998.

14. Mandlebrot L, Chenadec JL, Berrebi A, et al: Perinatal HIV-1 transmission: Interaction between zidovudine transmission and mode of delivery in the French perinatal cohort. *JAMA* 280:55–60, 1998.

15. Mandelbrot L, Mayauz M-J, Bongain A, et al: Obstetric factors and mother-to-child transmission of human immunodeficiency virus type 1: The French perinatal cohorts. *Am J Obstet Gynecol* 175:661–667, 1996.

16. Minkoff HL, O'Sullivan MJ: The case for rapid screening for HIV in labor. *JAMA* 279:1743–1744, 1998.

17. Hurley R, de Louvois J: Candida vaginitis. *Postgrad Med J* 55:645–647, 1979.

18. Witkin SS: Immunologic factors influencing susceptibility to recurrent candidal vaginitis. *Clin Obstet Gynecol* 34(3):662–668, 1991.

19. Roy S: Nonbarrier contraceptives and vaginitis and vaginosis. *Am J Obstet Gynecol* 165(4)[part 2]:1240–1244, 1991.

20. Masur H, Michelis MA, Wormser GP, et al: Opportunistic infections in previously healthy women: Initial mainifestations of a community-acquired cellular immunodeficiency. *Ann Intern Med* 97:533–539, 1982.

21. Rhoads JL, Wright C, Redfield RR, Burke DS: Chronic vaginal candidiasis in women with human immunodeficiency virus infection. *JAMA* 257(22):3105–3107, 1987.

22. Imam N, Carpenter CC, Mayer KH, Fisher A, Stein M, Danforth SB: Hierarchical pattern of mucosal candida infections in HIV-seropositive women. *Am J Med* 89(2):142–146, 1990.

23. Hawley P, Clayton D, Clayton A: *Correlation of CD4 counts in HIV serepositive women with and without vaginal candidiasis.* Amsterdam, the Netherlands, VIII International Conference on AIDS. 19-24 July. 1992. [abstract PoB3052].

24. Farizo KM, Buehler JW, Chamberland ME, et al: Spectrum of disease in persons with human immunodeficiency virus infection in the United States. *JAMA* 267(13):1798–1805, 1992.

25. Carpenter CCJ, Mayer KH, Stein MD, Leibman BD, Fisher A, Fiore TC: Human immunodeficiency virus infection in North American women: Experience with 200 cases and a review of the literature. *Medicine* (Baltimore) 70(5):307–325, 1991.

26. Farizo KM, Kelly JJ, Buehler JW, et al: Provision of gynecologic care at outpatient medical facilities serving HIV-infected persons. *J Womens Health* 1(3)193–196, 1992.

27. Just G, Streinheimer D, Schenellbach M, Bottinger C,

Helm EB, Stille W: Change of causative organisms under antifungal treatment in immunosuppressed patients with HIV-infections. *Mycoses* 32(Suppl)2:47–51, 1989.

28. Spinello A, Michelone G, Cavanna C, et al: Clinical and microbiologic characteristics of symptomatic vulvovaginal candidiasis in HIV-seropositive women. *Genitourin Med* 70:268–272, 1994.

29. Delhart DJ: HIV testing in women with vaginal candidiasis (letter). *AM J Med* 90:536, 1991.

30. Korn AP, Abercrombie PD: Gynecology and family planning care for the woman with HIV. *Obset Gynecol Clin North Am* 24:855–872, 1997.

31. Kutzer E, Oittner R, Leodolter S, Brammer KW: A comparison of fluconazole and ketoconazole in the oral treatment of vaginal candidiasis; Report of a double-blind multicenter trial. *Eur J Obstet Gynecol Reprod Biol* 29:305–313, 1988.

32. Seigal FP, Lopez C, Hammer GS, et al: Severe acquired immunodeficiency in male homosexuals manifested by chronic herpes simplex lesions. *N Engl J Med* 305:1439–1444, 1981.

33. Quinnan GV, Masur H, Rook AH, Armstrong G, et al: Herpesvirus infections in the acquired immune deficiency syndrome. *JAMA* 252:72–77, 1984.

34. Augenbraun M, Feldman J, Clarke L, DeHovitz J, Landesman S, Minkoff H: Increased genital shedding of herpes simplex virus type 2 in HIV-seropositive women. *Ann Intern Med* 123:845–847, 1995.

35. Bagdades EK, Pillay D, Squire SB, O'Neil C, Johnson MA, Griffiths PD: Relationship between herpes simplex virus ulceraton and CD4 cell counts in patients with HIV infection. AIDS 6:1317–1320, 1992.

36. Quinnan GV, Masur H, Rook AH, Armstrong G, et al: Herpes virus infections in the acquired immune deficiency syndrome. *JAMA* 252:72–77, 1984.

37. Quinn TC, Cannon RO, Glasser D, et al: The association of syphilis with risk of human immunodeficiency virus infection in patients attending sexually transmitted disease clinics. *Arch Intern Medicine* 150(6):1297–1302, 1990.

38. Augenbraum M, Minkoff H: Biologic false positive tests for syphilis in HIV-infected women. *Clin Infect Dis* 19:1040–1044, 1994.

39. Johns DR, Tierney M, Felsenstein D: Alteration in the natural history of neurosyphilis by concurrent infection with the human immunodeficiency virus. *N Engl J Med* 316(25):1569–1572, 1987.

40. Musher DM, Jammil RJ, Baughn RE: Effect of human immunodeficiency virus infection on the course of syphilis and on the response to treatment. *Ann Intern Med* 113(11):872–881, 1990.

41. Dowell ME, Ross PG, Musher DM, Cate TR, Baughn RE: Response of latent syphilis or neurosyphilis to ceftriaxone therapy in persons infected with human immunodeficiency virus. *Am J Med* 93:481–487, 1992.

42. Rolfs R, Gold M, Hackett K, et al: *Treatment of early syphilis in HIV-infected and uninfected patients: Preliminary report of the syphilis and HIV study group.* Presented at the IXth International Conference on AIDS. Berlin, 1993. Abstract PO-B111–1534.

43. El-Sadr W, Oleske JM, Aikens BD, et al: *Evaluation and management of HIV infection: Clinical practice guideline 7.* Rockville, MD: Agency for Health Care Policy and Research, Public Health Service, US Department of Health and Human Services, 1994, AHCPR publication no. 94-0572.

44. Rompalo AM, Cannon RO, Quinn TC, Hook EW III: Association of biologic false-positive reactions for syphilis with human immunodeficiency virus infection. *J Infect Dis* 165(6):1124–1126, 1992.

45. Glatt AE, Stoffer HR, Forlenza S, Alierie RH: High-titer positive nontreponemal tests with negative specific treponemal serology in patients with HIV infection and/or intravenous substance use. *J Acquir Immune Defic Syndr* 4(9):861–864, 1991.

46. Johnson PD, Graves SR, Stewart L, Warren R, Dwyer B, Luccas CR: Specific syphilis serologic tests may become negative in HIV infection. *AIDS* 5(4):419–423, 1991.

47. Haas JS, Bolan G, Larsen SA, Clemant MJ, Bacchetti P, Moss AR: Sensitivity of treponemal tests for detecting prior treated syphilis during human immunodeficiency virus infection. *J Infec Dis* 162(4):862–866, 1990.

48. Notenboom R, MacFadden DK: *Reliability of syphilis tests in patients with HIV.* Amsterdam, the Netherlands: VIII International Conference on AIDS. 1992 [abstract PoB3044].

49. Jacoby HM, Mady BJ: Acute gonoccocal sepsis in an HIV-infected woman. *Sex Trans Dis* 22:380–382, 1995.

50. Hoegsberg B, Abulafia O, Sedlis A, et al: Sexually transmitted diseases and human immunodeficiency virus infection among women with pelvic inflammatory disease. *Am J Obstet Gynecol* 163(4):1135–1139, 1990.

51. Centers for Disease Control: Pelvic inflammatory disease: Guidelines for prevention and management. *MMWR* 40:1–24, 1991.

52. Wright TC, Koulos J, Schnoll F, et al: Cervical intraepithelial neoplasia in women infected with the human immunodeficiency virus: Outcome after loop electrosurgical excision. *Gynecol Oncol* 55:253–258, 1995.

53. Mandelblatt JS, Fahs M, Garibaldi K, Senie RT, Peterson HB: Association between HIV infection and cervical neoplasia: Implications for clinical care of women at risk for both conditions. A review of 5 controlled studies comparing the association between HIV and CIN. *AIDS* 6:173–178, 1992.

54. Kreiss JK, Kiviat NB, Plummer FA, et al: Human immunodeficiency virus, human papillomavirus, and cervical intraepithelial neoplasia in Nairobi prostitutes. *Sex Transm Dis* 19:54–59, 1992.

55. Schafer A, Friedmann W, Mielke M, Schwartlander B, Koch MA: The increased frequency of cervical dysplasia-neoplasia in women infected with the human immunodeficiency virus is related to the degree of immunosuppression. *Am J Obstet Gynecol* 164:593–599, 1991.

56. Vermund ST, Kelly KF, Klein RS, et al: High risk of human papillomavirus infection and cervical squamous intraepithelial lesions among women with symptomatic human immunodeficiency virus infection. *Am J Obstet Gynecol* 165:392–400, 1991.

57. Minkoff H, Feldman J, DeHovitz J, Landesman S, Burke R: A longitudinal study of HPV carriage in HIV-infected and HIV-uninfected women. *Am J Obstet Gynecol* 178:982–986, 1998.

58. Anastos K, Dememberg R, Solomon L, Rein S: Relationship of CD4 cell counts to cervical cytologic abnormalities and gynecologic infections in 150 HIV-infected women. Amsterdam: Eighth International Conference on AIDS, 1992 [abstract TuB0532].

59. Fructer R Maiman M, Sillman FH, et al: Multiple recurrences of cervical intraepithelial neoplasia in women infected with the human immunodeficiency virus. *Am J Obstet Gynecol* 87:338–344, 1996.

60. Maiman M, Fructer R, Serur E, et al: Recurrent cervical intraepithelial neoplasia in HIV-seropositive women. *Obstet Gynecol* 82:170–174, 1993.

61. Williams A, Darragh T, Osmond D, Vranizan K, Moss AR, Palefsky J: Anal/cervical HPV infection and risk of anal/cervical dysplasia associated with HIV-1. Berlin: IX International Conference of AIDS, 1993 [abstract WSB175].

62. Feingold AR, Vermund SH, Burk RD, et al: Cervical cytologic abnormalities and papillomavirus in women infected with human immunodeficiency virus. *J Acquir Immune Defic Syndr* 3:896–903, 1990.

63. Kreiss JK, Kiviat NB, Plummer FA, et al: Human immunodeficiency virus, human papillomavirus, and cervical intraepithelial neoplasia in Nairobi prostitutes. *Sex Transm Dis* 19:54–59, 1992.

64. Palefsky J, Holly EA, Ahn DK: Progression of anal cytologic changes in men with group IV HIV disease. Berlin: IX International Conference on AIDS, 1993 [abstract WSB176].

65. Schwartz LB, Carcangiu ML, Bradham L, Schwartz PE: Rapidly progressive squamous cell carcinoma of the cervix coexisting with human immunodeficiency virus infection: Clinical opinion. *Gynecol Oncol* 41:255–258, 1991.

66. Relliham MA, Dooley DP, Burke TW, Berkand ME, Langfield RN: Rapidly progressing cervical cancer in a patient with human immunodeficiency virus infection. *Gynecol Oncol* 36:435–443, 1990.

67. Wright T, Chaisson MA, Ellerbrock T: Cervical intraepithelial neoplasia in women infected with HIV: Prevalence, risk factors and validity of Papanicoloau smears. *Obstet Gynecol* 84:591–597, 1994.

68. Conti M, Agaopssi A, Muggiasca M, et al: High progression rate of HPV and CIN in HIV-infected women. Amsterdam: Eighth International Conference on AIDS, 1992 [abstract PoB3050].

69. Rogo KO, Kavoo-Linge: Human immunodeficiency virus prevalence among cervical cancer patients. *Gynecol Oncol* 37:87–92, 1990.

70. Goedert JJ, Eyster ME, Biggar RJ, Blattner WA: Heterosexual transmission of human immunodeficiency virus: Association with severe depletion of T-helper lymphocytes in men with hemophilia. *AIDS Res Hum Retroviruses* 3:355–361, 1987.

71. Grossman C: Possible underlying mechanisms of sexual dimorphism in the immune response, fact and hypothesis. *J Steroid Biochem Mol Biol* 34:241–251, 1989.

72. Baker DA, Salvatore W, Milch PO: Effect of low-dose oral contraceptives on natural killer cell activity. *Contraception* 39:119–124, 1989.

73. Baker DA, Hameed C, Tejani N, et al: Lymphocyte subsets in women on low-dose oral contraceptives. *Contraception* 32:377–382, 1985.

74. Bisset LR, Griffin JFT: Humoral immunity in oral contraceptive users: I. Plasma immunoglobulin levels. *Contraception* 38:567–572, 1988.

75. Barnes EW, Loudon NB, MacCuish AC, Jordan J, Irvine WJ: Phytohaemagglutinin-induced lymphocyte transformation and circulating autoantibodies in women taking oral contraceptives. *Lancet* i:898–900, 1974.

76. Mulder JW, Jos Frissen PH, Krijnen P, et al: Dehydroepiandrosterone as predictor for progression to AIDS in asymptomatic human immunodeficiency virus-infected men. *J Infect Dis* 165:413–418, 1992.

77. Ben-Nathan D, Lachmi B, Lustig S, Feuerstein G: Protection by dehydroepiandrosterone in mice infected with viral encephalitis. *Arch Virol* 120:263–271, 1991.

78. Grossman CJ: Interactions between the gonadal steroids and the immune system. *Science* 227:257–261, 1985.

Other Infectious Diseases

Eileen Hilton
Leonard Rossoff

The Approach to the Febrile Patient

The approach to the febrile patient must begin with a thorough history and physical examination. An assessment should be made of how long the fever has been present, the maximum daily temperature spike and its timing, the presence of chills and rigors, and possible precipitating factors. The patient should be questioned regarding possible exposure to illness in others, foreign travel, and unexplained weight loss. Is there abdominal pain, nausea, vomiting, or diarrhea? If diarrhea is present, is it bloody, mucous, or watery? Has the patient taken antibiotics? If so, did they have any effect on the fever or the symptoms? Is there a cough, and is it productive? Does the patient report dysuria, hematuria, foul-smelling urine, urinary frequency, or urgency? A thorough reproductive health history, including a sexual history, is important. Has the woman had a prior sexually transmitted infection (STI)? Is there a possible recent exposure to an STI? Is the woman currently pregnant, or has there been a recent pregnancy? What is the most recent result of tuberculosis skin testing? Does the patient's household include pets? If so, are they healthy?

On physical examination, the skin should be carefully evaluated for rashes. Subconjunctival petechiae may be seen associated with endocarditis. The ethmoid, maxillary, and frontal sinuses should be palpated to identify the presence of tenderness or warmth. A pharyngeal examination should note the presence of exudates or vesicular lesions. Bulging of the tympanic membrane and redness of the canal should be noted on examination of the ear. The neck should be evaluated for stiffness, especially in the presence of headache. A careful lymph node examination should be performed. It is helpful to have the patient raise and slowly lower her arms while the examiner palpates for axillary nodes.

On lung examination, the apices should be auscultated anteriorly and above the clavicles. The right middle lobe is often overlooked on physical examination; one should also auscultate anteriorly and to the side of the breast. Auscultation of murmurs, especially those with a diastolic component, may suggest a diagnosis of endocarditis.

Complete abdominal and pelvic examinations are essential. Palpation of the spleen should be done with the patient lying on her right side; the examiner's hand should be placed below the edge of the rib cage. The patient should be asked to inhale deeply while the examiner feels for the spleen tip. On pelvic examination is there discharge from the cervical os, tenderness on cervical motion, or the presence of a pelvic mass?

Splinter hemorrhages under the fingernails should be viewed using a flashlight shining through the tip of the fingers. This enables the examiner to differentiate between superficial nail markings and signs of embolic phenomena. Unequal pulses are also suggestive of embolic episodes.

Differential Diagnosis and Evaluation of the Febrile Patient (Table 69-1)

Acute Fever

The differential diagnosis of the febrile patient includes infectious and noninfectious inflammatory diseases such as rheumatologic and granulomatous diseases (e.g., sarcoid and inflammatory bowel disease). It also includes malignancy, especially lymphomas and leukemias. Infectious causes of fever fall into two categories: prolonged or acute. Acute fever lasts for less than two or three weeks in duration and, in most cases, an extensive workup is not necessary as infection is usually the culprit. If the cause is viral, myalgias and sore throat are prominent as is a recent exposure to another individual with a "viral syndrome." In evaluating an acute bacterial infection, common etiologies include sinusitis, pharyngitis, cellulitis, lower respiratory tract, gynecologic, and urinary tract infections.

Chronic Fever

If a fever persists for longer than 3 weeks with no obvious source, it falls under the category of fever of unknown origin (FUO). In the past, infection accounted for about a third of all FUOs. With the increased empiric use of antibiotics, this percentage appears to be decreasing. The most common infectious causes of FUO include abscesses and infections of the kidney, bone, and heart valves. Human immunodeficiency virus (HIV) infection has led to an increase in tuberculosis as a cause of FUO. Viruses, such as Epstein-Barr and cytomegalovirus, may cause prolonged fever. If no evidence of infection is found, investigation for a noninfectious inflammatory disease, such as a vasculitis or mixed connective tissue disorder or neoplasm, should be considered.

Laboratory Studies

Initial blood tests should include a CBC, platelet count, and manual differential. An atypical lymphocytosis suggests a viral illness and a left shift suggests a bacterial infection. Anemia may be associated with more chronic infections. The value of the erythrocyte sedimentation rate (ESR) is underrated. It can be useful in the evaluation of a fever of unknown origin, because a viral illness is more likely to present with a normal and a bacterial infection with an elevated ESR. A sedimentation rate over 100 suggests a very long-standing infection, such as endocarditis, occult abscess, osteomyelitis, or a collagen vascular disease. Abnormalities in blood chemistries and liver function tests may provide clues as to the site of infection. If liver tests are abnormal and there is no other obvious etiology of the fever, imaging studies (CT scan, sonography, and HIDA) may reveal the source. Rheumatologic disorders are initially evaluated with an ANA and rheumatoid factor.

Blood cultures should always be obtained from a patient with prolonged fever. No more than six should be obtained. All blood cultures should be obtained with sterile skin preparation from different venipuncture sites. Any site that ap-

TABLE 69-1   Some Causes of Persistent Fever

Etiology	Diagnostic Aid
Infectious-inflammatory	
Abdominal	
Cholecystitis	
Cholangitis	HIDA, ultrasound
Abscess	
Diverticulitis	CT scan, MRI, gallium scan, In-labeled WBC scan
Appendicitis	
Genitourinary	
Pelvic inflammatory disease (PID)	Culture, ultrasound, CT, MRI, laparoscopy
Urinary tract infection (UTI)	
Intravascular	
Endocarditis	
Indwelling catheter	Blood cultures, echocardiogram
Other	
Sinusitis	Sinus films, CT scan
Osteomyelitis	Bone scan
Granulomatous	
Mycobacteria (typical/atypical)	Culture
Fungal	Biopsy
Nonbacterial	
Viral (Hepatitis, CMV)	
Rickettsial	
Chlamydial	Serology, culture, smear
Parasitic (amebiasis)	
Spirochetal (lyme, syphilis)	
Neoplasm	
Lymphoma	
Solid tumor (Renal cell, Hepatoma)	
Disorders of thermoregulation	
Brain tumor	
Stroke	
Encephalitis	
Seizure	
Heatstroke	
Malignant hyperthermia	
Miscellaneous	
Sacoidosis	ACE, biopsy
Inflammatory bowel disease	Endoscopy, biopsy
Drug reaction	
Radiation	
Thyroiditis	Thyroid function tests, scan
Hemolysis	Blood smear, serum haptoglobin/hemoglobin

pears inflamed or infected should be cultured. If the patient complains of a chronic cough, sputum cultures for pathogens should be taken. Sputum may be induced with a bronchodilator or nebulized 0.45% saline. If there is any history of tuberculosis exposure, early morning sputum for mycobacterial culture should be obtained on three consecutive days. An initial Gram stain is important to evaluate the presence of inflammatory cells and a predominant organism. All patients

with a fever of unknown origin should have a urine analysis and culture. Cultures of other areas should be based on history and symptoms.

Serological testing is used for the evaluation of viral illnesses such as Epstein-Barr virus, cytomegalovirus, and hepatitis infections. Occasionally, it may be useful for the diagnosis of a fungal illness such as coccidiomycosis.

Skin Testing

It is important to test for a positive reaction to a tuberculin skin test in patients with prolonged fever. Patients may be anergic in the face of overwhelming tuberculosis, malnutrition, and the immunocompromising states. Therefore, anergy testing using several immunoantigens such as *Candida*, streptokinase, and tetanus toxoid should be placed to assess cell-mediated immunity. The interpretation of a positive PPD is described in Table 69-2. The influence of a previous bacillus Calmette-Guérin (BCG) inoculation should be discounted.

Other Diagnostic Studies

A chest x-ray should be performed on all patients with a fever of unknown origin. Sinus and pa-

norex dental films may be useful if sinus or dental infection is suspected. Sonography is useful for suspicion of renal, biliary, retroperitoneal, and pelvic infections. In the evaluation for endocarditis, a transesophageal echocardiogram may reveal valvular lesions. CT scans are frequently helpful, especially in evaluating the retroperitoneum. MRI is most useful for evaluating soft tissue, brain, bones, and joints. Nuclear scans are occasionally useful. Technetium bone scans may show areas of osteomyelitis. Gallium scans are usually nonspecific, but may be useful in AIDS patients with pneumocystis pneumonia who present with a normal chest x-ray, and cough or hypoxemia. Gallium will also concentrate in the lung in interstitial pneumonitis. Indium-111-labeled leukocyte scanning has been found to be helpful in the diagnosis of abscesses.

Biopsies

Biopsies are recommended when less invasive testing has not revealed the diagnosis. If liver abnormalities are present, a biopsy of the liver might be indicated. Enlarged lymph nodes should be biopsied if other investigations are unrevealing. Bone marrow biopsy may clarify causes of anemia or reveal the presence of granulomatous disease. A needle biopsy aspiration of a suspicious area or collection guided by sonography, CT scan, or fluoroscopy may also be indicated. In patients unable to undergo surgery, drainage may be effected by percutaneously placed catheters. All biopsies should be sent for culture in addition to histology.

Empiric Therapy

In the absence of a clear source of infection, empiric trials of broad-spectrum antibiotics may be introduced. This may lead to confusion as patients may defervesce, leaving the clinician unsure about how long to continue treatment. Additionally, toxicities may be associated with antibiotics. If antibiotics fail, a course of antitu-

TABLE 69-2 Interpretation of a *Positive PPD*

5 mm is considered positive in a patient under these circumstances:
  Recent contact with infectious person
  CXR consistent with "old TB"
  Known or suspected HIV

10 mm is considered positive in a patient under these circumstances:
  Risk factor for TB
  Foreign-born in high-prevalence area
  High-risk population (African-American, Hispanic, Native American)
  Intravenous drug abuser
  High-prevalence locality

15 mm is considered positive in a patient under these circumstances:
  Anybody

berculosis therapy may be instituted while awaiting results of cultures.

Empiric corticosteroid therapy for presumed vasculitis or collagen vascular disease should be withheld unless the index of suspicion is very high. In many of these diseases, corticosteroids are not sufficient therapy and long-term immuno-suppressive drugs are required. The diagnosis should therefore be supported by suggestive serologic and histologic findings on the biopsy of an involved organ.

Common Infections

Upper Respiratory Tract Infections

A problem frequently seen in office practice is the upper respiratory tract infection. It usually begins with a feeling of malaise, sore throat, and myalgias. Cough may ensue, and the quality of the cough should be elucidated. By far the most common cause of upper respiratory tract infection is viral. The time of year and knowledge regarding community outbreaks may aid in the diagnosis. Occasionally, even after initial improvement, a bacterial superinfection may intervene with high fever and purulent nasal discharge and sputum. If a viral infection is probable, symptomatic therapy with decongestants may be given, but antipyretics should be avoided. Initial use of an antibiotic should be avoided to prevent unnecessary drug side effects and to diminish the development of resistant organisms in the community. If constitutional symptoms worsen and the sputum becomes purulent, the patient should be instructed to call back for additional investigation or empiric antibiotic prescription.

The therapy for superinfection of an upper respiratory tract infection may include erythromycin, a macrolide, or one of the respiratory quinolones. The optimal approach, which may be impractical, includes a Gram stain and culture of purulent fluids with treatment tailored to the pathogens recovered. In general, the macrolides or respiratory quinolones will cover most infections of the upper respiratory tract, including sinusitis, otitis, and pharyngitis. A failure to respond to empiric therapy should result in a determined effort to culture for specific pathogens.

Sinusitis

If in the course of an upper respiratory tract infection there is sinus pain and purulent discharge from the nostrils, a bacterial sinusitis should be considered and, if present, treated. However, persistent rhinitis and sinusitis are frequently allergic in etiology. If this is the case, there is no benefit to be derived from antibiotic therapy. The use of expensive imaging testing, such as a CT scan of the sinuses, should be reserved for patients with a persistent febrile course and sinus complaints.

Lower Respiratory Tract Infections (Table 69-3)

A frequent complaint of patients seen in office practice is cough. Symptoms of a lower respiratory tract infection with clinical or radiographic evidence of consolidation are labeled "pneumonia." If these findings are absent, particularly in a smoker, they are referred to as a "bronchitis," which may be acute or chronic. Thus, the critical determinant of the diagnosis of a pneumonia is the finding of a new or progressive infiltrate on chest radiograph. Other major findings are cough, sputum production, and an oral temperature exceeding 100°F. Less-frequent minor criteria include pleuritic pain, dyspnea, change in mental status, pulmonary consolidation, and a leukocytosis.

Any complaint of cough or pleurisy should prompt a detailed physical examination. There may be dullness on percussion (pneumonia or effusion) and tactile or auditory fremitus may be increased (pneumonia) or decreased (pleurisy). Fremitus should be tested with a resonant phrase such as "99" or "toy boat." The finding of crackles (rales, crepitations), tubular ("bronchial") breath sounds, and egophony or whispered pectoriloquy strongly support the diagnosis of

TABLE 69-3 Community-Acquired Typical and Atypical Pneumonia

	Typical	Atypical
Organism	Bacterial	Nonbacterial (viral, mycoplasma, chlamydia, legionella)
Onset	Abrupt	Insidious
Cough	Productive	Nonproductive
Sputum	Purulent	Scant, mucoid
Tachycardia	Frequent	Occasional
Gram stain	Polys and bacteria	Polys
Chest x-ray	Focal infiltrate Pleural effusion common	Diffuse infiltrate
Treatment: po	Penicillin, erythromycin, cefaclor	Erythromycin, doxycycline, clarithromycin, levofloxacin
Treatment: IV	Cefuroxime, penicillin, ampicillin-sulbactam, trimethoprim sulfate	Erythromycin, doxycycline, levofloxacin

pneumonia. Egophony represents the change in sound harmonics with transmission through consolidation; that is, an "EEE" to a bleating "AAA" sound. Whispered pectoriloquy refers to the clear transmission to the stethoscope of a whispered phrase such as "1-2-3."

Community-Acquired Pneumonia Despite the availability of a wide variety of antibiotics, pneumonia remains the sixth leading cause of death in the United States. There are over 4 million cases reported each year, with almost 1 million patients hospitalized.

A distinction is frequently made between a *typical* versus *atypical* presentation. A typical pneumonia is considered to be abrupt in onset, with severe constitutional complaints (high fever and rigors) and a cough productive of purulent mucoid sputum. There is more likely to be evidence of pulmonary consolidation on the physical examination. The Gram stain should have abundant bacteria, the white blood count is usually elevated with a left shift, and the chest radiograph reveals evidence of lobar consolidation. An atypical pneumonia is frequently described as subacute in onset with lower grade temperature, less severe constitutional complaints, and a nonproductive cough. The Gram stain may

have many white cells but rare bacteria, and the white blood cell count may be normal. Subtle and patchy infiltrates are seen on chest radiograph.

In the elderly, the presentation of the most common cause of pneumonia, pneumococcus, is frequently misleading. Fever, cough, and sputum production are often absent and leukocytosis is less common than in the younger patient. The presenting symptoms are malaise, dizziness, stupor, or other change in mental status. Radiographic evidence may be the first clue, and even then may be obscured by underlying pulmonary edema or chronic obstructive pulmonary disease (COPD). If evidence of a lower respiratory tract infection is lacking and cough persists, other causes should be considered. These include postnasal drip, "cough-equivalent" mild asthma, chronic bronchitis, gastroesophageal reflux, or even an occult lung malignancy.

There are no definitive guidelines regarding when to hospitalize a patient with pneumonia. Morbidity increases over age 65. Ninety percent of all reported pneumonia deaths occur in patients over this age. Other considerations include the presence of coexisting illness such as COPD, diabetes, congestive heart failure, chronic alco-

hol abuse, and malnutrition. Suspicion of swallowing disorders and aspiration, as well as alterations in immune status, should also be evaluated. If review of the chest radiograph shows more than two lobes involved, evidence of cavitation, or a pleural effusion, the risk of morbidity and mortality is higher. Significant leukocytosis ($>30 \times 10^9$/liter) or leukopenia ($<4 \times 10^9$/liter), or significant hypoxemia or hypercarbia should also prompt hospitalization.

Acute Bacterial Exacerbations of Chronic Bronchitis Forty-five million Americans smoke, and about 14 million are diagnosed with COPD; 12.5 million have clinical chronic bronchitis, and the rest have emphysema. In some populations, chronic bronchitis accounts for up to 20 percent of all physician contacts and 12 percent of all hospitalizations. Acute exacerbations of COPD may have a wide variety of causes, both infectious and noninfectious. Colonization of the tracheobronchial tree is common, often making cultures unreliable for identifying true pathogens. Bacterial infections may be acute or chronic, and the use of antibiotic therapy has been controversial. An exacerbation is defined as an increase in dyspnea, sputum volume, and purulence superimposed on evidence of chronic bronchitis. Recent studies have suggested potential benefits of antimicrobial therapy for acute bacterial exacerbations of chronic bronchitis. Short-term benefits may include a reduction in duration of symptoms, avoidance of hospitalization, earlier return to work, and possible prevention of progression to pneumonia. Putative long-term benefits of antibiotic therapy include prolongation of time between exacerbations and prevention of progressive airway damage.

Treatment of Lower Respiratory Tract Infection In the outpatient setting, a Gram stain and culture are not generally performed, and the clinical presentation is usually not diagnostic in distinguishing typical from atypical infection. Initial therapy is empiric, based on the knowledge of the prevalence of particular pathogens in the community. If patients are to be treated in an ambulatory setting, they must be able to take oral medications. If intravenous antibiotics are required, those with a bioequivalent oral form are most desirable. Increasingly, the attempt is to aim for early conversion to oral therapy as soon as the patient stabilizes (usually by days 2 to 4 of hospitalization).

In patients without comorbid illness who are under 60 years of age, the usual pathogens are *S. pneumoniae, M. pneumoniae, C. pneumoniae,* and *H. influenzae.* Recent studies using a variety of serological and other techniques suggest that atypical organisms represent a much larger proportion of these infections. In those patients who are older than 60 with coexisting illness, the organisms are much the same, but the relative frequency changes with more pneumococcus and gram-negative bacilli.

The microbiology of acute bacterial exacerbations of chronic bronchitis includes *Haemophilus influenzae, Haemophilus parainfluenzae, Streptococcus pneumoniae* and, increasingly, *Moraxella catarrhalis.*

Election of initial empiric therapy must take into account the age of the patient, suspected pathogens, history of drug allergies, comorbidities, and local resistance patterns. If pneumococcus is the most likely pathogen, penicillin remains the drug of choice. Increasingly, macrolides and the newer fluoroquinolones are being used as first line drugs for community-acquired pneumonia. The macrolides and fluoroquinolones are effective against the atypical organisms as well as pneumococcus.

Patients at high risk for lower respiratory tract infections should receive pneumococcal and seasonal influenza vaccines.

Tuberculosis

Tuberculosis is once again a major health problem in the United States. Patients with chronic cough, unexplained fever, weight loss, anemia, or other signs of chronic illness should be investigated for the possibility of primary or reactivation tuberculosis. This organism, the "great masquerader," may infect one or multiple body sites.

The lung is the most frequently involved in reactivation, usually the upper lobes, and frequently with a background of chronic changes (calcifications, scarring) suggesting the old infection.

New or "primary" TB is difficult to distinguish from other lower respiratory tract infections. The diagnosis rests on clinical suspicion and a positive stain for acid-fast organisms in the sputum. The ability to culture and type tuberculous organisms is rapidly improving. Sputum collections for this purpose should be obtained in the morning on three separate days.

TB Prophylaxis The healthy PPD converter should be viewed as infected with the tuberculosis bacillus. The risk of active TB developing in household contacts and new converters is 3 percent during the first year and 0.5 percent each year thereafter. If there are children in the household, immediate chemoprophylaxis should be instituted regardless of the results of the skin test. The test should be repeated in three months. If the skin test is negative, therapy may be discontinued. When evaluating the patient with a positive PPD, do the following: a careful exposure history, physical examination, CXR (PA and lateral), urine analysis, and serum and liver chemistries. If the urinalysis is abnormal, obtain urine for TB culture. If there are no signs of active infection, and conversion is suspected to have occurred within the last three or so years, therapy with INH for 6 to 9 months is advised. HIV-infected patients should be treated for a minimum of 1 year.

Patients should be followed at least bimonthly for evaluation of INH toxicity. At these visits, symptoms of abdominal discomfort, nausea, change in the color of the stool or urine, fevers or rashes, and signs of jaundice or liver tenderness should be elicited. The utility of routine liver function testing is controversial. Mild elevations in liver function tests should not discourage therapy, and most experts would not discontinue INH until liver enzymes rise to three times baseline. The risk of INH hepatitis increases with age and some choose not to use prophylaxis in patients over the age of 45 if the timing of PPD conversion is unclear. However, if conversion occurred within the last year, INH prophylaxis should be instituted at any age.

If a patient has a known exposure to a multiresistant strain of TB, there is no consensus as to the best form of prophylaxis and consultation with a local expert should be sought.

Therapy for Active TB Shorter course antituberculous regimens have proven effective. Infection with a resistant strain should prompt consultation with a specialist, because multiple second-line drugs of higher toxicity are likely to be used and the duration of therapy prolonged.

The routine short course treatment of a sensitive strain includes INH, rifampin, and pyrazinamide (Table 69-4). The pyrazinamide is given for the first two months then discontinued; the INH and rifampin are continued for a total of 6 to 9 months. Some clinicians continue with pyrazinamide until sputum is AFB-smear negative. All patients should be offered HIV testing. The recommended therapy for extrapulmonary tuberculosis varies depending on the site and severity of the infection, but most would treat for a minimum of one year. Follow-up should be monthly, with focus on the symptoms and signs of toxicity of the agents in use. Additionally, sputum samples should be obtained to document smear and culture conversion.

Isolation and Communicability Tuberculosis is communicable when the patient has pulmonary or laryngeal disease. The most contagious forms of tuberculosis occur when cavitary lesions are present. These cavities may be teeming with mycobacteria. Transmission usually occurs by droplets emitted during coughing, sneezing, or vocalizing. About two weeks after institution of therapy, the patient is considered noninfectious. Household and close contacts should have screening tuberculin (5tuPPD) skin testing.

Endocarditis

In most instances, endocarditis is treated in the inpatient setting. This discussion focuses on the

TABLE 69-4 Therapy for Tuberculosis

Condition	Drug	Duration	Potential Toxicity	Follow-up
PPD converter (HIV negative)	INH	6–9 mo	Hepatitis, neuropathy	Every 1–2 months
PPD converter (HIV positive)	INH	12 mo	Hepatitis, neuropathy	Every 1–2 months
Pulmonary TB	INH	9 mo	Hepatitis, neuropathy	Every 1–2 months
	RIF	9 mo	Hepatitis, flu-like syndrome	Every 1–2 months
	PZA	2 mo	Rash, arthralgia, high uric acid	Every 1–2 months
Extrapulmonary TB	INH	12 mo	Hepatitis, neuropathy	Every 1–2 months
	RIF	12 mo	Hepatitis, flu-like syndrome	Every 1–2 months
	PZA	2 mo	Rash, arthralgia, high uric acid	Every 1–2 months

NOTE: INH = isoniazid; RIF = rifampin; PZA = pyrazinamide; PPD = purified protein derivative (tuberculin)

outpatient diagnosis, follow-up, and prophylaxis of endocarditis.

The patient with endocarditis usually presents with fever. Occasionally, fever may not be present and nonspecific symptoms such as fatigue and weight loss may be the only clues. Recent dental manipulations or intravenous abuse of drugs are red flags.

The physical exam may reveal microembolic phenomena; that is, splinter hemorrhages and subconjunctival petechiae. Findings such as Roth spots and Osler's nodes are rare and usually associated with long-standing infection. Of paramount importance is careful evaluation of the heart sounds. A new murmur, especially one with any diastolic component, should alert the physician to the possibility of endocarditis.

Laboratory findings in endocarditis include an elevation in the white blood cell count and ESR, as well as microscopic hematuria and a false-positive rheumatoid factor. Sonography of the heart valves, especially with transesophageal echocardiography, may reveal valvular vegetations.

If the diagnosis of endocarditis is suspected, blood cultures should be obtained. Optimally, 2 to 4 cultures should be taken from different sites with at least 15 min between samples. This approach is aimed at decreasing contamination and the confusion that arises when two blood cultures

from the same venipuncture are positive with an organism of low pathogenicity. If prior antibiotics were given, the microbiology laboratory should be alerted to hold the cultures for a minimum of 14 days to maximize the possibility of isolation of an organism.

Treatment of endocarditis is based on the organism isolated. Once sensitivities are obtained, an antibiotic with a minimum of side effects and ease of administration should be selected. The latter is important as many patients are now discharged home on long courses of intravenous antibiotics. The microbiology laboratory is likely to provide two different sets of sensitivity tests: an inhibition zone test using discs impregnated with the antibiotic and the measurement of the minimum inhibitory concentration of each drug required to inhibit growth of the pathogen. The latter method is considered more accurate in predicting which antibiotic should be effective.

Rarely, blood cultures will be negative despite the strong suspicion of endocarditis. This may be due to previous antibiotic therapy or infection with a more fastidious organism such as *H. parainfluenzae.* Empiric therapy in these cases should address these possibilities. Possible regimens include ampicillin and an aminoglycoside or ampicillin, sulbactam, and an aminoglycoside.

The duration of therapy for endocarditis is 4 to 6 weeks of parenteral antibiotics. As previously

stated, outpatient therapy, usually after 2 weeks of hospitalization, is now common practice. Weekly follow-up in the office should include observation for signs of clinical deterioration such as a changing murmur, heart failure, embolic phenomena, and antibiotic toxicity or persistent infection. Electrocardiograms should be done to monitor for conduction abnormalities, as this may indicate myocardial abscess formation. Any serious clinical decompensation should prompt readmission to the hospital for further evaluation.

Patients with a history of endocarditis, mitral valve prolapse with regurgitation, aortic or mitral stenosis, or artificial heart valves should be given antimicrobial prophylaxis before dental, GU, or GI manipulations. Endocarditis prophylaxis is reviewed in Chaps. 60 and 83.

Urinary Tract Infections

A common medical problem that affects female patients is a urinary tract infection. Some women appear clearly predisposed to these infections, and an increasing number of host and bacterial factors are being identified. This discussion focuses on the practical aspects of diagnosis and treatment of lower and upper urinary tract infections.

Lower Urinary Tract Infection   Lower urinary tract infections involve the urethra and bladder. Symptoms of infection include frequency, burning, foul smelling urine, and hematuria. The most common causative organisms are *E. coli* and enterococcus. In chronically infected patients, or with the use of indwelling catheters, almost any organism may be implicated. Optimally, the work-up should include microscopy of the urinary sediment, Gram stain, and urine culture and sensitivity. In this age of cost containment, a more practical approach can be utilized. If on dipstick analysis of the urine the leukocyte esterase is positive and the pH is high, infection may be presumed. Empiric treatment should be initiated with an antibiotic likely to cover the most common pathogens. Good choices include

trimethoprim-sulfamethoxizole or a quinolone. These may be given in a single dose or for three days. The latter is preferred by many clinicians, because that is the usual time to symptomatic improvement. At the end of therapy, if a repeat urine culture is obtained, it should demonstrate bacterial eradication. Persistence of infection may represent either a resistant organism or an upper tract infection. Resistant organisms should be treated on the basis of their established antibiotic sensitivity.

Upper Tract Infection (Pyelonephritis)   Failure of short course therapy suggests an upper tract infection. Other signs and symptoms include fever, rigors, flank pain, nausea, and vomiting. Some patients may present acutely septic and hypotensive. A toxic presentation or inability to tolerate oral antibiotics should result in hospitalization. The organisms most commonly implicated in upper tract infections are similar to those found in the lower tract. Again, a chronically infected patient may have any causative pathogen. The work-up of an upper tract infection should include a urinalysis with microscopy, as well as culture and sensitivity. Initial antibiotics should be based on urine Gram stain results, if available, and subsequently modified with identification of the organism and its sensitivity. If a patient can tolerate oral agents, hospitalization may be deferred. If gram-negative rods are seen on Gram stain, therapy can be started with sulfa agents or one of the quinilones. Gram-positive cocci require coverage for enterococcus with ampicillin. Initial empiric parenteral antibiotic choices include ampicillin-sulbactam or piperacillin-tazobactam (pseudomonas suspected). A traditional, less expensive approach is ampicillin and an aminoglycoside pending final identification of the organism. Therapy should be continued for 2 weeks for an acute pyelonephritis, and 4 to 6 weeks for chronic infection.

Prevention   Some patients with frequent infections may benefit from long term, low dose antibiotic administration. Success has also been reported with thrice weekly dosing regimens. For the woman who notes infection after sexual inter-

course, a single prophylactic postcoital dose may prove helpful. All pregnant women should be screened for bacteriuria and treated even if they are asymptomatic.

Central Nervous System Infections

Bacterial Meningitis Bacterial infection of the central nervous system is a medical emergency. If unrecognized and untreated, patients can succumb to a bacterial meningitis infection in less than 24 h. The onset of a headache associated with a stiff neck and fever comprise the classical triad of bacterial meningitis. Unfortunately, not all of these symptoms and signs may be present. The best approach is to maintain a high degree of clinical suspicion.

Bacterial meningitis may be caused by pneumococcus, meningococcus, and, less frequently, other organisms depending on the clinical setting. Suspect group B streptococcus and *H. influenzae* in the very young, and pneumococcus and *H. influenzae* in the elderly. Immunocompromised patients and alcoholics may be infected by Listeria. AIDS patients should have cryptococcus and toxoplasmosis included in the differential diagnosis. Thus, the clinical setting is critical in the determination of the possible pathogen in bacterial meningitis.

The diagnosis of meningitis relies on an examination of the cerebrospinal fluid. If there is any evidence of papilledema or any focal neurological findings, a CT scan or MRI of the brain should be done to rule out a space-occupying lesion. If there is any question of central nervous system infection, a lumbar puncture should be performed immediately. This is normally done in an emergency room with access to a microscope for spinal fluid white blood cell count and interpretation of a Gram stain. In bacterial meningitis, white blood cells are found in the cerebrospinal fluid. Early in the course, there may be only a few cells. However, if they are polymorphonuclear cells, meningitis is likely. Additionally, chemistries of the fluid may reveal a glucose less than two-thirds of the simultaneous peripheral glucose. Gram stain of the fluid should be examined immediately for the presence of microbiota.

Treatment should be tailored to results of the Gram stain. If gram-negative or -positive cocci are seen, treatment with penicillin should be started. Gram-negative coccobacillary forms may be *H. influenzae,* and a later generation cephalosporin (cefuroxime or ceftriaxone) may be effective. Unfortunately, the Gram stain may be unrevealing, either because of technical problems, or a paucity of organisms, or previous therapy with antibiotics. In these cases, the clinical setting should help in choosing effective therapy. Unless there are unusual circumstances, therapy with a third generation cephalosporin with vancomycin, until resistant pneumococcus is ruled out, will be sufficient to cover most of the usual pathogens. Once the organism is isolated, therapy can be simplified. Treatment should be continued in the hospital for 10 days.

Aseptic Meningitis Aseptic meningitis is more common than the bacterial form. There are multiple causes of a sterile spinal fluid culture. The infectious causes, in order of likelihood, are: viral, partially treated bacterial, mycobacterial, syphilitic, Borrelia, fungal, leptospiral, and parameningeal foci. It should be noted that many of these entities require antimicrobial therapy; therefore, a vigorous attempt at diagnosis should be made.

Some patients can be observed while withholding antibiotics. A viral process is suggested if the patient is less than 45 years old; had a recent viral illness (in summer or fall); does not appear toxic; and the cerebrospinal fluid shows a predominance of lymphocytes, a normal glucose, and a negative Gram stain. If there is any question of a partially treated meningitis, the clinician should err on the side of treatment.

Patients with meningococcal and *H. influenzae* meningitis should be isolated for the first 24 h of therapy. The physician should notify appropriate health authorities. Prophylaxis is indicated only for close contacts, not co-workers or schoolmates. However, all contacts should be offered chemoprophylaxis if they report close exposure.

Chemoprophylaxis is with rifampin (*H. influenzae*: 20 mg/kg/day for 4 days; meningococcus: 10 mg/kg/twice a day for 2 days.)

Infections Requiring Surgical Intervention

There are a number of instances in which surgery should be considered as an essential part of management. These are discussed by organ system.

Head and Neck Infections of the sinuses usually do not require surgery. However, if there is pansinusitis, surgical drainage may prevent retrograde spread into the cavernous sinus or the cranium resulting in a brain abscess. The diagnosis of pansinusitis is suspected when erythema, warmth, and tenderness are noted over the maxillary and ethmoid sinuses. It is usually associated with a fever, significant toxicity, and confirmed by sinus films. In addition to drainage, parenteral antibiotics are given to cover pathogens including the pneumococcus and *H. influenzae*. Ampicillin-sulbactam or second to third generation cephalosporins are possible agents.

Ludwig's Angina or Infection of the Submandibular Spaces Deep fascial space infections are an emergency and require immediate surgery. These infections usually occur secondary to dental manipulations. Danger signs are bilateral involvement of the submandibular and sublingual spaces with rapid spread of cellulitis. Eating, swallowing, and eventually breathing may be impaired. In addition to surgical drainage, high doses of parenteral antibiotics are required. These should cover the usual mouth organisms and, hence, anaerobes. Appropriate agents include the carbepenems, clindamycin, ticarcillin-clavulanate, and ampicillin-sulbactam. If the patient is immunocompromised, an aminoglycoside should be added. Treatment should be continued until there is complete resolution of the cellulitis.

Abdominal Infections Infections in the abdominal cavity frequently require surgical intervention. In general, abscesses complicating diverticulitis, appendicitis, or microperforations of the bowel should be drained. Drainage may be attempted percutaneously by an "interventional" radiologist, or surgically, if more definitive therapy is required. Antibiotic treatment should be aimed at gastrointestinal organisms, including gram-negatives, gram-positives, and anaerobes. In the majority of cases, enterococcal coverage is not necessary in initial therapy. Enterococcal coverage should be added if an enterococcus has been isolated, or if the patient is not responding to initial coverage. Appropriate antibiotics include cefoxitin, cefotetan, clindamycin or metronidazole plus an aminoglycoside or, if enterococcal coverage is indicated, ampicillin-sulbactam, ticarcillin-clavulanate, the carbepenems, or piperacillin. Duration of therapy varies, and the abscess size should be followed with sonography or CT scanning.

Salpingo-oophoritis and other gynecologic infections are discussed in other chapters.

Acute Cholecystitis Acute cholecystitis usually follows obstruction of the cystic duct by a stone, and is frequently accompanied by bacterial infection. The diagnosis is suspected when there is a combination of right upper quadrant pain, tenderness (Murphy's sign), fever, and leukocytosis. The bilirubin is elevated in about one-half, and transaminases in about one-quarter, of patients with acute cholecystitis. Diagnostic imaging includes a radionuclide (HIDA) scan that may visualize the biliary tree but not the obstructed gallbladder. Ultrasonography may reveal a stone (9 of 10 cases). Although three-quarters of patients may initially be successfully treated medically, the recurrence rate is so high (60 percent in 6 years) that early surgery is usually indicated. Complications of acute cholecystitis (empyema, perforation) occur in one-quarter of cases and require urgent surgical intervention. Endoscopic surgery is gaining widespread acceptance. Antibiotics should cover the most common pathogens: *E. coli, Enterococcus,* and *Klebsiella.* Ampicillin-sulbactam or ampicillin and aminoglycoside represent good initial choices.

Diverticulitis Acute colonic diverticulitis is suggested by fever, left lower-quadrant pain, tenderness, and leukocytosis. The etiology is believed to be inflammation induced by fecal mate-

rial and bacteria (fecalith) entrapped in a diverticulum. These herniations of the mucosa through the muscularis occur most commonly in the sigmoid colon. Perforation may result in peritonitis, septic shock, or, if walled off, in an abscess. Appropriate antibiotics include those that cover bowel flora as discussed above.

Soft Tissue and Bone Infections Soft tissue infections may, under certain circumstances, require surgical debridement. A rapidly ascending infection of the fascia is a medical emergency especially when it occurs in a closed space such as the hand. An infection in a diabetic patient in the perineum or around the vulva is a synergistic mixed aerobic and anaerobic infection that requires immediate extensive debridement with the aggressive use of antibiotics. Antibiotic choices include ampicillin-sulbactam, imipenem, and ampicillin in addition to metronidazole and an aminoglycoside.

Osteomyelitis is another infection that may require debridement. It may present with fever, an elevated sedimentation rate, and pain over the affected area. A bone scan or indium-labeled white blood cell study should help to define the problem. Bone biopsy is essential for diagnosis, because cultures of the overlying area may not reflect the causative bacteria. In cases of chronic osteomyelitis, debridement may be indicated.

Therapy of osteomyelitis should be based on the results of biopsy or debridement cultures. Staphylococcus is a frequent pathogen and excellent coverage is provided by nafcillin, oxacillin, cephazolin, or vancomycin. Duration of therapy for osteomyelitis is between 4 to 6 weeks of parenteral antibiotics. Many clinicians opt for home antibiotic therapy. Office follow-up of the ambulatory osteomyelitis patient should include weekly monitoring for efficacy of treatment, as well as for drug toxicity. A normal bone scan and ESR support eradication of infection.

Hepatitis

Hepatitis, or inflammation of the liver parenchyma, may have multiple causes. Only viral hepatitis is discussed in this chapter. In the past, hepatitis A (infectious) and hepatitis B (serum) assays were the only agents to be identified serologically. Other agents of hepatitis include hepatitis C (previously called non-A, non-B) and hepatitis E (enterically transmitted non-A, non-B). There is also the potential for a superinfection with delta agent, which requires previous infection with hepatitis B to produce disease.

Hepatitis A In the United States, hepatitis A is most frequently found in food-borne outbreaks. It is, however, endemic in other parts of the world and should be a consideration in evaluating a returning traveler with illness. Spread is via the fecal-oral route, and the incubation period is 2 to 6 weeks. The case fatality rate is less than 0.5 percent, and it is not associated with chronic hepatitis. The diagnosis is made based on the history of possible exposure and an acute influenza-like illness with headache, myalgia, fever, and malaise. At the end of the prodromal phase, the stool appears clay colored and the urine darkens. At this point, the patient is clinically jaundiced with pruritus developing if there is substantial bilirubin deposition in the skin. The liver may be enlarged and tender. Serological testing will reveal elevated IgM antihepatitis A virus antibody. After about one month, an elevation of IgG antibody to the hepatitis A virus will appear.

The management of hepatitis consists of supportive care. Hospitalization is indicated for patients with evidence of hepatic failure, such as a prolonged prothrombin time. Bedrest with bathroom privileges is recommended, but once symptoms have abated, patients may resume normal activities. Alcohol and medications should be avoided. No specific treatment is recommended, and corticosteroids should be deferred unless there is fulminant hepatic failure and cholestatic hepatitis. Even in these circumstances, their use is controversial.

Hepatitis A is extremely contagious and is a reportable disease. Unfortunately, there is often a delay between the time of exposure and the diagnosis. Prophylaxis of intimate contacts

should be postponed until the identity of the agent is confirmed. Once confirmed, all family members and close contacts should quickly receive immune serum globulin at a dose of 2 to 5 ml. It is probably only effective within 7 to 14 days of exposure; however, it is usually given up to 4 weeks after exposure. Hospitalized patients should be in a private room with separate toilet facilities. At home, the patient should use a private toilet, if possible, and be instructed to avoid food preparation.

Hepatitis B   In the United States, acute hepatitis B infection is most commonly seen in intravenous drug abusers, sexual contacts of carriers, and health care workers. Because of the high rate of infection via sexual contact with carriers who are not suspected of being infected, there is currently a major initiative to immunize the large proportion of at risk individuals. In a significant number of patients, there is no obvious route of transmission.

The incubation period is 2 to 6 months, with a mean of 12 weeks. The fatality rate is 1 to 3 percent. Infection may become chronic in as many as 85 percent of neonates, 25 percent of children and of 10 percent of young adults. The onset of hepatitis B is more insidious than that of hepatitis A, but they cannot be differentiated on clinical grounds alone. A polyarthritis has been associated with the preicteric phase. Diagnostic serology reveals the hepatitis B surface antigen, which is found in almost all patients during the icteric phase. Occasionally, the patient may be in the "window" phase, which occurs before surface antigen rises. During this period, antibody to core antigen is found. The surface antigen usually disappears with convalescence; however, 5 to 10 percent of patients do not clear their surface antigen. These patients remain asymptomatic, but can transmit their infection to others. This chronic state should be suspected if the antigen titers do not disappear after 8 weeks of the illness. Patients who have past infection with hepatitis B may become infected with delta virus, with a mortality rate as high as 20 percent. This infection should be suspected in surface antigen-positive patients who present with a severe infection. Serological testing can confirm the diagnosis with the detection of anti-hepatitis delta agent antibody in the serum.

Hepatitis B is less contagious than hepatitis A. Prophylaxis is recommended for sexual contacts. Hepatitis B immune globulin at 5 ml should be administered as soon as possible and repeated in 1 month. Additionally, hepatitis B vaccine should be given simultaneously and repeated 1 and 6 months later.

Hepatitis C   Hepatitis C is the cause of most cases of transfusion-associated hepatitis. Unlike hepatitis B, the risk of transplacental transmission is low. Mothers who are carriers have about a 10 percent risk of transmission to the fetus. There is also some evidence of sexual transmission. The propensity to become a carrier is quite high—about 50 percent more likely than with hepatitis B. The incubation period is 6 to 12 weeks, with a mean of 8 weeks. Diagnosis is made serologically, with a positive antibody to hepatitis C detected in the serum. No vaccine is available and administration of immunoglobulin is not effective in prevention of hepatitis C.

Hepatitis E   Hepatitis E is referred to as enterically transmitted non-A, non-B hepatitis. It was first described in a 1955 Egyptian epidemic. In the 1980s, electron microscopy demonstrated the virus-like particle thought to be the cause of this disease. This type of hepatitis is a risk for foreign travelers. Outbreaks have occurred in India, Pakistan, Nepal, the Soviet Union, North Africa, sub-Saharan Africa, and Somalia.

Diagnosis is made on the basis of serology and typical symptoms of hepatitis. Pregnant females should be counseled not to travel to endemic areas as maternal mortality is very high. There is no evidence that immunoglobulin is effective for prevention, and there is no vaccine available.

Epstein-Barr Virus

Epstein-Barr virus (EBV) is a member of the herpes virus family that also includes cytomegalovirus and herpes simplex types I and II. Most

U.S. residents have been infected with this virus in their teens or 20s, with seroprevalence above that age approaching 90 percent. The symptoms of acute EBV include severe sore throat, fever, and lymphadenopathy. Other symptoms may be retro-orbital headaches, myalgias, and the sensation of abdominal fullness. Fever may take 10 to 14 days to resolve. A rash may be seen after the administration of ampicillin in over 90 percent of cases. A majority of the cases resolve spontaneously, but an unfortunate few are complicated by autoimmune hemolytic anemia, splenic rupture, or encephalitis.

Chronic fatigue syndrome is of unclear etiology. In the past, this syndrome has been linked with EBV because of elevations of the early antigens of EBV. These serologic abnormalities may represent a nonspecific activation of the immune system, the cause of which may be other infectious and inflammatory conditions. There are, however, those rare patients who suffer from what appears to be a reactivation of latent EBV. Their EBV serologies are markedly abnormal as compared to the previously mentioned group.

Varicella Zoster (Chickenpox and Shingles)

Varicella zoster, one of the herpes family of viruses, is the causative agent of chickenpox and, when reactivated, shingles. Most adults who have grown up in the United States have had chickenpox and are considered immune. However, there are some women who will not remember ever having had the disease. It is worthwhile to assess antibody status in these patients, especially if they are of childbearing age. This relatively benign disease of childhood may be life-threatening in adults and dangerous for a fetus. Chickenpox presents with vesicular, pustular, pruritic lesions on an erythematous base. The lesions are typically found at the hairline at the base of the scalp; they spread to other parts of the body. High fevers may precede the appearance of the lesions. The incubation period after exposure is from 10 to 21 days. In children, the disease causes irritability but little toxicity. In adults, however,

severe complications involving the respiratory tract may ensue. It is recommended that all adults with chickenpox be carefully observed for any respiratory symptoms. Any sign of respiratory involvement should prompt an immediate chest x-ray and an arterial blood gas measurement, with hospitalization if any abnormalities are found. Acyclovir and famciclovir have been used for therapy in V. zoster infections. Varicella immune globulin may be used to prevent the disease in patients with a compromised immune system and the newborn whose mother developed chickenpox within 5 days before or 2 days after delivery.

Chickenpox is highly contagious by the respiratory route. Spread may occur before the onset of skin lesions and may continue until all lesions have crusted over.

Like other herpes viruses, V. zoster may persist in a latent state. This virus prefers neural tissue, and, when reactivated, presents as a painful vesicular rash in a dermatomal distribution. Although reactivation is more common in the elderly, it may occur at any age. Shingles, or V. zoster reactivation, has been associated with decreases in cell-mediated immunity (malignancy, chemotherapy) but may also be seen in healthy patients.

V. zoster may reactivate in any dermatome, but is commonly seen on the thorax. Spread outside the dermatome suggests immunocompromise, and further work-up may be indicated. Facial zoster may be very debilitating, especially if there is involvement of the eye. Involvement of the tip of the nose should prompt aggressive examination of the cornea, as both areas are supplied by branches of the nasociliary nerve. In fact, all patients with facial zoster near the eye should be examined by an ophthalmologist to exclude corneal involvement.

The treatment of V. zoster is symptomatic. Acyclovir in doses as high as 15 mg/kg may be given to the immunocompromised patient to prevent dissemination. Topical acyclovir is not effective. The use of steroids to decrease postherpetic neuralgia is controversial and not recommended. V. zoster is also spread by contact with the in-

fected lesion, but this is only of concern in a person who has never had chickenpox. Contacts may contract chickenpox but not shingles.

A varicella vaccine is now available for use in children and nonimmune adults.

Measles (Rubeola)

Measles, a common childhood disease, may prove a serious illness in adults. Most adults are immune, but those born after 1956 have vaccine-induced immunity that may not be lifelong. This is suggested by recent reports of epidemics in colleges. This is a highly contagious virus with transmission by droplets from nasopharyngeal secretions, occurring from 5 days after exposure until 5 days after the initial appearance of skin lesions.

Manifestations of the disease include fever, malaise, cough, coryza, and conjunctivitis. The maculopapular rash occurs about 2 weeks after exposure, beginning on the forehead and spreading downward to the feet by the third day. In adults, fever and rash may be more severe. Additionally, like chickenpox, respiratory complications may be life-threatening. Any progression of respiratory complaints should be taken very seriously.

Measles may be prevented, or the course attenuated, by the administration of γ-globulin (0.25 ml/kg) within 6 days of exposure. There is no treatment for the measles virus. Bacterial superinfection should be treated based on the causative pathogen (usually pneumonia due to streptococcus, staphylococcus, or *Haemophilus influenzae*). All adults born after 1956 should have a booster vaccination for prevention of measles, especially if foreign travel is planned.

Rubella

Rubella (German measles) is usually a benign infection, but is a serious problem in pregnancy when it may lead to fetal malformations. The infection, less contagious than chickenpox or measles, is spread via nasopharyngeal secretions with an incubation period from 14 to 21 days.

After a prodrome of malaise, fever, headache, and conjunctivitis, a maculopapular rash begins on the forehead and spreads downward. Lymphadenopathy occurs, with postauricular and suboccipital involvement most characteristic. In young women, arthralgias and slight joint swelling may occur. The diagnosis of rubella is confirmed by virus isolation, or more easily with detected changes in antibody titers.

The prevention of congenital rubella is the aim of vaccination programs, as the disease itself is relatively benign. γ-Globulin can abort the clinical manifestations of the disease, but transmission to the fetus can still occur. Therefore, active immunization has been practiced since 1969. Women contemplating pregnancy should be screened for rubella antibodies, and immunized if they are not already immune. The rubella vaccine is a live-attenuated virus, and thus should be avoided during and for 3 months prior to a planned pregnancy because of the theoretical risk of fetal damage.

Mumps

Mumps, an acute viral disease, is transmitted via the respiratory route and has an incubation period of 12 to 25 days. It typically manifests with acute parotitis and a prodrome of malaise, anorexia, feverishness, and sore throat. There are few complications in adult females (up to 35 percent of adult males develop orchitis). Treatment is symptomatic. Prevention is with vaccination using a live-attenuated virus and should be avoided in pregnancy. Recommendations for MMR vaccination are further discussed in the chapter on immunization (Chap. 6).

Lyme Disease

Lyme disease, caused by the spirochete *Borrelia burgdorferi,* is the most common tick-borne infection in the United States. The disease is prevalent in the Northeast, Great Lakes region, and the Far West. Transmission is greatest during the warm weather months when people are more

likely to be outdoors. About 10 days after the bite of an infected tick, a flu-like illness may develop. About half of patients develop a rash, characteristically with a bullseye pattern, the hallmark of which is rapid enlargement. Left untreated, Lyme disease may progress to involve the heart (heart block, myocarditis), joints (arthritis), nervous system (aseptic meningitis, encephalopathy, neuropathy), and the eyes (uveitis, conjunctivitis). The disease, like syphilis, is protean in its manifestations. This is unfortunate, as diagnosis rests heavily on clinical judgment. Laboratory confirmation may be difficult, because many of the commonly used serological assays are unreliable. Thus, this disease has become a popular catchall diagnosis for those patients with nonspecific complaints.

The treatment of Lyme disease is based on the stage of disease. The duration of treatment is controversial, but in general these recommendations apply: Early Lyme (flu-like symptoms and rash) is treated with amoxicillin (500 mg tid) and probenecid (500 mg tid) or doxycycline (100 mg bid) for 21 to 28 days. Later Lyme disease may be treated with oral medication in the above doses or with parenteral ceftriaxone (2 g OD) for 4 to 6 weeks. If neurological involvement is suspected, a lumbar puncture and referral to a Lyme specialist should be considered. The Lyme spirochete may be transmitted transplacentally, and has resulted in fetal infections and death. Therefore, treatment for suspected disease in pregnancy should be aggressive.

Prevention involves avoidance of tick-infested areas and wearing protective attire. Tick repellents can be used on clothing, but not directly on the skin. Empiric treatment of a tick bite with antibiotics is not recommended. Vaccines seem effective and safe, but the duration of protection is still unknown.

International Travelers

Prevention

A patient traveling to an underdeveloped country should be counseled to avoid the local drinking water. In general, water is safe to drink if it has been boiled for over 10 minutes. If this is not possible, bottled water may be purchased, preferably with carbonation to avoid bottles illicitly filled with tap water and sold as pure to tourists. Foods to be avoided include salads and fruits and vegetables that have been peeled or prepared by someone else. The risk of waterborne infections includes hepatitis A and E, typhoid, cholera, and traveler's diarrhea (enterotoxigenic *E. coli, Clostridium perfringens, Campylobacter,* and viruses).

Pregnant women should be advised to postpone travel to high-risk areas until after delivery. Many of the antimalarials and treatments of tropical diseases are problematic during pregnancy. Hepatitis E may be prevalent in some regions and can be fatal in pregnancy. If travel to high-risk areas during pregnancy is unavoidable, a consultation with a travel medicine specialist is advised.

Preparation for foreign travel includes vaccination, especially for diseases particular to the area being visited. In general, patients should be up to date on their polio and tetanus vaccinations. Tetanus toxoid should be given every 10 years and polio vaccination as booster in adulthood for international travel. Other recommendations depend on the area visited (e.g., Africa: yellow fever, meningococcus, and typhoid; Asia: Japanese encephalitis and typhoid; South America: yellow fever and typhoid). Yellow fever injections are only obtainable at licensed centers.

The patient traveling or camping out in rural areas must be treated somewhat differently. Many underdeveloped areas have a high incidence of rabies, and vaccination for this disease may be indicated. If there is any question regarding current recommendations for vaccination, contact your local health department, the Centers for Disease Control and Prevention vaccination division in Atlanta, or a reputable local travel clinic.

Malaria is one of the leading causes of death in the world. International travelers visiting en-

demic areas should be given appropriate chemoprophylaxis. In the past, chloroquine was the preferred agent. Currently, there are many areas with chloroquine resistance (Africa, South America, and Asia). For these regions, mefloquine is now the drug of choice. These antimalarials are given for 1 to 2 weeks prior to international travel, and continued once weekly until 4 weeks after the patient leaves the malarious area. Side effects, including nightmares and worsening of depressive states, have been reported with mefloquine. Additionally, there is a question of drug interactions with calcium channel and β-blockers. Alternative antimalarials, such as doxycycline, should be chosen for these patients. There are some areas in southeast Asia that have mefloquine-resistant malaria. For patients traveling to mefloquine-resistant areas, doxycycline (100 mg daily) should be given.

The traveler should take stringent precautions to avoid mosquito bites, especially during the evening hours. If a patient has greater than 10 mosquito bites, she should be instructed to contact her physician upon return. One of the forms of malaria (*P. vivax*) has an autoinfectious cycle and a course of primaquine is indicated to eradicate the liver cycle. A G6PD deficiency should be assessed prior to giving primaquine.

Patients should be cautioned to avoid sexual contact with residents of developing countries. Hepatitis B and HIV are endemic in many parts of the developing world. Some countries require a certificate of HIV negativity prior to entry for extended periods of time.

Illness in the Returning Traveler

Fever in the returning traveler is usually self-limited and rarely related to the foreign travel. However, in view of the potential for life-threatening illnesses, it should be treated as a medical emergency. Along with the usual causes of fever, the clinician should evaluate the patient for malaria, enteric fever, and hepatitis. Screening procedures should include a history and physical exam, complete blood count, blood chemistries,

G6PD, urinalysis, hepatitis B surface antigen, syphilis screen, HIV testing, stool for ova and parasites and enteric pathogens, malaria smear, and schistosomiasis serology (if returning from endemic areas).

Even if the traveler took adequate antimalarial prophylaxis, malaria is still a possibility. The typical presentation of malaria includes fever, chills, headache, and myalgia. Diagnosis is made by smear examination, noting that a single negative smear does not exclude malaria. The incubation period for falciparum malaria is between 5 and 42 days. A clinical "pearl" is the presence of thrombocytopenia. If platelets are normal, it is unlikely that the patient has malaria. A patient with a high degree of parasitemia, anemia, or any signs of cerebral malaria should be admitted to the hospital for specialist consultation and treatment.

Enteric Infections

Diarrhea in the returning traveler may have numerous causes including bacterial (*Salmonella, Shigella, Campylobacter, E. coli* and *Yersinia enterocolitica*), protozoal (*Giardia lamblia, Entamoeba histolytica, Blastocystis hominis, Cryptosporidium,* and *Isospora belli*), *Strongyloides,* and schistosomiasis. Traveler's diarrhea is usually an acute illness caused by enterotoxigenic *E. coli* or Campylobacter. Stool cultures should be obtained to determine if any other of the above mentioned diarrheal pathogens are present. Another consideration is the possibility of *C. difficile* complicating treatment with previous antimalarials or antibiotics.

Empiric treatment of diarrhea should cover the usual bacterial pathogens. The quinolones (ciprofloxacin, ofloxacin, norfloxacin, etc.) afford excellent coverage for many of the possible causes. Once culture and sensitivity results are known, therapy can be changed to another agent if indicated. Treatment should continue until the diarrhea resolves. For illness caused by parasites, metronidazole treats amebiasis, giardiasis, and numerous other pathogens. If *C. difficile* toxin is

discovered, either oral metronidazole or vancomycin are used for therapy.

Complications of Antibiotics

The most frequently occurring adverse effects of antibiotics are mild, and include gastrointestinal distress (all antibiotics, but more commonly the erythromycins and tetracyclines), rashes, candidal vaginitis, and antibiotic associated diarrhea. Many of these problems may be treated symptomatically or by switching to another agent. Diarrhea associated with antibiotics may be caused by an overgrowth of a toxin-elaborating bacterium, *Clostridium difficile.* When this is suspected, stool for *C. difficile* toxin should be collected. The treatment of this diarrhea is oral metronidazole or vancomycin. Additionally, the causative antibiotic should be discontinued. If this is not possible, then oral metronidazole or vancomycin should be continued until the other antibiotics have been stopped, even if the diarrhea appears to have resolved.

Life-threatening reactions to antibiotics include anaphylaxis and severe dermatological problems such as Stevens-Johnson syndrome.

Patients who report antibiotic sensitivities should be questioned carefully regarding the nature of the reaction. A history of a rash is alarming if urticaria, desquamation, or mucosal involvement is reported. Any signs of bronchospasm should be regarded very seriously. If the antibiotic in question must be used, then an allergist should be consulted for skin testing and possible desensitization.

References and Selected Readings

1. American College of Obstetricans and Gynecologists Technical Bulletin: Hepatitis in pregnancy. *ACOG Bull* 174:1–9, 1992.
2. American Heart Association: Prevention of bacterial endocarditis: Recommendations by the American Heart Association. *JAMA* 164:2919–2922, 1990.
3. Bia FJ (ed): *Travel Medical Advisor: The Physician's Update on International Health.* Atlanta: American Health Consultants, 1993.
4. Wilson JD, Braunwald E, Isselbacher KJ, et al (eds): *Harrison's Principles of Internal Medicine,* 12th ed. New York: McGraw-Hill, 1991.
5. Centers for Disease Control: *Health Information for International Travel* Washington, DC: US Department of Health and Human Services, 1992. (HHS Publication No. [CDC] 92-8280).
6. Mandell GL, Douglas RG, Bennet JE (eds): *Principles and Practice of Infectious Diseases,* 3d ed. New York: Churchill-Livingstone, 1990.
7. New York City Department of Health: *City health Information, Bureau of TB Control.* New York City Department of Health, 2 (5), 1992.

Hematologic Disorders

Kanti R. Rai
Henny Billett

HISTORY AND PHYSICAL EXAMINATION
Symptoms • Physical Examination
DISORDERS OF ERYTHROCYTES
Anemia • Erythrocytosis
DISORDERS OF LEUKOCYTES
Leukopenia • Leukocytosis • Hematologic
Malignancies
**DISORDERS OF PLATELETS AND
    COAGULATION SYSTEM**
Coagulation Disorders • The
Antiphospholipid Syndrome •
Thrombophilia • Disseminated Intravascular
Coagulation • Thrombocytopenia •
Thrombocytosis
SPLENOMEGALY

History and Physical Examination

Physicians who provide primary health care to women should be knowledgeable about hematologic disorders that affect women of all ages—the elderly as well as the young, and among the latter, the nonpregnant as well as the pregnant. Special considerations in history taking and physical examination of patients with hematologic disorders are discussed below.

Symptoms

Thorough history taking is a requisite in the management of all medical problems. The following symptoms, however, deserve special emphasis when a hematologic disorder is suspected. Many of these symptoms may be the presenting symptoms, while others may only be elicited on direct questioning of the patient or a family member.

1. A sense of malaise, general weakness, easy fatigability. These symptoms may be present in a myriad of nonhematologic conditions, but they have a special significance in patients with anemia, leukemias, and bleeding disorders.
2. Bleeding history: Is the patient an easy bruiser? (This suggests the possibility of a platelet disorder and of congenital or acquired disorders of coagulation factors). Does she recall having bled excessively following a minor procedure (e.g., dental work) or major surgery? The extent and duration of bleeding during the menstrual cycle is a critical part of the history. It is necessary to determine whether the estimated iron loss far exceeds dietary and supplemental iron intake.
3. Does the patient have an increased frequency of infections? (This may be associated with neutropenia.).
4. Does the patient complain of dyspnea and/or palpitations on minor exertion (e.g., walking up a flight of stairs)? This may be suggestive of anemia of a relatively abrupt onset.

Other salient aspects of the history include:

1. Dietary and nutritional habits.
2. Past history of hemorrhoids; venous or arterial occlusions; or any hematologic complications of pregnancy or childbirth.

3. Current and past medications, birth control pills, antibiotics, psychiatric drugs.
4. History of previous transfusions.
5. Occupational history: exposure to radiation or organic chemicals.
6. History of bleeding disorders, anemia, frequent infections, or malignancies in the family.
7. Lifestyle history: prior or current recreational drug usage or sexual habits that may be risk factors for HIV infections.

Physical Examination

During the physical examination of a patient with a known or suspected hematologic disorder, special emphasis should be placed on the following: skin pallor and texture; hair; fingernails and evidence of clubbing; conjunctiva, tongue, and oral mucosa; fundi; lymphadenopathy; thyroid; spleen; liver; and bone tenderness.

Evidence of pallor of the skin and conjunctivae is a telltale sign of anemia. The presence of petechiae and ecchymoses indicates an abnormality of platelets or other bleeding disorders. Skin turgor is an indication of the state of hydration, as well as of overall nutritional status. Clubbing of the fingers may indicate an underlying chronic disease, such as sickle cell anemia or thalassemia. Fundi may reveal hemorrhages or sludging of vessels as seen with hyperviscosity syndromes, such as polycythemia, multiple myeloma, or Waldenström's macroglobulinemia. Enlargement of lymph nodes, spleen, or liver may suggest a wide range of disorders from infectious mononucleosis to leukemia and lymphomas, and bone tenderness may be indicative of hyperactivity in the bone marrow as is sometimes seen in leukemias or sickle cells crises, as well as in multiple myeloma.

In a majority of cases of hematologic disorder, the primary care physician can develop a very short list of differential diagnoses after a thorough history and physical examination. The next step is to formulate the plans for the most appropriate laboratory and radiologic tests to speedily establish the final diagnosis.

Hematologic disorders can be broadly classified in the following categories, although some diseases may involve more than one category:

Diseases Primarily Affecting the Red Cells
  Anemia
  Polycythemia

Diseases Primarily Affecting the Leukocyies
  Leukopenia
  Leukocytosis

Diseases Primarily Affecting Hemostasis
  von Willebrand disease
  Factor XI deficiency (hemophilia C)
  Presence of an inhibitor to the coagulation cascade
    or of a circulating anticoagulant
  Hypercoagulable state
  Disseminated intravascular coagulation (DIC)
  Thrombocytopenias and platelet abnormalities
  Thrombocytosis

Disorders of Erythrocytes

Anemia

The normal hemoglobin level for females is 12 to 14 g/dl and the range of normal mean red cell volume for women is 80 to 98 fl. After the age of 12, hemoglobin levels in women remain relatively stable. This is in contrast to males where the hemoglobin level rises until age 17 due to testosterone-induced hematopoiesis. Women who are runners may have hemoglobin levels that are somewhat below the norm, secondary to an increased plasma volume.

For convenience, the classification of anemias is often made on the basis of the reticulocyte count, as detailed in Table 70-1. Recently, the *reticulocyte count* has been replaced by the *absolute reticulocyte number*. This is a much better indicator of the true marrow response. A hypoproliferative anemia has a decreased absolute reticulocyte number, whereas a hemolytic anemia typically has an increased absolute reticulocyte number. The hypoproliferative anemias include the nutritional anemias of iron, B_{12}, and folate, and infiltrative anemias, both hematopoietic and nonhematopoietic.

TABLE 70-1 Differential Diagnosis of Anemia

Low or Normal Reticulocyte Count
  Low MCV
    Iron Deficiency
  High MCV
    Folate/B_{12} Deficiency
    Drugs
      Chemotherapy
      Immunosuppressives
    Liver Disease
  Normal MCV
    Chronic disease
    Renal disease
    Collagen vascular disease
    Diabetes and other endocrinopathies
    Myelodysplasia
    Myeloproliferative disease
    Marrow infiltration
      Tumor
      Infection
    HIV
    Aplastic
Increased Reticulocyte Count
  Low MCV
    Congenital Red Cell Disorders
    Hemoglobin Disorders
      Thalassemias
      β^0, β^+, HbH
      Hemoglobinopathies
      HbE and HbC syndromes
      Sickle cell syndromes
      SS, SC, $S\beta^0$ thalassemia
    Membrane—Spherocytosis
    Enzyme—G6PD, PK
  Acquired Red Cell Disorders
    Autoimmune hemolytic anemia
    Drug-induced hemolysis
    Microvascular
    Preeclampsia
    Thrombotic thrombocytopenic purpura (TTP)
    Hemolytic uremic syndrome (HUS)
    Disseminated intravascular coagulation (DIC)

Hypoproliferative Anemias *Iron Deficiency.* Our general recommendation is that the routine care of the nonpregnant female should include a yearly complete blood count. Hemoglobin levels below 11.5 g/dl in the nonpregnant female and hemoglobin levels below 10 g/dl at any time during pregnancy signal a nonphysiologic anemia. The most common cause of anemia in women is iron deficiency. Many menstruating women have decreased or absent iron stores, and some of these women develop an iron deficiency anemia during their lifetime, especially during pregnancy. Typically, the iron deficiency occurs as a result of further depletion of initially meager stores. Whereas good clinical protocol demands in men an investigation as to the *source* of bleeding that is causing an iron deficiency anemia, it is assumed that women who are iron deficient but who are still menstruating or who are only a few years postmenopausal are iron deficient *secondary* to menstruation and pregnancy, and do not always require further evaluation. A history of severe menorrhagia or menometrorrhagia should be sought and, if present, should prompt a detailed bleeding diathesis inquiry. For some women, the only manifestation of von Willebrand's disease is menorrhagia.

Iron deficiency should be the first diagnosis (but not the *only* diagnosis) suspected in women whose anemia is either microcytic or normocytic, but whose mean corpuscular volume (MCV) is lower than previously documented. Although the iron deficient blood smear usually demonstrates microcytic hypochromic cells, automated analyses may miss this population (especially during pregnancy when there is a mild increase in MCV of approximately 5 percent). The WBC count is normal and the platelet count may be normal, low, or high. The reticulocyte count is inadequate for the degree of anemia. Serum ferritin is diagnostic if it is low. However, *falsely normal* levels of ferritin may be seen secondary to a general increase in acute-phase reactive proteins in some patients and, therefore, a normal ferritin level does not exclude iron deficiency. Typically, the iron-deficient patient has a decreased serum iron and increased total iron-binding capacity (TIBC) levels, resulting in a decreased percent saturation. Again, however, a normal TIBC may occur even in the face of iron deficiency, so that a normal level of these proteins or a normal percent saturation does not exclude iron deficiency.

Bone marrow examination is not required to make the diagnosis in an otherwise healthy

female, pregnant or not pregnant. If, after the initial studies, there is still a question of etiology, a trial of iron therapy (60 to 180 mg/day) may be started, and the patient's response should be observed. An anemia that does not respond to iron with a reticulocytosis *within one week* or a demonstrable rise in hemoglobin within 2 to 3 weeks should prompt further investigation *and the discontinuation of iron therapy* until a diagnosis has been firmly established. At this time, a bone marrow examination may be appropriate. Iron supplementation (60 mg/day) may be routinely given to pregnant women to prevent the occurrence of iron deficiency.

Folate and B_{12}   Iron, B_{12}, and folate are required by an active hematopoietic system. Folate is necessary for amino acid synthesis and there is evidence that folate deficiency is associated with an increase in neural tube defects. Folate deficiency often occurs in periods of rapid growth (childhood), hemolytic anemias and hemoglobinopathies, in alcoholics who do not eat properly, and in late pregnancy when folate requirements are almost double that of the nonpregnant state. Folate requirements may be further increased in multiple gestations. Although normal pregnant women may increase their MCV during pregnancy, folate deficiency must be considered when the MCV rises.

Folate deficiency typically manifests itself as a macrocytic anemia *with* hypersegmentation of the neutrophils. There may be an accompanying leukopenia or thrombocytopenia. Folic acid deficiency may be silent, however, or it may yield a mixed peripheral blood picture due to an accompanying iron deficiency. Serum folate levels are often diagnostic, but in some patients redcell folate levels may be more helpful. These levels reflect the folate incorporated into the cell at the RBC's inception and represent, on average, the level of folate in cells about 6 to 8 weeks old. Therefore, red-cell folate levels may miss a relatively new folate deficiency. Folate therapy for the deficient state should be given at levels of 1 to 2 mg/day. A reticulocytosis may be seen in 1 week and a rise in hemoglobin levels should

be seen within 2 to 3 weeks. Given the ease of administration of folate and the lack of side effects, it is standard practice to prescribe prophylactic folic acid at levels of 0.4 mg/day to the pregnant female. In addition, if a woman has previously had an infant with a neural tube defect, she is given 4 mg/day of folic acid prior to and throughout early pregnancy. Megaloblastic anemia secondary to folic acid deficiency is not uncommon; megaloblastic anemia secondary to vitamin B_{12} deficiency is. Vitamin B_{12} deficiency typically occurs in the elderly, more Nordic population, but there is a subgroup of younger women (ages 30 to 50) with pernicious anemia. Vitamin B_{12} is also preferentially utilized by the fetus. The hematologic manifestations of the megaloblastic anemia—that is, a macrocytic anemia with hypersegmentation of the polymorphonuclear leukocytes—are similar in both B_{12} and folate deficiencies. Both may exhibit a pancytopenia and both will have bone marrow evidence of ineffective erythropoiesis and cytonuclear dissociation. However, the central nervous system sequelae, from peripheral neuropathy to a flagrant organic mental syndrome, occur only in vitamin B_{12} deficiency. Treating Vitamin B_{12}-deficient patients with folate ameliorates the anemia but leaves unchanged or may worsen the neurologic complications. Therefore, the diagnosis of B_{12} deficiency must be considered before ascribing all macrocytic anemias to folate deficiency.

Measuring B_{12} and folate levels are the easiest way to diagnose these deficiencies. Although B_{12} levels may decrease in pregnancy, they typically remain within normal limits. In B_{12} deficiency, the folate level is often elevated unless a malabsorptive picture is also present. In folate deficiency, the B_{12} levels are low. In the younger female population with B_{12} deficiency, an anti-intrinsic factor antibody is positive in about 50 percent of patients. When the anti-intrinsic factor (IF) is positive, a Schilling test need not be done. If the anti-IF is negative, a Schilling test helps differentiate between B_{12} deficiency secondary to malabsorption and pernicious anemia. Schilling tests are contraindicated in pregnancy because

they involve radioactivity. In severe megaloblastic anemia, the peripheral blood smear may be so abnormal as to be mistaken for a myelodysplastic syndrome. Treatment of pernicious anemia is simple with daily injections of B_{12} for 1 to 2 weeks and then monthly injections thereafter.

Intrinsic Marrow Dysfunction Anemia accompanies myelodysplasia, myeloproliferative diseases, and many tumors. This anemia can be secondary to marrow replacement and/or invasion by nonerythropoietic precursors, as well as a suppression of cytokine production and response. Many of the so-called chronic anemias that result from diabetes, chronic infections, HIV, collagen vascular diseases, and so forth, are multifactorial in etiology. HIV is the most common infectious cause of chronic anemias. Typically, these states do not require therapy, as the hemoglobin levels are usually not very low. If a severe anemia does result, however, many of these anemias respond to pharmacologic doses of erythropoietin. The prototype of an erythropoietin-responsive anemia is chronic renal disease, and all patients with anemia secondary to chronic renal failure should be on erythropoietin and iron. Even patients on chronic chemo- or immunotherapy often are able to mount an erythropoietin-induced red cell response.

Aplastic Anemia Some aplastic anemias are red cell aplasias. Of these, many are secondary to parvovirus B19, a virus that has a special predilection for the red cell series and that can cause total red cell suppression, especially in patients with increased hematopoietic needs. A transient disease, it can when necessary be treated with immune globulin. The majority of patients with aplastic anemia have suppression of *all* hematopoietic elements. Occasionally, this is due to drugs, radiation, or toxins; however, this rare disease is usually thought to be secondary to an immune-mediated phenomenon. There is an increased propensity to occur in females and during pregnancy, and to recur with each successive pregnancy. Depending on the degree of leukopenia and thrombocytopenia, therapy may be merely supportive. However, in the event that the degree of suppression is severe, therapy should be guided by a specialist who will decide if and when antithymocyte globulin and/or bone marrow transplantation will be necessary. The advisability of continuing a pregnancy where aplastic anemia has occurred is questionable, although there are reports of infants surviving both therapies.

Although less than 10 g/dl of hemoglobin signals an anemia that requires investigation, most pregnant women can tolerate hemoglobin levels as low as 8 g/dl. There is some evidence, however, that this moderate anemia in the pregnant woman may predispose to increased fetal morbidity. Hemoglobins less than 9 g/dl may require acute therapy if there is a question of fetal well being. This therapy can be vastly different depending on the etiology of the anemia. If a deficiency such as iron or folate is the cause, supplementation alone is typically sufficient. In contrast, a patient with a refractory hypoplastic anemia may be transfused earlier. A patient with an autoimmune hemolytic anemia, on the other hand, should avoid transfusions for as long as possible because the antibody is likely to destroy transfused cells and not yield any lasting benefit. A patient with a hemoglobinopathy may also tolerate a somewhat lower level of hemoglobin because tissue oxygenation may be adequate.

Hyperproliferative Anemias

Thalassemia Usually, the patient with thalassemia major or intermedia has been diagnosed in childhood and is under a regular schedule of care. These patients have severe anemias soon after birth and for many, bone marrow transplantation has been lifesaving. For others without an HLA-identical match, monthly transfusions with iron chelation is the rule. In caring for these women with thalassemia, therapy is directed against two fronts. Most patients with β^0-thalassemia (thalassemia major) are on a transfusion regimen that is aimed at hematopoietic suppression so that the level of hemoglobin is acceptable without allowing their own endogenous hematopoiesis to be so massive as to cause bone deformi-

ties. Pregnancy is not advisable if the patient is symptomatic from iron overload and has evidence of impaired cardiac, pulmonary, or liver function. However, patients with well-controlled thalassemia have delivered normal, healthy infants successfully. A more difficult issue is iron chelation. All patients on chronic transfusion regimens should be on chelation therapy in order to delay the consequences of hemosiderosis. A question exists whether or not to continue iron chelation therapy during pregnancy. There are no data concerning the safety of desferrioxamine therapy either during pregnancy or during breast-feeding. General consensus is to stop chelation therapy during pregnancy and to restart after delivery of the infant or when breast-feeding is discontinued.

Patients with Hb E-$\beta°$ often have a clinical course that is similar to thalassemia major, and require transfusion. Patients with β^+-thalassemia (thalassemia intermedia) or HbH disease (only one of the four α genes present) are not so symptomatic and should not be placed on chronic transfusion regimens. These patients can be followed on a routine basis, but care must be taken during viral illness because the hematosuppression that may occur during such illnesses may render these patients quite anemic.

For many patients, the first time they learn that they have thalassemia trait is on a routine blood screening when a mild anemia is seen with microcytic, hypochromic red cell indices accompanied by a relatively normal red cell count. Differentiating this group from patients with iron deficiency is usually not difficult *if* the diagnosis is entertained. Patients with β-thalassemia trait often have a mild degree of splenomegaly and the reticulocyte count may be increased. On hemoglobin electrophoresis, an increase in Hb A$_2$ is present. Hb F is usually normal. Patients with thalassemia trait typically do very well and require either no therapy or folate therapy if their folate intake is insufficient. If the diagnosis of β-thalassemia trait is made during pregnancy, patients must receive additional folate. If the hemoglobin is low and/or the patient is symptom-

atic, transfusion may be indicated. Hemoglobin testing of a mate is advisable. If there is a hemoglobin abnormality in a potential father (thalassemia trait, sickle trait, or other abnormal hemoglobins) genetic counseling is appropriate.

Hb E With the increasing Asian population, a higher proportion of patients are seen with microcytosis secondary to Hb E or Hb E trait. Patients with Hb EE may have a mild anemia but typically, whether homo- or heterozygous, these patients do not have ill effects. The same is not true for Hb E-$\beta°$, which has a clinical course as discussed above, more like a thalassemia major. Again, recognition of the potential severity of thalassemias such as Hb E-$\beta°$ should prompt investigation of the potential father's hemoglobin type.

Enzyme and Membrane Defects Other causes of congenital hemolytic anemia are uncommon. Glucose-6-phosphate dehydrogenase deficiency, a sex-linked disorder, is rare in women. Pyruvate kinase deficiency is an autosomal recessive disorder that is an uncommon cause of hemolytic anemia. Hereditary spherocytosis, when first seen in adulthood, is typically mild. The anemia seen in this syndrome, if requiring therapy, can be mitigated by splenectomy. Most patients with hemolysis have an increase in bilirubin gallstones. Typically, these are soft stones and do not cause the same symptomatology as cholesterol-based cholelithiasis. However, persistent symptomatic cholelithiasis may only be cured by cholecystectomy.

Sickle Cell Anemia The adverse effects of sickle cell anemia are well recognized. Patients with sickle cell disease may have episodes of painful crises with severe bone pain that can require hospitalization for analgesia therapy and that can recur with frequencies ranging from less than once a year to almost continual hospitalization. In addition, sickle cell patients may suffer from strokes, leg ulcers, kidney failure, aseptic necrosis, and frequent infections (especially pneumonias). Acute pulmonary vaso-occlusion, known as acute chest syndrome, can be a life-threatening emergency, and requires immediate transfusion

and intervention. Aplastic anemia, typically secondary to parvovirus B19, can cause a precipitous hemoglobin drop within one day, as can splenic and/or hepatic sequestration crisis. The pregnant woman with sickle cell disease has an increase in morbidity, typically in the form of increased infections (notably urinary tract and pulmonary) and vaso-occlusive and/or thromboembolic complications. Infants are often small for gestational age, or premature; an increase in miscarriages also occurs. Patients with Hb SC have less difficulty with pregnancy and painful crises, but may have more aseptic necrosis and CNS events. Care should be taken in all these groups to make certain that, when pregnant, they are placed in a high risk category and seen at frequent intervals. All patients should be on folate therapy. All pregnant patients with sickle cell disease should have their blood screened for the presence of alloantibodies, which is higher in this population than in other equivalently transfused groups. If possible, the father's blood type (ABO, Rh, Kell, and probably Duffy and Jka) and hemoglobin type should be ascertained to be prepared for potential problems. There is no evidence that routine transfusion of patients with sickle cell disease is necessary or even desirable. Patients should be transfused if their level of hemoglobin is too low for them (sudden decompensation, high output failure, failure to thrive, etc.) or if they experience acute chest syndrome. Some patients with *refractory* painful crises unresponsive to therapy may respond to transfusions. Patients with sickle cell disease who are to undergo surgery require transfusion to a level of approximately 10 g/dl. Nonpregnant and pregnant patients with sickle cell trait do not have any significant increased morbidity. Again, genetic counseling and hemoglobin electrophoresis of the father is desirable.

Immunohemolytic Anemias Autoimmune hemolytic anemia is more common in women than men and is often associated with collagen vascular diseases, the use of certain medications (especially Aldomet, penicillin, quinidine, and cephalosporin) or some hematoproliferative disorders.

These patients may present with a profound anemia for which compatible blood is unavailable (secondary to a panagglutinin). Although many of these anemias respond initially to steroids and/or intravenous γ-globulin, more than two-thirds eventually recur and approximately one-third ultimately require splenectomy as a means of controlling hemolysis. Other causes of hemolytic anemias associated with pregnancy, such as HELLP, preeclampsia, and DIC, are discussed under coagulation and platelet abnormalities.

Erythrocytosis

Patients with increased hemoglobin levels have erythrocytosis. Care should be directed to determining whether this is secondary (due to chronic lung disease or to aberrant erythropoietin production) or primary (polycythemia vera). An erythrocytosis can occur with uterine leiomyomas, renal cysts, hemangiomas, liver tumors, or high-affinity hemoglobins. Although patients with erythrocytosis have been shown to have increased fetal and neonatal morbidity during pregnancy, it is not clear whether this is due to a truly higher hemoglobin or to a decrease in plasma volume that occurs with certain illnesses such as toxemia. Patients who have secondary polycythemia are typically comfortable if their hematocrit levels are less than 60 percent. Polycythemia vera is usually accompanied by leukocytosis, thrombocytosis, and splenomegaly. The major morbidity for these patients is thrombosis that is directly correlated with the hematocrit. These patients should maintain their hematocrit levels at less than 45 percent. Phlebotomy is a simple means of lowering hemoglobin levels; for patients with p. vera who are not contemplating pregnancy, therapy with hydroxyurea may be more appropriate.

Disorders of Leukocytes

The total leukocyte count in the nonpregnant woman commonly ranges between 4.5 and

10.0×10^9/liter. It has been observed that these counts are generally somewhat lower in the normal African-American population. Approximately 60 percent of leukocytes are neutrophils. The most commonly encountered abnormalities are leukopenia and leukocytosis.

Leukopenia

A leukocyte count below 3500/μl on repeated examinations is defined as leukopenia. Although all types of white cells may be decreased (granulocytes, lymphocytes, monocytes), the most frequent clinically important abnormality is neutropenia, where the absolute neutrophil count is less than 1500/μl. It has been observed that some African-Americans and Yemenite Jews normally have a low neutrophil count. On occasion, a viral infection can cause a significant leukopenia. However, these events are transitory and blood counts tend to normalize on recovery from the acute infection. Patients with AIDS may also have leukopenia as a result of neutropenia, as well as a markedly reduced absolute lymphocyte count.

When a woman presents with a fever and sore throat, and is found to have a profound neutropenia, the physician should be immediately alerted to the possibility of drug-induced neutropenia or agranulocytosis. In agranulocytosis, the absolute neutrophil count is at a dangerously low level ($\leq$500/μl). Such a patient should be hospitalized and consultation with infectious disease and hematology specialists should be obtained to institute appropriate antibiotic therapy and to determine the cause of the problem. The infection in such a case can rapidly spread, resulting in substantial risk to the patient's life.

There are numerous drugs that can cause agranulocytosis or neutropenia. Generally, these drugs belong to one of these broad classes: nonsteroidal anti-inflammatory; anticonvulsants; antipsychotics; antidepressants; anxiolytics; antimicrobials; antiarrhythmics; diuretics; or antineoplastic agents. Examples of drugs prescribed in office-practice settings that are associated with agranulocytosis or neutropenia are imipramine, indomethacin, carbamazepine (Tegretol), clozapine, methimazole (Tapazol), and aminopyrine. The physician must formulate a complete list of all the medications a patient with neutropenia is currently taking or has taken in the recent past, and then thoroughly check to determine whether any of those drugs have neutropenia included in their toxicity profiles. The first step is to promptly discontinue those drugs. In certain cases, it may be necessary to substitute another drug that is free of such toxicity if an abrupt discontinuance of the medication suspected to cause agranulocytosis puts the patient at some other risk (especially patients with seizure disorders or schizophrenia). In nonsevere situations, when absolute neutrophil counts are between 1000 and 1500/μl, it may not be necessary to hospitalize the patient, but efforts to discover the drug causing neutropenia should be the same as in cases of agranulocytosis.

The mechanism of toxicity of various groups of drugs that cause neutropenia or agranulocytosis is not known in all cases. In some cases, it may be an abrupt idiosyncratic reaction, and it may be immunologic or direct suppression of bone marrow in others. Once the causative agent of neutropenia is discovered and eliminated, the blood leukocyte count generally starts to return toward normal in about 1 week, taking 3 or 4 weeks for its complete normalization. For severe neutropenia (especially associated with fever or overt infection), filgrastim (Neupogen) administered under the care of a hematologist is indicated. These patients should be monitored with blood counts at 3- to 6-month intervals for about 1 year to ensure that no other hematologic abnormality is being missed.

In addition to the above, a primary care physician should also keep in mind that conditions such as systemic lupus erythematosus, Hodgkin's disease, and leukemias may occasionally be associated with leukopenia. If a leukopenic picture persists after a suspected causative drug has been discontinued, consultation with a hematologist should be sought.

Leukocytosis

A leukocytosis (total leukocyte count in excess of 12,000/μl) with neutrophilia in a nonpregnant woman generally indicates an acute infection or inflammation. Sometimes, with an acute infection, the blood neutrophil concentration may be as high as 20,000 to 40,000/μl. There may be an associated increase in the band-forms, and metamyelocytes may be seen on the peripheral blood smear. Neutrophils may contain coarse cytoplasmic granules (toxic granules). This pattern is called a leukemoid reaction. With successful treatment of the underlying infection or inflammation, the blood count returns to normal.

Hematologic Malignancies

If the blood leukocytosis is persistent, or if there is no evidence of any obvious acute infection or inflammation, a hematology consultation should be obtained. Leukemias, lymphomas, and other bone marrow diseases manifest themselves with leukocytosis as well as other abnormalities in the blood counts. If the report of the blood count reveals the presence of blast forms (lymphoblasts or myeloblasts) accounting for more than 20 percent of all leukocytes, acute leukemia should be suspected. If, however, the differential count report shows a preponderance of mature cells, a diagnosis of chronic leukemia is very likely [morphologically mature-appearing lymphocytes in chronic lymphocytic leukemia (CLL); myelocytes, metamyelocytes, bands and polymorphonuclear neutrophils in chronic myelocytic leukemia (CML)]. A thorough physical examination may reveal the presence of palpable lymphadenopathy, hepatomegaly, or splenomegaly. Although leukemias and lymphomas may occur at all ages, CLL is generally a disease of the elderly, and CML generally has a bimodal age incidence—teenage and young adults and again the fourth and fifth decades. Hodgkin's disease and non-Hodgkin's lymphomas can occur at all ages, although the former is seen less frequently among the elderly. Palpable enlarged lymph nodes that are nontender, discrete, and nonad-

herent to the adjacent tissue, with splenomegaly, are the usual abnormal findings on physical examination in cases of lymphoma. A brief overview of malignancies involving the hemopoietic system is provided in the following section.

Acute Myelocytic Leukemia [syn. acute myeloblastic leukemia (AML), acute nonlymphocytic leukemia (AML)] is the most common form of acute leukemia affecting adults, and accounts for 80 percent of all cases of acute leukemia. Patients with congenital chromosomal abnormalities such as Down syndrome and Fanconi anemia have a higher risk of developing AML. Although all associated high-risk factors for AML are not known, there is an association with exposure to benzene, radiation, and chemotherapy. Based on morphologic and histochemical features of the leukemic blasts, AML has been classified by the FAB (French, American, British) system into acute myeloblastic, promyelocytic, myelomonocytic, monoblastic, and erythro- and megakaryocytic leukemias. The following are recognized as poor prognostic markers in AML: older age (especially older than 60), AML developing after a period of preleukemic syndrome, the presence of certain chromosomal abnormalities, and the inability to achieve a complete remission after one cycle of remission-inducting therapy. Disseminated intravascular coagulopathy may complicate the clinical picture of patients at the time of initial diagnosis of AML; however, the overall survival of such patients has markedly improved with today's improved chemotherapy agents and judicious use of clotting factors, heparin, and transfusions. Chemotherapy to induce remission requires hospitalization of the patients because bone marrow ablation (rendering it hypocellular or acellular) is a requisite before one can expect regeneration of normal cells in the marrow. Therefore, during the chemotherapy and for a few weeks thereafter, the patients are pancytopenic, requiring frequent transfusions of red cells and platelets and intravenous antibiotics. The major components of remission-induction are cytosine arabinoside by continuous intravenous infusion and an anthracycline drug (such as daun-

orubicin) given intravenously. Virtually all patients require central venous access (either a subcutaneously placed infusaport or Hickman catheter) to protect from extravasation of vesicant drugs. There is a significant morbidity associated with chemotherapy, including hair loss, mucositis, neutropenic fevers, sepsis, and bleeding. Generally, AML patients need to remain hospitalized for 4 to 6 weeks for the remission-induction therapy. A regular visit to the hospital by the primary care physician is helpful both for continuity of care and for general reassurance and psychological purposes. Such a visit protects patients from a sense of abandonment at a time when they are emotionally most vulnerable. Following an achievement of complete remission (CR), AML patients need continued chemotherapy as consolidation or maintenance regimens at intervals of 1 to 2 months. The overall median survival with AML has shown slow but clear improvement over the past 15 years, and today is about 3 years from diagnosis. Nearly 30 percent of those who achieve a CR are living beyond 5 years.

Acute Lymphocytic Leukemia [syn. acute lymphoblastic leukemia (ALL)] is the least common form of leukemia in the adult population. The FAB classification of ALL is based on the degree of maturity of lymphoblasts on morphologic grounds. The most primitive appearing undifferentiated lymphoblastic ALL and those with Burkitt morphological features are associated with poor prognosis. Other poor prognostic features include leukocyte counts higher than 50,000/μl, myeloid surface markers, older age, extensive hepatosplenomegaly or adenopathy, CNS involvement, presence of Philadelphia chromosome, and failure to achieve a CR after the first 4 weeks of remission induction therapy. Women in general, tend to have a better prognosis with ALL than men.

The major components of remission-induction therapy are vincristine, prednisone, L-asparaginase, cytosine arabinoside, and CNS prophylaxis with methotrexate. Maintenance therapy is given for about 2 years. Patients with ALL generally are hospitalized during the first 4 weeks of chemotherapy, and the subsequent therapy is provided on an outpatient basis. Adults with ALL have an overall median survival of approximately 2 years. Therefore, today there is an increasing trend toward encouraging patients less than 60 years of age with an available HLA-compatible sibling to undergo bone marrow transplant therapy, especially in those patients presenting with bad prognostic features.

Chronic Myeloctytic Leukemia [syn. chronic myelogenous leukemia (CML)] accounts for nearly 20 percent of all leukemias in the adult. Most patients have splenomegaly at the time of initial presentation. An increased blood leukocyte count with a preponderance of myelocytes, metamyelocytes, and polymorphonuclear cells with an increase in eosinophils and basophils, and the presence in the chromosome karyotype of the bone marrow (or peripheral blood) of an abnormality known as the Philadelphia chromosome (a translocation between chromosomes 9 and 22) are the diagnostic criteria for CML. Many patients present because of feeling of excessive fatigue. There are three recognizable phases of CML: chronic, aggressive, and blastic. Therapy is directed toward control of the leukocyte count, splenomegaly, and Philadelphia chromosome abnormality during the chronic phase. The three most effective agents for chronic phase CML are α-interferon, hydroxyurea, and cytosine arabinoside. Although the treatment is delivered and supervised by a hematologist-oncologist, the primary care physicians should know about it because the patients invariably ask for their advice and guidance. α-Interferon therapy is associated with considerable morbidity—fever, body-aches, chills, and malaise—that adversely impact on the overall quality of life of a patient who otherwise without treatment may feel quite well. However, α-interferon therapy (in combination with either cytosine arabinoside or hydroxyurea) is known to produce major, or complete cytogenetic remissions (elimination or $\geq$50 percent reduction of Philadelphia chromosomes in the bone marrow) that otherwise is achievable only with an alloge-

neic stem cell transplant from an HLA-compatible donor. Cytosine arabinoside therapy also is associated with nausea, vomiting, and bone marrow depression. Hydroxyurea has no major untoward side effects. In a relatively young woman in chronic-phase CML, if there is no sibling who is HLA compatible, it is advisable to accept short-term severe toxicity with a combination of cytosine arabinoside and α-interferon because this regimen offers the best chance of increasing the overall life expectancy. Hydroxyurea is easy to administer and is well tolerated for maintenance therapy after a remission has been achieved. There is no satisfactory therapy for the aggressive and blastic phases of CML, although treatment strategies generally used for AML are applied. Long-term (more than 10 years) survival is possible in 30 to 40 percent of patients who are less than 50 years of age and who have received bone marrow transplantation with HLA-compatible sibling marrow during the chronic phase of CML. The overall median survival with CML is about 6 years.

Chronic Lymphocytic Leukemia (CLL) is generally considered to be a disease of the elderly, but is now being diagnosed in increasing numbers in younger (40- to 50-year-old) patients. CLL is the most common form of leukemia in the adult. It occurs in women somewhat less frequently than in men. The diagnosis of CLL is suspected when a blood count reveals a high total leukocyte level with a preponderance of lymphocytes. To establish a diagnosis of CLL, these three criteria are considered: a sustained and absolute lymphocytosis in the blood ($>5000/\mu$l) with mature appearing lymphocytes; lymphocytosis in the bone marrow that is hypercellular or normocellular; and phenotypic features of blood lymphocytes showing monoclonal B-cell proliferation. Presenting symptoms and abnormal findings on physical examination may vary; some patients have no symptoms at all and there may be no abnormalities on physical exam, while others may have significant weakness, fever without sepsis, night sweats, and weight loss with generalized enlargement of lymph nodes and splenomegaly. A ma-

jority of patients present with features in between these two extremes. The survival of CLL patients also varies over a wide spectrum. Some patients die within 2 years after diagnosis while others remain alive and well for 10 to 15 years and may die of causes unrelated to CLL.

The Rai clinical staging system identifies patients according to their survival outlook: low-risk group patients have no abnormalities except for the minimum diagnostic features and have a long median survival time (>11 years); intermediate-risk patients have adenopathy and/or hepatosplenomegaly and have a median survival time of 6 to 7 years; high-risk patients have significant anemia (hemoglobin ≤11 g%) and/or thrombocytopenia (platelets $<100,000/\mu$l) and have a median life-expectancy of about 2 years. CLL patients are not started on cytotoxic therapy until they develop symptoms from their disease or the palpable organomegaly starts to become problematic. Treatment is based on the use of chemotherapy—fludarabine, chlorambucil, and cyclophosphamide. Fludarabine has emerged as a superior drug to chlorambucil for inducing a higher incidence of responses, but it has not resulted in a prolongation of life-expectancy in CLL. Fludarabine-induced remissions last longer than with chlorambucil; therefore, those patients have longer periods without requiring more chemotherapy. However, fludarabine is a potent immunosuppressive and myelosuppressive drug. Patients who were initially managed with chlorambucil respond quite well when switched to fludarabine when chlorambucil is no longer effective, but when fludarabine is used as the initial therapy and after a period of benefit loses its effectiveness, a switch to chlorambucil is of no benefit. We recommend choosing fludarabine as the first drug for CLL patients who are relatively young in age. We do not use prednisone in combination with fludarabine because of an increased risk of opportunistic infections. However, prednisone is used when autoimmune complications are present, and in those cases, if chemotherapy is necessary, chlorambucil or cyclosphosphamide is used. Radiation therapy to

an enlarged spleen or to large bulky lymphoid masses is of benefit in selected cases. Splenectomy has also been useful for control of hypersplenism. Patients with CLL are at an increased risk of bacterial infections, and sometimes intravenous immunoglobulin therapy can be very helpful in affording protection from such infections. Some CLL patients with anemia respond very well to injections of erythropoietin and can become independent of the need for frequent transfusions.

Hodgkin's Disease is a lymphoid malignancy that can affect all age groups in females as well as males. Often there is a painless enlargement of lymph nodes with no associated symptoms, but some patients present with what are known as "B" symptoms of lymphoma; night sweats, fever without infections, and weight loss of 10 percent or more of the baseline weight without trying. There may be palpably enlarged lymph nodes with or without enlargement of the spleen. Diagnosis is made by pathologic examination of a lymph node, spleen, or bone marrow that shows the characteristic Reed-Sternberg cell. The pathologic subtype of nodular sclerosing Hodgkin's is the most common (40 to 75 percent of cases), followed by mixed cellularity (20 to 40 percent), while lymphocyte predominance and lymphocyte depletion subtypes each account for 5 to 10 percent of all cases of Hodgkin's disease. The lymphocyte depletion type of Hodgkin's disease is associated with a poor prognosis. To establish the extent of disease, a staging work-up is necessary and consists of a chest x-ray; CT scans of the chest, abdomen, and pelvis; bone marrow examination; and, in selected cases, lymphangiogram and gallium scan. Splenectomy and exploratory laparotomy for biopsies of the liver and lymph nodes are done in selected cases of Hodgkin's disease. The Ann Arbor classification of extent of disease classifies stage I as involvement of a single lymph node region, stage II as involvement of two or more lymph node regions on the same side of the diaphragm, stage III as involvement of lymph node regions on both sides of the diaphragm, and stage IV as involvement of extralymphatic sites (i.e., bone marrow, liver, lungs). Each stage is further classified as either B (presence of classical symptoms of lymphoma) or A (absence of symptoms). Treatment strategies are governed by the staging; radiation therapy is appropriate for stages I and IIA. Some cases of stage IIIA are also treated with radiation therapy. Chemotherapy is used for all stage IIB, IIIB, and IV patients. For bulky mediastinal masses with stages II, III, and IV, both radiation therapy and chemotherapy are necessary to achieve a complete response. Chemotherapeutic drugs are used in combinations known by the acronyms MOPP [nitrogen mustard, vincristine (Oncovin), procarbazine, prednisone] and ABVD [doxorubicin (Adriamycin), bleomycin, vinblastine, and dacarbazine]. The combination of newer antiemetic drugs (ondansetron, granisetron) with older ones (prochlorperazine, lorazepam, diphenhydramine), has reduced chemotherapy-induced severe nausea and vomiting to a very large extent. Similarly, the use of filgrastim (Neupogen) has significantly reduced the incidence of chemotherapy-induced severe neutropenia. With these approaches to the therapy of Hodgkin's disease, an increasing proportion of patients are living 10 to 20 years without evidence of disease. Once the patients have completed their chemotherapy or radiation therapy, they can resume their follow-up with their primary care physician.

Primary care physicians must remain alert to the fact that long-term survivors of Hodgkin's disease may develop a second malignancy, including breast cancer and other solid tumors, leukemias, and lymphoma.

In a study of late effects of cancer treatment, 1380 children with Hodgkin's disease were followed for several years after their initial treatment (provided between 1955 and 1986) to determine the incidence of second neoplasms. In this cohort, there were 483 girls with a median age of 11 years (range: 1 to 16 years) at the time of diagnosis of Hodgkin's disease. Only 8 percent received chemotherapy alone, 23 percent had radiation alone, and 69 percent had both chemotherapy and radiation therapy. MOPP chemotherapy was given to 25 percent and ABVD to 75

percent; only 2 percent received radiation using orthovoltage techniques. This long-term follow-up study of 1380 children revealed a significantly elevated risk for all cancers combined, for leukemia, for non-Hodgkin's lymphoma, and for breast, thyroid, bone, central nervous system, colorectal, and gastric cancers. During the follow-up period the 483 young females developed 32 solid tumors, 8 leukemias, and 3 non-Hodgkin's lymphomas. Sixty-six percent of solid cancers developed in the group of patients who received both radiation and chemotherapy. A significantly higher risk of solid tumors (even 20 years after the diagnosis of Hodgkin's disease) was observed among women than in men (12.6 percent versus 3.9 percent, respectively). This increased incidence of second malignancies with solid neoplasms among women was almost wholly accounted for by 17 cases of breast cancers—8 occurred > 20 years, 1 between 16 and 20 years, 4 between 11 and 15 years, and 2 each between 6 and 10 and 0 and 5 years, respectively, during the follow-up period. Sixteen of the 17 breast cancers appeared within or at the margin of the radiation field. Five patients had bilateral breast tumors. The majority of the tumors were infiltrating ductal or lobular carcinomas. The median age of women at the time of diagnosis of breast cancer was 31.5 years (range: 16 to 42). The women in this cohort of survivors of Hodgkin's disease had a risk of breast cancer that was 75 times greater than the risk in the general population. The risk of breast cancer was elevated throughout the follow-up period, and the interval from the diagnosis of Hodgkin's disease to the diagnosis of breast cancer was less than five years in two cases. The estimated actuarial cumulative probability of breast cancer was 35 percent at 40 years of age. Multivariate analysis of all the risk factors revealed that an age of more than 10 years at the time of diagnosis of Hodgkin's disease and a higher radiation dose (>2000 cGy) were independently associated with increased risk of breast cancer. The risk of leukemia reached a plateau at 2.8 percent and the risk of non-Hodgkin's lymphoma plateaued at 1.1 percent. There were no cases of leukemia in the group treated only with radiation therapy. The cumulative probability of leukemia in patients receiving an alkylating agent-based MOPP chemotherapy was higher than with ABVD (2.9 percent versus 0.9 percent). Alkylating agent-based chemotherapy was the only significant independent risk factor for developing non-Hodgkin's lymphoma. These observations have forced the clinicians to seriously consider giving reduced dosage of radiation therapy and avoiding alkylating agent-based chemotherapy for Hodgkin's disease, especially for girls over 10 years of age. The high risk of breast cancer in women exposed to radiation at a young age raises important issues regarding enhanced screening programs, including physical examination of the breasts, and chemoprevention (e.g., tamoxifen) for survivors of Hodgkin's disease.

Non-Hodgkin's Lymphoma (NHL) is a diagnosis given to a heterogeneous group of lymphoid malignancies with either B-cell or T-cell monoclonal origin. Although all the etiologic factors of NHL are not known, there is a higher than expected rate of occurrence in immunosuppressed patients (renal transplantation, AIDS) and those exposed to radiation or various viruses (Burkitt's lymphoma and Epstein-Barr virus). Presenting symptoms and physical findings bear some resemblance to those seen in Hodgkin's disease. Diagnosis is established by pathologic examination of a biopsied enlarged lymph node or other involved tissue including the bone marrow. Pathologic subtyping was formerly done by the Rappaport criteria, but now the International Working Formulation (IWF) and the proposed Revised European American Lymphoma (REAL) classifications are used widely. IWF divides NHL into low-grade (small lymphocytic, follicular cleaved or mixed cell types); intermediate-grade (follicular large cell, diffuse small-, mixed-, or large-cell types); and high-grade (large cell, immunoblastic, lymphoblastic small noncleaved, or Burkitt or non-Burkitt cell types). The classification for extent of disease is similar to the Ann Arbor method described under Hodgkin's disease. However, NHLs present with extranodal involvement more often than Hodgkin's

and NHL tends to be more disseminated than Hodgkin's. The treatment and prognosis of NHL depends on a combination of both pathologic IWF subtype and Ann Arbor clinical stage. Generally speaking, chemotherapy is the mainstay of treatment in most cases of NHL. The choice of drugs varies from single-agent cyclophosphamide to combinations known by acronyms such as COP (cyclophosphamide, vincristine, prednisone) and CHOP (COP+doxorubicin). Some patients with NHL have a relatively indolent course and may be followed without instituting any cytotoxic therapy until "B" symptoms develop. Selected patients have benefited from radiation therapy to the involved lymphoid masses. Autologous bone marrow transplantation can be curative in selected cases of NHL as well as of Hodgkin's disease. With the improvements in chemoradiation therapy methods and in supportive therapies (antiemetic and protection from severe neutropenia), the overall survival in patients with NHL is improving continuously, but cures remain at relatively low frequencies.

Multiple Myeloma (syn. myeloma) and other malignancies involving plasma cells (Waldenström's macroglobulinemia, solitary plasmacytoma) are relatively rare B-cell neoplasms. The presenting features may vary from an accidental discovery of abnormally high total protein in the serum in an otherwise asymptomatic patient to symptoms of profound weakness, bone pain, and the discovery of pathologic fractures. The main diagnostic criteria are the presence of paraproteinemia, consisting of monoclonal immunoglobulin (IgG, IgA, and free light chains in myeloma, and IgM in Waldenström's macroglobulinemia), with marrow infiltration by plasma cells (myeloma) or lymphoplasmacytic cells (Waldenström's). These patients usually have anemia and an elevated sedimentation rate. They may have an increased vulnerability to infections and a bleeding diathesis. A hyperviscosity syndrome may result from severe paraproteinemia. The presence of renal insufficiency (elevated serum BUN and creatinine), hypercalcemia, and lytic lesions in the skeleton (with pathologic fractures)

portend a bad prognosis. The mainstay of treatment is chemotherapy (melphalan, prednisone, vincristine, doxorubicin, and dexamethasone). Radiation of painful skeletal lesions offers relief from symptoms. Therapeutic plasmapheresis is necessary prior to initiating chemotherapy when the serum viscosity is very high. The overall median survival of patients is 4 to 6 years.

Disorders of Platelets and Coagulation System

Coagulation Disorders (Table 70-2)

The most common congenital coagulation disorders in females are von Willebrand disease (vWD) and factor XI deficiency (hemophilia C). Factor VIII (hemophilia A) and factor IX (hemophilia B) deficiencies are sex linked and although they can occur in females, they rarely do. Patients with von Willebrand disease may present with easy bruisability and menorrhagia; patients with factor XI deficiency will more often present with a posttraumatic hemorrhage. On laboratory testing, both of these deficiencies demonstrate a prolonged PTT; typically the PTT of the patient with factor XI deficiency is longer than that of the patient with von Willebrand disease. The prolongation of PTT itself does not correlate with the degree of bleeding. Both these diseases can manifest widely disparate symptomatology and the best indicator for the patient's future prognosis is the family or the patient's prior surgical history. If the patient and/or the patient's family has no history of bleeding during previous surgical procedures, the patient is unlikely to bleed and should require no blood product. Thus, a patient with 5% factor XI who has bled from a previous operation will require plasma coverage in the next; a similar patient with 5% factor XI who has not bled should merely have plasma reserved for her in the blood bank. Similarly, many patients with vWD may be treated with desmopressin alone or desmopressin and amicar (epsilon aminocaproic acid); others may require treat-

TABLE 70-2   Coagulation Disorders

Congenital
  von Willebrand disease
  Factor XI deficiency
  Factor VII deficiency (rarely)

Acquired
  Antiphospholipid syndrome
  DIC

---

ment with a factor VIII product known to contain active functional von Willebrand factor (vWF) (such as Humate P). vWF increases greatly during pregnancy as do factor VIII and fibrinogen; the other factors increase somewhat. These increases often enable patients with mild von Willebrand disease and hemophilia A to be delivered without the need to resort to the administration of blood products. Levels of factor VIII and/or von Willebrand factor should be determined close to the delivery date to clarify whether a bleeding problem may likely be present during delivery. Although factor XI levels may increase somewhat during pregnancy, the increase is mild.

The Antiphospholipid Syndrome

Probably the most common abnormality seen in the female population is a prolonged prothrombin time (PT) and/or partial thromboplastin time (PTT) with *no* prior history of bleeding. Having discovered the prolonged clotting test, it becomes important to differentiate among an asymptomatic hemophiliac, a patient with a clotting diathesis, and a patient with a contact product abnormality with no significant clinical or prenatal sequelae. The first test to order for these women is a *mixing* or an *inhibitor* study to detect whether an inhibitor is present. Patients with congenital deficiencies who have not been previously transfused will correct their clotting tests (negative mixing tests). Other patients may have positive mixing studies that demonstrate the presence of an inhibitor to the coagulation cascade. Usually,

these are antiphospholipid antibodies (APA). Such patients may also have anticardiolipin antibodies present (ACL). When these tests are abnormal and there is a history of thrombosis or miscarriage, the patient is said to have the "antiphospholipid syndrome" (also known as "the lupus anticoagulant," although this more accurately refers to the clotting tests alone). In this condition, there is an increase in fetal wastage and in maternal and fetal obstetrical complications. APA positivity may be a more sensitive indicator of future thrombotic events and fetal loss, but there is no general consensus regarding which laboratory parameters are best to follow during pregnancy. The range of antibodies present may be highly variable and may change during the pregnancy. There is not unanimity of opinion regarding optimal therapy for this group. There is general agreement that no therapy is needed when the patient is asymptomatic. However, a woman with an antiphospholipid antibody who has had several miscarriages and is currently pregnant presents a difficult management problem. The poor prognosis may be mitigated by the use of anticoagulants (heparin) and/or aspirin in some cases. Laboratory documentation of decreases in antibody titer are not associated with improvement in outcome for many of these patients. There is some evidence that correlating Doppler studies with lupus anticoagulant clotting parameters is helpful in monitoring the disease and predicting outcome. Current recommendations include close monitoring and supportive care.

Thrombophilia

Many of the thrombotic episodes that occur in women (and men) under the age of 45 are due to congenital thrombophilias. Deficiencies in protein C, protein S, and antithrombin III (ATIII) all have been associated with an increased incidence of thrombosis or thromboses in various sites. Less commonly, problems with fibrinolysis, such as decreased plasminogen or

increased plasminogen activator inhibitor, have been documented. Patients with factor V Leiden, an abnormal factor V that binds well with the prothrombinase complex but poorly with protein C, is thought to be responsible for 20 to 40 percent of all thrombotic events in young Caucasians. This is thought to be the cause of resistance to activated protein C (APC). Another cause of thrombophilia has been determined to be secondary to an abnormal prothrombin protein, Prothrombin 20210.

When compared to nonpregnant females, pregnant women and, to some extent women taking oral contraceptives, have a "hypercoagulable state." Changes in coagulation factors in these patients include an increase in factor VIII, in von Willebrand factor, and in fibrinogen. For the nonpregnant, nonsmoker female taking birth control pills, these changes are unimportant. In pregnancy, many of these levels increase in the third trimester. This must be kept in mind when assessing coagulation parameters in pregnancy. These increases in coagulation proteins are accompanied by a decrease in ATIII and in fibrinolysis. These changes, plus the increased venous pressure from the pregnancy itself, cause a thrombotic diathesis. To date, no prophylaxis (for what is a normal physiologic state) is recommended, unless a thrombotic event has occurred.

Disseminated Intravascular Coagulation

Disseminated intravascular coagulation (DIC) typically occurs as a secondary event to a severe illness, be it sepsis, cancer, or another illness. It can also occur in pregnancy and is associated with such problems as amniotic fluid embolism, fetal demise, incomplete abortion, intra-amniotic saline injections, eclampsia, drugs, HIV, and sepsis. The laboratory features of schistocytes on smear, an increased PT, PTT, decreased platelet counts, relatively low fibrinogens, and positive D-dimers are usually characteristic. DIC must be differentiated from TTP and HUS (discussed below).

Thrombocytopenia (Table 70-3)

Thrombocytopenia, like anemia, can be divided into hypoproliferative or destructive etiologies. Sometimes thrombocytopenias are assumed to be destructive when the platelets visible on peripheral blood smear are large, and hypoproliferative when they are small. However, some congenital and dysplastic thrombocytopenias may display larger than normal-sized platelets and yet still be hypoproliferative in character. The final diagnosis rests on the marrow, and marrow examination may be necessary to determine the etiology of a thrombocytopenia if initial studies do not clarify the issue. For the majority of patients, a marrow evaluation is not necessary.

Hypoproliferative Thrombocytopenias The most common causes of a hypoproliferative thrombocytopenia are drugs, nutritional deficiencies, infections, and infiltrative disease. The drugs that are most often implicated are alcohol, chemotherapeutic agents, and antibiotics. Infection can cause a hypoproliferative thrombocytopenia secondary to suppressed hematopoiesis, but infection also can result in increased destruction secondary to immune complexes or DIC. Particularly, HIV has been associated with both a hypoproliferative and a destructive thrombocytopenia.

Occasionally, low platelets may be secondary to nutritional deficiency (B_{12} or folate), and

TABLE 70-3 Thrombocytopenia

Nonpregnant
  Drugs—chemotherapy, antibiotics
  Infection—viral, sepsis
  Immune thrombocytopenic purpura (ITP)
  Human immunodeficiency virus (HIV)
  B_{12}/folate deficiency
  Microvascular syndromes—TTP, HUS
  Marrow invasion and/or infiltration

Pregnant (all of the above plus)
  Incidental thrombocytopenia
  Preeclampsia (including HELLP)
  HELLP

rarely, they may be the presenting and predominant symptom. Tumor, myeloproliferative, or lymphoproliferative disease can all cause decreased platelet production secondary to invasion of the bone marrow. Typically, hypoproliferative thrombocytopenias when symptomatic (bleeding or platelet count <10,000) respond well to platelet transfusions.

Destructive Thrombocytopenias *Drugs* More commonly, the cause of thrombocytopenia is destructive. It sometimes seems that every drug created by every pharmaceutical company has thrombocytopenia listed as a potential side effect, making the differential diagnosis of a sick patient quite difficult. The more commonly incriminated drugs are the antibiotics and some of the cardiovascular drugs, especially quinidine, ticlopidine, and Reopro (abciximab).

ITP A troublesome and not uncommon thrombocytopenia is immune thrombocytopenic purpura. In its adult chronic form, it is recurrent and sometimes associated with collagen vascular disorders. Like autoimmune hemolytic anemia, it often responds to steroids or IVGG initially only to recur or recrudesce. Because the platelets are often quite large, making the surface area much higher, the platelet counts tolerated by this group before they experience bleeding are much lower than those of patients with hypoproliferative thrombocytopenias. Still, when platelet counts are less than 10,000, these patients have increased morbidity and an increase in CNS bleeds.

Thrombotic Thrombocytopenic Purpura (TTP) and Hemolytic Uremic Syndrome (HUS) TTP and HUS are diseases that have an increased incidence in women. Both TTP and HUS may occur in young women and are manifested by fever, a microangiopathic hemolytic anemia, and a thrombocytopenia. Renal vaso-occlusion is more prevalent in HUS, whereas CNS events are more common in TTP. There may be a recurrent form for both these illnesses, which suggests, to some, a congenital defect as the cause. TTP may be seen with increased frequency in pregnancy, typically in the second trimester. Therapy for

TTP is similar whether the patient is pregnant or not: an immediate plasma exchange or infusion with fresh frozen plasma is necessary. Plasma infusions, with or without exchange, aspirin, and/or steroids, ameliorate the problem in most patients, and mortality is less than 20 percent as compared to 60 to 80 percent without plasma exchange therapy. In contrast, HUS with its more prominent renal component, has a different prognosis in pregnant, as compared to nonpregnant, women. Women who are not pregnant respond to the same modalities used in TTP with generally the same frequency. HUS in pregnancy, however, typically occurs within the first month postpartum, is often associated with a premorbid gastroenteritis, and carries with it a 60 percent mortality even with therapy. An examination for retained products of conception may prove fruitful. This postpartum type of HUS often requires dialysis.

Thrombocytopenia and Pregnancy Thrombocytopenia in pregnancy is different from thrombocytopenia in a nonpregnant female because of the potential dangers of thrombocytopenia for the neonate. There are four separate categories: The first subset consists of pregnant women with thrombocytopenia in whom no abnormality could be found on either history or physical examination ("incidental thrombocytopenia"). These women have babies who do not have a rate of thrombocytopenia significantly different from women with normal platelet counts. Most of the women with this syndrome have platelet counts that are ≥100,000, although <150,000/mm³. In most cases there are no complications. It is not a clinically important entity other than to differentiate it from immune thrombocytopenic purpura (ITP) where the incidence of neonatal thrombocytopenia is high. The differential diagnosis rests on history. Although generally women with incidental thrombocytopenia have higher platelet counts than the group of mothers with ITP, the platelet count itself is not very helpful and the platelet-associated IGG is not useful in predicting neonatal thrombocytopenia. Thus, a woman with a history of ITP and a platelet count

of 250,000/mm^3 is still at risk of delivering a child with severe ITP.

The second group consists of the subset of women with hypertension syndromes. This group includes patients with preeclampsia and related syndromes. Preeclampsia is one of the more common causes of thrombocytopenia in the third trimester and occurs more often in those who are primigravida. Studies estimate that 9 to 50 percent of these women will have some decrease in their platelet count. Often the thrombocytopenia is associated with a hemolytic state and a true microangiopathic state can develop. Heparin is ineffective although aspirin has been tried with some success. The mainstay of treatment involves control of the preeclampsia, and early delivery. The vast majority of mothers with thrombocytopenia secondary to preeclampsia have normalized platelet counts within three days of delivery. A more serious problem associated with preeclampsia is the HELLP syndrome. In this entity, of Hemolysis, Elevated Liver enzymes and Low Platelets, the perinatal mortality is significant. DIC and abruptio placenta are frequent associations. Therapy is directed at early delivery when possible, although conservative attempts at waiting until fetal maturity is reached have been used. Fresh frozen plasma has had some success for bleeding episodes.

The third subset consists of patients with chronic diseases whose platelet counts have been previously low or low normal, who further decrease their platelet count during pregnancy. These are women with diabetes, hypersplenism, and primary hematologic diseases. Patients with insulin-dependent diabetes may have platelet counts that are at the lower end of the normal range; patients with gestational diabetes do not appear to be similarly affected. Therapy must be tailored to each patient based on maternal platelet count and the estimated danger of bleeding.

The last group includes women with preexisting ITP regardless of their present platelet count. ITP mothers comprise a much smaller group, approximately 1 : 10,000 pregnancies. The disease process may recrudesce or recur during pregnancy. The incidence of neonatal thrombocytopenia in this group is much higher, ranging from 5 to 60 percent in different studies. Factors determining the neonatal platelet count are many, including differences in functional maturity of the fetal reticuloendothelial system, fetal hematopoietic capability, and developmental differences in platelet membrane antigenic epitope exposure. Neonatal platelet counts cannot be predicted from maternal counts in ITP, and often the neonate will continue to decrease his/her platelet count for the first few days. If a woman has a history of ITP, there is a higher risk of thrombocytopenia in the neonate. The converse also is true. If there is no history of ITP, the chance of having an infant with severe neonatal thrombocytopenia is small.

Another type of autoimmune thrombocytopenia occurs in the group of pregnant women with antiphospholipid syndrome. This group has an increased risk of bleeding as compared to those patients with an antiphospholipid antibody who do not have thrombocytopenia, and therefore they need to be followed both for increased risk of miscarriage and possibly some increased hemorrhage at delivery.

The therapeutic options for pregnant women with ITP are similar to those for the nonpregnant patient. However, many of these options may benefit the mother without increasing the fetal platelet counts. Mothers with ITP may have their platelet counts increased by steroids or intravenous γ-globulin (IVGG), but this will not necessarily affect fetal platelet counts. We recommend treating ITP with steroids if the platelet count is low enough to be dangerous for the mother.

Thrombocytosis

Thrombocytosis is uncommon. Typically it is associated with bleeding, tumors, chronic inflammation, and postsplenectomy. It may also be secondary to a myeloproliferative syndrome, either essential thrombocythemia (ET) itself, or associated with polycythemia vera (PV) or chronic my-

elogenous leukemia (CML). Although the mye-loproliferative diseases tend to occur in the middle-aged (PV or CML) or the elderly (ET), there is a subgroup of ET that occurs in younger women and is associated with acrocyanosis, digital thrombosis, and ischemia. A mild thrombo-cytosis is not uncommon during normal pregnancy and may increase due to bleeding or trauma that occurs during delivery. Although typically thrombocytosis itself is not dangerous and requires no therapy, thrombocytosis secondary to myeloproliferative disease requires treatment with chemotherapeutic agents and/or aspirin, and needs close observation. A new drug, anagrelide, is approved for therapy of patients with essential thrombocythemia.

Splenomegaly

A physical examination should normally include palpation of the liver and the spleen. The technique of splenic palpation differs from that of liver palpation in that it requires merely light laying of hands just under the lateral lower left or midaxillary part of the rib cage. The hard palpation used for liver assessment often results in propelling the spleen away rather than its capture. Because lung sizes may be quite disparate, spleens may be enlarged but remain under the costal margin, or may be normal in size but palpable below the costal margin. True splenomegaly occurs in 2 to 5 percent of the U.S. population, but at much higher rates in tropical populations. When the spleen enlarges, "hypersplenism" may occur, resulting in an increased level of hematopoietic destruction within the spleen. Hyper-splenism may cause anemia, leukopenia, and/or thrombocytopenia. Typically, the bone marrow response is active but inadequate to meet the demand.

Overall, a large spleen does not require attention unless the cytopenia demands action or there is a potential for rupture. The etiology of true splenomegaly often helps determine whether therapy is or will be necessary (Table 70-4). Sple-

TABLE 70-4   Differential Diagnosis of Splenomegaly

Hepatitis
  CMV
  Hepatitis A, B, C
  Infectious mononucleosis
  Malaria
Infiltrative
  Infectious
  TB
  Histoplasma
Noninfectious
  Amyloid
  Gaucher's
Neoplastic and Hematologic
  Acute leukemias
  Chronic leukemias
  Myelodysplasia
  Polycythemia
  Myelofibrosis
  Hemoglobinopathies
  Thalassemia

nomegaly may be due to simple cysts and heman-giomas, or increased portal or splenic vein pressure from cirrhosis, idiopathic, or thrombotic causes. Infection typically causing both hepato-megaly and splenomegaly results from hepatitis (mononucleosis, malaria, CMV, hepatitis A, B, or C) or a chronic granulomatous infiltrative process (TB, histoplasma, echinococcus). Noninfec-tious infiltrative etiologies, such as amyloid, Gaucher's disease, and glycogen storage disease, typically have been present for long periods of time. Occasionally, diabetes may cause an enlarged spleen. Neoplasms may cause enlargement of the spleen either through infiltrative processes such as leukemias, diffuse lymphomas, or via invasion by metastatic tumors.

Connective tissue disorders, such as systemic lupus erythematosus, sarcoid, or rheumatoid arthritis, often have an accompanying spleno-megaly without liver enlargement. Acquired splenomegaly is associated with autoimmune syndromes such as autoimmune hemolytic anemias, chronic idiopathic thrombocytopenic purpura, and Felty's syndrome (neutropenia and splenomegaly).

Hematologic causes of splenomegaly may be congenital or acquired. Congenital etiologies of splenomegaly are usually due to increased hematopoietic demand secondary to hemoglobinopathies and thalassemias. In these diseases, the increased demand has been present since birth and has inhibited the natural repression of fetal splenic hematopoiesis. In the acquired disorders, the spleen may be enlarged in myelodysplastic ("preleukemic") syndromes, and in acute or chronic myeloid and lymphoid leukemias. Polycythemia vera may be differentiated from other causes of erythocytosis by the almost universal splenic enlargement, while some of the largest myeloproliferative spleens are seen in agnogenic myeloid metaplasia with myelofibrosis.

Surgical therapy is indicated only in cases of severe discomfort, potential rupture, or hypersplenism that outstrips hematopoietic capability. Although there is some question of an increased incidence of sepsis in splenectomized children, there are no data that splenectomy is harmful in the adult population. The peripheral smear in the splenectomized adult will typically show Howell-Jolly bodies (fragments of chromatin left within the red cells that would normally have been removed) and target cells; there may be thrombocytosis either acutely and/or chronically.

References and Selected Readings

1. Weatherall DJ: The hereditary anemias. *BMJ* 314:492, 1997.
2. Edlund M, Blomback M, Von Schoultz B, Andersson O: On the value of menorrhagia as a predictor for coagulation disorders. *Am J Hematol* 53:234–238, 1996.
3. Luscher JM: Screening and diagnosis of coagulation disorders. *Am J Obstet Gynecol* 175:778–783, 1996.
4. Goldstein KH, Abramson N: Efficient diagnosis of thrombocytopenia. *Am Fam Physician* 53:915–920, 1996.
5. Crowther MA, Burrows RF, Ginsberg J, Kelton JG: Thrombocytopenia in pregnancy. *Blood Rev* 10:8–16, 1996.
6. Petri M: Pathogenesis and treatment of the antiphospholipid antibody syndrome. *Med Clin North Am* 7(81):151–177, 1997.
7. Bhatia S, Robison LL, Oberlin O, et al Breast cancer and other second neoplasms after childhood Hodgkin's disease. *N Engl J Med* 334:745–751, 1996.
8. Donaldson SS, Hancock, SL: Second cancers after Hodgkin's disease in childhood. *N Engl J Med* 334: 792–794, 1996.

Clinical Neurology: Practical Office Evaluation and Treatment of Common Neurologic Disorders

Ronald Kanner

NEUROLOGIC HISTORY
NEUROLOGIC EXAMINATION
Mental Status • Cranial Nerves • Motor Examination • Sensory Examination • Reflexes • Coordination and Gait Examinations

COMMON CLASSES OF NEUROLOGIC DISEASE SEEN IN OFFICE PRACTICE
Episodic Loss of Consciousness • Loss of Intellect, Memory, or Language Function • Weakness • Disorders of Gait and Movement

Three factors stand out when addressing neurologic issues in women:

1. Certain neurologic disorders are much more common in women than in men (e.g., headache, multiple sclerosis);
2. Treatment of neurologic disorders is affected by pregnancy and normal hormonal fluctuations;
3. Oral contraceptive and hormone replacement therapy can affect the course of neurologic diseases.

Neurologic diseases are frightening and often devastating, affecting the very functions that make us human. The problem is further compounded by the commonly held belief that there is little in the way of therapeutic options for most neurologic disorders. While this latter statement may currently be true of some inherited/degenerative diseases of the nervous system, most of the problems seen in office practice can be addressed quickly and effectively.

Accurate diagnosis and treatment depend on a well-directed history, a careful neurologic examination, and the judicious selection of ancillary tests. This chapter discusses the neurologic history and physical examination, and the ancillary tests with each of the presenting problems. The orientation is around symptoms, rather than diseases, because that is the way patients present in the office. Gender differences in presentation and treatment are discussed, when germane.

Neurologic History

The neurologic history is more focused than a general medical history. Three major issues define the current complaint: location, onset, and progression. Location is the easiest point to obtain. The patient complains of a specific deficit (pain, weakness, or sensory loss) and can simply point to the area involved. The "geographic" pattern of impairment provides insight into the syndrome diagnosis (e.g., proximal weakness in myopathies; distal weakness in neuropathies; hemiparesis in cerebral disorders; radicular sensory loss in herniated discs). The temporal pattern (onset and progression) provides etiologic

insight (sudden and stable or improving in vascular disease; gradual and progressive in tumor or degeneration). Special attention should be paid to alterations in the temporal pattern associated with the menstrual cycle, pregnancy, or the use of oral contraceptives. These issues are addressed more fully in the sections that discuss the individual syndromes.

Neurologic Examination

An adequate neurologic examination can be performed in 5 min. Following a set pattern of examination, with emphasis on the area of complaint, can expedite the process. One possible approach is a "top to bottom" orientation, starting with mental status, then progressing to cranial nerves, motor, sensory, reflex, coordination, and gait examinations. The slight gender differences that have been described in olfactory perception and pain threshold are not clinically relevant.

Mental Status

The *level* of consciousness and the *content* of consciousness form the two main components of the mental status examination. Level of consciousness is purely descriptive. "Fully awake, alert, and oriented" and "comatose and unresponsive to all stimuli" represent ends of the spectrum that are easily understood. The problems lie in between. Vague terms, such as "lethargic," "stuporous," and "semicomatose" are not useful unless they are accompanied by an accurate description of the patient at rest, the stimuli that are required to arouse the patient, and the patient's best level of function when aroused.

Language function and memory are the two most important parts of the content of consciousness. A simple conversation and history-taking provide adequate language assessment in the majority of patients. If there is any doubt, the patient should be asked to follow some simple commands, repeat simple phrases, and name common objects. On the basis of these tests, the most commonly occurring aphasias can be classified (Table 71-1).

Memory function can only be tested after it is ascertained that the patient has adequate language function and attention. The level of education and sophistication should also be noted. The patient is asked to spell a five-letter word (e.g., world) and then spell it backwards (testing attention). Recent recall is then tested by asking the patient to recall three familiar objects after 5 min of distraction with other tasks (arithmetic function, reasoning, etc.). Remote recall should be tested using facts that can be verified (e.g., political events or family names when other members of the family are present).

Cranial Nerves

Cranial nerve (CN) I: *Olfactory* function is not always checked, but is important in cases of trauma and dementia. A familiar substance, such as coffee, should be passed under each nostril, with the other nostril blocked. Do not use alcohol, because it produces a noxious stimulus. Women may be slightly more sensitive than men to the perception of a specific odor, but this sensitivity is not clinically relevant.

CN II: *Optic nerve* function involves visual acuity, visual fields, and direct inspection of the nerve (funduscopic exam). Careful examination of the optic disc is imperative in women with headaches,

TABLE 71-1 Common Aphasias[a]

	Broca	Wernicke
Location	Anterior Inferior Frontal	Posterior Temporal
Type	Motor Expressive	Sensory Receptive
Output	Nonfluent	Fluent
Hemiparesis	Yes	No

[a]Most commonly, aphasias are mixed, showing characteristics of both anterior and posterior types. In a "global" aphasia, both components are fully represented, and the patient has neither comprehension nor significant output.

because of the possibility of pseudotumor cerebri, which is discussed in the section on headaches. The optic nerve is the afferent part of the pupillary light reflex. Visual acuity and visual fields should be checked before the fundi are examined, because the intense light of the funduscopic exam causes a large, artificial blind spot.

CN III, IV, and VI: *Oculomotor, trochlear, and abducens nerve* functions are tested together, first by observing the eye position on primary (straight ahead) gaze, then by having the patient track an object in all directions. When there is paresis of a muscle or nerve, diplopia is the resulting complaint. The false image is cast further out in the direction of movement of the paretic muscle. The oculomotor nerve is the efferent part of the pupillary light reflex.

CN V: The *trigeminal nerve* has a motor component that supplies the muscles of mastication (masseters, temporalis, and pterygoids [lateral movement of the jaw]), and three sensory divisions. V1 covers the area from the coronal suture to the upper lids and part of the cornea. V1 does not stop at the hairline, which is where hysterical or factitious sensory loss often stops. V2 covers the area of the zygomatic arches and cheeks. V3 covers the mandible, with the exception of the angle of the jaw.

CN VII: The *facial nerve* supplies motor function to the muscles of expression and, through the chorda tympani, supplies taste to the anterior two-thirds of the tongue. A branch to the stapedius dampens noise, and the greater superficial petrosal supplies the lacrimal glands.

CN VIII: The *statoacoustic nerve* subserves hearing and balance. Hearing can be tested either with a high-frequency tuning fork or by whispering a number in the patient's ear while rubbing the fingers near the other ear (to test the ear individually). Balance is tested by having the patient stand with feet together and arms outstretched. This testing is described further in the section on gait disorders.

CN IX and X: *Glossopharyngeal and vagal* functions are usually tested together, with the gag reflex. The glossopharyngeal nerve supplies sensation to the oropharynx. Voluntary and reflex (gag) elevation of the palate should be tested.

CN XI: The *spinal accessory nerve* supplies the trapezii (shoulder shrug) and the sternocleidomastoid muscles (contralateral head turning). Weakness is clinically manifest by shoulder droop.

CN XII: The *hypoglossal nerve* protrudes the tongue. When there is dysfunction, the tongue deviates toward the side of the weakness.

Motor Examination

Bulk, tone, and strength are the issues to be addressed. Muscles are checked visually for atrophy and fasciculations, indicative of lower motor neuron dysfunction. Benign fasciculations may occur in a cold environment. Facial myokymia (small twitches in the muscles around the eye) are common when patients are anxious, and may be mistaken for fasciculations. Tone is defined as involuntary resistance to passive stretch. It is generally increased in upper motor neuron lesions (spasticity) and decreased in lower motor neuron lesions. Specific types of increased tone may be diagnostic of certain disease states (e.g., cogwheel rigidity in parkinsonism). Strength is graded on a 0 to 5 scale. Zero is no flicker of movement; 1 = isometric contraction, without movement of the extremity; 2 = movement, but only parallel to the ground (not against gravity); 3 = movement against gravity; 4 = ability to overcome some resistance; 5 = full strength. In manual motor testing, the examiner should be positioned in such a way that the muscle being tested is put against an appropriate amount of force. That is, finger extensors should be tested against muscles of similar strength. Plantar flexion of the feet should be tested functionally, by having the patient try to stand on tiptoe, because manual testing cannot exert enough power to test the gastrocnemius muscles.

Sensory Examination

The sensory exam should be tailored to the individual complaint. Testing every sensory function in patients without sensory complaints is time-

consuming and confusing. Light touch, pin, vibratory, and position-sense testing usually suffices. Light touch and pin are self-explanatory. Vibration should be tested with a low-frequency tuning fork held against a toe or finger, with the examiner's finger beneath the patient's, using the examiner's sensation as normal. Position sense is tested by holding a distal phalanx on the side and displacing the digit a few millimeters.

Reflexes

Deep tendon reflexes are examined by tapping a muscle tendon where it crosses a joint, and looking for contraction of the muscle. Greater sensitivity can be obtained by holding the joint in the hand, with a finger over the tendon, and tapping the finger. Reflexes are generally increased in upper motor neuron lesions and decreased in lower motor neuron lesions.

The Babinski response, present in upper motor neuron lesions, is elicited by scratching the lateral aspect of the plantar surface of the foot and looking for extension of the great toe, with fanning of the others.

Coordination and Gait Examinations

The most important cerebellar functions can be tested by watching the patient walk and perform simple tasks. Appendicular dysfunction can be brought out by having the patient put her heel on her knee and run it down her shin, and by having her alternatingly touch her nose and the examiner's finger. Appendicular ataxia or dysmetria is caused by lesions in the cerebellar hemispheres or their connections in the brain stem. Truncal dysfunction can be brought out by having the patient tandem walk. Truncal ataxia is caused by lesions in the cerebellar vermis or its connections.

Common Classes of Neurologic Disease seen in Office Practice

Episodic Loss of Consciousness

Seizures and syncope are the two most common causes of episodic loss of consciousness. Syncope is usually preceded by a sense of "graying out," light-headedness, and diaphoresis. Recovery from syncope is usually rapid and complete, while seizures may be followed by postictal confusion, lethargy, and rarely, paralysis (Todd's). Occasionally, a patient may have some clonic movements during a syncopal event if the patient is maintained in an upright position. These jerks are due to transient global ischemia and are not harbingers of future epileptic seizures; they do not need to be treated. The movements are generally less prolonged and less violent than those seen in generalized seizures.

Seizures The most clinically useful classification of seizures is to divide them into generalized and focal (partial). Generalized seizures involve the entire brain from the onset and are associated with alterations of consciousness. The generalized major motor seizure, or "grand mal" is the most commonly recognized seizure type. An initial phase of tonic contraction lasts 10 to 20 s, and is followed by clonic movements of the extremities, gradually decreasing in frequency over 30 to 60 s. Tongue biting and incontinence often accompany the seizure. Absence seizures, another type of generalized epilepsy, involve loss of contact but no convulsive activity. When these seizures appear in childhood and are accompanied by a specific EEG pattern (three-per-second spike and wave), they are referred to as petit mal.

Partial seizures have a focal onset. The focal clinical symptomatology depends on the area of the brain affected. If a seizure is preceded by an aura, it is partial (focal). There may be focal motor or sensory signs. If there is no alteration of consciousness, these are called simple seizures; if there is clouding of consciousness, they are complex seizures. Partial complex seizures with psychomotor symptomatology usually originate in the temporal lobe (fewer than 10 percent may originate in the frontal lobe). These were previously referred to as temporal lobe or psychomotor seizures. Partial seizures can spread and evolve into generalized major motor seizures (secondary generalization).

When a patient presents in the office with a

first seizure, the decisions are how far to proceed with the clinical investigation, and whether to treat the first seizure. The type of seizure, the clinical circumstances in which it occurred, and the neurologic examination guide the physician's decisions. Partial (focal) seizures and/or focality on the neurologic exam necessitate imaging (MRI or contrast CT), EEG, and lumbar puncture (if there is no large mass), to rule out local pathology as the cause of the focal seizure. In the case of generalized major motor seizures with a clear etiology (head trauma, alcohol withdrawal, etc.), imaging and EEG are probably sufficient.

The decision of whether to treat a first seizure is more difficult. If there is a structural cause for the seizure, or there is an epileptic EEG, most clinicians would opt for treatment. Even in relatively benign seizures, the psychosocial impact of repeated seizures must be considered. In New York State, for example, epilepsy patients must be seizure-free for 1 year before being allowed to drive. Further, women using oral contraceptives must be cautioned that many antiepileptic drugs, including phenytoin, carbamazepine, and barbiturates can reduce the efficacy of the birth control pill. Reduced efficacy is the result of enzyme induction.

The most commonly used drugs for the various seizure types are listed in Table 71-2, along with side effects. Only adult doses are listed. If phenytoin is given without a loading dose, it will take nearly 1 week to reach therapeutic levels. An oral loading dose of approximately 15 mg/kg of body weight will achieve therapeutic levels within hours. Phenytoin is the only anticonvulsant in which a loading dose is routinely used to achieve levels rapidly. The other drugs must be titrated gradually. There are many new drugs on the market, but their teratogenicity has not been studied fully, and it is best for primary care physicians to manage drugs with which they are familiar.

There is a complex interaction among hormones, seizure frequency, and antiepileptic drugs. In experimental models of epilepsy, estrogen and progesterone appear to have opposing effects, with estrogen activating seizure foci and progesterone inhibiting them. These effects may be clinically significant, but they are difficult to quantify. While many women believe that they have increased seizure frequency during menses, true catamenial epilepsy probably occurs in less than 15 percent of epileptic women. The effects of hormonal fluctuations on antiepileptic drug activity have not been directly measured. Conversely, seizures and antiepileptic drugs alter hormonal function. Generalized seizures produce a marked increase in prolactin, and may affect other hormones as well. Both men and women on antiepileptic drugs are more likely than controls to have endocrine abnormalities, but it is unclear whether this is an effect on synthesis, release, activity, or metabolism.

The issue of epilepsy in pregnancy is a particularly complex one. Women with epilepsy are at risk for decreased fertility and, once they do become pregnant, the use of antiepileptic drugs requires in-depth discussion between the patient and the physician. More than 90 percent of pregnancies in epileptic women reach term without significant complications, but there is some increased risk of eclampsia. The effect of pregnancy on epilepsy is unpredictable in any given patient, but about one-third of all patients may have an increase in their seizure frequency and the ones most at risk for worsening are those with difficult seizures prior to pregnancy. A smaller number actually have a decrease in seizure frequency. Some increase in seizure activity may be related to an alteration in antiepileptic drug pharmacokinetics. These fluctuations are due to changes in protein binding, drug clearance, and volume expansion, requiring more careful monitoring of serum anticonvulsant levels.

In treating pregnant epileptic women, the balance to be struck is between the risk of seizures and the risk of medication to the fetus. All of the older-generation antiepileptic drugs have teratogenic potential, the most serious malformations being seen with carbamazepine and valproic acid (neural tube defects), but the effects

are most pronounced when these drugs have been taken during fetal morphogenesis. Approximately 4 to 6 percent of children born to treated epileptic mothers have major malformations, while minor abnormalities are present in 6 to 20 percent. Cleft lip and palate occur in about 1.8 percent of children born to mothers treated with phenytoin (0.7 percent in the general population). The greatest risk is associated with polypharmacy; the more drugs used, the greater the likelihood of malformations.

The question of whether to change drugs in a pregnant epileptic woman whose seizures are well controlled is very difficult and involves multiple issues, including whether the patient would consider termination of pregnancy if a neural tube defect were found, the patient's decisions regarding the risk/benefit ratio of changing, and the relative risks of increased seizures.

Prolonged maternal seizures with hypoxia have a deleterious effect on the fetus, and approximately one-third of mothers and one-half of fetuses do not survive status epilepticus. Five to 10 percent of pregnant mothers on antiepileptic drugs may develop vitamin K deficiency. This can lead to hemorrhagic complications in the newborn. It is suggested that women on antiepi-

leptic drugs take 20 mg of oral vitamin K daily, for the last two to four weeks of pregnancy.

Syncope The loss of consciousness due to lack of blood flow to the brain is called syncope. A feeling of faintness usually precedes it. The list of possible causes is legion, but the three most common broad category causes are loss of peripheral vascular resistance (vasovagal), loss of cardiac output (arrhythmias), and loss of blood volume (dehydration, blood loss, etc.). The neurologic examination is normal, and treatment is directed at the underlying cause.

Dizziness One of the most common and most difficult complaints is dizziness. The most important step in diagnosis is to determine what the patient really means by dizziness. Most often, it is light-headedness or a sense of giddiness. True vertigo, on the other hand, is the sensation that the patient or the environment is moving abnormally. If the patient cannot give a clear description, it may be helpful to have her hyperventilate for 3 min. This will produce mild light-headedness and swaying in most people. If that matches the patient's symptoms, a search for brain stem or peripheral causes of vertigo is unnecessary.

In cases of true vertigo, the issue is to differ-

TABLE 71-2 Commonly Used Antiepileptic Drugs

Drug (Generic) Dosing Schedule	Indication(s)	Side Effects
Dilantin (phenytoin) 300–500 mg/day[a]	Tonic-clonic Partial	Nystagmus, hirsutism, elevated LFTs[b], gingival hyperplasia
Luminal (phenobarbital) 30–60 mg tid[a]	Same	Somnolence
Tegretol (carbamazepine) 200 mg 3–6/day[a]	Tonic clonic Partial	Dizziness Agranulocytosis[c]
Klonopin (clonazepam)[d] 0.5–5.0 mg tid[a]	Absence	Somnolence

[a] Dosing ranges vary considerably with the individual and, when there are problems obtaining seizure control or there are questions of toxicity, serum levels should be checked. The average therapeutic ranges are 10–20 μg/ml for Dilantin, 10–40 μg/ml for phenobarbital, 4–10 μg/ml for Tegretol, and 0.01–0.07 μg/ml for Klonopin. These are mean effective ranges and should not be considered firm boundaries.

[b] These side effects appear even at therapeutic levels. A mild elevation of alkaline phosphatase does not necessarily represent toxicity. Gingival hyperplasia can be lessened with good oral hygiene.

[c] Agranulocytosis is a rare and idiosyncratic reaction to Tegretol, and not a true side effect. Blood counts should be checked weekly for the first month of therapy, and then monthly for two or three months.

[d] Klonopin is a benzodiazepine anticonvulsant that also has anxiolytic properties.

entiate between potentially lethal brain stem disease and relatively benign disorders of the peripheral vestibular system. Vestibular lesions produce vertigo that is sensitive to changes in position. There is a brief latency between the time the patient changes position and when she develops dizziness and nystagmus. The nystagmus tends to diminish with repeated exercises. One of the more successful ways of treating benign positional vertigo is with a series of exercises that has the patient reproduce the symptoms.

Loss of Intellect, Memory, or Language Function.

Dementia   Dementia is defined as a progressive decline in intellectual and cognitive function. Early signs of dementia may be so subtle that they go unnoticed. Commonly, patients progressively restrict their spheres of activity so that they continue to function well, but in a progressively more limited range. The dementia may not become apparent until the patient tries to function in a broader context, and gets lost or shows very significant confusion. The history should be directed at ascertaining what specific losses of cognitive function have occurred. Further clinical investigation is directed toward finding potentially curable causes of dementia, the most common of which is the "pseudodementia" of depression. Some screening for depression should be done in all patients presenting with a complaint of memory loss.

There have been some data to suggest that estrogen replacement therapy may improve cognition and delay the onset of dementia in postmenopausal women. These data must await appropriately controlled studies before definitive recommendations can be made. The same is true of recent reports regarding the use of nonsteroidal anti-inflammatory drugs.

In broad terms, the causes of dementia can be categorized in three groups: cases in which the brain is the target of a systemic illness (metabolic and nutritional disorders, infections, vascular, or inflammatory diseases); primary structural causes (tumors, other space-occupying lesions, or hydrocephalus); and primary degenerative diseases of the nervous system (senile dementia of the Alzheimer type, Pick's disease, or other syndromes). To clarify these issues, the initial workup for a presumed dementing illness should include a detailed neurologic history and clinical examination, an imaging procedure of the brain (noncontrast CT scan is usually sufficient), B_{12} and folate levels, thyroid function tests, and a serologic test for syphilis. In subtle cases, neuropsychometric testing may be needed.

Metabolic Causes of Dementia: B_{12} *deficiency* may produce a gradually progressive dementia that is accompanied by signs of combined systems degeneration (corticospinal tract and posterior column dysfunction) with some degree of spasticity and marked position sense loss. The CBC usually shows a macrocytic anemia. A Schilling test confirms the diagnosis.

Hypothyroidism rarely causes dementia without significant systemic signs of hypothyroidism, including weight gain, cold intolerance, sparse hair, and rough skin. Patients appear generally slowed, without any clear focal neurological deficit or specific area of intellectual dysfunction. With thyroid replacement in these cases, care must be taken not to precipitate an addisonian crisis. If patients are severely hypothyroid, steroid replacement should precede thyroid replacement.

CNS complications of syphilis had been becoming very rare. However, with the AIDS epidemic, the frequency is rising and, what formerly were considered late stages of the disease are appearing within one to two years. Patients may demonstrate confabulatory states and severe memory deficit. In suspected cases, lumbar puncture should be performed along with a serum RPR and FTA-ABS. CSF characteristically shows an elevated protein (50 to 200 mg/dL) and a lymphocytic pleocytosis. CSF VDRL is almost always positive, but it may require a number of LPs to demonstrate positivity. Serum FTA-ABS is invariably positive in neurosyphilis.

Recommended treatment is with aqueous crystalline penicillin G, 2 to 4 million units IV, every 4 hours, for 10 to 14 days. An approved alternative is procaine penicillin G 2.4 million units IM daily, for 10 to 14 days, along with probenecid 500 mg, po, 4 times a day.

In immunocompromised hosts, *opportunistic infections,* such as cryptococcosis, must be considered. Again, diagnosis is made by lumbar puncture.

Thiamine deficiency, when prolonged, can produce Korsakoff syndrome, which is primarily an amnestic syndrome. Patients have severe impairment of recent recall and are prone to confabulation. At this stage, thiamine replacement may stop progression of the disease, but usually does not reverse it fully.

Structural Lesions of the Central Nervous System: *Brain tumors* (particularly those located in the frontal lobes) and subdural hematomas may produce progressive dementia, with surprisingly little in the way of focal neurologic signs. Usually, there is a subtle hemiparesis associated with the dementia. The dementia tends to be more rapidly progressive than that seen in Alzheimer's disease, usually occurring over a matter of weeks to months. CT scan reveals the underlying lesion. In hydrocephalus, patients may show more slowness of response than true dementia. Along with cognitive impairment, gait disturbance and urinary incontinence form the typical triad of normal pressure hydrocephalus. Brain imaging confirms enlarged ventricles, out of proportion to any cerebral atrophy. When vascular disease causes dementia, a stepwise progression of impairment can usually be elicited, and there are signs of focal cerebral dysfunction.

Senile Dementia of the Alzheimer Type Previously called Alzheimer's disease, senile dementia of the Alzheimer type (SDAT) is the most common form of dementia. Incidence increases exponentially with advancing age. While some areas of cognition may be affected more than others early in the disease (recent recall more than distant), there is a gradual decline in all cognitive functions. In early cases, tacrine (an

ergot derivative) and donezepil (a cholinesterase inhibitor) may produce some benefit. There is no known cure, and the disease is progressive and fatal.

Pure memory loss Pure memory loss, without decline in other cognitive functions (amnestic syndrome), is unusual. Transient global amnesia is a syndrome in which there is brief (minutes to hours) loss of memory. The patient is fully awake and alert, but does not recognize her surroundings nor have any recall of how she arrived at the current place. It clears spontaneously, and there are usually no sequelae. It is believed to be due to bilateral mesial temporal lobe transient ischemia, but this has not been firmly established, and there are usually no further events. Korsakoff's psychosis is a pure amnestic syndrome that is caused by prolonged thiamine deficiency. It is most commonly seen in alcoholic patients, and is accompanied by confabulation and peripheral signs of thiamine deficiency (peripheral neuropathy). Occasionally, elderly patients have minor lapses of memory, such as forgetting names or where they put objects, with no further deterioration. This is called benign senile forgetfulness and is not a harbinger of future senile dementia of the Alzheimer type. Most commonly, however, memory loss in the elderly is only the start of the syndrome, and they then progress to other fields of cognitive impairment.

Aphasias Language function is predominantly in the left hemisphere in all right-handed patients and in more than half of left-handed patients. The left hemisphere is dominant for language in well over 95 percent of the population. Patients with language disorders (aphasias), have difficulty with all types of communication, not just the spoken word. Aphasias are broadly divided into two groups, anterior and posterior. The nomenclature and characteristics of the major aphasic syndromes are shown in Table 71-1. Broca's area is located in the inferior frontal gyrus of the left hemisphere. It is intimately related with the motor strip. Lesions in this area produce an expressive aphasia. Patients have trouble expressing themselves, they are nonfluent, and often

have accompanying motor signs. Wernicke's area is located in the posterior part of the left superior temporal gyrus. Lesions in this area produce difficulty in understanding language. Patients may be fluent, but their speech output makes no sense. Pure receptive aphasias may be associated with a field cut, but are usually not associated with a hemiparesis. The easiest way to remember the difference is that the motor strip is anterior to the sensory strip, so anterior aphasias are motor, expressive, nonfluent, and associated with motor paresis. Most commonly, aphasias are mixed, showing elements of both expressive and receptive aphasias.

Weakness

The approach to the patient with a complaint of weakness addresses three issues: localization (pattern), onset, and progression. The pattern of weakness can give an initial indication of what part of the nervous system is affected. Upper motor neuron lesions (brain or spinal cord) characteristically present with a hemiparesis or paraparesis. Rarely, a cerebral lesion may lead to a monoparesis. Muscle disease tends to be proximal, while peripheral neuropathy tends to be distal. Diseases of the neuromuscular junction, such as myasthenia, tend to be patchy and multifocal, often involving the ocular muscles. Weakness can occur with lesions virtually anywhere in the nervous system. It is useful to differentiate between upper motor neuron (central) and lower motor neuron (peripheral) lesions. The upper motor neuron is anywhere from the cortex to the synapse on the anterior horn cell in the spinal cord. From the anterior horn cell to the neuromuscular junction is the lower motor neuron. Lower motor weakness can occur anywhere in the path of the lower motor neuron. The course of the lower motor neuron, from proximal to distal, is anterior horn, root, plexus, nerve, neuromuscular junction, muscle. Increased tone, hyperreflexia, and Babinski's sign characterize upper motor neuron lesions. Decreased tone, decreased reflexes, atrophy, and fasciculations characterize lower motor

neuron lesions. Using this approach, some of the common neurologic disorders that present with weakness are discussed below.

Central Lesions Affecting the Brain

Cerebrovascular Disease   The discussion is limited to thrombotic and embolic cerebrovascular accidents (CVAs), because these account for the vast majority of strokes, and it would be unusual to manage hemorrhagic CVAs in the office. Clinically, strokes are characterized by the sudden onset of neurological dysfunction, limited to an area of the brain supplied by a specific artery. Deficits tend to resolve slowly, over weeks to months. If the deficits clear within 24 h, the event is technically considered a transient ischemic attack (TIA), although deficits lasting more than 1 h usually reflect an actual stroke. Even in completed strokes, the CT scan is often normal in the first 24 h and in small infarctions. If the patient's condition rapidly deteriorates, it is imperative to rule out superimposed hemorrhage, edema, or an incorrect diagnosis (tumor presenting as stroke). The greatest risk for postischemic brain swelling is between 48 and 72 h after the stroke.

Listing all of the possible stroke syndromes is beyond the scope of this book. Table 71-3 shows some of the common syndromes, and the arterial supplies that are responsible for them. When weakness occurs, it is usually in the form of a hemiparesis, with the extensors of the arms and the flexors of the legs being weaker than their antagonist muscles. Weakness is usually accompanied by hyperreflexia and Babinski's sign. The involvement of cranial nerves on one side with contralateral body involvement is indicative of brain stem disease. For office practice, stroke prevention is an even more important issue than stroke recognition and care.

Stroke prevention can be viewed in three ways: stroke prevention in the population with specific risk factors; stroke prevention in patients who have had transient ischemia; and prevention of recurrent stroke.

Hypertension is the most clearly recognized and easily treated risk factor. Good blood pressure control can greatly reduce the likelihood of

TABLE 71-3   Common Stroke Syndromes

Artery	Area Supplied	Clinical Syndrome
Anterior cerebral	Interhemispheric	Paresis of leg > arm Contralateral
Middle cerebral	Lateral hemisphere	Face > arm > leg Motor + sensory Aphasia, if dominant
Posterior cerebral	Occipital poles +/− temporoparietal	Hemianopsia +/− sensory
Vertebrobasilar	Brain stem	Crossed syndromes, with cranial nerves on one side and body findings contralateral

stroke. While diabetes is a risk factor, it is less clear that tight control of blood sugar alters the incidence of stroke. Atrial fibrillation is a clear risk factor for embolic CVA, and low-dose anticoagulation can reduce the risk. The vascular effects of smoking behoove us to advise patients to stop smoking. Young women who smoke and take oral contraceptives increase their stroke risk and should be cautioned against the combination. However, the newer oral contraceptives do not appear to be an independent risk factor. Patients with a history of migraine also have an increased risk of stroke when compared to age-matched controls, but the risk is still low and no specific prophylaxis is indicated.

Transient ischemic attacks (TIA) are a harbinger of stroke. Transient monocular blindness (amaurosis fugax) may be considered in the same category as a TIA and is usually due to platelet emboli from the carotid artery. Patients with TIA have about a 10 percent chance of suffering a CVA in the coming year. Aspirin can reduce this risk to about 5 percent. Other antiplatelet drugs, such as ticlopidine, are slightly more effective, but the side effect profile (e.g., reversible neutropenia) requires regular blood monitoring for the first three months of therapy. The data on anticoagulation are inconclusive. If a tight carotid stenosis (greater than 70 percent) can be demonstrated, there is clear benefit from carotid endarterectomy.

Patients who have had a stroke are more likely to have a second stroke than the general population is to have a first stroke. Prevention of that second stroke depends mainly on identifying the causes of the first one. There are experimental studies under way to determine whether aspirin, anticoagulation, or other drugs can prevent stroke recurrence.

Brain Tumors   Headache is the most common presenting complaint in patients found to have brain tumors. The "classic" brain tumor headache is described as worse in the early morning and improving with aspirin or as the day progresses. More commonly, the headache is more of a tension-type (see Chap. 77, on pain and headache), and the indications of a brain tumor are that the headache is progressive over weeks to a few months and that there may be focality on the neurological examination.

Weakness, when present, is most commonly in the form of a progressive hemiparesis. As in other upper motor neuron lesions, the extensors of the arm and the flexors of the leg are most affected. Severe, bilateral, progressive headaches are indicative of increased intracranial pressure and require emergency management. Other signs of decompensation requiring rapid attention include obtundation, nausea and vomiting, papilledema, and rapidly progressive neurologic deficits.

MRI scan with gadolinium demonstrates virtually all clinically significant brain tumors. If MRI is unavailable, contrast-enhanced CT is sufficient

in most cases. EEG and lumbar puncture add little or nothing to the diagnosis.

Treatment of metastatic brain tumors is directed at controlling intracranial pressure, reducing focal deficits, and lessening the tumor burden. Steroids (the equivalent of about 16 mg of dexamethasone/day) provide initial relief of most tumor symptoms, because the edema surrounding the lesions is vasogenic. For metastatic lesions, most commonly arising from lung, breast, melanoma, or colon primaries, surgical removal may be indicated for solitary lesions or those that are causing rapidly progressive deficits and are accessible. Radiation therapy is generally considered palliative and is rarely curative. Steroid therapy should be continued throughout the course of radiation, and tapered as tolerated. About 20 percent of patients with metastatic lesions will remain steroid-dependent until death.

Seizures occur in about 25 percent of patients with brain tumors, usually early in the course, and may be the presenting symptom. There is some disagreement about the need for prophylactic anticonvulsant therapy in patients who have not had seizures. Given that seizures tend to be an early occurrence and anticonvulsive therapy carries certain risks, many practitioners opt for treating only those patients who have had seizures or have undergone surgery.

Multiple Sclerosis Multiple sclerosis is a demyelinating disease that affects the central nervous system. While there are scattered reports of peripheral nervous system involvement, the brain and spinal cord are the two primary targets. The disease is defined clinically as "two lesions separated in space and time and not attributable to any other cause." This means that two different parts of the central nervous system are affected at two different times. It most commonly presents with gait difficulties that may be due to weakness, spasticity, or incoordination. While eye movement disorders, optic neuritis, and multifocal cerebral disorders are common, about one-third of cases are strictly spinal. It is the most common cause of asymmetric paraparesis in young adults. Onset is most commonly in the third or fourth

decade of life, and it is more common in women than in men. It usually takes an exacerbating-remitting course, but there are chronic progressive forms. Even with remissions, deficits usually tend to increase.

High doses of steroids or ACTH may shorten individual exacerbations but, until very recently, nothing had been definitely shown to alter the overall course of the disease. It has now been shown that two different types of interferon, as well as a copolymer, can decrease the frequency of attacks in exacerbating-remitting disease. About 25 percent of patients with multiple sclerosis are still working after 20 years. Poor prognostic factors include male sex, early age of onset, and presentation with primarily motor signs.

Compressive Myelopathies: Cervical spondylosis is a severe case of degenerative disease of the spine, mainly in elderly patients, in which there can be encroachment by disc material and overgrown bone on the cervical spinal cord. This generally has a very slow progression, associated with mild spasticity of the lower extremities. In cases in which the progression is rapid, or in which there is loss of bowel or bladder function, surgery is indicated to correct the compressive lesion. Many patients, however, can be followed conservatively.

Malignant epidural spinal cord compression affects 5 to 10 percent of patients with systemic cancer. Epidural spinal cord compression develops in these patients from a metastasis to the spinal column. Rarely, it can be the presenting symptom of the malignancy. The syndrome is characterized by severe back pain with a radicular radiation, followed by progressive paraparesis. Any patient with cancer and back pain should be suspected of having epidural cord compression. If there is a vertebral collapse on plain x-rays, it is more than 50 percent likely that the compression is at that level. These patients must be treated emergently, with high-dose steroids and radiation therapy.

B_{12} deficiency can also present with myelopathic features and is recognized by the marked position and vibratory sense loss in the toes,

added peripheral neuropathy, and megalocytic anemia.

Lower Motor Neuron Weakness Anything affecting the nervous system from the anterior horn cell in the spinal cord, to the muscle fiber, produces a "lower motor neuron" pattern of weakness.

Guillain-Barré Syndrome Guillain-Barré Syndrome (GBS) is an acute, demyelinating, polyradiculoneuropathy. Demyelination occurs from the nerve roots out to the nerves. The characteristic pattern is the development of a mild, distal paresthesia, following an upper respiratory tract infection. This is superceded by a rapidly progressive weakness and areflexia, reaching a maximum in a few days to a week. In fulminant cases, patients can go from normal to quadriplegic and respirator-dependent in a matter of hours. Early diagnosis is imperative. The syndrome should be suspected in anyone with progressive weakness and hyporeflexia. Sensory complaints are common, but sensory findings, when present, are minimal. Diagnosis can be confirmed early by showing markedly slowed nerve conduction velocities. The characteristic CSF picture of increased protein, but no cells, does not develop until 7 to 10 days into the disease. If GBS is suspected, the patient should be hospitalized immediately, in an Intensive Care Unit, with careful monitoring of vital capacity (VC). If VC drops below 1250 cc, or there is a marked deterioration in a few hours, the patient should be intubated and placed on a respirator.

Treatment is both supportive and etiological. The most common cause of death is respiratory failure, and patients may be respirator-dependent for weeks. With adequate care, 80 to 90 percent of patients make a full functional recovery.

Etiologic treatment is aimed at the presumed immune mechanism of demyelination and includes plasma exchange (plasmapheresis) and infusions of human immune globulin, both of which appear to shorten respirator time. The data on the use of steroids are less convincing.

The natural history of the disease is 7 to 10 days of progression, 2 to 4 weeks of stabilization, and many months of recovery. During the paralytic phase, passive range of motion of the joints must be performed to avoid contractures. With adequate care, 80 to 90 percent of patients make a full functional recovery.

Other Polyradiculopathies Nerve roots are formed by the motor and sensory fibers that leave or enter the spinal cord. The spinal cord itself ends at about the L1-L2 spinal column level. Below that, there are only lumbar and sacral roots. Roots can be affected by demyelination, compression, or inflammation. Single roots (monoradiculopathy) are most commonly affected by compressive lesions, such as herniated discs. The syndrome is marked by the sudden onset of pain after lifting or other strenuous movement. Pain radiates down the affected extremity in a dermatomal distribution, with the pattern and reflex changes depending on the root affected (Table 71-4). In most cases of lumbar radiculopathy, a few days of bedrest will bring about resolution. If there is significant motor impairment or sphincter involvement, surgical correction is indicated. With cervical discs, there is the added problem of cord compression. If signs of cord compression (paraparesis, hyperreflexia, Babinski's sign) appear, decompression should be considered. Further discussion of back pain and radiculopathy can be found in Chap. 77, on pain.

When systemic tumors metastasize to the meninges, they can affect multiple roots. The characteristic syndrome includes headache, along with involvement of cranial and/or spinal nerves. Diagnosis is made on lumbar puncture, which demonstrates increased protein and cells, with a cytology positive for malignant cells. Inflammatory processes, such as systemic lupus erythematosus, can also affect multiple roots in a similar fashion.

Plexopathies Brachial plexopathy is characterized by pain and weakness in the upper extremity. More than one root or nerve is involved. The course of the disease depends on the underlying cause. There are benign, idiopathic cases, in

TABLE 71-4 **Common Radicular Syndromes**

Root	Dermatome	Muscles[a]	Reflexes
C5	Cap of shoulder	Deltoids, biceps, brachioradialis	Biceps, brachioradialis
C6	Upper arm and thumb	+/− Biceps	Biceps
C7	Arm to middle finger	Triceps	Triceps
C8	Inner arm to fifth finger	Hand intrinsics	None
L2	Upper, inner thigh	Iliopsoas, quads, adductors[b]	Quadriceps
L3	Anterior to medial thigh	Same	Same
L4	Lateral thigh to medial knee	Same +/− Anterior tibial	Same
L5	Lateral hip to medial shin and foot	Anterior tibial	None[c]
S1	Posterior thigh to lateral foot	Plantar flexors, hamstrings	Achilles

[a]Only the major muscles are listed; not every one is innervated.

[b]The adductors are innervated by the anterior divisions of these roots, while the quadriceps are innervated
  by the posterior. If only one of the muscles is weak, the lesion is likely to be in the nerve, rather than in the root.

[c]Some neurologists test a posterior tibial reflex, but it is difficult to elicit.

which pain precedes the weakness and then diminishes as weakness progresses. These cases are self-limited and resolve in weeks. They are probably a form of localized demyelination. In endemic areas, a Lyme titer should be drawn. More ominous is a progressive, painful plexopathy that involves the lower roots (C8-T1) and is accompanied by Horner's syndrome (ptosis, myosis, and anhydrosis). This distribution is indicative of tumor in the apex of the lung, invading the brachial plexus (Pancoast's syndrome). Therapy must be directed quickly at the underlying tumor. Pain in the upper, inner aspect of the arm, radiating to the elbow, is rarely due to benign disease and should raise the suspicion of tumor.

Lumbar plexopathy is a neuropathy of the lumbar plexus, which is most often affected by processes in the retroperitoneal space. Tumors, such as renal cell cancer, lymphoma, and ovarian cancers commonly spread to this area and cause a progressive, painful plexopathy. In patients who are anticoagulated, the sudden onset of leg pain should raise the suspicion of a retroperitoneal hematoma with lumbar plexus involvement. Clinically, these both present as pain with weakness and patchy sensory and reflex loss in the leg. Retroperitoneal hematoma may resolve spontaneously but, if weakness progresses, exploration through laparotomy is indicated. Tumor involvement of the lumbar plexus requires direct therapy, either by surgery or radiation therapy.

Peripheral Neuropathies As with all other neurologic diseases, peripheral neuropathies can be defined by their onset, distribution, and progression. The main objective is to differentiate between mononeuropathies (in which individual nerves are affected) and diffuse polyneuropathies (in which peripheral nerves in general are affected). Mononeuropathies are usually compressive or inflammatory lesions, confined to one or a few nerves. The weakness, sensory loss, and reflex changes are confined to just that nerve distribution. In a polyneuropathy, however, there is more often symmetrical sensory loss and weakness, with a progression from distal to proximal. The mononeuropathies commonly seen in obstetrical and gynecological practices are:

Postpartum femoral neuropathy. In the dorsal lithotomy position, the femoral nerve can be

stretched, and the patient subsequently notices that she has trouble extending her leg at the knee (quadriceps weakness). The knee jerk is absent, and there may be sensory loss over the anterior thigh. Other muscles are intact, unless the obturator nerve has been stretched at the same time, causing weakness of the adductors of the thigh. Isolated obturator injury is uncommon. Both of these nerve injuries usually resolve spontaneously, but this may take many months, depending on the severity of the injury.

Sciatic neuropathy may occur from pressure from the fetal head. It is invariably on the side of repose of the head.

Intercostal neuropathy produces numbness and burning pain along the inferior part of the rib cage, late in pregnancy. It is believed to be due to stretching of the intercostal nerves at the junction with the spine.

The most common neuropathies seen in clinical practice are those due to diabetes. *Diabetic polyneuropathy* presents as a distal, symmetric sensory-motor loss that starts in the toes and ascends. Later in the disease, the fingers and hands may be affected. There is a shading of sensory loss from distal to proximal. In some cases, this neuropathy is quite painful, with burning dysesthesia. Low doses of tricyclic antidepressants may be effective for the burning pains. If they are lancinating pains, anticonvulsants may be useful. This subject is covered more fully in Chap. 77.

Occasionally, diabetes may present as a mononeuropathy, or mononeuropathy multiplex (multiple single nerves involved). The most common is a femoral neuropathy, in which there is pain in the anterior thigh and weakness in the quadriceps. It resolves spontaneously, over a period of months. The third and sixth cranial nerves are also occasionally involved. These are believed to be ischemic neuropathies. There is some debate about diabetic neuropathy in general, but it is believed that tight control of diabetes can forestall the appearance of neuropathic complications.

Other *nutritional neuropathies* that may be seen in clinical practice include B_{12} deficiency, which is characterized by peripheral neuropathy along with "combined systems disease" that includes signs of spinal cord dysfunction such as hyperreflexia and severe position sense loss. *Thiamine deficiency* produces a typical neuropathy but, in a florid picture, may be combined with Wernicke's encephalopathy. It is seen most commonly in alcoholics, but can present in anyone with severe nutritional deprivation over many months. Thiamine replacement will resolve the problem.

Pyridoxine (vitamin B_6), in very high doses, can produce a peripheral neuropathy. This has been seen in a number of women taking high doses of vitamin B_6 for premenstrual syndrome.

Myasthenia Gravis Myasthenia is a disease of the neuromuscular junction, characterized by weakness of many muscles (commonly starting with the extraocular and pharyngeal muscles) and fatigability. The most frequent initial complaints are double vision, lid ptosis, weakness, and fatigue. Muscles become weaker on repetitive testing.

The disease is most common in young women and elderly men, and is believed to be autoimmune in origin. The postsynaptic membrane of the neuromuscular junction is blocked by an autoantibody, so acetylcholine released from the presynaptic membrane does not bind adequately. Diagnosis is made when the clinical syndrome is drastically improved by the administration of edrophonium (Tensilon). Tensilon is a very short-acting cholinesterase inhibitor and makes more acetylcholine available at the neuromuscular junction, thus partially overcoming the blockade. The Tensilon test should not be undertaken in the office unless there is EKG monitoring and resuscitation equipment is available.

Treatment is directed at increasing acetylcholine availability with the use of cholinesterase inhibitors (Mestinon) or at modulating the immune system with plasmapheresis, steroids, thymectomy, or immunosuppressants. Decompensation can be precipitated by intercurrent illnesses or by incorrect medication dosing. When

Mestinon doses are too high, patients become cholinergic and have abdominal cramps and hypersecretion. The major cause of death in myasthenia is respiratory failure.

Myopathies Patients with myopathies present with proximal weakness. They complain of difficulty climbing stairs, or combing their hair, as a result of weakness of proximal muscles of the legs or arms; the reflex and sensory examinations are normal. The most common types seen in office practice are inflammatory myopathies, such as polymyositis, which can present with aching pain, and the metabolic myopathies, such as those associated with thyroid disease (hypo- and hyper-) or electrolyte imbalance (most commonly hypo- or hyperkalemia). Therefore, the initial approach to a patient who presents with proximal weakness, and shows the appropriate signs, is to check a serum CPK, thyroid function tests, and serum electrolytes. EMGs and muscle biopsy can confirm the diagnosis, and treatment is based on the underlying cause.

Disorders of Gait and Movement

Disorders of gait may be due to disorders of pyramidal function (weakness and spasticity), extrapyramidal function (increased tone and postural instability), sensory function (position sense loss), and cerebellar function (uncoordination). Weakness and spasticity are fairly obvious, but the other changes may be more subtle.

Spastic gait is characterized by "scissoring" of the legs, in which there is circumduction and crossing. It can be due to spinal or cerebral disease. Cerebral lesions that can cause spastic gait without arm weakness are usually midline (parasagittal tumors, hydrocephalus, etc.). Both intrinsic and extrinsic lesions of the spinal cord can also cause spastic gait. Structural lesions must be addressed first. If there are localizing signs (a sensory level, back pain, reflex changes), imaging should be directed at the area in question. Workup for demyelinating disease or metabolic problems is guided by the history and associated findings.

In Parkinson's disease, the most representative of the extrapyramidal disorders, the constellation of symptoms includes masked facies; bradykinesia; increased muscle tone with cogwheel rigidity; a characteristic "pill-rolling tremor;" postural instability; stooped posture; and a shuffling gait. Any one of the features may predominate in a given patient. Approximately 25 to 50 percent of patients develop dementia late in the disease. In many cases, it turns out to be senile dementia of the Alzheimer type. Depression is also very common.

The tremor of parkinsonism is a resting tremor, and attenuates briefly with volitional actions. The oscillations are slower than those seen in a nervous (adrenergic) tremor, and are differentiated from benign essential tremor because the latter occurs more with action.

Brain imaging should be performed to rule out the rare cases of structural lesions masquerading as parkinsonism (subdural hematomas, multiple CVAs, basal ganglia tumors).

The underlying pathophysiology of parkinsonism is a paucity of dopamine. Therapy is directed at replacing the deficit. Sinemet, a combination of levodopa and carbidopa, is the first line drug in most cases. L-Dopa is converted to dopamine within the central nervous system. Carbidopa prevents that conversion from taking place in the periphery, thus allowing more to be presented to the CNS. Dosing should be started low and titrated up gradually, as the patient needs and tolerates. The most common side effects are nausea and dizziness.

Anticholinergic agents and direct-acting dopamine agents can also be used. The first new class of antiparkinsonian drugs in many years was recently introduced. It is an inhibitor of COMT, an enzyme that metabolizes dopamine.

Gait disorders due to sensory impairment are usually the result of position sense loss. This can be tested by having the patient stand with her eyes open, and then close them. If the patient has severe sensory loss, she may be able to keep her balance by using visual cues, but will lose it with her eyes closed (positive Romberg). Cere-

bellar gait disorders, on the other hand, present with a broad-based gait and inability to tandem. These patients may lose their balance with their eyes open.

One of the most common abnormal movements seen in office practice is tremor. The defining points of tremor are its frequency, amplitude, and time of appearance (i.e., at rest or with movement).

Physiologic tremor can be seen in everyone. It may be irregular in frequency and amplitude, but is usually fine and fast. It is enhanced by anxiety and by maintaining an outstretched posture of the arms. A similar type of tremor can be caused by anticholinergic and adrenergic drugs, including caffeine, as well as by lithium and thyroid disease.

Familial, or benign essential tremor, is a coarse tremor that occurs during movement. It occurs mainly in the upper extremities, but the voice and head (titubation) may be affected. It can impair function, and usually responds to benzodiazepines or β blockers.

Intention tremor is not present at rest or during the first part of a movement. It is most pronounced during the terminal phase of a move-

ment, and may be interpreted as "end point dysmetria." It is most characteristic of hemispheric cerebellar dysfunction.

There are numerous other movement disorders that are beyond the scope of this book. References are provided for more in-depth reading.

References and Selected Readings

1. Donaldson JO: Neurology of pregnancy. 2nd ed. London WB Saunders, 1989.
2. Porter RJ: Epilepsy: 100 Elementary Principles. London: WB Saunders, 1984.
3. Adams RD, Victor M (eds): Principles of Neurology 5th ed. New York: McGraw-Hill, 1993.
4. Barnett HJM, Hachinski VC (eds): Cerebral Ischemia: Treatment and Prevention: Neurologic Clinics. Philadelphia: WB Saunders, 1992.
5. Yaffe K, Sawaya G, Lieberburg I, Grady D: Estrogen therapy in postmenopausal women: Effects on cognitive function and dementia. *JAMA* 279 (9):688–95, 1998.
6. Morrell MJ: Maximizing the health of women with epilepsy: Science and ethics in new drug development. *Epilepsia* 38 (Suppl 4): S32–S41, 1997.
7. Cudkowicz ME, Irizarry MC (eds): Neurologic Disorders in Women. Boston: Butterworth-Heinman. 1997.

Rheumatic and Musculoskeletal Disorders

Elise Belilos
Steven Carsons

APPROACH TO THE PATIENT WITH ARTHRITIS

Osteoarthritis • Evaluation of Low Back Pain • Rheumatoid Arthritis • The Spondyloarthropathies • Crystalline Arthropathies: Gout and Pseudogout • Septic Arthritis • Lyme Disease • Arthritis Associated with the Use of Oral Contraceptives

COMMON CONDITIONS THAT MIMIC ARTHRITIS

Polymyalgia Rheumatica and Temporal Arteritis • Fibromyalgia • Regional Disorders: Tendinitis and Bursitis

SYSTEMIC RHEUMATIC DISEASES

Systemic Lupus Erythematosus • Antiphospholipid Antibody Syndrome • Drug-Induced Lupus • Scleroderma and CREST Syndrome • Polymyositis and Dermatomyositis • Mixed Connective Tissue Disease • Sjögren's Syndrome • Vasculitic Syndromes • Behçet's Disease

Approach to the Patient with Arthritis

Several key factors help the clinician decide what type of arthritis a patient has. The first is the distribution of the joints involved. For example, rheumatoid arthritis (RA) tends to involve the wrists and the metacarpal phalangeal (MCP) and proximal interphalangeal (PIP) joints of the hands, while osteoarthritis (OA) tends to involve primarily the PIP and distal interphalangeal (DIP) joints of the hands and weight-bearing joints such as the hips and knees. The seronegative spondyloarthropathies tend to involve the low back or sacroiliac joints with an asymmetric oligoarthritis peripherally. The second factor is whether the arthritis is inflammatory or noninflammatory. In addition to objective inflammation in the joints, factors that suggest an inflammatory arthritis include morning stiffness (generally greater than 1 h) and gelling (stiffness after sitting for a prolonged period of time). The third factor is the duration of symptoms. For example, gouty arthritis tends to be episodic, with acute attacks generally resolving within 1 to 2 weeks, while RA and OA have more prolonged symptoms.

Physical examination reveals the presence or absence of objective synovitis in addition to assessing possible loss of range of motion of joints. The general medical evaluation is of extreme importance in discovering extra-articular features that may suggest a particular form of arthritis, such as nodules in RA, or psoriasis, and nail pitting in psoriatic arthritis.

Radiographs may be helpful in revealing characteristic changes of a particular form of arthritis, such as marginal erosions at the MCPs, PIPs, or ulnar styloid processes in RA, or sacroiliitis in the spondyloarthropathies. Laboratory data are often supportive of the clinical diagnosis, but

generally are not diagnostic. For example, older patients with clinical evidence of OA are often misdiagnosed as having RA simply on the basis of a positive rheumatoid factor. Examination of synovial fluid, if present, is helpful in differentiating inflammatory from noninflammatory effusions, to look for crystals, and to rule out infection.

Osteoarthritis

Osteoarthritis is the most common rheumatic condition; the prevalence currently is thought to exceed 60 million people in the United States. The incidence increases dramatically with advancing age, being less common before the age of 50 and estimated to exceed 50 percent by the age of 60.[1] Osteoarthritis of the hip is equally common in females and males, but OA of the knees and hands is more common in older females than in males of the same age. Polyarticular OA appears to be more common in women.[1] Many cases of OA are idiopathic, but in some cases predisposing factors may be elicited. Factors that may predispose patients to OA include genetic background, obesity or mechanical factors, previous trauma to the joint, or prior damage from other joint diseases.

Osteoarthritis is a degenerative arthritis with fissuring and wearing down of the cartilage, primarily of the weight-bearing surfaces. This leads to asymmetric joint space narrowing with secondary osteophyte or spur formation. As it is a disease of weight-bearing joints, it involves the hips, knees, feet, lumbosacral spine, lower cervical spine, and the PIP and DIP joints of the hands (from excessive use). It is generally a noninflammatory arthritis, but patients may at times have inflammation of one or more joints secondary to other causes, such as superimposed crystalline disease. The natural history of osteoarthritis is one of gradual progression of symptoms over time.

The chief complaint of a patient with osteoarthritis is usually joint pain. The patient's pain generally is worse after physical activity or at the end of the day. Patients often report that they have difficulty going up or down stairs. Morning stiffness, if present at all, generally lasts only a few minutes. In addition, patients may complain of a gradual progressive loss of joint function.

On physical examination, there is often evidence of bony swelling secondary to osteophyte formation. In the hands, this swelling is referred to as Heberden's nodes at the DIP joints and Bouchard's nodes at the PIP joints. The carpometacarpal (CMC) joint (at the base of the thumb) is often involved in osteoarthritis and may be tender on examination. While not commonly appreciated, the CMC is one of the most common sites of OA in persons who use their hands excessively. There may be hallux valgus (bunion) at the first MTP joint of the foot. The joints are generally cool without evidence of synovitis. There may be decreased range of motion in involved joints, and crepitus may be palpated.

Laboratory data generally are not helpful except in the sense that they are usually normal, including normal ESR and negative rheumatoid factor. If joint effusion is present, it generally will be noninflammatory with WBC counts of less than 2000 WBC/μl. Radiographs show asymmetric joint space narrowing of the weight-bearing surfaces (for example, the medial compartment of the knee is more commonly involved), and osteophyte formation. In addition, there may be evidence of subchondral sclerosis and cyst formation.

Treatment of osteoarthritis, like all diseases, begins with patient education. Physical therapy helps strengthen the structures around the affected joint(s) to relieve stress on the joint, and generally should be part of the therapeutic plan for all patients. Analgesics such as acetaminophen should be considered as first-line therapy in patients who require medical management. Muscle relaxants, such as cyclobenzaprine (Flexeril) or chlorzoxazone (Parafon Forte), may be helpful, especially in osteoarthritis of the cervical or lumbosacral spine where paraspinal muscle spasm may be contributing significantly to the patient's symptoms. Nonsteroidal anti-inflam-

matory drugs (NSAIDs) should be considered in those who do not respond to the above measures or who have evidence of inflammation. Examples of these are given in Table 72-1. The most common and worrisome side effects of NSAIDs include gastrointestinal (GI) intolerance or GI bleeding and renal toxicity. The risk of GI bleeding may be reduced by the coadministration of misoprostol (Cytotec) 100 to 200 μg tid-qid pc, in selected patients. Recently, more selective NSAIDs, such as celecoxib (Celebrex) and refecoxib (Vioxx), have been developed that preferentially inhibit cyclooxygenase-2, the form of the enzyme produced by inflammatory cells. This selectivity spares cyclooxygenase-1, which is largely responsible for the production of prostaglandins with protective effects on the GI tract. Varying degrees of hepatotoxicity may be seen with different NSAIDs. Thus, a CBC and renal and he-

patic profiles should be checked at baseline and approximately every 3 to 6 months while the patient is on an NSAID. Table 72-2 summarizes the instructions that should be given to all patients using NSAIDs. In addition, patients on these medications may develop fluid retention or hypertension, so that blood pressure should also be carefully monitored. NSAIDs also have an anticoagulant effect and, in most cases, should be avoided in patients on anticoagulant therapy. In general, NSAIDs should be withheld approximately one week prior to surgery to avoid enhanced bleeding due to antiplatelet effects.

In patients with symptomatic osteoarthritis of a single joint, intra-articular injection may be beneficial and can help avoid the use of systemic medication. In advanced OA, joint replacement should be considered, the timing of which should be determined by the degree of damage evident

TABLE 72-1 Examples of NSAIDs

Medication	Usual Starting Dose	Comments
Nonacetylated salicylates Choline magnesium trisalicylate (Trilisate) or salicyl salicylate (Disalcid)	750–1000 mg po bid pc	Less renal and GI toxicity; useful in the elderly when only a mild NSAID is needed May cause tinnitus
Ibuprofen (Motrin)	400, 600, or 800 mg po tid-qid pc (max dose = 3200 mg/day)	Inexpensive
Naproxen (Naprosyn)	375–500 mg po bid pc	
Diclofenac (Voltaren)	50–75 mg po bid pc	May have higher incidence of increased LFTs
Etodolac (Lodine)	200–300 mg po tid-qid pc	May have less GI toxicity
Nabumetone (Relafen)	500–750 mg (2 tabs po qd pc)	
Sulindac (Clinoril)	150–200 mg po bid pc	May have less renal toxicity May have CNS side effects
Indomethacin (Indocin)	25–50 mg po tid-qid pc	Very potent NSAID with frequent GI intolerance (best if used for short intervals such as acute gout attack) CNS side effects common, especially in the elderly
Piroxicam (Feldene)	10–20 mg po qd pc	Good in the younger patient for improved compliance (once a day) but should be used with caution in the elderly because of long half-life

TABLE 72-2 Instructions for Patients Using NSAIDs

Always take with food

Notify physician of any abdominal pain or change in bowel movement

Have your blood checked regularly while on the medication (every 3–4 months)

Avoid aspirin or other over-the-counter anti-inflammatory medications

radiographically, together with the patient's pain or limitation of daily activities, with the latter being the more important determinant.

Additional therapeutic considerations for degenerative joint disease of specific anatomic regions are discussed in the section below.

Osteoarthritis of the Hand Heberden's and Bouchard's nodes are often quite painful when they first appear, sometimes accompanied by significant erythema and swelling. However, these nodes generally become much less painful over time. Reassurance that symptoms will improve and that their arthritis will not cause severe deformities is very helpful to patients. In addition to analgesics or anti-inflammatory medications, local heat with hot soaks or paraffin baths may provide symptomatic relief during the initial painful phase.

Osteoarthritis at the base of the thumb (first CMC joint) is very common and deserves special attention. In addition to the above measures, use of a hand splint that immobilizes this joint may help. Severe pain in the first CMC joint may be treated with intra-articular steroid injection.

Osteoarthritis of the Hip In addition to the medical management of OA of the hip (see above), common sense measures to reduce stress on the joint should be employed. Obese patients should be encouraged to lose weight. Use of a walking aid such as a cane or walker is often helpful; a cane should be used on the contralateral side. The use of higher chairs and avoidance of activities such as climbing stairs, kneeling, squatting, or standing for prolonged periods also will reduce stress on the hip joint.[2] Nonweight-bearing exercises (such as swimming) are ideal for strengthening the structures around the joint. In advanced cases, total hip replacement should be considered; total hip replacement generally has excellent results, with relief of pain and restoration of hip motion.

Some patients who complain of "hip" pain actually have a trochanteric bursitis rather than a true hip problem. These patients have marked point tenderness of the upper lateral thigh (over the greater trochanter) and minimal symptoms on rotation of the hip. Trochanteric bursitis generally responds well to injection of steroid into the bursa.

Osteoarthritis of the Knee Similar to the treatment principles applied to OA of the hip, treatment of OA of the knee includes: avoidance of excessive stress on the joint; strengthening of the structures around the joint with specific exercises; medical management (see above); intra-articualar injection; and surgical management. Again, weight loss is essential in obese patients. Elastic supports or knee braces may help to stabilize the knee and relieve stress on the joint. Exercises to strengthen the quadriceps (such as leg lifts) are an essential part of the treatment plan.

Patients with OA of the knee commonly develop acute flares with joint effusion [sometimes secondary to superimposed calcium pyrophosphate dihydrate (CPPD) crystalline disease]. Joint aspiration with intra-articular steroid injection is especially helpful in this setting. Not uncommonly, a patient may develop an associated anserine bursitis (with point tenderness over the anserine bursa, which is located superficially at the inferomedial aspect of the knee); this also generally responds well to local steroid injection. Recently, purified polymers of hyaluronic acid for intra-articular injection were approved for use in OA of the knee. Usually administered as a series of three to five injections 1 week apart, viscosupplementation has been shown in clinical studies to provide pain relief lasting up to 6 months.

In advanced cases of OA of the knee, arthro-

scopic debridement may provide relief and allow the patient to postpone total knee replacement. ***Osteoarthritis of the Foot*** The most common cause of pain at the first metatarsal phalangeal (MTP) joint (at the base of the big toe) is osteoarthritis. The use of metatarsal pads or custom fit orthotics may be helpful in some patients. In severe cases, where conservative measures and medical management are ineffective, surgery may be required. Inflammation of the bursa medial to the first MTP joint may be helped by local steroid injection.

Evaluation of Low Back Pain

Low back pain is extremely common and accounts for up to one-third of all rheumatic complaints.[3] Heavy physical labor, anxiety, depression, cigarette smoking, and pregnancy are considered to be associated risk factors.[3] Degenerative disease is a common cause of low back pain in older patients, but there are numerous causes of low back pain. Both degenerative and nondegenerative causes are discussed in this section. In most cases, a careful history and physical examination together with appropriate imaging techniques can elucidate the eitology of low back pain.

The character of a patient's pain, together with aggravating or alleviating factors, can be important clues to the source of the pain. Spinal pain is felt locally, may be sharp or dull, and is typically aggravated by motion. Spinal pain secondary to degenerative disease is typically worse after exercise or at the end of the day, whereas patients with inflammatory spondyloarthropathies usually describe their pain as a stiffness that is worse in the morning or after periods of prolonged inactivity (see spondyloarthropathy section). Pain secondary to disc disease is worse with activities that increase intradiscal pressure such as lifting, bending, sitting, coughing, or the Valsalva maneuver. Nerve root pain is typically radicular and may be accompanied by numbness and paresthesias and occasionally motor weakness. It is usually exacerbated by maneuvers that stretch the

nerve root (such as bending) and relieved by rest. Sciatic pain (pain running from the buttock down the back of the leg) may arise from the lumbar spine (with impingement of nerve roots) or anywhere along the course of the sciatic nerve. Spinal stenosis, which may be congenital, or caused by degenerative disease and/or disc herniation, is suggested by claudication-like symptoms. Patients with spinal stenosis will report that their symptoms are worse with walking and relieved upon resting or sitting. In patients who have a history suggestive of peripheral vascular disease but lack objective abnormalities on vascular examination, spinal stenosis should be considered.

Low back pain may also be referred from abdominal or pelvic viscera and is usually a deep, aching pain felt in a dermatomal distribution. Referred pain generally is not affected by activity or rest. Gynecologic causes of referred back pain include endometriosis, myomata, pelvic infection, and invasive carcinoma of the uterus, cervix, or bladder.[3] Malignant invasion of the lumbosacral plexus may give rise to radicular symptoms. Sacral pain can occur with menstruation, and sacral pain on standing may be secondary to prolapse of the uterus.[3] Assessment of bowel, bladder, and sexual function should always be included in evaluating the patient with low back pain as they may be abnormal in patients with central disc herniations, conus tumors, and, occasionally, spinal stenosis.[3]

A history of fever or other constitutional symptoms may suggest infection of the vertebral body or disc space, or malignancy. Pyogenic vertebral osteomyelitis occurs via hematogenous spread. *Staphylococcus aureus* is the organism most commonly implicated, but gram-negative bacilli are increasingly involved, especially in the setting of genitourinary manipulations.[3] In patients with more indolent back pain and constitutional symptoms, tuberculosis (especially with involvement of L1) and other nontuberculous granulomatous infections of the spine should be considered.

On physical examination, simple observation will reveal normal lumbar lordosis and dorsal

kyphosis; the presence of scoliosis or straightening of the spine (which may be present with paraspinal muscle spasm) should be noted. Abnormalities in gait or posture may signify a low back problem; for example, the patient may flex her lower extremities to relieve root tension. Local tenderness or paraspinal muscle spasm may be palpable. Palpation may also reveal malalignment of the spinous processes secondary to spondylolisthesis (forward slippage of one vertebra on another). Range of motion of the lumbar spine should be tested with normal anterior flexion to 90 degrees, extension to 30 degrees, and lateral flexion to 30 degrees. Hyperextension may elicit pain from inflamed facet joints; asymmetric lateral bending may be a clue to unilateral root entrapment.[3]

Neurologic exam is extremely important in evaluation of patients with low back pain. L5-S1 and L4-L5 are the most common levels involved in disc herniations, followed by L3-L4.[3] Findings referable to the L4 root (L3-L4 disc) include absent or diminished patellar reflex, weakness of the quadriceps or tibialis anterior (inversion and dorsiflexion of the foot) muscles, or sensory findings including the medial aspect of the lower leg and foot. Involvement of the L5 root (L4-L5 disc) may lead to weakness of the extensor hallucis longus (raising big toe) or sensory findings including the lateral leg and dorsum of the foot. S1 root involvement may lead to a diminished Achilles tendon reflex, weakness of the peroneus longus and brevis (eversion and plantar flexion of the foot), or sensory findings including the posterior leg and lateral aspect of the foot. Certain maneuvers may be helpful in further evaluating the patient with low back pain. For example, the straight leg raise stretches the sciatic nerve and reveals problems originating at the nerve roots or along the sciatic nerve.

Laboratory data generally are not helpful in evaluating the patient with low back pain, with the exception of an abnormal CBC or elevated ESR, which may signal an underlying infection or malignancy.

Imaging studies, on the other hand, often are quite useful. Plain radiographs of the lumbosacral spine often are the first step in evaluating low back pain of almost any etiology and are particularly useful in evaluating patients for tumor, infection, or osteoarthritis. In degenerative disease, radiographs typically show loss of disc space, sclerosis, and osteophyte formation. Technetium-99 bone scanning is useful in detecting bony infection or malignancy and in detecting early sacroiliac disease in patients with spondyloarthropathies. Gallium-or indium-labeled leukocyte scans are useful for early diagnosis of infection. To evaluate patients with suspected disc herniations or spinal stenosis, imaging with CT or MRI is necessary. In patients with spinal stenosis, these techniques can reveal impingement on the cord or nerve root by bulging of the disc, thickening of the ligamentum flavum, or osteophytic entrapment from the facets.[3] CT scanning appears to be more than 95 percent reliable in detecting herniated discs.[3] MRI has the advantage of enhanced definition of soft tissue and neural structures. Myelography is not used as a diagnostic technique, but rather as a preoperative tool to help define the anatomy of a surgical lesion.

Treatment of low back pain depends on the etiology. In cases of suspected vertebral body or disc space infection, culture of the site either by CT-guided needle aspiration or open biopsy is essential. For vertebral osteomyelitis, treatment with appropriate antibiotics for six weeks is recommended.[3] For disc herniation, most cases can initially be treated conservatively with a combination of bedrest, antiinflammatory medications, analgesics, and muscle relaxants. Once the patient improves, a program of back protection and exercises should be started. Patients who do not respond to this regimen or have severe, recurrent symptoms may be candidates for surgery. Marked muscular weakness and progressive neurologic deficit in spite of conservative measures probably require surgery.[3] One absolute and emergent indication for surgery in patients with disc herniation is the cauda equina syndrome, where a midline herniation causes paralysis of

the sacral roots with bowel and bladder dysfunction and inability to walk.[3]

For patients with degenerative disease of the low back, a combination of anti-inflammatory medication or analgesics and an exercise program to strengthen the low back is the mainstay of treatment (see above). In patients with accompanying paraspinal muscle spasm, muscle relaxants may be a useful adjunct. For patients with spinal stenosis, similar measures may be helpful. If conservative measures are not helpful or symptoms are severe, surgical decompression generally provides good symptomatic relief in patients with spinal stenosis. Epidural steroid injections have also been used in the treatment of spinal stenosis.

Rheumatoid Arthritis

It is estimated that 1 percent of the adult population in the United States has rheumatoid arthritis.[4] It is two to three times more common in women than in men. The cause of rheumatoid arthritis remains unknown. There is, however, a genetic predisposition with a strong association of RA with the immunogenetic marker HLA-DR4. Rheumatoid arthritis is a symmetrical polyarthritis involving the wrists and the MCP and PIP joints of the hands, in addition to multiple other joints, including the MTP joints of the feet, ankles, knees, elbows, and upper cervical spine. The disease is inflammatory in nature, with prominent morning stiffness and gelling. Swelling of the joints usually is present for weeks to months, and should be present for at least 6 weeks before a diagnosis of RA can be made (see Table 72-3). It should be noted that there may be multiple patterns of onset, including an insidious onset (most common) over weeks to months, an acute onset, or an intermediate onset. Occasionally, the arthritis may begin in a more asymmetric fashion, but generally becomes more symmetric later on. Patients with RA can develop erosions and multiple joint deformities.

Unlike osteoarthritis, RA is a systemic illness, and patients may have constitutional symptoms

TABLE 72-3   Key Signs of Rheumatoid Arthritis

Symmetric polyarthritis especially small joints of hands and wrists

Prominent morning stiffness (>1 h)

Duration of symptoms >6 weeks

Nodules overlying elbows and other extensor surfaces

Positive rheumatoid factor (~80%)

Marginal erosions on x-ray

as well as extra-articular manifestations of their disease. Extra-articular manifestations include rheumatoid nodules; ocular involvement (scleritis, scleromalacia perforans); peripheral neuropathy or nerve compression syndromes such as carpal tunnel syndrome; pericarditis and other cardiac manifestations; vasculitis (which may be cutaneous or visceral); and pulmonary nodules (note: a single pulmonary nodule in a patient with RA should still be biopsied to rule out malignancy). Patients with RA may develop dry eyes, dry mouth, and salivary gland swelling consistent with secondary Sjögren's syndrome (see below). A small percentage of patients with RA (usually severe, erosive disease) may develop neutropenia and splenomegaly (Felty's syndrome).

The chief complaint of patients with RA is usually pain, swelling, and stiffness of multiple joints in a symmetrical pattern as described above. It is uncommon for RA to occur without wrist or hand (MCP/PIP) involvement. In addition to swelling, patients may note warmth or erythema of their joints. Patients report marked morning stiffness, usually lasting more than 1 h, and often lasting several hours or even all day. Patients will also describe gelling after sitting for prolonged periods of time. Their stiffness typically improves as they move around during the course of the day.

Examination of the joints reveals synovitis in multiple symmetric joint areas, including the MCPs, PIPs, and wrists. These joints will be warm, swollen, and tender, and painful on motion. Joint effusions are common and there may be decreased range of motion of the involved

joints. Characteristic deformities, such as ulnar deviation, swan-neck deformity (flexion at the MCP, hyperextension at the PIP, and flexion at the DIP), and boutonniere deformity (flexion at the PIP and hyperextension at the DIP) may be found. A careful search for rheumatoid nodules over extensor surfaces (most commonly over the olecranon processes, at the occiput, or over extensor tendons) should be performed. A thorough general medical examination should always be done to look for evidence of the extra-articular manifestations described above.

Laboratory studies may reveal a mild normochromic normocytic anemia, slight leukocytosis (with normal differential) or slight thrombocytosis, elevated ESR, and positive rheumatoid factor (positive in approximately 80 percent of cases). It should be noted that there are many possible causes for a false-positive rheumatoid factor and that 15 to 20 percent of cases of rheumatoid arthritis are seronegative. Thus, the rheumatoid factor should be used to support the clinical diagnosis of RA, but is not diagnostic. The presence of rheumatoid factor may have some prognostic significance in definite cases of RA, as patients with high-titer rheumatoid factor and nodules tend to have more severe erosive disease.

Analysis of rheumatoid synovial fluid reveals that it is inflammatory with WBC counts ranging from 5000 to 25,000 WBC/μl, usually with greater than 85 percent PMNs.[4] Crystal analysis and culture are negative.

Radiographs of the hands, wrists, and feet are often helpful in both establishing the diagnosis and evaluating patients for the presence or absence of erosive disease. Early on there may be evidence of soft-tissue swelling and periarticular osteopenia. Marginal erosions may be seen at the MCP, PIP, or MTP joints. Erosions are also commonly seen at the ulnar styloid, but may be seen in any joint involved in RA. With severe, long-standing disease, radiographs may show loss of joint space. Radiographs of the cervical spine should be part of the preoperative evaluation of the patient with RA, as possible C1-2 subluxation

is an important consideration in any patient undergoing general anesthesia.

Treatment of rheumatoid arthritis begins with patient education. As this usually is a chronic disease, it is critical that patients understand the disease and what they can do to minimize their disability. Physical therapy is important in maintaining range of motion of the joints; patients with rheumatoid arthritis must acheive a balance between rest and exercise. The first line of medical management generally is NSAID therapy (see Table 72-1).

Often patients will require treatment with second-line agents or disease modifying antirheumatic drugs (DMARDs), such as hydroxychloroquine, gold, methotrexate, or azathioprine. Recently, sulfasalazine was approved for use in RA. If a diagnosis of RA is suspected, the patient should be referred to a rheumatologist for evaluation and early intervention with these second-line agents in appropriate cases. In general, these medications require weeks to months before maximal effect is seen.

Arthrocentesis and local injection with corticosteroids may be a helpful adjunct with large or particularly symptomatic joint effusions (one should always be careful to rule out coexisting infection if a single joint appears inflamed out of proportion to the rest of the joints). Systemic corticosteroids should be used very sparingly in the smallest possible dose for the shortest possible period of time. The side effects of systemic steroids (especially with long-term use) are numerous and include edema and weight gain; hypertension; hyperglycemia; irregular menses; cataracts; glaucoma; aseptic necrosis of bone; GI bleeding; increased susceptibility to infections; pituitary axis suppression; and osteoporosis (with subsequent risk of fracture). All patients who are started on corticosteroids should be prescribed supplemental calcium and vitamin D if there are no medical contraindications. In addition, these patients should have a baseline bone mineral density study performed with additional treatment for osteoporosis as necessary. Patients who have been on chronic corticosteroids require

stress-dose steroids for surgery, trauma, or other major stresses.

In severely damaged joints with markedly restricted range of motion, joint replacement should be considered. The timing of surgery should be determined mostly by the patient's ability to function.

Rheumatoid Arthritis and Pregnancy Marked improvement of rheumatoid arthritis during pregnancy has been well described. Approximately 70 percent of patients with RA improve significantly during pregnancy, with improvement most commonly occurring in the first trimester and generally being sustained throughout pregnancy.[5] This improvement probably is even greater considering that second-line agents are generally discontinued during pregnancy and first-line anti-inflammatory medications are often reduced.[5] Unfortunately, greater than 90 percent of these patients will have a relapse of their rheumatoid arthritis within 6 to 8 months after delivery.[5] Women who experience significant improvement in their arthritis during pregnancy are likely to have similar improvement during subsequent pregnancies.[5]

Increased risk to the fetus during gestation in RA has not been conclusively demonstrated; most fetal complications in pregnant women with RA have been limited to those patients with severe active systemic disease or related to pharmacologic therapy.[5] In managing the pregnant patient with RA, all medications with known major toxicities should be discontinued as soon as pregnancy is known. Most authors recommend stopping all second-line agents. Methotrexate, chlorambucil, and cyclophosphamide may all cause congenital malformations and should ideally be stopped at least 4 months prior to conception.[5]

NSAIDs have not been shown to be teratogenic; therefore, prophylactic discontinuation of NSAIDs before pregnancy is not usually necessary. The smallest possible dose of aspirin or prednisone may be the safest alternatives to control symptoms during pregnancy.[5] Complications of aspirin use during pregnancy include an increased incidence of the postmaturity syndrome,

prolonged labor, increased peripartum hemorrhage, cephalohematoma, and intracranial hemorrhage in premature infants. For these reasons it is generally recommended that salicylates be discontinued in the final weeks of pregnancy.[5] Intra-articular corticosteroid injections offer the advantage of minimal systemic effects and no significant exposure to the fetus.[5]

In deciding whether to continue or begin disease-modifying agents in patients whose arthritis is resistant to the measures discussed above, the benefit to the mother must be weighed against the potential risk to the fetus. No evidence of fetal malformation has been demonstrated with gold or hydroxychloroquine therapy; however, clinical experience is limited. Extensive experience exists with regard to sulfasalazine in pregnancy because of its use in inflammatory bowel disease. No evidence of fetal malformation has been uncovered. Azathioprine is pregnancy category D.

The Spondyloarthropathies

The spondyloarthropathies are a group of related disorders that include ankylosing spondylitis (AS), psoriatic arthritis (PSA), Reiter's syndrome (RS) (reactive arthritis following genitourinary or gastrointestinal infection), and the arthritis associated with inflammatory bowel disease (IBD). As a group, the spondyloarthropathies are more common in men, but the incidence in women has probably been underestimated. In psoriatic arthritis, arthritis associated with IBD, and arthritis following enteric infection, for example, the female-to-male ratio is approximately 1:1.[7] In the spondyloarthropathies, there is usually a familial occurrence and a strong association with HLA-B27.

Clinically, the spondyloarthropathies are inflammatory in nature and are characterized by spinal and sacroiliac involvement, an asymmetric oligoarthritis peripherally, enthesopathy (inflammation at the site of tendon or ligamentous insertion onto bone), and the absence of serum rheumatoid factor. Extra-articular manifesta-

tions are common and vary in each syndrome. In ankylosing spondylitis, for example, aortic insufficiency, apical pulmonary fibrosis, or uveitis may be seen. As in IBD alone, a variety of cutaneous, mucosal, and ocular manifestations may occur in patients with arthritis associated with Crohn's disease or ulcerative colitis. In addition to skin lesions, nail pitting and onycholysis often are found in patients with psoriatic arthritis. Of note, some patients with psoriatic arthritis will have had psoriasis prior to the onset of the arthritis, some patients will have simultaneous psoriasis and arthritis, and still others will not develop psoriasis until months to years after their presentation with arthritis.

Reiter's syndrome typically follows infection with *Chlamydia trachomatis* of the GU tract or enteric pathogens in the GI tract. It is characterized by urethritis, conjunctivitis or other ocular involvement, painless oral or urogenital ulcerations, and, occasionally, skin lesions, such as keratoderma blennorrhagica (a hyperkeratotic skin lesion usually present on the soles of the feet in approximately 10 percent of patients with RS). Women with RS may have asymptomatic cervicitis as their only genitourinary manifestation. Thus, gynecologic examination with genital cultures or serologic testing for chlamydia may help establish the diagnosis. Salpingitis, vulvovaginitis, and asymptomatic cystitis also have been reported in RS.[8]

The history often reveals chronic low back symptoms, and swelling and warmth of one or more peripheral joints in an asymmetric fashion, with prominent morning stiffness and gelling. In addition to the musculoskeletal symptoms, a careful history should be taken to elicit any symptoms of rashes or psoriasis, recurrent eye inflammation, oral or genital ulcers, urethritis, or history of IBD. A family history of spondyloarthropathy or psoriasis should be sought.

Examination may reveal decreased range of motion of the spine (in both anterior and lateral directions), decreased chest expansion, or tenderness over one or both sacroiliac joints. There may be straightening of the spine with loss of the lumbar lordosis or an exaggerated stooped posture in more severe cases (especially in ankylosing spondylitis). Inflammation in one or more peripheral joints in an asymmetric distribution often is found. In psoriatic arthritis and Reiter's syndrome, diffuse swelling of an entire digit may be seen ("sausage digits"). The general medical examination should be comprehensive to search for extra-articular manifestations (see above), including a careful look at the nails and skin for evidence of psoriasis on the scalp, behind the ears, over the elbows and knees, and in the umbilicus and anal crease.

Laboratory tests are generally not helpful except to document the absence of rheumatoid factor. Although HLA-B27 is positive in a fairly high percentage of patients with spondyloarthropathy, it is not a useful screening tool because it is expensive and because it is present in 6 to 8 percent of normal individuals. Radiographs of the sacroiliac joints are much more helpful, as the presence of sacroiliitis on x-ray is highly suggestive of a spondyloarthropathy. Bone scan or MRI may be helpful in detecting early sacroiliac disease not yet apparent on plain radiographs. Radiographs of the lumbar spine may reveal nonmarginal bridging syndesmophytes or a "bamboo spine" appearance, especially in classic ankylosing spondylitis. Radiographs of involved peripheral joints may be helpful in evaluating for the presence of erosive disease (especially in psoriatic arthritis). Aspiration of joint fluid, if present, will reveal nonspecific inflammatory effusions.

Treatment of the spondyloarthropathies begins with patient education and an exercise program. For patients with spine disease primarily (as in ankylosing spondylitis), maintaining good posture is an important goal. For those with peripheral inflammatory arthritis, medical management usually starts with NSAID therapy (see Table 72-1). Individuals with reactive arthritis secondary to genitourinary or gastrointestinal infection should receive a course of appropriate antibiotics to eradicate the infecting organism. Treatment of chlamydial infections, in particular, appears to result in an improvement in arthritic

symptoms. Patients with erosive disease (as in psoriatic arthritis) are candidates for second-line agents (see treatment of rheumatoid arthritis) and should be evaluated by a rheumatologist early in their course for possible initiation of these medications. Local aspiration and injection with corticosteroids may be a helpful adjunct for peripheral joint disease.

Crystalline Arthropathies: Gout and Pseudogout

In the postmenopausal years, the incidence of gout in women rises dramatically and approximates that of men. In women, the prevalence of gout is approximately 640/100,000.[9] The risk of developing gout increases with age and serum uric acid levels.[9] Other risk factors for the development of gout include obesity, hypertension, and alcohol abuse. An acute attack may be precipitated by alcohol intake or abrupt shifts in fluid status, such as dehydration (or diuresis) or hydration in the hospitalized patient receiving intravenous fluid.

Gout is caused by the precipitation of uric acid crystals within the joint that subsequently causes an inflammatory response. A total body overload of urate may lead to extra-articular deposits of uric acid in tophi (most commonly in the olecranon bursae, over the extensor surfaces of the forearms, on the pinnae of the ears, or overlying joints) or to the development of urate nephrolithiasis.

Acute gouty arthritis is episodic in nature with attacks lasting for 1 to 2 weeks with symptom-free intercritical periods. It often begins as an inflammatory monoarthritis, commonly in the first MTP joint (large toe), ankle, or knee. Although podagra (gout of the first MTP joint) is a common presentation, the most common cause of first MTP pain is osteoarthritis. Later, the attacks may become polyarticular, with more frequent attacks or shorter intercritical periods. In more advanced cases, patients may develop chronic tophaceous gout with erosions and de-

forming arthritis that may mimic rheumatoid arthritis (although gout tends to be less symmetric).

On physical exam, a patient with an acute gout attack may have one or more swollen, warm, and erythematous joints that are markedly tender (gout is one of the most painful forms of inflammatory arthritis). Often there is marked warmth, erythema, and swelling of the surrounding soft tissue that may be confused with an infectious cellulitis and that has sometimes been referred to as "gouty cellulitis." In addition, patients with an acute attack of gout may also have fever. A careful search for tophi should be done; their presence will influence the long-term treatment plan for the patient.

Radiographs generally are not helpful in the initial attack. However, in long-standing disease, tophaceous deposits around the joint may lead to characteristic erosions with "overhanging edges."

Laboratory studies usually, but not always, reveal hyperuricemia; one can have an acute gout attack with a normal serum uric acid level. Additionally, there are patients who have hyperuricemia and arthritis but do not have gout. The only way to establish a definitive diagnosis of gout is to demonstrate the presence of intracellular monosodium urate (MSU) crystals in synovial fluid using a compensated polarized light microscope. MSU crystals are needle-shaped crystals that are slightly longer than the diameter of a WBC and are strongly negatively birefringent (they are bright yellow when parallel to the plane of compensated polarized light and bright blue in the direction perpendicular to this plane). Joint effusions are usually highly inflammatory with WBC counts ranging from 2000 to 100,000 WBC/μl.[8] A synovial fluid culture always should be ordered to rule out coexisting infection.

There are many possible therapeutic approaches to an acute gout attack. Which approach should be chosen depends on the patient's concomitant medical problems and the duration of symptoms. For example, intravenous or oral colchicine is most effective for an acute attack only if used within the first 24 to 48 h of the

attack. NSAIDs are useful for an acute attack of gout (see Table 72-1) if the patient has no contraindications to their use. If only one joint is involved, aspiration and local injection of corticosteroids is often the simplest and safest alternative. If multiple joints are involved and the patient is not a candidate for NSAID or colchicine therapy, a short, tapering course of moderate-dose systemic corticosteroids should be considered. Alternatively, ACTH gel may be given IM in dosages of 40 to 80 units IM every 12 h for 1 to 3 days. The major drawback of using either ACTH or systemic corticosteroids is that patients may have rebound flares when these medications are withdrawn; rebound flares may be minimized by giving low-dose prophylactic colchicine (0.6 mg/day) during and after therapy. The use of allopurinol during an acute gout attack is absolutely contraindicated; it may abruptly shift the uric acid levels and worsen an attack. Patients with chronic tophaceous gout, a history of urate nephrolithiasis, or frequent gouty attacks unresponsive to prophylactic NSAIDs or colchicine, and who are hyperuricemic, are candidates for urate-lowering agents such as allopurinol (once the acute attack resolves). Dosage of allopurinol should be adjusted for body weight and creatinine clearance.

Calcium pyrophosphate dihydrate deposition disease (CPPD), or pseudogout, is another crystalline arthropathy. The female-to-male ratio in this disorder is about equal, although some series indicate a female predominance.[10] CPPD disease often occurs in the setting of preexisting damage to a joint, as in osteoarthritis, and the incidence increases with age. CPPD disease sometimes is associated with an underlying metabolic disorder, such as hyperparathyroidism; hemochromatosis; hypomagnesemia; hypothyroidism; hypocalciuric hypercalcemia; hypophosphatasia; gout; diabetes; or amyloidosis.[10] There is also a hereditary form of this disorder that shows an autosomal dominant pattern (with variable penetrance) of inheritance.[10]

CPPD crystals set up an inflammatory re-sponse within the joint analogous to what happens in gout. Joints most commonly affected are the knee and the wrist. Attacks may be acute, subacute, or chronic, and may be monoarticular or polyarticular. CPPD disease may mimic gout (except for the noted absence of podagra) or, when polyarticular, rheumatoid arthritis.

The history and physical generally will suggest an inflammatory arthritis, commonly in the knee or the wrist. Radiographs may show evidence of chondrocalcinosis (linear-stippled calcification seen within the joint space). Like gout, the definitive diagnosis of CPPD disease is made by demonstration of the appropriate crystals in synovial fluid. CPPD crystals are rhomboidal in shape and are weakly positively birefringent (pale blue when parallel to the plane of compensated polarized light and pale yellow in the direction perpendicular to this plane). Laboratory tests are most helpful in screening for a possible associated metabolic disorder; all patients in whom a diagnosis of CPPD is made should have measurement of serum calcium, phosphorus, magnesium, alkaline phosphatase, glucose, and uric acid, and should have iron studies and thyroid function tests. Treatment of CPPD disease is symptomatic, with the use of NSAID therapy (see Table 72-1), local aspiration, and injection with corticosteroids, or a short, tapering course of low-dose systemic corticosteroids. Low-dose colchicine may occasionally be useful for prophylaxis in refractory recurrent cases, but usually this is not necessary as the attacks generally are spaced farther apart than those of recurrent gout.

Septic Arthritis

Septic arthritis should always be considered in an acutely swollen and warm joint, especially when associated with fever and chills. Prompt diagnosis and treatment of septic arthritis is of extreme importance, as infection with *S. aureus,* for example, can rapidly destroy a joint. Spread to the joint is usually via a hematogenous route; septic

arthritis is most commonly a monoarthritis, and the joint most commonly affected is the knee. Diagnosis is made by aspiration of synovial fluid with Gram stain and culture. Synovial fluid leukocyte counts are very high, generally above 50,000 WBC/μl, and synovial fluid glucose is often much lower than a simultaneous serum glucose. These findings are not specific, however, and can be seen, for example, in rheumatoid arthritis. The ultimate diagnosis rests on the results of the culture. The most common organism in septic arthritis is *S. aureus,* followed by streptococci and gram-negative bacilli. In young patients with one or more probable septic joints associated with tenosynovitis or skin lesions, gonococcal arthritis should be suspected. Gonococci are fastidious organisms and are difficult to grow from synovial fluid cultures. In suspected cases of gonococcal arthritis, cultures of the pharynx and genitourinary sites have a much higher yield and always should be performed. All cases of suspected septic arthritis should be treated with appropriate antibiotics (generally intravenously for at least 2 weeks followed by another 1 to 2 weeks of oral antibiotics) and thorough drainage of involved joints. Repeated arthrocentesis may be necessary to achieve adequate drainage.

Lyme Disease

Lyme disease is a multisystem illness caused by the spirochete *Borrelia burgdorferi,* which is carried by Ixodes ticks. Because of the small size of these ticks, many patients do not recall a tick bite. The initial manifestations of Lyme disease may include the characteristic rash, erythema chronicum migrans (ECM), which, when present, usually appears within a month of the tick bite. Lyme disease is discussed in Chap. 69. Early musculoskeletal manifestations generally consist of transient or migratory arthralgias. Later in the course (with a mean of about 6 months after onset), approximately 50 to 60 percent of patients develop frank arthritis.[11,12] The arthritis is most

commonly a monoarthritis or an asymmetric oligoarthritis, often involving the knee.

Arthritis Associated with the Use of Oral Contraceptives

Uncommonly, patients taking oral contraceptives may develop arthralgias, myalgias, or even a polyarthritis. Patients with this syndrome may complain of significant morning stiffness. In addition, patients may have positive tests for ANA or rheumatoid factor.[4] The syndrome resolves when oral contraceptives are discontinued.

Common Conditions That Mimic Arthritis

Polymyalgia Rheumatica and Temporal Arteritis

Polymyalgia rheumatica (PMR) is a fairly common clinical syndrome that occurs in patients over the age of 50, most commonly in Caucasians. It is more common in women, with a ratio of 2:1.[13] It is an inflammatory disorder characterized by pain and stiffness in the shoulder and hip girdle muscles, with prominent morning stiffness and gelling. Patients often complain of difficulty raising their arms to comb their hair or of difficulty arising from a chair. Physical examination reveals that the joints are normal. Weakness is absent.

Laboratory data reveals an elevated ESR of >40 to 50 mm/h (often >100 mm/h). Elevated α_2 globulins are often seen on serum protein electrophoresis. A mild normochromic, normocytic anemia may be noted. In addition, abnormalities of liver function tests may be seen, especially alkaline phosphatase. Thyroid function tests and CPK should be checked, and usually are normal. Radiographs are normal; however, because PMR is primarily a disease of the elderly, it is not uncommon to find incidental coexisting osteoarthritis on x-ray.

Treatment is with low doses of prednisone (10 to 15 mg/day), and the response of PMR to steroids is often dramatic. The response is usually so dramatic that if a patient suspected of having PMR does not respond to 15 mg/day of prednisone within 2 weeks, another diagnosis should be considered. In patients in whom it is preferable not to use steroids (for example, in diabetics) NSAIDs may also be tried (see Table 72-1). The natural history of PMR is that it is generally self-limited, resolving within several months to years. Steroids should be tapered to the lowest dose that will control the patient's symptoms.

The major concern in PMR is that approximately 15 percent of patients will develop an associated *temporal arteritis* (giant cell arteritis), a serious vasculitis that can lead to blindness. Patients with PMR should always be warned about this association; the symptoms of temporal arteritis should be reviewed and patients should be instructed to report any TA-like symptoms promptly. Individuals with temporal arteritis may develop headache (especially temporal headaches), visual changes, jaw claudication, or scalp tenderness. Examination may reveal thickened or tender temporal arteries, or diminished or absent temporal artery pulse on the involved side(s).

Laboratory data are similar to that seen in PMR, especially the marked elevation of the ESR. In cases of suspected temporal arteritis, a temporal artery biopsy should be performed. However, on pathologic examination, the lesion often is patchy and therefore may be missed on biopsy. Thus, if temporal arteritis is strongly suspected clinically, the patient should be treated, even after a negative biopsy.

Treatment of temporal arteritis is with high-dose steroids (1 to 2 mg/kg/day of prednisone in divided doses); treatment generally should be started as soon as the diagnosis is suspected. High-dose prednisone should be continued for at least 4 to 6 weeks. Thereafter, steroids may be tapered by approximately 10 percent per week.[13] It is more useful to follow the patient's symptoms (rather than the ESR) when tapering steroids.

Fibromyalgia

Fibromyalgia, or fibrositis, is a common disorder, that mostly affects women. Its prevalence was found to be 2.1 percent and 5.7 percent in a family practice and general internal medicine clinic, respectively.[14] The female predominance is striking; it has been reported that 80 to 90 percent of patients with fibromyalgia are women.[14] Accordingly, a great deal of attention has been directed toward the role of hormonal influences in the etiology of fibromyalgia. Recent studies have shown multiple abnormalities in the hypothalamic-pituitary-adrenal (HPA) axis in women with fibromyalgia. It has been hypothesized that gonadal hormones may play a role in HPA axis dysregulation. For instance, nearly all postmenopausal women develop HPA axis dysfunction during depression (which is known to be a contributing factor in fibromyalgia), whereas premenopausal women are resistant to HPA axis changes in depression.[15]

Fibromyalgia is characterized by reproducible, paired tender points or trigger points in the absence of arthritis. These tender points generally are accompanied by disturbed sleep or "nonrestorative" sleep. Fatigue is often a prominent symptom of fibromyalgia. Fibromyalgia and chronic fatigue syndrome are overlapping disorders.[14] Patients may also complain of morning stiffness that may mimic that seen in rheumatoid arthritis. Often patients have a history of irritable bowel syndrome or dysmenorrhea. Approximately 12 percent of patients with fibromyalgia have a "female urethral syndrome," which is defined as urinary frequency, dysuria, and suprapubic discomfort with negative urine cultures.[14] Although patients often complain of subjective swelling (especially in the hands), there is no objective evidence of swelling or inflammation on examination. Except for the characteristic

tender points, the physical examination is normal.

Patients have some or all of the following nine paired, symmetric tender points: insertion of the nuchal muscles into the occiput; upper trapezius (midportion); medial scapular border; low anterior cervical region; pectoralis muscle just lateral to the second costochondral junction; 2 cm below the lateral epicondyle; upper gluteal area; 2 cm posterior to the greater trochanter; inferomedial aspect of the knee.[16] Patients with fibromyalgia may present with costochondritis or an anterior chest wall syndrome.

Laboratory tests (including CBC, chemistries, ESR, RF, ANA, TFTs, and CPK) and radiographs should all be normal. Treatment of fibromyalgia is often difficult. Patient education and a program to improve physical fitness are extremely important. Medications that restore sleep [such as amitriptyline (Elavil) 10 to 25 mg po hs or cyclobenzaprine (Flexeril) 10 to 20 mg po hs] are helpful.

Regional Disorders: Tendinitis and Bursitis

Tendinitis often occurs in the setting of overuse, which may be a sports-related injury or may be occupational. Areas that are commonly affected include the supraspinatus and bicipital tendons of the shoulder and the lateral epicondyle (tennis elbow). Supraspinatus tendinitis is suggested by a painful arc from about 70 to 100 degrees of active shoulder abduction. Bicipital tendinitis is suggested by localized tenderness over the bicipital groove and by a positive Yergason's test (pain on resisted supination). Epicondylitis is suggested by point tenderness at or near the lateral epicondyle. Treatment of these disorders is by cessation of the offending repetitive motion; local injection of corticosteroids is often effective.

Bursitis may be caused by local irritation or trauma. Septic bursitis may occur when organisms are introduced by puncture wounds or overlying cellulitis. There are numerous bursae throughout the body, but common sites include

subacromial bursitis, trochanteric bursitis, olecranon bursitis, prepatellar bursitis, and anserine bursitis (inferomedial aspect of the knee). Treatment of bursitis (in the absence of infection) is by local injection of corticosteroids. Because it is an area that is susceptible to trauma in introduction of infection, the olecranon bursa is a common site for septic bursitis. Septic bursitis should be treated with aspiration (repeated drainage is often required) and appropriate antibiotics.

Systemic Rheumatic Diseases

Systemic Lupus Erythematosus

Systemic lupus erythematosus (SLE) is a complex disease that can involve multiple organ systems and is associated with the production of autoantibodies. The cause of SLE remains unknown; genetic, hormonal, and environmental factors have all been implicated. Estimates of prevalence of SLE have varied widely, from 4 to 250 cases per 100,000 population.[17] In the United States, the prevalence is higher among Asians and African-Americans than among Caucasians or Hispanics.[17] SLE is much more common in women, with a female:male ratio ranging from 8:1 to 13:1.[17]

Major clinical manifestations of SLE (Table 72-4) include rash (including malar or "butterfly"

TABLE 72-4 **Important Features of SLE**

Rash
Malar rash
Discoid lesions
Photosensitivity
Oral ulcers
Alopecia
Arthritis
Raynaud's
Pleuritis/pericarditis
Renal disease
CNS involvement

rash, photosensitivity, or discoid lesions); oral ulcers (which are typically painless); arthritis (which is often associated with morning stiffness but is typically nonerosive); serositis (including pericarditis or pleurisy); renal disease; CNS disease; Raynaud's phenomenon; or alopecia. Patients may also present with fatigue, fever, weight loss, or other constitutional symptoms, and may have hepatosplenomegaly or lymphadenopathy. Patients with renal or CNS disease have a worse prognosis. Renal disease is generally manifested by proteinuria (often nephrotic range), active urinary sediment, and later by renal insufficiency. A variety of renal lesions may be seen (with diffuse proliferative glomerulonephritis having the worst prognosis and requiring aggressive intervention), and renal biopsy may be helpful in selected cases. Countless manifestations of CNS lupus have been described, but the most common include seizures, psychosis, and migraine-type headaches. MRI may be helpful in evaluating patients for possible CNS lupus, but the findings are nonspecific. A subset of patients may give a history of previous thrombotic events (such as DVT, PE, or stroke) or multiple spontaneous abortions, and may have an associated "lupus anticoagulant" or antiphospholipid antibody (see below).

Physical examination will often give clues to the diagnosis. Alopecia may be noted, which may be diffuse or may manifest as short, broken hairs along the frontal hairline ("lupus hairs"). Discoid skin lesions will generally appear as rounded, slightly scaling lesions with a region of central atrophy; these lesions tend to scar. When discoid lesions involve the scalp, scarring can lead to permanent alopecia (other forms of alopecia are temporary and tend to fluctuate with disease activity). The malar rash typically appears on the cheeks and across the bridge of the nose, but characteristically spares the nasolabial folds. A livedo reticularis rash (a fine, lacy rash) may be noted, particularly in patients with an associated anticardiolipin antibody. Peripheral edema or hypertension may signify the presence of renal disease. Oral or nasal mucosal ulceration may be found; the patient may be unaware of these lesions, which tend to be painless. Examination of the chest may reveal evidence of pericardial or pleural involvement. The arthritis of SLE generally has less pronounced synovitis than that of rheumatoid arthritis; deformities (such as Jaccoud's arthropathy), if present, generally are completely reducible. In cases of severe Raynaud's phenomenon, the hands or feet may appear dusky and cool.

Laboratory data are extremely helpful in diagnosing and managing SLE (Table 72-5). The ANA is positive in greater than 95 percent of patients with SLE, and thus is a useful screening test. The major limitation of the ANA is its lack of specificity. More specific, but much less sensitive, tests for SLE include antidouble-stranded (anti-ds) DNA and anti-Smith antibodies. Some patients with SLE have hypocomplementemia, with decreased C3 and/or C4 levels. The presence of hypocomplementemia and high titers of anti-ds DNA antibodies may predict the onset of renal disease, and often fluctuate with disease activity. It is useful to follow serial measurements in patients with these abnormalities to assess disease activity and to help gauge therapy. Routine urinalysis should always be obtained at baseline and periodically in patients with SLE. Hematologic involvement in SLE is common, and patients may have evidence of a hemolytic anemia, leukopenia (especially lymphopenia), or thrombocytopenia. Patients may also have a false-positive VDRL (positive VDRL with negative FTA).

TABLE 72-5 Laboratory Findings in SLE

Anemia
Leukopenia
Thrombocytopenia
Abnormal urinalysis
Serologies
ANA (>95%)
Anti-native (ds) DNA
Anti-Smith (Sm)
BFP VDRL

Patients with an associated "lupus anticoagulant" may have an elevated aPTT, a positive dilute Russel viper venom time (DRVVT), a false-positive VDRL, IgG or IgM anticardiolipin and/or β_2-glycoprotein I antibodies.

Treatment of SLE is complex and depends on the specific manifestations of the disease. Avoidance of the sun and use of sunscreens should be advised. The arthritis of SLE often is managed initially with NSAIDs (see Table 72-1). Patients who have cutaneous disease, arthritis, and/or serositis as their major manifestations are candidates for treatment with the antimalarial hydroxychloroquine (Plaquenil) in dosages of 200 to 400 mg/day. Patients should be evaluated by an ophthalmologist at baseline and every 4 to 6 months while on this medication as they may (rarely) develop retinal changes. Screening for G6PD deficiency should also be performed prior to starting hydroxychloroquine; patients with G6PD deficiency may develop hemolysis on this drug. Topical steroid preparations may be a useful adjunct in patients with severe skin disease.

Systemic corticosteroids are generally used in two types of clinical settings in SLE. The first is in low doses (less than 10 mg prednisone/day) for patients with mild disease, such as arthritis or mild serositis, that is not controlled with NSAIDs or hydroxychloroquine alone. The second is in high dosages (prednisone 1 to 2 mg/kg/day) in patients who are severely ill with major organ involvement such as lupus cerebritis, lupus nephritis, severe autoimmune hemolytic anemia or thrombocytopenia, or systemic vasculitis.[18] In patients in whom there is any question of absorption, intravenous steroids should be used in equivalent doses.

Immunosuppressive agents such as azathioprine (Imuran) and cyclophosphamide (Cytoxan) may be necessary in patients with major organ involvement who fail to respond to corticosteroids. The use of intravenous cyclophosphamide is of significant benefit in class IV (diffuse proliferative) lupus nephritis. This drug is an alkylating agent with significant toxicity, including risk of subsequent malignancy, bone marrow suppression, leukopenia and risk of serious infection, hemorrhagic cystitis, premature ovarian failure, and infertility.[19] As SLE is a disease mainly of women of childbearing age, the risk of infertility with Cytoxan is a serious consideration. Loss of ovarian function may also contribute to osteoporosis and accelerated atherosclerotic disease, the latter especially in women on long-term corticosteroid therapy. In addition, cyclophosphamide is teratogenic; pregnancy should be ruled out before the drug is given and adequate contraception is mandatory during its use.

Azathioprine is used frequently as a steroid-sparing agent or for manifestations of SLE that are unresponsive to NSAIDs, hydroxychloroquine, or steroids alone. Azathioprine, although less toxic than cyclophosphamide, shares many of the same potential serious adverse effects, including bone marrow suppression, risk of serious infection, risk of subsequent malignancy, and premature menopause and infertility (which occurs much less frequently than with cyclophosphamide). In addition, patients on azathioprine may develop hepatitis.

SLE and Pregnancy Exacerbation of SLE occurs in 30 to 50 percent of pregnancies in women with this disorder, and there is an increased risk of fetal loss in SLE patients compared with normal populations.[20] Mothers with active disease at the time of pregnancy have worse pregnancy outcomes, with an increased risk of prematurity.[20] Furthermore, the risk of fetal death is increased in lupus patients with renal disease.[17] Exacerbations of SLE during pregnancy occur in all three trimesters (in approximately equal frequencies) and in the immediate postpartum period. However, the rate of exacerbation during and after pregnancy has been progressively decreasing over the past 30 years, possibly due to increased use of corticosteroids or improved care.[17] Consequently, pregnancy in women with SLE is considered high risk, but many women with SLE have successful pregnancies. Patients with SLE who are contemplating pregnancy should be advised that the optimal time for pregnancy is when their disease is quiescent or well controlled (especially

renal disease). Ideally, second-line or cytotoxic medications should be discontinued at least 4 months prior to conception; in most cases, the lowest possible dose of corticosteroids alone should be used to control their disease prior to and during pregnancy. In addition, screening for an associated antiphospholipid antibody syndrome (see below) and anti-Ro/La (SSA/SSB) should be done because of an associated risk of recurrent second and third trimester miscarriages[21-24] and congenital heart block, respectively.

Approximately 5 percent of SLE pregnancies are complicated by neonatal lupus, especially in mothers with anti-Ro/La antibodies (anti-SSA/SSB antibodies).[17] Infants with neonatal lupus often have a rash and some may have congenital heart block, necessitating pacemaker placement. Women with SLE who have infants with neonatal lupus have a 25 percent chance of having another child with neonatal lupus in subsequent pregnancies.[17]

SLE and Menstrual Abnormalities A small number of patients with SLE report a monthly flare in their symptoms around the time of their menses, most commonly manifested by increased joint pain, transient facial rash, or pleuritic chest pain.[25] Some women may have menorrhagia, possibly secondary to the use of NSAIDs, thrombocytopenia, or an inhibitor of one of the clotting factors.[25] In addition, women with SLE may have irregular menses secondary to their underlying disease or to the use of corticosteroids. Premature menopause may occur in patients treated with medications such as cyclophosphamide or azathioprine.

SLE and Estrogen Use Historically, the use of estrogens (oral contraceptives and estrogen replacement therapy [ERT]) has been avoided in patients with SLE, as their use was thought to be associated with exacerbations of the disease. However, this issue is being reevaluated. Recently, a prospective nurse's health study found a twofold relative risk of developing SLE in postmenopausal women who took ERT.[26] On the other hand, in a meta-analysis that included controversies related to pregnancy and hormonal therapy in SLE, Boumpas concluded that oral contraceptive use and postmenopausal ERT appeared not to cause clinical deterioration in lupus patients.[27] In a British retrospective study of 60 postmenopausal women with stable SLE, HRT appeared to be well tolerated and safe.[28] The issue of estrogen use in SLE is being further examined in an NIH-sponsored randomized, placebo-controlled study—SELENA (Safety of Estrogens in Lupus Erythematosus National Assessment).[29] Due to their prothrombotic properties, estrogens should not be used in SLE patients with associated clinical and/or laboratory evidence of the antiphospholipid antibody syndrome (see below).

Antiphospholipid Antibody Syndrome

The antiphospholipid antibody syndrome (APL) (or anticardiolipin antibody syndrome) may occur in association with other rheumatic diseases (most commonly with SLE, as discussed above) or may occur in the absence of any rheumatic disease (primary antiphospholipid antibody syndrome). It is characterized (Table 72-6) by recurrent venous and arterial thrombotic events (including DVT, PE, and stroke), recurrent spontaneous abortions (especially in the second trimester), and thrombocytopenia. Migraine-type headaches and a livedo reticularis rash are common. Patients may have abnormalities of phospholipid-dependent tests of coagulation, such as

TABLE 72-6 Features of the APL Syndrome

Arterial or venous thrombotic events
Recurrent fetal loss
Livedo reticularis
Migraine headache
Thrombocytopenia
Laboratory evidence of circulating anticoagulant
  ↑ aPTT
  DRVVT
  BFP VDRL
  Anticardiolipin antibody
  Anti-β_2-GPI

prolongation of the aPTT or the dilute Russel viper venom time (DRVVT). Sometimes this may be referred to as a "lupus anticoagulant," although this is a misnomer for two reasons. First, patients don't necessarily have lupus; second, patients are paradoxically hypercoagulable in vivo. Patients may also have a biological false-positive test for syphilis or IgG or IgM anticardiolipin antibodies (ACL). It should be noted that anticardiolipin antibodies are not entirely specific for the anti-phospholipid antibody syndrome and may be induced by infection and certain medications.

Recently, a glycoprotein cofactor, β_2-glycoprotein I (β_2-GPI) for anticardiolipin antibody reactivity was described. Antibodies to β_2-GPI appear to be more specific than other tests for the APL syndrome and may correlate more strongly with risk for thrombosis. Patients may have abnormalities in any one or any combination of these tests; it is thus useful to screen with all of these tests (aPTT, DRVVT, VDRL, ACL, and β_2-GPI) when this syndrome is suspected clinically. In pregnancy, the aPTT is often shortened; thus, the kaolin clotting time is a more sensitive test than the aPTT in the setting of pregnancy.[21]

Treatment of the antiphosphoplipid antibody syndrome should be individualized according to the specific clinical circumstances. In general, individuals with laboratory evidence but no clinical manifestations of the antiphospholipid antibody syndrome do not require treatment. In nonpregnant patients with this syndrome and recurrent thrombotic events, life-long anticoagulation with coumadin is warranted. In pregnant women who have had recurrent miscarriages or thrombotic events, a combination of subcutaneous heparin and low-dose aspirin may be used.

Drug-Induced Lupus

Patients taking certain medications may develop a syndrome similar to SLE. The medications most commonly implicated in drug-induced lupus include procainamide, hydralazine, INH, methyldopa, and chlorpromazine.[17] While drug-induced lupus may resemble SLE, there are several important differences. Patients with drug-induced lupus generally have arthralgias or arthritis, symptoms of pleuropericarditis, and constitutional symptoms; renal and CNS disease are distinctly uncommon. Unlike SLE, drug-induced lupus occurs with equal frequency in males and females and is rare in African-Americans.[17] As in SLE, ANAs are seen in approximately 95 percent of cases of drug-induced lupus, but patients with drug-induced lupus generally do not have anti-dsDNA or anti-Smith antibodies, and serum complement levels generally are normal. Approximately 90 percent of patients with drug-induced lupus will have antihistone antibodies (but these antibodies will also be present in approximately 25 percent of cases of native SLE).[17] Drug-induced lupus is treated by discontinuing the offending drug. Some patients will develop a positive ANA while on medication, but will not have any signs or symptoms of drug-induced lupus; in these patients, it is not necessary to discontinue that medication.

Scleroderma and CREST Syndrome

Systemic sclerosis (PSS; scleroderma) is a generalized disorder of connective tissue in which there is thickening and fibrosis of the skin that is associated with internal organ involvement. The etiology is unknown. Scleroderma commonly presents between the ages of 30 and 60. Female to male ratios have been reported to be as high as 7 to 12:1.[30]

Scleroderma may be rapidly progressive, with extensive skin and internal organ involvement (diffuse form), or may be more limited, with a more indolent course. Limited scleroderma has been termed the CREST variant (prominent features are Calcinosis, Raynaud's phenomenon, Esophageal dysmotility, Sclerodactyly, and Telangiectasias). Patients with CREST may have stable disease for many years (commonly with a long history of Raynaud's phenomenon) and tend to have involvement of the skin only of the distal extremities (up to MCPs or proximal forearms) and face. They generally do not have

other major organ involvement, with the notable exception of pulmonary hypertension. There is a co-occurrence of primary biliary cirrhosis in some patients with limited scleroderma. In contrast, patients with diffuse scleroderma have widespread involvement of the skin, including the skin of the proximal as well as distal extremities, the face, and the trunk (especially the anterior chest and abdomen). Early internal organ involvement is frequent, including involvement of the GI tract, lungs, heart, and kidneys.

The first symptoms of PSS are often in the hands, with either Raynaud's phenomenon, puffiness of the hands, and/or polyarthralgias. Generally, thickening of the skin of the hands follows several weeks or months later. Taut skin on the face may lead to decreased ability to open the mouth fully and a characteristic "pursed lip" appearance. Involvement of the GI tract most commonly takes the form of esophageal dysmotility, but other complications, such as malabsorption, pneumatosis intestinalis (air in the wall of the intestine), or wide-mouth diverticula, can occur. Patients with scleroderma may develop bibasilar pulmonary fibrosis, which may be evident on chest radiography. Pulmonary function tests may show decreased diffusing capacity or evidence of restrictive lung disease. Pulmonary hypertension occurs more commonly in patients with limited scleroderma. "Scleroderma renal crisis" is a major cause of death in patients with diffuse scleroderma, and generally presents with malignant hypertension (which may be associated with hypertensive encephalopathy) associated with proteinuria, microscopic hematuria, or worsening renal function. Therapy with angiotensin-converting enzyme inhibitors (ACE inhibitors) has dramatically improved survival in the acute setting in scleroderma renal crisis.

More than 90 percent of patients with scleroderma have positive ANAs.[31] Twenty to 40 percent of patients with diffuse scleroderma have antibodies to topoisomerase I (Scl-70); the majority of patients with limited disease have anticentromere antibodies. Nail fold capillary microscopy also is helpful in establishing the diagnosis, and may reveal dilated, tortuous vessels or capillary drop out.

Prognosis in patients with diffuse disease and early internal organ involvement is poor, but the disease course in scleroderma is extremely variable. Unfortunately, there is no drug or combination of drugs of proven value in treating patients with scleroderma.[31] Agents such as D-penicillamine have been used in the past with varying success. More recently, cyclophosphamide has been used in patients with interstitial lung disease and evidence of active inflammation on brochoalveolar lavage washings; stabilization of pulmonary function has been achieved in some patients.[32] Treatment with corticosteroids is generally of no benefit, except in associated inflammatory conditions such as inflammatory myositis or serositis. The use of high-dose steroid has been associated with the development of renal failure and other vaso-occlusive complications of the disease.[33]

Supportive measures are important in the overall management of patients with scleroderma. Patients with Raynaud's phenomenon should be instructed about common sense preventive measures such as keeping their hands and feet warm, and smoking cessation. Calcium channel blockers such as nifedipine often are helpful in managing Raynaud's. Meticulous skin care, especially in those who develop digital ulceration or other areas of breakdown, is of extreme importance. In patients with esophageal involvement, promotility agents, such as metoclopramide, may improve esophageal motility. Simple measures such as avoiding eating before bedtime and elevation of the head of the bed may minimize symptoms of esophageal reflux.

Polymyositis and Dermatomyositis

Polymyositis (PM) and dermatomyositis (DM) are inflammatory myopathies of unknown etiology. They are relatively uncommon, with an annual incidence of 0.5 to 8.4 cases per 1 million.[34] These disorders are more common in women than in men. Both are characterized clinically by

symmetric proximal muscle weakness; dermato-myositis has the additional feature of characteristic skin lesions. The heart, lungs, and GI tract also may be involved. An increased risk of malignancy has been reported in patients with PM and DM; all patients with these diagnoses should have a comprehensive history and careful physical examination, as well as routine screening procedures. More recent data suggest that gynecologic malignancies are particularly frequent in women with the paraneoplastic presentation of dermatomyositis. For example, Cherin found that ovarian carcinoma was present in 13 percent of women with dermatomyositis.[35] Thus, in addition to routine screening, women with dermatomyositis should have careful gynecologic evaluation including pelvic imaging where indicated.

Patients with PM/DM usually complain of symptoms referable to hip girdle or shoulder girdle weakness. They may report progressive difficulty arising from a chair or climbing stairs, or difficulty with activities that require raising their arms, such as combing their hair or putting heavy objects on a high shelf. Patients with involvement of the anterior neck flexors may complain of difficulty raising their head from their pillow. Less than half of the patients with PM or DM complain of pain in the hip or shoulder girdle muscles; weakness is generally the predominant symptom.

On physical exam, almost all patients have symmetric proximal muscle weakness. Tenderness of these muscles may be noted in some patients. In dermatomyositis, a variety of skin lesions may be seen, including diffuse erythema of the face, anterior neck and upper chest ("V sign"), or upper back and shoulders ("shawl sign"). Patients may have the classic "heliotrope" rash (purplish discoloration over the eyelids) and/or periorbital edema. Gottron's papules or Gottron's sign (violaceous or erythematous flat papules over the dorsal surface of the IP or MCP joints of the hands, elbows, knees, and/or medial malleoli) are skin findings considered to be pathognomonic of dermatomyositis.[34]

Laboratory data reveal elevated muscle enzymes, with CPK and/or aldolase being elevated in the majority of patients at some point during the course of their disease. Serum transaminases and LDH may also be abnormal. The remainder of routine laboratory tests generally are normal. A variety of autoantibodies have been described in patients with PM and DM, including antibody to Jo-1 (antihistidyl t-RNA synthetase), which is present in 20 to 30 percent of patients with polymyositis. The presence of Jo-1 antibody has been associated with an increased incidence of interstitial lung disease.

EMG studies show characteristic findings in patients with myositis and are often helpful in establishing the diagnosis. Demonstration of inflammation on muscle biopsy confirms the diagnosis and should be performed in almost all patients with suspected myositis before starting long-term and potentially toxic therapy.

The treatment of PM and DM is usually with high-dose daily oral corticosteroids (1 to 2 mg/kg/d prednisone). High-dose steroids are generally continued until normalization of muscle enzymes, which may require several months; steroids should then be gradually tapered to the lowest dose that controls the patient's disease. Patients who fail to respond to high-dose steroids, or who have unacceptable complications, require the addition of an immunosuppressive agent or intravenous gammaglobulin. In addition to medical management, patients with myositis should also receive physical therapy to help restore their strength.

Mixed Connective Tissue Disease

Mixed connective tissue disease (MCTD) occurs with a frequency similar to that of scleroderma; it is a disease mostly of women with a mean age of onset of 37 years.[36] It is characterized clinically by puffy hands, polyarthritis, Raynaud's phenomenon, and myositis. Patients often have pulmonary involvement, including pulmonary hypertension. In addition, patients often have features of other rheumatic disorders, especially SLE or systemic sclerosis (see above), and may eventually experience transition into these disor-

ders. Patients with MCTD generally have high-titer positive ANAs with a speckled pattern. MCTD is characterized by the presence of antibody to the extractable nuclear antigen ribonucleoprotein (anti-RNP) in the absence of other autoantibodies.

Treatment of this syndrome depends on the specific manifestations (see treatment of SLE, systemic sclerosis, and polymyositis). In general, inflammatory manifestations such as myositis respond to treatment with corticosteroids, whereas scleroderma-like disease and pulmonary hypertension do not. Raynaud's phenomenon should be treated with conservative measures (such as prevention of cold exposure) and calcium channel blockers (such as nifedipine), if needed. The prognosis for patients with MCTD is generally fairly good, with the exception of patients with scleroderma-like features or pulmonary hypertension.

Sjögren's Syndrome

Sjögren's syndrome has been estimated to affect 2 to 3 million people in the United States.[37] The majority of patients with this disorder are women (>90 percent) with an average age of onset of 50 years old.[37] Sjögren's syndrome may be primary, or it may be associated with other rheumatic conditions, most commonly RA, SLE, and systemic sclerosis. It is a disorder of unknown etiology in which there is lymphocytic infiltration of lacrimal and salivary glands. This leads to the clinical manifestations of keratoconjunctivitis sicca (dry eyes), xerostomia (dry mouth), and salivary gland swelling. Patients with primary Sjögren's syndrome may have extraglandular manifestations, including involvement of the lungs, kidneys, nervous system, and skin. Of importance, patients with primary Sjögren's syndrome have a significantly increased risk of developing lymphoma (approximately 40-fold) or other lymphoproliferative disorders.[38]

Patients with dry eyes often complain of a sandy or "gritty" feeling in their eyes or a "foreign-body sensation." Patients may also com-plain of dry, red, or painful eyes. It is important to ask the patient about use of medications that may cause dry eyes, such as cold remedies, antidepressants, and some antihypertensives. In addition, the normal production of tears and saliva decreases with age, and this decrease appears to be more common in women and to intensify after menopause.[38] Patients with dry mouth may complain of frequent thirst or inability to eat dry foods (such as a saltine cracker) without a drink. There may also be a sudden increase in dental carries secondary to decreased saliva. Patients with Sjögren's syndrome may also notice parotid gland swelling, which is usually bilateral. Women with Sjögren's syndrome may also complain of vaginal dryness, sometimes associated with a burning sensation or dyspareunia. Arthralgias, myalgias, and fatigue may also be reported. Hypothyroidism should always be ruled out in these cases, as it is relatively common in patients with Sjögren's syndrome.

On physical exam, dry or injected eyes may be noted. There may be decreased sublingual salivary pooling or evidence of poor dentition with accelerated dental caries. Fissuring of the tongue or corners of the mouth may be subtle signs of oral candidiasis. Enlargement of the parotid glands may be appreciated on palpation. A careful search for lymphadenopathy should be done in addition to a comprehensive general medical examination.

Laboratory data often reveal evidence of autoimmunity, including a positive ANA and/or RF. More specifically, patients with Sjögren's syndrome often have anti-Ro (SSA) and/or anti-La (SSB) antibodies, although these antibodies may be seen in other rheumatic disorders such as SLE. Women of childbearing potential who have SSA and/or SSB antibodies are at risk of having a child with neonatal lupus, including congenital heart block (see SLE and pregnancy, above). A mild normocytic normochromic anemia, leukopenia, or eosinophilia may be seen in some patients and an elevated sedimentation rate is common. Serum electrolytes and urinalysis may reveal evidence of renal tubular acidosis. In addi-

tion to routine laboratory screening, serum protein electrophoresis and immunoelectrophoresis should be performed to look for evidence of a monoclonal protein. Quantitative immunoglobulins should be performed at baseline and periodically, as a sudden change in immunoglobulin levels may indicate a transformation to lymphoma.

Schirmer's test (measurement of tear production/5 min using a small strip of filter paper) should be performed to provide more objective evidence of dry eyes. Additionally, patients should have ophthalmologic evaluation including a slitlamp exam and staining with rose bengal dye to demonstrate keratoconjunctivitis sicca.

Objective evidence of dry mouth can be obtained by salivary flow studies or salivary scintigraphy. In addition, minor salivary gland biopsy (lip biopsy) will demonstrate lymphocytic infiltration and help establish the diagnosis.

Treatment of Sjögren's syndrome is mostly symptomatic. Artificial tears (such as Tearisol, Liquifilm, or 0.5% methylcellulose) are helpful in patients with dry eyes.[37] Patients should be counseled on the need for fastidious dental care. Special toothpastes and oral preparations are available, although xerostomia is more difficult to treat. Recently, pilocarpine tablets (Salagen) have been approved for stimulation of salivary flow and may be helpful in cases where residual glandular function is present. Oral candidiasis should be treated with topical preparations such as clotrimazole or nystatin.[38] Hydroxychloroquine (Plaquenil) has been used to treat the arthralgias, myalgias, and fatigue associated with Sjögren's syndrome. Steroids generally are not used in the management of Sjögren's syndrome with the exception of life-threatening vasculitis, hemolytic anemia, and pleuropericarditis resistant to nonsteroidal anti-inflammatory drugs.[38]

Vasculitic Syndromes

The vasculitic syndromes, a group of disorders whose main pathologic feature is inflammation of the blood vessels, generally are classified by the dominant clinical and pathologic features, including the size of the vessels involved. Recent clinical use of the ANCA (antineutrophil cytoplasmic antibody) has improved our ability to identify and classify patients with these syndromes. Unlike most other rheumatic diseases, most of the vasculitic syndromes are more common in men. The cause of vasculitis is not known in most cases, but some cases have been associated with infections such as hepatitis B and HIV. Many clinical entities can mimic systemic vasculitis, including endocarditis, atrial myxoma, septicemia (especially gonococcemia, meningococcemia, and Rocky Mountain spotted fever), thrombotic thrombocytopenic purpura (TTP), the antiphospholipid antibody syndrome, and the multiple cholesterol emboli syndrome.[39] Hypersensitivity vasculitis is a fairly common disorder and is discussed in some detail. Other vasculitic syndromes are summarized in Table 72-7.

Small-Vessel Leukocytoclastic Vasculitis
Leukocytoclastic vasculitis is a pathologic diagnosis that describes infiltration of small vessel walls (especially postcapillary venules) with PMNs and subsequent fragmentation of the PMNs and destruction of the vessel wall.[39] It is found on biopsy of involved tissue in syndromes such as hypersensitivity vasculitis, Henoch Schönlein Purpura (primarily in children), mixed cryoglobulinemia, and urticarial vasculitis. In all these disorders, the skin manifestations (palpable purpura) are usually the most prominent clinical feature.

Hypersensitivity Vasculitis
Hypersensitivity vasculitis is a fairly common condition that may develop after exposure to various drugs or infectious agents. It may occur following exposure to a number of bacterial, parasitic, or viral agents. Although drug-induced hypersensitivity vasculitis most commonly occurs within the first few days of treatment, it may occur at any time after the start of a medication and is neither time nor dose dependent. The most commonly implicated medications are pencillin or its derivatives and sulfa drugs.

The key clinical finding in this disorder is palpable purpura. These slightly raised purpuric

TABLE 72-7 Vasculitic Syndromes

Syndrome	Key Clinical Findings	Laboratory Findings
Large and medium vessel		
Temporal arteritis	Age > 50	↑ ↑ ESR
	Association with PMR	↑ α_2 Globulin
	Headache, visual changes, fever, jaw claudication	↑ Alk phos.
	Tender TA with ↓ pulsation	Anemia
Takayasu's arteritis	Young Asian women	↑ ESR
	Claudication; UE > LE	Anemia
	Absent/unequal pulses or BP	Leukocytosis
Small-medium vessel		
Polyarteritis nodosa (PAN)	Multisystem including skin, joints, GI tract, kidney, nervous system	Hypocomplementemia
		Hepatitis B SAg
		p-ANCA (not specific)
Wegener's granulomatosis	Upper airway inflammation	c-ANCA (specific)
	Pulmonary involvement	
	Renal involvement	
Churg-Strauss angiitis	Multisystem including lung, skin, joints	Eosinophilia
	History of asthma and atopy	↑ IgE
		p-ANCA (not specific)

lesions do not blanch with pressure and are not related to thrombocytopenia. The lesions most commonly occur on the lower extremities or on dependent areas in bedridden patients. Individual lesions usually are fairly small, but may appear larger in areas where multiple lesions coalesce. They generally resolve in 1 to 4 weeks (sometimes leaving hyperpigmented areas or atrophic scars), but recurrent crops of skin lesions often occur.[39] Biopsy of these lesions will show leukocytoclastic vasculitis (see above). In addition to the skin manifestations, patients with hypersensitivity vasculitis commonly develop fever and other constitutional symptoms and arthralgias or, occasionally, arthritis.

Treatment of hypersensitivity vasculitis should start with a search for a possible inciting agent or medication. All suspect or nonessential medications should be discontinued. In mild cases, no further treatment is necessary. In more severe cases, or in patients with systemic involvement, corticosteroids usually are needed. Steroid dosage should be individualized based on the severity and extent of involvement (prednisone 20 to 60 mg/day or equivalent) and should be tapered to the lowest effective dose once symptoms are controlled.

Behçet's Disease

Behçet's disease occurs primarily in young adults (ages 25 to 35) and is slightly more common in women. The disease is more prevalent and more severe in Japan and eastern Mediterranean countries.[40] The cardinal manifestations of Behçet's disease include recurrent oral and genital ulcerations, ocular lesions, and cutaneous lesions. Oral aphthous ulcers usually are the initial manifestation and are present in almost all patients. They are most common on the lips, tongue, buccal mucosa, palate, and pharynx.[40] They are typically painful and appear as rounded or oval ulcerations with whitish or yellowish pseudomembranes and well-demarcated erythematous borders.[40] The lesions may be multiple and generally heal without scarring in 1 to 3 weeks.[40]

Genital ulcers are similar in appearance and also painful but tend to recur less frequently.

Women with Behçet's disease may have involvement of the vulva, perianal area, cervix, or vaginal mucosa. Recurrent anterior and posterior uveitis or retinal vasculitis may lead to blindness. The skin manifestations include erythema nodosum-like lesions, papules, pustules, folliculitis, ulcers, and cutaneous pathergy (formation of a pustule at the site of a sterile needle puncture 24 to 48 h later).[40] In addition to these features, patients may also have arthritis, GI lesions (ulcerations), vascular lesions (major vessel occlusion or aneurism, thrombophlebitis), and CNS lesions (cerebral vasculitis, aseptic meningitis).[40]

Laboratory tests in this disorder are nonspecific; acute phase reactants may be elevated in active disease, but may be normal in uveal disease.[40] Biopsy of lesions may reveal vasculitis (especially skin or vulva ulcerations). In patients with active CNS disease, CSF may show elevated protein and a mononuclear pleocytosis; MRI of the brain may show areas of increased signal in the periventricular white matter, brain stem, and cerebellum.[40]

Treatment of Behçet's disease with systemic corticosteroids may help some of the skin and joint inflammation, but is ineffective in controlling ocular or CNS manifestations. Cytotoxic agents, particularly chlorambucil and cyclophosphamide, are more effective.[40]

References and Suggested Readings

1. Solomon L: Clinical features of osteoarthritis, in Kelly WN, Harris ED Jr, Ruddy S, Sledge CB (eds): *Textbook of Rheumatology,* 5th ed. Philadelphia: WB Saunders, pp 1383–1393, 1997.
2. Brandt K: Management of osteoarthritis, in Kelly WN, Harris ED Jr, Ruddy S, Sledge CB (eds): *Textbook of Rheumatology,* 5th ed. Philadelphia: WB Saunders, pp 1394–1403, 1997.
3. Lipson SJ: Low back pain, in Kelly WN, Harris ED Jr, Ruddy S, Sledge CB (eds): *Textbook of Rheumatology,* 5th ed. Philadelphia: WB Saunders, pp 439–456, 1997.
4. Harris ED Jr: Clinical features of rheumatoid arthritis, in Kelly WN, Harris ED Jr, Ruddy S, Sledge CB (eds): *Textbook of Rheumatology,* 5th ed. Philadelphia: WB Saunders, pp 898–932, 1997.
5. Klippel GL, Cecere FA: Rheumatoid arthritis and pregnancy. *Rheum Dis Clin North Am* 15(2):213–239, 1989.
6. Ostensen M: Optimization of anti-rheumatic drug treatment in pregnancy. *Clin Pharmacokinet* 27:486–503, 1994.
7. Taurog JD: Seronegative spondyloarthropathies: Epidemiology, pathology, and pathogenesis, in Klippel JH (ed): *Primer on the Rheumatic Diseases,* 11th ed. Atlanta: Arthritis Foundation, pp 180–183, 1997.
8. Fan PT, Yu DTY: Reiter's syndrome, in Schumacher HR Jr (ed): *Primer on the Rheumatic Diseases,* 10th ed. Atlanta: Arthritis Foundation, pp 158–161, 1993.
9. Terkeltaub RA: Gout: Epidemiology, pathology, and pathogenesis, in Klippel JH (ed): *Primer on the Rheumatic Diseases,* 11th ed. Atlanta: Arthritis Foundation, pp 230–234, 1997.
10. Reginato AJ, Reginato AM: Diseases associated with the deposition of calcium pyrophosphate or hydroxyapatite, in Kelly WN, Harris ED Jr, Ruddy S, Sledge CB (eds): *Textbook of Rheumatology,* 5th ed. Philadelphia: WB Saunders, pp 1352–1367, 1997.
11. Steere AC: Lyme disease, in Kelly WN, Harris ED Jr, Ruddy S, Sledge CB (eds): *Textbook of Rheumatology,* 5th ed. Philadelphia: WB Saunders, pp 1462–1471, 1997.
12. Sigal LH: Lyme disease, in Klippel JH (ed): *Primer on the Rheumatic Diseases,* 11th ed. Atlanta: Arthritis Foundation, pp 204–207, 1997.
13. Hunder GG: Giant cell arteritis and polymyalgia rheumatica, in Kelly WN, Harris ED Jr, Ruddy S, Sledge CB (eds): *Textbook of Rheumatology,* 5th ed. Philadelphia: WB Saunders, pp 1123–1132, 1997.
14. Yunus MB, Masi AT: Fibromyalgia, restless legs syndrome, periodic limb movement disorder, and psychogenic pain, in McCarty DJ, Koopman WJ (eds): *Arthritis and Allied Conditions,* 12th ed. Philadelphia: Lea & Febiger, pp 1383–1405, 1993.
15. Crofford LJ, Demitrack MA: Evidence that abnormalities of central neurohormonal systems are key to understanding fibromyalgia and chronic fatigue syndrome. *Rheum Dis Clin North Am.* 22:267–284, 1996.
16. Freundlich B, Leventhal L: Signs and symptoms of musculoskeletal disorders: Diffuse pain syndromes, in Klippel JH (ed): *Primer on the Rheumatic Diseases,* 11th ed. Atlanta: Arthritis Foundation, pp 123–127, 1997.
17. Schur PH: Clinical features of SLE, in Kelly WN, Harris ED Jr, Ruddy S, Sledge CB (eds): *Textbook of Rheumatology,* 4th ed. Philadelphia: WB Saunders, pp 1017–1042, 1993.
18. Quismorio FP Jr: Systemic corticosteroid therapy in systemic lupus erythematosus, in Wallace DJ, Hahn BH (eds): *Dubois' Lupus Erythematosus,* 4th ed. Philadelphia: Lea & Febiger, pp 574–587, 1993.

19. Wallace DJ: Cytotoxic drugs, in Wallace DJ, Hahn BH (eds): *Dubois' Lupus Erythematosus,* 4th ed. Philadelphia: Lea & Febiger, pp 588–599, 1993.
20. Mintz G, Rodriguez-Alvarez E: Systemic lupus erythematosus. *Rheum Dis Clin North Am* 15(2):255–274, 1989.
21. Pattison NS, McKay EJ, Liggins GC, Lubbe WF: Anticardiolipin antibodies: Their presence as a marker for lupus anticoagulant in pregnancy. *N Z Med J* 100:61, 1987.
22. Hahn BH: Management of systemic lupus erythematosus, in Kelly WN, Harris ED Jr, Ruddy S, Sledge CB (eds): *Textbook of Rheumatology,* 5th ed. Philadelphia: WB Saunders, pp 1040–1056, 1997.
23. Dudley DJ, Branch DW: Antiphospholipid syndrome—A model for autoimmune pregnancy loss. *Infertil Reprod Med Clin North Am* 2(1):158, 149–164, 1991.
24. Asherson RA, Cervera R: Anticardiolipin antibodies, chronic biologic false-positive tests for syphilis and other antiphospholipid antibodies, in Wallace DJ, Hahn BH (eds): *Dubois' Lupus Erythematosus,* 4th ed. Philadelphia: Lea & Febiger, pp 233–245, 1993.
25. Rothfield NF: Systemic lupus erythematosus: Clinical aspects and treatment, in McCarty DJ, Koopman WJ (eds): *Arthritis and Allied Conditions,* 12th ed. Philadelphia: Lea & Febiger, pp 1155–1177, 1993.
26. Sanchez-Guerrero J, Liang MH, Karlson EW, et al: Postmenopausal estrogen therapy and the risk for developing systemic lupus erythematosus. *Ann Intern Med* 122(6):430–433, 1995.
27. Boumpas DT, Fessler BJ, Austin HA, et al: Systemic lupus erythematosus: Emerging concepts. Part 2: Dermatologic and joint disease, the anti-phospholipid antibody syndrome, pregnancy and hormonal therapy, morbidity and mortality, and pathogenesis. *Ann Intern Med* 123(1):42–53, 1995.
28. Arden NK, Lloyd ME, Spector TD, et al: Safety of hormone replacement therapy in systemic lupus erythematosus. *Lupus* 3(1):11–13, 1994.
29. Sammaritano LR, Lockshin MD: Personal communication (1997).
30. White B: Systemic sclerosis and related syndromes, in Klippel JH (ed): *Primer on the Rheumatic Diseases,* 11th ed. Atlanta: Arthritis Foundation, pp 263–266, 1997.
31. Medsger TA Jr: Systemic sclerosis (scleroderma), localized forms of scleroderma, and calcinosis, in McCarty DJ, Koopman WJ (eds): *Arthritis and Allied Conditions,* 12th ed. Philadelphia: Lea & Febiger, pp 1253–1292, 1993.
32. White B, Moore W, Wigley F, et al: Followup studies on pulmonary function in systemic sclerosis patients with alveolitis treated with cyclophosphamide, compared to untreated patients with alveolitis, patients without alveolitis, and controls. *Arthritis Rheum* 40(9):S123, 1997.
33. Seibold JR: Scleroderma, in Kelly WN, Harris ED Jr, Ruddy S, Sledge CB (eds): *Textbook of Rheumatology,* 5th ed. Philadelphia: WB Saunders, pp 1133–1162, 1997.
34. Olsen NJ, Wortmann RL: Inflammatory and metabolic diseases of muscle, in Klippel JH (ed): *Primer on the Rheumatic Diseases,* 11th ed. Atlanta: Arthritis Foundation, pp 276–282, 1997.
35. Cherin P, Piette JC, Herson S, et al. Dermatomyositis and ovarian cancer. A report of 7 cases and literature review. *J Rheumatol* 20:1897–1899, 1993.
36. Sharp GC, Singsen BH: Mixed connective tissue disease, in McCarty DJ, Koopman WJ (eds): *Arthritis and Allied Conditions,* 12th ed. Philadelphia: Lea & Febiger, pp 1213–1224, 1993.
37. Talal N: Sjögren's syndrome and connective tissue diseases associated with other immunologic disorders, in McCarty DJ, Koopman WJ (eds): *Arthritis and Allied Conditions,* 12th ed. Philadelphia: Lea & Febiger, pp 1343–1356, 1993.
38. Fox RI: Sjögren's syndrome, in Kelly WN, Harris ED Jr, Ruddy S, Sledge CB (eds): *Textbook of Rheumatology,* 5th ed. Philadelphia: WB Saunders, pp 955–968, 1997.
39. Valente RM, Hall S, O'Duffy JD, Conn DL: Vasculitis and related disorders, in Kelly WN, Harris ED Jr, Ruddy S, Sledge CB (eds): *Textbook of Rheumatology,* 5th ed. Philadelphia: WB Saunders, pp 1079–1122, 1997.
40. Conn DL, Hunder GG, O'Duffy JD: Vasculitis and related disorders, in Kelly WN, Harris ED Jr, Ruddy S, Sledge CB (eds): *Textbook of Rheumatology,* 4th ed. Philadelphia: WB Saunders, pp 1077–1102, 1997.

Allergy and Immunology

Peter LoGalbo
Vincent R. Bonagura

ALLERGIC RHINOCONJUNCTIVITIS
History • Physical Exam • Differential Diagnosis • Laboratory Evaluation • Treatment

ASTHMA
History • Physical Exam • Differential Diagnosis • Laboratory Evaluation • Treatment • Treatment in Pregnancy

DRUG ALLERGY
History • Physical Exam • Differential Diagnosis • Laboratory Evaluation • Treatment

FOOD ALLERGY
History • Physical Exam • Differential Diagnosis • Laboratory Evaluation • Treatment

ANAPHYLAXIS
History and Physical Exam • Differential Diagnosis • Laboratory Evaluation • Treatment

IMMUNODEFICIENCY DISEASES
History and Physical Exam • Differential Diagnosis • Laboratory Evaluation • Treatment

Allergic Rhinoconjunctivitis

History

Symptoms characteristic of allergic rhinoconjunctivitis are listed in Table 73-1. Ocular and nasal symptoms may be present simultaneously or in isolation. The disease exists in two forms: perennial, which is due to indoor substances such as house dust, mites, and animal dander; and seasonal ("hay fever") due to pollens. Ascertaining the time course of symptom exacerbations is therefore essential (Table 73-2). A history of fever, myalgia, or green nasal discharge (as opposed to clear) suggests infection. A complete list of over-the-counter, prescription, and illicit drugs used by the patient should be obtained. Frequently, patients with allergic rhinoconjunctivitis have concomitant eczema or asthma and a family history of allergies.

Physical Exam

The nasal mucosa is pale or cyanotic in up to 60 percent of patients with allergic rhinitis. Nasal white and firm polyps should be distinguished from pink and boggy swollen turbinates. Examination of the eyes may reveal injection of the conjunctivae and chemosis (swelling of the conjunctival tissue around the cornea).

Differential Diagnosis

Symptoms of perennial allergic rhinoconjunctivitis are present for more than nine months per year, whereas symptoms of seasonal rhinoconjunctivitis follow the allergy seasons outlined in Table 73-2. There are, in addition, several forms of nonallergic rhinitis.

Idiopathic or vasomotor rhinitis is a chronic rhinitis with symptoms almost identical to those of allergic rhinitis, although sneezing and itching

TABLE 73-1 Allergic Rhinoconjunctivitis: History

Symptoms
  Sneezing
  Rhinorrhea or ocular discharge
  Nasal or ocular pruritus or burning
  Nasal congestion
  Postnasal drip: nocturnal cough, throat-clearing

Time Course of Symptoms (season, diurnal pattern)

Symptom Triggers
  Irritants: e.g., smoke, perfume, pollution, cleaning fluids
  Emotion
  Exercise
  Food
  Specific allergens

Environmental Aeroallergens
  Pollens: e.g., seasonal symptoms, cut grass, raking leaves
  House dust mites: e.g., curtains, carpet, bedding
  Feathers: e.g., pillows, comforters
  Pets: e.g., cat, dog, birds
  Molds: e.g., basements, bathrooms, humidifiers, plants

Current Medications

Family History

TABLE 73-2 Allergy Seasons

Perennial
  House dust mites
  Indoor molds
  Pets
  Cockroaches
  Pyrethrum (insecticide)
  Feathers (pillows, comforters)

Seasons
  Weeds
    Mid-August through first frost (northeastern and northwestern U.S.)
    August through October (southern U.S.)
    July through October (Central Plains, California)
  Trees
    March through June (eastern U.S.)
    January through June (southern and northwestern U.S.)
    December through May (Central Plains, southwestern U.S.)
    January through May (California)
  Grasses
    Mid-May through mid-July (northeastern U.S.)
    March through September (southern U.S.)
    March through November (California)
    May through August (northwestern U.S.)
  Molds
    Autumn, spring, summer (warm and temperate climates)

are less common. In such individuals however, no allergic trigger can be identified; allergy skin tests are negative, serum IgE is normal, and there is no nasal eosinophilia. Symptoms are triggered by irritative stimuli such as strong odors, changes in temperature, cigarette smoke, or bright lights. Many individuals with allergic rhinitis have concomitant vasomotor rhinitis. This form of rhinitis responds poorly to the usual medication used to treat allergic rhinitis.

Rhinitis medicamentosa is caused by prolonged use of α-adrenergic nasal decongestants (e.g., oxymetazoline or phenylephrine). After as little as 5 days of regular use, rebound nasal congestion can occur upon withdrawal of the medication, and tachyphylaxis to the medication may develop. The nasal mucosa appears dark red and dry with small areas of bleeding. It is treated by weaning the patient from the medication over 1 week and administering topical steroids to reduce inflammation. Regular intranasal administration of cocaine also produces this syndrome.

Various prescription medications may cause rhinitis. Aspirin, nonsteroidal anti-inflammatory drugs, and a variety of antihypertensives are most commonly responsible. Hydralazine, prazosin, hydrochlorothiazide, nadolol, labetalol, clonidine, guanabenz, and reserpine have been associated with rhinitis.

Patients with nonallergic rhinitis with eosinophilia syndrome (NARES) have perennial symptoms and eosinophilia in the nasal secretions, but do not have specific allergic triggers. NARES is associated with chronic sinusitis and nasal polyps in up to two-thirds of patients.

Rhinitis may also be a symptom of a coexisting systemic disease. Nasal congestion is a common symptom in hypothyroidism. Nasal ischemia may cause a rhinitis in patients with diabetes or uremia. Several granulomatous diseases, such as sar-

coidosis, Wegener's granulomatosis, and midline granuloma, commonly involve the nose.

Rhinitis of pregnancy is a common syndrome that usually begins after the first trimester and that resolves spontaneously after delivery. Hormonal changes are responsible for producing nasal congestion and hypersecretion. Medical treatment is generally of limited benefit.

Although food allergy per se is rarely a cause of rhinitis, gustatory rhinitis is manifested as copious clear nasal discharge during eating, particularly spicy foods. It is due to a vagal reflex rather than an allergic mechanism, and may be treated with topical anticholinergics (e.g., ipratropium bromide, two sprays per nostril, qid prn).

Sinusitis is suggested by fever, green nasal discharge, headache, nocturnal cough, maxillary teeth pain when chewing, persistent halitosis, postnasal drip, and tenderness on exam. Not all symptoms need be present at one time. Three weeks of an appropriate antibiotic (e.g., trimethoprim-sulfamethoxazole, amoxicillin-clavulanate, clarithromycin), decongestants, and topical anti-inflammatory agents are indicated. A sinus CT scan, including coronal views, is indicated for recurrent or persistent sinusitis or when nasal polyps are suspected.

Laboratory Evaluation

A smear of nasal secretions should be obtained and examined for eosinophils under light microscopy with Wright's stain. Eosinophils are often present in abundance in allergic rhinoconjunctivitis and NARES. Total serum IgE elevation supports the diagnosis of allergic rhinoconjunctivitis. Although in vitro assessment of IgE antibody to specific allergens is readily available through the radioallergosorbent test (RAST), this method is less sensitive than allergic skin testing.

Treatment

Environmental control is an essential component of the treatment of allergic rhinoconjunctivitis. Pollens may be avoided by remaining indoors in an air-conditioned building and by driving in an air-conditioned automobile with the windows closed. Outdoor activities should be limited during the patient's allergy season. House-dust mite exposure is reduced by replacing curtains with window shades and by either removing carpeting from the home or vacuuming weekly with the patient out of the room. Vinyl dust covers may be used to cover pillows and mattresses. Such encasement of bedding permits regular cleaning and traps dust mites within the mattress. Washing bedding in hot water (130°F) for one hour also kills dust mites. Pets, especially cats, should be removed from the home. Mold may be reduced by thorough cleaning of warm, humid areas such as bathrooms, and by reducing humidity in the home.

The mainstay of medical treatment for allergic rhinoconjunctivitis is H_1-receptor antagonists (antihistamines). They relieve sneezing, itching, and rhinorrhea, but not nasal congestion. Several nonsedating antihistamines are currently available in the United States: loratadine (Claritin, 10 mg po qd); fexofenadine (Allegra, 60 mg po bid); cetirizine (Zyrtec); and astemizole (Hismanal, 10 mg po qd). Astemizole has a longer onset of action (days) and a longer half-life, making it less suitable as a prn medication.

Cases refractory to environmental control and antihistamines may be treated with topical anti-inflammatory drugs. Cromolyn sodium (e.g., Nasalcrom) is safe and relieves symptoms of sneezing, itching, and rhinorrhea, but must be used three to four times each day. Topical nasal steroid sprays are particularly effective for allergic rhinitis and may be used only once or twice daily; these include beclomethasone (Vancenase, Beconase), fluticasone (Flonase), budesonide (Rhinocort), and triamcinolone (Nasacort). Onset of action for both cromolyn and intranasal steroids is within several days, with peak effect obtained only after 1 to 2 weeks of regular use. Thus, these medications must be used regularly rather than as needed.

Decongestants are α-adrenergic agonists and are available as oral and topical preparations.

Oral forms include pseudoephedrine (Sudafed), phenylpropanolamine (Entex, Naldecon, Triaminic), and phenylephrine (Rynatan). They may be contraindicated in patients with hypertension or glaucoma, or in those taking monoamine oxidase inhibitors. Topical decongestants such as phenylephrine (Neo-Synephrine) and oxymetazoline (Afrin) should be used cautiously and for no longer than three days to prevent rhinitis medicamentosa. By keeping the mucosa moist, intranasal saline sprays (e.g., Ocean, NaSal) may provide safe symptomatic relief.

Immunotherapy is the administration of specific allergens to individuals with documented sensitivity in whom medical therapy is inadequate or intolerable. While not a cure for allergic rhinitis, it provides significant relief in over 85 percent of patients. Patients with a history suggestive of allergic triggers and symptoms refractory to simple treatment should be referred to an allergist for further evaluation.

Follow-up should be obtained within one month after initiating the use of a new medication to assess efficacy of treatment and side effects.

Asthma

History

Classic symptoms of asthma include wheezing, coughing, and shortness of breath. Exacerbations may be triggered by the allergens shown in Tables 73-1 and 73-2, by cold air, or by exercise. Symptoms may be seasonal or perennial. The patient may have coexisting allergic rhinoconjunctivitis or eczema, or a family history of allergic disease.

Many studies suggest that there is a subset of females with asthma who have increased symptoms in relationship to their menstrual cycle. In these individuals, worsening of chest tightness, wheezing, and dyspnea occur in the premenstrual or menstrual period. These may be accompanied by a fall in pulmonary function values such as peak expiratory flow rate. Skobeloff et al. have reported an increased occurrence of asthma ex-

acerbations during the perimenstrual period in a group of 182 women who presented to an emergency room.[10] One explanation for these findings is suggested by the work of Tan et al.[12] They demonstrated that female asthmatics had a paradoxical response to exogenously administered progesterone, which resulted in downregulation of lymphocyte β-adrenergic receptors, in contrast to nonasthmatic women who respond to progesterone by increasing the number of these receptors. This results in the loss of the normal cyclical pattern of a rise in the number of β-adrenergic receptors during the luteal phase of the menstrual cycle when progesterone levels are high.

Physical Exam

Wheezing, prolonged expiration time, and diminished air movement are characteristic of acute asthma, but may be absent in chronic stable disease. Intercostal or supraclavicular retractions with tachypnea suggest an acute exacerbation that requires emergency treatment. Signs of allergic rhinitis or conjunctivitis may coexist.

Differential Diagnosis

Extrinsic asthma is worsened by a specific, IgE-producing allergen, whereas intrinsic asthma is not. In reality, these two entities often overlap. A brief differential diagnosis of wheezing is presented in Table 73-3.

Laboratory Evaluation

Pulmonary function testing reveals obstructive disease (normal to low forced vital capacity [FVC], low forced expiratory volume in 1 second [FEV_1], diminished FEF_{25-75}, and diminished ratio of FEV_1/FVC) indicating air trapping and small airway obstruction. These abnormalities may be elicited by cold air provocation or by exercise. Improvement is seen after administration of a bronchodilator.

Asthmatic patients should be given a peak flow meter, which records peak expiratory flow rate.

TABLE 73-3 Brief Differential Diagnosis of Wheezing

α_1-Antitrypsin deficiency

Allergic bronchopulmonary aspergillosis (ABPA)

Asthma

Chronic obstructive pulmonary disease (COPD)
  Bronchiectasis
  Chronic bronchitis
  Emphysema

Chronic sinusitis

Congestive heart failure

Cystic fibrosis

Gastroesophageal reflux

Interstitial lung disease

Primary ciliary dyskinesia

Pulmonary embolism

Respiratory infections
  Bronchiolitis
  Bronchitis
  Pneumonia

Upper airway obstruction
  Foreign body
  Laryngeal edema

A patient's expected peak flow may be extrapolated based on sex, age, and height. A "personal best" peak flow should also be recorded during a symptom-free interval. The patient's peak flow during an exacerbation can be compared to the personal best peak flow to gauge the severity of that exacerbation. A value of 80 percent or greater of the personal best indicates that emergency treatment is not required; 50 to 80 percent of personal best indicates a moderate exacerbation requiring immediate home treatment; below 50 percent personal best warrants immediate emergency room evaluation if not rapidly improved with home or office treatment.

Severe asthmatics should be screened for cystic fibrosis with a sweat test. RAST or skin testing for specific allergens implicated by the patient's history may be useful in identifying allergic triggers. Markedly elevated serum IgE and peripheral eosinophilia may suggest allergic broncho-

pulmonary aspergillosis (ABPA). These patients should be referred to an allergist for further evaluation.

Treatment

Treatment of asthma begins with an inhaled β_2-agonist bronchodilator (e.g., albuterol) used as needed. Aerosolized bronchodilators are far more effective and have fewer side effects than the same medication given orally. Using a spacer device, such as the Aerochamber or InspirEase, may aid in drug delivery. β_2-Agonists are best used as needed, rather than as part of a fixed regimen. For patients with chronic moderate-to-severe symptoms, a newer long acting β-agonist is available, salmeterol (Serevent). This medication is used on a daily basis in conjunction with anti-inflammatory agents as described below. Because of its long duration of action, it is also useful in controlling nocturnal symptoms of asthma when given at bedtime.

If symptoms are not controlled adequately with a bronchodilator, an anti-inflammatory agent, such as inhaled cromolyn or an inhaled corticosteroid, is added. Either of these medications must be used regularly, as a therapeutic effect may not be observed until the second to fourth week of treatment. Cromolyn (Intal) has fewer side effects than steroids, and it can be delivered via a nebulizer for those unable to use a metered-dose inhaler. Nedocromil (Tilade) is a new anti-inflammatory drug with efficacy similar to cromolyn; it is delivered by metered-dose inhaler. Unlike cromolyn, nedocromil given together with aerosolized steroids may have an additive effect. Aerosolized steroids in common use include triamcinolone (Azmacort), flunisolide (Aerobid), beclomethasone (Vanceril, Beclovent), and fluticasone (Flovent). A new inhaled steroid, budesonide (Pulmicort), is delivered as a dry powder from an inhaler about the same size as a metered-dose aerosol inhaler. Any inhaled steroid aerosol should be used with a spacer device to reduce oral deposition and susceptibility to thrush.

The leukotriene antagonists are a new class of drugs that are available for management of patients with persistent asthma. The leukotrienes are produced from cell membrane arachadonic acid by the action of the enzyme 5-lipoxygenase following allergic or other triggers, and produce a variety of pathological effects, including airway edema, excess mucus production, and bronchospasm. Leukotriene antagonists can prevent these effects in two ways: either by blocking the leukotriene receptor or by inhibiting the enzyme 5-lipoxygenase. These medications are available only in oral form, and are taken one to four times each day. Three such medications are currently available: zafirlukast (Accolate), montelukast (Singulair), and zileuton (Zyflo).

Theophylline may be added to control symptoms in chronic moderate asthma. While its efficacy for treatment of acute asthma exacerbations is controversial, it is clearly effective in suppressing the symptoms of chronic disease. Sustained-release theophylline preparations (e.g., Slo-bid, Theo-Dur) may be useful in controlling nocturnal and early morning symptoms when given at bedtime. Once-daily preparations (e.g., Uniphyl) are available, but generally have not been shown to be effective in once-daily dosing. The average initial adult dosage of a long-acting preparation such as Theo-Dur is 300 mg bid. The serum theophylline level must be monitored initially until a therapeutic dose is established (serum concentration 10 to 20 μg/ml), and then checked every six months. Many patients, however, achieve therapeutic benefits with serum concentrations between 5 and 10 μg/ml. Theophylline clearance may be decreased and dosage reduction required in patients with heart failure or liver disease, or in those taking certain medications (e.g., cimetidine, erythromycin, ciprofloxacin). Because different theophylline preparations differ widely in their bioavailability and rate of release into serum, generic substitution should not be made without the knowledge of the physician. Signs and symptoms of theophylline toxicity include nausea, vomiting, agitation, tachycardia, seizures, and arrhythmias.

Severe asthmatics may require treatment with oral corticosteroids; for example, prednisone or methylprednisolone (Medrol). Side effects can be minimized by giving steroids every other day. A one-week course of prednisone or methylprednisolone (40 mg per day) during an asthma exacerbation may lead to rapid symptom improvement. Such a brief course of therapy causes few side effects and little adrenal suppression. Methylprednisolone has fewer mineralocorticoid side effects than does prednisone. Any patient requiring more than six courses per year of oral steroids should be considered for chronic steroid therapy.

Acute asthma exacerbations may be treated with a nebulized β_2 agonist (e.g., albuterol, 2.5 to 5.0 mg in 3-ml normal saline) or epinephrine (0.3 mg or 0.3 ml of a 1:1000 solution subcutaneously). Patients requiring treatments more frequently than every 4h should be referred to an emergency department. Although steroids are frequently prescribed during an acute exacerbation, onset of action takes several hours.

Immunotherapy also is effective in limiting the symptoms of extrinsic asthma. Patients with moderate or severe asthma, and those having suspected allergic triggers, should be referred to an allergist for further evaluation.

Routine follow-up of asthmatic patients should occur every three to four months—more frequently for those with severe disease. Ideally, an office visit should be scheduled at the beginning of a patient's "bad season" to assess the need for further therapy.

Treatment in Pregnancy

During pregnancy approximately one-third of asthmatic patients will worsen, one-third will improve, and one-third will remain unchanged. Peak asthma severity occurs between 29 and 36 weeks' gestation. Patients often experience a similar pattern of change in their asthma with each pregnancy. Effective asthma management is essential to prevent fetal hypoxia.

The Food and Drug Administration pregnancy categories for drugs (A, B, C, D, X) do not pro-

vide adequate information regarding the risks or usefulness of many asthma medications. Most asthma medications are either unrated or are pregnancy category C. Cromolyn and nedocromil, however, are category B.

Patients with chronic mild asthma are best treated with inhaled β-agonists used as needed. Terbutaline (Brethaire) is the inhaled β-agonist of choice in pregnancy. If the patient requires daily treatment or has a poor response to treatment, cromolyn or an inhaled steroid is added. Because it has had the largest experience in pregnancy, beclomethasone (Vanceril, Beclovent) is usually the inhaled steroid of choice during pregnancy. Patients with more severe chronic symptoms may require increased doses of inhaled steroids. A long-acting theophylline may also be used in this situation if serum concentrations are monitored carefully and maintained at a level of 8 to 12 μg/ml. Short courses of oral steroids or daily or alternate-day use may be required in those with the most severe chronic symptoms. Prednisone or methylprednisolone are preferred because they cross the placenta poorly. Systemic corticosteroids have not been demonstrated to cause fetal malformation; however, long-term use may cause decreased birthweight and increased incidence of premature delivery.

During an acute asthma exacerbation, inhaled β_2-agonists should be used first. Nonselective β-agonists, such as subcutaneous epinephrine, should be avoided because of the possibility of uterine vasoconstriction. Subcutaneous terbutaline (0.25 mg) has greater β_2 selectivity and is preferred over epinephrine. Systemic corticosteroids are frequently necessary in the management of acute asthma symptoms unresponsive to β-agonists alone.

Nonpharmacologic intervention, such as environmental control (especially smoke avoidance) and allergen avoidance, is crucial. Immunotherapy may be continued, but is not initiated during pregnancy.

Additional drugs that should be avoided during pregnancy include α-adrenergic compounds and iodides. Decongestants such as phenyleph-

rine, phenylpropanolamine, and ephedrine have α-adrenergic activity and could potentially compromise uterine blood flow, and so should be avoided during pregnancy. Pseudoephedrine, another α-adrenergic agonist, does not appear to produce this effect and is used during pregnancy. Mucolytic agents, such as potassium iodide, may increase cough and airway obstruction during acute exacerbations of asthma.

Drug Allergy
History

Drug allergies may be divided into three reactions: immediate (occurring in <1 h after drug administration); accelerated (1 to 72 h); and delayed (>72 h). Examples are anaphylaxis (immediate), rashes (accelerated), and serum sickness (delayed). Table 73-4 outlines a brief directed history. In general, drug allergies are not manifested within a week of the patient's first exposure to a drug. Furthermore, although a drug allergy may develop after months of asymptomatic chronic use of a drug, this is unlikely. Allergy to shellfish does not predispose one to allergy to radiographic contrast material; this is a common misconception. Allergy to multiple antibiotics can be familial.

Physical Exam

Urticaria, anaphylaxis, or angioedema may occur acutely. Urticaria consists of raised, erythematous, and pruritic lesions; it may have areas of central clearing. Bronchospasm and hypotension may be seen in anaphylaxis. Angioedema is characterized by swelling, usually involving the perioral and periorbital regions, tongue, extremities, or genitalia. It generally is not pruritic, although patients may report a burning sensation. Rashes are common in accelerated drug reactions, and usually manifest as hives or a pruritic maculopapular exanthem. Classic signs of serum sickness, a delayed reaction, include pruritic rash, fever, polyarticular arthritis, and lymphadenopathy.

TABLE 73-4   Drug Allergy: History

Symptoms
  Rash
  Wheezing
  Arthralgia
  Respiratory distress
  Pruritus
  Face/tongue swelling
  Trouble swallowing
  Lip/mouth pruritus
  Cough
  Fever
  Hives

Time course of symptom onset and resolution

Location of eruption

Medication history
  All medication taken in past month
  Temporal relation between medication and reaction
  New medications
  Topical agents
  Over the counter medications
  Latex exposure

Past history of allergy
  Type of allergic reaction
  Known allergies

Past medical history
  Thyroid disease
  Collagen vascular disease
  Malignancy
  Contact dermatitis

Family history of
  Drug allergy
  Food allergy
  Allergic rhinoconjunctivitis
  Asthma or autoimmune disease

Differential Diagnosis

Angioedema and urticaria also may be idiopathic or can be associated with occult malignancy, collagen vascular disease, hypothyroidism, hyperthyroidism, infection, physical stimulation (e.g., cold, sunlight, pressure), or food allergy. Certain medications, such as vancomycin and opiate analgesics, cause a nonspecific histamine release that can mimic an allergic reaction.

Patients demonstrating allergic reactions during surgery, in the hospital, or during physician contacts may have an allergy to latex. They may have similar reactions when exposed to balloons, condoms, latex gloves, or certain foods (e.g., avocado, bananas, chestnuts, figs).

Laboratory Evaluation

Skin testing detects only immediate IgE-mediated hypersensitivity reactions, and is not useful for predicting reactions such as fever or serum sickness. Testing is practical and reliable for only a very few drugs, including penicillin, insulin, streptokinase, latex, and other large-protein antigens.

A screen for nonallergic causes of urticaria and angioedema includes erythrocyte sedimentation rate, thyroid function tests, C4 level (the fourth component of complement), and complete chemistry profile.

Treatment

Most drug reactions resolve within one week after discontinuation of the drug. Symptoms may be relieved with an antihistamine, and, in severe cases, systemic steroids. Treatment of anaphylaxis is discussed separately. Concomitant use of β-blockers increases the severity of systemic reactions and makes patients more refractory to treatment. β-Blockers should be discontinued and another agent substituted in any patient having a systemic allergic reaction.

A protocol has been established to pretreat patients with anaphylactoid reactions to radiographic contrast who must undergo contrast studies. It involves administration of prednisone (50 mg po given 13, 7, and 1 h prior), diphenhydramine (50 mg IV or po 1 h prior), and ephedrine (25 mg if not contraindicated). Nonionic contrast should be used.

In cases where a life-threatening disease exists, treatable only by a medication to which the patient is allergic, desensitization may be possible. This is performed by an allergist in a hospital setting.

Food Allergy

History

Manifestations of food allergy include eczema, urticaria, angioedema, and anaphylaxis. Less commonly, there may be gastrointestinal manifestations, such as abdominal pain, nausea, vomiting, and diarrhea, or respiratory manifestations, such as bronchospasm. A reaction generally occurs within 2 h of ingestion. Symptoms occurring more than 48 h after ingestion are unlikely to be due to food allergy. The most common food allergens in adults are peanuts, tree nuts, fish, and shellfish. The type of allergic reaction to a particular food is usually consistent; the same food elicits the same kind of reaction with each exposure.

The history should include the type and severity of symptoms, the timing of symptoms in relation to food ingestion, the quantity of food ingested, and the relationship of symptoms to exercise. The patient should complete a food diary for the 24-h period prior to the reaction. The clinician should ascertain any prior history of food allergy or effort to eliminate certain foods from the diet.

Physical Exam

The primary role of the physical exam is to rule out other disorders, such as inflammatory bowel disease, that may be causing gastrointestinal symptoms. Any atopic features, such as rash or angioedema, are assessed. Note whether food intolerance or avoidance has affected the patient's nutritional status.

Differential Diagnosis

Oral allergy syndrome is swelling and itching of the mouth in response to food allergens. The syndrome tends to coexist with certain pollen allergies. For example, patients with ragweed allergy react to melon and bananas. Patients with birch tree allergy react to apples, carrots, potatoes, or hazelnuts.

Exercise-induced anaphylaxis occurs during or after exercise, and in some cases, depends on prior food ingestion. It may be associated with specific foods, particularly celery, shrimp, oysters, peaches, wheat, and chicken.

Nonallergic food intolerance must be differentiated from true food allergy: lactose intolerance causes diarrhea and cramps with milk ingestion due to lactase deficiency. Chinese restaurant syndrome is an adverse effect of the food additive monosodium glutamate (MSG). MSG can cause headache, burning dysesthesias, and facial and chest pain. Headache may be caused by the pharmacologic action of tyramine (in cheese and chocolate), histamine (in red wine), and nitrites (in smoked foods and cold cuts). Caffeine overdose or withdrawal also may cause headache.

Laboratory Evaluation

RAST or skin testing should be based on information gained from a food diary and thorough history. A negative test has a high negative predictive value. However, even when correlated with a good history, a positive test has a predictive value of only 40 to 50 percent. Therefore, these tests are commonly confirmed with a double-blind placebo-controlled food challenge.

Treatment

The best treatment is avoidance of foods to which the patient is allergic. Patients with anaphylaxis should carry an EpiPen for self-administration of epinephrine at the beginning of a reaction.

Any patient with a severe systemic reaction, frequent symptoms, or poor response to simple food avoidance should be referred to an allergist for further evaluation. Immunotherapy is contraindicated as a treatment for food allergy because of the risk of a serious allergic reaction.

Anaphylaxis

History and Physical Exam

Symptoms and signs of anaphylaxis may be cutaneous (urticaria, angioedema, flushing), respira-

tory (wheezing, chest tightness), gastrointestinal (nausea, vomiting, diarrhea), or cardiovascular (hypotension, shock). Most anaphylactic reactions occur within 2 h of allergen exposure, although a late reaction may occur hours after the initial event.

Differential Diagnosis

Medications, food, vaccines, blood products, latex, and insect stings are among the more common agents associated with anaphylactic reactions. Stings from Hymenoptera (wasps, hornets, yellow jackets, and bees) are particularly implicated and may be life-threatening. Patients with IgA deficiency are predisposed to anaphylactic reactions from blood products. Exercise-induced anaphylaxis may occur in isolation or in relation to food. The syndrome of idiopathic anaphylaxis is well described.

There have been reports of females who have cyclical anaphylaxis or urticaria in relationship to their menstrual cycle.[5] In these individuals, symptoms are commonly exacerbated or occur during the premenstrual phase of the menstrual cycle. In some, symptoms can be reproduced by the administration of progesterone, or skin test sensitivity to progesterone can be demonstrated, suggesting the possibility of an allergic sensitivity to endogenous progesterone. In this unusual condition, the use of luteinizing hormone-releasing hormone analogues to inhibit pituitary gonadotropin release and lower progesterone levels has been reported to be effective in some cases, as has oophorectomy.

Laboratory Evaluation

Patients experiencing anaphylactic reactions should be referred to an allergist for complete evaluation. Obviously, in the acute situation, emergency care must be rendered immediately.

Treatment

The mainstay of treatment for anaphylaxis is epinephrine (0.3 mg subcutaneously). Epinephrine may be given in the office or self-administered with an EpiPen. Antihistamines (e.g., diphenhydramine 25 to 50 mg qid) and prednisone (40 mg po qd) also may be given until symptoms resolve completely. A 1- to 2-week course is generally advisable. β-Blockers should be discontinued in patients at risk for anaphylaxis. They can increase the severity of the allergic reaction and hamper pharmacologic response to epinephrine.

Treatment for an acute reaction should be initiated immediately, and the patient should be transferred to an emergency department and observed for 24 h.

Immunotherapy is recommended for those with insect-sting anaphylaxis. A large local reaction to a sting—even swelling of an entire extremity contiguous with the sting site—does not warrant immunotherapy.

Desensitization to a medication that has caused an anaphylactic reaction may be attempted in the hospital in the case of a life-threatening illness when no other treatment options are available.

Immunodeficiency Diseases

History and Physical Exam

The hallmark of immunodeficiency is recurrent, persistent, or unusual infections (e.g., *Pneumocystis carinii* pneumonia). Excluding AIDS, which is discussed in Chap. 68, the diseases seen most often in adults are defects in humoral immunity. They generally predispose to bacterial sinopulmonary infections. Encapsulated organisms, such as *Streptococcus pneumoniae* and *Haemophilus influenze,* may predominate. Recurrent skin infections, meningitis, osteomyelitis, gastroenteritis, colitis, and bacteremia also are seen.

Differential Diagnosis

IgA deficiency is common, occurring in about one person in 400 in the general population. Its clinical significance is uncertain. Patients with

IgA deficiency are at risk for anaphylactic reactions from blood products.

Patients with common variable immunodeficiency (CVID) may present in young adulthood. Levels of IgG, IgA, and IgM are low, but not absent. B lymphocyte count is normal. CVID is associated with increased incidence of autoimmune diseases, such as rheumatoid arthritis. It is also associated with lymphoid malignancies, particularly non-Hodgkin's lymphoma.

Bruton's X-linked agammaglobulinemia is characterized by absent B lymphocytes and markedly reduced immunoglobulins of all classes.

Immunodeficiency with thymoma affects adults in their fourth decade or older. The thymoma usually is a benign spindle cell tumor. All immunoglobulins are decreased, as is the absolute B lymphocyte count.

Less common immune deficiencies may involve abnormalities of T lymphocyte or neutrophil function or complement deficiency.

Recurrent infections also may be caused by nonimmunologic mechanisms. For example, anatomic abnormalities hampering sinus drainage may predispose to recurrent sinusitis.

Laboratory Evaluation

An appropriate initial screen evaluates many components of the immune system. Serum immunoglobulins (IgG, IgA, IgM, IgE), total T and B lymphocytes, and T-cell subsets should be quantitated. Delayed hypersensitivity skin testing to PPD, mumps, and Candida, if positive, is evidence of functional cellular immunity. Specific antibody response to immunization should be demonstrated. Measuring antitetanus antibody evaluates response to protein antigen, while measuring antipneumococcal antibodies in a patient who has received the pneumococcal vaccine evaluates response to carbohydrate antigens.

Treatment

A patient suspected of having an immune deficiency should be referred to an allergist-immunologist for complete evaluation. Deficiencies of humoral immunity may be treated with infusions of gammaglobulin. In some cases, prophylactic antibiotics may be warranted.

References and Selected Readings

1. Bockner BS, Lichenstein LM: Anaphylaxis. *N Engl J Med* 324:1785–1790, 1991.
2. Buckley RH: Immunodeficiency diseases. *JAMA* 268:2797–3807, 1992.
3. Eghrari-Sabet JS, Slater JE: Latex allergy: A potentially serious respiratory disorder. *J Respir Dis* 14:473–482, 1993.
4. Lieberman P: Anaphylactoid reactions to radiocontrast material. *Clin Rev Allergy* 9:319–338, 1991.
5. Meggs WJ, Pescovitz OH, Metcalfe D, Loriaux DL, Cutler G Jr, Kaliner M: Progesterone sensitivity as a cause of recurrent anaphylaxis. *N Engl J Med* 311:1236–1238, 1984.
6. Naglerio RM: Allergic rhinitis. *N Engl J Med* 325:860–869, 1991.
7. National Asthma Education Program, Expert Panel Report: *Guidelines for the Diagnosis and Management of Asthma.* Bethesda, MD: National Heart, Lung and Blood Institute, National Institutes of Health, 1991. Publication No. 91–3042.
8. Patterson R, DeSwarte RD, Greenberger PA, Grammar LC: Drug allergy and protocols for management of drug allergies. *N Engl Reg Allergy Proc* 7:325–342, 1986.
9. Sampson HA, Metcalfe DD: Food allergies. *JAMA* 268:2840–2844, 1992.
10. Skobeloff EM, Spivey WH, Silverman R, Eskin BA, Harchelroad F, Alessi TV: The effect of the menstrual cycle on asthma presentations in the emergency department. *Arch Intern Med* 156:1837–1840, 1996.
11. Sneller MC, Strober W, Eisenstein E, et al: New insights into common variable immunodeficiency. *Ann Intern Med* 118:720–730, 1993.
12. Tan KS, McFarlane LC, Lipworth BJ: Paradoxical down-regulation and desensitization of beta-2 adrenoceptors by exogenous progesterone in female asthmatics. *Chest* 111:847–851, 1997.

Evaluation of Chronic Fatigue

Roy M. Pitkin

Complaints of protracted and disabling fatigue are commonly encountered in ambulatory practice. The sensation of tiredness may be either persistent or recurrent, but it can be severe enough that it comes to dominate the lives of those affected. Although it may be tempting to regard such individuals as casualties of the stresses of modern life, there is evidence that the problem is of much earlier origin. Hippocrates seems clearly to have recognized the various forms of muscular fatigue, observing that "fatigue pains" can occur in those out of training after the slightest exercise, but also in "trained bodies" after unusual exercises, and even after usual exercises "if they be excessive."

In the nineteenth century, "neurasthenia" was coined to relate chronic fatigue to a dissipation of energy in the nervous system. The term and the concept of nervous energy persisted until well into the twentieth century. Names used in more modern times include effort syndrome, fibrositis, fibromyalgia, myalgic encephalomyelitis, and postviral fatigue syndrome. Current thinking favors "chronic fatigue syndrome" even though the nature—and the existence—of a "syndrome" remain a contentious and emotional issue.

Regardless of whether a chronic fatigue syndrome exists as a specific and definable entity, conditions and diseases that may present primarily with complaints of abnormally persistent and severe fatigue are numerous and varied. For this reason, it is appropriate to consider first the differential diagnosis of chronic fatigue as a symptom.

Differential Diagnosis

When a patient complains of fatigue, several general medical conditions should be considered. The first condition that comes to mind is usually anemia. Because of the decreased oxygen-carrying capacity of the blood, an individual anemic for any reason will, especially if the anemia has developed fairly quickly, complain of tiredness with less than ordinary exertion. Malignancies, especially lymphomas and leukemias, occasionally are seen in patients whose primary complaint is feeling excessively tired.

Many endocrine-metabolic disorders can cause fatigue. Fairly often, fatigue heralds the onset of diabetes mellitus. Thyroid disease, more often hypothyroidism but occasionally hyperthyroidism, and hyperparathyroidism sometimes are characterized by malaise and weakness. Addison's disease and hypopituitarism also can present with chronic fatigue.

Lassitude accompanies many different infections and sometimes can dominate the clinical picture. Chronic infections, such as tuberculosis and brucellosis, are classic cases in point. On a

more modern note, weakness and inability to carry out ordinary activities probably are the most common early symptoms of the acquired immunodeficiency syndrome. Infectious mononucleosis and chronic pyelonephritis are notorious for presenting as fatigue.

The most difficult problems to differentiate are usually neurologic and psychiatric conditions. Fatigue is a prominent, and at times early, symptom of multiple sclerosis. Psychiatrically, the relevant disorder is depression; the distinction can be especially difficult because the chronic fatigue syndrome can include depression as well as forgetfulness, confusion, difficulty thinking, and inability to concentrate.

Chronic Fatigue Syndrome

Over the last 60 years, there have occurred throughout the world a number of apparent epidemics characterized by intense fatigue, myalgia, irritability and depression, and difficulty with memory and concentration. The clinical picture of what has come to be known as the chronic fatigue syndrome, though somewhat variable from epidemic to epidemic and in nonepidemic or sporadic cases, probably has enough consistency to merit designation as a syndrome.

There are three types of "normal" fatigue—that resulting from physical exertion unaccustomed in type or amount, that following sustained mental stress or effort, and that due to inadequate sleep—and the patient with chronic fatigue syndrome typically complains of perniciously exaggerated forms of all three. This is the primary and dominating symptom, and the affected individual complains of it bitterly and with a wide variety of descriptive illustrations. For research purposes, a duration of at least 6 months is required, a criterion that is also useful clinically to distinguish chronic fatigue syndrome from postviral syndromes such as those following influenza and infectious mononucleosis.

Muscle pain and tenderness is a common, though not invariable, accompaniment. The myalgia is generalized but seems to particularly involve the long muscles of the extremities. Patients complain of pain both with and without physical activities. Much of the time there is also arthralgia, but joint stiffness is somewhat less common. Examination may reveal tenderness at specific and consistent sites.

Nearly all patients with chronic fatigue syndrome experience an inexplicable decline in their ability to cope with the events and circumstances of everyday life. There may be an apparent personality change, inability to concentrate, and memory deficits. Depression, if present at all, is clearly secondary to concern about medical status. The presence of these mental and emotional symptoms raises the possibility of a primary psychological disorder, such as neurosis or hypochondriasis, but most authorities regard the weight of evidence as favoring a specific physical basis.

Definition and quantification are essential for research, and a case definition of chronic fatigue syndrome was first put forward in 1988 and subsequently revised in 1994 (Table 74-1). For a case to be acceptable for research purposes, there must be severe fatigue for at least 6 months and other chronic medical and psychiatric conditions must be excluded specifically. The fatigue must be severe, unrelieved by rest, and limit the individual's activities. Finally, there must be at least four of eight symptoms. Although intended to provide the kind of rigor in definition and quantification needed in research, these criteria also can be useful in clinical assessment. A diagnosis of chronic fatigue syndrome is warranted only if the criteria are met. Otherwise, idiopathic chronic fatigue should be used.

The etiology of the chronic fatigue syndrome is particularly controversial and, not surprisingly, theories of causation are both numerous and varied. They may be grouped conveniently under infectious, immunologic, neurologic and neuroendocrinologic, and psychological headings.

The most popular theories involve infections, usually viral. An infectious cause is suggested strongly by the well-described epidemics that

TABLE 74-1 **Case Definition of Chronic Fatigue Syndrome**

Severe fatigue that persists or relapses for 6 months, with all of the following excluded

  Active medical conditions that cause fatigue, such as hypothyroidism, sleep apnea, narcolepsy

  Previous medical conditions not fully resolved, such as treated malignancy, or unresolved hepatitis B or C, or viral infection

  Past or current manic depressive disorder with psychotic or melancholic features, including bipolar affective disorder, schizophrenia, delusional disorder, dementia, anorexia nervosa, and bulimia nervosa

  Alcohol or other substance abuse within 2 years before the onset of chronic fatigue and at any time thereafter

Classify as chronic fatigue if

  Fatigue is sufficiently severe; of definite onset (not lifelong); not alleviated by rest; and results in substantial reduction of occupational, educational, social, or personal activities

  Four or more of the following symptoms (all must have started after onset of fatigue) are concurrently present for 6 months

    Impaired memory or concentration

    Sore throat

    Tender cervical or axillary lymph nodes

    Muscle pain

    Multijoint pain

    Headache

    Unrefreshing sleep

  Postexertional malaise

Classify as idiopathic chronic fatigue if fatigue severity or symptom criteria for chronic fatigue syndrome are not met.

SOURCE: Modified with permission from Komaroff AL and Buchwald DS: Chronic fatigue syndrome: An update. *Ann Rev Med* 49:1–13, 1998.

have occured periodically over the last 50 to 60 years in various parts of the world. Much interest over the last decade has centered on the Epstein-Barr virus. However, most studies have failed to find a difference in antibody titers between patients who meet the criteria for chronic fatigue syndrome and those who do not, and few authorities believe Epstein-Barr virus to be a primary cause.

Enteroviruses and Coxsackie viruses also have been considered carefully. They are clearly capable of causing epidemic acute illnesses, and the enteroviruses probably were responsible for most of the "nonparalytic poliomyelitis" of former times. However, the issue of their causing a chronic and persisting form, especially involving the central nervous system, remains controversial. As with Epstein-Barr virus, antibody studies have not been rewarding.

The highest level of interest currently is centered on retroviruses that unquestionably can cause a chronic smoldering infection. About viruses generally, current thinking tends to assign them to a triggering role, rather than one of chronic infection.

Some sort of immunologic basis is suggested by a common history of allergy or atopy. Moreover, several laboratory test abnormalities, reported in individual studies although not often confirmed in independent research, suggest chronic immune abnormality. The abnormalities described include diminished natural killer cell function, impaired T-cell response to mitogenic or antigenic stimuli, and activated T-cell subsets. Both hyper- and hypogammaglobulinemia have been reported.

Neurologic origin is suggested by accompanying neurologic signs or symptoms (paresis, visual loss, or ataxia) in some patients who meet the criteria for chronic fatigue syndrome. Central nervous system diagnostic studies have been described as abnormal in some studies. For example, magnetic resonance imaging of the brains of patients with chronic fatigue syndrome reportedly demonstrates punctate areas of high signal in white matter and computed tomographics abnormalities are reported as more common. Several neuroendocrinologic abnormalities involving the hypothalamic-pituitary axis have been suggested. The function of corticotropin-releasing hormone neurons in the hypothalamus seems to be depressed, and disruptions of both serotonergic and nonadrenergic pathways have been reported.

The concept of a primary psychological basis has been particularly persistent. To be sure, most patients complaining of chronic fatigue will have

primary depressive illnesses or anxiety rather than chronic fatigue syndrome. Moreover, unraveling the temporal sequence in a patient who presents with complaints of "feeling tired all the time" but with obvious depression and anxiety can be a chicken–egg problem. Most patients with chronic fatigue syndrome *become* depressed and anxious within 1 or 2 months from the onset of this condition; for some, the depression is the most debilitating aspect of their condition. The question of whether there was evidence of a psychiatric disorder *before* the onset of chronic fatigue can be difficult to resolve by even the most careful history. Nevertheless, most authorities are persuaded by the sometimes epidemic nature and the laboratory abnormalities (even though not reported consistently) that a primary psychological cause is unlikely.

Under the circumstances in which the etiology is so unclear, it is not surprising that the number and variety of treatments are both extensive. The list of drugs tried and, at least in noncomparative reports or research involving open comparisons, found to offer some benefit, is a long one. Among the pharmacologic agents studied the most and in a controlled manner are acyclovir; liver extract, folic acid, and vitamin B_{12}; intravenous immunoglobulin; magnesium sulfate; essential fatty acids; tricyclic antidepressants; and nonsteroidal anti-inflammatory drugs. Although promising results have been reported in the case of each of these agents, subsequent independent studies generally have failed to confirm the initial positive outcome.

Clinical Assessment

History

In a patient presenting with complaints of chronic fatigue, a careful and detailed history is the first and most important step. The nature of the onset is often the most critical piece of information. It is usually abrupt in chronic fatigue syndrome, often accompanying or following a flu-like illness, whereas if the patient says she "has always been tired," the likelihood of an underlying psychiatric disorder is high. The duration of the illness should be sufficient to rule out recognized postviral conditions, and the research case definition of 6 months (Table 74-1) is probably useful clinically as well. Similarly, an effort to quantitate the disability, such as the 50 percent level suggested for research purposes, can be valuable.

Perhaps the most important, and at the same time the most difficult, distinction involves primary depressive disorders. Fatigability is a common complaint with depression and most chronic fatigue patients experience some secondary depression. A careful history is critical in determining whether depression preceded or followed the onset of the illness. Other features that point more to depression than to chronic fatigue syndrome include diurnal rhythm, terminal sleep disturbance, weight loss, and pervasive feelings of unworthiness and self-blame.

There may be a variety of other symptoms, of which unexplained generalized muscle pain is probably the most common. Weakness and arthralgias also may be present, as may sore throat, cervical adenopathy, and headache. Psychological complaints (difficulty concentrating, confusion, irritability, anxiety, and depression) are encountered commonly. As with the primary complaint of debilitating fatigue or easy fatigability, these other symptoms should be of new onset and should not have existed to any significant degree before the beginning of the present illness.

A complete listing of current and past medications is essential, because more than 250 drugs listed in the *Physician's Desk Reference* include fatigue as a side effect. There should be specific inquiry about various forms of substance abuse. Alcoholism per se may often lead to fatigue complaints, but alcoholics may invoke fatigue to try to cover up inadequate performance.

Past history is not generally remarkable in a patient with chronic fatigue syndrome, except possibly for an unusually frequent incidence of atopy or other allergies.

Physical Examination

A complete physical examination should be performed. Its major goal is to rule out other illnesses in the differential diagnosis. Particularly important is the neurologic examination.

Positive physical findings are infrequent in the chronic fatigue syndrome. Perhaps the most common, and present in approximately one-third of cases, are enlarged and/or tender lymph nodes in the cervical or axillary areas. Even when lymphadenopathy is present, the degree of nodal enlargement is modest, and nodes larger than 2 cm in diameter should suggest other causes.

The physical examination also offers an opportunity for assessment of intellectual capacity by, for example, evaluating the patient's orientation and ability to perform serial sevens. Individuals with chronic fatigue syndrome may have some degree of cognitive impairment, but severe forms are more consistent with primary psychiatric illness.

Laboratory Studies

There are no specific diagnostic laboratory tests in chronic fatigue syndrome, but some abnormalities are seen to occur with increased frequency in the condition. Moreover, carefully selected laboratory tests may be helpful in excluding other diseases. Table 74-2 lists those proposed as part of routine assessment, and others that are proposed to be done on specific indication.

A complete blood count is essential to rule out anemia and the more overt forms of infection. The erythrocyte sedimentation rate can help exclude infection and other inflammatory states. About 20 percent of patients with chronic fatigue syndrome have either leukocytosis or leukopenia, and a similar proportion exhibit minor elevation of the sedimentation rate.

Serum electrolytes, including calcium and phosphorus, should be measured, and liver function tests (transaminases and alkaline phosphatase) done as well. Urea nitrogen and creatinine measurements are important to evaluate renal status. All of these blood chemistry tests usually

TABLE 74-2 Laboratory Tests in Chronic Fatigue Syndrome

Standard tests
  Complete blood count with white blood cell differential
  Erythrocyte sedimentation rate
  Urinalysis
  Blood urea nitrogen, creatinine, and electrolytes; glucose
  Calcium and phosphorus
  Thyroid-stimulating hormone
  Alanine aminotransferase
  Alkaline phosphatase
  Total protein, albumin, and globulin

Optional tests
  Antinuclear antibodies
  Serum cortisol
  Rheumatoid factor
  Immunoglobulin levels
  Tuberculin skin test
  Lyme serology
  Human immunodeficiency virus serology

SOURCE: Modified with permission from Komaroff AL and Buchwald DS: Chronic fatigue syndrome: An update. *Ann Rev Med* 49:1–13, 1998.

can be performed by an automated technique as part of a panel. Routine urinalysis should be included, as well as some chemical or microbiological test for urinary tract infection. Thyroid evaluation should include measurement of thyroid-stimulating hormone; if this is abnormal, serum thyroxine and antithyroid microsomal antibodies should be tested.

Although the number of immunologic tests found to be positive in individual studies is large, few have been observed consistently in different investigations. Antinuclear antibody tests have been positive (usually weakly) and circulating immune complexes have been low, each in as many as one-half of patients with chronic fatigue. A similar proportion has been observed to have modest elevations in levels of one or another class of immunoglobulin (IgG, IgA, IgM).

Management

In a patient diagnosed as having chronic fatigue syndrome, with other causes of the complaint

ruled out, the important guiding principles of management are to provide compassionate emotional support and to avoid unproved and exotic remedies. The patient needs understanding and reassurance as she seeks to modify her lifestyle to come to terms with her chronic condition. She should eat a balanced diet and get sufficient rest, although she needs to understand that there is no evidence that prolonged rest is curative.

Chronic fatigue syndrome patients typically find that any physical activity leads to exacerbation of their symptoms, which leads to a vicious cycle of progressive physical deconditioning. This sequence can be broken by a specific program of very gradual graded exercise therapy, preferably under the direct supervision of an exercise therapist. Some success has been reported with cognitive behavior therapy, an approach that attempts to modify the individual's attitudes and perceptions regarding the symptoms. Pharmacologic treatment has a limited role, chiefly in treating specific symptoms. If depression is prominent, antidepressant medication with an agent that seems appropriate for the clinical picture and that the patient can tolerate may be given. Many clinicians find that very low doses of tricyclin drugs, such as amitriptyline 10 to 20 mg at bed time, improve sleep quality and reduce the fatigue syndrome. Some antidepressants have sedative side effects and generally should be avoided, except perhaps at bedtime. If anxiety or panic disorders occur, a drug such as alprazolam can be useful. For those in whom myalgias and arthralgias are troublesome, a nonsteroidal anti-inflammatory drug such as ibuprofen may give relief.

Referral is sometimes indicated for either diagnosis or management. Usually the proper consultant is a neurologist, although, depending on the individual clinical picture, a rheumatologist, psychiatrist, or other specialist may be appropriate. If the need is more therapeutic than diagnostic, referral to a psychologist or other counselor may be appropriate.

The prognosis for chronic fatigue syndrome, especially when diagnosed according to stringent criteria, is not very good. A recent systematic review of the literature found that a maximum of 10 percent of adults return to premorbid levels of functioning.

References and Selected Readings

1. Block GR, Whelan J (eds): *Chronic Fatigue Syndrome.* Chichester, UK: John Wiley (Ciba Foundation Symposium 173), 1993.
2. Buchwald D, Kornacoff AL: Review of laboratory findings for patients with chronic fatigue syndrome. *Rev Infect Dis* 13 (Suppl 1):S12–S18, 1991.
3. Dawson DM, Sabin TD (eds): *Chronic Fatigue Syndrome.* Boston: Little, Brown, 1993.
4. Holmes GP, Kaplan JR, Gantz NM, et al: Chronic fatigue syndrome: A working case definition. *Ann Intern Med* 108:387–389, 1988.
5. Joyce J, Hotopf M, Weasely S: The prognosis of chronic fatigue and chronic fatigue syndrome. *QJM* 90:223–233, 1997.
6. Komaroff AL, Buchwald DS: Chronic fatigue syndrome: An update. *Annu Rev Med* 49:1–13, 1998.
7. Thomas PK: The chronic fatigue syndrome: What do we know? *BMJ* 306:1557–1558, 1993.

Treatment of Obesity

Michael A. Hamilton
Cathy Nonas

Chapter 9 outlined in some detail the increasing prevalence of obesity in this country, particularly in higher body mass index (BMI) categories. Because of the known health risks associated with obesity, primary care clinicians should consider the weight of each patient as thoughtfully as blood pressure, fasting glucose, and cholesterol levels.

The clinician's attitude towards obesity is important. For example, women who are gaining weight, or who are already overweight or obese, need to be informed about the risks associated with their weight. But the manner in which this issue is brought to the attention of women is critical; too many clinicians project a judgmental attitude towards persons who are overweight or obese. Consequently, women may avoid or delay obtaining health care because of fear of criticism, and/or judgmental lectures on food intake, physical activity, and the virtues of willpower. One study showed that obese women were four times more likely to cancel their medical appointments when compared to non-obese women. A major reason: fear of the clinician's judgmental attitude.

Even if women make and keep their medical appointments, clinicians may be less inclined to perform a thorough examination on obese patients. One study of primary care physicians indicated that physicians were more reluctant to perform a gynecological examination on obese women when compared to non-obese women. Because obesity increases the risk of uterine cancer, it is a paradox that the very women who are at greatest health risk are the same women who may receive less preventive health care, either because they are reluctant to obtain health care or because they may be examined less thoroughly.

Most clinicians are seeing and treating patients with obesity, but most often they are treating the comorbidities of obesity, not the obesity itself. The reluctance of clinicians to consistently and actively become involved in treating obesity in their obese patients may stem from common misperceptions that obesity treatment is always unsuccessful, and that obesity is simply a disorder of willpower. Also, many clinicians do not appreciate the complex physiologic and metabolic processes that tie obesity, particularly visceral obesity, to the common problems encountered in primary care—diabetes, hypertension, dyslipi-

demia, coronary heart disease, and such varied problems as infertility, polycystic ovary syndrome, gallstone formation, and sleep apnea.

Health Consequences of Overweight and Obesity

Being overweight or obese increases the risk for a number of health problems (Table 75-1). A major concern, however, centers on the increased prevalence of diabetes and other cardiovascular risk factors, such as hypertension, and dyslipidemia. Although Jean Vague first described the association of diabetes, hypertension, and cardiovascular disease in those with upper-body obesity in 1947, it wasn't until the 1980s that his observations led to a serious research effort to understand this association. Since Vague's first obser-

vation, it has become accepted that visceral fat is a major depot that gives rise to these metabolic risks of obesity. For example, in a study of nonobese women and two groups of obese women matched for total body fat but with either high or low levels of visceral fat, those with high levels of visceral fat had higher triglycerides and lower HDL levels than obese women with low levels of visceral fat. Furthermore, women with high levels of visceral fat were found to have higher insulin levels in response to a glucose load, compared to obese women with lower levels of visceral fat. There may be ethnic variation in the health risk associated with different distributions of body fat; for example, subcutaneous abdominal fat may be a greater health risk in African-American women. However, upper-body obesity compared to lower-body obesity is a greater risk in all population groups.

It has also been found that men have twice the amount of visceral fat for a given body mass index as compared to premenopausal women. This observation is consistent with studies that show greater cardiovascular risk in men as compared to women. At menopause, however, women have as much as a 30 percent increase in visceral fat, even in the absence of an overall weight gain. At that point, women begin to approach men in terms of cardiovascular risk.

The metabolic problems associated with increased visceral fat are shown in Table 75-2.

TABLE 75-1   Medical Problems Associated with Obesity in Women

Insulin resistance

Hyperinsulinemia

Impaired glucose tolerance

Diabetes mellitus

Hypertension

Dyslipidemia

Coronary artery disease

Steatosis

Sleep apnea

Gallbladder disease

Gout

Osteoarthritis

Polycystic ovary syndrome

Menstrual irregularities

Infertility

Certain cancers
  Uterine
  Breast (in postmenopausal women with upper body
    obesity)
  Colon
  Gallbladder

TABLE 75-2   Major Findings in Women with Increased Amounts of Visceral Fat

Metabolic Changes
  Hyperinsulinemia
  Increased triglycerides
  Decreased HDL cholesterol levels
  Increased small, dense LDL particles
  Decreased sex hormone binding globulin
  Abnormal liver function tests
  Increased levels of androgenic steroids and testosterone
  Increased cortisol production
  Decreased fibrinolytic activity
  Increased plasminogen activator inhibitor

Obesity, Insulin Resistance, and Hyperinsulinemia

Development of Insulin Resistance To understand the role of insulin resistance and hyperinsulinemia in the development of the metabolic complications of obesity, two concepts are important:

1. Insulin has many actions besides its role in the cellular uptake of glucose (Table 75-3)
2. Resistance to the actions of insulin can be selective, affecting some of its actions more than others.

In cells that are normally sensitive to insulin, exposure to elevated concentrations of free fatty acids lowers the response to insulin. In an analogous manner, an increase in relative weight leads to increased free fatty acid levels in plasma, and this leads to a decrease in peripheral and hepatic insulin sensitivity. Upper-body obesity also decreases peripheral and hepatic insulin sensitivity, but to a greater extent than an increase in relative weight. Reduced hepatic insulin sensitivity in upper-body obesity results from an increased flow of free fatty acids from visceral fat cells through the portal system. In response to decreased sensitivity of peripheral and hepatic tissues to insulin, that is, insulin resistance, the pancreas is stimu-

lated to produce more insulin, which leads to hyperinsulinemia. The increased flow of free fatty acids through the liver in upper-body obesity also reduces the liver's capacity to extract plasma insulin. As a consequence, the amount of insulin exiting the liver to enter the systemic circulation is increased, contributing further to the hyperinsulinemia already resulting from insulin resistance. Genetic predisposition has a major role in modulating insulin resistance. Therefore, obese individuals will have varying degrees of hyperinsulinemia.

Diabetes Mellitus and Insulin Resistance Over time, with increasing duration of obesity and insulin resistance, the pancreatic beta cells in some individuals are less able to maintain sufficient insulin production to overcome the resistance to insulin. At this point, in affected women, blood sugar levels begin to rise and overt diabetes occurs. With further duration of obesity and insulin resistance, pancreatic insulin production may decline further and, in some, may eventually lead to insulin-dependent diabetes. However, because some endogenous insulin response usually remains, these patients do not generally develop ketosis.

Hypertension and Insulin Resistance Hypertension is approximately twice as common in the overweight and obese as in those who are nonobese. Here again, insulin resistance and hyperinsulinemia appear to play a role. In the hyperinsulinemic state that results from insulin resistance, the renal tubules remain sensitive to the sodium-retaining action of insulin and respond by reabsorbing more sodium, leading to greater plasma volume and increasing blood pressure. Insulin also activates the sympathetic nervous and renin-angiotensin systems, providing yet another mechanism for the hypertensive action of hyperinsulinemia. However, not all patients with hyperinsulinemia develop hypertension, again suggesting a significant genetic component in the development of obesity-related hypertension.

Dyslipidemia and Insulin Resistance Insulin resistance also plays a role in lipoprotein metabolism in obesity. The dyslipidemic profile of the

---

TABLE 75-3   Actions of Insulin

Increases glucose uptake by cells

Promotes uptake of amino acids by cells

Decreases hepatic production of sex hormone binding globulin

Promotes the cellular uptake of free fatty acids and inhibits the opposite (lipolysis)

Increases the reuptake of sodium by the kidney tubule

Increases sympathetic action

Decreases gluconeogenesis

Conversion of triglyceride from one lipoprotein particle to the other

Stimulates ovarian androgen production

obese person is most often characterized by high triglycerides, low HDL, and increased numbers of small, dense, atherogenic LDL particles. The elevated triglycerides result from the increased flux of free fatty acids from visceral fat cells through the liver, leading to greater production of triglyceride-rich VLDL particles. Because insulin resistance diminishes the action of lipoprotein lipase, there is a decrease in the peripheral breakdown of triglyceride-rich VLDL particles, which contributes to the development of increased concentrations of VLDL particles as manifested by elevated serum triglyceride levels. Because HDL particles exchange cholesterol for triglycerides from VLDL, HDL becomes triglyceride-enriched. These modified HDL particles undergo lipolysis by hepatic lipase, and as a result are more rapidly catabolized. In a similar manner, LDL particles become enriched with triglyceride. However, instead of more rapid catabolism, hepatic lipase simply removes triglyceride from the particles, leading to smaller dense LDL particles. Therefore, the patient with hyperinsulinemia can expect to have higher than normal triglyceride levels, lower HDL levels, and greater numbers of small, dense LDL particles. Because each LDL particle carries one apolipoprotein B molecule, the serum apolipoprotein B concentration may be a better reflection of atherogenicity than the LDL concentration.

Androgenicity and Hyperinsulinemia It has been suggested that insulin inhibits the production of sex hormone binding globulin (SHBG) by the liver. Indeed, SHBG levels are lower in obese women, particularly those with upper-body obesity and hyperinsulinemia. With lowered SHBG there is an increase in free testosterone concentrations. It has also been suggested that increased free testosterone leads to an inhibition of follicular maturation followed by anovulation and changes in ovarian morphology. Hyperinsulinemia may also stimulate ovarian androgen production. Thus, the androgenicity observed in women with obesity (particularly upper-body obesity) may in part be related to hyperinsulinemia.

Polycystic Ovary Syndrome and Hyperinsulinemia Although the underlying pathologic mechanism that leads to polycystic ovary syndrome is poorly understood, it has been observed that hyperinsulinemia and insulin resistance are common in women with polycystic ovary syndrome. Certainly, weight loss in women with the polycystic ovary syndrome may improve the menstrual cycle and, in some, restore fertility.

New Goals of Obesity Treatment

In the past, the success of obesity treatment was narrowly defined by one number, ideal body weight, based on the Metropolitan Life Tables. Today, the goals of obesity treatment are more realistic in terms of weight loss. A modest weight loss of only 5 to 10 percent loss from initial body weight has been shown to improve the metabolic complications of obesity—diabetes, hypertension, and dyslipidemia. Other measures of success include improvements in lifestyle with respect to nutrition and physical activity, and improvements in quality of life. Changes in body fat distribution, such as a reduction in waist circumference, may also reflect a less atherogenic profile or a decrease in insulin resistance. Even in the absence of weight loss, those who improve their diet or increase their level of physical activity are healthier. These lifestyle changes should be applauded, even though the number on the scale may not have changed. While quality of life is difficult to measure, studies support the observation that even a moderate weight loss in those who are severely obese creates opportunities for greater enjoyment of the activities of daily life. Weight loss, however, does not solve all problems, and may even create new ones—from changes in personal relationships to the cosmetic problem of sagging skin following weight loss.

Successful long-term treatment of obesity has been defined by the Institute of Medicine as a 5 percent decrease from initial body weight that can be maintained for at least a year. This level of success has been demonstrated with diet, exer-

cise, and behavior modification, and also with lifestyle change programs which include pharmacotherapy.

It is commonly said that weight loss programs are seldom, if ever, successful. However, studies show that current weight loss programs are achieving greater weight losses that are sustained for longer periods of time. One study has shown that 30 percent of patients undergoing an Optifast obesity treatment program were able to maintain a 10 percent loss from initial weight 5 years after completing the program. Other programs are beginning to show similar levels of success.

While there is no scientific consensus on an optimum weight loss goal, a weight loss of 5 to 10 percent from initial body weight is a reasonable and attainable goal for most people. However, most obese patients desire to lose much more weight than 5 to 10 percent from initial weight. In negotiating a weight goal with a patient, it is helpful to examine the weight history. Has the patient ever lost significant weight in the past? How much? What weight was the patient able to lose and maintain the longest—and was she still able to live a reasonable lifestyle that was not totally devoted to hours of daily exercise or severe caloric restriction? Did the patient's quality of life improve? If so, a past weight loss may be a reasonable basis for setting a new goal weight. On the other hand, goals based on previous weight losses that could only be maintained for a matter of days or weeks should probably be considered unrealistic. Because lean body mass and resting metabolic rate decline with age, the magnitude of a previous weight loss may not be attained at an older age. However, women who exercise minimize the loss of lean tissue with aging and therefore tend to maintain a higher metabolic rate. Finally, is the patient willing to make the necessary lifestyle changes to achieve and maintain a particular weight goal? If so, the goal has a much better chance of being achieved.

In general, acceptance of a reasonable weight loss goal coupled with an understanding that the lifestyle changes necessary to achieve that goal have important health benefits in themselves, should help to shift the focus from the scale to the other benefits of a weight loss program, that is, improvements in risk factors, improved sense of well-being and energy, and quality of life.

Assessment of the Overweight and Obese Patient

History

During the first interview, the clinician should assess the patient's motivation for weight loss. Are the reasons cosmetic? Are they realistic? If not, can the clinician tactfully bring more realism to her goals? Are there concerns about health problems commonly associated with obesity, and to what extent have these impacted the patient's ability to live a normal life. No matter what the patient's motivation for weight loss, it is the responsibility of the clinician to include the issue of health in the discussion. For example, an apparently healthy woman who is approaching a body mass index of 30 and who has a parent with diabetes, needs to clearly understand the risks of further weight gain and the benefits of even modest weight loss.

The medical history elicited from an overweight or obese patient differs little from the general medical history elicited from normal weight patients. However, diseases that are more commonly associated with overweight and obesity should receive emphasis, and the review of systems should focus on the symptoms of those diseases. Thus, questions should be asked about diabetes; hypertension; dyslipidemia; coronary artery disease; sleep apnea; gallstone disease; arthritis; menstrual irregularities; infertility; and her attention to preventive health procedures that screen for cancers more commonly observed with obesity, such as, breast, uterine, and colon cancers.

Although most obese women do not have a secondary cause for their obesity, the clinician should inquire about symptoms of hypothyroidism or the use of medications that promote weight gain (Table 75-4).

TABLE 75-4 Medications Associated with Weight Gain

Antihistamines
Tricyclic antidepressants
Glucocorticoids
Insulin
Sulfonylureas
Lithium
Valproic acid
Phenothiazines

The medication history should be complete, including over-the-counter preparations, as these may interact with medications that have been or will be prescribed. Medication requirements may change quickly after initiating a weight loss program, even before significant weight loss has occurred. For example, with a decrease in food intake and increased physical activity, medication requirements for diabetes and hypertension will usually decrease. Therefore, patients who are taking insulin, sulfonylurea drugs, or antihypertensive medications should be seen within days of initiating a diet and exercise program, and their dosages quickly reduced or discontinued if necessary. Close follow-up of blood pressure and blood sugar levels should continue until these parameters are stable.

Physical Examination

The physical examination of overweight and obese patients is not different from the examination given to other patients of similar age, etc. Blood pressure should be measured with a cuff appropriate to the size of the patient's arm (the width of the cuff bladder should cover 75 percent of the area between the shoulder and the elbow). The arm should be resting at the level of the heart. Systolic pressure should be recorded as the highest pressure at which two consecutive beats are heard, and diastolic pressure when no more beats can be heard.

Weight should be measured with a scale that is calibrated on a regular schedule. The patient should be weighed without shoes and in a light gown. A careful measurement of height, also without shoes, is important. Commercially manufactured stadiometers offer greater accuracy than the traditional metal measuring tape on the wall and a hand-held ruler positioned, perhaps incorrectly, on the head. Because weight is such a private matter for many women, the scale should be located in an area of the clinic offering privacy. An electronic scale is preferable because it is less time-consuming to use, and such scales can go beyond 350 pounds (there is nothing more demoralizing than to be told that one is too heavy for the scale). From weight and height, body mass index may be calculated. Waist circumference, measured standing at the level of the uppermost lateral border of the iliac crest, is an indirect indicator of visceral fat. Hip circumference, measured at the widest portion of the hips with the patient standing, enables one to calculate waist/hip ratio.

Population studies have shown that a waist/hip ratio greater than 0.8 in women is associated with significant visceral fat and therefore with an increased risk of diabetes, hypertension, dyslipidemia, and cardiovascular disease. However, recent data indicate that waist circumference alone is a better prognostic indicator of visceral fat. If the BMI is greater than 35 to 40, health risk is increased substantially, and the waist circumference assumes less importance as a predictor of risk.

Physical findings associated with hypothyroidism and hypercorticoidism should be looked for, but are rarely a cause of obesity. Young people may have deep, red stretch marks that suggest Cushing's syndrome. Follow-up tests rarely show hypercorticoidism.

Patients with diabetes, hypertension, and dyslipidemia need to be carefully screened for the complications of those diseases, as well as for coronary artery disease. The presence of additional cardiovascular risk factors, such as smoking, a family history of premature coronary disease, and a sedentary lifestyle, should prompt a careful assessment for underlying coronary dis-

ease, especially if an active exercise program is to be prescribed.

Because overweight and obese women may avoid regular preventive health care, the breast exam and mammograms, when indicated, along with a gynecological exam, should be performed or scheduled at an appropriate time.

The clinician should look for physical findings that are more commonly found in obese persons. Examination of the skin may reveal the presence of a fungal or bacterial infection in intertriginous areas, or there may be evidence of hyperinsulinemia, as demonstrated by acanthosis nigricans present over the extensor surfaces of the joints. The changes of chronic venous stasis are easily recognized and are often a major motivation for weight loss, especially if complicated by infection. The pharyngeal space may be narrowed due to enlargement of soft tissues in the throat. And, if the tongue is large and obscures a view of the posterior pharynx, sleep apnea may be present. Sleep apnea is a frequently missed diagnosis that should be suspected in anyone with daytime fatigue and somnolence.

Diagnostic Tests and Procedures

The laboratory assessment should include a CBC that may show increased hemoglobin and hematocrit in patients with hypoxia associated with obstructive airway disease and sleep apnea. Renal function as determined by the urinalysis, BUN, and creatinine, are important tests to obtain in patients with diabetes and hypertension. The urinalysis may reveal mild proteinuria, but greater amounts if the patient has diabetes. Because obese women may have difficulty in obtaining a clean-catch urine sample, the urinalysis may show an increase in white cells and/or bacteria. The presence of large numbers of epithelial cells suggests the sample was inappropriately collected or allowed to sit unrefrigerated prior to analysis. A second sample may be necessary. Because many women who are overweight or obese take diuretics for fluid retention, particular attention should be paid to the potassium, uric acid,

and blood sugar levels (diuretics can increase blood sugar and uric acid levels). Liver enzyme studies often reveal a modest elevation of liver enzymes secondary to fatty infiltration of the liver (steatosis). These will generally resolve with weight loss. The lipid profile characteristically shows an elevation of triglycerides and a decrease in HDL cholesterol levels with an increase of the total cholesterol/HDL ratio. LDL cholesterol levels may be normal, but do not necessarily mean that this lipid fraction is a healthy one, as obese patients, particularly those with visceral obesity, are more likely to have smaller, denser, more atherogenic LDL particles, not necessarily reflected by the LDL cholesterol level. Hemoccult tests on three different stool samples should be obtained; there is a somewhat increased risk of colon cancer in obese patients. A TSH should always be obtained to detect hypothyroidism. If indicated clinically, a 24-h urine for cortisol should be ordered.

An EKG for anyone over 40 years old should be obtained as a baseline, and to follow for possible prolongation of the QT interval, which is a risk factor for cardiac arrhythmias. If an active exercise program is to be encouraged and prescribed, an exercise stress test may be indicated for those with cardiovascular risk factors or for women over 40 to 50 years old, especially if there is a family history of premature coronary disease.

An overnight sleep study is indicated in anyone with a history of raucous snoring, daytime fatigue, and somnolence, especially if the bedroom partner has noted episodes of apnea during sleep.

Treatment

Diet

There are no compelling scientific data that can tell us what mix of nutrients best promotes weight loss on a long-term basis. The only uncontested truth is that to lose weight, the calories consumed must be less than energy expenditure.

For many, "diet" is a four-letter word that symbolizes food deprivation, tedious calorie-

counting, guilt over food lapses, and fear of failure. However, in the Greek language diet is a rather benign word that means "a way of life." It is in this sense of the word that we discuss diet. While many women diet for aesthetic reasons alone, diet is a fundamental component of medical care that serves two functions:

1. As therapy to control diseases such as diabetes, cardiovascular disease, renal failure, cirrhosis, or obesity;
2. To maintain health; e.g., diets low in saturated fats and cholesterol, or diets that provide calcium for prevention of osteoporosis

With respect to weight loss diets, three conditions must be met:

1. The diet must be healthy; i.e., adequate in all nutrients in spite of a reduction in calories;
2. The diet must minimize the loss of lean body mass that is normally associated with weight loss;
3. The diet must be sufficiently practical and palatable (even enjoyable) to promote long-term adherence by the patient.

As evidenced by the number of diets that continue to appear in bookstores and on television, Americans are still looking for a "magic diet" that will result in weight loss, preferably without an increase in physical activity or a decrease in food intake. Despite the popularity of these fad diets, the old truth remains: reduce fat, eat moderate to small portions, and increase physical activity.

A dietary prescription should be given in conjunction with a medical evaluation of the patient that includes a medical history and physical examination, a series of appropriate laboratory tests, and, very importantly, an assessment of the patient's eating patterns, food preferences, past dietary history, and weight loss goals, as well as an assessment of psychosocial and lifestyle factors.

Calories There is no reason to place patients on diets of less than 800 to 900 calories per day. In a study by Foster at the University of Pennsylvania, weight loss was not significantly different in subjects given three liquid-formula diets ranging from 420 to 800 calories per day. Furthermore, on a more liberal caloric intake, there is less risk of gallstone formation, gout, or electrolyte and fluid imbalances. The caloric level of the diet needs to be appropriate to the person's age, lifestyle, and medical condition. Does the person exercise? If so, a greater number of calories should be prescribed. Is the woman tall or short? If she is tall, she will probably lose weight quite nicely on a higher-caloric intake. A teenager requires more calories than an older adult. One approximate method to determine the caloric level of a weight-loss diet is to calculate the maintenance calories and then subtract the number of calories necessary for a given weight loss (a pound of weight loss or gain is roughly equivalent to 3500 kcal). Although there are many formulae for calculating maintenance calories without actually measuring metabolic rate, all result in very similar estimates of daily caloric requirements. The following three formulae give approximate estimates of daily caloric requirements in women. These equations tend to overestimate caloric requirements with increasing levels of obesity.

1. 10 calories per pound of body weight
2. Weight in kilograms $\times$ 0.95 $\times$ 24 h (for females)
3. A more elaborate formula that tends to overestimate caloric needs for obese people is the Harris-Benedict equation (for females): 655.096 + (9.563 $\times$ weight in kg) + (1.85 $\times$ height in cm) − (4.676 $\times$ age) = 24-h caloric needs

Actual requirements may vary from calculated caloric requirements by as much as 10 percent, in 60 percent of patients. The remaining 40 percent of patients will vary by even wider margins.

A moderate caloric restriction consists of a reduction of 500 calories from calculated mainte-

Color Plates*

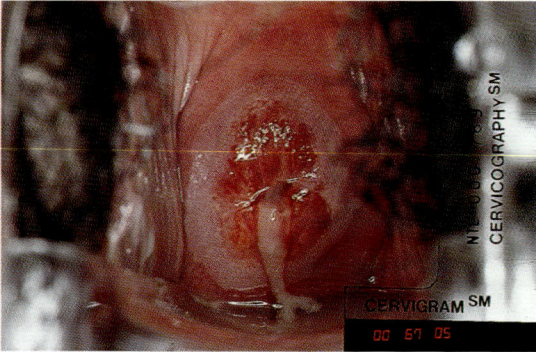

Plate 1 (Fig. 47-1) Normal transformation zone—columnar epithelium can be seen in the endocervical canal. Mature squamous epithelium is seen on the ectocervix. The metaplastic epithelium in the transformation zone in this woman is seen as a rim of acetowhite epithelium immediately surrounding the endocervical mucosa. A faint, mosaic pattern can be seen.

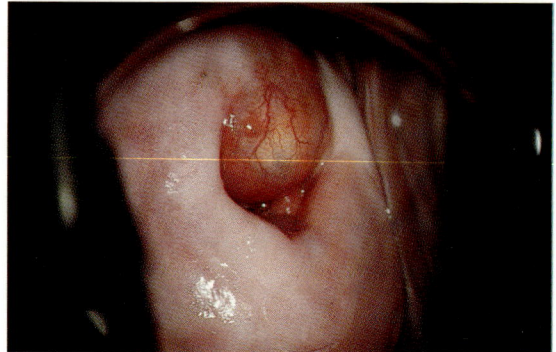

Plate 2 (Fig. 47-2) Nabothian cyst. Note the large blood vessels over the dome of the cyst. These can be distinguished from neoplastic vessels because they branch.

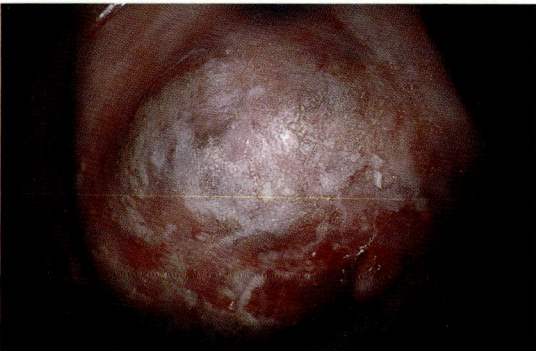

Plate 3 (Figure 47-3) Leukoplakia. A thick layer of keratin can be seen on the anterior lip of the cervix. The surface is white, shiny, and irregular prior to the application of acetic acid.

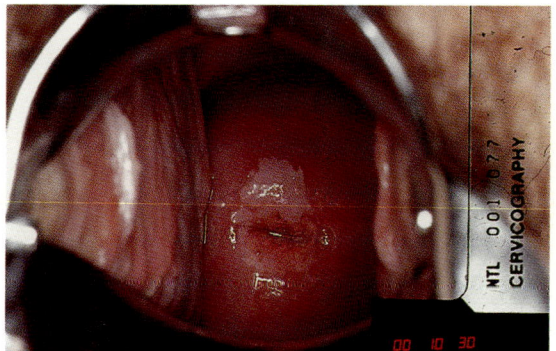

Plate 4 (Figure 47-4) Acetowhite epithelium—low grade. The lesion on the anterior lip of the cervix is snow-white in color and has an irregular geographic border. These are both characteristics of a low-grade dysplastic lesion.

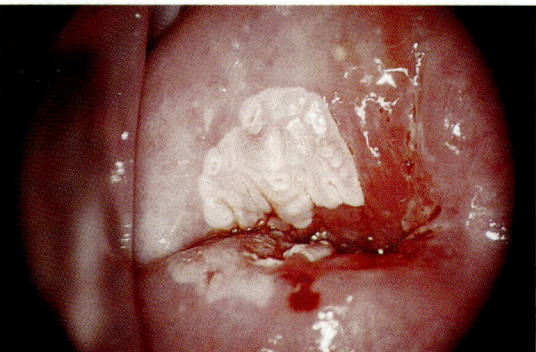

Plate 5 (Figure 47-5) Acetowhite epithelium—high grade. This is a well-demarcated, dense acetowhite epithelium on the anterior lip of the cervix. Note the straight edges of this high-grade lesion. Also, there is dense acetowhite epithelium extending into the endocervical canal on the posterior lip of the cervix.

*Each Plate is followed by the double-numbered figure in parentheses to indicate the chapter in which it is cited and the order of its citation therein.

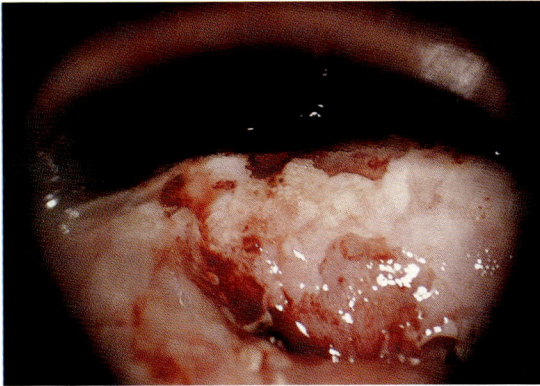

Plate 6 (Figure 47-6) Peeling margins. In high-grade lesions, the desmosomal attachment of the epithelium to the underlying stroma is weakened. The epithelium appears to peel away. At both the upper and lower portion of this lesion, the dense, high-grade acetowhite epithelium has been peeled away exposing the underlying stroma.

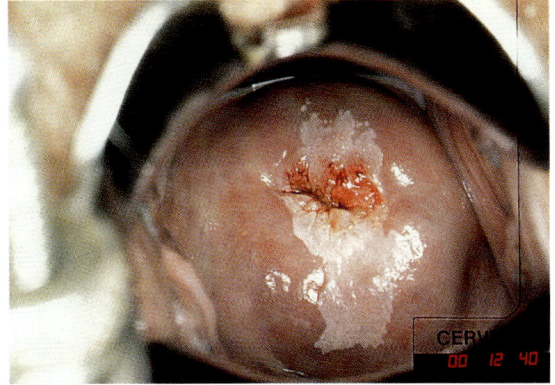

Plate 7 (Figure 47-7) Internal margins. A low-grade acetowhite lesion with a geographic border is seen on both the anterior lip and the posterior lip of the cervix. However, on the posterior lip of the cervix, within the larger lesion is a dense, oyster-shell white lesion with a clearly demarcated border. Such lesions with internal margins are almost always high-grade lesions.

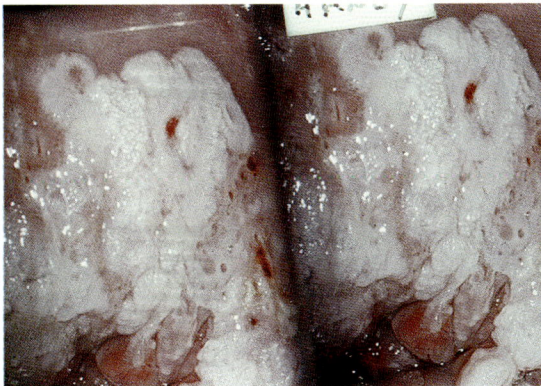

Plate 8 (Figure 47-8) Cervical condyloma. This is a raised hyperkeratotic acetowhite lesion with papillary features characteristic of overt cervical HPV infection.

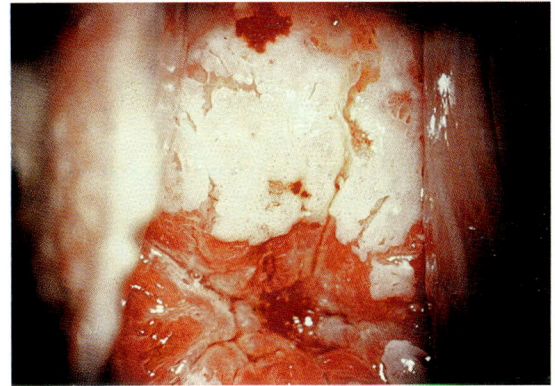

Plate 9 (Figure 47-9) Acetowhite epithelium. Biopsies should be taken from the inner margin of this dense acetowhite lesion. This is the most immature area and likely to be the highest grade lesion.

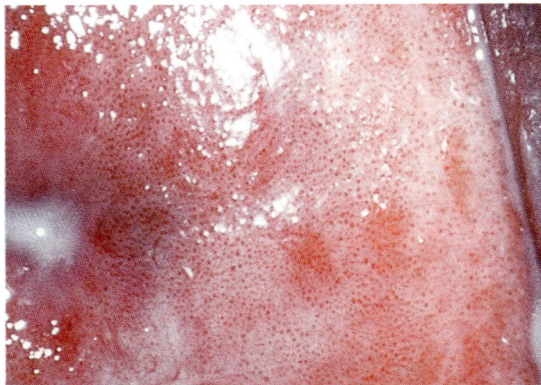

Plate 10 (Figure 47-10) Inflammatory punctations. The cervix is covered with intensely red punctations, but there is no well-defined acetowhite epithelium. This pattern is often found associated with vaginitis or cervicitis and is distinguished from true punctations because they are not found within an acetowhite layer.

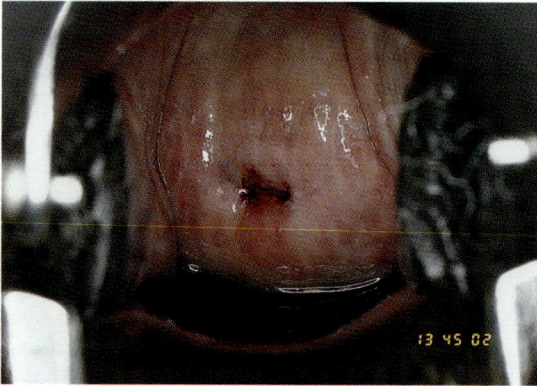

Plate 11 (Figure 47-11) Fine punctations. A faint acetowhite lesion is seen on the anterior lip of the cervix. Careful inspection will reveal fine punctations. This is characteristic of metaplastic or low-grade lesions.

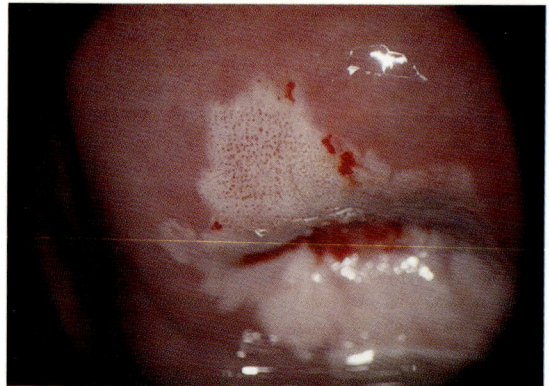

Plate 12 (Figure 47-12) Coarse punctations. Acetowhite epithelium with a coarse punctation pattern. Note that the dots vary in size and intensity, and their pattern is irregular. This is typical of a high-grade lesion.

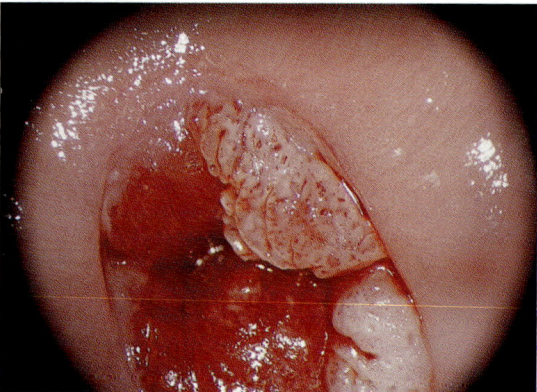

Plate 13 (Figure 47-13) Coarse punctations. In addition to having a large caliber and large intercapillary distances (distance between punctations), these punctations rise above the surface epithelium and are beginning to take on comma shapes suggestive of atypical vessels.

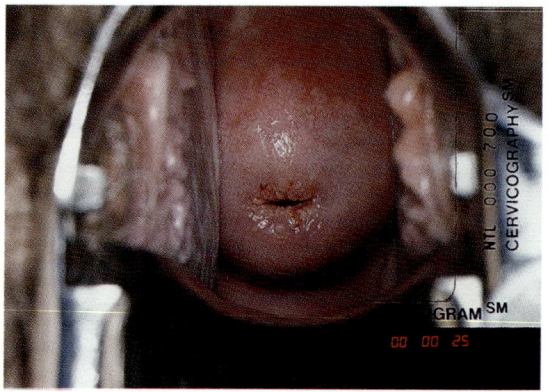

Plate 14 (Figure 47-14) Mosaic pattern. A large acetowhite lesion with a poorly developed mosaic pattern. Such a pattern is often seen in metaplastic epithelium.

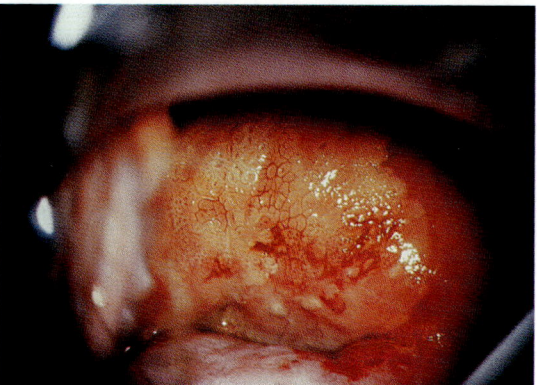

Plate 15 (Figure 47-15) Coarse mosaic. Acetowhite epithelium with a coarse mosaic pattern. Note that the mosaic tiles are large and irregular in size and shape. The vessels surrounding the mosaic tiles have a central vessel. This is highly suggestive of a high-grade lesion.

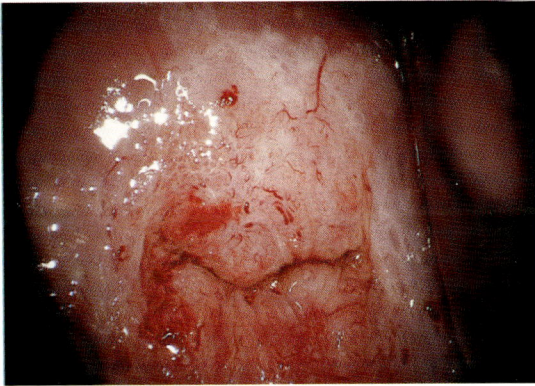

Plate 16 (Figure 47-16)   Atypical vessels. Atypical vessels have a variety of bizarre patterns. Sharp turns, comma-shaped vessels, and other bizarre patterns are seen in this colpophotograph. Several serpentine vessels are seen, which rise above the epithelium and then plunge below it only to resurface again. Although atypical vessels may be found in benign as well as malignant lesions, when they are seen, invasive cancer must always be excluded by a biopsy.

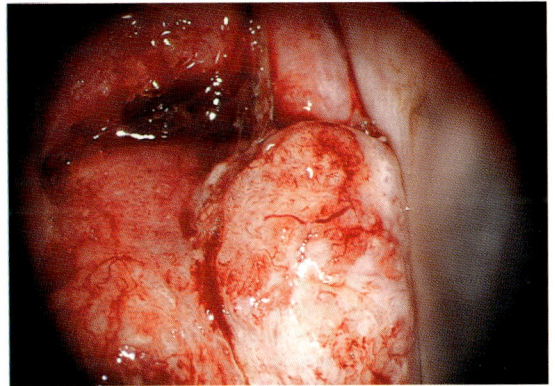

Plate 17 (Figure 47-17)   Atypical vessels. The prominent vessel in the center of the colpophotograph is one of several atypical vessels on this cervix. Note the varying caliber of this large vessel. Another characteristic of atypical vessels is that they do not branch.

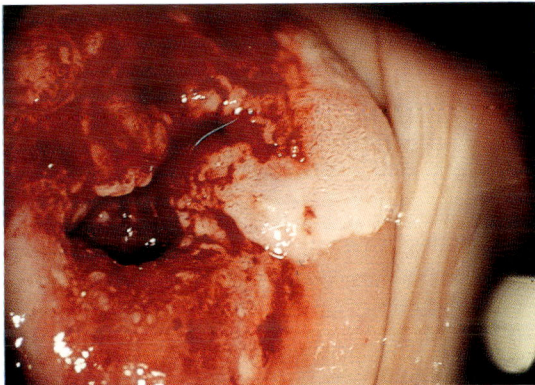

Plate 18 (Figure 47-18)   Invasive cancer. This is a bloody cervix with ulceration. There is a grossly visible acetowhite lesion with comma-shaped atypical vessels.

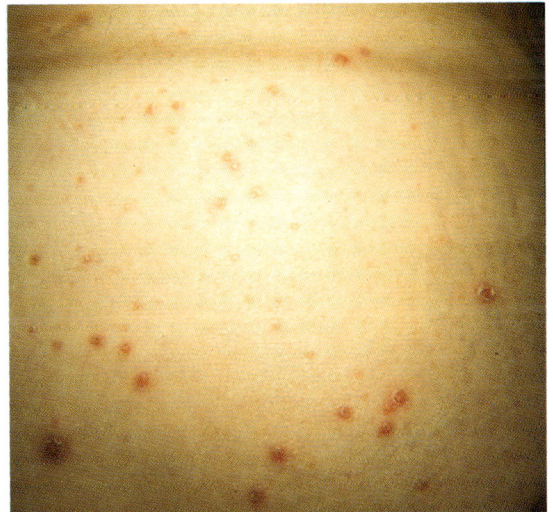

Plate 19 (Figure 80-1)   Folliculitis in a diabetic patient.

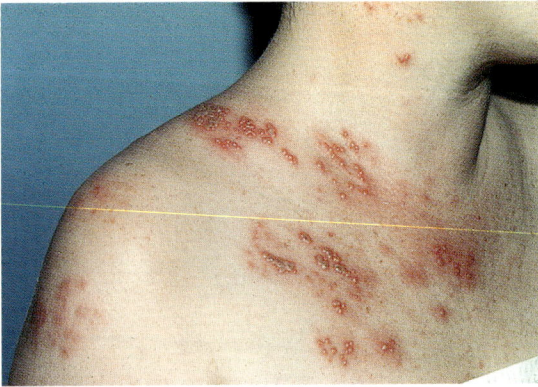
Plate 20 (Figure 80-2)   Herpes zoster.

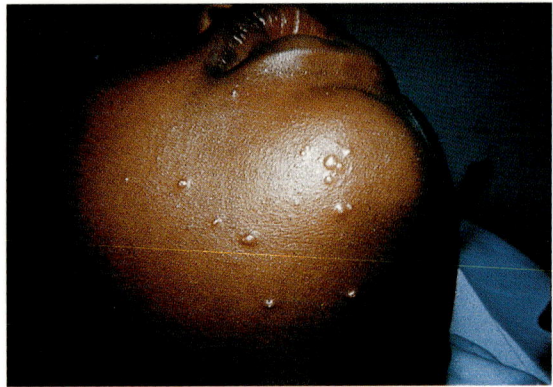
Plate 21 (Figure 80-3)   *Molluscum contagiosum.*

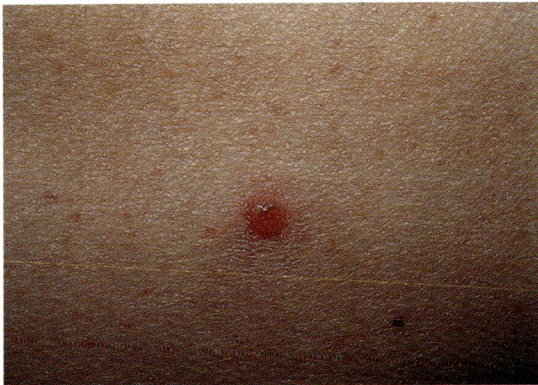
Plate 22 (Figure 80-4)   Insect bite.

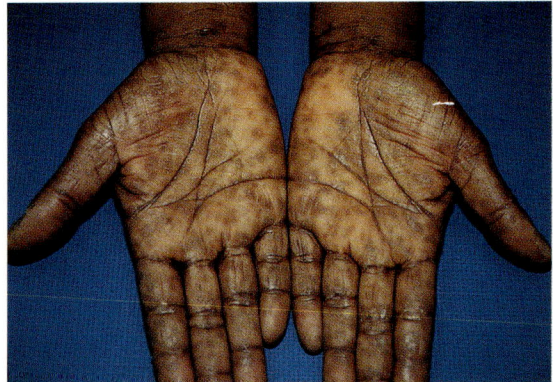
Plate 23 (Figure 80-5)   Secondary syphilis.

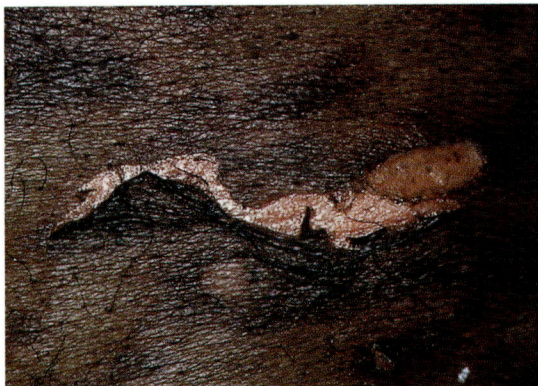
Plate 24 (Figure 80-6)   Toxic epidermal erythema multiforme.

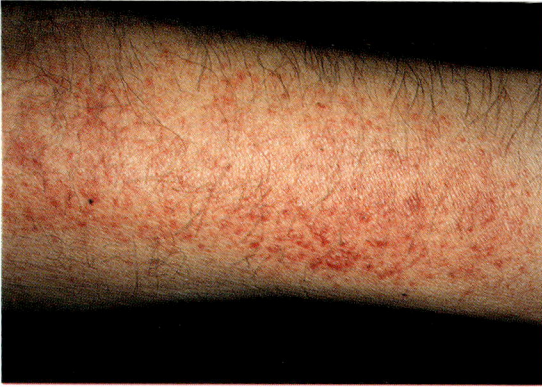

Plate 25 (Figure 80-7) Polymorphic light eruption.

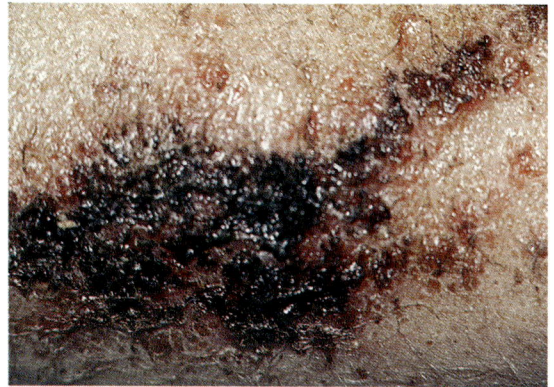

Plate 26 (Figure 80-8) Contact dermatitis from poison ivy.

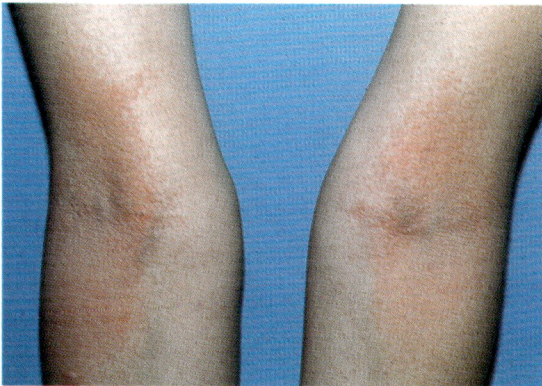

Plate 27 (Figure 80-9) Atopic dermatitis.

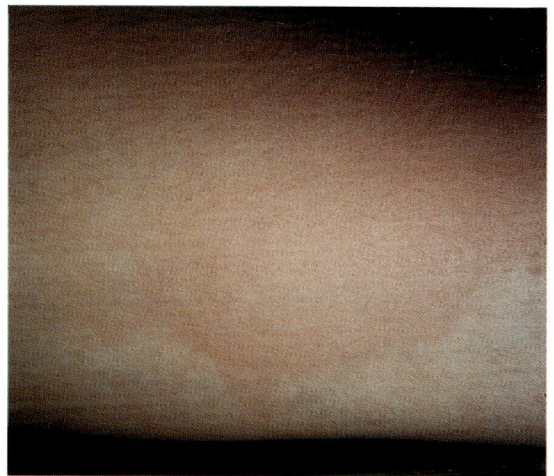

Plate 28 (Figure 80-10) Urticaria.

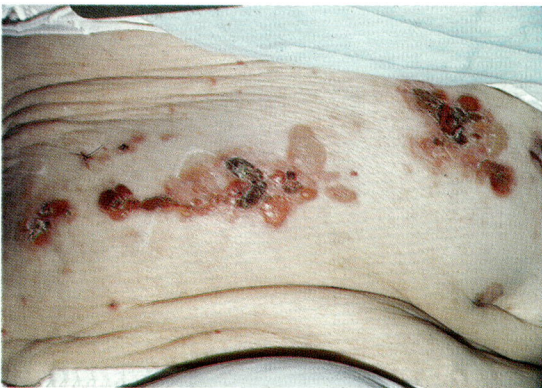

Plate 29 (Figure 80-11) Bullous pemphigoid flared by herpes zoster.

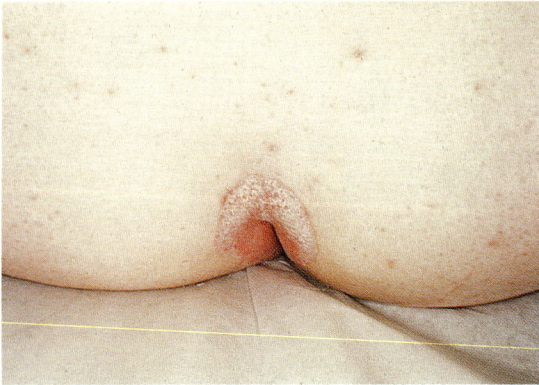

Plate 30 (Figure 80-12) Psoriasis.

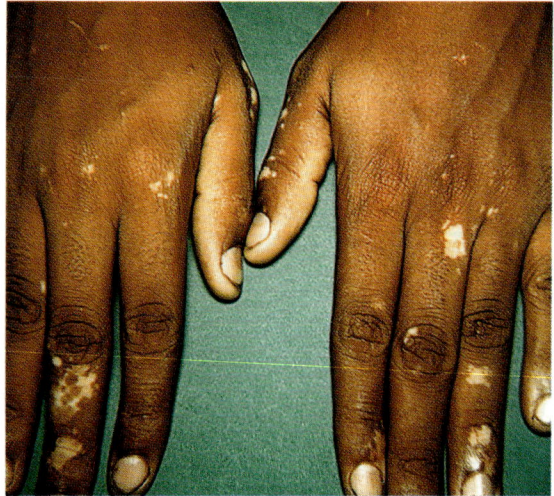

Plate 31 (Figure 80-13) Vitiligo.

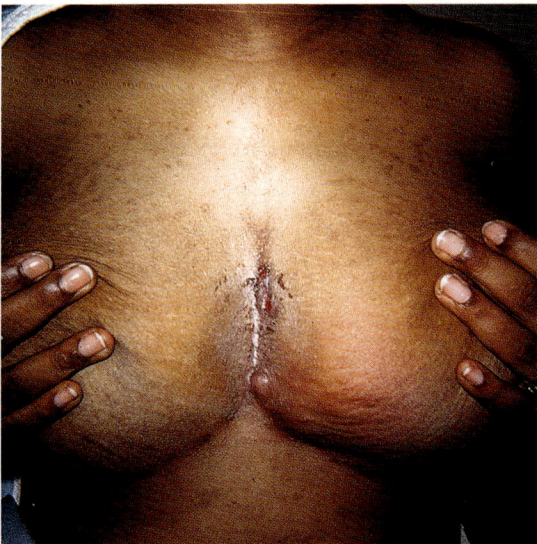

Plate 32 (Figure 80-14) Hidradenitis suppurativa.

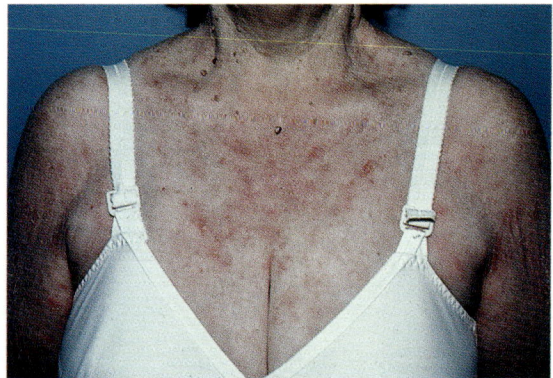

Plate 33 (Figure 80-15) Subacute cutaneous lupus erythematosus (drug induced).

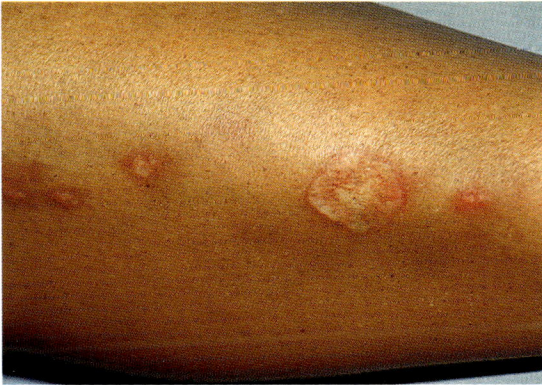

Plate 34 (Figure 80-16) Necrobiosis lipoidica diabeticorum.

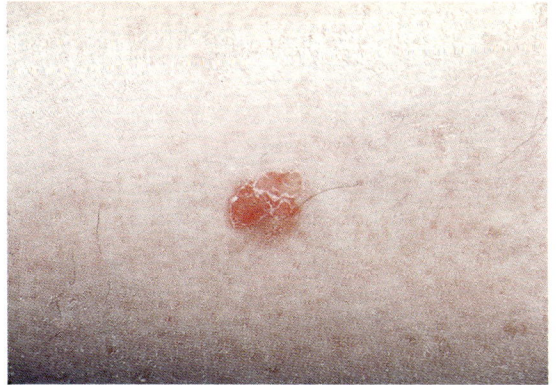

Plate 35 (Figure 80-17) Superficial squamous cell carcinoma.

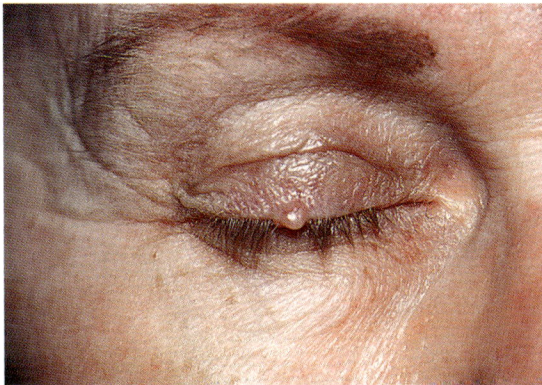

Plate 36 (Figure 80-18) Basal cell carcinoma.

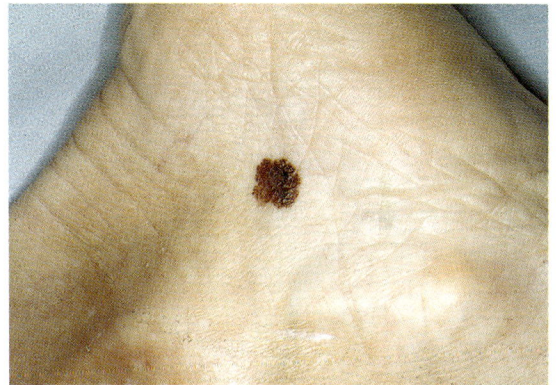

Plate 37 (Figure 80-19) Superficial spreading malignant melanoma.

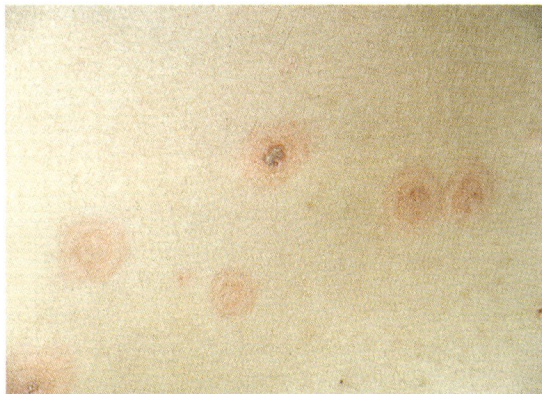

Plate 38 (Figure 80-20) Pemphigus gestationis—herpes gestationis.

nance requirements per day. This deficit should theoretically produce one pound of weight loss per week following the initial diuresis that occurs during the first several days to two weeks after starting a diet. The tissue composition of a safe weight loss should consist of 75 percent fat loss and no more than 24 percent loss of lean tissue. This generally occurs if the loss does not exceed 1 percent or less of initial weight per week.

Lack of significant weight loss may be due to several problems:

- Actual maintenance calories are lower than the patient's calculated maintenance calories;
- The patient has not been accurately estimating caloric intake;
- The diet is too restrictive and the patient is having difficulty in adhering to the diet;
- The diet is not restrictive enough; in other words, the diet allows food items that are excessively high in calories or can be consumed easily and quickly; e.g., the patient is eating too many low fat snacks or portion sizes are too liberal.

If the patient is not losing weight, this should be viewed as an opportunity to examine the possible reasons for the lack of weight loss. An important component of lifestyle counseling is to help the patient problem-solve—to learn what works and what doesn't, and to adjust accordingly. Therefore, the clinician must initially see the patient on a regular basis early in the course of the weight loss program to begin the process of identifying problems and their possible solutions.

Food Diary A food diary is an essential part of self-monitoring. However, many people abhor documenting what they do, and are unwilling to write down everything they eat, including portions, calories, and time, place, and emotions, associated with food intake. Self-monitoring does not have to be painful. The following are suggestions for easier food monitoring:

Ask the patient at which time of day she is most prone to overeating (at a restaurant, at home after dinner, at meal times, on weekends,

etc.). Tailor the diary to issues that are relevant to the patient:

- Record only restaurant meals;
- Record only nighttime eating or times when excessive eating usually occurs;
- Record hunger (no, a little, yes, famished);
- Record amount of vegetables during the day (to document a diet inadequate in vegetables);
- Record which meals were more satisfying than others and analyze the reason why;
- Record only foods that are high in fat and/or sugar.

Macronutrient and Micronutrient Composition Once a caloric level has been selected, the food choices must meet nutritional requirements. Although most nondieting Americans consume twice as much protein as needed (and therefore do not need more protein, even if exercising), when calories are reduced below maintenance calories, the dieter may need to increase protein intake to sustain nitrogen balance.

The RDA for protein from both plant and animal protein is 50g for women and 60g for men. Scientists suggest 72 to 80g per day during caloric restriction (or 1.0 to 1.5 g/kg ideal body weight).

Weight loss diets should contain no less than 125 g of carbohydrate per day to minimize ketosis. Although some suggest that ketosis reduces hunger, there is no consistent evidence in support of this theory. In addition, very low carbohydrate diets can induce electrolyte deficiencies, as well as elevations of the serum uric acid in those who are susceptible to gout.

Although guidelines suggest that no more than 30 percent of total calories should be from fat, we suggest that a goal of 20 percent is probably more appropriate for several reasons:

- Dietary fat is frequently underestimated in foods that do not appear to be fatty foods, for example, bran muffins (which may have more fat than a hamburger.)
- Fat contains more calories (9 calories per g, versus 4 calories per gr for protein and car-

bohydrates). Therefore, it is easier to consume more fat calories before reaching satiety.

- Research suggests that fat is preferentially stored, and that a higher fat intake results in greater storage of fat.
- Lower fat diets are associated with higher fiber intake.

If the weight loss diet is high in whole grains, fruits, and vegetables, it will seldom be inadequate in most vitamins and minerals. However, there are several micronutrients to which special attention must be paid. Calcium is frequently deficient in low-calorie diets, and therefore calcium supplementation should be considered during weight loss. Potassium supplementation is seldom warranted, but if the patient has a low-normal serum potassium, it may be wise to provide supplemental potassium. Dietary vitamin E can be deficient depending upon the fat intake, and 400 IU per day may be reasonable.

Physical Activity

Because exercise increases energy expenditure, it might be assumed that caloric restriction in combination with moderate exercise would result in greater weight loss. In fact, this is not the case. Weight loss is not significantly increased with exercise. Does this mean that exercise plays only a minor role in weight control? Emphatically no! Exercise provides important benefits during weight loss. Not only does exercise increase caloric expenditure and minimize the loss of lean tissue that normally occurs with weight loss, but it also improves the health profile by reducing blood sugar, serum lipids, and blood pressure. People who exercise generally move more easily and more often. Even small amounts of physical activity help—one study showed that fidgeting can increase energy expenditure by as much as 800 kcal/day! In addition, exercise is essential to the maintenance of weight loss.

The advice to exercise needs to be tailored to the individual's physical condition as well as the individual's willingness to be physically active. For example, a patient's heart rate may increase dramatically merely by walking 100 yards, while another patient can walk on a treadmill for 20 min at 4 miles/h without much fluctuation in heart rate. Because studies have shown that a person can achieve as much health benefit by exercising three times per day in 10-min sessions, as by exercising 30 min once per day, the exercise prescription can be adapted to the patient's lifestyle and level of conditioning.

The degree of overweight or obesity may influence the calories prescribed for a given level of recommended exercise. Patients who are only slightly overweight need more calories per pound to minimize the loss of lean tissue that occurs with weight loss. As a general principle, weight loss diets should be prescribed cautiously to patients who are only slightly or moderately overweight, especially if they plan to exercise vigorously. On the other hand, patients who are severely obese tolerate a greater caloric deficit with relatively less risk.

Pharmacology

In spite of recent concern about the safety of weight loss medications, pharmacologic agents can potentially improve the treatment of obesity in conjunction with lifestyle changes leading to healthier eating habits and increased physical activity. Phentermine and DL-fenfluramine were introduced in the United States more than 20 years ago, and together they became known as "phen/fen" following the 3.5-year study by Weintraub showing that the combination of these two drugs produced greater weight loss and maintenance compared to placebo. The rationale for the use of these two medications together was that they both decreased food intake but by different mechanisms, and therefore could be used in smaller doses, theoretically minimizing the side effects of each drug. In 1996, D-fenfluramine (Redux) was introduced, but then withdrawn in September 1997 because of reports of an increased incidence of valvular regurgitant lesions in those

taking either D-fenfluramine or DL-fenfluramine (Pondomin), which was also withdrawn from the market at that time. Sibutramine (Meridia) was introduced in the United States in 1997 and Orlistat (Xenical) was introduced in 1999. Phentermine (Ionomin, Fastin, Adipex), which was introduced in the United States in 1959, remains on the market, and is probably the most utilized of the several adrenergic agents.

All the commonly used weight loss medications achieve average weight losses of roughly 10 percent from initial weight. Most achieve this loss during the first 6 months of treatment. Those that have been found to maintain a significant weight loss from baseline at 1 year, nevertheless, show some regain from the maximum loss at 6 months.

While average weight loss is certainly useful in assessing the efficacy of a weight loss drug, it is more useful clinically to have an estimate of the patient's chance of achieving a defined weight loss. For example, what percentage of the treated group achieved a 5, 10, 15 or 20 percent loss from their initial weight versus placebo patients? This kind of information can help patients choose a weight goal that is realistic, based on the experience of different subsets of patients reported in clinical trials.

Adrenergic Agents Almost all the centrally acting drugs that decrease food intake are derivatives of β-phenylethylamine, and probably act by releasing norepinephrine from the presynaptic neuron. Mazindol is the exception; it is a tricyclic compound and probably acts by blocking the reuptake of norepinephrine by the presynaptic neuron.

Adrenergic weight loss medications should be used with care in patients with borderline or established hypertension or potential cardiovascular disease as suggested by the presence of risk factors. Patients with coronary heart disease or a history of a clinically significant arrhythmia should not be placed on these medications. The use of adrenergic weight loss medications in conjunction with other medications which have a stimulating effect on the cardiovascular system

should be avoided. If there is any doubt concerning the patient's cardiovascular health, an exercise tolerance test should be obtained prior to placing a patient on an adrenergic weight loss medication.

The major side effects of the various adrenergic appetite suppressants are headache, insomnia, nervousness, and dizziness. A rise in blood pressure, while rare, is possible. Therefore, monitoring for blood pressure, pulse, and other cardiovascular symptoms is necessary.

Phentermine Phentermine is the most commonly used adrenergic agent and has been on the market for 40 years. Given in doses of 15 to 30 mg, either as the resin form or as the HCL form, phentermine is an effective appetite suppressant that produced roughly twice the weight loss that a placebo produced in trials lasting between 6 and 36 weeks. Phentermine is usually given in the morning to minimize the insomnia associated with this and other adrenergic drugs that decrease food intake. A starting dose of the 15-mg resin form or a half-tablet of the 37.5-mg hydrochloride tablet is prudent, and may be sufficient for many people for prolonged periods. Some patients report that a dose every two or three days is effective. For those who do not respond to 15 mg, the dose can be increased to 30 mg of the resin or 37.5 mg of the hydrochloride form (both provide the same amount of the active drug).

Phenylpropanolamine Phenylpropanolamine is commonly used as a decongestant but has also been shown in clinical trials to achieve a small (approximately one-quarter pound weight loss per week) but significant weight loss compared to placebo. Like phentermine, it should be used carefully in patients with hypertension or cardiovascular disease.

Adrenergic/Serotonergic Agents The only weight loss medication in this category is sibutramine, a reuptake inhibitor of both serotonin and norepinephrine. Clinical trials in approximately 4500 patients have shown greater weight loss with 10 or 15 mg of sibutramine given once daily as compared to placebo. A statistically sig-

nificant number of patients achieved a weight loss of greater than 10 percent from initial body weight: 39 percent in the 15-mg sibutramine group and 30 percent in the 10-mg group, as compared to 8 percent of placebo patients.

As opposed to phentermine and the other adrenergic agents described above, sibutramine acts mainly to enhance satiety. Therefore, patients will continue to eat their meals, but will generally eat less while taking sibutramine. Sibutramine does not cause the central excitation seen with phentermine, or the profound loss of appetite seen in some patients early during treatment with that drug. Consequently, many patients report either little or no subjective sensation that they have been placed on sibutramine. Pharmacokinetic studies indicate that a steady state blood level is achieved in 3 to 4 days, but anecdotally, clinicians report that the full effect of the drug, that is, satiety enhancement, appears after only 10 days to 3 weeks of treatment.

The major side effect of sibutramine derives from its adrenergic action: a slight increase in pulse rate and blood pressure. In a minority of patients, significant increases in blood pressure have occurred. These changes in blood pressure and pulse tend to occur early in the course of treatment, and therefore frequent monitoring early in treatment is important. Patients with hypertension should be well-controlled with antihypertensive medications before considering treatment with sibutramine. As with phentermine, sibutramine should not be used in patients with suspected cardiovascular disease. In addition, sibutramine should not be used with other serotonergic agents and very cautiously with medications that can potentially increase blood pressure or stimulate the cardiovascular system.

Orlistat Orlistat is a weight loss medication that works by a completely different mechanism than the centrally acting weight loss medications. Orlistat is a nonsystemic agent that inhibits gastric and pancreatic lipase, and therefore prevents the breakdown of triglycerides into monoglycerides and free fatty acids, thus leading to a decrease in the absorption of fat, which is then excreted in the stool. With therapeutic doses, approximately one-third of ingested fat remains unabsorbed and is subsequently excreted. The most commonly reported adverse events with Orlistat derive from the excretion of greater amounts of fat in the stool.

Pulmonary Hypertension and Valvular Heart Disease The use of some appetite suppressants has been associated with the development of pulmonary hypertension. The most recent case control study estimated the potential risk of developing pulmonary hypertension at 1 in 50,000 with longer than 3 months' use of appetite suppressants. Most of the cases of pulmonary hypertension in that study were associated with the use of fenfluramine, primarily because fenfluramine had been the most widely prescribed weight loss medication in Europe where this study was conducted. Because pulmonary hypertension occurred primarily in patients taking monoamine releasing agents, there is a theoretical basis for suggesting that sibutramine, which is a reuptake inhibitor, will not be associated with pulmonary hypertension. To date, there have been no reports of pulmonary hypertension in patients taking sibutramine. Further usage of this drug will provide better information on this important question.

Valvular regurgitant lesions were first reported in 1997 in patients who had taken phentermine and fenfluramine. Subsequent echocardiographic surveys of patients taking fenfluramine led to the withdrawal of both DL-fenfluramine and D-fenfluramine. At present, sibutramine has not been associated with the development of valvular heart disease. In a study of 207 patients who were on either sibutramine or placebo for an average of 7.6 months, the incidence of valvular heart lesions was approximately 2.5 percent in both groups. Because less than one percent of administered Orlistat is absorbed, systemic complications affecting the cardiovascular, respiratory, and central nervous systems have not been observed in clinical trials for as long as two years.

Indications for the Use of Weight Loss Medica-

tions Weight loss medications should only be used after a thoughtful assessment of risks, benefits, and alternatives. In general, weight loss medications should not be used in patients with a body mass index less than 30 kg/m². However, patients with a body mass index as low as 27 kg/m² may be candidates for pharmacological treatment if they also have one or more of the comorbidities associated with obesity, such as, hypertension, dyslipidemia, diabetes, severe arthritis that interferes with mobility, etc. Every patient who is started on a weight loss medication must receive a thorough medical evaluation. Closer monitoring is indicated for patients taking medications than for those patients who are on diet and exercise alone, because medications may dramatically decrease food intake, requiring rapid adjustment of medications for diseases such as diabetes and hypertension.

Perhaps the most important advice to those considering the use of these agents is that they must be used in conjunction with a lifestyle modification program. Because these medications decrease food intake and thus promote weight loss, it is tempting for patients to simply take the medications without changing their choice of foods or making a plan to increase physical activity. When a plateau is reached or weight regain occurs, patients then assume that the drug has little value and is ineffective. This reasoning is analogous to suggesting that drugs for diabetes, hypertension, and dyslipidemia work magically by themselves, without the need for changes in diet and physical activity.

Surgery

In patients with severe obesity, that is, a body mass index greater than 40 kg/m² or 35 kg/m² with comorbidities, gastric surgery has been shown to be more successful than diet, physical activity, behavior modification, and medications. The two procedures that are commonly performed today are gastric restriction and gastric bypass. Gastric restriction creates a small pouch in the upper portion of the stomach with an extremely narrow outlet through which food can pass from the upper pouch into the distal stomach and then on through the intestinal tract. Overeating will cause fullness, discomfort, and possibly vomiting. The second procedure is gastric bypass, which also creates a small pouch in the upper portion of the stomach, but in this case the upper pouch is completely sealed or separated from the distal stomach. A gastrojejunostomy is also created, excluding most of the stomach, the duodenum, and a portion of the proximal jejunum from the process of food absorption.

Mortality for these operations is less than 1 percent in centers that have experience with these procedures. The success rate varies depending on patient selection and procedure, but in general, a 33 percent loss from initial weight can be achieved and maintained for at least 10 years after gastric bypass. Gastric bypass is a more extensive procedure and is associated with greater postoperative complications, such as, malabsorption of folic acid, vitamin B_{12}, and iron in approximately 25 percent of patients. However, it is considered to be the more effective of the two procedures. Both procedures are now being done laparoscopically in some centers.

In patients who are severely obese as defined above, the option of surgery should certainly be discussed. Referral to a conservative surgeon with a multidisciplinary team that includes a psychiatrist will enable the patient to make an informed decision regarding whether to pursue a surgical approach to weight control.

Community Resources

Although clinicians are seeing and treating many women who are overweight and obese, generally they are treating the comorbidities of obesity and not the obesity itself. This may be due to the wide array of needs of patients with diseases such as diabetes, hypertension, painful arthritis, and cardiovascular disease, as well as the significant commitment of time it takes to help patients

make the lifestyle changes necessary to lose weight. Also, most clinicians have not been trained to speak meaningfully and in practical terms about nutrition and physical activity. For those who do not have the time, the skills, or the interest in counseling about lifestyle modification, there are a variety of resources available in most communities upon which the clinician can draw. It should be relatively easy to identify community weight loss programs and exercise facilities, as well as individuals in a wide variety of disciplines such as psychology, social work, dietetics, and fitness who work with overweight and obese clients, individually or in groups. A dietician can be located in any community by calling (800) 366-1655. National weight loss organizations that are found in many communities include the following:

Overeater's Anonymous
Weight Watchers
Take Off Pounds Sensibly (TOPS)
Diet Center
Jenny Craig

For patients with severe obesity, especially if complicated by the comorbidities of obesity, there are a variety of programs that offer liquid diets under close medical supervision:

Health Management Resources
Medi-Fast
New Directions
Opti-Fast

For those who wish to enter an intensive lifestyle change program and are willing to spend 2 to 4 weeks away from home at considerable cost, there are several excellent residential programs that focus on nutrition, exercise, and behavior modification. Meals, supervised exercise, and educational sessions, individually and in groups, are scheduled throughout the day. While these programs can achieve significant results in terms of weight loss, their long-term objective is to pro-

vide an educational and motivational experience that enables patients to return home and practice the lifestyle habits they learned during their short but intensive intervention at these centers.

The major residential programs include:

Cooper Institute for Aerobics Research, Dallas, TX
Duke University Diet and Fitness Center, Duke Medical Center, Durham, NC
Pritikin Longevity Center, Miami Beach, FL
Pritikin Longevity Center, Santa Monica, CA
Structure House, Durham, NC
Renfrew Center, Coconut Creek, FL (treats obesity but is better known for its treatment of eating disorders)

Eating Disorders

The following disorders are rare compared to the prevalence of overweight and obesity. The primary care clinician will rarely have the skills to treat these disorders without the help of an expert. Therefore, the major task of the primary care clinician is to recognize these disorders and to refer patients to an appropriate health professional, often a psychologist or psychiatrist.

Binge Eating Disorder

Patients with binge eating disorder consume large quantities of food during a relatively short period of time. During these episodes, there is also a sense of lack of self-control, followed by feelings of guilt and shame. In addition, the binge episodes are often characterized by eating more rapidly than usual, eating until uncomfortably full, eating large amounts in the absence of physical hunger, and eating alone because of embarrassment. Such patients are usually on a strict diet or completely out of control. Therefore, there may be a history of repeated weight losses and gains. An emotional issue, depressed mood, or minor disturbing event can easily trigger a binge.

Binge eaters tend to be heavier on average

than other obese persons. For a given level of obesity, binge eaters are more likely to report feelings of desperation about their inability to control food intake. In addition, they are more likely to express feelings of self-loathing and disgust with their bodies. Binge eaters also tend to report higher levels of depression and anxiety, and more problems with their social and professional lives because of their weight.

Bulimia Nervosa

Patients with bulimia nervosa also experience binging episodes, but these are followed by a variety of compensatory behaviors. The most commonly noted compensatory behavior is purging via self-induced vomiting, laxatives, diuretics, or enemas. Nonpurging compensatory behavior may also occur and includes fasting or excessive exercise after binging.

Bulimic individuals are typically normal in weight, but feel that they are overweight. There is usually a history of chronic dieting and weight fluctuations. The individual is obsessively concerned about her body, and her self-esteem is unduly influenced by her perception of her body, Bulimia nervosa is discussed in Chap. 57.

Anorexia Nervosa

This eating disorder is discussed in Chap. 57.

References and Suggested Reading

1. Adams CH, Smith NJ, Wilbur DC, Grady KE: The relationship of obesity to the frequency of pelvic examinations: Do physician and patient attitudes make a difference?, *Women Health* 20(2):45–57, 1993.
2. Blackburn GL: Effect of degree of weight loss on health benefits. *Obes Res* 3 (Suppl 2): 211S–216S, 1995.
3. Connolly H et al: Valvular heart disease associated with fenfluramine-phentermine. *N Engl J Med* 337:581–588, 1997.
4. Després J-P: The insulin resistance-dyslipidemic syndrome of visceral obesity: Effect on patients' risk. *Obes Res* 6 (Suppl 1):8S–17S, 1998.
5. Després J-P, Moorjani S, Lupien PJ, et al: Regional distribution of body fat, plasma lipoproteins and cardiovascular disease. *Arterioscler Thromb Vasc Biol* 10:497–511, 1990.
6. Després J-P, Krauss R: Obesity and lipoprotein metabolism, in Bray G, Bouchard C, James WPT (eds): *Handbook of Obesity.* New York: Marcel Dekker, 1998, pp 651–675.
7. Drent ML, Larsson I, William-Olsson T, et al: Orlistat (Ro 18-0647), a lipase inhibitor in the treatment of human obesity: A multiple dose study. *Int J Obes Relat Metab Disord* 19:221–226, 1995.
8. Dunn AL, Blair SN: Exercise Prescription, in Morgan WP, (ed): *Physical Activity and Mental Health.* Washington DC: Taylor & Francis, 1997, pp 49–62.
9. Dunn AL, Marcus BH, Kampert JB, et al: Reduction in cardiovascular disease risk factors: 6-month results from project active. *Prev. Med,* 26:883–892, 1997.
10. Goldstein DJ: Beneficial effects of modest weight loss. *Int J Obes Relat Metab Disord* 16:397–415, 1992.
11. Greenway F L: Surgery for Obesity. *Endocrinol Metab Clin North Am* 25 (4): 1005–1021, 1996.
12. Kopelman P: Endocrine determinants of Obesity, in Bray G, Bouchard C, James WPT (eds): *Handbook of Obesity.* New York; Marcel Dekker, 1998, pp 475–489.
13. Kissebah A, Krakower G, Sonnenberg G, Hennes M: Clinical manifestations of the metabolic syndrome, in Bray G, Bouchard C, James WPT (eds): *Handbook of Obesity.* New York; Marcel Dekker, 1998, pp 601–636.
14. Lean ME: Sibutramine: A review of clinical efficacy. *Int J Obes Relat Metab Disord* 21(Suppl 1): S30–S36, 1997.
15. Marcus B, Pinto B, Clark M, et al: Physician-delivered physical activity and nutrition interventions. *Med Exerc Nutr Health* 4:325–334, 1995.
16. McCann UD, Seiden LS, Rubin LJ, et al: Brain serotonin neurotoxicity and primary pulmonary hypertension from fenfluramine and dexfenfluramine: A systematic review of the evidence, *JAMA* 278:666–672, 1997.
17. Pasquali R, Casimirri F: The impact of obesity on hyperandrogenism and polycystic ovary syndrome in premenopausal women. *Clin Endocrinol* 39:1–16, 1993.
18. Pi-Sunyer FX: Medical hazards of obesity. *Ann Intern Med* 119(7 pt 2):655–660, 1993.
19. Review: Long-term pharmacotherapy in the management of obesity. *JAMA* 276, (23): 1907–1915, 1996.
20. Stevens J, Plankey MW, Williamson DF, et al: The body mass index—mortality relationship in white and African-American women. *Obes Res* 6(4):268–277, 1998.

21. Stock MJ: Sibutramine: A review of the pharmacology of a novel antiobesity agent. *Int J Obes Relat Metab Disord* 21 (Suppl 1): S25–S29, 1997.

22. Troisi RJ, Wolf AM, Manson JE, et al: Relation of body fat distribution to reproductive factors in pre- and post-menopausal women. *Obes Res* 3:143–151, 1995.

23. Vague J: La Differenciation sexuelle: Facteur Determinant des formes de l'obesite. *Presse Med* 30:339–340, 1947.

24. Van Itallie TB: Health implications of overweight and obesity in the United States. *Ann Intern Med* 103 (6 pt 2):983–988, 1985.

25. Wadden TA: Treatment of obesity by moderate and severe caloric restriction: Results of clinical research trials. *Ann Intern Med* 119:688, 1993.

26. Weintraub M et al: Long-term weight control study, *Clin Pharmacol Ther* 51:586–646, 1992.

27. Wolf AM: What is the economic case for treating obesity? *Obes Res* 6(Suppl 1):2S–7S, 1998.

Sports Medicine and Minor Orthopedic Problems

David B. Hale
Melody Toth
Ralph W. Hale

During any physical activity there is a risk of injury. This may vary from a minor abrasion or strain to a severe spinal injury or death. In contact sports such as football, basketball, and soccer, or sports utilizing apparatus such as gymnastics, the risk of serious injury is far greater than for the individual who jogs 2 to 3 miles or participates in an aerobic dance class. This chapter concentrates on the more common and less severe problems of the type that are likely to be seen in a primary care office practice.

Exercise injuries usually occur in bone, muscle, tendon, ligaments, or skin, and often are the result of a misapplication of force or overuse. They also may occur from outside sources; for example, being hit by a bicycle while jogging. Whatever the cause, one of the major impacts of such injuries is the interruption of the exercise program, leading to a loss of conditioning or a failure to resume exercising. Therefore, it is important to recognize early injury and its potential effect as soon as possible. Complaints of a physical nature that are found in a routine health screen should be investigated further. In most instances, this requires very little additional time; when identified early, most problems are easily managed.

History Taking

During an initial health screen, the physician should always inquire whether the patient is pursuing an exercise program. If the answer is a negative, then one should be recommended. There are many pamphlets and local resources,

including the YWCA, local fitness centers, sporting goods stores, and so on. The physician can easily identify several sources in the community that can be recommended.

If the patient does have an exercise program, she should be asked about any problems. These may be acute or chronic. Whichever, the physician should attempt to determine their extent and severity. The following questions have proved very helpful and can serve as a guide. However, as with any question format, individual physicians need to develop their own routine. Following each question, an explanation of its purpose is included.

Do you participate in a regular exercise program? This establishes whether the patient is currently exercising or allows for recommendation of consideration of a program. If the answer is yes, the physician should continue with further questions.

What type of program do you use? This helps the physician understand the intensity level and to make a judgment regarding its effectiveness (see Chap. 10).

How often do you exercise and for how long? This further defines the level of exercise.

Have you ever had any injuries as a result of your exercise program? This gives a past history and can alert the physician to areas of potential chronic injury.

Do you currently have any injuries or problems as a result of your exercise program? If the answer is no, proceed to the last question. If the answer is yes, further questions about where, when, and other specifics are needed. Specific areas and the necessary investigations are discussed later in the chapter.

Do you have any questions about your exercise program? If the answer is no, then no further questions are needed. If the answer is yes, then a specific discussion regarding the concern should ensue.

These six questions are enough to identify and investigate the vast majority of injuries related to exercise. They can be easily presented, either orally as part of the clinical history or in a questionnaire given to the patient when she registers. The questionnaire format should require yes-or-no answers, with space for any explanations. Many physicians utilize the questionnaire approach because this is often the simplest method. For those who are still concerned about how these questions should be approached, substitute the word "contraception" for "exercise" and it will be noted immediately that the format is identical to a follow-up of contraception: Do you use contraception? What type? How often and for how long? Any history of problems? Any current problems? Any questions?

Physical Examination

Most physicians can readily examine any minor exercise injury without referral to an orthopedic surgeon. The principles are the same as with any other problem. However, when the basic examination fails to identify or diagnose the problem, a referral is warranted. As with all physical examinations, begin with observation. The following areas, which are not intended to be all-inclusive, need to be considered:

Color: Is there any discoloration?
Contour: Is there any obvious change in normal appearance? Any swelling?
Mobility: Is the patient having any difficulty moving the affected area? (This evaluation should include active and passive range of motion.)
Strength: Has there been a change, or is there a difference between the left and right side that indicates injury?

Following inspection, palpation is performed. Depending on the area of suspected injury, this may vary from simple palpation to establishing a range of motion.

Is there any palpable dislodgement or displacement?
Is there any pain on palpation?

If there is pain on palpation, is it point specific or diffuse?

Are there any limitations to the range of motion?

Is the area painful on motion?

Is the pain referred? If so, to where?

Are there any crepitations or effusions?

Is there any change in sensation? For example, is there numbness, a complaint of burning in the muscles or a joint, or any increase or decrease in sensation?

Obviously, when a specific site of injury is noted, a more direct examination of the site may be warranted.

Definitions

Before identifying specific complaints and their diagnosis and management, the physician needs to review several basic definitions.

Abrasion: A scraping of the epidermis that results in a mildly painful denuding of the skin.

Laceration: An incision into the skin that is usually described by length and depth. It is often contaminated if it occurs during exercise.

Strain: An injury to a muscle and/or tendon that usually occurs at the muscle tendon junction or at the tendinous insertion on the bone. Strains are classified into grades I, II, and III. Grade I: mild with minimal disability; Grade II: anything between grades I and III; Grade III: complete disruption of the muscle or tendon unit.

Sprain: An injury to a ligament. Usually this results in an unstable joint. The degree of injury is divided into three grades. Grade I: painful ligament but no instability; Grade II: painful ligament with partial instability; Grade III: painful ligament with complete instability including possible dislocation.

Contusion: A disruption of the blood vessels, usually veins, secondary to injury, resulting in extravasation of blood into the tissues (to the patient, a "bruise"). This term is used by some to indicate the blow or injury that caused the disruption as well as its appearance.

Ecchymosis: A small nonelevated discoloration of the skin. It is indistinguishable from a contusion and may lead to confusion because both terms are used in medical and lay literature.

Dislocation: The dislodgment of the articular surfaces of a joint such that the proximal and distal articular surfaces are no longer in apposition.

Avulsion: The tearing away of a part of a structure; for the patient, it is usually the complete loss of a portion of the skin.

Injury Evaluation

Most injuries associated with exercise are found in the head/neck or in one of the four extremities and their attachments to the trunk. Injuries to the trunk may occur but these are less frequent. However, injuries to the ribs, breast, and back have been described and must not be overlooked. It is not this chapter's purpose to review treatment or management of serious or severe injuries or fractures, some of which occur secondary to trauma, while others may occur during high-intensity exercise programs.

However, the diagnosis of a fracture or dislocation may be essential to minimize subsequent damage to surrounding tissues. Most fractures or dislocations are associated with the acute, sudden onset of pain in the area of the injury. It is critical for the physician to assess how the injury occurred, because this can be a key to diagnosis. Some patients may even describe a sudden popping or snapping.

Immediate assessment by observation and palpation to determine any obvious deformity of a bone or joint should be performed. Gross instability or inability to use a joint may indicate serious injury. Because the major diagnostic tool is an x-ray, when in doubt, treat any injury as a fracture and either order radiographs or refer the patient.

The initial treatment is immobilization of the bone or joint and restriction of weight-bearing

or use until the diagnosis is made. The general principles of first aid apply until definitive care is available.

One type of fracture to be aware of is the stress fracture. This is most common in the metatarsal, and is a result of extensive and prolonged intensive workouts. X-rays rarely reveal the fracture, and bone scans are necessary. If pain in the foot persists after conservative therapy, a stress fracture should be considered.

Treatment of Acute Minor Injuries

In general, acute minor injuries occurring with exercise should all be treated by *RICE,* either totally or partially. These initials refer to

R = rest
I = ice
C = compression
E = elevation

Rest allows the affected part to recuperate on its own, employing the body's own recuperative powers. If the injury is mild, the rest can be limited to a short time span. Recurrence or absence of pain can be helpful in determining the length of time necessary for rest.

Ice is the modality of choice for treating acute injuries. It decreases inflammation and swelling while providing pain relief. In the past, heat was applied for pain relief; now we know that in reality it increases the swelling and delays healing. Ice is best applied by either an ice pack or ice massage. In the former, the ice is wrapped in a protective coating, usually a plastic bag or towel, to avoid direct skin contact, and then applied to the injury site. In massage, ice can be applied directly but is moved constantly around the area to prevent skin damage. A styrofoam cup is an excellent method. As the ice melts the styrofoam is gradually peeled away. Ice therapy usually is applied for 15 to 20 min, or to the point of skin anesthesia. The frequency varies with the severity of the injury, but three to four times a day—

until the pain and swelling have disappeared—usually is adequate. For chronic injuries, many athletes apply ice to the affected area before and after exercise on a daily basis. Although there is some debate about the effectiveness of this approach, it appears to work for some athletes. An important aspect of ice therapy is to begin treatment as soon as possible after the injury. For reasons still completely unknown, immediate treatment with ice has resulted in a much more rapid recovery.

Compression with or without a support helps to reduce the swelling associated with acute injuries. An Ace bandage applied to the area also can be an excellent way to hold an ice bag in place. Bracing or support is required only when immobilization or support of a joint is indicated. Compression is rarely used in chronic injury rehabilitation. Elevation is essential in the early phases of acute injury. By changing the level of the injury, a reduction in swelling is facilitated. The reduced swelling facilitates healing.

Although not part of the RICE formula, the use of anti-inflammatory medications is an important aspect of treatment. For mild irritation or inflammation, acetaminophen is the drug of choice. For more severe irritation or inflammation, especially chronic cases, nonsteroidal anti-inflammatory drugs are indicated. However, these agents have been linked to problems with heat regulation, so they should be used with caution.

Rehabilitation is an essential component of any injury therapy program. This is best carried out by a certified athletic trainer or a physical therapist. Most minor injuries do not require this service. However, chronic injuries or repetitive injuries may benefit from this treatment.

Foot Problems

Most exercise programs involve use of the lower extremities. The frequency of walking, jogging, running, and aerobic dance make this area one of the most susceptible for injury. For conve-

nience, the lower extremity is described anatomically, although it is important to remember that it is a unit; problems in one area may result in difficulties in another (e.g., a contusion on the heel may alter running mechanics, causing excessive strain on the knee, ankle, or hip). It is only by remembering the mechanics involved that the underlying cause of some problems can be identified.

Tendons

Inflammation of a tendon (tendonitis) is extremely common. It often results from excessive pressure on the tendon during active flexion/extension of the extremity. As the tendon moves back and forth in its fascial sheath or canal, it creates friction and irritation. The most serious of these in the foot/ankle occurs in the Achilles tendon. This injury is usually disabling and markedly reduces the ability to exercise. It results in acute pain in the Achilles tendon, usually at about the level of the malleoli. When palpated, it is point-tender; when the foot is dorsiflexed, the pain is intensified. Occasionally, there is swelling in the posterior part of the ankle and slight crepitations may be felt. Other than the treatment described in the previous section, prolonged rest and anti-inflammatory drugs are indicated. Treatment is difficult, owing to the patient's inability to rest the tendon completely while participating in everyday activities. In the acute stages of Achilles tendonitis, a heel wedge may be added; this takes some of the stress from the tendon. Mild stretching exercises should be prescribed to keep full range of motion of the tendon. This can be accomplished by having the patient stand with her toes on a 2-in. block, heels down, for one minute and repeating this three times a day. In the extreme case, referral for cast immobilization is indicated, as well as modification of shoes.

Rupture of the gastrocnemius or soleus muscles can occur with forceful dorsiflexion (i.e., after missing a step during aerobics or "stepping"). The patient complains of pain. Physical exam does not always reveal a tendon defect or inability to plantar flex. Simply have the patient lie prone; then palpate the calf and the Achilles attachment on the foot. It is important to compare both sides to identify partial tears. Splinting often is effective when there has not been complete disruption. Occasionally, the Achilles tendon ruptures. This is an acute event, and may occur without warning. Examination reveals a defect in the tendon and an inability to plantar flex the foot. Treatment usually is surgical.

Another tendon injury of the foot/ankle is rupture of the tibialis posterior tendon. The patient complains of pain on the medial aspect of the ankle with point tenderness. This may be misdiagnosed as a sprain, but any sprain in this area with point tenderness and limited swelling should cause suspicion of a tendon rupture.

Fascia

One of the more common complaints of the foot/ankle occurs in the fascial sheath that covers the plantar surface. A fasciitis results from excessive weight-bearing on the arch of the foot. The constant pressure stretches the fascia, causing inflammation and swelling. The patient complains of pain; when pressure is applied to the plantar surface, a diffuse pain is elicited. Treatment is symptomatic and occasionally requires arch support. If fasciitis is left untreated, bone spurs may develop along the calcaneus. If this does happen, a spur pad will provide some comfort. Exercises such as toe raises and towel curls will be beneficial; they help redevelop the arch, thereby reducing the strain placed on the fascia by the falling arch.

Toe Raises: Stand with feet shoulder-width apart, rise up on toes, hold for three counts. Three sets of 10 should be performed daily.

Towel curls: Stand on the edge of a towel length-wise, moving only your toes; curl the towel up under your arches; keep going to the end of the towel. When the exercise becomes easy, add a weight. The exercise should be performed three to five times a day.

Rest for a short period is also helpful. The patient should be asked about her shoes and how long they have been used. Most running shoes should be changed every 500 miles or 6 months. One word of caution: mild plantar fasciitis may result in changes in running mechanics that result in excessive stress on the knee and lower extremities; this may be the patient's major complaint.

Others

Pain in and around the metatarsal area is not uncommon. It is usually due to excessive pressure on the toes, either by the type of exercise or the shape of the foot. It must be differentiated from plantar fasciitis, which is more diffuse. Metatarsalgia is point-specific. Treatment usually consists of changing the exercise pattern or padding the area with metatarsal pads. If the pain is localized to a specific metatarsal, Morton's neuroma or foot should be suspected. Initial treatment is with foot pads, followed by referral if no relief is obtained. Stress fractures always must be considered when foot pain is present. The diagnosis can be made only by x-ray or bone scan. When suspected, referral is indicated.

Ankle Injuries

The ankle is one of the most susceptible—and thus most often injured—anatomical areas. Because most exercise programs involve the lower extremity, this is not unexpected. The ankle itself contributes to the problem because it is composed of a series of nonarticulated bones that are held together by ligaments that sustain forces from all directions.

Strains and sprains are the usual injuries to the ankle. These injuries occur when the ankle bones are twisted or turned in such a fashion that abnormal stresses are placed on the ligaments and tendons. Frequently, this abnormal position occurs when the full weight of the body is placed on the ankle, thus creating tremendous forces. The resultant strain or sprain is graded as previously described. Treatment of the acute injury relies

on the RICE principle. To facilitate the healing process, range-of-motion exercises should be started as soon as possible. These exercises are nonweight-bearing and can be done in the early stages of RICE. If swelling can be controlled and range-of-motion exercises started within 24 h, recovery time will be dramatically decreased.

Range-of-Motion Exercises

A.B.C.: With the big toe, write the alphabet. Be sure that the ankle is used, not the leg. This should be repeated at least three to four times a day.
Towel stretch: Roll a towel up and place it around the ball of the foot. Hold the towel in both hands and gently plantar flex the foot. Next relax the pressure and let the foot fall. When the foot is relaxed, turn the foot inside and then outward. Repeat this exercise four to six times, several times a day.

As the injury heals, external support such as taping may be necessary. Once a sprain has occurred, the ankle is more susceptible to repeat injury, and many coaches insist that all ankles be taped once an injury has occurred. In severe injuries, such as grade III, casting and immobilization may be necessary.

Children (before closure of the growth plate) usually do not get ankle sprains. Rather, if they complain of pain around the ankle joint and if x-rays are negative, the injury should be treated as a Salter *T* fracture (fracture through the growth plate) with immobilization for 2 weeks and orthopedic referral.

Lower Leg Problems

The anterior fascial compartment of the tibia may swell during exercise. This swelling produces acute pain and limits use. The common term is "shin splints." Treatment consists of rest and ice. For some people the swelling is frequent and limits exercise activity. One common problem

that may increase shin splint pain in women is fallen arches. When shin splint pain is present, the physician should check first to see if the arch support is gone. If so, arch exercises should be initiated using toe raises and towel curls as noted previously. In addition, some type of arch support may be beneficial. For others, shin splints is only an occasional problem. Although the etiology is vague, an adequate warm-up prior to vigorous exercise is thought to be a beneficial preventive measure. If a young person continually develops lower calf pain with exercise, particularly running, this may indicate a more serious problem and an orthopedic referral should be made.

Cramping

The calf is a common site of cramps during exercise. Relief is obtained by gently stretching the calf muscle, by dorsiflexing the foot, and by massaging the calf. Relief occurs promptly. Although the etiology of cramping is attributed to lactic acid build up, this has not been clearly proven, and lactic acid levels may be only one of several contributing factors. Cramping usually occurs following prolonged exercise or with extreme heat. Recurrence is common if the exercise program is not interrupted. Mild stretching by flexing and extending the foot also helps relax and restore the leg to normal function. Usually after several minutes of light activity the muscle is able to function normally with no recurrence. It is important to recommend to the woman that she not bounce when stretching; also, she should not forcefully stretch, nor have someone else forcefully stretch, the muscles.

Knee Problems

Injuries to the knees are also common. The anatomy of the knee makes it extremely susceptible to injuries related to any application of external force. As a result, twisting or turning can be as responsible for problems as can blows to the knee. In addition, the knee, like the ankle, ab-

sorbs tremendous pressure when the weight of the upper body is transmitted through the distal femur to the proximal tibia. Because these two bones only rest on each other and do not form a true joint, the potential for injury is multiplied.

Ligament Injuries

Any history of injury during or as a result of twisting should suggest a ligamentous injury. In a typical history, the leg was planted down and the body turned with the foot in place. This would result in acute knee pain. Examination of the knee usually reveals swelling as well as pain on motion. This pain is accentuated by placing tension on the suspected ligament. Treatment requires referral to an orthopedic surgeon.

Meniscus

The meniscus serves as internal support to the knee. It is susceptible to injury by twisting. However, as opposed to ligament injury, this pain is more internal and is increased by flexing or extending the knee. The patient occasionally will complain that the knee locks or collapses unexpectedly. This is most frequent in chronic injuries, and the patient will indicate that while doing a normal activity her knee locked and she stumbled or actually fell. Treatment is surgical.

Inflammation

Occasionally the patellar tendon becomes irritated. When this occurs, the pain is in the ligament or under the patella. Motion of the patella is painful; occasionally there is crepitation on palpation. A similar problem occurs when the bursa is irritated. Often, careful palpation provides the only differentiation between bursitis and tendonitis. In this instance, a careful history is most helpful. Prolonged kneeling is a frequent preceding event. Treatment is conservative, with anti-inflammatory agents and ice. Occasionally, the bursa will swell to such a degree that it requires drainage.

Chondromalacia

Anterior knee pain is often a symptom of chondromalacia. In the usual history, the patient has been participating in jumping sports or exercise. The cause is related to the patella's constant motion over the anterior tibial and femoral surfaces. The pain is directly over the patella and may be reproduced by compressing the patella against the femur. Radiographs will confirm the diagnosis. Initial therapy includes rest, ice, and anti-inflammatory drugs. If significant improvement does not occur in a short time, referral is necessary, because physical therapy, bracing, and occasionally surgery may be indicated. In mild cases, a patellar brace that stabilizes the kneecap provides additional comfort and can be purchased at most sporting goods dealers. This helps in both tendonitis and chondromalacia.

The two most useful exercises to help strengthen and prevent tendonitis of the knee, chondromalacia, and even surgery, are quad sets and straight leg raises.

Quad sets: With the leg straight, tighten the thigh muscles. Hold for a count of three and relax. It is recommended that 200 be performed daily in sets of 10 done throughout the day.
Straight leg raises: While leaning against a table, place the leg straight out with the heel on the ground. Keeping the knee locked, raise the leg to waist level; then lower. Start at 3 sets of 25 daily, eventually increasing to 6 sets of 50 each day.

Hip and Thigh Injuries

Injuries to the thigh are almost always muscular. They result from excessive pressure on a major muscle or muscle group that results in tearing of either the tendon or muscle belly. These injuries occur most frequently in exercise or athletic events that require sudden explosive efforts, such as starts in a race. The most common area is the hamstring or quadriceps. Therapy is ice, compression, and rest. Stretching exercises and adequate preexercise warm-ups are helpful as preventive measures.

The hip joint is one of the most stable in the body. The ball and socket structure virtually guarantees limited injury. As a result, most injuries to the hip are either strains of the adjacent muscles or inflammations of the adjacent bursa. One of the most common hip injuries, caused by excessive running or by a direct blow, is greater trochanter bursitis. As the bursae become inflamed, the iliotibial band slips over it, instead of gliding smoothly, thus creating a snapping and giving-out sensation. It is easily cured. The therapy is rest, ice, and anti-inflammatory drugs. Occasionally, cortisone injections are indicated, but these are of limited value owing to their side effects.

Shoulder Injuries

The shoulder, like the knee, is composed of a large number of ligaments holding the bones in close approximation. As opposed to the hip, there is no deep ball and socket joint; the ligaments must support the joint against external as well as internal forces. This results in a potential for exercise injuries similar to that found in the ankle and knee.

Dislocations are commonly seen with pick-up football or city basketball league games. It is important to know that these injuries can have significantly morbidity. The best treatment is to place the arm in a sling so that the arm is in a position of comfort, and then obtain immediate referral. If an attempt is made to reduce the dislocation, it must be performed immediately. It is important to document neurovascular status before and after the procedure. Follow up x-rays should be obtained as soon as possible to demonstrate a successful reduction. If the physician is uncomfortable with an attempt at reduction, it should not be performed, as inappropriate manipulation can result in serious nerve or artery damage.

Bursitis

This common problem results in shoulder pain, especially when lifting the humerus above shoulder level. It is also called "impingement syndrome" and is seen most frequently in patients who participate in sports that require the arm to be lifted above the head. The etiology is the rubbing of the humeral head against the undersurface of the acromion. The rotator cuff then becomes compressed in this area, and the resultant inflammation and erythema cause pain. Therapy includes rest, anti-inflammatory drugs, and ice. Frequently cortisone injections are required. In the milder form of bursitis, conservative therapy often is all that is needed. However, for moderate to severe forms, referral is indicated.

Clavicle

The clavicle is susceptible to fractures and separations. Fractures usually result from falls during an exercise program. When they occur, pain and deformity result. It is rare for complete separation to take place. Treatment consists of shoulder immobilization for six weeks via a specially designed appliance and pain relief. Occasionally, the junction of the clavicle and the acromion separate as a result of a direct blow to the shoulder either from a collision or a fall, causing complete separation. Therapy is controversial, and referral is required. Minor separations can be treated conservatively with rest, immobilization, and analgesics.

Upper Extremities

The upper extremity, like the lower, is at risk for injury during exercise. This occurs primarily at the elbow and hand. Although injuries to the upper arm occur, they are unusual and most frequently are contusions or tendonitis.

Elbow

The most common cause of pain in the elbow is lateral epicondylitis. The etiology is the excessive torques produced at the elbow by the muscles of the forearm. Commonly called "tennis elbow," the pain occurs when the wrist is dorsiflexed. Treatment consists of rest, ice, anti-inflammatory drugs, and a tennis elbow strap. As a precaution, lifting of bulky or heavy items is to be avoided. Should the pain be unresponsive, more aggressive therapy is indicated.

Bursitis

Swelling of the olecranon bursa may cause an apparent distortion of the elbow. This condition is rarely painful, but cosmetically it creates much concern. Drainage may or may not be effective. Therapy with compression and anti-inflammatory medication should be initiated and careful follow-up should be obtained because some cases of bursitis are septic.

Ulnar Nerve

Exercise that requires repeated throwing can result in irritation of the ulnar nerve. This causes a paresthesia of the hand where the ulnar nerve innervates. Like hitting the "crazy bone," the paresthesia soon resolves. Treatment is rest of the elbow and anti-inflammatory drugs. If symptoms persist, they may be due to a condition called ulnar nerve entrapment. In severe cases, surgical intervention is required.

Dislocation

After dislocations of the fingers, elbow dislocations are the most common. This injury occurs most often with falling on an extended forearm. It is important to assess peripheral nerve and artery function as these structures are often injured as well. Radiographs must be taken, and immediate referral for early reduction is essential to minimize long-term sequelae.

Wrist

Most discomforts of the wrist are the result of repeated wrist actions. Except for ball sports or

grasping sports, such as gymnastics, the wrist is rarely a concern. Tendonitis may occur if repeated flexion-extension is performed. Ganglions are frequently seen, but rarely are exercise-related.

A specific entity of which the physician should be aware is *carpal tunnel syndrome*. The presenting complaint is a paresthesia of the palmar aspect of the hand and occasionally the wrist. It may also be associated with pain in the wrist or lower forearm, and occasionally with a sensory deficit or weakness in the fingers served by the median nerve. Although the pain may occur at any time, it is especially noticeable at night or in the late evening. The etiology is compression of the median nerve as it passes from the lower forearm and wrist into the hand. It is a relatively common occurrence, and has been reported more frequently in women. The antecedent events are those that require repeated wrist motion, especially if they are prolonged and require moderate to extensive force. This problem is common in office workers. A careful history is essential. Treatment consists of discontinuation of the task and occasionally use of splints to elevate the hand and relieve the compression. If this fails to relieve the symptoms, referral is indicated. Injection of corticosteroids or even decompression surgery may be required.

A common injury to the wrist is damage to the scaphoid bone. This most often results from falling on an outstretched hand, such as occurs in an attempt to brace or support the body. A symptom is pain in the anatomic snuff box. An x-ray is mandatory if this injury is suspected. If x-rays are negative, the hand can be immobilized with a thumb spica. An additional x-ray should be taken after two weeks, because nondisplaced fractures are difficult to identify on initial films. If pain persists, orthopedic referral is necessary.

Another common injury is fracture of the hamate. These are seen most often in golf, baseball, and tennis. They occur as a result of repeated stress on the hook of the hamate, and present as ulnar wrist pain. X-rays will confirm the fracture,

and referral to an orthopedic surgeon is usually needed.

Hand

A common injury to the fingers is "mallet" or "baseball" fingers. This injury results when the distal interphalangeal joint is forced into flexion and the extensor tendon is avulsed with or without bone. The diagnosis is simple as the patient cannot dorsiflex the distal phalanx. Treatment, after radiographic confirmation of lack of a fracture, consists of 6 to 8 weeks of splinting.

Other hand injuries are sprains and strains. These respond to rest, immobilization, and anti-inflammatory drugs. Occasionally, the patient will dislocate one of the distal interphalangeal joints. Immediate treatment is to grasp the digit and reapproximate the joint by pulling while slightly twisting the digit. If immediate replacement fails or if there is any possibility of a fracture, a radiograph must be taken before any further attempt at replacement.

The thumb is also very mobile, and dislocations at the base of the metacarpalphalangeal joint are quite common. It is also important to assess the collateral ligaments of the metacarpalphalangeal joint after relocation because treatment varies considerably if they are injured. Splinting is required for minor lateral instability, but more than 40 degrees of lateral instability may require surgery. This injury, which leads to the development of severe disability, is frequently missed. Remember, if there is a possibility of a fracture, radiographs should be taken *prior* to realignment.

Back Pain

Back pain is one of the most common complaints in the exercising patient. Its location is usually in the lower back between L4 and S1. Diagnosis is helped by a careful history of the activity that immediately preceded the onset of pain. When examining a patient with back pain, it is important to test the flexibility of the hamstrings. Low

back pain can be caused by hamstring tightness, especially in runners and very athletic persons. If the athlete is unable to touch her toes while in a sitting position or while standing with her leg straight, encourage a stretching program to increase flexibility in the hamstrings.

It is important to determine the site of the pain, whether it is constant or intermittent, and whether there is radiation, especially in the sciatic area. Pain in the midline should make the physician suspicious of a disk problem. Examination should consist of testing for range of motion, straight-leg raising, reflexes, motor and sensory effects. Most cases of midline pain or pain with sciatic radiation require referral. Often the first indication of scoliosis in a female is found during evaluation of back pain that occurs during exercise. Treatment of backache includes rest, Williams flexion exercises, anti-inflammatory drugs, muscle relaxants, heat, and ice. If the back pain persists or increases, it is best to refer the patient. Most back injuries require at least 2 weeks to recover.[3] A lengthier discussion regarding back pain is found in Chap. 72.

Bone Tumors

Bony prominences may appear throughout the body. They are most noticeable on the exposed long bones, but also may be noted with problems of fitting clothes or footwear. Because no two persons have identical bone structures, it is essential to determine whether these prominences are "normal" or the result of a bony tumor or exostosis. This is especially important if the prominence is increasing in size or causing pain. Causes vary from benign cysts or chondromas, to Paget's disease, to primary malignancy. Radiography is the primary diagnostic tool, and many of these "lumps" are found on radiographs obtained for other reasons. Referral is necessary unless the radiographic diagnosis is obvious.

Pregnancy

The same injuries that can occur to the nonpregnant woman can occur during pregnancy. How-

ever, there are a few special concerns about which the physician should be aware. During pregnancy the effect of progesterone causes a gradual relaxation of the ligaments. This occurs earlier in subsequent pregnancies than in the first. The resulting relaxation increases the risk of damage to ligaments of the ankle and knee during exercise. With the added weight of pregnancy, the patient should be cautioned to avoid sudden turning and twisting. Appropriate ankle support is also indicated, especially if there is a previous history of ankle injury. Instability of the pelvis in late pregnancy as the pubic symphysis changes can change running and walking mechanics. As a result, the patient increases her injury susceptibility. Finally, the marked lordosis that occurs with later pregnancy alters the body mechanics by changing the center of gravity. It becomes more difficult to stop forward motion as well as change direction. Any of these may increase the injury potential for a pregnant patient who is actively exercising. These factors should also be considered when a pregnant patient comes into the office with a nonspecific musculoskeletal complaint.

A frequent question that is raised when women who are pregnant exercise is, What is the effect on the fetus? Research in this area is ongoing, as this is a complex physiological interaction. Thus far, there is no evidence that exercise has a deleterious effect on the fetus.[2]

Team Physician

With the increasing emphasis on sports programs for women, many physicians are asked to serve as team physicians. There are three essentials for the physician who elects to take this role. First, establish a referral relationship with a knowledgeable orthopedic surgeon who is willing to take care of any patient whenever a problem arises that is beyond your expertise. Depending on the type of activity, this could be infrequent or usual. Second, become familiar with the common problems associated with the sport and develop

an expertise in their diagnosis and treatment. A certified athletic trainer who is associated with the team can be an invaluable resource in this area and probably can describe 90 percent of the problems that you will encounter. Finally, be available.

Summary

Most physicians can manage the common injuries and problems that occur during exercise. By taking a simple history and performing a brief examination, a diagnosis can be made. Treatment for almost all such injuries consists of rest, ice, and anti-inflammatory drugs. When the injury is beyond the scope of your expertise or when it requires a more specialized approach, a referral is appropriate and expected.

References and Selected Readings

1. American College of Obstetricians and Gynecologists Patient Education Pamphlet: *Women and Exercise: A Guide for Women.* Washington, DC: ACOG, 1992.
2. Richardson AB, Toth M: Orthopedic problems and office management of minor injuries of women who exercise, in Hale R (ed): *Caring for the Exercising Woman.* New York: Elsevier, 1991, pp 119–135.
3. Kardel KR, Kase T: Training in pregnant women: Effects on fetal development and birth. *Am J Obstet Gynecol* 178:280–286, 1998.

Office Assessment and Management of Pain

Ronald Kanner

This chapter presents a rational approach to a patient in pain, a means of conceptualizing pain syndromes, and some guidelines for the judicious selection of pain treatment modalities. It is not intended as a comprehensive review of pain pathophysiology, nor as a compendium of pain syndromes. Particular emphasis is placed on those pain syndromes that are either significantly more common in women than in men, or that have aspects of their presentation or treatment that may be different for women. In experimental pain situations, women have a lower threshold and tolerance for pain than men do, but this has never been shown to be clinically relevant. Women tend to have better sensory discrimination than men for other sensory modalities as well.

Pain is the most common symptom for which patients seek medical help. Intermittent headache is nearly ubiquitous, and over 75 percent of the general population has at least one episode of back pain. More than 50 percent of women suffer back pain during pregnancy, and many continue to have pain long after delivery. Unfortunately, physicians are often poorly trained to manage patients in pain. While they have an adequate knowledge of pharmacology, they often prescribe analgesics inadequately, and use a limited range of therapeutic modalities. The problem is further compounded by lack of clarity in terminology and in syndrome definitions.

Definitions

Pain must be conceptualized as both a sensory and an emotional experience. The International Association for the Study of Pain defines pain as "an unpleasant sensory and emotional experience which we primarily associate with tissue damage or describe in terms of such damage, or both." The two most important issues are that there is an emotional component to all pain, and that actual tissue damage is not necessary for the experience of pain.

Nociception is the perception of a noxious stimulus. Pain, therefore, is the conscious experience of nociception.

Dysesthesia is the experience of an abnormal noxious sensation. It differs from nociception in that it does not feel like a normal pain response to a stimulus. Patients describe burning, tingling, or tight feelings.

Allodynia is the perception of a non-noxious stimulus as painful. This commonly occurs in neuropathic pain syndromes, such as postherpetic neuralgia.

Hyperpathia is an exaggerated and abnormal pain response to a noxious stimulus. It is a type of dysesthesia in response to a noxious stimulus.

Hyperalgesia is similar to hyperpathia, but the response is aberrant only in magnitude, not in type. That is, the patient recognizes more intense pain than that expected from the stimulus.

Hypalgesia is diminished sensitivity to noxious stimuli.

Clinical Classification of Pain Syndromes

The most clinically relevant classifications of pain syndromes sort them according to location (topographic), time course (acute versus chronic), or presumed pathophysiology. Each has its advantages and disadvantages.

Topographic

Classification of pain syndromes by their location is useful in that it follows the manner in which patients present (e.g., with headache, backache, or abdominal pain). The drawback is the lack of specificity.

Temporal

Acute and chronic pain differ both in quality and in consequences. Acute pain is usually in proportion to tissue damage, and is expected to resolve with healing of the underlying process.

Pathophysiologic

Certain pain characteristics allow the clinician to infer the underlying pathophysiology and direct treatment accordingly. In broadest terms, pain syndromes can be divided into nociceptive and non-nociceptive. Nociceptive pain syndromes are due to ongoing tissue damage that stimulates normal pain perception pathways. Pain tends to be localized and aching in quality. Bone and muscle pains are typical examples of somatic nociceptive pain, while bowel obstruction is an example of visceral nociceptive pain.

The two most common types of non-nociceptive pain are neuropathic pain and psychogenic pain. Neuropathic pain syndromes are those in which injury to the peripheral or central nervous system sets up an abnormal, self-perpetuating pain that may be independent of the original stimulus. Pain is felt as dysesthetic and in the distribution of a nerve or nerves. Common examples are postherpetic neuralgia (shingles), diabetic peripheral neuropathy, and trigeminal neuralgia.

The term "psychogenic pain" implies a pain syndrome in which there is no underlying structural pathology, or the response to the pathology is far beyond what is expected for the lesion.

Approach to the Patient in Pain

Appropriate pain management requires a guided history and physical examination, a clear syndrome diagnosis, and a therapeutic plan based on that diagnosis.

Guided History

A guided history must elicit pain location, character, temporal characteristics, intensity, exacerbating and relieving factors, and functional impairment.

The *location* of the pain is the easiest part of the history for the patient to supply. If there is difficulty with the verbal description, she can stand and outline the pain with one hand. This

yields not only the location of the pain, but its radiation, if there is any. A drawing of the body outline may help some of the more concrete thinkers.

The patient should then be asked whether the pain is superficial or deep; comparing it to a muscle cramp or a sunburn can be helpful.

The next step is to decide whether the pain is due to local pathology or whether it is referred. Somatic pain is often accompanied by focal tenderness at the site of the lesion, whereas visceral pain is often referred to distant cutaneous sites.

When patients are entirely unable to describe the location of the pain, or the location is not in keeping with any anatomical possibility, the diagnosis of psychogenic pain should be entertained. The same is true when "total body pain" is the chief complaint.

The *character* of the pain is the most difficult part for the patient to describe, but verbal descriptors of pain are among the most important points in making an accurate diagnosis. Certain pain qualities are so characteristic that they are sufficient to imply a specific pathophysiology. Burning, dysesthetic pain that is superimposed on a numb or tight feeling is almost invariably neuropathic, as are sharp, lancinating jabs in a dermatomal distribution. Crampy, episodic pain is likely to be visceral, nociceptive pain. Localized, aching pain is likely to be somatic nociceptive. Pain that is described entirely in terms of emotional content (e.g., torturing, punishing, etc.) is likely to have a large psychogenic component. If, despite lists and guided questioning, the patient is still unable to describe the character of the pain, she should be asked to liken it to some past pain experience that can serve as a common language (e.g., toothache, stomach cramps, etc.).

The most significant *temporal characteristics* are onset, diurnal variation, and course. The onset of a change in character of pain is of equal importance. Posttraumatic pain is immediate. Weeks to months later, however, the pain may gradually change from an aching quality to a burning, dysesthetic one, heralding the start of reflex-sympathetic dystrophy (now called chronic regional pain syndrome). The true etiology and pathogenesis of this syndrome remain unclear.

Most patients with chronic pain state that the pain is more severe at night than it is in the morning or during the day. Certain pain syndromes have specific diurnal variations. The pain of rheumatoid arthritis is almost invariably worse in the morning and eases as the day progresses, while pain from osteoarthritis follows the opposite pattern. Cluster headaches may come on at a specific time each day, whereas brain tumor headaches are classically characterized by early morning awakening, and tension-type headaches may be present all day long.

Acute and chronic pain are separate entities, not only in their temporal patterns, but also in their pathophysiology. There is no clear temporal cutoff that determines when acute pain becomes chronic. It is more useful to decide when the concomitants of acute pain (response to a noxious stimulus, autonomic responses, anxiety, and appropriate pain behavior) give way to the concomitants of chronic pain (responses outlasting the stimulus, depression, and abnormal illness behavior).

Because pain is a subjective experience, efficacy of treatment is often judged by the patient's perception of changes in *intensity*. This can be done with numerical rating scales (using a 1 to 10 scale), verbal descriptors (none, mild, moderate, severe, intolerable), or visual analog scales (a 10-cm line on which the patient marks the level of intensity), as long as the type of evaluation remains constant for a given patient. Pain intensity ratings cannot be used to judge the severity of one person's pain compared to another's; they are used longitudinally, in a specific patient, to evaluate the efficacy of treatment.

Whether pain is constant, certain factors can make it more or less intense. A history of pain exacerbation with weather change is common in patients with arthritic disorders. Any form of the Valsalva meneuver (straining against a closed glottis) exacerbates pain from a herniated intervertebral disc. Patients with sympathetic-depen-

dent pain, as in reflex sympathetic dystrophy, causalgia, and some cases of postherpetic neuralgia, have marked exacerbations of pain with cold drafts. Other types of neuropathic pain are exacerbated by any light touch that would not normally be painful (allodynia).

There are a few other specific pain precipitants, such as alcohol in cluster headaches, tyramine-containing foods in patients taking monoamine oxidase inhibitors, and cutaneous triggers in patients with neuromata, but the majority of others (hot/cold, stress/relaxation, etc.) are nonspecific and idiosyncratic.

Functional impairment is one of the most important details is to determine on the initial visit: What is it that the patient cannot do because of the pain that she was able to do before it started? The degree of impairment may not correlate directly with pain intensity or with demonstrable clinical lesions. Recuperation of function may be the primary goal in cases in which complete pain control is not attainable. A small disc bulge may be of no importance to a typist, but completely disabling for a construction worker. A mild carpal tunnel syndrome would be just the opposite.

The medical history should be focused on three major issues: (1) possible medical explanation for the current pain syndrome; (2) possible contraindications for certain analgesic therapies (e.g., peptic ulcer disease with nonsteroidal anti-inflammatory drugs or arrhythmias with tricyclic antidepressants); and (3) prior painful illnesses.

The psychosocial history has two goals: to determine the factors that influence treatment (prior pain history, coping skills, support structures, history of substance abuse, and psychological profile), and to establish a working psychological diagnosis.

The goal of establishing a psychosocial profile is not simply to decide whether a pain complaint is "organic or functional," but to identify the patterns that may impede recovery and to address them specifically.

Anxiety is the most common psychological concomitant of acute pain and flare-ups of chronic pain. Patients who require progressively higher doses of analgesics for what appears to be a stable process may be suffering from anxiety and using analgesics for their sedating effects.

Depression is the most common concomitant of chronic pain, and may even have a similar neurophysiologic substrate. Patients may deny depression or claim that it is purely a result of the chronic pain. A careful history of premorbid affect may be revealing. A history of repeated postpartum depression or depressive reactions to other stressors should be sought. Questioning should address sleep pattern, appetite, and affect.

Hypochondriasis is defined as the fear of having, or belief that one has, a serious disease, based on the person's interpretation of physical signs or sensations as evidence of physical illness, despite medical reassurance to the contrary. It may also be considered more broadly in patients who overreact to minor illnesses. It is an emotional issue, not an attempt to deceive.

Somatization, or the somatoform pain disorder, is quite common. It is defined as the preoccupation with pain for at least six months, when appropriate medical investigation does not identify organic pathology, or the disability is far out of proportion to any pathology. This is the most common type of "psychogenic" pain. Patients are described as having alexithymia, which is the inability to express emotions in terms of emotions. They then "somatize" their emotions (unconsciously turn them into physical complaints).

Malingering is the false claim of pain, in hope of secondary gain (usually monetary). It is not a psychological syndrome, but a deliberate attempt to deceive.

Physical Examination

The two most crucial aspects of the examination are the inspection of the painful site and the demonstration of associated signs. Physical examination of the painful site serves three purposes: it reassures the patient that the complaint is being addressed directly; it provides informa-

tion on immediate causative and associated lesions; and it helps to determine whether the pain is local or referred.

The site is examined for direct causative lesions. This is also part of the functional assessment. The affected part should be inspected at rest, and then put through its full range of active and passive motion.

In somatic nociceptive pain, the causative lesion is usually at the site of the pain, whereas visceral nociceptive pain has cutaneous referral points that may be distant from the source. It may be necessary to reproduce the pain to determine the point of origin. Local tenderness usually indicates local pathology. With referred pain, on the other hand, pressure over the lesion may cause pain at the referred site. For example, pain from cholelithiasis may be felt in the right scapular region, but the scapula is not tender, and pressure in the right upper quadrant can cause pain in the shoulder.

Tenderness to percussion of the spine indicates a destructive lesion, while pain only on Valsalva is more compatible with disc protrusion. Tender points along the paraspinal muscles and trigger points in other muscles are characteristics of the myofascial pain/dysfunction syndrome, or fibromyalgia.

Sympathetically mediated neuropathic pain is associated with trophic changes in the skin and, sometimes, in the underlying bone. Temperature changes are almost invariably present, with the affected extremity appearing cooler than the healthy one.

Physical signs can be misleading in patients with psychogenic pain syndromes. The most difficult patients to assess are those who have some underlying organic lesion that is compounded by abnormal pain behavior. Just as the finding of psychological issues does not rule out the possibility of an organic lesion, the finding of a disease process does not mean that the psychological problems are not of primary importance. The issue is to decide whether the structural lesions can reasonably cause the pain complaint. "Psychogenic pain" implies a pain syndrome in which

there is no underlying structural pathology, or the response to the pathology is far beyond what is expected for the lesion.

Standard medical teaching has led us to regard pain as a signal of underlying disease and to direct our energies to finding the cause. The assumption was that the pain was a secondary issue that would take care of itself once the causative lesion was found. That model holds true for acute pain and pain due to malignant disease. However, in most of the common pain problems presenting to a general practice office, pain control is of paramount importance and the pain may be the disease.

The following pain syndromes were selected because of their frequency of presentation in a primary care setting. They are not an exhaustive list, but they do point out features that may be generalized to other pain syndromes.

Headache and Facial Pain

Headaches are the most common recurrent pain problem and, with the exception of cluster headaches, are far more common in women than in men. The vast majority are benign, and structural intracranial pathology accounts for less than 1 percent of headache visits. The most important issues in headache management are to make an accurate syndrome diagnosis and to recognize rapidly the few cases that require emergency treatment.

Benign headache syndromes tend to have a chronic, recurrent temporal pattern, are devoid of neurologic findings, and have stereotyped symptoms. More dangerous headaches are acute and progressive, and may present with stiff neck, papilledema, or a focal neurologic deficit; these require emergency intervention.

Chronic/Recurrent Headache Syndromes

These syndromes make up the vast majority of headache visits and, because they are rarely cured, require long-term management. If the correct diagnosis is made, most cases can be man-

aged easily in the office. The strongest historical datum leading to diagnosis is the temporal pattern of the headache.

Tension-Type Headache (aka Muscle Contraction) Episodic tension-type headache (ETTH) is the most common recurrent headache syndrome. A recent study demonstrated that nearly 40 percent of a randomly selected group had suffered from ETTH in the prior year; the figure became higher with higher levels of education. Chronic tension-type headache (CTTH), on the other hand, is less than one-tenth as common, and tends to decrease with increasing education levels.

The temporal pattern in ETTH may be vague. Most commonly, pain is gradual in onset and occurs late in the day. Pain is most often described as an aching or as a tight band around the head. While psychological stressors can often be identified, small daily hassles seem to be more important than major life stressors. When a tension headache pattern changes to become mainly a morning headache, analgesic rebound may be the culprit. In analgesic rebound, patients are taking a number of doses of analgesic during the day, have no analgesic intake during the night, and awken with a headache. This rebound pattern is particularly common in patients treated with compounds that contain either caffeine or a barbiturate. Frequent rebound headache may herald the onset of CTTH.

Physical examination is normal except for the occasional appearance of tender points in the muscles of the neck or in the muscles surrounding the temporomandibular joint.

Self-medication is the rule, but may actually perpetuate the headaches, as seen in the rebound phenomenon. Cognitive/behavioral techniques, such as relaxation training and biofeedback, can decrease the frequency and intensity of headaches. Simple relaxation techniques can be taught in the office. The role of self-medication in the perpetuation of headaches is a difficult concept for patients, and a great deal of explanation is needed to convince them to decrease their medication, rather than seek more medication.

Tricyclic antidepressants, such as amitriptyline, are usually considered the first-line drugs. They should be started in doses of 10 to 25 mg at bedtime and titrated up by similar increments every few days.

Migraine Migraine is an episodic headache syndrome characterized by throbbing or pounding pain that is usually unilateral and accompanied by photophobia, phonophobia, nausea, and anxiety. Untreated, attacks last from 4 to 72 h. The headache may be preceded by focal neurological symptoms (aura) that are most commonly visual (scotomata, fortification spectra, or photopsias), but may include numbness or weakness. Migraine with aura is what older classifications called "classic migraine."

The current theory of migraine pathogenesis holds that there is a unified neurovascular abnormality. There is an inherited predisposition to migraine, and any one of a number of factors may serve as a precipitant for a given attack. Following some type of as yet unidentified neural signal, a deficiency at the 5HT1-D receptor on blood vessels allows for the production of algogenic and vasodilatory substances, causing the painful throbbing associated with the acute attack. This receptor deficiency is the target of the newer abortive migraine therapies, as is discussed later.

Migraine is significantly more common in women than in men across all age groups, but the difference is most pronounced during the reproductive years, implicating hormonal fluctuations as a major cause. While many migraine sufferers believe that their headaches are worse around the time of menses, only a few percent have true catamenial migraine. This subgroup may not respond to the usual antimigraine measure and require hormonal manipulation. Gonadotropin-releasing hormone, bromocriptine, and estrogen stabilizers have all been suggested, but they require sophisticated control.

Migraine may begin in childhood, but the majority of patients have the onset in adolescence or early adult life. In susceptible patients, some specific foods may precipitate headaches and a

careful history may be sufficient to eliminate the provoking factors.

Serious complications of migraine are unusual, although women with migraine are at somewhat higher risk for cerebrovascular disease than are age-matched controls. Severe vomiting associated with prolonged migraine attacks can lead to dehydration that requires intravenous therapy.

There are three types of therapy for migraine: symptomatic, abortive, and prophylactic. Symptomatic therapy is aimed at pain relief and antiemesis. With sufficient doses of analgesics and antiemetics, patients may be able to retire to a darkened room (eliminating the photophobia) and sleep. If the patient is able to sleep, the attack is almost always dissipated upon awakening. Nonsteroidal anti-inflammatory drugs are most commonly used. Naproxen (375 to 1100 mg po) and ketorolac (60 mg IM) are nonsteroidal anti-inflammatory drugs that can abort acute migraine episodes. In severe or prolonged attacks, parenteral medications are needed. The combination of opioids and a phenothiazine provides symptomatic relief.

Ergot alkaloids were among the first specific abortive therapies for migraine. Ergotamine dosing is usually started with 2 mg orally, at the onset of the attack, followed by 1 mg every half hour, until the headache ceases or there is a maximum of 6 mg in a day or 12 mg in a week. Higher dosing raises the risk of producing ergotism or other vascular complications. It can also be used sublingually or rectally. Long-term use should be avoided because it may lead to tolerance and physical dependence, as well as chronic daily headache.

The newest specific treatments available are the triptans. These drugs are 5-HT1-receptor agonists and are assumed to work directly on the pathogenesis of migraine. Sumatriptan, the first one brought to market, is available as an autoinjector (for subcutaneous administration), as a tablet, and as a nasal spray. Subcutaneous doses of 6 mg effectively abort about 70 percent of attacks. Tablets are available in 25, 50 and 100-mg sizes and are approximately as effective,

but have a delayed onset of action and cannot be used if there is severe vomiting. Nasal spray is available in 5- and 20-mg sizes; the nasal spray avoids the problem of vomiting. These drugs are contraindicated in patients with angina, uncontrolled hypertension, and peripheral vascular disease. Naratriptan and rizatriptan are also effective. Naratriptan may have a longer duration of action; rizatriptan is available as a sublingual preparation.

Prophylactic agents are generally aimed at the vascular phase of migraine. The decision to use a prophylactic agent rather than an abortive one is usually based of the frequency of attacks. If patients are having more than one attack per week, they are at increased risk of complications from the abortive agents. A careful diary should be kept to track headache attacks and monitor therapy.

β-Adrenergic blockers (e.g., propranolol 10 mg qid) were among the first agents used for migraine prophylaxis, on the theory that eliminating the vasodilatory phase of migraine eliminates the pain. They are contraindicated in patients with asthma and congestive heart failure. Careful monitoring of pulse rate should be used to guide dose increases.

Methysergide may be effective in patients who are refractory to other ergots. Dosing is with one pill (2 mg) three to four times a day. It should not be used for more than a few months at a time because of the risk of retroperitoneal fibrosis.

Tricyclic antidepressants have been shown to decrease the frequency and intensity of migraine headaches. No one agent has demonstrated superiority over the others. Doses should be started low, at bedtime, and increased gradually.

Calcium channel blockers, such as verapamil, are also effective and are used in the same doses as those used to treat hypertension.

Nonpharmacologic measures, such as relaxation techniques and the elimination of identified dietary precipitants, can be helpful. Patients should be instructed to eat regularly and to avoid sleep deprivation.

Cluster Headaches Cluster is the only head-ache syndrome that is far more common in men than in women. Pain is piercing in nature, retro-orbital, and invariably unilateral. It is accompanied by nasal congestion, tearing, ptosis, and miosis. Pain reaches maximum intensity within a few minutes and lasts 20 min to 1 h. Alcohol and high altitudes precipitate attacks. The clinical picture is so stereotyped that no further testing is needed.

Prophylactic therapy can be started with meth-ysergide, as for migraine. Lithium is also quite effective, but the dose has to be adjusted carefully and can range from 300 to 1500 mg/day. During severe clusters, a brief course of oral steroids usually ends the cluster, while prophylactic medications are being started.

Chronic Daily Headache Chronic daily head-ache usually evolves from tension or migraine, as the result of frequent use of short-acting analgesics over a long period of time. The quality is similar to that of tension headache. Therapy is directed at withdrawing the offending agents and providing a regimen similar to that used for tension headache.

Temporomandibular Joint (TMJ) Disease Pain is described as aching and originating in the joint or ear. It is exacerbated by movement, and there may be evidence of jaw deviation or abnormal noises. It is probably best to consider it as a myofascial syndrome. Invasive therapies should be avoided and treatment should be based on conservative physical modalities, cognitive/behavioral techniques, and tricyclic antidepressants.

Acute or Progressive Headache Syndromes

These are the syndromes that are harbingers of serious neurological impairment and are more commonly seen in the emergency room than in office practice. The historical data that should raise suspicion are sudden onset and rapid progression of a new headache or a change in pattern of an existing headache syndrome.

Subarachnoid hemorrhage should be considered in an otherwise healthy person who presents with the sudden onset of a severe headache.

Headache frequently occurs during a Valsalva maneuver, as with coitus or straining at stool. Computed tomography must be performed immediately and will demonstrate blood in the subarachnoid space in more than 90 percent of cases. Lumbar puncture is confirmatory in the remainder.

Metastatic brain tumors present with headaches that are not qualitatively different from tension headaches. Only about 17 percent of patients with metastatic brain tumors present with classic brain tumor headaches (early morning pain, alleviation as the day progresses, response to aspirin and steroids, and increase with recumbency). The clinical differentiation is that the syndrome is progressive over weeks to months and is accompanied by an abnormal neurologic exam.

Pseudotumor Cerebri Also known as benign intracranial hypertension, pseudotumor cerebri is most commonly seen in obese young women. It may be precipitated by certain antibiotics and by intake of large doses of fat-soluble vitamins. The syndrome is characterized by headache and papilledema in a person with normal brain imaging. Lumbar puncture relieves the headache almost immediately and may be sufficient for treatment. Repeated taps may be necessary. Long-term treatment is aimed at lowering intracranial pressure. Acetazolamide is used most frequently, but other diuretics may be equally effective. Lumbar shunting is a last resort.

Low Pressure Headache This is the converse syndrome to pseudotumor cerebri. It usually occurs after inadvertent entry into the subarachnoid space during attempted epidural anesthesia. It is characterized by a markedly positional headache that is entirely relieved by recumbency. It is usually self-limited and responds to systemic fluid loading. In severe or protracted cases, intravenous caffeine infusions have been helpful. Epidural blood patch is a last resort.

Temporal Arteritis Temporal arteritis presents in elderly patients (it is very unusual in people under the age of 60), and is accompanied by jaw claudication and a general feeling of malaise.

Polymyalgia rheumatica (aching around the shoulders and hips) is a common concomitant. The diagnosis should be suspected in any elderly patient with a new headache and systemic symptoms. Tenderness around the temporal artery is variable. The erythrocyte sedimentation rate (ESR) is markedly elevated in the majority of patients and, if the clinical picture and elevated ESR appear together, treatment with prednisone 80 to 100 mg daily should be given emergently. Delay in treatment can lead to retinal artery occlusion and permanent blindness.

Low Back Pain

Accurate diagnosis depends on a directed history and physical examination, supplemented by the judicious selection of ancillary procedures. The first diagnostic branch point is to decide whether the pain is an acute, self-limited process or a symptom of more serious disease. The most crucial historical data include onset, distribution, exacerbating and relieving factors, and associated symptoms. Pain of acute onset, with radicular distribution, relieved by recumbency, and unassociated with any other symptoms, is likely to be due to benign root compression. On the other hand, pain of gradual onset with increasing severity, unrelieved by recumbency, and associated with systemic symptoms (fever or weight loss), is more ominous.

The spine should be examined at rest and in movement, checking for deformities and limitations in range. The vertical axis normally shows a gentle lordosis in the cervical and lumbar regions. These normal curvatures are obliterated by muscle spasm.

Normal anterior flexion of the lumbar spine should be about 40 to 60 degrees from the vertical; extension should be about 25 degrees. As a patient tilts laterally, the intervertebral foramen on the side toward which she is tilting closes, while the contralateral foramen opens. Increased pain with ipsilateral tilt is indicative of root compression; contralateral pain is more likely muscu-

lar. Pain originating in articular facets is exacerbated by extension of the spine; radicular disease is exacerbated by flexion and by straight leg raising. Pain from the hip can mimic radicular pain, but externally rotating the leg with the thigh flexed on the abdomen (Patrick's maneuver) reproduces hip, and not radicular, pain.

The paraspinal muscles should be palpated for areas of spasm or trigger points. When gentle pressure over muscles reproduces the clinical pain syndrome, massage or trigger-point injections may be helpful. Percussion tenderness of the spine itself should raise suspicion of collapse, metastatic disease, or infection, requiring immediate imaging.

Acute Low Back Pain

Acute low back pain is experienced by about 80 percent of the general population. It is usually self-limited and no specific diagnosis is made. Radiologic imaging is unnecessary in the vast majority of patients. However, if there is suspicion of tumor or infection, imaging should be performed immediately. The danger signals are point tenderness over the spine, pain that does not resolve with recumbency, focal tenderness, fever, or weight loss. Most acute back pain is presumed to be somatic nociceptive, unless there is a radicular component that produces neuropathic pain (usually felt as a shooting pain in a dermatomal distribution). In patients with a normal neurologic examination and no danger signals, pain resolves spontaneously within days to weeks, during which time simple analgesics usually suffice.

There is no evidence that more than 2 days of bedrest is beneficial for acute back pain, and lumbar traction plays no role in recovery. Prolonged bedrest may lead to deconditioning and further back problems. Epidural steroid injections may shorten the course of recovery from the acute phase, but such injections have no influence on long-term outcome.

Acute low back pain affects over 50 percent of pregnant women. Explanations for such a high

prevalence in such a young group include a forward shift in the center of gravity and laxity of pelvic ligaments. In patients with no prior history of back pain, posterior pelvic pain can be diagnosed by a specific maneuver: the thigh is flexed 90 degrees on the abdomen and direct downward pressure is exerted on the knee. Ipsilateral pain indicates posterior pelvic pain. This type of pain can be expected to subside within three months of delivery, whereas true lumbar pain may persist much longer.

Chronic Low Back Pain

The treatment of chronic low back pain considers the relative contributions of nociceptive, neuropathic, and psychological factors. A rehabilitative model is most likely to be successful.

Somatic Nociceptive Pain This type of pain is marked by an aching quality that is exacerbated by movement or weight bearing.

Degenerative Disease of the Spine Degenerative disease of the spine is an overused term that probably has little clinical relevance in chronic low back pain. Pain-sensitive structures in the spine (vertebral bodies, articular facets, joint capsules, and the annulus fibrosus of the intervertebral discs) are constantly subjected to physical stress. By age 40, most people demonstrate some evidence of degeneration of the spine, usually in the form of osteophytes or facet hypertrophy. These findings do not correlate with pain. However, disc space narrowing at multiple levels may be more predictive of pain.

A number of factors put women at risk for back pain. Osteoporosis produces recurrent low back pain. Although minor fractures may not be apparent on routine spine films, they can cause severe local pain. Bone scans are more sensitive than plain films in revealing fractures. The diagnostic hallmark is a marked exacerbation of pain with weight-bearing and complete resolution with recumbency. Unfortunately, prolonged recumbency increases osteoporosis and the patients must be encouraged to exercise through

the pain. Neurologic compromise from osteoporosis is very rare.

In chronic low back pain of presumed nociceptive origin, emphasis should be on restoration of function. Supportive orthoses may provide pain relief during exacerbations. Their influence on long-term results is unclear, and they may actually worsen outcome because of deconditioning. Exercises should be tailored to strengthen supporting muscles. This is particularly important in patients with osteoporosis, because chronic weight-bearing is important in treating the underlying bone loss.

Facet Disease Marked pain on dorsiflexion of the spine, and radiographs showing facet hypertrophy, suggest facet pathology, occasionally with encroachment on the lateral recess or the intervertebral foramina. A small subgroup of these patients may respond to injections of the facet joints with anesthetics or steroids.

Spondylolisthesis Elderly patients may show a small degree of anterior slippage of a vertebral body, usually as a result of degenerative spondylolysis. When pain is markedly exacerbated by movement, flexion-extension films are needed to check for instability, and bracing may provide dramatic temporary relief. Spinal fusion is reserved for cases characterized by severe slippage or neurologic compromise.

Fibromyalgia/Myofascial Pain Syndrome Back pain may be the predominant complaint in patients with widespread pain and tender points in muscles (fibromyalgia). There may also be functional disability, sleep disturbance, and depression. Management must address functional impairments, rather than pain per se.

Myofascial pain syndrome is a more localized pain syndrome, usually following a near-fall or intense exertion. Pain is deep and aching, without a radicular distribution. Range of motion is limited, and palpable "taut bands" are found in muscles. Local anesthetics or "spray and stretch" techniques may provide temporary relief, but should be coupled with a rehabilitation program.

Visceral Nociceptive Low Back Pain Disease in abdominal and pelvic organs and the retroperi-

toneal space can refer pain to the back. It characteristically has an episodic, waxing-waning quality, and treatment of the underlying cause is more urgent than pain control.

Neuropathic Low Back Pain Neuropathic pain syndromes present with dysesthetic or shock-like pains, in the distribution of a root or multiple roots. If an individual nerve is compromised in the lateral recess (a space formed by the pedicle, the edge of the vertebral body, and the superior articular facet), intermittent neuropathic pain may radiate down the leg (lateral recess syndrome). Dysesthesias predominate, straight leg raising is negative, and there is no spine tenderness. CT myelography can define the lesion and surgical decompression may be necessary if conservative measures fail.

Spinal Stenosis The hallmark of this disease is neurogenic claudication, in which walking produces bilateral leg pain that is relieved not just by resting but by bending forward. Epidural steroid injections may provide transient relief, but should be limited to fewer than three in any 6-month period, and coupled with an intensive rehabilitation program. Lumbar laminectomy should be reserved for severe, refractory cases because of the risk of spinal instability.

Lumbar Arachnoiditis This is most commonly an iatrogenic illness caused by repeated lumbar myelography or multiple surgeries. Pain is dysesthetic, covers a large, patchy area and is not exacerbated by straight leg raising. Complaints are often more severe than findings.

Adjuvant analgesics, such as the tricyclic antidepressants and anticonvulsants, may be helpful in treating the neuropathic components of the pain. Repeated surgery usually is unrewarding and a rehabilitative program is needed.

Failed Low Back Pain "Failed low back" describes patients who have not responded to standard therapies or to surgery, most commonly the latter. Incorrect patient selection and failure to address psychological factors are probably the most critical issues. The demonstration of a herniated disc by radiographic techniques does not necessarily assure that the disc was the cause of the pain syndrome or that its removal will relieve the pain.

The failed low back syndrome is often associated with psychological issues that appear to contribute to the pain, but arachnoiditis and spinal instability may be factors. Repeated interventions following failed surgery are a less than gratifying undertaking. Surgery should be reserved for those situations in which structural pathology can be defined and no significant psychological dysfunction complicates the picture. A multidisciplinary approach with emphasis on rehabilitation is more appropriate for most of these patients, and management by a single physician is extraordinarily difficult.

Other Neuropathic Pain Syndromes

These syndromes, caused by injury to the central or peripheral nervous system, are characterized by a stereotyped set of symptoms. Patients complain of dysesthetic pains that are burning, tingling, or vise-like, often unlike anything they have experienced in the past. Occasionally there is a stabbing or shooting, shock-like quality. Trigeminal neuralgia (tic douloureux) is usually purely stabbing, diabetic neuropathy purely dysesthetic, and postherpetic neuralgia is a combination.

Neuropathic pain syndromes are best treated with adjuvant medications (described below). Anticonvulsants are most often used for the stabbing pains. In particularly refractory cases, opioids may be given a trial, but should be prescribed by physicians who are well versed in their use and possible side effects.

Psychogenic Pain Syndromes

Purely psychogenic pain (delusional pain) is uncommon. More commonly, there are psychological factors that influence the patient's perception and experience of pain. Therefore, there is little or nothing to be gained by trying to decide whether pain is "real." With the exception of

malingering, all pain is real in that the patient is suffering.

If an accurate psychological diagnosis can be reached, specific therapies can be employed. Antidepressant medications for pain are more efficacious in depressed than in nondepressed patients, and the judicious use of anxiolytics may reduce dysfunction in distraught patients. Under no circumstances should the establishment of a psychiatric diagnosis be used as a confrontational tool, because that will reinforce abnormal illness behavior and destroy the physician-patient relationship. These are the cases in which treatment at a multidisciplinary pain center is very useful.

Analgesic Interventions

Adequate pain management requires appropriate coordination of pharmacologic, psychological, and physical measures. The systemic pharmacologic agents used for the treatment of pain fall into three groups: the nonopioid analgesics (primarily acetaminophen and the nonsteroidal anti-inflammatory drugs), opioid analgesics, and adjuvant drugs (primarily the antidepressants and anticonvulsants).

The characteristics of the nonopioid analgesics are their peripheral site of action, ceiling effect, and side effect profiles that mainly affect the gastrointestinal tract. The ceiling effect implies that there is a level after which further dose escalation will produce intolerable side effects without increased analgesia.

Acetaminophen and Nonsteroidal Anti-inflammatory Drugs

Acetaminophen and the nonsteroidal anti-inflammatory drugs (NSAIDs) are the most commonly used agents. Acetaminophen has an analgesic potency similar to aspirin, but is only minimally anti-inflammatory. It has fewer gastrointestinal side effects than aspirin, and does not affect platelet function. Total daily dosing should be kept below 4 grams to avoid the risk of analgesic nephropathy.

The nonsteroidal anti-inflammatory drugs are most effective in somatic nociceptive pain, presumably because of their antiprostaglandin activity and peripheral site of action. It is usually advisable to start with a loading dose to achieve serum levels quickly. The drug dosage should then be titrated until there are effects or side effects. The ceiling dose varies from drug to drug and from patient to patient, and must be established individually. Furthermore, patients unresponsive to drugs in a given group may be responsive to drugs in a different group (see Table 77-1).

The most appropriate drug is usually the one with which the physician is most familiar. Occasionally, one particular drug has been studied better than others for a given syndrome (indomethacin for chronic paroxysmal hemicrania and naproxen for migraine), but the analgesic profiles appear similar.

The major side effects of the NSAIDs are gastrointestinal, and they increase with the age of the patient and the duration of treatment. Misoprostol (Cytotec) can be used to avoid some of the gastric side effects, but may cause diarrhea, and has abortifacient properties. Renal impairment may occur with prolonged use at high levels. The main central nervous system side effects are dizziness and occasional confusion.

Most of the side effects of the NSAIDs are due to prostaglandin inhibition (as are their effects). A new group of drugs, the Cox-2 inhibitors, are about to be released. These drugs affect a different part of the arachidonic acid cascade, are reported to have similar analgesic efficacy to the older NSAIDs, and are relatively free of the prostaglandin-related side effects.

Opioid Analgesics

Opioid analgesics are the mainstay of treatment of pain associated with cancer. However, fears of addiction and abuse make many physicians reluctant to use opioid analgesics for patients with chronic pain of noncancer origin. In selected patients with refractory pain syndromes, opioids

TABLE 77-1   Nonopioid Analgesics

Group	Dose	Comments
Salicylates		
Aspirin	650 mg	q 4 h dosing; irreversible platelet inhibition; GI side effects
ChMg Trisalicylate (Trilisate)	1500 mg	q 12 h dosing; daily maximum 4 g, no platelet effects
Diflunisal (Dolobid)	500–1000 mg	q 12 h dosing; side effects similar to ibuprofen
Propionic Acids		
Ibuprofen (Motrin, etc.)	400–800 mg	qid dosing; precautions similar to aspirin
Naproxen (Naprosyn)	250–500 mg	bid-tid dosing
Fenoprofen	200–400 mg	Like ibuprofen
Acetic Acids		
Indomethacin (Indocin)	25–50 mg	tid dosing
Sulindac (Clinoril)	200 mg	bid-tid dosing
Fenamates		
Meclofenamate (Meclomen)	50–100 mg	q 4–6 h
Others		
Piroxicam (Feldene)	20–40 mg	daily
Nabumetone (Relafen)	1000–2000 mg	daily-bid
Ketorolac (Toradol)	10–40 mg	q 6 h
Diclofenac (Voltaren)	100–150 mg	bid-tid

can provide relief with an acceptable and manageable risk of side effects.

Constipation is the most common and troublesome side effect of opioid therapy, and requires prophylactic treatment. Stool softeners are not sufficient by themselves and all patients on opioids should also be given a laxative, such as one of the senna compounds. Severe somnolence and respiratory depression are extremely uncommon at therapeutic doses. Tolerance to respiratory depression and somnolence occurs fairly rapidly, while constipation is an enduring side effect.

Tolerance, physical dependence, and addiction are poorly understood and overly emphasized side effects. Tolerance is defined as decreased effectiveness of a drug caused by its prior administration. With analgesics, it is most commonly seen as a need for increasing dose amounts or shortened duration of action. As a practical matter, tolerance is not a significant problem after a stable and effective dose is reached. If rapidly escalating doses are required after stable analgesia is achieved, a search for progression of the underlying lesion or signs of aberrant behavior should be undertaken.

Physical dependence is a state in which withdrawal of the drug or administration of an antagonist precipitates an abstinence syndrome.

Addiction (substance abuse) is an aberrant behavioral syndrome in which there is preoccupation with securing the supply of a drug, an inordinate amount of time spent recovering from the effects of the drug or its withdrawal, medical or social harm caused by the drug, and continued use despite harm. It is very unusual in patients treated appropriately with opioid analgesics for pain.

Some opioids have specific side effects that are peculiar to the drug. Meperidine (Demerol), the most prescribed parenteral opioid analgesic, is metabolized to nor-meperidine, which can cause hyperreflexia, myoclonus, and seizures. The mixed agonist-antagonist narcotic analgesics, such as pentazocine (Talwin) and butorphanol (Stadol) can precipitate withdrawal in physically dependent patients and can have psychotomimetic effects in the elderly.

The important pharmacologic properties of the commonly used narcotic analgesics are shown in Table 77-2. The most significant issues are

TABLE 77-2 Opioid Analgesics

Drug	IM/po[a]	EQUI[b]	Half-Life	Comments
Morphine	3–6	10	3 h	Prototype of agonists; available as sustained-release
Hydromorphone	5	2	3 h	Similar to morphine
Levo-Dromoran	2	2	12–16 h	Long serum half-life; accumulation in elderly
Methadone	2	10	24–36 h	As above
Meperidine	4	75	3 h	Normeperidine toxicity. Not recommended po
Codeine		130[c]	4 h	Used orally for less-severe pain
				Constipation and nausea; ceiling dose
Oxycodone		15[c]	4 h	Used orally, in combination with ASA or APAP

[a]Relative analgesic potency of intramuscular injection compared to the same milligram dose given orally.
[b]Intramuscular dose (in milligrams) that provides approximately the same analgesia as 10 mg of morphine.
[c]Given orally.

differences in side-effect profiles, differences in duration of action, and p o/IM potency. All opioid analgesics are at least twice as potent when administered intramuscularly as when administered orally, due to a first-pass effect in the liver. Therefore, doses must be adjusted when the route is changed.

Opioids vary widely in their serum half-lives, from 2 to 3 h for hydromorphone (Dilaudid) to up to 54 h for methadone (Dolophine). Analgesic efficacy, however, does not directly parallel serum half-life. Even the long serum half-life drugs only provide 4 to 6 h of analgesia.

Controlled-release morphine preparations can provide gradual release of morphine over 8 to 12 h. Immediate release morphine may be used prn for breakthrough pain. There are similar preparations of oxycodone.

Adjuvant Medications

Adjuvant analgesic medications are drugs that were developed for a different purpose, but that have analgesic efficacy in certain clinical situations. Tricyclic antidepressants, anticonvulsants, anxiolytics, lidocaine derivatives (mexiletine), and steroids have all been used in specific pain states, primarily in neuropathic pain.

The tricyclic antidepressants are the most widely used and most adequately studied of the adjuvant medications for pain. While the most

recognized indication is for burning, neuropathic pain, they have also been used successfully in chronic low back pain, headache, and other pain syndromes. Although the analgesic effects are most evident in patients who have a concomitant depression, nondepressed patients also respond. Dosing of the tricyclic should be started at low levels (10 mg at bedtime in the elderly and 25 mg in the young) and titrated up every few days, by similar increments. Analgesic effects appear earlier and at lower doses than the antidepressant effects. Amitriptyline, a tertiary amine tricyclic, is the most widely used, but secondary amine tricyclics, such as nortriptyline and desipramine, are less anticholinergic and also have analgesic efficacy.

The newer, more selectively serotonergic antidepressants (fluoxetine and trazodone) are being studied, but do not seem as promising as the tricyclics, except in depressed patients.

Anticonvulsant drugs such as carbamazepine (Tegretol) and phenytoin (Dilantin) are the drugs of choice for trigeminal neuralgia and, by extrapolation, are used for other lancinating pains. Carbamazepine should be started at 100 mg twice daily, and titrated up to effect, which is usually at 200 mg three to five times a day. Phenytoin, on the other hand, can be started at 300 mg daily. Gabapentin (Neurontin) has demonstrated efficacy in postherpetic neuralgia and diabetic neuropathy, and the side effects are

relatively mild. It should be started at about 100 mg three times a day.

Anxiolytics should be used for the control of anxiety in patients with pain, particularly when anxiety is leading to increased analgesic intake. The evidence for a primary analgesic effect is not as strong as with the antidepressants.

Mexiletine, an orally administered lidocaine derivative, is currently under study for painful diabetic neuropathy and other types of burning, neuropathic pain.

Anesthesiological Procedures

Anesthesiological procedures can be used to provide regional blockade in somatic nociceptive syndromes, or sympathetic blockade in certain neuropathic syndromes. Temporary, short-acting blocks should always be used before any ablative therapy is considered.

Physical Techniques

There are no adequately controlled and blinded studies to demonstrate the efficacy of physical techniques for the treatment of pain. The existing studies on therapies as diverse as transcutaneous electrical nerve stimulation (TENS), massage, acupuncture, trigger-point injections, and traction are generally methodologically flawed. In anecdotal reports, all have been beneficial for a number of pain problems. Physical techniques should be adapted to the specific pain problem, such as trigger-point techniques for myofascial pain, support for articular derangement, and exercises for weakened or immobilized areas.

Psychological Techniques

Anxiety, immobility, and protective postures are often appropriate for acute pain, but may represent abnormal illness behavior in chronic pain. After an adequate psychosocial assessment, one of the main goals in the psychological management of chronic pain is to provide the patient with the tools to recognize and alter those behaviors that perpetuate her suffering. A pain diary is helpful to identify issues that may otherwise go unnoticed or unreported. Simple relaxation techniques can decrease the intensity and frequency of headaches and myofascial pain syndromes. Meetings with family members can identify interpersonal interactions that are perpetuating the pain. Patients who can recognize their role in pain treatment, and who believe that they are in control of their environment, are more likely to benefit from pain rehabilitation.

Some patients simply cannot be managed by an individual practitioner and require referral to a specialized pain center. In general, these are patients with combined psychosocial, medical, and pharmacological problems who need the multidisciplinary approach that can only be provided in a sophisticated center.

References and Selected Readings

1. Portenoy RK, Kanner RM: Definition and Assessment of pain, in Portenoy RK, Kanner RM (eds): *Pain Management: Theory and Practice.* Philadelphia: FA Davis, 1996.
2. Kanner RM: Headache and facial pain, in Portenoy RK, Kanner RM (eds): *Pain Management: Theory and Practice.* Philadelphia: FA Davis, 1996.
3. Kanner RM: Low back pain, in Portenoy RK, Kanner RM (eds): *Pain Management: Theory and Practice.* Philadelphia: FA Davis, 1996.
4. Portenoy RK, Kanner RM: Nonopioid and adjuvant analgesics, in Portenoy RK, Kanner RM (eds): *Pain Management: Theory and Practice.* Philadelphia: FA Davis, 1996.
5. Portenoy RK: Chronic opioid therapy in nonmalignant pain. *J Pain Symptom Manage* 5 (Suppl 1):S46–62, 1990.
6. Fillingim RB, Maixner W, Kincaid S, Silva S: Sex differences in temporal summation but not sensory-discriminative processing of thermal pain. *Pain* 75(1):121–127, 1998.
7. Vallerand AH: Gender differences in pain. *Image J Nurs Sch* 27(3):235–237, 1995.
8. Spierings El, Schroevers M, Honkoop PC, Sorbi M: Presentation of chronic daily headache: A clinical study. *Headache* 39(3):191–196, 1998.

9. Lipton RB, Stewart WF, Simon D: Medical consultation for migraine: Results from the American Migraine Study. *Headache* 38(2):87–96, 1998.

10. Lipton RB, Stewart WF: Migraine headaches: Epidemiology and comorbidity. *Clin Neurosci* 5(1):2–9, 1998.

11. Schwartz BS, Stewart WF, Simon D, Lipton RB: Epidemiology of tension-type headache. *JAMA* 279(5):381–383, 1998.

12. Scharff L, Marcus DA, Turk DC: Headache during pregnancy and in the postpartum: A prospective study. *Headache* 37(4):203–210, 1997.

13. Fettes I: Menstrual migraine: Methods of prevention and control. *Postgrad Med* 101(5):67–70, 73–77, 1997.

14. Scharff L, Marcus DA, Turk DC: Maintenance of effects in the nonmedical treatment of headaches during pregnancy. *Headache* 36(5):285–290, 1996.

15. Holm JE, Lokken C, Myers TC: Migraine and stress: A daily examination of temporal relationships in women migraineurs. *Headache* 37(9):553–558, 1997.

Common Medical Emergencies

Thomas G. Kwiatkowski
William Rennie

T his chapter describes the basic approach to the evaluation and treatment of some common traumatic conditions and medical emergencies encountered in the primary care setting.

Trauma is one of the most common causes of death and disability for all patients under age 40. Over 60 million injuries occur in the United States each year, with half of these injuries requiring some kind of medical treatment. As patients grow older, other medical problems may account for the majority of physician visits, but dealing with trauma of all types still plays a major role in the health care of every sector of the population. Of the 30 million injuries each year that require medical treatment, only 12 percent need in-hospital care; over 20 million patients are cared for in an ambulatory setting. The dramatic statistics of death and severe disability may not apply to these patients, yet real problems with temporary disability, loss of income, and occupational issues are often confronted in the primary care arena. In addition to treating trauma, primary care physicians can play a major role in reducing death and disability from trauma by emphasizing preventive issues.

The primary care clinician should be familiar with the management of patients with selected acute medical emergencies for whom they may need to provide care in a typical practice. Examples include environmental exposures such as smoke inhalation and insect stings, adverse drug reactions, and acute toxic ingestions. A thorough understanding of the approach to patients with these problems is important for establishing early treatment priorities and making appropriate referrals. Acute life-threatening conditions such as anaphylaxis and cardiac arrest can occur in the office setting as well. Understanding the general

approach to these life-threatening conditions will give the primary care physician the necessary skills to provide initial stabilization for these patients while definitive care is being arranged.

Minor Head Trauma

Head trauma is extremely common, with a spectrum of injuries ranging from trivial to life-threatening. More severely injured patients are transported to medical facilities or trauma centers, but patients with minor wounds or those seeking care at a time significantly delayed from the injury itself present to the primary care physician. It is important to assess these patients completely and to recognize the signs of more severe or occult injury.

Pathophysiology

The tightly closed bony calvarium provides good protection for the brain, but its rigidity also contributes to the injury patterns seen with head trauma. These injuries can be focal or diffuse. Focal lesions can occur within the brain itself or, more commonly, in the surrounding layers of tissue. These lesions begin with bleeding in a specific area. Then, as a hematoma forms and expands, intracranial pressure rises. The brain tissue is compressed as a result of this increased pressure giving rise to a continually worsening injury manifested by focal neurologic findings. Subdural, epidural, and parenchymal hematomas as well as cerebral contusions fall into this category. Diffuse injury usually is the result of rapid acceleration/deceleration, with the resultant energy shock being absorbed by the brain. This causes a temporary widespread loss of neurologic function. Brief periods of unconsciousness are seen in the milder forms of diffuse injury, while more severe diffuse axonal injury can produce prolonged coma and eventual death. Concussion is the most common form of diffuse injury.

Clinical Evaluation

In the primary care setting, the head-injured patient should be screened for any potentially serious injuries and treated and followed for the more common minor injuries. Typical patients present with recent minor injuries, often involving scalp lacerations or with previously sustained trauma that for one reason or another was not evaluated near the time of the injury. The clinician should always complete a thorough neurologic exam on all head-injured patients including an assessment of the patient's mental status.

Scalp Injuries

The layers of the scalp can be described by the letters S C A L P. The *skin* is followed by a layer of *connective tissue* containing nerves and vessels. Beneath this is the *aponeurosis,* a tough layer made up of fascia from the frontal and occipital muscles. *Loose areolar tissue* is below this and separates the aponeurosis from the *periosteum* of the skull. It is important to ascertain the depth of scalp injuries before attempting to repair them, because lacerations through the aponeurosis require an additional layer of closure. As with all wounds, thorough cleansing and debridement of foreign material is of primary importance. In addition, scalp wounds should be gently explored with a gloved finger to determine if any bony discontinuity is present. Skull films have been shown to be of little, if any, value in the evaluation of patients with head trauma. If mental status changes or focal findings are present, or if an examining finger detects depression, step-off, or crepitus of the underlying bone, the physician should immediately consider CT scanning and referral of the patient to an emergency care facility.

In cases of uncomplicated lacerations, closure of the aponeurosis can be achieved with interrupted absorbable suture (3-0 or 4-0) and skin closure can be accomplished with 3-0 nylon or other similar material. In general, not using pressure dressings and head wraps allows the patient to observe the wound for any complications,

which can then be reported quickly to the physician for management. A standard set of head-injury patient instructions should be given (Table 78-1) and should be discussed thoroughly with both the patient and a family member.

Loss of Consciousness

Most patients who have sustained a head injury significant enough to cause loss of consciousness are initially evaluated in an emergency department. Encourage patients who ask for telephone advice soon after sustaining such an injury to seek emergency evaluation. Many patients, for whatever reason, seek medical attention hours to days later, and report their previous loss of consciousness at that time. This can create a dilemma for the primary care physician, who must assess the significance of the injury. Obviously, one would like to be able to rule out potentially dangerous lesions quickly and with some measure of assurance.

The most devastating of focal injuries that cause loss of consciousness are subdural hematomas. These result from the tearing of venous structures, and are often associated with lacerations of the brain substance itself. For injuries this severe, a transient loss of consciousness is not unusual. The one exception to this rule is found in the elderly. These patients have longer and more vulnerable bridging veins, due to cerebral atrophy with age; damage to these vessels from a fall may result in subdural bleeding. Loss of consciousness may be only brief, with the slow bleeding giving rise to the so-called chronic subdural. Patients may experience a gradual deterioration of function, including mental status changes, over several days to weeks. It is important to consider this entity when evaluating any post-head trauma patient, particularly one who is elderly. Any changes in mood, clarity of thought, or motor function following such an injury should prompt the clinician to look for a subdural collection with CT scanning.

Epidural hematomas are characterized by rapid, arterial bleeding and do not present as chronic debilitation. They are usually associated with a fracture through the temporal bone, with subsequent disruption of the middle meningeal artery. Loss of consciousness is usual immedi-

TABLE 78-1   Head Injury Instructions

You have sustained a head injury, but do not require hospital admission at this time. Following head injury or concussion, you may develop headache, dizziness, or nausea, or vomit once or twice. If these symptoms continue over 48 h, you should return to the Emergency Department or to your personal physician for reevaluation.

Contact your personal physician or return to the Emergency Department immediately for:
1. Confusion, difficulty waking up, restlessness, or trouble with speech.
2. Persistent vomiting.
3. Continuing or increasing headache.
4. Weakness of arms or legs.
5. Stiff neck with or without a fever.
6. Seizure.
7. Clear or bloody fluid from ears or nose.
8. Fever over 101°F.
9. Pupils of unequal size.

There *must* be a responsible person with you for the next 24 h. You should be awakened every 2 h to check for the above symptoms.

For a headache you may use acetaminophen (Tylenol), 2 pills every 4–6 h, or ibuprofen (Advil), 1–2 pills every 4–6 h with food. Do *not* drink any alcohol. Take only medication prescribed by the doctor. Take only a clear liquid diet for the next 12 h.

ately after the blow to the head, but patients may regain consciousness for variable lengths of time before rapid deterioration takes place. This is the so-called lucid interval seen with epidural hematomas. Patients may present to the primary care physician during this interval, making recognition of this potentially fatal injury extremely important. The first thing for the clinician to realize is that the "lucid interval" is a misnomer. Patients may be able to function, but their mental status is never completely normal. This interval is also short-lived, unlike the pattern seen with chronic subdural hematomas, lasting only minutes to hours. The clinician should keep consideration of this injury at the forefront when any head trauma appears to involve the temporal bone above the ear. Signs of increasing intracranial pressure and compression of brain tissue may occur quickly. Tip-offs are a dilated or sluggishly reactive pupil on the side of the head lesion and muscular weakness on the contralateral side. If the timing of the injury and the clinical findings, especially abnormal mental status, suggest this as a possible injury, immediate neurosurgical and/or CT evaluations are necessary.

The most common injury producing a loss of consciousness is a cerebral concussion. This diffuse injury is always transient, with return to normal mental status occurring within minutes. The patient who has had loss of consciousness for less than 5 min and returns to normal following this can be safely observed at home, provided neurologic and mental status examinations are totally normal and that the patient is in a home environment conducive to observation over the next 24 h. In the immediate postinjury period, a patient who has had more than 5 min loss of consciousness, has an altered mental status, or who has an abnormal neurologic exam requires more indepth evaluation. Patients impaired by drugs or alcohol also fall into this category. Most of the time the additional evaluation consists of CT scanning and/or inpatient observation for 24 h. When patients present more than 24 h after the initial loss of consciousness, there is less concern

for significant occult injury. Usually such an injury will already have become apparent. The obvious exception is the elderly patient who may be harboring a chronic subdural hematoma. The evaluation for delayed presentation of loss of consciousness should consist of a thorough search for focal neurologic findings and a complete mental status exam. Individuals with normal exams may then be given standard head-injury instructions and followed as outpatients (see Table 78-1).

Summary

Head trauma is very common, and those patients with minor injuries are often the ones who present for care to the primary care physician. With proper evaluation and knowledge of the natural history of potentially serious injuries, these patients can be managed appropriately in this setting. Primary care physicians can also play a key role in preventing head and other injuries by emphasizing the importance of bicycle helmets, seat belt use, not driving while intoxicated nor being the passenger of an intoxicated driver, and so forth.

Neck and Spinal Injuries

Although it is unlikely that patients with spinal injuries will come to the primary care physician for evaluation and treatment, opportunities for preventing these injuries should not be overlooked. Injuries to the neck and spine occur most often from motor vehicle accidents and from falls. The elderly population is especially at risk for injury from falls, and "fall reduction" programs are now in place in many geriatric institutions. The primary care physician can help in the education of both patients and families by suggesting simple measures to be taken to guard against potentially debilitating falls. Inside the home, area rugs and small, low stools should be avoided, as they may easily contribute to unsure footing or stumbling. Particular attention should be paid to familiar paths within the house so

that they are kept clear of clutter. Any unsteady patient should have access to a walker or a quadcane to increase their stability. Open stairways should be avoided, and inclined ramps installed whenever possible.

If a family member calls to report that a patient has fallen, the physician should stress the importance of not hastily moving the patient. Any patient not fully awake after a fall should be kept in position until trained professionals (EMS) can move the patient safely. Likewise, any impairment of normal movement in any extremity requires that the patient be moved only after adequate spine immobilization. Fully alert patients who can move all their extremities and have no complaint of neck pain are the only ones who can be moved by untrained personnel. Immobilizing the head and neck can be done in the home, provided it does not interfere with the patient's ability to maintain an open airway. Heavy bags of sugar or flour can be placed on either side of the head to limit lateral motion, and a thick towel roll can be placed under the chin to prevent neck flexion. Most cervical spine injuries are more stable in extension than in flexion, so the motion to guard against is movement of the chin toward the chest.

As with all traumatic injuries, prevention is the key to reduction of morbidity and mortality from spinal injuries. Primary care specialists should take advantage of their ongoing relationships with patients and families to provide education aimed at the reduction of these and other potentially serious injuries.

Fractures and Soft Tissue Injuries

Fractures and soft tissue injuries are seen as the result of motor vehicle accidents, athletic injuries, and falls, and occur in all age groups. Evaluation of patients with complaints related to musculoskeletal trauma can be guided by knowledge of injury patterns and by diligently searching for those suspected injuries. Many simple soft tissue injuries can be treated and followed by the primary care physician, whereas most fractures are best referred to an orthopedist for management. Knowing how to sort out these problems from an unselected patient population is a challenge of primary care. There is an extensive discussion about this in Chap. 76. The problem is addressed here in a more abbreviated fashion, with a focus on a few common injuries.

Pathophysiology

Fractures occur when a direct impact, either applied externally or sustained from a fall, exceeds the ability of the bone to resist deformation. The history of injury as well as the radiographic appearance of the fracture usually gives information about the mechanism of injury. A direct blow to the shaft of a bone is likely to produce a transverse or oblique fracture. When associated with a twisting injury, a spiral fracture may be seen. Crush injuries or compression due to falls may produce fractures that are comminuted as the force of impact dissipates through the bony structure. Small avulsion fragments may be seen in fractures occurring from strain across a joint, with the often stronger ligamentous attachments remaining intact while the bone at the site of attachment gives way. The usual clinical triad seen in all types of fractures is pain, deformity, and disability.

Soft tissue injuries may also be characterized by the same clinical signs of pain and disability, but deformity is usually limited to generalized soft-tissue swelling. These injuries most often involve joints, as with sprains and strains, and the mechanism of injury is more often related to an overstressing of the particular joint than to a direct impact to the area.

Clinical Evaluation

Of primary importance in the evaluation of patients with traumatic injuries is a clear, concise history of the injury. Direct-impact injuries may lead the physician to suspect a fracture more than injuries sustained from stress across a joint. Age

is also an important factor. Older patients with osteopenic bones are less able to tolerate deforming forces than are younger patients with denser bone. The prevalence of osteoporosis in postmenopausal women, for example, is a significant contributor to bony injury. The clinician should maintain a high index of suspicion for fractures in this group of patients, even with seemingly minor mechanisms of injury.

Several general findings on physical exam can help the clinician differentiate between soft tissue injuries and fractures. Localized point tenderness is a hallmark of a fracture, while soft-tissue injuries may exhibit more diffuse pain. Likewise, crepitus in the area of injury suggests fracture. Ecchymosis of overlying tissue is common with fractures and more severe ligamentous injuries. Also, a fracture is less likely if both the patient and the examiner have difficulty in consistently localizing the pain. For lower extremity injuries, the ability to bear weight on the affected limb usually indicates soft-tissue injury.

Two of the most frequently encountered clinical scenarios involving musculoskeletal injury are the patient who has fallen on an outstretched hand, and the patient who has a twisting injury of the lower extremity with an associated fall. The evaluation of patients with these two presenting histories are illustrative of how the physician should approach upper and lower extremity injuries. In general, with ambulatory patients who have sustained injuries from these two mechanisms, the clinician should suspect fractures in the upper extremity and sprains and strains in the lower extremity.

Upper Extremity Injuries

The classic "fall on the outstretched hand" should be thought of as an impact injury. This history alone should raise the clinician's suspicion of a fracture. As the patient lands on the outstretched hand, the force of impact is transmitted through all bony structures from carpus to calvicle. This mechanism can be responsible for these fractures: scaphoid; distal radius; radial head (at the elbow); supracondylar humerus; surgical neck humerus; and clavicle. All these areas should be evaluated in a systematic way in a patient who has sustained such a fall. Soft tissue injuries associated with this mechanism of injury include lunate and perilunate dislocations, posterior elbow dislocation, dislocation of the shoulder, and tears of the rotator cuff.

When examining a patient who has fallen on her outstretched hand, the physician should first note how she is using or protecting the involved extremity. Most of the injuries mentioned above will cause the patient to present with the affected arm at her side, flexed at the elbow and being supported by the opposite arm. The only exception is a posterior elbow dislocation, which may be held away from her body. Keeping in mind all of the possible injuries, the physician should ask the patient which area is most painful, and begin the examination at a site removed from this area; this allows other injuries to be quickly ruled out.

From distal to proximal, the examination should include maneuvers to rule out the many possible fractures that can occur in such a fall. The soft-tissue injuries sustained from this mechanism of injury can be easily assessed at the same time.

Knowing the possible injuries from a classic "fall on the outstretched hand" will help in the quick office evaluation of patients injured by this mechanism. When asked for telephone advice from such patients, the possibility of fracture should be strongly considered. Patients should be instructed to apply ice packs to the affected area, to immobilize the arm in a sling if possible, and to come for examination as soon as possible. The patient describing significant deformity as a result of the injury should be referred to the emergency department. The clinician should anticipate the need for radiographic evaluation until a systematic exam reveals no areas of local pain or deformity and good range of motion of all joints involved.

Lower Extremity Injuries

A twisting of the lower extremity, usually accompanied by a fall, is a commonly described history of injury. Injuries sustained as a result of the twisting force are usually ligamentous and occur across joints. In the ankle, sprains occur from twisting such that the sole of the foot is either directed inward (inversion injuries, which are, by far, the most common) or outward (eversion injuries). Distal fibular and tibial fractures also may be encountered as a result of this mechanism. The knee can sustain the bulk of a twisting force, with both medial and lateral ligaments as well as cartilage at risk for injury. Finally, from the ensuing fall, both hip and pelvic fractures must be considered.

When evaluating patients with a twisting/falling mechanism of injury, the clinician must first note the patient's willingness to bear weight on the affected extremity. Fracture is much less likely if the patient, although in pain, is still ambulatory. Most lower extremity injuries are ligamentous, and evaluation should proceed in a systematic manner, both to confirm the suspected injury and to rule out possible associated skeletal injuries. In general, point tenderness over bony landmarks and crepitus in the involved area are indicative of fractures. Injuries to ligaments may cause point tenderness as well, but the painful area will be away from the nearby bony prominence. Ligamentous sprains are often classified as first-, second-, or third-degree sprains. First-degree sprains are characterized by stretching or microscopic tears to the ligament, and exhibit minimal tenderness and swelling. Second-degree sprains have definite point tenderness over the ligament, and some instabililty of the joint is noted when stressed by the examiner. A partial tear of the ligament has occurred with this degree of injury. Third-degree sprains are severe injuries with marked swelling and tenderness, often of more than one ligament surrounding a joint. The joint is very unstable, and more aggressive immobilization measures and timely orthopedic

involvement are necessary for complete treatment.

Hip and Pelvis Injuries

Younger patients tend to sustain ligamentous injuries from the twisting aspect of a "twisting and falling" injury, but older patients are at risk for fractures from the impact of the fall. This is especially true for fractures at the hip. With severe osteoporosis, however, the history may be a bit different. Instead of the hip fracturing on impact, the patient may describe a "crack" in the hip first, which represents a femoral neck fracture. The fall then occurs subsequent to this, as a result of instability. Patients with this injury cannot ambulate or even get up from the site of the fall. For this reason, it is unlikely that the primary care physician will see patients with this injury in the office or clinic. Telephone advice for family members who call to report the patient's condition should center on keeping the patient warm and relatively immobile until EMS workers can move her safely.

Classically, the patient with a fracture of the hip has a shortened and externally rotated appearance to the involved extremity, and pain in the hip is easily elicited by a simple heel strike.

A patient who gives a similar history of a fall, yet eventually is able to get up and come to the office for evaluation, should arouse suspicion of a pubic ramus fracture of the pelvis. She will have pain on compression of the pelvis and will exhibit no signs of hip involvement. Radiographs will confirm the diagnosis; urinalysis completes the evaluation to ensure that no associated bladder damage occurred. These patients can be treated with analgesia and allowed to bear weight as tolerated. They can be managed by a primary care physician, who should be cognizant of the complications of pain medications and prolonged bedrest. Most importantly, how the home environment may have contributed to the original fall should be explored. Older patients should be given a walker. Area rugs and other potential

obstacles should be removed from frequently traveled paths in the house (e.g., bedroom to bathroom). As always with older patients, a search for medical reasons for a fall should be diligent.

Minor Burns

Of the more than 2 million burns that occur annually in the United States, approximately 95 percent are treated in the outpatient setting. Though most minor burns heal uneventfully with minimal therapy, it is important for the primary care physician to recognize those burns that can be treated in the office, those that should be referred to a burn care specialist, and those that require hospitalization.

Classification

There are several ways to classify burn injuries. The most common form of burn injury is thermal injury, and these wounds are classified according to three major criteria: extent of body surface area (BSA) involved; depth of skin involvement; and anatomic location.

The simplest method to estimate the extent of a burn injury is to use the Rule of Nines. This method divides the adult body surface into 11 areas, each equal to 9 percent or multiples thereof (Fig. 78-1). The genitalia are assigned a value of 1 percent. Burn wounds may involve only the epidermis, or traverse all layers of the skin and involve deeper structures. Accordingly, burns are classified as first-, second-, third-, or fourth-degree.

First-degree burns are the mildest, and involve the epidermis only. Examples include most sunburns, brief exposures to hot liquids, or minor flash burns.

Second-degree burns are also referred to as partial-thickness burns, and are subdivided into superficial and deep partial-thickness injuries. They involve the epidermis and varying amounts of the dermis.

Superficial partial-thickness burns involve the

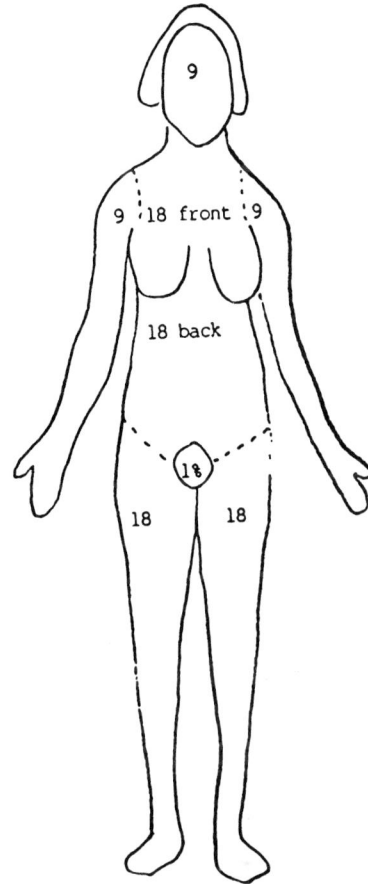

Figure 78-1 Rule of nines.

upper portion of the dermis or papillary dermis. On examination, these burns are red, moist, and blanch with pressure. Frequently there is blister formation, and the wounds are very painful. Deep partial-thickness burns involve the lower portion of the dermis or reticular dermis. On examination, the skin appears mottled or waxy-white. These burns are typically sensitive to pressure, but insensitive to pinprick. They may be very difficult to distinguish from full-thickness injuries.

Third-degree burns are also referred to as full-thickness injuries. They involve destruction of the epidermis, dermis, and a varying amount of the underlying subcutaneous tissues. The epithe-

lial appendages (hair follicles, sweat glands, sebaceous glands) are destroyed, so that epithelial regeneration cannot occur from these sites as with partial-thickness injuries. The burns appear white, black, or cherry-red, and have a dry, leathery texture.

Fourth-degree burns extend deeply beneath the skin surface, involving fascia, muscle, or bone. On the surface they may be difficult to distinguish from third-degree burns.

Accurate assessment of burn depth may not be possible on initial evaluation. Repeated observations over the first 1 to 3 days often are necessary for an accurate assessment.

The American Burn Association divides burn injuries into these categories: major—those requiring referral to a burn center; moderate—those that can be treated in a community hospital environment; minor—those that are amenable to outpatient treatment. Minor burns include partial-thickness burns covering less than 15 percent BSA of an adult or 10 percent BSA of a child; and small full-thickness burns covering less than 2 percent BSA of an adult.

Excluded from this definition are burns to critical areas (eyes, ears, face, hands, feet, perineum), inhalation injuries, electrical burns, and burns in patients who are at higher risk for complications (infants, elderly, patients with chronic diseases).

Treatment

The treatment of minor burn injuries has three primary objectives: relief of pain; prevention of infection and additional trauma; and minimizing scarring and contracture.

Home Management/Phone Advice Patients who sustain minor burn wounds should be instructed to cover the involved area with cool compresses. This not only will provide pain relief but also minimize edema. Any constricting jewelry, especially rings, must be removed to prevent vascular compromise. Home remedies such as butter, grease, or over-the-counter preparations should not be used; they will make physician evaluation more difficult, if not more painful.

In addition, they may promote bacterial growth. Prompt physician evaluation should be encouraged, except for trivial injuries, so that an appropriate treatment plan can be developed and followed.

Office Management The initial evaluation and management of the minor burn injury has these objectives: the safe and rapid removal of devitalized tissue through cleansing and debridement; the preservation of epithelial elements buried by the original injury; the provision of an optimal environment for epithelial regeneration; and the prevention of complications. After a complete history and physical exam, the burn wound should be approached as follows:

1. The extent and depth of the burn injury should be determined.
2. Tetanus prophylaxis should be provided for all minor burn wounds (Table 78-2). Patients without prior tetanus immunization require both tetanus immune globulin (TIG) and tetanus-diphtheria toxoid (Td) at the time of injury. They also require Td booster injections at three weeks and three months after injury to complete the immunization schedule.
3. The wound should be covered with cool compresses for patient comfort.
4. In preparation for cleansing and debridement, the patient should be given appropriate analgesics.
5. In a sterile manner, the burn should be

TABLE 78-2 Tetanus Prophylaxis

History of Tetanus Immunization	Administer Td[a]	Administer TIG[b]
Unknown or less than 3 doses	Yes	Yes
3 or more doses		
>5 years since last dose	Yes	No
<5 years since last dose	No	No

[a]Td dose is 0.5 cc IM.
[b]TIG dose is 250 units IM.

gently cleansed with a wet gauze pad. A mild detergent (e.g., Ivory, Hibiclens) may be utilized. Following cleansing, flush the wound with normal saline.

6. Perform debridement of remaining devitalized tissue with a forceps and scissors.
7. Treatment of blisters is controversial. The following is one recommended approach:
   a. Debride all ruptured blisters initially;
   b. Allow intact blisters to rupture spontaneously, at which point the dead skin should be debrided;
   c. After 5 to 7 days, debride all remaining blisters.

Burn Dressings With the open method, the burn wound is left exposed to air following initial cleansing and debridement. Wash wounds cared for in this manner 2 to 3 times daily. A topical antibacterial agent (e.g., bacitracin) is usually applied after each washing. This technique is especially useful for wounds of the face and neck where the closed method is cumbersome.

With the closed method, the burn wound is covered with one of several types of dressings. This is the most common method of treatment for minor burn injuries and is conducive to management in the ambulatory care setting. The application of dressings is also generally well-accepted by the patient because it provides protection for the injured area and allows her to wear her usual clothing. The following method can be utilized for the application of burn dressings:

1. After cleansing and debridement, cover the burn wound with a topical antibacterial agent, such as silver sulfadiazine, if indicated. Apply it with a sterile tongue blade and spread it to a thickness of 1/8 to 1/16 in.
2. Cover the wound with a nonadherent dressing; this will make subsequent dressing changes easier. If a topical antibacterial agent is used, a dry nonadherent absorbent dressing (e.g., Telfa) is very useful. If a topical antibacterial agent is not used, a petro-latum-based nonadherent dressing (e.g., Xeroform) can be utilized.
3. Cover the dressing with loose sterile gauze. For burns of the hands and feet, each digit should be separately padded to prevent maceration.
4. Wrap the entire dressing in a semielastic mesh bandage (such as Kerlix). It should be tight enough to hold the dressing in place but not so tight that it constricts the area.
5. Change the dressings of burn wounds treated with topical antimicrobial agents (e.g., silver sulfadiazine) twice daily. Take care to wash off all of the topical agent prior to the application of the new dressing. We advise that wounds treated without topical antimicrobial agents have their dressings changed daily, although some physicians believe that these dressings may be left in place for 48 to 72 h. Continue burn dressings until signs of epithelialization are evident on exam.

Follow-up Outpatient burn management requires close patient follow-up. Because patients will need to observe their wounds at home as well as perform dressing changes, complete step-by-step instructions and patient education must be provided (Table 78-3). Instructions must describe wound-cleansing techniques, wound dressing techniques, and signs and symptoms of wound infection.

The severity of the burn injury determines the frequency of patient follow-up. Most burns should be reevaluated within 24 to 48 h to assure that the patient is able to comply with outpatient management, to assess for signs of early infection, and to better appreciate the extent and depth of the burn injury. Most minor burn wounds should fully heal in 2 to 3 weeks.

Special Burns

Chemical and electrical burns are common, and patients may seek treatment for these injuries in the primary care setting. The clinician should be aware of the unique nature of these burns in

TABLE 78-3 Follow-up Care of Burn Wounds

1. Remove old dressing. If it adheres to your skin, soak in room-temperature water and gently remove.
2. Wash the wound gently with a mild soap and water.
3. Pat the wound dry with sterile gauze.
4. Look for signs of infection, including swelling, cloudy or foul-smelling drainage, pain, or increasing redness around the burn injury. If any of these are present, notify your doctor immediately.
5. If antibiotic cream (Silvadene) is prescribed by your doctor, apply it approximately ⅛-in. thick with a sterile tongue blade. If your injury does not require this treatment, proceed to step 6.
6. Apply the nonadherent dressisng in a single layer.

    ___ Telfa   ___ Xeroform

7. Cover generously with sterile gauze pads
8. Wrap with Kerlix just tight enough to hold the dressing in place.

order to provide appropriate initial management and subsequent referral.

Chemical Burns Substances causing injury can be most easily divided into acids and corrosive bases; identifying the nature of the substance is important for the prediction of its potential for serious injury. Regardless of the agent, first aid measures suggested to the patient by telephone or undertaken in the office or clinic should center on copious irrigation with water. A shower or garden hose is a much more effective decontamination device than is typical irrigation with normal saline. It is also of utmost importance to irrigate the injured area early, in the first few minutes following the burn. Telephone advice to chemically burned patients should direct them to accomplish at least 20 min of copious irrigation *before* going to the emergency department or traveling to the clinic or office for further evaluation.

Once adequate decontamination has been accomplished, the management of minor burns from chemical agents is not significantly different from that for thermal burns. Similar dressings and frequent wound checks are required. Indica-

tions for tetanus immunization and antibiotics are the same. However, because these can be devastating injuries and can be deceptive in their extent at first glance, the majority should be referred to a burn care specialist early in the course of treatment.

Electrical Burns Burns due to electricity may occur by three basic mechanisms: conduction injury, arcing, and flash burns. Secondary thermal burns also are seen when the victim's clothing is ignited as a result of the electrical exposure.

The most severe injuries result from the conduction of electricity through the body after contact with a high voltage source. Household current is normally considered low voltage, but common appliances and electronic equipment may include capacitors that store sufficient charge to cause extensive tissue damage. These patients are at risk for extensive tissue loss and complications involving virtually every organ system. Because of the risk of cardiac arrhythmias, patients should be transported from the primary care setting by ambulance in spite of what may appear to be a trivial injury.

Arcing occurs when two objects of different potential, usually a primary source and a "ground," are brought into proximity and a spark occurs between them. The temperature of this electrical arc is approximately 2500°C, and may therefore cause deep partial-thickness or full-thickness thermal burns at the point of skin contact. There is less propensity for deep tissue destruction with burns due to arcing alone than with conduction-type injuries.

Flash burns occur when current passes over the surface of the skin without any concentrated entrance point. These injuries usually result in only superficial partial-thickness burns. Normally one would consider treating this type of burn in a primary care setting; in practice, it often is impossible to determine the exact mechanism of injury causing a given patient's burn. It is therefore very difficult to determine which injuries are indeed minor and which will produce more severe complications. Even with minimal skin involvement and with a low-voltage source caus-

ing the injury, evaluation with ECG and urinary hemoglobin/myoglobin is a minimum requirement before considering the patient a candidate for outpatient management.

Electrical burns provide treatment challenges to even the most seasoned burn care specialists, yet patients sustaining these injuries may first present for treatment in a primary care setting. Any electrical burn must be considered a potentially serious injury and arrangements made for early involvement of qualified specialists.

Prevention

The primary care physician should take advantage of the office or clinic setting to provide a range of preventive medicine services for patients. Simple safety measures can be suggested in patient handouts or waiting room videotapes. Many offices rotate preventive literature by season, with burn-related handouts stressing barbecue safety, sun protection, and avoidance of overheated car radiator caps in summer months and fireplace and space heater safety in the winter. Also, specific patient groups can be targeted with educational information. New mothers, for instance, should be instructed to adjust the thermostat on home water heaters to the lowest possible setting to avoid scalding injuries to infants. Parents with toddlers should turn stovetop pot handles away from the room, and be sure that hot beverages are out of the reach of children. Electric cords should be kept from easy access to toddlers, and unused outlets should be plugged. Patients should be reminded to wear gloves when handling corrosive household chemicals, and all such agents should be kept in a childproof cabinet. Smoke detectors and fire extinguishers should be strongly recommended to all patients by medical professionals. Their importance is obvious and cannot be overemphasized.

One final area of preventive medicine concerning burn injuries involves the recognition and prevention of abuse. Although children and female spouses are most often considered as victims of abuse, there is increasing recognition of abuse of the elderly as well. Small, circular burns suggestive of cigarette burns, well demarcated extremity burns suggestive of immersion scalding, and historical details incompatible with the observed injury are all tip-offs to abuse for all ages. Also suggestive are frequent and variable injuries, delay in seeking medical attention, and known family stress. The astute clinician may help to prevent severe morbidity and possible mortality by recognizing and intervening in these circumstances.

Summary

The majority of burn injuries can be treated in the outpatient setting by primary care physicians. Although most of these injuries heal uneventfully, appropriate evaluation and management are necessary to minimize patient morbidity. Figure 78-2 outlines one approach to the management of these patients. Patient education efforts directed toward the prevention of all types of traumatic injury, including burns, is of major importance in the delivery of comprehensive medical care.

Smoke Inhalation/Carbon Monoxide Poisoning

Smoke inhalation—more specifically, carbon monoxide (CO) poisoning—is the most commonly reported toxicologic cause of death and the most common cause of fire-related mortality. In addition, CO poisoning is seen in many settings that have one thing in common: the improper combustion of carbon-containing materials in a closed space. Noteworthy examples include automobile exhaust in a closed garage, malfunctioning home space heaters (e.g., kerosene heaters), and the use of charcoal briquette barbecues or stoves in poorly ventilated areas. Because CO is a colorless, odorless, and nonirritating gas, accidental exposures are common. Patients often do not recognize the presence of the toxin, which accounts for the many exposure

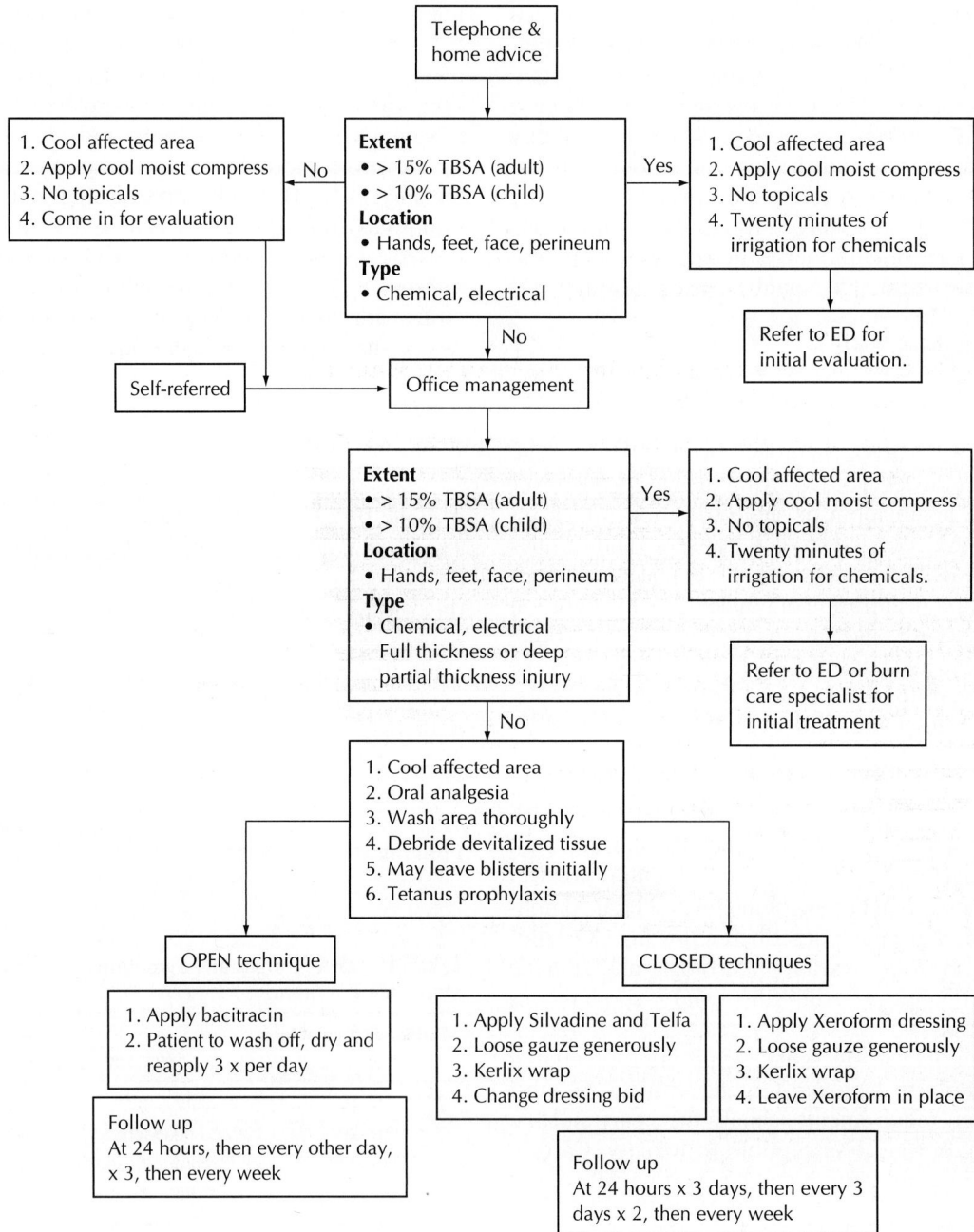

Figure 78-2 Management of minor burns.

deaths that occur during sleep. As is discussed subsequently, the manifestations of CO poisoning are protean and can mimic many other common illnesses. However, owing to the frequency of this exposure, its potential severe morbidity and mortality, and the high likelihood that patients with less severe exposures will present in the outpatient setting, it is important for the primary care practitioner to understand the pathogenesis and management of this syndrome.

Pathophysiology

Carbon monoxide exerts its toxic effects primarily through its combination with hemoglobin, forming carboxyhemoglobin (COHB). The higher the level of COHB in the blood, the lower is the hemoglobin oxygen saturation, which results in decreased oxygen transport and cellular hypoxia. The severity of the exposure depends on the concentration of inhaled CO, the duration of exposure, and various patient factors. Young children and household pets are more susceptible to severe toxicity because of their higher metabolic rates. Older patients with underlying vascular disease are more at risk because they are very sensitive to hypoxia.

Pregnant patients are also at increased risk because CO freely crosses the placenta, and fetal hemoglobin has an even higher affinity for CO than maternal hemoglobin. Several fetal complications have been described following CO exposure, including various neurologic and somatic abnormalities, stillbirth, and spontaneous abortion.

The clinical effects of CO poisoning are related primarily to hypoxia. Organs with the greatest oxygen requirements, chiefly the heart and the brain, are most susceptible to toxicity. Cardiac ischemia and arrhythmias and various neurologic disturbances are common with significant CO exposures.

Patient Evaluation

All patients with smoke inhalation or CO exposure require a thorough evaluation. Patients in high-risk groups should always be referred to the local emergency department for evaluation owing to their higher risk of toxicity. Signs and symptoms of CO poisoning are related to the percentage of COHB in the blood (Table 78-4). However, blood levels do not always reflect maximal COHB levels, making the patient's symptoms a much better predictor of CO toxicity. Because the early symptoms of CO toxicity are nonspecific, many exposures are misdiagnosed as viral syndromes. Clinicians must have a high index of suspicion for this syndrome, especially in the winter months and when cases occur in clusters (e.g., an entire family awakes in the morning with various nonspecific complaints).

Management

The treatment of CO poisoning includes removal of the patient from the source of exposure and therapy directed at the rapid reduction of the patient's COHB level. The half-life of COHB on room air is approximately 4 to 6 h; on 100 percent oxygen, approximately 90 min; and with hyperbaric oxygen therapy, 15 to 20 min.

Patients with minor symptoms (e.g., mild headache that quickly resolves) require no therapy other than removal from the source of exposure. Patients with more severe symptoms should be

TABLE 78-4   Signs and Symptoms of Carbon Monoxide Poisoning

Carboxyhemoglobin Level (%)	Signs and Symptoms
0–10	Usually none
10–20	Mild headache
20–30	Throbbing headache, exertional dyspnea
30–40	Severe headache, impaired sensorium
40–50	Lethargy, confusion, syncope, tachycardia, tachypnea
50–60	Seizures, coma
>60	Cardiorespiratory failure

placed on 100 percent oxygen and treated in the emergency department. A thorough evaluation including COHB level, arterial blood gas, electrocardiogram, and neurologic evaluation is required. The need for hyperbaric oxygen therapy will be determined based on the patient's symptoms, COHB level, age, and pregnancy status.

Prevention

Although CO poisoning in association with smoke inhalation is not always preventable, accidental exposure in the home can be minimized. Patients should be instructed regarding the proper use of space heaters that use fossil fuels. In addition, cooking with similar fuels or charcoal should be done only outside or in well-ventilated areas. Gas kitchen stoves should never be used to supplement home heating. And, most important, automobiles should never be allowed to run in a closed garage.

Drug Overdose/Toxic Ingestions

Drug overdose or poisoning by ingestion represents a leading cause of morbidity and mortality in the United States. For individuals under age 45, it is second only to motor vehicle injuries as a cause of death secondary to accidents. The epidemiology of toxic ingestion falls into two general categories: ingestions by children, which usually are accidental and typically have a good outcome; and ingestions by middle-aged and older adults, where the ingestion usually is intentional and more likely to result in an adverse outcome. Regional poison control centers make poison information and advice readily available to practitioners and the public. In addition, many public information campaigns have resulted in the introduction of childproof containers and improved product labeling that have reduced accidental ingestions. Recent data, however, show that drug overdoses, both accidental and intentional, continue to be common and serious problems in all age groups.

Pathophysiology

Drug ingestions cause a multitude of clinical syndromes depending on the class and amount of drug ingested. The most frequently involved substances include analgesics, cleaning substances, cosmetics, plants, and cough and cold preparations. In contrast, the categories of drugs with the largest numbers of deaths include antidepressants, analgesics, stimulants and street drugs, sedative/hypnotics, and cardiovascular drugs. Several poisoning syndromes or "toxidromes" are well described, and assist the clinician in determining the class or category of agent ingested. Many ingestions are nontoxic and require no specific therapy.

Patient Evaluation

Except for accidental nontoxic ingestions, all drug-overdose patients require a thorough clinical evaluation. In addition, all patients with intentional overdoses, regardless of clinical severity, require a complete psychiatric evaluation. Therefore, the vast majority of drug overdoses in adults require evaluation in an emergency department. Many drugs have delayed clinical manifestations (e.g., acetaminophen, methanol) so that the absence of symptoms shortly after ingestion does not rule out a serious or life-threatening ingestion.

This is especially true for intentional overdoses in depressed middle-aged adults who are less likely to give an accurate history regarding the agent ingested or the circumstances of the ingestion. Subtle, nonspecific clinical signs and symptoms, including minor vital sign abnormalities, change in sensorium, pupillary abnormalities, or change in the temperature or moistness of the skin and mucus membranes may herald the early manifestations of a serious drug ingestion.

Management

Adult patients who have intentionally or accidentally ingested a potentially toxic substance must be brought to the nearest hospital emer-

gency department. Following serious or life-threatening ingestions, they should be taken to the hospital via ambulance. Many communities are served by advanced emergency medical service systems whose emergency medical technicians can deliver both supportive care en route to the hospital and specific therapeutic interventions, including oxygen and airway maintenance, intravenous access, and the administration of specific medications such as glucose and naloxone (Narcan). In certain types of ingestions or exposures, specific therapy should be instituted prior to transporting the patient to the hospital. Included in this category are toxic exposures to the eyes or skin. Copious irrigation with tap water should be instituted immediately while awaiting ambulance transport. The routine use of syrup of ipecac to induce vomiting or the use of neutralizing substances (e.g., milk) is not recommended without professional advice. For potentially serious ingestions and in circumstances where transport to the nearest hospital is prolonged, patients should be instructed to contact their regional poison control center. If syrup of ipecac is recommended, the usual adult dose is 30 ml followed by 16 to 32 oz of water. Ipecac can be purchased in most pharmacies and does not require a prescription.

Prevention

Most poison-prevention activities are directed at accidental poisonings in children. The prevention of intentional ingestions in adults is much more difficult. However, the primary care physician has an important role in poison prevention. The physician's role involves patient education efforts, drug prescribing practices, and identification of patients at risk. Patients must be made aware of drug side effects and toxic symptoms.

As discussed in Chap. 55, it is important for the primary care physician to be alert to signs of depression. The physician should either treat or refer patients when appropriate. In addition, the physician should be prudent in her or his medication-prescribing practices for depressed patients.

This is especially important when giving a patient a prescription for a lethal amount of a potentially toxic medication.

Animal and Human Bites

Dog bites account for the vast majority of bite injuries in the United States, followed by cat bites and, less commonly, human and rodent bites. Most injuries occur in children and young adults, and typically involve the extremities. However, in children, because of their small size, facial injuries are not uncommon. The approach to most bite injuries is similar. However, certain types of bites require more intensive evaluation. For example, human bites—most importantly bites to the hand—often result in deep infections that require hospitalization. The risk of rabies transmission, especially from certain groups of wild animals, also must be determined, as is discussed later in this section.

Pathophysiology

Unlike lacerations, bites tend to produce deeper injuries; as such, they are classified as either puncture wounds or crush injuries. The oral cavity of animals and humans also harbors a multitude of organisms, frequently resulting in polymicrobial infections. Certain organisms are more common in one species than another. For example, *Pasteurella multocida* is very common in cat bites and less common in dog bites. Human bites are usually polymicrobial, including *Staphylococcus aureus, Eikenella corrodens,* Streptococcus species, and several anaerobic organisms.

In addition to infection, more serious bite injuries can result in fractures, tendon damage, lymphangitis, and osteomyelitis. Patient factors, including older age, diabetes mellitus, and immunosuppression, also can result in a greater likelihood of complications.

Patient Evaluation

All patients sustaining bite injuries require a thorough history. The age of the bite must be

determined because it influences subsequent management. It is also important to identify the source of the bite. For dogs and cats, a history of current rabies vaccination must be determined. For other animals, the risk of rabies transmission must be assessed (Table 78-5). Consultation with local public health officials will assist the practitioner in determining the need for rabies vaccination.

The physical exam must be directed at determining the extent and depth of the bite injury. Particular attention must be paid to the detection of associated injuries, including fractures, tendon lacerations, and the involvement of joints, especially of the hand. These complicated injuries are likely to require referral to a specialist.

Management

Because of the risk of infection, all bite wounds require meticulous management. This includes copious irrigation and the removal of devitalized tissue. The decision to close a bite wound is determined by its age, location, and source. Superficial wounds to the face, and to extremities other than the hand, that are evaluated within 8 to 12 h usually can be closed primarily and reevaluated in 24 to 48 h. For facial wounds with potential cosmetic deformities, primary closure may be attempted up to 24 h after the injury, provided that close follow-up can be obtained. Deep puncture wounds and wounds to the hand should be left open because of the high incidence of infection and the inability to cleanse deeper wounds thoroughly. This is especially true for human bite wounds to the hand, where infection rates are

TABLE 78-6 Antimicrobial Prophylaxis of Bite Wounds

Source	Likely Organisms	Antibiotic Choice
Cat	*Pasteurella multocida* S. aureus	Amoxicillin/ clavulanate, cefuroxime, or doxycycline
Dog	Viridans strep *Pasteurella multocida* S. aureus Eikenella Anaerobes	Amoxicillin/ clavulanate, or clindamycin + fluoroquinolone
Human	Viridans strep Staphylococci Corynebacterium Eikenella Anaerobes	Amoxicillin/ clavulanate or cephalexin

very high. If deeper structures (e.g., joints, tendons) are involved in the wound, these patients will require inpatient hospitalization for intravenous antibiotics, immobilization, elevation, and local wound care. All patients should receive tetanus prophylaxis if indicated (see Table 78-2), and all patients who have sustained animal bites should be evaluated regarding the need for anti-rabies prophylaxis.

The need for prophylactic antibiotics varies by the type of wound and its source. Because of the high risk of infection, all cat bites should be treated with antibiotics. Dog bites that are superficial do not require prophylaxis; however, those of the hand and all puncture wounds should be treated. Human bites that involve the hand, or a significant puncture wound elsewhere on the body, should also be treated. The choice of antimicrobial agent(s) is determined by the source of the bite and the most likely pathogenic organism (Table 78-6). All patients treated in the outpatient setting should be reevaluated in 24 to 48 h. High-risk patients (e.g., those with a history of diabetes, immunosuppression, peripheral vascular disease, and the elderly) should be considered for IV antibiotics and, if treated as outpatients, require close monitoring and frequent reevaluation.

TABLE 78-5 Risk of Rabies Transmission

High	Low
Skunks	Squirrels
Raccoons	Rats
Bats	Mice
Foxes	Rabbits
Woodchucks	Chipmunks
	Livestock

Prevention

Most preventive efforts directed at bite wounds involve control of rabies in domestic animals through vaccination programs. The control of rabies in wild animal populations usually is not possible. However, animals known to be common reservoirs of the rabies virus should be avoided and never kept as pets. In addition, houses and surrounding structures should be made "bat proof." If bats are found, they should be removed from the area.

Insect Bites and Stings

Insect bites are a common presenting complaint in the primary care physician's office. Most of these bites are mild and self-limited and require little treatment other than symptomatic medications and local wound care. Hymenoptera stings, in contrast, occasionally can cause serious systemic reactions, including anaphylaxis. They are the most common cause of fatalities in the United States, due to venomous bites or stings. Therefore, it is extremely important to differentiate between local and systemic reactions to insect bites and to identify patients at risk for more serious or fatal systemic reactions in the future. Such patients require referral to a specialist for skin testing and possible immunotherapy, and should be instructed in the use of other preventive measures, including the use of self-administered medications such as EpiPen.

The evaluation and treatment of local and systemic reactions to Hymenoptera stings are reviewed in this section, with special emphasis on the identification of patients at increased risk for the development of life-threatening systemic reactions.

Pathophysiology

The order Hymenoptera consists of three families of insects. Included are honeybees, hornets, yellow jackets, and wasps, found throughout the United States, and fire ants, which are primarily found in the southeast. Reactions to a sting are secondary to various proteins in the venom. The severity of a reaction ranges from no signs or symptoms to life-threatening systemic reactions and anaphylaxis.

The immunologic reaction to the venom appears to occur in two stages. In the first stage, the patient is sensitized through the production of antibodies of the IgE class. This occurs with the first exposure to the venom, i.e., the bite. On reexposure, the second stage of the immunologic reaction may occur. In this stage, the preformed IgE antibodies are activated. Through their interactions with basophils and mast cells, numerous mediators are released, including histamine and leukotrienes. Depending on host factors and the amount of venom absorbed, patients may develop only a local reaction (swelling and erythema) or full-blown anaphylaxis with pulmonary, cardiovascular, and gastrointestinal involvement.

Patient Evaluation

Hymenoptera stings may cause both local and systemic reactions.

Local Reactions Mild local reactions include a small area of redness, swelling, and pain. These symptoms are short-lived and resolve within 24 h. Severe local reactions involve a much larger area with more pronounced symptoms. Occasionally these patients also may complain of nausea and malaise, but there is no evidence of systemic involvement such as generalized urticaria or pruritus.

Systemic Reactions Systemic reactions also may be mild or severe. They usually occur within minutes of the sting. In their mildest form, the patient develops a generalized urticarial or erythematous rash that is usually pruritic. They may also develop gastrointestinal symptoms, including nausea, abdominal cramping, and diarrhea. Severe systemic reactions or anaphylaxis result in life-threatening pulmonary, cardiovascular, and other end organ dysfunction (Table 78-7).

Patients also occasionally develop delayed re-

TABLE 78-7 Anaphylaxis

End Organ	Signs and Symptoms
Skin	Generalized urticaria, erythema, pruritus, swelling
Pulmonary	
Upper Airway	Edema of tongue, larynx, upper airway with stridor, difficulty breathing
Lower Airway	Bronchospasm, coughing, dyspnea
Cardiovascular	Hypotension, arrhythmias, chest pain, shock
Gastrointestinal	Nausea, vomiting, abdominal cramping, diarrhea
Central nervous system	Confusion, altered mental status, occasionally seizures

actions to Hymenoptera stings. These reactions occur from several hours to several days after the bite. Patients typically present with a serum sickness-like reaction, including urticaria or erythema, arthralgias, and joint effusions.

Management

Local Wound Care Patients with a recent sting should have the area of the bite inspected for any remnants of the stinger because it may contain unabsorbed venom. The stinger should be removed with a mild and repetitive scraping motion, best accomplished with a scalpel blade held parallel to the skin. With this method, the stinger can be lifted away from the skin without squeezing the venom sac. The stinger should never be grasped and squeezed with tweezers or a forceps as this could result in increased venom release. Following removal of the stinger, the area should be cleansed with a mild soap or antiseptic.

Local Reactions Local reactions that are mild require little therapy other than wound care. Ice may be applied to the area. If significant pruritus is present, an oral antihistamine, such as diphenhydramine or hydroxyzine, can be prescribed. Severe local reactions with erythema and swell-

ing greater than 5 cm may benefit from more aggressive therapy. Though still somewhat controversial, recent studies suggest a potential additional benefit with the use of an H_2 blocker, such as cimetidine 300 mg qid. With severe swelling and erythema, an oral steroid may be prescribed. A recommended regimen is prednisone, 1 mg/kg per day (maximum 60 mg/day) for 5 days.

Systemic Reactions Patients with a very mild systemic reaction, such as urticaria only, may be treated in the office. Most of these patients respond to an initial 50 mg IM dose of diphenhydramine. If the patient is symptom-free after 1 h, she can be sent home on an oral antihistamine for 1 to 3 days.

All patients discharged from the office after treatment for a systemic reaction should be given appropriate instructions to go to the nearest emergency department if their symptoms recur or worsen. In addition, they should be referred to an allergist for a more thorough evaluation.

Patients with more severe systemic reactions (Table 78-7) require aggressive treatment in the emergency department. If they present in the office setting, emergency services should be called immediately as the reaction can progress rapidly, and can result in airway compromise and cardiac arrest. Initial office management should include subcutaneous epinephrine 0.3 to 0.5 ml (1:1000 solution), diphenhydramine 50 mg IM or IV, and IV fluids and oxygen if available. Epinephrine should be used cautiously in older patients and those with underlying heart disease.

Prevention

It is hard to predict which patients will develop severe systemic reactions or anaphylaxis to subsequent Hymenoptera stings. However, patients who have any type of systemic reaction are at greatest risk. Therefore, all patients who develop systemic reactions should be referred to an allergist for skin testing and possible immunotherapy (desensitization). In addition, an insect sting kit, such as EpiPen, should be prescribed and instructions given for its use. These patients should

avoid activities that place them at risk for subsequent stings.

Cardiopulmonary Arrest

Guidelines for cardiopulmonary resuscitation and emergency cardiac care were updated by the American Heart Association in 1992 and revised in 1997. Included are recommendations for both basic and advanced cardiac life support.

The practicing physician's familiarity with these guidelines depends on the type and extent of the physician's practice. At the minimum, a practicing physician should be familiar with the technique of CPR and preferably be certified in Basic Life Support (BLS) by the American Heart Association or the American Red Cross. Communities with a high level of citizen CPR education have improved survival rates for cardiopulmonary arrest when linked with an appropriate emergency medical service (EMS) system. Physicians should know the basics of CPR not only for the "health" of their communities, but also as a resource for their high-risk patients.

Universal Algorithm for Adults

Table 78-8 summarizes the Universal Algorithm for Adults. An important point to be stressed is

TABLE 78-8 Summary of the Universal Algorithm for Adults

1. Assess responsiveness
2. If unresponsive, activate EMS
3. Call for a defibrillator, if available
4. Assess breathing (open the airway, look, listen, and feel)
5. If not breathing, give two slow breaths
6. Check for a pulse
7. If no pulse, begin CPR
8. Defibrillate if ventricular fibrillation or ventricular tachycardia is present
9. If the rhythm is asystole or pulseless electrical activity, continue CPR while awaiting EMS arrival

No. 2, activation of the local EMS system. For patients in arrest, CPR has a very brief period of effectiveness. If advanced life support (ALS) is not available in 6 to 8 min, the chance of survival is near zero. Therefore, the institution of CPR without ready availability of ALS may not affect survival, although it certainly should be attempted if there is no alternative.

If a defibrillator is available, and the patient is in ventricular tachycardia or ventricular fibrillation, she should be defibrillated as soon as possible. This group of patients has the highest potential for survival following cardiac arrest, provided defibrillation is rapidly available. The initial defibrillator setting should be 200 J. If the patient does not respond, the next defibrillation should be at 300 J and, if unsuccessful, 360 J. These three defibrillations should be given in rapid sequence. If the patient still does not respond, more aggressive intervention is required, including intubation and the administration of medications, including epinephrine 1 mg and lidocaine 100 mg IV push.

For other types of cardiac arrest, such as asystole and pulseless electrical activity (formerly known as electrical-mechanical dissociation), the likelihood of success, even with readily available ALS, is much less than with ventricular fibrillation.

Recommendations for Primary Care Physicians

As previously stated, all practicing physicians should be certified in basic life support, especially those who treat high-risk patients. In addition, if a physician performs high-risk procedures in the office, including anesthesia or intravenous drug administration, adequate preparations for the possibility of cardiopulmonary arrest must be made. At the minimum, oxygen, intravenous access supplies, a defibrillator and basic cardiac arrest medications (e.g., epinephrine, lidocaine, and atropine), should be available. In addition, certification in advanced cardiac life support (ACLS) is desirable. Finally, the primary care

physician must be fully familiar with the local EMS system and how to access it. Should an emergency occur in the office, the ready availability of ALS and transport to the hospital are the only means to maximize patient survival.

Prevention

Primary care physicians must ensure that their high-risk patients and their families are familiar with CPR. This often entails having family members certified in BLS or CPR. These courses are readily available in most communities and usually are sponsored by local hospitals or the American Red Cross. These families must also know how to access the local EMS system to ensure rapid availability of ALS.

Finally, patients must be instructed on how to appropriately respond to high-risk symptoms. If a patient develops chest pain or shortness of breath, she should be told to call her local EMS number and not go to the hospital via private transportation. Patients often do not appreciate the risk they are taking. Ventricular fibrillation arrest may have a good outcome with ready availability of ALS. Primary care physicians must not be reluctant to send a patient who complains of chest pain or other high-risk symptoms from the office to the hospital via ambulance. Even if she is stable, her course is unpredictable, and appropriate monitoring en route to the hospital is mandatory.

References and Selected Readings

1. Committee on Trauma: *Advanced Trauma Life Support, Instructor Manual.* Chicago: American College of Surgeons, 1993.
2. Braen R (ed): *Minor Burns, Evaluation and Treat-ment.* American College of Emergency Physicians. Kansas City, MO: Place Marion Laboratories, 1979.
3. Centers for Disease Control: Compendium of animal rabies control, 1999. *MMWR* 48 (RR-3):1–9, 1999.
4. Crnkovich D, Carlson R: Anaphalyxis: an organized approach to management and prevention. *J Crit Illness* 8:332–346, 1993.
5. Swartz M: *Textbook of Physical Diagnosis: History and Examination,* 3rd ed. Philadelphia: WB Saunders, 1998.
6. Nelson L, Hoffman R: Toxic inhalations, in Rosen P, Barkin R, et al (eds): *Emergency Medicine—Concepts and Clinical Practice,* 4th ed. St. Louis: CV Mosby, 1998, pp 1443–1452.
7. Emergency Cardiac Care Committee and Subcommittees: Guidelines for cardiopulmonary resuscitation and emergency cardiac care. *JAMA* 268:2171–2302, 1992.
8. Goldfrank L, Flomenbaum N, Lewin N, et al: *Goldfrank's Toxicologic Emergencies,* 5th ed. Norwalk, CT: Appleton & Lange, 1994.
9. Hoppensfeld S: *Physical Examination of the Spine and Extremities.* Norwalk, CT: Appleton & Lange, 1976.
10. Kwiatkowski T, Rennie W: The outpatient management of minor burns. *Prim Care* 1(4):173–181, 1994.
11. Litovitz TL, Schitz BF, Holm KC: 1988 Annual report of the American Association of Poison Control Centers national data collection system. *J Emerg Med* 7(5):495–545, 1989.
12. Roberts J, Hedges J: *Clinical Procedures in Emergency Medicine,* 3d ed. Philadelphia: WB Saunders, 1998.
13. Rockwood CA, Green EP: *Fractures in Adults,* 4th ed. Philadelphia: JB Lippincott, 1996.
14. Rosen P, Barkin R, et al: *Emergency Medicine—Concepts and Clinical Practice,* 4th ed. St. Louis: CV Mosby, 1998.
15. Simon R, Koenigsknecht S: *Emergency Orthopedics: The Extremities.* Norwalk, CT: Appleton & Lange, 1995.
16. Sinkinson C, French R, Graft D, McLean D: Individualizing therapy for Hymenoptera stings. *Emerg Med Rep* 11(14):134–142, 1990.
17. Subcommittee on Advanced Cardiac Life Support: *Advanced Cardiac Life Support Manual.* Dallas, TX: American Heart Association, 1997.

The Role of the Physiatrist in Women's Health

Avital Fast
Audrey F. Sofair

APPROACH TO PATIENT ASSESSMENT AND TREATMENT

APPROACH TO CLINICAL PROBLEMS IN THE PATIENT WITH MULTIPLE SCLEROSIS
Spasticity • Weakness and Fatigue • Ataxia, Dysmetria, and Balance Problems • Bladder Dysfunction • Gastrointestinal Dysfunction • Pregnancy Care • Skin Care • Cognitive and Affective Problems

Occasionally primary care physicians have patients who will benefit from the input of the physiatrist and the physical medicine and rehabilitation (PM&R) team. It is, therefore, important that primary care physicians have an understanding of this discipline and its range.

This chapter provides an overview of the specialty. It then focuses on what the PM&R team can do to improve the well-being of patients by using the example of multiple sclerosis, a common disabling problem in women.

Approach to Patient Assessment and Treatment

Physical medicine and rehabilitation is an interdisciplinary specialty dealing with the diagnosis and management of patients with neurological and musculoskeletal conditions. Added to the patient's regular history and physical examination is a special emphasis on functional capacity. The physician questions the patient about mundane daily activities such as grooming, bathing, and dressing. The patient's mobility level is documented. Transfer and ambulation capacities are noted, and the need for assistive devices such as canes or crutches is determined.

The musculoskeletal examination includes range of motion assessment and detailed manual muscle testing. This portion of the examination requires an in-depth knowledge of the peripheral nervous system and the origins and insertions of the skeletal muscles. The finding of mild contractures, for example, helps provide an explanation of the patient's functional limitations, and a therapeutic program can then be tailored to address these limitations. Causes of limited range of motion include skeletal abnormalities (e.g., arthritis, heterotopic ossification or shortening of the soft tissues secondary to prolonged immobilization). In arthritis, the limited range may be permanent and not amenable to therapy; knowledge of special adaptive equipment is necessary.

A patient with deforming arthritis that leads to permanent contractures of the hands may have difficulty opening jars and bottles. Because the range of motion is not expected to increase in these circumstances, the patient should be provided with tools that increase her mechanical efficiency and enable her to preserve functional independence. In the case of soft tissue shorten-

ing, therapeutic efforts are directed toward reversing contractures and increasing range of motion. This is achieved via range of motion exercises and dynamic splinting. Prolonged stretching is most effective in achieving increased range. Prolonged stretching can be provided by the therapist or through spring-loaded splints. Semiquantitative grading of muscle strength also helps determine the patient's rehabilitative needs. Manual muscle scoring is used as depicted in Table 79-1.

This assessment method, albeit only semiquantitative, can be performed at the bedside, and does not require any special equipment. When assessing strength consider gender, body habitus, profession, and side dominance. Delineation of muscular weakness can aid in establishing the correct diagnosis, and may help develop the right therapeutic prescription. Maintaining strength, range of motion, and balance is of paramount importance, as it helps maintain higher levels of function and independence in activities of daily living.[11] Ask the patient to transfer and ambulate. Her balance and safety are assessed while she is standing and moving. Thus, an accurate evaluation of the patient's functional capacity and deficiencies are made.

Arrange a home visit to evaluate the adequacy of the patient's living quarters and to determine whether architectural changes are needed. A patient who is wheelchair-dependent may have to move if her apartment cannot be modified to accommodate a wheelchair. This would be extremely stressful for the patient and, often, financially unfeasible. Every effort, therefore, should be made to modify the patient's home.

At the conclusion of the physical examination, a prescription that is tailored specifically to the patient's needs is developed. The prescription may include instruction for the physical therapist, occupational therapist, and speech therapist.

The physiatrist, a board-certified specialist in PM&R, leads a team of professionals that includes physical therapists, occupational therapists, speech pathologists, psychologists, vocational counselors, social workers, and nurses. The team's primary assignment is to help the patient in the recovery process by making the adjustments necessary to maximize her level of function.

The essence of the rehabilitation process is to limit or abolish impairment (functional deficits), disability (reduction of ability to perform functional tasks such as walking, dressing), and handicap (reduction of ability to perform vocational or social tasks) as defined by the World Health Organization (Table 79-2).

The physiatric approach encompasses an interdisciplinary and holistic approach that evaluates the patient, and is not limited to specific body systems or specific disease entities. The patient's medical diagnosis does not necessarily predict the presence or absence of disability. Even when

Table 79-1 Manual Muscle Scoring

Zero—no voluntary contraction seen
Trace—some contraction of muscle is seen, but the muscle cannot produce any joint movement
Poor—the muscle can move the joint through its full range of motion when gravity is eliminated
Fair—the muscle can move the joint at full range of motion against gravity
Good—the joint can be moved against gravity and some resistance
Normal—normal strength

Table 79-2 World Health Organization Definitions

Impairment: Any loss or abnormality of psychological, physiological, or anatomical structure or function. (Decreased range of motion due to a contracture is an example of an impairment.)
Disability: Any restriction or lack resulting from an impairment of the ability to perform an activity in the manner or within the range considered normal. (Inability to perform the activities of daily living, i.e., dressing, undressing, bathing, cooking, due to the presence of contracture is an example of a disability.)
Handicap: A disadvantage for a given individual, resulting from an impairment or a disability, that limits or prevents the fulfillment of a role that is normal for that individual. (Any social or professional limitations due to dependency in activities of daily living is an example of a handicap.)

an impairment is permanent and cannot be modified (e.g., lower extremity amputation), disability and handicap may be minimized or eliminated altogether. This mandates disability assessment and evaluation that is based on the patient's functional capacity.

Special tools have been devised that enable simple and quick functional scoring. A well-known, standardized, and accepted scale is the Functional Independence Measure (FIM). Unlike other more specific scales, the FIM is applicable to many types of disabilities, and is not diagnosis or disability specific. The FIM score is rather simple to calculate, and requires limited time. Self-care activities, sphincter control, transferring abilities, locomotion status, communication, and social cognition are amongst the categories that are evaluated and scored. This enables the rehabilitation team to monitor the patient's progress and record it in a quantitative fashion.[5,9] The Barthel Index, another well accepted functional rating system, quantifies function by scoring 10 common activities. The scoring system has proved reliable, and allows rather accurate rehabilitation outcome measurement.

Approach to Clinical Problems in the Patient with Multiple Sclerosis

The following clinical example demonstrates the common problems that are encountered in patients with multiple sclerosis (MS) and emphasizes the role that the physiatrist and the PM&R team can play in helping such a patient. We chose MS as an example because it is a chronic disease that affects young women, involves multiple systems, and is the third most common cause of disabling illness.

Ms. S, a right-handed 36-year-old woman with a history of multiple sclerosis, presented to the office with difficulties in ambulation, urinary dribbling, a sensation of incomplete emptying of the bladder on voiding, and some functional deficits. She was diagnosed with MS 10 years earlier, and had various symptoms that have spontaneously resolved. She is married, has two children and stopped working after the birth of her second child. She has not been under any structured follow-up and has not been performing any therapeutic exercises. She is independent in most self-care activities, but has difficulties with overhead activities such as washing and brushing her hair. Her husband has to help her with buttons, and she has increasing difficulties putting her left upper-extremity through her shirt sleeve because of decreased range of motion and tightness. The patient admits to being depressed and feeling hopeless.

The abnormal findings on physical examination were mild dysarthric speech; mild weakness to good on manual muscle testing of all the extremities; and inability to walk on heels and toes. In addition, she had decreased sensation to pinprick in all limbs, general hyperreflexia, and bilateral unsustained ankle clonus accompanied with extensor plantar responses. Range of motion testing revealed a mild left elbow flexion contracture of 10 degrees, shortening of the finger flexors, and limited range of movements in the shoulder joints. Both ankles had 15 degrees of plantar flexion contractures. Hypertonicity was noted throughout. The spasticity was more noted in the elbow and finger flexors. The gait was narrow-based, with decreased heel strike. Occasional forefoot dragging was noted. The patient required assistance in transferring from supine to sit to stand. Urinary incontinence was also noted.

Multiple sclerosis is the third most common cause of severe disability, after trauma and rheumatologic diseases. It predominantly affects women in the most productive years of life[14], primarily young women in the second through fourth decades. It has an unpredictable course, and may leave many patients impaired or disabled. The disease affects the central nervous system and is characterized by areas of demyelination around axons, thus impeding electrical conduction within the central nervous system. As a result, many systems may be affected, leading to various cognitive, affective, and functional deficits. In the following paragraphs, we discuss

problems that MS patients frequently encounter and what the PM&R team can do to help patients with these problems. The medical management of multiple sclerosis is omitted from this discussion, as this is usually within the realm of neurologists.

Spasticity

Spasticity results from increased, uncontrolled muscle tone. It presents as increased muscle resistance to stretching, especially rapid elongation of muscles. It is accompanied by increased reflexes, clonus, and extensor plantar responses. Spasticity leads to slowing of voluntary movements, disturbed motor control, abnormal gait pattern, contractures, and impaired micturition. Very mild spasticity may be advantageous as it prevents muscle atrophy and may enhance strength in the lower extremities. In most cases, however, spasticity is an impediment to normal function. The gait may be scissoring (due to increased tone in the thigh adductors), and foot drop and toe dragging may develop due to shortening of the gastrocnemius muscles. The ensuing gait abnormalities increase the energy consumption of ambulation, and contribute to the general feeling of fatigue.

The physiatric approach to spasticity includes range-of-motion exercises of all joints, with special emphasis on the joints that are affected by spasticity. Stretching exercises are prescribed. Passive stretching (performed by the therapist) is performed at least twice a week, and the patient is instructed to perform stretching exercises on a daily basis. Several techniques may be utilized to achieve increased range of motion: deep heating (ultrasound) may be applied over shortened tendons prior to stretching, and ice massage may be administered over spastic muscles to reduce the amount of resistance. The antagonistic muscles can be facilitated and exercised to further decrease the tone in the spastic muscles.

In the patient described above, and in any MS patient with similar findings, the finger flexors, elbow flexors, and plantar flexors of the feet should be aggressively stretched. The upper limb may be immersed in ice water for a few minutes to decrease spasticity prior to stretching. Instruct the patient to assume positions that may help decrease the contractures. For knee tightness, instruct the patient to lie on her stomach with her feet protruding beyond the end of the bed so that gravity may help achieve full extension (small weights, e.g., sand bags of 2 to 4 lb, can be applied over the ankles).

Spring-loaded dynamic splints can be administered. These splints provide continuous forces over large skin surface areas, and are usually well tolerated by the patient. In patients with moderate spasticity, pharmacological intervention may be necessary. Baclofen (Lioresal), dantrolene sodium (Dantrium), or diazepam (Valium) are among the drugs most frequently used.[6] These medications have side effects and require some expertise.

In patients with severe spasticity that does not respond well to medications, stretching, and splinting, consider invasive procedures. The motor branch output of a peripheral nerve that is responsible for the spastic muscles can be decreased. In patients with adductor spasticity causing difficulties in ambulation and problems in hygiene maintenance, the obturator nerve can be injected and blocked via injections of 5% phenol. The injections require identification of the nerve location via electrical stimulation. The process is time-consuming, and requires special equipment and expertise. Phenol injections can be very effective in spasticity management. The effect is temporary, however, and may last for only a few months. An alternative approach is to induce muscular relaxation via motor-point injections with botulinum toxin (Botox) injections. Intrathecal baclofen administration may be helpful in selected patients. Once spasticity reduction is achieved, aggressive stretching should be maintained. At times, splints and orthoses are prescribed to maintain the increased range.

A common indication for orthotic use in MS

is foot drop. The modern ankle-foot orthotic is made of plastics and laminates, and is relatively light. The brace maintains the foot at a neutral position, prevents the foot from slapping during the stance phase, and facilitates clearance during the swing phase. These braces are cosmetically acceptable, and improve function and reduce energy consumption during ambulation.

Weakness and Fatigue

Our patient had diffuse muscle weakness that compromised her ability to function, slowed her down, and increased her fatigue. Indeed, weakness is a common complaint in MS patients. It usually involves the lower extremities, and presents as spastic paraparesis. Another common pattern affects the ipsilateral arm and leg. Respiratory muscle weakness due to abnormalities in the respiratory pathways also occurs in many patients and interferes with function. Weakness is due to upper motor-neuron lesions, demyelination, and disuse atrophy. The distribution of weakness has to do with the location of plaques. The pathophysiologic mechanisms responsible for fatigue are complex. Spasticity, demyelination, increased core temperature, moderate to intense exercises, and depression may all be related to the increased sense of fatigue.[7] Respiratory muscle weakness can also enhance fatigue, which may become overwhelming and exhausting.

The physiatric approach for fatigue reduction includes patient education, emphasizing attention to environmental set-up (e.g., making sure that the house, car, and workplace are all properly air conditioned). Bouts of fever should be aggressively managed, and the patient should remain out of the bed as much as possible during her illness. The patient is instructed to take short breaks during the day, and an afternoon nap followed by cold showers.

In addition, general conditioning exercises, such as swimming in a pool with cool water, may be prescribed to increase strength. The patient is instructed not to exercise to the point of fatigue. Short bouts of exercises are recommended. The swimming pool is the environment of choice for exercise. It provides mild resistance to a large number of muscles throughout the body and allows proper heat dissipation, thus preventing hyperthermia. In addition, the patient is instructed to slowly increase the level of resistive exercises to the involved extremities. Realistic goals should be set, with proper moral support and encouragement. Amantadine (Symmetrel) is frequently used to combat fatigue. The dose should be 100 mg twice a day, not to exceed 300 mg per day. Up to 50 percent of patients report some improvement with this medication.[4]

Antidepressants may be effective in many patients, because depression may be a cause of fatigue. In patients with mild-to-moderate depression, an herbal preparation such as *Hypericum perforatum* (St. John's Wort) is sometimes tried. It is generally considered a safe preparation, and has been shown to be efficacious. It works by regulating the serotonin system. This herb is very popular in Europe, and has been in use for decades.[3]

Promoting physical activity to patients with MS is a challenge. The fears of the patient, as well as the family, should be overcome. Both should be educated and made to understand the perils of inactivity and deconditioning. The natural tendency of family members to do everything for the patient should be dealt with. The benefits of staying active and independent should be stressed. The patient is referred to an occupational therapist who instructs her in energy preservation techniques. In patients with proximal lower extremity weakness, independent transfers may be preserved by providing the patient with high seating arrangements and increasing her bed's height. Assistive devices, such as canes and walkers, may help preserve independent ambulation. In debilitated patients, an electric scooter for outdoor ambulation may be required.

For upper extremity weakness, adaptive equipment is provided that facilitates functional independence. In addition, the patient is in-

structed in biomechanical principles and instructed on how to compensate for weakened muscles.

Ataxia, Dysmetria, and Balance Problems

Lesions located in the cerebellum, brain stem, spinal cord, and the connecting tracts may lead to ataxia and balance problems in many patients. Ataxic gait is very difficult to manage, and may lead to falls. The physiatric approach to balance problems includes exercises and assistive devices. Repetitive challenging of the patient's balance system leads to improvement. Static (sitting) as well as dynamic (transferring, walking) balance are assessed. To increase her confidence level, the patient practices getting up off the floor. Those with severe ataxia may be confined to a wheelchair. For indoor ambulation and transfers, they may be provided with a walker or with a weighted supermarket cart if their ataxia is severe. We find the heavy cart an excellent mobility device, as it provides stability and helps prevent sudden falls.

The physiatrist and therapists may conduct a home visit and recommend grab bars in critical locations, such as bathroom and toilet, to increase safety during transfers and ambulation. In bathrooms that lack a shower stall, a plastic bench may be provided to facilitate and increase the safety of bath transfers. Raising the toilet seat helps, especially in patients with proximal lower extremity weakness.

In patients with upper extremity ataxia and dysmetria, small weights in the form of wrist bands may decrease the oscillations of the forearm and hand when the patient is moving, and thus increase precision handling and function. Providing tools (such as kitchen accessories) with specially designed large handles may help compensate for weakness and dysmetria.

Incoordination of the palatal and labial muscles may lead to dysarthria in 20 to 25 percent of multiple sclerosis patients. This problem may present as slurred speech, hypernasal speech, or hypophonation. "Scanning speech," a speech pattern in which there is equal emphasis on each syllable, is not uncommon. Dysarthria may be very stressful to the MS patient, as it may have social and professional impact. Speech therapy may help ameliorate the problem. Treatment methods may include slowing the rate of speech so that the tongue can compensate for loss of control. In addition, exercising the muscles involved in speech, including the tongue, may be of benefit. In patients with severe dysarthria, communication boards are an option. From these boards, the patient may select words, phrases, pictures, or letters.

Bladder Dysfunction

Urinary complaints are quite common in MS patients. Fifty to 80 percent of MS patients complain of urinary symptoms during the course of their disease.[15] The majority of MS patients who remain asymptomatic as far as the urinary tract is concerned may have abnormal urodynamic studies. The most frequent complaints are concerned with urinary urgency and incontinence. These are especially bothersome in patients with decreased mobility and adductor spasticity. Bladder involvement is caused mainly by demyelination in the midbrain region where the micturition reflex is located, or of the lateral and posterior cervical spinal tracts that are the spinal pathways involved with normal bladder coordination and voiding.[1] Demyelination in these tracts leads to an unmasking of the sacral micturition center and results in a hypertonic bladder. At times the external sphincter becomes spastic, and may impede urination. Patients with detrussor-sphincter dyssynergy may be more difficult to manage and may be best treated with intermittent catheterization. Anticholinergic drugs may increase bladder capacity and compliance, but may lead to increased postvoid residuals. A hypotonic bladder results when there is involvement of the sacral center. Because multiple sclerosis may wax and wane or even remit spontaneously, urosurgical interventions are best

performed when the neurological status stabilizes.

Urologic or urogynecologic consultation should be obtained at an early stage. Management should be based on urodynamic studies and postvoiding residual urine determination. Remember, however, that there may be no significant correlation between urinary symptoms and urodynamic studies.[8,10] Whereas in the past, catheterization was required to determine postvoiding residuals, ultrasonic equipment now facilitates this task and allows noninvasive measurement. A normally innervated bladder does not have postvoid residuals. The goal in MS patients is to keep the residual urine volume well below 100 ml.

The mainstay of conservative management includes patient education, controlled fluid consumption, and scheduled voiding. The patient is taught to stop drinking 2 to 3 h before retiring for the night and to empty the bladder, regardless of the subjective need to void, prior to falling asleep. This may prevent nocturnal incontinence and lead to normal urine volume the following morning. Intermittent catheterization, external abdominal compression (Crede maneuver), and pharmacological interventions may be required in moderate to severe cases, and are decided upon based on the bladder status as portrayed in the urodynamic studies. Intermittent catheterization should be performed using an aseptic technique. This is effective and is proven to reduce the incidence of urinary infections.

The main goal of therapy is to preserve kidney function and interfere as little as possible with the patient's social and professional life. In patients managed with immunosuppressive medications, an effort should be made to identify urinary tract infections at an early stage and to treat them aggressively with the appropriate antibiotic medications.

Gastrointestinal Dysfunction

Swallowing disorders are not uncommon in MS. Less than 20 percent of patients experience dysphagia. Brain stem and corticobulbar involvement may affect the nuclei of the V, VII, IX, X, and XII nerves. As a result, weakness and sensory loss of the pharynx, larynx, and respiratory muscles may occur. This constellation of symptoms disrupts the timing and the sequence of swallowing. Food may stick in the throat and lead to choking and coughing during meals. Aspiration of liquids or solid food may lead to pneumonia, which can be life-threatening.

The physiatrist may elect to perform barium swallow testing (videofluoroscopy) to determine the etiology of the problem. The speech therapist may feed the patient barium-containing meals of various textures to help determine which food, if any, the patient can be fed. Swallowing techniques that improve swallow control are implemented. "Chin-tuck" exercises, which widen the vallecular space to allow food pooling without spilling over to the glottis, are demonstrated. This technique also provides time for the patient to gain control of the food in the mouth before moving it further. If the patient has a weak side, head tilts and turning may help by shifting the food to the stronger side, and by increasing the mechanical advantage. If safe swallowing cannot be achieved, feeding gastrostomy is advocated.

Expiratory muscle training should be considered in patients with aspiration pneumonia. These muscles are important for generating an effective cough, and thus may help prevent aspirations.[16] Some patients develop a neurogenic bowel and sphincter during their illness. These commonly result in decreased gastrointestinal motility and constipation. Fecal incontinence is relatively infrequent. The patient is instructed to consume adequate amounts of fluid and to increase the amount of fiber in her diet. Frequently, fiber supplementation and bulk-forming agents have to be utilized. Cascara sagrada or senna alexandrina are herbal products that may be effective in patients with constipation that does not respond to nutritional manipulations. Suppositories and, at times, Ther-Evac (mini-enemas) have to be added.

Pregnancy Care

Many MS patients, especially in the childbearing years, inquire about fertility and pregnancy. MS does not lead to infertility nor does it usually affect the course of pregnancy. Pregnancy, however, may affect the course of MS. It has been shown that during pregnancy there is usually a decrease in the incidence of MS relapses.[13] It is theorized that there is a state of relative immunosuppression during pregnancy in order to "tolerate" the immunologically foreign fetus. This state may explain the lower incidence of relapses during that period. Following delivery, however, between 20 and 40 percent of MS patients may expect to sustain a relapse or worsening of the disease.[2] In the postpartum period, a stressful time even for healthy women and a period that may lead to clinical depression, the MS patient should be monitored closely by an experienced neurologist and physiatrist.

Skin Care

Skin breakdown may become a major health problem in MS patients. Decubiti may lead to significant morbidity and, at times, mortality. Wheelchair-dependent patients and incontinent patients are at high risk to develop decubiti. Pressure sores develop due to prolonged immobility, which results in constant pressure that exceeds the capillary pressure. In addition, shearing forces that may develop when the patient slides forward in the chair or when she is sitting in bed also contribute to skin breakdown. Urinary or fecal incontinence also contributes to pressure-sore formation. Patient education (close monitoring of the skin combined with frequently performed "push-ups" in the wheelchair and weight shifting) and protective seating arrangements may be required. The patient or her family member should be trained to inspect the skin on a daily basis. Meticulous hygiene must be enforced. If skin breakdown occurs, the patient is instructed to avoid weight-bearing on the involved areas until the erythema disappears or the skin recovers.

Cognitive and Affective Problems

Cognitive dysfunction in MS is often not apparent without specific testing. The patterns of dysfunction that have been defined seem to implicate frontal lobe disease. The cognitive problems may not be apparent in the early course of the disease, but may be noticeable on formal psychometric testing. In later stages of the disease, cognitive and affective difficulties are more apparent, and may occur in up to 25 percent of the patients. Among the more common symptoms are attention, concentration, and memory deficits and slowing of information processing and executive functions, such as focusing, poor insight, and deficient problem-solving capacity. These changes may be accompanied by depression or euphoria. The latter symptoms may be very disruptive, as they lead to disease denial and intellectual malfunctions.

Counseling by cognitive rehabilitation therapists and social workers may be advisable. The burden of financial affairs should be removed if the patient cannot handle it. The patient's strategies in the kitchen should be evaluated and the patient should be counseled. A practical technique is the development of a memory book that is tailored to the patient's life. Simple activities should be practiced and the patient alerted to the correct sequencing. Family counseling about the personality changes should be conducted. Vocational counseling, when appropriate, may help keep the patient employed. At the appropriate time, application for disability assistance may help keep the family financially afloat.

Summary

We have described the role of the physiatrist and the rehabilitation team for patients with MS to provide an example of how important this team can be in improving the well-being of patients. It is clear that the best results in the management

of these complex patients can be achieved only with a well-coordinated team approach.

References and Selected Readings

1. Andrews KL, Husmann DA: Bladder dysfunction and management in multiple sclerosis. *Mayo Clin Proc* 72:1176–1183, 1997.
2. Birk K, Rudick R: Pregnancy and multiple sclerosis. *Arch Neurol* 43:719–726, 1986.
3. Britell CW: MS and cognitive function. *MSQR* 17:1–11, 1998.
4. Cohn RA, Fisher M: Amantadine treatment of fatigue associated with multiple sclerosis. *Arch Neurol* 46:667–680, 1989.
5. Deutsch A, Braun S, Granger CV: The functional independence measure (FIM instrument). *J Rehab Outcome Measurement* 1:67–71, 1997.
6. Erickson RP, Lie MR, Wineinger MA: Rehabilitation in multiple sclerosis. *Mayo Clin Proc* 64:818–828, 1989.
7. Freal JE, Kraft GH, Coryell JK: Symptomatic fatigue in multiple sclerosis. *Arch Phys Med Rehabil* 65:135–138, 1984.
8. Gallien P, Robineau S, Nicolas B, Le Bot MP, Brissot R, Verin M: Vesicourethral dysfunction and urodynamic findings in multiple sclerosis. A study of 149 patients. *Arch Phys Med Rehabil* 79:255–257, 1998.
9. Granger CV, Hamilton BB, Sherwin FS: *Guide for use of the Uniform Data Set for Medical Rehabilitation, Buffalo, 1986: Uniform Data System for Medical Rehabilitation.*
10. Hinson JL, Boone TB: Urodynamics and multiple sclerosis. *Urol Clin North Am* 23:475–481, 1996.
11. Judge JO, Schechtman K, Cress E, FICSIT group: The relationship between physical performance measures and independence in instrumental activities of daily living. *J Geriatr Soc* 44:1332–1341, 1996.
12. Kendall FP, Kendall H, McCreary E, Provance PG: Muscles: *Testing and Function,* 4th edition. Baltimore: Williams & Wilkins, 1993.
13. Korn-Lubetzki I, Kahana E, Cooper G: Activity of multiple sclerosis during pregnancy and puerperium. *Ann Neurol* 220–231, 1984.
14. Scheinberg L, Smith CR: Rehabilitation of patients with multiple sclerosis. *Neurol Clin* 5:585–600, 1987.
15. Shapiro RT: Symptom management in multiple sclerosis. *Ann Neurol* 36(suppl):S123–S129, 1996.
16. Smeltzer SC, Lavietes MH, Cook SD: Expiratory training in multiple sclerosis. *Arch Phys Med Rehabil* 77:909–912, 1996.
17. World Health Organization: The International Classification of Impairments, Disabilities, and Handicaps. A Manual of Classification Relating to the Consequences of Disease. Geneva: 1980.

Dermatologic Disorders

W. Kenneth Blaylock

The History and Physical Examination in Dermatologic Diagnosis

The clinical approach to a patient with a skin complaint should begin with a good history and

a thorough physical examination. Access to the skin by visual inspection, that is, seeing the gross pathology, is an advantage to the clinician. Special diagnostic procedures should be available, and are listed in Table 80-1.

The history of the skin eruption should include a description of the presentation of the first primary lesion type, the location, the configuration, and the type and duration of symptoms. The sequence of events in the progression of the eruption is important, and the relationship to drugs or other possible environmental flare factors can be very helpful in the evaluation process.

Cutaneous lesions are either primary or secondary. Primary lesions may present with fluid or be free of fluid (Table 80-2). The solid lesions are the macule, papule, nodule, tumor, and wheal. The fluid-filled lesions are vesicles, bullae, pustules, and cysts. Secondary lesions usually follow trauma to the primary lesions, or they may occur as manifestations of the healing skin. These secondary lesions include crusts, scales, erosions, and ulcers (Table 80-3).

The therapy for skin eruptions depends on the etiology and pathobiology of the disorder. Also, the location of the lesions can determine the need for a particular vehicle containing the medication. For example, lotions are more acceptable to the patient with an intertriginous lesion. Dosage, indications, adverse drug responses, and reaction possibilities should be obtained from the manufacturer's profile for each drug and discussed with the patient before prescribing.

Skin Infections: Bacteria (Table 80-4)

Impetigo

Impetigo (contagiosa) is the most common bacterial infection of the skin. It is caused by grampositive bacteria (i.e., coagulase-positive *Staphylococcus aureus,* or β-hemolytic *Streptococcus* spp., or both). These lesions are thin-walled subcorneal vesicles or pustules on erythematous bases that break easily and are seen most commonly on exposed areas of the skin. When the lesions rupture, they exude serum. There is usually peripheral extension, often developing a connected round pattern. Mixed infections are common.

Some strains of streptococci associated with impetigo and scabies with secondary impetigo can produce glomerulonephritis. Culture and Gram stain of exudate from a lesion are helpful in confirming the diagnosis of this bacterial infection and in assessing sensitivity to specific antibiotics.

Ecthyma

This is a deeper infection of the skin produced by β-hemolytic streptococcus organisms. The clini-

TABLE 80-1 · Cutaneous Diagnostic Procedures

Procedure Type	Procedure Supplies and Equipment	Clinical Condition Where Helpful
Hand lens or head magnification	Magnification 5–10×	Scabies; melanoma and other tumors
Potassium hydroxide (KOH)	KOH; glass slide; microscope	Tinea versicolor; tinea pedis; tinea corporis
Wood's light	360–400 nm wavelength light	Tinea versicolor; erythrasma
Skin biopsy	3 or 4 mm punch; formalin	Tumors; bullous diseases (adjacent skin or edge of lesion); nodules
Tzanck prep	Scalpel blade Glass slide Wright's stain	Herpes zoster; herpes simplex
Scabies prep	Scalpel blade (#15); oil	Papules or burrows; scabies or suspected scabies

TABLE 80-2 Primary Skin Lesions

Type	Definition	Examples
Macule	Flat; 1–30 mm	Freckle Viral eruption Purpura
Papule	Solid; elevated; 5 mm or less	Drug or viral eruption Psoriasis Purpura
Nodule	Solid; elevated; 5–20 mm	Panniculitis (subcutaneous) Sarcoid-sarcoidosis (dermal) Keloid (dermal)
Tumor	Solid; elevated; large nodule	Basal cell cancer; carcinoma; melanoma, etc. Dermatofibroma
Wheal	Elevated; fluid in dermis	Urticaria
Vesicle	Elevated; clear fluid; less than 5 mm	Eczema Herpes zoster Contact dermatitis
Bullae	Elevated; clear fluid; greater than 5 mm	Herpes zoster Erythema multiforme
Pustules	Round; elevated; white or yellow fluid	Impetigo Pustular psoriasis

cal lesions may initially resemble impetigo but later deeper ulcers occur in the skin, and associated lymphadenopathy may be present. Impetigo is common on the face and hands, whereas ecthyma is usually on the lower legs and follows dry fissures or insect bites. The diagnosis is established by the clinical picture, Gram-stained smear, and culture. Treatment is the same as for impetigo, although antibacterial therapy may need to be continued for as long as 2 to 4 weeks.

TABLE 80-3 Secondary Skin Lesions

Type	Definition	Clinical Example
Crust	Dried serum or exudate on surface	Healing wound or excoriation
Flake	Scales Stratum corneum	Seborrheic dermatitis
Plaque	Coalescing papules	Psoriasis Granuloma annulare
Fissure	Break or crack in epidermis	Ichthyosis or chronic eczema
Erosion or excoriation	Epidermis missing	Impetigo or scratching
Ulcer	Loss of epidermis and dermis	Venous stasis ulcer
Scar	Healing with dermal fibrosis	Acne
Atrophy	Loss of epidermis and dermis	Topical steroid abuse Sun damage

Erysipelas

This form of infection is produced by group A, β-hemolytic streptococci. The clinical manifestations are fever, malaise, and skin erythema, with distinct sharp borders, induration, and tenderness. This eruption usually occurs on the face, arms, or legs. Erysipelas is seen frequently in the elderly. Hospitalization is often indicated. Early intravenous antibiotic therapy may be replaced by oral therapy in two to three days, as disappearance of the redness occurs. Recurrences are common in the same site, particularly on the lower legs, where fissures between the toes may be the site at which pathologic organisms enter the skin. Venous insufficiency and lymphedema are frequently comorbid disorders. Antibiotic therapy in this setting should be followed by careful attention to any fungal infection of the feet.

Cellulitis

This infection closely resembles erysipelas. It is usually caused by β-hemolytic streptococci; however, *Staphylococcus aureus* can occasionally produce cellulitis. Recurrent cellulitis in the lower leg is treated with the same antibiotics as used for erysipelas. Recurrent cellulitis requires the prevention of tinea pedis between the toes.

Folliculitis

Folliculitis of the skin develops in skin that is traumatized as a primary infection. Bacterial folliculitis is characterized by inflammatory papules surrounding a central hair. *Staphylococcus aureus*-induced folliculitis has perifollicular erythema and pustule formation. A Gram's stain of the pustule contents usually shows the gram-posi-

TABLE 80-4   Skin Infections: Therapy

Infection	Organisms	Therapy
Impetigo	Group A β-hemolytic streptococcus, or S. aureus	Penicillinase-resistant penicillin, dicloxacillin 250–500 mg po qid, or erythromycin, 250–500 mg po qid
Ecthyma	Group A β-hemolytic streptococcus	Same as impetigo; antibiotic for 2–4 wks
Erysipelas	Group A β-hemolytic streptococcus	Systemic intravenous penicillin, such as nafcillin Hospitalization
Cellulitis	Group A, C, G streptococcus	Same as erysipelas (for severe cases) For mild cases: 500 mg erythromycin, or dicloxacillin, qid × 10 days and bedrest
Folliculitis	S. aureus	Moist heat and antiseptic cleansers In severe cases: erythromycin or dicloxacillin, 250–500 mg po qid × 10 days
	Pseudomonas	Stop exposure to contaminated water Local therapy and antibiotics as indicated
Furuncle	S. aureus	Erythromycin or dicloxacillin, a semisynthetic penicillin, 250–500 mg po qid × 7–10 days Moist heat, incision, and drainage Bacitracin or Mupirocin, bid × 7 days in nose
Toxic shock syndrome	S. aureus Toxic shock syndrome toxin-1	Managed in hospital

tive coccus. Folliculitis caused by *Pseudomonas aeruginosa* is associated with contaminated water in hot tubs or whirlpools. Folliculitis without infection may also occur in traumatized skin from rubbing or scratching (Fig. 80-1; see also color Plate 19).

Furunculosis

Furuncles and carbuncles are seen as painful, hot, erythematous nodules ("boils") that contain pus and that are usually caused by *S. aureus*. All fluctuant lesions should receive incision and drainage. Topically applied antibiotics in the nose may be indicated to prevent nasopharyngeal colonization and recurrence. Family members may need to be treated to reduce colonization of *S. aureus* in the nasopharyngeal and flexural skin folds.

Toxic Shock Syndrome

Although this is not a bacterial skin infection, there is a close relationship between toxic shock syndrome and infection with *Staphylococcus aureus*. Prolonged tampon use may support bacterial growth and precipitate this syndrome and

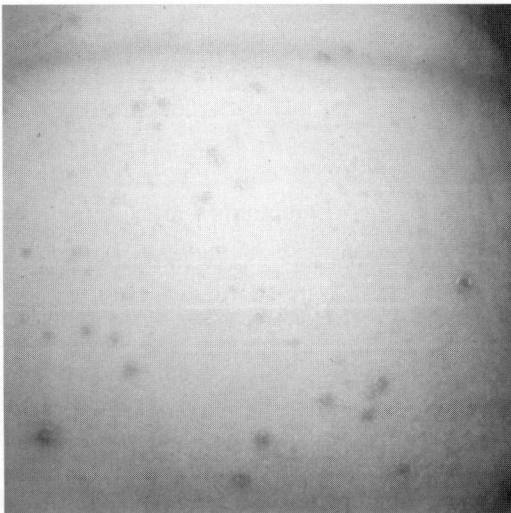

Figure 80-1 Folliculitis in a diabetic patient. (See color Plate 19.)

skin eruption. A proportion of the *Staphylococcus* isolates produce an antigen referred to as toxic shock syndrome toxin-1. This toxin can act as a superantigen.

Toxic shock syndrome evolves in a few days. Although it occurs in healthy menstruating women, it may also occur in nonmenstruating women and men. The syndrome begins with a sudden onset of high fever, with headache, myalgia, vomiting, diarrhea, and hypotension. The clinical criteria for the syndrome include temperature more than 38.9°C, hypotension, and an erythroderma of the palms and soles with subsequent desquamation. The mucous membranes may be inflamed. If organ failure occurs in three or more systems (such as the hepatic, renal, cardiovascular, or neurologic systems), with the skin signs and no evidence for other causes of sepsis, the syndrome is established.

The treatment includes hospitalization, volume expanders, appropriate antimicrobial drugs, and appropriate consultations. Death can occur with sepsis and multiorgan failure.

Skin Infections: Fungi and Yeast
(Table 80-5)

Dermatophyte infections, tinea versicolor, candidiasis, and erythrasma are common skin infections in this category.

Dermatophyte

Dermatophytic infections are the most common cutaneous fungal infections. These superficial infections occur in skin, hair, and nails, and are usually produced by Microsporum or Trichophyton organisms. Occasionally *Candida albicans* may produce this infection. All scaling eruptions should have a KOH examination performed to exclude a fungus or yeast infection. Hyphae on the slide are diagnostic for dermatophyte infection or Candida infection.

Tinea corporis is a dermatophyte infection involving glaborous skin areas other than the hands, feet, and groin. This infection produces a

TABLE 80-5   Cutaneous Fungal and Yeast Infections

Infection	Therapy
Tinea corporis Tinea cruris	Imidazole creams bid × 2 wks or until eruption is clear, then additional 1–2 wks
Tinea manum Tinea pedis	Imidazole creams bid × 2 wks or until clear, then additional 2 wks, or allylamine creams bid × 1–4 wks, or ciclopiroxolamine cream bid × 2 wks or until eruption is clear, then 1–2 wks
Tinea unguium Finger and toe nails	Terbinafine hydrochloride[a] Itraconzole
Tinea versicolor	Zinc pyrithione shampoo, imidazole creams: bid × 2–4 wks
Candidiasis	Imidazole cream bid until eruption is clear, then one additional week, keep the area dry

[a]I prefer these new oral antifungals because they are more effective and appear safer than previous therapies. The need for a specific drug for a designated infection, the drug's adverse effects, drug interactions, and different dosages require that a clinician familiar with each of these medications evaluate the patient before prescribing these drugs.

red, scaly patch with sharp, advancing borders and central clearing.

Tinea cruris is usually symmetric, and develops on the upper, inner surfaces of the thighs. This infection spreads peripherally with central clearing. The disorder flares in hot weather or with occlusion. Itching is common and severe. The organisms which may produce this eruption are *T. rubrum, T. mentagrophtyes,* or *Candida albicans.* When the eruption is produced by *Candida albicans,* small pustules may be observed at the border of the lesions.

Tinea manum is usually a dry, scaly, erythematous eruption that involves the palms and may extend to the dorsal surface of the hands. *Trichophyton rubrum* usually produces this eruption. *T. rubrum* can cause a dry infection on both feet as well, usually in a moccasin distribution. *T. mentagrophytes* infections generally produce an inflammatory, blistering eruption of hands and feet, and these lesions may become hemorrhagic.

Tinea faciale presents with scaling red patches, with scaling border, on the face. It must be differentiated from light eruptions, seborrheic eczema, and actinic skin damage.

Tinea pedis, or athlete's foot, is prevalent in warm weather, and is recurrent and commonly undertreated. Fissures between the toes, with maceration, is a common presentation. An erythematous, scaling eruption that covers the soles is an additional type of infection. A third form presents with cutaneous blisters that are occasionally hemorrhagic.

Tinea unguium, (onychomycosis), an infection of the nails, is usually caused by a *T. rubrum, T. mentagrophytes,* or *E. floccosum* infection, or by *Candida albicans. Trichophyton mentagrophytes* produces an invasion of the surface of the nail plate, resulting in white patches, while other organisms, such as *Trichophyton rubrum* and *Candida albicans,* produce a thick, yellow-brown discoloration of the nails with nail brittleness. Fungal cultures must be done to verify a fungal infection and the specific organism before oral therapy is prescribed.

Tinea Versicolor

This exceedingly common superficial fungal infection is caused by a lipophilic yeast, *Pityrosporum orbiculare,* which resides on the scalp and on the skin of the chest and back. Lesions appear as macules with slight scales. The infected areas do not pigment in a normal manner. As a result, this infection is quite apparent in summer, producing a white or semitanned appearance in pigmented persons. The lesions of tinea versicolor produce a gold fluorescence with the Wood's light examination. Diagnostic confirmation is easily made with a KOH preparation, fol-

lowing scraping with a scalpel blade or glass microscopic slide.

Candidiasis

Candidiasis (*Candida albicans*) is a common cutaneous infection today with the prevalence of diseases and drugs producing immunosuppression. This organism, which resides in the intestinal tract and on mucosal surfaces, thrives on damaged skin and in a moist, alkaline environment. Candidiasis is commonly flared by antibiotic therapy, especially in persons with immune defects (e.g., leukemia, lymphoma, AIDS), or in those persons receiving chemotherapy for cancer or inflammatory diseases. Severe atopic diseases—hay fever, asthma, and atopic dermatitis—enhance this eruption. Iron deficiency anemia and mild diabetes also promote candidiasis.

Erythrasma

This eruption is produced by a short, gram-positive rod, *Corynebacterium minutissimum*. The clinical eruption is a scaly, reddish or brownish, slightly thickened macule, seen in intertriginous areas such as the axillae, groin, and toe web spaces, especially between the fourth and fifth toes. The Wood's light examination reveals a coral pink fluorescence. Therapy includes topical antifungal creams, such as an imidazole, and oral erythromycin 250 mg po, qid for two weeks.

Viral Infections of the Skin

Vesicular Disorders

Herpes simplex The cutaneous lesions of herpes simplex infections are produced by HSV-1 (most commonly oral-facial) and HSV-2 (commonly associated with genital infection). Each of these viral types can infect any skin area. Recurrence in the genital area from type 1 infection is less common than from type 2 infection.

Recurrent herpetic infection is the most common clinical presentation of HSV-1, because primary HSV-1 infections are frequently subclinical. This reactivation of the latent herpes virus HSV-1 may be flared by sunlight, trauma, or immunosuppression. The first symptom of recurrence is skin fullness and burning. This is followed by small blisters in 12 to 24 h. The eruption usually occurs in the same area and resolves in 7 to 14 days. For perioral herpes labialis, or recurrent disease in the immunocompetent, a treatment of choice is penciclovir cream 1% applied every 2 h while awake for 4 days.

A systemic complication of recurrent herpes simplex infection is erythema multiforme, a serious bullous disorder. In individuals with atopic dermatitis, superimposed herpes simplex viral infection can occur as eczema herpeticum. These eruptions are best treated with oral acyclovir (Zovirax), a purine nucleoside analog. Intravenous acyclovir is a treatment of choice in recurrent mucocutaneous herpes simplex infection in immunocompromised adults, and in severe primary genital herpes in nonimmunocompromised patients. For suppression therapy for frequent recurrences, acyclovir, famciclovir, or valacyclovir taken orally are helpful in controlling the reactivation of the virus in the genital area.

Herpes zoster, which is becoming more common, especially in immunosupressed patients, is believed to develop with the reactivation of latent varicella virus. Following varicella (either overt or subclinical infection), the virus remains in a dormant state within sensory ganglia. This eruption may occur with normal immunity in middle age or later. When the eruption occurs in individuals less than 40 years of age, immunosuppression with AIDS or other diseases should be suspected. Herpes zoster is best treated with oral acyclovir, famciclovir, or valacyclovir. Adequate hydration and pain relief are important, as well as compresses for active blisters (Fig. 80-2; see also color Plate 20).

Solid or Wart Lesions

Molluscum contagiosum In this viral infection, papules erupt anywhere on the skin surface, but particularly in areas which are scratched, such as

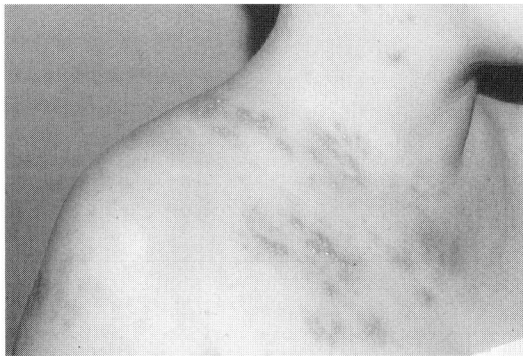

Figure 80-2 Herpes zoster. (See color Plate 20.)

the face, hands, and genital region. *Molluscum contagiosum* is frequently transmitted by sexual contact, and it may be quite extensive in the immunosuppressed patient and in patients with the atopic diseases. The lesions erupt as papules after an incubation period of two to seven weeks. These tiny papules grow to a final diameter of 2 to 5 mm. Occasionally, large lesions are seen. A curetted lesion can be examined with the microscope after Wright's stain has been utilized. A positive preparation reveals a characteristic inclusion body, which establishes the diagnosis. The best therapy is local curettage or cryosurgery. Gentle evacuation of the lesion with an 18-gauge needle and/or a Chalazion curette can also be helpful (Fig. 80-3; see also color Plate 21).

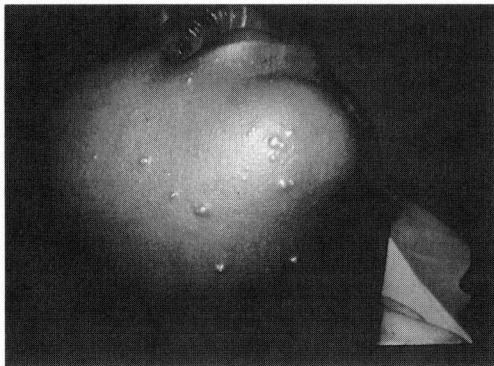

Figure 80-3 *Molluscum contagiosum.* (See color Plate 21.)

Warts caused by human papilloma viruses
The classical "warts" occur with the highest incidence in childhood or the teenage years, but are not uncommon among young adults. The clinical course is unpredictable, with the duration usually less than 3 years. Immunosuppressed patients, especially those who have undergone transplantation, are particularly susceptible to this eruption. Local trauma allows viral implantation, particularly on the fingers and plantar surfaces of the feet, and the genitalia.

The causative agent, human papilloma virus (HPV), is a spherical DNA virus. The human papilloma virus is host- and tissue-specific. There are more than 30 different types of HPV. Certain types of HPV infection have malignant potential. Spontaneous remission is immunological in nature.

The phenotypical appearance of warts depends on the location as well as secondary lesions, such as hyperpigmentation and scarring. The common verruca vulgaris presents as an elevated papule or nodule with a hyperkeratotic verrucous surface. Plane or linear lesions may occur in areas of trauma, especially on the face and on the lower extremities in those women who shave their legs.

Symptomatic warts should be treated. Wart destruction is the usual therapy. Liquid nitrogen freezing is the most useful technique in wart therapy. The lesion is frozen until the wart and a surrounding thin rim of normal-appearing skin turn white. A blister usually occurs in 24 to 48 h, followed by healing within three weeks. Cryotherapy may produce cutaneous nerve damage, scarring, and/or pigment loss or gain. Patients should be informed of this possibility. Freezing warts on the lower legs is not recommended because of the scarring potential.

Mild electrodesiccation and curettage can be useful in removing small warts from the skin surface. Caution is important because these physical modalities may produce scarring and other side effects as listed above. It is important that the physician does not overtreat a lesion that usually resolves without treatment in most patients.

Arthropod Bite Eruptions

Arthropod bites and stings by flying insects are common and produce many types of skin lesions. The clinical skin lesions are papular, urticarial, nodular, or tumor in type. The immediate effect of a sting is pain. In some patients, the symptoms from bites and stings are related to scratching the area of the bite. Later effects are usually allergic in nature. Insects are capable of transmitting a variety of infections, including Rocky Mountain spotted fever, Lyme disease, and Ehrlichiosis (Fig. 80-4; see also color Plate 22).

Most patients recognize the stinging or burning pain of an insect bite, including the erythema and edema that result. Most bites occur on exposed areas, especially the face and extremities. The lesions are usually red papules or nodules with a central opening in the epidermis. The best treatment includes eliminating the insect exposure and a low-strength topical steroid cream, plus a topical antibiotic if infection is suspected. Oral antihistamines can be very helpful in reducing itch.

Pediculosis

Pediculosis is caused by sucking lice such as *Pediculus humanus* var. *capitis* (head louse); *Pediculus humanus* var. *corporis* (body louse); and *Phthirius pubis* (pubic or crab louse). Each of these produces an infestation.

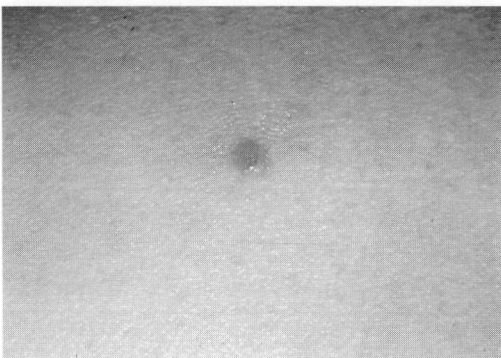

Figure 80-4   Insect bite. (See color Plate 22.)

Body lice are most common in adults, whereas head lice occur more often in children. Pubic and crab louse infestations usually occur in adults, and are sexually transmitted diseases. Patients with pubic lice should have other venereal diseases excluded. The adult louse attaches to the hair, and nits are distributed on these hairs. The pubic crab lice may also involve the eyebrows and eyelashes. Pruritus is extreme. The diagnosis of this infestation is frequently made by the patient. Topical therapy with lindane or permethrin is indicated.

Scabies

This disorder is caused by a small mite, *Sarcoptes scabiei*. Scabies occurs in individuals in all socioeconomic groups. The disease is spread by physical contact.

The female mite, after burrowing into the stratum corneum, deposits eggs in these burrows. The larvae, which emerge in three to five days, mature in about two weeks. With continued propagation of the organism, the infestation can persist indefinitely. The skin lesions are papules, excoriations, and burrows. The marked pruritus usually occurs at night.

The diagnosis is established by a mineral oil preparation from fresh skin scrapings. The papules and excoriations can mimic other skin conditions associated with pruritus, such as atopic dermatitis, contact dermatitis, or other arthropod bites. The best therapies are 1% lindane (Kwell) lotion and 5% permethrin (Elimite) cream. These preparations should not be used during pregnancy. For therapy a single application is applied from neck to toe and washed off the next morning. One application is recommended. Multiple applications of lindane may produce neurotoxicity. Treatment failures are not common when the correct diagnosis is made.

Sexually Transmitted Disease: Genital Ulcers (Table 80-6)

An extensive discussion of sexually transmitted diseases can be found in Chap. 28. The dermato-

TABLE 80-6 Sexually Transmitted Diseases: Genital Ulcers

Diagnosis	Organism	Diagnostic Methods
Genital herpes	Herpes simplex	Culture or Tzanck prep
Primary & secondary syphilis	*Treponema pallidum*	Dark field or immunofluorescence
Chancroid	*H. ducreyi*	Gram stain and culture from lesion; no aspiration
Granuloma inguinale	*Donovania granulomatis*	Donovan bodies: material from lesion edge Wright or Giemsa stain
Lymphogranuloma venereum	*C. trachomatis*	Culture from urethra, cervix, node, or rectum

logic manifestations of sexually transmitted diseases are discussed below.

Syphilis

Genital ulcers suggest venereal disease (i.e., syphilis, herpes, chancroid, or granuloma inguinale). Syphilis is caused by the spirochete *Treponema pallidum*. It can be detected in most of the primary and secondary skin lesions by darkfield examination. The most common mode of transmission is sexual contact. HIV infection must be excluded with any ulcerative sexually transmitted disease because, in addition to the fact that individuals with one sexually transmitted disease are at greater risk to have others, ulcer formation enhances the chance for this infection.

Syphilis is divided into three stages. In primary syphilis, a chancre with small ulcers develops in 1 to 4 weeks after contact with an infected source. Regional lymphadenopathy is present.

The secondary lesion, a papulosquamous lesion without ulcer, begins 2 to 12 weeks after onset of the chancre. Secondary lesions involve the body, the feet, and the hands, especially the ventral surface of the hands. Ulcers may be present on mucous membranes of the labial or buccal mucosa with secondary syphilis (Fig. 80-5; see also color Plate 23). The patient with these cutaneous features may have toxic symptoms—fever and malaise—as well as nontender lymphadenopathy. Secondary syphilis can produce alopecia. Condylomata lata, with papules and nodules found in intertriginous areas in the perineum,

are very contagious. Tertiary syphilis, occurring 2 years after the primary infection, is rare today because of the initial use of antibiotic agents.

Herpes Progenitalis

Primary genital herpes occurs following an incubation period of 3 to 7 days. Localized burning or paresthesia is followed by a typical eruption of grouped vesicles on the genitalia, followed by ulcer formation. Constitutional symptoms and lymphadenopathy occur with the primary infection. Healing occurs over a 2- to 3-week period. Secondary lesions are common, and heal within two weeks. Recurrent attacks become less frequent and less severe as time passes. Sexual contact should not occur while skin lesions are present on the skin or mucous membranes. Viral shedding occurs in some individuals after the resolution of all active lesions.

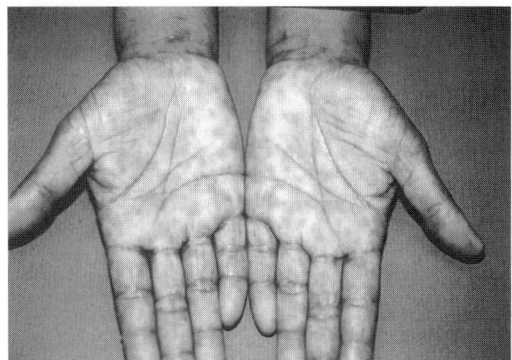

Figure 80-5 Secondary syphilis. (See color Plate 23.)

Chancroid

Chancroid is an infectious disease of the genitalia caused by a gram-negative bacillus, *Haemophilus ducreyi*. It is characterized by painful, nonindurated ulcers that develop after an incubation period of 3 to 5 days. Multiple lesions are common. A positive diagnosis requires the demonstration of the organism by means of smears or culture. Smears are taken after cleansing a lesion with normal saline, and securing material from the ulcer border. The sample is applied to a glass slide, heat-fixed, and then Gram stained. Clusters of gram-negative bacilli establish and confirm the diagnosis. It is difficult to culture the organism. Lymphadenopathy is present. The simultaneous presence of syphilis and/or HIV should always be excluded in these patients.

Lymphogranuloma Venereum

This sexually transmitted disease is caused by *Chlamydia trachomatis,* an intracellular parasite. The primary lesion is a small papule that rapidly ulcerates. Lymphadenopathy is present and prominent.

Granuloma Inguinale

Granuloma inguinale is a slowly progressive ulcerative disease caused by a gram-negative bacillus with features similar to Klebsiella. The disease begins as a papule or ulcer. Ulcers enlarge and spread from the labia minora to the inguinal region or perineum.

Condyloma Acuminatum

Condyloma acuminatum, a wart variant, occurs as a fleshy, papillomatous growth on genital skin and mucous membranes.

Common Drug Reactions

For an in-depth discussion of this issue, the reader is referred to Chap. 86. The discussion of drug reactions in this chapter focuses on the dermatologic manifestations.

Eruptions may occur in the skin and on mucous membranes following systemically administered drugs that have been utilized for establishing a diagnosis or for therapy. The eruption is not usually related to a therapeutic effect of the drug. The clinician must decide how the patient was exposed to the drug, and which of many drugs is producing the eruption. The clinical presentation and proposed mechanism for each drug reaction is helpful in deciding whether the drug should be discontinued.

The morphology of a drug eruption may resemble many other skin diseases. A drug may produce one or several different primary lesions. A drug can produce a localized urticarial response in one patient, while in another person, a blistering eruption may occur.

Topical or intradermal skin testing is not reliable except in the cases where penicillin allergy is suspected.

Anaphylaxis, a type 1 immunologic reaction, as a clinical syndrome can include urticaria, angioedema, laryngeal edema with hoarseness and stridor, and advancement to cardiovascular collapse. Severe bronchospasm may occur. This eruption can occur within a few minutes after a drug is administered.

Serum sickness typically develops 8 to 12 days after exposure to a drug, and is characterized by fever, urticaria or vasculitis, lymphadenopathy, splenomegaly, arthritis or arthralgias, and nephritis.

Delayed hypersensitivity, a type IV immune response, may produce a maculopapular eruption that can evolve into an exfoliative dermatitis. These reactions may result from systemic administration of a drug to which a patient has been previously sensitized by topical administration; thus, this type of reaction has the characteristics of systemic allergic contact dermatitis.

Among the most severe drug reactions are toxic epidermal necrolysis (TEN) and/or erythema multiforme (Fig. 80-6; see also color Plate 24). This usually begins as a macular erythema

Figure 80-6 Toxic epidermal erythema multiforme. (See color Plate 24.)

and progresses to bullae formation and desquamation of skin, leaving a raw, denuded surface. Mucosal erosions and conjunctivitis may also be present. Loss of fluid and electrolytes is a significant problem. Other evidence for systemic toxicity includes fever, lethargy, vomiting, and diarrhea. Death occurs in a high percentage of patients (25 to 30 percent) unless early intervention with grafting occurs. Toxic epidermal necrolysis must be distinguished from staphylococcal scalded-skin syndrome (SSSS). A skin biopsy can be very helpful.

Fixed drug eruptions, lichenoid eruptions, and vasculitis are less common manifestations of drug hypersensitivity (Table 80-7).

Photosensitivity (Phototoxicity and Photoallergy) (Table 80-8)

Many chemicals and drugs can combine with components of skin and allow the skin to respond excessively to ultraviolet light. This can result in a photosensitivity response, either phototoxicity or photoallergy. The usual wavelengths of light responsible for these reactions are between 290 and 400 nm. The 290 to 320 nm range is UVB, the spectrum that produces sunburn and skin cancers and some photoallergic reactions; the 320 to 400 nm range UVA light is responsible for most of the phototoxic and photoallergy drug eruptions.

Phototoxicity

This drug eruption is dose related. The erythema is similar to an exaggerated sunburn reaction occurring six to eight hours after exposure to sunlight. Tetracycline and many other drugs can produce phototoxicity in some patients.

Photoallergy

This drug reaction, which is secondary to a drug or chemical plus ultraviolet light, is due to an immune mechanism. Only small quantities of the drug are necessary to elicit a response. Photoallergic reactions can occur after topical or systemic administration of certain drugs. Photoallergic drug reactions have resulted from exposures to sulfonamides, chlorpromazine, sulfonylureas, and many other drugs.

Polymorphic light eruption is a photosensitivity eruption that occurs with sun exposure to the skin, which is immunologically mediated (Fig. 80-7; see also color Plate 25). It can be produced by ultraviolet light of any wavelength. The skin lesions appear within a few hours after sun exposure, and the eruption is not related to the length of exposure to the sun. Pruritus is common and the eruption usually occurs with first sun exposure in the spring. Edema, red papules, vesicles, or eczematous lesions are the usual skin lesions.

Eczematous Dermatoses

"Dermatitis," or "inflammation of the skin," is synonymous with the term "eczema," which refers to boiling. Eczema is characterized by a red papulovesicular eruption, with oozing and crusting, followed by scaling and thick skin (lichenification), with or without pigment loss. This eruption is markedly pruritic. The common forms of eczema are contact dermatitis, seborrheic dermatitis, atopic dermatitis, and stasis dermatitis.

Contact Dermatitis

Contact dermatitis is induced by a contact with an antigenic substance or irritant. Irritants, if ap-

TABLE 80-7   Drug Eruptions

Signs & Symptoms	Common Causes or Stimulus	Therapy
Urticaria Angioedema	Many drugs	Discontinue suspected drugs Hospitalization if anaphylaxis occurs Subcutaneous epinephrine Systemic steroids Antihistamines
Maculopapular	Many drugs	Discontinue offending drugs Cool or tepid baths Antihistamines for pruritus Topical steroids for severe eruptions
Exfoliative erythroderma	Many drugs	Stop suspected drug Topical corticosteorids Systemic steroids in severe cases
Fixed drug eruption	Barbiturates Tetracyclines Sulfonamides Anovulatory drugs	Discontinue suspected drug Topical steroid creams
Erythema multiforme	Sulfonamides Penicillins Many other drugs	Stop suspected drug or drugs Systemic steroids for severe cases Hospitalization
Toxic epidermal necrolysis	Allopurinol Sulfonamides Phenytoin	Do not use systemic steroids Stop suspected drug Hospitalization; skilled nursing care Skin grafting
Lichenoid eruption	Gold, thiazides, β-blockers	Antihistamines Topical corticosteroids Systemic steroids for severe cases
Lupus erythematosus	Related to manifestation of photosensitivity or immunological disorders	Protection from ultraviolet light Local steroids for cutaneous manifestations
Vasculitis	Allopurinol Penicillins Sulfonamides	Discontinue offending drug

plied in sufficient concentrations, will produce a dermatitis in any individual. Irritant dermatitis can be a dermatitis or a minimal burn. Allergic contact dermatitis is a T-cell-mediated immune response to an allergen that has followed a previous sensitizing contact with the chemical. Many chemicals and drugs can be both irritants and allergic sensitizers. The eczematous response in allergic contact dermatitis is vesicles or bullae in sites of exposure to the allergen.

Rhus dermatitis is usually produced by poison ivy, poison oak, or poison sumac, and is the most common form of contact dermatitis (Fig. 80-8; see also color Plate 26). The pattern of vesiculation is produced as the oleoresin from the plant strokes the skin. This resin attaches to the skin directly, at which point, the fingers can spread the oil. The antigen is similar in poison ivy, poison oak, and poison sumac. After the appearance of the dermatitis, the blister fluid from the lesion is not antigenic to other skin areas in the patient, and is not transferrable to other sensitive individuals.

Patients must be questioned at length about the history of any form of dermatitis. Other

TABLE 80-8 Photosensitivity Diseases

Type	Disease	Flare Factor	Therapy
Genetic	Erythropoietic photoporphyria	Sun	Sun screens Beta-carotene
Metabolic	Pellagra Sporadic porphyria Cutanea tarda	Alcohol/sun Drugs Hepatitis C	Niacin Phlebotomy Sun protection
Photoaggravated	Lupus erythematosus	UVB	Sun screens Topical steroids
Dermatoses	Atopic dermatitis or Lichen planus	UVB	Sun screens Topical steroids
Immunologic	Polymorphic light eruption	UVA UVB	Sun protection Topical steroids PUVA for hyposensitization

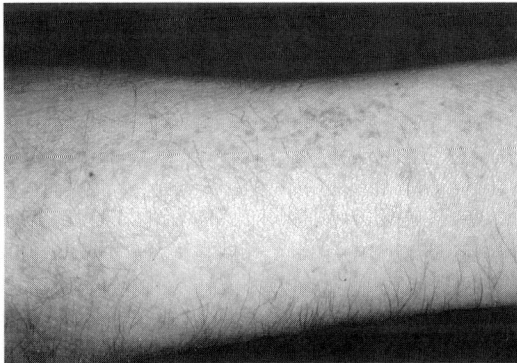

Figure 80-7 Polymorphic light eruption. (See color Plate 25.)

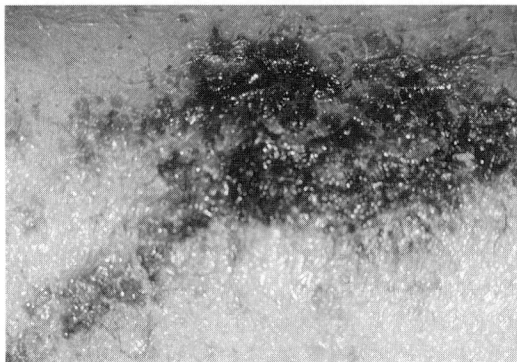

Figure 80-8 Contact dermatitis from poison ivy. (See color Plate 26.)

common causes of allergic contact dermatitis include nickel, potassium dichromate, paraphenylenediamine, rubber compounds, and formalin. To establish the cause when the history is nondiagnostic, careful skin testing should be done after the acute eruption has subsided. This should be done when the disease has cleared and when the patient has discontinued corticosteriods. Distinguishing irritant from allergic contact dermatitis is difficult. This problem frequently requires the help of an expert in dermatology. Skin biopsy is generally not helpful, except where psoriasis is to be excluded.

The therapy should begin with removal of the offending allergen. Topical soaks with cool water, or Burrow's 1/40 solution, and shake lotions are helpful. Prednisone, 1 mg/kg of body weight, for 4 to 5 days, with tapering over a 5- to 10-day period can also be very helpful. Antihistamines can be used to provide relief from itching, and antibiotics may be necessary for secondary infections.

Hand Eczema

This eruption occurs anywhere on the hands or feet, and is usually a localized form of either atopic or contact eczematous dermatitis. A history of atopy in the patient or family may be

helpful in determining the type of hand eczema (i.e., atopic or contact). The hands and feet may become sensitive to excess water, detergents, or other chemicals. The relationship to emotions is not clear. Allergic contact dermatitis may produce the eruption or flare underlying atopic dermatitis. Bacterial and yeast infections should be excluded in evaluating the condition. Chronically inflamed skin, especially when exposed to excess moisture and irritants, becomes dry and produces painful fissures.

The acute eruption is treated similarly to contact dermatitis. The chronic eczematous eruption that has not cleared with conservative topical therapy is best handled by a specialist in dermatology. Special attention must be given to the occupation and antigen exposure. Latex sensitivity may begin as pruritic swelling of the hands. This type I reaction should be evaluated and managed by an allergy specialist with an interest and expertise in evaluating and managing latex allergy.

Seborrheic Dermatitis (Table 80-9)

Seborrheic dermatitis or eczema involves the regions of the skin where many sebaceous glands are present. It is a common condition, and may produce regional scaling and mild exfoliation. It is often flared during a severe illness. Although seborrhea is associated with hypersecretion of sebum in most patients, there are individuals with a high output of sebum and no dermatitis. The therapy for this condition depends on the location of the eczema.

Stasis Dermatitis

Stasis dermatitis (eczema) is secondary to venous hypertension. Edema and infection are flare factors for the eruption. Diseases that produce edema and venous stasis—congestive heart failure, renal disease, and cirrhosis—flare the eruption in the susceptible individual. The medial surface of the lower leg is the most common site for the eruption. Fungal infection must be excluded

TABLE 80-9 Seborrheic Dermatitis

Location	Treatment
Scalp	Increase frequency of shampooing with shampoo containing selenium sulfide or zinc pyrithione; shampoo 2–3 times per week; low-strength topical steroid solution once daily for a few days, then 2–3 days per week
Face	1% Hydrocortisone cream, 2 × per day for 1 week, then once daily × 1 week, then discontinue. Avoid applying around the eyes.
Ears, neck, chest, and back	Hydrocortisone cream, bid for 1 week, then daily × 1 week, then discontinue. Nizoral cream bid for 3–4 weeks may be used for resistant eruptions.
Skin folds	1% Hydrocortisone cream, plus miconazole, or clotrimazole cream if *Candida albicans* infection exists.

by a KOH preparation and culture. Contact dermatitis to medications is common. Treatment should be directed toward reducing the edema and inflammation. Low-strength topical steroids, applied two times per day for two weeks, are helpful. Systemic prednisone may be required for the severe form of this dermatitis. Once the acute treatment is complete, in 4 to 7 days, the prednisone should be tapered gradually over a two-week period and discontinued. Support hose, limiting the standing position, and weight reduction are usually necessary for managing the chronic form of this eruption.

Atopic Dermatitis (Fig. 80-9; see also color Plate 27)

Atopic dermatitis is a form of eczema that can occur in all age groups. It is characterized by severe itching and a cutaneous papulovesicular eruption that is flared by scratching. The scratching can induce the physical findings, and the excoriations and bleeding promote bacterial infections followed by oozing and weeping, and more infection. The eruption occurs as a local or

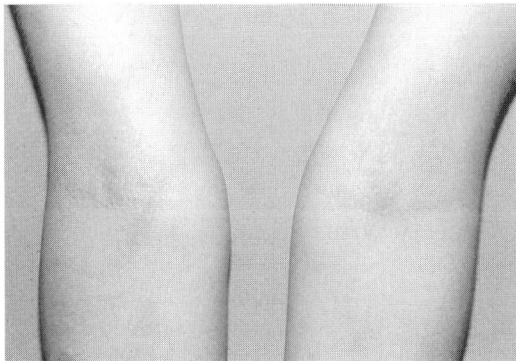

Figure 80-9 Atopic dermatitis. (See color Plate 27.)

generalized dermatitis. The flexural folds of skin and the hands and feet are the typical locations for the eruption.

This eczema usually occurs in persons with a personal or family history of asthma, hay fever, eczema, or urticaria. Patients with atopic dermatitis have increased sweating on the face, hands, and feet. There is increased itching, which is often followed by excessive scratching. The eruption often occurs from exposure to heat, sun, simple trauma, or stress. Severe skin infections may complicate this dermatitis.

The diagnosis of atopic dermatitis is established by the recognition of the cutaneous features, as well as by establishing an association with other components of the atopic state (asthma, hay fever, sinusitis) in the patient or the family members.

Most patients do not require hospitalization except during a severe flare of the dermatosis, which is usually followed by a severe secondary bacterial infection or exfoliative dermatitis. These patients are often carriers of *Staphylococcus aureus* in the nasopharynx and on the skin, and they are also at high risk for developing a generalized viral infection when exposed to the herpes simplex virus.

The management of this disorder includes reducing or eliminating all flare factors, especially dry skin and infection. The elimination of some foods, inhalant antigens, and other environmen-

tal antigens can be helpful. House dust can aggravate the condition in some individuals with atopic dermatitis, and some patients will clear the eruption with a change in the home environment.

Specific therapy for the dermatitis includes topical as well as systemic medication. Good topical therapy is most important because local therapy may prevent the need for systemic therapy, particularly systemic steroids.

Halogenated corticosteroid preparations are the most effective form of topical therapy. The delivery system in which the steroid is placed is quite important. A moisturizing agent, such as a hydrophilic or emollient cream to prevent dryness, is helpful. Emollients should be applied after each bath or water exposure. Soaps should be avoided if possible, and particularly should not be placed on red, inflamed, or fissured skin. The topical application of emollients containing a low concentration of coal tar can be helpful in the management of chronic, noninflamed atopic dermatitis.

If topical therapy is inadequate, consider light therapy or systemic therapy. The chronic unstable form of the eruption should be managed by a specialist in this disorder when light therapy or systemic therapy is required. Immunotherapy with inhalant extracts is not helpful.

Urticaria (Fig. 80-10; see also color Plate 28) (Table 80-10)

Urticaria is a common and troublesome pruritic eruption with wheals or generalized swellings in the skin or mucous membranes. It is generally a transient eruption, but it can be quite severe and very symptomatic and chronic.

Some agents can produce urticaria through a direct release of histamine or other mast cell mediators; examples include foods, such as shellfish, tomatoes, strawberries, and chocolate, and drugs, such as aspirin. Allergic urticaria is a type I, immunoglobulin E-mediated reaction.

The primary lesion in urticaria is a wheal, or red swelling, that may be annular (ring-shaped)

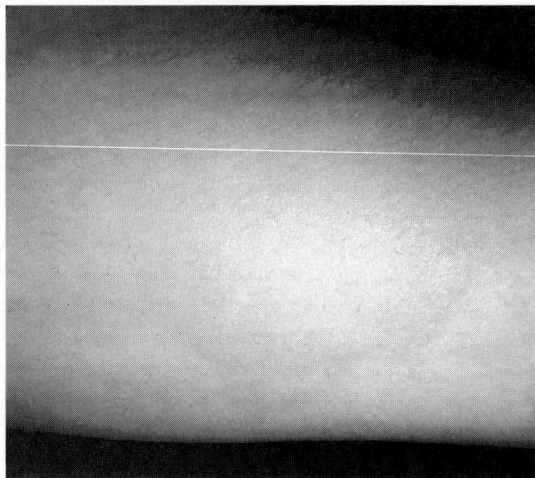

Figure 80-10 Urticaria. (See color Plate 28.)

or flat. Urticaria due to pressure may produce large and deep lesions with erythema. Itching, or stinging, or slight burning pain are the main symptoms, and each lesion may last as long as 24 h. New wheals come in crops as old lesions disappear. The eruption frequently occurs where there is pressure from clothing. The waistline is a common location.

Acute urticaria is six weeks or less in duration, while urticaria that remains longer than six weeks is considered chronic. There are several different forms of urticaria.

Skin Diseases with Blisters

Bullous Pemphigoid (Fig. 80-11; see also color Plate 29)

Bullous pemphigoid usually occurs in persons over age 60. This is a bullous eruption produced by an immune reaction involving the basement membranes. Bullous pemphigoid typically presents with large (2- to 5-cm in diameter), firm bullae on a red base on the trunk and extremities. They may also arise on otherwise normal-appearing skin. Mucous membrane lesions rarely occur. They are frequently seen in patients with pemphigus vulgaris.

TABLE 80-10 Urticaria Therapy

Type	Cause	Therapy
Urticaria (acute and chronic)	Drugs NSAIDs Food and food additives Insect bites Infection Emotions Physical trauma Systemic diseases	Nonsedating antihistamine therapy
Cold urticaria	Produced by cold environment	Cyproheptadine
Cholinergic urticaria	Induced by exercise challenges	Reduce hot showers Cool compresses Nonsedating antihistamine therapy
Solar urticaria	Exposure to defined wavelengths of sunlight	Nonsedating antihistamine therapy
Aquagenic urticaria	Tap water	Avoid water UVA light[a] Nonsedating antihistamine therapy
Angioedema	Drugs, or hereditary deficiency C^1 esterase inhibitor	Stop drugs For hereditary[b] angioedema Avoid trauma

[a]Should be given by dermatologist.
[b]Should be managed by rheumatologist or dermatologist.

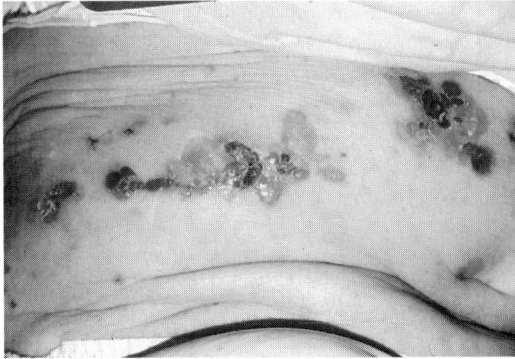

Figure 80-11 Bullous pemphigoid flared by herpes zoster. (See color Plate 29.)

A related disorder that occurs in elderly patients is benign mucous membrane or cicatricial pemphigoid. In this disease, bullae occur with frequency on the oral mucosa and on the eyelids. Skin involvement is less common. This disease causes scarring, which may occur on other mucous membrane surfaces, such as the vagina, larynx, or esophagus.

The lesions in bullous pemphigoid and benign mucous membrane pemphigoid differ from pemphigus vulgaris because the blisters are tense and not easily broken. The patients are usually healthy. The cutaneous blisters in bullous pemphigoid are similar to the lesions seen in erythema multiforme, although erythema multiforme is not chronic as is bullous pemphigoid.

Bullous pemphigoid is treated with systemic corticosteroids. The usual dose is 60 to 80 mg of prednisone by mouth each day. This dose is reduced to 5 to 10 mg over a 30-day period. In some patients, a low dose of oral prednisone is required for several months. A dermatologist should evaluate all patients with chronic bullous eruptions and should supervise the management of these patients.

Erythema Multiforme

In erythema multiforme, the blisters are tense and the skin is inflamed. This inflammatory reaction can be induced by several antigens. The severe forms of erythema multiforme are accompanied by constitutional symptoms—fever, malaise, and frequently upper respiratory symptoms. The initial lesion is a red macule, wheal, or an edematous papule. These lesions usually evolve to form an iris or target lesion.

Erythema multiforme is symmetrical and usually erupts on the palms and soles, and on the dorsal area of the hands and feet, as well as the arms and legs. The trunk is involved when the disease is generalized. Involvement of mucous membranes is usually present. The eyes, nose, mouth, rectum, and genitalia may be involved.

Lesions erupt in crops over a 2- to 4-week period. Eye involvement with blisters on the conjunctivae may occur, and corneal ulceration may be a problem. Toxic epidermal necrolysis, a variant of erythema multiforme, may evolve from erythema multiforme.

Many antigens trigger erythema multiforme, including bacterial, viral, and fungal infections; drugs; the collagen vascular diseases; inflammatory bowel disease; and malignancy.

The diagnosis depends upon the clinical recognition of the lesions. A drug history, chest film, and bacterial and viral cultures are a part of the evaluation process.

The best therapy is to eliminate the underlying cause and correct any abnormality produced by the disease. Any infection should be treated, and suspected drugs should be discontinued. Mild cases require only local treatment, such as compresses for blisters (1:20 Burrows solution, applied for 15 to 30 minutes qid). With a severe eruption, fluid and electrolyte balance must be maintained. Viscous xylocaine, applied locally, may help the patient to eat food. This medication should be rinsed over the mucous membranes for about 5 min and then removed from the mouth. Systemic steroids should be reserved for those patients who are extremely toxic, and should be given early in the disease process. If toxic epidermal necrolysis follows (Fig. 80-6), the systemic steroids should be withdrawn.

Papulosquamous Diseases and Ichthyosis

Psoriasis (Fig. 80-12; see also color Plate 30)
(Table 80-11)

Psoriasis is a papulosquamous eruption with a papule as the primary lesion. These papules are thickened and red with silver scales that bleed when the scales are physically removed. The degree of thickness of the scale is greatest when the disease is chronic, but minimal when the disease is active and inflammatory. The following help establish the diagnosis: (1) a positive family history; (2) a history of severe scalp eruption as an infant, with or without a severe diaper dermatitis; (3) prominent dandruff in the adolescent and adult; (4) nail changes including pinhead-size pits, brown spots, or oil drops, and subungal keratin deposition beneath a loose nail edge; (5) genital and intergluteal eruption; and (6) symmetrical disease. A history of a flare of the disease with an infection, such as streptococcal pharyngitis or a *Candida albicans* infection in the mouth, suggests psoriasis. Several drugs flare psoriasis, including lithium and β-blocking agents. Psoriasis must be differentiated from chronic eczema when the eruption involves the hands and feet. Psoriasis is frequently associated with arthritis.

In summary, a clinical diagnosis is not difficult

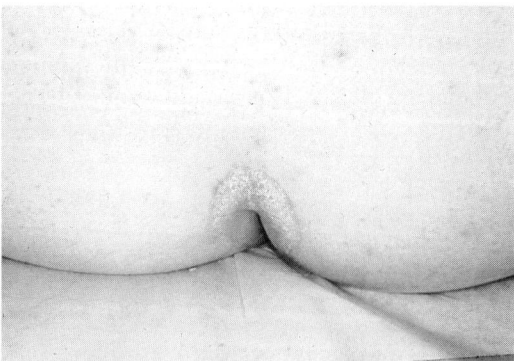

Figure 80-12 Psoriasis. (See color Plate 30.)

to establish if the patient has symmetrical papulosquamous lesions on the elbows and knees; scalp and nail involvement; and intergluteal and genital involvement. A biopsy of the skin may be helpful in some individuals when the hands are involved or where disease is minimal.

The treatment is sometimes difficult. The early management of this chronic eruption should include a discussion with the patient regarding the diagnosis and the morbidity of the disease, including the relationship of anxiety in aggravating the illness, the noncontagious nature of the eruption, and the possible impact on the family. Psoriasis is a dynamic disease process with fluctuations of the eruption throughout the patient's life.

The therapy of psoriasis can be enhanced if special attention is given to the control of infections of the tracheobronchial tree, sinuses, throat, and vagina. The eradication of any *Candida albicans* infection is frequently as helpful in controlling psoriasis lesions as is the use of topically applied therapies.

The use of any therapy for psoriasis and other generalized chronic skin disease requires an understanding of the dynamic aspects of the inflammatory process, training with the disease, and experience with the therapeutic modalities to be used. This can ensure the correct use and enhance the safety of the therapy. Any unstable inflammatory skin process usually requires the consultative expertise of a dermatologist, especially when therapies require UV light, retinoids, systemic steroids, and other chemotherapeutic agents.

Pityriasis Rosea

This is an acute, self-limited disease characterized by papulosquamous lesions on the body and extremities. The cause of pityriasis rosea is unknown, although a viral etiology is suspected because it is usually preceded by a fever or by upper respiratory symptoms.

The eruption occurs in males and females, usually between the ages of 20 and 40. Fever, cough,

TABLE 80-11 Psoriasis: Therapy

Type	Location	Management
Localized plaque psoriasis	Elbows, knees, scalp	Topical steroids (intermittent use of potent topical steroids[a]); 3% salicylic acid ointment[b]; UVB light with dermatologist supervision; topical vitamin D_3 calcipotriene[b]
Guttate generalized	Abdomen, back, arms, legs	Oral antibiotics when indicated for infection; topical steroids (as above); UV light (with dermatologist supervision)
Erythroderma exfoliative dermatitis	All skin areas	Acitretin[c], methotrexate (MTX)[d], or systemic steroids; consultation and supervision by a dermatologist
Pustular psoriasis, localized	Hands, feet	Acitretin[c] (retinoid); topical steroids; consultation with dermatologist
Pustular psoriasis, generalized	Entire body	MTX[d] or acitretin[c]; consultation with dermatologist

[a]Intermittent use for 2 weeks only.

[b]These preparations can be quite irritating to the skin, and low-strength topical steroids can reduce irritation. Expertise in using these preparations is recommended.

[c]A teratogen; it should not be used in women with childbearing capability.

[d]Hepatoxic; it should be monitored by a physician with expertise in MTX use.

or malaise may occur, but most patients are asymptomatic. The initial eruption is a round oval, scaly lesion, the herald patch. A generalized eruption occurs with smaller lesions on the trunk. The lesions generally disappear in six to eight weeks. Postinflammatory hyperpigmentation may occur. Recurrences are rare. The treatment of pityriasis rosea is symptomatic. A severe eruption with intense itch will respond to nonsedating antihistamine therapy.

Dry Skin and Ichthyosis

Patients with ichthyosis have very dry skin. Disorders in this category are associated with a retention of stratum corneum. There are four major types of inherited ichthyosis. The most common inherited form of the eruption is dominant ichthyosis vulgaris. Acquired, noninherited ichthyosis is seen as a manifestation of nutritional deficiency, sarcoidosis, AIDS, or an underlying malignancy.

In ichthyosis vulgaris, fine scaling occurs on the trunk and extremities, usually on the lower legs. Follicular hyperkeratosis is present over the lateral surface of the extremities, with increased palmar markings noted in the patient. The eruption is worse in dry winter weather. Many of these patients have an atopic disorder, such as hay fever or atopic dermatitis.

Many patients are helped by symptomatic therapy with emollients and bath oils. Emollient creams and lotions, free of allergic sensitizers, should be applied after a bath or shower while the skin is moist. Lotions, creams, or emollients containing alpha-hydroxy acids reduce dryness and improve skin texture and appearance.

Disorders of Pigmentation

Melasma

Melasma is a patchy form of overproduction of pigmentation occurring on the face. It occurs commonly in women who are pregnant or who

are taking oral contraceptives. Melasma is flared by sunlight.

Melasma can involve the forehead, face, upper lip, and chin. The pigmentation varies in intensity and shade related to the location of the pigment in the skin, epidermal-brown and dermal-gray. A Wood's light exam demonstrates superficial epidermal pigmentation. This eruption is difficult to manage. Experience with depigmenting agents is desirable. Topical bleaching agents containing a low concentration of hydroquinone 2 to 3% are frequently helpful. Sensitization can occur, as well as hyperpigmentation on the skin. Good sunscreens are absolutely necessary, especially sunscreens containing avobenzone.

Vitiligo (Fig. 80-13; see also color Plate 31)

Vitiligo is a hypopigmenting disorder that can produce a severe cosmetic defect. This patchy eruption is characterized by smooth complete depigmentation. Although the cause is unknown, there is evidence of an immune dysfunction. There is a familial tendency.

The pigment loss results in white macules that involve extensor surfaces and are bilateral and symmetrical. Depigmentation of the hair can occur. Depigmentation is noted in areas subjected to trauma including surgical trauma.

In persons with a dark complexion, vitiligo is especially noticeable, and results in a severe cosmetic problem. In persons with type I fair complexion, vitiligo is often not as noticeable. The lesions sunburn more easily than normal skin, and they never tan because of the loss of melanocytes. A Wood's light examination will demonstrate the difference between these lesions and postinflammatory hypopigmentation.

The treatment of vitiligo is difficult, and the results are not entirely satisfactory. Depigmentation therapy for small areas of hyperpigmentation and PUVA therapy to stimulate new pigment production should be monitored by an expert in dermatology and light therapy.

Oral Mucous Membrane Lesions

Aphthous Stomatitis

Aphthous stomatitis (canker sores) are common, recurrent, painful erosions of the oral mucosa. Although the cause is unknown, trauma is a definite flare factor. Herpes simplex must be excluded as a cause of any recurrent group of small mouth ulcers, but most aphthous ulcers are not due to herpes simplex infections.

The typical lesion occurring on the tongue and buccal mucosa begins as a tender spot that evolves into a round, shallow ulcer, surrounded by erythema. Multiple lesions can also occur. The size of a lesion is generally less than 1 cm in diameter. The pain in the lesion is quite severe, and new lesions are flared by rough foods and trauma from the teeth. A single ulcer clears in 10 to 14 days in most patients. Lesions similar to aphthous stomatitis occur with ulcerative colitis and Behçet's syndrome.

Topical steroid therapy, such as Kenalog in Orabase, is generally helpful in reducing pain with eating. Topical anesthetics can reduce the local pain.

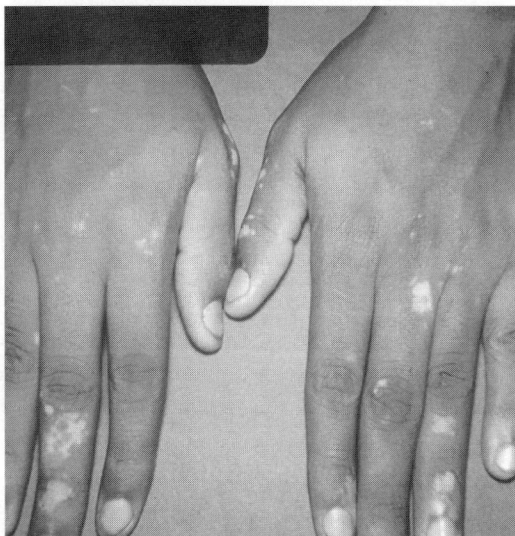

Figure 80-13 Vitiligo. (See color Plate 31.)

Mouth lesions produced by *Candida albicans* infections are white patches with crusting, and when the crust is removed, a red eroded area is noticed. Any white patch, plaque, or nodule in the mouth that is indurated requires a biopsy to exclude cancer.

Cheilitis

Cheilitis is an inflammatory dermatitis of the lips with mild exfoliation. The inflammation may be secondary to skin disease such as psoriasis or atopic dermatitis, or it may be allergy or irritation. An allergic contact reaction to food, metals, or cosmetics, such as lipsticks, may be present. Angular cheilitis results from accumulation of moisture at the mouth angle with fissuring. Topical allergens must be identified. Low-strength topical steroid preparations in an emolient base are helpful in managing an allergic cheilitis.

Acne

Acne Vulgaris

Acne vulgaris is not a diagnostic problem. A broad experience with the many topical and systemic preparations is helpful in managing this eruption. Adult sebaceous glands and follicles have wide openings on the skin surface and the sebaceous lobules are large. Obstruction due to hyperkeratinization occurs in the follicular neck of the pilosebaceous unit. Sebum is continually being generated. In addition, the anaerobic bacteria *Propionibacterium acnes* in sebaceous follicles reproduce in large numbers. Good therapy is aimed at these changes.

Acne occurs in families. Testosterone is implicated in the flare of acne at puberty. Although the level of the hormone in the serum is not elevated, follicular hypersensitivity is present.

Acne begins with closed comedones (usually white), and then proceeds to form pustules, nodules, or cysts over the face, neck, shoulders, chest, and back. Some patients have only nodulocystic acne from the beginning of the eruption, while others have only open and closed comedones. Cystic disease is the most severe form of the disease. Inflammatory nodules and deep cystic lesions scar.

Although most acne occurs in the adolescent, many cases begin in patients older than 20 years of age. When papular acne develops in women who are in their late 20s and early 30s and who have no prior history of the disease, cosmetics, hormones, and stress should be suspected as flare factors. Acne often flares premenstrually. Drugs such as corticosteroids, phenytoin, and lithium can flare acne.

The therapeutic objective is the control of the process until the condition enters a natural state of remission. The prognosis is good. An important management goal is patient education. The patient should recognize the chronicity of the condition, the flare factors, and should be motivated to properly manage the condition.

Topical retinoids are helpful in reducing hyperkeratinization in comedonal and papulopustular acne, as is benzoyl peroxide 2.5% or 5% solution. Gentle washing with a gentle skin cleanser should be done only twice daily.

Topical antibiotics are also helpful agents. Antibiotics work by reducing numbers of P. acnes. Benzoyl peroxide, tetracycline, minocycline, erythromycin, and clindamycin, as topical preparations, are useful in the management of papulopustular acne.

Oral antibiotics are the most helpful systemic form of acne therapy. Tetracycline and erythromycin are commonly used. The dose depends on disease activity. The usual dose is 250 mg administered 3 or 4 times a day for 2 weeks, followed by 500 mg per day for 3 to 6 months; 1.0 g per day may be necessary for the drug to be effective in the more severe nodulocystic forms of the disease.

Pseudomembranous colitis can occur following any orally administered antibiotic.

The oral retinoid Accutane (isotretinoin) is recommended in the management of severe no-

dulocystic acne that is resistant to other therapies. Pregnancy precautions are mandatory because of the teratogenic potential of this drug.

Rosacea (Acne Rosacea)

Rosacea is an inflammatory disease that affects adults. It commonly occurs in women over the age of 40 years. Although the cause of rosacea is unknown, the eruption is flared by many factors. Alcohol, coffee, tea, chocolate, and other food and beverage constituents are responsible for the flushing associated with drinking hot liquids. The use of fluorinated corticosteroids, applied over several weeks on the face, may produce a Rosacea-like eruption. The clinical presentation includes facial erythema, telangiectasia, and pustules. The most severe form of eruption is associated with red nodules and cysts. The best therapy is to avoid all flare factors, especially heat. Topical antibiotics, erythromycin or metronidazole, are important topical treatments for rosacea. In some patients, oral tetracycline, 250 mg three or four times a day, is required to control this eruption, although the usual dose for this problem is 250 to 500 mg of tetracycline a day.

Hydradenitis Suppurativa (Fig. 80-14; see also color Plate 32)

Hidradenitis suppurativa is a chronic, inflammatory eruption that occurs in the axillae, groin, and buttocks. The clinical eruption appears as red nodules that become painful. The nodules are elongated, and may or may not form an abscess. Draining fistulous tracts may develop. Initial cultures are sterile, but secondary infection may occur due to *Staphylococcus aureus*. Proteus and pseudomonas organisms can be grown from many of these lesions. The disease is persistent. The medical treatment includes oral antibiotics—tetracycline, erythromycin, or the cephalosporins. Surgical excision of the lesions may be necessary.

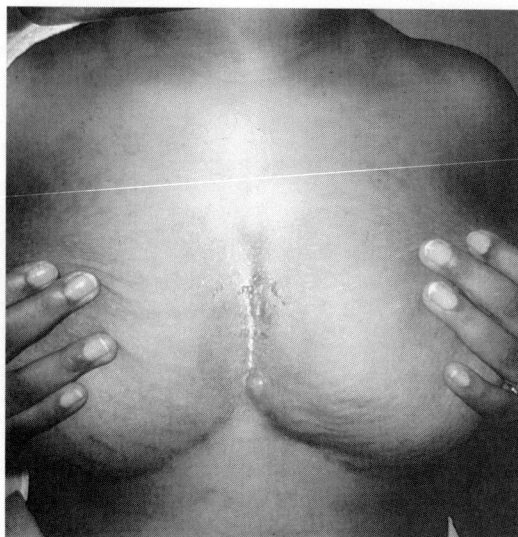

Figure 80-14 Hidradenitis suppurativa. (See color Plate 32.)

Hair Loss

Alopecia Areata

Alopecia areata, a form of acute hair loss that presents with patches of apparently complete hair loss, occurs without signs of inflammation and without scarring. Hairs at the periphery of the new patches can be easily plucked, and a clubbed hair root is noted with thinning of the hair shaft. There is usually spontaneous regrowth of hair after an interval of 2 to 6 months, and 90 percent of the hair is regrown in one year in most patients. There are some clinical features that indicate a poor prognosis for hair regrowth. These are extensive generalized and/or persistent hair loss, and a pattern of interlocking patches of alopecia involving the posterior scalp. The evaluation of treatment for alopecia areata is difficult because spontaneous remission is common. Oral corticosteroids for a short term may be considered in some patients with generalized hair loss, but their side effects should be discussed with the patient before using them. Topical corticosteroid therapy is generally not helpful. Intralesional corticosteroid therapy can be help-

ful for a small patch of alopecia, but skin atrophy can occur. Reassurance is the best therapy for a single lesion.

Androgenic Alopecia

This form of alopecia occurs in both males and females. This condition is genetic, with the onset occurring in patients usually between 20 and 30 years of age. Androgenic alopecia is associated with a short anagen (growth phase) in the hair cycle, and hairs plucked from involved regions show a high proportion of telogen (resting) hairs. A biopsy may be useful in separating this condition from other forms of alopecia. Topical minoxidil (Rogaine) applied bid can be helpful in some patients. Long-term treatment is required, and the hair falls out when therapy is discontinued. Hair transplantation is not usually necessary.

Telogen Effluvium—Loss of Resting Hairs (Telogen); Stress Alopecia

Telogen effluvium, loss of resting hairs, often occurs after pregnancy. Other stressful events may cause this form of hair loss. There is an excellent prognosis for hair regrowth. Telogen effluvium occurs when a higher than normal proportion of scalp hairs enter the telogen or resting phase. Several months of shedding may occur before there is hair regrowth. In addition to pregnancy, this form of hair loss may occur following a high fever, a severe illness, or sudden physical or emotional trauma. If the stress is resolved, the hairs return within 6 months.

Endocrine abnormalities can cause alopecia, and must be excluded when considering telogen effluvium. These conditions include hyper- and hypothyroidism. Hyperthyroidism is associated with dry, fine, thin hair; in hypothyroidism, the hair is coarse and brittle.

Traumatic Alopecia

Any injury to the hair and scalp can cause traumatic alopecia. Excessive handling, combing, and brushing, or frequent waving, can damage the hair.

Cutaneous Lesions with Systemic Disease

Lupus Erythematosus

There are three major forms of lupus erythematosus: discoid lupus erythematosus (DLE), subacute cutaneous lupus erythematosus, and systemic lupus erythematosus (SLE).

Discoid lupus erythematosus is generally limited to the skin. These patients may develop systemic manifestations. Patients with established SLE, especially when the eruption occurs early in life, may develop discoid skin lesions as part of their generalized disease. DLE begins as an erythematous papule that enlarges to form a plaque. Follicular plugging may be observed. The majority of these patients do not have a positive ANA. These patients can usually be managed with topical therapy such as sunscreens and medium-strength topical steroids. The more severe forms may require systemic anti-inflammatory drugs.

Systemic lupus erythematosus, a multisystem disease, may be mild to life-threatening. Women are affected more frequently than men. Cutaneous findings that are helpful in establishing the diagnosis of systemic lupus erythematosus include: mucosal ulcers; a malar erythematosus eruption; photosensitivity; and cold sensitivity in the hands and feet. The commonly affected organs include the joints, kidneys, and central nervous system. Renal disease is the most common cause of death in SLE. Systemic lupus erythematosus and subacute cutaneous lupus erythematosus can be caused by many drugs, including procainamide and hydralazine (Fig. 80-15; see also color Plate 33).

The diagnosis of SLE depends on clinical assessment and laboratory findings. A skin biopsy is important in the diagnostic process in most patients with possible lupus erythematosus. Light

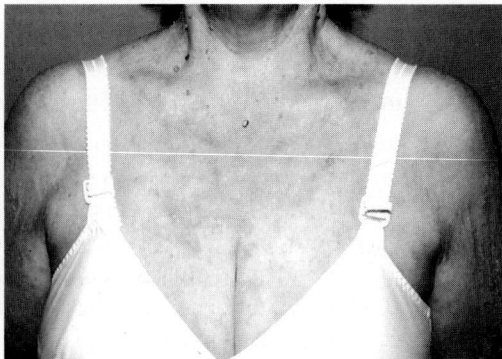

Figure 80-15 Subacute cutaneous lupus erythematosus (drug induced). (See color Plate 33.)

microscopy and immunofluorescent studies help to establish the diagnosis in the skin.

Dermatomyositis

Dermatomyositis is an inflammatory disorder that affects muscle and skin. It includes polymyositis (without cutaneous changes), myositis as a feature of other connective tissue disorders, and a dermatitis without myositis. Dermatomyositis may be acute with fever and toxicity, or may present with progressive muscle weakness accompanied by myalgia. The cutaneous findings are usually noted before the development of polymyositis. A red macular eruption that is photosensitive often appears over the face, neck, and upper trunk, and over the joints. Edema and scales may be present. Atrophy, telangiectasis, and pigmentation may be noted. Internal malignancy must be excluded.

Morphea

Morphea is a localized sclerosis of the skin of unknown cause. Although systemic scleroderma is rare in this condition, a generalized or linear form may be present. Morphea begins as a red macule that becomes a yellow-brown colored, indurated plaque, with pigment loss. The surface skin is not elevated. Some lesions have a characteristic violaceous border, while old lesions may

have postinflammatory hyperpigmentation. Topical steroids are helpful in the management of this condition. The linear form of the disease may have systemic manifestations that may require evaluation by a rheumatologist, or an orthopedic surgeon, or both.

Scleroderma

Hardening of the skin is a feature of systemic scleroderma, and the internal involvement may include the vascular system, the lungs, esophagus, and other organs.

In *progressive systemic sclerosis,* the cutaneous changes are regularly associated with systemic manifestations. Raynaud's phenomenon is usually present, and digital ulcers with gangrene may occur on fingers or toes, followed by loss of digits.

Erythema Nodosum

Erythema nodosum presents with tender erythematous nodules, 1 to 5 cm in diameter, on the anterior tibial area of the leg. Fever and arthralgias may be present. The skin lesions are short-lived, lasting a few weeks to several months. A chronic form of the disease may occur and persist. Erythema nodosum is a hypersensitivity phenomenon. The common precipitating factors include a streptococcal infection and/or drug sensitivity. Other causes include infectious diseases, such as deep fungi, sarcoidosis, and inflammatory bowel diseases, that is, ulcerative colitis or Crohn's disease. The best treatment is short-term bedrest, aspirin for pain reduction, support hose, and management of any underlying disease.

Sarcoidosis

Sarcoidosis is a systemic disorder characterized by granulomas in many organ systems. Sarcoidosis occurs in both sexes and in all races. One-third of patients with sarcoidosis develop skin lesions. In the acute form of the disease, patients may have erythema nodosum, fever, bilateral

hilar adenopathy, and polyarthralgia. In addition to erythematous nodules, other skin lesions may include papular eruptions of the face and extremities, cutaneous plaque formation, nodules, ichthyosis, and ulcers. These skin lesions will only resolve in a satisfactory manner when systemic therapy is given for the sarcoidosis.

Rheumatoid Arthritis (Rheumatoid Nodules)

Rheumatoid nodules occur on the skin in patients with rheumatoid arthritis, and they represent vasculitis. The nodules are seen in patients with high positive serum levels of rheumatoid factor. These nodules usually occur around the elbows, but may arise anywhere. Systemic therapy for the rheumatoid arthritis is the treatment of choice.

Cutaneous Manifestations of Diabetes Mellitus

There are a variety of skin eruptions that may occur in patients with diabetes (Table 80-12).

Tumors of the Skin (Tables 80-13, 80-14, and 80-15)

Benign Tumors and Cysts of the Epidermis

Epidermal tumors are common. When carefully examined, everyone has one or more of these tumors. Although they may occasionally resemble premalignant and malignant lesions, the recognition of these benign neoplasms enables the experienced clinician to reassure the patient about their benign nature. Their excision for cosmetic reasons is optional. Whenever there is any possibility of malignancy, a biopsy should be obtained.

Common epithelial cysts There are three types of epithelial cysts: the epidermal pilar cyst in the scalp, the milium that may occur anywhere on the face, and the epidermal inclusion cyst. Heat, erythema, and tenderness may be pronounced if a cyst has recently leaked or ruptured. The most effective treatment for epithelial and pilar cysts is surgical drainage or removal. It is often possible to make a small linear incision and remove the well-encapsulated cyst, or the cyst may be removed through a 3-mm biopsy site. Incision and drainage is usually temporary ther-

TABLE 80-12 Diabetes Mellitus

Cutaneous Eruptions	Morphology	Therapy
Diabetic dermopathy	1–2-cm patches, red-brown on legs	None
Diabetic bullae	Tense blisters, small or large, hands and feet	None, except avoid trauma
Thick skin scleroderma Diabeticorum scleroderma	Thick skin dorsal hands; marked increase in skin thickness, back and neck	No proven therapy; emollients for dryness of skin
Perforating disorders	Hyperkeratotic papules; elimination of dermal collagen elastin	Therapy for renal disease; emollients and peeling agents
Necrobiosis lipoidica diabeticorum[a]	Cutaneous marker for diabetes; annular plaque with elevated border; telangiectasia	Potent topical steroids applied at the periphery of the lesion

[a]See Fig. 80-16, which appears on page 1082. See also color Plate 34.

TABLE 80-13 Epithelial Tumors

Tumor	Location	Therapy	Prevention
Seborrheic keratosis	Face, body, leg	Cryosurgery, shave excision, or mild electrodesiccation	None
Sebaceous gland hyperplasia	Face	Electrodesiccation with epilating current and curettage	Sunscreens, protective clothing, hat
Actinic keratosis	Face	Cryosurgery or topical 5-fluorouracil or excision	Sun screens, hat
Keratoacanthoma	Any location	Surgical excision with adequate margin	Sun screens, hat
Cutaneous horn	Any location	Biopsy Surgical excision	Sun screens, hat
Bowen's disease	Any location	Surgical excision	Sun screens, hat
Squamous cell carcinoma	Any location	Surgical excision	Sun screens, hat
Basal cell carcinoma	Face, body	Surgical excision	Sun screens, hat

apy and may be followed by a recurrence of the cyst. Residual fragments may produce a foreign-body granuloma or serve as the nidus for a new cyst formation.

Milia are small (1- to 2-mm in diameter) superficial, white cystic lesions that may arise spontaneously or secondary to trauma. They are frequently found around the eye, and must be distinguished from sebaceous hyperplasia and syringomas. Milia may be successfully removed in a variety of ways. One method is to make a small nick in the overlying skin and then apply pressure to evacuate the contents with a comedone extractor.

Epidermal nevi Epidermal nevi are wart-like lesions that arise on the skin early in life. They may, however, begin in the adult. They are frequently noted on the face or behind the ear and on the neck. These lesions are usually brownish, hyperkeratotic papules that form a linear or swirling configuration. Localized epidermal nevi can be treated by local excision or dermabrasion, but a large lesion presents a distinct management problem and should be managed with cosmesis as the primary goal. Plastic surgery is usually required when the lesion is large. Local recurrence after surgery is not uncommon.

Seborrheic keratosis This common benign epithelial tumor arises in the skin in adult life. Many of these lesions are present in older adults, and they may occur on any area of skin on the body

TABLE 80-14 Nonepithelial Skin Tumors

Type	Location	Therapy
Skin Tags	Neck, axilla, groin	Cryosurgery or complete excision
Granuloma pyogenicum	Any area of the skin	Shave excision, followed by electrodesiccation of lesion base
Dermatofibroma	Any skin area	Cryosurgery
Lipoma	Any skin area	Simple excision or excision through a small punch biopsy of skin with pressure to the area to push the lipoma through the opening

TABLE 80-15 Cutaneous Characteristics of Pigmented Lesions

Type	Feature
Benign nevi	Small, uniform color, distinct border
Atypical nevi	Large, irregular border, several colors
Seborrheic kera-tosis	Flesh colored, brown, or black, with keratin
Pigmented basal cell carcinoma	Uniform color, distinct border, no keratin
Blue nevus	Small, blue, stable
Junctional nevus	Flat, distinct border
Malignant mel-anoma	Multiple colors, indistinct borders, rapid growth asymmetrical, over 5 mm in diameter

except the palms and soles. They may occasionally itch. The lesions vary in color from a normal flesh color to tan-brown or black, and they vary in size from a tiny papule (2 mm) to a large plaque or nodule, several centimeters in diameter. They usually have a warty surface and appear to be sitting on top of the skin. They can resemble a malignant lesion, such as Bowen's disease (squamous cell carcinoma in situ), pigmented basal cell carcinoma, or malignant melanoma. The pigmented seborrheic keratosis may require a biopsy to exclude malignant melanoma. Once malignancy has been ruled out, cryosurgery or mild electrodesiccation and curettage may be utilized if the patient wants the lesion treated for cosmetic reasons.

Adnexal tumors These tumors may resemble portions of cutaneous adnexal structures such as hair follicles, sebaceous glands, apocrine glands, and eccrine sweat glands. It is important to be knowledgeable about the more common adnexal tumors because they can resemble basal cell carcinoma. *Sebaceous gland hyperplasia* is a condition seen in fair-skinned adults who have a history of excessive exposure to ultraviolet light. The lesion is a yellow papule or a small nodule on the face. Telangiectasia and a central punctum can be similar to findings with a basal cell carcinoma. A biopsy distinguishes this lesion from a

basal cell carcinoma. A second adnexal tumor, the *trichoepithelioma,* is a solitary nodule that presents on the face. A third adnexal tumor is the syringoma, which is a flesh-colored papule that is frequently found in the skin just below the lower lid margin. A biopsy confirms the diagnosis in each case. The lesions may be surgically removed to produce a good cosmetic appearance by simple excision or electrodesiccation and mild curettage.

Common Nonepithelial Skin Tumors (Table 80-14)

Skin tags Skin tags, or squamous papillomas or skin polyps, are elevated, flesh-colored or tanned papular or filiform lesions that commonly occur in adults in the flexural areas of the neck, axillae, and groin. Obesity and local factors such as sweating and friction are flare factors. Patients are usually most concerned about the cosmetic appearance of these lesions, as well as bleeding from trauma.

Hypertrophic scars and keloids Injury to the skin below the epidermal basement membrane results in scarring. The size and appearance of a scar is dependent upon the injury, location on the body surface, and genetic factors. They may be tan to red-brown to black in color. Excess proliferation of fibrous tissue occurs in genetically susceptible individuals. Keloids are often difficult to manage (see Chap. 84).

Vascular Tumors

Hemangiomas The most common blood vessel tumors are varieties of *hemangioma.* They may be present at birth as a macular congenital form, that is *nevus flammeus,* or papular (strawberry), or cavernous in type. The acquired adult form of capillary hemangioma, the cherry angioma, is regularly seen on covered skin areas. This lesion is cosmetically unacceptable to many patients, but it is always benign.

Granuloma pyogenicum This common tumor represents an exuberant growth of vascular tis-

sue. The precise cause is unknown, but the lesions may be initiated by trauma or hormonal stimulation such as during pregnancy. Granuloma pyogenicum is red and usually presents as a solitary, polypoid lesion. The finger is a common location for this lesion, but it may occur anywhere following skin trauma.

Dermatofibroma The dermatofibroma is a common tumor of fibrohistiocytic origin. It occurs after trauma or infection. The tumor is a firm papule or nodule. Although it may occur anywhere, it frequently appears on the lower extremities.

Lipoma Lipomas are common and asymptomatic unless they have an angiomatous component. They present in a subcutaneous location, and must be distinguished from epithelial cysts and neurofibromas. Small lipomas are of no cosmetic importance and are best left untreated. Large lesions may be removed surgically.

Premalignant and Malignant Epithelial Tumors

The most common premalignant lesion occurring on the skin is actinic keratosis. Other lesions occurring in sun-damaged skin include cutaneous horns (keratoacanthoma), Bowen's disease, and basal cell and squamous cell carcinoma.

Actinic keratosis Actinic or solar keratoses are the most common precancerous skin lesions. They usually appear in the third or fourth decade of life in people who have a light complexion. Actinic keratoses range in color from pink or red to brown. The lesion size and the degree of accumulation of melanin pigment determines the color. They usually have a slight surface scale, and range in size from 0.2 to 1.5 cm in diameter. The lateral borders may be indistinct. The invasive malignant potential for these lesions is low; however, a firm hypertrophic lesion or a lesion with a small ulcer formation, or both, suggests malignancy with possible invasion of the dermis. A biopsy should be obtained when malignancy is suspected or when a lesion previously treated with cryosurgery returns on the skin surface to exclude invasive squamous cell cancer.

Keratoacanthoma This tumor is generally considered to be benign, although it may be hard to differentiate the lesion, clinically and pathologically, from squamous cell carcinoma. It is a lesion that is likely produced by excessive ultraviolet light exposure. Tar exposure and viral infection are possible flare factors. The usual history is a papule occurring on sun-exposed skin that evolves rapidly (in a matter of weeks) to form a nodule with a central crater filled with keratin. The lesion remains stationary for a 6- to 8-week period and then regresses. The major consideration in the differential diagnosis is squamous cell carcinoma.

Cutaneous horns are produced as a reaction to chronic sunlight exposure. The lesion is an elevated horny papule. These lesions have a malignant potential at the base. This lesion should be excised and evaluated histologically to exclude malignancy.

All persons who develop an actinic keratosis have sun-damaged skin and are likely to have many similar lesions in the future. Sun protection is mandatory and topical therapy is often indicated.

Bowen's disease (squamous cell carcinoma in situ of the skin) Bowen's disease is squamous cell carcinoma in situ of the skin. The epidermal malignancy is confined to the epidermis and has not invaded the dermis. It may occur anywhere on the skin surface, and the occurrence is not always related to the skin complexion or type, or to sun exposure. Bowen's disease can resemble psoriasis or nummular eczema. A biopsy should be done to establish the diagnosis.

Squamous cell carcinoma (Fig. 80-17; see also color Plate 35) Squamous cell carcinoma, a malignant epithelial tumor with a potential for metastasis, is commonly noted on the scalp, face, or lip. It should be considered a potentially dangerous skin malignancy, especially when it occurs in the T zone on the face, which includes the skin on the forehead, around the eyes, and over the nose. The ears, the oral mucosa,

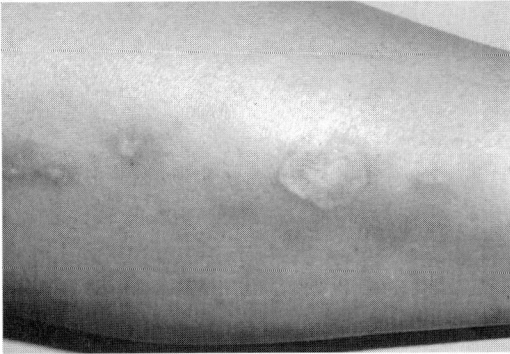

Figure 80-16 Necrobiosis lipoidica diabeticorum. (See color Plate 34.)

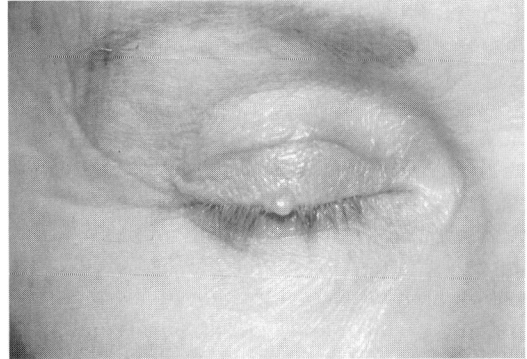

Figure 80-18 Basal cell carcinoma. (See color Plate 36.)

and any burn site are dangerous locations for metastases from these lesions.

Squamous cell carcinoma is usually related to chronic sun exposure. Arsenic exposure or radiation exposure may also be factors in causing squamous cell cancer. Squamous cell carcinomas are highly variable in appearance. Some are hyperkeratotic, some are verrucous nodules, and others form papules or plaques. Ulcer formation may occur in these lesions. The treatment of choice is surgical excision.

Basal cell carcinoma (Fig. 80-18; see also color Plate 36) Basal cell carcinoma is the most prevalent cutaneous malignancy. It is an epithelial tumor that arises as a consequence of an intrinsic defect in basal cells that prevents these cells from

maturing and forming normal keratin. Although local skin destruction and invasion are possible, this lesion rarely extends beyond the skin.

Lymphoma and Leukemia

Lymphoma of the skin presents with violaceous papules and nodules. Lymphomas of T-cell origin commonly begin in the skin.

Mycosis fungoides is an indolent T-cell lymphoma that originates in the skin and has an early course that resembles a persistent eczematous dermatitis or psoriasis. Erythematous, atrophic patches are frequently seen in the early or "patch" stage of the disease. As progression occurs, violaceous plaques and tumors develop in the skin. The diagnosis is made by frequent biopsies in several skin sites. Early therapies include topical nitrogen mustard and ultraviolet light A or B.

Melanocytic Tumors

Melanocytic lesions Melanocyte cell growth occurs within the epidermis or dermis. The *nevus cell* is a form of melanocyte and involves the epidermis, or dermis, or both. Benign epidermal melanocytic tumors include ephelis and lentigo. Nevus cell tumors are numerous and may be benign or malignant.

Ephelis (freckle) Freckles are especially numerous in many Caucasians. The freckles

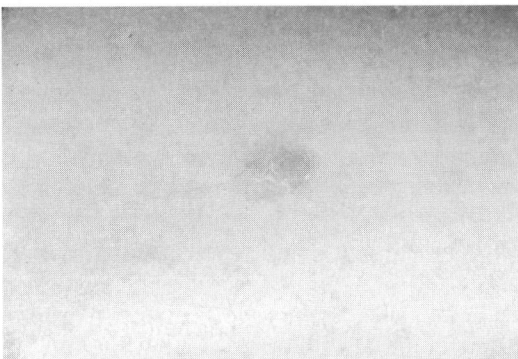

Figure 80-17 Superficial squamous cell carcinoma. (See color Plate 35.)

occur in sun-exposed areas. The melanocytes in freckles are normal, but appear larger than normal melanocytes. No therapy is indicated.

Lentigo Lentigines (pigmented macules) occur in young adults, with or without sun exposure. When they occur in older adults, the sun-exposed area is involved. In adults, lentigines occur on the face, neck, dorsa of the hands, shoulders, and back. Lentigos and seborrheic keratoses are the usual examples of "liver" spots. Lentigines, although benign, are a cosmetic problem and they can mimic malignant melanoma when the pigment is irregular. Suspicious lesions should be biopsied. Cosmetic therapy for benign lentigos can be accomplished with light cryosurgery.

Lesions composed of nevus cells Nevus cell nevi ("moles") occur in all human beings and are the most common tumors of the skin. Nevus cells are of melanocyte origin. Very few are clinically present at birth. Adults may have 60 or more nevi. As the patient advances in age, many of these lesions regress. Nevus cell nevi begin as nests of cells at the dermoepidermal junction (*junctional nevi*). When nevus cells are found solely in the dermis, the lesions are *intradermal nevi*. Nevi may be located anywhere on the body, including the palms, soles, and genitalia. Most nevi do not require excision. A nevus that has changed in color, shape, or size, or is symptomatic, or is merely suspicious to the patient or physician, should be biopsied to exclude malignant melanoma.

Malignant melanoma Malignant melanoma arises from melanocytes in the skin, as well as from melanocytes in other locations, such as the eye and the vagina. Only 1.5 to 3 percent of all skin cancers are melanomas. Melanoma occurs in any location on the skin surface, but is especially common on the head and neck, upper back, and lower extremities. Sunlight plays a role in the development of malignant melanoma and is a risk factor, especially when an acute sunburn occurs early in the life of the patient.

A majority of malignant melanomas arise spontaneously. Melanomas can arise in preex-

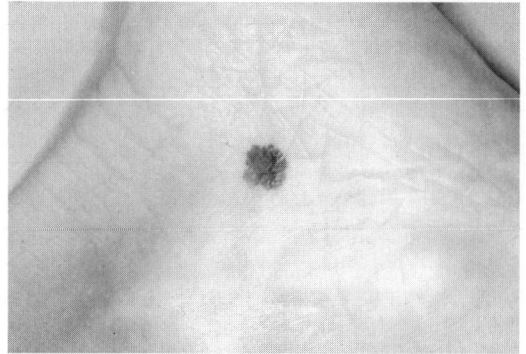

Figure 80-19 Superficial spreading malignant melanoma. (See color Plate 37.)

isting nevi, and especially in giant congenital nevi. The major risk factors for melanoma are a family history of melanoma, a personal history of melanoma, and an atypical mole in a patient with immunosuppression or who has a light complexion with a previous history of excess sun exposure.

Malignant melanomas are divided into four major clinical types. The *superficial spreading malignant melanoma* (Fig. 80-19; see also color Plate 37) is a slightly elevated lesion with an irregular, indistinct margin with irregular distribution of colors, including black, brown, red, and, occasionally, blue. The *nodular melanoma* is usually uniform in color and black. *Lentigo malignant melanoma* occurs in a sun-exposed area and

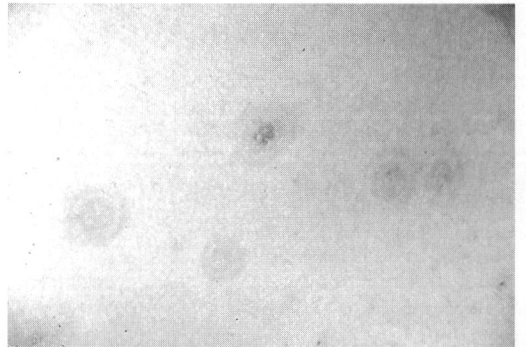

Figure 80-20 Pemphigus gestationis—herpes gestationis. (See color Plate 38.)

TABLE 80-16 Cutaneous Disorders in Pregnancy

Eruption	Type	Therapy	Prognosis
Hyperpigmentation	Physiologic	None	Good
Spider angioma and palmar erythema	Physiologic	None required	May recur
Pruritic papules and plaques of pregnancy (PUPPP)	Related to pregnancy	Should be minimal and should be prescribed by dermatologist and obstetrician	Resolves postpartum; does not recur
Pemphigus or herpes gestationis (Fig. 80-20)[a]	Related to pregnancy	Systemic steroids may be needed	Prognosis for mother good; prognosis for baby is variable; may recur

[a]Figure 80-20 appears on page 1083. See also color Plate 38.

usually begins as a lentigo maligna with gradual enlargement. A fourth variety of malignant melanoma is *acral lentigines melanoma*. This form of melanoma presents as an irregular, pigmented, macular or slightly elevated lesion on the palms, soles, or digits.

Early diagnosis and surgery present the only chance for a cure for any malignant melanoma (see Table 80-15). Periodic total body exams and biopsies of suspicious lesions are recommended.

Cutaneous Disorders in Pregnancy
(Table 80-16)

There are a variety of skin changes that can occur in pregnancy, many of which are physiologic. There are also cutaneous eruptions that occur in pregnancy, and skin diseases that are altered by pregnancy.

Natural Skin Aging and Photo-Induced Skin Damage

Skin dryness and loss of skin elasticity are natural occurrences in the skin in the elderly. Most of the changes that occur in the skin of the individual that are cosmetically unacceptable are related to long-term sun exposure or photoaging. Although skin moisturizers and emollients are help-ful for the skin dryness, the management of photoaging is far more difficult. It is much easier to prevent photoaging than it is to correct the problem once it has occurred. Those persons with a light complexion have a special risk for sun damage from chronic sun exposure, especially during the middle of the day. A sun avoidance and protection routine is the best mangement for preventing future sun damage in all age groups. Excellent sun protection from UVB and UVA light is available from hats and tightly woven fabrics in clothing, plus good sunscreens or sunblocks applied to exposed areas of skin.

Although previous sunscreens have been inadequate to protect the skin from UVA, products containing avobenzone filter adequate amounts of UVA light. Tretinon emollient cream 0.05% may be helpful in the management of fine wrinkles, mottled hyperpigmentation, and surface roughness. This product is a dermal irritant and some patients cannot tolerate it. Close dermatological supervision is required and complete knowledge of the manufacturer's prescribing information is necessary. The long-term safe use of this product has not yet been established.

References and Selected Readings

1. Arnold HL, Odom RB, James WD: *Andrew's Diseases of the Skin, Clinical Dermatology*. Philadelphia: WB Saunders, 1990.

2. Beutner KR: Human papillomavirus infection. *J Am Acad Dermatol* 20:114–123, 1989.
3. Bigby M, Jick A, Jick H, Arndt K: Drug-induced cutaneous reactions: A report from the Boston Collaborative Surveillance Program on 15,438 consecutive inpatients, 1975–1982. *JAMA* 256:3358–3363, 1986.
4. Borelli D, Jacobs PH, Nall L: Tinea versicolor: Epidemiologic, clinical, and therapeutic aspects. *J Am Acad Dermatol* 25:300–305, 1991.
5. Coskey RJ, Coskey LA: Diagnosis and treatment of impetigo. *J Am Acad Dermatol* 17:62–63, 1987.
6. Chuang TY: Condylomata acuminata (genital warts): An epidemiologic view. *J Am Acad Dermatol* 16:376–384, 1987.
7. Drake LA, Ceilley RI, Cornelison RL, et al: Guidelines of care for atopic dermatitis. *J Am Acad Dermatol* 26:485–488, 1992.
8. Drake LA, Ceilley RI, Cornelison RL, et al: American Academy of Dermatology guidelines of care for basal cell carcinoma. *J Am Acad Dermatol* 26:117–120, 1992.
9. Farber EM, Abel EA, Charuworn A: Recent advances in the treatment of psoriasis. *J Am Acad Dermatol* 8:311–321, 1983.
10. Fisher GJ, Wang ZQ, Datta SC, Varani J, Kang S, Voorhees JJ: Pathophysiology of premature skin aging induced by ultraviolet light. *N Engl J Med* 337:20, 1997.
11. Glass AG, Hoover RN: The emerging epidemic of melanoma and squamous cell skin cancer. *JAMA* 262:2097–2100, 1989.
12. Hanifin JM: Atopic dermatitis: New therapeutic considerations. *J Am Acad Dermatol* 24:1097–1101, 1991.
13. Hook EW, Hooton TM, Horton CA et al: Microbiologic evaluation of cutaneous cellulitis in adults. *Arch Intern Med* 146:295–297, 1986.
14. Howland WW, Golitz LE, Weston WL, Huff JC: Erythema muliforme: Clinical, histopathologic, and immunologic study. *J Am Acad Dermatol* 10:438–446, 1984.
15. Hughes BR, Murphy CE, Barnett J, Cunliffe WJ: Strategy of acne therapy with long-term antibiotics. *Br J Dermatol* 121:623–628, 1989.
16. Isselbacher KJ, Braunwold E, Wilson JD, Martin JB, Fauci AS, Kasper DL: *Harrison's Principles of Internal Medicine,* 13th ed. New York: McGraw-Hill, 1994.
17. Kaye FJ, Bunn PA, Steinberg SM, et al: A randomized trial comparing combination electron-beam radiation and chemotherapy with topical therapy in the initial treatment of mycosis fungoides. *N Engl J Med* 321:1784–1790, 1989.
18. Koh HK: Cutaneous melanoma. *N Engl J Med* 325:171–182, 1991.
19. Kwa RE, Campana K, Moy RD: Biology of cutaneous squamous cell carcinoma. *J Am Acad Dermatol* 26:1, 1992.
20. Landow K: The perennial scourge: Hand dermatitis. *Postgrad Med* 103:1, 1998.
21. Lowy FD: Staphylococcus aureus infections. *N. Engl J Med* 339(8):520–530, 1998.
22. Manders SM: Toxin-mediated streptococcal and staphylococcal disease. *J Am Acad Dermatol* 39(3):383–398, 1998.
23. The Medical Letter: Drugs for non-HIV viral infections 39(1006):, 1997.
24. Olsen EA, Katz HI, Levine N, et al: Tretinoin emollient cream: A new therapy for photodamaged skin. *J Am Acad Dermatol* 26(2 pt 1):215–224, 1992.
25. Physicians' Desk Reference: 53rd ed. 1999. Montvale, NJ: Medical Economics Company.

Otolaryngology

Gerald D. Zahtz
David Myssiorek

PHYSICAL EXAMINATION
Ears • Nose • Pharynx •
Larynx • Neck
NASAL OBSTRUCTION/SINUSITIS
DIZZINESS
HEARING LOSS
OTALGIA
HOARSENESS

The field of otolaryngology deals with disease processes involving the head and neck region. This chapter provides a broad overview of the diagnosis and office treatment of common otolaryngologic problems. Within the head and neck, very few disease processes are specific for women, except for hormonally related rhinitis, the increased incidence of cancer of the hypopharynx, otosclerosis, and Meniere's disease.

As in all fields of medicine, accurate history taking is essential for proper diagnosis and must be followed by a thorough physical examination.

Physical Examination

Ears

Initially, the external ear and postauricular areas should be inspected for swelling, erythema, cysts, and congenital malformations. After this inspection, the pinna is grasped and gently pulled superoposteriorly to straighten the ear canal as the otoscope is inserted. If the patient complains of pain during this maneuver, one must consider a diagnosis of otitis externa involving the external auditory canal. The normal ear canal should have no erythema or exudate. Cerumen should be removed gently by curettage or irrigation to allow proper evaluation, unless there are signs of infection or tympanic membrane perforation. The tympanic membrane is then visualized and should appear as an intact, pearly-white translucent membrane. Mobility of the tympanic membrane should be ascertained by pneumatic otoscopy. This is done using the insufflator bulb attachment of the otoscope. By blowing air through the head of the otoscope and into the ear canal, the mobility of the tympanic membrane can be evaluated.

Nose

Initial evaluation should begin with the examination of the external nose, with documentation of external deformities, as well as erythema or edema. Intranasal examination can be performed with an otoscope, but is best performed with a headlight and nasal speculum. The largest speculum should be placed into the patient's nostril carefully. Abnormalities in the position of the midline septum, the presence of masses, and the color and size of the turbinates should be noted, as well as the character of any intranasal secretions.

The intranasal examination should be performed twice, before and after the use of vasoconstrictors, such as oxymetazoline or phenylephrine. The postvasoconstrictor examination allows septal deformities, nasal masses, and purulent secretions to be easily diagnosed.

Pharynx

The entire oral cavity must be examined for mucosal and dental lesions. All bridgework and dentures must be removed. Optimal examination requires both a bright light and a tongue depressor to allow proper visualization of the oral mucosa and the posterior pharynx. The presence or absence of tonsils should be noted, as well as any asymmetric finding in the oral cavity. Careful attention should be given to the lateral borders of the tongue to examine for any suspicious lesions.

Larynx

The laryngeal examination is very important for the evaluation of hoarseness. This area is not easily accessible except by use of headlight and mirror or a fiberoptic nasopharyngoscope. This procedure is usually performed by the otolaryngologist.

Neck

The entire neck should be inspected for any masses, bruits, scars, or deformities, and should then be palpated. If any masses are found, their size, position, fluctuance, and mobility should be recorded. The contour (irregularity, lobularity) should also be noted. A careful evaluation of the thyroid gland is also essential as part of this examination.

Nasal Obstruction/Sinusitis

Nasal obstruction/sinusitis are common complaints in a general practice. Their evaluation requires an accurate history, physical exam, and, occasionally, diagnostic tests. Most nasal mucosal abnormalities cause bilateral disease with varying degrees of severity that can fluctuate over hours, days, or seasonally. Structural abnormalities are usually unilateral, fixed, and unchanging; however, their severity can vary.

The time of onset and duration of symptoms should be ascertained. Antecedent trauma, symptom laterality, and whether symptoms are intermittent or constant, seasonal or perennial, should be determined. If any factors seem to trigger the symptoms or relieve them, these should be recorded. The patient's hormonal status must be determined, as rhinitis of pregnancy, menopause, hypothyroidism, and hormonal therapy (e.g., replacement therapy or birth control pills) can also cause nasal obstruction.

The examination of the nose was previously discussed. Extra effort in the visualization of the nasal cavity will reward the practitioner with a proper diagnosis. Nasal obstruction usually can be divided into these categories: mucosal disease, structural abnormalities, and nasal masses. The differential diagnosis of mucosal disease includes acute rhinitis, allergic rhinitis, vasomotor rhinitis, atrophic rhinitis, rhinitis medicamentosa, hormonally related rhinitis, and sinusitis.

Acute rhinitis, also known as the "common cold," is the most common cause of nasal obstruction. It has no "cure," but is treated symptomatically with various drying agents, such as antihistamines, decongestants, antihistamine/decongestants, and topical decongestants. It can also be the first stage of an acute sinus infection. As the nasal mucosa becomes edematous, the sinus opening (ostium) becomes blocked and the oxygen saturation in the affected sinus decreases; bacteria begin to proliferate inside the sinus, causing an acute infectious process. The diagnosis of acute sinusitis is made as the patient's "cold" does not resolve over the normal 48 to 72 h; instead, the patient begins to develop purulent rhinorrhea. Swelling of the face, toothache, and facial pain may be associated with acute sinusitis. The patient suspected of having sinusitis should be sent for paranasal sinus x-rays to confirm the diagnosis. CT scans are necessary when an underlying etiology such as tumor or polyp is being sought. The CT also can distinguish fluid from solid tissue in the sinus. Culture of the nasal drainage may identify the infecting organism; however, approximately half the time, these cultures do not adequately represent the sinus pathogen. The most common organisms in adults

are Streptococci (including Pneumococci) and Haemophilus strains.

Treatment of sinusitis is similar for all the sinuses. Systemic nasal decongestants and short-term topical nasal decongestants (neosynephrine or oxymetazoline) should be started unless the patient is taking medications that preclude their use or has certain cardiac conditions. Humidification and warm compresses over the affected sinus help. If orbital complications are present referral to an otolaryngologist and an ophthalmologist usually is necessary.

Acute bacterial sinusitis should be treated aggressively with antibiotic therapy, as well as decongestant therapy to maintain drainage. The mainstay of antibiotic therapy is amoxicillin; however, in view of the increasing resistance of bacteria to this medication, one must consider change of therapy to amoxicillin/clavulanic acid, second/third-generation cephalosporins, quinolones, clarithromycin, or trimethoprim-sulfamethoxazole (for patients allergic to penicillin) if improvement is not seen. Patients who present with increasing pain, headache, or facial cellulitis should immediately be referred to an otolaryngologist for further therapy unless the primary care physician has substantial expertise with this problem.

Diagnosis of allergic rhinitis is based on the history of seasonal symptoms, nasal itching, paroxysmal sneezing and rhinorrhea. It can be exacerbated by exposure to antigens that trigger an allergic response. Nasal examination reveals clear, watery discharge with pale blue nasal turbinates. Further discussion of this problem can be found in Chap. 73.

Vasomotor rhinitis is a problem in which there is excessive swelling and congestion of the nasal mucosa in the absence of allergic disease. The findings on physical examination are the same as seen in allergic rhinitis except for the absence of response to skin tests and the lack of eosinophils on nasal smear. Factors causing symptoms include stress, changes in weather and humidity, and irritating fumes. The symptoms are treated using antihistamines, decongestants, antihistamine/decongestants, and topical intranasal steroids. Medical management is less successful in this disease, and patients may require surgical therapy of the turbinates for effective treatment of this problem.

Atrophic rhinitis is a rare disease caused by atrophy of mucosa and bone in the nasal cavity characterized by excessive crusting, foul-smelling rhinorrhea, epistaxis, and anosmia. Treatment is aimed at local therapy, with frequent cleaning of nasal crusts and debris, and moisturization of the nasal cavity.

Rhinitis medicamentosa is caused by the chronic use of topical nasal decongestants (e.g., oxymetazoline, phenylephrine, etc.). It is a rebound effect caused by the constant use of the topical vasoconstrictors. Its treatment requires the discontinuation of vasoconstrictor nose drops. Because these patients develop more congestion of the nose upon the termination of use of the vasoconstrictor, symptomatic therapy with the use of normal saline drops, systemic decongestants, topical intranasal steroids or occasional use of the systemic steroids may be necessary.

Other medications that can cause nasal obstruction include alcohol, antithyroid medications, aspirin, cocaine, estrogens and birth control pills, ephedrine, epinephrine, iodides, marijuana, reserpine, and tobacco.

The diagnosis of hormonally related rhinorrhea requires a good history. Each of these endocrine factors can play a role in nasal obstruction: pregnancy—especially the second and third trimester; menstruation—congestion can fluctuate with the woman's cycle; diabetes mellitus; and hypothyroidism—causes increased nasal congestion. In the latter two instances, control of the endocrine disease may be necessary to help control the congestion. These problems occasionally respond to topical intranasal steroids.

Structural abnormalities include extranasal deformities, deviated septum, nasal valve collapse, and choanal atresia. The most common nasal masses seen are nasal polyps, which usually are found in patients with severe allergies and asthma. Other neoplastic processes can be found

in the nasal cavity. Both the structural abnormalities and the nasal masses are disease processes that usually will require referral to the otolaryngologist.

Dizziness

The proper evaluation of the "dizzy" patient is one of the most difficult problems for the physician. Vertigo, with its sensation of motion, must be distinguished from disequilibrium, a sensation of imbalance not related to motion. Care must be taken when obtaining the history to decipher and define the patient's symptoms. Symptoms of visual disturbances, weakness in the legs, near-syncope, mild nausca, and spatial disorientation are not caused by inner ear disease.

Vertigo can be described by the patient as "things spinning around me" or "I am spinning around." It can also, on occasion, present with a tilting sensation. The association of symptoms with loss of hearing, ringing in the ears and pressure in the ears shift the diagnosis to a peripheral disorder; headaches, seizures, loss of consciousness, visual change, and lightheadedness shift the diagnosis away from peripheral disease. Other important questions concern the duration and frequency of the symptoms and the circumstances under which they occur (e.g., after meals or related to position), and response to medications. It must be remembered that the "balance mechanism" requires normal vestibular function, an intact optical system, as well as proprioception, which is then interpreted by the central nervous system as "balance." A breakdown in any one of these factors can cause "dizziness." Physical examination requires a brief neurologic examination of the cranial nerves, gait, and balance. Observation of the extraocular movement of the eyes for nystagmus is also important. Vertigo that can be elicited by change of position needs to be documented and distinguished from orthostatic changes.

With the above information, the physician should be able to differentiate dizziness caused by labyrinthine disease and that which is nonlabyrinthine in origin. Nonlabyrinthine disease requires further medical and neurologic evaluation.

The differential diagnosis of vestibular disease is divided into two types: peripheral disease and nonperipheral disease. Nonperipheral disease includes cerebellar or cerebellopontine angle tumors, multiple sclerosis, and temporal lobe epilepsy. These processes usually are diagnosed by eliminating peripheral causes and by direct imaging techniques of the brain using MRI. Vascular lesions causing brain stem ischemia usually have additional neurologic symptoms, such as slurred speech, visual problems, and difficulty swallowing. A whiplash injury to the neck can cause cervical vertigo, which is confirmed only by excluding all other forms of vertigo. Metabolic disorders, such as hypoglycemia, hypothyroidism, and syphilis, have all been associated with vertigo. These diseases are diagnosed by obtaining appropriate blood tests. Symptoms usually resolve with treatment of the underlying disease process.

Peripheral lesions of the labyrinth present with "true" vertigo. This differential diagnosis includes Meniere's disease, benign positional vertigo, vestibular neuronitis, labyrinthitis, ototoxicity, motion sickness, and multiple sclerosis (MS). Meniere's disease classically presents with episodes of vertigo, aural fullness, ringing, and fluctuating hearing loss. It is felt to be caused by endolymphatic hydrops, an increase of endolymphatic fluid in the inner ear due to an abnormality in the sodium-potassium pump of the inner ear. The classic episode lasts for hours, not days; however, unsteadiness may persist for some time after the episode. These attacks are episodic and may be separated in time by months or even years. An accurate history is very important in helping to make the diagnosis. Its treatment comprises a salt-restricted diet, diuretics, and the use of vestibular suppressants (meclizine, promethazine, diazepam). If symptoms continue, surgical therapy may be necessary.

Benign paroxysmal positional vertigo usually is described as a sudden onset of vertigo while

in a specific position (e.g., turning one's head, turning to one side in bed). Recent studies have shown that the pathophysiology of this disorder is related to an abnormality of the position of the inner ear otoconia. The otolaryngologist can mobilize the otoconia restoring normal function with the Epley maneuver.

Vestibular neuronitis presents with a sudden onset of vertigo lasting for hours that slowly abates. It has been related to antecedent viral diseases, but can occur at any time. The acute symptoms usually abate within 24 h; however, prolonged unsteadiness can persist for months. This disease has no aural symptoms and should not be confused with Meniere's disease or labyrinthitis. Vestibular suppressants and labyrinthine exercises also can be used for treatment of this problem.

Labyrinthitis presents with the same symptoms as noted above, except for the addition of hearing loss. This disease process must be monitored carefully, because it can be caused by bacterial infection and can lead to meningitis.

Perilymphatic fistula is a controversial area in otolaryngology. It is caused by a leak of "inner ear fluid" in the region of the round or oval windows. It presents with sudden vertigo, occasional hearing loss, and a history or antecedent barotrauma (e.g., scuba diving or airplane flight). It should be treated with bedrest and, if the symptoms do not improve, surgical therapy may be necessary.

Ototoxicity and vestibular toxicity can be caused by numerous medications that affect the vestibular and auditory system, including aspirin, aminoglycosides, loop diuretics, and antineoplastic agents. These problems can present at any time during therapy and have been reported to develop even months after discontinuing medication.

Motion sickness is distinguished by its direct causal effects, secondary to repetitive motions, such as experienced in ships, airplanes, and automobiles. Scopolamine patches are effective in the prevention and control of this problem.

Multiple sclerosis can present with vertigo in

10 percent of cases. Its diagnosis is based upon multiple presentations of various neurologic symptoms and signs. Approximately 30 percent of all MS patients have vertigo during the course of the disease.

Hearing Loss

Hearing loss is divided into two categories, conductive and sensorineural. Conductive loss is caused by abnormalities of the external ear, tympanic membrane and cavity, and the ossicles. It is this type of loss that is theoretically correctable either through medications or surgery. A sensorineural hearing loss implies damage to the auditory nerve caused by abnormalities in the cochlea or along its neural pathways to the brain.

A simple tuning fork test can help distinguish between these two types of hearing loss. A 512-Hz tuning fork is used to perform the Weber and Rinne test. Lower frequency tuning forks do not test hearing; they test vibrotactile sensation. In the Weber test, the examiner places a vibrating tuning fork on the midline of the forehead, bridge of the nose, or the midline on the teeth. Normally, the patient perceives the sound equally in both ears or is unable to localize the sound. In patients who have conductive hearing loss, the sound is louder in the ear with the conductive defect. In sensorineural hearing losses, the sound is greater in the opposite ear. Thus, if a patient notices the sound to be lateralized into one ear, it suggests either a conductive hearing loss in that ear or a sensorineural hearing loss in the opposite ear.

The Rinne test is then used to distinguish between a conductive hearing loss and sensorineural hearing loss. The vibrating tuning fork is placed along the ear and on the mastoid. In normal situations, and in sensorineural hearing loss, the patient perceives a louder noise when the tuning fork is placed alongside the ear (air conduction) versus placing it on the mastoid region (bone conduction). If the sound is louder when the tuning fork is placed on the mastoid, the

patient has a conductive hearing loss. Thus, once a patient has been shown to have an abnormal Weber test, each ear is then examined by the Rinne test, which distinguishes conductive from sensorineural hearing loss.

These tests can be used as a rough gauge to determine the type of loss, but this must be confirmed on audiometric evaluation. A physical examination of the ear, with removal of impacted cerumen for visualization of the tympanic membrane, to rule out perforations or fluid behind the ear, should be performed, as these are the most common causes of conductive hearing loss and are easily diagnosed. Treatment should be directed to the specific disease, and usually warrants referral to an otolaryngologist.

Some specific etiologies of hearing loss primarily affect women. Otosclerosis is an abnormality of the stapes, which becomes fixed, thus impeding the normal conduction mechanism of sound to the inner ear. It is frequently bilateral, has a genetic predisposition, and seems to present between the ages of 15 and 45 years, with a $2:1$ predominance in women. It is seen most frequently in Caucasian patients and is known to cause a rapid progression of hearing loss in younger women, during pregnancy, and in women taking estrogens. The diagnosis is made by a normal examination that has ruled out external and middle ear pathology, and by tuning fork tests, which show a conductive hearing loss. Audiometry is then used for confirmation. These patients should be referred to the otolaryngologist for definitive surgical therapy.

There are many other causes of hearing loss, including trauma, ototoxicity due to drugs, and presbycusis.

Otalgia

Otalgia (pain in the ear) may be due primarily to ear pathology, from local tissue inflammation or tumor (e.g., parotitis), temporomandibular joint syndrome, or referred from the throat. Approximately one-half of ear pain is nonotologic in origin. Sensory innervation to the ear is derived from the trigeminal, facial, glossopharyngeal, and vagal nerves. The greater auricular nerve (derived from C_3) provides sensation to the lower half of the auricle and its anterior canal wall. Consequently, if the patient has otalgia, it is not enough to examine only the ear.

In general, laboratory tests for otalgia are not necessary unless constitutional symptoms and signs are present. Appropriate cultures, complete blood count, and sedimentation rate may assist in determining treatment of infectious causes. Serologic tests in cases of Wegener's granulomatosis or relapsing polychondritis are needed to direct diagnostic investigation.

The most common source of ear pain over all age groups is infection. The patient should be questioned about recent trauma, upper respiratory tract infections, water exposure, travel, and instrumentation (cotton swabs, match sticks). Deeper trauma or spread of infection can lead to damage to the middle ear and/or inner ear. Symptoms to elicit include hearing loss, vertigo, tinnitus, and autophony (hearing one's self). During warm months, swimming quite often causes otitis externa. The physical examination of the external auditory canal will reveal swelling, erythema, and tenderness of the canal. The tympanic membrane (TM) may also be injected. If discharge or cerumen is noted in the canal, local care in the form of curettage or suctioning should be performed to allow the ear's pH to lower and humidity to decrease. If significant edema of the ear canal or TM exists, a Rinne test may show a bone conduction greater than air conduction. Nonototoxic, pH-buffered eardrops should be started and the ear kept dry. If the canal is very swollen, a wick should be placed to allow eardrops to enter the ear and prevent complete collapse of the canal. Attention should be turned to the preauricular lymph nodes. Enlargement of these nodes implies that the infection has spread beyond the local tissues and probably requires systemic antibiotics.

The middle ear and mastoid, when inflamed, also can cause otalgia. Acute otitis media may

occur at any age. In adults, the common predisposing factors include allergies, barotrauma, and upper respiratory infections. Symptoms include hearing loss, severe pain, and fullness. Some patients complain of tinnitus and/or dizziness. The patient should be asked if she has flown or scuba-dived recently. Previous ear surgery or trauma is significant, because these patients are more prone to the complications of otitis media. Unilateral otitis media should prompt an investigation of the nasopharynx because nasopharyngeal masses can obstruct the Eustachian tube orifices, resulting in otitis media. Unchecked, otitis media can result in TM perforation, sigmoid thrombophlebitis, meningitis, epidural/subdural abscess, and brain abscess.

The TM in otitis media appears thickened and red. The light reflex is absent and the drum will not move on pneumatic otoscopy. If the external ear is projecting from the head at a greater than usual angle ($\sim$30°) acute mastoiditis may be present. Obtaining cultures from draining ears may not necessarily reveal the infecting organism because the external auditory canal is usually colonized by *Pseudomonas aeruginosa.* Treatment for acute otitis media includes oral systemic antibiotics such as amoxicillin. Recent studies indicate the lack of efficacy of antihistamine decongestants in the treatment of otitis media. Recalcitrant otitis or suspected mastoid disease usually requires referral to a specialist.

If the ear exam is normal, pain may originate from facial structures such as the skin, teeth, or parotid gland. The skin should be examined for red, swollen, tender areas consistent with infection (abscess, acne). Gentle tapping of the dentition with an instrument handle may reveal a sensitive tooth, requiring evaluation by a dentist. The parotid gland should be palpated for irregularity, tenderness, and masses. Stensen's duct, which usually is opposite the second molar, is examined for stones, pus, and lack of saliva. Pus is indicative of a gland infection. Lack of saliva, particularly in an older, dehydrated patient, is suggestive of obstruction or Sjögren's syndrome. These patients need intravenous hydration, anti-

biotics for Staphylococcus species, and sialagogues.

If uncertainty persists, the pharynx and hypopharynx should be examined. Otalgia may be based on referred sensation via the glossopharyngeal nerve in patients with tonsillitis/pharyngitis or secondary to eustachian tube dysfunction caused by inflammation. If infected, the tonsils may appear red and cryptic with exudate. In mononucleosis, the exudate is thick and the tonsils are markedly red and enlarged. A peritonsillar abscess will deviate the uvula to the opposite side, cause trismus from pterygoid muscle involvement, and result in drooling from inability to swallow. Following tonsillectomy and/or adenoidectomy, pain in the ear is common.

Cancers in this region become painful when nerves or muscles are invaded or if the tumor becomes infected. One of the earliest symptoms of hypopharyngeal cancer is otalgia. Similarly, patients with laryngeal cancer or chondritis may experience otalgia. Again, the neck should be examined because a mass in the neck is also an "early" sign of hypopharyngeal carcinoma. Referral to an otolaryngologist is mandatory if a cancer is suspected or cannot be ruled out.

When no tumor or infection can be detected and a dental examination is normal, the temporomandibular joint (TMJ) should be suspected as the source of the pain. These patients may clench their teeth, grind them during sleep (bruxism), or have had recent dental manipulations resulting in spasm of the pterygoid musculature. The pain usually is described as dull, radiating to the scalp, neck, TMJ, face, or temple. It often is exacerbated by biting or chewing. Ask the patient about gum-chewing or holding her chin in her palm while sitting. During the examination, the joint should be palpated during opening and closing of the jaw. The mandible should be observed for unusual or unequal excursions as well. An intraoral digital examination may reveal tenderness over the pterygoid musculature. Disorders specific to joints should also be suspected; for example, the patient with rheumatoid arthritis may have TMJ arthritis. If the diagnosis of TMJ

syndrome is entertained, initial treatment with warm, moist heat, soft diet, and nonsteroidal anti-inflammatory drugs is indicated. If this fails, the patient should be evaluated by an oral surgeon who treats this entity, because an appliance may be necessary.

Hoarseness

Although hoarseness may have many etiologies, the most common site of pathology is the larynx. Occasionally the patient with poor pulmonary reserve or psychological difficulty develops hoarseness without laryngeal pathology. Speech is produced when a column of air passes through the vocal folds causing them to vibrate. This requires the coordination of the muscles of respiration, phonation, an intact laryngeal lining, and an intact cerebrum and brainstem. Hoarseness includes subjective complaints of breathiness, harshness, diplophonia (speaking in two pitches at the same time), change in pitch, or change in loudness.

The history should include the patient's age and sex, occupation, and the season. Certain avocations, (e.g., teachers, singers, and preachers) subject the voice to daily abuse. These people are usually extremely sensitive to subtle changes in their voices. Associated illnesses (sinusitis, neoplasm, and pneumonia) may change the voice. Trauma resulting in hoarseness may result in permanent vocal loss if not attended to early. Allergy, hormonal changes, and medication use (e.g., anticholinergic medications or hormonal therapy) can lead to hoarseness from their effects on the mucous membranes of the larynx, while substance abuse (tobacco/alcohol) additionally can cause tumor formation. Fluid retention during pre-and early menstrual days, as well as pregnancy, can cause hoarseness unresponsive to diuretic therapy. Reflux esophagitis may cause hoarseness by creating a chemical burn at the level of the arytenoids of the larynx. Specifically, the onset and duration of the voice change should be determined. Any previous treatment(s)

should be noted. Hemoptysis may be detected in supraglottic tumors or laryngeal tuberculosis. Constitutional symptoms of weight loss, shortness of breath and fatigue should be sought.

Hoarseness usually represents a vocal fold irregularity that does not allow this structure to vibrate correctly. Inspiratory stridor suggests that the patient has a mass at or above the level of the vocal cords. Expiratory stridor may represent a subglottic or extrathoracic tracheal lesion.

All patients with unexplained hoarseness of greater than two weeks' duration should be evaluated. Following a thorough head and neck examination, the external larynx should be palpated. Tenderness over the prominence (Adam's apple) in the face of laryngeal trauma is indicative of cartilaginous fractures.

The larynx should elevate during swallowing. Grasping the larynx and rocking it side to side should produce crepitus in the normal patient; however, it will glide smoothly in a patient with a cancer in the postcricoid region.

The larynx cannot be visualized in a routine examination without the proper equipment. For this reason, most physicians refer patients for evaluation of suspected laryngeal lesions. If a suspicious lesion is detected on physical examination, particularly in a patient who smokes, a biopsy performed in the operating room is indicated. A paralyzed vocal fold in the absence of trauma, thyroid surgery, or CVA requires systematic evaluation of the chest and skull base for lesions affecting the vagus nerve along its course. MRI or contrast CT scans of these structures and the neck should be performed to rule out lesions of the lung, esophagus, larynx, and thyroid gland.

When no lesion can be detected, or if adequate equipment is lacking, the patient should be referred to an otolaryngologist for further workup. The cause of hoarseness in the patient with no paralysis and no obvious lesion may be minor edema of the mucous membrane of the vocal cord itself, reflux, or misuse of the vocal organ. Voice rest is indicated (avoidance of screaming, singing, excessive speaking, whispering, grunting, and heavy weight lifting). An antireflux regimen

(no late meals, antacids, no acidic foods, head-of-bed elevation, nonrestrictive clothing), and hydration will help.

References and Selected Readings

1. Cummings CW, Fredrickson JM, Harker LA Krause CJ, Schuller DE, (eds): *Otolaryngology—Head and Neck Surgery.* CV Mosby, 1997.

2. English GM (ed): *Otolaryngology,* Revised ed. Philadelphia: JB Lippincott, 1992.
3. Goodhill V (ed): *Ear Diseases, Deafness, and Dizziness.* Hagerstown, Md: Harper & Row, 1979.
4. Josephson JS, Mattox DE (eds): Update in otolaryngology I. *Med Clin North Am* 75; 6, 1991.
5. Kimmelman CP (ed): Otolaryngologic office evaluation and management. *Otolaryngol Clin North Am* 25; 4, 1992.
6. Lee KJ (ed): *Essential Otolaryngology, Head and Neck Surgery* 6th ed. East Norwalk, CT: Medical Examination, 1995.

Eye Disorders

J. Stephen Hudgins

When faced with what they believe to be a medical problem with their eyes, many patients turn to their primary care physician for evaluation and treatment. This provider must therefore be comfortable in the assessment of ocular signs and symptoms, and in determining what conditions may be treated in his or her office, and what conditions need to be stabilized and referred.

Although the source of the patient's ocular problem may be obvious, eliciting a chief ocular complaint, a history of present illness, and a personal and family ocular history is usually time well spent. Likewise, a thorough ocular examination will help the clinician avoid missing unsuspected ancillary problems when the primary problem is known.

Diagnostic Equipment

The equipment needed for a screening ocular examination in the primary care setting includes:

- A visual acuity chart (Snellen)
- An occluder with pinhole
- A penlight or flashlight with a cobalt-blue filter
- A pair of loupes (optional, but useful)

- An ophthalmoscope
- A Schiotz tonometer
- Sterile saline irrigating solution
- Fluorescein strips
- Short-acting mydriatic agent (Tropicamide 1%)
- Topical anesthetic (proparacaine 0.5% or tetracaine 0.5%)

Ocular Symptoms

Decreased Visual Acuity

A rapid or significant decrease in visual acuity may be associated with a serious ocular condition and should be referred for ophthalmologic evaluation. More gradual reductions in vision, especially when visual acuity remains unchanged at some distances usually is indicative of a change in refractive error. A significant improvement in visual acuity when the patient is looking through a pinhole suggests either an error in focusing or a problem with the clarity of some part of the ocular media (e.g., cornea or lens).

Diplopia

When examining patients with double vision, the first priority is to determine whether the diplopia is monocular or binocular. In binocular diplopia, the patient's double vision goes away when either eye is covered. The etiology of this double vision is that the two eyes are aimed in different directions and therefore two different images are sent to the visual cortex. The images may be offset vertically, horizontally, or both, or even tilted. Ocular misalignment can arise from problems with the orbit, the extraocular muscles, the cranial nerves that innervate these muscles, or the brain. Ophthalmologic and sometimes neurologic evaluation is mandatory for adults complaining of binocular diplopia.

In monocular diplopia, the double vision persists in at least one of the eyes when the other eye is covered. This usually is the result of a

problem with the clarity of the ocular media (often the lens, frequently due to cataract formation).

Floaters

New-onset floaters, especially when accompanied by flashes of light seen in the periphery of vision at night, warrant prompt evaluation by an ophthalmologist. While these symptoms usually are attributable to a shifting of the vitreous jelly that fills the back of the eye, they may indicate the onset of a tear or detachment of the retina. Other serious causes of new-onset floaters include vitreous hemorrhage (often seen in diabetics) and inflammatory conditions involving the retina and vitreous.

Scotomas

A blind or blurry spot in the vision of one eye may be due to problems with the retina (e.g., macular hole, retinal hemorrhage, or aging macular degeneration) or optic nerve (e.g., glaucoma). Congruent scotomas in both eyes are presumed to be due to problems in the visual pathways or visual cortex. Migrainous auras, with or without the headache, may cause transient bilateral scotomas.

Photophobia

New-onset photophobia may be due to corneal abrasions or infections, or to intraocular inflammations such as uveitis. Increased glare caused by cataracts or other disturbances in ocular media clarity, or by problems associated with transition from dark to light (as seen with aging macular degeneration) may be confused with photophobia. When a patient complains that she has always been slightly sensitive to bright light, this usually does not suggest a significant problem.

Pain

Assessing the character, location, duration and severity of ocular pain symptoms can be quite

helpful in determining the etiology of the pain. Foreign-body sensation described as a "sharp, scratchy" pain may be associated with a foreign body or may be seen with corneal abrasions in the absence of a foreign body. A "dull, achy" pain that may be referred to the brow and may be associated with nausea is the hallmark of glaucomatous pain. Headaches often cause pain around or behind the eye, and on occasion may be attributed to the eye. Sinus pain also can be referred to the eye. Pain noted with movement of the eye is a serious symptom that may indicate involvement of the retrobulbar region by infectious or other processes.

Orbit

Orbital Cellulitis

Diagnosis Patients usually give a history of trauma to the lids or orbit, or sinus disease, or they may have a history of an infection elsewhere in the body. Symptoms may include orbital pain, pain with movement of the eyes, diplopia, decreased vision, fever, and malaise. Examination usually reveals swelling and rubor of the lids, hyperemia, and chemosis of the conjunctiva. Exophthalmos and restricted ocular motility may be seen.

Treatment Because of the risk of optic nerve injury and the risk of spread of the infection to the cavernous sinus or to the brain, treatment must be aggressive, with hospitalization, culturing of the infection if possible, appropriate IV antibiotics, urgent ophthalmological, and sometimes ENT evaluation, and often imaging of the orbit to look for suppuration.

Exophthalmos

Diagnosis If a patient reports onset of proptosis over a short period of time (not attributable to trauma), retrobulbar hemorrhage, or inflammation or extension of an adjacent sinus infection should be suspected. Proptosis developing over a few weeks is more consistent with orbital pseu-

dotumor or other more chronic inflammatory conditions. Proptosis developing over months is more consistent with thyroid orbitopathy or with an orbital neoplasm. An arteriovenous aneurysm of the cavernous sinus may cause proptosis and may have an associated bruit. Onset can be rapid or more gradual.

Because of the various etiologies of proptosis, imaging of the orbit usually is diagnostic. The urgency of ophthalmologic evaluation is related to the rapidity of onset of the proptosis.

Treatment After the etiology of the proptosis has been determined, treatment objectives are twofold: to treat the underlying cause of the proptosis and to protect the eye from the deleterious side effects of proptosis. The most common side effect is corneal and conjunctival exposure, and this should be treated aggressively with lubricating drops and ointments. Mild misalignments of the eyes sometimes can be treated with prism glasses. Optic nerve impingement can be serious and may require systemic corticosteroids or even orbital surgical decompression.

Eyelids

Blepharitis

Diagnosis Patients with blepharitis complain of ocular irritation (often described as burning or gritty), redness, and increased tearing. They also may report red, scaly lids that may be gummy or matted on awakening. Ocular examination reveals a red, sometimes scarred lid margin with telangiectatic vessels, lid margin debris, and conjunctival hyperemia.

Treatment Blepharitis may represent a chronic low-grade bacterial (usually staphylococcal or streptococcal) infection of the meibomian glands and lash follicles. In other patients, the etiology may be more akin to skin conditions such as seborrhea. In either case, the bulwark of the treatment is lid hygiene using warm compresses and some mild scrubbing action twice a day. When an infectious component is suspected, erythromycin or bacitracin ointment twice daily

to the lid margin after the warm soaks is useful. Lubricant eye drops during the day may be of symptomatic benefit.

Hordeolum (Stye)

Diagnosis Styes represent a localized infection of a lash follicle or meibomian gland at the lid margin. Examination reveals a localized area of redness, swelling, and tenderness at the lid margin. If the lesion has started to point, a whitish or yellowish area of induration may occupy the center of the lesion.

Treatment Drainage of the lesion is encouraged by application of warm compresses for 5 to 10 min, three to four times a day. Because the infecting organism is usually staph or strep, an antibiotic ointment with good gram-positive coverage such as erythromycin or bacitracin may be applied twice daily. Occasionally the lesions do not drain or clear and require surgical incision and drainage.

Chalazion

Diagnosis Meibomian glands located in the tarsal plates of the upper and lower lids produce oil that exits at the lid margin. When the gland's orifice is blocked, oil production is backed up; the gland is dilated; and a small, round, smooth, nontender mass may be noted in the lid. This stagnant collection of oily/waxy material is easily infected. When infected it becomes hot, red, irritated, and tender. Eversion of the lid may aid in diagnosis, especially if the lesion has started to point.

Treatment Treatment is similar to that of the stye, with warm compresses and topical antibiotics. Rarely, systemic antibiotics are required if a large region of the lid appears to be involved.

Preseptal Cellulitis

Diagnosis This condition simulates some of the signs and symptoms of orbital cellulitis with lid redness and swelling. Because this represents infection anterior to the orbital septum, proptosis, motility disorder, visual reduction, pain on ocular movement, and inflammation of the bulbar conjunctiva should never be seen.

Treatment If orbital cellulitis has been completely ruled out, the condition can be treated in compliant adult patients with systemic antibiotics on an ambulatory basis. Patients should be alerted to signs and symptoms that might indicate progression to orbital cellulitis and instructed to seek follow-up immediately if they occur.

Structural Lid Problem

Diagnosis Trauma, burns, chronic blepharitis, and aging can lead to lid abnormalities such as entropion, ectropion or lid margin irregularity or scarring. This, in turn, can lead to irritation of the globe either directly or due to poor distribution of tears and/or exposure.

Treatment Lubricating drops or ointments may be sufficient to prevent significant discomfort or damage. Epilation of inturned lashes and, in some cases, surgical correction are required.

Skin Cancers of the Lid

Diagnosis Skin cancers are not uncommon around the eyes. Basal cell carcinomas are the most common, but squamous cell carcinomas, melanomas, and even metastatic lesions are seen. Sun exposure and skin type are risk factors; the lower lid is most often involved.

Treatment Treatment of skin cancers of the lids must satisfy two objectives: complete removal of the lesion and maximum preservation of lid tissue and function.

Lacrimal Apparatus

Overflow Tearing

Diagnosis Epiphora may arise from excessive tear production, usually secondary to ocular irritation, structural abnormalities of the eyelid or lid margin, or from poor drainage of tears

through the tear ducts. Poor drainage may be due to blockage or stenosis of the duct passages or by a functional abnormality of its pumping action. Epiphora in adults is more often due to functional abnormalities or lid problems.

Treatment Congenital overflow tearing in children often spontaneously resolves with or without treatment. Treatment consists of lacrimal sac massage performed twice a day and antibiotic drops. When the symptoms persist, probing or placement of tubes in the tear ducts usually is effective. In adults, evaluation and treatment can be combined in irrigation and probing of the tear ducts. Occasionally, in children and adults, more definitive surgical treatment is needed.

Dacryocystitis

Diagnosis Ocular examination usually reveals pain, redness, swelling, and tenderness overlying the lacrimal sac. Massage of the lacrimal sac may express purulent material through the puncta (the opening of the lacrimal duct). Because the tear ducts are partly or totally obstructed, the patients may complain of epiphora.

Treatment Hot compresses over the lacrimal sac and systemic antibiotics are indicated. Culturing of the expressed purulent material during the initial evaluation often is useful. Unfortunately, these infections may be difficult to eradicate; even when stabilized, they may leave residual scarring and stenosis in the tear ducts.

Conjunctiva

Subconjunctival Hemorrhage

Diagnosis The cause of subconjunctival hemorrhage is the breakage of a small blood vessel in or under the conjunctiva. Patients often first notice the condition when they look in the mirror or when a friend or coworker asks what happened to their eye. Vision is usually unaffected; there is no discharge, and at most there is mild ocular awareness; there is never any pain. The history may reveal recent use of nonsteroidal anti-inflammatory medications. Onset is sometimes associated with coughing or sneezing, emesis, rubbing the eye, or straining while having a bowel movement. Ocular examination reveals that all or part of the conjunctiva is bright red. The redness stops at the corneal limbus and there is never blood in the eye.

Treatment The patient should be instructed not to rub her eye. Acetaminophen should be substituted for the nonsteroidal anti-inflammatory medication if possible. Cool compresses may help if the patient complains of ocular awareness.

Conjunctivitis

Conjunctivitis may have an allergic or infectious origin. Less frequently it may be due to a toxic reaction or have a systemic cause.

Allergic Conjunctivitis

Diagnosis Patients with allergic conjunctivitis, almost invariably complain of itch. Without significant itching, the primary care physician should not diagnose an allergic etiology. Patients also may complain of burning, increased tearing with a mucus discharge, and may report conjunctival redness and eyelid swelling. They usually give a history of allergies, and the symptoms often are seasonal. If the offending allergen is airborne or ingested, the condition usually is bilateral, although it may be asymmetric in intensity. However, if the causative allergen was touched with the finger before touching the eye, the condition may be unilateral.

Treatment There are two goals of treatment: alleviating the signs and symptoms of past and present exposure; and preventing future exposure. Ice-cold ocular compresses are quite effective in reducing redness, swelling, and itch. Topical vasoconstrictor/antihistamine drops are useful when not overused. Mast cell inhibitors, which are available in drop form, are effective agents for chronic treatment. The use of steroid eye drops should be restricted to ophthalmologists.

Infectious Conjunctivitis

Diagnosis Infectious conjunctivitis can be bacterial or viral in origin. Viral conjunctivitis proba-

bly is the most common. Patients with adenoviral conjunctivitis complain of a red, scratchy eye and increased tearing. Patients often have a simultaneous URI, and a preauricular node may be palpable. The condition eventually is bilateral in 80 percent of patients, but usually starts in one eye. Herpes conjunctivitis may present in a similar fashion; however, lid vesicles may be seen and the condition is more typically unilateral. Preauricular adenopathy may be seen with chlamydial conjunctivitis but usually not with other forms of bacterial conjunctivitis. A history of sexually transmitted chlamydia may be elicited with chlamydial conjunctivitis.

Treatment If chlamydial conjunctivitis is suspected, appropriate cultures should be obtained. Though topical antibiotics may provide symptomatic relief in chlamydial conjunctivitis, oral antibiotics usually are needed to effect a cure. As with other sexually transmitted chlamydial diseases, sexual partners may need to be treated. If bacterial conjunctivitis cannot be ruled out by history or exam, treatment with a broad-spectrum antibiotic such as topical ciprofloxacin or trimethoprim/polymyxin B should be initiated. Because these infections are usually due to gram-positive organisms, gentamycin (Garamycin) or tobramycin are not good first choices. Many organisms are now resistant to topical sulfonamides, so these also should be avoided. The high rates of allergic reaction to preparations containing neomycin should discourage their use.

Cornea

Pterygium

Diagnosis Patients with pterygia may be asymptomatic or may report mild chronic ocular irritation and sensitivity to dust and wind. Many patients will ask what is growing in their cornea. Ocular examination reveals a wing-like, whitish growth extending from the conjunctiva onto the cornea at 3 or 9 o'clock along the corneal limbus. The lesion may or may not appear inflamed. A small, yellow-whitish bump on the conjunctiva, called a pinqueculum, is usually the progenitive lesion.

Treatment Minimizing sun and wind exposure by using sunglasses, wearing a hat, or restricting time spent unprotected out of doors may slow the lesion's growth. Artificial tear supplements may decrease inflammation and increase comfort. When the lesions become large, they should be surgically removed, although they may grow back.

Keratoconjunctivitis Sicca

Diagnosis Patients with keratoconjunctivitis sicca (KCS) complain of dry, gritty eyes. In most patients, the symptoms are less on awakening and increase during the day, or with exposure to wind. Symptoms tend to be worse in the winter owing to lower humidity levels in the air. The eyes may be red, and vision may be normal or reduced. Paradoxically, some patients with dry eyes complain of episodic teariness, probably caused by chronic irritation triggering a short period of excess lacrimal secretion. Ocular examination may appear normal. Rose bengal staining by an ophthalmologist will often prove diagnostic by revealing mild to moderate exposure in the interpalpebral region.

Treatment Tear supplements are useful. When needed more than four times a day, preservative-free drops should be used. In more severe cases, closure of the tear ducts may be useful.

Infectious Keratitis

Diagnosis Patients with corneal infections complain of pain, photophobia, increased tearing, and often of decreased vision in the affected eye. When the infection is due to bacteria, the patients may have had prior corneal trauma or foreign bodies, or they may use contact lenses. Patients with fungal infections of the cornea often report trauma with vegetable material, such as being struck in the eye with a branch. Patients with herpes simplex infection may give a history of cold sores, blistering around the eye, or a past

similar infection in the same or other eye. Ocular examination reveals conjunctival hyperemia and a corneal lesion that stains with fluorescein. Mucoid material may be adherent to the lesion. A hypopyon (accumulation of white blood cells in the anterior chamber of the eye) may be present. ***Treatment*** Because of the risk of permanent visual loss or even loss of the eye, infectious keratitis should be treated only by an ophthalmologist. Antibiotics should not be started by the primary care physician because the lesion may need to be cultured. Ophthalmologic evaluation should be performed within a few hours if possible.

Glaucoma

Chronic Open-Angle Glaucoma

Diagnosis The great majority of patients with chronic open-angle glaucoma (COAG) never have any symptoms attributable to their glaucoma. Because of this, it is thought that up to half of the patients with COAG are unaware of their condition. COAG is thought to represent a mild to moderate elevation in intraocular pressure brought on by a chronic gradual reduction in outflow facility (at the iridocorneal angle). In other words, fluid flows into the eye, but outflow becomes more difficult over time and the fluid pressure then rises. The elevated pressure damages the optic nerve, with the fibers subserving peripheral vision being the most vulnerable and therefore the first destroyed. As the nerve is damaged, its appearance slowly changes, with the nerve head's anatomical cup becoming larger and larger over time. Asymmetric optic cups, large optic cups, and optic nerve head hemorrhages are all signs of possible glaucoma. The measurement of intraocular pressure, usually by Schiotz tonometer, is another way to detect glaucoma. Because intraocular pressure demonstrates significant fluctuation over time, a normal reading does not rule out glaucoma. Likewise, a high reading, especially if only mildly elevated, does not prove glaucoma, but is sufficient basis for ophthalmologic evaluation. The few patients who have symptoms prior to diagnosis may experience eye ache or headache, may see halos around lights, or may note decreased peripheral vision. Because these symptoms are associated with higher pressure levels or more advanced disease, more urgent evaluation and referral is indicated. ***Treatment*** Most, but not all, patients with glaucoma can achieve complete control of their disease with daily topical and/or oral medication. A few patients require laser treatments to reach good control and a very few require surgery. Regular ophthalmological follow-up with periodic visual field testing is usually required for the rest of the patient's life.

Angle-Closure Glaucoma

Diagnosis Unlike chronic open-angle glaucoma, patients with angle-closure glaucoma are almost always symptomatic. Patients often complain of a severe achy pain in the eye or brow and of ocular tenderness. Visual symptoms include halos around lights due to corneal edema and/or sudden loss of vision. The patients may have nausea and vomiting. Ocular examination reveals a red eye with limbal injection, corneal cloudiness, and a significant elevation in intraocular pressure. Other findings may include a shallow anterior chamber and/or a fixed mid-dilated pupil. ***Treatment*** Because the decrease in outflow facility, and therefore the pressure elevation, often is due to the peripheral iris tissue blocking the angle, constriction of the pupil with pilocarpine 2% is indicated. In patients for whom β-blockers are not contraindicated, Betoptic 0.5% may be instilled. Carbonic anhydrase inhibitors (e.g., acetazolamide [Diamox] 500 mg) given orally in patients for whom they are not contraindicated, aid in reducing pressure. Oral glycerin (or isosorbide for diabetics) also usually results in the reduction of pressure. Ophthalmological referral during the initial treatment or after the patient's condition is stabilized is recommended. Laser surgery is usually recommended and has been

generally effective in preventing recurrences of the angle-closure attack.

Secondary Glaucoma

Diagnosis Glaucoma can arise secondary to trauma, prolonged systemic or topical corticosteroid treatment, vascular disturbances in the eye or in the blood flow to the eye, or following cataract or other intraocular eye surgery. Uveitis, intraocular tumors, or even advanced cataracts can cause glaucoma.

Treatment Treatment involves simultaneous control of pressure and correction, if possible, of the underlying cause of the glaucoma.

Uveitis

Diagnosis Uveitis refers to inflammation of the uveal tissues that include the iris, ciliary body, and choroid. When the inflammation primarily affects the anterior uveal structures, patients complain of pain, photophobia, and possibly reduced vision; they report ocular redness. Ocular examination reveals circumcorneal injection. Adhesions from the iris to the lens may distort the pupillary opening. Intraocular pressure may be high, low, or normal. When the inflammation is more posterior in the eye, patients complain primarily of reduced vision and floaters. The external eye usually is quiet, and pain and photophobia may be minimal or absent.

Treatment Along with the treatment of the acute manifestations of the condition comes the search for and treatment of the underlying cause of the problem. Some causes, such as syphilis, tuberculosis, and Lyme disease, can be cured with antibiotics. Others, such as herpes zoster, herpes simplex, and toxoplasmosis have specific palliative treatments, but no cure. Still others, such as sarcoidosis and juvenile rheumatoid arthritis (JRA), while not curable, alert the practitioner to search for and treat systemic manifestations of the conditions. Because uveitis may present in many subtly different forms and because these different forms suggest different etiologies, early ophthalmic evaluation is mandatory. Likewise, because of the potentially serious nature of the condition and the risk of permanent eye damage, vision loss, and glaucoma, treatment should be initiated and followed by an ophthalmologist.

Lens

Cataract

Diagnosis Adult patients with cataracts report painless progressive loss of vision. Patients may also report loss of contrast and increased glare. Cataracts usually can be seen with the direct ophthalmoscope, viewing the eye from a distance of approximately one foot. Dilatation of the pupil aids diagnosis, but usually is not required.

Treatment Mild cataracts may be followed. Visually significant cataracts (best corrected visual acuities of 20/50 or worse attributable to the cataract) may be surgically removed. Surgical intervention also may be indicated with acuities greater than 20/50 when glare is significant or the patient's driving or work is affected. Rarely, cataracts grow and cause glaucoma, in which case prompt removal is indicated. If, as rarely happens, the cataract causes intraocular inflammation, rapid removal is indicated. There is some evidence of a protective effect of estrogen against the formation of cataracts.

Retina

Aging Macular Degeneration

Diagnosis Aging macular degeneration (AMD) is a leading cause of blindness in elderly Caucasian patients, and is more common in women than in men. The condition is painless and affects only the central vision; the peripheral vision is spared. Patients may notice blurring, distortion, or both in the center of their vision. The condition usually is bilateral, although the presentation and severity may be quite asymmetric. In mild cases, ocular examination may reveal

the loss of the foveal reflex or mild heterogeneity in the macular retinal pigment epithelium. Macular hemorrhage or scarring may be seen in more severe cases.

Treatment In the great majority of patients with AMD, the changes are gradual and untreatable. In 15 percent of patients, however, an acute worsening of the condition will be noted, usually secondary to subretinal hemorrhage and scar formation. In some of these patients, laser treatments may be of limited benefit in halting or reversing the acute exacerbation. Referral to an ophthalmologist is indicated.

Retinal Detachment

Diagnosis Unfortunately, there are no signs or symptoms pathognomonic for retinal detachment. The most reliable is the loss of part of the peripheral vision in one eye. The patient may report this as a shadow in the periphery of the vision. Floaters or flashes may be associated with retinal detachment, but usually are indicative of a posterior vitreous detachment without retinal detachment. Detachment of the macula results in significant unilateral vision loss. Confrontation visual field testing may be useful. Ophthalmoscopy through a dilated pupil may reveal vitreous hemorrhage or pigment, or the detachment itself may be seen. However, because much of the fundus cannot be visualized with the direct ophthalmoscope, nothing abnormal may be seen.

Treatment If retinal detachment is seen or suspected, the patient needs prompt referral for ophthalmological evaluation. Trauma, recent cataract or other intraocular surgery, or diabetes are risk factors and should raise the level of suspicion. Some small detachments can be treated with laser surgery. Larger detachments usually require placement of plastic devices called buckles on the outside of the eye. Some detachments also require intraocular surgery to repair.

Diabetic Retinopathy

Diagnosis Diabetes often leads to vascular changes in the retina. In mild or early diabetes, the retina may look normal. The first changes typically seen are microaneurysms and hemorrhage; this is designated "background retinopathy." Hard exudates and macular edema may result from the vascular changes, and these may mildly or markedly reduce vision. When vascular changes become more pronounced, areas of local retinal infarction called cotton-wool spots may develop. More severe changes produce abnormal new blood vessel formation called neovascularization. These vessels bleed easily and may contract, causing traction to—and sometimes detachment of—the retina. For patients with adult-onset diabetes, ophthalmological evaluation should be done at least once yearly, and more frequently as the severity of the condition increases. Pregnant diabetics should be seen at a minimum of every three months during pregnancy. Patients with juvenile-onset diabetes almost never develop problems during the first five years of their disease, but require yearly examination from then on.

Treatment The great majority of diabetic patients never require treatment for their diabetic retinopathy. However, most patients with neovascular changes eventually require a laser treatment called panretinal photocoagulation. Some patients with macular swelling and exudates can benefit from a different laser treatment called focal or grid treatment. Rarely, surgery is required. Good diabetic control has been shown to slow the onset of significant retinopathy and should be encouraged.

Retinal Vascular Occlusions

Diagnosis Patients with central retinal artery occlusion complain of painless unilateral blindness. If the patient is awake when the occlusion occurs, onset will be described as sudden; otherwise, it will be noticed on awakening. If one of the major retinal arterial branches is occluded, blindness in a part of the visual field is reported. If a smaller branch is occluded, the patient may be asymptomatic. Examination reveals retinal pallor in the area affected. Occasionally the ob-

structing plaque or emboli may be visualized. The affected retinal arteries may appear attenuated, and stagnant discontinuous segments of blood may be seen in the vessels. An afferent pupillary defect may be noted in the affected eye. Patients with venous obstructions report more gradual onset of less severe unilateral vision loss. Hemorrhages and edema are seen in the affected area of the retina, and the affected veins may appear distended.

Treatment Unless corrected within approximately one hour, retinal artery occlusion will result in permanent damage to the affected areas of the retina; therefore, this is a true ophthalmic emergency. No treatment works all the time, but intermittent massage of the eye and/or inhalations of 5% CO_2 have been recommended. An ophthalmologist may attempt an anterior chamber paracentesis to reduce intraocular pressure, and thereby may dislodge or move the obstruction. Evaluation to identify embolic sources or temporal arteritis is of utmost importance to prevent stroke and/or damage to the other eye. Becaue venous obstruction is usually seen in patients with hypertension, heart disease, diabetes, or peripheral vascular disease, a thorough history and physical examination usually is indicated. Although venous obstructions usually clear over a period of months, neovascular changes of the retina and iris and severe glaucoma can result. Therefore, the patient should receive periodic ophthalmic evaluations until the condition clears, and laser treatments if problems appear.

Optic Nerve

Optic Neuritis

Diagnosis Patients complain of decreased vision in one eye and may report problems with color vision or decreased color saturation. Occasionally there is pain with movement of the eye. Ocular examination may reveal visual acuity from 20/20 to the complete absence of light perception. An afferent pupillary defect is present in the affected eye, although it may be subtle when vision is only minimally affected. The eye appears quiet, and ophthalmoscopic exam may reveal blurring of the disk margin, nerve head hyperemia, peripapillary swelling, and hemorrhages and venous congestion.

Treatment Prompt referral to an ophthalmologist or neurologist is indicated.

Papilledema

Diagnosis Patients may complain of headache, blurring of vision, and brief obscurations of vision. Other neurologic signs or symptoms related to increased intracranial pressure may be present. Ophthalmoscopic examination of the optic nerves will show disk head elevation bilaterally.

Treatment Prompt neurologic evaluation is indicated.

Injuries

Ocular injuries can range from the trivial to the blinding. The extent of the injuries may not be immediately apparent; a careful examination and a complete history with detailed documentation almost always are indicated. If the history of injury includes possible chemical burns, irrigation should be initiated promptly (see ocular burns). In most other circumstances, a more detailed history may be obtained before initiating treatment. If the history suggests possible penetrating or perforating injuries to the eye, examination and manipulation of the eye should be minimized. A determination of visual acuity, pupillary response, extraocular motility, the location and extent of orbit and lid injuries, and the location(s) of any foreign bodies should be made. The presence or absence of conjunctival hemorrhage, laceration, corneal abrasion or laceration, and hyphema should be noted. If possible, direct ophthalmoscopy should be performed and the ease or difficulty of visualization recorded.

Superficial Foreign Bodies

Diagnosis Usually, but not always, the patient gives a history of "something in the eye." The

patient complains of a foreign body sensation, sometimes worse in certain gaze positions. The patient may report decreased visual acuity and/or photophobia. Inspection of the eye is greatly facilitated by instillation of a topical anesthetic. Visualization of foreign bodies may be enhanced with fluorescein staining. The upper and lower lids should be everted. Loupes will aid in locating small foreign bodies.

Treatment Many foreign bodies can be removed with a cotton-tipped applicator. More deeply embedded foreign bodies can be removed with the edge of a large-gauge hypodermic needle or foreign-body spud, although this should be done by a physician skilled in this procedure. Deeper foreign bodies or metallic foreign bodies that have rusted require removal by an ophthalmologist. If the eye is thought to be infected, prompt referral to an ophthalmologist is indicated. Otherwise, a topical antibiotic ointment such as erythromycin or bacitracin may be instilled, and, if the cornea is abraded, an eyepatch applied to keep the eyelid closed overnight.

Intraocular Foreign Bodies

When an intraocular foreign body is suspected, manipulation and examination should be minimized and the patient promptly referred to and seen by an ophthalmologist. A rigid shield should be placed over the eye. No ointment should be placed in the eye. In consultation with the ophthalmologist, broad-spectrum antibiotic therapy may be initiated.

Orbital Trauma

Trauma to the orbit from such injuries as falls, motor vehicle accidents, assaults, and industrial accidents often result in bruising and extravasation of blood in the adnexal region, leading to what is commonly known as a "black" eye. If this is the extent of the injury, treatment consists of cold compresses for 24 to 36 h and elevation to minimize swelling. Significant hemorrhage behind the eye as evidenced by exophthalmos, sub-

conjunctival hemorrhage, extraocular motility disorder, and/or decreased vision is potentially quite serious, and urgent ophthalmologic evaluation is indicated. Orbital trauma may result in fracture of the orbital rim or a blow-out fracture involving one or more of the bones that make up the orbit. Signs and symptoms may include enophthalmos, periorbital crepitance, diplopia, and numbness of the cheek. Work-up usually involves radiologic imaging of the orbit. When a blow-out fracture is suspected, prompt evaluation by an ophthalmologist or ENT specialist is indicated.

Lid Trauma

Lacerations of the eyelids are common. Repair of these lacerations, when indicated, must be done by an ophthalmologist in these circumstances:

- When there is significant tissue loss;
- When the lid margin is involved;
- When the lacrimal apparatus is potentially damaged;
- When the laceration is deep or when eyelid structures other than the skin may be involved.

Conjunctival Trauma

Subconjunctival hemorrhages are quite common and usually resolve without complication. However, subconjunctival hemorrhage may obscure deeper, more serious injuries. If this is a possibility, ophthalmologic evaluation is indicated. Because some conjunctival lacerations need to be repaired, ophthalmologic follow-up is indicated when these are diagnosed.

Corneal Trauma

Diagnosis Patients usually report pain and/or a foreign-body sensation, and may report photophobia or reduced vision. Corneal trauma often

is associated with a foreign body that may or may not be in the eye when the patient is seen. Damage to the corneal surface (e.g., corneal abrasion) may be demarcated after the instillation of fluorescein. Application of a topical anesthetic drop, such as proparacaine, improves patient comfort dramatically and facilitates evaluation.

Treatment If foreign bodies are seen, they should be removed as previously described. If there are signs of deeper corneal injury, such as a corneal laceration, or some indication or suspicion of corneal infection, the patient needs prompt ophthalmologic evaluation. Otherwise, instillation of an antibiotic ointment, such as erythromycin or bacitracin, followed by application of an eyepatch to keep the lid shut is indicated. In extreme abrasions, one drop of homatropine 2% may be instilled prior to patching to ease ciliary spasm. Next day follow-up with an ophthalmologist is indicated.

Intraocular Trauma

Intraocular trauma usually, but not invariably, causes decreased vision and often pain. Sometimes there are externally visible signs of inflammation, such as conjunctival hyperemia. Hyphemia, or blood in the anterior chamber, usually indicates trauma to the uveal structures. Because of the risk of elevated intraocular pressure, emergent ophthalmologic evaluation is indicated. A shallow anterior chamber, distortion of the pupil, and/or decreased clarity of the internal ocular media are all signs of potential intraocular injury and need ophthalmologic evaluation. Patient visual symptoms, such as new floaters, flashes, scotomas, or other new visual field defects, strongly suggest intraocular damage and should be specifically asked about when ocular trauma has occurred.

Ocular Burns

Chemical Burns

Diagnosis Significant ocular chemical burns produce mild to marked lid swelling, conjunctival hyperemia and chemosis, and corneal haze. This may be generalized or may be greater in the interpalpebral region. Because tearing tends to wash chemicals inferiorly, the inferior conjunctiva may be more affected. Sometimes lid swelling is so pronounced as to make examination and treatment quite difficult.

Treatment After instillation of several drops of a topical anesthetic agents, initiate irrigation of the eye with isotonic sterile saline. The present recommendation for chemical injuries due to caustic agents is to irrigate for one-half hour or more. The eyelids should be everted to facilitate irrigation under the lids and to allow for visualization and removal of material that may be lodged in the cul-de-sac. Except for the most trivial of chemical injuries, prompt ophthalmologic evaluation is indicated.

Thermal Burns

Diagnosis Thermal burns to the eyes are seldom seen in isolation; usually, facial or other burns are present. The skin of the eyelids may have suffered first-, second-, or third-degree burns. Lashes are often singed or absent. The conjunctiva usually is hyperemic and/or chemotic. Corneal haze and edema often are present.

Treatment Significant thermal lid or eye burns require prompt ophthalmologic evaluation.

Ultraviolet Burns

Diagnosis The patient usually gives a history of exposure to the light from arc welding, exposure to a tanning booth or bed, or sun exposure usually associated with reflection from snow or water. The light exposure usually precedes the typical symptoms of pain, increased tearing, decreased vision, and photophobia by 6 to 12 h. Examination reveals conjunctival hyperemia, corneal haze, and fluorescein uptake in a diffuse, often interpalpebral, pattern.

Treatment After instillation of a topical anesthetic agent, a mild antibiotic agent such as eryth-

romycin or bacitracin may be instilled, followed by patching to keep the lids shut. The patient should be informed that the pain usually recurs when the topical anesthetic wears off and that she may need oral analgesics until her eyes heal in a day or so. Because topical anesthetic agents may slow or prevent healing, their use after diagnosis should be minimized.

Contact Lenses

For many millions of women, contact lenses are a safe, effective, and, in some cases, superior alternative to spectacle glasses for the correction of refractive errors. Unfortunately, however, the use and misuse of contact lenses represents a risk factor for a wide variety of ocular conditions. Poorly fitted, damaged, or contaminated contact lenses may injure the surface of the eye. Improper insertion or removal, overwearing, or sleeping in contact lenses not meant to be slept in may lead to a red, irritated eye. The risk of corneal infection is greatly increased in contact lens wearers. In the presence of ocular irritation, redness, or decreased vision, the patient needs to know that the first step in treatment, and sometimes the only step needed, is to stop wearing the lenses. However, if the patient's symptoms do not quickly and completely resolve, ophthalmologic evaluation is needed.

Refractive Surgery

Surgery to correct nearsightedness, farsightedness, and astigmatism is a viable alternative to the use of glasses or contact lenses for many women. These procedures work by changing the refractive capacity of the cornea so that a sharper image is formed on the retina. In radial keratotomy (RK), a series of deep radial corneal incisions (typically four to eight cuts performed in one or two sessions) leads to a flattening of the corneal curvature. Risks include over or under-correction, increased glare, fluctuating refraction, and, rarely, infection or perforation of the eye. Photorefractive keratotomy (PRK) uses a device called an excimer laser to remove tissue from the surface of the cornea, changing its effective power. Risks include corneal haze and, less commonly, loss of best-corrected acuity. Laser assisted in situ keratomileusis (LASIK) uses the excimer laser to ablate and reshape the corneal stroma after a thin cap has been temporarily removed from the corneal surface. This procedure has risks, associated with removal and replacement of the corneal cap, but may have some advantages over PRK. All of these procedures are expensive and should never be portrayed to patients as completely and invariably safe and effective.

Physiologic Changes and Problems during Pregnancy

Physiologic ocular changes due to pregnancy include chloasma of the eyelids, decrease in intraocular pressure, transient loss of accommodation, changes in corneal thickness and sensitivity, and changes in the tear film. These latter changes may interfere with previous successful contact lens wear. Preexisting conditions potentially exacerbated by pregnancy include diabetic retinopathy, Graves' disease, and pituitary adenomas. Sarcoidosis may improve during pregnancy. Pathologic conditions that may develop during pregnancy include central serous retinopathy and ptosis. Toxemia of pregnancy can induce ocular changes, including retinal hemorrhages and ischemia, ischemic optic neuropathy, papilledema, and retinal detachment. Transient cortical blindness with eclampsia has been reported.

References and Suggested Readings

1. American Academy of Ophthalmologoy: Basic and Clinical Science Course, Sections 1-12 San Francisco: AAO; 1998–1999.
2. Berkow R: *The Merck Manual,* 16th ed. Rahway, NJ: Merck Research Laboratories, 1992.
3. Ewald G, McKenzie CR (eds): *The Washington Manual of Medical Therapeutics,* 28th ed. 1995.

4. MacCumber MW (ed): *Management of Ocular Injuries and Emergencies.* Philadelphia: Lippincott-Raven, 1998.

5. Summress JS: The Pregnant Woman's Eye. *Surv Ophthalmol* 32:(4), 1988.

6. Tasman W (ed): *Duane's Clinical Ophthalmology.* Philadelphia: JB Lippincott, 1998.

7. Trabe JD: *The Physician's Guide to Eye Care.* San Francisco: American Academy of Ophthalmology, 1993.

8. Wallach J: *Interpretation of Diagnostic Tests,* 6th ed. Little Brown & Co. 1996.

9. Yanoff M, Duker JS: *Ophthalmology.* Mosby, 1998.

Dental and Medical Interrelationships

Peter A. Mychajliw
James J. Sciubba

DENTAL CARE DURING PREGNANCY
DENTISTRY IN RELATION TO OTHER COMMON HEALTH CARE ISSUES
Oral Contraceptives • Endocarditis • Oral Cancer • Smoking and Alcohol Abuse • Trauma • AIDS

As advances in diagnostic technologies, research, and treatment modalities continue, the identification of patients who have residual problems and concurrent acute and/or chronic dental problems will increase. It is imperative that dentists and physicians manage these patients jointly and comprehensively based on their medical, dental, physical, and psychological findings. Although many women receiving medical care may seem to have adequate oral health, one must continually be aware of the intimate interrelationships between medicine and dental medicine. Appropriate referrals must be made for a wide array of conditions (Table 83-1).

After referral for dental evaluation, the physician should receive a comprehensive report detailing the patient's chief complaint, positive findings of the history, (limited) physical, laboratory, radiology, and clinical examinations. An overview of the proposed treatment plan, including any preventive/interceptive or emergent care, and an overall diagnosis also should be included. If the patient has or subsequently develops a medically related problem, the dentist and physician must agree on any modifications or contraindications to the proposed dental treatment based on those variables. The patient

should be counseled accordingly before beginning comprehensive dental treatment. Should the request for consultation originate from the dentist, the same scenario would apply.

Dental Care During Pregnancy

A classic example of the importance of coordinated care by the dentist and the physician is in the case of the pregnant patient. Therapeutic dental care must be rendered to the patient without endangering the fetus. The physician must provide an evaluation of the patient's current medical condition, a plan for prenatal management, a history of any previous pregnancies, and information regarding any complicating factors. A comprehensive treatment plan is formulated that stresses maintenance of optimal oral hygiene throughout the pregnancy, and tailors the treatment sequence to minimize or avoid exposure to such potentially harmful procedures as radiation, drugs, supine hypotension in late pregnancy, and breast milk transmission of drugs to the infant.

Radiographs crucial to an accurate dental diagnosis are best obtained in the second or early third trimester. Radiography is to be avoided, if possible, during the first trimester, as the fetus is particularly susceptible to damage from radiation at this time. Radiographic procedure precautions that must be in place include lead apron, high-speed film, collimation, filtration, long cone, and high voltage.

In some human and animal studies, exposures as high as 5 to 10 cGy total dose have shown no associated increase in gross congenital malforma-

TABLE 83-1 Conditions Likely to Benefit from Dental Medicine Consultation

1. Systemic diseases that may have oral manifestations/complications, e.g., AIDS, Sjögren's syndrome
2. Before cancer chemotherapy
3. Before head and neck cancer radiation therapy or extirpative oncological surgery
4. Before organ transplant
5. Before cardiac valve surgery
6. Oral complications of pregnancy
7. Eating disorders
8. Xerostomia
9. Infection suspected of soft/hard tissues in the head and neck region
10. Developmental or acquired physical or mental disabilities
11. Dentofacial deformities
12. Family/pregnancy planning

tions, intrauterine growth retardation, or abortion. A chest radiograph delivers an approximate fetal dose of 0.08 cGy. A complete diagnostic series of dental radiographs with a lead apron in place yields 0.0001 cGy fetal dose. A single dental radiograph taken with the precautions outlined, does not pose a substantial radiation risk to the fetus.[4, 16]

Ideally, no drug should be administered during pregnancy. Unfortunately, that is not always possible. Many of the drugs commonly used in dentistry may be used with relative safety. The current issues of the Food and Drug Administration *Drug Bulletin* and the *Physician's Desk Reference* (PDR) may need to be consulted, and the dentist should speak with the obstetrician prior to prescribing. The major concerns are fetal toxicity or teratogenicity and maternal problems that could result in fetal hypoxia. Local anesthetics, such as lidocaine and mepivicaine, and antibiotics, such as penicillin and the cephalosporins, may be utilized with relative safety during all trimesters. Tetracyclines are contraindicated owing to the potential for tooth discoloration and tooth

enamel hypoplasia in the developing dentition. Aminoglycosides, streptomycin in particular, also are contraindicated.

Oral complications of pregnancy commonly include gingival changes, exacerbation of existing gingivitis and periodontal disease, and a generalized increase in tooth mobility. An exaggerated inflammatory response to local factors, especially bacterial plaque secondary to hormonal influences and vascular changes, becomes readily apparent at the second month, progressing to a maximal effect at the eighth month, with resolution postpartum. The marginal gingiva and interdental papillae are most affected; these areas often become enlarged, painful, edematous, and bleed readily upon minimal provocation. Periodontal pseudopocketing also may occur secondary to interdental papillae hypertrophy. Pyogenic granulomas or pregnancy tumors occur in approximately 5 percent of pregnant women, usually appearing during the second trimester. The most common site is the labial gingiva of the anterior maxilla. They can be pedunculated or sessile, are usually painless, and bleed readily. These generally disappear after delivery, but may need surgical removal earlier if indicated. This would best be accomplished during the second trimester.

Outcomes of risk-assessment research involving periodontal disease suggest that periodontal disease may be a clinically significant risk factor for preterm low birthweight. It has been postulated that the mechanism for this might be through a systemic challenge to infection, triggering premature onset of labor or premature rupture of membranes. The mediators postulated as playing a possible role include lipopolysaccharides, endotoxin, prostaglandin E_2, and interleukin-1 β.[7,19]

Tooth mobility is believed to be associated with gingival disease and attachment apparatus disturbance or loss. It generally resolves postpartum. The "soft teeth" myth in pregnancy is predicated on the old belief that maternal teeth satisfy fetal calcium requirements. This is not the case, as the calcium in teeth is a crystalline type, un-

available to the systemic circulation or local eruptive mechanisms.[15,16,27]

The timing of dental treatment during pregnancy is relatively straightforward. During the first trimester, only plaque control therapy, including nonsurgical periodontal management, oral hygiene instruction, and emergency care should be rendered. Elective care should be deferred to the second and early third trimesters. As previously mentioned, the second trimester is the safest time to provide most elective dental care; however, anything that can be safely postponed until after childbirth should be. Plaque control and nonsurgical periodontal therapy may continue through the second and third trimester.[16]

The dentist should also seize these opportunities to educate the patient and her spouse, if possible, about the baby's dental development, dental disease and prevention, the importance of a good plaque control program, and fluoride supplementation, if warranted. Also, parents should be counseled to use only "pea size" amounts of a fluoride dentifrice when brushing the child's teeth. This is extremely important, as 1 gram of toothpaste contains 1 mg fluoride, and dentifrice ingestion plays a major role in contributing to tooth enamel fluorosis, especially during the first 3 years of life.[1] The American Academy of Pediatric Dentistry recommends an oral examination and preventive health education within 6 months of eruption of the first primary tooth, and no later than at 1 year of age.

Dentistry in Relation to Other Common Health Care Issues

Oral Contraceptives

As with pregnant patients, it is of paramount importance that the dentist who is prescribing certain medications be knowledgeable about drug administration to women taking oral contraceptives. Currently, there may be more than 10 million American women taking these agents. Numerous reports have implicated a wide variety of drugs that may cause reduction of contraceptive efficacy. These include ampicillin; penicillin; tetracyclines; clotrimazole; griseofulvin; phenytoin; phenobarbital; phenylephrine; phenylbutazone; phenacetin; diazepam; and cyclophosphamide, among others. The prescriber must advise the patient of potential reduction of effectiveness of the oral contraceptive owing to drug interaction.[29]

Endocarditis

Various forms of congenital heart disease; coarctation of the aorta; cardiac valve abnormalities; artificial cardiac valves; rheumatic heart disease; hypertrophic aortic stenosis; indwelling vascular catheter (right heart); hypertrophic cardiomyopathy; ventriculoatrial shunts for hydrocephalus; mitral valve prolapse with regurgitation; and mitral valve surgery may place patients at risk for infective endocarditis and/or endarteritis subsequent to bacteremia. Such exposure can be traced to many invasive procedures, including those of the upper respiratory, genitourinary, and gastrointestinal tracts, and to invasive dental treatment involving mucosal surfaces or contaminated tissues.[8,20] Prophylactic use of antibiotics is recommended for patients at risk for endocarditis when undergoing dental procedures likely to cause bacteremia with organisms commonly associated with endocarditis. Table 83-2 outlines the American Heart Association's most recent recommendations for the antibiotic prophylactic regimen for dental, oral, or upper respiratory tract procedures in patients who are at risk for infective endocarditis.[8]

In addition, well-coordinated medical-dental consultation is essential in establishing an appropriate comprehensive dental treatment plan for the patient at risk for endocarditis. The goal for these patients is to eliminate existing pathology, reduce gingival inflammation, and establish an effective prevention program. Patients who will be having cardiac surgery should have a preoperative dental evaluation and treatment prior to surgery, medical circumstances permitting.

TABLE 83-2 Prophylactic Antibiotic Regimens for Dental Procedures in Adults

Situation	Agent	Regimen
Standard general prophylaxis	Amoxicillin	2 g orally 1 h before procedure
Unable to take oral medications	Ampicillin	2 g intramuscularly (IM) or intravenously (IV) within 30 min before procedure
Allergic to penicillin	Clindamycin *or*	600 mg orally 1 h before procedure
	Cephalexin[a] or cefadroxil[a] *or*	2 g orally 1 h before procedure
	Azithromycin or Clarithromycin	500 mg orally 1 h before procedure
Allergic to penicillin and unable to take oral medications	Clindamycin *or*	600 mg IV within 30 min before procedure
	Cefazolin[a]	1 g IM or IV within 30 min before procedure

[a]Cephalosporins should not be used in individuals with immediate-type hypersensitivity reaction (urticaria, angioedema, or anaphylaxis) to penicillins.

Oral Cancer

A team approach to management is critically important for oral cancer patients undergoing surgery, radiation, or chemotherapy. The goal here is the same as for the cardiac patient. The dentist may also be called upon to help treat some of the acute and short- and long-term complications associated with cancer treatment, which include mucositis, opportunistic fungal infections, trismus, xerostomia, and surgical site prosthetic construction. These patients invariably require frequent follow-up visits and usually have continued dental needs. The benefit of early detection of the cancer by clinical and/or radiographic examination, with biopsy as necessary, cannot be overemphasized.

Smoking and Alcohol Abuse

Studies report an increased incidence of smoking among women. Alcohol abuse appears to be a growing problem as well.[18] These have been linked to an increased incidence of oral cancer. Smoking and smokeless tobacco also have been linked to many premalignant and benign oral and perioral conditions and diseases.[6] Maternal smoking during pregnancy may be a cause of general size reduction of primary teeth, and to

some degree may be associated with thinning incisal aspects of permanent mandibular teeth.[11,12] Smoking is another area in which medical-dental intervention is important.

Trauma

The physician may be the first consulted on trauma involving tooth avulsion. It is imperative to determine whether the tooth is a primary (baby) tooth or a permanent tooth, as reinsertion of primary teeth is contraindicated owing to inherent poor prognosis. Multiple variables must be considered when treating permanent tooth avulsions, including extraoral time lengths, wet or dry storage environment, type of preserving medium, and root development stage. Root surface periodontal ligament viability of a replanted tooth is the most important factor in prognosis.[24] Deterioration, desiccation, contamination, incompatible storage medium, and physical crushing of periodontal ligament cells on an avulsed tooth can compromise the viability of the periodontal ligament. As such, the root surface should not be manipulated; it should be cleansed by irrigation/soaking with an appropriate medium (0.05% doxycycline solution for 5 min for teeth with incomplete apical closure; pH-bal-

anced reconstituting medium for up to 30 min for teeth with complete apical closure).[10]

The tooth should be reinserted as soon as possible. The patient's tetanus immunization status should be evaluated, and systemic antibiotic and topical antimicrobial therapies are recommended. If reinsertion was achieved, the tooth should be held in place with finger or gauze pressure, and immediate dental consult is required to complete treatment. If the tooth could not be reinserted by the physician, it should be transported to the dentist in a pH-balanced cell-preserving solution, Hank's balanced salt solution, or Viaspan.[13,28] If these are not available, milk is superior to either saliva or tap water.[3] An immediate dental consultation is required, as the dentist will need to replant and stabilize the tooth with a nonrigid splint after treating the tooth with other mediums, and perform possible further dental procedures.[10] A tooth-preserving transport system (Emergency Tooth Preserving System)[14] consisting of Hank's balanced salt solution, a cushioning device, and an outer hard impemeable container is available, and would seem to be a prudent addition to the physician/dentist's armamentarium.

AIDS

The AIDS patient presents a complex challenge for the health care profession. As the patient becomes increasingly immunosuppressed, susceptibility to opportunistic infections, thrombocytopenia, and benign and malignant processes dramatically increases. The most common oral manifestations of AIDS include hairy leukoplakia, candidiasis, Kaposi's sarcoma, squamous cell carcinoma, lymphoma, periodontal disease, and xerostomia.[26] The AIDS patient does not need a referral to a hospital for dental treatment unless her health status is such that she requires the medical support of a hospital setting. The patient's dental treatment plan may need to be modified due to changes in her physical well being, degree of immunosuppression, and evidence of thrombocytopenia. The goal of treatment is

to prevent or eliminate infection and pain, and to deliver comprehensive dental care commensurate with the patient's ability to undergo the planned procedure. An aggressive oral home care protocol should be instituted with frequent office follow-up visits. Frequent medical or dental reconsultations as the disease progresses often are necessary.

There are many other instances in which the physician may wish to initiate a dental consultation, or the converse may apply. The patient can only benefit from this input.

References and Selected Readings

1. American Board of Pediatric Dentistry: *Reference Manual,* 1998–1999 Carmel, IN.
2. Berlin CM: Pharmacologic considerations of drug use in the lactating mother. *Obstet Gynecol* 58(suppl):175S–235S, 1981.
3. Blomlof L: Milk and saliva as possible storage media for traumatically exarticulated teeth prior to replantation (thesis). *Swed Dent J Suppl* 8:1–125, 1981.
4. Brent RL: The effects of embryonic and fetal exposure to x-ray, microwaves and ultrasound. *Clin Obstet Gynecol* 26:484–510, 1983.
5. Briggs GG, Freeman RK, Yaffe SJ: *Drugs in Pregnancy and Lactation,* Mitchell CW (eds) Baltimore: Williams & Wilkins, 1994.
6. Christen AG, McDonald JL, Christen JA: *The impact of tobacco use and cessation on nonmalignant and precancerous oral and dental diseases and conditions* Indiana University School of Dentistry Teaching [monograph]. Department of Preventive and Community Dentistry, Indianapolis, Indiana University School of Dentistry, IN: 1991.
7. Damarc SM, Wells S, Offenbacher S: Eicosavoids in periodontal diseases: Potential for systemic involvement. *Adv Exp Med Biol* 433:23–75, 1997.
8. Dajani AS, Taubert KA, Wilson W, et al: Prevention of bacterial endocarditis: Recommendations by the American Heart Association. *JAMA* 277(22):1794–1800, 1997.
9. Donahue AH: Women's health: A national plan for action. *J Dent Educ* 57(10):738–741, 1993.
10. Gehm SE, Crespi PV: Immediate treatment of dental avulsions. *J So Soc Pediatr Dent* 3(2):33–35, 1997.
11. Heikkinen T, Alvesalo L, et al: Maternal smoking and tooth formation in the fetus. III. Thin mandibular incisors and delayed motor development at 1 year of age. *Early Hum Dev* 47(3):327–340, 1997.

12. Heikkinen T, Alvesalo L, et al: Maternal smoking and tooth formation in the fetus II. Tooth crown size in the permanent dentition. *Early Hum Dev* 40(1):73–86, 1994.

13. Hiltz J, Trope M: Vitality of human lip fibroblasts in milk, Hank's balanced salt solution and Viaspan storage media. *Endod Dent Traumatol,* 7:69–72, 1991.

14. Krasner P, Person P: Preserving avulsed teeth for replantation. *JADA* 123:80–88, 1992.

15. Lamey PJ, Lewis MAO: Oral medicine in practice: The compromised patient. *Br Dent J* 168(10):389–394, 1990.

16. Little JW, Falace DA: *Dental Management of the Medically Compromised Patient,* 5th ed. St. Louis: CV Mosby, 1997.

17. Mason JO: A national agenda for women's health. *JAMA* 267(4):482, 1992.

18. Nicotine transdermal system, *Physicians' Desk Reference,* 52nd ed. Montvale, NJ: Medical Economics Data Production, 1998, pp 2787–2790.

19. Offenbacher S, et al: Periodontal infection as a possible risk factor for preterm low birthweight. *J Periodontol* 67(10):1103–1113, 1996.

20. Pallasch TJ: A critical appraisal of antibiotic prophylaxis. *Int Dent J* 39:183–196, 1989.

21. Pinkham J, et al: *Pediatric Dentistry: Infancy Through Adolescence,* Philadelphia: WB Saunders. 1988, pp 160–162.

22. Public Health Service: *Health United States 1991 and Prevention Profile.* Washington, DC: US Department of Health and Human Services, Public Health Service, Centers for Disease Control and Prevention. NCHS 1992: DHHS Publication No. (PHS)92-1232.

23. Public Health Service: *Women's Health Issues: A Presentation at the 159th Meeting of the National Heart, Lung and Blood Advisory Council.* Bethesda MD: US Department of Health and Human Services, National Institutes of Health. NHLBI, 1990.

24. Raphael SL, Gregory PJ: Parental awareness of the emergency management of avulsed teeth in children. *Aust Dent J* 35(2):130:130–133, 1990.

25. Redford M: Beyond pregnancy gingivitis: Bringing a new focus to women's oral health. *J Dent Educ* 57(10):742–748, 1993.

26. Regezi JA, Sciubba JJ: *Oral Pathology: Clinical-Pathologic Correlations.* Philadelphia: WB Saunders, 1999.

27. Tarsitano BF, Rollings RE: The pregnant dental patient: Evaluation and management. *Gen Dent* 41(3):226–231, 1993.

28. Trope M, Friedman S: Periodontal treating of replanted dog teeth stored in Viaspan, milk and Hank's Balanced Solution. *Endod Dent Traumatol* 8:103, 1992.

29. Zachariasen RD: Effect of antibiotics on oral contraceptive efficacy. *J Dent Hyg* 65(7):334–338, 1991.

Plastic Surgery

Frederick Neil Lukash

Women often request information from their primary care physicians regarding plastic or reconstructive surgery. In addition, there are situations in which it is clear to physicians that their patients would benefit from such information (e.g., a patient who is to have a mastectomy or one who has sustained severe facial trauma in an auto accident). Cosmetic surgery also may be beneficial to a patient's psychological well-being. It is therefore important for primary care physicians to be well informed about what is potentially available to their patients and the relative benefits and risks of the various procedures. This chapter discusses the most common types of cosmetic and reconstructive surgery procedures that primary care physicians are likely to discuss with their female patients.

Breast Surgery

Some women are quite concerned because they perceive their breasts to be different from the "societal" norms, and they may inquire about breast surgery. In addition, women who are facing possible mastectomy (or those who have had one) should be advised regarding the potential for breast reconstruction.

Breast Reduction

Overly large breasts can be problematic both physically and psychologically. Excessive weight of the breasts can result in back pain and poor posture. Pressure from brassiere straps can cause deep grooves in the shoulders and skin discoloration. Rashes often develop under large breasts from sweating and rubbing against the skin of the abdomen. Some women with pendulous breasts also may suffer psychological discomfort. Young women may be more likely to be stared at and commented on as sexual objects. Self-consciousness may lead to attempts at concealment, and they may shy away from sports or social events.

The ideal candidate for "reduction mammoplasty" is a person who has achieved a body weight appropriate for her size and has maintained it. Large weight swings up or down after surgery will influence breast size and alter the result. Age is not a barrier to reduction. Girls in their teens and older women many years beyond the menopause have successfully undergone this surgery. With younger patients an endocrine evaluation may be needed, and it is important to be certain that teenage breast development is essentially complete and that further breast growth after surgery is unlikely. Women contem-

plating pregnancy are encouraged to defer this procedure until their family is complete, because childbearing can markedly influence breast size and shape and the ability to breast-feed may be impaired.

Reduction mammoplasty usually takes three to four hours and is performed under general anesthesia. Because this is an elective operation that can result in blood loss, patients should be encouraged to donate their own blood for auto-transfusion if needed.

Two basic types of techniques are used to reduce the size of a breast. In women with moderate hypertrophy, the breasts can be reduced and recontoured while leaving the nipple-areolar complex attached to the remaining breast tissue. This preserves nipple viability and sensitivity. When dealing with very pendulous breasts, the nipple-areolar complex is detached from the breast and repositioned as a graft on the newly reshaped breast. This technique is the safest with overly large breasts, but results in temporary anesthesia to the nipples, which slowly regain sensation over a one-year period.

Breast Uplifts

Time, pregnancy, weight changes, and gravity can lead to sagging of the breasts. This condition is called "mammary ptosis." It can occur with both small and large breasts and represents a combination of decreased breast volume and increased skin stretching.

The diagnosis of breast ptosis is made by looking at the position of the nipple-areolar complex with respect to the inframammary fold. When the nipple is below the fold, ptosis is present.

In many patients, although there is significant sagging there is adequate breast volume, and an uplift alone will provide rejuvenation. In others, however, there is not enough breast tissue; here, an augmentation in combination with an uplift will be needed. Mastopexy is the procedure to correct mammary ptosis. Although it can be performed under local anesthesia, most patients elect general anesthesia. The procedure can eas-

ily be done on an ambulatory basis; it takes 2 to 3 h and is strictly a cosmetic operation.

Breast Augmentation

Each year over 100,000 women in the United States seek out cosmetic surgery for breast enlargement. Size-enhancement surgery has been performed since the 16th century; however, the modern age of breast augmentation began in 1960 with the creation of silicone sheeting. This allowed the creation of a bag that contained either silicone gel or saline. Since that time, many variations of the prototype have appeared, but the basic design has remained. There has been controversy over the safety and efficacy of silicone implants; however, the number of problems in relation to the total number of implants appears to be small. Ongoing studies are attempting to bring this issue to a conclusion and to allow patients to know the scientific status of silicone implants. Recently there have been some reassuring findings. At present, most surgeons are utilizing the silicone bag that is filled with physiologic normal saline.

Before undergoing breast augmentation, a woman should have a complete physical examination. Any history of collagen diseases, such as scleroderma and rheumatoid arthritis, should be specifically ascertained. (This would be a contraindication to implant surgery because it is believed that certain individuals may experience symptoms akin to these diseases many years following implantation.) Likewise, a mammogram should be performed to rule out occult malignancy and to establish a normal baseline. Obviously any problems with breast disease should eliminate surgical augmentation as an option and should be appropriately treated.

Augmentation mammoplasty is performed on an ambulatory basis under either local or general anesthesia. The incisions are small (2 to 3 cm). They are made either under the breast, around the lower portion of the areola, or in the axilla. Through these incisions a pocket is made either

beneath the breast itself or beneath the pectoralis muscle. The implant is then placed in the pocket.

Complications from breast implant and augmentation surgery can be divided into early, late, and very late categories. The early problems are very clear-cut and rectifiable. These include bleeding and infection. Implant removal usually is warranted in the presence of infection around the prosthesis. Late problems usually relate to what is called "capsular contracture." This hardening of the tissues around the implant is not really a complication but, rather, an exaggeration of the normal process of the body walling off foreign material. In 85 percent of patients this encapsulation process is minimal and the implants remain soft. In 15 percent, capsular contracture alters the esthetics of the breast. Current thinking is that if the contractures are a problem to the patient, the implants should be removed. Capsular contracture is not physically harmful, but can be frustrating to both patient and doctor. Finally, there is the issue of whether a woman who has had silicone breast implants is at higher risk for collagen vascular disease. This is currently under investigation.

Women who have had breast augmentation should have screening mammography, physician-performed breast examination, and breast self-examination utilizing the same schedule as patients who have not had this surgery. Mammography is somewhat more difficult to perform in these women, but innovative techniques have been described.

Breast Reconstruction following Mastectomy

Breast reconstruction following mastectomy is one of the most rewarding procedures that a plastic surgeon can perform. Reconstruction is quality-of-life surgery and has no influence on the outcome of the disease. The decision for reconstruction should rest with the affected individual.

There are many methods and timing sequences for reconstruction. Surgery can be immediate at mastectomy, or it can be delayed to any time convenient for the patient. Reconstruction also can utilize an implant or can involve transfer of the patient's own tissue from other areas, such as the abdomen. Most breast reconstruction surgery is staged. Whereas the mound can be part of the immediate surgical process, such refinements as fabrication of the nipple and areola and potential modification of the other breast (to match the reconstructed breast) are staged to allow for artistic precision. Most plastic surgeons who deal extensively with breast reconstruction like to see the patient as soon as the diagnosis of breast cancer is made. That way, assurances can be offered to allay her anxiety. It also provides the best opportunity to plan for the appropriate type and timing of the reconstruction, and to establish the plan with the oncologic surgeon. Breast reconstruction is not a purely "cosmetic" operation, but rather one that restores to normal tissues altered by disease and surgery.

The Aging Face

As people age, their skin elasticity decreases and the strong collagen fibers weaken. The firm fatty tissue beneath the skin shrinks. The skin "fits" more loosely, and lines appear where the facial muscles attach to the skin's undersurface. These are most apparent under the chin and around the mouth and eyes. Many factors play a role in the rate and degree of the aging process. First and foremost is genetics. People with thin, dry, fair skin will realize the signs earlier. Overexposure to sunlight and excessive use of tobacco and alcohol accelerate the aging process. The aging of skin involves wrinkling and sagging; therefore, rejuvenation procedures are aimed at these two processes.

Wrinkles

Facial wrinkling is the end result of constant muscle action on the skin. As the skin and underlying fat thin, the lines of facial expression become accentuated. These lines are predictable and are referred to as "crowfeet" (around the eyes),

"frown lines," and "laugh lines" (around the nose and mouth). The treatment of wrinkling is directed to the crease itself, and has no effect on sagging skin. Isolated wrinkles are currently managed by filling the creases with biocompatible materials or Botox. Most often this is accomplished with either collagen or fat. Collagen, a purified animal protein, is capable of incorporating with one's own collagen to elevate the depressed skin of a wrinkle. Any patient choosing this treatment requires a skin test to ensure that there is no allergy to the "foreign protein." If there is an allergy, this option is eliminated. Another option is fat taken from one's own body, which makes it totally compatible. The fat is harvested by liposuction techniques and then reinjected into the wrinkles. Both of these techniques render good short-term results, varying from 6 months to 2 years. By that time, the material has absorbed, and repeat procedures are needed. Botox is purified botulinum toxin, which when used in dilute amounts and injected into a muscle beneath a wrinkle, can smooth out that wrinkle. It is very effective, but results are not permanent and re-injections are periodically needed.

Generalized wrinkling is managed by various types of chemical treatments to the surface of the skin. The most superficial type of chemical "peel" utilizes the alpha-hydroxy acids. These compounds are derived from fruits and have been nicknamed "fruit peels." They act on the upper levels of the skin and work to improve the complexion and reverse the effects of sun damage. When used in combination with Retin-A, there is a noticeable improvement in superficial wrinkling (fine lines around the eyes). To maintain the benefits of alpha-hydroxy acid treatments, a home maintenance program is essential. Cessation of treatment results in a return to the pretreatment state.

The trichloroacetic acids are a group of chemicals that attack the middle levels of the skin and that can have a significant effect on improving wrinkling. The peel is performed in the doctor's office and requires no anesthesia. It takes about 4 days for the process to be completed. Strict compliance with protocol is necessary to avoid complications. The final group of compounds are in the phenol family. These attack the deeper layers of the skin and have the most profound effect on wrinkles. A side effect of phenol peels is a lightening of the skin. Therefore they are reserved for fair-complected people. As with the trichloroacetic acids, strict attention to protocol is mandatory, or disastrous complications such as scarring can occur.

Sagging Skin

Loose, sagging skin cannot be improved by chemical peels. Lifting procedures, such as face lifts and brow lifts, are necessary. The most dramatic results are seen with the loose skin of the neck, jowls, and the sagging eyebrows. Surgery of the face and brows can be performed on an ambulatory basis. Anesthesia can be either local or general, according to the patient's preference.

Lifting and peeling procedures produce significant improvement in the aging face. Many people have combination problems that require both techniques. Treatment, however, does not stop the aging process. Over time, the forces of elastic collagen degeneration and gravity work to cause further sags and wrinkles. At that time, many people seek out re-do surgery.

Surgery of the Eyelids and Eyebrows

Cosmetic plastic surgery of the eyelids is called a blepharoplasty. The procedure takes between 60 and 90 min, and most often is done under local anesthesia on an outpatient basis.

Prior to any surgery on the eyelids, careful medical and ophthalmologic examinations are essential. Conditions such as dry eye syndrome, glaucoma, thyroid disease, hypertension, and bleeding disorders are absolute contraindications. Most plastic surgeons practice conservatism when operating on the eyelids. A removal of too much skin can risk exposure and possible ulceration of the cornea.

Resuspension of the eyebrows is commonly referred to as a brow lift. This surgery is performed when there is an overhanging of skin on

the outside corners of the eye (hooding), and crowding of tissue at the nasal root and inner aspects of the eyes. Many patients who think they need a blepharoplasty are really in need of a brow lift.

The brow lift procedure, like a blepharoplasty, can be performed on an ambulatory basis and under local anesthesia. Blepharoplasty and brow lift often are performed together and may also be a part of additional facial rejuvenation procedures such as face lift and chemical peel.

Blepharoplasty and brow lift procedures are among the most frequently performed cosmetic surgery operations. Complications are unusual, but can occur. These include bleeding and infection. The most feared complication with a blepharoplasty is blindness. This is extremely rare, but has happened. Brow lift complications also include nerve injury and alopecia (spotty baldness).

Nasal Surgery

More than 70,000 people in the United States seek out cosmetic nasal surgery each year. Nasal plastic surgery is called rhinoplasty and can be performed any time beginning in the midteen years, when midfacial growth is complete. Surgery can be either under local or general anesthesia, and usually is performed on an ambulatory basis.

Chin Surgery

In some patients facial balance involves more than the nose itself. Not only may a nose be too large, but the chin can be too small and thus offset facial symmetry. An astute surgeon viewing the entire face will realize that more than refining the nose may be necessary, and in some situations may recommend chin augmentation as well.

Body Contouring

Perceptions of appropriate body image have changed drastically in recent times. Although diet and exercise remain the most important cornerstones for maintaining a healthy and fit body, there are indications for surgical assistance. When dealing with youthful elastic skin, liposuction is the ideal method to remold by removing isolated fat deposits. When the skin tone is poor from age, large weight losses, or from pregnancy, when stretching has destroyed the skin's elastic fibers, only redraping procedures will restore the desired contour.

Liposuction

This operation was endorsed by the American Society of Plastic and Reconstructive Surgery in 1982. The premise of liposuction is that once fat tissue is physically removed it will not return. Current medical theories agree that people are born with a certain number of fat cells. The number does not change, but rather the cells themselves increase and decrease in size. For many people this means a constant struggle with diet and exercise to overcome genetic predispositions. In spite of their best efforts, certain areas will not respond. These are commonly found under the chin, around the waist and hips, and on the upper, outer thighs. It is for these localized areas of fat that fail to respond to diet and exercise that liposuction deserves consideration. Liposuction is not a substitute for general weight control and is not a panacea to treat obesity.

The ideal candidates for liposuction are younger people with good skin tone. The elastic recoil of the skin is what allows for shrinkage and recontouring in the areas where fat has been removed. Liposuction in people with poor skin tone results in wrinkling and drooping of tissues, which may require additional surgical correction.

Depending on the size of the area to be recontoured, the operation can be performed in the office operatory, in an ambulatory facility, or it may require overnight hospitalization. Likewise, anesthesia may be either a local to the involved area, a regional, such as an epidural, or general anesthesia. Liposuction, as with any surgical procedure, is not without the risks and complications of bleeding and infection.

Body Contouring Surgery

When skin tone is poor, redraping surgery is the appropriate treatment for dysmorphias. The most common of these procedures is the abdominoplasty, or "tummy tuck." Thigh and buttock lifts are less frequent requests, but still remain an important aspect to body contouring.

Abdominoplasty is a major plastic surgical procedure designed to remove excess skin and fat between the umbilicus and the pubic hair line. The procedure takes between two and four hours, and is always done under general anesthesia in a hospital setting. As with most large surgical procedures, complications are possible. The most frequent is bleeding at the time of surgery. For this reason, patients should donate their own blood in advance for autotransfusion if needed.

Scars

The paramount role of a plastic surgeon regarding scars is to understand the biology of tissue injury and wound repair. This enables a plastic surgeon to sometimes revise and improve an unslightly scar, to tell patients what their scars might be like following various types of procedures— and periodically to give the unwelcome news that their existing scars are permanent and will remain as is.

All wounds, whether from accident or surgery, heal by the same basic mechanism—that of fibrous scar tissue. This applies to bones and internal organs as well as to skin. The main ingredient in wound repair is collagen. Following injury there are three phases of healing. The first lasts only a few days and involves the body's "signaling system" to manufacture collagen to "glue" the wound together. The next phase lasts about three weeks and is an intense period of wound healing in which collagen is manufactured and deposited into the wound. Scars during this period usually appear red and thick. The final phase of wound healing is called the "maturation" phase. This period starts at approximately the fourth week following injury and lasts more than

a year. During this time the body attempts to remodel the scar to make it as close to the original tissue as possible. It is during this final period that scars begin to soften and fade, but never totally disappear.

Many factors influence a scar's outcome. Foremost is location. There are areas of the body such as the eyelids where the skin is thin and soft; hence, incisions there heal very well. In other areas, such as the thick skin of the back and extremities, scars will be predictably wide and thick. Another factor is the direction of the scar. If a scar falls within a facial crease, or in one of the body's "relaxed skin tension lines," it will be more favorable than if it crosses perpendicular to these lines. Genetics and age also are extremely important in scar formation and healing. Fair-complected individuals tend to have better scars than do those individuals with darker complexions, and older skin scars better than younger skin, probably owing to a decrease in collagen production.

Keloids

A keloid is a metabolic disorder that affects collagen deposition and maturation. People affected by this problem experience scars that blossom out beyond the area of injury. A good plastic surgeon is skilled in solving wound-healing problems but cannot perform the miracle of scar erasure.

Cleft Lip and Palate

There is probably no joy greater than the birth of a child. When a child is born with a birth defect, apprehension and fear take over. Doctors, hospitals, and operations suddenly become part of the family lifestyle. Because obstetricians, family practitioners, and other primary care clinicians are the first to see the affected child, parents often seek their advice. This section provides familiarity with the reconstructive surgery available to correct these defects.

Clefts of the upper lip and palate are common

birth defects. They occur as a result of a failure of the middle third of the face to close during the fourth to seventh week of intrauterine life. Because the lip and palate close at different times during this period, it is possible to have only a cleft lip, only a cleft palate, or both. Also the severity can vary from small notches to complete splits, and can be unilateral or bilateral.

The timing of repair should be arranged to have minimal impact on future facial growth and yet carry the least risk from surgery and anesthesia. The lip usually is repaired at three months of age. At this time the child can easily withstand the 2- to 3-h procedure. The palate usually is closed shortly after the first birthday. This time is chosen because it is prior to the onset of sound formation and organized speech, for which an intact palate is needed. This procedure takes approximately 2 h. Both types of surgery require general anesthesia and a 2- to 3-day period of hospitalization.

What's New in Plastic Surgery

Probably the two most significant contributions to plastic surgery in the last 20 years are reconstructive microsurgery and cosmetic liposuction. These have provided tremendous hope to many and are the recent miracles of plastic surgery. Microsurgery allowed for the transfer of tissue from one part of the body to another without restriction. It opened the door to replantation of parts and to the future transplantation of parts from one person to another. Liposuction proved that fat could indeed be removed independently of other tissue, and resulted in the most popular operation in plastic surgery.

Other advances, such as endoscopic surgery, laser surgery, and ultrasonic-assisted liposuction, are refinements of already existing technology. They allow certain procedures to be performed more efficiently. They should not, however, be construed as miracles.

Endoscopic surgery has allowed for the lim-

iting of incisions in certain procedures such as brow lifts. Otherwise, the operation remains much the same. There remains debate as to whether open- or full-incision techniques or endoscopic procedures yield better results.

The laser has received much attention in the media as a panacea to facial rejuvenation. Various lasers do different things to the skin, but there is no such thing as "the laser surgery." The carbon dioxide laser serves as a more sophisticated form of dermabrasion, removing lines and wrinkles. Other lasers erase pigment and again are more sophisticated ways to remove tattoos and dark spots from the skin.

Ultrasonic liposuction is another adjunct to the specialty. There continues to be debate in plastic surgery circles regarding the benefit of this procedure versus the risks. It serves as an emulsifier of fat, thereby making it easier to remove the fat. There have been reported complications, such as burns, from the ultrasonic probe.

It is important with any new technique or technology to discuss with a board-certified plastic surgeon the risks, benefits, and outcomes.

A final note: The breast implant controversy may be beginning to resolve. Multiple worldwide studies are in progress. They appear to be reassuring so far. Hopefully, in the near future, the issue will be totally resolved so that both women with reconstructive problems and women with aesthetic issues will feel at ease in their decision regarding whether to use breast implants.

References and Selected Readings

1. Smith JW, Aston SJ (eds): *Grabb and Smith's Plastic Surgery,* 4th ed. Boston: Little, Brown, 1991.
2. Regnault P, Daniel R (eds): *Aesthetic Plastic Surgery.* Boston: Little, Brown, 1984.
3. Serafin D, Georgiade NG (eds): *Pediatric Plastic Surgery.* St Louis: CV Mosby, 1984.
4. Goldwyn R (ed): *The Unfavorable Result in Plastic Surgery.* Boston: Little, Brown, 1972.
5. Peck G (ed): *Complications and Problems in Aesthetic Plastic Surgery.* New York: Gower, 1992.

Occupational and Environmental Medicine

Arthur L. Frank

THE OCCUPATIONAL AND
ENVIRONMENTAL HISTORY
PRINCIPLES OF TOXICOLOGY
PREVENTION OF EXPOSURE
SOURCES OF INFORMATION

The role of women in the workplace continues to evolve rapidly. In many settings, the workplace has more women than men, and women are moving out of traditional roles into a wide range of occupational roles. Increasingly, children are born to women who are employed outside the home, and there continues to be significant recognition of potential reproductive hazards associated with workplace exposures. There is also an increasing awareness of the potential risks to reproduction from environmental exposures that transcend the workplace. Concerns regarding such topics as electromagnetic fields, lead in drinking water, pesticide exposure, and a wide range of other potentially noxious agents continue to receive attention. Perceived risks to workers are now also translated into concerns for potential offspring. There are a variety of issues regarding risks resulting from exposures including absolute or relative infertility in males and females, fetal loss, low birthweight infants, and children who may be born with malformations.[6-8,16]

Current data reveal that more than 60 percent of mothers in America between the ages of 15 and 44 worked for pay within six months of their most recent delivery. Full-time employment was held by 46 percent of these mothers, and part-time employment by more than 14 percent. Women are now also working later into their pregnancies. Compared to 1961, when only about half of working women stayed into their last trimester, and less than a quarter continued to work within one month of delivery, by the end of the 1980s about 80 percent of women worked into their third trimester and more than 50 percent were employed within one month of giving birth.

Among working women, over 40 percent were in technical, sales, or administrative positions, and slightly more than 25 percent were in managerial or professional occupations. Of the rest of the female workforce 17 percent were employed in service jobs, about 8 percent as operators or laborers, 2 percent in craft occupations, and about 1 percent in farming, ranching, and fishing. In addition, women who work are, as a group, more highly educated, have a higher income, start prenatal care earlier, and generally gain more weight during pregnancy than their nonworking counterparts. Full-time work does not appear to carry any different risk than part-time work.

Although most adult Americans, and most women, now work, clinicians traditionally have had little training in occupational and environmental medicine, and know little about obtaining information concerning exposure hazards. The continuing scientific uncertainty about many types of exposures further complicates matters, especially when an increasingly better-educated and more aware public asks questions of their caregivers. In the one-on-one setting of an office

practice, it can be extremely difficult to provide useful information to patients regarding potential hazards to pregnancy and to their own well-being from occupational and environmental exposure.[11] Although this may be true, primary care physicians, and obstetrician-gynecologists for many women, can have an important role in the prevention of adverse reproductive outcomes following such exposure.

The Occupational and Environmental History

Although traditionally poorly taught and almost never reinforced, taking an occupational and environmental history is an important aspect of the overall assessment of a woman's well-being and of any current or potential pregnancies. In their training, physicians are routinely reminded that the medical history is the most significant part of the patient-physician encounter, but the area of exposure assessment is often neglected. When taught, there is often insufficient experience to make use of information of this type when it is obtained in a patient's history.

The patient-physician encounter often puts the patient in a dependent role; however, when it comes to knowledge and experience about her workplace and environmental exposures, the patient is on a more equal footing with the professional, if not clearly more knowledgeable. When discussing workplace exposures, the patient, who is also the worker, is often the best source of information about what is used at the workplace and what occupational health hazards may exist. The worker can give her physician information about specific materials to which she has been exposed by providing access to Material Safety Data Sheets (MSDS), that are required by law to be available to workers for their own information, and for them to share with their health care providers. Clinicians should also know that there are a variety of specialists knowledgeable about workplace and environmental hazards and through such colleagues, which include occupa-

tional health physicians and nurses, industrial hygienists, and others, information can be obtained that may assist in dealing with individual patients. In this day of increasing computer access, searches through library databases, or to such agencies as the National Institute for Occupational Safety and Health (NIOSH), can also be valuable.

The taking of an occupational history originated about 1700 with Italian physician Bernardino Ramazzini, when he produced his great treatise on the diseases of workers, reminding physicians that it was incumbent upon them to ask what their patients did for a living.[14] In the modern world, this can be expanded to include additional exposures that may occur away from the worksite. There is an ever-increasing blurring of distinction between workplace and nonworkplace exposure. Toxins often leave the confines of the factory through air, water, and finished products. Other significant exposures, such as secondhand smoke, can be found in settings as private as one's own home.

Figure 85-1 is a framework for asking about occupational and environmental exposure hazards. Questions contained in the occupational and environmental exposure history need to be assessed along with other aspects of the patient's history, including her prior reproductive history, regular medical history, demographic background, and personal habits, such as cigarette smoking, drug ingestion, and alcohol consumption.[5]

When obtaining an occupational and environmental history the physician should ask what type of work the patient does, and then have the patient fully describe her work if the physician has any questions about the exact nature of a job or its exposures. It is useful to ask specifically about exposures to chemicals, dusts, fumes, vapors, radiation, or other similar exposures. Even noise has been suggested as a risk factor for reproductive outcomes in that fetal effects have been noted following exposure to loud noise.[2]

Continuing, the physician should specifically ask if the patient has any concerns about her

Current work: _____

How long at this job? _____

Description of work: _____

_____

Any contact with dust, fumes, chemicals, radiation, noise, etc?

_____ Yes _____ No   If yes, describe: _____

_____

Describe any adverse effects noted: _____

_____

Are any fellow workers ill? _____ Yes _____ No   If yes, describe: _____

_____

Do you use any protective equipment at work?   _____ Yes _____ No

Previous Job History	From	To	Exposures
1st regular job	_____	_____	
Next job	_____	_____	
Next job	_____	_____	
Vacation or temporary job	_____	_____	
Vacation or temporary job	_____	_____	

Military service or related exposures: _____

_____

Have you lived near an industrial facility or has a family member worked in a setting where hazardous materials have been

brought home? _____ Yes _____ No   If yes, describe: _____

_____

Hobby history:

Smoking history:

Alcohol and drug use history:

Comments:

Figure 85-1   Environmental and occupational exposure history.

health with regard to the workplace, whether any fellow workers are sick, and whether there are any known work-related health problems at her place of employment. It is important, as well, to ask whether the workers are required to wear any special protective equipment, such as a respirator, that might prevent inhalation or ingestion of substances that could be harmful.

There is merit in asking about former jobs in addition to current employment, and one should be prepared to undertake a comprehensive review of previous employment exposures. In some cases, health problems may persist from prior exposures and may not be attributable to the current job.

It is also important to ask about the spouse's

employment and the possibility that hazardous materials could affect one's spouse, or that a spouse might bring home on his work clothes or skin substances that could affect others. For example, if the spouse has been in the military, exposure to dioxins might be relevant, and there is an increasingly large body of data regarding male reproductive hazards.[9,15,18,20] Specific hazards, such as exposures to dibromochloropropane (DBCP) have received a great deal of attention.[13]

In addition to spousal exposures, it is also appropriate to ask if the patient knows of any local environmental contamination, or if she lives near a factory, hazardous waste site, or may be exposed to a contaminated water supply. Other relevant questions are related to exposures within the household. Potentially hazardous exposures can result from renovations or remodeling, installation of new home insulation with materials containing formaldehyde, off-gassing from carpeting and furniture, and even the use of certain household products. Also, it is appropriate to ask about the patient and spouse's hobbies, because they may be a source of potentially hazardous exposure.

An additional concern of growing interest is the matter of possible contamination of breast milk following industrial or other significant exposures.[1]

Further information regarding occupational history can be obtained from a variety of sources.[4,5,12,21]

Principles of Toxicology

The basic principles of toxicology govern reproductive outcomes, just as they can affect any other organ system. Important issues include the chemical and physical properties of possible toxins; exposure characteristics such as dose, route of entry, and metabolic fate; and other related factors. Issues of individual susceptibility and possible synergism may also be operative. Hazards to reproduction may come from both chemical and physical exposures, and may affect either

sex. Table 85-1 lists some of these exposures and their specific associated risk factors for adverse reproductive outcomes. These reproductive hazards cover a wide range of exposures from infectious agents, tobacco, medications, solvents, pesticides,[17] and heavy metals, to noise. Other factors still under study include electromagnetic radiation and the role of strenuous work in pregnancy outcome.

For some specific occupational groups, for instance, hospital personnel, there may be hazards from exposures such as waste anesthetic gases and chemotherapeutic agents. Among the infectious agents, there are risks from viruses, parasites, and some bacteria. There are case studies that more fully illustrate these hazards.[12,21]

A basic principle of toxicology that applies to

TABLE 85-1 Factors in Women That May Be Associated with Adverse Reproductive Effects

Risk Factors Associated with Menstrual Disorders
  Antineoplastics
  Carbon disulfide
  Chloroprene
  Fluorine
  Formaldehyde
  Tobacco
  Trinitrotoluene

Risk Factors Associated with Spontaneous Abortion
  Alcohol
  Medications
  Infections
  Smoking

Risk Factors Associated with Low Birthweight or Prematurity
  Alcohol
  Altitude
  Infections
  Noise (?)
  Smoking

Exposures That May Be Associated with Adverse Outcomes
  Anesthetic gases
  Heavy metals (e.g., lead, mercury)
  Ionizing radiation
  Pesticides (e.g., dibromochloropropane, dioxin)
  Solvents (e.g., carbon disulfide)

SOURCE: Adapted from Lemasters.[9]

reproductive hazards is the classic dose-response relationship, which states simply that as the dose escalates, the likelihood of a biological response also rises. Dose can be measured in different ways, including doses found in the environment, the internalized dose following a specific route of entry, the dose of a specific toxic agent following metabolism of a xenobiotic, or some combination of these various exposures. Potential complications are exposures to mixtures of materials, such as gasoline, or synergisms resulting from combinations of exposures either at the workplace or between workplace toxins and risky personal habits, such as the use of cigarettes or alcohol or drug ingestion.

Complicating our understanding of basic toxicology is the question of individual susceptibility. Susceptibility to toxins may vary by age, sex, nutritional status, genetics, current disease, hormonal and immunological status, or through possible synergisms with personal habits. Generally, all patients should be considered equally susceptible, because there is rarely any way, a priori, that one can judge who has a greater or lesser susceptibility to toxins.

Prevention of Exposure

Depending on the nature of exposure to toxins, there are a variety of basic approaches to eliminate or reduce such exposures before a woman becomes pregnant, during her pregnancy, or at all times, which is the best solution. For such personal habits as smoking, alcohol use, nutrition, and drug ingestion, each woman has considerable control over her own exposure.

At the workplace, exposure control can take several forms. As a basic principle, it is not ideal to have a woman who is pregnant, or who is trying to become pregnant, need to stop working. There may well be some unusual circumstances that require a woman to discontinue or curtail her normal activities, including work, but a ban on working is often the least acceptable alternative to the woman.

According to federal law, each worker is entitled to a safe and healthful workplace; this issue has been affirmed by the Supreme Court. Many companies have policies regarding workplace exposures and potential reproductive hazards, and some laws do exist. Discussion of such issues can be reviewed,[11] and to assist women and their caregivers in recognizing potential health hazards,[3] systems of labeling potentially dangerous substances have been developed.[19]

There are times, however, when administrative controls are necessary, including job transfer, restriction of physical hazards during pregnancy, or modification of a job assignment. Compared with engineering controls, which are the ideal way of reducing exposure, the least desirable alternative is a requirement to wear personal protective equipment as a major means of controlling harmful exposure. Although quite effective, the reality of using a respirator over a typical work shift is one of extreme difficulty. Similarly, a worker's use of a lead apron to minimize radiation exposure is far less acceptable than engineering modifications that do not allow for such exposure in the first place.

Sources of Information

The worker is often the best source of information regarding specific exposures, but most physicians have had little training in making use of such information. Assistance can be had from various government agencies such as NIOSH, the Agency for Toxic Substances and Disease Registry (ATSDR), and state or local health departments. Additional potential sources of information are university programs in occupational and environmental medicine and poison control centers. Increasingly, textbooks include some useful information, although it should be recognized that with the tens of thousands of potential chemical exposures in the workplace or the environment, considerable research may be needed to obtain specific information.

It should also be recognized that for very few

chemicals is there really much information about possible reproductive hazards. One database that does contain some recent references on reproductive data for over 800 chemicals and physical agents is Reprotoxline. The National Library of Medicine in Bethesda, Maryland, on the National Institutes of Health campus, has several computerized databases, including one on developmental reproductive toxicology, and various hazardous substances data banks, including Medline and Toxline. These are readily accessible from a desktop computer through the internet at www.nlm.nih.gov.

Given the large number of questions, and the relatively small database with good answers about potential reproductive effects, one is often left with the need to make individualized judgments with regard to a patient based upon limited amounts of information, recognizing that there is a complex set of factors that must be considered. These same limitations also apply in the area of regulatory toxicology, where still relatively few compounds or potentially hazardous exposures have been well studied. This lack of good scientific data, coupled with the potential anxiety of patients and the very real need to give good advice, is one of the great challenges to physicians, not only in the area of reproductive toxicology, but also with many similar issues of toxic exposure where reproduction is not an immediate or even a future concern.

References and Selected Readings

1. Byczkowski JZ, Gearhart JM, Fisher JW: "Occupational" exposure of infants to toxic chemicals via breast milk. *Nutrition* 10:43–48, 1994.
2. Etzel RA, Balk SJ, Bearer CF, et al: Noise: A hazard for the fetus and newborn. *Pediatrics* 100:724–727, 1997.
3. Feinberg JS, Kelley CR: Pregnant workers. A physician's guide to assessing safe employment. *West J Med* 168:86–92, 1998.
4. Frank AL (ed): ATSDR. *Case Studies in Environmental medicine: Taking an Exposure History.* Washington, DC, US Department of Health and Human Services, 1992, pp 1–56. No. 26.
5. Frank AL: The occupational and environmental history, in Rom WN (ed): *Environmental and Occupational Medicine.* Boston: Little, Brown, 1992, pp 29–34.
6. Gabbe SG, Turner LP: Reproductive hazards of the American lifestyle: Work during pregnancy. *Am J Obstet Gynecol* 176:826–832, 1997.
7. Gold EB, Tomich E: Occupational hazards to fertility and pregnancy outcome. *Occup Med* 9:435–469, 1994.
8. Gracoia GP: Reproductive hazards in the workplace. *Obstet Gynecol Surv* 47:679–687, 1992.
9. Lemasters GK: Occupational exposures and effects on male and female reproduction, in Rom WN (ed): *Environmental and Occupational Medicine.* Boston: Little, Brown, 1992, pp 147–170.
10. Morello-Frosch RA: The politics of reproductive hazards in the workplace: Class, gender, and the history of occupational lead exposure. *Int J Health Serv* 27:501–521, 1997.
11. Paul ME: Disorders of reproduction. *Prim Care* 21:367–386, 1994.
12. Paul M, Kurtz S: *Reproductive Hazards in the Workplace: Occupational and Environmental Reproductive Hazards Center.* Worcester: University of Massachusetts Medical Center, 1990.
13. Potashnik G, Porath A: Dibromochloropropane (DPCP): A 17-year reassessment of testicular function and reproductive performance. *J Occup Environ Med* 37, 1995, pp 1287–1292.
14. Ramazzini B: *Diseases of Workers (De Morbis Artificum Diatriba, 1713).* Wright WC, translator. New York: Hafner 1964.
15. Robaire B, Hales BF: Paternal exposure to chemicals before conception. *Br Med J* 307:341–342, 1993.
16. Sever LE: Congenital malformations related to occupational reproductive hazards. *Occup Med* 9:471–494, 1994.
17. Sever LE, Arbuckle TE, Sweeny A: Reproductive and developmental effects of occupational pesticide exposure: The epidemiologic evidence. *Occup Med* 12:305–325, 1997.
18. Steinberger E: Disorders of the male reproductive system, in Tarcher AB (ed). *Principles and Practice of Environmental Medicine.* New York: Plenum, 1992, pp 437–457.
19. Sullivan FM: The European Community Directive on the classification and labeling for chemicals for reproductive toxicology. *J Occup Environ Med* 37:966–969, 1995.
20. Tas S, Lauwerys R, Lison D: Occupational hazards for the male reproductive system. *Crit Rev Toxicol* 26:261–307, 1996.
21. Welch LS (ed): ATSDR. Case studies in environmental medicine: Reproductive and developmental hazards. Washington, DC, US Department of Health and Human Services, 1993, pp 1–41. No. 29.

Part VIII

Other Important Issues

Adverse Drug Reactions, Drug Interactions, and Cost-Effective Utilization of Drugs

Anne Y. F. Lin
Bruce G. Kay

ADVERSE DRUG REACTIONS
DRUG INTERACTIONS
Herbal Products
COST-EFFECTIVE UTILIZATION
   OF DRUGS

Adverse Drug Reactions

Adverse drug reactions, or side effects, can occur despite the most careful use of drugs. Although some authors differentiate between the terms "adverse drug reactions" and "side effects," they are used synonymously in this chapter. Many side effects are unavoidable, because they are an extension of the drug's pharmacologic effects and inseparable from its therapeutic actions. Such side effects are predictable on the basis of the drug's pharmacologic activity. Common examples of such reactions include chlorpropramide-induced hypoglycemia, captopril-induced hypotension, and diphenhydramine-induced urinary retention. There are, however, side effects that occur that are unpredictable because they are unrelated to the drug's pharmacologic activity. These effects can be subcategorized into allergic and idiosyncratic reactions.

Drug allergies account for approximately 20 percent of all adverse drug reactions. Although they are uncommon relative to predictable side effects, they are important because they may in-

crease patient morbidity and mortality. Allergic reactions cannot be predicted, are not related to a drug's pharmacologic activity, and generally are not dose-related. For example, based on the ability of penicillin to inhibit bacterial cell wall synthesis, one cannot predict that anaphylaxis will occur. All clinicians recognize a rash as a potential allergic reaction to a drug. However, allergic reactions can affect many organ systems. Heparin-induced thrombocytopenia, nafcillin-induced interstitial nephritis, and phenytoin-induced hepatitis are all examples of allergic reactions. Allergic reactions (synonymous with hypersensitivity) are immune mediated; as such, an induction period is required for the production of antibodies or T cells that recognize the specific drug. Therefore, reexposure or prolonged exposure is necessary for the development of allergic symptoms. Both humoral and cell-mediated immunity play a role in allergic reactions; while humoral immunity does not carry life-long memory, cell-mediated immunity does. Therefore, a patient who reports having developed a rash 5 days into treatment with penicillin 20 years ago may not develop a rash upon retreatment today. In contrast, reexposure to poison ivy after many years of exposure will still result in the development of contact dermatitis.

Upon obtaining patient medication histories, one question that always arises is whether

patients with drug allergies will react to drugs that are within the same or similar pharmacologic class. Unfortunately, cross-reactivity among drugs is not always predictable, because for most drug allergies we do not know what part of the chemical structure is responsible for the allergic reaction. This concept is best represented by patients with a sulfa allergy. The sulfur atom present in sulfa compounds is not the cause of the allergic reaction; if this were the case, such patients would have multiple allergies. It has been postulated that the para-amino group might be involved in this reaction. However, many compounds contain such a chemical group, and would present the potential for cross-reactivity with a large number of drugs if the postulate were correct. The small number of reported cases of cross-sensitivity among sulfonamides suggests that a unique metabolite or specific radical is the culprit. With the latter mechanism, cross-sensitivity would be limited to only a few drugs that are very similar in structure. This may explain why some patients are allergic to hydrochlorothiazide but can tolerate furosemide. On the other hand, the first mechanism may explain why some patients with sulfonamide allergies are allergic to all PABA compounds (e.g., sunscreens). Overall, although cross-sensitivity among sulfonamides does occur, it is impossible to predict its frequency. History of a sulfonamide allergy is not an absolute contraindication to the use of potentially cross-reacting drugs. The clinical manifestation of the allergic reaction would determine whether a potential cross-reacting agent should be used. The use of other sulfonamide drugs would be contraindicated in patients with a prior history of Stevens-Johnson syndrome or any adverse effect associated with high morbidity and mortality. If a patient reports having had a rash after using a sulfonamide antibiotic, it is prudent to use an alternative antibiotic. However, the use of thiazide diuretics or sulfonylureas may not be contraindicated.

Unfortunately, there are few confirmatory tests for drug allergy. Obtaining complete and accurate drug histories is critical to the diagnosis

of drug-induced allergic reactions, or of any adverse effect. Whether cross-reacting drugs can be used will depend on the type of allergic reaction elicited. For example, patients who develop a maculopapular rash after several days of treatment with penicillin can complete the course of therapy. Symptomatic management of the rash may be all that is necessary. Therefore, in such patients, a penicillin may be used again if medically necessary. However, for a patient with a history of a reaction that is associated with a high mortality rate, such as anaphylaxis, penicillin would be contraindicated.

Idiosyncratic reactions typically do not involve the immune system. An anaphylactoid reaction is an example of such an adverse effect. Although the clinical presentation of an anaphylactoid reaction is the same as that of anaphylaxis, it is different in that it does not involve the immune system. Drugs (e.g., skeletal relaxants, contrast media, opiates) that cause anaphylactoid reactions have the ability to cause the release of histamine directly, without antibodies. Therefore, an induction period is not needed and patients can develop this reaction on first exposure. Additionally, patients can be pretreated with antihistamines and/or corticosteroids to prevent or minimize the reaction.

Often physicians need to determine whether a drug can cause a specific side effect but the side effect may not be listed in the package insert or the *Physician's Desk Reference.* However, based on clinical judgment, it would appear that the drug, in fact, caused the problem. There are several reasons why Phase II and III clinical trials cannot determine the complete safety profile of any drug. First, the number of patients enrolled in such trials is relatively small in comparison with the number of patients who will use the drug after marketing. Therefore, rare side effects may not be detected in these initial trials. Second, these trials are mostly short-term; side effects that occur only after long-term use will not be detected. Finally, for the most part, study patients are relatively healthy, except for the disease being treated. Thus, the influence of other disease states and or-

gan dysfunction on the drug's safety profile is unknown at the time of initial marketing.

To determine if a patient is experiencing any adverse effect, five factors need to be considered: time sequence; serum drug concentrations; known response pattern; dechallenge; and rechallenge. The first two factors are self-explanatory. The known response pattern is the typical clinical presentation of the adverse effect in question. This information can be obtained from case reports in the literature and from the manufacturer. The amount of information given varies for each company. A manufacturer may have reports on file that have not been published. A drug information center, present in hospitals or colleges of pharmacy, can be contacted to determine what information is available in the literature. A comparison of the individual patient with this information will help the physician to determine causality. A positive dechallenge refers to resolution of the effect after the drug is discontinued, and a positive rechallenge refers to the reappearance of symptoms after the drug is restarted. In making this determination, one must keep in mind that patients may be taking more than one drug that could be associated with the side effect. One may not always be able to determine for certain which drug caused the problem; in other cases, the known response pattern will identify the responsible drug.

Using drugs only when they are medically necessary is the key factor in minimizing the development of adverse drug reactions. When drugs are used, obtaining complete and accurate medication histories is critical to avoiding the development of or effectively managing a drug-induced adverse effect. The following data should be obtained: names of all drugs (prescription and over-the-counter) and any "natural" remedies that the patient is taking; dosage regimen and duration of treatment; symptoms of adverse effects, including time of onset; how the adverse effect was managed (if it occurred in the past); and history of previous drug reactions—with all the above information, if possible. Patients who have drug allergies should be

treated with drugs that will not cross-react. However, the patient should be interviewed to determine if she did in fact have allergic symptoms. This would prevent the use of a less effective agent with a less desirable safety profile when it is not necessary to do so.

Drug Interactions

The documentation of a drug interaction does not necessarily contraindicate the use of the two interacting agents. To avoid adverse reactions that are due to drug interactions, the clinician needs to be aware of the mechanism of the drug interaction, the time course of the interaction, and how the effects of the interaction can be monitored and minimized.

As with adverse effects, drug interactions can be divided into two types: pharmacodynamic and pharmacokinetic. Pharmacodynamic interactions occur when the administration of a second drug alters the patient's clinical response to the first drug. For example, the administration of a diuretic increases the potential for hypotension in a patient who is also taking captopril. Pharmacodynamic interactions have been studied to a much lesser extent than pharmacokinetic interactions because in many cases it is difficult to quantify a patient's response to a drug. Additionally, it is difficult to assess the clinical significance of such interactions in clinical studies.

More commonly, pharmacokinetic drug interactions are studied prior to drug marketing. These interactions affect the absorption, distribution, metabolism, and elimination of a given drug. The resulting effects may or may not be clinically important. Usually, if a drug alters the rate of absorption of a medication given chronically, the interaction is clinically insignificant because the therapeutic serum concentration of the affected drug is not altered. For example, concomitant administration of theophylline and magnesium-aluminum hydroxide antacids decreases the rate but not the extent of theophylline absorption. Clinically, this has no impact on

patient management. In contrast, one would not want to delay the rate of absorption of morphine needed for immediate pain relief.

Interactions that occur as a result of one drug's ability to decrease the percentage of absorption of another drug may be clinically significant. Coadministration of digoxin and cholestyramine results in decreased serum digoxin concentration. This interaction may be clinically significant because, in essence, this decreases the digoxin dose. However, these two drugs may still be used concomitantly if one separates their administration by at least 1.5 to 2 h. Drug bioavailability also can be affected by changes in enterohepatic circulation, as in the interaction between penicillin and oral contraceptives. Disruption of the gastrointestinal flora by penicillin decreases or eliminates the hydrolysis of estrogen conjugates; this impairs the enterohepatic circulation of the pharmacologically active drug. The clinical significance of the interaction has not been determined, although there have been reports of unintended pregnancies.

Most acidic drugs are reversibly bound, to varying extents, to protein, primarily albumin. It is the free (unbound) drug that exerts the pharmacologic effects. Therefore, if a drug can be displaced from protein binding, there would not only be more free drug to exert its pharmacologic effect, but also more drug available for metabolism. However, the effects of drug displacement on drug metabolism are complex and variable, and depend on a number of factors.

Overall, changes in protein binding should result in a change in pharmacologic response. Generally, an interaction that occurs via this mechanism has potential clinical significance only for drugs that are highly protein-bound (>90 percent), such as warfarin. If a drug is bound to a lesser degree, any change in the percentage of free drug is not as great a relative change, and is not clinically significant. For example, if a drug is 50 percent protein-bound, drug displacement of 5 percent results in only a 10 percent change of free drug. In contrast, if a drug is 95 percent

protein-bound, an increase of 5 percent is a twofold increase in the amount of free drug.

Drugs also can alter the renal and hepatic elimination of other drugs. The offending drug must alter the major route of elimination of the affected drug for the interaction to be of potential clinical significance. In terms of metabolism, drugs may be either enzyme-inducers or enzyme-inhibitors. Generally, the effects of enzyme induction are slow and dose related. The clinical effect of this interaction is a decrease in efficacy of the affected drug. It may take up to 3 weeks before the maximal effects of the drug interaction are noted; corresponding to that, it would take some time for the effects of the drug interaction to dissipate. For example, the effects of enzyme induction by rifampin usually are seen within 2 to 4 days, with maximal effects occurring after approximately 6 to 10 days. Resolution of these effects occurs over two to three weeks. Therefore, a patient who is taking rifampin and was using oral contraceptives should continue to use alternative contraceptive methods for several weeks after the discontinuation of rifampin. At the extreme, the effects of enzyme induction by phenobarbital occur gradually, with maximal effects being observed in two to three weeks. Phenobarbital's effects may take one month or more to dissipate. The onset and dissipation of the effects of other enzyme-inducers probably lie somewhere between rifampin and phenobarbital. Other examples of enzyme-inducers that cause clinically significant drug interactions include other barbiturates, carbamazepine, primidone, and phenytoin.

In contrast, enzyme inhibition, which is one of the most common mechanisms responsible for drug interactions, occurs as soon as the enzyme inhibitor reaches a critical serum concentration. Generally, the effects of enzyme inhibition can be seen, and dissipate, within 24 h of drug administration and discontinuation, respectively. The primary effect of this drug interaction results in increased serum drug concentrations and pharmacologic response. The most recent example of

these interactions is the use of terfenadine and erythromycin. Erythromycin inhibits the metabolism of terfenadine and its carboxylic metabolite, resulting in cardiac dysrrhythmias. Concomitant administration of these two drugs obviously should be avoided.

As indicated, drugs also can affect the renal elimination of other drugs by altering the glomerular filtration, tubular secretion, or tubular reabsorption of a drug. The result of such an interaction can be used therapeutically. For example, probenecid competes for tubular secretion of penicillin and increases its therapeutic effects. On the other hand, probenecid can increase serum methotrexate concentration by two-to threefold, resulting in serious methotrexate toxicity.

In practice, one may not always be able to avoid the use of interacting drugs. However, several principles may be considered in order to minimize the potential for the development of subtherapeutic or toxic effects. First, the most critical time for monitoring the effects of any drug interactions is when the drug that causes the change is started or stopped. If the patient is already taking the drug that causes the change, the effects of an interaction may not be noticeable because the physician will be titrating the dose of the affected drug according to patient response. The time of onset of the effects, as well as the time to maximal effects, of the interaction must be taken into account, because this can influence when and if steps need to be taken to manage the interaction. For example, nonsteroidal anti-inflammatory agents can decrease the response of antihypertensive agents over a period of one to two weeks. Therefore, the short-term use of ibuprofen or naproxen for dysmenorrhea or headache does not require any change in the patient's antihypertensive therapy.

Additionally, the time of onset also determines when laboratory monitoring is needed. For example, erythromycin increases serum theophylline concentrations generally over 3 to 5 days, and in many patients beyond 5 days. Therefore, it would not be cost-effective to draw a theophyl-line level on the same day or the day after erythromycin is started. If this information is not available for a given set of drugs, the physician may be able to predict the time course by the drugs' half-lives.

Third, the drug interactions most likely to result in an adverse effect are those that affect drugs with a narrow therapeutic range. In the case of drugs for which there is a correlation between serum drug concentrations and pharmacologic response, the patient who is at the extremes of the therapeutic range has a greater potential to be affected by the drug interaction.

Fourth, because some drug interactions are dose-related, unless an adequate dose is used the interaction may not occur. On the other hand, a large dose of a drug may result in a faster onset of the interaction.

Fifth, a number of factors can affect a patient's response to the effects of the drug interaction. Factors such as age, genetics, and social habits (drinking, smoking) can increase the risk of drug interactions and can influence the extent of the effect.

Herbal Products

Given the tremendous increase in the interest and use of alternative medicine, and changes in the U.S. population, physicians will encounter many patients who will be taking alternative medicine, particularly herbal products. Whether one believes in the efficacy of such products is irrelevant, because physicians will be faced with having to determine whether there may be potential interactions with prescribed medications or adverse effects from their use. Many of these products are sold in health food stores as herbs, herbal teas, and food supplements. Because they cannot be legally labeled for use in the treatment of disease, many times claims are made regarding these products and information is placed next to the item on the shelf.

The difficulty with the use of these products is the scarcity of information that is available.

Much of the data that is currently available is from Germany, where the study of herbs has been more extensive than in the United States. The lack of scientific evidence for the safety and efficacy of herbal products is in part due to their use prior to our discovery of pharmacodynamics and pharmacokinetics, and prior to the requirement to demonstrate quality, safety, and efficacy. One major barrier to being able to provide evidence of safety and efficacy is that the active ingredients, in many cases, are unknown and there is a placebo effect associated with herbal use.

Due to the widespread use of herbal products, physicians obtaining a medication history should determine if the patient is taking any herbal products. If so, the following information is important: product name, product ingredients, and how it is taken. If the patient is using herbal tea, it is important to determine if tea bags are being used or if the patient is brewing the tea, in which case the brewing time and quantity of herb used are relevant. One should note that these products often list the common names of plants on the package, rather than the scientific name. This poses a problem because there are numerous common names for a particular plant. Additionally, these names are inexact and can refer to different species of the plant. The American Society of Pharmacognosy has recommended to the FDA that in addition to the scientific name, the part of the plant, country of origin (which can affect active constituent concentration), and lot number of the voucher specimen that is maintained for reference be listed on the package.

A drug information center located within a medical facility or school of pharmacy can be contacted for information regarding such products. One excellent reference that is published by Facts & Comparisons (*The Review of Natural Products*) provides the common name, botanical name, pharmacologic activity, and potential adverse effects of many plants. The reference cited at the end of the chapter by Tyler provides an overview of the subject matter, and the reference by Bisset provides information on 181 components of herbal teas.

Cost-Effective Utilization of Drugs

Physicians must consider drug costs when treating patients. Several factors must be taken into account aside from the cost of the drug itself. When many "me too" drugs exist in a given pharmacologic category, such as the β-blockers, it is important to determine if slight differences among the drugs are clinically significant in relation to patient management. If not, then the higher cost of the "new" and "better" drug is not worth the additional investment.

Second, if two drugs are equally effective, but one has a more risky side effect profile or requires additional laboratory monitoring, the additional cost of a drug without the latter two characteristics may be offset by the savings incurred from less laboratory monitoring and decreased potential for adverse drug reactions.

Third, a dosage regimen that lends itself to improved patient compliance (once a day versus four times a day, or shorter treatment duration), potentially can decrease cost. Noncompliance can increase the risk for treatment failure, thereby increasing the cost of treatment. For example, 3-day antibiotic regimens are usually as effective as 7-day regimens in the management of uncomplicated cystitis in women, and are associated with fewer side effects and lower costs. In many cases, once the patient becomes asymptomatic there is an increased potential for the patient not to finish the course of therapy.

Finally, the availability of generic drugs should be considered. Manufacturers of generic drugs that have provided data to the FDA to be considered "therapeutically equivalent" are also bioequivalent to the proprietary product. Use of generic drugs can decrease the overall cost of therapy. A list of therapeutically equivalent agents can be found in the FDA's *Approved Drug Products with Therapeutic Equivalence Evaluations*, which is updated annually.

Summary

The judicious use of drugs requires the physician to consider the therapeutic effects of the drugs,

and also to consider the potential for the development of adverse effects, to recognize and manage drug interactions and adverse effects, and to understand the costs of therapy. An understanding of some basic principles and the application of general guidelines, as outlined above, will aid the physician in the safe and effective use of medications.

References and Selected Readings

1. Assem E-SK: Drug allergy and tests for its detection, in Davies DM (ed): *Textbook of Adverse Drug Reactions*. New York: Oxford University Press, 1991, pp 689–732.
2. Bisset NG (ed): *Herbal Drugs and Phytopharmaceuticals*. Ann Arbor: CRC Press, 1994.
3. Boyd JR, Covington TR, Stanaszek WF et al: Drug defaulting, Part I. Determinants of compliance. *Am J Hosp Pharm* 31:362–367, 1974.
4. Burnham TH (ed): *The Review of Natural Products*. St. Louis: Facts & Comparisons.
5. Hoigne R, Malinverni R, Sontag R: Sulfonamides, other folic acid antagonists and miscellaneous antibacterial drugs, in Dukes MNG (ed): *Myler's Side Effects of Drugs*. New York: Elsevier, 1992, pp 715–725.
6. Hansten PD, Horn JR, Koda-Kimble MA, Young LY (eds): *Drug Interactions and Updates Quarterly*. Vancouver: Applied Therapeutics, 1993.
7. Patterson R: Diagnosis and treatment of drug allergy. *J Allergy Clin Immunol* 81(2):380–384, 1988.
8. Tyler VE: *Honest Herbal*. New York: Pharmaceutical Products Press, 1993.
9. Van Arsdel PP: Drug reactions: Allergy and near-allergy. *Ann Allergy* 57:305–311, 1986.
10. Witte KW, West DP: Immunology of adverse drug reactions. *Pharmacotherapy* 2:54–65, 1982.

Ethics

Kenneth J. Ryan

The practice of medicine is a thoroughgoing ethical enterprise. The physician has privileged access to intimate details of patients' lives and deals with judgments and actions that can significantly affect a patient's present and future well being. If anything, this is more true of primary care than of subspecialty branches of medicine, because primary care is concerned with all aspects of a patient's health in continuity over a lifetime. The primary care physician functions not only by the direct provision of medical care, but also as a gatekeeper for referral to other medical or health services, as an educator, a confidante, and a facilitator in matters related to the patient's medical and health needs.

The purpose of the renewed emphasis on medical ethics in medical school education and in practice during the past 25 years was to be sure that physicians recognize the ethical problems that modern society poses for medicine and the problems that advances in medical science and technology pose for society. Once an aspect of medical care is recognized as an ethical problem, the challenge for the physician is to reason about and deal with it so that the "right" choices are made.

The Hippocratic Oath and Ethical Theories, Principles, and Reason

The Hippocratic oath and writings have been the universal guides for generally defining a physician's duties and the ethical practice of medicine. Such admonitions as to help one's patients if possible and at least not harm them, to maintain confidentiality, to treat first and worry about the fee later, and to not take advantage of patients, are all timeless exhortations to the good doctor's conscience. Adherence to many but not all of the Hippocratic maxims is necessary, but not sufficient, to practice medicine today. The modern world has a different view of the rights of individuals and of civil and women's rights, of the physician's obligations, and of the limitations of the physician's authority, than that reflected in the Hippocratic corpus.

Modern bioethics began in the 1960s in the United States in the aftermath of the Holocaust and the Nuremberg code and the failure of medical ethics to protect human subjects of medical research from harm or exploitation, even in the post-World War II era. Advances in medical technology, organ transplantation, life support systems, and the public disputes over abortion all contributed to the interest in and expansion of medical ethics.

As a "foundation" for bioethics, several theories have been invoked, such as a Kantian respect for universal rules of conduct, or a John Millsian utilitarianism that bases ethics on the greatest

good for the greatest number. These two theories contrast the outcome of any medical action with the method used in achieving it. Ethical principles have also been promulgated that define ethical medicine in terms of respect for patients' rights and autonomy, of beneficent goals and outcomes for patients, and of seeking justice and fairness in the distribution and access of medical benefits.

The problem in the application of all these principles and theories in the real world is that they very often conflict, and decisions have to be made when the choices cannot easily be pigeonholed into unambiguous right or wrong. Decision-making then depends on experience and wisdom, and sometimes on compromise. In actual practice, we have to look at the ethical significance of both the outcomes and the means of our actions, and we need appropriate and convincing reasons for our choices. We all know that some reasons are better than others, and to function well we must justify our actions and decisions to our patients, to our colleagues, and to the larger community in which we live. There is also an inevitable ethical tension between the physician's obligation to the patient and the obligation with respect to resource allocation in society at large.

There are three general areas of medical practice where the new medical ethics has had a significant influence on the way physicians function: (1) The Art of Medicine has become more patient-oriented and the physician-patient interaction has been redefined. (2) The Goals of Medicine have been recast in keeping with the changed Social Uses of Medicine. (3) The Science of Medicine has set new standards by which to judge physician competence. Each of these is considered in turn.

Ethics of the Art of Medicine

The relationship between physicians and patients used to depend largely on the good intentions of the physician and the willingness of the patient to listen to the doctor and do as he or she was told. This essentially parent-child balance of power favored the physician, based on his or her social privilege and superior knowledge. Patients, according to the prevailing social theory, were to play the "sick role." In the 1960s, there was a change in the relationship of the public to institutions such as government and medicine. Discontent with the course of the Viet Nam War and concern over minority and women's rights brought challenge to the old ways of doing business. The challenge was for physicians to provide truthful and complete disclosure to their patients.

In the past, physicians might withhold information from their patients for the patients' "own good" and might not tell patients that they had cancer or a fatal illness. Physicians might offer patients only one course of action to combat a disease, and might not discuss other options and their consequences, including the possible value of no treatment at all. Patients might be used in research or for the education of medical or nursing students without their knowledge or consent. Physicians have had financial interests in laboratories or imaging centers and referred patients preferentially, and sometimes excessively, to these medical businesses from which they directly profited. Most of these practices are now seen as unethical or at least ethically problematical. Older physicians have had to change their ways and younger physicians who came of age in the 1960s and beyond grew into an environment that naturally accepted the need to respect patients' rights and what that entails.

The Patient Bill of Rights of the American Hospital Association codified many of these changes in physician and hospital duties, and while old ways die hard, patients are more apt today to insist on full disclosure and truth telling. This is especially true in the case of women's health care where, for example, women have insisted on more treatment options for breast cancer. Women now want more choice in medical care that affects their reproductive functions, and do not wish to be held captive to "male" percep-

tions of what is best, whether suggested by their physician, father, or spouse.

Research on women's medical problems had been systematically ignored or assumed to be the same as for men by the medical research community. Usually due to the possibility of a pregnancy or when pregnant, women had been excluded from research studies because of fear of harm to the fetus or fear of litigation. While men were studied for ways to avoid heart attacks and to deal with aging, women were simply ignored. This has made women medical orphans with respect to knowledge for dealing with illnesses during pregnancy, problems associated with the menstrual cycle, or for problems where their physiology differs markedly from men. Fortunately, in the 1990s this pattern has been reversed, and there is now a positive obligation by the Food and Drug Administration and federally funded medical research to involve women in their reproductive years and when pregnant in research on problems that are relevant to women's medical and health needs. From an ethical perspective, justice is now being done.

Ethics of the Goals and Social Role of Medicine

Of the innumerable ways that society influences and uses medicine, several are worth consideration in a chapter on the ethics of primary care of women. Among these are access to health care, restriction of services provided by HMOs, rationing, and care at the end of life including physician-assisted suicide and euthanasia. Of special interest in the primary care of women are ethical issues concerned with the reproductive functions, including parenting, contraception, abortion, and rape.

Access to Health Care, Health Care Insurance, HMOs and Rationing

In the United States, there is no universal health care insurance, and this distinguishes the U.S.

from Canada and most other industrialized nations. In seeking to provide wider access to health care, the objective has been to drive down and limit the rise of health care costs to that of general inflation. The creation of Health Maintenance Organizations (HMOs) was part of that strategy to regulate costs and conserve resources, and to stress disease prevention rather than simply respond to disease after it occurs with the more costly (in human and economic terms) curative services. HMOs have done only some of this, while creating a public backlash and political storm about their practices. A call has been made for a national Bill of Patients' Rights to protect against HMO excesses. Some of the proposed provisions are prevention of gag clauses in physicians' contracts (gag clauses keep physicians from advising patients about all treatment options including those the HMO might not allow); allowing for independent appeal for services denied by the HMO; requiring hospital stays of at least 48 h postdelivery should the patient request it; and coverage of any emergency room service if any prudent person would deem the need for care at that site urgent. At the time this chapter was written, at least 46 states and the District of Columbia had enacted laws to provide such safeguards.

There is an expectation by society that the primary care physician under health care reform and managed care is the agent of conserving resources and limiting inappropriate use of medical services. There is a belief by many that this is possible without denying needed care or jeopardizing the quality of care. Many believe that there is even an ethical mandate to husband resources in order to provide adequate care for all. Nonetheless, there will be an ethical tension between the individual patient's needs and wants and the limits society chooses to place on physicians. Where this has been tried, contraception, abortion, and pregnancy services have usually been included as being cost-effective, while many forms of infertility services have been denied. It has even been claimed that infertility is not an illness, but nothing could be further from the

truth. It is important that the physician not underestimate the incapacity, hurt, and need that infertility creates in patients, and that the physician advocates for these patients, where justified, to obtain help for those who have no children at all.

There are of course many ethical questions about the process of rationing itself, and whether those who can afford it should be allowed to purchase health services not available to others. The underlying assumption on the need for rationing is that in any society there are finite resources and that people will differ in how they might value and distribute them. Under National Health Insurance in England, there is rationing by disease type and age. The state of Oregon has tried a form of rationing under a special waiver from Medicaid to try to expand the population it can afford to serve. It is expected, however, that a fair health care system will provide all citizens with a decent level of essential health services and that in a free society, it should be possible and ethical to purchase additional health services as long as the basic needs of all are met.

Terminal Illness, Physician-Assisted Suicide, and Euthanasia

There may have been a time when one of the goals of medicine was to preserve life at all costs, but that is no longer tenable. The goal society seems to have for medicine today is to provide relief from pain and suffering and not to prolong life by delaying dying. The advent of the respirator and other life-support technologies has allowed preservation of vegetative life or the postponement of death, neither of which is highly prized by most patients. The change in public attitude evolved over time as various cases proceeded through the courts. In the case of Karen Ann Quinlan, the courts allowed the withdrawal of a respirator from a young woman who had been in a prolonged coma. Ironically, she continued to live for another 10 years. In the case of Brophy, it was a question of withdrawing food and fluid from a man in the persistent vegetative state. Finally, in the case of Cruzan, the United

States Supreme Court ruled that an individual had the right to have his or her preferences with respect to life support honored. Each of these cases were fought against by those who felt that even vegetative existence was sacred and should always be protected and maintained. Society, however, seems to accept the position that it is ethically permissible to give patients or their proxies a choice in the matter.

The advanced directive and living will are devices that allow patients to indicate their preferences on how to be treated if faced with terminal illness. Patient preferences are generally accepted by the courts, and may be required by some courts to withdraw therapies. It is the responsibility of the physician, and especially the primary care physician, to determine their patient's preferences and to honor them when the patient can no longer speak for herself. If physicians have a moral basis for disagreement, they should discuss this beforehand with their patients. When patients are referred to intensive care or coronary units, they very often lose all connections to their primary care doctor, and their preferences may be ignored unless forceful representation is made on their behalf. The same is true for cardiopulmonary resuscitation, which was designed to treat sudden, *unexpected* cardiac arrest. It was not designed, nor is it appropriate, to be applied to everyone in the hospital whose heart stops beating.

The Netherlands has been tolerating euthanasia by physicians for some time, and referendums in several of our states narrowly lost on legalizing euthanasia. From the ethical perspective, one is pitting the need for relief of suffering by the individual patient against the abhorrence of many to directly killing someone and the fear that the process is easily abused. It is further argued that one can generally provide relief of pain and suffering by adequate care and medication, and that good hospice services obviate the need for euthanasia. It is my judgement that our society and the medical profession will need a long time to discuss the need for and, the objectives and risks of euthanasia before considering its legalization. The same is true for assisted sui-

cide, which accomplishes the same goal, but makes the patient the active participant. This issue is particularly important to primary care physicians who care for women. Women are susceptible to depression that might not be readily recognized and that might masquerade as a justifiable despondency over living. Certainly, in these situations the aim is to effectively treat the patient for depression.

In cases where continued living is unbearably painful and can be relieved in no other way, carefully controlled and documented euthanasia might be morally acceptable, but the case for legalizing it should not be made prior to more study and societal review. Voters in the state of Oregon, in 1994 and again in 1997, supported a bill to allow physician-assisted suicide, and in 1998 the Health Services Commission of Oregon voted to pay for this under the (rationing) list of treatments covered by Medicaid. In the states of Washington and New York, laws were enacted that prohibited physician-assisted suicide, and these were challenged finally by appeal to the U.S. Supreme Court, which unanimously found that there is no constitutional right to assisted suicide. In the United States, the matter seems to be left to the state legislatures to decide. Oregon is the only state that allows physician-assisted suicide, while New York and Washington specifically prohibit it. In all of the court decisions, the distinction between withdrawing essential life support treatment (passive euthanasia) and active euthanasia has been maintained, although some philosophers have argued that there is no essential difference between the two actions, because both acts result in death of the patient.

Reproductive Function

For women over most of time, biology has been destiny and the social pressures have been for them to do what nature supposedly intended—to reproduce and mother. Anything that medicine could do to further this was generally acceptable, and it was often considered wrong for medicine to frustrate these goals. Infertility services and midwifery or obstetrics were accepted; contra-

ception and abortion generally discouraged. As civilization advanced, there developed a religious divide casting the issue in absolute terms. Starting with St. Augustine, for Catholics predominantly but not exclusively, the reproductive function was sanctified in marriage and natural coitus, and the fetus from conception had come to have an inviolable right to life. This limits practicing Catholics to abstinence from sex and the rhythm method for contraception, and prohibits abortion and the new assisted reproductive technologies such as in vitro fertilization. Others take a more naturalistic view of the reproductive process and have embraced the freedom from biological tyranny that contraception and abortion, as well as assisted reproduction for the infertile, have provided. Since abortion was legalized in the United States in 1973 by the Supreme Court's *Roe* v. *Wade* decision, the ethical debate has been divisive and strident. Most in our society accept contraception and some forms of assisted reproduction without much dissent. From an ethical perspective, it is my judgement that both sides to the abortion debate can adequately defend their positions depending on their religious beliefs in what God intended or requires. It is a true but rare instance of relativism in which both sides are correct for themselves but they live in separate worlds. There may be excessive rhetoric on both sides, but it is not useful or correct to vilify either position.

The ethical responsibility of physicians is to be clear in their own minds as to how they view these issues, and to be straightforward and fair to their patients when they seek advice or services in this area. It is a physician's duty to explain to the patient the extent to which the physician's own views on the matter influence the service or advice being provided. This is equally true with respect to questions about sexual orientation and lifestyle. No one expects physicians to perform abortions or give advice about sexual matters if they are morally opposed to them or are ignorant of such matters. Most would expect physicians to be consistent and make their positions clear to the patient, and to refer as necessary.

With assisted reproduction there are many so-

cial questions about who should parent, but in reality these cannot be much different than what pertains without medical assistance, except that by definition the assisted pregnancy is intended and usually wanted. Without going into all of the details of the issues raised by single-parenting and same-sex rearing parents, gamete donation, and surrogacy, I have a simple test for the ethical acceptability of infertility services and reproductive assistance. If the child is wanted and can be adequately cared for and no one (including any party to the process and the expected child) is exploited in the process, there should be a general presumption of moral acceptability. It is sad, but true, that most naturally occurring pregnancies cannot meet this simple moral test.

Abuse and Rape

Society has a sorry record in dealing with women's problems from rape and abuse. Male-dominated medicine may have been part of the problem. In the past, it was often assumed that women invited rape by their dress or behavior, which, in turn, justified the rape when it occurred. Often, complaining about a rape invited becoming even more of a victim in terms of loss of privacy and questioning of the victim's character and past sexual history by the police and courts. The idea that rape can occur in marriage is only now accepted and "date" rape is an all too frequent occurrence. Rape seems to be part of an overall abuse problem, but physical abuse and murder of women by their husbands or boy friends has become something of an epidemic in the United States. Just as society depends on pediatricians to alert authorities to child abuse, the gynecologist and primary care physician must fill that role for women. Physicians must be sensitive to the occurrence of abuse, and recognize the dependency that the woman often has on the abuser. Seeing the physician may be an important mechanism in seeking help if the physician is prepared to deal with these issues.

Ethics of the Science of Medicine

Patients have a right to expect their physicians to be competent and up-to-date with the latest preventive, diagnostic, and treatment modalities, and physicians have an obligation to meet those standards of competency. While much in medicine remains empirical, a good deal is now solidly grounded in carefully controlled, randomized clinical trials, meta-analyses, and outcomes research. The challenge to the physician is to remain current with respect to medical knowledge and to integrate that knowledge into everyday practice. For example, the value of periodic health examinations has been reviewed by a Canadian Task Force and a United States Preventive Service task force has looked at the effectiveness of 169 interventions and diagnostic tests. There have been meta-analyses of studies of what constitutes effective care in pregnancy, childbirth, and newborn care. It is clear that the primary care physician should be most knowledgeable about the need for periodic examinations, tests, counseling, and immunizations. While many recognize this as an essential component of practicing "good" medicine or being a "good" doctor, it should also be recognized as being an essential part of what medical ethics is all about.

References and Selected Readings

1. Evidence-Based Medicine Working Group: Evidence-based medicine. *JAMA* 268:2420, 1992.
2. Gostin LO: Deciding life and death in the courtroom. *JAMA* 278:1523, 1997.
3. Jonsen AR: *The Birth of Bioethics*. New York: Oxford University Press, 1998.
4. Kuttner R: Must good HMOs go bad: The commercialization of prepaid group health care. *N Engl J Med* 338:1558, 1998.
5. Kuttner R: Must good HMOs go bad: The search for checks and balances. *N Engl J Med* 338:1635, 1998.
6. Macklin R: Women's health: An ethical perspective. *J Law Med Ethics* 21:23, 1993.
7. Wear S: *Informed Consent*, Dordrecht, Germany: Kluwer Academic Publishers, 1993.

Preventive Ethics

Frank A. Chervenak
Laurence B. McCullough

INFORMED CONSENT AS AN
    ONGOING DIALOGUE
NEGOTIATION
RESPECTFUL PERSUASION
ADVANCE DIRECTIVES
ADVANTAGES OF PREVENTIVE ETHICS

Preventive health care is an essential dimension of primary health care for women. Preventive ethics is an essential, but sometimes overlooked, component of preventive health care. Preventive ethics describes a set of clinical skills aimed at developing an excellent physician-patient relationship by emphasizing communication and the prevention of ethical conflicts.[1,2] This chapter describes the basic strategies of preventive ethics that should be mastered by all obstetricians and gynecologists who provide primary health care for women. These strategies are: informed consent as an ongoing dialogue between the woman and her physician; negotiation; and respectful persuasion.

Informed Consent as an Ongoing Dialogue

There has been the tendency to equate informed consent with the patient's signature on operative or diagnostic permits. The signed consent form documents only the patient's agreement. Informed consent is a process, the goal of which is to develop and sustain a therapeutic alliance with the patient.[3] Utilizing the consent process in a preventive ethics approach to patient care contributes to this important goal.

The informed consent process—undertaken over time and in anticipation of potential ethically conflicting decisions—is the basic strategy of preventive ethics. The informed consent process should assist the patient in understanding the physician's evaluation of her condition and the alternatives for managing her condition, to evaluate those alternatives on the basis of her values, to express her value-based preferences, and to have the benefit of the physician's recommendations.[4,5] These goals can be achieved in the following steps:

1. The physician initiates the process by eliciting from the patient what she believes about her condition, its diagnosis, alternatives available to manage it, and her prognosis under each alternative.
2. The physician corrects factual errors and incompleteness in the patient's fund of knowledge. This does not require that the patient receive a complete medical education.
3. The physician provides and explains his or her clinical judgment about the patient's condition and all available management strategies (including watchful waiting).
4. The physician works with the patient, as needed or requested, to help her develop as complete as possible a picture of her condition and the alternatives available (including watchful waiting).
5. The physician works with the patient, as needed or requested, to help her identify her relevant values.
6. The physician, as needed or requested,

helps the patient, *in a nondirective fashion,* to evaluate her alternatives in terms of those values.

7. The patient undertakes to understand her condition, the available management strategies (including watchful waiting) and their prognoses, and expresses her value-based preferences.
8. The physician makes a recommendation, based on the clinical judgment already explained in step 3.
9. A mutual decision is reached and it is implemented.[2,6]

The nine steps of informed consent suggested here are a powerful antidote to the disturbing tendency to reduce the consent process to a signed form. To be sure, these nine steps can sometimes be time-consuming. However, building and sustaining a meaningful physician-patient relationship, which is assisted by this nine-step informed consent process, is worth the effort. Moreover, time spent on these nine steps will save time—and stress—in addressing ethical conflicts that may occur when these nine steps are not followed.

Negotiation

Negotiation should be the physician's first response to disagreement with the patient. Negotiation as a clinical strategy builds directly on informed consent.[1,2] Indeed, in the absence of ongoing informed consent, this strategy is likely to be much more difficult to implement.

Negotiation involves an ongoing dialogue in which a zero-sum game is not being played. A zero-sum game means that every advantage gained by one party occurs at the expense of or disadvantage to the other party.

Negotiation focuses primarily on the expression of values and then on their implications for shared clinical decision making. This simple step permits agreement on common values and mutual respect for different values. Common grounds between the pregnant woman and physi-

cian can frequently be found, something that may never be discovered if the two parties focus only on the conflict between differing decisions and on who will win the conflict. On the basis of this common ground, an atmosphere of good will and mutual respect can be fostered, thereby creating a context that encourages negotiation as a strategy for conflict resolution. An example is a physician who recommends cesarean section for failure to progress in labor but who agrees to extend a trial of continued labor for a specified period on the basis of the shared commitment to a healthy outcome of the pregnancy for both pregnant woman and fetus.

Respectful Persuasion

This kind of situation may become more difficult if the woman continues to refuse cesarean delivery after the specified period has elapsed. At this point, or shortly thereafter, obstetricians typically become very uncomfortable about permitting labor to continue. In this situation, the probability for ethical conflict between the physician and the pregnant woman increases. Respectful persuasion is the appropriate response to such situations in preventive ethics.[1,2] Respectful persuasion involves the physician in the following steps:

1. Remind the woman about previous discussions about general issues that may be applied to the specific issue at hand. Ideally, these should have occurred as a part of the ongoing informed consent process and prior negotiation.
2. Explain one's reasoning for taking the position.
3. Explain how other physicians may disagree.
4. Explain how one meets these objectives.
5. Show how the patient's values, including values she should reasonably adopt, support the recommendation.
6. Urge the patient to reconsider.

Identifying these elements of persuasion lets us draw the ethically significant distinction between

respectful persuasion and disrespectful persuasion. If any one or more of steps 2 to 5 are not followed, the physician is engaging in disrespectful persuasion.

Advance Directives

An important area of preventive ethics in the primary health care of women, especially older women, women with chronic diseases, and women facing gynecologic surgery, is advance directives.[2] These supplement the consent process. These legal instruments include the living will and a durable power of attorney for health care. The living will typically refuses life-prolonging intervention when the patient is terminally ill (as defined in applicable statutes) and not able to participate in the consent process. The durable power of attorney names someone to act as the patient's surrogate decision-maker when the patient cannot participate in the consent process. Both instruments guide clinical decision making, and having them can prevent ethical conflicts that arise in end-of-life care when the patient's prior wishes are unknown.

Physicians should take the lead in informing patients about advance directives and assure patients that they provide the means of articulating the patient's preferences. This information can then be used later, if it is needed.

Advantages of Preventive Ethics

There are a number of important advantages to the preventive ethics approach to primary health care for women.

First, preventive ethics focuses on underlying values of both physician and patient, rather than specific decisions. There is a greater likelihood of discovering areas of commonality and negotiating disagreements if values are the starting point of the informed consent process rather than specific decisions.

Second, this approach reduces the emotional stress and ethical risks of decision making in emergent situations wherein the woman is at risk for experiencing, all at once, the unexpected burdens of complicated clinical decisions. Complex matters require time and reflection if they are to be managed successfully and are therefore at high risk for being badly managed in a rush.

Third, preventive ethics focuses the patient-physician relationship on underlying matters of deep significance to both the physician and the patient. It furthers the aim of humanizing the primary health care of women by avoiding the steering of women's choices under a false banner of respect for autonomy. This can occur, for example, when the physician offers cesarean delivery as a valid alternative when it is not indicated. Respect for autonomy does not create a positive obligation on the physician's part to perform risky medical and surgical procedures when they are not indicated.

Fourth, like all primary care strategies it is hoped that preventive ethics in the primary care of women will reduce the incidence of ethical conflicts and of unresolved ethical conflicts.

Finally, a preventive ethics approach will enhance the opportunity for the early detection of irreconcilable value-based differences between a particular woman and a particular physician. In these cases, the physician will have ample time and opportunity to help the woman find a physician whose values are more compatible with her own and arrange for the transfer of her care with a minimum of bad feelings and a maximum of mutual respect, if she decides to choose another physician.

References and Selected Readings

1. Chervenak FA, McCullough LB: Clinical guides to preventing ethical conflicts between pregnant women and their physicians. *Am J Obstet Gynecol* 162:303–307, 1990.
2. McCullough LB, Chervenak FA: *Ethics in Obstetrics and Gynecology.* New York: Oxford University Press, 1994.
3. Wear S: *Informed Consent: Patient Autonomy and Physician Beneficence Within Clinical Medicine.* Dordrecht: Kluwer Academic Publishing, 1992.

4. The American College of Obstetricians and Gynecologists: *Ethical Dimensions of Informed Consent.* Washington, DC: ACOG 1992. ACOG Committee Opinion 108.

5. Faden R, Beauchamp TL: *History and Theory of Informed Consent.* New York: Oxford University Press, 1986.

6. McCullough LB: An ethical model for improving the physician-patient relationship. *Inquiry* 25:454–465, 1988.

Risk Management for Primary Care Physicians

Albert L. Strunk

Most physicians are well aware of the impact malpractice litigation has had on medicine.[1] Efforts at tort reform have been piecemeal at the state level and have not substantially alleviated the waste and cost of the present system. Several proposals have been made at the federal level, but have not been passed. A meaningful proposal to address issues of professional liability should be part of a comprehensive program of health care reform. Larger issues of tort and product liability cost U.S. taxpayers billions of dollars annually, and have resulted, for example, in the unavailability of important pharmaceutical agents (e.g., vaccines), the curtailment of athletic programs (e.g., football, soccer), the closing of municipal facilities (e.g., swimming pools), and, in some instances, the bankruptcy of local government.

Despite pressures to decrease the cost of health care, health care providers must find ways to maintain and improve the quality of care that they provide while simultaneously improving their ability to defend successfully against the almost inevitable, although often nonmeritorious, lawsuit(s). Risk management is a tool to assist health care providers in their own defense, as well as to assist patients. Risk management has been defined as "a style of practice wherein the physician minimizes the risk of lawsuits by practicing in a manner that reduces the possibility of actual error, ensures the best chance of obtaining desired results in patient care, and presents the most defensible treatment history." While risk management evolved in response to the malpractice litigation crisis, it is important to remember that the fundamental objective of risk management is quality assurance. The best and most defensible medicine is medical practice of the highest quality. If a patient chooses to assert a claim of negligent practice against her physician, there is no mechanism to prevent the filing of a complaint. However, risk management tremendously improves the health care provider's chance of defending successfully against such claims.

Risk management as part of the quality assurance process examines conformity to or deviation from accepted standards in the diagnosis and treatment of disease, whether medical or surgi-

cal. Physicians' training teaches that accepted medical standards are objectively ascertainable, are demonstrable to professional colleagues, and are readily accepted by the lay public. Indeed, important aspects of risk management are directed specifically to defining and elevating standards for the actual medical care received by the patient. But today, a significant impetus for litigation is a discrepancy between the patient's perception of her care and the actual care rendered. An equally important objective of risk management, therefore, is to increase the likelihood that the patient will understand and perceive that her care has been good. In the best of all worlds, both the actual care received and the patient's perception thereof will be good. Health care, formerly the practice of medicine, is now a consumer industry. How the health care consumer, formerly the patient, perceives her treatment is important. Finally, emotions such as fear and anxiety may significantly color a patient's perception of her care and treatment, most often in a negative manner.

The Health Care Consumer

The patient is interested in several things in her encounter with her physician. First, she wants to have good professional rapport. She hopes her physician will be easy to talk with. She hopes and expects that her physician will be genuinely concerned about her health and welfare. When appropriate, she hopes her physician will be concerned about her family as well. The ability of the physician to engage the patient and project real concern for her will likely improve the actual quality of care rendered and will certainly enhance the patient's perception of her care and treatment.

Second, the patient wants to have ready access to medical care. Putting aside the issue of whether the patient is willing to pay out-of-pocket for ready access, even for nonemergent problems, the patient increasingly has the expectation that she should be seen immediately upon

calling or nearly so. In other words, the patient wants physicians to be available in sufficient numbers, in sufficient specialties, and in sufficient geographical distribution that she can and will be seen when she wants to be seen. (From the patient's perspective the issue is not whether she has a condition for which immediate medical care is required as determined by accepted medical standards.)

Third, the patient is interested in the cost of services. The advent of managed care has demonstrated to physicians that economic realities are more compelling than the notion of loyalty to a long-established physician-patient relationship.

Fourth, the patient is interested in good care and, as previously noted, this has both a subjective and objective component. Board certified obstetrician-gynecologists and other primary care physicians and paraprofessionals are generally well trained and well equipped to deal with the objective reality of the patient's medical condition; risk management enhances the sensitivity of the health care team to the patient's subjective perception of her health care experience as well.

The Physician-Patient Relationship

While it is essential to the physician-patient relationship that adequate time be available for each patient encounter, and while physician time with the patient has sometimes been held out as a measurement of the quality of physician-patient interaction, it must be recognized that demands for greater efficiency in the delivery of health care may necessitate some curtailment of the physician component of the patient encounter. In other words, the patient will continue to seek a concerned physician who is easy to talk with, but it does not follow that the patient will be unwilling to accept the increasing involvement of certified nurse practitioners, midwives, physician's assistants, graduate nurses, and other paramedical personnel. If the use of such personnel enhances her access to the office, increases the quality of the history taking and documentation

of the office encounter, facilitates her diagnosis, speeds her treatment, meets or exceeds accepted standards of practice, and incurs less cost, the patient will usually believe that she has received excellent care and good value, even though her actual time with the physician may be less. The important thing is to avoid unnecessary delays in seeing the patient, to schedule in such a way as to minimize the impact of unexpected events on the physician's ontime availability in the office, and to be focused mentally and emotionally on the patient and her problems during the time available for direct physician-patient interaction.

Risk Management—A Team Effort

For such a schema to function effectively, the physician, paramedical personnel, and office staff must function as an integrated team. All personnel must understand their respective roles and responsibilities if delivery of the highest quality care is to be achieved. To that end, duties and responsibilities must be delegated according to ability, and must be well understood by all team members. Not infrequently, a lawsuit will arise because of an insensitive and uncaring act or remark by a staff member. Conversely, a well-trained team can handle unexpected events with care and concern, can detect complications, and can prevent injury.

Communication

The patient's initial encounter with the physician's office usually is by telephone. Effective risk management requires a review of procedures for handling telephone and written inquiries, the welcoming and integrating of new patients, and the scheduling of all patients whether established or new. Unfortunately, the telephone presents a significant liability risk because of the danger of misunderstanding and miscommunication. Telephone conversations should be clearly documented, and written notes and letters should be included in the patient's record, all in chronologi-

cal order. Often telephone answering services maintain computerized logs of after-hours calls that can be used to ensure the completeness of records of patients who call during nonoffice hours. Effective procedures for dealing with emergency situations must be in place. Patients should know what to do if telephone communications are temporarily interrupted. Likewise, coverage arrangements with other physicians must be clearly communicated to all patients.

Common sense dictates, when the physician is called away unexpectedly, that patients be told the reason for the delay beyond the blank statement that "the doctor has been called out." Some sense of the urgency or gravity of the situation must be conveyed if the patient is to understand and accept the notion that another patient's circumstance has a higher claim on the doctor's availability. Remember, the patient sees her time as no less valuable than that of her care providers.

Finally, though it may seem a small point, the office area where patients are received should be referred to as the "reception room," not the "waiting room." The latter connotes unnecessary delay and poor scheduling practices—factors that increase patient frustration, anxiety, and fear. Always ask yourself: Were I the patient, would I be pleased with the manner in which I was received in this office?[2]

Medical Records

A good medical record reflects not only the history of the present illness, but the medical, surgical, family, and social history as well. Checklists and patient-history forms are useful adjuncts and expedite the history-taking process. They may be utilized by a staff member, but at some point the physician must review the material and ask additional questions. The medical record is vital in documenting and defending the physician's diagnosis and treatment. A problem-oriented medical record (POMR) minimizes the likelihood that certain conditions or pathologies are addressed but others of equal or greater signifi-

cance are overlooked. Moreover, POMRs help avoid harmful drug interactions when multisystem disease necessitates polypharmacy. Good records suggest good care; poor records suggest poor care (even when this is not true), and may necessitate the settlement of an otherwise defensible case.

Never alter the medical record. If an error is made, draw a single line through the entry, date and sign in the margin, and write the corrected entry after the last entry with an explanation of the error. An altered medical record may convert a potentially defensible case into one that is difficult to defend. It is possible to defend a case with a less-than-optimal record; it is extremely difficult to defend a case once the record has been altered.

As to billing and financial records, keep these separate from the main chart. When patients or physicians request records, send only copies. Always retain originals. Obtain written authorizations for release of confidential information and, if there is uncertainty as to whether the patient understands the nature of the confidential information to be released, contact the patient before doing so, notwithstanding the previous written release.

Informed Consent

While informed consent has traditionally been more associated with hospital-based diagnostic and surgical procedures, primary care physicians are performing an increasing array of procedures in the office. Informed consent is often said to be a process rather than a form. In other words, the legal standard envisions that a patient will be educated about the specifics of her condition, the option(s) for treating the condition, the risks and benefits of the various methods of treatment, and the reasons for her physician's recommendation of a specific medical or surgical approach. The law further requires that all this be done at a level that the patient can understand. Moreover, most jurisdictions have replaced the "reasonable physician standard" (what a reasonable physician would have told the patient) with the "materiality" or "patient viewpoint" standard (what a reasonable person in the patient's position would want or expect to know under similar circumstances).

While it is true that failure to comply with the technicalities of an appropriate informed consent is not a frequent basis for recovery of an award in emergency circumstances, this is not true for elective procedures. In emergencies, juries simply do not believe a patient's contention that she would not have consented to emergency, often life-saving treatment. On the other hand, a large number of surgical procedures are elective. Diagnostic procedures are usually elective. Elective procedures require that the patient receive and understand the information necessary to make a fully informed decision about her treatment.[3]

Unrealistic Expectations

Most patients have little understanding of the pathophysiology of the disease or condition that leads them to seek medical attention. Most healthy pregnant patients, for example, have a very limited concept of the risks of pregnancy. Physicians, as well as members of the health care team, have an important task in educating patients about the realities of medical care and medical terminology. While health care providers certainly should not exaggerate the risk of a particular disease or condition to the patient, neither should they minimize its seriousness or the risks and complications of treatments and surgical procedures. By concentrating on the benefits of a test or treatment and minimizing or omitting its risks, physicians may contribute to a patient's unrealistic belief about her condition or about the result of medical or surgical intervention. On the other hand, patients must understand that perfect outcomes cannot be guaranteed and that a poor outcome, despite good quality care, is an inescapable reality for some conditions. Making the patient aware of the risks

inherent in the presenting condition, as well as the risks of treatment or nontreatment, will minimize patient surprise and disappointment. Audiovisual aids, printed materials, and paramedical personnel may be employed to facilitate these educational goals, reducing the likelihood of litigation arising from failed expectations, surprise, and disappointment.

Failure to Diagnose Cancer

The American College of Obstetricians and Gynecologists conducted its sixth national survey of professional liability in 1996.[1] While 60 percent of claims involved obstetrics, 40 percent were gynecology-related, and of these, two-thirds alleged failure to diagnose cancer. The focus here is on cancers of the breast, cervix, uterus, and ovary, as well as the nongynecologic lung and colon cancers.

Primary care physicians, including obstetrician-gynecologists, should be able to provide routine evaluation and counseling about cancer. Evaluation of a patient's risk for cancer is based on an assessment of high-risk habits, family history of cancer, and a review of symptoms pertinent to the organ system under scrutiny. As a cause of cancer death in women, lung cancer is the most common, followed by breast, colorectal, ovarian, and pancreatic cancers. The professional liability survey broke down the failure-to-diagnose cancer claims as follows: 67 percent breast, 14 percent cervix, and 8 percent ovary. An analysis of lung, colorectal, pancreatic, and endometrial cancer claims was not included in the survey.

Lung Cancer

Lung cancer killed approximately 66,000 women in 1997, reflecting a steady increase in the number of deaths. It is estimated that 79,800 women were diagnosed with lung cancer that year. It is the major cause of cancer death in women. There are no available techniques suitable for routine screening. Cessation of smoking is the only effective way to reduce mortality. Any persistent pulmonary complaint unresponsive to conservative therapy should lead to a chest x-ray within 30 to a maximum of 60 days. Occasionally the diagnosis of lung cancer is made on a sputum specimen, but most often it is made as a result of a chest x-ray. Lung cancers that compromise pulmonary function and produce blood-tinged sputum are usually advanced, with typical survivals of 6 to 18 months depending on cell type. Lung cancers associated with longer survivals tend to be the result of fortuitous discovery based on chest x-rays taken for other reasons, such as preadmission testing for surgery. Attention to the patient's personal and family history offers the only strategy for early diagnosis and risk management in the absence of pulmonary signs or symptoms. Risk factors include smoking; exposure to second-hand smoke or other pulmonary irritants (e.g., asbestos, fiberglass, chemicals, auto emissions); and advancing age.

Despite their lethal natures, lung cancer and ovarian cancer share the characteristic of low medicolegal risk based principally on the absence of available techniques suitable for routine screening and the advanced stage of the disease at the time of diagnosis.

Breast Cancer

The statistics concerning breast cancer are well known: 180,200 new cases were diagnosed in 1997; 43,900 women died of the disease. It is the most frequent cancer in women, and is second only to lung cancer as a leading cause of death from cancer in women. One in 50 women in the United States will develop breast cancer by the age of 50, 1 in 17 by age 65, and 1 in 8 over a lifetime.[4] Breast cancer represents 32 percent of all cancers in women in the United States each year.[5] Because of the greater opportunity for early detection, breast cancer warrants more lengthy and specific comment.

Risk factors These factors increase the risk of breast cancer:

1. Increasing age
2. Previous history of breast cancer
3. Nulliparity
4. Delayed childbearing
5. Early menarche
6. Late menopause
7. Family history of breast cancer
8. Biopsy-proven ductal or lobular hyperplasia
9. Higher socioeconomic status
10. Obesity

Breast and lymphatic examination Although there are many techniques of breast examination, a proper breast examination should include:

1. Visual inspection with the patient sitting or standing with hands on hips.
2. Palpation of the breast tissue with the patient in the upright and supine positions.
3. Evaluation of the nipple-areolar complex, including evidence of nipple discharge.

Specific mention should be made of:

1. Palpation of axillary and supraclavicular lymph nodes (enlargement, tenderness).
2. Symmetry and contour of breasts with description of any major disparity, evidence of inflammation, distortion of the skin surface, and presence of surgical scars.
3. Palpable masses.
4. Presence of nipple discharge, retraction, deviation, inflammation, or excoriation.

Screening mammography Screening mammography should be recommended according to an approved set of guidelines and the recommendation documented in the medical record. As always, treatment must be individualized and guidelines must be recognized as *merely* guidelines.

Terminology Most women have irregular breast tissue with diffuse nodality. The term "fibrocystic disease" is considered vague and inappropriate to describe nonhomogenous breast tissue. "Terms such as firm, lumpy, nodular, tender, and thickened should be used to describe the texture of the breast, and if they are the only findings in the absence of a dominant mass, it should be so stated. Terms that imply a dominant mass such as nodule, lump, or cyst should be reserved for masses that are truly dominant and the mass(es) should be measured."[5]

The palpable mass Persistent masses must be diagnosed. A palpable mass in a woman of reproductive age is considered persistent if it remains palpable and unchanged after the next menstrual period. If the patient is 35 or over (some would say 30 or over) and has not already had a mammogram, mammography should be performed. In addition, in women of all ages, ultrasound evaluation may be useful if the clinical assessment of a cystic lesion is in doubt. If a palpable mass is present, a diagnosis of that mass must be made even in the presence of a normal mammogram. Ten to 15 percent of women with breast cancer may have a normal mammogram.

The PIAA Breast Cancer Study[6] The June 1995 Breast Cancer Study is one of a series of special studies authorized by the Physicians Insurers Association of America. The studies are based on information from the PIAA Data Sharing Project that began in 1985. As of June 30, 1996, the PIAA data were based on 149,901 claims and suits, 40,228 of which were closed with indemnity payments totaling $5.94 billion. The average indemnity payment for all paid claims in all specialties reported was $147,862. In obstetrics and gynecology, breast cancer was the second most expensive condition in terms of indemnity dollars, second only to claims from neurologically impaired newborns.

The following points are summarized from the June 1995 PIAA Breast Cancer Study:

1. In 60 percent of cases, the patient herself discovered the lesion.
2. The most common presenting symptom was a painless mass (46.5 percent).
3. A mass was discovered on the initial exam in 57.2 percent of cases.
4. For those patients who had mammograms, 80 percent were negative or equivocal, including false-negatives and misread mammograms.
5. The most prevalent reason (35 percent of

all cases) for delay in diagnosis was the physician's failure to be impressed by the physical findings.

6. The average delay between the time the cancer could or should have been diagnosed and the actual diagnosis was 14 months.
7. In more than 63 percent of cases, there was no evidence of patient involvement in delaying diagnosis.

The PIAA Study is informative because it tells us in specific terms how we, as professionals, can improve the care for our patients in the important area of breast cancer surveillance.

Colorectal Cancer

In 1997, colorectal cancer claimed the lives of 27,900 women. Risk factors for colorectal cancer include the following:

1. Advancing age
2. History of unexpected rectal bleeding or change in bowel habits
3. History of anal intercourse, especially with multiple partners
4. Personal history of breast, ovarian, or endometrial cancer
5. Family history of colorectal cancer

Screening guidelines sometimes defer digital rectal exam until the age of 50. Despite the fact that women are more likely to have proximal disease and men to have distal or rectal disease, in most situations a properly performed pelvic examination should include digital rectal and rectovaginal evaluation. This is important not only for the proper assessment of the anus and rectum, but also for the complete evaluation of the ovaries, the parametrium, the rectovaginal septum, the cul-de-sac, and the posterior surface of the uterine corpus. Screening and surveillance techniques include digital rectal examinations, fecal occult blood testing, flexible sigmoidoscopy, double-contrast barium enema, colonoscopy, and genetic testing. It is noteworthy that 70 to 80 percent of cases of colorectal cancer occur in average-risk individuals.

Ovarian Cancer

Ovarian cancer is the leading cause of death from gynecologic malignancy. One in 70 women will develop ovarian cancer during her lifetime. Approximately 26,800 cases of ovarian cancer are diagnosed each year, and 14,200 women died of the disease in 1997. Eight percent of alleged failures to diagnose cancer involve ovarian cancer claims. Television, newspapers, and magazines sometimes seem to suggest to American women that ovarian cancer is a detectable disease and that current mortality rates may be attributable, inferentially, to negligence on the part of the physicians in not diagnosing the disease at an early stage. Nonetheless, the 1994 NIH Consensus Statement on Ovarian Cancer concluded that "there is no evidence available yet that the current screening modalities of CA-125 and transvaginal ultrasonography can be effectively used for widespread screening to reduce mortality from ovarian cancer nor that their use will result in decreased rather than increased morbidity and mortality."[7]

Despite the fact that ovarian cancer is the leading cause of death from pelvic gynecologic malignancy, the number of claims arising out of alleged failure to diagnose ovarian cancer is proportionally lower. Because there are fewer claims, we currently lack the type of detailed claims analysis that is available with respect to breast cancer. Accordingly, risk management strategies depend primarily on quality assurance considerations and some general principles relevant to most failure-to-diagnose claims.

The survival rate of women with early stage ovarian cancer is significantly higher than that of women with advanced stage disease, yet most women diagnosed already have advanced disease. While symptoms such as gastrointestinal discomfort, pelvic pressure, or pain are sometimes present, most women have mild, nonspecific symptoms or no symptoms at all. When

symptoms are present, the disease is usually already advanced. It has been suggested to women by nonphysicians that CA-125 markers and color Doppler imaging will enable physicians to detect early disease, but that view is currently unsupported by scientific evidence.

What elements of patient care would be scrutinized in a case alleging failure to diagnose ovarian cancer? An experienced lawyer will begin by looking where the physician properly begins, the personal and family history of the patient. Risk factors for ovarian cancer include

1. Advancing age
2. Family history of ovarian cancer
3. Personal history of endometrial, colon, or breast cancer
4. Nulliparity
5. North American or Northern European descent

Screening, although not cost-effective for the general population, may be considered for women with substantially increased risk.

Some gynecologic oncologists have suggested the regular screening of

1. Symptomatic women (including mild, nonspecific symptoms).
2. Women with one or more affected first-degree relatives.
3. Women who have taken infertility drugs.

In summary, these are some suggestions from a quality assurance and risk management perspective. Take a good personal and family history. Conduct a proper bimanual rectovaginal and abdominal examination. Transvaginal ultrasound/color Doppler imaging and CA-125 may be appropriate studies when the patient is in a high-risk group *or* the physical examination is abnormal.

Endometrial Cancer

In 1997, there were 34,900 new cases of endometrial cancer diagnosed and approximately 6000 endometrial cancer-related deaths. It is the most common pelvic gynecologic malignancy in women aged 45 and older. While an increase in the prevalence of endometrial cancer in the 1980s has been attributed to the longer life span of postmenopausal women, the use of unopposed estrogen therapy, and more stringent criteria for diagnosing early endometrial cancer, the prevalence has apparently stabilized in the 1990s. The most often-cited reason is the increased use of progestational agents with estrogen replacement therapy.

It has not been found cost-effective to screen asymptomatic women for endometrial cancer and its precursors. Accordingly, screening guidelines do not suggest or require endometrial sampling before or during estrogen-progestin therapy. The Pap test is not sufficiently sensitive to be useful as a screening technique for endometrial cancer.

The vagaries of a patient's history of bleeding may make it difficult for the physician to categorize it as normal or abnormal. Under the best of circumstances, obtaining an accurate menstrual history is difficult in the absence of a menstrual calendar. If a menstrual calendar cannot reasonably be obtained, the patient's history should establish, at a minimum, the duration, intensity, and character of the menstrual flow as well as a patient's specific denial of any intermenstrual or postcoital bleeding.

In women taking hormone replacement therapy (HRT), it is not uncommon to experience some irregular spotting. This is most common in continuous HRT regimens where there is no specific interval of withdrawal bleeding. In such cases, periodic measurement of endometrial thickness using ultrasound may provide the medical reassurance necessary to satisfy both the physician and the patient of normalcy, and to achieve necessary documentation in the medical record. Ultrasound measurements may be an adequate alternative to endometrial biopsy when the entire endometrium is scanned. However, myoma and other disorders may make it impossible to fully evaluate the endometrium with ultrasound.

Finally, consider etiologies for bleeding

other than anovulation/oligo-ovulation and menorrhagia/hypermenorrhea, such as coagulation disorders, medications (including oral contraceptives), and structural abnormalities. When neoplasia has not been ruled out, operative hysteroscopy with fractional D&C is necessary.

Cervical Cancer

Carcinoma of the cervix accounts for 4800 deaths in the United States each year. In 1997, 14,500 new cases were discovered. Fourteen percent of claims alleging failure to diagnose cancer involve cervical cancer.

Apart from the matter of false-negative Pap smears, the principal areas of liability exposure involve the failure to act in an appropriate and timely manner on an abnormal Pap result, and the failure to recognize that no report has been received from the pathology laboratory. Finally, it should be noted that one-quarter of all cervical cancers occur in women over 60.

Care of the Pregnant Woman

Care of the pregnant woman is an area of potentially high medical risk and equally high medicolegal risk. Reference has been made to ACOG's 1996 professional liability survey.[1] Data obtained therein revealed that 60 percent of all claims for obstetrician-gynecologists related to obstetrics, and 30 percent of these obstetrics claims involved neurologically impaired infants. The average indemnity payment for general obstetric claims was $328,614, but it was about twice that amount for claims involving neurologic impairment.

It has often been said that the high-risk obstetrics patient is easy to identify, but that the low-risk patient defies definition or categorization. This reflects the undeniable reality that seemingly low-risk mothers-to-be do convert, often with little or no warning, into high-risk categories. However, there are some risk management recommendations that may improve medical care and diminish medicolegal risk.

Among the many steps that can be taken, we review three that if met, may improve the quality of obstetric care and diminish vulnerability in the courtroom. First, ensure that the gestation is accurately dated. A caveat follows if the gestational age cannot be known with a high degree of accuracy: apply the entire range of possible gestational ages to each decision point in a treatment algorithm and document, as best one can, the risk-benefit analysis that led to a particular decision. It is more important to acknowledge a lack of precise dating and act with due regard for that crucial uncertainty than to "force" a precise date based on unreliable or conflicting data. Second, use a standardized antepartum record. Such a record may make it easier to identify and appropriately track high-risk patients. This type of record documents fetal age, validates assessment of fetal size, employs a method of validating risk analysis, and includes documentation of compliance/adherence issues and documentation of educational activities. It is estimated that 60 percent of malpractice cases are lost because of poor documentation. Third, choose an appropriate delivery date for high-risk patients and be prepared to respond promptly to the labor and delivery floor when needed.

Despite the fact that the rate of cerebral palsy (CP) has not changed in 25 years, and the evidence shows that only 8 to 10 percent of CP cases can be attributed to intrapartum hypoxia, infection, or obstetric mishaps, neurologically impaired infants account for 30 percent of obstetrics claims. The average indemnity payment in neurologically impaired infant cases is $609,117. In addition to the three previous recommendations, the following can be critical in defending CP cases: (1) carefully document the trial of labor; (2) monitor fetal heart rate and intrauterine pressure/contractions consistently; (3) obtain fetal scalp pH when indicated (but only if available personnel and equipment allow reliable results to be obtained from such testing); (4) obtain cord blood samples for blood gases and nucleated fetal red blood cells; and (5) in selected cases, consider evaluation of the placenta by a pathologist.

If a newborn is diagnosed with a neurologic

impairment, or if there is intrapartum injury of any type, do not withdraw from the patient and do not become defensive. Remain communicative and empathic at all times. Make certain that any expression of sorrow or sympathy is not understood as an apology for some alleged intrapartum act or omission. As the rabbi-author, Harold S. Kushner, noted in his book of similar title,[8] bad things *do* happen to good people. Physicians, accustomed to the retrospective inquiry of the clinical-pathologic conference (CPC) and the morbidity and mortality conference (MMC), must not fall victim to the logical fallacy that a bad outcome would have been avoided by using a different technique, method, or thought process. That a different approach might be suggested by hindsight, does not mean, ipso facto, that the initial approach was ill-conceived or negligent.

While the focus of this chapter is risk management rather than trial preparation, there must be some recognition of the special perils of the neurologically impaired or so-called "CP" baby cases at trial and in pretrial discovery. In that regard there are three points that, while important in all malpractice actions, are vital in defending neurologically impaired infant cases. First, take trial preparation very seriously and make time for your attorney. Do your homework. Second, while some attorneys caution their physician-clients not to acknowledge texts and other writings as "authoritative," a better practice is to learn a basic text and relevant ACOG publications before your deposition. Use an edition of the text that was *in effect when the birth occurred* to establish the relevant *standard of care.* Third, do not disqualify yourself on issues of causation. While neonatology and pediatric neurology are not your specialty, the defendant cannot afford to appear ignorant to the jury about these subjects. Study a leading, *current* text in pediatric neurology, especially regarding hypoxic-ischemic encephalopathy. While the standard of care is rooted at the time of the occurrence, the defendant should have up-to-date information on the causation issue. He or she must be able to negate hypoxic-ischemic enceph-

alopathy as a cause of the child's neurologic deficits.

Finally, in geographic areas where physician resources are scarce, it may be impossible for the obstetrician to be physically present in the hospital throughout all of active labor. If that is the case, however, antepartum identification of those patients who present special risks becomes even more important. Those patients may have to be sent to high-risk centers at the onset of labor in order to insure the continuous presence of physicians to provide urgent or emergency care.

It would be remiss not to mention briefly the issue of vaginal birth after a previous cesarean section (VBAC). VBAC exemplifies the conflict between good obstetrics and increased medicolegal risk. It has been suggested that VBAC has been almost exclusively responsible for decreasing the U.S. cesarean section rate to 22 percent in 1997 from 25 percent in 1989. It is also well-established that the risk of uterine rupture during a VBAC trial of labor is much lower than reported 20 years ago, although the exact percentage of trials that result in uterine rupture remains in dispute. Numbers ranging from 0.5 to 1 percent to 3 to 4 percent have been suggested. Whether a patient should undergo a trial of labor after a prior cesarean section is a decision that must be based on both clinical circumstances and an informed choice by the patient.

When approaching informed consent, it may be helpful to make use of available resources, (such as printed material) that may help you do a better job and save time. Those two goals are not mutually exclusive. Informed consent should be educational and patient-friendly, but it should also be honest and complete.

Use of Office Ultrasound in Pregnancy

The comments that follow relate to office-based ultrasound screenings undertaken by primary care physicians to confirm and date pregnancies, assess fetal growth, and screen for fetal develop-

mental anomalies. This discussion is not directed toward hospital-based scanning by radiologists or specialists in maternal-fetal medicine, nor is it directed toward independent, freestanding imaging facilities. The suggestions offered are intended to help the primary care physician who has an ultrasound machine in the office to use this equipment appropriately. It goes without saying that there should be a valid obstetric indication for scanning pregnant patients. The availability of office ultrasound carries with it special responsibility and increased risk of liability for improperly performed or read ultrasound scans.

The following risk management recommendations and observations are offered:

1. Do not perform office-based obstetric scanning without training.
2. Technicians, if employed, must be appropriately credentialed and supervised.
3. Basic scanning to establish gestational age by crown-rump length, biparietal diameter, femur length, and abdominal and head circumference can be competently performed by trained personnel.
4. Ultrasound guidance for amniocentesis can be competently performed by trained personnel; however, the amniocentesis should be performed by a physician.
5. Assessment of growth can probably be competently performed by trained personnel; however, assessment of growth in the last trimester may be hampered by poor resolution.
6. Fetal surveys for organ and organ-system anomalies present significant medico-legal risk; it is best not to perform such scans unless the physician and technician (both) have had specific training in targeted fetal ultrasound scanning. It is helpful to use a procedure-specific consent form that makes clear the specific objectives of the scanning procedure and the limitations thereof. Consent forms should state that ultrasound scanning cannot guarantee anatomic normalcy.
7. Credential your personnel, machine, and facility, if possible.

The scarcity of ultrasound diagnostic services in medically underserved areas does not lower the standard of care if a physician chooses to provide the service. The real issue is whether the quality of service allows the technique to achieve the diagnostic utility for which it is being offered.

Physician Impairment

According to some studies, between 10 and 30 percent of physicians may have some type of impairment. Chemical impairment is considered the most common. While alcohol abuse and self-prescription of scheduled substances predominate, the use of street drugs is undeniably present. Physical impairment refers to disabilities that develop with age or are due to injury. Frequently, physicians return to work too soon after injury or illness, thinking that they are capable of fulfilling their duties when, in reality, additional time for recuperation is needed. Psychiatric impairment can be acute or chronic. Suicide rates, while not as high as those of dentists, are significant. Fatigue is a factor that often exacerbates depressive symptoms and increases the risk for suicide. Sexual misconduct may be considered a type of physician impairment provided that the misconduct does not rise to the level of criminal offense. That is, education and remediation may be appropriate for some types of sexual impropriety or misconduct, whereas more egregious behavior may result in criminal liability and incarceration.

On this point, the ACOG *Code of Professional Ethics* applies as well to all members of the health care team[9]:

> II (6) The obstetrician-gynecologist should not practice medicine while impaired by alcohol, drugs, or physical or mental disability. The obstetrician-gynecologist who experiences substance abuse problems or who is physically or emotionally impaired should seek appropriate assistance to address these problems and limit his or her practice until the impairment no longer affects the quality of patient care.

As to the issue of sexual misconduct, the *Code of Professional Ethics* states:

I (4). Sexual misconduct on the part of the obstetrician-gynecologist is an abuse of professional power and a violation of patient trust. Sexual contact or a romantic relationship between a physician and a current patient is always unethical.

What is the obligation of a colleague who knows of an impaired member of the health care team who continues to practice? The *Code of Professional Ethics* places an obligation upon all physicians to "respond to evidence of questionable conduct or unethical behavior by other physicians through appropriate procedures established by the relevant organization" (Section II, Ethical Foundations). In exercising one's obligation to society as a whole, one must, of course, be mindful of the rights of the impaired person. Relevant guidelines include the following:

1. Do not engage in general publication of an impaired professional's or paraprofessional's behavior. Report such impairment to the responsible person in your hospital or county medical society.
2. Report only facts that you personally know to be true. Do not engage in accusations based on hearsay.
3. Keep in mind the perspective of the impaired individual. The objective here is acknowledgement of the problem by the impaired team member, followed by remediation. Retribution is not a goal.
4. If there is a perceived need for anonymity, or if one feels that the organization to which one would normally report cannot maintain confidentiality, it may be advisable to approach the matter through the hospital's attorney or through personal counsel. If procedures are unclear, consult with colleagues about proper procedures without disclosing the name of the involved person or details of improprieties.

The *Code of Professional Ethics* provides:

IV (4). The obstetrician-gynecologist should strive to address through the appropriate procedures the status of those physicians who demonstrate questionable competence, impairment or unethical or illegal behavior. In addition, the obstetrician-gynecologist should cooperate with appropriate authorities to prevent the continuation of such behavior.

Impact of Managed Care

Managed care has increased medicolegal risk for all members of the health care team. It has done so in many ways, five of which are considered here. First, by the terms of the provider's contract, managed care companies have fastened all of the liability for medical decision-making on the physician and the health care team. This remains so despite criteria for diagnosis and treatment that many observers believe make the HMOs' activities tantamount to practicing medicine. Second, reductions in reimbursements for services rendered and the need for more personnel to process managed care paperwork has generated significant pressure on the entire health care team to see greater numbers of patients in less time. This both decreases patient satisfaction with the health care experience and may increase the risk of actual medical error. Third, where tests or treatments are not deemed medically necessary by the HMO, the physician has the responsibility for being the patient's advocate in appealing such denials of care. Of course, the physician is not compensated for the sometimes very large amount of time that may be required to appeal a determination of lack of medical necessity. Fourth, patients are often ignorant of the provisions, limitations, and procedures of their plans. When a copayment is required or an examination cannot be performed because the patient has not obtained an appropriate referral, the patient's frustration and anger may be directed against the physician. This antagonism further derogates the quality of the patient's encounter and increases the opportunity for misunderstanding, unrealistic expectations, and medical error. All of this increases medicolegal risk. On this point, nothing more can be said than to encourage implementation of those policies and procedures set forth in the earlier sections of this chapter. Fifth, primary care physicians function

as gatekeepers in most managed care plans and referral responsibilities increase risk.

Unfortunately, in the face of managed care constraints, much of the risk management formulation tends to be defensive in nature. While the objective of improving health care quality and reducing actual medical error remains paramount, forcing the managed care enterprise to accept its share of liability for bad outcomes and negligent care is also a pressing objective. Concerning the nature of the provider contract, one recommendation is to try to negotiate through an IPA or other collective bargaining unit. As to the need to see more patients per unit time, paraprofessionals and skilled medical and office staff personnel offer the only means by which physicians can reduce actual time spent with the patient while maintaining quality of care and avoiding medical error. To build such a team can be a difficult task for any provider, and a Herculean task for solo practitioners.

An important point regarding managed care is that of patient advocacy. The physician should appeal a managed care determination that a particular test, procedure, or treatment is medically unnecessary if the physician disagrees. While immediate medical needs require telephone communication, correspondence provides better documentation and better legal defense against claims alleging the provider's failure to appeal for medically necessary care. This critical requirement bears repetition: the physician and the health care team must act as an advocate for the patient in appealing a managed care company's denial of services or treatment based on lack of medical necessity. The downside of this requirement is obvious: too many appeals or too vehement an appeal may result in a provider's removal from a managed care company's panel. While such removal would give rise to a cause of action by a physician against the managed care entity, a costly legal remedy offers little comfort. Unfortunately, the cost to the provider in time and staff expense of appealing a denial of treatment is not reimbursed. Lack of reimbursement, however, does not alleviate or mitigate the re-

quirement for appeal of a denial of treatment or for rendering the required care.

As gatekeepers, the primary care team may also have liability arising out of its referral responsibilities. The first issue is that of timely referral. In a case requiring specialized care, was the referral made in a timely manner or at all? Another area of potential liability arises concerning the qualification of the specialist. While in most cases it is acceptable to refer to a specialist in the panel, the mere fact of the specialist's membership does not obviate liability for the gatekeeper if the gatekeeper has knowledge that, despite paper qualifications, the specialist is not equipped by reason of training, experience, or demonstrated skill to deal appropriately with the problem for which referral has been made. Finally, the gatekeeper needs to obtain reports, laboratory information, and results of diagnostic studies from the specialist. Only in the event that the primary care person has effected a complete and unambiguous transfer of care to the specialist will potential liability be cut off.

An evolution of issues regarding liability in the managed care setting has resulted in the increasing extent to which managed care companies are found to be engaging, de facto, in the practice of medicine. Originally protected from liability by ERISA (Employee Retirement Income Security Act of 1974), an increasing number of legal cases have eroded the ERISA preemption.[10-13] Statutory attack on HMOs' attempts to be shielded by ERISA preemption began in 1997 with Texas' passage of a law allowing injured patients to sue managed care organizations for malpractice. The Texas Medical Association argued that HMOs routinely make medical decisions and that ERISA was not intended to protect health plans from negligence and malpractice claims. Missouri has also passed legislation allowing HMOs to be sued for malpractice. At the federal level, a bill was introduced in Congress to allow direct action against managed care organizations for negligence and medical malpractice. It may be just a matter of time before the ERISA preemption fails completely as

a defense for HMOs to avoid negligence-based liability. One must, however, be cognizant of the situation in one's own state.

Systems Approaches to Diminishing Risk

The National Patient Safety Foundation's purpose is to study the causes of medical error and then devise solutions to systems problems that threaten patient safety. Such an approach to safety is not new to the aviation industry, which has long been concerned with "cockpit error." As a consequence, the airline industry is a leader in the use of simulators and other methods that are intended to eliminate errors or reduce the impact of errors. The Anesthesia Patient Safety Foundation, established in 1984, has reduced patient mortality due to anesthesia from 1 in 10,000 to 20,000 to 1 in 200,000 over the past decade. Anesthesiologists interact with computerized dummies that bleed, breathe, and talk. When the dummy goes into cardiac arrest during surgery, participants are filmed while they react to the crisis. Subsequently, performance evaluations and retraining are carried out as students watch the videotape with clinical instructors.

But not all systems solutions are high-tech. Reference was made earlier to standardized antepartum records that, by their design, minimize the possibility that a significant maternal or fetal risk factor or problem will be overlooked. Patient consent forms specific to a procedure, but nevertheless standardized, help patients understand proposed tests/procedures and help physicians ensure that essential elements of an informed, risk-benefit discussion have not been omitted. Revisions of office schedules to more realistically reflect the time needed for patient-physician dialogue and/or the performing of required tests/procedures will improve patient care and satisfaction while lessening physician stress.

Many commentators and researchers have pointed out that the "blame-game" perpetuates

unreal expectations of infallibility. Error-free practice is not a realistic goal becasue the doctor rarely, if ever, controls all aspects of patient care. To the contrary, sources of error are often beyond the individual practitioner's control. When blame is assigned, meaningful investigation and comprehensive analysis of a clinical scenario stops, positions become defensive, and useful clinical information or perspective may disappear. Acknowledgement of error should ideally be a catalyst for independent investigation and analysis and should signify opportunity rather than crisis.

Conclusion

This chapter discussed in a broad fashion some of the principal elements in an effective program of risk management. However, the implementation of such a program requires detailed examination of the specifics of a medical practice. In addition to obtaining a thorough history and conducting a proper physical examination, one must critically evaluate such things as telephone communications, appointments and scheduling, patient relations, billing and collections, equipment and drugs, personnel management, and medical records—to name just a few.

As emphasis on primary care increases, and as managed care brings change to established physician-patient relationships, health care providers must remain alert to issues of professional liability. The concept that higher quality health care can be rendered to more citizens with increased efficiency at less cost remains untested in the marketplace of health care consumerism. No corresponding change is seen or anticipated in a tort system sorely in need of reform.

Risk management, as a means of improving patient care and responding as well to the challenges of our negligence-based system of determining professional liability, commends itself on several grounds. First, it is uniquely within our control and the obstacles to its

implementation can be significantly reduced through education of physicians. Second, professional liability insurance companies, whether physician-owned or privately owned, have the ability and motivation to collect data that enable us to identify areas of high medicolegal risk. Third, risk management is closely related to our attempts to monitor quality assurance and improve standards of care. As such, we have a starting point from which risk management strategies can be implemented. Fourth, a more sophisticated understanding of medicolegal risk and economic costs will be essential as managed care becomes more systematized and "treatment pathways" become the norm in health care. Fifth, emphasis on system failure rather than human error is more effective in improving patient care and diminishing medicolegal risk inasmuch as the very factors that cause health providers to err are often structural or organizational in character.

While health care personnel today may be providing care under increasingly challenging conditions, the professional ethos of healing remains strong. By introducing systems approaches to the delivery of primary care services, stress can be lessened, patient care and patient satisfaction improved, and documentation and data analysis made more accurate and timely. While human negligence can never be completely eliminated from any field of endeavor, the causes of medical error can be studied and solutions to those problems that threaten patient safety can be devised. Such an approach, it is believed, will provide the very best form of risk management.

References and Selected Readings

1. The American College of Obstetricians and Gynecologists: *Survey of Professional Liability.* Washington, DC: ACOG, 1997.
2. American Medical Association, Specialty Society: *Risk Management Principles and Commentaries for the Medical Office,* 2nd ed. Washington, DC: AMA/Specialty Society, 1995.
3. American College of Obstetricians and Gynecologists: *Litigation Assistant: A Guide for the Defendant Physician,* 2nd ed. Washington, DC: ACOG, 1998.
4. Fener EJ, Wun LM, Bering CC, et al: *J Natl Cancer Inst* 85:892, 1993.
5. The American College of Obstetricians and Gynecologists: *Guidelines for Women's Health Care.* Washington, DC: ACOG, 1996.
6. Physician Insurers Association of America: *Breast Cancer Study.* Rockville, MD: PIAA, 1995.
7. National Institutes of Health Consensus Statement: *Ovarian Cancer: Screening, Treatment, and Follow-up.* NIH Consensus Statement 12(3):1–30, 1994.
8. Kushner HS: *When Bad Things Happen to Good People,* 2nd ed. New York: Schocken Books, 1989.
9. The American College of Obstetricians and Gynecologists: *Code of Professional Ethics.* Washington, DC: ACOG, 1996.
10. *Dukes v United States Health Care Sys. Inc.,* 848 F. Supp. 39 (E.D. Pa. 1994), 57 F.3d 350 (3rd Cir. 1995).
11. *New York Conference of Blue Cross and Blue Shield Plans v Travelers Insurance Co.,* 115 S. Ct. 1671 (1995).
12. *De Buono v NYSA-ILA,* 117 S. Ct. 1747 (1997).
13. *Pacificare of Oklahoma, Inc. v Burrage,* 59 F.3d 151 (10th Cir. 1995).

Alternative Medicine

Ronald A. Chez

WHAT IS CAM?
THE MEDICAL DOCTOR'S ROLE
BECOMING INFORMED
THE IMMEDIATE FUTURE

Complementary and alternative medicine (CAM) can be defined as a medical system, practice, intervention, modality, profession, therapies, applications, theories, or claims that are currently not part of the dominant or conventional medical system. Allopathy is the dominant system in the United States.

Another definition of CAM is that it comprises those practices used for the prevention and treatment of diseases that are not taught widely in medical schools nor generally available in hospitals. Over time, a specific CAM practice or treatment may be reclassified to conventional medicine secondary to a change in prevailing societal attitudes, the emergence of supporting scientific data, or clinical experience with its use.

The use of CAM by American patients is not a passing fad, nor a medical side issue. It does reflect a genuine public need. The data supporting these statements were first published by Eisenberg et al. in *The New England Journal of Medicine* in 1993.[6] They collected data in 1990 from a phone survey of over 1500 people throughout the United States, and extrapolated the data to provide a national picture. At that time, 34 percent of Americans from all sociodemographic groups were using CAM. Almost all of these people were also seeing conventional doctors, but three of four did not tell their doctor that they were also using CAM.

Chronic or stress-related conditions were the major reasons patients sought CAM. The reasons included back problems, arthritis, headaches, digestive problems, depression, cancer, allergies, insomnia, and anxiety. In decreasing order, the interventions used were exercise, prayer, relaxation techniques, chiropractic, massage, imagery, spiritual healing, weight loss, herbal medicines, and megavitamins. Many of these interventions also are prescribed by conventional physicians. This explains some of the confusion as to what is defined as CAM and what is conventional medicine.

More recently, in 1997 Landmark Healthcare conducted a national survey of 1500 people in the United States. The use rate of CAM was 42 percent. Seventy-five percent of these people also were seeing physicians, and only two of five concealed that information from their physician. Interestingly, a similar survey of Canadian people in 1997 showed the same 42 percent use rate. In addition, patients with certain diagnoses tend to have a higher use of CAM. For instance, more than 60 percent of Americans who have cancer, AIDS, or Crohn's disease use this approach at some time.

Patients use CAM for a number of reasons. Most are seeking help in addition to that provided by their physician to prevent illness or injuries, to maintain wellness, or to obtain faster resolution of their disease. In doing so, they are accepting responsibility for their own health. Importantly, they are not expressing frustration with Western medicine, and they are not disillusioned with conventional medicine. Further, they are not harboring antiscience sentiments, nor are they disproportionately poor, seriously ill, or neurotic.

What is CAM?

There are over 350 modalities under the umbrella term CAM. One classification is shown in Table 90-1.

Mind-body interventions include biofeedback, meditation, yoga, and hypnotherapy. The category also includes guided imagery and the use of support groups.

Alternative systems of medical practice include traditional Chinese medicine, Native American medicine, homeopathy, ayurveda, naturopathy, and chiropractic. A system usually encompasses an organized approach to diagnosis, multiple approaches to treatment, a formulary, and a purposeful schedule of follow-up. For instance, traditional Chinese medicine is composed of herbal medicine, acupuncture, nutrition, acupressure massage, and qigong.

Pharmacological and biological treatments are large, diverse, and controversial areas. They include folk medicine products, medicinal plants, processed blood products, and vaccines. Apitherapy is also in this category. Phytomedicines are an increasingly active area of interest. Soy protein is one example. The isoflavins in soy have estrogen-like effects that include a positive effect on the lipid profile and coronary artery dilatation. They may possibly have a protective effect for breast or endometrial cancer risk, but, unfortunately, currently appear to have no effect on bone resorption or genitourinary epithelium.

Herbal medicine is another area that is large and controversial. Herbals that have been described in prospective, randomized clinical trials published in peer-reviewed medical journals include feverfew for migraines, hypericum (St. John's Wort) for depressive disorders, saw palmetto for benign prostatic hypertrophy, capsaicin for arthritis pain, and ginkgo biloba for circulatory disorders.

One of the conceptual difficulties physicians have with herbal medicine is that most herbal medicines do not require FDA approval. The Dietary Supplement Health Education Act of 1994 reclassified herbal remedies as dietary supplements; therefore, there is no requirement for premarket testing of safety or efficacy. Because they are not manufactured in a standardized fashion, one brand of an herb may be different in potency and efficacy than another brand of the same herb. Further, rather than the manufacturer being responsible to prove safety, the FDA must make a proactive effort if it wishes to prove a product is unsafe.

Diet and nutrition includes food elimination diets (gluten in patients with celiac disease), alternative diets (macrobiotic and vegetarianism), and lifestyle programs such as those advanced by Ornish and Pritikin. The Ornish program is composed of yoga, meditation, support groups, exercise, and diet; it has been found to be efficacious in patients with coronary artery disease.

Manual healing methods include physical therapy and massage, chiropractic and osteopathic manipulation, and biofield therapeutics. Biofield therapeutics is based on the premise that individuals have external energy fields surrounding them, a concept difficult for individuals trained in the classical sciences to accept. This category includes therapeutic touch, which is a misnomer because the patient is not actually touched, Reiki, polarity, and reflexology.

The last classification, bioelectromagnetic applications, includes the use of low-frequency thermal waves as used with diathermy, laser, and radio frequency surgery; nonionizing, nonthermal applications as with transcutaneous electrical nerve stimulation (TENS) for pain relief; and pulsed electromagnetic waves in the treatment of bone fractures.

TABLE 90-1 Classification of Alternative Medicine

Mind-body interventions
Alternative systems of medical practice
Pharmacological and biological treatments
Herbal medicines
Diet and nutrition
Manual healing methods
Bioelectromagnetic applications

There are common themes across many of the CAM interventions. They include the enhancement of wellness and prevention of disease, a focus on the person's wholeness versus individual symptoms, purposeful examination of the person's interaction with her environment and community, and the fostering of self-healing through the use of recuperative powers. Additional themes relating to mind-body-spirit relationships and the restoration or balancing of energy fields or the person's life force can be more difficult for allopathic physicians to understand and accept.

The Medical Doctor's Role

With this background, how does the allopathically trained physician respond when the patient asks questions such as, "I've been reading about XYZ alternative medicine. Is it okay for me to use it?" or "Is there an alternative care giver in the area to whom you can refer me?"

Each physician has to define his or her own sense of responsibility to the patient in considering answers. As a patient advocate, the physician has an ethical responsibility to promote the patient's well being and protect her from harm, to facilitate an informed choice, to honor her values in decision making, and to promote dialogue and a partnership in her care.

The concern about safety is one of the foremost issues with regard to CAM. There can be health risks associated with CAM. These include direct adverse effects from acute or delayed reactions from the medicant itself, or from the extraction process, route of delivery, nonstringent quality control, or toxic contaminants in a product. Indirect health risks can include patient delay in seeking conventional care, and the substitution of CAM interventions when more effective conventional therapy should be utilized.

However, there is a range to the safety of CAM and the physician can modify his or her response accordingly. For instance, it is unlikely that there will be adverse side effects from the patient using homeopathy, acupuncture, manipulation, bio-

feedback, or prayer. Thus, it would be appropriate for the physician to learn from the patient if there is an important psychological component to the intervention, if conventional care is failing her in some way, and if the CAM intervention can be continued in conjunction with appropriate conventional care.

There is a much greater likelihood that there can be safety issues associated with herbal preparations, intravenous hydrogen peroxide, high colonics with various substances added, and the administration of megadose vitamins and megadose minerals. In these instances, the physician should warn the patient of possible danger of direct toxic effects and discourage the patient's use of megadoses. This is also necessary if CAM prevents needed care, or when there is a more effective conventional treatment that can be used.

It can be difficult to respond to the patient who asks for a referral to a CAM provider. Allopathic physicians are defined by components of training, testing, certification, scope of practice, and audit. Licensure of health care professionals is the mechanism by which states exercise statutory protection through codified disciplinary actions. All states do license chiropractic providers, but fewer license acupuncturists, massage therapists, homeopathy practitioners, and naturopathy practitioners. There are national organizations to which these five CAM providers can belong. Most have membership requirements related to training, practice, and auditing, and thereby establish some criteria of credibility. Nevertheless, the ability to assess training and competence of a CAM provider is not as refined or rigorous a procedure as it is with medical specialists.

Reimbursement for services is a catalyst that is changing the landscape of health care. There now are a number of third-party payers and managed care organizations that reimburse for some CAM interventions in response to employees requesting their employers to offer this benefit.

Reimbursement can leave the impression that professional standards are in place for the CAM provider, that there are appropriate indications

for the use of the CAM intervention, and that there is a safe benefit-to-risk ratio with evidence of clinical and cost effectiveness. These criteria, all of which must be met for reimbursement of allopathic treatment, may not be present or required by a payer for CAM in any particular locale.

Becoming Informed

The physician's responsibility to be informed about various aspects of CAM is in keeping with the tenet of patient advocacy and concerns related to safety. Recent recommendations from the AMA's Council on Scientific Affairs state that stringently controlled research should be done to evaluate the efficacy of CAM, physicians should routinely inquire of their patients about its use, and physicians should educate themselves and their patients about the state of scientific knowledge of CAM.

The physician who wishes to be informed about CAM has to establish a knowledge base. Components of this knowledge base include obtaining information from the patient, self-study of journals and electronic reference databases, formal training in a specific CAM modality, and continuing medical education courses. An easy way to establish knowledge of CAM use in one's own practice is to routinely ask patients a question similar to, "Have you used or been considering other kinds of treatment, medications, supplements, or seeing nonphysician therapists for relief of your symptoms?" If the patient says yes, then it is appropriate to ask the patient questions related to when she decided to use it, what she was hoping to have happen, how she chose this particular modality, how long she has been doing it, and whether it has helped or caused harm.

It can be frustrating to access the published CAM literature because of the large number of therapies used and the lack of a readily available central library source. However, peer-reviewed English-language journals increasingly carry CAM-related articles. Table 90-2 lists some current peer-reviewed journals with a specific focus on CAM articles. Table 90-3 lists some newsletters that are sources for current information on CAM.

Table 90-4 identifies Web sites for readers who use a computer as a source of information. Medline has at least 23 MeSH headings under its CAM heading. Yahoo has over 300 such headings and is frequently used by the public. The Columbia University Web site provides access to at least 31 other CAM databases, as does the Pittsburgh University site. Herbalgram is the name of the Web site of the American Botanical Council in Austin, Texas. It is an excellent source for learning details about individual herbs. They also publish an English translation of the German Commission E-Monographs, the most authoritative source of information on herbals at the present time. The last two addresses on the list purposely focus on fraud and quackery.

The Immediate Future

It is highly likely that patients will continue to use CAM to obtain relief from chronic disease that is not being provided by conventional medicine. These patients will also continue with the expectation of reimbursement for CAM.

Separately, there is reason to believe that physicians increasingly will want to learn about CAM. Surveys indicate that medical students want familiarization with the subject. Many medical schools now offer CAM courses to their med-

---

TABLE 90-2 Complementary and Alternative Medicine Journals

Alternative Therapies in Health and Medicine

Integrative Medicine

Journal of Alternative and Complementary Medicine

Scientific Review of Alternative Medicine

Complementary Therapies in Medicine

Mind-Body Medicine

Focus on Alternative and Complementary Therapies

TABLE 90-3 Complementary and Alternative Medicine Newsletters

Complementary Medicine for the Physician
Alternative Medicine Alert
Andrew Weil's Self-Healing
NCA(H)F Newsletter
Complementary and Alternative Medicine at the NIH

nonconventional, traditional, nontraditional, orthodox, mainstream, alternative, complementary, holistic, natural, and new age. In the coming years, all of these adjectives may be replaced with the term "integrated medicine."

References and Selected Readings

ical students, and several family practice residencies instruct in CAM. Younger physicians exposed to this type of information will increasingly refer to CAM or learn to use some CAM interventions.

The multiple systems of medical care in the United States lend themselves to a number of different adjectives. These include conventional,

TABLE 90-4 Complementary and Alternative Medicine Web Sites

Medline
Yahoo
cpmcnet.columbia.edu/dept/rosenthal
pitt.edu/~cbw/altm.html
herbalgram.org
cgi.pathfinder.com/drweil
probe.nalusda.gov
healthy.net
altmed.od.nih.gov
quackwatch.com
hcrc.org

1. *Alternative medicine. Expanding Medical Horizons: A report to the National Institutes of Health on Alternative Medical Systems and Practices in the United States.* Washington, DC: US Government Printing Office, 1994. Publication No: 017-040-005377.
2. Brody H, Rygwelski J, Fetters MD: Ethics at the interface: Conventional western and complementary medical systems. *Bioethics Forum* 12:15–23, 1996.
3. Chez RA, Jonas WB: The challenge of complementary and alternative medicine. *Am J Obstet Gynecol* 1156–1161, 1997.
4. Chez RA, Jonas WB: One kind of medicine or many: The view from NIH. *Contemp Obstet Gynecol* 42:123–145, 1998.
5. Duke JA: *The Green Pharmacy.* Emmaus, PA: Rodale Press, 1997.
6. Eisenberg DM, Kessler RC, Foster C, Norlock FE, Calkins DR, Delbanco TL: Unconventional medicine in the United States; prevalence, costs and patterns of use. *N Engl J Med* 328:246–252, 1993.
7. Fugh-Berman A: *Alternative Medicine. What works.-* Baltimore: Williams & Wilkins, 1997.
8. Lerner M: *Choices in healing: Integrating the Best of Conventional and Complementary Approaches to Cancer.* Cambridge: MIT Press, 1994.
9. Micozzi MS: *Fundamentals of Complementary and Alternative Medicine.* New York: Churchill-Livingstone, 1996.
10. Newall CA, Anderson LA, Phillipson JD: *Herbal Medicines. A Guide for Health-Care Professionals.* London: The Pharmaceutical Press, 1996.

Patient Education in the Office

Ronald A. Chez
Lee A. Learman

ASPECTS OF PHYSICIAN-PATIENT
   COMMUNICATION
THE PEDAGOGIC MODEL
THE BEHAVIOR CHANGE MODEL
EDUCATIONAL MEDIA

P atient education is an essential component of comprehensive care. The medically educated and informed patient is better able to actively participate in her care, and more likely to have a rapid and favorable outcome.

The goals for educating and counseling patients include linking the patient's personal motivation and needs for medical care to an expected therapeutic outcome, reinforcing healthful behaviors, and modifying those behaviors that are associated with health risks. Another goal is to diminish professional medicolegal liability and incorporate risk management requirements.

There are at least two fundamental approaches to patient education. One is the pedagogic model. It involves the transfer of information to the learner based on the physician's belief of what the patient needs to know about her health, disease, or possible treatments. The other is the behavior change model. It assumes that the patient's ability to turn toward healthier behaviors is influenced by noncognitive factors that require identification and purposeful attention by the physician. The information is then presented in an effort to help motivate the patient to do so.

This chapter provides information about physician-patient communication, both models of patient education, and an overview of the media available to use as learning aids.

Aspects of Physician-Patient Communication

The crux of the doctor-patient relationship is the ability to communicate effectively. There are at least four important limitations in the way in which physicians communicate with patients. They can be categorized as limited time spent listening to the patient; patient reluctance to assert her needs for information; discrepancies between the type of information sought and the type given; and the use of complex language and medical jargon. Efforts to educate patients require attention to these limitations. Remedial actions include active listening; purposeful soliciting of requests for information; confirming that information given is the information sought; and using materials and media that communicate effectively.

Dialogue or conversation is the educational technique most frequently employed. Direct conversation assumes that the physician has the skills to identify the patient's reactions to what is being said, and that the physician will engage in a dialogue rather than a monologue. This includes the ability to speak in words and terms compatible with the patient's schooling and knowledge base, and consistent with the beliefs of the patient related to the diagnosis and treatment being discussed. As an active listener, the physician will convey through words and nonverbal actions that he or she has the time and interest to be supportive, repetitive, thorough, and complete relative to the patient's needs, hopes, and values.

The goal of meeting the patient's needs, hopes, and values can be impeded by intrinsic factors that are not readily identified or expressed. A

prominent one is the patient's underlying stress and fear about what is being or will be said by the physician. Other issues relate to the receiving of bad news in general, guilt, financial considerations, potential impact on lifestyle or potential disability, and an inadequate knowledge base. These may be influenced by patient embarrassment, concerns about appearing unintelligent, cultural beliefs related to the diagnosis or illness, attitudes of family and coworkers, and generic responses to authority figures that include an unwillingness to disagree or to interrupt. One result is less than effective communication with resultant incomplete understanding and misinterpretation.

The amount of time required for in-person communication for the purpose of education is another problem. Time is a priority in office practice, and an important objective of the workday is effective utilization of the physician's time. The physician's competence is in individualizing the information as pertinent to the patient once the patient has developed a fundamental base of knowledge. Much of the content that needs to be conveyed to patients is generic. It is a poor use of time to present repetitively this same standardized information from patient to patient. Thus, there is value in taking purposeful steps to formalize patient education activities in the office.

The Pedagogic Model

The first step in using this approach to patient education is to identify the clinical educational objectives for the individual patient. To ask, what is the goal of the learning? This can vary from health maintenance and disease prevention, to the need for diagnostic tests, to the exposition of treatment alternatives. The second step is to assess the patient's motivation for, preferences of, and expectations from the care received. This can be best accomplished through a series of three open-ended questions using these three terms. The result will be a mutually agreed upon goal of therapy or a specific outcome that is recognized as a shared responsibility.

The third step is to assess the patient's understanding and beliefs related to accomplishing this goal or outcome. An effective tool is "restatement" in which the patient is asked to verbalize the key elements of the information in her own words. Although this can require tact and itself can be time-consuming, it is necessary because it helps define the presence of barriers to learning. These can include less than adequate schooling and ability to comprehend, low literacy and English language proficiency, unrealistic fears and fantasies, and conflicts from traditional cultural interpretations of the problem or its treatment.

Additional barriers can emanate from staff. They include their own sense of priorities of time, territorial imperatives as to responsibility for educational activities, boredom from the tediousness of repetition, and negative personal attitudes about the content of the material. Patients are likely to detect this type of discomfort and avoid asking staff for information and clarifications.

The last step is to select the appropriate method and format. This can be considered analogous to writing an education prescription. The inevitable question is which approach is best? The answer is, it depends. Table 91-1 lists considerations that both enter into decision making related to the individual patient, and for the creation of a patient learning center with multiple learning aids and learning modules in the office environment. Its content is further expanded later in this chapter.

The Behavior Change Model

This approach to patient education is oriented toward encouraging patients to make healthier behavioral choices. Multiple theories and schemas have been advanced for the purpose of understanding why people behave in the ways that they do and for changing unhealthy behavior. Most of these models view information sharing as necessary but not sufficient to motivate and sustain changes in behavior.

TABLE 91-1 Checklist for Defining
Learning Aids

A. Environment
  1. Audience size:
     Groups or individuals
  2. Audience flow:
     Offered before, during, or after the visit
  3. Audience characteristics:
     Range of literacy
     Range of language
     Range of free choice and selected topics
     Presence of children requiring attention
  4. Time:
     Amount required
  5. Space:
     Site for the learning to take place
     Storage space for equipment and materials
     Requirement for privacy
     Requirement for ambient sound
     Requirement for ambient lighting
  6. Equipment:
     Portable hardware or permanent installation
     Need for theft precautions
     Durability of equipment
     Routine maintenance requirements
     Availability and expense of disposable supplies
B. Efficiency
  1. Cost:
     Initial and continuous
     Maintenance and replacement
  2. Staff time:
     Learn the method
     Setup of learning aid
     Patient orientation
     Patient requirements after using method
C. Effectiveness
  1. Content:
     Pretested
     Correct, credible, and authoritative
     Appropriate language, tone, and style
     Captures and maintains patient's attention
  2. Reinforcement:
     Materials available for review at home
     Plan for integration of content into care
     Plan for patient feedback
  3. Documentation:
     Written plan of care incorporates material
     Use of material recorded in medical record

Prochaska's stages of behavior change is one theory that has gained widespread acceptance among health care providers. Table 91-2 lists the defining characteristics of the stages of behavior change theory of Prochaska. Behavior change is a progression from thoughts to actions. The process begins when a patient who did not acknowledge the risks of a given behavior (*precontemplation*) does so and considers making a change (*contemplation*). Vague plans become more concrete and specific when the patient feels empowered to change (*preparation*). The change is implemented once there is a final commitment to do so (*action*). The patient then works actively to *maintain* the new, healthy behavior. *Relapse,* which can be considered inevitable for some patients, is framed as a temporary setback, and not as a permanent failure. The reasons for relapse are identified and used to guide future attempts at behavior change, beginning again with *contemplation.*

As listed in Table 91-3, the physician has several roles in facilitating change as a function of the patient's stage. Information about the risks of current behavior and benefits of changing it

TABLE 91-2 Prochaska's Stages of Change

Stage of Change	Defining Characteristics
1. Precontemplation	The patient is not considering a change. She does not accept the risks of continuing her current behavior or the benefits of changing it.
2. Contemplation	The patient is considering a change. She accepts the risks of continuing her current behavior and the benefits of changing it.
3. Preparation	The patient is making plans to implement a change in behavior.
4. Action	The patient has just implemented a change.
5. Maintenance	The patient is continuing the new behavior and working on strategies to prevent relapse.
6. Relapse	The patient returns to the unhealthy behavior.

TABLE 91-3 Prochaska's Stages of Change—Physician's Role

Stage of Change	Focused Interventions by the Physician to Promote Patient's Progress
1. Precontemplation	Provide information on the risks of the current behavior and the benefits of changing it.
2. Contemplation	Empower the patient to take control of her life and make change.
3. Preparation	Help the patient overcome ambivalence, make a commitment, and make specific plans to implement the change.
4. Action	Work on strategies to anticipate and prepare for high-risk situations in which relapse could occur. Help her develop a social support system for reinforcing her new, healthy behavior.
5. Maintenance	Support continuance of the positive, healthy behavior.
6. Relapse	Help her to overcome shame and guilt. Frame relapse as a common developmental stage. Identify factors leading to relapse and develop strategies for the future.

can help propel a patient into the *contemplation* stage. As a motivational coach, messages of empowerment can help a patient who is considering a change begin concrete *preparations*. As a negotiator, assistance in selecting a specific date can help prepared patients make the final commitment to take *action* and implement a change. Patients working to *maintain* a new behavior can be praised and supported by the physician as a friend as they work to identify strategies for confronting challenging situations. The physician may help support the patient who *relapses* by minimizing guilt and shame through purposeful exploration of the reasons for the relapse.

Focused questions help identify the patient's stage. As examples, these three questions are pertinent to a patient who smokes cigarettes: "You mentioned at the last visit that you smoke about a pack a day of cigarettes. How do you feel about that? Have you ever considered quitting? What happened?" If the patient does not accept that smoking is risky behavior, she is in the precontemplation stage. If she has considered quitting but has made no specific plans, she is in the contemplation stage. If she planned to quit on a specific date, but did not follow through, she is in the preparation stage. If she quit smoking since the last visit, she is in the action or maintenance stage. Once the patient's stage is defined, the physician can offer a specific message to support her forward progress. At subsequent visits, the same types of questions can be posed to monitor the patient's progress over time.

Educational Media

Both of these approaches to patient education emphasize the important contribution of basic information in helping patients obtain knowledge and understanding about their health and behaviors. Basic information can be learned through a variety of methods, none of which require direct physician time or effort. The content and style of each method can be honed to an appropriate educational level, medical terms can be defined, and the use of jargon can be minimized. Importantly, these methods can allow learning to take place when the patient is motivated and finds it convenient to do so. In this manner, these methods allow the patient to review, think, and digest the information at her own pace.

Techniques to educate patients encompass a wide range of activities from the printed word through contemporary electronic technology. The printed word is the most frequently used medium. Its format includes pamphlets, booklets, brochures, magazines, comic books, patient package inserts, and books. The sources range from those created by the physician to materials distributed by commercial sources, industry, government and nonprofit organizations to direct purchases by the patient.

The written approach enjoys many advantages. The method is portable, readily available, usually low in cost, and usually easy to reproduce in large numbers. Therefore, it lends itself to rapid creation from idea to final product. Desktop publishing computer software allows the individual office to produce professional-appearing newsletters and instruction sheets that reflect the philosophy and personality of the physician and staff. A variation on this approach is to purchase electronic computer files of generic information created by national organizations or commercial firms that allow the physician to personalize the content for the individual patient.

The disadvantages of the printed word relate to language and literacy. About one-fifth of Americans are illiterate and up to another one-fifth read at a grade five level or less. From a practical point of view, this means that written materials should be written at a sixth grade level in order to reach a majority of patients. There are formulas that can be applied to written prose to determine its grade or reading level. As an example, the Fry formula counts the number of sentences and the total number of syllables in three 100-word segments and uses a standardized graph to obtain a result.

Layout of the printed material is another consideration. It can be difficult to individualize a written piece without making it too lengthy. However, brevity may result in generic information with inadequate detail. A personal, active voice writing style, the use of illustrations, diagrams, and symbols to clarify instructions, and the purposeful use of color and font styles to highlight areas of importance are all ways to increase the likelihood that important information will not be missed.

An audiotape is relatively easy for the physician to create with his or her own voice. An inherent and potentially erroneous assumption of a taped message is that the patient is capable of learning at the same pace as the tape. There also is a shortened and limited attention span for learning detailed information using this method. Because it can be difficult for the learner to re-

view selected portions of an audiotape, it is necessary to provide the patient with the same information in a written brochure so that she may review and use it for purposeful recall without having to listen to the entire tape again. One frequent effective use of an audiotape is when a patient is required to follow a paced activity, such as a series of yoga exercises or stress-reduction relaxation techniques.

The motion medium, movie film and videotape, is a format that is particularly suited to demonstrate specific techniques, psychomotor skills, or actions important for the patient to learn. Because of the universal access to television, it is a medium that the public accepts and increasingly expects to receive as the learning aid.

There are considerable disadvantages to the method. It is extremely difficult for nonprofessional media personnel to create a product that does not look and sound amateurish. The message loses credibility for the patient when this occurs. Contributors to the lack of credibility include the type of background setting, the lighting and color, sound track quality, long periods of a person talking on screen without appropriate visuals, inability to identify with the persons on screen, and failure to emphasize primary and supporting messages with highlighted words.

The initial cost of a professional appearing tape or film can be high, and the finished product cannot be readily edited. And, similar to an audiotape, it makes the assumption that the learning is taking place at the same pace as the presentation and does not allow the learner to readily skip around to review the material.

The three-dimensional shape and form of models can facilitate the patient identifying with the object being depicted. This can be helpful in showing various aspects of normal and pathologic anatomy, demonstrating methods such as breast self-examination or self-injection of medicines, and in depicting the size of food portions as part of a diet.

However, the assumption that patients can interpret frontal and sagittal anatomical sections of the pelvis or abdomen, or the location of free-

standing organs such as a freestanding model of the uterus, should be questioned. Also, it may not be necessary to mimic exactly the texture, shape, or color of a model to demonstrate a point. For instance, the open end of an ankle sock and a tennis ball can be used to simulate the fetal head descending through a dilating cervix.

The computer with keyboard, mouse, or lighted pointer has a great deal of potential as a learning aid that possesses interactive communication capability. Hard drive or CD-ROM storage capacity for words, images, and pathways allows a high degree of individualization to take place when the method is used in a patient response manner. With appropriate programming, the patient can set the pace of learning, the level of literacy for the content, and the pathway they wish to take to learn.

As a tool for informed consent and risk management, the interactive computer program can be designed to require the patient to respond to questions related to benefit-risk learning objectives. According to the patient's answers, the program will continue forward to the next phase or require remedial learning before proceeding. At the end of such a session, the patient can be asked to verify completing the session by signature on a printout detailing the information presented and her answers.

The cost of hardware for this method revolves around a dedicated computer terminal, monitor, device players, and printer. Speakers or earphones are required if there is a soundtrack. Production costs for computer software are expensive and require skilled personnel. As with all learning aids, field testing and editing with revisions are also required. However, once a program is well accepted and purchased in large numbers by a national audience, the cost of one unit can be relatively modest.

The typical physician's office has a surfeit of patient learning aids available. Regardless of the source, the physician should read, view, or listen to everything that is being provided to the patient. It is imperative that the physician know if there is material with which the physician dis-

agrees, so that the patient can be told or the material can be hand-edited. Materials that are not usable should be discarded rather than displayed. It is also valuable to informally field test new learning material with staff and selected patients to validate that the message can be understood.

Summary

Patient education as an everyday, integral function in the physician's office serves a multitude of important roles. Some of these are purely pedagogic and aim to transmit clear and comprehensive information to patients about their health, illness, or treatment alternatives. To identify those that are most relevant to the patient's needs, it is necessary for the physician to actively listen, purposefully solicit requests for information, confirm that the information given is the information sought, and use materials and media that communicate effectively.

When behavioral change is the goal, educational materials can serve as the first step in encouraging patients to consider making this change. Helping patients implement and maintain healthy behaviors requires the physician to assume multiple interpersonal roles and to provide specific interventional messages according to the stage of change.

In both instances, appropriately designed learning aids will facilitate the education of a patient in an effective and efficient manner. As a valuable result, physician time can now be focused on individualized dialogue with the informed patient to bridge the gap between understanding and action.

References and Selected Readings

1. Aizen J, Fishbein M: *Understanding Attitudes and Predicting Social Behavior.* Englewood Cliffs, NJ: Prentice-Hall, 1980.
2. Bartlett EE: Contrasting views on patient education. *Patient Educ Newsletter* 4:63–64, 1981.
3. Becker MH, Maiman LA: Sociobehavioral determinants of compliance with health and medical care rec-

ommendations. *Med Care* 13:10–24, 1975.

4. DiMatteo MR: The physician-patient relationship: Effects on the quality of health care. *Clin Obstet Gynecol* 37:49–61, 1994.

5. Doak CC, Doak LG, Root JH: *Teaching Patients with Low Literacy Skills,* 2nd ed. Philadelphia: JB Lippincott, 1997.

6. Esdale A, Harris HL: Evaluation of a closed-circuit television patient education program: Structure, process and outcome. *Patient Educ Counsel* 7:193–215, 1985.

7. Festinger L: *A theory of Cognitive Dissonance.* Stanford, CA: Stanford University Press, 1957.

8. Learman LA: Helping your patients improve their health: A primer on behavior change for obstetricians and gynecologists. *Prim Care Update Obstet Gynecol* 5:130–135, 1998.

9. Olive DL, Olive KO: Patient education in a women's hospital: Attitudes of the medical and nursing staffs. *Obstet Gynecol* 65:686–690, 1985.

10. Prochaska JO, DiClemente CC, Norcross JC: In search of how people change: Applications to addictive behavior. *Am Psychol* 47:1102–1114, 1992.

11. Rosenstock IM: Why people use health services. *Milbank Q* 44:94–127, 1966.

12. Schwartz R: Quality assurance, standards, and criteria in health education: A review. *Patient Educ Counseling* 7:325–335, 1985.

13. Sledge WH, Feinstein AR: A clinimetric approach to the components of the patient-physician relationship. *JAMA* 278:2043–2048, 1997.

14. Wallace LM: Communication variables in the design of presurgical preparatory information. *Br J Psychol* 25:111–118, 1986.

Index

Index

Page numbers in *italics* refer to illustrations; those ending in the letter "t" refer to tables or charts.

for physically challenged, 361
Condyloma acuminata, 336, *483*, 1063
Conflict, defined, 587
Congenital adrenal hyperplasia,
836–838
amenorrhea and, 250
clinical presentation of, 836–837
corticosteroid therapy for, 185
diagnosis of, 187, 837
etiology and pathogenesis of, 836
hirsutism and, 185, 373, 836, 839
pseudohermaphroditism and, 187,
836
treatment of, 837–838
Congenital heart disease, pregnancy
and, 66t, 262, 367
Congenital rubella syndrome, 367
Congenital varicella syndrome, 367
Congestive heart failure, 684
classification of, 684t
diastolic dysfunction and, 688
hypertension and, 71
hypervolemic hyponatremia and,
739
management of, 688, 688t
pneumonia and, 726t
Conjugated equine estrogen, 79
Conjunctivitis, 1101–1102
Connective tissue diseases. *See specific
diseases, e.g.,* Systemic lupus
erythematosus.
pulmonary disorders and, 718–720
Conn's syndrome, 835
Consciousness, episodic loss of,
920–923
Consent, informed, 565, 1154. *See also*
Informed consent.
Constipation, 780–781
antidepressants and, 157
fibroids and, 324
opioid therapy and, 1017
treatment for, 781
urinary symptoms and, 436
Consumer Assessment of Health
Plans, 15
Contact dermatitis, 1064–1066, *1066*
Contact lenses, 1109
Continence mechanisms, 420–421. *See
also* Urinary incontinence.
Continuous positive airway pressure,
714
Contraception, 207–221. *See also*
Contraceptives.
counseling prior to use of, 137
emergency, 216–217
HIV infection and, 872–873
hormonal, 208–216
methods of, 208–221
barrier, 208, 217–219
cervical cap as, 220–221

condoms as, 208. *See also*
Condoms.
diaphragms as, 220–221
hormonal, 208–216. *See also* Oral
contraceptives.
implants as, 214–216
intrauterine devices as, 217–219
spermicides as, 219–220
sponge as, 219
physical disability and, 361–362
polycystic ovarian disease and, 301
screening prior to use of, 137
Contraceptives. *See also specific forms,
e.g.,* Oral contraceptives.
for adolescents, 134–135
for HIV-infected women, 872–873
oral. *See also* Oral contraceptives.
for renal transplant patients,
745–746
Contraceptive sponge, 219
Contusion, defined, 995
Conversion, defined, 587
Conversion disorder, 600
Cooper's ligaments, 794
Coordination examination, 920
COPD. *See* Chronic obstructive
pulmonary disease.
Core-needle biopsy, 540, *544*
Coronary angiography, 679, 681
Coronary artery bypass graft surgery,
69
Coronary artery disease, 396–398
chest pain in, 678
deaths from, 70, 396
diagnosis of, 679, 680, 681
gold standard for, 681
estrogen deficiency and, 396–397
estrogen replacement therapy and,
397
exercise and, 677
fat distribution as prognostic factor
for, 73, *73*
mortality from, 69, *70*
ovarian failure and, 397
plasma lipids and, 69, 73–74
postmenopause, 149, 396–398
risk factors for, 396–397
screening for, 35
sex variation in presentation of, 69
treatment of, 681–683
Cor pulmonale, 704
bronchiectasis and, 710
in COPD, 709
sleep apnea and, 714
Corticosteroid(s), 185
COPD and, 711–712
for Crohn's disease, 761
for dermatomyositis, 953
for idiopathic pulmonary fibrosis,
716
intranasal, 961

for polymyositis, 953
during pregnancy, 712, 965
for rheumatoid arthritis, 940–941
for sarcoidosis, 718
Costochondritis, 678
Cough, 702
blood produced by, 702
in gastroesophageal reflux disease,
722
nonpulmonary causes of, 702
physical examination for, 881–882
Coxsackie viruses, 973
Crab lice. *See* Pediculosis pubis.
Cranial nerves, 918–919
Creatinine, 744
Crest syndrome, 951–952
Crigler-Najjar syndrome, 772
Crohn's disease, 760–761
arthritis and, 942
clinical manifestations of, 760
differential diagnosis of, 761
extraintestinal signs of, 761
sigmoidoscopy for diagnosis of, 561
treatment of, 761
uropathy and, obstructive, 736
Cromolyn sodium, 712
Cryosurgery, 369, 489
Crystalline arthropathies. *See* Gout.
Culdocentesis, 790
Cullen's sign, 756
Cushing's disease, 373, 374, 728, 831,
834–835
Cyclobenzaprine, 934
Cyclophosphamide, 949
Cyproterone acetate, 840
Cyst(s)
Bartholin duct, 232–233
breast, 805
aspiration of, 805
palpable, 805
cervical, 322–323
dermoid, 306
epithelial, 1078–1079
hydatid, of Morgagni, 307
Nabothian, 322–323
ovarian. *See* Ovarian cysts.
paratubal, 307
pedunculated, 307
vaginal, 341
Cystadenomas, 306
Cystic fibrosis, 66t, 67t
bronchiectasis and, 709
chloride transport and, 10
genetic studies of, 282–283
incidence of, 709–710
infertility and, 10
screening for, 34
Cystitis, 438, 449, 942
Cystocele, 433, 449
Cystogram, 511